Australia

written and researched by

Margo Daly, Anne Dehne,
David Leffman and Chris Scott

with additional contributions by

Judith Bamber, Tim Dub, Adrian Proszenko,
Stephen Timblin, Rosie Waitt and Cameron Wilson

ROUGH
GUIDES

NEW YORK • LONDON • DELHI

www.roughguides.com

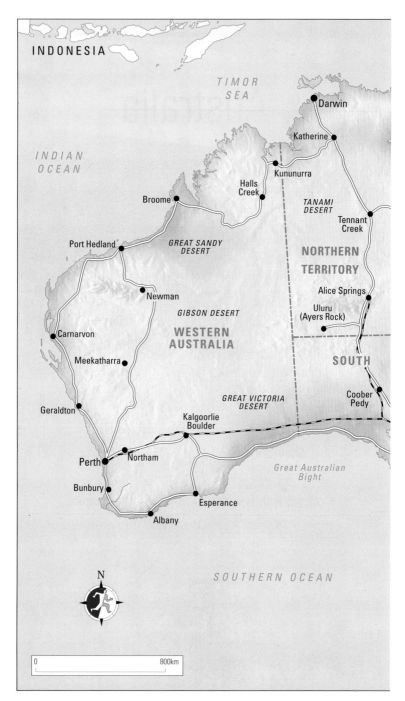

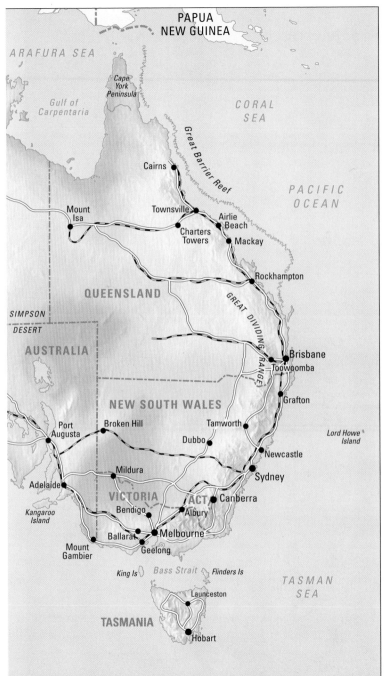

Introduction to
Australia

Australia is massive, and very sparsely peopled: in size it rivals the USA, yet its population is just under twenty million. It is an ancient land, and often looks it: in places, it's the most eroded, denuded and driest of continents, with much of central and western Australia – the bulk of the country – overwhelmingly arid and flat. In contrast, its cities – most of which were founded as recently as the mid-nineteenth century – express a youthful energy.

The most memorable scenery is in the aforementioned Outback, the vast desert in the interior of the country west of the Great Dividing Range. Here, vivid blue skies, cinnamon-red earth, deserted gorges and other striking geological features as well as bizarre wildlife comprise a unique ecology – one that has played host to the oldest surviving human culture for up to seventy thousand years (just ten thousand years after *Homo sapiens* is thought to have emerged from Africa).

The harshness of the interior has forced modern Australia to become a **coastal country**. Most of the population lives within 20km of the ocean, occupying a suburban, southeastern arc extending from southern Queensland to Adelaide. These urban Australians celebrate the typical New World values of material self-improvement through hard work and hard play, with an easy-going vitality that visitors, especially Europeans, often find refreshingly hedonistic. A sunny climate also contributes to this exuberance, with an outdoor life in which a thriving beach culture and the congenial backyard "barbie" are central.

While visitors might eventually find this *Home and Away* lifestyle rather prosaic, there are opportunities – particularly in the Northern Territory

v

Fact file

• With an area of eight million square kilometres, Australia is the **sixth largest country** in the world.

• The **population** stands at just under twenty million, of whom some 85% live in urban areas, mainly along the coast. About 92% of the population are of European origin, 2% Aboriginal and about 6% Asian and Middle Eastern.

• Much of Australia is arid and flat. One-third of the country is **desert** and another third is steppe or semi-desert. Only six percent of the country rises above 600m in elevation, and its **tallest peak**, Mount Kosciuszko, is just 2228m high.

• Australia's main **exports** are food, live animals, minerals, metals and fossil fuels, and its main **trading partners** are Japan and the US.

• Australia is a **federal parliamentary** state (formally a constitutional monarchy) with two legislative houses, the Senate and the House of Representatives. The chief of state is the British Monarch, represented by the Governor-General, while the head of government is the Prime Minister.

– to gain some experience of **Australia's indigenous peoples** and their culture, through visiting ancient art sites, taking tours and, less easily, making personal contact. Many Aboriginal people – especially in central Australia – have managed to maintain a traditional lifestyle (albeit with some modern accoutrements), speaking their own languages and living according to their law. Conversely, most Aboriginal people you'll come across in country towns and cities are victims of what is scathingly referred to as "welfare colonialism" – a disempowering system in which, supported by dole cheques and other subsidies, but with little chance of meaningful employment, they often fall prey to a destructive cycle of poverty, ill health and substance abuse. There's still a long way to go before black and white people in Australia can exist on genuinely equal terms.

Where to go

For visitors, deciding where to go can mean juggling with distance, money and time. You could spend months driving around the Outback, exploring the national parks, or just hanging out at beaches; or you could take an all-in two-week "Reef, Rock and Harbour" package, encompassing Australia's outstanding trinity of "must sees".

Both options provide thoroughly Australian experiences, but neither will leave you with a feeling of having more than scraped the surface of this vast country. The two big natural attractions are the two-thousand-kilometre-long **Great Barrier Reef** off the Queensland coast, with its complex of islands and underwater splendour, and the brooding monolith of **Uluru** (Ayers Rock), in the Northern Territory's Red Centre. You should certainly try to see them, although exploration of other parts of the country will bring you into contact with more subtle but equally rewarding sights and opportunities.

The **cities** are surprisingly cosmopolitan: waves of postwar immigrants from southern Europe and, more recently, Southeast Asia have done

Outdoor activities

Though there's fun to be had in the cities, it's really the great outdoors that makes Australia such a special place. Its multitude of national parks – around a thousand in total – embrace everything from isolated beaches and tropical rainforest, to the vast wildernesses of the bush and the Outback. Visitors are spoilt for choice when it comes to getting out and about, with a huge range of outdoor pursuits on offer – everything from diving off the Great Barrier Reef or white-water rafting Tasmania's Franklin River, to hot-air ballooning over Alice or even skiing in the Australian Alps. Perhaps the best way to see something of the great outdoors, and certainly the cheapest, is bushwalking. Extremely popular nationwide, you'll find trails marked in almost every national park. For more see p.62.

much to erode Australia's Anglocentrism. Each Australian state has a capital stamped with its own personality, and nowhere is this more apparent than in New South Wales where glamorous Sydney has the iconic landmarks of the Opera House and Harbour Bridge. Elsewhere, the sophisticated café society of Melbourne (Victoria) contrasts with the vitality of Brisbane (Queensland). Adelaide, in South Australia, has a human-scale and old-fashioned charm, while Perth, in Western Australia, camouflages its isolation with a leisure-oriented urbanity. In Hobart, capital of Tasmania, you'll encounter fine heritage streetscapes and get a distinct maritime feel. The purpose-built administrative centre of Canberra, in the Australian Capital Territory, often fails to grip visitors, but Darwin's continuing revival enlivens an exploration of the distinctive "Territory".

Away from the suburbs, with their peripheral shopping malls and quarter-acre residential blocks, is the transitional "bush", and beyond that the

Big things

Don't be surprised if, on a long, hot stretch of Queensland highway, you find yourself hitchhiking next to Captain Cook ... and no, that enormous pineapple on the horizon isn't an alien spacecraft – it's real. Real fibreglass, that is. Big Things are an Australian obsession, and a way for a small town to make a mark on the tourist map. As you travel around the country you'll find giant fruit – the Big Apple, the Big Banana, the Big Strawberry; animals – the Big Lobster, the Big Penguin, the Big Cow; and tourist attractions – the Big Gold Panner and even Big Ayers Rock. They're places to stop and get a drink or a bite, buy joyously tacky souvenirs and look at an exhibition – but above all they're places to take a photo. No Australian holiday is complete without at least one Big Thing in your album.

wilderness of the **Outback** – the quintessential Australian experience. Protected from the arid interior, the **east coast** has the pick of the country's greenery and scenery, from the north's tropical rainforests and the Great Barrier Reef to the surf-lined beaches further south. The east coast is backed by the Great Dividing Range, which steadily decreases in elevation as it extends from Mount Kosciuszko (2228m) in New South Wales north into tropical Queensland. If you have time to spare, a trip to often-over-looked **Tasmania**, across the Bass Strait, is worthwhile: you'll be rewarded with vast tracts of wilderness as well as landscapes almost English in their bucolic qualities.

When to go

A ustralia's **climate** has become less predictable in recent times, although like the rest of the planet the country has rarely had stable weather patterns over the last few thousand years. Recently observed phenomena, such as an extended drought in the eastern Outback, the cyclic El Niño effect, and even the hole in the ozone layer – which is disturbingly close to the country – are probably part of a long-term pattern.

Visitors from the northern hemisphere should remember that, as early colonials observed, in Australia "nature is horribly reversed": when it's winter or summer in the northern hemisphere, the opposite season prevails Down Under. Although this is easy to remember, the principle becomes harder to apply to the transitional seasons of spring and autumn. To confuse things further, the four seasons only really exist outside of the tropics in the **southern half of the country**. Here, you'll find reliably warm summers at the coast with regular, but thankfully brief, heatwaves in excess of 40°C. Head inland, and the temperatures rise further. Winters, on the other hand, can be miserable, particularly in Victoria, where the short days add to the gloom. Tasmania's highlands make for unpredictable weather all year round,

although summer is the best time to explore the island's out-door attractions.

In the **coastal tropics**, weather basically falls into two seasons. The best time to visit is during the hot and cloudless Dry (from

April to November), with moderate coastal humidity maintaining a pleasant temperature day and night and cooler nights inland. In contrast, the Wet – particularly the "Build Up" in November or December before the rains – can be very uncomfortable, with stifling, near-total humidity. As storm clouds gather, rising temperatures, humidity and tension can provoke irrational behaviour in the psychologically unacclimatized – something known as "going troppo". Nevertheless, the mid-Wet's daily downpours and enervating mugginess can be quite intoxicating, compelling a hyper-relaxed inactivity for which these regions are known; furthermore the countryside – if you can reach it – looks its best at this time.

Australia's **interior** is an arid semi-desert with very little rain, high summer temperatures and occasionally freezing winter nights. Unless you're properly equipped to cope with these extremes, you'd be better off coming here during the transitional seasons between April and June, or October and November.

In general, the **best time to visit** the south is during the Australian summer, from December to March, though long summer holidays from Christmas through January mean that prices are higher and beaches more crowded at this time. In the tropical north the best months are from May to October, while in the Centre they are from October to November and from March to May. If you want to tour extensively, keep to the southern coasts in summer and head north for the winter.

Aboriginal art

Aboriginal art has grown into a million-dollar industry since the first canvas dot paintings of the central deserts emerged in the 1970s. Though seemingly abstract, early canvases are said to replicate ceremonial sand paintings – temporary "maps" fleetingly revealed to depict sacred Dreaming trails. In the tropics, figurative bark and cave paintings are less enigmatic but much older, though until recently they were ceremonially repainted. The unusual x-ray style found in the Top End details the internal structure of animals. The Northern Territory – and Alice Springs in particular – are the best places to look; for tips on buying Aboriginal art as well as didgeridoos, see pp.672–673.

Average temperatures (°C) and rainfall (mm)

		Jan/Feb		Mar/Apr		May/Jun		July/Aug		Sept/Oct		Nov/Dec	
Adelaide	°C	28	27	25	22	18	16	14	15	17	21	22	25
	mm	20	20	25	45	65	70	65	60	55	40	25	20
Alice Springs	°C	36	35	32	27	22	21	19	21	25	30	32	35
	mm	35	40	25	20	25	25	20	20	10	25	30	35
Brisbane	°C	27	27	26	25	23	21	23	22	24	25	26	27
	mm	160	160	150	80	70	60	55	50	50	75	100	140
Cairns	°C	31	31	30	29	28	25	25	27	27	28	30	31
	mm	400	440	450	180	100	50	30	25	35	35	90	160
Canberra	°C	27	25	23	20	15	13	12	13	15	18	22	25
	mm	55	50	50	45	50	30	30	50	50	70	65	65
Darwin	°C	31	30	31	32	31	30	30	31	32	32	33	32
	mm	400	430	435	75	50	10	5	10	15	70	110	310
Hobart	°C	21	21	20	17	14	12	11	12	15	18	19	20
	mm	50	45	50	55	50	45	50	50	55	55	50	50
Melbourne	°C	26	26	24	21	16	15	14	15	17	19	21	20
	mm	45	50	55	60	55	50	50	50	55	65	55	55
Perth	°C	30	30	28	25	22	20	19	19	20	22	25	28
	mm	10	15	25	50	125	185	175	145	80	75	25	20
Sydney	°C	25	25	24	23	20	17	16	17	19	22	23	24
	mm	100	105	125	130	125	130	110	75	60	75	70	75

44

things not to miss

It's not possible to see everything that Australia has to offer in one trip — and we don't suggest you try. What follows is a selective taste of the country's highlights: great places to stay, outstanding national parks, spectacular wildlife — and even good things to eat and drink. Arranged in five colour-coded categories, you can browse through to find the very best things to see, do and experience. All highlights have a page reference to take you straight into the guide, where you can find out more.

01 Uluru (NT) Page **690** • Uluru, otherwise known as Ayers Rock, represents a sacred landmark for Aboriginal peoples, and a magnet to tourists the world over.

02 Wilpena Pound (SA) Page **879** • Fantastic hikes amid spectacular scenery at the famous elevated basin of Wilpena Pound in the Flinders Ranges National Park.

03 Mardi Gras (Syd) Page **182** • The irreverent Oxford Street parade, from dykes on bikes to the Melbourne marching boys, ends the summer season.

04 Humpback whales (Qld) Page **455** • Saved from extinction by a ban on whaling, humpback whales migrate up the Queensland coast each June–October to calve around the Whitsundays' warm tropical waters.

05 Kakadu National Park (NT) Page **633** • Australia's largest national park is a vast World Heritage-listed wilderness with an amazing diversity of wildlife.

06 **Giant termite mounds (NT)** Page **644** • These impressively huge towers – up to four metres tall – are a regular feature of the Top End.

07 **Sydney Opera House performance (Syd)** Page **116** • Take in a performance at one of the world's busiest performing arts centres – interval drinks certainly don't have such spectacular harbour views anywhere else in the world.

08 **Bondi Beach (Syd)** Page **152** • Beach, surf and café culture. The coastal walk around the headlands to Bronte Beach via Tamarama is stunning.

09 Aussie Rules match at the MCG (Melb) Page 911 •

Taking in a game at the venerable Melbourne Cricket Ground (MCG) is a must for sports fans.

10 Four-wheel-driving on Cape York (Qld) Page 552 •

The creeks and savannah of the Cape York Peninsula provide the setting for what is widely regarded as the most rugged 4WD adventure in the country

11 The Kimberley (WA) Page 777 •

Regarded as Australia's last frontier, the Kimberley is a sparsely populated, untamed wilderness that contains some stunning landscapes.

12 Kangaroo Island (SA) Page 837 •

Unspoilt Kangaroo Island boasts fantastic coastal scenery and excellent wildlife-spotting opportunities.

13 Tall Timber Country (WA) Page 730 •

The brooding, primeval karri forests of the so-called Tall Timber Country are one of WA's greatest natural sights.

15 Crocodiles (NT) Page **635** ● Head up north to see the Territory's fascinating and fearsome crocs.

14 Kings Canyon in Watarrka National Park (NT) Page **686** ● The hike around the canyon's rim takes you past exposed lookouts, domed outcrops and a secluded waterhole that's great for a dip on a hot day.

16 Climbing Sydney Harbour Bridge (Syd) Page **117** ● Scale the bridge for adrenaline thrills and great vistas – or walk or cycle across it for free.

17 Barossa Valley wineries (SA) Page **826** ● Australia's premier wine-producing region, just 50km from Adelaide, is a great place to stop over and unwind.

18 Skiing in the Snowy Mountains (NSW) Page 275 •
The Snowy Mountains have the best skiing in Australia.

19 Broken Hill (NSW) Page 368 • Historic Outback mining town and thriving arts centre.

20 Atherton Tablelands (Qld) Page 533 • With its majestic rainforest, crater lakes and abundant wildlife, you could spend days exploring the Atherton Tablelands.

21 Manly Ferry (Syd) Page 112 •
The short ferry trip from Circular Quay to the surfing Mecca of Manly takes in picture postcard views of Sydney Opera House and the Harbour Bridge.

ACTIVITIES | CONSUME | EVENTS | NATURE | SIGHTS |

22 Mutawintji National Park (NSW) Page 379 • Red,
barren earth laced with ancient galleries of Aboriginal rock art, secluded gorges and quiet waterholes.

23 The Great Ocean Road (Vic) Page 966 • On two wheels or
four, the 280-kilometre ride along the rugged, surf-battered cliffs bordering the Great Ocean Road comes straight out of a road movie.

24 The Strzelecki, Birdsville and Oodnadatta tracks (SA)
Page 881 • Making the most of the journey is what counts – the fabled Outback routes to Oodnadatta, Birdsville and Innamincka are still real adventures.

25 Aboriginal Dance Festival at Laura (Qld)
Page 549 • Electrifying celebration of Aboriginal culture, held in June in odd-numbered years.

ACTIVITIES | CONSUME | EVENTS | NATURE | SIGHTS

26 Melbourne Cup (Melb)
Page **60** • Melbourne's 130-year-old horse race brings the entire country to a standstill around the radio or TV.

27 The Sanctuary at Mission Beach (Qld) Page
517 • Rainforest retreat par excellence, with stilt cabins at tree level surrounded by fifty acres of steamy coastal jungle.

28 Fraser Island (Qld) Page **457** • The giant dunes, freshwater lakes and sculpted coloured sands of the world's largest sand island form the backdrop to exciting 4WD safaris.

29 Hiking through Carnarvon Gorge (Qld)
Page **571** • With its Aboriginal art sites and magical scenery, a day-hike into the Carnarvon Gorge takes some beating.

30 Bushtucker Page **49** •
Witchetty grubs and wattle seeds, possum-tail soup and rooburgers – a good few restaurants around the country are now experimenting with bushtucker.

31 **Birdsville Races (Qld)** Page **576** • *Birdsville Hotel* is the focus for the annual Birdsville Races, where five thousand people descend on the tiny desert township in Queensland's Outback for a weekend of drinking, horse racing and mayhem.

32 **Tree kanga- roos (Qld)** Page **538** • North Queensland's tropical rainforest is home to two species of tree kangaroo, which forage at night on the forest floor but spend the days crashed out in the canopy. Spot them at Yungaburra in the Atherton Tablelands.

33 **Boating on the Murray River (SA)** Page **854** • By far the best way to see the great brown Murray River is to get out on the water – hop on a paddle steamer, splash about in a canoe or rent a houseboat.

34 **Beer Can Regatta (NT)** Page **628** • Wacky boat races in sea craft made entirely from beer cans, held in early August.

35 **Coober Pedy (SA)** Page **872** • The underground homes, shops and churches of Coober Pedy – where temperatures soar to over 50°C in summer – are the most enduring symbol of the harshness of Australia's Outback.

36 **Karijini National Park (WA)** Page **766** • The dramatic water-carved gorges of the Karijini National Park remain one of WA's undiscovered gems.

37 **Diving at the Great Barrier Reef (Qld)** Page **470** • Come face-to-face with stunning coral and shoals of curious fish.

38 Overland Track in Cradle Mountain/Lake St Clair National Park (Tas) Page **1148** •

The eighty-kilometre Overland Track, attracting walkers from all over the world, is Australia's greatest extended bushwalk, spread over five or more mud- and leech-filled days of physical, exhilarating exhaustion.

39 The Franklin River (Tas) Page **1152** • White-water rafting is the only way to explore the wild Franklin River, one of the great rivers of Australia.

40 Sailing in the Whitsundays (Qld) Page **496** • There's fantastic sailing and diving – and whale-watching in season – in the idyllic white-sand Whitsunday Islands.

41 Blue Mountains (NSW) Page **220** • Now World Heritage listed, the Blue Mountains, just west of Sydney, get their name from the blue mist of fragrant eucalyptus oil hanging in the air all year round.

42 Lake Eyre (SA) Page **883** • This massive saline lake, topped by a glaring salt crust and walled by red dunes, creates a harsh, unforgettable landscape.

43 Canoeing up the Katherine Gorge (NT) Page **652** • Hop on a cruise or paddle a canoe through the dramatic orange cliffs of the Katherine Gorge – you won't have it to yourself, but it's still hugely enjoyable.

44 Wilsons Promontory National Park (Vic) Page **1028** • Victoria's most popular national park, "The Prom" boasts some superb coastal scenery and bushwalks.

Contents

Using this Rough Guide

We've tried to make this Rough Guide a good read and easy to use. The book is divided into five main sections, and you should be able to find whatever you want in one of them.

Front section

The front colour section offers a quick tour of Australia. The **introduction** aims to give you a feel for the place, with suggestions on where to go. We also tell you what the weather is like and include a basic country fact file. Next, our authors round up their favourite aspects of Australia in the **things not to miss** section – whether it's great festivals, amazing sights or a special hotel. Right after this comes the Rough Guide's full **contents** list.

Basics

You've decided to go and the basics section covers all the **pre-departure** nitty-gritty to help you plan your trip. This is where to find out which airlines fly to your destination, what paperwork you'll need, what to do about money and insurance, about Internet access, food, security, public transport, car rental – in fact just about every piece of **general practical information** you might need.

Guide

This is the heart of the Rough Guide, divided into user-friendly chapters, each of which covers a specific region. Every chapter starts with a list of **highlights** and an **introduction** that

helps you to decide where to go, depending on your time and budget. Likewise, introductions to the various towns and smaller regions within each chapter should help you plan your itinerary. We start most town accounts with information on arrival and accommodation, followed by a tour of the sights, and finally reviews of places to eat and drink, and details of nightlife. Longer accounts also have a directory of practical listings. Each chapter concludes with **public transport** details for that region.

Contexts

Read Contexts to get a deeper understanding of how Australia ticks. We include a brief **history**, articles about **indigenous peoples** and **wildlife**, together with a detailed further reading section that reviews dozens of **books** relating to the country.

Index + small print

Apart from a **full index**, which includes maps as well as places, this section covers publishing information, credits and acknowledgements, and also has our contact details in case you want to send in updates and corrections to the book – or suggestions as to how we might improve it.

Map and chapter list

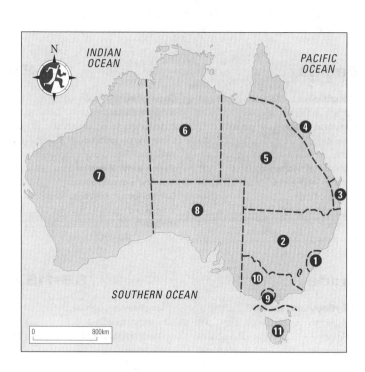

Contents

4

Contexts

Index and small print

Map symbols

maps are listed in the full index using coloured text

Main road		Conservation hut
Minor road		Chinese temple
Unpaved road		Lighthouse
Pedestrianized street (town maps)		Golf course
Steps		Bus stop
Path/track		Information office
Railway		Post office
Ferry route		Internet access
River		Campsite
State/territorial boundary		Accommodation
Chapter division boundary		Restaurant
Point of interest		Building
Mountain peak		Church/cathedral
Mountain range		Aboriginal land
Gorge		Prohibited area
Viewpoint		Beach
Waterfall		Cemetery
Reef		Marsh
Airport		Park
Cave		

Basics

Basics

Getting there

Few will be surprised to learn that flying is the main way of getting to Australia. You can fly pretty much every day to the main east-coast cities from Europe, North America and Southeast Asia. Airfares depend on the season, with the highest being the two weeks either side of Christmas, when the weather is best in the main population centres (note, however, that you can get a low-season-priced bargain if you fly on Christmas Day itself). Fares drop during the "shoulder" seasons – mid-January to March and mid-August to November – and you'll get the best prices during the low season, April to June. Because of the distance from most popular departure points, flying on weekends does not alter the price.

However, you can certainly cut costs by going through a **specialist flight agent** – either a consolidator, who buys up blocks of tickets from the airlines and sells them at a discount, or a **discount agent**, who in addition to dealing with discounted flights may also offer special student and youth fares and a range of other travel-related services such as travel insurance, rail passes, car rental, tours and the like. Some agents specialize in **charter flights**, which may be cheaper than anything available on a scheduled flight, but again departure dates are fixed and withdrawal penalties are high. One possibility is to see if you can arrange a courier flight, although you'll need a flexible schedule, and preferably be travelling alone with very little luggage. In return for shepherding a parcel through customs, you can expect to get a deeply discounted ticket. You'll probably also be restricted in the duration of your stay.

If Australia is only one stop on a longer journey, you might want to consider buying a **Round-the-World** (RTW) ticket. Some travel agents can sell you an "off-the-shelf" RTW ticket that will have you touching down in about half a dozen cities and Australia is frequently part of the regular eastbound RTW loop from Europe. Figure on £850/US$1300 for a RTW ticket including Australia.

Booking flights online

Many airlines and discount travel websites offer you the opportunity to book your tickets **online**, cutting out the costs of agents and middlemen. Good deals can often be found through discount or auction sites, as well as through the airlines' own websites.

Online booking agents and general travel sites

ⓦ**travel.yahoo.com** Incorporates a lot of Rough Guide material in its coverage of destination countries and cities across the world, with information about places to eat, sleep and so on.
ⓦ**www.cheapflights.com** Bookings from the UK and Ireland only. Flight deals, travel agents, plus links to other travel sites.
ⓦ**www.cheaptickets.com** Discount flight specialists.
ⓦ**www.etn.nl/discount.htm** A hub of consolidator and discount agent Web links, maintained by the non-profit European Travel Network.
ⓦ**www.expedia.com** Discount airfares, all-airline search engine and daily deals.
ⓦ**www.flyaow.com** Online air travel info and reservations site.
ⓦ**www.gaytravel.com** Gay online travel agent, concentrating mostly on accommodation.
ⓦ**www.geocities.com/thavery2000/** Has an extensive list of airline toll-free numbers and websites.
ⓦ**www.hotwire.com** Bookings from the US only. Last-minute savings of up to forty percent on regular published fares. Travellers must be at least 18 and there are no refunds, transfers or changes allowed. Log-in required.
ⓦ**www.lastminute.com** Offers good last-minute holiday package and flight-only deals.
ⓦ**www.priceline.com** Name-your-own-price

website that has deals at around forty percent off standard fares. You cannot specify flight times (although you do specify dates) and the tickets are non-refundable, non-transferable and non-changeable.

ⓦ**www.skyauction.com** Bookings from the US only. Auctions tickets and travel packages using a "second bid" scheme. The best strategy is to bid the maximum you're willing to pay, since if you win you'll pay just enough to beat the runner-up regardless of your maximum bid.

ⓦ**www.smilinjack.com/airlines.htm** Lists an up-to-date compilation of airline website addresses.

ⓦ**www. travelocity.com** Destination guides, hot Web fares and best deals for car rental, accommodation and lodging as well as fares. Provides access to the travel agent system SABRE, the most compre-hensive central reservations system in the US.

ⓦ**www.travelshop.com.au** Australian website offering discounted flights, packages, insurance and online bookings.

Getting there from Britain and Ireland

The market for flights between Britain and Australia is one of the most competitive in the world, and in real terms prices are still as low as ever. Modern aircraft can now reach the north Australian coast from London in just fifteen hours' flying time, though in practice the journey to Sydney or the other eastern cities takes a minimum of 21 hours including stopovers. If you break the journey in Southeast Asia or North America, getting to Australia need not be the tedious, seatbound slog you may have imagined. There are no direct flights from Ireland.

A word of warning: don't actually buy your ticket until you're sure that you've been granted a visa (see p.21 for more details). Visa in hand, you'll next need to decide where you want to fly to in Australia, where you would like to stop en route (or on the way back) and whether you want to use flights to get around once you're there. Sydney and Melbourne are served by the greatest number of airlines, and carriers such as Qantas offer the same price to fly to any east-coast city between Cairns and Adelaide; flights to Darwin and Perth are around £100 cheaper, but you'll spend at least that much on the overland journey to

the east coast. An **open-jaw ticket** (flying into one city and out from another) usually costs no more than an ordinary return.

Direct scheduled flights depart from London's two main airports, Gatwick and Heathrow, although Singapore Airlines has daily flights from Manchester to Singapore which connect with onward flights to Sydney.

There are relatively few traditional package holidays available – nobody's going to fly all the way to Australia just to spend a couple of weeks in a hotel by a beach – but if your time is short and you're reasonably sure of what you want to do, it may not be a bad idea to prebook some of your accommodation, tours and vehicle rental. Many companies offer minimal packages, consisting of a flight with some accommodation and a couple of tours. Full "see-it-all" packages can work out quite expensive and the pace can be rather tiring, but they aren't bad value, considering what you'd be spending anyway.

Many of the Australian specialists also offer such things as bus and train passes (see pp.35–37), discounted hotel vouchers and the like – all of which are worth considering. Some discount flight agents also arrange tours and accommodation – check out Austravel and Trailfinders, among others.

Fares

Note that all the fares quoted below are exclusive of **airport tax** – this is usually an extra £40–60. The cheapest fare you're likely to find is around £550 return, available during the **low-season** months of April to June, though special offers can go as low as £450; if you insist on flying with Qantas, BA or Singapore Airlines, expect to pay from around £800 for a flight in this off-peak period with special offers sometimes taking prices down to £600. In the two weeks before Christmas, you'd be lucky to find anything for less than £1000 return: to stand a chance of getting one of the cheaper tickets, aim to book at least six months in advance. Prices also go up from mid-June or the beginning of July to the middle of August coinciding with the peak European holiday times. In between times (the **shoulder seasons** of mid-Aug to Nov and mid-Jan to March) you should expect to pay around £700 (or up to £950 with one of the prestige airlines).

With Qantas you can fly from **regional airports** at Aberdeen, Belfast, Edinburgh, Glasgow, Manchester or Newcastle to connect with your international flight at Heathrow. There is no extra charge from Manchester, but you'll pay a **supplement** of £25 each way from the others.

An excellent alternative to a long direct flight is a **multi-stopover ticket**, which can cost the same or just a little more than the price of an ordinary return; check out the routing of the airlines detailed on pp.13–14 for some ideas. Unusual routes are inevitably more expensive, but it's possible to fly **via South America** with Aerolineas Argentinas, which offers stops in Buenos Aires and Auckland – at least £925 return – or **via Africa** with South African Airways, which offers return fares via Johannesburg to Perth and Sydney from around £1000, with the added bonus of discounted internal flights to Harare (Botswana), Victoria Falls, Nairobi and many other African destinations. You can also often get good deals **via Japan** on All Nippon Airlines and Japan Airlines.

More expensive, but even better value, **Round-the-World (RTW) tickets** incorporating Australia provide a chance to see the world on your way to and from down under. A good agent should be able to piece together sector fares from various airlines: providing you keep your itinerary down to three continents prices range from around £850 for a simple London–Bangkok –Sydney–LA–London deal to well over £1000 for more complicated routings. It's also possible to incorporate substantial overland segments for variety. A sample itinerary London–Nairobi–overland to Johannesburg –Perth overland to Broome–Alice Springs overland to Melbourne–Bali–Hong Kong –Bangkok–London costs from around £860.

Although most of the cheaper routings **from Ireland** involve a stopover in London and transfer to one of the airlines listed on pp.13–14, there are often good deals on Olympic Airways **from Dublin** via Greece. Singapore Airlines has flights ticketed through from Dublin, Shannon or Cork via London to Singapore and Sydney, while

Malaysia Airlines also goes from all three Irish airports via Kuala Lumpur. The three airports are also served by the affiliated British Airways and Qantas; all their flights to Australia have a Dublin–London add-on included in the price. Malaysia Airlines fares start from around €970 for an open one-year return in low season, up to €1640 in the Christmas period, while a Singapore Airlines ticket would cost around €1150 in the shoulder season. A low-season fare **from Belfast** with British Airways starts at £610, going up to £720 in the shoulder season. In high season fares average at around £1000. For youth and student discount fares, the best first stop is Usit (see p.14).

Airlines

Aerolíneas Argentinas ⊤ 020/7494 1001, ⓦ www.aerolineas.com.ar. London Heathrow to Madrid, changing planes for Buenos Aires and changing again for Sydney.
Air New Zealand ⊤ 020/8741 2299, ⓦ www.airnz.co.uk. Daily scheduled flights from London Heathrow to all major Australian airports via Los Angeles. Their popular Pacific routing gives you a choice of stopovers in Fiji, Western Samoa, the Cook Islands, Tahiti and New Zealand.
All Nippon Airways (ANA) ⊤ 020/7224 8866, ⓦ www.ana.co.jp. From London Heathrow to Tokyo, then on to Osaka, with connecting flights daily to Sydney.
Britannia Airways ⊤ 01582/424 155, ⓦ www.britanniaairways.com. Charter flights to most European holiday destinations, Australia, South Africa etc.
British Airways ⊤ 0845/77 333 77, Republic of Ireland ⊤ 1800/626 747, ⓦ www.britishairways .com. Daily scheduled flights from London Heathrow to all major Australian airports via Bangkok, Kuala Lumpur, Singapore or Hong Kong.
Emirates Airlines ⊤ 0870/243 2222, ⓦ www.emirates.com. Daily from London Heathrow and Manchester to Melbourne and every other day to Sydney. All flights via Dubai.
Garuda Indonesia ⊤ 020/7467 8600 or 0161/834 3747 in Manchester, ⓦ www .garuda-indonesia.co.uk. Three flights weekly from London Gatwick via Frankfurt flying into all the main Australian airports.
Japan Airlines ⊤ 0845/774 7700 or 020/7408 1000, ⓦ www.jal.co.jp. From London Heathrow, daily non-stop flights to Tokyo and five times weekly to Osaka, with connecting flights to Sydney from both

airports. Connecting flights to Brisbane and Cairns daily from Tokyo, three times weekly from Osaka.
KLM Royal Dutch Airlines ☎0870/507 4074, ⓦwww.klmuk.com. Daily flights to Amsterdam from just about every British airport except Gatwick and Luton but including London Heathrow, London City, Edinburgh, Manchester, Glasgow and Bristol, with connecting flights to Sydney via Kuala Lumpur.
Korean Air ☎020/7495 3377, ⓦwww .koreanair.eu.com. Five flights a week from London Heathrow to Sydney or Brisbane via Seoul.
Lauda Air ☎0845/601 0948, ⓦwww.laudaair.co.uk. Three flights weekly from Heathrow via Vienna and Kuala Lumpur to Sydney and two flights weekly to Melbourne.
Malaysia Airlines ☎0870/607 9090, Republic of Ireland ☎01/676 1561 or 676 2131, ⓦwww .mas.com.my. Daily flights from London Heathrow to Kuala Lumpur connecting daily to Sydney and Perth, four times weekly to Melbourne, five times weekly to Brisbane and twice weekly to Darwin and Cairns.
Olympic Airways ☎0870/606 0460, ⓦwww .olympic-airways.co.uk. Twice-daily flights from London Heathrow to Athens with three-times-weekly connecting flights to Sydney and Melbourne.
Qantas ☎0845/774 7767, ⓦwww.qantas.co.uk. Numerous flights daily from London Heathrow to all the mainland Australian state capitals and Cairns, via Singapore or Bangkok.
Royal Brunei Airlines ☎020/7584 6660, ⓦwww.bruneiair.com. London Heathrow to Darwin, Perth and Brisbane via Brunei.
Singapore Airlines ☎0870/608 8886 or 0161/830 8888 in Manchester, Republic of Ireland ☎01/671 0722, ⓦwww.singaporeair.com. Three-times-daily flights from London Heathrow, and once-daily flights from Manchester to Singapore, with connections to Adelaide, Brisbane, Melbourne, Perth and Sydney.
South African Airways ☎020/7312 5000, ⓦwww.flysaa.com. Daily flights to Johannesburg, with connecting flights three times weekly to Perth and Sydney.
Thai Airways ☎0870/606 0911, ⓦwww.thaiair.com. Daily flights to Bangkok from London Heathrow, with connections to Sydney, Melbourne and Perth.
United Airlines ☎0845/844 4777, ⓦwww.ual.com. Daily flights from London Heathrow to Los Angeles or San Francisco with a six-hour wait for connections to Sydney and Melbourne.

Courier flights

International Association of Air Travel Couriers UK ☎0800/074 6481 or 01305/216

920, ⓦwww.aircourier.co.uk. Agent for lots of companies.

Discount travel agents

Austravel ⓦwww.austravel.net. Specialists for flights and tours to Australia. Austravel also lays on audiovisual presentations all over the UK to help you make up your mind, aimed at independent travellers heading round the world via Australia. Issues ETAs and traditional visas for an administration fee of £16.
Bridge the World ☎0870/444 7474, ⓦwww.bridgetheworld.com. Specialists in RTW tickets, many with Australian components, with good deals aimed at the backpacker market.
Flightbookers ☎0870/010 7000, Glasgow ☎0141/204 1919, ⓦwww.ebookers.com. Low fares on an extensive range of scheduled flights.
Flynow.com ☎0870/444 0045, ⓦwww .flynow.com. Large range of discounted tickets.
Lee's Travel ☎020/7262 2665, ⓦwww .leestravel.com. Good deals on Korean Air flights as well as other as other airlines.
North South Travel ☎01245/608 291, ⓦwww.northsouthtravel.co.uk. Friendly, competitive travel agency, offering discounted fares worldwide – profits are used to support projects in the developing world, especially the promotion of sustainable tourism.
Quest Worldwide ☎0870/442 2699 or 020/8547 3322, ⓦwww.questtravel.com. Specialists in RTW and Australian discount fares.
STA Travel ☎0870/1600 599, ⓦwww.statravel.co.uk. Worldwide specialists in low-cost flights and tours for students and under-26s, though other customers welcome. Also has offices in Australia.
Trailfinders ☎020/7628 7628, ⓦwww.trailfinders.com. Excellent for multistop and RTW tickets, including some unusual routings via South Africa, the Pacific and the US. Well-informed and efficient – visa service available at the Kensington High St branch. Also has branches in Brisbane, Cairns, Melbourne, Perth and Sydney.
Travel Bag ☎0870/890 1456, ⓦwww.travelbag.co.uk. Well-established long-haul travel agent with a good reputation for Australian coverage. Direct and RTW flights on all the best airlines including Qantas, British Airways and Singapore, plus packages (see opposite).

Irish agents

Australia Travel Centre ☎01/804 7188. Specialists in long-haul flights.

Thomas Cook Dublin ☏ 01/677 1721, Belfast ☏ 028/9055 0232, ⓦ www.tcholidays.com. Mainstream package-holiday and flight agent, with occasional discount offers.

Trailfinders Dublin ☏ 01/677 7888, ⓦ www.trailfinders.ie. One of the best-informed and most efficient agents for independent travellers; produces a very useful quarterly magazine worth scrutinizing for RTW routes.

Travel Care ☏ 028/9047 1717 ⓦ www.travelcare.ie. Discount flight specialists.

Unijet ☏ 028/9031 4656, ⓦ www.unijet.com. Discount scheduled fares to major Australian cities; the best agent to contact for Malaysia Airlines ticket deals.

Usit Now Dublin ☏ 01/602 1600, ⓦ www .usitnow.ie. Student and youth specialists for flights and trains.

Discount travel websites

ⓦ **www.dialaflight.co.uk** Website useful for tracking down bargains, plus telephone sales for scheduled flights ☏ 0870/333 4488.

ⓦ **www.expedia.co.uk** Microsoft's venture into the Internet travel market, offering special fares and an online booking service.

ⓦ **www.flightline.co.uk** A telephone-based outfit (☏ 0800/036 0777), also offering online searches for cheap scheduled flights.

Package tours and specialist operators

Contiki ☏ 020/8290 6777, ⓦ www.contiki.com. Big-group, countrywide bus and 4WD tours for 18- to 35-year-olds "thriving on good times and loads of fun". All transport (excluding flights to Australia) and most meals covered; plenty of additional excursions (climbing, diving, etc) at extra cost. From £385 for a 7-day Alice and Rock; 25-day Sydney to Darwin via the east coast from £1199.

Explore Worldwide UK ☏ 01252/760 000, ⓦ www.explore.com. Bus and 4WD tours through Western Australia and the Northern Territory, ranging from a 15-day Outback Adventure (£745), to a 28-day East Coast and Territory Australian Explorer for around £1500.

Newmans Holidays ☏ 020/8879 1999, ⓦ www.newmans.com. New Zealand-based company offering self-drive tours of Australia; the smallest two-berth motorhome starts from £26 per day.

P&O ☏ 020/7800 2222, ⓦ www.pocruises.com. Once-yearly cruises to Sydney westbound on the *Aurora* (via Rio de Janeiro) or eastbound on the *Oriana* (via San Francisco). P&O's own price is from

£4568 on the *Aurora*, but you can get a cheaper price from a travel agent.

Qantas Holidays ☏ 0990/673 464, ⓦ www.qantas.com.au/qantasholidays. Quality packages from undoubted Australian experts. Car and campervan rental, accommodation and sightseeing passes, rail holidays, cruises, coach transport, city packages and tours can all be priced in.

Travelbag ☏ 020/7497 0515, ⓦ www.travelbag.co.uk. Everything from flights to car and campervan rental, farmstays and coach and 4WD tours all over the country. A 6-day Tropical North tour based in Port Douglas costs £318 per person twin share with 5 nights' accommodation and a Barrier Reef cruise. Several action and eco-oriented trips including Barrier Reef dive packages. Flights extra.

Travelmarvel ☏ 020/8879 3003, ⓦ www .aptours.com. Offers major bus tours Australia-wide, from 8 days in Tasmania (£795) through to the 24-day Grand Australian Explorer tour (£2985). All prices per person twin share. Accommodation and meals included; flights extra.

Travelmood ☏ 0870/500 1002, ⓦ www.travelmood.com. Flights, quality accommodation, car and campervan rental, tailor-made itineraries, bus passes, tickets and package tours.

Wildlife Worldwide ☏ 020/8667 9158, ⓦ www.wildlifeworldwide.co.uk. Tailor-made trips for wildlife and wilderness enthusiasts: includes a 7-day Jabiru Safari ex-Darwin for £1195, a 5-day Kimberley Wildlife ex-Broome from £750, and a 14-day London-to-London Wilderness Queensland trip for £2095.

World Expeditions ☏ 0800/074 4135, ⓦ www.worldexpeditions.co.uk. Australian-owned adventure company; small-group active wilderness holidays; cycling, canoeing, rafting, 4WD excursions, walking and camping. All expeditions are graded according to difficulty.

Getting there from the US and Canada

From Los Angeles it's possible to fly non-stop to Sydney in fourteen and a half hours. Qantas, United, Air Canada and Air New Zealand all operate direct to the east coast of Australia. Flying on an Asian airline will most likely involve a stop in their capital city (Singapore, Tokyo, Hong Kong, etc) and if you're travelling from the west coast of North America to the east coast of Australia you'll probably find their fares on the Pacific route somewhat higher than their American or

Australian competitors. However, if you're travelling from the east coast of North America with Perth, say, as your destination, a carrier such as Singapore Airlines or Malaysia Airlines with a transatlantic routing may offer the best value. Flights leave the west coast of the US in the evening, and there are good connections from most North American cities.

Many of the major airlines offer deals whereby you can make **stopovers** either at Pacific Rim destinations such as Tokyo, Honolulu or Kuala Lumpur or at a number of exotic South Pacific locations. Either there will be a flat surcharge on your ticket or they may offer you a higher-priced ticket allowing you to make as many stops as you like, within certain parameters, over a fixed period of time.

But the best deal, if you don't mind planning your itinerary in advance, will most likely be a **Circle Pacific** or a **Round-the-World** (RTW) ticket from a discount outfit (see p.17).

Fares

Sample lowest standard **scheduled fares** for low/high seasons are approximately as follows: **to Sydney or Melbourne** from Chicago or New York (US$1200/1900); Los Angeles or San Francisco (US$900/1500); Montréal or Toronto (CDN$1900/2500); Vancouver (CDN$1800/2000); **to Perth** from New York, Los Angeles or San Francisco (US$1250/1800); Vancouver, Toronto or Montréal (CDN$2500/4000). The price of an **open-jaw ticket** (flying into one city and returning from another) should be approximately the average of the return fares to the two cities. If your destination is on the west coast you might also want to check out Qantas' "Boomerang Pass" which offers coast-to-coast return flights in Australia starting at around US$300 (US$150 one-way); see "Getting Around", p.34, for more on these and other **internal air passes**.

Round-the-World (RTW) and **Circle Pacific** tickets can be very good value. A sample **RTW** itinerary would be: Los Angeles–Sydney–Bangkok–Delhi–Mumbai (Bombay)–London–Los Angeles (US$2500);

or New York–Tokyo–Hong Kong–Bangkok –Singapore–Jakarta–Yogyakarta–Denpasar (Bali)–Darwin, overland through Australia, Sydney–Kuala Lumpur–Amsterdam–New York (US$2700). Sample **Circle Pacific** routes are: Los Angeles–Tokyo–Kuala Lumpur–Singapore–Perth–Sydney–Los Angeles (US$1900); and New York–Hong Kong–Bangkok–Bandar Seri Begawan (Brunei)–Perth, overland through Australia, Sydney–Kuala Lumpur–Tokyo–Los Angeles/ New York (US$2100).

Charter flights to Australia, a more recent arrival on the scene, are offered by companies such as Jetset (who will only take bookings through a travel agent). Fares may slightly undercut those on scheduled flights, but this is offset by more restrictions to contend with, so check conditions carefully.

Airlines

Air Canada ☎1-888/247-2262, ⊛www.aircanada.ca. Daily flights to Sydney and Melbourne from Vancouver and Toronto via Honolulu; and from Montréal, via Toronto and Honolulu, or Chicago and Los Angeles.

Air New Zealand US ☎1-800/262-1234, Canada ☎1-800/663-5494, ⊛www.airnz.com. Daily non-stop flights from Los Angeles to Sydney plus sporadic service from Vancouver.

Cathay Pacific ☎1-800/233-2742, ⊛www.cathay-usa.com. Daily flights to Sydney via Hong Kong from New York, Los Angeles, San Francisco, Vancouver and Toronto.

Malaysia Airlines ☎1-800/552-9264, ⊛www.mas.com.my. Pacific and Atlantic route daily flights from Los Angeles and New York to Sydney or Perth, all via Kuala Lumpur.

Qantas Airways ☎1-800/227-4500, ⊛www.qantas.com. Two non-stop flights daily from Los Angeles to Sydney, and one daily to Melbourne, with connections available from other major cities. Special fares and Boomerang Passes available for travel within Australia – check Web fares too.

Singapore Airlines ☎1-800/742-3333, ⊛www.singaporeair.com. Daily flights via Singapore to Sydney and Perth from Los Angeles, San Francisco (both Pacific routes) and New York (via the Atlantic).

United Airlines international ☎1-800/538-2929, ⊛www.ual.com. Daily non-stop flights to Sydney from Los Angeles and San Francisco, with connections from many other cities.

Discount flight agents, travel clubs, courier brokers and consolidators

Air Brokers International ☎1-800/883-3273, 🖳www.airbrokers.com. Consolidator and specialist in Round-the-World and Circle Pacific tickets.

Air Courier Association ☎1-800/282-1202, 🖳www.aircourier.org or www.cheaptrips.com. Courier flight broker. Membership (1yr/$29, 3yr/$58, 5yr/$87) also entitles you to twenty percent discount on travel insurance and name-your-own-price non-courier flights.

Airtech ☎212/219-7000, 🖳www.airtech.com. Standby seat broker; also deals in consolidator fares and courier flights.

Airtreks.com ☎1-877-AIRTREKS or 415/912-5600, 🖳www.airtreks.com. Round-the-World and Circle Pacific tickets. The website features an interactive database that lets you build and price your own round-the-world itinerary.

Council Travel ☎1-800/2COUNCIL, 🖳www.counciltravel.com. Nationwide organization that mostly specializes in student/budget travel. Flights from the US only. Owned by STA Travel.

Educational Travel Center ☎1-800/747-5551 or 608/256-5551, 🖳www.edtrav.com. Student/youth discount agent.

International Association of Air Travel Couriers ☎308/632-3273, 🖳www.courier.org. Courier flight broker with membership fee of $45/yr.

Skylink US ☎1-800/247-6659 or 212/573-8980, Canada ☎1-800/759-5465, 🖳www.skylinkus.com. Consolidator.

STA Travel ☎1-800/781-4040, 🖳www.sta-travel.com. Worldwide specialists in independent travel; also student IDs, travel insurance, car rental, rail passes, etc.

TFI Tours ☎1-800/745-8000 or 212/736-1140, 🖳www.lowestairprice.com. Consolidator.

Travac ☎1-800/TRAV-800, 🖳www.thetravelsite.com. Consolidator and charter broker with offices in New York City and Orlando.

Travel Avenue ☎1-800/333-3335, 🖳www.travelavenue.com. Full-service travel agent that offers discounts in the form of rebates.

Travel Cuts Canada ☎1-800/667-2887, US ☎1-866/246-9762, 🖳www.travelcuts.com. Canadian student-travel organization.

Travelers Advantage ☎1-877/259-2691, 🖳www.travelersadvantage.com. Discount travel club; annual membership fee required (currently $1 for 3 months' trial).

Worldtek Travel ☎1-800/243-1723, 🖳www.worldtek.com. Discount travel agency for worldwide travel.

Package tours

Organized tours of Australia are usually tailored for those short on time and long on funds; that said, even independent travellers may want to build their stay around one or two planned activities arranged through a tour company. Several of the operators listed offer so-called **city stopovers/city modules**, providing, for instance, two nights' accommodation, and perhaps a day-tour, costing from US$180 to US$450 depending on the location and time of year. Though **fly-drive deals** don't always make sense in sprawling Australia, they're worth considering if you plan to explore just one part of the country closely. Typical prices for the smallest class of car work out at about US$75 a day. And even if a package tour is the furthest thing from your mind, before you leave home you may want to check out tour or specialist operators for **rail or bus passes** (see p.34 for some of the options).

Tour operators

AAT King's ☎1-800/353-4525, 🖳www.aatkings.com. Offers a wide selection of escorted and independent tours, the best of which are 4WD Wilderness Safari tours and camping adventures.

Abercrombie and Kent ☎1-800/323-7308, 🖳www.abercrombiekent.com. Offers 8- to 21-day high-end tours, ranging from basic tours (including Sydney, Melbourne and the Great Barrier Reef) to more extensive ones (including Tasmania and the Outback). Also specializes in family tours and customized itineraries. Extensions available to Papua New Guinea, New Zealand and Fiji.

Adventure Center ☎1-800/227-8747 or 510/654-1879, 🖳www.adventure-center.com. Customized tour service, offering excursions lasting 3 to 28 days. Tours include 4WD safaris, nature and wildlife tours, Aboriginal culture tours, 18-to-35 group tours, car rentals, camel safaris and rainforest lodges.

Adventures Abroad ☎1-800/665-3998 or 360/775-9926, 🖳www.adventures-abroad.com. Small-group cultural/historical/nature interest tours. A choice of multi-country South Pacific and Australia specific tours. Two weeks in Australia from US$3500 (land only).

Asia Transpacific Journeys ☎1-800/642-2742, 🖳www.southeastasia.com. Wide range of customized itineraries and group tours including nature, adventure and Aboriginal rock art.

ATS Tours ☎1-800/423-2880, ⓦwww
.atstours.com. Huge Australian and New Zealand
specialist; dive deals, fly-drives, city stopovers,
rail/bus passes, motel vouchers and other add-ons.

Australian Pacific Tours ☎1-800/290-8687 or
416/234-9676, ⓦwww.aptours.com. General
interest escorted tours along with cruising and safari
packages; specializes in coach tours
(US$1500–4000 land only) and fully independent
travel.

Contiki Tours ☎1-888/CONTIKI,
ⓦwww.contiki.com. 18- to 35-year-olds-only tour
operator. Their 14-day beaches and reefs tour starts
at $1500 (land only).

Cross-Culture ☎1-800/491-1148 or 413/256-
6303, ⓦwww.crosscultureinc.com. Well-balanced
all-inclusive group tours; a 15-day tour, including
flights from Los Angeles, starts at $5500.

Destination World ☎1-888/345-4669, ⓦwww
.destinationworld.com. Offers a wide variety of
tours, from budget to expensive. Off-the-beaten-
track tours include a pub-crawl on horseback and
motorcycle tours. Also offers a wheelchair-accessible
bus for disabled groups and motorhome rentals.

Goway Travel ☎1-800/387-8850, ⓦwww
.goway.com. Airfare deals, independent land
bookings, fully escorted tours, over-50s vacations,
bus tours, hostel passes, camping safaris, cruises,
rail, fly-drives and group arrangements.

**International Gay and Lesbian Travel
Association** ☎1-800/448-8550, ⓦwww
.iglta.org. Trade group with lists of gay-owned or
gay-friendly travel agents, accommodation and other
travel businesses.

Maupintour ☎1-800/255-4266, ⓦwww
.maupintour.com. Variety of South Pacific tours,
including 15 or 24 days in Australia (US$2900–4700
land only).

Nature Expeditions International
☎1-800/869-0639, ⓦwww.naturexp.com. 15-
day educational/nature-focused tour including
Sydney, Uluru, Great Ocean Road, Blue Mountains
National Park, Alice Springs and the Great Barrier
Reef, led by professional guides (US$3600 land
only).

Qantas Vacations US ☎1-800/252-4162,
Canada ☎1-800/268-7525,
ⓦwww.qantasvacations.com. Offers a variety of
special travel deals to cities (Sydney/Melbourne), the
Great Barrier Reef and the Outback, plus Fiji or New
Zealand extensions.

REI Adventures ☎1-800/622-2236,
ⓦwww.rei.com/travel. Adventure tours. Their 15-
day reef and rainforest trip includes diving,
whitewater rafting, hiking and mountain biking
starting at $2500 (land only).

Swain Australia Tours ☎1-800/227-9246 or
610/896-9595, ⓦwww.swainaustralia.com.
Customized tours to meet individual travel needs and
budgets, including tours specifically designed for
families.

Tauck World Discovery ☎1-800/788-7885,
ⓦwww.tauck.com. Upmarket guided group tours of
two to three weeks, with optional extensions to Fiji.

United Vacations ☎1-800/917-9246,
ⓦwww.unitedvacations.com. Varied assortment of
individual tours, city-break packages, and multi-city
excursions.

Wilderness Travel ☎1-800/368-2794 or
510/558-2488, ⓦwww.wildernesstravel.com.
High-end specialists in hiking and wildlife
adventures; a ten-day tour of Tasmania, including a
yacht cruise and luxury inns, starts at $3400 (land
only).

Getting there from New Zealand

New Zealand–Australia routes are busy and
competition is fierce, resulting in an ever-
changing range of deals and special offers;
your best bet is to check the latest with a
specialist travel agent (see p.19) or the relevant airlines' websites (see p.19). It's a relatively short hop across the Tasman Sea: flying time from Auckland to Sydney is around
three and a half hours.

All the **fares** quoted below are for travel
during low or shoulder seasons; flying at
peak times (primarily Dec to mid-Jan) can
add substantially to these prices. Ultimately,
the price you pay for your flight will depend
on how much flexibility you want; many of
the cheapest deals are hedged with restrictions – typically a maximum stay of thirty
days and a fourteen-day advance-purchase
requirement. The New Zealand, web-based
Freedom Air specializes in no-frills, low-cost
trans-Tasman air travel, with flights from Auck
land, Christchurch, Dunedin, Palm-erston
North and Wellington to Brisbane plus
Melbourne, Sydney or Gold Coast flights
from some destinations; there are few restrictions in how long tickets stay open and
advance purchase has little effect on ticket
prices, which are around $590 return. Only
Qantas, Air New Zealand, Freedom Air and
Aerolineas Argentineas offer tickets that stay
open for one year, while Polynesian and
Malaysia Airlines offer tickets open for up to
six months; there are also ninety-day

tickets that fall between the two extremes in price. The cheapest thirty-day return fare from Auckland to Sydney is usually with Aerolineas Argentineas or Polynesian Airlines (also to Melbourne) for $475–550 but flights tend to be heavily booked. Polynesian's six-month ticket is the cheapest long-stay ticket at $985. Qantas and Air New Zealand each have similarly priced daily direct flights to Brisbane, Melbourne and Sydney ($699–799), Cairns ($899) and Perth ($1119), and Malaysia Airlines regularly to Brisbane ($720). Whether you fly from Wellington or Christchurch generally makes no difference to the fare. Outside peak season, when the airlines often have surplus capacity, they may offer promotional fares, which can bring prices down to as low as $535 for a thirty-day return from Auckland to Brisbane.

Open-jaw tickets – which let you fly into one city and out of another, making your own way between – can save a lot of backtracking and don't add hugely to the total fare. For example, flying into Cairns and out of Sydney, or vice versa, with Qantas or Air New Zealand, costs from $850. There are also various internal flight deals available to buy with your main ticket (see "Getting Around", p.34, for details).

If you're taking in Australia at the beginning (or end) of your grand tour, you can usually add one or two Australian stops at negligible extra cost, since many airlines go via Australian gateway airports anyway.

Airlines

Aerolineas Argentinas ☎09/379 3675,
Ⓦwww.aerolineas.com.au
Air New Zealand ☎0800/737 000,
Ⓦwww.airnz.co.nz
Freedom Air ☎0800 600 500,
Ⓦwww.freedom.co.nz
Malaysia Airlines ☎09/373 2741,
Ⓦwww.mas.com.my
Polynesian Airlines ☎09/309 5396,
Ⓦwww.polynesianairlines.co.nz
Qantas ☎09/661 901, Ⓦwww.qantas.com.au
Thai Airways ☎09/377 3886,
Ⓦwww.thaiair.com

Specialist travel agents

Flight Centres 350 Queen St, Auckland ☎09/358 4310, Ⓦwww.flightcentre.co.nz, plus branches

nationwide. Competitive discounts on airfares and a wide range of package holidays and adventure tours.
Holiday Shoppe 27–35 Victoria St West, Auckland, plus 79 other branches around the country ☎09/379 2099,
Ⓦwww.holidayshoppe.co.nz. Long-established Budget Travel has now merged with Holiday Shoppe to form one of New Zealand's largest travel agencies. Still good for budget airfares and accommodation packages flies.
STA Travel Shop 2b, 187 High St, Auckland ☎09/309 0458, fastfare telesales ☎09/366 6673, ☎0508/782 872, Ⓦwww.statravel.co.nz, plus branches nationwide. Fare discounts for students and those under 26, as well as visas, student cards and travel insurance.
Student Union Travel 5 Victoria St East, Auckland plus branches in Hamilton and Christchurch ☎09/379 4224 or 0508/639 932, Ⓦwww.sut.com. Student/youth travel specialists.

Packages and tours

There's a huge variety of holidays and tours to Australia available in New Zealand; call any of the travel agents listed above. The holiday subsidiaries of airlines such as Air New Zealand and Qantas package short **city-breaks** (flight and accommodation) and **fly-drive deals** for little more than the cost of the regular airfare. On the other hand, if romping around the Outback is a high priority, check out any available **adventure tours** as they can be a good way of covering a lot of ground in a short time and getting you to remote places that would otherwise be inaccessible without your own transport. Itineraries range from 14 to 39 days and concentrate on exploring remoter regions, as well as classic rainforest-and-reef trips; prices (not including airfare from New Zealand) start at $1650 and go up to $4650 for extended journeys. A more economical option is offered by backpacker-oriented companies based in Australia, such as Oz Experience and Wayward Bus (see "Getting Around", pp.35–37), whose tours can be booked through STA offices in New Zealand if you want to plan ahead.

Getting there from Southeast Asia

A satisfying way of reaching Australia and really getting some impression of the distance you've come is to travel overland through Southeast Asia, or at least have a stopover en route. This is a very popular route for travellers en route to Australia from Europe, or vice versa, especially Australian backpackers heading in the other direction at the start of their trip. Southeast Asia isn't as straightforward or relaxing as Australia (and you'll need to take appropriate health precautions), but it's a fascinating region and is unlikely to make a big dent in your budget. It also shouldn't make too much of a difference to the price of your plane ticket, since many airlines stop in Bangkok, Singapore, Jakarta, Denpasar or Kuala Lumpur on the way to Australia, and breaking your journey is either free or possible for a small extra charge. If you want to go overland on the route detailed below between Bangkok and Bali, rather than just stop over, you could buy a Round-the-World ticket with an overland component. If you do buy a one-way ticket from Bali, you will still need to be in possession of a return ticket out of Australia to get through immigration, probably best routed via Bangkok.

Bangkok is a popular starting point for an overland route, with return flights available from around £400 in the UK and US$900 in the US. From Bangkok an inexpensive bus service leaves twice daily for the 2000-kilometre ride to **Singapore**, though it's a gruelling 48-hour trip unless you make a stop or two along the way; a more comfortable option is the International Express train from Bangkok to Pedan Besar on the

Thai–Malaysia border (1 daily; 23hr) and then the KMBT train from Butterworth in Penang to Singapore via Kuala Lumpur (4 daily; 6hr); you will usually need to stay overnight in Penang to connect with the KMBT train but at least a few days is recommended. Book both journeys a day or two in advance to be sure of a seat; the combined price for first class is UK£31/US$52, but considerably cheaper second- and third-class fares are available. Of course, you could instead go in luxury on the Eastern and Oriental Express, modelled on the original Orient Express; the 41-hour journey via Kuala Lumpur costs from US$1490 per person.

From Singapore, you can cross to the **Indonesian islands** of Sumatra or Kalimantan (Indonesian Borneo) and from there island-hop via local buses and ferries southeast through to Java and Bali, from where you can take a short flight to Darwin in Australia's Northern Territory. From Denpasar (Bali), Qantas flies to Darwin once weekly and Garuda has twice-weekly flights; one-way tickets cost US$235. Garuda also flies from Denpasar several times a week to Adelaide, Brisbane and Sydney and daily to Melbourne and Perth, while Qantas flies daily to Sydney and Brisbane from Denpasar and Jakarta.

Allow at least a month from Bangkok to Bali, but be aware that there is still political and social unrest right through Indonesia, including Bali, and travel through some of these regions may not be wise or even possible.

Red tape and visas

All visitors to Australia, except New Zealanders, require a visa or Electronic Travel Authority (ETA) to enter the country; if you're heading overland, you'll obviously need to check visa requirements for the countries en route.

You can get **visa application forms** from the Australian high commissions, embassies or consulates listed overleaf. Citizens of the US can get visa application forms from the Washington, Los Angeles and Ottawa offices and from the embassy Internet sites.

Nationals of the UK, Ireland, the US, Canada, Malaysia, Singapore, Japan and most European countries who intend to stay for **less than three months**, can get an **ETA** (Electronic Travel Authority), valid for multiple entry over one year. Applied for online, it replaces the visa stamp in your passport (ETAs are computerized) and saves the hassle of queuing or sending off your passport. ETAs can be applied for on the Web with a credit card for A$20 (see the Australian government websites below or go directly to ⓦ www.eta.immi.gov.au) or are available from travel agents and airlines at the same time as you book your flight. In this case an additional fee is levied on top of the cost of your ETA – in the UK around £16.

Citizens of other countries or visitors who intend to stay for longer than three months should apply for a **visitor visa**, valid for **three to six months**. You'll need to complete an application form and lodge it either in person or by post with the embassy or consulate. It costs A$65 (or the equivalent in your country) and takes up to three weeks to process. If you think you might stay more than three months, it's best to get the longer visa before departure, because once you get to Australia extensions cost A$160. Once issued, a visa usually allows multiple entries, so long as your passport is valid.

An important condition for all holiday-visa applications is that you have **adequate funds** both to support yourself during your stay – at least A$1000 a month – and eventually to get yourself home again. If you're visiting immediate family who live in Australia – parent, spouse, child, brother or sister – you can apply for a **Sponsored Family Visitor Visa** (A$65), which has fewer restrictions.

Twelve-month **working holiday visas** are easily available to British, Irish, Canadian, Dutch, German, Japanese and Korean single people aged 18–30, though exceptions are made for young married couples without children. Unless you see your future in planting sugar cane, it is not a chance to further your career, since the stress is on casual employment: you are meant to work for no more than three months at any one job. You must arrange the visa before you arrive in Australia, and several months in advance. Working visas cost A$160; some travel agents such as Trailfinders in the UK (see p.15) can arrange them for you. See p.67 for more on working in Australia.

Note that having a visa is not an absolute guarantee that you'll be allowed into Australia – immigration officials may well check again that you have enough money to cover you during your stay, and that you have a return or onward ticket. In extreme cases they may refuse entry, or more likely restrict your visit to a shorter period.

Australia has strict **quarantine** laws that apply to fruit, vegetables, fresh and packaged food, seed and some animal products, among other things; there are also strict laws prohibiting drugs, steroids, firearms, protected wildlife and associated products. Those over 18 can take advantage of a **duty-free allowance** on entry of 1 litre of alcohol and 250 cigarettes or 250g of tobacco.

Australian embassies and consulates abroad

UK
London Australian High Commission, Australia

House, Strand, London WC2B 4LA ☎ 020/7379 4334, ⓦ www.australia.org.uk
Manchester Honorary Consulate, First Floor, Century House, 11 St Peter's Square, Manchester M2 3DN ☎ 0161/273 9440, ⓕ 237 9135
Edinburgh Honorary Consulate, Melrose House, 69 George St, Edinburgh EH2 2JG ☎ 0131/624 3333, ⓕ 624 3701

Ireland

Dublin Australian Embassy, Fitzwilton House, Wilton Terrace, Dublin 2 ☎ 01/676 1517 or 662 3566, ⓦ www.australianembassy.ie

US

Atlanta Australian Consulate-General, 1 Buckhead Plaza, Suite 970, 3060 Peachtree Rd NW, Atlanta, GA 30305 ☎ 404/760-3400, ⓕ 760-3401
Chicago Australian Consulate-General, 123 North Wacker Drive, Suite 1330, Chicago IL 60606 ☎ 312/419-1480, ⓕ 212/419-1499
Honolulu Australian Consulate-General, 1000 Bishop St, Honolulu, HI 96813 ☎ 808/524-5050, ⓕ 531-5142
Los Angeles Australian Consulate-General, Century Plaza Towers, 19th Floor, 2049 Century Park E, Los Angeles, CA 90067 ☎ 310/229-4800, ⓕ 277-2258
New York Australian Consulate-General, 34th Floor, 150 E 42nd St, New York, NY 10017-5612 ☎ 212/351-6500, ⓕ 351-6501
San Francisco Australian Consulate-General, 625 Market St, Suite 200, San Francisco, CA 94105-3304 ☎ 415/536-1970, ⓕ 536 1982
Washington Australian Embassy, 1601 Massachusetts Ave NW, Washington, DC 20036 ☎ 202/797-3000, ⓕ 797-3331, ⓦ www.austemb.org

Canada

Ottawa Australian High Commission, Suite 710, 50 O'Connor St, Ottawa, ON K1P 6L2 ☎ 613/236-0841, ⓦ www.ahc-ottawa.org
Toronto Australian Consulate-General, Suite 316,

175 Bloor St E, Toronto, ON M4W 3R8 ☎ 416/323-1155, ⓕ 323-3910
Vancouver Australian Consulate, Suite 1225, 888 Dunsmuir St, Vancouver, BC V6C 3K4 ☎ 604/684-1177, ⓕ 684-1856

Netherlands

The Hague Australian Embassy, Carnegielaan 4, The Hague 2517 KH ☎ 0700/310 8200, ⓕ 365 2350, ⓦ www.australian-embassy.nl

New Zealand

Auckland Australian Consulate-General, 8th Floor, Union House, 132–138 Quay St, Auckland 1 ☎ 09/303 2429, ⓕ 377 0798
Wellington Australian High Commission, 72–78 Hobson St, Thorndon, Wellington ☎ 04/473 6411, ⓕ 498 7135, ⓦ www.australia.org.nz

Indonesia

Bali Australian Consulate, Jalan Prof Moh Yamin 4, Renon, Denpasar, Bali ☎ 0361/235 092-3, ⓕ 235 1990
Jakarta Australian Embassy, Jalan HR Rasuna Said Kav C15–16, Kuningan, Jakarta Selatan 12940 ☎ 021/2550 5555, ⓕ 522 7101, ⓦ www.dfat.gov.au/bali

Malaysia

Kuala Lumpur Australian High Commission, 6 Jalan Yap Kwan Seng, Kuala Lumpur 50450 ☎ 2146 5555, ⓕ 2141 4323, ⓦ www .malaysia.embassy.gov.au.

Singapore

Singapore Australian High Commission, 25 Napier Rd, Singapore 258507 ☎ 065/6836 4100, ⓕ 6737 5481, ⓦ www.singapore .embassy.gov.au

Thailand

Bangkok Australian Embassy, 37 South Sathorn Rd, Bangkok 10120 ☎ 02/287 2680, ⓕ 287 2029, ⓦ www.austembassy.or.th.

Information, websites and maps

Australian tourism abroad is represented by the Australian Tourist Commission, who produce *Australia, A Traveller's Guide,* an annual glossy publication which details the country region by region, offers travel tips and ways of getting around and has a useful directory of addresses. You can also get information at the Tourist Commission's website ⓦ www.australia.com.

More detailed information is available by the sackful once you're in the country. Each state or territory has its own **tourist authority**, which operates information offices throughout its own area and in major cities in other parts of Australia – some are even represented abroad (those with London offices are detailed below). A level below this are a host of regional and community-run **visitors centres** and **information kiosks**. Even the smallest Outback town seems to have one – or at the very least a pamphlet rack at the local service station – while larger places will often have two or more rival offices. Remember though, most of these associations only promote subscribing or advertising members – the information they supply is not comprehensive or impartial, as anyone in the tourist business is likely to be involved with a tourism association.

It's also worthwhile asking **fellow travellers** about places they've been to. **Hostels** tend to act as information points, with **notice boards** where you'll find local bus schedules, offers of cheap excursions or ride shares and comments and advice from people who've already passed this way.

Another thing that has cropped up in recent years are **travellers centres**, countrywide networks with branches in tourist hotspots. The most widespread of these organizations are Backpackers World Travel ⓦ www.backpackers-world.com.au; Backpackers Travel Centre ⓦ www.backpackerstravel.net.au; World Wide Workers ⓦ www.worldwideworkers.com; and Travellers Contact Point ⓦ www.travellers.com.au; all have branches in New South Wales, Victoria and Queensland. Once you've signed up with them, they can help find work and prebook travel and accommodation as you move

around; you also get discounted phone and Internet rates, cheap drinks at selected pubs, and use of mail services and notice boards. At around \$40 a year, this sounds like a bargain, and they can certainly help streamline a trip, but you'd be wise not to book everything in advance and lose your flexibility – you won't be able to get refunds if you change your plans.

Australian Tourist Commission offices

UK Gemini House, 10–18 Putney Hill, Putney, London SW15 6AA ("Aussie Helpline" charged at 50p a minute: ☏ 0990/022 000, ⓦ www.tourism.gov.au).
US Visitors should contact the "Aussie Helpline" for tour information (☏ 805/775-2000), or check out the tourist commission's website, ⓦ www.australia.com.
New Zealand Level 13, 44–48 Emily Place, Auckland 1 ☏ 09/379 9594.

Australia online

General

ⓦ **www.ozemail.com.au/atie/index.html** The Australian Travel Information Exchange gives an easy-to-read overview of key destinations, resorts, tour operators and transport services.
ⓦ **www.infoaustralia.com.au** This answers your questions, has history and photo gallery pages, and links to travel, recreation, government, weather and radio.
ⓦ **www.australianexplorer.com** Comprehensive travel information website.
ⓦ **www.travel.com.au** Book flights, get the basics on destinations and read all about others' experiences.
ⓦ **www.oztravel.com.au** Online database of hotels, tours, car rental and other travel services.

⊛ www.walkabout.fairfax.com.au Better-than-average directory including travellers' tales, links and not too much commerce.

⊛ www.ozramp.net.au/~senani/mainpage.htm Colourful site that's good for kids.

Newspapers

Try these sites for online versions of today's news – in fact, tomorrow's news if you're in Western Australia.

⊛ www.theage.com.au *The Age*
⊛ www.smh.com.au *Sydney Morning Herald*
⊛ www.news.com.au *The Australian*

Weather

Two sites for nationwide views of this time-less topic.

⊛ www.abc.net.au/news/australia/weather
⊛ www.bom.gov.au/weather

Gay and lesbian

All the info for a carefree holiday.

⊛ www.galta.com.au Gay and Lesbian Tourism Association
⊛ www.gaytravel.com Gay Travel

Maps

If you want to obtain maps before you go, the Rough Guide **map of Australia** (1:4500000) is handily printed on rip- and waterproof papers. Also finely produced are the GeoCenter (including NZ) and Nelles maps, both 1:4,000,000, with good topographical detail. The Bartholomew and the new Globetrotter (both 1:5,000,000) are the best of the rest. Any of the specialist map shops listed opposite should have all of these, together with a reasonable selection of more detailed local maps.

In Australia UBD, Gregory's, HEMA and AusMap produce national, state, regional and city maps of varying sizes and quality: the first three are the most widely available. HEMA (⊛ www.hemamaps.com) produces no less than 82 regional and themed maps and atlases covering the entire country many times over. Cities, states, national parks, fishing, 4WD and wine are some of the many themes covered. BP and the state motoring organizations have regularly updated **touring guides** to Australia, with regional maps, listings and details of things to see and do –

something for the back shelf of the car rather than a backpack.

If you're a member of a **motoring organization** or automobile association, there's a chance you'll have reciprocal rights with the Australian equivalent and be entitled to **free maps** and other discounted services. Each state has its own organization (they're listed in the Australian Tourist Commission's guide) and most are excellent – you'll need to bring proof of membership along to take advantage.

The whole country is now covered by 1:50,000 topographical sheets, suitable for hiking or travel in remote areas. You can get them at government mapping agency offices or official government bookshops (in major cities) or take a look at them at a library in the nearest major town; they're also available by mail from the **National Mapping Agency**, PO Box 31, Belconnen, ACT 2616.

Specialist book and map suppliers

UK and Ireland

Blackwell's Map and Travel Shop 50 Broad St, Oxford OX1 3BQ ☎ 01865/793 550, ⊛ maps.blackwell.co.uk

Easons Bookshop 40 O'Connell St, Dublin 1 ☎ 01/858 3881, ⊛ www.eason.ie

Heffers Map and Travel 20 Trinity St, Cambridge CB2 1TJ ☎ 01865/333 536, ⊛ www.heffers.co.uk

Hodges Figgis Bookshop 56–58 Dawson St, Dublin 2 ☎ 01/677 4754, ⊛ www.hodgesfiggis.com

The Map Shop 30A Belvoir St, Leicester LE1 6QH ☎ 0116/247 1400, ⊛ www.mapshopleicester.co.uk

National Map Centre 22–24 Caxton St, London SW1H 0QU ☎ 020/7222 2466, ⊛ www.mapsnmc.co.uk

Newcastle Map Centre 55 Grey St, Newcastle-upon-Tyne, NE1 6EF ☎ 0191/261 5622

Ordnance Survey Ireland Phoenix Park, Dublin 8 ☎ 01/802 5300, ⊛ www.osi.ie

Ordnance Survey of Northern Ireland Colby House, Stranmillis Ct, Belfast BT9 5BJ ☎ 028/9025 5755, ⊛ www.osni.gov.uk.

Stanfords 12–14 Long Acre, WC2E 9LP ☎ 020/7836 1321, ⊛ www.stanfords.co.uk

The Travel Bookshop 13–15 Blenheim Crescent, W11 2EE ☎ 020/7229 5260, ⊛ www.thetravelbookshop.co.uk

US and Canada

Adventurous Traveler.com US ☎ 1-800/282-3963, ⒲ adventuroustraveler.com
Book Passage 51 Tamal Vista Blvd, Corte Madera, CA 94925 ☎ 1-800/999-7909, ⒲ www.bookpassage.com
Distant Lands 56 S Raymond Ave, Pasadena, CA 91105 ☎ 1-800/310-3220, ⒲ www.distantlands.com
Elliot Bay Book Company 101 S Main St, Seattle, WA 98104 ☎ 1-800/962-5311, ⒲ www.elliotbaybook.com
Globe Corner Bookstore 28 Church St, Cambridge, MA 02138 ☎ 1-800/358-6013, ⒲ www.globercorner.com
Map Link 30 S La Patera Lane, Unit 5, Santa Barbara, CA 93117 ☎ 1-800/962-1394, ⒲ www.maplink.com
Rand McNally US ☎ 1-800/333-0136, ⒲ www.randmcnally.com. Around thirty stores across the US; dial ext 2111 or check the website for the nearest location.
The Travel Bug Bookstore 2667 W Broadway, Vancouver V6K 2G2 ☎ 604/737-1122, ⒲ www.swifty.com/tbug
World of Maps 1235 Wellington St, Ottawa, Ontario K1Y 3A3 ☎ 1-800/214-8524, ⒲ www.worldofmaps.com

New Zealand

Specialty Maps 58 Albert St, Auckland ☎ 09/307 2217

Insurance

If you're entitled to free emergency healthcare from Medicare (see p.26 for details of reciprocal arrangements), you may feel that the need for the health element of travel insurance is reduced, but check carefully what is included (ambulance trips, among other things, will not be reimbursed). In any case, some form of travel insurance can help plug the gaps and will cover you in the event of losing your baggage, missing a plane and the like.

A typical travel insurance policy usually provides cover for the loss of baggage, tickets and – up to a certain limit – cash or cheques, as well as cancellation or curtailment of your journey. Most of them exclude **"high-risk" activities** unless an extra premium is paid: depending on the insurer, these can include water sports (especially diving), skiing or even just hiking; check carefully that any policy you are considering will cover you in case of an accident. Many policies can be chopped and changed to exclude coverage you don't need – for example, sickness and accident benefits can often be excluded or included at will. If you do take medical coverage, ascertain whether benefits will be paid as treatment proceeds or only after return home, and whether there is a 24-hour medical emergency number. When securing baggage cover, make sure that the per-article limit – typically under £500 – will cover your most valuable possession. If you need to make a claim, you should keep receipts for medicines and medical treatment, and in the event you have anything stolen, you must obtain an official statement from the police.

Before spending out on a new policy it's worth checking whether you are already covered: some all-risks home insurance policies, for example, may cover your possessions against loss or theft when overseas, and many private medical schemes such as BUPA or PPP include cover when abroad, including baggage loss, cancellation or curtailment and cash replacement as well as sickness or accident. Bank and credit cards often have certain levels of medical or other insurance included and you may automatically get travel insurance if you use a major credit card to pay for your trip (check the small print on this, though, as it may not be of much use).

In Canada, provincial health plans usually provide partial cover for medical mishaps overseas, while holders of official student/teacher/youth cards in Canada and the US are entitled to meagre accident coverage and hospital inpatient benefits. Students will often find that their student health coverage extends during the vacations and for one term beyond the date of last enrolment.

Rough Guides travel insurance

Rough Guide offers its own low-cost travel insurance, especially customized for our statistically low-risk readers by a leading British broker, provided by the American International Group (AIG) and registered with the British regulatory body, GISC (the General Insurance Standards Council).

There are five main Rough Guides insurance plans: **No Frills** for the bare minimum for secure travel; **Essential**, which provides decent all-round cover; **Premier** for comprehensive cover with a wide range of benefits; Extended Stay for cover lasting two months to a year; and **Annual multi-trip**, a cost-effective way of getting Premier cover if you travel more than once a year. Premier, Annual Multi-Trip and Extended Stay policies can be supplemented by a **"Hazardous Pursuits Extension"** if you plan to indulge in sports considered dangerous, such as scuba-diving or trekking.

For a **policy quote**, call the Rough Guide Insurance Line: toll-free in the UK ℡0800/015 09 06 or ℡+44 1392 314 665 from elsewhere. Alternatively, get an online quote at www.roughguides.com/insurance

Health

Australia has high standards of hygiene, and there are few exceptional health hazards – at least in terms of disease. No vaccination certificates are required unless you've come from a yellow-fever zone within the past week. Standards in Australia's hospitals are also very high, and medical costs are reasonable by world standards. For general health information while in Australia, check out Ⓦwww.travmed.com.au.

The national healthcare scheme, **Medicare**, offers a reciprocal arrangement – free essential healthcare – for citizens of the UK, Ireland, New Zealand, Italy, Malta, Finland, the Netherlands and Sweden. This free treatment is limited to public hospitals and casualty departments (though the **ambulance** ride to get you there isn't covered); at GPs you pay up front (about $40 minimum) with two-thirds of your fee reimbursed by Medicare (does not apply to citizens of New Zealand and Ireland).

The whole process is made easier by the production of a **Medicare Card**, available from any Medicare Centre. Anyone eligible who's staying in Australia for a while – particularly those on extended working holidays – is advised to obtain one. Applicants need to bring their passport and the National Health documents of their country. Dental treatment is not included: if you find yourself in need of dental treatment in one of the larger cities, try the dental hospital, where dental students may treat you cheaply or for free.

The sun

Australia's biggest health problem for fair-skinned visitors is also one of its chief attractions: **sunshine**. A sunny day in London, Toronto, or even Miami, is not the same as a cloudless day in Cairns, and the intensity of the Australian sun's damaging ultraviolet rays is far greater. Whether this is because of Australia's proximity to the **ozone hole** is a matter of debate, but there's absolutely no doubt that the southern sun burns more fiercely than anything in the northern hemisphere, and you need to take extra care.

Australians of European origin, especially those of Anglo-Saxon or Celtic descent, could not be less suited to Australia's outdoor lifestyle, which is why two out of three Australians are statistically likely to develop **skin cancer** in their lifetime, the world's worst record. About five percent of these will develop potentially fatal **melanomas**, and about a thousand die each year. Looking at the ravaged complexions of some older Australians (who had prolonged exposure to the sun in the days before there was an awareness of the great dangers of skin cancer) should be enough to make you want to cover yourself with lashings of the highest factor sun block (SPF 35+), widely used and sold just about everywhere. Sunscreen should not be used on babies less than six months old: instead, keep them out of direct sunlight. What looks like war paint on the noses of surfers and small children is actually **zinc cream**; the thick, sticky waterproof cream, which comes in fun colours, provides a total blockout and is particularly useful when applied to protruding parts of the body, such as noses and shoulders.

These days, Australians are fully aware of the sun's dangers, and you're constantly reminded to "**Slip, Slop, Slap**", the government-approved catch phrase reminding you to slip on a T-shirt, slop on some sun block and slap on a hat – sound advice. Pay attention to any moles on your body: if you notice any changes, either during or after your trip, see a doctor; cancerous melanomas are

generally easily removed if caught early. To prevent headaches and – in the long term – cataracts, it's a good idea to wear **sunglasses**; look for "UV block" ratings when you buy a pair.

The sun can also cause **heat exhaustion** and **sunstroke**, so as well as keeping well covered up, stay in the shade if you can. Drink plenty of liquids: on hot days when walking, experts advise drinking a litre of water an hour – which is a lot to carry. Alcohol and sun don't mix well; when you're feeling particularly hot and thirsty, remember that a cold beer will actually dehydrate you.

Wildlife dangers

Although **mosquitoes** are found across the whole of the country, malaria is not endemic; however, in the tropical north there are regular outbreaks of similarly transmitted Ross River Fever and Dengue Fever, chronically debilitating viruses which are potentially fatal to children and the elderly. Outbreaks of Ross River Fever are now occurring as far south as Tasmania, which is reason enough not to be too blasé about mozzie bites. Aeroguard and Rid are the popular brands of insect repellent.

The danger from other **wildlife** is much overrated: snake and spider bites, and crocodile and shark attacks are widely publicized and an essential part of the perilous Outback myth – nonetheless, all are extremely rare. There are always scares, such as when a couple of people died from being bitten by flying foxes infected with the rabies-like lyssa virus in Queensland in 1996 – it's best not to handle bats, should you have the opportunity. Rabies itself is unknown in Australia.

The way to minimize danger from **saltwater crocodiles** (which actually range far inland; see p.635) is to keep your distance. If you're camping in the bush within 100km of the northern coast between Broome (WA) and Rockhampton (QLD), make sure your tent is at least 50m from waterholes or creeks, don't collect water at the same spot every day or leave any rubbish around, and always seek local advice. Four-wheel drivers should take extra care when walking creeks prior to driving across.

Snakes almost always do their best to avoid people and you'll probably never see one. They're more likely to be active in hot weather, when you should be more careful. Treat them with respect, and it's unlikely you'll be bitten: most bites occur when people try to catch or kill snakes. Wear boots and long trousers when hiking through undergrowth, collect firewood carefully, and, in the event of a confrontation, back off. **Sea snakes** sometimes find divers intriguing, wrapping themselves around limbs or staring into masks, but they're seldom aggressive. If **bitten** by a snake, use a crepe bandage to bind the entire limb firmly and splint it, as if for a sprain; this slows the distribution of venom into the lymphatic system. Don't clean the bite area (venom around the bite can identify the species, making treatment easier), and don't slash the bite or apply a tourniquet. Treat all bites as if they were serious and always seek immediate medical attention, but remember: not all snakes are poisonous, not all poisonous snakes inject a lethal dose of venom every time they bite, and death from snakebite is rare.

Two **spiders** whose bites can be fatal are the **Sydney funnel-web**, a black, stocky creature found in the Sydney area, and the small **redback**, a relative of the notorious black widow of the Americas, usually found in dark, dry locations. January and February are the months in which there is the greatest danger of bites by both. Treat funnel-web bites as for snakebite, and apply ice to redback wounds to relieve pain; if bitten by either, get to a hospital – antivenins are available. **Other spiders**, **centipedes** and **scorpions** can deliver painful wounds but generally only cause serious problems if you have allergies.

Ticks, **mites** and **leeches** are the bane of bushwalkers, though spraying **repellent** over shoes and leggings will help keep these pests away in the first instance. Ticks are poisonous and you may want to check yourself over after a hike, but you'll probably feel them – look for local stinging and swelling (usually just inside hairlines) and you'll find either a tiny black dot, or a pea-sized animal attached, depending on which species has bitten you. Kill the tick with kerosene and then, using tweezers, pull it off, while trying to avoid squeezing the animal's body, which will inject more venom. Some mites cause an infuriating rash known as "scrub itch", which characteristically appears wherever your clothes are tightest, such as around the hips and ankles. Unfortunately, there's not much you can do except dab on more kerosene to kill the mites, take antihistamines and wait a day or two for the itching to stop. Leeches are gruesome but harmless: insect repellent, fire or salt gets them off the skin, though bites will bleed heavily for some time.

More serious is the threat from various types of **jellyfish** (also known as stingers or sea wasps), which occur in coastal tropical waters through the summer months. Two to watch out for are the tiny irukandji and saucer-sized box jellyfish, though both are virtually invisible in water. Irukandji have initially painless stings, but their venom causes "irukandji syndrome" which can be fatal. Its symptoms are somewhat similar to those of decompression illness: elevated heart rate and increased blood pressure; in addition to that, excruciating pain, anxiety and an overwhelming sense of doom and dread. Box jellyfish stings leave permanent red weals, and the venom can cause rapid unconsciousness and even kill, by paralyzing the heart muscles, if the weals cover more than half a limb. Treat stinger victims by dousing the sting area (front and back) with liberal amounts of **vinegar** (never rub with sand or towels, or attempt to remove tentacles from the skin – both could trigger the release of more venom); apply mouth-to-mouth resuscitation if needed, and get the victim to hospital for treatment. Whatever the locals are doing, don't risk swimming **anywhere** on tropical beaches during the **stinger season** (roughly Oct to May) – stinger nets don't offer any protection against the tiny irukandji which pass through the mesh designed to stop the box jellyfish. Specific reef hazards are covered at the start of the chapter on Queensland's tropical coast (p.467).

For more background on Australian fauna, see "Wildlife" on p.1178.

Other health hazards

Australia has one of the lowest rates of **AIDS** infection in the world, largely because the population caught on very early to the need for safe sex, which has been promoted heavily. Infected needles are a danger, not only among intravenous drug users but also from ear-piercing and tattooing. You'll find AIDS helplines listed in the major cities in this guide.

Other health hazards are far less pressing. **Tap water** is safe to drink everywhere. It doesn't always taste good, but bottled water is commonly available. One thing to watch out for in the hot and humid north is **tropical ear**, a very painful fungal infection of the ear canal. Treatment is with ear drops and if you think you might be susceptible, use them anyway after getting wet.

Although you're unlikely to find yourself in the path of a raging **bushfire**, it helps to know how to survive one. If you're in a car, don't attempt to drive through smoke but park at the side of the road in the clearest spot, put on your headlights, wind up the windows and close the air vents. Although it seems to go against common sense – and your natural instincts – it's safer to **stay inside the car**. Lie on the floor and cover all exposed skin with a blanket or any covering at hand. The car won't explode or catch on fire, and a fast-moving wildfire will pass quickly overhead. If you smell or see smoke and fire while **walking**, find a cleared rocky outcrop or an open space: if the terrain and time permits, dig a shallow trench – but in any event, lie face down and cover all exposed skin.

Websites

🌐 **http://health.yahoo.com** Information on specific diseases and conditions, drugs and herbal remedies, as well as advice from health experts.
🌐 **www.tmvc.com.au** Contains a list of all Travellers' Medical and Vaccination Centres throughout Australia, New Zealand and Southeast Asia, plus general information on travel health.
🌐 **www.istm.org** The website of the International Society for Travel Medicine, with a full list of clinics specializing in international travel health.

🌐 **www.tripprep.com** Travel Health Online provides an online-only comprehensive database of necessary vaccinations for most countries, as well as destination and medical service provider information.
🌐 **www.fitfortravel.scot.nhs.uk** UK NHS website carrying information about travel-related diseases and how to avoid them.

Travel clinics in the UK and Ireland

British Airways Travel Clinics 213 Piccadilly, London W1 (Mon–Fri 9.30am–6pm, Sat 10am–5pm, no appointment necessary); 101 Cheapside, London EC2 (hours as above Mon–Fri only, appointment required) ☎ 0845/600 2236, 🌐 www.britishairways.com/travel/healthclinintro). Vaccinations, tailored advice from an online database and a complete range of travel healthcare products.
Communicable Diseases Unit Brownlee Centre, Glasgow G12 0YN ☎ 0141/211 1062. Travel vaccinations including yellow fever.
Dun Laoghaire Medical Centre 5 Northumberland Ave, Dun Laoghaire Co, Dublin ☎ 01/280 4996, 📠 01/280 5603. Advice on medical matters abroad.
Hospital for Tropical Diseases Travel Clinic 2nd Floor, Mortimer Market Centre, off Capper St, London WC1E 6AU (Mon–Fri 9am–5pm by appointment only; ☎ 020/7388 9600; a consultation costs £15 which is waived if you have your injections here). A recorded Health Line (☎ 09061/337 733; 50p per min) gives hints on hygiene and illness prevention as well as listing appropriate immunizations.
Liverpool School of Tropical Medicine Pembroke Place, Liverpool L3 5QA ☎ 0151/708 9393. Walk-in clinic Mon–Fri 1–4pm; appointment required for yellow fever, but not for other jabs.
Malaria Helpline 24-hour recorded message ☎ 0891/600 350; 60p per minute.
MASTA (Medical Advisory Service for Travellers Abroad) London School of Hygiene and Tropical Medicine. Operates a pre-recorded 24-hour Travellers' Health Line (UK ☎ 0906/822 4100, 60p per min; Republic of Ireland

AIDS organizations

ACON (AIDS Council of NSW), PO Box 350, Darlinghurst, NSW 2010 ☎ 02/9206 2000 or 1800 063 060, 🌐 www.acon.org.au; AIDS Trust of Australia, PO Box 1030, Darlinghurst, NSW 2010 ☎ 02/9310 1066; offices in other states.

℡01560/147 000, 75p per minute), giving written information tailored to your journey by return of post.

Nomad Pharmacy surgeries 40 Bernard St, London WC1; and 3–4 Wellington Terrace, Turnpike Lane, London N8 (Mon–Fri 9.30am–6pm, ℡020/7833 4114 to book vaccination appointment). They give advice free if you go in person, or their telephone helpline is ℡09068/633 414 (60p per minute). They can give information tailored to your travel needs.

Trailfinders Immunization clinics (no appointments necessary) at 194 Kensington High St, London (Mon–Fri 9am–5pm except Thurs to 6pm, Sat 9.30am–4pm; ℡020/7938 3999).

Travel Health Centre Department of International Health and Tropical Medicine, Royal College of Surgeons in Ireland, Mercers Medical Centre, Stephen's St Lower, Dublin ℡01/402 2337. Expert pre-trip advice and inoculations.

Travel Medicine Services PO Box 254, 16 College St, Belfast 1 ℡028/9031 5220. Offers medical advice before a trip and help afterwards in the event of a tropical disease.

Tropical Medical Bureau Grafton Buildings, 34 Grafton St, Dublin 2 ℡01/671 9200, ⓦhttp://tmb.exodus.ie.

In the US and Canada

Canadian Society for International Health 1 Nicholas St, Suite 1105, Ottawa, ON K1N 7B7 ℡613/241-5785, ⓦwww.csih.org. Distributes a free pamphlet, "Health Information for Canadian Travellers", containing an extensive list of travel health centres in Canada.

Centers for Disease Control 1600 Clifton Rd NE, Atlanta, GA 30333 ℡1-800/311-3435 or 404/639-3534, Ⓕ1-888/232-3299, ⓦwww.cdc.gov. Publishes outbreak warnings, suggested inoculations, precautions and other background information for travellers. Useful website plus International Travelers Hotline on ℡1-877/FYI-TRIP.

International Association for Medical Assistance to Travellers (IAMAT) 417 Center St, Lewiston, NY 14092 ℡716/754-4883, ⓦwww.sentex.net/~iamat, and 40 Regal Rd, Guelph, ON N1K 1B5 ℡519/836-0102. A non-profit organization supported by donations, it can provide climate charts and leaflets on various diseases and inoculations.

International SOS Assistance Eight Neshaminy Interplex, Suite 207, Trevose, USA 19053-6956 ℡1-800/523-8930, ⓦwww.intsos.com. Members receive pre-trip medical referral info, as well as overseas emergency services designed to complement travel insurance coverage.

MEDJET Assistance ℡1-800/863-3538, ⓦww.medjetassistance.com. Annual membership program for travellers ($175 for individuals, $275 for families) that, in the event of illness or injury, will fly members home or to the hospital of their choice in a medically equipped and staffed jet.

Travel Medicine ℡1-800/872-8633, ⓦwww.travmed.com. Sells first-aid kits, mosquito netting, water filters, reference books and other health-related travel products.

Travelers Medical Center 31 Washington Square West, New York, NY 10011 ℡212/982-1600. Consultation service on immunizations and treatment of diseases for people travelling to developing countries.

In Australia and New Zealand

Travellers' Medical and Vaccination Centres 27–29 Gilbert Place, Adelaide, SA 5000 ℡08/8212 7522; 1/170 Queen St, Auckland ℡09/373 3531 5/247 Adelaide St, Brisbane, Qld 4000 ℡07/3221 9066; 5/8–10 Hobart Place, Canberra, ACT 2600 ℡02/6257 7156;147 Armagh St, Christchurch ℡03/379 4000; 270 Sandy Bay Rd, Sandy Bay, Hobart, Tas 7005 ℡03/6223 7577; 2/393 Little Bourke St, Melbourne, Vic 3000 ℡03/9602 5788 45 Stirling Hwy, Nedlands, WA 6009 ℡08/9386 4511; Level 7, Dymocks Bldg, 428 George St, Sydney, NSW 2000 ℡02/9221 7133; Shop 15, Grand Arcade, 14–16 Willis St, Wellington ℡04/473 0991.

Costs, money and banks

If you've travelled down from Southeast Asia you'll find Australia expensive on a day-to-day basis, but fresh from Europe or the US you'll find prices comparable or cheaper, especially with the advantageous exchange rates. Australia is well set up for independent travellers, and with a student, YHA or a backpackers' card (see p.47) you can get discounts on a wide range of transport and entertainment.

Australia's currency is the Australian dollar, or "buck", divided into 100 cents. The colourful plastic notes with forgery-proof clear windows come in $100, $50, $20, $10 and $5 denominations, along with $2, $1, 50¢, 20¢, 10¢ and 5¢ coins. There are no longer 1¢ or 2¢ coins, but prices are regularly advertised at $1.99 etc and an irregular bill will be rounded up or down to the closest denomination, which can be confusing at first.

Exchange rates fluctuate around an over-the-counter rate of A$2.90 for £1; A$1.75 for US$1; A$1.15 for CDN$1; and A$0.95 for NZ$1.

Some basic costs

If you're prepared to camp you might get by on as little as $40 a day, but you should count on around $60 a day for food, board and transport if you stay in hostels, travel on buses and eat and drink fairly frugally. Stay in motels and B&Bs, and eat out regularly, and you'll need to budget $100 or more: extras such as scuba-diving courses, clubbing, car rental and tours will all add to your costs.

Hostel **accommodation** will set you back $15–25 a person, while a double room in a motel costs $50–95 and a moderate hotel costs $75–120. **Food**, on the whole, is good value: counter meals in hotels and café mains often start from $12; restaurants cost upwards of $30 for a reasonable three-course feed, and many let you BYO (Bring Your Own) wine or beer. Buying your own ingredients is not always the cheapest way to eat in the bigger cities, where there's sure to be a range of budget diners and Asian food halls, but overall you'll save; meat and

fresh seasonal produce are generally inexpensive. **Drinking** out will set you back around $3 for a small glass of draught beer, $4–6 for a bottled brew, and local wine by the glass starts at $4 for an ordinary drop but expect to pay at least $7 for something choicer. Beer is good value bought in bulk from a "bottle shop" – a "slab" of beer (24 cans) costs around $30; a decent bottle of wine will set you back from $14, with vin ordinaire from as little as $8.

Given the size of the country, **transport** can make a major dent in your budget and is perhaps the area in which you're most likely to overspend. **Pre-planning** helps – an open-jaw plane ticket, for example, saves you having to get back to where you started, or pay a little extra for an international flight that gives you some discounted internal fares. There is also a huge variety of **bus and train passes** available overseas (see "Getting Around", pp.35–37, for more on the options available). **Driving** yourself may not always save money but it does give you a great deal more flexibility. Finding passengers willing to share costs is one way to minimize expenses and is usually not too difficult – try the notice boards at hostels and other meeting places. Buying a used car will, realistically, set you back $4000 or more for a mechanically sound vehicle with a reasonable resale value (see p.41 for more advice), but even $2000 might buy something that will get you around – if not in the greatest of style. Renting a car costs $35–65 a day; the longer you rent for, the cheaper the price. Fuel, with substantial local variations, averages 88–98¢ a litre; cheaper than in the UK, dearer than the US, but vast distances see it used up fast.

Youth and student discounts

Once obtained, various official and quasi-official **youth/student ID cards** soon pay for themselves in savings. Full-time students are eligible for the International Student ID Card (ISIC, ⓦ www.isiccard.com), which entitles the bearer to special air, rail and bus fares and discounts at museums, theatres and other attractions. For Americans there's also a health benefit, providing up to $3000 in emergency medical coverage and $100 a day for 60 days in hospital, plus a 24-hour hotline to call in the event of a medical, legal or financial emergency. The card costs $22 for Americans; CDN$16 for Canadians; NZ$21 for New Zealanders; and £7 in the UK. If you're no longer a student, but are 26 or younger, you still qualify for the International Youth Travel Card, which costs the same price and carries the same benefits, while teachers qualify for the International Teacher Card (same price and benefits). All these cards are available in the US from Council Travel, STA, Travel CUTS and, in Canada, from Hostelling International (see pp.17 & 47 for addresses); in Australia and New Zealand from STA or Campus Travel; and in the UK from Campus Travel. Once you are in Australia, purchasing either an **International YHA Card** or **Backpacker Resorts VIP Card** will give you discounts on not just the relevant hostel accommodation, but a host of transport, tours, services, entry fees and even meals; they're worth getting even if you're not planning to stay in hostels. See pp.46–47 for prices and details.

Travellers' cheques

Travellers' cheques, such as those sold by American Express and Thomas Cook, are the best way to bring your funds into Australia, as they can be replaced if lost or stolen (remember to keep a list of the serial numbers separate from the cheques). Australian dollar traveller's cheques are ideal as theoretically they're valid as cash and so shouldn't attract exchange fees, though smaller businesses may be unwilling to take them, but you can always change them for free at the local offices – American Express have more outlets and agencies in Australia than Thomas Cook. Travellers' cheques in

US dollars and pounds sterling are also widely accepted, and banks should be able to handle all major currencies. It's worth checking both the rate and the commission when you change your cheques (as well as when you buy them), as these can vary quite widely – many places charge a set amount for every cheque, in which case you're better off changing relatively large denominations. You'll need your passport with you to cash travellers' cheques.

The usual fee **to buy travellers' cheques** is one or two percent, though this fee may be waived if you buy the cheques through a bank where you have an account. Make sure to keep the purchase agreement and a record of cheque serial numbers safe and separate from the cheques themselves. In the event that cheques are lost or stolen, the issuing company will expect you to report the loss forthwith to their head office in Australia; most companies claim to replace lost or stolen cheques within 24 hours.

Credit and debit cards

Credit cards are a very handy back-up source of funds, and can be used either in ATMs or over the counter. MasterCard and Visa are the most widely recognized; you can also use American Express, Bankcard and Diners Club. Remember that all cash advances are treated as loans, with interest accruing daily from the date of withdrawal; there may be a transaction fee on top of this. However, you may be able to make withdrawals from ATMs in Australia displaying the Cirrus-Maestro symbol and be able to pay for goods via EFTPOS (see p.33), using your debit card, which is not liable to interest payments, and the flat transaction fee is usually quite small – your bank will be able to advise on this. Make sure you have a personal identification number (PIN) that's designed to work overseas.

A compromise between travellers' cheques and plastic is Visa TravelMoney, a disposable pre-paid debit card with a PIN which works in all ATMs that take Visa cards. You load up your account with funds before leaving home, and when they run out, you simply throw the card away. You can buy up to nine cards to access the same funds – useful for couples or families travelling together – and it's a good idea to buy at least one extra as a back-up in case of loss or theft. There is also a 24-hour Australia-wide toll-free customer assistance number (☎1800 125 440). The card is available in most countries from branches of Thomas Cook and Citicorp. For more information, check the Visa TravelMoney website at ⓦwww.usa.visa.com/personal/cards/visa_travel_money.html.

Banks and exchange

The closure of local banks throughout much of Australia means you will no longer necessarily find a branch of one of the main **banks** in every town, though there will be a local agency which handles bank business – usually based at the general store, post office or roadhouse – though not necessarily a 24-hour ATM machine. The best policy is always make sure you have some cash on you before leaving the bigger towns, especially at weekends. The major banks, with branches countrywide, are Westpac (ⓦwww.westpac.com.au), ANZ (ⓦwww.anz.com.au), the Commonwealth (ⓦwww.commbank.com.au) and the National Australia Bank (ⓦwww.national.com.au); you can search their websites for branch locations.

Banking hours are Monday to Thursday 9.30am to 4pm, Friday 9.30am to 5pm (at the time of writing a change in the law has made Saturday opening legal, though it's not yet fully in practice). In country areas some banks may have more limited hours, such as lunch-time closures, or some agencies may be open later, and some big-city branches might also have extended hours. **ATMs** are generally open 24 hours.

Bureaux de change are only found in major tourist centres and airports; they are often open daily with more extended hours than banks, but due to their scarcity you should try to change money during banking hours. All **post offices** act as Commonwealth or National Australia Bank agents which means there's a fair chance of changing money even in the smallest Outback settlements – withdrawals at these places are often limited by a lack of ready cash, however,

though less remote post offices may have EFTPOS facilities (see below).

If you're spending some time in Australia, and plan to work or move around, it makes life a great deal easier if you **open a bank account**. To do this you'll need to take along every piece of ID documentation you own – a passport may not be enough, though a letter from your bank manager at home may help – but it's otherwise a fairly straightforward process. The Commonwealth Bank and Westpac are the most widespread options, and their **keycards** give you access not only to ATM machines but also anywhere that offers **EFTPOS** facilities (Electronic Funds Transfer at Point of Sale). This includes many Outback service stations and supermarkets, where you can use your card to pay directly for goods; some of them will also give you cash (ask for "cash back"). However, bear in mind that **bank fees and charges** are exorbitant in Australia; most banks allow only a few free withdrawal transactions per month (depending on who you bank with – it's well worth shopping around before you open an account), and there are even bigger charges for using a competitor's ATM machine, as well as monthly fees.

Wiring money

Having money wired from home is never convenient or cheap, and should be considered a last resort.

You can make arrangements with either TravelersExpress MoneyGram (☎1-800/777-750, ⓦwww.moneygram.com) through Thomas Cook foreign offices or Western Union (ⓦwww.westernunion.com) through American Express offices.

It's also possible to have money wired directly from a bank in your home country to a bank in Australia, although this is somewhat less reliable because it involves two separate institutions. If you go down this route, your home bank will need the address of the branch bank where you want to pick up the money and the address and telex number of the head office, which will act as the clearing house; money wired this way normally takes two working days to arrive, and costs around £25/US$40 per transaction.

Getting around

Australia's huge scale makes the distances, and how you conquer them, a major feature of any stay in the country. In general, public transport will take you only along the major highways to capital cities, the bigger towns between them, and popular tourist destinations; to get off the beaten track you'll have to consider driving, either by buying or renting your own vehicle. Regular long-distance bus, train and plane services can be found under "Travel details" at the end of each chapter, with local buses and trains covered in the main text.

However you decide to travel, check out the route on a map first, as it's very easy to underestimate **distances and conditions** – you may well be letting yourself in for a three-day bus or train journey, or planning to drive 500km on bad roads. Bear in mind what the **weather** will be doing too; you don't want to head into central Australia in a battered old car during the summer, or into the northern Outback in the wet season.

Planes

Flying, between major destinations has been shaken up with the collapse of Ansett in 2001 and the arrival of newcomer Virgin Blue, now grabbing an increasing share of Qantas' internal market. Elsewhere, **regional routes** are served by smaller airlines such as Regional Express, which covers New South Wales, Victoria, Tasmania and South Australia, and state-based companies such as Airlines of South Australia, Sunstate in Queensland and Skywest in WA. While these smaller airlines' fares appear costly, consider the time and money you'll spend on a long bus or train journey.

If you expect to be flying a fair amount, you can save costs **before you leave** home as some airfares to Australia allow you to buy a set number of internal flights at a substantial discount if booked with your international ticket. Qantas' **Boomerang Pass** which must be purchased before arrival, divides the country into three zones and requires you book at least two flights (and a maximum of ten) from £100/US$155 for single-zone fares, and £125/US$195 for multiple-zone flights across Australia. You pay according to how many zones your flight crosses. As long as you have purchased the minimum number of flights before arriving in Australia, you can purchase additional flights at the same rates, up to the maximum ten allowed. At the time of writing Virgin Blue was not offering any special air passes but check their website.

Even if you're not buying an air pass, great savings can be made **booking via the Internet**. The standard price for a Sydney–Perth one-way with Qantas is around $618, with Virgin Blue you pay $580: on the Web the same flight may be available for around $250 including the $10 online discount with Virgin Blue, or $260 with the Qantas "Red e-deal".

You may also be able to get further **student and pensioner reductions**. Qantas **backpacker fares** are available to anyone with a YHA or VIP card (see p.47); you buy a minimum of three flights and get a substantial discount – a useful adjunct to an open-jaw ticket.

Another type of flight offered all over Australia is brief **sightseeing** or joyrides. Everything is covered, from biplane spins above cities to excursions to the Great Barrier Reef and flights over well-known landscapes. A good example is a day flight from Alice Springs to Ayers Rock in a small plane which enables you to visit the Rock in a day, but also observe the impressive central Australian landforms from the air. **Aircruising Australia** (✆02/9693 2233, ⓦwww.aircruising.com.au) offers a twelve-day tour by air which takes in the main sights from A$9994 inclusive.

Trains

With the advent of concessionary fares and a new line linking Alice Springs with Darwin (see p.665), **trains** are at last becoming a good way to get around parts of Australia. The populous southeast has a reasonably comprehensive service: **interstate railways** link the entire east coast from Cairns to Sydney, and on to Melbourne and Adelaide. The two great journeys, though, are the twice-weekly coast-to-coast **Indian–Pacific** (Perth–Sydney; 67hr; student conc: one-way, seat only $252; sleeper $805; luxury sleeper with meals $1120) and the twice- weekly **Ghan** (Adelaide–Alice Springs; 20hr; student conc.: $105/$408/$578). Trainways (☎13 21 47; ⓦwww.trainways.com.au), which now runs the main transcontinental routes, finally decided to introduce **concessionary fares** for students which work out only around fifteen percent more than a bus. Now the two routes above, as well as the **"Overland"** Adelaide–Melbourne service (10hr; student conc: seat only $42, $89 with lunch and light dinner; reverse journey sleeper $139 with breakfast; return conc $84, with meals $221) are being used again. Remember though, this is not a European-style high-speed network; journey times are similar to those of buses. To qualify for the concessionary fare for **daynighter seats** you must produce an ISIC student card or a membership card of one of the reputable backpacker organizations (YHA, VIP, Nomads). The latter are easily obtained - you need never set foot in a hostel. However, the **student concession on sleeper and luxury sleeper cabins** only applies to ISIC card holders; a YHA, VIP or Nomads card only entitles you to a five percent discount off the full adult fare.

On the overnight Ghan and Indian–Pacific, a twin-share **"Red Kangaroo"** sleeper service provides washing facilities and converts from a day lounge into a sleeper, while "Gold Kangaroo" lays on an en-suite cabin and all meals for the full "Orient Express" treatment. Either of these options are well worth considering for the full two-and-a-half day trawl from Sydney to Perth if you have something against flying.

Other than these, there are a couple of inland tracks in Queensland – to Mount Isa, Longreach and Charleville, plus the rustic Cairns–Forsayth run and isolated Croydon–Normanton stretch – and suburban networks around some of the major cities. Only around Sydney does this amount to much, with decent services to much of New South Wales. There are no passenger trains in Tasmania.

The advantages of travelling by train rather than bus are comfort and (usually) a bar; disadvantages are the slower pace, higher price and potential booking problems – Queensland trains, for instance, travel at about 60kph and require a month's advance booking during the holiday season. The famous long-distance journeys can also be booked solid, so you'd be wise to reserve a place before you leave home if this is a major part of your plans (Rail Australia agents are listed on p.36).

Rail passes include Trainways' **Great Southern Rail Pass** (backpacker and student conc $450; full fare $590) which can be bought in Australia (show your overseas passport) then lets you loose on their routes described above for a six-month period. To be sure that you can make full use of your pass, it's advisable to book your route when you buy it. Western Australia, Victoria, New South Wales and Queensland also have their own passes available through main stations, but check any travel restrictions before buying – interstate routes do not overlap as far as passes are concerned.

Buses

With the attractive deals on train fares outlined above, as well as a long overdue appreciation of its limitations, **bus travel** amongst overseas travellers is in decline in Australia as more people rent or buy cars. It's almost certainly the cheapest way to get around but there's a lot to be said against spending much of your trip staring at the passing landscape from a cramped seat.

Major domestic airlines

Qantas ☎13 13 13,
ⓦwww.qantas.com.au
Regional Express (☎13 17 13,
ⓦwww.regionalexpress.com.au
Virgin Blue ☎13 67 89,
ⓦwww.virginblue.com.au

And even though the bus network reaches much further than the train network, it will still limit you to travelling from one town to another: routes follow the main highways between cities, and may mean arriving at smaller places in the middle of the night. And services are not daily as you might think, especially in Western Australia with only **three buses** a week to Adelaide. The buses are about as comfortable as they can be, with reclining seats, air conditioning, toilets and videos: the real problem is having all these things work for the entire duration of your trip. If possible, try and plan for a stopover after every twenty hours – if you try stoically to sit out a sixty-hour marathon trip, you'll need a day or more to get over it and the roadhouse food you'll have survived on. **Discounts** (ten percent, or fifteen percent if you buy your ticket before entering Australia) are available on many fares if you have a YHA, ISIC or recognized backpacker card such as VIP (see p.47), or if you are a pensioner.

The major **interstate bus company** on the mainland is **McCafferty's/Greyhound Pioneer** (☎13 20 30 or 13 14 99, ⓦwww .greyhound.com.au, ⓦwww.mccaffertys .com.au) which circuits the entire country. Along the east coast, there's also **Premier** (☎13 34 10; www.premierms.com.au), which calls in everywhere along the highway

between Melbourne and Cairns, Countrylink (☎13 22 32) which covers country and outback New South Wales, while in WA Integrity Coachlines (ⓦwww.integritycoachlines .com.au) runs from Perth as far as Broome. **Tasmania** is thoroughly covered by Tasmanian Redline Coaches and Tassie Link.

Fares vary according to the popularity of the route and quality and speed of the road, and, though competing companies offer similar rates, special offers can slash prices – it's always worth shopping around. Sample one-way fares from Sydney are: Adelaide $127, Alice Springs $304, Brisbane $93, Cairns $285, Darwin $498, Melbourne $65 and Perth $391. Return fares are, at best, only marginally cheaper than two singles.

A good value option for bus travellers is to buy a **pass**, though bear in mind that you won't save money over shorter routes, and that passes are **nonrefundable** – tie yourself into a specific schedule and you'll be unable to change your plans. McCafferty's/ Greyhound Pioneer offers a range of passes lasting between one and twelve months covering **preset routes**, on which you can break your journey as often as you like and travel in any direction, but are not allowed to backtrack. Sample fares include the Melbourne–Cairns "Sunseeker" pass for $456; a "Best of the East" pass which

---

Train and bus representatives abroad

Trainways

UK and Ireland Leisurail, PO Box 113, Peterborough PE1 1LE ☎0870/750 0222
US ATS Tours, Suite 325, 2381 Rosecrans Ave, El Segundo, CA 90245 ☎1-800/423-2880.
Canada Goway Travel Ltd, Suite 300, 3284 Yonge St, Toronto, ON M4N 3M7; Suite 1050, 1200 W 73rd Ave, Vancouver, BC V6P 6G5 ☎1-800/387-8850, ⓦwww.goway.com.

McCafferty's

UK and Ireland Contact one of the travel agents listed on pp.14–15, such as STA or Trailfinders.
US Austravel, 51 E 42nd St, Suite 616, New York, NY 10017 (☎1-800/633-3404, Ⓕ212/983-8376, Ⓔusinfo@austravel.com), with branches also in Boston, San Francisco, Los Angeles, Seattle, Chicago and Denver. Swain Australia Tours, 6 W Lancaster Ave, Ardmore, PA 19003 (☎1-800/227-9246, ⓦwww.swaintours.com).
Canada Goway Travel Ltd, Suite 300, 3284 Yonge St, Toronto, ON M4N 3M7; Suite 1050, 1200 W 73rd Ave, Vancouver, BC V6P 6G5 ☎1-800/387-8850, ⓦwww.goway.com.

circuits via everywhere between Adelaide, Uluru, Alice Springs, Mount Isa, Cairns, Sydney and Melbourne for $1173; and the "All Australian" pass for $2403. Year-long **kilometre passes** are more flexible, giving you unlimited travel up to 20,000 kilometres in any direction until you have used up the distance paid for – these work out upwards of just over 10¢ per kilometre. Tasmania has its own passes offered by Tassie Link (ⓦ www.tigerline.com.au). Their network covers all major destinations in the state, plus some of interest to bushwalkers. The Tassielink Explorer Bus Passes cost from $160 for seven days' travel within a ten-day period, to $260 for 21 days' of travel within a thirty-day period

One-way tours

The big bus companies exist to transport as many passengers as quickly as possible from A to B. If you want more than a fleeting look at what you're passing, a **one-way tour** may be a lot more fun, and operators such as **Wayward Bus** have routes that visit off-beat locations well outside the major bus companies' schedules. Some tours are quite small (ten to eighteen people) and the driver/guide might be a knowledgeable local. Some of these tours project a character which might either suit you or drive you mad, and you'd be well advised to ask around before plumping for a long-distance commitment. Other local one-way tours as well as conventional tours are listed throughout this Guide.

Safari and one-way tour operators

All Terrain Safaris ☏ 1800 633 456, ⓦ www.allterrain.com.au. Established Perth-based operator offering a range of adventure tours, with decent food and a comfortable purpose-built vehicle, but sleeping in swags. Runs up the west coast to Coral Bay and Karijini, and from Broome as far as the northern Kimberley and Bungles and all the way to Kakadu. Around $130 a day. Also cheap "returns" back to Perth.
Heading Bush ☏ 1800 639 933, ⓕ 08/8648 6655, ⓦ www.headingbush.com. Adelaide–Alice Springs in ten days, via Flinders Ranges, Oodnadatta Track, the Simpson Desert, Uluru, the Olgas, Kings Canyon and Alice ($1200). The tour is operated by *Andu Lodge* in Quorn (see p.877) and emphasizes

Aboriginal heritage. All buses are 4WD, with seating for a maximum of ten people, and all meals are vegetarian; departures every Mon. They also offer shorter excursions to the Flinders Ranges ($199–299 from Adelaide; $165–265 from Port Augusta).
Wayward Bus ☏ 1800 882 823, ⓦ www.waywardbus.com.au. The long-established Adelaide-based Wayward Bus continues to provide a good service with a series of one-way and circuit trips in eastern and central Australia. Depending on the trip, their buses seat 16–21 people and the price includes transport, tent or hostel accommodation (upgrades available on some routes for a surcharge), most or all meals, and national park entry fees. You can hop on and off where you like over a six-month period. Routes include Melbourne–Adelaide via the Great Ocean Road and the Coorong (3.5 days for $310), Adelaide–Alice Springs (8 days for $820, 10 days for $990).

Driving

Having **your own vehicle** really allows you to explore Australia, filling the public-transport void away from the cities and allowing you to get to the national parks, the isolated beaches and the ghost towns that make the country such a special place. If your trip is a long one – three months or more – then **buying a vehicle** may well be the cheapest way of seeing Australia. On shorter trips you should consider **renting** – if not for the whole time, then at least for short periods between bus rides, thereby allowing you to explore an area in depth.

Most foreign **licences** are valid for a year in Australia. An International Driving Permit (available from national motoring organizations) may be useful if you come from a non-English-speaking country. **Fuel prices** start at around 90¢ per litre unleaded, with diesel slightly cheaper: prices increase by ten to fifteen percent along the Outback highway and can double at remote communities or on stations. The **rules of the road** are similar to those in the US and UK. Most importantly, **drive on the left** (as in Britain), remember that seatbelts are compulsory for all, and that the **speed limit** in all built-up areas is 50kph or less. Outside built-up areas, maximums are around 110kph on long, isolated stretches – except in the Northern Territory, where common sense is your only limit between towns. Whatever else you do in a vehicle, avoid **driving when you are tired** – get out of the car every two hours and don't **drink alcohol**; random breath tests are common even in rural areas, especially during the Christmas season and on Friday and Saturday nights. One rule that might catch you out in town is that roadside parking must be in the same direction as the traffic – in other words don't cross oncoming traffic to park on the right.

Major **hazards** are boredom and fatigue, losing control on dirt roads, and the presence of animals on the road – a serious problem everywhere (not just in the Outback) at dawn, dusk and night time. Driving in the Outback is by far the most dangerous tourist pursuit in Australia and every year several people get killed in single-vehicle rollovers or head-on collisions, particularly Europeans on short see-it-all holidays in large rental vehicles. Beware of fifty-metre-long **road trains**: these colossal trucks can't stop quickly or pull off the road safely, so if there's the slightest doubt, get out of the way; only overtake a road train if you can see well ahead and are certain that your vehicle can manage it. On dirt roads be doubly cautious, or just pull over for a rest and let the road train get ahead.

Roads, Outback driving and breakdowns

Around the cities the only problem you'll face is inept signposting, but the quality of inter-state main roads – even Highway 1, which circles the country – isn't always great, and some of the minor routes are awful. **Conditions**, especially on unsealed roads, are unpredictable and some roads will be impassable after a storm, so always seek reliable advice (from the local police or a road-house) before starting out. Make it clear what sort of vehicle you're driving and remember that their idea of a "good" or "bad" road may be radically different from yours. Some "4WD only" tracks are often navigable in lesser transport as long as you take it easy – high ground clearance, rather than four driven wheels, is often the crucial factor.

Rain and flooding – particularly in the tropics and central Australia – can close roads to all vehicles within minutes, so driv-

ing through remote regions in the wet season – or even along the coastal highway – can be prone to delays. The stretches of highway between Broome and Kununurra and Cairns to Townsville are notorious for being cut by floods during the summer cyclone season; in late 2000 dozens of vehicles were stranded for weeks on the main Queensland–Northern Territory road waiting for floods to recede. Several remote and unsealed roads through central Australia (the Sandover and Plenty highways, the Oodnadatta, Birdsville and Tanami tracks, and others) are theoretically open to all vehicles in dry winter weather, but unless you're well equipped with a tough car, don't attempt a crossing during the summer, when extreme temperatures place extra strain on both driver and vehicle.

On **poor roads and dirt tracks**, the rules are to keep your speed down to 80kph, stick to the best section and never assume that the road is free from potholes, eroded cattle grids, sand, rocks or oncoming traffic. Long corrugated stretches can literally shake the vehicle apart – check radiators, fuel tanks and battery connections afterwards; reducing tyre pressures slightly softens the ride but can cause the tyres to overheat making them more prone to punctures. Windscreens are often shattered by flying stones from passing traffic, so slow down and pull over to the left. Fine "bulldust" obscures potholes and other hazards and invades the car. Dirt tracks are often deeply rutted, and exposed tree roots can burst tyres if you drive over them too fast.

At all times carry plenty of **drinking water and fuel**, and if you're heading Outback tell someone reliable your timetable, route and destination, so that a rescue can be organized if you don't report in. Carry a detailed, recent **map** and don't count on finding regular signposts. In the event of a **breakdown** in the Outback, always **stay with your vehicle**: it's visible to potential rescuers and you can use it for shade, and you risk finding it stripped when you return with a tow truck if you're stranded on an isolated road. As a last resort, burn a tyre or anything plastic – the black smoke will be distinctive from the average bushfire.

Car, 4WD and campervan rental

To **rent** a car you need a full, clean driver's licence; usually, a minimum age of 21 is stipulated by the major car-rental companies, rising to 25 for 4WDs. Check on any mileage limits or other restrictions, extras, and what you're covered for in an accident, before signing. The multinational operators Hertz, Budget, Avis and Thrifty have offices in the major cities, but outside the big cities lack of competition makes their **standard rates** expensive at $70–90 a day for a sedan: long-term rental, specials and even plain bargaining can bring this down to a more affordable level. National has offices in Melbourne, Brisbane, Cairns, the Gold Coast and Surfers Paradise, and Holiday has several branches throughout the country. **Local companies** – of which there are many in the cities – are almost always better value, and the bottom-line "rent-a-bomb" agencies go as low as $29 a day; however, these places often have restrictions on how far away from base you're allowed to go. A city-based non-multinational rental agency will supply new cars for around **$45 a day** with unlimited kilometres.

One-way rental might appear handy, but is usually very expensive: at least $200 extra for the drop-off fee (except in Tasmania where there is no surcharge). If you're simply trying to get from one place to another, you could try offering to relocate any vehicles they may have from other cities (ie returning someone else's one-way rental). They'll have regular drivers to do this, but being politely

---

Four-wheel driving: some hints

The Outback is not the place to learn how to handle a 4WD and yet this is exactly where many tourists attracted by driving a tough vehicle off-road, do so. In late 2002 a solo German tourist was rescued by chance after waiting for a week on the 1900-kilometre-long Canning Stock Route in WA, almost out of water and fuel. A novice four-wheel driver, he assumed his Maui bushcamper was an unstoppable, all-terrain machine until he got bogged in a salt pan through lack of experience. Take all the spares listed on p.42, plus a shovel, hi-lift jack and gloves. There are many "how to" manuals available in bookshops; if you're planning a long off-road tour, *Explore Australia by Four-Wheel Drive* (Viking) will suit recreational drivers. The following basic hints should help; see also the advice on creek crossings on p.552.

- Be aware of your limitations, and those of your vehicle.
- Know how to operate everything – including free-wheeling hubs (where present) and how to change a wheel – before you need it.
- Always cross deep water and very muddy sections on foot first.
- Don't persevere if you're stuck – avoid wheel spin (which will only dig you further in) and reverse out. Momentum is key on slippery surfaces such as mud, sand and snow – as long as you're moving forward, however slowly, resist the temptation to change gear, and so lose traction.
- Reducing tyre pressures down to 1 bar (15 psi) dramatically increases traction in mud and sand, but causes over-heating at higher road speeds and so risks punctures. Carry a compressor or reinflate as soon as possible.
- If stuck, clear all the wheels with your hands or a shovel, create a shallow ramp (again, for all wheels), engage four-wheel-drive lower pressures if necessary, and drive out in low-range second.
- Keep to tracks – avoid unnecessary damage to the environment. Driving on beaches can be great fun, but is treacherous – observe other vehicles' tracks and be aware of tidal patterns.
- Consider an inexpensive EPIRB rescue beacon or a rented satellite phone for remote travel.

persuasive and claiming previous experience might get you massive reductions. As a rule, cars are needed in the southern cities as the Wet hits the tropics towards the end of the year. To reserve a rental car from the UK, USA or Canada, contact the companies listed below.

Four-wheel drives are best used for specific areas rather than long term, as rental and fuel costs are steep, starting at around $120 a day. Some 4WD agents actually don't allow their vehicles to be driven off sealed roads, so check the small print first. **Campervans and motor homes** have really caught on in recent years as the idea of a big road trip across Australia becomes possible with rates from around $70 a day with unlimited kilometres – amazing value when you consider the independence, comfort and the saving on accommodation costs. And one-way rental is not necessarily penalized with campervan agencies. Like cars, campervans can be limited to sealed roads but they give you the chance to create your own tour of a lifetime across Australia. Vehicles are cleverly designed and converted – sometimes too cleverly; you can get pretty cranky spending all day *and* all night in the same compact vehicle. High-roof or pop-top models are more tolerable but don't expect to be happy to spend weeks on end in a campervan. Remember, too, that the sleeping capacity stated in the adverts is an absolute maximum, which you wouldn't want to endure for too long. Furthermore, in the tropics the interior will never really cool enough overnight unless you leave the doors open – which brings the bugs in. Consider sleeping outside under a mozzie dome or inner tent.

For **4WD campervans**, the high-roofed Toyota Troop Carriers used by Britz, Maui and Apollo to name a few are tough all-terrain vehicles fitted with 180-litre fuel tanks that will only be stopped off-road by your experience or the height of the roof. With these models it's important to understand the operation of the free-wheeling hubs on the front axle to engage 4WD. The only drawback with this popular model is the high fuel consumption. Lighter 4WD utes fitted with a cabin and a pop-up roof can't really take the same hammering but will be more economical, while the large Isuzu-based six-

berthers look chunky but would really be a handful off-road and use even more fuel. With all these 4WD campers it is vital to appreciate the altered driving dynamics of an already high vehicle fitted with a heavy body. In the hands of overseas renters they regularly topple when an inexperienced driver drifts off the road, overcompensates and rolls over.

Prices for 4WD campers start around $110 a day. For a long trip, May to June is the low season when prices drop by up to forty per cent with some operators. Branches of the big rental chains and local firms for all types of vehicles are detailed in "Listings" sections throughout the Guide.

Car reservations

Autos Abroad ⓦ www.autosabroad.co.uk – in the UK ☎ 020 7287 6000

Avis ⓦ www.avis.com – in the UK ☎ 0870/606 0100; in Eire ☎ 01/874 5844; in the US ☎ 1-800/230-4898; in Canada ☎ 1-800/272-5871; in New Zealand ☎ 09/526 2847

Budget ⓦ www.budget.com – in the UK ☎ 0800/181181; in Eire ☎ 0800/973159; in the US ☎ 1-800/527-0700; in New Zealand ☎ 09/375 2222

Hertz ⓦ www.hertz.com – in the UK ☎ 0870/844 8844; in Eire ☎ 01/676 7476; in the US ☎ 1-800/654-3001; in Canada ☎ 1-800/263-0600 or 416/620-9620

Holiday Autos ⓦ www.holidayautos.com – in the UK ☎ 0870/400 0011; in Eire ☎ 01/872 9366

Kemwel Holiday Autos ⓦ www.kemwel.com – in the US ☎ 1-800/678-0678

National ⓦ www.nationalcar.com – in the US ☎ 1-800/CAR-RENT

Campervan and motorhome reservations

Apollo Motorhome Holidays ☎ 07/3260 5466 or 1800 777 779, ⓦ www.apollocamper.com.au; agents around the world. A full range of 2–6 berth campervans and motorhomes and 4WD bushcampers.

Britz Campervan Rentals ☎ 03/9379 8990 or 1800 331 454, ⓦ www.britz.com; agents around the world. Long-established company whose high-roofed Bushcampers are a common sight all around the country. These 4WD models are built and equipped to a high standard with long-range fuel tanks and even a kitchen sink and outdoor shower. Britz also offer half-day 4WD training courses for around $200 that first-time off-roaders should consider good insurance. Also Koala and Maui (ⓦ www.maui-rentals.com) campervans and motorhomes holding 2–6 people.

Kea Campers ☎ 02/8707 5500, ⓦ www .keacampers.com. Sydney-based outfit with a range of campers and motorhomes.

Trailmaster Campervan Rentals ☎ 1800 651 202, ⓦ www.trailmaster.com.au. Rather cramped-looking converted 4WD utes with pop-up roofs as well as larger campervans and motorhomes.

Travel Hire Australia ☎ 02/9636 7191, ⓦ www.travelhire.com.au. Sydney-based Land Rover rental outfit. The Defender may be the classic Land Rover but an automatic Discovery is much more comfortable and drivable, nearly as capable off-road and fifty percent more economical than a Toyota Troop Carrier. Some vehicles come with easily-erected roof tents, but none are converted into campers so this requires some organization. However, they offer as much optional recreational gear as you can carry, including serious off-road recovery equipment that few others provide.

Buying a car

Buying a used vehicle needn't be an expensive business and a well-kept car should resell at about two-thirds of the purchase price at the end of your trip – if you're lucky, or a skilful negotiator, you might even make a profit. A good place to evaluate vehicle prices and availability on the Web is at ⓦ www.autotrader.com.au.

If you don't know your axle from your elbow but are not too gullible, **car yards** can provide some advice: in Sydney, they're the most common place to buy a used vehicle, and some even cater specifically to travellers (see p.194) – but don't forget you're dealing with used-car salesmen whose worldwide reputation precedes them; a **buy-back guarantee** offered by some car yards and dealers is usually a guarantee to pay you a fraction of the car's potential value. Assuming you have a little time and some mechanical knowledge, you'll save money by buying **privately**. Hostel notice boards in main exit points from Australia are the best places to look. One of the great advantages of buying from a **fellow traveller** is that you might get all sorts of gear thrown in – jerrycans, camping gear and many of the spares listed on p.42. The disadvantage is

Best secondhand buys

Big-engined, mid-1980s Holden Kingswood or Ford Falcon station wagons are popular travellers' cars: cheap, roomy, reliable, mechanically simple and durable, with spares available in just about any city supermarket, roadhouse or wrecker's yard. At the bottom end, $1500 plus some luck should find you some kind of old car that runs reliably. Chances are, if a vehicle has survived this long, there's nothing seriously wrong with it and you should be able to nurse it through a bit further. Real bargains can also be secured from travellers desperate to get rid of their vehicle before flying out. Ideally, though, you should plan to pay at least $4000 in total for a sound, and well-equipped vehicle. Manual transmission models are more economical than automatic, with the four-speed versions superior to the awkward, three-speed, steering-column-mounted models. Smaller and less robust, but much more economical to run, are old Japanese station wagons or vans, suitable for one or two people. Any city hostel notice board will be covered in adverts of vehicles for sale.

Four-wheel drives are expensive and, with poor fuel economy and higher running costs, worth it only if you have some serious off-roading planned – to do that you can't buy an old wreck. Toyota FJ or HJ Land Cruisers are Outback legends, especially the long-wheelbase (LWB) models: tough, reliable and with plenty of new and used spares all over the country. If nothing goes wrong, a diesel (HJ) is preferable to a petrol (FJ) engine, being sturdier and more economical – although all Toyota engines, particularly the six-cylinder FJs, seem to keep on running, even if totally clapped out. The trouble with diesels is that problems, when they occur, tend to be serious and repairs expensive. Generally, you're looking at $8000–16,000 for a reliable fifteen-year-old model.

BASICS | Getting around

41

that the car may have been maintained on a backpacker's budget.

A **thorough inspection** is essential. **Rust** is one thing to watch for, especially in the tropics where humidity and salt air will turn scratches to holes within weeks – look out for poorly patched bodywork. Take cars for a spin and check the engine, gearbox, clutch and brakes for operation, unusual noises, vibration and leaks; repairs on some of these parts can be costly. Don't expect perfection, though: worn brake-pads and tyres, grating wheel bearings and defective batteries can be fixed inexpensively, and if repairs are needed, it gives you a good excuse to haggle over the price. All tyres should be the same type and size, especially on 4WDs. If you lack faith in your own abilities, the various state automobile associations offer rigorous **pre-purchase inspections** for about $100, which isn't much to pay if it saves you from buying a wreck.

If you're buying privately (or from an unscrupulous dealer) you should also check the requirements of the state transport department: in most states you'll need a **roadworthiness certificate** to have the vehicle transferred from its previous owner's name to yours. This means having a garage check it over; legally, the previous owner should do this, and theoretically it guarantees that the car is mechanically sound – but don't rely on it. You then proceed to the local Department of Transport with the certificate, a receipt, your driver's licence and passport; they charge a percentage of the price as stated on the receipt to register the vehicle in your name. WA-registered cars are a special case because a new roadworthy certificate is not necessary when the car is sold, as is sensibly but expensively the case in other states. This means that cars with WA plates are much easier to sell on wherever you are (as long as you keep the WA registration).

If the annual **vehicle registration** is due, or you bought an interstate or deregistered vehicle ("as is", without number plates), you'll have to pay extra for registration, which is dependent on the engine size and runs into hundreds of dollars. Note that cars with interstate registration can be difficult to sell: if

possible, go for a car with the registration of the state where you anticipate selling. Registration includes the legal minimum third-party personal **insurance**, but you might want to increase this cover to protect against the theft of the vehicle (for around $95), or if you've bought something more flash go the whole way with comprehensive motor insurance. Joining one of the **automobile clubs** for another $60 or so is well worth considering, as you'll get free roadside assistance (within certain limits), and discounts on road maps and other products. Each state has their own association, but membership is reciprocal with overseas equivalents.

Equipping your car

Even if you expect to stick mostly to the main highways, you'll need to carry a fair number of **spares**: there are plenty of very isolated spots, even between Sydney and Melbourne. For ordinary cars, the cheapest place to **buy spares** is at a supermarket – head for the racks of any branch of K-Mart or Coles. A proper tow rope is vital; passing motorists are far cheaper than tow trucks. In addition – and especially if your vehicle is past its prime – you should have a set of spark plugs, points, fuses, fuel filters (for diesels), fan belt and radiator hoses – you need to check all these anyway and might want to replace them as a matter of course and keep the originals as back-ups. A selection of hose clamps, radiator sealant, putty for leaking tanks, water-dispersing spray, jump leads, tyre pump/compressor and a board to support the jack on soft ground will also come in handy. Again, if the car is old, establish its engine oil consumption early on; a car can carry on for thousands of kilometres guzzling oil at an alarming rate, but if the level drops too much the engine is ruined. If you're confident, get a *Gregory's* workshop manual for your vehicle; even if you're not, carry these spares anyway – someone who knows how to use them might stop. Whatever else, always carry jerrycans with enough water and fuel to get you to the next garage after a mishap.

Before you set off, check battery terminals for corrosion, and the battery for charge

– buy a new one if necessary, and don't risk money on a secondhand item. Carry two spare tyres. In fact, one of the best things you can do is start a long road trip with six new tyres, oil, filters, and radiator coolant, as well as points (if present) and plugs on a petrol engine. **Off-road drivers** in remote regions should add to the list a puncture repair kit, bead breaker and tubes – and know how to use them. Keeping tyres at the correct pressure and having a wheel balance/alignment will reduce wear.

Motorcycling

Motorbikes, especially large-capacity trail bikes, are fine for the Australian climate, although long distances place a premium on their comfort and fuel range. Japanese trail bikes, like Honda's NX650, sell for around $4000 and allow 100kph on-road cruising with adequate off-road agility and readily available spares. A **Honda** XL600V Transalp or Africa Twin is much more comfortable on the road and OK on gravel. The choice of tyres is crucial to off-road performance. Pirelli MT21 tyres are widely regarded as the best compromise tyre for road and track, but always carry a complete puncture repair kit and a spare tube or plugs for a tubeless tyre – and know how to use them. The *Adventure Motorcycling Handbook* (Trailblazer) is a definitive manual to motor-biking off the beaten track and includes a regional rundown of Australia's Outback biking highlights.

If it's likely that you'll return to your starting point, look out for dealers offering **buy-back** options, which guarantee a resale at the end of your trip; bikes can be more difficult to sell than cars. Whether you're planning to ride off or on the bitumen, **plenty of water**-carrying capacity is essential. Travelling alone can be risky, and **night-riding** is plain danger-ous, with poor surfaces hard to judge and kangaroos liable to bounce out of nowhere.

Motorbike **rental** – usually available only in the cities – is at least the same price as a car. A better alternative is a motorbike **tour**: these take various forms, with bikes supplied and a support vehicle (check out the bimonthly *Side Track* magazine once in Australia), to a quick blast on the back of a Harley Davidson (see "Listings" sections throughout the Guide for details of operators).

Cycling

Cycling is popular in Australia, and even if you're not a triathlete bent on pedalling between Sydney and Perth, bicycles are easily ferried between the places where you'd want to use them. Mountain bikes are ideal for rougher country, but lighter and more efficient tourers are better if you're attempting any long-distance travel on main roads. Most cities have well-defined cycle routes and bike lanes; helmets are compulsory, though the law is not always enforced in rural areas. **Renting** and **finding spares** is no trouble in the cities and larger country towns.

If you're **bringing your own bike**, international airlines usually overlook the odd extra kilo if the bike is properly packaged; ask first – though it's often the airport check-in counter which has the last word. On **internal flights** you'll need to have the handlebars and pedals turned in, the front wheel removed and strapped to the back, and the tyres deflated; some airlines consider bikes as two pieces of excess baggage and charge accordingly (excess baggage is usually insured against damage up to a maximum of $1600 damages, so you might want to extend this). **Trains** have fixed rates for carrying bikes (depending on the route) and you'll save on bus charges by disassembling

---

Useful motorcycling websites

Adventure Motorcycling ⓦ www.adventure-motorcycling.com. Not Australia-specific but compliments the *Adventure Motorcycling Handbook* with trip reports and the "Reef to Rock" video/DVD.

Bloke on a Bike ⓦ abc.net.au/bloke. Travels around Australia on a GS1150.

Net Bikes ⓦ www.netbikes.com.au. Check out bike prices and availability in Australia before you go with this classified ads site.

and packing your bike flat. See "Books" (p.1211) for specialist guides to cycling in Australia.

Hitching

The official advice is **don't**: with so many affordable forms of transport available, there's no real need to take the risk. If you must do it, **never hitch alone**, and always avoid being dropped in the middle of nowhere between settlements. In rural areas people seem more willing to stop, but long, isolated stretches of road don't make this the safest country to hitch in; as usual, **women** are at greatest risk. Remember that you don't have to get into a vehicle just because it stops: choose who to get in with and don't be afraid to ask questions before you do get in, making the arrangement clear from the start. Ask the driver where he or she is going rather than saying where you want to go. Try to keep your pack with you; having it locked

in the boot makes a quick escape more difficult.

A much better method is lining up lifts through **hostel notice boards** (though this means sharing fuel costs). This option gives you the chance to meet the driver in advance, and – as a fellow traveller – they will most likely be stopping to see many of the same sights along the way. In out-of-the-way locations, roadhouses are a good place to head, as the owners often know of people who'll be heading your way.

The best way to ensure your **safety**, apart from exercising your judgement and common sense, is to make concrete arrangements before your departure and stick to them. Hostel managers are well aware of the possible danger to young women departing across the Outback with new acquaintances or undertaking work on remote stations, and will gladly receive – or better still – make calls to ensure your safe arrival.

Accommodation

Finding somewhere to bed down is rarely a problem, even in the smallest of places. However, on the east coast it's a good idea to book ahead for Christmas and Easter holidays, and in some places (the Gold Coast, for instance) there are price rises and room shortages even at weekends.

Watch out for the term "**hotel**", which in Australia generally means a pub or bar. Although they were once legally required to provide somewhere for customers to sleep off a skinful – and many still do provide accommodation – the facilities are not necessarily luxurious. Those highlighted in this Guide do offer decent rooms, though the majority of them are still primarily places to drink, can be loud and drunken, and are not necessarily enticing places to stay.

The other side of this coin is that many places that would call themselves hotels anywhere else prefer to use another name –

hence the reason for so many motels and resorts, and in the cities "private hotels" or (especially in Sydney and Melbourne) "boutique hotels" that tend to be smaller and more characterful places to stay, run along guesthouse lines. There are also a growing number of bed and breakfast places (B&Bs) and farmstays where you can join in with farm life.

Other categories of accommodation worth looking into are the huge array of excellent hostels and "backpackers", caravan parks that offer accommodation in the form of permanent on-site vans and cabins or chalets as well as campervan facilities and tent spaces, and self-catering apartments or, in country areas, cabins and cottages.

Hotels and motels

Cheaper Australian **hotels** tend to be basic – no TV, and shared bathrooms and plain furnishings – and aren't always the best choice for peace and quiet. In country areas hotels are often the social centre of town, especially on Friday and Saturday nights. But with double rooms at around $50–70 and singles from $40 (often with breakfast included), they can be better value – and more private – than hostel accommodation. **Motels** are typically a comfortable, bland choice, often found en masse at the edge of town to catch weary drivers, and priced on average upwards of $70 for a double room with TV and bath, not including breakfast. They rarely have single rooms, but they may have larger units for families, often with basic cooking facilities.

In cities, you're far more likely to come across a hotel in the conventional sense. The cheaper of these may well describe themselves as "private hotels" to distinguish themselves from pubs, the decisive factor being the absence of a public bar. Some of these, especially in inner cities, can be rather sleazy, but others are very pleasant family-run guesthouses. Double rooms might cost anything from $60 and up, and there are often singles

available at about two-thirds of the price. More expensive hotels are much as you'd expect: in the cities most of them are standard places with all the usual facilities, aimed at the business community; in resorts and tourist areas they're more like upmarket motels. Prices might be anything from $150 to $300 or more in five-star establishments: a typical city three-star will probably cost you above $120. Similar places in a resort or country area charge $100 or more.

There are numerous nationwide hotel and motel chains that give certain guarantees of standards, among them familiar names such as Best Western and Travelodge, as well as Australian ones such as Budget, Golden Chain and Flag. All have directories of their members, which you can use to plan ahead. While you might find it rather restrictive to use them for your whole stay, they offer dependable facilities and can be used to ensure that you have a reservation on arrival, or at anywhere else you know you'll be spending some time.

Resorts and self-catering apartments

You'll find establishments calling themselves **resorts** all over Australia, but the term is not a very clearly defined one. At the bottom end, price, appearance and facilities may be

---

Accommodation price codes

All the accommodation listed in this book has been categorized into one of seven **price codes**, as set out below. These represent the cost of the cheapest available double or twin room in high season; single rooms are generally about two-thirds the price of doubles. However, there's a variety of different types of accommodation on offer – sometimes under the same roof: hostels and backpackers' accommodation mainly have beds in dormitories. Where this is the case the price stated is per dorm bed per night in high season. In addition, they quite often also have very inexpensive single and double rooms for which a price code is given. For units, cabins and vans the code covers the cost of the entire unit, which may sleep as many as six people.

In the lower categories, most rooms will be without private bath, though there's usually a washbasin in the room. From code ❹ upwards you'll most likely have private facilities. Remember that many of the cheaper places may also have more expensive rooms with en-suite facilities.

❶ Under $35
❷ $35–55
❸ $55–80
❹ $80–110
❺ $110–150
❻ $150–200
❼ $200 and upwards

little different to those of a motel, while top-flight places can be exclusive hideaways costing hundreds of dollars a night. Originally the name implied that the price was all-inclusive of accommodation, drinks, meals, sports and anything else on offer, but this isn't always the case. These places tend to be set in picturesque locations – the Barrier Reef islands swarm with them – and are often brilliant value if you can wangle a stand-by or off-season price.

Self-catering or self-contained units, apartments or country cabins can be a very good deal for families and larger groups. The places themselves range from larger units at a motel to purpose-built apartment hotels, but are usually excellent value. Cooking facilities are variable, but there'll always be a TV and fridge; linen (generally not included) can sometimes be rented for a small extra charge.

Farmstays and B&Bs

Another option in rural areas are **farmstays** on working farms and **B&Bs** or **guesthouses**, the last two predominantly in the south and east. Both offer a more homely atmosphere, though B&Bs especially can be anything from someone's large home to your own colonial cottage – ask what the "breakfast" actually includes. Farmstays are even more variable, with some offering very upmarket comforts while at others you make do with the basic facilities in vacant shearers' quarters; their attraction is that they are always in out-of-the-way locations, and you'll often get a chance to participate in the working of the farm, or take advantage of guided tours around the property on horseback or by 4WD.

Hostels

There's a huge amount of **budget accommodation** in Australia, and though the more shambolic operations don't survive for long, standards are variable. Official **YHA youth hostels** are pretty dependable – if often relatively expensive – and most of their depressingly regimented rules and regulations have been dropped in the face of competition, especially from the firmly established **Backpacker Resorts/VIP** network, whose membership card is as useful

and widely known as the YHA. Another established network of backpacker hostels is **Nomads** which also issues a membership card entitling holders to plenty of discounts.

At their best, hostels and backpackers' accommodation – both names are widely used, and don't necessarily imply membership of an organization – are excellent value and are good places to meet other travellers and get on the grapevine. There's often a choice of dormitories, double or family rooms, plus bike rental, kitchen, games room, TV, Internet access, a pool and help with finding work or organizing trips. Many have useful notice boards, organized activities and tours. At their worst, their double rooms might be poorer value than local hotel accommodation, and some are simply grubby, rapid-turnover dives – affiliation to an organization does not ensure quality. Hostels charge $15–28 or more for a dormitory bed, with doubles – if available – from around $40.

While it's a good idea to carry at least a sheet sleeping bag for hostels which don't provide linen, some hygienically minded establishments now prohibit the use of personal sleeping bags and instead provide all bedding needs.

Youth hostel associations

In England and Wales

Youth Hostel Association (YHA) Trevelyan House, 8 St Stephen's Hill, St Albans, Herts AL1 2DY ☎0870/870 8808, ⓦwww.yha.org.uk or www.iyhf.org. Annual membership £13; under-18s £6.50; family £26 (one-parent family £13); group £13; lifetime £190 (or five annual payments of £40).

In Scotland

Scottish Youth Hostel Association 7 Glebe Crescent, Stirling FK8 2JA ☎0870/155 3255, ⓦwww.syha.org.uk. Annual membership £6, under-18s £2.50.

In Ireland

An Óige 61 Mountjoy St, Dublin 7 ☎01/830 4555, ⓦwww.irelandyha.org.
Annual membership €15; under-18s €7.50; family €31.50; lifetime €75.
Hostelling International Northern Ireland 22–32 Donegall Rd, Belfast BT12 5JN ☎028/9032

4733, ⓦwww.hini.org.uk. Adult membership £10; under-18s £6; family £20; lifetime £75.

In the US

Hostelling International-American Youth Hostels (HI-AYH) 733 15th St NW, Suite 840, PO Box 37613, Washington, DC 20005 ☏202/783-6161, ⓦwww.hiayh.org. Annual membership for adults (18–55) is $25, for seniors (55 or over) is $15, and for under-18s and groups of ten or more, is free. Lifetime memberships are $250.

In Canada

Hostelling International/Canadian Hostelling Association Room 400, 205 Catherine St, Ottawa, ON K2P 1C3 ☏1-800/663-5777 or 613/237-7884, ⓦwww.hostellingintl.ca. Rather than sell the traditional one- or two-year memberships, the association now sells one Individual Adult membership with a 28- to 16-month term. The length of the term depends on when the membership is sold, but a member can receive up to 28 months of membership for just $35. Membership is free for under-18s and you can become a lifetime member for $175.

In Australia

Australia Youth Hostels Association 422 Kent St, Sydney ☏02/9261 1111, ⓦwww.yha.com.au. Adult membership rate $52 (under-18s, $16) for the first twelve months and then $32 each year after.

In New Zealand

New Zealand Youth Hostels Association 173 Gloucester St, Christchurch ☏03/379 9970, ⓦwww.yha.co.nz. Adult membership $40 for one year, $60 for two and $80 for three; under-18s free; lifetime $300.

Camping, caravan parks and roadhouses

Perhaps because Australian hostels are so widespread and inexpensive, simple tent **camping** is an option little used by foreign travellers. Australia has some remarkably hard ground, as well as lots of sand, so vital **equipment** includes ground mats and a range of pegs – some wide for sand, others narrow for soil. A hatchet for splitting fire-wood is light to carry and doubles as a

---

Hostel passes

If you're travelling on a budget, it's well worth laying your hands on at least one of the following **hostel passes**, which give you cheaper rates – around ten percent off – on accommodation at member hostels, and also entitle you to a wide range of other discounts on everything from bus tickets and tours to phone calls, museum entry fees and meals.

Probably of most use in Australia is a **Backpacker Resorts/VIP card**, which doubles as a rechargeable eKit phone card with a few dollars worth of phone calls factored into the price of the card ($32 for one year, $44 for two years). Anyone can obtain it from member hostels in Australia or over the Net at ⓦwww.backpackers.com.au (add $6 for postage and handling). At present there are around 140 member hostels around the country, and your card will also be valid at a score more in New Zealand and Fiji.

Another organization that works along similar lines is **Nomads**; their card, which also doubles as a rechargeable phone card, costs $29, and can be bought at their hostels in Australia) or on the Web at ⓦwww.nomadsworld.com. Their network comprises about 70 hostels in Australia, many of them in old pubs, a few of them "working hostels" in country areas specializing in harvest work, and there are also affiliated hostels in New Zealand, Fiji, and a few other countries.

Yet another option is an **International YHA card**, available through your national youth hostel association before you leave home, or you can purchase a one-year Hostelling International card in Australia for $32. Australian residents can, of course, also join in Australia but must pay $52. YHA Membership and Travel Centres can be found in Sydney, Darwin, Brisbane, Cairns, Adelaide, Hobart, Melbourne and Perth, at many YHA hostels, and on their website ⓦyha.com.au. Australian YHA hostels number about 140, with thousands more worldwide.

hammer. Fuel stoves are recommended, but if you do build a fire, make sure it doesn't get out of control – and always observe any fire bans. In national parks, **bushcamping** is often the only option for staying overnight: some park sites have hot showers, drinking water and toilets; others provide absolutely nothing. Prices depend on state policy and site facilities, and you'll usually need a permit from the local NPWS (National Parks and Wildlife Service) office, details of which are given throughout the Guide.

Camping rough by the road is not a good idea, even if you take the usual precautions of setting up away from the roadside and avoiding dry riverbeds. If you have to do it, try and ensure you're not too visible: having a group of drunks pitch into your camp at midnight is not an enjoyable experience. Animals are unlikely to pose a threat, except to your food – keep it in your tent or a secure container, or be prepared to be woken by their nocturnal shenanigans.

In towns, there's often a choice between basic council campsites and better-equipped private caravan parks, which will not only have space to pitch a tent but will also have powered hook-up facilities for campervans and probably a store; a lot also offer pools and all the facilities of a mini-resort. Many have on-site vans (caravans with cooking facilities but no toilet) or cabins (with bath or shower, often a TV, airconditioning and a heater): these can be very good value and are often available even when all the hotel and motel rooms have been filled up. The main problem is that linen – sheets, towels and so on – is usually not included, though you may be able to rent it. Expect to pay $10–18 per tent for an unpowered site, or $36–90 for a van or cabin, depending on its location, age, size and equipment. Highway roadhouses are similar, combining a range of accommodation with fuel and restaurants for long-distance travellers.

Eating and drinking

Australia is almost two separate nations when it comes to food. In the cities of the southeast – especially Melbourne – there's a range of cosmopolitan and inexpensive restaurants and cafés featuring almost every imaginable cuisine. Here there's an exceptionally high ratio of eating places to people, and they survive because people eat out so much – three times a week is not unusual. Remote country areas are the complete antithesis of this, where the only thing better than meat pies and microwaveable fast food are the plain, straightforward counter meals served at the local hotel, or a slightly more upmarket bistro or basic Chinese restaurant.

Traditionally, Australian food found its roots in the English overcooked-meat-and-three-veg "common-sense cookery" mould. Two things have rescued the country from its culinary destitution: immigration and an extraordinary range of superb, locally produced fresh ingredients that not even the most ham-fisted chef could ruin. Various ethnic cuisines are briefly discussed below, but in addition to introducing their own cuisine, immigrants have had at least as profound an effect on mainstream Australian food. "Contemporary Australian" cuisine is an exciting blend of tastes and influences from around the world – particularly Asia and the Mediterranean – and many not specifically "ethnic" restaurants will have a menu that includes properly prepared curry, dolmades and fettucine alongside steak and prawns. This healthy, eclectic – and above all, fresh – modern Australian cuisine has a lot in common with Californian cooking styles, and both go under the banner of "Pacific Rim cuisine".

Australian food

Meat is plentiful, cheap and excellent: steak forms the mainstay of the pub counter meal and of the ubiquitous **barbie**, or barbecue – as Australian an institution as you could hope to find. Even if no one invites you along to one, you can still enjoy a barbie: free or coin-operated electric barbecues can be found in car parks, campsites and beauty spots all over the country. As well as beef and lamb, you may also find **exotic meats**, especially in the more upmarket restaurants. Emu, buffalo, camel and witchetty grubs are all served, but the two most common are kangaroo, a rich, tender and virtually fat-free meat, and croco-dile, which tastes like a mix of chicken and pork and is at its best when simply grilled. At the coast, and elsewhere in specialist restau-rants, there's tremendous **seafood**: prawns and oysters, mud crabs, Moreton Bay bugs and yabbies (sea- and freshwater crayfish), lobsters, and a wide variety of fresh- and seawater fish – barramundi has a reputation as one of the finest, but is easily beaten by sweetlips or coral trout.

Fruit is good, too, from Tasmanian apples and pears to tropical bananas, pawpaw

Bushtucker

The first European colonists decided that the country was not "owned" by the Aborigines because they didn't systematically farm the land. As many frustrated pastoralists later came to realize, this was a direct response to Australia's erratic seasons, which don't lend themselves to European farming methods with any degree of long-term security. Instead, Aborigines followed a **nomadic lifestyle** within extensive tribal boundaries, following seasonal game and plants and promoting both by annually burning off grassland.

Along the coast people speared turtles and dugong from outrigger canoes, caught **fish** in stone traps, piled emptied oyster shells into giant middens, and even co-operated with dolphins to herd fish into shallows. Other animals caught all over the country were possums, snakes (highly prized), goannas, emus and kangaroos. These **animals** were thrown straight onto a fire and cooked in their own juices, and their skins, bones and fat were sometimes used as clothing, tools and ointment respectively. More meagre pickings were provided by honey and green ants, water-holding frogs, moths and various grubs – the witchetty (or witjuti) being the best known. Foot-long ooli worms were drawn out of rotten mangrove trunks and tiny native bees were tagged with strands of spider web and then followed to their hives for honey; another sweet treat was mulga resin, picked off the tree trunk.

Plants, usually gathered by women, were used extensively and formed the bulk of the diet. The cabbage palm, sea almond, mangrove seeds, pandanus and dozens of fruits, including tropical coconuts, plums and figs, all grew along the coast. Inland were samphire bush, wild tomatoes and "citrus", grasstree hearts, cycad nuts (very toxic until washed, but high in starch), native millet, wattle seeds, waterlily tubers, nardoo seeds (a water fern), fungi, macadamia nuts, quandongs, and bunya pine nuts – the last had great social importance in southern Queensland, where they were eaten at huge feasts. In Queensland's far north you'll find one of the few surviving traditional styles of cooking, the Torres Strait Islander *kup maori* – meat and vegetables wrapped in banana leaves and roasted in an underground oven.

It's tempting to taste some bushfoods, and a good few city **restaurants**, as well as the *Bushtucker Café* in the Grampians (see p.1009), are now experimenting with them as ingredients; otherwise you'll need expert guidance, as many plants are poisonous. A few **tours** and safaris (particularly in the Northern Territory) give an introduction to living off the land; for further reading, try *Bush Tucker: Australia's Wild Food Harvest* by Tim Low.

(papaya), mangoes, avocados, citrus fruits, custard apples, lychees, pineapples, passion fruit, star fruit and coconuts – few of them native, but delicious nonetheless. Vegetables are also fresh, cheap and good, and include everything from European cauliflowers and potatoes to Chinese choi sam and Indian bitter gourds. Note that aubergine is known as eggplant, courgettes as zucchini and red or green peppers as capsicums.

Vegetarians might assume that they'll face a narrow choice of food in "meatocentric" Australia, and in the country areas that's probably true. But elsewhere most restaurants will have one vegetarian option at least, and in the cities veggie cafés have cultivated a wholesome, trendy image that suits Australians' active, health-conscious nature.

Finally, a word on **eskies** – insulated food containers varying from handy "six-pack" sizes to cavernous sixty-litre trunks capable of refrigerating a weekend's worth of food or beer. No barbie or camping trip is complete without a couple of eskies. The brand name "Esky" has been adopted to describe all similar products.

Ethnic food

Since World War II wave after wave of immigrants have brought a huge variety of **ethnic cuisines** to Australia: first North European, then Mediterranean and most recently Asian.

Chinese

Chinese restaurants were on the scene early in Australia – a result of post-goldrush Chinese enterprise – and Sydney, Melbourne and Darwin have Chinese connections dating back to the 1850s. The Chinese restaurants you'll find in most of the country tend to be rather old-fashioned and heavily reliant on MSG, but they're often the only alternative to Australian food. In contrast, the Chinatown area of big cities will provide a chance to sample some regional Chinese dishes as well as the usual Cantonese fare.

Two specialities served in Chinese restaurants are *yum cha* (or dim sum), lots of little titbits such as steamed buns and dumplings served from trolleys; and steamboat, an Asian version of fondue. Both are tasty and

Infamous Australian foods

Chicko Roll Imagine a wrapper of stodgy dough covered in breadcrumbs, filled with a neutered mess of chicken, cabbage, thickeners and flavourings, and then deep fried. You could only get away with it in Australia.

Damper Sounding positively wholesome in this company, "damper" is the swagman's staple – soda bread baked in a pot buried in the ashes of a fire. It's not hard to make after a few attempts – the secret is in the heat of the coals and a splash of beer.

Lamington A chocolate-coated sponge cube rolled in shredded coconut.

Pavlova (pav) A dessert concoction of meringue with layers of cream and fruit; named after the eminent Russian ballerina. Made properly with fresh fruit and minimum quantities of cream and sugar, it's not bad at all.

Pie floater The apotheosis of the meat pie; a "pie floater" is an inverted meat pie swamped in mashed green peas and tomato sauce; found especially in South Australia. Floaters can be surprisingly good, or horrible enough to put you off both pies and peas for life.

Vegemite Regarded by the English as an inferior form of Marmite and by almost every other nationality with total disgust, Vegemite is an Australian institution – a strong, dark, yeast spread for bread and toast.

Witchetty grubs (*witjuti*) About the size of your little finger, witchetty grubs are dug from the roots of mulga trees and are a well-known Australian bush delicacy. Eating the plump, fawn-coloured caterpillars live (as is traditional) takes some nerve, so try giving them a brief roasting in embers. They're very tasty either way – reminiscent of peanut butter.

extremely good value for money – especially for a group.

Other Asian cuisines

Since the 1970s a new wave of immigrants from Southeast Asia has further energized Australian cuisine. **Vietnamese** restaurants not only offer some of the cheapest meals anywhere, they also come with the freshest of ingredients: with most meals a plate of red chillies, lemon wedges and crunchy beansprouts is served.

There are numerous **Malaysian** and **Indonesian** restaurants and market stalls, where hearty noodle soups and satays with hot peanut sauce are served up. Hawker-style stalls in city food courts often serve *laksa*, a huge bowl of hot and spicy coconut-milk-based soup full of noodles, tofu and chicken or prawns.

The biggest success of them all, however, are the **Thai** restaurants, and it's hard to believe that they've been around for less than twenty years. Dishes can be fiery, yet subtly flavoured, with ingredients such as basil, lemongrass, garlic, chilli and coriander.

Because so much fresh seafood is available in Australia, **Japanese** food is more accessible – and less expensive – that it is in many other countries. There may not be a large Japanese population, but there are a huge number of Japanese visitors, and plenty of places catering for them (you'll find lots on the Gold Coast and in Cairns, for example).

Mongolian barbecues sound like a short-lived novelty but in fact are quite good: an unusual, fast and inexpensive complement to the already diverse Asian food culture. Thinly sliced meat or seafood is added to a selection of sliced vegetables and stir-fried in a soy-type sauce before your eyes on a giant wok – a Mongol warrior's shield is said to have been the original cooking utensil.

Italian – and coffee

The **Italian** influence on Australian cooking has been enormous. Second in number only to the English as an ethnic group, the Italians brought with them their love of food, which was a perfect complement to the Australian climate and way of life, and from the 1950s pizzerias, espresso and *gelati* bars, and the then-exotic taste of garlic, were conquering palates countrywide. One particularly Australian metamorphosis is **focaccia**, now a staple of every city café and even beginning to make an appearance in country towns.

Australia can also thank the Italians for elevating coffee to a pastime rather than just a hot drink. Nowadays every suburban café has an espresso machine, and it's not just used to make cappuccino. Other styles of coffee have adopted uniquely Australian names: a "flat white" is a plain white coffee, a "cafe latte" is a milkier version usually served in a glass (like cappuccino without the froth), a "long black" is a regular cup of black coffee, and a "short black" is an espresso – transformed by a splash of milk into a macchiato. ("Espresso" is also a brand of instant coffee, so ask for a short black if you're after the genuine article.) A cappuccino costs around $3.

Other European and Middle Eastern

Melbourne is Australia's food capital, with its legendary **Greek** population among the many European influences in the city. As well as taverna-style Greek restaurants, souvlakia bars, with spiced lamb rotating on a spit, abound. **Turkish** and **Lebanese** takeaways use a similar ingredient for their spicy filled rolls, while some Turkish places also offer pides, small, simple but spicy variants on a pizza. Lebanese restaurants are especially good for vegetarians, with falafel rolls (pitta bread stuffed with chickpea patties, hummus and tabbouleh) making an inexpensive, filling meal.

Central European influences are most obvious in baking, particularly in Melbourne, where there is a large **Jewish** community made up of immigrants from prewar Poland, and there are also a few **Polish** restaurants serving solid, peasant-style dishes. **German** influences are most prominent around Adelaide – as well as at deli counters throughout the country, where you'll find an abundance of Australian-made small goods and sausages.

Places to eat

Restaurants are astonishingly good value compared with Britain and North America, particularly as many restaurants are **BYO** (bring your own): you buy your own wine or beer and bring it with you – you're rarely far from a **bottle shop** (the Australian term for an off-licence or liquor store). There may be a small corkage fee, but it's still better than paying inflated restaurant prices for your drink: even many licensed restaurants also allow you to BYO. You should have no problem finding an excellent two- or three-course meal in a BYO restaurant for $22 or less, though a main course at a moderate restaurant is around $15–19. There are also lots of excellent **cafés and coffee shops** – Italian ones (see p.51), continental patisseries/ bakeries, and places that serve English-style Devonshire (cream) teas and cakes. In the cities and resorts, cafés will be open from early in the morning until late at night, serving food all day; in the country, they may stick more or less to shop hours.

The hotel counter meal is another mainstay, and at times may be all that's available: if it is, make sure you get there in time – meals in pubs are generally served only from noon to 2pm and again from 6 to 8pm, and rarely at all on Sunday evening. The food – served at the bar – will be simple but substantial and inexpensive (usually around $12 or less): steak, salad and chips, and variations on this theme. Slightly more upmarket is the hotel bistro or restaurant in a motel, where you sit down to be served much the same food; these places often have a help-yourself salad bar, too, which is always a good alternative for vegetarians. Usually the most expensive thing on the menu is a huge steak for $12–15.

Fast food is widely available, with all the usual burger, pizza and chicken places offering a quick bite for as little as $5. Fish (usually shark or snapper) and chips can be excellent in coastal regions. In cities and bigger resorts you'll find fantastic fast food in food courts, often in the basements of office buildings or in shopping malls, where dozens of small stalls compete to offer Thai, Chinese, Japanese or Italian food as well as burgers, steaks and sandwiches. On the road, you may be reduced to what's available at the roadhouse, usually the lowest common denominator of reheated meat pies and microwaved ready meals.

Drinking

Australians have a reputation for enjoying a drink, and **hotels** (also sometimes called taverns, inns, pubs and bars) are where it mostly takes place. Traditionally, public bars are male enclaves, the place where mates meet after work on their way home, with the emphasis more on the beer and banter than the surroundings (see also "Women and sexual harassment" on p.79). While changing attitudes have converted many city hotels into comfortable, relaxed bars, many Outback pubs are still pretty spartan and daunting for strangers of either sex, but you'll find barriers will come down if you're prepared to join in the conversation.

Friday and Saturday are the serious party nights, when there's likely to be a band and – in the case of some Outback establishments – literally everybody for a hundred kilometres around jammed into the building. Opening hours vary from state to state; they're usually 11am to 11pm, but are often much later, with early closing on Sunday. Some places are also "early openers", with hours ranging from 6am to 6pm.

For take-out sales, liquor stores or offlicences are known as bottle shops. These are usually in a separate section attached to a pub or supermarket – in some states, you can't buy alcohol from supermarkets or grocery stores. There are also drive-in bottle shops attached to pubs where locals can load bulk purchases directly into the boot of their car; these solve the question of parking, though aren't totally the lazy option as you normally have to get out of the car to make your selection.

Beer

As anyone you ask will tell you, the proper way to drink **beer** in a hot country such as Australia is ice cold (the English can expect to be constantly berated for their warm beer preferences) and fast, from a small container so it doesn't heat up before you can down the contents. Tubular foam or polystyrene **coolers** are often supplied for **tinnies** (cans) or **stubbies** (short-necked bottles) to make sure they stay icy. Glasses are always on the small side, and are given confusingly different names state by state. The standard ten-ounce (half-pint) serving is known as a **pot** in Victoria and Queensland, and a **middie** in New South Wales and Western Australia, where the situation is further complicated by the presence of fifteen-ounce **schooners**. A **carton** or **slab** is a box of 24–30 tinnies or stubbies, bought in bulk from a bottle shop and always cheaper when not chilled (a "Darwin stubby", with typically Territorian eccentricity, is two litres of beer in an over-sized bottle).

Australian beers are lager- or pilsner-style, and even the big mass-produced ones are pretty good – at least once you've worked up a thirst. They're considerably stronger than their US equivalents, and marginally stronger than the average British lager at just under five percent alcohol. Each state has its own label and there are fierce local loyalties, even though most are sold nationwide: Fourex (XXXX; see p.410) and Powers in Queensland; Swan in Western Australia; Coopers in South Australia; VB in Victoria; Tooheys in New South Wales; and Boags in Tasmania. Almost all of these companies produce more than one beer – usually a light low-alcohol version and a premium "gold" or bitter brew. There are also a number of smaller "boutique" breweries and specialist beermakers: Tasmania's Cascade, WA's Redback or Matilda Bay, Cairns' Draught and Eumundi from Queensland are more distinctive but harder to find. Fosters is treated as a joke in Australia, something that's fit only for export. Larger bottle shops might have imported beers, but outside cities (where Irish pubs serve surprisingly authentic-tasting Guinness) it's rare that you'll find anything foreign on tap.

Wines and spirits

Australian wines have long been appreciated at home, and it's not hard to see why; even an inexpensive bottle (around $12) will be better than just drinkable, while pricier varieties compare favourably with fine French wines – though some critics complain that Australian reds have become a bit too "woody" in recent years. If you're new to Australian wines, you'll always find Yalumba, Lindeman's, Hardy's and Wolf Blass will give satisfaction, but the secret is to be adventurous: you're extremely unlikely to be disappointed. Even the "chateau cardboard" four-litre bladders or wine casks that prevail at parties and barbecues are perfectly palatable. Whatever the colour, a mid-range bottle of wine will set you back about $16.

The biggest wine-producing regions are the Hunter Valley in New South Wales (see p.214) and the Barossa Valley in South Australia (see p.826), but you'll find smaller commercial vineyards as far north as Kingaroy in Queensland and in southwest Western Australia; all are detailed in the text of the Guide. If you buy at these places you'll be able to sample in advance, though there's occasionally a charge for tasting to discourage overly enthusiastic visitors from just trying everything and then moving on elsewhere (see the box on "Wine tasting tips" on p.824). Most bottle shops will, in any case, have a good range of very reasonably priced options.

The Australian wine industry also makes port and brandy as a sideline, though these are not up to international standards. Two excellent dark rums from Queensland's sugar belt are well worth tasting, however: the sweet, deliciously smoky Bundaberg (see p.472) and the more conventionally flavoured Beenleigh. They're of average strength, normally 33 percent alcohol, but beware of "overproof" variations, which will have you flat on your back if you try to drink them like ordinary spirits.

Aussie wine on the Net

Boutique Wines
Ⓦ www.boutiquewines.com.au.
Links to all those vineyards you've probably never heard of.
Hardy's Ⓦ www.hardys.com.au.
Lindeman's Ⓦ www.lindemans.com.
Penfolds Ⓦ www.penfolds.com.au.
Wines of Distinction
Ⓦ www.australianwines.com.au.
Where to go and what to look for when making a selection.
Yalumba Ⓦ www.yalumba.com.

Soft drinks

Various colas, Sprite, 7-Up, Fanta and a couple of home-produced brands – Bundaberg ginger beer and Cascade's Tasmanian apple juice – are the **soft** alternatives to alcohol. Bottled **fruit juices** come in every style, and in the tropics (and trendy city cafés) you can often get freshly squeezed juices made from familiar and not-so-familiar fruits. There's also a range of **spring waters** from several sources along the Great Dividing Range – a relief at times from the heavily chlorinated tap water. Sickly **flavoured milk** is another national institution: every store's fridge will be packed with different-flavoured cartons.

Communications

Australia may be far away to some, but efficient international communication has enabled the visitor from abroad to be in contact wherever they are. To ensure you're not waking somebody up when phoning, see p.81 for the relevant time zone.

Mail

Every town of any size will have a **post office**, and where there isn't one there'll be an **Australia Post agency**, usually at the general store. Post offices and agencies are officially open Monday to Friday 9am to 5pm. Agencies might have an hour off during the day for lunch or close early, and big city GPOs sometimes open late or on Saturday morning. Out in the country it's rare to see postboxes, so you'll usually have to take your mail to the nearest post office or agency.

Domestically, the mail service has a poor reputation, at least for long distances: it will take a week for a letter to get from Wittenoom (WA) to Wagga Wagga (NSW), though major cities have a guaranteed express delivery service to other major cities – worth the expense for important packages. On the other hand, **international mail** is extremely efficient, taking five to ten days to reach Europe, Asia and the US, depending on where it's posted. **Stamps** are sold at some newsagents and general stores, as well as post offices and agencies. A standard letter or postcard within Australia costs 45¢; printed aerogrammes for international letters anywhere in the world cost 70¢;

postcards cost 95¢ to the US and Canada, $1 to Europe; regular letters start at $1.05 to the US and Canada, $1.20 to Europe. If you're sending anything bigger in or outside Australia, there are many different services; get some advice from the post office. Large **parcels** are reasonably cheap to send home by surface mail, but it will take up to three months for them to get there. Economy Air is a good compromise for packages that you want to see again soon – expect a fortnight to Europe.

You can receive mail at any post office or agency: address the letter to **Poste Restante** (add "GPO" or "Central Post Office" for cities, unless you have the address of a particular branch), followed by the town, state and post code. You need a passport or other ID to collect mail, which is kept for a month and then returned; it's possible to get mail redirected if you change your plans – ask for a form at any post office. Some smaller post offices will allow you to phone and check if you have any mail waiting.

Most **hostels** and **hotels** will also hold mail for you if it's clearly marked, preferably with a date of arrival, or holders of Amex cards or traveller's cheques can have it sent to American Express offices.

Phones, phonecards and mobile phones

The two major phone operators in Australia are Telstra and Optus – all public phones are Telstra-operated, their coverage is wider and their rates, on a day-to-day basis, are pretty similar. Post offices (but not agencies) always have a bank of **telephones** outside; otherwise head for the nearest bar or service station – you'll even find solar-powered, satellite-connected booths in the Outback. Public telephones take coins or **Telstra phonecards**, which are sold through newsagents and other stores for $5, $10, $20 or $50. You can make **international calls** from virtually any of them as from a private phone. Many bars, shops and restaurants have orange or blue **payphones**, but these cost more than a regular call box, and international dialling is not advised because they'll start to gobble money the moment you're connected, even if the call goes unanswered. Whatever their type, payphones do not accept incoming calls.

Creditphones accept most major credit cards such as Amex, Visa and Diners International, and can be found at international and domestic airports, central locations in major cities, and many hotels. You can make free **reverse charge** calls using 1800-REVERSE.

Rates for calls within Australia are cheapest in the evenings from Monday to Saturday, and all day Sunday. **Local calls** are untimed, allowing you to talk for as long as you like; this costs around 17¢ on a domestic phone, though public phones may charge 50¢. Many businesses and services operate **free call numbers**, prefixed ☏1800, while others have six-digit numbers beginning with ☏13 or 1300 that incur a one-off fee of ¢25 – however, both only apply to calls from within Australia. Numbers starting ☏0055 are private information services (often recorded), costing between 35¢ and 70¢ a minute, but with a minimum charge of 40¢ from public phones.

International calls are charged at a flat per-minute rate depending on the country

---

Operators and international codes

Operator services
Local Directory Assistance ☏1223
National Directory Assistance ☏12 455
International Directory Assistance ☏12 455

Operator ☏123
International Operator ☏1234

International calls
To call Australia from overseas dial the international access code (☏00 from the UK or New Zealand, ☏011 from the US and Canada), followed by ☏61, the area code minus its initial zero, and the number. **To dial out of Australia** it's ☏0011, followed by the country code, then the area code (without the zero, if there is one), followed by the number:

UK ☏0011 44
US and Canada ☏0011 1

Ireland ☏0011 353
New Zealand ☏0011 64

Country direct
UK
BT operator ☏1800 881 440
BT automatic ☏1800 881 441
Mercury ☏1800 881 417
Ireland
Telecom ☏1800 881 353
US
AT&T ☏1-800/881-011

LDDS Worldcom ☏1-800/881-212
MCI ☏1-800/881-100
Sprint ☏1-800/881-877
Canada
Teleglobe ☏1-800/881-490
New Zealand
Clear ☏1800 124 333
Telecom ☏1800 881 640

BASICS | Communications

called, whatever the hour or day of the week that the call is made. All incur a connection fee of 22¢, then it costs 37.4¢ per minute to the UK; 31¢ to the US; 44¢ for Canada; and 31¢ for New Zealand. If you plan to speak for a while, you can save money by buying half-hour blocks to all the above countries for $6.60 by dialling ☏0018 (instead of ☏0011), then the country code and number. Hang up within the first minute and you only pay a $2 connection fee, otherwise you'll be charged for the full half hour; speak for over thirty minutes and you'll pay double.

Phonecards can be a far cheaper way to call cross country or abroad. Various brands are available such as Say G'day or Go Talk, but all require a minimum of 40¢ to call the local centre, after which you key in your scratch number and telephone number. Rates are incredibly low, as little as 5¢ a minute with Go Talk, if you call from one of the urban centres listed on the card.

It's also possible to pop into Woolies and buy a **pre-paid mobile phone** for as little as $99 including a rechargeable SIM card with $25 credit that lasts three months. Or you can just buy the pre-paid SIM card alone in various denominations which slips into your own phone to give you an instant personal number once you've registered – very handy if you need to keep in touch when trying to get a job, for example. Telstra's communic8 network (ⓦwww.communic8.com.au) is the main provider. You'll need to check whether you own mobile is a GSM 900 or dual-band GSM 900/1800 (most are) and be warned that the phones are cheap but the rates are not so special: about 20¢ to connect and 77¢/minute thereafter. Texting is cheap at around 22¢ but by communic8's own

admission, texting overseas was "hit and miss" at the time of writing.

As with anywhere in the world, mobile phone reception drops off in remote areas. A solution offering guaranteed reception (but at call rates five times higher) is a **satellite phone**. Little bigger than a conventional GSM, they can be rented from ⓦwww .rentasatphone.com.au in Perth (among other places) from around $20/day and can run both GSM as well as the special satellite SIM cards.

The Internet

Public Internet access is now widespread across Australia. Wherever you travel in Australia, keeping in touch via the Web is easy, fast and cheap In the cities. **Internet cafés** are everywhere, typically charging $3–6 an hour with concessions as well as happy hours early in the morning. Many accommodation places– especially **hostels** – also provide terminals for their guests at similar rates (hotels will charge more) although some places – notably *Ayers Rock Resort* – still opt for the user-reviled coin-op booths, while at some YHAs you buy a card that works like a phonecard. The best machines and set-ups are what you'd want at home: modern, clean and fast with conventional controls and large screens. Otherwise, try **local libraries**, which almost always provide free access, though time is generally limited to one hour and you'll have to sign up in advance on a waiting list.

Even the smallest one-horse town will have a **Telecentre**, although opening times can be pretty provincial. Throughout the Guide, you'll find Internet locations have been identified, where available.

The media

The Murdoch-owned *Australian* is Australia's only national daily (that is, Monday to Saturday) newspaper; aimed mainly at the business community, it has good overseas coverage but local news is often built around statistics. The *Australian Financial Review* is the in-depth business and finance paper to buy. Each state (or more properly, each state capital) has its own daily paper, the best of which are two Fairfax-owned papers, the *Sydney Morning Herald* and Melbourne's venerable *The Age* – both available across the southeast (the two papers share similar content in their weekend-edition magazines). For the websites of these three papers, see p.24. There are also more leisurely populist Sunday-only papers in most capital cities, such as Sydney's *Sun-Herald*.

Local papers are always a good source of listings, if not news. You should be able to track down some **international papers**, or their overseas editions – British, American, Asian and European – in the state capitals. The weekly *Time Australia* and *The Bulletin* are the current-affairs **magazines**. The monthly *HQ* focuses on literature, the arts and current affairs from a younger but sophisticated international and Australian perspective, while *Juice* is an intelligent and amusing music/popular culture mag. If you're interested in wildlife, pick up a copy of the quarterly *Australian Geographic* (related only in name to the US magazine) for some excellent photography and in-depth coverage of Australia's remoter corners. There are some excellent glossy Australian-focused adventure travel magazines, too, like the quarterly *Wild*, while the beautifully produced and written quarterly *40° South* concentrates on all things Tasmanian (it's hard to track down; see ⓦwww.fortysouth.com.au for details). You'll find Australian versions of all the fashion mags, from *Vogue* to *Marie Claire*, plus enduring publications like the *Australian Women's Weekly* (now monthly) which is well-known for its excellent recipes, while the excellent *Australian Gourmet Traveller* celebrates both fine food and travel. Gossipy magazines like *Who Weekly* feature the lowdown on the antics of international and Australian celebs. On a different note, the Australian version of *The Big Issue*, produced out of Melbourne, is called *The Big Issue Australia* and has been operating since 1996. Vendors are homeless, ex-homeless or long-term unemployed and make half of the cover price.

Australia's first **television station** opened in 1956 and the country didn't get colour television until 1974 – both much later than other Westernized countries. Australian television isn't particularly exciting unless you're into sport, of which there's plenty, and commercial stations put on frequent commercial breaks – with often annoyingly unsophisticated advertisements – throughout films. There are Australian content rulings which mean that there are a good amount of Australian dramas, series and soap operas, many of which go on to make it big overseas, from *Neighbours* and *Home and Away* to *The Secret Life of Us*. However, there's a predominance of American programmes and lots of repeats. Australian TV is also fairly permissive in terms of sexual content compared to the programming of Britain or North America. There are three predictable commercial stations: Channel Seven; Channel Nine, which aims for an older market with more conservative programming; and Channel Ten, which tries to grab the younger market with some good comedy programmes including *Good News Week* and the irreverent talk show *The Panel*. In addition, there is also the more serious ABC – a national, advertisement-free station still with a British bias, showing all the best British sitcoms and mini-series – and the livelier SBS, a government-sponsored, multicultural station, which has the best coverage of world news, as well as interesting current-affairs programmes and plenty of foreign-language films. In more remote areas you won't be able to access all five channels and often only ABC and one commercial offering are receivable. There are two **pay TV** stations, Optus and the Murdoch-owned Foxtel, though the pay-TV culture is not firmly established yet as in other countries, and even expensive hotels often still only have terrestrial TV.

The best **radio** is on the various ABC stations, both local and national. ABC Radio National – broadcast all over Australia – offers a popular mix of arty intellectual topics, and another ABC station, 2JJJ ("Triple J"), a former Sydney-based alternative rock station, is aimed at the nation's youth and is available across the country in watered-down form.

Opening hours, holidays and festivals

Shops and services are generally open Monday to Friday 9am to 5pm and until lunchtime on Saturday. In cities and larger towns, many shops stay open late on Thursday or Friday evening – usually until 9pm – and all day on Saturday, and shopping malls, department stores and larger stores are now often open all day Sunday as well.

In remote country areas, **roadhouses** provide all the essential services for the traveller and, on the major highways, are generally open 24 hours a day. In tourist areas, even ones well off the beaten track, **tourist offices** are often open every day or at least through the week plus weekend mornings; urban information centres are more likely to conform to normal shopping hours.

Tourist attractions such as museums, galleries and attended historic monuments, are often open daily, though those in rural communities may have erratic opening hours. Practically without exception all are closed on Good Friday and Christmas Day. Specific opening hours are given throughout the Guide.

Holidays

Contrary to popular opinion and Australia's commendably relaxed interpretation of the work ethic, there are surprisingly few nationwide **public holidays** – and even when you add in the state ones (two or three per state), Australia lags behind most European countries in having official days off. State holidays are listed in the capital city accounts of each state or territory. National holidays are New Year's Day, Australia Day (26 Jan), Good Friday, Easter Monday, Anzac Day (25 April; see Canberra p.253), Queen's Birthday (10 June, except WA), Christmas Day and Boxing Day (26 Dec, except SA).

Watch out for **school holidays**, when seaside resorts can be transformed into bucket-and-spade war zones, national park campsites are full to overflowing, and the roads are jammed with station wagons full of holidaying families. Dates vary from year to year and state to state but all schools (except Tasmania) have four terms. Generally people are on the move for six weeks from a week before Christmas to the end of January or beginning of February (January is worst, as many people stay home until after Christmas), two weeks around Easter, another couple of weeks in late June to early July and another two weeks in late September to early October. The minor exceptions to this general pattern are Queensland and the Northern Territory, which both begin summer holidays a week earlier in mid-December, and far west New South Wales, where students return a week later than the rest of the state, in early February. The state with the greatest variation to this general pattern is Tasmania, which has an eight-week summer break, going back to school in mid-February. There are only three terms, with a short Easter break and two other fortnight-long holidays in early June and early September. January and Easter are the busiest periods when you are likely to find accommodation booked out.

Festivals

The nationwide selection of festivals listed below all include, necessitate and are in some cases the imaginative product of, prolonged beer-swilling. Why else would you drive to the edge of the Simpson Desert to watch a horse race (see p.576)? More seriously, each mainland capital tries to elevate its sophistication quotient with a regular celebration and showcase of art and culture, of which the biennial Adelaide Arts Festival is the best known.

Besides the major events listed below, there's a host of smaller, local events many of which are detailed throughout the Guide. Also, all cities and towns have their own agricultural "shows" which are high points of the local calendar. The Christmas and Easter holiday periods, especially, are marked by celebrations at every turn, all over the country.

January

Festival of Sydney NSW. Three weeks of festivities, with something for absolutely everyone (see p.188).
Melbourne Jazz Festival VIC. Australia's premier jazz festival, which takes place at venues all over the city over Australia Day weekend; book well ahead.
Tamworth Country Music Festival Tamworth, NSW. A week of Slim Dusty and his ilk, culminating in the Australian Country Music Awards.

February

Sydney Gay and Lesbian Mardi Gras NSW. Sydney's proud gay community's festival begins at the end of February and lasts three weeks, ending with an extravagant parade and an all-night dance party.
Festival of Perth WA. A month of "low-brow arts"

at venues all over the city.
Bindoon Rock Festival, Bindoon WA. WA's answer to Woodstock or Reading, with some visiting overseas bands.

March

Adelaide Arts Festival SA. The country's best-known and most innovative arts festival (biennial, in even years); not to be missed.
Australian Grand Prix Melbourne, VIC. Formula One street racing which follows a week of partying; formerly held in Adelaide, now relocated to Albert Park in Melbourne.
Womadelaide SA. Part of the Womad festival circuit, featuring world music, folk, blues and jazz.
Melbourne Moomba Festival VIC. Eleven days of partying, beginning and ending with fireworks and lots of fun in between.

April

Barossa Valley Vintage Festival SA. Biennial (odd years) Germanic festival set in the country's viticultural heart.
Melbourne International Comedy Festival VIC. Opening on April Fools' Day, comics from around the world gather for three weeks.

May

Bangtail Muster Alice Springs, NT. Wacky parades and Outback silliness (see p.672).

June

Melbourne International Film Festival VIC. The country's largest and most prestigious film festival, lasting two weeks.
Sydney International Film Festival NSW. Also an important film festival, running for over two weeks in June and based at the glorious State Theatre.
Barunga Sports Festival Beswick Aboriginal Land, NT. A rare and enjoyable chance to encounter Aboriginal culture in the NT. No alcohol.
Cape York Aboriginal Dance Festival QLD. Three-day, alcohol-free celebration of authentic Aboriginal culture. Biennial in odd-numbered years.

July

Camel Cup Alice Springs, NT. Camel-racing down the dry Todd River.
Darwin Beer Can Regatta NT. Mindil Beach is

the venue for the recycling of copious empties into a variety of seacraft. Also a thong-throwing contest; Territorian eccentricity personified.

August

Shinju Matsuri Festival Broome, WA. Probably the most remote big festival, which doesn't stop the town being packed for this Oriental-themed pearl festival.

Mount Isa Rodeo Mount Isa, QLD. Australia's largest rodeo – a gritty, down-to-earth encounter with bulls, horses and their riders.

September

Bathurst 1000 Road Races Bathurst, NSW. Australia's premier weekend of car and bike street racing.

Birdsville Races QLD. Once a year the remote Outback town of Birdsville (population 120) comes alive for a weekend of drinking and horse-racing – a well-known and definitive Australian oddity.

Warana Brisbane, QLD. Huge, two-week arts festival centred in the city's Botanic Gardens with food, wine, beer, music, writing and children's events topped off with fireworks and a crazy Concours de Decadence.

October

Henley-on-Todd Regatta Alice Springs, NT. Wacky races in bottomless boats running down the dry Todd riverbed; the event is heavily insured against the river actually flowing.

Manly Jazz Festival Sydney, NSW. Three-day jazz festival featuring artists from all over the world.

Melbourne International Festival of the Arts VIC. Two-week celebration of visual, performing and written arts in venues all over the city; lots of international and Australian "big names".

November

Melbourne Cup Flemington Racecourse, VIC. Australia's Ascot, a 130-year-old horse race which brings the entire country to a standstill around the radio or TV.

December

Sydney to Hobart Yacht Race Sydney, NSW. Crowds flock to the harbour to witness the start of this classic regatta which departs Sydney on Boxing Day and arrives in Hobart three days later. The Christmas holidays and New Year's Eve are celebrated with gusto everywhere.

Sports and outdoor pursuits

Australians are sports mad, especially for the ostensibly passive spectator sports of cricket, Aussie Rules football, rugby (league or union), tennis or any type of racing, from cockroach to camel. No matter what it is, it'll draw a crowd – with thousands more watching on TV – and a crowd means a party. Even unpromising-sounding activities such as surf lifesaving and yacht racing (the start of the Sydney to Hobart race just after Christmas is a massive social event) are tremendously popular.

It's hard to escape sport in Australia: people talk about it all the time; sporting news fills up the newspapers; events and commentary are constantly broadcast on TV and radio; and it's a huge source of national pride. The wintertime **football** (footy) season in Australia lasts from March to September; in summer **cricket** is played from October to March.

Footy comes in several varieties. Before World War II, **soccer** was played by British immigrants but with postwar immigration it was branded as "ethnic", as new clubs became based on the country of origin of the players: **Australian Rules** (see below) was considered the game "real Australians" played. More than fifty percent of Australia's twelve league soccer clubs evolved from communities of postwar immigrants – mainly Italians, Greeks and Yugoslavs – and the former chairman of Soccer Australia, David Hill, believed that their fervent nationalism marginalized the game; his mid-1990s ban on clubs that included national flags in their logos won support as well as accusations of the pursuance of a policy of "ethnic cleansing". **Rugby union**, despite the huge success of the Wallabies national team, is also very much a minority interest domestically. The introduction of a Super 12 competition, involving teams from Australia, New Zealand and South Africa, has generated a much greater interest in what was formerly an elitist sport.

Australian Rules ("Aussie Rules") football dominates Victoria, South Australia and Western Australia. It's an extraordinary, anarchic, no-holds-barred, eighteen-a-side brawl, most closely related to Gaelic football and known dismissively north of the Victorian border as "aerial ping pong". The ball can be propelled by any means necessary, and the fact that players aren't sent off for misconduct ensures a lively, skilful and, above all, gladiatorial confrontation. Aussie Rules stars have delightful sobriquets such as "Tugger" and "Crackers", and their macho garb consists of tiny butt-hugging shorts and bicep-revealing tank tops. The game is mostly played on cricket grounds, with a ball similar to that used in rugby or American football. The aim is to get the ball through the central uprights for a goal (six points). There are four 25-minute quarters, plus lots of time added on for injury. Despite the violence on the pitch (or perhaps because of it), Aussie Rules fans tend to be loyal and well behaved. Victoria has traditionally been the home of the game, and Victorian sides are expected to win the AFL Flag, decided at the Grand Final in September, as a matter of course.

In New South Wales and Queensland **Rugby League** attracts the fanatics, especially for the hard-fought **State of Origin** matches. The thirteen-a-side game is one at

which the Australians seem permanent world champions, despite having a relatively small professional league. Recently, the game has been split down the middle – there are now two rival competitions – the traditional Australian Rugby League (ARL) and the Murdoch-owned Super League. One of the sadder consequences of this media-inspired revolution has been the loss of some of the traditional inner-city clubs through mergers. The common view is that the game cannot support the number of teams required for two competitions. Many people also resent the way in which this one-time bastion of working-class culture has been co-opted by pay TV.

Summertime **cricket** is a great spectator sport – for the crowd, the sunshine and the beer as much as the play. Every state is involved, and the three- or four-day Sheffield Shield matches of the interstate series are interspersed with one-day games and internationals, as well as full five-day international test matches. Interest in the five-day matches has been revitalized by Australia's recent victories against all-comers: in 1998 they beat South Africa and England, but really consolidated their position of world champion when they beat Pakistan in Pakistan itself in 2001.

The international competition that still arouses greatest interest is that between Australia and England – **The Ashes**. Having been around for over 120 years, this is perhaps the oldest rivalry between nations in international sport. The "trophy" competed for has an interesting provenance: in 1882 an Australian touring side defeated England at the Oval in South London by seven runs, and the *Sporting Times* was moved to report, in a mock obituary, that English cricket had "died at the Oval... deeply lamented by a large circle of sorrowing friends". The funeral ceremony involved the cremation of a set of bails, which were then preserved in a funerary urn. Each time the two countries compete, this is the trophy that is up for grabs (though the urn itself never actually leaves Lord's cricket ground in London) and a new crystal trophy actually goes to the winners.

Minor sports are followed with no less avid attention, and there are plenty of them, including horse racing and trotting, motor racing, swimming, athletics, tennis – you name it. One peculiarly Australian institution is the **surf carnival**, when teams of volunteer lifesavers demonstrate their skills – this makes for a great day out on the beach. **Surfing** itself can also be a competitive sport, with the Eastertime World Championships held at Bell's Beach, southwest of Melbourne, and November's Margaret River Classic, south of Perth, both good opportunities to catch some waveriding action. Inland, many rural towns have a **speedway track** occupying a tract of wasteland, where at weekends motor-headed hoons demonstrate their dirt-tracking skills in souped-up utes or motorbikes; a dusty, noisy and merry focus for the entire community and passers-by.

Outdoor pursuits

Though the cities are fun, what really makes Australia special is the great outdoors: the vast and remote wilderness of the bush, the legendary Outback, and the thousands of kilometres of unspoilt coastline. There's tremendous potential here to indulge in a huge range of outdoor pursuits – hiking, fishing, surfing, diving, even skiing – especially in the multitude of national parks that cover the country. Further information on all of these is available from local tourist offices, which publicize what's available in their area; from Parks Australia, which has detailed maps of parks with walking trails, climbs, swimming holes and other activities; and from specialist books. In addition, virtually any activity can be done as part of an organized excursion, often with all the gear supplied. If you want to go it alone you'll find plenty of places ready to rent or sell you the necessary equipment. Before indulging in adventure activities, check your insurance cover (see pp.25–26).

As with any wilderness area, the Australian interior does not suffer fools, and the coast conceals **dangers** too: sunstroke and dehydration are risks everywhere, with riptides, currents and unexpectedly large waves to be wary of on exposed coasts. In the more remote regions isolation and lack of surface water compromise energetic outdoor activities such as bushwalking or mountain biking,

which are probably better practised in the cooler climes and more populated locations of the south.

Bushwalking

Bushwalking in Australia doesn't mean just a stroll in the bush, but refers to self-sufficient hikes, from a day to a week or longer. It's an increasingly popular activity nationwide, and you'll find trails marked in almost every national park, as well as local bushwalking **clubs** whose trips you may be able to join.

It's essential to be **properly equipped** for the conditions you'll encounter – and to know what those conditions are likely to be. Carry a **map** (often on hand at the ranger station in popular national parks), know how the trail is marked, and stay on the route. If your trip is a long one, let someone know where you're going, and confirm to them that you've arrived back safely – park rangers are useful contacts for this, and some will insist on it for overnight walks which may require registration. One point worth noting is that in national park areas the estimated duration of a given walk is often exaggerated – certainly in the Territory and WA (see p.722): you can comfortably divide the indicated time by half or more. On formed tracks a walking speed of 3–4kph is average. The essentials, even for a short walk, are adequate clothing including a wide-brimmed hat, enough food and, above all, **water**. Other useful items include a torch, matches or lighter, penknife, sun block, insect repellent, toilet paper, first-aid kit, and a whistle or mirror to attract attention if you get lost. A lot of this gear can be rented, or bought cheaply at disposal stores, which can often also put you in touch with local clubs or specialists.

Long-distance tracks exist mostly in the south of the country, with Tasmania's wilderness areas being perhaps the most rewarding bushwalking location; the eighty-kilometre **Overland Track** from Cradle Mountain to Lake St Clair is one of the country's best-known trails. On the mainland, the **Blue Mountains**, a two-hour train ride from Sydney, the **Snowy Mountains** further south, and Victoria's spectacular **Grampians**

are all popular regions for longer, marked walks.

South Australia's **Flinders Ranges**, 300km north of Adelaide, are accessible along the **Heysen Trail** from the Fleurieu Peninsula, the walk into the thousand-metre-high natural basin of Wilpena Pound being the highlight. In temperate southwestern WA, the 960-kilometre **Bibbulmun Track** (see p.723), an old Aboriginal trail passing through the region's giant eucalypt forests, was completed in 2002 from Albany to Kalamunda near Perth. In the same year the 220-kilometre **Larapinta Trail** (see p.678), along the McDonnell Ranges west of Alice Springs was also completed; an initially strenuous hike out of Alice that should only be attempted in winter. Queensland's rain-forested coastal strip offers plenty more opportunities for walks, including the **Lamington** area in the south, and around northern **Atherton Tablelands** and **Hinchinbrook Island**.

Water sports

The oceans and seas around Australia are a national playground and are not just for tanning or playing volleyball on the beach. Always take local advice on the waves, which must be treated with respect. If possible, **swim** from a patrolled beach, between the flags: raise one hand if you get into difficulty, and clear the water if a siren sounds – it could signal dangerous waves, a shark sighting or a swarm of bluebottles (stinging jellyfish).

Enjoying the water doesn't necessarily involve any special effort or equipment, but if you want it, there are plenty of activities on

Bush essentials

Four things above all:

Fire The driest continent on earth is covered by vegetation which has evolved with regular conflagrations, and is always at risk from bushfires. Three times in the last ten years Sydney was ringed with burning bushland, and during the terrible bushfire season of 2002/2003 a large part of the Alpine region in Australia's southeast was ablaze for almost two months, wreaking havoc on bush and forests, animals and people. Only a few human lives were lost, however, mainly owing to the skills, resilience and determination of the fire fighters and local residents. Even in wet years, there's a constant red alert during summer months. Always use an established fireplace where available, or dig a shallow pit and ring it with stones. Keep fires small and make absolutely sure embers are smothered before going to sleep or moving on. Never discard burning cigarette butts from cars. Periodic total fire bans – announced in the local media when in effect – prohibit any fire in the open, including wood, gas or electric barbecues, with heavy fines for offenders. Check on the local fire danger before you go bushwalking – some walking trails are closed in the riskiest periods (summer in the south; the end of the dry season – Sept/Oct – in the north). If driving, carry blankets and a filled water container, listen to your car radio and watch out for roadside fire danger indicators. If the worst happens, there are practical ways of surviving a bushfire. See "Health", pp.27–29, for potential bushwalking hazards and advice on how to deal with them – including ways to survive if caught in a bushfire.

Water Carry plenty with you and do not contaminate local water resources. In particular, soaps and detergents can render water undrinkable and kill livestock and wild animals. Avoid washing in standing water, especially tanks and small lakes or reservoirs.

Waste Take only photographs, leave only footprints. That means carrying all your rubbish out with you – never burn or bury it – and making sure you urinate (and bury your excrement) at least 50m from a campsite or water source.

Hypothermia In Tasmania, where the weather is notoriously changeable, prepare as you would for a walk in Scotland.

offer. Probably the easiest to get into is **surf-ing**, starting with body-surfing and progressing to boogie-boards (small boards that you lie on) and then on to full-scale surfboards. Surfing is popular everywhere, but don't expect the local surfie community to be too friendly at first – they're often very cliquey. Seaside hostels often have boards which they loan out free. **Windsurfing** and **sailing** are also extremely popular, and you'll be able to rent equipment and get instruction in almost any resort, though some of the best sailing in the country can be found around Queensland's Whitsunday Islands or off WA's West Coast. Other water sports include **white-water rafting**, **sea-kayaking** and **canoeing**.

The Great Barrier Reef is one of the world's great **scuba-diving** meccas, with some other lesser known but excellent sites around the country – such as West Australia's Ningaloo Reef – beginning to attract attention. Dive facilities in Australia are of a high standard, and scuba courses are not that expensive, though if you simply want to try it once there are plenty of people offering closely supervised "resort dives". Good **rental gear** is widely available, but if

you're bringing your own, check for compatibility problems; yokes are the Australian norm, so if your first-stage fitting is DIN (likely in Europe and the UK), you'll need an adaptor. **Snorkelling** is the low-tech alternative, and still allows you to get dramatically close to the aquatic life around a reef.

Fishing is an Australian obsession, conducted on rivers and lakes, off piers or small boats ("tinnies"), or out at sea where – if your cheque book is up to the challenge – marlin and other game fish are caught. Again, all the equipment – even boats – can be rented in most good fishing areas. Barramundi, renowned for its fighting qualities, is the thing to go for up north.

Other pursuits

Alice Springs' wide-open spaces make it the country's **hot-air-ballooning** capital and also the main base for **camel treks** into the surrounding desert.

More regular riding, on **horseback**, is offered all over the country – anything from a gentle hour at walking pace to a serious cattle roundup. **Cycling** and **mountain biking** are tremendously popular too, as well as

Australia's top dive sites

Bougainville Reef Coral Sea, QLD (see p.532). Exceptional in every way: kilometre-deep coral walls, clear water, and both reef and pelagic life in abundance. Live-aboard trips from Cairns and Port Douglas.

Cod Hole Great Barrier Reef, QLD (see p.532). Where the giant potato cod and divers meet. Live-aboard trips from Cairns.

Geographe Bay WA (see p.725). The *HMS Swan* was sunk to make a recreational diving wreck just off Cape Naturaliste, a couple of hours south of Perth.

Lord Howe Island NSW (see p.381). The world's southernmost reef surrounds one of the world's most beautiful islands. Flights from Brisbane and Sydney.

Ningaloo Reef WA (see p.760). Whale sharks come through from April to June, but there's great diving all year, in places right off the beach. Tours from Exmouth or Coral Bay.

Port Lincoln SA (p.868). South Australian waters are one of the last bastions for the poorly understood Great White shark. Trips out from Port Lincoln use shark cages.

Seal Rocks NSW (see p.292). Hosts a great grey nurse convergence every so often, a chance to be surrounded by these fierce-looking but largely harmless sharks. Trips from Foster or Tuncurry.

Yongala Shipwreck QLD (see p.504). Huge fish and the remains of a 100-metre-long passenger liner which went down in an early-twentieth-century cyclone. Trips from Townsville and Cairns.

being a good way of getting around resorts; just about all hostels rent out bikes, and we've listed other outlets throughout the Guide.

Australia's wilderness is an ideal venue for extended **off-road driving** or **motorbiking**, although permission may be needed to cross station- and Aboriginal-owned lands, and the fragile desert ecology should be respected at all times. Northern Queensland's Cape York and WA's Kimberley are the most adventurous destinations, 4WD-accessible in the dry season only. The great **Outback tracks** pushed out by explorers or drovers, such as the Warburton Road and Sandover Highway and the Tanami, Birdsville and Oodnadatta tracks, are actually two-wheel driveable in dry conditions, but can be hard on poorly prepared vehicles. Getting right to the tip of Queensland's eight-hundred-kilometre-long Cape York Peninsula will definitely require a 4WD or trail bike; while the Kimberley's notoriously corrugated Gibb River Road in WA is also popular in the Dry.

Finally, you may not associate Australia with **skiing**, but there's plenty of it in the 1500-metre-high Australian Alps on the border of Victoria and New South Wales, based around the winter resorts of Thredbo, Perisher, Falls Creek and Mount Hotham. Europeans tend to be sniffy about Australian skiing, and certainly it's limited, with a season that lasts barely two to three months – from the end of June until end of September, if you're lucky – and very few challenging runs. The one area where it does match up to Europe is in the prices. On the other hand it's fun if you're here, and the relatively gentle slopes of the mountains are ideal for **cross-country skiing**, which is increasingly being developed alongside downhill.

National parks

The **Australian Environmental Protection Agency** is split into federal and state bodies, the federal organization dealing with international problems such as whaling and how to make use of Antarctica, and occasionally arbitrating between the state-run **National Parks Wildlife Service** departments. These run the national parks themselves, though the departmental names vary from state to state. The thousand-odd **national parks** range from suburban commons to the Great Barrier Reef, and from popular hiking areas within striking distance of the big cities to wilderness regions which require days in a 4WD simply to reach. They protect everything within their boundaries: flora, fauna and landforms as well as Aboriginal art and sacred sites, although not always to the exclusion of mineral exploitation, as in Karijini in WA or Kakadu in the Territory.

Fees are variable. Some parks or states have no fees at all, some charge for use of camping facilities, while others require permits bought in advance. If you're camping you can usually pay on site, but booking ahead might be a good idea during the Christmas, Easter and school holidays (see p.58). Nearby resorts or alternative accommodation are always independently run.

Crime and personal safety

"Transportation across the seas", to which judges condemned the petty criminals of two centuries ago, seems to have been a successful policy; Australia today can pride itself on being a relatively crime-free country, although increasingly it is following the American trend in gun-related incidents.

This is not to say there's no petty crime, or that you can leave normal caution behind, but there is less violent crime and theft in Australia, even in the big cities, than in most of Europe or North America, and even "heavy" downtown areas can appear pretty tame. One place where **violence** is commonplace is at the ritual pub "blue" (fight), usually among known protagonists on a Friday or Saturday night. Strangers are seldom involved without at least some provocation.

You're more likely to fall victim to a fellow traveller or an opportunist: **theft** is not unusual in hostels and, so, many provide lockable boxes. But if you leave valuables lying around, or on view in cars, you can expect them to be stolen. Exercise caution, don't forget common-sense, streetwise precautions, and you should be fine; in cities at night stay in areas that are well lit and full of people, look like you know where you are going and don't carry excess cash or anything else you can't afford to lose.

Police and the law

Australia's **police** – all armed – have a poor public image and perhaps as a result tend to keep a low profile; you should have no trouble in your dealings with them. Indeed you'll hardly see them, unless you're out on a Friday or Saturday night when they cruise in search of drink-related brawls.

Things to watch out for, most of all, are drugs. A lot of marijuana is grown and its use is widespread, but you'd be foolish to carry it when you travel, and crazy to carry any other illicit narcotic. Each state has its own penalties, and though a small amount of grass may mean no more than confiscation or an on-the-spot fine, they're generally pretty tough – especially in Queensland.

When you **cross state borders** you may find that your vehicle will be **searched** – not just for "firearms, pornography or drugs" but also for fruit and fresh produce, which often cannot be carried from one state to the next, to minimize the spread of plant pests and viruses. Driving in general makes you more likely to have a confrontation of some kind, if only for a minor traffic infringement: **drunk driving** is regarded extremely seriously, so don't risk it – random breath tests are common around all cities and larger towns.

Lesser potential problems are **alcohol** – there are all sorts of controls on where and when you can drink, and taking alcohol onto Aboriginal lands can be a serious offence; **smoking**, which is increasingly being banned in public places; and nude or **topless** sunbathing, which is quite acceptable in many places, but absolutely not in others – follow the locals' lead.

If for any reason you are **arrested** or need help (and you can be arrested merely on suspicion of committing an offence), you are entitled to contact a friend or lawyer before answering any questions. You could call your consulate, but don't expect much sympathy. If necessary, the police will provide a lawyer, and you can usually get legal aid to settle the bill.

Prejudice, police and the traveller

Given Australia's record on its treatment of the Aboriginal population, the history of the

Emergencies

①000 is the free **emergency telephone number** which summons the police, ambulance or fire service.

White Australia policy, and the passing popularity of Pauline Hanson's One Nation party on a partly racist agenda, it comes as little surprise to find that this is a nation where **racial prejudice** is ingrained. As a **black traveller** you're likely to attract attention when you don't particularly want it, and be unable to get it when you do – even to the extent of being refused service in an Outback bar or being unable to flag down a cab in a city. Certainly in remote areas, where Aboriginal people are still treated as second-class citizens at best, black travellers may have an uncomfortable time.

Asians are generally more accepted (in Australia, "Asian" usually means Southeast Asian – the Indian and Pakistani populations are negligible). However, a strong undercurrent of anti-Asian feeling – never too far below the surface in Australia's European history – has recently come out into the open. Asians have always been a target of envy in Australia.

Nevertheless, Australia does have powerful anti-discrimination laws. Any racial discrimination can be reported to the **Human Rights and Equal Opportunities Commission** which has offices in each state capital (listed in the "Government" section at the front of the White Pages phone book). Although you might not have time (or the desire) to go through the lengthy complaints process, the threat is a useful one, as their powers are considerable. Just don't expect a country policeman to help you – many are part of the problem rather than its solution.

Work

Most visitors' visas clearly state that no employment of any kind is to be undertaken during a visit to Australia. However, if you've succeeded in getting a Working Holiday Visa (see "Visas and red tape", p.21) and are prepared to try anything – officially for no more than three months at a time – there are plenty of possibilities for finding work. Work Oz (ⓦwww.workoz.com) can help with paperwork and contacts. There are also organized work programmes – both paid and voluntary (see p.71)

In practice this means that the only jobs officially open to you are unskilled, temporary ones. The former Commonwealth Employment Service (CES) has been broken up into competing, semi-privatized employment agencies. One of the largest ones is **Employment National** (Mon–Fri 9am–5pm; ⓣ13 3444, Harvest Hotline ⓣ1300 720 126, ⓦwww.employmentnational.com.au). They will usually ask you to come in and register, or send a fax with all your details and a resumé. There are more than 200 branches all over Australia, including rural areas where there's a lot of seasonal work. What they offer will usually be either harvesting or farm-labouring jobs (see p.68), or in the cities, clerical, bar or restaurant jobs, or occasional factory work.

Aimed at backpackers with work visas, travellers' centres are scattered around eastern Australia, and can sort out all aspects of working, from organizing tax file numbers to actually getting you jobs. Each has links between their various branches, so you can check in advance about the likelihood of finding work where you are heading. Membership costs around $40 a year. See under "Information and maps" on p.23 for travellers' centres' contact details.

In addition, more specialized employment agencies are worth a try in the cities if you have a marketable skill (computer training, accountancy, nursing, cooking and the like). They might have better, higher-paid jobs on their books, though they may be looking for full-time or at least longer-term commitment. Newspaper job ads are also worth checking out, especially in smaller local papers. And finally, fellow travellers, hostel staff in smaller hostels, and notice boards may be the best source of all, especially in remote areas – some even run their own employment agency or have a permanently staffed employment desk. This is where you'll find out about local opportunities, and the hostels themselves may occasionally offer free nights in lieu of cleaning work – or even pay you for jobs that involve a bit more skill. Some of the hostels in the big cities or in country towns where there is a lot of harvesting work also arrange employment.

Significant long-term unemployment is prevalent in Australia, and the days of legendary wages for relentless hard work in mines, on the roads or on prawn trawlers are long gone. Nonetheless, plenty of people still manage to work illegally, though visa checks in the major harvest areas (they really do happen) and tax reforms have made this much harder than it used to be.

Seasonal picking and harvesting work

Listed below are the major **harvest seasons** around the country. Once you're into the harvest season it's possible to move with it around the country, from one product to another, as many people do. There may be lesser harvests and other work in all of these places at any time. Just remember that crop picking is hard work for low wages (which are paid on a commission basis) – if you're bad at it and don't pick much, you'll put in a lot of effort for virtually nothing.

New South Wales

Summer November–April, peaking in February, in the central eastern district around Bathurst, Dubbo and Orange; orchard and other fruits, cotton, onions and asparagus.
Year-round The north coast around Coffs Harbour; bananas.

Queensland

Summer December–March, around Warwick, inland on the NSW border; stone and orchard fruits, grapes.

May–December The central coast around Bowen; fruit and vegetables, especially mangoes at the end of the year.
May–November The northern coast around Ayr, Tully and Innisfail; sugar cane, bananas and tobacco.
Year-round The southern central coast around Bundaberg and Childers; all kinds of fruit and vegetables.

Western Australia

October–June The southwest; grapes and orchard fruits (February–April), plus tractor-driven grain harvesting.
March–November The west coast from Fremantle to Carnarvon; crayfish, prawn and scallop fishing and processing.
May–October The northeast around Kununurra; fruit and vegetable picking and packing.

South Australia

February–April The Barossa Valley; grapes.
Year-round The Riverland; picking, pruning and packaging citrus and soft fruits.

Victoria

Summer November–April, peaking in February, in central northern areas around Shepparton, and also along the Murray River (Mildura, Swan Hill and, to a lesser extent, Echuca); orchard fruits, tomatoes, tobacco, grapes and soft fruits.

Tasmania

Summer December–March; orchard and soft fruits, grapes.

Organized work programmes

To streamline the process of procuring a working visa, getting to Australia and orienting yourself on arrival, there are several packages aimed at working travellers. BUNAC organizes a **Work Australia** programme that can be combined with their North American programmes, with departures from London between August and December and from Los Angeles in September and October. Work Oz assists with the paperwork and arranges accommodation packages. See p.71 for contact details of these and other organizations.

Teaching English

There are two options: find or prepare for finding work before you go, or just wing it and see what you come up with while you're out there, particularly if you already have a degree and/or teaching experience. Teaching English – often abbreviated as ELT (English Language Teaching) or TEFL (Teaching English as a Foreign Language) – is the way many people finance their way around the greater part of the world; you can get a CELTA (Certificate in English Language Teaching to Adults) qualification before you leave home. Certified by the RSA, the course is very demanding and costs about £944 for the month's full-time tuition; you'll be thrown in at the deep end and expected to teach right away. The British Council's website, ⓦ www.britishcouncil.org/work/jobs.htm, has a list of English-teaching vacancies.

Useful publications and websites

Another pre-planning strategy for working abroad, whether teaching English or otherwise, is to get hold of Overseas Jobs Express (Premier House, Shoreham Airport, Sussex BN43 5FF; ☎ 01273/699 611, ⓦ www.overseasjobs.com), a fortnightly publication with a range of job vacancies, available by subscription only. Vacation Work also publishes books on summer jobs abroad and how to work your way around the world; call ☎ 01865/241 978 or visit ⓦ www.vacationwork.co.uk for their catalogue. Travel magazines like the reliable *Wanderlust* (every two months) have a Job Shop section which often advertises job opportunities with tour companies, while ⓦ www.studyabroad.com is a useful website with listings and links to study and work programmes worldwide.

Study and work programmes

From the UK and Ireland

BTCV 36 St Mary's St, Wallingford, Oxfordshire OX10 0EU ☎ 01491/839 766, ⓦ www.btcv.org.uk. One of the largest environmental charities in Britain, with branches across the country, also has a programme of national and international working holidays (as a paying volunteer), ranging from dry-stone walling in Japan to turtle monitoring in Turkey; comprehensive brochure available.

BUNAC (British Universities' North America Club) 16 Bowling Green Lane, London EC1R 0QH ☎ 020/7251 3472, ⓦ www.bunac.org. Organizes working holidays in Australia and New Zealand, among other countries, for students, typically training placements with companies.

Earthwatch Institute 57 Woodstock Rd, Oxford OX2 6HJ ☎ 01865/311 600, ⓦ www.earthwatch.org. Long-established international charity with environmental and archeological research projects worldwide (130 projects in around 55 countries). Participation is mainly as a paying volunteer (pricey) but fellowships for teachers and students are available.

Field Studies Council Overseas (FSCO) Montford Bridge, Shrewsbury SY4 1HW ☎ 01743/852 150, ⓦ www.fscoverseas.org.uk. Respected educational charity with over 20 years' experience of organizing specialized holidays with study tours visits worldwide. Studies have included ecology in the Canadian Rockies, flora of New Zealand, and plants and birds of Andalucia. Group size is generally limited to 10–15 people. *Overseas Experiences* brochure available.

International House 106 Piccadilly, London W1V 9NL ☎ 020/7518 6999, ⓦ www.ihlondon.com. Head office for reputable English-teaching organization which offers TEFL training leading to the award of a Certificate in English Language Teaching to Adults (CELTA), and recruits for teaching positions in Britain and abroad.

From the US

American Institute for Foreign Study River Plaza, 9 West Broad St, Stamford, CT 06902-3788 ☎ 1-800/727-2437, ⓦ www.aifs.com. Language study and cultural immersion for the summer or school year, as well as au pair and Camp America programs.

Association for International Practical Training 10400 Little Patuxent Pkwy, Suite 250, Columbia, MD 21044 ☎ 410/997-2200, ⓦ www.aipt.org. Summer internships for students who have completed at least two years of college in science, agriculture, engineering or architecture.

Bernan Associates 4611-F Assembly Dr, Lanham, MD 20706 ☎ 1-800/274-4888, ⓦ www.bernan.com. Distributes UNESCO's encyclopedic *Study Abroad*.

BUNAC USA PO Box 430, Southbury CT 06488 ☎ 1-800/GO-BUNAC, ⓦ www.bunac.org. Offers young US and Canadian students the chance to work in Australia, New Zealand or Britain. Visa support, flights, job information, help with setting up a bank account, and accommodation on arrival is provided.

Council on International Educational Exchange (CIEE) 205 E 42nd St, New York, NY 10017 ☎1-800/2COUNCIL, ⊕www.ciee.org/study. The non-profit parent organization of Council Travel, CIEE runs summer, semester and academic-year programs in Australia and New Zealand (among many other countries) and can also arrange six-month work permits for currently enrolled or recently graduated students in Australia. They provide leads, but it's up to you to find the work. CIEE also runs volunteer projects in more than 25 countries in Africa, Europe, Latin America, Asia and North America and publishes *Work, Study, Travel Abroad and Volunteer! The Comprehensive Guide to Voluntary Service in the US and Abroad.*

Earthwatch Institute 3 Clock Tower Place, Suite 100, Box 75, Maynard, MA 01754 ☎1-800/776-0188 or 978/461-0081, ⊕www.earthwatch.org. International non-profit organization with offices in Boston, Oxford (England), Melbourne and Tokyo. 50,000 members and supporters are spread across the US, Europe, Africa, Asia and Australia and volunteer their time and skills to work with 120 research scientists each year on Earthwatch field research projects in over 50 countries all around the world.

Elderhostel 75 Federal St, Boston, MA 02110 ☎1/877-426-8056, ⊕www.elderhostel.com. Runs an extensive worldwide network of educational and activity programs, cruises and homestays for people over 60 (companions may be younger). Programs generally last a week or more and costs are in line with those of commercial tours.

Experiment in International Living ☎1-800/345-2929, ⊕www.usexperiment.org. Summer program for high-school students.

HarperCollins Perseus Division ☎1-800/242-7737. Publishes *International Jobs: Where They Are, How to Get Them.*

Peace Corps 1111 20th St NW, Washington, DC 20526 ☎1-800/424-8580, ⊕www.peacecorps.gov. Places people with specialist qualifications or skills in two-year postings in many developing countries. Special Youth Program covers one four-month period in Australia, with an age restriction of 18–30 and a cost of US$365, through Work Experience Down Under, including two nights' accommodation in Sydney and work support. You have to pay the fee even if you have a job already lined up, and you have to fly on their specially arranged (and priced) twice-monthly flights from Los Angeles. The Australian embassy also

insists that you have US$500 a month available to you and proof of funds before departure.

Volunteers for Peace 1034 Tiffany Rd, Belmont, VT 05730 ☎802/259-2759, ⊕www.vfp.org. Non-profit organization with links to a huge international network of "workcamps", two- to four-week programs that bring volunteers together from many countries to carry out needed community projects. Most workcamps are in summer, with registration in April–May. Annual membership including directory costs $20. Programs worldwide.

World Learning Kipling Road, PO Box 676, Brattleboro, VT 05302 ☎802/257-7751, ⊕www.worldlearning.org. Its School for International Training (☎1-800/336-1616, ⊕www.sit.edu) runs accredited college semesters abroad, comprising language and cultural studies, homestay and other academic work. Programs in 40 countries.

In Australia

ATCV (Australian Trust for Conservation Volunteers) PO Box 423, Ballarat, VIC 3353 ☎03/5333 1483 or 1800 032 501, ⊕www.atcv.com.au. Volunteer work (unpaid) on conservation projects across Australia; $20 a day charged for food and accommodation. The projects are usually four to six weeks long.

Visitoz Springbrook Farm, MS 188 via Goomeri, 4601, Queensland ☎07/4168 6106, ⊕www.visitoz.org. Visitoz provides work on farms and stations and rural hospitality for all those who would like well-paid work in the bush and the experience of a lifetime. Previous experience is not required. There are more than 950 employers who provide work all over Australia throughout the year. Those coming in direct from overseas are met at the airport, have tax file numbers and other paperwork sorted out. There is an eight-day orientation course and during this period a job is chosen from a few suitable ones offered. On leaving Visitoz bus or air tickets are arranged to the jobs. Those already in Australia have a four-day course which they have to pass in order to be able to choose their job. Work is guaranteed. Driving licences are necessary for 95 percent of the jobs. Offices in the UK, Sweden, Germany, Holland, the USA and Canada.

Work Oz Kings House, 14 Orchard St, Bristol BS1 5EH ⊕www.work.oz.com. An organization owned and run in Australia and Britain by ex-Australian high commission staff, designed to assist 18–30 year old British, Irish, Canadian, Dutch, German, Japanese, Maltese and US citizens who want to work in Australia with a working holiday visa. They assist with visa application, employment in Australia, pre-book hostel accommodation prior to arrival, arrange pick-ups from the airport and arrange travel insurance.

WWOOF (Willing Workers on Organic Farms) Mount Murrindal Co-op, Buchan, VIC 3885 ☎ & ℱ 03/5155 0218, ⓦ www.wwoof.com.au. Their book *The Australian Organic Farm and Cultural Experience* lists about 1200 organic farms and 100 non-farm hosts (such as organic nurseries and greengrocers, alternative schools). You are expected to stay at least two nights and put in about half a day's work in exchange for full board and lodging; everything else is negotiable. As you

are not paid cash, a work visa is not required. By ordering the book you become a member; the membership includes a basic work insurance for one year ($50 single, $60 for a couple). The book is available over the Internet (add $5 for postage and handling) or from travel agents such as Backpackers' Travel Centres and branches of Student Uni Travel. WWOOF also publishes two other lists for people who would like to visit such places and stay there for a while without working: *WWOOF Australian Organic B&B List* ($11) and *Australian Organic Communities and Spiritual Retreats List* ($11) – both can also be ordered online.

B

BASICS | Travellers with disabilities

Tax

In recent years employers have been threatened with huge fines for offering cash-in-hand labour and, as a result, it's difficult to avoid paying **income tax**, which is levied at 29 percent for earnings under about $26,000 per annum and deducted at source. To become part of the system you'll need a **tax file number** (form available at post offices or taxation offices), which is pretty easy to obtain on presentation of a passport with relevant visa. Your employer will give you a couple of weeks' grace, but not much more – if you don't have a number, after that you'll be taxed at 49 percent. Nowadays it's hard to claim a tax **rebate**, no matter how little you earn; however, it's worth a try, and possibly a visit to a tax adviser.

Travellers with disabilities

The vast distances between Australia's cities and popular tourist resorts present visitors with mobility difficulties with a unique challenge but, overall, travel in Australia for people with disabilities is rather easier than it would be in the UK and Europe.

The federal government provides information and various nationwide services through the **National Information Communication Awareness Network** (NICAN) and the **Australian Council for the Rehabilitation of the Disabled** (ACROD) – see p.73 for contact details. The **Australian Tourist Commission** offices provide a helpline service and publish a factsheet, *Travelling in Australia for People with Disabilities*, available from its offices world-wide (see p.23 for addresses and phone numbers).

Disability needn't interfere with your sightseeing: the attitude of the management at Australia's major tourist attractions is excellent, and they will provide assistance where they can. For example, you'll find you can view the rock art at Kakadu National Park, do a tour around the base of Uluru (Ayers Rock), snorkel unhindered on the Great Barrier Reef, go on a cruise

71

around Sydney Harbour, and see the penguins at Phillip Island.

Planning a holiday

There are **organized tours and holidays** specifically for people with disabilities (including mobility, hearing, vision and intellectual restrictions). Some arrange travel only, some organize travel and accommodation, and others provide a complete package – travel, accommodation, meals and carer support. This last type, as well as catering fully for special needs, provides company for the trip. The contacts on pp.72–73 will be able to put you in touch with any specialists for trips to Australia; several are listed in the Australian Tourist Commission factsheet. If you want to be more independent, it's important to become an authority on where you must be self-reliant and where you may expect help, especially regarding transport and accommodation. It is also vital to be honest – with travel agencies, insurance companies and travel companions. Know your limitations and make sure others know them. If you do not use a wheelchair all the time but your walking capabilities are limited, remember that you are likely to need to cover greater distances while travelling (often over rougher terrain and in hotter temperatures) than you are used to. If you use a wheelchair, have it serviced before you go and carry a repair kit.

Read your **travel insurance** small print carefully to make sure that people with a pre-existing medical condition are not excluded. And use your travel agent to make your journey simpler: airline or bus companies can cope better if they are expecting you, with a wheelchair provided at airports and staff primed to help. A **medical certificate** of your fitness to travel (provided by your doctor) is also extremely useful; some airlines or insurance companies may insist on it. Make sure that you have extra supplies of medication – carried with you if you fly – and a prescription including the generic name in case of emergency.

Several **books** give a good overview of accessible travel in Australia, and include: *Smooth Ride Guides: Australia and New Zealand, Freewheeling Made Easy* (FT Publishing), which lists support organizations, airports and transport, specialist tour operators and places to visit and stay; *Easy Access Australia* (Easy Access Australia Publishing), which has information on all the states, with maps, and a separate section with floor plans of hotel rooms; and *A Wheelie's Handbook of Australia* (Program Print).

Useful contacts

ⓦ www.wheelabout.com and ⓦ e-bility.com/travel Both have lists of accommodation and transport in Australia for people with disabilities as well as Access Maps of major Australian cities.

In the UK and Ireland

All Go Here ⓦ www.everybody.co.uk. Provides information on accommodation suitable for disabled travellers throughout the UK, including Northern Ireland.
Holiday Care 2nd Floor, Imperial Building, Victoria Rd, Horley, Surrey RH6 7PZ ☎ 01293/774 535, Minicom ☎ 01293/776 943, ⓦ www .holidaycare.org.uk. Provides free lists of accessible accommodation abroad – European, American and long-haul destinations – plus a list of accessible attractions in the UK. Information on financial help for holidays available.
Irish Wheelchair Association Blackheath Drive, Clontarf, Dublin 3 ☎ 01/833 8241, ⓕ 833 3873, ⓔ iwa@iol.ie. Useful information provided about travelling abroad with a wheelchair.
RADAR (Royal Association for Disability and Rehabilitation) 12 City Forum, 250 City Rd, London EC1V 8AF ☎ 020/7250 3222, Minicom ☎ 020/7250 4119, ⓦ www.radar.org.uk.
Tripscope Alexandra House, Albany Rd, Brentford, Middlesex TW8 0NE ☎ 0845/7585 641, ⓦ www.justmobility.co.uk/tripscope. This registered charity provides a national telephone information service offering free advice on UK and international transport for those with a mobility problem.

In the US and Canada

Access-Able ⓦ www.access-able.com. Online resource for travellers with disabilities.
Directions Unlimited 123 Green Lane, Bedford Hills, NY 10507 ☎ 1-800/533-5343 or 914/241-1700. Tour operator specializing in custom tours for people with disabilities.
Mobility International USA 451 Broadway,

Eugene, OR 97401, voice and TDD ☎541/343-1284, ⓦwww.miusa.org. Information and referral services, access guides, tours and exchange programmes. Annual membership $35 (includes quarterly newsletter).

Society for the Advancement of Travelers with Handicaps (SATH) 347 5th Ave, New York, NY 10016 ☎212/447-7284, ⓦwww.sath.org. Non-profit educational organization that has actively represented travellers with disabilities since 1976.

Travel Information Service ☎215/456-9600. Telephone-only information and referral service.

Twin Peaks Press Box 129, Vancouver, WA 98661 ☎360/694-2462 or 1-800/637-2256, ⓦwww.twinpeak.virtualave.net. Publisher of the *Directory of Travel Agencies for the Disabled* ($19.95), listing more than 370 agencies worldwide; *Travel for the Disabled* ($19.95); the *Directory of Accessible Van Rentals* ($12.95); and *Wheelchair Vagabond* ($19.95), loaded with personal tips.

Wheels Up! ☎1-888/389-4335, ⓦwww.wheelsup.com. Provides discounted airfare, tour and cruise prices for disabled travellers, also publishes a free monthly newsletter and has a comprehensive website.

Australia

ACROD (Australian Council for Rehabilitation of the Disabled) PO Box 60, Curtin ACT 2605 ☎02/6282 4333; Suite 103, 1st Floor, 1–5 Commercial Rd, Kings Grove 2208 ☎02/9554 3666, ⓦwww.acrod.org.au. Regional offices provide lists of state-based help organizations, accommodation, travel agencies and tour operators.

DIRC (Disability Information Resource Centre) Adelaide, SA 5000 ☎08/8223 7522

Disability Advocacy Service Shop 1A, 63 Railway Terrace, Alice Springs, NT 0871 ☎08/8953 1422.

Disability Information Victoria PO Box 295, Malvern, Victoria ☎1300/650 865.

NICAN (National Information Communication Awareness Network) PO Box 407, Curtin, ACT 2605 ☎02/6285 3713 or 1800 806 769, ⓦwww.nican.com.au. A national, non-profit, free information service on recreation, sport, tourism, the arts, and much more, for people with disabilities. Has a database of 4500 organizations – such as wheelchair-accessible tourist accommodation venues, sports and recreation organizations, and rental companies who have accessible buses and vans.

Paraplegic and Quadriplegic Association 33–35 Burlington Rd, Homebush, NSW 2140 ☎02/9764 4166, ⓦwww.paraquadasn.au. Serves the interests of the spinally injured; offices in each state capital.

Travellers Aid Support Centre 2nd Floor, 169 Swanston St, Melbourne, VIC 3000 ☎03/9654 7690.

Accommodation

Much of Australia's tourist accommodation is well set up for people with disabilities, because buildings tend to be built outwards rather than upwards. New buildings in Australia must comply with a legal minimum **accessibility standard**, requiring that bathrooms contain toilets at the appropriate height, proper circulation and transfer space, wheel-in showers (sometimes with fold-down seat, but if this is lacking, proprietors will provide a plastic chair), grab rails, adequate doorways, and space next to toilets and beds for transfer. There are, of course, many older hotels which may have no wheelchair access at all or perhaps just one or two rooms with full wheelchair access. Most hotels also have refrigerators for medication which needs to be kept cool.

The best place to start looking for accommodation is the *A–Z Australian Accommodation Guide* published by the Australian Automobile Association (AAA) – the umbrella organization for state- and territory-based motoring associations that rate accommodation. They also offer some specialized services, a centralized **booking service** and a repair service for motorized wheelchairs, with reciprocal rights if you are a member of an affiliated overseas motoring organization. The guide is available from any of the state organizations; NICAN also has access to their database via computer, so you can choose your accommodation over the phone. Many travel shops and bookshops have accommodation guides which detail places that have wheelchair access.

The greatest range of accessible accommodation is found in the more densely populated areas of Australia – especially the east coast. In the **cities**, the big chain hotels have rooms with wheelchair access. Some of the smaller hotels do provide accessible accommodation, and a large proportion of suburban motels will have one or two suitable rooms. In the **country** there are fewer specially equipped hotels, but many motels have accessible units; this is particularly true of those that belong to a chain such as Flag – consult their directories for locations. The newest YHA **hostels** are all accessible, and there has been an effort to improve facilities throughout; accessible hostels are detailed in the YHA *Handbook*, or contact them direct (see p.46). **Caravan parks** are also worth considering, since some have accessible cabins. Others may have accessible toilets and washing facilities. Many **resorts** are also fully designed and equipped for wheelchair travellers, though in all cases, it's best to check in advance what facilities are available.

Transport

Interstate **buses** are generally not an option, though interstate **trains** can accommodate wheelchairs and give assistance for other disabilities; for enquiries about services in Queensland, New South Wales and Victoria call ☏ 13 2232, for elsewhere phone ☏ 1800 888 480. However, the most convenient ways of getting around are by plane and car. The two domestic airlines Qantas and Virgin Blue (see p.34) have services to help people with disabilities; Qantas staff undergo special disability-awareness training and on international flights their aircraft carry the sky chair and are equipped with a larger toilet cubicle.

Of the major car-rental agencies, Hertz and Avis offer **vehicles with hand controls** at no extra cost, but advance notice is

required. Reserved **parking** is available for vehicles displaying the wheelchair symbol (available from local council offices) in all major centres. There is no formal acceptance of overseas parking permits, but states will generally accept most home-country permits as sufficient evidence to obtain a temporary countrywide permit in Australia. Parking charges and designated spaces differ from state to state (call NICAN for further information). A specially adapted **taxi service** operates from all the major national airports, booked in advance on freecall ☏ 1800 043 187; in addition every capital city has wheelchair-accessible taxis. Some suburban rail services can be used with a wheelchair: Melbourne's *Met* leads the way – call (☏ 1800 800 120). Minibuses in some cities have either a hoist or a ramp for rental (call NICAN for further information – see p.73).

All capital cities and most regional centres produce **mobility maps** showing accessible paths, car parking, toilets and so on, which can be obtained from local councils. Other cities have gone further and their tourist authorities produce comprehensive books such as *Access Brisbane* and *Darwin City without Steps*, while ACROD in New South Wales publishes *Accessing Sydney* (available from them at 55 Ryde St, Ryde, NSW 2112). *Easy Access Australia – A Travel Guide to Australia* is a comprehensive guide written by a wheelchair-user for anyone with a mobility difficulty and is available over the Internet via ⓦ www.easyaccessaustralia.com.au ($45; includes postage and handling).

Travelling with children

Australians have an easy-going attitude to children and in most places they are made welcome. With plenty of beautiful beaches, parks and playgrounds, travelling with children in Australia can be great fun.

Getting around

Most forms of **transport** within Australia offer child concessions. Throughout the country, **metropolitan buses** and **trains** give discounts of around fifty percent for children and many allow children under 5 to travel free. Most **interstate buses** (see pp.35–37) offer around twenty percent off for children under the age of 14. Travel for infants is free if they are accompanied by two adults.

Long-distance train travel is limited in Australia (see p.35). It's also a slower and more expensive option, but if you're travelling with small children, it does have the advantage of sleepers and a bit more freedom of movement. **Domestic airlines** (see p.34) offer discounts of around fifty percent of the full adult fare, for children between 2 and 11 years. However, it's worth checking for adult discount deals which are likely to be even cheaper. Infants travel free of charge.

Otherwise, there's always the option of **self-drive**. Car rental is reasonably priced, and motorhomes and campervans are also available for rental (see p.39). They're an excellent way of seeing Australia and make it possible to camp rough in some spectacular national parks, as well as the many caravan parks, which offer power, amenities and often a pool and activities room. In most cases babies and very young children can camp for free. It's important to remember (especially when travelling with children) that Australia is a huge place and that driving outside of the major cities almost always involves long distances. Take plenty of activities for the car – tapes, books, magnetic games, cards and, if you don't like your children's taste in music, let them bring their own headsets. Stop regularly for breaks: most towns in Australia have public playgrounds which are a great way for young kids to let off steam.

Accommodation

Many **motels** give discounts for children and some offer a baby-sitting service – it's worth checking when you book. If you like the idea of a quiet whinge-free bushwalk or cocktails by the pool, most **resorts** and some motel chains (including Novotel ⓦ www.accor hotels.com.au/novotel/childrens_ club.asp) have kids' clubs, organized children's activities and a baby-sitting service.

Although initially more expensive, **self-contained accommodation** can prove cheaper in the long run as it's possible to cook your own meals. With young children this is often the best way to relax, without worrying about tired, grumpy behaviour in restaurants. Unless your children are older and very well-behaved, avoid **B&Bs** wherever possible. They're inevitably dotted with breakables and usually call for a quiet and restraint that isn't possible with young children.

These days **youth hostels** (see p.46) are not exclusively for young backpackers and most provide affordable family rooms – some en-suite. A few of the more modern hostels are positively luxurious, most are in fabulous locations, and in cities they're usually conveniently close to the city centre. They all have communal kitchens, lounge areas and television and there's usually plenty of books and games.

Aside from camping, the most economical way to see Australia is to stay in some of the thousands of **caravan parks** in Australia. Most have on-site vans or self-contained cabins at very reasonable rates for families. Check with information centres for caravan park listings.

Eating out

Things have moved on in Australia and, in the cities especially, many of the more atmospheric upmarket **restaurants** are welcoming to children, often providing high-chairs, toys, blackboards, drawing materials and a reasonable children's menu. Otherwise, there are still plenty of the standard fast-food outlets and children are allowed in the dining section of pubs for counter meals. Most country towns in Australia have pubs and some have RSL clubs (Returned Servicemen's League), which are a good cheap way to feed the family on basic pub food and make a welcome change from the greasy hamburgers, chips, meat pies and steak sandwiches sold practically everywhere.

Kids' gear

Car and van rental companies provide **child safety seats**. Taxis will also provide child seats if you request them when making a booking, although there may be a longer wait. Airlines will allow you to carry a pram or travel cot for free, and it's possible to rent baby equipment from some shops – check the local Yellow Pages for listings. When planning a sightseeing day that involves a lot of walking, check with the tourist attraction to see if they rent out push chairs, as this can make the difference between a pleasant and an awful day out.

Activities

Most tours and entry fees for tourist destinations offer **concession rates** for children and many also offer family tickets. If you have two or more children these will usually work out substantially cheaper. Museums often have special children's areas and during school holidays many run **supervised activities**, along with programmes that include storytelling and performances (check p.58 for school holiday dates). In most states the National Parks and Wildlife Service runs entertaining and educational ranger-led walks and activities during the school holidays. The walks are free, but there's usually a park entrance fee. Check at information centres or with NPWS in each state for timetables and fees.

Sun care

The Australian **sun** is ferocious, making it essential to combine outdoor activities with sensible skin care. A broad-spectrum, water-resistant sunscreen (minimum SPF of 30) is essential; see p.27 for more. There's a "no hat, no play" policy in school playgrounds and most kids wear legionnaire-style caps, or broad-brimmed sun hats, which are cheap and easy to find in surf shops or department stores. All sunglasses in Australia are UV-rated and most kids also wear UV-resistant lycra swim tops or wetsuit style all-in-ones to the beach. There are Cancer Council shops in most cities which sell a high-quality and colourful range of all these items.

Helpful publications

For general tips and anecdotes pick up the latest copy of Lonely Planet's *Travel With Children*, by Cathy Lanigan. In Sydney look for *Sydney's Child* (ⓦ www.sydneyschild .com.au), a free monthly paper listing kids activities in and around the city and advertising a range of services including babysitting. *Melbourne's Child* is a similar monthly paper and both can be picked up at libraries and major museums. *Lollipop* is a bi-monthly South Australian publication which lists activities for kids. In Tasmania, *It's a Kids Life* by Wendy Nielson and Avril Priem is available from bookstores for around $20. And in other states, most tourist information centres will be able to help with suggestions for planning a child-friendly itinerary.

Gay and lesbian Australia

Year by year Australia grows in popularity as a Queer destination. Even as far back as 1832 a Select Committee of the British Parliament noted the popularity of "alternative lifestyles" among the colonists. Today, the beautiful people flock down under, lured by the conducive climate and laid-back lifestyle and eager to hang out with the homeboys on balmy beaches and sun-kissed city streets.

Despite its reputation as a macho culture, Australia revels in a large and active **scene**: you'll find an air of confidence and a sense of community that is often missing in other countries – and, what's more, it's friendly and accessible.

The colonists transported English **law** to Australia, but in 1972 South Australia was the first state to enact **decriminalization**, followed the next year by the ACT and Northern Territory. Surprisingly, Victoria and New South Wales (generally thought of as liberal states) delayed similar legislation until the 1980s. Less surprisingly, Queensland took the plunge only in 1991, while it took a decade of constant petitioning from the Tasmanian Gay and Lesbian Rights Group, and pressure from the Federal Government and the UN Human Rights Committee for the law to change in Tasmania in 1997. In Western Australia there's still an age of consent of 21, whereas the ages of consent in ACT and Victoria (both 16), SA and Tasmania (both 17), are the same as the heterosexual age. In the Northern Territory and NSW, the homosexual age of consent is 18. In Queensland, the age of consent for homosexuals depends on the sexual act practised, with anal sex outlawed until 18 but otherwise 16. Sex between women is either not mentioned in state laws or is covered by the heterosexual age. The foreign partner in a de facto gay relationship can apply to immigrate to or permanently reside in Australia, a much better situation than in many countries, but the current battle the gay and lesbian lobby groups are waging is to make same-sex relationships completely equal in the eyes of the law as heterosexual ones, in terms of marriage, parenting, next of kin rights, superannuation and age of consent.

Today, Australia is testimony to the power of the pink dollar, and there's an abundance of gay venues, services, businesses, travel clubs, country retreats and the like.

Australia is definitely the place to watch Men At Work – and at play. **Aussie boys** get a lot of sun and sport – although the scene is a lot more diverse than simply tan and toned muscle, and the community is so large that there's bound to be something for everyone. One thing's for certain: you won't be bored. Just remember to pack your trunks, snorkel and fins, your clubbing gear and some barbecue tongs.

Australian **dykes** are refreshingly open and self-possessed – a relief after the more closed and cliquey scene in Europe. The flip side of their fearlessness is the predominance of S&M on the scene. Maybe the climate has something to do with it, but you'll see a good deal of tattoos and pierced flesh around. Dyke **scenes** are nothing if not mercurial, and Australia is no exception. We've done our best to list bars, clubs and meeting places, but be warned that venues open, change their names, change hands, shut for refurbishment, get relaunched at a new address and finally go out of business with frightening rapidity.

Where and how to go

Sydney is the jewel in Australia's luscious navel. Firmly established as one of the world's great gay cities – only San Francisco can really rival it – it attracts lesbian and gay visitors from around the world. And if this can be overwhelming at times (the gossip alone has been known to drive people to the other side of the continent), Australia has plenty more to offer. Melbourne closely follows the scene in Sydney, but for a change of pace, take a trip to Brisbane and the Gold Coast. Perth, Adelaide and Darwin all have smaller, quieter scenes.

Away from the cities, things get more discreet, but a lot of **country areas** do have very friendly local scenes – impossible to pinpoint, but easy to stumble across. Australians on the city scene are a friendly bunch, but in a small country town they get really friendly, so if there's anything going on you'll probably get invited along.

The **Outback** covers the vast majority of the Australian continent and is, in European terms, sparsely populated. Mining and cattle ranching are the primary employers and they help to create a culture not famed for its tolerance of homosexuality. Tread carefully: bear in mind that Ayers Rock may be 2000km from Sydney as the crow flies, but in many ways it's a million miles away in terms of attitudes.

Each chapter of this Guide has specific gay and lesbian listings, with a wealth of information – see in particular the box on pp.181–183, which has all you need to know to join in Sydney's Mardi Gras celebrations. Check out too **The Rough Guide to Gay and Lesbian Australia**, reviewed in our "Books" section on p.1200.

Gay and lesbian contacts

Personal contacts

Pinkboard ⓦ www.pinkboard.com.au. Popular long-running Australian website featuring personal ads and classifieds sections with everything from houseshares, party tickets for sale, employment and a help and advice section. It's free to run your own personal or classified.

Press and multimedia

Each major capital has excellent free gay newspapers, like the *Sydney Star Observer* (ⓦ www.ssonet.com.au) or Melbourne's *Brother Sister* (ⓦ www.brothersister.com.au; also available in a Brisbane edition) that give the local lowdown. Otherwise, check out:

ALSO Foundation ⓦ www.also.org.au. Based in Victoria (see p.935), they have a good website with an excellent nationwide business and community directory.

DNA ⓦ www.dnamagazine.com.au. A new national glossy – an upmarket lifestyle magazine for gay men.

Gay Australia Guide
ⓦ www.gayaustraliaguide.bigstep.com. Handy general guide. Information on where to stay, what to do, nightlife and community groups – covers Sydney and the state capitals.

LOTL (Lesbians on the Loose) ⓦ www.lotl.com. A monthly publication available at lesbian and gay venues.

Pink + Blue ⓦ www.pinkandblue.com.au. A useful online gay and lesbian lifestyle magazine.

The Pink Directory ⓦ www.thepinkdirectory .com.au or contact Pink Publishing Australia, PO Box 1005, Potts Point NSW 1335 ☏ 02/8356 9733, ⓕ 9225 9763. Launched in 2001, this is an online and print directory of gay and lesbian business and community information.

Tour operator

redOyster.com ATS Pacific Pty, Level 10, 130 Elizabeth St, Sydney, NSW 2000 ☏ 02/9268 2188, ⓦ www. redOyster.com. A gay- and lesbian-branded tour operator that can arrange packages for the Gay and Lesbian Mardi Gras,and other festivals and destinations, as can the lesbian-owned and -operated Silke's Travel, below.

Tourist services

GALTA (Gay and Lesbian Tourism Australia PO Box 208, Darlinghurst, NSW 1300 ☏ 02/8379 7498, ⓦ www.galta.com.au. A non-profit organization set up to promote the gay and lesbian tourism industry. Its website has links to accommodation, travel agents and tour operators, and gay and lesbian printed and online guides.

Q Beds ⓦ www.qbeds.com. An online accommodation directory and booking service for gay- and lesbian-owned, -operated or -friendly businesses.

Travel agents

Adelaide Parkside Travel, 70 Glen Osmond Rd, Parkside, SA 5063 ☏ 08/8274 1222, ⓔ parkside@harveyworld.com.au
Cairns Gay Cairns Travel, 28 Spence St, Cairns QLD 4870 ☏ 07/4041 1969, ⓦ www.gaycairns.com
Melbourne Tearaway Travel, 52 Porter St, Prahan, VIC 3181 ☏ 03/9510 6644, ⓦ www.tearaway.com

Perth Rainbow Worldwide Tours and Travel, Suite 11, 336 Churchill Ave, Subiaco WA 6008 ☏ 08/9382 4023, ✉ rbowtour@opera.iinet.net.au

Sydney Silke's Travel, PO Box 1099, Darlinghurst, NSW 1300 ☏ 02/8347 2000, ⓦ www.silkes.com.au

B

BASICS | Women and sexual harassment

Women and sexual harassment

The stereotyped image of the Aussie male is of a boozy bloke interested in sport, his car and his mates, with his girlfriend a poor fourth. And it's not that far wrong: the Australian ethos of mateship has traditionally excluded women – the hard, tough life of the early days of white settlement, when women were scarce, fostered a male culture that's to some extent still current. Another legacy of pioneering times is the reputation of Australian women for being robust and practical.

In the main **cities**, attitudes are generally enlightened and "new men" are gaining ground, but in the more remote **country and Outback** areas, the older attitudes are more tenacious and sexual harassment can be commonplace – if rarely threatening. Men driving by in cars, in particular, are notorious for shouting out crude comments and sexual remarks as a woman walks by, and catcalling from groups of men in the street can be intimidating.

Sexual equality and attitudes

In public life, Australia has one of the best records for **sexual equality** in the world. It was the second country to give women the vote (after New Zealand in 1893), and the fact that this happened a year after federation in 1901 shows that the intention was for women to take a full role in the new nation. In the 1970s and 1980s Australia kept pace with the worldwide **feminist movement** (indeed, with Germaine Greer, it helped lead it): the first big milestone – equal pay for equal work – was finally achieved in 1974. Equal opportunities legislation and affirmative action schemes for employment have been widely adopted: today, non-sexist language is the norm for newspapers and officialdom.

However, corresponding changes in attitudes have not always kept pace with all of this. At about the same time that women achieved equal pay, the **public bars** of hotels, which had traditionally refused to serve women, were being stormed by women's groups. Today, a woman can be served a drink anywhere in the country, but the way that Australian pubs are set up – with two separate bars – continues to reflect the old bias; you'll still see signs saying "Ladies' Lounge", and if you want to go to the women's toilets you'll have to walk a long way from the public bar. **Outback and country pubs** are still very much male bastions, and any woman travelling on her own would do well to avoid them, thus escaping the full blast of misogyny.

Travelling solo

Avoiding pubs is all very well, but **hotels** are often the cheapest and sometimes the only places to stay in **small towns**. The major drawback is that pub accommodation is often full of single male workers from other towns, or old men who are permanent boarders, so roaming corridors late at night in search of the toilet can be an unpleasant experience. That said, the management is usually friendly, and most country pubs are family-run. **Bed and breakfast** establishments and **guesthouses** provide a more homelike, friendly environment, unlike the inevitably impersonal **motels** where a stay can be a potentially lonely experience. **Caravan parks** and **campsites** tend to be safe, family-dominated environments and are a good bet if you have your own transport – and sleeping bag. In larger towns and cities, **hostels** are where you're most likely to meet like-minded women travelling alone. Easy-going Australian attitudes mean that dorms in backpackers' hostels (never YHA hostels) are often mixed sex. There's usually at least one female-only dorm and if this is really important to you, you should ask about it in advance or when you check in.

Best of all for making contact with locals and generally getting involved are **farmstays** (which needn't be expensive if you stay in shearers' quarters and the like) or the experience of being a WWOOF (Willing Workers on Organic Farms; see p.71). Before going to work or to stay on remote **Outback stations**, try to find out as much about the set-up as possible – you could end up being the only woman among a group of men.

Rape and serious trouble

If the worst happens, it's best to contact a **Rape Crisis Line** before going straight to the police; all major cities have them and there's always a free-call line if you're in the country. Women police officers form a large part of the force, and in general the police deal sensitively with sexual assault cases.

To **avoid** physical attack, don't get too relaxed about Australia's friendly, easy-going attitude. The usual defensive tactics apply. In the cities at night, buses or trams are generally safer than trains – on the train, always sit next to the guard in the carriage. Pick somewhere to stay that's close to public transport so you don't have to walk far at night – an area with busy nightlife may well be safer than a dead suburban backstreet. If you're going to have to walk for long stretches at night, take a cab unless the streets are busy with traffic, restaurants and people.

The 1992 "backpacker murders" of hitching travellers just outside Sydney prove that it's not only in remote areas or when travelling alone that **hitchhiking** is dangerous – and that even male company is no safeguard. Hitching is doubly inadvisable for women and, with the wide variety of inexpensive transport options available, is hard to justify. If you must do it, never do it alone – and heed the general advice and warnings given on p.43.

Women's contacts

All the major cities have good **women's contacts**, from resource centres and information lines to health centres where you can often get free pregnancy testing and other help. There's also a lively culture of women's galleries and bookshops; as well as stocking the works of the hundreds of great Australian women writers (see "Books" on pp.1200–1211), they'll have copies of feminist journals and good notice boards which often have information about **women-only accommodation**. Lesbian magazines also carry ads for women's bed and breakfasts and the like – you don't have to be gay to stay. In March, **International Women's Day** provides an excuse for a month-long series of women's events in the cities, culminating in enthusiastically attended street marches.

Specific women's contacts are listed in the city accounts of this Guide. For more, check out the White Pages under "Women"; alternatively, the Citizen's Advice Bureau in each city should be able to refer you to relevant organizations.

Directory

Electricity Australia's electrical current is 240/250v, 50Hz AC. British appliances will work with an adaptor for the Australian three-pin plug. American and Canadian 110v appliances will also need a transformer.

Emergencies Dial ☏000.

Gambling Australians are obsessive about gambling, though legalities vary from state to state. Even small towns have their own race-tracks and there are government TAB betting agencies everywhere; you can often bet in pubs too. Many states have huge casinos and clubs, open to anyone, with wall-to-wall one-armed bandits (poker machines or "pokies"); there are also big state lotteries.

Laundries Known as laundromats, these are rare outside urban centres. Hostels, motels and caravan parks will often have a laundry area with a washing machine (coin-op). Fancy hotels, of course, will do it for you.

Public toilets Towns and cities are very well supplied with public facilities in civic-minded Australia. They're found in parks and at council and tourist offices in country areas, and in shopping arcades, train stations and department stores in the cities. Most road-houses offer showers as well as toilets, usually for a small payment.

Seasons Don't forget that in the southern hemisphere the seasons are reversed. Summer lasts from November to February, winter from June to September. But of course it's not that simple: in the tropical north the important seasonal distinction is between the Wet (effectively summer) and the Dry (winter) – for more on their significance to travellers see p.619.

Student cards As an overseas student traveller, you need an International Student Identity Card (ISIC card) – well worth having (if you're eligible) for discounts on travel, tours, museum entry, etc. Backpackers of any age or status who can produce a YHA or VIP membership card (see p.47) are entitled to many of these discounts.

Tax A Goods and Services Tax (GST) of ten percent was introduced in 2000, and caused a general across-the-board price hike. Visitors can claim GST refunds for goods purchased in Australia as they clear customs, providing individual reciepts exceed $300 and the claim is made within thirty days of purchase.

Times zones Australia has three time zones: Eastern Standard Time (TAS, VIC, NSW, QLD), Central Standard Time (SA, NT) and Western Standard Time (WA). Eastern Standard Time is ten hours ahead of GMT (Greenwich Mean Time) and fifteen hours ahead of US Eastern Time. (When it's 10pm in Sydney, it's noon in London, 7am in New York and 4am in Los Angeles – but don't forget daylight saving, which can affect this by one hour either way.) Central Standard Time is thirty minutes behind Eastern Standard, and Western Standard two hours behind Eastern. Daylight saving (Oct–March) is adopted everywhere except QLD, NT and WA; clocks are put forward one hour.

Tips Tipping is not customary in Australia, and cab drivers and bar staff don't generally expect anything. In fact, cab drivers often round the fare down rather than bother with change. In cafés and restaurants you might leave the change – only very fancy establishments expect ten percent.

Weights and measures Australia has been fully metric since the early 1970s and is thoroughly adapted to kilometres, kilograms, litres and degrees Celsius. Shoe sizes are unique to Australia, while dress sizes are the same as in the UK (US 8 is equivalent to Australian 10).

Guide

Guide

Sydney and around

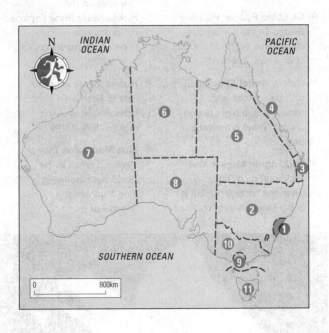

CHAPTER 1 # Highlights

✳ **Manly Ferry** The ferry trip out to Manly, with its unbeatable views of the harbour, is a must. See p.112

✳ **Opera House performance** Admire the stunning exterior of this Australian icon, or better still, take in a performance. See p.115

✳ **Climbing Sydney Harbour Bridge** Climb the famous coathanger for great harbour views. See p.116

✳ **Oxford Street** Crammed with bars, clubs and restaurants, a night out on Oxford Street is essential. See p.140

✳ **Paddington Market** Visit Paddington on Saturday, when the famous market is in full swing. See p.142

✳ **Bondi Beach** Big, brash Bondi is synonymous with Australian beach culture. See p.152

✳ **Mardi Gras** The biggest celebration of gay and lesbian culture in the world. See pp.182–183

✳ **Cruising on the Hawkesbury River** Explore the pretty Hawkesbury River on a leisurely cruise. See p.202

✳ **Hunter Valley wineries** One of Australia's most famous wine-growing regions. See p.214

✳ **Blue Mountains** Take a weekend break in the World Heritage-listed Blue Mountains. See p.220

1

Sydney and around

F lying into **Sydney** provides the first snapshot of Australia for most overseas visitors: toy-sized images of the Harbour Bridge and the Opera House, tilting in a glittering expanse of blue water. The Aussie city par excellence, Sydney stands head and shoulders above any other in Australia. Taken together with its surrounds, it's in many ways a microcosm of Australia as a whole – if only in its ability to defy your expectations and prejudices as often as it confirms them. A thrusting, high-rise business centre, a high-profile gay community and inner-city deprivation of unexpected harshness are as much part of the scene as the beaches, the bodies and the sparkling harbour. The sophistication, cosmopolitan population and exuberant nightlife of Sydney are a long way from the Outback, and yet Sydney has the highest Aboriginal population of any Australian city, and bushfires are a constant threat.

The area around – everything in this chapter is within day-trip distance – offers a taste of virtually everything you'll find in the rest of the country, with the exception of desert. There are magnificent **national parks** and native wildlife – Ku-Ring-Gai Chase and Royal being the best known of the parks, each a mere hour's drive from the centre of town – and beyond them stretch endless ocean **beaches**, great for surfers, and more enclosed waters for safer swimming and sailing. Inland, the **Blue Mountains**, with three more national parks, offer isolated bushwalking and scenic viewpoints. On the way are historic colonial towns that were among the earliest foundations in the country – Sydney itself, of course, was the very first. The commercial and industrial heart of the state of New South Wales, especially the central coastal region, is bordered by **Wollongong** in the south and **Newcastle** in the north. Both were synonymous with coal and steel, but the smokestack industries that supported them for decades are now in severe decline. This is far from an industrial wasteland, though: the heart of the coal-mining country is the **Hunter Valley**, northwest of Newcastle, but to visit it you'd never guess, because this is also Australia's oldest, and arguably its best-known, wine-growing region.

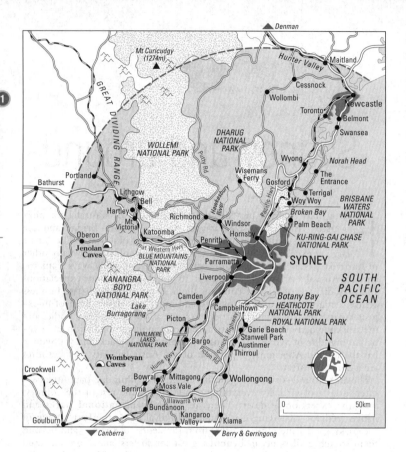

Sydney

The 2000 Olympics were a coming-of-age ceremony for **SYDNEY**. The impact on the city was all-embracing, with fifty years' worth of development compressed into four years under the pressure of intense international scrutiny. Transport infrastructure was greatly improved and a rash of luxury hotels and waterside apartments added themselves to the skyline. The City of Sydney Council spent $200 million to improve and beautify the city streets, public squares and parks, and licensing laws changed too, creating a European-style bar culture. Sydney now has all the vigour of a world-class city, with the reputation of its restaurants in particular turning the lingering cultural sneers to swoons. It seems to have the best of both worlds – twenty minutes from Circular Quay by bus, the high-rise office buildings and sky-scrapers give way to colourful inner-city suburbs where you can get an eyeful of sky and watch the lemons ripening above the sidewalk, while to the centre's north and south are corridors of largely intact bushland where many have built their dream homes. During every heatwave, however, bush-fires threaten the city, and sophisticated Sydney becomes closer to its roots than it sometimes feels. In the summer, the city's hot offices are abandoned for the remarkably unspoilt beaches strung around the eastern and northern suburbs.

It's also as beautiful a city as any in the world, with a **setting** that perhaps only Rio de Janeiro can rival: the water is what makes it so special, and no introduction to Sydney would be complete without paying tribute to one of the world's great **harbours**. Port Jackson is a sunken valley which twists inland to meet the fresh water of the Parramatta River; in the process it washes into a hundred coves and bays, winds around rocky points, flows past the small har-bour islands, slips under bridges and laps at the foot of the Opera House. If Sydney is seen at its gleaming best from the deck of a harbour ferry, especially at weekends when the harbour's jagged jaws fill with a flotilla of small vessels, racing yachts and cabin cruisers, it's seen at its most varied in its lively neigh-bourhoods. Getting away from the city centre and exploring them is an essen-tial part of Sydney's pleasures.

It might seem surprising that Sydney is not Australia's capital: the creation of Canberra in 1927 – intended to stem the intense rivalry between Sydney and Melbourne – has not affected the view of many Sydneysiders that their city remains the *true* capital of Australia, and certainly in many ways it feels like it. The city has a tangible sense of history: the old stone walls and well-worn steps in the backstreets around The Rocks are an evocative reminder that Sydney has more than two hundred years of white history behind it.

Some history

The early history of Sydney is very much the history of white Australia, right from its founding as a penal colony, amid brutality, deprivation and despair. In January 1788 the **First Fleet**, carrying over a thousand people, 736 of them convicts, arrived at **Botany Bay** expecting the "fine meadows" that Captain James Cook had described eight years earlier. In fact what greeted them was mostly swamp, scrub and sand dunes: a desolate sight even for sea-weary eyes. An unsuccessful scouting expedition prompted Commander Arthur Phillip to move the fleet a few kilometres north, to the well-wooded Port Jackson, where a stream of fresh water was found. Based around the less than satisfactory Tank Stream, the settlement was named **Sydney Cove** after Viscount Sydney, then Secretary of State in Great Britain. In the first three years of settlement, the new colony nearly starved to death several times; the land around Sydney Cove proved to be barren. When supply ships did arrive, they inevitably came with hundreds more convicts to further burden the colony. It was not until 1790, when land was successfully farmed further west at **Parramatta**, that the hunger began to abate. Measure this suffering with that of the **Eora Aborigines**: their land had been invaded, their people vir-tually wiped out by smallpox, and now they were stricken by hunger as the settlers shot at their game – and even, as they moved further inland, at the Eora themselves.

By the early 1800s Sydney had become a stable colony and busy trading post. Army officers in charge of the colony, exploiting their access to free land and cheap labour, became rich farm-owners and virtually established a currency based on rum. The **military**, known as the New South Wales Corps (or more familiarly as "the rum corps"), became the supreme political force in the colony in 1809, even overthrowing the governor (mutiny-plagued Captain

Bligh himself). This was the last straw for the government back home, and the rebellious officers were finally brought to heel when the reformist Governor **Lachlan Macquarie** arrived from England with forces of his own. He liberalized conditions, supported the prisoners' right to become citizens after they had served their time, and appointed several to public offices.

By the 1840s the transportation of convicts to New South Wales had ended, the explorers Lawson and Blaxland had found a way through the Blue Mountains to the Western Plains and **gold** had been struck in Bathurst. The population soared as free settlers arrived in ever-increasing numbers. In the Victorian era, Sydney's population became even more starkly divided into the **haves** and the **have-nots**: while the poor lived in slums where disease, crime, prostitution and alcoholism were rife, the genteel classes – self-consciously replicating life in the mother country – took tea on their verandahs and erected grandiloquent monuments such as the Town Hall, the Strand Arcade and the Queen Victoria Building in homage to English architecture of the time. An outbreak of the plague in The Rocks at the beginning of the twentieth century made wholesale slum clearances inevitable, and with the demolitions came a change in attitudes. Strict new vice laws meant the end of the bad old days of backstreet knifings, drunken taverns and makeshift brothels.

Over the next few decades, Sydney settled into comfortable **suburban living**. The metropolis sprawled westwards, creating a flat, unremarkable city with no real centre, an appropriate symbol for the era of shorts and knee socks and the stereotypical, barbecue-loving Bruce and Sheila – an international image which still plagues Australians. Sydney has come a long way since the parochialism of the 1950s, however: skyscrapers at the city's centre have rocketed heavenward and constructions such as the **Opera House** began to reflect the city's dynamism. The cultural clichés of cold tinnies of beer and meat pies with sauce have long been tossed out, giving way to a city confident in itself and its culinary attractions too. Today, Sydney's citizens don't look inwards – and they certainly don't look towards England. Despite this, when Sydney proudly beat Beijing and Manchester in the chase for the **Olympics** in the year 2000, no one would have guessed that Juan Antonio Samaranch, Olympic Chairman, would pronounce it the "best games ever". Thousands of immigrants from around the globe have given Sydney a truly cosmopolitan air and it's a city as thrilling and alive as any.

Arrival and information

The dream way to **arrive** in Sydney is, of course, by ship, cruising in under the great coathanger of the Harbour Bridge to tie up at the overseas passenger terminal alongside Circular Quay. The reality of the functional airport, bus and train stations is a good deal less romantic.

By air

Sydney's **Kingsford Smith Airport**, referred to as "Mascot" after the suburb where it's located, near Botany Bay, is 8km south of the city (international flight times ☎13 12 23). Domestic and international terminals are linked by a free shuttle bus (every 30min), or you can take the Airport Express bus for $3; see box opposite for **buses** into the city. You can take a train right into the centre: the **Airport Link** underground railway connects the airport to the

City Circle train line in around fifteen minutes (every 15min; one-way $10.60) However, as a suburban commuter service it can be crowded at peak hours, there is no dedicated space for luggage and it is more expensive than Airport Express buses, which will drop you off near your hotel. With three or more of you it can be cheaper to share a **taxi**, which will cost $30 to $35 from the airport to the city centre or Kings Cross.

Bureau de change offices at both terminals are open daily from 5am until last arrival with rates comparable to major banks. On the ground floor (arrivals) of the international terminal, the **Sydney Visitor Centre** (daily 5am until last arrival; ☎02/9667 6050) can arrange car rental and onward travel – it's licensed to sell train and bus tickets – and **book hotels** anywhere in Sydney and New South Wales free of charge and at stand-by rates. Most hostels advertise on an adjacent notice board; there's a freephone line for reservations, and many of them will refund your bus fare; a few also do free airport pick-ups.

Airport buses

State Transit
Airport Express ☎13 15 00. Buses (#300; green and yellow) run to Kings Cross via Central station, the city centre, The Rocks and Circular Quay (daily 5am–11pm; every 10min; $7, $12 return valid two months), picking up and setting down at various stops, including hotels and hostels. Tickets can be bought on board and at the Sydney Visitor Centre in the international terminal (see above), where you can also buy tourist bus passes – the Sydney Pass (see p.96) includes return airport–city transfer so it's best to buy it here.

State Transit also has a daily commuter route: the Metroline #400 goes frequently to Bondi Junction via Maroubra and Randwick in one direction, and to Burwood in the other (tickets cost a maximum of $4.70).

Shuttle services – Sydney area
Eastern Suburbs Airport Shuttle Bookings ☎0500 881 113, ⓦ www.supershuttle .com.au. Minibus service (quick call-out service) to and from the eastern beaches – Bondi, Coogee, Randwick, Clovelly and Bronte – and dropping off at all hostels, motels and hotels ($10 one-way).

Kingsford Smith Transport/Sydney Airporter ☎02/9667 3221 or 02/9666 9988 three hours before to book an accommodation pick-up, ⓦ www.kst.com.au. Private bus service dropping off at hotels or hostels in the area bounded by Kings Cross and Darling Harbour. Service leaves when the bus is full ($8 one-way, $13 return).

surfacetoair ☎02/9913 9912, ⓦ www.surfacetoair.com.au. Minibus service to the city and the northern beaches – including Manly, Whale Beach and Palm Beach – dropping off at accommodation. Book in advance by phone or email giving the day, time and flight and they will designate a waiting point. Manly $30, Palm Beach $49 (cheaper rates for couples and groups).

Coach and shuttle services – central coast and south coast
Bennetts Airport Shuttle ☎1300 130 557, ⓦ www.ben-air.com.au. Pre-booked door-to-door service to accommodation anywhere on the central coast ($47, cheaper rates for couples and groups).

Premier Motor Service ☎13 34 10, for bookings ☎02/4423 5244, ⓦ www.premierms .com.au. Departs daily at 9.45am and 3.30pm, plus Monday to Friday at 7.45am from the domestic terminal, fifteen minutes later from the international terminal, to south coast towns as far as Bega ($50), the 9.45am and 3.30pm services continuing on to Eden ($56). Bookings necessary.

By train and bus

All local and interstate **trains** arrive at **Central station** on Eddy Avenue, just south of the city centre. There are lockers and left luggage at the station, and showers at the volunteer-run **Travellers' Aid** (Mon–Sat 7.30am–2pm; shower $3, with towel $5). From here, and neighbouring **Railway Square** you can hop onto nearly every major bus route, and from within Central station you can take a CityRail train to any city or suburban station (see "City transport" on p.93).

All **buses** to Sydney arrive and depart from Eddy Avenue and Pitt Street, bordering Central station. The area is well set up with decent cafés, a 24-hour police station and a huge YHA hostel (see p.104), as well as the **Sydney Coach Terminal** (daily 6am–10pm), which also has luggage lockers ($6–9 per 24hr, depending on size) and oversize luggage storage (backpacks $10, bikes $14 per 24hr). The **Traveller's Information Service** (℡02/9281 9366) in the coach terminal can make hotel **accommodation bookings** at stand-by rates while a range of hostels advertise on an adjacent notice board with free phones for direct reservations; many of them provide free pick-ups (usually from Bay 14). You can purchase coach tickets and passes from the Information Service as well as Sydney Passes (see p.96), and arrange harbour cruises and other tours. Greyhound Pioneer and McCafferty's also have separate ticket offices/departure lounges on Eddy Avenue.

Information

The Sydney Visitor Centre at the international airport terminal (see p.91) offers the most comprehensive **information** service, with free maps and brochures – including *Sydney: The Official Guide* which is packed with useful maps – on-the-spot accommodation reservations at stand-by rates and transport bookings for Sydney and the rest of New South Wales. The main central tourist office is the **Sydney Visitor Centre** in The Rocks at 106 George St (daily 9am–6pm; ℡02/9255 1788 or 1800 067 676, ⓦwww.sydneyvisitorcentre.com; also see p.118), offering a similar range of literature; they also have a self-service budget accommodation booking board with free phone links to the listed hotels. Tourism NSW runs the **City Host Programme** with three green-coloured information kiosks at Circular Quay, Martin Place and Town Hall (all daily 9am–5pm) providing brochures, maps and face-to-face information. There's also the **Darling Harbour Visitor Information Centre** (see p.130), and the tourist office at Manly (see p.158). All the above sell the **See Sydney & Beyond Smartvisit Card** (℡1300 661 711, ⓦwww.seesydneycard.com) which comes in one-, two-, three- or seven-day versions with or without a transport option (one-day $59/$75, two-day $99/$130, three-day $129/$175, seven-day $189/$255) and includes admission to forty well-known attractions in Sydney and the Blue Mountains; as you would have to be a fast worker to make the pricey pass real value for money and because queues are not a huge problem in Sydney, there is no real advantage in purchasing it.

Several free monthly **listings magazines** are worth picking up at tourist offices: the weekly *Where Magazine* is best for general information; *This Month in Sydney* is also useful. The City of Sydney Council distributes a basic photocopied guide, *City Life*, every Wednesday to visitor centres and information booths, and also publishes the bimonthly *Official Sydney Events Guide* (free from the Town Hall, $3.25 from newsagents); similar information is available on their website, ⓦwww.cityofsydney.nsw.gov.au. *TNT Magazine* is the best of an array of publications aimed at **backpackers**, giving the low-down on Sydney on the cheap.

City transport

Sydney's public transport network is reasonably good, though the system relies heavily on buses, and traffic jams can be a problem. There are buses, trains, ferries, a light rail system and the city monorail to choose from, plus plenty of licensed taxis. Trains stop running around midnight, as do most regular buses, though several services towards the eastern and northern beaches, such as the #380 to Bondi Beach, the #372 and #373 to Coogee and the #151 to Manly, run through the night. Otherwise a pretty good network of **Nightride buses** follow the train routes to the suburbs, departing from Town Hall station (outside the Energy Australia Building on George St) and stopping at train stations (where taxis wait at designated ranks); return train tickets, Railpasses and Travelpasses can be used, or buy a ticket from the driver. For stays of more than a few days, a weekly **Travelpass** is a worthwhile investment (see box on p.96). For public transport information, routes and timetables call ☎13 15 00 (daily 6am–10pm; Ⓦwww.131500.com.au).

Buses

Within the central area, **buses**, hailed from yellow-signed bus stops, are the most convenient, widespread mode of transport, and cover more of the city than the trains. With few exceptions buses radiate from the centre with major interchanges at Railway Square near Central station, (especially southwest routes), at Circular Quay (range of routes), from York and Carrington streets outside Wynyard station (North Shore), and Bondi Junction station (eastern suburbs and beaches). **Tickets** can be bought on board from the driver and cost from $1.50 for up to two distance-measured sections, rising to $4.70; $2.60 (up to five sections) is the most typical fare. Substantial discounts are available with TravelTen tickets and other travel passes (see box on pp.96–97); these must be validated in the ticket reader by the front door. Bus **information**, including route maps, **timetables** and **passes** are available from handy booths at Carrington Street, Wynyard; at Circular Quay on the corner of Loftus and Alfred streets; at the Queen Victoria Building on York Street; at Bondi Junction bus interchange; and at Manly Wharf. For detailed timetables and route maps see Sydney Buses' website Ⓦwww.sydneybuses.nsw.gov.au.

Trains

Trains, operated by **CityRail** (see map p.94), will get you where you're going faster than buses, especially at rush hour and when heading out to the suburbs, but you need to transfer to a bus or ferry to get to most harbourside or beach destinations. There are six train lines, mostly overground, each of which stops at Central and Town Hall stations. Trains run from around 5am to midnight, with **tickets** starting at around $2.20 single on the City Loop and for short hops; buying off-peak returns (after 9am and all weekend) means you can save up to forty percent.

Automatic ticket machines (which give change) and barriers (insert magnetic tickets, otherwise show ticket at the gate) have been introduced just about everywhere. Fines for fare evasion exceed $150. All platforms are painted with

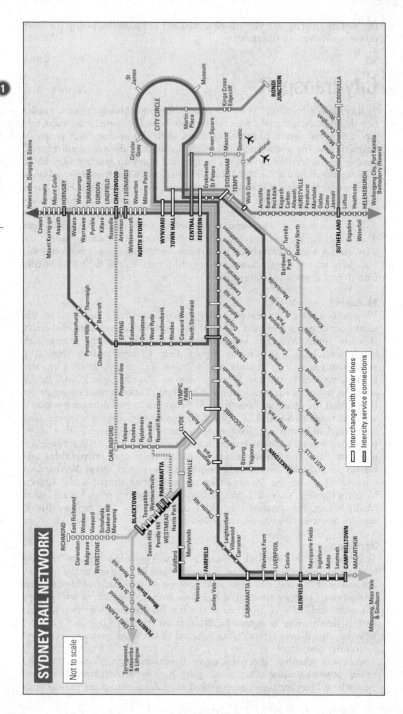

SYDNEY RAIL NETWORK

Not to scale

Interchange with other lines
Intercity service connections

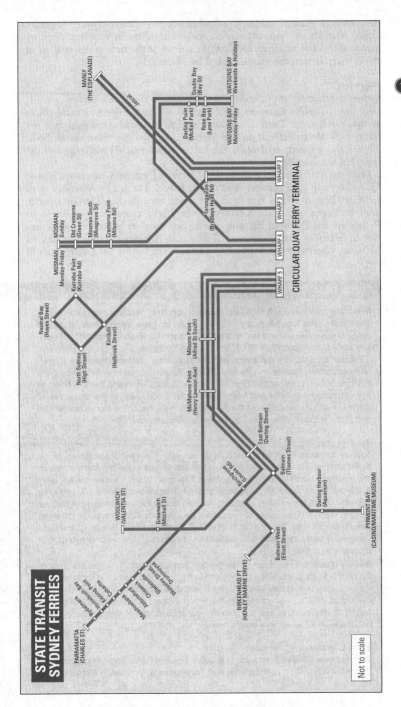

STATE TRANSIT SYDNEY FERRIES

CIRCULAR QUAY FERRY TERMINAL

WHARF 2
WHARF 3
WHARF 4
WHARF 5

MANLY
(THE ESPLANADE)

Jetcat

Darling Point
(McKell Park)
Rose Bay
(Lyne Park)
Double Bay
(Bay St)
WATSONS BAY
Weekends & Holidays
WATSONS BAY
Monday–Friday

Taronga Zoo
(Bradleys Head Rd)

MOSMAN
Sunday
Old Cremorne
(Green St)
Mosman South
(Musgrave St)
Cremorne Point
(Milsons Rd)

MOSMAN
Monday–Friday
Kurraba Point
(Kurraba Rd)

Neutral Bay
(Hayes Street)

North Sydney
(High Street)

Kirribilli
(Holbrook Street)

Milsons Point
(Alfred St South)

McMahons Point
(Henry Lawson Ave)

East Balmain
(Darling Street)

Balmain
(Thames Street)

Darling Harbour
(Aquarium)

PYRMONT BAY
(CASINO/MARITIME MUSEUM)

WOOLWICH
(VALENTIA ST)

Greenwich
(Mitchell St)

Birchgrove
(Louisa Rd)

Balmain West
(Elliott Street)

BIRKENHEAD PT
(HENLEY MARINE DRIVE)

PARRAMATTA
(CHARLES ST)
Rydalmere
Meadowbank
Abbotsford
Chiswick
Northam Bay
Kissing Point
Cabarita
Gladesville
Wolseley Street
Drummoyne

Not to scale

95

designated "nightsafe" waiting areas and all but two or three train carriages are closed after about 8pm, enforcing a cattle-like safety in numbers. Security guards also patrol trains at night. At other times, if the train is deserted, sit in the carriage nearest the guard, marked by a blue light.

Ferries

Sydney's distinctive green-and-yellow **ferries** are the fastest means of transport from Circular Quay to the North Shore, and indeed to most places around the harbour. Even if you don't want to go anywhere, a ferry ride is a must, a chance to get out on the water and see the city from the harbour. There's also a speedy **hydrofoil**, the JetCat, which reaches Manly in half the time, but with less charm.

There are ferries going off in various directions from the wharves at Circular Quay (see map p.95); cruises depart from Jetty 6. The last ferry service from Circular Quay to Manly is at 7pm after which time the faster JetCats operate until midnight, 11pm on Saturdays. Other ferry routes, such as those to Parramatta and Pyrmont Bay, also operate only until early evening, while ferries to locations including Neutral Bay and Balmain continue to around 11.30pm. Except for the Manly Ferry, services on Sunday are greatly reduced

Travel passes

In addition to single-journey tickets, there's a vast array of **travel passes** available. The most useful for visitors are outlined below; for more **information** on the full range of tickets and timetables, phone the Transport Infoline or check out their website (daily 6am–10pm; ☎13 15 00, ⓦwww.131500.com.au).

Passes are sold at most **newsagents** and at **train stations**; the more tourist-oriented Sydney Passes and Sydney Explorer Passes can be bought on board the Explorer buses, at the airport (from the Sydney Visitor Centre and the STA booth in the international terminal and from State Transit ground staff in the domestic), at State Transit Info booths, from the Sydney Visitor Centre in The Rocks (see p.118) and at some Countrylink offices as well as at train stations.

Tourist passes

Sydney Explorer Pass (one-day $30) comes with a map and description of the sights, and includes free travel on any State Transit bus within the same zones as the Explorer routes. The red **Sydney Explorer** (from Circular Quay daily 8.40am–5.22pm; every 18min) takes in all the important sights in the city and inner suburbs, via 26 hop-on-hop-off stops. The blue **Bondi Explorer** (daily from Circular Quay 9.15am–4.15pm; every 30min) covers the waterside eastern suburbs (19 stops include Kings Cross, Paddington, Double Bay, Vaucluse, Bondi, Bronte, Clovelly and Coogee). A **two-day ticket** ($50) allows use of both bus services over two days in a seven-day period.

Sydney Pass (three-, five- or seven-day passes within a seven-day period; $90/$120/ $140) is valid for all buses and ferries including the above Explorer services, the ferry and JetCat to Manly, the RiverCat to Parramatta and a return trip to the airport valid for two months with the Airport Express bus (buy it at the airport on arrival). It also includes four narrated harbour cruises, one of them in the evening, and travel on trains within a central area.

Buses, trains and ferries

Travelpasses allow unlimited use of buses, trains and ferries and can begin on any day of the week. Most useful are the **Red Travelpass** ($30 a week), valid for the city and often finish earlier. Timetables for each route are available at Circular Quay or on the Sydney Ferries website ⓦwww.sydneyferries.nsw.gov.au.

One-way **fares** are $4.30 ($5.40 for the Manly Ferry); return fares are doubled. The pricier JetCat to Manly and RiverCat to Parramatta are $6.70 and $6.40 respectively. Once again, the various Travelpasses and FerryTen tickets can be a good deal – see box below for details.

Monorail and Light Rail

The **Metro Monorail** (ⓣ02/9285 5600, ⓦwww.metromonorail.com.au) is essentially a tourist shuttle designed to loop around Darling Harbour every three to five minutes, connecting it with the city centre. Thundering along tracks set above the older city streets, the "monster rail" – as many locals know it – doesn't exactly blend in with its surroundings. Still, the elevated view of the city, particularly from Pyrmont Bridge, makes it worth investing $4 (day-pass $8) and ten minutes to do the whole circuit with its eight stops (see "Central Sydney" map on pp.102–103; Mon–Wed 7am–10pm, Thurs–Sat 7am–midnight, Sun 8am–10pm).

Metro Light Rail (ⓣ02/9285 5600, ⓦwww.metrolightrail.com.au) runs from Central station to the Pyrmont Peninsula (see "Central Sydney" map on

and inner suburbs, and inner harbour ferries (not the Manly Ferry or the RiverCat beyond Meadowbank); and the **Green Travelpass** ($38), which allows use of all ferries – except JetCats before 7pm. Passes covering a wider area cost between $42 and $52 a week, and monthly passes are also available.

DayTripper tickets ($13.40) are also available for unlimited travel on all services offered by CityRail, Sydney Buses and Sydney Ferries.

Buses and ferries

The **Blue Travelpass** ($27 a week) gives unlimited travel on buses in the inner-city area and on inner-harbour ferries but cannot be used for Manly or beyond Meadowbank; the **Orange Travelpass** ($34 a week) gets you further on the buses and is valid on all ferries; and the **Pittwater Travelpass** ($47 a week) gives unlimited travel on all buses and ferries. These Travelpasses start with first use rather than on the day of purchase.

Buses

TravelTen tickets represent a 45 percent saving over single fares by buying ten trips at once; they can be used over a space of time and for more than one person. The tickets are colour-coded according to how many sections they cover; the Brown TravelTen ($18.90), for example, is the choice for trips from Leichhardt to the city, while the the Red TravelTen ($23.50) is the one to buy if you're staying at Bondi.

Ferries

FerryTen tickets, valid for ten single trips, start at $26.50 for Inner Harbour Services, go up to $39.30 for the Manly Ferry, and peak at $55.80 for the JetCat services.

Trains

Seven Day RailPass tickets allow unlimited travel between any two nominated stations and those in between, with savings of about twenty percent on the price of five return trips.

pp.102–103) and on to Lilyfield in the inner west. There are fourteen stops on the route, which links Central station with Chinatown, Darling Harbour, Star City Casino, the fish markets at Pyrmont, Wentworth Park's greyhound race-course, Glebe (with stops near Pyrmont Bridge Road, at Jubilee Park and Rozelle Bay by Bicentennial Park) and Lilyfield, not far from Darling Street, Rozelle. The air-conditioned light rail vehicles can carry two hundred passengers, and are fully accessible to disabled commuters. The service operates 24 hours to the casino (every 10–15min 6am–midnight; every 30min midnight–6am) with reduced hours for stops beyond to Lilyfield (Mon–Thurs & Sun 6am–11pm, Fri & Sat 6am–midnight; every 10–15min). There are two zones: zone 1 stations are Central to Convention in Darling Harbour, and zone 2 is from Pyrmont Bay to Lilyfield. Tickets can be purchased at vending machines by the stops; singles cost $2.60/$3.60 for zone 1/zone 2, returns $3.90/4.90, a day-pass costs $8 and a weekly one $28, which includes the monorail. A TramLink ticket, available from any CityRail station, combines a rail ticket to Central station with an MLR ticket.

Taxis

Taxis are vacant if the rooftop light is on, though they are notoriously difficult to find at 3pm, when the shifts change over. The four major city cab ranks are outside the *Regent Hotel* on George Street, The Rocks; on Park Street outside Woolworths, opposite the Town Hall; outside David Jones department store on Market Street; and at the Pitt Street entrance to Central station. Drivers never expect a tip but often need directions – try to have some idea of where you're going. Check the correct tariff rate is displayed: tariff 2 (10pm–6am) is twenty percent more than tariff 1 (6am–10pm). See "Listings", p.196, for phone numbers.

Accommodation

There are a tremendous number of places to stay in Sydney, and fierce competition helps keep prices down. Finding somewhere to stay is usually only a problem just before Christmas and throughout January, in late February/early March during the Gay Mardi Gras, and at Easter: at these times **book ahead**. All types of accommodation offer a (sometimes substantial) discount for **weekly bookings**, and may also cut prices considerably during the **low season** (from autumn to spring, school holidays excepted).

The larger **international hotels** in The Rocks and the Central Business District (CBD) charge $200 and upwards for a double room. The least expensive hotels in the city centre, often above **pubs** and sharing bathrooms, start from $100. Rates in Kings Cross are much cheaper, with rooms in **private hotels** available for $55 (sharing a bathroom) and around $80 en suite and in three- or four-star hotels at around $130–160. **Motels**, such as ones we've listed in Glebe and Surry Hills, charge around $100. An increasing number of mid-range "boutique" hotels and **guesthouses** are smaller, more characterful places to stay, charging upwards of $150. **Serviced holiday apartments** can be very good value for a group, but are heavily booked.

Despite the number of **hostels** all over Sydney and the rivalry between them, standards are variable and, in Kings Cross especially, can be very low. As the scene changes rapidly, it's worth getting the latest news from other travellers. Rates (which should include bedding) can range from $20 to $30 depending on the number of dorm beds, the hostel standard and location. Rates rise in summer and fall in winter. Doubles average around $60, and $80 for an en suite; weekly rates usually save the cost of a night's stay. All hostels have a laundry, kitchen and common room with TV unless stated otherwise. Office hours are restricted, so it's best to arrange an arrival time.

For longer stays a **flat-share** can be an alternative to hotels or hostels. Saturday's real-estate section of the *Sydney Morning Herald* is the first place to look, or try café notice boards, especially in King Street in Newtown, Glebe Point Road in Glebe or Hall Street, Bondi Beach (the window of the health food store at 29 Hall St is crammed with house-share notices aimed at travellers). The average shared-house room price is $150 a week (usually two weeks in advance, plus a bond (deposit) of four weeks' rent; you'll usually need to get hold of at least your own bedroom furniture and linen). Sleeping With The Enemy, 373 Bulwara Rd, Ultimo (℡02/9211 8878, ⓦwww.sleepingwith-theenemy.com) organizes travellers' house-shares in fully equipped inner-city terraces but sharing a room with up to five others (from $135 per week for a one-month stay).

The nearest **campsites** to the centre are in the suburbs of Rockdale, 13km south of the city, and North Ryde, 14km northwest (see box below).

Where to stay

The listings below are arranged by area. For short visits, you'll want to stay in the **city centre** or the immediate vicinity: The Rocks, the CBD and Darling Harbour have the greatest concentration of expensive hotels and now also several backpackers' hostels, while the area around Central station and Chinatown, known as Haymarket, has some cheaper, more downmarket places and an ever greater concentration of hostels led by the huge YHA. **Kings Cross** is still hanging on as a travellers' centre, with more backpackers' accommodation and cheaper hotels than elsewhere. The area is falling out of favour as travellers head for the newer hostels in town to avoid the sleaze and the all-night partying. Despite this, Kings Cross remains a lively and convenient base; it's only a ten-minute walk from the city and has its own train station. The adjacent suburbs of **Woolloomooloo**, **Potts Point** and **Elizabeth Bay** move gradually

Campsites around Sydney

The three caravan parks listed below are the closest sites to the centre. Camping will cost from around $20–$22 for two people in an unpowered site to $24–29 for a powered site.

Lakeside Caravan Park Lake Park Rd, Narrabeen, 26km north of the city ℡02/9913 7845, ℗9970 6385, ⓦwww.sydneylakeside.com.au. Great spot by Narrabeen Lakes on Sydney's northern beaches. Free gas BBQs, camp kitchen and a nearby shop. Minimum two-night stay in cabins (all are en suite). Bus #190 or #L90 from Wynyard station and then a ten-minute walk. Cabins ⑥

Lane Cove River Caravan Park Plassey Rd, North Ryde, 14km northwest of the city ℡02/9888 9133, ℗9888 9322, ⓦwww.lanecoveriver.com. Wonderful bush location beside Lane Cove National Park, right on the river, in Sydney's northern suburbs. Great facilities include a bush kitchen (with fridge), TV room and swimming pool. Train to Chatswood then bus #550 or #551. En-suite cabins ④

Sheralee Tourist Caravan Park 88 Bryant St, Rockdale, 13km south of the city ℡02/9567 7161. Small park with camp kitchen. Train to Rockdale station and then a ten-minute walk. On-site vans ② upmarket, a little less accessible, but quieter. To the west, leafy and peaceful **Glebe** is another slice of prime travellers' territory, featuring several back-packers' and a number of small guesthouses.

For longer stays, consider somewhere further out, on the **North Shore**, where you'll get more for your money and more of a feel for Sydney as a city. **Kirribilli**, **Neutral Bay** or **Cremorne Point**, only a short ferry ride from Circular Quay, offer some serenity and affordable water views as well. Large old private hotels out this way are increasingly being converted into hostels, particularly on Carabella Street in Kirribilli. **Manly**, tucked away in the northeast corner of the harbour, is a seaside suburb with ocean and harbour beaches, just thirty minutes from Circular Quay by ferry. It has a concentration of hostels and also more upmarket accommodation; the beachside **eastern suburbs** of **Bondi** and **Coogee** offer similar places to stay and are closer to the city.

The Central Business District (CBD) and The Rocks

Hotels & B&Bs

Central Park 185 Castlereagh St, City ☎ 02/9283 5000, ⓦ www.centralpark.com.au. Small chic hotel in a great position in the midst of city bustle right near Town Hall and Hyde Park. Larger rooms have king-size beds and smart and spacious bathrooms with bathtub. Smaller standard rooms are still a good size although minus the tub; all come with sofa, desk, air-con and well-equipped kitchenette. Tiny daytime lobby café. 24hr reception. Light breakfast. ⑥–⑦

Corus 7–9 York St, City ☎ 02/9274 1222, ⓕ 9274 1230, ⓦ www.corushotels.com.au. Central position for both the CBD and The Rocks. This 22-storey four-star hotel has the usual motel-style rooms but excels with its spacious studios, which come with kitchen area, CD player, voicemail and safe. Small gym; 24hr room service; pleasant café-brasserie. Cheaper weekend packages available. Rooms ⑥, studios ⑦

Grand Hotel 30 Hunter St, City ☎ 02/9232 3755, ⓕ 9232 1073. Close to Wynyard station, with several floors of accommodation above one of Sydney's oldest (but not necessarily nicest) pubs, which opens until 3am Thurs–Sat. Rooms, sharing bathrooms, are fine – all brightly painted, with colourful bed covers, lamps, fridge, kettle, TV, fan, heating and ceiling fans. ④

Intercontinental 117 Macquarie St, City ☎ 02/9230 0200, ⓦ www.intercontinental.com. The old sandstone Treasury building forms the lower floors of this 31-storey, five-star property, with stunning views of the Botanic Gardens, Opera House and harbour. The café/bar is the perfect place for everything from champagne to afternoon tea, and there are three other eateries, a cigar divan, and a pool and gym on the top floor. All this comes at a price, of course: $275 city view and $345 harbour view. ⑦

Lord Nelson Brewery Cnr Argyle and Kent streets, The Rocks ☎ 02/9251 4044, ⓦ www.lordnelson.com.au. B&B in a historic pub dating from 1841. The ten very smart colonial-style rooms are mostly en suite and come with all mod-cons. Price varies according to size and position ($120–180): best is the corner room with views of Argyle St. Serves beer brewed on the premises, plus bar food daily and upmarket meals from its first-floor brasserie (lunch Mon–Fri, dinner Mon–Sat). Breakfast included. ⑤–⑥

Mercantile 25 George St, The Rocks ☎ 02/9247 3570, ⓔ merc@tpg.com.au. High-spirited Irish pub; bistro meals served at outdoor tables which are a fine spot to watch the weekend market crowds. Has a stash of fab rooms upstairs which are always booked out – get in early. Original features include huge fireplaces in several rooms, all furnished in colonial style. Several have bathrooms complete with spa baths. Cooked breakfast. ④–⑤

Old Sydney Holiday Inn 55 George St, The Rocks ☎ 02/9252 0524, ⓦ www.sydney.holiday-inn.com. Four-and-a-half star in a great location right in the heart of The Rocks, with impressive architecture: eight levels of rooms around a central atrium creates a remarkable feeling of space. The best rooms have harbour views but the rooftop swimming pool (plus spa and sauna) also gives fantastic vistas. 24hr room service. All this from $245. ⑦

Palisade 35 Bettington St, Millers Point ☎ 02/9247 2272, ⓦ www.palisadehotel.com. Magnificent tiled pub which manages to retain both old-style charm and simplicity – very down-to-earth downstairs bar, stylish contemporary restaurant upstairs. Clean, cute, shared-bath rooms have a bright old-fashioned feel, some have fantastic views over the inner harbour and Harbour Bridge. ⑤

The Russell 143A George St, The Rocks ☎ 02/9241 3543, ⓦ www.therussell.com.au.

Charming, small National Trust-listed hotel. Rooms have colonial-style decor; some are en suite but the small shared-bathroom options are very popular and a great price for the area. The priciest of the other rooms have views of the Quay. Sunny central courtyard and a rooftop garden, sitting-room and bar, and downstairs restaurant for continental breakfast. B&B ⑤–⑦

Hostels

Sydney Backpackers Victoria House, 7 Wilmot St, City ☎02/9267 7772 or 1800 88 77 66, ⊛www.sydneybackpackers.com. Very central choice off the George Street cinema strip (though you could find the alley-like street a bit scary at night). Clean and spacious, although lacking a little in atmosphere, staff encourage sociability and there's a comfortable, colourful common room with

cable TV, books and Internet access. Small but clean kitchen. Four-, eight-, ten- and twelve-bed dorms – one en-suite dorm on every floor – and spacious doubles and twins; all have air-con, cable TV, fridges and lockers. Modern but cramped bathrooms. Dorms $21–29, rooms ④

Wanderers on Kent 477 Kent St, City ☎02/9267 7718, ⊛www.wandererskent.com.au. Huge modern 360-bed hostel in a good location near Town Hall station. Though it's popular, facilities and atmosphere are somewhat lacking and bathrooms and kitchens are inadequate. Bustling ground-floor reception with a help- and job-search desk, Internet lounge, travel agency, café and bar. Well-furnished rooms and dorms (four-, six-, eight- and ten-bed), all air-con with shared bathrooms; fairly small doubles. Rooms over the bar can be noisy. Dorms $24–32, rooms ④

Around Central station: Darling Harbour, Haymarket and Ultimo

Hotels

Aarons Hotel 37 Ultimo Rd, Haymarket ☎02/9281 5555, ⊛www.aaronshotel.com.au. Large, three-star hotel right in the heart of Chinatown, with its own modern café downstairs. Comfortable en suites, all with TV and air-con. The least expensive are internal, small and box-like, with skylight only, while the pricier courtyard rooms have their own balconies. Cheaper midweek rates. ⑤

Capitol Square Capitol Square, Campbell and George streets, Haymarket ☎02/9211 8633, ⊛www.goldspear.com.au. One of the centre's most affordable four-stars (rooms from $165 but often specials at $110) and small enough not to feel impersonal – though service could be improved. Decor in the rooms is modern if a little chintzy. In an excellent location right next to the Capitol Theatre and cafés and across from Chinatown; in-house restaurant serves Asian and European food. Buffet breakfast. Parking $18. ⑥

The George 700A George St, Haymarket ☎ & ☏02/9211 1800, ⊛www.georgehotel.com.au. Budget private hotel on three floors opposite Chinatown. Bargain-priced rooms – all but two sharing bathrooms – are clean and acceptable. Facilities include a small kitchen/TV room and a laundry. ③–④

Glasgow Arms 527 Harris St, Ultimo, opposite the Powerhouse Museum ☎02/9211 2354, ☏9281 9439. Handily positioned for Darling Harbour, this accommodation is situated above a very pleasant pub with courtyard dining (Sat dinner only, closed Sun). The bar usually shuts around 10pm so

noise levels aren't a worry. The high-ceilinged rooms – nicely decorated down to the polished floorboards – are air-con and en suite with TV and radio. Light breakfast. ⑤

Hostels

Footprints Westend 412 Pitt St, Haymarket ☎02/9211 4588 or 1800 013 186, ⊛www.footprintswestend.com.au. Bright and contemporary hostel in a large renovated hotel close to Central station and Chinatown. Common areas are spic-and-span with funky furniture and there's a big modern kitchen and dining area, and a pool table. The young staff are local, clued-up and organize nights out and tours. All rooms have TV and/or mini fridge while dorms (four- and six-bed) come with lockers; all are en suite and with nice bedding. Many rooms have air-con: request these in summer, as there are no fans. In-house yoga classes ($5), travel centre and small café downstairs. 24hr reception. Dorms $28–$30, rooms ③

Maze Backpackers 417 Pitt St, Haymarket ☎02/9211 5115, ⊛www.nomadsworld.com. With charming original 1908 features, this huge hostel is a good choice if you're after a single room ($49); there are sixty of them although they're tiny, cubicle-like and dim. The atmosphere is sociable and all rooms and dorms (four- to six-bed) have ceiling fans, but stark fluoro lighting and shared bathrooms. Doubles have a wardrobe, chair and bedside table. The kitchens are small and lacking in facilities. Daily yoga classes. 24hr reception. Dorms $22–$24, rooms ③

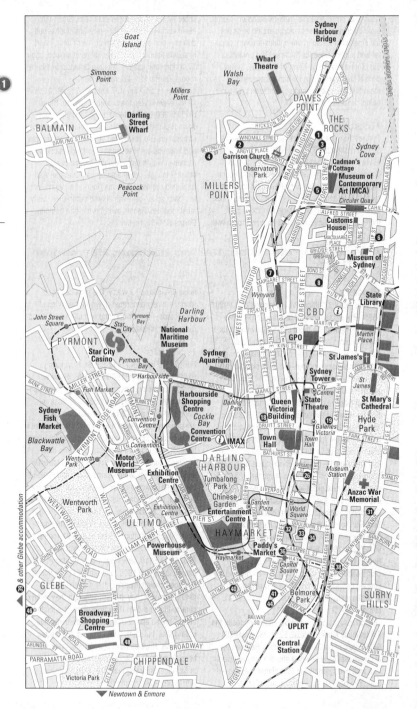

Goat
Island

Simmons
Point

Walsh
Bay

Sydney
Harbour
Bridge

Wharf
Theatre

DAWES
POINT

THE
ROCKS

Millers
Point

Darling
Street
Wharf

HICKSON RD

LOWER FORT ST

WINDMILL STREET

1

3

i

ARGYLE

Sydney
Cove

BALMAIN

DARLING STREET

BETTINGTON
ST

2

Argyle Place

4 Garrison Church

Observatory
Park

Cadman's
Cottage

Museum of
Contemporary
Art (MCA)

GEORGE STREET

5

Circular Quay

CAHILL EXP

CIRCULAR QUAY

Peacock
Point

MILLERS
POINT

KENT STREET

ALFRED STREET

Customs
House

PHILLIP ST

6

MACQUARIE
PLACE

LOFTUS ST

YOUNG ST

BRIDGE STREET

GRESHAM

Museum of
Sydney

HICKSON ROAD

SPRING ST

BOND ST

HIGH ST

State
Library

John Street
Square

Pyrmont
Bay

Star
City

Darling
Harbour

National
Maritime
Museum

MARGARET STREET

7

Wynyard

WESTERN DISTRIBUTOR

ERSKINE ST

HUNTER ST

8

O'CONNELL ST

PITT ST

i

PYRMONT

Star City
Casino

Pyrmont
Bay

Harbourside

MARTIN PL

Martin
Place

BANK STREET

MILLER STREET

Fish Market

Sydney
Aquarium

GPO

KING STREET

St James's

PYRMONT BRIDGE

Sydney
Tower

St
James

HARRIS ST

City
Centre

St Mary's
Cathedral

Sydney
Fish
Market

PYRMONT BRIDGE ROAD

Harbourside
Shopping
Centre

Darling
Park

Queen
Victoria
Building

State
Theatre

Hyde
Park

Blackwattle
Bay

Cockle
Bay

MARKET STREET

18

DRUITT STREET

19

Galeries
Victoria

Wentworth
Park

Convention
Centre

Convention
Centre

Convention
Centre

IMAX

Town
Hall

Town Hall

BATHURST STREET

Museum
Station

Motor
World
Museum

DARLING
HARBOUR

WILMOT

26

Anzac War
Memorial

Exhibition
Centre

Tumbalong
Park

LIVERPOOL ST

Garden
Plaza

World
Square

31

Wentworth
Park

Exhibition
Centre

Chinese
Garden

GOULBURN ST

32

WATTLE STREET

WILLIAM HENRY ST

PIER ST

Entertainment
Centre

HAYMARKET

33 **34**

38

Powerhouse
Museum

Haymarket

Paddy's
Market

36

SURRY
HILLS

GLEBE

MACARTHUR ST

40

Capitol
Square

41

44

Belmore
Park

ALBION STREET

39 & other Glebe accommodation

46

Broadway
Shopping
Centre

THOMAS STREET

MARY ANN ST

RAILWAY
SQ

48

ARUNDEL

GLEBE POINT ROAD

UPLRT

Central
Station

PARRAMATTA ROAD

BROADWAY

CHIPPENDALE

Victoria Park

CITY ROAD

REGENT ST

LEE ST

▼ Newtown & Enmore

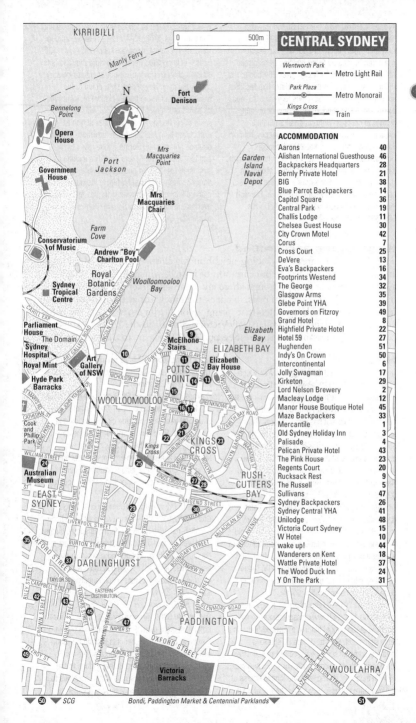

KIRRIBILLI

Manly Ferry

0   500m

CENTRAL SYDNEY

N

Fort
Denison

Bennelong
Point

Opera
House

Port
Jackson

Mrs
Macquaries
Point

Garden
Island
Naval
Depot

Government
House

Mrs
Macquaries
Chair

Farm
Cove

Conservatorium
of Music

Andrew "Boy"
Charlton Pool

Royal
Botanic
Gardens

Woolloomooloo
Bay

Sydney
Tropical
Centre

CAHILL EXP

Parliament
House

The Domain

Sydney
Hospital

Royal Mint

Hyde Park
Barracks

Art
Gallery
of NSW

NICHOLSON ST

Elizabeth
Bay

McElhone
Stairs

CHALLIS AVE

ELIZABETH BAY

Elizabeth
Bay House

POTTS
POINT

WOOLLOOMOOLOO

HUGHES ST

ORWELL ST

GREENKNOWE AVE

Cook
and
Phillip
Park

Kings
Cross

KINGS
CROSS

ROSLYN GARDENS

WILLIAM STREET

Australian
Museum

BAYSWATER

KINGS CROSS RD

RUSH-
CUTTERS
BAY

EAST
SYDNEY

CRAIGEND STREET

LIVERPOOL STREET

WOLLAHRA

BURTON STREET

OXFORD STREET

DARLINGHURST

TAYLOR SQ

EASTERN
DISTRIBUTOR

PADDINGTON

NAPIER ST

OXFORD STREET

ALBION ST

Victoria
Barracks

WOOLLAHRA

SCG   Bondi, Paddington Market & Centennial Parklands

Legend

Wentworth Park
----●---- Metro Light Rail

Park Plaza
---M--- Metro Monorail

Kings Cross
===■=== Train

Sydney Central YHA Cnr Pitt St and Rawson Place, opposite Central station ☏02/9281 9111, ⓔsydcentral@yhansw.org.au. Very successful YHA in a centrally located listed building transformed into a huge and snazzy hostel (over 550 beds); it's still the best choice in the area. Hotel-like facilities but still very sociable. Spacious four- and six-bed dorms and twins sharing bathrooms or en-suite twins and doubles. Wide range of amenities, including employment desk, travel agency, rooftop pool, sauna, and BBQ area. 24hr reception. Licensed bistro plus a cute, very popular basement bar, *Scubar*. Some parking available. Maximum stay fourteen days. For longer stays, the YHA also has a "working holidaymaker hostel" at Dulwich Hill (☏02/9550 0054, ⓕ9550 0570). Dorms $25–$31, rooms ❸–❹

wake up! 509 Pitt St, opposite Railway Square and Central station ☏02/9264 4121, ⓦwww.wakeup .com.au. The latest mega-backpackers' – over 500 beds – is almost too trendy. The vibrant interior sits inside a characterful turn-of-the-twentieth-century corner building. Very styled, right down to the black-clad staff in the huge intimidating foyer with its banks of Internet terminals, but with an impersonal edge. Rooms, which aren't as stylish as you'd expect, are light-filled and well furnished; only nine doubles are en suite. Dorms – four-, six-, eight- and ten-bed – have lockers. Facilities include a streetside café and an underground late-opening bar and eatery. The best feature is the huge modern kitchen, on a corner with gigantic windows overlooking busy Railway Square. Dorms $25–$30, rooms ❸–❹

Kings Cross and around

The Kings Cross area – including neighbouring Potts Point, Woolloomooloo and Elizabeth Bay – has a concentration of hostels, which are listed separately, as well as cheaper hotels, though there are some upmarket choices too. Some hotels also offer a few dorm beds, so check the hotel listings too. It's best avoiding any hostels or cheap hotels that spring up on Darlinghurst Road, the hardcore red-light strip; the parallel, leafy Victoria Street and the backstreets have a contrastingly pleasant atmosphere. See pp.144–145 for an account of the area.

Hotels

Bernly Private Hotel 15 Springfield Ave, Kings Cross ☏02/9358 3122, ⓦwww.bernlyprivate hotel.com.au. This clean budget hotel, which also has a few dorms, is just removed from the seedy heart of the Cross but has good security, 24hr reception, and courteous staff. Private rooms have air-con, TV, sink and fridge and are either en suite or have shared bathroom. There's a tidy kitchen, TV lounge and big sunroof with deck chairs and Harbour Bridge views. Good single rates. Dorms $22–$25, rooms ❸–❹

Challis Lodge 21–23 Challis Ave, Potts Point ☏02/9358 5422, ⓦwww.budgethotelssydney .com. Budget accommodation in a wonderful old mansion with polished timber floors throughout. In a great location on a quiet, tree-filled street that has three good cafés. All rooms have TV, fridge and sink; laundry but no kitchen. Rooms ❷, en suite ❸, with balcony ❹

Cross Court 201–203 Brougham St, Kings Cross ☏02/9368 1822, ⓦwww.crosscourthotel.com.au. Small, well-run budget hotel in a terraced house in a leafy side street. Smartly decorated spacious doubles, some en suite, plus a couple of self-catering apartments and some good-value small singles; all with fridge, TV, ceiling fans and lamps. Rooms at the rear have fantastic views over the city and the

self-catering rooms have big balconies at the front. The drawback is it's near a noisy, late-closing pub. Rooms ❸–❹, apartments ❺

DeVere 44–46 Macleay St, Potts Point ☏02/9358 1211, ⓦwww.devere.com.au. Comfortable three-star hotel in a great position close to cafés and restaurants. Third- and fourth-floor rooms have stunning views of Elizabeth Bay; studios with kitchenette available. Some rooms have balconies; all are air-con. There's also a breakfast room (buffet-style), guest laundry and 24hr reception. ❺–❻

Highfield Private Hotel 166 Victoria St, Kings Cross ☏02/9326 9539, ⓦwww.highfieldhotel.com. Swedish-run, very clean, modern and secure budget hotel well-located on Victoria Street. Rooms are well equipped with fans, heating and sinks. Also three-bed dorms. Tiny kitchen/common room with TV microwave, kettle and toaster; no laundry. Dorms $23, rooms ❷–❸

Hotel 59 59 Bayswater Rd, Kings Cross ☏02/9360 5900, ⓦwww.hotel59.com.au. Small hotel (just eight rooms) reminiscent of a pleasant European guesthouse; benefits include a friendly owner, small but tastefully decorated air-con rooms, a quiet leafy location that's close to the bustle, and a downstairs café where delicious full cooked breakfasts are served. Very popular, so book in advance. One family room (sleeps four) with small kitchenette. Outdoor courtyard. B&B. Rooms ❹–❺, studio ❺

Macleay Lodge 71 Macleay St, Potts Point ☏ 02/9368 0660, ⓦ www.budgethotels-sydney .com. Don't expect anything fancy from this budget option on four floors, but it's perfectly fine and in a fab spot in the midst of Potts Point's café and restaurant scene. All rooms (bar one) share bathroom and come with sink, plates, cutlery, kettle, fridge, cheap furniture and TV. Best rooms have access to the balcony area. ❸

Regents Court 18 Springfield Ave, Potts Point ☏ 02/9358 1533, ⓦ www.regentscourt.com.au. Small hotel, raved about by international style mags, and despite lots of arty guests, still very friendly and homey. Classic designer furniture, and each studio-style room has a sleek kitchen area. Instead of a bar, there's a well-chosen wine list downstairs (at bottle-shop prices), and help-your-self coffee and *biscotti*. Small rooftop kitchen and BBQ area, amongst potted citrus trees. Expect to pay between $220 and $255. ❼

Victoria Court Sydney 122 Victoria St, Kings Cross ☏ 02/9357 3200, ⓦ www .victoriacourt.com.au. Boutique hotel in two inter-linked Victorian terraced houses; very tasteful and quiet. En-suite rooms with all mod cons, some with balconies; buffet breakfast included and served in the conservatory. Secure parking a bonus. ❺

W Hotel The Wharf, 6 Cowper Wharf Rd, Woolloomooloo ☏ 02/9331 9000, ⓦ www .whotels.com. Luxury hotel with bags of colourful contemporary style and fantastic service and facili-ties, right on the water on a redeveloped wharf alongside an upmarket apartment complex and a marina. The lobby is spacious and striking in design; the lush *Water Bar* is one of Sydney's trendiest watering holes, and the rest of the wharf is lined with some of Sydney's best restaurants and cafés. 24hr room service; day spa, indoor heated pool and gym. From $288 to $363 for a loft room. ❼

Hostels

Backpackers Headquarters 79 Bayswater Rd, Kings Cross ☏ & ⓕ 02/9331 6180, ⓦ www .backpackershqhostel.com.au. In a quieter position close to Rushcutters Bay, this modern, light and clean hostel is well run by very courteous man-agement. Large, bright, partitioned dorms with firm mattresses, fans, heaters and mirrors; only two doubles. Usual amenities plus big-screen TV in the lounge area, sun deck and BBQ area on the rooftop. Excellent security. Dorms $22, rooms ❸

Blue Parrot Backpackers 87 Macleay St, Potts

Point ☏ 02/9356 4888, ⓦ www.blueparrot.com.au. In a great position in the trendy (and quieter) part of Potts Point and with helpful staff, this converted mansion is sunny, airy, brightly painted and taste-fully furnished. One of the best points is the huge courtyard garden out back with wooden furniture and big shady trees, looking onto a heritage build-ing. Mostly six- and eight-bed dorms; one four-bed dorm but no doubles or twins. Common room has cable TV and gas fire. Dorms $22.

Eva's Backpackers 6–8 Orwell St, Potts Point ☏ 02/9358 2185, ⓕ 02/9358 3259. Recommended family-run hostel away from Darlinghurst Road's clamour; feels safe and friendly. Colourful and clean rooms, well set up with fans, mirrors and lamps. Four-, six-, eight- and ten-bed dorms; four-beds are en suite. Peaceful rooftop garden with table umbrellas, greenery, BBQ area and fantastic views over The Domain. The guest kitchen/dining room, positioned at street level, feels like a café and is conducive to socializing, though this isn't a "party" hostel. Dorms $22, rooms ❸

Jolly Swagman 27 Orwell St, Kings Cross ☏ 02/9358 6400, ⓦ www.jollyswagman.com.au. Big, long-established hostel: colourful, clean and lively, with good notice boards and work connec-tions. Events range from sports teams to pub crawls; in-house travel centre. Along with the usual communal facilities, every room has its own fridge and lockers; four- to six-bed dorms. Cheap licensed café with Internet access out front. 24hr reception. Dorms $21, rooms ❸

The Pink House 6–8 Barncleuth Square, Kings Cross ☏ & ⓕ 02/9358 1689 or ☏ 1800 806 385, ⓦ www.pinkhouse.com.au. Attractive Art Deco mansion with big dorms – four-, six- and eight-bed – and a few doubles (some en suite), with fans and sinks. All the expected amenities plus cable TV in the common room and garden court-yards with BBQ. Friendly and very peaceful but also close to the action. Dorms $22–$24, rooms ❷, en suite ❸

Rucksack Rest 9 McDonald St, Potts Point ☏ & ⓕ 02/9358 2348. Small (thirty-bed), well-run private hostel in a lovely old terrace house, exud-ing a shabby charm. Friendly atmosphere, quiet leafy location and on-site local owner-manager. Facilities include a BBQ area and an outdoor kitchen perfect for summer. Three-bed dorms and doubles. Not a party hostel. Dorms $20, rooms ❷

The Wood Duck Inn 49 William St, East Sydney ☏ 02/9358 5856 or 1800 110 025, ⓦ www .woodduckinn.com.au. Hostel run by two switched-on brothers in a great spot right by Hyde Park and at the safer city end of William Street. Don't be put off by the dingy, endless flights of concrete steps:

they emerge into the nerve centre, a sunny rooftop with fantastic park and city views, all-day reception-cum-bar, outdoor tables and BBQ, a small but functional kitchen, laundry and a TV-cum-dining room with quirky surfboard tabletops. The accommodation below has polished floors, citrus-

coloured walls, high ceilings and fresh flowers in the hall. Spacious, clean dorms (mostly four- and six-bed) come with fans, good beds and cage lockers; doubles have TV. Lots of activities, including free lifts to the beach. Good security. Dorms $20–24, rooms ❸

Surry Hills, Darlinghurst, Paddington and Woollahra

BIG 212 Elizabeth St, Surry Hills ☎02/9281 6030, Ⓦwww.bigonelizabeth.com. Stylish new 140-bed part-hotel, part-hostel. Lousy location opposite the railway line but a five- to ten-minute walk to surrounding locations – Central station, Chinatown and Oxford Street. Sunny rooms have extra-thick glass, good curtains and contemporary decor in natural colours; all are air-con with TV and video but lack lamps and telephones. The ground-floor lobby, with designer lounges and Internet terminals, doubles as the common area with a high-tech guest kitchen to the side. An organic café serves breakfast through dinner (plus $5 specials). Four-, six- and eight-bed dorms; rates includes linen, towels and breakfast (pancakes, fresh scones, juice). Roof-terrace BBQ area. Guest laundry. Dorm $32.50, rooms ❺

City Crown Motel 289 Crown St, cnr of Reservoir St, Surry Hills ☎02/9331 2433, Ⓦwww.citycrownmotel.com.au. A fairly typical motel but in a great location. The en-suite units are air-con with free in-house movies. One self-catering unit, sleeping six, is available. Some parking space: enter on Reservoir St; it costs an extra $15 per night. Rooms ❹, apartment ❼

Hughenden 14 Queen St, Woollahra ☎02/9363 4863, Ⓦwww.hughendenhotel.com.au. Old-fashioned Victorian-era guesthouse, built in 1876, situated opposite Centennial Park. Expensive en-suite singles and doubles with rates ranging from $128 to $268, depending on size of room. Hot breakfast included. ❺–❼

Indy's On Crown 589 Crown St, cnr Cleveland St, above the Crown Hotel, Surry Hills ☎02/8300 8804 or 1800 889 449, Ⓦwww.indysbackpackers .com.au. In a lively locale but with a surprisingly relaxed and homey atmosphere. Cute and sunny kitchen with huge windows overlooking Crown Street. Sociable lounge with comfy couches,

cable TV and a big table. *Indy's* attracts working travellers; most end up as long-termers hence the shared-house atmosphere. Dorms (four- and six-bed) are better furnished than most with very comfortable beds; also two doubles. Handy supermarket across the road. Free Internet access and muesli. Dorms $23, rooms ❸

Kirketon 229–231 Darlinghurst Rd, Darlinghurst ☎02/9332 2011, Ⓦwww.kirketon.com.au. Top in the fashion stakes, thanks to the big name Australian designers who created the swish interiors. Stylish bars including *Fix*, and a top contemporary restaurant, *Salt*, beckon on the ground level, while the forty rooms (costing from $220 to $365) boast luxuries such as toiletries by Aveda, mohair throw rugs and CD players. Beautiful staff, slick service. Free pass to nearby gym and pool; free parking; room service. ❼

Sullivans 21 Oxford St, Paddington ☎02/9361 0211, Ⓦwww.sullivans.com.au. Medium-sized contemporary-style private hotel in a trendy location, run by staff tuned into the local scene (a walking tour of Paddington is thrown in). Comfortable, modern en-suite rooms with TV and telephones. Free (but limited) parking, garden courtyard and swimming pool, in-house movies, free Internet access, free guest bicycles, laundry, 24hr reception, tour-booking service, and a café open for breakfast. ❺

Y On The Park 5–11 Wentworth Ave, Darlinghurst ☎02/9264 2451, Ⓦwww.ywca-sydney.com.au. Great location just off Oxford St near Hyde Park for this YWCA (both sexes welcome); recently renovated, it's surprisingly stylish. Rooms have all you'd expect in a good hotel. En-suite, shared-bathroom or self-catering studios, good-value singles ($70) and four-bed dorms (made-up beds with towel, no bunks). No common kitchen, but facilities include a café (7am–8pm), and a laundry. Light breakfast. Dorms $32, rooms ❹–❺

Inner west: Glebe and Newtown

Alishan International Guesthouse 100 Glebe Point Rd, Glebe ☎02/9566 4048, Ⓦwww .alishan.com.au. Beautifully restored old villa in a

handy spot at the bottom of Glebe Point Road. Rather bland but very clean en-suite, motel-style rooms plus one furnished in Japanese fashion (minus an actual futon), and some four- and six-bed dorms that are getting a little shabby. Facilities include a kitchen, spa, an airy common room, garden patio and BBQ area. Internet access available. A spacious family room sleeps six. Dorms $27–$33, rooms ❹

Australian Sunrise Lodge 485 King St, Newtown ☏02/9550 4999, ℻02/9550 4457. Inexpensive and well-managed small, private hotel with kitchen. Sunny single and double rooms, all en suite with TV, fridge and toaster, most with balcony. Family rooms available. ❹–❺

Billabong Gardens 5–22 Egan St, off King St, Newtown ☏02/9550 3236, ⓦwww .billabonggardens.com.au. In a quiet street but close to the action, this purpose-built hostel is arranged around a peaceful inner courtyard with swimming pool. It offers clean dorms (up to six-bed; some en suite), and rooms and motel-style en suites. Undercover car park $5 per night. Dorms $20–$23, rooms ❸–❹

Glebe Point YHA 262 Glebe Point Rd, Glebe ☏02/9692 8418, ℮glebe@yhansw.org.au. Reliable YHA standard with helpful staff who organize lots of activities. The hostel sleeps just over 150 in a mix of private rooms – no en suites – as well as three-, four- and five-bed dorms. Facilities include the usual plus a pool table, luggage storage and roof terrace with city views. Dorms $23–27, rooms ❸

Glebe Village Backpackers 256 Glebe Point Rd, Glebe ☏02/9660 8133 or 1800 801 983, ⓦwww.bakpak.com/glebevillage. Three large old houses with a mellow, sociable atmosphere, more akin to that of a guesthouse than a hostel – the generally laid-back guests socialize in the leafy streetside fairy-lit garden. Staffed by young locals who know what's going on around town. Despite attempts at renovation it's still very shabby here, so come for the scene, not the clean factor.

Doubles and twins plus four, six-, ten- or twelve-bed dorms. Dorms $22–$24, rooms ❸

Rooftop Motel 146 Glebe Point Rd, Glebe ☏02/9660 7777, ℮reservations@rooftopmotel .com.au. Reasonably priced motel right in the heart of Glebe. On three floors (no lift), it has very light, spacious and clean air-con rooms with plain decor. Most have a double and a single bed. There's a rooftop courtyard with city views, BBQ and an L-shaped pool. 24hr reception. Parking included. ❹

Tricketts Bed and Breakfast 270 Glebe Point Rd, Glebe ☏02/9552 1141, ⓦwww.tricketts .com.au. Luxury B&B in an 1880s mansion. Rooms – en suite – are furnished with antiques and Persian rugs, and the lounge, complete with a billiard table and leather armchairs, was originally a small ballroom. There's also a fully self-contained one-bedroom garden apartment with its own verandah. Delicious, generous and sociable breakfast. ❻

Unilodge Cnr Broadway and Bay streets, near Glebe ☏02/9338 5000, ⓦwww.unilodge.com.au. Converted from a former department store with some striking original fixtures, this hotel, close to Sydney University, has a luxury feel, but rates are very reasonable for the facilities. Rooms are all studios, with small kitchenettes. Small gym, lap-pool, spa and sauna, rooftop running track and BBQ. 24hr reception, and 24hr convenience store and food court in the foyer. Children under 12 free. ❺

Wattle House Hostel 44 Hereford St, Glebe ☏02/9552 4997, ⓦwww.wattlehouse.com.au. Top-class small, cosy and clean privately owned hostel in a restored terrace house on a quiet street. Four-bed dorms and well-furnished doubles. Pretty gardens and an outdoor eating area make staying here extra pleasant, and there's even a library room. Rates include linen and towels. Very popular, so book in advance. Dorms $25, rooms ❸

Bondi Beach

Bondi Beachhouse YHA 63 Fletcher St, cnr Dellview St, Bondi ☏02/9365 2088, ℮bondi@intercoast.com.au. A former student boarding house, closer to Tamarama Beach than its namesake. International students stay here, hence the buffet-style breakfasts and dinners at cut-rate prices. Painted vibrant citrusy colours and with a sunny internal courtyard with BBQ, and a rooftop deck with fabulous ocean views. Spacious high-ceilinged dorms (four-, six- and eight-bed, with lockers) and rooms – some en suite, with fridges and kettles – all have ceiling fans. Bag a beach-view room which go for the same price.

Lots of local info; free surf talks. Dorms $26, rooms ❸, en suite ❹

Bondi Sands 252 Campbell Parade, Bondi Beach ☏02/9365 3703, ⓦwww.bondisands.com. Budget hotel across from the northern end of the beach. Fantastic views from its oceanfront rooms and the rooftop common area – with tables and chairs, a BBQ, and a handy kitchen and laundry. All rooms share bathrooms but have sinks; pricier ocean-fronts are well furnished and with queen-size beds. Very popular, so book in advance. ❸

Bondi Serviced Apartments 212 Bondi Rd, Bondi ☏02/9387 1122, ⓦwww.bondi

Gay and lesbian accommodation

You shouldn't encounter any problems booking into a regular hotel, but here are several places that are particularly gay friendly or close to Oxford Street in Darlinghurst. Other particularly welcoming places include *BIG* (p.106), *Cross Court* (p.104), *DeVere* (p.104), *Kirketon* (p.106), *Sullivans* (p.106) and *Victoria Court* (p.106). For **flat-shares** check the community press and café notice boards.

Chelsea Guest House 49 Womerah Ave, Darlinghurst ☎02/9380 5994, ⓦwww.chelsea.citysearch.com.au. Tastefully decorated terrace house in the quieter leafy backstreets of Darlinghurst. Doubles are en suite, singles ($94) share bathrooms but have sinks; all have fridge, kettle and TV. Light breakfast in the courtyard. B&B ❺–❻

Governors on Fitzroy 64 Fitzroy St, Surry Hills ☎02/9331 4652, ⓦwww.governors .com.au. Long-established gay B&B in a restored Victorian terrace a few blocks from Oxford Street. Rooms – big, individual and well-appointed – share bathrooms but have own basin. Guests – mostly men – can also meet and mingle in the dining room, garden courtyard or spa. Full cooked breakfast. B&B ❺

Manor House Boutique Hotel 86 Flinders St, Darlinghurst ☎02/9380 6633, ⓦwww.manorhouse.com.au. Grand mansion, once the residence of Sydney's first Lord Mayor, now gay-owned and run mostly for men. En-suite rooms with decks overlooking courtyard, heated pool and a spa. Licensed restaurant and bar. B&B ❻–❼

Pelican Private Hotel 411 Bourke St, Darlinghurst ☎ & ℻9331 5344, ⓦwww .pelicanprivatehotel.iwarp.com. Recently renovated, comfortable budget accommodation in one of Sydney's oldest gay guesthouses. The mid-nineteenth-century sandstone building's wonderful tree-filled garden is like an inner-city oasis. Communal kitchen and laundry out here makes it even more of a sociable hangout. Appealing, good-sized, well-furnished rooms have fans, TV and fridge, but share bathroom facilities. Help-yourself continental breakfast. B&B ❸

Wattle Private Hotel 108 Oxford St, cnr Palmer St, Darlinghurst ☎02/9332 4118, ⓦwww.sydneywattle.com. Long-running gay-friendly hotel, with stylish licensed café/bistro-cum-reception area open-fronted to the Oxford Street antics. Air-con en-suite rooms are spacious, clean and appointed with everything from telephones to ceiling fans and desks; well maintained but dated decor is now cutely retro. ❺

-serviced-apartments.com.au. Good-value serviced motel studio apartments halfway between Bondi Junction and Bondi Beach. Air-con units, recently decorated, with clean modern furniture, TV, telephone, kitchen and a balcony with sea view. Cheaper older-style apartments without views. Rooftop pool. Cheaper weekly or monthly rates. Parking included. ❹–❺

Indy's at Bondi 35A Hall St ☎02/9365 4900, ⓦwww.indysbackpackers.com.au. Spacious hostel that feels like a friendly student house-share – except it's well-organized with every amenity, including a pool table, outdoor area, excellent security, and free use of surfing and sporting equipment. Social events and trips organized; also travel bookings. The laid-back *Indy's at Coogee* is now only for longer-term stayers; enquire here for details. Dorms $26, rooms ❸

Noah's Backpackers 2 Campbell Parade, Bondi Beach ☎02/9365 7100, ⓦwww.noahsbondibeach .com. Huge hostel right opposite the beach. Fantastic ocean views from the rooftop deck with a BBQ area and a convenient kitchen. Beach-view rooms with sink, TV, fridge, fan, chair and lockable cupboard. Four-, six- and eight-bed dorms have sinks, lockers, table and chairs. Clean, well-run but with cramped bathrooms. On-site bar, TV room (wide-screen TV) and pool table; greasy-spoon food available. Excellent security. Dorms $21–25, rooms ❷–❸

Ravesi's Cnr Campbell Parade and Hall St, Bondi Beach ☎02/9365 4422, ⓦwww.ravesis.com.au. First-floor restaurant and also most rooms at this small hotel have glorious ocean views. The facade is pure 1914, but rooms have minimalist Asian-style decor. Most second-floor rooms have French windows onto small balconies; split-level and penthouse suites have spacious balconies. No views from smaller standard rooms, but great value at $120. Rooms have ceiling fans (plus air-con). Large, popular bar at ground level. ❹–❼

Holiday apartments

The following places rent out apartments, generally for a minimum of a week. All are completely furnished and equipped – though occasionally you're expected to provide linen and towels: check first. Many hotels (some called apartment hotels) and all hostels also have self-catering facilities – see main listings for details.

Enochs Holiday Flats ☎02/9388 1477, ℗02/9388 1353. One-, two- or three-bedroom apartments, all close to Bondi Beach, sleeping four to six people. $500–2000 weekly, depending on the size and season.

Manly National 22 Central Ave, Manly ☎02/9977 6469, ℗02/9977 3760. One- and two-bedroom apartments for up to four people; swimming pool; linen not supplied. One-bedroom $575–700 weekly, two-bedroom $745–1045.

Medina Executive Apartments Head office, Level 1, 155 Crown St, Surry Hills ☎02/9360 1699, ⓦwww.medinaapartments.com.au. Upmarket studio or one-, two- and three-bedroom serviced apartments with resident managers and reception in salubrious locales. Various locations in the city include Lee St near Central station, Kent St and Martin Place in the CBD, King St Wharf at Darling Habour; inner-city and eastern suburbs include Chippendale, Surry Hills, Paddington, Double Bay, Paddington, Randwick and Coogee, on the lower North Shore at Crows Nest, and at North Ryde. All include undercover parking. From $1085 weekly upwards.

The Park Agency 190 Arden St, Coogee ☎02/9315 7777, ⓦwww.parkagency.com.au. Several spacious, well-set-up studio and one-, two- and three-bedroom apartments near the beach from $700 per week for the smaller units, and $800–1000 per week for the larger properties. Cheaper quarterly leases also available. All fully furnished including washing machine and linen.

Raine and Horne 255 Miller St, North Sydney ☎02/9959 5906, ⓦwww.accommodationinsydney.com. Modern executive fully furnished apartments fitted out by interior designers, on the leafy North Shore: North Sydney, Kirribilli, Milsons Point and McMahons Point. Studios from $550, one-bed from $650, two-bed from $850, three-bed from $1200 per week. All have TV, video, CD player, telephone; several have spas, pools or gyms. One-off cleaning fee: $120 for studios and one-bedders, $220 for larger apartments.

Sydney City Centre Serviced Apartments 7 Elizabeth St, Martin Place ☎02/9233 6677, ℗02/9235 3432. Fully equipped, open-plan studio apartments sleeping up to three; kitchenette, laundry, TV, video, fans; basic, but in an excellent location. A good choice for long-stayers, as they rent out for a minimum of nine weeks. $300–$390 weekly.

Coogee and Randwick

Coogee Bay Boutique Hotel 9 Vicar St, Coogee ☎02/9665 0000, ⓦwww.coogeebayhotel.com.au. Newer hotel attached to the rear of a pub, the older, sprawling *Coogee Bay Hotel* . Rooms – all with balconies, half with ocean views – look like something from *Vogue Interior*; luxurious touches include marble floors in the bathrooms, minibars, in-room safes and data ports. Cheaper rooms in the old hotel are noisy at weekends but are just as stylish; several offer splendid water views. Parking included. 24hr reception. The pub has an excellent brasserie, several bars and a nightclub. ➍–➏

Dive 234 Arden St, Coogee Beach ☎02/9665 5538, ⓦwww.divehotel.com.au. Far from living up to its name, this is a wonderful small hotel in a renovated former boardinghouse opposite the beach. The hall features Art Deco tiling and high, decorative-plaster ceilings and there's a pleasant, bamboo-fringed courtyard (with BBQ and discreet guest laundry) that opens out from a spacious breakfast room for prepare-yourself breakfasts. Larger two rooms at the front have splendid ocean views; one at the back has its own balcony. All have funky little bathrooms, CD players, cable TV, queen-size beds and a handy kitchenette with microwave and crockery. Free Internet access. ➏–➐

The Royal 2 Perouse Rd, cnr Cuthill St, Randwick ☎02/9399 3006,

ⓦ www.royalhotel-sydney.com. Big, National Trust-listed pub with fairly upmarket rooms – TV, fridge, fan, telephone, kettle – but all with shared bathrooms. The stylish pub is a very popular drinking hole (open until very late nightly, but with no live music, so noise isn't a big problem) and has a traditional Italian restaurant. Good transport to the city and beaches. ❸

Surfside Backpackers Coogee 186 Arden St, Coogee ☎ 02/9315 7888, ⓦ www.surfside backpackers.com.au. On Coogee's main drag, above *McDonald's* and bang opposite the beach, Coogee's largest hostel tends to attract a drinking, party crowd – try elsewhere for quiet. Modern facilities and great views from its high balconies,

but a bit of a concrete tower-block feel, not as clean as it should be and dorms are mostly eight-, ten- or twelve-bed, though some four-beds are available. Doubles outside the peak periods only. Dorms $20–25, rooms ❸

Wizard of Oz Backpackers 172 Coogee Bay Rd ☎ 02/9315 7876, ⓦ www.wizardofoz.com.au. Top-class hostel run by a friendly local couple in a big and beautiful Californian-style house with a huge verandah and polished wooden floors. Spacious, vibrantly painted dorms with ceiling fans, and some well-set-up doubles. TV/video room, dining area, modern kitchen, good showers and big pleasant backyard with BBQ. Dorms $22–25, rooms ❸

North Shore

Cremorne Point Manor 6 Cremorne Rd, Cremorne Point ☎ 02/9953 7899, ⓦ www.cremornepointmanor .com.au. Huge restored federation-style villa. Nearly all rooms are en suite , except for a few good-value singles (from $52) which have own toilet and sink, and all have TV, fridge, kettle and a fan; some pricier rooms have harbour views. One family room has its own kitchen. Guest balcony also has great views. Communal kitchen and laundry. Light breakfast. Reception sells bus and ferry passes and books tours. ❺

Elite Private Hotel 133 Carabella St, Kirribilli ☎ 02/9929 6365, ⓦ www.elitehotel.com.au. Bright place surrounded by plants offering good rooms with sink, TV, fridge and kettle; some dearer ones have a harbour view and most share bathrooms. Small communal cooking facility but no laundry; garden courtyard. Only minutes by ferry from the city (to Kirribilli Wharf) and near Milsons Point train station. Cheaper weekly rates. ❸–❹

Glenferrie Lodge 12A Carabella St, Kirribilli

☎ 02/9955 1685, ⓦ www.glenferrielodge.com. Another made-over Kirribilli mansion: clean, light and secure with 24hr reception. Three-share dorms and single, double or family rooms (all shared bathroom). Some pricier rooms have their own balcony and harbour glimpses but guests can also hang out in the garden and on the guest verandahs. Facilities include a TV lounge, laundry and dining room; buffet-style $7 dinner. Light breakfast. Ferry to Kirribilli Wharf or train to Milsons Point. Dorms $32, rooms ❸

North Shore 310 Miller St, North Sydney ☎ 02/9955 1012, ⓦ www.smallanduniquehotels .com. Two-storey mansion with balconies in a quiet location opposite a park; within walking distance (10–15min) of the cafés and restaurants of North Sydney and Crows Nest (also bus from outside). En-suite rooms or family studios sleeping four, all with air-con, TV, fridge, hot drinks and telephone. Shared kitchen and laundry facilities; breakfast available. ❹

Manly and the northern beaches

Avalon Beach Hostel 59 Avalon Parade, Avalon ☎ 02/9918 9709, ⓔ gunilla@avalonbeach.com.au. This hostel, at one of Sydney's best – and most beautiful – surf beaches, has seen better days, but its location and atmosphere still make a stay worthwhile. Built mainly of timber, it has an airy beachhouse feel with breezy balconies and plenty of greenery and rainbow lorikeets to gaze at. Warming fireplaces make it conducive to winter relaxation as well. The hostel could be cleaner, however, and bathroom facilities are stretched at peak times. Dorms (four- and six-bed) and rooms have storage area and fans. Boat trips on Pittwater organized; surfboard rental available. Excellent

local work contacts. Dorms $20–22, rooms ❷

Boardrider Backpackers 63 The Corso, Manly ☎ 02/9977 6077, ⓦ www.boardrider.com.au. Brand-new hostel in a great spot on the lively pedestrianized Corso, en route to the surf beach. A balcony overlooks the action with views to the beach. Nearby pubs and clubs can make it noisy at night. Modern facilities include a large, well-equipped kitchen and dining area, big common room, lockers in the bedrooms and good security. Several rooms and dorms have balconies, some with ocean views; some en suites. Rooftop terrace with BBQ. Dorms $25, rooms ❸

Chateau Sur Mer 124 Pacific Palm Rd, Palm Beach ☎02/9974 4220, ⓦwww.palmbeachchateau .com.au. Mediterranean-style mansion perched on a hilltop with ocean views in one of Sydney's most sought-after streets. The three guestrooms are within the family home, much like a British B&B, but the friendly English couple who run it don't intrude on guests' privacy, and rooms have own bathroom and balcony. A fridge comes stocked with breakfast things and more goodies arrive on a tray in the morning. ⑥–⑦

Manly Backpackers Beachside 28 Raglan St, Manly ☎02/9977 3411, ⓦwww.manlybackpackers .com.au. Well-run, modern purpose-built two-storey hostel one block from the surf. One of the few hostels that manages to be both clean and fun, this place has a spacious well-equipped kitchen and outside terrace with BBQ. Attracts long-stayers. Twin and double rooms – some en suite – plus small three-bed dorms (six-bed is largest). Best dorm at the front with a balcony. Free boogie-boards. Dorms $21, rooms ②

Manly Beach Resort Backpackers 6 Carlton St, Manly ☎02/9977 4188, ⓔmanlybeachresort@ozemail.com.au. Hostel with a more upmarket motel section one block from the beach. Clean, four- to eight-bed, en-suite dorms and a few very reasonable doubles. Attached café is good for breakfast. 24hr reception. Dorms $24, hostel rooms ③, motel rooms B&B ⑤

Manly Pacific Sydney 55 North Steyne, Manly ☎02/9977 7666, ⓦwww.accorhotels.com. Beachfront, multistorey, four-star hotel with 24hr reception, room service, spa, sauna, gym and heated rooftop pool – all at a price: around $240, and more for an ocean view. ⑦

Periwinkle Guesthouse 18–19 East Esplanade, cnr Ashburner St, Manly ☎02/9977 4668, ⓦwww.periwinklemanlycove.com.au. Pleasant B&B in a charming, restored 1895 villa on Manly Cove, close to the ferry and shops. Rooms have fridge and fans; several en suites and larger family rooms available. Communal kitchen, laundry, courtyard with BBQ and car park. Light breakfast. ⑤–⑥

Sydney Beachhouse YHA 4 Collaroy St, Collaroy Beach ☎02/9981 1177, ⓦwww .sydneybeachhouse.com. Purpose-built beachside YHA hostel. Heated outdoor swimming pool, sun deck, BBQs, open fireplaces, video lounge and games and pool rooms. Four- to six-bed dorms plus several doubles (some en suite) and family rooms. Too far out for your entire Sydney stay (45min bus ride from the city), it's a good base for exploring the northern beaches – bikes are free for guests – or just relaxing by the beach for a few days. Free use of boogie- and surfboards with surfing lessons for weekly guests (or try their mechanical surf-board). Free parking. Dorms $20–$24, rooms ③

Cronulla Beach

Cronulla Beach YHA 40 Kingsway, Cronulla ☎02/9527 7772, ⓦwww.cronullabeachyha.com. Newish hostel in this unpretentious, surf-oriented suburb that's well situated for trips to the Royal National Park; the friendly live-in manager offers surf trips to Garie and drop-offs to Wattamolla. Surfboards, kayaks and bicycles for rent. Private rooms are en suite and there are four- and six-bed dorms, all with fans and lockers. Small and friendly. Dorms $25–27, rooms ③

The City

Port Jackson carves Sydney in two halves, linked by the Harbour Bridge and Harbour Tunnel. The **South Shore** is the hub of activity, and it's here that you'll find the **city centre** and most of the things to see and do. Many of the classic images of Sydney are within sight of **Circular Quay**, making this busy waterfront area on Sydney Cove a logical – and pleasurable – point to start discovering the city, with the **Opera House** and the expanse of the Royal Botanic Gardens to the east of Sydney Cove and the historic area of **The Rocks** to the west. By contrast, gleaming, slightly tawdry **Darling Harbour**, at the centre's western edge, was redeveloped for the Bicentenary in 1988 as a tourist and entertainment area.

Circular Quay

At the southern end of Sydney Cove, **Circular Quay** is the launching pad for harbour and river ferries and sightseeing boats, the terminal for buses from the eastern and southern suburbs, and a major suburban train station to boot (some of the most fantastic views of the harbour can be seen from the above-ground station platforms). Circular Quay itself is always bustling with commuters during the week, and with people simply out to enjoy themselves at the weekend. Restaurants, cafés and fast-food outlets stay open until late at night and buskers entertain the crowds, while vendors of newspapers and trinkets add to the general hubbub. The sun reflecting on the water and its heave and splash as the ferries come and go make for a dreamy setting – best appreciated over an expensive beer at a waterfront bar. The inscribed bronze pavement plaques of **Writers' Walk** beneath your feet as you stroll provide an introduction to the Australian literary canon. There are short biographies of writers ranging from Miles Franklin, author of *My Brilliant Career*, through Booker Prize winner

Harbour cruises

There's a wide choice of **harbour cruises**, almost all of them leaving from Jetty 6, Circular Quay and the rest from Darling Harbour. Apart from the running commentary (which can be rather annoying), most offer nothing that you won't get on a regular harbour **ferry** for a lot less. The best of the ordinary trips is the thirty-minute ride to **Manly**, but there's a ferry going somewhere at almost any time throughout the day. If you want to splash out, take a **water-taxi** ride – Circular Quay to Watsons Bay, for example, costs $52 for the first passenger and then an additional $7 for each extra person. Pick-ups are available from any wharf if booked in advance (try Water Taxis Combined on ℡02/9555 8888). One water taxi company, **Watertours**, located on Cockle Bay Wharf in Darling Harbour (℡02/9211 7730, ⊛www.watertours .com.au), even offer tours on their latest-model, bright yellow taxis, from $10 for a speedy ten-minute, one-way spin under the Harbour Bridge to the Opera House (every 15min).

The **Australian Travel Specialists (ATS)** at Jetty 2 and 6, Circular Quay, the Harbourside Shopping Centre at Darling Harbour and Manly Wharf (℡02/9211 3192; ⊛www.atstravel.com.au) books all cruises. Those offered by State Transit – **Harboursights Cruises** (℡131 500; ⊛www.sydneyferries.nsw.gov.au) – offer the best value: choose between the Morning Harbour Cruise (daily 10.30am; 1hr; $15), the recommended Afternoon Harbour Cruise to Middle Harbour and back (Mon–Fri 1pm, Sat & Sun 12.30pm; 2hr 30min; $22), or the Evening Harbour Cruise (Mon–Sat 8pm; 1hr 30min; $19). Buy tickets at the Sydney Ferry ticket offices at Circular Quay. STA cruises are also included in a Sydney Pass – see p.96.

Captain Cook Cruises at Jetty 6, Circular Quay (℡02/9206 1111, ⊛www.captaincook .com.au), the big commercial operator, offers a vast range of cruises on their very large boats including morning and afternoon "Coffee" Cruises into Middle Harbour (daily 10am & 2.15pm; 2hr 20min; $39), a lunch cruise (daily 12.30pm; 1hr 30min; buffet $52, one- or two-course $56–$66), a range of dinner cruises including the two-course Sunset Dinner (includes a drink; daily 5pm; 1hr 35min; $69) and Opera Afloat with opera singers accompanying a four-course dinner (daily 7pm; 2hr 30min; $99), and a Harbour Highlights Cruise (daily 9.30am, 11am, 12.45am, 2.30pm, 4pm; 1hr 15min; $20). Their hop-on-hop-off five-stop Sydney Harbour Explorer from Circular Quay (daily 9.30am–3.30pm; every 2hr; $22) circuits via the Opera House, Watsons Bay, Taronga Zoo and Darling Harbour.

Matilda Cruises, based in Darling Harbour (Aquarium Wharf, Pier 26; ℡02/9264 7377, ⊛www.matilda.com.au), offers various smaller-scale cruises on sailing catamarans (engines mostly used), with big foredecks providing great views. Departures are from Darling Harbour (either at the Aquarium or King Street wharves) with pick-ups from Circular Quay twenty minutes later. Morning and afternoon cruises include

Peter Carey and Nobel Prize awardee Patrick White, to the feminist Germaine Greer, and quotable quotes on what it means to be Australian. Notable literati who've visited Australia – including Joseph Conrad, Charles Darwin and Mark Twain – also feature.

Having dallied, read, and taken in the view and the crush of people, the next thing to do is to embark on a sightseeing **cruise** or enjoy a ferry ride on the harbour (see box below). Staying on dry land, you're only a short walk from most of the city-centre sights, along part of a continuous foreshore walkway beginning under the Harbour Bridge and passing through the historic area of Sydney's first settlement The Rocks, and extending beyond the Opera House to the Royal Botanic Gardens (see p.129). The Gardens boast some wonderfully picturesque picnic spots – all the necessaries, including bubbly and fresh

tea, coffee and biscuits (10am, 12.15pm & 3.05pm; 1hr 30min; $27); there's a buffet on the Lunch Cruise (12.15pm; 2hr; $56.20), while the pricey Dinner Cruise allows you to dine on the foredeck (7.30pm; 3hr 30min; $94.50). Their hop-on-hop-off **Rocket Harbour Express Cruise**, is a one-hour circuit stopping at Darling Harbour, the Opera House, Circular Quay West, Taronga Zoo and Watsons Bay (daily 9.30am–4.30pm; every hour; $20.50 includes refreshment; all-day ticket but one complete circuit only), while their ordinary ferry services include the Rocket Express, shuttling between Darling Harbour, the casino and Circular Quay ($4.50 one-way, $7.50 return).

There are also a number of more romantic sailing options. The **Bounty** (℡02/9247 1789, ⓦwww.thebounty.com), a replica of Captain Bligh's ship made for the film starring Mel Gibson, normally embarks from Campbells Cove, The Rocks, for various cruises daily. During 2003, the ship will be sailing in the Pacific and may be unavailable for cruises. **Svanen Charters'** (℡02/9698 4456, ⓦwww.svanen.com.au) sailing ship, built in 1922, is moored at Campbells Cove next to the *Bounty*, and offers harbour day-sails for $93.50, including morning tea and lunch, or longer overnight sails to Broken Bay or Port Hacking ($275). Sydney's oldest sailing ship, the **James Craig**, an 1874 three-masted iron barque, is part of the Sydney Heritage Fleet based at Wharf 7, Pirrama Rd, Pyrmont, near Star City Casino, and does six-hour cruises on Saturdays (9.30am–4pm; $190; over-12s only; morning and afternoon tea and lunch provided). **Sydney by Sail** (℡02/9280 1110, ⓦwww.sydneybysail .com), offers the popular small-group, three-hour Port Jackson Explorer cruise (daily 1–4pm; $120) on board a luxury Beneteau yacht, departing from the National Maritime Museum, Darling Harbour (free entry to the museum included).

There are several options for more thrills (but noise pollution for the locals). **Aussie Duck** (℡131 007, ⓦwww.aussieduck.com) combines a land and sea tour in an amphibious vehicle (Mon 2.30pm, Thurs & Fri 12.30 & 2.30pm, Sat & Sun 10.30am, 12.30pm & 2.30pm from Clocktower Square in The Rocks; 1hr 30min; $60). The brightly painted "coach" spends 45 minutes touring the city until a startling harbour "splash-down" transforms it into a jet-powered boat. Duck quackers and pumping themed music accompany the sights. **Ocean Extreme** (℡0414 800 046, ⓦwww.oceanextreme.com.au) offers a hair-raising, forty-minute, small-group (maximum ten) "Adrenaline Tour" (daily 11am & 1pm; $70) on *Extreme 1*, an RIB (Rigid Inflatable Boat). At speeds of more than 100kph, the harbour scenery is mostly a blur. **Harbour Jet** (℡1300 887 373; ⓦwww.harbourjet.com) offers the 35-minute "Jet Blast" (daily except Tues noon, 1.45 & 4.15pm from Convention Jetty, Darling Harbour; $50), on a boat which goes at speeds of 75kph, accompanied by blasting music.

prawns, can be purchased at the quay. Besides ferries, Circular Quay still acts as a passenger terminal for ocean liners; head in the opposite direction past the Museum of Contemporary Art to Circular Quay West. It's a long time since the crowds waved their hankies regularly from **Sydney Cove Passenger Terminal**, looking for all the world like the deck of a ship itself, but you may still see an ocean liner docked here; even if there's no ship, take the escalator and the flight of stairs up for excellent views of the harbour. The rest of the recently redeveloped terminal is given over to swanky restaurants and bars with fabulous views – *Aria*, *Wildfire* and *Cruise Bar and Restaurant* among them.

Leading up to the Opera House is the once-controversial **Opera Quays** development which runs the length of **East Circular Quay**. Locals and tourists have flocked to promenade along the pleasant collonnaded lower level with its outdoor cafés, bars and bistros, upmarket shops and Dendy Cinema, all looking out to sublime harbour views. The ugly apartment building above, dubbed "The Toaster" by locals and described by Robert Hughes, the famous expat Australian art critic and historian, as "that dull brash, intrusive apartment block which now obscures the Opera House from three directions", caused massive protests, but went up anyway, opening in 1999.

Customs House and the Justice & Police Museum

The railway and the ugly Cahill Expressway block views to the city from Circular Quay, cutting it off from Alfred Street immediately opposite, with its architectural gem, the sandstone and granite **Customs House**. First constructed in 1845, it was redesigned in 1885 by the colonial architect James Barnet to give it its current Classical Revival-style facade. On the fourth floor, the **City Exhibition Space** (daily 10am–5pm; free) keeps pace with the development of Sydney with an up-to-the-minute detailed 500:1 scale model of the city accompanied by history boards and video screens. Sydney Architecture Walks has various **walking tours** led by young architects leaving from here every Wednesday and Saturday at 10am and on the first and last Sunday of the month (first Sun 2pm, last Sun 10am; 2hr 30min; $22; bookings ☏02/9242 8555 ⓔinfo@sydneyarchitecture.org,). On the third floor, the **Centre for Contemporary Craft** shows free changing exhibitions of Australia's best artisans in the **Object Galleries** (daily 10am–5pm); Object Stores is the retail outlet on the ground floor (Mon–Fri 10am–5.30pm, Sat & Sun noon–5pm), selling beautifully designed glass, ceramics, woodwork and jewellery. There are several places to eat and drink, too: on the top floor, a pricey contemporary brasserie, *Cafe Sydney*, comes with wonderful Harbour Bridge views, while on the ground floor, take a coffee at *Caffe Bianchi*, or eat oysters and have a beer at *Quay Bar*, both with alfresco seating on Customs House Square out front.

A block east of Customs House, on the corner of Phillip Street, the **Justice & Police Museum** is housed in the former Water Police station (Jan daily except Fri 10am–5pm; Feb–Dec Sat & Sun only 10am–5pm; $7; ⓦwww.hht.net.au), an 1858 sandstone building with a particularly fine iron-work verandah. This social history museum focuses on law, policing and crime in New South Wales with several temporary themed exhibitions throughout the year. The permanent crime displays, including some truly macabre death masks and gruesome confiscated weapons, some of them murder implements, are shown within the context of a late-nineteenth-century police station and courtroom. There's also an interesting display on bushrangers.

Museum of Contemporary Art

The **Museum of Contemporary Art** (daily 10am–5pm; free; free tours Mon–Fri 11am & 2pm, Sat & Sun noon & 1.30pm; ☎02/9252 4033 for details of special exhibitions and events; ⓦwww.mca.com.au), on the western side of Circular Quay with another entrance on George Street (no. 140), was developed out of a bequest by the art collector John Power in the 1940s to Sydney University to purchase international contemporary art. The growing collection finally found a permanent home in 1991 in the former Maritime Services Building, provided for peppercorn rent by the State Government. The striking Deco-style 1950s building is now dedicated to international twentieth-century art, with an eclectic approach encompassing lithographs, sculpture, film, video, drawings, paintings and Aboriginal art, shown in themed temporary exhibitions. A selection of the permanent collection – which includes pieces by Julian Schnabel, Keith Haring, Bridget Riley, Jasper Johns, Beuys, Hockney, Duchamp, Tinguely and Rauchenberg is shown in special exhibitions twice a year. The museum's superbly sited, if expensive, café (Mon–Fri 11am–4.30pm, Sat & Sun 9am–4.30pm) has outdoor tables overlooking the waterfront.

The Opera House

The **Sydney Opera House**, such an icon of Australiana that it almost seems kitsch, is just a short stroll from Circular Quay, by the water's edge on **Bennelong Point**. It's best seen in profile, when its high white roofs, at the same time evocative of full sails and white shells, give the building an almost ethereal quality. Some say the inspiration for the distinctive design came from the simple peeling of an orange into segments, though perhaps Danish architect **Jørn Utzon**'s childhood as the son of a yacht designer had something to do with their sail-like shape – he certainly envisaged a building which would appear to "float" on water. Despite its familiarity, or perhaps precisely because you already feel you know it so well, it's quite breathtaking at first sight. Close up, you can see that the shimmering effect is created by thousands of white tiles.

The feat of structural engineering required to bring to life Utzon's "sculpture", which he compared to a Gothic church and a Mayan temple, made the final price tag A$102 million, ten times original estimates. Now almost universally loved and admired, it's hard to believe quite how controversial a project this was during its long haul from plan, as a result of an international competition in the late 1950s, to completion in 1973. For sixteen years, construction was plagued by quarrels and scandal, so much so that Utzon, who won the competition in 1957, was forced to resign in 1966. Some put it less kindly and say he was hounded out of the country by politicians – the newly elected Askin government disagreeing over his plans for the completion of the interior – and xenophobic local architects. Seven years and three Australian architects later the interior, which never matched Utzon's vision, was finished: the focal Concert Hall, for instance, was completely designed by **Peter Hall** and his team. However, Utzon will now have a chance to have final say: in 1999 he was appointed as a design consultant to prepare a Statement of Design Principles for the building, which will become the permanent reference for its conservation and development. At the time of writing Utzon was continuing his consultancy with the Opera House and the statement is intended to be publicly available by the end of 2003; check the Opera House website for the latest information.

"Opera House" is actually a misnomer: it's really a performing arts centre, one of the busiest in the world, with five performance venues inside its shells, plus two restaurants, several popular cafés and bars, an Aboriginal artists' gallery, and a stash of upmarket souvenir shops on the lower concourse. The building's initial impetus, in fact, was as a home for the Sydney Symphony Orchestra, and it was designed with the huge **Concert Hall**, seating 2690, as the focal point; the smaller **Opera Theatre** (1547 seats), is used as the Sydney performance base for Opera Australia (seasons June–Nov & Feb–March), the Australian Ballet (mid-March to May & Nov–Dec) and the Sydney Dance Company. There are three theatrical venues: the **Drama Theatre** and **The Playhouse**, both used primarily by the Sydney Theatre Company, and the more intimate **The Studio**. The last was added in 1999 and aims to draw in a younger audience, offering innovative Australian drama, comedy, cabaret and contemporary dance, with an adaptable theatre-in-the-round format. There's plenty of action outside the Opera House too, with the use of the Mayan temple-inspired **Forecourt** and Monumental Steps as an amphitheatre for free and ticketed concerts – rock, jazz and classical, with a capacity for around 5000 people. Sunday is also a lively day on the forecourt, when the **Tarpeian Markets** (10am–4pm), with an emphasis on Australian crafts, are held.

If you're not content with gazing at the outside – much the building's best feature – and can't attend a performance, there are **guided tours** available: the Front-of-House tour gives an overview of the site, looking at the public areas and discussing the unique architecture (daily 8.30am–5pm; every 30–40min; 45min; $17). Backstage tours run less frequently, about once or twice a week, and include access to the scenery docks, rehearsal rooms and technical areas (1hr 30min; $28; bookings on ☎02/9250 7250). It's only on these tours that you can see the small exhibition area in the foyer of The Playhouse where two original Utzon models of the Opera House are displayed, alongside a series of small oil paintings depicting the life of **Bennelong**, the Iora tribesman who was initially kidnapped as little more than an Aboriginal "specimen" but later became a much-loved addition to Governor Arthur Phillip's household; Phillip later built a hut for him on what is now the site of the Opera House.

The best way to appreciate the Opera House, of course, is to attend an evening **performance**: the building is particularly stunning when floodlit and, once you're inside, the huge windows come into their own as the dark harbour waters reflect a shimmering image of the night-time city – interval drinks certainly aren't like this anywhere else in the world. You could choose to **eat** at what is considered to be one of Sydney's best restaurants, *Guillame at Bennelong* overlooking the city skyline (see p.165) or take a **drink** at the *Opera Bar* on the lower concourse, with outside tables, an affordable all-day menu, wonderful views, and free Sunday jazz, plus there's a sidewalk cafe, a bistro and several theatre bars. **Packages** which include tours, meals, drinks and performances can be purchased over the Internet or on site (☎02/9250 7250, ◉www.soh .nsw.gov.au), and can be good value.

The Harbour Bridge

The charismatic **Harbour Bridge**, in the opposite direction from Circular Quay, has straddled the channel dividing North and South Sydney since 1932; today it makes the view from Circular Quay complete. The largest arch bridge in the world when it was built, its construction costs weren't paid off until 1988. There's still a toll ($3) to drive across, payable only when heading south; you can walk or cycle it for free. Pedestrians should head up the steps to the bridge from Cumberland Street, reached from The Rocks via the Argyle Steps off Argyle Street (see p.119), and walk on the eastern side (cyclists keep to the western side). The ever-increasing volume of traffic in recent years proved too much for the bridge to bear, and a harbour **tunnel** (also $3 heading south) also crosses the river, starting south of the Opera House.

The bridge demands full-time maintenance, protected from rust by continuous painting in trademark steel-grey. One of Australia's best-known comedians, Paul Hogan of *Crocodile Dundee* fame, worked as a rigger on "the coathanger" before being rescued by a *New Faces* talent quest in the 1970s. To check out Hoge's vista, you can follow a rigger's route and climb the bridge with **Bridge Climb**, who take small, specially equipped groups (maximum 12) to the top of the bridge from sunrise until after dark (minimum age 12; dawn, twilight, Sat & Sun daytime and Fri & Sat night climbs $175, Mon–Thurs & Sun nighttime and Mon–Fri daytime climbs $145; booking advised, particularly for weekends, on ☎02/8274 7777 or ⓦwww.bridgeclimb.com). Though the experience takes three and a half hours, only two hours is spent on the bridge, gradually ascending and pausing while the guide points out landmarks and offers interesting background snippets. The hour spent checking in and getting kitted up at the "Base" at 5 Cumberland St, The Rocks, makes you feel as if you're preparing to go into outer space, as do the grey *Star Trek*-style suits specially designed to blend in with the bridge. It's really not as scary as it looks – harnessed into a cable system, there's no way you can fall off. So that nothing be dropped onto cars or people below, cameras cannot be taken on the walk (only your glasses are allowed, attached by special cords), limiting scope for one of the world's greatest **photo opportunities**. Though one group photo on top of the bridge is included in the climb price, the group – of jolly strangers, arms akimbo – crowds out the background. To get a good shot showing yourself with the splendours of the harbour behind, you'll need to fork out $15.95 for one extra individual photo, $24.95 for an A4-size photo or $29.95 for four different small ones, taken by the guide.

If you can't stomach (or afford) the climb, there's a **lookout point** (daily 10am–5pm; $5; ⓦwww.pylonlookout.com.au; 5min walk from Cumberland St then 200 steps) actually inside the bridge's southern pylon where, as well as gazing out across the harbour, you can study a photo exhibition on the bridge's history.

The Rocks

The Rocks, immediately beneath the bridge, is the heart of historic Sydney. On this rocky outcrop between Sydney Cove and Walsh Bay, Captain Arthur Phillip proclaimed the establishment of Sydney Town in 1788, the first permanent European settlement in Australia. Within decades, the area had become little more than a slum of dingy dwellings, narrow alleys and dubious taverns and brothels. In the 1830s and 1840s, merchants began building fine stone warehouses here, but as the focus for Sydney's shipping industry moved from Circular Quay, the area fell into decline. By the 1870s and 1880s, the notorious Rocks "pushes", gangs of "larrikins" (louts), mugged passers-by and brawled with each other: the narrow street named **Suez Canal** was a favourite place to hide in wait. Some say the name is a shortening of Sewers' Canal, and indeed the area was so filthy that whole streetfronts had to be torn down in 1900 to contain an outbreak of the bubonic plague. It remained a run-down, depressed and depressing quarter until the 1970s, when there were plans to raze the historic cottages, terraces and warehouses to make way for office towers. However, due to the foresight of a radical building workers' union which opposed the demolition, the restored and renovated **historic quarter** is now

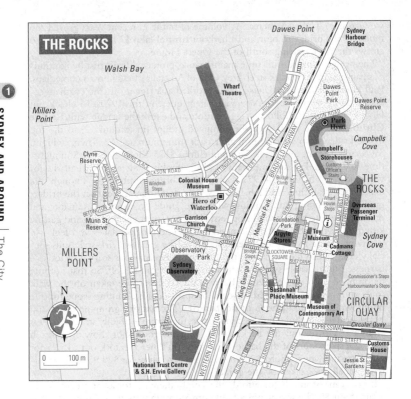

one of Sydney's major tourist attractions and, despite a passing resemblance to a historic theme park, it's worth exploring. It's also the best place, apart from the airport, to do tax-free shopping.

There are times, though, when the old atmosphere still seems to prevail: Friday and Saturday nights in The Rocks can be thoroughly drunken. New Year's Eve is also riotously celebrated here, to the backdrop of fireworks over the harbour. The best time to come for a drink is Sunday afternoon when many of the pubs here offer live jazz or folk music.

Information, tours and transport

The best place to start your tour of The Rocks is the **Sailors' Home**, at 106 George St, built in 1864 to provide decent lodgings for visiting sailors as an alternative to the brothels and inns in the area. The building housed sailors until the early 1980s but now contains the **Sydney Visitor Centre** (daily 9am–6pm; ☎02/9255 1788, ⓦ www.sydneyvisitorcentre.com), which at street level supplies tourist information (including a guided tour leaflet for $2.20). On the two galleried levels, information is provided about the history and sights of The Rocks along with a re-creation of the original sailors' sleeping quarters. A great introduction to the area is the long-running **The Rocks Walking Tours**, starting from Shop 4, Kendall Lane (Mon–Fri 10.30am, 12.30pm & 2.30pm, Jan 10.30am & 2.30pm only, Sat & Sun 11.30am & 2pm; 1hr 30min; $17.50; ☎02/9247 6678, ⓦ www.rockswalkingtours.com.au).

The small sandstone house next to the information centre, at 110 George St, is **Cadman's Cottage**, the oldest private house still standing in Sydney, built in 1816 for John Cadman, ex-convict and Government coxswain. It's now the **National Parks and Wildlife Service** bookshop and information centre (Mon–Fri 9.30am–4.30pm, Sat & Sun 10am–4.30pm; ☎02/9247 5033, ⓦwww.npws.nsw.gov.au), providing information about the Sydney Harbour National Park and taking bookings for trips to Fort Denison and other harbour islands that are part of the park.

The corner of Argyle and Kent streets, Millers Point, is a terminus for several useful **bus routes**; aim to walk to here through The Rocks and then catch a bus back: routes #431–434 go along George Street to Railway Square and from there to varying locations including Glebe and Balmain, while #339 goes to the eastern beaches suburb of Clovelly via George Street in the city and Surry Hills.

Exploring The Rocks: from Campbells Cove to the Argyle Cut

Just exploring the narrow alleys and streets hewn out of the original rocky spur is the chief delight of The Rocks, a voyage of discovery that involves climbing and descending several stairs and cuts to different levels. A set of steps alongside the Sydney Visitor Centre leads down to the waterfront and the Overseas Passenger Terminal (see p.114). Head north from here along the waterfront walkway to **Campbells Cove**, where the beautifully restored 1830s **Campbell's Storehouses**, once part of the private wharf of the merchant Robert Campbell, now house a shopping and eating complex. A replica of Captain Bligh's ship, the *Bounty*, is moored here between cruises (see box on p.113), adding a Disneyish atmosphere, while a luxury hotel, the *Park Hyatt*, overlooks the whole area. Climb the **Customs Officer's Stairs** from Campbells Cove to Hickson Road, from where it's a short walk to Dawes Point (see overleaf) beneath the Harbour Bridge, or browse in the road's **Metcalfe Stores**, another storehouses-turned-shopping complex, this time dating from around 1912. Exit onto George Street, where at weekends **The Rocks Market** (Sat & Sun 10am–5pm), takes over the entire Harbour Bridge end of the street with more than a hundred stalls selling bric-a-brac and arts and crafts mostly with an Australiana/souvenir slant.

There's more shopping at the **Argyle Stores**, on the corner of Argyle and Playfair streets, a complex of decidedly more tasteful and upmarket boutiques in a beautifully restored set of former bond stores arranged around an inner courtyard; on the top floor you can take in great views from the bar of *bel mondo* (see p.165), which can also be accessed from Gloucester Walk, see below. The Argyle Stores is just near the impressive **Argyle Cut**, which slices through solid stone to The Rocks' other half, Millers Point (see p.120). The cut took eighteen years to complete, carved first with chisel and hammer by convict chain gangs who began the work in 1843; when transportation ended ten years later the tunnel was still unfinished, and it took hired hands to complete it in 1859. Walk up the **Argyle Steps** and along the narrow, brick pedestrian walkway of peaceful **Gloucester Walk** – this was the very rocky spur the area was named after – to peep through greenery to gardens below. Remains of cottage foundations were discovered here and have been used as the basis for installations of sculptures of Victorian furniture in the tiny, delightful **Foundation Park**. En route back to the northern end of George Street have a drink at the *Mercantile*, one of Sydney's best-known Irish hotels (see p.100). Gloucester Walk also leads to the pedestrian entrance of the Harbour Bridge on **Cumberland**

Street, the location of a couple of fine old boozers, the *Glenmore* and the *Australian* (see pp.175 and 176). From the latter, head down **Gloucester Street**; at nos. 58–64 is the **Susannah Place Museum** (Jan daily 10am–5pm; Feb–Dec Sat & Sun 10am–5pm; $7; ⓦwww.hht.net.au), a row of four brick terraces built in 1844 and occupied by householders until 1990. It's now a "house museum" (including a re-created corner store), which conserves the domestic history of Sydney's working class.

The old wharves and Fort Denison

At the end of George Street, under the Harbour Bridge, **Dawes Point** separates Sydney Cove, on the Circular Quay side, from **Walsh Bay** and the old piers; the park here is a favourite spot for photographers. Looking out past the Opera House, you can see **Fort Denison** on a small island in the harbour: "Pinchgut", as the island is still known, was originally used as a special prison for the tough nuts the penal colony couldn't crack. During the Crimean Wars in the mid-nineteenth century, however, old fears of a Russian invasion were rekindled and the fort was built as part of a defence ring around the harbour. For those interested in Australian history, there are tours organized by the NPWS from Circular Quay. Tours are booked through and meet up at Cadman's Cottage (see p.119; ☎02/9247 5033). There are daytime tours (Mon–Fri 11.30am & 3pm, Sat 11.30am & 3pm, Sun 11.30am & 2.30pm; 2hr 30min; $22) and there are more leisurely weekend brunch tours with a cooked meal in the fort's café included (Sat 9am, Sun 9.15am; 3hr; $47).

Head a bit further along Hickson Road to the **Wharf Theatre** (Pier 4/5), home to the Sydney Theatre Company and the Sydney Dance Company as well as about twenty other smaller arts organizations. From the restaurant and its bar (see p.166) you can revel in the sublime view across Walsh Bay to Balmain, Goat Island and the North Shore, or get closer to the water (and relaxing dancers) at the cute little *Dance Café* on the ground floor. The exhibition of posters of past productions in the hallway leading to the theatre restaurant might tempt you to come back for a performance (see p.185). Guided tours, including the costume department and a peek at set construction, run on the last Thursday of the month (1hr–1hr 30min; $15; bookings ☎02/9250 1777, ⓦwww.sydneytheatre.com.au).

Millers Point and Observatory Park

Beyond the wharves, looking towards Darling Harbour, **Millers Point** is a reminder of how The Rocks used to be – with a surprisingly real community feel so close to the tourist hype of The Rocks, as much of the housing is government- or housing association-owned. Of course, the area has its upmarket pockets, like the very swish *Observatory Hotel* on Kent Street, but for the moment, the traditional street-corner pubs and shabby terraced houses on the hill are reminiscent of the raffish atmosphere once typical of the whole area, and the mostly peaceful residential streets are a delight to wander through.

Just for kids

There are two great **free attractions** in The Rocks aimed at children: **The Rocks Toy Museum**, just off Argyle Street on Kendall Lane (daily 10am–6pm; free), has two floors of collectable toys from the nineteenth through to the twentieth century, housed in a sandstone 1850s coachhouse; while next door, **The Puppet Cottage** puts on free weekend and school holiday puppet shows (11am, 12.30pm & 2pm).

Reach the area through the Argyle Cut (see p.119) or from the end of George Street, heading onto **Lower Fort Street**. The **Colonial House Museum**, 53 Lower Fort St (daily 10am–5pm by arrangement only on ℡02/9247 6008; $1), takes up the bottom two floors of a residential terrace house (1883) where local character Shirley Ball has lived for over fifty years; her collection – a labour of love rather than a commercial enterprise – is crammed into six rooms, and includes period furnishings, hundreds of photographs of the area, etchings, artefacts and models. Continue to wander up Lower Fort Street and stop for a drink at the **Hero of Waterloo** at no. 81 (see p.176), built from sandstone excavated from the Argyle Cut in 1844, then peek in at the place of worship for the military stationed at Dawes Point fort from the 1840s, the **Garrison Church** (daily 9am–5pm) on the corner of Argyle Street. Next to the church, the volunteer-run **Garrison Gallery Museum** (Tues, Wed, Fri & Sat 11am–3pm, Sun noon–4pm; free) is housed in what was once the parish schoolhouse and has a fascinating collection of turn-of-the-twentieth-century photographs of The Rocks. Beside the church, **Argyle Place** has some of the area's prettiest old terrace houses.

From here, walk up the steps on Argyle Street opposite the church to **Observatory Park** with its shady Moreton Bay figs, park benches and lawns, for a marvellous hilltop view over the whole harbour in all its different aspects – glitzy Darling Harbour, the newer Anzac Bridge in one direction and the older Harbour Bridge in the other, gritty container terminals, ferries gliding by – and on a rainy day enjoy it from the bandstand which dominates the park. It's also easy to reach the park from the **Bridge Stairs** off Cumberland Street by the Argyle Cut.

The Italianate-style **Sydney Observatory** from which the park takes its name marked the beginning of an accurate time standard for the city when it opened in 1858, calculating the correct time from the stars and signalling it to ships in the harbour and Martin Place's GPO by the dropping of a time ball in its tower at 1pm every day – a custom which still continues. Set amongst some very pretty gardens, the Observatory is now a **museum of astronomy** (daily 10am–5pm; free; ⓦwww.phm.gov.au). A large section is devoted to the Transit of Venus, a rare astronomical event occuring about twice every century; it was the observation of this which prompted Captain Cook's 1769 voyage. The extensive exhibition of astronomical equipment, both obselete and high-tech, includes the (still-working) telescope installed under the copper dome to observe the 1874 Transit of Venus. Another highlight, in the "Stars of the Southern Sky" section, are three animated videos of Aboriginal creation stories, retellings of how the stars came to be, from the Milky Way to Orion. Every evening you can view the southern sky through telescopes and learn about the Southern Cross and other southern constellations (times vary with season; 2hr tours include a lecture, film, exhibition, guided view of the telescopes and a look at the sky, weather permitting; $10; booking essential on ℡02/9217 0485, usually up to a week in advance); the small planetarium is only used during night visits when the sky is not clear enough for observation.

Also in the park is the **National Trust Centre**, located in the former military hospital (1815) south of the Observatory. The rear of the building, purpose-built as a school in 1850 in neo-Regency style, houses the **S. H. Ervin Gallery** (Tues–Fri 11am–5pm, Sat & Sun noon–5pm; free; entry to special exhibitions $6; ℡02/9258 0123 for details of special exhibitions, ⓦwww.nsw.nationaltrust.org.au), the result of a million-dollar bequest by Ervin in 1978; the changing thematic exhibitions, around eight each year, are of scholarly non-mainstream Australian art, focusing on subjects such as

Aboriginal or women artists. There's also a café (Tues–Fri 11am–3pm, Sat & Sun 1–5pm), and a National Trust bookshop (Tues–Fri 9am–5pm, Sat & Sun noon–5pm).

City Centre

From Circular Quay south as far as King Street is Sydney's **Central Business District**, often referred to as the **CBD**, with **Martin Place** as its commercial nerve centre. A pedestrian mall lined with imposing banks and investment companies (check out the splendid marbled interior of the National Australia Bank), Martin Place has its less serious moments at summer lunchtimes, when street performances are held at the little amphitheatre, and all-year-round stalls of flower- and fruit-sellers add some colour. The vast **General Post Office**, built between 1865 and 1887 with its landmark clock tower added in 1900, broods over the George Street end of the place in all its Victorian-era pomp. The upper floors have been incorporated into part of a five-star luxury hotel, the *Westin Sydney*; the rest of the hotel resides in the 31-storey tower behind. The old building and the new tower meet in the grand Atrium Courtyard, on the lower ground floor, with its restaurants, bars, classy designer stores, and the **GPO Store**, a gastronome's delight featuring a butcher, fish shop, deli, cheese room, wine merchant and greengrocer. The other end of Martin Place emerges opposite the old civic buildings on lower Macquarie Street (see p.126). The cramped streets of the CBD itself, overshadowed by office buildings, have little to offer as you stroll through, though a crowd often gathers outside the **Australian Stock Exchange** opposite Australia Square at 20 Bond St to gaze at the computerized display of stocks and shares through the glass of the ground floor. For a glimpse at how some of this wealth might be spent, stroll over to Sydney's most upmarket shopping centre, **Chifley Plaza**, on the corner of Hunter and Phillip streets, where you'll find Leona Edmiston, Max Mara and other exclusive labels; a huge stencil-like sculpture of former Australian Prime Minister Ben Chifley, by artist Simeon Nelson, stands on the pleasant palm-filled square outside.

Museum of Sydney

North of Martin Place, on the corner of Bridge and Phillip streets, stands the **Museum of Sydney** (daily 9.30am–5pm; $7; ℡02/9251 5988 for exhibition details, Ⓦwww.hht.net.au). The site itself is the reason for the museum's existence, for here from 1983 a ten-year archeological dig unearthed the foundations of the first Government House built by Governor Phillip in 1788 which was home to eight subsequent governors of New South Wales before it was

Sydney Sculpture Walk

The specially commissioned artworks of the **Sydney Sculpture Walk** – a City of Sydney Council initiative for the 2000 Olympics and the 2001 Centenary of Federation – form a circuit from the the Royal Botanic Gardens, through The Domain, Cook and Phillip Park, the streets of the CBD, Hyde Park and East Circular Quay. One of the most striking of the ten site-specific pieces is Anne Graham's *Passage*, at the eastern end of Martin Place. At timed intervals, a fine mist emerges from grilles marking the outlines of an early colonial home which once stood here, creating a ghostly house on still days. A map showing the sculpture sites is available from Sydney Town Hall (p.124) or the City Exhibition Space (p.114) or there are details at Ⓦwww.cityofsydney.nsw.gov.au.

demolished in 1846. The museum is totally original in its approach, presenting history in an interactive manner, through exhibitions, film, photography and multimedia, though you may come away feeling less well informed than you expected. A key feature of the museum are the special exhibitions – about four each year – so it's worth finding out what's on before you go.

First Government Place, a public square in front of the museum, preserves the site of the original Government House: its foundations are marked out in different coloured sandstone on the pavement. The museum itself is built of honey-coloured sandstone blocks, using the different types of tooling available from the earliest days of the colony right up to modern times: you can trace this development from the bottom to the top of the facade. Near the entrance, **Edge of the Trees**, an emotive sculptural installation which was a collaboration between a European and an Aboriginal artist, conveys the complexity of a shared history that began in 1788.

Inside, the **auditorium** on level 2 shows a fifteen-minute video explaining the background and aims of the museum. Back on level 1 a video screen shows images of the bush, sea and sandstone Sydney as it was before the arrival of Europeans, while on level 2, recordings of Aboriginal people are combined with video images to help the viewer reflect on contemporary experience. At the dark and creepy **Bond Store** on level 3, holographic "ghosts" relate tales of old Sydney as an ocean port. On the same level, a whole area is devoted to some rather wonderful **panoramas** of Sydney Harbour with views of the harbour itself from the windows.

There's also an excellent **gift shop** with a wide range of photos, artworks and books on Sydney. Quite separate from the museum is the expensive, licensed *MOS* **café**, on First Government Place; usually filled with lawyers at lunchtime, it's agreeably peaceful for a (reasonably priced) coffee at other times.

King Street to Liverpool Street

Further south from Martin Place, the streets get a little more interesting. The rectangle between Elizabeth, King, George and Park streets is Sydney's prime shopping area, with a number of beautifully restored **Victorian arcades** (the Imperial Arcade, Strand Arcade and Queen Victoria Building are all worth a look) and Sydney's two **department stores**, the very upmarket David Jones on the corner of Market and Elizabeth streets, established over 160 years ago, and the more populist but still quality-focused Grace Bros on Pitt Street Mall.

The landmark **Sydney Tower** (daily 9am–10.30pm, Sat until 11.30pm; viewing gallery and Skytour $19.80; ⓦ www.sydneyskytour.com.au), on the corner of Market and Pitt streets, a giant golden gearstick thrusting up 305m, is the tallest poppy in the Sydney skyline – and its observation level is the highest in the entire southern hemisphere, though management must ruefully admit the tower's height is just beaten by the spire of the Sky Tower in Auckland, New Zealand, which is 23m taller. The 360-degree view from the observation level is especially fine at sunset, and on clear days you can even see the Blue Mountains, 100km away. The observation deck is packaged with the **Skytour** on entry-lift level, a tacky "virtual ride" introduction to a clichéd Australia that lasts forty long minutes. Unfortunately, the addition of Skytour has doubled the entry price to Centrepoint Tower and no single ticket is available; the best advice is to steer clear of this assault to the intellect and the senses and go straight to the top. To see the same view, without the crowds, and help put the saved $20 towards a meal, there are a couple of **revolving restaurants** at the top of the tower; the tower revolution takes about seventy minutes and nearly all the tables are by the windows (bookings ☏02/8223 3800). It costs $75 for a three-course dinner in the level 1 restaurant (Tues–Sat from 5pm) or there is a daily buffet lunch or dinner on level 2 (Mon–Sat lunch $40, dinner and Sun lunch $50).

Nearby, several fine old buildings – the State Theatre, the Queen Victoria Building and the Town Hall – provide a pointed contrast. If heaven has a hallway, it surely must resemble that of the restored **State Theatre**, just across from the Pitt Street Mall at 49 Market St, host to the Sydney Film Festival (see p.187). Step inside and take a look at the ornate and glorious interior of this picture palace opened in 1929 – a lavishly painted, gilded and sculpted corridor leads to the lush, red and wood-panelled foyer. To see more of the interior, you'll need to attend the Sydney Film Festival or other events held here, such as concerts and drama, or you can go on a self-guided tour (Mon–Fri 11.30am–3pm; 1hr; $12). Otherwise, pop into the beautiful little *Retro Cafe*, attached, for a coffee.

The stately **Queen Victoria Building** (abbreviated by locals to the QVB), taking up the block bounded by Market, Druitt, George and York streets, is another of Sydney's finest. Stern and matronly, a huge statue of Queen Victoria herself sits outside the magnificent building. Built as a market hall in 1898, two years before her death, the long-neglected building was beautifully restored and reborn in 1986 as an upmarket shopping mall with the focus on fashion: from the basement up, the four levels become progressively upmarket (shopping hours Mon–Sat 9am–6pm, Thurs until 9pm, Sun 11am–5pm; building open 24hr). The interior is magnificent, with its beautiful woodwork, gallery levels and antique lifts; Charles I is beheaded on the hour, every hour, by figurines on the ground-floor mechanical clock. From Town Hall station you can walk right through the basement level (mainly bustling food stalls) and continue via the Sydney Central Plaza to Grace Bros Department Store, emerging on Pitt Street without having to go outside.

In the realm of architectural excess, however, the **Town Hall** is king – you'll find it across from the QVB on the corner of George and Druitt streets. It was built during the boom years of the 1870s and 1880s as a homage to Victorian England, and has a huge organ inside its Centennial Hall, giving it the air of a secular cathedral. Throughout the interior different styles of ornamentation compete for attention in a riot of colour and detail; the splendidly dignified toilets are a must-see. Concerts and theatre performances (details on the City Infoline Mon–Fri 9am–6pm; ☏02/9265 9007) set off the splendiferous interior perfectly.

Down to Chinatown

Between Town Hall and Central station, **George Street** becomes increasingly downmarket. Along the way you'll pass Chinatown, in the area known as **Haymarket**, and just beyond is Darling Harbour (see p.130). The short stretch between the Town Hall and Liverpool Street is for the most part teenage territory, a frenetic zone of **multiscreen cinemas**, pinball halls and fast-food joints; *Planet Hollywood* also attracts a keen stream of youngsters. The stretch is trouble-prone on Friday and Saturday nights when there are pleasanter places to choose to catch a film (see cinema listings, p.186). Things change pace at Liverpool Street, where Sydney's **Spanish corner** consists of a clutch of Spanish restaurants and the *Spanish Club*.

Sydney's **Chinatown** is a more full-blooded affair than Spanish corner. Through the Chinese gates, **Dixon Street Mall** is the main drag, buzzing day and night as people crowd into numerous restaurants, pubs, cafés, cinemas, food stalls and Asian grocery stores. Towards the end of January or in the first weeks of February, Chinese New Year is celebrated here with gusto: dragon and lion dances, food festivals and musical entertainment compete with the noise and smoke from strings of Chinese crackers. Friday nights are also a good time to visit, when a **night market** takes over Dixon and Little Hay streets (6pm–11pm). Just on the edge of Chinatown at the southern fringes of Darling Harbour, is the serene **Chinese Garden** (see p.132).

The area immediately south of Chinatown is enlivened every Friday, Saturday and Sunday by Sydney's oldest market, frenetic **Paddy's Market** (9am–4.30pm), in its undercover home at the corner of Thomas and Quay streets, next door to the Entertainment Centre. It's a good place to buy cheap vegetables, seafood, plants, clothes and bric-a-brac. Above the old market, the multilevel **Market City Shopping Centre**, has a very modern Asian feel and there's an excellent Asian food court (see p.166) on the top floor next to the Reading multiscreen cinema.

The historic precinct: Hyde Park, College Street and Macquarie Street

Lachlan Macquarie, reformist governor of New South Wales between 1809 and 1821, gave the early settlement its first imposing public buildings, clustered on the southern half of his namesake Macquarie Street. He had a vision of an elegant, prosperous city – although the Imperial Office in London didn't share his enthusiasm for expensive civic projects. Refused both money and expertise, Macquarie was forced to be resourceful: many of the the city's finest buildings were designed by the ex-convict architect Francis Greenway and paid for with rum money, the proceeds of a monopoly on liquor sales. Hyde Park was fenced off by Governor Macquarie in 1810 to mark the outskirts of his township, and with its war memorials and church, and peripheral museum and Catholic cathedral, is still very much a formal city park.

Hyde Park

From the Town Hall, it's a short walk east to **Hyde Park** along Park Street, which divides the park into two sections, with the Anzac Memorial in the southern half, and the Sandringham Memorial Gardens and Archibald Fountain in the north, overlooked by St James's Church across the northern boundary. From Queens Square, **St James's Church** (daily 9am–5pm; free tours 2.30pm) marks the entry to the park – the Anglican church, completed in 1824, is Sydney's oldest exisiting place of worship. It was one of Macquarie's schemes built to ex-convict Greenway's design, and the architect originally planned it as a courthouse – you can see how the simple design was converted into a graceful church. It's worth popping into the crypt to see the richly coloured **Children's Chapel** mural painted in the 1930s. Behind St James train station, the **Archibald Fountain** commemorates the association of Australia and France during World War I and near here is a **giant chess set** where you can challenge the locals to a match. Further south near Park Street, the Sandringham Memorial Gardens also commemorate Australia's war dead, but the most potent of these monuments is the famous **Anzac Memorial** at the southern end of the park (daily 9am–5pm; tours 11.30am & 1.30pm; free). Fronted by the tree-lined Pool of Remembrance, the thirty-metre-high cenotaph, unveiled in 1934, is classic Art Deco right down to the detail of Raynor Hoff's stylized soldier figures solemnly decorating the exterior.

College Street: the Australian Museum and St Mary's Cathedral

Facing Hyde Park across College Street, at the junction of William Street as it heads up to Kings Cross, the **Australian Museum** (daily 9.30am–5pm; 30min tours 10am–3pm on the hour; $8, special exhibitions extra; ⓦwww .austmus.gov.au) is primarily a museum of natural history, with an interest in human evolution and Aboriginal culture and history. The collection was founded in 1827, but the actual building, a grand sandstone affair with a facade of Corinthian pillars, wasn't fully finished until the 1860s and was extended in the 1980s. The core of the old museum is the three levels of the **Long Gallery**, Australia's first exhibition gallery, opened in 1855 to a public keen to gawk at the colony's curiosities. Many of the classic displays of the following hundred years remain here, Heritage-listed, contrasting with a very modern approach in the rest of the museum.

On the **ground floor**, the impressive **Indigenous Australian** exhibition looks at the history of Australia's Aboriginal people from the Dreamtime to more contemporary issues of the "stolen generation" and the freedom rides. The ground-floor level of the Long Gallery houses the **Skeletons** exhibit, where you can see a skeletal human going through the motions of riding a bicycle, for example. Level 1 is devoted to **minerals**, but far more exciting are the disparate collections on level 2 – especially the Long Gallery's **Birds and Insects** exhibit, which includes chilling contextual displays of dangerous spiders such as redbacks and funnelwebs. Past this section the **Biodiversity: Life Supporting Life** exhibition, looks at the impact of environmental change on the ecosystems of Australian animals, plants, and micro-organisms, around eighty percent of which do not naturally occur elsewhere, giving the country one of the highest levels of so-called biodiversity. In the newer section, **Search and Discover** is aimed at both adults and children, a flora and fauna identification centre with Internet access and books to consult, while the **Human Evolution** gallery traces the development of fossil evidence worldwide and ends with an exploration of archeological evidence of Aboriginal occupation of Australia. A separate section, **More Than Dinosaurs**, deals with fossil skeletons of dinosaurs and giant marsupials: best of all is the model of the largest of Australia's megafauna, the wombat-like Diprotodon, who may have roamed the mainland as recently as ten thousand years ago.

Stanley Street, off College Street just south of the museum, has a cluster of cheap Italian cafés and restaurants (see pp.169–171), and nearby Crown Street features Sydney's version of the *Hard Rock Cafe*. North up College Street is Catholic **St Mary's Cathedral** (Mon–Fri & Sun 6.30am–6.30pm, Sat 8am–6.30pm), overlooking the northeast corner of Hyde Park. The huge Gothic-style church opened in 1882, though the foundation stone was laid in 1821. In 1999 the cathedral at last gained the twin stone spires originally planned for the two southern towers by architect William Wardell in 1865. The cathedral also gained an impressive new forecourt – a pedestrianized terrace with fountains and pools – with the consolidation of two traffic-isolated parks into the large **Cook and Phillip Park**. Its **recreation centre** (Mon–Fri 6am–10pm, Sat & Sun 7am–8pm; swim $5) has a fifty-metre swimming pool, gym and an excellent vegetarian restaurant (see p.196). The remodelling also created a green link to The Domain.

Macquarie Street

The southern end of Governor Macquarie's namesake street is lined with the grand edifices that were the result of his dreams for a stately city: Hyde Park

Barracks, Parliament House, the State Library and the hospital he and his wife designed. The new Sydney – wealthy and international – shows itself on the corner of Bent and Macquarie streets in the curved glass sails of the 41-floor Aurora Place tower, designed by Italian architect Renzo Piano, co-creator of the extraordinary Georges Pompidou Centre in Paris. Macquarie Street neatly divides business from pleasure, separating the office towers and cramped streets of the CBD from the open spaces of The Domain and the Royal Botanic Gardens (see p.128).

Sandstone **Sydney Hospital**, the so-called "Rum Hospital", funded by liquor-trade profits, was Macquarie's first enterprise, commissioned in 1814 and therefore one of the oldest buildings in Australia. You can take a short cut through the grounds to The Domain and across to the Art Gallery of New South Wales (see p.128). One of the original wings of the hospital is now **NSW Parliament House** (Mon–Fri 9.30am–4pm; free guided tours: non-sitting days Mon–Fri 10am, 11am & 2pm, sitting days Tues 1.30pm; ℡02/9230 2111 or Ⓦ www.parliament.nsw.gov.au to check for parliamentary recesses), where as early as 1829 local councils called by the governor started to meet, making it by some way the oldest parliament building in Australia. Varied exhibitions in the foyer change about every fortnight – all represent community or public sector interests and range from painting, craft and sculpture to excellent photographic displays. You can listen in on question time (Tues–Fri 2.15pm) when the parliament is sitting. The other wing was converted into a branch of the **Royal Mint** in response to the first Australian goldrush, and for some time served as a museum of gold mining; most of the building has now been taken over by NSW Historic Trust offices, but a café (Mon–Fri 8am–4pm; licensed) extends onto the balcony looking over Macquarie Street, and some interpretive boards detail the Mint's history.

Next door, the **Hyde Park Barracks** (daily 9.30am–5pm; $7), designed by ex-convict Francis Greenway, was built in 1816, again without permission from London, to house six hundred male convicts. Now a museum of the social and architectural history of Sydney, it's a great place to visit for a taste of convict life during the early years of the colony: start at the top floor, where you can swing in re-creations of the prisoners' rough hammocks. Computer terminals allow you to search for information on a selection of convicts' history and background – several of those logged were American sailors nabbed for misdeeds while in Dublin or English ports (look up poor William Pink). Later the Barracks took in single immigrant women, many of them Irish, escaping the potato famine; an exhibition looks at their lives, and there's a moving monument in the grounds erected by the local Irish community. Look out too for the excellent temporary historical exhibitions (℡02/9223 8922 for details).

The **State Library of New South Wales** (Mon–Fri 9am–9pm, Sat & Sun 11am–5pm, Mitchell Library closed Sun; free guided tours Tues 11am & Thurs 2pm) completes the row of public buildings on the eastern side of Macquarie Street. This complex of old and new buildings includes the 1906 sandstone **Mitchell Library**, with an imposing Neoclassical facade gazing across to the verdant Botanic Gardens. Its archive of old maps, illustrations and records relating to the early days of white settlement and exploration in Australia includes the **Tasman Map**, drawn by the Dutch explorer Abel Tasman in the 1640s. The floor-mosaic in the foyer replicates his curious map of the continent, still without an east coast, and its northern extremity joined to Papua New Guinea. A glass walkway links the library with the modern building housing the General Reference Library. Free exhibitions relating to Australian history, art, photography and literature are a regular feature of its vestibules, while lectures, films and video shows take place regularly in the **Metcalfe Auditorium**, which holds free and ticketed events (℡02/9273 1770 or ⓦwww.slnsw.gov.au for details and bookings). The glass-roofed **café** on level 7 (Mon–Fri 10am–4.30pm, Sat & Sun 11am–3.30pm) is airy with masses of plants; it's a relaxing, inexpensive spot for lunch or just coffee and cake. It's also worth browsing in the library's **bookshop** on the ground floor, for an impressive collection of Australia-related books.

The Domain and the Royal Botanic Gardens

The Cook and Phillip Park fills in the gap between Hyde Park and **The Domain**, a much larger, plainer open space that stretches from behind the historic precinct on Macquarie Street to the waterfront, divided from the Botanic Gardens by the ugly Cahill Expressway and Mrs Macquaries Road. In the early days of the settlement, The Domain was the governor's private park; now it's a popular place for a stroll or a picnic, with the Art Gallery of New South Wales, an outdoor swimming pool and Mrs Macquaries Chair to provide distraction. On Sundays, assorted cranks and revolutionaries assemble here for **Speakers' Corner**, and every January thousands of people gather on the lawns to enjoy the free open-air concerts of the Sydney Festival (see p.188).

Art Gallery of New South Wales

Beyond St Mary's Cathedral, Art Gallery Road runs through The Domain to the **Art Gallery of New South Wales** (daily 10am–5pm; free general tours Mon & Sat 1 & 2pm, Tues–Fri hourly 11am–2pm, Sun 11am, 1 & 2pm; free except for special exhibitions, ℡02/9225 1744 or ⓦwww.artgallery.nsw.gov.au for details), whose collection was established in 1874. The original part of the building (1897) is an imposing Neoclassical structure with a facade inscribed with the names of important Renaissance artists, and principally contains the large collection of European art dating from the eleventh century to the twentieth; extensions were added in 1988, doubling the gallery space and providing a home for mainly Australian art. On level 1, the **Yiribana Gallery** was opened in 1994, devoted to the art and cultural artefacts of Aboriginal and Torres Strait Islanders; one of the most striking exhibits is the **Pukumani Grave Posts**, carved by the Tiwi people of Melville Island. A highly recommended half-hour performance here of dance and didgeridoo by an indigenous Australian (Tues–Sat noon), is well combined with the free one-hour tour of the indigenous collection (Tues–Sun 11am). Other highlights include some classic **Australian paintings** on level 4: Tom Roberts' romanticized shearing-shed scene *The Golden Fleece* (1894) and an altogether less idyllic look at rural Australia in Russell Drysdale's *Sofala* (1947), a depressing vision of a drought-stricken town. On level 5, the **photographic collection** includes Max Dupain's iconic *Sunbaker* (1939), an early study of Australian hedonism.

In addition to the galleries, there's an auditorium used for art lectures, an excellent bookshop, a coffee shop on level 2, and a restaurant on level 5 that attracts Sydneysiders for its food and atmosphere.

Mrs Macquaries Chair and "the Boy"

Beyond the Art Gallery, is the beginning of one of Sydney's most scenic routes – Mrs Macquaries Road, built in 1816 at the urging of the governor's wife, Elizabeth. The road curves down from Art Gallery Road to Mrs Macquaries Point, which separates idyllic Farm Cove from the grittier Woolloomooloo

Bay. At the end is the celebrated lookout point known as **Mrs Macquaries Chair**, a seat fashioned out of the rock. From here Elizabeth could admire her favourite view of the harbour on her daily walk in what was then the governor's private park. On the route down to the point, the **Andrew "Boy" Charlton Pool** is an open-air, saltwater swimming pool safely isolated from the harbour waters (daily Oct–April 6.30am–8pm; $4.50) on the Woolloomooloo side of the promontory, with views across to the engrossingly functional Garden Island Naval Depot. The "Boy", as the locals fondly call it, was named after the gold-medal-winning Manly swimmer, who turned 17 during the 1924 Paris Olympics. It's a popular hangout for trendy Darlinghurst types and sun-worshipping gays, even more so since its 2002 revamp. The much-glamourized pool now has its own café-restaurant, yoga classes and a regular Thursday night **biathlon** (running and swimming) open to all competitors.

The Royal Botanic Gardens

The **Royal Botanic Gardens** (daily 7am–sunset; free; ⓦ www.rbgsyd.gov.au), established in 1816, occupy the area between this strip of The Domain and the Opera House, around the headland on Farm Cove where the first white settlers struggled to grow vegetables for the hungry colony. While duckponds, a romantic rose garden and fragrant herb garden strike a very English air, look out for native birds and, at dusk, the fruit bats flying overhead (hundreds of the giant bats hang by day in the Palm Grove area near the restaurant) as the nocturnal possums begin to stir. There are examples of trees and plants from all over the world, although it's the huge, gnarled native Moreton Bay figs that stand out. The gardens provide some of the most stunning **views** of Sydney Harbour and are always crowded with workers at lunch time, picnickers on fine weekends, and lovers entwined beneath the trees.

Many **paths** run through the gardens. A popular and speedy route (roughly 15min) is to start at the northern gates near the Opera House and stroll along the waterfront path to the gates separating it from The Domain, through here and up the **Fleet Steps** to Mrs Macquaries Chair (see above). Within the northern boundaries of the park, the sandstone mansion glimpsed through a garden and enclosure is the Gothic Revival **Government House** (built 1837–45), seat of the governor of New South Wales, and still used for official engagements by the governor, who now lives in a private residence. The stately interior has limited opening hours (free guided tour every half hour Fri–Sun 10am–3pm; 45min; ⓣ02/9931 5222 or ⓦ www.hht.net.au for more details) but you are free to roam the grounds (daily 10am–4pm). Further south, just inside the gardens at the end of Bridge Street, the **Conservatorium of Music** is housed in what was intended to be the servants' quarters and stables of Government House. Public opinion in 1821, however, deemed the imposing castellated building far too grand for such a purpose and a complete conversion, including the addition of a concert hall, gave it a loftier aim of training the colony's future musicians. Conservatorium students have traditionally given free lunch-time recitals every Tuesday and Friday at 1.10pm during term time. A two-year renovation project, finished in 2000, uncovered an earlier convict-era site; the consequent archeological dig was incorporated into the redesign.

Below the Conservatorium, the remaining southern area of the gardens has a herb garden, a cooling palm grove, a popular café by the duckponds, and the **Sydney Tropical Centre** (daily 10am–4pm; $2.20), where a striking glass pyramid and adjacent glass arc respectively house native tropical plants and exotics. At an entrance to the park in the southeast corner is the **visitors** centre (daily 9.30am–5pm), where free **guided tours** of the gardens commence (daily 10.30am; 1hr–1hr 30min). If you're short of time, the **Trackless Train** runs through the gardens every twenty minutes (Mon–Fri 9.30am–5pm, Sat & Sun 9.30am–6pm; all-day hop-on-hop-off service $10) between the visitors centre and the entrance near the Opera House.

Darling Harbour and around

Darling Harbour, once a grimy industrial docks area, lay moribund until the 1980s, when the State Government chose to pump millions of dollars into the regeneration of this prime city real estate as part of the Bicentenary Project. The huge redevelopment scheme around Cockle Bay included the building of the above-ground monorail, which particularly irked environmentalists, but despite bitter protests the new shopping and entertainment precinct opened in 1988. In many ways it's a thoroughly stylish redevelopment of the old wharves around Cockle Bay – the glistening water channels that run along Palm Avenue are a great piece of modern design – and Darling Harbour and the surrounding areas of **Ultimo** and **Pyrmont** have plenty else to offer: museums, an aquarium, entertainment areas, a shopping mall, an IMAX cinema, a children's playground, gardens, a casino, and a convention and exhibition centre. However, it's only recently that Sydneysiders themselves have embraced it. Sneered at for years by locals as tacky and touristy, it took the recent Cockle Bay and King Street Wharf development – an upmarket café and restaurant precinct on the eastern side of the waterfront, with several lively bars and a huge nightclub (*Home*, see p.180) – to finally lure locals in to the much-maligned area.

Behind the development, and accessible from it, is **Darling Park**, with paths laid out in the shape of a waratah flower. The western side of Darling Harbour is dominated by rather ugly modern chain hotels ironically providing some of the view for the stylish Cockle Bay wharf diners.

It's only a five-minute walk from the Town Hall to **get to Darling Harbour**; from the Queen Victoria Building, walk down Market Street and along the overhead walkway. Further south there's a pedestrian bridge from Bathurst Street, or cut through on Liverpool Street to Tumbalong Park. Alternatively, the **monorail** (see p.97) runs from the city centre to one of three stops around Darling Harbour. Getting to the wharf outside the Sydney Aquarium by **ferry** from Circular Quay gives you a chance to see a bit of the harbour – STA ferries stop at McMahons Point and Balmain en route. Matilda Cruises's Rocket Express runs from the Commissioners Steps, outside the MCA, and goes via the casino at Pyrmont. By **bus**, the #443 goes from Circular Quay via the QVB, Pyrmont and the casino, or the #449 runs between the casino, the Powerhouse Museum, Broadway Shopping Centre and Glebe. The large site can be navigated on the dinky **People Mover train** (daily: Oct–April 10am–6pm; May–Sept 10am–5pm; every 15 min, full circuit 20min; $3.50). The **Darling Harbour Super Ticket** ($48) includes entry to the Aquarium and the Chinese Garden, a monorail ride, a one-hour Rocket Harbour Express Cruise, a meal at the Aquarium's café and discounts at the IMAX cinema, the Powerhouse Museum and on the People Mover train; purchase it at the Aquarium, see p.132.

There are always festivals and events here, particularly during school holidays. To find out what's on, visit the **Darling Harbour Visitor Information Centre** (daily 9.30am–5.30pm; ☎02/9281 0788, ⓦwww.darlingharbour .com.au), next door to the IMAX cinema.

Darling Harbour map showing: John Street Square, Star City, Foxtel, Darling Harbour, Pyrmont Bay, Maritime Heritage Centre, King St Wharf, Star City Casino, Pyrmont Bay Park, National Maritime Museum, Pyrmont Bay, HMAS Vampire, Sydney Aquarium, Ferry Wharf, King St, Harbourside, Harbourside Shopping Centre, Darling Park, Ferry Wharf, Cockle Bay, Marina, Fish Market, Sydney Fish Market, Cockle Bay Wharf, Darling Park, Convention Centre, Convention Centre, Motor World Museum, Convention, Western Distributor, Panasonic IMAX Theatre, Wentworth Park, PYRMONT, Wentworth Park, Darling Walk, Kiosk, Darling Park, Exhibition Centre, Tumbalong Park, Wentworth Park Greyhound Track, Exhibition Centre, Chinese Garden, ULTIMO, Wentworth Park, Entertainment Centre, Powerhouse Museum, Wentworth Park — Metro Light Rail, Haymarket — Metro Monorail, Haymarket, HAYMARKET, DARLING HARBOUR, University of Technology, Paddy's Market and Market City

Tumbalong Park and around

The southern half of Darling Harbour, just beyond Chinatown and the Entertainment Centre, is focused around **Tumbalong Park**, reached from the city via Liverpool Street. Backed by the Exhibition Centre, this is the "village green" of Darling Harbour and serves as a venue for open-air concerts and free public entertainment. The area surrounding it is perhaps Darling Harbour's most frenetic – at least on weekends and during school holidays – as most of

131

the attractions, including a free playground and a stage for holiday concerts, are aimed at children. For some peace and quiet head for the adjacent **Chinese Garden** (daily 9.30am–5pm; $4.50), completed for the Bicentenary in 1988 as a gift from Sydney's sister city Guangdong; the "Garden of Friendship" is designed in the traditional southern Chinese style. Although not large, it feels remarkably calm and spacious – a great place to retreat from the commercial hubbub to read a book, smell the fragrant flowers that attract birds and listen to the lilting Chinese music that fills the air. The balcony of the traditional tea-room offers a bird's-eye view of the dragon wall, waterfalls, a pagoda on a hill and carp swimming in winding lakes.

Beyond the children's playground, the Southern Promenade of Darling Harbour is dominated by the **Panasonic IMAX Theatre** (films hourly from 10am; 2-D films $16.20, 3-D $17.30; ☎02/9281 3300, ⓦwww.imax.com.au). Its giant eight-storey-high cinema screen shows a constantly changing programme from their 100-film library, with an emphasis on scenic wonders, the animal kingdom and adventure sports.

Sydney Aquarium

Beside the eastern side of **Pyrmont Bridge** – a pedestrian walkway across Cockle Bay, linking the two sides of the harbour – is the impressive **Sydney Aquarium** (daily 9.30am–10pm; $23, Aquarium Pass including STA ferry from Circular Quay $27.40; see also Darling Harbour Super Ticket, p.130; ⓦwww.sydneyaquarium.com.au). If you're not going to get the chance to explore the Barrier Reef, the aquarium makes a surprisingly passable substitute.

The entry level exhibits freshwater fish from the Murray–Darling basin, Australia's biggest river system, but speed past these to get to the two under-water walkways, where you can wander in complete safety among sharks and gigantic stingrays. Another area features exotic species from the Great Barrier Reef, including a mass of glowing, undulating Moon Jellyfish. The Great Barrier Reef Oceanarium finishes with a huge floor-to-ceiling tank where you can sit and be mesmerized by the movement and colour of the underwater world while classical music plays. Alongside all the fish, there are also platypus, seals and fairy penguins on display. Removed here after becoming lost or injured, the seals at least seem to be enjoying themselves in their glass-walled outdoor pool, but the sad-looking Fairy penguins appear most out of place.

The National Maritime Museum and around

On the western side of Pyrmont Bridge the **National Maritime Museum** (daily 9.30am–5pm, Jan until 6pm; $10, or with guided tours: of destroyers HMAS *Vampire* and HMAS *Onslow* $14, of barque *James Craig* $14, of destroyers and *James Craig* $20; ⓦwww.anmm.gov.au), with its distinctive modern architecture topped by a wave-shaped roof, highlights the history of Australia as a seafaring nation, but goes beyond maritime interests to look at how the sea has shaped Australian life, covering everything from immigration to beach culture and Aboriginal fishing methods in seven core themed exhibitions. Highlights include the "Merana Eora Nora – First People" exhibition, delving into indigenous culture, and "Navigators – Defining Australia" which focuses on the seventeenth-century Dutch explorers. Outside several vessels are moored: the navy destroyer, the *Vampire*, and a submarine, the *Onslow*, are permanently on display, while a collection of historic vessels, including a 1970s Vietnamese refugee boat, are rotated. The pleasant alfresco café here, which you don't have to enter the museum to use, has views of the boats. The bronze **Welcome Wall** outside the museum pays honour to Australia's six million immigrants.

Included in the museum entry is a behind-the-scenes tour of the **Maritime Heritage Centre** at Wharf 7, just beyond the museum off Pirrama Road and beside Pyrmont Bay Park, where conservation and model-making work takes place and some of the collection is stored. At the wharf, the Sydney Heritage Fleet's collection of restored boats and ships is moored, including the beautifully restored 1874 square-rigger the *James Craig* (cruises available; see p.112) and the replica of James Cook's *Endeavour*. Just nearby, the two-level **Harbourside Shopping Centre** provides opportunities for souvenir shopping: don't miss the first-floor **Gavala: Aboriginal Art & Cultural Education Centre** (daily 10am–7pm) a very spacious and relaxed store selling Aboriginal art, clothing, accessories and music, and the only fully Aboriginal-owned and -run store in Sydney, with all profits going back to the artists.

Ultimo: the Powerhouse Museum and around

From Tumbalong Park, a signposted walkway leads to **Ultimo** and its **Powerhouse Museum** on Harris Street (daily 10am–5pm; $10, free first Sat in month; free 45min tour daily 11.30am & 1.30pm; ⓦwww.phm.gov.au; monorail to Haymarket). Located, as the name suggests, in a former power station, this is arguably the best museum in Sydney, an exciting place with fresh ideas, combining arts and sciences, design, sociology and technology under the same roof – and even fashion, with the much-anticipated "Fashion of the Year" display every November. There are several big temporary exhibitions on each year, with themes as varied as "Star Wars: The Magic of Myth", "Tokyo Street Style" and "Bush Tucker Connections". The permanent displays are varied, presented with an interactive approach that means you'll need hours to investigate the five-level museum properly. The entrance level is dominated by the huge **Boulton and Watt Steam Engine**, first put to use in 1875 in a British brewery; still operational, the engine is often loudly demonstrated. The **Kings Cinema** on level 3, with its original Art Deco fittings, suitably shows the sorts of newsreels and films a Sydneysider would have watched in the 1930s. Judging by the tears at closing time, the **special children's areas** have proved a great success. On level 5, there's a licensed restaurant, with a more inexpensive courtyard cafeteria downstairs. The souvenir shop is also worth a browse for some unusual gifts.

Three blocks north, at 320 Harris St, the **Motor World Museum** (Fri–Sun, public holidays & daily during school holidays 10am–5pm; $11; monorail to Convention) houses just under two hundred vehicles on three levels. There's the usual mix of vintage cars and 1950s American-style cruisers, a comprehensive collection of Australian automobilia, plus the latest model cars, rally cars and motorcycles.

Pyrmont: Star City Casino and the Sydney Fish Market

Frantic redevelopment is taking place at **Pyrmont**, which juts out into the water between Darling Harbour and Blackwattle Bay. The once dilapidated suburb was Sydney's answer to Ellis Island in the 1950s when thousands of immigrants disembarked at the city's main overseas passenger terminal, Pier 13. Today the former industrial suburb, which had a population of only nine hundred in 1988, is being transformed into a residential suburb of twenty thousand with A$2 billion worth of investment. With the New South Wales government selling A$97 million worth of property, this has been one of the biggest concentrated sell-offs of land in Australia. The area has certainly become glitzier, with Sydney's casino, Star City, and two TV companies –

Channel Ten and Foxtel –based here. Harris Street has filled up with new shops and cafés, and the area's old pubs have been given a new lease of life. The approach to the spectacularly cabled **Anzac Bridge** (complete with statue of an Australian and New Zealand Army Corps soldier) – Sydney's newest – cuts through Pyrmont and saves between fifteen and twenty minutes' travelling time to Sydney's inner west.

Beyond the Maritime Museum, on Pyrmont Bay, palm-fronted **Star City** is the spectacularly tasteless 24-hour Sydney casino. As well as the casino, the building houses two theatres, fourteen restaurants, cafés and theme bars, souvenir shops, a convenience store and a nightclub. The casino interior itself is a riot of giant palm sculptures, prize cars spinning on rotating bases, Aboriginal painting motifs on the ceiling, Australian critters scurrying across a red desert-coloured carpet and an endless array of flashing poker machines. Dress code is smart casual. You can just wander in and have a look around or a drink, without betting. Nearby **Pyrmont Bay Park** is a shady spot to rest, and on the first Saturday of the month it hosts an early morning **Growers Market** (7–11am). To **get to the casino** bus #888 runs in a loop to and from Gresham Street in the city via the QVB to the casino and the Exhibition Centre in Darling Harbour, or the #443 runs from Circular Quay via Phillip and Market streets and the QVB. The Light Rail (see p.97) pulls in right underneath the casino.

The best reason to visit this area, though, is the **Sydney Fish Market**, on the corner of Pyrmont Bridge Road and Bank Street (daily 7am–4pm; ⓦwww.sydneyfishmarket.com.au), only a ten-minute walk via Pyrmont Bridge Road from Darling Harbour. The market is the second-largest seafood market in the world for variety of fish, after the massive Tsukiji market in Tokyo. You need to visit early to see the **auctions** (Mon–Fri only, with the biggest auction floor on Friday; buyers begin viewing the fish at 4.30am, auctions begin 5.30am, public viewing platform opens 7am); buyers log into computer terminals to register their bids.

You can take away oysters, prawns and cooked seafood and eat picnic-style on waterfront tables. Everything is set up for throwing together an impromptu meal – there's a bakery, a deli, a bottle shop and a grocer. Alternatively, you can eat in at *Doyles*, the casual and more affordable version of the famous *Doyles* fish restaurant in Watsons Bay; at the excellent sushi bar; or have dirt-cheap fish and chips or a crack-of-dawn espresso at the *Italian Fish Market Cafe* (Mon–Fri 4am–4pm, Sat & Sun 5am–5pm); retail shops open at 7am. The **Sydney Seafood School** (☎02/9004 1111) offers seafood cookery lessons, from Thai-style to French provincial, plus a two-hour, early-morning tour of the selling floor (first Thurs of month; $20 includes a coffee).

To **get to** the fish market, take the Light Rail from Central to Fish Market station on Miller Street. Bus #501 runs from outside the Electricity Australia Building, on the corner of George and Bathurst streets, to right outside the market on Bank Street; otherwise take bus #443 from Circular Quay or the QVB, and it's a five-minute walk from the corner of Harris Street and Pyrmont Bridge Road.

The inner west

West of the centre, immediately beyond Darling Harbour, the inner-city areas of **Glebe** and **Newtown** surround Sydney University, their vibrant cultural mix enlivened by large student populations. On a peninsula north of Glebe and west of The Rocks, **Balmain** is a gentrified former working-class dock area popular for its village atmosphere, while en route **Leichhardt** is a focus for Sydney's Italian community.

Glebe

Right by Australia's oldest university, **Glebe** has gradually been evolving from a café-oriented student quarter to more upmarket thirtysomething territory with a New Age slant. Indeed, it's very much the centre of alternative culture in Sydney, with its yoga schools, healing centres and organic food shops. **Glebe Point Road** is filled with a mix of cafés with trademark leafy courtyards, restaurants, bookshops and secondhand and speciality shops as it runs uphill from **Broadway**, becoming quietly residential as it slopes down towards the water of Rozelle Bay. The side streets are fringed with renovated two-storey terraced houses with white-iron lacework verandahs. Not surprisingly, Glebe is popular with backpackers and offers several hostels (see "Accommodation", p.106). The **Broadway Shopping Centre** on nearby Broadway, but linked to Glebe by an overhead walkway from Glebe Point Road opposite one of the

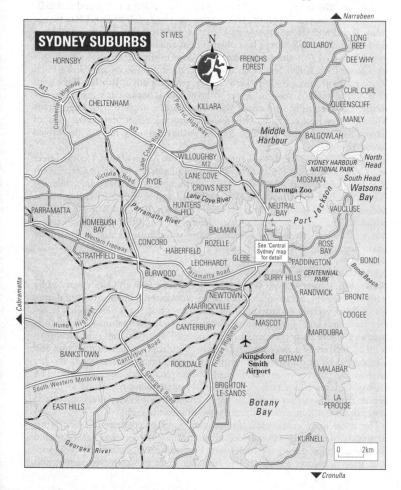

street's favourite cafés, *Badde Mannors* (see p.167), has begun to alter Glebe's laid-back, almost villagey feel, though it is handy if you're staying in the area, with its supermarkets, speciality food shops, huge food court, record, book and clothes shops and twelve-screen cinema.

Just before the beginning of Glebe Point Road, on Broadway, **Victoria Park** has a very pleasant, heated outdoor swimming pool (Mon–Fri 6am–7.15pm, Sat & Sun 7am–5.45pm; $3.50) with attached gym and a sophisticated café. From the park, a path and steps lead up into **Sydney University**, inaugurated in 1850; your gaze is led from the walkway up to the Main Quadrangle and its very Oxford-reminiscient clock tower and Great Hall. You're welcome to wander round the grounds.

Glebe itself is at its best on Saturday, when **Glebe Market**, which takes place on the shady primary school playground a couple of blocks up from Broadway, is in full swing. On sale are mainly secondhand clothes and accessories, plus plants, CDs, the inevitable crystals and a bit of bric-a-brac. At 49 Glebe Point Rd, you'll find the excellent **Gleebooks** – one of Sydney's best-loved bookshops (see "Shopping", p.191). The original, now selling secondhand and children's books only, is worth the trek further up at 191 Glebe Point Rd, past St Johns Road and Glebe's pretty park. Across the street and a couple of blocks further on is one of Sydney's best independent cinemas, the Valhalla (see p.186), established in 1976; stop for a coffee next door in the relaxed and very popular *Craven Cafe*. A few blocks on from here, the action stops and Glebe Point Road trails off into a more residential area, petering out at **Jubilee Park** with characterful views across the water to boats and Rozelle Bay's container terminal. The pleasantly landscaped waterfront park, complete with huge, shady Moreton Bay fig trees and a children's playground, offers an unusual view of far-off Sydney Harbour Bridge framed within Sydney's newest, the cabled Anzac Bridge.

Buses #431, #433 and #434 run to Glebe from Millers Point, George Street and Central station; #431 and #434 run right down the length of Glebe Point Road to Jubilee Park, with the #434 continuing on to Balmain, while the #433 runs half-way turning at Wigram Road and heads on to Balmain. The Metro Monorail (see p.97) runs between Central station and Rozelle stopping at the "Glebe" stop, just off Pyrmont Bridge Road, and the "Jubilee" stop at Jubilee Park. Otherwise it's a fifteen-minute **walk** from Central up Broadway to the beginning of Glebe Point Road.

Newtown and around

Newtown, separated from Glebe by Sydney University and easily reached by train (to Newtown station), is another up-and-coming, inner-city neighbourhood. What was once a working-class district – a hotchpotch of derelict factories, junkyards and cheap accommodation – has transformed into a trendy, offbeat area where body piercing, shaved heads and weird fashions rule. Newtown is characterized by a large gay and lesbian population, a rich cultural mix and a healthy dose of students and lecturers from the nearby university. It also has an enviable number of great cafés and diverse restaurants, especially Thai. The Dendy Cinema complex (see p.186), is a central focus, more like a cultural centre than just a film theatre, with its attached bookshop, excellent record store, and streetfront café, all open daily and into the night.

The main drag, gritty, traffic-fumed and invariably pedestrian-laden **King Street**, is filled with unusual secondhand, funky fashion and speciality and homeware shops; during the **Newtown Festival** (early Oct to early Nov) various shop windows let themselves be taken over by young, irreverent and in-your-face art, and the festival ends with a huge party in Camperdown Memorial Park, with hundreds of stalls and live music. Check out Gould's Book Arcade at no. 32, a vast and chaotic secondhand book warehouse that is a Sydney institution, browsable until midnight. Veer off King Street for Pretty Dog, at 1 Brown St, which is open daily for a good range of retro secondhand gear and over-the-top club and streetwear.

King Street becomes less crowded south of Newtown train station as it heads for a kilometre towards **St Peters** train station, but it's well worth strolling down to look at the more unusual speciality shops (buttons, ribbons, cacti, Chinese medicine amongst them), as well as some small art galleries and yet more retro clothes shops. It's also stacked with culturally diverse restaurants from Turkish to African, and closer to St Peters station are several colourful businesses aimed at the local Indian community. You'll also find a couple of theatres and a High School for the Performing Arts.

Enmore Road stretching west from King Street, opposite Newtown station, is a similar mix of speciality shops and evidence of a migrant population. Look out for the long-established Mocha Coffee at no. 16, which sells a big range of blends; Amera's Palace, at no. 83, stocking everything a belly dancer might need; Lemon Spread at no. 101, full of new and secondhand quirky collectable items; The Bead Company at no. 116; and Artwise Amazing Paper at no. 186. There's a range of restaurants, too, from Swedish to Thai. It's generally much quieter than Newtown, except when a big-name band or comedian is playing at the Art Deco **Enmore Theatre**, at no. 130. When it's closed, you can play boardgames at the cosy booths of the *Box Office Cafe*. At the end of Enmore Road, Enmore Park hides the **Annette Kellerman Aquatic Centre** and its tiny heated 33-metre pool (Mon–Sat 5.30am–8.30pm, Sun 8am–6pm; $3.50). Combine a swim with a home-made ice cream from Serendipity Icecream, just across the road at no. 333. Beyond here, the very multicultural, lively but down-at-heel **Marrickville** stretches out.

Erskineville Road, stretching from the eastern side of King Street marks the beginning of the adjoining suburb of **Erskineville**, a favourite gay address; the *Imperial Hotel* at 35 Erskineville Rd (see also p.181), has long hosted popular drag shows, and is famous as the starting point of the gang in the hit film *Priscilla, Queen of the Desert*.

Buses #422, #423, #426 and #428 run to Newtown from Circular Quay via Castlereagh Street, Railway Square and City Road. They go down King Street as far as Newtown station, where the #422 continues to St Peters and the others turn off to Enmore and Marrickville. Alternatively, catch a **train** to Newtown, St Peters or Erskineville stations.

Leichhardt to Rozelle

It's almost an hour from The Rocks to Balmain by the #440 bus, via **Leichhardt**, Sydney's "Little Italy", where the famous **Norton Street** strip of cafés and restaurants runs off ugly **Parramatta Road**. Leichhardt is very much up and coming – shiny, trendy, Italian cafés keep popping up all along the strip, though its focus is the upmarket cinema complex, The Palace (which hosts an Italian film festival in early Dec), with its attached record store, bookshop and Internet café and nearby shopping mall. Opposite, two-storey Beurkelow's bookstore sells both old and new books and has a café. Closer to Parramatta Road, the still-to-be-completed **Italian Forum** was meant to be a showcase for the Italian community. It is arranged around a central square, with two col-lonnaded levels surrounding it. Upmarket fashion shops, featuring Italian fash-ion of course, are on the top level, while downstairs there are hosts of mostly

Italian eateries, with alfresco tables on the square – heaving at lunch on a Sunday when the whole Forum is full of Italian families. An Italian Cultural Centre and a local library branch have been planned to open down here for years now, but the spaces still stand empty. However, the lively, much-loved and enduring *Bar Italia* (see p.168), a fifteen-minute walk further down Norton at the extent of the tempting array of eateries, is still the best Italian café in Leichhardt. The real heart of Italian Sydney, however, is a little further west on Ramsay St in **Haberfield**; one of Sydney's best pizzerias, *La Disfida* is here at no. 109; catch bus #436 from Leichhardt. As well as the #440 you can also take bus #436, #437 or #438 from George Street in the city.

From Leichhardt, the #440 bus continues to Darling Street, which runs from **Rozelle** right down to Balmain's waterfront. Rozelle, once very much the down-at-heel, poorer sister to Balmain is now emergently trendy with the Sydney College of the Arts and the Sydney Writers' Centre based here as well as lots of cafés, bookshops, speciality shops, gourmet grocers, restaurants, made-over pubs, and designer home-goods stores. There's also the ritzy Rozelle Bay Super Yacht Marina on James Craig Road; enjoy the views with a glass of wine at the bar-restaurant *Liquidity*, with its huge glassfront overlooking the water. A weekend **flea market** takes place in the grounds of Rozelle Primary School on Darling Street, near Victoria Road (Sat & Sun 9am–4pm).

To **get to Rozelle**, take bus #440 from George Street in the city or from Leichhardt. The Metro Light Rail from Central, Pyrmont or Glebe has a "Lilyfield" stop, about 500m from Balmain Road: follow Catherine Street and Grove Street to emerge opposite the Sydney College of the Arts campus.

Balmain and Birchgrove

Balmain, directly north of Glebe, is less than 2km from the Opera House, by ferry from Circular Quay to Darling Street Wharf. But, stuck out on a spur in the harbour and kept apart from the centre by Darling Harbour and Johnston's Bay, it has a degree of separation that has helped it retain its slow, villagey atmosphere and made it the favoured abode of many writers and filmmakers. Like better-known Paddington, Balmain was once a working-class quarter of terraced houses that has gradually been gentrified. The docks at White Bay are still important, though, and Balmain hasn't completely forsaken its roots. Darling Street rewards a leisurely stroll, with a bit of browsing in its speciality shops (focused on clothes and gifts), and grazing in its restaurants and cafés. It, and the surrounding backstreets, are also blessed with enough watering holes to warrant a pub crawl – two classics are the *London Hotel* on Darling Street and the *Exchange Hotel* on Beattie Street. The best time to come is on Saturday, when the lively **Balmain Market** occupies the shady grounds of St Andrews Church (7.30am–4pm), on the corner opposite the *London Hotel*. An assortment of books, handmade jewellery, clothing and ceramics, antiques, home-made chocolates, cakes and gourmet foods and organic produce are sold. The highlight is an eclectic array of food stalls in the church hall where you can snack your way from the Himalayas to Southern India.

On the Parramatta River side of Balmain, looking across to Cockatoo Island, Elkington Park is where you'll find the quaint **Dawn Fraser Swimming Pool** (Oct–April daily 6.30am–7.30pm; $3), an old-fashioned harbour pool named after the famous Australian Olympic swimmer, a Balmain local. For long, stunning sunsets and wow-worthy real estate, meander from here down the backstreets towards water-surrounded **Birchgrove** on its finger of land, where Louisa Road leads to Birchgrove wharf; from here you can catch a ferry back to Circular Quay, or stay and relax in the small park on Yurulbin Point.

Goat Island

Just across the water from Balmain East, **Goat Island** is the site of a well-preserved gunpowder magazine complex. The sandstone buildings, including a barracks, were built by two hundred convicts between 1833 and 1839. Treatment of the convicts was harsh: 18-year-old Charles Anderson, a mentally impaired convict with a wild, seemingly untameable temper who made several attempts to escape, received over twelve hundred lashes in 1835 – and if that wasn't enough, he was sentenced to be chained to a rock for two years in an attempt to control him, a cruel punishment even by the standards of the day. Tethered to the rock, which you can still see, his unhealed back crawling with maggots, he slept in a cavity hewn into the sandstone "couch". Sydneysiders would row up and tease him for entertainment. Eventually Anderson ended up on Norfolk Island (see p.388), where under the humane prisoner reform experiments of Alexander Maconochie, the feral, abused 24-year-old made a startling transformation. The island is looked after by the NPWS, who run various **tours** with Sydney Ferries leaving from Cadman's Cottage in The Rocks (bookings essential on ☎02/9247 5033), making the most of the island's gruesome history. Tours range from a Heritage Tour (Mon & Fri–Sun 1pm; 2hr 15min; $19.80), and a night-time **Gruesome Tales tour** (Sat 6pm depending on sunset; 3hr 20min; $24.20; over-12s only; supper included).

For a **self-guided tour** of Balmain and Birchgrove, buy a *Balmain Walks* leaflet ($2.20) from Balmain Library, 370 Darling St, or the well-stocked Pentimento Bookshop, at no. 275. To **get to** Balmain, you can catch a ferry from Circular Quay to Darling Street Wharf in Balmain East, where the #442 bus waits to take you up Darling Street to Balmain proper. Buses #433 and #434 run out to Balmain via George Street, Railway Square and Glebe Point Road and down Darling Street; faster is the #442 from the QVB, which crosses Anzac Bridge and heads to Balmain Wharf. Birchgrove can be reached via ferry from Circular Quay or on the #441 from the QVB.

The inner east

To the east, **Surry Hills**, **Darlinghurst** and **Paddington**, once rather scruffy working-class suburbs, have long been taken over and revamped by the young, arty and upwardly mobile. **Kings Cross** is home to Sydney's red-light district as well as many of its tourists, while in adjacent **Woolloomooloo** container ships tie up at the docks. Further east, the "Cross" fades into the more elegant suburbs of **Potts Point** and **Elizabeth Bay**, which trade on their harbour views.

Surry Hills

Surry Hills, directly east of Central station from Elizabeth Street, was traditionally the centre of the rag trade, which still finds its focus on Devonshire Street. Rows of tiny terraces once housed its original poor, working-class population, many of them of Irish origin. Considered a slum by the rest of Sydney, the dire and overcrowded conditions were given fictional life in Ruth Park's *The Harp in the South* trilogy (see "Books", p.1200), set in the Surry Hills of the 1940s. The area became something of a cultural melting pot with European postwar immigration, and doubled as a grungy, studenty, muso heartland in the 1980s. By the mid-1990s, however, the slickly fashionable scene of neighbouring Darlinghurst and Paddington had finally taken over Surry Hills' twin focal points of parallel **Crown Street**, filled with cafés, swanky restaurants, funky

Aboriginal Sydney

Just beyond Surry Hills, and only 2km from the glitter and sparkle of Darling Harbour, **Redfern** is Sydney's underbelly. Around the **Eveleigh Street** area, Australia's biggest urban Aboriginal community lives in **"the Block"**, a squalid streetscape of derelict terrace houses and rubbish-strewn streets not far from Redfern train station – the closest Sydney has to a no-go zone. The Aboriginal Housing Company, set up as a co-operative in 1973, has had problems paying for repairs and renovation work. Recently the company began knocking down derelict houses and relocating people, which has upset many residents who want to keep the community together.

clothes shops and designer galleries, and leafy **Bourke Street**, where a couple of Sydney's best cafés lurk among the trees. As rents have gone up, only **Cleveland Street**, running west to Redfern and east towards Moore Park and the Sydney Cricket Ground (see p.143), traffic-snarled and lined with cheap Lebanese and Turkish restaurants, retains its ethnically varied population.

A good time to visit Surry Hills is the first Saturday of the month when a lively **flea market**, complete with tempting food stalls, takes over the small Shannon Reserve, on the corner of Crown and Fouveaux streets, overlooked by the **Clock Hotel**. The hotel, which has expanded out of all recognition from its 1840s roots, is emblematic of the new Surry Hills, with its swish restaurant and cocktail bar. The artistic side of Surry Hills can be experienced nearby at the **Brett Whiteley Studio** at 2 Raper St (Sat & Sun 10am–4pm; by appointment Thurs & Fri ☎02/9225 1881; $7); walk about three blocks further south down Crown Street, and it's off Davies Street. Whitely was one of Australia's best-known contemporary painters with an international reputation by the time he died in 1992 of a heroin overdose at the age of 53; wild self-portraits and expressive female nudes were some of his subjects, but it is his sensual paintings of Sydney Harbour for which he is best known, painted from his home in Lavender Bay. In 1986 Whitely converted this one-time factory into a studio and living space, and since his death it has become a museum and gallery showing his paintings and memorabilia.

Surry Hills is a short **walk** uphill from Central (Devonshire St or Elizabeth St exit); take Fouveaux or Devonshire Street and you'll soon hit Crown, or it's an even quicker stroll from Oxford Street, Darlinghurst, heading south along Crown or Bourke streets.

Darlinghurst, Paddington and Woollahra

Oxford Street, from Hyde Park to Paddington and beyond, is a major amusement strip. Waiting to be discovered, here and in the side streets, is an array of nightclubs, restaurants, cafés and pubs. Around **Darlinghurst**, Oxford Street is the focus of Sydney's very active gay and lesbian movement. Hip and bohemian, Darlinghurst mingles seediness with a certain hedonistic style: some art students and clubbers never leave the district – save for a coffee at the Cross or a swim at the "Boy" in The Domain (see p.129). There's another concentration of cafés, restaurants and fashion on Liverpool Street, while Victoria Street is a classic pose strip with the legendary, street-smart *Bar Coluzzi* (see p.170). At 148 Darlinghurst Rd, the impressive **Sydney Jewish Museum** (Mon–Thurs & Sun 10am–4pm, Fri 10am–2pm; $10; ◎ www.sydneyjewishmuseum .com.au) is housed in the old Maccabean Hall, a Jewish meeting point for over seventy years. Sixteen Jews were among the convicts who arrived with

△ Paddington

the First Fleet, and the high-tech, interactive museum explores over two hundred years of Australian Jewish experience. An introductory fifteen-minute film discusses anti-Semitism through the ages, and the Holocaust is covered in harrowing detail with Australian survivors' videotaped testimony. You can pick up the pamphlet *Guide to Jewish Sydney* from the museum.

Paddington, a slum at the turn of the twentieth century, became a popular hangout for hipsters during the late 1960s and 1970s. Since then, yuppies have taken over and turned Paddington into the smart and fashionable suburb it is today: the Victorian-era terrace houses, with their iron-lace verandahs reminiscent of New Orleans, have been beautifully restored. Many of the terraces were originally built in the 1840s to house the artisans who worked on the graceful, sandstone **Victoria Barracks** on the southern side of Oxford Street, its walls stretching seven blocks, from Greens Road to just before the Paddington Town Hall on Oatley Road. **Shadforth Street**, opposite the entrance gates, has many examples of the original artisans' homes. Though the barracks are still used by the army, there are free guided tours (Thurs 10am) – complete with army band – while a small **museum** is open to visitors (Sun 10am–3pm). On the other side of Oxford Street the small, winding, tree-lined streets are a pleasant place for a stroll, and offer a chance to wander into the many small art galleries or to take some liquid refreshment. Head via Underwood and Heeley streets to **Five Ways**, where you'll find cafés, speciality shops and a typically gracious old boozer, the *Royal Hotel* (see p.172). There are more shops on Elizabeth Street running off Oxford Street, but the main action is, of course, on Oxford Street itself, most lively on Saturday from 10am to around 4pm, when the crowds descend on **Paddington Market** in the church grounds at no. 395. As well as being a prime spot to show off and hang out, it's a sure-fire source of great presents, with leather goods, jewellery and clothes – old and new – at the top of the list, and an emphasis on Australian-made products.

Woollahra, along Oxford Street from Paddington, is even more moneyed but contrastingly staid, with expensive **antique shops** and **art galleries** along **Queen Street** replacing the fashion and trendy lifestyle focus of Paddington's shops. Leafy Moncur Street hides *jones the grocer* (at no. 68), where Woollahra locals gather for coffee at the long central table; it sells stylishly packaged, outlandishly priced and utterly delicious groceries and gourmet treats.

Transport heading in this direction includes **buses** #380 and #382 from Circular Quay which both run up Elizabeth Street and along Oxford Street. The #378, from Central station, also heads along Oxford Street. Bus #389 from Circular Quay runs via Elizabeth and William streets in the city and along Glenmore Road and Hargrave Street, Paddington, to emerge on Oxford Street.

Centennial Parklands

South of Paddington and Woollahra lies the green expanse of **Centennial Parklands**, (daily sunrise to sunset; ⓦ www.cp.nsw.gov.au) opened to the citizens of Sydney at the Centennial Festival in 1888. With its vast lawns, rose gardens and extensive network of ponds complete with ducks it resembles an English country park, but is reclaimed at dawn and dusk by distinctly antipodean residents, including possums and flying foxes. The park is crisscrossed by walking paths and tracks for cycling, rollerblading, jogging and horse riding: you can rent a bike or rollerblades nearby or hire a horse from the adjacent equestrian centre and then recover from your exertions in the café with its popular outside tables (though packed and hideously slow on weekends, even for takeaways) or, in the finer months, stay on until dark and catch an outdoor film with the Moonlight Cinema (see p.186). Adjoining **Moore Park** is incorporated under the banner of Centennial Parklands and has facilities for tennis, golf, grass-skiing, bowling, cricket and hockey; it's also home to the Sydney Cricket Ground and Fox Studios (see below). Pick up a free map of the Centennial Parklands from the Park Office (Mon–Fri 8.30am–5.30pm; ☎02/9339 6699) near the café and easily reached from the Paddington gates off Oxford Street (opposite Queen Street).

To get to the park you can take a **bus** from Central station (#372, #393 or 395) or from Elizabeth Street in the city, before Museum station (#L90, #391, #394 or #396; #394 and #396 extend to and from Circular Quay). Alternatively you could take a bus to Oxford Street, Paddington and then walk in via the Paddington gates or further along at the Woollahra gates (opposite Ocean Street). There's plenty of free parking.

The Sydney Cricket Ground (SCG)

The venerated institution of the **Sydney Cricket Ground (SCG)** earned its place in cricketing history for Don Bradman's score of 452 not out in 1929, and for the controversy over England's bodyline bowling techniques in 1932. Ideally, proceedings are observed from the lovely 1886 Members Stand, while sipping an icy gin and tonic – but unless you're invited by a member, you'll end up elsewhere, probably drinking beer from a plastic cup. Cricket spectators aren't a sedate lot in Sydney, and the noisiest barrackers will probably come from "the Hill" – or the Doug Walters Stand, as it's officially known. Still the cheapest spot to sit, the concreted area was once a grassy hill where rowdy supporters threw empty beer cans at players and each other, but beer is now strictly rationed. The Bill O'Reilly Stand gives comfortable viewing until the afternoon, when you'll be blinded by the sun, whereas the Brewongle Stand provides consistently good viewing. Best of all is the Bradman Stand, with a view directly behind the bowler's arm, and adjacent to the exclusive stand occupied by members, commentators and ex-players. The Test to see here is, of course, **The Ashes** (see p.61); the Sydney leg of the five tests, each for five days, begins on New Year's Day. For information, scores, prices and times, call ☎02/9360 6601. You can buy tickets at the gates on the day subject to availability, or purchase them in advance from Ticketek (☎02/9266 4800). Die-hard cricket fans can go on a **tour** of the SCG on non-match days (Mon–Fri 10am & 1pm; 1hr 30min; $19.50; ☎02/9380 0383; ⓦwww.scgt.nsw.gov.au), which also covers the **Aussie Stadium** next door, where the focus is on international and national rugby league and rugby union: when the **State of Origin** rugby league competition (see p.61) is on here, its coverage produces some of the highest ratings on Australian television.

Fox Studios

Also within Moore Park, immediately southeast of the SCG, are the Murdoch-owned **Fox Studios** (ⓦwww.foxstudios.com.au), constructed at a cost of $A300 million within the old Showgrounds site, where the Royal Agricultural Society held its annual Royal Easter Show from 1882 until 1997; in 1998 the huge show took place for the first time at the A$380 million Sydney Showground at the Olympic site at Homebush Bay. The **Professional Studio**, opened in May 1998, takes up over half the site and has facilities for both film and television production, with six high-tech stages and industry tenants on site providing everything from casting services to stunt professionals. Films made here include *The Matrix*, *Mission Impossible II*, Baz Luhrmann's *Moulin Rouge*, and Episode I and II of the *Star Wars* saga. The **public areas** of the site opened in late 1999 and are focused around a state-of-the-art, twelve-screen **cinema complex**, complete with digital surround-sound and VIP lounges, and a smaller four-screen arthouse cinema; international film premieres are sometimes held here.

The old **Show Ring**, once the preserve of wood-chopping competitions and rodeo events, is now used for everything from open-air cinema and circuses, to the weekend market (Sat & Sun 10am–6pm) and the midweek Farmers Market (Wed noon–7pm). The **Bungy Trampoline** (Wed–Sun 10am–6pm; $10) here is designed to give you the thrill of a bungy jump without the danger.

The Show Ring is surrounded by the gleaming shops, cafés, restaurants and bars of pedestrianized **Bent Street**. The upmarket **shops** (casual clothing, beach, sports and fashion chains, a bookshop, record store and a bush outfitters), over twenty of them, stay open daily until 10pm. The two major **bars** are close to each other – the contemporary-styled but casual *Dog Gone Bar* and the traditional pub atmosphere of the *Fox and Lion* – by the big outdoor screen which shows music-video **Channel [V]**. The screen is outside the channel's live studio and there are often shows being taped both inside and out, which are free to attend; check the What's On page of their website ⓦ www.channelv.com.au for show times. Other bars include the stylish lounge atmosphere of *Arena Bar & Bistro*, and the action-focused **Sports Central** (Mon–Thurs & Sun noon to midnight, Fri & Sat noon–2am) with ten-pin bowling lanes ($6 before 5pm, $12.50 after 5pm), American pool tables ($3 per game), electronic games ($2 per game), and Fox Sports broadcasts. There's a stand-up comedy venue, the *Comedy Store* (see p.185) and a music venue, *City Live* (see p.179). Including the bars, there are fifteen **places to eat**: an eat-in gourmet deli, wood-fired pizza, Chinese seafood, noodles and classy contemporary Australian are among the choices.

The theme park area of Fox Studios, the Backlot, was a commercial failure, closing in 2001. However, there's still a lot to attract families including the mini-golf course by the old Backlot entrance (the film-themed murals are still there) and the indoor **Lollipops Playground**, pricey but perfect for a rainy day (Mon–Thurs 9.30am–7pm, Fri 9.30am–8pm, Sat 9am–8pm, Sun 9am–7pm; under-2s $7.90, 2–9 years $10.90, adults $4 includes a coffee). Just outside are two free playgrounds and a carousel ($2.50).

To get to Fox Studios catch buses #339, #392, #394 or #396 from Central, Wynyard, or Town Hall. There's plenty of parking, free for the first two hours.

Kings Cross and Potts Point

The preserve of Sydney's bohemians in the 1950s, **Kings Cross** became an R&R spot for American soldiers during the Vietnam war, and is now Sydney's red-light district, its streets prowled by prostitutes, drug abusers, drunks, strippers and homeless teenagers. It is also a bustling centre for backpackers and other travellers, especially around leafy and quieter Victoria Street; the two sides of "the Cross" (as locals call it) coexist with little trouble, though some of the tourists seem a little surprised at where they've ended up, and it can be rather intimidating for lone women. However, the constant flow of people makes it relatively safe, and it's always lively, with places to eat and drink that stay open all hours.

Heading up the rise of **William Street** from Hyde Park and past Cook and Phillip Park and the Australian Museum, **Kings Cross** beckons with its giant neon Coca-Cola sign. By day, William Street is hardly attractive with its streams of fast and fumey traffic heading to the eastern and western distributors and its car rental firms; at night, there are even fewer pedestrians as hardcore transvestite streetwalkers and kerb crawling patrons go about their business. However, with the development of the Cross City Tunnel, planned to be open to traffic by the end of 2004, there's a grand vision for William Street to become a European-style boulevard – tree-lined, traffic-calmed, and with wide pavements for café tables and strolling pedestrians. At the top of the hill, **Darlinghurst Road** is Kings Cross's "action zone". At weekends, an endless stream of suburban voyeurs emerge from the underground Kings Cross station, near the beginning of the Darlinghurst Road "sin" strip, and trawl along the streets licking ice creams as touts try their best to haul them into tacky strip-joints and sleazy nightclubs. The strippers and sleaze extend to the end of Darlinghurst Road at the El Alamein fountain in the paved Fitzroy Gardens, which though pleasant-looking, is the usual hangout of some fairly abusive drunks. It's much changed on Sundays when it's taken over by a small arts and crafts market. Generally, Kings Cross is much more subdued during the day, with a slightly hungover feel to it: local residents emerge and it's a good time to hang out in the cafés.

From Fitzroy Gardens, tree-lined **Macleay Street** runs through quieter, upmarket **Potts Point** with its tree-lined streets, apartment blocks, classy boutique hotels, stylish restaurants, buzzy cafés and occasional harbour glimpses over wealthier Elizabeth Bay (see p.147), just to the east; this is as close to European-living as Sydney gets. The area was Sydney's first suburb, developed land granted to John Wylde in 1822 and Alexander Macleay in 1826. The grand villas of colonial bureaucrats gave way in the 1920s and 1930s to **Art Deco** residential apartments and in the 1950s big splendid hotels were added to the scene. The area is set to go more upmarket and more residential with the conversion of all the large hotels into luxury apartments.

South Sydney Council has produced a free **Kings Cross Walking Tour** map available from the library off Fitzroy Gardens which points out some of the Art Deco architecture the area is known for and provides some background history.

You can get to Kings Cross by **train** or **bus** (#311, #324 or #325 from Circular Quay; #327 from Gresham St in the city), or it's not too far to walk. For a quieter route than William Street, you could head up from The Domain via Cowper Wharf Road in Woolloomooloo, and then up the McElhone Stairs to Victoria Street.

Woolloomooloo

North of William Street just below Kings Cross, **Woolloomooloo** occupies the old harbourside quarter between The Domain and the grey-painted fleet of the **Garden Island Naval Depot**. Once a narrow-streeted slum, Woolloomooloo is quickly being transformed, though its upmarket apartment developments sit uneasily side by side with problematic community housing, and you should still be careful at night in the backstreets. There are some lively pubs and some more old-fashioned quiet drinking holes, as well as the legendary **Harry's Café de Wheels** on Cowper Wharf Road, a 24-hour pie-cart operating since 1945 and popular nowadays with Sydney cabbies and hungry clubbers in the small hours.

Next door, the once picturesquely dilapidated **Woolloomooloo Finger Wharf**, dating from 1917, is now an upmarket complex comprising a marina, luxury residential apartments, the cool *W Hotel* (see p.105) and its funky *Water Bar*, and some slick restaurants with alfresco dining – *Otto* (see p.171), *Manta Ray* and *Shimbashi Soba* are the swankiest. The general public are free to wander along the wharf and even go inside: there's a free exhibition space with a changing theme in the centre. Anyone can afford a cake and pastry at the

Parisian-feel *Laurent Boulangerie Pâtisserie* (see p.171), or you can grab a pie from *Harry's* and sit for free on the other side of the wharf.

Woolloomooloo is best reached by foot from Kings Cross by taking the **McElhone Stairs** or the **Butlers Stairs** from Victoria Street; alternatively take bus #311 from Kings Cross, Circular Quay or Central station.

The Harbour

Loftily flanking the mouth of Sydney Harbour are the rugged sandstone cliffs of North Head and South Head, providing spectacular viewing points across the calm water to the city 11km away, where the Harbour Bridge spans the sunken valley at its deepest point. The many coves, bays, points and headlands of Sydney Harbour, and their parks, bushland and swimmable beaches are rewarding to explore. However, harbour beaches are not as clean as ocean ones, and after storms are often closed to swimmers (see pp.151–153). Finding your way by ferry is the most pleasurable method: services run to much of the **North Shore** and to harbourfront areas of the **eastern suburbs**. The eastern shores are characterized by a certain glitziness and are the haunt of the nouveaux riches, while the leafy North Shore is very much old money. Both sides of the harbour have pockets of bushland which have been incorporated into **Sydney Harbour National Park**, along with five islands, two of which – Goat Island and Fort Denison – can be visited on tours (see p.139 and p.120; the other three – Shark Island, Clark Island and Rodd Island – are bookable for picnics but you must provide your own transport. The NPWS publishes an excellent free map detailing the areas of the national park and its many walking tracks available from Cadman's Cottage in The Rocks (see p.119).

Elizabeth Bay to South Head

The suburbs on the hilly southeast shores of the harbour are rich and exclusive. The area around **Darling Point**, the enviable postcode 2027, is the wealthiest in Australia, supporting the lifestyle of waterfront mansions and yacht-club memberships enjoyed by some-time residents Nicole Kidman and Lachlan Murdoch. A couple of early nineteenth-century mansions, Elizabeth Bay House and Vaucluse House, are open to visitors, giving an insight into the life of the pioneering upper crust, while the ferry to **Rose Bay** gives a good view of the pricey contemporary real estate; the bay is close to beautiful **Nielson Park** and the surrounding chunk of Sydney Harbour National Park. At South Head, **Watsons Bay** was once a fishing village, and there are spectacular views from **The Gap** in another section of the national park. Woollahra Council (☎02/9391 7000, Ⓦwww.woollahra.nsw.gov.au) has walk brochures detailing three newly developed **waterside walks**: the 5.5-kilometre (3hr) **Rushcutters Bay** to Rose Bay harbour walk, which can then be continued with the eight-kilometre (4.5hr) walk to Watsons Bay, and the fascinating five-kilometre cliffside walk from Christison Park in **Vaucluse** (off Old South Head Road) to Watsons Bay and **South Head**, with shipwreck sites, old lighthouses and military fortifications along the way.

Buses #324 and #325 from Circular Quay via Pitt Street, Kings Cross and Edgecliff cover the places listed below, heading to Watsons Bay via New South Head Road; #325 detours at Vaucluse for Nielson Park. Bus #327 runs between Martin Place and Bondi Junction stations via Edgecliff station and Darling Point.

Elizabeth Bay and Rushcutters Bay

Barely five minutes' walk northwest of Kings Cross, **Elizabeth Bay** is a well-heeled residential area, centred on **Elizabeth Bay House**, at 7 Onslow Ave (Tues–Sun 10am–4.30pm; $7; bus #311 from either Railway Square or Circular Quay, or walk from Kings Cross station), a grand Regency residence with fine harbour views, built in 1832. Heading southeast, you're only a few minutes' walk from **Rushcutters Bay Park**, wonderfully set against a backdrop of the yacht- and cruiser-packed marina in the bay; the marina was recently revamped for the 2000 Olympics sailing competition. You can take it all in from the tables outside the very popular *Rushcutters Bay Kiosk*. The **tennis courts** at Rushcutters Bay Tennis Centre (daily 8am–9pm or 10pm; courts $20 per hour, $24 after 4pm and on Sat & Sun; racket rental $3; bookings ℡02/9357 1675) are popular, and if you don't have anyone to play, the managers will try to provide a hitting partner for you.

Double Bay and Rose Bay

Continuing northeast to **Darling Point**, McKell Park provides a wonderful view across to **Clarke Island** and **Bradleys Head**, both part of Sydney Harbour National Park; follow Darling Point Road (bus #327 from Edgecliff station). Next port of call is **Double Bay**, dubbed "Double Pay" for obvious reasons. The noise and traffic of New South Head Road are redeemed by several excellent antiquarian and secondhand bookshops (see p.191), while in the quieter "village", some of the most exclusive shops in Sydney are full of imported designer labels and expensive jewellery. Eastern suburbs' socialites meet on Cross Street, where the swanky pavement cafés are filled with well-groomed women in Armani outfits. Double Bay's hidden gem is **Redleaf Pool** (daily Sept–May dawn–dusk; free), a peaceful, shady harbour beach enclosed by a wooden pier you dive off or just laze on and there's an excellent café here. A ferry stops at both Darling Point and Double Bay; otherwise catch buses #324, #325 or #327.

The ferry to **Rose Bay** gives you a chance to check out the waterfront mansions of **Point Piper** as you skim past. Rose Bay itself is a haven of exclusivity, with the verdant expanse of the members-only Royal Sydney Golf Course. Directly across New South Head Road from the course, waterfront **Lyne Park**'s **seaplane** service has been based here since the 1930s (see "Listings", p.196). Rose Bay is also a popular **windsurfing** spot; you can rent equipment from Rose Bay Aquatic Hire (see p.196).

Nielson Park and Vaucluse

Sydney Harbour National Park emerges onto the waterfront at Bay View Hill, where the 1.5-kilometre **Hermitage walking track** to Nielson Park begins; the starting point, Bay View Hill Road, is off South Head Road between the Kambala School and Rose Bay Convent (bus #324 or #325). The walk takes about an hour, with great views of the Opera House and Harbour Bridge, some lovely little coves to swim in and a picnic ground and sandy beach at yacht-filled **Hermit Point**. Extensive, tree-filled **Nielson Park**, on Shark Bay, is one of Sydney's delights, a great place for a swim, a picnic, or refreshment at the popular café. The decorative Victorian-era mansion, **Greycliffe House**, built for William Wentworth's daughter in 1852 (see overleaf), is now the headquarters of Sydney Harbour National Park; if it's open (no regular hours) pop in for information on other waterfront walks. With views across the harbour to the city skyline, the park is a prime spot to watch both the New Years' Eve fireworks and the yachts racing out through the heads on Boxing Day.

Beyond Shark Bay, Vaucluse Bay shelters the magnificent Gothic-style 1803 **Vaucluse House** and its large estate on Wentworth Road (Tues–Sun & public holiday Mondays 10am–4.30pm, grounds open daily 10am–5pm; $7), with tearooms in the grounds for refreshment. The house's original owner, explorer and reformer William Wentworth, was a member of the first party to cross the Blue Mountains. In 1831 he invited four thousand guests to Vaucluse House to celebrate the departure of the hated Governor Darling – the climax of the evening was a fireworks display which burned "Down with the Tyrant" into the night sky. To get here, walk from Nielson Park along Coolong Road (or take bus #325). Beyond Vaucluse Bay, narrow **Parsley Bay**'s shady finger of a park is a popular picnic and swimming spot, crossed by a picturesque pedestrian suspension bridge.

Watsons Bay and South Head

On the finger of land culminating in South Head, with an expansive sheltered harbour bay on its west side, and the treacherous cliffs of The Gap on its ocean side, **Watsons Bay** was one of the earliest settlements outside of Sydney Cove. In 1790 Robert Watson was one of the first signalmen to man the clifftop flagstaffs nearby and by 1792 the bay was the focus of a successful fishing village; the quaint old wooden fishermen's cottages are still found on the tight streets around Camp Cove. It's an appropriate location for one of Sydney's longest-running fish restaurants, *Doyles*, by the old Fishermans Wharf (see p.172), now the ferry terminal (accessible by ferry from Circular Quay, or Rocket Harbour Express Cruise from Darling Harbour – see p.130). In fact *Doyles* has taken over the waterfront here, with two restaurants, a takeaway, and a seafood bistro in the bayfront beer garden of *Doyles Watsons Bay Hotel*.

Spectacular ocean views are just a two-minute walk away through grassy Robertson Park, across Gap Road to **The Gap** (buses terminates just opposite – the #324, #325, and faster #L24 from Circular Quay, and the #L82 from Circular Quay via Bondi Beach), whose high cliffs are notorious as a place to commit suicide. You can follow a walking **track** north from here to South Head through another chunk of **Sydney Harbour National Park**, past the HMAS Watson Military Reserve where you can detour up the road to look at the Memorial Chapel (daily 9am–4pm) and beautifully framed water views from its picture window. The track heads back to the bay side, and onto Cliff Street which leads to **Camp Cove**, a tiny palm-fronted harbour beach popular with families; a small kiosk provides refreshments.

Alternatively, reach Camp Cove by walking along the Watsons Bay beach and then along Pacific Street and through Green Point Reserve. From the northern end of Camp Cove, steps lead up to a boardwalk which will take you to **South Head** (470m circuit), the lower jaw of the harbour mouth affording fantastic views of Port Jackson and the city, via Sydney's best-known **nudist beach**, Lady Jane (officially "Lady Bay"), a favourite gay haunt. It's not very private, however: a lookout point on the track provides full views and ogling tour boats cruise past all weekend. From Lady Bay, it's a further fifteen minutes' walk along a boardwalked path to South Head itself, past nineteenth-century fortifications, lighthouse cottages, and the picturesquely red-and-white-striped Hornby Lighthouse.

The North Shore

The **North Shore** is generally more affluent than the South. **Mosman** and **Neutral Bay** in particular have some stunning waterfront real estate, priced to match. It's surprising just how much harbourside bushland remains intact here

– "leafy" just doesn't do it justice – and superbly sited amongst it all is **Taronga Zoo**. A ride on any ferry lets you gaze at beaches, bush, yachts and swish harbourfront houses and is one of the chief joys of this area.

North Sydney and around

North Sydney has been associated with pure fun since the 1930s – beside the Harbour Bridge on Lavender Bay at **Milsons Point**, you can't miss the huge laughing clown's face that belongs to **Luna Park**. Generations of Sydneysiders have walked through the grinning mouth, and the park's old rides and conserved 1930s fun hall, complete with period wall murals, slot machines, silly mirrors and giant slippery dips, have great nostalgia value for locals. Luna Park was closed down for several years from the late 1980s until a grand reopening in January 1995 with a new clown's face – the eighth since the park began – closely resembling the 1950s model. Unfortunately, the amusement park noise upset nearby residents, and the park promptly closed again. Back in business in 2000, it shut down again in early 2001 for yet another bout of redevelopment; the park is now set to reopen in the first half of 2004. The ferry to Milsons Point Wharf from Circular Quay or Darling Harbour pulls up right outside (or train to Milsons Point station). Beyond the park a boardwalk goes right around Lavender Bay.

Right next door to Luna Park is Sydney's most picturesquely sited public swimming pool, with terrific views of the Harbour Bridge – the heated **North Sydney Olympic Pool**, Alfred South Street (Mon–Fri 5.30am–9pm, Sat & Sun 7am–7pm; $4.20). Revamped in 2001, there's a new indoor 25-metre pool as well as the old fifty-metre outdoor pool, a gym, sauna, spa, café, and an expensive restaurant, *Aqua*, overlooking the pool (be prepared to be ogled as you swim your laps).

Beyond Luna Park and the pool, amongst North Sydney's impersonal corporate zone, is the Catholic Church-run **Mary MacKillop Place Museum**, 7 Mount St (daily 10am–4pm; $8.25; ⓦ www.marymackillopplace.org.au). Housed in a former convent, it provides a surprisingly broadminded look at the life and times of Australia's first saint-in-waiting (MacKillop was beatified in 1995 and is entombed here) and sainthood itself. For the full story, see the account in Coonawarra (on p.851), where the nun's charitable educational work began. Take the train to North Sydney station and head north along Miller Street for about five minutes.

Just east of the Harbour Bridge and immediately opposite the Opera House, **Kirribilli** and adjacent Neutral Bay are mainly residential areas, although Kirribilli hosts a great **market** on the last Saturday of the month in Bradfield Park (7am–3.30pm), the best and biggest of several rotating markets on the North Shore (see "Markets" p.192). On Kirribilli Point, the current prime minister, native Sydneysider John Howard, lives in an official residence, **Kirribilli House** (snubbing Canberra, the usual PM's residence), a sore point with ACT locals. Next door, Admiralty House is the Sydney home of the Governor General and where the British royal family stay when they're in town.

Following the harbour round you'll come to upmarket **Neutral Bay**. A five-minute walk from Neutral Bay ferry wharf via Hayes Street and Lower Wycombe Road is **Nutcote**, at 5 Wallaringa Ave (Wed–Sun 11am–3pm; $7), the former home for 45 years of May Gibbs, the author and illustrator of the famous Australian children's book, *Snugglepot and Cuddlepie*, about two little gumnuts who come to life; published in 1918, it's an enduring classic.

Bush-covered **Cremorne Point**, which juts into the harbour here, is also worth a jaunt. Catch the ferry from Circular Quay and you'll find a quaint

149

open-access sea pool to swim in by the wharf; from here, you can walk right around the point to Mosman Bay (just under 2km), or in the other direction, past the pool, there's a very pretty walk along **Shell Cove** (1km).

Mosman Bay: Taronga Zoo

Mosman Bay's seclusion was first recognized as a virtue during its early days as a whaling station, since it kept the stench of rotting whale flesh from the Sydney Cove settlement. Now the seclusion is a corollary of wealth. The ferry ride into the narrow, yacht-filled bay is a choice one – get off at Mosman Wharf – and fittingly finished off with a beer at the unpretentious *Mosman Rowers' Club* (visitors welcome).

What Mosman is most famous for, though, is **Taronga Zoological Park** on Bradleys Head Road, with its superb hilltop position overlooking the city (daily: Jan 9am–9pm; Feb–Dec 9am–5pm; $23, Zoo Pass including return ferry and entry $28.40; ⓦwww.zoo.nsw.gov.au). The wonderful views and the natural bush surrounds are as much an attraction as the chance to get up close to some animals. The zoo houses bounding Australian marsupials, native birds (including kookaburras, galahs and cockatoos), reptiles, and sea lions and seals from the sub-Antarctic region. You'll also find exotic beasts from around the world, including those frequently photographed giraffes, sticking their necks out across a sublime harbour view. Established in 1916, the zoo has come a long way from its Edwardian roots, and the animals now live in more natural habitats, rather than cages (though the enclosures are getting a little shabby). You can get close to kangaroos and wallabies in the **Australian Walkabout** area, and the **koala house** gives you eye-level views; to get closer, arrange to have your photo taken patting a koala. For a guaranteed **hands-on experience** with a native animal, a VIP Gold Tour (daily 9.15am & 1.15pm; 1hr 30min–2hr; $55 includes zoo entry; book 24hr in advance on ⓣ02/9969 2777) will give you and a small group a session with a zookeeper, guiding you through the Australian animals. Keeper talks and feeding sessions – including a free-flight bird show and a seal show – run through the day; details are on the map handed out on arrival.

The zoo is best reached by ferry from Circular Quay to Taronga Zoo Wharf (every half-hour). Although there's a lower entrance near the wharf on Athol Road, it's best to start your visit from the upper entrance and spend several leisurely hours winding downhill to exit for the ferry. State Transit buses still meet the ferries for the trip uphill, but a better option is to take the **Sky Safari** cable car included in the entry price. Bus #247 from Wynyard or the QVB also goes to the zoo.

Bradleys Head

Beyond the zoo, at the termination of Bradleys Head Road, **Bradleys Head** is marked by an enormous mast that once belonged to HMS *Sydney*, a victorious World War II battleship. The rocky point is a peaceful spot with a dinky lighthouse and, of course, a fabulous view back over the south shore. A colony of ringtailed possums nests here, and boisterous flocks of rainbow lorikeets visit. The headland comprises another large chunk of **Sydney Harbour National Park**: you can walk to Bradleys Head via the six-kilometre Ashton Park **walking track** which starts near Taronga Zoo Wharf, and continues beyond the headland to Taylors Bay and Chowder Head, finishing at **Clifton Gardens**, where there's a jetty and sea baths on **Chowder Bay**. The now defunct military reserve which separates Chowder Bay from another chunk of Sydney Harbour National Park on Middle Head is now open to the public (see below), reached by a boardwalk from the northern end of Clifton Gardens. NPWS offers a fortnightly two-hour **bush food tour** of Bradleys Head (1st & 3rd Sun of month 1.30pm; $13.20; bookings ☎02/9247 5033).

Middle Harbour

Middle Harbour is the largest inlet of Port Jackson, its two sides joined across the narrowest point at **The Spit**. The Spit Bridge opens regularly to let tall-masted yachts through – much the best way to explore its pretty, quiet coves and bays (see box pp.112–113). Crossing the Spit Bridge, you can walk all the way to Manly Beach along the ten-kilometre Manly Scenic Walkway (see p.158). The area also hides some architectural gems: the mock-Gothic 1889 bridge leading to **Northbridge**, and the idyllic enclave of **Castlecrag**, which was designed in 1924 by **Walter Burley Griffin**, fresh from planning Canberra and intent on building an environmentally friendly suburb – free of the fences and the red-tiled roofs he hated – that would be "for ever part of the bush". Bus #144 runs to Spit Road from Manly Wharf, taking in a scenic route uphill overlooking the Spit marina. To get to Castlecrag, take bus #207 from Wynyard.

Between Clifton Gardens and Balmoral Beach, a military reserve and naval depot at **Chowder Bay** blocked coastal access to both **Georges Head** and the more spectacular **Middle Head** by foot for over a century. Since the military's recent withdrawal from the site, walkers can now trek all the way between Bradleys Head and Middle Head. The 1890s military settlement is open to visitors as a reserve, and NPWS offers tours exploring its underground fortifications (2nd & 4th Sun of month 10.30am; 2hr; $13.20). You can reach the military reserve entrance from the northern end of Clifton Gardens (see opposite) or walk from Balmoral Beach.

The bush of Middle Head provides a gorgeous backdrop to **Balmoral Beach** on Hunters Bay. The shady tree-lined harbour beach is very popular with families. Fronting the beach, there's something very Edwardian and genteel about palm-filled, grassy Hunters Park and its bandstand, which is still used for Sunday jazz concerts or even Shakespeare recitals in summer. The antiquated air is added to by the pretty white-painted **Bathers Pavilion** at the northern end, now converted into a restaurant and café (see p.174). There are two sections of beach at Balmoral, separated by **Rocky Point**, a noted picnicking spot. South of Rocky Point, the "baths" – actually a netted bit of beach with a boardwalk and lanes for swimming laps – have been here in one form or another since 1899; you can rent sailboards, catamarans and take lessons from the neighbouring boat shed (see p.197).

On the Hunters Bay side of Middle Head, tiny **Cobblers Beach** is officially **nudist**, and is a much more peaceful, secluded option than the more famous Lady Jane at South Head (see p.148). The hillside houses overlooking Balmoral have some of the highest price tags in Sydney: for a stroll through some prime real estate, head for **Chinamans Beach**, via Hopetoun Avenue and Rosherville Road. To get to Balmoral, catch a ferry to Taronga Zoo Wharf then bus #238 via Bradleys Head Road, or the ferry to Musgrave Street Wharf, then bus #233 or #257 via Military Road (#257 originates from Wynyard).

Ocean beaches

Sydney's **beaches** are among its great natural joys, key elements in the equation that makes the city special. The water and sand seem remarkably clean –

people actually fish in the harbour, and don't just catch old condoms and plimsolls – and at Long Reef, just north of Manly, you can find rock pools teeming with starfish, anemones, sea-snails and crabs, and even a few shy moray eels. In recent years, humpback whales have been regularly sighted from the Sydney headlands in June and July on their migratory path from the Antarctic to the tropical waters of Queensland, and southern right whales even occasionally make an exciting appearance in the harbour itself – the three whales cavorting in July 2002 caused a sensation.

Don't be lulled into a false sense of security, however: the beaches do have **perils** as well as pleasures. Some beaches are protected by special shark nets, but they don't keep out stingers such as bluebottles, which can suddenly swamp an entire beach; listen for loudspeaker announcements that will summon you from the water in the event of shark sightings or other dangers. Pacific **currents** can be very strong indeed – inexperienced swimmers and those with small children would do better sticking to the sheltered **harbour beaches** or **sea pools** at the ocean beaches. Ocean beaches are generally patrolled by **surf lifesavers** during the day between October and April (all year at Bondi): red and yellow flags (generally up from 6am until 6 or 7pm) indicate the safe areas to swim, avoiding dangerous rips and undertows. It's hard not to be impressed as **surfers** paddle out on a seething ocean, but don't follow them unless you're confident you know what you're doing. Surf schools can teach the basic skills, surfing etiquette and lingo: see "Surfing" in the listing sections. You can check daily **surf reports** on Ⓦ www.realsurf.com.

The final hazard, despite the apparent cleanliness, is **pollution**. Monitoring shows that it is nearly always safe to swim at all of Sydney's beaches – except after storm water, when storm water, currents and onshore breezes wash up sewage and other rubbish onto harbour beaches making them (as signs will indicate) unsuitable for swimming and surfing. To check pollution levels, consult the Beachwatch Bulletin (Ⓣ 1800 036 677, Ⓦ www.epa.nsw.gov.au).

Topless bathing for women, while legal, is accepted on many beaches but frowned on in others, so if in doubt, do as the locals do. There are two official nudist beaches around the harbour (see pp.148 and 151).

Bondi and the eastern beaches

Sydney's eastern beaches stretch from Bondi down to Maroubra. Heading south from Bondi, you can walk right along the coast to its smaller, less brazen but very lively cousin **Coogee**, passing through gay favourite **Tamarama**, family-focused, café-cultured **Bronte**, narrow **Clovelly** and **Gordons Bay**, the latter with an underwater nature trail. Randwick Council has designed the Eastern Beaches Coast Walk from Clovelly to Coogee and beyond to more downmarket **Maroubra**, with stretches of boardwalk and interpretive boards detailing environmental features. Pick up a free guide-map detailing the walk from the council's Customer Service Office, 30 Francis St, Randwick (Ⓣ 02/9399 0999; Ⓦ www.randwickcitytourism.com.au), or from the beach-front Coogee Bay Kiosk, Goldstein Reserve, Arden Street opposite *McDonald's*.

Bondi Beach

Bondi Beach is synonymous with Australian beach culture, and indeed the mile-long curve of golden sand must be one of the best-known beaches in the world. It's the closest ocean beach to the city centre; you can take a train to Bondi Junction and then a ten-minute bus ride, or drive there in twenty minutes. Big, brash and action-packed, it's probably not the best place for a quiet sunbathe and swim, but the sprawling sandy crescent really is spectacular.

Christmas Day on Bondi

For years backpackers and Bondi Beach on **Christmas Day** were synonymous. The beach was transformed into a drunken party scene, as those from colder climates lived out their fantasy of spending Christmas on the beach under a scorching sun. The behaviour and litter began getting out of control, and after riots in 1995, and a rubbish-strewn beach, the local council began strictly controlling the whole performance, with the idea of trying to keep a spirit of goodwill towards the travellers while also tempting local families back to the beach on what is regarded as a family day. Nowadays alcohol is banned from the beach on Christmas Day, and police enforce the rule with on-the-spot confiscations. However, a big **beach party** is organized: a large area of sand is fenced off, with a bar, DJs, food and entertainment running from 11am to 8pm. Around 3000 revellers cram into "the cage", while thousands of others – including a greater proportion of the desired family groups – enjoy the alcohol-free beach outside. In 2002, tickets for **A Sunburnt Christmas** were $30 in advance from record stores or $33.20 from Ticketek (℡02/9266 4800).

Red-tiled houses and apartment buildings crowd in to catch the view, many of them erected in the 1920s when Bondi was a working-class suburb. Although still residential, it's long since become a popular gathering place for backpackers from around the world (see box above).

The beachfront **Campbell Parade** is both cosmopolitan and highly commercialized, lined with cafés and shops. For a gentler experience, explore some of the side streets, such as **Hall Street**, where an assortment of kosher bakeries and delis serve the area's Jewish community, and some of Bondi's best cafés are hidden. On Sunday the **Bondi Beach markets** (10am–5pm), in the grounds of the primary school on the corner of Campbell Parade and Warners Avenue facing the northern end of the beach, place great emphasis on groovy fashion and jewellery. Between Campbell Parade and the beach, **Bondi Park** slopes down to the promenade, and is always full of sprawling bodies. Along the promenade there are two board ramps for **rollerblading** and **skateboarding**. The focus of the promenade is the arcaded, Spanish-style **Bondi Pavilion**, built in 1928 as a deluxe changing-room complex and converted into a community centre hosting an array of workshops, classes and events, from drama and comedy in the theatre and the Seagull Room (the former ballroom) to daytime dance parties and outdoor film festivals in the courtyard (programme details on ℡02/9130 3325 Mon–Fri, ℡02/9368 1253 Sat & Sun, ☯www.waverley.nsw.gov.au). The pavilion is now also the base for the **Sydney Fringe Festival** in January. Downstairs in the foyer, photos of Bondi's past are worth checking out, with some classic beach images of men in 1930s bathing suits, and there's an excellent **souvenir shop** (daily 9.30am–5.30pm) which utilizes lots of old-fashioned Bondi imagery. There's even a community-access **art gallery** (daily 10am–5pm) featuring changing exhibitions by local artists. In September, the Festival of the Winds, Australia's largest **kite festival**, takes over the beach.

Surfing is part of the Bondi legend, the big waves ensuring that there's always a pack of damp young things hanging around, bristling with surfboards. However, the beach is carefully delineated, with surfers using the southern end of the beach – so you shouldn't have to fear catapulting surfboards. There are two sets of flags for swimmers and boogie-boarders, with families congregating at the northern end near the sheltered saltwater pool (free), and everybody else using the middle flags. The beach is netted and there hasn't been a shark attack for over forty years. If the sea is too rough,

Bondi's surf lifesavers

Surf lifesavers are what made Bondi famous; there's a bronze sculpture of one outside the Bondi Pavilion. The surf lifesaving movement began in 1906 with the founding of the Bondi Surf Life Bathers' Lifesaving Club in response to the drownings that accompanied the increasing popularity of swimming. From the beginning of the colony, swimming was harshly discouraged as an unsuitable bare-fleshed activity. However, by the 1890s swimming in the ocean had become the latest fad, and a Pacific Islander introduced the concept of catching waves or **bodysurfing** that was to become an enduring national craze. Although "wowsers" (teetotal puritanical types) attempted to put a stop to it, by 1903 all-day swimming was every Sydneysider's right.

The bronzed and muscled surf lifesavers in their distinctive red and yellow caps are a highly photographed, world-famous Australian image. Surf lifesavers (members of what are now called Surf Life Saving Clubs, abbreviated to SLSC) are volunteers working the beach at weekends, so come then to watch their exploits – or look out for a surf carnival; lifeguards, on the other hand, are employed by the council and work all week during swimming season (year-round at Bondi).

or if you want to swim laps, there is a seawater swimming pool (plus gym, sauna, massage service and poolside café) at the southern end of the beach under the **Bondi Icebergs Club** on Notts Avenue (Mon–Wed & Fri 6am–8pm, Sat & Sun 6am–6.30pm; $3.30). Part of the Bondi legend since 1929, members must swim throughout the winter, and media coverage of their plunge, made truly wintry with the addition of huge chunks of ice, heralds the first day of winter. The recently rebuilt clubhouse is a great place for a drink (see p.178). Below, Surf Lifesaving Australia offices have a small collection of memorabilia (Mon–Fri 10am–3pm; free).

Topless bathing is condoned at Bondi – a long way from conditions right up to the late 1960s when stern beach inspectors were on the lookout for indecent exposure. If you want to join in the sun and splash but don't have the gear, Beached at Bondi, below the lifeguard lookout tower, rents out everything from umbrellas, wetsuits, cozzies and towels to surfboards and boogieboards and has lockers for valuables.

Reach Bondi Beach on **bus** #380, #L82 or #389 from Circular Quay via Oxford Street and Bondi Junction, or take the train to Bondi Junction station, then transfer to these buses or to the #361, #381 and #382.

Tamarama to Gordons Bay

Many people find the smaller, quieter beaches to the south of Bondi more enticing, and the oceanfront and clifftop **walking track** to Clovelly (about 2hr) is popular – the track also includes a fitness circuit, so you'll see plenty of joggers en route. Walk past the Bondi Icebergs Club on Notts Avenue (see above), round Mackenzies Point and through Marks Park to the modest and secluded **Mackenzies Bay**. Next is **Tamarama Bay**, a deep, narrow beach favoured by the smart set and a hedonistic gay crowd ("Glamarama" to the locals), as well as surfers; there's a popular café here. Tamarama is a fifteen-minute walk from Bondi or a three-hundred-metre walk from the #380 bus stop on Fletcher Street, or take bus #360 or #361 from Bondi Junction.

Walk through Tamarama's small park and follow the oceanfront road for five minutes to the next beach along, **Bronte Beach** on Nelson Bay. More of a family affair with a large green park, a popular café strip and sea baths, it's easily reached on bus #378 from Central station via Oxford Street and Bondi Junction. The **northern end** has inviting flat-rock platforms, popular as fishing and relaxation spots, and the beach here is cliff-backed, providing some shade. The valley-like **park** beyond is extensive and shady with a **mini-train ride** ($2), here since 1947, and an imaginative children's playground. At the **southern end** of the beach, a natural rock enclosure makes a calm area for kids to swim in, and there are rock ledges to lie on around the enclosed sea swimming pool known as **Bronte Baths** (open access; free). Nearby, palm trees give a suitably holiday feel as you relax at one of the outside tables of Bronte Road's wonderful café strip (eight to choose from, plus a fish-and-chip shop).

From Bronte, it's a pleasant five-minute walk past the baths to **Waverly Cemetery**, a fantastic spot to spend eternity. Established in 1877, it contains the graves of many famous Australians, with the bush poet contingent well represented. **Henry Lawson**, described on his headstone as poet, journalist and patriot, languishes in section 3G 516, while **Dorothea Mackeller**, who penned the famous poem "I love a sunburnt country", is in section 6 832–833. Beyond here – another five-minute walk – on the other side of Shark Point, is the channel-like **Clovelly Bay**, with concrete platforms on either side and several sets of steps leading into the very deep water. Rocks at the far end keep out the waves and the sheltered bay is popular with lap-swimmers and snorkellers; there's also a free swimming pool. A grassy park with several terraces extends back from the beach and is a great place for a picnic. You can rent snorkels up the road at Clovelly (see "Diving" p.195). The divinely sited café is packed at weekends, and on Sunday afternoons and evenings, the nearby *Clovelly Hotel* is a popular hangout, with free live music and a great bistro, or get rock-bottom-priced drinks and fab views at the Clovelly Bowling Club. To get to Clovelly, take bus #339 from Millers Point via Central station and Albion Street, Surry Hills; #360 from Bondi Junction; or the weekday peak-hour X39 from Wynyard.

From Clovelly it's best to stick to the road route along Cliffbrook Parade rather than rockhop around to equally narrow **Gordon's Bay**. Unsupervised, undeveloped Gordons Bay itself is not a pretty beach, but another world exists beneath the sheltered water: the protected **underwater nature trail**, marked out for divers, is home to a range of sea creatures; diving and snorkelling gear can be rented at Clovelly (see "Diving", p.195). From here, a walkway leads around the waterfront to Major Street and then onto **Dunningham Reserve** overlooking the northern end of Coogee Beach; the walk to Coogee proper takes about fifteen minutes in all.

Coogee

While Coogee has a lively bar, café, restaurant and backpacker scene, and some big hotels, there's just something more laid-back, community-oriented and friendly about it compared to Bondi – and it's not totally teeming with trendies. With its hilly streets of Californian-style apartment blocks looking onto a compact, pretty beach enclosed by two cliffy, green-covered headlands, Coogee has a snugness that Bondi just can't match. Everything is close to hand: beachfront Arden Street has a down-to-earth strip of cafés that compete with each other to sell the cheapest cooked breakfast, while the main shopping street, Coogee Bay Road, running uphill from the beach, has a choice selection of coffee spots and eateries, plus a big supermarket.

The ugly high-rise *Holiday Inn* has spoilt the southern end of the beach, though its bar does have fabulous views over the water. Other 1990s developments were more aesthetically successful: the imaginatively modernized promenade is a great place to stroll and hang out. Between it and the medium-sized beach is a grassy park with free electric barbecues, picnic tables and shelters. The beach is popular with families (there's an excellent children's playground at the southern end) and travellers, as there's a stack of backpackers' hostels (see "Accommodation", pp.109–110). However, one of Coogee's chief pleasures are its baths, beyond the southern end of the beach. The first, the secluded McIvers Baths, traditionally remains for women and children only and is known by locals as **Coogee Women's Pool** and run by volunteers (noon–5pm; entry by donation). Opposite the entrance to the women's pool Grant Reserve has a full-on adventure playground. Just south of the women's pool, the unisex **Wylies Baths**, a saltwater pool on the edge of the sea, is at the end of Neptune Street (Oct–April 7am–7pm; May–Sept 7am–5pm; $2.50) with big decks to lie on, and solar heated showers; it's a fine spot for the excellent coffee made at its kiosk.

Reach Coogee on **bus** #373 or #374 from Circular Quay via Randwick, or #372 from Central station; journey time from Central is about 25 minutes. There are also buses from Bondi Junction via Randwick: #313 and #314.

Immediately south of Wylies, **Trenerry Reserve** is a huge green park jutting out into the ocean; its spread of big, flat rocks offer tremendous views and make a great place to chill out. Probably the most impressive section of Randwick Council's **Eastern Beaches Coast Walk** commences here. The council is attempting to regenerate the native flora, and the walk, sometimes on boards, is accompanied by interpretive panels detailing the surrounding plant- and birdlife. Steps lead down to a rock platform full of small pools – you can wander down and look at the life within, and there is a large tear-shaped pool you can swim in. It's quite thrilling with the waves crashing over – but be careful of both the waves and the blue-ringed octopus found here. At low tide you can continue walking along the rocks around Lurline Bay – otherwise you must follow the streets inland for a bit, rejoining the waterfront from Mermaid Avenue. Jack Vanny Memorial Park is fronted by the great cliffy rocks of Mistral Point, a great spot to sit and look at the water, and down by the water the **Mahon Pool**, a small, pleasant open-access sea pool, with waves crashing at the edge and surrounded by great boulders, has an unspoilt secluded feel. The isolated *Pool Caffe* across the road makes a wonderful lunch or coffee spot.

Manly and the northern beaches

Manly, just above North Head at the northern mouth of the harbour, is doubly blessed with both ocean and harbour beaches. When Captain Arthur Phillip, the commander of the First Fleet, was exploring Sydney Harbour in 1788, he saw a group of well-built Aboriginal men onshore, proclaimed them to be "manly" and named the cove in the process. During the Edwardian era it became fashionable as a recreational retreat from the city, with the promotional slogan of the time "Manly – seven miles from Sydney, but a thousand miles from care". An excellent time to visit is over the Labour Day long weekend in early October, for the **Jazz Festival** with free outdoor concerts featuring musicians from around the world. Beyond Manly, the **northern beaches** continue for 30km up to Barrenjoey Heads and **Palm Beach**. It's a

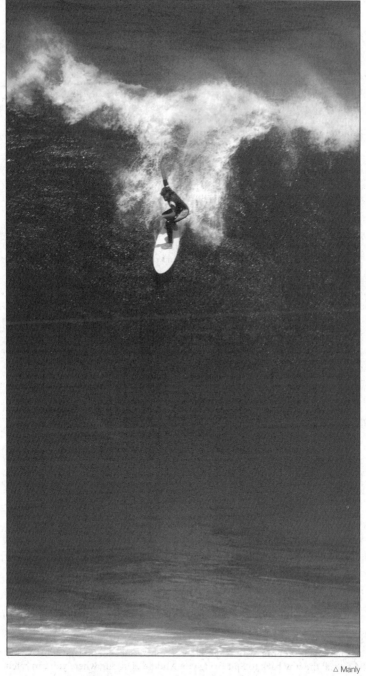

△ Manly

good idea to pick up the excellent and free *Sydney's Northern Beaches Map* from the Manly Visitor Centre (see p.158). The northern beaches can be reached by regular **bus** from various city bus terminals or from Manly ferry wharf; routes are detailed throughout the text below.

Manly

A day-trip to Manly, rounded off with a dinner of fish and chips, offers a classic taste of Sydney life. The ferry trip out here has always been half the fun: the legendary Manly Ferry service has run from Circular Quay since 1854, and the huge old boats come complete with snack bars selling the ubiquitous meat pie. Ferries terminate at Manly Wharf in Manly Cove, near a small section of harbour beach with a netted-off swimming area popular with families. Like a typical English seaside resort, **Manly Wharf** had always had a funfair until recently; now the wharf is all very grown-up and foodie with *Food Chain*, the **David Jones food hall**, a swathe of cafés and multi-cultural food stalls and a swish new pub, the *Manly Wharf Hotel*. You'll also find the **Manly Visitor Information Centre** (Mon–Fri 9am–5pm, Sat & Sun 10am–4pm; ⊤02/9977 1088, Ⓦwww.manlyweb.com.au; lockers $2) handily located here. The wharf is now a hub for adventure activity: three watersports companies based here offer parasailing, kayaking and rigid inflatable boat tours through crashing surf to North Head; ask at the tourist office for details.

From the wharf, walk along West Esplanade to **Oceanworld** (daily 10am–5.30pm; $15.90, discounted entry after 3.30pm; Ⓦwww.oceanworldmanly .com), where clear acrylic walls hold back the water so you can saunter along the harbour floor, gazing at huge sharks and stingrays. Divers hand-feed sharks three times weekly (11am Mon, Wed & Fri) and there's also a guided thirty-minute Shark Tunnel Tour (daily 2.30pm & Tues, Thurs, Sat & Sun 11am). You can organize dives amongst the sharks for half an hour (qualified diver $150; unqualified diver $195; bookings ⊤02/9949 2644). Opposite, the screams come from the three giant waterslides of **Manly Waterworks** (Oct to Easter Sat, Sun, school & public holidays 10am–5pm; 1hr $13.50, all day $19; over-6-year-olds only). Between the slides and Oceanworld, the **Manly Art Gallery and Museum** (Tues–Sun 10am–5pm; $3.50), has a collection started in the 1920s of Australian paintings, drawings, prints and etchings, and a stash of beach memorabilia including huge old wooden surfboards and old-fashioned swimming costumes.

Many visitors mistake Manly Cove for the ocean beach, which in fact lies on the other side of the isthmus, 500m down **The Corso**, Manly's busy pedestri-anized main drag filled with shops, cafés, restaurants and pubs. The ocean beach, **South Steyne**, is characterized by the stands of Norfolk pine which line the shore. Every summer, a beach-hire concession rents out just about any-thing to make the beach more fun, from surfboards to snorkel sets, and they also have a bag-minding service. A six-kilometre-long shared pedestrian and **cycle path** begins at South Steyne and runs north to Seaforth, past North Steyne Beach and Queenscliff. You can rent mountain bikes from Manly Cycles, a block back from the Beach at 36 Pittwater Rd (⊤02/9977 1189; 1hr $12, all day $25). For a more idyllic beach, follow the footpath from the south-ern end of South Steyne around the headland to Cabbage Tree Bay, with two very pretty, green-backed beaches at either end – **Fairy Bower** to the west and **Shelley Beach** to the east.

The **Manly Scenic Walkway** follows the harbour shore inland from Manly Cove all the way back to Spit Bridge on Middle Harbour, where you can catch bus #180 back to Wynyard station in the city centre (20min). The wonderful eight-kilometre walk takes you through a section of **Sydney Harbour National Park**, past a number of small beaches and coves, Aboriginal middens and some subtropical rainforest. The entire walk takes three to four hours but is broken up into six sections with obvious exit/entry points; pick up a map from the Manly Visitor Information Centre or NPWS offices (see "Parks and wildlife information" on p.196).

The streets between Manly Cove and the surf beach are lively and interesting with plenty of great places to eat or find the makings of a beachside picnic. There's the food hall and outlets at Manly Wharf (see opposite) but the nearby streets are also very quality-food-oriented: opposite the wharf, on the corner of Wentworth Street, is an organic food store. Head a block past this to the intersection with **Darley Road** to find upmarket delis, gleaming European-style cafés and an above-average supermarket. **Belgrave Street**, running north from Manly Wharf, is Manly's alternative strip, with good cafés, interesting shops, yoga schools and the Manly Environment Centre at no. 41.

Ferries leave Circular Quay for Manly twice an hour ($5.40) and take thirty minutes. The last ferry service from Circular Quay is at 7pm after which the faster JetCat catamarans operate until midnight. The JetCat ($6.70) goes twice as fast as the regular ferries but is about half as much fun. After it finishes, night bus #E50 runs from Wynyard station.

North Head

You can take in more of the Sydney Harbour National Park at **North Head**, the harbour mouth's upper jaw, where you can follow the short circuitous Fairfax Walking Track to three lookout points, including the **Fairfax Lookout**, for splendid views. A regular #135 **bus** leaves from Manly Wharf for North Head or if you have your own car you can drop in to the NPWS office (daily 9am–4.30pm), a kilometre or so before the lookouts, to pick up free information leaflets. Right in the middle of this national park is a military reserve with its own **National Artillery Museum** (Wed, Sat, Sun & public holidays 11am–4pm; $6) sited in the historic **North Fort**, a curious system of tunnels built into the headland – it takes up to two hours to wander through them by guided tour.

There's more history at the old **Quarantine Station**, on the harbour side of North Head, used from 1828 until 1984: arriving passengers or crew who had a contagious disease were set down at Spring Cove to serve a spell of isolation at the station, all at the shipping companies' expense. Sydney residents, too, were forced here, most memorably during the plague which broke out in The Rocks in 1900, when 1832 people were quarantined (104 plague victims are buried in the grounds). The site, its buildings still intact, is now looked after by the NPWS, which offers **guided history tours** (Mon, Wed & Fri–Sun 1.15pm; 1hr 30min–2hr; $11; booking essential on ℡02/9247 5033), giving an insight not only into Sydney's immigration history but the evolution of medical science in the 150 years, often in gory detail. The tours, which co-ordinate with the #135 bus from Manly Wharf (bus fare extra), provide the only opportunity to get out to this beautiful isolated harbour spot with its views across to Balmoral Beach. It's so beautiful that a hotel group has proposed to lease and run the site for 45 years and build a three-star hotel there, to local protest; at the same time the station has suffered two recent fires and consequent claims of NPWS mismanagement. The night-time **ghost tours** (Wed & Fri–Sun 7.15pm; 3hr 15min;

Wed $22, Fri–Sun $27.50 ; light supper included) are very popular; children under 12 have a less hair-raising, once-weekly Kids Ghost Tour (Fri 5.45pm; 2hr 15min; $13.20 child or adult; no supper). No public transport is available for the night-time visits.

Freshwater to Mona Vale

Freshwater, just beyond Manly, sits snugly between two rocky headlands on Queenscliff Bay, and is one of the most picturesque of the northern beaches. There's plenty of surf culture around the headland at Curl Curl, and a walking track at its northern end, commencing from Huston Parade, will take you above the rocky coastline to the curve of **Dee Why Beach** (bus #136, #146, #152, #158 or #169 from Manly Wharf; bus #178 from outside the QVB in the city). Dee Why provides consistently good surf, while its sheltered lagoon makes it popular with families. Beyond the lagoon, windsurfers gather around **Long Reef**, where the point is surrounded by a wide rock shelf creviced with rock pools and protected as an aquatic reserve – well worth a wander to peek at the creatures within. The long, beautiful sweep of **Collaroy Beach**, now with a popular YHA (see p.111), shades into **Narrabeen Beach**, an idyllic spot backed by the extensive, swimmable and fishable **Narrabeen Lakes**, popular with anglers and families; there's also a good campsite (see box on p.99). Both Collaroy and Narrabeen can be reached by bus #183 from Wynyard station and Manly Wharf; bus #190 from Central and Wynyard stations; and bus #155 from Manly Wharf. Several other buses also go to Collaroy including the #151 from outside the QVB and from Manly Wharf, the #187 from Millers Point in The Rocks, and the #156 and #159 from Manly Wharf.

Beyond Narrabeen, **Mona Vale** is a long, straight stretch of beach with a large park behind and a sea pool dividing it from sheltered **Bongin Bongin Bay**, whose headland reserve, and rocks to clamber on, make it ideal for children. Inland from Mona Vale at Ingleside, the domed **Bahá'í Temple** in extensive gardens on Mona Vale Road (daily 9am–5pm; ⓦ www.bahai.org) is one of only seven in the world; the Bahá'í faith teaches the unity of religion, and Sunday services (11am) read from texts of the world's main religions. To get to the temple, catch bus #159 from Manly Wharf or the #190 from Central or Wynyard stations.

The Barrenjoey Peninsula: Newport to Palm Beach

After Bongin Bongin Bay the Barrenjoey Peninsula begins, with calm Pittwater (see p.201) on its western side and ocean beaches running up its eastern side until it spears into Broken Bay. **Newport** boasts a fine stretch of ocean beach between two rocky headlands; on Sunday crowds gather to listen to live jazz in the beer garden of the *Newport Arms* (see p.175) on Kalinya Street, overlooking Heron Cove on Pittwater. Unassuming **Bilgola Beach**, next door to Newport, is one of the prettiest of the northern beaches. From Bilgola Beach, a trio of Sydney's best beaches, for both surf and scenery, run up the eastern fringe of the mushroom-shaped peninsula: Avalon and Whale beaches are less fashionable than Palm Beach, and are popular surfie territory.

Backed by bush-covered hills, and reached by three kilometres of winding road, small **Avalon Beach** has a suitably secluded feel and is indeed a slice of paradise on a summer's day. A pleasing set of shops and eateries run perpendicular from the beach on Avalon Parade; *Avalon Beach Cafe* at no. 23 is a good licensed café with a very contemporary feel, popular with the travellers who stay nearby at the hostel (see p.110). The people of Avalon memorably rejected the proposed filming of a series of *Baywatch* in early 1999, though the beach did feature in a tacky *Baywatch* special.

Whale Beach, 8km further north via Barrenjoey Road and Whale Beach Road, is much less of a settlement, with the beach fronted by the inevitable Surf Life Saving Club and the classy *Whale Beach Restaurant* (☏02/9974 4009; closed Mon), which dishes up six-course $85 menus alongside stunning views; it also has a much cheaper, very pleasant garden café. Continue following Whale Beach Road north to reach **Palm Beach** which, living up to its name, is a hangout for the rich and famous: you can even arrive by Hollywood-style seaplane from Rose Bay (see p.147). Palm Beach residents aren't as concerned about the film cameras as their Avalon neighbours: the ocean beach, on the western side of the peninsula, leads a double life as "Summer Bay" in the famous, long-running Aussie soap *Home and Away*, with the picturesque **Barrenjoey Lighthouse** and bushcovered headland – part of **Ku-Ring-Gai Chase National Park** – regularly in shot. Barrenjoey Adventures (see below) offers tours to the film set for fans. A steep walking path to the summit of **Barrenjoey Headland** from the carpark at the base takes twenty to forty minutes, rewarded by a stunning panorama of Palm Beach, Pittwater and the Hawkesbury River. The NPWS offers weekend tours of the sandstone lighthouse, which dates from 1881 (Sat & Sun 11.30am, 12.45 & 2pm; 1hr; $10; bookings ☏02/9247 5033).

The bulk of Ku-Ring-Gai Chase National Park (see p.200) is across Pittwater, and can be visited courtesy of Palm Beach and Hawkesbury River Cruises (☏02/9997 4815). The **ferries** leave from the Wharf on the eastern, Pittwater side of the peninsula (leaving at 11am, back at 3.30pm, with a one-hour lunch break at Bobbin Head; cruise $32); they also offers general transport to Patonga (see p.205). Alternatively, the Palm Beach Ferry Service (☏02/9918 2747 or 9973 2704) runs from Palm Beach Wharf via The Basin to Mackerel Beach reaching picnicking and camping spots on Pittwater (departing hourly 9–11am & 1–5pm, also noon Oct–May; Fri also 6pm, 7pm & 8pm; Sat & Sun also 6pm; $4 one-way, $8 return). You can also get out on the water with Barrenjoey Adventures (see below), who offers kayaking tours (2hr; $40), kayak rental ($16.50 per hour), surfing lessons (2hr; $40) and board rental ($20 per hour)

Beside the wharf, calm Snapperman Beach is fronted by yachts and a shady park. Across the road you can **eat** at the *Barrenjoey House*, an upmarket guesthouse and restaurant. You can also dine well at *Ancora*, but for less cash, get fish and chips from the excellent milk bar.

Bus #190 and #L90 run up the peninsula from Central via Wynyard to Avalon, continuing to Palm Beach via the Pittwater side; change at Avalon for bus #193 to Whale Beach. Bus #188 and #L88 go from Central and Wynyard to Avalon, and the #187 runs from The Rocks to Newport. Palm Beach Express, run by Barrenjoey Adventures (☏1800/23 23 30, ⌨www.sydneytrips.com; $18), pick up from the city, Kings Cross and eastern beaches in the morning, provide a map (and steer you in the direction of the *Home and Away* film set) and a drink at the *Newport Arms* on the way home in the late afternoon.

Botany Bay

The southern suburbs of Sydney, arranged around huge **Botany Bay**, are seen as the heartland of red-tiled-roof suburbia, a terracotta sea spied from above as the planes land at **Mascot**. Clive James, the area's most famous son, hails from

Kogarah – described as a 1950s suburban wasteland in his tongue-in-cheek *Unreliable Memoirs*. The popular perception of Botany Bay is coloured by its proximity to an airport, a high-security prison (Long Bay), an oil refinery, a container terminal and a sewerage outlet. Yet the surprisingly clean-looking water is fringed by quiet, sandy beaches and the marshlands shelter a profusion of birdlife. Whole areas of the waterfront, at **La Perouse**, with its associations with eighteenth-century French exploration, and on the **Kurnell Peninsula** where Captain Cook first put anchor, are designated as part of **Botany Bay National Park**, and large stretches on either side of the Georges River form a State Recreation Area.

La Perouse

At least, is there any news of Monsieur de Laperouse?

Louis XVI, about to be guillotined, 1793

La Perouse, tucked into the northern shore of Botany Bay where it meets the Pacific Ocean, contains Sydney's oldest Aboriginal settlement, the legacy of a mission. The suburb took its name from the eighteenth-century French explorer, **Laperouse**, who set up camp here for six weeks, briefly and cordially meeting Captain Arthur Phillip, who was making his historic decision to forgo swampy Botany Bay and move on to Port Jackson; after leaving Botany Bay, the Laperouse expedition was never seen again.

A monument erected in 1825 and the excellent NPWS-run **Laperouse Museum** (Wed–Sun 10am–4pm; $5.50), which sits on a grassy headland between the pretty beaches of Congwong Bay and Frenchmans Bay, tell the whole fascinating story. Tracing Laperouse's voyage in great detail, the museum displays are enlivened by relics from the wrecks, exhibits of antique French maps and copies of etchings by the naturalists on board. The voyage was commissioned by the French king Louis XVI in 1785 as a purely scientific exploration of the Pacific to rival Cook's voyages, and strict instructions were given for Laperouse to "act with great gentleness and humanity towards the different people whom he will visit". After an astonishing three-and-a-half-year journey through South America, the Easter Islands, Hawaii, the northwest coast of America, and past China and Japan to Russia, the *Astrolobe* and the *Boussole* struck disaster – first encountering hostility in the Solomon Islands and then in their doomed sailing from Botany Bay, on March 10, 1788. Their disappearance remained a mystery until 1828, when relics were discovered on Vanikoro in the Solomon Islands; the wrecks themselves were found only in 1958 and 1964. There is also an exhibition which looks at the Aboriginal history and culture of the area.

The surrounding headlands and foreshore have been incorporated into the northern half of **Botany Bay National Park** (no entry fee; the other half is across Botany Bay on the Kurnell Peninsula, see opposite). A **visitor centre** (☏02/9311 3379), in the same building as the museum, provides details of walks including a fine one past **Congwong Bay Beach** to Henry Head and its lighthouse (5km round trip). The idyllic verandah of the *Boatshed Cafe*, on the small headland between Congwong and Frenchmans bays, sits right over the water with pelicans floating about below. La Perouse is at its most lively on **Sunday** (and public holidays) when, following a tradition established at the turn of the twentieth century, Aboriginal people come down to sell boomerangs and other crafts, and demonstrate snake-handling skills (from 1.30pm) and boomerang throwing. There are also tours of the nineteenth-century fortifications on **Bare Island** (Sat, Sun & public holidays 12.30pm,

1.30pm, 2.30pm & 3.30pm; $7.70; no booking required, wait at the gate to the island), joined to La Perouse by a walkway; the island featured in *Mission Impossible II*. Across from the **Frenchmans Bay** beach and park there are a few places to eat on Endeavour Avenue, including the popular, casual and affordable *Paris Seafood Cafe* at no. 51; you can eat in or get take-away fish and chips and have them in the grassy park.

To **get to** La Perouse, catch bus #394 or #399 from Circular Quay via Darlinghurst and Moore Park, or #393 from Railway Square via Surry Hills and Moore Park, or the #L94 express from Circular Quay.

The Kurnell Peninsula and Cronulla

From La Perouse, you can see across Botany Bay to Kurnell and the red buoy marking the spot where Captain James Cook and the crew of the *Endeavour* anchored on April 29, 1770 for an eight-day exploration. Back in England, many refused to believe that the uniquely Australian plants and animals they had recorded actually existed – the kangaroo in particular was thought to be a hoax. **Captain Cook's Landing Place** is now the south head of **Botany Bay National Park**, where the informative **Discovery Centre** (Mon–Fri 10am–4pm, Sat & Sun 9.30am–4.30pm; car fee $7.50; ☏02/9668 9111) looks at the wetlands ecology of the park and tells the story of Cook's visit and its implications for Aboriginal people. Indeed the political sensitivity of the spot which effectively marks the beginning of the decline of an ancient culture has led to the planned renaming of the park to Kamay-Botany Bay National Park, "Kamay" being the original Dharawal people's name for the bay. Set aside as a public recreation area in 1899, the heath and woodland is unspoilt and there are some secluded beaches for swimming; you may even spot some parrots and honeyeaters. To get here, take the train to Cronulla and then Kurnell Bus Services route #987 (☏02/9524 8977).

On the ocean side of the **Kurnell Peninsula** is Sydney's longest beach: the ten-kilometre stretch begins at **Cronulla** and continues as deserted, dune-backed **Wanda Beach**. This is prime surfing territory – and the only Sydney beach accessible by train (surfboards carried free). Situated on a finger of land jutting into **Port Hacking**, Cronulla is blessed with both sheltered bay beaches and ocean frontage. Its modern residential and commercial developments can give it the feel of a Gold Coast resort, but at heart it's just a down-to-earth outer suburb. There are no trendies here, though with the opening of a purpose-built YHA hostel (see p.111), travellers have been added into the mix. Life revolves around the beaches and the shopping strip on **Cronulla Street**, which becomes a pedestrianized mall between Kingsway and Purley Place. The train station is at the southern end of this street, along with Cronulla's more interesting shops and a hip young café-bar, *Nulla Nulla*, at no. 75, which also has Internet access.

Serious surfing is done at the main beach, **North Cronulla**, straight down Kingsway. It's fronted by a commercial-looking eating precinct and the popular *Northies* pub across the road, with outdoor tables. Follow the concreted walkway, **The Esplanade**, south along the rock platform and past a couple of delightful sea pools to reach the smaller, more sheltered and less developed **South Cronulla** beach, fronted by shady Cronulla Park, sloping down to the water, a favourite sport for families. The waterfront *Cronulla Kiosk* is a magic spot for breakfast or lunch here while the unpretentious *Cronulla RSL Memorial Club* has ocean views from its wall-to-ceiling windows, which can be enjoyed with a cheap drink or meal. Keep following The Esplanade right around to Darook Park on sheltered **Gunnamatta Bay**, where you can catch a ferry to Bundeena in the Royal National Park (see p.236) from the Tonkin Street Wharf (Tonkin Street is just behind the train station, if you want to get to it quickly).

Eating and drinking

If the way its chefs are regularly stolen to work overseas is any indication, Sydney can be seen to have blossomed into one of the great restaurant capitals of the world, offering a fantastic range of cosmopolitan eateries, covering every imaginable cuisine. Quality is uniformly high, with the freshest produce, meat and seafood always on hand, and a culinary culture of discerning, well-informed diners. The restaurant scene is highly fashionable, and with so much choice, customers are correspondingly fickle: businesses rise in favour, fall in popularity and close down or change names and style at an astonishing rate. For a comprehensive guide, consider investing in the latest edition of *Cheap Eats in Sydney* or the *Sydney Morning Herald Good Food Guide*. All New South Wales' restaurants are **non-smoking**, except for reception areas and outside tables.

Most of the inner suburbs are just a few minutes away by bus, train, ferry or taxi, and there you'll generally find better, less expensive and more enjoyable places to eat and drink. Sydney's fully fledged **café culture** can be found most notably in Potts Point, Darlinghurst, Surry Hills, Glebe, Newtown, Leichhardt and the eastern beaches of Bondi, Bronte and Coogee.

There are many fascinating **ethnic** enclaves, representing Sydney's diverse communities, where you can eat authentic cuisines: Jewish on Hall Street, Bondi Beach; Japanese at Bondi Junction, Neutral Bay and Crows Nest; Chinese and Thai in Haymarket; Turkish and Indian on Cleveland Street, Surry Hills; Italian in East Sydney, Leichhardt, Haberfield and Five Dock; Portuguese on New Canterbury Road, Petersham; Greek in Marrickville, Earlwood and Brighton-Le-Sands; Indonesian on Anzac Parade, in Kingsford and Kensington. Much further out, all reached by train, there's Korean at Campsie, more Turkish at Auburn, Lebanese at Punchbowl and Lakemba, and Vietnamese at Cabramatta.

All restaurants in the following listings are open daily for lunch and dinner, unless otherwise stated, and the more specific café times are given (many are open early for breakfast, one of Sydney's most popular meals).

The Central Business District (CBD) and The Rocks

The cafés and food stalls in the business and shopping districts of the city centre cater mainly for lunch-time crowds, and there are lots of **food courts** serving fast food and snacks. Check out the selection in the basements of the **Queen Victoria Building** (see p.124), **Grace Bros Department Store** (see p.123) and the **MLC Centre** near Martin Place, and on the first floor of the **Hunter Connection** shopping arcade, 310 George St, opposite Wynyard station. The classiest is the foodie's paradise in the basement of the **David Jones** department store on Market Street. There are lots of great Italian espresso bars for quick coffee hits throughout the CBD. Many museums and tourist attractions also have surprisingly good **cafés** – notably the Museum of Contemporary Art, the Australian Museum, the Hyde Park Barracks and the Art Gallery of New South Wales.

There are several good **pubs** in The Rocks (see pp.175–176), many of which serve some kind of food, but for the most part the area around the harbour has a choice of expensive restaurants, popular for business lunches, or trading on fantastic views, such as *Cafe Sydney*.

Cafés and brasseries

Café Opera *Hotel Intercontinental*, 117 Macquarie St ☎02/9240 1260. The buffet offered by the five-star *Intercontinental's Café Opera*, groaning under the display of seafood, is legendary. Stuff yourself silly for $42 at lunch time ($59 Sun, with live jazz), $48 at dinner ($54 Fri & Sat, $52 Sun) or $28.50 at supper (10pm Fri & Sat).

Delizia 148 Elizabeth St. High-ceilinged Italian deli-café bustling with black-clad staff behind gleaming glass counters full of pasta and delicious salads; looks pricey, but nothing's over $10. A delightful secondhand literary bookshop is a haven out back, with café tables and sofas among the bookshelves. Popular for weekend breakfasts when most city cafés are closed. Mon–Fri 7am–6pm, Sat & Sun 8am–4pm.

Obelisk Café Shop 1, 7 Macquarie Place. Fabulous spot for an outdoor café on a historic square with big shady trees, close to Circular Quay. Attracts a working crowd who plunge in for great coffee, *pizzetta*, focaccia, pasta, steak sandwiches and healthy filled wraps. Mon–Fri 6am–5pm.

QVB Jet Cnr York and Druitt streets, City. Very lively Italian café/bar, on the corner of the QVB building looking across to the Town Hall, with big, glass windows and outdoor seating providing people-watching opportunities. Coffee is predictably excellent, and the menu is big on breakfast. The rest of the day choose from pasta, risotto and soups, salads and sandwiches. Licensed. Mon–Fri 8am–10pm, Sat 9am–10pm.

Rossini Between wharves 5 and 6, Circular Quay. Quality Italian fast food alfresco while you're waiting for a ferry or just watching the quay. *Panzerotto* – big, cinnamon-flavoured and ricotta-filled doughnuts – are a speciality. Pricey but excellent coffee. Licensed. Daily 7am–11pm.

Sydney Cove Oyster Bar Circular Quay East. En route to the Opera House, the quaint little building housing the bar and kitchen was once a public toilet, but don't let that put you off. The outdoor tables right on the water's edge provide a magical location to sample Sydney Rock Pacific oysters (around $15.50 for half a dozen), or just come for coffee, cake and the view. Licensed. Daily 11am–11pm.

Restaurants

bel mondo Level 3, the Argyle Stores, 12–24 Argyle St, The Rocks ☎02/9241 3700. Superior North Italian food comes with a fabulous vantage point over The Rocks and the harbour. A sophisticated crowd eats here, but for less cash you can get views and similar food at its fashionable *Antibar*. Very expensive; licensed. Restaurant closed Mon, Sat & Sun lunch.

Doyles on the Quay Overseas Passenger Terminal, Circular Quay West ☎02/9252 3400. Downtown branch of the Watsons Bay seafood institution (see p.172); pricey but excellent, with great harbour views from the outdoor waterside tables. Licensed.

Guillaume at Bennelong Sydney Opera House, Bennelong Point ☎02/9241 1999. French chef Guillaime Brahimi has fused his name with the Opera House's top-notch restaurant, housed in one of the iconic building's smaller shells; the huge windows provide stunning harbour views. For one splash-out, romantic meal in Sydney, come here. With mains at around $35 (elegant modern French fare), it's not *the* most expensive place in town and if you can't afford it you can opt for a drink at the bar. Lunch Fri only, dinner Mon–Sat.

Lillipilli in the Rocks 1 Globe St, cnr Nurses Walk, The Rocks ☎02/9251 6988. Authentic but upmarket bushtucker served among Aboriginal artwork; run by a Koori from the south coast. Expect vegetarian dishes like fettucine with wild spinach, bush mushrooms and bunya bunya nuts, or meatier meals like wallaby with local honey (mains $26–$28). Aboriginal dance performance Fri & Sat 8pm. BYO.

Rockpool 107 George St, The Rocks ☎02/9252 1888. Owned by top chef Neil Perry, the raved-about seafood – blue swimmer crab omelette, mud crab ravioli – and other contemporary creations here make sure this place is still rated as one of Sydney's best dining spots. With mains around $45, definitely splurge material. Licensed. Closed Sat lunch & Sun.

Sailors Thai Canteen 106 George St, The Rocks. Cheaper version of the much-praised, pricey downstairs restaurant (bookings ☎02/9251 2466), housed in the restored Sailors' Home (see p.118). The ground-level canteen with a long stainless-steel communal table looks onto an open kitchen, where the chefs chop away to produce simple one-bowl meals. Licensed. Daily noon–8pm.

Tetsuya's 529 Kent St, City ℡02/9267 2900, ℻02/9799 7099. Stylish premises – all Japanese timber interior, and a beautiful Japanese garden outside – of the internationally renowned chef Tetsuya Wakuda, who creates exquisite Japanese/French-style fare. The waiting list is a month ahead – worth it to sample his twelve-course *dégustation* menu ($170); wine teamed with each course starts from $60; book by phone

or fax. Licensed and BYO. Lunch Fri & Sat, dinner Tues–Sat.

The Wharf Pier 4, Hickson Rd, The Rocks, next to the Wharf Theatre ℡02/9250 1761. Enterprising modern food (lots of seafood), served up in an old dock building with heaps of raw charm and a harbour vista; bag the outside tables for the best views. Cocktail bar open from noon until end of evening performance. Expensive. Closed Sun.

Haymarket, Chinatown, Darling Harbour and around

The southern end of George Street has plenty of very cheap restaurants, of variable quality. Chinatown around the corner is a better bet: many places here specialize in *yum cha* (or dim sum as it's also known), and there are several late-night and all-night eating options. Inexpensive licensed Asian **food courts**, serving everything from Japanese to Vietnamese, and of course Chinese food, can be found in the Sussex Centre (1st Floor, 401 Sussex St; daily 10am–9pm); Dixon House (basement level, corner Little Hay and Dixon streets; daily 10.30am–8.30pm); the Harbour Plaza (basement level, corner Factory and Dixon streets; daily 10am–10pm); but the best is on the top floor of the Market City Shopping Centre, above Paddy's Market at the corner of Quay and Thomas streets (daily 8am–10pm). A few blocks from Chinatown back toward the city centre, there's a good array of Spanish eateries on Liverpool Street, while the Cockle Bay Wharf restaurant precinct harbours some gems. Beyond Darling Harbour, you can eat fantastically well at the Sydney Fish Market (see p.134).

Cafés, pubs and cheap eats

Grand Taverna *Sir John Young Hotel*, cnr Liverpool and George streets, Haymarket. Spanish food, including tapas, at the heart of the Spanish quarter. No-frills setting for some of the best paella and sangria in town.

Ippon Sushi 404 Sussex St, Haymarket. Fun, inexpensive Japanese sushi train downstairs, with a revolving choice of delectables from $2 to $5.50. Licensed and BYO. Daily 11am–11pm.

Mother Chu's Vegetarian Kitchen 367 Pitt St. Taiwanese Buddhist cuisine in suitably plain surrounds, and true to its name, it's family-run. Though onion and garlic aren't used, the eats here aren't bland. Don't try to BYO – there's a no-alcohol policy. Closed Sun.

Pho Pasteur 709 George St, Haymarket. Popular authentic Vietnamese cheap eat specializing in *pho* – rice noodle soup, served with fresh herbs, lemon wedges and bean sprouts. Most noodles (mostly pork, chicken and beef) are $7, and there's nothing over $10. Refreshing pot of jasmine tea included. BYO. Daily 10am–9pm.

Roma Caffe 191 Hay St, Haymarket. The veteran *Roma* offers fabulous coffee, great breakfasts and

a huge gleaming display of wicked Italian desserts, plus delicious focaccia and fresh pasta – try the home-made pumpkin tortellini. Mon–Sat 8am–6pm.

Tai Pei Shop 2, Prince Centre, 8 Quay St, Haymarket. Tiny, congenial and cheap Taiwanese eatery offering generous servings; great dumplings, and very tasty Mama Pho's tofu (with pork – like most things on the menu). Daily 11am–9pm.

Restaurants

BBQ King 18 Goulburn St, Haymarket ℡02/9267 2433. Unprepossessing but perpetually crowded Chinese restaurant specializing in barbecued meat. Surprisingly, there's a big vegetarian list on the menu too. Inexpensive to moderate; licensed. Daily 11.30am–2am (last orders 1.30am).

Blackbird Cockle Bay Wharf, Darling Harbour ℡02/9283 7835. Bar-restaurant with the feel of a funky American diner; sit on stools at the bar or couches out the back, or enjoy the water views from the terrace. Generous, good-value meals – from *dahl* to spaghetti, T-bone steaks, noodles, salads, pizzas from a hot-stone oven, and breakfast until 4pm. Licensed. Daily 7am–1am.

Capitan Torres 73 Liverpool St ☏02/9264 5574. Atmospheric and enduring Spanish place, specializing in seafood – a fresh display helps you choose – and paella; licensed. Sit downstairs at the bar or upstairs in the restaurant.

Chinta Ria – Temple of Love Roof Terrace, 201 Sussex St, Cockle Bay Wharf development, Darling Harbour ☏02/9264 3211. People queue to get in here (bookings lunch only) as much for the fun atmosphere – a blues and jazz soundtrack and decor which mixes a giant Buddha, a lotus pond and 50s-style furniture – as for the yummy Malaysian food. Licensed.

Kam Fook Sharks Fin Seafood Restaurant Level 3, Market City complex, cnr Quay and Haymarket streets, Haymarket ☏02/9211 8988. The long name matches the size of this Cantonese establishment, officially Australia's largest restaurant, seating 800. You can eat some of the best *yum cha* in Sydney here, and you'll still have to queue for it if you haven't booked, despite the restaurant's size. Moderate to expensive; licensed. *Yum cha* Mon–Fri 10am–5.30pm, Sat & Sun 9am–5.30pm, dinner nightly.

The Malaya 39 Lime St, King Street Wharf, Darling Harbour ☏02/9211 0946. Popular, veteran Chinese-Malaysian place now in swish water surrounds, serving some of the best, most authentic and spicy *laksa* in town. Moderately priced; licensed. Closed Sun.

Glebe

In Glebe you'll find both cheap and upmarket restaurants, ethnic takeaways, delis and a string of good cafés. **Glebe Point Road** is dominated by bookshops and cafés – with a cluster of particularly good cafés at the Broadway end. No one cuisine dominates: café fare is eclectic with plenty of choice for vegetarians, and Indian, Lebanese and Thai eateries rub shoulders. A delightful feature of Glebe cafés are their leafy courtyards and gardens.

Badde Manors 37 Glebe Point Rd. Veteran vegetarian corner café with a wonderful light-and-airy ambience, eclectic decor and laid-back staff; still one of Glebe's best cafés and always packed, especially for weekend brunch. Yummy cakes and ice cream, and inexpensive and generous servings – nothing over $12. Mon–Fri 8am–midnight, Sat 8am–1am, Sun 9am–midnight.

The Boathouse on Blackwattle Bay End of Ferry Rd, Glebe ☏02/9518 9011. Atmospheric restaurant located in a former boatshed, with fantastic views across the bay to Anzac Bridge and the fishmarkets, opposite. Fittingly, seafood is the thing here (and this is one of the best places to sample some), from the six different kinds of oysters to the raved-about fish pie with smoked tomatoes. Very expensive but worth it. Licensed. Closed Mon.

The Craven 166 Glebe Point Rd, next to the Valhalla Cinema. A great place to devour tasty titbits before or after the pictures, or plough into

more substantial North African and Mediterranean-style fare from the daily blackboard specials. Café atmosphere is friendly and relaxed, with plenty of space, light and air in the split-level shopfront building with big ceiling fans; if you don't mind bus fumes, there are on-street tables too. Mon–Fri 8am–10.30pm, Sat & Sun 9am–10.30pm.

Iku 25A Glebe Point Rd (also at 612A Darling St, Rozelle; 168 Military Rd, Neutral Bay; 279 Bronte Rd, Waverly; and 62 Oxford St, Darlinghurst). The original *Iku* at Glebe proved so popular it keeps branching out. Healthy – but delicious – macrobiotic meals and snacks, all vegetarian or vegan. Organic, pesticide-free coffee too. Meditative interior and outdoor dining area. Mon–Fri 11am–9pm, Sat 11am–7pm, Sun 12.30–7.30pm.

Well Connected 35 Glebe Point Rd. A popular Glebe hangout: choose from pavement tables, sofas, balcony seats or in front of the computers peppered about this colourful, funky cyber-café.

With breakfast served until 6pm, when dinner starts, people blow in and out all day. Simple good-value menu – Turkish-bread sandwiches, lasagne, soups and salads – with loads for vegetarians; generous servings. Moroccan vegetable curry and couscous is a dinner favourite. Internet access $1 per 10min to $5 per hour. Daily 7am–midnight.

① Newtown

On the other side of Sydney University from Glebe, **King Street** in **Newtown** is lined with cafés, takeaways and restaurants of every ethnic persuasion, particularly Thai.

Citrus 227 King St. A Newtown café favourite: vibrant walls, friendly service, huge servings of delicious food – the Mediterranean-inspired chicken-breast burger and the steak sandwich are stand-outs – with nothing much over $12. Big fold-back windows bring in light and views of Newtown's unconventional inner-city dwellers, while retaining a bit of a distance from the fumes and throng. BYO. Mon–Thurs & Sun 8am–10pm, Fri & Sat 8am–midnight.

Green Gourmet 115 King St. Loud and busy Chinese vegetarian eatery, which always has plenty of Asian customers, including the odd Buddhist monk. Buffet meals sold per 100g weight at dinner, or by the plate (around $8) at lunch; you can also order off the menu.

Kilimanjaro 280 King St. Long-running Senegalese-owned place serving authentic and simple dishes that span Africa – from West African marinated chicken to North African couscous. Casual and friendly atmosphere, with African art and craft adorning the walls. Inexpensive. BYO.

The Old Fish Shop 239 King St. This little corner place, decorated with strands of dried garlic and chilli, is pure Newtown: lots of shaven heads, body piercings, tattoos and bizarre fashions. Food is simple – mainly focaccia and mini pizzas – and the excellent raisin loaf goes well with a coffee. Daily 6am–11pm.

Steki Taverna 2 O'Connell St, off King St ☏02/9516 2191. Atmospheric and moderately priced Greek taverna, with live music and dancing at weekends – when you'll need to book. Dinner Wed–Sun.

Thai Pothong 294 King St ☏02/9550 6277. King Street's best Thai; excellent service and moderate prices. Essential to book on the weekend. Closed Mon lunch.

Thanh Binh 111 King St ☏02/9557 1175. With a celebrated original in Cabramatta, the Vietnamese food at this Newtown offspring is just as fresh, delicious and inexpensive. Roll-your-own rice-paper rolls are sensational (and fun); huge range of noodles to choose from. Licensed and BYO. Closed lunch Mon–Wed.

Balmain, Rozelle and Leichhardt

Further west is **Leichhardt**, Sydney's "Little Italy", which has a concentration of cafés and restaurants on **Norton Street**, while the **Darling Street** strip of restaurants runs from up-and-coming **Rozelle** to upmarket **Balmain**.

Bar Italia 169 Norton St, Leichhardt. Like a community centre with the day-long comings and goings of Leichhardt locals, positively packed at night. The focaccia, served during the day, comes big and tasty, and coffee is spot-on. Some of the best *gelato* in Sydney; pasta from $9, and the extra night-time menu includes more substantial meat dishes. Shady courtyard out the back. BYO. Sun & Mon 10am–midnight, Tues–Thurs 9am–midnight, Fri 9am–1am, Sat 10am–1am.

Canteen 332 Darling St, Balmain. Airy, high-ceilinged café with whitewashed walls inside the old Working Men's Institute. Simple fare: generous baguettes, burgers and salads, and big cooked breakfasts particularly popular on weekends when customers spill onto the sunny outside tables. Mon–Fri & Sun 7am–5pm, Sat 6am–5pm.

Frattini 122 Marion St, Leichhardt ☏02/9569 2997. One of the best Italian restaurants in Little Italy, run by a genial family. Modern, airy space but old-fashioned service. The fish is recommended, especially the whitebait fritters. BYO. Moderate. Closed Sat lunch and all Sun.

Harvest 71 Evans St, Rozelle ☏02/9818 4201. Established in the 1970s, this vegan and vegetarian restaurant has kept up with the times, dipping into Vietnamese, Japanese, Italian and a whole range of cuisines. Delicious, moderately priced food, decadent desserts and great coffee. BYO. Dinner only; closed Sun.

Surry Hills and Redfern

Just east of Central station, **Elizabeth and Cleveland streets** in Surry Hills, running down to Redfern, are traditionally the domain of Turkish and Lebanese restaurants, which are among the cheapest in Sydney, and almost all BYO. Several Indian restaurants have recently made an appearance too. **Crown Street** in Surry Hills harbours several interesting cafés and some upmarket restaurants.

Cafés, pubs and cheap eats

Almustafa 276 Cleveland St, Surry Hills. Very homey Lebanese place – relax on low couches in the traditional manner. Tasty home-style food – sample a wide range with a shareable mezze platter. Inexpensive. BYO. Closed lunch Mon–Wed; open until 12.30am Fri & Sat.

Café Niki 544 Bourke St, Surry Hills. Corner café with a relaxed ambience. Manages to feel groovy but not pretentious. Cheap and delicious food: best are their soups and focaccia plus excellent coffee. Mon–Fri 7am–10pm, Sat 8am–10pm, Sun 8am–4pm.

Erciyes 409 Cleveland St, Redfern ☎02/9319 1309. Among the offerings of this busy Turkish restaurant is delicious *pide* – a bit like pizza – available with a range of toppings, many vegetarian; take-out section too. Belly dancing Fri & Sat nights. BYO. Daily 10am–midnight.

Forresters Hotel 336 Riley St, Surry Hills. The *Forresters'* Sun–Wed steak and chicken specials (and until 6pm Sat) have become a legend: a 300g scotch fillet or T-bone steak or a chargrilled chicken breast with mash and Asian greens (and a different sauce each day), for $5 all day. There's not much of a catch – you must buy a drink. The steaks taste great and the three-levelled pub itself is very pleasant.

La Passion du Fruit 633 Bourke St, cnr Devonshire St, Surry Hills. Bright and friendly café serving one of the best brunches in town. Also interesting salads, sandwiches and light meals. Mon–Sat 8am–5pm.

Maltese Cafe 310 Crown St, Surry Hills. Café known for its delicious Maltese *pastizzi* – flaky pastry pockets of ricotta cheese, plain or with meat, spinach or peas – to eat in or take away; ridiculously cheap ($0.70 each) and satisfying. Mon 10am–6pm, Tues–Sun 8am–6pm.

Maya Masala 470 Cleveland St, Surry Hills. Fantastic, very cheap, authentic South Indian vegetarian food – *dosas*, thalis and more – served all day in a bustling cafeteria-style interior. Very popular with local Indian families, especially on weekends for the *chaat* (delicious snack) menu. A vast display of very sickly Indian sweets too. BYO. Daily 10am–10.30pm. The more upmarket version, *Maya da Dhaba* (☎02/8399 3785; closed lunch Mon–Thurs) opposite at no. 431, also serves meat dishes.

Mohr Fish 202 Devonshire St, Surry Hills. Tiny but stylish fish-and-chip bar, with stools and tiled walls, packs in the customers. BYO. Daily 10am–10pm.

Restaurants

Billy Kwong 355 Crown St, Surry Hills ☎02/9332 3300. Traditional Chinese cooking gets a stylish new slant. The space itself provides a similar contrast: all dark polished wood and Chinese antiques but brightly lit and with contemporary fittings. Mains start from $16. Licensed & BYO. Dinner nightly.

MG Garage 490 Crown St, Surry Hills ☎02/9383 9383. Flash restaurant which doubles as a car showroom, with MG cars sharing the dining room. A fun night out if you can afford it (mains start from $35); the modern Australian fare on offer is superb, by top chef Janni Kyritsis (closed Sun & lunch Sat). Next door, *Fuel* is the cheaper café/bistro version – phenomenally popular for weekend brunch from 8am (lunch Mon–Fri, dinner nightly) – or you can have a cocktail and some bar nibbles at the *Tow Bar* (daily 5.30pm–11pm).

Nepalese Kitchen 481 Crown St, Surry Hills ☎02/9319 4264. Speciality here is goat curry, served with freshly cooked relishes which traditionally accompany the mild Nepalese dishes. A whole range of vegetarian options, too. Cosy, calming atmosphere, with traditional music playing, or sit outside in the courtyard on a fine night. Dinner nightly. BYO.

Prasit's Northside Take-away 395 Crown St, and **Prasit's Northside on Crown** 415 Crown St, Surry Hills ☎02/9319 0748. Be prepared for some great Thai taste sensations amongst the bold purple colour scheme. Since entrees are available cheaply by the piece, you can attempt to work your way through their delicious repertoire; plenty of vegetarian options too. Takeaway branch can squeeze diners out front on stools, with a few more places upstairs. Both BYO. Takeaway closed Mon; restaurant open dinner Mon–Sat.

Sushi-Suma 421 Cleveland St, Surry Hills
☎02/9698 8873. That this small, noisy Japanese restaurant is extremely popular with Japanese locals and visitors says it all. Book a table to avoid disappointment. Moderate. BYO. Closed Mon & lunch Sat & Sun.

Darlinghurst and East Sydney

Oxford Street is lined with restaurants and cafés from one end to the other. **Taylor Square** and its surround is a particularly busy area, with lots of ethnic restaurants and several pubs. **Victoria Street** in Darlinghurst has a thriving café scene. East Sydney, where Crown Street heads downhill from Oxford Street towards William Street, has some excellent Italian restaurants and coffee bars – particularly on **Stanley Street**.

Balkan Seafood Restaurant 217 Oxford St, Darlinghurst ☎02/9331 7670. This long-running Croatian/Italian place is a Darlinghurst institution: fish and seafood is the best choice, but you can also get huge schnitzels and other continental meat dishes and Balkan specialities like *cevapci* and *razjnici*. Bustling atmosphere, moderate prices. Licensed and BYO. Tues–Sun dinner. There's another *Balkan Seafood* at Bent St, Fox Studios, Moore Park ☎02/9360 0097.

Bar Coluzzi 322 Victoria St, Darlinghurst. Famous Italian café: tiny and always packed with a characterful crew of regulars spilling out onto stools on the pavement. You can watch from a safe distance at the trendier, though equally tiny and very popular *Latteria* next door. Daily 5am–7.30pm.

Betty's Soup Kitchen 84 Oxford St, Darlinghurst. Soup is the speciality ($6.50), and makes for a cheap meal, served with damper, but there's also all the simple things your ideal granny might serve: stews, sausages or fish fingers with mash, pasta, salads and desserts too. Yummy home-made ginger beer or lemonade. Nothing over $11. Daily noon–10.30pm (11.30pm Fri & Sat). BYO.

Bill and Toni 74 Stanley St, East Sydney. Atmospheric, cheap Italian restaurant with balcony tables. Queue to get in. The café downstairs is a popular Stanley St local (daily 7am–midnight) and serves tasty Italian sandwiches. BYO.

bills 433 Liverpool St, Darlinghurst. This sunny corner café-restaurant in the quieter, terrace house-filled backstreets of Darlinghurst is one of Sydney's favourite breakfast spots: the ricotta hotcakes, huge muffins and deliciously creamy scrambled eggs top the morning list. Breakfast – until noon and all day Sat – isn't cheap ($14.50 for the hotcakes), but definitely worth it. The modern Australian lunch ranges from $17.50 to $23; BYO. The bistro-style *bills 2*, 359 Crown St, Surry Hills, also does dinner (plus breakfast and lunch; no bookings; licensed).

Bodhi in the Park Cook and Phillip Park, College St, East Sydney ☎02/9281 6162; another branch at Capitol Square, 730–742 George St, Haymarket. Top-notch Chinese vegetarian and vegan food, with the focus on delicious *yum cha*, which is served daily until 5pm. Organic and biodynamic produce is used. Licensed. Daily 11am–11pm.

fu-manchu 249 Victoria St, Darlinghurst; also a branch at Level 1, 80 Campbell Parade, Bondi Beach with fabulous ocean views. Perch yourself on red stools at stainless-steel counters and enjoy stylish but inexpensive Chinese and Malaysian noodles. BYO.

Govinda's 112 Darlinghurst Rd, Darlinghurst. Excellent, cheap Indian vegetarian restaurant, in the Hare Krishna centre. All-you-can-eat specials cost $15.90, with a film thrown in at the attached cinema (see p.186) for ten percent extra. Dinner nightly from 6pm.

Le Petit Crème 116 Darlinghurst Rd, Darlinghurst. Friendly and thriving French café whose speciality is huge, good-value filled baguettes. Also steak and *frites*, omelettes, home-made paté, *pain au chocolat* and big bowls of *café au lait*; bread and pastries are baked on the premises. Mon–Sat 7am–3pm, Sun 8am–3pm.

The Lounge 277 Goulburn St, Darlinghurst. Somewhere between a vegetarian café, bar, art gallery and music venue, this place yells "alternative". The menu is virtually all vegetarian and vegan with big servings and delicious recipes. By night, the atmosphere is more bar and music venue with DJs, open-mike nights, spoken-word performances, bands and projected images. Entertainment might be any night, but there's usually something happening on Fridays. Licensed. Tues–Thurs & Sun 9am–11pm, Fri & Sat 9am–midnight.

Oh! Calcutta! 252 Victoria St, Darlinghurst ☎02/9360 3650. Not your grungy neighbourhood Indian: the interior was fitted out by a star interior decorator. *Oh! Calcutta!* keeps getting suitably exclamatory reviews for its authentic – and occasionally inventive – food, and despite the decor, prices remain moderate. Licensed. Lunch Fri only, dinner Mon–Sat.

Onde 346 Liverpool St, Darlinghurst. French-owned restaurant in Darlinghurst's quieter back-streets, offering very good-value authentic bistro food: soups and patés to start, mains such as steak and *frites* or *confit* of duck, and decadent desserts. Portions are generous, service excellent, and it's invariably squeezed full of happy diners. Licensed, and all wine is available by the glass. Dinner nightly. No bookings, so be prepared to queue.

Tropicana Café 227B Victoria St, Darlinghurst. The birthplace of the Tropfest film festival (see box on p.187). Still a hugely popular place to hang out and pose, on the weekend especially. The huge but cheap Trop salad could fuel you all day. Daily 5am–11pm (Fri & Sat until midnight).

Una's Coffee Lounge 340 Victoria St, Darlinghurst. Cosy café that's been here for years dishing up schnitzel and other German dishes that are cheap, plentiful and tasty. The big breakfasts are very popular. BYO. Mon–Sat 6.30am–11pm, Sun 8am–11pm.

Kings Cross, Potts Point and Woolloomooloo

Many of the coffee shops and eateries in the Cross cater for the tastes (and wallets) of the area's backpackers, though there are also several stylish restaurants particularly in Potts Point. Many are also open late.

Cafe Hernandez 60 Kings Cross Rd, Potts Point. Veteran Argentinian-run 24hr coffee shop, open daily. Relaxed and friendly, you can dawdle here for ages and no one will make you feel unwelcome. Popular with taxi drivers and a mixed clientele of locals. Spanish food is served –*churros*, tortilla, *empanadas* and good pastries – but the coffee is the focus.

Laurent Boulangerie Pâtisserie The Wharf, 6 Cowper Wharf Rd, Woolloomooloo. Paris meets Sydney at this bakery-café: the gleaming glass counters hold a tempting array of pastries, filled baguettes and *croque monsieurs*, while the woven outdoor seats could have been stolen from the nearest *boulevard*. Daily 7.30am–8pm.

Otto The Wharf, 6 Cowper Wharf Rd, Woolloomooloo ☎02/9368 7488. *Otto* is the sort of restaurant where agents take actors and models out to lunch, and a well-known politician could be dining at the next table. Trendy and glamourous, with a location not just by the water but on the water, and serving top-of-the-range, very expen-

sive Italian cuisine, but with friendly service and a lively atmosphere. Licensed.

Venice Beach 3 Kellet St, Kings Cross ☎02/9326 9928. In a big Victorian terrace house with a courtyard and a cushion room, this is a seriously stylish cheap eat. All starters cost $6.90 except for the half-dozen oysters ($7.90), and mains range from pasta ($12.90) to steak ($15.90). A giant chargrilled seafood platter feeding two costs $49. Dinner nightly from 6pm. Licensed.

Wok Station 230 William St, Kings Cross. Tiny frenetic Thai café with friendly young staff cooking in the open kitchen to the sugary strains of Thai pop music. Food is inexpensive and delicious with an inventive line in daily specials.

Woolloomooloo Bay Hotel 2 Bourke St, Woolloomooloo. Big old pub popular for its bistro food, particulary the $35 seafood platters. Usual pub steaks and pasta also on offer, with mains under $20. Views across to the wharf and marina and over the bay from the outside tables and the big upstairs balcony.

Paddington

As **Oxford Street** continues through Paddington, it becomes gradually more upmarket; the majority of restaurants here are attached to gracious old pubs.

Arthurs 260 Oxford St, Paddington. Paddington pizza institution – queueing to get in is mandatory (no bookings). Pizzas here are the thin kind, with a huge range of toppings (from around $14 for a small), while the fresh pasta is nearly as much a star. Mon–Fri 5pm–midnight, Sat & Sun noon–midnight. BYO.

Grand National Hotel 161 Underwood St, cnr of

Elizabeth St ☎02/9963 4557. One of the best pub-restaurants in Sydney, dishing up imaginative fare but with old-fashioned attentive service. Booking essential at weekends. Expensive. Lunch Tues–Sun, dinner Tues–Sat.

Paddington Inn Bistro 338 Oxford St. Busy upmarket pub-bistro with an extensive and eclectic menu. Interior decor of textured glass, cushioned booths, polished concrete floors and fabric-lined walls. Packed on Saturdays, as it's opposite the market.

Royal Hotel Restaurant *Royal Hotel*, 237 Glenmore Rd, off Five Ways. Pub-restaurant serving some of the best steaks in Sydney, nonstop from noon to 11pm (9pm Sun). Smart interior and staff. Eating on the verandah is a real treat, with views over the art gallery and Five Ways action below, but places fill fast – and they don't take bookings. Wait to be called in the charming top floor *Elephant Bar* (from 4.30pm daily).

Sloanes Cafe 312 Oxford St. The emphasis in this veteran café is on good, unusual vegetarian food, moderately priced, but some meatier dishes have slipped onto the menu; the fresh juice bar has always been phenomenal. The stone-floored dining room opens onto the street to check out all the Saturday market action, or for more peace eat out back under vines in the delightful courtyard. Breakfast served all day. BYO. Mon–Sat 6.15am–5pm, Sun 7am–5pm.

Bondi and Watsons Bay

Bondi is a cosmopolitan centre with the many Eastern European and Jewish people giving its cafés a continental flair; there are also some fantastic kosher restaurants, delis and cake shops. The Bondi Beach area is full of cheap takeaways, fish-and-chip shops and beer gardens, as well as some seriously trendy cafés and restaurants. To the north, **Watsons Bay** is known for its famous seafood restaurant.

Bondi Tratt 34B Campbell Parade, Bondi Beach ☎02/9365 4303. Considering the setting, with outdoor seating overlooking the beach, not at all expensive. Come here to take in the view and the invariably buzzing atmosphere over breakfast, lunch and dinner, or just a coffee. Serves contemporary Australian and Italian food. Daily from 7am–11pm. Licensed and BYO.

Brown Sugar 100 Brighton Boulevarde, North Bondi. Groovy, relaxed little café tucked in a quiet residential street around the corner from the North Bondi set of shops. Music is funky, the staff suitably sweet. Locals straggle in for the very good breakfast menu: an interesting way with eggs, from green eggs (with pesto) to dill salmon eggs. Lunch on toasted Turkish sandwiches, salad or pasta. Great coffee. Daily 7.30am–4.30pm.

Burgerman 249 Bondi Rd, Bondi. Gourmet burgers to slaver over, at bargain prices. Vegetarian options, too. Busy takeaway service and small eat-in area. Daily noon–10pm. There's another branch at 116 Surrey St, off Victoria St, Darlinghurst.

Doyles on the Beach 11 Marine Parade, Watsons Bay ☎02/9337 1350; also **Doyles Wharf Restaurant** ☎02/9337 1572. The original of the long-running Sydney fish-restaurant institution is the first of these, but both serve great if overpriced seafood (but without the flair and inspiration of newer places) and have views of the city across the water. The adjacent pub serves pub-versions in its beer garden. A water taxi can transport you from Circular Quay to Watsons Bay. Expensive. Daily lunch and dinner.

Gelato Bar 140 Campbell Parade, Bondi Beach. The gleaming window display of indulgent creamy continental cakes and strudels lure in the beachgoers to this Hungarian-run place that's been serving up Eastern European dishes and huge portions of cake for over thirty years – and *gelato* too, of course (though the best is at *Pompei's*, round the corner on Roscoe Street). The coffee is among the best in Bondi. Old-fashioned coffee-lounge decor. Daily 8am–midnight.

Gertrude & Alice Cafe Bookstore 40 Hall St, cnr Consett Ave, Bondi Beach. Open daily from 7.30am until late into the night, it's hard to decide if *Gertrude and Alice*'s is more of a café or a second-hand literary bookshop. With small tables crammed into every available space, a big communal table and a comfy couch to lounge in, it can be hard for browsers to get to the books at busy café times. A homey hangout with generous, affordable serves of Greek and Mediterranean food, great cakes, great coffee and lots of conversation.

Hugo's 70 Campbell Parade, Bondi Beach ☎02/9300 0900. Smack amongst the parade of posers, surfers and travellers, this is contemporary Bondi – part café, part fine dining – with a casual, young and friendly flair. At weekends there's all-day brunch (9am–4pm; no bookings); while every night white tablecloths and softly glowing lamps appear and everyone seems to be having noisy fun. Service is wonderful and honed for your comfort, including blankets for those chilly sea breezes if you sit outside. Portions are generous modern Asian and Mediterranean-slanted creations. Expensive; licensed.

Lamrock Cafe 72 Campbell Parade, cnr Lamrock Ave. Stalwart Bondi café, always lively. The unpretentious local crowd come for the magnificent ocean views, the uncomplicated food – panini sandwiches, salads, pasta, burgers and fish and chips – and the breakfasts. You can even have a cocktail with your brunch – try the scarily named "Shark Attack", their version of a Bloody Mary. Umbrella-covered sidewalk tables outside, or cosy cushions inside. Licensed. Daily 7am–midnight.

The Red Kite 95 Roscoe St, Bondi Beach. Funky vegetarian café just back from Campbell Parade. Outside tables to catch the breeze. Fresh, imaginative food and freshly squeezed juices; yummy spiced Indian tea. Nothing over $10. Daily 8am–6pm.

Speedo's 126 Ramsgate Ave, North Bondi. Totally casual café bang opposite the north end of the beach, where the locals and their kids and dogs hang out, with no busy road in between you and the view. The walls are covered with vintage Speedo paraphernalia (the Australian cozzie in every surf lifesaver's wardrobe). The inexpensive breakfast specials are very popular. It gets so crowded expect long waits for your order, but there's always the big blue to gaze at. Daily 6am–6pm.

Yulla 1st Floor, 38 Campbell Parade, Bondi Beach ☎02/9365 1788. You could almost miss the discreet orange sign for *Yulla*, but this is no exclusive restaurant, though the beach views from the balcony are certainly million-dollar. Instead, you'll find a relaxed café atmosphere – colourful glowing walls, shining wooden floors and a window of blue sea – and very affordable contemporary Israeli food, which means a mix of Middle Eastern and North African dishes. An interesting breakfast served until noon. Licensed. Mon–Thurs 5.30pm–10pm, Fri noon–10.30pm, Sat & Sun 7am–10.30pm.

Bronte, Clovelly and Coogee

South of Bondi, **Bronte**'s beachfront café strip is wonderfully laid-back, and **Coogee** has a thriving café scene.

Barzura 62 Carr St, Coogee ☎02/9665 5546. Fantastic spot providing up-close ocean views. Both a café and a fully fledged restaurant, with wholesome breakfast until 1pm, snacks until 7pm, and restaurant meals – like seafood spaghetti or grilled kangaroo rump – served at lunch and dinner. Unpretentious though stylish service encourages a large local crowd. Moderate; licensed and BYO. Daily 7am–11pm.

The Beach Pit 211 Coogee Bay Rd, Coogee ☎02/9665 0068. Really enjoyable café-restaurant with Coogee's trademark informality and friendliness. Small but succulent menu has European and Asian influences and plenty of fish and seafood on offer; dishes are generous, well priced and presented. You can breakfast here at the weekend too. BYO. Closed Tues & Wed.

Sari Rasa 186 Arden St, above *McDonald's*, Coogee Beach ☎02/9665 5649. A mostly Indonesian menu, plus delicious Malaysian and Indian specialities, accompanied by ocean views – some tables outside on the balcony. Generous servings and low prices; BYO. Daily noon–3pm & 6pm–late.

Seasalt 1 Donnellan Circuit, Clovelly ☎02/9664 5344. Open-fronted café-restaurant, with fabulous views over the beach to cliffs, greenery and houses. *Seasalt* looks really smart, but it's the sort of casual beach place where you can come in sand-covered and have just a coffee, as well as the place to head for a full meal with wine. Cuisine is fresh and modern with a seafood basis; lunch mains range from $13 to $17, and summer-only dinner (fully clothed and groomed) starts from $16. Sophisticated, extensive breakfast packs them in at weekends. Takeaways from the small kiosk. Licensed. Mon–Fri 9am–5pm, Sat & Sun 8.30pm–5.30pm.

Sejuiced 487 Bronte Rd, Bronte. Delicious fresh juices, smoothies and frappés, combined with ocean and palm-tree views, make this tiny place a beauty to kick-start a summer's day. The "Morning Energiser" (beetroot, apple, ginger and carrot juice) ought to get you going, or there's all manner of other breakfast foods. Salads, soups and pasta are terrific too. If it's full, choose from several other great options on this wonderful café strip. Daily 6.30am–6pm.

North Shore and Manly

Military Road, running from Neutral Bay to Mosman, rivals and perhaps outdoes all the gourmet streets south of the harbour. The string of excellent restaurants tends to be expensive, but there are a number of bakeries, tempting pastry shops and well-stocked delis. **Manly** offers something for every taste and budget; there's an upmarket new food hall and food stalls on Manly Wharf, and loads of good cafés and restaurants on **Belgrave Street**, **Darley Street** and along **South Steyne**. **Miller Street**, which runs from North Sydney, has a great range of eateries around **Cammeray**.

Alhambra Cafe 54 West Esplanade, opposite Manly Wharf ☎02/9976 2975. With an owner from Spanish Morocco, the food served here is both authentic North African and Spanish – tapas, paella, merguez sausage, lamb and fish tagines, and couscous all feature. Flamenco dancers Thurs–Sun nights and a classical Spanish guitarist on Tues nights. Moderate. Licensed and BYO.

The Bathers Pavilion 4 The Esplanade, Balmoral Beach ☎02/9969 5050. Indulgent beach-house-style dining in the former (1930s) changing rooms on Balmoral Beach. The very pricey restaurant and café double act is presided over by one of Sydney's top chefs, Serge Dansereau. Fixed-price dinner menu in the restaurant starts from $87 for two courses (from $60 lunch time). Weekend breakfast in the café is a North Shore ritual – expect to queue to get in (the restaurant has Sunday breakfast only, for which you can book) – while the wood-fired pizzas are popular later in the day. Café daily 7am–midnight, restaurant lunch and dinner daily. Licensed.

Brazil Cafe 46 North Steyne, Manly ☎02/9977 3825. Classy surf-front café that's more Italian/eclectic than Brazilian, and transforms into a pricey restaurant in the evenings. A popular local hangout, particularly for the breakfasts and famed Sunday brunch. Licensed. Daily 8am–10pm.

Gourmet Pizza Kitchen 199 Military Rd, Neutral Bay ☎02/9953 9000. Spacious, busy place that's especially popular with families – how many other pizza joints provide pizza dough for the kids to play with? Inexpensive. Licensed.

Jipang 37 The Corso, Manly ☎02/9977 4436. Excellent Japanese noodle house; very inexpensive. BYO. Closed Mon.

Just Hooked 236 Military Rd, Neutral Bay ☎02/9904 0428. A small range of delicious fresh fish in a classy version of a classic fish shop, with white-tiled walls and high but comfortable stools. All sorts of inspired, often spicy things done with the seafood, from Thai curries to pasta dishes, but the simple fish and chips is just as popular. BYO. Dinner Mon–Sat.

Maisys Cafe 164 Military Rd, Neutral Bay. Cool hangout on a hot day or night (open 24hr), with funky interior and music. Good for breakfast – from croissants to bacon and eggs – or delicious Maltese *pastizzi* plus soups, burgers, pasta and cakes. Not cheap, but servings are generous. BYO.

Somi's 48 Victoria Parade, cnr South Steyne, Manly ☎02/9977 7511. Inexpensive Thai restaurant across from the beach – fantastic views – with an appropriately fresh and delicious range of spicy seafood dishes on the menu, and quite a few vegetarian dishes too. Inexpensive to moderate. Licensed and BYO. Daily noon–11pm.

Watermark 2A The Esplanade, Balmoral Beach ☎02/9968 3433. For a memorable Sydney meal, both for location and food, you can't go wrong here. Chef Kenneth Leung is well known for his fusion of Eastern and Western cooking styles and ingredients, plus there are views right across the water, a terrace to dine under the sun or stars (or sit by the fireplace in winter), a stylish interior and fabulous service. Very expensive; licensed.

Entertainment, nightlife and culture

To find out exactly **what's on** in Sydney, Friday's *Sydney Morning Herald* offers "Metro", a weekly entertainment lift-out, and the *Daily Telegraph* has the "Seven Days" pull-out every Thursday. In addition to these and the rather bland monthly programmes distributed by various tourist organizations (see p.92), there is a plethora of **free listings magazines** for more alternative goings-on – clubbing, bands, fashion, music and the like – which can be found lying around in the cafés, record shops and boutiques of Paddington, Glebe and Kings Cross: these include *Revolver* and *Drum Media* with their weekly band listings and reviews, and *3D World* and *Beat* covering the club scene. *City Hub*, a politically aware, free, weekly newspaper, also has an excellent events listing section. The Sydney Citysearch **website** (Ⓦwww.sydney.citysearch.com.au) has listings of film, theatre and music events.

Ticketek is the main **booking agency**, with branches located throughout Sydney, including 195 Elizabeth St, inside Grace Bros department store at the corner of George and Market streets, and within the Entertainment Centre (bookings ☎02/9266 4800, ⓦwww.ticketek.com.au). There's also Ticketmaster 7, at 13 Campbell St, Haymarket (Capitol Theatre) or 480 Elizabeth St, Surry Hills (bookings ☎02/9310 5020, ⓦwww.ticketmaster7.com). For theatre, concerts, opera and ballet you can always try for cheap, same-day tickets at the **Halftix** office at 91 York St (Mon–Fri 9.30am–5pm, Sat 10am–3pm; enquiries ☎02/9279 0855, bookings ⓦwww.halftix.com.au); they also sell regular tickets.

Pubs and bars

The differences between a restaurant, bar, pub and nightclub are often blurred in Sydney, and one establishment may be a combination of all these under one roof. The list below consists mainly of traditional old **hotels**, though at most of these there'll be some kind of food available, and they may even occasionally lay on entertainment. Sydney has many Art Deco pubs, a classic 1930s style notably seen in the tilework; we've mentioned some of the best below. For a guaranteed drink any time, head for Kings Cross. A recent relaxing of licensing laws also means many restaurants also have bars with identities in their own right where drinks can be served to non-diners, so also check out our restaurant listings.

The Rocks and CBD

Arthouse Hotel 275 Pitt St, City. A grand nineteenth-century School of Arts Building converted into a pub. The main bar, the *Verge*, is a converted chapel which makes for a dramatic drinks setting: high sky-lighted ceilings, polished wooden floorboards, beautiful Victorian-era design, fire-burning cauldrons and intriguing images projected onto a huge video screen. *Arthouse* lives up to its name with free life-drawing classes in the library, art exhibitions, short-film screenings and guest DJs. Restaurant prices are reasonable and lunch-time bar specials – like the Mon–Wed $5 steaks – are fantastic value.

Australian Hotel 100 Cumberland St, The Rocks. Convivial corner hotel with crowded outside tables

Legendary beer gardens

Many Sydney pubs have an outdoor drinking area, perfect for enjoying the sunny weather – the four listed below, however, are outright legends.

Doyles Watsons Bay Hotel 10 Marine Parade, Watsons Bay. Relaxing beer garden with views over Watsons Bay and good-value bistro meals, crowded at weekends with people enjoying a beer with their fish and chips.

The Mean Fiddler Cnr Commercial and Windsor roads, Rouse Hill. About an hour's drive from Sydney's CBD, near Windsor, the Fiddler is off the beaten track; you'll need your own transport to get here. It's well worth the effort though, evidenced by the huge crowds the 170-year-old pub attracts. An Irish pub with something for everyone – small intimate rooms, open fires, live televised sport in the sports bar, and one of the best beer gardens in Sydney: a big courtyard with cook-your-own-steaks and help-yourself salad bar by day and live entertainment at night.

Newport Arms Hotel 2 Kalinya St, Newport. Overlooking Pittwater. Sunday is the big day here, with free jazz outside (1–5pm); the bistro serves food from noon right through to closing.

The Oaks Hotel 118 Military Rd, Neutral Bay. The North Shore's most popular pub takes its name from the huge oak that shades the entire beer garden. Make use of the BBQ and cook your own (expensive) steak, or there's a gourmet pizza restaurant inside.

facing across to the lively basketball courts tucked beneath the Harbour Bridge. Inside, original fittings give a lovely old-pub feel. Known for its Bavarian-style draught beer brewed in Picton, plus gourmet pizzas with toppings which extend to native creatures – emu, kangaroo and crocodile.

Bridge Bar Level 10, 1 Macquarie St, City. Located near the infamous "Toaster" building, there's no better place to watch the sun go down. A see-through curtain drops down to minimise glare from the sunset and ensures an unspoilt view of the harbour. Despite the plush surrounds, the crowd's not as exclusive as you'd expect.

Establishment 252 George St. Deluxe bar. The huge main room boasts an extraordinarily long marble bar, white pillars, high decorative ceilings, and an atrium and fountain at the back. Despite the size, it gets jam-packed, particularly on Friday nights, when the door policy is very strict. On-site ballroom, restaurants (the world-class *est* , with top chef Peter Doyle) and *Tank* nightclub (p.180), and thirty-odd luxurious hotel rooms.

Forbes Hotel Cnr King and York streets, City. Atmospheric, turn-of-the-twentieth-century corner hotel with a lively downstairs bar. Upstairs is more sedate, with a pool table and plenty of window seating – the best spot is the tiny cast-iron balcony, with just enough room for two. Very popular Thurs & Fri nights. Fri & Sat to 3am.

Glenmore Hotel 96 Cumberland St, The Rocks. Unpretentious, inexpensive breezy pub perched over The Rocks, with great views from large windows in the public bar and spectacular ones from the rooftop beer garden. A handy refresher before or after the Harbour Bridge walk – it's opposite the pedestrian walkway entrance – and serving up reasonably priced pub grub.

Hero of Waterloo 81 Lower Fort St, Millers Point, The Rocks. One of Sydney's oldest pubs, built in 1843 from sandstone dug out from the Argyle Cut (see p.121), this place has plenty of atmosphere. Open fireplaces make it a good choice for a winter drink, and it serves simple meals.

Horizons Bar 36th Floor, *ANA Hotel*, 176 Cumberland St, The Rocks. Top-floor bar of the five-star *ANA* has a stunning 270-degree view – the Opera House, Darling Harbour, Middle Harbour and Homebush Bay to the Blue Mountains. Dress smart to get in. Mega-expensive but worth it for the view. Daily noon–1am (Sun until midnight).

Innc basement 244 Pitt St, City. A comfortable cocktail environment, with plenty of lounges and intimate mesh-curtained booths to relax in, moody lighting and funky lounge music. It's not cooler than thou, though: there are free pool tables and

pokies to play. A more style-conscious crowd on Saturday nights.

Marble Bar *Hilton Hotel*, 259 Pitt St, City. As much a sightseeing stop-off as a good spot for a drink amongst high Victorian decor featuring Italian marble. This was the original 1893 basement bar of the *Tattersalls Hotel*, which was replaced by the *Hilton* in 1973. The now-dated *Hilton* is undergoing massive refurbishment, but the iconic bar will remain the same (but shinier), re-opening in mid-2004.

Darling Harbour, Haymarket and around

Civic Hotel 388 Pitt St, cnr Goulburn St ✆ 02/8267 3186. Beautiful 1940s Deco-style pub, its original features in great condition. Upstairs, there's a glamorous dining room and cocktail bar. Handy meeting point for Chinatown and George Steet cinema forays. Stays open into the small hours Thurs–Sat. Closed Sun.

Pontoon Cockle Bay Wharf, Darling Harbour. Open-fronted bar with outside tables feels like one big lively beer garden, right on the water opposite the marina. Big umbrellas shade you from the sun for a daytime drink; pool tables inside. Attracts a young casual crowd, despite the upmarket restaurants surrounding it.

Scruffy Murphy's 43 Goulburn St. Rowdy, late-opening Irish pub with Guinness on tap, of course; phenomenally popular, particularly with travellers. Just around the corner from Central station. Closes around 3.30 or 4.30am most nights.

Slip Inn 111 Sussex St. On three levels overlooking Darling Harbour, this huge place has several bars, a bistro and a nightclub, *The Chinese Laundry*. A young style-conscious crowd still comes here, but it's dropped some of its past pretension (you can now get a Thai meal for just $7.50 Mon–Thurs). Front bars have a pool room, while downstairs a boisterous beer garden fills up on sultry nights, with the quieter, more sophisticated *Sand Bar* beside it. Excellent wine list, with lots available by the glass. Closed Sun.

Inner west: Glebe, Newtown and Balmain

Bank Hotel 324 King St, next to Newtown station. Smart-looking pub, always packed and open late. Pool table out front, cocktail bar out back and a great Thai restaurant, *Sumalee*, in the leafy beer garden.

Friend in Hand 58 Cowper St, cnr Queen Street, Glebe. Characterful pub in the leafy backstreets of Glebe, with all manner of curious objects dangling from the walls and ceilings of the public bar; a popular haunt for backpackers. Diverse entertainment in the upstairs bar (where you can also play pool) includes script-reading (Mon), poetry nights (Tues), and quizzes (Thurs). In the public bar, crab racing takes over Wednesday nights, and there's a piano player on Saturday nights. An Italian restaurant, *Cesare's No Names* (closed Sun lunch), with pasta from $9, is in the gazebo and beer garden.

London Hotel 234 Darling St, Balmain. Convivial British-style pub, with a high verandah overlooking the Saturday market. Attracts a typically mixed Balmain crowd.

Marlborough Hotel 145 King St, Newtown. A local favourite for a pre-dinner drink or to wind down after shopping along Newtown's upbeat retail strip on a Saturday. The "Marly" is benefiting from almost a decade of major structural work. The restaurant, *Bar Prego* has a diverse assortment of meals but with an Italian slant, and it's great value. Free music too – cover bands Tues & Sat and a funk band on Sun – plus trivia nights (Wed) and DJs (Thurs).

Monkey Bar 255 Darling St, Balmain. Stylish, crowded bar with an atrium restaurant. There's a small stage for the loud, free live music – blues, soul, jazz or acoustic rock (Tues 8–11pm and Sun 6–9pm). Inexpensive bar menu and a big selection of wine by the glass.

Nag's Head Cnr Lodge St and St Johns Rd, off Glebe Point Rd. Calling itself a "posh pub", this is a good place for a quiet drink – definitely no pokies. Decor and atmosphere is very much that of a British boozer: several imported beers on tap – Guinness, Boddingtons, Stella and Becks – and pints and half-pints available. Its bistro dishes up excellent steaks and other grills, and there's an extensive bar menu. For more action, there's a loft area upstairs with pool tables.

Darlinghurst and Kings Cross

Bourbon and Beefsteak Bar 24 Darlinghurst Rd, Kings Cross. Infamous 24hr Kings Cross drinking hole, which opened in 1968 to attract US soldiers on R&R. Undergoing massive changes at the time of writing, with the restaurant being converted into a bistro (you can still come here for a steak at 4am), the addition of a new terrace section upstairs and a lounge bar at the back, and the whole front section being opened up. Bands on every night (usually covers) and DJs playing retro four nights a week in the new downstairs Fandango Lounge. There may be a cover charge at weekends.

Burdekin 2 Oxford St, Darlinghurst. Well-preserved Art Deco pub with several trendy bars on four levels. The basement *Dug Out Bar* (from 5pm) is tiny and beautifully tiled, and has table service and generous cocktails; while the spacious, ground-level *Main Bar* sports dramatic columns and a huge round bar. See also p.181.

Darlo Bar *Royal Sovereign Hotel*, cnr Darlinghurst Rd and Liverpool St, Darlinghurst. Popular Darlinghurst meeting place, with a lounge-room atmosphere. Comfy colourful chairs, sofas and lamps have a 1950s feel, the crowd is mixed and unpretentious and drinks, including the house wines, aren't expensive. At night you can order from the menus of local eateries and they'll fetch the food for you.

Green Park Hotel 360 Victoria St, Darlinghurst. A Darlinghurst stalwart. Always lively, packed and cruisy at night with a crowd of young regulars. The stash of pool tables out back are a big part of the attraction.

Judgement Bar *Courthouse Hotel*, 189 Oxford St, Darlinghurst. Overlooking Taylor Square, the upstairs bar of this pub is often open 24hr. Totally undiscriminating – you may find yourself here in the wee hours among an assortment of young clubbers and old drunks – and drinks aren't pricey. Wakes up around 1am.

Lizard Lounge *Exchange Hotel*, 34 Oxford St. Stylish (mostly) straight bar in a gay strip (Tues night from 11pm is girls only). It has a spacious interior, wooden floorboards, changing art exhibitions on the walls and comfy leather couches in the corner (bag one of these early). Happy hour (Mon–Fri 5–8pm) gets them in, and as the crowd gathers and the music cranks up, posing becomes the main game. At weekends, after 11pm the bar becomes a club called *Stereo* (Fri $15, Sat $20) which leads through an entrance into *Q Bar* (see p.180). Otherwise the bar runs Mon–Sat 5pm to around 3am.

Middle Bar 1st Floor, *Kinsela's*, 383 Bourke St, Darlinghurst. Once a deluxe Art Deco funeral parlour, *Kinsela's* has long been transformed into an altogether lively drinking and dancing spot spread across three levels. The *Middle Bar* (Tues, Wed & Sun 5pm–1am, Thurs 5pm–3am, Fri–Sat 5pm–4am) is seriously sexy, from its lush decor and sunken seating area to the the young good-looking crowd who drink here. Gaze at the action in Taylor Square from the open-air balcony.

Savage 182 Campbell St, Darlinghurst. Just off Taylor Square. Upstairs above the restaurant of the same name (modern Australian fare), this new bar has a record store attached, and as you'd expect, a cool soundtrack to go with your drinks.

Soho Bar & Lounge *Piccadilly Hotel*, 171 Victoria St, Kings Cross. Trendy Art Deco pub on leafy Victoria Street, recently refurbished and looking better than ever. Ground-floor bar is the most Deco, but locals head for the upstairs lounge bar (Tues–Sun nights only) to hang out on the back balcony and play pool. The attached nightclub, *Yu*, runs on Fri and Sat nights.

Surry Hills, Paddington and Woollahra

Cricketers Arms 106 Fitzroy St, Surry Hills. Just down the road from the live music scene at the *Hopetoun* (see p.179), the *Cricketers* has an equally dedicated clientele. A young, offbeat crowd – plenty of piercings and shaved heads – cram in and fall about the bar, pool room, and tiny beer garden, and yell at each other over a funky soundtrack. Hearty bar snacks and a bistro (Tues–Sun 3–10pm).

Elephant Bar *Royal Hotel*, 237 Glenmore Rd, Paddington. The top-floor bar of this beautifully renovated, Victorian-era hotel has knockout views of the city, best appreciated at sunset (happy hour 6–7pm). The small interior is great too, with its fireplaces, paintings and elephant prints. As it gets crowded later on, people cram onto the stairwell and it feels like a party.

Grand Pacific Blue Room Cnr Oxford and South Dowling streets, Paddington. A cross between a bar, restaurant and club in a spacious Art Deco building. The surprisingly cosy bar fills the top corner, and diners eat below (Chinese/modern Australian menu). The chill-out lounge bar culture in Sydney began here and is still going strong. DJs get going at 11pm. Mon–Wed 6pm–1am, Thurs–Sat 6pm–3am.

Lord Dudley 236 Jersey Rd, Woollahra. Sydney's most British pub, complete with fireplaces, fox-hunting pictures, dark wood furniture – and a dartboard. Thirty-six beers on tap including Newcastle Brown Ale. The bistro serves up hearty British fare.

Mars Lounge 16 Wentworth Ave, Surry Hills. High ceilings, red and black dominated decor, moody lighting, heaps of seating – from hang-out-with-friends booths to meet-people stools – *Mars* is both comfortable and stylish. Music playing is eclectic; there's a different emphasis each night, from funky, retro-flavoured jazz, world grooves, latin, Seventies funk and uplifting house through to electronica. Mediterranean menu, including lots of shareable platters. Tues, Wed & Sun 5pm–1am, Thurs 5pm–1am, Fri & Sat 5pm–3am.

Bondi and Coogee

Beach Palace Hotel 169 Dolphin St, Coogee. Home to a young and drunken crowd, made up of locals, beach babes and backpackers. Features seven bars, two restaurants and a great view of the beach from the balcony under the distinctive dome.

Beach Road Hotel 71 Beach Rd, Bondi Beach. Huge, stylishly decorated pub with a bewildering range of bars on two levels and a beer garden. Popular with both travellers and locals for its good vibe. Entertainment, mostly free, comes from rock bands, DJs and a jazz supper club. Cheap Italian bistro, *No Names*, takes over the beergarden; upmarket contemporary Australian restaurant upstairs.

Bondi Hotel 178 Campbell Parade, Bondi Beach. Huge pub dating from the 1920s, with many of its original features intact. Sedate during the day but at night an over-the-top, late-night backpackers' hangout. Mon–Sat until 4am.

Bondi Icebergs 1 Notts Ave, Bondi Beach. Famous for its winter swimming club (see p.154), the Icebergs is a fantastic place to soak up the views and atmosphere of Bondi Beach. Though the clubhouse was recently rebuilt at a cost of $10 million, it's still surprisingly unpretentious – tourists mix with locals and enjoy the cheap drinks (still at club prices), live entertainment and fabulous view of the southern end of the beach, complete with surfers catching the waves. Cover bands play Wednesday to Sunday (except Thurs); trivia on Mondays. Meals at the *Sundeck Café*, with its open-air balconies, range from $5 to $20; pricey restaurant upstairs. Bring ID to show you're an out-of-towner. Daily 11am–11pm.

Live music: jazz, blues and rock

The live music scene in Sydney has passed its boom time, and pub venues keep closing down to make way for the dreaded poker machines. However, there are still enough venues to nourish a steady stream of local, interstate and overseas acts passing through every month, peaking in summer with a well-established open-air festival circuit. Pub bands and clubs are often free, especially if you arrive early; door charge is usually from $5, with $25 the uppermost price for smaller international acts or the latest interstate sensation. Early Sunday evenings (6–10pm) are a mellow time to catch some music, particularly jazz, around town.

The **venues for major events**, with bookings direct or through Ticketek or Ticketmaster (see p.175), are the Entertainment Centre at Haymarket near Darling Harbour (enquiries and credit-card sales ℡02/9266 4800); the Capitol Theatre, 13 Campbell St, Haymarket (℡02/9266 4800); the Enmore Theatre, 130 Enmore Rd, just up from Newtown (℡02/9550 3666); the centrally located Metro Theatre, 624 George St (℡02/9264 2666); *Selina's*, at the *Coogee Bay Hotel*, 212 Arden St, Coogee (℡02/9665 0000); and *City Live* (℡02/9358 8000) at Fox Studios.

There are now several big outdoor rock concerts throughout spring and summer but Homebake and the Big Day Out are still the best. **Homebake** (around $60; Ⓦ www.homebake.com.au) is a huge annual open-air festival in The Domain in early December with food and market stalls, rides and a line-up of over fifty famous and underground Australian bands from Killing Heidi to Grinspoon. The **Big Day Out**, on the Australia Day weekend (around $90; Ⓦ www.bigdayout.com), at the showground at Homebush Bay, features big international names like the Foo Fighters and PJ Harvey as well as local talent and attracts crowds of over fifty thousand. Also see Festivals, p.188, for other music events, including the Manly Jazz Festival.

Annandale Hotel Cnr Nelson St and Parramatta Rd, Annandale, just before Leichhardt ℡02/9550 1078. A showcase for indie bands, from up-and-comers to headline international acts, through rock, funk, metal and groove, with a capacity of 450. Music Tues–Sat nights (door $5–12).

The Basement 29 Reiby Place, Circular Quay ℡02/9251 2797. A great place to see jazz, acoustic and world music as well as a roster of the world's most renowned blues performers. The best way to take in a performance is to book a table and dine in front of the low stage.

Bridge Hotel 135 Victoria Rd, Rozelle ℡02/9810 1260. Legendary inner-west venue specializing in blues and pub rock, with some international but mostly local acts. Also good pub theatre and comedy nights.

Excelsior Hotel 64 Foveaux St, Surry Hills ℡02/9211 4945. Something of a muso's pub; jazz four nights a week, with residencies covering every style, from swing to avant garde (Mon–Wed; 8pm; $5). Sunday evening from 6pm is usually a jamming session. Bistro. Bar until 3am Fri and Sat.

Hopetoun Hotel 416 Bourke St, cnr of Fitzroy St, Surry Hills ℡02/9361 5257. One of Sydney's best venues for the indie band scene, "The Hoey" focuses on new, young bands: local, interstate and international all play in the small and inevitably packed front bar Monday to Saturday (from 7.30pm; cover charge depends on the act, though sometimes free), and on Sunday there are DJs (5–10pm; $5). Popular pool room, drinking pit in the basement, and inexpensive little restaurant upstairs (meals from $5–$8.50). Closes midnight.

Rose of Australia Hotel 1 Swanson St, Erskineville ℡02/9565 1441. Trendy inner-city types mix with Goths, locals and gays to sample some favourites of the pub circuit. Tuesday is Jazz and Soul Residency, Wednesday is popular local performer Bernie Hayes (laid-back Australian sounds). Bands play Fridays and Sundays on a rotational basis, so you can catch anything from an original rock act, through to a country and western cover band. Music starts from 8.30pm (from 6.30pm Sundays) and is always free. The bistro is cheap (from $5) and popular, with hundreds of thousands of Rose Burgers sold.

Sandringham Hotel 387 King St, Newtown ℡02/9557 1254. "The Sando" features local and interstate indie bands, who are no longer squeezed beside the bar but play on a new stage upstairs (Thurs–Sat 8.30pm–midnight, Sun 7pm–10pm; usually $5–$8, more well-known bands $12–$15).

Side On Cafe 83 Parramatta Rd, Annandale ℡02/9519 0055. Sydney's most interesting venue calls itself a "multi-arts complex". On Friday and Saturday nights you can hear jazz here in an inti-mate café atmosphere – everything from popular trios to the latest experimental fusions; Wednesday night is artist's residency; Thursday is world music/latin; Sunday night is cabaret. Also an art gallery and sometimes film screenings and script readings. Book if you want to dine (℡02/9516 3077); mains such as steak with roasted vege-tables cost around $20. Door charge $10–15.

Soup Plus 383 George St ℡02/9299 7728. This simple basement restaurant, near the Strand Arcade, has been serving up live jazz with its bowls of soup ($5) for over 25 years. Music Mon–Sat 7pm–11.30pm. Fri & Sat nights there's a cover charge of $25 which includes a two-course meal. Closed Sun.

Wine Banc 53 Martin Place ⊕02/9233 5399. Soft lighting and great jazz create a chill-out atmosphere at this upmarket venue. Live jazz Friday ($10) and Sat nights ($15) from 9pm. After midnight there's a "jam session", with jazz on Fridays and Latino music Saturdays. Delicious French-style meals at reasonable prices (mains around $16). Extensive, expensive wine list. Mon–Fri noon–11pm/midnight, Sat 6pm–2am. Closed Sun.

Clubs

Many of Sydney's best clubs are at **gay** or **lesbian** venues, and although we've listed these separately on pp.181–184, the divisions are not always clear – many places have specific gay, lesbian and straight nights scheduled each week. A long strip of thriving clubs stretches from Kings Cross to Oxford Street and down towards Hyde Park. The scene can be pretty snobby, with door gorillas frequently vetting your style. Admission ranges from $5 to $30; many clubs stay open until 5am or 6am on Saturday and Sunday mornings. The year's big dance party is **Vibes on a Summers Day** in the Bondi Pavilion at the end of January (around $90; ⓦwww.vibes.net.au). There are also good clubs attached to several of the drinking spots listed on pp.175–178.

BJs 195 Oxford St Mall, Bondi Junction. Lively club for lovers of South American sounds and salsa. A Latino band plays three sets through the night, while DJs offer up merengue, house and techno in two different club rooms. Sat 9.30pm–3am. $15.

Club 77 77 William St, Kings Cross. Rock venue which has post-band indie and alternative dance parties on Friday and Saturday nights until 5am. Popular with students. Drink prices aren't as high as at other clubs. $6.

Gas 467 Pitt St, Haymarket. One huge cutting-edge room downstairs where international DJs appear about once a month and a mezzanine level which acts as a viewing area over the dance floor, with chill-out lounges attached. Three bar areas. Thurs–Sun 10pm–6am. $15 Thurs, $20 Fri & Sat.

Globe 60 Park St, City. *Globe*'s cocktail-bar lounge is open 24 hours, and Thursday to Saturday from 10pm it's linked to a downstairs club section – you'll have to dress very cool to get past the door. Great place for soul, energetic house and hip-hop sounds Wed–Sat. $10–$15.

Home Cockle Bay Wharf, Darling Harbour. The first *really* big club venture in Sydney. The lavish *Home* can cram 2000 punters into its cool, cavernous interior. Also a mezzanine, a chill-out room, and outdoor balconies. Decks are often manned by name DJs, drinks are expensive, staff beautiful.Packed with a younger crowd on Fridays for its flagship night Sublime, with four musical styles across four levels. On Saturdays, Together at Home plays progressive and funky house. Fri & Sat from 11pm til late. $25.

Powercuts Reggae Club *Castles*, 114 Castlereagh St. DJs play "the smoothest reggae known to man" every Saturday night from 10pm until late. $10.

Q Bar 44 Oxford St, Darlinghurst. As the name suggests, this is a huge pool hall, but the main game is looking good in an elite crowd. An exclusive club which is difficult to penetrate, particularly if you're male and don't have a stunning babe on your arm. But it's worth trying to get into: it's another world altogether – entry is via a lift and the club is decked out with rich kid's toys, from arcade machines to a photo booth to capture insobriety. Daily 7pm til late (Fri from 5pm).

Rogues Cnr Oxford and Riley streets, Darlinghurst. Popular with the younger straight Oxford Street clubbing crowd, who can afford the hefty cover charge and $15 cocktails. Predominantly commercial dance and R&B at the weekends, although Eighties funk on Wednesday nights pulls an older crowd. Wed–Sat from 9pm. $16.50 Fri, $25 Sat.

Sugareef 20 Bayswater Rd, Kings Cross. After the sweaty writhing of *The World*, nearby *Sugareef* presents a more chilled, sophisticated atmosphere; deep house and breakbeat attract a regular crowd. Two rooms, two DJs and a popular pool table. Good on Tuesday nights, when there's not a lot happening elsewhere. Free Wednesday ("DJ Discovery" night), otherwise $5–15. Tues–Sun 9pm–6am.

Tank 3 Bridge Lane, off George St, City. This is for the glamorous industry crowd – fashion, music and film aficionados. If you don't belong, the style police will spot you a mile away. All very "funky" –

from the house music played by regular or guest DJs to the mirrors and wash basins in the toilets. Three amazing bars and a VIP section. Attire is smart casual to funky street wear, but attitude and good looks override the dress code. Fri & Sat 10pm–6am. $15–$20.

Tantra 169 Oxford St, Darlinghurst. Rotating resident DJs and live musicians/percussionists ensure that there's always something new happening. The younger crowd comes on Fridays for the high-octane beats, while Saturdays are pre-

dominantly 25- to 30-year-olds. Fri & Sat 10pm–6am. $10–$30.

The World 24 Bayswater Rd, Kings Cross. With cheap drinks on Friday and Saturday nights and a relatively relaxed door policy, *The World* is popular with a fun, party-loving crowd of travellers, who jive to a pleasing mix of funk and house grooves in a pleasant Victorian-era building with a big front balcony. The atmosphere throughout is lively, if a little beery in the front bar. Fri & Sat noon–6am, Sun–Thurs noon–4am. Free.

Gay and lesbian bars and clubs

One of the best things about Sydney's gay and lesbian scene is that it's all concentrated in two areas so it's easy to bar hop: in the inner east around Oxford Street, Darlinghurst, including Surry Hills and Kings Cross, and in the inner west in adjoining Newtown and Erskineville. Sydney never closes – there's always somewhere else to move on to. Entry is free unless otherwise indicated.

Arq 16 Flinders St, cnr Taylor Square, Darlinghurst. Huge nine-hundred-person capacity, state-of-the-art club with everything from DJs and drag shows to pool competitions. Two levels, each with a very different scene: the *Arena*, on the top floor, is strictly gay, while the ground-floor *Vortex* is a quieter, less crowded mix of gay and straights, with pool tables. Chillout booths, laser lighting, viewing decks and fishtanks add to the fun, friendly atmosphere. Sunday is the big night. Thurs–Sun from 9pm. Fri & Sat $15–20, Sun $5.

Bank Hotel 324 King St, next to Newtown station. This stylish bar is a dyke favourite on Wednesday nights when the long-running women's pool competition (8pm) draws large crowds to socialize and maybe even compete.

BumpHer Bar *Burdekin*, 2 Oxford St, Darlinghurst. On Friday nights (9pm–3am; $5) the lush *Lava Lounge* and the *Bat Bar* of this stylish hotel are taken over by a girls' cocktail and club night (gay friends welcome too).

DCM 33 Oxford St, Darlinghurst. Young, fast, mixed gay, lesbian and straight venue. A long-running but still-renowned nightclub, which like most Sydney clubs, doesn't really liven up till after midnight when you can be assured of a wild night of dancing. Thurs, Fri & Sun 10pm–6am, Sat 10pm–noon. $15–25.

Exchange Hotel 34 Oxford St, Darlinghurst. In the downstairs *Phoenix* bar, Saturday night's *Crash* underground "alternative" dance club is mostly gay men, but on Sunday nights there's a happy mix of gays and dykes (Sat & Sun from 10pm; $5 Sat, free Sun). In the upstairs *Lizard Lounge* (see

also p.177) on Tuesday nights from 11pm, *Furbar* is strictly for girls (free entry).

Flinders Hotel 63 Flinders St, Darlinghurst. A favourite pub haunt of young gay boys, quieter during the week; on weekends, a packed, wild late-night club playing commercial Hi-NRG dance.

Icebox 2 Kellet St, Kings Cross. Friday nights at this small club are usually gay and lesbian; no two nights are ever the same, but music is a mix of techno, house and hard house and the light show is lavish. The new decor is colourful and funky, but it's still kept cosily dark with candlight, and there are more intimate lounges to chill out in. Drinks aren't too pricey, dress is casual. Fri 10pm–6am. $10.

Imperial Hotel 35 Erskineville Rd, Erskineville ⊕ 02/9519 9899. Late-night gay and lesbian venue, with four bars including a popular, hot and sweaty dance floor in the basement (Fri & Sat progressive, commercial, Hi-NRG 11pm–6am for $5; "Go Girl" Thurs 10pm is a free, girls-only club night), and a riotous drag show line-up in the Cabaret Room (Wed–Sat; free; call for show times). The film *Priscilla, Queen of the Desert* both started and ended here; it was the *Imperial*'s finest hour, and the memories are kept alive in the photo-lined cocktail bar, the *Priscilla Lounge* (cabaret Fri & Sat 10.30pm; free). The drag shows are hilarious, inventive and constantly changing: expect anything from the gay-version of *Survivor* to the *Rocky Horror Drag Show*. Pool tables (free all day Mon) and music videos in the public bar. Mon–Thurs 3pm–2/3am, Fri & Sat 3pm–7am, Sun 3pm–midnight.

Sydney is indisputably one of the world's great gay cities – indeed, many people think it capable of snatching San Francisco's crown as the Queen of them all. There's something for everyone – whether you want to lie on a beach during the warmer months (Oct–April) or party hard all year round. Gays and lesbians are pretty much accepted – particularly in the inner-city and eastern areas. They have to be – there's too many of them for anyone to argue. A big drawcard is the **Sydney Gay & Lesbian Mardi Gras**; the festival lasts for four weeks, starting the first week of **February**, kicking off with a community fair day in Victoria Park and culminating in the parade and party on the last weekend of February or the first weekend of March. The first parade was held in 1978 as a gay-rights protest and today, it's the biggest celebration of gay and lesbian culture in the world. In 1992, an unprecedented crowd of four hundred thousand, including a broad-spectrum of straight society, turned up to watch the parade and two years later it began to be broadcast nationally on television. Mardi Gras turned 25 in 2003 but for a while it looked like it wouldn't make it. By 1999, the combined festival, parade and party was making the local economy $100 million dollars richer and the increasing commercialization of Mardi Gras was drawing criticism from the gay and lesbian community. Its bubble burst in 2002, after financial mismanagement saw the Mardi Gras organization in the red to the tune of $500,000. Instead of throwing in the towel, the fundraising organization was rebuilt as the "New Mardi Gras"; although less cash-rich and with fewer floats in the 2003 parade, New Mardi Gras is drawing on the resources and creativity of its talented community along with the desire to keep the festival going in order to revive the old Mardi Gras spirit.

But don't despair if you can't be here for Mardi Gras or the Sleaze Ball (the annual Mardi Gras fundraiser in late September/early October). The city has much more to offer. **Oxford Street** is Sydney's official "pink strip" of gay restaurants, coffee shops, bookshops and bars, and here you'll find countless pairs of tight-T-shirted guys strolling hand-in-hand, or checking out the passing talent from a hip, streetside café. However, the gay-straight divide in Sydney has less relevance for a new generation, perhaps ironically a result of Mardi Gras' mainstream success. Several of the long-running gay venues on and around Oxford Street have closed down and many remaining attract older customers, as younger gays and lesbians embrace inclusiveness and party with their straight friends and peers. **King Street**, Newtown, and nearby **Erskineville** are centres of gay culture, while lesbian communities have carved out territory of their own in **Leichhardt** (known affectionately as "Dykehart"). The bar and club listings have not been split into separate gay and lesbian listings, as the scene thankfully doesn't split so neatly into "them and us".

If you've come for the sun, popular **gay beaches** are Tamarama (see p.154), Bondi (see p.152), and "clothing optional" Lady Jane, at Watsons Bay (see p.148), while pools of choice are Red Leaf harbour pool at Double Bay (see p.129) and the appropriately named Andrew "Boy" Charlton pool in The Domain (see p.147). The Coogee Women's Baths, at the southern end of Coogee Beach (see p.156) is popular with lesbians.

Mardi Gras, Sleaze and PRIDE

From a Queer perspective the best time of year to visit Sydney is still February, when the **Sydney Gay & Lesbian Mardi Gras** takes over the city. Four weeks of exhibitions, performances and other events – including the ten-day **Mardi Gras Film Festival** in mid-February showcasing the latest in Queer cinema – represent the largest lesbian and gay arts festival in the world, paving the way for the main event, an exuberant night-time **parade** down Oxford Street, when up to a half-a-million gays and straights jostle for the best viewing positions, before the Dykes on Bikes, traditional leaders of the parade since 1988 roar into view. Participants devote months to the preparation of outlandish floats and outrageous costumes at Mardi

Gras workshops, and even more time is devoted to the preparation of beautiful bodies in Sydney's packed gyms. The parade begins at 7.30pm (finishing around 10.30pm), but people line the barricades along Oxford Street from mid-morning (brandishing stolen milk crates to stand on for a better view). If you can't get to Oxford Street until late afternoon, your best chance of finding a spot is along Flinders Street near Moore Park Road, where the parade ends. Otherwise, AIDS charity The Bobby Goldsmith Foundation (℡02/9283 8666, ⓦwww.bgf.org.au) has around 7000 grandstand seats on Moore Park Road, at $75 each.

The all-night **dance party** which follows the parade is held in several differently themed dance spaces at the old Showgrounds at Fox Studios in Moore Park (including a women's space, *G-Spot*). You have to plan ahead if you want to get a **ticket**: party tickets ($95) often sell out by the end of January. The purchase of tickets used to be restricted to "Mardi Gras members" to keep the event Queer, with special provisions for visitors from interstate and overseas, but as the New Mardi Gras is rebuilding the old memberships and procedures no longer exist, it's best to contact the **New Mardi Gras office** (℡02/9557 4332, ⓦwww.mardigras.org.au) for details of how to get hold of tickets. For credit-card bookings for festival events visit ⓦwww.ticketek.com.au. Your local gay-friendly travel agent can also organize tickets. The **Sydney Gay & Lesbian Mardi Gras Guide**, available from mid-December, can be picked up from bookshops, cafés and restaurants around Oxford Street or at the Mardi Gras office.

Sydney just can't wait all year for Mardi Gras, so the **Sleaze Ball** is a very welcome stopgap in late September or early October and acts as a fundraiser for the Mardi Gras organizers. Similar to the Mardi Gras party, it's held at the former Showground site, and goes on through the night. Tickets, which cost around $95, are organized by New Mardi Gras. The community centre **PRIDE** (℡02/9331 1333; ⓦwww.pridecentre.com.au), have been organizing a similarly priced and over-the-top **New Year's Eve party** for the past decade, usually at Fox Studios.

Groups and information

Information The Bookshop, 207 Oxford St, Darlinghurst (℡02/9331 1103), is a good starting point for getting to know gay Sydney, with a complete stock of gay- and lesbian-related books, cards and magazines. The staff are friendly and ready to help in any way they can. You can pick up the free gay and lesbian weeklies *Sydney Star Observer* and *SX* and the monthly lesbian-specific *LOTL* (*Lesbians on the Loose*) from here and other venues and gay-friendly businesses in the eastern suburbs and inner west. These magazines will tell you where and when the weekly dance parties are being held, and where you can buy tickets.

Support networks Gay & Lesbian Counselling Service (daily 4pm–midnight; ℡02/9207 2800). AIDS Council of NSW (ACON), 9 Commonwealth St, Surry Hills ℡02/9206 2000. Albion Street Centre, 150–154 Albion St, Surry Hills ℡02/9332 1090; counselling, testing clinic, information and library. Anti-Discrimination Board ℡02/9318 5444.

Travel agents

Friends of Dorothy Travel 96 Crystal St, Petersham NSW 2049 ℡02/9569 5331. Offers special tours designed for gay men and lesbians, and can advise about travel during Mardi Gras.

Silke's Travel PO Box 1099, Darlinghurst, NSW 1300 ℡02/8347 2000. Offers advice and bookings for domestic and international travel, and accommodation from a gay and lesbian perspective. Lots of experience with backpacker tours.

See also p.108 for gay- and lesbian-friendly **places to stay**, and pp.181 and 184 for a lowdown on the **club scene** and listings of specifically gay and lesbian venues.

Midnight Shift 85 Oxford St, Darlinghurst. "The Shift", running for over twenty years, is a veteran of the Oxford Street scene. The *Shift Video Bar* is a large drinking and cruising space to a music-video backdrop; pool tables out back. Upstairs the revamped weekend-only club is a massive space with everything from a waterfall to a cutting-edge laser light show. It hosts drag shows (usually Fri nights), DJs and events; cover charge upwards of $5. Mainly men. Bar daily noon–6am, club Fri & Sat 11pm–7am.

Newtown Hotel 174 King St, corner Watkin Street, Newtown. A stalwart of the Sydney scene. Laid-back mix of Newtown lesbians and gays (though predominantly male), drag shows (Tues–Sat 10pm & 11pm, Sun 8.30pm & 9.15pm), and pool tables (free on Mon nights). A tiny dance floor – nightly DJs means its always in action. The well-regarded *Linda's Backstage Restaurant* (Mon–Sat from 6pm) serves up delicious, very reasonably priced modern Australian fare. Upstairs, *Bar 2* is a quiet intimate space. Mon–Sat 11am–midnight, Sun 11am–10pm; *Bar 2* Wed–Sun 6pm–midnight.

Oxford Hotel 134 Oxford St, Darlinghurst. The ground-floor bar, open 24 hours, is the macho pillar of the gay community, with dim lights, hard music and a packed crowd after 11pm – particularly busy on Friday and Saturday nights. On the first floor, *Gilligans* is a very different scene, a popular cocktail bar which attracts a mixed crowd of gay boys, lesbians and the straight party set; happy hour 5–7pm; daily 5pm–3am. On the second floor,

Gingers is a quieter, more women-friendly bar – decor is plush, and several small cosy rooms provide intimacy; open Thurs–Sat from 6pm.

The Red Room *Lansdowne Hotel*, 2–6 City Rd, Chippendale. Upstairs on Saturday nights (8pm–3am), this classy funk and soul night is strictly for girls, including the female DJs and special guests. The motto is "dress to impress", but from cargo pants to sequinned splendour, anything goes. Entry $5.

Stonewall Hotel 175 Oxford St, Darlinghurst. With three action-packed levels, this pub is a big hit with young gays and lesbians and their straight friends. Theme nights like karaoke, celebrity drag, or dating games and DJs in the various different bars Wednesday to Saturday. Downstairs bar plays commercial dance music, the cocktail bar above accelerates on uplifting house, while the top-floor, weekend-only VIP Bar gets off on campy, "handbag" sounds (Fri & Sat 11pm–6am; free). Natural light and outside tables at ground level, where you can order a meal from the neighbouring café, *The Californian*.

Taxi Club 40 Flinders St, Darlinghurst. Last stop. It's a Sydney legend, but don't bother before 2 or 3am, and you'll need to be suitably intoxicated to appreciate it fully. There's a strange blend of drag queens, taxi drivers, lesbians and boys (straight and gay) to observe, and the cheapest drinks in gay Sydney. An upstairs dance club (free) operates Friday and Saturday from 1am. Bring ID to show you're from out of town. 24hr except for a clean from 6am–9am.

Classical music, theatre and dance

Sydney's **arts scene** is vibrant and extensive. Half-price same-day tickets are available from Halftix (see p.175). The Sydney Symphony Orchestra plays at the Town Hall, St James's Church or the Opera House while the Australian Ballet performs at the Opera House and the Capitol Theatre. The free outdoor performances in The Domain, under the auspices of the Sydney Festival, are a highlight of the year, as crowds gather to enjoy the music with a picnic.

Concert halls

Conservatorium of Music Royal Botanic Gardens, off Macquarie St ℡ 02/9351 1263. Conservatorium students have traditionally given free lunch-time recitals every Tuesday and Friday at 1.10pm during term time. Staff and students also give other concerts, both free and ticketed (up to around $30) at various venues around town; a programme is available from the concert department. See p.129 for more details.

Sydney Opera House Bennelong Point ℡ 02/9250

7777. The Opera House is, of course, *the* place for the most prestigious performances in Sydney, hosting not just opera and classical music but also theatre and ballet in its many auditoriums. Forget quibbles about ticket prices (classical concerts from $40, opera from $90) – it's worth going just to say you've been. See pp.115–116 for more details.

Town Hall Cnr Druitt and George streets ℡ 02/9265 9189. Centrally located concert hall. See p.124 for more details.

Theatre and dance

Bangarra Dance Theatre Pier 4, Hickson Rd, Millers Point, The Rocks ☎02/9251 5333. Formed in 1989, Bangarra's innovative style fuses contemporary movement with the traditional dances and culture of the Yirrkala Community in Arnhemland. Based at the same pier as the Wharf Theatre but performing at other venues in Sydney and touring nationally and internationally – call for the latest details.

Belvoir St Theatre 25 Belvoir St, Surry Hills ☎02/9699 3444. Highly regarded two-stage venue for a wide range of contemporary Australian and international theatre.

Capitol Theatre 13 Campbell St, Haymarket ☎02/9320 5000. Built as a deluxe picture theatre in the 1920s, the theatre was saved from demolition and beautifully restored in the mid-1990s. The 2000-seater now hosts big-budget musicals and ballet, watched from beneath its best feature, the deep-blue ceiling spangled with the stars of the southern skies.

Ensemble Theatre 78 McDougall St, Milsons Point ☎02/9929 0644. Australian contemporary and classic plays.

The Footbridge Theatre Parramatta Rd, University of Sydney, Glebe ☎02/9692 9955. Rich and varied repertoire, from *Cabaret* to Shakespeare.

Lyric Theatre Star City Casino, Pirrama Rd, Pyrmont ☎02/9657 9657. The place to see those big musical extravaganzas imported from the West End and Broadway. The casino's smaller theatre, the Star City Showroom, puts on more off-beat musicals – such as the *Rocky Horror Picture Show* – and comedy.

Marian Street Children's Theatre 2 Marian St, Killara ☎02/9498 3166. Bookings are essential for the popular 1pm Saturday matinee for kids (aged 3–10; also school holidays Mon–Fri 10.30am & 1pm).

NAISDA Dance College 3 Cumberland St, The Rocks ☎02/9252 0199. Established in 1976, this famous training company for young Aboriginal and Islander dancers, based in The Rocks, puts on mid-year and end-of-year performances at the NAISDA Studios at the college; call for times.

The Playhouse , Drama Theatre and The Studio Sydney Opera House, Bennelong Point ☎02/9250 7777. The three theatrical venues at the Opera House. The Playhouse and Drama Theatre show modern and traditional Australian and international plays mostly put on by the Sydney Theatre Company, while the Studio, the Opera House's smallest venue (and most affordable ticket prices), is flexible in design with a theatre-in-the-round format, and offers an innovative and wide-ranging programme of contemporary performance: theatre, cabaret, dance, comedy, and hybrid works.

Theatre Royal MLC Centre, King St, City (bookings through Ticketek ☎02/9266 4800). Imported musicals and blockbuster plays.

Wharf Theatre Pier 4/5, Hickson Rd, Millers Point, The Rocks ☎02/9250 1777. Home to the highly regarded Sydney Theatre Company, producing Shakespeare and modern pieces, and to the Sydney Dance Company. Atmospheric waterfront location, and a well-regarded restaurant (see p.166), bar and café.

Fringe theatre, comedy and cabaret

As well as the venues listed below, also see the *Bridge Hotel* (p.179) which has Monday comedy nights and Tuesday improv and cabaret runs, and *The Imperial* (p.181) for its brilliant free drag shows.

Comedy Store Fox Studios, Driver Ave, Moore Park ☎02/9357 1419. International (often American) and Australian stand-up comics Tuesday to Saturday. Bar open from 4pm, show 8.30pm. Meals aren't available inside, but the sleek *Arena Bar & Bistro* offers meal discounts for Comedy Store ticket holders. Bookings recommended. Entry Tues–Thurs $15, Fri & Sat $27.50.

New Theatre 542 King St, Newtown ☎02/9519 3403. Professional and amateur actors (all unpaid) perform contemporary dramas with socially relevant themes. Entry $22.

NIDA Studio 215 Anzac Parade, Kensington ☎02/9697 7613. Australia's premier dramatic training ground – the National Institute of Dramatic

Art – where the likes of Mel Gibson, Judy Davis and Colin Friels started out, also offers student productions for talent-spotting. Tickets $27.

The Performance Space 199 Cleveland St, Redfern, opposite Prince Alfred Park ☎02/9698 7235. Experimental performances.

Stables Theatre 10 Nimrod St, Darlinghurst ☎02/9361 3817. Theatre with a mission to develop and foster new Australian playwrights.

Theatresports ☎02/9518 4014, bookings ☎02/9699 3444. Improvised genius with teams competing against each other. The theatrical games are at Belvoir St Theatre most Sunday evenings (see above), or occasionally at other venues around town.

Cinemas

The commercial movie centre of Sydney is two blocks south of the Town Hall at 505–525 George Street where you'll find the three big chains – Hoyts (℡02/9273 7431), Greater Union (℡02/9267 8666) and Village (℡02/9273 7409) – under one roof. This is mainstream, fast-food, teenager territory and there are much nicer places to watch a film, especially at the locals in the list below. Other more pleasantly located Hoyts can be found at the Broadway Shopping Centre, on Broadway near Glebe (℡02/9211 1911), and at Fox Studios (℡02/9332 1300), which incorporates the less mainstream Cinema Paris (℡02/9332 1633) and upmarket screening room La Premiere (℡02/9266 4887). Another mainstream multiplex is bang in Chinatown, Reading Cinemas, at Level 3, Market City Shopping Centre, Haymarket (℡02/9280 1202). Standard tickets cost around $14, but Tuesdays are reduced-price (around $9.50) at all of these cinemas and their suburban outlets, and Monday or Tuesday at the arthouse and local cinemas listed below.

In the summer, two open-air cinemas open up: from November to mid-February the **Moonlight Cinema**, in the Centennial Park Amphitheatre (Oxford Street, Woollahra entrance; Tues–Sun, films start 8.45pm, tickets from 7.30pm or via Ticketek on ℡02/9266 4800; $14), shows classic, arthouse and cult films; and throughout January as part of the Sydney Festival, the **Open Air Cinema** (tickets from 6.30pm or bookings on ℡13 61 00; $17.50) is put up at Mrs Macquaries Point in the Royal Botanic Gardens for a very picturesque film screening – mainly mainstream recent releases and some classics. See box opposite for details of Sydney's annual film festivals.

Chauvel Twin Cinema Paddington Town Hall, cnr Oatley Rd and Oxford St, Paddington ℡02/9361 5398. Varied programme of Australian and foreign films plus classics at this Australian Film Institute Cinema. Discount on Mon and Tues.

Cremorne Orpheum 380 Military Rd, Cremorne ℡02/9908 4344. Charming heritage-listed, four-screen cinema built in 1935 with a splendid Art Deco interior and old-fashioned friendly service. The main cinema has never dispensed with its Wurlitzer organ recitals preceding Saturday and Sunday night films. Mainstream, and foreign new releases. Discount on Tues.

The Dendy MLC Centre, 19 Martin Place ℡02/9233 8166. Trendy single-screen cinema, café, bar and pool room complex (daily noon–midnight). Also the four-screen Dendy Newtown, 261 King St (℡02/9550 5699), with attached café, bar and bookshop; and the newest, superbly sited, addition – the three-screen Dendy Opera Quays, 2 East Circular Quay (℡02/9247 3800). All showing prestige new-release films. Discount on Mon.

Govinda's Movie Room 112 Darlinghurst Rd, Darlinghurst ℡02/9380 5155. Run by the Hare Krishnas (but definitely no indoctrination), Govinda's shows two films every night from a range of classics and recent releases in a pleasantly unorthodox cushion-room atmosphere. The movie and dinner deal (all-you-can-eat vegetarian buffet) is popular – $15.90 for the meal with an extra tenpercent to see a movie –and you may need to book (see p.170).

Palace Cinemas Chain of inner-city cinemas showing foreign-language, arthouse and new releases: Academy, 3A Oxford St, cnr South Dowling St, Paddington (℡02/9361 4453); Verona, 17 Oxford St, cnr Verona St, Paddington (℡02/9360 6099), with a bar; Norton, 99 Norton St, Leichhardt (℡02/9550 0122), the newest with a bookshop and cybercafé. Discount Mon.

Panasonic IMAX Theatre Southern Promenade, Darling Harbour ℡02/9281 3300. State-of-the-art giant cinema screen showing a choice of four films designed to thrill your senses; $15 for 2-D version, $17 for 3-D.

Valhalla 166 Glebe Point Rd, Glebe ℡02/9660 8050. The beloved Valhalla, Sydney's first alternative cinema (established in 1976), shows documentaries, foreign films, new-release independents and Australian film. Also hosts specialist evenings – including short film nights – which draw in local filmmakers for screenings and discussions.

Film festivals

The **Sydney Film Festival**, held annually for two weeks in **early June**, is an exciting programme of features, shorts, documentaries and retrospective screenings from Australia and around the world. Founded in 1954 by a group of film enthusiasts at Sydney University, the festival struggled with prudish censors and parochial attitudes until freedom from censorship for festival films was introduced in 1971. From the early, relaxed atmosphere of picnics on the lawns between screenings and hardy film-lovers crouching under blankets in freezing prefabricated sheds, it has gradually moved off-campus, to find a home from 1974 in the magnificent State Theatre (see p.124). Films are also shown at the wonderfully sited three-screen Dendy Quays in Circular Quay. The festival was once mainly sold on a subscription basis, but subscriptions now only apply to screenings at the State Theatre; the more provocative line-up of films at the Dendy Quays aims to attract a new, younger audience on a single or packaged ticket basis. Single **tickets** cost around $12, packages of four around $44 or ten around $100; **subscriptions** for the State programme start from $110 for one week daytime only unreserved stalls seating, and go up to $250 for two weeks reserved dress circle night-time screenings. For more information, call or drop into the festival office at 405 Glebe Point Rd, Glebe (Mon–Fri 9am–5pm; ⓣ02/9660 3844 or 9660 0252, ⓦwww.sydfilm-fest.com.au).

There are also two short film festivals in the summer with the sort of irreverent approach which once fuelled the Sydney Film Festival. Stars above and the sound of waves accompany the week-long **Flickerfest International Short Film Festival** (single ticket $13.50, season pass $110; ⓣ02/9365 6888, ⓦwww .flickerfest.com.au), held in the amphitheatre of the Bondi Pavilion in early January, and showcasing foreign and Australian productions, including documentaries. The **Tropfest** (ⓣ02/9368 0434, ⓦwww.tropfest.com.au) is a competition festival for short films held annually around the end of February; its name comes from the *Tropicana Cafe* (see p.171) on Victoria Street, Darlinghurst, where the festival began almost by chance in 1993 when a young actor, John Polsen, forced his local coffee spot to show the short film he had made. He pushed other filmmakers to follow suit, and the following year a huge crowd of punters packed themselves into the café to watch around twenty films. These days the entire street is closed to traffic to enable an outdoor screening, while cafés along the strip also screen the films inside. The festival has grown enormously over the years, and the focus of the event has moved to The Domain, with huge crowds turning up to picnic and watch the free 8pm screening (plus live entertainment from 3pm). The judges are often famous international actors and Polsen himself, still the festival's director, has made it as a Hollywood director with his recent film *Swimfan*. Each state capital also screens the event simultaneously in venues ranging from cafés to parks. Films must be specifically produced for the festival and be up-to-the-minute – an item is announced a few months in advance of the entry date which must feature in the shorts. In 2003 it was "rock" – however you wanted to interpret it.

Other film festivals include a **Women on Women Film Festival** held over three days in October at Cinema Paris, Fox Studios (ⓦwww.wift.org/wow); and a **gay and lesbian film festival** in late February as part of the Gay and Lesbian Mardi Gras (see p.182).

Art galleries and exhibitions

The Citysearch Sydney website (ⓦwww.sydney.citysearch.com.au) has comprehensive listings of art galleries and current exhibitions, while Friday's "Metro" section of the *Sydney Morning Herald* offers reviews of recently opened shows. Galleries tend to be concentrated in Paddington and there are several small ones on King Street, Newtown.

Artspace The Gunnery Arts Centre, 43–51 Cowper Wharf Rd, Woolloomooloo ⓣ02/9368 1899. In a wonderful location, showing provocative young artists with a focus on installations and new media. Tues–Sat 11am–6pm.

Australian Centre for Photography 257 Oxford St, Paddington ⓣ02/9332 1455. Exhibitions of photo-based art from established and new international and Australian artists in two galleries. Emerging photographers are showcased on the Project Wall. There's a specialist bookshop plus the French-style *Bistro Lulu*. Tues–Sat 11am–6pm.

Australian Galleries: Painting & Sculpture 15 Roylston St, Paddington ⓣ02/9360 5177. Serene gallery exhibiting and selling contemporary Australian art, including works by Gary Shead, Jeffrey Smart and John Coburn. Tues–Sat 10am–6pm.

Australian Galleries: Works on Paper 24 Glenmore Rd, Paddington ⓣ02/9380 8744. Works for sale here include drawings by William Robinson, Brett Whiteley and Arthur Boyd, as well as prints and sketches by young Australian artists. Tues–Sat 10am–6pm, Sun noon–5pm.

Hogarth Galleries Aboriginal Art Centre 7 Walker Lane, Paddington ⓣ02/9360 6839. Extensive collection of work by contemporary Aboriginal artists, both tribal and urban, and special exhibitions. Tues–Sat 10am–5pm.

Ivan Dougherty Gallery Cnr Albion Ave and Selwyn St, Paddington ⓣ02/9385 0726. This is the exhibition space for the College of Fine Arts, University of NSW. The ten shows per year focus on international contemporary art with accompanying forums, lectures and performances. Mon–Sat 10am–5pm.

Josef Lebovic Gallery 34 Paddington St, Paddington ⓣ02/9332 1840. Renowned print and graphic gallery specializing in Australian and international prints from the nineteenth and twentieth centuries, as well as vintage photography. Tues–Fri 1–6pm, Sat 11am–5pm.

The Performance Space 199 Cleveland St, Redfern, opposite Prince Alfred Park ⓣ02/9698 7235. Experimental multimedia and plastic arts: installations, sculpture, photography and painting. Wed–Fri noon–6pm.

Ray Hughes Gallery 270 Devonshire St, Surry Hills ⓣ02/9698 3200. Influential dealer with a stable of high-profile contemporary Australian and New Zealand artists. Openings monthly, with two artists per show. Tues–Sat 10am–6pm.

Roslyn Oxley 9 Gallery 8 Soudan Lane, off Hampden St, Paddington ⓣ02/9331 1919. Avant-garde videos and installations among the Australian and international offerings. Tues–Fri 10am–6pm, Sat 11am–6pm.

Festivals and events

The Sydney year is interspersed with festivals and events of various sorts that reach their peak in the summer. The City of Sydney Council has a **City Infoline** (Mon–Fri 9am–5pm ⓣ02/9265 9007, ⓦwww.cityofsydney.nsw.gov.au) for details of events year-round.

The **New Year** begins with a spectacular **fireworks** display from the Harbour Bridge and Darling Harbour. There's a brief hiatus of a week or so until the annual **Sydney Festival** (ⓣ02/8248 6500, ⓦwww.sydneyfestival.org.au), an exhaustive and exhausting arts event that lasts for most of **January** and ranges from opera-in-the-park, concerts, plays and outdoor art installations to circus performances. About fifty percent of the events are free and are based around urban public spaces, focusing on Circular Quay, The Domain and Darling Harbour; the remainder – mostly international performances – can cost a packet. The general programme is usually printed in the *Sydney Morning Herald* in October while a full eighty-plus-page programme is available nearer the time. There's also the **Sydney Fringe Festival** based at the Bondi Pavilion (see p.153). From Boxing Day to the end of January, Darling Harbour hosts its own festival, linked with the Festival of Sydney. Most of the attractions are aimed at children, but there's also a free promenade jazz festival.

Australia Day on January 26 is a huge celebration in Sydney, with activities focused on the water. There's the Coca-Cola Amatil Marathon, where Sydney's passenger ferries race from Fort Denison to the Harbour Bridge, the Tall Ships Race from Bradleys Head to the Harbour Bridge, a 21-gun salute fired from

There are horse-racing meetings on Wednesday, Saturday and most public holidays throughout the year, but the best times to hit the track are during the **Spring and Autumn Carnivals** (Aug–Sept and March–April), when prize money rockets, and the quality of racing rivals the best in the world. The venues are well maintained, peopled with colourful racing characters, and often massive crowds. Principal **racecourses** are: Royal Randwick (Alison Rd, Randwick), which featured in *Mission Impossible 2*; Rosehill Gardens (James Ruse Drive, Rosehill); and Canterbury Park (King St, Canterbury), which has midweek racing, plus floodlit Thursday-night racing from September to March. Entry is around $8, or $15–20 on carnival days. Contact the Australian Jockey Club (℡02/9663 8400) for details of many other picturesque country venues to choose from. Every Friday the *Sydney Morning Herald* publishes its racing guide, "The Form". Bets are placed at TAB shops; these are scattered throughout the city, and most pubs also have TAB access.

the Man O'War steps at the Opera House, and an aerial display of military planes. The **Australia Day Regatta** takes place in the afternoon, with hundreds of yachts racing all over the water, from Botany Bay to the Parramatta River. There are also events at The Rocks and Hyde Park, and at Darling Harbour, where the day culminates at around 9pm with a fireworks display. In addition, many museums let visitors in for free. Besides all this, there are at least two outdoor rock concerts to choose from: **Survival**, which celebrates Aboriginal culture and acts as an antidote to the mainstream white Australia Day festivities, is held at Waverly Oval near Bondi; while the **Big Day Out** is usually held that day at the Showground at Homebush Bay, featuring around fifty local and international acts.

An entirely different side of Sydney life is on view at the impressive summer **surf carnivals**, staged regularly by local surf lifesaving clubs; check the newspapers for details.

At the end of **February** the city is engulfed by the **Sydney Gay & Lesbian Mardi Gras** (see box on pp.182–183). Another big event is the **Royal Easter Show**, an agricultural and garden show in late **March/early April**, based at the Sydney Showground at Homebush Bay. For twelve consecutive days (with the second weekend always the Easter weekend) the country comes to the city for a frantic array of amusement-park rides, fireworks, parades of prize animals, a rodeo and wood-chopping displays.

The **International Film Festival** takes over many of the city's screens in **June** (see box on p.187); and the **City to Surf Race**, an eight-kilometre fun run from the city to Bondi, happens every **August**. In **spring**, from September to early October, **Carnivale** celebrates ethnic diversity and "vibrant collaborations in the fields of theatre, music and dance". The Labour Day weekend in early **October** is marked by the **Manly International Jazz Festival**, with several free outdoor, waterfront events and a few indoor concerts charging entry. This is followed by the very Italian **Blessing of the Fleet** at Darling Harbour. Every alternate (even-numbered) year, the **Biennale of Sydney** takes place over six weeks from mid-September until early November, with provocative contemporary art exhibitions at various venues and public spaces around town.

The year is brought to a close by the **Sydney to Hobart Yacht Race**, when it seems that half of Sydney turns up at or on the harbour on December 26 to cheer the start of this classic regatta and watch the colourful spectacle of two hundred or so yachts setting sail for a 630-nautical-mile slog.

Shopping

Sydney's main shopping focus is the city centre, in the stretch between Martin Place and the Queen Victoria Building. Apart from its charming old nineteenth-century arcades and two **department stores**, David Jones and Grace Bros (see p.123), the city centre also has several modern multilevel **shopping complexes** where you can hunt down clothes and accessories without raising a sweat, among them Skygarden (between Pitt and Castlereagh streets) and Centrepoint on Pitt Street Mall, on the corner of Market Street. Much of the area from the QVB to the mall is linked by underground arcades which will also keep you cool.

Most stores are **open** Monday to Saturday 8.30am to 5.30pm, with Thursday late-night shopping until 9pm. Many of the larger shops and department stores in the city are also open on Sunday 10am to 5pm, as are shopping centres in tourist areas such as Darling Harbour. If you've run out of time to buy presents and souvenirs, don't worry: the revamped **Sydney Airport** is attached to one of the biggest shopping malls in Sydney, with outlets for everything from surfwear to R.M. Williams bush outfitters, at the same prices as the downtown stores. The Rocks is the best place for souvenir and duty- and GST-free shopping.

Fashion

Oxford Street in Paddington (see p.140) is the place to go for interesting fashion, along with the Strand Arcade (see p.142) in the city; for striking street fashion check out Crown Street in Surry Hills, with places such as Wheels & Doll Baby at no. 259 and Dangerfield at no. 330; and for cheaper styles, retro clothes and other interesting junk, try King Street in Newtown (see p.136). If you want to peek at expensive Australian **designer fashion**, head for David Jones (see p.142) or the Strand Arcade. To go with the outfits, funky Australian **jewellery** can be found in the Strand Arcade at Dinosaur Designs (also at Argyle Stores, The Rocks, see p.119, and 330 Oxford St, Paddington), and at Love and Hatred, both on Level 1.

For Australian **workwear** head for Gowings, a delightfully old-fashioned **menswear** department store on the corner of Market and George streets. The beloved Sydney institution, in business for over 125 years, it has everything a bloke (and often a sheila) could want, from Bonds T-shirts to Speedo swimwear, Blundestone boots and a range of felt hats at the best prices in town – plus cheap haircuts. Two other branches are at 319 George St, near Wynyard station and 82 Oxford St, Darlinghurst. The quality **bush outfitters** R. M. Williams, 389 George St (also at Chifley Plaza; Fox Studios; Darling Walk, Darling Harbour; and the airport), is great for moleskin trousers, Drizabone coats and superb leather riding boots. For the widest range of Akubra hats, check out Strand Hatters in the Strand Arcade. If it's interesting **surfwear** you're after, head for Mambo, 105 George St, The Rocks (also at Market City, Hay St, Haymarket; 17 Oxford St, Paddington; Shop 80, The Corso, Manly; and 80 Campbell Parade, Bondi Beach).

Arts and crafts

The Rocks is heaving with **Australiana** and **arts and crafts** souvenirs, from opals to sheepskin. Tourists flock to Ken Done's emporium here at 123 George St and 1–5 Hickson Rd (in the restored Australian Steam and Navigation Building) to buy his colourful designs, which feature Sydney's harbour, boats and flowers; there's a Ken Done store at the airport, too.

The Rocks is also a focus for **Aboriginal art** (see also "Art Galleries and exhibitions", p.187): the Aboriginal and Tribal Art Centre, 1st Floor, 117 George St, has a huge collection of traditional Aboriginal art from around Australia; the Dreamtime Gallery, Shop 35, The Rocks Centre, 12–24 Playfair St (also a branch at the Opera House), sells traditional Aboriginal art including didgeridoos (live didj played at weekends). However, the best place to buy Aboriginal art and craft is the Aboriginal-owned and -run Gavala, in the Harbourside Shopping Centre in Darling Harbour (see p.133). A great place to buy **boomerangs** is The Boomerang School, 200 William St; the boomerangs sold here are mostly authentic, made by Aboriginal artisans from around Australia. The owner, Duncan MacLennon, has been giving free boomerang-throwing lessons every Sunday in Yarranabbe Park near Rushcutters Bay (10am–noon) since 1958.

Music and books

For a take-home sample of the **Australian music** scene in all its variety, from Aboriginal through to indie and jazz, head for Sounds Australian, Shop 33, The Rocks Centre, 12–24 Playfair St – the retail arm of the Australian Music Centre with very knowledgeable staff.

One of the biggest **bookshops** in the city is the long-running, Australian-owned Dymocks, 428 George St, open daily, on several floors with an impressive Australian selection and a café. New book superstores include Kinokuniya in Galleries Victoria, on the corner of George and Park streets; Borders, 77 Castlereagh St, between King and Market streets; and Collins Superstore, Level 2, Broadway Shopping Centre near Glebe (see p.135). Nearby, Gleebooks, 49 Glebe Point Rd, Glebe, is one of Australia's best bookshops, specializing in academic and alternative books, contemporary Australian and international literature, and is open daily until 9pm; book launches and other literary events are regularly held. Ariel has two large, lively and hip branches, one at 103 George St, The Rocks and the other at 42 Oxford St, Paddington; both branches open daily until midnight. Macleay Bookshop, 103 Macleay St, Potts Point (daily until 9pm), is a tiny and peaceful choice. **The Travel Bookshop** at 175 Liverpool St (closed Sun) is the place to head for maps, guides and travel journals, plus a good selection of Australiana. **Secondhand books** can be found at Glebe and Paddington markets, at Gleebooks Second Hand Books, 191 Glebe Point Rd (daily until 9pm); upstairs at Lesley McKays Bookshop, 346 New South Head Rd, Double Bay (the ground level, for new books, is open until midnight); and in the secondhand bookshops on King Street, Newtown – in particular check out the amazingly chaotic piles of books at Gould's Book Arcade, 32–38 King St, Newtown (daily 7am–midnight).

Food and drink

There are several handy **supermarkets** in the city centre with extended opening hours: one is in the basement of Woolworths on the corner of Park and George streets, above Town Hall station (Mon–Wed 7am–8pm, Thurs & Fri 7am–9pm, Sat 9am–6.30pm, Sun 10am–5.30pm); and another, Coles Express, is on Level 2, Wynyard station (daily 6am–midnight). The Coles Express in Kings Cross, at 88 Darlinghurst Rd, is also handy for travellers (daily 6am–midnight). In the suburbs, large supermarkets such as Coles stay open daily until about 10pm, and there are plenty of 24-hour 7-Eleven convenience stores in the inner city and suburbs. For **delicatessen** items, look no further than the splendid food hall at David Jones (see p.123). The **Australian Wine Centre**, cnr George and Alfred streets, Circular Quay

(Mon–Sat 9.30am–6pm, Sun 11am–5pm), sells more than a thousand **wines** from around Australia.

Markets

The two best **markets** are the Paddington Market and Balmain Market, both on Saturday (see p.142 and p.138, respectively), while the relaxed Glebe Market (see p.136), also on a Saturday, and flea market at Rozelle (Sat & Sun 9am–4pm; see p.138) are also worth a look. The Rocks Market on George Street (Sat & Sun 10am–5pm; see p.119), is more touristy but worth a browse, while Paddy's Market (Thurs 10am–6pm, Fri–Sun 9am–4.30pm; see p.124), in Haymarket near the Entertainment Centre and Chinatown, is Sydney's oldest, selling fruit and veg, deli products, meat and fish, plus large quantities of bargain-basement clothes and toys. There's also a series of alternating Saturday markets on the North Shore; Kirribilli Market (fourth Sat of month; see p.149) is the most well known – call ☎02/9936 8197 for details of the others. The latest addition to Sydney's market scene is a series of **produce markets**: at Pyrmont Bay Park in front of the Star City Casino (first Sat of month 7–11am); at Fox Studios on Bent St (Wed noon–7pm); and at Northside Produce Market at the Civic Centre, Miller St, North Sydney, between Ridge and McClaren streets (third Sat of month 8am–noon).

Listings

Airlines (domestic) Aeropelican (☎02/4945 0988) to Belmont, nr Newcastle; Qantas, see address opposite (☎13 13 13), Australia-wide including Albury, Armidale, Ballina, Canberra, Coffs Harbour, Dubbo, Grafton, Kempsey, Lord Howe Island, Moree, Narrabri, Newcastle, Norfolk Island, Port Macquarie and Tamworth; Regional Express (☎13 17 13) to Albury, Ballina, Bathurst, Canberra, Dubbo, Griffith, Lismore, Merimbula, Mildura, Moruya, Narrandera, Orange, Parkes, Traralgon and Wagga Wagga; Sydney Harbour Seaplanes, Lyne Park, Rose Bay (☎02/9388 1978), charter flights to destinations on the Hawkesbury River and the Central Coast, as well as Palm Beach, Newcastle and Port Stephens; Virgin Blue (☎13 6789), Australia-wide to all state capitals as well as much of coastal Queensland, and Coffs Harbour.

Airlines (international) Aeroflot, 44 Market St ☎02/9262 2233; Aerolineas Argentinas, Level 4, 189 Kent St ☎02/9252 5150; Air Canada, Level 12, 92 Pitt St ☎02/9232 5222; Air New Zealand, Level 4, 10 Barrack St ☎13 24 76; Alitalia, 64 York St ☎02/9244 2400; British Airways, Level 19, 259 George St ☎02/9258 3200; Cathay Pacific ☎13 17 47; Continental, 64 York St ☎02/9244 2242; Delta, Level 9, 189 Kent St ☎02/9251 3211; Finnair, 64 York St ☎02/9244 2299; Garuda, 55 Hunter St ☎02/9334 9900; Gulf Air, 64 York St ☎02/9244 2199; Japan Airlines, Level 14,

201 Sussex St ☎02/9272 1111; KLM, 115 Pitt St ☎02/9231 6333; Korean Air ☎02/9262 6000; Lauda Air, Level 2, 1 York St ☎02/9251 6155; Malaysia Airlines, 16 Spring St ☎13 26 27; Olympic, 3rd Floor, 37–49 Pitt St ☎02/9251 1048; Qantas, 70 Hunter St, cnr Phillip St, and 468 Oxford St, Bondi Junction ☎13 13 13; Scandinavian Airlines, Level 15, 31 Market St ☎1300 727 707; Singapore Airlines, 17–19 Bridge St ☎02/9350 0100; Swissair, Level 3, 117 York St ☎1300 724 666; Thai International, 75 Pitt St ☎02/9251 1922; United, Level 5, 10 Barrack St ☎13 17 77.

American Express Outlets include Level 1, 124–130 Pitt St (Mon–Fri 8.30am–5.30pm; ☎1300 139 060); Shop 4, Quay Grand Circular Quay Concourse (Mon–Fri 9am–5pm, Sat & Sun 11am–4pm); and within the Travel Bookshop, Shop 3, 175 Liverpool St (Mon–Fri 9am–5pm, Sat 10am–1pm). Lost or stolen traveller's cheques ☎1800 251 902.

Banks and foreign exchange Head offices of banks are mostly in the CBD, around Martin Place; hours are Mon–Thurs 9am–4pm, Fri 9am–5pm, with some suburban branches open later and on Saturday. Money can also be exchanged at the airport; American Express (see above); Thomas Cook, 175 Pitt St (Mon–Fri 9am–5.30pm; ☎02/9231 2901) and at the Queen Victoria Building outlet at Shop 64, Lower Ground Floor

(Mon–Fri 9am–6pm, Sat 10am–3pm); Singapore Money Exchange, Eddy Ave (Mon–Fri 8am–5.30pm; ℡02/9281 4118); Travelex Australia, 37–49 Pitt St (Mon–Fri 9am–5.15pm, Sat 10am–2.45pm; ℡02/9241 5722).

Bus companies Bennetts Airport Shuttle (℡1300 130 557), pre-booked service from the airport to the Central Coast and back; Firefly Express (℡02/9211 1644), to Melbourne and Adelaide; Great Lakes Coaches (℡02/4983 1560), daily to Forster via Newcastle; Greyhound Pioneer (ticket office at Eddy Ave, Central station; ℡02/9212 1500, nationwide reservations ℡13 20 30). Australia-wide: Keans Travel Express (Sydney ℡02/9211 3387, Muswellbrook ℡02/6543 1322), daily Sydney to Hunter Valley including Cessnock, Muswellbrook and Scone; McCafferty's (ticket office at Eddy Ave, Central station; ℡02/9212 3433, nationwide reservations ℡13 14 99), to Melbourne and Adelaide, Brisbane and Queensland; Murray's (℡13 22 51), to Canberra three times daily from Central or Strathfield; Pioneer Motor Service, 490 Pitt St, near Central station (℡13 34 10), Sydney to Cairns via the north coast with stops including Byron Bay, and to Melbourne via the south coast (a pass is available – see p.37); Port Stephens Coaches (℡02/9281 9366 or 1800 045 949), daily to Port Stephens at 2pm from Central via Newcastle outskirts; Premier Motor Service (℡13 34 10), daily to Bega via the south coast, with one service daily continuing on to Eden, and the service is also available from the airport; Prior's Scenic Express (℡02/4472 4040 or 1800 816 234), five times weekly from Campbelltown train station to the Southern Highlands including Kangaroo Valley, thence to Moruya or Narooma via the south coast; Selwoods (℡02/9281 9366) once daily to Orange via the Blue Mountains, Lithgow and Bathurst; Kings Bros (℡02/4983 1560 or 1800 043 263) daily Sydney to Taree via Newcastle, Tea Gardens, Hawks Nest, the Great Lakes and Foster-Tuncurry.

Bus terminal Sydney Coach Terminal, cnr Eddy Ave and Pitt St, next to Central station (daily 6am–10pm; ℡02/9281 9366).

Bus tickets Make bookings at the Traveller's Information Service at the bus terminal (℡02/9281 9366), at Backpackers Travel Centres listed under "Travel agents" p.197, or direct with the bus companies listed above.

Campervans and 4WD rental All Seasons Campervans, 77 Planthurst Rd, South Hurstville (℡02/9547 0100), offers a wide range of campervans, motorhomes, four-door sedans plus camping equipment, including free delivery to airport or accommodation, linen and sleeping bags;

Australian Outback 4 Wheel Drive Hire Co, 184 Elizabeth St, City (℡02/9281 9676; Britz Australia, 263 Coward St, Mascot (℡02/9667 0402 or 1800 331 454), campervans, 4WDs and camping gear, available one-way to Adelaide, Alice Springs, Brisbane, Cairns, Darwin, Melbourne and Perth; Travel Car Centre, 54 Orchard Rd, Brookvale (℡02/9905 6928), hatchbacks, stationwagons, campervans and 4WDs available for long- or short-term rental; Travellers Auto Barn (℡02/9360 1500; see "Cars: buying and selling" box on p.194), budget campervan rental.

Camping equipment and rental Kent Street in the city behind the Town Hall is nicknamed "adventure alley" for its preponderance of outdoor equipment stores; the best known is the high-quality Paddy Pallin at no. 507. Cheaper options include army surplus stores at the downtown ends of George and Pitt streets near Central station (try Boss Disposals, 708 George St) and suburban K-Mart stores (closest stores to the city are at Spring St, Bondi Junction and at the Broadway Shopping Centre, Bay St) or hostel notice boards. Only a few places rent gear, mostly based in the suburbs: try Alpsport, 1045 Victoria Rd, West Ryde (℡02/9858 5844) with weekend rental of a backpack for around $32, sleeping bag from $29, and tent from $30.

Car rental The big four car-rental companies, with expensive new model cars, charge from around $50–70 per day for a small manual: Avis, airport (℡02/9353 9000) and 220 William St, Kings Cross (℡02/9357 2000); Budget, airport (℡13 27 27), and 93 William St, Kings Cross (℡02/9339 8888); Hertz (℡13 30 39), airport and elsewhere including cnr William and Riley streets, Kings Cross; Thrifty, airport (℡1300 367 227) and elsewhere, including 75 William St, Kings Cross. Also at the airport, Network (℡02/9317 3223), offers good-value one-way rentals. There are cheaper deals with Bayswater, 180 William St, Kings Cross (℡02/9360 3622), which has low rates but limited kilometres; Kings Cross Rent-a-Car, 169 William St, Kings Cross (℡02/9361 0637), which is open daily and has low rates; Daytona Rentals, 164 Parramatta Rd, Ashfield (℡02/9716 8777), which has slightly older cars at very good rates for weekly rentals all inclusive of insurance, and Apollo Car Rental, 33 Pittwater Rd, Manly (℡02/9977 5777), which has new model cars and also incorporates Rent-a-Ruffy, for cheap, older-model cars; both have limited kilometres. Travellers Auto Barn, 177 William St, Kings Cross (℡02/9360 1500), does cheap one-way rentals to Brisbane or Cairns.

Sydney is the most popular place to buy a car or campervan in which to travel around Australia; the information below is specific to buying a car in NSW – for general background on buying and selling a car, see Basics pp.40–42.

Before you start looking for wheels, it's a good idea to join New South Wales' motoring association, the NRMA which has offices at 74 King St, City, or 183 Oxford St Mall, Bondi Junction (☎13 21 32). If you're a member of a motoring association overseas, you'll already have reciprocal membership (otherwise there's a $99 initial joining fee, then the annual charge is $55), which entitles you to roadside assistance and a $120 inspection and appraisal of a potential purchase (call ☎02/9892 0355 to book a vehicle inspection). The *Weekly Trading Post*, out every Thursday (or check the web version at ⊛www.tradingpost.com.au), has a big secondhand car section and it's worth checking through this to get a general idea of prices of cars bought direct from sellers; it's good also if you know a fair bit about cars and want to go it alone, though you would probably need to rent a car to get to most of the far-flung suburban locations. The *Sydney Morning Herald's* Friday edition has a "Drive" supplement which has full-page ads for secondhand dealers (most of which are on Parramatta Rd from Annandale onwards) and private used cars for sale at the pricier end of the secondhand market. Demand to see the pink slip (certificate of roadworthiness), as it proves the car is safe. In NSW the seller is under no obligation to show a certificate of roadworthiness but the buyer is entitled to ask to see one. If you're seriously thinking about buying, call REVS on ☎02/9633 6333 to check the validity of NSW-registered cars; quote registration, engine and chassis numbers and they will inform you of any payments owing or unpaid parking fines (you can also do this via the web on ⊛www.revs.nsw.gov.au). Call the Roads and Traffic Authority (RTA; ☎13 22 13) to double-check that the registration has not been cancelled.

As Sydney is the first place where most tourists arrive, the city is well equipped with dealerships who will arrange to **buy back** the vehicle they've sold you at the end of your trip for a thirty to fifty percent buy-back (see "Getting around" in Basics for general advice). Two of the of the longest running are **Auto Becker**, 752 Parramatta Rd, Lewisham (☎02/9568 4455, ℻02/9337 4202), who also offer a twelve-month warranty on many cars, and **Travellers Auto Barn**, 177 William St, Kings Cross (☎02/9360 1500, ⊛www.travellers-autobarn.com.au), who get hold of as many station wagons, vans and campervans as they can – the preferred forms of travellers' transport; they also have offices in Brisbane and Cairns.

The **Backpackers Car Market**, Kings Cross Car Park, Level 2, Ward Ave (daily 9am–6pm; ☎02/9358 5000 or 1800 808 188, ⊛www.carmarket.com.au) is the only place where it's legal for travellers to resell their cars at the Cross – selling on the street is not allowed. Dealers are barred, and fees for sellers (if you have a pink slip) are set at $20 per day or $40 per week; inspection reports for the seller cost around $30 – call the car market for recommended mechanics. One of the advantages of the **car market** for sellers is that it's one of the few places where you will be able to sell a car registered in another state. If you're thinking of buying here, get in early for the best choice. Many of the vehicles come ready equipped with camping gear and other extras at good prices. The guys will advise you and help with the paperwork, and will oversee the exchanging of the contract to make sure everything's done properly, and arrange third-party property **insurance** ($210 for 3 months, $375 for 12 months) – the NRMA refuses to provide cover for overseas travellers. It's worth checking their website, where sellers can advertise for $20. Another car market is held on Sunday at Flemington Market opposite Flemington station, Austen Avenue entrance (8am–4pm; ☎1900 921 122 $1.10 per minute), but is better for buying than selling: if you're trying to sell a vehicle that's travelled around Australia, particularly if the clock is past 200,000km, local buyers won't be interested; besides, fees for sellers are steep at $60 per day (no bookings required).

Consulates Embassies are all in Canberra (see p.268), and it's usually easier to call them when in difficulty than to go to the consulates in Sydney: Canadian, Level 5, 111 Harrington St ☎02/9364 3000; New Zealand, 55 Hunter St ☎02/8256 2000; UK, Level 16, Gateway Building, 1 Macquarie Place ☎02/9247 7521; US, Level 59, MLC Centre, 19–29 Martin Place ☎02/9373 9200. For visas for onward travel, consult "Consulates and Legations" in the *Yellow Pages*.

Cycling Bicycles are carried free on trains outside of peak hours (Mon–Fri 6–9am & 3.30–7.30pm) and on ferries at all times. The Roads and Traffic Authority (☎02/9218 6888) produces a handy fold-out map, *Sydney Cycleways*, showing both off-road paths and suggested bicycle routes, which they will post out. The best source of information, however, is the organization Bicycle NSW, based at Level 2, 209 Castlereagh St, cnr Bathurst St (Mon–Fri 9am–5.30pm; ☎02/9283 5200). Two useful publication are *Bike It Sydney* ($13) which has inner-city bike routes and is good for people new to Sydney and *Discovering NSW and Canberra Bike and Walking Paths* ($18.50). Popular cycling spots are Centennial Park (see p.142) and the bike path which runs from Manly (see p.158). The international cycling activist group Critical Mass has a Sydney movement; on the last Friday of the month meet at the Archibald Fountain in Hyde Park between 4.30pm and 5.30pm for an hour-long mass ride through the city. Recommended central bicycle shops include Clarence Street Cyclery, 104 Clarence St (☎02/9299 4962); Woolys Wheels, 82 Oxford St, Paddington (☎02/9331 2671); and Inner City Cycles, 31 Glebe Point Rd, Glebe (☎02/9660 6605). The cheapest bike rental is at Cheeky Monkey Cycle Co, 456 Pitt St, City (open daily; mountain bikes $25 day; ☎02/9212 4460), and they also sell bikes and rent and sell cycle-touring equipment. Clarence Street Cyclery also rents mountain bikes ($65 per day, $100 per weekend), as does Inner City Cycles (open daily; $33 per 24hr, $55 per weekend). For a leisurely ride in the park, Centennial Park Cycles, 50 Clovelly Rd, Randwick (open daily; ☎02/9398 5027) rents bikes at hourly rates (mountain bikes $9 per hour, $20 per 4hr, bikes for kids $7 per hour, $16 per 4hr).

Disabled travellers ACROD NSW, Suite 103, 1st Floor, 1–5 Commercial Rd, Kingsgrove, NSW 2208 ☎02/9554 3666, ⓦwww.acrod.org.au; People with Disabilities NSW, 52 Pitt St, Redfern, NSW 2016 ☎02/9319 6622. Randwick Council (☎02/9399 0999) has installed wheelchair accessible ramps at Clovelly and Malabar beaches; they also publish a series of mobility maps which they

will post out. The Australian Quadriplegic Association publishes the very useful *Access Sydney* ($24.95; ☎02/9661 8855). Most national parks have wheelchair-accessible walks; check ⓦwww.npws.nsw.gov.au. Post-Olympic improvements include many wheelchair-accessible train stations; check ⓦwww.cityrail.nsw.gov.au. All taxi companies take bookings on behalf of Wheelchair Accessible Taxis; for numbers, see "Taxis" on p.196.

Diving One of the best places to dive is at Gordon's Bay in Clovelly, and off the North and South Heads. Prodive Coogee, 27 Alfreda St, Coogee (☎02/9665 6333), offers boat and shore dives anywhere between Camp Cove and La Perouse (double boat dive $135, double shore dive $105), plus dives all over Sydney. Cronulla Dive Centre, 40 Kingsway, Cronulla (☎02/9523 7222), does local shore dives (free but gear rental costs $50 per day) and also organizes dives and week-ends away up and down the New South Wales coast. Dive Centre, 10 Belgrave St, Manly (☎02/9977 4355), offers shore dives to Shelley Beach, Fairlight, and Little Manly plus Harbord if conditions are good, and boat dives off North and South Head and Long Reef (single boat dive $85, double $130, single shore dive $75, double $95). They also have a Bondi branch at 192 Bondi Rd (☎02/9369 3855) offering shore dives at Camp Cove (Watsons Bay) and North Bondi (double dive $95) and boat dives to South Head and Maroubra where there's a chance to see sharks.

Gyms Most of the swimming centres listed on p.196 also now have gyms available for casual visits.

Hospitals Sydney Hospital, Macquarie St ☎02/9382 7111; St Vincents Hospital, cnr Victoria and Burton streets, Darlinghurst ☎02/8382 1111.

Immigration Department of Immigration, 26 Lee St, near Central station, City ☎13 18 81.

Internet access You can surf the Net for free at the State Library, Macquarie St (see p.127), but can't send emails. Many backpackers', hostels have Internet terminals, and dedicated Internet places have sprung up all over Sydney, with a glut of cheap places around Kings Cross offering an hour's access for as low as $3. Global Gossip has several offices ($3.95 for 30min–1hr), including 770 & 790 George St (both daily 9am–11pm); 415 Pitt St, 14 Wentworth St, next to Hyde Park, City (daily 9am–midnight); 111 Darlinghurst Rd, Kings Cross (daily 8am–midnight); 37 Hall St, Bondi (daily 8am–midnight); they also offer cut-rate international calls and postage. *Phone.Net Cafe*

73–75 Hall St, Bondi (daily 8am–10pm; from $3.30 for 1hr) is a lively café haunt in its own right, as is the *Well Connected Cafe* on Glebe Point Road ($3 per hour; see p.167).

Left luggage Cloakrooms at Town Hall station and Central station (country trains) are both open daily 6.30am–9.30pm ($8/$6/$4 per 24hr depending on size); also lockers at the airport and the Sydney Coach Terminal ($6– $9 per 24hr).

Libraries See the State Library, p.127.

Maps Map World, 371 Pitt St, City ⊤02/9261 3601; see also "Parks and wildlife", on below.

Medical centres Broadway Medical Centre, 185–211 Broadway near Glebe (⊤02/9212 2733), general practitioners open Mon–Fri 9am–7pm, Sat & Sun 11am–5pm, no appointment necessary; Skin Cancer Centre, ground floor, 403 George St (⊤02/9262 4877); Sydney Sexual Health Centre, Nightingale Wing, Sydney Hospital, Macquarie St (⊤02/9382 7440), free tests, counselling and con- doms; Travellers Medical and Vaccination Centre, 7th Floor, 428 George St (⊤02/9221 7133).

Motorbikes Wentworth Avenue in the city has a concentration of motorbike salerooms for new models. For secondhand motorbikes there's Bikescape, 191 William St, Kings Cross (⊤1300 736 869), with scooters from $65 per day and motorbikes from $95. Maverick Motorcycles, 133 Parramatta Rd, Homebush, NSW 2140 (⊤02/9746 2005), specializes in selling and exchanging trav- ellers' motorbikes.

NRMA 74–76 King St, City (⊤13 21 32, ⓦwww.nrma.com.au). Road maps of New South Wales and other states, and a useful map of Sydney and other cities. The maps are free to members of associated organizations plus lots more information. The useful accommodation directories they publish range from $5.50 to $7.50.

Parks and wildlife information The NPWS, Cadman's Cottage, 110 George St, The Rocks (⊤02/9247 8861, ⓦwww.npws.nsw.gov.au) is the information centre for Sydney Harbour National Park and books tours to its islands; they do not arrange camping permits. For these and informa- tion on other national parks around Sydney, go to the National Parks Centre, 102 George St, The Rocks (⊤02/9253 4600). The Sydney Map Shop, part of the Surveyor-General's Department, 23–33 Bridge St (⊤02/9228 6111) sells detailed National Park and bushwalking maps of New South Wales.

Pharmacy (late-night) Crest Hotel Pharmacy, 60A Darlinghurst Rd, Kings Cross (daily 8.30am–midnight; ⊤02/9358 1822).

Police Headquarters at 14 College St (⊤02/9339 0277); emergency ⊤000.

Post office The General Post Office (GPO) is in Martin Place (Mon–Fri 8.15am–5.30pm, Sat 10am–2pm). Poste restante is located at the post office in the Hunter Connection shopping mall at 310 George St (Mon–Fri 8.15am–5.30pm), oppo- site Wynyard station. Log your name in the com- puter to see if you have any post before queueing. Poste Restante, Sydney GPO, Sydney, NSW 2000.

Public holidays In addition to the Australia-wide public holidays (see Basics, p.58), the following are celebrated only in New South Wales: Bank Holiday – first Monday in August; Labour Day – first Monday in October; Queen's Birthday – first Monday in June.

Scenic flights Sydney Harbour Seaplanes, Rose Bay (⊤02/9388 1978) can take you on a 15min scenic flight over Sydney Harbour and Bondi Beach ($110 per person, min 2, max 8), or the harbour and the Northern beaches ($190), or drop you off to lunch at Palm Beach or one of the Hawkesbury River restaurants ($335 including lunch).

Surfing The two best surf schools in Sydney, offering both individual and group lessons are Lets Go Surfing (⊤02/9365 1800) which also has its own surf store renting and selling boards at 28 Ramsgate Ave, North Bondi; and Manly Surf School (⊤02/9977 6977) which covers the northern beaches.

Swimming pools Most pools are outdoors and unheated, and open from the long weekend in October until Easter. Those detailed in the text, with times and prices given, are: Cook and Phillip Park Aquatic and Leisure Centre, near Hyde Park (p.125); Andrew "Boy" Charlton in The Domain (see p.129); North Sydney Olympic Pool, North Sydney (p.149); Victoria Park, City Rd, next to Sydney University (p.136); the Annette Kellerman Aquatic Centre in Enmore (p.137); and the pool of champions, the Sydney International Aquatic Centre at Homebush Bay (p.218).

Taxis ABC ⊤13 25 22; Legion ⊤13 14 51; Premier ⊤13 10 17; RSL ⊤13 15 81; St George ⊤13 21 66; Taxis Combined ⊤02/8332 8888. For harbour water taxis call Taxis Afloat ⊤02/9955 3222.

Telephones The unattended Telstra Pay Phone Centre, 231 Elizabeth St, City (Mon–Fri 7am–11pm, Sat & Sun 7am–5pm) has private booths; BYO change or phonecard. Global Gossip (see "Internet access" on p.195) offers discount- rate international calls and Backpackers Travel Centre (see opposite) sells their own rechargeable discount phonecard.

Trains All out-of-town trains depart from the country trains terminal of Central station (informa- tion and booking 6.30am–10pm; ⊤13 22 32).

There are Countrylink Travel Centres at Central station (☎02/9379 3800); Wynyard station (☎02/9224 4744); in the Queen Victoria Building Arcade at Town Hall station (☎02/9379 3600); and at Circular Quay (☎02/9224 3400) and Bondi Junction station (☎02/9379 3777). The Indian Pacific, the Ghan and the Overland are now managed by Great Southern Railway; booking office on Eddy Avenue alongside Central station (☎13 21 47). Interstate trains should be booked as early as possible, especially the Indian Pacific and Brisbane–Cairns trains.

Travel agents Backpackers Travel Centre, Shop 33, Imperial Arcade, off Pitt St Mall (☎02/9231 3699), does everything from international flights to bus passes; offices also at 488 Pitt St in the Premier Coaches office (☎02/9212 2880), 412 Pitt St inside Hotel Bakpak (☎02/9280 1519), 155 Oxford St, Bondi Junction (☎02/9369 1331), 37 Hall St, Bondi Beach (☎02/9300 0505), 194 Coogee Bay Rd, Coogee (☎02/9315 7751). Flight Centre, 52 Martin Place (☎02/9235 0166), also at several other locations, offers cheap domestic and international air tickets. STA Travel has many branches, including Shop 205, Broadway Shopping Centre, Bay St, Broadway (☎02/9211 2563). Trailfinders is at 8 Spring St (☎02/9247 7666). YHA Travel, 422 Kent St, behind the Town Hall (☎02/9261 1111) also has a branch at *Sydney Central YHA*, 11 Rawson Place off Eddy Ave (☎02/9281 9444), and offers an excellent range of Sydney tours. For details of tours from Sydney see p.198.

Water sports Rose Bay Aquatic Hire, just near the waterfront at 1 Vickery Ave, Rose Bay (☎02/9371 7036), rents out catamarans ($25 first hour, $15 thereafter), kayaks ($15 per hour) and motorboats (weekends $50 for the first two hours, $15 for each subsequent hour). Balmoral Windsurf, Sail and Kayak School, open all year at the Balmoral boatshed, southern end of the Esplanade (☎02/9960 5344), rents out sailboards (from $27 per hour), offers sailboarding lessons (beginners $200 per 5hr lesson) and a dinghy sailing course (4hr; $200). Northside Sailing School, Spit Bridge, Mosman (☎02/9969 3972) specializes in weekend dinghy sailing courses on Middle Harbour during the sailing season (Sept–April); tuition is one-on-one ($120 per 3hr lesson). Teamsail, based at the Royal Prince Alfred Yacht Club, Mitala St, Newport (☎02/9999 3047), offers all-year yachting courses on Pittwater (2-day course $405; maximum 4), and follow-up twilight sails (summer Mon & Thurs; 2hr) and Sunday sails (last Sun of month; 4hr), both $35, can further develop skills. Sydney by Sail (☎02/9280 1110), has Learn To Sail programmes for yacht sailing throughout the year,

from a Level 1 Introductory Course (12-hour 2-day course; $450) to a Level 4 Inshore Skipper Course (2-day, 2-night live-aboard; $660). Experienced sailors can charter the yachts from $345 half-day. For other sailing courses and yacht rental contact the NSW Yachting Association (☎02/9660 1266). Natural Wanders Sea Kayak Adventures (☎02/9899 1001) arrange sea-kayaking in the harbour: their most popular trip is the Bridge Paddle ($75; 4hr; suitable for beginners), from Lavender Bay near Luna Park, under the Harbour Bridge and exploring the North Shore; picnic brunch included.

Western Union Office in Travelex, 37–49 Pitt St (Mon–Fri 9am–5pm, Sat 10am–2pm; ☎02/9241 5722).

Women The big events are around International Women's Day in March. Contact the Women's Information and Referral Service (Mon–Fri 9am–5pm; ☎1800 817 227) for information on this and women's organizations, services and referrals, or try The Women's Library, 8–10 Brown St, Newtown (Tues, Wed & Fri 11am–5pm, Thurs 11am–8pm, Sat & Sun noon–4pm), which lends feminist and lesbian literature. Jesse Street National Women's Library, housed in the Town Hall, 456 Kent St (Mon–Fri 10am–2pm), is an archive collecting literature detailing Australian women's history and writing. The Feminist Bookshop is in Orange Grove Plaza on Balmain Rd, Lilyfield (☎02/9810 2666).

Work If you have a working holiday visa, you shouldn't have too much trouble finding some sort of work, particularly in hospitality or retail. Offices of the government-run Centrelink (☎13 28 50) have a database of jobs; the most central offices are at 140 Redfern St, corner of George St, Redfern; 151 Crown St, Darlinghurst; and 231 Oxford St, Bondi Junction. Centrelink also refers jobseekers to several private "Job Network" agencies, including Employment National (☎13 34 44). The private agency Troy's (Level 11, 89 York St; ☎02/9290 2955), specializes in the hospitality industry. If you have some office or professional skills, there are plenty of temp agencies that are more than keen to take on travellers: flick through "Employment agencies" in the *Yellow Pages*. For a whole range of work, from unskilled to professional, the multinational Manpower is a good bet (☎13 25 02). Otherwise, scour hostel notice boards and the *Sydney Morning Herald*'s employment pages – Saturday's bumper edition is best. **YHA New South Wales** 422 Kent St, behind the Town Hall (Mon–Fri 9am–5pm, Thurs until 6pm, Sat 10am–2pm; ☎02/9261 1111). Membership and travel centre.

Around Sydney

If life in the fast lane is taking its toll, Sydney's residents can easily get away from it all. Right on their doorstep, golden beaches and magnificent national parks beckon, interwoven with intricate waterways. Everything in this part of the chapter can be done as a day-trip from the city, although some require an

Tours from Sydney

Tours from Sydney span the range from a day spent staring out the window of a bus to two days canyoning in the Blue Mountains. Listed below are a couple of regular bus-tour operators, but you'll almost certainly have a better time with one of the outfits who specialize in small-group tours, quite often with an emphasis on physical activities such as bushwalking, horse riding, white-water rafting or abseiling.

One-way tours can be the next best thing to going by car: small groups in minibuses travel from Sydney to Melbourne (for example), taking detours to attractions along the way that you'd never be able to reach on public transport.

As well as booking direct on the numbers given, most of the tours listed below can be booked through YHA Travel (℡02/9261 1111 or 9281 9444, ⓦwww.yha.com.au).

Return tours

AAT Kings ℡02/9518 6095, ⓦwww.aatkings.com. One of the largest operators, its big-group, sedentary bus tours cover city sights, wildlife parks, the Blue Mountains, Jenolan Caves, the Hawkesbury River and the Hunter Valley. Admissions and hotel pick-ups and drop-offs included in the price.

Blue Mountains Canyon Tours ℡ & ℻02/9371 5859, ⓦwww.canyontours.com.au. Exploring the Blue Mountains' deep canyons requires a thrilling mixture of abseiling down waterfalls, swimming through cave slots, bushwalking and rock-climbing. Wet canyoning is offered Oct–April, dry canyoning is available all year. Depending on the area or the number of abseils, trips range from $150 to $210. The most popular wet-canyoning trip is to Fortress Creek (grade 2; $150), near Leura, picking up Sydney 7am and returning 7pm.

CityRail ℡13 15 00, ⓦwww.131500.com.au. Day-trips by rail can be very good value, generally covering all transport and entry fees – trips include the Blue Mountains, and the Hawkesbury River (which includes a cruise). Details and tickets from any CityRail station.

Oz Trek ℡02/9666 4662, ⓦwww.oztrek.com.au. Recommended active full-day tours to the Blue Mountains ($54), with a choice of three bushwalks (30min–1hr 30min). Small groups (max 21). The trip can be extended to overnight packages with either horse riding ($209), abseiling ($209), or a Jenolan Caves visit ($179–199). Coogee, Bondi, Kings Cross, Central and Glebe pick-ups.

Waves Surf School ℡0414 682 228 or 1800 851 101, ⓦwww .wavessurfschool.com.au. One- or two-day "Learn To Surf" trips in the Royal National Park (one day with lunch $65; two days with meals, bushwalking and camping or sleep-on-board bus $169). Bondi, Coogee, Kings Cross and city pick-ups.

Wildframe Ecotours ℡02/9314 0658, ⓦwww.wildframe.com. Two full-day tours to the Blue Mountains. The Grand Canyon Eco-tour ($76) is for fit walkers, as it includes a small-group bushwalk (max 16) through the Grand Canyon (5km; 3hr); BYO lunch in Katoomba. The Blue Mountains Bush Tour ($86) is more relaxed with short bushwalks and lunch at a mountain lodge. Kangaroo spotting and overnight stay to explore more fully. See the box below for some of the huge variety of tours on offer.

North of Sydney the Hawkesbury River flows into the jagged jaws of the aptly named **Broken Bay**, which streaks across the map like a bolt of lightning. The entire area is surrounded by bush, with the huge spaces of the **Ku-Ring-Gai Chase National Park** in the south and the **Brisbane Waters National Park** in the north. Beyond Broken Bay, the **Central Coast** between Gosford and Newcastle is an ideal spot for a bit of fishing, sailing and lazing around. **Newcastle** is escaping its industrial city tag and the attractive

boomerang-throwing practice promised on both trips. Kings Cross and city pick-ups.

WonderBus ☎02/9555 9800 or 1800 669 800, ⓦwww.wonderbus.com.au. Three good-value day-tours to the Blue Mountains. The Eco Tour includes wildlife-watching and a two- to three-hour bushwalk ($70) while the Discovery Tour includes Featherdale Wildlife Park and lunch ($95). The unique Walkabout Aboriginal Tour is an all-day, off-the-beaten-track bush roam (around 10km) between Faulconbridge and Springwood led by an Aboriginal guide; expect to look at Aboriginal rock carvings, swim in waterholes in summer, and eat a bushtucker lunch ($95; own train journey to Faulconbridge and ex-Springwood).

One-way tours

Ando's Outback Tours ☎02/6842 8286 or 1800 228 828, ⓦwww.outbacktours .com.au. Popular five-day tour from Sydney to Byron Bay but getting well off the beaten track inland via Coonabarabran and Lightning Ridge ($460 all inclusive); includes a stay on the rural property of the family who run the tours. Sydney return for $35. Finding farm work is a common bonus.

Aussie Surf Adventures ☎02/4396 1007 or 1800 113 044, ⓦwww.surfadventures .com.au. Fun five-day surfing trip, catching the waves from Sydney to Byron Bay, learning surfing technique and etiquette and beach safety, with a chance to spot wildlife. Price ($590) includes gear, lessons, meals, and beachside cabin accommodation. Trips run Oct to mid-May; optional return coach to Sydney included.

Autopia Tours ☎03/9326 5536 or 1800 000 507, ⓦwww.autopiatours.com.au. This excellent, long-established Melbourne-based tour company, has an ex-Sydney tour, the three-and-a-half-day Highland Explorer to Melbourne via the Blue Mountains, Jenolan Caves, Canberra, the Snowy Mountains and Victoria's Alpine Way ($180; shortened version to Canberra $80; transport only). Small-seater buses with the driver acting as guide.

Oz Experience 761–763 George St, near Central station ☎02/9213 1766 or ☎1300 300 028, ⓦwww.ozexperience.com. A cross between transport and tours that go a little off the beaten track, with a hop-on-hop-off component lasting six months; accommodation not included. Scheduled routes include Sydney to Cairns in nine days ($386); and Sydney to Melbourne in three days via the south coast, Canberra, the Snowy Mountains and Phillip Island ($194). A day-trip to the Blue Mountains ($75) also takes in a wildlife park and the Hawkesbury River.

Pioneering Spirit ☎02/6685 7607 or 1800 672 422, ⓦwww.pioneeringspirit.com.au). Another tour (max 21 passengers) that heads to beach-heaven Byron Bay. This three-day, two-night excursion goes inland via the Hunter Valley for wine-tasting, back on the coast to Hat Head National Park, inland again to the Dorrigo World Heritage Area, returning to the coast at Coffs Harbour ($285 including breakfast, dinner, accommodation and entry fees; extra $30 for a Sydney return).

beach metropolis is coming up in the world, with a surfing, student, café and music culture all part of the mix. Immediately beyond are the wineries of the **Hunter Valley**.

To the **west**, you escape suburbia to emerge at the foot of the beautiful World Heritage-listed **Blue Mountains**, while the scenic Hawkesbury–Nepean river valley is home to historic rural towns such as **Windsor**.

Heading **south**, the **Royal National Park** is an hour's drive away, while on the coast beyond are a string of small, laid-back towns – Waterfall, Stanwell Park, Wombarra – with beautiful, unspoilt **beaches**. The industrial city of **Wollongong** and neighbouring Port Kembla are impressively located between the Illawarra Escarpment and the sea, but of paltry interest to visitors, although more interesting spots cluster around. Inland, the **Southern Highlands** are covered with yet more national parks, punctuated by pleasing little towns such as **Bundanoon** and **Berrima**.

North

The **Hawkesbury River** widens and slows as it approaches the South Pacific, joining Berowra Creek, Cowan Creek, Pittwater and Brisbane Water in the system of flooded valleys that form **Broken Bay**. The bay and its surrounding inlets are a haven for anglers, sailors and windsurfers, while the surrounding bushland is virtually untouched. Three major national parks surround the Hawkesbury River: **Ku-Ring-Gai Chase** in the south, **Brisbane Waters** facing it across the bay, and **Dharug**, inland to the west.

The **Pacific Highway** up here, partly supplanted by the Sydney–Newcastle Freeway, is fast and efficient, though not particularly attractive until you're approaching Ku-Ring-Gai Chase; if you want to detour into the park or towards Brooklyn, don't take the freeway. The **rail** lines follow the road almost as far as Broken Bay, before they take a scenic diversion through Brooklyn and Brisbane Waters to Woy Woy and Gosford.

Ku-Ring-Gai Chase National Park

Ku-Ring-Gai Chase is much the best known of New South Wales' national parks and, with the Pacific Highway running all the way up one side, is also the easiest to get to. The bushland scenery is crisscrossed by walking tracks, which you can explore to seek out Aboriginal rock paintings, or just to get away from it all and see the forest and its wildlife. Only 24km from the city centre, the huge park's unspoilt beauty is enhanced by the presence of water on three sides: the Hawkesbury, its inlet Cowan Creek, and the expanse of **Pittwater**, an inlet of Broken Bay. From Palm Beach you can take a boat cruise (see p.161) through all these waters to the park's most popular picnic spot at **Bobbin Head**, with a colourful marina. At the **Kalkari Visitor Centre** (daily 9am–5pm), on the Ku-Ring-Gai Chase Road, you can pick up information about walks in the park or take a guided walk. The Birrawanna Walking Track leads from here for 1.5km to the park headquarters, which can also be approached by car further along Ku-Ring-Gai Chase Road. The NPWS **Bobbin Head Information Centre** (daily 9am–4pm; ☎02/9472 8949) is located inside the Art Deco *Bobbin Inn* which also has a very pleasant restaurant, popular for weekend breakfasts and Sunday afternoon jazz. There are four road entrances to the park and a $10 entrance fee for cars. Without your own transport, take a ferry to the Pittwater side from Palm Beach, or a train to

Turramurra station and then Hornsby Bus #577 (☎02/9457 8888 for times) to the Bobbin Head Road entrance; some buses continue down to Bobbin Head itself.

Pittwater

From West Head at the northeastern corner of Ku-Ring-Gai Chase, there are superb views across Pittwater to the Barrenjoey Lighthouse at Palm Beach (see p.161). The **Garigal Aboriginal Heritage Walk** (3.5km circuit) heads from West Head Road to the Aboriginal rock engravings and hand art, the most accessible Aboriginal art site in the park. The only place to **camp** is The Basin (☎02/9451 8124 for bookings) on Pittwater, reached via the Palm Beach Ferry Service. Facilities at the site are minimal so bring everything with you.

If you want to stay in the park in rather more comfort, there's a very popular **YHA hostel** (☎02/9999 5748, ℮pittwater@yhansw.org.au; dorms $19–22, rooms ❸ ; bookings essential and well in advance for weekends) at **Halls Wharf**. It's one of New South Wales' most scenically sited – a rambling old house surrounded by bush and with a verandah where you can feed rainbow lorikeets and look down onto the water; sailing lessons can also be arranged. You must bring everything with you – the last food (and bottle) shop is at Church Point where the **ferry** departs to Halls Wharf (last departure Mon–Fri 7pm, Sat & Sun 6.30pm; ☎02/9999 3492 for times; $7.50 return).

Two direct buses run to Church Point: #E86 from Central station or #156 from Manly Wharf; it's then a ten-minute uphill walk. Alternatively the 24-hour Pink Water Taxi operates from Newport (☎018 238 190); bus #190 from Wynyard runs up the coast to Newport.

Cuddly koalas

It is no longer legal to physically pick up and hold a koala in New South Wales' wildlife parks, but photo-opportunity "patting" sessions are still on offer. Below are several hands-on wildlife experiences around Sydney.

The **Koala Park Sanctuary** (daily 9am–5pm; $17; ⓦwww.koalaparksanctuary .com.au) was established as a safe haven for koalas in 1935 and has since opened its gates to wombats, possums, kangaroos and native birds of all kinds. Koala-feeding sessions (daily 10.20am, 11.45am, 2pm & 3pm) are the patting and photo-opportunity times. Around 25km north of Sydney, not far from the Pacific Highway on Castle Hill Road, West Pennant Hills; train from Central station to Pennant Hills then bus #651 or #655 towards Glenorie (Mon–Sat).

At **Featherdale Wildlife Park** (daily 9am–5pm; $16; ⓦwww.featherdale.com.au), patting koalas is the special all-day attraction. Located at 217 Kildare Rd, Doonside, 30km west of Sydney off the M4 motorway between Parramatta and Penrith; train to Blacktown station then bus #725.

Wonderland Sydney (daily 10am–5pm, wildlife park from 9am; wildlife park $17.60, whole complex plus rides and events $48.40; ⓦwww.wonderland.com.au) is a huge family entertainment complex encompassing shows, giant waterslides, three roller-coasters and other theme park rides (queues of up to an hour on a busy day), plus the **Australian Wildlife Park**, where the "meet the animals" experience includes koalas, kangaroos and echidnas. Wonderland Sydney is on Wallgrove Road, Rooty Hill, just off the M4 approaching Penrith. Train to Rooty Hill station then Busways service (☎02/9625 8900 for times) from outside the Commonwealth Bank. AAT Kings (☎02/9518 6095) offers a bus, transfer and admission package.

The Hawkesbury River

One of New South Wales' prettiest rivers, with bush covering its banks for much of its course and some interesting old settlements alongside, the **Hawkesbury River** has its source in the Great Dividing Range and flows out to sea at Broken Bay. For information about the many national parks along the river, contact the the NPWS in Sydney (☎02/9247 8861) or at 370 Windsor Rd in Richmond (☎02/4588 5247). Short of chartering your own boat, the best way to explore the river system is to take a cruise (see box below); the River Boat Mail Run is the most interesting.

Upstream: Wisemans Ferry

The first ferry across the Hawkesbury River was opened by ex-convict Solomon Wiseman ten years after he was granted two hundred acres of river frontage in 1817, at the spot now known as **WISEMANS FERRY**. The crossing forged an inland connection between Sydney and the Hunter Valley via the convict-built Great North Road. Unfortunately, travellers on this isolated route were easy prey for marauding bushrangers and it was largely abandoned for the longer but safer coastal route. Today it's a popular recreational

---

Exploring the Hawkesbury River system

Brooklyn, just above the western mass of Ku-Ring-Gai Chase National Park, and easily reached by train to Brooklyn station from Central station in Sydney and from Gosford, is the base for Hawkesbury River Ferries (☎02/9985 7566), whose River Boat Mail Run still takes letters, as well as tourists, up and down the river. Departures are from Brooklyn Wharf on Dangar Road (Mon–Fri 9.30am excluding public holidays; 4hr; $35 including morning tea; booking essential). Also on offer are two-hour coffee cruises towards the mouth of the river (Mon–Thurs 11am & 1.30pm; $20), which can be used as transport to Patonga (see p.205; $10 one-way).

Gosford's Public Wharf is the starting point for the MV *Lady Kendall* (☎02/4323 1655, ⓦwww.starshipcruises.com.au), which cruises both Brisbane Water and Broken Bay (Mon–Wed, Sat & Sun, daily during school & public holidays, 10.15am & 1pm; 2hr 30min; $21; bookings essential).

Windsor is the base for the Hawkesbury Paddlewheeler (☎02/4575 1171, ⓦwww.paddlewheeler.com.au) which has a good-value Sunday afternoon Jazz Cruise: live jazz and a BBQ lunch for $28 (12.30pm–3pm; advance bookings essential).

Woy Woy is also a port of call for the MV *Lady Kendall* (see above) at 10.35am and 12.10pm.

Boat and houseboat rentals

The Hawkesbury River Marina Boat Hire, on Dangar Road, opposite the railway station in Brooklyn (☎02/9985 7252) hires out **boats** which comfortably seat six people (from $70 half-day, $95 full day, more at weekends) and are perfect for fishing expeditions around the mouth of the Hawkesbury or Dangar Island. The centre has a fishing shop and sells bait supplies; you'd need to buy rather than rent rods here. **Houseboats** can be good value if you can get a group together, with prices starting from $560 a weekend and $1040 a week for four people. The Sydney Visitor Centre in Sydney (☎02/9667 6050) has details of operators, or try Able Hawkesbury River Houseboats, on River Road in Wisemans Ferry (☎02/4566 4308 or 1800 024 979, ⓦwww.hawkesburyhouseboats.com.au), or Ripples Houseboats, 87 Brooklyn Rd, Brooklyn (☎02/9985 7788, ⓦwww.ripples.com.au) .

spot for day-trippers – just a little over an hour from Sydney by car, and with access to the **Dharug National Park** over the river by a free 24-hour car ferry. Dharug's rugged sandstone cliffs and gullies shelter Aboriginal rock engravings which can be visited only on ranger-led trips during school holidays; there's a camping area at Mill Creek (Gosford NPWS ☎02/4324 4911 for details of walks and camping; bookings for both essential at weekends and holiday periods). Open to walkers, cyclists and horse riders but not vehicles, the **Old Great North Road** was literally carved out of the rock by hundreds of convicts from 1829; you can camp en route at the Ten Mile Hollow camping area.

The settlement of Wisemans Ferry was based around Wiseman's home, Cobham Hall, built in 1826. Much of the original building still exists in the blue-painted *Wisemans Ferry Inn* on the Old Great North Road (☎02/4566 4301, ☞02/566 4780; motel ❸, pub ❹), with characterful **rooms** upstairs sharing bathrooms, and en-suite, motel-style rooms outside at the back. Bistro meals are served daily and there's entertainment on Sunday afternoons. Other accommodation in the surrounding area includes *Del Rio Riverside Resort* (☎02/4566 4330, ☜www.delrioresort.com.au; en-suite cabins ❹), a campsite in Webbs Creek reached via the Webbs Creek car ferry, 3km south of Wisemans Ferry; facilities include a Chinese restaurant, swimming pool, tennis court and golf course. *Rosevale Farm Resort*, 3km along Wisemans Ferry Road en route to Gosford (☎ & ☞02/4566 4207; vans ❷, en-suite cabins ❸), has less expensive camping and cabins – cheaper weekdays – in extensive bushland close to Dharug National Park.

Taking the ferry across the river from Wisemans Ferry, it's a scenic nineteen-kilometre river drive north along Settlers Road, another convict-built route, to **ST ALBANS**, where you can partake of a cooling brew (or stay a while) at a pub built in 1836, the hewn sandstone *Settlers Arms Inn* (☎02/4568 2111, ☞02/4568 2046; en-suite rooms ❺). The pub is set on two and a half acres and much of the vegetables and herbs for the delicious home-cooked food is organically grown on site (lunch daily, dinner Fri–Sun).

The Upper Hawkesbury: Windsor

About 50km inland from Sydney and reached easily by train from Central station via Blacktown, **WINDSOR** is probably the best preserved of all the historic Hawkesbury towns, with a lively centre of narrow streets, spacious old pubs and numerous historic colonial buildings. It's terrifically popular on Sundays, when a **market** takes over the shady, tree-lined mall end of the main drag, George Street, and the *Macquarie Arms Hotel* on Thompson Square, the grassy village green opposite, which claims to be the oldest pub in Australia, puts on live rock 'n' roll. Next door to the pub, the **Hawkesbury River Museum and Tourist Information Centre** (daily 10am–4pm; museum $2.50; ☎02/4577 2310, ☜www.hawkesburyweb.com) doles out local information. A Sunday cruise leaves from from the jetty across the road from the tourist office (see box opposite). From Windsor, Putty Road (Route 69) heads north through beautiful forest country, along the eastern edge of the Wollemi National Park, to Singleton in the Hunter Valley (see p.213).

From Richmond, just 7km northwest of Windsor, the **Bells Line of Road** (Route 40) goes to Lithgow via Kurrajong and is a great scenic drive; all along the way are fruit stalls stacked with produce from the valley. There's a wonderful view of the Upper Hawkesbury Valley from the lookout point at **Kurrajong Heights**, on the edge of the Blue Mountains. Another scenic drive from Richmond to the Blue Mountains, emerging near Springwood (see p.225), is south along the Hawkesbury Road, with the **Hawkesbury Heights Lookout** halfway along providing panoramic views. Not far from the lookout, the modern solar-powered *Hawkesbury Heights YHA* (☎02/4754 5621; dorms $18), has six twin rooms with beds at dorm rates and more views from its secluded bush setting.

The Central Coast

The shoreline between Broken Bay and Newcastle, known as the **Central Coast**, is characterized by large **coastal lakes** – saltwater lagoons almost entirely enclosed, but connected to the ocean by small waterways. The northernmost, **Lake Macquarie**, is the biggest saltwater lake in New South Wales. People in a hurry can bypass the Central Coast altogether on the Sydney–Newcastle Freeway which runs some way inland, but to see a bit more of the coastal scenery and the lakes, stay on the older Pacific Highway which heads to Newcastle via Gosford and Wyong. A further detour would take you from Gosford to **Terrigal** and then right along the narrow coastal strip via **The Entrance** and **Budgewoi** to rejoin the Pacific Highway after Lake Munmorah. The fit and intrepid can get here by bike: from Manly, head up the northern beaches, hop on a ferry service from Palm Beach (see p.161) to **Ettalong** (ex-Palm Beach: 8 Mon–Fri 6.30am–5pm, 7 Sat, Sun from 9am; ex-Ettalong: 8 Mon–Fri 6am–5.40pm, Sat from 8am, Sun from 9.40am; $7.50 one-way; ☎02/9918 2747, ⓦwww.palmbeachferry.com.au), then continue up through Woy Woy and Gosford to the coast. You can also reach **Patonga** by ferry with Palm Beach and Hawkesbury River Ferries (☎02/9997 4815, ⓦwww.sydneysceniccruises.com), departing Palm Beach daily at 11am (also 9am & 3.45pm holidays & weekends; $6.50 one-way) and returning from Patonga at 4.15pm (also 9.30am & 3pm holidays & weekends) and from Brooklyn with Hawkesbury River Ferries (see box on p.202). Otherwise, you can take a very scenic **train** route to Gosford or Woy Woy from Central station in Sydney, or come direct from Sydney airport with Bennetts Airport Shuttle (see "Airport buses" box on p.91).

Central Coast Tourism (☎1800 806 258, ⓦwww.cctourism.com.au) offers **tourist information** on the whole region and accommodation bookings. Within the Central Coast area a well-developed **bus service** run by the private Busways (☎02/4392 6666) and The Entrance Red Bus Services (☎02/4332 8655). For **taxis**, call Central Coast Taxis (☎13 10 08).

Gosford and around

To get anywhere on the Central Coast, you need to go through **GOSFORD**, perched on the north shore of Brisbane Water and just about within commuting distance of Sydney. Its proximity to the city has resulted in uncontrolled residential sprawl along much of the Central Coast, which has put a great strain on the once-unspoilt lakes. Although there's plenty of accommodation in and around Gosford – details from **Central Coast Tourism**, near the train station at 200 Mann St (Mon–Fri 10am–4pm, Sat 10am–12.30pm; ☎02/4385 4074, ⓦwww.cctourism.com.au) – there's not much incentive to stay.

Brisbane Waters National Park, immediately south of Gosford, is the site of the **Bulgandry Aboriginal engravings**, which are of a style unique to the Sydney region, with figurative outlines scratched boldly into sandstone. The site, no longer frequented by the Guringgai people – whose territory ranged south as far as Sydney Harbour and north to Lake Macquarie – is 7km southwest of Gosford off the Woy Woy road. Tiny **Bouddi National Park** is 20km southeast along the coast, at the northern mouth of Broken Bay, and is a great spot for bushwalking, with camping facilities at Putty Beach, Little Beach and Tallow Beach: book through the NPWS office at 207 Albury St, Gosford (☎02/4324 4911), which also has information on both parks. You can visit the rock-art sites with Coastal Eco-Tours (☎02/4344 3392, ⓦwww.coastalecotours .com.au), who offer excellent small-group, expert-led bushwalking tours in both national parks focusing on bush medicine, bushtucker and bush skills ($110 includes picnic lunch and Woy Woy station pick-ups).

Surrounded by Brisbane Waters National Park, friendly, undeveloped **PEARL BEACH**, just over a 25-kilometre drive from Gosford via Woy Woy and Umina, is a small community which expands on weekends. There are holiday houses to rent, but no other accommodation. Besides the popular *Sit 'n' Chats Beach Cafe* (live jazz Sun noon–4pm) and a restaurant, *Pearls on the Beach* (licensed and BYO; bookings ☎02/4342 4400; closed Mon–Wed, no dinner Sun), there's a general store (daily 8am–6pm) also selling petrol, a real estate agent who can arrange holiday lets (☎02/4341 7555, ⓦwww .pearlbeachrealestate.com.au; from $700 per week in peak season), and some tennis courts. The very pretty, sheltered beach, popular with families, has a relaxing open-access saltwater pool at one end. You can walk from the end of Crystal Avenue to the neighbouring beach settlement of **PATONGA** visiting a lookout and the **Crommelin Native Arboretum** en route. The 45-minute walk is best undertaken on the last Sunday of the month when the **Patonga Beach market** is held (8am–4pm); by road from Pearl Beach, it's 2km southwest. Ocean Planet, 25 Broken Bay Rd, Ettalong Beach (☎02/4342 2222, ⓦwww.oceanplanet.com.au; kayak rental from $30 half-day), does **kayaking trips** on Patonga Creek (8km; 7hr; $92.50) with pick-ups from Woy Woy station.

To get to Pearl Beach or Patonga, take the Busways **bus** (☎02/4392 6666) from Woy Woy station or the **ferry** to Patonga from Palm Beach or Brooklyn.

Terrigal

Twelve kilometres southeast of Gosford, beautiful upmarket **TERRIGAL**, backed by bush-covered hills, is one of the liveliest spots on the Central Coast, a thriving beach resort with a strong café culture. The big curve of beach has a picturesque sandstone headland, and the sheltered eastern end, The Haven, where the boats moor, is popular with families. Much of the social life revolves around the five-star *Crowne Plaza Hotel*, with its grand marble lobby and pricey boutiques, which dominates one end of **The Esplanade**.

Terrigal is a popular spot for **water-based activities** and operators include Erina Sail 'n' Ski (☎02/4365 2355; sailboarding lessons and rental); Learn To Surf (☎02/4332 0523; 1hr lesson $20); Central Coast Charters (☎0427 665 544; ocean and river cruises, deep-sea and game fishing); Kincumber Water-ski School (☎0414 685 005; first-timer $50 sessions); and Terrigal Dive School (☎02/4384 1219; five-day diving courses $385, shore or boat dives $60/$80).

Central Coast Tourism at Rotary Park, Terrigal Drive (daily 9am–5pm, May–Sept closed Sun; ☎02/4385 4430, ⓦwww.cctourism.com.au), is a good source of information on the whole region, and can make free **accommodation** bookings. If you're after a holiday unit (from around $400 weekly) contact Hunters Real Estate, 104 Terrigal Esplanade (☎02/4384 1444, ⓔhuntrs@ozemail.com.au). *Crowne Plaza Hotel*, on the corner of Pine Tree Lane (☎02/4384 9111, ⓦwww.crowneplaza.com; ❼), has three restaurants, two bars, a nightclub, a pool, gym and tennis courts; all this costs from $285 per night, including buffet breakfast and champagne. The pleasant YHA-affiliated *Terrigal Beach Backpackers Lodge*, 12 Campbell Crescent ⓣ & ⓕ02/4385 3330, ⓦwww.terrigalbeachlodge.com.au; dorms $24, rooms ❸), is only one minute's walk from the beach; boogie-boards are provided free. *Terrigal Beachhouse Motel*, 7 Painters Lane, off the northern end of The Esplanade (ⓣ02/4385 9564, ⓦwww.accommodationterrigal.com; share bathroom ❷, ensuite ❸–❹) feels like a cross between a motel and a backpackers'. It's seriously old but comfortable, brightly painted and has a common room but no kitchen; rooms are small and old-fashioned but very clean. They also run the more upmarket motel *Tiarri* (all rooms with own courtyard ❹), and rent apartments ($350 to $895).

Terrigal has plenty of **cafés**: *Louvres*, 60 The Esplanade (daily 8am–9pm), is beachy but sophisticated with a lovely plant-filled courtyard; *Aromas on Sea* has the best position (and great coffee, or drinks from the hotel bar with your food), on the breezy terrace of the *Crown Plaza* looking right over the beach (daily 8am–5pm, Fri & Sat to 9pm) while the local favourite is the tiny *Patcinos*, a block back from the beach at 17 Church St, near the hostel. The best fish and chips are from *Fish Bonez*, 90 The Esplanade (take away or eat in), while *The Break*, on Pine Tree Lane behind the *Crowne Plaza*, specializes in gourmet pizzas; its fun, intimate bar is a good alternative to the *Crowne's* packed beer garden – the *Florida Beach Bar* – or its posh *Lord Ashley Lounge* upstairs. The **restaurant** scene is dominated by Thai eateries: two of the best are the stylish *Al-Oi Thai*, near the *Crowne Plaza* at 3 Kurrawyba Ave (ⓣ02/4385 6611) and the cheap and cheerful *N Thai Sing*, 84 The Esplanade (ⓣ02/4385 9700).

To get to Terrigal, take Busways #80, #81 or #82 from Gosford station.

Avoca Beach and The Entrance

Six kilometres to the south of Terrigal, and altogether quieter, **AVOCA BEACH** is especially popular with surfers. A large, crescent-shaped and sandy beach between two headlands, it has its own surf lifesaving club and a safe children's rock pool. West of the beach are the still waters of **Avoca Lake**. Avoca's pleasant small-town atmosphere is enhanced by the Avoca Beach Theatre near the beach on Avoca Drive (ⓣ02/4382 2156), a little-changed, early-1950s cinema. You can **learn to surf** here with Central Coast Surf School (ⓣ02/4382 1020; 1hr lesson $25) or Aquamuse (ⓣ02/4368 4172), by the bridge in Heazlett Park, rents out pedal boats, bikes, kayaks and surf-skis to use on the lake. Limited overnight **accommodation** in Avoca includes self-contained cabins and villas in an upmarket, garden-set holiday resort, *The Palms*, Carolina Park, off The Round Drive (ⓣ02/4382 1227, ⓦwww.palmsavoca .com.au; ❹), which has swimming pools, spa, and games room. Otherwise, the best bet is to rent a holiday unit (from $450 per week) – call George Brand Real Estate (ⓣ02/4382 1311) for listings. For **eating**, grab fish and chips, gourmet and veggie burgers and Turkish bread sandwiches from the groovy, colourful *Prawn Star Seafood Cafe*, at the end of the main set of shops at 168 Avoca Drive (8.30am–9.30pm, closed Tues & Wed, daily school holidays), or there's fine dining at the expensive French-run *Feast* at Shop 3, 85 Avoca Drive (ⓣ02/4381 0707), at the end of the beach near the SLSC, with an open deck right over the beach. **To get here**, take Busways #79 from Gosford station; #81 also links Terrigal and Avoca Beach.

Further north, Tuggerah and Munmorah lakes meet the sea at **THE ENTRANCE**, a beautiful spot with water extending as far as the eye can see. It's a favourite fishing spot with anglers – and with swarms of **pelicans**, which turn up for the afternoon fish-feeds daily at 3.30pm (free) at Memorial Park, near the visitor centre (see below). The beaches and lakes along the coast from here to Newcastle are crowded with caravan parks, motels and outfits offering the opportunity to fish, windsurf, sail or water-ski: although less attractive than places further north, they make a great day-trip or weekend escape from Sydney. Pro Dive Central Coast, 96 The Entrance Rd (☎02/4334 1559), arranges **scuba-diving** lessons, daily boat dives and rents out snorkelling and dive gear. The **Entrance Visitors Centre**, Marine Parade (daily 9am–5pm; ☎02/4385 4074 or 1300 13 0708, ⓦwww.cctourism.com.au), has a free **accommodation** booking service. To get here by **bus**, take The Entrance Red Bus Services #21–23 from Gosford station or #24–26 from Tuggerah or Wyong stations.

Newcastle

NEWCASTLE was founded in 1804 for convicts too hard even for Sydney to cope with, but the river is the real reason for the city's existence. Coal was brought down it from the fields of the Hunter Valley, to be exported around the country and the world, and the proximity of the mines encouraged the establishment of other **heavy industries**. The production of steel here ceased in late 2000 and most of the slag heaps have been worked over, but the docks are still functional, particularly with the through traffic of coal from the Hunter Valley.

New South Wales' second city, with a population of around a quarter of a million, Newcastle has long-suffered from comparison with nearby Sydney. However, for a former major industrial city, it is surprisingly attractive, a fact which is now being more widely recognized. The city is experiencing a **real estate boom**: hundreds of apartments and hotels are going up, and old icons are being redeveloped, such as the once grand *Great Northern Hotel*, first built in 1938 and undergoing a $3 million facelift. Years of accumulated soot has been scraped off the city's stately buildings, riverside gardens have been created in front of the city centre, and an old wharf has been converted into a water-side entertainment venue. The once blue-collar town is now taking to tourism in a big way, trading particularly on its **waterside location** – the surf beaches are wonderful, and there are some more sheltered sandy beaches around the rocky promontory at the mouth of the Hunter River; the extraordinary dunes of Stockton Beach are just a ferry ride away. An alternative feel is provided by a big dose of **surf culture** – many surfwear- and surfboard-makers operate here, several champion surfers hail from the city, and the big contest is Surfest in March – and the large and lively student community. You might not choose to spend your entire holiday here, but it can be a good base for excursions, particularly for the wineries of the nearby Hunter Valley.

Arrival, public transport and information

If you're not driving, you'll arrive by train at Newcastle **train station**, right in the heart of the city on Scott Street, or by bus at nearby Watt Street.

Heading west from Newcastle train station, Scott Street eventually becomes Hunter Street, the city's main thoroughfare. Newcastle's hub is the pedestrianized, tree-lined Hunter Street Mall, with its department store, shops, fruit stalls and buskers, linked by a footbridge across to the harbour foreshore. From the mall, continuing west along Hunter Street, Civic train station marks the city's cultural and administrative district focused around City Hall and Civic Park. A short walk south of here, Cooks Hill is focused on café- and restaurant-lined Darby Street. It's easy to get around using Newcastle's **public transport**

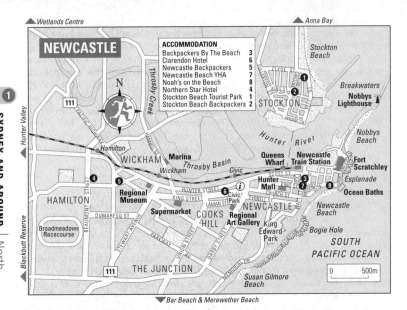

system. Newcastle Bus and Ferry Services (☎02/4961 8933) has an information booth at the west end of Hunter Street Mall on the corner of Perkins Street; ask here about the free city loop bus which was trialing at the time of writing. Bus fares are time-based, allowing transfers (1hr $2.50; 4hr $4.90; all-day bus and ferry $7.60); all tickets can be bought on board. The one ferry operating goes to Stockton, departing from Queens Wharf (Mon–Sat 5.15am–11pm/midnight, Sun 8.30am–8.30pm; $1.80 one-way). Two passenger train lines have several suburban stops, the most useful heading towards Sydney, with handy stops at Civic for Darby Street and Hamilton for Beaumont Street (fares from $2.20 single). Weekly train-bus-ferry passes, available from selected newsagencies, start from $34.

You can familiarize yourself with the city sights on **Newcastle's Famous Tram** (Mon–Fri hourly 10am–1pm & 1.45pm, Sat & Sun hourly 10am–3pm; 45min; $10; ☎02/4963 7954), the usual twee coach-done-out-as-a-tram deal, departing from Newcastle station; or get shown around Newcastle Harbour with **Moonshadow Cruises** (Nov to mid–May only: Mon, Wed, Fri 10.30am, Sat & Sun 1.30pm; 1hr 30min; $15; licensed kiosk; ☎02/4984 9388, Ⓦwww.moonshadow.com.au), based at the new Newcastle Cruising Yacht Club Marina, Hannel Street, Wickham, next to the Fisherman's Co-op; train to Wickham station, then a short walk.

The very helpful **Newcastle Visitors Information** (Mon–Fri 9am–5pm, Sat & Sun 10am–3.30pm; ☎02/4974 2999 or 1800 654 558, Ⓦwww .newcastletourism.com) at 361 Hunter St, opposite Civic station, can provide other local information and maps.

Accommodation

Backpackers By The Beach 34 Hunter St ☎02/4926 3472, Ⓦwww.backpackersbythebeach .com.au. A fun and sociable hostel, with a street-

level kitchen-cum-common room with big windows and outdoor tables set on an already lively, café-filled corner. Reached by utilitarian metal steps, there are three floors of very clean dorms (four- and eight-bed, some en suite) and rooms, all with fans and colourful curtains. Free boards and bikes; loads of computers for Internet access. Dorms $22, rooms ❷

Clarendon Hotel 347 Hunter St ☎02/4927 0966, ⓦwww.clarendonhotel.com.au. This central 1930s Art Deco pub has been recently, and beautifully, renovated and shows its original features in the bar downstairs. The really stylish, vibrantly coloured rooms are totally contemporary and offer great value. Suites have kitchenettes. The bright café-bistro with its huge courtyard does good-value meals from breakfast on. Free parking. ❺

Newcastle Backpackers 42 and 44 Denison St, Hamilton ☎02/4969 3436 or 1800 333 436, ⓦwww.newcastlebackpackers.com. A home-style hostel (with own heated pool) in two houses run by a friendly family. One more upmarket house has doubles, while the other has dorms (four- and six-bed plus one twelve-bed). Located 3km from the city centre and beach but only a few minutes' walk from lively Beaumont Street; bus #260 from the city runs for a free pick-up. The owner runs people down to the beach most days and offers free surfing lessons (boogie-boards free, surf-boards $15 per day). Dorms $21, rooms ❷

Newcastle Beach YHA 30 Pacific St, cnr King St ☎02/4925 3544, ⓔyhanewcastle@hunterlink.net.au. Fantastic hostel in an impressively restored, spacious old building complete with ball-room, huge staircases and a lounge with a fire-place and leather armchairs, a pool table and courtyard with BBQ, plus the usual facilities. Four-bed dorms, doubles, twins and family rooms. Just

50m from the surf and right in the centre of town; free surfboards and boogie-boards. Dorms $23–24, rooms ❸

Noah's on the Beach Cnr Shortland Esplanade and Zaara St ☎02/4929 5181, ⓦwww.noahsonthebeach.com.au. Upmarket, modern multi-storey motel right opposite Newcastle Beach. Most rooms have ocean views. Room service. ❺

Northern Star Hotel 112 Beaumont St, Hamilton ☎02/4961 1087, ⓦwww.northernstarhotel.com.au. Pub accommodation in a great location on this restaurant- and café-lined street – though with bands downstairs nightly, this is not the place for light sleepers. All double rooms are en suite, spacious, clean and have fridges, TV, tea and coffee facilities and ceiling fans; cheaper shared-bath singles available for $50. ❹

Stockton Beach Backpackers 68 Mitchell St, Stockton Beach, 250m from Stockton Wharf ☎02/4928 4333, ⓦwww.stocktonbeachbackpackers.com.au. A former Art Deco picture theatre trans-formed into a fantastic, spacious hostel. Facilities include the usual, plus split-level lounge areas, free spa and sauna, rooftop deck with water views, games room, huge courtyard with BBQ, and masses of showers and toilets. Clean and bright four- and six-bed dorms with lockers, share bathroom and en-suite rooms, some quite large (families are wel-come). Dorms $25, rooms ❸ , en suites ❹

Stockton Beach Tourist Park Pitt St, Stockton Beach ☎02/4928 1393. Picturesquely sited camp-ground right on the extensive beach; two camp kitchens. Two-minute ferry ride from the city. Cabins ❷ , en-suite cabins ❹

The City

Newcastle has whole streetscapes of beautiful **Victorian terraces** that would put Sydney's to shame – pick up a free *Newcastle City of Heritage and Enterprise* map from the tourist office, or the *Newcastle Town Walk*, to guide you around some of the old buildings. A couple of buildings in **Newcastle Harbour Foreshore Park** show the trend for the city's wealth of disused public archi-tecture: on one corner of the park stands the beautiful Italianate brick **Customs House**, now a popular pub. Nearby is the wooden two-storey **Paymasters House**, where you can sit with a coffee in its fine verandah café and contemplate the water. The restored **Queens Wharf**, a landmark with its distinctive observation tower, is located on the south bank of the Hunter River. It's linked to the city centre by an elevated walkway from Hunter Street Mall and boasts *The Brewery*, a popular and stylish waterfront drinking spot (see p.212).

Besides Newcastle's waterside attractions, a few other places might be of interest. The **Newcastle Regional Museum**, 787 Hunter St (Tues–Sun 10am–5pm, daily during school holidays; free), housed in what began as a brewery in the 1870s, focuses on the history of the mining and steel industries of the area; attached is the Supernova hands-on science centre, much the best thing about the museum (along with the **free Internet access** in the café on weekdays). If you're at a loose end, the **Newcastle Regional Art Gallery**, on Laman Street near Civic Park (Tues–Sun 10am–5pm; free), usually has an interesting temporary exhibition in addition to its permanent display.

Beaches and wildlife reserves

The city centre, positioned on a narrow length of land between the Hunter River to the west and the Pacific Ocean to the east, has several popular and pleasantly low-key beaches close by. **Newcastle Beach**, only a few hundred metres from the city on Shortland Esplanade, has patrolled swimming between flags, a sandy saltwater pool perfect for children, shaded picnic tables and good surfing at its southern end. At the northern end, the beautifully painted Art Deco-style free **Ocean Baths** houses the changing pavilions for the huge saltwater pool, which has its own diving board.

Overlooking the water north of Newcastle Beach, **Fort Scratchley**, built in the 1880s, houses a maritime and military museum (generally Tues–Sun noon–4pm but check on ☎02/4929 2588 as it's volunteer-run; free). Beyond the fort is the long, uncrowded stretch of **Nobbys Beach**, with a lovely old beach pavilion. A walkway leads to Nobbys Head and its nineteenth-century lighthouse.

If you follow Shortland Esplanade south from Newcastle Beach, you'll come to the huge expanse of King Edward Park, with good walking paths and cliff views over this rocky stretch of waterfront. One section of the rock ledge holds Australia's first man-made ocean pool, the **Bogie Hole**. Chiselled out of the rock by convicts in the early nineteenth century for the Military Commandant's personal bathing pleasure. The cliffs are momentarily intercepted by **Susan Gilmore Beach** – secluded enough to indulge in some nude bathing – then further around the rocks is **Bar Beach**, a popular surfing spot that's floodlit at night. The longer **Merewether Beach** next door has a fabulous ocean baths at its southern end and a separate children's pool; overlooking the beach is the *Merewether Hotel*, a fine place for a drink.

Just two minutes by ferry from Queens Wharf across the Hunter River, the beachside suburb of **Stockton** is the starting point for the extensive, extraordinary **Stockton Beach**, which extends 32km north to **Anna Bay**. Two kilometres wide at some points and covered in moving sanddunes, some of which are up to 30m high, Stockton Bight, as its officially known, looks strikingly like a mini desert and has been the location for a Bollywood film. It's become something of an adventure playground in recent years, with thrilling quad-bike tours offered by Sand Safaris (2hr; $110, pick-ups from Stockton ferry; ☎02/4965 0215, ⊛www.sandsafaris.com.au) which also take in the 1974 shipwreck, the *Sygna Bergen*. You can sandboard down the dunes on the 4WD beach tours offered by Dawsons Scenic Tours (from $20; 1hr 30min tour; pick-ups from Anna Bay) or explore them on horseback with Horse Paradise Tours, based at Williamtown (☎02/4965 1877, ⊛www.users.bigpond.com/horseparadise; from 1hr beginner, $35).

Inland, **Blackbutt Reserve** is a large slab of bushland in the middle of Newcastle suburbia in New Lambton Heights about 10km southwest of the city (daily 9am–5pm; free; koala talks Sat & Sun 11.30am & 2.30pm, koala feeding daily 2–3pm); consisting of four valleys, it includes a remnant of rainforest, creeks, lakes and ponds and 20km of walking tracks to explore them. En route you'll see kangaroos, koalas, wombats, emus and other native animals in the reserve's wildlife enclosures. To get there from the city, take bus #262 to the Carnley Avenue entrance; for the entrances on Lookout Road you can take bus #363; the tourist office produces a helpful free map. Northwest of the city, the **Wetlands Centre**, Sandgate Road, Shortland (daily 9am–5pm; donation), is situated on the wetlands of Hexham Swamp by Ironbark Creek and is home to a mass of birdlife. There are walking and cycling trails here, and you can rent canoes from tourist information. Reach the Wetlands Centre by train from Newcastle to Sandgate, from where it's a ten-minute walk.

Eating

The two streets to head for are **Darby Street**, close to the city centre, which has a multicultural mix of restaurants and some very hip cafés – *The Grind Coffee Co* at no. 127 and *Longbench* at no. 161 are currently in vogue – as well as some secondhand bookshops and retro clothes stores to browse in between coffees; and **Beaumont Street** in Hamilton, 3km northeast of the city centre (train to Hamilton station or bus #260), with a concentration of Italian places, as well as Turkish, Lebanese, Japanese and Indian; it's jam-packed Friday and Saturday nights. Another good spot in the city centre is *Market Square Foodcourt*, upstairs in the Hunter Street Mall, with a range of food bars. Newcastle has the only franchise of the Sydney legend, *Harry's Cafe de Wheels*, an all-day, **late-night** pie-cart (Mon, Tues & Sun to 11pm, Wed & Thurs to 1am, Sat & Sun to 4am) stationed on Wharf Road near *The Brewery* (see overleaf).

Al-Oi-Thai 133 Darby St ☎02/4929 3610 & 50 Beaumont St, Hamilton ☎02/4969 1434. Delicious traditional Thai food served in stylish surrounds. Justifiably popular. Lunch Wed–Sat, dinner Tues–Sun; BYO.

George's 79 Beaumont St, Hamilton. The popular *George's* has a spacious (and very trendy) interior and also outside tables to check out the busy street action, but it still gets packed: the portions of great contemporary Australian food are huge, coffee is good and you can just come here for a drink. Licensed (and BYO). Daily 8am–10pm.

Goldbergs Coffee House 137 Darby St. This perennially popular Darby Street institution is big, buzzy and airy with modish green walls and polished wooden floors. The emphasis is on the excellent coffee, plus very reasonably priced eclectically modern meals. Also outside courtyard. Daily 7am–midnight. Licensed.

The Last Drop Espresso Bar 37 Hunter St. Great little café near the YHA which serves excellent coffee, fresh juices, frappés and smoothies and tasty gourmet sandwiches. Mon–Fri 7am–4pm, plus Nov–Feb Sat & Sun 7am–3pm.

Little Swallows Café Restaurant 54 Beaumont St, Hamilton ☎02/4969 2135. Simple place, a favourite daytime coffee hangout for Italian locals.

Captures the earthy feel of a traditional Italian trattoria, with suitably generous portions. You can also dine outside on the square. Inexpensive. BYO. Daily 9am–10pm.

Salar Couch Cafe 54 Watt St. Quirky, comfortable and relaxed café on the bottom floor of a terrace house: long communal tables, lounging couches and cushions, a fireplace, good music (good live performances Sun from 3pm and every second Thurs night; ☎02/4927 5329 for details), free Internet access, books and games . Delicious food – nothing over $15 – from a spicy international menu. Tues & Wed 11am–5pm, Thurs 11am–10pm, Fri 11am to late, Sat 10am to late, Sun 10am–10pm.

Scott Street Restaurant 19 Scott St ☎02/4927 0107. Smart, minimalist restaurant close to Newcastle Beach. The small seasonal dinner changes every six weeks, with contemporary-style dishes such as king prawn risotto with coriander and chilli. Licensed & BYO. Dinner Tues–Sat.

Shalimar 100 Beaumont St, Hamilton ☎02/4961 3862. Stylish Indian restaurant but with inexpensive to moderate prices. A small well-chosen menu covers regional cuisines with a modern Australian slant, such as Tandoori Rainbow Trout; lots of fish and vegetarian options. BYO. Lunch Mon–Fri, dinner daily.

Entertainment and nightlife

The area known as "the cultural precinct", near Civic Park on King, Hunter and Auckland streets, is the location for three refurbished Art Deco venues; pick up a monthly calendar from the tourist office for details of what's on. The **Civic Theatre**, 375 Hunter St (☎02/4929 1977) hosts mainly big-budget musicals and theatre productions. At the **University Conservatorium of Music** on Auckland Street (℡02/4921 8900), there are often free lunch-time concerts as well as evening performances, while the grand **City Hall**, 290 King St (℡02/4974 2948) has occasional classical music events such as the Australian Chamber Orchestra. Mainstream **cinema** is on offer at the three-screen Greater Union nearby at 183 King St (discount Tues $9; ℡02/4926 2233). Both arthouse and mainstream releases are shown around the corner at the small, single-screen Kensington Cinema, 299 Hunter St, opposite Civic station (℡02/4929 3893), or the three-screen Showcase City Cinemas, 31–33 Wolfe St, off Hunter Street Mall (℡02/4929 5019); the two co-owned cinemas price every session at a discount $10.50.

For **nightlife listings**, check out the listing supplement "TE" in Wednesday's *Post* or the fortnightly free music mag, *U Turn*. During term time, the students of Newcastle University add a lot of life to the city but there is always a thriving **live music** scene. One of the best venues in town for live bands is the uni's **Bar on the Hill** at Callaghan (℡02/4921 5000; bus #260) and the **Cambridge Hotel** 789 Hunter St, Newcastle West (℡02/4962 2459) is also a big venue for touring interstate and international bands. On Friday and Saturday nights the city pubs on Hunter Street and parallel King Street are lively and there are two popular, young **nightclubs** – *Surf City* and *The Mercury* – on perpendicular Watt Street.

Beaches Hotel Opposite Merewether Beach ℡02/4963 1574. With a huge beachfront beer garden this is popular all weekend and is *the* place to go on Sun nights when there are live bands.

The Brewery 150 Wharf Rd. Popular waterfront drinking hole – grab tables right on the wharf or on the upstairs balcony. Food from the busy bistro can be eaten outside (weekend breakfasts too). Live music or DJs Wed–Sun.

Crown & Anchor 189 Hunter St. Well-known city boozer recently renovated with colourful feature walls and opened up to the light. Pavement tables alongside the classic, beautifully tiled exterior. Popular balcony upstairs, overlooking the street. The nightclub, *Frost Bites* (Wed–Sun; free), specializes in lethal sno-cone alcoholic drinks.

The Kent 59 Beaumont St, cnr Cleary St, Hamilton ℡02/4961 3303. Beautifully renovated old pub and music venue, which is busy most nights – pool comps, quizzes, karaoke, a rock duo Friday to Sunday nights, and Sunday afternoon jazz (4.30pm–8.30pm) – but with several refuges, including a plant-filled beer garden and a great bistro. No cover charge.

Finnegan's Cnr Darby and King streets. Newcastle's obligatory Irish theme pub. Inevitably lively and popular, especially with travellers as they often put on free food nights to pack them in.

Northern Star Hotel 112 Beaumont St, Hamilton ℡02/4961 1087. Music in the back bar nightly from folk to jazz, blues and rock but Friday and Saturday are the big nights for up-and-coming Australian bands (10.30pm–1am; $6–10); other nights mostly free.

Sydney Junction Hotel 8 Beaumont St, Hamilton ℡02/4961 2537. "SJs" as the locals call it, is a young and lively pub in an equally animated strip – open to 1am most nights and until 4am Friday and Saturday. Bands – local and touring – and CD launches Thurs–Sat nights. Usually free but entry up to $15 for major gigs.

Listings

Banks and exchange American Express, 49 Hunter St ℡1300 139 060. Commonwealth Bank, 136 Hunter Street Mall (℡02/4927 2777), has foreign exchange.

Car rental A.R.A ℡02/4962 2488; Thrifty ℡02/4942 2266.

Internet access Internet Cafe, 58 Lindsay St, off Beaumont St, Hamilton; daily 10am–10pm; $6.60 per hour); *Salar Couch Cafe* (see p.211); Newcastle Regional Museum (see p.209).

Left luggage At the train station (daily 8am–5pm; $1.50 per article).

Post office Newcastle GPO, 96 Hunter St, NSW 2300 (Mon–Fri 8am–5pm).

Supermarket Bi-Lo, cnr King and National Park streets; open 24hr.

Taxi Taxi Services Co-Op ℡02/4979 3000.

Travel agent Newcastle Travel, 68 Hunter St ℡02/4926 1855.

The Hunter Valley

In Australia (and, increasingly, worldwide) the **Hunter Valley** is synonymous with fine **wine**. The first vines were planted 150 years ago and are mainly the two classic white-wine varieties of Semillon and Chardonnay, with Pinot Noir and Shiraz dominating the reds. In what seems a bizarre juxtaposition, this is also a very important **coal-mining region**: in the upper part of the valley especially, the two often go hand-in-hand. By far the best-known area, however, is in the Lower Hunter Valley around the main town of Cessnock – even the town's jail has its own vineyard, and the prisoners have produced some prize-winning wines. One of the appeals of the Hunter Valley wine country is the bush and farming feel of the place with the vast plantings of vineyards

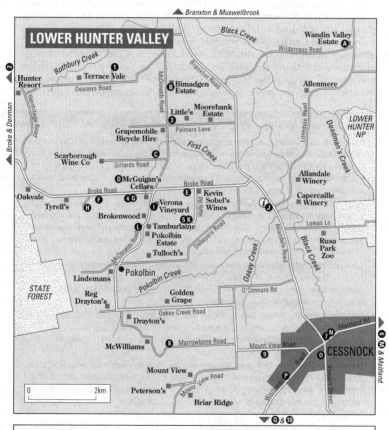

seemingly lost among bushland, forested ridges, red-soiled dirt tracks, and paddocks with grazing cattle.

CESSNOCK is uninteresting in itself, and surprisingly unsophisticated given the wine culture surrounding it, though at the time of writing the rather ugly main drag, Vincent Street, was being landscaped in an attempt to improve things. Its big old country pubs are probably its best feature and staying in one provides a taste of Australian rural life. Most of the **wine-tasting** is around the area called **Pokolbin** (no town to speak of), at the centre of the vineyards, 12 to 15km northwest of Cessnock, alongside some very salubrious accommodation and a fine-dining scene. For overnight stays with your own transport you'd be better off basing yourself out here, and in Cessnock if you've come on the coach.

Pick up the excellent free *Hunter Valley Wine Country* guide with a handy fold-out map in the centre from the Sydney Visitor Centre in The Rocks (see p.118) or the brand-new **Hunter Valley Wine Country Visitor Information Centre** (Mon–Sat 9am–5pm, Sun 9am–4pm; ℡02/4990 4477, ⓦwww.winecountry.com.au), Main Road, Pokolbin, scenically sited amongst vineyards and with the very pleasant, affordable *Wine Country Cafe*. If it's closed you can still pick up the free guides from a rack outside. Try to tour the wineries during the week; at weekends both the number of visitors and

Hunter Valley wineries

More than sixty wineries cluster around the Hunter Valley, almost all of them offering tastings. The most visited are in the lower part of the valley, near Pokolbin, but there are also a few gems in the upper valley, around Wybong and Denman, west of Muswellbrook. See the box on p.824 for some wine-tasting tips. Below are a few of our favourites and some that offer tours.

Allandale Winery Lovedale Rd, Pokolbin ℡02/4990 4526. Picturesque, small winery established in 1978. Set on a hill, with great views overlooking the vineyard and the Brokenback Range. They're happy for you to visit during vintage time, when you can see the small operation in action; try their prize-winning Chardonnay. One of the best. Mon–Sat 9am–5pm, Sun 10am–5pm.

Cruikshank Callatoota Estate Wybong Rd, Wybong, Upper Hunter Valley, 18km north of Denman ℡02/6547 8149. Winemaker John Cruikshank is a real character who has been making red wine here since 1974. Vineyard BBQ and picnic facilities, or light lunch available. Daily 9am–5pm.

Drayton's Family Wines Oakey Creek Rd, Pokolbin ℡02/4998 7513. Friendly, down-to-earth family winery, established for over 150 years and well known for their ports. BBQ and picnic facilities; children's play area. Tours Mon–Fri 11am. Mon–Fri 8am–5pm, Sat & Sun 10am–5pm.

Hermitage Road Cellars and Winery Hunter Resort, Hermitage Rd, Pokolbin ℡02/4998 7777. The largest commercial winery, lacking in atmosphere but offering informative wine tours (9am, 11am & 2pm; booking essential; $5.50 which is refunded if you buy a bottle of wine) or a two-hour "Wine School" tutorial (daily 9am; $25). Daily 9am–5pm.

Kevin Sobel's Wines Cnr Broke and Halls roads, Pokolbin ℡02/4998 7766. The welcome at this small, simple winery is wonderfully down-to-earth, and includes a greeting by Bacchas, the resident St Bernard. The circular timber-and-glass building itself is a real treat, with a home-made, wonky feel. Picnic tables outside. Daily 9am–5pm.

Lindemans McDonalds Rd, Pokolbin ℡02/4998 7684. One of the Hunter's best-known names; Dr Lindeman first planted vines in the valley in 1842. Its museum has a collection of winemaking paraphernalia. Daily 10am–5pm.

accommodation prices go up. In February, when the place is flooded with wine-lovers enjoying the Dionysian delights of the **Hunter Valley Vintage Festival**, accommodation is impossible to find, but summer is normally quieter as it's so very hot inland. Another lively time is October, when Wyndham Estate hosts **Opera in the Vineyards** (℡02/4938 3444), followed by the **Jazz in the Vines Festival** (℡02/4993 7000) based at Tyrell's.

Getting there and around

To get to Cessnock, catch a train from Central to Maitland or Newcastle and then a bus to Cessnock with Rover Motors (℡02/4991 1967). Alternatively, Keans Travel Express (Sydney ℡02/9211 3387; Muswellbrook ℡02/6543 1322) goes direct from Sydney to the Hunter Valley once daily (terminating at Scone), taking just over two hours with stops including Kurri Kurri, Neath, Cessnock, Pokolbin and Muswellbrook.

If you're without transport (there's no public transport to the wineries) – or don't want to meander unintentionally off-road after excessive wine-tasting – **vineyard tours** are a good option. Many are exhausting return trips from Sydney (see box on pp.198–199), but several local operators offer day-trips from within the valley: Shadows Wine Tours (℡02/4990 7002) does good-value, day-long (7hr) wine tours of the Hunter Valley visiting five wineries, with pick-ups

Rosemount Estate Rosemount Rd, Denman, Upper Hunter ℡02/6549 6400. Producer of some of Australia's best-known, award-winning wines, and with an excellent vineyard brasserie (Tues–Sun 10am–3pm). Daily 10am–4pm.

Scarborough Wine Co Gilliards Rd, Pokolbin ℡02/4998 7563. Small, friendly winery specializing in Chardonnay and Pinot Noir. Pleasantly relaxed sit-down tastings are held in a small cottage on Hungerford Hill with wonderful valley views. Daily 9am–5pm.

Small Winemakers Centre Verona Vineyard, McDonalds Rd, Pokolbin ℡02/4998 7668. Sells wines produced by several other small vineyards; the tasting charge levied on some wines is usually refunded on purchases. Excellent *Harry's Sandwich Bar* downstairs or BYO *Cafe Max* upstairs, with balcony views and an eclectic menu to team with your wine (Wed–Sun 11am–4pm). Daily 10am–5pm.

Tamburlaine Wines McDonalds Rd, Pokolbin ℡02/4998 7570. The jasmine-scented garden outside gives a hint of the flowery, elegant wines within. Only a small range of wines – too small even for the domestic market, so you must buy here. Tastings are well orchestrated and delivered with a heap of experience. Daily 9.30am–5pm.

Tyrrell's Family Vineyard Broke Rd, Pokolbin ℡02/4998 7509. The oldest independent family vineyards, producing consistently good wines. The tiny ironbark slab hut, where Edward Tyrell lived when he began the winery in 1858, is still in the grounds, and the old winery with its cool earth floor is much as it was. Beautiful setting against the Brokenback Range. Mon–Sat 8am–5pm, with free tour 1.30pm.

Wandin Valley Estate Cnr Wilderness and Lovedale roads ℡02/4930 7317. One of the most picturesquely sited wineries, set on a hundred acres of vineyards with a creek and magnificent views across the Wategos and the Brokenback Ranges, shared by the great little *Cafe Crocodile* (weekend brunch, lunch Wed–Sun, dinner Fri & Sat; wine at cellar-door prices and by the glass). Very friendly, relaxed cellar door and tours Sat & Sun 11am. Daily 10am–5pm.

from Newcastle, Maitland, Cessnock and the vineyards ($40 or $60 with restaurant lunch). Hunter Vineyard Tours (☎02/4991 1659, ⓦwww .huntervineyardtours.com.au) runs small-group bus tours visiting ten well-chosen wineries over six hours, all offering tastings ($45, pick-up from Cessnock; Newcastle or Maitland pick-ups $5 extra; restaurant lunch $20 extra or BYO). The more expensive Hunter Valley Day Tours (☎02/4938 5031, ⓦwww.huntertourism.com/daytours) offers a small-group wine-and-cheese tasting tour ($80 for pick-ups from Cessnock, Pokolbin and Maitland; $95 for Newcastle pick-ups). Pedal power is also popular: **rent bikes** from Grapemobile, on the corner of McDonalds Road and Palmers Lane, Pokolbin (☎ & ⓕ02/4990 7002 or 0500 804 039, ⓦwww.grapemobile.com.au; $30 per day, $22 half-day). Finally, there's always a **taxi**: call Cessnock RadioCabs (☎ 02/4990 1111).

Hunter Valley accommodation

Since the Hunter Valley is a popular weekend trip for Sydneysiders, accommodation **prices** invariably rise on Friday and Saturday nights when most places only offer two-night deals; we have indicated the weekday prices. If you're going to be here at a weekend, or during the February vintage festival, advance **booking** is essential.

Belford Country Cabins 659 Hermitage Rd, Pokolbin ☎02/6574 7100, ⓦwww.belfordcabins .com.au. Family-run, fully equipped two- and four-bedroom wooden bungalows (sleeping up to four or eight). Great bushland location, small pool and playground. ❹

Bellbird Hotel 388 Wollombi Rd, Bellbird, 5km southwest of Cessnock ☎02/4990 1094, ⓕ02/4991 5475. Great classic country pub, circa 1908, with wide iron-lace. Public bar is full of country characters. Eat inexpensive no-frills bistro food in the very pleasant vine-covered and flower-filled beer garden; adjacent children's playground. All rooms share bathrooms. Mid-week light breakfast or weekend cooked breakfast included. ❸

Cessnock Hotel ☎02/4990 1002, ⓦwww.huntervalleyhotels.com.au. This recently renovated pub is now very much city-style, with a great bistro-cum-bar, the *Kurrajong Cafe*, taking over most of downstairs (breakfast through dinner; modern Australian plus meaty pub favourites, mains average $14; couple of vegetarian options). Rooms all share bathrooms but they are huge with high ceilings, fans and really comfy beds. Big verandah for guests to hang out on; cooked breakfast served in the café. ❹

Elfin Hill Motel Marrowbone Rd, Pokolbin ☎02/4998 7543, ⓔelfinhill@hunterlink.com.au. Friendly, family-run hilltop motel with extensive views. Comfortable air-con units in timber cabins, plus a saltwater pool and BBQ area. ❹

Hunter Valley Gardens Broke Rd, Pokolbin ☎02/4998 7854, ⓦwww.hvg.com.au. Modern combined motel and hotel complex overlooking the

vineyards, complete with an Irish pub, *Harrigan's*, bistro, pool, spa, tennis courts and three standards of accommodation: four-and-a-half-star in *The Lodge* ❼; motel-style in *Harrigan's* ❻; or in self-contained one- and two-bedroom cabins at *Grapeview Villas* ❺. One room is accessible to disabled guests.

Neath Hotel Cessnock Rd, Neath, 6km east of Cessnock ☎02/4930 4270, ⓦwww .huntervalleyhotels.com.au. B&B in a nicely furnished big old country pub, listed by the National Trust; all rooms share bath. Friday and Saturday night rates ($130) include a cooked breakfast and a three-course meal in *Baron's*, the antique-filled restaurant. Restaurant Sat nights only; cheaper bistro rest of week. Mid-week rates include a light breakfast ❹

Peppers Convent Halls Rd, Pokolbin ☎02/4998 7764, ⓦwww.peppers.com.au. The swankiest place to stay in the Hunter Valley, with a price to match (from $310 per night). The guesthouse, converted from an old convent, has heaps of cosy cachet, fireplaces and low beams, and is part of the Peppertree winery. Attached fine-dining restaurant, *Robert's* (☎02/4998 7330; licensed) in a charming 1876 wooden farmhouse filled with flowers; French rustic-style food emerges from wood-fired ovens.

Pokolbin Cabins Palmers Lane, Pokolbin ☎02/4998 7611, ⓕ02/4998 7873. In the midst of the wineries, this extensive complex has two- and three-bedroom log cabins and six-bedroom homesteads, fully equipped with everything from linen to CD player to firewood. Swimming pool and tennis court in the shady grounds. ❹–❺

Sussex Ridge Off Deaseys Rd, Pokolbin
℡02/4998 7753, ⓦwww.sussexridge.com.au.
Guesthouse in a classic two-storey, tin-roofed
homestead among extensive bushland, with great
views from the balcony. En-suite rooms. Two communal lounge areas with open fires; outdoor BBQ
area; swimming pool. Cooked breakfast. ❺

Valley Vineyards Tourist Park Mount View Rd,
2km northwest of Cessnock ℡ & ⓕ02/4990
2573, ⓦwww.valleyvineyard.com.au. High-
standard camping site with camp kitchen,
portable BBQs and pool. Cabins have external
en suites, cottages internal. Cabins ❸, cottages
❹

Eating and drinking

Most of the many excellent (and pricey) Hunter Valley restaurants are attached
to the various wineries or are among the vineyards, rather than in the towns
(see the box on pp.214–215 for some listings), while the Hunter's large old
pubs dish out less fancy but more affordable grub (see "Accommodation"
opposite). Every year over a mid-May weekend eight wineries along and
around the very scenic Lovedale and Wilderness roads team up with local
restaurants to host the **Lovedale Long Lunch** (℡02/4930 7611,
ⓦwww.lovedalelonglunch.com.au), with wine and gourmet food served
amongst the vines. You can taste free samples of The Hunter Valley Cheese
Company's handmade wares, or buy some to accompany a picnic, at the
McGuigan Bros Winery, Broke Road, Pokolbin.

Amicos 138 Wollombi Rd, Cessnock ℡02/4991
1995. A few kilometres from the town centre, this
is a very popular cheap eat with the locals. Serves
Italian and Mexican food, and has a lively, colourful
atmosphere. Licensed & BYO. Daily from 6pm.
Café Enzo Peppers Creek Antiques, Broke Rd,
Pokolbin ℡02/4998 7233. Courtyard café with a
light Mediterranean menu and excellent Italian-
style coffee. Wed–Sun 10am–5pm.
Chez Pok *Pepper's Guesthouse*, Ekerts Rd,
Pokolbin ℡02/4998 7596. Highly regarded restaurant stylishly using local produce including fresh-
picked herbs. The views overlooking vineyards are
very pretty as is the antique-filled cottage interior.
Expensive. Daily from 7am breakfast to dinner.
Esca Bimbadgen Lot 21, McDonalds Rd, Pokolbin
℡02/4998 4666. With a squint this winery, complete with bell tower, could be in Europe. Its
modern restaurant, however, is all timber and
glass, reached via the working winery, and with
wonderful vineyard views from the balcony. Food,
with mains around the $30 mark, is contemporary

European, with veal, spatchcock and roast duck all
on the menu. Licensed. Lunch daily, dinner
Wed–Sat.
The Hoot Café 115 Vincent St, Cessnock. Bright
and airy café with ceiling fans whirring and soul
music playing. Gourmet sandwiches, filo pastries,
samosas, nachos, delicious stuffed potatoes, tasty
cakes, and good coffee. Mon–Fri 8am–4pm, Sat
8am–1pm.
Il Cacciatore Hermitage Lodge, cnr McDonalds
and Gilliards roads, Pokolbin ℡02/4998 7639.
Excellent upmarket Northern Italian restaurant with
a wide choice, including fish dishes. Desserts such
as chocolate pasta ensure that the place is
packed. Dinner nightly plus lunch Sat & Sun.
Licensed and BYO.
Mulligans Brasserie Cypress Lakes Resort,
McDonalds Rd, Pokolbin ℡02/4993 1555.
Gourmet sandwiches, salads, tortillas and burgers
accompanied by pleasant courtyard views looking
out over the resort's pool and verdant golf course.
Licensed. Daily 6.30am–10pm.

West

For over fifty years, Sydney has been sliding ever westwards in a monotonous
sprawl of shopping centres, brick-veneer homes and fast-food chains, along the
way swallowing up towns and villages, some of which date back to colonial
times. The first settlers to explore inland found well-watered, fertile river flats,
and quickly established agricultural outposts to support the fledgling colony.
Parramatta, **Liverpool**, **Penrith** and **Campbelltown**, once separate communities, have now become satellite towns inside Sydney's commuter belt. Yet,

despite Sydney's advance, bushwalkers will find there's still plenty of wild west to explore. Three wildlife parks keep suburbia at bay, and the beauty of the **Blue Mountains** are a far cry from the modernity of Sydney. Heading west, however, now starts for many travellers with a visit to the Olympic site at **Homebush Bay**.

Sydney Olympic Park at Homebush Bay

The main focus of the 2000 Olympic events was **Sydney Olympic Park** at **Homebush Bay**, a down-at-heel working-class area in the city's west, far removed from the glamour of Sydney's harbour. Virtually the geographical heart of a city that sprawls westwards, Homebush Bay also already had some heavy-duty sporting facilities – the State Sports Centre and the Aquatic Centre – in place. The **Sydney Olympic Park Authority** is turning Sydney Olympic Park into an entertainment and sporting complex with family-oriented recreation in mind, with events such as outdoor movies and an Aboriginal arts festival. For details call ☎02/9714 7888 or check ⓦwww.sydneyolympicpark .nsw.gov.au.

The A$470 million Olympic site was centred around the 110,000-seat **Telstra Stadium** (previously called Stadium Australia), the venue for the opening and closing ceremonies, track and field events, and marathon and soccer finals. Since, a A$68 million overhaul reduced the number of seats to 80,000, a more realistic number for its use as an Australian Rules Football, cricket, rugby league, rugby union, soccer and concert venue. Tours of the stadium, with commentary, are available daily in one hour or half-hour versions (hourly 10.30am–3.30pm; 30min tour $15, 1hr $26; turn up at Gate C but check it's a non-event day first by calling ☎02/8765 2360; ⓦwww.telstrastadium .com.au).

Just south of the stadium is the **State Sports Centre** (daily 9am–5pm; ☎02/9763 0111, ⓦwww.sscbay.nsw.gov.au), where you can visit the **NSW Hall of Champions**, devoted to the state's sporting heroes (same hours as centre; free; the Hall of Champions is closed when events are being held at the the State Sports Centre, so call the latter before setting out); and the **Sydney International Aquatic Centre** (Nov–March Mon–Fri 5am–8.45pm, Sat & Sun 6am–7.45pm; April–Oct Mon–Fri 5am–8.45pm, Sat & Sun 6am–6.45pm; swim & spa $5.80, with steam and sauna $11.50, also including gym and fitness classes $14; tours daily noon, 1pm & 2pm; 1hr; $16; ☎02/9752 3666, ⓦwww.sydneyaquaticcentre.com.au). A SuperPass ($34.95) is available which gives a guided tour of the stadium and swimming centre (includes admission for swimming) and a visit to the observation deck at the *Novotel*.

On the south side of the site, you can watch tennis tournaments or rent a court at the **Sydney International Tennis Centre** (☎02/8746 0777, ⓦwww.sydneytennis.com.au), while on the north side, the **Sydney Superdome** (tours Mon–Fri 11am & 3pm; 45min; $15.40; ☎02/8765 4321, ⓦwww.superdome.com.au), which hosted the basketball, rhythmic gymnastics and paralympic basketball, is Sydney's basketball stadium. The Royal Agricultural Society Showground, taking up an extensive area at the very north of the site, hosts the annual Easter Show (see p.189).

Opposite the Olympic site, is the huge **Bicentennial Park**, opened in 1988; more than half of the expanse is conservation wetlands. The park's own visitor centre (Mon–Fri 10am–4pm, Sat & Sun 9.30am–4.30pm; ☎02/9714 7545) at the Australia Avenue entrance can give details of around 8km of cycling and walking tracks, and of the "Explorer Train" that tours the wetlands (Sun 12.30pm; 1hr 30min; $4.40).

Further north, the green-friendly Athlete's Village consisted mostly of modular dwellings, which have been moved and reused elsewhere; it is now incorporated into a new solar-powered suburb, **Newington**.

To get an overview of the site, there is an **observation centre** on the 17th floor of the *Novotel Hotel* (daily 10am–4pm; $4; ⓦwww.sydneyolympicpark hotels.com.au), on Olympic Boulevard between the Telstra Stadium and the Aquatic Centre. The *Novotel* is the social focus of the Olympic Park, with several places to eat and drink including a *McDonald's* and the popular *Homebush Bay Brewery*.

Visiting the venues

The nicest way to get out to Olympic Park is to take a ferry up the Parramatta River: the **RiverCat** from Circular Quay ($5.40 one-way to Homebush Bay) stops off frequently en route to Parramatta. The second best option is the direct **train** from Central to Olympic Park station (at the centre of Sydney Olympic Park on Dawn Fraser Avenue, a few minutes' walk to the Telstra Stadium on Olympic Boulevard), which runs four times daily on weekdays (otherwise and at weekends change at Lidcombe station from where trains depart every 10min). You can also take a more direct route to some of the venues from Strathfield train station: **buses** #401–404 run regularly from Strathfield to the Homebush Bay Olympic Centre, the State Sports Centre and the Athletic Centre. Parking is available at several parking stations for $2 per hour ($10 per day); to find out how to pre-book on event days or to check availability, call ☏1900 95 7275 ($0.55 per min).

Tours of the ex-Olympic venues leave from the **Olympic Park Visitor Centre**, set within a pleasant garden at 1 Herb Elliot Avenue, near the train station (daily 9am–5pm; ☏02/9714 7958). The hop-on-hop-off STA-run **Explorer Bus**, with tour commentary, does a circuit of the venues, picking up from the visitor centre (daily 9.17am–3.47pm; every 30min; $10). Another bus, without commentary, the **People Mover** operates continuously between Olympic Park station and the venues (daily 10am–5pm; all-day ticket $11, one-way $2.20, return $5.50). Entry fees to the venues are not included in the price of either bus.

Parramatta and Penrith

Situated on the Parramatta River, a little over 20km upstream from the harbour mouth, **PARRAMATTA** was the first of Sydney's rural satellites – the first farm settlement in Australia, in fact. The fertile soil of "Rosehill", as it was originally called, saved the fledgling colony from starvation with its first wheat crop of 1789. It's hard to believe today, but dotted here and there among the malls and busy roads are a few remnants from that time – eighteenth-century public buildings and original settlers' dwellings that warrant a visit if you're interested in Australian history. Today Parramatta is the headquarters of many government agencies and has a multicultural community and a lively restaurant scene on its main drag, Church Street.

You can call in to Parramatta on your way out of Sydney – a rather depressing drive along the ugly and congested Parramatta Road – or endure the dreary thirty-minute suburban train ride from Central station. But much the most enjoyable way to get here is on the sleek RiverCat ferry from Circular Quay up the Parramatta River (1hr; $6.40 one-way). The wharf at Parramatta is on Phillip Street, a couple of blocks away from the helpful visitor centre within the **Parramatta Heritage Centre**, on the corner of Church and Market streets (Mon–Fri 10am–4pm, Sat 9am–1pm, Sun 10.30am–3.30pm;

☎02/9630 3703, ⊛www.parracity.nsw.gov.au), which hands out free walking route maps. From the ferry wharf, you can walk to the centre in around ten minutes along the colourful paved Riverside Walk, decorated with Aboriginal motifs and interpretative plaques which aim to tell the story of the Burramatagal people. Alternatively, STA run a hop-on-hop-off, weekend-only **Parramatta Explorer bus**, with commentary, leaving from Parramatta Wharf (Sat & Sun 10am–4.30pm; every 20min; $10), visiting the places listed below.

Parramatta's most important historic feature is the National Trust-owned **Old Government House** (Mon–Fri 10am–4pm, Sat & Sun 10.30am–4pm; last admission 3.30pm; $7) in **Parramatta Park** by the river. Entered through the 1885 gatehouse on O'Connell Street, the park – filled with native trees – rises up to the gracious old Georgian-style building, the oldest remaining public edifice in Australia. It was built between 1799 and 1816 and used as the Viceregal residence until 1855; one wing has been converted into a pleasant teahouse. A few streets away, the aptly named **Experiment Farm Cottage** at 9 Ruse St (Tues–Fri 10.30am–3.30pm, Sat & Sun 11am–3.30pm; $5.50), another National Trust property, was built on the site of the first land grant, given in 1790 to reformed convict James Ruse. On parallel Alice Street, at no. 70, **Elizabeth Farm** (daily 10am–5pm; $7) dates from 1793 and claims to be the oldest surviving home in the country. The farm was built and run by the Macarthurs, who bred the first of the merino sheep that made Australian wealth "ride on a sheep's back"; a small café here serves refreshments. Nearby **Hambledon Cottage**, 63 Hassel St (Wed, Thurs, Sat & Sun 11am–4pm; $3), built in 1824, was part of the Macarthur estate.

One block south of the visitor centre, the area around the corner of Church and Phillip streets has become something of an **"eat street"** with around twenty cafés and restaurants , from Filipino through Chinese and Malaysian to Japanese, reflecting Parramatta's multicultural mix.

Continuing west, the Western Highway and the rail lines head on to **PENRITH**, the most westerly of Sydney's satellite towns, in a curve of the Nepean River at the foot of the Blue Mountains (on the way out here you pass a couple of wildlife parks; see box on p.201). Penrith has an old-fashioned Aussie feel about it – a tight community that is immensely proud of the Panthers, its boisterous rugby league team. From Penrith station, you can't miss the huge lettering announcing the **Museum of Fire** on Castlereagh Road in a former power station (daily 10am–3pm, closed last fortnight Dec; $7); the museum has an extensive collection of fire-fighting vehicles (fifty in all) and memorabilia. Penrith is also the home of the extensive International Regatta Centre on Penrith Lakes, spreading between Castlereagh and Cranebrook roads north of the town centre, and used in the Olympics; at **Penrith Whitewater Stadium** here you can go on a thrilling one-hour beginners' **white-water rafting** session ($60.50; bookings ☎02/4730 4333, ⊛www.penrithwhitewater.com.au). You can take in the splendour of the spectacular **Nepean Gorge** from the decks of the paddle steamer *Nepean Belle* (range of cruises from $13 for 1hr 30min; bookings ☎02/4733 1274), or head 24km south to the **Warragamba Dam**. The dam has created the huge reservoir of **Lake Burragorang**, a popular picnic spot with barbecues and a kiosk, and some easy walking trails through the bush.

The Blue Mountains region

The section of the Great Dividing Range nearest Sydney gets its name from the blue mist that rises from millions of eucalyptus trees and hangs in the mountain air, tinting the sky and the range alike. In the early days of the colony, the **Blue Mountains** were believed to be an insurmountable barrier to the west. The first expeditions followed the streams in the valleys until they were defeated by cliff faces rising vertically above them. Only in 1813, when the explorers Wentworth, Blaxland and Lawson followed the ridges instead of the valleys, were the mountains finally conquered, allowing the western plains to be opened up for settlement. The range is surmounted by a plateau at an altitude of more than 1000m where, over millions of years, rivers have carved deep valleys into the sandstone, and winds and driving rain have helped to deepen the ravines, creating a spectacular scenery of sheer precipices and walled canyons. Before white settlement, the Daruk Aborigines lived here, dressed in animal-skin cloaks to ward off the cold. An early coal-mining industry, based in Katoomba, was followed by tourism which snowballed after the arrival of the railway in 1868; by 1900 the first three mountain stations of Wentworth Falls, Katoomba and Mount Victoria had been established as fashionable resorts, extolling the health-giving benefits of eucalyptus-tinged mountain air. In 2000 the Blue Mountains became a **World Heritage Listed** site, joining the Great Barrier Reef; the listing came after abseiling was finally banned on the mountains' most famous scenic wonder, the **Three Sisters**, after forty years of clambering had caused significant erosion. The Blue Mountains stand out from other Australian forests, in particular for the recently discovered **Wollemi Pine** (see p.226), a "living fossil" which dates back to the dinosaur era.

All the villages and towns of the romantically dubbed "**City of the Blue Mountains**" – Glenbrook, Springwood, Wentworth Falls, Katoomba and Blackheath – lie on a ridge, connected by the Great Western Highway. Around them is the **Blue Mountains National Park**, the fourth-largest national park in the state and to many minds the best. The region makes a great weekend break from the city, with stunning views and clean air complemented by a wide range of accommodation, cafés and restaurants. But be warned: at weekends, and during the summer holidays, Katoomba is thronged with escapees from the city, and prices escalate accordingly. Even at their most crowded, though, the Blue Mountains always offer somewhere where you can find peace and quiet, and even solitude – the deep gorges and high rocks make much of the terrain inaccessible except to bushwalkers and mountaineers. Climbing schools offer courses in rock-climbing, abseiling and canyoning for both beginners and experienced climbers, while Glenbrook is a popular mountain-biking spot.

Transport, tours and information

Public transport to the mountains is quite good but your own vehicle will give you much greater flexibility, allowing you to take detours to old mansions, cottage gardens and the lookout points scattered along the ridge. **Trains** leave from Central station for Mount Victoria and follow the highway, stopping at all the major towns en route (frequent departures until about midnight; 2hr; $11.40 one-way to Katoomba, $13.60 off-peak day return). If you're dependent on public transport, Katoomba makes the best base: facilities and services are concentrated here, and there are **local buses** to attractions in the vicinity and to other centres. Mountainlink (☏02/4782 3333) has five commuter routes from Katoomba: to Medlow Bath, Blackheath and Mount Victoria; to Echo Point; to Leura and Gordon Falls; and to North Katoomba; and to the Katoomba Aquatic Centre, the scenic railway, Leura, Wentworth Falls, Bullaburra, Lawson, Hazelbrook and Woodford; buses run daily between about 7am and 6pm, roughly half-hourly, and it costs $2.20, for example, to get to Echo Point, while an all-day bus pass, valid on all routes, including the Trolley

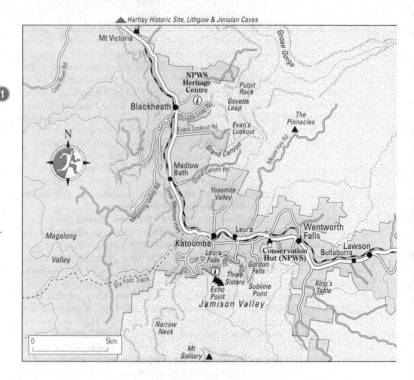

Tour minibus detailed below, costs $12. All buses leave from Katoomba Street outside the *Carrington Hotel*.

There are also a couple of Katoomba-based, hop-on-hop-off **tours**. **Trolley Tours** (℡1800 801 577, Ⓦ www.trolleytours.com.au) is a minibus decked out like a tram, which takes the scenic route from Katoomba to Leura around Cliff Drive, and continues to the Three Sisters and the Skyway cable car (8 daily roughly 9.30am–4.15pm ; $12 all-day pass). The **Blue Mountains Explorer Bus**, run by Fantastic Aussie Tours, 283 Main St, Katoomba, by the train station (℡02/4782 1866 or 1300 300 915, Ⓦ www.fantastic-aussie-tours .com.au), links Katoomba and Leura with all attractions, including the Edge Maxvision Cinema, Three Sisters, the Skyway, Wentworth Falls, Narrow Neck and other lookouts over thirty stops, in a red double-decker bus (departs Katoomba half-hourly 9.30am–4.30pm, last return 5.15pm; $25 all-day pass). Although the Explorer Bus is pricier, it is more frequent, has a wider route with more stops, and comes with a 32-page guidebook which gives substantial discounts on entry fees to other attractions.

The **Blue Mountains Information Centre** (Mon–Fri 9am–5pm, 8.30am–4.30pm; ℡1300 653 408, Ⓦ www.bluemts.com.au) is on the Great Western Highway at Glenbrook (see opposite), the gateway to the Blue Mountains. The centre has a huge amount of information on the area, including a couple of useful free publications: the *Blue Mountains Wonderland Visitors Guide*, which has several detailed colour maps, and *This Month in the Blue Mountains*. The other official tourist information centre is at **Echo Point**, near Katoomba (see p.226); both offices can **book accommodation**.

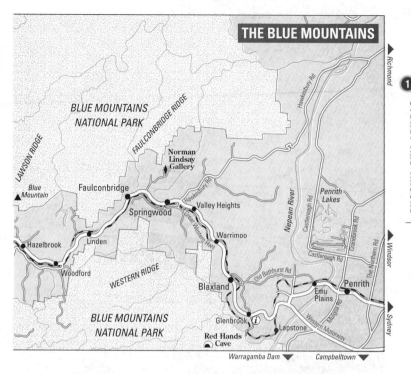

BLUE MOUNTAINS
NATIONAL PARK

FAULCONBRIDGE RIDGE

LAWSON RIDGE

Norman
Lindsay
Gallery

Blue
Mountain

Faulconbridge

Springwood

Valley Heights

Hawkesbury Rd

Great Western Hwy

Nepean River

Warrimoo

Hazelbrook   Linden

Woodford   WESTERN RIDGE

Penrith
Lakes

Castlereagh Rd

Cranebrook Rd

The Northern Rd

Castlereagh Rd

BLUE MOUNTAINS
NATIONAL PARK

Blaxland

Old Bathurst Rd

Emu
Plains

Penrith

Glenbrook ⓘ

Red Hands
Cave

Lapstone

Western Motorway

Mulgoa Rd

Warragamba Dam ▼   Campbelltown ▼

Richmond ►

Windsor ►

Sydney ►

The **NPWS** has ranger stations at Wentworth Falls (see p.225) and Blackheath (see p.228) where you can get comprehensive walking and camping information – there are NPWS camping and picnic sites reached by car near Glenbrook, Woodford, Wentworth Falls, Blackheath and Oberon and bush camping is allowed in most areas. The only point where vehicle entry must be paid is at Glenbrook ($6).

Glenbrook to Wentworth Falls

Once you're off the busy highway and further on from the information centre (see opposite), **GLENBROOK** is a pleasant village arranged around the train station, with a great cinema and lots of cafés and adventure shops; the section of the **Blue Mountains National Park** here is popular for **mountain-biking** along the **Oaks Fire Trail** (it's best to start the thirty-kilometre trail higher up the mountain in **WOODFORD** and head downhill ending up in Glenbrook; bike rental is only available at Katoomba, see p.226). The park entrance (cars $6) is just over a kilometre from the train station following Burfitt Parade then Bruce Road alongside the railway line as it heads back towards Sydney; about 200m before the entrance you'll cross a railway bridge. There are two bushwalks to two swimmable waterholes, **Blue Pool** and **Jellybean Pool**, not far within the park while several walking trails start from the Causeway, just under a kilometre into the park via a winding hilly road). One of the best walks from here is to see the Aboriginal hand stencils on the walls of **Red Hands Cave** (3hr return; medium difficulty). With a car or bike you can get there via road and

△ Paddington

continue to the grassy creekside Eoroka picnic ground (also camping) where there are lots of eastern grey kangaroos.

Eleven kilometres northwest of Glenbrook, **SPRINGWOOD** is home to many of the artists who have settled in the mountains with numerous shops selling antiques and arts and crafts. There are also bushwalks in Sassafras Gully. Further west is **FAULCONBRIDGE**, where it's well worth visiting the exhibition of paintings and drawings at the **Norman Lindsay Gallery**, a National Trust property set amongst extensive gardens at 14 Norman Lindsay Crescent (daily 10am–4pm; $8). The controversial artist and poet (1879–1969), whose nude studies scandalized Australia in the 1930s and whose story was told in the 1994 film *Sirens*, spent the last part of his life here. He is also famous for his humorous children's tale, *The Magic Pudding*, made into a film in 2001.

The small village of **WENTWORTH FALLS**, further west, was named after William Wentworth, one of the famous trio who conquered the mountains in 1813. A signposted road leads from the Great Western Highway to the **Wentworth Falls Reserve**, with superb views of the waterfall tumbling down into the Jamison Valley. You can reach this picnic area from Wentworth train station by following **Darwin's Walk** – the route followed by the famous naturalist in 1836. Most of the other bushwalks in the area start from the NPWS **Valley of the Waters Conservation Hut** (daily 9am–5pm; ☎02/4757 3827), about 3km from the station at the end of Fletcher Street. Bus services are infrequent; there are taxis waiting outside the train station. The hut is in a fantastic location overlooking the Jamison Valley, and from its wonderful *Conservation Hut Cafe* you can take full advantage of the stupendous views through the big windows or from the deck outside; in winter an open fire crackles in the grate. A wide selection of bushwalks, detailed on boards outside, range from the two-hour **Valley of the Waters track**, which descends into the valley, to an extended two-day walk to **Mount Solitary**. One of the most rewarding is the quite strenuous, six-kilometre **National Pass**, a one-way walk which will conveniently get you back to the train station and takes in Wentworth Falls en route.

Leura

Just two kilometres east of Katoomba, the more upmarket **LEURA**, packed with great cafés, art galleries and small boutiques, retains its own distinct identity and a real village atmosphere. Leura is renowned for its beautiful **gardens**, some of which are open to the public during the **Leura Gardens Festival** (early to mid-Oct; $12 for visits to around eight gardens, or $3 per garden; more details from the tourist office). Open all year round, though, is the beautiful National Trust-listed **Everglades Gardens** (daily 9am–sunset; $6), situated in the grounds of an elegant mansion at 37 Everglades Ave. There are enjoyable views from its formal terraces, with a colourful display of azaleas and rhododendrons, an aboretum, and peacocks strutting among it all. Not far from the village, the flowers give way to the bush: less tame scenery, such as **Leura Cascades**, can be viewed from the picnic area on Cliff Drive; to see it at closer quarters, take the two- to three-hour walk to the base and back. Other waterfalls in the area include the much-photographed **Bridal Veil Falls**, accessible from the Cascades picnic area, and **Gordon Falls**, which you can walk to from Lone Pine Avenue. To the east of Gordon Falls, Sublime Point Road leads to the aptly named **Sublime Point** lookout, with panoramic views of the Jamison Valley. A popular walking track from Leura Falls is the Federal Pass, which skirts the cliffs between here and **Katoomba Falls** (6km one-way; 2hr 30min).

Katoomba and around

KATOOMBA, the biggest town in the Blue Mountains and the area's commercial heart, is also the best located for the major sights of Echo Point and the Three Sisters. It has a lively café culture on the main drag, **Katoomba Street**, which runs downhill from the train station; the street is also full of vintage and retro clothes, secondhand bookstores, antique dealers and giftshops. When the town was first discovered by fashionable city dwellers in the late nineteenth century, the grandiose **Carrington Hotel** prominently located at the top of Katoomba Street, was the height of elegance (an in-house historian gives 1hr tours of the hotel; $7.50 on demand). It's recently been returned to its former glory, with elegant sloping lawns running down to the street, half of which will soon be taken over by a new **town square**. Katoomba also boomed during the era of **Art Deco** and lots of cafés and restaurants feature the style, notably the famous **Paragon Cafe** at 65 Katoomba St (closed Mon); it's also known for its fabulous handmade chocolates and sweets.

Across the railway line (use the foot-tunnel under the station), a stunning introduction to the ecology of the Blue Mountains can be had at the **Edge Maxvision Cinema**, at 225–237 Great Western Highway (☏02/4782 8928), a huge six-storey cinema screen created as a venue to show *The Edge – The Movie* (daily 10.20am, 11.05am, 12.10pm, 1.30pm, 2.15pm & 5.30pm; $13.50). The highlight of the forty-minute film is the segment about the "dinosaur trees", a stand of thirty-metre-high **Wollemi Pine**, previously known only from fossil material over sixty million years old. The trees – miraculously still existing – survive deep within a sheltered rainforest gully in the **Wollemi National Park**, north of Katoomba, and they made headlines when they were first discovered in 1994 by a group of canyoners. Since the discovery, the first cultivated Wollemi Pine was planted in 1998 at Sydney's Royal Botanical Gardens (see p.129) and at the Mount Annan and Mount Tomah botanic gardens (see p.241 and p.228 respectively).

A 25-minute walk south from the train station down Katoomba Street and along Lurline Street and Echo Point Road (or by Mountainlink or tour bus from outside the Savoy Theatre; see p.221) will bring you to **Echo Point**, the location of the **information centre** (daily 9am–5pm; ☏1300 653 408). From here you have breathtaking vistas that take in the Blue Mountains' most famous landmark, the **Three Sisters** (910m). These three gnarled rocky points take their name from an Aboriginal Dreamtime story which relates how the Katoomba people were losing a battle against the rival Nepean people: the Katoomba leader, fearing that his three beautiful daughters would be carried off by the enemy, turned them to stone, but was tragically killed before he could reverse his spell. The Three Sisters are at the top of the **Giant Stairway**, the beginning of the very steep stairs into the three-hundred-metre-deep **Jamison Valley** below, where there are several walking tracks to places with such intriguing names as **Orphan Rock** and **Ruined Castle**. There's a popular walking route, taking about two hours and graded medium, down the stairway and part way along the **Federal Pass** to the **Landslide**, and then on to the Scenic Railway and Sceniscender (see opposite), either of which you can take back up to the ridge.

If you want to spare yourself the trek down into the Jamison Valley – or the walk back up – head for the tacky **Scenic World complex** at the end of Violet Street, where you can choose between two modes of transport. The **Scenic Railway** (daily 9am–5pm; every 10min; last train up leaves at 4.50pm; $6 one-way; ⓦwww.scenicworld.com.au), originally built in the 1880s to

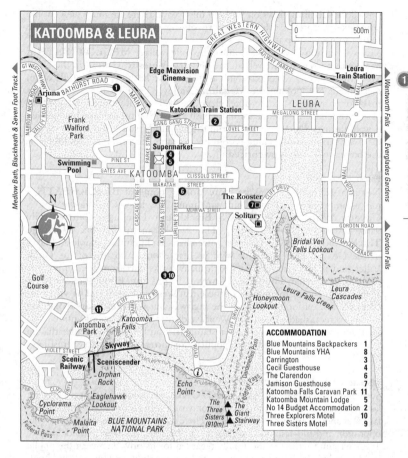

KATOOMBA & LEURA

0   500m

Edge Maxvision
Cinema

Leura
Train Station

Katoomba Train Station

LEURA

MEGALONG STREET

LOVEL STREET

Frank
Walford
Park

Arjuna

GT WESTERN ROAD

NARROW NECK ROAD

BATHURST ROAD

VALLEY ROAD

MAIN ST

GANG GANG STREET

PARKE STREET

PINE ST

CRAIGEND STREET

Supermarket

Swimming
Pool

GATES AVE

KATOOMBA

CLISSOLD STREET

WARATAH   STREET

CASCADE STREET

KATOOMBA STREET

LURLINE STREET

MERRIWA STREET

The Rooster

Solitary

CLIFF DRIVE

GORDON ROAD

Bridal Veil
Falls Lookout

OLYMPIAN PARADE

THE MALL

ELURA MALL

THE MALL

Golf
Course

CLIFF   FALLS RD

CLIFF DRIVE

ECHO POINT ROAD

Honeymoon
Lookout

Leura Falls Creek

Leura
Cascades

Katoomba
Falls

Katoomba
Park

Skyway

VIOLET STREET

Scenic
Railway

Sceniscender

Orphan
Rock

Eaglehawk
Lookout

Cyclorama
Point

Malaita
Point

Federal Pass

BLUE MOUNTAINS
NATIONAL PARK

Echo
Point

Federal Dardanelles Pass

Federal Pass

The
Three
Sisters
(910m)

The
Giant
Stairway

ACCOMMODATION

Blue Mountains Backpackers   1
Blue Mountains YHA   8
Carrington   3
Cecil Guesthouse   4
The Clarendon   6
Jamison Guesthouse   7
Katoomba Falls Caravan Park 11
Katoomba Mountain Lodge   5
No 14 Budget Accommodation   2
Three Explorers Motel   10
Three Sisters Motel   9

Medlow Bath, Blackheath & Seven Foot Track

GT WESTERN HIGHWAY

RAILWAY PARADE

Wentworth Falls

Everglades Gardens

Gordon Falls

N

carry coal, is a funicular that glides down an impossibly steep gorge to the valley floor. Even more vertiginous, but not as nail-bitingly thrilling, is **Sceniscender** (same price and hours), an A$8 million, high-tech cable car (wheelchair accessible). With floor-to-ceiling windows, the views as the car drops 545m are really spectacular. At the base, there's a 330-metre elevated boardwalk through forest to the base of the Scenic Railway via the entrance to the **old coal mine**, where an audio-visual display tells the story of the mine at the time when the funicular railway still hauled coal.

Back up on the ridge, you can get your legs trembling again with **Skyway** (daily 9am–5pm; $10), a rickety-looking cable-car contraption that starts inside the Scenic World complex next to the Scenic Railway and travels 350m across to the other side of the gorge and back again – you can't actually get off – giving those who can bear to look a bird's-eye view of Orphan Rock, Katoomba Falls and the Jamison Valley. The **Scenic World** complex also features a **Scenic Cinema** which shows a seventeen-minute film, *Rapture in Blue* ($4.40), of the mountain sights, designed to satisfy visitors who have missed the fabulous views on wet and misty days. There are more views at the complex's overpriced, cafeteria-style **revolving restaurant** (9am–5pm daily), with a souvenir shop next door.

One train stop beyond Katoomba, the quiet village **MEDLOW BATH** is based around the distinctively domed **Hydro Majestic Hotel** (on the Great Western Highway) which was built as an exclusive health resort in 1904 on an escarpment overlooking the **Megalong Valley**. The hotel had a meticulous make-over by the Mercure hotel chain in 2000, and it's worth a stop-off to gaze at the interiors and the stunning bush views from the balcony beer garden – walk through the Megalong Room to get outside; you can take a drink out there anytime. The Megalong Room has the same view from its windows, but the buffet-style café is overpriced.

Blackheath

North of Katoomba, there are more lookout points at **BLACKHEATH** – just as impressive as Echo Point and much less busy. One of the best is **Govetts Leap**, near the NPWS **Blackheath Heritage Centre** (daily 9am–4.30pm; ☎02/4787 8877). The two-kilometre **Fairfax Heritage Track** from the NPWS Centre is wheelchair- and pram-accessible and takes in the Govetts Leap Lookout with its marvellous panorama of the Grose Valley and Bridal Veil Falls. Although many walks start from the centre, one of the most popular, **The Grand Canyon**, begins from Evans Lookout Road at the south end of town, west of the Great Western Highway. The village of Blackheath itself looks dull from the highway, but **Govetts Leap Road** and its cross street, shady, tree-lined Wentworth Street, have lots of antique and craft shops and great cafés and restaurants. Southwest of Blackheath, the beautiful **Megalong Valley** is popular for **horse riding** (see "Listings" p.233).

Mount Victoria and around

Secluded and homely **MOUNT VICTORIA**, 6km from Blackheath and the last mountain settlement proper, is the only one with an authentic, unspoilt village feel and is very peaceful and leafy. There's a great old pub, the *Imperial* (see opposite), and old-fashioned scones at the *Bay Tree Tea Shop* (closed Mon & Tues). Mount Victoria is also fondly regarded for its tiny cinema in the public hall (see p.232). Worth a browse are several antique shops and secondhand book stores. Some short **walks** start from the Fairy Bower Picnic area, a ten-minute walk from the Great Western Highway via Mount Piddington Road: get details from any Blue Mountains tourist office, or ask at the *Victoria and Albert Guesthouse* (see p.230).

Beyond Mount Victoria, drivers can circle back towards Sydney via the scenic **Bells Line of Road**, which heads back east through the fruit- and vegetable-growing areas of Bilpin and Kurrajong to Richmond, with growers selling their produce at roadside stalls. On the way you'll pass **Mount Tomah Botanic Garden** (daily: Oct–March 10am–5pm; April–Sept 10am–4pm; $4.40; ☎02/4567 2154 for details of free guided tours, ⓦwww.rbgsyd.gov.au), an outpost of Sydney's Royal Botanic Gardens since 1987. The popular *Garden Restaurant* at the visitors centre (lunch daily; licensed; ☎02/4567 2060) has fantastic north-facing views over the gardens, Wollemi National Park and the orchards of Bilpin. Main courses – contemporary Australian – cost a pricey $30 but the views make it worthwhile; book for a balcony table at weekends. Cheaper light lunches (sandwiches, pies) are also available and there's a kiosk. There is no public transport to the gardens. By car, you can continue west along the Bells Line of Road to the Zig Zag Railway at Clarence, just over 35km away (see p.233).

Accommodation

Accommodation rates rise on Friday and Saturday nights, so you should aim to visit on weekdays when it's quieter and cheaper. Prices given below are for the cheapest double room available on a weekday in the high season. The tourist offices at Glenbrook and Echo Point (see p.226) can both book accommodation. **Katoomba** is the obvious choice if arriving by train, particularly for those on a budget since it has several **hostels** to choose from, but if you have your own transport you can indulge in some of the more unusual and characterful guesthouses in **Blackheath** and **Mount Victoria**. Blue Mountains Budget Accommodation Group (☏02/4782 2652; ⓦwww.pnc.com.au/~ivanhoe) offers a range of good-value, self-catering holiday homes and cabins in Katoomba and Blackheath. There are also lots of pricier bush-set cabins and retreat-style places to stay on Evans Lookout Road just beyond Blackheath, backing onto the national park including *Jemby-Rinjah*, p.230. To get even closer to nature, you can **camp** in the bush at several NPWS sites (see p.223). Or for more comfort, there are two **caravan parks**: Katoomba Falls Caravan Park, at Katoomba Falls Rd (☏ & Ⓕ02/4782 1835; en-suite cabins ❹) and Blackheath Caravan Park at Prince Edward St (☏02/4787 8101; cabins ❷, en suite ❸), and you can camp in the grounds of Blue Mountains Backpackers (see p.230).

Hotels, motels and guesthouses

Carrington Hotel 15–47 Katoomba St, Katoomba ☏02/4782 1111, ⓦwww.thecarrington.com.au. When it opened in 1882, the *Carrington* was one of the region's finest hotels and it has been fully restored. Original features include stained-glass windows and open fireplaces, a splendid dining room and ballroom, cocktail bar, snooker and games room, library and guest lounges. The spacious, well-aired rooms are beautifully decorated in rich heritage colours. Budget rooms, which share bathrooms, are very good value and there are masses of very private bathrooms (with baths) to use. ❹, en suite ❺–❻

Cecil Guesthouse 108 Katoomba St, Katoomba ☏02/4782 1411, ⓦwww.ourguest.com.au. Very central choice, set back from the main drag; peaceful and surrounded by greenery and with great views over the town and Jamison Valley from the common areas and some bedrooms (these ones go first). Shabby but charming – an old-fashioned 1940s atmosphere with log fires, games room and tennis courts, plus modern touches such as the spa (and the sometimes surly service). Most rooms share bathrooms. Good single rates. Cooked breakfast included; dinner served if booked in advance. ❹

The Clarendon Cnr Lurline and Waratah streets, Katoomba ☏02/4782 1322, ⓦwww.clarendonguesthouse.com.au. Classic 1920s guesthouse with its own cocktail bar and restaurant, and cabaret weekends. Also swimming pool, sauna, gym, open fires, games room and garden. The guesthouse rooms are best – avoid the fairly unattractive, 1970s-style motel rooms. Mostly en suites but budget rooms without bathroom also available. ❹–❺

Glenella 56 Govett's Leap Rd, Blackheath ☏02/4787 8352, Ⓕ02/4787 6114. Guesthouse in a charming 1905 homestead with a well-regarded restaurant (dinner Fri & Sat; licensed). Rooms are furnished with antiques. Rates vary with size of room. Most are en suite, but there are a few cheaper share-bathroom options. ❹–❺

Imperial 1 Station St, Mount Victoria ☏02/4787 1233, ⓦwww.bluemts.com.au/hotelimperial. Nicely restored country pub with beautiful lead-lighting. Good-value, filling and tasty bistro meals. B&B, with some en-suite rooms. ❹–❺, en suite ❻–❼

Jamison Guesthouse 48 Merriwa St, cnr Cliff Drive, Katoomba ☏ & Ⓕ02/4782 1206. Built as a guesthouse in 1903 and still going strong, this is a seriously charming place in a great spot giving it amazing, unimpeded views across the Jamison Valley. The feel is very much that of a small European hotel, added to by the French restaurant downstairs, *The Rooster*, in a gorgeous dining room full of original fixtures (dinner nightly, lunch Sat & Sun; set price menus $52/$64) and with big picture windows. Upstairs, a breakfast room gives splendid views – provisions (and an egg cooker) come with the room – and there's a sitting room with a fireplace. All rooms en suite. ⑤

Jemby-Rinjah Lodge 336 Evans Lookout Rd, Blackheath ℡02/4787 7622, ⓦwww.jembyrinjah lodge.com.au. Accommodation in distinctive one- and two-bedroom timber cabins (with own wood fires) in bushland near the Grose Valley. There's also a big licensed common area whose focal point is the huge circular "fire pit" ; a restaurant operates in here Friday and Saturday nights (Fri Italian buffet $29, Sat two-course meal $40). Bushwalks organized for guests. Cabins sleep two to six people. ⑥

Kanangra Lodge 9 Belvedere Ave, Blackheath ℡ & ⒻP02/4787 8715, ⓦwww.kanangralodge.com. Spacious, elegant and peaceful B&B with four large guest rooms decorated in warm, inviting colours, all en suite. Open fireplaces in its cosy, sociable lounges and all rooms overlook the beau- tiful large garden outside. Owner has local know- ledge. Full hot breakfast. ⑥

Peppers Fairmont Resort 1 Sublime Point Rd, 2km southeast of Leura ℡02/4782 5222, ⓦwww.peppers.com.au. Huge four-and-a-half-star resort (over 200 rooms) in peaceful grounds with fantastic recreational facilities. There's a large indoor pool and spa, but a wintry swim in the heated outdoor pool and a dip in the steaming spa is quite magical. Also a gym, and squash and tennis courts. At least $240 a night. Room service. ⑦

Three Explorers Motel 197 Lurline St, Katoomba ℡02/4782 1733, ⓦwww.bluemts.com .au/3explorers. Well-run, three-star place a cut above the usual charmless motel, on two levels with tastefully decorated units. Spa rooms plus large family suites. Great spot near Echo Point. ④

Three Sisters Motel 348 Katoomba St, Katoomba ℡02/4782 2911, ⒻP02/4782 6263. Small, old- style, red-brick motel units, but clean, well- equipped and run by an amiable couple. Excellent location near Echo Point. ③

Victoria and Albert Guesthouse 19 Station St, Mount Victoria ℡02/4787 1241, ⓦwww .ourguest.com.au/victoria.albert.html. Built in 1914, this traditional guesthouse has lovely origi- nal fixtures. Rooms are large though a little run-down. Cheaper rooms share bathroom. Cooked breakfast. The café at the back overlooks the lovely garden with pool, spa and sauna; bar and restaurant. B&B ③, en suite ⑤

Hostels

Blue Mountains Backpackers 190 Bathurst Rd, Katoomba ℡02/4782 4226 or 1800 624 226, ⓦwww.kacadventures.com/bmb. Colourfully painted, very homey and comfortable bungalow near the station, with dorms sleeping six to ten and doubles. Separate TV/video rooms, games to play, a small kitchen, free tea and coffee and lots of info on and lifts to bushwalks. Linen included for doubles and twins only. They also have tent and van sites for $13. Dorms $19, rooms ②

Blue Mountains YHA 207 Katoomba St, Katoomba ℡02/4782 1416, Ⓔbluemountains@yhansw.org.au. Huge 200-bed YHA hostel right in the town centre. The former 1930s guesthouse has been modernized but retains its charming, beautiful, leadlighted win- dows, Art Deco decor, huge ballroom and an old- fashioned mountain retreat ambience, with an open fire in the reading room, a separate games room (with pool table), Internet access and a very pleasant courtyard. Most rooms and some of the four-bed dorms are en suite, there are also eight- share dorms available. Mountain-bike rental for guests and abseiling and Jenolan Caves trips; other tours can be booked. A dedicated informa- tion room comes complete with topographic maps and the friendly staff on reception are very helpful. Dorms $19–23, rooms ③

Katoomba Mountain Lodge 31 Lurline St, Katoomba ℡ & ⒻP02/4782 3933, ⓦwww.bluemts.com.au/kmtlodge. Central budget accommodation with great views over the town from its verandah, TV room and some bedrooms. Four- and six-bed dorms and attractive doubles (all share bathrooms) with window seats. Small kitchen, and large dining room with free tea and coffee. Cheap breakfast and dinner available. Dorms $16–20, rooms ②

No 14 Budget Accommodation 14 Lovel St, Katoomba ℡02/4782 7104, ⓦwww.bluemts .com.au/No14. This relaxed hostel in a charming restored former guesthouse – polished floors, cosy fire, and original features – is like a home away from home, run by an informative, friendly young couple who put in a lot of effort. Mostly twin and double rooms, some en suite, plus four-share dorms with comfy beds instead of bunks; all centrally heated. Peaceful verandah surrounded by pretty plants and valley views. Dorms $20, rooms ③

Eating and drinking

Cuisine in the Blue Mountains has gone way beyond the ubiquitous "Devonshire teas", with some well-regarded restaurants, and a real **café cul- ture** in Katoomba and Leura; on Katoomba Street check out *Fresh* at no. 181,

The Elephant Bean at no. 159 and *Cafe 123* (see below). Don't forget the NPWS-run *Conservation Hut Cafe* (see p.225), with tremendous views over the Jamison Valley. There are also several fine **bakeries**, most open daily: best are the German *Patisserie Schwarz* at Wentworth Falls, opposite the station (closed Tues); *Hominy Bakery*, 185 Katoomba St, Katoomba and *Bakehouse on Wentworth*, 105 Wentworth St, Blackheath. See also the accommodation listings for hotel restaurants open to non-guests. The salubrious little cocktail bar of the *Clarendon* (see p.229) also hosts music and cabaret. On the other side of the railway line, the late-opening *Gearins Hotel* has several bars where you can play pool and see bands; it's lively but can sometimes get a little rough.

Arjuna 16 Valley Rd, just off the Great Western Highway, Katoomba ☎02/4782 4662. Excellent, authentic Indian restaurant. A bit out of the way – think taxi or own car – but positioned for spectacular sunset views, so get there early. Good veggie choices too. BYO. Evenings from 6pm; closed Tues & Wed.

Avalon Restaurant 18 Katoomba St ☎02/4782 5532. Stylish restaurant with the ambience of a quirky café, located in the dress circle of the old Savoy Theatre, with many Art Deco features intact. Beautiful views down the valley too – coming here for lunch is high on the agenda. Moderately expensive menu, but generous servings and to-die-for desserts. BYO & Licensed. Separate bar, so you can come here just for a drink and soak up the atmosphere. Lunch & dinner Wed–Sun.

Blues Café 57 Katoomba St, Katoomba. Bakery and cosy, mostly vegetarian café – this place has been going for years. Daily 9am–5pm.

Carrington Hotel 15–47 Katoomba St, Katoomba ☎02/4782 1111. The *Carrington* has a host of bars in and around the grand old building on Katoomba Street. Within the old hotel, *Champagne Charlies Cocktail Bar* has a decorative glass ceiling dome and chandeliers. You can order an understandably pricey drink and take it into one of the classic Kentia-palm filled lounges or out onto the wonderful front verandah overlooking the lawns. Its really splendid *Grand Dining Room* has columns and decorative inlaid ceilings; the high tea buffet here is a treat (3–5pm; $12.50). Cheaper drinks and a more lively atmosphere are found in the modern annexe next door, the *Carrington Bar* (jazz on Sat nights), and the more down-to-earth public bar, *The Sporters*, has a separate entrance on Main Street opposite the train station; there's a nightclub above, *The Attic* (Fri & Sat 10am–3am; $5).

Cafe 123 123 Katoomba St. White, bright modern place with a couple of outside tables and a counter with stools indoors does simple, inexpensive food that's as fresh and healthy as the decor: excellent juices, organic wheat-grass shots, sandwiches, focaccia and muffins. Coffee is freshly roasted. Daily 8.30pm–6pm.

Cafe Bon Ton 192 The Mall, Leura. Upmarket corner café with an extensive and inviting garden terrace out front, shaded by some impressive old trees, which makes a very pleasant spot for good coffee, fresh cakes, lunch or weekend breakfast on a fine day. Food ranges from filled baguettes through pasta and salads to interesting modern Australian main meals (average $17). Mon–Fri 11.30am–5pm, Sat & Sun 8am–5pm, plus dinner nightly except Tues. BYO.

Cozzi Nostri 189 Katoomba St, Katoomba ☎02/4782 3445. Stylish and congenial little place with a lighter, less meaty menu than most Italian restaurants; lots of fish on the menu. Pasta ranges from $14 to $16, and mains are around the $20 mark. Dinner Wed–Sun. BYO.

House of Penang 183 Katoomba St, Katoomba. Popular Chinese and Malaysian fast-food joint with a few eat-in tables. Delicious *laksa* noodle soups for $6–10 and even cheaper lunch specials. Separate, extensive vegetarian menu. Daily 10am–10pm.

Il Postino 13 Station St, opposite the train station, Wentworth Falls ☎02/4757 1615. Great relaxed café in the original old post office – the cracked walls have become part of an artfully distressed, light and airy interior; outside tables on a street-facing courtyard. Menu is Mediterranean- and Thai-slanted, with plenty for vegetarians, with nothing over $14. Excellent all-day breakfast featuring lots of different kinds of pancakes. Daily 8.30am–6pm, plus pricier dinner Fri & Sat (bookings essential). BYO.

The Mountain Deli 134 The Mall, Leura. A big range of food at reasonable prices makes this a popular one with the locals, and the big window overlooking the street means all-day people-watching. Good-value sandwiches, yummy home-baked cakes, and friendly staff. Mon–Fri & Sun 9am–6pm, Sat 8am–6pm.

Parakeet Café 195B Katoomba St, Katoomba. Eclectic, colourful café, its walls covered with paintings by mountains' artists is a big favourite with the locals for the simple, inexpensive food and hearty soups and down-to-earth atmosphere. Daily 8am–9pm, later Sat night when there's live music, usually blues.

Siam Cuisine 172 Katoomba St, Katoomba ☎02/4782 5671. Popular inexpensive Thai restaurant with cheap lunch-time specials. BYO. Tues–Sun 11.30am–2.30pm & 5.30–10pm.

Solitary 90 Cliff Drive, Leura Falls ☎02/4782 1164. Perched on a hairpin bend on the mountains' scenic cliff-hugging road, the views of the Jamison Valley and Mount Solitary from this former kisok, now modern Australian restaurant, are sublime. Expect beautifully laid tables, eager service, a well-chosen and reasonably priced wine list, jazz on the soundtrack, and fine food. There's a fireplace in the back room, and picnic tables outside which are popular for the weekend breakfast. Moderate to expensive. Lunch Sat & Sun, dinner Tues–Sat. Licensed.

Treis-ilies Greek Cypriot Taverna 110 Bathurst Rd ☎02/4782 1217. This open-fronted, tile-floored place has a very lively authentic taverna feel and a great atmosphere and serves all the Greek favourites, plus pizza and pasta (lunch Wed–Sun, dinner nightly). Servings are meagre and over-

priced and the wine list isn't great but it's fun and opposite is the *Triselies Nightclub* (☎02/4782 4026; Thurs–Sun 7pm–3am) with live music – world, blues, rock – or DJs Thurs–Sat (cover charge $5–10) plus food .

Victory Cafe 17 Govetts Leap Rd, Blackheath ☎02/4787 6777. A very pleasant space in the front of an old Art Deco theatre now converted into an antiques centre; the café also houses a book stall. Gourmet sandwiches ($8.50)and café favourites (from $6 to about $13.50) with an interesting spin; special mains such as Greek-style fish, and all-day breakfast, with also plenty for vegetarians. The Friday and Saturday night dinner menu (bookings essential) goes Asian – Indian, Thai, Indonesian and Malaysian all feature – otherwise open daily 8.30am–5pm. BYO.

Vulcan's 33 Govetts Leap Rd, Blackheath ☎02/4787 6899. Bookings are essential at this raved about restaurant housed in an early-twentieth-century bakery, where the wood-fired oven is put to use to produce sensational, seasonal food. Fantastic desserts too, such as the trademark chequerboard liquorice and pineapple ice cream. Lunch & dinner Fri–Sun. Moderate. BYO.

Listings

Adventure activities Australian School of Mountaineering (at Paddy Pallin, 166 Katoomba St; ☎02/4782 2014, ⦿www.asmguides.com or www.canyons.com.au), Katoomba's original abseiling outfit, offers daily day-long courses ($119 including lunch), plus canyoning (daily Oct–May; lunch included $135), rock-climbing and bushsurvival courses. Canyoning is the big thing with Katoomba Adventure Centre,1 Katoomba St, opposite the station (☎02/4782 4009 or 1800 824 009, ⦿www.kacadventures.com), with beginners' full-day canyoning and abseiling trips in the Grand Canyon or Empress Canyon ($139, includes lunch), rock-climbing and mountain biking and serious off-track adventure walks and camping trips. High 'n' Wild Mountain Adventures, 3/5 Katoomba St (☎02/4782 6224, ⦿www.high-n-wild.com.au), has a consistently good reputation for its beginners' courses in abseiling (full day $119 including lunch, half-day $75), canyoning, ($139), and rock-climbing (2 days; $259) and half-day mountain biking ($99). If the weather is bad, you can train at Blackheath Climb Centre, Shed 4, 134 Station St, Blackheath (Mon & Tues 4pm–8pm, Wed–Fri 1pm–8pm, Sat & Sun 1pm–6pm; $10; ☎02/4787 5771).

Bike rental Cycle Tech, 182 Katoomba St, Katoomba (☎02/4782 2800), has mountain bikes

from $27.50 half-day, $49.50 full day.

Bookshops There are several interesting secondhand bookshops on Katoomba St, Katoomba, and in the other villages. New books can be bought at the very literary Megalong Books, 183 The Mall, Leura.

Bus services Mountainlink ☎02/4782 4213.

Camping equipment If you haven't got your own gear, you must rent it in Sydney before you come up (see Sydney "Listings", p.193). Alternatively, Paddy Pallin, 166 Katoomba St (☎02/4782 4466), sells camping gear and a good range of topographic maps and bushwalking guides, as does Katoomba Adventure Centre, see opposite, or for cheap gear go to K-Mart (next door to Coles supermarket, see p.233).

Car rental Thrifty, 19 Edward St, Katoomba ☎02/4782 9488.

Cinemas The Edge Maxvision Cinema, 225–237 Great Western Highway, Katoomba (☎02/4782 8928), shows new-release feature films on a giant screen ($11.50; cheap tickets $8.50 all day Tues), as well as *The Edge – The Movie* (see p.226). Mount Vic Flicks, Harley Ave, off Station St, Mount Victoria (☎02/4787 1577), is a quaint local cinema in an old hall showing a fine programme of prestige new releases and independent films (Thurs–Sun, daily during school holidays; cheap tickets Thurs).

Festivals Blue Mountains Music Festival ⓦwww.bmff.org.au. Three-day mid-March festival of folk, roots and blues features Australian and international musicians on several indoor and outdoor stages; includes food and craft stalls and kids' entertainment; $110 whole weekend, $75 day ticket.

Horse riding Blue Mountains Horse Riding Adventures ℡02/4787 8688, ⓦwww.megalong.cc. A variety of escorted trail rides in the Megalong Valley and along the Coxs River from a beginners' one-hour Wilderness Ride ($35) to an experienced riders', all-day adventure ride, or helping to drive cattle along the river ($165). Pick-ups from Blackheath. Werriberri Trail Rides (℡02/4787 9171), offers horse riding for all abilities and pony rides for children in the Megalong Valley. Their two-hour ride, including pick-up from Katoomba, costs $55.

Hospital Blue Mountains District Anzac Memorial, Katoomba (℡02/4782 2111).

Internet access *Barcode 6ix*, 6 Katoomba St, Katoomba, opposite the station, has twelve terminals ($2.50 15min, $5.50 1hr); it's also a cheap Thai eatery.

Laundry The Washing Well, K-Mart car park, Katoomba. Daily 7am–7pm.

Meditation Australian Buddhist Vihara, 43 Cliff Drive, Katoomba (℡02/4782 2704), offers free meditation sessions Sunday 8am–11am and one-hour sessions daily 8am & 6pm.

Pharmacies (late-night) Blooms Springwood Pharmacy, 161 Macquarie Rd, Springwood (Mon–Fri 8.30am–9pm, Sat 8.30am–7pm, Sun 9am–7pm; ℡02/4751 2963); Greenwell & Thomas, 145 Katoomba St, Katoomba (Mon–Fri 8.30am–7pm, Sat & Sun 8.30am–6pm; ℡02/4782 1066).

Post office Katoomba Post Office, Pioneer Place opposite Coles supermarket, off Katoomba St, Katoomba, NSW 2780.

Supermarket Coles, Pioneer Place off Katoomba St, Katoomba (daily 6am–midnight).

Swimming pool Katoomba Aquatic Centre, Gates Ave, Katoomba (Mon–Fri 6am–8pm, Sat & Sun 8am–8pm, winter weekends closes 6.30pm; ℡02/4782 1748; swim $3.80), has outdoor, heated Olympic-sized and children's pools, plus an attached complex which is open all year with heated indoor pool, sauna, spa and gym.

Taxis Taxis wait outside the main Blue Mountains train stations to meet arrivals; otherwise call Katoomba Radio Cabs (℡02/4782 1311) or Blue Mountains Taxi Cab (℡02/4759 3000).

Tours Most tours of the Blue Mountains start from Sydney; see box on pp.198–199. There are two hop-on-hop-off tour services offered from Katoomba of the immediate area, run by Mountainlink and Fantastic Aussie Tours (see p.222). Fantastic Aussie Tours also does large-group coach tours: there's a day-tour to the Jenolan Caves (daily from $75) and a combined bushwalk and cave visit ($105), plus adventure caving ($130). A small-group, half-day 4WD tour takes in the Blue Mountains National Park ($92); all prices include entry fees. Tread Lightly Eco Tours (℡02/4788 1229; ⓦwww.treadlightly.com.au) offers recommended small-group, expert-guided, off-the-beaten-track half-day and full-day bushwalk and 4WD tours from Katoomba; the popular two-hour morning Wilderness Walk ($25) takes in some of the Six Foot Track (see p.234).

Trains Katoomba station general enquiries ℡02/4782 1902.

Travel agent Backpackers Travel Centre, 283 Main St, Katoomba ℡02/4782 5342, ⓦwww.backpackerstravel.net.au. Bookings for domestic buses, trains, flights and tours.

The Zig Zag Railway

LITHGOW, on the Great Western Highway 11km northwest of Hartley, is a charming coal-mining town nestled under bush-clad hills, with wide leafy streets and some imposing old buildings. Situated about 13km east of the town on the Bells Line of Road, by the small settlement of Clarence, is the **Zig Zag Railway**. In the 1860s engineers were faced with the problem of how to get the main western railway line from the top of the Blue Mountains down the steep drop to the Lithgow Valley, so they came up with a series of zigzag ramps. These fell into disuse in the early twentieth century, but tracks were relaid by rail enthusiasts in the 1970s. Served by old steam trains, the picturesque line passes through two tunnels and over three viaducts. You can stop at points along the way and rejoin a later train. The Zig Zag Railway can be reached by ordinary State Rail train on the regular service between Sydney and Lithgow, by requesting the guard in advance to stop at the Zig Zag platform; you then walk across the line to Bottom Point platform at the base of the Lithgow Valley. To catch the Zig Zag Railway from Clarence, which is at the top of the valley, you'll need to have your own transport, or take the Fantastic Aussie Tour (see p.222). Zig Zag trains depart from Clarence daily (11am, 1pm & 3pm; from the Zig Zag platform add 40min to these times; $17; no bookings required; ⓦwww.zigzagrailway.com.au). There are plenty of **motels** in and around Lithgow – and the helpful **Lithgow Visitor Information Centre**, 1 Cooerwull Rd (daily 9am–5pm; ☎02/6353 1859; ⓦwww.tourism.lithgow .com), can advise on accommodation.

Kanangra Boyd National Park and the Jenolan Caves

Kanangra Boyd National Park shares a boundary with the Blue Mountains National Park. Further south than the latter, much of it is inaccessible but you can explore the rugged beauty of **Kanangra Walls**, where the Boyd Plateau falls away to reveal a wilderness area of creeks, deep gorges and rivers below. Reached via Jenolan Caves, three **walks** leave from the car park at Kanangra Walls: a short lookout walk, a waterfall stroll and a longer plateau walk – contact the NPWS in Oberon for details (☎02/6336 1972; $6 car entry). Boyd River and Dingo Dell camping grounds, both off Kanangra Walls Road, have **free bush camping** (pit toilets; no drinking water at Dingo Dell). You can get to **Oberon**, a timber-milling town and the closest settlement to Kanangra, by Countrylink bus from Mount Victoria (3 weekly).

The **Jenolan Caves** lie 30km southwest across the mountains from Katoomba on the far edge of the Kanangra Boyd National Park – over 80km by road – and contain New South Wales' most spectacular limestone formations. There are nine "show" caves with prices for a guided tour of each cave ranging from $15 to $27.50 depending on the cave (guided tours various times daily 10am–5pm; 1hr 30min–2hr). If you're coming for just a day, plan to see one or two caves: the best general cave is the Lucas Cave ($15; 1hr 30min), and a more spectacular one is the Temple of Baal ($22; 1hr 30min) while the extensive River Cave, with its tranquil Pool of Reflection, is the longest and priciest ($27.50; 2hr). Buying a ticket for two more caves works out to be a better deal: for example, the Lucas combined with the Temple of Baal is $29.50. The system of caves is surrounded by the **Jenolan Karst Conservation Reserve**, a fauna and flora sanctuary with picnic facilities and walking trails to small waterfalls and lookout points. It and the caves are looked after by The Jenolan Caves Trust (☎02/6359 3311, ⓦwww.jenolancaves.org.au), which also offers **adventure caving** in various other caves (3hr tour $60.50, 7hr tour $187.50). There's no public transport to the caves but you can get here from Katoomba with Fantastic Aussie Tours (see p.222) or many other tours are available from Sydney (see box on pp.198–199).

You can actually **walk** from Katoomba to the Jenolan Caves; the 42-kilometre-long **Six Foot Track** through the bush begins at the Explorers Tree next to the Great Western Highway about 2.5km west of Katoomba train station; you'll need to allow two to three days for the walk, and you're advised to carry plenty of water. There are four basic **campsites** along the way, plus well-equipped cabins at Binda Flats, *Jenolan Cottages*, reached by car from Jenolan Caves Road, sleeping six to eight people (❹; BYO linen). Book the cabins through Jenolan Caves Trust (see above), who will also supply details and **information** on the walk and camping. Glenbrook NPWS information centre (see p.223) can provide more information on camping. Fantastic Aussie

Tours (T02/4782 1866 or 1300 300 915; Wwww.fantastic-aussie-tours.com.au), offers good-value, three-day, two-night fully catered and supported **guided walks** along the Six Foot Track (departs 9.30am first and third Wed of month; $315; tent camping). If you're going it alone, the same company provides a daily transfer service for bushwalkers to the start of the track and then a return service a few days later from the Jenolan Caves ($47); you can leave your car in their depot. The same service will get you from Katoomba to the Jenolan Caves (2hr 15min; departs Katoomba 10.30am; departs Jenolan Caves 3.45pm), designed as an overnight rather than a day-return service; otherwise the same company offers day-tours from Katoomba, as do several other operators (see "Listings" p.233), or there are many tours from Sydney (see pp.198–199).

The focus of the area, apart from the caves themselves, is the rather romantic *Jenolan Caves House*, a charming old hotel which found fame as a honeymoon destination in the 1920s and is now part of the *Jenolan Caves Resort* (T02/6359 3322, Wwww.jenolancaves.com). In the old hotel, which also has a good restaurant, there are recently refurbished en-suite rooms (6–7), and cheaper share-bathroom versions (5). The newer annexe, the *Mountain Lodge*, has motel-style rooms and two- to three-bedroom units without the character (5); family rooms sleep four to six in the *Gatehouse* (4; BYO linen), which has shared communal areas, including a kitchen. The Jenolan Karst Conservation Park (see p.198) has a spacious simple campsite (no powered sites), in a rural and secluded spot 1.6km from the caves along the Jenolan River from where you can walk back to the caves. Other **places to stay** in the area include *Jenolan Cabins*, 42 Edith Rd, 4km west of Jenolan Caves on Porcupine Hill (T & F02/6335 6239, Wwww.bluemts.com.au/jenolancabins; 4), whose very reasonably priced, well-equipped, modern, two-bedroom timber cabins with wood fires accommodate six (BYO linen) – all with magnificent views over the Blue Mountains National Park, Kanangra Boyd National Park and the Jenolan Caves Reserve.

South

Once you escape Sydney's uninspiring outer suburbs, the journey south is very enjoyable. Beyond Botany Bay and Port Hacking, the Princes Highway and the Illawarra railway hug the edge of the **Royal National Park** for more than 20km. South of the park, the railway and the scenic Lawrence Hargrave Drive (Route 68) follow the coast to **Wollongong**. Between here and Nowra, the ocean beaches of the Leisure Coast are popular with local holidaymakers, while fishermen, windsurfers and yachtsmen gather at **Lake Illawarra**, a huge coastal lake near Port Kembla. A few kilometres further down the coast is the famous, and often lethal, blowhole at **Kiama**.

Inland, west of Wollongong, Sydney's drinking water is stored in the Cataract and Cordeaux **reservoirs**, surrounded by picnic and leisure areas. Further southwest, past **Kangaroo Valley**, the softly rolling hills of the **Southern Highlands** are dotted with old country towns such as **Berrima** and **Bundanoon**, the latter overlooking the wild and windswept crags of **Morton National Park**.

Transport down south is good, with a frequent train service operating between Sydney and Nowra, stopping at most of the coastal locations detailed below. The main bus service is Pioneer Motor Service, which stops at

Wollongong and Kiama en route to Bega and Eden (℡02/4423 5233). Greyhound Pioneer (℡13 20 30) has a daily Sydney–Melbourne coastal route which also stops at Wollongong and Kiama. There are also several local bus companies in the region detailed in the accounts below.

① The Royal and Heathcote national parks

The **Royal National Park** is a huge nature reserve right on Sydney's doorstep, only 36km south of the city. Established in 1879, it was the second national park in the world (after Yellowstone in the USA). The railway between Sydney and Wollongong marks its western border, and from the train the scenery is fantastic – streams, waterfalls, rock formations and rainforest flora fly past the window. If you want to explore more closely, get off at one of the stations along the way – Loftus, Engadine, Heathcote, Waterfall or Otford – all starting points for walking trails into the park. On the eastern side, from Jibbon Head to Garie Beach, the park falls away abruptly to the ocean, creating a spectacular coastline of steep cliffs broken here and there by creeks cascading into the seas and little coves with fine sandy beaches; the remains of **Aboriginal rock carvings** are the only traces of the original Dharawal people. The ultimate trek is the spectacular 26-kilometre **Coastal Walk**, taking in the entire coastal length of the park. Give yourself two days to complete it, beginning at either Otford or Bundeena, camping overnight at the officially designated bushcamp at North Era (several other campsites were closed at the time of writing; check availability with the NPWS). The walk is gruelling as you mostly have to carry your own water; water is available at Wattamolla and Garie but it must be purified. Undertaking part of the route is also satisfying, such as the popular trail from **Otford** down to beachfront **Burning Palms** (2hr oneway; no camping). A good book to buy is the *Royal National Park on Foot* by Alan Fairley, and try to get a copy of the *Royal National Park* map; both are available at the NPWS Visitor Centre (see below).

You can also drive in at various points (\$10 car entry; gates open 24hr except at Garie Beach where gates close at 8.30pm). Coming in at the northern end, turning off the Princes Highway south of Loftus, you can visit the **NPWS Visitor Centre** (daily 8.30am–4.30pm; ℡02/9542 0648, ⓦ www.npws.nsw.gov.au), 2km from Loftus train station. The easy one-kilometre track from here to the Bungoona Lookout boasts panoramic views and is wheelchair-accessible. Cars are allowed right through the park, exiting at **Waterfall** on the Princes Highway or **Stanwell Park** on Lawrence Hargrave Drive. Not far south of the NPWS centre, **Audley** is a picturesque picnic ground on the Hacking River, where you can rent a boat or canoe for a leisurely paddle and where you'll find another **NPWS Visitor Centre**. Deeper into the park, on the ocean shore, **Wattamolla** and **Garie beaches** have good surfing waves; the two beaches are connected by a walking track. There are **kiosks** at Audley, Wattamolla and Garie Beach.

There's a small, very basic but secluded YHA **youth hostel** inside the park 1km from Garie Beach (book in advance at any YHA hostel; key must be collected in advance; dorms \$11, rooms ①), with no electricity or showers. There is also the **bushcamp** at North Era which requires a permit from the visitor centre; often full weeks in advance on weekends, you'll need to book and the permit can be posted out to you (which can take up to five days), or you can purchase it before leaving Sydney at the NPWS centre at 102 George St, Sydney (see p.196).

An interesting way to get here is by **ferry** to Bundeena from the southern beachside suburb of Cronulla (see p.163) at the Tonkin Street Wharf just below the train station: Cronulla and National Park Ferries (Mon–Fri hourly 5.30am–6.30pm, except 12.30pm but continuous during school holidays; Sat & Sun: Sept–March 8.30am–6.30pm, April–Oct to 5.30pm; returns from Bundeena hourly: Mon–Fri 6am–7pm, except 1pm; Sat & Sun: Sept–March 9am–7pm; April–Aug to 6pm; $3.30; narrated cruises 10.30am: Sept–May daily; June–Sept Mon, Wed, Fri & Sun; 3hr; $15; cruise bookings ☎02/9523 2990, ⊛www.cronullaandnationalparkferrycruises.com) take 25 minutes to cross Port Hacking to the small town of **BUNDEENA** at the park's northeast tip. To begin the Coastal Walk from Bundeena, follow The Avenue and Lambeth Walk 1km to the national park gate. A shorter option is the pleasant half-day walk to pretty sheltered **Little Marley Beach** for a swim and a picnic (2hr one-way) – or head down a pathway to **Jibbons Beach**, a thirty-minute stroll which will take you past some Dharawal rock engravings, where faint outlines of a kangaroo, stingrays, whales and a six-fingered man can be seen (pick up the *Jibbon Aboriginal Rock Engravings Walk* map and leaflet from the café near the wharf). Just west of the town on the shores of the Hacking River is a NPWS **campsite**, the *Bonnie Vale Camping Ground* (no powered sites) but for more comfort, try *Bundeena Caravan Park*, south of the wharf on Scarborough Street (☎02/9523 9520; cabins ❷, en suite ❸). There are a couple of great cafés and a sheltered little beach next to the ferry wharf.

Heathcote National Park, across the Princes Highway from the Royal National Park, is much smaller and quieter. This is a serious bushwalkers' park with no roads and a ban on trail bikes. The best **train** station for the park is Waterfall, from where you can follow a twelve-kilometre trail through the park, before catching a train back from Heathcote. On the way you pass through quite a variety of vegetation and alongside several swimmable pools, the carved sandstone of the **Kingfisher Pool** making it the most picturesque, and there is a small, six-site, very basic camping ground beside it (no drinking water; $3 per adult), and another one at Mirang Pool. **Camping** permits are available from the Royal National Park NPWS Visitor Centre (see p.236) or at The Rocks NPWS office (see p.196). By **car**, you can reach the picnic area at Woronora Dam on the western edge of the park: turn east off the Princes Highway onto Woronora Road (free entry).

South down the coast

For a **scenic drive from Sydney**, for bush, coast and cliff views and beautiful beaches, follow the Princes Highway south, exiting into the Royal National Park after Loftus onto Farnell Drive; the entry fee at the gate is waived if you are just driving through without stopping. The national park route emerges above the cliffs at **Otford** beyond which follow **Lawrence Hargreave Drive** (Route 68) to Thirroul. A few kilometres from Otford is the impressive clifftop lookout on Bald Hill above **Stanwell Park**, where you're likely to see the breathtaking sight of **hang-gliders** taking off and soaring down. You can join in with the Sydney Hang Gliding Centre (☎02/4294 4294, ⊛www.hanggliding.com.au), which offers tandem flights with an instructor for around $180 during the week, $195 weekends (available daily depending on the weather); the centre also runs courses (from $195 per day). At **Clifton** the *Imperial Hotel* is a must for an en-route drink, as it sits right on the cliff's edge.

By the time you get to **AUSTINMER** you're at a break in the stunning cliffs and into some heavy surf territory. The down-to-earth town has a popular, very clean, patrolled surf beach that gets packed out on summer weekends. Across the road from the beach, there's delicious fish and chips at *Ann's Quality*

Foods (but expect long weekend waits), or good coffee and more upmarket eats at the big and airy BYO bakery-café, *Cov*, next door.

There's impressive cliff scenery again as you pass through **Scarborough** (best seen from the historic *Scarborough Hotel*), **Wombarra** and **THIRROUL**. Thirroul is the spot where the English novelist D.H. Lawrence wrote *Kangaroo* during his short Australian interlude; the town and the surrounding area are a substantial part of the novel, though he renamed the then-sleepy village Mullumbimby. Thirroul is now gradually being swallowed up in the suburban sprawl of Wollongong; it's busy, with plenty of shops and cafés, including the excellent and appropriately literary *Oskar's Wild Bookstore & Coffee Bar* at 289 Lawrence Hargrave Drive. At the southern end of the beach, **Sandford Point**, as it's known (it's actually Bulli Point on maps) is a famous surfing break. A sixty-kilometre cycle track runs from Thirroul south along the coast through Wollongong to Lake Illawarra. *The Beaches Hotel*, 272 Lawrence Hargrave Drive (T02/4267 2288, F02/4268 2255, rooms ❸, apartment ❺), is a modern, stylish pub complex that has one good-value spacious, colourful two-bedroom apartment, plus cheaper share-bathroom **rooms**; you can barbecue your own steaks in the the popular beer garden or eat in the bistro; weekend bands (when accommodation can be noisy) and pool tables provide entertainment.

After Thirroul, Lawrence Hargrave Drive joins up with the Princes Highway going south into Wollongong (Route 60) or heading northwest, uphill to a section of the forested **Illawarra Escarpment** and the **Bulli Pass**. There are fantastic views from the Bulli Lookout, which has its own café, and further towards Sydney at the appropriately named **Sublime Point Lookout**. You can explore the escarpment using the **walking tracks** which start from the look-outs, and another extensive part of the **Illawarra Escarpment State Recreation Area**, about 10km west of Wollongong's city centre on Mount Kembla and Mount Keira.

Wollongong

Although it's New South Wales' third-largest city, **WOLLONGONG** has more of a country-town feel; the students of Wollongong University give it extra life in term time and it has a big dose of surf culture as the city centre is set right on the ocean. Eighty kilometres south of Sydney, it's essentially a working class industrial centre – Australia's largest steelworks at nearby Port Kembla looms unattractively over Wollongong City Beach but the **Illawarra Escarpment** (see above) rises dramatically beyond the city and provides a lush backdrop.

There's not really much to see in the **city centre** itself (concentrated between Wollongong train station and the beach), which has been swallowed up by a giant shopping mall on **Crown Street** but the regional art centre, the **Wollongong City Gallery**, on the corner of Kembla and Burelli streets (Tues–Fri 10am–5pm, Sat & Sun noon–4pm; free), shows changing exhibitions and has a permanent collection with an emphasis on contemporary Aboriginal and colonial Illawarra artists. If you continue east down Crown Street and cross Marine Drive, you'll hit **Wollongong City Beach**, a surf beach which stretches over 2km Most locals choose the more salubrious **North Wollongong Beach** (bus #23 or #24 from the Gateway bus interchange near City Mall). But in between the two beaches, sheltering beside Flagstaff Point, is the city's highlight, **Wollongong Harbour**, with its fishing fleet in Belmore Basin, a fish market, a few seafood restaurants, and a picturesque nineteenth-century lighthouse on the breakwater; there's also gentle swimming from its beach.

Away from the centre, science and religion provide the most interest. North of the city centre, near the University of Wollongong at the southern end of **Fairy Meadow Beach** and next to Brandon Park, is the new $6 million **Science Centre** on Squires Way (daily 10am–4pm; $9.50; ⓦwww.uow.edu.au/science_centre; train to Fairy Meadow station, then a 10–15min walk), Attractions include the state's best **planetarium** (daily shows noon & 3pm; 30min; laser concert Sat, Sun & school holidays 1pm; $2 extra per show; planetarium-only $6) and over a hundred themed kid-friendly hands-on exhibits. South of the centre the vast **Nan Tien Buddhist Temple**, the largest in Australia, is on Berkeley Road, Berkeley, reached from Sydney by train to Unanderra station and a twenty-minute walk, or by bus from Wollongong station with John J. Hill Bus Co (☎02/4229 4911). The Fo Guang Shan Buddhists welcome visitors to the temple (public holiday Mon & Tues–Sun 9am–5pm) and offer a good-value $7 vegetarian lunch, monthly two-day meditation retreats and a peaceful and surprisingly upmarket guesthouse accommodation (☎02/4272 0600, ⓦwww.ozemail.com.au/~nantien; ❹).

Practicalities

The best and cheapest way to get to Wollongong from Sydney by public transport is the frequent **train** from Central station which hugs the coast and stops at most of the small towns en route; Wollongong station is right in the centre just off Crown Street. Pioneer Motor Service has three to four services on weekdays and two a day at weekends, while Greyhound Pioneer runs one daily bus service, leaving Sydney at 11.30am and returning from Wollongong at 11.50am. **Wollongong Tourist Information Centre**, near the mall at 93 Crown St (Mon–Fri 9am–5pm, Sat 9am–4pm, Sun 10am–4pm; ☎02/4227 5545, ⓦwww.tourismwollongong.com), provides information and can advise on **accommodation**. The central *Boat Harbour Motel*, on the corner of Campbell and Wilson streets (☎02/4228 9166, ⓦwww.boatharbour-motel.com.au; ❺), has comfortable and spacious rooms with balconies, some with sea views; more upmarket, and also with water views, is Wollongong's four-and-a-half-star *Novotel Northbeach*, 2–14 Cliff Rd, North Wollongong (☎02/4226 3555, ⓦwww.novotelnorthbeach.com; ❼). The really friendly, colourful and home-like *Keiraleagh House*, 60 Kembla St (☎02/4228 6765, ⓔbackpack@bigpond.net.au; dorms $18, rooms ❷), in an old converted mansion a few blocks back from the beach, has dorms (up to six-bed) as well as singles, and doubles (some en suite); rooms are comfy and clean with desks and an armchair. A garden with a barbecue area makes for happy mingling between the students, surfers and travellers who all stay here; free surfboards. A **YHA hostel** was set to open at the time of writing at the Art Deco-style *Crown Hotel*, 309–311 Crown St, right near the train station (☎02/4229 7444, ⓔcitypac@1earth.net; four- and six-bed dorms $20, en-suite rooms ❸). There's nowhere central to **camp**, but the two caravan parks to the north are right on the beach: *Corrimal Beach Tourist Park* is on Lake Parade in Corrimal, 6km north at the mouth of Towradgi Lagoon (☎02/4285 5688; en-suite cabins ❸); while *Bulli Beach Tourist Park* is 11km north of town on Farrell Road, Bulli (☎02/4285 5677; bungalows ❷, en-suite cabins ❸–❹).

Wollongong isn't really renowned for its **food**. There's a concentration of cafés on Crown Street near the tourist office (*Flame Tree Music Cafe* at no. 89 and *Santana Books & Coffee* at no. 53 are both worth checking out) and Corrimal and Keira streets, both intersecting Crown. *Namik's*, on the corner of Crown and Corrimal streets, is one of the best. Around the corner, *Litani's*, at 120 Corrimal St, is a relaxed BYO restaurant and coffee shop serving Lebanese and other Mediterranean dishes; its street-side courtyard is very popular On Keira Street, well-regarded *Lorenzo's Diner* at no. 119 (℡02/4229 5633; lunch Thurs & Fri, dinner Tues–Sat; licensed & BYO), serves top-notch contemporary Italian food, at surprisingly moderate prices, in a bold and stylish interior.

Kiama and around

Of the coastal resorts south of Sydney, **KIAMA** is probably the most attractive – though if you want more than a day- or overnight trip to the beach, you'd be better off continuing down to Nowra and beyond (see p.281). A large resort and fishing town, Kiama is famous for its star attraction, the **Blowhole**, a five-minute walk from the **railway station** on Blowhole Point. Stemming from a natural fault in the cliffs, the blowhole explodes into a waterspout when a wave hits with sufficient force. It's impressive, but also potentially dangerous: freak waves can be thrown over 60m into the air and have swept several over-curious bystanders into the raging sea – so stand well back. The **Kiama Visitor Information Centre**, nearby on Blowhole Point Road (daily 9am–5pm; ℡02/4232 3322 or 1800 803 897, ⓦwww.kiama.com.au), supplies details of other local attractions such as **Cathedral Rocks**, a few kilometres to the north, whose rocky outcrops drop abruptly to the ocean. About 15km south of Kiama is **Seven Mile Beach**, a stunning sweep of sandy beach with its own small oceanfront **national park** which includes a **camping ground** at its northern end, with toilets and cold showers (bookings Nowra NPWS ℡02/4423 2170).

West of Kiama, a steep road leads to **Mount Saddleback Lookout**, from where on a clear day you can get an incredible view of the entire coast – from the Royal National Park in the north to Jervis Bay in the south. Beyond the lookout you can head north to join the Illawarra Highway, and follow that inland to **Macquarie Pass**, the gateway to the Southern Highlands. The **Macquarie Pass National Park** is one of the southernmost stands of Australia's subtropical rainforest; there's a car park on the road from where the Cascades Walk takes you on a two-kilometre loop through the forest to Cascades Waterfall. Alternatively, Jamberoo Mountain Pass Road heads to Robertson on the Illawarra Highway via the **Budderoo National Park** where the **Minnamurra Rainforest Centre** (park daily 9am–5pm, centre and *Lyrebird Cafe* 9am–4pm; boardwalk closes 4pm, track closes 3pm; ℡02/4236 0469; car entry $10 at Minnamurra only), has a wheelchair-accessible elevated loop boardwalk from the centre (1.6km return; 30min–1hr) through subtropical and temperate rainforest – you'll see cabbage tree palms, staghorn ferns and impressive Illawarra fig trees – and a viewing platform to **Minnamurra Falls**. You can continue half way on a paved walk with some steep sections leading to the upper falls (2.6km return; 1.5–2hr). The impressive **Carrington Falls**, also within the park, are 8km east of Robertson by road, and are worth a detour: a turn-off from the Jamberoo Mountain Pass Road leads to lookout points over the waterfalls. Free **bushcamping** is possible in both Macquarie Pass and Budderoo national parks.

Otherwise if you want to **stay** in this area you'll find plenty of the usual motels strung out along the highway. There's an abundance of B&Bs and self-catering holiday units too; the tourist office (see above) has a comprehensive list and can book accommodation for free. Budget alternatives in Kiama include *Kiama Backpackers*, 31 Bong Bong St, very close to the train station and right near the beach (☎ & ⓕ02/4233 1881; dorms $20, rooms ❷), though it sometimes closes down in winter; and the *Grand Hotel*, on the corner of Manning and Bong Bong streets (☎02/4232 1037; ❸), which has budget-priced, old-fashioned share-bathroom pub accommodation – the pub restaurant serves decent filling meals lunch and dinner daily. The closest campsite to the centre is at *Blowhole Point Holiday Park* right near the blowhole (☎02/4232 2707; ⓦ www.kiama.net/holiday/blowhole; vans ❷, en-suite vans ❸), while *Easts Beach Caravan Park*, a couple of kilometres south of Kiama (☎02/4232 2124 or 1800 674 444, ⓦ www.kiama.com.au/eastpark; en-suite cabins ❹–❺), on the beach with safe, sheltered swimming; the grassy park has a camp kitchen, playground and tennis courts. There are plenty of **places to eat** – Thai, Chinese, Italian and lots of cafés – with a concentration on Manning and Terralong streets. For a great coffee, the smart *esse*, 55 Collins St (dinner bookings ☎02/4232 2811; from 10am, closed Tues, dinner Thurs–Sat; licensed & BYO) is a café by day and modern Australian restaurant by night. Sunday lunch is hugely popular at the relaxed *Zumo Restaurant*, 127 Terralong St (☎02/4232 2222; lunch Sun only, dinner Wed–Sun; licensed & BYO), housed in an old building with lots of greenery and outdoor seating; food is adventurous and eclectic.

GERRINGONG, 10km south of Kiama, is wonderfully scenic, set against green hills with glorious sweeping beach views. Budget accommodation includes a **YHA hostel**, *Nestor House*, on Fern Street, just 250m from Werri Beach (☎ & ⓕ02/4234 1249; dorms $20, rooms ❸), or there's the *Werri Beach Holiday Park* (☎02/4234 1285; vans ❸, en-suite cabins ❹–❻), which benefits from a great location at the northern end of Seven Mile Beach, between Crooked River and the sand. The best café in town is *Gerringong Gourmet Deli*, 133 Fern St, which does divine fish and chips and gourmet burgers. Non-meat eaters should head for the *Perfect Break Vegetarian Cafe*, further along at no. 115.

Inland: the road to Canberra

If you want to take your time getting to Canberra, there are a number of worthwhile diversions off the speedy South Western Motorway (M5), the main road inland which eventually joins up with the Hume Highway (Route 31). Camden Valley Way heads west from the motorway to **CAMDEN** on the Nepean River, where John Macarthur pioneered the breeding of merino sheep in 1805. The town still has a rural feel and several well-preserved nineteenth-century buildings, the oldest of which dates from 1816. En route, you'll pass **Mount Annan Botanical Garden** (daily: April–Sept 10am–4pm; Oct–March 10am–6pm; $4.40; ⓦ www.rbgsyd.gov.au). Actually the native-plant section of the Royal Botanic Gardens in Sydney, this outstanding collection of flora is the largest of its kind in Australia. Within the grounds, you can eat well at the idyllically sited *Gardens Restaurant* at outside tables surrounded by trees. A major attraction, it makes sense to book if you intend to dine (☎02/4647 1363); there's also a kiosk in the park. The garden is 57km south-west of Sydney and can be reached from the M5 (Camden exit, then follow Tourist Drive 18 and look for signs) or by a combination of CityRail train to Campbelltown, and then Busways (☎02/4655 7501).

From Camden, Remembrance Drive leads to **PICTON**, a small farming town cradled by hills; you can get here by train from Sydney or with Picton Coaches (☎02/4677 1564) from Campbelltown or Wollongong, via Bargo, Tahmoor and Thirlmere. Picton is a good spot for a drink in the shady beer garden of the 1839 sandstone *George IV Inn*, which brews its own beer by a traditional German method (and also serves up legendary seafood platters). Eleven kilometres south of Picton, the five connected freshwater lakes that make up **Thirlmere Lakes National Park** are named in the language of the Gandangarra Aborigines. Lake Couridjah is best for swimming, surrounded by unspoilt bushland and plenty of birdlife. Continuing along Remembrance Drive, it's 8km to the **Wirrimbirra Sanctuary** at **Bargo** (daily 8am–5pm; free; ☎02/4684 1112, ⓦwww.stonequarry.com.au/wirrimbirra), a peaceful bushland spot run by the National Trust, with a field studies centre, a native-plant nursery, a visitor information centre and café (daily 7am–5pm), bushwalking trails, and pools to swim in, where you can engage in a bit of platypus-spotting at dawn or dusk if you stay over in the bunk-style cabins ($15 per person) or camp. You might also see wallabies, kangaroos, wombats, brush-tailed possums and goannas, along with 150 different species of birds. Without your own **transport**, you can get here by train from Sydney to Bargo and then walk a couple of kilometres.

The Southern Highlands

From Bargo, you can detour onto the Old Hume Highway, through the picturesque **Southern Highlands**, a favourite weekend retreat for Sydneysiders since the 1920s; the pretty Highlands towns are full of cafés, restaurants, antique shops and secondhand bookstores and there's an emerging wine industry. The Southern Highlands is well served by **transport**, with a frequent train service between Sydney and Canberra stopping at Picton, Mittagong, Bowral, Moss Vale, Bundanoon and Goulburn. Priors Scenic Express (☎02/4472 4040 or 1800 816 234) from Campbelltown train station on Sydney's western fringes also goes to Mittagong, Bowral and Moss Vale while Berrima Coaches provides a local bus service (☎02/4871 3211).

Marking the beginning of the Highlands is **MITTAGONG**, a small agricultural and tourist town 110km south of Sydney, mostly visited on the way to the limestone **Wombeyan Caves** (daily 8.30am–5pm; guided tours: one cave $15; two caves $21; all caves $26; 1hr 30min for each cave) in the nearby hills. The route to the five caves begins 4km south of the town off the highway and winds upwards for 65km on a partly unsealed road. The associated **campsite** near the caves (☎02/4843 5976, ⓦwww.jenolancaves.org; vans ❷, cabins ❸–❹, cottages ❹) is well run. For more on accommodation in the area – and a free booking service – contact **Tourism Southern Highlands** (daily 8am–5.30pm; ☎02/4871 2888, accommodation bookings on ☎1300 657 559, ⓦwww.highlandsnsw.com.au) in Winifred West Park on the Hume Highway; room rates in the area rise considerably on Friday and Saturday nights. Tourism Southern Highlands also has masses of information on bushwalks of varying lengths. Neighbouring **BOWRAL**, 6km southwest, is a busy, well-to-do town; its main strip, Bong Bong Street, is full of upmarket clothes and homeware shops and it has a good bookstore and a cinema. It was also the birthplace of cricket legend Don Bradman and cricket fans should check out the **Bradman Museum** (daily 10am–5pm; $7.50), on Jude Street, in an idyllic spot between a leafy park and the well-used cricket oval and club. It has a pleasant café with a garden terrace. Other good **places to eat** include *That Noodle Place*, 279 Bong Bong St (☎02/4861 6930; lunch Tues–Sun, dinner Wed–Sun), a colourful and funky retro-styled place that serves really yummy Vietnamese, Thai and Chinese food (including *yum cha*); and further down the same street, on a lane beside the Empire Cinema complex, you can have the best coffee in town at slick, city-style *Coffee Culture*. The picturesque village of **BERRIMA** is 7km on from Bowral. The *Surveyor General Inn*, one of an excellent complement of well-preserved and restored old buildings, has been serving beer here since 1835. Inside the 1838 sandstone **courthouse**, on the corner of Argyle and Wiltshire streets (daily 10am–4pm; $5), is the **Berrima Visitor Centre** (same hours; ☎02/4877 1505), while across the road the still-operational **Berrima Gaol** once held the infamous bushranger Thunderbolt – and also has the dubious distinction of being the first place in Australia where a woman was executed. Continue up Wiltshire Street from the courthouse to get to the **River Walk**, the end of which is marked by a fine reserve with picnic tables – and camping too. Other **accommodation** includes a slather of B&Bs in pretty, old stone cottages such as *Berrima Glen* (☎02/4877 1164; ❺), and the *White Horse Inn* in the Market Place (☎02/4877 1204, ⓦwww.highlandsnsw.com.au/whitehorseinn; ❹), a large, old 1832 sandstone hotel with accommodation in modern motel units in the garden. Three kilometres north of Berrima on the Old Hume Highway in the direction of Mittagong and worth a look is *Berkelouw's Book Barn & Café*, for secondhand and rare books and good **food** and coffee in a vast converted barn set amongst fields.

Five kilometres from **Moss Vale** on the Old Hume Highway is the turn-off south to **BUNDANOON**, famous for its annual April celebration of its Scottish heritage. Exploiting the autumnal atmosphere of mist and turning leaves, Bundanoon becomes Brigadoon for a day, overtaken by Highland Games – Aussie-style. But a nearby commmunity of Thai Buddhist monks at the **Sunnataram Forest Monastery** (visitors welcome; ☎02/4384 4262 or ⓦwww.sunnataram.org for details and directions) are providing a different cultural input. Bundanoon is in an attractive spot set in hilly countryside scarred by deep gullies and with splendid views over the gorges and mountains of the huge **Morton National Park** (car fee $6) which extends from Bundanoon to near Kangaroo Valley (see p.244). The park, and Bundanoon, have traditionally been a **cycling** mecca, with the long-established Ye Olde Bicycle Shop renting out bikes at very reasonable rates (Mon–Fri 10am–4.30pm, Sat & Sun 9.30am–5pm; $10 per hour, $16.50 half-day, $25 full-day; ☎02/4883 6043). A recommended evening activity – set off at sunset, armed with a torch – is a visit to **Glow Worm Glen**; after dark the small sandstone grotto is transformed by the naturally flickering lights of these creatures. It's a 25-minute walk from town via the end of William Street, or an easy forty-minute signposted trek from Riverview Road in the park.

At the northeast edge of Morton National Park, 17km from Kangaroo Valley, **Fitzroy Falls** is a must-see. A short boardwalk from the car park takes you to the waterfall plunging 80m into the valley below, with glorious views of the Yarrunga Valley beyond. The **NPWS Visitor Centre** (daily 9am–5.30pm; ☎02/4887 7270; entry fee $3 site visit, $6 all-day visit) includes a buffet-style café with a very pleasant outside deck. Detailed information about walking tracks and scenic drives in the surrounding area is available and the office issues **camping** permits for the nearby bushcamp at Yarrunga Creek and the Gambells Rest camping ground near Bundanoon, which has flush toilets and hot showers but no drinking water.

The *Bundanoon YHA* **hostel**, Railway Avenue (☎02/4883 6010, ☏02/4883 7470; dorms $20, rooms ❷), is a spacious Edwardian-era guesthouse complete with open fireplaces and an outdoor spa (extra charge), and set on extensive grounds where you can also camp. A good-value **motel** with great facilities is the central *Bundanoon Holiday Resort* on Anzac Parade (☎02/4883 6068, ☏02/4883 6068; ❸). For more style, the elegant, antique-furnished *Tree Tops Country Guesthouse*, 101 Railway Ave (☎02/4883 6372, ⓦwww.treetopsguesthouse.com.au/guesthouse;

B&B ❺), dates from 1910. Recommended **places to eat** are the *Old Post Office Cafe*, on Railway Parade, which doubles as a modern Australian restaurant on Saturday nights (dinner bookings ☎02/4883 6354; otherwise Wed–Sun 9am–5pm). The best coffee in town is served at the cute *Cafe de Railleur* attached to Ye Olde Bicycle Shop (see p.243). The *Bundanoon Hotel*, on Erith Street, opposite the station – on the other side of the railway tracks – is a very cosy British-style pub which serves up plain, affordable food in its tiny *Thistle* bistro (book Fri–Sun on ☎02/4883 6005; no food Mon & Tues).

Kangaroo Valley

Between Nowra on the coast and Moss Vale on the inland road, **Kangaroo Valley** is a popular spot for weekenders from Sydney – a lovely, hidden valley situated between the lush dairy country of Nowra and the Southern Highlands. Coming from the coastal end, a narrow, winding country road climbs 700m up Cambewarra Mountain, with suberb coastal panoramas along the way. In **KANGAROO VALLEY** village itself, Moss Vale Road has several craft, antique and gift shops and a bookstore, plus lots of cafés – two of the best are *Cafe Bella*, at no. 151 and *Bounce* at no. 165 – but is dominated by the characterful old pub, the *Friendly Inn Hotel* at no. 159, which is overflowing on weekends. A kilometre further on, the picturesque old sandstone Hampden Suspension Bridge crosses the Kangaroo River; beside it there are tearooms and the **Pioneer Settlement Museum** (daily 9.30am–4.30pm; $3.50) with an attached bushwalk and a **market** held in the grounds on the last Sunday of the month. A service station here sells groceries. The very pleasant *Kangaroo Valley Tourist Park* is just beside the bridge (☎1300 559 977, ⓦwww.kangaroovalleyescapes.com.au; ❹–❺), is a great place to camp, complete with camp kitchen, or the en-suite timber cabins have everything from video to air-con; mountain bikes, canoes and kayaks for rent. But this is above all **B&B** territory: *Tall Trees Bed and Breakfast*, 8 Nugents Creek Rd, 1km east from the Kangaroo Valley village (☎ & ⓕ02/4465 1208, ⓦwww.talltreesbandb.com.au; ❹), has log fires and great views across the valley from its patio; the self-contained studio has a spa, wood fire and kitchen

You can get to Kangaroo Valley from Campbelltown train station on the outskirts of Sydney on Priors Scenic Express (☎02/4472 4040 or 1800 816 234); a half-hour stop is scheduled at Fitzroy Falls (see p.243).

Travel details

Sydney is very much the centre of the Australian transport network, and you can get to virtually anywhere in the country from there on a variety of competing services. The following list represents a minimum; as well as the dedicated services listed below, many places will also be served by long-distance services stopping en route.

Trains

Sydney to: Adelaide (Indian Pacific 2 weekly, Mon & Thurs 2.40pm; 27hr 30min); Brisbane (1 daily; 16hr); Canberra (3 daily; 5hr); Dubbo (1 daily; 6hr 40min); Goulburn (8–10 daily; 3hr); Katoomba (22–30 daily; 2hr); Maitland (1 daily; 2hr 30min); Melbourne (1 daily; 10hr 20min; plus daily bus/train Speedlink via Albury; 12–13hr); Murwillumbah (1 daily; 13hr 35min); Newcastle (20–25 daily; 2hr 30min); Perth (2 weekly, Mon & Thurs 2.40pm; 60hr); Richmond

(18–25 daily; 1hr 15min); Windsor (18–25 daily; 1hr 15min); Wollongong (15–25 daily; 1hr 40min).

Buses

Sydney to: Adelaide (2–3 daily; 20hr); Albury (2 daily; 8hr 30min); Armidale (2 daily; 8hr 30min); Batemans Bay (3 daily; 5hr 20min); Bathurst (2–3 daily; 4hr); Bega (2–3 daily; 8hr); Bowral (5 weekly; 2hr 35min); Brisbane (8–12 daily; 15–17hr, with connections to Cairns and Darwin); Broken Hill (2–3 daily; 15hr 30min); Byron Bay (8 daily; 12hr 30min); Canberra (3 daily; 4hr); Cessnock (1 daily; 2hr 20min); Coffs Harbour (8 daily; 8hr 30min); Eden (4 daily; 8hr 30min–9hr 30min); Forster (1 daily; 5hr 30min); Glen Innes (2 daily; 10hr); Grafton (2 daily; 10hr); Melbourne (5 daily; 12–18hr); Mildura (2–3 daily; 16hr); Mittagong (5 weekly; 2hr 30min); Moss Vale (5 weekly; 2hr 45min); Muswellbrook (1 daily; 3hr 30min); Narooma (4 weekly; 8hr); Newcastle (8 daily; 3hr); Nowra (3 daily; 3hr–4hr 20min); Orange (1 daily; 4hr 15min); Perth (2–3 daily; 52–56hr); Port Macquarie (8 daily; 7hr); Port Stephens (1 daily; 4hr); Scone (1 daily; 3hr 50min); Tamworth (2 daily; 7hr); Taree (5 daily; 6hr); Tenterfield (2 daily; 11hr 30min).

Flights

Sydney to: Adelaide (20 daily; 2hr 30min); Albury (4–6 daily; 1hr 20min); Alice Springs (4 daily; 2hr 40min); Armidale (4–8 daily; 1hr 10min); Ballina (1–7 daily; 1hr 35min); Bathurst (2–4 daily; 40min); Brisbane (20 daily; 1hr 15min); Broken Hill (6 weekly; 2hr 30min); Cairns (15 daily; 2hr 40min); Canberra (15–20 daily; 1hr 20min); Coffs Harbour (4–6 daily; 1hr 15min); Cooma (1–2 daily; 1hr); Darwin (3 daily; 4hr); Dubbo (4–7 daily; 1hr); Glen Innes (1–3 daily; 1hr 25min); Grafton (4–6 daily; 1hr 45min); Griffith (3–4 daily; 1hr 40min); Hobart (8 daily; 1hr 30min); Inverell (1–3 daily; 2hr 15min); Lismore (2–3 daily; 1hr 35min); Lord Howe Island (6 weekly; 2hr 20min); Melbourne (20 daily; 1hr 10min); Mudgee (2–3 daily; 1hr); Newcastle (Mon–Fri 4 daily; 40min); Orange (3–4 daily; 45min); Parkes (1–4 daily; 1hr); Perth (10 daily; 4hr); Port Macquarie (3–4 daily; 1hr 25min); Port Stephens (Mon–Fri 1 daily; 1hr); Tamworth (4–6 daily; 1hr); Taree (3–4 daily; 1hr); Uluru (2 daily; 3hr); Wagga Wagga (2–4 daily; 1hr 5min).

New South Wales and ACT

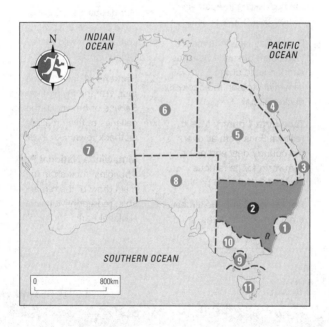

CHAPTER 2

Highlights

* **New Parliament House, Canberra** The angular contours of the New Parliament House show contemporary Australian design at its best. See p.260

* **Snowy Mountains** Fine bushwalking in summer, and the best skiing in Australia in winter. See p.274

* **Byron Bay** New Age mecca with 30km of sandy beaches and fantastic diving – an essential stop on the backpacker circuit. See p.313

* **Tamworth Country Music festival** Fans from all over the country descend on Tamworth for its famous annual festival. See p.330

* **Bald Rock** Climb the largest granite monolith in the world for unbeatable views. See p.336

* **Warrumbungle National Park** The rugged Warrumbungle National Park is especially beautiful in spring, when the wild flowers are in bloom. See p.347

* **Gunnedah** You stand a good chance of spotting koalas in the wild at Gunnedah. See p.348

* **Broken Hill** Take a mine tour, visit the Flying Doctors Service or browse in the art galleries of this gracious Outback town. See p.368

* **Mutawintje National Park** Aboriginal rock art is the main draw of the remarkable, red-earth Mutawintje National Park. See p.379

New South Wales and ACT

New South Wales is Australia's premier state in more ways than one: it's not only the oldest of the five states, but it's the most densely populated too. Including Sydney, New South Wales covers an area about twice the size of Britain, with roughly a tenth of its population; not a very big state by antipodean standards, but its six and a quarter million residents constitute one-third of the country's population. Their distribution is wildly uneven: few live in the Outback or the rural regions, and the vast majority are absorbed by the urban and suburban sprawl on the coast. The state's Aboriginal population is about forty thousand, approximately one-fifth of the total living in Australia. This chapter also covers the Australian Capital Territory (ACT), which was carved out of New South Wales at the beginning of the twentieth century as an independent base for the new national capital, Canberra.

When Lieutenant James Cook claimed New South Wales for Great Britain in 1770, naming it after a land that he'd apparently never visited – and to which it bears strikingly little resemblance – he could have hardly foreseen what would become of it. And indeed the early years, of penal settlement and timid encroachment into the fringes of the coastal area around Sydney, were not a promising start. But with the discovery of a passage through the Blue Mountains in 1813 (see p.223), the rolling plains of the west were opened up. Free (non-convict) settlers – **squatters** – appropriated vast areas of this rich pastureland, making immense fortunes off the backs of sheep. When **gold** was discovered near Bathurst in 1851, and the first goldrush began, New South Wales' fortunes were assured. Although penal transport ceased the following year, the population continued to increase rapidly and the economy boomed as fortune-seekers arrived in droves. At much the same time, Victoria broke off to form a separate colony, followed by Queensland in 1859. The much-reduced borders that New South Wales has today were defined in 1863.

There are over a thousand kilometres of **Pacific coastline** in New South Wales, from subtropical **Tweed Heads** in the north to temperate **Eden** in the south. The year-round mild climate, together with the ocean and the **beaches**, draws visitors pretty much all the time – though it's the summer holiday season that brings thousands of Australians to the coast to enjoy the extensive surf

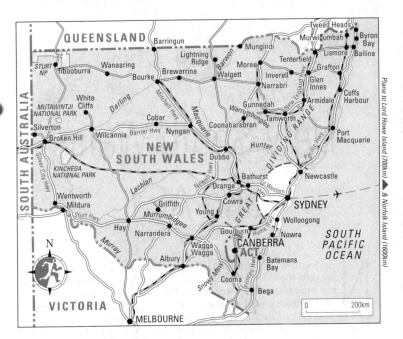

beaches and the numerous more sheltered waters, in bays, river mouths and inlets, and in a series of salt lagoons or "coastal lakes", protected behind a narrow spit from the force of the ocean waves. **South of Sydney** the coast is relatively undeveloped, and there's a string of low-key family resorts and fishing ports, great for water sports and fishing. To the **north** the climate gradually becomes warmer, and the coastline more popular – the series of big resorts up here includes **Port Macquarie** and **Coffs Harbour**, but there are also less-developed places where you can escape it all. One of the most enjoyable beach resorts in Australia is **Byron Bay**, which is just about managing to retain its slightly offbeat, alternative appeal, radiating from the still-thriving hippie communes of the lush, hilly **North Coast Hinterland**.

The **Great Dividing Range** runs parallel to the coastline – often very close – splitting the state in two. In the north, the gentle **New England** stretch of the range comprises tablelands ideal for sheep- and cattle-farming; where this plateau falls away steeply towards the coast are some of the few remaining pockets of dense – at times impenetrable – primeval **forest**: the Big Scrub that drove the early settlers to despair. To the south is the Australian Capital Territory where **Canberra**, the nation's capital and a city struggling to shed its dull image, is the gateway to the **Snowy Mountains**. Here the range builds to a crescendo as **Mount Kosciuszko** (Australia's highest at 2228m) marks the peak of the Australian Alps. In winter there's skiing here, but the mountains are perhaps even better in summer, when the national park that covers most of them offers some unbeatable hiking. Unsurprisingly, it's not so warm up in the mountains of the Great Dividing Range: in summer the cooler days and the drop in temperature at night offer a welcome respite from the coastal heat and humidity. In winter, however, it can be genuinely freezing, with snow even falling near the Queensland border in Tenterfield.

West of the range, rich agricultural country gradually fades into desert-like **Outback** regions where the mercury can climb well above the 40°C mark in summer, while mild winter days are followed by very cold, frosty nights. West of Canberra, between the three rivers of the Murrumbidgee, the Darling and the Murray (the last dividing New South Wales from Victoria), is the fertile **Riverina**. Beyond New England, the flat, black-soiled plains of the **northwest** head through cotton country to the opal-mining town of **Lightning Ridge**. It's a uniquely Australian experience to leave Sydney, cross the extraordinarily scenic Blue Mountains and be gradually sucked into this vast emptiness, where the "**back o' Bourke**" is synonymous with the Outback. The mining settlement of **Broken Hill**, almost at the South Australian border, is the obvious destination, a gracious city surrounded by the desert landscape of *Mad Max* and home to the classic Outback institutions of the School of the Air and the Flying Doctor Service.

We've also included in this chapter the Pacific islands far off the north coast of New South Wales: subtropical **Lord Howe Island**, 700km northeast of Sydney and roughly parallel to Port Macquarie, and **Norfolk Island**, 900km further northeast and actually closer to New Zealand, inhabited by the descendants of the mutiny on the *Bounty*.

New South Wales still has a fairly extensive **rail** network, although Countrylink (Ⓦ www.countrylink.info), as it's called, has replaced many services with buses. A one-month Backtracker pass ($198) will get you just about anywhere in the state on this system (call Ⓣ 13 22 32 for reservations).

Parks and wildlife

Throughout the state there are magnificent **national parks** and wilderness areas. Before European settlement, the **northeastern** corner of New South Wales was covered by dense subtropical rainforest. It's this that you can visit along the escarpment of the Great Dividing Range, though often only the very edge of these national parks or forests can be reached by road or track, while the interior is accessible only to hardy bushwalkers. These forests are inhabited by many types of parrots and, occasionally, by bell birds and bower birds, brush turkeys, and marsupials such as ringtail possums, bandicoots and padimelons. **Further south**, the slightly higher altitudes and the plateaus are dominated by eucalypt forest with a more open canopy, and by less-dense eucalypt woodland – the preferred habitat of wombats, wallabies, other types of possum, koalas and a few small marsupials, as well as echidnas and platypuses, kookaburras, magpies and parrots. The **Snowy Mountains** are covered by snow gums, a slow-growing, cold-resistant eucalypt and in the summer clusters of delicate wild flowers cover the mountain hillsides and meadows. Where the forest is not protected, lumber is still big business in New South Wales, and is the source of fierce clashes between environmentalists and the towns that make their living from the timber trade. To the **west**, kangaroos, wallabies and emus roam the wide plains, and with a bit of luck a wedge-tailed eagle can be sighted. Parks here tend to encompass vast areas of desert or places marked out by extraordinary geological formations. The far southwest corner is part of the **Mallee** – a sandy, semi-arid area covered by the eucalypt shrubs that lend the area its name. Here the mallee fowl build the incubation mounds for their eggs in the sand.

The **National Parks and Wildlife Service** (NPWS) has **entrance fees** to many of its parks – usually $6–15 per car and $4 for motorcyles (often on an honour system when there is no ranger station). If you intend to go bush often in New South Wales you can buy an **annual pass** for $60 ($30 for motorbikes), which includes all parks except Kosciuszko. Because of its popularity as a skiing destination, entrance to Kosciuszko is a steep $15 per car per day, perversely levied in summer too – so if you plan on spending any length of time here, or are going to visit other parks as well, consider the $80 annual pass which covers entry to all parks, including Kosciuszko. Passes can be bought in person at NPWS offices and some park entry stations, over the phone using a credit card (☎02/9253 4600 or 1300 361 967) or online (Ⓦwww.npws.nsw .gov.au); you can also download an order form from the website and send it (include your vehicle type and its registration number) by fax (Ⓕ02/9251 9192) or by mail to the National Parks Centre, PO Box N429, Grosvenor Place, NSW 1220.

You can **camp** in most national parks. Bushcamping is generally free, but where there is a ranger station and a designated campsite with facilities, fees are charged, usually around $6 per site. If the amenities are of a high standard, including hot showers and the like, or if the spot is just plain popular, fees can be as high as $18 per tent. Open fires are banned in most parks and forbidden everywhere on days when there is high danger of fire, and while there are often electric or gas barbecues in picnic areas, you'll need a fuel stove for bush camping.

Australian Capital Territory

In the 1820s the first European squatters settled in the valleys and plains north of the Snowy Mountains and established family dynasties on their prosperous grazing properties. Until 1900, however, this remained a remote rural area. When the Australian colonies united in the **Commonwealth of Australia** in 1901, a capital city had to be chosen, with Melbourne and Sydney the two obvious and eager rivals. After much wrangling, and partly in order to avoid having to decide on one of the two, it was agreed to establish a brand-new capital instead: Melbourne was to be the seat of the provisional government until the new capital was completed and the government departments had moved there. A provision in the Constitution Act decreed that the seat of government was to be in the state of New South Wales and not less than one hundred miles from Sydney. In 1909 Limestone Plains, a plain south of Yass surrounded by mountain ranges, was chosen out of several possible sites as the future seat of the Australian government. An area of 2368 square kilometres was excised from the state of New South Wales and named the **Australian Capital Territory** (ACT). The ACT officially included an adjunct at Jervis Bay (see p.281), on the coast south of Nowra, to give Australia's capital its own access to the sea and a naval base. The name for the future capital was supposedly taken from the language of local Aborigines: **Canberra** – the meeting place.

Canberra is situated on a high plain (600m above sea level) and, unlike the coastal cities, experiences four distinct **seasons**. In summer, the average temperatures are 27°C maximum during the day and 12°C minimum at night; in winter they drop from an average of 12°C maximum during the day to freezing point (and below) at night. Spring and autumn can be really delightful, though. The mountain ranges to the west and south of the city rise up to 1900m and are snow-covered in winter.

Canberra

In 1912 Walter Burley Griffin, an American landscape architect from Chicago, won the international competition for the design of the future Australian capital: his plan envisaged a garden city for about 25,000 people, which took into account the natural features of the landscape. There were to be five main centres, each with separate city functions, located on three axes: land, water and municipal. Roads were to be in concentric circles, with arcs linking the radiating design. Construction started in 1913, but political squabbling and the effects of World War I prevented any real progress being made. Little building had been done, in fact, by the time Griffin left the site in 1920, and only in 1927 was the provisional parliament building officially opened. By 1930 some one thousand families had settled in the capital. Then the Depression set in, World War II broke out and development slowed again. After more years of stagnation, the National Capital Development Commission (NCDC) was finally established in 1958, and at last growth began in earnest.

In 1963 the Molonglo River was dammed to form a lake 11km wide, the artificial **Lake Burley Griffin** that is the centrepiece of modern **CAN-BERRA**. Numerous open spaces and public buildings came into existence, as a real city started to emerge. Slowly, the **Civic Centre** near London Circuit began to live up to its name. The **population** grew rapidly, from fifteen thousand in 1947 to over one hundred thousand in 1967; today, it is more than three hundred thousand. This population growth has been accommodated in satellite towns with their own centres: **Woden**, 12km south of the Civic Centre, was built in the mid-1960s; five years later **Belconnen** was added in the northwest; and in the mid-1970s **Tuggeranong** in the south. It was this sprawl that fostered Canberra's image as "a cluster of suburbs in search of a centre".

Inevitably, modern Canberra is mainly a city of civil servants and administrators. There are plenty of service industries – especially ones aimed at feeding and watering all those politicians and visitors – but little real industrial activity. Canberra gained self-government in 1989, with only the Parliamentary Triangle – the area bounded by Commonwealth Avenue, Kings Avenue and Lake Burley Griffin – remaining under federal control; the self-financing responsibilities that this entails have placed a premium on tourism revenues. And indeed, the main reason to come to Canberra is for the **national museums and institutions** you can visit – top of the list is the **National Gallery**, and the stunning **New Parliament House**, opened in 1988 and certainly one of the principal tourist sights, with its original architecture intended to blend into the landscape. Canberra is also trying very hard to present an image to counter its reputation as the domain of dull bureaucrats. It hasn't succeeded yet: most Australians still regard Canberra as "pollie city" – a frosty, boring place where politicians and public servants live it up at the expense of the hard-done-by Australian taxpayer. They also complain about its concentric circular streets, which can make driving here seem like a Kafkaesque nightmare, and about the contrived, neat-as-a-pin nature of the place.

But the image-makers have a point, and Canberra is a far more pleasant place than it's usually given credit for. The city has wide open spaces and many **parks** and gardens, with the impressive architecture housing the national institutions set in astonishingly well-groomed surroundings, so that you can pad barefoot through the grass from the National Gallery to the National Library, peacefully admiring the gum trees. Right on its doorstep are forests and **bushland**, with unspoilt wilderness just a bit further afield in the Brindabella Ranges and the

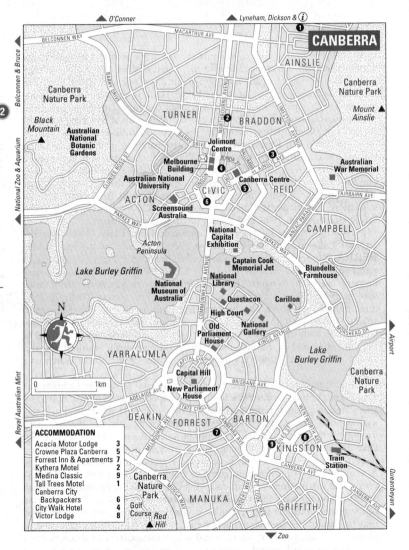

▲ O'Conner   ▲ Lyneham, Dickson & ⓘ

CANBERRA

BELCONNEN WAY   MACARTHUR AVE

Belconnen & Bruce

National Zoo & Aquarium

Canberra
Nature Park

Black
Mountain

Australian
National
Botanic
Gardens

AINSLIE

Canberra
Nature Park

Mount ▲
Ainslie

TURNER

BRADDON

Jolimont
Centre

Melbourne
Building

Australian National
University

ACTON

Screensound
Australia

Canberra Centre

CIVIC

REID

Australian
War Memorial

FAIRBAIRN AVE

CAMPBELL

National
Capital
Exhibition

Acton
Peninsula

Lake Burley Griffin

Captain Cook
Memorial Jet

National
Library

National
Museum of
Australia

Questacon

High Court

Old
Parliament
House

National
Gallery

Blundells
Farmhouse

Carillon

N

YARRALUMLA

Capital Hill

New Parliament
House

Lake
Burley Griffin

Canberra
Nature
Park

Airport

0   1km

DEAKIN

FORREST

BARTON

Royal Australian Mint

Queanbeyan

ACCOMMODATION

Acacia Motor Lodge	3
Crowne Plaza Canberra	5
Forrest Inn & Apartments	7
Kythera Motel	2
Medina Classic	9
Tall Trees Motel	1
Canberra City Backpackers	6
City Walk Hotel	4
Victor Lodge	8

KINGSTON

Train
Station

Canberra
Nature Park

Golf
Course   Red
▲ Hill

MANUKA

GRIFFITH

▼ Zoo

Namadgi National Park; skiing in the Snowy Mountains or surfing on the coast are only a few hours away. Sadly, in late 2002, this natural bush setting, combined with extreme drought conditions, precipitated Canberra's worst **bushfires** for fifty years. The area to the west of the city was hardest hit. Mount Stromlo Observatory was completely gutted and in all over five hundred homes were destroyed and four residents were left dead. Remarkably, though the CBD was covered in a pall of smoke for several weeks, none of its buildings was damaged by the fires.

Canberra's **nightlife** is also a great deal better than you might expect considering its reputation, in term time at least: the two universities here (and the Duntroon Military Academy for officer material) mean there's a large and lively **student population** (good news for those who have student cards, as most attractions offer hefty discounts). The city is said to have more **restaurants** per capita than any other in Australia – which is saying something – and there are plenty of pubs and nightclubs to choose from, too. Many of them, though, are tucked away in hidden corners of the city or in the satellite towns. Surprisingly perhaps, Canberra also holds the dubious title of Australia's **porn** capital, due to its liberal licensing laws, which legalize and regulate the sex industry.

Arrival and information

Canberra's **airport**, about 7km east of the city, handles domestic flights only. Bus #80 runs on weekdays between the airport and the city centre, otherwise expect to pay around $15 for a taxi. The main **train station** is located southeast of the centre, on Wentworth Avenue in Kingston, and from here taxis are again the easiest way to get where you're going; trains also stop at the suburb of Queanbeyan, in New South Wales, where there's some cheap accommodation. Most interstate **buses** drop and pick up at the handy **Jolimont Centre**, downtown at 65–67 Northbourne Ave; the modern centre has showers, lockers (free if you can find one that works), a TV room, snack bar, post office, Internet kiosk and a travel bookshop, which also offers everything from Australia-wide tours to Canberra city bus tickets, as well as some tourist information and maps. Additionally, the centre has ticket offices for the train, airline and bus companies. There is a free direct telephone line to the tourist office (see below), to taxi companies and to accommodation.

The **Canberra Visitor Information Centre**, the main tourist office, is inconveniently located about 2km north of the centre, at 330 Northbourne Avenue in Dickson (Mon–Fri 9am–5.30pm, Sat & Sun 9am–4pm; ☎02/6205 0044 or 1800 026 166, ⓦwww.canberratourism.com.au), reached by bus #380; it books tours, transport and accommodation. More central is the **tourist information booth** on the ground floor of the Canberra Centre, a shopping mall on Bunda Street (Mon–Thurs & Sat 9am–5.30pm, Fri 9am–7.30pm, Sun 10am–4pm); it provides maps and information but doesn't make bookings.

City transport

To appreciate the city, you ideally need a vehicle of some kind – things are very spread out, and at the weekend especially (when many residents leave and the city is quite dead) public transport is extremely limited. You'll find that the dispersed nature of Canberra means that you can easily park your car, often for free, at the main sights. Cycling is very popular and renting a bike – to take advantage of the excellent network of bike paths – is strongly recommended (see "Listings" on p.268). An alternative to your own transport is the tourist office's handy **hop-on-hop-off double-decker bus**, which does a circuit of the major sights and routes; buses depart from 9am until 5pm (every 40min) at the Melbourne Building on Northbourne Avenue. Your $25 ticket is valid for 24 hours, and includes obligatory running commentary from the driver; call ☎02/6282 2385, or see ⓦwww.city-sightseeing.com for further information. Note, however, that unless you are planning a relentless sightseeing spree, municipal route #34 actually covers many of the major tourist haunts for a fraction of the cost.

Municipal buses are run by Action. The **Off-Peak Daily**, purchased from the driver, offers enormous savings; it's valid for as many journeys as you like and costs $4.40 (valid Mon–Fri 9am–4.30pm after 6pm, Sat, Sun & public holidays all day). Other buses cover all of Canberra, including the satellite towns: for details, contact Action **timetable information** (☎13 17 10, ⓦwww.action.act.gov.au).

Most Action buses start at the City Bus Interchange, at East Row just across Northbourne Avenue from the Jolimont Centre; you can buy tickets at the Newslink shop behind stance 9, or at most other newsagents. For ticketing purposes, the city is divided into three zones: North, South and Central – most sights are situated within the central zone. Besides the day-trip ticket (valid for all zones), you can pay a single zone, flat-rate fare ($2.30) or a single, all-zone fare ($5.40), both of which can also be bought on board; a ten-journey Faresaver ticket costs $18.40 one zone ($36.80 all zones), or a weekly ticket costs $19.80 ($38).

For a bit of kitsch fun, check out the very popular Love Bus **tours of the adult entertainment industry**, which include the National Museum of Erotica (information and bookings on ☎02/6262 9266, ⓦwww.lovebus.com.au).

Accommodation

Staying in Canberra, on the whole, is not cheap, but most places are modern and clean. Location is problematic, as most accommodation is in the nearby suburbs rather than the centre. One of the best locations is **Kingston**, a salubrious, café-filled suburb close to the train station, and also within walking distance of the Parliamentary Triangle attractions. **Hotels** and **motels** rarely charge less than $65 for a double, although guesthouses often have more reasonable rates. Canberra has a couple of excellent, modern **youth hostels**, and out-of-term inexpensive B&B is available in several student halls of residence.

Hotels, motels and guesthouses

Acacia Motor Lodge 65 Ainslie Ave, Braddon ☎02/6249 6955, ⓦwww.acaciamotorlodge.com. Very central motel in a leafy street near the war memorial. A light breakfast is included. Bus #33 or #38. ❹

Blue & White Lodge 524 Northbourne Ave, Downer, 5km north of the city ☎02/6248 0498, ✉blueandwhitelodge@bigpond.com. Newly refurbished B&B with well-equipped, en-suite rooms – TV, fridge, heating, air-con and tea-making facilities. Cooked breakfast included. Bus #39 or #50. ❺

Crowne Plaza Canberra 1 Binara St, Civic ☎02/6247 8999, ⓦwww.crowneplaza.com. Central, four-star hotel with all the conveniences you'd expect, including room service, swimming pool, sauna and gym. ❼

Forrest Inn and Apartments 30 National Circuit, Forrest ☎02/6295 3433, ⓦwww.forrestinn.com.au. Modern motel in the embassy area next to the pretty Serbian church offering air-con units. Bus #35 or #36. ❹

Kythera Motel 98–100 Northbourne Ave, Braddon ☎02/6248 7611, ⓦwww.kythera.com.au. Well-equipped rooms with heating and air-con, and a

swimming pool to cool off even further. Bus #33 or #72. ❸

Medina Classic 11 Giles St, Kingston ☎02/6239 8100, ⓦwww.medinaapartments.com.au. Upmarket one-, two- or three-bedroom, self-catering serviced apartments with fully equipped kitchens (except for a couple of smaller apartments), popular with families. Facilities include reception, swimming pool, spa, gym and undercover parking; bike rental available. Bus #39 or #84. ❼

Parkview Lodge 526 Northbourne Ave, Downer, 5km north ☎02/6249 8038, ⓦwww.mirandalodge.com.au. A recommended nonsmoking B&B near Southall Park; rooms with TV, fridge, heating and tea-making facilities, all en suite and some with whirlpool. Bus #39 or #50. ❹

Tall Trees Motel 21 Stephen St, Ainslie ☎02/6247 9200, ⓦwww.bestwestern.com.au. Pleasant, upmarket motel in quiet shady grounds. Laundry. Bus #38. ❹

Hostels and college accommodation

ANU student accommodation ⓦwww.anu.edu.au. Bruce, Burton and Garran Halls ☎02/6267 4700, ℱ6267 4450. Fenner Hall

△ Lake Burley Griffin, Canberra

☎02/6295 0123, ⓕ6295 7871. Ursula College ☎02/6279 4300, ⓕ6279 4320. Located around the Australian National University campus in Acton, just west of the city centre; most rooms are singles, but there are also a few twins. Dorms $35.
Canberra City Backpackers 7 Akuna St, Civic ☎02/6229 0888, ⓕ6229 0777. With facilities that would put many a palace to shame, Canberra's latest and most central hostel heralds a new backpacking dawn. The megalith could be daunting to lone travellers, but boasts TV-chef kitchens, licensed bar, rooftop BBQ garden, laundry, Internet café, sauna, bike rental, cable TV, lockers in every room and 24hr check-in. Dorms $22, rooms ❸
Canberra YHA Hostel 191 Dryandra St, O'Connor ☎02/6248 9155, ⓔcanberra@yhansw.org.au. Canberra's YHA is a friendly, modern hostel with excellent facilities, situated about 4km out of town in a gorgeous bush setting. There's a small shop, Internet access and super-cheap bike rental; rates include linen. The congenial staff at reception (7am–10pm) run regular minibus pick-ups from town (call beforehand); otherwise it's a ten-minute trip on bus #35. Dorms $19, rooms ❸
City Walk Hotel 2 Mort St, City ☎02/6257 0124, ⓦwww.citywalkhotel.citysearch.com.au. Just across the road from the bus station, this passable establishment is clean and relatively safe. Its biggest draws are location and the excellent Irish bar downstairs; guests often get discounted beer. Facilities include kitchen, Internet access and a common room with TV. Dorms $22, rooms ❸

Victor Lodge 29 Dawes St, Kingston, 4km southwest ☎02/6295 7777, ⓦwww.victorlodge.com.au. A small, friendly, very popular family-run hostel/guesthouse, situated in a lovely area. Clean, bright rooms with heating, washbasin, and desks in the singles; rates include linen and duvets. There's also a well-equipped kitchen and outside BBQ area, laundry, TV room with Internet station and the opportunity to soak in a long, hot bath. Very reasonable bike rental; city pick-ups and drop-offs. Bus #39, #80 or #84. Dorms $23, rooms ❸

Camping and caravan parks

Canberra Carotel Motel and Caravan Park Federal Highway, Watson, 6km north ☎02/6241 1377, ⓦwww.carotel.com.au. Park with a swimming pool and café. Campsites and holiday apartments (for up to six people). Bus #36. On-site vans ❷, cabins ❸
Crestview Tourist Park 81 Donald Rd, Queanbeyan, 14km east ☎02/6297 2443, ⓦwww.crestview.contact.com.au. Facilities include a swimming pool and shop. Camping space, plus cabins. ❷
White Ibis Tourist Village and Caravan Park 47 Bidges Rd, off the Federal Highway, Sutton, 12km north ☎02/6230 3433, ⓦwww.sydneycaravanparks.com.au. Good site with pool, tennis court and kiosk selling the essentials. Cabins ❹

The City

Strictly planned as it is, Canberra is a straightforward place to find your way around – though distances are such that only in the very centre will you want to do much walking, and even there it can be something of a test of fitness. The eleven-kilometre-wide **Lake Burley Griffin** pretty much marks the heart of the city, with several lakeside places of interest both north and south, including the **National Museum of Australia** right on the lake on the Acton peninsula. North of the lake is the city centre proper, the **Civic Centre**, or "Civic" for short, which houses shops, restaurants, cafés, pubs, cinemas and theatres, as well as the GPO. Like many Australian cities, drug use is on the increase in Canberra, and Civic can get a little dangerous at night. The campus of the **Australian National University** (ANU) is just to the west of the centre in the suburb of Acton, as is **Screensound Australia**, the old National Film and Sound Archive. Beyond Acton, the **National Botanic Gardens** sit at the flanks of the 806-metre **Black Mountain**, topped by the distinctive Telstra Tower and just one of many scattered sections of the **Canberra Nature Park**. East of the centre is the **Australian War Memorial**, solemnly gazing back along monument-lined **Anzac Parade** to the **Parliamentary Triangle**, south of the lake, with the old Parliament House overlooked by the New Parliament House on Capital Hill. This political quarter, linked to the city centre by the **Commonwealth Avenue Bridge**, is where you'll find the government offices and national cultural institutions, and is the part of Canberra that is of most architectural interest. Fronting the lake, strung along King Edward Terrace, are four impressive modern public buildings: the **National Library**, **Questacon** (the National Science and Technology Centre), the **National Gallery** and the **High Court**. Most of the foreign embassies – intended to resemble the vernacular architecture of their home countries – cluster around Yarralumla and Forrest.

Questacon and the National Library

Crossing the Commonwealth Avenue Bridge from the city centre, you turn left onto King Edward Terrace. Immediately before you is **Questacon** – the National Science and Technology Centre (daily 9am–5pm; $10; ⓦ www .questacon.edu.au), a "hands-on" museum opened in 1988 as a joint Australian/Japanese bicentennial project. The centre's six galleries are arranged around a 27-metre-high drum at the core of the building, and are linked by a continuous spiral walkway. There are some free interactive exhibits in the foyer if you just want a taste, but it's a good place to keep children occupied.

Looming behind the science centre is one of the country's most important institutions, the **National Library** (Mon–Thurs 9am–9pm, Fri & Sat 9am–5pm, Sun 1.30–5pm; ⓦ www.nla.gov.au), whose Reading Room has a comprehensive selection of overseas newspapers and magazines. There are also exhibitions of rare books in the foyer, and usually some kind of interesting temporary display, including a selection from the pictorial collection comprising about forty thousand items; you can view any of those not on display via an interactive touch-screen system in the foyer. The library's *Brindabella Bistro* is a good place to stop for a cappuccino and a snack – it's open until half an hour before the library closes.

The High Court of Australia

From the library, it's a pleasant walk about 500m east along lakefront Parkes Place to the **High Court of Australia** (daily 9.45am–4.30pm; free), the highest authority in the Australian judicial system, set in an appropriately grandiose, glass-fronted edifice with a stylized waterfall running alongside the walkway up to the entrance. Its functions are to uphold and interpret the constitution and to hear cases referred from the lower courts, which involves delivering about seventy judgments a year. Visitors can watch a short video that explains the court's function and examines two of its landmark cases: its 1983 ruling that saved Tasmania's wild Franklin River from damming as part of a hydroelectric scheme; and its finding on the 1992 land rights case Mabo versus Queensland – a momentous decision that overturned the British legal concept of *terra nullius* whereby Australia was considered uninhabited prior to white settlement in 1788. The Great Hall and three courtrooms are also worth looking at – and there's a licensed café upstairs.

The National Gallery

One of the major attractions in Canberra is the **National Gallery** (daily 10am–5pm; free; ⓦ www.nga.gov.au), situated on Parkes Place immediately east of the High Court, to which it is linked by a footbridge. Occupying twelve galleries spread over three floors, the collection explores the art of Africa and the Americas, Asia and Europe from ancient to modern (with a fairly good collection of modern European and North American art, including works by Monet, de Chirico, Magritte and Tanguy), but the core of the national collection is Australian. There are also regular special exhibitions and international touring shows (admission charge).

For most visitors, the highlight is the **Art of Aboriginal Australia and Torres Strait Islands** gallery on the entrance level; the collection is extensive and every six months a new display is mounted, ranging from traditional bark paintings from the Northern Territory to politically aware contemporary work in different media. On permanent display is the **Aboriginal Memorial 1988**, which pays homage to the Aboriginal people who since 1788 have lost life, land and culture; the memorial comprises two hundred termite-hollowed logs representative of the culture's log coffins, painted with totemic designs by over forty artists from around Ramingining in Central Arnhemland.

On the upper level, the **Australian Art** gallery explores the country's visual arts, from colonial to contemporary. Most striking are the 25 bushranger paintings in Sidney Nolan's celebrated *Ned Kelly* series, painted in the 1940s. Other works on permanent display include Russell Drysdale's *The Drover's Wife* (1945), probably his best-known painting and American artist Jackson Pollack's *Blue Poles* (1950). The National Gallery's most valuable foreign work of art, *Blue Poles* was bought by the Labor government in 1973 for A\$1.3 million. It has been loaned to MoMA in New York to feature in a Pollack retrospective as one of the artist's most significant works and despite recent offers touching \$70 million, the painting is resolutely not for sale. These works are probably the only permanent features of an ever-changing "permanent" collection, only three percent of which is on show at any one time.

Outside is a living fern-tree sculpture by Australian artist Fiona Hall, and a **Sculpture Garden** overlooking Lake Burley Griffin. Also visible and audible from here is the **Carillon** stranded on Aspen Island, whose three bell towers with 53 bronze bells were a gift from the British government to mark Canberra's fiftieth birthday. It's pleasant to sit on the lawns under a shady tree by the lake and listen to the recitals (Tues & Thurs 12.45–1.35pm, Sat, Sun & public holidays 2.45–3.35pm). On summer evenings, concerts and other events, such as open-air film screenings, sometimes take place here to coincide with special exhibitions (ask at the tourist office for details).

The Old and New Parliament houses

Away from the lake, on King George Terrace at the foot of Capital Hill, is the **Old Parliament House** (daily 9am–5pm; \$2; ⓦ www.oldparliamenthouse .gov.au), whose grounds became the site of a live-in Aboriginal protest for land rights (dubbed the **Tent Embassy**) for over six months in 1972. Twenty years later a second tent embassy was erected, to protest the fact that Aboriginal land rights had still not been achieved, and it remains there still, flying the Aboriginal flag.

The simple white Neoclassical building was the seat of government from 1927 until 1988, but it was only ever meant to be a provisional parliament house for fifty years; a **tour** of the "wedding cake" – either before or after seeing the New Parliament House to allow comparisions – provides a fascinating insight into how crowded and inconvenient the building actually was. Presently, the **National Portrait Gallery** (ⓦ www.portrait.gov.au) uses the building for exhibitions, making it something of a treasure trove to visit. Outside, you can wander in the **Senate Rose Garden** or visit the National Archives of Australia on Queen Victoria Terrace, which has socio-historical exhibitions (daily 9am–4pm; free).

Merging onto Capital Hill itself is the **New Parliament House**, with its grass-covered contours (daily 9am–5pm; free; ⓦ www.aph.gov.au). The stunning angular design of the exterior, topped by a sputnik-like flagpole, is matched by the interior, which represents the best in Australian art and design. You can wander about inside unattended but the excellent guided tours are recommended, helping you to come to grips with the amount of work that went into a building which employs three people just to change the lightbulbs. The first-floor theatre screens hourly films about the construction of the building, including interviews with architects and artisans. There's an excellent café (daily 10am–4.30pm) with an outdoor area with views across to Old Parliament House.

An **international competition** for a new Parliament House was launched in 1980, the brief being to create a building true to Walter Burley Griffin's vision of a city nestling in the natural folds of the land. The resulting building (opened in May 1988) was the startling design of Romaldo Giurgola, an American-based Italian architect. Visitors and locals are generally impressed, but the unnecessarily large edifice still causes many an Aussie cheek to burn, not least that of former president Malcolm Fraser, who in 1997 described the building as "an unmitigated disaster" and "my one very serious political mistake". Whatever your views on the architecture and scope of the thing, you're free to walk over, loll on, and even roll down the grassy ramps covering the building. Outside the ground-floor entrance level is a **mosaic** by the Aboriginal artist Michael Tjakamarra Nelson – a piece that conveys the idea of a sacred meeting place. Inside, the impressive **foyer** is dominated by grand marble staircases and over forty columns clad in grey-green and rose-pink marble, representing a eucalypt forest; all the marble in the foyer is sourced from Europe, itself meant to symbolize the pioneering spirit of the early European settlements. The floors are made of native woods, and the walls feature marquetry panels detailing native plants.

Beyond the foyer, the **Great Hall** is dominated by a vast twenty-metre-high tapestry based on a painting of the same dimensions by **Arthur Boyd**; in a richly symbolic landscape, the opposing forces of life and death meet in blackened trees set against a powerful sky. Other chambers are adorned with paintings by artists such as Albert Tucker, Sidney Nolan and Ian Fairweather, as well as portraits of political figures, photographs and ceramics. Important documents in the country's political history are also on display, as is an exhibition on Federation and a display outlining the Australian political system.

When Parliament is in session – usually from seventy to eighty days a year – you can sit in the public gallery and watch the proceedings in the House of Representatives (the lower chamber of Parliament) or the Senate (the upper chamber of the legislature); **Question Time** in both chambers starts at 2pm, with the House of Representatives making for better (and therefore more popular) viewing; to guarantee a seat, book in advance on ☎02/6277 4889.

The diplomatic quarters and the mint

After visiting the New Parliament House, a trip among the upmarket suburban homes in Canberra's diplomatic quarters – **Yarralumla** and **Forrest** – completes the political sightseeing tour. The consuls and high commissions were asked to construct buildings that deployed the typical architecture of the countries they represent. The result is an international compendium of architectural styles. Some of the eye-catching national designs worth looking out for include the American Embassy's plantation-style mansion, and the embassies of Thailand, Indonesia (with a small cultural centre), the People's Republic of China and Papua New Guinea.

At the **Royal Australian Mint**, a few kilometres to the southwest on Denison Street, Deakin (Mon–Fri 9am–4pm, Sat, Sun & public holidays 10am–4pm; free), you can watch money being "made" on weekdays and acquire a few items for your coin collection at the Collectors' Shop.

Lake Burley Griffin

Back across the Commonwealth Avenue Bridge, the northern shores of Lake Burley Griffin have plenty to offer. At the far western end of the lake, by the Scrivener Dam on Lady Denman Drive, is the **National Zoo and Aquarium** (daily 9am–5pm; $10; ⓦ www.zooquarium.com.au). Visitors walk through tunnels of acrylic glass while sharks, stingrays and other creatures glide past, only an arm's-length away; outside there's a bear park, a monkey island, and kangaroos, emus and dingoes.

On the Acton Peninsula, the prime lakefront site of the old Royal Canberra Hospital is now home to the **National Museum of Australia** (daily 9am–5pm; free; ⓦ www.nma.gov.au). The $100 million museum finally opened in March 2001 – 25 years after it was first proposed – to coincide with celebrations for the centenary of the Federation. Melbourne architectural firm Ashton Raggat McDougall won the competion to design the building, given the brief that it was to be "anti-monumental". The controversial result, a postmodern riot of differing colours, building materials and quirky features such as the orange metal structure looping above, is considered vibrant and playful by some, mediocre and crass by others. The exhibitions, which range over five permanent galleries (plus an outdoor section and three temporary exhibition halls), offer an interesting look at what it means to be Australian, warts and all, with the claim from some quarters that white Australia has been trivialized and Australian kitsch celebrated: the **Nation: Symbols of Australia gallery** features Victa lawnmowers and Hills Hoists (revolving clothes lines), while the bleak symbolism of an arid, treeless country is presented in the concrete **Garden of Australian Dreams**. There has been discomfort, too, at the **First Australians gallery**, which goes beyond boomerangs and canoes to tell the story of the "massacre" of Aboriginal people, the reserve system, black deaths in custody, and the "stolen generations". In the **Eternity gallery**, the inclusion of an outfit worn by baby Azaria Chamberlain has been considered bad taste by some, though without doubt her disappearance at Ayers Rock in the 1980s and the subsequent miscarriage of justice suffered by her mother, Lindy, live deep in the national psyche. The **Tangled Destinies gallery**, focusing on the environment, explores the relationship between land and people in Australia, while the **Horizons gallery**, subtitled "The Peopling of Australia since 1788" looks at the nation's migrant history.

Just east of the Commonwealth Avenue Bridge, you'll pass the **National Capital Exhibition** at Regatta Point (daily 9am–5pm; free), comprising a small theatre, displays and models depicting Canberra's development from the cattle and sheep pastures of the nineteenth century to its modern incarnation as capital city. There's a great view from the terrace, though on windy days you have to beware of the spray from the **Captain Cook Memorial Jet** (10am–noon & 2–4pm, also 7–9pm during daylight saving), which spurts a column of water 140m into the air. The jet, built in 1970 to mark the bicentenary of Captain Cook's "discovery" of Australia, costs over $130 an hour to run – hence the limited operating times.

Further east is one of the few historic buildings in the city: **Blundells Cottage**, on Wendouree Drive in Kings Park (daily 11am–4pm; $2), serves as a reminder of the farming industry that flourished here before Canberra became the capital. Built in 1860, this simple farmhouse once housed workers from a sheep station, and has been preserved as a small museum.

The Australian War Memorial and Mount Ainslie

To the east of the city, the massive, domed building perched at the base of Mount Ainslie, at the far end of **Anzac Parade** (its length lined with smaller war memorials), is the **Australian War Memorial** (daily 10am–5pm, school public holidays from 9am; free; Ⓦ www.awm.gov.au). At the same time as commemorating the 102,000 Australian soldiers who lost their lives in seven wars in the last hundred years, most movingly in the Hall of Memory, this is also a military museum, depicting war through miniature battle dioramas and old aircraft. Although it's the most visited museum in Australia, with an average of about a million visitors a year – many of them motivated by patriotism – this mixture makes for slightly uneasy viewing: it's an unquestioningly heroic past

---

The Anzacs

Travelling around Australia you'll notice almost every town – large or small – has a war memorial dedicated to the memory of the Anzacs, the **Australia and New Zealand Army Corps**.

When war erupted in Europe in 1914, Australia was overwhelmed by a wave of pro-British sentiment. On August 5, 1914, one day after Great Britain had declared war against the German empire, the Australian prime minister summed up the feelings of his compatriots: "When the Empire is at war so Australia is at war." On November 1, 1914, a contingent of twenty thousand enthusiastic volunteers – the **Anzacs** – left from the port of Albany in Western Australia to assist the mother country in her struggle.

In Europe, Turkey had entered the war on the German side in October 1914. At the beginning of 1915, military planners in London (Winston Churchill prominent among them) came up with a plan to capture the strategically important Turkish peninsula of the Dardanelles with a surprise attack near **Gallipoli**, thus opening the way to the Black Sea. On April 25, 1915, sixteen thousand Australian soldiers landed at dawn in a small bay flanked by steep cliffs: by nightfall, two thousand men had died in a hail of Turkish bullets from above. The plan, whose one chance of success was surprise, had been signalled by troop and ship movements long in advance; by the time it was carried out, it was already doomed to failure. Nonetheless, Allied soldiers continued to lose their lives for another eight months without ever gaining more than a feeble foothold.

In December, London finally issued the order to withdraw. Eleven thousand Australians and New Zealanders had been killed, along with as many French and three times as many British troops. The Turks lost 86,000 men.

Official Australian historiography continues to mythologize the battle for Gallipoli, elevating it to the level of a national legend on which Australian identity is founded. From this point of view, in the war's baptism of fire, the Anzac soldiers proved themselves heroes who did the new nation proud, their loyalty and bravery evidence of how far Australia had developed. It was "the birth of a nation", and at the same time a loss of innocence, a national rite of passage – never again would Australians so unquestioningly involve themselves in foreign ventures.

Today the legend is as fiercely defended as ever, the focal point of Australian national pride, commemorated each year on April 25, **Anzac Day**. To outsiders, it may seem rather odd that a futile battle in someone else's interests occupies such a central place in the country's conscience, but the ceremony – akin to Britain's Remembrance Day and the USA's Veterans' Day – is a solemn occasion, when one is asked to reflect on the sacrifices made by those who fought in all wars.

that's constructed here, with the Anzac legend as its most illustrious episode. However, the museum does have some intriguing temporary exhibitions – past ones have looked at the Boer War, for example – which do make the point about Australians fighting for interests which were actually remote to them. For something more life-affirming, the picnic grounds in bushland behind the memorial yield the beginning of a walk to the summit of Mount Ainslie – really a large round hill and part of Canberra Nature Park (see opposite) – where a lookout provides a perfect view over the city and the Parliamentary Triangle.

ANU and Screensound Australia

The green, spacious **Australian National University** (ANU) campus, just west of the city centre in **Acton**, is a pleasant place to wander. The two small **anthropological museums** at the Hope Building on Ellery Crescent are open to the public (Mon–Fri 9am–4pm; free), and there are also the usual student activities, concerts and plays: for information about current and forthcoming events call ☎02/6125 5736 or see ⓦwww.anu.edu.au. Within the grounds of the ANU campus, on McCoy Circuit, **Screensound Australia**, the old National Film and Sound Archive, is the most comprehensive collection of Australian sound and screen recordings in existence, dating back to the 1890s. One of the highlights of a visit here is an interactive exhibition (Mon–Fri 9am–5pm, Sat, Sun & public holidays 10am–5pm; free; ⓦwww .screensound.gov.au), where special headphones tune in to the frequency of each display as you pass. A highlight of the exhibits is the yellow car that split in two in the 1986 film *Malcolm* (see "Australian film", p.1186); the scene is replayed on a video screen. A wild-card display of Australian TV ads features some real humdingers from the 1970s, and you can watch fascinating snippets from old newsreels in a small projection room.

Black Mountain and around

The **National Botanic Gardens** (daily 9am–5pm, till 8pm Jan & Feb; free; free guided tours leave from the visitor centre daily at 11am & 2pm; ⓦwww .anbg.gov.au), on the flanks of Black Mountain, are well worth a diversion from the city centre – beautiful in themselves and an excellent introduction to Australian flora. About six thousand species of native plants have been planted here in ecological niches, including an example of Sydney Basin flora, some mallee shrubland, and rainforest species growing in a shady, watered gully. There are hundreds of different types of eucalypts, banksias and proteaceas, as well as tree ferns and even an Aboriginal trail. The main entrance is on Clunies Ross Street, beyond the university area, and there's a **visitor information centre** (daily 9.30am–4.30pm) with leaflets for self-guided tours, displays and videos, and a small bookshop; nearby there's a pleasant coffee shop (same hours).

While you're here, you should take the opportunity to drive or walk up to Black Mountain, which rises about 200m above Canberra. On clear days, the panoramic view of Canberra and across the ACT from the 58-metre-high viewing platform at the **Black Mountain Telstra Tower** (daily 9am–10pm; $3.30) is magnificent. The tower also has a café and a revolving restaurant (advance booking recommended on ☎02/6248 1911), serving smorgasbord.

A couple of kilometres north of Black Mountain, the **Australian Institute of Sport** (AIS), on Leverrier Crescent in Bruce (daily 9am–5pm; tours 10am, 11.30am, 1pm & 2.30pm; $10.80; ⓦwww.aisport.com.au; bus #431), is a manifestation of Australia's craze for sport. The ultramodern, multimillion-dollar complex was established in 1981 with the aim of churning out world-class athletes, and a visit is particularly relevant in the wake of the Sydney 2000 Olympics. The Sportex interactive sports exhibition gives you the chance to test your sporting prowess, and there's a café and a shop selling souvenirs and sports clothing – just in case you decide to take advantage of the facilities (at an extra charge): a heated pool, spa and sauna, and indoor and outdoor tennis courts.

Canberra Nature Park

The bush hills and ridges that intersperse Canberra's suburbs make up the **Canberra Nature Park**, which has many walking tracks to explore. You can pick up maps and guides from the ACT Government Information Shop Front, Saraton Building, East Row, Civic, or call the park headquarters for more information on ☎02/6207 2113 (north) or 6207 2087 (south) or check their website ⓦwww.environment.act.gov.au/general. The park actually comprises many sites, one of the most accessible being the Bruce/O'Connor Ridge section, across Belconnen Way from the Black Mountain area of the park; from here, several walking tracks head through bushland, including one that runs right behind the well-positioned youth hostel.

Eating and drinking

All cuisines imaginable are represented somewhere in Canberra and the surrounding suburbs, and if you have the time it's well worth getting out of the centre to explore some of them. Woolley Street in **Dickson** is the best suburban street to head for, crammed as it is with a variety of Asian restaurants and supermarkets. The well-off areas of **Manuka** and **Kingston**, near New Parliament House, have gourmet café-delis and fine restaurants. **Civic** itself is well served with places to eat, especially in the pedestrian mall around Garema Place. In addition to the restaurants listed here, Canberra's many clubs (see p.268) also serve very inexpensive meals in a typical Aussie atmosphere. **Cafés** are plentiful around the centre, with a particular concentration on Bunda Street, near the cinemas. On the ground level of the City Market shopping mall, on the corner of Bunda Street and Ainslie Avenue, there's an excellent **food court**, with cafés and specialist stores serving a wide variety of cuisines, as well as a large **supermarket**. Healthy vegetarian ingredients can be bought from Mount Creek Wholefoods, 14 Barker Street, Griffith. Most local buses go from the City Bus Interchange to the suburbs listed below (see "City transport", p.255, for details).

Cafés

Ali Baba Cnr Garema Place and Bunda St. A simple Lebanese takeaway with outside tables. Daily to 10pm, very late Fri & Sat.

ANU Union Union Crescent, Acton. The students' union has a restaurant, a café and a super-cheap bistro specializing in Asian food. BYO. Mon–Fri lunch and dinner.

The Blue Olive 56 Alinga St. Home-baked speciality breads and cakes, toasted Turkish sandwiches and ice-cold beer from the in-house bottle shop. Mon–Sat 7am–late.

The Café Barrine Drive, west of the Commonwealth Avenue Bridge, next to Mr Spokes

Bike Hire. In a lovely spot by the lake. Daily from 9am.

Café Essen Garema Arcade. A much-loved gourmet coffee house with enormous, cheap and unusual brunches for health freaks and carbo-junkies alike. Live music at the weekend. Daily from 7.30am.

Caffe della Piazza 19 Garema Place. A lively, people-watching place spilling out into the square, with pavement tables. Award-winning Italian coffee, focaccia, pizza and pasta. Licensed.

Gus' Café Bunda St, next to Center Cinema. Canberra's best café serves inexpensive light meals, and fresh soups with lots of choice for vegetarians. Tables outside under vines and a huge tree; magazines and newspapers to read. Popular with students and an arty crowd. Daily 7.30am–10.30pm, later at the weekend.

Iridium Cnr Northbourne Ave and London Circuit. This is a beautifully designed space with interesting breakfast and dinner choices, and an all-day menu featuring the scrumptious artistry of its very own pastry chef. Perfect for post-club munchies. Mon–Thurs 7am–midnight, Fri–Sun 24hr.

Zydeco 173 City Walk. This airy café/restaurant offers a comprehensive breakfast menu, great coffee, and an Australian twist to the omnipresent focaccia. Tables outside. Mon–Sat 10am–late, Sun noon–6pm.

Restaurants

Barocca Café Shop 6, 60 Marcus Clarke St ☏ 02/6248 0253. Modern Australian cuisine is the order of the day at this reasonably priced award-winning restaurant. Bookings advised for evenings. Mon–Fri lunch and dinner.

Bernadette's Ainslie Shops, Wakefield Gardens, Ainslie ☏ 02/6248 5018. A friendly, sunny BYO vegetarian café with a pleasant terrace, in an unassuming suburb about ten minutes' walk from the main tourist office. The menu features huge focaccia sandwiches, pizzas (with vegan alternatives) and salads, as well as home baking to die for. Booking advised at night. Tues–Fri 11am–10pm, Sat & Sun 9am–10pm.

Chairman and Yip 108 Bunda St ☏ 02/6248 7109. A stylish, good-humoured Chinese restaurant, much more congenial than most of its Civic neighbours. The walls are adorned with Mao paraphernalia and a "workers lunch" costs $12.50. Lunch Mon–Fri, dinner daily.

Delicateating O'Connor Shopping Centre, Macpherson St. Trendy, delicatessen-style place tending towards Italian cuisine, and conveniently

located near the Canberra YHA hostel. Mellow-yellow walls and tables outside. BYO. Mon–Fri 10am–10pm, Sat & Sun 9am–10pm.

Fringe Benefits Brasserie 54 Marcus Clarke St ☏ 02/6247 4042. Stylish French restaurant with an extensive wine cellar. Licensed. Closed Sun.

Kingsland Vegetarian Restaurant Shop 5, Dickson Plaza, 28 Challis St, Dickson ☏ 02/6262 9350. Earthy, reasonably priced veggie cuisine situated near the visitor information centre. Mon–Fri & Sun 11am–2.30pm & 5–10pm, Sat 5–10pm.

Lemon Grass Thai Restaurant 65 London Circuit ☏ 02/6247 2779. Award-winning Thai restaurant with an imaginative menu that is strong on fish and vegetarian dishes.

Little Saigon Cnr Alinga St and Northbourne Ave ☏ 02/6230 5003. Large, busy, cheap and tasty Vietnamese restaurant, with $5 lunch-time specials. Advisable to book on weekends. Daily 9am–3pm & 5–10.30pm.

Mama's Trattoria 7 Garema Place. Decent, usually crowded, Italian restaurant with outside tables. Daily 10am–late.

Montezuma's 197 London Circuit, next to *Canberra City Backpackers*. Loud, accommodating and popular Mexican, with live entertainment Fri–Sun. Licensed. Mon–Sat 5pm–late, also open for lunch Wed–Fri.

Tilley's Devine Café Gallery Cnr Brigalow and Wattle streets, Lyneham. Wonderful platefuls of comfort food – salads, big melts and special carrot cake – in a gorgeous, candlelit locale.

Tosolini's Cnr Franklin and Furneaux streets, Manuka ☏ 02/6232 6600. Very popular, award-winning modern Australian eatery in the most glitzy of neighbourhoods. Sunday brunch on the terrace is a must. Tues–Sun noon–3pm & 6–10.30pm, plus weekend breakfast 8.30–11.30am.

Entertainment and nightlife

Despite the eerie quiet that invades Civic after working hours, there's quite a vibrant and even experimental entertainment scene in Canberra. For current events, the daily *Canberra Times* is your best bet: the most extensive **listings** are published every Thursday in a cultural and entertainment supplement, *Good Times*. For details of bands and clubs, pick up a copy of *BMA*, a free monthly music magazine. The visitor information centre and most hotels also distribute the quarterly booklet *Canberra What's On*, which lists major cultural events. Up-to-date **information** can be found by calling the "Today and Tonight" events hotline on ☏ 02/6257 4347.

Nightclubs and pubs

There are several chart-oriented **nightclubs** in Canberra, including *Babylon*, on the corner of Alinga St and East Row, with two floors of dance music, disco and easy rock; and *Insomnia*, above *ICBM*, 50 Northbourne Ave, where the city's public servants let their hair down. Of several **bars** and **dance venues**, *In Blue*, at the corner of Mort and Alinga streets, is worth a visit – downstairs is a vodka and cocktail bar, upstairs a small mezzanine-level dance floor.

In the centre, the best **pub** for a drink is the tiny *Phoenix Pub*, 23 East Row, which attracts a grungey crowd and has feral live bands. Frequented by locals and tourists alike is the large Irish theme pub *P.J. O'Reilly's Irish Pub*, at the corner of West Row and Alinga Street, which also has a reasonable restaurant and snack menu. Similarly popular, and rather less forced, are *King O'Malleys* at 131 City Walk, with outside tables, nightly live music (see ⓦwww .kingomalleys.com.au for details) and a hearty bill of fare; and *Filthy McFaddens* on Green Square in Kingston. Another good Kingston pub is *The Holy Grail*, also on Green Square; catering for a slightly older crowd, it hosts live music (Wed–Fri) and has a nightclub.

Live music

The *ANU Union Bar* on Childers Street at the ANU campus in Acton, entertaining six thousand or so students, is invariably the best place for **rock bands** of all sorts, with live performances at least a couple of times a week during term time (☎02/6249 2446 or ⓦwww.anuunion.com.au for details), while the *Canberra Workers Club* (☎02/6248 0399) hosts big touring bands, with cheap drinks until midnight.

However, the music you're most likely to hear in Canberra is **jazz**. *Déjà Vu*, the upstairs bar at the *Casino Canberra*, 21 Binara St (☎02/6257 7074), regularly hosts big-name jazz bands. For something more intimate, jazz can be heard on Sunday night from 7pm at the gay-friendly *Tilley's*, an ambient café/bar/gallery in Lyneham on the corner of Brigalow and Wattle streets (☎02/6247 7753); more mainstream jazz is played on Thursdays and Sundays at *All Bar Nun*, near the YHA in O'Connor, and at the *Wig & Pen* on Alinga Street on Saturday nights.

Weekends see **folk and blues** at the *Pot Belly Bar*, Weedon Close, Belconnen; there's nightly **hardcore rock** and ear-splitting **metal** at *Rock Ape* in the Northside Fitness Centre, 20 Dickson Place, Dickson (☎02/6257 8195), and anything from **world music** to **jungle** at the self-consciously cool *Mombasa*, 128 Bunda St (ⓦwww.clubmombasa.com.au). The *Canberra Yacht Club*, Coronation Drive, Yarralumla, has more middle-of-the-road lounge-style entertainment on Friday night, featuring a singer and guitarist. **Classical music** performances are staged sporadically at the Canberra Theatre Centre, London Circuit (☎02/6257 1077, ⓦwww.canberratheatre.org.au), and regularly at the Canberra School of Music, Llewellyn Hall, Childers St (☎02/6249 5700, ⓦwww.anu.edu.au).

Theatre and cinema

The main **drama** venue in the capital is the impressive Canberra Theatre Centre on London Circuit (☎02/6257 1077, ⓦwww.canberratheatre.org.au). In addition to a broad range of plays, its several theatres also host concerts, dance performances and readings – it's always worth finding out what's going on here. Other, less mainstream, options include The Street Theatre (☎02/6247 1519, ⓦwww.thestreet.org.au) on the corner of Childers Street and University Avenue, and a number of active independent theatre groups based at the Gorman House Community Arts Centre on Ainslie Avenue, Braddon (☎02/6249 7377, ⓦwww.gormanhouse.com.au). *Tilley's* in Lyneham (see p.266 and p.267) also hosts cabaret programmes, as does the *School of the Arts Café*, 108 Monaro St, Queanbeyan (℡02/6297 6857), worth checking out for its new plays by fringe theatre groups, as well as its live music, bush poetry and comedy acts – all from Thursday to Saturday.

As for **cinemas**, the Center Cinema on Bunda Street (℡02/6249 7979, ⓦwww.ronincinemas.com.au) is probably the best of the regular commercial choices, with a well-considered programme and interesting Saturday late shows at 11pm, while the Electric Shadows Cinema, Akuna Street (℡02/6247 5060, ⓦwww.electricshadows.com.au), shows the best in world cinema, and has a bookshop and café-bar.

Clubs

Numerous **clubs**, most of which admit visitors, are one of the features of Canberra life. They often serve inexpensive meals, and may also organize live music, film evenings, parties or comedy shows – all in the hope of luring visitors to gamble their money away on the one-armed bandits. One of the biggest is the *Canberra Workers Club* on Childers Street (℡02/6248 0399): it boasts a bistro serving meals every day, regular discos, and darts and pool as well as pokies. The *Canberra Tradesmen's Union Club*, 2 Badham St, Dickson (℡02/6248 0999, ⓦwww.ctuc.asn.au/dickson.htm), has a sauna, gym and squash courts, an observatory with an astronomical officer on duty (dusk until about 12.30am), and a Bicycle Museum (daily 9am–midnight); you can even dine in a restored tram, or have your hair cut in a 1920s-style barber shop. The attractions are all free, but children have to leave by 8pm, when the sinful poker machines rev up. The *Canberra Labor Club*, Chandler Street, Belconnen (℡02/6251 5522), serves meals daily and offers bingo as well as occasional disco or rock nights.

Listings

Airlines Qantas ℡13 13 13; Regional Express ℡13 17 13; Virgin Blue ℡13 67 89.

American Express Centerpoint Arcade, cnr City Walk and Petrie Plaza ℡02/6247 2333.

Banks The city branches of the bigger banks are open Mon–Thurs 9.30am–4pm, Fri until 5pm: ANZ, 25 Petrie Plaza; Commonwealth Bank, cnr London Circuit and Northbourne Ave; National Australia Bank, cnr London Circuit and Hobart Place; Westpac, 53 Alinga St.

Bike rental A pleasurable bicycle path goes all the way around Lake Burley Griffin. To rent a bike the most convenient place to head for is Mr Spokes Bike Hire (℡02/6257 1188; $10 per hour), right on the water at Barrine Drive, Acton. You can also check out Row 'n' Ride, c/o Canberra South Motor Park, Canberra Ave ℡02/6228 1264; $30 per half-day, $40 per day.

Books Smiths Alternative Bookshop is the antithesis of all things Canberrian, stocking interesting fiction and cultural theory, as well as radical and left-leaning publications.

Buses For local bus information phone Action timetable information (℡13 17 10), check out their website (ⓦwww.action.act.gov.au) or call at the kiosk at the City Bus Interchange, 11 East Row. Long-distance services, including state-owned Countrylink, use the Jolimont Centre, 65–67 Northbourne Ave, as their terminal. You can buy tickets here from the Jolimont Centre for direct services with Countrylink to Cooma, Eden and Cootamundra (℡13 22 32); McCafferty's/Greyhound Pioneer to Sydney, Brisbane, Melbourne and Adelaide (℡02/6249 6006); and Murrays Coaches to Wollongong and south coast (℡13 22 51).

Car rental Inexpensive deals are available from Network Car & Truck Rentals, 117 Redfern St, Macquarie (℡02/6251 6626) and Rumbles Rent-a-Car, 11 Paragon Mall, Gladstone St, Fyshwick (℡02/6280 7444). Others, mostly clustered on Lonsdale St in Braddon, with additional locations at the airport, are: Avis ℡02/6249 6088, airport ℡02/6249 1601; Budget ℡13 27 27; Hertz ℡02/6257 4877, airport ℡02/6249 6211 or 13 30 39; and Thrifty ℡02/6247 7422, airport ℡1300 367 227.

Embassies and high commissions There are over 70 in Canberra (all the following are in Yarralumla, unless otherwise stated): Britain,

Commonwealth Ave ⓣ02/6270 6666; Canada, Commonwealth Ave ⓣ02/6270 4000; Germany, 119 Empire Court ⓣ02/6270 1911; Indonesia, 8 Darwin Ave ⓣ02/6250 8600; Ireland, 20 Arkana St ⓣ02/6273 3022; Malaysia, 7 Perth Ave ⓣ02/6273 1543; Netherlands, 120 Empire Circuit ⓣ02/6273 3111; New Zealand, Commonwealth Ave ⓣ02/6270 4211; Norway, 17 Hunter St ⓣ02/6273 3444; Papua New Guinea, 39–41 Forster Crescent ⓣ02/6273 3322; Singapore, 17 Forster Crescent ⓣ02/6273 3944; Sweden, 5 Turrana St ⓣ02/6270 2700; Switzerland, 7 Melbourne Ave, Forrest ⓣ02/6273 3977; Thailand, 111 Empire Circuit ⓣ02/6273 1149; US, 21 Moonah Place ⓣ02/6214 5600.

Environmental contacts The Environment Centre, Kingsley St, Acton (ⓣ02/6247 3064, ⓦwww.ecoaction.net.au), is a library and archive on environmental topics as well as a book and gift shop (Mon–Fri 9am–5pm). The Wilderness Society Shop, 16 Garema Place (ⓣ02/6249 8011), is a book and gift shop with information about the local environment.

Festivals The big event of the year is the Canberra Festival – the anniversary of the city's foundation – celebrated with concerts, theatre, exhibitions, street parades and fireworks for ten days from the beginning of March. The Royal Canberra Show is an agricultural fair lasting three days over the last weekend in February, while the Floriade is a spring festival marked by floral displays, theatre and music, from mid-September to mid-October. Even more popular, though less feted by the tourist board, is the annual Summernats Car Festival in January (details on ⓣ02/6241 8111 or at ⓦwww.summernats.com.au), when revheads convene in Exhibition Park to compare modified street machines and compete at the world's only purpose-built burnout facility.

Galleries Good private galleries include the Chapman Gallery, 31 Captain Cook Crescent, Griffith (Wed–Sun 11am–6pm; ⓣ02/6295 2550), specializing in Aboriginal art; and the Beaver Galleries, 81 Denison St, Deakin (daily 10am–5pm; ⓣ02/6281 1315), for paintings, sculpture, jewellery and furniture.

Gay and lesbian Canberra Gayline ⓣ02/6247 2726 (nightly 6–10pm); Gay Contact ⓣ02/6257 2855 (same hours); Gaywaves Radio Mondays 92.9 FM.

Golf Royal Canberra Golf Club, Westbourne Woods, Yarralumla ⓣ02/6282 7000.

Horse riding Brindabella Valley Trails, 19 Sabine Close, Garran (ⓣ02/6281 6682), offers riding in the Brindabella Ranges close to Kosciuszko National Park.

Hospitals John James Memorial Hospital, Strickland Crescent, Deakin ⓣ02/6281 8100.

Internet access *On Line Café Canberra*, cnr London Circuit and Akuna St ⓣ02/6262 7427.

Markets Gorman House Markets, Gorman House Arts Centre, Ainslie Ave, Braddon (Sat 10am–4pm; bus #302, #303 or #385), is a community market where items such as pottery, hand-painted T-shirts, bric-a-brac and secondhand clothes are sold; Belconnen Markets, Lathlain St (Wed–Sun 8am–6pm), is a large fresh-food market featuring an organic grocery, seafood and poultry outlets, organic veggies, home-made jams, health foods, a naturopath and several cafés. Old Bus Depot Markets, Wentworth Ave, Kingston Foreshore (Sun 10am–4pm), is the big market in town – high-quality handcrafts, great food, musicians and other entertainment make this a must if you're here on a Sunday.

Nature reserves Information on ACT parks and reserves from Canberra Nature Park (north ⓣ02/6207 2113, or south ⓣ02/6207 2087) and Environment ACT (ⓣ02/6207 9777, ⓦwww.environment.act.gov.au/general).

NRMA (National Roads and Motorists Association), 92 Northbourne Ave, Braddon, or Belconnen Mall, Belconnen ⓣ13 11 1. Publishes a very useful map of Canberra and the ACT, free to members.

Police ⓣ02/6256 7777.

Post office Alinga St, Canberra, ACT 2600 (Mon–Fri 9am–5pm; ⓣ02/6209 1680).

Rape Crisis Centre 59 Majura Ave, Dickson ⓣ02/6247 2525 (24hr).

Scenic flights Canberra Flight Centre (ⓣ02/6257 6331) charges from about $60 per person for 30min–1hr.

Shopping Shopping hours are Mon–Thurs 9am–5.30pm, Fri 9am–9pm, Sat 9am–4pm, Sun 10am–4pm. In the city centre the shopping focus is on Bunda St and surrounding area, with department stores such as David Jones and Grace Bros, and the Canberra Centre shopping mall. There are late-opening supermarkets in the shopping centres of the satellite towns.

Taxis Canberra Cabs (ⓣ13 22 27) has wheelchair-accessible cabs; Queanbeyan Taxi Co-operative (ⓣ02/6297 3000). There is a taxi rank on Bunda St outside the Center Cinema.

Tours and cruises Murrays, the Jolimont Centre, 65–67 Northbourne Ave (ⓣ13 22 51), has half- or full-day bus tours around Canberra and to the Snowy Mountains; Go Bush Tours (ⓣ02/6231 3023, ⓦwww.gobushtours.com.au) offers tours for small groups around the city, to the Snowy Mountains and to Namadgi National Park; Harley Rides 'r' Us (ⓣ02/6231 7231 or 1800 242 753), offers sightseeing trips in and around Canberra from the back of a Harley-Davidson from $60; Wild Things Tours (☎02/6254 6303) runs six-hour tours into Namadgi National Park for guaranteed eastern grey kangaroo spotting and to see indigenous rock art ($80, including light lunch, park entrance, pick-ups and drop-offs); Southern Cross Cruises (☎02/6273 1784, ⌨www.cscc.com.au) offers one-hour scenic cruises, plus lunch and dinner cruises on Lake Burley Griffin; and Dawn Drifters (☎02/6285 4450, ⌨www.dawndrifters.com.au) will fly you over the city in a balloon (Mon–Fri $185 per person, weekends & holidays $215 per person), and then feed you breakfast when safely aground.

Trains The Xplorer train links Canberra and Sydney (3 daily; 4hr) via Queanbeyan, Bungendore, Goulburn, Bundanoon, Moss Vale, Bowral and Mittagong. Ticket sales and information at the Countrylink Travel Centre, Jolimont Centre, 65–67 Northbourne Ave, and at the train station in Kingston (all enquiries ☎13 22 32).

Travel agents Flight Centre, Lower Ground Floor, Canberra Centre (Mon–Thurs 9am–5.30pm, Fri 9am–8pm, Sat 10am–3pm; ☎13 16 00); STA Travel, 13 Garema Place, Civic (Mon–Thurs 9am–5pm, Fri till 7pm, Sat 10am–2pm; ☎02/6247 8633).

Women Women's Information and Referral Centre, 6th Floor, FAI Insurance Building, 197 London Circuit (Mon–Fri 9am–5pm; ☎02/6205 1075, ⌨www.act.gov.au/womensinfo).

Around Canberra

The residents of Canberra live with nature right on their doorstep: the numerous **picnic grounds** and **bushwalking trails** in the state reserves and national parks are only about half an hour's drive from the city centre. Be warned, though, that at the height of summer, when there is a high risk of bushfires, a total fire ban is declared and all the nature reserves and national parks are closed (call ☎02/6207 8600 to check). Bushland aside, the environs of the capital can also lay claim to historic **homesteads and villages**, private zoos, a former gold-mining town and a few **wineries**, some of them across the border in New South Wales.

South

Leaving the city behind, the Tharwa Road follows the course of the **Murrumbidgee River** as it approaches Tharwa. Thirty-two kilometres from Canberra, at the southern end of the Tuggeranong Valley, the convict-built **Lanyon Homestead** (Tues–Fri 10am–4pm, Sat & Sun 10am–5pm; $6, admission to grounds free) dates back to the earliest European settlement of the region. Thoroughly refurbished by the National Trust, it now houses a small display outlining the history of the area before Canberra existed, but the real reasons to come are the house itself and the **Sidney Nolan Gallery** (same hours as homestead; $3.50) next door, where works by the famous Australian painter are on permanent display alongside changing exhibitions of contemporary Australian art. There's no public transport out here.

Beyond the Lanyon Homestead and Tharwa, old cottages on the Naas Road, overlooking the river, house the galleries and antique shops of the **Cuppacumbalong Craft Centre** (Wed–Sun & holidays 11am–5pm). Nearby, a small, licensed café serves hearty meals and local cider, and there's also a spot where you can swim in the river.

Namadgi National Park

Namadgi National Park occupies almost half of the ACT, largely made up of wilderness areas in the west and southwest. Its mountain ranges and high plains, rising to 1900m, have a far more severe climate than low-lying Canberra and give rise to the Cotter River and many smaller streams. In the northwest, the Corin Road leads to Corin Dam, while in the south the partly surfaced Bobyan Road cuts right through the national park, emerging beneath the Snowy Mountains in the south (the park abuts the Kosciuszko National Park along the state border). There are picnic grounds and bush campsites by the Orroral River and near Mount Clear in the south.

The **Namadgi Visitors Information Centre**, 3km south of Tharwa on the Naas Road (Mon–Fri 9am–4pm, Sat, Sun & public holidays 9am–4.30pm; ☎02/6207 2900, ⓦwww.environment.act.gov.au/general), has displays and videos about the park, and also provides guided tours on request as well as detailed information on bushwalking tracks and emergency shelters in the remote areas.

West: Tidbinbilla Nature Reserve and Cotter Reserve

The small **Tidbinbilla Nature Reserve**, to the southwest of the city (daily 9am–6pm, later during daylight saving; $8.50 per car; ⓦwww.environment .act.gov.au/general), is an enjoyable place with relatively easy walks, and some wheelchair-accessible paths. In the area around the park entrance and **information centre** (Mon–Fri 9am–4.30pm, Sat & Sun 9am–5.30pm; ☎02/6205 1233) kangaroos and wallabies roam in spacious bush enclosures, and you can also see koalas and lots of birds. Picnic grounds are dotted all along the sealed road that leads through the reserve, and on long weekends and during the school holidays it's a busy place, especially popular with families. The **Canberra Space Centre** on Discovery Drive in Tidbinbilla (visitors centre open daily 9am–5pm, till 8pm in summer; free; ⓦwww.cdscc.nasa.gov) sounds like every child's dream, though in fact the displays of spacecraft and highly sensitive communications equipment are not as exciting as you might have hoped. Operated in conjunction with NASA, the purpose of the station is to pick up even the most obscure signals from outer space; there are only two others in the world with the same range as Tidbinbilla – one near Madrid, the other in Goldstone, California.

Southwest of here, Corin Road turns off the Tidbinbilla Road towards the **Corin Forest** (Sat, Sun & holidays 10am–5pm; also weekdays during school holidays 10am–4pm; ⓦwww.corin.com.au) and reservoir, a popular recreation spot in the hills, with many walking trails, year-round bobsledding, picnic grounds and barbecue facilities. In winter you can ski on artificial snow and during school holidays special activities are organized for children.

Cotter Reserve

The **Cotter Reserve**, near the Cotter Dam, 22km west of the city, was badly hit by the 2002 bushfires. This has traditionally been a popular spot for short weekend outings, though the devestation that the fires wreaked meant that the reserve remained out of bounds at the time of writing; for latest details, contact the tourist office. On the way to the Cotter Reserve you pass the remains of the **Mount Stromlo Observatory** (ⓦwww.mso.anu.edu.au/msovc), about 16km from Canberra, whose main dome housed the ANU's Department of Astronomy; historical records and several important telescopes were lost in the fires and, at the time of writing, the future of the complex remained uncertain.

North

Leaving Canberra by the Barton Highway to the north, the first place of interest is **GINNINDERA**, approximately 9km out. It's a rather consciously touristy village with a few arts and crafts shops and *The Green Herring* restaurant in a log hut. Just before Ginninera, on Gold Creek Road, the **National Dinosaur Museum** (daily 10am–5pm; $8.50; @ www.nationaldinosaur museum.com.au) is not a big, government-run museum as the name might suggest, but rather a private collection of replica skeletons and some bones and fossils. Other local tourist attractions include **Cockington Green** (daily 9.30am–4.30pm; $11.50; @ www.cockington-green.com.au), a miniature model English village; and the **Artgems Gallery** (daily 10am–5pm) in the village, with exhibits of paintings, gems (especially opals and crystals), and local arts and crafts. **HALL**, 3km north of Ginninera, is a similar village with a few shops and a restaurant, and another Artgems Gallery.

More or less opposite the turn-off for Hall, the Wallaroo Road heads west towards the New South Wales border. Not far down the road, at Woodgrove Close, is Brindabella Hill Wines (☎ 02/6230 2583), where you can sample some of the local "cool climate" vintages. There are more **wineries** around **MURRUMBATEMAN**, north along the Barton Highway into New South Wales between Canberra and the large country town of Yass (see p.352); full lists are available from the tourist office.

The Federal Highway

Northeast of Canberra, the Federal Highway crosses into New South Wales shortly after leaving the city. The first of the sights along this way is the **Bywong Gold Mining Town** (daily 9.30am–4.30pm; $8; bookings essential for groups ☎ 02/6236 9183, @ www.bywonggold.citysearch.com.au), where a brief goldrush at the end of the nineteenth century has left shafts and some old mine workings. The gold-diggers' camp has been reconstructed with some serious attention to historic detail, and it's well worth stopping in if you're passing by; you can also try your hand at panning, and there are picnic and barbecue areas. The mining village is on Bungendore Road, further down which lies the attractive village of **BUNGENDORE**, with a pottery, woodturner, café and shops arranged around the village green. Heading on, you can circle back round to Canberra via Queanbeyan, or strike east, a scenic drive that takes you through **BRAIDWOOD** – which has more antiques and crafts shops, and a fine old hotel – towards the coast at Batemans Bay (see p.284).

Southern New South Wales

There are two quite separate parts to the southern half of New South Wales, just as there are to the state as a whole: the coast, and the mountains and hinterland beyond them. The **south coast**, with its green dairylands, is delightful in a quiet sort of way – an area for fishing or surfing or relaxing on the beaches, with no huge resorts or commercial developments. Inland, the **Snowy Mountains** constitute the Dividing Range's highest peaks; they have Australia's best skiing and, in summer, some fine bushwalking. Beyond the mountains, the southwest is dull farming country – you're better off crossing to the riverlands of Victoria, or driving straight through.

The direct route from Sydney to Melbourne is via the inland **Hume Highway**, from which you can easily detour to Canberra or the Snowy Mountains. There's a four-lane freeway from Sydney to Moss Vale, and the rest of the way it's a normal two-lane road with occasional overtaking lanes, but very winding between Yass and Albury. It is also very busy, with heavy truck traffic, and most of the time quite boring – a potentially lethal combination. It takes roughly twelve hours to drive straight through from Sydney to Melbourne, which is fine if you're sharing the driving, but otherwise allow two days.

The coastal route, the **Princes Highway**, is slightly longer but much more attractive in terms of scenery. Give yourself two or more days if you want to appreciate the surf, the sandy beaches, and the mountains, valleys and forests that back this beautiful stretch of the coast. Most **buses** run via the Hume Highway, usually with a detour to Canberra; the **train** follows largely the same route.

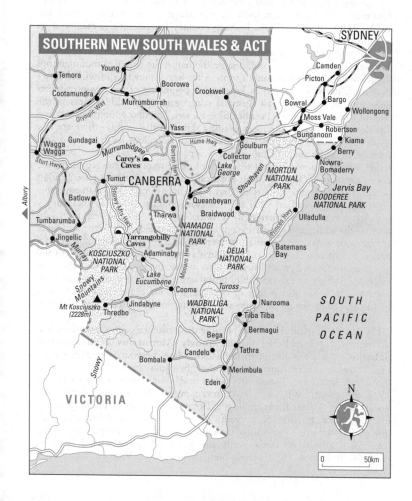

The Snowy Mountains

The **Snowy Mountains** are just one section of the alpine highlands that spread across the southeast corner of the Australian continent. The Australian Alps sprawl from Mount Buller, Mount Bogong and Mount Beauty in northeast Victoria via the Crackenback Range in New South Wales to the township of Cooma; though it's a continuous massif, only the New South Wales section is strictly known as the Snowy Mountains. **Mount Kosciuszko**, at 2228m the highest mountain in mainland Australia, is located close to the Victorian border in the far southeast. It was named in 1840 by the Polish-born explorer Paul Strzelecki after the Polish freedom fighter General Tadeusz Kosciuszko, and, although Strzelecki stressed he was "in a foreign country and on a foreign ground", he couldn't resist giving it its name "amongst a free people who appreciate freedom". The **Kosciuszko National Park**, which surrounds the peak, includes most of the Snowy Mountains region and almost everything of interest. To the north and east of **Cooma** – the main approach to the range – the treeless, brownish-yellow **Monaro High Plain** is sheep country famous for the quality of its merino wool.

Compared to the high mountain ranges of other continents, the "roof of Australia" is relatively low and, despite the name, the flattened mountaintops lie below the line of permanent snow. After heavy snowfalls in winter, however (roughly from the end of June to the beginning of Oct), winter-sports fans from all over southeast Australia congregate at the **ski resorts** in the Mount Kosciuszko area – Perisher Blue Resort, Thredbo, Mount Selwyn and Charlotte Pass. It's not the most exciting skiing in the world – there are few challenging runs – and prices are hiked up to ridiculous levels as the resorts attempt to make their living during a very short season. Selwyn, a family resort, which is generally half the price of other resorts in the region, is one cheap alternative. Only the most fanatical European winter-sports enthusiast would come here especially to ski, but if you're passing it can be an enjoyable diversion. This is also an ideal area for cross-country skiing, an increasingly popular pursuit. In **summer** it's a different story: price levels return to normal, the towns and resorts are not quite so crowded, even sleepy, and there are fabulous walks and mountain scenery to be enjoyed. Perisher and Selwyn almost completely close down, but Thredbo operates ski-lifts throughout the year, transporting hikers and sightseers to mountaintops from where they can embark on short or extended bushwalks across the wildflower-covered high country. There are also plenty of opportunities for horse riding, mountain biking and trout fishing or white-water rafting in the crystal-clear mountain streams.

The system of roads that made possible the existence of the townships and ski resorts was established by the **Snowy Mountains Hydroelectric Scheme**, which was begun in the 1950s. Many postwar immigrants from middle and southern Europe found their first jobs on the "Snowy"; some lost their lives here. Twenty-five years and about $800 million later, in 1974 the project was completed: seven power stations now utilize the waters of the Upper Murrumbidgee, Tumut and Snowy rivers to generate electricity and provide New South Wales, the ACT and Victoria with power. The scheme's generating capacity is about eighteen percent of the total for southeast Australia, while the water of the redirected rivers is used for irrigation right across New South Wales, Victoria and South Australia.

Skiing in the Snowy Mountains

The easiest option for **skiing in the Snowy Mountains** is to arrange a **ski package** departing from Sydney – always check exactly what's included in the price. Recommended operators include: Kosciuszko Accommodation Centre (℡02/6456 2022 or 1800 026 385), who can put together a low-season basic weekend package including transport by bus, national park entry, ski rental, lift and lessons, and two nights' accommodation, dinner and breakfast for around $350; and Ski Kaos (℡02/9976 5555, ⓦwww.skikaos.com.au) who offer similar deals and some more basic packages for slightly less.

A one-day **ski-lift pass** starts from about $45 at Selwyn, $70 at Charlotte Pass and $75 at Thredbo and Perisher Blue, and beginners' one-day group lessons cost around $90. Resorts are generally child-friendly, particularly at Charlotte Pass where the homely and old-fashioned *Kosciuszko Chalet* (℡1800 026 369) offers free child-care throughout the ski season; Paddy Pallin at Jindabyne (℡02/6456 2922 or 1800 623 459) has several cross-country skiing sessions, including an easy three-hour introduction aimed at family groups.

Another good source of information on the latest deals is Inski, a popular ski shop with its own attached ski travel agency, Alpine World, at 46 York St, Sydney (℡02/9906 2744, ⓦwww.alpineworld.com.au).

Getting there and around

The most important of the area's roads is the **Snowy Mountains Highway**, which leads straight across the mountain ranges and through the national park from Cooma to Tumut and Gundagai. If you want to see more of the alpine scenery, head along the fully sealed **Alpine Way**, which offers a spectacular circuit, turning off the highway at Kiandra in the heart of the park and heading via Khancoban and Geehi to Thredbo. In winter, check road conditions before driving anywhere, even on the Snowy Mountains Highway; on the Alpine Way and on Kosciuszko Road (after Sawpit Creek) **snow chains** must be carried between June and October, and the roads might be closed altogether.

Bus services are far more frequent in winter than in summer – a **rental car** is strongly recommended for summer sojourns. McCafferty's/Greyhound (℡13 20 30) has summer services four times weekly from Canberra to Cooma, Jindabyne, and Thredbo. Backpacker busline Autopia Tours operates a year-round Melbourne–Sydney route (℡02/9326 5536 or 1800 000 507, ⓦwww .netspace.net.au/~autopia; $180) via the Alpine Way, picking up and dropping off in Jindabyne. Additional winter-only bus services include Adaminaby Bus Service (℡02/6454 2318) between Cooma, Adaminaby and Mount Selwyn ski resort. Perisher Blue Skitube (℡02/6456 2010, ⓦwww.perisherblue .com.au; see p.277 for more details) is a **railway** specially designed for skiers, but it also operates for bushwalkers in the summer months, linking the ski areas of Bullocks Flat, Perisher Valley and Mount Blue Cow. Countrylink (℡13 28 29) has a daily train from Sydney, with a coach connection on to Cooma.

Cooma

Because of its location at the intersection of two highways – the Monaro Highway south from Canberra and the Snowy Mountains Highway from the coast to the high peaks – **COOMA** is the obvious base for trips into the Snowy Mountains. Although it functions mainly as a service centre for skiers, it's also an attractive place in its own right, with a number of fine old buildings, notably on Lambie and Vale streets – the visitors centre (see below) has a brochure detailing buildings of interest.

The town has really come into its own since the 1950s, when it took on the mantle of administrative centre for the hydroelectric scheme. Many of the migrants who worked on the Snowy – particularly those who arrived from central Europe – ended up settling here, making it a fairly cosmopolitan town. If you're interested in the history of the project and the technical details, check out the **visitors centre** of the Snowy Mountains Authority, on the Monaro Highway in North Cooma (Mon–Fri 8am–5pm, Sat & Sun during school holidays 8am–1pm; ☎1800 623 776 for details of guided visits to various power stations, ⓦ www.snowyhydro.com.au). The Snowy Mountains are traditionally regarded as prime **horse-riding** country. The long-established Yarramba Trail Riding at Berridale, 34km southwest of Cooma (☎02/6453 7204), offers escorted rides at $25 per hour or full-day picnic rides ($75), as well as extended camping safaris ($180 for two days).

Practicalities

The helpful **Cooma Visitors Centre**, Centennial Park (daily: June–Oct 7am–6pm; Nov–May 9am–5pm; ☎02/6450 1742 or 1800 636 525, ⓦ www.visitcooma.com.au), has detailed information on Kosciuszko National Park, plus farmstays, horse riding and fishing safaris, and offers a free accommodation booking service. Pick up a copy of the free monthly *Snowy Times*, which has detailed resort information and maps, plus listings of skiing prices and packages. Harvey World Travel, 96 Sharp St (☎02/6452 4677), is a helpful **travel agency** that can book flights out, provide details of bus services and arrange local tours; **car rental** is available from Thrifty, 60 Sharp St (☎02/6452 5300).

Accommodation can be hard to come by in the ski season, when everything, especially the motels, is booked up pretty early, but the rest of the year you shouldn't have too many problems. Good options include the inexpensive and central *Royal Hotel*, on the corner of Lambie and Sharp streets (☎02/6552 2132; ❷): built in 1858, it has loads of character – many of the rooms have French windows opening onto the huge balcony. The family-run *Bunkhouse Motel*, 28–30 Soho St (☎02/6452 2983, ⓦ www.bunkhousemotel.com.au; dorms $20, rooms ❷), is a guesthouse-style backpackers' with dorms and lots of en-suite singles. The good-value *Swiss Motel*, 34 Massie St (☎02/6452 1950; ❷), also has holiday apartments on offer (❹) – there are plenty of other motels nearby, and a great value B&B, the *Alpine Country Guesthouse* (☎02/6452 1414; ❷), just next door. *Snowtels Caravan Park*, 286 Sharp St (☎02/6452 1828, ⓦ www.snowtels.com.au; on-site vans ❷, cabins ❸, apartments ❹), with a tennis court and communal kitchen, is probably the best of the campsites.

Cooma's not really a foodie sort of town. The best place to **eat** is the licensed *Sharp Food*, 122 Sharp St, a lovely cosy place with outdoor dining in a pleasant courtyard at the back, serving delicious soups and sandwiches.

Kosciuszko National Park and around

The largest national park in New South Wales, **Kosciuszko National Park** extends 200km north to south, from Tumut to the Victorian border, encompassing an area of some 6500 square kilometres. The scenery includes almost all of the high country, with ten peaks above 2100m, forested valleys and a treeless plateau with glacial lakes, as well as the headwaters of Australia's biggest river system, the Murray–Murrumbidgee. The main centres are the lakeside resort of Jindabyne, just outside the eastern boundary of the park, and the ski resort of Thredbo, 30km further west along the scenic Alpine Way, actually in the national park. Perisher and Mount Blue Cow can be reached via the Skitube from Bullocks Flat, roughly midway between Jindabyne and Thredbo.

If you're driving through, note that there's a **fee** of $15 per car per day – so if you plan to stay more than a day or two and especially if other national parks are on your itinerary, the annual national park pass ($80) may be a good investment (see p.251 for details). Arriving by bus, you'll still have to fork out a one-off payment of $6. Note that **parking** is heavily restricted throughout the park, and can reach crisis point in Thredbo – if you've come by car it might be worth paying extra for accommodation with space to park.

The **NPWS** has its headquarters in Jindabyne (daily: summer 8am–6pm; winter 7am–7pm; ☎02/6450 5600, ⓦwww.npws.nsw.gov.au), a $5.4 million complex featuring red-gum interiors and including a tourist information office, cinema, café and bus station. It offers a comprehensive service, with leaflets about walking trails in the national park, activities such as ranger-guided tours, details of campsites, as well as maps for sale and a display on the natural features of the park. There are also NPWS **ranger stations** at Perisher Valley (☎02/6457 5214; winter only), Khancoban (☎02/6076 9373), Yarrangobilly (☎02/6454 9597) and Tumut (☎02/6947 7000).

Bushwalking in the park

Some of the country's most interesting and beautiful **bushwalking tracks** pass through the area. One of the most accessible of these is the walking trail around **Mount Kosciuszko**. The **chair-lift** from Thredbo (see below) will take you up to Crackenback station on the edge of the plateau; the actual summit is about 6km from here, though it seems barely higher than the surrounding country, or you can walk 2km to **Mount Kosciuszko Lookout** for panoramic views. Another good way up to the high country is to take the **Skitube** from Bullocks Flat on the Alpine Way, a funicular railway that leads uphill and through a tunnel to Perisher Valley and Mount Blue Cow (which has a bistro and art gallery), where more fine trails await. Even if you plan only a brief walk of an hour or so, bear in mind that the weather up here is very fickle, and pack a sweater and some rain protection.

Jindabyne and Thredbo

A resort town at the man-made lake of the same name, **JINDABYNE**, 63km west of Cooma, is the jumping-off point for the ski resorts of Thredbo, a further 30km west, and Guthega, or up the Kosciuszko road to Smiggin Holes and Perisher Valley (these two are also accessible by the Skitube – ☎02/6456 2010, ⓦwww.perisherblue.com.au; $17–25 return). Jindabyne itself is entirely new, having been relocated when the Snowy Mountains Scheme dammed the Snowy River and drowned the first settlement, and the lake is now its main attraction: there's good fishing, and in summer you can also swim and sail – most equipment is available to rent in the town. The **Snowy Region Visitor Centre** is within the NPWS headquarters here (daily: summer 8.30am–5pm; winter 8am–5.30pm; ☎02/6450 5600).

From Jindabyne, the Alpine Way continues into the national park and up to **THREDBO**, a compact and attractive village, squeezed into a narrow valley beside the road and the Crackenback River, with alpine-style houses huddled against the mountainside. In winter it offers the best and most expensive skiing in Australia, but unlike the other resorts, it is also reasonably lively in summer and – with its Crackenback **chair-lift** (daily 8.30am–4pm; $20 return) giving easy access to the high country – makes a good base for bushwalking and other explorations. The **Thredbo Resort Centre**, Friday Drive (☎1800 020 589, ⓦwww.thredbo.com.au), can advise on chair-lift timetables and provide other tourist information. There are several annual events in the Thredbo calendar. Musical highlights include the three-day Thredbo **Blues Festival** in mid-January, the three-day **Global Music Festival** in March and the four-day **Jazz Festival** in early May.

Yarrangobilly Caves and Kiandra

The **Yarrangobilly Caves**, a system of about sixty limestone caves at the edge of a rocky plateau surrounded by unspoiled bushland, are one of the few specific sights in the park; they're 6.5km off the Snowy Mountains Highway near Kiandra, 113km northwest of Cooma and 70km south of Tumut. There are several guided tours daily to the **North Glory**, **Jersey** and **Jillabenan Caves** (the last is wheelchair-accessible; all $11; ☎02/6454 9597 for tour times). A fourth cave, the **Glory Hole Cave** (daily 10am–4pm; $3), can be explored on a self-guided tour. From walking trails along the edge of the rock plateau there are panoramic views of the Yarrangobilly Gorge, and a steep trail leads from the Glory Hole car park to a thermal pool at the bottom of the gorge near the Yarrangobilly River. The spring-fed pool, which you can swim in (for free), has a year-round constant temperature of 27°C.

KIANDRA itself is a ghost town, but the detailed interpretive boards of the Heritage Trail will help you find your way through the remaining ruins on this desolate, windswept spot – the extensive plains in the northern part of the park are too cold for any trees to survive. It's hard to believe that fifteen thousand prospectors camped here during the goldrush of 1860; the short-term rush left behind a town of about three hundred people who eked out a living mining and grazing.

Accommodation

In winter, **rooms** are at a premium – despite the plethora of holiday apartments and motels, accommodation is almost impossible to come by without a reservation. In summer, the situation is less dire, and you should have little difficulty finding somewhere in one of the resorts, or at motels on the fringes of the park, such as at Tumut in the north or even back in Cooma (see p.276). Most accommodation in Thredbo can be **booked** through the Thredbo Resort Centre (see above) or Thredbo Accommodation Services (☎1800 801 982, ⓦwww.thredboproperties.com.au); the Snowy River Information Centre in Jindabyne (☎02/6456 2444) also handles accommodation bookings, and there is extensive information and a booking service online at ⓦwww.thredbo.com.au. Note that prices given below are for high season (winter), and that prices can drop dramatically in summer.

Alpine Inn Alpine Way, Khancoban ☎02/6076 9471. The *Alpine Inn* offers motel-style accommodation attached to a great pub and restaurant. Parking. ❸

Banjo Patterson Inn 1 Kosciuszko Rd, Jindabyne ☎02/6456 2372, ⓔbanjopatterson@ski.com.au. Tastefully decorated en-suite rooms with disabled access, balconies, cable TV and fridges. The inn itself has open fires, a laundry, bistro and communal cooking facilities. ❼

Fishermen's Lodge Alpine Way, Khancoban

☎02/6076 9471. Under the same management as the *Alpine Inn*, this lodge caters to backpackers with inexpensive single rooms, plus activities such as horse riding and white-water rafting; they also rent out fishing gear, boats and canoes. ❶

Kasees Lodge Banjo Drive, Thredbo ☎02/6457 6370, ⓦwww.kasees.com.au. One of several lodges and motels along Banjo Drive, this one is particularly cosy and boasts a pool, sauna, log fires and bargain summer rates. Parking. ❺

Kosciuszko Mountain Retreat Sawpit Creek,

near the park headquarters ⓣ02/6456 2224, ⓔjindre@acr.net.au. Tent sites, and cabins and chalets sleeping six, set among a forest of snow gums. Advance booking recommended, especially in winter when prices rise. Two-night minimum stay in high season; dramatically lower rates in low season. Chalets for two high season ❼, low season ❸

Jindy Inn 18 Clyde St, Jindabyne ⓣ02/6456 1957, ⓦwww.jindyinn.com. Friendly place with great views of the lakes from its verandah. Rates include breakfast. Parking. ❹

Snowline Caravan Park Junction of Alpine Way and Kosciuszko Rd, Jindabyne ⓣ02/6456 2099, ⓦwww.snowline.com.au. Camping or cabins, and good facilities, including spa, sauna, café-restaurant and boat rental. Dorms $19, cabins ❸

Snowy Mountain Backpackers 7 Gippsland St, Jindabyne ⓣ02/6456 1500, ⓦwww.snowybackpackers.com.au. This friendly, purpose-built hostel is a backpacker haven: facilities include an Internet lounge, a good café with tasty food, massage, laundry, a tour-booking desk and fantastic kitchens and common areas. Full disabled access. Dorms $25, rooms ❸

Thredbo Alpine Hotel Friday Drive, Thredbo ⓣ02/6459 4200, ⓦwww.thredbo.com.au. Large luxury hotel complex in the centre of the village, close to the chairlift. Wine bars and the resort's only nightclub. ❺

Thredbo YHA Lodge 8 Jack Adams Pass, Thredbo ⓣ02/6457 6376, ⓔthredbo@yhansw.org.au. A luxury purpose-built lodge in the heart of Thredbo village. Cosy atmosphere with open fires and great views across the mountains. Dorms $21, rooms ❷

The south coast

The **south coast** of New South Wales is relatively quiet and relaxed, its numerous bays, coastal lakes and inlets interspersed with unspoiled, sandy beaches, small fishing villages and seaside resorts. During the summer months, especially from Christmas to the end of January, a lot of holiday-makers escape here from the "big smoke" up north, or come up from Victoria: the towns can get busy then, especially the **Shoalhaven area** around **Nowra**, **Batemans Bay**, and **Merimbula**. But don't expect resort hotels and entertainment Queensland-style – it's all rather low-key and family-oriented. There are a few wildlife and amusement parks to keep the children happy, and plenty of opportunities for traditional outdoor pursuits. (One of the region's highlights is the awesome **Pebbly Beach**, 20km from **Ulladulla**, where a tame kangaroo colony lives right on the sand dunes.) Exposed parts on this stretch of the coast are battered by powerful waves that are perfect for **surfing**, while the calmer waters of the numerous coastal lakes, bays and inlets are suited for **swimming**, windsurfing, sailing or paddling your own canoe. There's great **fishing** too, in the rivers and lakes, as well as the inevitable deep-sea season, when game-fishers set out to tussle with marlin. Away from the ocean there's some superb, rugged scenery and great bushwalking and horse riding in the forest-clad, mountainous hinterland. When summer holidays are over, even the bigger towns revert back to an unassuming, laid-back lifestyle, and the weather is mild enough to enjoy them pretty much year-round.

Most of the way down the coast from Sydney, the **Princes Highway** runs a few kilometres inland. Away from the towns, apparently obscure turn-offs from the highway often lead to beautiful and secluded beaches – it's worth taking some time to make your own discoveries. From **Canberra** there are three main routes to the coast: through Kangaroo Valley (see p.244), via Goulburn and Moss Vale (or Bundanoon); the Capital Highway to Batemans Bay; and the Snowy Mountains Highway to Bega via Cooma.

Transport links from Sydney, Canberra and Melbourne to the south coast include **train** from Sydney as far as Bomaderry on the South Coast rail line and from Canberra to Eden with Countrylink (ⓣ13 22 32); and **bus** along the

Princes Highway from Sydney with Premier Motor Services (☎13 34 10) and Murray's (☎13 22 51).

Berry and Nowra-Bomaderry

Sixteen kilometres north of Nowra along the Princes Highway, and easily reached by train on the Sydney–Nowra route, **BERRY** is a charming small town with many National Trust-classified buildings, in a scenic spot surrounded by dairy country and green hills. Its main **Queen Street** is packed with antique and secondhand shops, around a dozen cafés, a variety of restaurants, and a couple of lively country pubs. All this combined with characterful places to stay both within town and in the surrounding countryside, and the beach just 6km away at Gerringong (see p.241), makes Berry a favourite weekend getaway for Sydneysiders. So much so that it can be almost unbearably crowded on fine weekends, especially when the monthly market is on in the showgrounds (first Sun of month).

The town's two **pubs** are attractions in themselves, at opposite ends of Queen Street. You can't miss the *Great Southern Hotel* at no. 95, an Outback-style bungalow pub with two rowing boats on its tin roof. The wrap-around verandah, hung with pretty flowerbaskets, is a great place to relax, or the beer garden is a dream if you have kids, with a fantastic enclosed children's playground. Inside, the pub is quirkier still and there's a pool room, live music on Friday nights, and DJs on Saturday nights. The typical pub bistro is moderately priced. The old *Berry Hotel*, at no. 120 is a more traditional country pub and also popular; the pleasant covered courtyard is a good choice for an affordable tasty meal, from char-grilled steaks to meze plates, and there's a tapas bar out front.

You can **stay** at both pubs. The attached motel units of the *Great Southern Hotel* (☎02/4464 1009, ☞4464 1118; ❸) are all as wackily decorated as the pub itself and make a fun and cheap place to stay, especially if you want to hang out at the pub. The accommodation at the *Berry Hotel* (☎02/4464 1011, ✉berrypub@shoal.net.au; ❸–❹) gets booked out on Saturday nights, even the huge four-bedroom flat upstairs and the two-bedroom house (with kitchen) out the back. Other rooms, which are well furnished, share bathrooms. A more upmarket option is *The Bunyip Inn* next door at 122 Queen St (☎02/4464 2064, ☞4464 2324; B&B ❺), in an imposing two-storey, National Trust-classified former bank. The lovely garden with its huge hedge encloses a swimming pool. The decor is elegant olde-worlde and every room is different (nearly all are en suite); the stables accommodation includes a wheel-chair accessible unit and one with a kitchen. There are lots of places in the surrounding area that are popular **gay and lesbian** weekend retreats including *Spotted Gums Cottage* (☎02/4464 1779, ✉spotgum@shoalhaven.net.au; ❺), a one-bedroom self-contained cottage 3km out of town set on five acres of native gardens (with a barbecue), which has its own spa; expect champagne when you arrive and a breakfast basket for the morning.

There's a big choice of **places to eat** in town, including the pubs detailed above. Opposite the *Berry Hotel*, *The Emporium Food Co* at 127 Queen St is a deli-café which serves affordable gourmet sandwiches, savoury pies and pastries and excellent coffee. The delicatessen *Delicious Food By Lisa* also has an excellent reputation but is harder to find, tucked away on the corner of Alexander and Albert streets behind the main street. Also on Alexander Street, on the corner with Queen Street, vegetarians could head to the early-closing *Thai Berry* (noon–8pm, Fri & Sat to 9pm, closed Tues), where there are several non-meat choices on the spicy menu. *Cavese Trattoria* at 65 Queen St, is an authentic Italian place offering wood-fired pizzas and operating as a café in between meal times (T02/4464 3909; Wed–Sun 10am–9pm; BYO). **Around Berry** there are several wineries, some with attached restaurants. Most highly regarded is the fine-dining *Silos* at **Silos Winery** on the Princes Highway at Jaspers Bush (wine-tasting daily 9am–5pm; restaurant bookings T02/4448 6160; lunch & dinner Wed–Sat, lunch Sun).

Straddling the wide Shoalhaven River, some 20km south of Berry, the twin town of **NOWRA–BOMADERRY** is the main administrative centre of the Shoalhaven holiday region: Bomaderry is situated north of the river, Nowra to the south. The river here is great for sailing, windsurfing and boating in general, while the coast, 13km away, is dotted with popular holiday settlements and numerous beaches. **Shoalhaven Heads** north of the river mouth, **Greenwell Point** in the south, **Huskisson** at Jervis Bay (see p.282) and **Sussex Inlet** are all easily accessible on good roads, although public transport doesn't run out this way. Local **tour companies** such as Southcoast Scenic Bus Tours (T02/4455 1862) run short tours of the area, as does Down Under Close Up Tours (T02/4454 3226), which runs two- to four-day guided tours to more remote parts of the south coast.

For further information on the beaches and how to get to them, and on local accommodation, stop first at the **Shoalhaven Tourist Centre**, at the corner of the Princes Highway and Pleasant Way, just after the road bridge between the two towns (daily 9am–5pm; T02/4421 0778 or 1800 024 261, W www.shoalhaven.nsw.gov.au). **Accommodation** includes an abundance of motels, and an ever-increasing choice of guesthouses, hostels and boutique B&Bs. The old-fashioned, welcoming *M & M's Guesthouse* at 1A Scenic Drive in Nowra (T02/4422 8006, W www.mmguesthouse.com; dorms $25 rooms ❸, including breakfast) offers four-person dorms as well as private rooms. One of the better motels, the *Riverhaven Motel*, is next door, on a riverfront landscaped property but only one block from the shops, by the bridge (T02/4421 2044, F 4421 2121; ❸); facilities include a kitchen and swimming pool. You can camp at the central, riverside *Shoalhaven Caravan Village*, Terrara Road, Nowra (T02/4423 0770; cabins ❸), with its own pool and tennis courts and bikes available to rent. There's not much by way of **restaurants** or **nightlife** in Nowra, but it does have one alternative hangout, the *Tea Club*, 46 Berry St (T02/4422 0900; closed Sun & Mon), a veggie café with a bohemian feel, exhibitions and artworks for sale, drumming workshops (Thurs) and alternative show nights (Sat). They also run monthly poetry and philosophy evenings (call for details). If you need a seafood fix without the showtime thrills, the Co-op next to Shoalhaven River Bridge sells oysters caught by Jimmy Wildes, the reigning world oyster-opening champion.

Jervis Bay

Just southeast of Nowra, the sheltered waters of **Jervis Bay**, by a political quirk, are technically part of the ACT, in order to provide Canberra with access to the sea. The beautiful coast of **Booderee National Park**, at the southeast arm of the bay, is very popular, with its rugged cliffs facing the pounding ocean and tranquil beaches of dazzling white sand and clear water within the confines of the bay, while inland heaths, wetlands and forests offer strolls and bushwalks; details are available from the **visitor centre** (T02/4443 0977) as you enter the park. Note that the park is privately run by Wreck Bay Aboriginal Community and Environment Australia, and NPWS passes are not valid. There are a couple of **campsites** (bookings, essential in summer, are made through the visitor centre): the more secluded and small *Cave Beach* on Wreck Bay is the most sought-after site, despite its cold showers; the larger, more expensive *Greenpatch*, on a creek by Jervis Bay, has the benefit of hot showers, and cars can be parked at each tent site. Holiday-unit accommodation is available on Ellmoos Road, right next to the beach, at *Kullindi Homestead* (⊤ & ⑤02/4441 2897; ❺ two-night minimum).

The **Wreck Bay Aboriginal Community** organizes a summer cultural interpretation programme, Wreck Bay Walkabouts (bookings and information through the visitor centre), which covers diet and medicines, archeology and wildlife; plus there's the recommended Barry's Bushtucker Tours (⊤02/4442 1168). **Jervis Bay Botanic Gardens** (Mon–Fri 8am–4pm, Sun & holidays 10am–5pm; free), on Cave Beach Road, are an annexe of Canberra's Australian National Botanic Gardens and have specimens of plants from around Australia, including a pleasantly cool rainforest gully. Ten kilometres south of Nowra, down the turn-off for Huskisson, is **Marayong Park Emu Farm**, 132 Jervis Bay Rd (Wed–Sun 10am–4pm; ⊤02/4447 8505).

On the western shores of Jervis Bay, 21km southeast of Nowra, **HUSKISSON** is an old town that's a popular tourist spot, with several beach-side campsites, including the council-run *Huskisson Beach Tourist Resort*, Beach Street (⊤02/4441 5142 or 1300 733 027; cabins ❸), which has a playground and tennis courts, and *Huskisson White Sands Tourist Park*, on the corner of Nowra and Beach streets (⊤ & ⑤02/4441 6025; cabins ❺). On the opposite corner of Nowra and Beach streets, overlooking the beach itself, is the elegant and tastefully decorated beach-house-style *Jervis Bay Guesthouse* (⊤02/4441 7658, ⓔinfo@jervisbayguesthouse.com.au; ❻), with just four en-suite rooms, all with verandahs, two with beach views and one with its own spa bath. Another friendly option is *Huskisson B&B* at 12 Tomerong St (⊤02/4441 7551; ❹). For something a little out of the ordinary, however, consider *Paper Bark Camp Eco Resort* at 605 Woollamia Rd (⊤02/4441 6066 or 4441 7299, ⓦwww.paperbarkcamp.com.au; full-board in tents ❼, or B&B in lodge ❼; often midweek and low-season deals available), a luxury resort modelled on permanent tented camps in South Africa: accommodation is in beautiful en-suite tents with huge beds, private verandahs and solar powered lighting, and modern bush tucker is provided for meals. The focus of the town itself is the beachfront *Huskisson Hotel*, which has a good bistro and plenty of pool-playing opportunities. **Sealife-watching tours** are available all year, and there's an eighty percent success rate of seeing whales and other marine life with Dolphin Watch Cruises, 50 Owen St (⊤02/4441 6311 or 1800 246 010, ⓦwww.dolphinwatch.com.au). Huskisson is also a good base for **diving** into the pristine waters of the bay. In fact, it is the second most popular dive spot in Australia, after the Great Barrier Reef. For details of one-off dives and packages, contact ProDive at 64 Owen St (⊤02/4441 5255) or Seasports, 47 Owen St (⊤02/4441 5012).

Ulladulla

In the 1930s many Italian fishermen settled in the small fishing village of **ULLADULLA**, and they're still a strong influence on the atmosphere of this tranquil outpost: the traditional Blessing of the Fleet continues to be celebrated every Easter at the harbour breakwater. It's a beautiful area, dominated by the sandstone plateau of the **Morton National Park**, rising steeply to the west of town. Mostly this is an inaccessible barrier, but there's a good bushwalk to the top of the 719-metre-high **Pigeon House Mountain** in the Budawang Range; the walk there and back takes about four hours and is accessed from the Princes Highway, via a turn-off 8km south of Ulladulla. Along the coast in both directions are attractive river mouths, beaches and lakes: among those worth visiting are pretty **Lake Conjola**, 10km to the north; **Lake Burrill**, 5km to the south; and **Lake Tabourie**, 13km to the south – all are popular with fishermen, canoeists and campers. Around Ulladulla there are also some quaint country towns worth visiting. **Mollymook**, 3km to the north, has some sensational surfing sites and hiking trails and a few kilometres further on there's lots to see and do in the village of **Milton**, home to numerous antique shops, craft shops and cafés. This region provides a relaxing weekend escape from Sydney or a worthwhile stopover en route to or from Melbourne, but you really need your own transport to appreciate the area and to get off the main roads on to some of the scenic drives.

Tourist information is available from the Civic Centre on the highway (daily 9am–5pm; ☎02/4455 1269, ⓦwww.shoalhaven.nsw.gov.au). **Places to stay** include the elegant *Ulladulla Guesthouse*, near the harbour at the corner of Burrill and South streets (☎02/4455 1796, ⓦwww.guesthouse.com.au; ❺), which has a spa, sauna, beautiful palm-fringed, heated, saltwater swimming pool and a restaurant serving top-notch French cuisine; *Quiet Garden Motel* on a rocky promontory at 2 Burrill St (☎02/4455 1757, ⓕ4454 3090; ❹); and the *South Coast Backpackers*, 63 Princes Highway (☎02/4454 0500, ⓦwww.southcoastbackpackers.com.au; dorms $20, rooms ❷), a small hostel which can provide lifts to Pigeon House Mountain, Jervis Bay or Murramarang National Park, and also have bikes and canoes for rent. The *Beach Haven Holiday Resort*, on Princes Highway in Ulladulla South (☎02/4455 2110 or 4455 1712; on-site vans ❷, holiday apartments ❸, cabins ❸), boasts a beachfront location, complete with swimming pools, spa and tennis courts. There's also a council-run caravan park on South Street, close to the beach: *Ulladulla Headland Tourist Park* (☎02/4455 2457; tent site ❶, six-person cabins ❹).

In terms of **activities**, there's swimming at the free seawater pool by the wharf, or open-water scuba courses run by Ulladulla Divers Supplies, Watson Street (☎02/4455 5303). The local Budamurra Aboriginal community has also constructed an interesting cultural trail, the **Coomee Nulunga** (☎02/4455 5883, ⓦwww.budamurra.asn.au); access is via Deering Street, opposite the Lighthouse Oval car park. The track meanders through eucalypts and heath flowers to a viewing platform over the ocean, and then on to a secluded beach. Guided tours ($10) are offered by the Budamurra people, and include tips on boomerang throwing, didgeridoo playing and fire making, as well as some bush tucker.

There are a couple of good Italian places to **eat** in the town, including *Tory's Seafood*, 30 Watson St, by the wharf (☎02/4454 0888, daily for dinner plus Sun lunch). *Café Alfresco*, 10 Watson St, offers great home-made soups, interesting salads and sandwiches daily; while the *Harbourside Restaurant*, 84 Princes Highway (☎02/4455 3377), specializes in modern Australian cuisine and fresh seafood open daily and is licensed and BYO. For Thai, head for *Supreeya's* restaurant at the corner of Deering and St Vincent streets (☎02/4455 4579), which also offers takeaway and has a good selection of vegetarian options. *Ulladulla Guesthouse's* wonderful licensed restaurant, *Elizans* (bookings essential; see above), is open to non-residents and serves breakfasts and superb three-course evening meals accompanied by a carefully chosen wine list featuring local wines.

Batemans Bay and around

BATEMANS BAY, at the mouth of the Clyde River and the end of the highway from Canberra, is a favourite escape for the landlocked residents of the capital, just 152km away. It's not the most exciting place on the coast, but since it's a fair-sized resort, there's plenty to do. Around Batemans Bay itself you can take a **cruise** on the Clyde River with one of several companies, including Merinda Cruises (℡02/4472 4052); tours depart daily from the wharf and prices start at around $25 for a three-hour tour, including a lunch stopover upriver in the historic township of **Nelligen** with arts-and-crafts shops and a nice café. Alternatively, you can board one of the little trains that run through the woodlands of the **Birdland Animal Park**, 55 Beach Rd (daily 9.30am–4pm; $11), for a closer look at the birds and native animals – the wombat display is among the best in the country. In the **Murramarang National Park** (℡02/4423 2170), a small coastal strip just north of town, there are campsites at **Pretty Beach**, **Pebbly Beach** and **Durras Beach** – popular not only with campers but also with kangaroos, which come here at dawn or dusk to frolic on the beach. Rumour has it that they even enjoy body surfing. You can stay at *Murramarang Resort* (℡02/4478 6355, ⓦwww.murramarangresort.com; cabins and on-site vans ❸), where there's bike and canoe rental available, plus organized geology walks, lake rides and fishing cruises.

From **MOGO**, 10km to the south, you can visit the open-air **Old Mogo Town** museum (daily 9am–5pm; $12; ⓦwww.oldmogotown.com.au), a reconstruction of a mid-nineteenth-century goldrush town near an old gold mine. The best time to come is Sunday morning when there's a bric-a-brac **market** held here. Twenty-five kilometres south of Batemans Bay, just before **Moruya**, a small, unsealed road turns off the highway to the west, heading through a pretty valley and then up over hills at the edge of the remote **Deua National Park** to the former goldrush town of **Araluen** where, between 1868 and 1872, about fifteen thousand prospectors congregated in the hope of striking it lucky.

Batemans Bay Tourist Information is on Princes Highway, at the corner of Beach Road (daily 9am–5pm; ℡02/4472 6900 or 1800 802 528, ⓦwww.naturecoast-tourism.com.au). As you'd expect of a resort, **accommodation** consists mainly of motels and a wide range of holiday units; most of the latter require a minimum week's booking during peak summer times. However, there are also two hostels: *Shady Willows Holiday Park* (℡02/4472 4972, ⓦwww.shadywillows.com.au; dorms $21, cabins ❷), is close to town (but not the beach), with a YHA hostel section attached, while *Beach Road Backpackers Hostel*, at 92 Beach Rd (℡02/4472 3644, Ⓔbrbph@dynamite .com.au; dorms $23), is a small independent place; the owner here will book tours and cruises. Otherwise, try *Bay Surfside Holiday Flats*, 7km out of town at 662 Beach Rd (℡02/4471 1275; ❹), whose units sleep up to six and have all mod cons. There's **camping** at eight caravan parks including the upmarket *Coachhouse Marina Resort*, by the beach on Beach Road 1km south of town (℡02/4472 4392 or 1800 670 715, Ⓔbookings@coachhouse.com.au; cabins ❺, on-site vans ❷), with a pool and tennis court; or the excellent *River Breeze Caravan Park* (℡02/4474 2370, ⓦwww.riverbreeze.com.au; dorms $22, 4-person cabins ❸), a five-minute walk from the coach stop on the Princes Highway in Moruya. *Mogendoura Farm*, on Hawdons Road, 8km west of Moruya on the Moruya River (℡02/4474 2057, ⓦwww.southcoast.com.au /mogendoura; ❹), offers week-long cottage **farmstays** with horse riding, canoeing and bushwalking opportunities; occasionally overnight stays are also possible.

There's a range of **restaurants** in Batemans Bay, mainly with fish- and seafood-based menus. Cheap and healthy luncheon fare – mugs of coffee and home-made savouries and cake – can be found at the *Good Food Café* on 45 Orient St. *Rafters*, 28 Beach Rd (☎02/4472 4288; closed Mon), has a relaxing, intimate atmosphere, with à la carte dining, vegetarian options and BYO. On the Esplanade, *Seagulls* serves rather overpriced seafood and steaks, but the sweeping waterfront views make it worth the extra expense (☎02/4472 0253; closed Tues), while the trendy and popular *Starfish Deli* also has a marine panorama with a modern menu, including a variety of wood-fired pizzas and many veggie dishes. *Jameson's on the Pier*, on the opposite side of the bay, by the bridge on Old Punt Road (☎02/4472 6405), offers fine dining on fresh fish and is set on its own jetty.

Narooma and around

A small but expanding fishing village surrounded by beautiful beaches, bays and coastal lakes, **NAROOMA** lies at the heart of an area famous for its succulent **mud oysters**. You can canoe and windsurf on the **Wagonga Inlet** or sail to **Montague Island** – an offshore sanctuary for sea birds, seals and penguins. If you actually want to disembark at the island, you'll have to join a tour organized by the NPWS in Narooma (tours daily: winter 3.30pm; summer 6.30pm, though 9.30am tours are sometimes available; 3hr; $70; ☎02/4476 2888, ☞4476 2757), since it's a protected wildlife reserve. Southern right and humpback **whales** have begun to reappear in the bay between September and November, and tour operators also organize whale-watching tours in the event of any sightings; you can book at the **Narooma Visitors Centre** on the highway (daily 9am–5pm; ☎02/4476 2881, ⓦwww.naturecoast-tourism.com.au). Non-landing **cruises** cost from around $50 for a two-hour trip, including a visit to Montague Island to see the seal colonies. The visitors centre also books scenic cruises aboard the *Wagonga Princess*, a century-old pine ferry which winds its way in and out of secluded bays on the river, stopping off for a guided rainforest walk and oyster-tasting session ($22 for a 3hr tour). **Diving** can be found off Montague Island all year, organized by Ocean Hut, 123 Princes Highway (☎02/4476 2278; $55 for one dive, $65 for two; Jan–April grey nurse sharks and tropical fish; Aug–Dec mainly seal-spotting).

In Narooma there's the *Narooma Blue* YHA **hostel**, 8 Princes Highway (☎02/4476 4440, Ⓔnaroomayha@narooma.com; dorms $21, rooms ❷). Accommodation is in well-equipped wooden cabins, surrounded on three sides by lakes and bay; there is also a very reasonable Internet lounge, cheap bike and canoe rental and free fishing gear. Steve, the ever-helpful owner, will happily dispense advice and book local tours for his guests. Good **motels** and resorts include *Forsters Bay Lodge*, 55 Forsters Bay Rd (☎ & ☞02/4476 2319; ❸), and *Tree Motel*, 213 Princes Highway (☎02/4476 4233; ❸), which has air-conditioned suites, a pool and barbecue. The beachside *Island View Beach Resort*, on the highway 3km south of town (☎02/4476 2600 or 1800 465 432, ⓦwww.islandview.com.au; camp sites ❶, cabins ❹) has luxury cabins (with Jacuzzis) as well as more basic accommodation, a heated pool, tennis courts and a barbecue area. *Pub Hill Farm*, Scenic Drive, 8km west of Narooma (☎ & ☞02/4476 3177, ⓦwww.pubhillfarm.com; ❹), is a farm-style B&B that has four en-suite rooms (including one private, garden room with log fire – ❺), and offers a baby-sitting service. The beautifully located *Clark Bay Farm* (☎02/4476 1640, Ⓔamethyst@sci.net.au; ❹) offers disabled-access accommodation sleeping up to six, with electronically activated doors and beds.

Local favourites for **dining** include *Lynch's Restaurant* on Princes Highway (☏02/4476 3002), serving excellent contemporary Australian cuisine and local oysters. There are several **bistros** at the marina on Riverside Drive at Forsters Bay, including the *Quarterdeck Marina* (☏02/4476 2723). *Rockwall Restaurant*, 107 Campbell St, has well-priced à la carte seafood specials (☏02/4476 2040; closed Sun & Mon), while *Casey's Café* at the top of the town's hill, on the corner of Canty and Wagonga streets (☏02/4476 1241), is a bright, cheery establishment, serving healthy, hearty food with many veggie options and the best coffee in town. For something more special, you could try the oyster bar overlooking Forsters Bay in the Narooma Oyster Supplies shop on Riverside Drive (☏02/4476 1256).

Narooma's **nightlife** doesn't extend much beyond the vast *Golf Club* on Ballingalla Street (daily 10am–10pm), with pool tables and poker machines, serving the latest drink in town. If you're in need of a film fix, worth visiting is the delightfully preserved, National Trust-classified Kinema picture theatre – an original 1920s **cinema** screening modern movies on Friday and Saturday evenings and Sunday matinees (during school holidays and the Dec/Jan holiday season, shows run daily except Monday).

A thriving local **Koorie** community run their own Umbarra Aboriginal Cultural Centre (☏02/4473 7232, @umbarra@acr.net.au) at **Wallaga Lake**, 25km south of Narooma. They operate daily tours to local sacred sites, including Gulaga (Mount Dromedary), with hands-on activities such as painting with ochres, building bark huts and sampling bush tucker and traditional medicine. (As some of their tours traverse Aboriginal lands, special permits are required for external visitors planning on visiting these areas independently.) They also have a cruise with commentary on Wallaga Lake, one of the largest saltwater lakes on the Australian coast. The lake's black duck is the sacred totem for the local indigenous people. Entry to the centre is free; activities and tours range from $7 to $45.

Central Tilba and Tilba Tilba

On your way south you can take a break in the picturesque mountain villages of **CENTRAL TILBA** and **TILBA TILBA**, just off the highway, 10km south of Narooma, where time seems to have stood still – and various craft shops and workshops are ready and willing to exploit the olde-worlde ambience. It's an

Burnum Burnum: Aboriginal activist

Wallaga Lake is the birthplace of one of Australia's most important Aboriginal figureheads, the elder named **Burnum Burnum**, an ancestral name meaning great warrior. He is best known for his flamboyant political stunts, which included planting the Aboriginal flag at Dover to claim England as Aboriginal territory in Australia's bicentennial year, 1988, highlighting the dispossession of his native country. He was born under a sacred tree by Wallaga Lake in January 1936. His mother died soon afterwards and he was taken by the Aborigines Protection Board and placed in a mission at Bomaderry, constituting one of the "stolen generation" of indigenous children removed from their families in this period. After graduating in law and playing professional rugby union for New South Wales, he became a prominent political activist in the 1970s. He was involved in various environmental and indigenous protests, including erecting the "tent embassy" outside the Federal Parliament in Canberra (see p.260), and standing twice, unsuccessfully, for the senate. Burnum Burnum died in August 1997 and his ashes were scattered near the tree where he was born.

area famous for its cheeses, and is also a little-known wine-growing region: Central Tilba's hundred-year-old **ABC Cheese Factory** is open for visits and free tastings (daily 9am–5pm); and you can follow this up with some wine tasting at **Tilba Valley Winery**, signposted off the Princes Highway, 5km north of town (Mon–Sat 10am–5pm, Sun 11am–5pm). Situated on Corunna Lake, the working family vineyard and winery is an idyllic spot for a ploughman's lunch on the terrace or a picnic in the grounds, overlooking a lake. Try the unusual local mead made at the winery.

The *Dromedary Hotel*, on Bates Street in Central Tilba (℡02/4473 7223, Ⓕ4473 7229; ❸), is a historic pub with open fires; counter **meals** are served and **B&B** accommodation is available. The nearby *Rose & Sparrow Café* is the most atmospheric of several places offering cream teas and light meals. If you're feeling energetic, follow the walking trail which starts from Pam's Store in Tilba Tilba and leads through a forest to the summit of **Mount Dromedary**, at almost 800m. The hike there and back is about 11km, and you should allow five to six hours – or take a **horse** from Mount Dromedary Trail Rides (book through the Narooma Tourist Information Centre – see p.285).

Bermagui

Not long after the turn-off from the highway for Central Tilba and Tilba Tilba, there's a delightful scenic detour along the coast via **BERMAGUI**, 8km southeast from the highway, on both the Bermagui River and sheltered Horseshoe Bay. (The road runs from Wallaga Lake – see opposite – to Tathra – see p.288). Bermagui attracts quite a few **game-fishing** fanatics, thanks to its associations with Zane Grey, the American writer of Westerns and a legendary marlin fisherman. There are several big-game fishing tournaments annually, and charter boats offer trips to catch black marlin, yellow-fin tuna and other big fish. In addition to several **motels**, there's the pleasant old *Bermagui Hotel* on Lamont Street (℡02/6493 4206; ❸), which serves good meals; *Flats Elite*, 84 Murrah St (℡02/6493 4274; ❹), which only takes weekly bookings; or the central *Zane Grey Caravan Park* on Lamont Street (℡02/6493 4382; cabins ❹). Bermagui has its own, tiny, **Information Centre** by the *Bermagui Hotel* (daily 10am–4pm; ℡02/6493 4206 or 1800 645 808). **Eating choices** include a Thai restaurant and a pizzeria, but the *Saltwater Seafood Restaurant* (℡02/6493 4328) is the best place to try Bermagui's legendary fish catches.

For a quieter alternative to the highway, you can continue south along the coast road to Merimbula via Tathra (see p.288). Not far out of Bermagui, unsealed tracks branch off the coast road to **Mimosa Rocks National Park**, where there are opportunities for bushwalking and swimming. There are NPWS **campsites** at Middle Beach, Picnic Point and Argannu Beach (details and bookings on ℡02/4476 2888).

Bega and around

Lush green meadows, munching cows, wide valleys and mountains in the background – you could almost mistake this pastoral scenery for somewhere in the foothills of the Swiss Alps. Certainly the area around **BEGA** is prime dairy country: at the **Bega Cheese Heritage Centre**, Lagoon Street, North Bega (daily 9am–5pm; ⓦwww.begacheese.com.au), you can watch the famous local cheese being made, and try a few samples. Scenery and cheese apart, there's no great reason to come here, but it's a convenient stopover, handy for the junction of the Princes Highway with the Snowy Mountains Highway. In town, the **Bega Family Museum**, on the corner of Bega and Auckland streets

(Mon–Fri 10am–4pm), has regional memorabilia and photos. For more on local attractions, including the Grevillea Winery, check out the **Bega Tourist Information Centre**, 91 Gipps St (Mon–Sat 9am–5pm, Sun 9am–3pm; ☎02/6492 2045, ✉begatic@acr.net.au).

Accommodation can be found at the *Grand Hotel*, 236 Carp St (☎02/6492 1122; ❷), which has motel-style pub **rooms**, as well as counter **meals** during the week; at the *Pickled Pear*, a beautifully restored and comfortably furnished three-room 1870s guesthouse on the main street (☎02/6492 1393, ⓦwww.ausac.com/ppear; ❹); and at *Bega Caravan Park* on the Princes Highway (☎02/6492 2303; cabins and units ❸, on-site vans ❷).

Tathra

From Bega, you can peel off the Princes Highway to pick up the coast road at the small holiday and fishing village of **TATHRA**. **Accommodation** in Tathra ranges from the motel-style units at the *Tathra Hotel Motel* on Bega Street (☎02/6494 1101; ❸), to the *Tabja Rural Retreat* on Barrabooka Road (☎02/6494 0220, ⓦwww.tanjaruralretreat.com.au; ❻), an artist-owned B&B with an emphasis on good food and relaxation. Alternatively, try the timber cottages at *Kianinny Cabins Resort* on Tathra Road, Tathra Beach (☎02/6494 1990 or 1800 064 225, ⓦwww.kcr.com.au; ❻), a family-oriented place with a saltwater pool; at peak times, only weekly bookings are accepted. There's a **tourist information centre** at Tathra Wharf (daily 9am–5pm; ☎02/6494 4062), an all-purpose place that also rents out fishing, diving and surfing gear, and has a decent café; there's a **maritime museum** upstairs (daily 8am–5pm; $1.50).

Just south of Tathra, coastal **Bournda National Park** features stunning beaches, brackish lagoons and freshwater lakes: there are NPWS **campsites** at Hobart Beach on the southern end of Wallagoot Lake (book well ahead from Dec to Easter; ☎02/6495 5000).

Merimbula

The pretty township of **MERIMBULA** attracts a lot of holiday-makers from Victoria because of its accessibility, year-round temperate climate and good beaches. Between tanning sessions, you can cruise Merimbula Lake (actually the wide mouth of the Merimbula River) and Pambula Lake with several different companies for around $20 for two hours: Sinbad Cruises (book at the tourist centre) is recommended for their interesting commentary on Aboriginal history and oyster cultivation, while Merimbula Marina (☎02/6495 1686) offers dolphin-watching and, from September to early December, whale-watching tours. Cruises and boat rental can both be arranged at the **Tourist Information Centre** on Beach Street (daily 9am–5pm; ☎02/6497 4900, ⓦwww.sapphirecoast.com.au).

There are several places to **eat** out, including the renowned *Waterfront Café*, on the promenade by the tourist office, which has a seafood and snack menu (☎02/6495 2211). Also on the promenade, the *Lakeside Café* serves assorted fish dishes and some veggie options. *Wheelers*, across the road from the Golf Club on the south side of town (☎02/6495 6330), serves excellent local oysters. There are several good Asian restaurants, including *Bahn Thai* at 17 Merimbula Drive (☎02/6495 4555) and, in the shopping centre on Princes Highway, *Saigon Palace* (☎02/6495 3255). Opposite *Saigon Place*, *Pedro's* serves good Mexican meals. Booking is recommended for all restaurants in the evenings.

Accommodation

Though there are dozens of **motels** (❸) and **holiday apartments** in Merimbula, all of them can be heavily booked during the summer holidays, when many places hike their rates considerably and holiday apartments accept only weekly bookings. The places listed below may have space at short notice. If you're stuck, try the free **phone booking service** run by the local Chamber of Commerce (☎1800 150 457), which covers all grades of accommodation.

Mandeni Resort Sapphire Coast Drive, 7km north ☎02/6495 9644 or 1800 358 354, ⓦwww .mandeni.com.au. Fully equipped timber cottages in a bushland setting, sleeping a maximum of six. Facilities include tennis courts, two swimming pools, a golf course and many walking trails. Nightly rates available on request. Weekly rate per cottage $1000.

Merimbula Beach Cabins Short Point, Merimbula ☎02/6495 1216 or 1800 825 555, ⓦwww.beachcabins.com.au. Bushland cabins by the beach, with half-court tennis, laundry and BBQ. Weekly rate per cabin $425.

South Haven Caravan Park Elizabeth St, between Merimbula Lake and the beach ☎02/6495 1304, ⓦwww.southhaven.com.au. Sauna, heated pool,

tennis and squash courts. Cabins ❸

Wandarrah Lodge YHA 8 Marine Parade ☎02/6495 3503, ⓕ6495 3163. A modern, purpose-built youth hostel close to both the beach and lake. Facilities include two lounges, Internet access and a BBQ area. Generous free breakfast, lots of organized activities and outings (including free canoe rental), friendly, knowledgeable staff and free pick-up service. $2 discount per night for three nights' stay or more. Dorms $21, rooms ❷

Woodbine Park Holiday Cabins Sapphire Coast Drive, 7km north ☎ & ⓕ02/6495 9333, ⓦwww.woodbinepark.com.au. Award-winning wooden cabins in a bushland setting, sleeping a maximum of six. Swimming pool, tennis court and golf course. ❺

Eden and heading inland

EDEN, on Twofold Bay, is pretty much the last seaside stop before the Princes Highway heads inland towards Victoria. In 1818 the first whaling station on the Australian mainland was established here, and **whaling** remained a major industry until the 1920s. For information on the local area, call in at the **Tourist Information Centre** on the highway (Mon–Fri 9am–4pm, Sat & Sun 9am–noon; ☎ & ⓕ02/6496 1953, ⓦwww.sapphirecoast.com.au).

Today Eden is touristy in a quiet sort of way, with good fishing, and there are plenty of reminders of the old days, the best of which is the **Killer Whale Museum** on Imlay Street (daily 9.15am–3.45pm; $5; ⓦwww.killerwhale museum.com.au); as well as whaling, it looks at the fishing and timber industries which still contribute to Eden's livelihood. At the information centre you can also book **cruises** on Twofold Bay and further out to sea – with luck, penguins, dolphins and, in winter, even whales might be sighted. Cat Balou Cruises (☎02/6490 2027) offers excellent year-round dolphin-spotting cruises ($25 for 2hr 30min), and seasonal whale-watching trips ($50 for 4hr); student discounts are available.

As you head south from Eden, you become increasingly surrounded by the vast temperate rainforests that characterize southeastern Australia. Roads lead off the highway in both directions into the magnificent **Ben Boyd National Park** (☎02/6495 5000), which hugs the coast to the north and south of Eden, offering good camping, walking and beaches. Inland, the summit of **Mount Imlay** can be reached by a three-kilometre walking track that starts at the picnic grounds at Burrawang Forest Road, 14km south of Eden. The steep, strenuous ascent is rewarded by a panoramic view over the coast and across the dense forests of the hinterland onto the Monaro plain. Camping and park passes can be obtained from the visitors centre in Eden.

Accommodation

Australasia Hotel 160 Imlay St, Eden ☏02/6496 1600, ℱ6496 1462. Budget, basic accommodation in an old pub, catering mostly to backpackers; counter meals available. Dorms $20, rooms ❷

Bayview Motor Inn Princes Highway, Eden ☏02/6496 1242, ℮azalea@asitis.net.au. Deluxe motel with room service, swimming pool and spa. ❺

Crown & Anchor Inn 239 Imlay St, Eden ☏02/6496 1017, ℮www.acr.net.au/~crown anchor. A much talked-about Eden sleep-haven in an 1840s building that is full of character. Gourmet breakfasts, sea views, and complimentary port by the open fire. Ten percent discounts for stays of three nights or more. ❹

Seahorse Inn just off the Princes Highway in Boydtown ☏02/6496 1361. A mock-Tudor inn offering B&B, with a tennis court, tearooms and restaurant. ❹

Twofold Beach Resort 7km south of Eden ☏02/6496 1572, ℮2fold@austernet.com.au. Beachside location with pool and hospitable management. Cabins and on-site vans ❸

Wonboyn Lake Resort 40km south of Eden ☏02/6496 9162, ℮www.wonboynlakeresort .com.au. A scenic location off the beaten track at Lake Wonboyn. Swimming pool, spa, shop, boat-ramp, canoe and boat rental; beach nearby. Cottages ❹

Northern New South Wales

Northern New South Wales may have nothing to match the majesty of the Snowy Mountains, as the Dividing Range falls away to the lower slopes that protect the **New England Plateau**, but the World Heritage-listed temperate and subtropical areas of the range's northeast end harbour sixteen pockets of rainforest that more than compete in terms of natural beauty. In many ways the north is more varied than the south, offering a taste of everything: big resorts and empty beaches on the coast, with alternative-lifestyle villages and communes in the hinterland beyond; lovely parks and forests on the steep slopes behind the coast; and further inlands quietly attractive agricultural country, dotted with interesting old towns.

The roads are generally in fairly good condition, but the busy **Pacific Highway** is not the best of them. Though it's gradually being upgraded and widened, with the addition of much-needed overtaking lanes, sections of this winding coastal road are still alarmingly narrow considering the weight of traffic and the big trucks that use it; bus services on the highway almost invariably run late. The inland route on the **New England Highway** via Muswellbrook, Tamworth and Armidale is a faster alternative if you're heading straight for Brisbane – many buses go this way too.

The north coast

The coast from Sydney north to the Queensland border is more densely populated and much more touristy than the southern coast. Popular holiday destinations are strung up the coast north from Newcastle (see p.207). **Port Stephens**, **Port Macquarie**, **Coffs Harbour** and the twin city of **Tweed Heads**–Coolangatta, straddling the state line, attract local tourists as well as overseas visitors. The subtropical part of the coast, from Coffs Harbour north, is more attractive: since the 1970s the area around **Lismore**, **Byron Bay** and

Murwillumbah has been a favoured destination for people from the southern cities seeking an "alternative" lifestyle. This movement has left in its wake not only disillusioned hippie farmers (as well as a few who've survived with their illusions intact), but also a firmly established artistic and alternative scene.

As in the south, the **coastline** consists of myriad inlets, bays and coastal lakes, interspersed by white, sandy beaches and rocky promontories. Parallel to the coast, the rocky plateaus of the **Great Dividing Range** rise up from the plain; so steep is the eastern edge of this range that it defied even the efforts of the early foresters, so that to this day the hills remain densely wooded. A handful of townships still depend on the timber industry, but most **forest** areas are now protected as either national parks or state forests. From the highlands, numerous streams tumble down from the escarpment in mighty waterfalls, and once on the coastal plain they flow together to form short, very wide and fast-flowing rivers. In the fertile river valleys the predominant agricultural activity is cattle breeding, while in the north subtropical and tropical agriculture takes over, especially the cultivation of bananas.

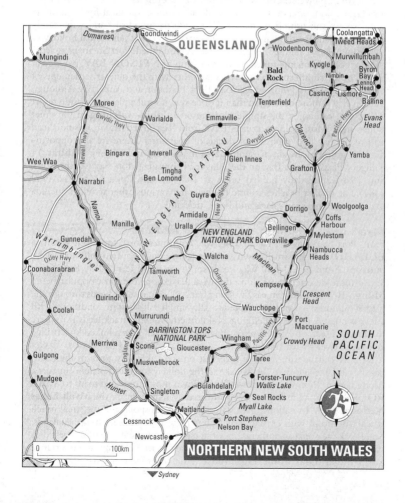

NORTHERN NEW SOUTH WALES

0   100km

▼ Sydney

In essence, the further you go, the better this coast gets – the northeast corner is one of the most scenic areas in the state and its remote country roads are well worth exploring. If the bigger coastal resorts are too touristy for your liking, there's no shortage of quiet, even lonely, beaches as you head further up, along with small fishing villages and sleepy hamlets inland that are virtually undiscovered. For bushwalkers there are vast areas of totally remote, rugged, wild terrain to explore in the national parks of the Great Dividing Range.

Getting up the north coast is easy, with frequent **train** and **bus** services between Sydney and Brisbane stopping en route. There are also some excellent one-way tours from Sydney to Byron Bay (see box on p.198). In addition, Kirklands (℡02/6622 1499) runs between Brisbane and Lismore via Surfers Paradise (see p.428), Tweed Heeds, Murwillumbah, Brunswick Heads, Byron Bay, Lennox Head and Ballina.

Port Stephens and the lakes

Just north of Newcastle, the wide bay of **Port Stephens**, which extends inland for some 25km, offers calm waters and numerous coves ideal for swimming, water sports and fishing, while the ocean side has good surf and wide, sandy beaches. In January, thousands of families arrive to take their annual holiday in the "Blue Water Paradise", as the area has been dubbed. Port Stephens is actually the collective name for the main township of **NELSON BAY**, perched at the tip of the southern arm of the bay, together with the quieter settlements of Shoal Bay, Soldiers Point, Fingal Bay, Boat Harbour and Anna Bay. Although Nelson Bay is more developed than it once was, it's still a pleasant seaside resort where you can enjoy the simple pleasure of **dolphin-watching** in the quiet waters here. Most dolphin cruises leave from **Tea Gardens** on the northern arm of the bay (see opposite for details of operators). There are also opportunities to go on bushwalks to spot **koalas** in the wild at **Tilligery Habitat**, 14 Tilligery Plaza, Tanilba Bay, on the Tilligery Peninsula (Mon–Sat 9.30am–4pm, Sun 10am–2pm; daily guided tours at 10.30am and 2pm; $11; ℡02/4982 4441). The smaller beaches around the bay offer various other activities, including sea-kayaking, sand safaris and horse trekking.

Myall Lakes National Park and around

From Port Stephens the Pacific Highway continues north for about 40km to **BULAHDELAH**, a small town surrounded by bush-covered hills and rocky outcrops. From here, Myall Way heads south via a toll ferry (daily 8am–6pm; $3) to more deserted spots along the Myall lakeshore, the most popular being **Mungo Brush**, where an easy walking track (30min return) heads through the littoral rainforest – a variant adapted to salty and harsh seafront conditions, with a low canopy. A more challenging 21-kilometre walking track leads from here to **Hawks Nest**, on Port Stephens Bay and the Myall River, linked by a bridge across the river to Tea Gardens.

Just after Bulahdelah, you can turn east on the Lakes Way towards the coast, past Myall Lake and then Wallis Lake to the holiday town of Forster–Tuncurry. Along here, at Bungwahl, a turn-off leads down mostly unsealed roads to **SEAL ROCKS**, a remote fishing village and the only settlement in the **Myall Lakes National Park**. Its national park status means it's unspoilt, and the small beach is truly beautiful with crystal-clear waters marooned between two headlands. Seal Rocks' seasonal agglomerations of nurse sharks make it one of the best dive sites in New South Wales; contact Forster Dive Centre (see opposite) to arrange a trip. **Sugar Loaf Point Lighthouse**, built in 1875, is a ten-minute stroll away; the grounds (Tues & Thurs 10am–noon & 1–3pm) offer a fantastic view along the coast, and the lookout below leads down to a deserted, rocky beach with a view of the 4WD track that extends through the national park.

North of Seal Rocks, the tiny **Booti Booti National Park** is located between Cape Hawke and Charlotte Head. The park encompasses many beaches, oceanside forests and – on the western boundary – Wallis Lake, an excellent boating and fishing spot. There's also a secluded camping site on the coastline near Seal Rocks. Ten kilometres further north, a bridge connects the twin cities **FORSTER–TUNCURRY** on the spit of land that separates **Wallis Lake** from the ocean. The lake is very pretty, surrounded by trees and with bush-covered **Corrie Island** at its centre. Forster is famous for its **oysters**, and for its playful resident **dolphins**. The lake itself is superb for fishing and swimming – you can rent houseboats as well as dinghies, canoes and windsurfers. The abundant seafood made the spot attractive to the local Aboriginal people, the Wallamba, and their descendants can take you on a tour of significant sites.

Practicalities

Port Stephens, Forster–Tuncurry and Myall Lakes National Park are not the easiest places to reach on public **transport**. Only a few long-distance Sydney–Brisbane buses, such as McCafferty's/Greyhound Pioneer stop at Bulahdelah. However, there are reasonably good connections to and from Newcastle and Sydney with Port Stephens Buses (☎02/4982 2940, ⓦwww.psbuses.nelsonbay.com), which stop daily at Nelson Bay, Shoal Bay and Fingal Bay, from where local buses run to Boat Harbour, Anna Bay and Soldiers Point. In addition, Great Lakes Coaches (☎1800 043 263) runs weekdays only from Newcastle to Tea Gardens, Hawks Nest, Bulahdelah, Forster and on to Taree.

Both the **Port Stephens Visitors Centre** at Victoria Parade in Nelson Bay (daily 9am–5pm; ☎02/4981 1579 or 1800 808 900, ⓦwww.portstephens .org.au) and the well-organized **Great Lakes Visitors Centre** at Little Street in Forster (daily 9am–5pm; ☎02/6554 8799 or 1800 802 692, ⓦwww.great lakes.org.au), can provide you with stacks of information and can book accommodation and tours (including those run by local aborigines). The **NPWS** office is on Teramby Road in Nelson Bay (☎02/4984 8200). **Dolphin-watching** jaunts are organized by Dawson's Scenic Cruises (☎02/4982 0444, ⓦwww.portstephens-multimedia.com.au/dawsoncruises; 2hr; $16) at Nelson Bay; Amaroo Dolphin Watch (☎0419 333 445, ⓦwww.amaroocruise.com.au; 2hr 30min; $30) at Forster; and Simba Luxury Cruises (☎02/4997 1084, ⓔsimba@myallcoast.net.au) at Tea Gardens (daily 10am; 3hr; $18) and Nelson Bay (Wed & Sun 11am; 2hr; $14). Much more satisfying than a motor cruise, however, are the environmentally aware dolphin- and whale-watching trips ($20/$49 respectively) aboard *Imagine*, a fifteen-metre catamaran moored at Nelson Bay (☎02/4984 9000, ⓦwww .portstephens.org.au/imagine). Forster Dive Centre at 15 Little St in Forster (☎02/6555 4477) arranges **diving trips** at Seal Rocks.

A good place to **eat** in Forster–Tuncurry is the *The Oyster Rack* on Wharf Road, which serves great seafood (bookings advised ☎02/6557 5577). *Merret's Restaurant* (☎02/4984 2555) in Peppers Anchorage, just outside Kallaroo, is well worth the detour for its award-winning modern cuisine. As for **accommodation**, there are scores of motels and even more holiday apartments to choose from in the area, though many insist on weekly bookings during the holiday season. If you want to stay within the national park itself, **camping** is the way to go. **Houseboats** are also an option: try Myall Lakes Houseboats, 90 Crawford St, Bulahdelah (☎02/4997 4221, ⓦwww.myalllakeshouseboats .com.au), or Tea Gardens Houseboats, 22 Marine Drive, Tea Gardens (☎02/4997 0555); weekly rates range from $550 to more than $2000, weekends from $390 to $1160.

Accommodation

Dolphin Lodge YHA 43 Head St, Forster ☎ & ⓕ02/6555 8155, ⓔdolphin_lodge@hotmail.com. Just three minutes from the beach and the ocean baths, this lodge/hostel has plenty of en-suite doubles, as well as dorms. Facilities include communal kitchens, a BBQ area and laundry. Free use of bikes, fishing gear and surf- and boogie-boards. Dorms $21, rooms ❸

Halifax Holiday Park Beach Rd, Little Beach, 2km east of central Nelson Bay ☎02/4981 1522 or 1800 600 201, ⓔhalifax@beachsideholidays .com.au. A well-outfitted beachside campsite with camp kitchen, BBQs and kiosk. Cabins ❷

Myall Shores Ecotourism Resort Bombah Point, 16km east of Bulahdelah in the Myall Lakes National Park ☎02/4997 4495, ⓔresort @myallshores.com.au. Campsite with restaurant, shop and boat ramp; bushwalks, 4WD tours and cruises on offer. Sites ❶, cabins ❹

Samurai Beach Bungalows Frost Rd, cnr Robert Connell Close, Anna Bay ☎02/4982 1921, ⓔsamurai@nelsonbay.com. A gorgeous backpackers' hostel in an idyllic bushland setting; cabins are arranged around an undercover "bush" kitchen. Free use of boards and bikes; campfires,

surfing excursions to nearby beaches and other social activities also available. Port Stephens Buses from Sydney or Newcastle stop outside. Dorms $17, rooms ❷

Seal Rocks Camping Reserve Seal Rocks ☎02/4997 6164 or 1800 112 234. Small site just across from the beach; all sites unpowered. Bookings essential during school holidays. Sites ❶

Shoal Bay Backpackers YHA/Shoal Bay Motel 59–61 Shoal Bay Beachfront Rd, Shoal Bay ☎02/4981 0982, ⓔshoalbaymotel@bigpond.com. Beachfront motel with sauna and spa that also runs a small YHA section – nonmembers welcome. Advance booking recommended. Dorms $19, rooms ❸

Smuggler's Cove Holiday Village 45 The Lakes Way, 2km south of Forster ☎ & ⓕ02/6554 6666, ⓦwww.smugglerscove.com.au. Lakeside campsite with camp kitchen, pool and children's playground. Cabins ❷

Thurlow Lodge Thurlow Ave, Nelson Bay ☎02/4981 1577. Central self-catering units available by the week and sleeping up to six, with a communal swimming pool. Good discounts outside of high season. $400–800 per week.

A detour inland: Barrington Tops

There's equally attractive scenery inland, and the drive from Forster via Nabiac, Krambach and Gloucester to the World Heritage-listed **Barrington Tops National Park** ($7.50 entry per car; ⓦwww.barringtons.com.au) makes an enjoyable day-trip. On the way up to the country town of Gloucester it's gently hilly farming country; from here, unsealed roads lead to various scenic spots in the national park – the Barrington Road towards Scone (see p.329), or the Gloucester Tops road to the park's southwestern section. You can also approach it via the Hunter Valley from Maitland via Dungog. The closest you'll get to the park with public transport is on the train from Sydney or Newcastle to Dungog or Gloucester; *The Barringtons Country Retreat* (see opposite) does free pick-ups from Dungog.

The Barrington Tops themselves are two high, cliff-ringed plateaus, Barrington and Gloucester, which rise steeply from the surrounding valleys. The changes in altitude within the park are so great – the highest points are Mount Barrington (1555m) and Polblue Mountain (1577m) – that within a few minutes you can pass from areas of subtropical rainforest to warm and cool temperate rainforest, and then to high, windswept plateaus covered with snow gums, meadows and subalpine bog. Up on the plateau, snow is common from the end of April to early October, while heavy fogs and rains are possible at virtually any time.

The **Great Lakes Visitors Centre** in Forster (see p.293) can help with specific routes or organized 4WD tours into the national park. There are plenty of picnic grounds and scenic **lookouts** in the park, plus several **campsites**, some of which are accessible only by 4WD. The main camping area, reached by car, is in the Gloucester River area, with barbecues, toilet (but no shower) and water ($5 per site). You don't need to book, but for more information contact the NPWS at 59 Church St, Gloucester (⊺02/6538 5300, ⓔgloucester@npws.nsw.gov.au). Otherwise, **accommodation** in the area is of the pricier, and plusher, kind, with one of the closest places to the park itself being in Salisbury, 40km north of Dungog – the *Salisbury Lodges*, 2930 Salisbury Rd (⊺02/4995 3285, ⓔbookings@salisburylodges.com.au; ❻), offers self-contained lodges, with spa, fire, cooking/dining area and private balcony, and more basic chalets, also with self-catering facilities (though meals are available with both types of accommodation for an additional fee), in a gorgeous rainforest setting. A cheaper alternative is *The Barringtons Country Retreat* on Chichester Dam Road, 23km north of Dungog (⊺02/4995 9269, ⓔinfo @thebarringtons.com.au; cabins ❸, lodge ❹), which has a pool, spa and horse riding on offer (meals or self-catering deals are also available).

The Manning Valley: Taree and around

TAREE, on the Pacific Highway north of Forster–Tuncurry, is a quiet riverside town and the main centre of the fertile, scenic Manning Valley. Served by trains and buses from Sydney and Brisbane, it's a pleasant alternative to the touristy hustle and bustle of Port Macquarie, the next stop north (see p.296), and especially good as a base for some gentle exploration of the hills, forests and deserted beaches.

The very helpful **Manning Valley Visitor Information Centre**, on the old Pacific Highway in Taree North (daily 9am–5pm; ⊺02/6592 5444 or 1800 182 733, ⓦwww.retreat-to-nature.com), has detailed leaflets describing forest drives, most of which lead to the high plateau where waterfalls abound. Taree's main attraction, **river cruises**, are organized by Manning River Marina and Boat Hire (3hr; $15; ⊺02/6553 2683). There's the usual abundance of **motels** along the highway, including the wheelchair-friendly *Pacific Motel*, 500m north of town (⊺02/6552 1977; ❸), which has air-conditioned rooms and a swimming pool. For a bit more character, try the *Fotheringham's Hotel* at 236 Victoria St (⊺02/6552 1153; ❷), a pleasant old pub and restaurant. The *Twilight Caravan Park*, Pacific Highway, 3km north of town (⊺02/6552 2857, ⓔtwilight@tsn.cc; on-site vans ❶, cabins ❷), has a saltwater pool, barbecues and kiosk. If you want to stay aboard a **houseboat**, contact Manning River Holidays Afloat (⊺02/6552 6271), who have moored and moving boats available for rent.

Along the route from Taree to Port Macquarie, there are a number of worthwhile detours. One of the most impressive waterfalls on the whole coast is the 160-metre-high **Ellenborough Falls**, about an hour's drive northwest of Taree beyond Wingham on the Bulga Forest Drive – unsealed much of the way. From the main Pacific Highway at Moorland, a road turns off to the small **Crowdy Bay National Park**, situated between Crowdy Head and the lofty Diamond Head, whose landscape includes heathlands, swamp, lagoons, woodlands, forests and sand dunes, all enlivened by prolific birdlife. Back on the Pacific Highway, there is a convenient gateway tourist office fuelling drivers with free tea and coffee at **Kew**, between Taree and Port Macquarie; turn right at the *Kew Hotel* for the more interesting route that hugs the coast.

Port Macquarie

PORT MACQUARIE, at the mouth of the Hastings River, was established in 1821 as a place of secondary punishment for convicts who had committed offences after arrival in New South Wales, as well as for hardened criminals from Britain. By the late 1820s, however, the spread of population meant that this was no longer an isolated outpost, so the penal settlement was closed and the area was opened up to free settlers. The convicts who were still considered incorrigible were sent off either to Moreton Bay in the Brisbane area, or to remote Norfolk Island (see p.388).

As with many other northern coastal ports, the **harbour** was unreliable and its approaches difficult, so for more than a century the town failed to live up to its early promise of commercial success. Prosperity and expansion finally came only with the tourism boom, which started in the early 1970s and shows no signs of abating; with a population of about forty thousand, Port Macquarie is now one of the fastest-growing towns on the north coast of New South Wales, particularly popular with older people from the southern cities who want to spend their retirement years in a sunny place with what the CSIRO meteorologists have declared "Australia's best year-round climate". If you approach from the south, you'll see the town's featureless **suburbs** sprawling along the beaches, encroaching further on the bush. Once you reach the town itself, however, you'll see that there are obvious scenic attractions – long, sandy beaches that start right in town and extend far along the coast, and forests and mountains in the hinterland– as well as plenty laid on in and around the town itself: amusement parks, mini-zoos, nature parks, cruises on the Hastings River and connecting waterways, horse riding and, above all, water sports and fishing.

Arrival and information

As a popular resort, Port Macquarie is well served by transport from Sydney, Tamworth (see p.330) and Brisbane, although not all **buses** make the detour from the Pacific Highway, so check carefully. Buses drop you off outside the tourist information office. Countrylink **trains** stop in Wauchope, 22km west, from where there's a connecting bus service (3 daily; ℡13 22 32).

You can also **fly** into Port Macquarie from Sydney with Qantas (℡13 13 13); the airport is about 6km west of town. Horton Street is the main downtown street, running north to the Hastings River. The helpful and friendly **tourist information office** (Mon–Fri 8.30am–5pm, Sat & Sun 9am–4pm; ℡02/6659 4400 or 1300 303 153, ⓦwww.portmacquarieinfo.com.au), on Clarence Street paralleling the river, will also mind your bags free of charge. The town's attractions and beaches are far flung, and transport isn't the best. You can get around town on Port Macquarie Bus Service (℡02/6583 2161), which has five different routes running mainly in the daytime Monday to Friday, with some services on Saturday. Only bus #334 to Wauchope runs every day of the week. Waits are long between buses (often an hour or more), so a timetable – available from the tourist information office – is vital. There's a limited local bus service run by Kings Brothers, otherwise the best option is **cycling** (see "Listings" on p.299).

Accommodation

With sixty motels and holiday apartments in town, you're not going to be hard-pressed to find somewhere to stay; the cheaper, older motels are mostly found on Gordon Street, with the average double costing from around $60.

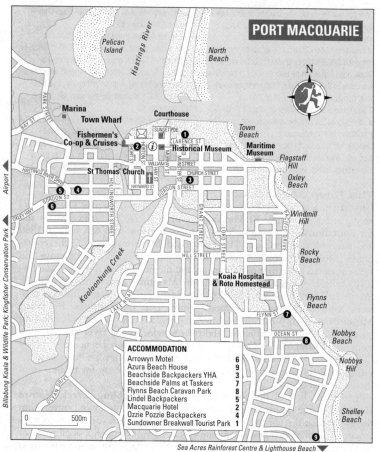

PORT MACQUARIE

N

Pelican Island

Hastings River

North Beach

Marina
Town Wharf
Courthouse
SUNSET PDE
Fishermen's
Co-op & Cruises
CLARENCE ST
Historical Museum
St Thomas' Church
CHURCH STREET
HAYWARD ST

Town Beach
Maritime Museum
Flagstaff Hill
Oxley Beach

Airport

Billabong Koala & Wildlife Park; Kingfisher Conservation Park

HASTINGS RIVER DRIVE
GORDON ST
OXLEY HWY
HOLLINGWORTH STREET
GORDON STREET
GRANT STREET
LORD STREET
HILL STREET
LAKE ROAD
OCEAN DRIVE
Kooloonbung Creek
PACIFIC DRIVE

Windmill Hill
Rocky Beach

Koala Hospital
& Roto Homestead

Flynns Beach
FLYNN ST
OCEAN ST
Nobbys Beach
Nobbys Hill
Shelley Beach

0   500m

ACCOMMODATION

Arrowyn Motel	6
Azura Beach House	9
Beachside Backpackers YHA	3
Beachside Palms at Taskers	7
Flynns Beach Caravan Park	8
Lindel Backpackers	5
Macquarie Hotel	2
Ozzie Pozzie Backpackers	4
Sundowner Breakwall Tourist Park	1

Sea Acres Rainforest Centre & Lighthouse Beach ▼

Arrowyn Motel 170 Gordon St ☎02/6583 1633, @howlettc@bigpond.com. Simple, inexpensive motel with a communal kitchen/dining area and outside BBQ. Within walking distance of the river and Town Beach. ❹

Azura Beach House 109 Pacific Drive ☎ & ℱ02/6582 2700, ⓦwww.azura.com.au. A great B&B near the beach with modern, elegant rooms designed to blend with private rainforest views, balconies, a guest lounge, comfy library and heated pool. Complimentary travel transfers. ❹

Beachside Backpackers YHA 40 Church St ☎ & ℱ02/6583 5512, @portmaqyha@hotmail.com. Central, family-run, friendly YHA hostel, with kitchen/TV/video room and BBQ on the patio. Free pick-up from the bus terminal. Small gym area; free bikes, boogie- and surfboards, with free surf

lessons every morning. Dorms $20, rooms ❷

Beachside Palms at Taskers 14 Flynn St, opposite Flynns Beach ☎02/6583 1520. Nice, shady complex with pool, children's playground and BBQ. Cabins ❹

Flynns Beach Caravan Park 22 Ocean St, 2.5km from the centre ☎02/6583 5754. A good camping option for people with no transport, as they will pick up travellers from the bus terminal. On-site vans ❷, cabins ❸

Lindel Backpackers Hastings River Drive, cnr Gordon St ☎02/6583 1791 or 1800 688 882, @lindel@midcoast.com.au. Pleasant hostel in an 1888 Victorian Gothic building. Clean, friendly and family-run, with a BBQ area and swimming pool, plus free use of bikes, surfboards and fishing gear. Book in advance for free pick-up service from the bus terminal; free trips by shuttle-bus to the koala hospital and beaches. Dorms $22, rooms ②

Macquarie Hotel Clarence St, opposite the post office ☎02/6583 1011, ⓦwww.pubstay.com.au. Clean, good-value rooms with or without bath, in a pub close to the river; some cheap singles available. Good beer garden and bistro. ③

Ozzie Pozzie Backpackers 36 Waugh St ☎ & ⓕ02/6583 8133, ⓦwww.nomadsworld.com. The best hostel in Port Macquarie, and one of the friendliest in New South Wales. Free pick-ups and drop-offs, free use of bikes and boogie-boards, comfortable dorms, separate video and games

rooms and free chilli (Wed) and $6 pizza (Thurs). Dorms $20, rooms ②

Rainbow Beach Holiday Village Beach St, Bonny Hills, about 23km south ☎02/6585 5655 or 1800 045 520, ⓦwww.sydneycaravanparks .com.au. Spacious, beachside camping complex in a bushland setting, with solar-heated pool, playground, BBQ and shop. On-site vans ②, cabins ③, cottages ④

Sundowner Breakwall Tourist Park Right on the riverfront ☎02/6583 2755 or 1800 636 452, ⓦwww.sundowner.net.au. Park offering shops, amenities, free Internet access for guests and a palm-fringed pool. Sites ①, cabins ②

The Town and around

Port Macquarie has a history of destroying reminders of its past. The few surviving remnants include **St Thomas' Church** (1824–28) on Hay Street and the **courthouse** on Clarence Street (Mon–Sat 10am–4pm; $2), built in 1869 and refurbished accordingly. The **Historical Museum**, opposite the courthouse (Mon–Sat 9.30am–4.30pm, Sun 1–4pm; $4.50), has an extensive and well-presented collection of documents and memorabilia dealing with the history of the Hastings River area; while the **Maritime Museum**, 6 William St (Mon–Sat 11am–3pm; $2), offers a history of the early navigators through artefacts, nautical paintings and model ships. The 1890s **Pilots Boatshed Museum** at Town Wharf (Mon–Sat 9am–3pm; $1) also has a small collection covering the history of maritime and river wrecks. Several **river cruises** leave from the **Fishermen's Co-op** at the beach end of Clarence Street (see "Listings", p.299). The river foreshore provides a pleasant place for a peaceful sunset stroll and you can watch the pelican colony begging for tiddlers from the local anglers.

Perhaps the best of the attractions is the **Kooloonbung Creek Nature Reserve**, a large bushland reserve remarkably close to the town centre. From the entrance at the corner of Horton and Gordon streets, you step onto trails among casuarinas, mangroves and eucalypts, or sweat through a small patch of rainforest, and it's amazingly easy to believe that you're lost in the wilderness of the Australian bush, rather than minutes from the main road. The eastern part of the nature reserve is accessible to wheelchairs, and at the **old cemetery** near the main entrance a few graves of pioneer settlers have been preserved.

On the ocean-facing side of town, Port Macquarie's three flagged, patrolled **beaches** are Town Beach, Flynns and Lighthouse. The **Sea Acres Rainforest Centre** (daily 9am–4.30pm; $10; free guided walks at regular intervals), south of the town on Pacific Drive, is impressive, conveying an urgent environmental message about the fast-disappearing coastal rainforest of New South Wales, which you can learn about in the ecology display room and enviro-theatre. The centre comprises three different types of rainforest, which can be inspected at close quarters from a boardwalk (again wheelchair-accessible).

Back towards the town centre, on Lord Street, **Roto House** is a fine nineteenth-century homestead, with Australia's oldest **koala hospital** in its grounds (both open Mon–Fri 10am–4pm, Sat & Sun 9am–1pm; free, donations welcome; check feeding times on ☎02/6584 1522). Run and financed by volunteers, the hospital takes in disease-stricken koalas, as well as the inevitable road casualties. For yet more cuddly animals, the **Billabong Koala & Wildlife**

Park, 61 Billabong Drive (daily 9am–5pm; $8.50), advertises cute kangaroos that can be hand-fed and koalas that can be patted and embraced.

Eating, drinking and nightlife

As you'd expect in a resort of this size, there are plenty of places to **eat**, particularly fast-food outlets; not surprisingly, seafood and fish predominate and the local oysters really must be tried. *Macquarie Seafoods*, centrally located on the corner of Clarence and Short streets, is the best place for takeaway fish and chips. You can also buy fresh fish and seafood from the **Fishermen's Co-op** at the end of Clarence Street in the Town Wharf area and cook it yourself. *Scampi's*, at the marina on Park Street, just west of the town centre (℡02/6583 7200; nightly dinner plus lunch in summer; BYO), is one of the most enjoyable of several seafood restaurants, while *Coolenberg* (℡02/6584 3770), at the corner of Lake Road and Hill Street, is an award-winning modern Australian establishment in a historic building just out of town. *Toro's Mexican Cantina* at 22 Murray St has build-your-own burritos and tacos in the evenings, while *Spicy Kruathai* on the corner of Clarence and Hay streets (℡02/6583 9043) serves reasonably priced Thai seafood and stir-fries. On the waterfront at 74 Clarence St, *Crays* is a pricey restaurant with decent lunch-time deals, while the *Macquarie Hotel* has an affordable bistro. In the Port Central Shopping Centre, behind the tourist information office on Clarence Street, you'll find a good-value food court on the second floor; choices include fresh, healthy fare from the *Pure and Natural Food Co*, and excellent coffee and cakes at *The Coffee Club* – both open daily. *Signatures Bar & Café* at the bottom of Clarence Street, close to Town Wharf, offers good-value seafood platters, plus steaks and pizzas.

The space-age *RSL Club* on Short Street (℡02/6583 4018) offers a cocktail bar, an auditorium and **live music** at the weekends, when it's open for 24-hour drinking (and, regrettably, for its pokies). More central and tackier (but good-naturedly so) is *Finnians Irish Tavern* at 97 Gordon St; they also have live music at the weekend, and serve decent grub. Opposite the tourist information office, the streets leading down to the river offer several good drinking spots, notably the *Beach House*, right on the river front. Of the nightclubs, *Down Under*, on Short Street next to Coles supermarket, is a perennial favourite – a tiny underground place for the over-30s.

There are also a few **wineries** in the area: Cassegrain Winery, on the Hastings River on Fernbank Creek Road off the Pacific Highway south of town (daily 9am–5pm; ℡02/6583 7777), has a particularly pleasant restaurant on a veran-dah overlooking the vineyards.

Listings

Airlines Qantas ℡13 13 13.
Bike rental Gordon Street Cycles, Shop 3, 163 Gordon St ℡02/6583 3633.
Boat rental Settlement Point Boatshed (℡02/6563 6300), next to the Settlement Point Ferry, 2km north of the CBD on the Hastings River, rents out boats from $20 per day; they also rent out party boats, complete with BBQ, beer cooler and toilet, to groups.
Buses Kings Bus Service (℡02/6562 4724) runs between Port Macquarie and Tamworth via Kempsey, Macksville, Nambucca Heads, Urunga, Coffs Harbour, Bellingen, Dorrigo, Armidale, Uralla

and Walcha three times a week. As well as running around town, Kings Brothers (℡1300 555 611) also serves Wauchope and Kempsey.
Camel safaris Port Macquarie Camel Safaris ℡ & ℻02/6583 7650, ✉pmqcamels@telstra.easymail.com. Offers rides of up to an hour from Lighthouse Beach.
Car rental Hertz, 73 Hastings River Drive ℡02/6583 6599; Thrifty, at the airport ℡02/6584 2122.
Cruises *Port Venture* cruises up the Hastings River ($20–35; ℡02/6583 3058); Pelican River Cruises goes to the everglades in Limeburners Creek National Park and an oyster farm for tastings

($24–41; ☎0418 652 171); and the Waterbus Everglade Tours offers a dolphin-spotting cruise in their glass-sided boats ($22–50; ☎02/6582 5009).
Hospital Port Macquarie Hospital, Wright's Rd ☎02/6581 2000.
Internet access Port Surf Sub, 57 Clarence St ☎02/6584 4744.
Police ☎02/6583 0199.
Post office Port Macquarie Post Office, Clarence St, NSW 2444.

Surfing The Paradise Surf Centre at 49 Horton St (☎02/6583 6062) sells surfboards and gear.
Taxis Port Macquarie Taxicabs ☎02/6581 0081; Wauchope Radio Taxicabs ☎02/6585 2100. There is a taxi rank on Horton Street.
Water sports Several companies operate para-sailing, fishing charters and jet-ski tours on the river and ocean, including Watersports World (☎02/6583 9777), Port Water Sports (☎0412 234 509) and Sea Quest (☎02/6583 3463).

Heading inland: Wauchope

Surrounded by forest, the pretty little village of **WAUCHOPE** (pronounced "war-hope"), 22km west of Port Macquarie, makes an enjoyable contrast to the coast. Through working exhibits, the open-air museum of **Timbertown**, 3km from the village on the Oxley Highway (daily 9.30am–3.30pm; free), depicts life as it must have been in the isolated timber settlements 150 years ago. Timber logs are pulled over muddy roads to saw-pits, where they are cut and shaped, the bakery bakes and sells bread fresh from the oven, and many other aspects of Victorian life are re-enacted. North of Wauchope, the **Wilson River Rainforest Reserve**'s picnic grounds are a popular destination for day-trippers from Port Macquarie. Another feature of Wauchope is the large separatist lesbian community that lives in the vicinity – something strangely absent from the tourist literature.

Basic pub **accommodation** and counter meals can be had at the *Hastings Hotel*, on the corner of High and Cameron streets (☎02/6585 2003; ❶), and there are slightly fancier rooms at the *Wauchope Motel*, 84 High St (☎02/6585 1933, ☎6586 1366; ❸). You can get to Wauchope daily with Kings Brothers (☎1300 555 611).

The coast north to Nambucca Heads

The coastline between Port Macquarie and Nambucca Heads, 115km north, has some magic spots. **KEMPSEY**, though not one of them, is an important, large service town on the Macleay River, 49km from Port Macquarie, and springboard for sights further on. It is home to a prominent Aboriginal population, the **Dunghutti** people. The first white settlers moved into the region five years after the explorer John Oxley entered the Macleay River area in 1818. Between 1830 and 1850 the Dunghutti put up resistance to the settlers, and several Aboriginal massacres resulted. By the 1850s resistance was so widespread that native police (see p.1165) were called in to stop the fighting. In the following decade Aboriginal reserves were established, and a degree of self-determination existed from the 1890s when several Aboriginal farms were set up, but the people were pushed off the farms after World War I. The Dunghutti were still holding traditional ceremonies as late as the 1940s. Their ability to demonstrate continuous links with their land led in 1996 to a successful claim for native title for a portion of land at **CRESCENT HEAD**, 21km southeast from Kempsey along a good sealed road, although they held title only temporarily and have since received compensation for losing their native title rights to property developers in the area. The agreement was the first recognition of native title by an Australian government on the mainland and the first time that an Australian government negotiated an agreement with indigenous people to acquire their land. There are some wonderful waterfront **campsites** here: *Crescent Head Holiday Park* (☎02/6566 0261), which also has some very pleasant verandah-fronted wooden chalets (❸); and *Delicate Nobby Camping Ground* (☎02/6566 0144), which is in extensive but secluded bushland, ten minutes' drive from the township. Meandering back and then away from the Pacific Highway, you come to the coastal **Hat Head National Park** and the small town of **SOUTH WEST ROCKS**, perched on a picturesque headland. Three kilometres east on **Trial Bay**, the **Arakoon State Recreation Area** has as its centrepiece **Trial Bay Gaol** (daily 9am–4.15pm; $4). Classified as a public works prison in which prisoners could learn a trade, the gaol was considered progressive when it was established in 1886. Built from local granite, it's certainly an impressive construction – the massive outer walls surround an extensive complex of buildings and are supported by high buttresses with four watchtowers. The prison was closed in 1903, but reopened during World War I when it was used as an internment camp for over five hundred prisoners of war, including some Buddhist monks from Ceylon, though most of those held here were German.

Further north, back on the Princes Highway and just before you reach the turn off for Nambucca Heads, you'll pick up signs for **TAYLORS ARM**, famous for its pub, *The Pub with no Beer* (☎02/6564 2100, ⓦwww.pub withnobeer.com.au) from the popular Australian folk song; the pub, though still looking as it did when Slim Dusty and Gordon Parsons penned the song, now promises to always have the coldest and freshest beers regularly on tap. It also serves up lunches daily and evening meals at weekends and has rooms available (❹). Nearby is the wonderful *Bakers Creek Station* (☎02/6564 2165, ⓦwww.bcstation.com.au; bunkhouses ❶, cabin tents ❷, cabins ❻), which offers luxury cabins, bunkhouses and camping in its massive grounds. As well as accommodation, the station offers horse riding, canoeing and fishing as well as tennis and bushwalking; it also has its own restaurant, the *Billabong*, overlooking the eighteen-acre lake.

Nambucca Heads and around

About 100km away, via the Pacific Highway, the casual resort town of **NAMBUCCA HEADS** makes a good base for trips to the rivers, mountains and forests of the hinterland; it's also a great place to break the long haul from Sydney to Brisbane – whether you're travelling by car, bus or train (the train station is on Bowra Street, about 3km north of the centre). From the headlands near the town centre there are fantastic views of the mouth of Nambucca River, and of the seemingly endless sweep of sandy beaches that stretch both north and south from here. There's fishing, windsurfing and canoeing available to take advantage of the gentler waters at the river mouth, and some excellent surf on the ocean beaches. From vantage points at **Scotts Head**, a popular surfing spot, whales can sometimes be sighted during their southern migration (Aug–Oct).

For information on these and other activities around town (including white-water rafting and horse riding), call in at the **visitor information centre**, just off the Pacific Highway on Riverside Drive, at the southern entrance to town (daily 9am–5pm; ☎02/6568 6954, ⓦwww.here.com.au). You can book **accommodation** here; motels and apartments are generally better value here than in Port Macquarie or Coffs Harbour. Perhaps the cosiest place of all to stay is *Beilby's Beach House* at 1 Ocean St (☎02/6568 6466, ⓦwww .midcoast.com.au/~beilbys; ❸), a great, homely B&B with a pool, good-value rooms and a great location overlooking the dramatic coastline, just a ten-minute walk from the shops. Alternatively, try *Scotts Guesthouse*, 4 Wellington Drive (☎02/6568 6386, ℱ6569 4169; ❹), or the equally attractively located *White Albatross Holiday Centre*, just up the road (☎02/6568 6468; ❷), with a tennis court, tavern, café and children's playground. The cheapest option is the pleasant *Nambucca Backpackers*, 3 Newman St (☎02/6568 6360; dorms $20, rooms ❷), a small, cosy, family-run hostel with free use of boogie-boards, snorkelling and fishing gear, and free pick-up from the bus terminal or train station. The main drag, Bowra Street, has several good takeaway places, selling sandwiches and barbecued chicken among other choices, plus there's *Byll's Café* (weekdays till 5pm, Sat till late; BYO) at the top of the street, which serves breakfast, afternoon tea, baguettes, burgers and salads as well as more substantial meals. *Nirvana Sawadee*, opposite the tourist office, is a traditional Thai restaurant that makes good use of fresh local seafood. Ten kilometres south of town in Macksville, is the very popular *Bridge Café* – a Fifties-style milk bar offering burgers, sandwiches and home-made chocolates.

Nambucca Heads is on the main Sydney–Brisbane bus and train routes. Kings Brothers (☎1300 555 611) runs to Macksville, Coffs Harbour and Bellingen daily. All Countrylink services along the north coast call at Nambucca Heads.

Heading inland from Nambucca, it's about half an hour's drive to the picturesque former timber town of **BOWRAVILLE**, where you can rest up in the old pub, now renovated to its former glory, and browse in a few arts-and-crafts shops and the jumble of Gleeson's Second Hand Store. *The Phoenix Gallery & Tea Rooms* is a pleasant refreshment stop. From here, you can travel on unsealed forest roads to the small, alternative town of Bellingen (see below), although it's more easily reached on the sealed road that turns off the Pacific Highway after Urunga.

The Bellinger River and around

URUNGA, 20km north from Nambucca Heads, is a pleasant beachside spot where the Bellinger and Kalang rivers meet the sea. From here you can walk right along the beach to nearby **MYLESTOM** (the turn-off is 7km further down the highway), which occupies a stunningly beautiful spot on the wide Bellinger River. You can take advantage of its riverside setting at the **Alma Doepel Reserve**'s sheltered, sandy river beach, which has changing rooms and showers. Two minutes' walk to the east is a gorgeous sweep of surf beach – often gloriously deserted – which is patrolled on summer weekends and school holidays. You can walk along the beach to **Bundagen**, an alternative, environmentally friendly community that welcomes visitors and hosts frequent music and spoken-word evenings.

A great **place to stay** in Mylestom is the haphazard *Riverside Lodge*, on River Street facing Tuckers Island (☎ & ℱ02/6655 4245; ❶). Although there's no transport here, Sandy, the friendly owner, will pick guests up from Urunga or Coffs Harbour. The lodge has the comfortable, relaxed feel of an Indonesian guesthouse; all the rooms are well furnished with desks, lamps and armchairs. You can use the lodge's boat and kayaks, ride one of their bicycles through Bongil Bongil Floral Reserve. Other **facilities** in Mylestom are limited: a post office with supplies and EFTPOS, a decent Chinese **restaurant**, and a swanky riverfront brasserie called *Beaches* (with a handy bottle shop).

Bellingen

Just after Urunga, the turn-off west heads through the verdant Bellinger River valley for 12km to **BELLINGEN**, a relaxed little town with a strong alternative bent, full of arts-and-crafts outlets and workshops, cafés and thriving small businesses. Just before town, the **Old Butter Factory** (☎02/6655 9599), a renovated dairy, holds a complex of several craft shops where you can check out the work of local artisans, plus a chilled-out café and a massage and float-tank centre ($65 for a 2hr combo pamper). In town, The Yellow Shed, Hyde St (daily 9am–5pm), is a crafts outlet worth a peek, although it sells some of the Old Butter Factory products at an inflated price. Bellingen also has an interesting monthly **market**, held on the third Saturday of the month (7am–2pm) in Bellingen Park, with buskers, crafts and organic food stalls. There's more shopping at the **Hammond and Wheatley Emporium** on Hyde Street, a glorious old restored department store with an Aladdin's cave of locally produced jewellery, artefacts and artworks. Each year Bellingen hosts a lively **jazz festival** (☎02/6655 9345, ⓦwww .midcoast.com.au/~belljazz) over the third weekend in August, followed by the three-day Global Festival of world music over the October long weekend. For a cooling break from crafts and culture, you can swim in the waterholes of the Bellinger and Never Never rivers.

More **information** on the town and surrounding area is available at Traveland on Hyde St (☎02/6655 2055), which has details of rafting, bushwalking and other tours, and acts as an agent for Countrylink; you can also check out ⓦwww.bellingen.com. The creekfront *Bellingen YHA Backpackers*, 2 Short St (☎02/6655 1116, ⓔbelloyha@midcoast.com.au; dorms $22, rooms ❸), is one of the best **hostels** around, a beautiful two-storey building with a huge balcony facing a rainforest island full of jacaranda trees that come alive at dusk with the stirrings of fruit bats; you can even sleep outdoors under a gazebo, or camp out the back if you prefer. Free pick-ups from Urunga train station are available, as are weekly trips to Bundagen (see opposite) and lifts to Dorrigo for $10. They also offer canoes and bikes for rent, plus barbecues and frequent shenanigans round the campfire. Otherwise, there's the gay-friendly *Rivendell Bed and Breakfast*, centrally located at 12 Hyde St (☎ & ⓕ02/6655 0499, ⓦwww .midcoast.com.au/~rivendell; ❹), where there's a pool. The *Koompartoo Retreat* (☎ & ⓕ02/6655 2326; ❺), at the corner of Rawson and Dudley Streets at the southern edge of town, is another good option; tucked away in five acres of gardens and rainforest, its four self-contained chalets, built from local hardwood and each with own balcony, are superb. You can **camp** at the *Bellingen Caravan Park* on Dowle Street, North Bellingen (☎02/6655 1338).

The town is full of great **cafés**. *Lodge 241*, an art gallery-cum-café on Short Street serves some of the best coffee in town and delicious, wholesome lunches. The light and airy *Carriageway Café*, 75 Hyde St, serves affordable city fare – melts, burgers and gourmet sandwiches, plus dinner at the weekend; at the back, a polished wooden staircase heads upstairs to an art gallery. On Church Street, the spacious *Cool Creek Café* (open Mon & Thurs–Sun for dinner, plus Sat lunch) has a folky ambience and an extensive veggie menu, as well as live music and poetry readings. Next door is *The Good Food Shop*, a real find for wholefood picnic supplies and good lunches, and next door to that the early-opening *Swiss Patisserie & Bakery*. Finally, there's *McNally House* on Hyde Street (☎02/6655 0344; Tues–Sat dinner only), a BYO restaurant in a cute cottage, with a distinctly European menu. The town has only one **pub**: the animated heritage-listed *Federal Hotel* on Hyde Street, with live music (usually free) from Thursday to Sunday.

Interstate **buses** do not detour into Bellingen; the nearest drop-off point is Coffs Harbour or Urunga from where Kings Brothers (☎1300 555 611) runs here daily.

Inland to Dorrigo

The Dorrigo road from Bellingen follows the beautiful Bellinger River, with bewitching green hills in the distance and fat cows grazing in lush riverside fields, passing through **THORA**, and its roadhouse with the pleasant *River Bend Café* attached. Beyond Thora, the scenic road winds ever more steeply through the **Dorrigo National Park**, a startlingly beautiful rainforest remnant of an area that was once similarly heavily forested; the lure of the valuable Australian cedar – "red gold" – left most of the plateau cleared by the 1920s. The ultramodern **Dorrigo Rainforest Centre** (daily 9am–5pm; ☏02/6657 2309) has a detailed interpretive display that goes through this sorry saga, with some insights into the life of the north coast Aboriginal people, and some examples of red cedar furniture. The *Canopy Café* here, with wonderful views, serves light lunches and afternoon teas until 4pm. Starting at the visitor centre, the **Skywalk** is easily the most spectacular of the walks through the park and also the least strenuous; a wooden walkway stretches out high over the rainforest canopy, enabling you to look down on the forest and out over the surrounding landscape and distant hills. The walkway is open 24 hours, to allow observance of the forest's nocturnal creatures. Other trails will take you to some of the park's best features, including a number of beautiful waterfalls; try the Wonga Walk, a 5.8-kilometre stroll through the rainforest past two waterfalls, or there are comprehensive information boards and leaflets at the centre.

DORRIGO itself is an old settlement on the eastern edge of the New England Plateau, a small country town with artistic leanings and an old-fashioned air typified by the kitsch 1950s Formica fittings of *Nick's Café* on Hickory Street, which serves scones and pots of tea. There's plenty of **accommodation** here: the wide-verandahed *Hotel Dorrigo* (☏02/6657 2016; ❷) has basic hotel and fancier motel-style rooms, some of them en-suite; while *Dorrigo Mountain Resort*, 1 Bellingen Rd (☏02/6657 2564, ✉managers@dorrigo-mountainresort.com.au), close to the national park, has camping and a range of cabins (❷). There are also plenty of farmstays in the area; full details are available from the **tourist information** service at 36 Hickory St (daily 10am–4pm; ☏02/6657 2486).

The only way to get to Dorrigo on **public transport** is with Kings Brothers (☏1300 555 611), which runs via Bellingen. The bus follows the road west from Dorrigo cutting cross-country, past several more national parks, towards Armidale (see p.332).

Coffs Harbour and around

Back on the main coastal highway, **COFFS HARBOUR** – or "Coffs" – divides neatly into two separate parts. One half is a modern town snuggled close to the hills near the Pacific Highway – this is the centre of town, with the shopping mall, post office and all other facilities. The other part is the jetty area around the train station and the man-made harbour. For years the dramatic coastline managed to hold at bay the suburban sprawl, but retirement homes, holiday apartments, hotels and motels are gradually encroaching on the area's natural beauty. There is still a lot to admire, though: at this point on the coast the mountains and hills of the Great Dividing Range fall almost directly into the South Pacific Ocean, and glorious white, sandy **beaches** stretch endlessly, from the town shores of Boambee Beach and Jetty Beach through Park Beach and Diggers Beach, up to northern strands such as Emerald (see p.309). There are several small islands offshore with fringing coral reefs designated as marine reserves; the plethora of fish surrounding them makes diving a popular activity. In summer, the cool, rainforest-clad mountains with crystal-clear creeks and tumbling torrents offer a welcome respite from the heat and humidity of the coast.

Arrival and information

All long-distance buses stop at the new **bus station**, on the corner of Maclean Street and the Pacific Highway; the **train** station (☎13 22 32) is by the harbour. You can also fly into Coffs with Qantas (☎13 13 13); the airport is about 5km south and you can rent a car at one of the airport desks, take a **taxi** into town (about $9) or, if you've booked accommodation, you can probably arrange to be picked up. Given the split of Coffs into two halves, the distances you have to cover are considerable, and the **local bus service**, which runs

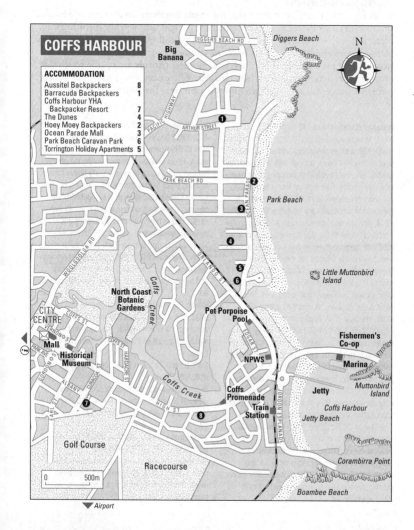

COFFS HARBOUR

ACCOMMODATION
Aussitel Backpackers	8
Barracuda Backpackers	1
Coffs Harbour YHA Backpacker Resort	7
The Dunes	4
Hoey Moey Backpackers	2
Ocean Parade Mall	3
Park Beach Caravan Park	6
Torrington Holiday Apartments	5

Big Banana
DIGGERS BEACH RD
Diggers Beach
N
PACIFIC HIGHWAY
ARTHUR STREET
PARK BEACH RD
 OCEAN PARADE
Park Beach
WOOLGOOLGA RD
ORLANDO ST
Coffs Creek
Little Muttonbird Island
North Coast Botanic Gardens
CITY CENTRE
COFFS ST
VERNON ST
Mall
Historical Museum
COFFS ST
HARDARE ST
GORDON ST
PARK AVE
ALBANY
EARL ST
ORARA ST
HIGH ST
Coffs Creek
Pet Porpoise Pool
NPWS
Coffs Promenade
Train Station
JORDAN ESPLANADE
Fishermen's Co-op
Marina
Jetty
Muttonbird Island
Coffs Harbour Jetty Beach
Golf Course
Racecourse
Corambirra Point
0   500m
Boambee Beach
Airport

between the town centre, Coffs Jetty and Park Beach (Kings Brothers ☎1300 555 611; timetables from the visitor information centre), is barely adequate, so you may find yourself having to take taxis. Alternatively, you could rent a bike or car – see "Listings" on p.308 for details.

The City Centre Mall, right in the centre off Grafton Street (as the Pacific Highway is called in town), is very much the heart of Coffs and most facilities and much of the accommodation are nearby. The **visitor information centre** (daily 9am–5pm; ☎02/6652 1522 or 1300 369 070, ⓦwww.coffscoast.com.au) is a few minutes' walk south of here, also on Grafton Street, at the junction with Mclean Street. The NPWS has an office down at the marina (☎02/6651 0900), providing information on the marine reserve and rangers tours of Muttonbird Island.

Accommodation

Coffs has everything from international resort hotels to caravan parks. During the summer and Easter holidays the place is packed, and weekly **bookings** are preferred and sometimes compulsory. As trains and buses from Sydney arrive in the late evening, it's wise to book in advance in any case, especially as the **hostels** will pick you up if notified. The cheapest **motels** are on the south side of town; **resorts** sometimes have bargain off-season rates, too. The visitor information centre can book accommodation over the phone.

Aussitel Backpackers 312 High St ☎02/6651 1871, ⓦwww.aussitel.com. Large, well-equipped hostel with a clean communal kitchen and heated pool; free use of bikes, boogie- and surfboards and canoes, and lots of activities including an inexpensive dive course. Free pick-up from the bus terminal and train station. Dorms $22, rooms ❷

Barracuda Backpackers 19 Arthur St ☎02/6651 3514, ⓦwww.nomadsworld.com. Another popular hostel, affiliated to the Nomads network and situated near bars, restaurants and a cinema complex. Facilities include Internet access, free linen, a laundry and a pool. Heaps of organized activities, free pick-ups and drop-offs and free use of fishing gear, as well as boogie- and surfboards. Three-night deals available. Dorms $20, rooms ❷

Coffs Harbour YHA Backpacker Resort 110 Albany St ☎ & ⓕ02/6652 6462. Friendly, busy hostel, handy for the town centre with lifts every morning to the beach and other attractions. Kiosk with basic foodstuffs, garden with a pool, BBQ, plus bike rental, free boogie- and surfboards and fishing gear. Surf lessons and special-rate dive courses arranged. Free pick-up from bus terminal, train station and airport. Dorms $21, rooms ❷

The Dunes 28 Fitzgerald St, off Ocean Parade ☎02/6652 4522 or 1800 023 851, ⓦwww.dunes.com.au. A luxurious complex of one-, two- and three-bedroom serviced apartments near Park Beach, with a heated pool, tennis courts, spa and sauna. Good Internet specials often available. ❹

Hoey Moey Backpackers Ocean Parade ☎02/6652 3833, ⓔhoey@hoeymoey.com.au. This VIP/Backpackers hostel in a converted old pub has the best location in town, fronting the activity-centred Park Beach. More of a party hostel than a relaxing place to stay, dorms are cramped but features include a BBQ area, pool competitions with free pizza, free beer on arrival and frequent live music. Use of boogie-boards, surfboards and mountain bikes is free. Dorms $25, rooms ❷

Moonee Beach Caravan Park 12km north off the Pacific Highway ☎02/6653 6552. Magic camping spot in bush surroundings, with beach, estuary and headlands to explore. On-site vans ❷, cabins ❸

Ocean Parade Mall 41 Ocean Parade ☎02/6652 6733. Opposite Park Beach Bowling Club, with views across to Park Beach, this leafy motel makes for a peaceful stop right in the heart of things. ❹

Park Beach Caravan Park Ocean Parade ☎02/6652 3204, ⓦwww.parkbeachcaravanpark.com.au. Huge, well-run beachfront campsite, with BBQ facilities and children's playground. Cabins ❹, on-site vans ❷

Torrington Holiday Apartments 27 Boultwood St ☎02/6652 7546 or 1800 118 112, ⓔholiday@torrington.com.au. On a quiet street close to Park Beach. Fully self-contained apartments ideal for families, with a playground, swimming pool, spa and sauna. ❸

The Town

The small **Historical Museum**, at 191 High St (Mon–Fri & Sun 10am–4pm; $3), has a collection of relics and tools owned by early pioneers and cedar-getters, as well as local Aboriginal artefacts of the **Gumbaingirr** people, whose territories extended from the Nambucca River north to the Clarence River, and inland to the foothills of the Great Dividing Range. From the museum, it's only a short distance to the magnificent **North Coast Botanic Gardens**, with an entrance on Hardacre Street, just off High Street (daily 9am–5pm). These delightfully tranquil subtropical gardens are located on a triangle of land surrounded on two sides by **Coffs Creek** and feature a mangrove boardwalk and a slice of rainforest. A charming **creek walk** and **cycle trail** begin in the town centre, just off Coffs Street and head 5.4km to Muttonbird Island (see below); the final thirty minutes are along the northern breakwater – detailed maps are available from the visitor information centre. **Coffs Promenade**, along the creek walk, off the High Street at the Coffs Jetty end, contains crafts and speciality shops as well as an ice-cream parlour, a café and restaurant, the last two with outdoor tables overlooking the tranquil, tree-lined creek. You can rent bikes here (see "Listings" on p.308), as well as canoes ($15 an hour, $30 half-day).

The **Fishermen's Co-op**, on the northern breakwater of the harbour, sells fresh fish; the wharf here is also the departure point for most cruises from Coffs (see p.308). Beyond the boat-filled marina is **Muttonbird Island Nature Reserve**, high enough to offer fantastic views of Coffs Harbour and the southern and northern beaches. There's plenty of birdlife too, with an interpretive walk describing the lifestyle of the oily, migratory birds that come here to nest in summer. The best time to come is at sunset, when you can watch the muttonbirds return to their nests. You can sometimes see dolphins frolicking close to the island. If you want to see domesticated dolphins and seals being put through their paces, visit the misleadingly named **Pet Porpoise Pool**, between Coffs Jetty and Park Beach (performances 10.30am & 2.15pm; 1hr 30min; $18), which seems stuck in a 1970s time warp; there's also a small aquarium with sharks, other marine animals and a reef tank.

Banana plantations indicate that at Coffs you're entering a subtropical climatic zone. The cultural influence of nearby Queensland becomes apparent, too, in tourist attractions such as the **Big Banana** (daily 9am–5pm; Ⓦ www.bigbanana.com), a huge, bright-yellow concrete banana, 3km north of Coffs on the Pacific Highway, advertising a "horticultural theme park". It's free to walk through the banana and look at displays dealing with early pioneer life in the district and Coffs Harbour's $70-million-a-year banana industry. There are monorail tours of the plantation (1hr 30min; $12), which show you packing sheds and hydroponics glasshouses, as well as a space station and an Aboriginal Dreamtime Cave. A newer attraction is a toboggan ride ($6), which whizzes 720m down through the steep hillside plantations. For the complete banana experience, stop in at the milk bar, which serves bananas in every conceivable way.

Eating, drinking and nightlife

For **coffee** and gourmet **snacks** and cakes, head to the creek for the *Up the Creek Café*, on the Promenade. In town, good city fodder – focaccia, large breakfasts and decent cups of coffee – can be had at *Zigges on the Mall*, in the City Centre Mall.

For more extensive **eating** try High Street, at either end – around the City Centre Mall and nearby Grafton Street or down in the block or so before Coffs

Harbour Jetty. At the ocean end of High Street, on the corner of Camperdown Street, the *Pier Hotel* has a bistro with good, inexpensive counter meals (daily 7–9am, noon–2pm & 6–9pm), while the *Tahruah Thai Kitchen*, 368 High St (✆02/6651 5992), is recommended for its spicy stir-fries. *Tandoori Oven*, nearby at no. 384 (✆02/6652 2279), has tasteful, marine-inspired decor and a menu to match, along with good-value vegetarian thalis. *Maria's*, at no. 368, is an Italian BYO with pasta, pizza and seafood chowders, while Chinese food is available at the *Golden Crown* at no. 374 (✆02/6651 6787; Tues–Sat dinner only), which also offers takeaway. Innovative, international food with a hefty price-tag can be found at *Passionfish Brasserie*, 384A High St (✆02/6652 1423; Tues–Sat). Down at the marina, the *Tide & Pilot Brasserie* (✆02/6651 6888) has excellent, though expensive, seafood specials with waterfront views, while the *Fisherman's Co-op* does fish and chips to die for for just $8, but closes at 5.30pm.

Nightlife in Coffs is lively in summer, but very mainstream. There are generally **live bands** playing cover versions at some venue around town from Wednesday to Sunday, usually with free entry. On Friday and Saturday nights the *RSL Club*, on the corner of Vernon and Grafton streets, has two live bands, free entry and very cheap drinks until 2am. The *Plantation Hotel*, 88 Grafton St, puts on live music at weekends. For a more sedate drink, the *Greenhouse Tavern*, on the corner of Bray Street and the Pacific Highway, lets you sip in a reasonable approximation of tropical rainforest surroundings in its gazebo – they also serve tasty, good-value food. For a contemplative drink overlooking the ocean, the verandah at the yacht club bar in the marina is hard to beat.

Listings

Banks Commonwealth, 92 City Centre Mall; National, 42 City Centre Mall; Westpac, 137 High St.

Bike rental Promenade Leisure Hire, Coffs Promenade, Coffs Creek, 321 High St (✆02/6651 1032), charges $25 a day; weekly rates are negotiable.

Buses Besides the interstate services, there's: Ryan's Buses (✆02/6652 3201), with services to Woolgoolga and Grafton; and Kings Brothers (✆1300 555 611), with services to Urunga, Bellingen and further afield.

Canoeing Bellingen Canoe Adventures (✆02/6656 9955) organizes half- and full-day canoeing trips on the Bellinger River ($44/$88), including gourmet lunch; they also rent out canoes to those who would sooner go it alone (from $11 per hour).

Car rental Delta Europcar ✆02/6651 8558; Coffs Harbour Rent-a-Car ✆02/6652 5022; Hertz ✆02/6651 1899; Thrifty ✆02/6652 8622.

Cinema Coffs Cinema, Bray St , in the CBD ✆02/6651 6444.

Cruises Pacific Explorer (✆02/6652 7225, ⓦwww.pacificexplorer.com.au) runs whale-watching cruises on a sailing vessel June–Nov; regular cruises Dec–May.

Diving The Solitary Islands Marine Reserve, five islands and several islets north of Coffs, is the largest marine reserve in New South Wales; the mingling of tropical and temperate waters means that there's a huge variety of sealife, described in a range of excellent leaflets, available from the visitor information centre or the Fisheries office at the marina. Jetty Dive Centre, 398 High St, at the harbour (✆02/6651 1611), offers dives for beginners and experienced divers costing from $107 for two dives for PADI qualified divers and from $185 for four-day PADI courses for the unqualified. All hostels arrange inexpensive snorkelling expeditions and scuba courses.

Horse riding Valery Trails, 20km southwest of Coffs, off the Pacific Highway at Bonville ✆02/6653 4301; rates include pick-up and return to Coffs. Closer to Coffs, Bushland Trails (✆02/6649 4491) offers horse rides and overnight treks.

Hospital 345 Pacific Highway, opposite the junction with Isles Drive ✆02/6656 7000.

Internet access *Happy Planet* (closed Sun), 13 Park Ave.

Laundry Marina Laundrette (daily 8am–8pm) at the jetty has the best views whilst you wait for your whites.

Markets Sunday-morning markets are held at the Jetty Village Shopping Centre, at the jetty (8am–2pm), and in the Big W car park, cnr Castle and Vernon streets (same hours).

Police ☎02/6652 0299.

Post office In the Palms Centre, off High St, NSW 2450.

Sky diving Coffs City Skydivers (☎02/6651 1167, ⓦwww.coffsskydivers.com.au) offers dives from 10,000ft for $241.

Surfing East Coast Surf School, based at Diggers Beach (☎02/6651 5515, ⓦwww.eastcoast surfschool.com.au), is an excellent place to learn to surf in small groups. An introductory two-hour lesson costs $40 and five classes cost $160; includes surfboard and wetsuit. They also do excellent-value weekend (two-night) courses.

Taxi ☎13 10 08.

Tours Mountain Trails 4WD Tours (☎02/6658 3333) is the main operator in town and runs half- and full-day 4WD adventures along remote tracks to banana plantations, waterfalls and the rainforest, weekend trips to Dorrigo and mountain country, and wildlife tours at night; also has "bush tucker and Dreamtime" tours hosted by Mark Flanders, local Aboriginal tour guide. Discovery Tours (☎02/6651 1223) is another great local outfit, with good-value half- and full-day tours into the rainforest, all of which include meals. Those heading north, might be interested in their one-way trip to Byron Bay: two days 4WD via national parks and along beaches, with all accommodation included.

Travel agent Kelly Travel, cnr High and Moonee streets (☎02/6651 2747, ⓔkellytravel@key.net.au), is a discount flight agent for Qantas and STA Travel.

White-water rafting Coffs Harbour is one of the few areas on the east coast where you can go rafting, though after a dry winter the rivers can be low. The best outfit is WOW, based a few kilometres inland at 1448 Coramba Rd, Coramba (☎02/6654 4066), with trips at around $139 per day.

Around Coffs Harbour

An hour's drive inland from Coffs, on Bushmans Range Road at Lowanna, 42km northwest, is **George's Gold Mine** (Wed–Sun 10am–5pm, daily during school holidays; $10), where you can take a tour of a gold mine and look at the old stamper battery that was used to crush the ore. There are also picnic grounds, barbecues and walking trails through the rainforest.

To the north of Coffs is a string of fantastic sandy beaches. **Sapphire Beach**, 9km north, has an **environment centre** (daily 10am–5pm) with a relaxing café. **Moonee Beach Reserve**, 3km further, is in beautiful bush surroundings with a winding creek that has safe swimming – but beware of strong currents at its mouth. The reserve has plenty of shade, picnic tables and barbecues. There's a caravan park here (see "Accommodation", p.306), and little else except for a small shop selling basic supplies, good fish and chips and hamburgers. About 8km further on, the relatively unspoilt **Emerald Beach** is popular with surfers; it's very picturesque, with a small island offshore.

At **WOOLGOOLGA**, another 10km or so north on the Pacific Highway, a gleaming white **temple** is evidence of the large Sikh population that settled here in the early 1970s. Woolgoolga is also a popular seaside holiday resort, with excellent surfing on the ocean beach, while the calmer waters of **Woolgoolga Lake** to the north offer swimming and boating opportunities. Eight kilometres north of Woolgoolga, **Corindi Beach** is the site of the **Yarrawarra Aboriginal Cultural Centre** (phone for opening hours and to book guided walks on ☎02/6649 2669), which provides a focus and employment for the **Gumbaingirr** people in the area. There's an arts-and-crafts shop, bush-tucker café, and a native bush-tucker medicine nursery with plants for sale. After Corindi Beach, the road turns inland towards Grafton; for more beaches, take the first turn off the Pacific Highway and follow a short road northeast for 6km to reach the coast again at **Red Rock** and the beginning of the **Yuraygir National Park** (see p.311).

Grafton and around

Between Woolgoolga and Ballina the Pacific Highway runs inland, and the unspoilt coast between the two towns consists of a series of national parks to which access is gained by a few intermittent side roads. **GRAFTON**, an 83-kilometre drive along the Pacific Highway from Coffs Harbour, is a peaceful district capital on a bend of the wide **Clarence River**, which almost encircles the city and occasionally floods it. The "Big River" is the largest river system on the north coast and, with its tributaries, drains a vast area of northern New South Wales. You can while away a very pleasant afternoon sitting on the balcony of the *Crown Hotel*, sipping a beer and watching the majestic river roll by. Northeast of Grafton, the river widens as it approaches the ocean and branches out into a network of waterways and channels. There are more than a hundred river islands, on many of which sugar cane is grown.

Grafton is proud of its wide, tree-lined streets and has the air of a genteel, old-fashioned town. In spring, when the jacaranda and flame trees are ablaze with purple, mauve and red blossoms, they even have a **Jacaranda Festival** to celebrate them (last week of Oct and first week of Nov). Out of festival time this is a quiet place, where the main attraction is cruising on the river or visiting some of the historic buildings preserved by the National Trust. **Schaeffer House**, 192 Fitzroy St (Tues–Thurs & Sun 1–4pm; $3), has a collection of beautiful china, glassware and period furniture donated to the Trust over the years; on the same street at no. 158 is the **Grafton Regional Gallery** (Tues–Sun 10am–4pm; donation), which has a pretty garden café.

Practicalities

Call in at the **Clarence River Visitor Information Centre**, on the Pacific Highway at the corner of Spring Street, South Grafton (daily 9am–5pm; ☎02/6642 4677, ⓦwww.clarencetourism.com), which can give you information on scenic drives, river cruises and the national parks that surround Grafton. Countrylink **train** services along the north coast stop at Grafton station, close to the river crossing in South Grafton, while **long-distance buses** stop nearby, close to the visitor information centre. Harvey World Travel, 54 Prince St (☎02/6640 3910), can provide timetables and make reservations, as can the Countrylink office at the train station. Kings Brothers (☎1300 555 611) runs local bus services. There's plenty of **accommodation**: try the *Roches Family Hotel*, 85 Victoria St (☎02/6642 2866; ❶), a friendly pub offering cheap accommodation and good food on a leafy street close to the western bend of the river, by Susan Island; or the *Crown Hotel-Motel*, 1 Prince St (☎02/6642 4000; ❸), for hotel rooms with a river view or ground-level motel units. If you want a swimming pool, spa and all the mod-cons, check out the more expensive *Fitzroy*, 27–29 Fitzroy St (☎02/6642 4477, ⓕ6643 1828; ❹), now part of the Comfort Inn chain, 500m east of the centre. For **camping**, head for the well-equipped *Gateway Village Holiday Park*, just north of Grafton at 598 Summerland Way (☎02/6642 4225, ⓔgateway@hotkey.net.au; cabins ❹). A good place to **eat** is *Crabba Jack's Takeaway*, 79 Fitzroy St, for fresh fish and chips and seafood, or try *Georgie's Café* (closed Sun & Mon), at the Regional Art Gallery.

Around Grafton

From Grafton it's 47km northeast on the Pacific Highway, paralleling the Clarence River, to **MACLEAN**, a small delta town which proclaims its Scottish heritage with street signs in Gaelic. From the Maclean lookout on Wharf Street, 2km from the centre, panoramic views of the coast, bushland, canefields, river islands and the town itself can be enjoyed – while you are here, sample some of the much-feted local prawns from the Co-op. A few kilometres further north, you can turn east off the highway in the direction of the twin towns of **YAMBA** and **ILUKA** – increasingly popular holiday spots facing each other across the mouth of the river. Clarence River Ferries shuttles between the two communities (4–5 daily; $4; ☎0408 664 556) and also cruises along the river. In Yamba, the *Yamba Pacific Backpackers*, 1 Pilot St (☎02/6646 2466, ✉pachotel@nor.com.au; dorms $17.50, rooms ❷), is in a great old pub right on the beach, and offers very cheap singles and twins and also live music on Thursday to Sunday nights; ask about lifts to Byron Bay. You can get to Yamba on several daily public transport routes with Kings Brothers (☎1300 555 611).

A few kilometres south of Yamba is **Yuraygir National Park**, with several basic but attractive NPWS campsites (details from Grafton Visitor Information Centre) surrounded by isolated beaches and placid lake systems. North of Iluka, between the town and Bundjalung National Park, the **Iluka Nature Reserve** contains within it a World Heritage-listed **rainforest remnant**, one of sixteen such areas in northern New South Wales. **Bundjalung National Park** itself has a long coastline on the Coral Sea, as well as the sheltered inland waterways of the Esk River; **camping** is available at Woody Head, a spacious, modern site very popular with anglers (☎02/6646 6134, bookings advised). Just north of Bundjalung, the town of **EVANS HEAD** has a range of accommodation and shops, plus boat rental outlets. The tropical climate begins to make its presence felt here, with sugar cane growing by the roadside.

West from Grafton, the **Gwydir Highway** takes you to Glen Innes, 160km away on the New England Plateau. En route it passes the rugged and densely forested adjoining **national parks** of Gibraltar Range and Walshpool. **Gibraltar Range** is an elevated plateau 1200m above sea level, scattered with huge granite outcrops and intersected by deep gorges, and is famous for its wild-flower displays of Christmas bells and waratahs in late summer. There's a **visitors centre** on the highway at Dandahra Picnic Area and a gravel road leads from here into the park, where you'll find walking tracks, lookout points and waterfalls. **Walshpool National Park** is very remote, a wilderness park on the eastern escarpment of the New England Tableland. Its **rainforest** is worth visiting, and there are picnic facilities, walks and camping at Coombadjha Creek – reached via the Coombadjha Road off the Gwydir Highway, 88km from Grafton.

Ballina

The old port of **BALLINA**, at the mouth of the Richmond River, experienced a short-lived goldrush in the 1880s, but it has few reminders of this era and is now mostly a holiday town, with some pleasant beaches and the opportunity to take river trips to Lismore (see p.322) and other destinations. Neither has it escaped the clutches of the "big things", with the **giant prawn** marking the entrance to town, just off the highway from Grafton. It's a fairly conservative cousin to nearby Byron Bay, although the fact that you're entering New Age territory is obvious by the outskirts of Ballina, where the **Thursday Plantation** (daily 9am–5pm; free; ⊛www.thursdayplantation.com), 4km north on Gallans Road, east of the Pacific Highway, was the first commercial **tea tree** plantation, producing the all-healing tea tree oil and its products. One of the highlights of the town is a lively **market**, held here on the third Sunday of the month.

There's a cycling and walking track from the centre of town along the sea wall to the beach, a twenty-minute walk. In Las Balsas Plaza, on River Street, is a small **maritime museum** (daily 9am–4pm; donation), whose exhibits include the *Atzlan*, a balsa raft that made it across the Pacific from Ecuador in 1973 as part of the Thor Heyerdahl-inspired Las Balsas expedition. The **tourist information centre** (Mon–Fri 9am–5pm, Sat & Sun 9am–4pm; ℡02/6686 3484, ⓦwww.discoverballina.com) is in the same plaza, and can book lodging, river cruises and other tours. **Accommodation** includes the lovely *Ballina Manor*, a luxurious B&B at 25 Norton St (℡02/6681 5888, ⓦwww .ballinamanor.com.au; ❻), and the *Ballina Travellers Lodge Motel*, 36 Tamar St (℡02/6686 6737; dorms $19, rooms ❸), with a pleasant YHA hostel section; it's modern and family-run, with a swimming pool and free use of bicycles, fishing rods, boogie- and surfboards. *Ballina Central Caravan Park* (℡02/6686 2220, ⓦwww.tropicalnsw.com.au/ballinavanparks; cabins ❷) is situated right by the Richmond River and has disabled access, but if you have a car, the prime spot to pitch a tent is at *Flat Rock Tent Park* (℡02/6686 4848), on the coast road 5km east of Ballina; right on the beach, this unspoilt site is for tents only and there's no electricity, so it's very peaceful – solar-heated hot showers supply a touch of comfort.

For tasty alfresco **food**, try the *Shattered Plate* on Moon Street (℡02/6686 7119; open till late Fri & Sat, closed Sun). The best place for brunch – with great ocean views and healthy, creative cooking – is *Shellys on the Beach* at Shellys Beach: follow the bridge and sea wall 2km out of town. Ballina has quite a lively summer **nightlife**: *Rous Tavern*, on River Street, has a popular café and hosts occasional bands, while the *Australian Hotel*, on the corner of Cherry and River streets, is more sedate, with jazz, piano music and a pleasant beer garden. Backpacker types tend to gravitate towards the nightly *craic* on offer at *Paddy McGintys* on River Street.

Qantas (℡13 13 13) and Regional Express (℡13 17 13) fly direct to Ballina from Sydney. By land, the town is connected by the long-distance Kirklands **bus** (℡02/6622 1499) to Brisbane via Lismore, Lennox Head and Evans Head. **Local** services include Blanch's (℡02/6686 2144) to and from the airport east of town, and to Lennox Head, Byron Bay and Mullumbimby. To get around, you can rent a **bike** from Jack Ransom Cycles, 16 Cherry St (℡ & ℻02/6685 3485). Rental **cars** are available from Budget (℡13 27 27) and Avis (℡02/6681 4036); both operators have offices on Southern Cross Drive and at the airport.

Lennox Head

The best of the **surf beaches** are those around the small town of **LENNOX HEAD**, 11km north of Ballina, a relaxed resort with a small shopping centre, some good cafés and restaurants and a lively pub. Lennox rates among the top ten **surfing** spots in the world and professionals congregate here for the big waves in May, June and July. Adding to Lennox Head's appeal is the calm, fresh water of **Lake Ainsworth** close to the beach; stained dark by the tea trees around its banks, it's a popular swimming spot for families seeking refuge from the crashing surf, and the soft, practically medicinal water (it's effectively diluted tea tree oil) is wonderful for your skin.

Ideally situated between the lake and the beach, *Lennox Head Beach House YHA*, 3 Ross St (℡02/6687 7636, ⓔlennoxbacpac@hotmail.com; dorms $22, rooms ❷), is a relaxed place where massage, reflexology and Bowen therapy are available in-house; there's unlimited use of boards and fishing gear, bikes, windsurfers and paddle-skis for $5 for the duration of your stay. Also in a prime position is the *Lake Ainsworth Caravan Park* on Pacific Parade (☎02/6687 7249, ⓦ www.tropicalnsw.com.au/ballinavanparks; cabins ❸). *Café de Mer* is great for coffee, smoothies and lunches. The cheap but excellent pizza, pasta and salad available at *Lennox Head Pizza* on Ballina Street (☎02/6687 7080) is popular with surfies, as is the delicious grub at *Mi Thai* a few shops further down. The *Lennox Point Hotel* serves excellent modern Australian food in a convivial atmosphere with water views; it also plays host to bands on Thursday, Friday and Saturday nights.

Since Lennox Head is off the Pacific Highway, few long-distance **bus** services call here; the closest drop-off with McCafferty's/Greyhound Pioneer is at nearby Ballina, from where the YHA will pick up guests free of charge. Premier, which runs services right along the east coast, stops in Ballina three times daily and there are local services to and from Byron Bay.

Byron Bay and around

Situated at the end of a long sweeping bay, the township of **BYRON BAY** boasts 30km of almost unbroken sandy beaches. Formerly a working-class coastal town of dilapidated weatherboard cottages, best known for its abattoir, it's now a thriving resort, first discovered by the surfies, then the hippies and more recently by better-heeled travellers – these days Byron is as much of a "must do" on the backpacker circuit as the Whitsundays and Uluru. In summer it can seem like Sydney-by-the-sea, as half of Paddington and Darlinghurst arrive en masse, fleeing the city only to form another urban jungle further up the coast. It's a pity, because what once made the place special – the small-community feel, the free-for-all atmosphere, the barefoot hippies and the herbalists – is fast disappearing. Byron these days is still beautiful and undeniably good fun, but the ever-encroaching chain stores and the profusion of competing tie-dye therapies combine to make it, in summertime at least, about as subversively alternative as MTV.

Arrival and information

If you come by **train**, you'll arrive right in the heart of town on **Jonson Street**, the main thoroughfare. Not all north-coast **buses** stop at Byron Bay; those that do will also drop you here, or else a little way north near the junction of Jonson and Lawson streets (see "Listings" for details of bus companies and booking agents, on p.319). The closest **airports** are at Ballina, 39km south (from where you can get a bus connection with Kirklands, see opposite), or Coolangatta, 109km north in Queensland (see p.435); Byron Bay Connection buses link up with Coolangatta and Brisbane airports (☎02/6685 7447; from $27).

Check out the helpful **Byron Bay Tourist Information Centre**, staffed by volunteers at 80 Jonson St, next to the train station (daily 9am–5pm; ☎02/6680 9271, ⓦ www.visitbyronbay.com). You'll be able to pick up an excellent range of printed information here about accommodation (free booking service), eating, national parks, scenic drives, sights, activities and tours. A *Disabled Access Guide* is also available. An alternative for information is the **Byron Bus & Backpacker Centre**, next to the information centre (daily 7am–7pm; ☎02/6685 5517, ⓔ bustop@lismore.com.au), which books tours, activities, accommodation, bus tickets, car rental (from $49 a day including 100km mileage), provides currency exchange and arranges freight. There are other "information centres" along the street, but they're really geared up for selling adventure activities and tours.

Tours from Byron Bay

There are many **tours** to the rainforest, waterfalls and national parks in the hinterland around Byron Bay (see "Far North Coast Hinterland", p.321, for details of destinations mentioned). All tours and activities can be booked at Byron Bus & Backpacker Centre, next to the tourist office (daily 7am–7pm; ℡02/ 6685 5517). Below are listed some of the more specialist and unusual tour operators.

Byron Bay Motorcycle Tours ℡02/6685 6762, ✉soundwav@norex.com.au. Whizz around the beaches and hinterland on the back of a Harley-Davidson (20min $35, 2hr $115; summer only).

Byron Bay Sea Kayaks ℡02/6685 5830, ⓦwww.byronbayadventureco.com. Dolphin-watching from sea level in two-person boats, leaving at 8.30am & 1.30pm ($45 including breakfast or afternoon tea).

Byron Bay Walking Tours ℡02/6687 1112, ✉walknorth@mullum.com.au. These ten- to fifteen-kilometre hikes change daily, leaving at 8.30am to take in the likes of Nightcap National Park, Minyon Falls and the Angourie coast ($46–88 per person including lunch).

Jim's Alternative Tours ℡02/6685 7720. Tours aimed at presenting a positive, accurate portrayal of the hinterland "back to the land" movement. The tours visit Nimbin and Minyon Falls, with opportunities for swimming ($25). They can also help transport you to the Sunday markets at The Channon ($10) and Bangalow ($5), with more flexible times than other operators.

Mick's Bay to Bush Tours ℡02/6685 6889. The longest-established of Byron Bay's alternative tours, offering the popular Rainbow Trip which takes in Nimbin and Minyon Falls ($30).

Nimbin Explorer Tours ℡02/6689 1577. Yet another tour operator doing the Nimbin thing, but this time via Protestors Falls, with an emphasis on the environment ($30 including lunch).

Rockhoppers Mountain Bike Adventures ℡0500 881 881, ⓦwww.rockhoppers .com.au. One of several tours by this operator (champagne breakfast on the Mt Warning Sunrise Trek is one other popular option), this tour offers exhilarating, 24-speed, environmentally aware, mountain biking through rainforest, taking in swimming holes, waterfalls and lookouts. They are licensed by the NPWS, and the cost ($70) includes drinks, snacks and a BBQ lunch.

Accommodation

There are plenty of places to stay in Byron Bay, but that doesn't mean it's easy to find a bed. During December and January especially, demand for accommodation in all categories far exceeds supply, and it's essential to book well in advance. There's a dedicated **accommodation** desk in the tourist information centre (same hours as centre; ℡02/6680 8666, ⓦwww .byronbayaccom.net). The **hostels** in Byron Bay are among the best in Australia, but prices and stress levels rise dramatically in summer, and choosing the wrong kind of hostel could ruin your stay. If you're part of a group, **holiday apartments** (booked through the accommodation desk at the tourist office and real estate agents in town) might be a more practical option. If all places in town are full, you may strike it lucky in the surrounding area – either towards **Brunswick Heads**, about 18km further up the coast (see p.317), or in the quiet town of **Mullumbimby** – known for its very potent marijuana – just inland at the foot of Mount Chincogan on the Brunswick River.

Motels, hotels, guest-houses and apartments

Beach Hotel Cnr Jonson and Bay streets ☎ 02/6685 6402, ⓦ www.beachhotel.com.au. This luxury waterfront hotel is a favourite amongst visiting Aussie celebs. Spacious, tasteful units with patios or balconies. Outdoor heated pool and spa set among greenery. **❼**

Byron Bay Beach Resort Bayshore Drive, 3km north on the road to the Pacific Highway, turn off at the Byron Bay Industrial Estate ☎ 02/6685 8000, ⓦ www.byronbaybeachresort.com.au. Lovely complex of serviced wooden chalets with self-contained cooking facilities and TV. The resort-style extras include a pool, bar, restaurant, tennis courts and golf course. **❼**

Byron Bay Rainforest Resort Broken Head Rd, Suffolk Park, 3.5km south, opposite the golf course ☎ 02/6685 6139, ⓔ holiday@rainforestresort .com.au. A prize-winning resort designed to be completely accessible to people with disabilities. Private one- or two-room cabins, fully equipped (linen is provided), with verandah and TV, set in a rainforest with easy access to the beach; there's also a swimming pool with ramp. Cheaper weekly rates available. Cabins **❼**

Byron Sunseeker Motel 100 Bangalow Rd, 1.5km south ☎ 02/6685 7369, ⓦ www.byronsun .com.au. Cottage-style motel units with balconies or verandahs. Saltwater pool, playground and BBQ. All units sleep six and have limited cooking facili-ties. Close to Tallow Beach. **❺**

Great Northern Hotel Cnr Jonson and Byron streets ☎ 02/6685 6454. No-frills pub rooms in an excellent location on the main street. The noise from the bands playing below make this place one for confirmed night owls. Cheap single rates, par-ticularly off-season. **❸**

Lord Byron Resort Motel 120 Jonson St ☎ 02/6685 7444, ⓔ lbyron@nor.com. Central loca-tion, with amenities including a swimming pool, spa, sauna and tennis court. All units air-con. Some serviced apartments available (with fans only). **❻**

Hostels

Aquarius Backpackers Motel 16 Lawson St ☎ 02/6685 7663 or 1800 028 909, ⓦ www .aquarius-backpackers.com.au. Close to Main Beach, this swanky backpacker motel offers self-contained units with kitchenettes as well as dorms. Pool, BBQ area, café, bar, free use of bikes and boogie-boards. Internet and currency exchange facilities are also available. Dorms $25, units **❸**

Arts Factory Backpackers Lodge Skinners Shoot Rd ☎ 02/6685 7709, ⓦ www.artsfactory .com.au. More an experience than an establish-ment, the *Arts Factory* attracts those who value a social scene and sleepless nights over space and security – most guests either love it immediately or desperately want to leave. The wooden lodge is situated in a bushland creek setting, with a choice of dorms, tepees and canvas huts by the creek; there's also a camping area. Facilities include pool and free bikes, as well as New Age workshops and classes. No children allowed. Advance booking required for pick-ups from train or bus station, and expect to pay a deposit for everything. Dorms $23, huts **❷**

Backpackers Holiday Village 116 Jonson St ☎ 02/6685 8888 or 1800 350 388 (reservations only), ⓕ 6685 8777. One of the most central and long-established hostels, this place is clean, friendly and well equipped, with a solar-heated swimming pool, spa and BBQs. Free bikes, boards and luggage storage. Dorms $25, rooms **❸**

Backpackers Inn on the Beach 29 Shirley St ☎ 02/6685 8231, ⓦ www.byron-bay.com /backpackersinn. Arranged around a central court-yard. Facilities include a communal kitchen, swim-ming pool, BBQ and volleyball court. Free bikes and boards. Dorms $23, rooms **❸**

Belongil Beach House Childe St ☎ 02/6685 7868, ⓔ info@belongilbeachhouse.com. Beautiful complex in the style of a Balinese resort, with spacious, cool, high-ceilinged timber cottages around a landscaped garden. Single travellers may find it a little remote. Parking, free bikes and boards available, plus there's an excellent café, *Switch*, next door. Dorms $25, rooms **❸**, apart-ments **❹**

Blue Iguana Beachhouse 14 Bay St ☎ 02/6685 5298. In a lovely old bungalow with a wooden verandah, this is perfect for lone travellers and those needing a touch of home. It's small enough to feel personal – a place to relax, listen to music and BBQ on the deck among the hibiscus, before swimming at the beach opposite. Double, twin and four-share rooms, all en suite. Couples might like to try sleeping in the honeymoon suite parked out-side – a converted double decker bus. Dorms $25, rooms **❸**

Byron Bay Bunkhouse 1 Carlyle St ☎ 02/6685 8311 or 1800 241 600, ⓔ byronbay@org.com.au. Large, rowdy, laid-back hostel with dorms only. Free pancakes, but the place is not for the faint at heart. Dorms $23.

Cape Byron YHA Hostel Cnr Middleton and Byron streets ☎ 02/6685 8788, ⓔ byronyha@nrg.com.au. Large, central hostel that feels more like a resort hotel, except you have

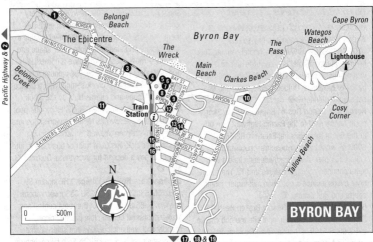

BYRON BAY

ACCOMMODATION					
Aquarius Backpackers Motel	9	Blue Iguana Beachouse	6	Cape Byron YHA Hostel	12
Arts Factory Backpakers Lodge	11	Broken Head Holiday Park	19	Clarkes Beach Holiday Park	10
Backpackers Holiday Village	15	Byron Bay Beach Resort	2	First Sun Holiday Park	4
Backpackers Inn on the Beach	3	Byron Bay Bunkhouse	13	Great Northern Hotel	8
Beach Hotel	5	Byron Bay Rainforest Resort	17	J's Bay YHA Hostel	14
Belongil Beach House	1	Byron Sunseeker Motel	18	Lord Byron Resort Motel	16
				Nomads Main Beach Backpackers	7

to pay a deposit on crockery. Facilities include a pool and basketball court; also free pancakes, bikes and boogie-boards, and two BBQ nights a week. Some rooms en suite. Dorms $22, rooms ❸

J's Bay YHA Hostel 7 Carlyle St ℡02/6685 8853 or 1800 678 195, ✉jbay@nor.com.au. Bright, airy resort-style hostel with two central courtyards, one with BBQ and outdoor eating area, the other with heated saltwater pool. Good-value social pizza evenings, and a weekly pub crawl. Extras include free boards and bikes and a TV room with videos. Dorms range from small to immense; many rooms are en suite. Dorms $22, rooms ❸

Nomads Main Beach Backpackers Cnr Lawson and Fletcher streets ℡02/6685 8695, ⓦwww.nomadsworld.com. Safe and pleasant old Council chambers converted into a hostel, complete with pool, car parking, Internet access and secure lockers in every room. Dorms $22, rooms ❸

Campsites

Broken Head Holiday Park Beach Rd, Broken Head ℡02/6685 3245. Great location at the southern end of Tallow Beach. Sites ❶, cabins ❹

Clarkes Beach Holiday Park Off Lighthouse Rd ℡02/6685 6496, ⓦwww.bshp.com.au/clarkes.

Only 1km west of town, and right on the beach. All cabins are fully self-contained, with showers and toilets. Sites ❶, cabins ❺

Ferry Reserve Holiday Park Pacific Highway, Brunswick Heads ℡02/6685 1872, ⓦwww .bshp.com.au/ferry. Pleasant campsite near the river, with a kiosk and BBQ. Self-contained and basic cabins as well as campsites. Sites ❶, cabins ❸

First Sun Holiday Park Lawson St ℡02/6685 6544, ⓦwww.bshp.com.au/first. Very central, overlooking Main Beach. Cabins range from fully self-contained to basic. Sites ❶, cabins ❹

Maca's Camping Ground Main Arm Rd, near Mullumbimby ℡02/6684 5211. Campsite in the bush. Communal kitchen and dining room, plus laundry. Tents for rent. Vans ❶, sites ❶

Suffolk Park Holiday Park Alcorn St, Suffolk Park, 5km south ℡02/6685 3353, ⓦwww.bshp.com.au/suffolk. Good location in a shady setting on Tallow Beach. Self-contained cabins with shower and toilet. Cabins ❹, sites ❶

Terrace Reserve Holiday Park Fingal St, Brunswick Heads ℡02/6685 1233, ⓦwww .bshp.com.au/terrace. Shady spot by the river, near the beach. Cabins come with shower and toilet and are fully self-contained. Sites ❶, cabins ❹

The Town and around

There's plenty of opportunity to soak up local atmosphere – and the often bizarre mix of counter-cultures as surfie meets soap starlet meets hippie – simply by wandering the streets. Probably the best place to take it all in is on the first Sunday of each month at the **market**, on Butler Street behind the train station, a huge affair containing everything from leather handbags to organic veggies. If you want to explore, one of the first places to visit is the **lighthouse** on the rocky promontory of **Cape Byron**, where there's a small nature reserve (8am–5.30pm). The cape includes the easternmost point of the Australian mainland and is a popular spot to greet the dawn, but don't worry if you're not an early riser – the views from the cape and the lighthouse reserve are fabulous anytime, and there's an excellent circular **walking track** from the lighthouse. With a bit of luck you'll see **dolphins**, who like to sport in the surf off the headland, **humpback whales**, which pass this way heading north to warmer waters in June or July and again on their return south in September or October, and maybe some **sharks**.

Main Beach in town is as good as any to swim from, and usually has relatively gentle surf. One reason why Byron Bay is so popular with surf freaks is because its beaches face in all directions, so there's almost always one with a good swell; however, you can usually find somewhere for a calmer swim.

East of Main Beach, you can always find a spot to yourself on the less sheltered stretch of **Belongil Beach**, from where there's sand virtually all the way to **BRUNSWICK HEADS**, a quieter, more family-oriented resort located between the mouth of the Brunswick River and Simpson's Creek, with a long crescent of beach on the ocean side. The grassy riverfront area is a good spot for children, with several playgrounds and picnic areas.

Back in the other direction, Main Beach curves round towards Cape Byron to become **Clarkes Beach**. This and neighbouring **Wategos Beach** – beautifully framed between two rocky spurs – face north, and they usually have the best surfing. On the far side of the cape, **Tallow Beach** extends towards the **Broken Head Nature Reserve**, 6km south of the town centre at Suffolk Park; there's good surf at Tallow just around the cape at Cosy Corner, and also at Broken Head. From the car park here, a short stroll through rainforest leads to the secluded, nudist **Kings Beach**, one of several isolated stretches of sand out this way.

The diversity of marine life in the waters of Byron Bay makes it second only to the Great Barrier Reef as a place to **dive** on the east coast. Tropical marine life and creatures from warm temperate seas mingle at the granite outcrop of **Julian Rocks Aquatic Reserve**, 3km offshore; by far the most popular spot here is the **Cod Hole**, an extensive underwater cave inhabited by large moray eels and other fish. Between April and June is the best time to dive, before the plankton bloom (see "Listings" on p.320 for information on dive schools).

Eating

There's a multitude of places selling food in Byron Bay, and the standard is generally pretty high. Lots of alternative **cafés** offer delicious health foods and vegetarian dishes – although they don't usually stay open late, even in summer – and there are plenty of takeaways and fish-and-chip shops, as well as **restaurants** that serve everything from kebabs to gourmet seafood. Most have extended opening hours in the peak summer period.

Bay Kebabs Cnr Jonson and Lawson streets. Generous falafel rolls and gourmet kebabs are the thing to have here. Eat sitting on the stools inside, or take away. Daily 10am until late.

Byron Bay offers a truly wide variety of alternative therapies, extensive browsing in New Age bookshops, a wealth of crystals, and a future foretold through palmistry and tarot readings – all underlaid with a good dose of capitalism as prices for massages and tarot readings are hiked up during the lucrative summer months. The alternative culture attracts artists and artisans in droves, and galleries and artists' studios abound.

Alternative therapies

The **Community Centre**, at 69 Jonson St (℡02/6685 6807, ✉bbcc@mullum .com.au; closed Sun), opposite the train station in a brand new building, has great notice boards packed with information on everything from Celtic Shamanism to Tibetan healing workshops. At the rear of the *Belongil Beach House* on Childe Street, the Relax Haven (℡02/6685 8304) has a **floatation tank** (1hr float $25) and **massage** available (float and massage $40); or the more central Samadhi Flotation Centre, 107 Jonson St (℡02/6685 6905), offers the same, plus classes, workshops and a resident naturopath and homeopath. Quintessence, Shop 8, 11 Fletcher St (℡02/6685 5533), offers **aromatherapy** massage and **reflexology** ($40). Ambaji Wellness Centre at 6 Marvel St (℡02/6685 6620, ⊛www.ambaji.com.au) offers a wide range of treatments from **homeopathy** and **yoga** to **tarot readings**.

Arts and crafts

The **Byron Bay market**, held on the first Sunday of each month on Butler Street, behind the train station, is the best way to become acquainted with the arts and crafts of the area (if you miss it, there's others at The Channon on the second Sunday, Mullumbimby on the third Saturday, Uki on the third Sunday and one at the showground at Bangalow, 13km southwest, on the fourth Sunday of each month). The **Arts Factory**, on Skinners Shoot Road, has several artists' workshops that you can visit (Tues–Sun 10am–3pm), and the **Byron Craft Market** is held here every Saturday (8.30am–3pm) with a courtesy bus (9.30am–3.30pm) from the community centre on Jonson Street. **The Epicentre**, on Border Street, near Belongil Beach, has several outlets and resident artists and craftspeople, plus a large art gallery showing the work of local artists (open shop hours; $1 donation). Beyond here, 3km northwest of town, signposted off Ewingsdale Road (the road to the Pacific Highway), **Byron Bay Industrial Estate** has a host of artisans producing everything from leathergoods to glassware. Back in town, Jonson Street is lined with shops selling crystals and locally made crafts, particularly jewellery.

Byron Bay is host to an Australian **Writers' Festival** during the last week of July featuring readings and signings by established and budding writers; contact the Northern Rivers Writers' Centre, PO Box II41, Lismore, NSW 2480 (℡02/6622 3599, ⊛www.byronbaywritersfestival.com.au).

The Beach Café Clarkes Beach. A good place for breakfast after a morning stroll, open from 7.30am. Serves eclectic dinner choices in the summer.

Byron Juice Bar Jonson St. Delicious smoothies and fantastic freshly squeezed juices are almost a meal in themselves at this popular place. They offer healthy snacks, too, if you need something more than a liquid lunch.

Café D.O.C. 7 Middleton St. Far from the madding crowds in a local bit of town, this great café is the best in the centre for huge bowls of muesli with fruit and other breakfasty things.

Earth 'n' Sea Pizzas Lawson St. Recently moved to new premises, this is a perennial favourite in Byron. Toppings are unusual and imaginative: try "Mullumbimby Madness", with mushrooms, of course. Generous and affordable pasta too, or there's a $10 all-you-can-eat special on Wed nights. BYO and licensed. Daily from 5.30pm.

Fins At the *Beach Hotel*, cnr Jonson and Bay streets ℡02/6685 5029. A hugely popular and very pricey brasserie with an extensive people-watching verandah overlooking the ocean. Mainly fish and vegetarian dishes, with Moroccan and southern European twists. Booking advised.

Fresh 7 Johnson St. A very funky place to try oriental salads, excellent slices and juices or simply to hang out over a coffee. Evening meals are a delight.

The Piggery Supernatural Food Arts Factory, Skinners Shoot Rd ☎ 02/6685 5833. Don't be fooled by the name – this is a popular vegetarian place in a vast setting, retaining the open rafters of the building's early days as – ironically – a meatworks. Cheap and candlelit. BYO.

The Rails Bistro At the train station. Great food and ambience at this popular spot. Food served throughout the day.

The Raving Prawn Feros Arcade, off Jonson and Lawson streets ☎ 02/6685 2481. Great-value seafood restaurant offering some of the freshest and best-cooked catch in town.

Switch Childe St, next to *Belongil Beach House*. Another great oceanfront place for breakfast, lunch and dinner, though the sea view is behind beachfront bush. There are outside tables, and frequent avant-garde spoken word, cinema and music nights. BYO. Daily 8am–9pm.

Thai Noodle Bar Feros Arcade, off Jonson and Lawson streets. Moderately priced fresh noodles wok-fried; you select the added ingredients. Also Malaysian-style laksa (noodle soup). Good selection of vegetarian dishes. Small bar-style eating area, but primarily a takeaway place. Mon–Sat 10am–6pm.

Entertainment and nightlife

The weekly free community newspaper, *The Byron Shire Echo*, has a comprehensive gig guide. There's plenty of activity in summer: **New Year's Eve** is such a big event that the council has taken to closing the town off – so come early. The huge outdoor **Annual Byron Bay Arts and Music Festival** is normally held for three days in early January but may be moving to February; it takes over Belongil Fields with several stages, a rave field, an all-night cinema, a food fair, market stalls and workshops; to find out exact dates, call the tourist information centre (☎ 02/6680 9271). Tickets can be bought in advance from independent record outlets around Australia. At Pighouse Flicks, Old Piggery, Skinners Shoot Road (☎ 02/6685 5828), **"The Byron Cinema Experience"** shows a hand-picked bill of latest-release films with the emphasis on the quirky and the first-rate, with two to three films nightly and deck chairs or sofas for seating. The price is $10.50 per film, or $12 with a meal and drink thrown in from their great vegetarian restaurant.

Beach Hotel Cnr Jonson and Bay streets ☎ 02/6685 6402. Owned by John Cornell, who played Paul Hogan's sidekick in a 1970s Australian comedy series, this big and smart pub is superbly sited right opposite Main Beach with a huge terrace beer garden, bistro and restaurant, and attracts a cross-section of locals. Live music (often free), including jazz sessions on Sunday afternoon.

The Cheeky Monkey 115 Jonson St ☎ 02/6685 5886. Popular backpackers' hang out. Cheap food, loud music and a happy hour after 10pm. Closes 3am.

Great Northern Hotel Jonson St ☎ 02/6685 6454. Something for everyone: a front room with pool tables, a typically blokish public bar and *The Backroom*, a large stylish space that doubles as an Italian restaurant and a music venue with big-name Australian bands playing three or four times a week. Open till 1am nightly.

La La Land Lawson St. If the hair wraps and tie-dye brigade are making you ill, then try this Byron Bay branch of a Melbourne institution; a place for sipping cocktails and wearing black. Sushi, dips and pizza available for "grazing". Daily 7pm–1am.

Listings

Bike rental Many hostels have either free or rentable bikes for guests; otherwise try Byron Bay Bicycle, 93 Jonson St, opposite Woolworths (☎ 02/6685 6067), which charges around $20 a day for a mountain bike and also has rollerblades; or Byron Bay Bike Hire, opposite (☎ 0500 856 985). A cycling track runs from Byron to Suffolk

Park via Broken Head nature reserve (8km one-way).

Buses Booking for McCafferty's/Greyhound Pioneer, Kirklands and Premier, through Byron Bus & Backpacker Centre, 84 Jonson St (☎ 02/6685 5517). Kirklands goes daily to Brisbane, and to Ballina (with stops at Murwillumbah and Tweed

Heads), also daily to Lismore and Casino. Blanch's Coaches (℡02/6686 2144) runs south to Ballina via Suffolk Park, Bangalow and Lennox Head, and north to Mullimbimby – buy your ticket on the bus.

Car rental Budget at *Dolphins Motel* ℡02/6680 9577; Earth Car Rental, Middleton St ℡02/6680 9708; Hertz, Marvel St ℡02/6680 7925; Thrifty, Shirley St ℡02/6685 7925.

Diving Most dive schools offer complete scuba-diving courses, together with more affordable one-day courses and daily snorkelling trips (around $30). Byron Bay Dive Centre, 9 Marvel St (℡02/6685 8333 or 1800 243 483, ⓦwww .byronbaydivecentre.com.au), does a good-value, one-day course for $125 including all equipment; Sundive, Middleton St (℡02/6685 7755), is a small, friendly outfit. If you're already trained, one dive at Julian Rocks, with gear, costs from $75, two dives $105.

Environment Byron Bay Environment Centre, in the kiosk opposite the tourist information centre (same hours), at the train station.

Gay and lesbian information Tropical Fruits is a social group for gays and lesbians, holding dance parties every few weeks in halls around the area; the Fruitline (℡02/6622 6440, ⓦwww .tropicalfruits.org.au) gives recorded information on upcoming events.

Hang-gliding Tandem take-offs and lessons from $104 for 30min with the excellent Byron Airwaves (℡02/6629 0354).

Horse riding Pegasus Park (℡02/6687 1446) charges from $45 for one hour. Combined riding and canoeing trips cost $55 per hour. Seahorses Riding Centre (℡02/6680 8155) offers lessons from $70 per half-day. Rides include beach, rain-forest, sunrise and sunset tours.

Hospital Wordsworth St, off Shirley St ℡02/6685 6200.

Internet access Facilities are available all over town, but *Global Gossip*, by the tourist information centre on Lawson Street (daily 8am–midnight), has the most reliable connection and the best rates.

Laundries You can use the laundry at most accommodation; otherwise try Byron Dry Cleaners and Laundrette, 42 Jonson St (daily 7am–7pm), with both self-service and service washes avail-able, or the unattended self-service laundry on Marvel St (daily 7am–7pm).

Left luggage Byron Bus & Backpacker Centre, next to the tourist information centre, will mind bags for 24 hours for $5 (daily 7am–6.30pm).

Police 2 Shirley St ℡02/6685 9499.

Post office Next door to the Community Centre on Jonson St (postcode NSW 2481).

Surfing Many hostels provide free boards. For surf lessons, one of the best outfits is the Byron Bay Surf School, at 84 Jonson St (℡0500 853 929), which rents out surf gear and offers 3hr lessons from $40 with free pick-ups daily (classes 9am, 11am, 1pm & 3pm).

Taxi Byron Bay Taxi & Limousines ℡02/6685 5008, ⓦwww.byronbaytaxis.com. There's a taxi rank on Jonson St, opposite the *Great Northern Hotel*.

Travel agents There are a string of specialist out-fits along Jonson Street who can book adventure tours. Byron Bay Travel Centre, Shop 4, 52 Jonson St (Mon–Fri 9am–6pm, Sat & Sun 9am–4pm; ℡02/6685 6733), is a good general travel and STA agent which deals with bus bookings and passes; also sells YHA and VIP membership. Jetset, Marvel St (same hours; ℡02/6685 6554), can revalidate tickets and book international and domestic flights.

Tweed Heads

From Brunswick Heads, the Pacific Highway heads around 30km inland to Murwillumbah (see p.326) and then a further 30km to the coast at **TWEED HEADS**. Although officially still part of New South Wales, Tweed Heads – the twin city of Coolangatta in Queensland (see p.435) – is for all practical pur-poses part of the **Gold Coast**. It certainly looks the part: high-rise buildings, concrete apartment blocks and shopping centres vie for space with grandiose club buildings and a roadscape of advertising billboards in gaudy colours. From the shore, the jagged skyline of Surfers Paradise can be seen in the distance.

In its favour, it does have lots of places to stay (motels are cheaper here than further north), and even more opportunities to eat and drink – not to men-tion the opportunity to **gamble**, an activity that was once banned in Queensland. **Clubs** and casinos opened up just across the border to cash in: one of the biggest, brightest and longest-established of these is the *Twin Towns RSL Club* (℡07/5536 2277) on Wharf Street, whose special offers on cheap food and drink can be a good deal, so long as you don't lose too much in the machines along the way.

One of the few other attractions is the **Minjungbal Aboriginal Cultural Museum**, on Kirkwood Road in South Tweed Heads (daily 10am–4pm; $6), where detailed exhibits and videos illustrate how Aboriginal people lived off this stretch of the coast; near the museum, a signposted boardwalk leads past an old bora ring – a sacred site used in initiation ceremonies. Ironically, the **Captain Cook Memorial Lighthouse** on **Point Danger** celebrates the very event that signalled the demise of Aboriginal culture in these parts: right at the state border, it was erected for the Cook bicentenary celebrations in 1970. Cook gave Point Danger its name after nearly running aground on it, and **Mount Warning** (see below) got its name at the same time – as a landmark to help sailors navigate around the point.

Practicalities

The **Tweed Heads Visitors Centre** is in the Tweed Mall, at the corner of Wharf and Bay streets (Mon–Sat 9am–5pm; ☎1800 674 414, ⓦwww.tweed-coolangatta.com); they also have information on the rest of the Gold Coast. From Coolangatta airport, **buses** generally make a beeline for the resort strip in Queensland; **long-distance buses** stop on Bay Street, near Tweed Mall; Surfside Buslines (☎13 12 30) runs local services up and down the Gold Coast, and to Murwillumbah.

Should you want to **stay**, there are dozens of motels, caravan parks and holiday apartments strung out along the highway, though there's even more choice over the border and you're probably better off continuing on to Surfers Paradise (see p.428) for the full Gold Coast experience – if that's what you're after. For something less crass, head 20km south down the Coast Road to **Cabarita Beach** near Bogangar where you'll find the *Emu Park Lodge* (☎02/6676 1190, ⓔemupark@norex.com.au; dorms $21, rooms ❷), a good **hostel** which has Internet access, a swap library, laundry, free use of bikes and boards, surfing lessons and trips to Mount Warning; pay for two nights and you get the third free. The village has a pub and several eating places. Back in Tweed Heads itself, it's not hard to find something to **eat**: if the clubs don't appeal, head for oceanfront Marine Parade, where there's everything from takeaway pizza to seafood restaurants.

Far North Coast Hinterland

The beautiful area inland from the far north coast, between artist-filled **Lismore** in the fertile Richmond River valley to the south, and staid **Murwillumbah** in the even lusher valley of the Tweed River near the Queensland border, is known as the **Far North Coast Hinterland**. But pioneers dubbed this region – once covered in **rainforest** that included species of flora extant from the era of the ancient supercontinent of **Gondwanaland** – the Big Scrub. The Hinterland's three national parks, plus several reserves, are World Heritage-listed, protecting pockets of rainforest that the settlers never managed to log, and which protestors helped to save in the first successful anti-logging demonstration in Australia, in 1979.

Mount Warning – Wollumbin or "cloud catcher" to the Bandjalung Aborigines – is what remains of the central magma chamber of a four-thousand-square-kilometre, shield-shaped volcano; from this 1157-metre peak, where the sun's rays first strike Australia, dazzling views reveal the area's geographic features. **Mount Warning National Park** rises in the middle of a massive **caldera** eroded on the eastern side into a huge bowl, where the Tweed River flows to the sea through the mostly agricultural patchwork of the valley floor. The northwest rim section consists of the McPherson and Tweed ranges, in the **Border Ranges National Park**; the southern section is within the **Nightcap National Park**, near counter-cultural **Nimbin**, and **The Channon** – one of many villages in "the hills" and famous for hosting the largest, most colourful **market** in the area.

Kirklands (℡ 02/6622 1499) is based at Lismore and the area is well served by **buses** from the coast, although there is no regular service on to Nimbin. A special shuttle bus runs three times daily to Nimbin from Byron Bay (℡ 02/6680 9189; $14).

Lismore and around

On the Bruxner Highway 65km inland from Ballina, **LISMORE** is the principal town of northeast New South Wales and the commercial focus of the fertile Richmond River valley, surrounded by prosperous dairy and farming country. This is one of the most densely populated rural areas in Australia, and has been since the early days of the colony. In the nineteenth century Lismore was an important river port for the **timber** trade, as lumberjacks cut their way through the dense forest of the valley – the so-called Big Scrub – before moving up to the steep slopes of the McPherson Ranges near the Queensland border. Local red cedar, especially, was much sought after. There's still a fair amount of forestry in the region, but these days the economic mainstay is dairy farming and cattle breeding, along with a rapidly growing tropical agriculture sector: bananas, sugar cane, avocados, tropical fruit and macadamia nuts. The Rainbow Region organic market takes place at the Lismore Showground on Tuesdays and Thursdays.

For all the intense agriculture, however, this is not your typical Ocker backwater; the city of 42,000 even has its own **Southern Cross University**, which includes a Koala Hospital on its grounds. Since the alternative-lifestyle seekers discovered the northeast in the 1970s, **cultural life** has flourished and jewellers, potters, painters, graphic artists, sculptors and other arts-and-crafts people who have settled here have established a whole network of shops and galleries where they can sell their work. Every other weekend they all come together for the region's **Art and Craft Expo**; at other times the **Regional Art Gallery**, 131 Molesworth St (Tues–Fri 10am–4pm, Sat & Sun 10.30am–2.30pm; free), is the best place to get an overview. The **Historical Museum**, on the same street at no. 165 (Mon–Fri 10am–4pm; $2), houses an interesting, if somewhat motley, collection of pioneer relics and photographic records of the region's history. There are several festivals throughout the year, the most popular being the **Lantern Festival** in June and the **Herb Festival** in August.

Practicalities

Lismore is the home base of Kirklands **buses** (℡ 02/6622 1499), which, along with Premier (℡ 13 34 10) and McCafferty's (℡ 13 20 30), stops here on the Sydney–Brisbane route; their terminal is on Molesworth Street. Lismore is also on a branch line of the Sydney–Murwillumbah **train** route; trains from Brisbane call in at Casino, 31km southwest (see p.324), from where there's a connecting bus. You can **fly** from Sydney with Regional Express (℡ 13 17 13) and if you've booked accommodation, you'll normally be picked up from the airport; there are **car rental** desks here, as well as branches of the usual multinational agencies on Dawson Street. For details of what's going on locally, head for the **Lismore Visitor Information Centre**, at the corner of Molesworth and Ballina streets (Mon–Fri 9.30am–4pm, Sat & Sun 10am–3pm; ☎02/6622 0122, ⓦwww.liscity.nsw.gov.au), which also offers Internet access ($5/hr) and has an indoor rainforest display, a cultural gallery with the works of a hundred artists and craftspersons and a history exhibit; ask here about **river cruises**.

There's a wide range of **accommodation** choices in the Lismore region, including hostels, hotels, motels, B&Bs and caravan parks, most of which can be booked through the Visitor Information Centre. The friendliest place to stay is the *Carrendina Lodge Backpackers Hostel*, 14 Ewing St (☎02/6621 6118, ⓔcurrendi@nor.com.au; dorms $25, rooms ❷), a pleasant hostel that will pick you up from the bus, train station or airport, or from Byron Bay by arrangement; they also organize tours to the surrounding national parks, and take WWOOF volunteers. Note that no smoking or drinking is permitted in the hostel. An alternative is the newly renovated *Civic Hotel* at 210 Molesworth St (☎02/6621 2537; ❷). A couple of kilometres south of town, the *Lismore Lake Caravan Park*, Bruxner Highway (☎02/6621 2585; cabins ❷), has inexpensive campsites, a pool, barbecue, children's playground and small shop. For a bit more luxury, head for *Melvill House*, 267 Ballina St (☎ & ⓕ02/6621 5778; ❸), a lovely, relaxed guesthouse, with a heated outdoor pool, offering a home-from-home in the heart of town; some rooms are en suite, and one has a four-poster bed.

Lismore isn't a bad place to **eat**, and has a couple of excellent cafés and cosmopolitan restaurants. The favoured haunt of artists is *Caddies Coffee Company*, at 20–24 Carrington St, which has excellent bagels, panini, salads and coffee, while retro fans should head for the *Mecca Café* in the mall on Magellan Street, for tasty lunch-time snacks. Vegans and juice freaks will love *20,000 Cows Café*, 58 Bridge St, and *Dr Juice*, a vegetarian healthy heaven, just round the corner at 142 Keen St. If meatballs are more tempting than mushrooms, head for one of a number of fine Italian establishments, including *Paupiettes* on Ballina Street (☎02/6621 6135) for à la carte dining and *Café Giardino* on Keen Street (☎02/6622 4664). *Thai Lotus* at 207 Ballina St (☎02/6622 0062) is also recommended.

The presence of students means there's some **nightlife** in Lismore. Most of the pubs feature live bands throughout the week, and the area is developing a bit of a reputation for its local musical talent: *Maggie Moore's* pub at 29 Molesworth St hosts bands on Thursdays, Fridays and Saturdays, and *Mary Gilhooley's Irish Pub & Restaurant* at the corner of Keen and Woodlark streets is also very popular. The town's **nightclub**, *Powerhouse*, is on Molesworth Street. For other diversions, there's a four-screen **cinema** in town, on the corner of Keen and Zadoc streets (☎02/6622 4350).

Around Lismore

To explore the country **around Lismore** you really need your own vehicle, though tours do depart from Byron Bay (see p.314). Most Sundays there's a **market** in at least one of the villages, providing a taste of the area's colourful alternative lifestyle – the big ones are in the hilltop village of The Channon on the second Sunday of the month, and in Nimbin on the last (see p.324). The halls in the various towns have dances and live music, and you may be lucky enough to be invited to a legendary hill party involving live bands, fire-eaters and drumming and dancing till dawn – there's usually one happening somewhere every weekend, normally in the same place as the market.

CASINO, around 30km southwest of Lismore, is a small country town on the Richmond River from where route 91 follows the rail lines south towards Grafton, or north through KYOGLE, with its Buddhist temple and retreat, into Queensland. One of the most scenic drives in New South Wales is the short round-trip over the mountainous, winding country roads north and northeast of Lismore to Nimbin, The Channon (see p.326), and Clunes, and then via Eltham and Bexhill, with superb views from the ridges and hilltops. Accessible via Nimbin, with the peak of Mount Nardi (800m) visible 12km beyond the town, is **Nightcap National Park**, a World Heritage-listed park with several walking trails from the summit.

Nimbin and around

NIMBIN, site of the famed Aquarius Festival that launched Australian hippie culture in 1973, is understandably more reluctant than most towns to move out of its 1970s time warp. Its house facades and shopfronts are painted in bright, psychedelic designs, its small stores sell health food, incense sticks and patchouli oil, and many of its 1300 locals have stuck to their 1970s dress code, too. Yet the range of Nimbin's cafés and restaurants marks it as a place of the new millennium – counter-culture style. Not to everyone's taste, Nimbin is somewhere that will appeal to the hippy in you, if there is one. Invariably, you'll be offered dope as soon as you set foot in town – and you'll see it smoked openly on the streets – but a simple "no thanks" is enough to deter would-be pushers; and while there is not really any great danger, lone travellers may find this threatening. This aside, though, Nimbin can be a fun place to spend a day or two. And set as it is on the southern edge of the Mount Warning caldera, there is stunning scenery and abundant wildlife to explore when the town's life gets too much.

Something akin to a "hippie hall of fame", the **Nimbin Museum** at 62 Cullen St (hours as they please but usually daily; ☎02/6689 1123; $2 donation) is certainly worth a visit. It's a weird and wonderful living museum run by hippies, with plenty of local history relating to the Aquarius Festival, Bundjalung Aboriginal culture, and a huge stone phallus in the centre of one room. Ask here about the **Annual Hemp Mardi Grass and Drug Law Reform Festival** (ⓦwww.nimbinmardigrass.com), held on the first weekend in May; the place is booked up well in advance so be prepared to camp. If you have affinities with the Green movement, the **Nimbin Environmental Centre**, also on Cullen Street, might interest you: they publicize and campaign on environmental issues, and can also arrange visits to the **Permaculture Centre**, a showcase for a system of sustainable agriculture that is gaining ground worldwide but especially in developing countries. The **Hemp Embassy** (again, opens as it pleases; ☎02/6689 1123, ⓦwww.nrg.com.au/~hemp) down the lane next to the pub is worth a visit too for its display on the uses of hemp; its owners also run the *Hemp Bar* next door, and organize the town's Mardi Grass.

Practicalities

Nimbin has its own, small, **tourist information centre**, Nimbin Tourist Connexion at 8 Cullen St (daily 9am–5pm; ☎02/6689 1764, ⓦwww.nimbin australia.com), which can book accommodation and bus and train tickets; it also rents out bikes and has three Internet terminals ($5/hour). They also have details of the **shuttle bus** up from Byron Bay (☎02/6680 9189; $14).

There are a number of **places to stay** in and near Nimbin. The pick of the hostels is the new *Nimbin Rox YHA*, 74 Thorburn St (☎ & ⓕ02/6689 0022,

△ Nightcap National Park

@www.nimbinroxhostel.com; ❶), a small, cosy hostel with doubles, dorms and tepees – plus a flotation tank and massage room in its fruit garden – in a superb hilltop location just outside town. The next plot along is home to another hostel, the *Rainbow Retreat* (☎02/6689 1262; dorms $15, rooms ❷), sharing a stretch of the Goolmanger Creek with the resident platypus – there's a swimming hole nearby, too. *Granny's Farm Backpackers & Camping* (☎02/6689 1333; dorms $15, rooms ❷), also within a short walk of town but in a peaceful farm setting, is an easy-going place with log fires for cool winter nights; it also has two swimming pools for use year-round. Right in town, the very comfortable, beautifully decorated *Grey Gum Lodge*, 2 High St (☎ & ℱ02/6689 1713; ❷), is a relaxed guesthouse with its own saltwater swimming pool. The *Klassic Lodge*, 413 Crofton Rd (☎02/6689 9350; ❸), 4km north of town near Nightcap National Park, also has a small pool.

Nimbin's main strip, Cullen Street, is full of good **places to eat** – though the once-legendary *Rainbow Café* closes (and opens up again) every couple of months. For great Indian veggie food, try *The Cave* opposite the tourist office on Cullen Street. The *Nimbin Café*, which invites its visitors to come "experience the joint", has lots of tasty munchies – yummy savouries, hot chocolate, coffee and cakes, while *The E-Bar* offers Italian coffee, smoothies and excellent breakfast fare, as well as Internet access. Finally, the *Nimbin Trattoria & Pizzeria* serves up generous servings of pizza, pasta and salad nightly from 5pm (BYO). In terms of **nightlife and entertainment**, Nimbin has just one drinking hole, the *Nimbin Hotel and Backpackers* (no phone; dorms $13) on Cullen Street, which sees plenty of action (the bistro also serves good counter meals). The cultural heart of town, though, is the small Bush Theatre (☎02/6689 1111), located in an old butter factory over the bridge opposite *Granny's Farm* hostel. It hosts small rep shows, serves fabulous food and is home to the town's "Movie House" – films are shown here at weekends; call or check town notice boards for details.

The Channon

THE CHANNON, a 26-kilometre drive south of Nimbin, is a pretty village on the banks of **Terania Creek** with a well-known monthly market, and a tavern, teahouse, craft shop and art gallery in an old butter factory. A fourteen-kilometre drive along the unsealed Terania Creek Road brings you to **Protestors Falls**, perhaps the Nimbin area's most famous environmental attraction, saved by a 1979 protest that was dubbed a "hippie guerrilla struggle" by a *Rolling Stone* article of the period. The first successful anti-logging campaign in Australia saved this rainforest valley filled with ancient brush box trees. The falls, named after the dispute, are a seven-hundred-metre walk from the picnic area, and the waterhole underneath is perfect for swimming. You are permitted to **camp** for one night only at Terania Creek – but no open fires are allowed; otherwise you can head back to The Channon, where you can stay at the village campsite on the banks of the creek (☎02/6688 6321) or at *Terania Park* (☎02/6688 6121; cabins ❸), a scenic caravan park with cabins and campsites. Terania Creek is near the western edge of **Whian Whian State Forest**. On the forest's southeastern edge (reached via Mullumbimby or Dunoon), further watery delights are provided by the one-hundred-metre cascade of **Minyon Falls**.

Murwillumbah and around

After Ballina and Byron Bay, the next major stop on the Pacific Highway is **MURWILLUMBAH**, a quiet, inland town on a bend of the Tweed River, a little over 30km north of Byron Bay, which makes a good base for exploring some of the beautiful Tweed Valley and the mountains that extend to the Queensland border.

Murwillumbah is the terminus of the coastal branch **rail** line from Sydney (one train daily in each direction, with onward bus services to Tweed Heads with Countrylink), and almost all buses on the north coast route stop here. The **tourist information** office is located in the **Rainforest Heritage Centre** on Alma Street (Mon–Sat 9am–4.30pm, Sun 9.30am–4pm; ☎02/6672 1340, ⓦwww.tweed-coolangatta.com), and has information on the immediate area and on several other magnificent national parks in the vicinity. It's worth dropping by the **Tweed River Regional Art Gallery** on Tumbulgum Road, by Nicholls Park on the river (Wed–Sun 10am–5pm; free). It displays the winners of the Doug Moran National Portrait Prize, which originated here, as well as the work of local artists and travelling exhibitions.

The Tweed Valley and the surrounding area close to the Queensland border are among the most beautiful in New South Wales, ringed by mountain ranges that are actually the remains of an extinct volcano. Some twenty million years ago a huge shield **volcano** (a flat, shield-shaped landform rather than a cone-shaped peak) spewed lava through a central vent onto the surrounding plain. Erosion carved out an enormous bowl around the centre of the resultant mass of lava, while the more resistant rocks around the edges stood firm – these are now the **Nightcap**, **Border**, **Tweed** and **McPherson ranges**, the outer rim of a vast bowl. Right at its heart is **Mount Warning** (1150m), the original vent of the volcano, whose unmistakeable, twisted profile rises like a sentinel from the Tweed Valley. A well-marked **bushwalking track** leads to the top from a car park just off the national park access road, itself a turn-off from the road to Uki, southwest of town. The path is extremely steep in its final stages (allow at least 4hr there and back) but you're rewarded by a sweeping view over the ranges of the volcanic rim and across the Tweed Valley to the Pacific.

There's a less strenuous, signposted 64-kilometre scenic drive through the **Tweed Valley**, which takes in some of its best features. A patchwork of sugar-cane fields and tropical fruit plantations is testimony to the fertility of the volcanic soil; there's even a tea plantation. Between the villages of Tumbulgum and Duranbah, the **big avocado** lures the wild-at-heart towards **Avocado Adventureland** on Duranbah Road (daily 10am–5pm; free admission, train and bus rides extra), a plantation that grows avocados, macadamia nuts and many kinds of tropical fruit, and has been turned into a miniature theme park where you can ride through the plantation in open-air buses and miniature trains, or cruise around on man-made "tropical canals". There are canoes and aqua-bikes for rent, an animal park and playground, a restaurant and café, as well as a fruit market selling plantation produce. Slightly less commercial are the tours given during the cane-harvesting season at **Condong Sugar Mill**, on the Tweed River about 5km north of Murwillumbah (guided tours July–Nov Tues–Thurs 9am–3pm; $7). The turn-off for the **Tree Tops Environment Centre** (daily 10am–5pm; free) is opposite the sugar mill; the centre is the home of Griffith Furniture, which creates beautiful designs from salvaged native timber such as red cedar, using traditional timber-working techniques that you can observe in the workshop. Halfway between Nimbin and Murwillumbah, **UKI** is a pretty little village with views of Mount Warning; there's a small, relaxed **market** here on the third Sunday of each month. A stall sells locally grown organic coffee, or you can sample some at the *Uki Trading Post* (daily 9am–5pm).

Practicalities

Places to stay in Murwillumbah include the recently restored, candy pink *Imperial Hotel* at 115 Main St (☎02/6672 1036; ❸), a grand old building right in the centre of town with good-value singles, an excellent bistro and a guest kitchen. *Mount Warning Riverside YHA Backpackers*, 1 Tumbulgum Rd (☎02/6672 3763, ✆mbahyla@norex.com.au; dorms $23, rooms ❷), is a truly wonderful find – a cosy hostel in an old sea-captain's home leaning over the river, where free ice cream is served every evening at 8pm. The hostel has private access for swimming; you can also rent their bikes or use their canoes or rowing boat for free. Alternatively, make the most of the countryside by staying in rural or **farmstay** accommodation: *Midginbil Hill Holiday Farm* (☎02/6679 7158, ✆midhill@norex.com.au; bunkhouses ❶, lodges ❻, plus camping), is a cattle station 30km west near Mount Warning, offering activities such as horse riding, canoeing and archery. *Mount Warning Forest Hideaway* on Byrill Creek Road, near Uki (☎02/6679 7277, ⓦwww.foresthideaway .com.au; ❺), consists of small, motel-style units each with a double bed and bunks, fridge and cooking facilities, and there's a swimming pool too.

Places to eat include the old-fashioned *Austral Café*, an eat-in bakery on Main Street. *Margherita's Cantina*, also on Main Street, serves salads, lunches and breakfast from 7.30am. The *Imperial Hotel* on Main Street serves the best bistro food in town.

The New England Plateau

The **New England Plateau** rises parallel to the coast in the northeast of New South Wales, extending from the northern end of the Hunter Valley to the Queensland border. At the top it's between 1000m and 1400m above sea level, and on the eastern edge an escarpment falls away steeply towards the coast. This eastern rim consists of steep slopes and precipitous cliff faces, deep gorges and thickly forested valleys, and because of its inaccessibility has remained a largely undisturbed wilderness. Streams and rivers from the highlands tumble over the rocks, and numerous mighty waterfalls pour into narrow gorges. On the plateau itself the scene is far more peaceful, as sheep and cattle graze on the undulating highland. Because of the altitude, the **climate** up here is fundamentally different from the subtropical coast, a mere 150km or so away: winters are cold and frosty, with occasional snowfalls, while in summer the fresh, dry air can offer welcome relief after the heat and humidity of the coast. Even during a summer heatwave, when the daytime temperature might reach 30°C, the nights will be pleasantly cool. Perhaps it was this that attracted the mainly Scottish immigrants who – despite the name – transformed the New England highlands into pastures in the nineteenth century.

The **New England Highway**, one of the main links between Brisbane and Sydney, runs north through New England, passing all the major towns – **Tamworth**, **Armidale**, **Glen Innes** and **Tenterfield**. From any of these, good, sealed roads branch off towards the coast, and it's these minor roads that are especially worth exploring, with turn-offs leading to gorges, waterfalls and scenic lookouts. The area around Glen Innes and Inverell is rich in gemstones, yielding industrial diamonds, zircons and, above all, sapphires.

Farms and stations all over the highlands provide **farmstay accommodation**, offering horse riding and other activities. The area is well serviced by **bus**: McCafferty's/Greyhound Pioneer has daily services between Sydney or

Canberra and Brisbane and between Brisbane and Melbourne, both via New England; Keans Travel (☏1800/043 339) operates daily between Sydney and Tenterfield via the Upper Hunter Valley; and Kings Brothers (☏02/6562 4724) runs three times a week between Port Macquarie and Tamworth via Nambucca Heads, Coffs Harbour, Bellingen, Dorrigo, Armidale, Uralla and Walcha. There is also a daily **train** service between Sydney and Armidale via Tamworth.

The Upper Hunter Valley

The upper end of the Hunter Valley is Australia's main horse-breeding and thoroughbred area – indeed it claims to deal in as much horseflesh as anywhere in the world, with at least thirty stud farms. There are cattle- and sheep-breeding stations up here, too, while the fertile soils of the Upper Hunter also yield a harvest of cereals and fruits including, of course, grapes – see the box on p.214 for a sampling of Hunter Valley wineries.

The pretty township of **SCONE** is at the centre of the Hunter Valley horse trade, and you can get further details of the business from the **Scone Tourist Information Centre** on the corner of Susan and Kelly streets (daily 9am–5pm; ☏02/6545 1526, ✉stic@scone.nsw.gov.au), where you'll also find an excellent Internet café. The best time to visit, when everything's open, is during **Scone Horse Festival** – ten days in the middle of May – which features local prize specimens in horse shows, rodeos and races, along with more general cultural and artistic events. If you're planning to be in town at this time, be sure to book accommodation way in advance.

Lake Glenbawn, 15km east of Scone, makes a pleasant excursion. The dam holds back the waters of the Upper Hunter, storing up to 750,000 million litres for irrigation purposes. **Recreation facilities** at the reserve here include accommodation and boat rental: the lake is great for water-skiing, canoeing, sailing and fishing. Next to the kiosk, a small **museum** (open by appointment only – ask at the tourist information centre) exhibits relics from early pioneering days in the Hunter Valley. For a fine day-trip you can continue past the dam and climb to the plateau of the Barrington Tops (see p.294) to the national park of the same name, or you can go on towards the coast via Gloucester (about 150km from Scone).

Northeast of Scone is polo country, the haunt of mega-rich Australians such as the media mogul Kerry Packer. If you fancy watching the elitist sport in action, there are polo grounds at **GUNDY** and at **ELLERSTON**. At Gundy, you can have a drink at the classic green-tin-roofed *Linga Longa Hotel*. In between Gundy and Ellerston, **Belltrees** is the family estate of the White family, who gave the world the Nobel prize-winning novelist **Patrick White**. Belltrees Station is a collection of buildings, including the 1832 Semphill Cottage, set among pepper trees; there's even a small school established in 1879. Further along is the White mansion where the family still live, and if you can afford it you can stay at the country house next door, or in the mountain retreat where in later life Patrick White used to escape when he returned home to visit; there are also a couple of cheaper self-contained **cottages** sleeping four people (country house from $198 per person per night, including breakfast, dinner and tour of the property; mountain retreat $245 per person per night, including all meals and 4WD transfers; cottages $70–110 per person per night; ☏02/6546 1123, ⊛www.belltrees.com); polo tuition can be arranged as part of your stay.

Heading on towards the heart of the New England Plateau, you pass **Burning Mountain** about 20km north of Scone, near the village of Wingen.

The smoking vents do not indicate volcanic activity but rather a seam of coal burning 30m under the surface: the fire was ignited naturally, perhaps by a lightning strike or spontaneous combustion, over a thousand years ago. The area, protected as a nature reserve, can be reached via a signposted **walking trail** that starts at the picnic grounds at the foot of the hill, just off the New England Highway; pick up the informative NPWS guide to the area's walking tracks from any NPWS office; the nearest one is in Scone. Fourteen kilometres north of Wingen, **MURRURUNDI** marks the end of the Upper Hunter Valley. It's a pretty spot, enclosed by the Liverpool Ranges; the *Café Telegraph* here makes a cheerful refreshment stop, with seats outside in the garden with the creek flowing past.

Practicalities

Countrylink **trains** run twice daily from Sydney to Scone and McCafferty's **buses** pass through. **Places to stay** in this area are widely scattered. Right in Scone the *Royal Hotel-Motel*, St Aubins St (℡02/6545 1722; ❶–❸), offers simple pub accommodation or fancier motel units – it also serves good counter meals. About halfway to Glenbawn Dam, at 115 Segenhoe Road, is a delightful YHA **hostel** (℡02/6545 2072, ✉yhascone@hunterlink.net.au; dorms $18, rooms ❷) in a former school; you can rent bikes here to explore the countryside. Right at the lake, the *Lake Glenbawn Holiday Village* (℡02/6543 7752; ❸) has camping and three-bedroom cottages. In nearby Aberdeen, a few kilometres south on the New England Highway, a recommended B&B is the *Segenhoe* at 55 Main Rd (℡02/6543 7382, ⓦwww.segenhoebandb.com.au; ❺), a charming sandstone edifice from the early 1800s. If you're hungry for scones in Scone, then head to *Asser House Café* on Kelly Street – they also serve excellent coffee and tea. For entertainment, Scone's **Civic Theatre** (℡02/6545 1569) is an Art Deco movie palace with displays of memorabilia in the foyer.

Tamworth and around

TAMWORTH is the first city on the New England Plateau proper, a fair-sized place that's proud of its public buildings, parks and gardens. It also likes to refer to itself as the "City of Lights", having been the first in Australia to be fitted with electric street lighting, in 1888. To most Australians, however, Tamworth means **country music** – it's a sort of antipodean Nashville. The twelve-metre-high golden guitar in front of the **Golden Guitar Complex** (daily 9am–5pm; $6; ⓦwww.biggoldenguitar.com.au), on the southern edge of town, sums up the town's role as the country-and-western capital of Australasia. Inside the centre, you'll find waxwork figures of the great Australian country stars such as Chad Morgan, Buddy Williams, Smoky Dawson and his horse Flash, Slim Dusty, Reg Lindsay and Tex Morton. There's also a slightly incongruous collection of gems and minerals from the region – no rhinestones though. Afterwards, the *Longyard Hotel* next door is a handy place to weep in your beer for a while and, once a year, for a week at the end of January, it becomes the focus of the **Tamworth Country Music Festival** when fans from all over the country descend, packing out camping spots. Every pub, club and hall in town hosts gigs, record launches and bush poetry, culminating in the presentation of the Australian country music awards – further information and bookings from Rural Press Events (℡02/6762 2399, ⓦwww.country music.asn.au) or the visitors centre (see opposite). The final piece of the country puzzle is found at the corner of Brisbane Street and Kable Avenue, where the **Hands of Fame** cornerstone bears the palm-prints of more country greats. A glorious spoof, the Noses of Fame memorial, can be savoured over a beer at the *Tattersalls Hotel* on Peel Street.

Don't give up on Tamworth entirely if country music isn't your thing. The **Powerstation Museum** at 216 Peel St (Tues–Fri 9am–1pm; $2.20), celebrates those pioneering street lights, and there are numerous art galleries and crafts studios around town: the **Tamworth City Gallery**, housed in the Guy Kable Building on Marius Street (Mon–Fri 10am–5pm, Sat 10am–1pm, Sun 1–4pm; free) has a surprisingly good permanent exhibition. Natural attractions include the **Oxley Lookout and Nature Reserve** at the end of White Street, with panoramic views of the city and the Peel River Valley, and **Lake Keepit**, 56km northwest of the city, where you can rent boats and mess about on the water.

The former gold-mining township of **NUNDLE** lies some 60km southeast of town in the "hills of gold" – people still visit with picks, shovels and sieves in the hope of striking it lucky, and you can join them for a day. You no longer need to buy a fossicking licence but it's still worth dropping by the General Store on Jenkins Street; they'll point you in the right direction to start digging.

Practicalities

The big, guitar-shaped **Tamworth Visitor Information Centre** (daily 9am–5pm; ☎02/6755 4300, ⓦwww.tamworth.nsw.gov.au) is on the corner of Peel and Murray streets. Tamworth is well serviced by **bus**: McCafferty's runs daily between Sydney and Brisbane and between Brisbane and Melbourne. **Local buses** can get you to Nundle (check with the tourist office), while Countrylink runs a daily train service from Sydney.

As you drive into Tamworth you'll pass a string of **motels** on the New England Highway – the only time you might have trouble finding a room is during the festival, when everything's booked out. An excellent choice is the friendly Tamworth YHA **hostel** at 169 Marius St, opposite the railway station (☎02/6761 2600, ⓔtam_yha@yahoo.com.au; dorms $20, rooms ❷), which has Internet access, a laundry and two lovely guest lounges; alternatively, the *Tamworth Hotel* on Marius Street, in the centre of town, offers simple pub accommodation and good counter meals (☎02/6766 2923, ⓕ6766 2847; ❷). If, however, you feel like staying somewhere a little more luxurious, the *Flag Inn*, on the New England Highway 1.5km northeast of the centre (☎02/6765 7022 or 1800 028 889, ⓕ6765 8818; ❺), is the place to head; it has four-star facilities, including room service, gym, swimming pool and sauna. The closest place for **campers** and caravanners is the *Paradise Caravan Park*, Peel Street (☎ & ⓕ02/6766 3120; on-site vans ❷, cabins ❸), on the river about five minutes' walk from the main part of town. Further out, 4km from town but right on the riverfront off the New England Highway, is the award-winning *Austin Caravan Park* (☎02/6766 2380, ⓕ6766 6257; cabins ❷), with a pool and children's playground. In **Nundle** there are rooms and meals on Jenkins Street: at the historic *Peel Inn* (☎02/6769 3377, ⓕ6769 3307; ❷), where they also organize gold-panning, and at the very special *Jenkins Street Guest House* (☎ & ⓕ02/6769 3239; ❻), where you'll find polished wood floors, fresh flowers in all rooms and an excellent local chef. If you want a taste of Australian country living, head to *Leconfield*, 50km east of Tamworth (☎02/6769 4328, ⓦwww.leconfield.com), which offers a five-day residential **Jackeroo and Jilleroo school** ($375), where you learn to ride and groom horses, shear and throw fleeces, lassoo, whip crack and go out mustering. They can also arrange pick-ups from Tamworth YHA. New kid on the block, also offering the Jackeroo/Jilleroo experience, is **Dag Sheep Station** over at Nundle (☎02/6769 3234, ⓦwww.thedag.com.au; three nights' full board, gear and training $373); to get to Dag direct from Sydney, there's a package available through Countrylink (☎13 28 29), which includes bus transfers from Tamworth.

Eating, drinking and entertainment

There's a profusion of good but pricey Sydney-style **cafés** in Tamworth, and two of the best are on Peel Street: the *Old Vic Café* at no. 261 (Mon–Wed 7.30am–6pm, Thurs–Sat 7.30am–11pm, Sun 10am–4pm) and the *Inland Café* at no. 407 (Mon–Wed 7am–6pm, Thurs–Sat 7am–11pm, Sun 9am–5pm). For larger portions of perfectly good tucker, try the *Longyard Hotel* on the New England Highway (daily noon–2.30pm, Mon–Fri 6–8.30pm, Sat & Sun 6.30–8.30pm). Outside festival time, you'll be disappointed if you think the town's **clubs and pubs** constantly resound to country-and-western twangings, but you can catch some acts on Thursday evening at the *Tamworth RSL Club* on Kable Avenue, and on the first Friday and third Sunday of the month in the *Tamworth Hotel*.

Armidale and around

The university city of **ARMIDALE**, halfway between Sydney and Brisbane, is something of a rarity in Australia, where most universities are based in the state capitals. About four thousand students are enrolled at the **University of New England**, which, together with a couple of famous boarding schools, provides an unexpected academic aspect in a place so far "up country". Armidale is a city of some natural beauty, especially in autumn when, with its church spires and many parks, it is embedded in a sea of red and golden leaves. At around 1000m, the climate is unpredictable and can be decidedly brisk in winter.

Beardy Street, the town centre's pedestrian mall, is flanked by quaint Australian country pubs with wide, iron-lace verandahs, and is an excellent place to start exploring. On the last Sunday of the month the mall comes alive with a 150-stall market complete with buskers, and the mall's cafés open their doors. One of the best ways to get around town is by **bike**: there's a signposted city tour, as well as a bike path to the **university campus**, 5km northwest of the city, where there are two small specialized museums (both free), a kangaroo and deer park, and the historic Booloominbah homestead, built in the 1880s as a fashionable gentlemen's residence and now housing the principal administration office. Back in the city centre, the **New England Regional Art Museum** on Kentucky Street (Mon–Fri 10.30am–5pm; free) is worth a visit for its two collections of Australian art. Foremost is the Hinton Collection, a group of paintings from the 1880s to the 1940s that includes works by Arthur Streeton and Tom Roberts. The Coventry Collection, focusing on the second half of the twentieth century, also has some important works, among them a wild self-portrait by Brett Whitely. Next door, the arresting modern building with the distinctive ochre-coloured tin roof is the Aborigine-run **Aboriginal Centre and Keeping Place** (Mon–Fri 10am–4pm; $3), an educational, visual and performing arts centre that aims to foster the renewal and continuity of Aboriginal culture. Artefacts and interpretive material are on permanent display, and special exhibitions are shown. You might also want to visit the Armidale **Folk Museum**, at the corner of Rusden and Faulkner streets (daily 1–4pm; donation), which has a collection of artefacts from the New England region and displays on local history, or take a two-hour **free bus tour** of the city with Heritage Tours (Mon–Fri 10am, Sat & Sun 10.30am, departing from the visitor information centre; free).

The Myall Creek massacre

In the first decades of the nineteenth century, when European settlers started to move up to the highlands and to use Aboriginal-occupied land on the plateau as sheep and cattle pasture, many of the local Aborigines fought back. Time and again bloody skirmishes flared up. The **Myall Creek massacre** is one of the few that has found a place in the history of white Australia, while innumerable others were never mentioned in genteel pioneer circles and have subsequently been erased from public memory.

For Aboriginal people, expulsion from the lands of their ancestors amounted to spiritual as well as physical dispossession, and they resisted as best they could: white stockmen staying in huts far away from pioneer townships or homesteads feared for their lives. In 1837 and 1838, Aborigines repeatedly ambushed and killed stockmen near the Gwydir and Namoi rivers. Then, during the absence of the overseer at Myall Creek Station, near present-day Inverell, twelve farm hands organized a raid in retribution, killing 28 Aborigines. In court, the farm hands were acquitted – public opinion saw nothing wrong with their deed, and neither did the jury. The case was later taken up again, however, and seven of the participants in the massacre were sentenced to death on the gallows.

Practicalities

Armidale has a helpful **Visitor Information Centre** at 82 Marsh St (Mon–Fri 9am–5pm, Sat 9am–4pm, Sun 10am–4pm; ☎02/6772 4655, ⓦwww.new-england.org/armidale), which has information on accommodation, local sites and the area's national parks. The **bus** terminal is just by the information centre. Plenty of places offer **car rental**, among them Budget, at Ian Yates Service Centre, 2/270 Mann St (☎02/6771 1535), and Realistic Car Rentals, at Armidale Exhaust Centre, corner of Rushden and Marsh streets (☎02/6772 3004). **Bikes** can be rented from Armidale Bicycle Centre, 244 Beardy St (☎02/6772 3718). For **taxis**, call Armidale Radio Taxis (☎13 10 08).

For **accommodation**, the *Tattershall Hotel*, 147 Beardy St (☎02/6772 2247; ❷) offers inexpensive rooms. There are over twenty motels in Armidale: the information centre has the full list with prices. The most central upmarket choice is the *New England Motor Inn*, 100 Dumaresq St (☎ & ⓕ02/6771 1011, ⓦwww.newenglandmotorinn.com.au; ❹). For a taste of tranquillity, *Glenhope* on Red Gum Lane is an elegant B&B homestead set in a valley 4km northwest from the city (☎02/6772 1940, ⓔglenhope@bluepin.net.au; ❹). Alternatively, try *Poppy's Cottage* (☎02/6775 1277, ⓔpoppyscottage@bluepin.net.au; ❹), a private farm cottage just five minutes' drive from town, with free port and chocolates, a well-stocked bookcase and an optional gourmet three-course dinner ($45 with wine). *Pembroke Tourist and Leisure Park*, 39 Waterfall Way, 2km east of town (☎02/6772 6470, ⓔpembroke@mail.northnet.com.au; dorms $20, on-site vans ❷, cabins ❸), is also home to YHA hostel accommodation; the complex has its own swimming pool and tennis court.

Good, inexpensive **counter meals** are served at many of the grand old pubs on Beardy Street, including the *New England Hotel* and the *Imperial*. Amongst the town's better **restaurants** are the BYO *Jean Pierre's*, on Beardy Street, and the award-winning, modern Australian restaurant, *Jitterbug Mood* at 115 Rusden St (☎02/6772 2201). There are several Chinese restaurants in town, including the *Mandarin Restaurant* at 213 Beardy St; *Eagle Boys Pizza* on Rusden Street (eat in or takeaway) is open until late. The student population contributes to a **café** society of sorts: the light and airy *Café Midalé*, in the Beardy St Mall, serves up Italian-style food – focaccia, panini and pasta of the day – while *Rumours on the Mall*, further down, offers good, inexpensive meals and sandwiches, plus a decent breakfast served until noon.

For an evening's **entertainment** visit the Belgrave Twin Cinema (☎02/6773 3833), which screens mainstream and alternative films, and has a café open until late.

Around Armidale

Surrounded by national parks and wild mountain scenery, Armidale makes a good base to stop over for a few days and explore, or perhaps try your hand at a spot of fossicking. The **New England National Park**, 85km east on the Waterfall Way, and the several patchwork sections of the **Oxley Wild Rivers National Park**, exploit the beauty of the eastern edge of the plateau; gorges and spectacular waterfalls abound, although the falls may diminish to a trickle during prolonged dry spells. The most impressive of them are the **Wollomombi Falls**, just over 40km east of Armidale, off the road to Dorrigo; among the highest in Australia, they plunge 225m into a gorge. Nearby are the Chandler Falls, while **Ebor Falls**, a stunning double drop of the Guy Fawkes River in the national park of the same name, can be viewed from platforms just off Waterfall Way, another 40km beyond Wollomombi. Between Wollomombi and Ebor, **Point Lookout** in the New England National Park offers a truly wonderful panoramic view across the forested ranges. The road to the lookout is unsealed gravel, but is usually in reasonable condition, and there are simple **cabins** and bush **campsites** where you can stay overnight: phone the NPWS in Armidale (☎02/6776 4260) for further information – it's essential you book in advance. The rest of the park is virtually inaccessible wilderness.

On the way back to Armidale, you could detour through the goldrush ghost town of **HILLGROVE**, where the old school has been converted into the **Rural Life and Industry museum** (daily 10am–5pm; $2) displaying old mining equipment and trying to re-create the lifestyle of the once-prosperous settlement. **URALLA**, 22km south of Armidale, is another old gold town, though in this case it has managed to hang on, with a population of a couple of thousand. The Historic Building Walk will take you past the town's highlights, including **McCrossin's Mill Museum** (daily noon–5pm; $4), an old three-storey flour mill on Salisbury Street. Fossicking is still possible at the old Rocky River diggings: enquire at the **Uralla Visitor Information Centre**, New England Highway (daily 9.30am–4.30pm; ☎02/6778 4496, ⓦnew-england.org/uralla); or you can go on a tour with **Uralla Goldfield Tours** (☎02/6778 4850). Gold apart, Uralla's other claim to fame is that **Captain Thunderbolt**, the bushranger who terrorized the New England region in the nineteenth century, was shot dead here in 1870, after a furious battle in the swampy country southeast of Uralla – an event commemorated by the bronze statue of Thunderbolt and his horse on the corner of Bridge and Salisbury streets.

Southeast of Armidale, towards Walcha, **Dangars Lagoon** is a wetland region visited by more than a hundred different kinds of bird; a hide is provided for spotters. **Dangars Falls** and a network of twenty walking tracks and lookouts around **Dangars Gorge** are only 22km from Armidale on a minor road. Beyond these, about 20km east of Walcha, a turn-off from the Oxley Highway leads to **Apsley Gorge** and two more waterfalls in another section of the Oxley Rivers park. In **WALCHA** itself, 65km southwest of Armidale, there are the usual pioneer museums, but more interesting is the **Amaroo**

Museum and Cultural Centre on Derby Street (Mon–Fri 9am–5pm; donation), which displays arts and crafts made by local Aboriginal people.

West of Armidale, 27km along the Bundarra Road, is the Mount Yarrowyck Nature Reserve where an **Aboriginal cave-painting site** can be accessed via a three-kilometre circuit walk.

Glen Innes and around

GLEN INNES, the next major stop north on the New England Highway, about 100km from Armidale, is another pleasant town in a beautiful setting. Although agriculture is still important up here, you begin to see more and more evidence of the gemfields – sapphires are big business, as, to a lesser extent, is tin mining. In the centre, on Grey Street especially, numerous century-old public buildings and parks have been renovated and spruced up. There's some fine country architecture including a couple of large corner pubs, their verandahs decorated with iron lace. The **Land of the Beardies History House** (Mon–Fri 10am–noon & 2–5pm, Sat & Sun 2–5pm; $5), in the town's first hospital on the corner of Ferguson Street and West Avenue, displays pioneer relics, period room settings and a reconstructed slab hut. The name alludes to the two hairy men who settled the area in the nineteenth century, and it's a title the town's proud of, along with the Scottish connections reflected in the name of the town itself and in many of its streets, which are rendered in both English and Gaelic. The local granite **Australian Standing Stones** at Martins Lookout, Watsons Drive, are based on the Ring of Brodgar in Scotland, and are intended to honour the "contribution of the Celtic races to Australia's development"; there's a great picnic and barbecue area with granite seats and tables, echoing the stones themselves. The strongly Celtic nature of Glen Innes is counterbalanced by the town's department store, Kwong Sing & Co, which has been run by the same family of Chinese origin since 1886. While you're in the area, you might also consider a **horseback pub crawl** with Great Aussie Pub Crawls on Horseback (☏02/6732 1599); despite the name, this is really a six-day trekking adventure with overnight stops at traditional Aussie pubs, and no drinking is permitted during the five to six hours of riding each day.

In early November, Glen Innes celebrates the **Land of the Beardies Festival**, with everything from a beard-growing contest and shopping-trolley derby to dances, street parades and arts-and-crafts exhibits. More details, including help with rooms, are available from the **Glen Innes & District Visitors Centre**, 152 Church St, as the New England Highway is called when it passes through town (Mon–Fri 9am–5pm, Sat & Sun 9am–3pm; ☏02/6732 2397, ⊛www.gleninnestourism.com). Good **accommodation** options include the air-conditioned *Central Motel* on Meade Street (☏02/6732 2200; ❸); the fancier (though not air-con) *Rest Point Motel* on Church Street, 1km south of the centre (☏02/6732 2255, ⓕ6732 1515; ❹), with a swimming pool and extensive landscaped grounds; and the well-equipped *Blue Sapphire Caravan Park*, 1km north of town off the New England Highway (☏02/6732 1590; on-site vans ❶, cabins ❸). For a homely semi-splurge try *Diarmid's B&B* at 15 Torrington St (☏ & ⓕ02/6732 5701; ❹) – a lovely guesthouse with a log fire in the guest lounge and bedrooms decorated in old Scottish and Irish style. Fresh flowers abound, and included in the price are a high tea – with shortbread, apple cake and home-made preserves – and a tour of the Australian standing stones. For sustenance in the town, try the *Tea and Coffee Shop* on Grey Street, a cosy **tearoom** with loads of choice including Dutch pancakes, an array of interesting sandwiches, savoury croissants and hot breakfasts. If it's all getting a bit too olde worlde for you, head for Grey Street's *Café Heritage*, a modern brasserie with a menu to match, or the *One Eighty Nine Coffee Lounge*, at 189 Grey St, which has an even more down-to-earth menu, designed to cure even the worst hangover.

Inverell

The area between Glen Innes and **INVERELL**, 67km to the west, is one huge gemfield. Industrial diamonds, garnets, topaz, zircons and three-quarters of the world's sapphires are mined in the area. Inverell is also known as "Sapphire City", and at the **Dejon Sapphire Centre**, on the Gwydir Highway, 18km east of town, you can watch the gems being mined, washed, sorted and cut (daily 9am–5pm, mine tours 10.30am & 3pm; free). The showroom has a display of sapphires in 155 colours, from pale blue and green, to gold, lemon and pink. To try your own luck, you'll need to contact the **tourist office** on Campbell Street (Mon–Fri 9am–4pm, Sat 9am–noon; ℡02/6722 1693, ⓦwww.inverell-online.com.au), which can direct you to the designated areas. If you want to **stay** over and wait for that big strike, try the newly refurbished *Royal Hotel*, 260 Byron St (℡02/6722 2811; ❸), which has clean rooms with shared facilities, open fires and air conditioning, and serves counter meals; or *Sapphire City Caravan Park* on Moore Street (℡02/6722 1830; on-site vans ❷, cabins ❸).

Tenterfield and around

Less than 20km from the Queensland border, **TENTERFIELD** marks the northern end of the New England Plateau. Although only a small town, it has a confirmed place in Australian history, being the birthplace of the Australian Federation, and in 2001 it played host to many centennial celebrations. Its title was earned when, in 1889, the Prime Minister of New South Wales, Sir Henry Parkes, made his famous Federation speech here, advocating the union of the Australian colonies; twelve years later the Commonwealth of Australia was inaugurated. A small **museum** (Wed–Sun 10am–4pm; $2) in Centenary Cottage recalls the occasion and displays other items of local interest.

As throughout the region, however, the real attractions of Tenterfield lie outside town – undulating pastures and orchards, remnants of stands of eucalypt and rainforests, and rugged granite hills. **Bald Rock**, in a national park of the same name near the Queensland border, about 30km northeast of Tenterfield, is Australia's second-largest monolith, after Uluru (see p.690), but a grey-granite version, 213m high. It can be climbed from its northeast side, and from the summit there are breathtaking panoramic views taking in both states. The excursion to Bald Rock fits in nicely with a visit to 210-metre-high **Boonoo Boonoo Falls**, set in the national park of the same name, 32km north of Tenterfield. Access is via an unsealed road that can be a bit rough, but it's worth it (as long as you're not in a rented car), and there's a beautiful picnic area. The NPWS occasionally offers tours to both national parks: details are available from the **Tenterfield Visitors Centre**, 157 Rouse St (Mon–Fri 9.30am–5pm, Sat 9.30am–4.30pm, Sun 9.30am–4pm; ℡02/6736 1082, ⓦwww.tenterfield.com). Perhaps the best way to climb the rock, however, is with Woollool Woollool Aboriginal Cultural Tours (book through the visitors centre; $70); these are conducted by trained Aboriginal guides who, as well as escorting you up the monolith, will guide you through rock-art sites, the falls and the ghost town of Boonoo Boonoo. The daily tours also include lessons in boomerang throwing, and free pick-ups and drop-offs from most accommodation in town.

Accommodation in Tenterfield includes the very cheap and central *Commercial Hotel*, 288 Rouse St (℡02/6736 1027; ❶), which has a beer garden, shared cooking facilities and counter meals.

West of the Great Dividing Range

Western New South Wales is a very different proposition from the other parts of the state. For a start, there's hardly anyone living here. Beyond the Great Dividing Range are a few towns with a pioneer heritage, such as **Bathurst** and **Dubbo**, where there are still small agricultural communities and green fields; beyond them it begins to get increasingly desolate and arid, and even apparently large towns turn out to be tiny communities.

Out beyond the Blue Mountains, the **Great Western Highway** takes you as far as Bathurst; from there the **Mid-Western Highway** goes on to join the **Sturt Highway**, which heads, via Mildura on the Victorian border, to Adelaide. Any route west is eventually obliged to cross the **Newell Highway**, the direct route between Melbourne and Brisbane that cuts straight across the heart of central New South Wales. The most exciting Outback routes head north and west, though, passing through Dubbo, at the junction of the Newell and **Mitchell** highways, and then plunging into real isolation: north to **Lightning Ridge** or **Bourke** and western Queensland, or west on the **Barrier Highway**, right across the state to **Broken Hill**, almost at the South Australian border. **Public transport** out here is limited, but Dubbo, Lightning Ridge and Bourke are all accessible on Countrylink services.

Bathurst, Dubbo and the central west

The central west of New South Wales is much underrated, seldom visited but often passed through. Its rich, fertile land lends itself to cherry trees and undulating green hills – providing both seasonal work and ripe picnicking spots for travellers – and the intermittent towns have their own rewards, not least **Mudgee** with its surrounding vineyards. **Dubbo** is the region's major city, and while it's not the most appealing of places, it proves an excellent base from which to start a road trip to Broken Hill and the Outback.

Bathurst and around

The gracious city of **BATHURST**, elegantly situated on the western slopes of the Great Dividing Range 209km west of Sydney, is Australia's oldest inland settlement. Its beautifully preserved nineteenth-century architecture makes it worth a weekend visit from Sydney, to browse the antique shops and mellow out in one of the city's many cafés. The settlement was founded by Governor Macquarie in 1815, but Bathurst remained nothing more than a small convict and military settlement for years, only slowly developing into the main supply centre for the surrounding rich pastoral area. It was the discovery of **gold** nearby at the Lewis Ponds Creek at Ophir in 1851 (see p.342) and, later the same year, on the Turon River, which resulted in a goldrush that changed the life of the town and the colony forever. Soon rich fields of alluvial gold were discovered in every direction and, being the first town over the mountains for those on the way to the goldfields, Bathurst prospered and grew. The population increased dramatically: in 1885 Bathurst was proclaimed a city, and in the late 1890s it was even proposing itself (needless to say, unsuccessfully) as the site for the capital of the new Commonwealth of Australia.

Although there's still the odd speck of gold and a few gemstones (especially sapphires) in the surrounding area, modern Bathurst has reverted to its role as a community in the centre of some of the richest agricultural land in New South Wales, a pastoral and fruit- and grain-growing district. It's also a tertiary education centre, with many students attending the Mitchell campus of Charles Sturt University. For anyone heading west, it's still the first stop beyond the mountains, and the gateway to the Outback. In October and November, visitors are also drawn to the big annual motor-racing meeting – centred on the famous **F.A.I. 1000** endurance race – at the Mount Panorama Racing Circuit.

The City

Because of its cool climate – proximity to the mountains means it can be cold at night and sometimes snowy in winter – and a scattering of grand nineteenth-century buildings, the town has a very different feel to anywhere on the coast or on the baking plains further west.

Pick up a map from the modern visitor information centre (see opposite) to help you find some of the stately mansions scattered around that bear testimony to Bathurst's former wealth; one of their pamphlets outlines an entertaining self-guided walk through the historic city centre. The old **courthouse** on Russell Street, built in 1880, makes a good place to start exploring, and there's also an interesting little **museum** tucked away in the east wing (Tues, Wed, Sat & Sun 10am–4pm; $3), which displays relics and archives of regional pioneer history along with some interesting Aboriginal artefacts. The **Regional Art Gallery**, 70–78 Keppel St (Tues–Sat 10am–5pm, Sun & public holidays 2–5pm; free), is a fine provincial art collection which has very good ceramics and paintings by Lloyd Rees, as well as regular special and travelling exhibitions. **Machattie Park**, further north up Keppel Street, on the corner of William Street, offers a chance to relax amid landscaped Victorian-era gardens with duck ponds and spreading shady trees; there's also a Fern House, and a Begonia House, which has an impressive display from mid-February to Easter. Look out, too, for the **Chifley Home** at 10 Busby St (Sat, Sun & Mon 11am–3pm; $4), once the residence of Bathurst's most famous son, who was born to a blacksmith and his wife in south Bathurst in 1885, and was prime minister of Australia between 1945 and 1949.

Further afield, a drive up to **Mount Panorama** and its famous racing circuit provides, as you might expect, panoramic views of the city: there's the **National Motor-Racing Museum** at Murray's Corner (daily 9am–4.30pm; $7), at the beginning of the racing circuit, featuring famous racing cars and bikes, along with photographs and memorabilia from the races. **Sir Joseph Banks's Nature Park** (daily 9am–3.30pm; $3.30) occupies the summit of the hill, enabling native birds and animals, including wallabies, kangaroos and koalas, to enjoy the vistas from a large area of bushland; the visitors centre houses an aquarium and a reptile collection. Not far away, the **Bathurst Goldfields** at 428 Conrod Straight (Mon–Fri 10am–4pm; guided tours $7.50) a reconstruction of a former gold-mining area, are worth a visit if you're not going to make it to one of the actual gold towns further out. Goldrush mining methods are demonstrated and explained, and you can even take individual lessons in gold-panning. A bit further out, the **Bathurst Sheep and**

Cattle Drome on Limekilns Road, 8km northeast of the city, has an educational and entertaining show (daily at 11.30am, extra shows during school holidays; $11, children $6.60) covering everything you always wanted to know about sheepshearing and milking cows.

Practicalities

Trains and long-distance **buses** run here from Sydney, with onward services to Broken Hill. **Bathurst Visitor Information Centre** is at 28 William St (daily 9am–5pm; ℡02/6332 1444 or 1800 681 000, Ⓦwww.bathurst.nsw.gov.au). **Accommodation** is relatively expensive here, but try the *Park Hotel* at 201 George St (℡02/6331 3399; ❸) for comfortable B&B and motel-style units. There are a dozen or more motels along the highway, as well as holiday units at *Rossmore Park Farm Holidays*, at the Bathurst Sheep and Cattle Drome (see above; ℡02/6337 3634, Ⓦwww.rossmorepark.com.au; ❺), and **camping** at *East Bathurst Holiday Park*, on the highway in Kelso, 5km east (℡02/6331 8286, Ⓦwww.eastholidayparks.com.au; cabins ❷). For comfortable B&B, head for *The Russells* at 286 William St (℡ & Ⓕ02/6332 4686, Ⓔrussell@ix.net.au; ❹), a small, family home offering comfortable rooms, log fires and generous cooked breakfasts. Staying at the lavish *Royal Apartments* further along at 108 William St (℡02/6332 4920, Ⓦbathurstheritage.com.au; ❻), the town's jewel-in-the-crown heritage building is a real treat; apartments are fully serviced.

There's a variety of **restaurants** in the city centre, including Thai, Indian and modern Australian cuisine. Most of the town's pubs also serve counter meals or have bistros at the back. For à la carte dining, try *Lamplighters* at 126–130 William St (℡02/6331 1448; closed Sun), with blackboard specials and old world charm. In the *Royal Apartments* building, the *Heritage Royal Coffee House* has superb coffee and cakes, while *Crêpes Royale*, serves French-inspired dishes from morning tea to dinner (closed Mon). *The Crowded House Café* at 1 Ribbon Gang Lane (℡02/6334 2300; closed Sun), offers good lunches and great Modern Australian cuisine in the evenings, in the neo-Gothic Old School House; you can eat inside, or out in the leafy courtyard.

Due to the presence of so many students, Bathurst has a reasonable **nightlife**, centering mainly on the pubs close to the university. Particularly popular is the *Oxford Tavern* on the corner of William and Piper streets, opposite the enormous *Leagues Club*. Friday is club night, featuring guest DJs at the *Site* on George Street ($7.50 entry).

Around Bathurst

The area **around Bathurst**, heading towards the Mudgee wine country, is dotted with semi-derelict villages and ghost towns dating back to the gold-rushes of the nineteenth century. A scenic drive to the north via Peel and Wattle Flat leads to the tiny, picturesque village of **SOFALA**, 35km north of Bathurst on the Turon River, en route to Mudgee. Gold was found in the river here in 1851, just three weeks after the very first gold strikes in Australia, and today the narrow, winding main street still follows the course of the river. A good spot for a drink is the *Sofala Royal Hotel*, a very atmospheric, classic wooden pub with a big balcony; they also offer meals with a period flavour.

From Sofala, a very narrow, bone-rattling unsealed road follows the Turon River towards **HILL END**, an even more important goldrush site located on a plateau above the Turon Valley, 86km from Bathurst. In 1870, Hill End was the largest inland centre in New South Wales, a booming gold-mining town with a population of about twenty thousand, with 53 hotels, plus all the accoutrements of a wealthy settlement. Within ten years, however, gold production had faltered and Hill End had already become a virtual ghost town. It stayed that way until 1967, when the area was proclaimed a historic site and huge efforts were made to restore and preserve the town. You can pick up a leaflet at the NPWS **visitors centre** in the old hospital (daily 9.30am–12.30pm & 1.30–4.30pm; ☎02/6337 8206), where there is also a small museum ($3), and take a self-guided walk around the village, or rent some equipment and try your hand at panning or fossicking. There's an underground **mine tour** daily at 1pm ($6) and a gold-panning tour at 11am ($4). You can **stay** in the *Royal Hotel* here (☎02/6337 8261, ⓕ6337 8393; ❷) and **eat** in the restaurant. There is also a B&B, as well as **camping** areas run by the NPWS.

Another enjoyable excursion from Bathurst takes in the former gold-mining towns of Rockley, 35km south of Bathurst, and Trunkey Creek, and then continues to the spectacular **Abercrombie Caves**, 72km south of Bathurst in the middle of a large nature reserve. The principal and most impressive cavern, the **Grand Arch** (self-guided tours daily 10am–4pm; $11), is 221m long, about 39m wide at the north and south entrances, and in some places over 30m high – it's said to be the largest natural limestone arch in the southern hemisphere. More than eighty other caves are dotted around the reserve. In one of them, miners constructed a dance floor more than a century ago, and concerts or church services are still held here occasionally. Also within the reserve are old gold mines, and swimming holes in **Grove Creek**, which runs right through the reserve, plunging more than 70m over the Grove Creek Falls at the southern edge. There's a **camping area** on the shore (☎02/6336 1972; cabins ❷), complete with a public fossicking ground.

Mudgee and the wine country

The large, old country town of **MUDGEE** (in the Kamilaroi language meaning "the nest in the hills") is the centre for an often-overlooked wine region about 120km north of Bathurst. The town is set along the lush banks of the Cugewong River, and the countryside appears to have more grazing cows and sheep than vineyards. The wines, once referred to as "Mudgee mud", have improved in the past few years: the Cabernet Sauvignon and Shiraz wines are the tastiest, although the area's Chardonnays are gaining a good reputation. You can reach Mudgee via Hill End, but it's a bumpy unsealed route, and you're better off approaching via Sofala on an 88-kilometre sealed road (except for a small section) – watch out for sheep.

Countrylink runs a **bus** and **train** service to Mudgee from Sydney, changing at Lithgow, just east of Bathurst. The useful **tourist information centre** is at 84 Market St (Mon–Fri 9am–5pm, Sat 9am–4pm, Sun 9am–3pm; ☎02/6372 1020, ⓦwww.mudgee.nsw.gov.au) to pick up a copy of the *Mudgee Region Visitors' Guide*, which has detailed winery information and maps. Mudgee's proximity to Sydney means that **accommodation** is booked out at weekends, when it's best to call in advance. Some places worth targeting are the *Federal Hotel* at 34 English St (☎02/6372 2150, ⓔaussie@winsoft.net.au; ❷); the central but more upmarket *Wanderlight Motel*, 107 Market St (☎02/6372 1088; ❹), which has a pool and spa and some units adapted for disabled travellers; and the gay-friendly *Parkview Guest House*, 99 Market St (☎02/6372 4477 or 1800 621 531; ❺), a quiet, centrally located B&B built in 1859. Other heritage houses worth staying at for the charm factor include *Bleak House*, 7 Lawson St (☎02/6372 4888, ⓔbleakhousemudgee@bigpond.com; ❻), with private verandahs overlooking the Cugewong River, and the *Lauralla Historic Guesthouse*, at the corner of Lewis and Mortimer streets (☎02/6372 4480, ⓦwww.lauralla.com.au; ❺), a classic Victorian-style home offering "murder

Botolabar Botolabar Lane (Mon–Sat 10am–5pm, Sun 10am–3pm; ℡02/6373 3840). An organic winery with self-guided tours (40min). Tastings on a shady terrace; picnic area and BBQs.

Huntingdon Estate Wines Cassilis Rd (Mon–Fri 9am–5pm, Sat 10am–5pm, Sun 10am–3pm; ℡02/6373 3730). A rather bland and functional building producing some of the region's most delicious wines. Particularly recommended are the young Semillons and the intense, heady Cabernet Sauvignon from 1995. An excellent annual chamber music festival takes place here in November.

Miramar Wines Henry Lawson Drive (daily 9am–5pm; ℡02/6373 3874). Atmospheric tastings among old cobwebbed casks. The well-respected wine-maker, Ian MacRae, established the winery in 1977; he's serious about his wines, and specializes in delicious whites.

Pieter Van Gent Black Springs Rd (Mon–Sat 9am–5pm, Sun 11am–4pm; ℡02/6373 3807). Tastings in a delightful setting: beautiful nineteenth-century choir stalls on cool earth floors, overshadowed by huge old barrels salvaged from Penfolds. Try their Pipeclay Port, a tawny port aged in wood, a blend of various vintages. The winemaker is Dutch, and the herbs he uses in his traditional vermouth are specially imported from the Netherlands.

Poet's Corner Craigmoor Rd (Mon–Sat 10am–4.30pm, Sun 10am–4pm; ℡02/6372 2208, ⓦwww.poetscornerwines.com). Incorporating Craigmoor, Montrose and Poet's Corner wines. The original 1859 cellar, a vast space with a huge open fire-place, has a tin roof held up by tree-trunk beams. Upstairs is an equally character-ful, expensive restaurant (daily lunch, Fri & Sat dinner), while outside, views of hills and vineyards are fronted by a perfect cricket pitch and peaceful lawns fragrant with flowers.

mystery" and wine weekends. **Campers** should head for the *Mudgee Riverside Caravan and Tourist Park*, 22 Short St (℡02/6372 2531, ⒻFAX6372 7189; sites ❶, cabins ❷), which has cabins as well as campsites and offers multi-night stay dis-counts and bike rental. With the exception of the award-winning *Grape Vine Restaurant* at *Lauralla Historic Guesthouse* (bookings essential; set meals $30), Mudgee isn't really a town in which to **eat** out, so your best bet is the pub food at places such as the *Red Heifer Grill and Carvary* at the *Lawson Park Hotel*, a great old country pub on Church Street, which does roasts on Monday and Tuesday and pasta specials on Wednesday night. You could also lunch at one of the wineries (see box above); or try the tearooms (Thurs–Sun 10am–4pm only) attached to the *Parkview Guest House*, for refreshments on the verandah or in the courtyard.

Orange, Forbes and Parkes

ORANGE, on the Mitchell Highway en route from Bathurst to Dubbo, is a small city on the eastern slopes of Mount Canabolas; coming from Bathurst, the drive is a pleasant one through undulating countryside, with the valley opening up before you. Orange is a pretty place full of trees, including many European varieties; it claims to have four distinct seasons, and the chilly winter always sees one or two snowfalls. Its major industry is **apple growing**, based in the apple orchards southwest of the town. You can find apple-picking **work** here from late February or early March for a period of about six weeks, while cherry picking takes place from late November to early January; contact the Employment National (see p.343). Many growers have rough accommodation on their properties but demand often outstrips supply, so bring a tent. The **Orange Visitors Centre** on Byng Street (daily 9am–5pm; ℗02/6393 8226, ⓦwww.orange.nsw.gov.au) has information on local attractions, which include the **Ophir diggings**. The first gold field in Australia, established in 1851 and only 30km north of Orange, the site remains much as the diggers left it – beware of open shafts.

Orange prides itself on being rather cosmopolitan, and it has quite a **café** society and some well-regarded **restaurants**. *Scottys on Summer* at 202A Summer St prepares gourmet sandwiches, while the *Union Bank Café* at 84 Byng St has a good range of vegetarian dishes and *Café 48*, at 48 Sale St (BYO), offers praiseworthy Southeast Asian curries. For something a little more special, *Sloozi's* on Summer Street (℗02/6563 1314; dinner Tues–Sat) serves tasty food in a convivial, casual atmosphere, whilst *Selkines* on Anson Street (℗02/6361 1179; dinner Tues–Sat) offers the opportunity of an expensive foray into modern Australian cuisine. A recommended place both to **stay** and eat is the *Metropolitan Hotel* at 107 Byng St (℗02/6362 1353; ❷), just up from the tourist office. It's a huge old-fashioned country pub built in 1872, with a wooden verandah where you can sit and eat barbecued dishes, baked potatoes, damper and salad. Hotel rooms are clean and nicely decorated, and all have TV but no en-suite facilities, while the more expensive motel suites come with all mod cons. There are two **caravan parks**, both a few kilometres from the centre: to the north, the *Colour City Caravan Park* on Margaret Street (℗02/6362 7254; cabins ❶); and to the east, the *Canabolas Caravan Park*, 166 Bathurst Rd (℗02/6362 7279; cabins ❷).

Forming a triangle, with Orange at the apex, Forbes and Parkes to the west are also important regional towns. **FORBES**, on the Lachlan River, is a graceful old town famous as the stomping ground of the nineteenth-century bushranger **Ben Hall**, who is buried in the Forbes Cemetery. **PARKES**, 33km to the northwest along the Newell Highway, is well known for its **Observatory**, which has a 64-metre radio telescope. The observatory's visitor centre (daily 8.30am–4.15pm; ℗02/6861 1777, ⓦwww.parkes.atnf.csiro.au) has a 25-minute audiovisual presentation, *The Invisible Universe* (daily 8.30am–3.30pm, every 30min; $3). Just east of Forbes lies the small township of **ELLGOWRA**, where in 1962 Frank Gardiner and his gang pulled off the biggest gold heist in Australian history. They took a total of $3700 in cash and 77kg in gold from a mailcoach – worth an impressive $1.3 million at today's rates.

Cowra

COWRA, on the banks of the Lachlan River, 107km southwest of Bathurst along the Mid-Western Highway, is famous as the location of the **Cowra Breakout** during World War II. August 5, 1944 saw the escape of 378 Japanese prisoners of war armed with baseball bats, staves, home-made clubs and sharpened kitchen knives – those who were sick and remained behind hanged or disembowelled themselves, unable to endure the disgrace of capture. It took nine days to recapture all the prisoners, during which four Australian soldiers and 231 Japanese died. The breakout was little known until the publication of Harry Gordon's excellent 1970s account *Die Like the Carp* (republished as *Voyage of Shame*; see "Books", p.1204).

You can see the site of the POW camp, now just ruins and fields, on Sakura Avenue on the northeast edge of town. The graves of the Japanese, who were buried in Cowra, were well cared for by members of the local Returned

Servicemen's League, a humanitarian gesture that touched Japanese embassy officials who then broached the idea of an official **Japanese War Cemetery**. Designed by Shigeru Yura, the tranquil burial ground is further north, on Doncaster Drive. The theme of Japanese–Australian friendship and reconciliation continued in Cowra with the establishment of the **Japanese Garden** (daily 8.30am–5pm; $8) in 1979 with funding from Japanese and Australian governments and companies. The large garden, designed by the internationally known Ken Nakajima to represent the landscape of Japan, is set on a hill overlooking the town, on a scenic drive running north off Kendal Street, the main thoroughfare. Cherry and other flowering trees blossom and their leaves change colour with the autumn, mirroring the northern hemisphere's change of seasons. It's very peaceful and idyllic here: cooling on a hot day, with the shade and the sound of the stream burbling through the garden. A further anti-war symbol in Cowra is the **World Peace Bell** in Civic Square, and the planting of an avenue of cherry trees connecting the war cemeteries, the POW camp site and the Japanese Garden. The introduction of the **POW Theatre**, at the Cowra Visitors Centre, is another attraction explaining the war years, the breakout and the reconciliation process since then.

For more information on the town, and **accommodation** options, head for the very helpful **Cowra Visitor Information Centre**, at the junction of Grenfell, Young and Boorowa roads on the Mid-Western Highway (daily 9am–5pm; ☎02/6342 4333, ⓦwww.cowratourism.com.au), near the large riverside park. An interesting alternative to the usual motels and campsites is offered at *Riverslea Station* (☎02/6385 8433, ⓦwww.backpackersfarmstay.com.au; dorms $65 per person, doubles $75 per person including all meals; camping and self-catering options also available) in nearby Wyangala Waters State Park; their five-day packages (from $370 per person) include a day's horse riding in serene countryside.

There are lots of **vineyards** in the Cowra area – actually more than in Mudgee – but no wineries; instead, grapes are sent off to large wineries elsewhere to be made into wine. Their origin is often revealed by their names, such as Richmond Grove Cowra Wine. The region is best known for Chardonnay: to taste the product of the local grapes, head for the Quarry Cellar, 4km from Cowra on the Boorowa Road (Tues–Sun 10am–4pm; ☎02/6342 3650, ⓦwww.cowraregionwines.com); the attached restaurant (lunch Wed–Sun, dinner Fri & Sat) also does Devonshire teas and inexpensive light lunches of pasta and salads. If you're interested in the possibility of some **grape-picking** work, contact the Employment National (see below).

Young

Seventy kilometres southwest of Cowra along the Olympic Way, the hilly town of **YOUNG** is a good spot to pick up some **cherry-picking** work during the season (approximately six weeks from the first week of Nov). Being monotonous rather than strenuous, the work attracts a genteel crowd and is popular with retired Queenslanders. To just pick your own and have a look at some orchards and packing sheds, head to any one of a number of places on the way into town from Cowra; you could also contact the Employment National on Boorowa Street (☎02/6340 2900). The long weekend in October generally coincides with the time when the **cherry blossoms** are in full bloom – a glorious sight. There's even a Cherry Festival each year, in late November/early December. There are also several vineyards on the slopes of the undulating area, which is becoming known as the Hilltops wine region; one worth visiting is the small, family-run **Lindsays Woodonga Hill Winery**, 10km north of Young on the Olympic Way (daily 9am–5pm; ☎02/6382 2972).

Young also has some significance as the site of the notorious **Lambing Flat Riots**, described in every Australian history book. A former gold-mining centre known then as Lambing Flats, the town was the site of racist riots against Chinese miners in June 1861. As the gold ran out, European miners resented what they saw as the greater success of the more industrious Chinese. Troops had to be called in when the Chinese were chased violently from the diggings, beaten, their pigtails cut off, and their property destroyed. Carried at the head of the mob was a flag, painted on a tent flysheet, with the Southern Cross in the centre, and "Roll Up, Roll Up, No Chinese" lettered in the manner of a circus flyer. You can see the original flag, and other exhibits relating to the riots, in the **Lambing Flat Historical Museum** (Mon–Sat 10am–4pm, Sun 10.45am–4pm; $2) in the Community Arts Centre, Campbell St. For more information, including lists of accommodation and where to eat, contact the **Young Visitor Information Centre**, 2 Short St (Mon–Fri 9am–5pm, Sat, Sun & public holidays 9.30am–4pm; ☎02/6382 3394, ⊛www.young.nsw .gov.au). A recommended **farmstay** outside town is *Old Nubba School House* (☎02/6943 2513, ✉nubba@dragnet.com.au; ❸), halfway between Young and Cootamundra on the Olympic Highway; the peaceful self-contained accommodation, a former schoolhouse in the grounds of the friendly family farm, sleeps up to eight and breakfast provisions are included.

Dubbo

DUBBO, an Aboriginal word meaning "red earth", is a self-styled "Wild West" country city on the banks of the Macquarie River, 420km northwest of Sydney and about 200km from Bathurst. The regional capital for the west of the state, it supports many agricultural industries and is located at a vital crossroads where the Melbourne–Brisbane **Newell Highway** meets the **Mitchell Highway** and routes west to Bourke or Broken Hill.

As such, it's well used to people passing through, but not staying long. If you do stop, drop by the **Western Plains Zoo** on Obley Road, 5km south of town off the Newell Highway (daily 9am–5pm; $23; 2hr zoo walks for an additional $3 Sat, Sun & public holidays at 6.45am; ⊛www.zoo.nsw.gov.au). The vast, open-range zoo features expansive landscaped habitats, through which many Australian animals are free to roam; other animals from five continents are kept in natural surroundings, separated from the public by moats or creeks rather than fences wherever possible. The zoo is crisscrossed by walking and cycling paths: especially during the hot months, the best idea is to get up early in the morning and set off early – by noon, the temperatures can become unbearable and the animals sometimes slink off out of sight into the shade. There is no public transport to the zoo, so cycling there, and around the zoo itself, is a good option: Wheeler Cycles, 193 Brisbane St (☎02/6882 9899), rents out bikes; electronic carts and bikes can also be rented at the zoo itself. To walk there, follow the pleasant cycle track along the river – around an hour on foot from the city centre. Otherwise, take a taxi (Radio Cabs ☎13 10 08).

The state's largest **Livestock Market**, 3km north out of town on the Newell Highway, auctions sheep and cattle every Monday, Thursday and Friday (unloading from 8.30am). It's worth a visit just to see the local farmers decked out in their Akubra hats and Drizabone coats, and to get the authentic smell of country life. The YHA gives lifts to the market to its guests on request.

In the centre of town, **Old Dubbo Gaol** on Macquarie Street (daily 9am–4.30pm; $7) is worth an hour or so of your time. A hundred years ago, this fortress-style building housed some of the most notorious criminals of the west, and today it glories in the details of nineteenth-century prison life, with loving attention to the macabre: the gallows, the hangman's kit and the careers of some of those who were executed here. In the cells, life-size (and convincingly lifelike) animatronic models of convicted criminals tell the stories of their lives and condemned futures. The **Dubbo Museum** at 234 Macquarie St (temporarily closed for renovation; for latest check with tourist office) has an extensive and somewhat chequered collection of items of regional history. There are agricultural and transport exhibits, a colonial kitchen, musical instruments, a dentist's surgery and a re-creation of a village square complete with drapery store, bootmaker, barber and blacksmith. Also worth a look-in is the National Trust property **Dundullimal Homestead** (daily 9am–5pm), 2km past the zoo on Obley Road. An 1840s slab house with stone stables, it now houses a craft shop and mini farm, and you can sometimes see the odd jackeroo riding oxen rodeo-style. A visit here is best combined with a "hayride" on a truck and cruise on the Macquarie River, stopping in at the property for afternoon tea. Tours cost from $16; book through the visitors centre.

The Dubbo **Regional Gallery** at 165 Darling St (Tues–Sun 11am–4.30pm; free) has a kitsch collection of animals represented in art, including, surprisingly, an exceptional painting of a fox by the noted Australian artist Arthur Boyd. They also have a rotating cultural programme, including indigenous works at times.

Practicalities

As it's a crossroads, Dubbo's 24-hour **bus** terminal, at the junction of the Mitchell and Newell highways, is busy with daily connections to Brisbane, Sydney, Melbourne, Adelaide, Canberra, Newcastle and Port Stephens. Just across the railway line is the **train station**, terminal for the XPT to and from Sydney. Countrylink (☎13 22 32) buses leave here for Bourke and Lightning Ridge. You can also **fly** to Dubbo with Regional Express (☎13 17 13) and Qantas (☎13 13 13) from Sydney. The tiny airport is 5km northwest of town. Regional Express also flies to Broken Hill and Coolangatta from here. Thrifty (at the train station) **rents cars** from $50 a day. The helpful **Dubbo Visitors Information Centre** (daily 9am–5pm; ☎02/6884 1422, ⓦwww .dubbotourism.com.au) is set in a riverside park at the corner of Erskine and Macquarie streets, just off the Newell Highway.

As you'd expect, there are plenty of **motels**, with the majority on the Mitchell Highway (called Cobar Street as it passes through town). A couple of the better-value ones are the *Merino Motel*, 65 Church St, 200m south of the city centre (☎02/6882 4133, ⓕ6684 3528; ❸), and the budget *Formule 1* on Whylandra Street (☎02/6882 9211, ⓕ6682 9311; ❷). Two old **hotels** downtown offer a bit more character: the *Pastoral*, 110 Tabralgar St (☎02/6882 4219; ❷), has a huge verandah and the cheapest rooms in town, or there's the *Castlereagh Hotel*, on the corner of Brisbane and Tabralgar streets (☎02/6882 4877, ⓕ6684 1520; ❸). The most salubrious pub-hotel in town is the *Amaroo Hotel*, 83 Macquarie St (☎02/6882 3533, ⓕ6684 2601; ❸), which has smart rooms and includes a cooked breakfast. *Mayfair Cottage*, 10 Baird St (☎02/6882 5226, ⓕ6684 4273, ⓔdonjstephens@bigpond.com; ❹), is another good breakfast-included choice, and has a separate guest wing and a pool. The only hostel in town is the *Dubbo Backpackers YHA* at 87 Brisbane St (☎ & ⓕ02/6882 0922, ⓔyhadubbo@hwy.com.au; dorms $19, rooms ❷), a slightly down-at-heel, family-run place with a drab common area and overgrown verandahs; it's within walking distance of the train station and the city centre, although the owner suggests taking a cab (see p.344) if you arrive at night. **Campsites** include *Dubbo City Caravan Park* on Whylandra Street, 2km west (☎02/6882 4820, ✉ddcp@dubbo.nsw.gov.au; on-site vans ❶, cabins ❷), and *Poplars Caravan Park*, overlooking the river near the city centre on Lower Bultje Street (☎ & ℱ02/6882 4067; on-site vans ❶, cabins ❷).

Dubbo has developed a bit of a **café society**. The self-consciously trendy *Echidna Café* at 177 Macquarie St (closed Sun & Mon), serves expensive contemporary Australian cuisine, but you can just drop in for an excellent coffee. The *Grapevine Café*, 144 Brisbane St, is more low-key – a relaxing place with a lovely, leafy courtyard, generous portions and breakfast served until noon at the weekend. For fresh bread and cakes, try the *Village Hot Bake* on Darling Street, by the railway station, a bustling bakery on two levels, also serving pies, fries and pizzas. If you crave the usual country-town fare, head to the *Amaroo Hotel* which has the best **bistro** in Dubbo. There are also several **restaurants** at the bottom end of the main shopping area, including the *Darbar* at 215 Macquarie St (☎02/6884 4338), a tandoori house located in an old sandstone basement.

The northwest

From Dubbo the **Newell Highway**, the main route from Melbourne to Brisbane, continues through the wheat plains of the northwest, their relentless flatness relieved by the ancient eroded mountain ranges of the **Warrumbungles**, near Coonabarabran, and **Mount Kaputar**, near Narrabri, with the **Pillaga Scrub** between the two towns. Clear skies and the lack of large towns with their attendant lights make the area ideal for the **telescopes** that stare into space at both **Coonabarabran** and **Narrabri**. The thinly populated northwest has a relatively large percentage of Aborigines, peaking in the largest town of **Moree**. In 1971 Charles Perkins, an Aboriginal activist, led the **Freedom Ride**, a group of thirty people – mostly university students – who bussed through New South Wales on a mission to root out racism in the state. The biggest victory was in Moree itself when the riders, facing hostile townsfolk, broke the race bar by escorting Aboriginal children into the public swimming pool.

The **Namoi Valley** – extending from **Gunnedah**, just west of Tamworth, to Walgett – with its rich black soil, is **cotton country**. Beyond Walgett, just off the sealed Castlereagh Highway that runs from Dubbo, is **Lightning Ridge**, a scorching-hot, opal-mining town relieved by the hot **artesian bore baths** which are a feature of the northwest.

Coonabarabran and the Warrumbungles

COONABARABRAN is a touristy little town on the Castlereagh River, 160km north of Dubbo via the Newell Highway, and 465km northwest of Sydney. People come here to gaze at stars in the clear skies, or for bushwalking and climbing in the spectacular Warrumbungles, an ancient mountain range 35km to the west.

By virtue of its proximity to the **Siding Spring Observatory Complex** (daily 9.30am–4pm; $5.50), perched high above the township on the edge of the Warrumbungle National Park, Coonabarabran considers itself the astronomy capital of Australia. The skies are exceptionally clear out here, due to the dry climate and a lack of pollution and population. The giant 3.9-metre optical telescope (one of the largest in the world) can be viewed close up from an observation gallery, and there's an astronomy exhibition, complemented by hands-on exhibits and a video show. There's no public transport here, but the school bus passes by – ask at the visitors centre (see below). You can't actually view the stars at Siding Spring, but the **Skywatch Observatory** (daily, opening times vary; $7.70, night show $12.10; book before dusk on ☏02/6842 3303; ⓦhwy.com.au/~skywatch) on Timor Road, 2km from town on the way to the Warrumbungles, has night viewing through its modern telescope, plus a planetarium and computer space-simulation programs.

Warrumbungle National Park

The rugged **Warrumbungles** are ancient mountains of volcanic origin with jagged cliffs, rocky pinnacles and crags jutting from the western horizon. The dry western plains and the moister environment of the east coast meet at these ranges, with plant and animal species from both habitats coexisting in the park. Warrumbungle means "crooked mountains" in an Aboriginal language, and the park was in fact bordered by three different language groups – the Kamilaroi, the Weilwan and Kawambarai. Evidence of past Aboriginal habitation here is common, with stone flakes used to make tools indicating old campsites. The **Warrumbungle National Park** is spectacular, especially in spring when the wild flowers in the sandstone areas are in bloom. The most popular months with visitors are April, September and October: it's really just too hot for walking here in summer, and the cold winters sometimes bring snow. If you do come in the hot months, remember to take plenty of water when you go walking, and something warm for the nights, which get quite cool.

The **National Park Visitors Centre**, in Coonabarabran at 56 Cassilis St (daily 9am–4pm; ☏02/6825 4364), has hands-on displays and detailed maps of walking tracks. The wheelchair-accessible bitumen **Gurianawa Track** makes a short circuit around the centre and overlooks the flats where eastern grey Kangaroos gather at dusk. Another good introduction to the park is the short **White Gum Lookout Walk** (1km), with panoramic views over the ranges that are particularly dramatic at sunset. However, the ultimate – for the reasonably fit only – is the 14.5-kilometre **Grand High Tops Trail** along the main ridge and back. The walk begins at the kangaroo-filled Camp Pincham and follows the flat floor of Spirey Creek through open forests full of colourful rosellas and lorikeets, and lizards basking on rocks. As the trail climbs, there are views of the three-hundred-metre-high Belougery Spire, and more scrambling gets you to the foot of the **Breadknife**, the park's most famous feature, thrusting 90m up into the sky. From here the main track heads on to the rocky slabs of the Grand High Tops, with tremendous views of most of the surrounding peaks and with the possibility of spotting a wedge-tailed eagle soaring above. Experienced walkers could carry on to climb Bluff Mountain and then head west for Mount Exmouth (1205m), the park's highest peak; both are great spots from which to watch the sunrise. The Warrumbungles are very popular with **rock climbers**, who are allowed to climb anywhere except the Breadknife; permits are required. There isn't any public transport to the Warrumbungles, so you'll need your own.

Practicalities

In addition to the National Park Visitors Centre on Cassilis Street (see above), Coonabarabran has its own **Visitor Information Centre** on John Street (daily 9am–5pm; ☎02/6842 1441 or 1800 242 881, ⓦwww.lisp.com.au /coonabarabran), which can organize special visits to out-of-the-way places, including Aboriginal sites.

Accommodation in the national park itself is limited to campsites, some of which have hot showers, electric barbecues and fireplaces (note that wood is not supplied, and while plenty of places sell it, there's a fine for collecting it in the park), and *Balor Hut*, an eight-bunk hut adjacent to the Breadknife. Bookings aren't necessary for any of the sites, but you may need to book the hut; mattresses are not provided, and bookings and the key are available from the National Park Visitors Centre. Anyone planning to stay in the park will need to bring provisions. Between the park and Coonabarabran, the *Warrumbungles Mountain Motel & Cabins* on Timor Road, 19km from town (☎02/6842 1832, ⓦwww.warrumbungles.lisp.com.au; cabins ❷, rooms ❸), is set in bushland on the Castlereagh River. Rooms (BYO linen) have extra bunks and kitchens, so are good for families or small groups; there's also a small saltwater pool and a playing field. Also along Timor Road (16km from town), nestled under Bulleamble Mountain, is the *Tibuc* farm (☎02/6842 1740; ❸), where self-contained cabins vary from posh to extremely basic. There are reductions for longer stays and B&B is available; mention when booking if you're not bringing your own linen. There are plenty of alternative **accommodation options in town**: on John Street you'll find the *All Travellers Motor Inn* (☎02/6842 1133, ⓕ6842 2505; ❸–❺), with air conditioning and wheelchair-accessible rooms, or the excellent *Imperial Hotel* (☎02/6842 1023; ❶), which has a guest lounge, kitchenette, very reasonable singles and a huge verandah with tables and armchairs for warm spring nights. Along the Newell Highway you'll find the pleasant and well-equipped *Castlereagh Village Holiday Units* (☎02/6842 1706; ❷) and on the Oxley, the shady *John Oxley Caravan Park* (☎02/6842 1635; on-site vans ❶, cabins ❷).

Good **places to eat** in town include the wonderful *Woop Woop*, which has excellent, modern cuisine in a cosy room of exposed brick and iron girders, situated in an alleyway just off John Street. Other establishments are all on John Street itself: the bright and airy *Jolly Cauli*, at no. 30, offers a wide choice of dishes, delicious coffee and home-made cakes, and also serves as the town's Internet café. *The Lunch Box* does inexpensive midday meals, the *Imperial Hotel* has the best counter meals, and the *Golden Sea Dragon* serves up reliable Chinese food.

The Namoi Valley: cotton country

On the Oxley Highway, 76km west of the New England city of Tamworth, **GUNNEDAH**, with a population of eight thousand, is one of the largest towns in the northwest. The town's claim to fame is as the inspiration for the Australian poet Dorothea MacKellar (1885–1968) and her patriotic verse *My Country*, in which she pledged her undying love for what was then – and still is now – a drought-stricken land. The opening stanza is familiar to most Australians, who learnt it by rote at school:

I love a sunburnt country
A land of sweeping plains
Of ragged mountain ranges
Of drought and flooding rains...

Gunnedah has one of the healthiest **koala populations** in the state, and there is a semi-permanent resident bear in a eucalypt opposite the **information** centre in Anzac Park (Mon–Fri 9am–5pm, Sat & Sun 10am–3pm; ⓣ02/6740 2230, ⓦwww.infogunnedah.com.au). The staff put out a "koala today" sign when he's home, so you'll know if you're in luck; otherwise you still have a high chance of seeing some on the Bindea Walking Track, a 7.4-kilometre walk from the information centre, or a 4.5-kilometre trek through the bush from the car park at Porcupine's Lookout; you'll also see wild kangaroos, and maybe even an echidna, but be careful because the track is quite overgrown and it's easy to get lost. Should you want **to stay** in Gunnedah, try the friendly *Regal Hotel* at 298 Conadilly St (ⓣ02/6742 2355; ❷), which has a laundry, a guest lounge with an open fire and entertainment on Friday and Saturday nights. The nearest **caravan park** is 1km east of town on Henry Street (ⓣ02/6742 1372; cabins and on-site vans ❶). Besides the usual pub bistros you can **eat** in more style at the rather swish *Fiorella's Italian Restaurant* at 378 Conadilly St (ⓣ02/6742 5004). *Pantry Creations, Classic Visions Café* and *Redgum Outdoor*, all on Conadilly Street, are good for coffee, cake and healthy luncheon fare – *Redgum* also serves smoothies.

While Gunnedah does have some cotton crops, **NARRABRI**, 97km northwest via the communities of Boggabri and Baan Baa, is recognized as the commercial centre of cotton growing. A little smaller than Gunnedah, the town has a prosperous feel. The **tourist information centre**, on Tibbereena Street (Mon–Fri 9am–4pm, Sat & Sun 9am–1pm; ⓣ02/6792 3583 or 1800 659 931), can give you the times to go and see the five linked dishes of the **Australia Telescope** complex (ⓣ02/6790 4070), 20km west on the Yarrie Lake road. Opening times depend on what they're tracking, but the centre is staffed Monday to Friday from 8am to 4pm, entry is free and there are lots of computer models to play with. The other main attraction around Narrabri is **Mount Kaputar National Park**. The drive from the park to the 1524-metre **lookout** – with its panoramic views encompassing the vast Pillaga Scrub, the Warrumbungles and the New England Tablelands – is steep, narrow and partly unsealed (call ⓣ02/6792 1147 to check road conditions). There are eleven marked bushwalking trails in the park, with brochures available from the **NPWS office**, 100 Maitland St in Narrabri (ⓣ02/6799 1740). There are **camping** facilities at *Dawsons Spring*, with hot showers, and a couple of cabins sleeping a maximum of six, with bathroom, kitchen and wood stove (reservations via NPWS; cabins ❸). The most striking geological feature of the park is **Sawn Rocks**, a basalt formation that looks like a series of organ pipes; it's reached via the northern end of the park on the unsealed road heading to Bingara. If you want to **stay** in Narrabri itself, or grab something to **eat**, try the good-value *Tourist Hotel* at 142 Maitland St (ⓣ02/6792 2312; ❶), which offers homely and clean rooms, and has its own restaurant, *Thurlows* (Mon–Sat 9am–3pm & 6–9pm; ⓣ02/7672 1125).

The drive from Narrabri to **WEE WAA**, roughly 40km west, warns of your entry into redneck territory – the roadside glitters with shattered bottles thrown from speeding cars. Wee Waa was where the Namoi cotton industry began in the 1960s, and the large cotton "gins" or processing plants are located here. During the picking and growing season (April–July) free guided tours leave Namoi Co-op (daily 10.30am & 2.30pm; 1hr 30min–3hr 30min), but you'll need your own car to get around the various areas. If you can stand the rather raw, dispirited town and the blazing summer heat, you could earn some cash from the **cotton-chipping** work that's here in abundance in December and January; ask at one of the two pubs on Rose Street, the main drag, and someone will send you in the right direction. From Wee Waa you can head west to Walgett and on to Lightning Ridge.

Lightning Ridge

The population of **LIGHTNING RIDGE**, 74km north of **Walgett** on the Castlereagh Highway (the road is fully sealed, but note that there's no place to stop for fuel between the two), is officially 4000 but unofficially it's reckoned to be about 10,000. It's a transient place, where people in their hordes pitch up in town lured by the town's one attraction: opal. Amid this harsh landscape scarred by holes and slag heaps, Lightning Ridge's opal fields are the only place in the world where the extremely valuable **black opal** can consistently be found. This lone enticement is heavily exploited by opal galleries and **mines** you can visit, among them the Big Opal, 3 Mile Rd (daily 9am–5pm; tours 10am, $12), which has demonstrations of opal-cutting and guided tours of an underground mine; and the Walk-in Mine, 1 Bald Hill Rd (daily 9am–4pm; tours $7.50), which has a mining display and tours to an underground mine. There's even an opal and gem **festival** in late July, which sees the population shoot up by another few thousand souls. The effects of the opal obsession can be seen all over town, in the faces of the residents and the glorious, crazy constructions of the few who do strike it rich; check out the **Bottle House** at 60 Opal St, a bizarrely beautiful cottage and matching dog kennel built entirely from wine bottles set in stone.

There are clearly demarcated fossicking areas where you can try your luck at finding opals – but don't do it anywhere else, or you may stray onto others' claims. Recover afterwards in the 52°C water of the hot **artesian bore baths** on Pandora Street (open 24hr; free). More cooling is the Olympic Pool on Gem Street (end Sept to Easter daily 10am–8pm), particularly appealing in the scorching heat since parts of the pool are shaded from the sun. The **Goondee Aboriginal Keeping Place** on Pandora Street (call ☎02/6829 2001 for opening times) has Aboriginal artefacts and information on bush tucker.

Practicalities

Countrylink runs **buses** here from Sydney and Dubbo daily. The **tourist information centre** in Lightning Ridge is in the Miners Associated building on Morilla Street (☎02/6829 1466 or 1800 639 545, ⓦwww.lightningridge .net.au) and has opal-buying rooms attached – ask for the useful booklet *Walgett Shire and the Lightning Ridge Opal Fields*, which contains a handy guide to buying opals. The centre can also fill you in on **accommodation** possibilities (all have air-con rooms), which include the *Black Opal Motel* on Opal Street (☎02/6829 0518, Ⓕ6829 0884; ❸), the *Wallangulla Motel*, on the corner of Morella and Agate streets (☎02/6829 0542, Ⓔwgulla@turboweb.com.au; ❸), and *Lightning Ridge Hotel Motel* on Onyx Street (☎02/6829 0304, ⓦwww.lightning-ridge-hotel-motel.com; ❸), which also has cabins (❷) and van and tent sites (❶). The best place to **camp**, though, is *Crocodile Caravan and Camping Park*, Morilla Street (☎02/6829 0437, Ⓕ6829 2049; vans ❶, cabins ❷), which has a pool and spa and air-cooled cabins. Fossicking backpackers might also like to try the *Tram-o-tel* at 2 Morilla St (☎02/6829 0448, ❶), which has basic bunk units and is within 300m of two opal mines. Full **banking** facilities are available at Westpac on Morilla Street, and **Internet** access at Harrisons secondhand bookstore at 48 Morilla St.

The Hume Highway and the Riverina

The rolling plains of southwestern New South Wales, spreading west from the Great Dividing Range, are bounded by two great rivers: the Murrumbidgee to the north and the Murray to the south, the latter forming the border with the state of Victoria. This area is known as the **Riverina**, a name that conjures up a certain rural romance, suggesting a country Australia little visited by tourists – except those en route to Melbourne along the **Hume Highway**, which cuts a fume-filled swath through the region. If you're looking for work on the land, you've a reasonable chance of finding it here. The land the explorer John Oxley described as "uninhabitable and useless to civilized man" began its transformation to fertile fruit bowl when the ambitious **Murrumbidgee Irrigation Scheme** was launched in 1907, and the area around **Griffith** and **Leeton** now produces ninety percent of Australia's rice, most of its citrus fruits and twenty percent of its wine grapes. The capital of the central Riverina is **Wagga Wagga**, Australia's largest inland city. Along the Upper Murray, the main towns are on the Victorian side of the river (and are covered in the Victoria chapter), but you may drop into **Albury** en route to Melbourne on the Hume, or into **Wentworth** as a day-trip from Mildura or on the way to or from Broken Hill on the Silver City Highway. There are several interesting **festivals** in the region, including the Wagga Wagga Jazz Festival in September and the Festival of Griffith, an orgy of Aussie wine, food and culture held every May (℡02/6964 1866).

The Hume Highway: Goulburn to Albury

If you want a quick route to Melbourne from Sydney, or vice versa, you'll inevitably end up on the rather tedious **Hume Highway**, which passes through the Southern Highlands, the Riverina and across the Murray River. Over the years the highway has been improved, but though this is one of Australia's main arteries between its two largest cities, it still narrows to one lane either way in parts. Choked with trucks, particularly at night, accidents are not infrequent, so keep your wits about you. While the highway itself may seem dreary, some of the nearby towns are truly and typically Australian; rich in food, wine, flora and fauna and friendly locals, they can be well worth a day or so of your time. Following are the main stopping points along the way in New South Wales (for Sydney to Goulburn, see p.351) and some suggestions for food, accommodation and breaks.

Goulburn and around

Now bypassed by the Hume Highway, **GOULBURN** is still the traditional stop-off point en route to Canberra. It's a large regional centre for the surrounding area, and for a quality **wool industry**, which was established in the 1820s. The town, with its wide streets, has a conservative country feel, but boasts city facilities and some large and impressive public buildings. Goulburn's connection to sheep, and one kind in particular, is made obvious to the public with the **Big Merino** (daily 8am–8pm). Another of Australia's unashamedly tacky "big things", the fifteen-metre-high sheep proudly stands next to the Ampol service station on the Old Hume Highway; the first floor has a wool industry display, and on the third level you can look out over the town through the sheep's eyes. Spare a thought for the poor beast as you traverse his insides, though; he was emasculated in the name of shop space. To get closer to the real thing, head for the long-established **Pelican Sheep Station** on Braidwood Road, 10km south of town (℡02/4821 4668, ⊛www.pelicansheepstation .com.au; bunkhouses ❷, cabins ❸, plus camping), which has been in the same family since 1827. Tours include a shearing demonstration and the chance to see some sheepdogs being put through their paces.

The Hume and Hovell Walking Track

This long-distance walk starts at **Gunning**, on the Hume Highway 50km east of Goulburn, and runs over 400km southwest **to Albury**, retracing as closely as possible the route taken on foot by the two eponymous explorers in the spring and summer of 1824 on their expedition from Sydney to Port Phillip, the site of what was to become Melbourne. The walk takes about fifteen to twenty days but the layout – a Bicentenary project – allows for half-day, full-day and weekend walks. There are several free leaflets detailing different chunks, available from the Department of Conservation and Land Management in Sydney (℡02/9228 6111), Goulburn (℡02/4823 0665) and Wagga Wagga (℡02/6921 2503); the *Hume and Hovell Walking Track Guidebook* by Harry Hill (Crawford House Press, Bathurst, $19.95) is also useful.

There are several historic places to visit in Goulburn, including the National Trust property **Riversdale**, an 1840 coaching inn on Maud Street (mid-Sept to mid-July Sat, Sun & public holidays 10am–4.30pm, at other times by appointment on ℡02/4821 9591), but the most interesting is the **Old Goulburn Brewery** on Bungonia Road (daily 9am–5pm), which has been brewing traditional ales and stouts since 1836. Details of other old properties can be obtained from the **Goulburn Visitors Centre** opposite the shady, flower-filled Belmore Park, at 201 Sloane St (daily 9am–5pm; ℡02/4823 0492, ⓦ www.igoulburn.com); they also have a list of accommodation.

The classic place to **eat** in Goulburn, is the *Paragon Café*, at 174 Auburn St, open daily for lunch and dinner. A bastion of good, filling food including inexpensive breakfasts, great hamburgers, steaks, fish, veal, pasta and pizza, it's been here for around fifty years and retains its 1940s-era fittings; it's also licensed.

The most intriguing place to **stay** in the area is at the **Gunningbar Yurt Farm**, 20km out of town on Grabben Gullen Road (℡02/4829 2114; $20 as a helper with four-hours' work per day required, but all meals included; or as part of a WWOOF placement, see p.67). A yurt, in its original form, is a Mongolian round leather tent, and the concept was enthusiastically adopted and adapted by Californian New Agers. The ones here are mostly of wood and are portable prefab buildings in the Californian mould – solar-powered, naturally lit and wood-heated. Essentially a sheep property, the "yurt village" has several yurts, each with a different function, providing an educational centre for groups of children to help them become more self-sufficient and environmentally aware. If you want to stay, you must call in advance; if you don't have your own transport, someone can pick you up. In town, *Tattersalls Hotel*, 74 Auburn St (℡02/4821 3088, Ⓕ4822 3505; $19), is a Nomad-affiliated hostel offering good, if basic, accommodation in dorms.

The **Bungonia State Recreation Area**, 25km east of Goulburn, covers a rugged strip of the Southern Tablelands containing some of the deepest **caves** in Australia. The spectacular limestone Bungonia Gorge and the Shoalhaven River are two of its physical attractions.

Yass and the Burrinjuck Waters State Park

YASS dates back to 1821 when Europeans first entered the area. Prior to this, the area had a high Aboriginal population, who gave the town its name, "yharr", meaning running water. On the outskirts of Yass as you exit the Hume Highway onto the Yass Valley Way from Goulburn (87km away) is the National Trust-owned **Cooma Cottage** (Mon & Thurs–Sun 10am–4pm; $4), the former home of the famous explorer **Hamilton Hume**, set in rolling countryside stocked with sheep. The well-preserved, nineteenth-century homestead's architectural interest is outweighed by the excellent interpretive material it contains on Hume and his expeditions. Hume was different from many of his contemporaries in that he was born in Australia – in Parramatta, to free settlers in 1797. His explorations relied on his knowledge of the bush: he befriended Aborigines who taught him their skills and language, which made him infinitely better prepared than those equipped only with romantic notions. His first expedition was at the age of 17, accompanied by his brother and his Aboriginal friend Doual, and the trio discovered prime grazing lands in the Southern Highlands. Three years later he led the Goulburn Plains expedition, and pushing further afield in 1821 he discovered the rich and productive Yass Plains, where he settled in later life. Hume's best-known exploration was when he paired with Hovell, an English sea captain, to head for Port Phillip Bay; you can follow in their footsteps on the Hume and Hovell Walking Track (see box opposite). He also assisted Sturt in tracing the Murray and Darling rivers. The **Visitors Centre** (Mon–Fri 9am–4.30pm, Sat & Sun 9am–4pm; ℡02/6226 2557, ℮yasstourism@interact.net.au) has maps outlining a two-kilometre informative walk, and the **Hamilton Hume Museum** (call ℡02/6226 2557 or ask at Visitors Centre to confirm opening times; $2), which is run by volunteers and contains displays on what the town looked like back in the 1890s.

Continuing along the Hume Highway you'll reach a turn-off for the **Burrinjuck Waters State Park** after 27km, and from here it's a 25-kilometre drive on a sealed road to the bushland park set around Burrinjuck Dam, with camping and picnic areas filled with kangaroos and chirping rosellas (℡02/6227 8114; on-site vans, units and tent sites ❷, cottages ❹). There is a **riverboat cruise** most weekends in summer on the *Lady BJ* (2hr; $16; ℡02/6227 7270) up to the dam and across the main basin. **WEE JASPER** is a picturesque village located on the backwaters of Burrinjuck Dam, with a basic **campsite** (℡02/6227 9626). From here you can visit **Carey's Caves** and see some of Australia's most spectacular limestone rock formations (Mon & Fri–Sun tours at noon & 1.30pm; $8; ℡02/6227 9622).

Turning off the Hume Highway at **Bowning** brings you to the peaceful village of **Binalong**. Australia's best-known poet, Banjo Patterson, spent much of his childhood here, attending the local school. Binalong railway station was used to transport gold from nearby Lambing Flats (Young), which made it a lucrative area for bushrangers. The grave of the daring bushranger "Flash" Johnny Gilbert, a member of a local outlaw gang is along the side of the road to Harden.

Gundagai and Holbrook

One hundred and four kilometres from Yass, **GUNDAGAI** sits on the banks of the Murrumbidgee, at the foot of the rounded bump of Mount Parnassus. The town was once situated on the alluvial flats north of the river, despite warnings from local Aborigines that the area was prone to major flooding. Proving them correct, old Gundagai was the scene of Australia's worst flood disaster in 1852 when 89 people drowned. The relocated Gundagai, on the main route between Sydney and Melbourne (until bypassed by the Hume Highway), became a favoured overnight stopping point, with the bullock wagons that took the pioneers into the interior favouring a camping spot out of town at Five Mile Creek. A large punt was the only means of crossing the Murrumbidgee from 1849 until the **Prince Alfred Bridge** was erected in

1867; although now closed to traffic, the pretty wooden bridge can still be crossed by pedestrians. Gold was eventually discovered here, and by 1864 Gundagai had become a boom town, preyed upon by the romantically dubbed bushranger **Captain Moonlight** who was eventually captured and tried at the Gundagai courthouse in 1879.

Perhaps this colourful history and the road-much-travelled appeal of Gundagai explains why the town features so often in Australian verse and folk song, finding immortality through a Jack Moses' poem, in which "the dog sat on the tuckerbox, nine miles from Gundagai" – and stubbornly refused to help its master pull the bogged bullock team from the creek. Somehow the whole image became elevated from that of a disobedient hound and a fed-up, cursing teamster to a symbol of the pioneer with a faithful hound at his side. As a consequence, a **statue** of the dog was erected at Five Mile Creek (Moses erroneously referred to it as being nine miles from town): it's actually a very pleasant place to take a break from the rigours of the road, with a shady picnic area and undulating fields and hills beyond. Inside the **tourist centre** here, there's a range of cheerfully tacky souvenirs plus the rare opportunity to send a postcard with a special "dog on the tuckerbox" postmark.

In the town itself, the **Gundagai Tourist Information Centre** (Mon–Fri 8am–5pm, Sat & Sun 9am–noon & 1–5pm; ℡02/6944 0250, ℮ztc1 @gundagaishire.nsw.gov.au) can help you find somewhere to stay if need be, and also sells a tape of several folk songs featuring Gundagai, including *Along the Road to Gundagai*, from which every Australian remembers only the tuneful snatch "There's a track winding back, to an old-fashioned shack, along the road to Gundagai". Also at the information centre, you can see (for $2) the **miniature Baroque cathedral** by Frank Rusconi, the sculptor who created the statue of the noble dog. The cathedral, a project that required complete patience and precision, took 28 years to build; constructed with absolutely no plans of any sort, it is made from thousands of pieces of twenty different kinds of New South Wales marble.

Sixty-eight kilometres south of Gundagai, **HOLBROOK** is a recommended food break on the drive to Melbourne (or Sydney), with two excellent bakeries on the Hume Highway as it heads through town. The *Holbrook Bakery* dishes out delicious beef and curry pies, and the *Scrummy Buns Bakery* across the road sells more unorthodox pies filled with crocodile, emu, kangaroo and rabbit – plus cappuccino and continental cakes. Perhaps these great bakeries are a legacy of a German past: settled by Germans in the 1860s, Holbrook was called Germantown right up until World War I, when anti-German feeling warranted a name change.

Albury and around

The small city of **ALBURY** on the Murray River is a major stopover point on the route between Sydney and Melbourne, being roughly halfway. It's twinned with Wodonga across the river in Victoria, and although Albury is the major centre, the principal information centre is on the Wodonga side – **Albury Wodonga Visitor Information Centre** on the Hume Highway (daily 9am–5pm; ℡02/6041 3875 or 1300 796 222, ℮www.alburycity .nsw.gov.au). You can also pick up tourist information from the **Albury Regional Museum** (daily 10.30am–4.30pm; free; ℡02/6021 4550) on the Hume Highway in what was once the *Turks' Head Hotel* – opportunistically sited here when the river was crossed by punt; changing exhibitions now focus on the social history of the region. The museum is set in **Noreuil Park**, a peaceful spot looking across to a bush-covered riverbank in Victoria. People lie about under the large gum trees – one of which was marked by the explorer Hovell at the point where he and Hume crossed the Murray – and swim in the river. You can also take to the water with a **cruise** on a replica paddle steamer (mid-Sept to mid-April Wed–Sat, daily during school holidays, 10.30am, 12.30pm & 3pm; from $9; ℡02/6041 5558). Another pleasant place to stretch your legs is in the **Albury Botanical Gardens** at the Dean Street end of Wodonga Place. Established in 1877, the gardens hold some impressive old trees, including a huge 41-metre Queensland kauri pine; palm trees and flowerbeds fill a small grassy park, and the short fern walk is pleasantly cooling. The **Albury Regional Art Centre** is at 546 Dean St (Mon–Fri 10.30am–4pm, Sat & Sun 10.30am–5pm; free), in the decorative old town hall. The gallery's speciality is photography, but it also has a sizeable collection of Russell Drysdale's sketches and studies for paintings; the Australian artist (1912–81) lived in the area in the 1920s and married into a local family.

Albury has a good range of places to **stay** for the night, which the tourist office can book for you. There are two **hostels**; the comfortable *VIP Albury Backpackers*, near the train station at 452 David St (℡02/6041 1822, ℮thecanoeguy@hotmail.com; dorms $16, rooms ❷), is a slightly shambolic place, reminiscent of a student flat (with the social life to match). The friendly owner rents canoes (half-day $18, full day $25) and arranges overnight **canoe trips** ($55) down the mighty Murray. He can also help line up **fruit-picking and farm work**, as well as get you involved with **conservation volunteers**. The second hostel, the *Albury Motor Village YHA*, 372 Wagga Rd (Hume Highway), Lowington (℡02/6040 2999, ℮albury@yhavic.org.au; dorms $18.50, rooms ❷), is situated at a caravan park with a pool, but it's 5km out of town. If the hostels don't appeal but you're on a tight budget, try *The New Albury* (℡02/6021 3599, ℮matthewsheridan@hotmail.com; ❸); one of the best-value central hotels, this place has its own Irish bar, and is blissfully situated off the highway at 491 Kiewa St. The most upmarket places to stay are the *Carlton Country Comfort*, on the corner of Dean and Elizabeth streets (℡02/6021 5366, ℮ccalbury@dragnet.com.au; ❺), with a swimming pool, sauna, gym, spa and room service; or for a little lost grandeur, you could try *Gondowring B&B* (℡02/6041 4437, ⊛www.gundowringbb.com.au; ❺), a restored Federation residence, with full country breakfasts served on the verandah. **Campers** are catered for at *Trek-31 Tourist Park*, 8km north on the highway (℡02/6025 4355, ℮trek31@bigpond.com; cabins ❷).

Dean Street is lined with interchangeable, ever-changing cafés and is very much the main street for **food**: if you are ravenous and broke, head for *The Commercial Club* which serves up one of the best deals in Australia, with all the pasta, steak, seafood and salad you can eat for $10. For something a little less functional, the retro *Electra Café* on the corner of Dean and Macaley streets serves a variety of internationally influenced meals on kitsch crockery (Mon–Sat 10am–10pm, Sun 10am–3pm; live music on Tues), while *Café L'Espresso*, opposite the cinema, serves excellent coffee and has **Internet** access. An alternative way of getting a feed is to visit the **Hume Weir Trout Farm**, a pleasant spot with landscaped gardens and waterfalls off the Riverina Highway (daily 9am–dusk; free; ⊛www.humeweirtrout.com.au), where you're provided with rods so that you can catch your own freshwater trout; there are barbecues here to cook the fish, although you must pay for the catch by the kilo.

About 10km north of Albury on the Hume Highway, the larger-than-life **Ettamogah Pub** is a parody of an Outback pub, straight out of a sketch by the Aussie cartoonist Maynard, although the precariously askew hotel really does serve drinks. Walk up the slanting staircase to the veering verandah where there are great views of the surrounding countryside. A touristy tin shack in the back flogs souvenirs.

The Murrumbidgee Irrigation Area

Irrigation has transformed the area northwest of Albury, between the Lachlan and the Murrumbidgee rivers, into a fertile valley full of orchards, vineyards and rice paddies, cut through with irrigation canals. The **Murrumbidgee Irrigation Area** (or **MIA**) extends over two thousand square kilometres, a mostly flat and – from ground level at least – featureless landscape that nonetheless is responsible for producing most of Australia's rice, approximately eighty percent of New South Wales's wine grapes, and sixty percent of its citrus fruits. The water for the irrigation area is stored in Burrinjuck and Blowering dams and flows over 400km down the Murrumbidgee River to Berembed Weir, before being diverted into the main canal, which is 155km long and feeds a network of 1450km of supply canals.

Probably the main reason you'll visit this off-the-beaten-track area is to find **work**, which there is in abundance for the intensive fruit picking throughout the year (this is the largest citrus-growing area in Australia). At the peak season there are up to three thousand jobs going begging. The season starts in August with oranges, which are picked right through to March, then onions in November, and stonefruit, prunes and melons from December to March, overlapping with the grape harvest in February and March. Pay is calculated according to the amount picked and, basing yourself in Griffith or Leeton, you'll need your own transport – if only a bicycle – since the orchards are up to 10km outside town. To avoid the possibility of a wasted trip, due to a late season or a poor crop, it's essential to check with Employment National (see p.67) before turning up.

Griffith

Citrus orchards line the way into **GRIFFITH**, with a range of low hills in the background. The major centre of the MIA, it's known for its large **Italian population** and its enduring cultural life, despite the fact that some of the families arrived here around the time of World War I. More came in the 1920s, having already tried mining in Broken Hill, and the area attracted post-World War II Italian immigrants as well. Needless to say, a string of excellent Italian cafés and restaurants line the tree-filled main street of Banna Avenue, and the majority of **wineries** are run by Italian families. Designed by Walter Burley Griffin, the landscape architect from Chicago who was responsible for Canberra, the city has since grown beyond his plan.

For free maps and information, head for the **Griffith Visitors Centre**, on the corner of Jondaryan and Banna avenues (Mon–Fri 9am–5pm; ☎02/6962 4145, ⓦ www.griffith.nsw.gov.au). They can arrange for you to hop on a school bus-run (7–9am & 3.30–5pm) to see the surrounding district, its rice paddies, citrus and stonefruit orchards and vineyards, for around a dollar. An even better way to get an overview of the area is to head for **Scenic Hill**, the escarpment that forms the northern boundary of the city. The **Sir Dudley de Chair's Lookout** gives a panoramic view of the horticultural enterprises below. Immediately beneath this rocky outcrop, is the **Hermit's Cave** where Valerio Recetti, an Italian immigrant, lived alone and quite undetected for ten years, working only at night and early in the morning to create his home in the caves. One cave contained a small shrine where you can still see a painted cross. During World War II he was interned in Hay (around 150km to the west of

Griffith) – as were most of the local Italians – and in 1952 he returned to Italy, where he died.

Pioneer Park, in an extensive bushland setting 1.5km west of the lookout and 2km from the city centre (daily 9am–4.30pm; $7), has 36 buildings re-creating the era of the early MIA. The most interesting part is "Bagtown", a reconstruction of an early makeshift town built in 1910 to meet the needs of the Murrumbidgee Irrigation Area canal workers and pioneer farmers, and so-called because the homes were made of hessian cement bags with corrugated-iron roofs.

There are sixteen **wineries**, many Italian-run, in the area surrounding Griffith. Eleven are open to the public (some by appointment only); all are detailed in the *Griffith Visitors' Guide* booklet available from the visitors centre. The very first winery, McWilliam's, was established in 1913 and holds tastings in a building resembling a wine barrel (Mon–Sat 9am–5pm); there are barbecues in the grounds. Several other wineries have been around for more than fifty years, dating from the post-World War I influx of Italian immigrants. One of these is Rossetto Wines on Rossetto Road, off Leeton Road (Mon–Sat 8.30am–5.30pm). Still run by the same family, it's a down-to-earth, friendly concern known for its muscats and ports.

The *Pioneer Park* has bunkhouse **accommodation** for backpackers and fruit-pickers (℡02/6962 4196; dorms $13, cheap weekly rates), but it's a long uphill walk out of town, with no public transport. There's also a very basic back-packers, *Griffith International Hostel*, at 112 Binya St (℡02/6964 4236, ⓦwww.griffithinternational.com.au; dorms $15), but don't expect luxury. Most pickers camp or stay in cabins at the *Griffith Tourist Caravan Park*, 919 Willandra Ave, 2km south of the centre (℡02/6964 2144, ⓕ6964 1126; cabins ❷) or the cheap and basic campsite at the showground on the edge of town. For a bit more comfort, the popular *Victoria Hotel*, 384 Banna Ave (℡02/6962 1299, ⓕ6962 1081; ❷, cheap weekly rates), has basic rooms, but there's a TV lounge with tea and coffee provided, a cool, covered courtyard, counter lunches downstairs, live entertainment (Wed–Sat) and quality bistro meals from Tuesday to Saturday.

There's no shortage of good Italian places to **eat and drink** on Banna Avenue, with the pavement tables of the hugely popular *Bassano Café* being a good place to sample excellent coffee and delicious focaccia; you can also get pasta, home-made *gelati*, pastries and biscuits. The much cheaper bakery-style *Bertoldo's Pasticerria* has budget-priced and filling pasta dishes. For gourmet picnic supplies, *Riverina Grove* on Whybrow Street is a fantastic deli stocking a wide range of regional produce. Casual meals are served at the *Belvedere Restaurant and Pizza. Romeo & Giulietta Pizza Restaurant*, 40 Mackay Ave (Thurs–Sun dinner), uses a wood-fired oven for its delicious pizzas. For drinking, the town convenes at the *Gemini Hotel* on Banna Avenue, where you can sip a cocktail or down a schooner while listening to live music at the weekends.

Around Griffith

Twenty-five kilometres northeast of Griffith is the **Cocoparra National Park** in the woodland-covered Cocoparra Range. Enquire about camping and bushwalking at the NPWS office at 200 Yambil St in Griffith (℡02/6966 8100). Much further away, on the flat plains 185km northwest of Griffith, is **Willandra National Park**, reached via **Hillston** (64km from Griffith) on the unsealed Hillston–Mossgiel road. The park was created in 1971 from a section of the vast Big Willandra pastoral station, a famous stud merino property that had operated since the 1860s, and now has several temporary wetland areas. As well as enabling you to experience the semi-arid riverine plains country at close quarters, a visit to the 1918 **homestead** gives an insight into station life and the wool industry. Wet weather makes all the roads to Willandra impassable, so check before you head out with the **park office** in Hillston (℡02/6967 8159). You can also contact the park office about **accommodation bookings**, with shared rooms available in shearers' quarters (●) – take extra supplies in case you get rained in.

Fifty-nine kilometres southeast of Griffith, **LEETON** is the third-largest town in the MIA, with a quarter of its population of Italian extraction; like Griffith, it was designed by Walter Burley Griffin. For information on the area and details of visiting its **rice mill**, head for the **Leeton Visitor Information Centre**, 10 Yanco Ave (Mon–Fri 9am–5pm, Sat & Sun 9.30am–12.30pm; ℡02/6953 6481, ⓦwww.leeton.nsw.gov.au). There are two **caravan parks**, both 2km southeast: the *Leeton Caravan Park*, on Yanco Avenue (℡ & ℉02/6953 3323), caters best for fruit-pickers with basic bunkrooms (●), but also has on-site vans (●) and en-suite cabins with TV (❷); while *An Oasis Caravan Park* on Corbie Hill Road (℡02/6953 3882, ℉6953 6256; vans ●, cabins and spacious cottage ❷), caters more for tourists with a better range of facilities. The large, tree-filled property at *Gilgal* is also a great spot to pitch a tent, with cheap rates for pickers. Despite the Italian population, Leeton feels less cosmopolitan than Griffith, but you can nevertheless enjoy an Italian **meal** at the *MIA Social Club* on Racecourse Road (daily from 3pm; ℡02/6953 4357).

Narrandera

Thirty kilometres southeast of Leeton, at the junction of the Sturt and Newell highways, **NARRANDERA** is a popular overnight stop en route from Adelaide to Sydney, or Melbourne to Brisbane. It's actually a very pleasant place to take a break, set on the Murrumbidgee River with streets lined with tall native and deciduous trees owing to the foresight of the pioneer settlers; its white cedars, which blossom in November, are particularly beautiful.

A good place to cool down is **Lake Talbot**, a willow-surrounded expanse of water flowing from the Murrumbidgee River. Right next to the lake, with just a grassy bank between them, is the splendidly sited Lake Talbot Pool (Nov–April Mon–Fri 6am–9pm; adults $2.40, children $1.30). The complex is family-friendly, with picnic areas and barbecues, various watery slides, children's pools and an Olympic-sized **swimming** pool. Nearby, a reserve along the river has been declared a **koala regeneration area** for a disease-free colony of koalas; to get there, follow the **Bundidgerry Walking Track** around Lake Talbot and the Murrumbidgee River. Free maps of the track are available at the friendly **Narrandera Tourist Information Centre**, in Narrandera Park on the Newell Highway (daily 9am–5pm; ℡02/6959 1766 or 1800 672 392, ⓔtourist.centre@narranderra.nsw.gov.au). Fishing fanatics could try out the lake or river for some Murray cod, yellowbelly or silverbeam; fish abound in the river and, 5km east of Narrandera, off the Sturt Highway, the **John Lake Centre** at the Inland Fisheries Research Station (Mon–Fri 9am–4pm; guided tours 10.30am; ℡02/6959 1488), which carries out research into the species of the Murray, Murrumbidgee and Darling rivers, can provide further details.

The best place to **stay** in Narrandera is the *Historic Star Lodge*, 64 Whitton St (℡02/6959 1768, ⓦwww.historicstarlodge.com.au; ❹), a fine B&B with an award-winning restaurant. Classified by the National Trust, the building retains many of its original 1916 features and is run by a friendly couple. If that's a little beyond your budget, head for East Street, the main street for hotels and motels, with several classic country hotels, complete with iron-lace balconies, all offering very reasonably priced accommodation. The most appealing of these is the *Murrumbidgee Hotel* at 159 East St (☎02/6959 2011; ❶), or try the *Mid Town Motor Inn*, situated off the highway on the corner of East and Larmer streets (☎02/6959 2122, ℗6959 3271; ❸), which has a swimming pool. Another good spot is the shady *Lake Talbot Caravan Park*, well positioned above the lake and pool (☎02/6959 1302, ✉ltcp@webfront.net.au; cabins and on-site vans ❷). Aside from the *Historic Star Lodge* (lunch Thurs–Sat, dinner Tues–Sat), the best place for a **good meal** is the reliable *Ex-Servicemen's Club* opposite the information centre on Bolton Street.

Wagga Wagga

WAGGA WAGGA, known simply as "Wagga" to the locals, is the most populous inland city in Australia with around 58,000 inhabitants, but it still has the appearance of a slow and solid country town. Its curious name comes from the Widadjuri, the largest of the New South Wales Aboriginal peoples: Wagga means crow and its repetition signifies the plural. Set on the Murrumbidgee River just under 100km east of Narrandera, with a beautiful sandy river beach to swim from, close to the main street, it is the capital of the Riverina region. The city has a **university**, Charles Sturt, boasting a well-regarded wine course and its own on-campus **winery**, which is open for tastings and cellar-door sales on Coolamon Rd (Mon–Fri 11am–5pm, Sat & Sun 11am–4pm; ☎02/6933 2435); an ABC radio station; and a regional theatre.

Wagga's main attractions, though, are on the edge of the city. To the south, about a half-hour hike by foot, are the impressive **Botanic Gardens** (daily: summer 7.30am–8pm; winter 7.30am–4.15pm; free) at the base of Willans Hill, a huge place with such attractions as a walk-through bird aviary where over three hundred species flit about, a children's petting zoo, bush trails and picnic areas, specialist gardens of cacti and succulents, and a Chinese-style garden, plus a kiosk café. On the first and third Sunday of each month, a model train takes children around about for $0.80 a ride. There's a **Historical Museum** (Tues–Sat 10am–5pm, Sun 2–5pm; free) on Lord Baden Powell Drive, by the Botanic Gardens, with a hotchpotch collection of old farm machinery, printing presses and a display of over 200 door knockers. Further to the south, the artificial **Lake Albert** is a popular spot for water-skiing. Canoe cruises are also available down by the Murrumbidgee River (2hr; $12; ☎02/6925 5807).

Back in the centre, the **Wagga Wagga Regional Art Gallery** on Baylis Street (Mon–Sat 10am–5pm, Sun noon–4pm; free) is home to the National Art Glass collection, a stunning array of contemporary glass pieces, and the Carnegie Print Collection, with over five hundred originals from innovative Australian printmakers from 1940 on; if you're lucky, Sally Robinson's vivid *Kakadu* series might be on display. The adjacent **Museum of the Riverina** (Tues–Sat 10am–5pm, Sun 2–5pm; free) often hosts exhibitions on indigenous artists and local crafts.

On Sunday mornings a bit of life is sparked by the **markets** (7.30am–noon) at the Grace Bros car park on O'Reilly Street, which have secondhand clothes and books, crafts, local produce and cakes on sale. The **Ngungilanna Culture Centre**, 11 Gurwood St (call to check opening hours on ☎02/6921 8982), is also worth checking out: run by the Wagga Advancement Aboriginal Corporation, it sells locally made crafts and clothes, as well as books, cards and paintings from around Australia.

Practicalities

Roughly halfway between Sydney (470km) and Melbourne (435km), Wagga is just off the Sturt Highway, the main route between Adelaide and Sydney. Interstate McCafferty's/Greyhound Pioneer **buses** heading to and from Brisbane, Sydney, Adelaide, Melbourne and Canberra all pass through, stopping at the train station, a little out of town. To **get around**, you can rent bikes from Kidson's Cycles at 107 Fitzmaurice St (☏02/6921 4474), or a car from Avis, on the corner of Edward and Fitzharding streets (☏02/6921 9977). Baylis Street, the main strip (and Fitzmaurice St, its continuation), extends from the train station to the bridge spanning the Murrumbidgee River.

The **Wagga Wagga Visitors Centre**, on Tarcutta Street, close to the river (daily 9am–5pm; ☏02/6926 9629, ⓦwww.wagga.nsw.gov.au or ⓦwww.tourismwaggawagga.com.au), dispenses free handy driving maps. It doesn't book **accommodation**, but does have information about **farmstays** in the surrounding countryside. In town, the old *Romano's Hotel*, on the corner of Sturt and Fitzmaurice streets (☏02/6921 2013, ⓕ6921 8357; ❷), has been beautifully renovated; rooms are decorated in late-nineteenth-century style, and some have baths. The *Victoria Hotel*, 55 Baylis St (☏02/6921 5233, ⓦwww.vichotel.net; ❶), has no-frills pub doubles and reasonable singles, while *The Manor*, 38 Morrow St (☏02/6921 5962; ❹), is a good B&B with excellent weekly rates for singles, next to the beautiful riverfront park. The best-situated **caravan park** is the shady and peaceful *Wagga Beach Tourist Park*, 2 Johnston St (☏02/6931 0603; en-suite cabins ❸), with a free gas barbecue and a backpackers' room right on the town beach, five minutes' walk from the main shops.

One of the best places to **eat** is the *Wagga Wagga Winery* (☏02/6922 1221), fifteen minutes' drive out of town on the Oura road. The wines themselves are nothing special, but the excellent local food and the setting, in an old pine log building (with disabled access), a large verandah and a garden area, combine to make a very pleasurable experience. In the town centre, the Baylis/Fitzmaurice strip and its side streets provide fertile eating ground. *Sugars Coffee Lounge* at 16 Forsyth St has fresh and healthy focaccia and American-style bagels, as well as excellent coffee and a wide range of breakfast fare. *Romano's Hotel* (see above) has a modern and very stylish café/bar that makes a decent espresso and serves breakfast all day, and the slick *Victoria Hotel* (see above) has an extensive, quality bistro menu and upstairs balcony open Friday and Saturday nights. For Mexican, try *Montezuma's* cosy wooden cantina at 85 Baylis St (lunch Wed–Fri, dinner Tues–Sun). The *Tourist Hotel* at 97 Fitzmaurice St has a great place to eat out back – *Bernie's Veggie Restaurant* (lunch Wed–Fri, dinner Wed–Sat), serving an array of sumptuous, cheap meals, in a room with an open-fire and retro decor.

Wagga also has several huge **clubs** providing free courtesy buses. *Wagga RSL*, on the corner of Dobbs and Kincaid streets, also has a Chinese restaurant and Friday-night piano bar, while the *Wagga Leagues Club*, Gurwood Street, has a good brasserie and live entertainment every Saturday. For drinking and dancing, the town's most popular spot is the newly refurbished and ever-lively *Victoria Hotel*, whilst *Maddison's* at 146 Fitzmaurice St (Wed–Sat) is Wagga's venue for bands and irresponsible student shenanigans. The *Black Swan Hotel* (alias "The Muddy Duck") in North Wagga, close to the university, is eternally popular with the student population.

The lower Murray: Albury to Wentworth

Following the **lower Murray River** between Albury (see p.354) and the South Australian border, there's little of interest on the New South Wales side until the old port town of **Wentworth** and its surrounding storehouse of ancient Aboriginal history around **Lake Victoria** and in the remote **Mungo National Park**. The main centres are on the Victorian side of the river, Mildura (see p.1016) and Echuca (see p.1022) chief among them, although the New South Wales riverside towns of **Tocumwal** and **Corowa**, not far from Albury, are pleasant enough.

Corowa and Tocumwal

Following the river, it's 56km from Albury northwest to **COROWA**, across the Murray from Victoria's **Rutherglen wine region** (see p.1043). Blue flags flying all over town proclaim it to be the birthplace of Federation, since the Federation Conference of 1893 was held at Corowa's courthouse. The **Corowa Tourist Information Centre** is at 88 Sanger St (daily 9am–5pm; ℡02/6033 3221, ⓦwww.corowa.nsw.gov.au). There are stacks of **motels** in town offering very reasonable accommodation, such as the *Murray View* at 193 River St (℡02/6033 2144, ⓔsandrall@bigpond.com; ❸), with a swimming pool, spa and barbecues (some rooms have a private garden courtyard). **Campers** could try the *Ball Park Holiday Retreat*, by the Murray on Bridge Road (℡02/6033 1426; cabins and vans ❷). There are several places on the main street where you can get a **meal**, including the *Star Hotel*, which does a good-value roast of the day; the *Royal Hotel*, which serves up decent counter food; and the *Old Corowa Bakehouse*, a popular café/bakery that opens early.

On the way to Tocumwal, which is just under 80km from Corowa, there's a **boomerang factory** at **BAROOGA** called the Binghi Boomerang, where you can watch boomerangs being made and try them out yourself (call ℡03/5873 4463 for times). **TOCUMWAL** itself ("Toc" to locals) is a small, pleasant river town: its **Foreshore Park**, just behind the main street, is peaceful and shaded by large gum trees, and there's a sandy river beach only ten minutes' walk away. In front of the park, there's a rather tacky fibreglass model of a huge Murray cod, and alongside is the **Tocumwal Visitor Information Centre** (daily 9am–5pm; ℡03/5874 2131, ⓕ5874 3300), which provides information about the area and can book rides in a glider that flies over the Murray.

Tocumwal has some classic old **country hotels**, most notably the *Tocumwal Hotel* on Deniliquin Street (℡03/5874 2025; ❸), a single-storey hotel built in 1861, with self-contained motel units and an iron-lace verandah; rates include breakfast. Next door is Central Store Antiques, which has good tearooms at the back serving scones, jam and cream or reasonably priced sandwiches and light meals. The best place to **camp** is the riverfront *Bushlands on the Murray Holiday Park* (℡03/5874 2752, ⓕ5874 2202; cabins ❸), right on the swimming beach.

Wentworth and Lake Victoria

Once a thriving river port, **WENTWORTH** is now a sleepy old town overshadowed by nearby Mildura, 31km back along the Sturt Highway and across the Murray River in Victoria. Located at the junction of the Murray and the Darling, the "two rivers" town was for seventy years the centre of river trade between New South Wales, Victoria and South Australia. The extension of the railway at the turn of the century bypassed Wentworth, however, and at the same time killed off much of the river trade. Nowadays the town makes a pleasant stopover en route to or from Broken Hill, 261km north on the sealed **Silver City Highway**, or a brief excursion from Mildura (in Victoria). Enquire at the **Wentworth Visitor Information Centre**, 28 Darling St (Mon–Fri 9.30am–4pm, Sat & Sun 10am–2pm; ℡03/5027 3624, ⓦwww .wentworth.nsw.gov.au/tourism), about river cruises on the MV *Loyalty*, built around 1914 (or direct on ☎03/5027 3224; $14). You could visit the **Old Wentworth Gaol** on Beverly Street (daily 10am–5pm; $5), built of handmade bricks in 1879, but the interpretive displays consist of bits of curling cardboard and dejected dummies, making it hardly worth the entrance fee. Opposite, **Pioneer World** (daily 10.30am–5pm; $4) is a folk museum exhibiting items related to Aboriginal and European history of the area, and very tacky models of large animals. You can also take a tour through citrus groves at **Orange World** in Mourquong, back towards Mildura (Mon–Fri & Sun 10am–4pm; guided 1hr tractor tours 10.30am & 2.30pm; $6).

The Aboriginal land council in Wentworth organizes visits to significant **Aboriginal sites** around Lake Victoria to the west, and Mungo National Park (see below) among the dry salt lakes to the northeast. The tours are run by Harry Nanya Tours at Shop 10, Wentworth Place, Sandych Street (☎03/5027 2076), and are accompanied by accredited Barkindji guides. In 1994, ancient Aboriginal graves were discovered at **Lake Victoria** – the Barkindji had always spoken of their existence. The partial draining of the eleven-square-kilometre lake revealed skeletons buried side by side and in deep layers; some of the estimated ten thousand graves date back six thousand years, in what is believed to be Australia's largest pre-industrial burial site – surpassing any such finds in Europe, Asia or North and South America. The site also challenges the premise that Aboriginal lifestyles were solely nomadic, suggesting that here at least they lived in semi-permanent dwellings around the lake.

Among the places to **stay** in Wentworth, the luxury apartments at the *Red Gum Lagoon Holiday Apartments*, 210 Adams St (☎03/5027 2063; ❹), are wonderful, offering free use of canoes and rowboats on the lagoon itself. Another good waterfront choice is the *Willow Bend Caravan Park* on Darling Street (☎03/5027 3213; on-site vans ❶, cabins ❷), right near the shops but also at the confluence of the Darling and Murray rivers, where there are plenty of trees – watch out for ferocious possums, though. You can get out on the water by renting a **houseboat** from *Twin Rivers Houseboats* at 1 William St (☎03/5027 3626 or 1800 037 047; sleeps up to 6; $730–1500 per week off-peak, $1055–1750 peak). If you're looking for employment in the area, perhaps the best accommodation option is *Urumba Backpackers* at 81 Darling St (☎02/5027 2499, ❶), who can help with finding work.

Mungo National Park

Mungo National Park, in the far southwest of New South Wales, is most easily reached from the river townships of Wentworth (see above) or Mildura (over the Victorian border, about 110km away – see p.1016); organized tours run from both towns. If you want to tackle it on your own, you'll need a 4WD. The park is part of the dried-up **Willandra Lakes System**, a designated UNESCO World Heritage area in recognition of its Aboriginal legacy and record of past climates preserved in the landscape. The Willandra Lakes contain the longest continuous record of Aboriginal life in Australia, dating back more than forty thousand years. During the Ice Ages, between forty thousand and fifteen thousand years ago, the system formed a vast chain of freshwater lakes strung along Willandra Creek, then the main channel of the Lachlan River, flowing into the Murrumbidgee. The waters teemed with fish, attracting waterbirds and mammals, while Aborigines camped at the shores of the lake to fish and hunt, and buried their dead in the sand dunes. When the lakes started drying out fifteen thousand years ago, Aborigines continued to live near soaks along the old river channel. The park covers most of one of these dry lake beds, and its dominant feature is a great, crescent-shaped dune (a lunette), at the eastern edge of the lake, commonly referred to as the **Walls of China**. Elsewhere, the vegetation consists of saltbush on the lake floors and mallee (a low-growing, scrubby type of eucalypt) on the dune fields. Casuarinas grow on the sand plains, and western grey and red kangaroos can sometimes be seen.

There's an NPWS office (☎03/5021 8900) on the corner of the Sturt Highway at Buronga near Mildura, Victoria. The official **visitors centre** is by the southwest entrance to the park, and has a very informative display about the geological and Aboriginal history of the national park; nearby the impressive old **Mungo Woolshed** is open for inspection. From there it's a short drive to the lookout point on the rim of the lake, the former shore, from where you can look across the dry lakebed to the Walls of China. A signposted track takes you on a return trip across the lake floor to the Walls of China, then over the dune and to the northwest part of the park. At sunset, or on nights with a full moon, the scenery takes on an eerie, otherworldly quality.

For **accommodation** nearby, beds in the former shearers' quarters, or at NPWS campsites in the park, can be booked in advance through the visitors centre. Otherwise, try *Mungo Lodge* on the Mildura road (☎03/5029 7297; ❸), which has motel units and self-contained cottages as well as a licensed restaurant.

Back o' Bourke: the Outback

As you travel beyond Dubbo into the northwest corner of New South Wales you'll be struck by the red plains that make the area the quintessential Australian Outback. The searing summer heat makes touring uncomfortable from December to February, and you'd be well advised to visit at a cooler time of year. **Bourke**, about 370km along the sealed **Mitchell Highway**, is generally considered the turning point; venture further and you're into the land known as "Back o' Bourke" – the back of beyond.

En route to Bourke, the Mitchell passes through **NYNGAN**, at the geographical centre of New South Wales and 133km from Dubbo, where the sealed **Barrier Highway** heads west for 584 sweltering kilometres, through Cobar and Wilcannia, to Broken Hill. Flood-prone Nyngan, on the eastern bank of the Bogan River, is a sizeable (compared to what you'll find beyond), old-fashioned country town where you can refuel and freshen up. There's a small, shady park on Main Street where you can slump at picnic tables; *Arnold's Take Away* at 133 Main St – a spacious café where generous pots of tea help to quench thirst and a ceiling fan manages to circulate a bit of air – is another option here. For more on the area, see ⓦ www.outbacknsw.org.au.

Bourke and around

BOURKE is mainly known for its very remoteness, and this alone is enough to attract tourists; once you've crossed the North Bourke Bridge that spans the **Darling River**, you're officially "out back". If you want to have a drink in the "Back o' Bourke" without pressing too far into the endless, scarcely populated plains all around, try the *North Bourke Hotel*, a shabby, wooden, green-tin-roofed Outback pub where bush poets congregate once a year during the annual **Mateship Festival** weekend normally held in late September (details from the information centre). The lively festival began in 1993 to mark the centenary of the poet **Henry Lawson**'s stay in Bourke during a particularly harsh drought. Discovering mateship in hardship was but a microcosm for the fierce nationalism that arose in 1890s depression and drought-struck Australia.

Work was scarce and Lawson often slept out in the town's Central Park, where a plaque is dedicated to him and to two other bush poets who lived in the area at around the same time – Will Ogilvie and **Breaker Morant**, the latter executed during the Boer War. Another famous resident was the well-known ophthalmologist **Fred Hollows**, who began working here in the 1970s with local Aborigines suffering from cataract blindness. As a result of his work the number of cases of incurable blindness among Aboriginal peoples throughout Australia has been halved. Hollows was buried in the town in 1993.

Bourke was a bustling river port from the 1860s to the 1930s, and there are some fine examples of riverboat-era architecture, including the huge reconstructed **wharf**, which can be explored – from here a track winds along the magnificent, tree-lined river. A new port with paddle-steamer cruises is promised, but has been "under development" for a number of years. Thanks to irrigation with Darling River water, crops as diverse as cotton, lucerne, citrus, grapes and sorghum are successfully grown here despite the 40°C summer heat, while Bourke is also the commercial centre for a vast sheep- and cattle-breeding area: to the north there are rich grazing lands across the Queensland border around Cunnamulla and Charleville.

With a population of three thousand (approximately twenty-five percent Aboriginal), Bourke acts as a base for regional services and welfare. Unfortunately, there is sporadic trouble involving alcoholism and aimless youngsters, and after dark the atmosphere can be somewhat intimidating. Visitors are best off drinking in the very pleasant *Port of Bourke Hotel* (see below), the *Oxley Club* or *Bowling Club*, and avoiding the *Post Office Hotel*.

Practicalities

The **information centre** is inside the former train station on Anson Street (Easter–Oct daily 9am–5pm; Nov–Easter Mon–Fri 9am–5pm; ☎02/6872 2800, ✉tourinfo@lisp.com.au). It can provide "**Mud Maps**", roughly drawn maps marking places of interest off the beaten track in the surrounding area: but bear in mind that these destinations could be as far as 200km away. It can also arrange Back o' Bourke tours (Mon–Sat 9.30am–1pm; 3hr tour covering orchards and vineyards in summer, historical buildings and cotton farms in winter; $10). An ongoing project to seal the roads in this corner of New South Wales has made it much more accessible than in previous times, but many lesser-travelled routes remain little more than dirt tracks. Up-to-date information for visitors can also be found at Ⓦwww.backobourke.com.au.

Countrylink buses arrive here from Dubbo four times weekly, and you can also fly here with Airlink, four times weekly, from Sydney via Dubbo. **Accommodation** in town includes the pleasant *Port of Bourke Hotel* on Mitchell Street (☎02/6872 2544; ❸), which has air-conditioned rooms, some sharing a bath, some en suite, but all opening out on to a sociable verandah, and the *Bourke Riverside Motel*, 3 Mitchell St (☎02/6872 2539, Ⓕ6872 1471; ❹), boasting deluxe heritage cottages with king-size beds and a communal swimming pool. An ideal way to see how life is lived out here is to stay on an **Outback station**; the information centre has details of those that welcome visitors, among them *Comeroo Camel Station* (☎02/6874 7735; prices on application, but in the region of $20 per person self-catering and $50 full board in the homestead), a unique experience with artesian hot bores, river waterholes with yabbying and fishing opportunities, and resident buffalo and ostriches. For those interested in **employment** in Bourke – harvesting tomatoes, onions and grapes between November and February and cotton-chipping between December and February – *Kidman's Camp Tourist Park* (☎02/6872 1612,

ⓕ6872 3107), 8km north of town on the Darling River, may be able to point you in the right direction.

The *Port of Bourke Hotel* is the best place in town for **food** and **drink**: their excellent bistro meals (Thurs–Sat) are fresh and healthy, or you can eat counter meals (Mon, Tues & Wed) out in the shady beer garden. A palatable alternative is the Chinese food proffered at the *Bowling Club* on the corner of Mitchell and Richard streets, and there's good coffee at *Gecko Café* on Oxley Street. **Internet** facilities are available in the library on Mitchell Street (Mon–Fri 9am–5pm), where there is also a reasonable supermarket.

West and north of Bourke

West of Bourke, it's 193km to the small settlement of **WANAARING**, past a reconstruction of **Fort Bourke**, built by Major Mitchell in 1835 as a secure depot to protect his stocks from Aboriginal people, while he explored the Darling River. Near Fort Bourke is the kibbutz-like **Cornerstone Community**, a cotton-farming operation and teaching centre run by Christians; they put a lot of effort into the local community, including running the tourist office, and visitors are welcome.

Northwest, the road runs 215km to **HUNGERFORD**, on the Queensland border, and the **Dingo Fence** (see p.380). The state border bisects Hungerford, which consists of little more than a couple of houses, a post office and a pub but was made famous (amongst Australians) by a Henry Lawson short story of the same name. Make sure you shut the steel dingo-proof fence behind you when you drive through: there's a $1000 fine if you don't. The heart of the town is the corrugated-iron *Royal Mail Hotel* (ⓣ07/4650 4093; ❷) just near the fence in Queensland: you can buy fuel, bread, milk and meat here, excellent **meals** are served until 9pm, and the friendly owners are happy to give advice. You can also **stay** in the bedrooms running along the front veranda, the caravan or bunkroom in the back, or camp.

Heading directly **north** from Bourke, the sealed Mitchell Highway goes right up to just past Charleville in Queensland (see p.573). If you're passing this way, **BARRINGUN**, on the border 135km from Bourke, is worth a stop-off just to have a drink at the remarkably genteel *Tattersalls Hotel*, set amid a flower-scented garden, once frequented by Breaker Morant. The hotel serves only snacks and doesn't have any accommodation. Across the road and closer to the border is the painted tin shed that comprises the *Bush Tucker Inn* (ⓣ02/6874 7584; ❶), which has **meals**, rooms, fuel and camping space.

South and east of Bourke

Because the empty, featureless plains seem to extend in all directions, the elongated rise of **Mount Gunderbooka** (498m), about 70km **southwest** of Bourke en route to Cobar, likened to a mini-Ayers Rock, is striking. It was also of great cultural significance to the Aboriginal people of the area, with semi-permanent waterholes and caves; several **cave paintings** can be seen, contact the NPWS on Oxley Street in Bourke for details (ⓣ02/6872 2744).

Twenty-eight kilometres **east** of Bourke, en route to Brewarrina, is a turn-off south to **Mount Oxley**, climbed by the explorers Sturt and Hume in 1829 to herald the white settlement in the area. It's on private property, so you must first pick up a key from the information centre in Bourke. The town of **BRE-WARRINA** (locals call it "Bree"), 100km east of Bourke on the Barwon River, has a large Aboriginal population. The abundant fish stocks in the river made the area a natural fishery for the original population and the **fish traps** – large, partly submerged boulders – can still be seen in the river. The excellent **Aboriginal Cultural Museum** (Mon–Fri 9am–4.30pm; $6), located near the ancient fisheries in an award-winning, earth-covered building similar to an Aboriginal shelter, explains the history of the area's Ngemba people and offers walkabout **tours**. One of the guides is a teenager whose grandfather recorded over two hundred tapes of his tribe's language, thus saving it for posterity; these days she is entrusted with educating others in the tongue.

Cobar

Since copper was discovered here in 1869, **COBAR**, just under 160km south of Bourke and the first real stop on the Barrier Highway between Nyngan and Broken Hill, has experienced three mining booms. Today, it's home to the vast **CSA Mine**, said to be the most highly mechanized in Australia, extracting about 850,000 tonnes of copper every year. Earlier booms resulted in a number of impressive public buildings, among them the 1882 **courthouse** and the police station, as well as the *Great Western Hotel* on Marshall Street, whose iron-lace verandahs are said to be the longest in the state. Cobar's most recent industry is **emu farming**: as more and more restaurants serve up bush tucker, the big birds are in demand. Most people only stop here to refuel before the monotonous 250-kilometre stretch to Wilcannia, and the town offers little to entice you otherwise. There is, however, a lovely picnic spot in Drummond Park, just off the highway on Linsley Street.

For more about the town, head for the **Great Cobar Outback Heritage Centre** (Mon–Fri 8.30am–5pm, Sat & Sun 9am–5pm; $5.50) on Marshall Street, which is also the local **tourist office** (☎02/6836 2448, ⓦwww .outbacknsw.org.au/cobar). They can tell you about above-ground tours of the CSA mine and provide Mud Maps showing places of interest around Cobar that are difficult to reach. Chief of these, and arguably one of the most significant **Aboriginal rock-art** locations in New South Wales, is the **Mount Grenfell Historic Site**, a 72-kilometre drive northwest of town. The rocky ridge contains three art sites with over a thousand motifs – human and animal figures, including the emus that you're still likely to see around the site, plus abstract designs and hand stencils. Older layers are visible beneath the more recent pigments, but there's no way to tell exactly how old the art is. The adjacent semi-permanent waterhole explains the significance of the site for the **Wongaibon people**. The NPWS in Cobar, at 19 Barton St (☎02/6836 2692), hands out a leaflet detailing the site, with its picnic and barbecue areas, toilets and limited water, plus a five-kilometre signposted return **walk** to the top of the ridge. To reach the site, head west along the Barrier Highway for 40km, then 32km north along a gravel road past Mount Grenfell Homestead to the picnic site.

There are a number of **motels** along the highway in Cobar; one to try – with air conditioning and pools is the *Cross Roads Motel*, at the corner of Bourke and Louth roads (☎ & ⓕ02/6836 2711; ❸); alternatively, there's the *Cobar Caravan Park* (☎02/6836 2425; on-site vans ❶, cabins ❷), or the tourist office can advise on **Outback bush stays**, including a recommended one on Trilby Station (☎02/6874 7420, ⓔliz@lisp.com.au).

Wilcannia and around

The next major town on the Barrier Highway is **WILCANNIA**, 260km west of Cobar. The former "Queen City of the West" was founded in 1864 and up until the early 1900s was a major port on the Darling River, from where produce was transported by paddle steamers and barges down the Darling–Murray river system to Adelaide. Droughts, the advent of the railways and the motor car put an end to the river trade, and today the ruins of the docks and the old lift-up bridge, along with a few impressive public buildings – the post office, police station, courthouse, Catholic convent and Council Chambers, which houses the **tourist centre** (daily 9am–5pm; ☎08/8091 5909) – are reminders of the once-prosperous era. Nowadays Wilcannia survives as a service centre for a far-flung Outback population, with its banks, shops, motels and service stations, though problems with unemployment and alcoholism combine to make it, while not exactly threatening, perhaps not the most welcoming place to stay.

Heading north or south of Wilcannia you can follow the river along one of Australia's last great 4WD adventures – **The Darling River Run** – 829km of Outback history, heritage and landscape running between Brewarrina and Wentworth. Further information on the run is available from Bourke Information Centre (see p.364).

You can travel the Darling River upstream **northwest** of Wilcannia all the way to Bourke (see p.363), just under 300km, on unsealed roads that closely follow the east and west banks with crossings at the settlements of Tilpa and Louth. Station properties dot the riverfront, including Mount Murchison Station, on the west side of the river 30km north of Wilcannia, said to have once been managed by the son of Charles Dickens. At **TILPA**, 130km north of Wilcannia, there's a classic Outback pub, the 1890s *Tilpa Hotel* (☎02/6837 3928, @tilpapub@bigpond.com.au; **1**), where you can find **meals** (the steak sandwiches come highly recommended), **accommodation** and **fuel**, and for a $2 donation towards the Royal Flying Doctor Service, you can immortalize your name on the pub's tin wall. Ninety-three kilometres further on, at **LOUTH**, *Shindy's Inn* sells diesel and petrol and has basic accommodation in miniature cabins (☎02/6874 7422; **2**).

White Cliffs

From Wilcannia, you can branch off the Barrier Highway, heading north along a road partly sealed for 30km, and then graded gravel for the final 67km to the **opal fields** at **WHITE CLIFFS**, 97km away. Besides opals, White Cliffs is famous for the extraordinary summer heat, and for the way in which the miners have avoided it since the 1890s (when about four thousand lived here) – many of the approximately two hundred residents live underground in so-called "dug-outs", where it's cool in summer and warm in winter. There are all sorts of underground attractions, as well as a high-tech attempt to exploit the climate in the form of an experimental solar power station. For the authentic underground experience, there are two places to stay: the original and very friendly *White Cliffs Underground Motel* (☎08/8091 6647 or 8091 6677, @underground.motel@telstra.com; **4**), which comes complete with licensed restaurant and outdoor swimming pool; and the only subterranean B&B, *PJs* (☎08/8091 6626, @pjsunderground@bigpond.com; **5**), where you have to share a bathroom and take off your shoes. Cheaper, above-ground options are the *White Cliffs Hotel* (☎08/8091 6606; **2**) and the *White Cliffs Family Inn* at the post office (☎ & ℻08/8091 6645; **3**). If you can bear the heat, there's also **camping** (with hot showers) to consider at *Opal Pioneer Reserve*, close to town (☎08/8091 6688). **Tourist information** is available on Keraro Road at the White Cliffs General Store (daily 8am–7pm; ☎ & ℻08/8091 6611).

There are several **tours** to White Cliffs from Broken Hill (see box on p.378); otherwise you'll need your own transport to get here. The only fuel stop between Wilcannia and Broken Hill is at the *Little Topar Hotel*, roughly halfway along the 195-kilometre stretch of the Barrier Highway.

Broken Hill and around

The ghosts of mining towns that died when the precious minerals ran out are scattered all over Australia. **BROKEN HILL**, on the other hand, celebrated its centenary in 1988, and its famous "**Line of Lode**", one of the world's major lead–silver–zinc ore bodies and the city's *raison d'être*, still has a little life left in it after being mined continuously for over 110 years. Inevitably, Broken Hill revolves around the mines, but in the last decade it has also evolved into a thriving arts centre, thanks to the initiative of the **Brushmen of the Bush**, a painting school founded by local artists Pro Hart, Hugh Schulz, Jack Absalom, John Pickup and the late Eric Minchin. Diverse talents have been attracted to Broken Hill, and their works are displayed in galleries scattered all over town. Some may be a bit on the tacky side, but others are excellent, and it's well worth devoting some time to gallery browsing. The city was also the memorable location for several scenes of the drag-queens-run-riot-in-the-Outback film *The Adventures of Priscilla, Queen of the Desert*, which was shot here in 1993.

Almost 1200km west of Sydney and about 500km east of Adelaide, this surprisingly gracious Outback mining town, with a feel and architecture reminiscent of the South Australian capital, and with a population of around 21,000, manages to create a welcome splash of **green** in the harsh desert landscape that surrounds it. Extensive revegetation schemes around Broken Hill have created grasslands that, apart from being visually pleasing, help contain the dust that used to make the residents' lives miserable. It's aided by a reliable water supply – secured for the first time only in 1953 – via a one-hundred-kilometre-long pipeline from the Darling River at Menindee. The city is also a convenient base for touring far northwest New South Wales and nearby areas in South Australia.

Remember to adjust your watch: Broken Hill operates on South Australian **Central Standard Time**, half an hour behind the rest of New South Wales. All local transport schedules are in CST, but you should always check.

Arrival, information and accommodation

Arriving in Broken Hill by bus or train, you'll be pretty centrally placed. The **bus terminal** (℡13 20 30) is behind the useful **tourist information centre**, at the corner of Bromide and Blende streets (daily 8.30am–5pm; ℡08/8087 6077, Ⓦwww.murrayoutback.org.au), where you can pick up a map ($3) for a self-guided Heritage Walk along Argent and Blende streets, or get information on the guided walking tour which delves into the city's history (Mon, Wed, Fri & Sat 10am, no tour late Dec to early Feb; 1hr 30min–2hr; donation). The **train station** is on Crystal Street, just a block below Argent Street, although most Countrylink services arrive in town by bus. The **airport** is about 5km south of town; there is no shuttle bus – a taxi costs around $10 and there are usually a few waiting; alternatively you can arrange to have a rental car waiting (see p.376).

Accommodation

Black Lion Inn 34 Bromide St ℡08/8087 4801. If the hostel is full this is a good budget option near the bus station. Basic but clean rooms in a separate half of the lively hotel away from the pub noise; ceiling fans but shared bathrooms. Single rates of $20 are comparable to a dorm price. ❶

The Imperial 88 Oxide St ℡08/8087 7444, Ⓔimperial@pcpro.net.au. Pricey four-star home-from-home in a beautiful old building with huge verandah. The five rooms have all mod-cons; there's also a kitchenette, a billiard room, a guest lounge and a garden. ❺

Lake View Caravan Park 1 Mann St, 3km north-east ℡ & Ⓕ08/8088 2250. A large site with

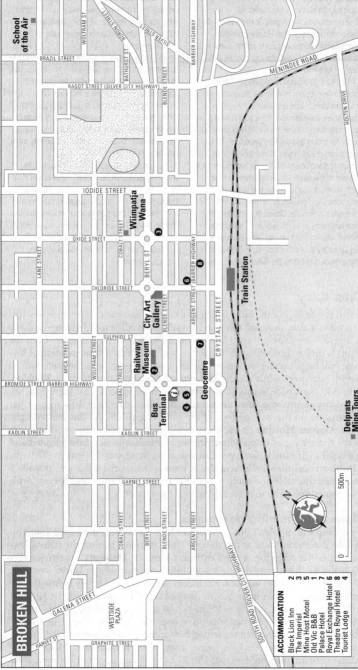

BROKEN HILL

School of the Air

Afghan Mosque ▲

▲ Barrier Highway

WOLFRAM ST

BORAN STREET

SILVER STREET

BRAZIL STREET

BATHURST ST

BARRIER HIGHWAY

MENINDEE ROAD

BAGOT STREET (SILVER CITY HIGHWAY)

BLENDE STREET

HOLTEN DRIVE

▼ South Mine & Photographic Recollections

IODIDE STREET

Wiinpatja Wana

COBALT STREET

③

OXIDE STREET

LANE STREET

BERYL ST

ARGENT STREET (BARRIER HIGHWAY)

⑧

◄ ❶

CHLORIDE STREET

BLENDE STREET

City Art Gallery

⑥

CRYSTAL STREET

Train Station

SULPHIDE ST

MICA STREET

WOLFRAM STREET

Railway Museum

② ⑦

COBALT STREET

❶

▲ Sculpture Symposium & Pro Hart Gallery

BROMIDE STREET (BARRIER HIGHWAY)

Bus Terminal

ⓘ ⑤

Geocentre

④

KAOLIN STREET

KAOLIN STREET

Delprats Mine Tours

▲ Silverton and Daydream Mine & White's Mineral Art and Mining Museum

GARNET STREET

N

500m

0

GALENA STREET

COBALT STREET

BERYL STREET

BLENDE STREET

ARGENT STREET

SOUTH ROAD (SILVER CITY HIGHWAY)

WESTSIDE PLAZA

HARVEY ST

GRAPHITE STREET

ACCOMMODATION
Black Lion Inn	2
The Imperial	3
Mine Host Motel	5
Old Vic B&B	1
Palace Hotel	7
Royal Exchange Hotel	6
Theatre Royal Hotel	8
Tourist Lodge	4

Royal Flying Doctor Service & Airport

disabled-access, en-suite cabins, a swimming pool and kiosk. On-site vans ❶, cabins ❷

Mine Host Motel 120 Argent St ☏ 08/8088 4044. Modern decor and comfort including air-con; there's also a swimming pool to splash about in. Central location right near the bus station, and close to clubs and pubs. ❹

Old Vic B&B 230 Oxide St ☏ 08/8087 1169. A comfortable guesthouse in an old bungalow with a wide verandah; a light breakfast is served and all rooms share the bathroom. It's a 15min walk from the centre, though there are a couple of good pubs nearby for eating and drinking opportunities. ❸

Palace Hotel 227 Argent St ☏ 08/8088 8169, ✉ mariospalace@bigpond.com.au. Vast corner pub with one of the largest hotel balconies in New South Wales, it also has to be one of the state's most eccentric. Featured to hilarious effect in *The Adventures of Priscilla, Queen of the Desert*, this place has every available wall and ceiling space covered with murals of Australian bush scenes plus an outburst of a Botticelli-style *Birth of Venus* ceiling mural painted by the Italian owner. The rooms are a kitsch-lover's dream; the most extreme, with its own mural, was where the drag gang stayed in *Priscilla*. All rooms have air-con, a fridge and a sink and some are en suite. ❷, *Priscilla* suite ❸

Royal Exchange Hotel 320 Argent St, cnr Chloride St ☏ 08/8087 2308, ✆ 8087 2191. An old pub with some en-suite rooms, but mostly the usual pub accommodation. Breakfast is included. ❸

Theatre Royal Hotel 347 Argent St ☏ 08/8087 3318, ✆ 8087 3511. Nineteenth-century drinkers' pub with simple rooms, which are air-conditioned and come with TV. Cheap singles and weekly rates available. ❷

Tourist Lodge 100 Argent St ☏ 08/8088 2086, ✉ mcrae@pcpro.net.au. YHA-affiliated hostel near the tourist information centre and bus terminal. The budget air-con guesthouse rooms are popular with older Australians and young families; shared kitchen/dining/TV room and common room. YHA section with mostly twin, double and triple accommodation. Solar-heated swimming pool; bikes available for rent. ❶

The City

Green it may be, but the huge slag heap towering over the city centre leaves you in no doubt that, above all, this is still a mining town. Even the streets – laid out in a grid – are mostly named after minerals: Argent Street (from the Latin for silver) is Broken Hill's main thoroughfare, with the highest concentration of historic buildings; parallel, on either side, are Crystal Street, with the train station, and Blende Street, while at right angles across the centre run Bromide, Sulphide, Chloride and Oxide streets. If you want to get an idea of what there is to see in the city centre, stop in at the tourist office for a Heritage Walk map or get information on the walking tour of the town (see p.368). An unexpected sight is the **Afghan Mosque** on the corner of Williams and Buck streets, on the site of the former camel camp where Afghan and Indian camel drivers loaded and unloaded their camel teams; you can visit it on Sunday at 2.30pm.

Public transport in Broken Hill is poor – the tourist office can provide a combined timetable and route map of the Broken Hill Town Bus Service, with four routes operating infrequently within the city only.

Mines and mining museums

One thing you shouldn't miss in Broken Hill is an underground mine tour. You can do it right in town at the disued Delprats mine, behind the railway station, or nearer Silverton at the Daydream Mine. At **Delprats** (tours Mon–Fri 10.30am, Sat 2pm, more during school holidays, arrive 10min before start; 2hr; $26; ☏ 08/8088 1604) you don a miner's hat, boots and a heavy belt with batteries for your helmet light, before descending in the miners' cage – jammed with thirty or more people – 130m below the surface. Here, former miners working as guides will take you on a tour through the system of tunnels (stopes), describing and demonstrating how miners used to work in the bad old days, and how the work is done now. The **Daydream Mine** (daily 10am–3.30pm; tours on demand; 1hr; $12.10), which operated between 1882

Mining and unionism in Broken Hill

The story of Broken Hill began in 1883 when a German-born boundary rider from Mount Gipps Station, Charles Rasp, pegged out a forty-acre lease of a "broken hill" that he believed was tin. A syndicate of seven was formed, founding the **Broken Hill Proprietary** (BHP) to work what turned out to be rich silver, lead and zinc deposits. Broken Hill's mines, dominated by BHP until they withdrew operations in 1939, have contributed greatly to the wealth of Australia: the deposit, more than 7km long and up to 250m wide, is thought originally to have contained more than three hundred million tonnes of sulphide-rich ore. Even now there's said to be ten years left in the "Line of Lode", though only one mining company, **Pasminco**, is currently working it.

In the early years, living and working **conditions** for the miners were atrocious. The climate was harsh, housing was poor and diseases such as typhoid, scarlet fever and dysentery – to say nothing of work-related illnesses such as lead poisoning and mining accidents – contributed to a death rate almost twice as high as the average in New South Wales. The mine and the growing town rapidly stripped the landscape of timber, leaving the settlement surrounded by a vast, bleak plain. Dust storms were common. Not surprisingly, perhaps, Broken Hill was at the forefront of **trade union** development in Australia, as the miners, many of them recent immigrants, fought to improve their living and working conditions. It was their ability to unite that ultimately won them their battles, above all in the Big Strike of 1919–20, when, after eighteen months of holding out against the police and strikebreakers, major concessions were won from BHP. Not that the trade union movement at Broken Hill should be viewed through too-rosy glasses. The union, which effectively ran the town in conjunction with the mine companies, was also a bastion of racism and male supremacy, though the interpretive boards at the tourist information centre glorify this as "mateship". Non-white persons were not tolerated in town, nor were working women who happened to be married. Even now, these attitudes have not altogether disappeared.

Despite the life left in Broken Hill's mineral deposits, the future is none too certain. With modern mining technology the ore is removed faster, and the numbers employed are lower. Between 1970 and 1975, about 4000 people were employed in the mines. By the early 1980s this number had been reduced to 2500, and less than 700 work there now. The population continues to decrease gradually and every few years another of the city's many pubs closes down.

and 1889, is 20km out of Broken Hill on the Silverton Road – turn right at the sign and follow the dirt road for 13km; tours here are similar, but half as long and a little tamer. Daydream can be booked through the tourist information centre, but without your own transport, you'll need to go on a bus tour (see box on p.378); Delprats must be booked direct.

If you can't face going underground, take an overground tour of the old **South Mine**, which commenced operations in 1888 and closed in 1972. Accessed via Eyre Street in Broken Hill South, the site is being developed for visitors with a $4.6 million Federal Government grant. Ambitious plans include a miners' memorial site and cable car to go right across the old opencut workings, with only part of the restoration complete at the time of writing. For the moment, the twice-daily, two-hour tours (10am & 2pm; $11; ☎08/8088 6000, ⓦwww.lineoflodebrokenhill.org.au or the tourist office for details) – which concentrate on the old ambulance room and BHP's rather horrific safety record – are rather haphazard and not particularly value-for-money. If you've proven your interest in mining history by making it out to South Mine, you might like to combine it with a visit to the nearby

△ Sculpture Symposive, Broken Hill

Photographic Recollections, also on Eyre Street (Mon–Fri 10am–4.30pm, Sat & Sun 1–4.30pm; $4.40). This privately run exhibition provides a pictorial history of Broken Hill, with over six hundred photographs accompanied by well-researched text that delves into mining, union and social history. The location itself, in the former Central Power Station, tells a story of the city's very Outback past; from the 1930s Broken Hill produced all its power here until as late as 1986 when it finally went on the national grid.

There are three other mining-related attractions in the city. A visit to the bizarre but wonderful **White's Mineral Art and Mining Museum**, 1 Allendale St (off Silverton Rd; daily 9am–6pm; $4), might well be the next best thing to going underground. The art section is pretty extraordinary, consisting mainly of collages of crushed minerals depicting Broken Hill scenes, and at the back there's a walk-in underground mine, re-created so convincingly that it genuinely looks and feels like the real thing: inside, you're given an entertaining lecture, with videos and models, on the history of Broken Hill and its mines. A shop at the front of the museum sells minerals, opals, jewellery and pottery. The **Railway, Mineral and Train Museum** (daily 10am–3pm; $2), opposite the tourist information centre, features an extensive mineral collection as well as old railway machinery and memorabilia including the fittings from the bedroom of the *Maidens Hotel* in Menindee where the explorers Burke and Wills stayed on their ill-fated expedition (see p.575). Finally, the **Geocentre**, in a nineteenth-century bond store on the corner of Bromide and Crystal streets (daily 9am–5pm; $4), looks at Broken Hill's geology, mineralogy and metallurgy. At the back is an example of a tin-miner's shed – you can imagine what the heat must have been like in summer, or experience it yourself if you're foolhardy enough to come out here at that time of year.

Art galleries and sculpture parks

There's not only indoor art in galleries in Broken Hill; the city is full of public murals and outdoor sculpture. Pick up the Broken Hill Art Trail fold-out poster ($2), which has colour photographs and maps, from the **Broken Hill City Art Gallery** (Mon–Fri 10am–5pm, Sat & Sun 1–5pm; $2), in the Entertainment Centre on Chloride Street, where there's an excellent representative collection of artists from Broken Hill. Established in 1904, it's the second-oldest gallery in the state – after the Art Gallery of New South Wales in Sydney – with a small collection of nineteenth- and early-twentieth-century paintings. It's the recent work that's interesting, though, including a Sidney Nolan and a great John Olsen, as well as the works of the "Brushmen of the Bush" (though sometimes these might be moved to make way for special exhibitions). One of the highlights of the gallery is the spectacular **Silver Tree**, a 68-centimetre-high figurine, wrought of pure silver from the Broken Hill Mines, depicting five Aborigines, a drover on horseback, kangaroos, emus and sheep gathered under a tree. Also on display are sculptures created by artists who participated in the 1993 Sculpture Symposium at The Living Desert (see p.374).

The **Pro Hart Gallery**, at 108 Wyman St (Mon–Fri 9am–5pm, Sun 1.30–5pm; $4), should also not be missed. Pro Hart is a former Broken Hill miner turned artist and national celebrity who claims that his only artistic influences were the colours and subjects he saw on his family's sheep station where he grew up, which he then turned into illustrations that decorated his correspondence lessons. His trademark humorous Outback scenes depict events such as race meetings or backyard barbecues, all featuring lively figures in a caricature style. The gallery's three cramped levels are said to hold the largest private art collection in Australia, with a truly astounding amount of the artist's own work as well as works by other Australian painters – Tom Roberts, Sidney Nolan and Albert Namatjira among them – although not necessarily their best. A collection of Hart's sculptures is in a lot across the road – you can check them out for free. Hart's daughter Raylee Marie has her studio just next door to her father's gallery, and his sister runs the **Ant Hill Gallery** – the only place in Broken Hill where you can actually buy a Pro Hart – at 24 Bromide St (Mon–Sat 9am–5pm, Sun 1.30–5pm), just opposite tourist information. Also in the centre is the **Art of Broken Hill Gallery**, at 219 Argent St (Mon–Fri 10am–6pm, Sat 10am–1pm, Sun 1–5pm), which, like the Ant Hill Gallery, displays a variety of local artists' works.

Six kilometres out of town, the **Sculpture Symposium** in **The Living Desert Reserve** is the most stunning of Broken Hill's art exhibits, a reserve in the eroded Barrier Ranges desert region that contains a group of sculptures carved from Wilcannia sandstone boulders. The twelve artists involved in their creation were part of a sculpture symposium in 1993 and were drawn from diverse cultures – two from Mexico (including an Aztec Indian), two from Syria, three from Georgia (in the Caucasus), and five Australians, including two Bathurst Islanders – and this is reflected in the variety of their works. The pieces from the Georgian artists are particularly fine: Badri Sulushia's *Outback Madonna and Child*; Valerian Jiiya's Cubist interpretation; and Jumber Jikiya's horse's head, a tribute to the rare breed of Georgian horses slaughtered under Stalin's orders. Nastra Luna of Mexico badly injured his hands and his piece became a collective effort, depicting a soaring eagle, with the hands of the other sculptors who helped him imprinted in the rock. The Aboriginal artist Badger Bates, from Broken Hill, was inspired by the stone carvings of his ancestors, and his piece shows two rainbow serpents travelling north. The best time to visit the sculptures is at sunset on a clear evening, when the light is magical and the rocks glow crimson, and you can really soak up the atmosphere. It's a pleasant fifteen-minute walk up the hill from the car park to the sculptures; you can also drive right up, but because of unfortunate bouts of vandalism in the past you must first go to the tourist information centre in town, get a key to the gate ($10 deposit) and pay $5.50 per car. A $1.10 information brochure about the sculptures is available from the tourist office.

The Royal Flying Doctor Service and the School of the Air

Broken Hill offers an excellent opportunity to visit two Australian Outback institutions, the **Royal Flying Doctor Service** (RFDS) and the School of the Air. The RFDS, at Broken Hill Airport, offers guided tours (Mon–Fri 9am–5pm, Sat & Sun 10am–4pm; $3.30; it's best to buy your ticket in advance from the tourist office as places are limited; ℡08/8080 1777, ⊛www .rfds.org.au), with an accompanying video and talk. In the headquarters you'll see the radio room where calls from remote places in New South Wales, South Australia and Queensland are handled before going out to the hangar to see the aircraft. The popularity of the tours is due to the Australian television series *The Flying Doctors*, which is shown worldwide, and since a third of the annual budget of $30 million has to come through fund-raising – the rest of the money is from the State and Federal governments – whatever you spend on the tour and at the souvenir shop here is going to a good cause.

In many ways the **School of the Air** is also indebted to the RFDS: lessons for children in the Outback, in a transmission area of 1.8 million square kilometres, are conducted via RFDS two-way radio. The service was established in 1956 to improve education for children in the isolated Outback, and today visitors listen to the first hour's transmission in a schoolroom surrounded by childrens' artwork (Mon–Fri, term time only 8.30am; book in advance at the tourist centre; $2.20). It's frighteningly like being back at school, with jolly primary-school teachers hosting singalongs; what comes out of the radio is a static squawk, but the children in the far-flung areas seem to enjoy it.

Eating, drinking and nightlife

There are several good **cafés and bakeries** on Argent Street where you can get something to eat and drink – restaurants aren't really Broken Hill's style. *Ruby's Coffee Lounge*, at no. 373, near the corner of Oxide Street (closed Sun), places the emphasis on healthy food, with a few vegetarian dishes always on offer and lots of baked goodies. At no. 198, the friendly *Jonathan's Café* serves almost exclusively veggie fare, while Cosy *Charlotte's* at no. 317, opposite the post office, is reckoned to serve the town's best cappuccino and has a well-assorted range of cakes, muffins and slices to accompany your foamy brew. *Café Alfresco* at no. 343 (closed Sun) is a city-style café with big open doors and wooden floors, but unfortunately the standard of its coffee doesn't match the interior. Their open toasted sandwiches, however, are huge, tasty and cheap; a separate, pricier night-time restaurant menu features grills, pasta and salads. For **grocery** supplies, visit the well-stocked, late-opening IGM behind the police station on Blende Street, or the out-of-town Westside Plaza, Galena Street (open daily), which proffers both an enormous Woolworths (with liquor) and a cheaper Big W supermarket.

Broken Hill still has the proverbial **pub** on every corner – most of them serve inexpensive counter meals as well as ice-cold beer on tap. The city has always been a legendary drinking hole, once having over seventy hotels. Many have been converted to other uses, but there are still more than twenty licensed establishments and a pub crawl is highly recommended. Some places to include for an early drink are the kitsch-crammed *Mario's Palace*, 227 Argent St, which memorably featured in *The Adventures of Priscilla, Queen of the Desert*; the *Rising Sun*, 2 Beryl St (ⓣ08/8087 4856), popular with younger locals on Friday nights when live bands play; the *Black Lion Inn*, 34 Bromide St (after midnight Tues–Sat but Fri & Sat till 4am), good any time but especially during happy hour at the cocktail bar done out like an underground mine; and the *Mulga Hill Tavern*, on the corner of Oxide and Williams streets.

Another option is to sample the local culture at one of the numerous **clubs**. These make most of their money out of gambling – with snooker tables, darts and endless parades of one-armed bandits – and they're happy to draw their customers in and keep them playing by tempting them with large portions of cheap food, and quite often live entertainment. Best known is the *Barrier Social Democratic Club* (*Demo Club* to the locals) at 214 Argent St (ⓣ08/8088 4477), with daily meal specials including a well-assorted salad bar plus great, inexpensive breakfasts (7–9am). You could also try the *Broken Hill Legion Club*, 166–170 Crystal St (ⓣ08/8087 4064); or the *Broken Hill Musicians Club*, 276 Crystal St (ⓣ08/8088 1777), which has inherited Broken Hill's famous **Two Up School**, once an illegal back-lane gambling operation.

Listings

Airlines Qantas ⓣ13 13 13; Regional Express ⓣ13 17 13.

Bike rental Johnny Windham, 135 Argent St (ⓣ08/8087 3707), rents mainly mountain bikes: $5 per day, $25 per week, plus obligatory helmet $2; closed Sat & Sun. The *Tourist Lodge* rents bikes to guests at similar rates.

Bookshops ABC Centre, 309 Argent St, specializes in local history and the Outback (℡08/8088 1177). For secondhand books, try W Book Exchange, 320 Chloride St, cnr Thomas St (℡08/8087 3383).

Car rental Avis, 121 Rakow St ℡08/8087 7532; Budget, 338 Crystal St ℡13 27 27; Hertz, at the tourist information centre ℡08/8087 2719; and Thrifty, 190 Argent St ℡08/8088 1928; all have desks at the airport too. Cheaper deals are available at Holmes' Hire, 475 Argent St (℡08/8087 2210), with older cars from $60 per day and 4WDs from $110.

Cinema Village Silver City Cinema, 41 Oxide St ℡08/8087 4569.

Hospital Broken Hill Base Hospital and Health Services, 176 Thomas St ℡08/8080 1333.

Internet access Bizbyte, 435 Argent St (Mon–Fri 9am–5.30pm, $3/30min); PC Professionals, 387 Argent St (Mon–Fri 9am–5.30pm, Sat 9am–12.30pm; $3/30min). There is also free

access at the library, on the corner of Blende and Chloride streets, but you have to book.

Laundry Oxide Street Laundrette, 241 Oxide St ℡08/8088 2022. Service washes available, with free pick-up and delivery.

Pharmacies Amcal Chemist, Westside Plaza, Galena St, has an after-hours emergency number (℡08/8088 4800), but the most central pharmacy is Peoples CP Chemist, 323 Argent St.

Post office Cnr Argent and Chloride streets, NSW 2880.

Swimming pools There are two municipal outdoor pools: Alma Pool, Voughtman St, South Broken Hill (mid-Nov to late March daily 9am–6pm; $1); and North Pool, north of the centre on McCulloch St (daily: April–Oct 6am–6pm; Nov–March 6–10pm; $2), which is heated in winter.

Taxi Yellow Radio Cabs ℡08/8088 1144.

Tours See box on p.378.

Around Broken Hill

The ghost town of **SILVERTON**, just 25km northwest of Broken Hill on a good road, makes a great day out. Note that there is no fuel available at Silverton. If the scene looks vaguely familiar, you probably have seen it before: parts of *Mad Max II* were shot around here, and the **Silverton Hotel** (daily 8.30am–9.30pm, though they often close earlier) has appeared as the "Gamulla Hotel" in *Razorback*, the "Hotel Australia" in *A Town Like Alice*, and "Juanita's Diner" in *Fiddlers Green* with Don Johnson. It also seems to star in just about every commercial – usually beer-related – that features an Outback scene. The stark impact of the pub, with barren, red earth stretching endlessly to the horizon, has been somewhat diminished by the greening of the desert, but it's still the ultimate Outback image and makes a great photo. The pub has its own photo collection, the lower walls covered with snapshots from the various film shoots, the upper walls piled high with an assortment of beer cans and old bottles. In some ways it feels like a milk bar, with a fridge full of cold soft drinks, a tea urn, and the only available food some limp sandwiches, pies and pasties, rather than the usual counter meals. But in the tradition of all Outback pubs, it has its own in-jokes; you'll find out what all the laughter is about if you ask to "take the test".

Taking the **Silverton Heritage Trail**, a two-hour stroll around town marked by white arrows, is a good way to work up a thirst. But it's far too hot to attempt in the summer, and is best undertaken during the cooler months. Along the way it'll take you past the old **Silverton School Craft Centre**, and the 1889 vintage **Silverton Gaol Museum** (daily 9.30am–4.30pm; $2.50), with the usual collection of relics from pioneer days and Outback stations, plus mining equipment. There's a burgeoning art scene here, too, with four galleries to browse through. **Peter Browne's Gallery** (daily 9am–5pm; Ⓦwww .outbackgalleries.com.au), in an 1884 house on a hill, is worth a look for its uniquely original decoration and the humorous paintings of bush scenes, koala-shearing, kookaburras boiling the billy, and Browne's trademark emus with huge, saucer-shaped eyes. Also interesting is Albert Woodroffe's and Bronwen Woodroffe-Standley's **Horizon Gallery** (daily 9am–6pm;

Ⓦwww.brokenhillartists.com), opposite the pub. The husband and wife team paint in a similar style, creating their trademark horizon paintings, mainly in pastels and acrylics – finely detailed works that really capture the sense of space and the seemingly endless skyline.

One of the most enjoyable things to do while in Silverton is to go on a camel tour. The Cannard family who run the **Silverton Camel Farm** (☎08/8088 5316, Ⓔsilverton@datafast.net.au) come from a long line of camel trainers and have forty working camels. You can't miss the farm on the way into Silverton, with the shapes of camels looming like desert mirages. You can hop on for fifteen minutes ($5), or trot for an hour along the nearby creek ($20), but the best experience is the sunset trek (2hr; $40), a ride to the Mundi Mundi Plain to look at the setting sun and a return trip under the night stars accompanied by a pack of lively dogs. Longer safaris into the desert are also on offer, from one to three days ($150–300).

Beyond Silverton, the road continues a further 14km to the **Umberumberka reservoir**, Broken Hill's only source of water until the Menindee Lakes Scheme was set up. There's a signposted lookout area that makes a nice picnic spot. A few kilometres further on you reach the **Mundi Mundi Plains Lookout**. Here, the undulating plateau you have been driving across descends gradually to a vast plain, and on clear days you can see in the distance the blurred outline of the northern Flinders Ranges in South Australia. This spot is where, at the end of *Mad Max II*, Mel Gibson tipped the semi-trailer.

If you want to stay in Silverton, your only choice is to **camp** at Penrose Park, where there's a shower, toilets and barbecue; rates are around $3 – ask at the house there or call ☎08/8088 5307.

Kinchega National Park and the Menindee Lakes

Flat **Kinchega National Park** is situated among the **Menindee Lakes**, near the township of **MENINDEE**, southeast of Broken Hill. There's a sealed road for the 110km to Menindee and the park entrance, and gravel roads thereafter; before you go, visit the Broken Hill NPWS to get information about road conditions (183 Argent St; ☎08/8088 5933), or ask at the **Menindee Tourist Information Centre** (Mon–Fri 9am–5pm, Sat & Sun 10am–1pm; ☎08/8091 4274), where a detailed, hand-drawn "Mud Map" of the lakes area, showing areas of interest, is available free of charge. The Menindee lakes are an extensive, natural oasis, feeding the Darling and Murray rivers and, most importantly, supplying water to Broken Hill; they're also a big recreation area, with facilities for camping, powerboating, water-skiing, sailing, swimming and fishing. The waters protected by the Kinchega National Park, **Menindee Lake** and **Cawndilla Lake**, are a haven for **waterbirds**; a common sight are little black cormorants (commonly known as shags), floating in feeding flocks alongside pelicans, with whom they hunt co-operatively. There's an **information** shelter 5km into the park and a normally unmanned visitor information centre about 10km further on near the **Kinchega Woolshed**. Kinchega Station was one of the first pastoral settlements in the area in 1850 and was worked until 1967; you can explore it by following the signposted woolshed **walk**. Accommodation is available in the shearers' sheds here (❶; book at Broken Hill NPWS, or at the thirty river campsites ($5 payable on site) scattered throughout the river-red-gum woodland along the river – including the site of Burke and Wills' base camp from late October 1860 until late January 1861 (a tree marks the spot). The main camping area, with toilets, is on the shores of Cawndilla Lake, with its sandy beaches and good swimming.

There is a big range of tours on offer, from scenic flights to 4WD tours, all of which can be booked from the tourist information centre (see p.368). Most include a pick-up and return service to and from your accommodation.

Air charters and scenic flights

If you have a bit of cash to spare, small aircrafts are an excellent way of getting around, covering the enormous distances rather quickly and in relative ease and comfort.

Crittenden Air Airport Terminal ℡08/8088 5702. Tour flights to Tibooburra ($360), White Cliffs ($250), over Lake Eyre and South Australia's Flinders Ranges ($550) as well as several more local scenic tours. Minimum of four people or equivalent per person price.

Bus tours

These tend to be overpriced, given that many tours merely provide transport to places that could be more enjoyably visited with a rental car or bike, or even by taxi. Tours are more frequent between early April and the end of November, and have reduced schedules during the hot summer months.

Broken Hill Outback Information and Safari Tours ℡08/8087 8574, ⓦwww .bhoutbacktours.com.au. Half-day tours ($45) to Silverton, the Daydream Mine, Delprats Mine, or city art galleries plus the Sculpture Symposium; a day-tour is also offered to Menindee Lakes and Kinchega National Park ($96).

Silver City Tours ℡08/8087 6956, ⓔsctbhq@ruralnet.net.au Excursions include Royal Flying Doctor Service ($17), School of the Air ($17), White's Mineral Art and Mining Museum ($17); half-day tours of city sights ($35), art galleries ($21), sunset Sculpture Symposium ($30), Silverton ($37); day-tours, including lunch, to White Cliffs ($119), Menindee Lakes, Kinchega National Park and Tandou Irrigation Farm ($95), and Mutawintji National Park ($106).

Four-wheel-drive tours

Broken Hill's Outback Tours ℡08/8087 7800 or 1800 670 120, ⓦwww.outback tours.net. Amongst these long-haul fully inclusive tours are a four-day/three-night trip to all three national parks detailed in the following pages ($1185), and a six-day excursion to Flinders Ranges ($1395). They will happily provide customized tours too.

Corner Country Adventure Tours ℡08/8087 5142. Longer 4WD trips, including a four-day/three-night trip to Kinchega, Mutawintji and Sturt national parks ($1060), or tailor-made excursions as far afield as the Birdsville Track (see p.577).

Goanna Safari ℡08/8087 6057, ⓦwww.goanna-safari.com.au. Heartily recom-mended tours with a well-informed, uniquely qualified and interesting guide who is never in too much of a rush; maximum four people in the group. One-day tours ($95) to: Poolamacca Station, a sheep station 60km north of Broken Hill; Menindee Lakes and Kinchega National Park; Mutawintji National Park including the Aboriginal art sites; the Dingo Fence; or closer to home a round-up of the Royal Flying Doctor Service, Silverton, and the Sculpture Symposium. Two-day safari to White Cliffs, staying in a dug-out motel ($340), or extending to three days and including Mutawintji ($510). Tibooburra and Camerons Corner are taken in on another two-day trip (also $340). Short trips out to The Living Desert sculpture site (minimum $10, cheaper depending on numbers) are also available.

Tri-State Safari ℡08/8088 2389, ⓦwww.tristate.com.au. Tours ranging from sunset sculptures and wine ($38), to one-day trips to Kinchega ($125) and mammoth Burke and Wills or desert tours, between four and ten days in length.

Burke and Wills stayed in Menindee at the *Maidens Hotel*, Yartla Street (☎08/8091 4208; ❶), on their ill-fated trip north in 1860 (see box on p.575). Unfortunately the room in which they stayed is now full of poker machines, but there is some interpretive material in the hotel (the room's fittings are now in the Railway Museum in Broken Hill; see p.373), and the green courtyard's a good place for a drink or a counter meal. Otherwise, you can stay at the *Burke & Wills Motel* opposite (☎08/8091 4313, ℻8091 4406; ❸), or camp in relative comfort at the *Menindee Lakes Park* on Lakes Shore Road, 5km northwest of town (☎08/8091 4315, ℻8091 4325; on-site vans ❶), which has a kiosk and grocery store. If you don't have transport, you can take a **day-tour** out here from Broken Hill; the best is with Goanna Safari (see box opposite).

Scotia Sanctuary

Halfway between Broken Hill and Wentworth, 163km south along the Silver City Highway, then 30km southwest, is **Scotia Sanctuary**, which protects the rare Mallee fowl in an environment of Mallee sand dunes. There are opportunities to see the birds, as well as other native wildlife and flora, on guided tours (from $15 per person), and you can stay here (providing your own sheets; ☎03/5027 1200, ✉scotia@ruralnet.net.au; ❶) in the well-equipped homestead and more basic shearers' quarters – or choose to camp.

Mutawintji National Park

Mutawintji National Park, 130km northeast of Broken Hill in the Bynguano Ranges, has totally different and perhaps even more fascinating scenery to offer: secluded gorges and quiet waterholes that attract a profusion of wildlife. The main attractions of the park are the ancient galleries of **Aboriginal rock art** in the caves and overhangs; you can only visit these accompanied by an Aboriginal tour guide (Wed & Sat 11am Eastern Standard Time; 2hr; $15; bookings required; special tours by arrangement on ☎08/8088 7000) – there are no tours in the hot summer months. While on the tour you get to visit the **Mutawintji Cultural Resource Centre**, an amazing multimedia collaboration between indigenous Australians and the NPWS which tells of tribal history and myth in sound and pictures. There's a **camping** area at Homestead Creek, among river red gums at the entrance to Homestead Gorge (camping is payable on site; $6) and a number of **walking trails** (including the short wheelchair-accessible Thakaaltjika Mingkana Walk). Access to and within the park is via unsealed gravel roads, and you'll need to bring extra fuel as none is available here. It's normally fine for 2WD vehicles, but check locally, as the roads can quickly become impassable after even a light rain; bring extra food just in case. The NPWS office in Broken Hill can provide other information. You can also get here from Broken Hill with Goanna Safari; a bushwalk (2hr 30min) is part of their excellent tour (see box opposite).

Corner Country: Tibooburra and the Sturt National Park

A remote Outback settlement in the far northwest corner of New South Wales, 337km from Broken Hill, **TIBOOBURRA** can be reached by normal vehicle on a well-maintained dirt road from Broken Hill – the Silver City Highway. You can also reach it from Bourke (see p.363), 454km west along various unsealed and mostly deserted roads. After rain, roads may become impassable, and it's important to find out about road and weather conditions before you set out; it's also crucial to carry extra food, water, fuel and spare vehicle parts in case you get stranded later on. (Refer to the tourist information office in Broken Hill or Bourke for advice before leaving.) Tibooburra has been settled for over a hundred and ten years: several stone buildings from the 1880s still remain, the result of a flurried goldrush, which add a bit of architectural charm to the tiny township. The nearby granite outcrops – worthy of a sunset stroll – from which the stone was quarried, gave the town its former name of Granites. Outback institutions are well represented here: there are some classic pubs (the *Family Hotel* and *Tibooburra Hotel* are detailed below), a hospital serviced by the Royal Flying Doctor Service, and a **School of the Air** similar to the one in Broken Hill; visitors can witness the on-air education service on schoolday mornings from 9am ($2). The **NPWS office** in the town (☎08/8091 3308), attached to the old courthouse (with a display about the town's history), provides visitor information, including the latest on the roads and weather, and camping permits for the national park.

In nearby **Sturt National Park**, a network of roads and tracks is maintained by the NPWS to 2WD standard, but check with the rangers at Tibooburra before setting out. The park's 3500 square kilometres are cut in two by the Grey Range: to the west are the rolling red sand dunes of the Strzelecki Desert, and to the east the stone-covered, so-called gibber plains extending for hundreds of kilometres. The area supports a number of red and grey kangaroos, emus and lizards.

At the edge of the park, the border between Queensland, New South Wales and South Australia is delineated by the 1.8-metre-high **Dingo Fence**. This, the world's longest fence (4850km), was originally constructed by the Queensland government to stop the invasion of rabbits from the south; it's now maintained to keep dingoes out of sheep-grazing land. The point where the three states meet is known as **Cameron's Corner** and is marked by a post: it's a popular target for travellers, so much so that there's even a shop here, the wittily named *Corner Store* (☎08/8091 3872). As well as dishing up the ubiquitous meat pies and other typical Aussie fillers, they have fuel and can give you useful road advice.

There are a couple of pleasant **hotels**, with welcome air conditioning, on Briscoe Street in Tibooburra: the *Family Hotel* (☎08/8091 3314; ❷) is marginally the fancier with a wall mural by the Australian artist Clifton Pugh, while the two-storey *Tibooburra Hotel* (☎08/8091 3310; ❷) vies for attention with its wall full of old hats. Both also serve decent counter meals. *The Granites Caravan Park*, at the corner of Brown and King streets (☎08/8091 3305; on-site vans ❶, cabins ❷), has a refreshing pool.

Pacific Islands: Lord Howe and Norfolk

Lord Howe Island, 700km northeast of Sydney, and roughly in line with Port Macquarie, is actually a far-flung part of New South Wales, on the world's southernmost coral reef. Its nearest neighbour is **Norfolk Island**, 900km further northeast – an external independent territory of Australia, though geographically closer to New Zealand. The approach to tourism of the two subtropical islands couldn't be more different: Lord Howe is the perfect ecodestination, attracting outdoor types, and is very sophisticated in terms of food and accommodation, while Norfolk Island mostly disregards its natural beauty to concentrate first on its status as a tax haven and a magnet for Australian pensioners who come for its duty-free shopping, and second on its fascinating history as a tough convict settlement and then as the home for many of the descendants of the *Bounty* mutineers after they had left Pitcairn Island.

Getting there

It's not cheap to get to **Lord Howe Island**: you can **fly** with Qantas (☎13 13 13) from Sydney four times weekly, and from Coffs Harbour and Brisbane once weekly, for about $600 return; flights via Newcastle and Ballina may be available in peak summer months. It's much easier to go on a **package tour**, but the lowest you can expect to pay for five nights is about $850 in winter, rising to a steep $1600 in summer: try Fastbook Pacific Holidays (☎02/9212 5977, ⓔreservations@fastbook.com.au) or Talpacific Holidays (☎13 27 47, ⓦwww.talpacific.com); both operators also fly to Norfolk Island. Overseas visitors can fly to Lord Howe as an add-on sector fare on an air pass (see p.34).

The Qantas-linked Norfolk Jet Express (☎1800 816 947) flies to **Norfolk Island** from Sydney and Brisbane at weekends, while Flight West (☎1300 130 092, ⓦwww.flightwest.com.au) operates four flights a week from Brisbane and Sydney. Note that there's a $25 departure tax from Norfolk. **Packages** offer the best value, costing from $890 for five days. Air New Zealand flies twice weekly **from Auckland and Christchurch** to Norfolk Island, and a code-share agreement with Flight West means the destination can now be a stop-over between New Zealand and Australia.

Lord Howe Island

I would strongly urge preserving this beautiful island from further intrusions of any kind...

Government Expedition, 1882

On the UNESCO World Heritage list since 1982 because of its rare birds and plant life, and its coral reef in unpolluted and virtually untouched waters, **LORD HOWE ISLAND** is the ultimate destination for ecotourists. The island's preservation was assured by Victorian-era descriptions of "this gem of the sea" when reports were brought back to the Australian mainland regarding the progress of the multiracial settlers who had arrived in the 1830s. Even today only a tenth of the land has been cleared for cultivation or grazing, and two-thirds of the island is designated as **Permanent Park Reserve**. Only 11km long and just under 3km across at its widest point, the crescent-shaped subtropical island is covered with **kentia palm plantations**, which represent the island's only industry other than tourism. With a population of just 300, the island can be visited by no more than 400 visitors at any one time; to enforce this limit, accommodation has to be booked in advance. There is only one short road and, although some locals have vehicles, people get around mainly by bicycle, boat or on foot.

As you fly in, you have a stunning view of the whole of the volcanic island: the towering summits of rainforest-clad **Mount Gower** and **Mount Lidgbird** at the southern end, the narrow centre with its idyllic lagoon and a **coral reef** extending about 6km along the island's west coast, and a group of tiny islets off the coast at the lower northern end of the island providing sanctuary for the prolific **birdlife** – the island's 32 species make this a heaven for ornithologists.

One of the first things you notice about the island is how easy-going and laid-back the local people are: many prefer to go barefoot. The emphasis is on tranquillity and visitors are mostly couples and families – there are no rowdy nightclubs here. Though it's expensive to get to the island, once here you'll find that cruises, bike rental and eating out are all relatively affordable. The island's **climate** is subtropical, with temperatures rising from an average low of 16°C to 19°C in winter, 26°C in the summer, and an annual rainfall of 1650mm. It's cheaper to visit in the winter, though many places are closed and there's usually a lot more rain and wind.

Some history

Although the ship *Supply* discovered Lord Howe Island in 1778 on a journey from Sydney to found a colony on Norfolk Island, the island was not actually

Lord Howe ecology

Seven million years ago a volcanic eruption on the sea floor created Lord Howe Island and its 27 surrounding islets and outcrops – the island's boomerang shape is a mere remnant of the massive shield volcano, mostly eroded by the sea. While much of the **flora** on the island is similar to that of Australia, New Zealand, New Caledonia and Norfolk Island, the island's relative isolation has led to the evolution of **new species** – of the 241 native plants found here, 105 are endemic, including the important indigenous **kentia palm** (see opposite).

Similarly, until the arrival of settlers, fifteen species of **land birds** (nine of which are now extinct) lived on the island, undisturbed by predators and coexisting with migrating seabirds, skinks, geckos, spiders, snails and the now-extinct giant horned turtle. However, in the eighteenth century Lord Howe became a port of call for ships en route to Norfolk Island, whose hungry crews eradicated the island's stocks of **white gallinule** and **white-throated pigeon**. The small, plump and flightless **woodhen** managed to survive, protected on Mount Gower, and an intensive captive breeding programme in the early 1980s more than doubled numbers of the species to 66. About one million **seabirds** – fourteen species – nest annually: and it is one of the few known breeding grounds of the **providence petrel**; the island also has the world's largest colony of **red-tailed tropic birds** and is the most southerly breeding location of the **sooty tern**, the noddy tern and the masked booby.

The cold waters of the **Tasman Sea**, which surround Lord Howe, host the world's southernmost **coral reef**, a tropical oddity that is sustained by the warm summer currents that sweep in from the Great Barrier Reef. There are about sixty varieties of brilliantly coloured and fantastically shaped coral, and the meeting of warm and cold currents means that a huge variety of both tropical and temperate fish can be spotted by snorkellers in the crystal-clear waters. Some of the most colourful species include the yellow **moon wrasse** and the yellow-and-black **banner fish**. Unique to Lord Howe is the **doubleheader**, with its bizarre, bulbous forehead and fat lips. Beyond the lagoon, the water becomes very deep, with particularly good **diving** in the seas around the **Admiralty Islets**, which have sheer underwater precipices and chasms. The diving season lasts from May to September (for information on dive companies, see p.387).

settled for another 55 years. These first **settlers**, who arrived in 1833, were three white men, with Maori women and boys, and the group earned their livelihood by providing whaling vessels with provisions. Other settlers arrived in the 1840s, but in 1853 two white men came with three women from the Gilbert Islands, and it is from this small group that many of Lord Howe's present population is descended. In the 1840s and 1850s the island continued to serve as a stopover for **whaling ships** from the US and Britain, with as many as fifty ships a year passing through. In 1882 a government expedition from the mainland recommended that, in order to preserve the island, no one other than the present "happy, industrious" leaseholders and their families be allowed to make permanent settlement.

With the decline of whaling, economic salvation came in the form of the "thatch" palm, one of the four endemic species of the **kentia palm**. Up to this time used as roofing for the islanders' homes, it now began to be exported to Europe and the USA as a decorative interior plant, which helped to boost the island's economy. Then, in 1918, the kentia industry was devastated by the introduction of **rats**, which escaped onto the island from a ship. **Tourism**, though, was eventually to become the mainstay of the island. Lord Howe had been a popular stopover on the cruise-ship circuit before World War II, and after the war it began to be visited by holiday-makers from Sydney, who came by seaplane.

Today, rats still pose a hazard to the palms, but the **kentia industry** is nonetheless in resurgence, run by the Lord Howe Island Board under the auspices of the government of New South Wales, with profits going towards the preservation of the island's unique ecosystem. Seeds are no longer exported but instead cultivated in the Lord Howe Island Board's own **nursery**, which sells two and a half million plants annually, mainly to Europe and North America; they also grow seedlings here for regeneration around the island. You can visit the nursery on guided walks with Ron's Rambles (☎02/6563 2010) or Jim's Tours (☎02/6563 2263); both can be booked at Thompson's General Store, see below.

Arrival, information and transport

There's no official transport from the **airport**, located in the narrow central part of the island, but wherever you're staying, you'll be met on arrival by the lodge-owner. The island's **visitors centre** (Mon–Fri & Sun 9am–4pm; ☎02/6563 2114 or 1800 240 937, @www.lordhoweisland.info) is located inside the Lord Howe Island Museum at the junction of Lagoon and Middle Beach roads; the centre runs an excellent twenty-minute audiovisual presentation on the island, gives out advice on weather conditions, and also has plenty of free brochures about wildlife and plants, as well as basic walking maps. A good buy for walkers is the useful *Ramblers Guide to Lord Howe Island* ($8), which covers all the walks on the island in much greater detail and is available from the visitors centre.

Crossing the centre of the island to the north, Ned's Beach Road has a cluster of **shops** and **services**, including Thompson's General Store (☎02/6563 2155), where you can book most activities – it's advisable to sign up in advance for cruises. You'll also find a **post office** (Mon–Fri 9am–1pm & 2–5pm) on this road, which acts as a Commonwealth Bank agent (no fee up to $200), as well as a Westpac **bank** (Mon–Fri 10am–noon & 2–4pm) and a community hall-cum-summer cinema. There are no ATMs on the island, although in emergencies some establishments, including Larrups clothes and beachwear

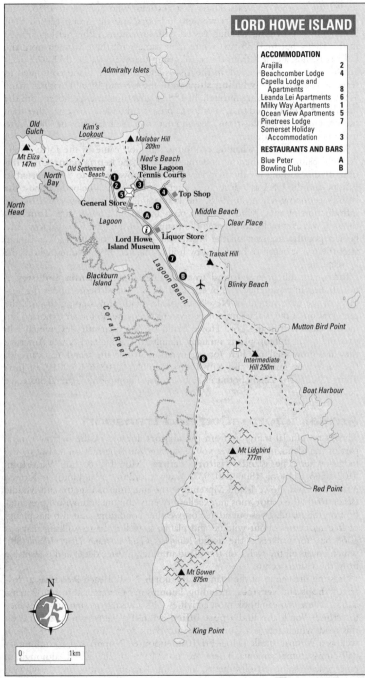

LORD HOWE ISLAND

ACCOMMODATION

Arajilla	2
Beachcomber Lodge	4
Capella Lodge and Apartments	8
Leanda Lei Apartments	6
Milky Way Apartments	1
Ocean View Apartments	5
Pinetrees Lodge	7
Somerset Holiday Accommodation	3

RESTAURANTS AND BARS

Blue Peter	A
Bowling Club	B

Admiralty Islets

Old Gulch

Kim's Lookout

Malabar Hill 209m

Mt Eliza 147m

Ned's Beach

Blue Lagoon Tennis Courts

Old Settlement Beach

North Bay

North Head

General Store

Top Shop

Lagoon

Middle Beach

Clear Place

Lord Howe Island Museum

Liquor Store

Transit Hill

Blackburn Island

Lagoon Beach

Blinky Beach

Coral Reef

Mutton Bird Point

Intermediate Hill 250m

Boat Harbour

Mt Lidgbird 777m

Red Point

Mt Gower 875m

King Point

N

0   1km

Balls Pyramid (23 km)

shop on Ned's Beach Road and *Blue Peter* café, may give cash out on EFTPOS or credit cards to customers.

There are three places to buy **groceries** on the island: Thompson's General Store with a good selection of refrigerated items and the only freshly baked bread on Lord Howe; the erratically stocked and somewhat overpriced Joy's Shop (daily 9am–7pm), opposite *Leanda Lei Apartments* on Middle Beach Road, which also sells liquor and cigarettes (though the cheapest place to get alcohol is the Liquor Store, off Lagoon Road further east); and the Top Shop (Mon–Fri 9am–12.30pm & 4.30–6pm, Sun 9am–12.30pm), favourite of the locals, tucked away on Skyline Street off Mutton Bird Drive – here you can get fresh meat and vegetables, which are flown in daily from Port Macquarie.

Transport

The island has only one **road** and relatively few cars. There are no streetlights so you'll need to bring a torch with you, or buy one from Joy's Shop, if you want to venture out at night. There's no regular bus service, but lodge hosts and restaurants will usually pick up and drop off customers. Otherwise, Wilson's (see below) can do pick-ups and drop-offs. The most common ways to get around are by **bicycle**, boat or just plain walking. There are plenty of places to **rent bikes** and most lodges offer them to guests, but the drawback is that they don't have lights either, so if you want to ride at night attach a torch. If your lodge has exhausted its supply, then try Wilson's Hire Service, opposite Lagoon Beach (℡02/6563 2045; $8 per day; closed Sat). Both Wilson's and *Leanda Lei Apartments* (℡02/6563 2195) rent **cars** ($50–60 per day); pre-booking is essential.

Accommodation

Since you need to have an accommodation booking before you can buy a flight, package tours are the most convenient option. Most of the accommodation on Lord Howe Island is **self-catering** (otherwise full board is available) and of a good standard, including TV and usually a laundry. All the lodges are centrally located, with the exception of *Capella Lodge*, where privacy, views and atmosphere more than compensate.

Arajilla ℡02/6563 2002 or 1800 063 928, ⓦwww.arajilla.com.au. Ten individual suites with private verandahs nestling in among the kentia forest. The rooms are a minimalist's dream: spacious, airy, comfortable and very Zen. The on-site restaurant is by far the island's best. **❼**

Beachcomber Lodge ℡02/6563 2032, ⒻF6563 2132. Studio apartments including breakfast (some larger suites available with self-catering facilities) in a central location amongst palm trees. Owned by long-established island family; suitable for couples with kids. **❼**

Capella Lodge and Apartments ℡02/9544 2273, ⓦwww.lordhowe.com. Towards the southern end of the island, above Salmon Beach and overlooked by Mount Gower and Mount Lidgbird. Nine stylish, breezy rooms with fantastic views, hip *Mambo* furnishings and interior design and large bathrooms. TVs, torches and mountain bikes also

provided. Top-class restaurant and cocktail café-bar, with stunning views over the mountains. **❼**

Leanda Lei Apartments ℡02/6563 2195, ⓦwww.leandalei.com.au. Studio or one- or two-bedroom self-catering apartments in the middle of the island by Lagoon Beach, set in nicely manicured grounds with BBQs. The friendly owners can rent you a bike or a car. **❹**

Milky Way Apartments ℡02/6563 2012, ⓦwww.lordhowe.net. Set amid native forests by Old Settlement Beach at the northern end of the island. One of the best spots, surrounded by bird-filled green forests. All units have balconies. **❼**

Ocean View Apartments ℡02/6563 2041, ⒻF6563 2122. Very pleasant, old-fashioned place, with a sunny garden, tennis court, a common room with pool tables and the island's only swimming pool. There is a view of the sea at the end of the driveway, but not from the rooms. **❹**

Pinetrees Lodge ☎02/9262 6585, ⓦwww
.pinetrees.com.au. The island's original guesthouse, set in extensive grounds filled with native
palms and 100-year-old Norfolk Island pines. A
pleasant, old-fashioned homestead with a guest
lounge, verandah, courtyard and tennis court. Units
are motel-style, each with a small verandah. The
newer, self-catering garden cottages ("Palm

Haven"; $435) are better, with courtyards, sepa-
rate bedrooms and living rooms. The lodge has its
own boatshed and deck on Lagoon Beach. ⓻
Somerset Holiday Accommodation ☎02/6563
2061, ⓦwww.lordhoweisle.com.au. The largest
self-contained apartment complex on the island,
with kitchenettes, BBQs and private verandahs.
⓻

The island

At the island's **northern end**, you can walk, stopping at various lookout
points, all the way from Old Settlement Beach on the western side to Ned's
Beach on the east. Relaxed, educational half-day **guided walks** are available
for around $15 from personable local resident Ron or island biologist Ian
Hutton (book at Thompson's Store for both). However, if you simply want to
take in the scenery, it's very easy to do it yourself. From the streamside picnic
area at **Old Settlement Beach**, it's just over 2km to the summit of **Mount
Eliza** (147m). If you want to save time, you can take a boat to **North Bay**
with Islander Cruises (see opposite) and begin the walk from there – the return
walk will then take only an hour. The summit is the most accessible place to
see **sooty terns** in their southernmost breeding grounds. When the colony
visits the island between August and March each female lays a single speckled
egg on the bare ground, which means that the actual summit has to be closed
for the birds' protection. Back at the base, a short five- or ten-minute walk
through forest from **North Beach** (good for swimming and snorkelling on
North Reef) leads to **Old Gulch**, a beach of boulders, where at low tide you
can rock-hop to the **Herring Pools** at the base of the cliff front and examine the colourful marine life. From **Ned's Beach** (see opposite) the walk to
Malabar Hill (209m) gives access to one of the world's largest nesting concentrations of **red-tailed tropic birds**, who between September and May
make their homes in the crannies of the cliff face below, laying only one egg
and looking after the chick for twelve weeks until it can fly. It's fascinating to
watch the white-and-red birds' unusual and rather balletic backwards-dancing
through the air. From here, you can head along the cliff edge to **Kim's
Lookout** (182m), which provides a good view of the settlement and the
lagoon beaches and islets at this end of the island, and from where it's just over
a kilometre back to Old Settlement Beach (or you can continue on to North
Beach and Mount Eliza).

In the **centre of the island** there are other walks to take: from Middle
Beach to Clear Place; from Blinky Beach, the island's main surfing spot, to
Transit Hill (121m); and from near the airstrip to the summit of
Intermediate Hill (250m); and two longer walks from the base of
Intermediate Hill to **Boat Harbour** or to the base of **Mount Lidgbird**
(777m). Less energetic, but no less rewarding, is a trip to the **Lord Howe
Island Museum**, opposite Lagoon Beach on the corner of Middle Beach and
Lagoon roads, which details the history of the island from its discovery to the
present day.

The ultimate view on the island is at its **southern end**, where the lofty
summit of **Mount Gower** (875m) gives vistas over the whole island and out
to sea towards **Balls Pyramid** (548m), a rocky outcrop 23km from Lord
Howe. The mountain is high enough to have a true **mist forest** on its summit,
with a profusion of ferns, and tree trunks and rocks covered in mosses. This

very strenuous walk can be undertaken only with a licensed **guide** (Jack Shick ℡02/6563 2218; $30; BYO lunch). The track to the top was blazed by botanists in 1869, who took two days to get there, but they were rewarded with the discovery of a plant seen nowhere else on earth – the **pumpkin tree**, bearing fleshy orange flowers. You can see other rare endemic plants here, such as the island apple and the blue plum, as well as birds such as the providence petrel and the woodhen. On average, the return walk takes eight hours; it's graded medium to hard and you'll need to be fit and have a good pair of walking boots. It's not for the faint-hearted: one section of the walk runs precariously along a narrow cliff face above the sea, and in parts the track is so steep that you must haul yourself up by ropes. To join the walk, you have to be at the Little Island gate on the south of the island by 7.30am: transport there is available for an extra $5.50 round-trip from Whitfield Bus Tours (℡02/6563 2115), or it's about a half-hour cycle ride from the north of the island.

Slightly less energetic activities are available at the *Blue Lagoon Lodge*'s **tennis courts** on North Beach Road (balls and rackets available to rent from Thompson's Store), and the nine-hole **golf course** near *Capella Lodge*, which operates on an honesty system ($15 with your own clubs, $25 with theirs; balls $1); there's a chicken run competition held here on Friday afternoons, and an eighteen-hole competition on Sundays.

Water-based activities

Besides bushwalks, the island has some sensational swimming, snorkelling and diving sites. The water's combined temperate and tropical sealife make local double-headed wrasse, lobsters and angelfish a common sight. Among the cruises on offer, the **glass-bottom boat cruises** from Lagoon Beach, which take about twenty passengers, are particularly good value at $20 for two hours (book at Thompson's General Store); included are opportunities to snorkel at **Erscotts Hole**, with gear and wet suits provided, and hand-feeding of fish, including a friendly old double-headed wrasse – you also see much more than on other, motorboat excursions. Islander Cruises (℡02/6563 2021, ✉islander cruises@bigpond.com.au) can take you to North Bay, combining a **snorkelling** excursion around the 1965 wreck of the *Favorite* (where three-stripe butterfly fish have made their home) with bushwalks up to Old Gulch or up to the summit of Mount Eliza (Sept–June 10am–4pm; $28 including morning and afternoon tea, BYO lunch).

There's more stunning snorkelling at Sylphs Hole, off Old Settlement Beach, and on the east side of the island at Ned's Beach, where slightly musty snorkelling sets can be rented on an honesty-box system ($2 for 1hr, $4 half-day, $6 full day, $30 per week; wet suit $3 for 30min, $6 for 1hr); sets are also available from most lodges, and Thompson's Store. Every day at 5pm for the last fifteen years, Ned's Beach has been the site of a **fish-feeding** frenzy, when a local man throws fish scraps into the water, attracting a throng of big trevally and reef sharks; the beach is also home to a venerable sea turtle. Stay here until dusk and you can observe **muttonbirds** en masse darkening the sky as they come home to roost. This experience can be a bit frightening, as they fly low through a forest of enormous **banyan trees** whose tangle of aerial roots descends to the ground.

Fishing trips can be arranged with Lulawai (℡02/6563 2195; $50 half-day), who guarantee you some fish, which the crew will prepare for you to barbecue later. Thompson's Store provides rods, reels, tackle and bait for those who already know what they're doing. If you're interested in **diving** in the waters around Lord Howe, contact Howea Divers (℡ & ℻02/6563 2290,

@howeadivers@bigpond.com.au), a recommended outfit run by a local. As well as advanced dives and tuition, they offer novices the chance to dive either off boats or from the shore for $80, and they also host sensational dive trips to nearby Ball's Pyramid, the world's tallest monolith. Pro-Dive also has an outlet on the island, with packages bookable through their Sydney central reservations (℡02/9281 5066 or 1800 820 820, Ⓦwww.prodive.com.au).

Eating and drinking

Bookings are necessary at all **eating** places for evening meals. An essential **lunch** or snack stop is the *Blue Peter* (daily 10am–5pm), a summer-only café on Lagoon Road, which offers affordable salads, speciality burgers, focaccia and daily fish specials. Thompson's General Store also does inexpensive takeaway fish and beef burgers at lunch time. The best **restaurants** on the island are the restaurant at the *Arajilla* resort (℡02/6563 2002) and *White Gallinule* (at *Capella Lodge*; ℡02/6563 2008). Both serve deliciously innovative modern Australian cuisine, with the emphasis on local ingredients and excellent fish dishes, while *White Gallinule* offers the best views, and has the advantage of an extensive cocktail list. There's no pub on the island, but the closest thing to a **bar** is the *Bowling Club*, where the locals hang out (daily 4.30–8pm); there's also a very popular disco held here every Friday night (8pm–midnight).

Norfolk Island

Just 8km long and 5km wide, tiny, isolated **NORFOLK ISLAND**, an External Territory of Australia located 1500km due east of Brisbane, nevertheless has had an eventful history, linked with early convict settlements and later with the descendants of Fletcher Christian and other "mutiny-on-the-*Bounty*" rebels and their Tahitian wives who had outgrown Pitcairn Island. It's a beautiful, unique island, forested with grand indigenous pine trees, and with a mild subtropical climate ranging between 11°C and 18°C in the winter and from 19°C to 28°C (with high humidity) in the summer. Nowadays the island's **tax-haven** status makes it a refuge for millionaires, with thirteen of them living on the island including the Australian novelist Colleen McCullough. The island's history is exploited to the full for Norfolk's tourists, who spend a fortune in the numerous duty-free stores; there's a big philatelic industry too.

The island mainly attracts honeymooners or retired Australians and New Zealanders lured by the quiet life and the inexpensive shopping (known collectively as the "newly weds and nearly deads"). Even the most frequent visitors require a passport to visit the island, which has its own government, a nine-member Legislative Assembly, and an administrator appointed by the Australian Governor General. A thirty-day **visitor permit**, extendable to 120 days, is granted automatically on arrival. The island has no income tax, finances being raised from sources such as departure tax ($25) and a road levy included in the price of petrol. There's a $500 fine for working illegally for non-residents of the island. Many of the 1800 residents (who are not entitled to unemployment benefit) hold down two or three jobs, and employment for school-leavers is guaranteed, often in the two tacky sound-and-light shows that tell the story of the mutiny on the *Bounty* and the convict era. Most of the local people remain unaffected by tourism, maintaining their friendly, good-humoured attitude, their ridiculous nicknames and the remnants of their dialect, **Pitcairn**, a mixture of old West Country English and Tahitian (see p.390).

Much of the land is cleared for cultivation, as islanders have to grow all their own fresh food to keep the island disease-free; cattle roam freely on the green island and are given right of way, creating a positively bucolic atmosphere. At the centre of the island is its only significant settlement, **BURNT PINE** and on the south coast, contrastingly picturesque **KINGSTON** is the sightseeing focus of the island. Scenic winding roads provide access to the **national park** and the **Botanic Garden** in the northern half of the island, which together cover twenty percent of Norfolk's area. It's here that you get an idea of how the entire island originally looked, as you roam through the best of the remaining subtropical rainforest. Norfolk Island is also an ornithologist's paradise, with nine endemic **landbird** species, including the endangered **Norfolk Island green parrot** with its distinctive chuckling sound. The two small islands immediately south of Norfolk, Nepean and Phillip islands, are important **seabird** nesting sites.

Some history

A violent volcanic eruption three million years ago produced the Norfolk Ridge, extending from New Zealand to New Caledonia (Norfolk Island's closest neighbour, 700km north), with only Norfolk Island and the smaller adjacent and uninhabited **Phillip** and **Nepean islands** remaining above sea level. **Captain Cook** "discovered" the island in 1774, but it's now believed that migrating Polynesian people had lived here for hundreds of years prior to his visit. Cook recommended that the island be secured for the British Crown, seeing value in its vegetation: the tall **Norfolk pines** he thought would make fine ships' masts, with accompanying sails woven from the native **flax**. Norfolk Island was settled in 1788, only six weeks after Sydney, with the idea of establishing a free settlement – of the 23 original settlers, 15 were convicts. However, plans to use the fertile island as a base to grow food for the starving young colony of Australia foundered when, in 1790, a First Fleet ship, the *Sirius*, was wrecked on a reef off the island, highlighting the problem, which still exists today, of its lack of a navigable harbour. This **first settlement** was judged a failure when its wood proved not to be strong enough for masts and it was finally abandoned in 1814. Most of the buildings were destroyed to discourage settlement by other powers, and many free settlers were granted land in New Norfolk in Tasmania (see p.1089).

Norfolk's isolation was one of the major reasons for its **second settlement** (1825–55) – as a **prison** rather than a productive island, described officially as "a place of the extremest punishment short of death". Some of the imposing stone buildings designed by Royal Engineers still stand in **Kingston**, on the southern coast of the island. There were up to two thousand convicts on the island, overseen by sadistic commandants who had virtually unlimited power to run the settlement and inflict punishments as they saw fit. Only under the command of the enlightened reformer Captain Maconochie (1840–44) was there some improvement in prisoners' conditions.

Norfolk Island was again abandoned in 1855, but this time the buildings remained and were used a year later during the **third settlement**, which consisted of 194 Pitcairn Islanders (the entire population of the island), who left behind their overcrowded conditions to establish a new life elsewhere. The new settlers had only eight family surnames among them – five of which (Christian, Quintal, Adams, McKoy and Young) were the names of the original mutineers of the *Bounty*. These names – especially Christian – are still common on the island, and today about one in three islanders can claim descent from the mutineers. The building of an airport during World War II and the arrival of television have helped greatly to reduce Norfolk's linguistic isolation, though these descendants still speak some Pitcairn to each other. Listen for expressions such as "Whataway?" ("How are you?") and "Webout you gwen?" ("Where are you going?"). **Bounty Day**, the day the Pitcairners arrived, is celebrated in Kingston on June 8.

Information, transport and tours

The island's **airport** is on the western side of the island, just outside **Burnt Pine**, the main service town; the island's information centre, banks and post office are all in Burnt Pine. For information and bookings in advance, contact **Norfolk Island Tourism**, PO Box 211, Norfolk Island 2899 (℡6723/22147, ⓦwww.norfolkisland.com.au), or consult ⓦwww.pi-travel.com/norfolkisland – the most comprehensive of the many island information websites. All tourist facilities are based in the main town of **Burnt Pine**. Here, in the Bicentennial Complex on Taylor's Road, you'll find: the **Norfolk Island Visitor Information Centre** (Mon–Fri 8.30am–5pm, Sat 8.30am–1pm, Sun 8.30am–3pm; ℡6723/22147, ⒡23109), which can book tours and activities; the liquor bond store, which sells discounted alcohol on production of your airline ticket; the **post office**; and the Communications Centre, where you need to go to make international **phone calls**. There are two **banks** on the main street, Westpac and Commonwealth; the Commonwealth has an ATM.

There's no public transport on Norfolk Island, so getting around by **car** is much the best option. Many accommodation places offer a car as part of the package or give you a big discount on **car rental**. It's very cheap anyway, from just $25 (plus insurance) at the airport. No one's bothered about seat belts or even driving mirrors, and the maximum speed limit is only 50kph (40kph in town). There are also a limited number of **bikes** for rent, which can be arranged through the tourist office.

Tours

For **tours**, Pinetree Tours (℡6723/22424, ⓦwww.pinetrees.com.au), with an office on the main street next to the Commonwealth bank, offers a slew of pricey tours, including an extensive introductory half-day bus tour of the island ($18). Bounty Excursions (℡6723/23693, ⓦwww.bountyexcursions.com) covers a range of cultural and historic sites, including a Convict Ruins Tour (Mon 1pm & Fri 3pm; 3hr; $20) and a panoramic Norfolk Discovery Tour (Mon & Thurs–Sun; 3hr; $20). Culla & Co, on Rooty Hill Rd (℡ & ⒡6723/22312), offers horse-drawn carriage rides of the island.

The island is surrounded by a coral reef and pristine waters, so at least one waterborne tour is a must. There are several glass-bottomed **boat cruises** on Emily Bay, including on the *Emily Queen* (℡6723/22225) and *Christian's Glaas Bohtam Boet* (℡6523/23258). For fishing trips, ask at the tourist office. Bounty Divers at the Village Centre (℡6723/22751, ⓦusers.nf/bountydivers) runs PADI courses and has **dive** charters ($79 per dive, including gear); **snorkelling** and **diving** gear, and **fishing** rods, are all available for rent here, too.

Accommodation

A lot of **accommodation** is in 1970s-style motels, but the island is gradually upgrading its image and now boasts some quaint, faithfully restored five-star cottages. A central online **booking service** is available at ⓦwww.norfolkislandaccommodation.com, or call ℡6723/22255, or fax ⒡22909.

The two most stunning places to stay are: *Christians* of Bucks Point (☎02/9525 7724, ⓦwww.christians.nf; ❼), a well-renovated historic property on the southeast coast, sleeping up to six, with floorboards and wooden doors from the original convict quarters in Kingston and car rental included in the price; and *Tintoela of Norfolk* (☎ & ⓕ6723/22946, ⓔtintoela @ni.net.nf; ❼), a large, luxury wooden house, and adjacent cottage sleeping up to ten, with panoramic views of Cockpit Valley and the ocean. *Anson Bay Lodge* (☎6723/22897, ⓔansonbaylodge@norfolk.nf; ❹), a smaller property for two to four people, is reasonably priced and located on Bullock's Hut Road. Some of the more attractive **motels** include: *Whispering Pines Luxury Cottages* on Grassy Road (☎6723/22114, ⓦwww.norfolk-pines-group.nf; ❼), which offers two-bedroom units with garden views over the sea; *Shearwater Scenic Villas* (☎ & ⓕ6723/22539, ⓦwww.shearwater.nf; ❺), with upmarket self-contained accommodation on extensive grounds overlooking the water near Bumbora Reserve; and the well-appointed *Crest Apartments*, near Kingston (☎6723/22280, ⓕ22977; ❺), which have fully equipped kitchens and excellent views over to Phillip Island. The *South Pacific Resort* (☎6723/23154, ⓦwww.southpacificresort.nlk.nf; ❻) is a recommended hotel close to Burnt Pine, with a bar, restaurant and swimming pool set in pleasant green grounds.

The island

BURNT PINE is a fairly modern affair crammed with shops selling everything from Lancôme cosmetics through to Sanyo stereos, all at duty-free prices; most shops are closed on Wednesday and Saturday afternoons and all day Sunday.

KINGSTON is Norfolk's administrative centre, with the Legislative Assembly meeting in the military barracks and the old colonial Government House now home to the island's Administrator. There is an excellent view from the **Queen Elizabeth Lookout** (opened by the Queen in 1974, the bicentenary year of the "discovery" of the island) over the **Kingston and Arthur's Vale Historic Area** and the poignant seafront **cemetery**, containing a number of graves from the brutal second settlement. You can wander freely around the cemetery and the grounds, which have detailed interpretive boards, but it's expensive to visit the remaining buildings and their museums: you can tour the buildings separately ($6) or with a combined ticket ($18) which allows multiple access to all sites spread over several days.

Quality Row bears some of the world's most impressive examples of Georgian **military architecture**, and looking at the buildings now it's difficult to imagine the suffering that took place behind their walls. Here is the place to come for a taste – or a surfeit – of Norfolk Island history; there are four museums housed under the umbrella of the **Norfolk Island Museum** (daily 11am–3pm; $6 per museum, $18 combined ticket; ⓦwww.museums.gov.nf). The **Archeological Museum**, where ongoing research is carried out, is located in the basement of the former Commissariat and was built in 1835; the upstairs was converted by the Pitcairners to All Saints Church. Close by, in the **No. 10 House Museum**, there are examples of Norfolk pine furniture made by convicts. The worthwhile **Social History Museum** is located in the pier store and outlines the story of the island through its three settlements. Perhaps most interesting, though, is the **Maritime Museum**, in what was once the Protestant chapel; various artefacts recovered from the 1790 wreck of the *Sirius* are on display, including its huge anchor, but more compelling is the *Bounty*-related paraphernalia brought here by Pitcairners, including the ship's cannon and even the kettle that was used on Pitcairn Island for everything from fermenting liquor to boiling sea water for salt. Near the museum you can watch cargo being towed ashore to the small jetty – even cars have to come this way, as there are no wharves. The Kingston area is also the site of the sports oval, the golf course and the island's main swimming **beaches**, protected by a small reef. Immediately in front of the walls of the ruined barracks, which local people use for shade and wind shelter while picnicking, is **Slaughter Bay**, which has a sandy beach dotted with interestingly gnarled and eroded basalt rock formations; the small bit of coral reef is excellent for **snorkelling**. At low tide you can take a cruise in a glass-bottomed boat (see "Tours", p.390) from nearby Emily Bay, which is also a safe swimming area, backed by a large pine forest.

In **Bumbora Reserve**, just west of Kingston, reached by car via Bumbora Road, you can see the natural regrowth of Norfolk pines; from the reserve you can walk down to Bumbora Beach, a shady little beach where you'll find some safe pools for children to swim in at low tide. There's another track down to **Crystal Pool**, which has more swimming and snorkelling.

West of Burnt Pine, along Douglas Drive, you'll find the exquisite **St Barnabas Chapel**, once the property of the Melanesian Mission (Anglican), which relocated gradually here from New Zealand between 1866 and 1921 with the aim of educating Western Pacific people in trades and education. The chapel's rose window was designed by William Morris, some of the others were designed by Sir Edward Burne-Jones, with the altar carved by Solomon Islanders.

On the **west coast** there's a scenic picnic area with tables and barbecues high over **Anson Bay**, from where it's a satisfying walk down to the beach. Immediately north of here, the **national park** has 8km of walking trails, many of them old logging tracks. Many walks start from **Mount Pitt** (320m), a pleasing drive up a fairly narrow and winding sealed road surrounded by palms and trees – worth it for the panoramic views. The most enjoyable walk from here is the three-kilometre route to the **Captain Cook Memorial** (1hr 45min), which starts as a beautiful grassy path but soon becomes a downward-sloping dirt track with some steps. Just south of the national park, on Pitt Road, the rainforest of the **Botanic Gardens** is worth a tranquil stroll. Here you can observe the forty endemic plant species including the pretty native hibiscus, the native palm, and the island's best-known symbol, the **Norfolk pine**, which can grow as high as 57m with a circumference of up to 11m. Both parks are permanently open, but camping is not allowed in either. The island also has an ecotourism attraction, **A Walk in the Wild**, at Taylor's Road, Burnt Pine (daily 2–5pm; free), educating visitors about the fragile, disappearing rainforest and its birdlife.

Eating, drinking and entertainment

Norfolk Island **food** is plain and fresh, with an emphasis on locally caught fish and home-grown seasonal produce. Tahitian influence remains in the tradition of the big fish fries, and in some novel ways of preparing bananas. As most accommodation is self-catering, you'll want to head to the Foodland Supermarket in Burnt Pine (daily to 6pm); most of the products on the shelves are from New Zealand, and the small range of fruit and veg available reflects what is grown on the island – you won't find the variety you would elsewhere. On Sunday afternoon fresh fish is sold at the Kingston pier.

The best, and most expensive, **restaurant** is *Mariah's*, at *Hillcrest Gardens Hotel* on Taylor's Road (℡6723/22255), for à la carte dining with spectacular views of Phillip Island. *James' Place* at New Cascade Road in Burnt Pine (℡6723/23039) has innovative, Asian-influenced and vegetarian dishes. The *South Pacific Resort* puts on big fish fries, smorgasbord nights, roast carveries and musical shows at various times during the week; on other nights an ordinary brasserie menu is available from 5.30pm. A superb spot for lunch is the extremely popular *Café Pacifica* (℡6723/23210) on Cutters Corn Road, set in a leafy nursery and serving exquisite brunches and afternoon teas.

The **clubs** on the island provide good places to eat, drink and mingle with the locals. Facing each other across Burnt Pine's main street are the *Sports and Workers Club* and the *Norfolk Island Bowling Club*. The *Golf Club* in Kingston has a popular bar that also serves meals, while the nearby Royal Engineers Office has a café serving tea and cakes. The only **pub** is the *Brewery*, opposite the airport, with local ales such as "Bee Sting" and "Bligh's Revenge", pool tables and a rough, late-night crowd that can be a bit intimidating for single women.

Travel details

Most public transport in New South Wales originates in Sydney, and the main services are outlined in the "Travel details" at the end of Chapter 1 on p.244.

Trains

There are ten main train routes departing from Sydney that pass through the region covered in this chapter; all trains are run by Countrylink, which extends its network with additional bus services. For full details see ⓦ www.countrylink .nsw.gov.au or call ℡13 22 32.

- Sydney–**Broken Hill** (3 daily; 13hr), via **Condoblin** (6hr 40min).
- Sydney–**Albury** (2 daily; 7hr 20min), via **Cootamundra** (5hr) and **Wagga Wagga** (6hr).
- Sydney–**Armidale** (1 daily; 8hr 10min), via **Tamworth** (6hr 15min).
- Sydney–**Brisbane** (1 daily; 14hr 10min), with stops including **Taree**, **Coffs Harbour** and **Grafton**.
- Sydney–**Canberra** (3 daily; 4hr 10min), via **Goulburn** (2hr 35min).
- Sydney–**Dubbo** (2 daily; 6hr 30min), via **Bathurst** (3hr 30min).
- Sydney–**Melbourne** (2 daily; 10hr 20min), with stops at **Cootamundra** and **Wagga Wagga**.
- Sydney–**Moree** (1 daily; 9hr), via **Scone** (4hr 20min), **Gunnedah** (6hr 20min) and **Narrabri** (7hr 45min).
- Sydney–**Murwillumbah** (1 daily; 13hr 45min), via **Taree** (5hr 20min), **Wauchope** (6hr 30min), **Coffs Harbour** (8hr 40min), **Grafton** (10hr),

Lismore (12hr) and **Byron Bay** (13hr).
- The New South Wales leg of the Indian Pacific linking Sydney and Perth via Adelaide takes in **Condoblin** (10hr 35min from Sydney), **Ivanhoe** (13hr 50min), **Menindee** (16hr 10min) and **Broken Hill** (18hr 55min).

Buses

Albury to: Canberra (2 daily; 4hr); Corowa (3 weekly; 1hr); Cowra (1 daily; 4hr); Dubbo (1 daily; 8hr 30min); Echuca (3 weekly; 4hr 15min); Melbourne (3 daily; 4hr); Tamworth (1 daily; 12hr 20min); Yass (2 daily; 3hr 20min).

Armidale to: Brisbane (6 daily; 7hr 45min); Port Macquarie (3 weekly; 6hr 15min); Melbourne (2 daily; 18hr 45min); Sydney (4 daily; 8hr); Tamworth (3 daily; 1hr 45min); Tenterfield (2 daily; 2hr 20min).

Bourke to: Dubbo (3 weekly; 4hr 45min).

Broken Hill to: Adelaide (2 daily; 7hr); Cobar (3 daily; 5hr 20min); Dubbo (5 daily; 9hr 30min); Mildura (3 weekly; 4hr); Sydney (1 daily; 17hr 40min).

Byron Bay to: Ballina (3–8 daily; 35min); Brisbane (10–11 daily; 2hr 15min); Coffs Harbour (6 daily; 3hr 50min); Murwillumbah (4–8 daily; 50min); Port Macquarie (4 daily; 6hr); Surfers Paradise (6–7 daily; 1hr 5min); Sydney (6 daily; 12hr 15min).

Canberra to: Albury (1 daily; 4hr 10min);

Bairnsdale (3 weekly; 7hr); Batemans Bay (1–2 daily; 2hr 30min); Bega (1 daily; 3hr 30min); Bombala (3 weekly; 3hr 30min); Cooma (1–2 daily; 1hr 50min); Eden (1 daily; 4hr 20min); Griffith (1 daily; 6hr 35min); Melbourne (6 daily; 8hr 30min); Moruya (1–2 daily; 3hr 25min); Narooma (1–2 daily; 4hr 30min); Nowra (1 daily; 4hr 45min); Wagga Wagga (2 daily; 3hr); Wollongong (1 daily; 3hr 25min).

Coffs Harbour to: Byron Bay (6 daily; 3hr 40min); Grafton (5 daily; 1hr 10min); Nambucca Heads (6 daily; 50min); Tweed Heads (1 daily; 6hr 10min).

Coonabarabran to: Adelaide (3 daily; 12hr); Brisbane (4 daily; 19hr); Canberra (3 daily; 5hr 40min); Melbourne (5 daily; 7hr 30min); Sydney (5–6 daily; 8hr 30min–10hr).

Cootamundra to: Dubbo (1 daily; 4hr 15min); Gundagai (6 weekly; 45min); Tumbarumba (6 weekly; 2hr 45min).

Dubbo to: Albury (1 daily; 9hr); Bathurst (1 daily; 2hr 45min); Bourke (3 weekly; 4hr 45min); Brewarrina (3 weekly; 5hr 45min); Broken Hill (5 daily; 8hr 30min); Canberra (4 weekly; 6hr 10min); Cobar (3 daily; 3hr 30min); Coonabarabran (3–5 daily; 1hr 50min); Cootamundra (3 weekly; 4hr 15min); Cowra (1–2 daily; 3hr 20min); Forbes (2 daily; 2hr 35min); Griffith (2 daily; 4hr 45min); Gunnedah (1 daily; 4hr); Lightning Ridge (1 daily; 4hr 50min); Moree (3 daily; 4hr 20min); Narrandera (1 daily; 5hr 15min); Orange (1 daily; 2hr 40min); Parkes (2 daily; 2hr 10min); Tamworth (3–5 daily; 4hr); Wagga Wagga (2 daily; 6hr).

Griffith to: Canberra (1 daily; 6hr 15min); Cootamundra (1 daily; 2hr 35min); Hay (1 daily; 3hr 50min); Leeton (1–2 daily; 50min); Narrandera (1–2 daily; 1hr 15min); Wagga Wagga (1–2 daily; 2hr 40min).

Lismore to: Ballina (1–3 daily; 45min); Brisbane (3–5 daily; 3hr); Byron Bay (4–6 daily; 1hr 15min); Casino (2 daily; 25min); Murwillumbah (3–5 daily; 2hr); Nimbin (2–3 daily; 25min); Tweed Heads (3–5 daily; 2hr 45min).

Lithgow to: Bathurst (3–6 daily; 1hr); Coonabarabran (6 weekly; 5hr 30min); Cowra (6 weekly; 2hr 40min); Dubbo (6 weekly; 4hr 30min); Mudgee (1 daily; 2hr 30min); Orange (2–5 daily; 1hr 45min–2hr).

Murwillumbah to: Tweed Heads (4–11 daily; 30min).

Port Macquarie to: Armidale (3 weekly; 6hr 15min); Ballina (5 daily; 6hr); Bellingen (3 weekly; 3hr 15min); Brisbane (5 daily; 10hr 30min); Coffs Harbour (5–6 daily; 2hr 40min); Dorrigo (3 weekly;

3hr 50min); Grafton (5 daily; 4hr 10min); Scone (3 weekly; 10hr 20min); Surfers Paradise (5 daily; 9hr); Tamworth (3 weekly; 8hr 30min).

Tamworth to: Armidale (1 daily; 1hr 40min); Cessnock (1 daily; 4hr); Dorrigo (3 weekly; 4hr 10min); Gunnedah (2 daily; 1hr); Inverell (1 daily; 3hr 40min); Port Macquarie (3 weekly; 8hr 30min); Scone (2 daily; 2hr 15min); Tenterfield (2 daily; 4hr 30min).

Flights

Armidale to: Brisbane (1–2 daily; 1hr 10min); Coolangatta (3 weekly; 50min); Sydney (1–3 daily; 1hr 10min).

Ballina to: Brisbane (1–3 daily; 45min); Sydney (2–5 daily; 1hr 10min).

Broken Hill to: Adelaide (1–4 daily; 1hr 40min); Dubbo (6 weekly; 2hr), Sydney (2–4 daily; 3hr 45min).

Canberra to: Ballina (2–3 daily; 4hr 40min); Dubbo (1–2 daily; 2hr 15min); Grafton (1–2 daily; 2hr 30min); Lismore (1–4 daily; 4hr 10min); Moree (1–2 daily; 3hr 55min); Narrabri (1–2 daily; 3hr 15min); Newcastle (3–4 daily; 2hr 10min); Port Macquarie (3–9 daily; 2hr 25min); Sydney (25–30 daily; 35min); Tamworth (4–8 daily; 2hr 25min).

Coffs Harbour to: Brisbane (2 daily; 45min); Sydney (3–5 daily; 55min).

Dubbo to: Brewarrina (3 weekly; 1hr); Broken Hill (6 weekly; 2hr); Brisbane (2 weekly, 2hr 10min) Cobar (1–3 a day, Sun–Fri; 1hr); Coolangatta (2 weekly, 1hr 35min); Lightning Ridge (1–2 a day, Mon–Fri; 1hr 40min); Nyngan (4 weekly; 30min); Sydney (3–13 daily; 1hr); Walgett (5 weekly; 1hr 10min).

Lismore to: Brisbane (2–3 daily; 25min); Sydney (5–8 daily; 1hr 50min).

Lord Howe Island to: Brisbane (6 weekly; 2hr); Sydney (6 weekly; 2hr).

Norfolk Island to: Brisbane (6 weekly; 2hr 10min); Sydney (5 weekly; 2hr 30min).

Port Macquarie to: Brisbane (3–6 daily; 1hr); Coffs Harbour (2–3 daily; 25min); Sydney (6 daily; 55min).

Tamworth to: Brisbane (4–12 daily; 2hr 20min); Cobar (8 weekly; 1hr); Melbourne (2–3 daily; 3hr 20min); Mildura (6 weekly; 1hr 30min); Sydney (3–8 daily; 1hr).

Taree to: Port Macquarie (1–2 a day, Mon–Sat; 20min); Sydney (3 daily; 55min).

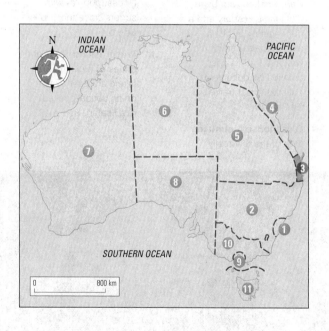

Southeast
Queensland

CHAPTER 3   # Highlights

✳ **Gold Coast nightlife**
The bars, clubs and theme parks of Australia's prime domestic holiday destination provide raucous entertainment around the clock. See p.427

✳ **Lamington National Park** Packed with beautiful jungle scenery and a huge variety of plants and animals, Lamington National Park is crisscrossed by dozens of enticing forest trails. See p.440

✳ **Glasshouse Mountains** One of the few really special places on the Sunshine Coast, it's worth climbing at least one of the dramatic pinnacles for the fantastic views. See p.444

✳ **Surf at Noosa** Catch the waves at exclusive Noosa, popular with surfers since the 1960s. See p.447

✳ **Fraser Island** The giant dunes of beautiful Fraser Island are best explored on an action-packed 4WD safari. See p.457

3

Southeast Queensland

S outheast Queensland comprises the 800-kilometre stretch between the New South Wales border and Fraser Island, and contains many of the classic features that lure visitors to Australia's second-largest state. **Surf** rolls in to long, sandy beaches, backed by vibrant towns in exotic settings; behind them, the land rises a thousand metres or more to lush, rainforest-clad plateaus. It's one of Australia's busiest tourist venues, a factor that will be central to your impressions of the region: some love the hype and pace of it's higher-profile attractions; others loathe it for the same reasons and despair of ever finding an untramped corner.

However, though parts of Southeast Queensland undoubtedly live up to their glitzy reputations, there's far more to the region than its popularity on the "drunken backpacker" trail would suggest. Set down towards the border, the state capital **Brisbane** is an attractive, relaxed city with good work opportunities and a lively social scene, with some very underrated scenery within easy reach – the best of which are the giant, wooded, sand islands of shallow **Moreton Bay**. South of Brisbane, the **Gold Coast** is Australia's prime domestic holiday destination; while its reputation was founded on some of Queensland's best surf, this now takes second place to a belt of beach-front high-rises, **theme parks**, and the host of bars and nightclubs surrounding **Surfers Paradise**. But even here there are quieter corners, such as the often almost empty beaches at the Gold Coast's southernmost town, **Coolangatta**. An hour inland, the Scenic Rim's green heights provide the perfect antidote to coastal concretions, with a chain of national parks packed with wildlife and endless hiking trails. Heading north of Brisbane, fruit and vegetable plantations behind the gentle **Sunshine Coast** benefit from rich volcanic soils and a subtropical climate. **Noosa** is the hub here, an up-and-coming resort town with more beaches and famous surf. Beyond looms **Fraser Island**, whose surrounding waters host an annual whale migration and where huge forested dunes, freshwater lakes and sculpted coloured sands form the backdrop for exciting 4WD safaris.

In a way, Queensland's popularity as a holiday hotspot is surprising, as this is eastern Australia's most **conservative** state, often lampooned – somewhat unfairly – as being slow and regressive. There are, however, very physical and social divisions between the densely settled, city-oriented southeastern corner and the large, rural remainder, which is given over to primary industries such

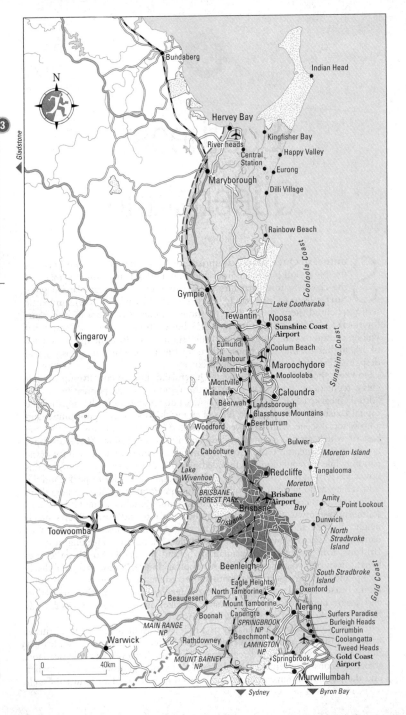

as mining and farming. These divisions date back to when Brisbane was chosen as capital on Queensland's separation from New South Wales in 1859; the city proved an unpopular choice with the northern pioneers, who felt that the government was too far away to understand, or even care about, their needs. These needs centred around the north's sugar plantations and the use of Solomon Islanders for labour, a practice the government equated with **slavery** and finally banned. Ensuing demands for further separation, this time between tropical Queensland and the southeast, never materialized, but the remoteness of northern settlements from the capital led to local self-sufficiency, making Queensland far less centralized than other states.

The darker side of this conservatism has seen Queensland endure more than its fair share of extreme or simply dirty politics. During the 1970s and early 1980s, the stranglehold of a strongly conservative National Party government, led by the charismatic Sir **Johannes Bjelke-Petersen** (better known as "Joh"), did nothing to enhance the state's image. Citing issues of law and order to justify granting the police sweeping powers, Joh created a repressive and domineering government, characterized by his own peculiar, slippery oratory. He finally became the victim of his own devices after initiating the Fitzgerald Inquiry – an investigation into government corruption – which implicated his cabinet in a variety of offences and forced him from office. But the following left-wing government was not without controversy, though state Labor leader Peter Beatty was re-elected as Premier with a huge majority in 2001. The late 1990s were also blighted by the emergence from Southeast Queensland of **Pauline Hanson** and her One Nation Party, whose shallow, racist outbursts won favour with a fair number of Australians who felt ignored by the main parties and threatened by a slowing economy and immigration issues.

As a major tourist destination, Queensland's south coast seldom presents travel or accommodation problems, and in many places the only trouble is making some sort of choice between the vast array of options. However, during **busy periods** – the Easter and Christmas holidays, and at weekends – there are room shortages and price hikes in all accommodation except hostels. This is most pronounced on the Gold Coast, though you'll find a degree of seasonal inflation throughout the region. Book in advance whenever possible, and don't be afraid to bargain outside the peak times.

Brisbane and around

By far the largest city in Queensland, **BRISBANE** is not quite what you'd expect from a state capital with almost one-and-a-half million residents. Although there is urban sprawl, and high-rise buildings, slow-moving traffic, crowded streets and the other trappings of a business and trade centre, there's little of the pushiness that usually accompanies them. To urbanites used to a more aggressive approach, the atmosphere is slow, even backward (a reputation the city would be pleased to lose), but to others the languid pace is a welcome change and reflects relaxed rather than regressive attitudes.

Seen from the river or the top of Mount Coot-tha, it is an attractive enough place, with the typical features of any Australian city of a comparable age and

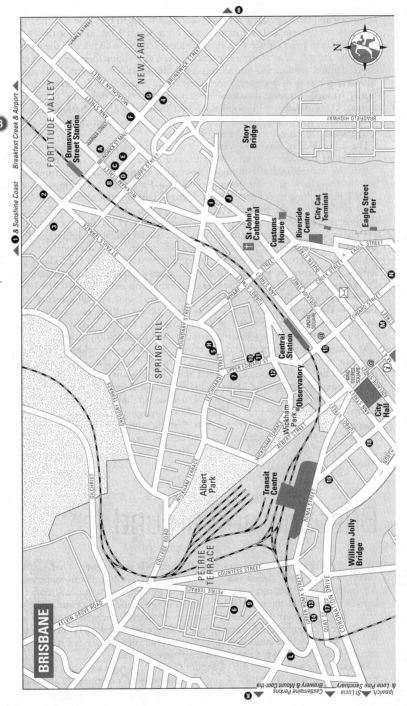

BRISBANE

FORTITUDE VALLEY

NEW FARM

SPRING HILL

PETRIE TERRACE

Albert Park

Wickham Park

Story Bridge

St John's Cathedral

Customs House

Riverside Centre

City Cat Terminal

Eagle Street Pier

Brunswick Street Station

Central Station

Observatory

City Hall

Transit Centre

William Jolly Bridge

Anzac Square

King George Square

▶ Ipswich

▶ Gold Coast

ACCOMMODATION	
Acacia	10
Annie's Shandon Inn	11
Astor	12
Aussie Way Hostel	6
Balmoral House	2
Banana Benders	9
Brisbane	
Backpackers' Resort	20
Central Brunswick	4
Apartment Hotel	
City Backpackers	13
Dorchester Inn	7
Econo Inn	3
Explorers Inn	18
Homestead	8
Palace Backpackers	15
Somewhere to Stay	21
Sportsmans Hotel	5
Stamford Plaza	19
Tinbilly	16
Tourist Guest House	1
Yellow Submarine	17
YHA Brisbane City	14

RESTAURANTS	
Asian House	D
Café The Hague	O
Caffé Tempo	V
California	F
Casablanca	L
Chez Laila	W
Cosmopolitan Coffee	A
Cristo's Café	T
e'cco	I
Govindas	P
Hunan	E
Jameson's	J
Kado Ya	Q
King Ahiram	X
King of Kings	C
New Asia	U
Paddo Tavern	K
Pane e Vino	R
Sushi Station	M
Three Monkeys Coffee	
Shop	S
Tibetan Kitchen	G
Topolino's	H
Victory Hotel	N
The Vietnamese	B

KANGAROO POINT

SHAFSTON AVENUE

WELLINGTON RD

MAIN STREET

Ferry Terminal

Botanic Gardens

BRISBANE CITY

Old Government House

Queensland Club

Parliament House

The Mansions

Harris Terrace

Science Centre

Commissariat Store

Treasury

Myer Centre

ALICE STREET

MARGARET STREET

CHARLOTTE STREET

MARY STREET

ELIZABETH STREET

ALBERT STREET

WILLIAM STREET

GEORGE STREET

Captain Cook Bridge

SOUTH EAST EXPRESSWAY

Maritime Museum

STANLEY STREET

Brisbane River

Ferry Terminal

RIVERSIDE EXPRESSWAY

City Cat Terminal

Lone Pine Ferry & North Quay

Performing Arts Complex

State Art Gallery

State Library

Queensland Museum

VICTORIA BRIDGE

South Bank Parklands

GREY STREET

MELBOURNE STREET

GREY STREET

South Brisbane Station

Convention Centre

MERIVALE STREET

CORDELIA STREET

RUSSELL STREET

EDMONDSTONE STREET

SOUTH BRISBANE

STEPHENS ST

Vulture Street Station

GLADSTONE ROAD

BLAKENEY ST

GLADSTONE RD

VULTURE STREET

BRIGHTON RD

VULTURE ST

FRANKLIN ST

BOUNDARY STREET

WEST END

BOUNDARY STREET

20

21

T

S

U

V

X

0   300m

401

size: a historic precinct, museums and botanic gardens. There's a confused blur of old and new, crammed in side by side rather than split into distinct districts, while new suburbs are blithely added to the shapeless edges as the need arises. The residents, too, have a spontaneous manner, partly because many are new to the area. In the early 1990s, economic malaise in Australia's southern states resulted in a steady northward migration of people seeking **work** – or at least finding Queensland a better place to be unemployed – and Brisbane was the obvious first stop. It's still a fairly easy place to find casual, short-term employment, and there's a healthy, unpredictable social scene, tempting many travellers to spend longer here than they had planned. As for exploring further afield, you'll find empty beaches and surf on **North Stradbroke Island** and **Moreton Island** – both easy to reach from the city – as well as subtropical woods in **Brisbane Forest Park**, a twenty-minute drive from the centre.

Some history

In 1823, responding to political pressure to shift the "worst type of felons" away from Sydney and the southeast – the further the better – the New South Wales government sent the Surveyor General **John Oxley** north to find a suitable site for a new prison colony. Sailing into **Moreton Bay**, he encountered three shipwrecked convicts who had been living with Aborigines for several months; they introduced Oxley to a previously unknown river. He explored it briefly, named it "Brisbane" after the governor, and the next year established a convict settlement at **Redcliffe** on the coast. This was immediately abandoned in favour of better anchorage further upstream, and by the end of 1824 today's city centre had become the site of Brisbane Town.

Twenty years on, a land shortage down south persuaded the government to move out the convicts and free up the Moreton Bay area to settlers. Immigrants on government-assisted passages poured in and Brisbane began to shape up as

Aboriginal Brisbane

John Oxley recorded that the **Brisbane Aborigines** were friendly; they had looked after the shipwrecked convicts and, in the early days, even rounded up and returned runaways from the settlement. In his orders to Oxley on how to deal with the indigenous peoples, Governor Brisbane admitted, though in a roundabout way, that the land belonged to them: "All uncivilized people have wants . . . when treated justly they acquire many comforts by their union with the more civilized. This justifies our occupation of their lands."

But future governors were not so liberal in their views, and things had soured long before the first squatters moved into the Brisbane area and began leaving out "gifts" of poisoned flour and calling in the Native Mounted Police to disperse local Aborigines – a euphemism for exterminating them. Bill Rosser's grim account in *Up Rode the Troopers – The Black Police in Queensland* tells the story through dialogues with the grandson of one of the last tribal members in the Brisbane area, and gives a good idea of how communities were split up and scattered by Queensland's **Protection Act**, which remained in force until the 1970s.

A trace of Brisbane's Aboriginal past is found at the **Nudgee Bora Ring** about 12km north of the centre at Nudgee Waterhole Reserve, at the junction of Nudgee and Childs roads. Last used in 1860, two low mounds where boys were initiated form little more than an icon today, and you'll probably feel that it's not worth the trip. More rewarding are the several **Aboriginal walking trails** at Mount Coot-tha; the City Hall information desk has leaflets on these which explain traditional uses of the area (see p.421).

a busy **port** – an unattractive, awkward settlement of rutted streets and wooden shacks. As the largest regional settlement of the times, Brisbane was the obvious choice as capital of the new state of Queensland on its formation in 1859, though the city's first substantial buildings were constructed only in the late 1860s, after fire had destroyed the original centre and state bankruptcy was averted by Queensland's first **gold** strikes at Gympie (see p.454). Even so, development was slow and uneven: new townships were founded around the centre at Fortitude Valley, Kangaroo Point and Breakfast Creek, gradually merging into a city.

After World War II, when General Douglas MacArthur used Brisbane as his headquarters to co-ordinate attacks on Japanese forces based throughout the Pacific, Brisbane stagnated, earning a reputation as a dull, underdeveloped backwater – not least thanks to the Bjelke-Petersen regime. As if to remove all trace of his rule, Brisbane underwent a thorough facelift before hosting the 1988 **World Expo**; not least for locals, who treated it as something of a coming-out party, the Expo provided a real boost after years of tedium. Since the 1990s, the city has become an increasingly busy and pleasant place to spend some time.

Arrival, information and city transport

Brisbane Airport is located 9km northeast of the centre, at the end of Kingsford Smith Drive. You'll find banks (including ATMs) and luggage lockers at both the domestic and the international terminals. To get **to Brisbane** from either terminal, there's the speedy **Airtrain** ($9 one-way, $15 return; ⓦ www.air-train.com.au), which takes just fifteen minutes to reach Brisbane's Transit Centre; or the **Coachtrans bus** ($9 one-way, $15 return; ⓣ07/3238 4799, ⓦ www.coachtrans.com.au), which takes up to forty minutes but delivers direct to central accommodation as well as the Transit Centre. A taxi into the city costs around $30 for the half-hour trip. For the **Gold Coast**, buses delivering direct to accommodation include Coachtrans (ⓣ1300 664 700) and Suncoast Pacific Coaches (ⓣ07/5443 1011), which both charge $33 one-way, $54 return.

Long-distance buses and trains all end up at Brisbane's **Transit Centre**, located in the heart of the city on Roma Street. On the highest of the three levels are the **bus offices**, luggage lockers and a hostel information desk (Mon–Fri 7am–6pm, Sat & Sun 8am–5pm). The middle floor has fast-food joints, a bar, toilets and showers, a medical centre and ATMs, while on the ground floor is the arrival and departure point for local and interstate **trains**.

During the day, reaching your accommodation seldom poses any problems as **local buses** and **taxis** leave from just outside the Transit Centre, and most hosteliers either meet buses or will pick you up if you call them. You can't always rely on a pick-up late at night, however, when it's best to take a taxi. While Brisbane is not as dangerous as most European or American cities of its size, it's still not a good idea to wander around after midnight with your luggage in tow. If you simply must get somewhere and don't have the cab fare, it's worth considering leaving your luggage in the lockers.

Information

Accommodation is well geared up to providing general information, and there are also **booths** providing city information at the airport (Mon–Fri 8.30am–4.30pm, Sat 10am–1pm), halfway down Queen Street Mall (Mon–Thurs 9am–5pm, Fri 9am–7pm, Sat 9am–4pm, Sun 10am–4pm) and in the City Hall foyer (Mon–Fri 8.30am–4.30pm, Sat 10am–1pm). There's also a

budget accommodation counter – aimed mostly at backpackers – on the top floor of the Transit Centre, staffed daily from 8am to 5pm.

City transport

Brisbane's centre is small and possible to cover on foot, but as the only Queensland city with a comprehensive transport system, it offers a level of luxury that's worth taking advantage of. Anywhere further afield is relatively easy to reach with private or public transport.

Buses, trains and ferries

All **bus and train fares** are calculated by zone – the more zones you cross, the more you pay. For example, a single bus fare in the central zone is $1.80, while a ride out to the suburbs costs around $3.80. One-way tickets can be bought on your journey (bus drivers give change); for several journeys and longer stays it's cheaper to buy a book of tickets or a **pass** from agencies around the city – look for the yellow-and-white flags outside participating shops. Some passes give discounts for day or off-peak travel – for example, the **Day Rover** ($8.40) offers unlimited bus, ferry and train travel for a day, ending at midnight; an **Off-Peak Saver** ($6.40) gives the same benefits Monday to Friday 9am to 3.30pm and after 7pm, and throughout Saturday and Sunday. A **Ten-Trip Saver** is a book of ten single fares for the price of eight.

Buses run from about 5am to 11pm, with most travelling via Queen Street Bus Station (below the Myer Centre), where platforms are named after native animals: platypus, koala, etc. There's also an information office (Mon–Fri 8.30am–5pm). The **City Sights bus** tours a preset route through the centre with a guide from 9am to 5pm daily – look for the specially marked stops. Tickets cost $20, are valid all day, and also allow unlimited use of bus and ferry services.

The electric **Citytrain** network provides a faster service than the buses, but it's not as frequent or comprehensive. Trains through central Brisbane run every few minutes, but for the more distant suburbs you may have to wait an hour. The last trains leave Central Station on Ann Street at about 11.45pm – timetables are available from ticket offices. You can buy tickets and passes at most stations.

Brisbane's **ferries** are a quick way of getting across the city. Running every ten to thirty minutes between 5.50am and 10.30pm, there are a couple of easy cross-river connections, but the Inner City and City Cat services are the most useful, the latter running at a bracing 27 knots between the University of Queensland campus in the southwest to Bretts Wharf, up towards the airport on Kingsford Smith Drive. Fares start at around $1.60 for a single crossing, and most bus passes are also valid. The central departure points for Inner City and City Cat are from South Bank Parklands, Eagle Street Pier and North Quay, next to Victoria Bridge.

Taxis, cars and bikes

After dark, **taxis** tend to cruise round the clubs and hotels; during the day Roma Street is a good place to find one. To call a taxi, try B&W Cabs (☎13 10 08) or Yellow Cabs (☎13 19 24).

Driving is not much fun until you get your bearings. Unfortunately, signs just at junctions, rather than well before them, are typical not only of Brisbane but of all of Queensland, and you'd be well advised to get some sort of street directory as soon as possible. Once familiar with the city, there are no great

For all bus, train or ferry **information** call ☎13 12 30.

problems, although parking is expensive and in short supply in the centre. For details of car-rental agencies, see "Listings", p.419.

Cyclists have a good number of bike routes from which to choose. Maps are available from some information sources (see p.403), libraries and city council offices. A few hostels loan bikes, or they can be easily rented elsewhere – again, see "Listings".

Accommodation

Brisbane's inner-city **accommodation** is varied and excellent value. The most expensive places are in the city centre, though there are also some first-rate **motel** deals here. If you're staying for a while, ask about **weekly rates**, which might amount to one free night in seven; for stays of a month or more contact Brisbane City Apartments (℡1800 627 538) which rents out one-bedroom apartments that sleep three for $280 per week. Beds are scarce only during major sports events and the **Royal Queensland Show** (the "Ekka") in August, a big agricultural expo with fairground attractions, stock shows, and wood-chopping competitions; the show sees around half a million visitors descend on the RNA Showgrounds over the weekend event. Prices at more upmarket places may also drop at weekends and outside peak season, due to the scarcity of business customers and competition from the Gold Coast.

Brisbane's abundant **backpackers' hostels** are scattered right across town and out to the coastal suburb of Manly. Many have entertainment, cheap meals, Internet facilities, bikes for rent or loan, pools and courtesy buses on arrival (and sometimes departure), and can arrange work connections.

City centre and Petrie Terrace

Petrie Terrace is a ten-minute walk from the Transit Centre – or take bus #144 from opposite the Transit Centre to stop 5.

Acacia 413 Upper Edward St ℡07/3832 1663, ℻3832 2591. Pleasant and central motel-like B&B with shared and en-suite rooms. ❸

Annie's Shandon Inn 405 Upper Edward St ℡07/3831 8684, ℮anniesshandoninn@hotmail .com. A cosy family-run B&B with single, double, and en-suite rooms just a 5min walk from the city centre. ❸

Astor 193 Wickham Terrace ℡07/3144 4000, ℗www.astorhotel.com.au. Boutique hotel in a smart, renovated nineteenth-century colonial building with a range of en-suite rooms and fully serviced apartments. Doubles ❹, suites ❺, two-bedroom apartments ❻

Aussie Way Hostel 34 Cricket St ℡07/3369 0711, ℮aussieway15@hotmail.com. Renovated nineteenth-century town house with quiet ambience, large pool, verandahs, balcony and period decor. Dorms $22, rooms ❷

Banana Benders 118 Petrie Terrace ℡07/3367 1157, ℮bbenders@bigpond.net.au. A small, friendly hostel with a homely, easy-going feel. There's a

small kitchen and BBQ area, a casual TV-and-video lounge, deck-space for dining, and free entry to the local public pool. Dorms $20, rooms ❷

City Backpackers 380 Upper Roma St ℡07/3211 3221, ℗www.citybackpackers.com. One of Brisbane's biggest hostels, this busy and well-run place has clean facilities, fair-sized rooms, own bar with budget meal deals and BBQ nights, and swimming pool. Dorms $16, en-suite rooms ❸

Dorchester Inn 484 Upper Edward St ℡07/3831 2967, ℮dorchesterinn@bigpond.com.au. Comfortable, self-contained, serviced apartments. Singles/doubles ❸, triples ❹

Explorers Inn 63 Turbot St ℡07/3211 3488, ℗www.powerup.com.au/~explorer. Smart, friendly boutique hotel comfortably located halfway between Queen Street Mall and the Transit Centre; standard rooms are a bit small but superior rooms have plenty of space and comfortable furnishings. ❸–❹

Palace Backpackers Cnr Ann and Edward streets ℡1800 676 340, ℗www.palacebackpackers.com.au. Huge hostel, purpose-built in 1911 but completely revamped (except for the ancient lift). Bang in the centre of town – which means that there's no parking space – with a restaurant and rowdy *Down Under Bar*, whose noise prompts some travellers to move elsewhere for some sleep. Poky singles, high-ceilinged and spacious doubles, and three- to nine-bed dorms. Dorms $20, rooms ❷

Sportsmans Hotel 130 Leichhardt St, Spring Hill ☎07/3831 2892. Gay-friendly pub with rooms; predominantly male clientele but both sexes welcome. ❷

Stamford Plaza Edward St ☎07/3221 1999, ⓦwww.stamford.com.au. Top-notch hotel with a grand mix of colonial and modern buildings overlooking the river and Botanic Gardens. ❼

Tinbilly Cnr George and Herschel streets

☎07/3238 5888, ⓦwww.tinbilly.com. Modern party hostel and bar almost directly opposite the Transit Centre; facilities are good though doubles are expensive and the noise level can build through the evening. Dorms $20, rooms ❸

Yellow Submarine 66 Quay St ☎07/3211 3424. Small, comfortable hostel in a refurbished 1860s building. Full kitchen facilities, laundry, BBQ and pool. The friendly owners put on boat trips around the bay and free BBQs, ensuring a sociable atmosphere, and the staff can help out with work connections. Dorms $21, rooms ❷

YHA Brisbane City 392 Upper Roma St ☎07/3236 1004, ⓦwww.yha.com.au. Sterile but with excellent facilities, including a first-rate budget canteen (open to nonguests). Dorms $24.50, rooms ❸

Fortitude Valley and New Farm

The Valley's accommodation is well placed for clubs but the area can be seedy late at night, although the surrounding area of New Farm is quiet enough. Most buses travelling up Adelaide Street pass through the Valley, or you can take the train to Brunswick Street Station. For New Farm, take a bus (#177, #178, #167 or #168) from Adelaide Street.

Balmoral House 33 Amelia St, Fortitude Valley ☎07/3252 1397 or 1800 066 202. A very quiet, secure and clean hostel, with new self-contained apartments, both handy for Chinatown and Brunswick Street; not for partying. Dorms $16, rooms ❸

Central Brunswick Apartment Hotel 455 Brunswick St, Fortitude Valley ☎07/3852 1411, ⓦwww.strand.com.au/brunswick.html. Gay-friendly accommodation in a sparkling modern building. Rooms are very comfortable, all with own bath, TV etc, some apartment-style with kitchen facilities. Shared amenities include spa and gym. ❹

Econo Inn 55 Brunswick St, Fortitude Valley ☎1800 655 381, ⓦwww.econoinn.com.au. Only a

short walk to Brunswick Street Mall and Chinatown, this modern place has spacious rooms and communal kitchen and BBQ areas. ❸

Homestead 57 Annie St, New Farm ☎1800 658 344. A large house converted to a hostel, with a pool shaped like a shamrock and plenty of outdoor space. There is free use of bikes and the hostel arranges trips to Mt Coot-tha and buses to North Stradbroke Island. Tends towards a party atmosphere. Dorms $19, rooms ❸

Tourist Guest House 555 Gregory Terrace, Fortitude Valley ☎1800 800 589, ⓦwww.touristguesthouse.com.au. One of Brisbane's converted Queenslanders (see p.409), this is a clean, quiet place with parking space, bar, laundry, and kitchen. Dorms $19, rooms ❸

South of the river and Manly

Brisbane Backpackers' Resort 110 Vulture St ☎07/3844 9956 or 1800 626 452, ⓦwww.home.aone.net.au/brisbanebackpackers. Massive, soulless hostel complex with round-the-clock reception, video surveillance and all facilities, including a licensed travel agent. Booking is essential, and be clear about what you're getting: some low-rate rooms are in a dilapidated old house across the road. Courtesy bus into town and

free pick-up. Dorms $20, rooms ❷

Moreton Bay Lodge 45 Cambridge Parade, Manly Harbour Village, Manly ☎1800 800 157. A 30min train ride from central Brisbane, this well-furnished antique pub out at Manly, on Moreton Bay, has great views of the bay and islands. It's just a stone's throw from Manly harbour and well geared up for sailing and island trips; there are plenty of shops and places to eat nearby. Pick-up from town

or airport, or a 5min walk from Manly train station. Dorms $19, rooms ②–③
Somewhere to Stay 45 Brighton Rd ☎07/3846 4584 or 1800 812 398, ⓦ www.somewhere tostay.com.au. Reasonable facilities, but noncha-

lant staff; building and furnishings are showing distinct signs of wear. Pay the extra and get a room with a view over Brisbane's skyline rather than one of the basic dorms. Courtesy bus into town and free pick-up. Dorms $18, rooms ③

The City

The **city** is focused around the meandering loops of the **Brisbane River**, with the triangular wedge of the business centre on the north bank surrounded by community-oriented suburbs. At its heart are the busy, upmarket commercial and administrative precincts around **Queen Street** and **George Street**, an area of glass towers, cafés and century-old sandstone facades that extends to the **Botanic Gardens** on the river. Radiating **north**, the polish gives way to less conservative shops, accommodation and eateries around Spring Hill, Fortitude Valley and New Farm, and the aspiring suburbs of Petrie Terrace and Paddington. To the **west** is a blaze of riverside homes at Milton and Toowong and the fringes of Mount Coot-tha and Brisbane Forest Park. **Across the river**, the major landmarks are the Cultural Centre and the convention centre, and **South Bank Parklands**, which stretch to Kangaroo Point. Beyond are the open, bustling streets of **South Brisbane** and the **West End**, more relaxed than their northern counterparts.

Downtown

Queen Street is Brisbane's oldest thoroughfare, its southern section between George and Edward streets a pedestrian mall with the **Myer Centre** – a multistoreyed shopping complex – as its focus. Outside, the **mall** is always busy with people running errands, eating at any number of cafés, window shopping or just socializing. There's usually some kind of entertainment too: either informal efforts – acrobats, buskers and the occasional soap-box orator – or more organized events such as Aboriginal and Torres Strait Islander dancing or jazz sessions on the small stage about halfway down the street.

City Hall, the Observatory and the business district

North from the mall along Albert Street, you arrive at **City Hall**, facing King George Square: in front of the fountains are bronze sculptures of swaggies, native wildlife and what look like large pieces of futuristic circuitry. A stately 1920s building ruined by an ugly clock tower, there's a reflection of former policies in the triangular sculpture over the portico, which depicts the Aboriginal way of life "dying out before the approach of the white man". The City Art Gallery (daily 10am–5pm; free) inside has a smattering of paintings, pottery and glassware, though it's worth checking to see if there are any temporary exhibitions of work by Australian artists, or if there are any screenings at the tiny cinema. The clock tower is open, too, if you want a view of the city centre (Mon–Fri 10am–3pm, Sat 10am–2pm; $2); access is through the City Hall foyer.

Further up Albert Street is **Wickham Park** and the grey cone of Brisbane's oldest building, a windmill known locally as the **Observatory**, built by convicts in 1829 to grind corn for the early settlement. The original wooden sails were too heavy to turn but found use as a gallows until being pulled off in 1850, and all grinding was done by a treadmill – severe punishment for the convicts who had to work it. After the convict era the building became a signal station and now stands locked up and empty, held together with a cement glaze.

East of here lies Brisbane's business district, which was heavily developed in the 1990s and left with a legacy of glassy high-rises sprouting alongside the restaurants and shops of the Riverside Centre; the few surviving old buildings are hidden among the modern ones. The copper-domed **Customs House** (daily 10am–4pm; free) at the north end of Queen Street, built in 1889, harbours a small collection of Chinese antiques and hosts free concerts given by the Queensland University Orchestra every month, while neo-Gothic **St John's Cathedral** (Mon–Sat 9.30am–4.30pm, Sun 11am–4.30pm; donation) on Ann Street, has some elegant stained-glass windows and the only fully stone-vaulted ceiling in Australia. Sunday morning is made lively by the **Eagle Street Markets** between the river and the road – too trendy for bargains, but not bad for jewellery and leatherwork, clothing and $20 massages.

The historic precinct

The area between Queen Street and the Botanic Gardens contains some of Brisbane's finest architecture, dating from the earliest days of settlement until the late nineteenth century. Between Elizabeth and Queen streets, occupying an entire block, is the former **Treasury** with its classical facade. Built in the 1890s, its grandeur reflects the wealth of Queensland's gold mines (though by this point most were on the decline) and was a slap in the face to New South Wales, which had spitefully withdrawn all financial support from the fledgling state on separation some forty years previously, leaving it bankrupt. With a twist typical of a state torn between conservatism and tourism, the building is now – appropriately enough – Brisbane's **casino**.

South along William Street, the **Commissariat Store** is contemporary with the windmill, though in considerably better shape. Originally a granary, it is now a museum (Tues–Sun 10am–4pm; $4) and headquarters of the Royal Historical Society of Queensland; the knowledgeable staff pep up an otherwise dusty collection of relics dating back to convict times. Brisbane's **Science Centre** (daily 10am–5pm; $8), whose entrance is one block over on George Street, is more interesting to visit. A hands-on approach makes it great fun, especially for children, and very therapeutic if you like to prod and dismantle exhibits instead of merely peering at them through a protective glass case. Favourites include the various optical illusions – try the "swinging bridge", guaranteed to induce nausea though it remains stock-still – and the "Thongophone", a set of giant pan pipes played by whacking the top with a flip-flop. It's all good rainy-day material.

Further south along George Street you pass **Harris Terrace** and **The Mansions**, two of the city centre's last surviving rows of Victorian-era terraced houses, the latter guarded by stone cats on the parapet corners. Nearby, on the corner of George and Alice streets, the **Queensland Club** was founded in 1859, just four days before the separation of Queensland from New South Wales. Heavy walls, columns and spacious balconies evoke a tropical version of a traditional London club; entrance and membership – women are still not allowed to join – are by invitation only. Diagonally opposite, **Parliament House** (Mon–Fri 9am–5pm when Parliament not in session, Sun 10am–2pm; free) was built to a design by Charles Tiffin in 1868 and presents an appealingly compromised French Renaissance style which incorporates shuttered north windows, shaded colonnades and a high, arched roof to allow for the tropical climate. You can see the grand interior on an hour-long guided tour, and there's access to the chambers when there's no debate in progress.

South of Parliament House, George Street becomes a lane along the western side of the Botanic Gardens. Here you'll find **Old Government House** (Mon–Fri 9am–4pm; $4), the official residence of Queensland's governors and premiers between 1862 and 1910. Another of Tiffin's designs, the building has been comprehensively restored to its stately early-twentieth-century condition, and is well worth a look for its furnishings. The National Trust offices are in the upper storey.

The Botanic Gardens

Bordered by Alice Street, George Street and the river, Brisbane's **Botanic Gardens** overlook the cliffs of Kangaroo Point and, while more of a park than a botanic garden, provide a generous arrangement of flowers, shrubs, bamboo thickets and green grass for sprawling on, all offering an easy escape from city claustrophobia. Free **guided tours** (Tues–Sun 11am & 1pm) leave from the rotunda, 100m inside the gardens' main entrance, halfway along Alice Street. Once a vegetable patch cultivated by convicts, formal gardens were laid out in 1855 by Walter Hill, who experimented with local and imported plants to see which would grow well in Queensland's then untried climate. Some of his more successful efforts are the oversized **bunya pines** around the Edward Street entrance at the east end of Alice Street, planted in 1860, and a residual patch of the **rainforest** that once blanketed the area, at the southern end of the park. Mangroves along the river, accessible by a boardwalk, are another native species more recently protected. During the day, cyclists flock to the park, as it's at one end of a popular cycling and jogging track that follows the north bank of the river south to St Lucia and the University of Queensland. At the southern end of the gardens, an open-air stage gets used for **classical music recitals** in the summer, beyond which there's a new **pedestrian bridge** over the river to South Bank Parklands.

The northern suburbs

North of the river, just beyond Brisbane's business district, are several former suburbs which have been absorbed by the city sprawl: Paddington and Petrie Terrace to the west, Spring Hill and Fortitude Valley to the north, and New Farm to the east. Houses in these areas are popular with Brisbane's aspiring professional class, and while office buildings and one-way streets are beginning to encroach, there's also an older character reflected in the high-set Queenslander-style houses (see box on below) still standing around Spring Hill and Petrie Terrace.

Queensland houses

There can hardly be a more typical image of rural Queensland than a high-set "Queenslander" surrounded by green fields of sugar cane. A response to the northern climate, these houses come in all shapes and styles but the basic design is a wooden box on piles with a verandah or balcony – the idea being to have a cool flow of air underneath the house to reduce the humidity inside. Traditional colours, now more commonly seen in cities where it's becoming popular to renovate Queenslanders, are cream, red or green, while older buildings may have corrugated-iron awnings, red "bull-nosed" roofs and wooden latticework on porches and eaves. In Brisbane they're generally low-set, but tend to be raised further off the ground as you move up into the tropics – the exception to the rule is at Redcliffe, 12km north of Brisbane, where the pole houses have supports 10m high to compensate for a steep hill.

The Castlemaine Perkins Brewery

Just down the hill from Petrie Terrace, the **Castlemaine Perkins Brewery**, Milton Road, Milton (☎07/3361 7597), has been making Queensland's own beer since 1878. Their famous yellow-and-red XXXX emblem is almost part of the Queensland landscape: splashed across T-shirts and the roofs of Outback hotels, or on labels on countless discarded bottles and cans that litter everywhere from roadsides to the depths of the Barrier Reef. For enthusiasts, the brewery opens its gates for **tours** (Mon–Wed 11am, 1.30pm & 4pm; $8.50; bookings essential and you must wear fully-enclosed shoes), which incorporate a thirty-minute rundown on the brewing process, followed by fifteen minutes swilling beer.

Fortitude Valley

While the other areas are mainly residential, **Fortitude Valley** – better known as just "the Valley" – is a tangled mix of shops, restaurants, bars and clubs, comprising Brisbane's unofficial centre of artistic, gastronomic and alcoholic pursuits. An eclectic mix of the gay, the groovy and the grubby, the Valley is now in stage two of inner-city gentrification, which sees the urban-poor make way for hipsters, artists and students. Stage three – the arrival of yuppies and inflated real-estate prices – is looming, but in the meantime you can enjoy an evening out among Brisbane's young, fun and adventurous. In less than a kilometre, the main thoroughfare of Brunswick Street has a dozen nightclubs, an Irish pub, a compact **Chinatown** complete with the usual busy restaurants and stores, and a burgeoning European street-café scene. It's best at weekends; on Saturday there's a secondhand **market** in the mall and the cafés are buzzing. After dark the Valley's streets can be somewhat menacing, with an element of drug-related petty crime. Although there are usually crowds around until very late, if you've any distance to go on your own after the pubs close, take a taxi.

Breakfast Creek

Named by John Oxley, who tucked into a morning meal here in 1823 on his voyage of exploration upstream, **Breakfast Creek** has shops and a hotel marking an acute traffic bottleneck where the road bridges the creek between the upper reaches of Fortitude Valley and the route to the airport. A pretty, if noisy, spot, looking out over usually placid water to inactive wharves, the real estate in nearby Hamilton and Ascot is becoming quite exclusive. If you're out this way – perhaps going to the airport or heading north – consider looking around **Newstead House** (Mon–Fri 10am–4pm, Sun 2–5pm; $4.40), Brisbane's oldest residence. A low, solid brick-and-stone building with a slate roof, it was constructed as a private home in 1845 by convict labour, and became the Government House twelve years later. Enlarged by the governor, the house was the focus of social gatherings, and on the nights that balls were held armed police protected it from attacks by Aborigines. Restored and now open as a museum, both house and grounds are remarkably quiet. As you stand surrounded by century-old furniture, taking in the views across the creek from one of the elegant windows, it's easy to forget how close you are to the city. The house is off Breakfast Creek Road just south of the bridge; to get there by public transport, take bus #117, #190 or #160 to stop 12.

South Brisbane

Across the river from the city centre, the **Cultural Centre** and its environs – comprising the state museum, library, gallery, performing arts complex,

△ Castlemaine

convention centre and South Bank Parklands – is Brisbane's most obvious tourist attraction. Immediately south of Victoria Bridge (itself a continuation of Queen Street), it's easily reached by train to South Brisbane Station, while plenty of buses from all parts of the city stop outside the station on Melbourne Street.

Beyond here, the **West End** is South Brisbane's answer to Fortitude Valley, with Boundary Street a similar ethnic mix – Asian, Greek and Italian – but with a more genteel atmosphere. There are no sights here as such, but it's worth a visit for the cluster of Asian stores and continental delicatessens, and for an escalating number of inexpensive restaurants and cafés around the hub at Boundary Road and Vulture Street, popular with students from the University of Queensland across the river at St Lucia; see pp.414–416 for details.

Queensland Museum

The **Queensland Museum** (daily 9.30am–5pm; free, except for special exhibitions) is essentially a natural history museum, but it benefits from a bias towards unorthodox methods of presentation. Wedge-tailed eagles hover overhead, koalas climb the walls and, in the foyer, there's the unsettling experience of walking underneath full-scale models of a family of humpbacked whales suspended from the ceiling. There's an overview of the state's marine environment and western Queensland's fossil beds, including a reconstruction of Queensland's own Muttaburrasaurus and a section of the **Lark Quarry dinosaur trackways**. Above swings a furry pterodactyl, reflecting recent theories that Australia was subject to a cold climate during the era of the dinosaurs. Upstairs, the more recently extinct **megafauna** from the Darling Downs, just west of Brisbane, unexpectedly come to life – a breathing, twitching model of a marsupial lion lounging on a rock at the top of the escalators catches everyone by surprise. Rock hounds and prospective gem hunters will also be interested in the museum's **mineral collection** – dozens of multi-coloured rocks from around the state together with information on identifying them in the field.

Ethnographic displays mostly relate to traditional life in New Guinea and Melanesia, with the glaring omission – apart from a handful of tools and a small section on the rainforest tribes from the north – of anything on Queensland's Aboriginal and Torres Strait Islander history. The displays are rounded off by miscellaneous items, including bits and pieces from aviation history and an eclectic collection of period furniture.

State Art Gallery and Library

Queensland's **State Art Gallery** (daily 10am–5pm; free, except for special exhibitions) provides a large, airy space for its wide-ranging collection, which includes a sizeable exhibition of twentieth-century painters. As well as works by visionaries such as Brett Whitely, Arthur Boyd and Sidney Nolan, there are some unusual (and very European) watercolour landscapes by **Aboriginal artists** Walter Ebataringa and Albert Namatjira (for more on the latter, see p.681) alongside a few functional tribal items – dilly bags, headwear and shields – labelled as "art" but somehow out of place here. One of the most interesting pieces in the gallery is a nineteenth-century stained-glass window depicting a kangaroo hunt – an Australian theme executed in a very European medium. Other Australian works include the romantic paintings of Tom Roberts and the Impressionistic canvases of Frederick McGubbin. Sculpture is scattered throughout the gallery in a somewhat offhand manner, and there's a small collection of high-quality glass hidden away in the back.

Next door, the **State Library** (Mon–Thurs 10am–8pm, Fri–Sun 10am–5pm) is best known for its **John Oxley Library** (closed Sat) up on level four, which records every aspect of Queensland's past in endless books, journals and photographs. Level three is devoted to music and art; they lend scores and there's even a piano room available for practice. Film buffs should head to level two to sample the video collection and check out the cinema's programme.

The South Bank Parklands

The **South Bank Parklands** date back to just 1988 and were built on the former Expo site. Despite this, they're one of the nicest parts of the city – you can promenade under shady fig trees along the riverfront; picnic on lawns under rainforest plants and bamboo, lining the banks of shallow, stone-lined "streams" (which are convincing enough to have attracted large, sunbathing water dragons and birds); or make use of the artificial beach and accompanying saltwater pool. **Bands** play most Saturday nights on the outdoor stage, or at the *Plough Inn*, a restored, century-old pub in the reconstructed, cobbled high street; other attractions include exhibits at the **Maritime Museum** (daily 9.30am–4.30pm; $6), including a 90-year-old Torres Strait pearling lugger and the World War II frigate *Diamantina*, on show in the dry dock. Ferries and the City Cat stop at the Parklands, and there's also a pedestrian bridge from the Botanic Gardens to the Maritime Museum.

Along the river

The sluggish, meandering **Brisbane River** is four hundred million years old, one of the world's most ancient waterways. It flows from above Lake Wivenhoe – 55km inland – past farmland, into quiet suburbs and through the city before emptying 150km downstream into Moreton Bay, behind Fisherman Island. Once an essential trade and transport link with the rest of Australia and the world, it now seems to do little but separate the main part of the city from South Brisbane; though it's superficially active around the city centre, with ferries and dredgers keeping it navigable, most of the old wharves and shipyards now lie derelict or buried under parkland.

If the locals seem to have forgotten the river, it has a habit of reasserting its presence through **flooding**. In February 1893 cyclonic rains swelled the flow through downtown Brisbane, carrying off Victoria Bridge and scores of buildings: eyewitness accounts stated that "debris of all descriptions – whole houses, trees, cattle and homes – went floating past". This has since been repeated many times, notably in January 1974 when rains from Cyclone Wanda completely swamped the centre, swelling the river to a width of 3km at one stage. Despite reminders of this in brass plaques marking the depths of the worst floods at **Naldham House Polo Club** (1 Eagle St, near the markets), some of Brisbane's poshest real estate flanks the river, with waterfront mansions at Yeerongpilly, Graceville and Chelmer. They're all banking on protection from artificial Lake Wivenhoe, completed in 1984, which should act as a buffer against future floods.

Of the various ways to explore the river, the easiest is simply to take a return ride on the City Cat (though Fort Lytton and Lone Pine below are not on the Cat route) – such a popular, if unofficial, sightseeing trip that the service can be severely overcrowded during holidays.

Fort Lytton National Park

Surrounded by the pipes and chimneys of the Ampol oil refinery at Wynnum, **Fort Lytton National Park** (Sun and public holidays only 10am–4pm;

$4.40) is a product of the colonial struggles around the Pacific Rim at the end of the nineteenth century. Only a few days away from French forces on Nouméa (New Caledonia), Queensland felt threatened by competing European empires and developed a string of coastal defences during the 1880s. Brisbane received the best of these: by 1900, the river mouth at Fort Lytton bristled with artillery and a barrage of floating mines. However, the defences were never put to the test and modern warfare made them obsolete. The fort was downgraded to a secondary line of defence after World War I and abandoned altogether in 1945.

As a piece of military history, the buildings look the part: austere concrete bunkers dug into slopes and capped in grass, gun ports trained on the river and an underground tunnel for checking the mines running down to the water. The best time to visit is when the **Brisbane Garrison Battery** dresses up in period costume and fires the massive gun at Easter, and again on the Queen's birthday. The fort is at the end of Lytton Road, west of Wynnum at the mouth of Brisbane River; it is not possible to get here on public transport.

Lone Pine Sanctuary

Lone Pine Sanctuary on Jesmond Road, Fig Tree Pocket (daily 8am–5pm; $19), has been a popular day-trip upstream since first opening its gates in 1927. Here you can see a large number of native fauna in their natural state which, in the case of the sanctuary's hundred-odd **koalas**, means being asleep for eighteen hours a day. At close quarters they're revealed as grey cushions wedged into convenient forks in the trees, occasionally waking up for long enough to chew eucalyptus leaves and blink myopically at the crowds. In nearby cages you'll find other slumbering animals: Tasmanian devils, fruit bats, blue-tongued lizards and dingoes. Indeed, about the only lively creatures you'll see are birds and a colony of hyperactive sugar gliders in the nocturnal house. Alternatively, head for the outdoor paddock where tolerant wallabies and kangaroos allow themselves to be petted, fed and occasionally roughed up by visitors.

You can catch **bus** #430 from outside the Myer Centre on Elizabeth Street to Lone Pine, but the best way there is to take a ninety-minute **river cruise** past Brisbane's waterfront suburbs with Mirimar Cruises (daily departure 10am from Queens Wharf Rd beside Victoria Bridge, return 2.50pm; $22, not including entry to Lone Pine). Free pick-up from your central accommodation is usually possible (for bookings call ☎07/3221 0300).

Eating

Brisbane has no gastronomic tradition to exploit, but there's a good variety of bars and restaurants all over the city, with a trend towards "Modern Australian" (creative use of local produce, with Asian and Mediterranean influences). Fortitude Valley has a dense grouping of Asian restaurants (and a fashionable café society), while South Brisbane's Boundary Street has more of a European flavour.

Counter meals and unlimited buffets at hotels are the cheapest route to a full stomach – aim for lunch at around noon and dinner between 5 and 6pm – or try one of the scores of **cafés** in the centre catering to office workers. The city's **restaurants** open from around 11am to 2pm for lunch, and from 6 to 10pm or later for evening meals; many are closed for one day a week (often Monday).

City centre

Café the Hague Myer Centre, Level A. Dutch-style coffee house, a cut above the fast-food joints opposite. Try the *poffertjes* – sweet pancakes – and a gourmet coffee for breakfast.

e'cco 100 Boundary St ☎07/3831 8344, ⓦwww.eccobistro.com. Boasts an impressive awards list, not to mention publishing their own cookbook – you'll have to book, sometimes days ahead. Not cheap but good value, with local favourite steamed mussels $15, and mains $20–30. Open for lunch Tues–Fri, dinner Tues–Sat.

Govindas Elizabeth St. Hare Krishna-run vegetarian food bar, with a $7.50 all-you-can-eat menu. Open for lunch Mon–Sat 11.30am–2.30pm, dinner Fri 5.30–7.30pm; there's a $4 banquet every Sunday (5–7pm), but you'll have to sit through a lot of chanting before you actually get to eat.

Jameson's 475 Adelaide St ☎07/3831 0077. Ostensibly a wine bar, Jameson's reputation rivals that of *e'cco*. Billed as "Modern Australian", the menu features dishes such as Woodside goat's cheese, snail and parsley soufflé, and breast of wood pigeon, all complemented by wine from what is reputed to be Brisbane's most satisfying and extensive cellar. It's one of the only places open late in the city (till 3am) and has live nightly entertainment (from jazz to hip-hop). Restaurant bookings essential; open Mon–Sun 10am–3am.

Kado Ya Elizabeth Arcade, between Elizabeth and Charlotte streets. Most popular of several Asian fast-food restaurants in the arcade, serving up Japanese soups, noodle dishes and sushi rolls from about $7.

Pane e Vino Cnr Charlotte and Albert streets. Smart Italian café-restaurant with pavement tables, catering mainly to nearby office executives. Pastas from $12, main courses (lots of fish, chicken and lamb) around $21.

Sushi Station 142 Elizabeth St, next to *McDonald's*. One in a chain of Japanese sushi bars where the selection of dishes parades around the tables on the back of a model train, featuring low-priced soups, rice, fish, seaweed and green-tea ice cream.

Topolino's 124 Leichhardt St. Cavernous budget Italian restaurant with huge pizzas, small but filling pasta favourites and very average salads. Pasta dishes under $11; pizzas $9–19.

Victory Hotel 127 Edward St. Nice beer garden with braziers taking the chill off in winter. The bistro meals are popular with the local business folk.

Petrie Terrace

Casablanca 52 Petrie Terrace. Inexpensive brasserie and café serving the young and preten-

tious. Tapas is served at the bar for around $12, and the food is excellent and mouthwateringly spicy, with genuine leanings towards North African cuisine. Taped Brazilian music or live bands provide atmosphere and there's an "open" jam (mostly jazz/funk) on Monday nights.

Paddo Tavern 186 Given Terrace. Respectable pub lunches served every day for only $1.95, leaving you with enough money for a beer or two.

Fortitude Valley

Asian House 165 Wickham St. Good, filling Chinese food at very reasonable prices – most mains, such as roast pork or greens in oyster sauce, are under $10.

California 376 Brunswick St. 1950s diner with original coffee cups, Formica-covered tables and hulking jukebox. Few people have managed to finish their legendary "truckie's breakfast" of five eggs, steak, liver, bacon, sausage and tomato ($20); a regular cooked breakfast costs $10. Open daily 7am–4pm.

Cosmopolitan Coffee 322 Brunswick St Mall. Relaxed place, something of an institution with Brisbane's café society; opens early for breakfast and is less pretentious than the surrounding competition.

Hunan Duncan St (halfway up Chinatown Mall, on the left). Stick to the "chef's suggestions" on the menu and you'll enjoy Brisbane's most authentic Chinese cuisine – though be warned, Hunanese cooking can use copious amounts of chilli and garlic. Try steamed beef in lotus leaf, fish in bamboo, or Mao's sliced pork – apparently a favourite dish of the late Chairman. Big portions; mains $12–17.

King of Kings 169 Wickham St. Two restaurants with separate entrances, though in the same building; the upstairs hall is popular with the local Chinese community thanks to its fine late-morning *yum cha* selection. Come prepared to queue at weekend lunch times. Open daily for lunch and dinner.

Tibetan Kitchen 454 Brunswick St ☎07/3358 5906. It's hard to resist any place that advertises "traditional Tibetan, Sherpa, Nepalese foods", and luckily the food here, including the Valley's best samosas ($4.90 for four) and curries, is tasty and cheap, and served in a very attractive setting. Mains $10–14. Open daily for dinner only; booking advisable at weekends.

The Vietnamese 194 Wickham St ☎07/3252 4112. With an interior as plain and unassuming as the name over the door, this is no-frills, genuine Vietnamese cuisine – the steamboat is excellent, as are the chicken salad and Vietnamese spring rolls (self-assembled using a boiled rice-noodle wrapper). Most mains cost around $9; two can eat well for $30. Open daily 11am–3pm & 5–10.30pm; you'll need to book at the weekend.

South Brisbane

Caffé Tempo 181 Boundary St. Great Italian-style home cooking, with fresh salads and fine seafood pasta – even humble sandwiches come with a salad big enough to be a meal in itself. Most expensive dish costs around $15, and they stay open until the last customer leaves.

Chez Laila On the Boardwalk, South Bank Parklands. Smart, open-plan restaurant and bar with fine river views and Lebanese cuisine. Upmarket falafel, kebabs and *kibbi*, along with side dishes of stuffed vine leaves, hummus, and *baba ghanouj* (grilled aubergine and tahini puree). Mains around $17.

Cristo's Café Cnr Melbourne and Boundary streets. Popular spot, sporting minimalist decor and Mediterranean colours inside, but with an open front that gives the feeling of pavement dining. Food is eclectic – tapas, antipasta, risotto, polenta and Moroccan lamb, alongside Asian noodles and spiced quail. Mains around $20.

King Ahiram 88 Vulture St. A long-running Lebanese takeaway and restaurant; not worth crossing town for, but good for kebabs and sticky Mediterranean desserts if you're in the area.

New Asia 153 Boundary St. Forget flashier Vietnamese restaurants in the neighbourhood, this is the best – prawns grilled on sugar cane, deep-fried quail, rice-noodle dishes – all for less than $8 a dish.

Three Monkeys Coffee Shop 58 Mollison St. Decorated with a funky assortment of African oddments; serves average coffee, awesome cakes, and effortlessly achieves the sort of bohemian atmosphere most coffee shops merely aspire to. Greek-influenced menu with plenty of vegetarian/lentil options, and nothing over $10. Open daily 9.30am–midnight.

Nightlife and entertainment

The city's entertainment horizons consist of an ever-fluctuating range of clubs, and a sound, if unadventurous, arts scene. The best cross-section of attractions are north of the river in **Fortitude Valley**, which throbs with the nightclub crowd.

Pubs, clubs and live music

Brisbane nights were once a byword for boredom: the few places that offered after-dark entertainment were either illegal or lifeless and closed early, and locals headed to the coast for their weekends. Things have changed, however, and Brisbane has seen a recent explosion of home-grown musical talent, with bands such as Savage Garden, Regurgitator, Custard and Powderfinger putting the city firmly on the Australian pop-culture map. On Friday and Saturday evening the centre is crowded, but the big push is out to the clubs, bars and restaurants (many with quality entertainment) of a reinvented and revamped Fortitude Valley. Live-music venues, however, are on the decline and tend to open and close in the blink of an eye; places listed below might be here to stay, but check with music stores such as Rocking Horse, 101 Adelaide St, or weekly **free magazines** for up-to-the-minute reviews and **listings**: *rave* for general info, *Time Off* for rock and live bands, and *Scene* for dance. There's no standard charge for club entry, and many places offer free nights and special deals.

City centre

Down Under Bar At *Palace Backpackers*, cnr Ann and Edward streets. Hugely popular and often overtly sexist get-drunk-throw-up-and-fall-down venue for travellers.

Jameson's 475 Adelaide St. Restaurant with nightly entertainment in the bar varying from live jazz and Wednesday's "songwriters night" to DJs playing hip-hop and acid jazz on Friday and Saturday.

Gay and lesbian Brisbane

Queensland has long had a reputation for repressive attitudes towards gays and lesbians, though anti-discrimination legislation is in force and Brisbane's gays and lesbians are revelling in a loud and energetic scene which gets better every year. In June the Pride Collective hosts the annual **Pride Festival**, a diverse event, with a street march, fair, art exhibitions, a film festival, sports events, general exhibitionism and a dance party – the **Queen's Birthday Ball**. At the **Sleaze Ball** in November there's another opportunity to indulge.

The gay scene is largely clustered around the suburbs of Spring Hill, Fortitude Valley, New Valley, New Farm and Paddington. For up-to-the-moment **information**, listen to Queer Radio, station ZZZ 102.1FM (Wed 6–9pm) or pick up a copy of *Qnews* (ⓦwww.qnews.com.au) or *Queensland Pride* from gay nightclubs, street distributors and some coffee shops.

For gay-friendly **accommodation**, try *Central Brunswick Apartment Hotel*, or the *Sportsmans Hotel* (see p.406); nightlife focuses on *The Beat*, *Options*, *The Wickham Hotel*, *Sportsmans Hotel* and the *Cockatoo Club* – all listed under "Pubs, clubs and live music".

Support groups and information

AIDS Gladstone Road Medical Centre, 38 Gladstone Rd, Highgate Hill (ⓣ07/3844 9599), medical services and counselling; Queensland AIDS Council, 32 Peel St, South Brisbane (ⓣ07/3017 1777, ⓦwww.quac.org.au).

Books Bent Books, cnr of Vulture and Boundary streets, West End, is the longest established gay bookshop in Brisbane.

Medical Brunswick Street Medical Centre, 665 Brunswick St, New Farm (ⓣ07/3358 1977). Gay and Lesbian health service, open Mon–Sat from 8am.

The Pride Collective Organizers of the Pride Festival – contact them through ⓦwww.prideawards.org.au.

Queensland Pride PO Box 8151, Woolloongabba, QLD 4102 (ⓣ07/3392 2922). Free monthly publication covering Brisbane and the rest of the state.

Petrie Terrace and Spring Hill

Options At the *Spring Hill Hotel*, cnr Leichhardt and Little Edward streets. Two-level gay and lesbian nightclub with bar, dance floor, coffee shop and cabaret stage. Events include drag shows, karaoke, strip nights and sausage sizzles. Young crowd, with women's nights every Friday, when there's a $5 cover charge; free entry on Sunday for cheap drinks, free wine and a floor show. Closed Mon & Tues.

Paddo Tavern 186 Given Terrace. Band and disco on Friday night with a crowded beer garden early on in the evening.

Sportsmans Hotel 130 Leichhardt St. Gay, lesbian and straight crowds fill the two floors; pool tables, pinball, bands, bottle shop and bistro. Their *Mineshaft Bar* is men only.

Fortitude Valley and New Farm

Arena 201 Brunswick St ⓣ07/3252 5690 for band info. Long-established venue hosting popular DJs and dance parties as well as local and international touring bands.

The Beat 677 Ann St. Small, crowded and sweaty, with a beer garden outside where you can recharge your batteries on bar food. $10 cover charge is a bit off-putting, but it's one of the best techno/dance venues in town, and open until 5am. Upstairs is the *Cockatoo Club*, a stridently gay venue featuring both indoor and outdoor bars, with a penchant for 1980s music. Open Wed–Sun.

Dooley's Cnr Brunswick and McLachlan streets. Rowdy, popular Irish pub hosting bands of variable quality; territorial male behaviour is the norm in the big pool-hall upstairs, and the police seem to get called in on a regular basis.

The Healer 27 Warner St. A renovated 90-year-old church, which has remained true to its origins by putting the stage at one end and the bar at the other, with rows of seats in between; feels just right for its menu of quality live blues, soul, and R&B.

The Press Club In the *Empire Hotel*, cnr Brunswick and Ann streets. "Members only" club (whatever that means); if you make it past the door gorillas, you'll find leather lounges, big "pouf" cushions to rest your feet on and a huge glam/industrial fan as the centrepiece, all of it enveloped in a relaxed and funky dance beat. Rather a "fabulous" crowd, out to see and be seen, with drinks prices to match. Closed Mon.

Queen's Arms Hotel 64 James St, New Farm. Tuesday night Comedy Club, bands Thursday, Saturday and Sunday, and DJ sets Friday and Saturday. Closed Mon.

Ric's Bar 321 Brunswick St. Narrow, crowded place – getting to the bar takes some effort – very popular with the young, slightly affluent crowd. Nightly mix of live Aussie bands downstairs and DJ-driven techno upstairs at the *Upbar*.

Waterloo Hotel Cnr Ann St and Commercial Rd. Manages to attract some big-name Australian touring bands, but almost always has good local talent Friday and Saturday nights.

The Wickham Hotel Cnr Wickham and Alden streets. Reputedly Queensland's most popular gay pub. Men-only nights on Thursday, women-only Friday and Sunday, but DJs every night, with cabaret and drag shows as a regular feature.

Zoo 711 Ann St. A hectic night out featuring dub or local bands, and swing sessions on Sunday; Wed–Sun 5pm–late.

Film and theatre

Compared with the rest of the state, which tends to get only mainstream commercial successes, Brisbane has a varied programme of films. The Dendy, 346 George St (☎07/3211 3244), Palace Centro, 39 James St, Fortitude Valley (☎07/3852 4488), and Schonell, University of Queensland, St Lucia (☎07/3377 2229), all show contemporary and vintage foreign-language and "offbeat" films. Even the multiscreen Hoyts cinema, upstairs at the Myer Centre, and the luxurious Regent, further down the mall, are worth checking for unexpected offerings. In August the **Brisbane International Film Festival** is in town with a bundle of goodies from around the world shown over a week – contact one of the cinemas for details.

Big **theatrical productions** are staged at the Performing Arts Complex (☎13 62 46) on the south bank in the Concert Hall, Optus Playhouse (home of the Queensland Theatre Company), Cremorne, or Lyric theatres; look out for lower-key, lunch-time performances, workshops and foyer exhibitions. The University of Queensland's Cement Box Theatre, over the river at their St Lucia campus (☎07/3377 2240), offers more down-to-earth repertory fare, and there's also a newer venue in town at the Powerhouse, on the river next to New Farm Park in eastern Brisbane. A former power station, this once derelict building opened in May 2001 as a centre for the performing arts, including the long-established La Boite Theatre and Vulcana Womens' Circus. Contact information outlets for performance details.

Drinks for women: the Regatta Hotel

Though Australian pubs tend towards being all-male enclaves, women were once legally barred to "protect" them from the corrupting influence of foul language. On April 1, 1965, Merle Thornton (mother of the actress Sigrid Thornton) and her friend Rosalie Bogner chained themselves to the footrail of the **Regatta Hotel** bar at Toowong in protest; the movement they inspired led to the granting of "the right to drink alongside men" in the mid-1970s. The pink-and-white colonial hotel is now a trendy place for a drink after work on Fridays. It's on the west bank of the river along Coronation Drive, about 2km from the city centre towards St Lucia.

Sports and activities

Queensland's sporting obsession revolves around **rugby league**, though the Brisbane Broncos have lost their edge a little since their glory days in the early 1990s. Their stomping ground is at the ANZ Stadium, west of the city, and the event of the year is the State of Origin series in May or June. **Cricket** matches are played at "The Gabba", Vulture Street, and the Queensland Reds **rugby union** team play at Ballymore oval. Tickets are usually easy to get at the games.

For something more hands on, Bay Dolphin (℡07/3207 9620, 🌐www .baydolphin.com.au) offers a full-day **sailing** between the mainland and North Stradbroke Island for $75. **Surfing** trips are covered by Dust Tours (℡1800 111 262, 🌐www.surftours.com.au), who offer all-inclusive two-day tours ($199) and four-day surf safaris ($299) for everyone from complete novices upwards. Finally, for some plain Aussie weirdness, head west of town to the Australian Woolshed at 148 Samford Rd, Ferny Hills (℡07/3351 5366), where you can watch a highly polished performance including **trained sheep** (a rarity in itself), a shearing demonstration, morning tea and sheepdogs putting startled flocks through their paces. Shows start at 8am, 9.30am, 11am, 1pm & 2.30pm, and entry costs $15.

Listings

Airlines Air New Zealand, 133 Mary St ℡13 24 76, 🌐www.airnewzealand.com.au; Air Niugini, 99 Creek St ℡1300 361 380, 🌐www.airniugini .com.pg; Air Vanuatu, Floor 5, 293 Queen St ℡07/3221 2566, 🌐www.airvanuatu.com.au; Alliance ℡07/3212 1212, 🌐www.flightwest .com.au; British Airways, 313 Adelaide St ℡07/3238 2900; Garuda, 288 Edward St ℡1300 365 331; Gulf Air, 217 George St ℡07/3407 7282; Japan Airlines, Level 14, 1 Waterfront Place, Eagle St ℡07/3229 9922; KLM ℡1300 303 747; Korean Air, 400 Queen St ℡07/3860 6000; Malaysia Airlines, 17th Floor, 80 Albert St ℡13 26 27; Qantas, 247 Adelaide St ℡13 13 13; Royal Brunei, 60 Edward St ℡07/3017 5000; Singapore, 344 Queen St ℡13 10 11; Thai International, 145 Eagle St ℡07/3215 4700; United, 400 Queen St ℡13 17 77; Virgin Blue, Level 7, Centenary Square, 100 Wickham St, Fortitude Valley ℡07/3295 3000 or 13 67 89.

Banks Queensland banking hours are Mon–Fri 9.30am–4pm; major branches in the centre are around Queen and Edward streets.

Bike rental Valet Cycle Hire (℡0408 003 198, 🌐valetcyclehire.com) delivers bikes direct to your accommodation ($50 for one day, $70 for two, and $10 for each day thereafter).

Bookshops American Book Store, 173 Elizabeth St; Dymmocks, near the post office in Queen St;

and Borders, near the Myer Centre, Elizabeth Street, all have a broad selection.

Buses All ticket desks are on the third floor of the Transit Centre, Roma Street. Coachtrans (Gold and Sunshine coasts; ℡07/3236 4165); Crisp's (Toowoomba, Warwick, Stanthorpe, Goondiwindi and Tenterfield; ℡07/3236 5266); Greyhound Pioneer (Queensland and interstate; ℡13 14 99); Kirkland's (Gold Coast, Byron Bay and Lismore; ℡1300 367 077); McCafferty's (Queensland and interstate; ℡13 14 99); Premier (all highway destinations between Melbourne and Cairns; ℡13 34 10).

Camping supplies K2, 140 Wickham St, Fortitude Valley ℡07/3854 1340; Kathmandu, 144 Wickham St ℡07/3252 8054; and Mountain Designs, 120 Wickham St ℡07/3216 1866, for top-quality camping gear and information.

Car market Brisbane Backpackers Car Market, 22 Judge St, Petrie Terrace ℡07/3236 5213, 🌐www.backpackercarmarket.com. Open daily 8.30am–4.30pm if you're looking for, or wanting to sell, a budget car.

Car rental You'll pay around $40 for a single day's car rental; longer terms work out from $25–29 a day. Camper vans start at $59 a day for long-term rental. Shop around and read rental conditions before signing. Most places will deliver; minimum age is 21. Abel (℡13 14 29); Integra, for campervans and one-way rentals to Melbourne, Sydney or Cairns (℡1800 067 414, ⓦwww.integracar.com .au); Travellers Auto Barn, 2 Maud St, Newstead (℡07/3252 2638, ⓦwww.travellers-autobarn .com), have campers for $60 a day and station wagons for $25 a day; U-Drive Impulse (℡1800 673 067); Wicked (℡1800 246 869, ⓦwww.wickedcampers.com.au) specializes in discount long-term campervan rentals.

Consulates Britain, Level 26, 1 Eagle St ℡07/3223 3200; Indonesia, 123 Eagle St ℡07/3309 0888; Japan, 12 Creek St ℡07/3221 5188; Papua New Guinea, Level 3, 320 Adelaide St ℡07/3221 7915; Philippines, 126 Wickham St, Fortitude Valley ℡07/3252 8215; Thailand, 87 Annerley Rd ℡07/3846 7771.

Hospitals/medical centres Roma Street Medical Centre, Level 2, Transit Centre (Mon–Fri 8am–5.30pm, free dental consultations Tuesdays; ℡07/3236 2988); Royal Brisbane, Herston Rd, Herston (℡07/3253 8111; buses #126, #144 or #172 from outside City Hall); and Travellers' Medical Service, Level 1, 245 Albert St (Mon–Fri 7.30am–7pm, Sat 8am–5pm, Sun 10am–4pm; ℡07/3211 3611, Ⓕ3221 3771), for general services, vaccinations and women's health.

Internet access Most hostels have terminals where you can log on from around $5 an hour; Backpackers' Employment Service on the top floor of the Transit Centre charges $6.

Left luggage At the airport and Transit Centre; $5–7 per day per locker.

Maps The Royal Automobile Club of Queensland's series, free to members, or $5.50 each from the RACQ centre at 261 Queen St, covers everything from major highways to almost invisible 4WD-only tracks; and World Wide, 187 George St, stocks a comprehensive range of maps, atlases and travel guides for Queensland and beyond.

Markets Eagle Street (Sun until 3pm) and Brunswick Street Mall (Sat until 4pm) for bits and pieces; South Bank Parklands (Fri night, Sat & Sun until around 4pm) for clothing, arts and crafts and a family atmosphere; while the Riverside Centre (Sun only) is more "arty" than the rest.

NPWS (Naturally Queensland) 160 Ann St ℡07/3227 8186. Plenty of fluffy toys, brochures, books and general information about the state's national parks.

Pharmacies Transit Centre Pharmacy (daily 7am–5pm); and Day & Night Pharmacy, Queen Street Mall (Mon–Sat 8am–9pm, Sun 10am–5pm).

Police Queensland Police Headquarters is opposite the Transit Centre on Roma St ℡07/3364 6464.

Post office 261 Queen St (℡13 13 18 poste restante); bring photo ID to collect poste restante. Mon–Fri 7am–6pm.

RACQ 261 Queen St (℡13 19 05 breakdown service).

Scenic Flights Possum Air Tours (℡07/3397 0033, ⓦwww.possumairtours.com.au) depart daily at 5.45am for a spin over the city followed by a champagne breakfast. $214 per person, includes pick-up and return to accommodation.

Tours from Brisbane

Most **tours** from Brisbane are pretty straightforward day-trips by bus to take in the highlights of Lamington, Tamborine Mountain, the Sunshine Coast or Gold Coast. Allstate Scenic Tours (℡07/3285 1777) has been running day-trips to Green Mountain at Lamington National Park for years (daily except Sat; $45), and you can arrange to be dropped off on one day and picked up another. Australian Day Tours (℡07/3236 4155) has a dozen or so day-tours to the Sunshine Coast, Gold Coast theme parks, or Lamington and Tamborine Mountain for $50–80; Coachliner (℡07/3236 1239) goes to Tamborine Mountain, Green Mountain or the Sunshine Coast ($45–90); while Far Horizons (℡07/3284 5475) operates day-trips to Lamington, the Glasshouse Mountains, or Hinterland cattle stations from around $60.

If you want a bit more depth to your trips, or to visit more distant regions, try the highly recommended Rob's Rainforest Explorer (℡07/3357 7061 or 0409 496 607, ⓦwww.powerup.com.au/~frogbus7) for day-trips to various parts of the Scenic Rim or Glasshouse Mountains, featuring plenty of wildlife, rainforests, bush tucker and swimming holes ($48); or Sunrover Expeditions (℡07/3203 4241, ⓦwww .sunrover.com.au), for one- to three-day 4WD safaris to Moreton and North Stradbroke islands. Moreton Bay Escapes (ⓦwww.moretonbayescapes.com.au) offers one- to three-day tours of Moreton Island (see p.424), and organizes one-day sailing trips out on the bay for $95.

Telephones International payphones are located in the arcade beside the GPO at 261 Queen St; cheap international rates are also available through the Internet places near *Palace Backpackers* on Edward St, and the Backpackers Travel Centre at 138 Albert St.

Trains Queensland and interstate trains leave from the Transit Centre's ground floor; the ticket office and information centre there is open Mon–Fri 9am–5pm. For rail information call ☏ 13 22 32.

Travel agents Discounted air fares and other travel arrangements are available from: Flight Centre, 181 George St ☏ 07/3229 0150; cnr Creek and Queen streets ☏ 07/3227 1777; STA, 111 Adelaide St ☏ 07/3221 5722; Student Uni Travel, 201 Elizabeth St ☏ 07/3003 0344,

ⓔbrisbane@sut.com.au; Trailfinders, 91 Elizabeth St ☏ 07/3229 0887. There's also the Backpackers Travel Centre at 138 Albert St (☏ 07/3221 2225, ⓦwww.backpackerstravel.net.au), and a YHA office opposite the Transit Centre at 154 Roma St (Mon–Fri 8.30am–5pm, Sat 9am–3pm; ☏ 07/3236 1680).

Work Popular with job-hunters, Brisbane offers fairly good employment prospects, if you're not too choosy. Many hostels run effective ad hoc agencies for their guests, or try Backpackers' Employment Services, on the top floor of the Transit Centre in Roma St (Mon–Fri 9am–3pm; ⓦwww.workandtravel.com.au). Brisbane's WWOOF office is at 118 Petrie Terrace (☏ 07/3367 1165).

Outer Brisbane and Moreton Bay

With the grossly hyped Gold Coast and Hinterland for competition, it's not surprising that few people bother with the country immediately surrounding Brisbane. Only 5km to the west, the city is hemmed in by **Mount Coot-tha**'s botanic gardens and the foothills of **Brisbane Forest Park**, which covers the green, wet heights of the D'Aguilar Range and stretches to the edge of Lake Wivenhoe.

In the opposite direction, coastal suburbs provide access to the shallow waters of **Moreton Bay**, famous throughout Australia as the home of the unfortunately named Moreton Bay Bug, which is actually a small, delicious lobster-like crustacean. While Brisbane is hardly noted for its beach life, with muddy shorelines attracting mangroves rather than sun worshippers, the largest of the bay's islands, **Moreton** and **North Stradbroke**, are generously endowed with sand, and are just the right distance from the city to make their beaches accessible but seldom crowded. The island of **St Helena** is not somewhere you'd visit for sun and surf, but its prison ruins recall the convict era and are an interesting daytrip. In the bay itself, look for dolphins, dugong (sea cows) and humpbacked whales, which pass by in winter en route to their calving grounds up north.

For organized **transport and tours** into the area, check the following individual accounts, as well as the box opposite.

Mount Coot-tha

The lower slopes of **Mount Coot-tha** are the setting for Brisbane's second botanic gardens, a popular place for a Sunday picnic located on Sir Samuel Griffith Drive (Mon–Sat 8am–5pm; free; bus #471 from Adelaide St runs hourly 9.15am–3.15pm). Careful landscaping and the use of enclosures create varying climates – dry pine and eucalypt groves, a cool subtropical rainforest complete with waterfalls and streams, and the elegant **Japanese Gardens**. In summer, the **tropical plant dome** seems an unnecessary feature in an already sweltering climate; inside, the floor is almost completely occupied by a pond – stocked with tropical lotus lillies and fish – and is overshadowed by tropical greenery dripping with moisture.

The other dome in the gardens does duty as a **planetarium** ($10.50; call ☏07/3403 2578 for programme and timetable of events). While the foyer display is dry and dated, the show itself, which you view lying back under the dome's ceiling, is an interesting observation of the key features of Brisbane's night sky.

After visiting the botanic gardens most people head up the road to the summit for panoramas of the city and, on a good day, the Moreton Bay islands. Walking tracks from here make for moderate hikes of an hour or two through dry gum woodland, and include several **Aboriginal trails** – the best of which branches off the Slaughter Falls track and points out plants and their uses as food, artefacts and hunting poisons. Pamphlets on the tracks are available from the botanic gardens library (Tues–Fri 9.30am–4.30pm, Sat 10am–noon) and the information desk in the foyer of Brisbane's City Hall.

Brisbane Forest Park

If your plans don't include seeing any other forests in the southeast, take advantage of **Brisbane Forest Park**'s proximity to the city. Covering approximately 280 square kilometres to the west of Brisbane, the park contains substantial tracts of virgin forest, and is well stocked with wildlife, pretty lookouts and easy walking tracks. A day is ample time to look around, or you could make the park the first stage of a scenic circuit from Brisbane via Lake Wivenhoe and Toowoomba (see p.564).

Highway 31 runs from the city centre via The Gap right through the park, with a half-dozen places to stop off and explore along the way. First of these is **Bellbird Grove** (4km into the park), containing another of the city's Aboriginal trails with an outdoor museum of bark huts and information on traditional plant uses. Around 12km along is **Boombana**'s one-kilometre rainforest circuit of moss-covered logs and towering buttressed trees, with the tiny township of **MOUNT NEBO** just beyond. From here it's a long run through gum woodland to similarly-sized **MOUNT GLORIOUS**, and then you're at **Maiala National Park** (30km into the park), a fascinating tract of subtropical forest, where palms, figs and other giant trees compete for light, vines tangle up the forest floor and gullies guide fast-flowing creeks. Both townships sport tearooms.

There's plenty of **wildlife** to be encountered along the park's many kilometres of walking tracks. Catbirds snarl at each other in the rainforest, while dark-blue male **satin bowerbirds** woo females with an elaborate tunnel made from grass and decorated with blue objects – seeds and flowers are the natural choice, though given the opportunity the birds are happy to raid picnic tables and dustbins for blue plastic clothespegs, straws, and even *Bushell's* teabags, which have a blue paper label attached to the string (Queensland dairies changed the colour of their plastic bottle-lids when it was suggested that bowerbirds might throttle themselves on them). At night, you'll see wallabies on verges, glider possums around flowering trees in open woodland, echidnas scraping through leaf litter for ants, and possibly the bandy-bandy, a timid, mildly poisonous snake boldly striped in black and white, which forms vertical hoops with its body when frightened.

Lake Wivenhoe was created in the late 1970s to stop the Brisbane River flooding the city – the last of a series of floods struck in 1974. Its southern end is just visible from an outlook on the western edge of the **D'Aguilar Range**, about 10km west of Maiala, that gives a sweeping view down wooded hills to the drier country of the southwest. A road links the park with the Brisbane Valley Highway and if you're heading west, you can get to Toowoomba (see p.564) via the Wivenhoe Dam (140km) – a slower-paced, far more scenic route than the alternative Warrego Highway.

Practicalities

In general, spring (Sept–Oct) is the best time to visit Brisbane Forest Park; animals are active, many plants are in flower and rain is infrequent. It can be cold and damp at night in winter, while fire bans can close sections of the park during prolonged dry spells (most frequently in November).

The park entrance and headquarters are at **Walkabout Creek Freshwater Study Centre** (Mon–Fri 8.30am–4.30pm, Sat & Sun 9am–5pm; ℗07/3300 4855), about 12km west of the city. You can reach Walkabout Creek by bus from the Myer Centre #385 (hourly Mon–Fri 9am–5pm, Sat & Sun 9am–4pm). Coming by car – the only way to explore more of the park unless you walk – follow College Road west onto Route 31, and stay on it until you reach Walkabout Creek. Walkabout Creek makes a good first stop for free **maps**, information, details of bushwalking tours and, if you want to **camp** rough (there are no formal campsites), a permit. The Study Centre itself (daily 9am–4.30pm; $3.50) is an idealized creek system where lungfish, turtles, snakes and frogs coexist with few of the stresses they'd encounter living this close together in the wild. Everything is well labelled and it's unlikely you'll ever get better views of crayfish mincing over the gravel at the bottom of the stream or water dragons sunning themselves on rocks. The centre also has a noisy walk-through aviary, as well as a collection of platypuses and a nocturnal house, and there's a smattering of wildlife in the surrounding gum forest.

Accommodation in the park needs to be booked in advance. At Mount Nebo, the *Railway Carriage* (℗07/3289 8120; chalet ❸, car ❹) offers a night in a restored 1930s sleeper car, with bed, kitchen and en-suite, or a similarly equipped but more conventional chalet. At Mount Glorious, *Mt Glorious Getaways* (℗07/3289 0172; ❹) has several nicely designed and fully furnished self-catering cottages.

St Helena Island

Small, low and triangular, **St Helena Island** sits 8km from the mouth of the Brisbane River. Once the hunting ground of local tribes, the island took its name after an Aborigine known as Napoleon who was dumped here in 1828 when he became too troublesome for the jail at Dunwich on North Stradbroke Island. Forty years later, the spectre of overcrowding in mainland prisons prompted the government to turn St Helena Island into a penal settlement, and after clearing rainforest for timber and to prevent escapes, gardens were planted and houses built from coral blocks and clay. In some respects it was a model system, though conditions were still severe for the inmates: prisoners were taught a trade and were even paid for their labour, and there were only three escapes in 65 years. The government found it particularly useful for political troublemakers, such as the leaders of the 1891 shearers' strike and, with more justice, a couple of slave-trading "Blackbirder" captains.

A **tour** of the prison island, endearingly tagged the "Hell Hole of the South Pacific" during its working life, leaves you thankful you missed out on the "good old days". A clue to why there were so few escapes is provided by the rusty swimming enclosure at the jetty, which was constructed to protect warders from the sharks whose presence was actively encouraged around the island. Evidence of the prisoners' industry and self-sufficiency is still to be seen in the stone houses, as well as in the remains of a sugar mill, paddocks, wells and an ingenious lime kiln built into the shoreline. The Deputy Superintendent's house has been turned into a bare museum (reached from the jetty on a mini-tramway), displaying a ball and chain lying in a corner and photographs from the prison era. Outside, the gardens that once produced prize-winning olive oil are now sparse, and the two cemeteries have been desecrated: many headstones were carried off as souvenir coffee tables, the corpses dug up and sold as medical specimens. The remaining stones comprise simple concrete crosses stamped with a number for the prisoners, or inscribed marble tablets for the warders and their children. The last inmate left in 1933.

Cat-o'-Nine-Tails (☎07/3893 1240, ⓦwww.sthelenaisland.com.au) offers **day-trips** (Mon–Fri departing 9.30am and returning 2.15pm, Sat & Sun departing 11am and returning at 4pm; $65 including lunch) and **night tours** (departs some Friday and Saturday nights; $75 includes three-course meal), the latter including a theatrical sound-and-light show on the island. Advance bookings are essential. Boats leave around 15km east of the city from the public jetty in the suburb of **Manly**, a ten-minute walk from Manly train station – from Brisbane, you can reach Manly direct from Roma Street, Central, South Brisbane and Vulture Street train stations.

Moreton Island

A 38-kilometre-long, narrow band of stabilized, partly wooded sand dunes 20km east of Brisbane, **Moreton Island**'s faultless beaches are distinctly underpopulated for much of the year – making it perfect for a day or two of surfing, fishing or camping. Most people cross to mid-point **Tangalooma Resort** on the daily **ferry** (departs 10am, leaves the island 3pm; $38 open return) which leaves from the terminal 8km from the city at the end of Holt Street, off Kingsford Smith Drive at Pinkenba. They also offer extended day-trips to take in **dolphin feeding** ($85; returns after dark) and, from mid-June to late October, **whale-watching** tours ($140). A **courtesy bus** to the ferry terminal leaves daily at 9am from the McCafferty's coach bay on the third floor of the Roma Street Transit Centre, and returns you there afterwards (though extended day-trips return too late to catch it back and you'll need a taxi).

To **take your own vehicle** to the island, whose sand tracks are 4WD-only, contact the *Combie Trader* **vehicle barge** (☎07/3203 6399 for timetables and departure point), which crosses to the tiny settlement of Bulwer on the island's north – it costs at least $150 return. The road rules are the same as on the mainland; check tide times before driving on the beach, and be aware that pedestrians may not hear you above the sound of the surf. Alternatively, Sunrover Expeditions (☎07/3203 4241, ⓦwww.sunrover.com.au) and Moreton Bay Escapes (ⓦwww.moretonbayescapes) run excellent **tours** from Brisbane lasting from one to three days ($120–300 per person).

If you're planning to stay a while, note that **supplies** on the island are expensive, so you need to be self-sufficient and have enough water if you are camping. There are no banks. And before you go in the sea, remember that the beaches aren't patrolled and there are no shark nets. The worst times to visit are at Christmas and Easter, when up to a thousand vehicles crowd onto the island all at once.

The island has designated **campsites** at Tangalooma and Ben-Ewa (3km towards Bulwer) on the west coast, and Blue Lagoon and Eagers Creek on the east side; you can also camp anywhere along beaches except where there are signs asking you not to, but you should first obtain a permit, available from barge operators or at the sites for $4 per person per night.

Around the island

TANGALOOMA, midway along the island's west coast, is fronted by a set of wrecks, deliberately sunk to create an artificial harbour but now swamped in sand – a fine **snorkelling** site at high tide. Nearby is *Tangalooma Resort* (☎07/3408 2666, ⊛www.tangalooma.com; code), a casual, upmarket affair with a range of rooms and units that incorporate parts of a former whaling station; they also organize daily **dolphin feeding** for wild dolphins who rock up every evening for a handout. Pleasantly shaded and busy at weekends and holidays, it's the only place on the island that has a **restaurant** and serves cold drinks – respectable dress required. There's also an NPWS campsite here (with water, showers and toilets), which gets as crowded as anywhere on the island. A three-kilometre track heads south from Tangalooma to the Desert, where the dunes are a great place to try **sand-tobogganing**. The resort lays on a short 4WD tour and sand-tobogganing trip for $16.

With your own vehicle, or if you don't mind hiking, take the ten-kilometre track from Tangalooma across to Moreton's more attractive **eastern side**; generally less crowded, the beach also has good surf. You end up at **Eagers Creek**, where there's another campsite and a five-kilometre return trip up sandy **Mount Tempest**'s 280-metre peak – an exhausting climb. Head 10km north up the beach, and you'll find **Blue Lagoon**, the largest of the island's freshwater lakes, only 500m from the beach and adjacent to the smaller, picturesque **Honeyeater Lake**. Blessed with shady trees, the dunes behind the beach make an ideal place to camp, and the site is supplied with water, showers and toilets. Dolphins come in close to shore – a practice that Moreton's Aborigines turned to their advantage by using them to chase fish into the shallows. Writing in the 1870s about his life in Brisbane, Tom Petrie reported that the Ngugi men would beat the surf with their spears, and:

> By and by, as in response, porpoises would be seen as they rose to the surface making for the shore and in front of them schools of tailor fish. It may seem wonderful, but they were apparently driving the fish towards the land. When they came near, [they] would run out into the surf, and with their spears would jab down here and there at the fish, at times even getting two on one spear, so plentiful were they.

Moreton's **northern end** is about 9km wide, covered in ferns, grasstrees, paperbark and banksias around the shore, and dense scrub inland. The landing point here is **BULWER**, a cluster of weatherboard "weekenders" and a store stocking fuel and beer and providing basic **accommodation** in six-person units (☎07/3203 6399 or 3408 2202; ⑤). The beach is the only "road" south to Tangalooma, while vehicle tracks cut across to Honeyeater Lake and to the island's northeastern corner, **North Point**, where adjacent dunes form near-vertical cliffs, and fresh water, brown with tannin, seeps out into lagoons. Around from North Point, rocky Cape Moreton is capped by a red-and-white **lighthouse**, built between 1857 and 1928 and still operating. There's a museum in the house below and fine views down the east coast from adjacent cliffs.

The **south** of the island mostly consists of exposed dunes, some covered in scrub and others forming white "blows", which are destabilized, shifting hills that slowly roll over forests. Right at Moreton's southern tip, **KOORINGAL** is a sleepy version of Bulwer and has a **store** offering fuel, supplies and drinks from their bar (daily 8am–midnight), as well as **holiday units** that sleep up to six (☎07/3409 0298 or 3409 0105; ⑥–⑦). From Kooringal, diversions include the twelve-kilometre return trip to **Big and Little Sandhills** via Toompani beach and eerie, long-dead stands of trees in the wake of the dunes. Take plenty of water.

North Stradbroke Island

North Stradbroke Island is, at 40km long, the largest and most established of the bay's islands, with sealed roads and the fully serviced townships of Dunwich, Amity and Point Lookout. Ninety percent of "Straddie" is given over to mining **rutile** (titanium oxide), and the majority of the 3200 residents are employees of Consolidated Rutile Ltd. The mine sites south of Amity, and in the central west and south, are far from exhausted but their future is precarious, thanks to an oversupply on the world market. Other industries focus on timber, a by-product of preparing land for mining, and, increasingly, tourism.

Transport to the island leaves from Toondah Harbour at Cleveland, with Stradbroke Ferries (☎07/3286 2666) crossing to Dunwich eleven times daily (return fares $15 per person by water-taxi; $75 per car by barge). You can reach Cleveland by train from Brisbane, then catch the courtesy bus "Bessie" to the harbour from the station – phone Stradbroke Ferries for details. Also, watch out for package deals from various sources, such as the free courtesy bus (not including ferry fare) from Brisbane run on Monday, Wednesday and Friday by *Stradbroke Island Guesthouse* – call them first to book.

To **get around** the island, the Dunwich–Point Lookout **bus** connects with all water-taxis and costs $9 return, and various operators offer 4WD **safaris**: Sunrover Expeditions (☎07/3203 4241; ⓦwww.sunrover.com.au) and Straddie Kingfisher Tours (☎07/3409 9502) both come recommended. Some roads on Stradbroke are open to mining vehicles only, so drivers should look out for the signs. Off-roading through the centre is ill-advised: quite apart from the damage caused to the dune systems, the sand is very soft and having your vehicle pulled out will be very expensive.

Dunwich to Main Beach

Unless you need to fuel up or visit the bank, there's little to keep you at **DUN-WICH**, Straddie's ferry port. Two sealed roads head out of town, east through the island's centre towards **Main Beach**, or north to Amity and Point Lookout. The road through the centre passes two **lakes**, the second and smaller of which, Blue Lake, is a national park and source of fresh water for the island's wildlife, which is most plentiful early in the morning. Beyond Blue Lake you have to cross the **Eighteen Mile Swamp** to reach Main Beach and, though there's a causeway, the rest of the route is for 4WDs only. You can **camp** behind the beach anywhere south of the causeway (north of it is mining company land), but be prepared for the mosquitoes that swarm around the mangroves; the southernmost point, looking over to South Stradbroke Island (see p.434), is an angling and wildlife mecca, with birdlife and kangaroos lounging around on the beaches.

The Top End

Heading north from Dunwich, it's 10km to where the road forks left to Amity and right to Point Lookout: **AMITY** is a sleepy place built around a jetty, while **POINT LOOKOUT** is where most visitors end up if they don't want to camp. Nineteen kilometres from Dunwich, Point Lookout spreads out around Stradbroke's single rock headland, overlooking a string of beaches. Stretched out along the road are a pub, takeaway pizza place, a store, some cafés and various types of **accommodation**. Top of the range are *Ocean Beach Resort* (☎07/3409 8555, ⓦwww.whalewatchresort.com.au; ❻), a comfortable, motel-like option, and *Samarinda* (☎07/3409 8785; ❻), with motel rooms and two-bedroom units. At the other end of the scale, *Stradbroke Island Guesthouse* (☎07/3409 8888, ⓦwww.stradbrokeislandscuba.com.au; dorms $17, rooms ❷) has dorm beds, plus free loans of surfboards, bikes and fishing gear; they also organize 4WD, walking and trail-riding trips. Long-running *Straddie Hostel* (☎07/3409 8679, ⓔstraddiehostel@hotmail.com; dorms $17, rooms ❷) is a low-key alternative. *Stradbroke Tourist Park* (☎07/3409 8127; tent $15, four- to six-person cabins ❸) is the best of the local **caravan parks**, or you can camp on the foreshore west of Rocky Point's beach access road, at the northwest corner of the island.

The **beaches** here are good. **Flinders** runs west of Amity; **Home** and **Cylinder** between here and Cylinder Headland are both patrolled and, therefore, crowded during holiday weekends. If you don't mind swimming in unwatched waters, head for **Deadman's Beach** or **Frenchman's Bay**. On the headland above, there are fine views and the chance to see loggerhead turtles and dolphins; from the walking track around North Gorge down to Main Beach you might see whales – if you have binoculars. Stradbroke's **diving** – organized through *Stradbroke Island Guesthouse* – is renowned for congregations of the increasingly rare grey nurse shark, along with moray eels, dopey leopard sharks, and summertime manta rays.

The Gold Coast

Beneath a jagged skyline shaped by countless high-rise beachfront apartments, the **Gold Coast** is Australia's Miami Beach or Costa del Sol, a striking contrast to Brisbane, only an hour away. Aggressively superficial, it's not the place to go if you're seeking peace and quiet: the endless succession of nightclubs, bars and theme parks provide raucous, relentless entertainment. It can be enjoyable for a couple of days – perhaps as a weekend break from Brisbane – but there's little variation on the beach and nightclub scene and if you're concerned that this will leave you jaded, bored or broke you would be better off avoiding this corner of the state altogether.

The coast forms a virtually unbroken beach 40km long, from **South Stradbroke Island** past **Surfers Paradise** and **Burleigh Heads** to the New South Wales border at **Coolangatta**. Surfers Paradise has the highest concentration of people and skyscrapers; as you head south through the strip of motels and shops the pace slows (relatively) and it's easier to find some unoccupied sand. The beaches are still touted as the main attraction, though they've become a backdrop to more commercial interests, and they swarm with bathers and board-riders all year round. **Surfing** blossomed here in the 1930s and still pulls in veterans and novices; Coolangatta, Burleigh Heads and South Stradbroke have the best waves and definitely the more serious surfies, but you'll find rideable swell all the way along the coast.

With around three hundred days of sunshine each year there's little "off-season" as such. **Rain** can, however, fall at any time during the year, including midwinter – when it's usually dry in the rest of the state – but even if the crowds do thin out a little, they reappear in time for the Gold Coast **Indy car race** in October, and then continue to swell, peaking over Christmas and New Year. The end of the school year in mid-November also brings on the phenomenon of **Schoolies Week**, when thousands of high-school leavers ditch exam rooms and flock to Surfers for a few days' of hard partying, causing a budget accommodation crisis.

Getting there and around

From Brisbane, local **buses** from Roma Street Transit Centre to the Gold Coast include Kirkland's (☏ 1300 367 077), which runs about eight times daily to Southport, Surfers, Burleigh Heads, and Coolangatta; and Coachtrans (☏ 07/5506 9777), which runs about four services daily – both cost around $15. Coachtrans also organizes theme park transfers (☏ 07/3236 1000) from central Brisbane accommodation to Carrumbin Sanctuary, Dreamworld, Movie World, Wet 'n' Wild and Sea World. **Driving** from Brisbane, head down Vulture Street onto the Gold Coast Highway, where there's a detour at **BEENLEIGH** to Queensland's oldest rum distillery at the *Beenleigh Tavern* (tours at 11am, noon, 1pm & 2pm; ☏ 07/3287 2488), which started in 1860 as a pirate business on the Albert River.

Coming up **from New South Wales**, the coastal highway enters Queensland at Coolangatta, where you'll also find the **Gold Coast airport**. Airport Transit **shuttle buses** (book in advance on ☏ 1300 655 655) run to all points between the airport and Surfers Paradise for $11 one-way, $16.50 return.

Getting around, the Gold Coast Highway from Tweed Heads and Coolangatta to Surfers Paradise, and all the theme parks, are covered by a **24-hour bus service** run by Surfside Shuttle and Surfside Buses, with up to seven services an hour between Surfers and Coolangatta. Their **passes** give unlimited travel for between one and fourteen days ($10–60). Otherwise you'll need to take a taxi or rent a vehicle; there are more details in accounts of the individual resorts.

Surfers Paradise

Spiritually, if not geographically, **SURFERS PARADISE** is at the heart of the Gold Coast, the place where its aims and aspirations are most evident. For the residents, this involves making money by providing services and entertainment for tourists; visitors reciprocate by parting with their cash. All around and irrespective of what you're doing – shopping for clothes, sitting on the beach, partying in one of the frenetic nightclubs or even finding a bed – the pace is brash and glib. Don't come here expecting to be allowed to relax; subtlety is nonexistent and you'll find that enjoying Surfers depends largely on how much it bothers you having the party mood rammed down your throat.

Surfers' beaches have been attracting tourists for over a century, though the town only started developing along commercial lines during the 1950s when the first multistoreyed **beach-front apartments** were built. The demand for views over the ocean led to ever-higher towers which began to encroach on the dunes (not to mention shading them from mid-afternoon); together with the sheer volume of people attracted here, this soon caused serious **erosion** problems along the entire coast. Attempts to stabilize the foreshore with retaining walls, groynes and sand pumping from offshore have had little long-term success. But none of this really matters. Though Surfers Paradise is a firm tribute to the successful marketing of the ideal Aussie lifestyle as an eternal beach party, most people no longer come here for the beaches but simply because everyone else does.

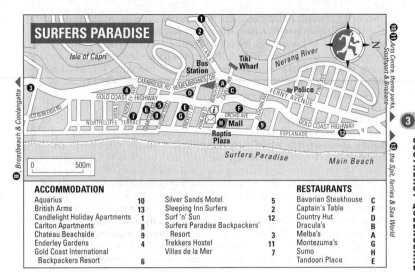

SURFERS PARADISE

Isle of Capri

Bus Station

Tiki Wharf

Nerang River

Police

Broadbeach & Coolangatta

GOLD COAST HIGHWAY

OLD BURLEIGH RD

NORTHCLIFFE TERRACE

Raptis Plaza

Mall

GOLD COAST HIGHWAY

ESPLANADE

Surfers Paradise

Main Beach

0   500m

Arts Centre, theme parks, Southport & Brisbane

the Spit, ferries & Sea World

ACCOMMODATION		RESTAURANTS	
Aquarius	10	Silver Sands Motel	5	Bavarian Steakhouse	C
British Arms	13	Sleeping Inn Surfers	2	Captain's Table	F
Candlelight Holiday Apartments	1	Surf 'n' Sun	12	Country Hut	D
Carlton Apartments	8	Surfers Paradise Backpackers'		Dracula's	B
Chateau Beachside	9	Resort	3	Melba's	A
Enderley Gardens	4	Trekkers Hostel	11	Montezuma's	G
Gold Coast International		Villas de la Mer	7	Sumo	H
Backpackers Resort	6			Tandoori Place	E

Arrival, information and security

Surfers' **bus station** (6am–10pm) is on Beach Road on the corner of the high-way, one street down from Cavill Avenue. Here you'll find **luggage lockers**, **bus company desks** and an **accommodation information** counter. If the hostel you want isn't listed, call them for a free pick-up, and don't be surprised if, while walking around with your luggage, hostel minibuses stop for you as they pass. The **tourist information office** is an open-air booth on Cavill Avenue (Mon–Fri 8am–5pm, Sat 9am–5pm, Sun 9am–3.30pm; ☎07/5538 4419).

Surfing the Gold Coast

As locals will tell you, the Gold Coast has some of the **best surfing** beaches in the world. And in terms of consistency this might be true – on any given day there will be rideable surf somewhere along the coast – with 200-metre-long sand-bottom point breaks and rideable waves peaking at about four metres in prime conditions.

The area is known for its **barrels**, particularly during the summer cyclone season when the winds shift around to the north; in winter the swell is smaller but more reliable, making it easier to learn to surf. A rule of thumb for finding the best surf is to follow the wind: north when the wind blows from the north, south when it comes from the south. Generally, you'll find the best swell along the southern beaches, and on South Stradbroke Island. Sea **temperatures** range between 26°C in December and 17°C in June, so a 2–3mm wetsuit is adequate. Hard-core surfies come for Christmas and the cyclone season, though spring is really the busiest time. On the subject of **general safety**, all beaches as far north as Surfers are patrolled – look for the signs – and while sharks might worry you, more commonplace hostility is likely to come from the local surfies who form tight-knit cliques with very protective attitudes towards their patches.

For expert **tuition**, tours, or advice anywhere on the Gold Coast, contact locally based Surfaris (☎1800 634 951, ⊛www.surfaris.com) or Gold Coast Surfing Schools (☎1800 787 337, ⊛www.australiansurfer.com) – beginners pay around $45 for a two-hour session. **Competitions** or events are held somewhere along the coast on most weekends, advertised through local surf shops.

Security is worth bearing in mind. Many people migrate to Surfers in search of an easier life, only to find themselves homeless and hard up. Others come to prey deliberately on tourists, especially around Christmas and Easter, or on teenagers during Schoolies Week in November. Don't leave vehicles unlocked at any time, don't take valuables onto the beach, and don't wander alone at night; muggings are common, especially around nightclubs – so take advantage of the courtesy buses run by hostels.

Accommodation

You need to book all **accommodation** in advance, and be prepared for slightly above-average room rates everywhere. Typically quiet early on, the **hostels** come to life late in the day and you won't be left in peace until you've signed up for trips to nightclubs, parties and beach events. Most have struck deals with various clubs for cheap entry and drinks, and all have much the same facilities – Internet at $5 an hour, pool, dormitories, kitchen, TV and loans of surfboards. Many places don't encourage long stays, but it may be worth asking about weekly rates. **Motels and apartments**, on the other hand, often insist on a minimum three-day stay – during quieter times bargaining may get you a reduced rate. Peak-season motel rates range from $55 to a few hundred dollars a night; during off-season and midweek, rooms are considerably cheaper. Expect to pay more for ocean views. There are simply too many possibilities to give a comprehensive list; those below are central and good value. If you want to **camp**, you'll have to head south to the quieter sections of the Gold Coast – though all campsites get booked solid through the Christmas break.

Aquarius 44 Queen St, Southport ☎ 07/5527 1300 or 1800 229 955, ⓦ www.aquariusback packers.com.au. A hostel with tiny TV lounge on each floor, pool and communal kitchen; price includes free basic breakfast. Small four- and six-bed dorms. Dorms $20, rooms ❷

British Arms 70 Seaworld Drive ☎ 07/5571 1776 or 1800 680 269, ⓦ www.britisharms.com.au. A YHA property, close to Sea World about 5km north of the centre. Good facilities, plus a lively English bar and grill serving up pub fare, occasional entertainment and a range of beers till late. Dorms $20, rooms ❷

Candlelight Holiday Apartments 22–24 Leonard St ☎ 07/5538 1277, ⓔ canlight@bigpond.com. Very pleasant, self-contained one-bedroom units in a quiet street close to the bus station; very helpful and friendly owners. ❺

Carlton Apartments Cnr Northcliffe Terrace and Clifford St ☎ 07/5538 5877. Self-contained double units in a seven-storey building on the beach. ❺

Chateau Beachside Cnr Esplanade and Elkhorn Ave ☎ 07/5538 1022, ⓔ chateau@strand.com.au. Right in the heart of Surfers and overlooking the beach, this modern tower block is a great mid-range deal – rooms are a good size, and suites come with cooking facilities. ❺

Enderley Gardens 38 Enderley Ave ☎ 07/5570 1511, ⓔ enderley@strand.com.au. Self-contained

units, one block away from the beach, ten minutes from the heart of Surfers; facilities include pool, spa and tennis court. ❻

Gold Coast International Backpackers Resort 28 Hamilton Ave ☎ 07/5592 5888 or 1800 801 230. Secure, purpose-built hostel, with safe car park; facilities include a small kitchen and a bar, but there's no pool and the place feels a bit sterile. Four-bed dorms $22, tiny doubles ❷

Silver Sands Motel 2985 Gold Coast Highway ☎ 07/5538 6041. Low-rise and pleasant, despite a location on the main highway. One hundred metres from the beach, plus there's a pool. ❺

Sleeping Inn Surfers 26 Whelan St ☎ 07/5592 4455 or 1800 817 832, ⓦ www.sleepinginn.com.au. Close to bus station; nicely furnished, quality budget accommodation in self-contained units, all with TV and free in-house videos. Dorms $20, rooms ❷

Surf 'n' Sun 3323 Gold Coast Highway ☎ 07/5592 2363 or 1800 678 194. Noisy party hostel, with cramped rooms and ordinary facilities, but it's close to the beach and centre. Five-bed dorms $20, twins ❷

Surfers Paradise Backpackers' Resort 2837 Gold Coast Highway ☎ 07/5592 4677 or 1800 282 800, ⓦ www.surfersparadisebackpackers.com.au. Purpose-built, sparklingly clean and efficient, with spacious rooms; the price per bed covers everything, including use of washing machines. Dorms $22, rooms ③

Trekkers Hostel 22 White St, Southport ☎07/5591 5616 or 1800 100 004. Beautifully restored old house 3km from the centre; comfortable, and with heaps of deals and trips. Staff are particularly friendly and welcoming, and their weekly BBQ is cheap and good fun. Price includes a basic breakfast, with cheap meals at the nearby RSL club. They have a courtesy bus, or you can catch local transport to the hostel. Dorms $20.

Villas de la Mer Cnr Markwell Ave and Northcliffe Terrace ☎07/5592 6644, ⓕ5592 6324. Attractive apartments in a three-storey security complex, with ocean views from upper levels. Rooms are simple but modern and well furnished. Two- and three bedroom apartments. ⑥

The City and theme parks

Downtown Surfers Paradise is a thin ribbon of partially reclaimed land between the ocean and the **Nerang River** which – as the Broadwater – flows north, parallel with the beach, past **the Spit** and South Stradbroke Island into the choked channels at the bottom end of Moreton Bay. Reclaimed land in the river forms islands whose names reflect the fantasies of their founders – Isle of Capri, Sorrento, Miami Keys – and which have become much-sought-after real estate.

From its dingiest club to its best restaurant, Surfers exudes entertainment, and at times – most notoriously at New Year and Christmas – you can spend 24 hours a day out on the town. Another thing you'll spend is money; the only free venue is the beach and with such a variety of distractions it can be financial suicide venturing out too early in the day. The city is full of tourists staggering around at noon, with terrible hangovers and empty wallets, complaining how expensive their holiday has become. The area around **Cavill Avenue** is a bustle of activity from early morning – when the first surfers head down to the beach and the shops open – to after midnight, when there's a constant exchange of bodies between **Orchid Avenue**'s bars and night-clubs. If you spend any length of time in town, you'll get to know the district intimately. The block between the sea and Orchid Avenue is a **mall**, given over to snack bars, coffee houses and shopping arcades; you can pick up a cheap T-shirt or play a game of chess at one of the outdoor tables. **Raptis Plaza** here is a collection of upmarket fast-food joints overlooked by a replica of Michelangelo's *David*, with an indoor rock-climbing wall tucked away in the Plaza's basement.

Surfers **tower-block** cityscape makes an immediate impression, but the stakes in who can build highest and so block their neighbours' view of the beach have just been upped considerably: on the highway near the corner of Hamilton Avenue, a site has been cleared for what is planned to be the **world's tallest residential building**, which will be almost double the height of the surrounding architecture – check this space to see if it actually goes ahead.

Across the Esplanade, the **beach** is all you could want as a place to recover from your night out. In early afternoon, the sun moves behind the apartment buildings, but you can escape the shadows by moving up to **Main Beach**. If you're feeling energetic, seek out a game of volleyball or head for the surf: the swell here is good in a northerly wind, but most of the time it's better for boogie-boards. North of Main Beach, the Spit's attractions include the world's first "Versace hotel" – a six-star edifice fitted out with all things Versace – and **Sea World** (daily 10am–5pm; $52, family rates; ⓦ www.seaworld.com.au; access on the Surfside Bus from the highway), the longest running of the Gold Coast's theme parks. Besides various stomach-churning rides, the park features immaculately trained dolphins and killer whales, and helps rehabilitate stranded wild dolphins for later release.

The other theme parks are north out of town, all located on Surfside and Gold Coast Shuttle bus routes. **Dreamworld** (daily 10am–5pm; $52, family rates; ⓦ www.dreamworld.com.au), on the Pacific Highway at Coomera, 17km north of Surfers Paradise, has a violent double-loop roller-coaster and a fairground atmosphere, as well as a collection of hand-reared tigers in a large enclosure; this may be as close as they'll get to the wild, but at least they're protected from poachers. **Movie World** (daily 10am–5pm; $52, family rates; ⓦ www.movieworld.com.au), also on the Pacific Highway, 14km north of Surfers, is a slice of Hollywood featuring studio tours, and western and stunt shows. Near Movie World, **Wet 'n' Wild** (daily 10am–4.30pm or later; $32; ⓦ www.wetnwild.com.au) has a series of pools linked by vicious water slides – the back-breaking "twister" and the 25-metre-tall, high-speed slide alone are worth the entrance fee.

Eating

Surfers has somewhere to eat wherever you look, though most places are pretty forgettable. Some resorts offer bargain all-you-can-eat **breakfasts**, while during the rest of the day there's always something to eat at the **cafés** and snack bars along Cavill Avenue and the Esplanade. **Restaurants** range from fast-food to Asian and modern Australian; some places offer discounts on evening meals if you get in before a certain hour. More and more people are heading to convenient takeaway and burger joints out of Surfers to eat – south to the area around Broadbeach Mall, or north to Broadwater or Tedder Avenue, in Southport, where there's usually a Porsche or two parked along the trendy café strip. For **supplies**, there's a supermarket downstairs in the Paradise Centre (on Cavill Ave mall) and a 24-hour Night Owl store on the highway near Trickett Street.

Bavarian Steakhouse Cnr Gold Coast Highway and Cavill Ave ⓣ07/5531 7150. Wood-panelled theme restaurant on several floors, where you can wolf down steins of beer and plates of beef while staff dressed in leather and lace pump away on Bavarian brass instruments. Good fun if you're in the mood, and fair value; about $19 for steak, salad and fries.

Captain's Table 26 Orchid Avenue ⓣ07/5531 5766. Award-winning restaurant with excellent seafood and Australian bush game meats. A plate of delicious barbecued Moreton Bay Bugs is $18.50, though their mud crabs in lemon butter sauce cost almost three times as much, but are also good – get in before 6.30pm for a discount.

Country Hut Gold Coast Highway. Small place with rough-cut "Outback" furniture and a menu featuring crocodile and kangaroo steaks – portions are large and the food well cooked.

Dracula's 1 Hooker Blvd, Broadbeach ⓣ07/5575 1000, ⓦwww.draculas.com.au. Well-designed and fun Gothic cabaret restaurant. Open Tues–Sat from 6pm; $55 per head

($60 on Sat); advance booking essential.
Melba's 46 Cavill Ave ⓣ07/5592 6922. Ambitious café-restaurant attached to the nightclub of the same name, with a mix of Mediterranean-style light meals and snacks served, unusually for Surfers, at pavement tables. Their chicken and avocado fettucine, turkey bagel, and Cajun fish salad are all good, and their prices are reasonable, with nothing over $17.50. Opens at 7am for breakfast.

Montezuma's 8 Trickett St, under the Aloha Tower ⓣ07/5538 4748. A cramped Mexican restaurant hung with luridly coloured, papier-mache fiesta dolls, but serving fresh and spicy food. $18 will fill you up; open for lunch and dinner.

Sumo Raptis Plaza. Tiny Japanese takeaway known for its fair prices and large portions, from seafood tempura ($10.45) down to humble buckwheat noodle soup ($5.50).

Tandoori Place 7–9 Trickett St ⓣ07/5592 1004. Fast-food ambience, but actually better than first impressions would suggest; their sweet curries are engagingly different, and they have a limited vegetarian menu. Most main dishes cost around $15.

Entertainment

Find out **what's on** through accommodation or by word of mouth; the free weekly magazines *Today Tonight Tomorrow* and *Wot's On* are simply business directories. For those desperate for an injection of culture amid all the brash goings-on, check out the programme at the **Arts Centre**, 135 Bundall Rd (☎07/5581 6900), where there's a theatre, gallery, restaurant and bar. You'll find **cinema** complexes on the corner of Clifford Street and Gold Coast Highway (☎07/5575 3355), as well as inside Pacific Fair Shopping Centre, Mermaid Beach (☎07/5575 3355), and Australia Fair shopping centre, Southport (☎07/5531 2200).

Realistically, though, it's Surfers **clubs** that provide most of the nightlife. Initially, particularly if you're staying at a hostel or have picked up a **free pass** somewhere, your choice will most likely be influenced by the various deals on entry and drinks; check out the latest events at ⓦwww.goldcoastclubbers.com. The places listed below have a dependable reputation; none is especially chauvinistic, though places do change. Opening times are from around 6pm until 3am or later.

Berlin Bar On a lane off Orchid Ave. A bit discreet and stylish for Surfers, with a more civilized scene than you find elsewhere; well-heeled 20–35 crowd being slinky and sexy to Seventies disco and funk tunes. Pricey drinks, no cover charge.

Cocktails and Dreams Orchid Ave. Seventies nights on Tuesday from 8pm; nightly R&B at the *Bourbon Bar*, cheap drinks and extended happy hours. Closed Wed.

Fever 26 Orchid Ave. Best place for house and dance on the coast, with an ever-changing array of local and international DJs.

Meeting Place 26 Orchid Ave. Gold Coast's sole gay nightclub – though anyone is welcome – in the same building as *Fever*.

Melba's 46 Cavill Ave. Big and relatively upmarket nightclub, with nightly happy hour until 10pm.

Palladium 7–9 Trickett St ☎07/5570 2100. Surfers live-music mainstay, often attracting major Australian touring bands. There's also a packed and sweaty nightclub here on Friday and Saturday nights.

The Party At *The Mark*, Orchid Ave. Live rock bands on Friday and Sunday (often with a $5 cover charge); DJs for the rest of the week.

Rose and Crown Raptis Plaza, Cavill Ave. Surfers "local" pub; entertainment varies from decent local bands to DJs and strip shows (male and female).

Shooters Right beside *Cocktails and Dreams*. Crowds heading for more serious dance spots start out here for a game of pool and a few drinks.

Sugar Shack Orchid Ave. Venue of the moment; popular pool sessions and live bands most weekends.

Surfers Beergarden Cavill Ave, opposite Orchid Ave. Live music with local and interstate band talent on Thursday and Saturday nights.

Gold Coast tours and cruises

Some hostels organize **tours** to the Scenic Rim, or try the following for day-trips to the **Hinterland** (Lamington, Natural Bridge, Tamborine Mountain and Binna Burra), **Sunshine Coast** (Noosa, The Big Pineapple or Mooloolaba) and **Brisbane**. Most offer free pick-ups. Bushwacker Ecotours (☎07/5525 1653, ⓦwww.bushwacker-ecotours.com.au), highly recommended, day and night wildlife-spotting tours to Hinterland national parks; Coachliner (☎07/5534 9977); Coachtrans (☎1300 361 788); Mountain Coach Company (☎07/5524 4249); Pacific Tours (☎07/5596 0350); Scenic Hinterland Tours (☎07/5545 2030 or 5531 5536). Southern Cross (☎1800 067 367) runs 4WD day-tours around the Hinterland.

The following explore the **Nerang River** and **seafront** on one-hour to half-day cruises. Adventure Duck (☎07/5557 8869, ⓦwww.adventureduck.com), a unique amphibious bus, departs several times daily from Orchid Avenue for an hour-long trip ($45); Gold Coast Cruises (☎07/5557 8888, ⓦwww.shangrila.com.au); Tall Ship (☎07/5532 2444), from two-hour calm-water cruises for $31.90 to day-trips to South Stradbroke at $99. See p.434 for more on trips to South Stradbroke Island.

Listings

Banks and exchange Banks and ATMs are located right throughout Surfers, with most main branches around the Cavill Ave-Highway intersection. There are also several bureaux de change in Cavill and Orchid avenues, giving pretty much the same rates as the banks.

Buses Coachtrans to Brisbane (☎07/5574 5111); Greyhound Pioneer (☎07/5538 2700); Kirkland's to Brisbane, Byron Bay and Lismore (☎1300 367 077); McCafferty's (☎07/5538 2700); Premier (☎13 34 10).

Car rental Competition keeps prices low, but advertised prices are often for long rentals, and exclude insurance and mileage charges: CY Rent a Car (☎07/5570 3777), from $29 a day; East Coast Car Rentals (☎07/5592 0444 or 1800 028 881), from $27 a day; Holiday Car Rentals (☎07/5598 2955), new cars from $35 a day; Kanga Car and Moped (☎07/5527 6088), old model cars from $19 a day; Red Back Rentals, inside the bus station, Beach Rd (☎07/5592 1655), from $30 a day; Red Rocket (☎07/5538 9074 or 1800 673 682), old model cars from $15 a day.

Hospitals and medical centres Gold Coast Hospital, Nerang St, Southport ☎07/5571 8211; Gold Coast Medical Centre, Paradise Centre, on Cavill Avenue ☎07/5538 8099.

Internet There are many Internet cafés around the bus station on Beach Road and Gold Coast Highway charging upwards of $3.50 an hour.

Pharmacy Galleria Shopping Plaza, cnr Elkhorn Ave and Gold Coast Highway (7am–midnight).

Post office The main post office is in the Paradise Centre on Cavill Avenue.

Surf rental Surfworld, Paradise Centre, on Cavill Avenue ☎07/5538 4825. Typical prices are $25 a day for board rental, plus credit-card deposit. For tuition see the box on p.429.

Taxis ☎13 10 08.

South Stradbroke Island

South Stradbroke Island is a twenty-kilometre-long, narrow strip of sand, separated from North Stradbroke Island by the 1896 cyclone and, as apartment buildings edge closer, doomed to become an extension of the Gold Coast. For now, though, South Stradbroke's relatively isolated and quiet beaches offer something of an escape from the mainland, though most day-trippers come over simply to get plastered in the bar at **South Stradbroke Island Resort** (☎07/5577 3311; ⓦwww.southstradbrokeislandresort.com.au; rooms ❺, cabins ❻). Alternative accommodation is available at the new **Couran Cove Resort** (☎07/5597 9000, ⓦwww.couran.com; cabins and rooms ❼), which offers a much more exclusive atmosphere, and doesn't welcome day-guests. There's also fine **surf** to enjoy along the southeast shore (though local surfies are notoriously protective), along with **fishing** in the Jumpinpin Channel between here and North Stradbroke.

Day-cruises to the resort depart Tiki Wharf on Cavill Avenue and cost around $80 including lunch, with evening booze cruises about $55; operators include Island Queen (☎07/5557 8800, ⓦwww.islandqueen.com.au) and Shangri-La (☎07/5557 8888, ⓦwww.shangrila.com.au). A cheaper alternative is the **resort ferry** ($49, includes lunch at the resort) which departs daily 10.30am from Runaway Bay Marina, 5km north of Surfers on Bayview Street, and returns between 2.45pm and 5pm depending on the day – bookings are essential.

Surfers Paradise to Currumbin

The central section of the Gold Coast lacks any real focus. Haphazardly developed and visually unattractive, it exists very much in the shadow of Surfers Paradise, but can't match its intensity. The highway is just a continuous maze of crowded, multi-lane traffic systems and drab buildings which lose momentum the further south you drive, but once you leave the road there are fine beaches, two **wildlife sanctuaries** and – unbelievable amid all the commotion and noise – a tiny **national park**, which preserves the coast's original environment.

Burleigh Heads

Around 7km south of Surfers, **BURLEIGH HEADS** consists of a traffic bottleneck where the highway dodges between the **beach** and a rounded headland; there can be very good **surf** here but the rocks make it rough for novices. Fifty years ago, before the bitumen and paving took over, this was all dense eucalypt and vine forest, the last fragment of which survives as **Burleigh Head National Park**. Entrance is on foot from the car park on the Esplanade, or turn sharply at the lights below the hill just south of the headland for the visitors **information centre** (daily 9am–4pm; ℡07/5535 3032).

Geologically, Burleigh Heads stems from the prehistoric eruptions of the Mount Warning volcano (p.327), 30km to the southwest. Lava surfaced through vents, cooling to tall hexagonal basalt columns, now mostly tumbled and covered in vines. Rainforest colonized the richer volcanic soils, while stands of red gum grew in weaker sandy loam; along the eastern seafront there's a patch of exposed heathland bordered by groups of pandanus, and a beach along the mouth of Tallebudgera Creek. This diversity is amazing considering the minimal space, but urban encroachment has seriously affected the wildlife. **Butterflies** and **birds** are the most obvious inhabitants – on the heathland look out for the fairy wren's telltale black and red plumage – but the gums also support a small **koala** population (though, notoriously sensitive to disturbance, they often make themselves scarce). The area's natural resources once attracted Yugumbir Aborigines, indicated by a few mounds of half-buried shells up on the headland, whose history is brought to life on a "Kaila" tour – book through the park visitors centre, or phone ℡07/5528 9744.

More of the same awaits you 2km inland at **David Fleay Wildlife Park**, West Burleigh Rd (daily 9am–5pm; $13; ℡07/5576 2411; take the Surfside Bus). The late David Fleay was the first person to persuade **platypus** to breed in captivity and the park has a special section devoted to this curious animal, along with crocodiles, koalas, plenty of birds and smaller animals. The free guided tours are worthwhile; take advantage of their night spotlight and, Sunday to Wednesday, their Aboriginal talk.

Currumbin Beach and Sanctuary

A further 6km past Burleigh Heads, **CURRUMBIN BEACH** is a nice, relatively undeveloped stretch of coast between Elephant Rock and Currumbin Point, and with a breeze there are usually some decent rollers to ride. Just to the north, **PALM BEACH** is more sheltered. *Vikings*, in the surf-club building below Elephant Rock, serves Chinese food, or you can fill up on regular pub fare at the *Palm Beach Surf Club*.

Currumbin Sanctuary, on Tomewin Street (daily 8am–5pm; $20; night tours by arrangement ℡07/5534 1266, ⓦwww.currumbin-sanctuary.org.au), was started in 1946 by Alex Griffiths, who foresaw the decline of the coastal environment and developed the seventy-acre park as a wildlife refuge. Forest, lake and grassland fairly bustle with native fauna. There are the usual feeding times and tame kangaroos but the park's strongest point is the beautiful natural surroundings, best experienced from the elevated walkways through the forest, where you'll see koalas, tree kangaroos and birds at eye-level.

Coolangatta

On the Queensland-New South Wales border 10km south of Currumbin, **COOLANGATTA** merges seamlessly with Tweed Heads (in New South Wales; see p.435) along Boundary Road. With only a giant concrete plinth just off the main road marking the border, you'll probably make the crossing between states without realizing it. Unless it's New Year, when everyone takes advantage of the one-hour time difference between the states to celebrate twice, most travellers bypass Coolangatta completely; in doing so, they miss some of the best surf, least crowded beaches and the only place along the Gold Coast which can boast a real "local" community.

Coolangatta is set out one block back from the beach along **Griffith Street**, where you'll find banks, shops and little in the way of high-density development. Even the motel towers on Point Danger are well spaced, and the general ambience is that of a very small seaside town. Marine Parade fronts the shore, the view north over sand and sea ending with the jagged teeth of the skyscrapers on the horizon at Surfers Paradise.

Straddling the border at Point Danger, the **Captain Cook Memorial Lighthouse** forms a shrine where pillars enclose a large bronze globe detailing Cook's peregrinations around the southern hemisphere (see also p.1163). Twenty-five metres below, surfers in their colourful wet suits make the most of Flagstaff Beach's swell – at weekends this area is very crowded.

Coolangatta's daytime action is in the **surf**, the best being between Point Danger and Kirra Point (the latter nominated by world surfing champion Kelly Slater as his favourite break), or at Flagstaff, across the state border in Tweed Heads – exactly where depends on the wind. **Greenmount**, effectively Coolangatta's town beach, is fairly reliable and is a good beach for beginners; Snapper Rocks and Point Danger further down the peninsula are for the more dedicated. For sun worshippers, **Coolangatta beach**, just north of Greenmount, is fine if you're staying nearby, but the six-kilometre stretch of sand further up, beyond Kirra Point, is wider and less crowded. **Surfing supplies and rentals** are available from Pipedream, Griffith Street (☎07/5599 1164), the best place for gear and information about local conditions and competitions, and from Mount Woodgee, 122 Griffith St (☎07/5536 5937). Surfboard and ski rental is around $20 a day plus credit-card deposit. All shops have decent secondhand boards for sale, though local boards tend to be too thin and lightweight to use elsewhere. You might also find a bargain in one of the pawnbroker's shops on Griffith Street. For **tuition**, see the box on p.429.

Practicalities

Griffith Street (the Gold Coast Highway) and the parallel, seafront **Marine Parade** run south for about a kilometre from the edge of town to the border, with a handful of short streets connecting them. At the border, Griffith Street kinks sharply inland as it enters Tweed Heads, while Boundary Street continues south (uphill) to Point Danger.

The **long-distance bus stop** is actually 150m over the border in Tweed Heads, just off the highway at Golden Gateway Travel, 29 Bay St (Mon–Sat 7.30am–5.30pm, New South Wales time; ☎07/5536 1700) – there's no station as such, and if Golden Gateway is closed, you just get set down on the pavement. The **Gold Coast airport** (flight information on ☎13 13 00) is 3km north of Coolangatta, from where Airport Transit shuttle buses (book in advance on ☎1300 655 655) run to Coolangatta and all points to Surfers Paradise for $11 one-way and $16.50 return. Coolangatta's helpful **information centre** (Mon–Sat 8am–5pm, Sun 10am–2pm; ☎07/5536 7765, Ⓦwww.tweed-coolangatta.com) is on the corner of Warner and Griffith streets, about halfway down Griffith towards the border. **Taxis** can be booked on ☎13 10 08 while **car rental** is available through Thrifty (☎07/5536 6954), at the Gold Coast airport, with prices starting at $35.

Accommodation

Accommodation is strung out along the highway at Bilinga and Kirra, while the more expensive places are in the apartment buildings overlooking the sea on Marine Parade and Point Danger. For **camping**, try *Kirra Tourist Park*, Charlotte Street, Kirra (℡07/5581 7744).

Calypso Plaza 87–105 Griffith St ℡07/5599 0000 or 1800 062 189. Modern and expensive resort hotel, with suites and two-bedroom penthouse apartments, right across from Greenmount Beach. **❼**

Kirra Beach Hotel Across from the beach at Kirra Point ℡07/5536 3311. Ideal location for boardriders. Some rooms are quite spacious, and all have bath, TV & fridge; cheap meals available in the pub bistro. **❸**

On the Beach 118 Marine Parade, Greenmount Beach ℡07/5536 3624. Single or double rooms

and singles in self-contained apartments. Tidy and well placed for the town and the beach. **❹**

Sunset Strip Budget Resort 199 Boundary St ℡07/5599 5517. Good facilities, including family rooms and singles, huge kitchen and living areas (with three TVs), 20m pool and sun deck; no dorms. **❸**–**❹**

YHA 3km up the coast at 230 Coolangatta Rd/Gold Coast Highway, Bilinga, near the airport ℡07/5536 7644. Helpful management and nicely located for the quieter beaches, though a bit far from Coolangatta itself. **❷**

Eating, drinking and nightlife

If you're doing your own cooking, there's a 24-hour **convenience store** inside the Beach House complex beside the *Coolangatta Hotel* (corner of Griffith and Warner streets), and bigger supermarkets across the border at the main shopping centre on Wharf Street, in Tweed Heads (for further information on Tweed Heads, see p.320). There are plenty of snack bars along Griffith Street, while **restaurants** include *Little Malaya Restaurant*, right at the northern end of Marine Parade near the *Coolangatta Sands Hotel*, which does an unforgettable crispy-fried whole fish in sour chilli sauce for $25 (enough for two), and *Café Uno* on Marine Parade, with sea views, pavement tables and a slightly overworked "Mediterranean" menu featuring mains from $19. The Surf Lifesaving Club down near the border at Greenmount Beach has good-value burgers, salads, sandwiches and cold drinks.

Coolangatta's **nightlife** centres around the pubs – you'll have to rely on posters to find out what's on. Best are live music sessions at the *Coolangatta Sands Hotel*'s fairly relaxed bar (corner of Griffith and McLean streets) and the *Coolangatta Hotel*'s nightclub, which also has live music and pool competitions.

The Hinterland and Scenic Rim

Inland from the coast's jangling excesses, the **Scenic Rim** forms a barrier between the coastal flatlands and the pastoral Darling Downs, encompassing a series of mountainous **national parks**. Here you'll find Queensland's largest expanse of subtropical rainforest and – the main attraction – the **Lamington Plateau**, packed with powerfully beautiful scenery, animals and birds. Whether you're a day-tripper, veteran hiker or just fancy camping in the same spot for a few days, it's not to be missed. Closest to the coast, **Springbrook**'s waterfalls or the rainforest suburbia at **Tamborine Mountain** make easy day-trips and are thus the most-visited destinations, while tough tracks at the region's extremes in the **Main Range** remain the prerogative of experienced bush-walkers.

The Eastern and Central Rim

The **Tamborine Mountain-Lamington** area is covered with a network of graded, well-trodden paths, so you don't have to be particularly skilled at bush-walking to enjoy the experience. Come prepared, though – tackling the longer or steeper routes requires some degree of **fitness**; test your endurance on shorter walks first. **Paths** are often well marked but sometimes narrow and slip-pery with little fencing along cliffs and waterfalls, so footwear should have a good grip and, ideally, be waterproof. **Rain** is a year-round possibility; the most comfortable weather conditions occur between June and November, though everything looks its best in the middle of the wet season with waterfalls in full flood and the greenery shockingly intense. If you do visit during the Wet (Jan–March), you'll have to endure rain, deep and fast-flowing rivers, occa-sionally closed paths and an unwelcome abundance of **leeches**.

Accommodation is largely limited to resorts and campsites, so if you're on a tight budget you'll need a tent. Nights in winter (July–Sept) are always cool enough to warrant a sleeping bag and pullover, though after-dark temperatures can drop even in midsummer. **Campsites** have water and stores nearby, but you'll save money by bringing your own supplies. A fuel stove is a good idea – collecting firewood in national parks is forbidden, although there are often bar-becues with wood supplied. Access to the area is easy enough in itself but because of local geography there are few interconnecting roads, making back-tracking unavoidable if you want to visit more than one place. If you can, get hold of a vehicle – only Lamington and Tamborine Mountain have a regular bus service – and make sure you take a good **road atlas** along, as signposts to the parks are few and far between. Tours visit most locations – see accounts below and also the boxes on p.420 and p.433.

Tamborine Mountain

Tamborine Mountain is a rainforested mountain top, about 40km inland as the crow flies from the Gold Coast, interspersed by the upmarket, compact satellite suburbs of northerly **Eagle Heights**, adjoining **North Tamborine** and **Mount Tamborine**, about 5km south. Once the haunt of the Wangeriburra Aborigines, Tamborine Mountain's forests were targeted by the timber industry in the late nineteenth century until locals succeeded in getting the area declared Queensland's **first national park** in 1908. Today, six parks protect a surprisingly diverse range of native forests from development.

Most of the parks surround North Tamborine. Just east between here and Eagle Heights, walking tracks at **Joalah National Park** head downstream through woodland to a (cold) swimming hole; look for giant epiphytic ferns in the canopy along the way and the Albert lyrebird, with its fantastically shaped tail and liquid song. There's more of the same – and fine views to the north-west – immediately north of North Tamborine at **Knoll National Park** (also a good place for a picnic). To the west are **Witches Falls**, where a three-kilometre track slaloms downhill through open scrub and rainforest. It's an easy walk, but is more rewarding for the views from the mountain than for the falls themselves, which are only a trickle that disappears over a narrow ledge below the lookout. Far more impressive is **Cedar Creek Falls**, another good swimming spot off the Brisbane road, though possibly the best park is **Palm Grove** near Eagle Heights, with views through the canopy of the Gold Coast, a few small creeks, and a limpid, eerie gloom created by an extensive stand of elegant piccabean palms. Hidden 20m up in the canopy are elusive wompoo pigeons, often heard but seldom seen – despite their vivid purple-and-green plumage and onomatopoeic call. Finally, down near Mount Tamborine, there's a stand of primitive, slow-growing cycads (see box on p.510) and a relatively dry climate at **Lepidozamia National Park**.

Practicalities

Ideally, you'll have your own transport for the mountain. Coming up **from Brisbane**, you'll be travelling either via Beenleigh and Oxenford to Eagle Heights, or via the lowland settlement of Tamborine township to North Tamborine; **from Surfers Paradise**, you ascend via Nerang to Mount Tamborine. The sole **bus service** to the mountain is with the Mountain Coach Company (℡07/5524 4249), which picks up daily from points along the Gold Coast between 8 and 9am and charges $42 for a day-trip, or $25 each way if you want to go up one day and back another. Once up here, you can get around with the Mountain Shuttle Service, which runs between settlements from 10am to 5pm on Saturday and Sunday only ($10 for the day).

　　NORTH TAMBORINE has most of the area's services, including a general store, post office, garage, ATMs (there are **no banks** up here) and a **visitors' information centre**, which has maps of walking trails; **EAGLE HEIGHTS** has another post office and a **tourist office** (daily usually 8.30am–5pm; ℡07/5545 1161); while **MOUNT TAMBORINE** is mostly residential. There's abundant **accommodation** on the mountain, generally of a romantic-getaway nature, including cosy rooms at *The Polish Place*, 333 Main Western Rd, North Tamborine (℡07/5545 1603; self-contained chalet **❼**); *Maz's on the Mountain*, 25 Eagle Heights Rd, North Tamborine (℡07/5545 1766, **Ⓦ**www.mazsretreat.com; **❻**) which has suites with four-poster beds, plus a pool and surrounding forest; *The Cottages*, 23 Kootenai Drive, North Tamborine (℡07/5545 2574; **❻**); the very stylish wooden pole-frame buildings at *Pethers Rainforest Retreat* (℡07/5545 4577, **Ⓦ**www.pethers.com.au; **❼**); and *Tambourine Mountain Bed and Breakfast*, Witherby Crescent, Eagle Heights, which offers sweeping views (℡07/5545 3595; **❺**).

Springbrook National Park

Close to the coast along the New South Wales border, **Springbrook**'s three parks (Mount Cougal, Purling Brook Falls and Natural Bridge) feature abundant waterfalls and swimming holes; though grouped together, access to each section is by a different road. **Mount Cougal** is at the end of a road 21km west of Currumbin. Rainforest flanks the upper reaches of Currumbin Creek, and a path follows the stream to an abandoned sawmill, past pools and pretty cascades. For higher drama and a short, moderately demanding walk, head for **Purling Brook Falls**, a thirty-kilometre drive from Burleigh Heads via Mudgeeraba. There's a **campsite** outside the forest, near the top of the falls, with a store about 4km back along the main road. The 109-metre falls are very impressive after rain has swollen the flow; a four-kilometre track zigzags down the escarpment and into the rainforest at the base of the falls before curving underneath the waterfall (expect a soaking from the spray) and going back up the other side. In the plunge pool at the foot of the falls, the force of the water is enough to push you under; swimming is more relaxed in a couple of pools downstream, picturesquely encircled by lianas and red cedar. A ten-kilometre drive beyond the falls brings you to **Best of All Lookout** and a broad vista south to Mount Warning from the very edge of the Rim. On the lookout road, *Springbrook Mountain Lodge* **youth hostel** (☏07/5533 5366, ✉springbrooklodge@ion.tm; dorms $29, rooms ❸) has a good fireplace for cold winter nights and a fair claim to being the first place in Australia to see the sun each day – note that you should phone ahead for $20 transfer from the Gold Coast, and bring all your own supplies.

At **Natural Bridge** a collapsed cave ceiling beneath the riverbed has created a subterranean waterfall. An exciting but very dangerous leap down the falls will take you into the cave: several people have been killed trying it, and the recommended method is simply to walk in through the mouth, 50m downstream. From the back of the cave the forest outside frames the waterfall and blue plunge pool, surreally lit from above; **glow worms** illuminate the ceiling at night. The park is 49km from Burleigh Heads or Southport via Nerang and about 27km from Purling Brook. For a different tour of the area, Numinbah Valley Adventure Trails is highly recommended for half-day **horseback** rides from the base near Nerang to otherwise inaccessible volcanic caves ($55, pick-up from Surfers accommodation extra; book on ☏07/5533 4137, ⓦwww.numinbahtrails.com.au).

Lamington National Park

Lamington National Park occupies the northeastern rim of a vast caldera centred on Mount Warning, 15km away in New South Wales. An enthralling world of rainforest-flanked rivers, open heathland and ancient eucalypt woods, Lamington's position on a **crossover zone** between subtropical and temperate climes has made it home to a staggering variety of plants, animals and birds, some forming isolated populations of species found nowhere else.

There are two possible bases: **Binna Burra** on the drier northern edge, and **Green Mountain** (also known as **O'Reilly's Guesthouse**) in the thick of the forest. Routes come in from Canungra to Green Mountain (37km) and from Beechmont to Binna Burra (10km) – these are narrow, twisting roads cutting through patches of forest and cleared grazing land. From the Gold Coast, turn off at Nerang – roads to both Binna Burra and Green Mountain diverge from here; from Brisbane, leave the highway at Beenleigh – you pass through Canungra to reach Beechmont this way.

Buses run from the Gold Coast or Brisbane, although groups will find it's cheaper to rent a car. When you buy your bus ticket, make it clear whether you want to return the same day or another day: it's also possible to walk between Binna Burra and Green Mountain (see opposite for details), so you might want to arrange to be dropped at one end and collected at the other. Green Mountain can be reached daily from Surfers Paradise with Mountain Coach Company (☏07/5524 4249, call first to arrange pick-up; $45 return) and from Brisbane's Transit Centre with Allstate Scenic Tours (☏1300 30 700; $44 return; no Sat service). Binna Burra's only bus is the Mountain Lodge's Gold Coast service (☏1800 074 260 for details).

Once here, Lamington has to be explored **on foot**: most of the tracks described below are clearly signposted and **free maps** are available from local NPWS ranger stations. If you're experienced and want to head off along less-defined paths, contact the rangers first for advice.

Binna Burra

It's some time since guests had to walk the last few kilometres through the steep forest to **Binna Burra** with their luggage on a horse. Today, upmarket *Mountain Lodge* (℗07/5533 3622, ⓦwww.binnaburralodge.com.au; tent $10 per person, on-site tents ❷, cabins ❻) has wooden cabins with log fires, along with **on-site tents** and a **campsite** with hot showers up the road. Other facilities include a tearoom aimed at day-trippers, but bread and some basic provisions are also sold. Don't leave food unattended at the campsite – it's infested with brazen scrub turkeys. Hikers can **bushcamp** between February and November; for details contact the **park ranger** (daily 8am–4pm; ℗07/5533 3584) at the station, 1.5km before the lodge.

Both lodge and campsite overlook the Numinbah Valley from woodland on the crown of Mount Roberts, and **walking** anywhere always leaves you with an uphill return journey. The lethargic can simply wander 500m between the campsite and the lodge at night with a torch to be rewarded by the sight of groups of wallabies grazing on the verges; commotion in the trees betrays the presence of brushtail possums foraging for flowers and leaves. Try the lodge's unique **senses trail**: blindfolded and following a rope you become aware that there's more to the forest than just a blaze of green – you sense a drop in temperature under the canopy, feel the textures of bark and leaves, and receive wafts of scent from the forest floor.

Of the **longer walks**, try the easy five-kilometre **Caves Circuit**, which follows the edge of the Coomera Valley past the white, wind-sculpted Talangai Caves to remains of Aboriginal camps, strands of psilotum nudum, a rootless precursor of the ferns, and a hillside of strangler figs and red cedar. Plunging into another forest below the campsite, the harder **Ballunji Falls track** is a typical compromise between access and terrain, with occasional vertical drops to test sure-footedness. Features on the way include views of Egg Rock from Bellbird Lookout, at its most mysterious when shrouded in dawn mists, and a stand of majestic forty-metre-tall box brush trees. Dedicated walkers can extend the track out to **Ships Stern**, an arduous and dry 21-kilometre return (allow a minimum of 8hr) with some wonderful views off the escarpment. **Dave's Creek Circuit** is similar but about half as long, crossing bands of rainforest and sclerophyll before emerging onto heathland. Look for tiny clumps of red sundew plants along the track, which supplement their nitrogen intake by trapping insects in sticky globules of nectar.

Other longer tracks can be joined together, allowing you to spend days hiking without ever returning to base. Most popular of these is the **Border Track**; a relatively easy 21-kilometre/nine-hour (one-way) path through rainforest linking Binna Burra with Green Mountain. If you need road transport between the two, the lodge usually runs a free weekly service to *O'Reilly's* for its guests, and will often take others for a fee if there's room – departures depend on demand, so all arrangements have to be made on site.

Green Mountain

Green Mountain's forests are Lamington at its best. With so much to dazzle the senses here the initial experience is confused, but gradually the various types of plants and trees become familiar, as do the distinct layers between the rainforest floor and canopy. Random rustles and trills resolve into wallabies thumping around tree roots, scrub turkeys scratching up leaf litter and a whipbird's cracking call; it's easy to become lost in the environment's complex structure.

The road from Canungra to **Green Mountain** ends at *O'Reilly's Guesthouse* (℗07/5544 0644, ⓦwww.oreillys.com.au; ❼), a splendid and comfortable place opened in 1926 – bookings are advised at weekends and during holiday periods. The guesthouse has a very limited store (with EFTPOS facilities) and a moderately priced restaurant for meals and snacks throughout the day. There's also an exposed NPWS campsite with showers; call ☎13 13 04 for essential advance booking. If you can't get in here, about 7km down the road the rustic *Mt Cainbable Cabins* (☎07/5544 9207, ⓦwww.cainbable.com; ❺) offers bed and breakfast in four-person cabins, or try the *Canungra Motel* (☎07/5543 5155; ❹) at the bottom of the range.

The **birdlife** around *O'Reilly's* is prolific and distracting: you can't miss the chattering swarms of crimson rosellas mingling with visitors on the lawn, and determined twitchers can clock up over fifty species without even reaching the forest – most spectacular is the black-and-gold regent bowerbird. But it's worth pushing on to the **treetop walk** just beyond the clearing, where a suspended walkway swings 15m above ground level. At the halfway anchor point you scale a narrow ladder to vertigo-inducing mesh platforms 30m up the trunk of a strangler fig to see the canopy at eye level. Soaking up the increased sunlight at this height above the forest floor, tree branches become miniature gardens of mosses, ferns and orchids. By night the walkway is the preserve of possums, leaf-tailed geckoes and weird stalking insects.

If you manage only one day-walk at Lamington, make it the exceptional five-hour **Blue Pool–Canungra Creek track** (15km), which features all the jungle trimmings: fantastic trees, river crossings and countless opportunities to fall off slippery rocks and get soaked. The first hour is dry enough as you tramp downhill past some huge red cedars to Blue Pool, a deep, placid waterhole where **platypuses** are sometimes seen on winter mornings; this makes a good walk in itself. After a dip, head upstream along Canungra Creek; the path traverses the river a few times (there are no bridges, but occasionally a fallen tree conveniently spans the water) – look for yellow or red **arrows** painted on rocks that indicate where to cross. Seasonally, the creek can be almost dried up; if the water is more than knee-deep, you shouldn't attempt a crossing and will need to retrace your steps. Follow the creek as far as **Elabana Falls** and another swimming hole, or bypass the falls; either way, the path climbs back to the guesthouse.

Another excellent trail (17.5km) takes six hours via **Box Creek Falls** to the eastern escarpment at **Toolona Lookout**, on the Border Track to Binna Burra; rewards are a half-dozen waterfalls, dramatic views into New South Wales, and encounters with clumps of moss-covered **Antarctic beech trees**, a strange Gondwanan relict also found in South America. For seasoned, well-equipped walkers, there's a chance to delve into local history by way of an overnight hike to the **Stinson Wreck**. In February 1937 a plane bound for Sydney crashed into dense forest and the survivors were only located due to the incredible efforts of Bernard O'Reilly who, on his own, hiked from the plane to Green Mountain and returned with a rescue party. Nearby is **Westray's grave**, the burial place of one of the passengers who died looking for help, but it's difficult to reach. Today most of the wreck has been carted off by souvenir hunters or covered by jungle, but the guesthouse and park rangers can give you advice on the walk and may be able to put you in touch with bushwalkers who've been there.

The Western Rim

In contrast to the obvious charms of the Eastern Rim, the drier **Western Rim** is mainly given over to open eucalypt woods, with the steep peaks covered in heath. With few facilities, it's a place for serious bushwalkers; even "easy" routes are fairly demanding, with few neat paths or signposts – so come equipped, don't walk alone, and carry plenty of water. Access is along the Cunningham and Mount Lindesay highways from Boonah or Beaudesert in the east and **Warwick** (see p.566) from the west; there's no public transport.

Mount Barney, Main Range and Mount Mistake

Mount Barney's multiple peaks – the taller of which is a respectable 1359m above sea level – form an extremely rough region along the New South Wales border, 45km southwest of Beaudesert. From wherever you're approaching, aim for Rathdowney and then take Barney View Road past Bigriggen to Yellowpinch. You can stay south of Rathdowney at *Mt Barney Lodge*, an excellent old homestead at the foot of Mount Barney with camping, cabin and house **accommodation** (☎07/5544 3233; tent sites with hot showers $9 per person, cabins ❺; 2- to 8-person house $280 per weekend). The nearest supplies and alternative camping are at Rathdowney and Bigriggen.

From the car park 5km from Yellowpinch there's a distinct, hour-long track to the **Lower Portals**, a pool on Barney Creek flanked by vertical cliffs. The only other marked hike (though even for this you might need a topographic map) is the misleadingly named "tourist trail" along the south ridge to the saddle between Mount Barney's peaks: be prepared for an exhausting seven-hour return trip from Yellowpinch. Experienced walkers, with permits and advice from the NPWS about current conditions (write to PO Box 121, Boonah; ☎07/5463 5041), could camp in the saddle at **Rum Jungle** and climb the peaks in the morning; the eastern peak is the easier of the two and has the better views across to Mount Lindesay's tor, poking above wooded slopes.

Main Range's precipitous terrain and sharp, progressively higher peaks are most directly accessible along the Cunningham Highway at Cunningham's Gap, between Brisbane and Warwick, about 90km from Boonah. Here you'll find some of the easier trails: tracks through rainforest along West Gap Creek and ascents of Bare Rock and Mount Mitchell, which you could complete in a couple of hours or a day, depending on your inclination. There's an NPWS **campsite** at the Gap (☎07/4666 1133); call in advance to check on conditions. **Mount Mistake** is an undeveloped park on the junction of three mountain ranges which form the northernmost extent of the Scenic Rim. Walking is said to be tricky but well worth the effort; if you're tempted, contact the NPWS on ☎07/4666 1133.

The Sunshine Coast

The **Sunshine Coast**, stretching north of Brisbane to **Noosa**, is a more pedestrian version of the Gold Coast, where largely domestic tourist development is tempered by, and sometimes combined with, agriculture. Much local character is due to the lack of death taxes in Queensland – something which, together with the pleasant climate, attracts retirees from all over Australia. The towns tend to be bland places, lively enough at Christmas, but out of season you may be hard pushed to find much to do after dark. Even so, the beaches and surf are good, improving as you go further north and providing an excuse to linger for a few days. And though you'll find the hinterland far tamer than it is down south, it still has some arresting landscapes and scattered hamlets rife with Devonshire cream teas and weekend markets.

Without your own **transport**, the easiest way through the area is by **bus** – Sunshine Coast Sunbus (℡07/5492 8700), and Suncoast Pacific from Brisbane (℡07/5443 1011) are the local alternatives to the national operators – or on a tour from Brisbane or the Gold Coast. Brisbane's **Citytrain** network can also take you into the region, with stops at the **Glasshouse Mountains**, **Woombye**, **Nambour** and **Eumundi**, from where there's a connecting bus to Noosa. There's also the **Sunshine Coast airport** just north of Maroochydore, serving Brisbane, Sydney and Melbourne. Once here, "the other car rental company" (℡07/5447 2831, ⓦwww.noosacarrental.com) has the best in **car rentals** in the region, from runarounds to 4WDs for Cooloola and Fraser Island. Alternatively, Adventures Sunshine Coast (℡07/5444 8824, ⓦwww.adventuressun.com.au) organizes day-trips **climbing** in the Glasshouse Mountains, **bushwalking** the Obi Obi gorge in the Blackall Range, or **canoeing** the Mooloolah River south of Maroochydore (from $155 per person, including lunch and pick-up from lodgings along the coast).

Woodford, Australia Zoo and the Glasshouse Mountains

Caboolture marks the start of the Sunshine Coast, 40km north of Brisbane. Though there's nothing to detain you here, 20km inland is the two-street town of **WOODFORD**, which draws thousands for the annual **folk festival** in December, and north from Caboolture are the **Glasshouse Mountains**: nine dramatic, isolated pinnacles jutting out of a flat plain, visible from as far away as Brisbane. Another reason to head up this way is **Australia Zoo**, at the northern end of the mountains between the hamlets of Beerwah and Landsborough (daily 8.30am–4pm; $21; ℡07/5494 1134, ⓦwww.crocodile hunter.com), made famous by the antics of zoo director Steve Irwin, otherwise known for his screen persona, "Crocodile Hunter". The best way into the area is along the old highway 16km north from Caboolture or off the new one 10km north of Beerburrum; **Citytrain** stops at Beerburrum (where zoo visitors can get a free pick-up, arranged in advance) and Glasshouse Mountains. Noosa Hinterland Tours (℡07/5474 3366, call to arrange door-to-door pick-ups), and Australian Day Tours from Brisbane (℡07/3236 4155) offer regional **tours**. The most convenient **accommodation** in the area is at *Log Cabin Caravan Park* (℡07/5496 9338; cabins ❸), south of Glasshouse Mountains township at the foot of Mount Tibrogargan.

Catching sight of the Glasshouse Mountains from the sea, Captain Cook named them after their shape and "elevation", a resemblance that's obscure today. To the Kabi Aborigines, the mountains are the petrified forms of a family fleeing the incoming tide; their names for the peaks – Tibrogargan, Tibberoowuccum and Beerwah, for instance – are far more evocative than Cook's. The peaks themselves vary enormously: some are rounded and fairly easy to scale, while a couple have vertical faces and sharp spires requiring competent climbing skills. It's worth conquering at least one of the easier peaks; the views are superb and the mountains are one of the few really special places on the Sunshine Coast. **Beerburrum**, overlooking the township of the same name, and **Ngungun**, near Glasshouse Mountains township, are two of the easiest to climb, with well-used tracks; the latter's views and scenery outclass some of the tougher peaks and it will take you only two hours there and back, though the lower parts of the track are steep and slippery. **Tibberoowuccum** must be climbed from the northwest, and you'll need a map; ask at the *Log Cabin Caravan Park* for directions. The taller mountains – **Tibrogargan** and **Beerwah** (the highest at 556m) – are at best tricky, and **Coonowrin** should be attempted only by experienced climbers after contacting the NPWS, 61 Bunya Rd, Maleny (☎07/5494 3983), for more information.

Caloundra, Mooloolaba and Maroochydore

Coastwards and a little north of the Glasshouse Mountains, **CALOUNDRA** just manages to hold on to its small seaside-town atmosphere, and as such is unique along the Sunshine Coast where busy highways and beachfront over-development have long put paid to this elsewhere. Even so, there are plenty of towering apartment blocks, though central **Bulcock Street** has only low-rise buildings and is lined with trees. Caloundra's **beaches** are very pleasant: the closest is Deepwater Point, just two streets south of Bulcock Street. **Shelley Beach** and **Moffat Beach**, about a kilometre distant, are much better however. The **bus terminal** is on Cooma Terrace, one street south of Bulcock, where there's also an **information centre** (Mon–Fri 8.30am–5pm; ☎07/5491 0202). For **accommodation** try *Caloundra City Backpackers*, 84 Omrah Ave (☎07/5499 7655; dorms $19, rooms ❷), which is clean, well run, and just two minutes from Deepwater Point. *Estoril*, 38 McIlwraith St (☎07/4591 5988, ⓦwww.estoril.com.au; ❹), offers self-catering apartments in a high-rise block right next to Moffat Beach and has a huge pool.

The stretch of coast north of Caloundra is taken up with Mooloolaba, Alexandra Headland, and Maroochydore, three beach-side suburbs which are gradually filling the foreshore between the Mooloolah and Maroochy rivers with an amoeba-like blob of high-rise units. **MOOLOOLABA** features the kitsch, touristy Mooloolaba Wharf – from where you can organize sixty-minute **canal cruises** ($10), taking in some rather opulent waterfront real estate – and the pedestrianized seafront **Esplanade**, thick with boutique shops and restaurants. Nearby, on Parkyn Parade, **Underwater World** (daily 9am–6pm, last entry at 5pm; $22) has superb saltwater and freshwater tanks where barramundi – fish revered by Queensland anglers for their taste and legendary fighting spirit – and sharks, turtles and inoffensive freshwater crocodiles stare blankly at you through huge windows. For the real thing, Scuba World (☎07/5444 8595, ⓦwww.scubaworld.com.au), just around the corner on Parkyn Parade, can train you or take you **diving** to local sandstone terrain, where you'll find nudibranch, soft corals and bottom-dwelling sharks, or up to **Wolf Rocks** – one of the best dive sites in Southeast Queensland – for bigger game.

For **budget accommodation** in Mooloolaba, head to *Mooloolaba Beach Backpackers*, about 250m back from the waterfront at 75 Brisbane Rd (☎07/5444 3399, ⓦwww.mooloolababackpackers.com.au; dorms $19), which organizes tours of the Sunshine Coast region (including abseiling in the Glasshouse Mountains and surfing tuition). Most of the **other accommodation** options are 3km north of Mooloolaba, past Alexandra Headland, at **MAROOCHYDORE**. At the bottom end of the market, *Cotton Tree Caravan Park* on Cotton Tree Parade, Maroochydore (☎07/5443 1253, Ⓕ5443 8807; tent sites $15, cabins ❸) is right on the beach; for hostels there are *Suncoast*

Backpackers Lodge at 50 Parker St, Maroochydore (℡07/5443 7544; dorms $19), and the *YHA* close to the Maroochy River on Schirrmann Drive (℡07/5443 3151; dorms $21), both of which offer a free pick-up from Maroochydore, free loans of surfboards, bikes and fishing gear, and trips to Hinterland towns and the Sunshine Coast Brewery for tours and tasting. **Motels** include *Sunshine Motor Inn*, 122 Alexandra Parade, Alexandra Headland (℡07/5443 6899; ❹), and *Blue Waters Motel*, 64 Sixth Ave, Maroochydore (℡07/5443 6700; ❺), both with spacious rooms, sea views and easy access to the beach. **Eating** options are everywhere, though *Mooloolaba Surf Club's* smart café, bar and restaurant on the Esplanade (daily noon–2pm & 6pm–late, Sun from 8am) is worth a visit for views out over the surf, and *Karakas* at 59 Esplanade, has fiery Mexican cooking and live music through the week. *Mooloolaba Hotel*, also on the Mooloolaba Esplanade, hosts rock bands every Friday and Saturday, and opens its doors as a nightclub on Sundays; the *Alexandra Hotel*, on the highway at Alexandra Headland, is another venue for big-name bands.

Nambour, the hinterland, and on to Noosa

Bisected by tramways from surrounding sugar plantations, **NAMBOUR** sits inland from Maroochydore in the centre of the Sunshine Coast's farming community. Five kilometres south between the highway and **Woombye** lurks the Sunshine Plantation (daily 9am–5pm; free except rides; ℡07/5442 1333) overshadowed by its renowned, ridiculous **Big Pineapple**; activities include trips around the plantation on a cane train and, of course, climbing the fibreglass fruit. Woombye is a stop on Brisbane's Citytrain network, or Sunshine Coast Coaches can bring you here from Nambour.

A two-hour circuit drive from Nambour into the **hinterland** along the Blackall Range takes you into a rural English-like idyll quite unexpected in subtropical Queensland – fields dotted with herds of pied dairy cattle, and occasional long views out to the coast. Several settlements – such as **Montville** and **Mapleton** – have dolled themselves up as "villages" and suffer from an overdose of potteries and twee tearooms, though it's worth stretching your legs to reach a couple of respectably sized **waterfalls** up here: Kondalilla, 3km from Montville, with swimming holes along Obi Obi Creek; and Mapleton Falls, just west of Mapleton, where the river plunges over basalt cliffs.

A much more genuine place is **MALENY**, whose ageing hippy population and single street of **cafés** (the *Upfront Club* has good food and live bands at weekends), a co-operative supermarket, and a short river walk all create a pleasantly "alternative" atmosphere. About 5km south out of town, **Mary Cairncross Park** (winter 10am–4pm, summer 9am–5pm; voluntary donation) is a small patch of **rainforest** inhabited by snakes, wallabies and plenty of birds; there's a fantastic view south over the Glasshouse Mountains from the entrance. Maleny's **accommodation** options include the fairly central *Maleny Palms Tourist Park* (℡07/5494 2933; tent sites $17, cabins ❸) and the wonderfully friendly and often full *Maleny Hills Motel* (℡07/5494 2551; ❸), which is about 5km out of town on the Montville road.

Back down near Nambour, you can reach Noosa by turning coastwards at **EUMUNDI**, a tiny town also on the Citytrain line best known for its Saturday **market**, reputed to be the biggest and best in Australia, and as the original home of Eumundi Beer (now shifted elsewhere). An appealing place to overnight here is *Taylor's Damn Fine B & B* (℡07/5442 8685; ❼), an old Queenslander home filled with an extraordinary array of European "kitsch" and collectables – one separate guestroom is a beautifully renovated railway caboose. Otherwise, the turn-off for **Cooroy** sees you entering Noosa along the river via **Tewantin**. Approaching from Maroochydore up the coastal road, the journey is half as long, passing unevenly spaced townships; coming this way, *Coolum Beach Budget Accommodation* at 1862 David Low Way, Coolum (☏07/5471 6666; dorms $20, rooms ❸), is a very clean and well laid-out place to pull up for a couple of days of beach life.

Noosa

The exclusive end of the Sunshine Coast and an established celebrity "des-res" area, **NOOSA** is dominated by an enviably beautiful headland, defined by the mouth of the placid **Noosa River** and a strip of beach to the southeast. Popular since surfers first came in the 1960s to ride fierce waves around the headland, the setting compensates for any neon and concrete in town. It's also a starting point for trips to **Cooloola National Park** and **Fraser Island** directly north (see p.451), attractions that tend to overshadow Noosa's own sand, pleasant river scenery and tiny national park.

"Noosa" is a loose term covering a seven-kilometre-long sprawl of merging settlements stretched along the south side of the Noosa River, culminating at **NOOSA HEADS**. This forms the core of the town, with a chic and brash shopping-and-dining enclave along beach-side **Hastings Street**, and a far more down-to-earth area of shops, banks, and cafés, 1km south along **Sunshine Beach Road**. Immediately east of this is the headland itself and **Noosa National Park**, worth a look for its mix of mature rainforest, coastal heath and fine **beaches** – Granite Bay and Alexandria Bay ("swimwear optional") have good sand pounded by unpatrolled surf – all reached along graded paths. These start from the picnic area at the end of Park Road (a continuation of Hastings Street), where you'll probably see **koalas** in gum trees above the car park. South of the headland and national park is the discreet suburb of **SUNSHINE BEACH**, which features Noosa's longest and least crowded stretch of sand. All three suburbs are connected by a **bus service** (Sunbus), which goes by every twenty minutes or so between 5am and 9pm, with service extended to midnight at weekends.

West from Noosa Heads, **NOOSAVILLE** is a mainly residential district along the riverfront. In the late afternoon, half of Noosa promenades along **Gympie Terrace** as the sinking sun colours a gentle tableau: mangroves on the opposite shore, pelicans eyeing anglers for scraps and landing clumsily midstream, and everything, from cruise boats to windsurfers and kayaks, out on the water. With a spare day you can cruise or canoe (if you're energetic and start early enough) upstream to shallow lakes Cooroibah and Cootharaba (see p.452), or just paddle around, fish at the river mouth or rent a jet ski and have fun getting soaked (see box on p.449 for rental outlets). If you just want to take a quick ride along the river and don't want to fork out for a tour, hop on the **Noosa ferry**, which runs six times daily (10am–6pm) from the Sheraton Noosa Jetty off Hastings Street upstream to the suburb of **Tewantin**; it costs $8.50 for the hour-long return journey, or $12.50 for an all-day pass.

Information and accommodation
There are **information booths** all over Noosa, particularly along and around Hastings Street and Sunshine Beach Road, though most guard their knowledge jealously, and to receive any help you have to appear interested in booking a tour through them. Alternatively, accommodation may be able to help with information, though expect a certain bias towards favoured tours.

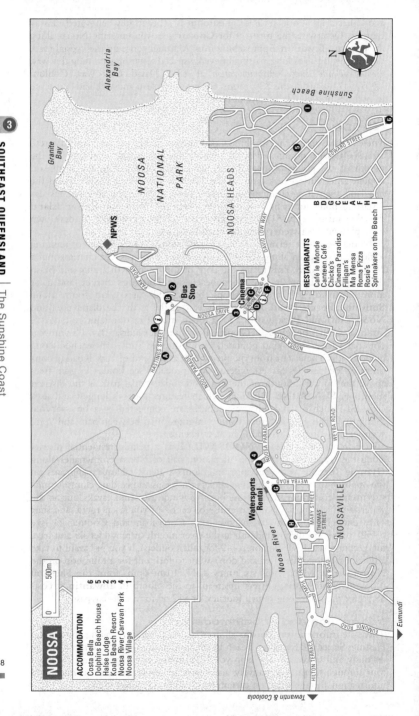

NOOSA

ACCOMMODATION
Costa Bella	6
Dolphins Beach House	5
Halse Lodge	2
Koala Beach Resort	3
Noosa River Caravan Park	4
Noosa Village	1

RESTAURANTS
Café le Monde	B
Canteen Café	D
Chicko's	G
Cinema Paradiso	C
Filligan's	E
Ma Mensa	A
Roma Pizza	F
Rosie's	H
Spinnakers on the Beach	I

N

Alexandria Bay

Granite Bay

NOOSA NATIONAL PARK

NOOSA HEADS

Sunshine Beach

NPWS

Bus Stop

Cinema

Watersports Rental

Noosa River

NOOSAVILLE

HASTINGS STREET

PARK ROAD

NOOSA DRIVE

NOOSA PARADE

DAVID LOW WAY

EDWARD STREET

WEYBA ROAD

MARY STREET

THOMAS STREET

HILTON TERRACE

GYMPIE TERRACE

GIBSON ROAD

EDMUNDI ROAD

0   500m

▼ Tewantin & Cooloola

▼ Eumundi

Noosa activities

Noosa's original reason to be was the **surf**, and if you know what you're doing you'll find all the necessary gear at Surf World, 34 Sunshine Beach Rd, Noosa Heads (☎07/5447 3538). If the only surfing you've ever done is on the Net, find out what the real thing is like with Learn to Surf (☎0418 787 577) or Wavesense (☎07/5474 9076) – they can be hard to get hold of, but are worth the effort.

Cruising the Noosa River is a more sedate way to pass time in the area. Blue Laguna (☎07/5449 0799) and Noosa River Cruises, Gympie Terrace, Noosaville (☎07/5449 7362), have day-tours on the river and lakes for around $60. To get as far as Lake Cootharaba, Beyond (☎1800 657 666, ⊛www.beyondnoosa.com.au) and Everglades Waterbus, Harbour Town Complex, Tewantin (☎07/5447 1838, ⊛www.evergladeswaterbus.com.au), have half-day cruises upriver for around $55, six-hour cruises including lunch for $70–80, and full-day tours for $130 including a cruise and a 4WD run along Rainbow Beach.

For **water sports**, Pelican Boat Hire, on the river bank at Gympie Terrace (☎07/5449 7239), has canoes and surf skis at $12 for the first hour ($6 per hour after that); Pro Ski (☎07/5449 7740), in the same place, has water-skiing at $75 for thirty minutes, $120 for an hour, including instruction for novices, and jet skis at $55 for thirty minutes. Kingfisher Boat Hire (☎07/5449 9353), at the Harbour Town Complex in Tewantin, rents out fishing boats with fuel, rods, bait pumps, crab pots, ice boxes and the rest, for around $18 an hour. In a different line, Kayanu, at the Noosa River Shopping Centre on Gympie Terrace (☎0438 788 573, ⊛www.kite-surf.com.au), has two-hour **kite surfing courses** ($95), and also rents out canoes.

Hostels have courtesy buses for the beach, town and nightclubs, and all accommodation will help organize activities and tours, from surfing lessons to Cooloola and Fraser Island trips. **Motels** are concentrated along the river between Noosa Heads and Noosaville; some offer weekly rates which might add up to a free night, but prices double during school holidays. A group of four staying a week or two may get better value – and a slice of luxury – by checking with Accom Noosa (☎07/5447 2224, ⊛www.accomnoosa.com.au) about deals on furnished apartments outside holiday periods.

Costa Bella 7 Selene St, Sunshine Beach ☎1800 003 663, ⊛www.melaluka.com.au. A well-appointed high-rise development with excellent, self-contained apartment accommodation – one of the best deals in town. ❸

Dolphins Beach House 14 Duke St, Sunshine Beach ☎07/5447 2100, ⊛www.dolphinsbeachhouse.com. Self-contained units about a 5min walk from the sea; offers use of bikes and surfboards. ❹

Gagaju Call ahead for directions or pick-up ☎07/5474 3522, ⊛www.travoholic.com/gagaju. This is an authentic bush camp near Noosa, with a dozen bunk beds and space for campers. Created as an eco-friendly "bush experience", everything is built from recycled timber. Canoes and camping equipment, advice on hikes and canoe trips, and fireside bush-poetry readings are among the attractions. Their three-day canoe trip is highly recommended as an independent adventure experience. Camping $11 per person, dorms $17.

Halse Lodge (YHA) 17 Noosa Drive, Noosa Heads

☎1800 242 567, ⊛www.halselodge.com.au. Giant, sprawling, immaculate 1888 Queenslander building in large grounds close to Noosa Beach; definitely not for partying. Often full despite quantity of rooms, so book in advance. Dorms $22, rooms ❸

Koala Beach Resort 44 Noosa Drive, Noosa Heads ☎07/5447 3355 or 1800 357 457, ⊛www.koalaresort.com.au. Central budget accommodation in dorms and motel units. Nowhere near the beach, and not especially clean, but the party atmosphere and pool, restaurant and bar might compensate. Dorms $19.

Noosa River Caravan Park Russell St, Noosaville ☎07/5449 7050. Large campsite and van park with splendid river views, but with no cabins or on-site vans. Tent sites $15.

Noosa Village 10 Hastings St ☎07/5447 5800, ⊛www.noosavillage.com.au. Very good-value, unpretentious motel in the heart of Noosa's glitz; rooms are quiet but not huge, and some have balconies. ❺

Eating, drinking and nightlife

Noosa's three communities – surfers, retirees and tourists – seldom share the same enthusiasms; evenings tend to be spent with your own crowd. This doesn't seem to affect the **nightlife**, though, and eating out in particular is pursued as a serious pastime. Hastings Street has long been the place to dine and be seen in Noosa, but soaring rents have seen some excellent eateries relocate to Noosaville, where you'll now find lots of casual diners checking out the places clustered along Gympie Terrace and Thomas Street.

Café le Monde Hastings St, Noosa Heads ☎07/5449 2366. Slightly snobbish street atmosphere and a mainly international menu – try the le Monde salad at $13.50. Open 7am for cappuccino; happy hour Mon–Fri 4–6pm; live music in the evenings except Mon & Wed.
Canteen Café Sunshine Beach Rd, Noosa Heads. Somewhere to slump over a sandwich and good strong coffee, rather than be seen; late-risers will appreciate the breakfasts served till 4pm.
Chicko's 281 Gympie Terrace, Noosaville. Unquestionably the place for fish and chips; open daily 9am–8pm.
Cinema Paradiso Sunshine Beach Rd, next to the cinema, Noosa Heads. Outdoor eating and good-sized portions of sirloin, rack of lamb and salads from around $13; check out the $17 meal-and-film deal.
Filligan's 9 Russell St, Noosaville ☎07/5449 8811. Fish and a variety of other tasty dishes with a slight Asian influence (most main courses around

$17–22). With an appealingly casual, holiday ambience it's extremely popular, so book ahead. Open for lunch and dinner every day.
Ma Mensa Hastings St. Obligatory Italian bistro with outdoor tables; inexpensive for location. Very fine steamed mussels and lamb shanks (around $16); also specializes in pasta dishes ($12).
Roma Pizza 36 David Low Way, Noosa Heads. Good-value takeaway pizzeria, plus a trattoria-style restaurant featuring used chianti-bottle decorations and inexpensive pizza and pasta meals.
Rosie's Gympie Terrace, near the corner of Albert St, Noosaville ☎07/5449 7888. Tiny and intimate BYO place, with a new menu every week. Popular with locals; mains around $17.
Spinnakers on the Beach Sunshine Beach Surf Club ☎07/5474 5177. Recently refurbished surf club, with a bar, restaurant and unbeatable views. Seafood, steaks, pasta and salad – big servings, all in the $10–15 range.

Listings

Banks Located along Sunshine Beach Rd, Noosa Heads.
Bike rental Noosa Bike Hire and Tours (☎07/5474 3322, ⊛www.noosabikehire.com) rents bikes from $25 a day ($80 per week), and runs guided half-day cycle tours ($55); will also deliver to your door.
Buses There's no actual bus station for long-distance buses. Drop-off and pick-up points are at the "Transit Centre" – just a bus shelter – at the junction of Noosa Parade and Noosa Drive.
Camping supplies and rental Outdoor Store, 28 Sunshine Beach Rd, Noosa Heads (☎07/5447 2688), has all you'll need for Fraser Island and Cooloola.
Car rental Allterrain, 91 Noosa Drive, Noosa Heads (☎07/5449 0877), Sunrover Rentals, at the marina in Tewantin (☎07/5449 7833), and

Sunshine 4WD (☎07/5447 3702), next to the Noosa post office, have five-seater 4WDs from $155 per day plus deposit. For a conventional runaround vehicle, try Virgin (☎07/5474 5777) or Henry's (☎07/5447 3777).
Cinema Sunshine Beach Rd, Noosa Heads ☎07/5449 2255.
Internet Internet Café, 9 Sunshine Beach Rd, has terminals from $5 an hour.
NPWS Park Rd, at Noosa National Park's picnic area ☎07/5447 3243.
Pharmacy Noosa Heads Day and Night Pharmacy, Hastings St. Daily until 9pm.
Police 48 Hastings St ☎07/5474 5255 or 5447 5888.
Post office Noosa Drive, Sunshine Beach Rd end (Mon–Fri 9am–5pm, Sat 9am–12.30pm).
Taxis ☎13 10 08.

The Cooloola Coast and Fraser Island

Halfway between Brisbane and the tropics, the **Cooloola Coast** and **Fraser Island** between them cover over 190km of the coastline north from Noosa, forming a world of giant dunes, forests, coloured sands and freshwater lakes where fishing and four-wheel driving take precedence over the more usual beach activities. But it doesn't have to be a macho tangle with the elements: for once it's relatively easy and inexpensive to rent tents and a 4WD and set off to explore in some comfort.

Europeans were initially unimpressed with this part of the coast, but abundant fresh water, seafood and plants must have supported a very healthy **Aboriginal population**; campfires along the beach allowed Matthew Flinders to navigate Fraser Island at night in 1802. Flinders labelled the region as "the **Great Sandy Peninsula**" on his maps, though he suspected that Fraser Island was in fact separated from the mainland. The Queensland government declared the area an Aboriginal reserve in the early 1860s but, with the discovery of **gold** at Gympie in 1867, Europeans flocked into the region in their thousands. This influx, and the economic boom that went with it, saved the fledgling Queensland from bankruptcy, but brought the usual racial conflicts, and the reserve gradually became little more than a holding pen for tribal survivors from all over the state. They were devastated by disease, and the last few were relocated to other reserves around Queensland at the start of the twentieth century so the area could be opened up for recreation.

Sand mining and **logging** are other incendiary topics here and there's a predictable split between conservationists and those people who count on local industries for their livelihood. **Forestry** is a particularly bitter issue; the mainland town of Maryborough was built on timber felling, and logging bans have aroused fury at what is seen as a sell-out to the Green movement. Locals, too, once drawn to the area for its natural appeal, now feel crowded out by regulations made to protect the coast from overuse by 4WDs and by drunken campers leaving piles of garbage behind them. While it's unlikely that visitors will become too entangled in these issues, a balance between protection and "development" – a word with almost religious connotations in Queensland – is far from being established.

Orientation and access

The first thing to decide is where to start. Cooloola comprises two regions: the inland region around **Cooroibah and Cootharaba lakes**, and the beach running north for 40km towards the lower end of Fraser Island and the small township of **Rainbow Beach**. The lakes and the southern end of the beach can be accessed directly from Teewantin, on the river 7km west of Noosa. Unless you drive up the beach from here – for which you'll need a 4WD – Rainbow Beach and northern Cooloola can only be reached 75km off Highway 1 from the inland town of Gympie, itself around 60km from Noosa. **Access to Fraser Island** is by ferry from Rainbow Beach (Inskip Point) in the south, or from the town of **Hervey Bay** in the north, 90km beyond Gympie.

Tours around the area run from Noosa, Rainbow Beach and Hervey Bay, though given the grand scale of the region they're inevitably rushed. The wildlife and overall serenity of the area are elusive, to say the least, unless you get away from the more popular places, camp for the night and explore early on in the day. Assembling a group and **renting a 4WD** is one way to do this, with hostels in Hervey Bay well experienced in arranging this type of tour for Fraser Island. Another is simply **walking**, an alternative ignored by almost all visitors, but one which allows unequalled access and intimacy with the region.

Unless you're on a tour, you'll definitely need **maps**, with many available from local garages and newsagents. Relevant sheets on national parks, available from the NPWS, supplement these. Drivers need **tide timetables**, as most beaches are only reliably negotiable at low tide. Rain won't ruin your stay – in fact it makes driving on sand far easier and enhances the colours – though in rough conditions services to Fraser might be cancelled, leaving you stranded.

The Cooloola Coast

The southern end of the **Cooloola Coast** is dominated by features of the Noosa River which pools into lakes Cootharaba and Cooroibah as it nears Tewantin, while stands of commercial timber and dry sclerophyll woodland cover the interior, rising to dunes along the beach stabilized by scrubby heath. The beach runs straight north from Tewantin to **Double Island Point** and then curves west to Rainbow Beach township, where it's backed by vertical, coloured-sand cliffs whose weathered contours and tones constantly change with the shifting sun. Below, the windswept strip of sand separating land from sea becomes a 4WD highway at low tide, with brightly coloured flashes of canvas marking where the cliffs are low enough to form a protective foreshore suitable for camping. Most of the beach and interior north of Cootharaba is **national park**, as is the lake's shoreline.

Before you head in, note that **4WD** is essential for the beach, and the access roads leading to it – see Noosa "Listings", p.450 for car rental. Conventional vehicles can manage the lake road from Tewantin in the south, and Rainbow Beach from Gympie in the north – both of which are good places to use as bases for day-walks if you don't have the right vehicle. **Hiking**, you'll find the easiest path along the beach, but it makes things more interesting if you head inland at some stage. For the well equipped, walking tracks head upstream from Elanda Point, past the top of Lake Cootharaba and along the forty-kilometre **Cooloola Wilderness Trail**, or towards the coast – contact the NPWS first for maps and an idea of conditions. For **tours** of the region, check operator details in the Noosa and Hervey Bay accounts.

The lakes

Cooroibah and its larger and more northerly neighbour **Cootharaba** are joined by a winding six-kilometre stretch of the Noosa River. Placid, and fringed with paperbarks and reedbeds, the lakes look their best at dawn before there's any traffic; they're saltwater and average just 1m in depth, subject to tides. At Cootharaba's top end, Kin Kin Creek and the Noosa River spill lazily into the lake through thickets of mangroves, hibiscus and ti-trees – the so-called **Everglades**. A boardwalk from **Kinaba**'s information centre at the northern end of the lake leads to a hide where you can spy on birdlife, and there's more on nearby Fig Tree Lake. The picnic area here is a former corroboree ground, which featured in the saga of Eliza Fraser (see p.458).

Beyond here, there's a footpath – or it's an easy paddle – on up the **Narrows** to **Harry Spring's Hut**. A campsite on the edge of the forest here is a gateway to Cooloola's interior: about another 8km upstream are navigable by canoe, and walking tracks mark the start of the Cooloola Wilderness Trail, a three-day hike up to the road at Rainbow Beach. Shorter trails also head across the river from here – you'll have to swim – and through forested dunes to the beach: an exhausting day-trip.

To reach the lakes from Tewantin, turn off the main road onto Werin Street at the school – there is a sign, but it's easy to miss – then turn left again and follow the signposts. The twenty-kilometre-long road follows the western side of the lakes to Kinaba, with turn-offs along the way to **Boreen Point** and **Elanda Point** townships, both on Cootharaba. **Accommodation** is at campsites in either, or there's bushcamping at Harry Spring's Hut (see above); at Boreen Point, *Lakeside Lodge* (℡07/5485 3127; ❸) has comfortable doubles. **Supplies** are available at Boreen Point – where there's fuel, a general store, hotel and telephones – or at Elanda Point's small general store. The township's campsites also **rent canoes** or flat-bottomed tinnies, or you can link up with a river tour from Noosaville (see box on p.449).

The coast

To reach the southern end of the beach from Tewantin, catch the **vehicle ferry** from the top of Moorindil Street (daily 6am–10pm; cars $4 one-way, pedestrians free), which lands you about five minutes' drive from the sea. There's **accommodation** 2km along near Lake Cooroibah's otherwise inaccessible eastern shore at *Lake Cooroibah Holiday Park*, PO Box 220, Tewantin (℡07/5447 1225 or 5447 1706; tent sites $9.50 per person, caravans ❸, suites/cottages ❻); family-oriented, and with every activity from horse riding to canoeing and tennis, they offer camping and caravans, as well as suites and cottages for up to eight people, plus all the associated facilities.

Otherwise, press on to the beach. The powdery foredunes at the end of the road look too small to worry about, but even in a 4WD you won't be the first to get stuck driving through them; a basic **campsite** here has fine views of Noosa, but this close to town things can get busy. From here you have a straight, 40-kilometre run of uninterrupted sand, backed by steep, forested dunes to play with. Just make sure you know what the local tides are doing, and remember that steep dunes mean that there are no exits off the beach until you reach the **Freshwater Creek campsite** (where there's a boggy patch of quicksand to be avoided), 30km along. For most of the way there's little to look out for in particular, though **coloured sands** are a feature of the region – particularly the northern end of the beach – caused by minerals leaching down the cliffs from above leaving broad bands of orange, red and white. There's also the **shipwreck** of the *Cherry Venture*, grounded just north of Freshwater Creek in 1973 and now eroded down to a rusting frame and funnel.

From Freshwater Creek you can reach Rainbow Beach by either negotiating a rutted, scarred track which runs up off the beach and inland through gum woodland to the township; or by carrying on up the beach, around it's northern extremity at **Double Island Point** – when Fraser Island first fills the horizon – and then turning west along the sand for the final 5km or so.

RAINBOW BEACH itself is a small, slowly developing township and access point for Fraser's southern reaches at the end of the sealed road to Gympie and the highway. There's a post office, service station and shops, and **accommodation** at *Rainbow Beach Holiday Village* (☎07/5486 3222; tent sites $13.50, villas ❹), with tents, on-site vans, one-bedroom villas and two-bedroom chalets; *Rainbow Beach Hotel* (☎07/5486 3125; ❸) has motel rooms; and *Rainbow Beach Backpackers* (☎07/5486 3288; dorms $16) and *The Rocks* (☎07/5486 3711; ❷) both offer budget beds. Accommodation can line up **Fraser Island safaris** from Rainbow Beach lasting one to three days, or contact Sun Safari Tours (☎07/5486 3154, ⓦwww.fraser-is.com), who run day-trips to Central Station and Lake Birrabeen ($99). For **4WD rental**, many places to stay also rent out vehicles, or Safari (☎07/5486 3485) offers five-seater off-roaders from about $100 per day, and can sort out packages including all vehicle permits for Fraser Island – for more on which, see p.459.

Heading on, Gympie and the highway are 80km away; if you don't have your own transport, there's a very slow local **bus** to Gympie (Mon–Fri 7.30am & 3.45pm, returning 6am & 1.30pm). The **Fraser Island ferry** leaves Inskip Point, 10km north of Rainbow Beach, for the fifteen-minute crossing to Hook Point on the island's south coast (daily, first ferry leaves Inskip Point 7am, last ferry leaves Fraser 6pm; $55 per vehicle, $12 for foot passengers; ☎07/5486 3227): drivers should note that this is a very difficult landing and should only be attempted if you have sound 4WD experience. You'll also need a **permit** for the island from the NPWS on the Rainbow Beach road (daily 7am–4pm; ☎07/5486 3160; see p.459 for more about Fraser Island permits and practicalities), and your own transport to Inskip Point.

Hervey Bay

Back on the highway and heading north, it's a couple of hours to Hervey Bay past **GYMPIE** and **MARYBOROUGH**, historic gold and timber communities and now healthy market towns with handsome stone and wooden period buildings in their centres testifying to their wealthy past. **HERVEY BAY**, a rapidly expanding sprawl of coastal suburbs – known locally as "God's Waiting Room" due to the large number of retirees living here – has no such pretensions, and the only reason to visit is to join the throng crossing to **Fraser Island**, or to venture into the bay to spot **whales** in the spring.

Orientation, arrival and information

Pialba is the centre, with shops strung along the **Esplanade** as it runs 7km from here east through **Scarness** and **Torquay** to **Urangan Harbour** and Marina; **barges and tours to Fraser Island** leave from here and from **River Heads**, 17km south. Approaching Hervey Bay from the south, turn off at Maryborough; from the north, leave the highway at Howard. The **bus station** is at Bay Central shopping complex, just off the main road into town about 1km from Pialba; the **airport** is about 5km south of Urangan off Booral Road, on the way to River Heads. Hervey Bay has a decent **local bus** service, circuiting around town from Bay Central between about 6am and 6pm, though you'll need a **taxi** for the airport (☎13 10 08; $10–15). Almost every place to stay provides information and makes bookings, but you'll get more reliable, pressure-free help from the **tourist information office** right next to the bus station (Mon–Fri 6am–5.30pm, Sat & Sun 6.30am–1pm; ☎07/4124 8244).

Whale-watching from Hervey Bay

Humpbacked whales are among the most exciting marine creatures to encounter: growing to 16m long and 36 tonnes, they make their presence known from a distance by their habit of "breaching" – making spectacular, crashing leaps out of the water – and expelling jets of spray as they exhale. Prior to 1952 an estimated ten thousand whales made the annual journey between the Antarctic and tropics to breed and give birth in shallow coastal waters; a decade later whaling had reduced the population to just two hundred animals. Now protected, their numbers are increasing and you're fairly likely to see one if you put out to sea between Brisbane and the Whitsundays during the **whale-watching season**. In Hervey Bay, this lasts only from late July until October; the whales follow the coast, and because Fraser Island leans outwards they're deflected away from Hervey Bay coming up from the south, but get funnelled into its constricted waters when returning.

The town makes the most of their visit with an August **Whale Festival**, and operators are always searching for new gimmicks to promote day-cruises and flights. In perfect conditions you'll see whales breach, swim directly under the boat and raise their heads out of the water, close enough to touch. You might also, of course, see nothing at all. Whether all this voyeurism disturbs the animals is unclear, but they seem at least tolerant of the attention paid to them.

For **flights**, try Air Fraser Island (☏07/4125 3600); the cost is from $55 per person (depending on the number of passengers) for a thirty-minute buzz. **Cruises** last for a morning or a full day, costing upwards of $65–80 per person, and are booked through an agent; some get very crowded – check the boat size and how many will be going. *Princess II* (the cheapest vessel), *Tasman Venture II*, *Hombre*, *Whalesong* and *Volante III* all come recommended, while *Spirit of Hervey Bay* (the most expensive) has the bonus of being a glass-bottomed vessel. For the added pleasure of sailing out to the whales, make arrangements with the yacht *Stefanie* through your accommodation or the information centre, or call ☏1800 650 776.

Accommodation

Accommodation is packed during the whale-watching season (July–Oct) and at Christmas and Easter (when motel prices can double). Most places will pick you up from the bus station, and all can organize tours to Fraser, with the hostels specializing in putting together budget self-drive packages. If you're **camping**, the best van parks are on the Esplanade at Torquay ($15 per tent), and the huge *Pialba Caravan Park* on the corner of Main Street and the Esplanade on the foreshore in Pialba (☏07/4128 1399; $15 per tent).

Bay Bed & Breakfast 180 Cypress St, Urangan ☏07/4125 6919. Hugely friendly, home-style accommodation with excellent rooms and discounted weekly rates. ❹

Bayview Motel 399 Esplanade, Torquay ☏07/4128 1134. Not much to look at from outside, but the rooms are spotless and the friendly owners can't do enough for you. ❸

Beaches 195 Torquay Rd, Torquay ☏07/4124 1322, ⓦwww.beaches.com.au. Busy party hostel with lively bar/bistro and cheerful staff, one street back from the Esplanade. Dorms $18.

Beachside Motor Inn 298 Esplanade, Scarness ☏07/4124 1999. Comfortable motel units with beach views. ❹

Colonial Backpackers Resort (YHA) Cnr Pulgul St and Boat Harbour Drive, near Urangan Harbour, Urangan ☏07/4125 1844 or 1800 818 280. Tidy, comfortable and well run, though even double rooms are pretty bare, and you have to leave deposits for everything except the bed. Spacious grounds, with a bar, pool and restaurant, plus tame wildlife, might compensate. Dorms $20, rooms ❸

Fraser Roving 412 Esplanade, Torquay ☏07/4125 6386, ⓦwww.oziroving.com.au. Barracks-like but clean and efficient backpackers with own bar and pool, specializes in Fraser trips. Dorms $18.

Friendly Hostel 182 Torquay Rd, Scarness ☏07/4124 4107. Very homely, secure guesthouse, with small dorms and nice, family atmosphere. Dorms $18, rooms ❷

Koala Backpackers 408 Esplanade, Torquay ☎07/4125 3601 or 1800 354 535, ⓦwww.koalaresort.com.au. Recently renovated rooms, large grounds, and party atmosphere; close to the shops. Dorms $18, rooms ❸

Oceanic Palms 50 King St, Urangan ☎ & ⓕ07/4128 9562. Quiet, small and welcoming bed and breakfast, with a pool and orchid-laden garden. ❺

Palace 184 Torquay Rd, Scarness ☎07/4124 5331 or 1800 063 168, ⓔisland@palacebackpackers.com.au. Excellent, purpose-built hostel with its own fleet of 4WDs; all units are roomy and

come complete with kitchen and TV, and there's a pool too. Dorms $18, rooms ❸

Playa Concha 475 Esplanade, Torquay ☎07/4125 1544, ⓕ4125 3413. Comfortable, beachfront motel surrounded by palms and ferns, with a mix of single and double rooms and excellent-value serviced apartments sleeping up to six people. ❹–❺

Woolshed 181 Torquay Rd, Scarness ☎07/4124 0677. Unusual place, with dorms done up in corrugated iron and timber, and hung with Outback iconography. There's a bit of a garden and plenty of off-road parking, and it's all much more roomy than appears from the road. Dorms $16, rooms ❸

Eating

Apart from snack bars and fast-food joints in Pialba, most of the places to eat and spend the evening are along the Esplanade at Torquay.

Beachside Hotel Cnr Esplanade and Queens St, Scarness. Great bar with open front for sea views, DJ Friday and Saturday nights.

Black Dog Café Cnr the Esplanade and Denman Camp Rd, Scarness. An odd name for what is actually a small, smart restaurant with heavy Asian leanings – mostly Japanese. Udon soup, sushi, and beef teriyaki, sit strangely alongside Cajun fish and Caesar salad. Good value, with mains at $11–15.

Curried Away 174 Boat Harbour Drive, Pialba ☎07/4124 1577. Half-a-dozen tables, 1960s musak, and takeaway ambience, but the food – genuine Sri Lankan curries – will get your mouth watering. Medium portions of rutu chicken, vegetable samosas, dhal, raita and chutney – enough for two – will set you back $22; most mains are around $10. Dine in, take away or have it delivered for free.

Gringo's 449 Esplanade, Torquay. Good Mexican menu of enchiladas, chilli con carne and nachos,

spiced to individual tolerances and with bean fillings as an alternative to meat. Main courses $17. Open daily from 5.30pm.

Le Café Near cnr of the Esplanade and Queens St, Scarness. Inexpensive, cheerful service, with the best coffee in town, and budget "backpackers' specials" such as shepherds pie for around $6. Open 6.45am–2pm & 5–8.30pm.

O'Reileys 446 Esplanade, Torquay. Savoury pizza, pasta and crepes, but best for fruit pancakes and cream. From $10.

Sails Cnr Fraser St and Esplanade, Torquay ☎07/4125 5170. Moderately upmarket Mediterranean/Asian brasserie, and a good place to splash out a little. Good choices are the Singapore noodles, seafood risotto, or seafood marinara, at around $15–18; some decent vegetarian options too, along with good old Aussie steaks. Alternatively, just plump for their tapas platter and a cocktail. Open for lunch Thurs & Fri, and from 6pm Mon–Sat.

Listings

Airlines Air Fraser Island (☎07/4125 3600); Sunstate (☎07/4125 3488) for flights to Fraser and Brisbane. For Lady Elliot Island, contact the resort direct (see p.475).

Banks Most banks are in Pialba, with a few scattered along the Esplanade at Torquay.

Bicycles Rayz Pushbike Hire (☎0417 644 814) rents out bikes at $12 a day, with free delivery and pick-up.

Camping equipment Some 4WD operators also rent camping equipment.

Car rental Nifty, 463 Esplanade (☎1800 627 583), has decent runarounds from $29 a day. For 4WDs expect around $90 per day for two-seaters such as a Suzuki, $155 per day for an eight-seater Landrover or Toyota Landcruiser, including insurance. Note that older Landrovers, while mechanically sound, are uncomfortable and best avoided unless you're trying to save money. Aussie Trax, 56 Boat Harbour Drive, Pialba (☎07/4124 4433, ⓕ4124 4965, ⓦwww.aussietrax.com), is probably the most clued-up, longest-running operator in

Not surprisingly, all **tours** from Hervey Bay involve **Fraser Island**; day-trips start around $75, overnight camping trips at about $170. Top Tours (T07/4125 3933 or 1800 624 677) is a little pricey, but gives the best one-day tour, with BBQ lunch, new vehicles and first-rate guides – it also seems to work out of phase with rival tours' schedules, so you don't keep bumping into busloads of other visitors. Alternatively, Fraser Venture Tours (T07/4125 4444) scores slightly higher for its overnight trips with accommodation at Eurong ($165). Otherwise try Wilderness Adventure (T07/4120 3333, F4120 3326), a two-day tour including accommodation at *Kingfisher Bay Resort* ($220); and Sand Island Safaris (T1800 246 911) for three days' worth covering most of the island (including accommodation at *Eurong Beach Resort*; $250).

Cruises include Stefanie Yacht Charters (T1800 650 776, W www.stefanie -charters.com.au), which spends two days or longer cruising around Fraser's western side, with the chance to see dolphins year-round, do some kayaking and land on the island. The cost is dependent on the number of passengers and the exact itinerary. Outside the whale season, Whalesong (T07/4125 6222, W www .whalesong.com.au) spends four hours around the bay looking for dolphins, turtles and – with real luck – dugong (sea cow) at $70 per person. Alternatively, Krystal Clear (T07/4124 0066) allows four to five hours for snorkelling, coral viewing, and a BBQ lunch on a small sand island in the bay for $65. For whale-watching operators see box on p.455.

Hervey Bay and puts together good-value all-inclusive packages; Bay 4WD Centre, 54 Boat Harbour Drive, Pialba (T07/4128 2981, F4124 2723), has been going nearly as long as Aussie Trax and offers much the same deal; Heritage Island Explorers, 104 Boat Harbour Drive, Pialba (T07/4124 3770); Safari (T1800 689 819, W www.safari4wdhire.com.au). For information abour 4WD rental for Fraser Island, see box on p.459.

Internet access Several hostels can oblige, as can the tourist information near the bus station at Pialba's Bay Central shopping complex ($4 an hour).

Laundry Cnr Esplanade and Frank St, behind *Dot's Food Bar*, Scarness (daily 7am–7pm).

Pharmacy Day and Night Pharmacy, 418 Esplanade, Torquay (daily 8.30am–8pm).

Police 146 Torquay Rd, Scarness T07/4128 5333.

Post office On the Esplanade, Torquay.

Scooter rental Horny's Scooter Hire (T0408 249 455) has scooters for $50 a day plus $100 deposit.

Taxi T13 10 08.

Vehicle lock-up Fraser Coast Secure Vehicle Storage, 629 Esplanade, Urangan T & F07/4125 2783, W www.users.bigpond .com/parkingsafe. Somewhere to leave your vehicle safe and sound if you're heading over to Fraser or Lady Elliot for a while.

Watersports Torquay Beach Hire, on the Esplanade at Torquay (T07/4125 5528), offers surf skis to windsurfers and outboard-driven tinnies for a day's fishing.

Fraser Island

With a length of 123km, **Fraser Island** is the world's largest sand island, but this dry fact does little to prepare you for the experience. Accumulated from sediments swept north from New South Wales over the last two million years, the scenery ranges from silent forests and beaches sculpted by wind and surf, to crystal-clear streams and dark, tannin-stained lakes. The east coast forms a ninety-kilometre razor-edge from which Fraser's tremendous scale can be absorbed as you travel its length; with the sea as a constant, the dunes along the edge seem to evolve before your eyes – in places low and soft, elsewhere hard and worn into intriguing canyons. By contrast, slow progress through the forests of the island's interior creates more subtle impressions of age and permanence – a primal world predating European settlement – brought into question only when the view opens suddenly onto a lake or a bald blow.

The idyllic mood, however, is sobered by a number of factors, most alarming of which is the volume of traffic tearing along the beach and main tracks. In many ways the island has become the epitome of Queensland's environmental conflicts, with conservationists, tour operators, foresters and Aboriginal groups vying for control of resources – though the big problem of garbage-strewn foredunes has been solved by the introduction of large metal skips. At present, Fraser's north end is a World Heritage-listed **national park**, with the rest in private hands.

To the Kabi Aborigines, Fraser Island is **Gurri** (or K'gari), a beautiful woman so taken with the earth that she stayed behind after creation, her eyes becoming lakes that mirrored the sky and teemed with wildlife so that she wouldn't be lonely. The story behind the European name is far less enchanting. In 1836, survivors of the wreck of the *Stirling Castle*, including Captain Fraser and his wife Eliza, landed at Waddy Point. Though runaway convicts had already been welcomed into Kabi life, the castaways suffered "dreadful slavery, cruel toil and excruciating tortures", and after the captain's death Eliza was presented as a prize during a corroboree at Lake Cootharaba two months later. She was rescued at this dramatic point by former convict John Graham, who had lived with the Kabi and was part of a search party alerted by three other survivors from the *Stirling Castle*. The exact details of Eliza's captivity remain obscure as she produced several conflicting accounts, but her role as an "anti-Crusoe" inspired the work of novelist Patrick White and artist Sidney Nolan.

Practicalities

There are several ways to **get to Fraser**. If you're just after a quick day-trip and don't want to find yourself too far from civilization, take the **fast ferry** from Urangan Marina to *Kingfisher Bay Resort* on the island's west side ($35 includes return fare, lunch and brief ranger-guided walk; at least five trips daily between 8.45am and 4pm, with return ferries departing from Kingfisher Bay 7.40am–5pm).

For more serious explorations, you'll be crossing on one of three **barges**, which leave from Urangan Harbour, River Heads or Inskip Point (see p.454 for the latter), and you need to make arrangements for these in advance. The **Urangan Harbour–Moon Point** (central west coast) barge leaves at 8.30am and 4pm, returning at 9.30am and 5pm. The Moon Point landing is very difficult, however – unless you have sound 4WD experience, leave from River Heads. The **River Heads–Wanggoolba Creek** barge (access to Central Station) departs daily at 9am, 10.15am and 3.30pm, returning at 9.30am, 2.30pm and 4pm. Unless on an organized tour, you need a **barge ticket** (returns are $82 for vehicle and driver, plus $5.50 for passengers; pedestrians pay $16.50 each way), **vehicle permit** for the island if driving ($30.80), plus you'll have to pay **camping fees** in advance for national park sites if you're planning to camp ($4 per person a night). All these can be obtained where you rent your vehicle – and are usually covered in package deals – or from barge offices at Urangan and River Heads. It's essential to **prebook** barge services (☎07/4128 9800, ℉4125 3357). Note that you can use return tickets only on the same barge; if you're planning a different exit from the island, you'll have to buy two one-way tickets.

There are a couple of **safety points** to bear in mind. As there have never been domestic dogs on the island, Fraser's **dingoes** are considered to be

Australia's purest strain, and they used to be a common sight. Following the death by mauling of a child in 2000, however, dingoes which frequented public areas were culled and you'll probably not see many. If you do encounter some, keep your distance, back off rather than run if approached, and – despite their misleadingly scrawny appearance – don't feed them, as it's the expectation of hand-outs which makes them aggressive. You should also be aware that sharks and severe currents make Fraser a dangerous place to get in the sea; if you want to **swim**, stick to the freshwater lakes. Pack **insect repellent**.

Getting around

Driving requires a **4WD vehicle**. The east beach serves as the main highway, with roads running inland to popular spots. Other tracks, always slower than the beach, crisscross the interior; main tracks are often rough from heavy use, and minor roads tend to be in better shape. General advice is to **lower your tyre pressures** to around 12psi to increase traction on the sand, but this isn't generally necessary (if you get bogged, however, try it first before panicking). Rain and high tides harden sand surfaces, making driving easier. Most **accidents** involve collisions on blind corners, rolling in soft sand (avoid hard braking or making sudden turns – you don't have to be going very fast for your front wheels to dig in, turning you over), and trying to cross apparently insignificant creeks on the beach at 60kph – 4WDs are not invincible. Don't drive your vehicle into the surf; you'll probably get stuck and, even if you don't, this much saltwater exposure will rust out the bodywork within days (something the rental company will notice and charge you for). Noise from the surf means that pedestrians can't hear vehicles on the beach and won't be aware of your presence until you barrel through from behind, so give them a wide berth. Road rules are the same as those on the mainland.

Walking is the best way to see the island. There's only one **established circuit**, and even that is very underused, running from Central Station south past lakes Birrabeen and Boomanjin, then up the coast and back to Central Station via lakes Wabby and McKenzie; highlights are circumnavigating the lakes, chance encounters with goannas and dingoes, and the energetic burst up Wongi Blow for sweeping views out to sea. A good three-day hike that by each sundown

---

Renting a 4WD for Fraser Island

Fraser Island is simply too large and varied to appreciate fully on a day-trip, and with competition in Hervey Bay keeping prices to a minimum it's a great opportunity to learn to handle a 4WD. See p.456 for some recommended outfits, but from whomever you rent your vehicle, the company should take the time to protect both it and you with a full briefing on the island and driving practicalities.

Conditions include a minimum driver age of 21 and a $500 deposit, payable in plastic or cash – note that advertised prices are normally for renting the vehicle only, so tents, food, fuel, and **ferry** and **vehicle permit** for the island are extra, available separately or as part of a **package**. To help cut costs, you'll want to form a **group** of between five and eight, and the easiest way to arrange this is by staying at one of the hostels; they'll organize numbers and provide everything except food and fuel – a three-day, two-night trip works out to about $125 a person. A popular option at present is to pay a little bit extra for a "You Drive, We Guide" tour, where the rental agency or hostel provide a guide to accompany your group and point you in the right direction.

renders you all but unconscious after all that walking across sand, it requires no special skills beyond endurance and the ability to set up camp before you pass out.

Accommodation and supplies

Accommodation needs to be booked in advance. Top of the range is the plush *Kingfisher Bay Resort* (☎07/4125 5511 or 1800 072 555, Ⓦwww .kingfisherbay.com; ❼) on the west coast; the more down-to-earth *Fraser Island Retreat* at Happy Valley on the east coast (☎07/4125 2343, Ⓦwww.seefraser island.com; doubles ❹, 5-bed lodge ❻) provides comfortable cabins and good food; while *Yidney Rocks Cabins* (☎07/4127 9167; ❺), just to the south, has basic self-contained, three-bedroom units aimed at fishing groups renting on a weekly basis. Further south, *Eurong Beach Resort* (☎07/4127 9122, Ⓦwww.eurongbeach.com; ❹) has motel-style rooms, while *Dilli Village* (☎07/4127 9130; ❹) has self-contained, four-bed bunkhouses.

With a permit, you can **camp** anywhere along the eastern foreshore except where signs forbid, or if you need tank water, showers, toilets and barbecue areas, use the **national park campsites** at Wathumba on the west coast, or at Lake Allom, Dundubara and Waddy Point (the last two can be booked through most NPWS offices in the region) on the east. Elsewhere there are sites at Central Station, Lake Boomanjin and Lake McKenzie (which is often full by noon). There are **privately run campsites** at *Cathedral Beach Resort* (☎07/4127 9177) and the nicer *Dilli Village* (see above).

For **supplies**, the east coast settlements of **HAPPY VALLEY** and **EURONG** have stores, telephones, bars and fuel; there's another store at *Cathedral Beach Resort* but no shops or restaurant at *Dilli*. You'll save money by bringing whatever you need with you – and make sure you take the empties home.

Around Central Station

Most people get their bearings by making their first stop at **Central Station**, an old logging depot with campsite, telephone and information hut under some monstrous bunya pines in the middle of the island, directly east of River Heads on the mainland. From the station, take a stroll along **Wanggoolba Creek**, a magical, sandy-bottomed stream so clear that it's hard at first to see the water as it runs across the forest floor. It's a largely botanic walk past some prehistoric angiopteris ferns to **Pile Valley**, where satinay trees humble you to insignificance as they reach 60m to the sky. They produce a very dense timber, durable enough to be used as sidings on the Suez Canal – and are consequently in such demand that the trees on Fraser have almost been logged out.

There are several **lakes** around Central Station, all close enough to walk to and all along main roads. Nine kilometres north (track distance), **McKenzie** is the most popular on the island, and often very crowded: ringed by white sand with clear, tea-coloured water reflecting a blue sky, it's a wonderful place to spend the day. To the south, **Birrabeen** (8km) is mostly hemmed in by trees, while **Boomanjin** (16km) is open and geologically "perched" in a basin above the island's water table. There's a fine campsite and communal fireplace here, attended by tame goannas.

East Beach

Seventy-Five Mile Beach on the east coast is Fraser's main road and camping ground, one of the busiest places on the island. Vehicles hurtle along, pedestrians and anglers hug the surf, and tents dot the foredunes; this is what beckons the crowds over from the mainland. Sights along the way include **sand** in all its different forms: **Hammerstone Blow**, 6km north of Eurong, is slowly engulfing **Lake Wabby**, a small but deep patch of blue below the dunes with excellent swimming potential – another century and it will be gone. At **Rainbow Gorge**, about 5km south of **Happy Valley**, a short trail runs between two blows, through a hot, silent desert landscape where sandblasted trees emerge denuded by their ordeal. Incredibly, a dismal spring seeps water into the valley where the sand swallows it up; "upstream" are the gorge's stubby, eroded red fingers.

Six kilometres north of Happy Valley you cross picturesque **Eli Creek**, where water splashes briskly between briefly verdant banks before spilling into the sea. Sand-filtered, it's the nicest swimming spot on the island, though icy-cold. Back on the beach, another 4km brings you to the **Maheno**, wrecked in 1935 and now a skeleton almost consumed by the elements. More striking are the coloured cliffs known as the **Cathedrals**, which run north from the wreck. About 5km up the beach from here is the **Dundubara campsite**, behind which is the tiring, hot four-kilometre walk up **Wungul Sandblow** through what may as well be the Sahara; turn around at the top, though, and the glaring grey dunescape is set off by distant views of a rich blue sea.

Approximately 20km north from Dundubara, **Indian Head** is a rare – and pretty tall – rocky outcrop, the anchor around which the island probably formed originally. It's not a hard walk to the top, and on a sunny day the rewards are likely to include views down into the surf of dolphins, sharks, and other large fish chasing each other; in season you'll certainly see pods of whales too, breaching, blowing jets of spray, and just lying on their backs, slapping the water with outstretched fins. From here there's a tricky bit of soft sand to negotiate for a final nine-kilometre run around to **Champagne Pools**, a cluster of shallow, safe swimming pools right above the surf line which mark as far north as vehicles are allowed to travel.

The interior, west coast and far north

Fraser's wooded **centre**, a real contrast to the busy coast and popular southern lakes, gets relatively few visitors. It encloses **Yidney Scrub**, the only major stand of rainforest left on the island, and although the name doesn't conjure up a very appealing image, the trees are majestic and include towering kauri pines. There's a circuit through Yidney from Happy Valley, taking in **Boomerang** and **Allom** lakes on the long way back to the beach near the Maheno. You can **camp** at Allom, a small lake surrounded by pines and cycads, and completely different in character from its flashy southern cousins. Further north, another road heads in from Dundubara township to **Bowarrady**, a not particularly exciting body of water famed for turtles who pester you for bread – if you can't imagine being pestered by a turtle, try refusing to hand it over.

The island's **west coast** is a mix of mangrove swamp and treacherously soft beaches, both largely inaccessible to vehicles. Rough tracks cross the island via Lake Bowarraddy and Happy Valley to where the Urangan barge lands at Moon Point, though there's a better road to *Kingfisher Bay Resort* from the Central Station area.

Travel details

Trains

Main train routes out of Brisbane follow the Queensland coast north, covered at least daily by the *Sunlander*, *Queenslander*, and high-speed tilt train to Cairns, the *Spirit of the Tropics* to Townsville, and the *Spirit of Capricorn*, to Rockhampton. Southbound interstate services to Sydney also run daily. For Outback destinations from Brisbane, there's the *Westlander*, which heads inland twice a week to Toowoomba, Roma, and Charleville, and the *Spirit of the Outback*, another twice-weekly service via Rockhampton to Emerald and Longreach. For the twice-weekly *Inlander* to Charters Towers and Mount Isa, change at Townsville. All tickets – especially for sleepers – need to be booked as far in advance as possible.

Brisbane to: Ayr (6 weekly; 22hr 30min); Beenleigh (every 20min; 55min); Bowen (6 weekly; 21hr); Bundaberg (at least 1 daily; 4–6hr); Caboolture (every 20min; 1hr); Cairns (4 weekly; 31hr); Charleville (2 weekly; 16hr 25min); Cleveland, for Stradbroke Island (8 daily; 50min); Emerald (2 weekly; 15hr 15min); Eumundi (2 daily; 2hr 10min); Gladstone (at least 1 daily; 6–8hr); Glasshouse Mountains (every 2hr; 1hr 15min); Gympie (2 daily; 3hr); Ingham (4 weekly; 26hr 30min); Longreach (2 weekly; 24hr); Mackay (6 weekly; 16hr 30min); Maryborough (at least 1 daily; 3hr 45min–5hr); Proserpine (6 weekly; 19hr); Rockhampton (at least 1 daily; 7–12hr); Roma (2 weekly; 10hr 30min); Sydney (1 daily; 14hr); Toowoomba (2 weekly; 3hr 45min); Townsville (6 weekly; 24hr); Tully (4 weekly; 27hr 30min); Woombye (1 daily; 3hr).

Buses

The three main long-distance bus operators in Queensland are McCafferty's/Greyhound Pioneer and Premier, who all follow the coastal highway; in addition, McCafferty's/Greyhound Pioneer also run inland from Brisbane to Longreach and Mount Isa. Local operators include Kirkland's, which runs between Brisbane and Byron Bay via the Gold Coast; Suncoast Pacific Coaches, which runs between Brisbane and Noosa via the Sunshine Coast; and Crisp's, which runs due west from Brisbane to Toowoomba, Stanthorpe, Warwick and Goondiwindi.

Brisbane to: Airlie Beach (7 daily; 18hr); Ayr (8 daily; 21hr 30min); Beenleigh (8 daily; 40min);

Bowen (8 daily; 19hr 30min); Bundaberg (5 daily; 6hr); Burleigh Heads (8 daily; 1hr 50min); Byron Bay (12 daily; 2hr 30min); Cairns (7 daily; 28hr 30min); Caloundra (8 daily; 2hr); Cardwell (7 daily; 24hr); Charleville (1 daily; 11hr); Childers (7 daily; 7hr); Coolangatta (8 daily; 2hr 10min); Gladstone (5 daily; 11hr); Gympie (10 daily; 4hr); Hervey Bay-Pialba (10 daily; 4hr 40min); Ingham (7 daily; 23hr 30min); Innisfail (7 daily; 27hr); Lamington National Park (1 daily; 3hr); Longreach (1 daily; 17hr); Mackay (8 daily; 15hr 30min); Maroochydore (5 daily; 2hr 5min); Maryborough (11 daily; 4hr); Mission Beach (5 daily; 26hr 25min); Mount Isa (1 daily; 25hr); Nambour (9 daily; 1hr 30min); Noosa Heads (7 daily; 2hr 50min); Rockhampton (7 daily; 12hr); Roma (2 daily; 7hr 45min); Surfers Paradise (every 30min; 1hr 30min); Sydney (10 daily; 16hr); Toowoomba (8 daily; 2hr 15min); Townsville (8 daily; 21hr 30min); Tully (7 daily; 25hr 30min); Winton (1 daily; 19hr).
Hervey Bay to: Airlie Beach (6 daily; 12hr 20min); Brisbane (8 daily; 4hr 40min); Bundaberg (5 daily; 1hr 40min); Cairns (6 daily; 22hr); Mackay (7 daily; 10hr); Mission Beach (5 daily; 20hr 30min); Noosa (5 daily; 3hr 15min); Rockhampton (7 daily; 5hr 30min); Townsville (7 daily; 16hr 25min).
Noosa to: Airlie Beach (4 daily; 15hr 50min); Brisbane (6 daily; 2hr 50min); Bundaberg (1 daily; 5hr); Cairns (2 daily; 25hr 45min); Hervey Bay (7 daily; 3hr 10min); Mackay (4 daily; 13hr 20min); Maroochydore (4 daily; 35min); Mission Beach (2 daily; 24hr); Rockhampton (4 daily; 9hr) Townsville (4 daily; 20hr).
Surfers Paradise to: Brisbane (every 30min; 1hr 30min); Burleigh Heads (every 10min; 30min); Coolangatta (every 10min; 1hr); Lamington National Park (2 daily; 1hr 30min); Sydney (8 daily; 15hr 30min); Tamborine Mountain (1 daily; 1hr); Toowoomba (2 daily; 3hr 30min).

Ferries

Brisbane to: Moreton Island (2 daily; 2hr); North Stradbroke Island (11 daily; 30min); St Helena (3 or more weekly; 2hr).
Hervey Bay to: Fraser Island (8 daily; 30min–1hr).
Rainbow Beach/Inskip Point to: Fraser Island (continually on demand; 15min).
Surfers Paradise to: South Stradbroke Island (3 or more daily; 30min).

Flights

The following are direct flights only.
Brisbane to: Adelaide (many daily; 3hr 30min);

Alice Springs (2 daily; 4hr 30min); Bundaberg (2 daily; 50min); Cairns (many daily; 2hr 10min); Canberra (many daily; 2hr); Charleville (1 daily; 2hr); Darwin (2 daily; 3hr 40min); Emerald (2 daily; 1hr 40min); Gladstone (4 daily; 1hr 15min); Hervey Bay (2 daily; 1hr 15min); Hobart (many daily; 3hr 50min); Longreach (1 daily; 3hr); Mackay (9 daily; 3hr); Maroochydore-Sunshine Coast (many daily; 30min); Melbourne (many daily; 2hr 25min); Mount Isa (2 daily; 4hr); Norfolk Island (4 weekly; 3hr 45min); Perth (many daily; 5hr); Proserpine (2 daily; 1hr 50min); Rockhampton (4 daily; 1hr 5min); Roma (1 daily; 1hr 10min); Sydney (many daily; 1hr 35min); Townsville (6 daily, 1hr 50min).

Gold Coast-Coolangatta to: Adelaide (many daily; 3hr 35min); Canberra (12 daily; 2hr 40min); Melbourne (many daily; 3hr 35min); Sydney (many daily; 1hr 15min).

Hervey Bay to: Brisbane (2 daily; 1hr 15min); Lady Elliot Island (2 daily; 35min).

Sunshine Coast-Maroochydore to: Brisbane (many daily; 30min); Melbourne (1 daily; 3hr); Sydney (1 daily; 1hr 45min).

Tropical Queensland and the reef

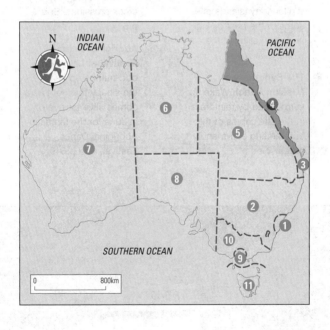

CHAPTER 4

Highlights

* **Great Barrier Reef**
Scuba diving is the best way to explore one of the world's most beautiful coral complexes. **See p.470**

* **The Whitsundays** Lying just off the Great Barrier Reef, the rainforested peaks and long white beaches of the Whitsunday Islands offer some of the best diving and snorkelling in the world. **See p.492**

* **The Sanctuary at Mission Beach** Wake up surrounded by rainforest in the stilt cabins of this outstanding eco-friendly retreat. **See p.517**

* **Atherton Tablelands**
The magnificent rainforest of the Atherton Tablelands brims with wildlife. **See p.533**

* **Four-wheel driving on Cape York** The Cape York Peninsula has some of the most challenging 4WD territory in Australia – watch out for crocs on creek crossings. **See p.544**

* **Aboriginal Dance Festival at Laura** In odd-numbered years, the sleepy town of Laura comes alive for two days in June for the fantastic Aboriginal Dance Festival. **See p.549**

Tropical Queensland and the reef

The move towards, and into, Queensland's **tropical coast** is more obvious than simply passing the Tropic of Capricorn marker at **Rockhampton**. North of Hervey Bay the landscape begins to brown as the temperature rises, and though there's still an ever-narrowing farming strip hugging the coast, the Great Dividing Range edges coastwards as it progresses north, dry at first, but gradually acquiring a green sward which culminates in the steamy, rainforest-draped scenery around **Cairns**. Along the way are scores of beaches, archipelagos of **islands** and regularly spaced cities, including **Townsville**, north Queensland's largest. There's also a wealth of **national parks**, some – such as Hinchinbrook Island – with superb walking trails, and others where you might encounter rare or unusual wildlife. Several places along the way are well set up for those with work visas to recharge their bank balances by **fruit and vegetable picking**; the best organized spots for this are the towns of Bundaberg, Bowen, Ayr and Innisfail. Moving north of Cairns, rainforested ranges ultimately give way to the savannah of the huge, triangular **Cape York Peninsula**, a sparsely populated setting for what is widely regarded as the most rugged 4WD adventure in the country.

Offshore, the onset of the tropics is marked by the appearance of the **Great Barrier Reef**, among the most beautiful and extensive coral complexes in the world. The reef, which begins to make its presence felt round the latitude of Bundaberg, drastically changes the nature of the coastline by blocking incoming surf and producing currents that deflect ocean-borne sand far out to sea. As a result, most **islands** north of Fraser are continental, formed when the peaks of ranges were drowned by rising waters at the end of the last Ice Age, creating abrupt coastlines and coral rubble beaches entirely different in character from the southeast's sandy formations. On the reef's outer edge, however, small isolated **cays** (sand islands) form, which tend to become encircled by fringing coral reef – these are particularly a feature of the southern reef. Further north, the cays thin out, while the main body of the reef thickens into thousands of individual shoals as it ventures nearer the coast. Whether cay or continental, many of these islands are close enough to ports for a day-trip, but for a real change of pace, try camping on one for a week or splashing out on a comfortable resort. **Divers** are well catered for, but novices needn't miss out on the best of the coral, which is within snorkelling range of the surface.

Access is along the more-or-less coastal Bruce Highway to Cairns, which is then briefly replaced by the Cook Highway, until notions of "main roads" begin to fall apart north of Mossman. Beyond here lie the jungles of the **Daintree**, the outpost of **Cooktown** and the beginnings of seasonal roads, humble tracks and the savannah wilderness of the Cape York Peninsula. Frequent **bus** and **train** services stop at all centres between Bundaberg and Cairns, but ideally you'll either be driving or willing to hitch to those places that the travel brochures have overlooked. Among the region's peculiar hazards are the slow, endless **sugar cane trains** that cross roads during the crushing season (roughly June–Dec); crossings are often (but not always) marked by flashing red lights.

Winters are dry and pleasant, but the summer climate (Dec–April) can be oppressively humid, with unpredictable **cyclones** bringing torrential rain and devastating storms, making roads on Cape York impassable and frequently even severing the coastal highway. To avoid the worst of the **crowds** at key places such as the Cairns region or the Whitsunday Islands, come as soon as the wet season is over (late April).

The Southern Reef

A string of cays about 80km offshore marks the southernmost section of the Great Barrier Reef: **Lady Musgrave Island** makes for a good day-trip, while there are resorts on **Heron** and **Lady Elliot** islands, and completely undeveloped campgrounds on several others. This section of the reef contains some of the better coral: being the furthest from land and surrounded by cool, deep water, it has suffered least from pollution and the El Niño-induced coral bleaching of recent years. Access is either from the ports of **Bundaberg** and **Gladstone**, or from the relatively remote coastal settlements of **Agnes Water** and **1770**. Bundaberg – along with the nearby hamlet of **Childers** – also lies at the heart of a rich sugar cane, fruit and vegetable farming area, and both are popular places to find short-term picking **work**.

Bundaberg lies 50km off the Bruce Highway from Childers (south) or Gin Gin (north); Agnes Water and 1770 can be reached either from Bundaberg or the highway; and Gladstone is 20km off the highway about 170km north of Gin Gin. Both Bundaberg and Gladstone are on the **train** line.

Childers

CHILDERS is a pretty, one-horse highway town, sadly known for the terrible fire which burned down the old *Palace Backpackers* in 2000, killing fifteen. The town has moved on, however: the site has been rebuilt as a tasteful, low-key memorial and **information centre** (Mon–Fri 9am–4pm, Sat 9am–1pm, Sun 10am–2pm), and there's a new backpacker hostel planned on an adjacent block. Childers' core of old buildings offers an excuse to pull up and stretch your legs; these include the photogenic *Federal Hotel*, a wooden pub built in 1907, and the musty, bottle-filled and slightly dull **Childers Pharmaceutical Museum** (Mon–Fri 8.45am–4.30pm, Sat 8am–noon; $5). Just west of Childers, Flying High (daily 9am–4.30pm; $11) is a huge **aviary** with just about every type of Australian parrot and finch zipping around, squawking, or chewing the furnishings.

If you're after **farm work**, ask at the information centre for contacts, though the new hostel will presumably cater to workers; in addition, the *Sugar Bowl*

The **Great Barrier Reef** is to Australia what rolling savannahs and game parks are to Africa, and is equally subject to the corniest of representations. "Another world" is the commonest cliché, which, while being completely true, doesn't begin to describe the feeling of donning mask and fins and coming face to face with extraordinary animals, shapes and colours. There's so little relationship to life above the surface that distinctions normally taken for granted – such as that between animal, plant and plain rock – seem blurred, while the respective roles of observer and observed are constantly challenged by shoals of curious fish following you about.

Beginning with Lady Elliot Island, out from Bundaberg, and extending 2300km north to New Guinea, the Barrier Reef follows the outer edge of Australia's continental plate, running closer to land as it moves north: while it's 300km to the main body from Gladstone, Cairns is barely 50km distant from the reef. Far from being a continuous, unified structure, the nature of the reef varies along its length: the majority is made up by an intricate maze of individual, disconnected **patch reefs**, which – especially in the southern sections – sometimes act as anchors for the formation of low sand islands known as **cays**; continental islands everywhere become ringed by **fringing reefs**; and northern sections form long **ribbons**. All of it, however, was built by one animal: the tiny **coral polyp**. Simple organisms, related to sea anemones, polyps grow together like building blocks to create modular colonies – corals – which form the framework of the reef's ecology by providing food, shelter and hunting grounds for larger, more mobile species. Around their walls and canyons flow a bewildering assortment of creatures: large rays and turtles "fly" effortlessly by, fish dodge between caves and coral branches, snails sift the sand for edibles, and brightly coloured nudibranchs dance above rocks.

The reef is administered by the **Marine Parks Authority**, which battles against – or at least attempts to gauge – the effects of overfishing, pollution, environmental fluctuations, and tourism. A popular villain, the polyp-eating **crown of thorns starfish**, also causes severe destruction during cyclic plagues. All these things, sadly, are beginning to have a serious affect on the reef: the scorching, El Niño-inspired summer of 2001 saw extensive and widespread **coral bleaching** and subsequent die-back which, coupled with other stresses mentioned above, reduced many former colourful coral gardens to weed-strewn rubble. As of 2003, most badly hit areas were recovering, but it is becoming clear that if drastic measures are not taken soon to protect fish stocks, control agricultural runoff from sugar cane and banana farms, and reduce urban waste from being washed out to sea, the reef may have been irreversibly damaged within a generation. Don't let this put you off going – the reef is still unquestionably worth seeing, and if the government realizes how much tourism will be lost if the reef dies, they may get more involved in protecting it. In order to minimize damage, visitors should never stand on or hold onto reefs when snorkelling or diving; even if you don't break off branches, you'll certainly crush the delicate polyps.

Diving and other ways of seeing the reef

Scuba diving is the best way to come to grips with the reef, and **dive courses** are on offer right along the coast. **Five days** is the minimum needed to safely cover the course work – three-days' pool and theory, two days at sea – and secure you the all-important C-card. The quality of training and the price you pay vary. Cheaper courses use island reefs or shore diving, instead of taking you to the main reef – though this isn't always a bad thing, as some of these sites are good. Before signing up, ask others who have taken courses about specific businesses' general attitude and whether they just seem concerned in processing as many students in

THREDBO
ALPINE
HOTEL

Van ⇌ SYD
Th July 20   Dpt
Sat Aug 19   Rtn

$1990⁻

↳ Dpt. Wed. July 26 $1790⁻

Qantas

Congress Code   WFOT2000

LZ
Dpt J22 Ac 33 Arr 24
Rtn A5

as short a time as possible – you need to know that any problems you may encounter while training will be taken seriously. Another consideration is whether you ever plan to dive again: if this seems unlikely, **resort dives** (a single dive with an instructor) will set you back only $50 or so, and they're usually available on day-trips to the reef and island resorts. While the extra weight is a drag between dives, **qualified divers** can save on rental costs by bringing some gear along; tanks and weightbelts are covered in dive packages but anything else is extra. You need an alternative air source, timer, C-card and log book to dive in Queensland (the last is often ignored, but some places insist, especially for deep or night-time dives).

Snorkelling is a good alternative to diving: you can pick up the basics in five minutes and with a little practice the only thing you sacrifice is the extended dive time that a tank allows. If you think you'll do a fair amount, buy your own mask and snorkel – they're not dramatically expensive – as rental gear nearly always leaks. Look for a silicone rubber and toughened glass mask and ask the shop staff to show you how to find a good fit. If getting wet just isn't for you, try **glass-bottomed boats** or "subs", which can still turn up everything from sharks to oysters.

Reef hazards

Stories of shark attacks, savage octopuses and giant clams all make good press, but are mostly the stuff of fiction. However, there are a few things at the reef capable of putting a dampener on your holiday, and it makes sense to be careful. The best protection is simply to look and not touch, as nothing is actively out to harm you.

Seasickness and **sunburn** are the two most common problems to afflict visitors to the reef, so take precautions. **Coral and shell cuts** become badly infected if not treated immediately by removing any fragments and dousing with antiseptic. Some corals can also give you a nasty **sting**, but this is more a warning to keep away in future than something to worry about seriously. Animals to avoid tend to be small. Some dangerous **jellyfish** (see warning on p.28) are found at the reef during summer – wear a protective Lycra "stinger suit" or full wetsuit with hood. Conical **cone shells** are home to a fish-eating snail armed with a poisonous barb which has caused fatalities. Don't pick them up: there is no "safe" end to hold them. Similarly, the shy, small, **blue-ringed octopus** has a fatal bite and should never be handled. **Stonefish** are camouflaged so that they're almost impossible to distinguish from a rock or lump of coral. They spend their days immobile, protected from attack by a series of poisonous spines along their back. If you tread on one, you'll end up in hospital – an excellent argument against reef-walking. Of the larger animals, **rays** are timid, flattened fish with a sharp spine capable of causing deep wounds – don't swim close over sandy floors where they hide. At the reef, the most commonly encountered **sharks** are the black-tip and white-tip varieties, and the bottom-dwelling, aptly named carpet shark, or wobbegong – all of these are inoffensive unless hassled.

Reef tax

The Marine Parks Authority levy a **reef tax** (currently $4.50 per person per day, though some tour operators add $1 extra for administration) to help fund monitoring and management of human impact on the reef. On most tours and boat trips, you will be required to pay the reef tax in addition to the cost of the tour. You may feel a little annoyed at having to fork out the extra money, especially if you've already paid quite a lot for your trip, but this is simply a "user-pays" system to help ensure that the reef is maintained for everyone to experience and enjoy.

Caravan Park (℡07/4126 1521; cabins ❷) has contacts with local farms, though its management has drawn bad press from some travellers. Otherwise, *Hotel Childers* (℡07/4126 1719; ❷) is a great place to **stay**, with very cute "country-style" rooms, a spacious beer garden, and the best **meals** in Childers – though *Laurel Tree Cottage*, at the Bundaberg end of town, comes a close second.

Bundaberg and around

Surrounded by canefields and fruit farms, **BUNDABERG** is famous for its **rum**, though the town is otherwise a humdrum place whose value as a jumping-off point for trips to Lady Elliot and Lady Musgrave **islands** is scarcely advertised. The adjacent coast is, however, an important place for **marine turtles**, who mass in huge numbers every summer to lay their eggs on the beaches; and those wanting **work** are virtually guaranteed seasonal employment (mostly Feb–Nov) picking avocados, tomatoes, snow peas and zucchini on farms in the area.

"Bundie" is synonymous with dark rum throughout Australia and if you believe their advertising pitch, the town's **rum distillery** on Whittered Street, about 2km east of the town centre along Bourbong Street (tours Mon–Fri 10am–3pm, Sat & Sun 10am–2pm; $7.70), accounts for half the rum consumed in Australia each year. A distillery **tour** allows fans to wallow in the overpowering pungency of raw molasses and ends, of course, with a free sample – though you probably won't need to drink much after inhaling the fumes in the vat sheds, where cameras are prohibited in case a flash ignites the vapour.

Flying 1270km from Sydney to Bundaberg in 1921, **Bert Hinkler** set a world record for continuous flight in a light aircraft (his flimsy wire and canvas Baby Avro), demonstrating its potential as transport for remote areas and so encouraging the formation of Qantas the following year (see p.583). In 1983, the **house** where Hinkler lived at the time of his death in England was transported to Bundaberg and rebuilt in the Botanic Gardens, 4km from the centre over the Burnett Bridge towards Gin Gin, sharing its desirable surroundings with a Sugar Museum, Historical Museum and a steam train (all daily 10am–4pm; $5 for house). Outside the house, landscaped gardens flank ponds where Hinkler was supposedly inspired to design aircraft by watching ibises in flight.

Mon Repos Beach and the turtle rookery

Mon Repos Beach is 15km east of Bundaberg, reached by initially following Bourbong Street out of town towards the port and looking out for small brown signposts for the beach (or larger ones for the *Turtle Sands Caravan Park*). Once the site of a French telegraph link to New Caledonia, today its reputation rests on being Australia's most accessible **loggerhead turtle rookery**. From October to March, female loggerheads clamber laboriously up the beaches after dark, excavate a pit with their hind flippers in the sand above the high-tide mark, and lay about a hundred parchment-shelled eggs. During the eight-week incubation period, the ambient temperature of the surrounding sand will determine the sex of the entire clutch; 28.5˚C is the change-over point between male and female. On hatching, the endearing, rubbery-brown youngsters stay buried in the nest until after dark, when they dig themselves out en masse and head for the sea. In season, about a dozen turtles lay each night, and

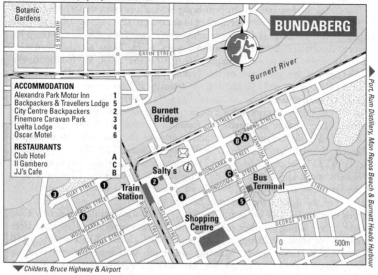

1770, Mystery Craters & Gin Gin

BUNDABERG

N

Botanic Gardens

HINKLER ST

GAVIN STREET

Burnett River

ACCOMMODATION
Alexandra Park Motor Inn   1
Backpackers & Travellers Lodge   5
City Centre Backpackers   2
Finemore Caravan Park   3
Lyelta Lodge   4
Oscar Motel   6

RESTAURANTS
Club Hotel   A
Il Gambero   C
JJ's Cafe   B

Burnett Bridge

QUAY STREET

BOURBONG STREET

TANTITHA STREET

WALLA STREET

Salty's ℹ

WOONGARRA STREET

TARGO STREET

Bus Terminal

Train Station

QUAY STREET

BOURBONG STREET

WOONGARRA STREET

WOONDOOMA STREET

BURRUM STREET

McLEAN STREET

Shopping Centre

GEORGE STREET

0   500m

Childers, Bruce Highway & Airport

Port, Rum Distillery, Mon Repos Beach & Burnett Heads Harbour

4

TROPICAL QUEENSLAND AND THE REEF | Bundaberg and around

watching the young leave the nest and race towards the water like clockwork toys is both comical and touching – your chances of seeing both laying and hatching in one evening are best during January. The loggerhead's future does-n't look too bright at present: since 1980 Mon Repos' rookery population has halved, most likely due to net-trawling offshore. The NPWS runs nightly guided **tours** ($4) from November to March, when the beach is otherwise off limits between 6pm and 6am; most accommodation places can book you on a tour and transport package ($38.50), or contact Footprints Adventures (℡07/4152 3659, ⓦwww.footprintsadventures.com.au).

Practicalities

Bundaberg lies south of the **Burnett River**, with the coast and quiet satellite suburbs – Bargara, Innes Park, Elliot Heads – about 15km to the east. Bourbong Street, the main thoroughfare, runs parallel to the river and is where you'll find several banks, the post office, and **Internet** cafés. The **bus termi-nal** is on Targo Street, and the **train station** (℡07/4153 9724, bookings ℡13 22 32) is 500m west on McLean Street. The **airport**, for departures to Lady Elliot amongst other places, is 4km from the centre on the Childers Road; the **port**, for Lady Musgrave ferries, is 10km east of the centre. The **tourist infor-mation** office (Mon–Fri 8.30am–4.45pm, Sat–Sun 10am–1pm; ℡07/4153 9289) is at 186 Bourbong St.

Salty's, at 208 Bourbong St (℡07/4151 6422, ⓦwww.saltys.net), offers prob-ably the cheapest four-day **dive course** in Australia ($169), though this uses shore dives with poor visibility and few fish; for $580 you get boat diving around reefs and Lady Musgrave Island (qualified divers can get the same trip for $495 plus equipment rental). Bundaberg Coach Tours (℡07/4153 1037) runs day-tours featuring the rum distillery and other sights twice a week ($75), and twice-weekly day-tours to Agnes Water and 1770 ($75).

Central **accommodation** options include the *Backpackers & Travellers Lodge*, opposite the bus terminal on Targo Street (℡07/4152 2080; dorms $20), and

City Centre Backpackers, at 216 Bourbong St near the train station (☎07/4151 3501, ✉ccbackpackers@interworx.com.au; dorms $20) – note that these are dedicated workers' hostels and probably won't appeal if you're not looking for work. Another budget option is the quiet *Lyelta Lodge* on the corner of Maryborough and Woondooma streets (☎07/4151 3344, ℱ4151 6626; ❷). Most motels are just west of the centre: *Oscar Motel* at 252 Bourbong St (☎07/4152 3666, ℱ4152 6626; ❸) is friendly and has a pool and barbecue area; *Alexandra Park Motor Inn* at 66 Quay St (☎07/4152 7255, ✉alex.park motorinn@bigpond.com; ❸) is a modern Queenslander-style place with huge rooms. The closest **campsite** is *Finemore Caravan Park* on Quay Street (☎07/4151 3663; cabins ❷), which overlooks the river. At **Mon Repos Beach**, the first-rate beachfront *Turtle Sands Caravan Park* (☎07/4159 2340, ℱ4159 2737; camping $16.50 per 2 people, cabins ❷) is right next to the turtle rookery and a kilometre of beach. All places fill up over the Christmas holidays, and the two workers' hostels are reluctant to take advance bookings except in the quieter months from January to March.

For **eating**, *JJ's Café* on Bourbong Street opens early, while the nearby *Club Hotel* serves filling counter meals for lunch and evening, and sports a beer garden. For sound Italian pizza, pasta, and grills for under $15 a serving, try *Il Gambero*, on Targo Street. **Moving on**, trains and long-distance buses – Greyhound Pioneer (☎13 20 30), McCafferty's (☎13 14 99) and Premier (☎13 34 10) – head up the coast to Gladstone and down to Childers and beyond; Greyhound Pioneer and McCafferty's also run to Agnes Water and 1770 once a day (though note that there is no bus service from Agnes Water or 1770 to Bundaberg).

Lady Elliot Island

The southern outpost of the Great Barrier Reef, **Lady Elliot Island** is a two-kilometre-square patch of casuarina and pandanus trees stabilizing a bed of coral rubble, sand, and – in common with all the southern cays – a thick layer of **guano**, courtesy of the generations of birds which have roosted here. The elegant **lighthouse** on Elliot's west side was built in 1866 after an extraordinary number of wrecks on the reef; on average, one vessel a year still manages to come to grief here. Wailing shearwaters (muttonbirds) and the occasional suicide of lighthouse staff didn't endear Lady Elliot to early visitors, but a low-key **resort** and excellent reef have now turned the island into a popular escape.

Shearwaters aside, there's a good deal of **birdlife** on the island; residents include thousands of black noddies and bridled terns, along with much larger frigatebirds and a few rare red-tailed tropicbirds – a white, gull-like bird with a red beak and wire-like tail which nest under bushes on the foreshore. Both loggerhead and green **turtles** nest on the beaches too, and in a good summer there are scores laying their eggs here each night. The main reason to come to Lady Elliot, however, is to go **diving and snorkelling**: the best spots for diving are out from the lighthouse, but check on daily currents with the dive staff before getting wet. The Blowhole is a favourite with divers, with a descent into a cavern (make sure you see the "gnomefish" here), and there's also the 1999 wreck of the yacht *Severence* to explore. You've a good chance of encountering harmless leopard sharks, sea snakes, barracuda, turtles and gigantic manta rays wherever you go. Shore dives cost $29 per person, while boat dives are $39 ($49.50 for night dives), plus gear rental.

Lady Elliot can only be reached **by air** on daily flights from Hervey Bay or Bundaberg (day-return $225, including use of resort facilities, snorkelling gear and glass-bottom boat; resort guests $175; book through the resort). **Accommodation** on the island is with the comfortable *Lady Elliot Island Resort* (℡1800 072 200, ⓦwww.ladyelliot.com.au; ❼), which has basic four-person tented cabins as well as motel-like suites with private bathrooms and ocean views. Breakfast and dinner (but not lunch or flights) are included in the rates; or enquire about discounted longer-term packages – but if you're not interested in underwater activities, a day or two is ample time to see everything and unwind.

Lady Musgrave Island

Lady Musgrave Island is another tiny, low island, this time covered in soft-leaved pisonia trees which host the usual throng of roosting birdlife, ringed by a coral wall which forms a large turquoise lagoon. Diving the inside of the lagoon here is safe but pretty tame (though snorkelling is good) – the outside wall is more exciting. Relatively easy, inexpensive access means that Lady Musgrave is the best of the southern cays on which to **camp** – there is no resort on the island, nor any facilities – though the island itself is off-limits during the tern nesting season (Oct–April).

From Bundaberg, *MV Lady Musgrave* departs from the Port Marina, about thirty-minutes' drive from town (Mon, Tues, Thurs, Sat & Sun 8.30am; $135 single or day-return), taking three hours to reach the island. The booking office is at the marina (℡07/4159 4519, ⓦwww.lmcruises.com.au) and staff can organize a bus pick-up from your accommodation ($9). The island is also visited on Salty's dive trips (see Bundberg "Practicalities", p.473). Alternatively, you can reach Lady Musgrave **from 1770** (see below) with the same company, whose ferry zips over to the island in just over an hour (Tues, Wed, Fri, Sat & Sun; $128 single or day-return). **Diving** from either vessel costs $30 for one dive or $40 for two, plus gear rental. **Campers** need camping **permits** from the Gladstone NPWS (see p.476); you can arrange for fresh provisions to be brought over by either ferry if you're planning a long stay – for practical details, see the "Island camping" box on p.477.

Agnes Water and 1770

On the coast 100km north of Bundaberg along the Rosedale road (or an additional 65km from the highway via **Miriam Vale**), the tiny settlements of **Agnes Water** and nearby **1770** mark where Captain Cook first set foot in Queensland on May 24, 1770. It's a pretty area, and one of the few undeveloped places along the Queensland coast that can be reached without a 4WD. If you don't have your own transport, there's one northbound **bus** (McCafferty's/Greyhound Pioneer) from Bundaberg daily, though no return service, as all southbound buses stick to the main highway. Nearby attractions include the mangrove, fan palm and paperbark wetlands at **Eurimbula National Park**, and the coast at Agnes Water, which has Queensland's northernmost official **surfing** beaches – though the beach is good, even if you haven't come to ride the waves. 1770 is also the closest point on the mainland to the southern cays, with regular transport to several reefs.

AGNES WATER itself consists of a service station, a few **stores** at Endeavour Plaza, and the *Agnes Water Tavern* – which does excellent **meals** – set a few hundred metres back from the sea, while **1770** is even smaller, occupying the foreshore of a narrow promontory some 6km to the north.

For **Eurimbula**, head 10.5km back towards Miriam Vale from Agnes Water, where you'll see the track and national park sign to the north of the road. You can bushcamp about 15km inside the park in the dunes behind Bustard Beach – ask at the Agnes Water service station for directions. You'll need high clearance or 4WD for the park. Alternatively, you can **tour** the region aboard *The Larc* (☎07/4974 9422; full day $88, sunset cruise $20), an amphibious bus which spends the day exploring the coastline and reaches of the otherwise impenetrable **Deepwater National Park**, south of Agnes Water. **Reef boats** leave from the marina; *Reef Jet* runs day-trips according to conditions to either Pancake Reef ($100) or Fitzroy Reef lagoon ($125). See p.475 for details of how to reach **Lady Musgrave Island**.

Accommodation at Agnes Waters includes the smart homestay-style *Pacific Crest* (☎07/4902 1770, ⓦwww.barrierreef.net/pacificcrest; ❺), which has spa pools and ocean views (just); and *Agnes Water Caravan Park* (☎07/4974 9193), which fronts onto the beach. In 1770, *1770 Getaway* (☎07/4974 9329, ⓔgetaway1770@bigpond.com; ❹) has comfortable units and a laid-back atmosphere; budget alternatives include the *Captain Cook Holiday Village* (☎07/4974 9219; dorms $18, rooms ❸), which has a store, bar and bistro; *Cool Bananas* (☎07/4974 7660, ⓦwww.coolbananas.biz.com; dorms $18); or *1770 Campgrounds* (☎07/4974 9286; cabins ❷), also on the beach.

Gladstone and nearby islands

GLADSTONE is a busy port, and also the site of the Boyne Island processing plant, which refines aluminium from ore mined at Weipa on the Cape York Peninsula. Glaringly hot, there's no reason to stop here unless you're trying to reach the reef – if you're planning to camp on any of the southern cays, Gladstone is where you need to make arrangements through the **NPWS office**, at 136 Goondoon St (Mon–Fri 8.30am–5pm; ☎07/4972 6055, ⓕ4972 1993); if booking by post, mail the office at PO Box 5065, Gladstone. If you've time to spare, the **Tondoon Botanic Gardens**, about 7km south of town, comprise a part-wild spread of wetlands, woodlands, forests, and native shrubs, all expertly laid out – you'll probably clock up wallabies and birdlife here too.

The main strip is Goondoon Street, where there's a "mall" – just the usual high-street shops, post office and banks – plus a couple of hotels and motels. You'll find a helpful **information centre** (Mon–Fri 8.30am–5pm, Sat–Sun 9am–5pm) inside the **ferry terminal** at the marina, about 2km north of the centre on Bryan Jordan Drive. *Gladstone Reef Hotel*, 38 Goondoon St (☎07/4972 1000; ❹), has ordinary motel rooms and good views from a rooftop pool. **Places to eat** on Goondoon include the *Grand Hotel*, which offers straightforward grills, and *Swaggy's*, where you can spoil yourself with native cuisine – emu, crocodile, kangaroo – though at gourmet prices.

Diving can be arranged through Last Wave Watersports, 16 Goondoon St (☎07/4972 9185), which runs irregular trips to Lamont, Llewellyn and Fitzroy reefs south of Heron. For longer trips, *Mikat* (☎07/4972 3415, ⓦwww.mikat.com.au) caters to more serious divers and covers much of the southern reef from Lady Musgrave to Northwest islands.

Masthead and Northwest islands

Remote both in feel and location, **Masthead and Northwest islands** remain virtually undisturbed, with limited numbers of campers permitted at any one

Campers intending to stay over on one of the undeveloped southern reef cays need to organize camping permits and transport well in advance, particularly for the Easter and September holiday periods, and to contact the boat operator a few days before departure to check on weather conditions – rough seas can suspend services to the islands. Note, too, that Lady Musgrave, Northwest and Masthead islands are **closed** to camping during the tern nesting season, between mid-October and mid-April. **Camping permits** cost $3.85 per person per night, and are only issued by the Gladstone NPWS (see opposite). You need to be entirely self-sufficient: take food, at least five litres of water per person per day, a fuel stove (wood fires are prohibited), waterproof tents and sand pegs, shovels, first-aid kit, a radio (for weather forecasts), spare batteries, garbage bags and emergency rations for at least two extra days.

time. Both cays are around 500m long and 100m wide, with a good covering of pisonias; as the usual crowd of seabirds and turtles nest here, both are also closed during the nesting season (Oct–April). Even at other times, the ruckus generated can be quite disturbing, but in the right frame of mind this all becomes part of the experience. Don't overlook the reef's **snorkelling** or **fishing** if you have the gear, though bear in mind that certain sections of reef are protected zones where fishing is prohibited – check first with the NPWS in Gladstone.

The only way to reach Northwest and Masthead from Gladstone is by **charter boat**, and at $3000 minimum, you'll need to get a group together for it to be financially viable: operators include Robert Poulsson (☎07/4972 5166) and Curtis Endeavour (☎07/4972 6990), or contact the NPWS for leads on other boats. Check the "Island camping" box above for practical details.

Heron Island

Famous for its diving, **Heron Island** escaped the depredations of guano hunters in the early twentieth century, though a turtle-canning factory operated on the island for several years. Small enough to walk around in an hour, half the cay is occupied by a comfortable **resort** and **research station**, the rest covered in groves of pandanus, coconuts and shady pisonias, whose sticky seeds are unwittingly spread between islands on the backs of birds. Patches of long grass hide ground-dwelling rails (moorhen-like birds) which rocket from underfoot. Herons also stalk around the coral tops at low tide, fishing the pools – they're typically white, but a black form also frequents the area.

You can literally walk off the beach and into the reef's maze of coral, or swim along the shallow walls looking for action. The eastern edges of the lagoon are good for snorkelling at any time, but **diving** must be arranged through the resort (see p.478), which charges $48 for a standard dive, and $75 to venture out at night; equipment is extra. Dive **packages** save a few dollars if you're staying long enough to take advantage of them, and you can make two dives daily for free during June. A drift along the wall facing Wistari reef to Heron Bommie covers about everything you're likely to encounter. The coral isn't that good but the amount of life is astonishing: tiny boxfish hide under ledges; turtles, cowries, wobbegong, reef sharks, moray eels, butterfly cod and octopuses secrete themselves among the coral; manta rays soar majestically, and larger reef fish gape vacantly as you drift past. The Bommie itself makes first-rate **snorkelling**, with an interesting swim-through if your lungs are up to it, while the Tenements along the reef's northern edge are good for bigger game – including sharks.

There's a price to pay for all this natural wonder, namely no day-trips and no camping. The P&O-owned resort (reservations ☎13 24 69; island reception ☎07/4972 9055; ❼) is excellent, but its rates, coupled with the ferry charge ($164 return) place it well outside the budget bracket. **Ferries** leave from Gladstone Marina daily at 11am, except at Christmas; there's a car lockup here ($9 a day) operated by the tackle shop (8am–5pm).

The Tropics: Rockhampton to Cape York

Rockhampton marks the start of the tropics, but with the exception of the Mackay region, it's not until you're well past the line and north of **Townsville** that the tropical greenery associated with north Queensland finally appears. Then it comes in a rush, and by the time you've reached **Cairns** there's no doubt that the area deserves its reputation: coastal ranges covered in rainforest and cloud descend right to the sea. **Islands** along the way lure you with good beaches, hiking tracks and opportunities for snorkelling and diving: the **Keppels** near Rockhampton, the **Whitsundays** off Airlie Beach, **Magnetic Island** opposite Townsville, and **Hinchinbrook** and **Dunk** further north. Cairns itself serves as a base for exploring highland rainforest on the **Atherton Tablelands** and coastal jungles in the **Daintree**, and for trips onto the **Cape York Peninsula** and, of course, out to the most accessible sections of the **Great Barrier Reef**.

Rockhampton

Straddling the Tropic of Capricorn, 100km north of Gladstone, **ROCK-HAMPTON** was founded after a false goldrush in 1858 left hundreds of miners stranded at a depot 40km inland on the banks of the sluggish **Fitzroy River**; their rough camp below **Mount Archer** was adopted by local stockmen as a convenient port. The iron trelliswork and sandstone buildings fronting the river recall the balmy 1890s, when money was pouring into the city from central Queensland's prosperous cattle industry and the gold and copper mines 40km west at **Mount Morgan**. Today, however, despite hosting a large university campus, Rockhampton feels a bit despondent: the mines have closed (though before they did, they managed to fund the fledgling BP company), the beef industry is down in the dumps and the summers, unrelieved by coastal breezes, are appallingly humid. Bearing this in mind, the city is best seen as a springboard for the adjacent Capricorn Coast (see p.481), but with half a day to spare it's worth catching the Aboriginal version of history at the

Dreamtime Cultural Centre; and there are a group of **limestone caves** to the north to poke around in.

The City and around

It doesn't take long to look around the city. The **Tropic Marker**, 3km south of the river at Rockhampton's southern entrance, is just a spire informing you of your position at 23° 26' 30" S. And, apart from a riverside stroll to take in the turn-of-the-twentieth-century architecture or the brown-stained boulders in mid-stream that gave the city its name, there's very little to detain you.

About 5km north of town on the Bruce Highway, the **Dreamtime Cultural Centre** (daily 10am–3.30pm; tours with an Aboriginal guide from 10.30am; $14) offers a good introduction to central Queensland's Aboriginal heritage. Inside, chronological and Dreamtime histories are intermingled, with a broad dissection of the archeology and mythology of Carnarvon Gorge (see p.570). Outside, surrounded by woodland, gunyahs (shelters of bark and branches) and stencil art, you'll find an unlikely walk-through dugong (sea cow), and the original stone rings of a **bora ground** which marked the main camp of the Darumbal, whose territory reached from the Keppel Bay coastline inland to Mount Morgan. The tour also introduces plant usage, plus boomerang, dance and didgeridoo skills – audience participation is definitely encouraged.

Etna Caves and Capricorn Caverns

The limestone hills 25km north of Rockhampton are riddled with an interesting **cave system** discovered in the 1880s. The caves have few classic stalagmites and stalactites, which need continuous dripping water to form; instead,

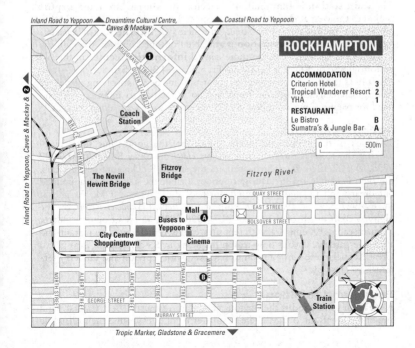

there are tree roots encased in stone after forcing their way down through rocks, "cave corals" and "frozen waterfalls" – minerals deposited by evaporation after annual floods. The **ghost bat** (Australia's only carnivorous species) and the **little bent-winged bat** – both now endangered – seasonally use the caves for roosts, and you might catch the odd group huddled together on the ceilings, eyes peering down at you over leaf-shaped noses.

There are two sets of caverns open to the public, both reached by turning off the Bruce Highway at **The Caves** township: cross the rail line and bear left, and Etna Caves National Park is straight on past a council depot and around to the right; for Capricorn Caverns, turn right after the hotel and follow the billboards. The **Etna Caves** are undeveloped but none too extensive; between February and June you can explore on your own (6am–8pm; take a torch and durable shoes); between November and February you can go on a bat tour (four evenings a week; $7.20) with the NPWS – contact them for details (see opposite). The **Capricorn Caverns** (daily 9am–4pm; guided tour $15, caving tour $40; ⓦ www.capricorncaves.com.au) are impressive, with plenty of spotlights illuminating their interiors. Bus tours to the Caverns leave at 9.30am on Monday, Wednesday and Friday from near the *Leichhardt Hotel* on Bolsover Street (book first on ⓣ07/4934 2883; $32).

Practicalities

Rockhampton is divided by the Fitzroy River, with all services clustered directly south of the **Fitzroy Bridge** along Quay Street and East Street; the Bruce Highway runs right through town past two pairs of fibreglass bulls (repeatedly "de-balled" by pranksters). **Long-distance buses** stop at the coach station just north of the bridge on the highway; **local buses** to or from Yeppoon and the coast set down, amongst other places, along Bolsover Street. The **train station** is 1km south of the centre on Murray Street; the **airport** is 4km to the west at the end of Hunter Street. Banks, the post office and other services are mostly along East Street, and there's an **Internet** bar at *Sumatra's* (see p.481). **Tourist information** is available from the booth on the highway at the Tropic Marker, or at the more central **information centre** in the old customs house on Quay Street (Mon–Fri 8.30am–4.30pm, Sat–Sun 9am–4pm; ⓣ07/4922 5339). Recent reports of nasty incidents involving gangs of Aboriginal teenagers are unfortunately too numerous to ignore; there's no need for paranoia, but do follow local advice and don't walk alone at night.

Accommodation

The pick of the **accommodation** choices are the good-value suites overlooking the river at the historic *Criterion Hotel* on Quay Street (ⓣ07/4922 1225, ⓕ4922 1226; ❸), which occupies the site of Rockhampton's first pub, the *Bush Inn*, built in 1857. **Budget** options include the YHA's well-appointed but dreary and isolated compound north of the river at 60 MacFarlane St (ⓣ07/4927 5288, ⓕ4922 6040; $20); or the *Tropical Wanderer Resort*, on the highway 3km north of the river (ⓣ07/4926 3822, ⓦwww.tropicalwanderer .com.au; cabins ❷, units ❸), with tent sites, cabins, motel units, a restaurant, and attractive gardens. If your only reason for being in Rockhampton is to get to Great Keppel, there's little reason to stay over, with Yeppoon and the ferry terminals so close by.

Eating and drinking

A **steak** of some kind is the obvious choice in Australia's "Beef Capital", and any of the hotels can oblige. There's a smattering of cafés around the mall, while the more upmarket *Le Bistro*, at 152 Quay St (Mon–Sat 6.30pm–late), serves huge slabs of meat for about $28. A perch at the *Criterion*'s bar is recommended for less flamboyant steak and beer, along with elbow-to-elbow closeness with a few locals. *Sumatra's* and the associated *Jungle Bar*, on the corner of East and William streets, is a popular café-restaurant-bar which stays open late and serves sandwiches and light meals for under $10.

Listings

Airlines Virgin and Qantas fly daily to Brisbane.

Buses Local buses serve the Capricorn Coast: Young's buses (☎07/4922 3813; 6–12 daily) run from the stop beside the car park in Bolsover St, near the junction with William, to Yeppoon, Emu Park, and Rosslyn Bay. McCafferty's/Greyhound Pioneer (☎07/4927 2844) and Premier (☎13 34 10) services all depart from the main bus terminal.

Car rental Network, cnr George and Archer streets (☎1800 077 977); Rockhampton Car Rentals, south on the Bruce Highway (☎07/4922 7802).

Diving Capricorn Reef Diving, 189 Musgrave St, North Rockhampton (☎07/4922 7720), gives certification courses from around $450 and offers dive courses around the Keppels.

Farmstays Myella Farm, The Eather Family, Myella, Barabala (☎07/4998 1290,

Ⓦwww.myella.com), and Kroombit-Lochenbar, Valentine Plains Rd, Biloela (☎07/4992 2186, Ⓦwww.kroombit.com.au), are both a couple of hours out of town and offer accommodation, meals and participation in farm life from $240 for three days.

Hospital Base Hospital, Canning St, South Rockhampton ☎07/4920 6211.

NPWS The helpful NPWS office (☎07/4936 0511) is situated 5km out of town on the Yeppoon–Rockhampton road.

Pharmacy CQ Pharmacy, 150 Alma St (daily 8am–10pm; ☎07/4922 1621).

Police 212 Quay St ☎07/4938 4880.

Shopping City Centre Plaza on Bolsover St.

Taxi ☎07/4922 7111.

Trains Murray St ☎07/4932 0211.

The Capricorn Coast

Views from volcanic outcrops overlooking the **Capricorn Coast**, east of Rockhampton, stretch across graziers' estates and pineapple plantations to exposed headlands, estuarine mudflats and the **Keppel Islands**, 20km offshore. The coastal townships of **Yeppoon** and **Emu Park**, settled by cattle barons in the 1860s, were soon adopted by Rockhampton's elite as places to beat the summer heat, and retain a pleasantly dated holiday atmosphere, though **Great Keppel Island** is the coast's main draw.

Rockhampton to Yeppoon

First stop on the road to Yeppoon is about 25km from Rockhampton at **Koorana Crocodile Farm** (tours daily at 10.30am and 1pm; $15), where estuarine crocs are bred (koorana means "giving birth") to supply the leather industry and restaurants. If this doesn't bother you, the tours are interesting – despite a certain amount of showmanship involved in the feeding and meeting of Koorana's "stars". Some of the crocs are penned individually, but most are viewed en masse from the safety of protected boardwalks, raised over the mudflats and ponds where the reptiles bask. With luck you might see babies hatching, bleating as they squeeze themselves out of tiny eggs.

The sea appears suddenly at **EMU PARK**, a beach and breezy hillside covered by scattered Queenslander houses, where the wind howls mournful tunes through the wires of the **Singing Ship**, a peculiar monument to Captain Cook. **Budget beds** in a smart century-old building are offered at *Emu Park Beach House*, 88 Pattison St (☎07/4939 6111, bookings ☎1800 333 349; dorms

$16, twin rooms and cabins ❷) – they also offer discount packages to Great Keppel from $47, and can collect from Rockhampton. A good alternative is the more motel-like *Endeavour Inn* on Hill Street (℡07/4939 6777; ❸). One place to note between here and Yeppoon is **Rosslyn Bay**, where the cliffs have been weathered into hexagonal columns behind the **island ferry terminal** and **marina** (for details of getting to the islands, see below). Further on, **COOEE BAY** is virtually a suburb of Yeppoon, with an annual "Cooee Competition" when competitors give their tonsils a good airing from Wreck Point.

Yeppoon

YEPPOON's quiet handful of streets faces the Keppel Islands over a blustery expanse of sand and sea. All services are on **Normanby Street**, at right angles to seafront Anzac Parade. **Buses** pull into the depot on Hill Street, which also runs off Anzac Parade parallel with Normanby; the Young's Coaches **office** is just opposite. For **accommodation**, *Driftwood Motel*, 7 Todd Avenue (℡07/4939 2446, ℻4939 1231; ❸), has self-contained rooms overlooking the beach, while friendly *Yeppoon Backpackers*, 30 Queen St (℡07/4939 8080; $17), has four-bed dorms and an attractive pool area, and operates a daily courtesy bus to Rockhampton to meet evening arrivals; call ahead to check exact times. The *Strand Hotel* (℡07/4939 1301; ❸), on the corner of Anzac Parade and James Street, offers basic, four-bed units, while the *Poinciana Tourist Park* (℡07/4939 1601; cabins ❸), just south of town off the Emu Park road, has self-contained cabins and shady tent sites.

For **eating**, *Latitude 23*, on Anzac Parade, is a popular but pricey restaurant-wine bar specializing in seafood; the nearby *Keppel Bay Sailing Club* has a cheaper bar with with long views of the islands, while their restaurant offers budget all-you-can-eat lunches and dinners. Otherwise there's a legion of **cafés** to choose from along Normanby Street – *Shore Thing* has an awful paint job, good coffee, and set-price curry nights. For weekend **entertainment**, try the *Strand Hotel* or *Bonkers Nightclub*, one road back from Anzac Parade on Hill Street.

The Keppel Islands

The eighteen **Keppel Islands** comprise a series of windswept hillocks covered in casuarinas and ringed by white sand so fine that it squeaks when you walk through it, while the sea is an invitingly clear blue – just right for a few days of indolence. Most of the islands are national parks and, with the exception of North and Great Keppel, are very small. Easy access, coupled with a resort and associated facilities, has made Great Keppel the most popular, but there are also reefs to snorkel and isolated camping spots on the other islands.

All access is from **ROSSLYN BAY**, just off the main road about 8km south of Yeppoon on the coastal route to Rockhampton, with departures from both the **ferry terminal** and the nearby **marina**. For **Great Keppel**, *Reef Cat* (℡07/4933 6744) from the terminal and *Freedom Fast Cat* (℡07/4933 6244) from the marina run a total of seven daily return services (the last leaves Great Keppel at 4.30pm), plus an additional late service on Fridays; both charge $30 return. The marina is the place to find transport to **other islands** or **cruises**: *Prince Regal* is available for charter from $479 for two days; *Funtastic* is a sailboat which offers day-cruises around the islands (departs Fri–Sun at 9.30am; $98) – for either call ℡1800 336 244. The ferry terminal and marina both have exposed **free parking**, though for protection from salt spray, leave your car undercover at Great Keppel Island Security Car Park (℡07/4933 6670; $9 a day), opposite the Rosslyn Bay junction on the main road.

Great Keppel

Arriving at **Great Keppel**, the ferry leaves you on a spit near several **accommodation choices**; most offer packages or last-minute discounted packages (standby) if you ask for them. Closest to the spit, the YHA-run *Backpackers Village* (☎07/4927 5288, ⓕ4933 6429; $22) is a tent village; facilities are basic, and the place feels a bit stark and military. Nearby, *Great Keppel Island Holiday Village* (☎07/4939 8655, ⓦwww.gkiholidayvillage.com.au; dorms $24, tent cabins ❷, cabins ❹) is a spruce and very friendly place with a first-rate kitchen, and accommodation in self-contained cabins, tents or dorms.

Along the beach, *Keppel Lodge* (☎07/4939 4251, ⓕ4939 8251; ❹) is a pleasant, **motel**-like affair; further down you come to the *Great Keppel Island Resort* (☎07/4939 5044 or 1800 245 658; ❽). This place changes its style on a regular basis; at present it's an 18–35 Contiki resort, with a lively bar and pool which may be open to non-guests. For **food**, there's a tearoom at the Shell House on Fisherman's Beach. There's also a late-opening pizza shack – much frequented after the bar closes.

The main **beaches**, Putney and Fisherman's, are remarkably pleasant considering the number of people lounging on them at any one time, but a half-hour walk will get you to some more secluded spots. Reached on a woodland path past the resort, **Long Beach** attracts sun-worshippers, while snorkellers make the short haul over sand dunes at the western end to shallow coral on **Monkey Beach**. Middens (shell mounds) on Monkey Beach were left by Woppaburra Aborigines, who were enslaved and forcibly removed to Fraser Island by early settlers.

Other Keppels

Emu House in Emu Park (see p.481) can set up trips to other islands, or contact the marina and enquire about boat charters (see opposite). None has provisions or reliable drinking water, so take your own. NPWS camping permits can be picked up at the Rockhampton (see p.481) or Rosslyn Bay offices. If you want to **scuba dive** around the islands, or simply get certified, contact Keppel Island Dive Centre, near the *YHA* on Great Keppel (☎07/4939 5022, ⓦwww .keppeldive.com) – most dive sites are less than 15m deep, and there are abundant rays, turtles, and sea snakes. Alternatively, *Reef Cat* (☎07/4933 6744) runs daily snorkelling and sightseeing **island cruises** from Great Keppel for $55.

North Keppel is an undeveloped version of Great Keppel. There's an NPWS **campsite** on the west side of the island, behind the dunes at Considine Bay, with showers, toilets and a sporadic supply of tank water; take precautions against sandflies, which are abundant in sheltered spots here, and note that wood fires are banned. A walking track from the group of cabins at the southern end of Considine Beach leads to the reef at Maisy Bay.

Middle Island is lightly wooded, with an NPWS camping area and **underwater observatory** complete with scenic Taiwanese junk. It's only a short hop from Great Keppel, and ferries run trips daily for about $10 return. **Humpy Island**, also off Great Keppel, is popular for fishing and has the best snorkelling reef of all the islands. The hump doesn't do much to protect it from the southeasterlies, which are the main problem with camping here; facilities are similar to those on North Keppel.

Mackay and around

Some 360km north of Rockhampton along a famously unexciting stretch of the Bruce Highway, the fertile **Pioneer Valley** makes the **MACKAY** area a pleasant break from the otherwise dry country between Bundaberg and Townsville. Despite encounters with aggressive Juipera Aborigines, John Mackay was impressed enough to settle the valley in 1861, and within four years the city was founded and the first **sugar cane plantations** were established, attracting the migrant communities common to north Queensland – it's not unusual to hear English, Islander Pidgin and Maltese spoken within earshot of each other in town. Sugar and servicing mining operations centred inland on the Bowen Basin coalfields remain the core industries today, though both are facing uncertain futures: drought and viruses are ravaging crops, and the mines are gradually following new coal seams south and out of the region.

Mackay provides some welcome relief from the east coast "backpackers' pub crawl", and though it's only mildly geared up for tourism, the town's proximity to the delightful **Eungella** and **Cape Hillsborough** national parks makes it well worth a visit.

Practicalities

Mackay's centre straddles the crossroads of Victoria Street and Sydney Street, with the **bus station** just off Victoria on Macalister Street. Both **trains** (station on Connors Road, 3km south off Milton Street along Boundary Road or Paradise Street) and **planes** arrive south of town; a **taxi** into town from either terminal will set you back around $8. Mackay Travelworld at the bus station (℡07/4944 2144) is **ticket agent** for bus, train, and air travel. The **tourist information** centre (℡07/4952 2677) is badly informed and poorly located 3km south of town along the Nebo Road (Bruce Highway); if you need information, ask the staff at wherever you're staying.

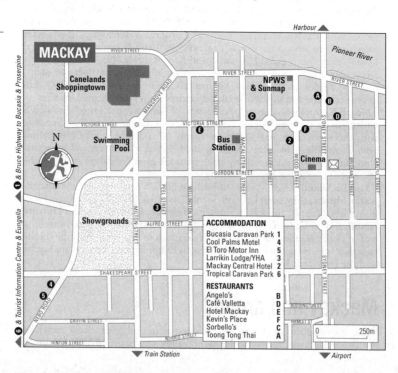

Accommodation

Most **accommodation** is either located in town or south along the Nebo Road, though for sun and sand, you need to take the highway towards Townsville and then turn off and follow the signs for **Bucasia**.

Bucasia Caravan Park Bucasia Esplanade, Bucasia ☎07/4954 6375. Beachfront camping and units with nice island views. Few amenities, although there's a nearby store. Units ❷

Cool Palms Motel 4 Nebo Road ☎07/4957 5477, ⓕ4951 4660. Closest motel to town, quiet and inexpensive. ❸

El Toro Motor Inn 14 Nebo Rd ☎07/4951 2722 or 1800 687 186. Not too far from the centre, with a friendly atmosphere and pool. ❹

Larrikin Lodge/YHA 32 Peel St ☎07/4951 3728, ⓔlarrakin@mackay.net.au. Low-set, comfortable Queenslander house with a laid-back atmosphere,

two-minutes' walk from the bus station; also run their own bus to Eungella. Phone ahead to arrange check-in outside the office opening hours (7–10am & 5–10pm). Dorms $19, rooms ❷

Mackay Central Hotel 64 Wood St ☎07/4957 7286. Smack in the centre of town, with pleasant doubles and twins, with TV and shared bathrooms, and a huge communal balcony right over Mackay's downtown action. Can get noisy on weekends. ❷

Tropical Caravan Park Nebo Road ☎07/4952 1211. Two kilometres from the centre, a tidy van park with self-contained units in a garden setting. ❸

Eating

Mackay has plenty of good, cheap **places to eat**. Several downtown pubs and restaurants also offer filling weektime lunch specials for around $5–10.

Angelo's 27 Sydney St. Mediterranean cooking and genuine wood-fired pizzas.

Café Valletta Victoria Street. Daytime café hugely popular with local Maltese for its fresh breads and salads.

Hotel Mackay Victoria Street. As well as the usual grills, the hotel restaurant here has tasty Indian food, though the choices are limited – a meal here costs around $15 a head.

Kevin's Place Cnr Wood and Victoria streets ☎07/4953 5835. Singaporean–Chinese restaurant with fixed-price lunches (try the laksa – a colossal

bowl of noodles, seafood and spicy coconut soup) and à la carte dinners – around $22 – featuring five-spice squid and whole fried fish. Closed Mon evenings.

Sorbello's 168 Victoria St. Good choice for pastas and other Italian dishes for around $20 per person. Lunch specials Mon–Fri; open for dinner daily.

Toong Tong Thai 10 Sydney St. Long-established Thai restaurant and takeaway with authentically hot and spicy food. Lunchtime specials are good value, or it's around $25 a head for a full meal.

Listings

Airlines Virgin and Qantas have direct flights from Mackay to all the major cities between Cairns and Brisbane.

Banks Branches of all major banks are located around the intersection of Sydney and Victoria streets.

Camping equipment Mackay Camping World, 54 Gregory St.

Car rental Europcar, at the airport (☎07/4944 1188), offers the best rates in town.

Hospital Mackay Base Hospital, Bridge Rd

☎07/4968 6000.

NPWS Cnr Wood and River streets ☎07/4951 8788.

Pharmacy Day and Night Pharmacy, 65 Sydney St (daily 8am–9pm; ☎07/4957 3360).

Police Sydney St ☎07/4968 3444.

Post office Sydney St.

Shopping Canelands Shoppingtown, across the road from the bus station, has everything you'll need.

Taxi ☎13 10 08.

Cape Hillsborough National Park

Cape Hillsborough, about an hour's drive north of Mackay, is the site of a pretty beachfront national park with tame wildlife, though you'll need your own vehicle to reach it. Head first up the highway towards Townsville and then take the signposted Seaforth road from **The Leap**, a small township at the base of a distinctively shaped hill which takes its name from events of 1866, when a settler was killed by Aborigines and the police drove an Aboriginal woman over the cliff during reprisals. The woman turned out to be holding a baby, which survived and was adopted by a local family. *The Leap*, one of Mackay's oldest **hotels**, is right underneath, and you can contest the details of the story over a cold beer if you're interested. From here the road passes the inevitable canefields on the way to Mount Jukes, before descending to coastal flats and turning off to Cape Hillsborough a couple of kilometres before **Seaforth** township.

The national park

The main area of the national park is set around a broad two-kilometre beach bounded by the wooded cliffs of Cape Hillsborough to the north and Andrews Point to the south; the shallow bay is good for swimming outside the stinger season. Local fauna include bush turkeys, pretty-face wallabies and some butch kangaroos – they're often on the beach in the early morning, males flexing muscles and chasing does in a parody of the stereotypical Aussie male. There's a ranger station here, with a small exhibition giving the rundown on local history and geology, but it's often closed. Hidden in bushland at the end of the road, the *Cape Hillsborough Resort* (℡07/4959 0152; ❹) has **tent sites and cabins**, plus an expensive and limited **store** (which closes at 6pm) and a restaurant. A good walk heads out 2km past here to **Hidden Valley**, a patch of cool, shady forest on a rocky beach where you'll find the outline of an Aboriginal fish trap; keep your eyes peeled for dolphins, turtles and pelicans out in the bay.

Sugar cane on the Tropical Coast

Sugar cane, grown in an almost continuous belt between Bundaberg and Mossman, north of Cairns, is the tropical coast's economic pillar of strength. Introduced in the 1860s, the crop subtly undermined the racial ideals of British colonialists when farmers, planning a system along the lines of the southern United States, employed **Kanakas** – Solomon Islanders– to work the plantations. Though only indentured for a few years, and theoretically given wages and passage home when their term expired, Kanakas on plantations suffered greatly from unfamiliar diseases, while the recruiting methods used by "**Blackbirder**" traders were at best dubious and often slipped into wholesale kidnapping. Growing white unemployment and nationalism through the 1880s eventually forced the government to ban blackbirding and repatriate the islanders. Those allowed to stay were joined over the next fifty years by immigrants from Italy and Malta, who mostly settled in the far north and today form large communities scattered between Mackay and Cairns.

After cane has been planted in November, the land is quickly covered by a blanket of dusky green. Before cutting, seven months later, the fields are traditionally **fired** to burn off leaves and maximize sugar content – though the practice is dying out. Cane fires often take place at dusk and are as photogenic as they are brief; the best way to be at the right place at the right time is to ask at a mill. Cut cane is then transported to the mills along a rambling rail network. The **mills** themselves are incredible buildings, with machinery looming out of makeshift walls and giant pipes which belch out steam around the clock when the mill is in operation. Cane is juiced for raw sugar or molasses, as the market dictates; crushed fibre becomes fuel for the boilers that sustain the process; and ash is returned to the fields as fertilizer. **Farleigh Mill** (℡07/4953 8400), north of Mackay, is open for **tours** (including a very popular evening tour) during the crushing season (June–Nov).

Five hundred metres back up the road towards Mackay, an excellent two-kilometre-long trail follows a **boardwalk** through coastal mangroves (bring insect repellent) and then snakes up to a ridge for views out over the area from open gum woodland peppered with grevillias, cycads (see box on p.510) and grasstrees – the latter identified by their tall, spear-like flower spike. There's also a huge **midden** up here, the remains of Aboriginal shell-fish feasts, plus plenty of reptiles sunning themselves around the edges of the path.

Eungella National Park

At the end of the bitumen, 80km west of Mackay, magical rainforest and rivers would make **Eungella National Park** (pronounced "young-g'lla") worth the journey even if you weren't almost guaranteed to see **platypuses**. There are two separate sections: lowland swimming holes at **Finch Hatton Gorge** and highland forest at **Broken River**. Finch Hatton's rainforest is authentically tropical, while Broken River's plants are more closely allied with subtropical forests; isolation has produced several unique species, including the Mackay tulip oak, the Eungella honeyeater and the much-discussed but probably extinct **gastric brooding frog**, known for incubating its young in its stomach.

Day-trips to both sections of the park can be arranged with Reeforest Tours from Mackay (℗07/4953 1000; $80) or the *Larrikin Lodge*'s bus (see p.485; $80); with prior arrangement, either operator might be able to bring you up on one day and take you back on another. With your own vehicle, head south down the Nebo Road/Bruce Highway to Mackay's city limits and follow the signs; if you're coming south down the highway from Proserpine, follow the signs just south of tiny **Kuttabul**, around 30km from Mackay.

Finch Hatton Gorge

The Eungella road passes through prime cane country as it runs the length of the **Pioneer Valley**; 35km along, call in at **Illawong Fauna Park** (daily 8am–5pm; $17) for a close look at a big slice of the local wildlife, from croco-diles and dingoes to koalas and the bizarre tawny frogmouth. Feeding time is 2.15pm, there's a pool to cool off in, a **campsite**, and tickets are valid for unlimited entry all day.

Some 60km from Mackay, signposts just before Finch Hatton township mark the turn-off to **Finch Hatton Gorge**, 12km from the main road across sev-eral **fords** – access depends on the season, though generally it's negotiable by all vehicles. Immediately across the first creek, *Platypus Bush Camp* (℗07/4958 3204; dorms $18), provides **camping** space and **accommodation**: mattress, pillow, amenities and kitchen are supplied; the rest (including food) is up to you. This is the most authentic rainforest experience you can have anywhere in Queensland: you'll see an astonishing array of bird- and animal-life (includ-ing the elusive platypus), sit by a fire under the stars, shower in the rainforest amidst fairy-like fireflies, and be lulled to sleep by a gurgling creek. About a kilometre and three creeks further you'll find *Finch Hatton Gorge Cabins* (℗07/4958 3281; six-person cabins with showers, toilets and shared barbecue area ❹) and a small **tearoom**. This is also the pick-up point for **Forest Flying** (advance booking essential on ℗07/4958 3359), which can take you for a ride 25m up through the tree tops (and a flying fox colony) on a wire-and-sling affair – much more secure than it sounds, and offering as close a view of the forest canopy as you'll ever get.

Another kilometre past the tearoom, the road ends at a picnic area, with **walking tracks** leading off into the forest. The gorge winds down the side of Mount Dalrymple as a rocky creek pocked with **swimming holes** and over-shadowed by a hot jungle of palms, vines and creepers. **Araluen Falls** (1.5km from the picnic area), a beautiful, if icy, swimming hole and cascade, is the perfect place to spend a summer's day; further up (3km from picnic area) is an even more attractive cascade at the **Wheel of Fire Falls**, where you can sit up to your neck in the water.

Eungella township and Broken River

Past Finch Hatton township, the main road makes an unforgettably steep and twisting ascent. Take an immediate left at the top and stop for a drink or meal at *Eungella Chalet* (℡07/4958 4509; twins and doubles with shared bath ❸, suites ❹, five-person cabins ❻), whose back-lawn beer garden and swimming pool sit just metres away from a 700-metre drop into the forest, with a fantastic panorama down the valley. They've also installed a **hang-glider ramp** next to the pool that's used for the sporadically staged North Queensland Hang-gliding Championships (ask locally for dates). Around the corner, a general store, chip shop and couple of cafés form the rest of **EUNGELLA** township, while 5km further on, through patches of forest and dairy pasture, is **Broken River**. There's **accommodation** here at the excellent *Broken River Mountain Retreat* (℡07/4958 4528, ℻4958 4564; doubles or four-person self-contained cabins with fireplaces ❺) – they also run free guided **night walks** for their guests – or across the river at the NPWS **campsite** (hot showers and barbecues). Book in advance and pick up free maps at the ranger's office (daily 8–9am, 11.30am–12.30pm & 3.30–4.30pm; ℡07/4958 4552). Next door is a **kiosk** open daily for snacks and minimal supplies. Be prepared for rain: Eungella translates as "Land of Cloud".

Crowded during holidays and weekends, at other times the forest is quiet and cool, its interior chock full of wildlife and unusual plants. The best vantage points for **platypus-watching** are upstream from the road bridge on the purpose-built platform, or from the bridge itself. Normally fairly timid creatures, here they've become quite tolerant of people, and you can often see them right through the day. Wander around the picnic area after dark with a torch to see other **wildlife**: feathertail gliders, bettong, possums, grey kangaroos and owlet nightjars. Down by the river you're more likely to come across frogs, cane toads and platypuses in the evening, while squirrel gliders are sometimes seen in the huge gum trees up along the main road, and pythons use the warm verges to recover energy before a night's hunting.

The real star of Broken River, though, is the **forest** itself, whose ancient trees with buttressed roots and immensely high canopies conceal a floor of rich rotting timber, ferns, palms and vines. Local **cabbage palms**, with their straight trunks and crown of large, fringed leaves, along with huge, scaly-barked **Mackay cedar** and **tulip oaks**, are all endemic; many other shrubs and trees here are otherwise only found further south, indicating that Eungella may have been once part of far more extensive forests. It can be difficult to see animals in the undergrowth but the sun-splashed paths along riverbanks attract goannas and snakes, and you'll certainly hear plenty of birds. The best two **walking tracks** are either following the river upstream to Crediton, and then returning along the road (16km); or heading through the forest and down to the *Eungella Chalet* (13km return). If you're not that dedicated, there's also an easy forty-minute circuit from the picnic grounds upstream to **Crystal Cascades**.

On to Whitsunday

PROSERPINE, 123km north of Mackay, is a workaday sugar town on the turn-off from the Bruce Highway to Whitsunday, and a major transit point for the Whitsunday region. **Trains** and **planes** both make stops in town, as do the main **long-distance buses** – though they also have services which detour daily to Airlie. Just south of town on the highway, **Whitsunday Information** (℡07/4945 3711) provides a fairly unbiased view of the area, something somewhat lacking at similar operations elsewhere in Whitsunday. If you wind up in town, Whitsunday Transit (℡07/4946 1800) runs a **local bus** about five times daily between Proserpine and Whitsunday; contact them in advance to arrange pick-ups from the train station or airport (which is 10km south of town). Late arrivals can stay at the *Proserpine Motor Lodge*, 184 Main St (℡07/4945 1788; ④), or the van park on Jupp Street.

Twenty kilometres east off the highway, **WHITSUNDAY** is the cover-all name for the increasingly sprawling communities of **Cannonvale**, **Airlie Beach** and **Shutehaven** (aka Shute Harbour). Until the early 1980s these were known only to locals and yachties, though following the discovery of the **Whitsunday Islands** (see p.492) by the mass tourist industry, the area boomed. Despite this, even now nobody comes to Whitsunday to spend time in town; it's just a place to be while deciding which island to visit. Airlie Beach and Cannonvale are the service centres; Shutehaven, from where island ferries generally leave, is 10km on from Airlie, past Cape Conway National Park. Other cruise and dive boats leave from **Abel Point Marina** between Cannonvale and Airlie. Whitsunday Transit runs a daily bus from the Wildlife Park (see below) through Cannonvale to Airlie and Shutehaven roughly once an hour from around 6am to 10pm.

Cannonvale, Airlie Beach and Shutehaven

Coming from Proserpine, Whitsunday's first community is **CANNONVALE**, a scattering of modern buildings fringing the highway for about a kilometre or so, overlooked by luxury homes set higher up on the wooded slopes of the Conway Range. Just around the headland past Abel Point Marina, **AIRLIE BEACH** is nestled between the sea and pine forests, with just about everything crammed into one short stretch of **Shute Harbour Road** and the hundred-metre-long **Esplanade**. Despite the name, Airlie Beach has only a couple of gritty stretches of sand which get covered at high tide – though the view of the deep turquoise bay, dotted with yachts and cruisers, is very pretty. To make up the shortfall, there's a fine open-air landscaped **pool**, complete with showers, changing rooms, and a little sand, between Shute Harbour Road and the sea, which has gained local notoriety thanks to its nocturnal popularity with couples.

The main preoccupation in Whitsunday is organizing a **cruise**, but you can also rent **watersports** gear from the kiosk on the beach at Airlie; organize half-day to six-day **sea-kayaking** expeditions with Salty Dog (℡07/4946 1388, ⓦwww.saltydog.com.au); or hop on the courtesy bus to the **Wildlife Park** (daily 9am–4.30pm; $15), a small zoo 7km towards Proserpine, which has an excellent reptile collection. Otherwise, **Conway National Park** comprises a mostly inaccessible stretch of forested mountains and mangroves facing the islands, but there's a small picnic area on the roadside about 7km from Airlie on Shute Harbour Road, from where an easy walking track climbs **Mount Rooper** to an observation platform giving views of the islands' white peaks jutting out of the unbelievably blue sea. A final 3km on, **SHUTEHAVEN** (Shute Harbour) comprises a cluster of houses overlooking the islands from wooded hills above Coral Point; it's one of Australia's busiest harbours, and most of the island ferries and bareboat charters depart from here. Those with cars will find limited **parking space** here; undercover facilities are available behind the Shell garage ($7 a day, or $12 for 24hr); there's an open-air grid at the harbour itself ($8 a day), and a free (but unguarded) area up the hill from the Shell garage overlooking the harbour.

The Reef

The **Barrier Reef** sits about 50km northeast of Airlie and contains some good sections – though if you're heading north, you'll find much better-value daytrips to the reef available from Cairns. For a very easy couple of hours of snorkelling or diving, head for the pontoon at **Hardy reef** with Fantasea (℡07/4946 5111, Ⓦwww.fantasea.com.au; $145 plus dive gear). The popular **Bait reef** is visited by Reefjet (℡07/4948 1212, Ⓦwww.reefjet.com.au; $180 plus dive gear), though the lagoon here has been very hard hit by coral bleaching; bommies (isolated coral outcrops) on the outer edge make for better drift diving, and manta rays are occasionally seen too. The best sites – which are only visited by live-aboard dive boats (see "Listings", p.492) – are **Elizabeth**, **Seagull** and **Fairey**; Elizabeth and Seagull have great visibility, swarms of mackerel, trevally, humpheaded wrasse, sharks, and juvenile reef fish hiding in the coral, while Fairey's strong currents make for exhilarating drift dives. Don't discount the fringing reefs around the islands either – see the island accounts for details of these.

Before heading out to the reef, make sure you catch **Reef Discovery**, a ninety-minute slide show and talk about the reef and its inhabitants given by local divers. Shows are held daily except Saturday at 6.15pm ($10) in the Reef Discovery building, towards the Shutehaven end of Shute Harbour Road; times are posted on the door.

Practicalities

Airlie's **long-distance bus terminal** is at the eastern end of town, off the Esplanade past the *Airlie Beach Hotel*. Staff at the town's hotels, hostels and other places offer limitless **information**, though don't expect it to be unbiased; the information office, airliebeach.com, up at the Cannonvale end of Airlie (℡07/4946 5299, Ⓦwww.airliebeach.com) is probably the most objective source, but it's a good idea to ask other visitors about which cruises they recommend before making a decision.

Accommodation

Unless you're in town during the September **Whitsunday Fun Race**, Christmas or New Year, you'll have little trouble finding **accommodation**. All places act as tour agents, offering reductions or free nights if you book through them, although competition is ruthlessly cut-throat and some places eject guests found making bookings through other agents. Hostels are all cramped, but a pool, kitchen and room fridges are standard amenities. Motels and resorts often offer discounted rates of ten to twenty percent during the low season (roughly Feb to Easter and Oct to mid-Dec). For a campsite or cabins, try *Airlie Cove Van Park*, 3km towards Shutehaven on Shute Harbour Road (℡07/4946 6727; cabins ❸).

Airlie Beach Hotel On the Esplanade, Airlie ☎07/4964 1999, ⓦwww.airliebeachhotel .com.au. This formerly seedy motel is now one of the smartest places to stay in Airlie. Refurbished older motel rooms ❹, new beachfront hotel rooms ❺

Airlie Beach YHA 394 Shute Harbour Rd, Airlie ☎07/4946 6312. Tidy dorms and doubles, generally busy and somewhat crowded. Dorms $22.50, rooms ❷

Airlie Waterfront Backpackers Near the *Airlie Beach Hotel*, Airlie ☎07/4948 1300, ⓔawbpack@airlie.net.au. Apartments above a boutique shopping complex with private bedrooms and shared bathrooms and kitchens, sleeping six; also has dorms. Dorms $20, apartment rooms ❸

Airlie Waterfront Bed and Breakfast Cnr Broadwater and Mazlin streets, Airlie ☎07/4946 7631, ⓦwww.airliewaterfrontbnb.com.au. One- or two-bedroom serviced apartments in a modern timber house with fantastic bay views; rooms are comfortably furnished; some have outdoor spa baths. ❺

Backpackers By The Bay 12 Hermitage Drive, Airlie ☎07/4946 7267, ⓔbythebay @whitsunday.net.au. Small, comfortable place that's quieter than those in the centre of town and has nice bay views. Dorms $17, rooms ❸

Beaches 362 Shute Harbour Rd, Airlie ☎07/4946 6244 or 1800 636 630. Brash backpackers' hostel, with plenty of bunks and double rooms available. Dorms $15, rooms ❷

Coral Point Lodge 54 Harbour Ave, Shute Harbour ☎07/4946 9500, ⒻBund4946 9469. A bit hard to find – turn up the hill immediately after the Shell garage and keep going to the end – but worth it for the best views from any Whitsunday

accommodation. There's a good café-restaurant here too, even if you're not staying. ❹

Coral Sea Resort 25 Oceanview Ave, at the Cannonvale end of Airlie ☎07/4946 6458, ⓦwww.coralsearesort.com. Airlie's newest, most exclusive accommodation; rooms (some with ocean views) are all very smart, and there's a private jetty and a popular bar and pool area too. ❻

Koalas Shute Harbour Rd, at the Canonvale end of Airlie ☎07/4946 6001 or 1800 800 421. Basic six-bed dorms, each with bathroom and TV. Facilities include a communal kitchen, volleyball court and large pool in pleasant landscaped grounds; you can also camp here. Dorms $15, rooms ❸

Magnums By the bridge on Shute Harbour Rd, Airlie ☎07/4946 6266 or 1800 624 634. Tidy cabins with own bathrooms, pleasantly sheltered lawns, and a loud bar next door. Dorms plus dinner $15, rooms ❷

On the Beach Shute Harbour Road, Cannonvale end of Airlie ☎07/4946 6359, ⓔthebeach @whitsunday.net.au. Unpretentious central motel with self-contained serviced units looking over Airlie's artificial pool to the bay. ❹

Reef Oceania Village Resort ("Reef O's") 147 Shute Harbour Rd, Cannonvale ☎07/4946 6137 or 1800 800 795. The cheapest beds in town, with 4-, 6- and 8-bed units, some with kitchen and air-con. Rates includes breakfast and a regular shuttle-bus to town (6am–midnight), and there's also a pool, inexpensive bar/bistro with live music, and a poorly equipped communal kitchen. Dorms $10, rooms ❶

Whitehaven Holiday Units 285 Shute Harbour Rd, Airlie ☎07/4946 5710, Ⓕ4946 5711. Extraordinarily quiet, given its central location. Rooms are simply furnished and face out to sea. ❹

Eating and entertainment

You'll find a variety of places to **eat** in the area, though the majority of restaurants, as well as the liveliest nightclubs, are in Airlie, with a string of places along the Esplanade or Shute Harbour Road. Many of the smaller cafés open early and offer cheap breakfast specials. For self-caterers, there's a supermarket near the bridge .

Airlie Beach Hotel On the Esplanade, Airlie. Smartly renovated, incorporating *Mangrove Jack's Café* and *Capers* restaurant, with a tropics-style menu and wood-fired pizzas, though the ambience is entirely ruined by the poker machines and TAB betting window at rear of pub.

Café Mykonos Near the *Airlie Beach Hotel* on Shute Harbour Rd, Airlie. Cheap and cheerful kebabs, souvlakia, dolmades and salads, with nothing over $7. Basically a takeaway, but there

are a few tables and chairs if the nearby beach doesn't appeal.

Chatz Shutehaven end of Shute Harbour Rd, Airlie. Bar and brasserie serving mammoth helpings of grilled and basted meats for around $22. Top-value lunchtime deals for $6–10.

The Courtyard 301 Shute Harbour Rd, across from Chatz. Award-winning BYO restaurant, highly rated by locals, with a seasonal menu (around $30 per person). Dinner only (Tues–Sun).

Hog's Breath Café Shute Harbour Rd, Airlie. The original of this chain of Tex-Mex grill restaurants, still serving good grub. Main courses around $18.

Juice Bar Cannonvale end of Shute Harbour Rd. Nightly grind 10pm–late.

KC's 50 Shute Harbour Rd, Airlie. Blowout on char-grilled steak, kangaroo, croc and seafood in noisy comfort; stays open until 3am and often has live bands. Mains around $20–25.

Morocco's Shute Harbour Rd, at the Cannonvale

end of Airlie. Cheerful place with a huge video screen, a superb view from the terrace and excellent lunch specials. Coral trout recommended for dinner, and the Mediterranean salad for lunch. Open daily 7am–midnight.

Paddy Shenanigan's Below the *Juice Bar*. Popular place to down a few and set the mood before heading upstairs.

Sailing Club Up past the bus stop off the Esplanade. Bar and good pub food from 10am until late, with views out over the bay.

Listings

Airlines Island Air ☎07/4946 9933; Qantas ☎07/4945 1613 or ☎13 13 13.

Airports Long-distance flights use Proserpine; local flights to or around the islands depart from Whitsunday Airport, about halfway between Airlie and Shutehaven.

Banks NAB and Commonwealth in Airlie; ANZ and Westpac in Cannonvale.

Boat charters Unless you know exactly what you want, bookings are best made through an agent. Bareboat charters should be undertaken by experienced sailors only: average wind velocity in the Whitsundays is 15–25 knots, which means serious sailing. Five-person yachts start at around $400 a day; add another $100 during holiday seasons. Australian Bareboat Charters ☎07/4946 9381, ℮ABCcharters@bareboat.com.au; Whitsunday Rent-a-Yacht ☎07/4946 9232, ℮rentayacht@bareboat.com.au; and Queensland Yacht Charters ☎07/4946 7400 have been going for years and are thoroughly reliable.

Car and scooter rental Airlie Beach Budget Autos, 285 Shute Harbour Rd, Airlie ☎07/4948 0300; Tropic Car Hire, 10 Commercial Close, Airlie ☎07/4946 5216.

Car lockup If you need to leave your vehicle in safe hands for a few days, contact Whitsunday Car Security, near the Whitsunday Airport between Airlie and Shutehaven (☎07/4946 9955).

Diving Airlie's two most established operators are Oceania Dive, 257 Shute Harbour Rd ☎07/4946 6032, ℗www.oceaniadive.com; and Reef Dive, in the centre of town, near the post office ☎07/4946 6508, ℗www.reefdive.com.au. Both offer training (around $350 for a four-day open-water course, or

$600 for a five-day course with up to eight dives) and live-aboard outings for qualified divers – three days and three nights work out at about $530 for ten dives. Weather, tides and currents will determine the most promising sites on any given day, but check first on how long is spent at the reef – often a couple of dives will be around an island. Island cruises and day-trips can often accommodate divers too – see the box on pp.496–497.

Doctor Opposite *McDonald's*, Shute Harbour Rd, Airlie (daily 8am–7pm; 24hr phoneline ☎07/4948 0900).

Flea market By the creek, for local produce and souvenirs (Sat 8am–noon).

Flights Island resort transfers aside, Air Whitsunday (☎07/4946 9111, ℗www.great barrierreef@bigpond.com) offers a seaplane trip out to the reef and Whitehaven Beach (4hr; $235).

Internet If your accommodation can't help out, airliebeach.com, up near the *Hog's Breath* at the Cannonvale end of town, has a stack of terminals.

Left luggage There's a set of lockers with 24hr access on the corner of Shute Harbour Road and the Esplanade ($4–6 per day).

NPWS Shute Harbour Rd, 3km out towards Shute on the left of the road (Mon–Fri 9am–5pm, Sat 9am–1pm; ☎07/4946 7022). Island camping permits and a small environmental display.

Pharmacy Airlie Day and Night Pharmacy (daily 8am–8pm).

Police Shute Harbour Rd, Cannonvale ☎07/4948 8888.

Post office In the centre of town, right behind *McDonald's*.

Taxi ☎13 10 08.

The Whitsundays

The **Whitsunday Islands** look just like the mountain peaks they once were before rising sea levels cut them off from the mainland six thousand years ago. They were seasonally inhabited by the Ngaro Aborigines when Captain Cook sailed through in 1770; he proceeded to name the area after the day he arrived, and various locations after his expedition's sponsors. Today, dense green pine forests and roughly contoured coastlines give the islands instant appeal, and the surrounding seas bustle with yachts and cruisers. Resorts first opened here in the 1930s and now number eight, but the majority of islands are still undeveloped and controlled by the NPWS, which maintains campsites on thirteen of them. Resorts aside, the few islands left in private hands are mainly uninhabited and largely the domain of local yachties. Those covered below all have regular connections to the mainland.

There are two ways to explore the Whitsundays: staying on the islands or cruising around them. **Staying** allows you to choose between camping and resort facilities, with snorkelling, bushwalks and beach sports to pass the time. **Cruises** spend one or more days around the islands, perhaps putting ashore at times (check this if it's the islands themselves you want to see) or diving and snorkelling. Don't miss the chance to do some **whale-watching** if you're here between June and September, when humpbacks (for more on which see p.455)

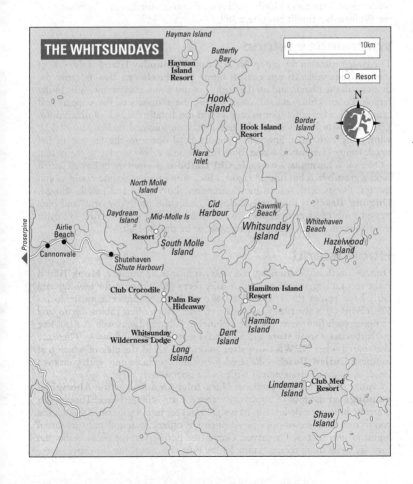

arrive from their Antarctic wintering grounds to give birth and raise their calves before heading south again.

If you're planning to make use of the 32 **island campsites**, you'll first need to arrange transport, then obtain **permits** from the Whitsunday NPWS office (see "Listings", p.492; $4 per person a night). At most, campsite facilities comprise a pit toilet, picnic tables, and rainwater tanks, so take everything you'll need with you, especially insect repellent, a fuel stove (wood fires are prohibited) and **drinking water** – if you're planning a long stay, you can arrange for cruise boats to ferry in supplies. **Resorts** sometimes have a higher profile than the islands they're built on; though staying is often beyond most budget travellers' means, stand-by deals can slash prices and polite bargaining is always worth a try. Most, in any case, allow day-trippers to use their facilities.

The resort islands all offer relatively expensive return **ferry transfers** to and from the mainland. If you'd like to see more than one island, or plan to camp away from a resort, it's cheaper to choose some sort of a **cruise** – for details, see the box on pp.496–497. Once you've arranged everything else, check your **departure points**; most cruises and dive boats leave from Abel Point Marina, while resort ferries and island transfers tend to use Shutehaven – both stops on the Whitsunday Transit bus (see p.489).

Whitsunday Island

The largest island in the group, NPWS-run **Whitsunday Island** is also one of the most enjoyable. Its east coast is home to **Whitehaven Beach**, easily the finest in all the islands, and on the agenda of just about every cruise boat in the region. Long, white, and still clean despite the numbers of day-trippers and campers, it's a beautiful spot so long as you can handle the lack of distractions. The **campsite** here is above the tide line, with minimal shelter provided by whispering casuarinas. Snorkellers should head down to the far end of the beach facing Hazelwood Island. Blue Ferries runs a daily service to the beach.

Over on Whitsunday's west side, **Cid Harbour** is a quieter hideaway which lacks a great beach but instead enjoys a backdrop of giant granite boulders and tropical forests, with several more campsites above coral and pebble shingle. **Dugong Beach** is the nicest, sheltered under the protective arms and buttressed roots of giant trees; it's a twenty-minute walk along narrow hill paths from Sawmill Beach, where you're likely to be dropped off.

Hook Island

Directly north of Whitsunday, and pretty similar in appearance, **Hook Island** is the second largest in the group. A daily **ferry** ($32) runs to the low-key and fairly basic **resort** (℡07/4946 9380, ⓦ www.hookislandresort.com.au; dorms $20, cabins ❹) at the island's southeastern end, which offers cabins, dorms, and camping with fine views over the channel to Whitsunday, as well as a bar, free gas barbecues, a small **store** and a cafeteria serving meals and snacks. There are also several other **NPWS campsites** around the island, the pick of which is at southern **Curlew Beach** – sheltered, pretty and accessible only with your own vessel or by prior arrangement with a tour operator.

Cruises often pull into southern **Nara Inlet** for a look at the **Aboriginal paintings** on the roof of a small cave above a tiny shingle beach. Though not dramatic in scale or design, the art is significant for its net patterns – though the connection here seems obvious – which are otherwise found only at central highland sites such as Carnarvon Gorge (see p.570). On the rocks below the cave are some more recent graffiti, left by boat crews over the last thirty years.

Snorkelling on the reef directly in front of the resort is a must; snorkelling gear and surf skis are free (with deposit) to guests. The water is cloudy on large tides, but the coral outcrops are all in fairly good condition and there's plenty of life around, from flatworms to morays and parrotfish. Day-cruises run from Airlie to the snorkelling spots and visit the top-rate fringing coral at **Manta Ray Bay**, **Langford Reef** and **Butterfly Bay** on the northern and north-eastern tips of the island – visibility can be poor here, but on a good day these sites offer some of the best **diving** in the islands.

Hayman Island

The extremely high price of accommodation at the **Hayman Island resort** (℡07/4940 1244, Ⓦwww.hayman.com.au; ➐), pales into insignificance when compared with the resort's building costs, which topped $300 million. Guests indulge in lush rooms with extravagant and genuine Baroque and Renaissance furnishings, and staff move about through underground tunnels so that they don't get in the way. Not surprisingly, day-trippers aren't allowed anywhere near the place, although cruises and some dive trips stop off for a look at the coral off **Blue Pearl Bay** – which isn't actually that exciting – on the island's west coast.

The Molles and nearby islands

South Molle Island was a source of fine-grained **stone** for Ngaro Aborigines, a unique material for tools that have been found on other islands and may help in mapping trade routes. The slightly shabby **resort** (℡1800 075 080; ➏) in the north of the island offers heaps of extras – such as guided walks, and all sports and facilities – along with stand-by rates. **Walking tracks** from behind the golf course lead to gum trees and rainforest, encompassing vistas of the islands from the top of Spion Kop and Mount Jeffreys, and some quiet beaches at the south end. Blue Ferries and Whitsunday All Over run ferries daily from Shute Harbour ($32 return) if you just want a day out. South Molle's resort can sometimes organize a lift to the campsite on uninhabited **North Molle Island**, only 2km away (or contact Camping Whitsunday; see box on p.496); the beach here is made up of rough coral fragments, but the snorkelling is fairly good. There are another couple of campsites on **Mid-Molle Island**, joined to South Molle by a low-tide causeway about half a kilometre from the resort.

Daydream Island is little more than a tiny wooded rise between South Molle and the mainland, with a narrow beach running the length of the east side and coral to snorkel over at the north end. The **resort** (℡07/4948 8488; ➐) offers fine food and hospitality, but its regimental lines dominate views of the island from the sea and detract from an otherwise very pretty scene. At present, day-trippers aren't allowed on the island, though this could change in the near future.

Tiny **Planton**, **Tancred** and **Denman** islands are just offshore from South Molle – with no facilities and limited camping at NPWS sites, they're about as isolated as you'll get in the Whitsundays. All three are surrounded by reef, but be careful of strong currents. Again, you may be able to arrange with Camping Whitsundays or cruise boats bound for Whitsunday Island to drop you off here.

Long Island

Long Island is exactly that, being not much more than a narrow, ten-kilometre ribbon almost within reach of the mainland forests. There are a few

Island transfers are offered by Fantasea-Blue Ferries and Whitsunday All Over, which between them operate daily ferry circuits between about half a dozen popular destinations; and Camping Whitsunday, which offers more remote drop-offs for campers. **Day-cruises** usually take in two or more islands, and offer the chance to experience the thrills of **boomnetting** – sitting in a large rope hammock stretched above the water at the front of the boat so that you can catch the full soaking force of the waves – and do some snorkelling; others may concentrate on a single theme, such as whale-watching, fishing or lazing on Whitehaven Beach. **Multi-day cruises** cover much the same territory but at a slower pace, and may give sailing lessons. Experienced groups might consider a **bareboat charter** (see "Listings" on p.492 for operators).

The list below is not exhaustive; word of mouth is the best method of finding out about who is still in business, what the current deals are and if operators live up to their advertisements. Check the length of trips carefully – "three days" might mean one full day and two half-days – along with how much time is actually spent cruising and at the destination, how many other people will be on the cruise, and the size of the vessel. There are scores of beautiful boats, so you'll be swayed by your preference for a performance racing yacht or a fun trip with lots of deck space on which to lounge. Bear in mind that a cheerful (or jaded) crew can make all the difference, and that weather conditions can affect destinations offered. Finally, if you want to save money, shop around as close to departure times as possible, when advertised prices tend to drop.

Island transfers

In addition to the following services, some island resorts have their own ferries or flights for guests.

Camping Whitsunday ☎07/4946 9330 or 0417 759 743. Return runs to beach campsites at North Molle, South Molle, Denman and Planton islands ($40 per person for a minimum of two people); they also offer good deals for transfers to campsites on Hook and Whitsunday and give free loans of water containers and snorkelling gear.

Fantasea-Blue Ferries Shute Harbour ☎07/4946 5111, ⓦwww.fantasea.com.au. Runs ferries several times daily to resorts on Hamilton, South Molle, and Daydream, and to Whitehaven Beach – see island accounts for prices.

Day-trips: sailing
The following cost $70–85.

Illusions ☎07/4946 5255, ⓦwww.illusions.net.au. Catamaran trip to Hayman's Blue Pearl Bay includes snorkelling and boomnetting; scuba diving also available. Lunch is optional at $10 extra.

Maxi Ragamuffin ☎1800 454 777, ⓦwww.maxiaction.com.au. 24-metre-long racer to Blue Pearl Bay (Mon, Wed & Sat) and Whitehaven Beach (Tues, Thurs & Sun), for snorkelling; diving available. Lunch included.

Day-trips: powered vessels
The following cost $70–80; includes lunch unless otherwise stated.

worthwhile hikes through the rainforest to Sandy Bay (where there's an NPWS **campsite**) or up Humpy Point, as well as three **resorts** on the island. *Club Crocodile Long Island* (☎07/4946 9555, ⓦwww.clubcroc.com.au; packages including meals and transfers ❼), at Happy Bay, and *Peppers Palm Bay* (☎07/4946 9233, ⓦwww.peppers.com.au; cabins and bungalows ❼), half a

Jetstream ☎1800 454 777, ⓦwww.maxiaction.com.au. Trips in a fast, open-sided speedboat, spending a couple of hours' R&R at Whitehaven before zipping up to suitable diving and snorkelling sites around Hook Island. A good price, but can feel crowded, and there's no deckspace for lounging – although most of the day is spent on the beach or in the water.

Mantaray ☎1800 816 365, ⓦwww.mantaraycharters.com. Fast and relatively roomy boat out to Whitehaven, where you spend around three hours at leisure before zipping north to Mantaray Bay and some good snorkelling.

Whitehaven Express ☎07/4946 7172, ⓦwww.whitehavenexpress.com.au. Trips to Whitsunday Island, stopping for scenery at Hill Inlet, before a snorkel and beach BBQ at Whitehaven.

Whitsunday Island Adventure Cruises ☎07/4946 5255. After a mandatory stop at Whitehaven Beach, this cruise proceeds to the resort areas at Hook and South Molle islands. Lunch $10 extra, or eat at the resorts.

Longer trips

The following cost $300–450 for two-night, three-day outings; trips departs at around 9am from Abel Point Marina, returning on day three about 4pm. The basic itinerary is to visit Hook Island via Nara Inlet, then move round to Whitehaven Beach on Whitsunday. There are two major sailboat companies in town, fronting for the majority of vessels: **Aussie Adventure Sailing** (☎1800 359 554, ⓦwww.aussiesailing.com.au) specializes in classic tall and vintage-style ships; **Southern Cross** (☎1800 675 790, ⓦwww.soxsail.com.au), puts the emphasis on maxi-yacht racers. Another large stable is owned by **Tallarook** (☎1800 331 316, ⓦwww.tallarookdive.com.au), with a varied bag of vessels all offering diving for certified divers.

Anaconda ☎1800 466 444. The 25-metre-long maxi *Anaconda II* usually visits Whitsunday. *Anaconda III* is the largest yacht in the Whitsundays, and fantastically comfortable; it heads to Whitehaven and then the reef.

The Card A 26-metre-long Whitbread Round-the-World racer, this is one of the best of the Southern Cross boats. Can hold twenty passengers, but is quite roomy even when full.

Derwent Hunter Contact Aussie Adventure Sailing. Ninety-foot schooner built in 1945 and totally refitted with timber decking and fittings after years spent as a research vessel, a film set and dubious activities in the South China Seas.

Iceberg ☎1800 677 119, ⓦwww.airliebeach.com. Modern, fifteen-metre cruising yacht with a maximum of twelve passengers and an enthusiastic crew.

Schooner Friendship Beautiful, romantic wooden schooner run by Aussie Adventure Sailing, and carrying just ten passengers.

Siska A 25-metre-long ocean maxi yacht owned by Southern Cross, winner of races between the UK and Australia.

Southern Cross The company's flagship: a high-speed, 21-metre-long America's Cup challenger accommodating fourteen passengers.

Waltzing Matilda A more modern design than most of Aussie Adventure Sailing's fleet, this eighteen-metre ketch is not that roomy, but has a great atmosphere.

kilometre south at the island's waist, have similar attractions (a disco, parasailing, water-skiing and a dozen other sports). Whitsunday All Over runs daily **ferries** from Shute Harbour to *Club Crocodile* and *Peppers* ($32 return). For a real escape, *Whitsunday Wilderness Lodge* (☎07/3221 7799, ⓦwww.south longislandcom; ❼) offers self-contained waterfront cabins, superb food and attentive service. It's only accessible by helicopter: contact the *Lodge* for package deals and transfers.

Hamilton and Lindeman islands

The apartment buildings dominating the view on **Hamilton Island** are the Gold Coast revisited, and it's interesting to speculate about what will happen to them during the next big cyclone. An enormous colony of fruit bats lives in the trees behind the waterfront and, apart from the flocks of cockatoos, seems to be the only native wildlife here. The island is privately owned, and its businesses operate under a lease: development includes a quaint colonial waterfront with hotel, bakery and various other stores, the *Hamilton Island Resort* (☎1800 075 110, ⓦwww.hamiltonislandresort.com; ❼), a small zoo, and so many restaurants, pools, gift shops and sports facilities that the original character of the island has long since vanished. The twin towers of the resort loom over the beach complex, and give the best view of the whole area from one of the external glass lifts taken up to penthouse level. Inside the beach complex you'll find one of the pricier places to eat, and lots of signs in Japanese. Blue Ferries runs a daily service from Shute Harbour ($45 return).

Lindeman Island suffered as a victim of feral goats, though their eradication has seen native plants making a comeback in a small melaleuca swamp and on the wooded northeast side. Mount Oldfield offers panoramic views, while other walking tracks lead to swimming beaches on the north shore. The *Club Med* **resort** (☎1800 801 823, ⓦwww.clubmed.com; ❼), Australia's first, has all the services you'd expect; Whitsunday All Over runs transfers from Shute Harbour for guests.

Bowen and the route to Townsville

BOWEN, a quiet seafront settlement 60km north of Proserpine, was once under consideration as the site of the state capital, but it floundered after Townsville's foundation. Today, stark first impressions created by the sterile bulk of the saltworks on the highway are offset by a certain small-town charm and some pretty beaches just off to the north. The other attraction is the prospect of seasonal **farm work**: Bowen's mangoes and tomatoes are famous throughout Queensland, and there's a large floating population of itinerant pickers in town between April and January. The backpackers' hostels (see below) can help with finding work, though nothing's guaranteed.

Bowen's centre overlooks **Edgecumbe Bay**, at the harbour end of Herbert Street, where you'll find the usual range of services and a couple of old colonial exteriors on the *Grand View Hotel* and the Harbour Office; the **train station** is a few kilometres west of town near the highway, and **buses** stop outside Bowen Travel (☎07/4786 2222), just off Herbert on Williams Street, which can organize **tickets** for either. Budget **accommodation** – which should be booked in advance – consists of *Barnacles* (☎07/4786 4400; dorms $18, rooms ❷), on Gordon Street; and *Trinity's at the Beach* (☎07/4786 4199; dorms $20), located near the beaches at 93 Horseshoe Bay Rd – both offer pick-ups from the centre. Both serve as a base for workers and aren't particularly inspiring; if you don't plan to work, you're unlikely to stay long. **Mid-range** options include *Castle Motor Lodge*, 6 Don St (☎07/4786 1322; ❸), about the closest to the centre of town, and the pleasant *Skyview Motel*, on the way to the beaches at 49 Horseshoe Bay Rd (☎07/4786 2232; ❸). You can **eat** at the *Grand View Hotel*, down near the Harbour Office on Herbert, or *McDees Café*, on the corner of Herbert and George streets; alternatively, stock up at Magees Supermarket on Williams Street and at the town's numerous fruit and vegetable stalls.

Bowen's attractive **beaches** lie a couple of kilometres north of the town centre. **Queens Beach**, which faces north, is sheltered and has a stinger net for the jellyfish season, but the best is **Horseshoe Bay**, small, and hemmed in by some sizeable boulders, with good waters for a swim or snorkel. *Horseshoe Bay Resort* (℗07/4786 2564; units ❸) makes an excellent base, two-minutes' walk from the sea.

With your own transport, it might be worth skipping Bowen in favour of the ranch-style *Bogie River Bush House* (℗07/4785 3407, ⓦwww.bogiebush house.com.au; dorms $20, rooms ❸), about 60km inland from town towards Collinsville. This splendid retreat has a range of accommodation, from rooms through to backpacker dorms, as well as a pool and the chance to go horse riding, fishing, or play with tame wildlife; you can also organize **farm work** here.

The Burdekin River, Ayr and Mount Elliot

Further on up the highway, 115km past Bowen, are the towns of **Home Hill** and **Ayr**, separated by a mill, a few kilometres of canefields and the iron framework of the **Burdekin River Bridge**. The river, one of the north's most famous landmarks, is still liable to flood during severe wet seasons, despite having to fight its way across three weirs and a dam. On the northern side, **AYR** is a compact farming town which is becoming another popular stop on the **farm work** trail. The highway – which runs through town as Queen Street – is where you'll find the bus stop and all essential services, as well as two workers' hostels which can find you employment picking and packing capsicums, amongst other things – *Ayr Backpackers* (℗07/4783 5837; phone in advance for pick-up; $18) is definitely the better option.

North of Ayr, **Mount Elliot** looms on the horizon, the only accessible section of the fragmented **Bowling Green Bay National Park**; turn off from the highway when you see the signs for **ALLIGATOR CREEK**, about 55km from Ayr. There's a NPWS ranger station and **campsite** (℗07/4778 8203), in a valley at the end of the road (note that the road is open 6am–6pm only), from where the creek widens into a chain of rock pools and deeper channels. The pools become more private the further you get from camp and though swimmers might attract cruising eels and nibbles from freshwater shrimp, it's pretty idyllic.

Townsville

Hot and stuffy **TOWNSVILLE** sprawls around a broad spit of land between the isolated hump of Castle Hill and swampy Ross Creek. While cynics describe its two biggest attractions as **Magnetic Island** (just offshore) and Cairns, Townsville has undergone some tasteful development in recent years, and does have its moments – above all in its visible maritime history, in the sea views from the Strand promenade, and in the muggy, salty evening air and old pile houses on the surrounding hills, marking down Townsville as the coast's first really tropical city.

Townsville was founded in 1864 by John Melton Black and Robert Towns, entrepreneurs who felt that a settlement was needed for northern stockmen who couldn't reach Bowen when the Burdekin River was in flood. Despite an inferior harbour, the town soon outstripped Bowen in terms of both size and prosperity, its growth accelerated by **gold** finds inland at Ravenswood and Charters Towers (for more on which see p.590). Today, it's the gateway to the far north and transit point for routes west to Mount Isa and the Northern Territory; it's also an important military centre, seat of a university and home to substantial Torres Strait Islander and Aboriginal communities.

Arrival and information

Townsville's roughly triangular city centre is hemmed in by Cleveland Bay on the north, Ross Creek to the south and Castle Hill to the west. Oriented northeast and parallel with Ross Creek, **Flinders Street** is the main drag, sectioned into a downtown pedestrian **mall** before running its last five hundred metres as Flinders Street East. The **airport** is 5km northwest; a shuttle bus (book in advance on ☎07/4775 5544; $7 single, $11 return) meets most flights, stopping at points around town. **Long-distance buses** stop at the **Transit Centre** on the south side of Ross Creek on Palmer Street, while the **train station** is on the north side of the creek and east of the centre on Flinders Street.

Public **transport** serves the suburbs rather than the sights, though much of what there is to see is central; some hostels have bikes available. A very helpful **information** booth, with a separate counter handling (and booking) diving, cruises and tours, is located in Flinders Street Mall (Mon–Fri 9am–5pm, Sat & Sun 9am–1pm).

Accommodation

Lodgings are concentrated around the city centre and near the Transit Centre, but hostels and caravan parks might collect you from further afield if you call ahead.

Civic Guesthouse 262 Walker St ☎1800 646 619, ⓦ www.backpackersinn.com.au. Clean and helpful, if not wonderfully modern, with a well-equipped kitchen, spa pool, and free Friday night BBQs. Deals on dive courses with Diving Dreams (next door) and a sunset bus ride to Castle Hill lookout, or trip to Alligator Creek available. Dorms $20, rooms ❷

Globetrotters Palmer St, just down from the Transit Centre ☎07/4771 3242, ⓔ globetrotters @austarnet.net.au. Small, peaceful hostel with pool and simple rooms; almost always full. Dorms $18, rooms ❷

Great Northern Hotel Cnr Flinders and Blackwood streets ☎07/4771 6191. Old Queenslander pub; the downstairs bar has lots of character, and serves huge meals from $10. Rooms have fan or air-con and shared bath. ❸

Holiday Inn Flinders Street Mall ☎1300 666 747, ⓦ www.townsville.holiday-inn.com. Comfortable and bland business venue set in a building resembling a giant sugar-shaker. ❻

Plaza Cnr of Flinders and Stanley streets ☎07/4772 1888, ⓦ www.plazahotels.com.au. Downtown motel-like apartments, modern, friendly, and with a bit more panache than the nearby Holiday Inn. ❹

Reef Lodge 4–6 Wickham St ☎07/4721 1112, ⓔ reeflodgetownsville@bigpond.com. The cheapest place in town, friendly enough and a bit cramped but freshly renovated. Dorms $16, rooms ❷

Rowes Bay Caravan Park Heatleys Parade ☎07/4771 3576, ⓕ 4724 2017. Off The Strand, 3km north of the centre towards Pallarenda, overlooking Magnetic Island across the bay; take bus #7 from the mall. Very popular cabins and campsites, so worth booking in advance. Cabins (with or without en suite) ❷–❸

Strand Park Hotel 59–60 The Strand ☎07/4750 7888, ⓦ www.jasons.com.au. Small boutique motel in Townsville's prettiest area, offering self-contained double rooms and suites with either garden or sea views. Rooms ❺–❻

Yongala Lodge 11 Fryer St ☎07/4772 4633, ⓦ www.historicyongala.com.au. A welcoming place, named after the city's most famous shipwreck, with roomy if slightly shabby motel rooms joined to a historic old Queenslander with original furnishings. ❹

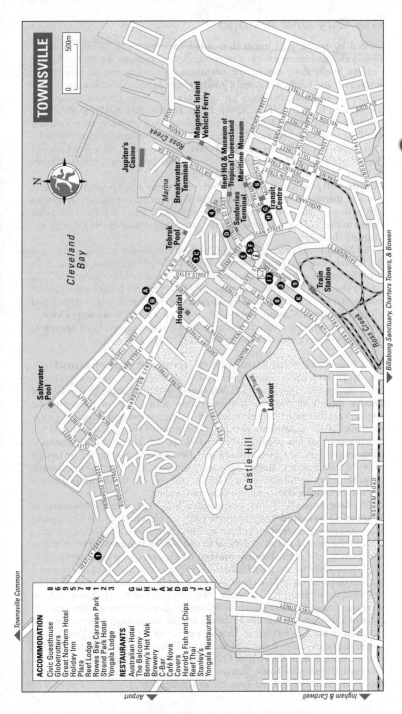

TOWNSVILLE

0   500m

N

Townsville Common ▲

Airport ▲

Ingham & Cardwell ▲

Billabong Sanctuary, Charters Towers, & Bowen ▶

Cleveland Bay

Saltwater Pool

Ross Creek

Magnetic Island Vehicle Ferry

Jupiter's Casino

Marina

Breakwater Terminal

Tobruk Pool

Reef HQ & Museum of Tropical Queensland

Maritime Museum

Sunferries Terminal

Transit Centre

Hospital

Castle Hill

Lookout

Train Station

ACCOMMODATION
Civic Guesthouse   8
Globetrotters   6
Great Northern Hotel   9
Holiday Inn   5
Plaza   7
Reef Lodge   4
Rowes Bay Caravan Park 1
Strand Park Hotel   2
Yongala Lodge   3

RESTAURANTS
Australian Hotel   G
The Balcony   E
Benny's Hot Wok   H
Brewery   F
C-Bar   A
Café Nova   K
Covers   D
Harold's Fish and Chips B
Reef Thai   J
Stanley's   I
Yongala Restaurant   C

501

The City and around

Funded by inland gold mines during the late nineteenth century, some of Townsville's architecture is quite imposing. A stroll through the mall and along Flinders Street East, among the unimaginative assortment of pharmacies, newsagents and banks, will reveal a good number of stylishly solid stone facades and iron wraparound balconies on buildings that were formerly shops and warehouses. In the mall itself, the **Perc Tucker Art Gallery** (Mon–Fri 10am–5pm, Sat & Sun 10am–2pm; free) is one such building, now featuring travelling exhibitions of mainly antique art. More offbeat, modern work by local artists is on view at the **Umbrella Gallery**, 222 Sturt St (Mon–Fri 9am–5pm, Sat & Sun 9am–1pm). On Sunday the mall hosts **Cotters Market** (8.30am–2pm), which has good local produce.

Castle Hill looms over the city centre, an obvious target if you're after clear views of the region. There's a road to the top from Stanley Street; on foot go along Gregory Street to Stanton Terrace and join a walking path of sorts that climbs to the lookout for vistas over the city to the distant Hervey Range and Magnetic Island.

The Strand runs northwest along Cleveland Bay, lined with more old houses and fig trees looking out to Magnetic Island. The busy waterfront strip here is a beautiful stretch of palms, beach, shady lawns and free hotplates for picnics, plus cafés, a children's waterpark, and a specially built jetty for fishing from. Off the eastern end you'll find Townsville's **marina** (where most dive trips depart) and adjacent **Jupiter's Casino**; right down the western end is **Kissing Point**, a grassy headland with a stretch of sand and accompanying enclosed **saltwater pool** below – very welcome during the scorching stinger season.

The Reef HQ and Museum of Tropical Queensland

The **Reef HQ**, on Flinders Street East (daily 9am–5pm; aquarium $19.50, Imax theatre $12, combined $29.50), houses a terrific aquarium and **Imax theatre** (hourly shows), which projects films with a popular science theme onto a domed ceiling to create an overwhelming, wraparound image. The huge live tanks in the **aqaurium** contain re-creations of the reef, where you can watch schools of fish drifting over coral, clown fish hiding inside anemones' tentacles and myopic turtles cruising past. Between the main tanks are smaller ones for oddities: sea snakes, deep-sea nautiluses, baby turtles and lobster. Upstairs, videos about the reef are shown, and you can handle some inoffensive invertebrates – tiny clams, sea slugs and starfish.

Next door to the Reef HQ, an innovative building houses the **Museum of Tropical Queensland** (daily 9am–5pm; $9), which showcases the Queensland Museum's marine archeology collection. The centrepiece is a full-sized, cut-away replica – figurehead and all – of the front third of the **Pandora**, a British frigate tied up in the tale of the **Bounty mutiny**, which sank on the outer reef in 1791 (see box opposite for the full tale). Accompanying artefacts salvaged off the wreck since its discovery in 1977 include water jars and bottles, tankards owned by the crew, and the surgeon's pocket watch, with glass face and finely chased gold and silver mountings. Dioramas re-create life on board, with views into the cramped captain's cabin, and a dramatic reconstruction of the sinking; while a life-sized blueprint of the *Pandora's* upper deck is mapped out on the carpet. You can also join in the twice-daily "Running Out the Gun", the loading and mock firing of a replica cannon from the *Pandora*. Other sections of the museum cover Outback Queensland's extensive **fossil** finds (including several life-sized dinosaur models), and touch on Aboriginal and Torres Strait Islander history.

The Bounty and the Pandora

In 1788, the British Admiralty vessel *Bounty* sailed from England to Tahiti, with a mission to collect **breadfruit** seedlings, intended to provide a cheap source of food for Britain's plantation slaves in the West Indies. But the stay in Tahiti's mellow climate proved so much better than life on board the *Bounty* that on the return journey in April 1789 the crew **mutinied**, led by the officer **Fletcher Christian**. Along with eighteen crew who refused to join in the mutiny, **Captain William Bligh** was set adrift in a longboat far out in the Pacific, while the mutineers returned to Tahiti, intending to settle there.

Things didn't go as planned, however. After an incredible feat of navigation over 3600 nautical miles of open sea, in June Bligh and all but one of his companions reached the Portuguese colony of Timor, emaciated but still alive, from where Bligh lost no time in catching a vessel back to England, arriving there in March 1790. His report on the mutiny immediately saw the Admiralty dispatch the frigate *Pandora* off to Tahiti under the cold-hearted **Captain Edwards**, with instructions to bring back the mutineers to stand trial in London.

Meanwhile in Tahiti, Christian and seven of the mutiny's ringleaders – knowing that sooner or later the Admiralty would try to find them – had, along with a group of Tahitians, taken the *Bounty* and sailed off into the Pacific. Fourteen of the *Bounty*'s crew stayed behind on Tahiti, however, and when the *Pandora* arrived there in March 1791, they were rounded up, clapped in chains and incarcerated in the ship's brig, a three-metre-long wooden cell known as "Pandora's Box".

Having spent a fruitless few months island-hopping in search of the *Bounty*, Captain Edwards headed up the east coast of Australia where, on the night of August 29, the *Pandora* hit a northern section of the Great Barrier Reef. As waves began to break up the vessel on the following day, Edwards ordered the longboats to be loaded with supplies and abandoned the ship, leaving his prisoners still locked up on board; it was only thanks to one of the crew that ten of them managed to scramble out as the *Pandora* slid beneath the waves.

In a minor replay of Bligh's voyage, the *Pandora*'s survivors took three weeks to make it to Timor in their longboats, and arrived back in England the following year. Edwards was castigated for the heartless treatment of his prisoners, but otherwise held blameless for the wreck. The ten surviving mutineers were court-martialled: four were acquitted; three hanged; and three had their death sentences commuted. Captain Bligh was later made Governor of New South Wales, where he suffered another mutiny known as the "Rum Rebellion" (see "History", p.1061). And the *Bounty*'s whole project proved a failure; when breadfruit trees were eventually introduced to the West Indies, the slaves refused to eat them.

Seventeen years later, the American vessel *Topaz* stopped mid-Pacific at the isolated rocky fastness of **Pitcairn Island** and, to the amazement of its crew, found it settled by a small colony of English-speaking people. These turned out to be the descendants of the *Bounty* mutineers, along with the last survivor, the elderly **John Adams** (also known as Alexander Smith). Adams told the *Topaz*'s crew that having settled Pitcairn and burned the *Bounty*, the mutineers had fought with the Tahitian men over the women, and that Christian and all the men – except Adams and three other mutineers – had been killed. The other three had since died, leaving only Adams, the women, and their children on the island. After Adams' death, Pitcairn's population was briefly moved to Norfolk Island in the 1850s (see p.388), where some settled, though many of their descendents returned and still live on Pitcairn.

The Maritime Museum

You'll find more about shipwrecks at the **Maritime Museum** (Mon–Fri 10am–4pm, Sat–Sun 1–4pm; $5), across Ross Creek near the Transit Centre on Palmer Street. Material here focuses on local shipwrecks. Most attention is given to the story of the **Yongala**, a hundred-metre-long passenger liner which went down with all hands during a cyclone in 1911, and was finally located intact in 1958; exhibits here are a must-see for scuba divers planning to dive the wreck (see below). Other wrecks covered include the Blackbirder vessel *Foam*, and the *Gothenburg*, a gold-miners' transport which sank near Bowen in 1875; ghoulish salvagers recovered the captain's safe and, assuming that corpses loaded with bullion had been eaten by sharks, began to fish for them, spurred on by the prospect of recovering gold from the carcasses.

Townsville Common and Billabong Sanctuary

The **Townsville Common Environmental Park** (daily 7.30am–7.30pm; free) is 6.5km north of the centre, on the coast at Pallarenda. The Bohle River pools into **wetlands** below the Many Peaks Range, a habitat perfect for wildfowl including the brolga, the stately symbol of northern marshes. Less popular – with rice farmers anyway – are huge flocks of magpie geese that visit after rains and are a familiar sight over the city. You need a vehicle to reach the park, but once there you can get about on foot, although a car or bike makes short work of the less interesting tracks between lagoons. Camouflaged **hides** at Long Swamp and Pink Lily Lagoon let you clock up a few of the hundred or more bird species: egrets stalk frogs around waterlilies, ibises and spoonbills strain the water for edibles and geese honk at each other, undisturbed by the low-flying airport traffic. Bring binoculars.

Seventeen kilometres south of Townsville on the highway, **Billabong Sanctuary** (daily 8am–5pm; $19.80; call in advance about transfers from town or the airport ☏07/4778 8344) is a well-kept collection of penned and wild Australian fauna laid out around a large waterhole. Amongst the free-ranging wildlife you'll find wallabies and flocks of demanding whistling ducks on the prowl for handouts; things you'll probably be happier to know are caged include saltwater crocs, cassowaries (bred for release into the wild), dingoes, wedge-tailed eagles and snakes. A swimming pool and accompanying snack bar make the sanctuary a fine place to spend a few hours, and you can also tour the grounds with an Aboriginal guide and get an introduction to bush foods.

Diving and reef trips from Townsville

The pontoon at **Kelso Reef** – a pretty but shallow dive site – is the day-trip destination of Reef and Island Tours (☏1800 079 797, ⓦwww.reefislandtours.com.au), whose fast catamaran leaves from the Barrier Reef HQ jetty, picking up from Magnetic Island en route ($136). Sunferries (☏1800 447 333, ⓦwww.sunferries.com) also runs a day-trip to **John Brewer Reef** for more of the same ($109). Diving and snorkelling gear is also available from both vessels. Townsville's best dive destination is the coral-encrusted **Yongala**, in 15–30m of water some distance offshore; this is a fabulous dive, particularly at night. However, tricky anchorage means that dives can only be made in good weather, and be aware that this is a demanding site – deep, with strong currents and startlingly big fish; it's best not to go unless you are an advanced diver with at least twenty dives. Operators include: Diving Dreams, 252–256 Walker St (☏07/4771 2500, ⓦwww.divingdreams.com), who offer both day-trips to the *Yongala* (two dives, $175 plus gear) or multi-day excursions including the *Yongala* (from $395); and Tropical Diving (☏1800 776 150, ⓦwww .tropicaldiving.com.au), who do day-trips to the *Yongala* aboard their fast boat *Gladiator* (two dives, $175 plus gear). Both also offer dive courses from $215 to $550, depending on whether you opt for a live-aboard vessel or dive from shore.

Eating, drinking and entertainment

There are plenty of good **eating** options in Townsville, with restaurants grouped in three main areas: in the centre on Flinders Street; south near the Transit Centre on Palmer Street; and out along The Strand. For evening entertainment, many of the town's hotels cater to the sizeable military and student presence and have regular live music, for which you might have to pay a cover charge; check *This Month in Townsville*, the local free magazine, for listings.

Cafés and restaurants

Australian Hotel Palmer Street. This old wooden hotel is the place of choice for a decent steak and a drink in their attractive beer garden.

The Balcony Flinders Street Mall. Mediterranean-style salads and grills; also good coffee and cakes and a great view over the mall from upper-storey balcony tables. Mains $12–20.

Benny's Hot Wok Palmer St. Stylish and popular Singaporean and Asian café-restaurant, with tasty bowls of noodle soup for around $12, and Indonesian or Thai curries for about $18.

Brewery Cnr of Denham and Flinders. Café, bar and boutique brewery housed in the old post office building. The beer and ambience are good, though the outdoor tables are a bit noisy thanks to the adjacent main road.

C-Bar The Strand. One of the several café-restaurants in the area – right on the seafront with outside tables and a bar overlooking Magnetic Island. Good for anything from a coffee or beer to succulent char-grilled steak or lamb kebabs and salad. Happy hour daily from 5pm to 6pm, with live local bands on Sun evenings. Mains around $18.

Café Nova Cnr of Blackwood and Flinders streets, near the station. A student venue, with generous helpings and meals for under $15. Serves huge and tasty salads. Tues–Fri 10.30am–midnight, Sat & Sun 6pm–midnight.

Covers Upstairs at 209 Flinders St East ☎07/4721 4630. A café-bar-restaurant that's primarily somewhere to go to be seen. The menu features decent-sized grills including Australian game meats, such as crocodile and kangaroo, for around $25. Tues–Sun from 6pm.

Harold's Fish and Chips The Strand, opposite the *C-Bar*. If you can't catch your own from the nearby fishing jetty, console yourself with a take-away from this excellent establishment.

Reef Thai Flinders St. Seafood green curry, satays and the chilli-packed beef dish known as "crying tiger". Mains around $11. Daily 5.30–10pm.

Stanley's Cnr Flinders and Stanley streets. Airy café and bistro serving early breakfasts, pasta, ornate sandwiches, and grills.

Yongala Restaurant 11 Fryer St, in front of the *Yongala Lodge* ☎07/4772 4633. Historic, authentically furnished surroundings where you can enjoy live music and good, Greek-influenced food. Appropriately, the building's architect was on the *Yongala* when it sank.

Pubs, bars and clubs

Bank Flinders St East. Drunken mix of military and locals makes this a sometimes heavy nightclub sporting Corinthian columns, spiked iron railings and bars on the windows.

Exchange Hotel Flinders St East. A real locals' watering-hole in a run-down pub, with occasional live bands.

Mad Cow Flinders St East. Pool tables and dancing to "Top 40" tunes – packed on weekends.

Molly Malones Flinders St East. Standard Irish bar with stout on tap. Happy hour Mon–Fri 5–6pm, live bands Wed & Sat, and Irish dancing on Sun evenings.

Listings

Airlines Virgin flies to Brisbane, and Qantas to everywhere else.

Banks All located on Flinders Street Mall; there are ATMs in most pubs and at the Transit Centre.

Bookshops Mary Who?, 414 Flinders St, has a fine range of everything.

Buses Greyhound Pioneer ☎07/4772 5100; McCafferty's ☎07/4772 5100; Premier ☎13 34 10.

Car and scooter rental Independent, 25 Yeatman St (☎1800 678 843), has basic models from $30 a day; Townsville Car and Scooter Rentals, 12 Palmer St (☎07/4772 1093), starts at $28 per day for a car, $7.15 for a scooter, and $10 for a push-bike; Europcar (☎13 13 90) is the cheapest of the major car rental companies.

Hospital Townsville General Hospital, Eyre St ☎07/4781 9211.

Internet access At the Transit Centre, and next to Perc Tucker Gallery in the Mall ($5–6 per hour).

Left luggage At the Transit Centre and airport.

NPWS Information on regional parks at the Reef HQ (Mon–Sat 9am–5pm; ☎07/4721 2399).

Police 30 Stanley St ☎07/4760 7777.

Post office Behind the Mall in Sturt Street, near the junction with Stanley Street.

Swimming Tobruk Swimming Pool, The Strand, in the parkland on the north side of the road, about 1km west of the junction with Wickham St.

Taxi There's a stand at Flinders Street Mall ☎13 10 08.

Tours Townsville Tropical Tours (☎07/4721 6489, ⓦwww.townsvilletropicaltours.com.au) runs small, personalized 4WD day-tours to rainforest at Paluma ($110), the old gold-mining town of Charters Towers ($130), and more forest and waterfalls at Wallaman Falls ($130).

Magnetic Island

Another island named by Captain Cook in 1770 – after his compass played up as he sailed past – **Magnetic Island** is a beautiful triangular granite core about 12km from Townsville. There's a lot to be said for a trip: lounging on a beach, swimming over coral, bouncing around in a moke from one road-side lookout to another, and enjoying the sea breeze and the island's vivid colours. Small enough to drive around in half a day, but large enough to harbour several small settlements, Magnetic Island's accommodation and transfer costs are considerably lower than on many of Queensland's other islands, and if you've ever wanted to spot a **koala** in the wild, this could be your chance – they're often seen wedged into gum trees up in the northeast corner of the island.

Seen from the sea, the island's apex of **Mount Cook** hovers above eucalypt woods variegated with patches of darker green vine forest. The north and east coasts are pinched into shallow sandy bays punctuated by granite headlands and coral reefs, while the western part of the island is flatter and edged with mangroves. A little less than half the island is designated a **national park**, with the settlements of **Picnic Bay**, **Nelly Bay**, **Arcadia** and **Horseshoe Bay** dotted along the east coast. Shops and supplies are available on the island, so there's no need to bring anything with you.

Arrival, island transport and diving

At present, **Sunferries** (☎07/4771 3855) leaves from the Flinders Street East terminal and the Breakwater terminal for Picnic Bay at the island's southern-most point at least ten times daily, with extra departures at weekends ($16.95 return); pick up a **timetable** from any information booth. There's no need to book, just buy a ticket at the jetty and hop on board. There's also a **car ferry** (☎07/4772 5422; $123 return for a car and up to six passengers; pedestrians $17 return), to Geoffrey Bay, Arcadia, at least four times daily from Ross Street, a ten-minute walk east along Palmer Street from the Transit Centre. A **new marina** is being built further up Magnetic Island's east coast at Nelly Bay, and when this opens (nobody knows exactly when; the project has been plagued by delays) both ferries will probably run direct to this new marina instead; prices are also expected to rise.

The island has 35km of road, including a dirt track to West Point and a sealed stretch between Picnic and Horseshoe bays. **Magnetic Island Bus Service** (☎07/4778 5130) meets all ferries and runs between Picnic Bay and Horseshoe Bay more or less hourly between 7.40am and 7.20pm; their day pass

($11) allows unlimited travel. For your **own transport**, Moke Magnetic at Picnic Bay mall (℡07/4778 5377) rents out fun mini-mokes for a flat $65 a day, plus $100 deposit; MI Wheels at Horseshoe Bay (℡07/4778 5491) seems cheaper at $42 a day, though here you pay an additional $0.33 per kilometre and have to return the car with a full fuel tank. Both require a minimum driver age of 21, and ask that you stick to sealed roads. Various places on the island, including accommodation, rent out **bicycles** for about $14 a day, while Road Runner (℡07/4778 5222), in the mall at Picnic Bay, has scooters from $30 a day. For a **tour**, plump for a day out in a 4WD with Tropicana (℡07/4758 1800, ⓦwww.tropicanatours.com.au; $125); the cost seems steep, but you get very well fed and looked after, plus you'll see just about all the island's beaches and bays. You could also spend a day **sailing** to hard-to-reach beaches and bays with *Jazza* (℡1800 808 002, ⓦwww.jazza.com.au; $75), including snorkelling, lunch and afternoon tea; or try your hand **sea-kayaking** with Magnetic Island Sea Kayaks (℡0/4778 5424; $45, including breakfast).

Relatively murky waters don't make Magnetic Island the most dramatic place to learn to **scuba dive**, but with easy shore access it's very cheap – certification courses start at $199 – and on a good day there's some fair coral, a couple of small shipwrecks and decent fish life. Operators include Pleasure Divers (℡1800 797 797), and Dive Shack (℡07/4778 5690), both near *Arkie's Resort* at Arcadia; both can also arrange dives on the *Yongala* (see p.504).

Accommodation

Magnetic Island's **accommodation** is ubiquitous, with options for all budgets. Most lodgings have **Internet**, rent out snorkelling gear, bikes, beach gear and watersports equipment, can make tour bookings and might pick you up if you call in advance.

Picnic Bay and Nelly Bay

Dunoon The Esplanade, Picnic Bay ℡07/4778 5161, ⓦwww.dunoon.au.com. Huge pool and shady palm garden surround fairly simple, fully furnished one- and two-bedroom apartments, some with sea views. ❺

Magnetic Island Tropical Resort Yates St, Nelly Bay ℡07/4778 5955, Ⓕ4778 5601. Clean and comfortable chalet-style cabins with bathroom, in a lovely bush setting. Good-value evening bistro, pool, kitchen, BBQ, plus lots of friendly birdlife. Dorms $18, cabins ❸

Palm View Chalets 114 Sooning St, Nelly Bay ℡07/4778 5596. Self-contained and very private A-frame units surrounded by palms and views; advance booking essential. ❹

Travellers Backpacker Resort *Picnic Bay Hotel*, The Esplanade, Picnic Bay ℡1800 000 290, ⓦwww.travellers-on-maggie.com. Comfortable units and four- to six-bed dorms, plus a large pool, beer garden, kitchen and BBQ. The downside is the various nightly events laid on by the hotel, designed to draw local customers eager to see backpackers behaving badly. Dorms $12, units ❷

Arcadia

Arkie's Resort 7 Marine Parade ℡1800 663 666. Motel-style units set around a pool, with a good bistro, plus a bar that aspires to be the island's main nightclub – though, again, resident backpackers are used as entertainment to increase bar custom. Dorms $15, doubles ❷

Beaches Bed & Breakfast 39 Marine Parade ℡07/4778 5303, Ⓔbeaches@tpgi.com.au. Small, quiet timber guesthouse with cool slate floors, a pool, gardens and just two rooms, right across the road from the beach. ❸

Centaur House ℡1800 655 680, ⓦwww.bpf.com.au. Restored 1940s beach house, with fine bedrooms and shared bathrooms, helpful owners and a very relaxing atmosphere, plus good snorkelling just across the road in Geoffrey Bay. The kitchen is best avoided, though. Fifth night free. Dorm $18, rooms ❷

Magnetic North Apartments 2 Endeavour Rd ℡07/4778 5647, Ⓔmagneticnorth@iprimus.com.au. Large apartments sleeping up to six; nothing flash, but good value. ❹

Marshall's 3 Endeavor Rd ℡07/4778 5112. Very

friendly B&B with a family atmosphere and quiet garden; facilities are nothing special, but the owners more than make up for it. Three-day discounts are available. ❸–❹

Horseshoe Bay

Geoff's Place 40 Horseshoe Bay Rd ☎1800 285 577, ⓦ www.geoffsplace.com.au. Busy and crowded hostel, with a party atmosphere, pool, bar and campsite. The owner feeds hundreds of wild lorikeets every afternoon. Dorms $17.60, rooms ❷

Maggie's Beach House Pacific Drive ☎07/4778 5114, ⓦ www.maggiesbeachhouse.com.au. Large,

purpose-built backpackers' complex overlooking the sea, with its own pool, budget restaurant, Internet facilities and bar. The place is well run, although you can't help feeling that this sort of high-density accommodation misses the whole point of Magnetic Island. Dorms $21, rooms ❸

New Friends Bed & Breakfast Horseshoe Bay Rd ☎07/4758 1220. Spacious, well-furnished apartments in large grounds a five-minute walk from the beach. ❺

Sails 13 Pacific Drive ☎07/4778 5117, Ⓕ4778 5104. Secluded, self-contained apartments with all mod-cons, including pool and outdoor BBQ area. One-bedroom apartments ❻, villas ❼

The island

Set on the southernmost tip of the island, **PICNIC BAY** is a languid spot, well shaded by surrounding gum woodland and beachfront fig trees, and offering a welcome contrast to Townsville's parched environment. Picnic Bay's **beach** has a swimming enclosure and is pretty enough, but most people head off after sorting out transport. The bay's focus is a hundred-metre-long pedestrian **mall** where you'll find a cluster of shops, including a **bank**, **post office** and Dee Jay's **store**. For somewhere to **eat**, *Mermaid's* and *Feedja Café* (which uses only organic ingredients) serve tasty meals in a courtyard setting, while *Crusoe's* (closed Mon) has more upmarket grills; all are on the mall and like everywhere else to eat on the island, they shut by 8pm.

Nelly Bay, Arcadia and the Forts

On the east coast, north of Picnic Bay, **NELLY BAY** comprises a sprawl of houses fronted by a good beach with a little reef some way out, though the **new marina** under construction here will probably draw many businesses away from Picnic Bay when it opens. Two streets back is a shopping complex with a supermarket, Mexican **restaurant** and coffee shop, while the **aquarium** (daily 9am–5pm; $3) just around the corner has tanks of giant clams – all part of a research project, and only open to the public as an afterthought. Alternatively, there's a **walking track to Arcadia** from here, though it can be hot work – start early and take plenty of water. A little further along the coast, **ARCADIA** surrounds **Geoffrey Bay** and counts the good-value *Banister's Seafood Restaurant* among its attractions. At Arcadia's northern end is the perfect swimming beach of **Alma Bay**, hemmed in by cliffs and boulders, and with good snorkelling over the coral just offshore. **Diving** here is marred by low visibility, but there are plenty of fish and brain coral, and a disintegrating shipwreck. A walking track from the end of Cook Road leads towards Mount Cook and the track to Nelly Bay, or up to **Sphinx Lookout** for sea views. At dawn or dusk you might see the diminutive island **rock wallaby** on an outcrop or boulder near Arcadia's jetty.

North of Arcadia the road forks, with the right branch (prohibited to rental vehicles) leading via tiny **Florence Bay** – one of the prettiest on the island – to **Radical Bay**, and the main road carrying on to Horseshoe. Leave your car at the junction and continue uphill on foot to **the Forts**, built during World War II to protect Townsville from attack by the Japanese. The walking track climbs gently for about 1.5km through gum-tree scenery to gun emplacements (now just deserted blockhouses) set one above the other among granite boulders and pine trees. The best views are from the slit windows at the command centre, right at the pinnacle of the hill. The woods below the Forts are the best place to see **koalas**, introduced to the island in 1930. They sleep during the day, so tracking them down involves plenty of wandering around – although if you hear ferocious pig-like grunts and squeals, then some lively koalas are not far away.

Horseshoe Bay and around

The road ends in the north at **HORSESHOE BAY** on the island's longest beach, with views north across a blue sea to distant Palm Island. The cluster of shops at the road's eastern end feature a **general store**, bakery, and the *Marlin Bar and Grill*, while a couple of beachfront operators here **rent** out jet skis, kayaks, surf skis and boats. Other diversions include **horse rides** with the experienced Bluey's Horseshoe Ranch ($48 for the popular beach ride, $66 for a half-day ride; advance bookings necessary on ☎07/4778 5109). **Walking tracks** lead over the headland to Radical Bay by way of tiny **Balding Bay**, arguably the nicest on the island; you can spend a perfect day here snorkelling around the coral gardens just offshore and cooking on the hotplate provided. **Radical Bay** itself is another pretty spot, half a kilometre of sandy beach sandwiched between two huge, pine-swathed granite fists.

Townsville to Cairns

Just an hour to the north of Townsville the arid landscape that has prevailed since Bundaberg transforms into dark green plateaus shrouded in cloud. There's superlative scenery at **Wallaman Falls**, inland from **Ingham**, and also near Cairns as the slopes of the coastal mountains rise up to front the **Bellenden Ker Range**. Forests here once formed a continuous belt almost to Cooktown, but logging has thinned them to a disjointed necklace of plantations and national parks. Even so, it seems that almost every side-track off the highway leads to a waterhole or falls surrounded by natural jungle – this is where it really pays to have your own vehicle. There's also a handful of islands to explore, including the wilds of **Hinchinbrook**, as well as the **Mission Beach** area between **Tully** and **Innisfail**, where you might find regular **work** on fruit plantations or further opportunities to slump on the sand.

Paluma and Jourama Falls

The change in climate starts some 60km north of Townsville, where the Mount Spec road turns west off the highway and climbs a crooked 21km into the hills to **Paluma** township. Halfway there, a solid stone **bridge**, built by relief labour during the Great Depression in the 1930s, spans **Little Crystal Creek**, with some picnic tables and barbeque hotplates by the road, and deep **swimming holes** overshadowed by rainforest just up from the bridge – beware of slippery rocks and potentially strong currents. Look out too for large, metallic-blue Ulysses **butterflies** bobbing around the canopy.

PALUMA itself consists of a handful of weatherboard cottages in the rainforest at the top of the range. A couple of **walking tracks** (from 500m to

2km in length) take you into the gloom, including a ridgetop track to **Witt's Lookout**; keep your eyes open for **chowchillas**, plump little birds with a dark body and white front which forage by kicking the leaf litter sideways; you'll also hear whipbirds and the snarls of the black-and-blue **Victoria riflebird**, a bird of paradise – they're fairly common in highland rainforest between here and the Atherton Tablelands, but elusive. For a good glimpse of these head for *Ivy Cottage Tearooms* (Tues–Sun 10am–4pm), whose garden and birdtable is the local riflebird population's favourite afternoon haunt; their Devonshire cream teas aren't bad either. They also offer B&B **accommodation** (℡07/4770 8533; ❹); alternatives include self-contained cabins at *Misthaven Units* (℡07/4770 8520; ❹), and two cottages for rent (℡07/4770 8520; ❺).

Past Paluma the range descends west, leaving the dark, wet coastal forest for open gum woodland. *Hidden Valley Cabins* (℡07/4770 8088, ⓦwww .hiddenvalleycabins.com.au; ❷–❹), 24km beyond Paluma on a dirt road, provides everything you'll need: spa, pool, beer, meals and packed lunches. Nearby is **the Gorge**, a lively section of river with falls, rapids and pools – drive down in a 4WD or walk the last kilometre.

Back on the coastal highway heading north, you pass the *Frosty Mango* roadhouse (daily 8am–6pm), whose exotic fresh cakes and ice creams are made from locally grown fruit, before encountering more aquatic fun at **Jourama Falls**, 30km from the Paluma road. After turning west off the highway, the five-kilometre unsurfaced road to Jourama ends at a low-key NPWS campsite (contact Ingham NPWS for booking details) set amongst gum and wattle bushland peppered with huge **cycads**. From here an hour-long walking track follows chains across the rocky riverbed to more swimming holes surrounded by gigantic granite boulders and cliffs, finally winding up at the falls themselves – which are impressive in full flood but fairly insignificant by the end of the dry season.

Ingham and around

Home to Australia's largest Italian community, the small town of **INGHAM**, 110km north of Townsville, is well placed for trips inland to **Lumholtz National Park** – home to Australia's highest waterfall – and also gives access to the tiny port of **Lucinda**, the southern terminus for ferries to Hinchinbrook Island (p.512). Pasta and wine are to be had in abundance during the May **Italian Festival**, but the town is better known for events surrounding the former *Day Dawn Hotel* (now *Lee's Hotel*) on Lannercost Street, the legendary "**Pub with No Beer**". During World War II, Ingham was the first stop for serviceman heading north from Townsville, and in 1941 they drank the bar dry, a momentous occasion recorded by local poet Dan Sheahan and later turned into a popular ballad.

Cycads

Cycads are extremely slow-growing, fire-resistant plants found throughout the tropics, with tough, palm-like fronds – relics of the age of dinosaurs. Female plants produce bright orange seed cones which, in Australia, are eaten (and thus distributed) by emus. Despite being highly toxic to humans – almost every early Australian explorer made themselves violently ill trying them – these seeds were a staple of Aborigines, who detoxified flour made from the nuts by prolonged washing. They also applied "fire-stick farming" techniques, encouraging groves to grow and seed by annual burning.

The highway curves through town as Herbert Street, though most services are located slightly to the west along Lannercost Street. Interstate **buses** stop ten times daily just where the southern highway meets Lannercost Street; **trains** stop 1km east on Lynch Street – you can buy tickets at Ingham Travel on Lannercost. Information is available at the well-informed **Hinchinbrook Visitor Centre** (Mon–Fri 8.45am–5pm, Sat & Sun 9am–2pm; ⓦwww .hinchinbrooknq.com), on the corner where the highway from Townsville meets Lannercost Street; they also stock brochures on local national parks.

Accommodation options include *Palm Tree Caravan Park* (☎07/4776 2403; cabins ❸); straightforward pub rooms at *Lee's Hotel* (☎07/4776 1503; ❷, including hot breakfast); or basic dorm beds at the *Royal Hotel* (☎07/4776 2024; $12) on Lannercost Street. *Lee's* does filling budget **meals** – lunches are just $3.50 from Monday to Wednesday – and the bar hasn't run out of beer since the 1940s. The *Olive Tree Coffee Lounge*, just a few doors along from the Visitor Centre, is a great Italian place, with home-made pizza and pasta. For the various sections of Lumholtz National Park, turn west down Lannercost Street and follow the road to **Trebonne** (lucidly marked, "This road is not Route 1"); for Lucinda, follow the signs for Forest Beach and Halifax from the town centre.

Lumholtz National Park

Several disconnected areas of wilds west of Ingham together form **Lumholtz National Park**, named after the nineteenth-century Danish ethnographer Karl Lumholtz, who passed through in the 1880s. The road from Ingham divides 20km along at Trebonne, with separate routes from here to either Mount Fox or Wallaman Falls. For **Mount Fox**, stay on the road for 55km as it crosses cattle country to the base of this extinct volcano cone; the last two kilometres are dirt and can be quite rough. A rocky, unmarked path climbs to the crater rim through scanty forest; it's hot work, so start early. The crater itself is only about 10m deep, tangled in vine forest and open woodland. With prior permission, you might be able to **camp** at the nearby township's cricket grounds – either ask at the school, or call ☎07/4777 5117.

The signposted **Wallaman Falls** route is a dusty 40km run along a mostly sealed road up the tight and twisting range. Tunnelling through thick rainforest along the ridge, the road emerges at a bettong-infested NPWS **campsite** before reaching the falls **lookout**. The falls – at 280m, Australia's highest – are spectacular, leaping in a thin ribbon over the sheer cliffs of the plateau opposite and appearing to vaporize by the time they reach the gorge floor. A walk down a narrow and slippery path from the lookout to the base dispels this impression, as the mist turns out to be from the force of water hitting the plunge pool. If you're staying the night, walk from the campsite along the adjacent quiet stretch of Stoney Creek at dawn or late afternoon to see **platypuses**.

Cardwell

Some 50km north from Ingham lies the modest little town of **CARDWELL** – just a quiet string of shops on one side of the highway, with the sea on the other – though it's made attractive by the outline of Hinchinbrook Island, which hovers just offshore, so close that it almost seems to be part of the mainland. In recent years, Cardwell has become a bit of an environmental battleground as a result of the controversial **Port Hinchinbrook Marina**, which was built during the 1990s just south of town in a "protected" mangrove zone and dugong (sea cow) sanctuary. The resulting increase in marine traffic and the uncontrolled access to Hinchinbrook could be disastrous for this fragile area, and the numbers of once-common dugongs, and the sea-grass beds on which they feed, have already declined drastically.

Cardwell spreads for about 2km along the highway, with banks, the post office, supermarket, and hotel all near or south of the **old jetty**, itself about halfway along the road. **Buses** pull up beside the BP service station and *Seaview Café* at the "Transit Centre" – actually just an open-sided bus shelter; the **train station** is about 200m further back. You can buy **tickets** at the agent next to the *Seaview Café* or, if they're closed, in the café itself (open daily 8am until late). Just north of the jetty, the NPWS-run **Rainforest and Reef Centre** (Mon–Fri 8am–4.30pm, Sat & Sun 8am–noon; free; ☎07/4066 8601) issues **island permits** and has a walk-through rainforest and mangrove display.

The best of the **accommodation** is north of the jetty at the *Kookaburra Holiday Park*, 175 Bruce Highway (☎07/4066 8648, ⓦwww.kookaburra holidaypark.com.au; dorms $18.50, cabins ❷, motel rooms ❸), which has motel rooms, tent sites and a self-contained backpackers' block, plus free use of bikes and fishing gear. Alternatively, try the *Cardwell Beachfront Motel*, 1 Scott St (☎07/4066 8776, ⓕ4066 2300; ❸), a low-key, standard place which faces the sea. For **food**, *Annie's Kitchen*, just up the highway from the bus stop, opens early and is the best of the town's numerous cafés; fish and chips can be had from *Cardwell Seafood* – the last building at the north end of town; if you're self-catering, head for DA's Supermarket.

As well as running to Hinchinbrook Island, Hinchinbrook Ferries (see Hinchinbrook Island "Practicalities" on p.513) also runs day-trips ($85) to the reef around **Garden** and **Gould islands** – you can camp on either. **Bareboats** from Hinchinbrook Rent a Yacht (☎07/4066 8007) work out at around $90 per person per day in a group of six.

Hinchinbrook Island

Across the channel from Cardwell, **Hinchinbrook Island** looms huge and green, with mangroves rising to forest along the mountain range that forms the island's spine, peaking at **Mount Bowen**. The island's drier east side, hidden behind the mountains, has long beaches separated by headlands and the occasional sluggish creek. This was Giramay Aboriginal land, and though early Europeans reported the people as friendly, attitudes later changed and nineteenth-century "dispersals" had the same effect here as elsewhere. The island was never subsequently occupied, and apart from a single resort, Hinchinbrook remains much as it was two hundred years ago.

The island's main attraction is the 32-kilometre-long **Thorsborne Trail**, a moderately demanding hiking track along the east coast which takes in forests, mangroves, waterfalls and beaches. More adventurous, unmarked routes scale **Mount Straloch** – site of a USAF B24 plane wreck from World War II – and Mount Bowen; you'll need advice from the NPWS in Cardwell (see above) if you want to tackle these.

The Thorsborne Trail

The 32-kilometre **Thorsborne Trail** is manageable in two days, though at that pace you won't see much. **Trailheads** are at Ramsay Bay in the north and George Point in the south, and the route is marked with orange triangles (north to south), or yellow triangles (south to north). The difficulties are pretty much the same whichever direction you choose to travel; the advantage to ending up in the north is that the pick-up with Hinchinbrook Ferries includes a welcome few hours unwinding at the *Hinchinbrook Island Wilderness Lodge*'s bar and pool.

Boats **from Cardwell** take you through the mangroves of Missionary Bay in the north to a boardwalk that crosses to the eastern side of the island at **Ramsay Bay**. The walk from here to **Nina Bay**, which takes a couple of hours, is along a fantastic stretch of coast with rainforest sweeping right down to the sand and Mount Bowen and Nina Peak as a backdrop. If long bushwalks don't appeal, you could spend a few days camped on the forest's edge at Nina instead; a creek at the southern end provides drinking water and Nina Peak can be climbed in an hour or so. Otherwise, continue beyond a small cliff at the southern end of Nina, and walk for another two hours or so through a pine forest to **Little Ramsay Bay** (drinking water from Warrawilla Creek), which is about as far as you're likely to get on the first day.

Moving on, you rock-hop over boulders at the far end of the beach before crossing another creek (at low tide, as it gets fairly deep) and entering the forest beyond. From here to the next camp at **Zoe Bay** takes about five hours, following creek beds through lowland casuarina woods and rainforest, before exiting onto the beach near Cypress Pine waterhole. A clearing and pit toilets at the southern end of Zoe Bay marks the campsite, and water bottles can be filled just beyond. This is one of those places where you'll be very glad you brought insect repellent.

Next day, take the path to the base of **Zoe Falls** – the **waterhole** here is fabulous – then struggle straight up beside them to the cliff top, from where there are great vistas. Across the river, forest and heathland alternate: the hardest part is crossing **Diamantina Creek** – a fast-flowing river with huge, slippery granite boulders. **Mulligan Falls**, not much further on, is the last source of fresh water, with several rock ledges for sunbathing above a pool full of curious fish. Zoe to Mulligan takes around four hours, and from here to George Point is only a couple more if you push it, but the falls are a better place to camp and give you the chance to backtrack a little to take a look at the beachside lagoon at **Sunken Reef Bay**.

The last leg to **George Point** is the least interesting: rainforest replaces the highland trees around the falls as the path crosses a final creek before arriving at unattractive Mulligan Bay. The campsite at George Point has a table and fireplace in the shelter of a coconut grove but there's no fresh water and nothing to see except Lucinda's sugar terminal, and little to do except wait for your ferry.

Practicalities

If you're not interested in a serious hike, Hinchinbrook Ferries (T 1800 777 021, W www.hinchinbrookferries.com.au) offers an excellent **day-trip** ($85) from the marina at Cardwell, cruising after dugong and stopping for a three-kilometre beach and rainforest walk before winding up with a dip in the pool at the *Hinchinbrook Island Wilderness Lodge* (T 1800 777 021, W www.hinchin brookresort.com.au; four-person cabins ❻, units ❼), which is where you'll find the island's only proper **accommodation**. The lodge is set on Cape Richards at Hinchinbrook's northernmost tip and makes a comfortable retreat, with either self-contained cabins or luxury treehouse units.

The Thorsborne Trail needs some **advance planning**. As visitor numbers to the island are restricted, the trail is usually booked solid: for the Christmas and Easter holidays, aim to book at least four months in advance. Also note that there are no ferries through February and March. The Cardwell NPWS office hands out trail **maps**, practical details, and **camping permits** ($4 per person per night), which can also be registered online at ⓦ www.epa.qld.gov.au. Since different **ferries** service the north and south ends of the island, you'll need to make two separate bookings if you're planning to enter and exit from separate ends of the trail. Hinchinbrook's north is served by Hinchinbrook Island Ferries from Cardwell's marina ($59 one way). For the south, contact Bill Pearce at Hinchinbrook Wilderness Safaris in Lucinda (ⓣ07/4777 8307; $46 one way, and $58/65 for a pick-up from the island plus a bus back to Ingham/Cardwell). Both operators also offer return fares for their ends of the island; contact them for prices.

Optimum hiking **conditions** are during winter (June–Oct), though it can rain throughout the year. Essentials include water-resistant footgear, pack and tent, a lightweight raincoat and insect repellent. Although streams with **drinking water** are fairly evenly distributed, they might be dry by the end of winter, or only flowing upstream from the beach – collect from flowing sources only. Wood fires are prohibited, so bring a fuel stove. Accommodation and booking agents in Cardwell rent out limited **camping gear**. White-tailed rats and marsupial mice will gnaw through tents to reach food; the NPWS has installed metal food stores at campsites, though hanging anything edible from a branch may foil their attempts. Snakes are also common, if seldom encountered, and you should beware of crocodiles in lowland creek systems.

Edmund Kennedy National Park, Murray Falls and Tully

In May 1848, the **Edmund Kennedy expedition** landed just a few kilometres north of where Cardwell was later to be founded, and set off to walk to Cape York. Thick vegetation forced them to abandon their one hundred sheep and three carts, and, harassed by local tribes, the party gradually ran out of food; by December, Kennedy had left the others while he raced the last 100km with his Aboriginal companion, **Jackey-Jackey Galmarra**. Kennedy was killed by Jadhaigana Aborigines while negotiating a river within sight of the cape; Jackey managed to reach the waiting schooner *Ariel*, which set off down the coast to find only two of the other expedition members still alive. The little **Edmund Kennedy National Park**, down a short road off the highway 22km from Cardwell, marks the spot where the doomed expedition struck inland, and you have to ponder the wisdom of trying to manoeuvre carts through the paperbark and mangrove thickets – romantically described by Kennedy's informant as "wooded hills and green valleys". There are boardwalks and trails through the park, and views across to Dunk and Hinchinbrook islands from the beach.

The road to the small but attractive **Murray Falls**, off the highway 10km further north, heads 20km inland past banana plantations to the edge of the Cardwell Range and the falls themselves. It's really just worth a look to break your journey, but there are also two free **camping areas** here and tracks through the forest to permanent swimming holes and lookouts across the bowl of the valley. The nearest source of supplies is the store on the approach road, some distance from the falls.

Some 45km north of Cardwell, **TULLY** lies to the left of the highway on the slopes of **Mount Tyson**, its 450-centimetre annual rainfall the highest in Australia. Settled by Chinese, who pioneered banana plantations here at the beginning of the twentieth century, it's a stopover for **white-water rafting** day-trips out of Cairns and Mission Beach on the fierce Tully River, 40km inland, but otherwise nothing special: cultivated lawns and flowerbeds back onto roaring jungle at the end of Brannigan Street, a constant reminder of the colonists' struggle to keep chaos at bay. Though most people drive the extra thirty minutes to Mission Beach (see below), there's **accommodation** here at *Green Way Caravan Park* (℡07/4068 2055; cabins ❸); while the well-managed *Banana Barracks* hostel at 50 Butler Street (℡07/4068 0455, ⓦwww .bananabarracks.com) has excellent **work** connections, plus free weekend beach trips and barbecues.

Mission Beach and Dunk Island

After branching east off the Bruce Highway a couple of kilometres past Tully, a loop road runs 18km through canefields and patches of rainforest to **Mission Beach**, the collective name for four peaceful hamlets strung out along a four-teen-kilometre stretch of sand – the area owes its name to the former **Hull River Mission**, destroyed by a savage cyclone in 1918. Aside from the lure of the beach, forests here are a reliable place to spot **cassowaries**, a blue-headed and bone-crested rainforest version of the emu, whose survival is being threat-ened as their habitat is carved up – estimates calculate that there are only a couple of thousand birds left, all in tropical Queensland. Many larger trees rely on the cassowary to eat their fruit and distribute their seeds, meaning that the very makeup of the forest hinges on the bird's presence. Unlike the emu, cas-sowaries are not at all timid and can attack if they feel threatened: if you see one, remain quiet and keep a safe distance.

Right down at the bottom end of the beach, **SOUTH MISSION** is a quiet, mostly residential spot, with a long, clean beach. Signposted off the main road on Mission Drive is a monument to the original site of the Hull River Mission; after the cyclone, the mission was relocated to safer surroundings on Palm Island. At the end of beachfront Kennedy Esplanade, the **Kennedy Walking Track** weaves through coastal swamp and forest for a couple of hours to the spot where Edmund Kennedy originally landed near the mouth of the Hull River – a good place to spot coastal birdlife and, most likely, crocodiles.

Heading 4km north of South Mission takes you to **WONGALING BEACH**, a slowly expanding settlement based around a shopping centre and Mission's only **pub**. A further 4km lands you at **MISSION BEACH** itself, a cluster of shops, boutiques, restaurants, banks, and a post office one block back from the beach on Porter Promenade. Inland between the two, a six-kilometre-long walking track weaves through **Tam O'Shanter State Forest**, a dense maze of muddy creeks, vine thickets and stands of licula palms (identified by their frilly, saucer-shaped leaves). If you don't see cassowaries here – sometimes leading their knee-high, striped chicks through the undergrowth – you're very unlucky. Continuing 6km north of Mission township past **Clump Point** – a black basalt outcrop with views south down the beach sitting above **Clump Point Jetty** – the road winds through sleepy **BINGIL BAY** and then heads back to the highway.

Mission Beach practicalities

Long-distance buses set down outside the post office at Mission Beach, from where your accommodation might collect you if forewarned. Alternatively, a local **bus** (℡07/4068 5468) plies between South Mission and Bingil Bay roughly eight times daily between 8.30am and 8.30pm (restricted service Sat); for a taxi call ℡07/4068 8155. The **Visitor Information Centre** (Mon–Sat 9am–5pm, Sun 9am–1pm) is just north of Mission Beach township along Porter Promenade. Behind the centre, the **Environmental Information**

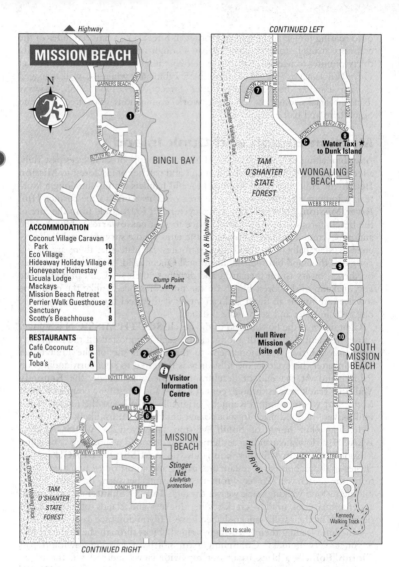

MISSION BEACH

N

BINGIL BAY

ACCOMMODATION

Coconut Village Caravan Park	10
Eco Village	3
Hideaway Holiday Village	4
Honeyeater Homestay	9
Licuala Lodge	7
Mackays	6
Mission Beach Retreat	5
Perrier Walk Guesthouse	2
Sanctuary	1
Scotty's Beachhouse	8

RESTAURANTS

Café Coconutz	B
Pub	C
Toba's	A

Clump Point Jetty

Visitor Information Centre

MISSION BEACH

Stinger Net (Jellyfish protection)

TAM O'SHANTER STATE FOREST

CONCH STREET

SEAVIEW STREET

BOYETT ROAD

CAMPBELL ST

Tully & Highway

TAM O'SHANTER STATE FOREST

Water Taxi ★ to Dunk Island

WONGALING BEACH

WEBB STREET

MISSION CIRCLE

Hull River Mission (site of)

SOUTH MISSION BEACH

Hull River

JACKY JACKY STREET

Kennedy Walking Track

Not to scale

Centre (daily 10am–5pm) has a display on local habitat, along with a nursery growing seeds collected from cassowary droppings, with the aim of safeguarding the food supply for future generations of this giant bird. There are stores and places to **eat** at all four hamlets, though only Mission Beach has a comprehensive range – the best of the **restaurants** here are *Toba*'s eclectic "Asian" menu, and stylishly presented grills at *Café Coconutz*, which also has a bar.

There are also a few local **tours** worth looking out for. Skydive Mission (☎1800 638 005, ⍟www.jumpthebeach.com) can take you to eight thousand feet for freefall fun ($235), and also offers skydiving plus Tully River white-water rafting packages ($348). If it's riverine wildlife you're after, Hinchinbrook Explorer (⊕07/4088 6154) runs four-hour croc-spotting trips with dinner thrown in ($40), or you can go paddling with Coral Sea Kayaking (⊕07/4068 9154, ⊛www.coralseakayaking.com; $89).

Accommodation

Places to stay are fairly evenly distributed along the coast and cover everything from camping to resorts. All can provide information and book you on white-water rafting and other tours in the area. **Campsites** include the tidy *Coconut Village Caravan Park* at South Mission (⊕07/4068 8129; units ❷), and the *Hideaway Holiday Village* at Mission Beach (⊕07/4068 7104; cabins ❸).

Eco Village Clump Point ⊕07/4068 7534, ⊛www.ecovillage.com.au. Smart, motel-like accommodation set just back from the beach amongst pandanus, native nutmeg trees and tropical gardens. Luxury rooms have Jacuzzi and private pool. ❺

Honeyeater Homestay 53 Reid Rd, Wongaling ⊕07/4068 8741, ⊜honeat@znet.net.au. Delightful, Balinese-inspired house, with lush tropical gardens surrounding the pool making the place look far larger and more secluded than it actually is. Only takes a maximum of six people. ❸

Licuala Lodge 11 Mission Circle, Mission Beach ⊕07/4068 8194, ⊛www.licualalodge.com.au. A tropical-style B&B with airy wooden verandahs and traditional, high-ceilinged interior; the landscaped garden and pool are worth a stay in themselves, and the huge breakfast will keep you going all day. ❺

Mackays 7 Porter Promenade, Mission Beach ⊕07/4068 7212, ⊛www.mackaysmission beach.com.au. Standard Australian resort complex, with comfortable modern units arranged around gardens and a pool. ❹

Mission Beach Retreat Mission Beach ⊕1800 001 056, ⊕07/4088 6111. New backpackers' joint right next to the shops and bus stop in Mission Beach, close to the beach and with a decent-sized pool. Dorms $19.

Perrier Walk Guesthouse Perrier Walk, Mission Beach ⊕07/4068 7141, ⊛www.perrierwalk.nq.au. Vivid tropical architecture, with a mix of Thai, Indonesian and Mexican elements in the guesthouse design and decor; friendly and very comfortable too, with pleasant gardens. Each room has its own verandah and outdoor shower. ❹

Sanctuary Holt Rd, Bingil Bay ⊕07/4088 6064, ⊛www.sanctuaryatmission.com. An outstanding operation set in fifty acres of thick rainforest. There's abundant wildlife – including cassowary – and a 700m forest track down to a beach. Huts are on stilts (and walled with fine-meshed netting, so you wake up surrounded by greenery), while cabins have verandahs; there's a bar, yoga lessons, and an excellent-value restaurant. Note that hut access paths follow steep slopes, and some find the wildlife's proximity unsettling. Advance booking essential. Dorms $29.50, hut ❸, cabin ❺

Scotty's Beachhouse 167 Reid Rd, Wongaling ⊕1800 665 567, ⊜scottysbeachhouse @bigpond.com. A popular backpackers' party place right across from the beach at Wongaling, with bunkhouses, a pool and a fine restaurant offering cheap meals. Dorms $19.

Dunk Island and the Reef

In 1898 Edmund Banfield, a Townsville journalist who had been given only weeks to live, waded ashore on **Dunk Island**. He spent his remaining years – twenty-five of them – as Dunk's first European resident, crediting his unanticipated longevity to the relaxed island life. A tiny version of Hinchinbrook, Dunk attracts far more visitors to its resort and camping grounds. While there's a reasonably satisfying track over and around the island, it's more the kind of place where you make the most of the beach – as Banfield discovered.

Vessels from the Mission Beach area put ashore on or near the jetty, next to a beach rental shop and **canteen** selling sandwiches and hot meals; there's no store on the island. On the far side is the shady NPWS campsite (⊕07/4068 8199 for permits and details), with toilets, showers and drinking water. Five

△ Dunk Island

All the ferries below run daily to Dunk for $29 return.

Dunk Island Ferry & Cruises Clump Point Jetty ☏07/4068 7211. Departs 8.45am and 10.30am, and can also provide a coach pick-up from Cairns or Innisfail. For an extra $10 they provide a barbecue lunch at Dunk, and for a flat $69 you get the trip to Dunk, barbecue lunch, and an afternoon boomnetting around Bedarra Island.

Quick Cat Clump Point Jetty ☏07/4068 7289. Departs 10am; after dropping passengers at Dunk, continues out to Beaver Cay on the Barrier Reef for coral viewing, snorkelling and diving ($140; two dives $90 extra). On Wednesday and Sunday they also run a budget boat direct to the reef for $80.

Water Taxi Wongaling Beach ☏07/4068 8310. Departs 9.30am, 11am, 12.30pm, 2.30pm and 4.30pm; last boat leaves Dunk 5pm. Free bus from Mission Beach accommodation available on request.

minutes along the track is the **resort** (☏07/4068 8199, ⓦwww.poresorts .com.au/dunk; ➐), a low-key affair well hidden by vegetation. The best places to relax are either on **Brammo Bay**, in front of the resort, or **Pallon Beach**, behind the campsite. Note that the beaches are narrow at high tide and the island is close enough to the coast to attract box jellyfish in season, but you can always retreat to the resort pool.

Before falling victim to incipient lethargy, head into the interior past the resort and Banfield's grave for a circuit of the island's west. The full 9km up **Mount Cootaloo**, down to **Palm Valley** and back along the coast is a three-hour rainforest trek, best tackled clockwise from the resort. You'll see green pigeons and yellow-footed scrubfowl foraging in leaf litter, vines, trunkless palms and, from the peak, a vivid blue sea dotted with hunchbacked islands.

Ferries to Dunk cost $29 (see box above for details of operators), though occasional price wars between operators might save a few dollars; book directly or through your accommodation. The island is 5km – barely fifteen minutes – offshore, but even so the tiny water taxis are not really suitable if you have much luggage. **Camping gear** can be rented from the complex next to the post office in Mission Beach; you can also leave surplus equipment with them.

Some distance northeast of Dunk is **Beaver Cay**, the local section of the Barrier Reef, with a sand island and some very pretty coral gardens that make for easy **snorkelling** or **diving**. Aside from *Quick Cat* (see box above), you can dive with Mission Beach Dive Charters, near the post office in Mission Beach (☏07/4068 7277); they charge $140 plus gear rental for two dives and lunch, though they don't provide hot drinks or free drinking water, and their vessel gives a rough ride.

Paronella Park, Innisfail and the Bellenden Ker Range

Back on the highway around 25km north of Tully, tiny **Silkwood** marks the turning inland for the 23-kilometre run through canefields to **Paronella Park** (daily 9am–5pm; $17; ☏07/4065 3225, ⓦwww.paronellapark.com.au). This extraordinary estate was laid out by **José Paronella**, a Spanish immigrant who settled here in 1929 and constructed a **castle** complete with florid staircases, water features and avenues of exotic kauri pines amongst the tropical forests. Left to moulder for twenty years, the park was reclaimed from the jungle and restored during the 1990s, and now forms a splendidly romantic theme park, with half-ruined buildings artfully part-covered in undergrowth, lush gardens and arrays of tinkling fountains – all gravity-fed from the adjacent Mena Creek. A former walk-through aquarium has become the roost of endangered little bent-winged bats, and native vegetation includes a bamboo forest and dozens of *angiopteris* ferns, rare elsewhere. You need a good couple of hours to do the place justice, and it's possible to **camp** here and explore after dark – phone ahead for details. There's a **restaurant** on site, or you can eat across Mena Creek at the old pub.

The Paronella Park road and highway converge again 25km on at **INNISFAIL**, a busy town on the Johnstone River and a good spot to look for **work** picking bananas: *Innisfail Budget Backpackers*, on the highway just on the northern side of town (℡07/4061 7833; dorms $18), can help if you stay with them. Alternatively, try the much smarter *Codge Lodge* near the bright pink Catholic church on Rankin Street (℡07/4061 8055; dorms $19, rooms ❸). Innisfail is worth a quick look anyway as a reminder that modern Australia was in no way built by the British alone: there's a sizeable **Italian community** here, represented by the handful of delicatessens displaying herb sausages and fresh pasta along the central Edith Street. The tiny red **Chinese Joss House** (and huge longan tree next to it) on Owen Street was first established in the 1880s by migrant workers from southern China, who cleared scrub and established market gardens here; and many of Innisfail's banana plantations have been bought up recently by **Hmong** immigrants from Vietnam.

Just beyond town, the Palmerston Highway turns off across the bottom end of the Atherton Tablelands, and at about the same point you begin to see the **Bellenden Ker Range**, which dominates the remaining 80km to Cairns. This coastal area of the tablelands includes Queensland's highest mountain, **Bartle Frere**. While the two-day return climb through **Wooroonooran National Park** to the 1600-metre summit is within the reach of any fit, well-prepared bushwalker, you should contact the park ranger (℡07/4067 6304) or the Cairns NPWS in advance (see "Listings", p.528) for accurate information about the route. To reach the start of the track, leave the highway 19km north

Cane toads

Native to South America, the huge, charismatically ugly **cane toad** was recruited in 1932 to combat a plague of greyback beetles, whose larvae were wreaking havoc on Queensland's sugar cane. The industry was desperate – beetles had cut production by ninety percent in plague years – and resorted to seeding tadpoles in waterholes around Gordonvale. They thrived, but it soon became clear that toads couldn't reach the adult insects (who never landed on the ground), and they didn't burrow after the grubs. Instead they bred whenever possible, ate anything they could swallow, and killed potential predators with poisonous secretions from their neck glands. Native wildlife suffered: birds learned to eat non-toxic parts, but snake populations have been seriously affected. Judging from the quantity of flattened carcasses on summer roads (running them over is an unofficial sport), there must be millions lurking in the canefields, and they're gradually spreading into New South Wales and the Northern Territory – Kakadu received its first arrivals around 2000. Given enough time, they seem certain to infiltrate most of the country.

The toad's outlaw character has generated a cult following, with its warty features and nature the subject of songs, toad races, T-shirt designs, a brand of beer and the award-winning film *Cane Toads: An Unnatural History* – worth seeing if you come across it on video. The record for the largest specimen goes to a 1.8-kilogram monster found in Mackay in 1988.

of Ingham at one-house Pawngilly and continue for 8km, past Bartle Frere township, to **Josephine Falls**. Even without going any further, the falls – wonderfully enclosed jungle waterslides – are worth the trip. Marked with orange triangles, the climb to the peak passes through rainforest, over large granite boulders and out onto moorland with wind-stunted vegetation. Much of the summit is blinded by scrub and usually cloaked in rain, but there are great views of the tablelands and coast during the ascent.

Further along the highway, there's a detour at **BABINDA** township – dwarfed by a huge sugar mill – to another waterhole at **the Boulders**, where an arm of Babinda Creek forms a wide pool before spilling down a collection of house-sized granite slabs. Cool and relatively shallow, the waterhole is an excellent place to swim, though it also has a more sinister reputation. Legend has it that an Aboriginal girl was raped here and in reprisal she cursed the pool against men; several deaths have been caused by subtle undertows dragging people over the falls – be very careful and stay well clear of the falls' side of the waterhole. You can also **camp** here for free.

Nearing the end of the range is **Gordonvale**, the place where the notorious **cane toad** was first introduced to Australia (see box opposite). From here, the tortuous Gillies Highway climbs from the coast to lakes Barrine and Eacham on the Atherton Tableland (for more on these see p.538). Marking the turn-off is **Walsh's Pyramid**, a natural formation which really does look like an overgrown version of its Egyptian counterpart. From here, the last section of the Bruce Highway carries you – in thirty minutes – through the suburbs of Edmonton and White Rock to Cairns.

Cairns and around

CAIRNS was pegged out over the site of a sea-slug fishing camp when gold was found to the north in 1876, though it was the Atherton Tablelands' tin and timber resources that established the town and kept it ahead of its nearby rival, Port Douglas (see p.540). The harbour is the focus of the north's fish and prawn concerns, and tourism began modestly when **marlin fishing** became popular after World War II. But with the "discovery" of the reef in the 1970s and the appeal of the local climate, tourism snowballed, and high-profile development has now replaced the unspoiled, lazy tropical atmosphere which was what everyone originally came to Cairns to enjoy.

For many visitors primed by hype, the city falls far short of expectations. However, if you can accept the tourist industry's shocking glibness and the fact that you're unlikely to escape the crowds, you'll find Cairns a good base with a great deal on offer, and easy access to the surrounding area – the Atherton Tablelands, Cape York and, naturally, the Great Barrier Reef and islands.

Arrival and information

Downtown Cairns is the grid of streets behind the Esplanade, overlooking the harbour and Trinity Bay. **Buses** arrive at the end of the Esplanade at Trinity Wharf Transit Centre – though note that the bus terminal will eventually be relocating to near the train station on Bunda Street. The **train station** is 750m away under the Cairns Central development between Bunda Street and McLeod Street. The **airport** is about 7km north, along the Cook Highway. A taxi from the airport into Cairns costs $12–15; a shuttle bus ($7)

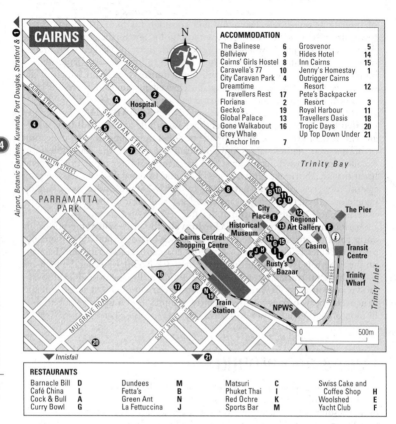

CAIRNS

N

ACCOMMODATION

The Balinese	6	Grosvenor	5
Bellview	9	Hides Hotel	14
Cairns' Girls Hostel	8	Inn Cairns	15
Caravella's 77	10	Jenny's Homestay	1
City Caravan Park	4	Outrigger Cairns	
Dreamtime		Resort	12
Travellers Rest	17	Pete's Backpacker	
Floriana	2	Resort	3
Gecko's	19	Royal Harbour	11
Global Palace	13	Travellers Oasis	18
Gone Walkabout	16	Tropic Days	20
Grey Whale		Up Top Down Under	21
Anchor Inn	7		

Trinity Bay

ESPLANADE

DIGGER STREET

CAIRNS STREET

Hospital

SHERIDAN STREET

McLEOD ST

GROVE ST

MARTYN STREET

UPWARD STREET

PARRAMATTA
PARK

SEVERIN STREET

MINNIE STREET

GRAFTON STREET

FLORENCE STREET

LAKE STREET

ABBOTT STREET

ESPLANADE

City
Place

Historical
Museum

Cairns Central
Shopping Centre

Cairns Central
Shopping Centre

APLIN STREET

SHIELDS STREET

The Pier

Regional
Art Gallery

Casino

Transit
Centre

Rusty's
Bazaar

BUNDA STREET

SPENCE STREET

McLEOD STREET

Trinity
Wharf

Train
Station

NPWS

WHARF STREET

Trinity Inlet

MULGRAVE ROAD

DRAPER STREET

SCOTT STREET

0   500m

▼ Innisfail

RESTAURANTS

Barnacle Bill	D	Dundees	M	Matsuri	C	Swiss Cake and	
Café China	L	Fetta's	B	Phuket Thai	I	Coffee Shop	H
Cock & Bull	A	Green Ant	N	Red Ochre	K	Woolshed	E
Curry Bowl	G	La Fettuccina	J	Sports Bar	M	Yacht Club	F

connects with most flights and delivers to all central accommodation. If you're staying in a hostel, you'll usually be **picked up** at the Trinity Wharf Transit Centre, and possibly from the train and airport if you give advance notice.

Cairns' official **Information Centre** is at 93 Esplanade (☎07/4301 1751, ⓦwww.barrier-reef-holidays.com), though it's geared towards the upmarket end of things. Several **backpackers' contact points** also help out with accommodation, bookings, work contacts, and cheap phone and Internet deals; two close to each other at City Place on Shields Street are Backpackers World/World Wide Workers (☎07/4041 0999, ⓦwww.worldwideworkers.com) and Travellers Contact Point (☎07/4041 4677, ⓔcairns@travellers.com.au).

Sunbus, the **local bus** service, is based at the **Transit Mall** on City Place (Lake St), and serves several beaches north as far as Palm Cove; daily, weekly and monthly **passes** are available, and you can get free timetables from the driver. You may also be able to **rent bikes** at your accommodation, or check out the rental outfits in "Listings" on p.528. If you want to buy or sell a **secondhand car**, head for the Esplanade, scene of an informal trade amongst backpackers; cars for sale are also advertised on notice boards outside *Johno's* on the corner of Aplin and Abbott streets, and in an arcade beside the museum at City Place.

Accommodation

Cairns has a prolific number of **places to stay**, and the following is just a selection of the best places. **Luxury** places favour views overlooking the sea, especially along the lower end of the Esplanade, an area which used to be the core of the city's **budget accommodation**. These are now spreading elsewhere; in particular, the area west of the train station is a focus for a number of smaller hostels, of which *Dreamtime*, *Gone Walkabout* and *Tropic Days* are the pick. The nearest **campsite** to the centre is the *City Caravan Park*, at 14 Little St (℡07/4051 1467), though you can also camp at *Tropic Days* hostel.

Expect seasonal **price fluctuations** at all accommodation, with Christmas and Easter as the busiest times, and February to March as the quietest; book ahead but beware of committing yourself to a special deal on a longer stay until you've seen the room – you probably won't be able to get a refund. All hostels have kitchens, most have a courtesy bus service, laundry and a pool, and offer special meal deals, usually at the *Woolshed*. Note that hostels make most of their profits through commissions, not beds, so don't admit to making tour bookings elsewhere if you want your room to remain available.

For a change of pace, **farmstays** in the Cairns region include *Mount Mulligan Station* (℡1800 359 798, ℮owenrankine@hotmail.com; three-day packages $145 per person), and *Springmount Station* (℡1800 333 004, ⓦwww.springmountstation.com; $110 per day per person), where you can horse ride, camp out under the stars, swim in bush waterways or bushwalk – both get good reviews and provide a free pick-up from Cairns.

Hotels, motels and guesthouses

The Balinese 215 Lake St ℡07/4051 9922, ℉4051 9822. Stylish motel with carved wooden doors, bamboo blinds and lots of tiling. There's a small pool, satellite TV, inclusive breakfast and airport courtesy bus. ❹

Floriana 183 Esplanade ℡07/4051 7886, ⓦwww.cairnsinfo.com/floriana. Amiable old guesthouse with sea views and Art Deco decor in the reception. Rooms overlooking the Esplanade are good, as are the self-contained "flats"; the cheaper rooms have no windows and get pretty stuffy. Rooms ❸–❹, flats ❹

Grey Whale Anchor Inn 19 Gatton St ℡07/4051 9249. Fully self-contained rooms in an older, quiet house, with very friendly owners. ❸

Grosvenor 188 Mcleod St ℡1800 629 179, ⓦwww.grosvenorcairns.com.au. Bright and cheerful motel offering self-contained apartments and deluxe units; not very central but close to the highway. Apartments ❹, units ❻

Hides Hotel Cnr Lake and Shields streets ℡07/4051 1266, ⓦwww.clubcroc.com.au. One of the oldest hotels in town (and formerly the roughest), now under the *Club Crocodile* banner. The higher-priced motel rooms have been totally revamped; cheaper hotel rooms are unadorned

pub rooms, with original fittings. ❸–❹

Inn Cairns 71 Lake St ℡07/4041 2350, ⓦwww.inncairns.com.au. Smart boutique apartments slap in the centre of town, with pool and BBQ area, plus rooftop views out to the reef. ❺

Jenny's Homestay 12 Leon Close, Brinsmead ℡07/4055 1639, ⓦwww.jennysbandb.com. Very friendly B&B accommodation, with big rooms, about 10km northwest of the city on a regular bus route; free pick-up available. ❸

Kewarra Beach Resort ℡07/4057 6166, ⓦwww.kewarrabeachresort.com.au. Luxury getaway on the seafront 25km north of town, with private cabins and units (and a pool) set amidst forest, beach and landscaped gardens, with as much activity or inactivity as you desire. ❼

Outrigger Cairns Resort 53–57 Esplanade ℡07/4046 4141, ⓦwww.outrigger.com.au. Plush high-rise hotel in a prime location close to the casino, restaurants, shops and the new "beach". ❻

Royal Harbour 73–75 Esplanade ℡07/4080 8888, ⓦwww.breakfree.com.au. Self-contained hotel apartments with sea views – it feels surprisingly secluded given the location. Minimum two-night stay. ❻

Hostels

Bellview 85 Esplanade ☏ 07/4031 4377, ℻ 4031 2850. The best organized hostel on the Esplanade, with motel-like facilities and a range of rooms. Dorms $18, rooms ❷

Cairns' Girls Hostel 147 Lake St ☏ 07/4051 2016, ⓦ www.girlshostel.webprovider.com. Renovated 1930s Queenslander, now a secure, cool and quiet place to stay with relaxed management and low prices. Can be hard to locate; look for the adjacent laundry. ❶

Caravella's 77 77 Esplanade ☏ 07/4051 2159. Busy and long-established place on the Esplanade, with small dorms and a warren of dark corridors and passages. Dorms $18.

Dreamtime Travellers Rest 4 Terminus St, behind the train station ☏ 07/4031 6753, ⓦ www.dreamtimetravel.com.au. Small, friendly hostel with a keen owner about ten minutes' walk from the centre. They also offer Atherton Tableland tour/accommodation packages with their sister hostel at Yungaburra (see p.538). Dorms $19, rooms ❷

Gecko's 187 Bunda St ☏ 07 4031 1344, ℻ 4051 5150. Large hostel with wooden floors and dated furnishings in a restored 1920s house opposite the new bus station site; it's developing into a bit of a party venue. Dorms $17, rooms ❷

Global Palace City Place, Lake St ☏ 07/4031 7921, ℻ 4031 3231. Enormous backpackers' place right in the centre of town, the first of a new wave of super-hostels springing up around Cairns.

Well organized with good facilities, but also expensive. Dorms $22, rooms ❸

Gone Walkabout 274 Draper St ☏ 07/4051 6160, ⓦ www.gonewalkabout.com.au. One of the longest-running hostels in Cairns, with a well-informed owner and staff who can't do enough for guests. Recently refurbished and kept spotlessly clean, and there's also a spa pool and small garden. Dorms $18, rooms ❷

Pete's Backpacker Resort 242 Grafton St ☏ 1800 122 123, ⓦ www.petescairns.com.au. Nice, family-run hostel in an old Queenslander house with a huge landscaped pool and decent-sized rooms. Dorms $20, rooms ❷

Travellers Oasis 8 Scott Street ☏ 07/4052 1377, ⓦ www.travoasis.com.au. Low-key newcomer to the local owner-operated scene, garnering plenty of good feedback. Dorms $18, rooms ❷

Tropic Days 28 Bunting St ☏ 07/4041 1521, ⓦ www.tropicdays.com.au. Though a little bit out of town, this is one of the best hostels in Cairns, with a big pool, nice gardens, good rooms and highly sociable atmosphere. There's a small campsite too, and a courtesy bus through the day. Dorms $19, rooms ❷

Up Top Down Under 164 Spence St ☏ 07/4051 3636. Quite a way from the centre, but otherwise the best of Cairns' bigger hostels, with cheap meals, helpful staff, a huge pool and enough space to relax. Dorms $18.

The City

Cairns' strength is in doing, not seeing: there are few monuments, natural or otherwise. This is partly because the Cape York goldfields were too far away and profits were channelled through Cooktown, and partly because Cairns was remote, lacking a rail link with Townsville until 1924; people came here to exploit resources, not to settle. Your best introduction to the region's heritage is at the **Cairns Historical Museum**, at the junction of Shields and Lake streets (Mon–Sat 10am–3pm; $5), which uses photos and trinkets to explore maritime history, the Tjapukai and Bama Aborigines from the tablelands, and Chinese involvement in the city and Palmer goldfields.

At **City Place**, the open-air pedestrian mall outside the museum, you'll find Cairns' souvenir-shopping centre, with a rash of cafés, and shops selling didgeridoos, T-shirts, paintings and cuddly toy koalas. Local performers do their best at the small **sound shell** here from time to time, and there are often more professional offerings in the evenings. Between Grafton and Sheridan Streets, towards Spence Street, **Rusty's Bazaar markets** (Fri afternoon, Sat & Sun morning) sell a great range of local produce from crafts to herbs, fruit and veg, coffee and fish; the site is being developed but the markets seem set to remain. Moving from the mall area down towards Trinity Wharf, the shops become more upmarket, though they're still selling essentially the same things; an increasing number of signs target the many Japanese visitors. **Trinity Wharf** itself is a collection of dormant offices, due for redevelopment, but the adjacent **cruise terminals** are where most sea trips out of Cairns begin. The glass-domed **casino** faces **The Pier**, a flashy shopping complex where many tour and cruise operators have booking offices ready to tempt you with brochures and videos of their activities. An **aquarium** (daily 8am–8pm; $12.50) here has regular feeding shows and big tanks full of hulking reef fish such as maori wrasse, sharks and potato cod, but somehow lacks punch.

Through the day and into the night, the **Esplanade** is packed with people cruising between accommodation, shops and restaurants. Grabbing an early-morning coffee here, you'll witness a quintessentially Australian scene: fig trees framing the waterfront, a couple of trawlers and seaplanes bobbing at anchor in the harbour, and drunks languishing on the benches. Joggers jog, and others promenade along the edge at low tide and watch birds feeding in the shallows – there's an identification chart in the park. Though originally fringed in mangroves and mud flats, developers have, after years of wrangles, created an **artificial beach** near the Pier; it's actually way above the tide-line, but encloses five equally artificial, landscaped **lagoons**. The Esplanade's **night market** (daily 5pm until late), which runs through to Abbott Street, has a mix of fast-food courts, trendy tack and good-quality souvenirs, plus a good location near plenty of bars. Just around the corner from the Esplanade on Shields Street, **Cairns Regional Art Gallery** (Mon–Fri 10am–5pm, Sat & Sun 1–5pm; $4) is worth a look if Cairns' crasser commercial side is beginning to grate; exhibitions include both local artists' work and travelling shows.

Heading out of the centre, the city's natural attractions include the **Botanic Gardens** (Mon–Fri 8.30am–5.30pm; free) and the adjacent **Mount Whitfield Environmental Park** on Collins Avenue, off the highway near the airport (bus #7 from the City Place transit mall, or a dull forty-minute walk). Ringed by suburbia, the rainforest is dense enough for wallabies, and a raised boardwalk track through the wonderfully cool and tranquil atmosphere makes a fine escape from the city. Also worth a look are the **mangrove walks** on the airport approach road, whose boardwalks and hides give you a chance to see different varieties of mangrove trees, mudskippers and red-clawed, asymmetric fiddler crabs. Take some repellent or else you'll end up giving the flies a free lunch.

Eating and nightlife

Cairns has no shortage of places to **eat**. Least expensive are the takeaways between the Esplanade's hostels serving Chinese food, falafel, kebabs and pasta. Some open early while others, such as *La Pizza* on the corner of Aplin Street, never close, switching from fast food during the day and evening to coffee and croissants at dawn. The night market also houses a fast-food plaza, with a choice ranging from fish and chips to pizza or sushi; alternatively, you can stock up at the **supermarkets** on Abbott Street or in Cairns Central.

Openly **drinking** on the streets is illegal in Cairns, but the pub and club culture thrives undaunted. Clubs open around 6pm, most charging $5 entry for bar and disco; more if there's a band playing. Many pubs also feature live music once a week – reviews and details are given in Cairns' free weekly **listings magazine**, *Barfly*; for some indigenous sounds, try to catch one of the up-and-coming local **Torres Strait Islander** performers, such as Seaman Dan (who had moderate UK success with his CD *Steady Steady*). Try not to make yourself an obvious target for **pickpockets** and **bag-snatchers** who work the nightclubs, though the steady reports of drink-spikings, rapes and muggings are more worrying – don't hang around outside venues and get a taxi home.

Cafés and restaurants

Barnacle Bill 65 Esplanade ☎07/4051 2241. Popular seafood restaurant, where you choose your lobster and Moreton Bay bugs from the live tank. Food is good, but it's the Esplanade location which really pulls in the crowds. Main courses for around $28. Daily from 5pm.

Café China Cnr of Spence and Grafton streets. Two sections here catering to the increasing numbers of Chinese visitors to Cairns: an inexpensive noodle house on Spence Street with most dishes under $10, and a more sophisticated Cantonese restaurant on Grafton, with great roast meat or seafood dishes from $15, and daily *yum cha* sessions (best selection at weekends).

Cock & Bull 6 Grove St, cnr Grafton St. Keg Guinness, good-quality and huge counter meals (from around $15) and a pleasant garden atmosphere.

Curry Bowl In the arcade between Grafton and Lake streets, just south of Shields St. Very ordinary-looking fast-food counter, but the portions of (mostly vegetarian) Sri Lankan dahls and curries are large, cheap and pretty authentic.

Dundees Spence St. Popular upmarket grill restaurant, with leanings towards native fauna – kangaroo, emu, crocodile – and seafood. Best dishes are the kangaroo satay, and seafood platter (includes crays and mud crab). Mains around $28.

Fetta's Abbott St. Very reasonably priced Greek restaurant with particularly good seafood. Most main dishes around $25; vegetable dishes from $18.

Green Ant Bunda St. Cheap, cheerful and tasty evening meals and drink deals, with mains – such as spicy chicken salsa or meat grills served with rice or chips – for around $10, and burgers which remind you what burgers used to be like before fast-food versions appeared. Thurs–Sun only.

La Fettuccina 41 Shields St ☎07/4031 5959. Superb home-made pasta and sauces for around $18, though very popular, so get in early or book – their "small" servings would be enough for most people.

Matsuri Next to the night-market entrance on Abbott St. Best place for sushi, noodle soups or other Japanese light meals in an authentic environment – popular with Japanese tourists. Most meals around $15. Closed Mon, and often on Tues.

Phuket Thai Grafton Street ☎07/4031 0777. Thai seafood and curries, with mains under $20 – highly rated by locals, and full most nights.

Rattle and Hum Esplanade. Smart bar and grill serving huge platters of steak and seafood. The neon-lit pool tables are popular too. Mains $19 or less.

Red Ochre 43 Shields St ☎07/4051 0100. Long-running restaurant with Outback decor and a menu revolving around truly Australian ingredients such as kangaroo and crocodile – although emu meat seems to have been replaced by ostrich. Tasty, but some dishes a bit overworked. Mains $25 and up.

Sports Bar Spence St. Competition for the *Woolshed* at this bar, with light, good-value meals, and plenty of satellite sport channels playing on the video screen. Evening specials on meals and drinks via vouchers from backpacker accommodation.

Swiss Cake and Coffee Shop 93 Grafton St. Top-notch patisserie with crisp strudels, rich cakes and fine coffee.

Woolshed 22 Shields St. Budget backpackers' diner, with huge and inexpensive meals, beer by the jug and party fever. Hostels give out vouchers for various discount meal deals here; it's worth "upgrading" these for a couple more dollars and getting a full-blown feed.

Yacht Club Esplanade. Opens 11am for drinks and good-value grill-and-salad meals at around $13; their "Sunset Special" (5.30–6.30pm) is a bucket of prawns and a beer for $15.

Nightlife

Cairns City Club Abbott St. Competition for the nearby *Johno's*, with a range of local and international jazz and funk bands.

Casa De Meze Cnr Aplin St and the Esplanade. Open nightly, but best to come for Sun afternoon jam sessions of Latin and jazz.

Club Nu Trix 53 Spence St. Gay club. Wed–Sun 9pm–late.

Johno's Cnr Abbott and Aplin streets. Traditional backpackers' haunt, with a huge video screen and a youngish clientele. Live music, including international bands, most nights, and it's even worth catching Johno and the house band – they've been a Cairns' institution for decades.

P.J.O'Brien's City Place, next to Hides, Shields St. Irish bar with mix of locals and tourists – a popular place to meet and warm up before later club sessions. Best on Fri, Sat, and Sun nights.

Playpen Cnr Lake and Hartley streets. Nightclub and disco, with action on most nights and live bands some weekends.
XS 10 Shields St. Cairns' newest gay bar.

Activities

In addition to the tours covered in the box below, several operators offer more activity-led excursions. For **bushwalking**, Wooroonooran Safaris (☎1300 661 113, ⓦwww.wooroonooran-safaris.com.au) spends a moderately strenuous day hiking through thick rainforest just north of Bartle Frere, where you're guaranteed to see wildlife and get wet crossing creeks ($119 all-inclusive, or $89 with your own gear and lunch); The Adventure Company (☎07/4051 4777) spends two days in similar conditions ($225). If it's just **wildlife** you're after, Wildscapes Safaris (☎07/4057 6272, ⓦwww.wildscapes-safaris.com.au) visits the Atherton Tablelands to spot platypus and rare nocturnal marsupials (day-tour $95, night-tour $120), as does Wait-a-While Spotlighting Tours (☎07/4033 1153, ⓦwww.waitawhile.com) and Currawong (☎07/4093 7287, ⓦwww.australiawildlifetours.com; $98–148).

Bicycle tours around the Atherton Tablelands are on offer four times a week with Bandicoot (☎07/4055 0155; $98), or you can get stuck into some moderate to extreme off-road biking around Cairns and Cape Tribulation ($75–120) with Dan's Mountain Biking (☎07/4032 0066) – both come highly recommended. Cairns' **bungee-jumping** venue is a purpose-built platform surrounded by rainforest in the hills off the coastal highway 5km north of Cairns; contact A.J. Hackett (☎07/4057 7188; $109). **White-water rafting** is organized on the Tully River near Tully, the Barron River, behind Cairns, and the remote Johnstone River near Innisfail, and is wild fun despite being a conveyor-belt business: as you pick yourself out of the river, the raft is dragged back for the next busload. A "day" means around five hours rafting; a "half-day" about two. Agents include RnR (☎1800 079 039, ⓦwww .raft.com.au; day-trips $83–145, multi-day expeditions $630–1200); Wildside (☎07/4031 3460; half-day $65); and Extreme Green (☎07/4030 7990; half-day $65).

Tours from Cairns

Before exploring locally or around the Atherton Tablelands, Port Douglas and Cape Tribulation, bear in mind that the cheapest day-tours will set you back $80 per person, while it costs as little as $50 per day to rent a four-seat car – though you'll miss out on a tour guide's local knowledge. For the **Atherton Tablelands, the Daintree and Cape Tribulation**, the following come highly recommended: Uncle Brian ☎07/4050 0615; Cape Trib Connections ☎07/4053 3833; Tropical Horizons ☎07/4058 1244, ⓦwww.tropicalhorizonstours.com.au; the backpacker-oriented Jungle Tours ☎07/4032 5600, ⓦwww.jungletours.com.au; Queensland Adventure Safaris ☎07/4041 2418, ⓦwww.qastours.com; and Trek North Safaris ☎07/4051 4328, ⓦwww.treknorth.com.au. Wilderness Challenge ☎07/4055 6504, ⓦwww .wilderness-challenge.com.au visits the Daintree, Cape Tribulation and Mossman Gorge, and also goes to Cooktown and the Aboriginal rock-art sites around Laura. For **Cape York**, the following organize trips to the tip by 4WD, boat and plane, and enjoy reliable reputations: OZtours ☎07/4055 9535, ⓦwww.oztours.com.au; Billy Tea Bush Safaris ☎07/4032 0077, ⓦwww.billytea.com.au; and Exploring Oz ☎1300 888 112, ⓦwww.exploring-oz.com.au.

4

TROPICAL QUEENSLAND AND THE REEF | Cairns and around

Finally, two good places to arrange a spot of small-scale **fishing** for barramundi and other estuary fish are Paradise Sportfishing (℡07/4055 0027) and All Tackle (℡07/4034 2550) – both charge around $75 per person for a full day of shore-based fishing, or $140 from a boat.

For **diving**, see the box on pp.530–531.

Listings

Airlines Air New Zealand ℡ 1800 221 111; Air Niugini, 4 Shields St ℡07/4035 9888; Cape York Air Services, at the airport ℡07/4035 9399; Cathay Pacific ℡07/4013 1747; JAL, 15 Lake St ℡1800 177 884; Malaysia, 15 Lake St ℡07/4013 1627; Qantas ℡13 13 13; Singapore, 15 Lake St ℡07/4013 1011; Sunstate ℡07/4086 0457; Virgin Blue ℡13 67 89.

Banks and exchange Banks are scattered throughout the city centre, mostly around the intersection of Shields and Abbott streets and in Cairns Central. Some booths around the Esplanade also offer bureau de change facilities, though rates are lower than at the banks.

Bike rentals Bandicoot Bicycle Hire & Tours, 59 Sheridan St ℡07/4055 0155; bike rental $16.50 a day.

Books Exchange Book Shop, 78 Grafton St, has an excellent range of secondhand books to buy or exchange.

Buses The main operators are Greyhound Pioneer (℡07/4051 5899); McCafferty's (℡07/4051 5899); and Premier (℡13 34 10). At the time of writing, public bus services to the Atherton Tablelands, Cooktown, and the Gulf of Carpentaria were in limbo following the demise of Coral Coaches and White Car Coaches – ask around for the latest information, as it's possible that new services will begin.

Camping equipment Adventure Equipment, 133 Grafton St (℡07/4031 2669), stocks and rents out all types of outdoor gear and even kayaks; City Place Disposals, cnr Shields and Grafton streets; Geo Pickers, 108 Mulgrave Rd, cnr Draper St; and Wolfies Disposals, 56 McLeod St, all have basic equipment and secondhand gear.

Car rental All the following offer discounts on long rentals; on a day-by-day basis, you're looking at around $50 for a four-person runaround. Best of the bunch for general purposes is Minicar Rentals, 150 Sheridan St ℡07/4051 6288, ⓦwww.minicarrentals.com.au. Alternatively, try: A1 Car Rental, 141 Lake St ℡07/4031 1326; All Day, 151 Lake St ℡07/4031 3348, ⓦwww .cairns-car-rentals.com; Britz, 411 Sheridan St ℡1800 331 454, ⓦwww.britz.com, for 4WDs, motorhomes and campervans; or Cairns Tropical ℡07/4031 3995.

Cinemas There are multi-screens at 108 Grafton St and in Cairns Central.

Hospital and medical centres Cairns Medical Centre, cnr of Florence and Grafton streets (℡07/4052 1119) is open 24hr for vaccinations and GP consultations (free if you have reciprocal national health cover). Hospitals include Base Hospital, northern end of the Esplanade (℡07/4050 6333), or, if you have insurance, Calvary Private Hospital (℡07/4052 5200).

Internet access If your accommodation isn't connected, try the travellers' information centres at City Place, or the net cafés around the corner on Abbott Street ($4 per hour).

Left luggage At the airport, train and bus stations; around $5 a day.

NPWS At the southern end of Sheridan, just past the police station – look for the building with green and yellow trim (Mon–Fri 8.30am–4.30pm; ℡07/4046 6601). Staff are very helpful, and have plenty of free brochures on regional parks, plus books for sale on wildlife and hiking.

Pharmacy Cairns Day and Night Pharmacy and Medical Centre, 29b Shields St ℡07/4051 2466 (daily 8am–9pm).

Police 5 Sheridan St ℡07/4030 7000.

Post office 13 Grafton St, and upstairs in Orchid Plaza off the Transit Mall, Lake St.

Scenic flights Cairns Seaplanes offers spins over the reef and islands for $299; Cape York Airlines charges just $200.

Shopping Tourist-oriented shops are concentrated close to the Esplanade and around City Place and Lake St, where Aboriginal art galleries have sprung up in profusion, though little is truly local – didgeridoos on sale here might have been made in Indonesia. Moving down Shields St the shops become more general, preparing you for what's on offer at the modern air-conditioned shopping complex in the Cairns Central development. Many shops don't open on Saturdays or Sundays.

Taxis The main cab rank is on Lake St, west of City Place. Alternatively, ring Black and White Cars on ℡13 10 08.

Trains Bunda St, under Cairns Central ℡13 22 32. Trains head south down the coast to Brisbane, up to Kuranda on the Atherton Tablelands (p.531), and west to Forsayth in the Gulf (p.605).

Travel agents For budget travel and tours try: Flight Centre, 24 Spence St ☎07/4052 1077; STA, 9 Shields St ☎07/4031 4199; Trailfinders, next to *Hides Hotel*, Shields St ☎07/4041 1199.
Work You may be able to work a passage on barges going to Cape York; check "General Notices" in the Cairns Post for openings. For more regular employment try the backpacker contact

points listed in the Cairns' "Arrival" section (p.522); there are often WWOOF placements available on the Atherton Tablelands.
Yacht Club 4 Esplanade ☎07/4031 2750. Worth contacting for hitching/crewing north to Cape York and the Torres Strait, south to the Whitsundays and beyond, and even to New Guinea and the Pacific.

Around Cairns

There's a fair amount to see and do **around Cairns** (unless otherwise stated, the areas below can be reached on Sunbus services from City Place; see p.524). About 12km northwest near Redlynch, **Crystal Cascades** (Wongalee Falls) is a narrow forest gorge gushing with rapids, small waterfalls and swimming opportunities – somewhere to picnic rather than explore. Don't leave valuables in your car, and heed warnings about the large, pale-green, heart-shaped leaves of the **stinging tree** (also known locally as "Dead man's itch"), common on the sides of the paths here; the stories may seem apocryphal but if stung you'll believe them all. Backtracking through **Kamerunga** township – as far as you'll get on the bus – there's a marked, fairly steep track through the **Barron Gorge National Park** up through forests to Kuranda (see p.534).

About 10km north of Cairns, the township of **Smithfield** marks the starting point for the Kennedy Highway's ascent to Kuranda in the Atherton Tablelands. Shortly before, a large complex on the roadside houses both the Kuranda Skyrail cable-car terminus (see p.533) and the **Tjapukai Aboriginal Centre** (daily 9am–5pm; various packages $28–91, plus transfers). The centre's hefty admission price isn't bad value, as it includes entry to boomerang and didgeridoo displays, a fine museum, and three separate theatre shows featuring Dreamtime tales and dancing; it's not eye-opening stuff, but does offer a good introduction to Aboriginal culture.

Cairns' variously developed **beaches** start 20km north of town: **Palm Cove**'s beach is spotlessly clean, and the nearby **Wild World** zoo (daily 8.30am–5pm; $24) offers close views of Australia's often-elusive fauna – their **night tour** (Mon–Thurs & Sat 7–10pm; $99 including transfers) is particularly recommended. Further north, **Trinity** and **Yorkeys Knob** attract campers and day-tripper crowds with a van park, shops and watersports gear for rent. If you want to escape for a few days, however, get out to **Ellis Beach**, thirty minutes north on the way to Port Douglas (and unfortunately beyond the reach of bus services). You couldn't ask for a finer place to camp, with tent sites and cabin accommodation at *Ellis Beach Caravan Park* (☎07/4055 3538; cabins ❸).

The Reef and diving

Seeing the **Great Barrier Reef**, either on a cruise or as a diver, is what attracts many visitors to Cairns, and there are so many ways to do this that making a choice can be almost impossible. Broadly speaking, the reef can be classified into **three regions** – inner, outer and fringing – each somewhat different in character. The **inner reef**, a sheltered patchwork of coral and sea between the outer walls and Cairns, is flat and fairly shallow, a good place for novices. The **outer reef** borders the open sea, so has more dramatic appeal in the shape of walls, canyons, deeper water and bigger fish. **Fringing reef** surrounds **Green Island** and **Fitzroy Island**, and again has safe, easy access.

Reef trips and dive schools

The **reef cruises** and **diving** listings given below are not mutually exclusive – most outfits offer diving, snorkelling (usually free), or just plain sailing. **Prices** can come down by as much as thirty percent during the low seasons (Feb–April & Nov) and **standbys** on live-aboard boats can save even more. All dive schools run trips in their own boats, primarily to take students on their certification dives – experienced divers may want to avoid these. Paddy Colwell, a **marine biologist** at Reef Teach (see p.532), can organize a day-trip to the reef and accompany you on your dives ($200, all inclusive). Beware of **"expenses only"** boat trips offered to backpackers, which usually end up in sexual harassment once out at sea. If in doubt, find out from any booking office in town if you're dealing with an authorized, registered operator.

Reef cruises
SAIL BOATS
Day-trips $66–110; three days (two nights) $380–500

Ecstasea ☎07/4041 3055, ⓦwww.reef-sea-charters.com.au. Modern yacht taking a maximum of twenty guests for trips to Upolu Cay, just south of Michelmas; good food, and they'll let you have a go at sailing, too.

Falla ☎07/4051 7699. The last wooden pearling lugger built in Australia (in 1956), now restored for top-value day-trips to the inner reef, including snorkelling and storytelling.

Ocean Free ☎07/4041 1118, ⓦwww.oceanfree.com.au. Day-trips to the reef around Green Island aboard a nineteen-metre rigged schooner.

Passions of Paradise ☎07/4050 0676. Roomy sail catamaran (very stable), cruising out to Upolu Cay.

Santa Maria ☎07/4031 0558, ⓦwww.reefcharter.com. Replica nineteenth-century, twenty-metre rigged schooner for overnight trips to Thetford and Sudbury reefs.

POWERBOATS
$85–160 (day-trips only)

Great Adventures ☎07/4044 9944, ⓦwww.greatadventures.com.au. Trips on a large, fast catamaran via Green Island to a private reef pontoon.

Osprey V ☎1800 079 099, ⓦwww.downunderdive.com.au. Speedy vessel to Norman and Hastings reefs; comfortable boat, great crew, and the best meals of any day-trip.

Reef Magic ☎1300 666 700, ⓦwww.reefmagic.com.au. High-speed catamaran to Thetford or Moore reefs for snorkelling and glass-bottom boat trips.

Reef Quest ☎1800 612 223, ⓦwww.divers-den.com. Stable, well-equipped catamaran which covers any number of sites depending on weather conditions.

Sunlover Cruises ☎1800 810 512, ⓦwww.sunlover.com.au. Fast catamaran to Moore and Arlington reefs and Fitzroy Island; also offers packages including reef trips and overnight stays on Fitzroy.

Diving
DAY-TRIPS
$70–145; diving upwards of $50 for two dives, including gear rental.

Compass ☎07/4031 7217, ⓦwww.reeftrip.com. Visits to a good selection of reefs in a broad, stable budget vessel for windy weather. Departs 8am, giving you five hours at the reef; price includes snorkel gear and a glass-bottomed boat trip.

Noah's Ark II ☎07/4050 0677. Real budget diving at Michaelmas Cay and Hastings Reef; great value, but don't expect many creature comforts.

Sea Quest ☎1800 612 223. Very comfortable and speedy vessel running to Norman Reef.

Seastar II ☎07/4033 0333. Long-established family-run business with permits for some of the best sections of Hastings Reef and Michaelmas Cay – the top-value trip allows a good long time in the water.

Super Cat ☎1800 079 099. Another good-value budget option, though a faster, newer vessel than most in the price range.

Tusa ☎07/4031 1248, ⓦwww.tusadive.com. Purpose-built vessel holding a maximum of 28 passengers; a roving permit means each trip could go to any of ten separate reefs.

LIVE-ABOARDS

Live-aboard trips cater to more serious divers, last from three days upwards and cover the best of the reefs. Prices vary seasonally, with cheaper rates from February to June; standby rates only become available 48 hours or so before departure and have to be booked direct with the operator. All costs below include berth, meals and dives, but not gear rental. Remember that weather conditions can affect the destinations offered. For unbiased advanced **information**, check out Diversion Travel (ⓦwww.diversionoz.com), based in Cairns.

Diversity ☎4087 2100, ⓦwww.quicksilverdive.com.au. Speedy and very comfortable catamaran for trips to Cod Hole and Coral Sea. Two days $929; three and a half days $1749.

Mike Ball ☎07/4031 5484, ⓦwww.mikeball.com. Luxury diving with one of Queenslands' best-equipped and longest-running operations; venues include Cod Hole and the Ribbons, Coral Sea sites and minke whale-watching expeditions, plus the *Yongala* near Townsville (see p.504). From $1050.

Nimrod Explorer ☎07/4031 5566, ⓦwww.explorerventures.com. Motorized catamaran with basic or plush cabins; four- to seven-day Cod Hole and Coral Sea trips cost $995–1995.

Serica ⓦwww.sericadiveaustralia.com. Luxury 22-metre sailboat to remote and pristine sections of the northern reef and Coral Sea. Five nights from $2700.

Spirit of Freedom ☎07/4040 6450, ⓦwww.spiritoffreedom.com.au. Huge 33-metre vessel with superlative facilities sailing to Cod Hole, the Ribbons and Coral Sea. Three days from $950; four days from $1050.

Taka II ☎07/4051 8722, ⓦwww.taka.com.au. Refurbished trawler with fair facilities, including photographic equipment rental and E-6 processing on board. Four days at the Cod Hole and Ribbon reefs $930; five days (including Coral Sea sites) $1045.

Undersea Explorer ☎07/4099 5911, ⓦwww.undersea.com.au. Scientific research vessel where guests are allowed to participate in ongoing projects; destinations include Osprey Reef, Cod Hole and the Ribbons, and occasional trips to the historic *Pandora* wreck (see p.503). Seven days $2450.

DIVE SCHOOLS

As always, ask around about what each **dive school** offers, though training standards in Cairns are pretty uniform. You'll pay around $300 for a budget Open-Water Certification course, diving lesser reefs whilst training and returning to Cairns each night; and $550–620 for a four- or five-day course using better sites and staying on a live-aboard at the reef for a couple of days doing your certification. The following schools are long-established and have a sound reputation; certification dives are either made north at Norman, Hastings and Saxon reefs, or south at Flynn, Moore and Tetford.

CDC 121 Abbott St ☎07/4051 0294, ⓦwww.cairnsdive.com.au.

Deep Sea Divers Den 319 Draper St ☎07/4046 7333, ⓦwww.divers-den.com.

Down Under Dive 287 Draper St ☎07/4052 8300, ⓦwww.downunderdive.com.au.

Pro-Dive Cnr Abbott and Shields streets ☎07/4031 5255, ⓦwww.prodive-cairns.com.au.

All regions are visited on **cruises**, with vessels ranging from old trawlers to racing yachts and high-speed cruisers; if you want to stay longer, check into an island **resort** or take an extended **dive trip**. One way to choose the right boat is simply to check out the **price**: small, cramped, slow tubs are the cheapest while roomy, faster catamarans are more expensive – though often better value. To narrow things down further, find out which serves the best **food**. Generally, if this is going to be your only visit, it's worth paying the extra. Before going (or even if you're not) take in the superb two-hour **Reef Teach** slide show in Cairns at the Bolands Centre, 14 Spence St (Mon–Sat 6.15pm; $13; Ⓦ www.reefteach.com.au), at which eccentric marine biologist Paddy Colwell gives more essential background than the dive schools and tour operators have time to impart – this is the most worthwhile thing you can do in Cairns.

You might be a little taken aback by the state of the Cairns **coral**: years of agricultural run-off and recent coral-bleaching events – not to mention the sheer number of visitors – is beginning to have a visibly detrimental effect. This is less apparent on the more remote sites, but becomes quite marked the closer you get to the coast. Having said that, even the most visited sites are still stocked with marine life, ranging from tiny gobies to squid, turtles, and big pelagic fish – though seasoned divers might come away disappointed.

Dive sites

The dozen or more **inner reef** sites are much of a muchness. Concentrated day-tripping means that you'll probably be sharing the experience with several other boatloads of people, with scores of divers in the water at once. On a good day, snorkelling over shallow outcrops is enjoyable; going deeper, the coral shows more damage, but there's plenty of patchily distributed marine life. **Michaelmas Cay**, a small, vegetated crescent of sand, is worth a visit: over thirty thousand sooty, common and crested terns roost on the island, while giant clams, sweetlips and reef sharks can be found in the surrounding waters. Nearby **Hastings Reef** has better coral, resident moray eel and Napoleon maori wrasse, as well as plenty of sea stars and snails in the sand beneath. The two are often included in dive- or reef-trip packages, providing shallow, easy and fun diving. Another favourite, **Norman Reef**, tends to have very clear water, and some sites preserve decent coral gardens with good marine life.

One of the cheaper options for diving the **outer reef** is to take an **overnight trip** (sleep on board) to nearby sections such as **Moore** or **Arlington** reefs, which take between ninety minutes and two hours to reach – rather generalized terrain, but the advantages over a simple day-excursion are that you get longer in the water plus the opportunity for night dives. **Longer trips** of three days or more venture further from Cairns into two areas: a circuit north to the Cod Hole and Ribbon reefs, or straight out into the Coral Sea. **Cod Hole**, near Lizard Island (see p.548), has no coral but is justifiably famous for mobs of hulking potato cod which rise from the depths to receive hand-outs; currents here are strong, but having these monsters come close enough to cuddle is awesome. **The Ribbons** are a two-hundred-kilometre string with some relatively pristine locations and good visibility, as are **Coral Sea** sites; these are isolated, vertically walled reefs some distance out from the main structure and surrounded by open water teeming with seasonal bundles of pelagic species including mantas, turtles and seasonal **minke whales**. The most visited Coral Sea sites are **Osprey** and **Holmes** reefs, but try to get out to **Bougainville Reef**, home to everything from brightly coloured anthias fish to fast and powerful silvertip sharks.

Green Island and Fitzroy Island

Heart-shaped, tiny and sandy, **Green Island** is the easiest of any of the Barrier Reef's coral cays to reach, making it a near-essential, if expensive, day-trip from Cairns. This, combined with the island's size, means that it can be difficult to escape other visitors, but you only need to put on some fins, visit the **underwater observatory** ($5; free admission with some ferry tickets) or go for a cruise in a glass-bottomed boat to see plentiful coral, fish and turtles. The five-star rooms at the **Green Island Resort** (☎07/4031 3300, ⓦwww .greenislandresort.com.au; ➐) attract long-term guests, and there's a restaurant and pool open to day-trippers, plus plenty of sand to laze on. Daily **ferries** include *Big Cat* (☎07/4051 0444, ⓦwww.bigcat-cruises.com.au; $54) from the Pier Marketplace; and Great Adventures (☎07/4044 9944; $46) from Trinity Wharf. Both leave Cairns around 9am and return about 5pm, and run courtesy buses which will collect you from your accommodation. Day-trippers should bring their own **lunches**, as the resort's restaurant is very expensive.

Fitzroy Island is a continental island, not a cay like Green Island, and sports a YHA-run **resort** (☎07/4051 9588, ⓦwww.fitzroyislandresort.com.au; bunkhouse $31, cabins ➐) set in forest near the shore, from where you can dive on the island's reef. There's also a council-run **campground** here, which charges $13 per tent per night. Fitzroy is actually quite large and, away from the resort, there are some good walks through highland greenery where you can escape the sunbathing hordes. Sunlover (☎07/4050 1333, ⓦwww.sunlover.com.au) operates daily ferries from Trinity Wharf to the island from Cairns (55min each way; $34 return), and also offers overnight package deals.

The Atherton Tablelands

The **Atherton Tablelands**, the highlands behind Cairns, are named after **John Atherton**, who made the tin deposits at Herberton accessible by opening a route to the coast in 1877. Dense forest covered these highlands before the majority was felled for timber and given over to dairy cattle, tobacco and grain. The remaining pockets of forest are magnificent, but it's the understated beauty that draws most visitors today, and though **Kuranda** and its markets pull in busloads from the coast, there are several quieter national parks brimming with rare species. You could spend days here, driving or hiking through rainforest to crater lakes and endless small waterfalls, or simply camp out for a night and search for wildlife with a torch. For a contrast, consider a side trip west to the mining town of **Chillagoe**, whose dust, limestone caves and Aboriginal art place it firmly in the Outback.

Drivers can reach the tablelands on the **Palmerston Highway** from Innisfail, the twisty **Gillies Highway** from Gordonvale, or the **Kennedy Highway** from Smithfield to Kuranda. Two stylish and unforgettable ways to ride up to the tablelands are by **train** from Cairns to Kuranda, which winds through gorges and rainforest; and in the green gondolas of the **Kuranda Skyrail** cable car, with a fantastic seven-kilometre (40min) aerial view of the canopy between Smithfield and Kuranda – either method costs $33 one way or $54 return, and a "Skyrail up & train back" package is $69. Numerous **tours** run from Cairns (see box on p.527), and there are rumours of a **Kuranda bus service** costing just $1, though you really need your own transport to explore at leisure.

Kuranda and the Barron Gorge

A constant stream of visitors arriving from the coast has turned **KURANDA** into a stereotypical resort village – something, ironically, this once atavistic community was keen to escape. But despite overdevelopment and market-day tourism, it's hard not to like the place. The road comes in at the top of town, while **trains** and the **Skyrail** cable car arrive 500m down the hill, with essential services – post office, store (EFTPOS), bank, cafés – laid out between them along Coondoo Street. **Cafés** are legion, though pricey: *Annabel's Pie Shop*, across from the main markets, has excellent pasties and pies; the nearby Honey House has an on-site **bee hive** and sells its honey, and if you're staying the night, *Billy's* at the *Middle Pub* (halfway down Coondoo) does tasty charcoal grill and salad fare.

Given its accessibility from Cairns, Kuranda isn't a place where many people stay overnight – it's virtually a ghost town after the markets close – and there's little **accommodation**. Just up from the cable-car terminus and orchid-shrouded train station, you'll find the quiet *Kuranda Backpackers' Hostel*, 6 Arara St (☎07/4093 7355; dorms $18), with a plentiful supply of bunks, large grounds (where you can **camp**), kitchen and laundry. Around the corner is *The Bottom Pub and Motel* (☎07/4093 7206; ❸), whose bar has more than a little atmosphere on Friday nights.

The main **market times** are 8.30am to 3pm on Wednesday, Friday and Sunday, though some stalls open daily. The markets are best for crafts and clothes, but are not what they used to be, with a growing number of stallholders shying away from the regulated atmosphere here in favour of similar events at Yungaburra and Port Douglas. Nearby, forest fauna can be seen close up at the **Butterfly Sanctuary** (daily 10am–3.15pm; $12), a mix of streams and "feed trees" where giant ulysses and birdwing butterflies are the most obvious of the dozen local species protected by the breeding programme. **Birdworld**, behind the markets (daily 9am–4pm; $11), is a superb aviary with realistically arranged vegetation and nothing between you and a host of native and exotic rarities such as ecclectus parrots. Tucked away down a backstreet, the **Aviary** (daily 10am–3.30pm; $11) is partly a replay of Birdworld with purely Australian species, but they also have a collection of snakes and frogs, and a freshwater crocodile.

Kuranda sits at the top of the **Barron Gorge**, spectacular in the wet season when the river rages down the falls, but otherwise tamed by a hydroelectric dam upstream. Cross the rail bridge next to the station and take a path leading down to the river, where 45-minute **cruises** ($14) depart five times a day; the

---

Wet tropics and World Heritage

Queensland's **wet tropics** – the coastal belt from the Paluma Range, near Townsville, to the Daintree north of Cairns – has been nominated under UNESCO **World Heritage** listing as containing one of the oldest surviving tracts of **rainforest** anywhere on earth. Whether this listing has benefited the region is questionable, however; logging has slowed, but the tourist industry has vigorously exploited the area's status as an untouched wilderness, constantly pushing for more development so that a greater number of visitors can be accommodated. The clearing of mangroves for a marina and resort at Cardwell is a worst-case example; Kuranda's Skyrail project was one of the few cases designed to lessen the ultimate impact (another highway – with more buses – was the alternative). Given the profits to be made, development is inevitable, but it's sadly ironic that a scheme designed to promote the region's unique beauty may accelerate its destruction.

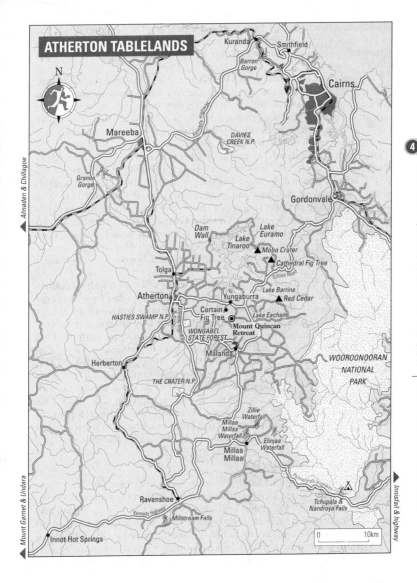

cruise operators often rent out canoes too. On foot, a newly prepared **walking track** descends to cold swimming spots along the railway and river from the lookout at the end of Barron Falls Road, 2km from town. Other trails follow the road beyond the falls through the **Barron Gorge National Park** and down to Kamerunga, near Cairns – see p.529 for details.

Mareeba

West of Kuranda, rainforest quickly gives way to dry woodland and tobacco plantations, quite a change from the coast's greenery. **Davies Creek** is at the end of a track branching off the road after 25km; paths lead from a campsite to where falls pour over a granite rock face to a pool surrounded by boulders and scrub.

The main road continues to **MAREEBA**, a quiet place and the tablelands' oldest town, founded in the 1900s after the area was opened up for tobacco farming, though with the tobacco industry now under attack, local farmers face an uncertain future. Coffee is another local industry, and at Coffee Works on Mason Street at the south exit of town (daily 9am–4pm) you can take a tour ($5.50), buy fresh beans, or try a brew at their café.

The **Mareeba Wetlands**, a beautiful pocket of grass-fringed lagoons 13km northwest of town via Biboohra (Wed–Sun 10am–4pm; $8; ℡07/4093 2514), attracts seasonal flocks of brolgas, jabiru storks and black cockatoos, along with resident wallabies and goannas. You can rent **canoes** here ($11 an hour), or book twilight ranger-led **tours** ($30) in advance. Another spot you could spend a few hours at is **Granite Gorge**, 14km southwest of town off the Dimbulah road; the last kilometre is a dirt track and entrance costs $2. At the gorge, a small river flows between a mass of house-sized granite boulders, creating plenty of swimming holes and opportunities for short hikes.

Back in Mareeba, Byrnes Street has all the shops and banks, with the **information centre** (daily 8am–4pm) at its southern end, marked by a memorial to James Venture Mulligan, the veteran prospector who discovered the Palmer River Goldfields (see p.549). Most of the **places to stay** are also at the southern end of town, including the *Golden Leaf Motel*, 261 Byrnes St (℡07/4092 2266, ℻4092 2207; ❸) and the pleasant *Tropical Tablelands Caravan Park* (℡07/4092 1158). Alternatively, *Arriga Park* (℡07/4093 2114, ⓦwww.bnbnq.com.au/arriga; ❺) is a colonial-style homestead and fruit farm about 15km west of town towards Chillagoe. After dark you can tangle with the farming fraternity in one of the hotels, or at *Jimmy D's Night Club* (Thurs–Sat 7pm–3am) on Byrnes Street. **Leaving**, Atherton is 30km south, while the Peninsula Developmental Road heads north to Mount Molloy. For Chillagoe, follow signs from the northern end of town for Dimbulah.

West to Chillagoe

The 150-kilometre road to Chillagoe mysteriously alternates between corrugated gravel and isolated sections of bitumen, but poses no real problem during the dry season. Look for graffiti on boulders ("Top Cat Pass" is a gem) and enticing adverts for the *Almaden Hotel*, whose cool, mirrored, well-supplied bar and beer garden are an incredible oasis in ramshackle, dilapidated **ALMADEN**. From here until Chillagoe's inactive smelter chimney appears from behind an outcrop of rock, the road passes blocks of cut marble awaiting shipment to Italy.

CHILLAGOE dates from 1887, when enough copper ore was found to keep a smelter running until the 1950s; now a gold mine 16km west at Mungana seems to keep the place ticking over. Red dust, hillocks, a service station, oversized hotels and general store complete the picture. The **NPWS office** (℡07/4094 7163) is in the post office down the main street, and can arrange **tours** of Chillagoe's caves (see below; daily 9am & 1.30pm) – though check well in advance as the tours may be closed during the wet season and numbers are limited. They can also arrange **camping**: there are two campsites (tank water and pit toilets), one close to town, the other 7km out near the caves themselves. If you need more comfortable **accommodation**, the *Chillagoe Lodge Motel*, 7 King St (℡07/4094 7106; ❹), has a pool and serves meals, while *Chilagoe Cabins*, on the Mareeba edge of town (℡07/4094 7206, ⓦwww.chillagoe.com; ❹) has self-contained cabins, a pool, small garden, and a nice atmosphere.

The caves

Chillagoe's **caves** are ancient coral reefs, hollowed out by rain and broken up into fluted masses half-buried in the scrub. Guides can take you through some, while you can explore others on your own, with instructions from the ranger. The caverns are varied by natural **limestone sculptures** deposited by evaporation and, unusually for the location, some large stalagmites; the best formations are at **Royal Arch**, **Donna** and **Trezkinn**. Wildlife here includes grey swiftlets and agile pythons, which somehow manage to catch bats on the wing. A footpath leads through grassland between the caves, where you'll find echidnas, kangaroos, black cockatoos and frogmouths, the last odd birds whose name fits them perfectly. This is prime snake country, so wear solid shoes and trousers. **Balancing Rock** offers panoramic views, with the town hidden by low trees, while obscure Aboriginal paintings and engravings have been found near the **Arches**, west at Mungana. Past here, the road continues 500km to Normanton, Karumba and tracks up western Cape York – but it doesn't improve, and there's no fuel or help along the way.

Atherton

Thirty kilometres south of Mareeba and centrally placed for forays to most of the tablelands' attractions, **ATHERTON** is the largest town in the tablelands. It was founded in part by Chinese miners who settled here in the 1880s after being chased off the goldfields: 2km south of the centre, the corrugated iron **Hou Wang Temple** (daily 10am–4pm; $7) is the last surviving building of Atherton's old **Chinatown**, a once-busy enclave of market gardens and homes which was abandoned after the government gave the land to returning World War I servicemen. The temple was restored in 2000, with an accompanying **museum** containing photographs, and artefacts found on site.

The other main reason to come to Atherton is to catch the authentically grubby 1920s **steam train** to Herberton, which leaves from Platypus Park, just south of town (Wed, Sat & Sun 10.30am; $27.50 return); along the way you get to look at tunnels, forest and the pretty Carrington Falls, and then have an hour or so to look around Herberton (see p.539) before the return trip. Otherwise, you can clock up local birdlife at **Hasties Swamp**, a big waterhole and two-storey **observation hide**, about 5km south of town. While nothing astounding, it's a peaceful place populated by magpie geese, pink-eared ducks, swamphens and assorted marsh tiggets.

Atherton's banks, shops and early-opening **cafés** – *Chatterbox* is best – can be found along Main Street, with a supermarket right at the south end past the post office. There's a friendly **information centre** (daily 9am–5pm) just south of the centre. **Accommodation** includes green and spacious **campsites** at the *Woodlands Tourist Park*, just at the edge of town on Herberton Road (℡07/4091 1407); the heavily tiled and hospitable *Atherton Travellers Lodge*, 37 Alice St, off Vernon Street (℡07/4091 3552, ⓔathertonguesthouse @hotmail.com; $18), which specializes in finding **farm work**; and the very pleasant *Atherton Blue Gum* at 36 Twelfth Ave (℡07/4091 5149, ⓦwww .athertonbluegum.com; ❹–❺), a modern timber B&B place which also runs regional tours.

Yungaburra and around

Just 13km east of Atherton at the start of the Gillies Highway to Gordonvale, the self-conciously pretty village of **YUNGABURRA**, consisting of the old wooden *Lake Eacham Hotel*, a store and a handful of houses, makes another good base to explore the tablelands. The village is also the venue for a huge **market** held on the last Sunday of each month. Considering its diminutive size, Yungaburra has plenty of **places to stay**. The pine-and-slate *On the Wallaby Hostel*, 37 Eacham Rd (☎07/4050 2031; dorms $14, rooms ❷), is very clued up on the area and organizes canoe and wildlife-spotting trips. The upmarket cottages at *Eden House* (☎07/4095 3355, ⓦwww.edenhouse .com.au; ❺), and well-appointed motel rooms at the *Kookaburra Lodge* (☎07/4095 3222, ⓦwww.kookaburra-lodge.com ❹) are other good bets, or treat yourself to a weekend at the romantic *Mt Quincan Crater Retreat*, on the Peeramon Road about 8km southeast of Yungaburra (☎07/4095 2255, ⓦwww.mtquincan.com.au; ❼); the self-contained wooden units here come with spa baths and are built on tall poles looking into an extinct volcano crater; the place is also infested with tree kangaroos. For **eating**, *Flynn's Café* does an excellent breakfast, or try the bratwurst and rosti at *Nick's Swiss Italian Restaurant* (closed Mon). *Eden House* has an "Australian contemporary" menu and good-value set dinners; while the popular *Burra Inn* (☎07/4095 3657) offers eclectic gourmet treats, from Tuscan lamb to kangaroo pie.

The **platypus-viewing platform**, set above a stream just on the edge of Yungaburra, is best in the early morning and late afternoon, when the crowds have dispersed. Another good place for wildlife spotting is the **Curtain Fig Tree**, an extraordinarily big parasitic strangler fig a couple of kilometres south-west on a minor road; the base is entirely overhung by a stringy mass of aerial roots drooping off the higher branches. Come here in the late afternoon or early morning to see **tree kangaroos** hopping along the branches, or well after dark to glimpse rare possums.

Lakes Tinaroo, Eacham and Barrine

Northeast from Atherton and north of Yungaburra, **Lake Tinaroo** is a con-voluted reservoir which was formed by pooling the Barron River's headwa-ters. Following the fifteen-kilometre access road off the Atherton to Yungaburra road lands you near the **dam wall** at *Lake Tinaroo Holiday Park* (☎07/4095 8232, Ⓕ4095 8808; cabins ❷), which also rents out canoes at $33 a day. Past here, a gravel road runs 25km around to the Gillies Highway, 15km east of Yungaburra, passing five very cheap **campsites** on the north shore before cutting deep into native forests. It's worth stopping along the way for the short walks to bright-green **Mobo Crater**, the spooky **Lake Euramo**, and the **Cathedral Fig**, another giant tree some 50m tall and 43m around the base; the thick mass of tendrils supporting the crown have fused together like melted wax.

A few kilometres east of Yungaburra at the start of the Gillies Highway down to Gordonvale on the coast are the **crater lakes**, or "maars", of Barrine and Eacham – blue, still circles surrounded by thick rainforest. **Lake Eacham** has an easy four-kilometre trail around its shores, taking you past birds and insects foraging on the forest floor, along with inoffensive **amethystine pythons** – Australia's largest snake – sunning themselves down by the water. There's **accommodation** near the lake at *Lake Eacham Caravan Park* (☎07/4095 3730; cabins ❸), and cosy *Crater Lake Rainforest Cottages* (☎07/4095 2322, ⓦwww.craterlakes.com.au; ❻), with four self-contained themed cottages set in a forest clearing. Some 5km further east on a dirt road, **Red Cedar** is another forest giant, a valuable timber tree somehow overlooked by nineteenth-century loggers; the tree's support roots are thicker than an average tree, and its straight, 35-metre-high trunk is two metres in diameter. For its part, **Lake Barrine** is relatively developed, with a **tearoom** overlooking the water serving good cream teas and canteen-style meals, and a **cruise boat** (daily at 10.15am, 2pm & 3.15pm; $10) which spends an hour circuiting the lake. To get away from the crowds, head for the two enormous kauri pines which mark the start of an underused six-kilometre **walking track** around the lake; keep your eyes peeled for spiky-headed water dragons, and hordes of musky rat-kangaroos, which look exactly as you'd expect them to.

The Southern Tablelands

The Kennedy Highway continues 80km down from Atherton to Ravenshoe, the highlands' southernmost town, past easy walking tracks through **Wongabel State Forest**, and **the Crater** at Mount Hypipamee, a 56-metre vertical rift formed by volcanic gases blowing through fractured granite that's now filled with deep, weed-covered water. Picnic tables are on the site, as are ridiculously tame Lewins honeyeaters, but camping is prohibited. An alternative road from Atherton – and the train (see p.537) – circles west via **HERBERTON**, a quaint, one-time timber town without a modern building in sight. During the 1880s there were 30,000 people here (a century before Cairns achieved this population), and the railway from Atherton was built to service the town. Just south of Herberton, the **Historic Village** (daily 10am–4pm; $10) comprises a meticulous but lifeless collection of about thirty pioneer buildings relocated from elsewhere, including a schoolroom, bishop's residence, hotel, Chinese relics and bottle dump – you name it. If you're in Herberton at lunchtime on Sunday, there are huge outdoor **barbecues** at the *Royal Hotel*'s beer garden.

RAVENSHOE is mainly notable for the *Tully Falls Hotel*, Queensland's highest pub, and **Millstream Falls**, Australia's broadest waterfall, 5km away. There's also another **steam railway** here, with a train departing Saturday and Sunday at 2.30pm to the tiny siding of Tumoulin, Queensland's highest train station (call ☎07/4091 4871 for details). Ravenshoe's **Visitor Centre** (daily 9am–4pm, ☎07/4097 7700) is also very informative, with a small natural history display. If you get stuck here overnight, the *Kool Moon Motel* (☎07/4097 6407; ❸) and *Tall Timbers Caravan Park* (☎07/4097 6325; tent sites $13.50, motel rooms ❸) offer decent **accommodation**. Northeast, the road back to Atherton takes you past a blustery hillside sprouting an array of twenty long-stemmed **windmills**, part of a wind-generator power scheme. Southwest, the road drops off the tablelands past **Innot Hot Springs** – with its huge anthills and steamy upwellings behind the *Hot Springs Hotel* – and the township of **Mount Garnet**, to the start of the Gulf Developmental Road (see p.602).

Malanda, Millaa Millaa and the Palmerston Highway

About 25km southeast of Atherton, the **dairy** at **MALANDA** provides milk and cheese for the whole of Queensland's far north, plus most of the Northern Territory and even New Guinea. In the centre of town, the *Malanda Hotel* (☎07/4096 5488; ❷) was built in 1911 to sleep 300 people and claims to be the **largest wooden building** in the southern hemisphere; its old furnishings and excellent *1911* restaurant are worth a look even if you're not staying here, though the bar is so cavernous it always feels empty. Back about a kilometre towards Atherton, there's a roadside swimming hole and short rainforest walk at **Malanda Falls Environmental Park**; the display at the **information centre** here (daily 10am–4pm; $1) gives a run-down on the tableland's geology and its Aboriginal and settler history.

From Malanda it's about 20km south to **MILLAA MILLAA**, a quiet, 500-metre-long street with the usual hotel and general store. A waterfall circuit starts 2km east of the town, where a fifteen-kilometre road passes three small cascades: **Millaa Millaa Falls** consist of a ten-metre-high cascade over basalt collumns into a cold, shallow pool, framed by gingers and tree ferns; **Zillie Falls** has good views from the top; and **Elinjaa Falls** has grassy picnic grounds and a short track through forest to the base of the falls. Past Millaa Millaa, the Palmerston Highway descends to the coastal highway near Innisfail; the road was named after **Christie Palmerston**, a fugitive who hid with Aborigines on the tablelands in the 1870s and pioneered the route. The **Palmerston section** of Wooroonooran National Park, which includes the Bellenden Ker Range (see p.520), occupies a huge area north of the highway and is worth a stopover to explore the most extensive, undisturbed spread of Atherton's rainforest, though you'll need some protection from summer flies. There's a NPWS **campsite** ($4 per person per night) about 27km from Millaa Millaa, from where the best of the walking tracks lead to mossy **Tchupala Falls** and the impressive **Nandroya Falls**, while the highway descends 40km past the park to Innisfail.

Cairns to Cape Tribulation

Just a couple of hours' drive **north of Cairns** on the Cook Highway are the Daintree and Cape Tribulation, the tamed fringes of the Cape York Peninsula. The highway initially runs within sight of the sea to **Port Douglas** and **Mossman**, a beautiful drive past isolated beaches where hang-gliders patrol the headlands. North of Mossman is **the Daintree**, Australia's largest and the world's oldest surviving stretch of tropical rainforest. World Heritage listing hasn't saved it from development: roads are being surfaced, land has been sub-divided, and there's an ever-increasing number of services in place, undermining the wild and remote brochure image. While this disappoints some visitors, the majestic forest still descends thick and dark right to the sea around **Cape Tribulation**, and you can explore paths through the jungle, watch for wildlife, or just rest on the beach.

Tours from Cairns will show you the sights, but you really need longer to take in the rich scenery and atmosphere – without your own transport, Cape Trib Connections (℡07/4053 3833, bookings essential) runs a daily **shuttle bus** from Cairns to Cape Tribulation, picking up at Port Douglas and Mossman along the way.

Port Douglas and Mossman

Massive development in recent years has seen the once pretty fishing village of **PORT DOUGLAS**, an hour north of Cairns, turned into an upmarket tourist attraction, with a main street full of boutiques, shopping malls and holidaying hordes. However, the town does have a huge **beach**, along with plenty of distractions to keep you busy for a day or two, and it's getting to be as good a place as Cairns to pick up a regional tour or dive trip to the reef – though prices are steeper.

The town comprises a small grid of streets centred around Macrossan Street – which runs between Four Mile Beach and Anzac Park – with the **marina** a couple of blocks back. As in Cairns, a prolific number of businesses offer tourist **information** – the Port Douglas Tourist Information Centre at no. 23 (daily 8.30am–5.30pm; ☎07/4099 5599) can sort out everything from Aboriginal-guided tours of Mossman Gorge to sailing trips and buses to the Daintree. Between the end of Macrossan Street and the sea, **Anzac Park** is the scene of an increasingly busy Sunday morning **market**, good for fruit, vegetables and souvenirs. Near the park's **jetty** you'll find the whitewashed timber church of **St Mary's by the Sea**, built after the 1911 cyclone carried off the previous structure. Behind, at **Ben Cropp's Shipwreck Museum** (daily 9am–5pm; $5.50), bronze cannon, teapots and the results of twenty years salvaging are piled around a continuously playing video of Ben's exploits.

Out to sea, the Low Isles, Chinaman, Tongue and Opal **reefs** are all decent enough, though in much the same condition as popular sites off Cairns. *Quicksilver*, based at the marina (☎07/4099 5500, ⑩www.quicksilver-cruises.com), runs a sailing boat to the Low Isles ($135), while its high-speed catamaran will whisk you to the Agincourt Reef for the day ($165). You can organize **diving** with them, but more serious divers should contact Poseidon Cruises, 34 Macrossan St (☎07/4099 4772, ⑩www.poseidon-cruises.com.au), or *Silverblue* (☎07/4099 4544, ⑩www.silverblue.com.au), two smaller vessels which make day-trips to less touristed sections for between $175 and $200.

The best of the town's **accommodation** options is the huge *Mirage Resort* (☎07/4099 5888; ⑩www.mirageresort.com.au; ❼), off Davidson Street on the way into town, which hosted former US president Bill Clinton during his 1996 visit. Less flamboyant lodgings include *4 Mile Beach Caravan Park* on Reef Street (☎07/4099 4222; cabins ❸); the pleasant *Port O'Call Lodge/YHA* about 700m from town on Port Street (☎07/4099 5422, ⑩www.portocall.com.au; dorms $20, rooms ❷); and the central, multi-story *Parrotfish Lodge* backpackers on Warner Street (☎07/4099 5011, ⑩www.parrotfishlodge.com; dorms $23, rooms ❸). There are also two motel options just back from Four Mile Beach: *Whispering Palms Resort*, on Langley Road (☎07/4098 5128, ⑩www.whisperingpalms.com.au; ❺), and *Mango Tree Apartments*, 91 Davidson St (☎07/4099 5677; ❺).

Places to eat abound along Macrossan Street. Near the information centre, *EJ Seamarket* is a licensed fish-and-chip shop, so you can grab a cold beer while waiting for your meal to crisp. The *Iron Bar* has rough-cut timber furniture and a mid-range surf 'n' turf menu, while *Mango Jam Café* across the road opens late for wood-fired pizza, and the nearby *Star of Siam* has moderately priced Thai fare. *Catalina*, around the corner on Wharf Street (Tues–Sun 6.30pm–late; ☎07/4099 5287), occupies a beautiful setting, with a verandah shaded by two ancient mango trees, and serves sophisticated delicacies such as coral trout grilled in banana leaves. The seafood-oriented *Starfish* restaurant on Macrossan Street (☎07/4099 4077) does a superb charred snapper for around $25.

Mossman

MOSSMAN, 14km past Port Douglas, is a quiet town which has hardly changed in the last thirty years; rail lines between the canefields and mill still run along the main street. Ten minutes inland, **Mossman Gorge** looks like all rainforest rivers should; the boulder-strewn flow is good for messing around in on a quiet day, but attracts streams of tour buses and car break-ins in peak season. Kuku Yalangi, the local community, put together the **Aboriginal walking trail** here and conduct **tours** (Mon–Fri 10am, noon & 2pm; $16.50;

bookings on ☎07/4098 2595) of the gorge explaining its history and local plant usage. If you want **to stay** somewhere plush in the area, book in at the exclusive *Silky Oaks Lodge* (☎1800 737 678, ⓦwww.poresorts.com.au; ❼), 12km from town through the canefields; there's not much rainforest here, but you get very well looked after.

Continuing north, the road splits left to Daintree township or right for the Daintree Ferry to Cape Tribulation. Backtracking southeast lets you leave the highway and climb to **Mount Molloy** and the **Peninsula Developmental Road** – the easier, inland route to Cooktown.

The Daintree

Set off the Mossman to Cape Tribulation road, the riverside **DAINTREE** township – a former timber camp – is now more or less just one big pub, a general store and a campground, though experienced 4WD hands can test their mettle on the **CREB Track** from here to Cooktown; erroneously marked as a proper road on some maps; you'll need tyre chains for steep, slippery gradients, and some practice at manouvering over large granite boulders. Most people skip all this, however, and instead follow the road to the **Daintree River Ferry** (6am–midnight; pedestrians $1 each way, vehicles $8) and the start of the mostly sealed 35-kilometre Cape Tribulation road. The river crossing can be very busy, with the cable ferry taking a dozen cars and tour coaches every fifteen minutes or so; you might want to take a **crocodile-spotting tour** with Bruce Belcher (☎07/4098 7717; $22) or Nice n Easy (☎07/4098 7456; $22), who prowl through the local mangroves in search of prey.

Across the river, it's 8km through rainforest over the convoluted Alexandra range to the **Jindalba Environmental Centre** (daily 8.30am–5pm; $15), which features a five-level, 27-metre-high **tower** with identification charts for the plants and birds you're likely to see at each stage – the top also provides a fabulous view over the canopy. Trails head off into the forest from the car park beneath. Just up the road, **FLORAVILLE** has the regional **pub**, a café, and unexpected French cuisine – using Australian game meats – at *Le Bistrot* (☎07/4098 9016); past here, a six-kilometre side road from the airstrip heads straight to the coast at **Cow Bay**, where there's an excellent **beach**. **Accommodation** along the Cow Bay road includes the open-plan, laid-back *Epiphyte Bed and Breakfast*, off a short track about 4km along (☎07/4098 9039; ❷); and the jungle-clad cabins of *Crocodylus Village/YHA*, about 2km along (☎07/4098 9166; dorms $20, rooms ❸) – meals here are good and inexpensive, and they arrange night walks, kayak trips to Snapper Island, and diving at the local reef.

Back on the Cape Tribulation road, another few kilometres lands you at **ALEXANDRA BAY** township, which has a **campsite**, cabins and self-contained units at *Lync-Haven Retreat* (☎07/4098 9155, ⓦwww.lynchaven .com.au; ❸–❹), and *Fanpalm Café*, which marks the start of a **boardwalk** through a forest of fan palms. Moving on past a tea plantation, there's further **accommodation** up against the forest fence at *Deep Forest Lodge* (☎07/4098 9162; ❺), which has well-furnished, self-contained cabins; and, inland off the main road in "boutique cabins" at *Heritage Lodge* (☎07/4098 9138, ⓔheritage@c130.aone.net.au; ❼), which also sports a fancy restaurant and more walking trails along Cooper Creek. The next stop is 4km on at sandy **Thornton Beach**, where you'll find a licensed kiosk at *Café on Sea*; then it's another few kilometres to where concrete paths and boardwalks follow the creek through a mixture of forest to mangroves at the river mouth on the

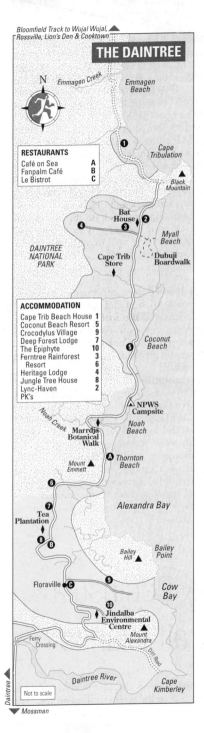

THE DAINTREE

Bloomfield Track to Wujal Wujal,
Rossville, Lion's Den & Cooktown

Emmagen Creek

Emmagen Beach

N

Cape Tribulation

Black Mountain

RESTAURANTS

Café on Sea	A
Fanpalm Café	B
Le Bistrot	C

Bat House

Myall Beach

Cape Trib Store

Dubuji Boardwalk

DAINTREE NATIONAL PARK

Coconut Beach

ACCOMMODATION

Cape Trib Beach House	1
Coconut Beach Resort	5
Crocodylus Village	9
Deep Forest Lodge	7
The Epiphyte	10
Ferntree Rainforest Resort	3
Heritage Lodge	4
Jungle Tree House	8
Lync-Haven	2
PK's	

NPWS Campsite

Noah Creek

Marrdja Botanical Walk

Noah Beach

Mount Emmett

Thornton Beach

Alexandra Bay

Tea Plantation

Bailey Hill

Bailey Point

Floraville

Cow Bay

Jindalba Environmental Centre

Mount Alexandra

Ferry Crossing

Dirt Road

Daintree River

Cape Kimberley

Not to scale

Daintree

Mossman

Marrdja Botanical Walk at **Noah Beach**. Look for spiky lawyer cane, lianas twisted into corkscrew shapes where they once surrounded a tree, and the spherical pods of the cannonball mangrove – dried and dismembered, they were used as puzzles by Aboriginal peoples, the object being to fit the irregular segments back together. The NPWS has a **campsite** here in woodland behind the beach; it's big but prone to be muddy and is closed during the wet season.

Just up the road is the exclusive beachfront *Coconut Beach Resort* (☏07/4098 0033, ⊛www .coconutbeach.com.au; ❼), with an extensive array of facilities including a huge A-frame restaurant ("smart tropical dress" required). North of here, the **Cape Trib Store** has a café and supplies, and is also the base for Mason's Tours (☏07/4098 0070, ⊛www.masonstours.com.au), which organizes 4WD safaris and local day and night walks. Plants close in again a couple of kilometres beyond at **Dubuji Boardwalk**, a 1.2-kilometre-long replay of Marrdja, though with a greater variety of forests. Aside from fan palms, rainforest cycads and vines, look out for the very odd peppermint stick insect, which hides in pandanus leaves alongside the path; they're a strange blue-green colour, and squirt out a mint-scented spray when disturbed.

Cape Tribulation

Cape Tribulation ("Cape Trib") – a forty-minute drive from the ferry crossing – was named when Captain Cook's vessel hit a reef offshore in June 1770. The cleared area below the steep, forested slopes of **Mount Sorrow** has a café, store, a boardwalk onto the beach and a **Bat House** (daily 10.30am–3.30pm; $2), worth a visit to handle tame orphaned flying foxes. **Beds** and **campsites** are available at the often noisy and overcrowded *PK's* hostel (T 1800 232 333, W www.pksjungle village.com; camping $12, dorms $25, rooms ❸); alternatively, there's the upmarket *Ferntree Rainforest Resort* (T 07/4098 0000, W www.ferntree.com; ❻), and the *Jungle Treehouse* B&B (T 07/4099 5651, W www.jungletree housecapetrib.com.au; ❺), both set 200m up in the hills, as well as the friendly beachfront *Cape Trib Beach House*, 2.5km north (T 07/4098 0030, W www.capetribbeach.com.au; dorms $25, cabins ❸), which has dorms as well as beds. All can organize horse riding, sea-kayaking and guided forest walks.

The area is best explored on foot – for the simple pleasure of walking through the forest with the sea breaking on a beach not five minutes distant. A **path** runs out to the cape, where you may see brilliantly coloured pittas (small, tailless birds with a buff chest, green back and black and rust heads) bouncing around in the leaf litter, or even a crocodile sunning itself on the beach. One way to penetrate the undergrowth away from the paths is to follow small creeks: **Emmagen**, about 6km north, runs halfway up Mount Sorrow and is recommended for its safe swimming holes.

The Bloomfield Track

The scene of vicious confrontations in 1984 between construction crews and environmentalists who tried unsuccessfully to stop this alternative road to Cooktown being built through virgin forest, the **Bloomfield Track** is completely impassable after rain and otherwise requires a 4WD. Spanning 80km from Cape Tribulation to where the track joins the Cooktown Road at **Black Mountain**, the exciting section with drastic gradients lies below the halfway mark of the tidal **Bloomfield River**, which has to be crossed at low water. Beyond **Wujal Wujal Aboriginal community** on the north side, the road flattens out to run past *Bloomfield Cabins and Camping* (T 07/4060 8207, W www.bloomfieldcabins.com; ❹), where there's plentiful camping space and three basic cabins; and *Home Rule Rainforest Lodge* at **ROSSVILLE** (T 07/4060 3925; ❸), which offers kitchen facilities and inexpensive meals. Alternatively, you could fork out for the reclusive *Bloomfield River Lodge* (T 07/4035 9166, W www.bloomfieldlodge.com.au; ❼), though at a minimum of two nights at $586 per person – including transport from Cairns – it's not for everyone. Moving on, it's not far now to the more down-to-earth *Lions Den* pub at **Helenvale** near Black Mountain (see p.546), about thirty minutes from Cooktown.

The Cape York Peninsula and Torres Strait Islands

The **Cape York Peninsula** points north towards the Torres Strait and New Guinea, and tackling the rugged tracks and hectic river crossings on the "Trip

To The Tip" is an adventure in itself – besides being a means to reach Australia's northernmost point and the communities at **Bamaga** and **Thursday Island**, so far removed from southern attitudes that they could easily be in another country. But it's not all four-wheel driving across the savannah: during the dry season the historic settlement of **Cooktown**, the wetlands at **Lakefield National Park** and **Laura**'s Aboriginal heritage are only a day's journey from Cairns in any decent vehicle. Given longer you might get as far as the mining company town of **Weipa**, but don't go further than this without off-road transport; while some have managed to reach the Tip in family sedans, most who try fail miserably.

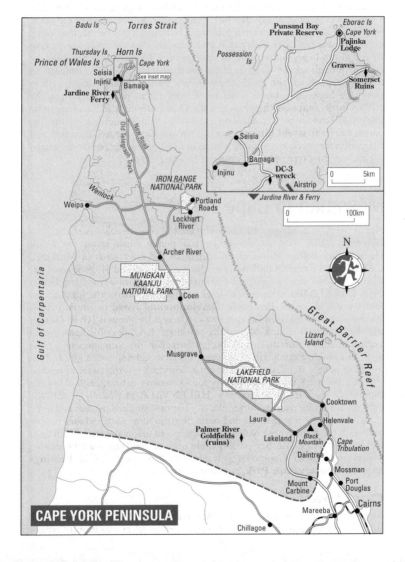

With thousands making the overland journey between May and October, a **breakdown** won't necessarily leave you stranded, but the cost of repairs will make you regret it. **Bikers** should travel in groups and have off-roading experience. Those without their own vehicle can take overland **tours** right to the Tip; see box on p.526. From Cairns, it's also possible to **cruise** up to Thursday Island, aboard the *Trinity Bay* passenger ferry (☏07/4035 1234, ⓦwww.seaswift.com.au; one-way $325). You can also **fly** to various places on the Cape with Cape York Air (☏07/4035 9399, ⓦwww.capeyorkair.com.au), which also does a one-day return postal run up to Thursday Island, stopping briefly at remote stations along the way.

You'll find a few roadhouses and motels along the way, but north of Weipa **accommodation** on the Cape is mostly limited to camping, and it's inevitable if you head right to the Tip that one night at least will be spent in the bush. Settlements also supply meals and provisions, but there won't be much on offer, so take all you can carry. Don't turn bush campsites into rubbish dumps: take a pack of bin liners and remove all your garbage. **Estuarine crocodiles** are present throughout the Cape: read the warning under "Wildlife dangers" in Basics (p.27) and see also p.635. There are few **banks**, so take enough cash to carry you between points – some roadhouses accept plastic. In Cairns, the NPWS stocks **maps** and brochures on the Cape's national parks, and might be able to fill you in on current road conditions. Vehicles heading to the Tip should carry a **first-aid kit**, a comprehensive tool kit and spares, extra fuel, and a tarpaulin for creek crossings. A winch, and equipment for removing, patching and inflating tyres may also come in handy.

Mossman to Cape York

Not as pretty as the coastal Bloomfield track but considerably easier, the 260-kilometre inland road to Cooktown and points north leaves the Cook Highway just before Mossman and climbs to the drier scrub at **MOUNT CARBINE**, a former tungsten mine whose roadhouse and *Wolfram Hotel* (❷, with simple but clean rooms) fulfil all functions. The road beyond is sealed as far as **LAKELAND**, whose café, hotel and fuel stop marks the junction for routes north along the **Peninsula Developmental Road** to Laura (p.549), but the way to Cooktown lies east, past cataracts at the **Annan River Gorge**, and the mysterious **Black Mountain**, two huge dark piles of lichen-covered granite boulders near the road. Aborigines reckon the formation to be the result of a building competition between two rivals fighting over a girl, and tell stories of people wandering into the eerie, whistling caverns, never to return.

At this point it's worth making the four-kilometre detour south along the Bloomfield Track to the *Lions Den* at **HELENVALE**. The *Den* is an old-style pub playing up for tourists during the day, but one hundred percent authentic at night, from the iron sheeting and beam decor to those nasty exhibits in glass bottles on the piano. Those with 4WD vehicles can follow the track south from Helenvale to Cape Trib (see p.543), while back on the main road it's another twenty minutes to Cooktown past birdlife-filled waterholes at **Keatings Lagoon Conservation Park**, just 5km short of town.

Cooktown

After the *Endeavour* nearly sank at Cape Tribulation in 1770, Captain Cook landed at a natural harbour to the north, where he spent two months repair-

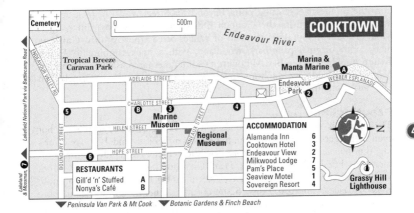

COOKTOWN

Cemetery

Endeavour River

Tropical Breeze
Caravan Park

Marina &
Manta Marine

ADELAIDE STREET

Endeavour
Park

CHARLOTTE STREET

Marine
Museum

HELEN STREET

Regional
Museum

HOPE STREET

ACCOMMODATION
Alamanda Inn   6
Cooktown Hotel   3
Endeavour View   2
Milkwood Lodge   7
Pam's Place   5
Seaview Motel   1
Sovereign Resort   4

Grassy Hill
Lighthouse

RESTAURANTS
Gill'd 'n' Stuffed   A
Nonya's Café   B

0   500m

Lakefield National Park via Battlecamp Road

ENDEAVOUR VALLEY RD

BOUNDARY STREET

Lakeland & Mossman

WALKER STREET

FURNEAUX STREET

WEBBER ESPLANADE

▼ Peninsula Van Park & Mt Cook   ▼ Botanic Gardens & Finch Beach

ing the vessel, observing the "Genius, Temper, Disposition and Number of the Natives" and – legend has it – naming the kangaroo after an Aboriginal word for "I don't know". Tempers wore thin on occasion, as when the crew refused to share a catch of turtles with local Aborigines and Cook commented: "They seem'd to set no value upon any thing we gave them."

The site lay dormant until gold was discovered southwest on the **Palmer River** in 1873, and within months a harbour was being surveyed at the mouth of the **Endeavour River** for a tented camp known as **COOKTOWN**. A wild success while gold lasted, the settlement once boasted a main street alive with hotels and a busy port doing brisk trade with Asia through thousands of Chinese prospectors and merchants. But the reserves were soon exhausted and by 1910 Cooktown was on the decline. Today, the town's main drag, Charlotte Street, is neat but quiet, good for random wandering past the old wharves and **Endeavour Park**, the site of Cook's landing, now graced by a statue of the great navigator. Among monuments on the lawn are the remains of defences sent from Brisbane in the nineteenth century to ward off a threatened Russian invasion: one cannon, three cannonballs and two rifles. At the far end, the marina, Manta Marine (℡07/4069 5601, ℮mantam@bigpond.com) organizes two-hour **cruises** through the Endeavour River's mangroves ($25) and **fishing and diving** trips. Just outside town, 500m along Endeavour Valley Road, the half-wild **cemetery**'s Jewish, Chinese, Protestant and Catholic sections gives a glimpse of how cosmopolitan the town once was. The cemetery's most famous resident is **Mary Watson** of Lizard Island (see p.548), whose grave near the entrance is decorated with seashells and a painting of a pietà.

The best **views** of the town and river are from the top floor of the old Sisters of Mercy Convent, now a **regional museum** (daily 9.30am–4pm; $5.50) containing a bit of everything: artefacts jettisoned from the *Endeavour*; a reconstructed joss house; a display on pearling around Thursday Island; and an account of the "hopelessly insolvent" Cooktown–Laura railway. Not far away on the corner of Helen and Walker streets, the **Marine Museum** (daily 8.30am–5.30pm; $5.50) details the 1899 cyclones Mahina and Nachon, which collided north of Cooktown, sinking 76 vessels and killing 350 people.

There are more views of the district from the red-and-white corrugated-iron cone of **Grassy Hill Lighthouse**, reached on a concrete track from the end of Hope Street. **Mount Cook** is a rather tougher proposition, a two-hour return hike through thick forest on meagre paths – follow the orange triangles from the nondescript starting point beyond Ida Street (you can pick up free maps of the route from the Council Offices next to the post office, open Mon–Fri 9am–4.30pm). At the end of Walker Street, the **Botanic Gardens** merge into original paperbark woodland, with a track running to **Finch Beach** on Cherry Tree Bay. Although it's sometimes rated as a safe swimming beach, you should heed the home-made warning signs in pidgin: "Dispela Stap Hia" and a picture of a croc.

Practicalities

The June **Discovery Festival** tends towards being a thorough piss-up, but even then **accommodation** shouldn't be too difficult to find. If you're camping, the *Tropical Breeze Caravan Park* near the cemetery is handy for town, or there are budget beds at *Pam's Place*, Charlotte Street (☎07/4069 5166, ⓦwww.cooktownhostel.com; dorms $19, rooms ❷). For something a bit more lavish, *Alamanda Inn* (☎07/4069 5203; ❸) offers quiet motel rooms and a big pool; the two-storey *Seaview Motel* (☎07/4069 5377; ❸) is central and tidy; *Endeavour View* (☎07/4069 5676, ⓕ4069 6642, ❹) has self-contained wooden cabins; while the lavish *Sovereign Resort* (☎07/4069 5400; ❺) has a pool and café-bar-restaurant. Two kilometres out of town on a secluded hillside, *Milkwood Lodge* (☎07/4069 5007, ⓦwww.milkwood-lodge.com; ❹) offers self-contained cabins with verandah views out over the valley. There's good **food** with an Asian twist at *Nonya's Café*, or riverside views from *Gill'd 'n' Stuffed*, a chip shop at the marina; the *Cooktown Hotel* (also known as the *Top Pub*) is the best spot for drink and bar meals. The **supermarket** is the last source of fresh provisions before Weipa, and the ATM at the **bank** here is the only one on the Cape.

Those continuing **up the Cape** have two options: vehicles other than 4WDs have to head southwest to Lakeland for Laura and points north; stronger sets of wheels can reach Lakefield National Park more directly by heading towards Hope Vale community and then taking the Battlecamp Road. The last **fuel** this way until Musgrave is about 33km from Cooktown at the *Endeavour Falls Tourist Park* (☎07/4069 5431; self-contained units ❸), a nice spot in itself with a neighbouring waterfall, forest and an apparently croc-free swimming hole – though don't swim here without advice from the tourist park.

Lizard Island

Lizard Island is one of the most isolated resorts in Australia, a granite rise covered in stunted trees and heath, 90km north of Cooktown, and within sight of the outer reef – divers rave about the fringing coral here. The only regular access is on **flights** from Cairns with Qantas (around $500 return); those unable to afford the **lodge** (☎07/4060 3999; ❼) – which has a bar and restaurant and comfortable, if simple, units – can use the NPWS **campsite** (permits from Cairns; see p.528) down on Watson Beach. Campers should be self-sufficient in food and carry charcoal beads for cooking (gas cylinders and fuel are not allowed on the plane); unless in serious emergencies the lodge is off limits, with the exception of its bar. There are far worse places to spend a few days in a tent, however, and there's sometimes fresh fish on sale to bulk out your supplies. The lodge can arrange diving for its guests.

Shell middens show that Lizard was regularly visited by Aboriginal peoples, but the island was uninhabited when **Robert Watson** built a cottage and started a sea-slug processing operation here in the 1870s, accompanied by his wife **Mary** and two Chinese servants. Aborigines attacked the house while

Robert was at sea in October 1881, killing one of the Chinese and forcing Mary, her baby and Ah Sam to flee in a water tank; they paddled west for five days before dying of thirst. Her painfully matter-of-fact diary is kept at Brisbane's John Oxley Library, while the tank is on display at the Museum of Tropical Queensland in Townsville.

Quinkan Country: Laura and around

Back on the Peninsula Road, 60km north of Lakeland, **LAURA**'s store-cum-post office and roadhouse support the two-day **Aboriginal Dance Festival**, an electrifying assertion of Aboriginal identity, held in June of odd-numbered years. At any time of year you can visit the sandstone caves and ridges at **Split Rock**, 13km south of town, where a steep track leads to a two-hour gallery circuit. Paintings depict animals and startling spirit figures associated with sorcery: spidery, frightening **Quinkan** with pendulous earlobes, and dumpy Anurra, often with their legs twisted upwards. Other sites show scenes from post-Contact life, depicting horses, rifles and clothed figures; some caves were probably in use until the 1930s. You can find out more through the *Ang-Gnarra Aboriginal Corporation Caravan Park* (℗07/4060 3200) or from Trezise Bush Service/Quinkan Tours (℗07/4060 3236), which has a camp west in the scrub at Jowalbinna, about an hour's drive from Laura (4WD only; for reservations call ℗07/4051 4777, ⓦwww.adventures.com).

Sites along the **Palmer River**, 80km (8hr) southwest of Laura along a terrible 4WD track, recall the gigantic 1873 **goldrush**. Mining life was volatile: Aborigines waged guerrilla warfare, and race riots erupted between whites and the Chinese – who at one time outnumbered the entire European population of Queensland and infuriated whites by doggedly extracting gold from "exhausted" claims. The settlements at Maytown and German Bar were abandoned once the gold had gone and today there's virtually nothing left except atmosphere; the Cairns NPWS (see p.528) stocks maps and permits.

Lakefield National Park

Ideally you'd take at least a week to absorb **Lakefield National Park**'s fifty thousand square kilometres of savannah and riverine flats, but even a single night spent here will give you a feel for the Cape's most accessible wilderness area. Apart from the **Old Laura Homestead** – built between 1892 and 1940 and standing abandoned in the scrub on the Laura River – the park's pleasures revolve around outdoor pursuits, fishing and exploring lagoons for wildlife. Lakefield's **crocodile-conservation** programme means you might see both fresh- and saltwater types; birdlife is plentiful and plenty of kangaroos put in an appearance. "**Magnetic**" **anthills** are a common landmark: the ants build flattened towers aligned north–south to prevent overheating in the noonday sun.

Vehicles other than 4WDs can sometimes manage the rough 170-kilometre track through the park between Laura township and Musgrave Roadhouse (see p.550), but only if there hasn't been any rain for a good while. High clearance is essential for other routes, including the Battle Camp road to Cooktown. **Ranger stations** (℗07/4060 3271) are located along the road at New Laura, at the southern end of the park, 50km from Laura; at Lakefield (central, 80km); and at Bizant (north, 100km). Popular places to camp and watch wildlife are **Horseshoe Lagoon** beyond Old Laura, **12 Mile Hole** near New Laura (4WD only), **Kalpowar Crossing** (near Lakefield, with showers and toilets) and **Hann Crossing**, in the north of the park.

Laura to Iron Range and Weipa

Following the main road, the 300km that stretches between Laura and Archer River passes in a haze of dust, jolts and roadhouses supplying fuel, food, beds and drink. First on the list is **MUSGRAVE** (135km from Laura; ☎07/4060 3229 for road condition check), a converted homestead where the track from Lakefield National Park joins the road; there's accommodation about 10km in towards the park at *Lotus Bird Lodge* (☎07/4059 0773, ⓦwww.cairns .aust.com/lotusbird; ❼), whose spacious wooden cottages are surrounded by much the same scenery as you'll find in the national park. Back on the road north, the next two hours are a wild roller-coaster ride – look out for "Dip" signs warning of monster gullies – down to **COEN**'s (S)*Exchange Hotel*, 107km from Musgrave. Coen's Ambrust General Store handles **camping**, provisions, fuel, post office business and EFTPOS. The *Homestead Guest House*, on Regent Street, has **beds** (☎07/4060 1157; ❸) and can provide meals, while you can have any car problems fixed at Clark's workshop.

Some 25km further north, a 4WD track west heads into the dry woodland and rainforest of the **Mungkan Kaanju National Park**; the ranger station lies 75km along at Rokeby station (☎07/4060 1137), with camping at undeveloped bush sites. Back on the main road north, it's 45km from the park turn-off to the **Archer River Roadhouse** (☎07/4060 3266), which has a camp-site and accommodation in units (❸), as well as the last reliable **fuel** on the main road before Bamaga, 400km away. Beyond are routes east to Iron Range (155km) and west to Weipa (190km) – covered below.

Iron Range

There's nothing else in Australia quite like the magnificent jungle at **Iron Range National Park**, a leftover from the Ice Age link to New Guinea, which hides fauna found nowhere else on the continent – the nocturnal green python and brilliant blue-and-red eclectus parrot are the best-known species. Four hours bouncing along a 110-kilometre 4WD track from the main road should bring you to a clearing where the army simulated a nuclear strike in the 1960s – fortunately using tons of conventional explosives instead of the real thing. Turning right at the junction here takes you past the **ranger station** (☎07/4060 7170) to **LOCKHART RIVER**, an Aboriginal mission and fishing beach; supplies and fuel are sold here during weekday trading hours. The road left passes two **bush campsites** near the Claudie River and Gordon's Creek crossings before winding up at **PORTLAND ROADS** – a few houses (though there are no stores or any public services here) overlooking a monument to Edmund Kennedy (see p.514) and the remains of a harbour used by US forces in World War II. There's further camping a few kilometres back towards the junction at **Chilli Beach**, a perpetually blustery, tropical setting backed by forest and coconut palms.

Next day, you have the chance to experience something unique on the mainland – sunrise and sunset over different seas – by taking **Frenchman's Road** to Weipa. This starts 30km back from the Lockhart/Portland junction, crosses the difficult Pascoe and Wenlock rivers, and emerges on the Peninsula Developmental Road, 2km north of **Batavia Downs**. Head through Batavia and cross more creeks, which look worse than they are, to the main Weipa road; the trip coast to coast might take six to eight hours.

Weipa

Those without a 4WD will have to give Iron Range a miss, but can still take the road from Archer River to **WEIPA**, a town of red clay and yellow mining trucks dealing in kaolin and bauxite. The area was one of the first in Australia to be described by Europeans: Willem Janz encountered "savage, cruel blacks" here in 1606, a report whose finding were subsequently reiterated by Jan Carstensz, who found nothing of interest and sailed off to chart the Gulf of Carpentaria instead. Apart from a mission built at **Mappoon** in the nineteenth century, little changed until aluminium ore was first mined here in the 1950s, and Comalco built the town and began mining.

All traffic in Weipa gives way to the gargantuan mine vehicles and stays out of the restricted areas. The town comprises mostly company housing, but it does offer long-forgotten luxuries: you can pick up **spares** for your vehicle at the auto wreckers and service station on the way into town; and there's a **supermarket** and **post office** just in front of *Weipa Camping Ground* (☎07/4069 7871), a large campsite featuring hot showers and a laundry, where you can unwind and swap tales about the rigours of the trip; fishing trips and mine tours can be arranged at the campsite office. The *Albatross Hotel* (☎07/4069 7314; ④) up the road has rooms and bungalows, and its beer deck looks out over the western sea. Hardened **bikers** should try to catch the August **Croc Run**, Australia's richest and most challenging endurance race, which weaves its way through mangroves and creeks.

Around town, the library's **Cape York Collection** contains a unique collection of books and documents relating to the area, while the **Uningan Nature Reserve**, situated on the Mission River, preserves sixteen-metre-high **middens** composed entirely of shells left over from Aboriginal meals – some have been dated to sixteen hundred years ago. Driving is the only way to get here, and guidebooks are available from the campsite. Keep an eye out for crocs while walking around the reserve.

Leaving, there's a barge to Normanton (see p.605) in the Gulf once a week, and occasional services to Thursday Island – contact Gulf Freight Services (☎07/4069 7309 or 1800 640 079). Note that there is no reliable **fuel** between Weipa and Bamaga (340km).

North of the Wenlock

The seasonally deep, fast-flowing **Wenlock River**, an hour north of the Weipa junction on the main road, marks the start of the most challenging part of the journey north, with road conditions changing every wet season. Formerly requiring some skill and a bit of luck to cross safely, the Wenlock River itself has been tamed by a bridge. The road divides 42km further on, where die-hards follow the **Old Telegraph Track**, which has all the interesting scenery and creek crossings, though the telegraph lines have been dismantled, and many of the poles have been robbed of their ceramic caps by souvenir hunters. The first travellers of the year build simple rafts and log bridges to cross the creeks; as tracks dry and traffic increases, jarring corrugations and potholes are more likely to pose a problem, constituting a serious test of vehicle strength. There are some fine creeks on this route: **Bertie's** potholes are large enough to submerge an entire vehicle; **Gunshot's** three-metre vertical clay banks are a real test of skill (use low range first, and keep your foot off the brake); and the north exit at **Cockatoo** is deceptively sandy. Dozens wipe out on Gunshot every season; for the cautious there's a 24-kilometre detour via open scrub at **Heathlands** to the north side.

Those less certain of their abilities avoid the Old Telegraph Track and take the longer **New Road** to the east, consisting of 200km of loose gravel and bulldust. The two routes rejoin one another briefly after 75km, after which the

Crossing creeks by 4WD

While Cape York's crocs make the standard 4WD procedure of walking creek crossings before driving them potentially dangerous, wherever possible you should make some effort to gauge the waters' depth and find the best route. Never blindly follow others across. Make sure all rescue gear – shovel, winch, rope, etc – is easy to reach, outside the vehicle. Electrics on petrol engines need to be waterproofed. On deep crossings, block off air inlets to prevent water entering the engine, slacken off the fan belt and cover the radiator grille with a tarpaulin; this diverts water around the engine as long as the vehicle is moving. Select an appropriate gear (changing it in midstream will let water into the clutch) and drive through at walking speed; clear the opposite embankment before stopping again. In deep water, there's a chance the vehicle might float slightly, and so get pushed off-track by the current – though there's not much you can do about this. If you stall, switch off the ignition immediately, exit through windows, disconnect the battery (a short might restart the engine) and winch out. Don't restart the vehicle until you've made sure that water hasn't been sucked in through the air filter – which will destroy the engine. If you have severe problems, recovery will be very expensive; see Basics, p.39.

New Road diverges left for 54km to the Jardine River Ferry ($80 return, including use of the Injinu campsite at Bamaga), while the Telegraph Track ploughs on past beautiful clear green water and basalt formations at **Twin Falls**' safe swimming holes, through the deep Nolans Brook, before reaching the hundred-metre-wide **Jardine River**. This spot was once the only crossing point on the Jardine, but the river's width makes the crossing extremely testing, and the likelihood of crocodiles adds to the risks. However, it's worth the trip to camp (assuming you have enough fuel) before heading back to the ferry. From there, the last hour to Bamaga passes the remains of a **DC-3** that crashed just short of the airstrip in 1945.

Bamaga

BAMAGA, a community of stilt houses and banana palms founded by Saibai islanders in 1946, owes nothing to suburban values. Around the intersection you'll find a workshop and service station selling **fuel** (Mon–Fri 9am–5pm, Sat 9am–12.30pm, Sun 1.30–3pm), airline offices, a hotel and a **shopping centre** (fresh veggies, National Australia Bank agent, telephones, café and post office). For **accommodation**, there's the central *Resort Bamaga* (☏07/4069 3050, Ⓦwww.resortbamaga.com.au; ❷–❹), which has motel rooms and no-frills bungalows; turn left at the junction to **Injinu campsite** (Cowall Creek), or right past the shopping centre to the coast at **SEISIA** (Red Island Point). You can stay here in tents or cabins at the **Seisia Village Resort** (☏07/4069 3243, Ⓔseisiaresort@bigpond.com; cabins ❹), under palms near the jetty, and take advantage of showers, laundry facilities, a canteen and fishing safaris. Other services in Seisia include a roadhouse, tackle shop, taxi (☏07/4069 3333) and 4WD rental.

Cape York and Somerset

To make local contacts, stay around Bamaga. To keep with the overland crowd, head 16km north to a road junction, then bear left for 11km to the idyllic beach at **Punsand Bay Private Reserve** (☏07/4069 1722; camping $18, prefab tents ❹), a just reward for the trials of the journey, with prefab tents, camping, meals, basic provisions, and a limited repairs service (but no fuel). Around here you might spot the rare **palm cockatoo**, a huge, crested black parrot with a curved bill. You could spend a day recuperating on the beach, or return to the junction and take the seventeen-kilometre road past the Somerset fork to its end at another **campsite** (shower, water and kiosk) and the luxurious, Aboriginal-owned **Pajinka Lodge** (☎07/4069 2100, bookings ☎1800 802 968; ❼). Follow the footpath through vine forest onto a rocky, barren headland and down to a turbulent sea opposite the lighthouse on Eborac Island. A sign concreted into an oil drum marks the tip of mainland Australia and the end of the journey.

Somerset

Established on government orders in 1864 to balance the French naval station in New Caledonia, **Somerset** was founded by John Jardine, who was succeeded by his son Frank the following year. Frank became a legend on the Cape and tales of his exploits assume larger-than-life proportions (fearless pioneer to some, brutal colonial to others). Though envisaged as a second Singapore, Somerset never amounted to more than a military outpost under constant attack from termites and local tribes. In 1877, after the pearling trade in the Torres Strait erupted into lawlessness, the settlement was abandoned in favour of a seat of government closer to the problem at Thursday Island.

Today, only a few cannon, machine parts and mango trees testify to Somerset's former inhabitants; the buildings succumbed to white ants or were moved long ago. Frank and his wife Sana are buried on the beach directly below (standing up, say locals), next to a Chinese cemetery and traces of a jetty into the Adolphus Channel. Dogged exploration of the dense undergrowth above the beach to the left will uncover remains of a **sentry post** and a **cave** with stick-figure paintings, presumably Aboriginal. Past Somerset, a track continues onto another beach before circling back towards the main road.

The Torres Strait

Beyond Cape York, the 200-kilometre-broad, obstacle-strewn **Torres Strait** separates Australia from New Guinea; the strait was named after Luís Vaez de Torres, who navigated its waters in 1606. Prior to European contact, the Strait's islands had developed trade links with Australia and highland New Guinea, which supplied outrigger canoes – no suitable trees grow in the Strait – in exchange for oyster and trochus shell, and heads. Warfare between islands pervaded all aspects of life, and the eastern cult of Malo required human jaws as tribute. The early nineteenth century saw the first trade with Europeans, who soon discovered the Strait's rich pearl beds and occupied the islands as bases for the industry, decimating the islanders through violence and disease. Then on July 1, 1871, the **London Missionary Society** landed on Darnley Island. Once the islanders realized that the mission protected them from the more piratical whites, they converted to Christianity at a speed that amazed even the missionaries. The advent of Christianity (known here as the "Coming of the Light") stabilized communities but also heralded the end of traditional life, as cults were undermined and wages and stores replaced the barter network. Another influential group were **South Sea Island** teachers, who brought their own dance styles and crops, and gradually intermarried with the locals.

The church created **island councils**, but Queensland held the real power with its **segregation laws**, which prevented emigration to the mainland. The only job in the Strait was pearling (for mother-of-pearl), and white boat-owners would have lost their labour pool if Islanders went south. Until World War II the islands made the best of it, but army service overseas gave return-ing recruits a better understanding of what they deserved from the govern-ment, and pressure removed some barriers to migration. The advent of plastics led to the collapse of the mother-of-pearl industry, and the unemployment that followed forced the government to drop all protectionist policies, with the result that by the mid-1970s half the Strait's former population was living on the mainland. The remainder formed a movement to establish an **Islander Nation**, which bore its first fruit on June 3, 1992, when the **Mabo Decision** acknowledged the Merriam as traditional owners of Murray Island, thereby setting a precedent for mainland Aboriginal claims and sending shock waves through the establishment.

Ferries cross regularly between Cape York and **Thursday Island**, the Strait's administrative centre – which, even on a brief visit, offers a fascinating glimpse into an all-but-forgotten corner of Australia. Travel beyond Thursday (except to neighbouring islands) is generally expensive, but many other islands do have guesthouses.

Thursday Island

A three-square-kilometre speck within sight of the mainland, between Prince of Wales, Hammond and Horn islands, **Thursday Island** wears a few aliases: coined "Sink of the Pacific" for the variety of peoples who passed through in pearling days, the local tag is Waiben or (very loosely) "Thirsty Island" – once a reference to the availability of drinking water and now a laconic aside on the quantity of beer consumed. The hotel clock with no hands hints at the pace of life and it's only for events like Christmas, when wall-to-wall aluminium punts from neighbouring islands make the harbour look like a maritime supermar-ket car park, that things liven up. Other chances to catch Thursday in carnival spirit are during the Coming of the Light festivities on July 1, and for the full-bore Island of Origin rugby league matches later in the same month – in one season 25 players were hospitalized, and one killed.

In town there are traces of the old **Chinatown** district around Milman Street, and a reminder of Queensland's worst shipping disaster in the **Quetta Memorial Church**, way down Douglas Street, built after the ship hit an uncharted rock in the Adolphus Channel in 1890 and went down with virtu-ally all the Europeans on board. The Aplin Road **cemetery**, where two of the victims are buried, has tiled Islander tombs and depressing numbers of **Japanese** graves, all victims of pearl diving. As a byproduct of the industry, Japanese crews had accurately mapped the Strait before World War II and it's no coincidence that the airstrip was bombed when hostilities were declared in 1942; fortifications are still in place on Thursday's east coast. Bunkers and naval cannon at the **Old Fort** on the opposite side date from the 1890s.

Practicalities

There are **ferries** to Thursday Island every weekday morning from Punsand Bay (1hr 30min) and Seisia (1hr 15min); prices are $80 return. Passing **Possession Island** on the way over, you come within sight of a plaque com-memorating James Cook's landing here on August 22, 1770, when he planted the flag for George III and Great Britain. Then it's into the shallow channel between Horn Island (see below) and **Prince of Wales Island**, the Strait's largest island, stocked with deer and settled by an overflow population unable to afford Thursday's exorbitant land premiums.

The wharf on Thursday sits below the colonial-style **Customs House**, a minute from the town centre on Douglas Street. Here you'll find a post office with payphones, a **bank**, cafés and two of the island's **hotels**: the *Torres* just beats the neighbouring *Royal* as Australia's northernmost bar. Facing the water on Victoria Parade, the *Federal* (T07/4069 1569; ❹) is fractionally quieter as lodgings on a busy night, while on Douglas Street, *Mura Mudh* (T07/4069 2050; ❶) is a good-value **hostel** run by Thursday Islanders. Other facilities include *Café Gallery*, and a pharmacy and laundry on Douglas Street. Peddell's Buses (T07/4069 1551) meets incoming ferries for a ninety-minute tour of the island ($18).

Other islands

Though you generally need permission from the local council, it's possible that you may be privately invited to other islands in the Strait. While some are within outboard range – "one drum trips" – you're looking at $400 or more each way to charter a five-seater plane to anywhere more distant. Torres Strait Tours on Thursday Island (T1800 420 666, F07/4069 1408) can arrange **water taxis** and island transfers if needed.

Just a few minutes from Thursday's wharf by water taxi ($15), **Horn Island** is another small chunk of land surrounded by mangroves and coral, the site of an open-cut gold mine and the regional **airport** (with regular flights to and from Cairns). The main reason to trip across is to visit the **pearling museum**, run by an ex-diver and stocked with his memorabilia – including an old-fashioned bronze dive helmet. He also owns Horn's sole place to **stay and eat**, the *Gateway Torres Strait Reso*rt (T07/4069 2222; ❹).

Of the remoter islands, eastern **Murray Island** (Mer) is enticing for its importance in island history; it was the centre for pre-contact religion, and it was over a land-claim here that the Mabo Decision was handed down. To the north are **Badu**, centre of the Strait's burgeoning crayfish industry, and **Saibai**, a low deltaic island just 16km from the New Guinea mainland – the only place in Australia from where you can see another country.

Travel details

Trains

Bundaberg to: Ayr (6 weekly; 16hr); Bowen (6 weekly; 14hr); Cairns (4 weekly; 25hr); Gladstone (6 weekly; 2hr 30min); Ingham (4 weekly; 18hr); Innisfail (4 weekly; 21hr); Mackay (6 weekly; 11hr); Proserpine, for Airlie Beach (6 weekly; 13hr 30min); Rockhampton (6 weekly; 4hr 30min); Townsville (6 weekly; 17hr); Tully, for Mission Beach (4 weekly; 20hr).
Cairns to: Ayr (4 weekly; 9hr); Bowen (4 weekly; 11hr); Bundaberg (4 weekly; 25hr); Forsayth (1 weekly; 11hr 15min); Gladstone (4 weekly; 22hr); Ingham (4 weekly; 5hr); Innisfail (4 weekly; 2hr);

Kuranda (1–2 daily; 1hr); Mackay (4 weekly; 13hr 20min); Proserpine, for Airlie Beach (4 weekly; 11hr 30min); Rockhampton (4 weekly; 19hr); Townsville (4 weekly; 4hr 40min); Tully, for Mission Beach (4 weekly; 3hr 15min).
Ingham to: Ayr (4 weekly; 3hr 30min); Bowen (4 weekly; 5hr); Bundaberg (4 weekly; 18hr); Cairns (4 weekly; 5hr); Gladstone (4 weekly; 16hr); Innisfail (4 weekly; 3hr); Mackay (4 weekly; 9hr); Proserpine, for Airlie Beach (4 weekly; 7hr); Rockhampton (4 weekly; 15hr); Townsville (4 weekly; 2hr); Tully, for Mission Beach (4 weekly; 2hr).
Mackay to: Ayr (6 weekly; 5hr); Bowen (6 weekly; 3hr); Bundaberg (6 weekly; 11hr); Cairns (4

weekly; 13hr 20min); Gladstone (6 weekly; 8hr); Ingham (4 weekly; 9hr); Innisfail (4 weekly; 12hr); Proserpine, for Airlie Beach (4 weekly; 2hr 30min); Rockhampton (6 weekly; 5hr 30min); Townsville (6 weekly; 7hr); Tully, for Mission Beach (4 weekly; 10hr 30min).

Proserpine to: Ayr (6 weekly; 2hr 40min); Bowen (6 weekly; 2hr); Bundaberg (6 weekly; 13hr 30min); Cairns (4 weekly; 11hr 30min); Gladstone (6 weekly; 10hr); Ingham (4 weekly; 7hr); Innisfail (4 weekly; 9hr 30min); Mackay (4 weekly; 2hr 30min); Rockhampton (6 weekly; 7hr 40min); Townsville (6 weekly; 4hr 40min); Tully, for Mission Beach (4 weekly; 8hr).

Rockhampton to: Ayr (6 weekly; 11hr); Bowen (6 weekly; 8hr 20min); Bundaberg (6 weekly; 4hr 30min); Cairns (4 weekly; 19hr); Gladstone (6 weekly; 1hr 30min); Ingham (4 weekly; 15hr); Innisfail (4 weekly; 18hr); Longreach (2 weekly; 12hr 30min); Mackay (4 weekly; 5hr 30min); Proserpine, for Airlie Beach (6 weekly; 7hr 40min); Townsville (6 weekly; 12hr); Tully, for Mission Beach (4 weekly; 16hr).

Townsville to: Ayr (6 weekly; 1hr 30min); Bowen (6 weekly; 3hr); Bundaberg (6 weekly; 17hr); Cairns (4 weekly; 4hr 40min); Gladstone (6 weekly; 14hr); Ingham (4 weekly; 2hr); Innisfail (4 weekly; 5hr); Mackay (6 weekly; 7hr); Mount Isa (2 weekly; 19hr); Proserpine, for Airlie Beach (6 weekly; 4hr 40min); Rockhampton (6 weekly; 12hr); Tully, for Mission Beach (4 weekly; 4hr).

Tully to: Ayr (4 weekly; 5hr 30min); Bowen (4 weekly; 7hr); Bundaberg (4 weekly; 20hr); Cairns (4 weekly; 3hr 15min); Gladstone (4 weekly; 18hr); Ingham (4 weekly; 2hr); Innisfail (4 weekly; 1hr 15min); Mackay (4 weekly; 10hr 30min); Proserpine, for Airlie Beach (4 weekly; 8hr); Rockhampton (4 weekly; 16hr); Townsville (4 weekly; 4hr).

Buses

Airlie Beach to: Ayr (7 daily; 2hr 20min); Bowen (7 daily; 1hr); Bundaberg (7 daily; 11hr 30min); Cairns (7 daily; 9hr 45min); Gladstone (7 daily; 10hr); Ingham (7 daily; 6hr); Innisfail (7 daily; 8hr 30min); Mackay (7 daily; 3hr); Mission Beach (5 daily; 8hr); Rockhampton (7 daily; 8hr 30min); Townsville (7 daily; 3hr 30min).

Bundaberg to: Airlie Beach (7 daily; 11hr 30min); Agnes Water/1770 (2 weekly; 2hr); Ayr (8 daily; 15hr); Bowen (8 daily; 13hr 30min); Cairns (8 daily; 21hr); Gladstone (8 daily; 3hr); Ingham (8 daily; 18hr); Innisfail (8 daily; 21hr); Mackay (8 daily; 9hr); Mission Beach (5 daily; 19hr); Rockhampton (8 daily; 4hr); Townsville (8 daily; 14hr 30min).

Cairns to: Airlie Beach (6 daily; 9hr 45min); Ayr (8 daily; 7hr 30min); Bowen (8 daily; 9hr); Bundaberg (8 daily; 21hr); Cape Tribulation (1 daily; 4hr); Gladstone (8 daily; 19hr 30min); Ingham (8 daily; 3hr 15min); Innisfail (8 daily; 1hr); Kuranda (1 daily; 35min); Mackay (8 daily; 12hr); Mission Beach (5 daily; 1hr 55min); Mossman (1 daily; 1hr 45min); Port Douglas (1 daily; 1hr 45min); Rockhampton (8 daily; 17hr); Townsville (8 daily; 4hr 45min).

Mackay to: Airlie Beach (7 daily; 3hr); Ayr (8 daily; 5hr); Bowen (8 daily; 4hr); Bundaberg (8 daily; 9hr); Cairns (8 daily; 12hr); Gladstone (8 daily; 6hr); Ingham (8 daily; 9hr); Mackay (8 daily; 11hr); Mission Beach (5 daily; 23hr); Rockhampton (8 daily; 4hr); Townsville (8 daily; 5hr 15min).

Mission Beach to: Airlie Beach (5 daily; 8hr); Ayr (5 daily; 5hr 30min); Bowen (5 daily; 7hr); Bundaberg (5 daily; 19hr); Cairns (5 daily; 1hr 55min); Gladstone (5 daily; 16hr); Ingham (5 daily; 2hr); Innisfail (5 daily; 2hr 45min); Mackay (5 daily; 23hr); Rockhampton (5 daily; 15hr); Townsville (5 daily; 4hr).

Rockhampton to: Airlie Beach (7 daily; 8hr 30min); Ayr (8 daily; 10hr); Bowen (8 daily; 10hr); Bundaberg (8 daily; 4hr); Cairns (8 daily; 17hr); Gladstone (8 daily; 1hr 15min); Ingham (8 daily; 10hr); Innisfail (8 daily; 16hr); Longreach (3 weekly; 9hr); Mackay (8 daily; 4hr); Mission Beach (5 daily; 15hr); Mount Morgan (14 weekly; 2hr); Townsville (8 daily; 9hr 30min); Yeppoon (3 daily; 1hr 30min).

Townsville to: Airlie Beach (7 daily; 3hr 30min); Ayr (8 daily; 1hr); Bowen (8 daily; 3hr); Bundaberg (8 daily; 14hr 30min); Cairns (8 daily; 4hr 45min); Charters Towers (3 daily; 1hr 30min); Gladstone (8 daily; 13hr); Ingham (8 daily; 1hr 30min); Innisfail (8 daily; 3hr 45min); Mackay (8 daily; 5hr 15min); Mission Beach (5 daily; 4hr); Mount Isa (3 daily; 11hr 30min); Rockhampton (8 daily; 9hr 30min).

Ferries

Airlie Beach/Shute Harbour to: Daydream Island (1–2 daily; 45min); Hamilton Island (1–3 daily; 1hr); Hook Island (1–2 daily; 1hr 30min); Lindeman Island (2 daily; 1hr 30min); South Molle Island (2 daily; 45min); Whitsunday Island (1 daily; 2hr).
Cairns to: Thursday Island (1 weekly; 36hr).
Cape York to: Thursday Island (Mon–Fri 3 daily; 1hr 15min–2hr).
Cardwell to: Hinchinbrook Island (2 daily; 1–2hr).
Mission Beach to: Dunk Island (10 or more daily; 15min).
Rosslyn Bay to: Great Keppel Island (4–5 daily; 45min–1hr).

Townsville to: Magnetic Island (10 or more daily; 45min).
Weipa to: Normanton (1 weekly; 24hr).

Flights

Bundaberg to: Brisbane (3 daily; 1hr); Cairns (1 daily; 50min); Gladstone (1 weekly; 35min); Lady Elliot (daily; 45min); Mackay (1 daily; 2hr); Rockhampton (1 daily; 50min).
Cairns to: Bamaga (1 daily; 1hr 45min); Bundaberg (3–5 daily; 3hr 30min); Cooktown (1 daily; 45min); Dunk Island (1 daily; 45min); Lizard Island (2 daily; 1hr); Mackay (2 daily; 2hr 45min); Proserpine (6 weekly; 2hr); Rockhampton (2 daily; 3hr); Thursday Island/Horn Island (1–2 daily; 2hr); Townsville (2 daily; 1hr); Weipa (1 daily; 1hr 15min).
Gladstone to: Bundaberg (1 weekly; 35min); Rockhampton (5 weekly; 25min).
Mackay to: Cairns (2 daily; 2hr 45min); Rockhampton (2 daily; 45min); Townsville (4 daily; 1hr).
Rockhampton to: Cairns (2 daily; 3hr); Gladstone (5 weekly; 25min); Great Keppel Island (3 daily; 25min); Mackay (2 daily; 45min); Townsville (2 daily; 1hr 50min).
Townsville to: Cairns (2 daily; 1hr); Mackay (4 daily; 1hr); Rockhampton (2 daily; 1hr 50min).

TROPICAL QUEENSLAND AND THE REEF | Travel details

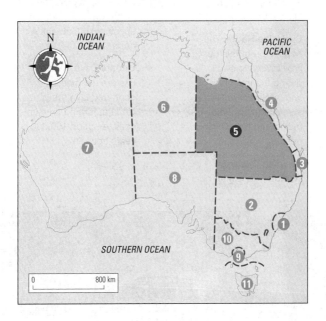

Outback Queensland

5

OUTBACK QUEENSLAND

CHAPTER 5

Highlights

* **Artesian hot spa at Mitchell** The hot springs in single-street Mitchell make an enjoyable wallow on a cold winter's morning. See p.569

* **Carnarvon Gorge** Reach fantastic Aboriginal art sites with a hike through the verdant Carnarvon Gorge. See p.570

* **Birdsville Races** The population of this dusty little township swells during the infamous annual Birdsville Races, a weekend of horse racing and free-flowing beer. See p.576

* **Crayfish Derby at Winton** The winner nets $1500 and the runner up gets to eat all the competitors at the biennial Australian Crayfish Derby, held in September in the archetypal frontier town of Winton. See p.585

* **Lawn Hill Gorge** Taking to the water is a wonderful way to explore the lush Lawn Hill Gorge, a spectacular Outback oasis. See p.600

* **Undara Lava Tubes** Explore the massive contorted lava tubes at Undara, formed by a volcanic eruption 190,000 years ago. See p.603

Outback Queensland

Outback **Queensland**, the west of the state, is thinly populated by tenacious farming communities swinging precariously between famine and survival, and seems hard to reconcile with the lushness of the wet tropics. The population is concentrated in the relatively fertile highlands along the **Great Dividing Range**, running low behind the coast; on the far side, featureless plains slide over a hot horizon into the fringes of South Australia and the Northern Territory. Almost untouched by overseas visitors, the only places attracting tourists in any numbers are the **Stockman's Hall of Fame** at Longreach, the oases of **Carnarvon Gorge** in the Central Highlands, and the northwest's **Lawn Hill Gorge**. But elsewhere the opportunities for exploration are immense, with **precious stones**, **fossils**, waterholes and **Aboriginal art** in abundance.

Choosing where to go is often determined by the most convenient starting point. **Main roads** and **trains** head west from the coast at Brisbane, Rockhampton and Townsville; interstate **bus services** from Townsville are good, but otherwise the highways are only partially covered. If you're **driving**, your vehicle must be sound and you should carry essential spares, as even main centres often lack replacements.

Unless you're experienced and well equipped, you'll find that western **summers** effectively prohibit travel, with searing temperatures and violent flash floods that can isolate regions (especially in the Channel Country on the far side of the Great Dividing Range) for days or weeks on end. Consequently, many tour companies, information offices and motels simply shut up shop between November and March, or at least during January and February. On the other hand, water revives dormant seeds and fast-growing desert flowers, which cover the ground to the horizon in good years. At other times, expect hot days and cool nights, plenty of dust and sparse landscapes.

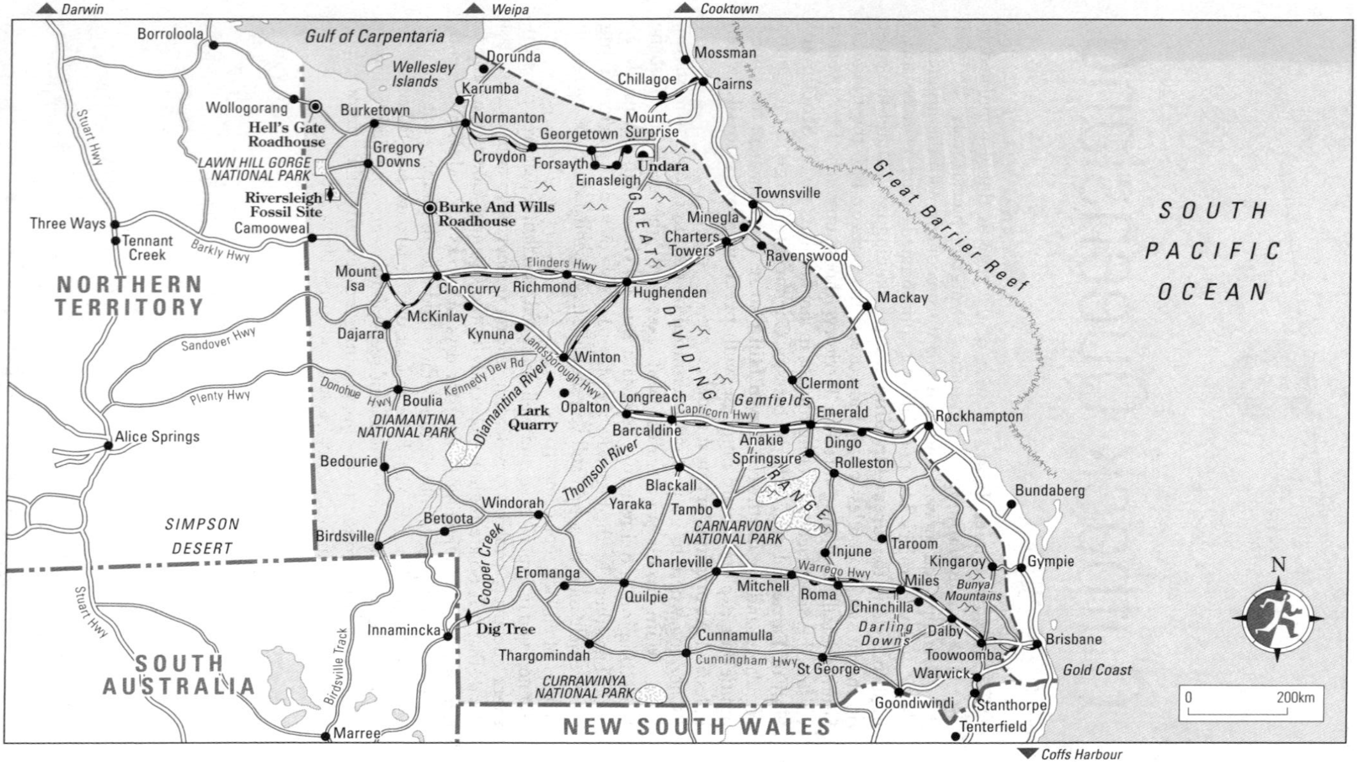
Darwin
Weipa
Cooktown
Coffs Harbour
Gulf of Carpentaria
Wellesley Islands
SOUTH PACIFIC OCEAN
Great Barrier Reef
NORTHERN TERRITORY
SOUTH AUSTRALIA
NEW SOUTH WALES
SIMPSON DESERT
GREAT DIVIDING RANGE
Gemfields
Darling Downs
Bunya Mountains
LAWN HILL GORGE NATIONAL PARK
DIAMANTINA NATIONAL PARK
CARNARVON NATIONAL PARK
CURRAWINYA NATIONAL PARK
Borroloola
Wollogorang
Hell's Gate Roadhouse
Riversleigh Fossil Site
Burke And Wills Roadhouse
Lark Quarry
Dig Tree
Undara
Three Ways
Tennant Creek
Alice Springs
Camooweal
Burketown
Gregory Downs
Dorunda
Karumba
Normanton
Croydon
Georgetown
Forsayth
Einasleigh
Mount Surprise
Chillagoe
Mossman
Cairns
Townsville
Minegla
Charters Towers
Ravenswood
Mackay
Mount Isa
Cloncurry
Richmond
Hughenden
McKinlay
Dajarra
Kynuna
Winton
Opalton
Boulia
Longreach
Barcaldine
Clermont
Emerald
Anakie
Springsure
Dingo
Rolleston
Rockhampton
Bundaberg
Bedourie
Birdsville
Betoota
Windorah
Yaraka
Blackall
Tambo
Taroom
Injune
Charleville
Mitchell
Roma
Miles
Kingaroy
Gympie
Chinchilla
Dalby
Toowoomba
Brisbane
Gold Coast
Eromanga
Quilpie
Innamincka
Thargomindah
Cunnamulla
St George
Warwick
Goondiwindi
Stanthorpe
Tenterfield
Marree
Stuart Hwy
Barkly Hwy
Sandover Hwy
Plenty Hwy
Donohue Hwy
Kennedy Dev Rd
Flinders Hwy
Landsborough Hwy
Capricorn Hwy
Warrego Hwy
Cunningham Hwy
Birdsville Track
Diamantina River
Thomson River
Cooper Creek
N
0
200km

Brisbane to Cooper Creek and Birdsville

The thousand-plus-kilometre haul from the coast's comforts to Queensland's remote southwestern corner dumps you tired and dusty on the South Australian border, with some exciting routes down the Birdsville and Strzelecki tracks or through the hostile red barrier of the Simpson Desert yet to come (see p.886). There are two ultimate targets: the outpost of **Birdsville**, with its annual horse races, and the Dig Tree at Nappa Merrie on **Cooper Creek**, monument to the Burke and Wills tragedy (see box on p.575). The highway scenery is as bleak as you'd expect: after crossing the fertile disc of the **Darling Downs**, the country withers and dries, marooning communities in isolation and hardship. Detour north through Queensland's **Central Highlands**, however, and you'll find a landscape peppered with forested sandstone gorges and Aboriginal sites at **Carnarvon National Park** – worth the journey even if you don't go any further.

The most practical route into the area from Brisbane is on the **Warrego Highway**, through Toowoomba, Roma and Charleville towards Quilpie. Roma is the jumping-off point for the Highlands; from Quilpie there are largely unsurfaced roads to Birdsville and the Dig Tree. The twice weekly Westlander **train** runs in this direction to Charleville, as do daily buses en route from Brisbane to Mount Isa.

Running parallel to the Warrego to the south, the **Cunningham Highway** crosses the Downs between Warwick and Goondiwindi (the limit of the **bus** service in this direction), then heads out to Cunnamulla. West of Cunnamulla you're on your own, heading across oil, gas and opal fields towards the Dig Tree; 4WD is preferable **beyond the bitumen** and is generally essential for reaching the Dig Tree.

The Darling Downs

The **Darling Downs**, a broad spread of prime agricultural land first explored by **Ludwig Leichhardt** in the 1840s, sprawl westwards from the back of the Great Dividing Range behind Brisbane down to the state's southern boundaries. The Warrego Highway climbs a steep escarpment to **Toowoomba** and the Northern Downs, while the Cunningham Highway cuts through Cunningham's Gap to **Warwick** and the south. Highway towns west of Toowoomba – Dalby, Miles and Chinchilla – are unadorned farming centres with no specific sights, and it's more the scenery along the Downs' fringes, particularly north at the **Bunya Mountains** or around the southeasterly **Granite Belt** (where there are also **wineries** and the possibilty of farm **work**), that warrants a visit. But even if you tear across the Central Downs without stopping, you'll notice that the flat grasslands are clear evidence of Aboriginal custodial practices: created by controlled burning designed to clear woodland and increase grazing land for game, they perfectly suited European pastoral needs. The Downs are relatively fertile and stud farms, dairy, cotton, wool and cereal farming have all been successfully tried at one time or another. Even unwanted plants thrive. During the 1920s millions of acres were infested by **prickly pear**, a South American cactus finally brought to heel by the tiny parasitic cactoblastis moth in 1930 – a success story of biological control in Queensland to match the later failure of the introduction of the cane toad (see box on p.520).

Toowoomba

TOOWOOMBA is a stately but staid university city perched on the edge of a six-hundred-metre escarpment, a promising setting that it can't quite live up to. To be fair, though, Toowoomba's side streets and numerous gardens are pleasant, the stylish houses and blaze of late-nineteenth-century sandstone architecture along central Main and Ruthven streets a reminder of its former business wealth. There's a September **flower festival** during which the **tourist office** in Ruthven Street (daily 9am–5pm; ☏1800 331 1155) hands out lists of exhibition gardens to visit. At other times the main attraction is the **Cobb & Co. Museum**, 500m northeast of the centre across spacious Queens Park at 27 Lindsay St (daily 10am–4pm; $5), recalling days when these intrepid coaches bounced across the Outback delivering mail and passengers between the 1860s and 1924. Amongst the exhibits are coaches (including one emblazoned with a Royal Mail badge), two-wheeled sulkys and a two-tier omnibus from Brisbane; there's also a working **smithy** out the back. If you've any spare time, **Picnic Point** at the top of Tourist Road 2.5km east of the centre, is a pleasant spot on a warm day, offering a café, bar and restaurant as well as picnic space, all with splendid views of the escarpment.

Downtown Toowoomba is a compact area based around the intersection of north–south oriented **Ruthven Street** and east–west **Margaret Street**, around which you'll find shops, **restaurants**, banks and a post office. The **bus station** is one block east of here on Neil Street (☏07/4690 9888 for all companies); while the **train station** is 500m northwest on Railway Street. **Accommodation** prospects include the *Jolly Swagman Caravan Park*, 47 Kitchener Rd (☏07/4632 8735; tent sites $15, cabins ❸) about 1km southeast of the centre; *Range Motel*, on Tourist Road (☏07/4632 3133; ❸), near the plateau's edge and with fine views; and the fairly quiet and central *Park Motel* at 88 Margaret Street (☏07/4632 1011; ❹). **Moving on** from Toowoomba, the New England Highway runs north to Kingaroy, plied by Polleys Coaches, and south to Warwick and Stanthorpe (Greyhound Pioneer and Crisps). Goondiwindi is three hours southwest with McCafferty's, which also follows the Warrego Highway west across the Central Downs.

Around Kingaroy: the Northern Downs

KINGAROY is a small town in the heart of peanut country, on the very fringes of the Downs, a couple of hours' drive from Toowoomba and Dalby to the south or Gympie on the coast. A cluster of castle-like **peanut silos** in the middle of town aptly symbolize the fame Kingaroy owes to **Johannes Bjelke-Petersen**, who farmed nuts here before taking Queensland under his thumb in 1968. His equally charismatic wife Flo made it onto postcards featuring her pumpkin scone recipe, and with a dam, bridge, road and sportsground named after him, not to mention his ominous catch phrase "Don't you worry about that" still on everyone's lips, Joh is in no danger of obscurity. To get in touch with what Kingaroy is all about, take the free fifty-minute tour at **Kingaroy Toasted Peanut Factory** (Mon–Fri 10.30am), 1km south of the centre on Kingaroy Street, where the scent of roasting is so seductive that you'll want to head back to the **Peanut Van** outside Lions Park between the factory and town, which sells roasted nuts by the kilo. The last few years has also seen a rash of **wineries** springing up around Kingaroy, most open for tasting – and of course, buying – Tuesday to Sunday, with guided tours twice daily. Stuart Range Estates, just northeast of the centre at the end of William Street (℡07/4162 3711), has definite potential, though at present the wine is still a little green.

Kingaroy's tiny centre is built around the intersection of **Haly Street** and parallel **Youngman** and **Kingaroy** streets, which run north–south through town. The peanut silos are just east along Haly, facing the **tourist information office** (Mon–Fri 9am–4.30pm; ℡07/4162 3199), which hands out a wineries map. For **somewhere to stay**, there's *Kingaroy Caravans*, 1km south near the peanut factory on Walter Road (℡07/4162 1808; camping $12.50, cabins ❸); or rooms at either the *Kingaroy Hotel-Motel* on the corner of Youngman and Haly streets (℡07/4162 1966; ❸) or the central *Club Hotel* on Kingaroy Street (℡07/4162 2204; ❸). The latter also offers occasional live music. Polleys Coaches leaves daily from Kingaroy to Gympie and Toowoomba, while drivers can also take the Bunya Highway to Dalby.

The Bunya Mountains

Southwest of Kingaroy, a sixty-kilometre section of road twists through the **Bunya Mountains** before you reach **Dalby** (see p.568), back on the Warrego Highway. Among the mountains' general greenery and clusters of unlikely flowers, you'll find stands of enormous **bunya pines**, which once covered the mountains and whose seeds were a valuable food source for local Aborigines, who seasonally gathered to gorge themselves. On his trip across the Downs in 1844, the indefatigable **Ludwig Leichhardt** (see p.1164) witnessed the collection and roasting of nuts at such a feast and persuaded the government to make the area an Aboriginal reserve, free from logging or settlement. The decree was revoked in 1860 but today the Bunya Mountains retain a significant stand of pines, along with orange-flowering **silky oaks** and ancient **grass trees**, with their three-metre-high, spear-like flower heads.

Two NPWS-run sites along the road at Burton's Well and Westcott make for good **bushcamping**, with another wallaby-infested site at the hamlet of Dandabah, where you'll also find the ranger's office (daily 9am–4pm; ℡07/4668 3127; advance booking essential during holiday periods). Less frugal accommodation is also on hand about 500m north along the main road at *Rice's Log Cabins* (℡07/4668 3133; ❹), and the nearby elegant *Bunya Mountain Lodge Guest House* (℡07/4668 3134; ❼). Note that the mountains are generally several degrees cooler than the plains below, and it gets cold in winter. **Walking tracks** between the three campsites lead through the forest to orchid-covered lookouts and waterfalls; satin bowerbirds (see p.422) and paradise riflebirds, with their deep blue-black plumage and long curved beaks, are both fairly common here.

The Granite Belt

The southeastern edge of the Darling Downs along the New South Wales border, known as Queensland's **Granite Belt**, is a major **wine-** and **fruit-growing** area which regularly records the state's coldest temperatures – on a winter's night it drops well below freezing here. Heading south from Toowoomba, you pass through the one-horse town of **NOBBY**, whose former resident **Steele Rudd** created archetypal Australian country characters in his "Dad and Dave" tales – commemorated at the *Nobby Hotel* in paintings and farm bric-a-brac.

Around 85km south of Toowoomba, **WARWICK** makes a fine base for exploring the region, and is known state-wide for its **cheese**, though you can't tour the factory. Services are centred around Grafton and Palmerin streets, where sandstone buildings – which give the town a distinct "New South Wales" feeling – date back to the time when Warwick graziers competed fiercely with Toowoomba's merchants to establish the Downs' premier settlement. The October **rodeo** is about the only time you might experience trouble finding **accommodation**: try *Warwick Tourist Caravan Park*, 18 Palmer Ave, north of town on the highway (☎07/4661 8335; camping $13, cabins ❸), *Warwick Motor Inn*, 17 Albion St (☎ 07/4661 1533, ⓕ4661 8400; ❸), or *Country Rose Motel* (☎07/4661 7700, ⓕ4661 1591; ❸). Alternatively, ask at the **tourist office** and art gallery halfway down Albion Street (daily 8.30am–5pm; ☎07/4661 3122).

The **Condamine River**, unimpressive where it flows through town, is part of Australia's longest river system. Originating from the highlands east of Warwick, it joins the Murray/Darling before emptying into the ocean near Adelaide. At **Queen Mary Falls**, 43km from Warwick beyond **Killarney**, a tributary exits the forest in a plunge off the top of the plateau. A two-kilometre-long track climbs to the escarpment at the head of the falls from the road, with a kiosk, **accommodation** and lunches provided by *Queen Mary Falls Tourist Park* (☎07/4664 7150, ⓕ4664 7122; camping $12.50, cabins ❹); you need your own transport to get here.

Heading on from Warwick, the New England Highway (served by Crisps Coaches and Greyhound Pioneer) runs south to Stanthorpe then over the border to Tenterfield. The Cunningham Highway continues 200km west to Goondiwindi and the banks of the Macintyre River, which marks the state border with New South Wales.

Stanthorpe and Girraween National Park

Sixty kilometres south of Warwick along the New England Highway, **STANTHORPE** was founded in the 1880s around a **tin mining** operation on Quart Pot Creek, but really kicked off in the 1940s after Italian migrants started up the **fruit farms** and **wineries** that now throng the region. Today it's a miniature version of Warwick, central **Maryland Street** sporting a couple of sandstone facades while retiree bungalows sprout on the hills above, and with good opportunities for wine sampling and – in season – **fruit-picking work**.

To start a **wine** tour, Heritage Wines (☎07/4685 2197), 15km north on the New England Highway – worth a visit alone for its huge, antique-laden reception room – and Ballandean Estate, the region's oldest vineyard, 20km southwest of town (☎07/4684 1226) both produce excellent wines and are open daily. A full list of wineries – and advice on the best – is available at the **tourist office**, overlooking the river just south of the centre on Leslie Parade (daily 7.30am–5pm). Staff can also help if you want to try **fossicking for topaz** (a semi-precious stone found near tin deposits) 13km northwest of Stanthorpe at **Swiper's Gully**; permits are available from the *Blue Topaz* van park.

Stanthorpe has a good range of **accommodation**. For camping, *Blue Topaz Caravan Park*, 5km south along the highway (☎07/4683 5279, ⓕ4683 5280; tent site $14, cabins ❷) can provide mining permits; *Top of Town*, on the highway 2km north of town (☎07/4681 4888, ⓕ4681 4222; tents $13.20, dorms $16.50, cabins ❸) has huge grounds; there are hostel beds at the new and excellent *Backpackers of Queensland*, 80 High St (☎07/4681 0999, ⓦwww .backpackersofqueensland.com.au; dorms $16.50); while *Stannum Lodge Motor Inn* (☎07/4681 2000, ⓔstannumlodge@halenet.com.au; ❸) on Wallangarra

Road is a central motel. If you're after **farm work**, contact the hostel or *Top of Town*, though some people have found the latter's management difficult to deal with.

The hills around Stanthorpe are granite, exposed as fantastic monoliths at **Girraween National Park**, 30km south down the New England Highway. Surrounding woodland suffered an apalling **bushfire** in October 2002, though as most plants in the region are fire-adapted, and regeneration had already begun at the time of writing, the park remains a worthwhile stopover. There's an NPWS **campsite** and ranger's office here (℡07/4684 5157) with showers and toilets – and the chance of seeing small, shy, active sugar gliders just after dark. Listen for claws clattering over bark and then shine your torch overhead to catch a glowing set of eyes in the spotlight.

With more energy than skill, you can climb several of the giant hills with little risk, as long as rain hasn't made them dangerously slippery – trails are well marked and free **maps** are available from the ranger's office. **Castle Rock** (2hr return) is entertaining: initially a gentle incline past lichen-covered boulders in the forest, the track follows a dotted white line into a fissure – look up and you'll see loose rocks balanced above you – before emerging onto a thin ledge above the campsite. Follow this around to the north side and clamber to the very top for superb views of the Pyramids, Sphinx and Mount Norman poking rudely out of the woods. **The Sphinx** and **Turtle Rock** are another thirty minutes from the base of Castle. Sphinx is a broad pillar topped by a boulder, while Turtle's more conventional shape means a scramble, with no handholds on the final stretch. But pat yourself on the back if you make it to the top of the completely bald **South Pyramid** (2hr return) without resorting to hands and knees. Take a well-earned rest at the top and look across to the unscaleable North Pyramid from below Balancing Rock, an oval boulder teetering so precariously on its narrow end that you can see underneath to where the support is surely only a few years away from collapse. **Mount Norman**, the park's 1267-metre apex, lies an hour beyond Castle Rock and should only be attempted by experienced climbers; check details with the ranger at Girraween.

Goondiwindi and St George

Before European settlers put weirs on the Macintyre River in the **GOONDI-WINDI** area (pronounced "gundawindee"), right on the New South Wales border some 180km west of Stanthorpe or 220km southwest of Toowoomba, it was little more than a string of waterholes and lagoons, attracting a lot of birdlife and inspiring the Aboriginal name Goonawinna – "birds' resting place". The irrigation weirs now supply the huge demands of the local cotton and wheat industries, but this hasn't dented the varied birdlife, despite the constant stream of road train transports rumbling through at all hours.

Goondiwindi is best known in Australia for the racehorse Gunsynd, alias the **Goondiwindi Grey**, who won over half of his races through the early 1970s. There's a monument to him at the southern end of McLean Street, close to where the **Macintyre River** marks the state boundary. Nearby, also on McLean Street, the **Old Customs House Museum** (daily except Tues 10am–4pm; $2) has an eclectic gathering of anything old, from preserved snakes to steam engines. It predates the rest of the town and even the wood-paved **Border Bridge** over the river.

The main road east–west through town is Marshall Street, with shops, **banks**, a post office and most services nearby. You'll find a **tourist informa-tion centre** with brochures galore and **Internet** facilities just around the corner on Bowen Street (daily 9am–5pm; ℡07/4671 2653). Inexpensive central **accommodation** can be found at *Devon's Caravan Park*, near the information centre at 3 DeLacy St (⊕07/4671 1383; camping $12, cabins ❷); *Gunsynd Motor Inn* on McLean Street (⊕07/4671 1555; ❸); and at the *Border Motel*, 126 Marshall St (⊕07/4671 1688; ❹). Be aware that during the November **cotton–chipping season** places to stay are in very short supply. **Eat** at the *Victoria Hotel* on Marshall Street, whose $12.50 counter meals feature a half-kilo steak buried under a mountain of vegetables.

Two hundred kilometres further west on the Barwon Highway, **ST GEORGE** sits on the banks of the Balonne River and is the administrative centre for the tranquil shire of Balonne. From St George, roads leave in almost every direction, and on your way through the shire every town offers a taste of farming history, wildlife and a relaxed atmosphere. **Information** on the region is available from the Council Offices under the clock tower in the town centre (Mon–Fri 9am–4.45pm; ⊕07/4625 4996), and you can **stay** at the *Australian Hotel* (⊕07/4625 5000; ❷) on the river bank. At the back of the Balonne Sports Store, a few doors down from the Council Offices, the proprietor has combined the woodcarving skills of his native Greece with the Aboriginal tradition of emu egg-carving and the wonders of electric lighting to produce a unique display of carved, illuminated emu eggs (daily 9am–5pm; $2).

The Central Downs and around

To break the unexciting journey northwest across the Downs from Toowoomba to Dalby, call in at **Jondaryan Woolshed** (daily 9am–4pm; $10), 3km south of the highway from Jondaryan and about 45km from Toowoomba, to look around the collection of old buildings – all relocated from elsewhere, with the exception of the shed itself. Exhibits worth a closer look include a document, dating from 1880, which itemizes some of the schoolmistress's tasks – including splinting broken legs, wallpapering buildings to keep out snakes and being able to fight off swaggies trying to sleep in the schoolhouse. Make sure you catch one of the **tours** (Mon–Fri 1pm, Sat, Sun & holidays 10.30am & 1.30pm) when the smithy is working, and you can watch sheep shearers at work beneath the vast emptiness of the handcrafted woolshed roof, lit by a bare bulb – a very surreal tableau.

The next stops over the following 200km are **Dalby**, **Chinchilla** and **Miles**, rural centres devoid of much in the way of attractions but with the usual complement of places to stay. One place worth stopping at, however, is *Possum Park* (⊕07/4627 1651; camping $12.50, carriages ❸), some 20km north of Miles. A motel sited in WWII ammunition bunkers in prime bushland, **accommodation** here is in restored train carriages or your own tent, and you'll have to provide your own meals too.

Roma and Mitchell

ROMA, 140km west of Miles, was founded by settlers eager to occupy country made available by the opening up of the Darling Downs in 1862. Today, the town thrives on farming, supplemented by the **oil** and **gas fields** which have been exploited intermittently since the 1900s. Roma was also the venue for the 1871 trial of the audacious **Captain Starlight** (also known as Harry Redford), who stole a thousand head of cattle from a nearby property and drove them down through the South Australian deserts to Adelaide for sale. An unusual white bull in the herd was recognized and Redford arrested, but his pioneering of a new stock route won such popular approval that the judge refused to convict him.

Roma is a typical inland town: tidy, with streets lined with **bottle trees** (not only bottle-shaped but also full of sugary water for emergency stock-watering), and a slightly dated air lent by the iron decorations and wraparound balconies of its hotels. A useful place to stock up before heading north to Carnarvon National Park (see p.570), it also has a reputation for its **cattle markets**, and every Easter there is a rodeo and carnival. Romavilla Winery has been producing prize-winning **wine** since 1863 – it's an eccentric, overgrown place about a kilometre north of town on the Carnarvon road, at Quintin Street (Mon–Fri 8am–5pm, Sat 9am–noon & 2–4pm; ☎07/4622 1822).

The Warrego Highway runs through Roma as Bowen Street, and it's here on the eastern side of town you're greeted by the **Big Rig**, a drilling tower left as a monument to the oil boom of the 1920s, and beside it the **information centre** (daily 9am–5pm; ☎07/4622 4355). A landscaped bend in the river behind makes a good picnic spot if you just want a rest; for supplies, most of the town's shops, banks and businesses are one block north of Bowen on parallel **McDowall Street**. Roma's **accommodation** choices include the *Starlight Motor Inn* (☎07/4622 2666, ℉4622 2111; ❹), with standard motel beds; the less pricey *Bottle Tree Gardens*, corner of Bowen and Charles streets (☎07/4622 6111, ℉4622 6499, ❸); and the *Big Rig Caravan Park*, 4 McDowell St (☎07/4622 2538), near the Big Rig, which has hot showers, welcome during sub-zero winter nights. **Restaurants** in Roma are fairly basic, though *Deano's*, at 77 Quintin St, does good steaks.

The train station is one block south of the highway on Station Street at the corner of Charles Street (☎07/4622 9411), and the **bus terminal** is on Bowen Street by the more central BP roadhouse (there are two of them). The **airport** is a small strip a few kilometres outside town. Tickets for all these can also be obtained from Maranoa Travel, 71 Arthur St (☎07/4622 1416). Heading north, the Carnarvon Developmental Road (take Quintin St from the town centre) gives access to Carnarvon National Park; otherwise the next stops west along the highway are Mitchell and Charleville.

Mitchell

MITCHELL is a delightful, single-street town right on the western rim of the downs beside the Maranoa River, 88km west of Roma on the Warrego Highway. As at Roma, Mitchell has its local outlaw legend; the protagonists this time were the two **Kenniff Brothers**, who raided the district for cattle and horses in the early 1900s. After killing a policeman during one arrest attempt they were finally ambushed south of town and dragged off for trial in Brisbane; unlike Captain Starlight, they were sentenced to death, though one brother had this commuted to a prison term.

There are two reasons to stop at Mitchell: either to follow the two-hundred-kilometre-long track north to Mount Moffat in Carnarvon National Park (p.570); or to make use of the town's **hot artesian springs**, which have been thoughtfully channelled into an open-air swimming pool and spa (daily 8am–7pm; $5.50) in the grounds of the old Kenniff Courthouse – good, steamy fun on a cold winter's morning. The courthouse itself now houses an **information centre** (daily 8am–7pm; ☎07/4623 1133), incorporating the *Healthy Byte Café*, an **Internet** terminal and a weekend cinema, where you can arrange hour-long river cruises ($8.80), or 4WD day-tours to Mount Moffatt (minimum of four; contact Brian McCarrol, ☎07/4623 1323). For somewhere to **stay**, the excellent council-run campsite back across the Maranoa allows you to pitch a tent free for two nights ($5.50 per tent a night thereafter); the *Mitchell Motel* (☎07/4623 1355; ❸), on the western side of town, is the alternative. The central *Blue Pub* is a good place to eat and offers Friday night **meal** specials for about $10.

Moving on, all transport and the Warrego Highway continue a further 180km west to Charleville; the **train station** is 500m from the courthouse at the western side of town, and the main-street newsagent doubles as the **bus** agent.

Carnarvon National Park

North of Roma and Mitchell, Queensland's Central Highlands consist of a broad band of weathered sandstone plateaus along the Great Dividing Range, thickly wooded and spectacularly sculpted into sheer cliffs and pinnacles. It's an extraordinarily primeval landscape, and one still visibly central to Aboriginal culture, as poor pasture left the highlands relatively unscathed by European colonization. Covering a huge slice of the region, **Carnarvon National Park** includes **Carnarvon Gorge**, **Mount Moffatt** and other remoter sections further west. Most people head for Carnarvon Gorge, where you'll find the main facilities, the highest concentration of **Aboriginal art** and arguably the best scenery. For the more adventurous, Mount Moffatt can usually be reached in a non-4WD vehicle, but requires high clearance – and often 4WD – to get around once there.

As there is **no public transport** to the park, you'll need your own vehicle: **access** to Carnarvon Gorge is from Roma or Emerald (p.579); and to Mount Moffat from Roma or Mitchell. All these roads involve some stretches of dirt, making them impassable after heavy rain (most likely Nov–May). Always carry extra rations in case you get stranded for a while and, unless you're desperately short of supplies, stay put in wet weather – you'll only churn the road up and make it harder for others to use. Note too, that it is not possible to drive directly between the gorge and Mount Moffat sections (though you can hike with permission and advice from the rangers). Summer **temperatures** often reach 40°C, while winter nights will be below freezing. Gathering firewood is prohibited inside the park, so stop on the way in or bring a gas stove. The **NPWS district headquarters** are in Emerald (℡07/4982 4555), and regional offices are detailed below.

Carnarvon Gorge

To reach Carnarvon Gorge **from Roma**, head 199km north along the Carnarvon Developmental Road, past Injune, then 45km west along a gravel access road to the ranger station, at the mouth of the gorge. **From Emerald**, the same access road is 230km south along the Gregory/Dawson highways through Springsure and Rolleston. Either way, the **Consuelo Tableland** stands out magnificently above dark forests as the road crosses the plains below, rising gradually to the foothills on the park's edge before terminating at the mouth of the gorge. The ranger station here (daily 8am–5pm; ℡07/4984 4505) has a payphone, an orientation model of the gorge, **free maps** and a library on the highlands and its wildlife.

Accommodation – best booked well in advance – is available either 2km before the ranger station at *Carnarvon Gorge Wilderness Lodge* (℡1800 644 150, ⓦwww.carnarvon-gorge.com; ❼), where comfortable rooms are surrounded by a neat lawn and respectably sized cycad palms; or a further 2km away at the creekside *Takarakka* (℡07/4984 4535, ⓦwww.takarakka.com.au; camping $8, canvas cabins ❸), which has canvas-sided "cabins" and a big campsite. The lodge

Boomerangs

Curved throwing sticks were once found throughout the world. Several were discovered in Tutankhamen's tomb, Hopi Indians once used them and a 23,000-year-old example made from mammoth ivory was recently found in Poland. Since that time the invention of the bow and arrow superseded what Aborigines call a **boomerang** or karli, although they seem to be the only people to have invented returning boomerangs; they were originally used as children's toys but were then modified into decoys for hunting wildfowl. The non-returning types depicted in Carnarvon Gorge show how sophisticated they became as hunting weapons. Usually made from tough acacia wood, some are hooked like a pick, while others are designed to cartwheel along the ground to break the legs of game. Thus immobilized, one animal would be killed while another could be easily tracked to meet the same fate. Besides hunting, the boomerang was also used for digging, levering or cutting, as well as banging pairs together for musical or ceremonial accompaniment. At Carnarvon Gorge the long, gently curved boomerangs stencilled on the walls in pairs are not repetitions but portraits of two weapons with identical flight paths; if the first missed through a gust of wind, for instance, the user could immediately throw the second, correcting his aim for the conditions. For the definitive book on the subject, check out Philip Jones' nicely illustrated *Boomerang: Behind an Australian Icon* (Wakefield Press).

also has a bar and a **store** selling basics, fuel and LP gas refills. If both these are full, *Warremba Farmstay and Camping* (℡07/4626 7175; camping $10, homestay ❸), on the access road 57km east of the gorge, has all-weather access, **homestay** accommodation and a campsite with hot showers, toilets, and big kitchen area.

Along the gorge

Carnarvon Creek's journey between the vertical faces of the gorge has created some magical scenery, where low cloud often blends with the cliffs, making them look infinitely tall. A three-kilometre trail heads downstream from near the lodge (see opposite), crossing the creek a few times by means of stepping stones and fallen trees. If you're not prepared to get wet, you can't get past the frigid **swimming hole** here. **Baloon Cave**, in woodland behind the *Lodge*, shelters some stencil art of hands and boomerangs – easy to reach if unimpressive compared with other sites in the park. Before setting off to find them, climb **Boolimba Bluff** from the *Takarakka* campsite for a rare chance to see the gorge system from above; it's a tiring climb but the views from the "Roof of Queensland" make the three-kilometre track worth the effort.

The day-walk (19km return) **into the gorge** takes some beating, with intriguing side gorges: best are the **Moss Garden** (3.5km), a vibrant green carpet of liverworts and ferns lapping up a spring as it seeps through the rockface; the awesomely quiet, claustrophobic **Amphitheatre** (4km), open to the sky and reached by a long ladder from the gorge floor; and **Alijon Falls** (5km), concealing the enchanting **Wards Canyon**, where a remnant group of angiopteris ferns hang close to extinction in front of a second waterfall and gorge, complete with bats and blood-red river stones.

Carnarvon's two major **Aboriginal art sites** are the Gallery (5.6km) and Cathedral Cave (at the end of the trail, 9.3km from the *Takarakka* campsite), both on the gorge track, though if you keep your eyes open there are plenty more to be found. These are Queensland's most documented Aboriginal art sites, although an understanding of their significance is limited to representational terms. A rockface covered with engravings of vulvas lends a

5

pornographic air to the **Gallery**; other symbols include kangaroo, emu and human tracks. A long, wavy line might represent the rainbow serpent, shaper of many Aboriginal landscapes. Overlaying the engravings are hundreds of coloured stencils, made by placing an object against the wall and spraying it with a mixture of ochre and water held in the mouth. Always personal and striking, hands – including children's – form the bulk of the designs, but there are also artefacts, boomerangs and complex crosses formed by four arms. Goannas and mysterious net patterns at the near end of the wall have been painted with a stick. **Cathedral Cave** is larger, with an even greater range of designs, including seashell pendant stencils – proof that trade networks reached from here to the sea – and engravings of animal tracks and nests of emu eggs.

Beyond Cathedral Cave, there's a **bush campsite** (contact the ranger for information) and a number of little-visited canyons to explore plus, with advice and permission from the rangers, the possibility of hiking right through to Mount Moffatt.

Mount Moffatt

Mount Moffatt is part of an open landscape of ridges and lightly wooded grassland at the top of a plateau to the west of Carnarvon Gorge. The area was the Kenniff Brothers' stomping ground (see p.569), and it was here that they murdered a policeman and station manager in 1902, events which were to lead to their being run to earth by a group of vigilantes. Years later in 1960, archeological excavations at their hideout, **Kenniff Cave**, were the first to establish that Aboriginal occupation of Australia predated the last Ice Age, and – though the cave is currently closed due to instability – there's plenty of evidence of previous Aboriginal tenure through the area.

From Roma, it's a 248-kilometre drive to the park boundaries via Injune; **from Mitchell** it's 220km direct. Although the park perimeter can often be reached in 2WD vehicles, you'll need to rely on a 4WD or walking to get around once there. As there is **no fuel** or supplies of any kind available in the park, make sure you have enough before arrival; last sources for either are at Injune (150km) or Mitchell. There are four bush **campgrounds** in the park, two of which have drinking water.

Mount Moffatt's attractions are spread out over an extensive area. Entering from the south, the **Chimneys** area has some interesting sandstone pinnacles and alcoves which once housed bark burial cylinders – look for the stencil of an entire body, arms spread-eagled. Around 6km on from here the road forks, and the right track procedes 10km to the **ranger station** (℡07/4626 3581, ℗4626 3651) where you can collect your **map** of the area, plan any bushwalking and book a site. The left track, meanwhile, runs 6km past **Dargonelly campsite** to **Marlong Arch**, a sandstone formation decorated with handprints and engravings. Five kilometres northeast from here, a trail leads to **Kookaburra Cave**, named after a weathered, bird-shaped hand stencil. A further 5km beyond the cave is **Marlong Plain**, a pretty expanse of blue grass surrounded by peaks, and another sandstone tower known as **Lot's Wife**. Ten kilometres north of Marlong Plain, a lesser track leads to several sites associated with the Kenniff legend, including the **murder scene**, and the rock where they are believed to have burned the evidence.

Finally, for pure scenery, head 15km due east of Marlong Plain to the **Mahogany Forest**, a stand of giant stringybark trees. Mount Moffatt itself and pink-walled Devils Canyon, in the park's southeast, are more difficult to reach – you need to carry reliable maps and have bushwalking skills.

Charleville to Cooper Creek and Birdsville

The last place of any size on the journey west from Roma is **CHARLEVILLE**, terminus for the **train** and a compact, busy country town with broad streets, shaded pavements and some solid buildings constructed when the town was a droving centre and staging post for Cobb & Co. (see p.556). It's well known as a victim of contradictory weather – in November 1947 a typical hot summer afternoon was interrupted for twenty minutes as the temperature plummeted and a blast of massive hailstones stripped trees, smashed windows and roofs and killed pets and poultry. In 1990 the town centre was inundated by five-metre-deep floodwaters from the **Warrego River** – a dramatic end to years of drought. At the turn of the twentieth century, attempts were made to end another dry spell with **Stiger Vortex Guns**, giant conical contraptions supposed to seed rainclouds. During trials, two of the six guns exploded and the meteorologist who recommended them was run out of town. Only two have survived: one is in the Queensland Museum in Brisbane and the other is outside the Scout Hut on Sturt Street, heading south towards Cunnamulla.

Around town, the NPWS complex and **fauna park**, east at Park Street on the Warrego Highway from Mitchell (Mon–Fri 9am–4pm; free), is dedicated to studying and breeding populations of rare local fauna such as the absurdly cute **bilby** (for more on which see Currawinya National Park, p.574) and the graceful **yellow-footed rock wallaby**, both of which are on show. The **Historic House** on Galatea Street (Mon–Sat 9am–3.30pm; $4.50), originally a bank, is now a museum with some rooms decorated in period style and showing elegant architectural touches. **Anglers** can try their luck along the river where the prize catch is large Murray cod, though perch and freshwater catfish are more likely.

The town is small but laid out in a confusing grid pattern. The **bus stop** (two services daily in each direction) is next to *Corones Hotel* on kilometre-long **Wills Street**, and the **train station** is at the street's southern end (two trains a week to Brisbane); most services – banks, shops, and post office – are also on this street. The **tourist information centre** (Mon–Fri 9am–5pm; ☎07/4654 3057, ℱ4654 3970), a kilometre south of town on Sturt Street, also organizes nightly stargazing sessions at the **Skywatch Observatory** ($8.80), which is being completely rebuilt at present, and previously featured two powerful telescopes and an astronomy chart to guide you. **Motel** rooms can be found at the *Charleville Motel*, near the train station on King Street (☎07/4654 1566; ❸), or *Corones Hotel* on Wills Street (☎07/4654 1022, ⓦwww.hotelcorones.com; bed in the hotel $35, motel doubles ❸). To **camp**, head for *Cobb & Co. Caravan Park*, on the eastern side of town off Alfred Street (☎07/4654 1053; tent sites $7.50, cabins ❷), a pleasant spot, with hot water, barbecues and a small shop (6am–8pm). There are the usual coffee shops, and generous **meals** at the *Corones Hotel*, whose dining rooms have been refurbished to original 1925 condition. **Moving on** from Charleville, roads head north to Blackall and Longreach (covered by Brisbane–Mount Isa buses), south via Cunnamulla to New South Wales, and further west to Quilpie. **Flights** to Brisbane leave from the tiny strip outside town. All transport bookings can be made with *Western Travel Service*, 37 Wills St (☎07/4654 1260).

Cunnamulla and Currawinya National Park

CUNNAMULLA, a nondescript handful of service stations and motels 200km south of Charleville, is a trucking stop on the long run down the Mitchell Highway to Bourke in New South Wales. The town received recent noteriety thanks to Dennis O'Rourke's 2000 **documentary** *Cunnamulla*, which focused rather obsessively on the relationships of the town's more off-beat characters – universal topics were used in this case to stereotype an Outback settlement. Though the documentary annoyed plenty of locals, not everyone here is shy of its themes, and you can visit some of the film's locations on the daily two-hour **Gossip Tour** (℡07/4655 2222; $12). There's also a helpful **information** centre (daily 9am–3pm; ℡07/4655 1416) in the old schoolhouse on central Jane Street; **accommodation** is just around the corner at the *Cunnamulla Hotel* on Stockyard Street (℡07/4655 1102; ❸), or a short way south at *Jack Tonkin Caravan Park* (℡07/4655 1421; tent site $7.50, cabins ❸). Cunnamulla's Council Offices, on the corner of Stockyard and Louise streets (℡07/4655 2481, Ⓦwww.paroo.info) is the place to arrange a **miner's right** ($14.50) if you're planning to head 160km west to the **Yowah Opal Fields**, where shallow deposits yield much-sought-after Yowah Nuts – opalized ironstone nodules. At the fields, beware of unfenced vertical shafts, which are practically invisible until you're on your way down: always look where you're going and never step backwards. Yowah has bore water, fuel and a **caravan park** (℡07/4655 4953; cabins ❷).

Two hundred kilometres southwest of Cunnamulla on minor roads, **Currawinya National Park** features lakes, wetlands and associated wildlife in contrast to the semi-arid land more typical of the region. One animal to benefit is the highly endangered **bilby**, which, with its long ears and nose, looks like a cross between a rabbit and a bandicoot. Feral cats, rabbits, and grazing cattle have brought the bilby close to extinction, but a recently completed **fence** at Currawinya will keep all these pests out, allowing the new bilby population – reintroduced from the NPWS fauna centre in Charleville – to prosper. You can **camp** at Currawinya, but check on road conditions and practicalities with the NPWS ranger first (℡07/4655 4001). Past Currawinya is the tiny border town of **Hungerford**, and from there it's a 200-kilometre run southeast on a largely unsealed road to Bourke (see p.363).

Quilpie and the road to the Dig Tree

QUILPIE is a compact, dusty farming community 200km west of Charleville. The **visitor centre** is on Brolga Street (Mon–Fri 9am–4.30pm; ℡07/4656 2166); amenities include a supermarket, baker, butcher, fuel depot, the *Channel Country* **caravan park** at 21 Chipu St (℡07/4656 2087; tent sites $8, cabins ❷) and **beds** at the *Quilpie Motor Inn* (℡07/4656 1277; ❸). The *Imperial Hotel* serves evening **meals** between 6 and 7.30pm, and there are a couple of cafés in town which close at about 5.30pm.

As there are few signposts, a **map** is essential if you plan to drive from Quilpie to the Dig Tree at Nappa Merrie, 50km from Innamincka in South Australia. The last place to get fuel on the 490-kilometre, largely unsealed route lies an hour west of Quilpie at **EROMANGA**, a maintenance depot with a population of eighty souls whose *Royal Hotel* (℡07/4656 4837; ❸) offers beer, food, information, and four **motel rooms**. From here you're heading across the stony plains above the huge **gas and oil** reserves of the Cooper Basin, past the cattle stations of Durham Downs and Karmona, lonely "nodding donkeys" and unaccountably healthy-looking droughtmaster cattle, to the **Dig Tree** on **Cooper Creek**.

The Burke and Wills saga

In 1860, the government of Victoria, then Australia's richest state, decided to sponsor a lavish expedition to make the first south–north crossing of the continent to the Gulf of Carpentaria. Eighteen men, twenty camels (shipped, along with their handlers, from Asia) and over twenty tons of provisions started out from Melbourne in August, led by Robert O'Hara Burke and William John Wills. Problems had already begun by the time the party reached Cooper Creek in December: Burke had impatiently left the bulk of the expedition and supplies lagging behind and raced ahead with a handful of men to establish a base camp on Cooper Creek. Having built a stockade, Burke and Wills started north, along with two other members of their team (Gray and King), six camels, a couple of horses and food for three months. Four men remained at camp, led by William Brahe, waiting for the rest of the expedition to catch up. In fact, most of the supplies and camels were dithering halfway between Cooper Creek and Melbourne, unsure of what to do next.

As Burke and Wills failed to keep a regular diary, few details of the "rush to the Gulf" are known. They were seen by Kalkadoon Aborigines following the Corella River into the Gulf, where they found that vast salt marshes lay between them and the sea. Disappointed, they left the banks of the Bynoe (near present-day Normanton) on February 11, 1861, and headed back south. Their progress slowed by the wet season, they killed and ate the camels and horses as their food ran out. Gray died after being beaten by Burke for stealing flour; remorse was heightened when they staggered into the Cooper Creek stockade on April 21 to find that, having already waited an extra month for them to return, Brahe had decamped that morning. Too weak to follow him, they found supplies buried under a tree marked "Dig", but failed to change the sign when they moved on, which meant that when the first rescue teams arrived on the scene, they assumed the explorers had never returned from the Gulf. Trying to walk south, the three reached the Innamincka area, where Aborigines fed them fish and nardoo (water fern) seeds, but by the time a rescue party tracked them down in September only King was still alive. The full, sad tale of their trek is expertly told by Alan Moorehead in his classic work *Cooper's Creek*, a book well worth tracking down in your library (see "Books", p.1204)

The site of Burke and Wills' stockade (see box above), Depot Camp 65 is a beautiful shaded river bank alive with pelicans and parrots, and it's hard to believe that anyone could have starved to death nearby. The Dig Tree is still standing and protected by a walkway, but the three original blaze marks reading "BLXV, DIG 3FT NW, DEC 6 60–APR 21 61" have been cemented over to keep the tree alive. Burke's face was carved into the tree on the right by John Dickins in 1898, and is still clearly visible.

Pressing on, you'll be relieved to know that **Innamincka**'s pub is only 50km away at the top of the Strzelecki Track in South Australia (see p.881). If you've made it this far you shouldn't have much trouble with the road.

Quilpie to Birdsville

The long road from Quilpie to Birdsville is a relatively easy journey, manageable in good conditions without a 4WD, though depth markers along the road give an idea of how saturated this **Channel Country** becomes after rain. First stop is **WINDORAH**, a limp settlement of a dozen buildings offering fuel, a post office and an amazingly well-provisioned store. The *Western Star Hotel* (☎07/4656 3166, ⓕ4656 3103; ❹) is hard to pass by for a cold drink and a look at its collection of old photos; they have tidy air-conditioned **rooms** and might let you **camp** out the back.

Ruins of the *John Costello* hotel lie 80km further on towards Betoota, opposite a windmill. Tired of riding 30km every morning to round up his stockmen from the bar, the manager of a nearby station had the local liquor licence transferred from the *JC* to his homestead in the 1950s. He pulled the roof off the hotel for good measure, and there's now little left beyond the foundations and some posts.

BETOOTA, 220km from Windorah, is also on the verge of crumbling back into the dust, its tiny, century-old adobe **hotel**, with its sole occupant, opens only once a year for the races and gymkhana. Even then they don't provide beds but there's plenty of room to pitch a tent along the river banks behind. Beyond Betoota the country turns into a rocky, silent plain, with circling crows and wedge-tailed eagles the only signs of life, and it's hard to imagine what the occasional fenceline or grid is keeping apart. Look for red sand dunes, distant outposts of the Simpson Desert. Driving can be hazardous here – you'll pass plenty of wrecks and shredded tyres – but with care (and luck), the Diamantina River and Birdsville are just three hours away.

Birdsville and beyond

Famous for the **horse races** on the first weekend in September, when a few thousand beer-swilling spectators pack out the dusty little settlement, at other times **BIRDSVILLE** promises to be something of an anticlimax, a handful of buildings where only the hotel and roadhouses seem to be doing business. But unless you've flown in, you'll very probably be glad simply to have arrived intact. The **caravan park** (℡07/4656 3214) comprises a large patch of scrub by the creek with an amenities block, or you can camp for free along the artesian overflow where huge flocks of raucous corellas seem to justify the township's name – though it's actually a corruption of "Burt's Ville", after the first storekeeper. Given the lack of alternatives, don't be surprised to find the comfy **accommodation** at the *Birdsville Hotel* full (℡07/4656 3244, ⓔbirdsville hotel@bigpond.com; ④); during race weekend, all beds are reserved for the bar staff anyway, so you have to camp. For more on the **race weekend**, check out ⓦwww.birdsvilleraces.com, which gives a good breakdown of what to expect: alcohol and ponies in that order; the hotel trades over 50,000 cans of beer in just two nights. **Provisions** and snacks can be bought from the general store. If you're organizing your own food, prepare the next day's meals after dark when the flies have settled down. You owe yourself at least one **drink** in the hotel's mighty bar; order by 5.30pm if you want a full evening meal – the "seven-course takeaway" is a pie and a six-pack.

The **Wirrarri Information Centre** on Billabong Boulevard (Mon–Fri 9am–4pm; ℡07/4656 3300, ⓔwirrarri@hotmail.com) will give you the lowdown on the state of the various Outback tracks if you're planning to use them, or ask at the **fuel station** (℡07/4656 3226), across from the hotel. The Information Centre can also direct you to another tree blazed by Burke and Wills across the Diamantina, otherwise hard to locate among the scrub, or to attractions in town such as the old hospital; originally built as a hotel and now just a stone shell, it operated as the original Australian Inland Mission between 1923 and 1927. The **Birdsville Working Museum**, as its name suggests, is more than just a collection of old stuff; all the exhibits, from petrol pumps and farm machinery to a complete blacksmith's shop are fully restored and regularly operated.

Outside Birdsville there's a stand of slow-growing, old and very rare **Waddi trees**, 14km north on the Bedourie road. They're about 5m tall and resemble sparse conifers wrapped in prickly feather boas with warped, circular seed pods; the wind blowing through the needles makes an eerie noise like the roar of a distant fire. For something more dramatic, head out 33km west to **Big Red** at the start of the Simpson Desert crossing. Simpson's largest dune may seem unimpressive from below, but your opinion will change radically if you walk up or try to plant a 4WD on the top. If you're having a hard time getting up the long western face, there is a less steep track immediately on the right, which has a couple of quick turns near the summit. Two-wheel-drive vehicles can often reach the base (check with the police before setting off) and it's worth it to see the dunes, flood plains and stony gibber country on the way.

North of Birdsville, the next substantial settlement, Mount Isa (see p.595), is a lonely 700km further on, with fuel available about every 200km. Those heading west **across the Simpson Desert** to Dalhousie Springs in South Australia need a Desert Parks Pass ($80) from the Birdsville NPWS office on Jardine Street (℡07/4656 3272). Feasible in any sound vehicle during a dry winter, the 520-kilometre **Birdsville Track** heads from the racecourse down to Marree in South Australia – see p.883 for details of this and the Simpson Desert crossing.

Rockhampton to Winton

Heading west from Rockhampton, the **Capricorn** and **Landsborough highways** run through the heart of central Queensland to Winton and, ultimately, Mount Isa. There's a lot to see here: just a couple of hours from the coast you'll find magical scenery atop the forested, sandstone plateau of the **Blackdown Tablelands**; while the town of **Emerald** offers the chance of seasonal farm work, as well as a gateway to Carnarvon Gorge and the **Gemfields'** sapphire mines. Continuing inland, both **Barcaldine** and **Longreach** are historically important towns, the latter hosting the archetypal Outback museum in the **Stockman's Hall of Fame**. For its part, **Winton** sits surrounded by a timeless, harsh orange landscape, with close access to some remote bush, unexpectedly imprinted with a dramatic set of dinosaur footprints at **Lark Quarry**.

Buses connect Rockhampton with Winton, and all main-town settlements west of Barcaldine are also on the Brisbane–Mount Isa bus run. Alternatively, you can catch the twice-weekly *Spirit of the Outback* **train** from Rockhampton as far as Longreach.

Into the Northern Highlands

As you move inland the coastal humidity is left behind and the gently undulating landscape becomes baked instead of steamed. Passing the white rubble moonscape atop **Mount Hay**, where you can stay at the van park and fossick for agates, the road loops over low hills before adopting a pattern that becomes ever more familiar: straight for miles and then an unexpected bend. Bottle trees, with their bulbous, thick grey trunks and spindly, thinly leaved branches, herald the drier climate. Gradually, the deep-blue platform of the **Blackdown Tablelands** emerges from the horizon, and, by the time you reach **DINGO**, dominates the landscape. Dingo is somewhere to stock up: there's a hotel, van park, fuel station and store, and a bronze monument to the town's namesake.

The Blackdown Tablelands

Floating 600m above the heat haze, the **Blackdown Tablelands'** gum forests, waterfalls and escarpments are a delight, a scenic refuge from the dry, flat lands below. A corrugated, unsealed twenty-kilometre access road is signposted on the highway 11km from Dingo. National Park campsite bookings can be made through the NPWS in Rockhampton or Emerald, or with the local **ranger** (☎07/4986 1964, ℱ4986 1325). Outside school holidays you could well have the place to yourself. There's no public transport into the park, but call in advance and catch the McCafferty's bus to Dingo, and **Namoi Hills Cattle Station** (☎07/4935 9121, ℱ4935 9234), set at the base of the tablelands, will pick you up at the drop-off point on the highway. They offer accommodation-and-meal packages, run tours round the station and onto the tablelands and regularly cater to the tour-bus crowd – phone ahead for costs and to check which days are booked if you want peace and quiet.

The access road from the highway runs flat through open scrub to the base of the range; the climb is steep, twisting and slippery, as "pea gravel" puts in an appearance. Views over a haze of eucalypt woodland are generally blocked by the thicker forest at the top of the plateau, but at **Horseshoe Lookout** there's a fabulous view north and, after rain, **Two Mile Falls** rockets over the edge of the cliffs. From here the road widens and runs past Mimosa Creek **campground** ($3.85 per person per night), dead-ending at the **Rainbow Falls** car park. The campground is excellent, shaded by massive stringybark trees with tank water, tables, toilets, fire pits and a creek to bathe in. At night the air fills with the sharp scent of woodsmoke, and the occasional dingo howls in the distance; with a torch, you might see **greater gliders** or the more active brush-tail possum. Watch out for pied currawongs (crows) that raid unattended tables, tents and cars for anything, edible or not. Temperatures can reach 40°C on summer days, and drop below zero on winter nights.

Walks in the park include the short trip to **Officers Pocket**, a moist amphitheatre of ferns and palms with the facing cliffs picked out yellow and white in the late afternoon; a **circuit track** along Mimosa Creek, past remains of cattle pens and stock huts, to some beautifully clear **ochre stencils** of hands and weapons made by Gungaloo Aborigines a century ago; and the park's finest scenery at **Rainbow Falls**, 6km past the campsite. At its glorious best around dawn, this track leads from the car park through an eerie gum forest to the top of the gorge, then follows around to where the creek seeps down steps into the greenery. From the edge you can spy on birds in the rainforest beneath; explosive thumps from below signal rock wallabies tearing across ledges hardly big enough for a mouse. A long staircase descends into a cool world of spring-fed gardens, ending on a large shelf about halfway into the gorge where Rainbow Falls sprays from above into a wide, clear pool. It may be pretty, but the water's paralyzingly cold; for a warmer dip, climb back up the stairs and follow the path to the top of the falls, where the creek runs in full sun and the bed has handy, bath-sized holes to sit in.

Emerald and around

The road west of Dingo crosses the lower reaches of the **Bowen Basin coal-fields** at **Blackwater**, then moves into **cotton country**, signalled by fluffy white tailings along the roadside around **YAMALA**, where there's a **cotton gin** to tour (by appointment ☏07/4982 3888).

EMERALD is a misleadingly named place. This close to the Gemfield towns of Sapphire and Rubyvale, you'd think its origins could be traced to precious stones, but in fact the area was named Emerald Downs by a surveyor who saw the grassland here, atypically rich and green after heavy rains. A dormitory town for the Bowen Basin coal **mines** to the north, and set at the junction of routes north to Mackay and south to Carnarvon Gorge, Emerald is a busy place at the heart of a soundly productive district: the rich soil supports sunflowers, citrus trees, grape vines, lychees and rockmelons, all of which attract swarms of seasonal **fruit-pickers**. Despite being around 100 years old, the town appears quite modern due to rebuilding after a series of disastrous fires in the 1950s.

Most essential services are on the Capricorn Highway, here called **Clermont Street**, where the main feature is the pristine train station, built in 1901 and restored in 1986. One road back from this is Egerton Street, where 250-million-year-old fossil tree trunks outside the town hall are preserved in great detail, right down to the texture of the bark. The **tourist information booth** at the west end of Clermont Street (Mon–Sat 9am–5pm, Sun 10am–2pm; ☏07/4982 4142) has leaflets on local attractions; at the other end is McCafferty's **bus station** (☏07/4982 2755). **Accommodation** is plentiful, though during the April harvest or November cotton-chipping season there may be very little room available. The *Central Inn*, near the station on Clermont Street (☏07/4982 0800; ❸), has a big kitchen, simply furnished rooms, and offers good advice for either farm work or visiting the Gemfields; the *Meteor Motel*, on the corner of Opal and Egerton streets (☏07/4982 1166; ❹), has a pool and a good steak restaurant; and the *Explorers Inn Motel* (☏07/4982 2822; ❹) is in a quiet spot at the edge of town – it's newer than the rest with comfortable, well-appointed rooms and a saltwater pool.

South to Springsure

Ten kilometres south of Emerald, **Lake Maraboon** has been created by the Fairbairn Dam as the region's main water supply, though this being Australia you can also induldge in water sports, fishing and bird-watching here. All modern amenities and **accommodation** are provided by the *Lake Maraboon Holiday Village* (☏07/4982 3677, ✉lakemaraboon@bigpond.com; camping $12, cabins ❸), including fuel, a store (8am–6pm), a **restaurant** and a grassed camping area, which is pleasantly situated among trees by the lake.

The Carnarvon Gorge lies a further 200km or so south via the town of **SPRINGSURE**, set below the dramatic orange cliffs of Mount Zamia, also known as Virgin Rock – though weathering since it was named means you can barely see the likeness of the Madonna and Child. If you wind up here for the night, the *Zamia Motel* (☏07/4984 1455; ❸) is a comfortable **motel** and **café**, and it's worth pausing in the area to detour 10km southwest to **Rainworth Fort** (Mon–Wed & Fri 9am–2pm, Sat & Sun 9am–5pm; $6) to see how, from the moment this district was settled, Aborigines put up a strong resistance. The fort is a squat stockade of basalt blocks and corrugated iron built by settlers for protection after "the **Wills Massacre**" when, on October 17, 1861, Aboriginal forces stormed Cullin-la-ringo station and killed nineteen people in apparent retaliation for the slaughter of a dozen Aborigines by a local squatter. White response was savage, spurred on by vigilantes and a contingent of Native Troopers; newspapers reported that "a great massacre has been made among the blacks of the Nogoa [river district]". The fort and later structures of Cairdbeign School and Homestead at the same site house a few relics of the period. Back on the Carnarvon road, it's 70km from Springsure to **Rolleston**, the last source of fuel, supplies and accommodation before the Gorge (see p.570).

The Gemfields

The country an hour west of Emerald is sparse and always hot, the scrub interrupted only by ugly cleared patches covered in rubble from mining operations. This wasteland masks one of the richest **sapphire fields** in the world and, with hard work, the chances of finding some are good – though you're unlikely to get rich. The easiest fields to reach are the **Anakie Fields**, with facilities at Anakie, Sapphire and Rubyvale. Anakie township is off the highway about 45km from Emerald; Sapphire is 9km north of Anakie, and Rubyvale a further 8km. Though well worked, the Anakie Fields are the best place for the newcomer to pick up tips; old hands proceed directly to **the Willows** (see opposite), 27km west of Anakie along the Capricorn Highway.

ANAKIE (a local aboriginal word for "permanent water") has no gemfields itself, but gave its name to those at Sapphire and Rubyvale. Unusually pretty, it comprises a **van park** (T & F 07/4985 4142; cabins ❷) with hot showers by the waterhole and a small shop open every day, backing onto a **pub**, post office and store. The **information centre** near the highway has fuel, licences, rough maps and advice.

In contrast, the country around **SAPPHIRE** looks like a war zone. You'll find a post office and houses scattered along the road and an elbow of **Retreat Creek**, where the first gems were found. *Sunrise Cabins* (T 07/4985 4281; ❸) has cabins and tent sites across the road from the medical centre, in sight of the creek, and *Blue Gem Caravan Park* (T 07/4985 4162) has a **store**, fuel, and fast food, or try a meal at *Thai & Chinese* next door. Towards Rubyvale is Pat's Gem Park (T 07/4985 4544) with a café, jewellery and craft displays and **fossicking lessons** for beginners; and Forever Mine (T 07/4985 4616), which charges a seemingly steep $50 to fossick, though for this you get a tractor-scoop (about four buckets of wash) to pick through.

RUBYVALE has several shops, service stations and a few **mines** to look around: tour groups tend to visit Miner's Heritage (open daily; $5 per person), but equally interesting is Bobby Dazzler (daily; $5) on the hill as you approach town. The ground beneath each new development here has to be mined first; outdoor tennis courts and the surfaced road were built only after years of wrangling over whether the ground had given up all its treasures. Rubyvale also seems to be the place to pick up on apocryphal stories, such as the one about the largest star sapphire ever found being used as a doorstop. You'll also hear plenty more during the annual **August Gemfest** which includes, in odd-numbered years, a **Wheelbarrow Race** when, in imitation of the first pioneering miners, all comers push their one-wheeled transport laden with pick and shovel up the eighteen-kilometre track from Anakie to Rubyvale, pausing only at Sapphire to take on board a bucket of dirt. There's fuel, a general store, and a good **van park** in Rubyvale (T 07/4985 4118; tent sites $10, cabins ❸) with camp sites and cabins; the *New Royal Hotel* nearby is a smart stone and timber building, with a mighty fireplace and tasty **food**.

Gem mining

Gems were first discovered in 1870 near Anakie but until Thai buyers came onto the scene a century later operations were low-key, and even today there are still solo fossickers making a living from their claims. Formed by prehistoric volcanic actions and later dispersed along waterways and covered by sediment, the **zircons**, **rubies** and, especially, **sapphires** found here lie in a layer of gravel above the clay base of ancient riverbeds. This layer can be up to 15m down, so gullies and dry rivers, where nature has already done some of the excavation for you, are good places to start digging.

Looking for surface gems, or **specking**, is best after rain, when a trained eye can see the stones sparkle in the mud. It's erratic but certainly easier than the alternative – **fossicking** – which requires a pick, shovel, sieve, washtub full of water and a canvas sack before even starting (this gear can be rented at all of the fields). Cut and polished, local zircons are pale yellow, sapphires pale green or yellow to deep blue, and rubies are light pink, but when they're covered in mud it's hard to tell them from gravel, which is where the washing comes in: wet gems glitter like fragments of coloured glass.

You have to be extremely enthusiastic to spend a summer on the fields; the mercury climbs steadily to 42°C, topsoil erodes and everything becomes filmed in dust. The first rains bring floods as the sunbaked ground sheds water, and if you're here then you'll be treated to the sight of locals specking in the rain, dressed in Akubras and Drizabones and shuffling around like mobile mushrooms. Conditions are best as soon after the wet season as possible (around May), when the ground is soft and fresh pickings have been uncovered – not surprisingly, this is also the busiest period.

If this all seems like too much hard work, try a **Gem Park** such as Pat's (see opposite), where they've done all the digging for you and supply all the necessary gear for about $10. All you have to do is sieve the wash, flip it onto the canvas and check it for stones. There's an art to sieving and flipping, but you're pretty sure to find something, since park owners lace the wash with rejects. Gem parks will also value and cut stones for you. Another break from the business end of a pick is to pay $5, take a **mine tour** and see if the professionals fare any better. In some ways they do – the chilled air 5m down is wonderful – but the main difference is one of scale rather than method or intent.

You need a **fossicker's licence**, available from shops and gem parks, which allows digging in areas set aside for the purpose or on no-man's-land. The $7.25 licence is valid for two months and gives you no rights at all other than to keep what you find and to camp at fossick grounds. To stake a claim and keep others away you need a **Miner's Right** from the field officer in Emerald (Department of Minerals and Energy, Clerana Centre, Clermont St; ☎07/4982 4011); this also carries obligations to restore the land to its original state and maintain it for two years after quitting the site.

The **Willows Gemfield** is still in the making, part mining camp, part township. The immaculate *Willows Caravan Park* (☎ & ℱ07/4985 5128; cabins ❷) is well shaded, has wangled a liquor licence and acts as a bank agent as well as supplying fuel and digging equipment. The gemfields are just down the track from the park.

Over the Range to Winton

Vistas from the rounded sandstone boulders at the top of the Great Dividing Range west of the tiny railway stop of **Boguntungan** reveal a dead-flat country beyond; rivers flow to the Gulf of Carpentaria or towards the great dry lakes of South Australia, while unsealed roads run north to Clermont and south to Charleville. You'll notice an increase in temperature; flies appear from nowhere, tumbleweeds pile up on fences and trees never seem closer than the horizon. In terms of numbers, sheep are the dominant mammal in these parts, though there are some cattle and even a few people out here. Next stop on the road or rail line is the pleasant township of **Alpha**, where you can find fuel and a café or two, and **JERICHO**, which is one of the last places in Queensland with a **drive-in movie theatre** (films showing on Saturday nights).

Barcaldine and Blackall

The only place of any size on the way to Longreach is **BARCALDINE**, 300km from Emerald, an unassuming grid of quiet streets belying an important niche in Australian history. It was near here during the 1885 drought that geologists first tapped Queensland's **artesian water**, revolutionizing Outback development. The town further secured its place in history during the 1891 **shearers' strike** which, though a failure itself, ultimately led to the **formation of the Labor Party**. On the highway, outside the station which became the focus of the dispute, is a granite monument – sculpted to resemble the tips of a pair of shears – to shearers arrested during the strike. Right next to it, the sagging silver trunk of the **Tree of Knowledge**, a rallying point for shearers, struggles gamely to improve on its 170 years.

The **Australian Workers' Heritage Centre** (Mon–Sat 9am–5pm, Sun 10am–5pm; $9.90) is unmissable underneath a yellow and blue marquee on Ash Street. With an expanding collection of displays concentrating on the history of the workers' movement after the shearers' strike, as well as videos, artefacts and plenty of sepia-tinted photos covering themes including Outback women and Aboriginal stockmen, the museum rounds out Longreach's Stockman's Hall of Fame (see opposite). On the highway the **information centre** (Mon–Fri 8.30am–4.30pm; ☎07/4651 1724) will direct you to other attractions such as the self-styled **Mad Mick's Funny Farm** (open most mornings April–Sept or by arrangement ☎07/4651 1172; adults $7.70, children $4.40), which has been restored to its turn-of-the-twentieth-century condition and is inhabited by friendly, hand-reared animals; admission includes a ride in a Ford Model-T and tea and damper. For a closer look at Outback caves, waterholes, and **Aboriginal art** – much of it on private property – with a tall tale or two thrown in, contact *Artesian Country Tours* (☎07/4651 2211, ℱ4651 2499); their day-long "Aramac & Graceville" **tour** (Wed & Sat; $129 including all transport, lunch and tea) is highly recommended.

Banks and other services are mostly on Box Street, which runs south off the highway. **Accommodation** options include the *Ironbark Inn* (☎07/4651 2311; ❹), an "Outback"-style motel with attached steakhouse; *Barcaldine Motel* (☎07/4651 1244; ❹); and *Homestead Van Park* (☎07/4651 1308; camping $12, cabins ❷), all on Box Street. Barcaldine has a disproportionate number of hotels, probably due to the hot summers – the *Artesian*, *Commercial* and *Union* hotels are three highway establishments all offering cold **drinks** and pub **meals**.

Blackall

One hour south of Barcaldine on the Landsborough Highway (and covered by Brisbane–Mount Isa buses), a sign at **BLACKALL** welcomes you to Merino Country. It was near here in 1892 that **Jackie Howe** fleeced 321 sheep in under eight hours using hand shears, a still-unbroken record. If you want to visit a **sheep** station to see modern shearers in action, it can be arranged by the **tourist office** just off Shamrock Street on Short Street (daily 9am–noon & 1–5pm; ☏07/4657 4637). There's more on the industry at the steam-driven woolscour (the plant where the freshly sheared fleeces are vigorously washed and cleaned), built in 1908 and in operation for seventy years; it has been restored recently and runs daily, with guides on hand to show you around (8am–4pm; $7.70).

In town, you could also track down the famous **black stump**, a surveying point used in pinpointing Queensland's borders in the nineteenth century and now the butt of many jokes; the original stump has been replaced by a more interesting fossilized one. Otherwise, pass time at the new **artesian spa** (Mon–Sat 9–11am & 2–6pm, Sun 2–6pm; $1.50), a large pool along the line of Mitchell's (p.569) at the town's Aquatic Centre on Salvia Street. Around 100km southwest of Blackall, **Idalia National Park** preserves one of Queensland's last population of yellow-footed rock wallabies in the wild – more easily seen at the fauna park in Charleville if you're heading that way (see p.573). For details of access to Idalia, and possible guided **night tours** of the park, contact the ranger on ☏07/4657 5033.

Blackall town sits on the banks of the often dry (but occasionally five-metre-deep) **Barcoo River**; two-hundred-metre-long Shamrock Street, shaded by palms and bottle trees, is the main road on which you'll find banks, supplies and a few **places to eat** – if your dress is reasonably smart you can savour good food at the *Blackall Club*. The most central **place to stay** is the smart *Accacia Motor Inn* (☏07/4657 6022; ❹), and at *Blackall Caravan Park* (☏07/4657 4816; on-site vans ❷) on Hart Lane you can yarn with other travellers around a huge campfire and be fed pot roasts, billy tea and damper for an extra fee. Long-distance **bus tickets** are available from Blackall Travel (☏07/4657 4422).

Longreach

LONGREACH, 110km west of Barcaldine and right on the Tropic of Capricorn, is different from other western towns: it's doing more than surviving. This is mainly due to the **Stockman's Hall of Fame**, an ambitious museum which pulls in busloads of tourists. Yet even before the museum, Longreach was an enterprising settlement with a firm place in history. Ever since the discovery of artesian water it has been a stronghold of cattle- and sheep-farming, but it really took off as the original headquarters of **Qantas** – their first hangar, full of replica aircraft, still stands at the airport, and mid-2002 saw the arrival – by air – of a decommissioned Qantas **jumbo jet**, currently being prepared as a museum.

Qantas

There's always been contention between Longreach and Winton as to which was the birthplace of **Qantas** (the Queensland and Northern Territories Aerial Service). Though the company officially formed at Winton, the first joy-flights and taxi service actually flew from Longreach in 1921, pioneered by Hudson Fysh and Paul McGuiness. Their idea – that an airline could play an important role by carrying mail and passengers, dropping supplies to remote districts and providing an emergency link into the Outback – inspired other projects such as the Flying Doctor Service. Though the company's headquarters moved to Brisbane in 1930, Qantas maintained their offices at Longreach until after World War II – during the war US Flying Fortresses were stationed here – by which time both the company and its planes had outgrown the town.

The Stockman's Hall of Fame

On the highway 2km from the town centre, **The Stockman's Hall of Fame** (daily 9am–5pm; $20.70) is a masterpiece, not just in architectural design – a blend of aircraft hangar and cathedral – but in being an encyclopedia of the Outback right in its heart. Since opening in 1988 its success has silenced critics who underestimated the Outback's widespread appeal. A minor complaint might be that the displays themselves are fairly ordinary, but once you're here the Hall of Fame has achieved its dual aim of bringing people out west and providing background to the development of a vast portion of Australia.

Inside the museum, the Outback is romanticized through videos, slide shows, photographs and exhibits – but this is not just another local museum where anything more than five years old is shown for its own sake. History starts in the Dreamtime and moves on, via a directory of those on the First Fleet (see p.1163), to early explorers and pioneers (including a large section on women in the Outback), ending with personal accounts of life in the bush. Among more day-to-day features are some offbeat selections; if you thought barbed wire was just something to get stuck on, then check out the collection here, with over a hundred types – from the old hook design to modern razor wire. You'd be hard pushed not to find something of interest, be it boxing kangaroos, rodeos, bark huts or tall stories. The library and exhibitions by Outback artists (displayed in the art gallery) are also worth a browse.

Practicalities

Longreach is a more active version of Barcaldine, with plenty of spruce old buildings and a further abundance of watering holes. The main drag is south off the highway along **Eagle Street**, where you'll find hotels, cafés, banks, a cinema and a well-stocked **supermarket**. The **airport** is off the highway between town and the Hall of Fame; **trains** terminate at the station at the junction of Galah Street and the highway; and **buses** set down on Eagle Street at Longreach Outback Travel Centre (℡07/4658 1776, Ⓔcrums@outback qld.net.au), which can arrange all tickets – they also offer **tours** of nearby sheep stations, and waterway **cruises** on a paddle boat. The **tourist office** (April–Oct Mon–Fri 9am–5pm & Sat–Sun 9am–1pm; Nov–March Mon–Fri 9am–5pm; ℡07/4658 3555) is in a replica of Qantas's original office on the corner of Eagle and Duck streets, opposite the post office.

There are two **campsites**: *Gunnadoo Van Park*, on Thrush Road looking across to the Hall of Fame (℡07/4658 1781), and *Longreach Caravan Park* on Ibis Street (℡07/4658 1770). *Hallview Lodge*, 81 Wompoo St (℡07/4658 3777; ❸–❹), is a friendly B&B; or you can indulge in **motel** comforts at the *Albert Park Motel*, Hudson Fysh Drive (℡07/4658 2411, Ⓕ4658 3181; ❹), or *Longreach Motor Inn*, Galah Street (℡07/4658 2322; ❹). For **meals**, the Longreach RSL Club welcomes visitors; you can dine in their inexpensive restaurant (noon–2pm & 6.30–8.30pm) or just settle into a chair in the lounge-bar. Of Eagle Street's half-dozen hotels, try the *Lyceum* for counter food, or *Starlight's Hideout Tavern* for meals and nightlife.

Winton and beyond

Scenery doesn't come blander than on the 173-kilometre-long Longreach–Winton stretch: your only worry as a driver is to keep your foot down and stay awake as the car cruises the empty Mitchell Plains. At the far

The first public performance of "Banjo" Paterson's ballad **Waltzing Matilda** was held in April 1895 at Winton's *North Gregory Hotel*, and has stirred up gossip and speculation ever since. Legend has it that **Christina MacPherson** told Paterson the tale of a swagman's brush with the law at the Combo Waterhole near Kynuna (p.588) while the poet was staying with her family at nearby Dagwood Station. Christina wrote the music to the ballad, a collaboration which so incensed Paterson's fiancée, Sarah Riley, that she broke off their engagement. While a straightforward "translation" of the poem is easy enough – "Waltzing Matilda" was contemporary slang for tramping (carrying a bedroll or swag from place to place), "jumbuck" for a sheep, and "squatters" refers to landowners – there is some contention as to what the poem actually describes. The most obvious interpretation is of a poor tramp, hounded to death by the law, but first drafts of the poem suggest that Paterson – generally known as a romantic rather than social commentator – originally wrote the piece about the arrest of a union leader during the shearers' strike, and later toned it down. Either version would account for the popularity of the poem, which was once proposed as the national anthem – Australians readily identify with an underdog who dares to confront the system.

end, **WINTON** is a real frontier town, and an excellent base for exploring this corner of the Outback; dust devils blow tumbleweeds down the streets, and the main change over the last fifty years is that 4WDs have superseded the horse as a means of getting around. As Queensland's largest cattle-trucking depot, Winton has a constant stream of road trains rumbling through it, and conversations in hotel bars tend to revolve around problems of stock management. Winton has its share of history, too: Qantas was founded here in 1920 and **Waltzing Matilda**, that evergreen ballad, premiered at the *North Gregory Hotel* (see box above). The surrounding countryside is an eerie world of windswept plains and eroded **jump-ups** – flat-topped hills layered in orange, grey and red dust – complete with **opal deposits** at Opalton and a stunning set of **dinosaur footprints** at Lark Quarry.

Winton's central drag is **Elderslie Street**, where you'll find banks, a post office and service stations. If there's a film on, treat yourself to a session in the **open-air cinema**, complete with canvas seats and original projector, at the corner of Elderslie and Cobb streets; the café here stays open until after dark. A few doors down, next to the *North Gregory Hotel*, the immense **wooden Corfield & Fitzmaurice building** (Mon–Fri 9am–5pm, Sat 9am–12.30pm; $5) opened as a store in 1916 and now houses a vast collection of rocks and fossils from around the world, along with a life-size diorama of the Lark Quarry dinosaurs – garbage bins around town are also shaped as dinosaur feet.

Further down Elderslie Street, opposite a tepid swimming pool and bronze statue of the jolly swagman, the **Waltzing Matilda Centre** (daily 8.30am–5pm; $15; ☎07/4657 1466) has some unusual items, including an indoor billabong, a fine display of Aboriginal artefacts featuring an entire tree with a boomerang half-carved out of its trunk, and a bottle collection covering everything from poisons to schnapps. The centre also doubles as an **information office** and sorts out **tours** to local sights – check with them too about road conditions before visiting Opalton, Lark Quarry, or national parks. For some really ludicrous fun, the **Australian Crayfish Derby**, part of the Outback Festival held in September in odd-numbered years, has to be worth a look; the owner of the winning crustacean nets $1500, and the runner up gets to eat all the competitors. In April the **Waltzing Matilda Festival**

△ Kookaburra

involves a rodeo and arts events attracting bush poets to compete with "Banjo" Paterson.

Winton's **accommodation** prospects include the *Matilda Country Tourist Park* on Chirnside Street, about 700km from Elderslie Street where the Landsborough Highway kinks into town (☎07/4657 1607; camping $7.50, cabins ➌); the nearby neat and trim *Banjo Motel* on Manuka Street (☎07/4657 1213; ➌); and the *North Gregory Hotel* (☎07/4657 1375; dorms $17, rooms ➋), which has en-suite and shared bathrooms as well as some basic budget beds in the old shearers' quarters. The *North Gregory* is also one of the best places to **eat** in town, with the early-opening *Twighlight Café* opposite. Leaving, there are two **buses** daily in each direction along the Landsborough Highway towards Mount Isa and Brisbane; the Gift and Gem Centre on Elderslie Street is the pick-up point and sells **tickets**.

Bladensburg National Park, Opalton and Carisbrooke

South of Winton, a 120-kilometre-long unsealed road runs down through the beautifully stark jump-ups, spinifex scrub, grassland and thin woods of Bladensburg National Park to the mining settlement of Opalton. The borders of **Bladensburg National Park** start just 8km from town, from where a rough track – generally negotiable in a conventional vehicle in dry weather – runs 15km in to **Skull Waterhole**, named after the "dispersal" of the Goa Aborigines by the Native Mounted Police in the late 1800s. Despite this sad history it's an interesting spot, as the water attracts kangaroos, budgerigars and ring-necked parrots. A further 10km south, via a **bush campsite**, is the southern boundary of the park near a waterhole and the twenty-metre-high **Logan Falls**. Contact the **ranger** (☎07/4657 1192) before visiting and take all supplies, including ample drinking water, with you.

OPALTON is a multicultural shanty town, with Yugoslav and Czech miners, as well as deserters from Coober Pedy in South Australia (see p.872), reworking century-old diggings with Chinese and Korean finance. You need to be entirely self-sufficient here: the only modern feature is a solar-powered telephone and there isn't any drinking water. During the summer there won't be any miners either – hotels in Winton are easily preferable to Opalton's 40°C-plus temperatures. Fossicking zones have been established where you can pick over old tailings for scraps. There is a **camping** and caravan area, "washing water", and a small **store** that's open most days from 10am to 2pm – they don't sell fuel, however.

If you don't have your own transport, it's worth seeing the area on a **day-tour** from Winton to **Carisbrooke Station**, 85km southwest of Winton (by arrangement, minimum of four passengers; $125; ☎07/4657 3984), where you can also spend the night in renovated shearer's quarters. The trip includes visits to an opal mine and to caves covered in Aboriginal paintings – some abstract, others recognizable outlines of boomerangs and club-like nulla-nullas.

Lark Quarry

It takes about two hours to drive the 120km southwest on the Jundah Road from Winton to **Lark Quarry**, dodging kamikaze kangaroos and patches of bulldust, and once you've arrived there's no doubt that this is the rough heart of the Outback. Nor is it surprising to find **dinosaur remains** here: the place looks prehistoric, swarming with flies and surrounded by stubby hills where stunted trees and tufts of grass tussle with rocks for space. A hundred million years ago this was a shrinking waterhole across which a carnivorous dinosaur chased a group of various turkey-sized herbivores through the mud to a rockface where it caught and killed one as the others fled back past it. Over three thousand **footprints** have been found recording these few seconds of action, excavated in the 1970s and now protected by an awning and walkway around them (though the awning collapsed onto the footprints in 2002 and had to be rebuilt). Indentations left by small, amazingly sharp, three-clawed feet – some very light as the prey panicked and ran on tiptoe – stream in all directions, while those left by the larger predator go only one way. Paths lead around to other, buried tracks where the chase ended.

West from Winton

The main route out of Winton follows the Landsborough Highway 340km northwest to Cloncurry (p.593) on the Townsville–Mount Isa road. Heading this way, the **Combo Waterhole**, 165km from Winton and just shy of Kynuna, provided the inspiration for "Banjo" Paterson's classic ballad "Waltzing Matilda". It's a fairly typical muddy soak, decorated by trees and beer cans, and with some solid stone weirs built at the turn of the twentieth century by Chinese labourers. **KYNUNA**'s low-slung *Blue Heeler Hotel* (⊤07/4746 8650; ❸) is also worth a stop, not least for its ice-cold beer; it's possible to camp here too. The other feature on the journey is the *Walkabout Creek Hotel* at **McKINLAY**, 75km past Kynuna, which you might recognize as the rowdy Outback pub in the film Crocodile Dundee. Since the film was shot, the whole building was moved 400m in order to make it more visible to passing tourists.

Heading due west of Winton the Kennedy Developmental Road leads to Boulia, around 350km away. The journey is a continuation of the Winton landscape, with fuel available every 150km and the chance to see the enigmatic **Min Min Light**, an unexplained glowing oval reputedly seen bobbing around the bush at night; in case you miss it, thoughtful townspeople have erected a larger-than-life Min Min model. **BOULIA** consists of a hotel (⊤07/4746 3144), van park and roadhouse; if you need a reason to visit, make it the annual **camel races** in July, when the town gets lively and inordinate quantities of beer are consumed. At quieter times of the year, drop in to the **Fossil Museum** (Mon–Fri 9am–4pm; $5) displaying regional finds, and the **Min Min Encounter Centre** (Mon–Fri 9am–4pm; $11), a cross between a museum and sound-and-light show. Boulia's **information office** is here, too (daily 9am–5pm; ⊤07/4746 3386), along with *Encounter's Café*, which claims to serve the Outback's best cappuccino – there's certainly no competition for a good many miles around. Some 200km southeast of Boulia, **Diamantina National Park** is a huge, pristine area with two **campsites**, rivers and waterholes, sand dunes, claypans, and heaps of wildlife, including **bilbies**; the park is very remote so come fully prepared and note that you might need 4WD – contact the **ranger** in Winton first (⊤07/4657 3024)

From Boulia, Mount Isa is 300km north on bitumen, and Birdsville is 400km south on a mostly reasonable road. If you're really enjoying the ride, Alice Springs is 800km west on the Donohue-Plenty "highways" – a long stretch of dust and gravel. There's fuel every 250km or so, and track conditions improve once you're over the border into the Northern Territory.

Townsville to Lawn Hill

All the major settlements along the Townsville to Lawn Hill route are **mining** towns, spaced so far apart that precise names are redundant: **Mount Isa** becomes "the Isa", **Cloncurry** "the Curry", **Charters Towers** "the Towers", as if nowhere else existed. Scattered across the vast tracts between are geological treasures waiting to be discovered, as well as traces of those who've tried before, and there's plenty to see as you head into the Northern Territory. Most people never stop to find out, grimly tearing along as fast as possible between Townsville and Three Ways along the Flinders/Barkly Highway. It's a shame, because even if time is limited and you're relying on public transport, Charters Towers' century-old feel and Mount Isa's strange setting are worth a stopover. With the freedom of your own vehicle, there's untramped bush at the **Great Basalt Wall** and **Porcupine Gorge** and the spectacular oasis of **Lawn Hill Gorge**, all a lifetime away from the coast's often banal spirit. With the highway forming the main link between Queensland and the Northern Territory, the major **bus lines** have at least daily services interstate, or there's the twice-weekly *Inlander* **train** between Townsville and Mount Isa.

Gold country

There's little scenic variation over the two-hour journey from the coast to the heights of the inland range at the community of **Mingela**, but dry scrub at the top once covered seams of ore which had the streets of both **Charters Towers** and **Ravenswood** bustling with lucky-strike miners. Those times are long gone – though gold is still extracted from old tailings or sporadically panned from the creek beds – and the towns have survived at opposite extremes: connected by road and rail to Townsville, Charters Towers became a busy rural centre, while Ravenswood, half an hour south of Mingela, was just too far off the track and wasted to a shadow. Detours (☎07/4721 5977) runs day-trips from Townsville to one or the other for about $55.

Ravenswood

As wind blows dust and dried grass around the streets between mine shafts and lonely old buildings, **RAVENSWOOD** fulfils ideas of what a ghost town should look like. Gold was discovered here in 1868 and within two years there were solid brick houses, a frenetic atmosphere and seven hundred miners on Elphinstone Creek working seams of gold, silver and lead ore: "every building in the main street was either a public house and dance house or public house and general store".

The main attraction is to wander between the restored buildings, trying to imagine how the others must have looked; the curator of the **Court House Museum** (daily except Tues 10am–3pm) gives entertaining **tours** of the museum, town and – with sufficient notice – current mining efforts (☎07/4770 2047 to book). Built in 1879, the **post office** today doubles as the town's store and fuel supply. Unsurprisingly, the two most complete survivals are hotels, though how they both keep going with a scattered population of barely a hundred souls is anybody's guess. You'll probably end up in one as the day heats up; the *Railway* (☎07/4770 2131; ❸) seems to be the more popular, but though the *Imperial* (☎07/4770 2131; ❸) looks the worse for wear it has original wood panelling, mirrors and swing doors on the bar; **accommodation** and counter meals are available at either.

Charters Towers and around

Once Queensland's second-largest city, and often referred to in its heyday simply as "the World", **CHARTERS TOWERS** is a showcase of colonial era architecture. An Aboriginal boy named **Jupiter Mosman** found gold here in 1871 and within twelve months three thousand prospectors had stripped the landscape of trees and covered it with shafts, chimneys and crushing mills. At first, little money was reinvested – the **cemetery** is a sad record of cholera and typhoid outbreaks from poor sanitation – but by 1900, despite diminishing returns, Charters Towers had become a prosperous centre. There's been minimal change since then and the population, now mainly sustained by cattle farming, has shrunk to about a third of what it was in its prime. Good times to visit are for the May Day weekend **Country Music Festival**, and the Easter **Rodeo**.

The town itself is worth about an hour of your time, with plenty of spruce old buildings along Gill and Mosman streets: the pink-and-white headquarters of the *Northern Miner* on Gill Street, one of Queensland's oldest surviving newspapers; the classical elegance of the post office and the **World Theatre**; and the shaded country arcades outside the stores. The courtyard and glass roof at the former **Stock Exchange** and Assayer's Office now front some quiet shops and a lifeless **mining museum** (daily 9am–4pm; $3). Next door, the solid facade of the town hall betrays its original purpose as a bank, which stored gold bars smelted locally; and the next bank along is now a grand facade for the World Theatre and Cinemas. Just down Mosman Street is the **Zara Clark Museum** (daily 10am–3pm; $4.40), housing an absorbing jumble of everything from old wagons to a set of silver tongs for eating frogs' legs. Further along the road there's plenty of shade under giant fig trees at **Lissner Park**, whose Boer War memorial recalls stories of **Breaker Morant**, a local soldier executed by the British after shooting a prisoner.

The **Venus Gold Battery**, 5km out of town down Gill Street (**tours** daily 10am & 2pm; $4.40), is a fascinating illustration of the monumental efforts

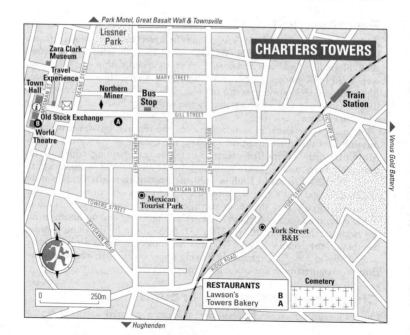

needed to separate gold from rock. Abandoned in 1972 after a century of operations, the battery is a huge, gloomy temple to the past, its machinery lying silent and piecemeal around the place. The intention is to restore it to full working order, presumably without re-creating the actual conditions – it was a hideous place, a sweatbox filled with noxious fumes and noise. Ore was ground to a powder in one of the seven massive crushers, mixed with water and passed over a mercury screen. Any gold formed an amalgam and adhered to the mercury, which was then heated in a crucible to leave a pitted nugget and later re-melted with flux to absorb any impurities. Sludge from the mercury screens was soaked in cyanide to leach out more gold, and then the cyanide was neutralized with sulphur and piled up outside. These mounds are now being reprocessed using modern methods to extract the last vestiges of the precious metal.

Practicalities

The main streets are Gill and Mosman, where you'll find everything from supermarkets to banks; **trains** stop at the far end of Gill Street, **buses** halfway along by the Caltex service station; **tickets** for either can be arranged through Travel Experience, 13 Gill St (℡07/4787 2622). For **accommodation**, the *Mexican Tourist Park*, at the corner of Church and Mexican streets (℡07/4787 1161; on-site vans and cabins ❷) on the site of the once-busy Mexican Mine, is shaded and central. In tune with the local atmosphere is *York Street B&B* at 58 York St (℡07/4787 1028, ⓔyorkstreetbb@httech.com.au; ❷), a nicely restored old timber building with wide verandahs and a pool. The *Park Motel*, on the corner of Mosman and Deane streets (℡07/4787 1022; ❹), is also central and comfortable. For **food**, the hotel dining rooms do cheap meals, though *Towers Bakery*, 114 Gill St, has award-winning meat pies, and *Lawson's Restaurant*, next to the World Theatre on Mosman, is a pricey place with an eclectic modern Australian menu. There's a Sunday morning **market** in the Stock Exchange building. The helpful **information** centre (daily 9am–5pm; ℡07/4752 0314), on Mosman, facing down Gill Street, has rough maps and advice on gold-panning **tours** in the area, while Gold Nugget Scenic Tours packs the town sights into three hours (Mon–Sat; $22; ℡07/4787 4115) and makes longer excursions by arrangement.

The Great Basalt Wall

About thirty minutes north of Charters Towers, the Gregory Developmental Road crosses the eastern side of a hundred-kilometre-long overgrown **lava flow** known with some justification as **the Great Basalt Wall**. Central sections form an impenetrable band of black boulders, riddled with gullies and caves; aerial surveys show dense vegetation weighed down beneath rubber vines, hiding colonies of fruit bats and hundreds of unconnected saline waterholes. Compasses don't work properly around basalt and those who've entered the maze are not short on tales about promptly getting lost and wandering around for hours. If you want to linger in the area, *Bluff Downs* (℡07/4770 4084; cabins ❷, homestead ❻) is a working **cattle station** offering **accommodation** and activity tours of the property, and is also one of the most significant **fossil sites** in Queensland.

You can also get an impression of what the region is like on the fringes of the wall, at Big Bend and Red Falls. **Big Bend**, 33km north of the Towers and then 2km east, is best reached in a high-clearance vehicle, though it's not far to walk from the main road. This is where the Burdekin River was diverted as lava edged into it, forming a concave cliff and swimming spot at Echo Hole. The flows covered an ancient coral reef and you can still pick out some shapes in the limestone rocks where the lava has worn away. At **Red Falls**, 40km along the Developmental Road and then 44km west down a dry-season track, the river runs at right angles to the lava flow; water pours into an Olympic-sized swimming hole and then down a sandy creekbed lined with paperbark trees and overlooked by a bush **campsite**. Walking about 200m further upstream to swim at Silent Hole, you'll see that the riverbed is pocked by the frozen impressions of burst bubbles where gases erupted through the solidifying rock.

Dalrymple National Park

Dalrymple National Park, 46km north of Charters Towers and then 2.5km on a track, marks the site of the now-vanished **Dalrymple township**, founded in 1864 as the first official inland settlement in northern Australia. A gold-mining town, finds were rich enough to support five hotels during Dalrymple's very brief heyday; having been completely demolished by a flood in 1870, today the remains include only the traces of pavements, foundations, and gravesites.

Dinosaur country

HUGHENDEN, 245km west of Charters Towers along the highway, looks big compared with some of the places you pass on the way here. A dozen wide streets, a supermarket, a couple of hotels and **banks** all conspire to make you feel that you've arrived somewhere. There are two places to spend time: the swimming pool on Resolution Street and the **Dinosaur Museum** and **information centre** on Gray Street, just past the hotel (daily 9am–5pm; $3; ☎07/4741 1021). The display here focuses on the swamp-dwelling Muttaburrasaurus, bones of which were found south of town in 1963 and assembled into a ten-metre-long skeleton after souvenir hunters handed over pieces to the Queensland Museum in Brisbane. Though this family of dinosaurs was formerly believed to be vegetarian, Muttaburrasaurus' needle-like teeth have prompted a rethink about their possible diet. The *Grand Hotel* on Gray Street (☎07/4741 1588; ❷) offers filling **meals** and budget **beds**, but the *Rest Easi Motel* (☎07/4741 1633; ❹) is quieter and you can also **camp**. *Pete's Country Café*, before the tracks on the other side of town, has good **burgers** and doubles as the **bus stop**. Routes head out of Hughenden in all directions – aside from the highway west, there's the road north to Porcupine Gorge, or long stretches south to Winton or Longreach – and you should fuel up before leaving town.

Porcupine Gorge is 70km north of Hughenden along the partially surfaced Kennedy Developmental Road, accessible only if you have your own vehicle (and you can usually scrape by without a 4WD). A deep gash completely invisible among the drab brown scrub until you're virtually in it, it's best seen at the start of the dry season (May–July) before the **Flinders River** stops flowing, when good swimming holes, beautifully coloured cliffs and flowering bottlebrush and banksia trees reward the effort of getting here. A **campsite** at the top of the gorge has limited cold water, toilets and nothing else. Look for wallabies on the walk into the gorge, which leads down steps and becomes an increasingly steep, rough path carpeted in loose stones. The white riverbed has been moulded by water into soft, elongated forms, curving into a pool below the orange, yellow and white bands of **Pyramid Rock**. This is the bush at its best: sandstone glowing in the afternoon sun against a deep-blue sky, with animal calls echoing along the gorge as the shadow of the gorge wall creeps over distant woods.

Richmond

More on the regional fossil record is on show 115km west of Hughenden along the highway at **RICHMOND**, whose **Fossil Museum** (daily 8.30am–4.45pm; $8) displays the petrified remains of hundred-million-year-old fish, long-necked elasmosaurs, and models of a kronosaur excavated in the 1920s by a team from Harvard University and now on show in the USA. Pride of the collection are a complete skeleton of a seal-like pliosaur – the most intact vertebrate fossil ever found in Australia – and the minmi ankylosaur, with its armour-plated hide.

Not many people hang around in Richmond, though it's by no means an unpleasant place – just very small. A roadside park makes a good spot to stretch your legs, with an original **Cobb & Co. coach** (see p.564) and views out across the Flinders River. There's **accommodation** at the *Richmond Caravan Park* (☎07/4741 3772; camping $8, dorms $15, cabins ❷), which has tent sites, "backpacker" rooms with a communal kitchen, and cabins; or *Entriken's Pioneer Motel* (☎07/4741 3188; ❸). The museum's **café** is the only one in town; otherwise head to the old wooden *Federal Palace Hotel* or one of the service stations for a feed.

Cloncurry and around

CLONCURRY, 280km west of Richmond, is caught between two landscapes, where the flat eastern plains rise to a rough and rocky plateau. Besides being the place where Australia's highest temperature (53.1°C) was recorded, Cloncurry offers glimpses into the mining history that permeates the whole stretch west to the larger and less personal settlement of Mount Isa. Copper was discovered here in 1867 but as the town lacked a rail link to the coast until 1908, profits were eroded by the necessity of transporting the ore by camel to Normanton. This meant that Cloncurry never reflected the quality of its mines: there are no traces of a wealthy past because there never was one. Even the current resurgence in mining hasn't had much effect on Cloncurry (aside from raising motel rates); miners are flown in from the coast to the mines, work their two-week shifts, then head home again, all without spending more than a couple of hours in town.

Buildings at the **Mary Kathleen Memorial Park Museum** (Mon–Fri 7am–4pm, Sat & Sun 9am–3pm; $5) were salvaged from Mary Kathleen, a short-lived uranium mining town between Cloncurry and Mount Isa (see p.595). The museum is primarily of geological interest, a comprehensive catalogue of local ores, fossils and gemstones arranged in long cases, though Aboriginal tools and Burke's water bottle add some historical depth. The office gives out information on old mining camps and fossicking details if you feel inspired to try your luck hunting for garnets, copper and Maltese crosses (hard, reddish-brown staurolite crystals paired at right angles).

A positive side to Cloncurry's isolation is that it inspired the formation of the **Royal Flying Doctor Service**. Over on the corner of King and Daintree streets, John Flynn Place (Mon–Fri 7am–4pm, closed Dec 1–Feb 1; $8.50) is a monument to the man who pioneered the use of radio and plane to provide a "mantle of safety over the Outback". The exhibition explains how ideas progressed with technology, from pedal-powered radios to assistance from the young Qantas, resulting in the opening in Cloncurry of the first Flying Doctor base in 1928. A very different aspect of Cloncurry's past is also evident in the two foreign **cemeteries** on the outskirts of town. To the south of the highway, before you cross the creek on the way to Mount Isa, a hundred overgrown plots recall a brief nineteenth-century goldrush when the harsh conditions took a terrible toll on Chinese prospectors; equally neglected are the unnamed graves of Afghans at the north end of Henry Street, all aligned with Mecca. Afghans were vital to Cloncurry's survival before the coming of the railway, organizing camel trains which carried the ore to Normanton whence it was shipped to Europe – a role now largely forgotten.

Practicalities

The highway runs through town as McIlwraith Street in the east, and **Ramsay Street** in the west; most services – the usual banks, supermarket, half-dozen **bars** and a post office – are along Ramsay or the grid of streets immediately north. Cloncurry's **train station** is a couple of kilometres southeast of the centre, while **buses** drop off along Ramsay; buy **tickets** for either at Cloncurry Agencies, 45 Ramsay St (⊕07/4742 1107). The best **campsite**, *Gilbert Park Tourist Village*, is on the eastern edge of town off McIlwraith (⊕07/4742 2300; camping $7.50, cabins ❸) and has decent cabins; otherwise seek **accommodation** at the central *Wagon Wheel Motel* on Ramsay (⊕07/4742 1866; ❸), founded in 1867 with both older pub rooms and a new motel block; or the trendily eco-conscious *Gidgee Inn* on McIlwraith (⊕07/4742 1599, Ⓔgidgeeinn@bigpond.com.au; ❹), built from recycled timber and rammed earth. The bars have counter **meals**, though *Cuppa's*, a café on Ramsay, is cool and spacious, and serves up strong coffee and good-value food. For entertainment, there's an **open-air cinema** one block north of Ramsay on Scarr Street, which fires up once or twice a week.

Moving on, the highway, buses and trains continue west for 118km to Mount Isa, while the **Burke Developmental Road** heads 380km north past forest of anthills and kapok trees to Normanton (see p.605) via the one-pub settlement of **Quamby** (which also has races and an underwear-throwing competition in May), and the **Burke and Wills Roadhouse**. Aside from being a welcome break in the journey, with fuel pumps and a bar and canteen selling drinks, sandwiches and burgers, the roadhouse also marks the turning west on a sealed road to **Gregory Downs**, gateway to the oasis of Lawn Hill Gorge (p.600).

Onwards to Mount Isa: Mary Kathleen

The rough country between Cloncurry and Mount Isa is evidence of ancient upheavals which shattered the landscape and created the region's extensive mineral deposits. While the highway continues safely to Mount Isa past the **Burke and Wills monument** and the **Kalkadoon/Mitakoodi tribal boundary** at Corella Creek, forays into the bush will uncover remains of less fortunate mining settlements. About halfway to Mount Isa, a short and steadily crumbling road north to **MARY KATHLEEN** is marked with a small plaque. By all accounts, **uranium** was found here by accident when a car broke down; while waiting for help the driver and his friends tried fossicking and found ore. The two-street town was built in 1956 and completely dismantled in 1982 when export restrictions halted mining. Since then, once-manicured lawns have run riot, and an occasional bougainvillea and an unkempt row of casuarinas tangling along the access road are the only signs that there were gardens here; in a few years it will all have gone. About a kilometre past the old town the road becomes a dirt track and splits; a kilometre along the right fork a bumpy uphill track leads to the terraces of the opencast **mine**, now reminiscent of a flooded Greek amphitheatre. On a cloudy day you can be sure that the alarming blue-green colour of the water is not simply a reflection of the sky. Locals maintain it's safe to swim here, and some even claim health benefits.

Mount Isa and around

As the only place of consequence for 700km in any direction, the smokestacks, concrete paving and sterile hills at **MOUNT ISA** assume oasis-like qualities on arrival, despite being undeniably ugly. Though the novelty might have worn off by the time you've had a cold drink, the city has a few points to savour before heading on. There's evidence of the area's **Aboriginal heritage**, a couple of unusual **museums**, tours of the mines themselves, Australia's largest rodeo every August and, not least, the fascinating situation and the community it has fostered.

The largest city in the world in terms of surface area – its administrative boundaries stretch halfway to Cloncurry – Mount Isa sits astride a wealth of zinc, silver, lead and copper, and owes its existence to these reserves and the need for a staging post for interstate travellers. The city's founding father was **John Miles**, who discovered ore in 1923, established **Mount Isa Mines** (MIM) the next year and began commercial mining in 1925. Originally a settlement of canvas and scrap wood, the city enjoyed a forty-year boom under the hegemony of MIM until the late 1980s saw a decline in profits. Developments such as the Hilton Mine, north of the city, keep business ticking over, but mines further afield, as at Cloncurry, tend to be staffed by workers who live on the east coast and fly in for their shifts, staying on site until they take their money home, completely bypassing the Isa.

Arrival, information and accommodation

With its two huge chimneys illuminated at night – the Rotary lookout on Hilary Street gives a good view – **MIM** is the city's major landmark, west of the often dry **Leichhardt River**. The Barkly Highway runs through town as Marian and Grace streets, with the city centre immediately south between Simpson and West streets; it then crosses the river and joins the Camooweal road in front of MIM. All **buses** pull in across the river at Campbell's Coach Terminal; **trains** terminate at the station below MIM; and the **airport** is 7km to the north, where taxis meet arrivals. The **tourist information office** (daily 8.30am–5pm; ☎07/4749 1555) is in the Riversleigh Fossils Interpretive Centre on Marian Street, and can make all tour bookings.

Accommodation

There's plenty of **accommodation** scattered all over Mount Isa. If you're **camping**, the best spots are *Mount Isa Van Park*, on the eastern side of town just off Marian Street (☎07/4743 3252; camping $10, cabins with/without bathroom ❸/❷); or *Moondarra Caravan Park*, 4km from the city off Camooweal Road (☎07/4743 9780; tent sites $10), which is close to a creek that draws plenty of local birdlife. For **hostel** beds, *Traveller's Haven*, on the corner of

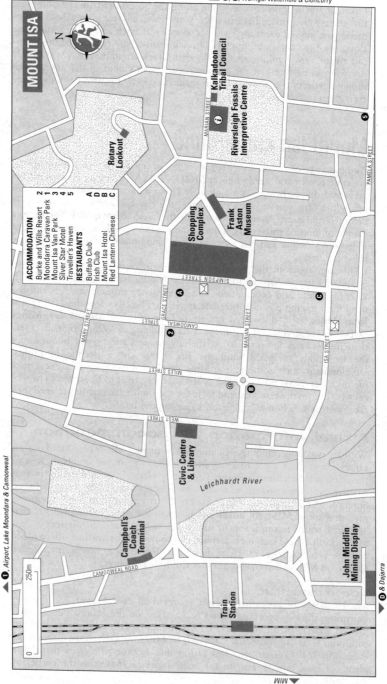

MOUNT ISA

N

▲ ❸ ❹ Warrigal Waterhole & Cloncurry

Kalkadoon
Tribal Council

MARIAN STREET

❶

Riversleigh Fossils
Interpretive Centre

PAMELA STREET

❺

Rotary
Lookout

Shopping
Complex

Frank Aston
Museum

ACCOMMODATION
Burke and Wills Resort   2
Moondarra Caravan Park   1
Mount Isa Van Park   3
Silver Star Motel   4
Traveller's Haven   5
RESTAURANTS
Buffalo Club   A
Irish Club   D
Mount Isa Hotel   B
Red Lantern Chinese   C

SIMPSON STREET

GRACE STREET

Ⓐ

MARR STREET

CAMOOWEAL STREET

Ⓐ
②

MILES STREET

MARIAN STREET

ISA STREET

Ⓒ

WEST STREET

ⓐ

Ⓑ

Civic Centre
& Library

Leichhardt River

▲ ❶ Airport, Lake Moondara & Camooweal

Campbell's Coach
Terminal

CAMOOWEAL ROAD

Train
Station

John Middlin
Mining Display

▼ ❶ & Dajarra

MIM ▼

250m

0

Spence and Pamela streets (☎07/4743 0313; dorms $18, rooms ❷), is cool and quiet and staff can pick you up from train and bus stations. **Motels** include the upmarket and central *Burke and Wills Resort*, on the corner of Grace and Camooweal (☎07/4743 8000 or 1800 679 178; ❻), and the *Silver Star Motel*, to the east on the corner of Marian Street and Doughan Terrace (☎07/4743 3466; ❸).

The City

Having passed so much mining heritage consigned to history on the way here from the coast, there's novelty value in exploring Mount Isa's active mines. The **surface tour** ($19.80) includes a stint looking at videos and pieces of machinery at the **John Middlin Mining Display** on Church Street (daily 9am–4pm; $7.50) and a bus ride around surface operations. Underground tours, from which women were once barred as harbingers of bad luck, have now been discontinued, but a new display, recreating the tunnels and offering a close look at mining machinery, is under construction beside the **Frank Aston Museum** on Shackleton Street (currently closed), with which it will merge.

Mount Isa's geological wonders are not confined to minerals, however. Over 400km northwest, the lime-saturated waters of the Gregory River at Riversleigh Station (see p.600) have been encapsulating a fossil record since Australia was a teeming tropical forest. Paleontologists working there since the 1980s have discovered an incredible record of marsupial and mammalian evolution and environmental change between ten thousand and twenty million years ago, all magnificently displayed at the **Riversleigh Fossils Interpretive Centre** on Marian Street (Mon–Fri 9am–4pm, Sat & Sun 9am–2pm; $9.50). Imaginative, life-sized dioramas and an informative video re-create the region at a time when it was a lush wetlands populated by ancestral platypus and koalas, giant snakes and emus, carnivorous kangaroos and the enigmatic "thingadonta". You can also visit the **laboratory** out the back, where fossils are being prepared by soaking boulders collected at Riversleigh in weak acid, dissolving the rock but leaving bones, beaks and teeth intact. It's all essential viewing, particularly if you're planning to head out to Riversleigh itself.

(see p.600)

MIM

The **Mount Isa Mines** complex is a land of trundling yellow mine trucks, mountains of slag, intense activity and miles of noisy vibrating pipelines. Above all this the two chimneys trail Mount Isa's signature across the sky, marking the copper mine to the south and separate silver, lead and zinc deposits. Ore is mined almost 2km down by a workforce of 1200; it is roughly crushed, and hoisted to the surface before undergoing a second crushing, grinding and washing in flotation tanks, to separate ore from waste rock. Zinc is sold as it is, copper is smelted into ingots and transported to Townsville for refining while four-tonne ingots of lead/silver mix are sent to England for the few ounces of silver to be separated. Power for the mines and the entire region comes from MIM's own plant; surplus is sold to the state grid.

The scale of the process will be brought home to you if you stand under one of the mountains of tailings awaiting future treatment – next to which are humble mounds of green copper ore, bought from a local miner and representing maybe a year's effort – or look down into the depths of the open-cut mine, worked simply for rubble to fill in old shafts. At the edge of the mine the last ridge of the original Mount Isa, and site of the first finds seventy years ago, has been left as a memorial.

Eating and drinking

Mount Isa boasts inhabitants of over fifty nationalities, many of whom have their own **clubs** with **restaurants** and bars. One in which you'll almost certainly end up is the *Irish Club*, on Buckley Avenue 2km south of the centre, where everyone converges for weekend night bands and inexpensive food. The other mainstay is the central and flashy *Buffalo Club* ("The Buffs"), which hosts an Oktoberfest and has a comfy, and heavily air-conditioned, bar and bistro serving the best steaks in town. Both offer **courtesy buses** to and from accommodation (℡0413 126 666). **Hotels** are the alternatives – the bulky *Mount Isa Hotel*, on the corner of Marian and Miles streets, sets the standard for cheap lunch-time specials, or try the *Red Lantern Chinese*, on the corner of Simpson and Isa streets.

Listings

Airlines Air Mount Isa ℡07/4743 2844; North Western Air ℡07/4743 7720.

Bus station For all enquiries, contact Campbell's Coach Terminal (℡07/4743 2006, ⓦwww .campbellstravel.com.au). Greyhound Pioneer and McCafferty's between them cover routes to Townsville, Tennant Creek and Brisbane. The tourist office at the Fossils Interpretive Centre can also make bookings.

Car rental Avis, Marian St (and at the airport) ℡07/4743 3733; Four Wheel Drive Hire Service, Simpson St (℡07/4743 6306, ⓦwww.4wdhire.com.au), which provides five-day vehicle and camping gear packages for $275 per person; Thrifty, cnr of Patricia and Miles streets ℡07/4743 2911.

Cinema Cnr Marian and West streets.

Hospital 30 Camooweal St ℡07/4744 4444; Gemini Medical Centre, across from shopping centre and next to post office on Simpson Street ℡07/4743 4533.

Internet access Back of Mt Isa Newsagent at 25 Miles St; $5.50 an hour.

Pharmacy Corner Pharmacy, cnr Marian and Miles streets.

Police 7 Isa St ℡07/4744 1111.

Post office For poste restante, Isa St (℡07/4743 2454); there is another office on Simpson Street opposite the shopping complex.

Taxi ℡07/4743 2333.

Tours Campbell's (℡07/4743 2006, ⓦwww.campbellstravel.com.au) runs day-tours to local mines and Aboriginal sites for around $40, as well as three-day safaris to Lawn Hill Gorge between April and October ($495). Book through the bus station, tourist information office or your accommodation. True North (℡07/4749 1555) offers half-day adventure tours through the bush, including a helicopter ride and abseiling, for $175.

Trains For information and bookings, call ℡07/4744 1202. There are two services each week back to Townsville.

Kalkadoon country

The scrub around Mount Isa is thick with abandoned mines, waterholes and Aboriginal sites. Either take a tour (see above) or, if you're doing your own driving, check at the tourist office for the latest news on road conditions.

The city marks the centre of the territory of the **Kalkadoons**, a tribe often compared with the Zulus for their fierce opposition to white invasion in the nineteenth century. After hounding squatters for ten years with guerrilla tactics, they were decimated in a pitched battle with an army of local settlers and Native Mounted Police near Kajabbi in 1884. Kalkadoon bones littered the battleground for years, but their stand gained them respect for their organized resistance to Europeans.

Numerous sites around Mount Isa attest to the Kalkadoons' abilities as prolific toolmakers and painters, and it's worth paying the token entry fee to visit their **Tribal Council office** (Mon–Fri 9am–5pm; $1; ℡07/4749 3838), next to the Riversleigh Centre on Marian Street in Mount Isa, and talk to the staff. Bear in mind that, although it's against the law to alter Aboriginal sites in any way, many local sites have been vandalized and you might find the council evasive.

Warrigal Waterhole, Poison Hole and Lake Moondarra

You need high clearance or great care to reach **Warrigal Waterhole**: drive 7km towards Cloncurry from the Tribal Council office on Marian Street in Mount Isa, turn south through the gate and bear left along a very rough track to reach a parking area 3.4km later, from where you walk past "ripple rocks" to the waterhole. One red figure with strange hair outlined in yellow on the left seems to have escaped damage; not so other figures and symbols, which have melted to ochre smears. The waterhole itself is hemmed in by sheltering rocks, which makes for a cool retreat from the sun.

A flooded open-cut mine, **Poison Hole**'s name comes from the surreal appearance of the water, coloured green by copper, but it's actually safe to swim in. Tracks there change each year, but the hole is about ten minutes from the highway, and the turn-off should be roughly 25km back towards Cloncurry; look for signs spray-painted on the road. **Lake Moondarra**, 20km along on a good road (follow the signs from the highway heading towards Camooweal), is less offensively toned, and packed out at weekends with windsurfers and boats. During the week it is nearly deserted and other animals are attracted to the water – goannas, wallabies and flocks of pelicans. Beyond the dam wall at the north end of the lake, the unexpectedly green and shady **Warrina Park** is the unlikely home of peacocks and apostlebirds.

Camooweal and Lawn Hill

West of Mount Isa, the **Barkly Highway** continues to Camooweal and the Northern Territory, with an unsealed road, a little over halfway to the state border, heading north off it leading, via Gregory Downs, to **Lawn Hill Gorge National Park** and **Burketown**. If you're making for Lawn Hill, ensure you have a **campsite** booked (see overleaf for details) and check the latest **road conditions** – the route via Riversleigh is sometimes 4WD-only or closed, while the Gregory Downs road is fine for most cars if it's dry. Wherever you're driving, fuel up; it's two hundred monotonous kilometres to Camooweal and the fringes of the black-soil **Barkly Tablelands**, and at least twice that to Lawn Hill.

Camooweal and the Caves

There's no way to avoid **CAMOOWEAL** but you might wish there were; the township's atmosphere of lazy aggression is exacerbated by a total lack of charm. The highway from Mount Isa forms the main street, built in 1944 by American servicemen whose names are painted on a rock at the edge of town. You'll find a roadhouse, mechanic, general store (and Westpac agent), post office and hotel – a risky place for a last drink in Queensland. The store's old decor is worth a peek, and murals at the *Camooweal Roadhouse* (☎07/4748 2155; cabins ❸) should raise a chuckle; around the back are **cabins** and a **campsite** with thick grass to raise a tent over. Otherwise, fuel up and move on.

The best features of the surrounding area are dolomite sinks known as **the Caves**; drive 8km down the Urandangie road south of Camooweal, then turn left and follow the dirt track for about thirty minutes. There's an NPWS **campsite** here with toilets and a fence to keep out marauding cattle. Flocks of gibbering green budgerigars congregate around the creek and, if you can put up with their racket, it's preferable to a night in town. The park's nine caves are intriguing terraces, spiralling down 10m before tapering to vertical shafts. The district is riddled with them; one is a roost for **ghost bats**, and another has become famous for its coolabah trees. Caused by tunnels into the water table collapsing at the surface, the shafts continue straight down for anything between 18m and 75m before levelling out into an uncharted system. Instability makes approaching the mouths dangerous, so don't even think about exploring underground.

Heading on from Camooweal there's another track north to Lawn Hill, while 200km south beyond the Caves is **Urandangie** and a 650-kilometre, 4WD "short cut" across to Alice Springs. West, it's a mere ten minutes' drive to the cattle grid separating Queensland from the Northern Territory's time zone and better roads. Next fuel is at the Barkly Homestead, 275km away.

Gregory Downs and Lawn Hill Gorge National Park

Hidden from the rest of the world by the Constance Range and a hot ocean of bleached grass, the red sandstone walls and splash of tropical greenery at **Lawn Hill National Park** seem outrageously extravagant. There's little warning: within moments a land which barely supports scattered herds of cattle is exchanged for palm forests and creeks teeming with wildlife. There are two places to aim for: **Riversleigh Fossil Site** and **Lawn Hill Gorge**, connected to each other by a seventy-kilometre track; most people base themselves at the gorge, which has the easiest access and the best facilities and scenery, though it is definitely worth making a trip to Riversleigh.

For Lawn Hill Gorge, routes from Cloncurry, Camooweal and Burketown all converge at **GREGORY DOWNS**, a pub providing cold drinks, fuel, mechanical repairs, and a wild **canoe race** down the Gregory River on the May Day weekend. From here, the gorge is 76km west along a decent gravel road via the controversial **Century Zinc mine**, where work was halted when local Aborigines claimed traditional ownership of the region; after several years of negotiations they finally accepted a substantial payment for use of the land and the mine reopened. While the situation has exacerbated the frustration felt by mining companies and farmers over the legal ambiguities surrounding the 1992 Mabo Decision (see Contexts, p.1173), it's evidence that the wishes of Aboriginal communities are now being taken far more seriously.

Riversleigh Fossil Site

The Gregory Downs–Camooweal road to Riversleigh crosses the **Gregory River** three times around Riversleigh Station, which is why you need a 4WD on this route; the crossings are a foretaste of Lawn Hill – sudden patches of shady green and cool air in an otherwise hostile landscape. You can **camp** near the station from April until the end of October at *Campbell's Riversleigh Camp* (satellite phone ⊕014 511 6441), where you'll also find on-site double tents (❸), hot showers, toilets and a barbecue area; they also rent out canoes ($5.50 per hour) and organize various guided tours.

Like Lawn Hill, **Riversleigh** was once cloaked in rainforest supporting many ancestral forms of Australian fauna. The **fossil finds** here cover a period from twenty million to just ten thousand years ago, a staggering range for a single site and one which details the transitional period from Australia's climatic heyday to its current parched state. Riversleigh may ultimately produce a fossil record of evolutionary change for an entire ecosystem, but don't expect to see much *in situ* as the fossils are trapped in limestone boulders which have to be carefully blasted out and treated with acid to release their contents (see p.600). A roadside shelter houses a map of the landscape with fossil sites indicated on a rock outcrop nearby where, with some diligence, you can find bones and teeth protruding from the stones.

The Riversleigh Fossil Site lies halfway along an eighty-kilometre, 4WD-only track between Lawn Hill Gorge and the unsealed, 220-kilometre-long Gregory Downs–Camooweal road. Coming southwest from Gregory Downs on this road, the Riversleigh track starts 65km along; or it's 155km northeast from Camooweal.

Lawn Hill Gorge

When **Lawn Hill Creek** started carving its forty-metre-deep gorge, the region was still a tropical wetland but, as the climate began to dry out, vegetation retreated to a handful of moist, isolated pockets. Animals were drawn to creeks and waterholes and people followed the game – middens and art detail an **Aboriginal culture** at least 17,000 years old. The NPWS **campsite** (tank water, showers, toilets) occupies a tamed edge of the creek at the mouth of the gorge and is booked solid between Easter and October (bookings on ℡07/4748 5572). An alternative campsite is at the pleasant **Adels Grove** (℡07/4748 5502; camping $8.50, tent rental $20, tent and all meals ❸), a Savannah Guides post 5km from the gorge and run by Barry Kubala, an expert on the gorge's vegetation.

Canoes ($5 per person per hour) let you explore the gorge from the inside. An easy hour's paddle over calm green water takes you from the NPWS campsite between the stark, vertical cliffs of the Middle Gorge to **Indari Falls**, an excellent swimming spot with a ramp to carry your gear down. Beyond here the creek relaxes, alternating between calm ponds and slack channels choked with vegetation before slowing to a trickle under the rockfaces of the Upper Gorge. Saltwater crocs are absent from the gorge, but you'll certainly see plenty of **birds** – egrets, bitterns and kites all put in an appearance. **Freshwater crocodiles** are hard to spot: since visitor numbers have increased, this timid reptile has retreated to the **Lower Gorge** – a sluggish tract edged in waterlilies and forest where goannas lounge during the day and rare **purple-crowned fairy wrens** forage in pandanus leaves.

In the creek itself are turtles, shockingly large catfish, and sharp-eyed **archer fish** that spit jets of water at insects above the surface. Just how isolated all this is becomes clear from the flat top of the **Island Stack**, a twenty-minute walk from the camp. A pre-dawn hike up the steep sides gives you a commanding view of the sun creeping into the gorge, highlighting orange walls against green palm-tops which hug the river through a flat, undernourished country. The rocks along the banks of the Lower Gorge are daubed with designs relating to the Dingo Dreaming, while fuel drums, tins and middens inside an overhang demonstrate that Lawn Hill has only recently been abandoned by Aborigines. This fact was rammed home when a group of fifty people from local communities staged a month-long sit-in at the park in October 1994, demanding joint management. The case is still being milled through the legal system, but it's possible that Aboriginal tour guides may one day be on hand to show you around.

The Gulf of Carpentaria

The great savannahs and intricate river systems of western Cape York and the **Gulf of Carpentaria** were described in 1623 by the Dutch explorer Jan Carstensz as being full of hostile tribes – not surprising, since he'd spent his time here kidnapping and shooting any Aborigines he saw. The Gulf was ignored for centuries thereafter, except by Indonesians gathering sea-slugs to sell to the Chinese, but interest in its potential was stirred in 1841 by **John Lort Stokes**, a lieutenant on the *Beagle* (which had been graced by a young Charles Darwin on an earlier voyage) who absurdly described the coast as "Plains of Promise":

A vast boundless plain lay before us, here and there dotted with woodland isles. . . I could discover the rudiments of future prosperity and ample justification of the name which I had bestowed upon them.

It took Burke and Wills' awful 1861 trek (see box on p.575) to discover that the "woodland isles" were deficient in nutrients and that the black soil became a quagmire during the wet season. Too awkward to develop, the Gulf hung in limbo as settlements sprang up, staggered on for a while, then disappeared; even today few places could be described as thriving communities. Not that this should put you off visiting: with few real destinations and plenty to see, the Gulf is a perfect destination for those who just like to travel. On the way, and only half a day's drive from Cairns, the awesome lava tubes at **Undara** shouldn't be missed, while further afield there are **gemstones** to be fossicked, the coast's birdlife and exciting **barramundi** fishing to enjoy, and the Gulf's sheer remoteness to savour.

Two sealed roads head through the region to Normanton and Karumba: the **Gulf Developmental Road**, which starts southwest of Ravenshoe on the Atherton Tablelands, and the **Burke Developmental Road** from Mount Isa. At the time of writing, Gulfland Coaches in Cairns (℡07/4055 3452) was planning a bus service from Cairns to Mount Isa via Undara, and the Gulf Developmental Road to Normanton and Karumba, and then down the Burke Developmental Road to Mount Isa, linking up with regional rail services. The Cairns–Normanton "road", via Chillagoe, is a shattering, unserviced, five-hundred-kilometre track best tackled by well-equipped off-road transport only – as are all the Gulf's remoter stretches. In the wet season, flying is the sole option for any travel. **Safaris** run from Cairns (see box on p.527) if you don't have the right vehicle, or you could get at least part of the way around on the Gulf's two rustic railways (see box opposite).

Most visitors to the Gulf need to be reasonably self-sufficient, as there are few banks and **accommodation** is largely in campsites or pricey motels. For **information** before you go, contact Gulf Savannah Tourism at 74 Abbott St, Cairns (℡07/4031 1631, Ⓦwww.gulf-savannah.com.au), which offers brochures and advice, though doesn't make bookings. Once in the region, you'll find the local NPWS is joined by the **Savannah Guides**, a private ranger organization recently voted the best of its type in the world, which runs campsites with guides to show you around. On a more alarming note, you might also come face to face with the Gulf's two **crocodile** species – take care.

Undara Lava Tubes

The **Undara Lava Tubes** are astounding, massive tunnels running in broken chambers for up to 35km from the side of the volcano's low cone. It wasn't until 1989 that the majority of the caves were located and mapped and Undara declared an area of scientific interest, currently run by the Savannah Guides but NPWS-owned. Undara is on **Yarramulla Station**, 16km south off the Gulf Developmental Road, 130km from Ravenshoe. **Accommodation**, bar and **restaurant** at the *Lava Lodge* (℡07/4097 1411, ⓦwww.undara.com.au; prefab tents $18 per person, camping $6 per person, cabins ❺) are in eleven restored railway carriages brought over from Mareeba and set up amongst a thin wattle forest – an eccentric but comfortable idea. Their swimming pool is an almost essential place to spend time during summer.

Because the tunnels are hard to enter – and some host a virulent lung fungus – you must take a **tour**. Although not cheap ($33 for a 2hr introduction, $63 for a half-day, $93 full day), these are good value considering that, as well as the chance to explore the tubes, you get an intimate rundown on local geology, flora, fauna and history from a member of the Collins family, who've lived on the station for more than a century. You can, however, make plenty of good short walks through woodland and up to lookout points in the low hills above the *Lava Lodge*, where you'll find wallabies and parrots during the day and plenty of nocturnal insects and reptiles.

Tubes and caves

When the Undara volcano erupted 190,000 years ago, the liquid lava followed rivers and gullies as it snaked northwest towards the Gulf. Away from the cone, the surface of these lava rivers hardened, forming insulating tubes which kept the lava inside in a liquid state and allowed it to run until the tubes were drained. These were then covered by later accumulations, and they'd still be unexplored if hot gases hadn't popped holes in the tube ceilings which eventually collapsed, creating a way in.

The edge of the flow is marked by darker soil and healthier vegetation; at cave mouths this becomes rampant, successfully concealing the entrances and making your first view of the tubes something of a shock – what looks like a bush at ground level turns out to be the top of a giant fig tree growing from the cave floor. The caves are decked in rubble and remnant pockets of thick

---

Gulf trains

Two unconnected, anachronistic **railways** still operate in the Gulf region, mostly as tourist attractions. For advance bookings on either, call in to the relevant stations, or contact Queensland Rail (℡13 22 32). It's also worth checking whether Gulfland Coaches (℡07/4055 3452) has started up connecting bus services for both trains.

The Savannahlander runs every Wednesday morning from Cairns to Almaden on the Chillagoe road (p.536), where it overnights before continuing south to Forsayth, arriving Thursday afternoon. Friday morning it leaves Forsayth for Mount Surprise, arriving back in Cairns on Saturday evening. You spend the snails-pace journey being hauled over rickety bridges in carriages with corrugated-iron ceilings and wooden dunnies – a pastiche of Outback iconography. The trip costs $100 each way; you'll need to bring extra for hotel accommodation and meals.

The Gulflander runs once a week each way along an isolated stretch of line between Croydon and Normanton, a journey that takes a mere four hours (departs Croydon Thurs 8.30am, departs Normanton Wed 8.30am; $38 each way).

prehistoric vegetation quite out of place among the dry scrub on the surface. Tool sites around the cave mouths show that Aborigines knew of their existence, though there's no evidence that they ever ventured in.

Once **inside**, the scale of the 52 tubes is overpowering. Up to 19m high and 900m long, their glazed walls bear evidence of the terrible forces that created them: coil patterns and ledges formed by cooling lava, whirlpools where lava forged its way through rock from other flows, and "stalactites" made when solidifying lava dribbled from the ceiling. Some end in **lakes**, while others are blocked by lava plugs. Animal tracks in the dust indicate the regular passage of kangaroos, snakes and invertebrates, and seasonally you'll encounter twittering colonies of bats clinging to the ceiling, but the overall scale of the tubes tends to deaden any sounds or signs of life.

Mount Surprise and around

MOUNT SURPRISE, 40km from Undara, reputedly takes its name from the shock of the local Aborigines when they first saw whites. Aside from being a stop for the Savannahlander train on its weekly return leg to Cairns (see box on p.603), there's little more here than the *Jo & Joe's Caravan Park* (℡07/4062 3193; cabins ❷), a gem shop/service station (℡07/4062 3153) and **hotel** (℡07/4062 3118; ❸). The main attraction lies a bumpy 40km north at **O'Briens Creek Topaz Field** (check in Mount Surprise on road conditions), where you can camp at a waterhole known as **the Oasis**, and then organize fossicking with Pete and Pam at *Diggers Rest* (℡07/4062 5241; a few snacks available), who also rent out all the gear you'll need and can point you in the right direction. You might find a handful of topaz in a couple of hours, and while it's not very valuable, there's pleasure in the hunt – and it's beautiful when cut.

Beyond Mount Surprise the main road, which is the worst in all Queensland for stray cattle, crosses **the Wall**, where expanding gases in a blocked subterranean lava tube forced the ground above it up 20m into a long ridge. The same gaseous expulsion also seems to have cracked open a much deeper seam at **Ambo Springs** on Tallaroo Station (Easter–Oct daily until 4pm; $9; ℡07/4662 1221). Formed by water 3km down becoming heated and forcing its way to the surface, the clear blue, sulphurous pools gradually accumulate a crusty grey collar around their vent from dissolved lime, which eventually closes the outflow – until the build-up of pressure explodes through to create a new spring. The water emerges at 92°C, but there are some cooler spas that are more comfortable for soaking in.

South of the main road near Ambo, there's a forty-kilometre detour down to **EINASLEIGH**, an ordinary handful of weatherboard and iron houses, made memorable by the huge, delicious evening meals served at the *Central Hotel* (℡07/4062 5222; ❸), and summer dips in **Einasleigh Creek**'s deep basalt gorge. If you don't have your own vehicle (and you might need 4WD after rain), the Savannahlander **train** also passes this way.

Georgetown, Forsayth and around

Back on the main road about 90km west of Mount Surprise, **GEORGE-TOWN** is a similarly scaled, tidy town, home to the *Midway Caravan Park* (℡07/4062 1219; tent sites $7, cabins ❷), and the rather plusher, pink *Latara Resort Motel* (℡07/4062 1190; ❹), along with a couple of shops and **hotels** (*Wenaru* has the best meals). The area around Georgetown has a reputation as somewhere to fossick for **gold** nuggets, and you can get information on likely places to try from the Shire Offices, just south of the main road (Mon–Fri 9am–5pm; ☎07/4062 1233).

Forty kilometres south off the highway down a decent gravel road is **FORSAYTH**, terminus for the Savannahlander **train** and home to the *Goldfields Hotel* (☎07/4062 5374; ❹ including dinner); it's also the last place to stock up before heading bush to two unusual locations. Two hours south in a 4WD through the scrub, the basic camp at **Agate Creek** (☎07/4062 5335; Easter–Oct) caters to agate hunters who scour the creek banks after each wet season and rate this the best site in the world for these semiprecious stones. This may be a matter of opinion but the colours, ranging from honey through to delicate blue, justify the time spent grubbing around with a pick looking for them. **Cobbold Gorge**, at Robinhood Station (Easter–Oct), 50km south of Forsayth on a passable dirt road, is a recently discovered and starkly attractive oasis inhabited by freshwater crocs and crayfish and surrounded by baking hot sandstone country. You can **camp** or stay in **cabins** here at *Cobbold Camping Village* (☎07/4062 5470, ⓦwww.cobboldgorge.com.au; camping $5.50 per person, cabins ❸), which also organizes **tours**, including a 4WD trip around the station, fossicking for agates, lunch, and a scout up the kilometre-long gorge in a motorized punt ($110) – an excellent way to experience a very remote corner of the Outback.

Croydon

CROYDON, 150km west of Georgetown along the main road, was the site of Queensland's last major **goldrush** after two station hands found nuggets in a fence-post hole in 1885. For a brief period the region received the attention it had always craved: within five years the railway was built and lucky miners whooped it up at Croydon's 36 hotels, but by 1900 chaotic management had brought operations to a close. Today, despite rumours of a new gold strike near town, the place is pretty sedate and most buildings predate 1920: the *Club Hotel* (last of the 36), the general store and the restored old courthouse all have their original fittings and offer directions to other scattered relics. If you're tempted to stay, there's the hotel (☎07/4745 6184; ❹) or you can pitch a tent at *Croydon Gold Van Park* on the Georgetown side (☎07/4745 6238; tent sites $12).

Moving on, buses and the main road plough on to Normanton, 154km west, as does the Gulflander **train** (see box on p.603); which leaves Croydon on Thursday mornings from the station on Helen Street. When the rails and sleepers were unloaded at Normanton's wharves in the nineteenth century they were meant to form the first stage of a line to Cloncurry, but this was redirected to Croydon when gold was found. At the height of the gold rush the service carried 200 passengers a week.

Normanton

Founded on the banks of the Norman River in 1868, **NORMANTON** was the Gulf's main port, connected to the Croydon goldfield by rail and Cloncurry's copper mines by camel train, though today the town lacks an expected air of faded splendour. Set in gritty, flat country, Normanton's fortunes declined along with regional mineral deposits, and today there's only a thin collection of stores and service stations, a bank and post office, with shop awnings and a handful of trees providing scant shade. A worthy survivor of former times is the **Burns Philp Store**, whose timber shell, built in the 1880s, covers almost an acre and remains upright (if empty) despite the attentions of over a century of termites. The **train** still runs once a week to Croydon (see box on p.603) from the station just outside town, and also makes day-trips (June–Sept; $25) to a local waterhole for tea and damper.

Fishing for barramundi (book with Norman River Cruises ☎07/4745 1347, @normfish@tpg.com.au) is beginning to brighten the area's prospects, celebrated by the *Gulfland Motel* (☎07/4745 1290; campsites $6.60, rooms ❸) under the sign of the "Big Barra" at the south entrance to the town; the **motel** has pleasant rooms and a **campsite**. Alternative **accommodation** is at Normanton's lurid and recently refurbished *Purple Pub* (☎07/4745 1324, ⓕ4745 1626; ❸); this is also a good place to **eat**, with a beer garden and tasty char-grilled steaks and fish. The town's other two hotels, the *Albion* and *Middle Pub*, are pretty raw watering holes. When you've had enough boozing, Karumba and routes on to western Cape York lie north, and Cloncurry is 400km south via the Burke and Wills Roadhouse (p.594). To the west is the fuelless, 220-kilometre Burketown road, with features along the way including the site of Burke and Wills' northernmost camp near the Bynoe River, and the often difficult **Leichhardt River** crossing where the pocket-sized **Leichhardt Falls** contrasts with the aridity of the surrounding sand dunes, deposited each year when the river is in spate.

Karumba and the Gulf

Reached from Normanton across 70km of cracked, burning saltpan, patrolled by saurus cranes and jabiru storks, **KARUMBA**'s tidy gardens are, given the setting, ridiculously suburban. Set near the mouth of the **Norman River** and once an airforce base for Catalina flying boats moving between Brisbane and Singapore, today the town is overlooked by huge **sheds** storing slurry from the Century Zinc Mine near Lawn Hill Gorge (p.600); the slurry is fed through pipes to Karumba, then shipped overseas for refining. Mostly, however, Karumba survives on prawn trawling and fishing; declining stocks of barramundi in the Gulf have inspired the **Barramundi Farm**, 2km from town along the river (daily 8.30–10.30am & 2.30–5pm; $3), which raises fish for release into the wild. One thing that you'll probably register is that there are few Aborigines in town; they shun the area, as many died in a tribal battle nearby.

Karumba comprises two separate areas: central Karumba itself, and Karumba Point, a couple of kilometres downstream near the estuary. The **centre** is along Yappar Street on the Norman River's south bank, with a supermarket, the *Karumba Café* (serving good barraburgers) and a post office. For **accommodation**, *Gulf Country Van Park* (☎07/4745 9148; tent sites $8.50, cabins ❸) is a shady campsite; *Matilda's End* (☎07/4745 9368; ❹) has tidy units; or try the *Karumba Lodge* (☎07/4745 9121; ❹), which started life as the airforce mess; the ramp that runs alongside the lodge down to the river was where the Catalina aircraft berthed. The *Lodge* has two **bars**: the ordinary *Suave Bar* and the infamous *Animal Bar* – which you should probably avoid unless you're extremely serious about drinking and occasional bouts of hand-to-hand combat. **Karumba Point** overlooks mudflats and mangroves along the river mouth and has a pool, campsites, and a twice weekly free fish barbecue at the *Karumba Point Tourist Park* (☎07/4745 9306; tent sites $10, cabins ❸). For outstanding sunsets, meals and ice-cold beer, head to the riverside *Sunset Tavern*.

To spot crocodile and birds, or **catch** something for the pot, contact Y-Not (☎07/4745 9316) or Katherine MII Fishing Charters (☎07/4745 9449). If you have your own tackle, Gulf Hire Boats (☎07/4745 9148) rents out four-metre-long tinnies from $55 for a half-day.

The Wellesleys and western Cape York

Gulf Freight Services on Yappar Street, Karumba (℡07/4745 9333) operates a weekly **barge** from Karumba to Weipa (see p.551 for more on Weipa itself). The journey takes around thirty hours, leaving on Friday and returning Tuesday. A one-way trip costs $285 including meals and cabin; prices for vehicles, which must be containerized, start at $490. Erratic services also go to the **Wellesley Islands**, which comprise two dozen windswept islands north of Burketown with excellent fishing around fragmented coral rubble. Never settled by whites, today they are **Aboriginal communities**, with an expensive but basic **resort** on **Sweers Island** (℡07/4748 5544, ℱ4748 5644; ❼), catering to serious fishermen. Transfers ($160 per person, minimum of four) can be booked with Gulf Line Aviation on Yappar Street, Karumba (℡1800 458 458), which can also fly you to Lawn Hill for the day ($250 per person, minimum of four).

Off-road drivers after wildlife might be tempted by superb **wetlands** on the western edge of the Cape York Peninsula, accessed from the Normanton–Karumba road off a 4WD-only, 500-kilometre track which ultimately takes you to Chillagoe (see p.536). Detouring north from it, you'll find the coast thick with creeks, waterholes and animals. **Dorunda Station** (food, drink and limited fuel supplies; ℡07/4745 3477; units ❺), about 180km up the road, is a working cattle property which arranges hunting safaris with cameras or .303s – targets are pigs, fish, birds and crocodiles. There's more of the same even further north at **Mitchell and Alice Rivers National Park**, via the Aboriginal community of **Kowanyama**. You'll need to take all supplies for this, an NPWS permit and permission from the community (contact Cairns NPWS on ℡07/4052 3096 for details).

Burketown and on to the Territory

Set on the Albert River some 230km west of Normanton, **BURKETOWN** balances on the dusty frontier between grassland and the Gulf's thirty-kilometre-deep, unfriendly coastal flats. Styled Queensland's "Barramundi Capital" after the delicious sports fish, it has a huge road maintenance depot employing most of its 235 inhabitants. Despite lukewarm fame for providing background to Nevil Shute's *A Town Like Alice*, there's little beyond the welcoming and historic *Burketown Pub* (℡07/4745 5104; units ❹), *Burketown Caravan Park* (℡07/4745 5118; tent sites $6.50, cabins ❸), a hot artesian spring, a store, a couple of **fuel** pumps and a post office which also acts as the **tourist information office** and agent for day-flights to the Wellesley Islands (Mon–Fri 9am–5pm; ℡07/4745 5111). Accommodation can also organize **barra fishing**, or head 16km west to **Escott Barra Lodge** (℡07/4748 5577, ℮ escottbarralodg@austarnet.com.au; units ❺) where you can also go riding or mustering, or tour one of the Gulf's precarious cattle stations. There's a restaurant and bar at the *Lodge*, but no store.

The Hell's Gate Track

The best road from Burketown heads south for about 120km to **Gregory Downs** and routes to Lawn Hill and Cloncurry (see p.593). If you're serious about **fishing** and have a 4WD, however, head 170km west from Burketown via *Tirranna Roadhouse* (food and fuel facilities) and the Aboriginal community at **Doomadgee**, to the **Hell's Gate Roadhouse** (℡07/4745 8258), 50km from the Northern Territory. Fishing information and guided tours can be obtained from the Savannah Guides here, or you could try **Massacre Inlet**, reached from *Wollogorang Station* (℡08/8975 9944; ❻) just on the Territory border; they will supply you with a $12 fishing permit as well as camping, motel rooms, meals, beer and the last fuel before Borroloola (see p.659). Giant anthills, pandanus-frilled waterholes and irregular tides are the rewards – and the area is stacked with wildlife, including **saltwater crocs**.

The road on from Hell's Gate improves inside the Territory and once there you shouldn't have any trouble reaching Borroloola, 266km down the track.

Travel details

Trains

Barcaldine to: Emerald (2 weekly; 6hr); Longreach (2 weekly; 2hr); Rockhampton (2 weekly; 10hr).

Cairns to: Almaden (1 weekly; 6hr 30min); Forsayth (1 weekly; 2 days).

Charleville to: Brisbane (2 weekly; 17hr); Mitchell (2 weekly; 3hr 30min); Roma (2 weekly; 5hr); Toowoomba (2 weekly; 12hr).

Charters Towers to: Cloncurry (2 weekly; 11hr 30min); Hughenden (2 weekly; 5hr); Mount Isa (2 weekly; 20hr); Richmond (2 weekly; 7hr); Townsville (2 weekly; 2hr 30min).

Cloncurry to: Charters Towers (2 weekly; 11hr 30min); Hughenden (2 weekly; 8hr); Mount Isa (2 weekly; 4hr); Richmond (2 weekly; 5hr 30min); Townsville (2 weekly; 15hr).

Croydon to: Normanton (1 weekly; 4hr).

Emerald to: Barcaldine (2 weekly; 6hr); Longreach (2 weekly; 8hr); Rockhampton (2 weekly; 4hr 30min).

Forsayth to: Cairns (1 weekly; 2 days); Mount Surprise (1 weekly; 5hr 15min).

Hughenden to: Charters Towers (2 weekly; 5hr); Cloncurry (2 weekly; 8hr); Mount Isa (2 weekly; 11hr); Richmond (2 weekly; 2hr 10min); Townsville (2 weekly; 6hr).

Longreach to: Barcaldine (2 weekly; 2hr); Emerald (2 weekly; 8hr); Rockhampton (2 weekly; 12hr 30min).

Mitchell to: Brisbane (2 weekly; 14hr); Charleville (2 weekly; 4hr); Roma (2 weekly; 2hr); Toowoomba (2 weekly; 10hr).

Mount Isa to: Charters Towers (2 weekly; 15hr 30min); Cloncurry (2 weekly; 4hr 15min); Hughenden (2 weekly; 11hr); Richmond (2 weekly; 9hr); Townsville (2 weekly; 19hr).

Mount Surprise to: Cairns (1 weekly; 11hr).

Normanton to: Croydon (1 weekly; 4hr).

Richmond to: Charters Towers (2 weekly; 7hr); Cloncurry (2 weekly; 5hr 30min); Hughenden (2 weekly; 2hr 10min); Mount Isa (2 weekly; 9hr); Townsville (2 weekly; 9hr).

Roma to: Brisbane (2 weekly; 10hr 20min); Charleville (2 weekly; 5hr 10min); Mitchell (2 weekly; 2hr); Toowoomba (2 weekly; 11hr 40min).

Toowoomba to: Brisbane (2 weekly; 3hr 30min); Charleville (2 weekly; 12hr 30min); Mitchell (2 weekly; 10hr); Roma (2 weekly; 6hr 40min).

Buses

Barcaldine to: Anakie (2 weekly; 4hr); Blackall (1 daily; 1hr 15min); Brisbane (1 daily; 17hr); Chaleville (1 daily; 6hr); Cloncurry (1 daily; 8hr); Dingo (2 weekly; 6hr); Emerald (2 weekly; 4hr); Longreach (2 weekly; 2hr); Mitchell (1 daily; 13hr); Mount Isa (1 daily; 10hr); Rockhampton (2 weekly; 8hr); Roma (1 daily; 8hr); Toowoomba (1 daily; 13hr); Winton (1 daily; 6hr).

Charleville to: Barcaldine (1 daily; 6hr); Blackall (1 daily; 4hr 10min); Brisbane (2 daily; 10hr 40min); Cloncurry (1 daily; 13hr 30min); Longreach (1 daily; 6hr 30min); Mount Isa (2 daily; 15hr); Roma (2 daily; 3hr 40min); Toowoomba (2 daily; 8hr); Winton (1 daily; 9hr).

Charters Towers to: Camooweal (2 daily; 13hr); Cloncurry (2 daily; 8hr); Hughenden (2 daily; 3hr); Mount Isa (2 daily; 10hr); Richmond (2 daily; 5hr); Townsville (2 daily; 1hr 40min).

Cloncurry to: Camooweal (2 daily; 4hr 30min); Hughenden (2 daily; 5hr); Mount Isa (2 daily; 1hr 30min); Richmond (2 daily; 3hr 40min); Townsville (2 daily; 10hr).

Emerald to: Anakie (2 weekly; 35min); Barcaldine (2 weekly; 3hr 40min); Dingo (1 daily; 1hr 35min); Longreach (2 weekly; 5hr 30min); Mackay (6 weekly; 4hr); Rockhampton (1 daily; 3hr 30min).

Goondiwindi to: Brisbane (2 daily; 5hr); Toowoomba (2 daily; 3hr); Warwick (1 daily; 2hr 30min).

Longreach to: Anakie (2 weekly; 5hr); Barcaldine (1 daily; 1hr); Blackall (1 daily; 3hr 15min); Brisbane (1 daily; 16hr 10min); Charleville (1 daily; 6hr 30min); Cloncurry (1 daily; 6hr 30min); Dingo (2 weekly; 7hr 30min); Emerald (2 weekly; 5hr 30min); Mitchell (1 daily; 8hr); Mount Isa (1 daily;

7hr 50min); Rockhampton (2 weekly; 9hr 30min); Roma (1 daily; 10hr 25min); Toowoomba (1 daily; 14hr); Winton (1 daily; 2hr).

Mitchell to: Barcaldine (1 daily; 7hr); Blackall (1 daily; 5hr); Brisbane (2 daily; 9hr); Charleville (1 daily; 2hr 10min); Cloncurry (1 daily; 15hr); Longreach (1 daily; 8hr); Mount Isa (1 daily; 16hr); Roma (2 daily; 1hr); Toowoomba (2 daily; 6hr); Winton (1 daily; 11hr).

Mount Isa to: Barcaldine (1 daily; 9hr); Blackall (1 daily; 11hr 10min); Brisbane (1 daily; 25hr 20min); Charleville (1 daily; 14hr 40min); Charters Towers (2 daily; 9hr 50min); Cloncurry (2 daily; 2hr 35min); Hughenden (2 daily; 7hr); Longreach (1 daily; 8hr); Mitchell (1 daily; 16hr); Richmond (2 daily; 6hr); Roma (1 daily; 18hr 20min); Toowoomba (1 daily; 23hr); Townsville (2 daily; 12hr); Winton (1 daily; 6hr).

Richmond to: Charters Towers (2 daily; 5hr); Cloncurry (2 daily; 3hr); Hughenden (2 daily; 2hr); Mount Isa (2 daily; 4hr 30min); Townsville (2 daily; 7hr).

Roma to: Barcaldine (1 daily; 8hr); Blackall (1 daily; 7hr); Brisbane (2 daily; 7hr); Charleville (1 daily; 3hr 30min); Cloncurry (1 daily; 16hr 20min); Longreach (1 daily; 10hr); Mitchell (2 daily; 1hr); Mount Isa (1 daily; 18hr); Toowoomba (2 daily; 4hr 30min); Winton (1 daily; 12hr).

Stanthorpe to: Brisbane (1 daily; 5hr); Toowoomba (2 daily; 2hr 30min); Warwick (2 daily; 40min).

Toowoomba to: Barcaldine (1 daily; 13hr); Blackall (1 daily; 12hr); Brisbane (8 daily; 1hr 50min); Charleville (1 daily; 8hr); Cloncurry (1 daily; 21hr 30min); Goondiwindi (2 daily; 3hr);

Kingaroy (1 daily except Fri; 3hr); Longreach (1 daily; 14hr 30min); Mitchell (2 daily; 6hr); Mount Isa (1 daily; 23hr); Rockhampton (1 daily; 12hr 45min); Roma (2 daily; 5hr); Stanthorpe (2 daily; 2hr 30min); Surfers Paradise (2 daily; 3hr); Warwick (2 daily; 3hr); Winton (2 daily; 16hr 30min).

Warwick to: Brisbane (2 daily; 3hr); Goondiwindi (1 daily; 2hr 30min); Stanthorpe (2 daily; 40min); Toowoomba (2 daily; 3hr).

Winton to: Barcaldine (1 daily; 3hr); Blackall (1 daily; 5hr 15min); Brisbane (1 daily; 19hr 25min); Charleville (1 daily; 9hr 20min); Cloncurry (1 daily; 4hr 30min); Longreach (1 daily; 2hr); Mitchell (1 daily; 11hr); Mount Isa (1 daily; 6hr); Roma (1 daily; 12hr 25min); Toowoomba (1 daily; 17hr).

Flights

Emerald to: Brisbane (2 daily; 2hr); Cairns (1–2 daily; 6hr 40min); Mackay (5 weekly; 5hr); Maroochydore (1 daily; 4hr 35min); Rockhampton (1–2 daily except Sun; 4hr); Townsville (1 daily except Sat; 4hr).

Longreach to: Brisbane (1 daily; 2hr 25min); Roma (5 weekly; 2hr).

Mount Isa to: Brisbane (1–2 daily; 2hr 15min); Burketown (1 weekly; 1hr 35min); Cairns (1–2 daily; 5hr 20min); Mackay (1 daily except Sun; 8hr); Mornington Island (5 weekly; 1hr 50min); Rockhampton (1–2 daily; 4hr); Townsville (1–3 daily; 2hr).

Roma to: Brisbane (1–2 daily; 1hr 10min); Longreach (4 weekly; 2hr).

Winton to: Townsville (2 weekly; 1hr 25min).

Northern Territory

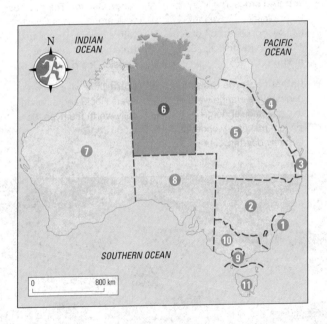

N

INDIAN
OCEAN

PACIFIC
OCEAN

SOUTHERN OCEAN

0   800 km

CHAPTER 6   # Highlights

* **Aboriginal culture** You won't get all the answers, but the Territory is the best place to ask. See p.616

* **Kakadu National Park** Discover the best of the park, including the fascinating ancient rock art and the gorge swim to Twin Falls. See p.633

* **Top End crocs** The Mary River Wetlands have the highest concentration of crocodiles in Australia. See p.635

* **Katherine Gorge** Cruising beneath the orange walls of this spectacular gorge system makes a wonderful, leisurely day-trip. See p.652

* **Shopping for Aboriginal art in Alice** A cluster of galleries in and around Todd Mall make finding a special souvenir easy. See p.672

* **Four-wheel driving in the Red Centre** A network of dirt tracks and destinations spread out from Alice Springs. See p.682

* **Kings Canyon** The two-hour walk around Kings Canyon, with a swim in a secluded waterhole halfway, is a classic. See p.686

* **Uluru** Otherwise known as Ayers Rock, and emphatically worth the hype. See p.690

6

Northern Territory

Far in the north of Australia lies a little-known land, a vast half-finished sort of region, wherein Nature has been apparently practising how to make better places. This is the Northern Territory of South Australia . . . The decline and fall of the British Empire will date from the day that Britannia starts to monkey with the Northern Territory.

A.B. ("Banjo") Paterson, 1898

This rather ominous prophecy by the bush balladeer "Banjo" Paterson, author of "Waltzing Matilda", is still the way many Australians view the frontier lands of the **Northern Territory**, usually known as "the Territory", or simply "NT". Even the name conjures up a distant, untamed province and, to an extent, this is so: with around one percent of Australians (198,000) living in an area covering nearly twenty percent of the continent. Until recently this tiny population and lack of economic autonomy explained why the Territory never achieved full statehood. There was talk that by the new millennium the NT would have become the **seventh Australian state** (with a few strings still held by the federal government) but provincial politics has put this in the same basket as Australia becoming a republic. Incidents like the failed euthanasia bill (quickly quashed by Canberra) and extremes like mandatory sentencing (since repealed by the first NT Labor government since the 1970s), gave southern liberals the impression that some Territorian necks are redder than Ayers Rock at sunset.

Territorians relish this tough, maverick image, as well as the extremes of climate, distance and isolation that mould their temperaments. In this utmost corner of the country, drifters get washed up, fugitives cower and failed entrepreneurs pursue another abortive venture or end up in politics. That great Australian institution of the "character" is in his element here, propping up the bars and bolstering the mythology of the Territory's recent lawless frontier history in what Xavier Herbert once described as the "Land of Ratbags". His classic 1938 novel, *Capricornia*, remains a scathing allegorical saga of the early Territorian years, based on Herbert's experience in 1930s Darwin. Recent episodes such as the 2002 croc attack on a tourist in Kakadu augment the Territory's wild, Outback mystique.

Within the Territory's boundaries there's evidence of the most recent colonial presence set among the oldest-occupied Aboriginal sites in Australia. **Darwin**, the Territory's capital, is a prospering tropical town – a year-round temperature in the low thirties compelling a laid-back lifestyle. Travellers the world over flock here to explore the **Top End** (as tropical NT is known), primarily **Kakadu National Park**'s wildlife, waterways and Aboriginal art sites. Adjacent **Arnhemland**, to the east, is also Aboriginal land – and out of bounds

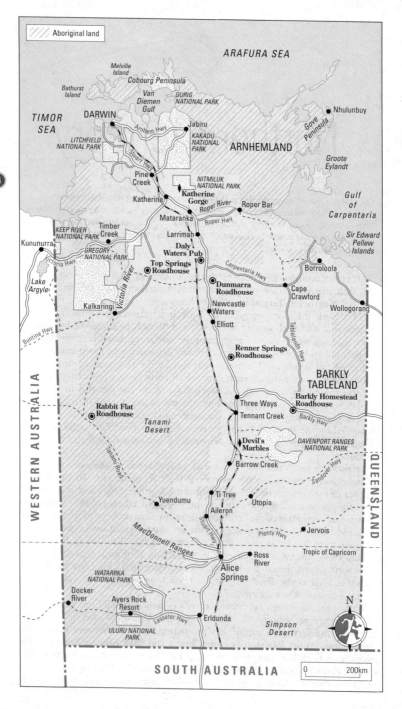

Aboriginal land

ARAFURA SEA

*TIMOR
SEA*

Melville
Island

*Bathurst
Island*

Cobourg Peninsula

Van
Diemen
Gulf

GURIG
NATIONAL PARK

Nhulunbuy

DARWIN

Jabiru

Arnhem Hwy

KAKADU
NATIONAL
PARK

*Gove
Peninsula*

LITCHFIELD
NATIONAL PARK

Stuart Hwy

ARNHEMLAND

*Groote
Eylandt*

Pine
Creek

NITMILUK
NATIONAL PARK

Katherine

Katherine
Gorge

Roper River

Roper Bar

*Gulf
of
Carpentaria*

Mataranka

Roper Hwy

KEEP RIVER
NATIONAL PARK

Timber
Creek

Larrimah

*Sir Edward
Pellew
Islands*

Kununurra

GREGORY
NATIONAL PARK

Daly
Waters Pub

Victoria Hwy

Victoria River

Top Springs
Roadhouse

Carpentaria Hwy

Borroloola

*Lake
Argyle*

Dunmarra
Roadhouse

Cape
Crawford

Wollogorang

Buntine Hwy

Kalkaringi

Newcastle
Waters

Elliott

Tablelands Hwy

Renner Springs
Roadhouse

BARKLY
TABLELAND

WESTERN AUSTRALIA

Rabbit Flat
Roadhouse

*Tanami
Desert*

Three Ways

Barkly Homestead
Roadhouse

Tennant Creek

Barkly Hwy

QUEENSLAND

Tanami Road

Devil's
Marbles

DAVENPORT RANGES
NATIONAL PARK

Barrow Creek

Sandover Hwy

Yuendumu

Ti Tree

Utopia

Aileron

Jervois

Plenty Hwy

MacDonnell Ranges

Stuart Hwy

Tropic of Capricorn

Ross
River

WATARRKA
NATIONAL PARK

Alice
Springs

Docker
River

Ayers Rock
Resort

Lasseter Hwy

Erldunda

*Simpson
Desert*

ULURU NATIONAL
PARK

N

SOUTH AUSTRALIA

0   200km

to casual visitors, although a couple of tours visit this never-colonized wilderness of scattered communities. Heading south, you arrive at **Katherine**, where nearby gorges within the **Nitmiluk National Park** are the town's principal attraction. At Katherine, the **Victoria Highway** reaches west, past the Gregory National Park to Western Australia.

By the time you reach **Tennant Creek**, 650km south of Katherine, you're out of the interminable light woodland and passing pastoral tablelands on the way to the central deserts surrounding **Alice Springs**. By no means the dusty Outback town many expect, Alice makes an excellent base to explore the natural wonders of the region, of which that famous monolith, **Ayers Rock** – or **Uluru** – 450km to the southwest, is but one of many. This is one of the best areas to try to learn about the Aborigines of the western desert, among the last to come into contact with European settlers.

Darwin and the Top End

Darwin, the Territory's capital, lies midway along Australia's convoluted northern coast. Most tourists end up spending no more time here than it takes to visit nearby **Kakadu** and **Litchfield national parks**, continue their Australian circuit or fly on to Indonesia. Until recently the city had little appeal to short-term visitors, but nowadays Darwin is beginning to mature into a worthwhile destination in itself. Besides the two well-known parks mentioned above, there are two less accessible areas in the Top End: the **Mary River Wetlands** offer a chance to explore an exciting environment, where you'll find some huge, wild crocs; while on the east side of Kakadu sits beautiful **Arnhemland**. In the southwest, the **Daly River region** is comprised of small Aboriginal communities and riverside fishing haunts.

Darwin and around

Establishing a European settlement on Australia's remote northern shores was never going to be easy. It took four abortive attempts over a period of 45 years before **DARWIN** (originally called Palmerston) was surveyed in 1869 by the new South Australian state keen to exploit its recently acquired "northern territory". The early colonists' aim was to pre-empt foreign occupation and create a trading post, a "new Singapore", for the British Empire.

Things got off to a promising start with the arrival in 1872 of the **Overland Telegraph Line** (OTL), following the route pioneered by explorer **John McDouall Stuart** in 1862, that finally linked Australia with the rest of the world. **Gold** was discovered at Pine Creek while pylons were being erected for the OTL, prompting the inevitable goldrush, and the construction of a southbound railway. After the goldrush subsided, a cyclone flattened the depressed town in 1897, but by 1911, when Darwin adopted its present name, the rough-and-ready frontier outpost had grown into a small government centre, servicing the mines and properties of the Top End. Yet even by 1937, after being

Aborigines in the Northern Territory

Over a quarter of the Territory's inhabitants are Aborigines, a far higher proportion than anywhere else in Australia. Most modern maps show that half of the Territory is now "**Aboriginal land**", commercially unviable and returned to nominal Aboriginal control following protracted land claims. This uniquely Territorian demography is the result of a formerly sympathetic federal government's co-operation with the politically powerful Land Councils within the NT, established following the Land Rights Act of 1976. Excepting the national parks, most Aboriginal land is out of bounds to visitors without a permit or invitation, although some roads which cross them are exempt.

While the overwhelming majority of non-Aboriginal people tend to live in the two major urban centres of Darwin and Alice Springs, most Aborigines live in Outback communities, or occasionally in still more remote **outstations**: small satellite communities supporting a couple of families. While outstations replicate a nomadic, pre-Contact social group, the communities have been less successful, mixing clans who may have been enemies for eons.

Although snazzy interpretive centres in the national parks tend to concentrate on the eco-trendy close bond with nature, the truth is that Aboriginal society in the Territory and elsewhere in the north is imploding. The Territory is Australia's murder capital, chiefly led by men whose self-esteem as family providers and custodians of the Law (or even once poorly paid but respected stockmen) has been eliminated. The fact that Aboriginal men make up a disproportionately high percentage of the prison population is not solely due to widely assumed racism – although such attitudes may have driven them there in the first place. Furthermore the conditions in which many Aboriginal people live, along with their health, is worse than in many developing nations.

You will be reminded of these thorny and complex issues as you encounter the depressing spectacle of the Aboriginal fringe dwellers staggering around Katherine, Tennant Creek and Alice. Alienated from the affluent white society that busies itself around them, these people are the casualties of the clash of cultures which, in the Territory, is still within living memory. This chasm between two different cultures is actually far greater than most visitors realize. The failure of assimilation – the naive policy of the 1950s and 1960s – has been followed by the current failure of self-determination, while talk of Reconciliation or even land rights is merely symbolic and does little to improve actual living conditions.

razed by a second cyclone, the town had a population of just 1500. The first boom came with WWII after **Japanese air raids** destroyed Darwin once again – this time at a human cost of hundreds of lives (more bombs were dropped on Darwin than Pearl Harbour, a fact long concealed from the jittery nation). The fear of invasion, and an urgent need to get troops to the war zone, led to the swift construction of the Stuart Highway, the first reliable land link between Darwin and the south of the country.

Three decades of guarded postwar prosperity followed until Christmas Day, 1974, when **Cyclone Tracy** devastated Darwin. By 3am the worst was thought to be over as winds that had raged since midnight began to abate. Instead, the becalmed eye of the storm was passing over the part-ruined city, only to return with even greater fury from the opposite direction. Lampposts were bent flat along the ground, houses were ripped from their piers, and at the Yacht Club mangled remains of boats filled the car park. Mercifully, a low tide meant that only 66 people lost their lives, but Tracy marked the end of old Darwin, psychologically as well as architecturally. For many residents this was

Yet looking at the galleries of Alice Springs and the droning forests of didgeridoos, it would appear that Aboriginal **culture** is thriving. Some communities are inviting responsible tour operators to visit their settlements, or are setting up their own operations, so allowing you to experience something of their current and former way of life. It must be remembered, however, that even in the Territory no Aborigines live in or off the bush as they once did, although hunting and gathering is still a pastime to supplement conventional food sources.

Despite the often depressing realities, for those interested in getting to the heart of the enigmatic Australian wilderness, the Northern Territory offers enriching and memorable travel, providing an introduction to a land that has sustained a fascinating and complex culture for at least sixty thousand years.

Aboriginal tours

The term "**Aboriginal tour**", while seeming to offer the promise of a privileged insight into the culture of indigenous Australians, can be misleading. Some tours will simply be focused on Aborigines and their culture, some will be offered by white-managed agencies but led by Aboriginal people (sometimes coerced into the role of guide), and some will be run by Aboriginal-owned organizations. Tours can often be no more than an opportunity for the operator to charge tourists over the odds to learn Aboriginal secrets and laws. Yet this secrecy, which was one of the pillars that supported traditional Aboriginal society, is exactly that, and what you learn on a tour can be a very watered-down version of the truth, from people reluctant to give away closely guarded customs.

As a tourist, meeting Aboriginal people by chance and getting to know them is difficult or takes some nerve, especially as Aboriginal land is, for the most part, out-of-bounds. Meaningful contact with Aborigines for the short-term visitor is therefore unlikely. Many Aborigines are weary of endless questions, well-meaning though they are, and an entirely different strategy in social dealings renders most exchanges awkward and superficial. In many cases then, it is from a knowledgeable and sympathetic non-Aboriginal guide (as well as from older, pre-PC-era books on the subject) that you can learn more about Aboriginal life and culture than which berries make good eating.

The message here is that you should not expect the earth by hopping onto an Aboriginal tour. In most cases they will only scrape the surface of a complex and arcane way of life, an experience that cannot easily be bought across a travel desk.

the last straw and having been evacuated they never returned. Indeed, the myth of Darwinian resilience is just that: the town has always accommodated a transient population, happy to "give it a go" for a couple of years and then move on. The surrounding land is agriculturally unviable and Top End beef is among the poorest in Australia; most is exported as live cattle to Asia.

But since the mid-Nineties Darwin has been making a concerted effort to take itself seriously as Australia's commercial "gateway" into Asia. With the help of the tourist boom, kicked off by Kakadu's exposure in the film *Crocodile Dundee*, as well as some thoughtful refurbishments in Mitchell Street and the Mall, Darwin has shaken off the bland feel of a company town armoured against the climate. A spate of cool new outdoor eateries now allow you to appreciate the tropical ambience so that where once the city centre had all the life of a late night CBD, now it can be as lively as any other Australian capital. The long talked about **Darwin rail link** with Alice and Adelaide has finally become a reality, with the first freight due to run in 2004, followed hopefully by a passenger service (see box on p.665).

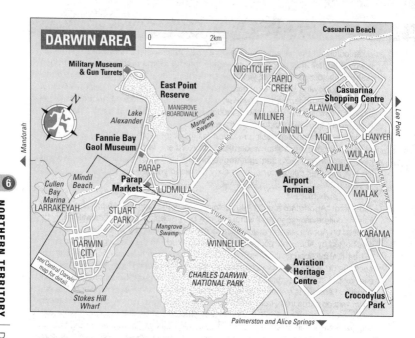

DARWIN AREA

0   2km

Casuarina Beach

Military Museum & Gun Turrets

East Point Reserve

MANGROVE BOARDWALK

Lake Alexander

Mangrove Swamp

NIGHTCLIFF

RAPID CREEK

Casuarina Shopping Centre

ALAWA

TROWER ROAD

MILLNER

JINGILI

MOIL

LEANYER

WULAGI

ANULA

MCMILLANS ROAD

LEE POINT ROAD

VANDERLIN DRIVE

BAGOT ROAD

Fannie Bay Gaol Museum

PARAP

Parap Markets

LUDMILLA

Airport Terminal

MALAK

Mindil Beach

Cullen Bay Marina

LARRAKEYAH

STUART PARK

DARWIN CITY

Mangrove Swamp

STUART HIGHWAY

WINNELLIE

KARAMA

see Central Darwin map for detail

CHARLES DARWIN NATIONAL PARK

Aviation Heritage Centre

Stokes Hill Wharf

Crocodylus Park

◄ Mandorah

▲ Lee Point

Palmerston and Alice Springs ▼

Day-trips from Darwin include the popular Litchfield Park (see p.644) as well as the Aboriginal-owned Bathurst and Melville islands, a thirty-minute flight from town. Also worth a visit are either Crocodylus Park on the edge of Darwin or the Darwin Crocodile Farm south of town which makes a good day out when combined with the Territory Wildlife Park (see pp.643 and 644). It takes more than a day to appreciate Kakadu; for tours there see p.627.

Arrival and information

All flights arrive at **Darwin Airport**, 12km northeast of the city centre. A **shuttle bus** service (☎08/8981 5066 or 1800 358 945; $7.50) meets international flights and drops you off at all major hotels or delivers you to the **Transit Centre** behind 69 Mitchell St; a **taxi** (☎13 10 08) to town from the airport costs about $20. Given the proximity of Indonesia, Darwin is the cheapest place from which to leave Australia (see "Listings", p.630, for details).

On the other hand, Darwin is a long way from anywhere in Australia – the bus journey from Cairns takes a gruelling day and a half, including changes, and coming direct from Sydney, Melbourne or Perth, you'd do much better to fly. **Interstate buses** arrive behind the Transit Centre, where you can make reservations for onward journeys. Don't expect to be able to take a **train** from Adelaide to Darwin before 2005 at best and even then only a weekly service is planned. The new rail link is primarily for freight; see ⓦwww.aarc.com.au for more details.

Five minutes' walk up Mitchell Street, the **Visitors Information Centre** (Mon–Fri 9am–5pm, Sat 9am–3pm, Sun 10am–3pm; ☎1300 138 886, ⓦwww.ntholidays.com.au or ⓦwww.tourismtopend.com.au) is the official tourist information outlet and has plenty of material on national parks throughout the NT. It's also worth noting that local rental cars booked through

Top End weather

There is a certain amount of misunderstanding about the **tropical climate** of the Top End, usually summed up as the hot and humid "Dry" and the hotter and very humid "Wet". Give or take a couple of weeks either way, this is the pattern: the **Dry** begins in April when rains stop and humidity decreases – although this always remains high in the maritime tropics, whatever the season. It may take a couple of months for vehicular access to be restored to all far-flung tracks, but the bush never looks greener, while engorged waterfalls pound the base of the escarpments. From now until October skies are generally cloud-free with daily temperatures reliably peaking in the low thirties centigrade, though August nights might cool down to 10°C – sheer agony for seasoned Top Enders but bliss for unacclimatized tourists.

From October until the end of the year temperatures and humidity begin to rise – the dreaded **Build Up**. Clouds accumulate to discharge brief showers, and it's a time of year when the weak-willed or insufficiently drunk can flip out and go "troppo" as the unbearable tensions of heat, humidity and dysfunctional air-con push them over the edge. Around November storms can still be frustratingly dry but often give rise to spectacular lightning shows; Darwin is the world's most lightning-prone city. While rain showers become longer and more frequent towards Christmas – the onset of the **Wet** – access on sealed roads is rarely a problem.

Only when the actual **monsoon** commences at the turn of the year do the daily afternoon storms quickly rejuvenate and then saturate the land. This daily cycle lasts for at least two months and is much more tolerable than you might expect, with a daily thunderous downpour cooling things off from the mid- to the low-thirties. Along with Queensland's Cape York, Darwin's proximity to the equator gives it a true monsoon. Two hundred kilometres south the rains are much less heavy, though a Wet is experienced along the coast as far southwest as Derby, WA and Townsville on the north Queensland coast.

Cyclones, sometimes just a week apart, occur most commonly at either end of the Wet and can dump 30cm of rain in as many hours, with winds of 100kph and gusts twice that speed. Frequent updates on the erratic path and intensity of these tropical depressions are given on national and state radio, so that most people are fully prepared if and when the storm actually hits. Some fizzle out or head back out to sea; others can intensify and zigzag across the land, as nearly every community between Exmouth, WA (1999) and Darwin (1974) has found to its cost.

the visitors information centre may still come with unlimited kilometres. All around town you'll find several other independent tourist information offices, all competing for their slice of commission; shop around before you shell out a couple of hundred dollars on a tour. The free booklets *This Week In Darwin* and *Darwin and the Top End Today*, which can be picked up all around town, are mostly rose-tinted advertorials, but are handy for **maps**, including bus routes (see below). A five-hundred-metre radius around Smith Street Mall encompasses Darwin's city centre, catering for most of your needs; there are few attractions in the sea of suburbs spreading towards the north and the east.

City transport

The city's inexpensive **bus service** can deliver you to most corners of Darwin. Services operate daily from around 7am to 8pm, with some routes running until after 11pm on Friday and Saturday. "Multirider" tickets are available, giving you ten trips from $11.80. Another alternative is the "Tourcard" which gives unlimited travel for seven days for $25. One-day cards cost $5. The **bus terminal** (☏08/8924 7666) is on Harry Chan Avenue, at the bottom of

Renting and buying a vehicle: some tips

The hit-and-run pace and variable guide quality of many Kakadu tours has made renting a car or campervan big business in Darwin. The advantages of **driving yourself** are obvious and with a group of three or four you can end up paying less than with a tour. At the bottom end of the trade, a car can cost as little as $50 a day in Darwin (still comparatively expensive compared to the other capitals) plus a typical surcharge rate of 25¢ for each kilometre. Alternatively you can pay up to $60 with 100 free kilometres – handy for a day round town – or around $70 a day with unlimited kilometres. The older the cars the company offers, the lower their charges.

Seemingly **special deals** for the standard Kakadu/Litchfield run (eg $200 for three days with 1000km free) are commonly offered, but note that this trip will easily clock up 1200km and clued-in operators price accordingly.

It's important to understand the limitations of your **insurance** and **where you can drive** conventional cars. Basically, with one or two clearly defined exceptions, you cannot take your $50-a-day sedan on unsealed roads, and any underbody, roof, windscreen and water damage is down to you. Your **insurance obligations** are not something that all rental agencies spell out, but be assured that if you damage their car you end up paying. An additional premium of a few dollars a day can reduce this liability to a few hundred dollars. Local operators know too well that European drivers are unused to the vagaries of driving on cambered dirt roads and that sliding off into the scenery are common accidents. If you get tempted to take to the dirt, remember that even with the windows shut and air-con on recycle, fine dust will leave a clear message of where you've been. Bear in mind, though, that whatever you drive and whatever you pay in surcharges, most rental vehicles – even 4WDs – are uninsured off the bitumen. If you have an accident here, you pay dearly. It's a way of ensuring that people take it easy on the dirt roads or don't leave the highway at all.

Wherever you go from Darwin **distances** are long. The Territory has Australia's highest death rate on the roads and many of these are overseas travellers – in one month alone in 2002 five tourists were killed in four separate accidents in the NT. New laws and speed traps are desperately trying to reduce this, but the problem is not merely speed but concentration on long boring drives and controlling relatively top-heavy 4WDs and campervans when they wander onto the shoulder. Avoid trying to pack in a Katherine and Kakadu run in a couple of days, take it easy if driving cumbersome 4WDs on dirt roads and avoid driving at night in rural areas. There's more on the perils of Outback driving in Basics on p.37.

Self-contained **campervan** rentals have boomed across Australia over the last few years and in Darwin they are available from $120 a day, although most companies specify a few days' minimum rental. The smallest models can get crowded with more than two people, but the savings in accommodation and the independence offered make them a great way to see the parks or even the whole country. Like ordinary cars, campervans must stick to sealed roads unless you opt for the 4WD models.

Many visitors assume a **4WD** will allow them to really see Kakadu but it's not essential. Built to take a beating, a Toyota Land Cruiser will cost around $140 a day and use twice as much fuel as an ordinary car, although the only road in Kakadu where you need a 4WD is the Jim Jim/Twin Falls track (see p.640). Several vehicles have been lost here over the years and even in a "four-wheeler" some rental companies may still exclude this track so make sure you ask.

If you're looking to **buy a vehicle**, hostel notice boards are the best starting-point. The semi-squatted lot on Mitchell Street behind the night markets where private buyers sold their vehicles has been closed down, but ask around, as it may have located elsewhere.

Cavenagh Street, plus there's also a major interchange in the shopping centre at Casuarina, in the northern suburbs. Buses leave the city for the suburbs along Cavenagh Street and come back in along Mitchell and Smith streets. They head out as far as Palmerston, Howard Springs and, on school days, Humpty Doo, 50km from town on the Kakadu road.

Most hostels and some hotels rent out **bicycles** for around $16 a day. Although Darwin is flat, it's also hot and humid, so East Point Reserve, 8km from the centre, is about as far as you'd want to ride for fun. A "twist and go" **scooter** is much more fun; at present there's one operator opposite the Transit Centre offering 50cc scooters (car licence required, no passengers, $40 a day) or 125s which can carry a pillion rider (motorcycle licence required, $70 a day). Unless you want to ride two-up, a 50 will be fine around Darwin. Along Mitchell and Smith streets, a few local **car rental** outfits do battle, with prices starting at around $50 a day, plus a kilometre fee (see box opposite and "Listings", p.630, for more). **Taxis** work out at about a dollar a kilometre and there are plenty cruising around: either hail one on the street or give them a call on ☎13 10 08.

Accommodation

Darwin has plenty of **accommodation**, from luxury hotels to hostels galore, and most of it is conveniently central. During the Wet (Jan–March) prices in the upmarket establishments can take a dive, with half-price weekend packages frequently available. Contact the visitors information centre which deals with specials. In the hostels the price has settled at around a rather high $20 a bed, but in the middle of the Wet, brief price wars can flare up to fill beds.

Hotels, motels and apartments

Most **hotels** and **motels** are right in the city centre, with the more prestigious examples found along the Esplanade offering views of the bay. If you're looking for self-catering accommodation, there are several **apartment-hotels** in the centre, but for the most part they're further out.

Atrium Novotel 100 Esplanade ☎08/8941 0755, ⓦwww.noveldarwin.com.au. Upmarket hotel along the Esplanade with a foliage-draped atrium, bars, restaurants, a gym and pool as well as a sea view. ❻

City Gardens Apartments 93 Woods St ☎08/8941 2888, ⓦwww.citygardensapts.com.au. Spacious, centrally located family units with a pool. Two minutes' walk from Frogshollow Park, five minutes from town. ❹

Darwin Central Hotel Knuckey St ☎08/8944 9000, ⒻGreat 9100, ⓦwww.darwincentral.com.au. Luxury, high-rise modern hotel right by the Mall with spacious

rooms and a choice of restaurants and bars. ❻
Palms Motel 100 McMinn St ☎08/8981 4188, Ⓕ8981 4415. Good-sized rooms, pool and off-street parking make this one of Darwin's better-value motels. ❸
Top End Hotel Cnr Mitchell and Daly streets ☎08/8981 6511 or 1800 626 151, Ⓕ8981 1253. Well-kept, low-rise, motel-style rooms in Darwin's "party pub", complete with garden and pool. ❺
Value Inn 50 Mitchell St ☎08/8981 4733, ⓦwww.valueinn.com.au. Set price, no-frills motel with small en-suite rooms (TV, air-con and fridge) that sleep up to three – a real squeeze but a good deal and there's a pool too. ❹

Hostels

Backpackers' **hostels** in Darwin have improved in recent years with the standards reaching those of the East Coast, although the prices aren't as low. Note that some establishments offer a free pick-up on the airport shuttle if you book with them in advance. Air-con is not essential at night, but a fan certainly is.

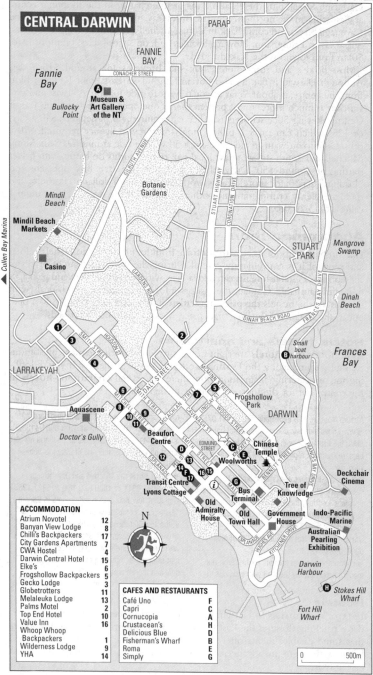

Fannie Bay Gaol Museum & East Point ▲

Aviation Heritage Centre & Crocodylus Park ▲

CENTRAL DARWIN

PARAP

FANNIE BAY

Fannie Bay

CONACHER STREET

Bullocky Point

Ⓐ ■ **Museum & Art Gallery of the NT**

GULBUTH AVENUE

Mindil Beach

Botanic Gardens

STUART HIGHWAY

CORONATION DRIVE

STUART PARK

Mangrove Swamp

◀ Cullen Bay Marina

◆ **Mindil Beach Markets**

■ **Casino**

GARDENS ROAD

FRANCES BAY DRIVE

Dinah Beach

DINAH BEACH ROAD

Ⓑ *Small boat harbour*

Frances Bay

Ⓐ

Ⓑ

LARRAKEYAH

SMITH ST

HOUSTON ST

DALY STREET

MITCHELL STREET

MANTON STREET

LINDSAY STREET

WOODS STREET

Frogshollow Park

Aquascene

Ⓒ

Ⓗ

Ⓓ Ⓘ Ⓙ

Ⓚ

Doctor's Gully

Beaufort Centre

MCLACHLAN STREET

CAVENAGH ST

SMITH STREET

EDMUND STREET

KNUCKEY ST

BENNETT STREET

DARWIN

Ⓖ

Ⓔ

Chinese Temple

Ⓒ Ⓔ **Woolworths**

ESPLANADE

Ⓛ

Ⓜ

Ⓝ Ⓕ

Ⓞ Ⓟ

Transit Centre

Lyons Cottage

i

Ⓖ **Bus Terminal**

Tree of Knowledge

Deckchair Cinema

Old Admiralty House

Old Town Hall

Government House

Indo-Pacific Marine

Australian Pearling Exhibition

ESPLANADE

HUGHES AVE

KITCHENER DRIVE

FRANCES BAY DRIVE

Darwin Harbour

Ⓗ *Stokes Hill Wharf*

Fort Hill Wharf

N

ACCOMMODATION

Atrium Novotel	12
Banyan View Lodge	8
Chilli's Backpackers	17
City Gardens Apartments	7
CWA Hostel	4
Darwin Central Hotel	15
Elke's	6
Frogshollow Backpackers	5
Gecko Lodge	3
Globetrotters	11
Melaleuka Lodge	13
Palms Motel	2
Top End Hotel	10
Value Inn	16
Whoop Whoop Backpackers	1
Wilderness Lodge	9
YHA	14

CAFES AND RESTAURANTS

Café Uno	F
Capri	C
Cornucopia	A
Crustacean's	H
Delicious Blue	D
Fisherman's Wharf	B
Roma	E
Simply	G

0   500m

Banyan View Lodge 119 Mitchell St ☎ 08/8981 8644 or 1800 249 124, ℮ bookings@travel -ys.com. Quiet with well-kept twin rooms with fans and fridge and big recreational rooms. Dorms from $18, rooms ❸

Chilli's Backpackers 69A Mitchell St ☎ 08/8949 9722 or 1800 351 313, ℉ 8941 9835. The old YHA half knocked down and cleverly redesigned with airy decks to eat, chat or sunbake by the pool, Internet café and travel shop. Dorms from $20, rooms ❹

CWA Hostel 3 Packard Place ☎ & ℉ 08/8941 3305. Not a backpackers' place but a small, shady house in its own grounds for women, couples and families only. Dorms from $20, rooms ❹

Elke's 112 Mitchell St ☎ 08/8981 8399 or 1800 808 365, ⓦ www.elkesbackpackers.com.au. Friendly old house at the quiet end of Mitchell Street, with a shady pool, free pick-ups from the airport, and a good tour desk. Dorms from $16, rooms ❸

Frogshollow Backpackers 27 Lindsay St ☎ 08/8941 2600 or 1800 068 686, ℮ frogs@octa4.net.au. Attractive, tropical building opposite Frogshollow Park, away from the Mitchell Street ghetto and with a mix of fans and air-con. Free breakfast. Dorms from $18, rooms ❸

Gecko Lodge 146 Mitchell St ☎ 08/8981 5569 or 1800 811 250, ℉ 8981 3680. At the far end of Mitchell St, a small hostel with a pool and with an annexe *Whoop Whoop Backpackers* a few doors down at 151 Mitchell St (℮ whoopwhoop @ozemail.com). Free breakfast pancakes, airport pick-ups and nightly lifts uptown. Dorms from $18, rooms ❸

Globetrotters 97 Mitchell St ☎ 08/8981 5385, ⓦ www.globetrotters.com.au. Ex-motel with a pool and licensed bar with live European football on TV and music jam sessions, making up for shabby rooms. Dorms from $16, rooms ❺

Melaleuka Lodge 52 Mitchell St ☎ 08/8941 3395 or 1800 623 543. Well-run, popular and well-equipped warren of rooms and courtyards right opposite the Transit Centre. Air-con in all rooms. Dorms from $15, rooms ❹

Wilderness Lodge 88 Mitchell St ☎ 08/8941 8363 or 1800 068 886, ⓦ www.wildlodge.com.au. Breezy outdoor feel with pool, BBQ, pick-ups and air-con dorms. Dorms from $18, rooms ❹

YHA 69 Mitchell St ☎ 08/8981 3995, ℉ 8981 6674. Modern, clean and thoughtfully designed hostel resort right by the Transit Centre. Outdoor dining area overlooks the pool. Dorms from $20, rooms ❸

Camping and caravan parks

The following **camping** and **caravan parks** are both along the Stuart Highway in Winnellie, between 7km and 14km from the centre. Comments by visitors at the visitors centre have not been kind to Darwin's caravan parks and Winnellie itself is a rather godforsaken light-industrial suburb, lying along the southern edge of the airport. Many of Darwin's caravan parks are pitched at long-term stays or touring retirees. Buses #5 and #8 run here from the central bus terminal. From the airport it's only a five-minute taxi ride.

Overlander Caravan Park Cnr Stuart Highway and McMillans Rd, Berrimah ☎ 08/8984 3025. Plenty of shade and lawns and close to shops. On-site vans ❸

Shady Glen Caravan Park Cnr Farrell Crescent and Stuart Highway ☎ 08/8984 3330. Pool and kiosk with tent sites. On-site vans ❹

The City

Present-day Darwin projects north from the end of a stubby peninsula where a settlement was originally established in 1869 on the lands of the Larrakeyah Aborigines. Over the years, the suburbs have spread across the flat, mangrove-fringed headland, but for the visitor most of the points of interest lie between the Wharf Precinct and East Point, 9km to the north. Tropical vegetation apart, it's by no means a good-looking city: huge tides create a warm, sludge-filled sea devoid of waves, while repeated destruction from cyclones, air raids and termites has left any surviving colonial architecture discreet and intermittent.

If you don't mind the heat the city's attractions can all be reached on foot. Other than renting a car or a scooter, you could take the **Tour Tub** (daily

9am–4pm; day–ticket $25; ☎08/8985 6322), which is a fun way to see most of the places detailed below over a day. Departing on the hour from Smith Street Mall, opposite the old Woolworths, the minibus trundles along its route allowing you to hop on and off as you please.

The City Centre

The city's commercial heart is **Smith Street Mall**, or the Mall as it's known these days. A **walk-through fountain** tempts passers-by with a quick soaking and your willpower will be much depleted after a good session at the **Hotel Victoria** – as the erstwhile *Vic*, it was once Darwin's answer to a Wild West saloon. All along and off the Mall several art galleries and gift shops entice you to buy Aboriginal crafts or Australiana.

There are more old buildings further along Smith Street. The **Old Town Hall**, built in 1883, was demolished by Cyclone Tracy, but its ruins occasionally host outdoor performances by the theatre group based in the stone building, **Brown's Mart**, opposite. In the park behind Brown's Mart is a huge banyan tree known as the **Tree of Knowledge**, while nearby stands the ornate **Chinese Temple** (Mon–Fri 8am–4pm, Sat & Sun 8am–3pm) on Woods Street, near the corner of Bennett Street. Another post-cyclone restoration, using the altar and statues from the 1887 original, this still serves Darwin's Chinese population – considerably diminished since the early days of white settlement, when Chinese labourers were responsible for building virtually everything, including the former railway down to Pine Creek.

At the other end of the Mall, a left turn down Knuckey Street leads to the Esplanade. On the left corner is the former **Admiralty House** (Mon–Sat 10am–5pm; free), a tropical-style house elevated on stilts that has survived cyclones and air raids. Opposite, **Lyons Cottage** (daily 10am–5pm; free), a stone bungalow, also dates from the 1920s; inside are displays of early Territorian history focussing on the Overland Telegraph Line (OTL). For a diversion step round to the so-called **Mitchell Street Tourist Precinct** (aka the Transit Centre). Formerly a backpackers' ghetto, it has been redefined with the help of a few long-overdue outdoor bars and cafés, night markets (see p.630) and occasional entertainment into somewhere to linger rather than loiter.

A pleasant walk along the lawns of the **Esplanade** leads to Daly Street, which marks the very end of the Stuart Highway. From here it's a straight 1500-kilometre run to Alice Springs with less than half a dozen traffic lights on the way. Otherwise, a left turn down Doctor's Gully leads to the ever-popular **Aquascene** (see ⓦwww.aquascene.com.au for tide-dependent opening hours or call ☎08/8981 7837; $5.50), where at high tide scores of catfish, mullet and metre-long milkfish come in to be hand-fed on stale bread (supplied free).

The Wharf Precinct

Hesitant development is refashioning **Stokes Hill Wharf** at the southern end of town into a new tourist precinct. A few souvenir shops and alfresco cafés have sprung up along the pier, which comes to life every evening. Well worth a visit is the live coral display at **Indo-Pacific Marine** (daily: April–Oct 10am–5pm; Nov–March 9am–1pm; $16; ☎08/8999 6573, ⓦwww.indopacific.com.au). In the right frame of mind, you could spend hours observing these marine environments, and the regular informative talks will set you straight about corals – the Timor Sea north of Darwin is one of the world's richest and most diverse coral environments, obscured from view by tidal silt. The night tours are excellent and include dinner, with wine (bookings essential). In the same building, the **Australian Pearling Exhibition** (Mon–Fri 10am–5pm, Sat & Sun 10am–5.30pm; $6) is a similarly imaginative display, entertainingly describing Darwin's part in northern Australia's pearling exploits.

Round the other side of the harbour, a stairway up the cliff just past the Oil Storage Tunnels (on the Tour Tub itinerary, but about as interesting as they sound) leads up to a viewing point and to **Government House**, built in 1883 after the original residence was devoured by white ants. Rarely open to the public, it's nevertheless a good example of an elegant, though much restored, tropical building.

Cullen Bay Marina and the Fannie Bay museums

Walking north down the full length of Smith Street will bring you to a small roundabout and a sign leading down to **Cullen Bay Marina**. Right by the roundabout you'll notice the so-called **Mylill Point Heritage Park**, a couple of pre-Tracy tropical houses. Like most marinas around the world there's not much to do here except observe yachties fiddling with their boats, poke around the "speciality" shops, and enjoy a meal or a drink in one of a good selection of waterside eateries, all within two minutes' walk of each other (see p.628). Harbour cruises or the jet shuttle (℡08/8978 5015; $16 return) over the harbour to Mandorah's deserted, although not that special, beaches leave from here. You'll find a small **beach** in the northeast corner of the marina overlooking Fannie Bay.

From the marina roundabout it's a short walk north to the **Botanic Gardens** (daily 7am–7pm; free), Darwin's main park, housing a large collection of palms as well as a separate Plant Display House (daily 7.30am–4pm). A further kilometre north brings you to the excellent **Museum and Art Gallery of the NT** (Mon–Fri 9am–5pm, Sat & Sun 10am–5pm; free) on Conacher Street, overlooking Fannie Bay. An excellent museum and art gallery, it's particularly notable for its Southeast Asian perspective, in pleasing contrast to the usual focus on recent white achievements. With an absorbing display of Aboriginal art by the Tiwi people of Bathurst and Melville islands as well as Top End bark paintings and the familiar pointillist style of the Central deserts, there's just enough here to keep your attention without seeing dots yourself. Elsewhere the stuffed remains of "Sweetheart", a five-metre-long rogue crocodile with a taste for outboard engines, are particularly alarming, while the massive boat shed is a mariners' paradise, with boats as diverse as pearling luggers, Indonesian *praus*, Polynesian outriggers and the simplest of bark canoes. There's also an imaginatively designed exhibition commemorating Darwin's destruction by Cyclone Tracy.

Short tours from Darwin

Darwin's **harbour** may not be the world's most picturesque inlet but there are a number of ways of making it an enjoyable experience. At Stokes Hill Wharf a **sea plane** and **helicopter** stand by, waiting to fly you over the city, while down at the Small Boat Harbour off Frances Bay Drive a **hovercraft** can take you for a spin around the bay. But the best options are the **yacht**, **catamaran** or **pearl lugger** based at Cullen Bay Marina. A sunset cruise brings you back in time to enjoy an evening meal by the waterfront and in the meantime you'll get an amusing commentary as well as drinks and snacks for your two-hour trip.

Fannie Bay Gaol Museum (daily 10am–5pm; free; bus #4 or #6), further north along the bay, 5km from the city centre, served as Darwin's prison for nearly a hundred years until 1979. The old cells are still there but hardly edifying – more interesting is a display on the long-proposed Darwin rail link, and now they have something to celebrate.

On to East Point

Right by the Gaol Museum, the main route (and buses #4 and #6) curves right, while East Point Road continues straight up to the **East Point Reserve**, an area of largely natural bushland that's home to around two thousand wallabies. After a kilometre you pass **Lake Alexander**, a recreational saltwater lake suitable for year-round swimming and, nearby, a **mangrove boardwalk** takes you into the tidal environment.

The road ends 3km from the former prison at the **Military Museum** (daily 9.30am–5pm; $5) and **gun turrets**. Most visitors – and quite a few Australians – are unaware that Darwin was repeatedly bombed by the Japanese in 1942; at the time, news of both the air raids and the thirty thousand enemy troops massed on Timor, awaiting the order to invade, was suppressed. The museum commemorates these events with a short video and some rather staid displays of uniforms, medals and other wartime memorabilia, while in the grounds a collection of neglected World War II guns, aircraft engines and associated hardware quietly rusts away. At the top of East Point, the guns themselves were never actually fired and the huge barrels were eventually sold ten years later as scrap to – ironically – the Japanese. East Point is also an ideal spot to watch the striking hues of Darwin's multichrome sunsets; if driving, watch out for roadside wallabies on the way back.

Aviation Heritage Centre, Crocodylus Park and Charles Darwin National Park

Set in a hangar off the Stuart Highway, on the southeastern edge of the airport, the non-profit **Aviation Heritage Centre** (daily 9am–5pm; $11; bus #5 or #8) is easily dominated by the huge bulk of a B52 bomber on loan from the US Air Force. The museum offers an alternative history to Southeast Asia and the Top End through the engaging story of civil and military aviation in the region.

Further down the Stuart Highway, and taking a left at the Berrimah traffic lights, leads you to the crocodile research facility and farm of **Crocodylus Park** (daily 9am–5pm; tours 10am, noon & 2pm; $22; bus #5) on McMillans Road. No visit to Australia is complete without a close look at these prehistoric-looking beasts and in the croc-filled lagoon you can get within kissing distance of a three-metre man-eater should one happen to doze off right by the fence. These usually dormant reptiles are coaxed into action during daily feeding sessions, which coincide with tours led by guides, and there's an absorbing museum giving you the lowdown on the world of crocs.

Returning along Tiger Brennan Drive you can pay a visit to the **Charles Darwin National Park**, designated to protect an area of natural bushland against a rash of surrounding development. Along with views onto the city and a few wartime storage hangars, **mangroves** is what it's all about down here. Although not much to look at, mangroves provide a crucial and biodiverse coastal habitat. Nearly eighty percent of the world's many species are found in tropical NT. The trees' salt-tolerant root systems inhibit coastal erosion, filter the water and provide shelter to everything from mud crabs and crocs to pesky sandflies which can waltz through mosquito nets five abreast. Altogether the park's a nice spot for a picnic, a walk or a traffic-free cycle: just don't forget some repellent for the insects.

Darwin's beaches

Several factors exclude Darwin from being the beach resort you might have hoped for. A high tidal range, the fierce tropical sun, sheets of mangroves and the seasonal but deadly menace of stinging box jellyfish (from Oct to May)

Tours from Darwin to the Top End

For the visitor, Darwin itself isn't a destination of enduring interest compared to the surrounding countryside. **Kakadu** is the obvious, sometimes overrated, draw, and for many is the primary reason for visiting the Top End, but **Litchfield Park** is nearer and has croc-free swimming holes. While Litchfield remains a popular day-trip, most Kakadu tour operators offer two- to five-day tours, the latter providing a less hurried way of enjoying the park.

Note that the Territory and especially the Top End do not always attract the cream of **tour guides** – a guide led a group to a croc-filled billabong in Kakadu in 2002 where one woman was killed. Operators listed below are recommended but be aware that the quality of the guides working for them can vary. Expect to pay around $130 a day. Most of these tours include the $16.25 Kakadu park entry fee.

Aussie Overlanders ℡1300 880 118, ⓦwww.aussieoverlanders.com. Small-group three-day Kakadu tours including Twin Falls, as well as five-day tours including a dip into Arnhemland and a five-day trip visiting Katherine Gorge and Litchfield Park.

Billy Can ℡1800 813 484, ⓦwww.billycan.com.au. Catering for the older end of the market who enjoy their comforts, with accommodated options. Small groups, forward-facing seats with tours from two to five days right up to the Cobourg Peninsula with a flight back ($2125).

Coo-ee Tours ℡08/8981 6116. Enjoyable twelve-hour waterfall hop through Litchfield and Reynolds River with a dinkum Aussie family.

Darwin Day Tours ℡08/8947 4060 or 1800 811 63. Day- and half-day tours (essentially a bus service plus a cuppa) to the croc farms, Territory Wildlife Park as well as the jumping croc cruise and a visit to Fogg Dam, all for $110.

Desert Ventures ℡1800 078 119. Cairns-based bus doing Darwin in five days for $400 plus $80 kitty.

Kakadu Adventure Safaris ℡08/8947 2677. Two or three full days in a packed 4WD for the fun-hearted and budget-minded; a longer tour includes Twin Falls.

Kakadu Dreams 50 Mitchell St ℡1800 813 266, ⓦwww.kakadudreams.com.au. Low-cost full-on fun and games in another packed 4WD. "No oldies allowed." Park fee extra.

Keetleys ℡08/8947 2472. Established tour operator for those who prefer not to rough it too much. One-day Litchfield and Katherine tours or two-day Kakadu tours.

Travel North ℡08/8972 3989. Variety of well-organized trips south to Katherine and Kakadu.

Wild Thing ℡08/8941 9494. All-out one- and two-day action and adventure in Litchfield.

Wilderness 4WD Adventures ℡1300 666 100, ⓦwww.wildernessadventures .com.au. Competitively priced two- to five-day tours through Kakadu and Litchfield. Plenty of fun and action with the longer tours always a better deal.

Xplore ℡1300 136 133, ⓦwww.xploretours.com.au. Cheap and cheerful, similar to Kakadu Dreams; "only fun-loving organisms should apply". Three-day Kakadu tours and five-day tours with Katherine and Litchfield.

mean that, despite its few beaches, you're rarely pushed for a spot to roll out your towel. Traps in the harbour regularly capture *most* of the crocodiles. **Fannie Bay**'s beaches (bus #4 or #6) are closest to the town centre, have a kiosk and water-craft rental and are not at all bad when the tide's out. However, the **Casuarina Coastal Reserve** (bus #4 or #10; 40min), capping the northern suburbs, has the city's best sandy stretches, including a "free beach" for nudists. A good place to splash about is **Lee Point**, mainly used by sunset dog walkers and found at the end of Lee Point Road, directly north of the airport.

Eating

There have been big improvements in the ambience of Darwin's restaurants in the last few years, and they've finally realized that whatever you're eating, sitting in an open-air tropical environment with a few palms flapping about is far more agreeable than inside an air-con box. For a city of this size, there's a wide selection of good-quality options for every budget – certainly enough to keep your taste buds busy. Adventurous carnivores can tackle exotic meats such as **kangaroo**, **buffalo**, **camel** and **crocodile**, though they're often more memorable running about in the bush than on a plate. Ironically, the climate makes it likely that **seafood** will have been frozen, and so might as well be from Cape Cod as from the Timor Sea. That said, anglers are drawn to the Top End hoping to catch **barramundi**, a bland-tasting and overrated "fighting fish"; **snapper** (aka Red Emperor) is much more flavoursome.

City centre and the wharf area

Cafe Uno Mitchell St. Pleasant Mediterranean-style menu with pasta and focaccia from $8. Groovy cocktail bar at the back.

Capri 37 Knuckey St. City-centre coffee bar serving good-value big brekkies and meals with a Mediterranean theme.

Crustacean's Stokes Hill Wharf ☎08/8981 8658. At the end of the pier, offering swish steak and fish from $24.

Delicious Blue 84 Mitchell St. Airy inside and outside tables with $5 breakfast from 7.30am and Asian-influenced meals from $12.

Fisherman's Wharf Small Boat Harbour, Frances Bay Drive. A long-time Darwinians' select getaway for cheap seafood and chips.

Roma Cavenagh St. This classic, Italian-inspired coffee bar serving tasty meals and breakfasts is an old favourite with Darwinites.

Simply Star Arcade, The Mall. Town centre veggie and health food joint.

Cullen Bay, Fannie Bay and East Point

Buzz Cafe Marine Blvd, Cullen Bay. Inexpensive large portions of seafood and chips.

Cornucopia MAGONT Complex, Conacher St ☎08/8981 7791. Sunset views from the terrace and a contemporary Australian menu. Moderate prices.

Dos Amigos Marine Blvd, Cullen Bay. Huge serves of authentic and moderately priced Tex-Mex food with good bar and outdoor tables.

Lemongrass Cullen Bay. Thai restaurant plus seafood and steak staples.

Pee Wees at the Point East Point Rd. Tucked away in the trees on a grassy terrace overlooking the bay serving up steak and seafood at around $20 plus.

YOTS Shop 4, 54 Marine Blvd, Cullen Bay. One of a dozen or so restaurants in the marina, this one has a varied and reasonably priced seafood menu and pleasant location. Ideal for a post-cruise evening meal.

Drinking, nightlife and entertainment

Darwin's thirst for alcohol is legendary, with statistics for **beer** consumption averaging out at around 230 litres per year per person – fifty percent more than in the rest of Australia, although consumption of soft drinks is also well above the national average: if it's not a VB then it will be the other favourite, a chocolate milk. In recent years, consumption among the non-indigenous community has eased off but beer-drinking is still considered a prerequisite or indeed the main way of having a good night out in Darwin.

Pubs and bars

Many **pubs** have transformed their functional frontier-town interiors into something more conducive to public servants and tourists. The atmosphere that may once have been at home in the Wild West is long gone, in the centre of Darwin at least. The *Hotel Victoria*, on the Mall, is the looser venue in Darwin's CBD, but even this place is calming down in its old age.

Don't turn down any invitations to the "members only" *Yacht Club* in Fannie Bay, a fine spot to watch the sun set over the Timor Sea. Next to the Transit Centre the Guinness-serving *Shenanigan's* brought "Oirishness" to the Territory and has struck the right chord with both locals and visitors. There's also *Kitty O'Shea's* at the top of Mitchell Street creating the same sort of hooley but serving food as well. Over the road, *Rourkes Drift* is very popular, featuring a bit of wood and brass instead of the ubiquitous "galvo".

Clubs and live music

Like Darwin's transient population, things change quickly on the city's **club scene**, if it can be called that, which is centred on Mitchell Street, with several options stretching up to the *Top End Hotel*; just walk along it and see what takes your fancy. The **casino** (see below) hosts several diversions, including *Crystals*, a straightforward disco, while karaoke crooning takes off in the early hours at the *Sweethearts Bar*. On Sunday afternoons "Jazz on the Lawn", behind the casino, is strictly middle of the road.

Theatre, cinemas and the casino

For **theatrical performances**, see what Brown's Mart Community Arts (℡08/8998 5522) is up to, or check out the programme at the Performing Arts Centre (℡08/8198 1222) on Mitchell Street, which hosts top acts and shows from all over the country and even international ones. The five-screen **Cinema Darwin**, just over the road, has cheap tickets on Tuesday; for an alternative to mainstream films, see what's on at the outdoor **Deckchair Cinema**, on Frances Bay near Stokes Hill Wharf (closed Nov–March).

Down on East Point Road the **casino** (open nightly) is a sawn-off pyramid designed to withstand 350kph winds – and filled with a variety of distractions aimed at emptying your wallet. Don't be put off by the jet-setting image of European casinos; the Australian's love of **gambling** means that anyone can fit in comfortably as long as they're presentable.

Festivals and events

The Dry season sees an upsurge in popular activity as the city shakes off the languor of the Wet. As well as agricultural shows, rodeos and racing, August's **Festival of Darwin** sees bands, plays, parades and all sorts of happenings around the city, and is well worth catching. Early August is the time for the famous **Beer Can Regatta** in Fannie Bay – wacky boat races in sea craft made entirely from beer cans. A genuine manifestation of Territorian eccentricity, interest has picked up after a few slow years, but it's not the alcohol-fueled celebration it used to be. Also in August, there is more nuttiness during the barefoot **Mud Crab Tying Competition**, a speed event that can cost you your digits.

Markets

Every Thursday night from 5.30pm (May–Oct only) **Mindil Beach Markets** attracts thousands of locals who park, unpack their eskies and garden furniture, and settle in for the sunset. A mouthwatering array of sizzling food stalls from all corners of the earth (but mostly Asia) torments your nostrils, and New Age remedies, handicrafts and teeming humanity round off Darwin's one unmissable event. It's a three-kilometre walk from town through the Botanic Gardens, or a short ride on a #4 or #6 bus from the city centre. **Parap's Saturday morning market**, on Parap Road (bus #6), or **Rapid Creek market**, off Trower Road on Sunday (bus #6 or #10), are good year-round substitutes, with a smaller food selection, old books and knick-knacks. There is also the recently developed **night markets** which have spiced up Mitchell Street.

Listings

Airlines The Flight Centre (☎13 16 00) is on Knuckey Street near the corner with Smith Street and the promisingly named Backpackers Discount Centre is on Smith Street near the corner with Knuckey St. Both offer deals to Bali for around $550.

Banks All major banks are located in or near Smith Street Mall.

Bookshops Readback Book Exchange is on the Mall near Star Arcade.

Buses McCafferty's, Transit Centre, 69 Mitchell St ☎08/8911 8700.

Camping equipment The NT General Store, 42 Cavenagh St, has everything you need for going out into the bush, from a new pair of Blunnies to mozzie nets, eskies and billies.

Car rental Advance, 86 Mitchell St ☎08/8981 2999; Network, 90 Mitchell St ☎08/8924 0000; Thrifty Rental Cars, 64 Stuart Highway (☎08/8981 8400), is out of town but has a big fleet of vehicles.

Consulates Indonesia, 18 Harry Chan Ave (Mon–Fri 9am–1pm & 2–5pm; ☎08/8941 0488).

Hospital Royal Darwin Hospital, Rocklands Drive, Casuarina ☎08/8922 8888.

Internet access The best rates are at Didjworld in Harry Chan Arcade off Smith Street; there are also places on Mitchell Street.

Permits for Aboriginal Land Northern Land Council, PO Box 42921, Casuarina 0811 ☎08/8920 5100.

Pharmacy 46 Smith St Mall (daily 9am–9pm; ☎08/8981 9202).

Police The main police station is at West Lane, behind Knuckey St ☎08/8981 1866.

Post office 48 Cavenagh St, cnr Edmunds St. Open on Saturday morning and with a well-organized poste restante service.

Swimming The nearest decent-sized pool is at Ross Smith Ave, Parap (☎08/8981 2662); take bus #6 or #10 from the city centre. Or try Lake Alexander at East Point.

Vaccinations Contact the Travel and Immunization Service, 43 Cavenagh St (☎08/8981 7492), for vaccination service if you're heading for Asia.

Bathurst and Melville islands

Around six thousand years ago, rising sea levels created **Bathurst and Melville islands**, 80km north of Darwin. Home of the **Tiwi** Aborigines, the islands are often collectively known as the Tiwi Islands. Differing significantly from mainland Aborigines, with whom they had limited contact until the nineteenth century, the Tiwi people's hostility towards all intruders hastened the failure of **Fort Dundas**, Britain's first north Australian outpost (on Melville Island), which lasted just five years until 1829. The Tiwi word for white men, *murantani* or "hot, red face", probably originates from this time.

In just two generations, since a Belgian missionary cautiously established the present-day town of **NGUIU**, on Bathurst, the Tiwi have moved from a hunter-gatherer lifestyle to a commodity-based economy with much less difficulty than mainland Aborigines, but still not without social problems. Running their own tours and manufacturing their own crafts and garments,

△ Melville Island

they are now seen as an offshore model for successful Aboriginal self-determination.

The **Tiwi Land Council** (☎08/8947 1838) issues permits for visitors to the islands, but doesn't allow individual tourism. Without an invitation, **tours** are the only way to see the islands. Tiwi Tours (☎1800 183 630, ⓔaussieadventure@attglobal.net) offers small-group tours of the islands, from $298 for a day-trip, including return flight and permit. It's a bit of a shopping trip, inspecting Tiwi art and craft outlets such as Bima Wear's showroom, but lunch at Taracumbie Waterfall and a visit to an overgrown burial ground, where lopsided crosses mingle with carved *pukamani* burial poles, add some flavour – as does the thirty-minute flight over Van Diemen Gulf. At $564 the **overnight tours** are much more worthwhile. You'll get a chance to go food-gathering with local Tiwi, either offshore or through the bush, making it a refreshingly spontaneous encounter.

The Mary River Wetlands

The **Arnhem Highway**, which runs east towards Kakadu, parts company with the main southbound Stuart Highway 10km after Howard Springs. It passes through a region that has come to be known as the **Mary River Wetlands**, a proposed national park which allows visitors to explore one of the difficult-to-access habitats found in adjacent Kakadu. Few Darwin-based tours stop here, such is their rush to get you to Kakadu, and yet it possesses the greatest variety of wildlife, including what is probably the biggest concentration of crocodiles on the Australian mainland.

On your way into the wetlands you'll see the turn-off to **Fogg Dam Conservation Reserve**. Originally established in the late 1950s as an experimental rice- and cotton-growing area which was to transform the Territory's economy, for various "operational" reasons, not least the passing birds which tucked in with beaks adrool, the whole scheme was a flop. Since then the dam has become more successful as a bird sanctuary: early morning or twilight are the best times for spotting jacanas, egrets and geese, as well as pythons who feed on the water rats, goannas and wallabies. There's also a 3.6-kilometre signposted boardwalk through the adjacent woodland and another leading into the lagoon itself.

Back on the highway you'll spot the distinctive observation platform of the **Windows on the Wetlands Visitors Centre** (daily 7.30am–7.30pm), which overlooks the Adelaide River flood plain from the top of Beatrice Hill. On the top floor you can play with interactive displays describing the surrounding ecology and look out onto the flood plain through binoculars. Unfortunately, what you have, in the words of one ranger, is a window on the weedlands. The floodplain has been infested by something called the "giant sensitive plant", an exotic triffid-like shrub which is choking all other plant life out.

Adelaide River Crossing

Seeing crocodiles in their natural habitat is one of the Top End's undoubted highlights but at the **Adelaide River Crossing**, 64km east of Darwin, you can go one better and sign up for a **jumping crocodile cruise**. The *Adelaide River Queen* cruises ($35 for a 90min cruise; up to 4 times daily; check times and availability of seats in advance on ☎08/8988 8144) involve enticing the river's numerous salties with bits of boney offal, making the business of snapping stunning photographs straightforward and safe. All the crocs are wild but have been trained to draw up and grab the morsels, and many have adopted personalities, but the six-metre Hannibal, Marrakai or Aggro are the ones you will hope to snap in action. Sea eagles sometimes swoop in to snatch the meat from the crocs' maw and, whatever your thoughts on the methods or wisdom of encouraging crocodiles to jump 2m out of the water, they are an amazing spectacle.

The Mary River

Continuing along the Arnhem Highway, 12km past the *Bark Hut Inn*, the **Old Darwin Road** (also known as the Jim Jim Rd) leads southeast into Kakadu. Another 6km further on, the unsealed Point Stuart Road turns north into the proposed **Mary River National Park**, ending at the point where explorer Stuart actually reached the sea in 1862. It's an opportunity for those with their own vehicle to explore a wetlands environment no less impressive for not being in Kakadu. Try and locate the Mary River Wetlands **brochure/map** in the "Discovery Trails" series produced by the visitors centre in Darwin. A good base to explore this region is right on the highway at *Mary River Park* (☏1800 788 844, ⓦwww.maryriverpark.com.au; tents $8, dorms $23, en-suite cabins ❻). The McCafferty's **bus** from Darwin to Jabiru stops here and there's a range of cabin accommodation for all budgets among the lawns and palms, an airy covered dining area as well as crocodile or sunset **cruises** on the river and tours up into the wetlands which are especially popular with birdwatchers. It was here that legendary bushman Tom Cole made his living for a while, shooting crocs and buffalo, a tough life described with typical stoicism in his book, *Riding the Wildman Plains*.

North of the highway you can follow the Point Stuart Road passing the Wildman Ranger station (☏08/8978 8986) to **Rock Hole**, a lush billabong similar to the better-known Yellow Waters near Cooinda. Another 25km up the road is *Point Stuart Wilderness Lodge* (☏08/8981 7263, ⓔnttours@adventure-tours.com.au; units ❹), with a pool, boat tours, gear rental and, with advance notice, meals available.

Kakadu National Park

A hundred and fifty kilometres east of Darwin you reach the western boundary of **KAKADU NATIONAL PARK**, an area of largely unspoilt wilderness. On UNESCO's World Heritage List, it was brought to worldwide attention when used as a backdrop in the film *Crocodile Dundee*. The park derives its name from the Gagudju language group of Aborigines, who number among the area's traditional custodians; the Gagudju Association, the Aboriginal owners, jointly manage the park with the assistance of Environment Australia, a government agency (ⓦwww.ea.gov.au/parks/kakadu). Many of the traditional owners also claim a royalty from the **uranium** mined in Kakadu: along the eastern border with Arnhemland lies fifteen percent of the world's known reserves, and the Ranger Uranium Mine near Jabiru yields around $10 million a year for the association. The huge sums of money generated by the mine they never wanted have if anything been squandered and so worsened the living conditions of many of the park's traditional occupants.

It was the environmental debate over the proposed mining in the late 1970s that was instrumental in the establishment of the park. Mining of a new site at **Jabiluka** located close to Ubirr, one of the park's most beautiful spots, was

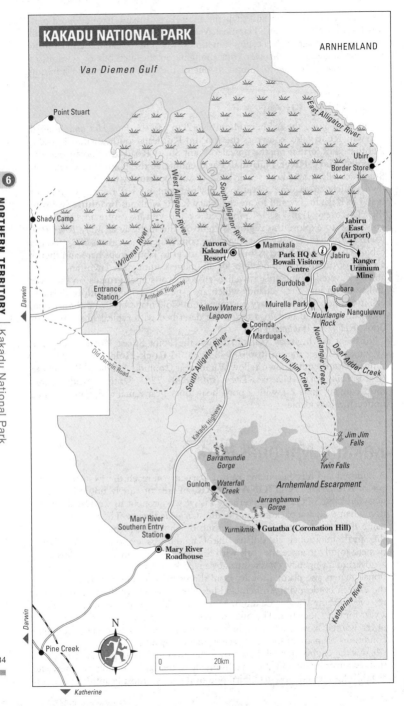

KAKADU NATIONAL PARK

ARNHEMLAND

Van Diemen Gulf

Point Stuart

East Alligator River

Ubirr
Border Store

Shady Camp

West Alligator River

South Alligator River

Wildman River

Jabiru East (Airport)

Aurora Kakadu Resort

Mamukala

Park HQ & Bowali Visitors Centre

Jabiru

Ranger Uranium Mine

Entrance Station

Arnhem Highway

Burdulba

Gubara

Yellow Waters Lagoon

Muirella Park

Nanguluwur

Cooinda

Nourlangie Rock

Mardugal

South Alligator River

Old Darwin Road

Jim Jim Creek

Nourlangie Creek

Deaf Adder Creek

Kakadu Highway

Jim Jim Falls

Barramundie Gorge

Twin Falls

Gunlom
Waterfall Creek

Arnhemland Escarpment

Jarrangbammi Gorge

Yurmikmik ▼ Gutatba (Coronation Hill)

Mary River Southern Entry Station

Mary River Roadhouse

Darwin

Pine Creek

N

0   20km

Katherine River

Katherine

proposed in 1998, creating widespread controversy as protestors occupied the site. In the end mining was suspended, but only because demand for uranium has dropped in recent years.

The park's 20,000 square kilometres encompass the entire catchment area of the **South Alligator River**, misnamed by an early British explorer after the river's prolific crocodile population. In its short run to the sea, the river passes through, and creates, a number of varied topographical features. Ravines in the southern sandstone escarpment, itself topped with plateau **heathlands**, shelter scattered pockets of monsoonal **rainforest**, while downstream the more commonly seen **eucalypt woodlands** merge into the paperbark **swamps** and tidal **wetlands** and **mangroves** of the coastal fringe.

Within these varied habitats an extraordinary diversity of flora and fauna thrives. Included are 2000 different **plants**, over 10,000 species of **insect**, half the Territory's species of **frog**, a quarter of Australia's **freshwater fish** and over 75 different **reptiles** – more than you'll find in Europe and some, such as the freshwater (or Johnston) crocodile, unique to Kakadu. A third of Australia's **birds** can also be found in Kakadu, including the elegant Jabiru stork, the similarly large brolga, with its curious courting dance, lily-hopping jacanas, white-breasted sea eagles, which build lifelong nests from heavy sticks, as well as galahs and magpie geese by the thousand. **Mammals** include kangaroos, wallabies,

Crocodiles

Two distinct types of crocodile inhabit the Top End. Bashful **Johnston** or **freshwater** crocodiles ("freshies") grow up to 3m in length, and are almost exclusively fish-eaters, living in freshwater rivers and billabongs. Unique to Australia, and distinguishable by their narrow snouts and neat rows of spiky teeth, they look relatively benign and are considered harmless to man. Some swimming areas in Kakadu are known to harbour freshies.

Estuarine, or **saltwater** crocodiles ("salties"), can inhabit both salt and fresh water and are the world's biggest reptiles. Once fully mature (up to 6m long and 1000kg in weight), they have no natural predators other than each other and have been known to "take" (the approved euphemism) buffaloes trapped in the mud. Their broad, powerful snouts and gnarled jawline embody a fascinating and gruesome profile that has changed little since the time of the dinosaurs – only then salties were four times bigger than they are now. They are opportunistic hunters, catching their prey in sudden, short bursts of speed and then resuming their customary inactivity for days if not weeks at a time. Apart from the jumping crocs at Adelaide River, most you'll see are inactive, sunning themselves in the mud or cooling off underwater.

Aborigines have lived alongside crocodiles, and eaten them or their eggs, for thousands of years, but in the early twentieth century crocodiles were hunted close to extinction – either for sport, as vermin, or for their skin. Legislation reversed this trend in the late 1960s and even with current conservation, farming and elimination of rogue crocs, the Top End will not see the return of the really huge crocs again.

The absence of **warning signs** does not guarantee safe swimming, nor does the *apparent* absence of salties. Hard enough to spot even when they're above water, crocodiles can lie submerged for hours. Fatalities are surprisingly rare but in October 2002 a Kakadu tour group ignored warning signs and took a midnight swim in Sandy Billabong. The timing could not have been worse: crocs are most active at night and this was the breeding season when males become aggressive. A few hours later a 4.5-metre saltie was harpooned by rangers with the body of a German woman still in its jaws. It's the latest grisly story to join every tour guide's repertoire and become firmly entrenched in Territorian folklore.

wallaroos, 26 bat species, and dingoes – a barkless and incorrigibly wild dog introduced from Indonesia by Aborigines some five thousand years ago.

With so many interdependent ecosystems, maintaining the park's natural balance has become a full-time job. The **water buffalo**, brought in from Timor early in the nineteenth century and one of a dozen or so **feral species** found in the park, proliferated so successfully that its wallowing behaviour soon turned the fragile wetlands into saltwater mudbaths. However, concerted bovine eradication in the Top End has left other problems in its wake, not least the aptly named **salvinia molesta weed**. With no buffaloes to eat it, the exotic weed has invaded vast areas of the wetlands, creating a thick, sunlight- and oxygen-depleting mat that chokes all other plant and fish life. The arrival of the **cane toad** in the park is also a cause for concern; by the 2002–03 Wet it had reached Jabiru and Cooinda and scientists are currently trying to develop a genetically engineered block. But it is in fact exotic **grasses** blown in from the east which pose the greatest ecological threat to the park, due to the temperature at which they burn. **Burning off** has long been recognized as a technique of land management by Aborigines who lit small, controllable fires as an aid to hunting and to stimulate new plant growth. Today, rangers imitate age-old Aboriginal practice, burning off the drying speargrass during June to preclude bushfires at the end of the Dry, when the desiccated countryside could be devastated by an early electrical storm. These exotic grasses burn at a far higher temperature than indigenous varieties and destroy rather than singe the woodlands.

Visiting the park

It must be stressed that Australia's largest national park is a difficult place to appreciate in one short visit. Access to the park's diverse features is limited, and those expecting to find the bush humming with wildlife will be disappointed. Furthermore, at the most popular times of year for visitors, Kakadu is much drier than might be imagined, and most of the wildlife is active only during the early morning, in the evening or at night. The danger from crocodiles and of inadvertent desecration of sacred Aboriginal sites, as well as the harsh terrain, means that the wetlands and especially the escarpment country are best appreciated from a small aircraft, something which can be arranged in Jabiru (see p.638) or through the *Gagudju Lodge* in Cooinda, with thirty-minute scenic flights from $100.

Ancient rock art

Up to five thousand **Aboriginal art sites** cover the walls of Kakadu's caves and sheltered outcrops, ranging from thirty to over twenty thousand years in age. Most of them are inaccessible to visitors, and many are still of spiritual significance to the three hundred or so Gagudju and other language groups who live in the park. The paintings include a variety of styles, from hand prints to detailed cross-hatched depictions of animals and fish from the rich **Estuarine period** of six thousand years ago. At this time, rising sea levels submerged the land bridge by which Aborigines crossed into Australia. It is not unusual to see paintings from successive eras on one wall: **Contact period** images of seventeenth-century Maccassan fishing *praus* and larger European schooners might be superimposed over depictions of ancient and bizarre spirit-beings. Though partially understood at best, Kakadu's rock art provides a fascinating record of a culture that, as excavations at Jinmium on the NT/WA coastal border suggest, might have inhabited the Top End for over 100,000 years.

Although Kakadu's Aborigines distinguish six **seasons** throughout the year, to most people it's either the Wet, with up to 1600mm (just over five feet) of torrential rainfall between December and March, or the Dry, an almost complete drought. The **dry-season months** of June, July and August are the most popular times to visit the park, with acceptable humidity and temperatures and fairly conspicuous wildlife. Towards the end of the Dry, birdlife congregates around the diminishing waterholes, while November's rising temperatures and epic electrical storms – known as the Build Up – herald the onset of the Wet. To see Kakadu during the **Wet** or the early Dry is, some say, to see it at its best. Water is everywhere and, while some sights are inaccessible and the wildlife dispersed, the land demonstrates the kind of verdant splendour that people often expect, but fail to find, in the most visited months.

Getting there

The **Arnhem Highway** leaves the Stuart Highway 43km south of Darwin, following which it's a fairly dull 210-kilometre drive to the Park HQ near Jabiru (see below). On the way you'll pass the **park entrance station**, where you pay the $16.25-per-person entrance fee; tickets are valid for a week, and you can leave and re-enter the park as many times as you like during this period. From Jabiru the sealed **Kakadu Highway** heads southwest through to Pine Creek on the Stuart Highway (an alternative entry point into the park if approaching from the south), passing Cooinda, which is pretty much at the heart of the park. Along this road you'll encounter many of Kakadu's best features.

The **Old Darwin Road** (or **Jim Jim Rd**), unsealed, but usually passable for robust 2WD cars in dry conditions, is a good alternative to slogging the full length of the Arnhem Highway. It starts 12km east of the **Bark Hut Inn** on the Arnhem Highway and joins the Kakadu Highway near Cooinda, 100km further on. Entering the park this way you should pay at the Cooinda resort, or at the Park HQ near Jabiru; for both, see below.

Without your own transport you'll have to rely on a **tour** (see box, p.627 for some recommended Darwin-based operators, or p.651 out of Katherine). There are **buses** into the park: McCafferty's operates daily between Darwin, Jabiru and Cooinda, and the Kakadu Parklink (☎1800 089 113) runs between the main accommodation centres of the Kakadu Resort, Jabiru and Cooinda. But make no mistake, those trying to see the park using only their bus passes may end up frustrated. To make the most of using the bus, try to organize some day-tours out of Jabiru or Cooinda, although this can take some planning. You're probably going to be in Kakadu only once, so do it properly: rent a car or join a tour. If you find yourself in the park and suddenly decide you need a car, **rental** can be arranged through the Thrifty office at the *Gagudju Crocodile Hotel* in Jabiru (☎08/8979 2552). The **map** you're given when you enter the park is handy, but details only the most popular areas; for the whole picture get yourself a copy of the HEMA 1:400,000 *Kakadu National Park* map.

The Park Headquarters and Bowali Visitors Centre

At the eastern edge of the park, 250km from Darwin, near the junction of the Arnhem and Kakadu highways, you arrive at the **Park Headquarters and Bowali Visitors Centre** (daily 8am–5pm; ☎08/8938 1123). The visitors centre is a masterpiece of thoughtful and relevant landscaping and design and should not be missed. Here you can get an official *Visitors' Guide* that suggests how to make the most of your visit, while for further information, *Park Notes*, covering all aspects of the park, are available at the desk. A *What's On* pamphlet has details of the informative ranger-led walks at many of the sites covered below, and the programme of evening slide shows at the caravan parks and resorts.

An innovative walk-through exhibition takes you through a condensed Kakadu habitat, passing across underfloor snakes and under a croc's belly. There's also a range of **videos**, shown near the main desk. A café and gift shop round off the facilities.

Accommodation

Within Kakadu there are resorts near the **South Alligator River** and at **Cooinda**, and a hotel and caravan park at **Jabiru**. There are also thirteen free basic camping areas in the park, some accessible only along deliberately unmaintained tracks where 4WD is best. There are also four better-equipped camping areas ($5.40 per person) at **Mardugal** near Cooinda, **Muirella Park** near Nourlangie Rock, **Merl** at Ubirr and at **Gunlom**. In the Dry season, booking ahead at the Park HQ is advisable.

Aurora Kakadu Lodge and Caravan Park Jabiru ℡08/8979 2422, ℮kakadu@aurora-resorts .com.au. Caravan park (camping available) surrounding a grassed pool and bar area, with plain, four-bed, air-con rooms, shared facilities and basic kitchen (extra charge for linen). Close to Jabiru and Park HQ. Dorms ❶, rooms ❼

Aurora Kakadu Resort Arnhem Highway, 2.5km west of South Alligator Bridge ℡08/8979 0166, ℮kakadu@aurora-resorts.com.au. Attractively landscaped resort with café, restaurant, and pool area visited by birds and wallabies. Has its own Gungarre nature trail on the doorstep. Motel rooms with camping available. ❼

Gagudju Crocodile Holiday Inn Jabiru ℡08/8979 2800, ℉8979 2707, ℗www.gagudju

-crocodile.holiday-inn.com. Overpriced crocodile-shaped hotel popular with coach parties. ❼
Gagudju Lodge Cooinda ℡08/8979 0145, ℉8979 0148, ℗www.gagudjulodgecooinda .com.au. Well-positioned resort near Yellow Waters and Warradjan Cultural Centre; good campsite, decidedly cramped air-con cabins which are supposedly YHA, and motel units. Nightly all-the-veggies-you-can-add-to-your-meat/fish bistro from $16. Cabins ❶, motel units ❼
Kakadu Hostel Next to the Border Store near Ubirr ℡08/8979 2232. An old lodge past its prime but with all facilities; the cheapest bed in Kakadu but popular with mosquitoes too. Open all year subject to access. Dorms from $18, rooms ❸

Around the park

If your visit to Kakadu is short, seeing **Ubirr** or **Nourlangie Rock**, taking a **cruise** at Guluyambi or Yellow Waters and checking out the Bowali Visitors Centre or Warradjan Cultural Centre will give you a taste of the park, and can just about be fitted into a long day. However, you can easily spend a week visiting all the spots detailed below, ideally followed by a return visit six months later to observe the seasonal changes. All the following places are reached off the **Kakadu Highway** which runs southwest from Jabiru out of the park, joining the Stuart Highway at Pine Creek. Unless indicated, all roads below are sealed and so accessible to rental cars.

Jabiru and the Ranger Uranium Mine

JABIRU, a couple of kilometres east of the Park HQ, is a company town, originally built to serve Kakadu's uranium-mining leases before the park was established. There are four mine leases in the park (and another in Arnhemland) but only one or two are operating at present. As a result, Jabiru is less than half-full of mineworkers and park employees. There is a **tourist information centre** (℡08/8979 2548), a small **supermarket**, a takeaway, bakery, post office and Westpac bank, all found in the **shopping plaza**. You'll also find a **health and dental clinic** (τ08/8979 2018) and a swimming pool (daily 9am–7pm; $3).

Kakadu Air (τ1800 089 113) operates out of the airport (6km east of Jabiru), offering thirty-minute **scenic flights** along the escarpment and wetlands from $80. Helicopter rides cost from $145 for twenty minutes. From Kakadu Air's office you can also take a one-hour tour of **Ranger Uranium Mine**. However, the mine is nothing more than a pit, pipelines and mysterious-looking buildings where the ore is processed, while the tour itself is largely a public-relations litany.

Ubirr and the Guluyambi Cruise

The rock-galleries at **Ubirr**, 43km north of the Park HQ, illustrate the rich food resources of the wetlands. Fish, lizards, marsupials and the now-extinct Tasmanian tiger or thylacine are depicted, as well as stick-like Mimi spirits, mischievous beings said to inhabit cracks in the rock. The **Lookout** offers one of the park's most beautiful views across the East Alligator River to the rocky outcrops of Arnhemland and should not be missed, while the six-kilometre return **Rockholes Walk** along the East Alligator River is one of the few longish walks in the park – a good way to escape the crowds.

Right by the start of the Rockholes Walk you can take a ninety-minute **Guluyambi Cruise** ($30; 4 daily; τ1800 089 113) along the East Alligator River. A local Aboriginal guide takes you upstream to view the towering escarpment and rock paintings while demonstrating some canny bush trickery and even gives you a chance to set foot, albeit briefly, on Arnhemland. The dramatic scenery makes it an enjoyable, if not superior, alternative to the better-known Yellow Waters option at Cooinda and one of the most informative guided tours in the region.

Nourlangie Rock Area

Nourlangie Rock, Kakadu's most accessible and therefore most visited site, is 31km south of the Park HQ. It includes the **Anbangbang Rock Shelter**, where the dry ground preserves evidence of occupation stretching back twenty

---

Bushwalking in Kakadu

One of Kakadu's biggest disappointments is the lack of long-distance marked trails. A leaflet at the Park HQ lists twenty marked trails in the park, but most are short **nature trails**, such as the six-kilometre **Rockholes Walk** near Ubirr. Only the twelve-kilometre **Barrk Walk** – a three-hour trek (the sign claiming "allow 6–8 hours" can only exist to put people off) through Nourlangie Rock's backcountry – offers any challenge: a half-hour slog up the rock which you then cross, descend and circumnavigate. Although the trail is marked, it should not be undertaken lightly and is best done in the cool of early morning. No less energetic is the little-advertised two-hour walk up to the top of **Jim Jim Falls** for fine views across the escarpment (the scramble to the top of nearby Twin Falls having been closed).

In the often-overlooked southwest of the park near Gunlom, the **Yurmikmik** area on the edge of the escarpment offers a similar challenge in the unmarked **Motor Car Creek Walk** (11km) and **Motor Car and Kurrundie Creek Circle Walk** (14km; overnight stop recommended). Ask for the *Yurmikmik Park Notes* at the visitors centre. You're more than likely to have the faint track to yourself.

Experienced bushwalkers can apply to Park HQ with proposed itineraries, which need to be approved before a permit is given. Willis Walkabouts (τ08/8985 2134) in Darwin organizes extended bushwalks up in the escarpment country.

thousand years; dimples on boulders show where ochre was ground and then mixed with blood for painting. The **Anbangbang Gallery**, nearby, depicts the dramatic figures of Nabulwinjbulwinj, Namarrgon (the Lightning Man) and his wife Barrkinj. Unusually vivid, they were in fact repainted (a traditional and sometimes ritual practice) between 1963 and 1964 over similar but faded designs. The **Lookout** over the Arnhemland escarpment, to the home of Namarrgon, is also the beginning of the twelve-kilometre **Barrk Walk** (see box p.639). Other places in the Nourlangie Rock area, all signposted, and marked in the *Visitors' Guide*, include **Nanguluwur**, a less popular but fascinating art site 1.5km from the Nourlangie car park, which includes images from the Contact period when Aborigines first encountered explorers and settlers. **Nawulandja Lookout** has views onto the imposing hulk of Nourlangie Rock itself, which looms over **Anbangbang Billabong**, a *Crocodile Dundee* location. During the Dry, a two-and-a-half-kilometre track circumvents the billabong.

Gubara or Burdulba Springs, an unsealed 13km off the Nourlangie road, is a string of small pools along a palm-shaded creek, itself a hot forty-minute walk from the car park.

Jim Jim Falls and Twin Falls

Although over 100km south of Park HQ, ending along a slow bumpy track, these two falls are definitely worth visiting, especially the latter. Allow two hours for the sixty-kilometre drive from the Kakadu Highway or get an operator like *Kakadu Gorge and Waterfall Tours* to take you there for the day (T08/8979 0145; around $130) from Jabiru or Cooinda. **Jim Jim Falls** tip 215m straight off the escarpment and are best caught in the early Dry, as soon as the road reopens – they stop flowing later and will certainly look less impressive. A rocky, one-kilometre trail leads alongside the large pool to the base of the falls and a new track leads up to the top, but it's quite a slog – ask at the Bowali Centre.

Twin Falls is a bumpy and sandy ten-kilometre drive from Jim Jim and includes the crossing of Jim Jim Creek, which genuinely does require a 4WD and not just high clearance. The base has been cobbled but it's subsiding and should be taken extremely slowly. From the Twin Falls car park it's a short walk and then a swim up the gorge for another kilometre – an airbed or waterproof containers help here (most day tours supply these, or even canoes). This little bit of adventure is rewarded by the sight of Twin Falls cascading into a pool edged by an idyllic sandy beach, a beautiful and now very popular spot to while away the day. The climb up the vegetated gully to the top is no longer allowed but some tour guides have found a way to the top by a less severe path from the car park.

Yellow Waters and the Warradjan Aboriginal Cultural Centre

As Jim Jim Creek begins meandering into the flood plains close to the Cooinda resort, 50km southwest of Jabiru, it forms the inland lagoon of **Yellow Waters**. From the car park here, a short walk leads along the edge of the billabong, from where popular **cruises** (5 daily; book in advance on T08/8979 0145) weave through the lushly vegetated waterways. The early morning cruise (2hr; $28) catches the lagoon and wildlife at their best: heat-of-the-day tours are thirty minutes shorter and a few dollars cheaper.

The turtle-shaped **Warradjan Aboriginal Cultural Centre** (daily 9am–5pm), on the Cooinda access road, offers unusually designed interpretive displays on the culture and lore of the local Aborigines, together with an arts and crafts shop. Interesting though it is, it has to be said that the display is not particularly effective at communicating its message and, unless you have some previous understanding of Aboriginal culture, you've forgotten much of what you've seen soon after leaving.

Barramundie Gorge, Gunlom and other beauty spots

Robust cars can manage the twelve-kilometre corrugated track from the Kakadu Highway to **Barramundie Gorge** (also known as Maguk), the best of Kakadu's few swimming holes, 57km southwest of Cooinda. From the car park, a path leads along the creek to the large pool, possibly still the home of a harassed freshie; for its sake rather than yours, keep away from the left bank. The top of the waterfall and more rock pools can be reached by clambering up the tree roots to the right of the falls.

Gunlom (also known as Waterfall Creek) is another *Crocodile Dundee* location, on a corrugated track 36km off the Kakadu Highway, close to the park's southwestern exit. Although the falls don't flow all year, it's a lovely paperbark-shaded swimming spot, and as you can camp here comfortably it's well worth the diversion if entering or leaving via Pine Creek (if your car can take it). The steep path to the top of the falls reveals still more pools inviting you for a dip.

A right turn at the junction that leads to Gunlom follows on through Koolpin Creek to a locked gate and **Koolpin** or **Jarrangbammi Gorge**. The key is available, if you leave a $50 deposit, from the Southern Entry Station (☎08/8975 4859) on the Pine Creek road, but you must also get a permit from Parks HQ which limits the number of visitors to forty vehicles per day. The track to the gorge crosses the creek again and requires 4WD. You can camp here or follow the escarpment on foot to the northwest for 3km to the narrow chasm of **Freezing Gorge** which, you'll be pleased to discover, lives up to its name. Five kilometres past the locked gate is Gutatba, a picnic site on the South Alligator River. Also known as Coronation Hill, this is the site of a former uranium mine. To local Jawoyn Aborigines this area is traditionally "Sickness Country", suggesting that even in its natural state uranium proved harmful to human health.

Arnhemland

ARNHEMLAND is essentially the continuation of Kakadu east to the Gulf of Carpentaria but without the infrastructure. Never colonized and too rough to graze, it was designated an Aboriginal reserve in 1931 and has stayed in Aboriginal hands since that time. Individual tourist access is virtually impossible and by and large, the three thousand Aborigines who live here, whose supplies come in by sea or air, like it that way. Little disturbed for over forty thousand years, Arnhemland like Kakadu features thousands of unseen rock-art sites and burial grounds.

In 1963 the Yirrkala of northwestern Arnhemland appealed against the proposed mining of bauxite on their land. It was the first such protest of its kind, and included the presentation of sacred artefacts as well as a petition in the form of a bark painting to the government in Canberra. Although it didn't help in this particular case, their actions brought the issue of Aboriginal land rights to the public eye and paved the way for subsequent successful land claims.

The **Northern Land Council** (Darwin ☎08/8920 5100; Jabiru ☎08/8979 2410) issues free permits to drive the 4WD Central Arnhem Road but only allows a maximum of fifteen tourist vehicles in at any one time. The only major settlement is **NHULUNBUY**, also known as Gove, in the northeast corner, a mining town of little appeal to tourists. Most visitors are fishermen heading up to **Smith Point** on the Cobourg Peninsula (see below), an approved destination for which permits are booked up months in advance. Arhhemland has the allure of a forbidden and mysterious place offering a potentially authentic Aboriginal experience. It's something that tour operators have capitalized on and prices reflect this exclusivity. Billy Can Tours (☎1800 813 484, ⓦwww .billycan.com.au) drives you out and flies you back for a five-day tour of Arnhemland costing $2185 per person twin share. Davidson's Arnhemland Safaris (☎08/8927 5240, ⓦwww.arnhemland-safaris.com) is another established operator offering expensive tours in the Mount Borradaile area for at least $600 a day with flights. Lord's Kakadu (☎08/8979 2970, ⓔlords @austrarnet.com.au) offers a day-hop into Arnhemland from the Border Store in Kakadu just so you can say you've been there. Highly recommended is the Dreamtime Safari visiting central Arnhemland from Katherine (see p.651).

The Cobourg Peninsula

The **Cobourg Peninsula** – encompassing the **Gurig National Park** and **Cobourg Marine Park** – is a largely inaccessible headland clinging to northwestern Arnhemland by a slender isthmus. Although you have to drive through Arnhemland to get there, the peninsula is not part of the Aboriginal-owned reserve. With the failure of Fort Dundas on nearby Melville Island, the British tried again to establish a foothold, first at **Raffles Bay** and later at **Port Essington** (from 1838 to 1849), where the explorer Ludwig Leichhardt arrived in 1844 after his epic overland trek from Moreton Bay in Queensland. Port Essington was abandoned after eleven years due to malarial epidemics, harassment by Aborigines and Indonesian pirates, and – more tellingly – the peninsula's severe climatic extremes, being hotter and wetter than anywhere else in the Territory.

On the peninsula is **Seven Spirit Bay** (☎03/9826 2471, ⓦwww.seven spiritbay.com), an exclusive low-key eco-resort reached by boat or light aircraft offering five-star service and cuisine, with various activities at your disposal. At over $390 per person per night for twin-share habitats (minimum, and flights cost extra), it's the place to politely ignore film stars trying to get away from it all. Alternatively, you can visit this area under your own steam with a 4WD. It's about 260km from the Border Store in Kakadu to **Smith Point**, where you will find *Cobourg Beach Huts* (☎08 8979 0030, ⓦwww.cobourg.gurig.com.au; ❻) on the other side of the inlet from *Seven Spirit Bay*. You can get fuel and check in with the ranger at the Gurig Store at **Black Point** (daily 3–5pm; ☎08/8979 0263).

Along the Stuart Highway

From Darwin the **Stuart Highway** passes early mining and pastoral outposts and is bordered intermittently by overgrown, but still commemorated, airstrips dating from World War II. Along its length are a number of attractions which can be visited either as excursions from Darwin or as diversions on the journey to Katherine, 320km to the south. On the **bus** (or the train when it starts operating) don't expect to get to any of the places off the Highway without organizing local transport.

Darwin Crocodile Farm

South of the Arnhem Highway turn-off, 40km from Darwin, is the **Darwin Crocodile Farm** (daily 10am–4pm; $12) where crocodiles are both studied and bred for their skins and meat as they are at Crocodylus Park near Darwin (see p.626). The lucky ones get scarred at an early age, rendering themselves unsuitable for conversion into belts and handbags and become breeding stock.

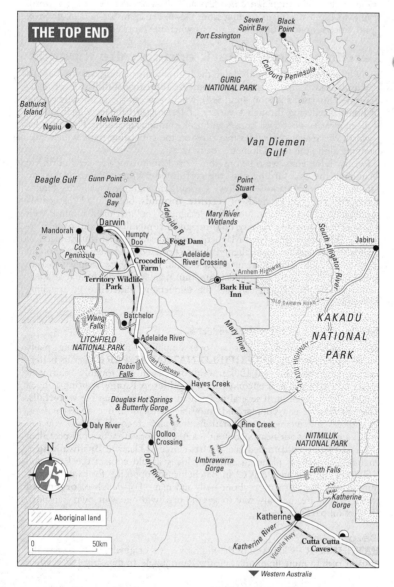

THE TOP END

Seven Spirit Bay
Black Point
Port Essington
Cobourg Peninsula
GURIG NATIONAL PARK

Bathurst Island
Nguiu
Melville Island

Van Diemen Gulf

Beagle Gulf
Gunn Point
Shoal Bay
Point Stuart
Mandorah
Darwin
Humpty Doo
Adelaide R.
Mary River Wetlands
Cox Peninsula
Fogg Dam
Crocodile Farm
Adelaide River Crossing
Arnhem Highway
South Alligator River
Jabiru
Territory Wildlife Park
Bark Hut Inn
OLD DARWIN ROAD
Wangi Falls
Batchelor
KAKADU NATIONAL PARK
LITCHFIELD NATIONAL PARK
Adelaide River
Mary River
Robin Falls
Stuart Highway
Hayes Creek
KAKADU HIGHWAY
Douglas Hot Springs & Butterfly Gorge
Daly River
Oolloo Crossing
Pine Creek
NITMILUK NATIONAL PARK
Daly River
Umbrawarra Gorge
Edith Falls
N
Katherine Gorge
Aboriginal land
Katherine
Cutta Cutta Caves
0   50km
Katherine River
Victoria Hwy

Western Australia

Rogue crocs that harass local communities, as well as the sixty-odd caught annually in the traps around Darwin Harbour, are also relocated here. If you haven't been to Crocodylus Park in Darwin, this is a good place to learn the difference between salties, freshies and alligators. Besides, nowhere else could you get as close to such a monster as Burt, the five-metre star of *Crocodile Dundee*, and live to tell the tale.

Souvenirs (including photo opportunities to cradle baby salties) and croc burgers are available at the shop, and **guided tours** set off on the hour, when some of the eight thousand crocodiles and alligators also get fed. It's worth trying to catch the main feeding time (Mon–Fri 2pm, Sat & Sun noon & 2pm), since it's one of the few occasions when the crocs actually move.

Territory Wildlife Park and termite mounds

Eight kilometres further south down the highway, the turning west to the Cox Peninsula leads to the four-square-kilometre **Territory Wildlife Park** (daily 8.30am–6pm, last admission 4pm; $18), where you can spend a happy couple of hours wandering through a variety of Territorian habitats, which include walk-in aviaries, nocturnal houses and walk-through aquariums. The entry fee – worth every cent – includes free rides on the circulating train, which saves trudging along the four-kilometre roadway.

Twenty kilometres west before the Cox Peninsula road veers north to Mandorah there's a turning onto the corrugated northern approach track to Litchfield National Park (see below). Crossing through the usually dry Finniss River, this track passes fields of **termite mounds**, both fluted "cathedral" mounds, up to 4m high, and so-called "magnetic" or "meridian" mounds. Not often seen in the same vicinity, both designs accomplish their aim of regulating the internal temperature. Magnetic mounds are unusual things: made of digested grass, they're always aligned along a polar axis, and were once thought to be in tune with the earth's magnetic field. In fact, they are arranged so as to present a knife edge to the midday sun, thus maintaining the habitat at a termite-preferred 30°C; you can feel the temperature difference by touching either side of the mound.

Litchfield National Park

"Kaka-don't, Litchfield-do" is an over-simplified quip expressing many people's preference for **LITCHFIELD NATIONAL PARK** over its better-known neighbour. Situated 100km south of Darwin, and roughly 16km west of the Stuart Highway, it encompasses the **Tabletop Range**, a spring-fringed plateau from which gush several permanent and easily accessible **waterfalls**. The whole park is a popular and enjoyable destination, free of restrictions, long drives and intangible expectations. It is also crocodile-free, so you can splash around to your heart's content – a much more attractive prospect than some of the sterile dammed lake resorts closer to Darwin. **Bushwalking** is encouraged: walkers planning extended hikes should contact the Parks and Wildlife Commission (P&WC) in Batchelor (see opposite) for camping permits, as well as information about trails and maps. For details of **organized tours**, which are the only way to see the park without your own transport, see box on p.627.

Batchelor

BATCHELOR – 8km west of the highway – was originally built to serve the postwar rush to mine uranium at nearby Rum Jungle. In the early 1970s, when large-scale mining ceased, the townsfolk managed to resist Rum Jungle's closure. The establishment of the national park in the 1980s gave the town a new lease of life, though don't expect much here; just about the only sight of note is a replica of the Gothic **Karlstein Castle**, next to the police station, built by a homesick Czech immigrant. The local **P&WC** (T08/8976 0282) gives out information on Litchfield National Park. There are a couple of **caravan parks** around Batchelor, but **camping** in the park is generally more appealing (some of the best sites are detailed in the text below). For those who don't want to rough it, try the *Rum Jungle Motor Inn* (T08/8976 0123, F8976 0230; **5**), on Rum Jungle Road in Batchelor, a comfortable **motel** with a decent restaurant, or the *Jungle Drum Bungalows* (T08/8976 0555, Wwww.jungledrumbungalows.com.au; **4**) nearby, which have cabin-style rooms to yourself or to share between four.

Into the park

There's no admission fee to enter the park, and no visitors centre either, so get all the information you need (including a map) from the P&WC at the visitors centre in Darwin or Batchelor. Heading into the park from Batchelor you'll pass black-soil plains dotted with grey, tombstone-like termite mounds. **Buley Rock Holes**, down a right turn, 38km from Batchelor, are nothing more than a couple of rock pools, but a five-kilometre trail follows the creek from here to **Florence Falls**. A high lookout surveys the twenty-metre falls, which can be reached along a path leading from the car park down to the plunge pool. There's not much room to spread out picnics, but the water is beautifully cool, and a 4WD track leads back to the Batchelor road. **Camping** is permitted at both the rock holes and the falls.

The **Lost City**, off the main road through the park, 6km after the Florence Falls turn-off, is a jumble of unusually weathered sandstone columns. These are interesting enough in themselves, but getting to them is the real highlight, as they're at the end of an increasingly difficult, eight-kilometre 4WD track which should not be visited in rented vehicles unless you know how to drive over steep rock steps without damage. The rarely used track, which continues on to Blyth Homestead and Sandy Creek (see below for more on these – and an easier way of getting to them), gets trickier still after the Lost City. Back on the main road through the park, the pool below **Tolmer Falls** is closed to the public, to grant the rare orange horseshoe bat some seclusion. However, the long, slender falls can be appreciated from a fine lookout (signposted off the main road). A two-kilometre path leads from here to an area of pools and minor cascades at the top of the falls, which are swimable in the Wet, before heading back to the car park.

From the park road a track leads south to **Blyth Homestead** and **Sandy Creek** (aka Tjaynera Falls). The abandoned homestead adds some token historic interest to the park, while Sandy Creek (accessible by 4WD only) is a series of falls and a pool surrounded by rainforest, with a **campsite** less than 2km away. From Sandy Creek, the 4WD track continues (with several steep creek crossings) to the Reynolds River – back in crocodile country – and halfway between Daly River (see p.646) and the Stuart Highway.

Green Ant Creek is the latest destination carved out of the bush. From the car park by the road a stiff one-hour return walk leads to the top of **Tjaetaba Falls**, with a pool to cool off in right on the lip of the cascade.

The park's most popular waterfall, with easy access to tree-shaded lawns and a large pool, is **Wangi Falls**, 55km east of Batchelor. There is a sun-warmed natural spa pool near the base of the left-hand cascade, once a sacred site for

Aboriginal women and forbidden to men. Strangely enough, several men, including some trying to save drowning women, have perished at Wangi; trilingual signs now warn of the danger, and the pool closes in the Wet when abnormal **undertows** develop. A trail leads through a rainforest boardwalk (the initial section of which is wheelchair-accessible), up over the falls and down the other side via a **lookout** – a good way to work off lunch. Wangi tends to get overcrowded at weekends and in school holidays, since it has the best-equipped **campsite** in the park.

A corrugated dirt road leads north from Wangi out of the park, past *Pethericks Rain Forest* (waterfalls and quiet **camping**) and across the Finniss River (where "Sweetheart" the crocodile once roamed before falling prey to the taxidermist at the museum in Darwin) and on to the Territory Wildlife Park.

Adelaide River and the Daly River Region

Established during the construction of the Overland Telegraph Line, the town of **ADELAIDE RIVER** was the supply head for Darwin's defence during World War II and consequently suffered sporadic Japanese bombing after 1942. Today the town, 110km south of Darwin, provides little more than a lunch-stop along the Stuart Highway, or you could visit the town's **war cemetery** where many of the victims of the air raids are buried. Officially, 243 people died as a result of the eighteen months of Japanese bombing, which began in February 1942, but the cemetery has twice as many graves. The *Mobil Roadhouse* has **camping**, or try the *Adelaide River Inn* for rooms, dorms and a **restaurant**.

Just south of town, the old highway forks west along a rolling 75-kilometre **scenic drive** before rejoining the main road at *Hayes Creek* roadhouse. After the first 17km you'll come to the turn-off for **Robin Falls**, a pretty little cascade reached after a ten-minute scramble up the creek bed from the car park, while a further 17km marks the turn-off for Daly River.

The Daly River Region

A quiet backwater, 120km southwest of Adelaide River, the **Daly River Region** is best known as an excellent fishing spot. Apart from a twenty-kilometre section, the road is sealed all the way from the highway to the Aboriginal community of **DALY RIVER** (Nauiyu) – beyond that it's dirt in all directions. It wasn't always so pleasant: in 1884, local Aborigines killed four copper miners. The *Northern Territory News* was apoplectic with indignation, but calmed down enough to reassure its readers that "the right class of men are now on the tracks of the Daly River natives, but we do not expect to hear many particulars of their chase; the less said the better". Two years of punitive "bush riding" followed until the Wilwonga Aborigines were all but wiped out.

There are no banks or shops here, but you'll find **accommodation** spread out along both sides of the river. The pick of the crop is the *Daly River Mango Farm* (℡08/8978 2464), signposted a few kilometres over the causeway and offering cabins (❹), safari tents with linen (❷) as well as a pool, small bistro, dinghy rental, river cruises and "24-hour power", something to boast about in these parts. Its most outstanding feature, however, is the stand of mature **mango trees** which arch over the whole compound like the vaulting of a Gothic cathedral; in season you'll be woken repeatedly by the thud of mangoes dropping onto the tin roofs. Another good place to stay is the *Woolianna Tourist Park* (℡08/8978 2478; cabins ❹), on the other side of the river about 30km downstream, with more boats to rent, a pool and **camping**, while the main attraction at the *Daly River Roadside Inn* (℡08/8978 2418; ❹), in what might be called the "town centre", is a four-metre-long pet saltie called Boris.

Douglas Hot Springs and Butterfly Gorge

Back on the scenic route from Adelaide River, a turn-off leads 35km south-west to **Douglas (Tjuwaliyn) Hot Springs**, where water bubbles at 40°C out of the sandy creek bed – very agreeable, but often crowded during school holidays. **Camping** costs just $4, but you'll need to collect your firewood on the way in, as the nearby woods have been picked clean. From the springs, a 4WD track leads another 17km to the secluded **Butterfly Gorge**. When you can drive no further, follow the creek upstream on foot, past massive paperbarks and over rocky outcrops to the beautiful, orange-walled gorge and sandy beach. Here you can swim in several rock pools.

Pine Creek and around

Site of the Territory's first goldrush, the small town of **PINE CREEK**, 230km from Darwin, has retained its colonial appearance, making it an unusually appealing stop along the highway. Gold was discovered while digging holes for the Overland Telegraph Line pylons in 1871, and fools rushed in, hoping to pan their way to fortune. Unfortunately the gold was in the rock, not the riverbeds, requiring laborious crushing with heavy stamp batteries, which, for most prospectors, was too much like hard work for unpredictable returns. The subsequent labour shortage was solved by importing Chinese workers who kept the progressively poorer-quality ore coming for a couple of years until fears of Asian dominance (the Chinese labourers outnumbered Europeans eight-to-one by this time) led to their being banned from the Territory in 1888, a shot in the foot for gold production. A modern gold mine now goes at it hammer and tongs, as new technology extracts the remaining deposits.

Around the town, the various time-worn buildings, such as the 1889 **Old Playford Hotel** and **Old Bakery**, may lead you to contemplate the crucial role of corrugated iron, or "galvo", in the pioneering colonial process. The **Miners Park**, at the northern end of town, displays the crude mining hardware from a hundred years ago and there's a **museum** (Mon–Fri 1–5pm; $2) on Railway Terrace, near the police station, and an old locomotive on the old train station itself. For accommodation there's a **caravan park** with camping, or the *Pine Creek Diggers Rest Motel* (℡08/8976 1442, ℻8976 1458; ❹) on Main Street and the *Pine Creek Backpackers* at the back of town on Wilcox Street (℡08/8976 1076; dorms $20). **Places to eat** amount to the pub and the *Hard Rock Café*, presumably an ore-crushing pun, next to it. Ah Toys general store on Main Terrace is still run by the descendants of its original Chinese owner.

From Pine Creek it's 200km along the sealed **Kakadu Highway** to Jabiru, in the heart of Kakadu National Park, passing the majority of the park's highlights on the way (see pp.633–641). At **Umbrawarra Gorge**, 22km southwest of Pine Creek along a corrugated track with several dry creek crossings, you can camp and walk up the shaded gorge which has pools throughout the year. **Edith Falls**, however, halfway to Katherine, 20km east of the highway, are more impressive. It's also possible to walk to Katherine Gorge from here, along a 66-kilometre trail (see p.652).

CONSERVATION COMMISSION

NORTHERN   TERRITORY

△ Crocodile warning

Katherine to Alice

An obligatory stopover (at least for a couple of days) for visitors to the Top End, **Katherine** is a small but rapidly growing regional centre on the southern banks of the Katherine River. It's just 30km to **Katherine Gorge**, the town's primary tourist attraction and itself part of the larger **Nitmiluk National Park**.

West of Katherine, the **Victoria Highway** leads for 500km west to the WA border, passing Timber Creek and the entrance to **Gregory National Park** on the way. South of town is a vast touristic no-man's-land until you reach Alice. A dip in **Mataranka**'s thermal pool and a couple of "bush pubs" are the highlights of the 670km to **Tennant Creek**. South of Tennant Creek, only the rotund boulders of the **Devil's Marbles** brighten the string of roadhouses along the Stuart Highway, which stretches for just over 500km to Alice Springs.

Katherine

Traditionally home of the Jawoyn and Dagoman people, the **Katherine River** area must have been a sight for explorer John McDouall Stuart's sore eyes as he struggled north in 1862. Having reached here, he named the river after a benefactor's daughter, Catherine, and within ten years the completion of the Overland Telegraph Line (OTL) encouraged European settlement, as drovers and prospectors converged on the first reliable water north of Alice Springs. In 1926 a railway from Darwin finally spanned the river and "Kathrhyne", as the die-hard locals still call the town of **KATHERINE**, became established on its present site. It's essentially a "one-street" town, with Tennant Creek the only other place of consequence in the 1500km between Darwin and Alice.

The flood of '98

As you cross the road bridge into Katherine from the north you'll pass a height scale on the redundant rail bridge alongside. The scale ends at 18m above the river but by the evening of January 26, 1998, following an Australia Day few in the town will forget, the engorged Katherine river peaked at a record 20.5m.

This staggering volume of water was the result of **two cyclones** dumping their load over southern Arnhemland – a Wet season's worth of rain dropped over a few days – and was exacerbated by a king tide from the Timor Sea which backed up the water inland. Just about every business in town was under 2m of water, four lives were lost and a crocodile was spotted cruising lazily past the semi-submerged Woolworths. Within two days the waters dropped away as quickly as they had risen and the evacuated townsfolk returned to their ruined homes and businesses to begin the clean-up. Knee-high silt was shovelled out of shops and motel rooms, while the stench of rotting food and drowned cattle enveloped the town. And yet, with voluntary help from other communities and government aid, the town was on its feet within just a couple of weeks.

Recent years have seen erratic but **record Wets** in the Top End – partly the consequence of La Niña, El Niño's less well-known deluge-bringing sibling.

Arrival, information and transport

The **airport** is 8km south of town; a **taxi** from there to Katherine will cost about $20 (℡08/8972 1777 or 8972 1999). All buses arrive at the **Transit Centre**, at 6 Katherine Terrace (daily 7.30am–6.30pm; ℡08/8972 1044), next to the 24-hour *BP Roadhouse*. Katherine is a busy interchange for buses, with at least one daily arrival or departure for Darwin, Kununurra (WA) and Alice Springs. Just over the road you'll find the **tourist information centre** (Mon–Fri 8.30am–6pm, Sat & Sun 10am–3pm; ℡1800 653 142, ⓦkrol.com.au) with shelves groaning with leaflets. For more detailed information on Nitmiluk, Gregory and Keep River national parks call in at the **Parks and Wildlife Commission** on Giles Street, just over a kilometre from town, past O'Shea Terrace (℡08/8973 8770). There's **Internet** at the Katherine Art Gallery at 12 Katherine Terrace and also at the better-equipped Didj Café round the corner. Alternatively, you'll always find a free machine at the *Katherine River Lodge*, 2km up the road to the gorge.

To **rent a car** call Thrifty (℡08/8972 3183), Hertz Rent-A-Car (℡08/8971 1111) or Delta Car Rentals (℡13 13 90). **Bikes** can be rented from most accommodation.

Accommodation

Thanks to the immense popularity of Katherine Gorge, there's plenty of choice for places to stay in town. The tourist information centre provides a list and current prices of all the town's accommodation; the best options and all the hostels are detailed below.

Motels

Beagle Motor Inn 2 Fourth St ℡08/8972 3998, ⓕ8972 3725. The best choice for a cheap motel in town. ❸
Mercure Inn Katherine Stuart Highway ℡08/8972 1744, ⓔmercurekatherine@bigpond.com.au. Good-value resort 4km south of town, with pool, bar and restaurant. ❺
Paraway Motel Cnr O'Shea and First streets ℡08/8972 2644, ⓕ8972 2720. The most comfortable motel in the town centre. ❹

Hostels

Kookaburra Lodge Cnr Lindsay and Third streets ℡08/8971 0257 or 1800 808 211, ⓦwww.kookaburrabackpackers.com.au. Well-converted motel units in spacious grounds with eight-bed air-con dorms and twins, making this Katherine's best backpackers' choice. Also table tennis, free breakfast, small pool and Transit Centre drop-offs. Dorms from $19, rooms ❸
Palm Court Backpackers Cnr Giles and Third

streets ℡08/8972 2722 or 1800 626 722, ⓦwww.travelnorth.com.au. Old motel with a cramped kitchen and small pool. Dorms are mostly four-bed with fridge and en suite; when they're full it's up to nine per room. Free breakfast and 20min use of the Internet. Dorms from $19, rooms ❸
Victoria Lodge 21 Victoria Highway ℡1800 808 875, ⓔvictorialodge@bigpond.com. Post-flood renovations make this place better than expected, with eight- and four-bed dorms, plus twins. Dorms from $18, rooms ❸

Caravan parks

Katherine Low Level Shadforth Rd ℡08/8972 3962. Close to the Low Level Nature Reserve, with plenty of shady, grassed sites. Cabins ❺
Knotts Crossing Resort 4km down Giles Rd. Well-appointed resort with all sorts of cabins and units, motel rooms and camping. Cabins ❺
Nitmiluk Gorge Caravan Park Nitmiluk National Park ℡08/8972 3150, ⓦwww.travelnorth.com.au. Right by the gorges but 30km from Katherine. Makes a good base for exploring the park on foot.

The Town and around

The Stuart Highway becomes **Katherine Terrace**, the main street, as it passes through town. Along it lie most of the shops and services, including a big

Woolworths, as well as a surprising number of galleries proferring anything from traditional Aboriginal to modern art, giving Katherine a compact – and unexpectedly busy – feel. The **Railway Museum** (Mon–Fri 1–3pm; $2), housed in the old station on Railway Terrace, isn't really worth the bother. If you want the full story on the town head 3km up Giles Street to the **Katherine Museum** (Mon–Fri 10am–4pm, Sun 2–5pm; $6), just before the old town site at Knotts Crossing, where a few original OTL pylons still remain upright. Inside are displays relating to Katherine's colonial history, including early medical instruments and a biplane from the time when the building did duty as a Flying Doctor base.

Three kilometres down Victoria Highway are some decidedly **warm springs** first right after the *Red Gum Caravan Park*. From here, it's just a short walk to the **Low Level Nature Park**, a pleasant spot for a stroll, swim or canoe along the pandanus-fringed river, seasonal floods permitting. **Springvale Homestead**, at the end of Shadforth Road, 8km west of the town centre, is a tourist resort based around the oldest homestead in the Territory, built in 1884. The station was at one time run by Ted Ronan, a writer of the wry and romantic school, who helped mythologize the Outback with novels such as *Vision Splendid*. There are free, half-hourly tours of the homestead (May–Oct daily 10am & 2pm).

Cutta Cutta Caves, 27km south of town, offer guided tours (hourly 9–11am & 1–3pm; closed at the height of the Wet; $9.50; ☎08/8972 1940) of the Limestone Cave and Cutta Cutta. These caves display extraordinary subterranean karst features as diverse as they are delicate. Cutta Cutta is the more visually impressive and is also the home of the rare orange horseshoe bat and rather alarming stalactite-climbing brown snakes. A bus leaves daily for the caves at 9am from outside the tourist information centre, returning at 11.30am ($20).

Eating, drinking and nightlife

With the gradual improvement in tourist services it is no longer mandatory to go to a hotel to get a good feed, which is just as well, because the pubs' front **bars** are rough and sometimes rowdy places.

Tours from Katherine

Campbells Trail Rides (☎08/8972 1394) and **Brumby Tracks** (☎08/8972 1425) both offer horse rides from a few hours to a few days.

Dreamtime Safari ☎08/8975 4277, ℻8975 4277. Two days and three nights based in a remote but well-appointed Central Arnhemland bushcamp with a guide who's lived among the Aboriginal people since the 1980s. Thought-provoking and forthright, it raises issues rather than distracts you with bush lore. Special backpacker deals via the YHA in Darwin (see p.623).

Gecko Canoe Tours ☎1300 555 542. Two- to twelve-day canoeing trips on the Katherine River downstream of town costing around $310 per day. Suitable for beginners and in many ways far more satisfying than the rather crowded Katherine Gorge.

Kakadu Tours ☎1800 808 211. Katherine to Darwin over three days, all the sights including Twin Falls and no back tracking for $370.

Manyallaluk ☎08/8975 4727. Long-established Aboriginal culture tours; a fun day out with didge playing, painting, spear throwing and fire lighting, all for $132 or $99 self-drive.

Restaurants and cafés

Buchanan's *Paraway Motel,* cnr O'Shea and First streets ☎ 08/8972 2644. Sharing the honours, with *Mercure Inn,* as the best restaurant in town. Around $22 a head.
Croc Room *Beagle Motor Inn,* 2 Fourth St ☎ 08/8972 3998. Serves up its namesake, baked,

at moderate prices.
Jade Café Katherine Terrace. One of the few lunch spots in town, serving wholesome snacks.
Mercure Inn Stuart Highway, 4km south of town. Eat your heart out from an à la carte menu of steak and seafood for $20–25 a meal.

Nitmiluk National Park

The central attraction of the **Nitmiluk National Park** is the magnificent twelve-kilometre **Katherine Gorge**, carved by the Katherine River through the Arnhemland plateau. Often described as thirteen gorges, it is in fact one continuous cleft, turning left and right along fault lines and separated during the Dry season by rock bars. The spectacle of the river, hemmed in by orange cliffs, makes for a wonderful **cruise** or canoe trip and, unlike Kakadu, Nitmiluk also welcomes bushwalkers along its many marked **trails**.

Travel North (☎ 1800 089 103) operates **shuttle buses** along the sealed road between Katherine and the gorge for $19 return. Once at the gorge the **Park Visitors Centre** (daily 8am–7pm) has interpretive displays on the park's features from the local Jawoyn Aborigines' perspective (they own the park), and provides maps and further information on the trails, including the *Guide to Nitmiluk National Park* ($6.55) with topographical walking maps. It also includes a restaurant, gallery and a model of the gorge system which puts it all in perspective. As you sit on the terrace overlooking the river below, consider that in January 1998 you would have been under a metre of water.

Bushwalks include the 66-kilometre **hike to Edith Falls**, in the park's northwestern corner, for which you'll need at least three days, a minimum of two people and a $50 returnable deposit. The falls drop to a large, forest-encircled pool in three stages, around which an adventurous five-kilometre loop **walk** has been completed. You can **camp** at the falls.

Away from the gorge itself, the terrain is rough and very dry; be sure to wear sturdy footwear and a hat, and carry plenty of water. As a safety precaution, all walkers must **register** ($3.30; overnight stays $20 refundable deposit) with the rangers at the visitors centre: those on day-hikes must check in again by 6pm.

Exploring Katherine Gorge

Buses from Katherine terminate at the new canoe ramp and jetty designed to save canoeists tangling with the cruise boats heading **up the gorge**. Tickets for cruises are sold at the visitors centre. They've also sorted out safe swimming access, too, and you'll be pleased to know that saltwater crocs are virtually unknown in the gorge. While waiting for a cruise, you might want to take the steep, four-hundred-metre walk leading from the jetty to a superb clifftop **lookout** up the river (no need to register for this short walk).

Cruises ply the gorge in a series of boats. Travel North (☎ 1800 089 103) offers somewhat rushed two-hour cruises to the second gorge for $37, a four-hour cruise to the third gorge (the limit during the Wet season, when a more powerful jet boat is brought in) for $53, and an eight-hour "safari", which includes some rock-hopping that demands secure footwear, for around $92. The relaxed safari cruise includes a barbecue lunch, refreshments, plenty of time for swimming and a peep at the sixth gorge; it gets away from the rather busy downstream sections and is highly recommended. There are also exhilarating **helicopter flights** up the gorge from as little as $60 per person for fifteen minutes (☎08/8972 1253).

Canoeing up the gorge is an option for the more energetic, but don't expect to paddle up to the "thirteenth" in a day; canoeing is hard work for unaccustomed arms and shoulders, especially against the breeze which wafts down the gorge, but is a definite alternative to the sedate cruises. Nitmiluk Tours (☎1800 089 103) rents solo canoes for $41 a day, $29 per half-day – add about fifty percent for two-person canoes (easier to control and a shared load for beginners). Waterproof containers are provided. The rental period is 8.30am to 4.45pm; overnight trips cost a bit less than an extra day's rental. Alternatively, put your own canoe on the river, for a small fee payable at the visitors centre. Expect long sections of canoe-carrying over boulders and successively shorter sections of water as you progress up the gorges. Those determined to reach the thirteenth gorge (which, scenically speaking, is not really worthwhile) will find it easier to leave the canoe at the fifth and swim/walk the last couple of kilometres.

The first permissible overnight **campsite** is Smith's Rock in the fifth gorge (or anywhere upstream from there) – this is regarded as a fair day's paddling and portaging. The best time to canoe the gorge is early in the Dry season, when small waterfalls run off cliff walls and the water level is still high enough to reduce the length of the walking sections.

The Victoria Highway to Western Australia

The **Victoria Highway** stretches for 510km southwest of Katherine to Kununurra in Western Australia. South of the highway is the legendary **Victoria River Downs (VRD) station** once the country's biggest cattle station. Known colloquially as the "Big Run", VRD was established in the great droving days of the 1880s when mobs of cattle were driven overland from Queensland over several months or even years. These days, like many unmanageable properties, it is now owned by a business consortium better able to weather the market. VRD still operates over a massive, semi-arid area, with the homestead more like a small township, incorporating a post office and shop. The station is also the base of Australia's biggest **heli-mustering** outfit, which pursues the daredevil practice of mustering widely dispersed stock with single-seater helicopters.

Around 150km from Katherine the Victoria Highway enters a picturesque spur of the Gregory National Park (see p.655). Just after the Victoria River crossing is the *Victoria River Wayside Inn* (❷–❹) which runs **river cruises** (daily April–Oct; 3hr; $40) on the Victoria River.

Timber Creek

Although little more than a pair of roadhouses/bars with adjacent campsites, **TIMBER CREEK** makes a welcome break on the long run to Kununurra, 300km west of Katherine. Lying on the Victoria River, a century ago it was known as the "Depot", when the inland port supplied the vast pastoral properties being established throughout the region. But this remote outpost was soon the scene of bitter disputes between Aborigines and the settlers. In 1885

6

End of the line for the Big Runs

The iconography of the **Australian cattle industry** is etched deep in the nation's psyche, as evinced by the popularity of the Stockman's Hall of Fame in Longreach, Queensland (see p.583). The romance of the gritty station owner in a crumpled Akubra, his kids educated from the remote homestead by the School of the Air, while triple-trailer road trains drag tornadoes of dust across the plains, creates a stirring idea of the modern-day pioneer battling against the elemental Outback.

Australia remains the world's largest exporter of beef, but in recent years shrewd business interests from the **USA and Japan** (the latter Australia's biggest overseas market) have bought into the trade – lock, stock and barrel – including everything from stations to abattoirs, packers and shipping companies. This has enabled them to control the price of beef and drive marginal stations over the edge into bankruptcy.

Indeed, the days of old-fashioned station dynasties have come to an end, and the extravagance of maintaining thousand-kilometre fences and mustering over a vast area with helicopters has been put to the test. Despite the glory associated with the great drovers such as Nat Buchanan and the Duracks, the semi-arid interior and tropical Top End of the Northern Territory run less than a tenth of the stock that could be supported on the same area in New South Wales. Western Australia's Kimberley region similarly glorifies in its great stations (Derby has its eyes set on its own hall of fame), but it's the worst land in the country, cut with seasonal torrents, and with boulder-strewn plains prone to fires and flooding. Many stations only bother to muster enough to make ends meet and keep within the terms of their pastoral leases, leaving their stock to run feral; you'll come across some huge and essentially wild bulls in the Kimberley.

It's far simpler to keep the beasts in enclosed and well-watered paddocks munching decent grass rather than leave them roaming the semi-desert for years. In fact most Territory beef which does not end up getting exported live to Indonesia heads south or east to these paddocks for fattening up on good feed prior to slaughter.

Only slowly are consumer's eyes being opened to "non-traditional" meats. **Kangaroos**, now a plague in Australia, have meat leaner than anything a cow can produce, and taste virtually the same. Meanwhile, Ian Conway, the half-Aboriginal owner of Kings Creek station near Uluru, raises **camels**, descended from those introduced from Afghanistan in the nineteenth century and which were released to roam free with the advent of rail and roads. Cattle owners who detest them, shoot them on sight; a thirsty mob can drain a tank and run through bovine fences with impunity. Yet one of Conway's disease-free camels can fetch ten times the price of a cow when sold to a private zoo in America or a racing cartel in Arabia. When the station gets low on stock they simply drive out into the Gibson Desert for more, capitalizing on a resource which prospers in the Australian desert rather than turning it into a dust bowl.

---

a police station was set up at Timber Creek, staffed by two policemen and a black tracker whose task was to patrol an area the size of Tasmania. Diana Bell's harrowing book *Hidden Histories* describes the ruthless pastoral occupation of the area from an Aboriginal perspective.

The **museum** (Mon–Fri 10am–noon; $2.20) is housed in an early police station, west of the town. It's a familiar display of miscellaneous pioneering relics, dragged out of the surrounding undergrowth or abandoned homesteads and used to illustrate a pithy historical commentary about the region. On a different note, the town has the easternmost examples of the curious, bottle-trunked **boab trees**, similar to Africa's baobabs and according to Aboriginal mythology a once-arrogant tree turned upside down to teach it a lesson in humility.

Behind one such tree, a twin-trunked boab on the south side of the highway 4km west of town, lies the miserable **grave** of Tom Lawler (or Lander). He was not the first disillusioned inhabitant of Timber Creek to seek solace in alcohol, and in 1906, a bullet through his brains, but he is one of the few to get a marked grave. The explorer Gregory inscribed another boab, Gregory's Bottle Tree, on the banks of the Victoria River, in 1856. A short distance upstream, his ship ran aground and he was forced to make repairs here, giving Timber Creek its name.

Practicalities

Tourist information is dispensed from the Max River Cruise office between the two pubs (daily 8am–6pm; ☎08/8975 0850). You'll find one of the finest selections of crocobilia north of the twenty-sixth parallel. Of special note is a rubber "Rude Croc" – squeeze one and see. A four-hour afternoon boat tour (daily 4pm; $40) runs 40km down the Victoria River to come back for sunset on the crags, meeting a few crocs, both polite and rude, on the way.

    Accommodation can be found at the grandly named *Timber Creek Hotel* (☎08/8975 0772; ●), incorporating the *Circle 'F' Caravan Park* and Fogarty's Store, which has camping, cabins and motel rooms. The *Wayside Inn* (☎08/8975 0732; ●) also has camping and cabins, with shared bathrooms. The *Shell Roadhouse* here is open 24 hours. **Eating** options include whatever's going on at either of the two roadhouses or what you can dig up at the store next to Max's.

Gregory National Park

Gregory National Park, the Territory's second-largest park, is most easily entered off the Victoria Highway, 11km east of Timber Creek. Carved out from unviable pastoral leases, the park exhibits sandstone escarpments and limestone hills covered in light woodland. Because of its remoteness and rough terrain, it can only be explored in a suitable **4WD vehicle**, and it's a good idea to call at the **P&WC** office in Timber Creek (turn right just before Watch Creek, west of town; ☎08/8975 0888) to study the large map and get information about conditions. Voluntary **self-registration** is encouraged but not compulsory; you have to ring a call centre on ☎1300 650 730. They take your credit card details and if you de-register on time they won't charge you and won't come looking for you.

    Conventional cars with good clearance and up for a hammering can get as far as **Limestone Gorge**, on a corrugated road 47km south of the highway. Here you'll find a 25-minute marked walking trail looping up onto the surrounding escarpment, a croc-free billabong and a **campsite**. The stockyards and old homestead at Bullita, along with the ranger at Bullita Outstation (☎08/8975 0833), are another 9km south of the Limestone Gorge turn-off where there's a phone to self-register. The seventy-kilometre **Bullita Stockroute** loops back northwards, crossing a couple of rivers and crawling over some extremely rocky terrain which will chew up your tyres. This takes a full day and scenically it's not worth it, although **camping** is permitted at designated spots along the way.

    Alternatively, 4WDs can choose to leave the park south along the **Humbert River Track** – another rocky drive, allow at least six hours for the 112km to the park's eastern boundary, from where you can head east along station tracks. For another route continue circuitously south to the **Buntine Highway** and Kalkaringi via the **Broadarrow** or **Wickham tracks**. Both the stockroute and this route are **one-way** only from Bullita, and are closed from December to March.

Keep River National Park and the WA border

West of Timber Creek, the land flattens out into the evocatively named **Whirlwind Plains**, where the East and West Baines rivers frequently cut the Victoria Highway in the Wet. **Keep River National Park** lies just before the Western Australia border, 185km from Timber Creek. Accessible to all vehicles, it's an easily explored area of dissected sandstone ridges, shallow gorges and Aboriginal art sites, the best of which is **Nganalam**, 24km from the park entrance. Marked trails start from the two **campsites** in the park, and the ranger station (☎08/9167 8827), 3km from the highway, supplies details on longer walks and other attractions.

By now you can hardly have failed to get the message that Western Australia does not want any infested Territorian livestock, produce or honey. The intensively irrigated agricultural area around Kununurra is hoping to remain free from pests found elsewhere in Australia, so eat up your fruit and veg before the border or throw it away. If you're not sure what to get rid of the guys at the checkpoint will put you right; the regulations are not as severe as they seem. Note too that WA is an hour and thirty minutes behind the Territory.

At the **border**, Kununurra (see p.783) is just 40km away.

South to Alice

The 1100km from Katherine, south down the "**Track**" (as the Stuart Highway is known) to Alice Springs, are regarded as something of a **no-man's-land** for travellers. A flat, arid plain rolls from the Top End's big rivers to the waterholes of the Red Centre. The white population in this region is sparse, and consists largely of individuals who are either unusually tenacious, transient or slowly going "troppo" in a ring of empty beer cans. West of the Track, the vast Aboriginal lands of the Warlpiri and neighbouring groups just about occupy the entire **Tanami Desert**, while to the east are the grasslands of the **Barkly Tableland**, a declining pastoral region extending north to the seldom-visited coast of the **Gulf of Carpentaria**. **Tennant Creek**, just over halfway, can come as an anti-climactic break to a night-time bus journey, and even car drivers tend to press on down the Track before something breaks or wears out. The landscape as seen from the Stuart Highway encourages a kind of agoraphobic urgency (or just plain boredom), while the mind churns repetitively over such imponderables as "just how many anthills *are* there in the Northern Territory?"

Mataranka and the Roper River Region

MATARANKA – just over 100km from Katherine – is a small town, the capital of the tediously hyped "Never Never" country named after Jeannie Gunn's 1908 novel of a pioneering woman's life, *We of the Never Never*, set and later filmed in the region. Site of despised Administrator John Gilruth's planned Northern Territory capital, today the town is practically eclipsed by the nearby **Mataranka Homestead** resort, which lures in buses and passing tourists (see opposite). South of town the **Elsey National Park** leads to the often-overlooked freshwater wetlands of the **Roper River**.

There's not much to the town itself. Outside the Stockyard Gallery you can feed a dollar into the statue of **The Fizzer** to hear the tale of the punctual postman, Henry Peckham of "Never Never" fame, who was drowned in action. Tom Coles' account of his escapades in the Top End between the wars, *Hell West and Crooked*, describes the hair-raising river crossings with pack horses while delivering mail in the Wet season. Invariably the post would be delivered with barely a smudge.

All **accommodation**, along with the supermarket, roadhouses, museum, café and craft shop, is lined up along **Roper Terrace**, the main highway. Both the *Shell* and *Mobil* roadhouses have basic on-site cabins but at the town **pub**, the *Old Elsey Roadside Inn* (☎08/8975 4512; ❸), you'll find motel rooms. The *Territory Manor*, on Martins Road (☎ & ℻08/8975 4516; ❹), is a plush motel set in its own landscaped grounds, catering for bus tours: it also boasts a caravan park (with camping) as well as the town's only licensed **restaurant**.

Mataranka Homestead

Mataranka Homestead, 6km from town (☎1800 975 454, ⓦwww .travelnorth.com.au), was established by Gilruth to raise sheep and horses and is now a resort. The palm-shaded **thermal pool**, actually in Elsey National Park but seemingly part of the resort, is the main, if not only, attraction here: it's free, always open, teeming with people and the water is a pleasant 34°C. A replica of the *Elsey Homestead*, used in the 1981 film of *We of the Never Never*, is open for daily tours. The original "Old Elsey Homestead" site and cemetery are south of town, just past the Roper Highway turn-off – of interest only to Jeannie Gunn devotees.

The resort has a **bar** and **bistro**, and free nightly entertainment (April–Sept only) as well as a tour-booking service. **Accommodation** includes rooms and self-catering cabins (❹) plus motel rooms, and three-bed en-suite rooms with air-con (❺). There is also a backpackers' (dorms $17) and a campsite. Overland **buses** stop at the homestead, which is signposted south of Mataranka.

Elsey National Park and the Roper River

A twelve-kilometre road into **Elsey National Park** (turn off just before the homestead) leads to a more secluded **campsite** with less of a holiday-camp atmosphere, offering canoe rental and swimming in the (almost croc-free) upper Roper River, as well as a small kiosk.

The **Roper River** itself is difficult to appreciate without your own boat, since it's barely developed, yet it's as scenic as the wetlands of Kakadu. Someone may still be operating **cruises** along the Roper wetlands in the season – ask around. If this is the case you'll be able to explore the river's so-called **Pandanus Avenue** and some "African Queen"-type channels into the beautiful **Red Lily Lagoon**, the most extensive freshwater wetland in the Territory.

The Roper Highway

A couple of kilometres south of Mataranka, the **Roper Highway** leads east for 185km (the bitumen ends after 140km) to the remote community store at **ROPER BAR**. It was here in 1844, during his five-thousand-kilometre trek from Queensland, that explorer **Ludwig Leichhardt** dined on fruit bat and built a "bar" (ford) across the Roper River. You may drive across the slippery bar, but beyond is Aboriginal land – off-limits without a permit. The store provides the local Aboriginal community and visiting barramundi fishermen with pricey fuel, food and the biggest selection of cheap toys and gobstoppers for 200km. Up behind the store are some self-catering **cabins** (❷) or there's a

campsite 2km back towards the highway. If you go boating or fishing here, take care because you're back in "saltie waters" again.

If you've got this far, you'll have seen the turn-off to Borroloola, 380km away (see p.659). Corrugated enough to test the calmest temperaments, this rarely used route to the Gulf of Carpentaria and Queensland is passable in the Dry for regular cars in good shape.

Down the Track to Three Ways

LARRIMAH, 72km south of Mataranka, was where the old Darwin railway terminated until 1976 when it closed for good, due to a lack of maintenance following Cyclone Tracy. Up until then, Larrimah had been a busy road-rail terminus, receiving goods brought up from Alice Springs. Now it's just a fuel stop on the highway with a bit more history than most.

The *Larrimah Hotel* is a typical **bush pub**, full of eccentricity, old bottles and half-melted Spitfire engines; you can **camp** here for free but there's a $2.50 charge for showers. The hotel should have received some long overdue renovation by now; otherwise expect to pay backpacker prices for basic rooms.

Another 89km south brings you to the **Daly Waters Pub**, situated 3km off the highway. Having held a "gallon licence" since 1893, it positively drips with memorabilia including money and women's underwear pinned to the walls: you're welcome to contribute. If you need a break there are cheap and basic **rooms** (❷). During the 1930s, when Qantas's Singapore flights refuelled here, world-class aviators used to pop in for a pint, and these days tourists come to marvel at the nutty quaintness of it all and buy the famous tea towels.

Just beyond here, the **Carpentaria Highway** (technically the circumnational Highway 1) heads off east to Borroloola, 414km away (see p.659); the turn-off is at the *Highway Inn Roadhouse* (open 24hr). There's a second turn-off, further down the Track, just before *Dunmarra Roadhouse*, where the **Buchanan Highway** heads west to *Top Springs Roadhouse* (185km) and ultimately, if you turn off south, Halls Creek in Western Australia (see p.780) along almost 800km of mostly unsealed road suitable for sound vehicles only. **Dunmarra**'s drive-through drudgery was livened up a few years ago when it received a bizarre shower of fish; the hoped-for cloud of chips with vinegar never materialized.

Further down the Track, **Newcastle Waters** can't seem to make up its mind whether it's a historic droving township wanting to encourage tourists or a semi-abandoned ghost town. Right up to the 1950s, when road trains replaced the great cattle drives, it was the junction (hence the *Junction Hotel*) of the Barkly and Murranji stockroutes. However, it's of little interest today except to nostalgic drovers.

Further south, **ELLIOTT** is little more than a string of roadhouses with cheap **camping** at the *Mobil Roadhouse* and slightly better facilities at the *Midland Caravan Park* (also the local post office). The *BP Roadhouse* and the *Elliott Hotel* (☏08/8969 2018; ❸) both offer simple **rooms**. There are a few shops serving the Jingili Aboriginal communities at either end of town, but apart from filling up with fuel or a counter meal at the pub, there's no earthly reason to stop.

As you leave town to the south, the trees which have blocked the horizon for days recede into shrubs and soon disappear altogether as you approach the deserts of Central Australia. **RENNER SPRINGS** is a roadhouse built after World War II from bits of ex-army junk; you can camp here, and eat the same sort of food you were offered at the last roadhouse.

On the way to the roadhouse at **THREE WAYS** (open 24hr) watch out for the turn-off to a rocky profile of Churchill's Head and also the **Attack Creek Memorial** – where explorer Stuart was repelled by Aborigines on one of his expeditions. At Three Ways, the **Barkly Highway** heads east to Camooweal, Mount Isa and eventually Townsville, all in Queensland; it's 210km on the highway to the *Barkly Homestead* (6am–1am;), a better-than-average roadhouse with all the usual services. From Three Ways, Tennant Creek (see p.660) is just 26km down the road.

Cape Crawford, Borroloola and the Tablelands Highway

Cape Crawford is nothing more than a highway junction where the *Heartbreak Hotel* roadhouse stands (☎08/8975 9928; ❸), 113km southwest of Borroloola. In between the two you'll find the **Caranbirini Conservation Reserve**, with a couple of walks through weird rock formations and a bird-filled lagoon. From the roadhouse the single-width **Tablelands Highway** is a bitumen alternative to the Gulf route, leading to western Queensland via the *Barkly Homestead* roadhouse.

Borroloola

Situated on the croc-infested **MacArthur River**, **BORROLOOLA** has a colourful history which reads like an exaggerated version of the familiar boom, bust and dribble pattern of so many Outback towns. The explorers Leichhardt and Gregory came this way in the mid-nineteenth century, reporting good pasture, and the cattle followed in droves. By the early 1880s, when Tennant Creek and Katherine were still just shacks on the Overland Telegraph Line, the settlement was a wild outpost that even the missionaries avoided. Ships that formerly supplied the OTL came upriver with provisions for the hard-living drovers, who were helping stock the pastoral leases right across the north of Australia.

Borroloola was proclaimed, or "gazetted", in 1885 and a new police station was established in an attempt to control the town's lawless urges. Although well watered, the **Great Coast Route** which Borroloola serviced fell victim to the bovine disease of Red Water Fever, after which the southern stockroute (today's Barkly Highway) became the favoured droving route. By the turn of 1900, just a handful of Europeans remained in "The 'Loo" and, with their frenzied passing, the four local Aboriginal groups comprising the Yanyuwa (see "Books", p.1202) have reclaimed the town and surrounding land, which now serves their communities.

The only original building to have survived the punch-ups, white ants and cyclones is the **Old Police Station**, now a museum (Mon–Fri 10am–4pm; free). With Borroloola's exceptional white history (see box overleaf), the museum couldn't fail to be fascinating. Read, for example, E. Gaunt's hair-raising account of "The Birth of Borroloola", recalling the sporadic insanity of the early days; it seems the toxic home-brew known as "Come Hither", whose label showed a red-eyed Lucifer beckoning malevolently, was to blame. Not surprisingly, the coverage of local Aboriginal history is lightweight. All this history may tickle your fancy but don't be mislead, Borroloola is a rough and depressing Aboriginal welfare town of interest only to those needing fuel and a feed on the coastal Gulf route.

There are a couple of basic **campsites** along the main road (cabins ❸–❺) and rooms in the pub (❺) which from the outside looks as inviting as a detention centre. By road, Borroloola is easily accessible along the

The classics library and hermits of Borroloola

There are a number of more or less unlikely explanations for Borroloola's improbable **classics library**, including one which starts with a bored policeman's request for reading matter to New York's Carnegie Foundation. In truth, it was a gradual acquisition of nearly two thousand literary classics by the town's MacArthur Institute at the beginning of the twentieth century. Termites tucked into the library, a cyclone destroyed the remains and only a handful of books survived, many in "private collections", gathering what must be enormous overdue fees.

In 1963 a boyish David Attenborough made a TV documentary about three **hermits** who had chosen to retreat to the 'Loo. Jack Mulholland came across as a slightly jaded recluse when pressed about "loneliness and... women", and the reputedly aristocratic "Mad Fiddler" was too deranged to face the camera, but **Roger Jose** was, and looked like, the real thing. Having devoured the library ahead of the ants, he lived in a water tank with his Aboriginal wife and was a humane if eccentric "bush philosopher" who once observed that "a man's riches are the fewness of his needs". He is buried at the end of the airstrip in Borroloola.

Carpentaria Highway, via the *Heartbreak Hotel* at Cape Crawford (see p.659). Depending on who you ask, the **dirt road** to **Wollogorang** (a roadhouse with access to coastal inlets) and Hells Gate in Queensland (see p.607) is either terrible or not bad, but it's bound to be an adventure; the Queensland gulf towns are by no means renowned for their sobriety. The dirt road up to Roper Bar is good until Nathan River, where the corrugations will turn your brain into a froth for about 100km.

Tennant Creek

Visitors expect to be disappointed by **TENNANT CREEK**, lying 26km south of Three Ways, and indeed its appeal to tourists is not immediately apparent. However, hang around and you'll discover an unpretentious Outback town, defying stagnation and hoping for prosperity.

John McDouall Stuart came through in the early 1860s, followed by the Overland Telegraph Line ten years later. Pastoralists and prospectors came from the south and east, and in 1933 Tennant Creek was the site of the last major **goldrush** in Australia. This was the time of gritty "gougers", such as Jack Noble and partner Bill Weaber (with one eye between them), who defied the Depression by pegging some of the town's most productive claims. Modern methods of gold retrieval have caused a revival in recent years, although tenacity and luck still have much to do with striking it rich.

Arrival and information

Tennant Creek is 504km from Alice and 664km from Katherine. The **airport** is about 3km from the centre, at the end of Davidson Street; for a **taxi** into town from the airport, call ☎08/8962 2522 or your chosen accommodation may pick you up. The new Darwin railway link may have passenger services stopping here too (see p.667). On Paterson Street (the town's main street – essentially the Stuart Highway) you'll find the Transit Centre where interstate **buses** pull in – some buses come through at 3.30am, which doesn't exactly encourage stopovers. There's **Internet** at Switch next to the Transit Centre.

The **visitors centre** at **Battery Hill** (May–Sept Mon–Fri 9am–5pm & Sat 9am–noon; ☎08/8962 3388, ⓦwww.tennantcreektourism.com.au) is on an old mine site 1.5km east along Peko Road.

Accommodation

El Dorado Paterson St North ℡ 08/8962 2402, ℻ 8962 3034. One of the town's better motels, with a licensed restaurant and nice pool area. ❹

Outback Caravan Park Peko Rd ℡ 08/8962 2459. Shady and comfortable caravan park with shop and pool. On-site vans ❷, cabins ❸

Safari Backpackers Davidson St ℡ 08/8962 2207. Clean block with four-bed dorms, doubles, kitchen, TV and functional air-con. Dorms $16, rooms ❷

Safari Lodge Motel Davidson St ℡ 08/8962

2207. Comfortable motel rooms right in town with *Fernanda's* (see below) right next door. ❹

TC Caravan Park Next to the Shell service station, Paterson St ℡ 08/8962 2325. Good deals for camping; backpackers' bunkhouse and roomy cabins also available. Dorms $25, cabins ❷

Tennant Creek Tourist's Rest Leichhardt St ℡ 08/8962 2719. This former youth hostel is still hanging on, with an ageing row of two- and three-bed rooms with rattly air-con, a pool and an authentic "Tennant" feel. Dorms $16, rooms ❷

The Town and around

With one or two free days on your hands, the limited prospects of Tennant Creek are spread before you. In town, the **museum** (daily 3.30–5.30pm; $2), across the road from the *Memorial Club*, minutely details the history of Tennant Creek, using a chronological time scale starting from the year 0 "AS" (After Stuart) and displaying plenty of pioneering relics. The Ngalipanyangu Cultural Centre Aboriginal Arts and Crafts Gallery (Mon–Fri 8.30am–5pm) on Davidson Street is one of three galleries in town where you'll find a selection of local dot **paintings and crafts**, a bit cheaper than those in Alice Springs. If you're heading to the visitors centre at Battery Hill you might as well take the sixty-minute **tour of the mine site** (up to 4 daily; $13), which includes an entertaining stroll through a specially built show mine. There's also a chance to savour the din of the old stamp battery (2 tours daily; $13). Without your own vehicle, that's about it, although a couple of kilometres north of town is an old telegraph station, restored as a historic exhibit (℡ 08/8962 3388 for opening times). If you've come down the Track and not seen an OTL station yet, here's your chance.

Eating

Tennant Creek's **eating** opportunities are limited. Besides those listed below, there are functional restaurants in the *El Dorado* and *Bluestone* motels (the latter at the south end of Paterson St).

Fernanda's 1 Noble St ℡ 08/8962 3999. Mediterranean flavour and the best seafood, albeit cooked from frozen, in Tennant Creek.

Memorial Club Schmidt St. At the "Memo" you can sign in and get a decent counter meal to eat

in (or take away) for around $12 plus have a quiet drink afterwards. Meals noon–2pm & 6pm until late.

Tennant Creek Hotel Paterson St. Good restaurant attached to one of the town's more tranquil pubs.

Drinking and nightlife

Dedicated drinkers are well looked after, as the town boasts around thirteen licences and two **pubs**. The fortnightly "Thirsty Thursday" sees takeaway sales banned in an effort to curb excessive waste of Aborigines' welfare cheques (issued on Thurs). Like a lot of pubs in Outback towns, front bars can become intimidating arenas of flying bottles and vitriol, while the carpeted back bars are for games of pool and benign socializing. Pubs are generally open from 10am to midnight.

Goldfields, on Paterson Street, has a cleared front bar where you can get a good swing at your neighbour without breaking any of the fittings; the back bar is the place to take your mum for a sherry. Over the road, the *Tennant*

Creek Hotel has a blues-proof (punch-ups, not John Lee Hooker) front bar and a tamer back bar for a quiet drink, and *The Shaft*, the town's only **disco** (Thurs–Sat 11pm–3am), enables licensed drinking into the night. *Jackson's Bar* is where the legendary beer cart got mired on the way to the original settlement near the telegraph station, sixty years ago. The beer cart wouldn't budge, so the settlement relocated around it, drank it dry and the rest is history.

If you just want a quiet drink don't forget the "Memo" (see p.661) or "Sporties" clubs (the latter on Ambrose Street); at either you can easily sign in as a guest and enjoy the tame if somewhat suburban atmosphere.

Towards Alice and the Centre

If you're feeling a bit "Top Ended" then the 505km from Tennant to Alice offer some respite as the land opens out into the subtle hues of the central deserts. Only the Devil's Marbles are worth breaking the journey, and if you've not got your own transport then they can be visited on a day-tour from Tennant Creek with Devil's Marbles Tours (℡0418 891 711; $55, 2 people minimum).

The first thing to catch your eye will be a sign announcing the proposed **Davenport Ranges National Park**. You'll need a 4WD and two or three days to get any impression of the park, which is essentially a track passing the north of the Ranges, visiting various waterholes of which Old Police Station Waterhole is the pick, followed by a rougher track south of the Ranges, back to the highway. These perennial waterholes tucked into the creeks of the escarpment are what makes the Ranges special, a sanctuary to wildlife. There are at least seven types of fish here that are cut off from the outside world, although there is little chance that they're aware of this cruel ecological misfortune.

Back on the Track, the **Devil's Marbles**, just over 100km south of Tennant Creek, are a genuine geological oddity, a scattering of huge rounded boulders thought by the local Warumungu Aborigines to be the eggs of the Rainbow Serpent. They're well worth a look, as they're just off the highway and any excuse for a break is welcome.

A short drive from the Marbles is the comfortable old roadhouse/pub of **WAUCHOPE** (pronounced "walkup"). **WYCLIFFE WELL**, a little further south, has a good foreign beer selection, a nice park and lake round the back, an alien spaceship parked in the forecourt, camping and rooms (❹). See the box below for details of Wycliffe Well's UFO activity.

Area 51 – Downunder

For decades there have been sightings of UFOs in the skies over Wycliffe Well. While the roadhouse has capitalized on this to the full with some kitsch alienobilia, scores of newspaper articles in the restaurant attest to the regular sightings of UFOs, if not necessarily bug-eyed ETs. The location has certain parallels with Nevada's Area 51, a sparsely populated semi-desert, and the shady goings-on at the Pine Gap US military base near Alice Springs are just 400km to the south. Of course that's no distance at all for the latest remote orbiter prototypes fitted with the second generation plasma drives. Rationalizations of the sightings include that they are merely "glowing birds" or the "Min Min Light" (see p.558). Whatever the truth is, it would be unfair to suggest that Wycliffe Well's astonishing selection of over 130 beers from around the world has any connection with the phenomenon, but it gives you something to do while you watch the skies and wait.

BARROW CREEK, 60km further on, is one of the oldest roadhouses on the Track, originally a telegraph station, and remembered as the site of the **Barrow Creek Massacre** in 1874. It's never quite clear to whom the word "massacre" applied – the two dead and several wounded during an attack on the two-year-old station by the local Kaitej, or those who perished in the two months' "speedy and severe" retribution demanded by the *Northern Territory News*. The pub itself (℡08/8956 9753) has walls daubed in coarse humour, as well as old-fashioned rooms (❹) and cheaper cabins (❷–❸) out back.

At **TI TREE**, an Aboriginal community close to the middle of the continent, a couple of galleries sell keenly priced artefacts and paintings produced by the local Anmatjera and communities further afield. After another 43km, the **AILERON** roadhouse (❺) has the last fuel before Alice and also sells Aboriginal art; the first beer in the bar is free to backpackers staying overnight.

The Plenty Highway and Tanami Road

Heading towards Alice, the land finally begins to crumple as you near the MacDonnell Ranges. The **Plenty** and **Sandover highways**, which run off the Stuart Highway 66km south of Aileron, head northeast towards Queensland through the scenic Harts and Jervois ranges. Both are passable with sound, well-equipped conventional cars – the Plenty (which becomes the Donohue Highway in Queensland) is generally the busier and better maintained. If you're heading down to Birdsville or Winton (both in Queensland) this way, the Donohue Highway short cut down to Boulia isn't half as bad as maps suggest.

Twenty kilometres north of Alice, the **Tanami Road** leads 1040km northwest to Halls Creek in Western Australia. The track is a dirt freeway up to the Granites mines just before the WA border where things can get a little rough and sandy. If you're heading for the Bungles, the Tanami is quicker than the bitumen via Katherine, but pretty boring. The longest section without fuel is the 322km from Yuendumu to **Rabbit Flat** roadhouse (closed Tues–Thurs), with the next section to Billiluna station in WA nearly as long at 292km. You can also pop into the art gallery at the Aboriginal community of **Balgo Hills**, which sometimes has fuel, 31km south of the Tanami (the turn-off is about 88km on the WA side of the track); their garish and splodgy school of dot paintings is highly distinctive.

Before embarking on either route, it's worth checking out the condition of the tracks; phone RACQ for the Queensland sections (℡07/4775 3600), Emergency Services in Alice Springs (℡08/8951 6688) or the Main Roads Dept, Halls Creek (℡08/9168 6007); you can also read daily **print-outs** of the track conditions at the tourist information office in Alice Springs or check out up-to-date road conditions of desert tracks at ⓌWww.exploreoz.com. Although they shouldn't be considered a time-saving short cut, the Plenty and Tanami tracks are both perfectly feasible in a tough, well-equipped 2WD vehicle.

Alice and the Centre

Set in what is just about the geographical centre of the continent, **Alice Springs** has a population of just 25,000, yet is still the largest settlement of the

Australian interior. A clean, modern and compact town in the midst of the MacDonnell Ranges, it makes an excellent base from which to plan trips into the surrounding countryside.

The **Red Centre**, a marketing term coined to describe the area to the south, west and east of Alice Springs, is a historically rich and scenically spectacular region. It includes the lands inhabited by the "Anangu", the tourist-friendly epithet for the Aborigines from the Uluru region. The **Aborigines of the central deserts** were fortunate in being among the last to come into contact with white settlers, by which time the massacres and exterminations of the nineteenth century had passed their peak. As a result of this, and the strict tribal law needed to survive in the desert, their traditional way of life is historically much closer. These factors are said to have made their adjustment to modern Australia less successful than Top End Aborigines.

Ayers Rock – known to the Anangu as **Uluru** – is Australia's most famous and most visited natural spectacle, and still the primary reason why most people come to the Centre. At first sight, even jaded "seen-it-all" cynics will find it hard to take their eyes away from its awesome bulk. But there's much more in the area than just the Rock, and it's rare in Outback Australia to find such a large region crammed with worthwhile and accessible places of interest. The **West MacDonnells**, a series of rugged ridges cut at intervals by slender chasms or enormous gorges, start right on Alice's doorstep. In the other direction, the **Eastern MacDonnells** are less visited but no less appealing, with the remote tracks of the **Simpson Desert** to the south attracting the intrepid. To the west, **Palm Valley**, now linked to **Kings Canyon** via a good dirt road, can add a few days to a trip which, including the Rock, makes for probably the most memorable tour in the Outback. While most of these places certainly don't need a 4WD vehicle to get to, there are a few enjoyable and easy off-road tracks that can be fun in a rented 4WD; they're detailed in the box on pp.682–683.

When to go and what to take

The aridity of the Centre results in extremes of temperature that are best avoided, if at all possible. In the midwinter months of July and August the air is lovely and clear although **freezing nights**, especially around Uluru, are not uncommon. But there's no escaping the **summer heat**: in December and January the temperature may have already reached 40°C by 10am and doesn't drop below 30°C all night. The transitional seasons of autumn (April–June) and Spring (Sept & Oct) are ideal times to explore the region in comfort.

Rain is a rare and wonderful thing in the Centre. Whenever you visit, a sudden storm may temporarily transform the desert into a garden of exquisite flowers as well as cut off access along even the main roads; as a rule it is midsummer storms which bring the most rain.

Out here a **wide-brimmed hat** is not so much a fashion accessory as a life saver, keeping your head and face in permanent shadow. All but the shortest of walks will also require a **water bottle** and loose, long-sleeved clothing plus lashings of **sun block** on any exposed skin. Australia's many venomous but rarely seen snakes and, more relevantly, rocky tracks and the carpet of prickly spinifex grass that covers a fifth of the continent, make a pair of **covered shoes or boots** the final elementary precaution to safe and comfortable tramping around the Centre.

Alice Springs and around

Most visitors are surprised by the modern appearance of **ALICE SPRINGS**. The bright, clear desert air gives the Outback town and its people a charge you don't find in the languid, tropical north. In Alice, the shopping centre is actually in the middle of town and not in some peripheral suburb, and so allusions to Nevil Shute's flyblown *A Town Like Alice*, or even Robyn Davidson's ockersome observations in *Tracks*, have long been obsolete.

The area has been inhabited for at least thirty thousand years by Aranda Aborigines, who moved between the waterhole of Alice Springs (Tjanerilji) and other reliable water sources in the MacDonnell Ranges. But, as elsewhere in the Territory, it was only the Overland Telegraph Line's arrival in the 1870s that led to a permanent settlement here. Following **John McDouall Stuart**'s exploratory journeys through the area in the early 1860s, it was the visionary **Charles Todd**, then South Australia's Superintendent of Telegraphs, who saw the need to link Australia with the rest of the empire. The town's river and its tributary carry his name, and the spring that of his wife, Alice.

With repeater stations needed every 250km from Adelaide to Darwin to boost the OTL signal, the site just north of today's town, with its permanent "spring" (actually a billabong on the Todd River), was ideal as a place to erect the necessary buildings. When a spurious ruby rush led to the discovery of gold at Arltunga in the Eastern MacDonnells, **Stuart Town** (the town's seldom-used official name in its early years) became a jumping-off point for the long slog to the riches out east. Arltunga's goldrush fizzled out under desperate conditions, but the township of Stuart remained, a collection of shanty dwellings serving a stream of pastoralists, prospectors and missionaries.

In 1929 the **railway line** from Adelaide finally reached Stuart Town. Journeys that had once taken weeks by camel from Oodnadatta could now be undertaken in just a few days and by 1933, when the town officially took the name Alice Springs, the population had mushroomed to nearly five hundred Europeans. In 1942 the bombing and subsequent evacuation of Darwin saw Alice Springs become the Territory's administrative headquarters and a busy military base, supplying the war zone in the north. After the hostilities ceased, some of the wartime population stayed on and Alice's fortunes continued to grow slowly, boosted by the establishment of the Pine Gap US military base just south of town in the mid-Sixties. The secret activities at the base have conjured up many Roswell-esque theories (see box on p.662), but it's probably not used for anything more mysterious than satellite tracking. The continued presence of around three hundred well-financed American families in town has helped give Alice a purposeful, cosmopolitan feel as well as greatly aiding the local service economy.

With the reconstruction of the poorly built rail link from Adelaide and the sealing of the Stuart Highway in the mid-1980s, Alice has only recently attained its present size. A **tourist boom** at that time, helped in no small measure by the massive publicity surrounding Azaria Chamberlain's canine abduction at the Rock, comes and goes over the years, but Alice still remains the undisputed "capital" of the Outback. Even so, the population remains tiny: within a thousand-kilometre radius of "the Alice", as it's known, there are fewer than forty thousand inhabitants. The town has embraced tourism wholeheartedly and despite the famously overpriced *Ayers Rock Resort* Alice still seems set to succeed, primarily because both the town and surrounding area have much to offer, even without the obligatory visit to the Rock.

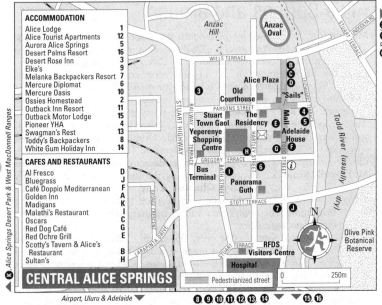

▲ *Telegraph Station & Tennant Creek*   ▲ *Telegraph Station*

ACCOMMODATION

Alice Lodge	1
Alice Tourist Apartments	12
Aurora Alice Springs	5
Desert Palms Resort	16
Desert Rose Inn	3
Elke's	9
Melanka Backpackers Resort	7
Mercure Diplomat	6
Mercure Oasis	10
Ossies Homestead	2
Outback Inn Resort	11
Outback Motor Lodge	15
Pioneer YHA	4
Swagman's Rest	13
Toddy's Backpackers	8
White Gum Holiday Inn	14

CAFES AND RESTAURANTS

Al Fresco	D
Bluegrass	J
Café Doppio Mediterranean	F
Golden Inn	A
Madigans	K
Malathi's Restaurant	I
Oscars	C
Red Dog Café	G
Red Ochre Grill	E
Scotty's Tavern & Alice's Restaurant	B
Sultan's	H

Alice Springs Desert Park & West MacDonnell Ranges

CENTRAL ALICE SPRINGS

Pedestrianized street   0   250m

Airport, Uluru & Adelaide ▼

Arrival, information and transport

The **airport** is 14km south of town. The airport shuttle (☎08/8953 0310) meets incoming flights and costs $10, or $18 return, while a taxi (☎08/8953 0979) will be about $25. **Buses** arrive at the Coles Complex at the western end of Gregory Terrace. Some of the keener hostels send minibuses to meet incoming buses (as well as some incoming flights). Alice's **train station** – open only when trains are due to arrive – is on George Crescent on the west side of the Stuart Highway, just off Larapinta Drive, about a fifteen-minute walk (or $5 taxi ride) from the town centre. See the box opposite about the possibility of passenger services north to Darwin on the new rail link.

The **tourist information office** (Mon–Fri 8.30am–5.30pm, Sat & Sun 9am–4pm; ☎08/8952 5800 or 1800 645 199, ⓦwww.centralaustralian tourism.com) is at the river end of Gregory Terrace by the library and council offices. It features a well-organized range of brochures detailing the mind-boggling possibilities in Alice and around.

Transport

The centre occupies a compact area between the Stuart Highway and Leichhardt Terrace, along the dry Todd River, bordered to the north and south by Wills Terrace and Stott Terrace respectively. Bisecting this rectangle is **Todd Mall**, once the main street, now a relaxing pedestrian thoroughfare lined with alfresco cafés, galleries and souvenir outlets.

The town's sights are scattered, but you can still get around them all in a couple of days on foot. An alternative is to use the green and yellow **Alice Wanderer** (☎08/8952 2111; day-ticket $25), a hop-on-hop-off bus service with commentary, visiting most of the places of interest every seventy minutes. The Yeperenye Shopping Centre, on Hartley Street, is the terminus for the

Alice to Darwin by rail

Under proposal ever since the railway reached Alice from Adelaide in the 1920s (and a condition set by the British on federation in 1901), suddenly in 1999 the decision was made to build the AustralAsia railway, funded by the Commonwealth, South Australian and Territory governments. By mid-2002 work was already months ahead of schedule, with over two-thirds of the 1420-kilometre line cleared, track laying underway and half of the 97 bridges built. To minimize the construction time the railway is being built out in both directions, from depots near Tennant Creek and Katherine where two milliion termite-proof concrete sleepers are being cast.

Part of the rationale in what will probably be a $1.5 billion project is that commodities from Southeast Asia which currently ship down to the conurbations of southeastern Australia could be offloaded at Darwin and railed to their markets. Some see little advantage in this, the cost of delivering freight being largely in the loading/offloading, not the actual transportation. But with reduced freight costs coming up from the south, benefits for the Top End, where locals complain about the cost of living, should be clearer. The rail link will also provide a "land bridge" serving mining and cattle stations through the middle of the Territory.

Initially a daily service commencing in 2004 will only carry freight, but from the following year there should be a weekly passenger service to Darwin and back to Adelaide. AustralAsia Railway Corporation's website, ⓦwww.aarc.com.au, has the full story and progress reports on what is being called the "Steel Snowy", a reference to the similarly monumental Snowy River Irrigation Project of the 1960s.

suburban bus network. This is tailored for shoppers and schoolchildren, which means you'll have to plan your ride around a timetable (available from the tourist office or the council offices on Gregory Terrace) rather than just turning up at a bus stop and waiting; of the four main routes, #1 West and #4 South are the most useful. Otherwise your best bet is to rent a **car** (see "Listings", p.674), or a **bicycle** from any of the hostels, for around $20 a day. There's an enjoyable seventeen-kilometre **paved cycle track** through the bush to Simpson's Gap, starting at Flynn's Grave, 7km along Larapinta Drive, west of the town centre.

Accommodation

In Alice most places (except the campsites) are either in the central area or along **Todd Street** and its southern continuation, **Gap Road** – a fifteen-minute walk from the Mall. Booking ahead is advisable during the winter school holidays (June & July) or during special events. Note that the price codes given for self-contained apartments are for a unit sleeping between four and six people; they often work out a better deal all round than a motel and are certainly more spacious.

Motels

Aurora Alice Springs 11 Leichhardt Terrace ☎08/8950 6666 or 1800 089 644, ⓔasp@aurora-resorts.com.au. About as central as they get and better than it looks. Covered parking, in-house movies and adjacent *Red Ochre Grill* on the Mall. ❺
Desert Rose Inn 15 Railway Terrace ☎08/8952 1411 or 1800 896 116, ⓔinfo@desertroseinn

.com. Budget motel in town, with cooking facilities in some rooms, backpacker twins ($40), a BBQ area and off-street parking. ❹
Mercure Diplomat 15 Gregory Terrace, cnr of Hartley St ☎08/8952 8977, ⓔmercureinn .diplomat@bigpond.com.au. Right in town, a large four-star motel with a better than average restaurant; popular with coach groups. ❺
Mercure Oasis 10 Gap Rd ☎08/8952 1444,

ⓔ mercureoasis@bigpond.com.au. Nicely laid-out motel with landscaped pool area, comfortable rooms and a fine restaurant/bar. ⑥

Outback Inn Resort Stephens Rd ☎08/8952 6100 or 1800 810 644. Well-equipped, modern four-star hotel tucked under the MacDonnell Ranges with a pool, tennis courts and a good restaurant. ④

Self-contained apartments

Alice Tourist Apartments Cnr Gnoilya St and Gap Rd ☎08/8952 2788, ⓕ8953 2950. Large, well-equipped apartments at the far end of Gap Rd. ④

Desert Palms Resort 74 Barrett Drive ☎08/8952 5977 or 1800 678 037,
ⓦwww.desertpalms.com.au. Well-equipped apartments in palmy setting just over the river. ④

Outback Motor Lodge South Terrace ☎08/8952 3888 or 1800 896 133, ⓕ8953 2166. Among the best deals in this category, with more room than many more expensive motels. ③

Swagman's Rest 67–69 Gap Rd ☎08/8953 1333 or 1800 089 612, ⓦwww.theswagmansrest .com.au. Another good-value, self-contained option on Gap Rd. ④

White Gum Holiday Inn 17 Gap Rd ☎08/8952 5144 or 1800 896 131, ⓕ8953 2092. Nearest self-contained apartments to town centre. ④

Hostels

Alice Lodge 4 Mueller St ☎08/8953 1975 or 1800 351 1925. Often-overlooked converted house in a quiet, residential area on the east side of the river, with no parking problems. Long-stay deals, nice garden and pool. Converted caravans are a good option. Dorms $20, rooms ②

Elke's 39 Gap Rd ☎08/8952 8134 or 1800 633 354, ⓕ8952 8143. Former self-contained apartments with various-sized air-con rooms from twins to eights, each sharing a bathroom and small kitchen with TV. Nice pool area, scooters ($50/day) and free breakfasts make up for the lack of a good communal area. Dorms $18, rooms ②

Melanka Backpackers Resort 94 Todd St ☎08/8952 4744 or 1800 896 110,
ⓦwww.melanka.com.au. Huge complex of central but ageing motel buildings popular with unfussy young backpackers. Has a popular bar/cafeteria with cheap meals, a pool and even beach volley-ball. Avoid the four-bed dorms unless you're a sardine; the eights have more room. Dorms $17, rooms ②

Ossies Homestead 18 Warburton St ☎08/8952 2308 or 1800 628 211, ⓔossies@ossies.com.au. Small and friendly hostel in quiet residential street no further than the Gap Rd options, with two pet 'roos, pool and horse rides too. Mixed dorms plus some four- and twin-bed rooms. Dorms $13, rooms ②

Pioneer YHA Todd River end of Parsons St ☎08/8952 8855, ⓔalicepioneer@yhant.org.au. The most central location by far, just half a minute from the "Sails" awning (though parking can be a problem). Four-bed air-con dorms, two eight-beds and even one with sixteen, plus a pool and a clean and spacious kitchen. Dorms $16–22.

Toddy's Backpackers 41 Gap Rd ☎08/8952 1322, ⓕ8952 1767. Popular, large (but friendly) resort next to *Elke's* with very simple mixed, eight-bed dorms, smaller dorms and "de luxe" double rooms with bath, fridge and TV. Bargain evening meals with bar, BBQs and free breakfast, plus pick-ups and 24hr Internet. Dorms from $14, rooms ②

Campsites and caravan parks

Macdonnell Range Holiday Park Palm Place ☎08/8952 6111. Camping and cabins in a leafy setting on the south edge of town with all mod-cons and airport pick-ups. Cabins ③

Stuart Tourist Park Opposite Araluen Centre, Larapinta Drive ☎08/8952 2547. Most central caravan park about 2km west of town with regular camping and powered sites. On-site vans ③

Wintersun Caravan Park Stuart Highway, 3km north of town ☎08/8952 4080. Regular camping and powered sites. On-site vans ③

The Town

Start your tour of town by nipping up to **Anzac Hill** (off Wills Terrace) for a great view over Alice to the Heavitree Ranges beyond. In town, on Parsons Street is the **Old Courthouse** (daily 10am–5pm; $2.20) now home of the National Pioneer Women's Hall of Fame, a stirring photographic exhibit detailing the achievements of women such as Olive Pink (see opposite). Across the street is the **Residency** (Mon–Fri 9am–4pm, Sat 10am–4pm; free), a neat period dwelling and good place to cool off. Inevitably, a bit further down

Parsons Street comes the **Stuart Town Gaol**, Alice's oldest building, dating from 1909.

From the "Sails" awning, a short stroll down the mall will take you past **Adelaide House** (March–Nov Mon–Fri 10am–4pm, Sun 10am–noon; $4), an ingenious convection-cooled building designed by the Reverend John Flynn, founder of the Royal Flying Doctor Service (RFDS). Adelaide House was the first hospital in Central Australia, and also the site of Flynn and Alf Treager's innovative radio experiments using portable, pedal-generated electricity. Inside you'll come across early medical and RFDS memorabilia. If you want to find out more about the RFDS, head down Hartley Street to the **RFDS Visitors Centre** (March–Nov Mon–Sat 9am–4pm, Sun 1–4pm; $5.50) on Stuart Terrace, which has half-hourly tours including a film describing the work of this unique medical organization, still subsidized by charitable donations.

Next door to Adelaide House is the **John Flynn Memorial Church** and, at 65 Hartley St, you'll find **Panorama Guth** (Mon–Sat 9am–5pm, Sun noon–5pm; $5.50), a museum and art gallery displaying scores of Henk Guth's oiled landscapes, as well as original Albert Namatjira watercolours (see box on p.681 for more on Namatjira's life and the Hermannsburg school of painting he initiated). Much more curious is the collection of rare Aboriginal artefacts found here, including some sacred and totemic objects (*tjuringas*) that you'll rarely see elsewhere. The panorama, from which the gallery takes its name, is a novel if unremarkable painting, 60m in circumference, showing the area around Alice, but the gallery below is a wonderfully comfy and congenial place to snooze through the regional home movies on show.

When you've had enough of artefacts and memorabilia, head out to the **Olive Pink Botanical Reserve** (daily 10am–6pm; donation), just across the causeway on Tuncks Road. Olive Pink, whose life story was made into a film, was a passionate defender of Aboriginal rights long before the issue became fashionable. Like Ted Strehlow (see overleaf), with whom she worked, Pink practised a kind of fanatical "inverted eugenics", working solely for the welfare and preservation of "full-blood" tribal Aborigines and their lore, while dismissing those of mixed blood as a lost cause. She also found time to collect native flora from the surrounding lands, all of which can be seen neatly labelled along pathways winding up through the reserve. Displays in the **visitors centre** (daily 10am–4pm) explain the various strategies the plants use to survive in the desert.

The Telegraph Station and School of the Air

The old **Telegraph Station** (daily 8am–5pm, picnic grounds until 9pm; $6.50) is tucked in the hills just to the north of town. Fully restored and accessible along a three-kilometre riverside walk from Wills Terrace (or off the Stuart Highway, 4km north of town), the historic reserve – situated right by the pool from which the town derives its name – faithfully re-creates the settlement's earliest years. There are free and informative thirty-minute **tours** (April–Oct 8.30am–4.30pm; Nov–March 10am–3pm) further detailing pioneering life at the telegraph station. All in all, it's a pleasant place to while away a quiet afternoon, with the surrounding picnic area giving a taste of the Outback on the edge of a city. The station is also the starting point of the **Larapinta Trail** bushwalk to Standley Chasm in the Western MacDonnells (see p.677).

On the other side of the Stuart Highway is the **School of the Air** (Mon–Sat 8.30am–4.30pm, Sun 1.30–4.30pm; closed during school holidays; $3.50), at 80 Head St. Explanatory sessions are offered every thirty minutes on this famous Outback institution, through which children living on remote stations are taught over the radio. It's mostly visited by overseas schoolchildren and teachers, though visiting British royalty have taken a nodding interest at various times, too. From town, take bus #3 and alight at stop 5 or 11.

Along Larapinta Drive to the Alice Springs Desert Park

Larapinta Drive heads out through the western suburbs to the **Alice Springs Cultural Precinct** (daily 10am–5pm; $7), some 2km from the town. The walk to the precinct isn't too bad, but check out the bus service if you're continuing to the Alice Springs Desert Park.

The precinct has brought together some of Alice's best attractions. The **Araluen Centre for Arts and Entertainment**, for example, is the focal point for the performing arts in the region with a 500-seat theatre, cinema, and art galleries that always have something on that is worth checking out. **The Central Australian Aviation Museum**, located in the Old Connellan Hangar, houses many of the aircraft that pioneered travel in the Outback and has a special memorial to the "Coffee Royale Incident" of 1929, in which rescuers searching for missing aviator and national hero Charles Kingsford-Smith crashed and perished in the northern Tanami Desert. Kingsford-Smith was accused of cynically staging the crash for publicity purposes, though this was never proved; the memorial poignantly displays the wreckage of the long-lost *Kookaburra* used in the search.

The **Museum of Central Australia** contains local fauna, including the largest bird that ever lived and an impressive display of locally found meteorites. In the same building is the **Strehlow Research Centre**; Ted Strehlow was the son of a Hermannsburg missionary and an initiate of the Aranda tribe. He devoted much of his life to studying the tribe, producing a comprehensive account of Aboriginal life in the desert. In later years Strehlow disclosed his secret knowledge and collection of sacred *tjuringa* objects to his second wife, Kathleen (also a student of Aboriginal culture), and a battle is still seething for the return of the objects locked in the Research Centre's vaults. *Tjuringas* should only ever be seen by their initiated Aranda owners, none of whom now exist, for, as Strehlow suggested, the passing on of Aranda ceremonial knowledge effectively ended the moment the young men came into contact with Europeans. Interestingly, the Research Centre has put a new spin on its mission, explaining that the sacred objects, chants and Strehlow's extensive family trees are used to support native title claims and reunite members of the Stolen Generation (see p.1175).

For an introduction into Strehlow's work, his sixty-page article *Central Australian Religion*, published in 1964, is available at the Centre. It's a good taster before seeking out his absorbing *Aranda Traditions* and his less accessible magnum opus, *Songs of Central Australia* (both possibly available in libraries, or try asking at the Research Centre). In libraries you may also track down interesting and politically unfashionable reports by Kathleen Strehlow which reflect the feminist politics of her time.

Around the corner on Memorial Drive is the **Alice Springs Memorial Cemetery**, which includes the graves of pioneer aviator Eddie Connellan, artist Albert Namatjira and the reburied remains of the legendary, luckless prospector Harold Lasseter, after whom the town's casino is rather ironically named.

Continuing from the precinct on Larapinta Drive you will come to one of Alice's premier attractions, the **Alice Springs Desert Park** (daily 7.30am–6pm;

$18), phase one of which opened in March 1997. Set right beneath the ranges topped by Mount Gillen, the park is an example of a thoughtful and imaginative design displaying various natural environments of the Territory. Allow yourself at least two hours to fully appreciate the centre's ecology. Shown on the hour, the twenty-minute **film** is actually a little over-portentous, and the real highlight, after you've wandered through various **aviaries** and creek, sand-dune and wood-land habitats, is the large **nocturnal house** where the Territory's varied, but rarely seen, fauna can be seen scurrying around in moonlit action. The park succeeds in blurring the boundary between the surrounding bush and the fenced interior – there's as much birdlife darting about outside the aviaries as in and now it's beginning to grow into itself it's better than ever.

Eating

For a town with the population of a couple of New York precincts, the **eating opportunities** in Alice aren't at all bad. And some places can turn a meal into an event, such as the dinners served on the old Ghan train once or twice a week (℡08/8955 5047), or a ride out into the bush to crack whips and throw boomerangs, while the damper bakes, with the *Camp Oven Kitchen* (℡08/8953 1411). Alternatively, start the day with a gourmet **champagne breakfast**, having just watched the sunrise from a thousand metres up in a hot-air balloon (see "Tours from Alice" box, p.675).

Otherwise, Todd Mall is lined with **cafés** providing outdoor seating, and the **pubs** (see "Drinking, nightlife and entertainment", below) supply counter meals for well under $10. Besides the places listed below, some of the **hotels** have good restaurants.

Cafés and snack bars

Alice Plaza Todd Mall. Food halls with Asian- and Italian-inspired lunches.

Cafe Doppio Mediterranean Fan Arcade, Todd Mall. Mouthwatering concoctions of trans-Adriatic and Asian dishes with pitta or rice.

Red Dog Café Todd Mall, south end. Along with *The Cafetière* next door, a good spot for breakfast croissants and early morning people-watching.

Restaurants

Al Fresco Todd Mall, next to the cinema. Delicious pasta and salad dishes with movie-and-meal deals on Monday night.

Bluegrass Stott Terrace. Latest name for this distinctive old building serving "bush meat", seafood and veggie meals.

Golden Inn Undoolya Road. A Chinese that's better than it looks.

Madigans Alice Springs Desert Park, Larapinta Drive. Top-quality bush tucker with a great setting (noon–3pm & 6.30pm–late).

Malathi's Restaurant 51 Bath St. Possibly the world's first Irish–Indian restaurant, with a bar that is a popular alternative to the town's more raucous pubs.

Oscars Todd Mall Cinema Complex. A classy Italian restaurant offering surprisingly good-value and large portions.

Red Ochre Grill Todd Mall. Creative native Australian food with a couple of imaginative veg options.

Scotty's Tavern and Alice's Restaurant Todd Mall. Bar and restaurant serving typical Territorian food (including emu). Seven-dollar schnitzels with all the veg you can eat on Thursday nights.

Sultan's Cnr Gregory Terrace and Hartley St. Good-value traditional Turkish food where you can BYO.

Drinking, nightlife and entertainment

Like the surrounding desert, night-time Alice initially appears lifeless. However, something can be found going on somewhere most nights, particularly in the latter half of the week. The fortnightly freebie, *Pulse*, or Alice's daily *Centralian Advocate*, carry details of what's going on.

The *Todd Tavern*, at the top of Todd Mall, is the town's landmark **drinking** spot, complete with "unofficial" segregated bars. Thursday night at the enduringly popular *Bojangles Saloon* on Todd Street is all action. There's **jazz and blues** at *Scotty's* on Sunday afternoon from 1pm. *Sean's Irish Sibin* at *Malathi's Restaurant* (see p.671) is a quieter option, while homesick Brits can head for the *Firkin and Hound*, on Hartley Street, a British theme pub that shows just what can be done with a multilevel car park and a little imagination. If nothing else tempts you, there's always the **cinema** at the top of Todd Mall, with cheap nights on Tuesday. Check the programme at the **Araluen Centre for Arts and Entertainment** (℡08/8952 5022) on Larapinta Drive: you'll usually find a worthwhile play, film or concert. And if you're feeling lucky, *Lasseters Hotel Casino* on Barrett Drive along the river's east bank can accommodate you – but not in thongs and a tatty singlet.

Events

The more energetic activities tend to occur in the cooler months, starting with the **Bangtail Muster** on the first Monday in May, followed by May's **Heritage Week** celebrating Alice's history, a colourful and irreverent parade of silliness. The **Camel Cup races** in mid-July are Australia's biggest camel race meeting, ending in a huge fireworks display. The string of **rodeos** along the Track hits Alice in late August, while the town's most famous event, the wacky **Henley-on-Todd Regatta** kicks off in early September. Bottomless boats are run down the dry riverbed; needless to say, the event is heavily insured against the Todd actually flowing. On the last Sunday in November there is the **Corkwood Festival**, a celebration of art, music and dance, with food and craft stalls in Todd Mall. There's also a rather uninspiring **market** every Sunday in the mall.

Shopping for Aboriginal art

Alice has become the country's foremost centre for the art and crafts produced by Aboriginal people, and Todd Mall is full of galleries selling a vast range of high-quality work. Most common are the **dot paintings**, canvas depictions of the temporary sand paintings formerly used to pass on sacred knowledge during ceremonies of the Central Desert tribes. The modern manifestation of this school of art originated in the early 1970s at Papunya, northwest of Alice, under the encouragement of a local teacher, Geoff Bardon. What was intended as a kind of constructive graffiti for youngsters was actually taken up by the elders. Clifford Possum and Billy Stockman were among the earliest of the Papunya artists to find fame, and their paintings are free of the clumsy flashiness of some contemporary work. There are half a dozen lavish books offering a compilation of Central Desert art, such as *Songlines and Dreamings* by Patrick Corbally Stourton (Lund Humphries) – you'll find it in Alice's bookshops.

While it's more difficult to recommended a single **gallery**, you'd do well starting your search at the Original Dreamtime Gallery, 63 Todd Mall, the Aboriginal Art and Culture Centre, 86 Todd St (still a gallery despite the name), Gallery Gondwana, 43 Todd Mall, and Red Sand next door; all are attractive galleries full of good-quality work with Red Sand displaying some lovely Indonesian artefacts too. Less fancy in appearance but loaded with quality unframed canvases is the Aboriginal-owned Papunya Tula Artists, at 78 Todd St, and the similar Warumpi Arts round the corner on Gregory Terrace; you certainly won't save money by buying direct but you might feel happier

Buying and playing a didgeridoo

Didgeridoos, the simple wooden instruments whose eerie drone perfectly evokes the mysteries of Aboriginal Australia, have become phenomenally popular souvenirs, and even a New-Age musical cult to some. Authentic didges are created from termite-hollowed branches of stringybark, woollybark and bloodwood trees which are indigenous across the Top End, from the Gulf to the Kimberley. Most commonly they are associated with Arnhemland, where they were introduced around 2000 years ago and are properly called *yidaka* or *molo* by the Yolngu people of that region. "Didgeridoo" is an Anglicized name relating to the sound produced.

Minuscule, bamboo and even painted pocket didges have found their way onto the market, but a real didge is a natural tube of wood with a rough interior. Painted versions haven't necessarily got any symbolic meaning; plain ones can look less tacky and are less expensive. Branches being what they are, every didge is different but if you're considering playing it rather than hanging it over the fireplace, aim for one around 1.3m in length with a 30–40mm diameter mouthpiece. Beeswax is often used to bring an oversize didge's mouthpiece down to an operable size, but a didge with a body of the right diameter and without wax can feel nicer to use. The bend doesn't affect the sound but the length, tapering and wall thickness (ideally around 10mm) does. Avoid cumbersome, thick-walled items which get in the way of your face and sound flat.

You'll be surprised that making the right sound instead of an embarrassing raspberry will take only a few minutes of persistence; the key is to hum while letting your pressed lips flap, or vibrate, with the right pressure behind them – it's easier using the side of your mouth. The tricky bit – beyond the ability of most uninitiates – is to master circular breathing; this entails refilling your lungs through your nose while maintaining the sound from your lips with air squeezed from your cheeks. A good way to get your head round this concept is to blow or "squirt" bubbles into a glass of water with a straw, while simultaneously inhaling through the nose. Unless you get the hang of circular breathing you'll be limited to making the same lung's worth of droning again and again.

Most outlets that sell didges also sell tapes and CDs and inexpensive "how to" booklets which offer hints on the mysteries of circular breathing and how to emit advanced sounds using your vocal chords.

The Sounds of Starlight show in Todd Mall (April–Nov Tues–Sat 7.30pm; $20) features Alice didge impresario Andrew Langford and friends and gives you a good chance to hear what can be done with a didge as well as being an entertaining night out. You'll also be given a free lesson afterwards, if you want.

And finally, remember that there is nothing magical about a didgeridoo; it's your lips that make the sound, which resonates through the tube – any tube. A length of grey 40mm PVC pipe from Mitre 10 may not have the same kudos or eerie timbre but produces a similar sound at around $5 a metre.

about who benefits from the proceeds. Another place offering mediocre but inexpensive paintings and didgeridoos is The House of Oz, opposite *Melanka Backpackers Resort*, but in the end it's just a matter of spending half a day or more looking for what you want at a price that you find acceptable. The more you spend, the more chance there is of making a deal, with free overseas postage and insurance usually offered at the bigger places. If you're heading north, the galleries in Aileron, Ti Tree (see p.663) and Tennant Creek (p.660) have a much smaller range of Aboriginal art on sale, but often at lower prices than that in Alice's galleries.

Listings

Bookshops Arunt a Bookshop, Todd St, is very good for local history plus Aboriginal art and culture. Bookworm, Colacag Plaza (in the block between Gregory and Stott terraces), buys and sells secondhand books.

Camping supplies Alice Springs Disposals, Reg Harris Lane, off Todd Mall.

Car rental Advance Car Rentals (☎08/8953 3700) has good deals. Outback Rentals (☎08/8952 1405 or 1800 652 133), at 78 Todd St opposite the council offices, has mopeds and Suzuki 4WD jeeps, as well as special deals, as does Thrifty (☎08/8952 9999), on the corner of Hartley St and Stott Terrace. For 4WDs, Britz/Maui (☎1800 331 454) on the Stuart Highway north of Alice and has Toyota Bushcampers and larger trucks. With an advance booking Travel Hire Australia (☎02/4754 5817, ⓦ www.travelhire.com.au) can have a bush-equipped Land Rover waiting for you.

Fuel 24hr service and marginally cheaper fuel than in town at the Shell truckstop on the Stuart Highway north.

Hospital Gap Rd ☎08/8951 7777.

Internet access Fast connections are found at Didjworld in Spring Plaza, just north of the "Sails" in Todd Mall. There are a couple more places on Todd Street opposite the council lawns.

Maps The Map Shop, Alice Plaza, first floor (☎08/8951 5393) for detailed maps of the Centre.

Permits for Aboriginal Land Central Land Council, 33 North Stuart Highway, PO Box 3321, Alice Spings 0871 ☎08/8951 6211.

Police Parsons St ☎08/8951 8888.

Post office Hartley St ☎08/8952 1020.

Trains The Ghan leaves Alice Springs each Tuesday and Friday at 2pm and arrives in Adelaide at 10am the next day, with the return leg to Alice departing Adelaide on Monday and Thursday at 2pm and arriving at 10am. Coach class (no bed or meals) costs $170 ($136 from Port Augusta); first class costs over three times as much, with a sleeper and meals included. If you opt for "holiday class" you get a four-berth sleeper for around $351, but no meals. Change at Port Augusta to connect with the Indian-Pacific line to Sydney or Perth. By 2005 there may be a weekly service to Darwin (see box on p.665).

Sights south of Alice

Several sites of interest are located beyond **Heavitree Gap**, a couple of kilometres south of town. The museum, date garden and camel farm described below are within range of the #4 bus, which terminates at the **Old Timers Folk Museum** (April–Nov daily 2–4pm; $2), just off the Stuart Highway, yet another display of pioneering memorabilia. The remainder are easily reached by bike, or on the Alice Wanderer bus route.

Out on Palm Circuit, the **Mecca Date Garden** (Mon–Fri 9am–5pm, Sat 9am–1pm; free) was Australia's first commercial date farm, set up in the 1950s. Dates themselves are believed to be the first plant to be cultivated by man, and the farm now produces around 4000kg of the fruit a year from trees introduced in the nineteenth century by Afghan cameleers. You are offered a free sample on arrival. Tours of the farm – basically rows of date palms with an informative commentary – start on the hour.

A farm of a very different sort is just a couple of kilometres down the Ross Highway. The **Frontier Camel Farm** (daily 8am–5pm; $6) offers short rides on camels, plus a camel and cameleering museum. Back down the Stuart Highway just before the airport, about 10km south of town, the **Ghan Preservation Society** (daily 9am–5pm; $5.50) at MacDonnell Siding features a converted old train station housing a **museum** of Alice Springs' early rail years, and is also involved in the refurbishment of old Ghan locomotives and rolling stock, which are used for **train rides** (☎08/8955 5047) along a short section of track. Next door the **National Transport Hall of Fame** (9am–5pm; $6) features a collection of old cars, trucks and motorbikes, including a cute red Fiat Tipo, something called the "Mulga Express" (not your average touring Kingswood) as well as the

Tours from Alice

A large number of **tour operators** offer adventurous, cultural or historic tours throughout the area – some recommended operators are listed below. Just about every hostel and hotel offers a tour-booking service or you can try any of a number of travel shops which specialize in selling tours; there are a few around the corners of Todd Street and Gregory Terrace.

Austour ⓣ1800 335 009. Day-trips to Uluru, but you'll regret such a short visit. Also offers Eastern and Western MacDonnell tours.

Ballooning Downunder ⓣ1800 801 601; **Outback Ballooning** ⓣ1800 809 790; **Spinifex** ⓣ1800 677 893. Alice is Australia's ballooning capital and any of these will take you up, up and away – and back down to a champagne breakfast (around $170 for 5hr). Don't wear your best clothes.

Frontier Camel Tours ⓣ08/8953 0444, ⓦwww.cameltours.com.au. Short camel rides down the Todd River, two-and-a-half-day West Mac jaunts from *Glen Helen Resort* (see p.679), and five-day Simpson Desert treks.

Ossie's Outback Horse Treks ⓣ08/8952 2308. Day, sunset and overnight rides up the Todd River's east bank from $60. Beginners welcome; discounts for YHA/VIP members.

Outback Experience ⓣ08/8955 2666. Trips to Chambers Pillar and other spots in the northern Simpson.

Outback Quad Adventures ⓣ08/8953 0697. Fun quad-bike rides using automatic machines: all you have to do is turn the throttle and steer. Dress for extreme dust. Also at Curtin Springs (see p.687) and with another operator at Kings Creek Station (p.685).

Rockayer ⓣ08/8956 2345; **Australian Outback Flights** ⓣ08/8952 4625. Flights to the Rock and back in a day for around $300. Don't underestimate a flight like this, with a bit of luck you'll get some great scenery on the way.

Rod Steinert ⓣ08/8955 5095. Several Aboriginal culture tours in the Alice area, including the excellent, half-day Dreamtime tour. While the apparently solemn "corroboree" will bore or embarrass you, the rest of the tour is unusually informative, educational and provocative.

Sahara Outback Tours ⓣ08/8953 0881. Offers two-, three- and five-day camping tours through the West MacDonnells, to Kings Canyon and Uluru. As is often the case, the longer tours are the best value.

Wayoutback ⓣ1300 551 510, ⓦwww.wayoutback.com.au. Popular and inexpensive three-day Rock and Canyon tours packed into a Troopcarrier.

original 8WD road train that used to slog up to Darwin during the 1930s at a hot and noisy 30kph.

The MacDonnell Ranges

The **MacDonnell Ranges** are among the longest of the parallel ridge systems that corrugate the Centre's landscape. Their east–west axis, passing right through Alice Springs, is broken in many places by gaps carved through the ranges during better-watered epochs. It is these striking ruptures, along with the grandeur and colours of the rugged landscape – particularly west of Alice – which make a few days spent in the MacDonnells so worthwhile. The expansive **West MacDonnell Ranges National Park** is best appreciated with at least one overnight stay at any of the campsites mentioned, while the often-overlooked

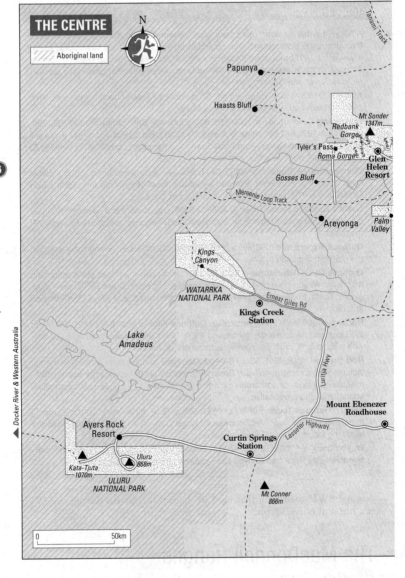

Eastern MacDonnells have a more compact, intimate feel; a better bet if your time is limited. Both ranges can be visited as part of a tour (see box on p.675) or with your own vehicle. Although some tracks are unsealed, 4WD vehicles are mostly unnecessary. However, because most rental companies forbid the driving of conventional cars on corrugated tracks, you may end up renting one. If you do, then make the most of its all-terrain capabilities; check out the box on pp.682–683 as well as the off-road driving advice in Basics (p.39).

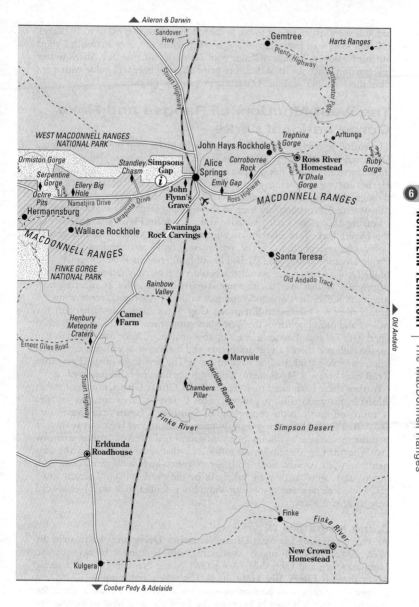

A better way still to get in touch with the West Macs is to do part of the **Larapinta Trail**, a long-distance footpath following the ranges, which was finally completed in 2002. It starts at the Telegraph Station north of Alice (see p.669) and ends 223km to the west on the 1347m summit of Mount Sonder. The walk is divided into around a dozen sections, but these sections do not necessarily delineate a day's walk. Trailside water tanks are situated no more than two days' walk or 30km apart. As a rule the more impressive but also more arduous sections are nearer town. Section 2 from Simpson's Gap to Jay Creek is 25km long – an overnight stop is advised, while the next section is a short but hard 14km to Standley Chasm with 350m of climbing. See Alice's tourist information office for latest details or print off the whole trail guide with maps from the PWCNT website: Ⓦ www.nt.gov.au/ipe/pwcnt.

The West MacDonnell Ranges and Finke Gorge national parks

The **route** described below follows an anticlockwise loop out along Larapinta Drive and then Namatjira Drive to *Glen Helen Resort*, from where a 110-kilo-metre part-dirt road brings you past Gosses Bluff to the turn-off for Palm Valley, Hermannsburg and back to Alice – a total distance of 370km. The track passes through **Aboriginal land** on its return section, but no permit is required (unless stated), providing you keep to the road and camp at designated sites.

Leaving Alice along Larapinta Drive, you reach **John Flynn's Grave**, just past the Desert Park, 7km from town. Situated beneath Mount Gillen, a granite boulder set on a plinth marks the spot where John Flynn, founder of the Royal Flying Doctor Service (RFDS), had his ashes interred in 1951. Originally one of the Devil's Marbles (see p.662), the boulder was recently claimed back by the Aborigines of that area, a rather mean-spirited land claim considering how much the RFDS has done and continues to do for Aboriginal communities. A little further is a turning to **Simpsons Gap** (gates open daily 8am–8pm), the nearest and most popular of the West Macs' gaps, where a white, sandy riverbed lined with red and ghost gums leads up to a small pool. Agile rock wallabies live on the cliffs and there's a **visitors centre** and barbecues, as well as a seventeen-kilometre cycle track leading back to town. The first stage of the **Larapinta Trail** ends here – a 24-kilometre walk from the Telegraph Station in Alice.

Further along Larapinta Drive are the **Twin Ghost Gums**, immortalized in Albert Namatjira's definitive painting of the Centralian landscape, and just after is a turn-off north to the tourist trap of **Standley Chasm** (daily 8am–6pm; $6), 50km from Alice. Situated on Iwupataka Aboriginal land, this is another popular spot, where a walk up the cycad palm-lined riverbed leads to a narrow chasm formed by the erosion of softer rock that once lay between the red-quartzite walls. Around noon both eighty-metre-high walls reverberate with "oohs" and "ahhs" as they are briefly lit by the overhead sun. There is also a café with a terrace and a souvenir shop; black-footed rock wallabies are fed here daily at 9.30am.

Along Namatjira Drive

Another 6km along Larapinta Drive, **Namatjira Drive** turns north amid the West MacDonnell Ranges; continuing on Larapinta brings you to Hermannsburg and Palm Valley (see p.680). Along Namatjira Drive, a scenic 42km ahead is **Ellery Big Hole** (barbecues, toilets and camping; $2.20), the deepest – and thus most permanent – waterhole in the area, and at times the coldest. Nevertheless, caught between the brief ebb and flow of visiting bus tours, it's a pleasant spot, and your stealth may be rewarded by glimpses of wildlife quenching their thirst. Eleven kilometres to the west is **Serpentine Gorge** (toilets but no camping): the only way to appreciate this gorge is to swim across the small pool which sometimes blocks the entrance to the gorge (or climb high over the ridge to the right). Few bother to exert themselves, but rock-hopping upstream brings you to a flooded chasm. As with many con-cealed and perennial pools in Central Australia, the Aranda have nurtured a myth about the pool being the home of a fierce serpent, and even today they visit the place reluctantly and never enter the water; Mutujulu waterhole beneath Uluru has a similar legend. In this way the myth acted as a superstitious device to ensure that the pool – a droughtproof source of water – was never polluted or carelessly used.

With an interpretation shelter and a great walk to **Inarlanga Pass** (actually a narrow gorge), the **Ochre Pits**, signposted off Namatjira Drive, also make an interesting diversion. The ochre, particularly the red variety, became a highly valued trading commodity and is still used by the Aranda for ceremonial purposes. The **two-hour walk** to the pass along rounded ridges and through wooded valleys is most enjoyable. Once at Inarlanga you may find the egg-like kernels of cycads on the boulder-strewn creek bed, which is itself framed by acutely twisted beds of rock; altogether a lovely spot lacking only a waterhole.

Fourteen kilometres further west, **Ormiston Gorge** and **Pound National Park** (barbecues and camping) are also worth the effort. One of the most spectacular and easily accessible spots in the West Macs, the short ascent up to **Gum Tree Lookout** (the walk continues down into the gorge) gives a great view over the 250-metre-high gorge walls rising from the pools below – home to ducks and even the odd black swan. The three-hour **Pound Walk** includes some rock-hopping, and longer overnight walks can be undertaken by those who are properly equipped – ask the rangers at the Park Information Centre in the car park, who also organize occasional free slide show evenings for campers.

Just west of Ormiston is **GLEN HELEN**, another wide chasm with a perennial waterhole in the bed of the ancient **Finke River**, which – on the rare occasions when it flows – can reach Lake Eyre in South Australia. *Glen Helen Resort* (☎08/8956 7489, ⓦwww.melanka.com.au; dorms from $22, rooms ❺) is a nice place to spend a comfortable night out in the West Macs and sells fuel. Helicopter flights over the nearby sites cost from around $5 per minute per person. If you're heading towards Kings Canyon along the **Mereenie Loop Track** (see p.682) you're supposed to get your permit here ($2.20) but they are seldom checked. Make sure you have enough fuel for the entire journey of at least 250km.

Roma Gorge, Redbank Gorge and Gosses Bluff

Beyond Glen Helen the bitumen ends, but the natural spectacles continue. If you intend to complete the loop, it's about 107km to Hermannsburg (part-sealed), and another 126km east along Larapinta Drive to Alice. Providing you stay on the road, it's easily done by 2WD vehicles at a sensible pace in dry conditions.

The turn-off for **Roma Gorge** is around 13km from Glen Helen. A curious spot formerly only known to some locals, it has become open to the public in recent years. The small gorge is 10.5km from the road (4WD clearance needed) and it takes about 25 minutes to get there, despite what the sign indicates. The track follows a stony creek bed to a basic campsite just before the gorge. From there a short walk leads to the gorge where you'll have little difficulty spotting the scores of arcane **engravings** on the rocks; the well-known concentric circles are here, as well as feather-like depictions. To be honest, Roma and its mysterious engravings sound more interesting than they are to look at, but the drive in adds to the experience.

Keeping the distinctive outline of **Mount Sonder** (another classic Namatjira silhouette) in view to the north, the turn-off for **Redbank Gorge** is 20km from Glen Helen, with a further 10km to the car park, passing one of the exposed **campsites** on the way. Redbank is the longest and narrowest cleft along the MacDonnells, its slippery walls no more than a metre apart in places and rarely warmed by direct sunlight. To get a full impression of the gorge you'll need an airbed and a pair of trainers to swim the 400m to the other end, which involves crossing countless freezing pools and some awkward scrambling.

Seventeen kilometres from the Redbank turn-off, you keep straight on for **Tyler's Pass**, passing the Haasts Bluff and Papunya turn-off to your right. The road can be rough until you're over the pass, from where a short ascent to the radio mast gives a great view of **Gosses Bluff**. From the pass mysterious forces have seen fit to re-align the road and then seal it as far as the Hermannsburg track; if nothing else it can give your suspension a break. A bumpy track (flooding apart, not 4WD as stated) leads to the interior of this extraordinary two-kilometre-wide crater, known to the Western Aranda as *Tnorula*. Inside, the majority is a fenced-off ceremonial site where once male miscreants paid the penalty just short of death for sexual indiscretions. When you consider the magnitude of this comet impact 140 million years ago, it makes you wonder whether this might not have been the climate-shifting cataclysm which caused the extinction of the dinosaurs around the same time (give or take 20 million years). The interpretive displays don't speculate quite so daringly, instead explaining how the crater is actually the frayed relic of a dome created by rebounding rock strata. The interior of the crater is rather less satisfying than the view from outside, or better still from the air, and a good way to appreciate the wonder of it all is to scramble up to the rim; there's no path, it's less steep on the outside slope and it's all probably not allowed, but from this vantage point the impact which created the two-hundred-metre-high circular ridge is made a little more comprehensible.

South of the bluff, you reach the Hermannsburg–Mereenie Loop junction and you're back on the dirt. Left leads to Palm Valley and Alice, right to Kings Canyon and close encounters of the corrugated kind (see p.682).

Finke Gorge National Park

The popularity of **FINKE GORGE NATIONAL PARK** is founded on its prehistoric cycads and unique red cabbage palms which have survived in the park's sheltered **Palm Valley** for over ten thousand years. Despite the difficult 4WD road leading to the valley it's on every tour's itinerary, though it doesn't quite live up to the hype. The pleasant forty-minute loop walk is the valley's highlight; visiting the rest of the park requires a 4WD vehicle and seems discouraged, as does the route along the Finke riverbed from Hermannsburg (see box on pp.682–683). On the way in or out of the valley, you can climb up to the once-sacred **Initiation Rock**, giving a fine view over the **Amphitheatre**, a cirque of sandstone cliffs. The park has barbecues, toilets, solar-heated showers and camping.

HERMANNSBURG was originally a Lutheran mission established in the 1870s, making it among the oldest communities in the Centre. Unusually, you are able to visit the town, or more specifically the **Historic Precinct** (daily 9am–4pm; $5) which features the original mission buildings converted into tearooms and an art gallery (tours $3.50). Your guide will rattle off his spiel on the history of the mission and the life and work of Albert Namatjira who was born here (see box opposite), although any observation about the "totemic faces" concealed in Namatjira's paintings should be taken with a pinch of salt. There is also a supermarket and fuel (cash only), but no accommodation.

Back towards Alice Springs, passing the **Albert Namatjira Memorial**, you reach the small community of **WALLACE ROCKHOLE**, offering sixty

Albert Namatjira 1902–1959

Born on the Hermannsburg Lutheran mission in 1902, Albert, who added his father's name to appease Eurocentric propriety, was the first of the Hermannsburg mission's much-copied school of landscape watercolourists. Although without much previous painting experience, Namatjira assisted Rex Battarbee on his painting expeditions through the Central Australian deserts in the 1930s. His talent soon became obvious to Battarbee, who later became Namatjira's agent. Like all NT Aborigines at that time, Namatjira was forbidden to buy alcohol, stay overnight in Alice Springs or leave the Territory without permission, but at the insistence of southern do-gooders – and against his wishes – he was the first Aborigine to be awarded Australian **citizenship**, in 1956. This meant he could travel without limitations, but needed a permit to visit his own family on Aboriginal reserves, while the house in Alice he longed for was denied him for fear of the entourage he might have attracted. Following the success of his first exhibition in the south, which sold out in three days, he became a reluctant celebrity, compelled to pay taxes on his relatively huge earnings which were further depleted by the "share-it-all" kinship laws that still hamper successful Aboriginal artists today. A shy and modest man, much respected for his earnestness and generosity, he died in 1959 following a sordid conviction and short imprisonment for supplying alcohol to fellow Aborigines.

Critics could never make up their minds about his work, but his popular appeal was undoubted: exhibitions in the southern cities, which he rarely attended, persistently sold out within hours of opening, and today his paintings remain among the most valuable examples of Australia's artistic preoccupation with its landscape.

-minute tours (☎08/8956 7415; $10) of the nearby Aboriginal petroglyphs as well as a shop, fuel and camping. From here, it's 117km of bitumen back to Alice Springs.

The Eastern MacDonnells and the northern Simpson Desert

Heading out of Alice through the **Heavitree Gap** and along the Ross Highway, you soon reach **Emily Gap**, Alice's nearest waterhole, 10km from town. This is one of the most significant Aranda sacred sites, the start of the Caterpillar Dreaming trail. There are engravings on the far side of the soupy pool, and plenty of darting birds and irksome flies; camping or open fires are not permitted. **Jessie Gap**, a little further east, is similar in appearance, but usually dry and of limited appeal. **Corroborree Rock** (camping), 45km east of Alice, is an unusual, fin-like outcrop of limestone with an altar-like platform and a crevice whose polished appearance suggests that, if not Aranda initiates, then plenty of tourists have squeezed through in a rite of passage. Known as *Antanangantana* to the Aranda, it was once a repository for sacred *tjuringa* objects.

John Hayes Rockhole and Trephina Gorge

John Hayes Rockhole and Trephina Gorge, by far the most satisfying of the accessible destinations in the Eastern MacDonnells, are just 80km from Alice. Both offer superb scenery and a selection of enjoyable walks, and there's a four-hour ridge walk linking the two. **John Hayes Rockhole** (limited camping space), reached along a rocky four-kilometre track requiring a high-clearance vehicle, is a series of pools linked by (usually dry) waterfalls along a canyon. The ninety-minute "Chain of Pools" walk takes you to the top of the gorge

Some 4WD tracks in the centre

While most us have little need to own a heavy, fuel-guzzling 4WD, renting one for a few days of off-road driving is fun and can get you to some beautiful corners of the central deserts visited only by other intrepid "four-wheelers". Below are some **4WD-only** routes close to Alice, which will give you a chance to fiddle with the transmission levers and which could all be linked into a memorable week in the dirt. Remember that 4WD vehicles are not invincible: when driven carelessly they can easily get stuck, become uncontrollable or damaged. They can also make a mess of the terrain if driven off main tracks; avoid wheel spins and tearing up vegetated ground which takes years to recover. Finally, make sure the outfit you're renting from understands and approves your proposed 4WD itinerary and, at the very least, read the advice and carry the gear recommended in "Basics", p.39. Ask at Alice's tourist office for the *4x4 Guide* booklet, which details other routes in the area. For recommended 4WD rental agents see the "Listings" for Alice, p.674. One problem with renting is that you're rarely supplied with any recovery gear; even a tow strap or second spare tyre have to be prised out of rental companies (Travel Australia Hire is an exception here, even providing compressors for sand driving) and yet they encourage you to take your vehicle off-road. Although most of the rental cars are in good shape, it is in your own interest to make sure you are appropriately equipped, especially for travelling in remote areas, which may mean actually buying or renting gear.

Mereenie Loop Track

The main appeal of the Mereenie, linking the West Macs with Kings Canyon (around 200km, allow 3–4 hours), is that it avoids backtracking on the usual "Canyon and Rock" tour. But scenically from the junction west of Palm Valley it's nothing special and the corrugations west of Areyonga can be fearsome. A further irritation is that, according to the mandatory permit issued either at Glen Helen or Kings Canyon, you're not allowed to stop, let alone camp, except for one so-so look-out just before the descent to the Kings Canyon Resort.

Finke River Route

With a day to spare and minimal experience with a 4WD, following the Finke riverbed from **Hermannsburg** down to the **Ernest Giles Road** offers an adventurous alternative to the highway and also saves some backtracking from Kings Canyon. Rewards include stark gorge scenery, a reliable waterhole and the likelihood that you'll have it all to yourself. Before you set off, seek out the ranger at Palm Valley (℡08/8956 7401) who'll fill you in on the state of the track and provide a handy **map** that clarifies all the junctions. When on the route follow the small signs for "Kings Canyon".

The hundred-kilometre track starts immediately south of Hermannsburg and after 10km of corrugated road, you descend into the riverbed. From now on it's slow driving along a pair of sandy or pebbly ruts – you must deflate your tyres to at least 25psi/1.7bar and keep in the ruts to minimize the risk of getting stuck. The sole designated campsite is at **Boggy Hole**, much nicer than it sounds and around two hours (28.5km) from Hermannsburg. The campsite looks out from beneath river red

and down through the pools – an ideal way to get hot, but with plenty of opportunities to cool off. Alternatively, the lower pools are accessible from the car park.

Trephina Gorge, perhaps the most impressive spot in the eastern part of the range, is a beautiful, sheer-sided sandy gorge whose rich red walls support slender, white-barked ghost gums and a pool. There is a pleasant **campsite** and the gums to permanent reed-fringed waterholes, best seen at dawn as the sunlight creeps across the gorge and the ponds are alive with birdlife.

Beyond Boggy Hole, the track crisscrosses rather than follows the riverbed before the roller-coaster ride to the Giles Road across some low dunes thinly wooded with desert oaks – beware of oncoming traffic on blind crests. Boggy Hole to the Giles Road is 65km, so allow three hours. If you fancy taking the direct route to the Ernest Giles Road from the Tempe Downs station track, keep straight over the dunes just after a salt pan instead of turning sharply east; subsequent dunes can be avoided but the Palmer River crossing can be very sandy and may require further tyre deflation. Back on the road, keep speeds down until you can reflate your tyres.

Arltunga to Ruby Gap

The same sensible precautions are required for this route; make sure you're well equipped and see the ranger at the **Arltunga Visitors Centre** (☏08/8951 8211), 101km east of Alice, for the latest track conditions. It's a very scenic, if bumpy, 53-kilometre drive (allow two hours) through the ranges and including some steep creek crossings until you reach the sandy riverbed of the Hale and the **Ruby Gap Nature Park**. From here keep to the sandy ruts and inch carefully over the rocks for 7km to **Glen Annie Gorge**, a dead end with maroon red cliffs, bright green reeds and off-white sand.

Cattlewater Pass and the Harts Ranges

A less difficult track heads north from Arltunga past Claraville station and up over the Harts Ranges through the **Cattlewater Pass** to the Plenty Highway, 67km or three hours from Arltunga. It's a worthwhile and no less scenic way of returning to Alice from Ruby Gap via a different route and you're bound to see some hopping marsupials along the way. Once you reach the Plenty Highway it's an easy dirt road via Gemtree to the Stuart Highway and Alice, 150km away.

The Finke and Old Andado Tracks

More ambitious than the above and a satisfying 750-kilometre loop into the fringes of the Simpson Desert are the **Finke** and **Old Andado tracks** whose routes diverge at Alice's airport and rejoin at **Mount Dare station** just over the South Australian border. At Alice airport the westerly Finke branch follows the route of the old Ghan railway past Ewaninga Rock Carvings and Maryvale (fuel), where you can take an 88-kilometre return diversion to Chambers Pillar (more on these three places overleaf). After Maryvale it's a straight run to Finke (fuel) with the sandy or corrugated track being fun and mostly 2WD. On the way you'll pass stands of desert oak, shrubs and claypans and you might even see some feral camels. Just as things seem to be getting too easy the track sometimes gets sandier soon after Charlotte Waters towards Mount Dare, where you can buy fuel, provisions and a beer at the bar. Heading back to Alice (433km, no fuel) towards Old Andado, the track can again be sandy, but from the old homestead the going gets much easier as you cross the low ranges bringing you past the Santa Teresa community and the road back to the airport. For an outline of the Simpson crossing itself, from Mount Dare to Birdsville, see p.577.

"Gorge" and "Panorama" walks (both taking about 30min) are well worth the effort.

Ross River Homestead and Arltunga Historical Reserve

Five kilometres beyond Trephina Gorge, the Ross Highway peters out into two tracks: 8km to the southeast (90km east of Alice Springs) is the **Ross River Homestead**, an Outback resort (℡08/8956 9711 or 1800 241 711, ℱ8956 9823; bunkhouse ❷, cabins ❼, camping also available), which offers "dude ranch" activities such as camel, horse and wagon rides, boomerang throwing, whip cracking and billy tea with damper. It's a comfortable, if relatively busy, base for a few days' stay in the Eastern MacDonnells, and has a popular bar, pool and restaurant.

The other track, a 35-kilometre corrugated dirt road heading east, leads to **ARLTUNGA**, the site of Central Australia's first goldrush. The road here may be long overdue for a grading, but a whole heap of money has been spent on restoring the ghost town and providing it with a fancy **visitors centre** (daily 8am–5pm; ℡08/8951 8211). All the place needs now is some visitors. Arltunga's story began in the 1890s, in the midst of the country's first economic depression, when gold was discovered by the miners originally drawn to the garnets at Ruby Gap (see p.683). Over the next fifteen years they regularly pushed barrows the 600km from Oodnadatta railhead to grope in desperate conditions for pitiful returns. Arltunga was never a particularly rich field and remains an abandoned testament to pioneering optimism.

Ruby Gap and Glen Annie Gorge

From Arltunga it's a fairly rough 4WD out to Ruby and Glen Annie gorges, both of them beautiful and wild places. Back in 1885 the explorer Lindsay discovered "rubies" while in the process of digging for water, thereby initiating the customary rush for what turned out to be worthless garnets. Crossing the sandy Hale riverbed leads into **Ruby Gap** and then **Glen Annie Gorges** (no facilities except camping). At the end of the day, even with the flies handing over to the mozzies, it's one of the most tranquil places you'll find in Central Australia.

The Old South Road and the northern Simpson Desert

Just 14km out of Alice, shortly after the airport turn-off, a sign indicates "Chambers Pillar (4WD)". This is the **Old South Road**, which follows the abandoned course of the Ghan and original Overland Telegraph Line to Adelaide, 1550km away; these days the sandy and corrugated route has become one arm of a loop which takes adventurous four-wheel drivers through the northern Simpson Desert past Finke settlement and Old Andado homestead (see box on p.683).

Ordinary cars can easily manage to cover the 35km to **Ewaninga Rock Carvings**, a jumble of rocks by a small claypan (a dried-up pool). Their meaning, like that of other petroglyphs in the area, remains unknown but their age, estimated at 35,000 years, suggests that they certainly predate occupation of the Centre by today's Aborigines – something countered by PW&C's more tourist-friendly claims that it is a sacred Aboriginal site, part of the Rain Dreaming, but that the meaning of the symbols are too dangerous to reveal.

Heading on past the store at **MARYVALE** (shop and fuel), you'll need a 4WD vehicle and to be in the mood for a thorough hammering to get across the Charlotte Ranges and subsequent sand ridges on the way to **Chambers Pillar** (toilets, barbecues and camping), a historic dead-end, 165km from Alice. Named by Stuart after one of his benefactors (who had natural features named after him and his family all the way to the Arafura Sea), the eighty-metre-high sandstone pillar was used as a landmark by early overlanders heading up from the railhead at Oodnadatta, in South Australia. The plinth is carved with their names as well as those of many others (including a certain J. Hendrix), and can be seen from the platform at the pillar's base. If you don't fancy renting your own vehicle, Outback Experience in Alice (☎08/8955 2666) has full-day tours to this area which include Chambers Pillar. For an outline of the Finke and Old Andado tracks, see p.683.

South to Kings Canyon

Kings Canyon is 320km southwest of Alice Springs, of which the hundred-kilometre section from the Stuart Highway turn-off towards Stockyard Homestead/Wallara is unsealed. From Stockyard, it's bitumen all the way to the Watarrka National Park which envelops Kings Canyon. If you're heading straight down the Track from Alice there's an increasingly barren run of nearly 700km to Coober Pedy (itself no oasis, see p.872) in South Australia.

Most **tours** of two days or more departing from Alice include Kings Canyon on their see-it-all itineraries, providing the easiest and cheapest way to enjoy the canyon. There are daily McCafferty's bus services from Alice Springs to Kings Canyon, or from Ayers Rock Resort with AAT Kings (see p.875).

The Stuart Highway to Kings Canyon

Around 76km from Alice, the turn off to **Rainbow Valley** (camping, but no water or firewood) follows a twenty-kilometre dirt track (the very last bit may be sandy), to the "valley", actually a much-photographed outcrop set behind claypans which are said to produce rainbows following rain. More commonly, sunset catches the red-stained walls spectacularly and it's a wild place to spend the night, best followed in the morning by a climb up the crag.

You soon reach the Ernest Giles Road, where you turn off right for Kings Canyon; note that the first hundred kilometres are unsealed though easy in a 2WD. Not far along this road there's another turn-off, to **Henbury Meteorite Craters**. The extra-terrestrial shower that caused these twelve depressions, 2–180m in diameter, may have occurred in the last twenty thousand years, given that one of the Aranda's names for the place translates as "sun walk fire devil rock". A walk with interpretive signs winds among the craters, long since picked clean of any unearthly fragments. There is camping, barbecues and toilets.

The Ernest Giles Road heads west, sandy at times, joining the sealed Luritja Highway linking Ayers Rock Resort to Kings Canyon. Around here you'll see some nice shady groves of desert oak, the largest of the casuarina desert trees. The bitumen road continues west, past **Kings Creek station** (☎08/8956 7474, ⓦ www.kingscreekstation.com.au; canvas cabins ❷ with breakfast), 35km from the canyon. Unlike most other pastoral properties in Australia, Kings Creek has taken to rounding up and raising the feral camels which other station owners regard as vermin (see box on p.654). As meat they fetch the same as cattle but as a racing camel sold to Arabia they are worth six times as much. The only problem is you can't fit as many into a double-decker, triple-trailer road train which makes transportation expensive. There are various activities you can do at Kings Creek: quad rides along a twisty, sandy circuit, helicopter flights over the canyon or beyond, and camel rides at sunrise or sunset. You'll also find a well-equipped campsite, pool, fuel and a shop/café with preternaturally good coffee.

Watarrka National Park (Kings Canyon)

As you cross the boundary of the **Watarrka National Park**, you'll see the turning to **Kathleen Springs**, a sacred Aboriginal waterhole, an easy twenty-minute stroll away. It was once used to corral livestock and is now a good place to catch sight of colourful birdlife.

Another twenty minutes down the road is **Kings Canyon** itself. The big attraction here is the two-hour, six-kilometre **walk** up and around the canyon's rim. Undertaken in the preferred clockwise direction, it starts with a steep ascent from where the trail leads through the **Lost City**, a maze of domes resembling giant petrified cowpats stacked at random. Don't miss the vertiginous **look-outs** onto the two-hundred-metre-high southern wall before you clamber down into the **Garden of Eden**, a palm-filled chasm bridged by an impressive array of staircases. On the far side there's an easily missed detour downstream to the waterhole where you can cool off and beyond the pool, reach the classic view of the canyon wall from the brink of the dry waterfall. The rest of the walk descends gradually to the car park, passing the 22-kilometre overnight "Giles Track" to Kathleen Springs.

There have been some long-overdue improvements in facilities here (including a kiosk) but there is still no **camping** at Kings Canyon itself, although you can camp elsewhere in the park with a ranger's permit. Ten kilometres past the canyon, the *Kings Canyon Resort* (℡08/8956 7442, ✉kcr@austranet.com.au) is a small **resort** with a neat, grassy campsite, a bunkhouse with four-bed dorms $22) but only barbecues to cook on. Away from the rabble, the much more expensive *Lodge* (❼) offers a pool and great views. The daytime café (6am–9am & 10am–2pm), by the service station and pricey shop (daily 7am–7pm), serves meals for about $15; in the evening you can enjoy a barbie in the adjacent grill/bar, otherwise try the $45 buffet at *Carmichaels Restaurant* at the lodge. Lilla Tours (book at the lodge's reception) offers a personal look at the region though Aboriginal eyes. A **shuttle bus** ($20) operates daily from the resort reception to the canyon.

Uluru–Kata Tjuta National Park and Ayers Rock Resort

Uluru–Kata Tjuta National Park encompasses **Uluru** (the Anangu name for **Ayers Rock**) and **Kata Tjuta** (or the **Olgas**). The park is the most visited single site in Australia and if you're wondering whether all the hype is worth it, then the answer is, emphatically, yes. The Rock, its textures, colours and not least its elemental presence is without question one of the world's natural wonders. Overt commercialization has been controlled within the park and other tourists can be avoided, especially if you choose not to undertake the climb.

Kata Tjuta (meaning "many heads") lies 45km west from the park entry station. A cluster of rounded domes divided by narrow chasms and valleys, it is geologically quite distinct from Uluru. Public access is limited to the "Valley of the Winds" walk and none of the domes, including Mount Olga, actually 200m higher than Uluru, are permissible to climb.

You can't camp, let alone so much as pick a flower in the park, nor can you go anywhere other than Uluru and Kata Tjuta or the Cultural Centre and the few roads and paths linking them. Instead the **Ayers Rock Resort**, part of the settlement of Yulara, just outside the park, takes care of all tourists' needs.

Getting there

It's 210km from Alice to **ERLDUNDA**, a busy roadhouse (camping and cabins; ❹) on the Stuart Highway, from where the **Lasseter Highway** heads to Ayers Rock Resort, 247km to the west. After 56km is *Mount Ebenezer Roadhouse* and later the turning for the **Luritja Highway**, which leads up to the Kings Canyon road. Following several rollovers and head-ons on this arrow-straight, if narrow, bitumen road (most caused by overseas tourists in rented vehicles), there is now a speed limit of 100kph.

The next thing to catch your eye will be the flat-topped mesa of **Mount Conner**, sometimes mistaken for Uluru. *Curtin Springs Station* (☎08/8956 2906), 11km west of Mount Conner, was the original roadhouse serving the Rock before Yulara and the tourist boom. Only settled following World War II on land riddled with salt lakes, its grizzled owner Peter Severin made the headlines when he refused to sell alcohol to Aborigines. Expensive court cases ensued, lawyers got rich and now his liquor licence has been revised to exclude Aboriginal people. Many Territorians, including those concerned with Aboriginal affairs, feel that such drastically unconstitutional discrimination, rather than locally imposed "dry days" and "one cask per person", is much needed. Curtin Springs is the last inexpensive accommodation (dustbowl camping free with $1 charge for showers; rooms ❷–❹) before Ayers Rock Resort. There's also a shop, fuel, bar and a collection of furry and feathered near-roadkill refugees out back. You-know-what is now only 80km away.

Ayers Rock Resort (Yulara)

Purpose-built twenty years ago, **AYERS ROCK RESORT** (aka Yulara) is far from the eyesore it could have been. It's low impact design was well ahead of its time and over the years it has aged well, helped along by the refurbishments and additions carried out in 2002.

Practicalities

All the town's facilities branch off a central ring road called Yulara Drive around which a **free bus** circulates every twenty minutes from 10.30am to 6pm and 6.30pm to midnight. Within this ring is a duned area crisscrossed with tracks and the Imalung Lookout, scanning the Rock and Kata Tjuta on the horizon. In the **Shopping Square**, off the north side of Yulara Drive, you'll find a post office, supermarket (daily 8.30am–9pm), newsagent and an ANZ **bank** (Mon–Thurs 9.30am–4.30pm, Fri 9.30am–5pm) with an ATM, as well as cafés and restaurants. Apart from hotel bars, the only alcohol outlet is the **bottle shop** at the *Outback Pioneer Lodge* (see overleaf), where you'll also find the only **laundry**. There is also the all-important **Tours and Information Centre** (7.30am–8.30pm; ☎08/8957 7377) where you can rent a car and book everything that's going – see box overleaf for some ideas. In here, as well as at a couple of other locations in the resort, you'll find some of those execrable, coin-operated **Internet machines** which sum up the resort's attitude to tourists.

Buses will either drop you off at your chosen accommodation, where you'll be given a town map, or at the Shopping Square which is the hub of the resort. All incoming **flights** to Connellan Airport, 6km from town, are met by a free shuttle bus – **taxis** (☎08/8955 2152) cost about $10. The main **Uluru–Kata Tjuta Cultural Centre** (daily 7am–6pm; ☎08/8956 3138) is located within the park, but just as worthwhile is the rather misnamed **visitors information centre** (daily 8am–8pm), tucked out of the way between the Shopping Square and the *Desert Gardens Hotel*. In here you'll find absorbing visual displays on the geology, ecology and Anangu connections with Uluru – well worth an hour's browse and much more broadly informative than the Cultural Centre in the park.

Accommodation

Wherever you stay, you're advised to **book ahead** unless camping or visiting in mid-summer. All accommodation is run by the Sydney-based Ayers Rock Resort (☎1300 134 044, ✉reservations@voyages.com.au). To ring the actual hotels call ☎08/8957 7888, and ☎08/8956 2055, ✉campground@voyages .com.au for the campground. All the places below are situated off Yulara Drive, none more than fifteen minutes' walk from the Shopping Square. Accommodation in the resort is expensive, and prices drop less than ten percent in summer; the places below are listed in order of expense, cheapest first.

Ayers Rock Campground Electric BBQs, small shop, swimming pool and well-kept grassy sites for tents. Air-con cabins with microwave, fridge and TV cost $145.

Outback Pioneer Lodge Most distant from the Shopping Square but with its own dining options and a bottle shop. Beds in the crowded twenty-bed backpacker dorms go for $32. The cheapest room is the small and plain budget option with two bunk beds and air-con, TV, fridge, tea and coffee, and costs $162; the same unit with a bathroom costs $172. There are also conventional en-suite motel rooms with all the usuals, plus in-house movies, costing $365.

Emu Walk Apartments Under refurbishment at the time of this update and possibly since re-named, these will probably still be well-equipped and spacious self-contained apartments with either one ($365) or two bedrooms ($485).

Lost Camel Hotel Right behind the Shopping Square and refurbished as a trendy boutique hotel, the *Lost Camel* features small one-bedroom units (sleeping three at a pinch; $365) with en-suite bathrooms and music centres but no TV, all set around an attractively tiled courtyard with a heated pool. The foyer has soft furnishings, a large TV screen and a small bar.

Desert Gardens Hotel Four-star hotel with a floral theme and well-appointed studio rooms ($410), which actually measure up pretty well compared to the *Lost Camel* and certainly the *Pioneer Lodge*. The pricier deluxe rooms (with verandah and bath tub) cost $480.

Sails in the Desert Hotel Until recently this was the resort's five-star flagship with à la carte restaurants and galleries. The *Sails* is the choice of upmarket package tour operators who are probably paying a lot less than the $487 rack rate.

Longitude 131° At $1350 per night (single $950) at a minimum of two nights, you won't be turning up here off the cuff. In fact you couldn't if you tried as this bank of super luxury tented modules are hidden among the dunes with no signed access

---

Uluru National Park tours from Ayers Rock Resort

AAT Kings Bus tours to the park, sunrise, the climb and sunset suppers (from $25). There's also an Uluru Express shuttle serving the Rock and Kata Tjuta.

Anangu Tours Variety of tours accompanied by local Aboriginal guides; sunset and sunrise tours cost from $20.

Ayers Rock Helicopters and Scenic Flights Fifteen-minute helicopter rides or half-hour flights around the Rock, with longer options as far as Kings Canyon available. From £150.

Discovery Ecotours Personalized walking tours around Uluru and Kata Tjuta with local experts from $35.

Frontier Camel Tours Camel rides at sunrise and sunset. From $45.

Uluru Motorcycle Tours Pillion rides round the Rock on the back of a throbbing Hog. From $40.

All tours can be booked at the Tours and Information Centre (see p.687).

from the resort. Each is individually themed after a Centralian pioneering identity and with a direct view of the Rock. The aim is not to interact with Yularans by being delivered by 4WD direct from the airport across a dune to this exclusive retreat.

Meals are eaten communally in the central Dune House and all tours and other activities are thrown in. Realistically, you're likely to enjoy your room so much you may want to skip the tour program or stay an extra day or two.

Eating and drinking

Listed below are the moderately priced eating options at the resort. For the half-dozen, à la carte, expense-be-damned alternatives head to the restaurants, grills and bars at the *Sails* or *Desert Gardens* hotels.

Geckos Shopping Square. Mediterranean-style restaurant serving wood-fired pizzas, pastas, seafood and steak, all from around $15–25. Open 10am–10pm.
Outback Pioneer Lodge Yulara Drive. The kiosk (11am–9pm) here has various offerings, including fish and chips or burgers from around $7, as cheap a feed as you'll get here. A better deal is the cook-your-own BBQ (6.30–9.30pm) for around

$16–20 including unlimited salad (note that they may insist on covered shoes). Opposite the pool is the *Bough House Restaurant* with an all-you-could-ever-want-to-eat buffet with countless meats, fish, salads and wobbling deserts for around $40 a head. A wheelbarrow back to your room is extra.
Quick Bites Shopping Square. Sandwich bar with an ice creamery nearby too. Open 9am–9pm.

Uluru–Kata Tjuta National Park

Even with our bus tours and our fully automatic cameras and our cries of "Oh, wow!", we still couldn't belittle it. I had come expecting nothing much, but by the power of the thing itself I had, like some ancient tribesman wandering through the desert and confronting the phenomenon [sunset on Uluru], been turned into a worshipper. Nobody was more surprised than I.

Geoff Nicholson, *Day Trips to the Desert*

The entry fee for **ULURU–KATA TJUTA NATIONAL PARK** (daily from one hour before dawn to one hour after dusk; $16.25, under 16s free) permits unlimited access for up to three days, though it's easily extendible. Besides the two major sites of Uluru and Kata Tjuta, the park is also home to over 500 species of plants, 24 native mammals and no less than 72 species of reptiles. It incorporates the closed Aboriginal community of Mutujulu, near the base of the Rock, once the original pre-Yulara tourist resort.

The **Uluru–Kata Tjuta Cultural Centre** (daily: April–Oct 7.30am–5.30pm; Nov–March 7am–6pm; ☎08/8956 3138), situated 1km before the Rock, opened in 1995, on the tenth anniversary of the so-called "hand back" of Uluru to its traditional owners. The centre also houses a café, souvenir shop and gallery, and all together you'd want to allow yourself two hours to have a look around. As in the Kakadu equivalent at Cooinda, the strikingly innovative design doesn't conceal the fact that you're getting a sanitized and superficial coverage of Aboriginal life. You pass an exposition of the dramatic mythical events at the dawn of creation, a baffling film including an *inma* (ceremony) and end with a display of men's and women's artefacts. In the next hall you can play with buttons to learn the right pronunciation of words such as "Anangu" or "Uluru". You leave saturated with the usual Dreamtime myths, information on care for the land and bushtucker know-how, while interesting if sensitive questions such as how significant, if at all, are age-old spiritual values to contemporary Aboriginal people are not considered. A look around nearby Mutujulu or any Aboriginal community in the Centre would certainly threaten this rose-tinted message.

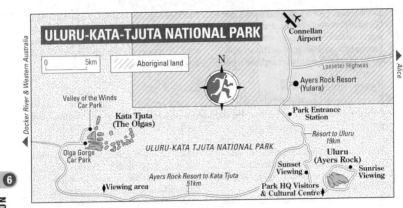

There are free, ninety-minute **tours** of the cultural centre and a free ranger-guided **Mala Walk** (daily: April–Oct 10am; Nov–March 9am; 90min) which takes you from the centre to the base of the Rock and is a good introduction to Anangu perceptions and beliefs. Anangu Tours (see box on p.688) offers a chance to explore the park accompanied by an Aboriginal guide.

Otherwise, leaflets are available at the information desk on the park's geology, flora and fauna, as well as informative *Park Notes* on various topics and issues. The *Tour Operator's Workbook* is the definitive official handbook to the park, with as comprehensible an explanation of Anangu culture as you'll find here. Around the back, the outdoor Maruku Gallery sells arts and crafts from local artisans.

Uluru

Uluru straddles what were the ancestral lands of the Yankunytjatjara and Pitjantjatjara tribes, who survive in this extremely arid environment in small mobile groups moving from one waterhole to another. Water was their most valued resource and so any site like Uluru, with its near permanent waterholes, was of vital significance.

The first European to set eyes on Uluru was the explorer Ernest Giles, in 1872, but it was William Gosse who followed his Afghan guide up the Rock and so completed the first ascent by a European a year later, naming it **Ayers Rock** after a South Australian politician. With white settlement of the Centre came relocation of its occupants from their traditional lands to enable pastoralists' stock to overgraze the fragile desert environment.

In 1958 the national park was excised from what was then the Petermann Aboriginal Reserve but was subsequently returned, with much flourish, to the Yankunytjatjara and Pitjantjatjara groups in 1985, following a ten-year battle. Reclaimed, and renamed, as **Uluru**, the site was initially unchanged under Aboriginal ownership, since it was a condition of hand back that the park was leased straight back to Parks Australia (part of the Department of Environment and Heritage that administer the park). Tourism continued unaffected but since that time, changes assisted by Aboriginal input have manifested themselves with characteristic subtlety, guiding the park's development.

Anangu mythology

Uluru, Kata Tjuta and the surrounding desert are bound to a culture whose holistic cosmology sees the People – *anangu* – as having the Land and the Law – *tjukurpa* – as their central tenet of belief. A little confusingly, *tjukurpa* can also refer to the Time of Creation or Dreamtime. The Anangu are thought to have occupied this area for around twenty thousand years and *Uluru* is actually the name of one of the many temporary waterholes near the summit. Like all religious mythology (and traditional fairy tales for that matter), the *tjukurpa* seeks to provide its adherents with a connection with the past, and a code of strict rules by which to live and behave correctly.

While Uluru is a key intersection along many "dreaming trails" (or Songlines, as Bruce Chatwin's book described them) – principally those of the **Mala** (hare wallaby), **Liru** (poisonous snake), **Kuniya** (python) and **Kurpany** (monster dog) – it is not as some imagine, a shrine to which Aborigines flocked from around the country to pay their respects. A muddy waterhole 200km away may be as significant. Uluru was once important to the Anangu as a reliable source of water and food and as one of many landmarks incorporating ceremonial and burial sites along the trails created by the Anangu's Dreamtime ancestors.

Geology

The reason Uluru rises so dramatically from the surrounding plain is because it is a **monolith** – that is, a single piece of rock. With few cracks to be exploited by weathering, and the layers of very hard, coarse-grained **sandstone** tilted to a near-vertical plane, the Rock successfully resists the denudation of the landscape surrounding it. If one can visualize the tilted layers of rock, then Uluru is like a cut loaf, its strata pushed up to near-vertical slices so that from one side you look at the flat ends (the classic, steep-sided sunset profile). Elsewhere the separate vertical layers or slices are clearly evident as eroded grooves – the pronounced fluting and chasms along the Rock's southeast and northwest flanks. Brief, but spectacular, waterfalls stream down these channels following storms. In places, the surface of the monolith has peeled or worn away, producing bizarre features and many caves, mostly out of bounds. The striking orangey-red hue, enhanced by the rising and setting sun, is merely skin deep, the result of oxidation ("rusting") of the normally grey rock.

Up and around Uluru

You can appreciate Uluru in any number of ways on various tours but to climb or not to climb… that is the question. "Anangu don't climb" is the oft-repeated message found at the base of the climb, along with the plea that "Anangu feel sad" when someone hurts themselves or dies on the Rock. That said, the Anangu have exclusive access to many more culturally significant sites along the base of the Rock than the summit climb (which, if they really had power over their land, would have been closed long ago).

Regardless of Anangu sentiment, most visitors to the Rock do attempt the hour-long **climb** to the summit, but make no mistake, if you do decide to climb it will be the greatest exertion you will undertake during your visit to Australia. Probably a third give up and, on average, one tourist a year dies, usually from a heart attack, with scores more needing rescuing. If you slip or collapse you'll roll straight back to the car park. But with a firmly attached hat, plenty of water, secure footwear and frequent rests, you'll safely attain the end of the chain from where the gradient eases off considerably and continues up and down gullies to the **summit**, often a windy spot, especially in the morning. Most people hang around only long enough for their legs to "dejellify" and then climb back down; the daunting view into the car park can cause some freak outs. But the summit plateau is quite an interesting place. Gnarled trees survive in wind-scooped gullies and, while obviously maintaining caution near the edges, it's satisfying to explore the area away from the throng before they put signs up forbidding it. And before you ask, yes your mobile will work from the summit.

If you're at all unfit or are nervous about heights and exposed places, do not attempt the climb. These days the climb is regularly closed during high winds and by 8am when the temperature that day is expected to rise above 35°C, as it does every day in summer.

Far less strenuous, no less satisfying and certainly more in keeping with the spirit of the place is the nine-kilometre **walk around the Rock**, which takes an easy three hours. It offers a closer look at some Anangu sites (though most are closed – heed any warning notices) as well as the extraordinary textural variations. At the very least, the five-minute walk from the car park to **Mutitjulu**, a secluded pool, low-grade art site and scene of epic ancestral clashes marked by gashes in the rock, is recommended.

Kata Tjuta and on to WA

The "many heads", as **Kata Tjuta** – or the **Olgas** – translates from the local Aboriginal language, are situated 51km from the resort or Uluru. This remarkable formation may have once been a monolith ten times the size of Uluru, but has since been carved by eons of weathering into 36 "monstrous domes", to use Giles' words, each smooth, rounded mass divided by slender chasms or broader valleys. The composition of Kata Tjuta, very different from Uluru's fine-grained rock, can be clearly seen in the massive, some-times sheared, boulders set in a conglomerate of sandstone cement. Access to this fascinating maze is limited to just two walks, in part because of ear-lier problems with over-ambitious tourists. Furthermore, the east of Kata Tjuta is said to be a site sacred to Anangu men and is not accessible to the public.

The first of the permitted walks, the **Olga Gorge Walk**, is a rather point-less one-kilometre stroll into the dead-end chasm flanking Mount Olga (which, at 1070m, is the highest point in the massif). Better by far is the **Valley of the Winds Walk**, a seven-kilometre loop trail which takes about two hours, or the five-kilometre "there and back" walk to a **pass** between two domes. This is as much as you can see of Kata Tjuta's interior without a permit. It's worth knowing that the large tour buses tend to visit the Rock in the early morning and Kata Tjuta in the afternoon. By reversing this trend you can avoid the worst of the crowds and enjoy this magical place in reasonable solitude.

From Kata Tjuta a track leads to the WA border at Docker River and from there along the **Warburton Road** (or part of the continent-spanning Outback Highway from Queensland to WA) to Laverton, north of Kalgoorlie (see p.746). Though no one checks, the need for slowly issued **permits** (see "Listings", p.674 and p.710 for WA) to cross Aboriginal land still remains to put people off. A 4WD is not necessary but the usual pre-cautions for driving on the dirt should be taken: spare fuel, tyres and water, especially in summer. Travelabout Tours (☎08/9244 1200; ⊛www .travelabout.com.au) does a fast, three-day return to Perth via the Warburton Road ($329), leaving Tuesday mornings from Alice with an Ayers Rock Resort pick-up at 3pm.

Travel details

Trains

Alice Springs to: Adelaide (Tues & Fri; 20hr); Port Augusta (Tues & Fri; 17hr; change for Sydney or Perth). See also p.665.

Buses

Alice Springs to: Adelaide (3–4 weekly; 27hr); Darwin (1 daily; 19hr); Katherine (1 daily; 15hr; change here for WA); Tennant Creek/Three Ways Roadhouse (1 daily; 6hr–6hr 30min; change at Three Ways for Queensland destinations); Yulara (1 daily; 5hr).

Darwin to: Alice Springs (1 daily; 19hr); Katherine (2 daily; 4hr; change for WA); Tennant Creek/Three Ways Roadhouse (2 daily; 13hr–13hr 30min).

Katherine to: Alice Springs (1 daily; 15hr); Darwin (2–3 daily; 4hr); Kununurra (2 daily; 6hr 30min); Tennant Creek/Three Ways Roadhouse (2–3 daily; 9hr 30min).

Tennant Creek to: Alice Springs (1 daily; 6hr); Darwin (2 daily; 13hr); Katherine (2–3 daily; 13hr); Townsville (1 daily; 12hr).

Domestic flights

Alice Springs to: Adelaide (1–2 daily; 3hr); Brisbane (1–2 daily; 3hr); Darwin (1–2 daily; 2hr); Melbourne (1–2 daily; 3hr); Sydney (1–2 daily; 3hr); Yulara (1–2 daily; 40 min).

Darwin to: Alice Springs (1–2 daily; 2hr); Brisbane (1–2 daily; 4hr); Broome (1 daily; 2hr); Cairns (1 daily; 3hr); Perth (1 daily; 4hr 30min).

International flights

Darwin to: Brunei (2 weekly), Denpasar, Bali (3 weekly); Kuala Lumpur, Malaysia (1 direct weekly, or change at Singapore); Kupang and Dili, East Timor (4 weekly); Singapore (5–6 weekly).

Western Australia

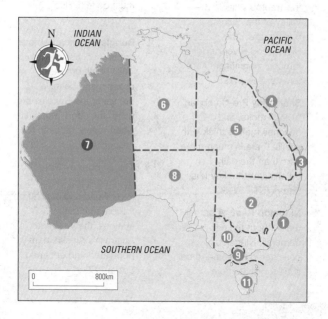

CHAPTER 7

Highlights

＊ **Fremantle** Eclectic, authentic and alive: it's worth staying here instead of Perth, rather than making the usual day-trip. See p.711

＊ **Tall Timber Country** Take the Treetop Walk in the Valley of the Giants, paddle down the Blackwood River or drive through magnificent karri forests. See p.730

＊ **Shark Bay** Pre-Cambrian "living" rocks, and beaches metres thick with shells: there is much more here than the daily dolphins at Monkey Mia. See p.754

＊ **Ningaloo Reef** "A barrier reef without the barriers", Ningaloo is considered by some to be superior to its more famous cousin in Queensland. See p.760

＊ **Karijini National Park** The legendary "Miracle Mile" was described by FHM magazine as "one of the hundred things a man must do in his life". See p.766

＊ **Bungle Bungles** Remote, hot and accessible only by 4WD or air, but the chasms and beehive domes of the Bungles are worth the effort, especially when topped off with a helicopter ride. See p.781

＊ **The Kimberley** Gorge-hopping along the Gibb River Road and staying on million-acre cattle stations, the Kimberley is Australia's Alaska, barely populated and untamed. See p.777

Western Australia

W **estern Australia** (WA) covers a third of the Australian continent; nearly the size of India, yet with less than half a percent of that country's population. Always revelling in its isolation from the more populous eastern states, WA is like them, primarily a suburban state: almost all of its 1.8 million inhabitants live within 200km of Perth and most of the rest live in communities strung along the coastline.

Perth itself retains the leisure-oriented vitality of a young city, while the port of **Fremantle** resonates with a largely European charm. South of Perth, the wooded hills and trickling streams of the **Southwest** support the state's foremost wine-growing and holiday-making area, and the giant **eucalypt forests** around Pemberton further soften a land fed by heavy winter rains. East of here is the state's intensively farmed **wheat belt**, an interminable man-made prairie. Along the Southern Ocean's storm-washed coastline, **Albany** is the primary settlement, part-holiday, part-retirement resort with the dramatic granite peaks of the **Stirling Ranges** just visible from its hilltop lookouts. Further east, past Esperance on the edge of the Great Australian Bight, is the **Nullarbor Plain**, while inland are the Eastern Goldfields and **Kalgoorlie**, sole survivor of the century-old mineral boom on which WA's prosperity was originally built.

While the temperate southwest of WA has been tamed by colonization, the north of the state is where you'll discover the raw appeal of the **Outback**. The virtually unpopulated inland deserts are blanketed with spinifex and support remote Aboriginal communities, while the west coast's winds abate once you venture into the tropics north of **Shark Bay**, home of the amicable dolphins at **Monkey Mia**. From here, the mineral-rich **Pilbara** region fills the state's northwest shoulder with the often-overlooked gorges of the **Karijini National Park** at its core. Visitors are also discovering the submarine spectacle of the **Ningaloo Reef**, lapping the North West Cape's beaches – some consider it superior to Queensland's Barrier Reef.

Northeast of the Pilbara, **Broome**, once the world's pearling capital, is indeed a jewel in the cyclone-swept coastline of the rugged "Nor'west", and an ideal preliminary to the **Kimberley**'s wilderness and hard-won cattle country. Cut off by floods in the wet season, the Kimberley is regarded as Australia's last frontier, its convoluted and inaccessible coasts washed by enormous tides and inhabited only by a handful of Aboriginal communities and crocodiles. On the way to the Northern Territory border, the surreal enigma of the **Bungle Bungle** massif is one of WA's greatest natural wonders, carefully protected by minimal development.

If you hope to explore any significant part of the state's million-and-a-half square kilometres, and in particular the remote Northwest, your own vehicle

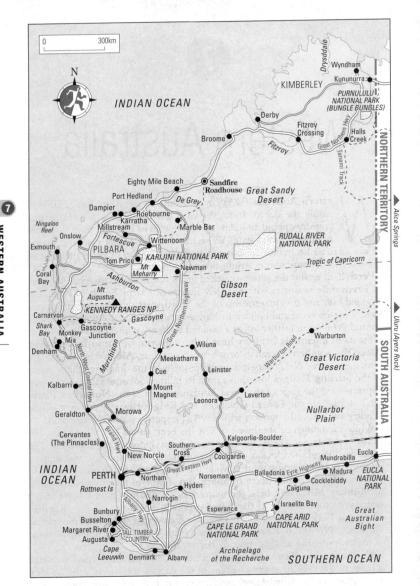

is essential, although you'll get to the most interesting places by combining buses with local **tours**. Either way, WA offers an essential mix of Outback grandeur, albeit more dispersed than elsewhere, and it's beginning to attract tourists from the more popular "Eastern States", as the rest of Australia is known in these parts.

WA's **climate** is a seasonal mix of temperate, arid and tropical. **Winters** are cool in the south and very wet in the southwest corner, while in the far northern tropics the temperature sits around 32°C but with no rain and tolerable humidity: this is the dry season. Come the **summer**, the enervating "Wet" (from Dec to March) washes out the north while the rest of the state, particularly inland areas, crackles in the mid–40s heat. The southern coast is the only retreat for the heatstruck, although the temperate west coast is cooled by dependable afternoon sea breezes – in Perth known as the "Fremantle Doctor".

Some history

Aborigines had lived all over WA for thousands of years by the time the seventeenth-century traders of the **Dutch East India Company**, and probably the **Portuguese** before them, began bumping into the west coast on their way to the East Indies. A Dutch mariner, **Dirk Hartog**, was among the first of these when, in 1616, he left an inscribed pewter plate on the island off Shark Bay which now bears his name. Recent evidence was also found hereabouts to suggest that the **French** claimed the whole continent just a few years before Cook. For the next two hundred years, however, impressions of WA's barren and waterless fringes remained – commercially at least – uninspiring to European colonists.

France's subsequent interest in Australia's southwest corner at the beginning of the nineteenth century, which left a legacy of attractively named coastal features, led the **British** hastily to claim the unknown western part of the continent in 1826. Fredrickstown (Albany) was established on the south coast in that year and the Swan River Colony, today's Perth, two years later. The **new colony**, initially rejecting convict labour and so struggling desperately in its early years, had the familiar effect on an Aboriginal population that was at best misunderstood and at worst annihilated. Aborigines and their lands were cleared for agriculture: these days black faces are rarely seen south of Perth.

Economic problems continued for the settlers until stalwart explorers in the mid-nineteenth century opened up the country's interior, leading to the goldrushes of the 1890s which propelled the colony into autonomous statehood in less than a decade. This **autonomy**, and growing antipathy towards the Eastern States, led to a move to secede from the federation in the depressed 1930s, when WA felt the rest of the country was dragging it down. But following World War II the whole of white Australia, and especially WA, began to thrive, making money from wool and, later, from huge mineral discoveries that continue to form the basis of the state's wealth. In fact, so prosperous is the state that at present its wealth accounts for a quarter of the nation's economy. Meanwhile, many of WA's forty thousand Aborigines continue to live in squalid and remote communities, as if in another country

Perth and the south

South of the **Great Eastern Highway**, which joins Perth to Kalgoorlie, is the most climatically benign portion of Western Australia, supporting intensive agriculture and seaside towns, and with all points well connected to **Perth**, the modern face of the state's wealth. East of the state capital, the **Darling Ranges** offer a number of appealing day-trip destinations, while south of Perth, the

Margaret River Region's mellow landscape is especially attractive, supporting orchards, wineries and numerous homey holiday hideaways in the giant karri forests around **Pemberton**. Both **Albany** and **Esperance** are engaging resort towns on the Southern Ocean's rugged coastline, where sea breezes take the edge off the summertime heat. They make ideal bases for exploration of their adjacent national parks, while the dreary **Wheatlands**, north of the coast, is a region to pass through rather than head for. **Kalgoorlie**, at the heart of the once-thriving **Eastern Goldfields**, is a colourful caricature of an Outback mining town and certainly deserves a stop if you're travelling east.

Perth

Although its lack of urban grime creates a favourable first impression, it's hard to get too excited about **PERTH**. Western Australia's modern capital of 1.5 million people has a reputation for sunshine, youthfulness and an easy-going lifestyle – after work, people often go sailing or swimming. It is perhaps because of this complacency that Perth lacks the substance and charisma, and the tension, of diverse wealth and ethnicity, that make a really great city something more than just a group of modern skyscrapers and people enjoying the good life.

In the 1980s mineral prosperity and a spate of cocky, self-made wheeler-dealers (now largely bankrupt or disgraced) set off a mini-boom which continues with development almost for development's sake. But although upbeat campaigns have managed to attract some people back into the city centre outside office hours, apart from shopping and some museums and galleries, the CBD has little to offer tourists bar the adjacent restaurant and club district of **Northbridge**. If you're looking for action, imitate the locals and head for the hills, the beaches, the western suburbs of Leederville, Subiaco, Claremont and Cottesloe, or cruise on down to the port of Fremantle, 20km from Perth.

Arrival and information

Perth's **international airport** is 16km east of the city centre and the **domestic** one a few kilometres closer. **Shuttle buses** (international $13, domestic $11; ☎08/9475 2999) meet arrivals at both airports and take you to your chosen accommodation; don't let them undermine your preference. Poorly signposted, but directly opposite the Qantas domestic terminal, you can also catch a green Transperth bus #200, #201, #202, #208 and #209 to the city, at least every forty minutes ($2.90). Otherwise, a trip by **taxi** to or from the international airport will take thirty minutes and cost around $25, or a bit less and a bit quicker from the domestic terminal (call ☎08/9333 3333 or 9444 4444). An airport shuttle runs to **Fremantle** ($18 one-way; ☎08/9383 4115) once an hour. Interstate **trains** and Westrail country **buses** arrive at the **East Perth Rail and Bus Terminal**, three train stops from the central Transperth **Perth Train Station** and the adjacent **Wellington Street Bus Station**. To confuse matters further there is also the **City Busport** on Mill St (see overleaf), although there is talk of centralizing all bus services from an expanded Wellington Street station.

The main **tourist office** (Mon–Fri 8.30am–6.30pm, Sat 9am–1pm; ☎1300 361 351 or 1800 812 808, ⓦwww.westernaustralia.net) is just across the road from the Transperth station, in Forrest Chase precinct, and has numerous free city guides and maps, tour information and statewide promotional videos. The **Travellers' Club Tour and Information Centre** (Mon–Fri 9am–5.30pm, Sat 10am–4pm; ☎08/9226 0660, ⓦwww.travellersclub.com.au), just round the

CENTRAL PERTH

ACCOMMODATION

All Seasons Chateau	21
Billabong Resort	3
Britannia International YHA	11
Brownlea Holiday Apartments	2
City Waters Lodge	26
Coolibah Lodge	6
Criterion	19
Exclusive Backpackers	25
Globe Backpackers	15
Goodearth	24
Governor Robinsons	9
Grand Central Backpackers	17
Hay Street Backpackers	22
Hotel Northbridge	5
Kings Park Motel	16
Mad Cat Backpackers	12
Melbourne	13
Miss Maud European Hotel	20
Northbridge YHA	10
Perth City	23
Red Back Packers	1
River View on Mount Street	14
Royal Hotel	18
Shiralee	7
The Witch's Hat	4
Underground Backpackers	8
Wentworth Plaza	14

RESTAURANTS

Annalakshmi	M
C Restaurant	L
Café Universal	J
Dusit Thai	H
Hans Café Noodle Bar	F
Lotus Vegetarian	I
Maya Masala	E
Meads Mosman Bay	K
Siena Pizzeria	A
Sparrows	G
The Street Café	C
Villa Italia	D
Woodpeckers	
Woodfired Pizza	B

WESTERN AUSTRALIA | Perth

701

corner at 499 Wellington St, offers a specific information service for backpackers and budget travellers as well as providing **emailing** facilities. See p.707 for listings magazines.

City transport

Transperth is the city's excellent and inexpensive **suburban transport** network, with frequent trains to Fremantle and the northern, eastern and southern suburbs of Joondalup, Midland and Armadale, and a fleet of buses filling the gaps in between. The city centre has two **bus stations**, one on Wellington Street, next to the central **train station** and, for services south of the river, the City Busport ten minutes' walk south at the bottom of Mill Street. Any bus from Horseshoe Bridge goes to the Busport. There are helpful Transperth **information offices** at both bus stations (Mon–Fri 7.30am–5.30pm, Sat 8am–1pm; ☎13 22 13) and also in the city centre at Plaza Arcade, Hay Street Level (Mon–Fri 8am–5.30pm, Sat 8am–5pm, Sun noon–5pm; same number).

Outside the FTZ (see box below), Perth is divided into eight concentric zones – zones 1 and 2 ($2.90) are the most useful to visitors, incorporating Fremantle, the northern beaches and Midland. **Tickets** are available from bus conductors or vending machines at all (mostly unstaffed) stations; they are valid for up to two hours' (some for 1hr 30min) unlimited travel within the specified zones on Transperth buses, trains and the ferry to South Perth from Barrack Street Jetty. All-zone day-passes ($7.30) and ten-trip MultiRiders ($25) are also available from certain newsagents.

The tourist-oriented **Perth Tram** (daily 8am–5.10pm; day-ticket $15; ☎08/9322 2006), running every ninety minutes and most conveniently caught at Barrack Street Jetty, allows you to jump off at points of interest and reboard a later tram.

Perth's web of **bicycle** lanes, which spread from the city out to the suburbs, can also make bike rental a pleasant and viable option; Bikewest (☎08/9216 8000) can provide more information.

Accommodation

There's a full range of **accommodation** around the centre of Perth, all of it – from backpackers' hostels to hotels and apartments – inexpensive, presentable and conveniently close to, or even right in, the city centre. Self-contained apartments can be great value for groups of four or more. The nearest campsites are 7km from the city. Booking ahead for motels and apartments is advisable in summer if you want to stay at the first place on your list.

Free transport in central Perth: the FTZ

Both of Perth's central bus stations, as well as the local train stations one stop on either side of the main train station, are within the **Free Transit Zone**, or **FTZ**. Most buses passing through the FTZ offer free travel within it, as do the snazzy **"CAT"** (Central Area Transit) buses serving the city centre. You can board the buses at special CAT stops to take you along two circular CAT routes; press a button and a voice tells you when the next bus is due. The **Blue CAT** runs north–south from Barrack Street Jetty up to Aberdeen Street and then down William Street back to the river, while the **Red CAT** runs east–west along St Georges Terrace and back along Wellington Street. Both routes run from Monday to Thursday 7am to 6pm, Friday 7am to 1am, Saturday 8.30am to 1am and Sunday 10am to 5pm, with intervals of fifteen minutes at the most.

Hotels and motels

All Seasons Chateau 417 Hay St ☎08/9325 0461, ⓕ9221 2448. Right in the centre of town, with parking, restaurant, bar and pool. ❹

Criterion 560 Hay St ☎08/9325 5155, ⓕ9325 4176. Very central grand-era hotel. ❻

Goodearth 195 Adelaide Terrace ☎08/9492 7777. Superior motel right in the city centre. ❻

Hotel Northbridge 210 Lake St ☎08/9328 5254, ⓔhotelnb@delron.com.au. Excellent refurbished old-style hotel for those on a budget, as well as good value four-star alternatives with a spa in every room. Off-street parking and three-bar pub below. ❸–❺

Kings Park Motel 255 Thomas St, Subiaco ☎08/9381 0000, ⓕ9381 4159. Good-value modern motel, five minutes from the city, on the edge of Kings Park. Restaurant, and spas in some rooms. ❹

Melbourne Cnr Hay and Milligan Sts ☎08/9320 3333, ⓕ9320 3300. Renovated federation-era boutique hotel, close to the centre with breakfast included. ❺

Miss Maud European Hotel 97 Murray St ☎08/9325 3900, ⓦwww.missmaud.com.au. A pleasant variety of rooms, an interior with a Swedish/Alpine flavour and a popular buffet breakfast included. ❹

Perth City 200 Hay St ☎08/9220 7000, ⓦwww .perthcityhotel.com.au. Newly built, good-value hotel with fair-sized rooms, parking, breakfast café and the trendy adjacent *Kilo* restaurant. ❹

Royal Cnr Wellington and William streets ☎ & ⓕ08/9324 1510, ⓔwentpert@fc-hotels .com.au. One of central Perth's bargains, a tidy grand-era hotel (mostly shared facilities) with some big rooms better and cheaper than the *Wentworth* next door. ❸

Wentworth Plaza 300 Murray St ☎08/9481 1000, ⓔwentpert@fc-hotels.com.au. Plusher version of its sister, the *Royal* (above) with same central location, mix of en-suite and basin-only rooms plus 24hr reception and lifts. ❸–❺

Self-contained apartments

Brownlea Holiday Apartments 166 Palmerston St ☎08/9227 1710, ⓔbrownlea@iinet.net.au. North of Northbridge with a spa, pool and bargain rates. ❸

City Waters Lodge 118 Terrace Rd ☎08/9325 1556, ⓔperth@citywaters.com.au. Small one- and two-bedroom apartments close to the river and ten minutes' walk from the centre. ❸

River View on Mount Street 42 Mount St ☎08/9321 8963, ⓦwww.riverview.au.com. Comfortable, well-equipped units between the city centre and Kings Park. ❹

Hostels

The best of central Perth's **hostels** are listed below, including boutique backpackers' and the new breed of licensed "backpacker resorts", though even these are conversions rather than purpose-built. Most are located in Northbridge, Perth's restaurant and nightlife district which is ideally central, though there are quieter and more spacious options further north towards Mt Lawley and along the eastern end of Hay Street. The keener (but not necessarily recommended) hostels meet incoming trains and buses at East Perth and will also collect you from the airports. Free on-street **parking** is no longer possible within Northbridge, but private parking is available at some accommodation and this is indicated in the reviews; there are plenty of inexpensive central car parks. Not before time, there are plans to build a new YHA on Wellington Street; perhaps it's just the competition that the tired backpackers' ghetto of Northbridge, needs. All of these hostels offer weekly rates which work out at one free night or more.

Northbridge and City Centre

Britannia International YHA 253 William St ☎08/9328 6121, ⓔbritannia@yhawa.com.au. Huge, three-storey warren in the heart of Northbridge, a stone's throw from the clubs and cafés but also affected by late-night noise. Not much ambient communal space, although you do get little lounges here and there; many singles available, but some rooms have no windows. 24hr reception, free breakfast. No parking. Eight-share dorms from $11, rooms ❷

Globe Backpackers 497 Wellington St
☏ 08/9321 4080, ⓦ www.globebackpackers
.com.au. Big old hotel opposite the railway station
converted into another maze of rooms – from
eight-bed dorms right down to singles for $200
a week – with a dingy outdoor area but some
parking. Free breakfast and cheap Internet. ❷
Grand Central Backpackers 379 Wellington St
☏ 08/9421 1123, ⓔ grandcentralbp@hotmail.com.
Similar block to the *Globe*, one minute from the
station. Lack of a good, non-TV communal area
made up for by a coffee bar and banks of computers. Some doubles with en suites. Eight-share
dorms from $11, rooms ❷
Mad Cat Backpackers 55 Stirling St ☏ 08/9228
4966, ⓦ www.madcatbackpackers.com.au. A bit
out in No Man's Land but near the station and better
than it looks. Spacious and clean inside and with
more improvements on the way. Mostly dorms from
$11 with a couple of doubles and some parking. ❷
Northbridge YHA 46 Francis St ☏ & ⓕ 08/9328
7794, ⓔ northbridge@yhawa.com.au. Tinkering
with this old house has been taken as far as it will
go over the years, with decent outdoor areas
making up for small kitchens and pokey bathrooms.
Either join in or bring ear plugs against late-night
partiers and early morning "garboes". A few twins
but mostly six- and eight-bed dorms $11–18. ❷

Along Newcastle Street

Red Back Packers 496 Newcastle St ☏ 08/9227
9969, ⓦ www.club-red.com.au. Detached houses
a bit far out, but with a bar, mini-shop, free
breakfast and occasional bread, plus apricots in
season. More outdoor space than most and some
parking. Eight-share dorms from $11, rooms ❷
Underground Backpackers 268 Newcastle St
☏ 08/9228 3755, ⓔ underground@iinet.net.au.
Mega-hostel with spacious foyer and a new block
out the back by the pool which makes up for some
windowless rooms. Free breakfast, bar, cheap
Internet, air-con rooms and video lounge, plus 24hr
reception. Parking may be possible on vacant lot
opposite. Eight-share dorms from $11, rooms ❷

North of Newcastle Street

Billabong Resort 381 Beaufort St ☏ 08/9328
7720, ⓦ www.billabongresort.com.au. Former

Caravan parks

Central 38 Central Ave, 7km east of Perth
☏ 08/9277 5696. Located in Redcliffe, by the
domestic airport. Closest good caravan park to the
city centre. Cabins ❺

students' digs converted into a vast palmy
mega-resort. Like most places, the four- to
eight-bed dorms (from $11) may not be where
you want to spend your time, but just about
every possible need, short of tucking you in at
night, is catered for, including a pool and a bar.
Close to Mt Lawley shops and with masses of
parking. ❷
Coolibah Lodge 194 Brisbane St ☏ 08/9328
9958, ⓦ www.coolibahlodge.com.au. Well-kept
pair of colonial-era houses close to *Hotel
Northbridge* but just a touch too cramped for comfort. Very limited parking. Eight-share dorms from
$11, rooms ❷
Governor Robinsons 7 Robinson Ave ☏ 08/9228
3200, ⓦ www.govrobinsons.com.au. An old colonial house, beautifully converted from the ground
up with plenty of warm wood, plus a kitchen and
bathrooms that won't make you squirm. Six-bed
dorms ($15) with large lockers but mostly doubles,
some en suite. No TV. ❷
Shiralee 107 Brisbane St ☏ 08/9227 7448,
ⓔ shiralee@global.net.au. Nicely converted small
old house retaining a bit of space plus winter log
fires and summer air-con. Four-bed dorms from
$16, rooms ❷
The Witch's Hat 148 Palmerston St ☏ 08/9228
4228 or 1800 818 358, ⓔ witchs_hat@hotmail
.com. Distinctive heritage building away from the
throng with wood interior and attractive communal
area plus small doubles, "real beds", but part-time
reception. Some parking. Eight-share dorms from
$12, rooms ❷

East of the Centre

Exclusive Backpackers 158 Adelaide Terrace
☏ 08/9221 9991, ⓕ 9362 5872. An attractive
jarrah-wood interior, balcony and spacious dorms
offer a touch of class. Off-street parking and a nice
café next door to supplement the inadequate
kitchen. Five-bed dorms from $14 and comfortable
twins or doubles. ❷
Hay Street Backpackers 266–268 Hay St
☏ 08/9221 9880. Well positioned on the Red CAT
route, *Hay Street* comprises nicely converted and
well-maintained adjoined houses with two
kitchens, small pool and some parking. Four- to
six-bed dorms from $12 with air-con and
twins/doubles in the back. ❷

Scarborough Starhaven 18 Pearl Parade
☏ 08/9341 1770. Situated in a popular beach
suburb, a 35min bus ride from the centre. On-site
vans ❻

The City

The compact and walkable **central area** of Perth, from Wellington Street down to St Georges Terrace, and bounded vaguely by Hill Street to the east and Milligan Street to the west, is an easy-to-negotiate grid. Much of your time will be spent exploring the links between **Hay Street** and **Murray Street**, both of which are pedestrianized between William and Barrack streets and connected by numerous, glittering arcades: the mock-Tudor **London Court** and its idealized "Olde English" imagery is much photographed. William Street runs north over the railway at **Horseshoe Bridge** and on into lively Northbridge, while Barrack Street runs south to the **Barrack Street Jetty** on Perth Water, site of the millennial **Swan Bells Tower** (10am–5pm; $6). The distinctive tower houses the 280-year-old bells of London's St Martin-in-the-Fields church, presented to WA on the 1988 bicentenary. Perth Water is a lagoon on the **Swan River** formed by the bridged **Narrows** and popular with windsurfers, sailors and jet-skiers. As an urban recreation area it's rather wasted but may be due for development. From the jetty a Transperth ferry regularly crosses the Narrows to Mends Street Jetty on the south shore, while tourist ferries ply the river upstream to the Swan Valley wineries and downstream to Fremantle and Rottnest Island (see box on p.708).

Museums and Old Perth

Situated just over the tracks in Northbridge, at the end of James Street, the **Perth Cultural Centre** comprises the **Art Gallery of Western Australia** (daily 10am–5pm; free) and the state **museum** (daily 9.30am–5pm, closed Good Friday; free), as well as the state library. The gallery's constantly changing displays include Aboriginal art, and other contemporary and classic works by Western Australian artists. There's always something worth seeing, the air-con is blissful in summer, and free guided tours (Tues–Sun 1pm) provide good information about the work displayed. The museum, part of the same complex, is housed in a collection of old and new buildings. It includes a floor devoted to Aboriginal culture, plus exhibitions of vintage cars, stuffed marsupials, a 25-metre whale skeleton, meteorites, a diorama of a swamp, and a reconstruction of an old jail.

Perth's old buildings, popular with many sightseeing tours, are colonial survivors on the endangered list while the city fathers remain obsessed with continual renewal and development, where even modern soaring skyscrapers, barely twenty years old, are not safe from demolition in the name of progress. In a westward sweep from the manicured perfection of **Queens Gardens**, at the east end of Hay Street, start with the **Perth Mint** (Mon–Fri 9am–4pm, Sat & Sun 9am–1pm; free), on the corner of Hill and Hay streets. Operating from its original 1899 base, Australia's principal specialist mint still trades in precious metals in bar or coin form and displays some large-scale replicas of gold nuggets and alluring 400-ounce ingots. Visitors can also take a tour ($5) to observe minting operations in the refurbished foundry.

Further down are the **Stirling Gardens**, on the corner of St Georges Terrace and Pier Street, with their "Ore Obelisk" sculpture symbolizing WA's mineral diversity, and also a group of big bronze kangaroos. The **Old Courthouse** (Tues & Thurs 10am–2.30pm; free), the colony's oldest surviving building, is also in the gardens and houses the less than electrifying **Francis Burt Law Museum**, while other sights in the area include the **Deanery** on the corner of Pier Street, the **Cloisters** – now an office – and the **Old Perth Boys' School**, at 139 St Georges Terrace, now a café and wine bar. Barely discernible at the far end of the terrace is the **Barracks Archway**, the remains of an 1860s structure not really worth closer inspection unless you're heading up that way to Kings Park. Easily missed on the corner of Hay and Barrack streets is the neo-Jacobean facade of the **Town Hall**, dating from the 1870s.

The **Old Mill** (daily 10am–4pm; $3; Transperth ferry from Barrack Street Jetty), situated at Mill Point, south of the Narrows and in the shadow of the Kwinana Freeway bridge, is an early building that has managed to retain its charm. A quaint, fairy-tale relic, the mill ground the colony's first flour and now houses a collection of pioneering bull-carts and period artefacts in its own attractive grounds.

Perth Zoo and Kings Park

Perth Zoo (daily 9am–5pm; $13.20; Ⓦwww.perthzoo.wa.gov.au), on Labouchere Road a short walk from the Old Mill (see above), is a hundred-year-old park where animals are not confined to small cages, in keeping with the trend away from traditional zoos. There is enough indigenous and exotic wildlife here to make a great afternoon out.

Perhaps the city's best attraction is the mostly wild, five-square-kilometre expanse of **Kings Park**, a two-kilometre walk west of the centre down Mount Street, turning off at the end of St Georges Terrace (or take bus #33 or #5 from St Georges Terrace, free FTZ). Created with great foresight in 1872, the park remains Perth's premier recreational area (other than the river), enlivened by various flora and fauna, and no visit would be complete without a wander around. Although the park is small enough to enjoy on foot, you can rent **bicycles** from Koala Cycle Hire (Mon–Fri 9.30am–4pm, Sat & Sun 9.30am–6pm) in the main car park on the park's east side, where there's a fine, tree-framed view over the city. There's a trail leading through the native bushland, a botanic and an aromatic garden, playgrounds, picnic areas and free guided tours from the **information centre** (daily 9.30am–3.30pm; Ⓣ08/9480 3600) by the car park, which also provides maps of the park.

Eating and drinking

To eat well and inexpensively in Perth, stick to **Italian** and **Asian** places; these two cuisines cater for ninety percent of eateries and both dominate the **food courts**, where you can easily get a decent meal for as little as $7. In Northbridge there's the Asian *Shang Hai* on James Street, while in the city you'll find the *Metro* and the cosmopolitan *Carillon* off Hay Street Mall. At the other end of the scale, some of the better seafood restaurants may cost you $30 or more per head – still great value unless you're a local. **Northbridge**, especially around James and Lake streets, is the heart of Perth's tourist café and restaurant scene, with over forty establishments crammed into a square kilometre. Except for Sunday and Monday Northbridge is very busy in the evenings, as people wander from place to place, eating and drinking until late.

It's also worth exploring options elsewhere, such as the strip of restaurants along Beaufort Street in Mt Lawley, north of Northbridge, lively Leederville to the west, Subiaco on the west side of Kings Park or of course Fremantle (see p.711). All are fun places to dine without the congested, frenetic feel of Northbridge.

Cafés, snack bars and inexpensive restaurants

Café Universal 251 William St, Northbridge. Trendier place than most to enjoy cappuccinos, beers and street life along with Italian dishes. A Northbridge institution.

Dusit Thai 249 James St, Northbridge. Authentic Thai food on the edge of Northbridge and cheaper than elsewhere in Perth, with main courses for around $9. Closed Mon.

Hans Café Noodle Bar Cnr Francis and William streets, Northbridge. Unpretentious Southeast Asian dishes in a central location. Noodle dishes from $7, rice from $8.

Lotus Vegetarian 220 James St, Northbridge. Inexpensive vegetarian dishes.

Sparrows 434A William St, Northbridge. Good-value and friendly Indonesian.

The Street Café 78 Lake St, Northbridge. Serves smooth cappuccinos and cheap, tasty pasta every day. Opens early.

Villa Italia Cnr Aberdeen and William streets, Northbridge. Jazzy Italian café with lunch specials.

Restaurants

Annalakshmi 12 Esplanade, Perth CBD ✆08/9221 3003. Odd location in the CBD but with a selection of vegetarian Indian dishes overlooking the Swan River.

C Restaurant Level 33, St Martin's Tower ("AAPT"), 44 St Georges Terrace, Perth CBD ✆08/9220 8333. Revolving restaurant with a matchless view and a top class, cosmopolitan menu.

Maya Masala Cnr Lake and Francis streets, Northbridge. One of Perth's few Indian restaurants offering curries from $12.

Meads Mosman Bay 115 Johnson Parade, Mosman ✆08/9383 3388. Top-class seafood restaurant situated on the upmarket northern shore of the Swan, north of Fremantle.

Siena Pizzeria 500 Beaufort St, Mt Lawley ✆08/9227 6991; also 115 Oxford St, Leederville ✆08/9444 8844. Deservedly busy with mouth watering, wood-fired pizzas and all your other Italian favourites.

Woodpeckers Woodfired Pizza 372 Hay St, Subiaco ✆08/9388 1122. Gourmet pizza and pasta. Open from 6pm.

Entertainment and nightlife

As with food, **Northbridge** is the focal point of after-dark action, with plenty of **pubs**, **bars** and teeming **dance clubs** concealed in improbable buildings. In view of Perth's famed isolation, a night in Northbridge is the hottest spot for thousands of kilometres in any direction but there are also some lively bars in the city and inner suburbs. Perth's nightlife centres around alcohol and although the city is attempting to curb intoxicated revellers and promote responsible behaviour, the many pubs and bars offering **free beer**, happy hours and other value-added incentives to get you loaded, means it is to little avail. Late at night Northbridge can have an edge to it that some might find intimidating.

The free *Wax* newspaper available outside various central outlets has comprehensive **listings**, as well as a useful "vibe guide" so you won't stumble into trance when you wanted hard house. Alternatively, check out the entertainment section of Thursday's *West Australian* newspaper. For the lowdown on the **gay and lesbian scene**, see the box on p.710.

Pubs and bars with music

Aberdeen Hotel 84 Aberdeen St. Ever-popular meeting place in Northbridge, with a long-established gay night on Sundays.

Brass Monkey Cnr William and James streets. Enduringly popular pub with a good atmosphere in the heart of Northbridge. Live entertainment and a range of local beers.

Leederville Hotel Oxford St, Leederville. The Sunday sessions are all the rage but you need to be smartly dressed. Mainstream bands and DJs.

Moon & Sixpence 300 Murray St. Popular English theme pub in city centre.

Mustang Bar 46 Lake St. Big screen sports, and Wild Wednesdays with free pool, cheap food and monthly karaoke.

Northbridge Hotel 198 Brisbane St. Quiet piano lounge and restaurant which does good breakfasts. Rowdier public bar with Internet facilities.

Queens 520 Beaufort St, Mt Lawley. One of Perth's best bars, away from the Northbridge mania with a great atmosphere, locally brewed beers and a

WESTERN AUSTRALIA | Perth

good restaurant for a Sunday morning breakfast. **Spirit Sound Bar** Murray St. Popular pre-club meeting place with DJs at weekends.

Subiaco Hotel Cnr Rokeby and Hay streets. Mixed and unpretentious crowds, popular on Thursdays and at weekends.

Clubs

Connections 81 James St. Perth's established gay and lesbian nightspot offers the best dance music for all sexual preferences. Closed Mon.
The Deen 84 Aberdeen St. Monday backpackers' night with "a Saturday feel" plus free pick-ups and meals.
The Globe 393 Murray St. Live international alt-rock acts and DJs for an otherwise mainstream crowd.

Hip-E-Club Cnr Anzac Rd and Oxford St, Leederville. Still dishing out retro-psychedelia and famed Tuesday backpackers' nights.
The Post Office 133 Aberdeen St. Long-established club which also has specials for backpackers on Wednesdays and live bands on Thursdays.

⑦ Cinemas, theatres and live music

Most of Perth's mainstream movie **cinemas** are located in the arcades off Hay

---

River cruises and tours from Perth

As well as commercial **ferry** operators, all based at Barrack Street Jetty and offering cruises up and down the Swan River from as little as $10 to Fremantle or $70 for a full-day upriver, **bus and 4WD** tours leave daily in all directions from Perth. Popular day-tours include the curious Pinnacles, near Cervantes (see p.749), the wineries of the Upper Swan Valley (see p.720) and New Norcia and Toodyay (p.720). Longer excursions reach up to the Ningaloo Reef around Coral Bay and Exmouth (via Monkey Mia), right up to Broome or Darwin or through WA's diverse Southwest region including Margaret River wineries. Bookings for all tours can be made at your accommodation, at the official tourist office in Forrest Chase (℡08/9483 1111), or at any of the tour shops such as the YHA, 235 William St, or others around Wellington and Barrack streets.

River cruises and Rottnest ferries
Captain Cook Cruises ℡08/9325 3341, ⓦwww.captaincookcruises.com.au. Offers a whole medley of cruises including upriver to some wineries ($65–99 with lunch) down to Fremantle ($15; 3 daily) and evening dinner cruises ($62–75) on the Swan.
Golden Sun Cruises ℡08/9325 1616. Cruises upriver to visit the National Trust property at Tranby House, faintly historic Guildford, and a day-cruise and bus tour around the Swan Valley wineries. Also downriver cruises to Fremantle from $11 or $18 return.
Oceanic Cruises Perth ℡08/9325 1191; Fremantle ℡08/9430 2666, ⓦwww .oceaniccruises.com.au. Five daily Perth–Rottnest cruises from $53 and three daily from Fremantle from $40, as well as all-in island tours for $84 and overnight backpacker deals from $55. Also day-tours to Carnac Island including lunch and snorkel to meet the sealions ($79 from Perth, $69 from Fremantle).
Rottnest Express ℡08/9335 6406, ⓦwww.rottnestexpress.com.au. Up to ten Fremantle departures daily from $40, with overnight packages at the YHA from $55.

Tours
All Terrain Safaris ℡1800 633 456, ⓦwww.allterrain.com.au. One of WA's leading and longest-established tour operators offering a full range of professionally run adventure tours, with decent food and a comfortable purpose-built vehicle, but

and Murray streets in the city centre. Tuesday nights are cheap, with matinees also discounted at some places. Art-house cinemas close to the centre include Cinema Paradiso, in James Street's Galleria complex; a little further out, the Art Deco-style Astor, at Mt Lawley on the corner of Beaufort and Walcott streets; and the Luna on Oxford Street, Leederville, both a fifteen-minute walk west of Northbridge.

Any out-of-the-ordinary **shows** that visit Perth tend to set the city astir and are advertised and patronized heavily. The *Burswood Resort and Casino* (℡08/9362 7777), just over the Causeway, southeast of the centre, is a do-it-all leisure complex comprising a five-star hotel, numerous restaurants and a huge dome hosting all sorts of sporting and show-business events. Otherwise try the Perth Concert Hall on St Georges Terrace (℡08/9325 9944) or Her Majesty's Theatre (℡08/9322 2929) on the corner of King and Hay streets. International bands play at the monolithic and somewhat suburban Metropolis Club by the railway station at 146 Roe St.

sleeping in swags. Runs up the coast doing all the usuals to Coral Bay, as well as inland to Karijini and from Broome right into the northern Kimberley and the Bungles, continuing all the way to Kakadu. Around $130 a day. Also cheap "return the bus" runs back to Perth.

Easyrider Backpacker Tours 114 William St, Northbridge ℡08/9226 0307. Hop on and off the yellow bus, from three days up to six months, as far as Broome via Coral Bay and Karijini or down to Albany from as little as $70 per day, but not including meals and accommodation.

Feature Tours ℡08/9479 4131. Regular coach tours from Perth along the Swan Valley.

Out and About Tours ℡08/9377 3376. Offers small-group Swan Valley day-tours visiting several wineries and including lunch. Tours run Thursday to Sunday and cost $72.

Pinnacles Tours and Travel Centre 16 Irwin St, cnr Hay St ℡08/9221 5411. One-day non-backpacker coach tours to the Pinnacles (4WD option), Wave Rock and Margaret River, plus longer runs as far afield as Coral Bay (5 days), together with seasonal whale-watching and wildflower tours. From $80 per day.

Planet Perth Tours ℡08/9225 6622, ⊛www.planettours.com.au. Accommodated tours into the Southwest and up to Exmouth and Broome from around $100 a day. Weekly departures.

Redback Safaris ℡08/9275 6204, ⊛www.redbacksafaris.com.au. Similar to Planet Perth, this outfit offers popular four-day Monkey Mia tours and the preferable five-day one-way to Exmouth, with sandboarding plus optional abseiling, catamaraning and wine-tasting with accommodation in backpackers' or farm stays. From around $100 a day.

Travelabout ℡9244 1200, ⊛www.travelabout.com.au. Similar outfit to All Terrain, with four- to six-day Monkey Mia and Southwest tours, eleven-day trips up the coast via Exmouth and Karijini to Broome, and an eight-day Kimberley and Bungles tour to Darwin. Also offers an unusual six-day Perth to the Rock and Alice via the Warburton Road, all at around $140 a day.

Western Travel Bug ℡1800 627 488, ⊛www.travelbug.com.au. Day-tours to the Pinnacles, Wave Rock and Margaret River under $100, as well as longer tours of the Southwest offering plenty of activities and a lively atmosphere.

Gay and lesbian Perth

Perth has a robust, self-sufficient and extremely friendly gay and lesbian scene. The heart of the action is **Northbridge**, but neighbouring Highgate, Mt Lawley and especially Leederville all have more than their share of gay residents, while lesbians seem to opt for a relaxed lifestyle down in Freo. As usual, the quickest way to plug into the scene is to pick up the community paper: in Perth it's the fortnightly *Westside Observer* (*WSO*; ⓦ www.wso.com.au) and *Women Out West* (*WOW*; ⓦ www.womenoutwest.com.au), both free at gigs or available for $1 at the Arcane Bookshop, 212 William St, Northbridge (Mon–Fri 10am–5.30pm, Sat 10am–5pm; ☎ 08/9328 5073), which has plenty of other gay, lesbian and feminist literature.

October heats up with **Perth Pride** (ⓦ www.pridewa.asn.au), celebrated with the usual array of fun and games, including a night march and dance party. Also in October, lesbians march to **Reclaim The Night** (☎ 08/9381 3706). Every November competitors get set to "go for glory" at the **Western Australia Gay Olympics**. At other times of year, outdoor organizations such as GAGS and Team Perth (see below) can put you in touch with other pink athletes.

The main **community organizations** for gays and lesbians in Perth are the Gay Activities Group Services (GAGS), PO Box 8234, Perth 6849, which is responsible for the Gay Olympics and other sporting events; the Gay Outdoor Group, PO Box 263, Cottesloe, Perth 6011 (☎ 08/9270 7181); Team Perth, PO Box 3234 Stirling Street, Perth 6849 (☎ 0412 599 577), a lesbian and gay sports group; and Wednesday Women (☎ 08/9328 9044), a lesbian social group.

For gay- and lesbian-friendly **accommodation**, try the *Court Hotel* (50 Beaufort St, ☎ 08/9328 5292) or the beachside *Swanbourne Guest House* (see p.719). **Nighttime venues** include *Connections*, *Court Hotel* and the *Red Lion* at the *Aberdeen Hotel* on Sundays (see p.707).

Listings

Airline Skywest ☎ 1300 660 088, ⓦ www.skywest.com.au. Daily flights to the Goldfields, Esperance and Albany, Exmouth and Karratha.

Buses McCafferty's, 554 Wellington St (☎ 13 14 99 or 08/9321 6211), goes up along the coast to Darwin every day, less frequently to Port Hedland via Newman on the inland route, and only once a week to Adelaide and the east coast; Integrity Coach Lines (☎ 08/9226 1399 or 1800 226 339, ⓦ www.integritycoachlines.com.au) also heads north via Coral Bay/Exmouth (4 weekly) and as far as Broome (Mon & Fri); South West Coach Lines (☎ 08/9322 5173) has daily services to the Margaret River Region as far as Augusta; and Westrail (☎ 13 10 53) operates daily bus services as far as Esperance and, less frequently, north to Kalbarri and Meekatharra via Mullewa. They do a four-week Southern Discovery Pass for around $120.

Car rental Ace Rent-a-Car, 311 Hay St, East Perth (☎ 08/9221 1333, ⓦ www.acerent.com.au; Atlas Rent-a-Car, 36 Milligan St, West Perth (☎ 08/9481 8866; M2000, 228 Lord St, East Perth (☎ 08/9227 0709, ⓦ www.m2000car.com.au. The cheapest new cars with unlimited kilometres cost around $45 a day, with restricted kilometres from around $28.

Car purchase For used cars, backpackers' notice boards and many Internet cafés and travel shops have private sales. Used car lots specializing in backpackers' vehicles are found on the edge of the city, up around Beaufort Street in Mt Lawley and the west end of Newcastle Street. Delving further into the suburbs for private sales may unearth better deals, but without gear thrown in. Be careful who you hand your money over to as not all dealers are reputable.

Disabled travellers ACROD, Unit 9, 189 Royal St, East Perth (☎ 08/9222 2961), provides information for disabled visitors to WA. For information about accessible accommodation, call the Para Quad Association (☎ 08/9381 0173), or use the fairly reliable RACWA Touring Guide (see opposite).

Hospitals Royal Perth, Victoria Square ☎ 08/9224 2244; Fremantle, Alma St ☎ 08/9321 3333.

Internet access The city library (see p.705) has several somewhat clunky computers free for surfing up to an hour a day. If your accommodation has no machines then you'll find several Internet cafés on Barrack Street and William Street, between Murray Street and Wellington Street.

Maps Perth Map Centre, 900 Hay St (☎08/9322 5733), has a full range of topographic and touring maps.

Motoring associations RACWA, 228 Adelaide Terrace (☎08/9421 4444), offers a complete range of services, as well as maps.

Permits for Aboriginal Land Aboriginal Affairs Department, 197 St Georges Terrace ☎08/9235 8000, ⓦwww.dia.wa.gov.au/Land/Permits/.

Police 2 Adelaide Terrace ☎08/9222 1111.

Post office Forrest Chase, opposite the train station, with a mail collection service.

Taxis ☎08/9333 3333 or 9444 4444.

Trains The Indian-Pacific rail service (☎13 21 47, ⓦwww.trainways.com.au) has finally reduced prices to 10–15 percent above an equivalent bus fare and has great deals such as the Great Southern Rail Pass (see p.35) although it is no faster in crossing the width of the country. Services leave on Wednesday, getting to Sydney or Melbourne two days later. Westrail also has daily rail services south to Bunbury and twice on week-days to Kalgoorlie. Both have offices at the Wellington Street Bus Station or tickets can be booked at the office on the ground floor at the adjacent City railway station.

Around Perth

While Perth may not be all it's cracked up to be, the area around the city offers some compensation. The port of **Fremantle**, at the mouth of the Swan River, should not be overlooked, nor should a day-trip to **Rottnest Island**, an eighty-minute ferry ride from the city or half that from Fremantle. Perth's **beaches** form a near-unbroken line north of Fremantle, just a short train or bus ride from the centre, while with your own vehicle you can escape to the **national parks** northeast of Perth, atop the **Darling Ranges**, which parallel the coast. Patchily forested hills, just half an hour's drive east of the city, they offer a network of cool, scenic drives and marked walking trails among the jarrah woodlands.

Further afield **Toodyay** and **New Norcia** can make a satisfying day-trip with a tour or in a rented car, as can a visit to **Mundaring Weir** and the old colonial settlement of **York**.

Fremantle

Although long since merged into the metropolitan area's suburban sprawl, Perth's port of **FREMANTLE** – "Freo" – retains a character all of its own. It's small enough to keep its energy focused with a lively, working harbour instead of a fake marina and an eclectic, arty ambience without any upmarket preten-sions.

Much of the convict-built dock, dating from the 1890s, was spruced up for the 1987 Americas Cup yacht race for an eagerly anticipated tourist boom that never quite materialized. Before that makeover Freo was as rough as any port: the period hotels were then "bloodhouses" full of brawling sailors. Even today though, the jazzed-up "latte and deck shoes" image, so popular with metro-politan visitors, takes a knock as an unmistakable ovine pong settles over the whole town when streams of "baa-ing" road trains load up live sheep freighters bound for Arabia.

Freo's relaxed, Mediterranean ambience attracts hordes of weekenders to its famed arty **markets** (worth planning your visit around) and "cappuccino strip", as the café-lined **South Terrace** is known. In fact, many other attrac-tions are only open Friday to Sunday. It's also worth noting that in the heat of summer Fremantle is often a breezy 5°C cooler than Perth, a mere 25 minutes away by train.

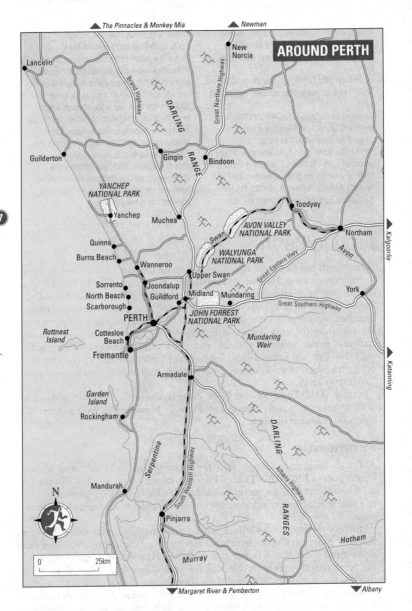

Arrival and information

Fremantle Station is located at the top end of Market Street, five minutes' walk north of the town centre. **Buses** (routes #102–106 and #151 from Perth's City Busport) also stop here; local **taxis** can be called on ☎08/9335 3944. **Ferries** to Rottnest and Perth leave from the B Shed, behind the E Shed, ten minutes' walk from the station along Phillimore Street (see box on p.708 for details and prices). The free orange **Fremantle CAT** bus service runs roughly every ten minutes along a figure-of-eight route which covers all places in the description below. You could also consider hopping aboard the **Fremantle Tram** which offers informative commentaries on its various tours (daily 10am–4pm; hourly; $10), and departs from outside the Town Hall on Kings Square. There's a small **tourist office** in the Town Hall on Kings Square (Mon–Sat 9am–5pm, Sun noon–4.40pm; ☎08/9431 7878).

Accommodation

Fremantle has enough conveniently central accommodation to entice you to stay rather than visit. There are no less than five **hostels** all within a kilometre of each other, plus a caravan park. Grand-era hotels have been splendidly refurbished, their only drawback being shared bathrooms for most rooms.

Backpacker Inn 11 Packenham St ☎08/9431 7065, ⓔbpinn_freo@hotmail.com. The best backpackers' in Freo until *Sundancer* rewrote the book. More spacious than anything you'll get in Perth with massive kitchen, banks of computers and more than one spot to sit and chill. No parking. Four-, six- and eight-bed dorms from $16, rooms ❷

Fremantle Hotel Cnr High and Cliff streets ☎08/9430 4300, ⓕ9335 2636. Right by the Round House, this unpretentious hotel has rooms with shared and en-suite facilities. ❹

Fremantle Village Caravan Park Cnr Cockburn and Rockingham roads, South Fremantle ☎08/9430 4866. The nearest campsite to the centre of town. On-site vans ❷

His Majesty's Hotel Cnr Phillimore and Mouat streets ☎08/9336 4681, ⓕ9336 4691. One of Freo's many federation-era hotels refurbished to a high standard. Nearly all rooms have shared bathrooms. Restaurant and bar. ❸

Norfolk Hotel 47 South Terrace ☎08/9335 5405, ⓕ9430 5909. Non-pub central hotel with mostly en-suite rooms; at the end of the strip. ❹

Old Fire Station Backpackers 18 Phillimore St ☎08/9430 5454, ⓦwww.firestation.fdns.net. Popular with young ravers just two minutes from the station and big on security. Battling the competition with free Internet, breakfast, bikes, parking and $3 curries from the in-house Indian. A huge common room and women-only lounge and dorms, but a bit rough out back. Four- to twelve-bed dorms from $16, rooms ❷

Pirates Backpackers 11 Essex St ☎ & ⓕ08/9335 6635. Old hostel, with a small kitchen but cosy lounge and outdoor area, plus a bar. No parking. Dorms from $16, twins/doubles ❷.

Sundancer Backpacker Resort 80 High St ☎08/9336 6080 or 1800 061 144, ⓦwww .sundancer-resort.com.au. A stunningly refurbished old pub and club you could bring your mother to, featuring lashings of jarrah, arty colour and space, plus a touch of class in the rooms and even a spa and bar. Fee parking. Eight-bed dorms $16, rooms ❷–❸

Tradewinds Hotel 59 Canning Highway ☎08/9339 8188, ⓕ9339 2266. Good-looking, federation-era hotel with well-equipped, self-contained apartments, close to the river and 2km from the centre. ❺

The Town

Exploring Fremantle on foot, with plenty of streetside café breaks, is the most agreeable way of visiting the town's compactly grouped sights. If you're feeling worthy and want to comb through all of Freo's tourist sites, start your appraisal on the relatively dull east side, moving down to the ocean to end up at the Fishing Boat Harbour, ready for a sunset seafood dinner. If Freo's sedate sights don't appeal, it's just as rewarding to simply follow your nose and wander through the livelier town centre.

The **Fremantle Arts Centre and Museum** (daily 10am–5pm; free) is on the corner of Finnerty and Ord streets, although the small museum's local history displays are not very exciting. The Arts Centre itself, in an attractive building with a gallery, is a popular rendezvous for the arty set and a venue for live performances on summer Sunday afternoons. The gallery has a variety of local offerings, but can't compare with the collection of the Art Gallery of Western Australia in Perth.

At the end of Quarry Street, 500m from the Arts Centre, **World of Energy** (Mon–Fri 9am–5pm; $4), at 12 Parry St, is a rather stodgy, educational exhibition of power-generating apparatus with a few "hands-on" displays. Continuing down Parry Street brings you to the hillside enclosure of **Fremantle Prison** (daily 10am–6pm; $14.30; @ www.fremantleprison.com), whose entrance is in The Terrace. Built by convicts in 1855, soon after the struggling colony found it couldn't do without their labour, it's now one of the biggest tourist-attraction jails in the country. The high admission charge is offset by free tours (every 30min) of the prison buildings, sometimes guided by ex-wardens. The building was only decommissioned as late as 1991 and there is now talk of a future "master plan" to make something more of the place, possibly even offering accommodation.

Not far from the prison, **Fremantle Markets** (Fri 10am–9pm, Sat & Sun 10am–5pm), on the corner of Henderson Street and South Terrace, are a hub of activity. A real locals' market, not aimed at tourists, it's well worth a browse for some fresh food, unusual souvenirs from the many arts-and-crafts stalls, or cosmic accessories. Moving down **South Terrace**, Fremantle's main street, you can revive your aching feet with some refreshment in one of the many inviting, alfresco **cafés** that give the town its Mediterranean atmosphere.

Suitably re-caffeinated, head towards the "**West End**", as the old shipping office and freight district of Freo is known. A left down High Street leads past various art-and-crafts galleries and knick-knack shops inviting you for a browse. At the end of the street is the **Round House** (10am–5pm; donation), the state's oldest building and original jail, with fine views back down into town and out to sea.

From here you can't have failed to miss the striking new building housing the **West Australian Maritime Museum** on Victoria Quay (Mon–Sun 9.30am–5pm; $10). The museum, with architectural overtones of the Sydney Opera House, opened in December 2002 and features the *Australia II* yacht which won the Americas Cup, as well as galleries about the Swan River and the navy. The **submarine** *Ovens* is nearby (Fri–Sun 11am–4pm; $8.80, possibly to be included in museum entry).

Outside the Fremantle Port Authority building there's a statue to C.Y. O'Connor who masterminded the rebuilding of the docks in the 1890s as well as the construction of the vital water pipeline to Kalgoorlie (see p.743). Nearby, where the Rottnest ferries berth, the **E Shed markets** (Fri 10am–9pm, Sat & Sun 10am–5pm) offer a similar range of stalls and a food hall as found at the better-known Fremantle Markets.

The original maritime museum is back on Cliff Street, just past the Round House, and has now been redesignated as the **Shipwreck Museum** (daily 9.30am–5pm; $10). Pride of place goes to the *Batavia* display, the Dutch East Indiaman wrecked off present-day Geraldton over 360 years ago. As well as the ship's reconstructed stern, the exhibit includes the stone portico bound for the Company's unfinished fort at Batavia (Jakarta) and numerous corroded artefacts, together with a fascinating video about the extraordinary drama and subsequent salvage of the wreck. The rest of the museum has collections from other Dutch vessels which regularly struck Australia's west coast on their way to the East Indies.

Coming out of the Shipwreck Museum you find yourself on the grassy esplanade facing the numerous seafood restaurants on **Fishing Boat Harbour** – see "Eating", below.

Eating

Fremantle is a fun place to eat. **Seafood** restaurants overlook the Swan River or jut out into the Fishing Boat Harbour by the Esplanade. In town, South

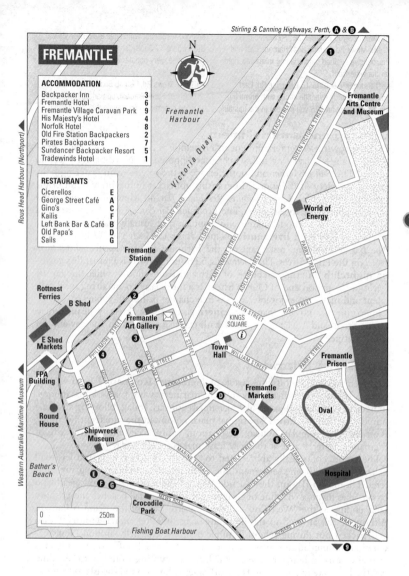

FREMANTLE

ACCOMMODATION

Backpacker Inn	3
Fremantle Hotel	6
Fremantle Village Caravan Park	9
His Majesty's Hotel	4
Norfolk Hotel	8
Old Fire Station Backpackers	2
Pirates Backpackers	7
Sundancer Backpacker Resort	5
Tradewinds Hotel	1

RESTAURANTS

Cicerellos	E
George Street Café	A
Gino's	C
Kailis	F
Left Bank Bar & Café	B
Old Papa's	D
Sails	G

Terrace and its adjacent streets are lined with predominantly **Italian** or **Asian** cafés and restaurants, none of them expensive and all adding to Freo's distinctive ambience. At the **Food Halls** on Henderson Street (Thurs–Sun noon–9pm), next to the markets, an array of global, but mostly Asian "pop foods" is served up.

Cicerellos Fishing Boat Harbour. One of the best fish-and-chip places in town.

George Street Café 73 George St, East Fremantle. Pleasant, small café, an east-side alternative to the central Freo coffee "strip".

Gino's 1 South Terrace. Enduringly popular and unpretentious, serving great coffee and inexpensive food. After a "cappucho" at *Gino's* and lunch at *Cicerellos* you've done the "Fremantle thing". **Kailis** Mews Rd, Fishing Boat Harbour. Fast and inexpensive seafood cafeteria and takeaway, right on the waterfront.

Left Bank Bar & Café 15 Riverside Rd, East Fremantle. Trendy riverside venue with brimming subs, or for around $25 you can eat in the upstairs seafood restaurant which has great river views.

Old Papa's 17 South Terrace. Local legendary Italian café, very popular with locals, serving up cheap meals.

Sails 47 Mews Rd, Fishing Boat Harbour ☎08/9430 5050. Elegant, upmarket, harbourside seafood specialities for around $25 per person.

Drinking and entertainment

Like the town itself, entertainment in Fremantle is generally a laid-back, easy-going affair – a jazzy or folksy scene, as opposed to Northbridge's techno venues. The *Sail & Anchor* on South Terrace is the town's main watering hole, serving a variety of "boutique" **beers** (this upmarket home-brew trend originated in Fremantle). *Little Creatures Restaurant Bar*, 40 Mews Rd, is also good and not a bad place to eat, either. The *Left Bank Bar & Café*, on Riverside Road in East Freo, is a good-looking and popular spot, usually packed on sunny weekends. Bars with **live music** include *Rosie O'Grady's* on William Street; *The Bar* at *Lombardos* restaurant on the harbour; and the spruced-up *Orient Hotel* on the High Street. The *Metropolis*, 52 South Terrace, is Fremantle's gigantic **nightclub**, offering a choice of bars and dance floors while the *Fly By Night*, at the prison end of Queen Street, is a musicians' co-op airing local **folk** talent and makes an enjoyable, smoke-free change from pub venues.

Fremantle has no less than four **cinemas**, on Essex Street, William Street, Collie Street and Adelaide Street, all with cut-price tickets on Tuesday and for some matinees.

Rottnest Island

Eighteen kilometres offshore, west of Fremantle, **Rottnest Island** was so named by seventeenth-century Dutch mariners who mistook its unique, indigenous **quokkas**, beaver-like marsupials, for rats. Today, following an ignominious period as a brutal Aboriginal penal colony in the nineteenth century, Rottnest is a popular holiday destination, easily accessible from Perth or Fremantle by ferry and, at the very least, makes for a fun day out.

The island, colloquially abbreviated to "Rotto", is 11km long and less than half as wide, with one settlement, the main resort, stretching along the sheltered Thompson Bay on the east side. West of the settlement, a low heathland of salt lakes meets a coastline of clear, scalloped bays, small beaches and offshore reefs ending at the "West End", as the seaward "tail" of the island is known. Although well attuned to the demands of its 400,000 annual visitors, Rotto gets packed out during school summer holidays, especially around New Year when accommodation can be hard to find. Motorized traffic on the island is virtually non-existent, a real treat which makes **cycling** from bay to sparkling bay the best way to appreciate Rotto. Besides riding around the island, you can take a **train ride** up to Oliver Hill (5 trips daily, allow 2hr; $12), or get underwater with the Dive Shop (daily 7.30am–6pm; ☎08/9292 5111), which organizes **dive trips** and rents out everything from a snorkel and fins to a full scuba rig. The diving and snorkelling off Rotto's beautiful coves are unlike anywhere on the adjacent mainland and a couple of days spent here, especially midweek when it's less busy, are well worth the excursion from Perth.

Practicalities

There are at least three **ferry** operators that service Rotto from the B Shed in Fremantle and Perth's Barrack Street Jetty. Prices have stabilized at around

$40 day-return from Freo and $50 from Perth (see p.708). The trip from Perth takes about eighty minutes, half as long from Fremantle. You can also **fly** to Rotto in twenty minutes from Jandakot airport, about 20km south of Perth, with the Rottnest Air Taxi (T 1800 500 006; from $60 if the 4–6 seater is full; city pick-ups). Rottnest Airport is a fifteen-minute walk from the settlement.

Ferries arrive at the jetty in Thompson Bay right in front of the island's **information office** (Mon–Sat 8.30am–5pm, Sun 10am–4.30pm; T 08/9372 9752, W www.rottnest.wa.gov.au), which has maps and bus timetables. The office is also a **post office** with Commonwealth and Westpac bank agencies. Daily two-hour **bus tours** depart from the bus stop behind the information office at varying times throughout the day ($13.20). The more-or-less hourly Bayseeker **bus service** (Oct–April daily 9am–5pm; $5.50 per trip) also takes you to the island's bays as far as the isthmus, Narrow Neck, 3km from the West End. The settlement has a general **store** (daily 9am–5.30pm; with ATMs), bakery, takeaway and **bistro**, with **bike** rental (daily 9am–1pm & 2–5pm; from $15 per day; T 08/9372 9722) behind the hotel, a couple of minutes south of the information office.

Accommodation is found along Thompson, Longreach and Geordie bays, all adjacent to each other at the developed northeast end of the island and linked by an hourly bus service (daily 8am–5pm; $2). A small YHA-associate **hostel** (T 08/9372 9780, E rottnest@yhawa.com.au; booking essential; dorms $18) is located in Kingstown Barracks, at the southeastern end of Thompson Bay, 1km from the shops. **Camping** is available just behind the settlement (T 08/9372 9730): tents and mattresses can be rented (❶) or there are four- and six-bed self-contained cabins (❸); note that camping is not permitted elsewhere on the island. The *Rottnest Lodge Resort* (T 08/9292 5161, F 9292 5158; ❻–❼) is a prison converted into first-class motel units.

Perth's beaches

Perth's closest **beaches** extend along the Indian Ocean's **Sunset Coast**, 30km of near-unbroken sand and coastal suburbs stretching north of the Swan River and cooled by afternoon sea breezes. There are also **inshore beaches** along the Swan River at Crawley, Nedlands, Peppermint Grove and Mosman Bay on the north shore, and Como, Canning Bridge and Applecross on the south – all are calm and safe for kiddies.

Cottesloe Beach, 7km north of Fremantle, is the most popular city beach, with safe swimming in the lee of a groyne, although in the summer of 2000 a swimmer was killed by a shark and summertime air patrols are still being debated. There are ice-cream vendors, cafés and watercraft-rental outlets all just a ten-minute walk from Cottesloe train station. North of here, **Swanbourne Free Beach**, cut off by army land in both directions but accessible from the road, has nude bathing. Further north, the surf and currents are more suited to wave-riding and experienced swimmers, with fewer beachside facilities, which tends to reduce crowds.

Scarborough Beach, dominated by the *Rendezvous Observation City Hotel*, is as much a holiday resort as a somewhat dowdy beachside suburb with a love of concrete. Popular with surfers and their groupies, the suburb has an easy-going air of "Californian tan-upmanship", plus enough services, inexpensive accommodation and activity to sustain a few days out of central Perth. **Bus** #400 leaves from Perth's Wellington Street Bus Station for the 35-minute journey.

△ Cottesloe Beach, Perth

Beachside accommodation

The accommodation at Scarborough Beach is mostly self-catering, suited to extended stays. The *Western Beach Lodge* serves backpackers in a converted house at 6 Westborough St (℡08/9245 1624; dorms from $18) or try *Sunset Coast Backpackers*, 119 Scarborough Beach Rd (℡08/9245 1161; dorms $17). The *Mandarin Gardens Holiday Resort*, at 20 Wheatcroft St (℡08/9431 5431, Ⓔmandarin@crystal.com.au; ❹), has backpacker accommodation (dorms $19) as well as motel rooms, plus it offers free pick-ups from the airport. Further south in **Swanbourne**, the excellent and welcoming *Swanbourne Guest House*, 5 Myera St (℡08/9383 1981; ❹), is great for couples, as well as being gay- and lesbian-friendly. The *Cottesloe Beach Chalets*, 6 John St (℡08/9383 5000, Ⓦcottesloebeachchalets.com.au; ❺), have self-contained apartments sleeping five right by the beach that are suitable for families or small groups. On the corners of Marine Parade and Eric Street is *Ocean Beach Backpackers* (℡08/9384 5111, Ⓦwww.obh.com.au/backpackers; dorms from $19, twins/doubles ❸).

New Norcia and Toodyay

One of WA's most unusual architectural sights is the nineteenth-century monastic community of **NEW NORCIA**, 130km northeast of Perth on the Great Northern Highway. This unexpected collection of Spanish-style buildings, bizarrely out of place in the Australian bush, is part of a community founded by Benedictine monks in 1846. **Dom Rosendo Salvado** established the mission (named after St Benedict's birthplace in Italy) with the aim of converting the local Aborigines to the "twin blessings" of agriculture and Christianity, and to escape persecution back home. Nowadays it's a popular tourist attraction, which tends to compromise the monastic tranquillity its ageing inhabitants seek, and yet pays for the upkeep of their remarkable endowment.

The community has a roadhouse with a restaurant, a **tourist office** (Aug–Oct daily 9.30am–5pm; Nov–July daily 10am–4.30pm; ℡08/9654 8056) and a **museum and art gallery** (daily 9.30am–5pm; $5) describing the Benedictines' motivations in coming here and displaying a fine collection of religious art. The tourist office also runs two-hour tours of the town that leave at 11am and 1.30pm ($12.50). The **rooms** in the *New Norcia Hotel* (℡08/9654 8034, Ⓕ9654 8011; ❸) don't quite match the building's grand exterior, but they still offer an old-fashioned treat. The two-kilometre New Norcia **heritage trail** (guide leaflet available from the tourist office or museum; $3.50) begins here and takes you on a circuit past the community's impressive buildings.

The two most ornate buildings, on either side of the cemetery, are **St Gertrude's Residence for Girls** and **St Ildephonsus's for Boys**, the latter with striking Moorish minarets. Both were built by the mission's second abbot, Bishop Torres, at the beginning of the twentieth century. You can also visit the **Flour Mills** and the **Abbey Church** – relatively ordinary by comparison. The **monastery** is still the residence of New Norcia's few remaining monks and is closed to the public, although its guesthouse (℡08/9654 8002; $40 per person for full board) gives the opportunity to experience Benedictine hospitality. From here an eight-hundred-metre marked trail leads down to the old wells and Bishop Torres' gazebo-like **Beehouse** by the Moore River; on the way back there are great views of St Ildephonsus's turreted roofline poking through the trees.

Several bus-tour companies offer **day-tours** from Perth to New Norcia, which is otherwise served only three times a week by Westrail's rural bus service.

Toodyay

The charming old town of **TOODYAY**, set among the wooded hills of the Avon Valley, 85km northwest of Perth, makes an agreeable diversion on the way to or from New Norcia. The town was founded in 1836, making it one of the earliest inland settlements of the Swan River Colony, and many buildings survive from that era. The unembellished bulk of **Connors Mill** on the main road, Stirling Terrace, is now a **museum** (Mon–Sat 9am–5pm, Sun 10am–5pm; $2), featuring, among the usual relics, displays on the exploits of the local bushranger known as "Moondyne Joe". The **Old Newcastle Gaol** on Clinton Street is also a local history museum (daily 10am–3pm; $2). Other historic buildings include **St Stephen's Church**, opposite the mill, and the **Mechanics' Institute**, on Stirling Terrace, which features unusual scissor trusses supporting the roof.

These aside, the town is an attractive place for a stroll, with antique and country crafts outlets, a couple of **tearooms**, pleasant parks and riverside walks. The **Avon Valley** and **Walyunga national parks** (CALM fee; see box on p.722) follow the Avon River southwest of town and make a further scenic diversion on the road to Perth.

Guildford and the Swan Valley

North of the town of **GUILDFORD**, a thirty-minute drive from Perth, is the **Upper Swan Valley**, WA's oldest wine-growing region. Set at the foot of the Darling Ranges, it makes for a pleasant day's **wine-tasting**, although the wines produced here don't match those of the Margaret River Region (see p.726). Guildford itself is a historic town dating back to the earliest years of the colony, with several federation-era grand hotels to admire and Guildford Village Potters, at 22 Meadow St, acting as the town's **tourist office** (Mon–Fri 10am–3pm, Sat & Sun 10am–4pm; ☏08/9279 9859). If you're heading up the valley, pick up the *Swan Valley Drive – Route 203* guide from here, which details the area's attractions and its dozen or so wineries.

The Swan Valley Drive

Heading north from Guildford Village Potters, a clearly marked thirty-kilometre drive follows the west side of the river. A turn-off left down Banera Road leads to **Pinelli Wines** on Bennett Road (Mon–Sat 9am–6pm, Sun 10am–5pm), offering two-litre flagons of decent table wine from $15. Back on the West Swan Road, the simply named **Wines** (Mon–Sat 10am–5pm, Sun 11am–4pm) has some of the valley's best bottles, but you'll probably be more impressed by their Margaret River selection. (All of WA's wines are rather pricey, while being no better than Australia's eastern equivalents.) Further up Route 203, the **Little River Winery & Café** (daily 10am–5.30pm) is a small, independent winery with some award-winning wines and a pleasant café in which to enjoy them.

Coming down the valley's east side, several more wineries tempt you: **Talijancich Wines** (Sun–Fri 11am–5pm), produces a rich muscat, which can be bought rather than tasted, while **Houghton's**, on Dale Road (daily 10am–5pm), is the area's biggest and most diverse producer of wines, with an art gallery and tended lawns on which to contemplate your tastings. The route returns to Guildford via Midland and thence to Perth passing the Toodyay Road (see opposite) winding up into the Darling Ranges. Various tour operators offer **bus and boat tours** (see box on p.709) of the valley.

Mundaring Weir and around

At the crest of the Darling Ranges, 40km from Perth and 7km south of the town of Mundaring on the Great Eastern Highway, is **Mundaring Weir**, a dam constructed in the 1890s to provide water for the Goldfields Water Scheme. At the time, desperate water shortages were hampering development of the Eastern Goldfields and the dam was part of a scheme devised by the colony's chief engineer, C.Y. O'Connor, to raise water the 400km up to Kalgoorlie with the aid of pumping stations. His radical idea was ridiculed and O'Connor struggled to secure funds for his scheme, eventually committing suicide on Fremantle Beach just months before water finally gushed into Kalgoorlie's reservoir in 1903. Today, the Goldfields are still fed by an upgraded version of the pipeline and pumping stations which parallel the Great Eastern Highway to Kalgoorlie.

At the base of the dam wall is the **C.Y. O'Connor Museum** (Mon & Wed–Fri 10.30am–3pm, Sun noon–5pm; $5), housed in the primary steam pumping station. Inside are early versions of the pitch and wood pipeline, at that time the longest in the world, and details of O'Connor's other public works, as well as a biographical video on his achievements.

The **John Forrest National Park** (CALM fee; see box overleaf) lies north of the Great Eastern Highway between Mundaring and Midland, right on the edge of the Darling escarpment and a mere thirty minutes' drive from Perth. An area of natural bushland with swimming spots, waterfalls, and walking and riding trails, as well as barbecues and a restaurant, it's among the best of the nearby parks.

York

Stranded in the Avon Valley, 97km from Perth via the Great Southern Highway, **YORK** looks like a film set for an Australian western. The town is the state's most complete pioneering settlement, filled with attractive and well-preserved early architecture. The commercial centre of the Avon Valley until the railway – and with it the Great Eastern Highway – bypassed it 30km to the north, York is now an agricultural centre but also plays a historic role as a venerable museum of ornate nineteenth-century public buildings, coaching inns and churches. Be warned though, this inland region regularly bakes at 40°C in mid-summer.

The **Old York Gaol & Courthouse** (Tues–Sun noon–4pm; $4) on Avon Terrace harks back to its pioneer history while the **York Motor Museum** (daily 9.30am–4pm; $7), opposite the tourist office on Avon Terrace, capitalizes on York's antiquarian charisma with a large collection of vintage and classic vehicles – from a hundred-year-old single-cylinder tricycle to Ossie Cranston's 1936 Ford V8 racer. At the north end of the terrace are the **Sandalwood Yards** where the perfumed wood, once prolific in WA and highly prized in the Orient, was stored during York's heyday. Near here you can take a walk down to the wobbly **suspension bridge** spanning the generally sluggish Avon River and have a look at the 1854 **Holy Trinity Church**, with its modern stained-glass designs by Robert Juniper, one of WA's foremost artists.

Recrossing the river, passing the Shire Offices and old cemetery, a left turn down the southern end of Avon Terrace leads to **Balladong Farm** (daily

CALM (the government department of Conservation and Land Management) levies an **entry fee** or "pass" to the most-visited national parks in WA. The prices of the various passes are listed below. Throughout this chapter those CALM parks that require an entry fee have the phrase "CALM fee" placed in brackets after their names. You can obtain a pass from the entry station (often unattended), local CALM offices and some tourist offices.

Day Pass: $9 per car, $3 per motorbike. For any number of WA parks visited on that day; useful in the Southwest.

Annual Local Park Pass: $20, giving unlimited access for a year to parks in a given area.

Holiday Pass: $25 per vehicle, allowing entry into all WA parks for four weeks.

Annual All Parks Pass: $55, allowing entry into all WA parks for a year.

Walking times

Right across the state (if not the entire country) signs for short walking trails consistently exaggerate a suggested duration time to the point where it probably dissuades many from even trying. Experience has shown that you can comfortably halve the indicated times and still factor in a picnic and a siesta. Where shown, this chapter gives **actual walking times**: the *minimum* time it takes to complete the walk at a normal pace without stops.

10am–5pm; $5), restored by the National Trust. At a time when York was a key inland settlement and jumping-off point for treks into the interior, the farm played a pivotal role in the region, and today it still employs machinery and husbandry techniques from that era. An elevated view of York and the Avon Valley can be enjoyed from **Mount Brown Lookout**, signposted 2km to the east of town.

Practicalities

York's **tourist office** (daily 9am–5pm; ☏08/9641 1301, ⓦ www.yorktourist bureau.com.au) is at 105 Avon Terrace, the main road on which most of York's fine old buildings are located. A **town map** and information sheet is available here, which locates and briefly describes all of these structures as well as places to stay and eat. The *Imperial Inn*, 83 Avon Terrace (☏08/9641 1010, Ⓕ9641 2201; ❹), is a restored, century-old **hotel** full of old-world charm, while the pricier *Castle Hotel* (☏08/9641 1007; ❹) is even more splendid. There are several upmarket B&Bs in and around town; ask at the tourist office or check out their website.

The Southwest

The region south of Perth and west of the Albany Highway, known as **the Southwest**, is the temperate corner of the continent, where the cool Southern and warm Indian oceans meet to drop heavy winter rains. North of **Bunbury**, 180km from Perth, is a knot of industrial installations and satellite towns such as Rockingham and Mandurah, suburbs which offer little of interest to the visitor compared to what's ahead.

South of Bunbury things improve greatly. The **Margaret River Region** is WA's most popular holiday destination and is famed for its wineries and surf.

To the southeast is the so-called **Tall Timber Country**: towns set amid the remnants of the giant karri forests, offering a chance to experience one of the world's last stands of temperate old-growth forests.

At its best in spring and outside school holidays, the Southwest's lush bucolic scenery is all the more appealing in that it can be enjoyed without necessarily clutching a hat, waterbottle and sunblock. Along with all the tourist infrastructure, the moderate temperatures and prolific shade can inspire a relaxation that would not be possible in the Outback of the north. This experience is augmented by several commendably untacky **galleries** and **woodcraft studios** displaying the quality works of local artisans, from boardroom tables to salad tongs – and at prices (even with overseas shipping) that are worth serious consideration.

There is also more, better-quality and varied **accommodation** in this region than the rest of the state put together and, hostels apart, the recommendations given below barely scratch the surface. Make the most of the visitors centres and the large portfolios many of them have illustrating local places to stay.

South West Coach Lines (in Busselton ☎08/9752 1500; in Perth, at City Bus Port, ☎08/9324 2333) serves Augusta via Margaret River and Busselton and Bunbury, as well as Collie, Donnybrook, Bridgetown and Manjimup. Westrail has a similar provincial **bus** service as well as 28-day, unlimited-travel **bus passes** for around $120.

The best way to get about is, of course, with a **car**, making use of Perth's inexpensive rental agencies. Expect to cover at least 2000km in a week's tour as far as Albany on the Rainbow Coast (see p.732), and note that some attractions and scenic drives take in unsealed roads – make sure these are permitted in your rental contract and keep speeds down to 40kph to prevent stone damage.

An alternative is to follow the recently completed **Bibbulmun Track** long-distance path which winds down over 963km from Kalamunda southeast of Perth to Albany. It's unlikely you'll have the time to undertake the full trek, taking six weeks or more, but some of the best sections of the track are found between the coastal inlets around Walpole and the forests and pastures south of Bunbury. There's more on the "Bib Track" at ⓦwww.bibbulmuntrack.org.au.

Bunbury and Wellington National Park

Described as the capital of the Southwest, **BUNBURY**, the state's second-largest population centre, is clearly prosperous and content, but not the sort of place you've crossed oceans to see. A day's dallying here on the way south offers a chance to commune with the **dolphins** (found around The Cut on Leschenault Inlet) and is a lot more fun, if less predictable, than traipsing all the way up to Monkey Mia (see p.756). They've made a better interpretive job of the Dolphin Discovery Centre too, situated on the beach off Koombana Drive (daily 8am–5pm; $2; ☎08/9791 3088). Tours allow interaction from a boat ($27) or even by swimming with the dolphins ($99), and there are also whale-watching trips in the summer months ($45).

Daily **bus services** from Perth (3hr) drop you at the well-stocked **tourist office** (Mon–Sat 9am–5pm, Sun 9.30am–4.30pm; ☎08/9721 7922) in the old train station on Carmody Place. Shuttle buses operate from the new **train station**, 3km from the centre, during the day and otherwise usually meet evening arrivals. The train from Perth takes two hours and costs around $22.

Accommodation includes the *Wander Inn* at 16 Clifton St (☎08/9721 3242, ⓔwanderinnbp@yahoo.com; dorms $17 rooms ❷), off Victoria Street, the main road, a nice backpackers' to hang out in after the dolphins have gone

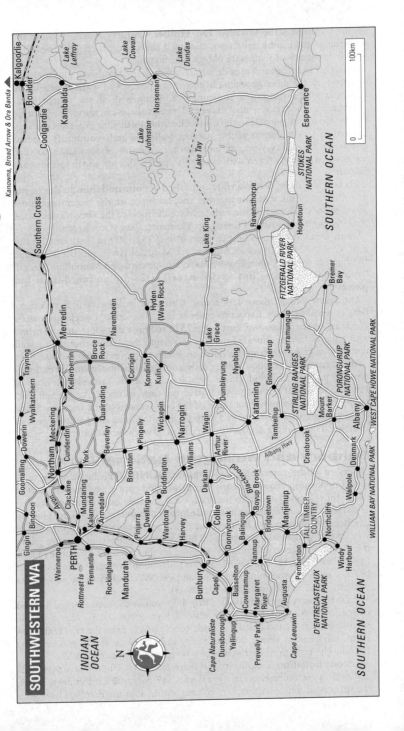

SOUTHWESTERN WA

INDIAN OCEAN

N

100km

0

SOUTHERN OCEAN

to bed, with bikes, boogie-boards and local tours. In this street, on the corner with Molloy Street, you'll also find the federation-era-style *Clifton* (T08/9721 4300, Wwww.theclifton.com.au; ❹), while the elegant *Rose Hotel* (T08/9721 4533; ❺) on Victoria Street boasts a reasonable restaurant and a large range of boutique beers. There are plenty of sidewalk **cafés** and **restaurants** along Victoria Street.

Wellington National Park

A fifteen-minute drive along the Collie road east from Bunbury leads to Dardanup, an old logging town. Just before town a sign points left to **Wellington Discovery Forest**, part of the eponymous national park. The nineteen-kilometre drive to the Discovery Forest passes through some lovely countryside, with lush grassy pastures that Outback cattle only dream about. The last few kilometres are a gravel road leading to the Wellington Forest visitors centre – actually an unstaffed shelter with a couple of interpretive boards. From here a couple of trails take off into the surrounding jarrah woodlands which typify the drier northern reaches of the Southwest. Jarrah, once known as "Australian mahogany", has been logged since the beginning of colonization in WA. Indeed, with indigenous stocks all but depleted, it has been said that the European voyages of discovery were partly driven by a need for new sources of timber. Jarrah, famously strong and termite proof, found its way back to Europe and America as railway sleepers, road cobbles as well as supports for the early London Underground. At the park you can take a wander through mostly regrown forests along the one-kilometre **Jarrah Trail**, or a longer walk to the **Total Forest Trail** (doing both takes about 1hr 30min). On the way to the latter trail you'll find a few huge original, old-growth jarrahs which managed to escape the loggers' axes. In the woodcraft galleries of the Southwest you'll find many beautiful artefacts made from fallen old-growth or jarrah reclaimed from demolished old buildings.

Geographe Bay to Cape Naturaliste

South of Bunbury the Bussell Highway curves west around **Geographe Bay** to **BUSSELTON**, named after a prominent pioneering family. The town, sheltered from the ocean's currents and swells, is a popular "bucket and spade" resort where parents can be sure their kids won't be swept away or dashed onto the rocks. There's a **museum** (Mon & Wed–Sun 2–5pm; $5) in the Old Butter Factory, off Peel Terrace, and the town's famously long **jetty** (at nearly 2km it's the longest in the southern hemisphere) can be fun to walk along or ride down on the back of a little train. With over a century of marine growth and soft corals there are plans for an underwater observatory here. Until then it's a great place for snorkelling or diving – see p.64.

After Busselton, the highway turns south towards Margaret River, though continuing west brings you to **DUNSBOROUGH**, 21km from Busselton, a holiday resort with a YHA **hostel** (T & F08/9755 3107, Edunsborough @yhawa.com.au; dorms $17 rooms ❸), 2km southeast of town (get off the bus at Quindalup) and right on the beach. The *Dunsborough Inn*, 50 Dunn Bay Rd, (T08/9756 7277, Edunsinn@wn.com.au; dorms $20, rooms ❷–❹), has good-value, self-contained units and motel rooms. A step up in quality is the *Mercure Inn* (T08/9756 7711, Emercure@netserve.net.au; ❹) which is also the town's only **pub**. *Café Ibis*, across the road from the post office, has interesting if pricey **meals** while *My Thai*, next to the service station, gives Dunsborough's best impersonation of Bangkok. With its shelter and minimal tides, Geographe Bay is ideal for **diving** – all the more so since the sinking of the *Swan* warship in 1997 which has left a prepared dive wreck in 30m of water. Cape Dive, 222 Naturaliste Terrace, Dunsborough (☎08/9756 8778, ⓦwww.capedive.com), is one of the dive outfitters visiting this and other dive sites in the bay.

Cape Naturaliste itself, 14km northwest of the resort, is the less impressive of the two capes which define the Margaret River Region. Its truncated **light-house** (Mon & Wed–Sun 9.30am–4.30pm; $3.50) is open for inspection, and along the way there are turn-offs to secluded beaches, with the **Sugarloaf** offering particularly fine views.

Along Caves Road to Margaret River and Cape Leeuwin

South of Dunsborough you head into the **Margaret River Region** proper, characterized by caves, wineries, choice restaurants and snug hideaways all interspersed with woodcraft galleries, glass-blowing studios and potteries. Passing **Ngilgi Cave** (see box on p.728) you come to the turn-off for **YALLINGUP**, a small seaside resort with a lovely clean beach where surfers wait for the big one. Caves Road leads south from here passing the Gunyulgup Gallery (daily 10am–5pm) with a particularly fine selection of pottery, glass, paintings and furniture by local artisans, and a lovely restaurant overlooking a lake. *Yallingup Forest Resort* (☎08/9755 2550, ⓦwww.yallingupforestresort .com.au; ❺) on Hemsley Road off Caves Road would suit an extended stay in the area, offering large, self-contained chalets with the use of a pool and tennis court. The site also hosts the **Wicked Ale Brewery** (daily 10am–5pm; ☎08/9755 2848) where chocolate beer is on tap. *Caves House Hotel* (☎08/9755 2131, ⓦwww.caveshouse.com.au; ❺) is an inviting lodge dating from the 1930s and in the middle of town.

Back on Caves Road a right turn leads 3km to **Canal Rocks**, where the waves relentlessly pound the pink-granite outcrops into curious, scalloped forms. Further south are more turn-offs to the winery at **Abbey Vale Estate** (daily 10.30am–5pm) and **Bootleg Brewery** (daily 10am–4.30pm) which cheekily calls itself "a beer oasis in a desert of wine". Those intent on visiting some of the 65 wineries (and breweries) in the region should pick up the *Margaret River Regional Vineyard Guide* or the *Regional Map and Guide* from the Margaret River visitors centre (see opposite).

Another turning west off Caves Road leads 4km to **Quininup Beach**, accessible only to high-clearance vehicles, and 17km further on, a right turn leads to **Ellenbrook House**, a Bussell homestead dating from 1857 – not necessarily worth the small entry fee but in a lovely quiet spot by the brook. From here it's a thirty-minute walk up to the luxuriant **Meekadarribee Falls** which, unusually, manage to spiral underneath themselves.

Down Caves Road you come to the crossroads leading inland 5km to Margaret River township (see opposite), while a right turn takes you to the resort of **PRE-VELLY PARK**, on the estuary of the Margaret River. The Greek **Chapel of St John** will certainly catch your eye: a memorial to the Preveli Monastery on Crete which sheltered Allied soldiers, Australians among them, in World War II. The turning opposite leads down to the blustery beach where November's annual Margaret River Classic **surfing** championships are held, so long as sponsors continue to support the event. The surf here is legendary among WA board-riders, probably as much for its accessibility as anything else: the entire coast between the two capes (and north of Perth for that matter) is surfable.

Back at the chapel, the road continues down into the **resort**, where a boom in seaview property over the last few years has seen private houses outnumber holiday chalets and caravan parks. Check out the *Café Gnarabup* (Nov–Feb daily 8.30am–sunset), overlooking the sea and offering the mouthwatering aroma of sizzling fish or just coffee and cakes. The modern *Surfpoint Lodge*, on Reidle Drive (℡08/9757 1777, ⓦwww.surfpoint.com.au; dorms $18, en-suite rooms ❸), is one of WA's best-keep secrets. Free pick-ups are on offer from Margaret River if you call ahead.

Margaret River

The town of **MARGARET RIVER** is the capital of the eponymous region which has come to symbolize every stress-worn Perthian's dream to escape the rat race, set up a craft boutique or a sylvan getaway, and claim their share of the good life. Full of a mix of holiday-makers, partying wave-riders and tourists drawn in by the hype, the crowded town is presumably what you've come down here to get away from, although it's handy for shopping, eating out and browsing. The **visitors centre** (daily 9am–5pm; ℡08/9757 2911, ⓦmargaretriver.com), at the downhill end of the main road, can line you up with accommodation, tours and wineries. Westrail and South West Coach Lines **buses** visit daily from Perth. Local wine-tasting **tours** ($48 half-day, $75 full day) can save your licence, while Cave & Canoe Bushtucker Tours (℡08/9757 1084; $40) offer just that from the river mouth on Prevelly Beach.

Apart from the two main backpackers', the range of **accommodation** is daunting, with over seventy options in the immediate vicinity, but the woodland settings out of town are the ones to go for; the tourist office has big portfolios full of ideas. The *Inne Town* **backpackers'** (℡08/9757 3698 or 1800 244 115; dorms $16 rooms ❸), down the road from the visitors centre is a traditional small hostel. Two kilometres out of town the purpose-built *Margaret River Lodge* on Railway Terrace (℡08/9757 9532, ⓦwww.mrlodge .com.au; dorms $17, en-suite rooms ❹), has a vast array of rooms plus a pool and volleyball and is set in spacious grounds. You can also sample backpacker luxury at *Surfpoint Lodge* out on the beach (see above). For those whose dorm-stays are behind them, the self-contained *Margaret River Chalets* situated by the forest 2km south of town (℡ & ℻08/9757 2905; ❺), sleep up to six with everything provided. The *Margaret River* (℡08/9757 2180; on-site vans ❸) and the *Riverview* (℡08/9757 2270; on-site vans ❸) **caravan parks** are both just a kilometre out of town.

The countryside surrounding Margaret River is dotted with charming **restaurants**, often attached to wineries or galleries. In town and all situated along the main road, the best places to eat include *Goodfellas* for wood-fired pizzas, *Mammas* or *Margaret River Fish and Chips*. *VAT 107* is the town's premier gourmet restaurant for local seafood dishes or you can join the young crowd at *Settlers*, the town's main **pub**, which puts on live music in summer. There's an **Internet café** behind the Challenge bank on Bussell Highway, the main road through town.

Augusta and Cape Leeuwin

Five kilometres southwest of Margaret River, on Boodjidup Road, one of the more interesting attractions vying for your attention is **Eagles Heritage** (daily 10am–5pm; $8), a fascinating collection of birds of prey. Aviaries house huge wedge-tail and white-breasted sea eagles, peregrine falcons and a few owls – a rare menagerie of impressive flying hunters.

Margaret River caves

A band of limestone passing through the cape has created some 350 **caves** around Margaret River, four of which are open to the public. Most involve guided tours to avoid damage and accidents, with relatively high entrance fees and shuffling crowds rather detracting from the cavernous spectacle. Nevertheless, a visit to the region would be incomplete without seeing at least one. All are humid and include some long, stepped ascents, with temperatures around 17°C. Tours are less frequent from May to August – for more details about all except Ngilgi Cave, enquire at the Margaret River or Augusta visitors centres. The Cave Works Interpretive Centre at Lake Cave (see below) sells a **Grand Tour pass** for $36, which includes entry to Lake, Jewel and Mammoth caves; it also offers special discount options to visit all the caves except Ngilgi.

Jewel Cave (daily 9.30am–4pm, 7–12 tours per day; 60min; $15; ☎08/9758 4541). The best cave, featuring extraordinary and fragile formations such as five-metre "helictites" (delicate, straw-like formations) protected by breeze-proof doors. Also includes a two-hour tour of **Moondyne Cave** (daily 2pm; $20, with equipment supplied; maximum 10 people), a mildly adventurous and less rushed excursion with some belly crawling, although you won't miss any amazing features by not taking the tour. Enclosed footwear is compulsory.

Lake Cave (daily 9.30am–4pm, 7–12 tours per day; 45min; $15). A collapsed cavern, overgrown with huge karri trees, is the impressive entrance to the cave where a unique "suspended table" hangs over the subterranean lake. The cave is also the site of the **Cave Works Interpretive Centre** (daily 10am–5pm; $3; ☎08/9757 7411), dealing with all things speleological.

Mammoth Cave (daily 9am–4pm, self-guiding; $15). Large cavern and easy access with some bones and fossils of extinct creatures; it would really be your last choice.

Ngilgi Cave (daily 9.30am–4.30pm; $15). Not visited on the cave tours but with plenty of nooks to explore and delicate features to admire.

Rejoining Caves Road, having passed the turning for the **Leeuwin Winery** (daily 10am–4.30pm) with its art gallery and restaurant, you head south into the silvery-barked **karri forest**. It's a magnificent sight, well worth taking some time to appreciate now if you're not planning to visit Pemberton. Down the road are Mammoth and Lake caves (see box above). If you have visited the latter cave and have noticed the stream that trickles out of its subterranean lake, you can catch up with it at the spring on **Cowup Bay** beach, 4km from the cave entrance along a dirt road, and with a campsite on the way. Back on Caves Road, Boranup Drive takes an off-road detour through the **Boranup Forest**, a great place for biking and riding, while *Boranup Gallery and Chalets* (☎08/9757 7585, ☎9757 7527; ❼) sells local art and gorgeous **furniture** made from local timbers and offers accommodation in self-contained, rammed-earth **chalets** in bushland settings.

South of the forest, the Brockman Highway leads 90km east to Nannup, while continuing 3km south down Caves Road brings you to a turn-off to the old timber port of **Hamelin Bay**, which has a clutch of shipwrecks ideal for snorkellers and scuba divers. There's a beachside **caravan park** (on-site vans ❸) offering bikes for rent.

Passing **Jewel Cave**, the Bussell Highway takes you 8km further to the small town of **AUGUSTA**, on the estuary of the Blackwood River – Western Australia's oldest settlement after Albany and Perth. Little remains from those days, although the **museum** (daily: June–Sept 10am–noon; Oct–May 9am–5pm; $2), on Blackwood Avenue, the main road, retains some old relics and is more absorbing than you might expect. The **visitors centre** (daily: June–Sept 10am–noon; Oct–May 9am–5pm; ☎08/9758 0166) is on Ellis Street. The *Augusta Motel* (☎08/9758 1944, ⓦwww.augusta-resorts.com.au; ❸) on Blackwood Avenue has great river views as well as budget rooms. The pristine *Baywatch Manor Resort YHA* (☎08/9758 1290, ⓔaugusta@yhawa .com.au; dorms $18, rooms ❸), also on Blackwood Avenue, offers quality back-packers' accommodation and rents bikes and canoes. The owners also offer self-contained chalets at *Augusta Homes for Holidays* (❹). *Doonbanks Caravan Park* (on-site vans ❸) is up the road, and there are two more caravan parks south of town. You can **eat** at the *Colonial Restaurant* on the main road, or at the *Augusta Moon* Chinese restaurant on Allnutt Terrace.

Cape Leeuwin, 9km south of town, is probably why you've come this far, and it's worth the journey, giving a bleak, windswept "land's end" feel to this continental corner, especially on a mean and moody day. A Dutch captain named the cape after his ship 370 years ago, and Matthew Flinders began the onerous task of mapping Australia's coast right here in 1851. From the top of the still working **lighthouse** (daily 9am–4pm; $6), built in 1895, you can con-template your position – halfway between the equator and the Antarctic coast. Nearby, an **old water wheel**, originally constructed for the lighthouse builders and now petrified in salt, is a well-known landmark.

Hikers may want to consider the 140-kilometre Cape Leeuwin to Cape Naturaliste **coastal walk**, though even the less adventurous can tackle its five sections individually. The CALM office in Busselton (☎08/9752 1677) has detailed information on this, while the Cape Leeuwin lighthouse store has maps and advice.

Tall Timber Country

Sandwiched between the popular tourist areas of Margaret River and Albany's Rainbow Coast, the forests of the so-called **Tall Timber Country** are one of WA's greatest sights. Along with the sinuous **Blackwood River** (ideal for sedate canoeing, especially downstream of Nannup), the highlight of the region is the brooding, primeval majesty of the **karri forests**, known not as much for their arboreal gimmicks – of which the "climb-if-you-dare" **Gloucester Tree** near Pemberton is the best-known – as they are for the raw, elemental nature of the unique forest environment. Since old-growth logging was banned in 2001 (see box on p.730), towns like Pemberton are having to adjust from an economy based around logging to one more reliant on tourism. Check out ⓦwww.southernforests.com.au for further details on this area as far as Walpole.

The Blackwood River Valley and south

The northern part of the forest country is watered by the **Blackwood River** and divided by scenic roads through forests linking the riverside mill towns. An idyllic example is **NANNUP**, on the Vasse and Brockman highways, 60km southeast of Busselton, a cluster of wooden cabins nestling quietly among wooded hills. The **visitors centre** (daily 9am–5pm; ☎08/9756 1211, ⓦwww .compwest.net.au/~nannuptb/) is on Brockman Street and has a portfolio of local **accommodation**. Set in a glorious permaculture garden, the *Black Cockatoo Travellers Retreat* on Grange Rd (☎08/9756 1035; dorms $20 rooms ❷) is a laid-back haven in a class of its own. On the hill behind the *Cockatoo* is the smart and child-free *Holberry House* (☎08/9756 1276, ⓕ9756 1394; ❹), while lost among the jarrah 6km northwest of town, the *Nannup Bush Cabins* (☎ & ⓕ08/9756 1170; ❹) are enchantingly situated hideaways.

Logging in Tall Timber Country

After a century and a half, the controversial logging of the Southwest's irreplaceable **old-growth forest** officially came to an end in 2001. Public debate over logging and the sell-off of old-growth forests by CALM (the government department of Conservation and Land Management which looks after WA's parks) to logging mills had grown ever more intense throughout the 1990s, with even celebrities getting behind the cause. Campaigners criticized CALM's sell-off as a display of mind-boggling environmental short-sightedness, pointing out that the centuries-old trees of old-growth forest predate colonization, and support a complex ecological system. Quick to capitalize on a vote-winning issue, Labor won the 2001 state election promising to outlaw the logging of old-growth forests. Loopholes remain, but since that time the recession predicted in the logging industry has not materialized, and fast-growing plantations of blue gum (aka Tasmanian oak) have been found to offer a viable future to sustainable plantation logging in WA.

Hamish's Café on the corner of Grange Road facing the **Telecentre** opens all day and evening for local fish or big breakfasts. *Nannup Furniture Gallery* on Warren Road, past the pub, can undertake a one-off commission using local timber and even ship it home for you. If you want to try out some paddling, Blackwood Canoeing (T08/9756 1209) offers **canoe trips** on the lower Blackwood River for $35 a day.

From Nannup, a **scenic drive** winds 41km along the river to unremarkable Balingup, while the equally tree-lined Brockman Highway heads east 46km to **BRIDGETOWN**, a busy mill town with a large **tourist centre** (daily 9am–5pm; T08/9761 1740) on Hampton Street. Despite some token tea and craft shops, Bridgetown is really a place to get your ute serviced or chainsaw sharpened. By the river, where some pleasant bankside walks begin, the National Trust property of Bridgedale House (Mon & Thurs–Sun 10am–4pm; $4) rents out **canoes**.

Thirty-seven kilometres south of Bridgetown, **MANJIMUP** is the region's commercial centre, handy for shopping and other services but, apart from a visit to the **Timber Park** (daily 9am–5pm), behind the **visitors centre** (daily 8.30am–5.30pm; T08/9771 1831) on Rose Street (both celebrating the local timber industry), it has little appeal. Graphite Road is a picturesque forest drive heading west 22km to **One Tree Bridge** and, after another couple of kilometres, to the magnificent **Four Aces**, a quartet of huge, 350-year-old karri trees standing in a row. With a detailed map it's possible to spend all day driving around these gravelly, winding logging roads, but should you head south to Pemberton along the tarmac road you'll pass a turn-off to the **Diamond Tree**, where you can climb a fifty-metre lookout tree for free.

Pemberton and around

PEMBERTON is the most central base for Tall Timber touring. You'll find the **tourist information** office halfway up the hill on Brockman Street (daily 9am–5pm; T08/9776 1133, Wwww.pembertontourist.com.au), where you can pick up the excellent *Pemberton–Northcliffe* map and guide ($1), as well as information on **horse riding**, **canoe** and **bicycle rental**, and local **tours**. Round the back is the interactive Karri Forest Discovery Centre (daily 9am–5pm; donation), which replicates the forest environment.

On Dickinson Street, Fine Woodcraft is one of the best **craft galleries** in the Southwest with everything you see, including the building itself, made from old-growth timber, either reclaimed or rejected as too small for the mills, which would otherwise be burned or left to rot. A fun way of enjoying the surrounding forest is to take the **tram** (☎08/9776 1322, Ⓦwww.pemtram.com.au; from $15) from Pemberton to Warren Bridge (2 daily; 1hr 45min return). The diesel tram rattles noisily along the old logging railway, over rustic timber bridges spanning tiny creeks, and visits the local beauty spot, the **Cascades** (also accessible by road) – an enjoyable excursion. In summer there's also a weekend **steam train** service up to Lyall Sidings, north of town.

The region's single most popular attraction is the **Gloucester Tree** (CALM fee; see box on p.722), situated on a clearly signposted road 3km southeast of town. At 61m, it's the world's tallest fire-lookout tree and its platform is accessible by climbing a spiral of horizontal stakes. Only a quarter of those who visit the tree actually climb up to the platform – the climb itself being more satisfying than the actual view.

The countryside all around is crisscrossed with peaceful walking trails and enchanting forest drives cutting deep into the wonderful karri woodlands. **Beedelup National Park**, on the Vasse Highway 20km west of town, has a short walk to a wobbly suspension bridge over **Beedelup Falls**, while the drive through the native karri forests of the **Warren National Park**, 10km southwest of town, will leave you in awe of these huge trees. The specially signed, 86-kilometre **Karri Forest Explorer** is a scenic drive that winds past many of the above attractions on a mixture of dirt and sealed roads. Otherwise Pemberton Hiking Company (☎08/9776 1559) or Pemberton Discovery Tours (☎08/9776 0484) can take you out for a day which includes "river tubing" and the D'Entrecasteaux dunes from $80.

As for **accommodation**, the *YHA Forest Stay* at Pimelea (☎08/9776 1153, Ⓔpemberton@yhawa.com.au; dorms $17 rooms ❷), 10km northwest of town, is a clutch of basic woodman's cabins with free pick-ups from town as well as bike rental and pet 'roos. In town *Pemberton Backpackers* (☎08/9776 1105; dorms $17, rooms ❸), right by the bus stop, has comfy doubles and a self-contained cottage (❸). Both hostels can give you details and **maps of day-hikes** in the area including part of the Bibbulmun Track (see p.723). Otherwise, besides the couple of motels in town (❹), the surrounding countryside abounds in tranquil woodland retreats, like *Karri Valley Hideaway Cottages* (☎ & Ⓕ08/9776 2049, Ⓦwww.karrivalleyhideaway.com.au; ❺), 21km west of town, or *Treenbrook Cottages* (☎08/9776 1638, Ⓦwww.treenbrook.com.au; ❹), 5km west. Campers can stay at the town's central **caravan park** (☎08/9776 1300; on-site vans ❸) or at any of the CALM-approved **campsites** in the surrounding forests. There are a couple of restaurants and cafés in town, but for trout or marron (freshwater crayfish), both local delicacies, try the restaurant at the *Eagle Springs Trout Hatchery*, signposted north of town.

Northcliffe and D'Entrecasteaux National Park

Thirty kilometres south of Pemberton, **NORTHCLIFFE** is a small, untouristed logging town and to the southwest is the long spread of coastal heathland and inland dunes making up the mostly inaccessible **D'Entrecasteaux National Park**. South of Northcliffe you emerge from the forest and onto the heathland, passing a short steep walk up 187-metre **Mt Chudalup** for views of the Southern Ocean breaking against Sandy Island just off **WINDY HARBOUR**, 30km south of Northcliffe. The tidy but seemingly deserted settlement has about fifteen permanent residents, no services and a few dozen clapboard holiday homes, although there is talk of building a national park visitors centre at the Salmon Beach turn-off just as you come into the hamlet.

As long as you're suitably equipped, a grassy **campsite** in the centre of the hamlet makes an inviting stopover. West of the main bay you can walk to a broader, slightly more sheltered beach, also accessible from a car park off Old Lighthouse Road, a dead-end which leads west out of the settlement. From here it's possible to walk the 2km up the clifftop to **Point D'Entrecasteaux**, where a platform hangs out over the pounding surf below. You can also reach the Point in your car by following the Salmon Beach turn-off just before Windy Harbour. **Salmon Beach** itself (no camping) is a wild exposed strand below Point D'Entrecasteaux facing the prevailing southwesterlies and good for a hair-tussling stroll.

❼ Albany, the Rainbow Coast and inland

The alternating sheltered bays and rugged headlands of the **Rainbow Coast** around **Albany** were the site of WA's original colonial settlement. As elsewhere in the Southwest, the temperate climate here creates a rural antipodean-English idyll – unknown in the rest of WA – attracting retirees and lotus-eaters.

Albany, 410km from Perth, is an agricultural centre and holiday destination, while **Denmark**, 54km to the west, is a twee, arty hamlet; **Walpole**'s bays and tingle forests mark the Rainbow Coast's limit. An hour's drive north of Albany lie the burgeoning wine-making region of **Mount Barker** and the mountainous **Porongurup** and **Stirling Ranges national parks**.

Perth's radial **bus services** to the main centres run on a frequent basis, but moving around requires some planning to avoid inconvenient delays. Westrail buses depart from Perth for Albany at least daily, either directly down the Albany Highway (6hr) or four times a week via Bunbury and twice weekly via Pemberton (8hr). **Car rental**, or shared lifts, are clearly a better option and **tours**, despite their breathless pace, will at least show you it all, however briefly.

Albany

In 1826, two years before the establishment of the Swan River Colony, the British sent Major Lockyer and a team of hopeful colonists to settle the strategic **Princess Royal Harbour**. It was a pre-emptive response to French exploration of Australia's Southwest, and the small colony, originally called Fredrickstown, was allowed to grow at a natural pace – avoiding the vicissitudes of Swan River Mania that plagued Perth in the 1880s, when thousands of starry-eyed colonists poured into the shanty town. Prior to the building of Fremantle Harbour in the 1890s, **ALBANY** was a key port on the route from England to Botany Bay, a coaling station in the age of steamers. It was also the last of Australia that many Anzacs saw on their way to Gallipoli in 1914.

Now serving the southern farming belt, Albany has also become the centre of one of the Southwest's main holiday areas. Factors such as weekend proximity to Perth, moderate summer temperatures, a surfeit of natural splendour and historical kudos all combine to make an agreeable and genuine destination, largely bereft of bogus tourist traps.

Arrival, information and accommodation

Westrail **buses** arrive near the old train station on Lower Stirling Terrace, the location of the **visitors centre** (daily 9am–5.30pm; ☎08/9841 1088 or 1800

644 088, ⓦwww.albanygateway.com.au), which dispenses a handy local and regional **map**. Loves Bus Service (timetables at the tourist office, or call ☎08/9841 1211) offers in-town **public transport**: the #301 route between York Street, the town's main road, and Middleton Beach/Emu Point is particularly useful (Mon–Fri 9am–3pm, Sat 9.15–11am).

Albany offers several **guesthouses** and **B&Bs**, especially along Shirley Terrace near the harbour, as well as the customary range of highway-side motels and self-contained units, the latter found in the Middleton Bay area, 3km east of the centre. In the countryside, farmstays mix with classy cottages and other pastoral hideaways. The visitors centre has a detailed photographic portfolio of the town's accommodation options. Note that prices drop by 15–50 percent in winter, especially for apartments.

Motels, units, hostels and guesthouses

Albany Backpackers Cnr Stirling Terrace and Spencer St ☎08/9841 8848. The energetic owners provide a lively atmosphere and plenty of activities with rooms painted in individual themes. Free breakfast and Internet. Dorms $17, rooms ❸
Bayview YHA 49 Duke St ☎ & ⓕ08/9842 3388, ⓔalbany@yhawa.com.au. Old wooden building 5min from the centre with dorms, twins, barbies and some parking. Dorms $18, rooms ❸
Coraki Holiday Cottages Lower King River, 11km east of town ☎08/9844 7068, ⓔcoraki@albanyis.com.au. Great-value cottages in their own gardens by Oyster Harbour. ❹
Discovery Inn 9 Middleton Rd ☎08/9842 5535, ⓦwww.discoveryinn.net.au. An especially agreeable old guesthouse and restaurant, close to Middleton Beach, with breakfast included. ❹
Dog Rock Motel 303 Middleton Rd ☎08/9841 4422, ⓕ9842 1027. Good-value rooms close to town and the shops, plus there's a restaurant. ❹

Dolphin Lodge 1 Golf Links Rd, Middleton Beach ☎08/9841 6600, ⓦwww.dolphinlodge.com.au. Inexpensive family units. ❹
Norman House 28 Stirling Terrace ☎ & ⓕ08/9841 5995. Plusher sort of guesthouse, close to town, with disabled access and bright rooms. ❸
Travel Inn 191 Albany Highway ☎08/9841 4144, ⓕ9841 6215. Albany's best motel, with large comfortable rooms. ❺

Caravan parks

Emu Beach Emu Point, 7km from the town centre ☎08/9844 1147. Not a bad spot to stay for a few days. Amenities include trampolines and mini-golf. On-site vans ❸, cabins ❹
Middleton Beach Flinders Parade, Middleton Beach ☎08/9841 3593. Right on the weekend-posing drag and the sometimes windy beach. Cabins and on-site vans ❸
Mount Melville 22 Wellington St ☎08/9841 4616. Has a useful camp kitchen and is just 1km from town. On-site vans ❷, chalets from ❸

The Town and around

Albany's attractions are spread between the Foreshore, where the original colonists set up camp, and the calm beaches around **Middleton Beach** and Emu Point on the still waters of Oyster Harbour. Driving around the harbour brings you after 40km to the idyllic nature reserve at Two Peoples Bay, while the features and attractions on the **Torndirrup Peninsula**, 20km from town, along Frenchman's Bay Road, are also well worth a look.

On the **Foreshore** there's a replica of the *Amity* (daily 9am–5pm; $3), the brig that landed its three-score colonists here on Boxing Day, 1826, after six months at sea. Nearby is the **Old Gaol** (daily 10am–4.30pm; $4), with the usual bare cells and barred doors. The **Albany Residency Museum** (daily 10am–5pm; donation) is much more interesting, with meticulous displays of the town's maritime history, a section on Aboriginal bush medicines, an annexe with an obsolete lighthouse lens that was too good to throw away and, upstairs, an educational see-and-touch gallery for children.

Heading towards Middleton Beach, the curious tower on top of **Mount Melville Lookout**, off Serpentine Road, is colloquially known as "the spark plug". One of two lookouts in Albany, this one offers the better seaward vista. From here, backtrack to York Street, turn left and head 2km down Middleton Road to **The Old Farm**, Strawberry Hill (daily 10am–5pm; closed June; $3.30), tucked behind modern houses in its own enchanting gardens. Reminiscent of an English cottage, the farm (WA's first) provided the colonists with fruit and veg, while the 1836 building here housed visiting Governor Stirling and today offers Devonshire teas and displays of domestic accoutrements.

Middleton Beach itself is dominated by Albany's pride and joy, the presti-gious *Esplanade Hotel*, and the town's main beach. From the beach, head up Marine Drive and turn right towards **Mount Clarence Lookout**, with its Anzac memorial and, on a clear day, a view as far as the Stirling Ranges, 80km to the north. On the way down you pass **The Princess Royal Fortress** (daily 9am–5pm; $3.30), an impressively restored naval installation dating from the end of the nineteenth century.

Southeast of town, Frenchman Bay Road curls round Princess Royal Harbour to **Whaleworld** (daily 9am–5pm, hourly tours 10am–4pm; $11), the site of Australia's last whaling station until operations finally ceased in 1978. The informative tours begin with a gory video and move on to the crude and sickening whale-dismembering machinery and towering *Cheyne IV* whale chaser, before an upbeat, eco-ending in the skeleton shed.

Returning along the Torndirrup Peninsula, check out the view at **Stony Hill** and, if the swell's up see how the **Blowholes** are doing. You won't get the reli-able geysers as found near Carnarvon (see p.757), but the sound of the spray blasting out at 187kph could well make you jump. **The Gap** and **Natural Bridge** are well worth a look; there's something mesmeric about watching the Southern Ocean pound into the Gap's boxed walls and rebound, frothing, in all directions, while the Natural Bridge satisfies those who get excited about "freaks of nature". This area has claimed several lives, many by **king waves** (unexpectedly huge waves indistinguishable in the swell) that well up imper-ceptibly onto the shore here; play it safe, and don't walk under the bridge.

Eating

Fortunately, Albany shares the rest of the Southwest's laudable preoccupation with quality eating; several independent **restaurants** fill the gap between fast-food franchises and dreary motel dining rooms in a most appetizing way. The sometimes lively *Earl of Spencer* and *White Star* **pubs** on Spencer Street also have counter meals.

Al Fornetto York St. Italian-style steak and seafood, as well as pizzas from $12. Daily 6pm–late.
Argyle's 42 Stirling Terrace. Overlooking the bay, with meals for around $15 and Internet access. Wed–Sun 11.30am–late.
Beachside Cafe 2 Flinders Parade, Middleton Beach. Right on the beach, inexpensive alfresco by day and à la carte steak and seafood by night from $20. Daily 5.30pm–late.
Curry Pot 30 Spencer St. Unpretentious all-you-can-eat curries from $14. Daily 6pm–late.
Dylan's on the Terrace 82 Stirling Terrace. Burger and pancake dispensary; good for early breakfast. Mon–Sat 7am–midnight, Sun 7am–10pm.
Rookleys Cnr Peels Place and York St. Deli-style café with focaccia and half-decent coffee. Mon–Sat 8am–5.30pm.
Shamrock Café 184 York St. Full "Irish" breakfast from $7, meals from $10. Mon–Sat 8am–8pm.

Listings

Bus Westrail ☎13 10 53.
CALM (Department of Conservation and Land

Management), 120 Albany Highway (Mon–Fri 9am–5pm; ☎08/9841 7133). Information and passes to local national parks (see box on p.722).

Post office Cnr Grey and York streets ☎08/9841 1811.

Taxi ☎08/9844 4444.

Tours and cruises Albany Whale Tours (☎0409 107 180) takes a catamaran into King George

Sound for two hours from $36. Escape Tours (☎08/9844 1945) have day- and half-day tours around the region in a minibus; Wild West Adventures (☎0418 929 517) do adventure activity tours; and Silver Star Cruises (☎08/9841 3333) offer cruises in King George Sound for around $22.

Along the Rainbow Coast

West of Albany, **West Cape Howe National Park** is a coastal wilderness best suited to exploration by 4WD, while **William Bay National Park**, west of Denmark, has many inviting coves accessible to regular vehicles. Just before Walpole, the **Valley of the Giants** is the home of the now-famous **Tree Top Walk** and marks the edge of the giant tingle tree country. Westrail buses run on Monday and Friday between Albany and Perth (via Bunbury; 6hr), but you won't see much along this way – renting a car or arranging a lift is a better bet.

Denmark and William Bay National Park

DENMARK, set on the river of the same name that leads into Wilson Inlet, is a cute little town, a great spot to enjoy a pleasant lunch, wander around some galleries, and take a stroll or boat up the river. If you want to get to the coast, give the anaemic Wilson Inlet a miss and head west to **William Bay National Park**, through the hills along **Shadforth Scenic Drive**. Once there, you'll find **Green Pool** to be one of the prettiest spots along the coast, with Madfish Bay and Waterfall Bay also worth a visit.

Denmark's **tourist office** (daily 9am–5pm; ☎08/9848 2055), on the corner of Strickland and Bent streets, can advise you on the array of **places to stay** in the vicinity and has a comprehensive free guide to the area. The pristine *Edinburgh House* (☎08/9848 1477; ❷) is in the centre of town, while on Inlet Drive you'll find *Denmark Waterfront Motel and Cottages* (☎08/9848 1147, Ⓦwww.denmarkwaterfront.com.au), an idyllic hideaway on the water with shared budget rooms ($18), motel-style accommodation (❸) and great-value studios (❹). For a **meal**, the natty *Fig Tree Café*, off Strickland Street, and the friendly *Blue Wren* on the main road, are good alternatives to fast food.

The Valley of the Giants' Tree Top Walk and Walpole

About 40km west of Denmark you can turn south to **Peaceful Bay**, a pleasant lunch stop with a **caravan park**. The forest of massive tingle and karri trees that make up the **Valley of the Giants** is now much better known for its **Tree Top Walk** (daily 8am–5pm; $7), an amazingly engineered six-hundred-metre walkway (accessible to wheelchairs), which sways on half a dozen pylons among the crowns of the karris, 40m above the ground. Ironically, the most exciting aspect of the walk is not the scrutiny of the tree canopy – which isn't especially dense, close or teeming with anything more exotic than crows – but rather the fairground thrill of actually treading on the quivering walkway. To gain a better impression of the surrounding forest, take the **Ancient Kingdom Walkway** which winds through the forest floor.

Back on the coastal highway, you pass through **Nornalup**, remarkable for having no arts-and-crafts outlets. You'd do better to take the track 6km west of town leading to the lovely **Conspicuous Beach**. **WALPOLE**, 10km down the road, is the hub of many scenic drives to more towering forests, oceanic lookouts and sheltered inlets. Light **meals** are served at the *South Coast Café*, or try the *Top Deck Café* next to the Glassblower's Gallery. There are a couple of **caravan parks** on Walpole and Nornalup inlets, but for more creature comforts try *Hideaway Cottage* (☎08/9840 1138; ❹), 10km north of town, or *Che Sara Sara Chalets*, 15km north (☎ & ℻08/9840 8004; ❺). Backpackers head for the *Tingle All Over YHA* (☎08/9840 1041, ℮walpole@yhawa.com.au; dorms $17), at the west end of town or *Walpole Backpackers* on Pier Street (☎08/9840 1244; $17) which does meal deals with the local pub and tours. Just east beyond Walpole you'll pass the turn-off to **Nuyts Wilderness**, where several walking trails pass through groves of jarrah and karri on to secluded coastal coves where camping is permitted.

From Walpole, the **South Western Highway** begins its scenic run northwest through more colossal forests to Northcliffe (100km) and Pemberton (138km) at the heart of the Tall Timber Country (see p.730).

The Porongurups, the Stirling Ranges and Mount Barker

North of Albany lie the ancient granite highlands of the Porongurups and the majestic thousand-metre-high Stirling Ranges, 40km and 80km from Albany respectively. Both have been designated as **national parks** (CALM fees; see box on p.722) and CALM in Albany (see p.734) provides further information and maps. To the west are the youthful vineyards of **Mount Barker**, whose viticultural potential continues to spread and which may one day merge with Margaret River as a homogeneous wine-making region. Several small **wineries** open their cellar doors for tasting and prospective purchases; details are available from the tourist office in Albany.

The Porongurups

The **Porongurups**, said to be the oldest hills in the world, feature a dozen wooded peaks with bald summits and an elevation of over 600m. The fifteen-kilometre-long ridge catches any coastal moisture to support its isle of karri forests, thereby leaving the loftier Stirlings to the north dry and treeless.

Most people are happy to do no more than take the five-minute stroll to the **Tree in a Rock**, a natural oddity near the park's northern entrance, but if you want to get your teeth into a good walk, head up the marked trail to **Devil's Slide** (671m) and, if you're up to it, return via Nancy and Hayward peaks; the full route needs at least half a day, stout footwear, water and a hat. **Balancing Rock**, at the eastern end of the park, can be reached in 45 minutes from the car park, with a cage on the exposed outcrop of Castle Rock providing safe viewing. There's no camping in the park, but half a dozen establishments offer **accommodation** close to the northern entrance, among them bunkhouse accommodation at the *Porongurup Range Tourist Park* (chalets and on-site vans ❸) and the nearby *Karribank Country Retreat Chalets* (☎08/9853 1022, ⓦwww.karribank.com.au; ❹), which has a restaurant.

The Stirling Ranges

Taking the Chester Pass Road north towards the looming **Stirlings**, the distinctive profile of Bluff Knoll will, if you're lucky, reveal itself from the cloud banks which often obscure its summit. Avid hillwalkers could spend a few days "peakbagging" here and come away well satisfied – the mild weather makes the Stirlings WA's best mountain-walking area, although five peaks are over 1000m and sometimes receive winter snow. Less strenuous activities are also catered for: the unsealed 45-kilometre Stirling Range **scenic drive** winds amid the peaks to Red Gum Pass in the west, where you can turn around and go back the same way (with superior views) or continue down to Mount Barker. **Bluff Knoll** (1073m), the park's highest and most popular ascent, has a well-built path involving a three-hour-return slog. The weather can often surprise you from the unseen, southeast side: no matter how hot you may feel in the car park before beginning the climb, take a sweater with you. There are better views looking onto the park's eastern summits from the west: **Talyuberup** (800m), halfway along the scenic drive is a short, steep ascent to great views, while **Toolbrunup** (1052m) is among the harder climbs in the park, with some exposed scrambling – allow a tough half-day to get there and back. Many other **trails** wander between the peaks and could link up into overnight walks. Before heading off, discuss your plans with the **ranger** (☎08/9827 9230 or 9827 9278) at his residence by the park campsite off Chester Pass Road.

There are basic facilities at the **campsite**, or much better options at the *Stirling Range Retreat* (☎08/9827 9229, ⓦwww.stirlingrange.com.au; on-site vans ❸, four-bed chalets ❸), just outside the park's northern boundary, opposite the Bluff Knoll turn-off.

Mount Barker

MOUNT BARKER is at the centre of a small wine-growing region and makes a pleasant day out from Albany, driving around the lanes sampling the fruits of the vine. There are over twenty wineries around the town and a couple more near Porongurup. **Plantagenet Wines** (Mon–Fri 9am–5pm, Sat & Sun 10am–4pm), on Albany Highway, is the region's most established, and undertakes bottling for the lesser wineries in the vicinity. The atmosphere is civilized and amiable, with tastings as well as informal behind-the-scenes **tours**. Wine-tasting apart, Mount Barker, on the old mail-coach route between Albany and Perth, is just another country town, although **St Werburgh's Chapel**, built in 1873 on a hillside a few kilometres west of town (get directions from the **visitors centre** in the old railway station, 57 Lowood Rd; ☎08/9851 1163) is worth a look – an unexpected relic of Mount Barker's God-fearing pioneers.

Esperance and the south coast

Esperance, 721km southeast of Perth, is at the western end of the **Archipelago of the Recherche**. Both town and archipelago are attractively named after French ships which visited the area in the late eighteenth century and whose persistent nosing around precipitated the hasty colonization of WA by the nervous British. The archipelago is a string of haze-softened granite isles bobbing in the inky blue Southern Ocean, presenting an almost surreal seascape common to coasts washed by cold currents. The mild summer weather (rarely exceeding 30°C), fishing possibilities (especially the local snapper) and surrounding national parks make the town a popular destination for heat-sensitive holiday-makers.

Southeast of Esperance are **Cape Le Grand** and the much less visited **Cape Arid National Park** (both charge CALM fees; see box on p.722) on the edge of the Great Australian Bight, while 130km north of town is the undeveloped Peak Charles National Park – a hill in the middle of nowhere. Back towards Albany, the **Fitzgerald River National Park** offers a shrubby wilderness of rare flora. Care should be taken all along this restless coastline, as **king waves** frequently sweep away the unwary from exposed, rocky shores, most recently at Cape Le Grand.

You can get to Esperance from Kalgoorlie with Westrail's **bus service** (3 weekly; 5hr) or direct from Perth on the *Spirit of Esperance* service (6 weekly; 10hr). Albany, nearly 500km to the east along the South Coast Highway, can only be reached from Esperance direct on Mondays and Thursdays (connecting buses on Tues & Fri). To get from Albany to Esperance, it's best to arrange a **lift** with fellow travellers.

Esperance and around

The town of **ESPERANCE**, which prospered briefly as a supply port during the heyday of the Eastern Goldfields, was revived after World War II when its salty soils were made fertile with the addition of missing trace elements. Now an established farming and holiday centre, the town lacks the charm promised by its name, but makes an ideal base from which to enjoy a westward exploration of WA's often spectacular and storm-washed southern coast.

Dempster Street is the town's main road and site of the arts-and-crafts vending cabins which comprise the **Museum Village**. Nearby, the actual **museum** (daily 1.30–4.30pm; $4), on James Street, is a surprisingly good repository of local memorabilia – diverse enough momentarily to engage most visitors. It's very proud of its Skylab display: the satellite disintegrated over Esperance in 1979 and NASA was reputedly fined $400 for littering.

Besides a walk along the Norfolk pine-lined Esplanade and a round of mini-golf or go-karting, there's not much else to do in Esperance, so rent a bike or a car and head out along the 36-kilometre **scenic loop** west of town. Travelling clockwise, you'll come first to the **Rotary Lookout** which overlooks the captivating seascape. You'll spot the **windfarm**, a modest experiment in alternative energy generation, on the way to **Twilight Beach**, an idyllic and sheltered spot, much prettier than the town's more exposed beaches. From here it's more windswept grandeur to **Observation Point Lookout** and a free (nudist) beach, before the road turns inland towards **Pink Lake**, sometimes coloured a lurid shade by salt-tolerant algae, whose marine cousins give the coastline its enchanting turquoise hue.

The approximately one hundred islands of the romantically named Archipelago of the Recherche, known as the **Bay of Isles** around Esperance, are chiefly occupied by colonies of seals, feral goats and multitudes of seabirds. Dolphins may also be seen offshore and southern right whales are commonly observed migrating to the Antarctic in spring. Mackenzies Island Cruises, 71 The Esplanade (℡08/9071 5757), offers daily trips with the possibility of overnight stays on **Woody Island** (summer only), which is equipped with enough facilities to cast yourself away in comfort.

Practicalities

Westrail **buses** stop in the town centre, with **taxis** available on ℡08/9071 1782. The **visitors centre** (Mon–Fri 8.45am–5pm, Sat & Sun 9am–5pm; ℡08/9071 2330), in the Museum Village on Dempster Street, provides detailed town maps and takes care of bookings for local tours and onward travel. The **post office** is on the corner of Dempster and Andrew streets, with a **shopping centre** up Andrew Street, over the roundabout. CALM, at 92 Dempster St (℡08/9071 3733), provides information and passes to the national parks around Esperance. **Bicycles** are rented out from the visitors centre or along the Esplanade. For inexpensive **car rental**, try Hollywood Hire (℡08/9071 3144) for old bangers or try the usual agencies. Esperance Diving and Fishing, 56 The Esplanade (℡08/9071 5111), takes care of **dive** charters and courses, while Aussie Bight Tours (℡08/9071 7778) offers half-day **tours** to Cape Le

7

Grand and beyond. Both hostels (see "Accommodation", below) have 4WDs for making informal runs along the coast if there's enough in-house interest.

Accommodation

There are plenty of **places to stay** around town, although the self-contained units will almost certainly be booked out during school holiday periods; air-con is rarely necessary in Esperance.

All Seasons Esplanade Apartments 73 The Esplanade ☎08/9071 2257. The cheapest units in town and fully equipped; book ahead. Each unit sleeps up to four. ❹

Bayview Motel 31 Dempster St ☎08/9071 1533, ⓕ9071 4544. Motel with some self-contained units. ❸

Blue Waters Lodge YHA Goldfields Rd ☎ & ⓕ08/9071 1040, ⓔesperance@yhawa.com.au. Sprawling old hospital transplanted from Kalgoorlie and situated right on the bay, with pick-ups, bikes and the largest hostel kitchen in the southern hemisphere. Can get inundated with school groups. Dorms $17, rooms ❸

Captain Huon Motel 5 The Esplanade ☎08/9071 2383, ⓕ9071 2358. Excellent small motel with some self-contained units, bike rental. ❹

Esperance Backpackers 14 Emily St ☎08/9071 4724. The town's livelier hostel, with all mod-cons, tours and pick-ups. Dorms $17, rooms ❸

Esperance Bay Caravan Park Cnr The Esplanade and Harbour Rd ☎08/9071 2237. So close to town you feel like you're camping in someone's garden. On-site vans and cabins ❷, chalets ❸

Esperance Seafront Caravan Park Goldfields Rd ☎08/9071 1251. The best choice for camping close to the town and beach. On-site vans ❸

Jetty Motel 1 The Esplanade ☎08/9071 3333, ⓕ9071 5540. Well-appointed, two-storey motel with ocean views. ❹

Old Hospital Motel William St ☎08/9071 3587, ⓕ9071 5768. "Boutique" establishment offering an antidote to motel sterility with considered and tasteful decor. ❸

Orleans Bay Caravan Park Cape Le Grand National Park ☎08/9075 0033. Located at Duke of Orleans Bay, reached along a turn-off about 88km from Esperance, this site is ideal for those in search of seclusion. On-site vans ❷, chalets ❸

Restaurants

Besides the counter lunches at the *Pier* and *Esperance* **hotels** along the foreshore there are a couple of interesting **restaurants** to match the mouthwatering seascapes.

Ollies on the Esplanade 32 The Esplanade. Coffee house with an all-day menu. Attractive sea views. Daily 7am–8pm.

Peaches Restaurant *Bay of Isles Motel*, 32 The Esplanade ☎08/9071 3999. Top-quality à la carte cuisine for around $22 a meal and with a view to match. Daily 6–9pm.

Taylor Street Tearooms Taylor St. By the jetty, with an open fire, seafood and pasta and not as stuffy as it sounds.

Village Café Museum Village. A convenient little lunch spot for seafood and chips. Daily 9am–5pm.

Cape Le Grand and Cape Arid national parks

A visit to **Cape Le Grand National Park** (CALM fee; see box on p.722) is well worth the expense of renting a car or taking a tour; it's essentially a climb up a hill and a beach-hop – but on a good day they're the sort of beaches you want to roll up and take home with you. Once in the park, the climb to the summit of **Frenchman's Peak** (262m) is not as hard as it looks, and well worth the half-hour's exertion in a sturdy pair of shoes. The secret of the distinctive, hooked summit is an unexpected hole that frames the impressive view out to sea. Just after the Frenchman's Peak turn-off, a track leads to **Hellfire Bay**; sheltered coves don't come any more perfect than this. From here you can take a tough, three-hour walk to **Le Grand Beach** (limited camping) to the northwest which is also accessible right along the beach in a 4WD from Wylie

Bay at the end of Bandy Creek Road if the tide is right. There is also a less demanding two-hour trek to **Thistle Cove**, from where an easier trail leads to the broad arc of **Lucky Bay** (camping and water), with more sheltered swimming and unbelievable colours. **Rossiter Bay**, 6km east, is distinctly unimpressive by comparison and not worth the trip.

If you're still having trouble getting away from it all, keep heading east to **Cape Arid National Park** (CALM fee; see box on p.722). This is best explored in a 4WD, but ordinary cars can make it as far as **Yokinup Bay**, **Thomas River** and **Sandy Bight**, where there's camping; all visitors must bring their own **fresh water**. East of the park is **Israelite Bay**, well worth a visit if you've come this far, with another impossibly blue seascape, the remains of an old telegraph station and a track up to Balladonia on the Eyre Highway.

Esperance to Albany

From Esperance, the **South Coastal Highway** leads 479km to Albany with just a couple of small farming settlements along the way; it's a fairly dull day's drive with only the military museum and rabbit-proof fence at Jerramungup to perk you up.

RAVENSTHORPE, 186km along the highway west of Esperance, is a farming community that was formerly a mining town. **Accommodation** options here include a couple of motels (❸) or the caravan park at the east end of town. **HOPETOUN** is a picturesque holiday and fishing spot and most usefully a place to get into the adjacent national park. If you want to **stay the night**, the best deals are at the *CWA Cottages* (☏08/9838 3106; ❸) on Canning Street or the cushy **caravan park** on Spence Street (on-site vans ❸). Otherwise, pamper yourself at the *Hopetoun Motel* (☏08/9838 3219; ❹) on Veal Street, and tuck in at the rather pleasant *Starboard Café* (daily 7am–2pm & 4–8pm) right in the middle of town.

Just outside Hopetoun, a road leads west, across the causeway separating the ocean from Culham Inlet – where the explorer John Eyre observed Aborigines fishing in 1841 – and up towards **East Mount Barren**. This marks the eastern edge of the **Fitzgerald River National Park**, one of two parks in WA designated by UNESCO as a World Heritage Biosphere. Nearly two thousand species of wild flower are protected in the park, including the curious, flame-like hakae and scores of orchids, seventy of which are found nowhere else in the world. Access is limited due to the presence of the tropical fungus known as dieback, the root-rotting spores of which are easily spread by wheels and boots. Four-wheel-drive vehicles can reach the sea at **Quoin Head** and camping for all is provided at **Four Mile Beach**, at the foot of East Mount Barren. In the western half of the park (you have to return to the South Coast Highway), **Point Ann**, 64km south of the **ranger's residence** (☏08/9835 5043) along Quiss Road, is the spot to head for; the magnificent view across the sea alone is worth the corrugations. Think twice before descending the sandy track to the campsite here if you're in a 2WD.

The Eastern Goldfields

Five hundred kilometres east of Perth, at the end of the **Great Eastern Highway**, lie the **Eastern Goldfields**. Just over a century ago, gold was found in what still remains one of the world's richest gold-producing regions. Lack of fresh water made life very hard for the early prospectors, driven by a national economic depression into miserable living conditions, disease and, in most cases, premature graves. Nevertheless, boom towns of thousands, boasting grand public buildings, several hotels and a periphery of hovels, would erupt and collapse in the length of time it took to extract any payable ore.

In 1892 the railway from Perth reached **Southern Cross**, just as big finds turned the rush into a national stampede. This huge influx of people accentuated the water shortage, until the visionary engineer C.Y. O'Connor oversaw the construction of a 556-kilometre **pipeline** from Mundaring Weir (see p.721) to Kalgoorlie in 1903. By this time many of the smaller gold towns were already in decline, but the Goldfields' wealth and boost in population finally gave WA the economic autonomy it sought in its claim to statehood.

In the years preceding the goldrush, the area was briefly one of the world's richest sources of **sandalwood**, an aromatic wood greatly prized throughout Asia. Supplies in the Pacific had become exhausted so that, by 1880, the perfumed wood was WA's second-largest exportable commodity after wool. Exacerbating the inevitable over-cutting came the goldrush's demand for timber to prop up shafts or to fire the pre-pipeline water desalinators. Today the region is a pit-scarred and prematurely desertified landscape, dotted with the scavenged vestiges of past settlements, while at its core the Super Pit gold mine in Kalgoorlie gets wider and deeper every year.

Moribund **Coolgardie** may have been the original goldrush settlement, but the Goldfields are now centred around the rich reef of gold adjacent to the twinned towns of **Kalgoorlie–Boulder**, with Kalgoorlie being the thriving, energetic hub; this is Australia's richest town after Canberra. Even if you're not planning to pass through the Goldfields, there's enough to see in Kalgoorlie to make a couple of days excursion from Perth worthwhile – if for nothing else than the novelty of riding on the **Prospector**, the daily rail link between Perth and Kalgoorlie. Overland **buses** depart with similar regularity (and journey times).

The Great Eastern Highway

Heading from Perth to the Goldfields, there's precious little to detain you until you reach Coolgardie, or even Kalgoorlie. **MECKERING**, 132km east of Perth, was destroyed by an earthquake in 1968 and a gazebo off the main road commemorates the event. **CUNDERDIN**, 24km further east, has a pioneering **museum** (daily 10am–4pm; $2), housed in one of the eight steam pumping stations that once propelled the water to Kalgoorlie at a little over 1.5km per hour. **KELLERBERRIN**, not far beyond Cunderdin, was one of the earliest settlements along the Great Eastern Highway, and dates from 1861. It also has a **museum** (Mon–Fri 8.30am–5pm; $2), located in a historic building, and inexpensive **rooms** at the *Ampol Roadhouse Motel* (☎08/9045 4007; ❸) on the highway. **MERREDIN** is a bigger wheat and wool town than most, with a **museum** (daily 9am–3pm; $2) housed in an old train station, built from bricks of Kalgoorlie clay that are said to contain gold of mineable grade.

East of Merredin the country becomes drier and, by the time you get to **SOUTHERN CROSS**, 370km from Perth, you have passed through the Wheatbelt. It was here in 1887 that small traces of gold precipitated the country's largest and most fruitful goldrush, and with the arrival of the railway in 1892, the town became a jumping-off point for the greater finds to the east. Nowadays Southern Cross has that moribund feel so familiar to rural settlements with prosperous pasts; the disproportionately wide streets, common to all the goldrush towns, allowed camel trains to turn round. Local goldrush history is recounted in the **Yilgarn History Museum** (Mon–Sat 9am–noon &

1.30–4pm, Sun 1.30–4pm; $1) on Antares Street, while **accommodation** is available at the *Southern Cross Palace Hotel* (☎08/9049 1555, ☏9049 1509; ❸), near the museum, or the *Southern Cross Caravan Park* (on-site vans ❷), on the eastern edge of town.

Coolgardie

Rather too tidy and intact to carry the name "ghost mining town", **COOL-GARDIE** is more of a museum to itself, a town which, at its peak, had twenty-three hotels, three breweries and six newspapers serving a population ten times greater than its present fifteen hundred. Arthur Bayley increased the pitch of the gold fever when he returned to Southern Cross – then the easternmost extent of the rush – in 1892 with nearly sixteen kilograms of gold. The ensuing wave of prospectors started within hours – ten thousand men rushed out of Southern Cross, culminating in a fourfold increase in WA's population by the end of the century.

The imposing **Wardens Court Building** on Bayley Street is a good point from which to start an appraisal of Coolgardie's numerous gold-boom relics. The building houses the **tourist office** (daily 9am–5pm; ☎08/9026 6090) and has one of the most extensive provincial **museums** in WA (daily 9am–5pm; $3.30), filling the grand upper floors with an especially comprehensive collection of bottles. It rewards a prolonged browse, giving you a feel for the dramatic effect the goldrush had on the area.

Outside the museum is an index to the 155 **historic markers** set around the town, and right opposite you can't miss the varied miscellany and just plain old junk comprising **Ben Prior's Open-Air Museum** (free). Half a kilometre up Hunt Street, at the end of McKenzie Street, **Warden Finnerty's Residence** (Mon–Wed 1–4pm, Sat & Sun 10am–noon & 1–4pm; $2) is the finely restored 1895 residence of the man whose unenviable job it was to set the ground rules for mining at the height of the rush.

On the way back to Bayley Street, a left down Woodward Street leads to the **Railway Station Museum** (daily 9am–5pm, closed Wed; donation welcome), housed in a station used until 1971, when the railway was rerouted north of town. Featured is the drama of the 1907 Varischetti mine rescue and the story of the once-thriving sandalwood industry. There's accommodation and places to eat in town but a far better range is available at Kalgoorlie, 40km down the road.

Wave Rock

WA's best-known natural oddity is **Wave Rock** ($4 per car), 3km from the tiny farming settlement of **HYDEN**, at the eastern edge of the Wheatlands prairie. At 15m high and 110m long, the formation resembles a breaking wave, an impression enhanced by the vertical water stains running down the overhanging face. While the rock, formed by wind and rain, is certainly unusual (though not unique) it's not worth the long day-trip from Perth. Even as a diversion south of the Great Eastern Highway (Merredin is 185km away and Southern Cross is 178km), its appeal is still overrated.

At the base of the rock a marked, twenty-minute trail leads to another outcrop, **Hippo's Yawn**, while 21km from Wave Rock, on the way to Southern Cross, **Bates Cave** features Aboriginal hand paintings.

You can stay at the *Wave Rock Caravan Park* (☎08/9880 5022; chalets ❸) 5km east of town. In Hyden itself, try the *Hyden Wave Rock Hotel* on Lynch Street (☎08/9880 5052; ❹).

Kalgoorlie-Boulder

Whichever way you approach **Kalgoorlie**, the bustling gold capital of Australia and twinned with **Boulder**, it comes as a surprise after hundreds of kilometres of desolation. It possesses the idiosyncratic appeal of similar places such as Coober Pedy (in South Australia) or Las Vegas. All three blithely disregard their isolation and bleak surroundings, so devoted is their attention to the pursuit of earthly riches – which, in Kalgoorlie's case, is **gold**.

Kalgoorlie

In 1893 **Paddy Hannan** (then 53 years old) and his mates, Tom Flannigan and Dan O'Shea, brought renewed meaning to the expression "the luck of the Irish" when a lame horse forced them to camp by the tree which still stands at the top of Egan Street in **KALGOORLIE**. With their instincts highly attuned after eight months of prospecting around Coolgardie, they soon found gold all around them: as the first on the scene, they enjoyed the unusually easy pickings of surface gold. Ten years later, when the desperately needed water pipeline finally gushed into the Mount Charlotte Reservoir, Kalgoorlie was already established as the heart of WA's rapidly growing mineral-based prosperity, a position it still retains. As sole survivor of the original rush, revitalized by the 1960s nickel boom, Kalgoorlie has benefited from new technology that has largely dispensed with slow and dangerous underground mining. Instead, the fabulously rich "**Golden Mile**" reef east of town – which Boulder was originally built to serve – is being devoured wholesale by machinery and explosives to create the vast, open-cast "Super Pit".

Proud of its history and continued prosperity, Kalgoorlie is one of the most parochial towns in a country that's full of them. Although the last decade has seen the encroachment of a suburban "shopping mall" lifestyle, "Kal" is first and foremost a Working Man's Town of twelve-hour, seven-day shifts, a dinky-di testament to the ethos of hard work and hard play that flourished in Australia's Anglo-Celtic heyday. A pub without a "skimpy" barmaid is the exception and in the sniggeringly louche red-light district of Hay Street, three of the infamous "tin shack" brothels remain conspicuously in business.

Start your tour of the town by taking a walk up to the top of Hannan Street, where the bright red head-frame immediately attracts your attention. This is the impressive entrance to the **Museum of the Goldfields** (daily 10am–4.30pm; donation), right next to the spot where Paddy and his crew found their first, auspicious nuggets. Inside is a modern display of Goldfields artefacts and history, with the very stuff that keeps the town going viewable in the basement vault. Aboriginal history and the sandalwood industry are also covered in this excellent introduction to the area, and there's a lookout over the town from the top of the red-head frame. Next door is the **British Arms** pub, now a coffee shop but better known as Australia's narrowest ex-pub.

Hannan Street itself is one of Kalgoorlie's finest sights, with its superbly restored **federation-era architecture**, imposing public buildings and numerous flamboyant hotel facades. You're welcome to inspect the grandiose interior of the **town hall** (Mon–Fri 9am–4pm; free), with its splendid hall and less impressive art gallery. It's only when you stop to reflect that this is a remote, 100-year-old town in the West Australian desert that the stunning wealth of the boom years, which still continues, is brought home to you. Outside, a replica of a bronze **statue** of Paddy himself invites you to drink from his chrome-nozzled waterbag – the much vandalized original is now safely in the Mining Hall of Fame in Boulder (see overleaf).

If your curiosity has drawn you to Hay Street then *Langtrees 181* at no. 181 has found a novel and very successful way of perking up business in the quiet daylight hours by offering **brothel tours** (1hr 30min; $25). Although prostitution is illegal in WA, Kalgoorlie's special needs see a local policy of "containment" tolerated in a usually sordid industry that is made more palatable by the exclusion of male control or investment to the sole benefit of entrepreneurial "madames". The tour itself leads you through the dozen or so themed rooms, some of which are more popular than others, while relating some of the not so lighthearted history of prostitution in WA, and answering all the questions you dare to ask.

Boulder and around
BOULDER, 5km south of Kalgoorlie, is much quieter and smaller – a place to visit rather than stay in. It was originally set up as a separate settlement to serve the Golden Mile but Boulder's heyday passed as Kalgoorlie's suburbs slowly expanded around it.

Boulder has a similar collection of grand old buildings which, as in Kal, have received a face-lift, along with the pubs. One thing worth coming to Boulder for is a ride on the **Golden Mile Loopline**. Departing daily (Mon–Sat 10am & 11.45pm; $9.90) from the former train station at the top of Burt Street, the "Rattler", as it is known, once delivered workers to their pits and served all shifts round the clock. Now it will take you to a massive abandoned power station on the edge of the Super Pit with an intriguing commentary on the way. The highlight of the ride is the **Super Pit Lookout** where you can marvel at the mind-boggling scale of the operation. The "little" yellow dump trucks crawl in and out of the pit round the clock, hauling two hundred tons of ore at a time; interpretive boards at the lookout remind you why this exceptional mineral is sought after for more than just jewellery.

Just north of town are a couple more attractions without which a visit to Kalgoorlie–Boulder would not be complete. The **Mining Hall of Fame** (daily 9.30am–4.30pm; $20, surface only $10) is an old mine site now transformed into a theme park. Inside you can have a crack at gold panning or take a guided underground tour, led by former miners. It's probably as long as you'd want to spend down a mine – especially when you're given a brief demonstration of the pneumatic "air leg" drill. Pride of place goes to the new Hall of Fame building. Not all of the presentations in the galleries were completed on our visit, but after viewing a comprehensive display of rocks and minerals just past the entrance, the **Prospectors Gallery** is fascinating, chiefly due to the life stories of Mark Creasly and Lang Hancock. Creasly was a lone prospector who doggedly scoured WA in his battered ute (displayed), scraping by until one day he finally struck it rich and sold a claim for millions. Lang Hancock is a better known figure who established WA's iron ore boom in the Pilbara half a century ago by prospecting from the air in a light plane, a replica of which hangs in another gallery. Conspicuous by its absence is the not-so-glorious blue asbestos chapter in WA's mining history with which Hancock was also involved (see p.768). Allow about two and a half hours for your visit.

Practicalities
Perth–Goldfields Express (☎1800 620 440) and McCafferty's (☎08/9021 7100) **buses** arrive at Forrest Street in Kalgoorlie, opposite the **train station** (Westrail; ☎08/9021 2923). **Taxis** (☎13 10 08) meet daily trains, which are no quicker than buses. Kalgoorlie's **tourist office** (Mon–Fri 8.30am–5pm, Sat & Sun 9am–5pm; ☎08/9021 1966, ⓦwww.kalgoorlieandwagoldfields.com.au) is

at 250 Hannan St, on Kalgoorlie's main thoroughfare, and gives out informative sketch maps pinpointing Kal's dispersed attractions. There is an **Internet café** in the adjacent St Barbara's Square and a **post office** just up the road at 204 Hannan St.

A local **bus service** operates between the two towns every 25 minutes (Mon–Sat 8am–6pm; $1.80), with timetables available from Kalgoorlie's tourist office or the town hall. **Car rental** is expensive, though Halfpenny Rentals, 544 Hannan St South (℡08/9021 1804), is an exception. **Bikes** can be rented at Johnstons Cycles, 78 Boulder Rd (℡08/9021 1157). Goldrush Tours (℡1800 620 440, Ⓦwww.goldrushtours.info) is the main local tour operator whose two-hour "History and Heritage" tour ($25) is recommended.

Accommodation

Although it's unlikely that Kalgoorlie will maintain your interest for more than a couple of days, the town does get busy with holiday-makers in the winter school holidays, when it's best to check room availability in advance. The many splendid hotel facades along Hannan Street deteriorate alarmingly inside, but they all offer inexpensive rooms with either shared or en-suite facilities. You'll also find a couple of *Mercures* and *Best Westerns*.

Australia Hotel 138 Hannan St ℡08/9021 1320, Ⓦwww.theaustralia.com.au. Federation-era hotel in better shape than most. ❹

Gold Dust Backpackers 192 Hay St ℡08/9091 3737, Ⓦwww.kalgoorliebackpackers.com. Purpose-built hostel with air-con rooms, pool, bike rental, help with employment in the area and free pick-ups. Dorms $17, rooms ❸

Golden Village Caravan Park 406 Hay St ℡08/9021 4162. The caravan park closest to town. On-site vans ❸

Hannan's View Motel 430 Hannan St ℡08/9091 3333, Ⓔhvm@emerge.net.au. Motel units with pool, cheap breakfasts and some wheelchair-accessible, self-contained units. ❹

Kalgoorlie Backpackers 166 Hay St ℡08/9091 1482. Former brothel close to centre with big

kitchen, dorms and twins plus pool and bikes. Dorms $17, rooms ❸

Midas Motel 409 Hannan St ℡08/9021 3088 or 1800 813 088, Ⓕ9021 3125. Motel with night-club, pool, self-contained rooms and *Amalfi* restaurant. ❺

Prospector Holiday Park Great Eastern Highway, 3km west of town ℡08/9021 2524. Excellent park with pool, playground, kitchen and grassy sites. On-site vans ❷, cabins ❸

Sandalwood Motel Lower Hannan St ℡08/9021 4455 Ⓕ9021 3744. Well-priced and comfortable motel with air-con, TVs and en-suite bathrooms. ❹

York Hotel 259 Hannan St ℡08/9021 2337. Probably the best-looking facade on Hannan St. Shared bathrooms, but rates include breakfast. ❸

Eating and drinking

Starting at the cheap end, treat yourself to a good old **counter meal** at the *Star and Garter* pub on upper Hannan, or try *Basil's*, 268 Hannan St, for Italian home-style cooking and something to read, or the *Kalgoorlie Café* (10.30am–3pm & 6pm–1am) on the other side of the road, which has more of a family atmosphere. Also at the top of Hannan, the spacious *Martys Café* is open round the clock. The current in place to eat is the *Akudjura* restaurant at the south end of Hannan serving seafood and steaks in a classy setting. There's also a **food hall** near Coles/K-Mart, and *Health Works*, 75 Hannan St, caters for veggies. Next door is the *Top End Thai* (6pm–late; ℡08/9091 4027) with another Thai joint opposite.

For most locals, Kal's **nightlife** revolves around scantily clad pub barmaids laying on the beer, so there's no better way to mingle than by having a crack at the "**Kal pub crawl**"; T-shirts available at the tourist office are printed with a map linking the 32 pubs in Kalgoorlie-Boulder area. These days the roughest of the rough is the *Foundry*, 148 Boulder Rd, with the *De Benares' Tavern*, on Hannan Street, imposing dress regulations for customers and staff. Otherwise there is a **cinema** complex on Oswald Street, halfway to Boulder.

The Goldfields Highway

North of Kal are a number of mining and also Aboriginal communities along the 726km stretch to Meekatharra, itself halfway up the Great Northern Highway (the last 180km from Wiluna are dirt). Scenically the Goldfields Highway hasn't got much to commend it, but it is useful if you're heading up the Warburton Road to Alice or if you want to get from the Eyre Highway to northern WA in a hurry. It's worth knowing that most **ghost towns** in this area, especially the ones closer to Kalgoorlie, are mere stumps of long-since ruined buildings as any abandoned structure was quickly scavenged for use elsewhere. Nevertheless, in 2003 the **Golden Quest Discovery Trail** was established to allow tourists to self-guide through the region as far as Leonora and Laverton – ask for the free map and guide at Kalgoorlie visitors centre.

Though it once boasted twelve thousand residents, two breweries and an hourly train to Kalgoorlie, give the rubble remains of **Kanowna** a miss. Even the two ghost towns of **BROAD ARROW** and **ORA BANDA** (respectively 38km and 66km from Kalgoorlie) have only a "bush pub" each to show for themselves. Broad Arrow is just a couple of dilapidated shacks and a **pub** covered with inane graffiti that's popular with weekending Kal–Boulderians looking for a change of pub interiors. The historic *Ora Banda Hotel* may have been rebuilt by now after it was bombed by a biker gang. At **Kookynie**, a short distance off the highway, is another bush pub, the *Grand Hotel* (❷), standing alone in the desert.

LEONORA, 237km north of Kalgoorlie, is a century-old mining town that survives with a federation-era main street and a couple of hotels (❹). Just south of town is the reconstructed **Gwalia** ghost town – an evocative scattering of galvo hovels and a general store – plus a museum (daily 10am–4pm; $3) at the top of the hill. Right alongside is the pit of the Sons of Gwalia mine which took off where the original mine left off.

A sealed road also branches northeast to Laverton where the **Warburton Road** is now being touted as part of the transcontinental "Outback Highway", a straightforward if desolate track (often confused with the long-unmaintained Gunbarrel Highway to the north) leading 1160km to Yulara, NT (see p.687). Permits from Aboriginal Land Councils are technically required for both the WA and NT stretches, which puts most people off this useful short cut to the Centre (see Alice and Perth "Listings" for details of obtaining permits, see p.710 and p.674). Back on the Goldfields Highway **LEINSTER** is another one of those bizarrely suburban-looking company towns, with a supermarket and a motel (❹), while **Wiluna** (hotel: ❷) is the polar opposite, a century-old settlement that's now an Aboriginal welfare "ghost" town of quite intimidating desolation. Fueling up is the only reason you'd want to stop here.

From Wiluna the long unmaintained **Gunbarrel Highway** winds east towards Alice while the Canning Stock Route runs northeast across the Great Sandy Desert for 1900km to Halls Creek; both routes are serious 4WD expeditions. Meekathara (see p.765) is 180km to the west along a dirt road.

The Eyre Highway to South Australia

South of Kalgoorlie the Great Eastern Highway runs down to Norseman, at the western end of the **Eyre Highway**. The highway is named after the explorer John Eyre, who crossed the southern edge of the continent in 1841, a gruelling five-month trek which cost his companion's life and would have cost his own but for some Aborigines, who helped him locate water. Eyre crawled into Albany on his last legs but set the route for future crossings, the laying down of the telegraph lines and, most recently, the highway.

NORSEMAN was named after a prospector's horse which kicked up a large nugget in 1894 – a real case of lucky horseshoes; a bronze statue of the nag now stands proudly on the corner of Roberts and Ramsay streets. Arrivals from South Australia may be eager to pick up their Nullarbor certificate from the **tourist office** (daily 9am–5pm; ☎08/9039 1071) on Roberts Street with a telecentre next door. For an **overnight stay** try the *Norseman Eyre Motel* (☎08/9039 1130 or 1800 094 824; ❸), next to the 24-hour BP roadhouse on Roberts Street. More modest accommodation is available at the caravan park (on-site vans ❸) next to the motel, or there are budget rooms on Princep Street (the main Kal–Esperance road) at *Lodge 101* (☎08/9039 1541; dorms $18) nearby.

If you've come from the east and are in a quandary about which route to take to Perth, the inland road, after a stop in Kalgoorlie–Boulder, is fast and fairly dull while the coast road via Esperance can be made into a week-long scenic dawdle. For the best of both worlds, nip up to Kal and then return south and west along the coast.

Following the Eyre Highway, it's about 730km to the South Australian border and another 480km from there to Ceduna, where the bleak **Nullarbor** section ends (see p.870). That still leaves 800km before you reach Adelaide – a solid, two-day drive of legendary monotony. Although the road has been sealed for over twenty years and the longest stretch without fuel is only around 200km, do not underestimate the rigours of the journey in your own vehicle. Carry reserves of fuel and water, take rests every two or three hours and beware of kangaroos and other beasts, especially between dusk and dawn. There are no banks between Norseman and Ceduna, and both towns have a quarantine checkpoint where a large range of prohibited animal and vegetable goods must be discarded.

BALLADONIA, 193km from Norseman, is the first settlement on the way to the border, with the *Balladonia Hotel* (☎08/9039 3453; ❹) and adjacent caravan park your choice for an overnight stop. Then, 200km further, mostly along a 145-kilometre section of dead-straight road, you reach **CAIGUNA**, which has a motel and caravan park (☎08/9039 3459; on-site vans ❸, motel units ❹), and then **COCKLEBIDDY**, another 66km further on (motel ❹). On the coast near here, 16km east of town and 32km south of the highway along what becomes a 4WD track, are the remains of an old **telegraph station** that once linked WA with the rest of Australia. Today it houses the *Eyre Bird Observatory*, where you can stay overnight if you book in advance (☎08/9039 3450; ❹, plus $30 for pick-up and return). Overlooking **Twilight Cove** on the Great Australian Bight, this is a great spot to break a Nullarbor crossing. The place to stay in **MADURA**, 92km east of Cocklebiddy and halfway between Perth and Adelaide if you're still counting, is the *Madura Pass Oasis Motel* (☎08/9039 3464; ❹), while **MUNDRABILLA**, 116km further on and where you rise up into the actual Nullarbor plain, has a combined motel and campsite, the *Mundrabilla Motor Hotel* (☎08/9039 3465; ❸).

EUCLA, just 12km from the border, was re-established up on the escarpment after sand dunes exposed by overgrazing engulfed the original settlement by the sea. Only 4km away, the old telegraph and weather station are still visible above the sands, an eerie sight well worth a stroll. From **Eucla National Park**, the vertical cliffs can be seen extending east for hundreds of kilometres along the coast of South Australia. For accommodation, Eucla has a **caravan park** (bunkhouse ❶, on-site vans ❷) and the *Eucla Motor Hotel* (☎08/9039 3468; ❹). Right on the border there's the *Border Village* (☎08/9039 3474; ❸) and the western edge of a 200-kilometre line of cliffs which drop dramatically into the Southern Ocean. For the South Australian section of this route, see p.870.

From Perth to Kununurra

The 4400-kilometre haul up Highway 1 along Western Australia's arching coastline from Perth to Broome, across the Kimberley and on to Darwin in the Northern Territory, is one of Australia's great road journeys. Even without detours it's a huge, transcontinental trek between the country's two most isolated capitals, fringing the barely inhabited wilderness that separates them. From the **WA–NT border** 40km east of Kununurra, it's still another 730km to Darwin. This final stretch, along the Victoria and Stuart highways, which meet at Katherine, is covered on pp.653–656.

If any single trip across Australia benefits from independent mobility, it's this one: a car enables you to explore intimately or linger indefinitely. While some days in WA's **Northwest** will be punctuated by nothing more than road trains, road kills and roadhouses, there are several places where the climate, scenery and ambience will collectively conspire to subdue your road fever for a few days. If you're interested in discovering the wayside attractions, allow at least three to four weeks for the journey right through to Darwin; otherwise a fortnight will let you whizz through the highlights; anything less and you may as well fly.

The route is sealed all the way, but a glance at any map clearly shows the long distances between roadhouses, let alone settlements. Your vehicle should be in sound condition, particularly the tyres and the cooling system, both of which will be working hard in the heat and dirt-road detours of the Northwest. If you're undertaking the trip between January and March, once you get **north of Exmouth** you can expect **storms**, flooding and even cyclones. Following damage, roads and bridges on Highway 1 are repaired amazingly quickly, but if rain persists, routes can be closed for weeks. When it has reception, a **radio** is a handy aid to keeping track of cyclones, similarly troublesome "rain-bearing depressions" and the status of roads.

If you don't have a car, the rigid schedules and butt-numbing sectors of long-distance **bus** travel require a certain equanimity. McCafferty's and Integrity Coachlines offer a range of good-value **regional passes** up the coast to Exmouth, Broome and Darwin. It should be noted that by doing the journey from Perth, schedules generally match connections to places off the highway with little delay. In the opposite direction, you are travelling "against the flow" of the timetable and can expect long waits on roadhouse forecourts unless heading directly back to Perth.

Up the coast to Broome

Ironically, nowhere along the 2400-kilometre drive along the North West Coastal Highway to Broome will you glimpse vistas of frothing surf breaking temptingly onto golden beaches or taste the salt in the air. The highway takes a more sheltered inland course, with access to the ocean limited by private land, not to mention the sheer impenetrability of some of the terrain. The myth of beach-camping your way up a deserted coast is unfortunately just that, but there are just about enough attractions to make up for this deficiency. High points along the route include the spooky **Pinnacles** near Cervantes, the idyllic resort of **Kalbarri**, and the **Shark Bay** Peninsula, with its chummy dolphins. Further north, the **Ningaloo Reef** running down the North West Cape should not be missed.

The Brand Highway

Travelling the **Brand Highway**, there's an all but obligatory detour to view the remarkable Pinnacles in **Nambung National Park**, 250km from Perth and 70km off the highway. A young crayfishing town, beaten by strong winds in summer, **CERVANTES** is the closest overnight stop. There are two caravan parks here, with tent sites and on-site vans (❷), plus *Pinnacles Beach Backpackers*, at 91 Seville St (☎08/9652 7377; dorms $18, rooms ❷), which has kitchen facilities, a laundry, TV/video lounge and barbecue, and books tours. For greater comfort, try the *Cervantes Pinnacles Motel* (☎08/9652 7145; ❹). You can eat at the *Tavern* or the *Thirst Point* pizzeria. Minibus **tours** of the park leave daily (1pm plus 9.45am & 4.15pm, depending on demand; $15; ☎08/9652 7041) from the *Pinnacle Country Café*, which is also the **tourist information centre** (daily 8am–6pm), next to the Shell service station. Better still, Happyday Tours (☎08/9652 7244) do **pick-ups** from the McCafferty's bus on the highway and next morning takes you for a two-hour stroll ($35) through the Pinnacles on the way back to the bus.

Otherwise, in the park (CALM fee; no camping; see box on p.722) there's access to the ocean at **Kangaroo Point** and **Hangover Bay** but the **Pinnacles** are the main attraction: a patchy forest of limestone columns up to three metres high, formed by subsurface erosion and since exhumed like a terracotta army by the perennial southwesterlies. A three-kilometre drive winds among them, but however lazy you're feeling, you'll find it hard not to park and wander around this eerie expanse, sometimes enhanced by a "mist" of fine, windblown sand. Most day-tours from Perth arrive around midday, missing the evening sun's long shadows, which add still further to the Pinnacles' photogenic qualities.

After the Pinnacles there's really very little of interest until you get to the tiny coastal resort of **GREENOUGH**, 400km north of Perth. The **Greenough Historical Hamlet** (daily 9.30am–4.30pm; $3 including guided tour; ☎08/9926 1140) is an unusually well-restored nineteenth-century farming community that would make an ideal period-film location. Up the road you'll see Greenough's strange **leaning trees** – some bent almost flat against the ground by the prevailing salt-laden winds – as well as the imposing, three-storey bulk of **Clinch's Mill**, the **Pioneer Cemetery** and the **Pioneer Museum** (daily except Fri 10am–4pm; ☎08/9926 1058; $1.50), recording the area's heritage.

The *Greenough Rivermouth Caravan Park* (☎08/9921 5845) is a better-than-average facility offering tent spaces, on-site vans (❸) and cheap fuel. The

△ Pinnacles Desert

nearest **backpackers'** (☎08/9927 1581; dorms $18) is at 32 Waldeck St, Dongara, 40km to the south.

Geraldton

Situated in the middle of the **Batavia Coast**, **GERALDTON** is a crayfishing, mining and pastoral centre whose downtown feels more like a busy Perth suburb than a country town. In fact it's the state's second-largest city as well as a **windsurfing** haven.

The **tourist office** is in the Bill Sewell Complex (Mon–Fri 8.30am–5pm, Sat & Sun 9am–4.30pm; ☎08/9921 3999) on Chapman Road, 2km north of town, and will happily sort out all accommodation bookings. McCafferty's and Integrity **buses** arrive here daily and Westrail buses alight at the old train station, just down the road. The modern town has little of interest except for a museum and an extraordinary cathedral. The **Maritime Museum** (Mon–Sat 10am–4pm, Sun 1–5pm; donation) on Marine Terrace, by the yellow submarine, focuses on the fascinating tragedy of the *Batavia* and the many other shipwrecks off the treacherous Batavia Coast, as well as describing the contemporary "treasures" of the crayfishing industry.

St Francis Xavier Cathedral on Cathedral Drive, built over a 25-year period and completed in 1938, was the crowning glory of Monsignor John Hawes' career. He was a qualified architect before taking up the cloth, and there are half a dozen examples of his unique Romanesque–Byzantine architectural style in the vicinity, of which the cathedral is his masterpiece, just as stunning and bold inside as out. There are free tours on Mondays at 10am and Fridays at 2pm. If you're sufficiently impressed, ask at the tourist office about the **John Hawes Heritage Trail**, which leads you around some of his other works.

Of Geraldton's other attractions, the city's **beaches** aren't particularly appealing and are often windy, like much of the west coast. There's the obligatory **Old Gaol**, now a craft centre, next to the Bill Sewell Complex, and a **lighthouse** at Point Moore, while the old **Keepers' Cottage** (Thurs 10am–4pm; donation welcome), off Chapman Road, 5km north of town, is fastidiously maintained in its original state.

Accommodation

Batavia Backpackers Bill Sewell Complex, Chapman Rd ☎08/9964 3001. Spacious and clean former hospital with wards for dorms. Dorms $18, rooms ❸
Batavia Motor Inne Fitzgerald St ☎08/9921 3500. Close to the city centre and with restaurant and pool. ❹
Foreshore Backpackers 172 Marine Terrace ☎08/9921 3275, ✉foreshorebp@hotmail.com.

Right in the town centre and close to the harbour. YHA discounts and free pick-ups. Dorms $17, rooms ❸
Mercure Inn Brand Highway ☎08/9921 2455 or 1800 642 244, ✆9921 5830. Customary motel-chain comforts. ❹
Sun City Tourist Park Sunset Beach, 6km north of town ☎08/9938 1655. Geraldton's best caravan park but rather a long way out. On-site vans ❸

Eating and drinking

Geraldton has a fair selection of places to eat, and if you're heading north this will be your last chance to sample a choice of decent food rather than take what you are offered. For **drinks** and **live bands**, the *Geraldton Hotel* on Lester Avenue is the place to go, with the *Freemasons* on Marine Terrace offering a more refined alternative.

Boat Shed 357 Marine Terrace. Quality seafood from around $20. Daily from 6pm.

Go Health Café Marine Terrace. Breakfasts and lunches with vegetarian options and big burritos.

Lemon Grass 18 Snowdon St. The town's best choice for Thai food.
Montego's Marine Terrace. Dinner seven days with the best views of the bay.

Skeetas George Rd. Very popular garden restaurant, an ideal place for salad lunches in the sun.
Topollini's 158 Marine Terrace. Stylish and affordable Italian lunch spot in the town centre.

Kalbarri and around

Situated at the mouth of the Murchison River, whose sandbar shelters its beach, **KALBARRI** is the best of the west coast's resorts. Without so much as a dreary old jail to shuffle through, this small town is simply a great place to do as much or as little as you like. With the dramatic scenery of the Kalbarri National Park on its doorstep, few resorts can boast such an ideal location, together with good, inexpensive accommodation and a host of activities.

The area's history holds a few wonders of its own. In the 1920s a stockman discovered the remains of a **castaway's camp** on the clifftops north of Kalbarri and excavation revealed the wreck of the Dutch trader, *Zuytdorp*, at the base of the cliff, but no human remains. The fate of the survivors had been a three-hundred-year-old mystery until the diagnosis of the rare Ellis van Creveld Syndrome (endemic in seventeenth-century Netherlands) among local children of Aboriginal descent suggested that some of the *Zuytdorp*'s castaways survived long enough to pass the gene on to the Aborigines of the area.

Arrival, information and getting around

McCafferty's **buses** from Perth drop passengers at the **Ajana turn-off** on the highway, to be met by a shuttle bus on Monday, Thursday and Saturday only. Westrail buses from Perth come right into town in the middle of the night on Sunday, Monday, Wednesday and Thursday. The **tourist office** (daily 9am–5pm; ☎08/9937 1104, ⊛tourismmidwest.com.au) is in the Allen Centre on Grey Street; many of the local activities and tours can be booked here. The small **shopping centre** on Porter Street includes a bakery, supermarket and **post office**, with bank agencies and cash machines at various outlets around town. Suzuki **4WD jeeps** can be rented from *Kalbarri Backpackers*; mileage is unlimited in Kalbarri and in the national park, and the drive up River Road at the town's northern end will give you a chance to fiddle with the transmission levers.

Accommodation

In the school holidays when Kalbarri is busy, most holiday units insist on a minimum one-week's booking.

Kalbarri Backpackers 2 Mortimer St ☎08/9937 1430, ⓔkalbarribackpackers@wn.com.au. No competition but still spacious and tidy. Mixed dorms $18, rooms ❸
Kalbarri Beach Resort Off Clotsworthy St ☎08/9937 1061. Large resort with a pool, sauna and the *Zuytdorp Restaurant*. ❹
Kalbarri Seafront Villas 37 Grey St ☎08/9937 1025, ⓕ9937 1525. Well-equipped units, some with ocean views and a free dinghy provided. ❹
Murchison Park Grey St ☎08/9937 1005. Well-shaded caravan park right opposite the Foreshore.

On-site vans ❸
Murchison View Apartments Cnr Grey and Rushton streets ☎08/9937 1096, ⓕ9937 1522. Quality two- and three-bedroom units with a pool and some sea views. ❹
Palm Resort 8 Porter St ☎08/9937 2333 or 1800 819 029. Good-value spacious rooms with pool, tennis courts and restaurant. ❸
Pelican's Nest Cnr Mortimer and Wood streets ☎08/9937 1430, ⓕ9937 1563. The town's only other budget option with two-bedroom apartments suitable for groups. ❸

The Town and around

You don't have to be a parrot lover to flock to **Rainbow Jungle** (Tues–Sat 9am–5pm, Sun 10am–5.30pm; $10), 4km south of town. A minor architectural work of art, it's filled to bursting with tropical fauna, has a superb display of stunningly colourful parrots and includes a walk-through aviary.

For those not content to laze on **Chinaman's Beach** all day, there are plenty of more active pursuits on offer. An easy way to get yourself going is to take a **cruise** up the Murchison River on the *Kalbarri River Queen* (℡08/9937 1104) or rent all sorts of **watercraft** on the Foreshore from Kalbarri Boat Hire & Canoe Safaris (℡08/9937 1245), who can also take you up the lower Murchison to Gregory's Rock for a morning's canoeing, with a traditional bush breakfast on the way, for $40. Big River Ranch, 4km inland from Kalbarri (℡08/9937 1214; pick-ups available), runs very popular **horse-riding** trips for beginners and the experienced alike; the three-hour sunset ride ($35), through the river, along the beach and back again, is the memorable highlight. **Scenic flights** with Kalbarri Air Charter (℡08/9937 1130; enquire at the gift shop, 28 Grey St) start from just $35 for the short but spectacular Coastal Cliffs run, and go up to $140 for the Grand Tour or a five-hour visit to Monkey Mia. Kalbarri Sports and Dive (℡08/9937 1126) can organize **dives** if you ask, while the *Reef Walker* (℡08/9937 1356) sets off on a variety of coastal cruises with diving or fishing opportunities.

Eating and drinking

Don't leave Kalbarri without checking out *Finlay's Fish BBQ* (daily 11.30am–2pm & 5.30–8.30pm; ℡08/9937 1260) on Magee Crescent. With plate-spinning Captain Finlay's fresh fish, salad and damper for $10, and an unusual setting in an old ice works (plus occasional fireside ballads), *Finlay's* on a balmy night is a treat.

All the other **restaurants** can seem rather ordinary by comparison; the *Zuytdorp* (daily 6–10pm) at the *Kalbarri Beach Resort* is a close rival, with a $17 smorgasbord, while in the same place *Jacks* is less formal. The *Black Rock Cafe* (daily 10am–8pm), on Grey Street, has views and seafood lunches, and *Rivers Café* (daily 10am–8pm), opposite the wharf, has takeaways and more fresh seafood. *Kalbarru Pizza* (Tues–Sun 5.30pm–late), behind the *Gilgai Tavern* on Porter Street, serves average pizzas from $8, and there's a good health-food café inside the shopping centre. Of the two **pubs**, the *Kalbarri Hotel* on Grey Street is where the locals hang out, while the livelier *Gilgai Tavern* on Porter Street also serves meals.

Kalbarri National Park

Kalbarri National Park (CALM fee; see box on p.722), which surrounds the town, has two popular attractions: the serpentine **river gorge** of the upper Murchison River, reached off the Ajana road east of town, and the **coastal gorges** created by lesser creeks, a few kilometres south of Kalbarri, just about within cycling range. Kalbarri Coach Tours (℡08/9937 1161) visits both areas several times a week for around $45, with a range of more adventurous options available too.

The **coastal gorges** are accessible by tracks and short walks off the Kalbarri–Northampton road, which begins just before *Red Bluff Caravan Park*. **Red Bluff** is the prominent butte overlooking Jakes Corner (good surfing) and the site of some barely discernible, prehistoric crustacean fossils. **Rainbow Valley** has some intriguing features exposed by weathering, as well as a coastal walk up to **Mushroom Rock**, the most interesting part of the coastline. Pot Alley is another lookout and Eagle Gorge has a tiny secluded beach, but the view from the cliffs above **Natural Bridge** (at 16km, the furthest from town) gives the impression that you are indeed perched on the edge of a vast continent.

Eleven kilometres east of Kalbarri, a corrugated road turns north for 25km to the **gorge** along the Murchison River, where at a junction you can go a few kilometres further north to **the Loop**, or south to **Z Bend**. It's possible to walk round the Loop (a horseshoe bend in the Murchison River) in about two hours although this may be prolonged by the abundance of swimming opportunities, birdlife and the odd, mean-looking feral pig; the walk is best undertaken early in the morning. Z Bend is the most dramatic lookout over the Murchison River far below, accessible down a steep track. You can abseil or rap jump down if you dare and climb up Z Bend's cliff; enquire at *Kalbarri Backpackers* – no experience is necessary. Back on the Ajana road, heading inland for 30km from the Loop turn-off, Hawks Head and Ross Graham Lookout, both a few kilometres off the road, are less impressive but worth stopping for on the way out of Kalbarri if you're driving.

It is possible to **walk** from Z Bend to the Loop over a couple of days and from Ross Graham Lookout to the Loop in four days, but both are demanding walks and you should speak to the **park ranger** (☎08/9937 1140) first.

Shark Bay

Shark Bay is the name given to the two prongs of land and their corresponding lagoons which comprise Australia's westernmost point, forming a roughly W-shaped coastline. **Denham**, the only settlement, is on the west side of the Peron Peninsula, while at **Monkey Mia Dolphin Resort**, on the sheltered east side of the peninsula, a family of dolphins has been coming in almost daily to meet people for the past forty years. The shallow, aquamarine waters of Shark Bay have earned it a World Heritage listing as a remarkable **ecological habitat**, a fact that tends to be overshadowed by the visits of the dolphins. It's worth noting that dolphins also "interact", albeit less reliably, at Rockingham and Bunbury south of Perth (see p.723).

McCafferty's **bus** runs to Monkey Mia from Perth twice daily on Monday, Thursday and Saturday (12hr): if you plan to visit, make sure your bus pass includes this excursion. Otherwise, if it's just the dolphins you want to see consider flying up from Perth with Skywest (☎08/9948 1247). Shark Bay **Taxi** Service (☎08/9948 1331) connects with interstate buses at the *Overlander Roadhouse*, which marks the turning off the highway to Shark Bay, charging $30 to Denham and $36 to Monkey Mia.

The roads to Monkey Mia and Steep Point

It's 150km to Monkey Mia from the *Overlander Roadhouse*, a drive that is much like the rest of the coastline in this area – it's rather dull through dense mulga scrub but punctuated with some unusual sights along the way. **Hamelin Pool**, 5km off the Denham road, is home to a uniquely accessible colony of **stromatolites**, colonies of sediment-trapping algae which are direct descendants of the earth's earliest life forms, dating back over three billion years. We can thank their ancestors for the diligent oxygenating of the earth's atmosphere which eventually begat the more complex life forms from which humans evolved. Viewed from a platform the 3000-year-old examples in Hamelin Pool flourish because no potential predator can handle the pool's hyper-saline water. Nearby, the **Old Telegraph Station** (daily 8.30am–5.30pm; $6) has a display, video and a pet "stromie" in a tank which can be more interesting than the actual colony unless the tide is right out. There are also some old telecommunications relics and an interesting gift shop and café with a small **camping ground** (☎08/9942 5905).

Fourteen kilometres further along the Denham road, a turn-off leads to the salt and gypsum mine at Useless Loop: this road divides again with the left fork, accessible by 4WDs only, leading to **Steep Point** ($20 entry fee; camping allowed), Australia's most westerly mainland extremity. **Dirk Hartog Island**, off the north end of Steep Point, is where the first European is known to have set foot on what is now Australian soil, 150 years before Captain Cook. The Dutch mariner Hartog left a pewter plate inscribed "Anno 1616" on the island.

Continuing towards Denham, you'll pass *Nanga Bay Resort* (☎08/9948 3992, ⓔ nangabay@wn.com.au; dorms $18, rooms ❺), where there are accommodation units, cabins and dorms; it's a popular fishing spot but otherwise uninspiring. Across the isthmus – now divided by an electric fence, which emits a recording of barking dogs (an attempt to scare feral animals off the peninsula) – is **Shell Beach**, composed of millions of tiny shells several metres deep. Where they've consolidated they're cut into blocks for local buildings. Twenty kilometres before Denham, **Eagle Bluff** is an impressive clifftop lookout where, if you're lucky, you might spot dugongs, dolphins and manta rays in the clear waters of Freycinet Reach below.

Denham

A small prawning port and holiday resort, **DENHAM** thrives in the lee of Monkey Mia's unflagging popularity. Between here and Monkey Mia (25km away), **François Peron National Park** (CALM fee; see box on p.722) is part of the Eden project which, with the help of the electric fence is intended to

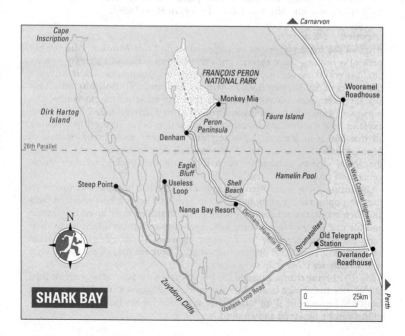

return native species to the park once the destructive ferals, most significantly the cat, have been eliminated with poison. The CALM office (℡08/9948 1208) on Knight Terrace has more information about the park and other natural features in the Shark Bay area.

The **tourist office** (daily 8am–6pm; ℡08/9948 1253, ℮bayjet@wn .com.au) is on the town's main road at 71 Knight Terrace, and there's another one a few doors down. The town also has a post office and a couple of supermarkets. **Buses** for Monkey Mia leave daily at 8am ($10).

As for **tours and cruises**, the MV *Explorer* (℡08/9948 1246; from $80) operates cruises around Shark Bay, offering a good chance to see some of the clear-water bay's submarine wildlife. Shark Bay Charter Service's luxurious catamaran (℡08/9948 1773) offers a great day out, and the company also offers **scenic flights** from $50.

It is important to call ahead when staying in the Shark Bay region as it can occasionally fill quickly if a coach tour arrives in town. **Places to stay** include *Bay Lodge*, 109 Knight Terrace (℡08/9948 1278, ℮baylodge@wn.com.au; ❹), the *Tradewinds Holiday Village* (℡08/9948 1222, ℱ9948 1161; ❹), with units that sleep up to six people, and the *Heritage Resort* (℡08/9948 1133, ℱ9948 1134; ❺), on the corner of Durlacher Street, which is the town's best with a very pleasant bar. Of the three **caravan parks** in town, the *Shark Bay Caravan Park* (℡08/9948 1387; vans and cabins ❷–❸), 4 Spaven Way, is your best bet and has a big pool.

The only notable **restaurant**, apart from the one in the *Heritage Resort*, is the *Old Pearler* opposite, built from shell block and with an attractive maritime interior; meals cost around $15. Other than that, there are a couple of cafés, a pizza bar and a bakery along Knight Terrace. Note that **water** is very precious in the Shark Bay area since rain rarely falls: salty bore water is used as widely as possible but locally desalinated, fresh public drinking water is available at a tap just as you come into town after the information board.

Monkey Mia

After all the hype, you might be surprised to find that **Monkey Mia** ($9 per person) is nothing more than an attractive caravan park and a jetty by a pretty beach overlooking the inauspiciously named Disappointment Reach. It is here that scores of day-trippers flock to witness the almost daily **dolphin** visits (usually for three feeds between 8am and 1pm and most reliably in winter). An intriguing video in the **Dolphin Information Centre** (daily 7.30am–4pm) explains how the entirely unprompted interaction began in the 1960s. Almost all that has been learned about dolphins has been gleaned from studies of Monkey Mia's regular troupe of visitors, each one known by name, although the actual visitors number between three and six females and their third-generation progeny.

Unfortunately, as is so often the case, the place has become a victim of its massive popularity for both dolphins and tourists. The dolphins' repeated visits and their spontaneous familiarity seem to take a toll on their breeding patterns and for this reason calves, which lack immunity to human infections in their early weeks, are kept away from visitors. However, if you push into the right spot you do have a great opportunity to get a close up shot of a dolphin, even if it is really no more wild than a cat.

More satisfying is a spin around the bay in one of the two catamarans berthed at the jetty, the choice being the stripped-down *Shotover* with **cruises** starting from $30 for an hour. With luck plenty of marine life (including prancing dolphins) can be observed and enjoyed.

The *Monkey Mia Dolphin Resort* (☎08/9948 1320, ⓦwww.monkeymia
.com.au) is right on the beach: it has grassed campsites and, for backpackers,
cramped old **caravans** with ancient kitchens (❷) or, a better option, safari tents
(❹). There are also basic cabins (❹) and motel **rooms** (❺), plus a pool and spa,
a restaurant and a small shop with basic groceries and takeaways.

Carnarvon and around

A centre for prawning fleets and the sheep stations of the Upper Gascoyne
region, tropical **CARNARVON** also supports a large agricultural zone, thanks
to the seemingly dry Gascoyne River's retrievable subterranean water. The
town continues to battle against a reputation for drink-related violence and
crime, largely down to a couple of feuding Aboriginal clans, and it's the only
place between Perth and Katherine where you'll regularly see police cars on
the prowl.

There's little in town to detain a passing traveller anyway, but a couple of
diversions up the coast can make a fun day out. Six kilometres east of
Carnarvon a bridge crosses the riverbed, passing the 65°C thermal well of
Bibbawarra Bore, joins the sealed Blowholes Road, which leads to the
Blowholes at Point Quobba, 65km from town. On all but the calmest days,
incoming waves compress air through vents in the low cliff to erupt like geysers up to 20m into the air, a sight and sound well worth the detour. A couple
of kilometres to the south is a basic campsite (no water) with sheltered
snorkelling in the bay. Heading north past *Quobba Homestead* (camping; basic
rooms ❷) and occasional tracks down to shell-lined beaches, you cross the
private road linking the Dampier Saltworks at Lake MacLeod with the jetty
at Cape Cuvier. Just north of the cape is the wreck of the *Korean Star*,
beached here during a cyclone in 1988. It was here, too, that a "**fish feeding frenzy**" caught the world's attention in 1992, when several species of
shark and whale appeared to co-operate in devouring a glut of small fry.
North of here is Red Bluff Beach (camping, shop and restaurant) and
Gnaraloo Homestead (camping), the domain of beach fishermen and white-
knuckle windsurfers.

Practicalities

The new **tourist office** (daily 9am–5pm; ☎08/9941 1146) is on the corner
of Robinson Street and Camel Lane. **Buses** also arrive here, and the **post
office** is just opposite.

Accommodation in town includes the *Gateway Motel* on Robinson Street
(☎08/9941 1532; ❻) and the *Hospitality Inn* (☎08/9941 1600 or 13 17 79,
ⓕ9941 2405; ❻) on West Street. *Carnarvon Backpackers*, on the foreshore, left
at the end of Robinson Street (☎08/9941 1095; dorms $19), is the only choice
in hostels and as good as you'd expect for this town. There are no fewer than
seven **caravan parks** close to town catering for itinerant workers, and cara-
vanners seeking the winter sun.

Inland to the Kennedy Ranges

East of Carnarvon, a dirt road following the Gascoyne River inland may now
be sealed to **GASCOYNE JUNCTION**, a former droving settlement where
the outlaw Ned Kelly (see p.1040) was reputed to have once hidden out. The
Junction Hotel is all that's left, a century-old relic with a small general store and
fuel. East of here, a good dirt road makes reaching Meekathara from the coast
possible in a day. North of town, another track leads along the escarpment of

the **Kennedy Ranges National Park**, basically three short walks leading into gorges cut back into the weathered ranges. Drapers Gorge is probably the most satisfying, with a waterhole and some basic engravings on the way, and more pools further up. The problem with exploring this area, especially on to Mount Augustus is that tracks don't connect readily with the Karijini Park or the North West Cape, both much more worthwhile destinations.

For what it's worth, **Mount Augustus** (set in Burringurrah National Park) claims to be the world's largest monadnock (a residual hill), trumpeted as being "bigger and older than Uluru (Ayers Rock)". Many hills can also claim this and Mount Augustus lacks even a fraction of Uluru's majesty and is not worth the four-hundred-kilometre diversion.

The North West Cape

Back on Highway 1, 141km north of Carnarvon is the *Minilya Roadhouse* (dorms $20), from where a turning 6km later leads to the **North West Cape**. This hot and arid spike of land is notable for the 250-kilometre **Ningaloo Reef** which fringes its western edge, never more than 7km offshore, and is, in places, accessible right off the beach; "WA's barrier reef without the barriers" as some call it. **Exmouth** is the main settlement on the cape, but the tiny resort of **Coral Bay** is not only more convenient and more pleasant, but the easiest place from which to view the reef. It's near here that those blue "Save Ningaloo Reef" bumper stickers (Ⓦwww.save-ningaloo.org) you'll have seen all over the state are helping highlight a proposed (and by now possibly approved) marina resort at Mauds Landing.

Buses leave from Carnarvon, stopping at Coral Bay on the way to Exmouth before returning to Carnarvon each afternoon. If you're heading further north after an excursion to the Cape, you might as well go all the way back to Carnarvon and catch the bus you'd otherwise wait for at *Minilya* – it's certainly more comfortable that way. Skywest flies between Perth and Exmouth (daily except Sat; 6hr), a better way of making an excursion to the Cape if you don't want to make the 1600-kilometre drive from Perth.

Coral Bay

CORAL BAY is a small beach resort 12km off the Exmouth road and, school holidays excepted, is a lovely, quiet spot. Here you can enjoy all the activities offered at Exmouth but without having to drive a single metre if you don't want to. Little more than a couple of caravan park/motels and a mini shopping centre, the lack of fresh water and available land has held back large-scale development, though this doesn't seem to have stopped the proposed resort at Mauds Landing, just north of town. Coral Bay's **water** comes from a hot and salty bore, making it suitable for cooking and washing but not for drinking; make sure you drink from freshwater taps.

Two **glass-bottomed boats** operate daily cruises over the reef (times depend on the tides and snorkelling gear can be kept for the rest of the day). Coral Bay Charters' version (Ⓣ08/9942 5932; from $35) is the better of the two, especially the four-hour cruise, which takes you snorkelling on the more impressive outer reef, as well as visiting the Manta rays round the headland. But even without getting wet you'll see an amazing variety of soft and hard coral that's slowly recovering from the last cyclone in 1999. Other fun **activities** at Coral Bay include catamaran cruises, resort dives or full PADI courses, scenic flights and even quad treks inland and over the dunes. Your accommodation or either Coral Bay Adventures (Ⓣ08/9942 5955, Ⓦwww.coralbayadventures

.com.au) or Coastal Adventure Tours (☎08/9942 5865) next to each other behind the information bay can organize it all for you. In the shopping arcade on the right, by the *Ningaloo Club*, you'll also find **Internet** access costing around $6 per hour.

The *Bayview Coral Bay* **motel** (☎08/9942 5932; ❺) forms a large resort that also offers camping, on-site vans (❸) and various configurations of chalets and cabins (❸), as well as a small shop and a restaurant. The better positioned *Ningaloo Reef Resort* (☎08/9942 5934, ✉whaleshark@bigpond.com; ❹), offers motel accommodation plus a **bar**, restaurant/takeaway and a grassed pool area with a great view over the small bay. The awful backpackers' annexe round the back (dorms $18) is destined to take nothing more than the disappointed over-spill from the new *Ningaloo Club Backpackers* (☎08/9948 5100; dorms $18, rooms ❸). On the right as you come into town, it's not the most innovative design, but has a pool, plenty of space and a proper kitchen. Book ahead for this one.

Exmouth

On the way up to Exmouth, you pass the now sealed Burkett Road which cuts 150km from the journey if you're coming from the north. A worthwhile overnight stopover along this road is *Giralia Station* (☎08/9942 5937, ✉giralia@aol.com) a working sheep station which offers caravans and camping ($17), backpacker rooms (❷), or boutique private rooms with en-suite bath (❺). Continuing towards Exmouth, two roads lead up onto the emerging **Cape Range**: the Charles Knife Road climbs precipitously to the top of the range, 311m above sea level. From here it's possible to walk to the head of Shothole Canyon (allow 2hr), also accessible off the Exmouth road, though a far less dramatic introduction to the range.

EXMOUTH was built in 1967 to serve a former US VLF Communications Station and has since become a tourist base for visits to the Cape Range National Park and Ningaloo Marine Park. Cloud-free days make the town a popular winter holiday-makers' resort with numbers increasing as the wonders of the Ningaloo reef become more widely known. Though far from being a west-coast Cairns, diving and fishing charters, as well as marine wildlife-spotting tours (see box below) and other recreational activities vie for your attention. Unlike Cairns, however, it's a few kilometres to the ocean (a necessary cyclone precaution), with the town's so-called Sunrise Beach now a marina. The nearest place to see the reef is in a glass-bottomed boat off **Bundegi Beach**, 14km north of Exmouth, opposite the towering antennae of the naval station, but the best of the reef and beaches are 50km away on the other side of the Cape. Recently the naval base was vacated with much of the infrastructure handed over to the town; they've tried to sell it as a new resort area but the razor wire and functional architecture don't fool anybody and the best that remains is the **drive-in cinema**.

Ningaloo marine-spotters' calendar

Turtle hatching – January to March
Coral spawning – March to April
Whale sharks – April to June
Whale-watching – June to October
Manta rays – all year, Coral Bay
Turtle nesting – November to January

Practicalities

Overland **buses** stop outside the new **tourist office** (Mon–Fri 8.30am–5pm, Sat & Sun 9am–4pm; ☎08/9949 1176, ⓦwww.exmouth–australia.com) on the main Murat road, where you can begin to get your head around the range of offshore charters and tours offered. Note that if you are coming up to swim with the whale sharks, you can expect to pay a couple of hundred dollars a day for the privilege.

The actual town centre is based around Maidstone Crescent a bit up the road on the left. Here you'll find banks and the post office, plus the main **shopping centre** and the *Ningaloo Blue* **Internet** café round the back. A bus runs twice a week to Coral Bay and back (☎08/9949 4623; $50 return) and another service runs round the Cape once a day to just past the national park visitors centre (see below).

Accommodation is available at a couple of resorts including the *Ningaloo Lodge* off Maidstone Crescent (☎08/9949 4949, ⓦwww.ningaloolodge .com.au; ❹) or the *Potshot Hotel Resort* (☎08/9949 1200, ⓦwww.potshot resort.com; ❹), the town's main motel with restaurants and a pool. *Excape Backpackers* round the back of the *Potshot* (entrance in Payne St, ☎08/9949 1201; dorms $18) is the usual budget effort with small dorms and a basic kitchen but also access to the resort's facilities. *Pete's Backpackers*, 2km down Murat Road (☎08/9949 1101, ⓦwww.exmouthvillage.com; $18), flies the YHA flag but is really a spacious caravan park offering cramped cabins and organizing tours, cruises and rental jeeps. Opposite the tourist office (and much more central) is *Winstons Backpackers* (☎08/9949 2377, ⓦwww.exmouth resort.com; dorms $18) a small block of four-bed dorms, part of the *Ningaloo Caravan Resort* (cabins from ❹), with a better pool and some shaded camping too. There's also the new *Marina Beach Retreat* (☎08/9949 1500; dorms $18, cabins ❸) right by the town beach (and further away from town), with cabins and tents, a pool, bar and the promise of full-moon festivities. It's associated with the upmarket camping at *Ningaloo Chase* (☎08/9949 1500, ⓦwww.ningaloochase.com.au; $120 per person all inclusive) on the other side of the Cape, just south of Yardie Creek.

When it comes to **eating** there's precious little to get excited about: *Whalers Café* behind the shopping centre is good, with a baker and two **supermarkets** just over the road. The *Rock Café*, behind the Ampol service station, is worth a try too, while the *Potshot* accommodates the town's main **pub**.

Cape Range and Ningaloo parks

These parks are adjacent land- and sea-conservation areas on the western edge of the North West Cape: to explore them from Exmouth, you really need a vehicle or to join one of the many tours sold around town. The proximity of the continental shelf is what gives the **Ningaloo Marine Park** a stunning variety of marine life: over five hundred species of fish and 220 species of coral have been recorded here. **Cape Range National Park** (CALM fee; see box on p.722) is essentially a coastal drive past several bays, lagoons and rather congested campsites (book ahead or at the park entrance). For snorkelling, the reef comes closest at the south point of Turquoise Bay where the wind and current tend to drift you north across the bay. Oyster Stacks, just to the south, is an alternative snorkelling venue, but you can pick pretty much any turn-off to enjoy a pristine beach and the sight of a few emus along the way.

The **Milyering Visitors Centre** (daily 10am–4pm), 52km from Exmouth, is a solar-powered complex with videos and displays on the local ecology, and enthusiastic, helpful staff. Another 30km past various bays and campsites brings you to **Yardie Creek**, a steep-walled canyon just a kilometre from the ocean. This is as far south as 2WDs can get in the park but the walk up along the gorge's cliffs is worth the effort. The mouth of the creek silted up in 2001 and, as long as this does not change, 4WDs can easily continue south through the park past Ningaloo Homestead, enjoying beach camping or picnics all the way to Coral Bay, a drive that otherwise takes about half a day.

To Dampier and Karratha

Back on the North West Coastal Highway, it's over 500km from Carnarvon to the industrial twin towns of Dampier and Karratha, with nothing but the occasional roadhouse along the way. At *Nanutarra Roadhouse* a road heads east via the pristine company towns of **Parabardoo** (sealed road), **Tom Price** (70km dirt road) to the fabulous Karijini National Park (see p.766). Further up the highway a road leads north 80km to the cyclone-battered **ONSLOW** (camping and motel ❹), an old coastal settlement bypassed by the highway and most travellers too.

The two young towns of **DAMPIER** and **KARRATHA** are a major industrial conurbation and the Northwest's largest population centre. Dampier is the port for Hamersley Iron's mines at Tom Price, Paraburdoo and Marandoo, linked by a 350-kilometre railway. Karratha was established in 1968 when Dampier's boulder-strewn environs were deemed unsuitable for further expansion, growing dramatically when the **North-West Shelf Natural Gas Project** got underway in the early 1980s. The project collects gas from an offshore platform 135km northwest of Dampier, from where it's piped 1500km to Perth or liquefied for export to Japan and lately China in a huge deal that further guarantees the success of the project. Offshore on the Montebello Islands the Brits experimented with another energy source in the 1950s; several hydrogen bombs were detonated before tests moved down to South Australia.

While being well equipped for shopping, vehicle repairs and other services, the two towns hold little of interest to the traveller apart from tours of the industrial installations or as a launchpad for a mission into Karijini. For those keen and determined enough, exploration of the prolific **Aboriginal engravings** on the **Burrup Peninsula** is possible (enquire at CALM, see p.722). Snappy Gum Safaris (☏08/9185 2141) organizes **day-tours** from Karratha/Dampier to the Roebourne, Cossack and Point Samson area, and further afield to Millstream–Chichester National Park (see overleaf) and Karijini. There is a host of **motels** in Karratha: the *Mercure Inn* (☏08/9185 1155; ❹) is on Searipple Road and the *Karratha International Hotel* is on Millstream Road (☏08/9185 3111; ❹). *Karratha Backpackers* (☏08/9144 4904; dorms $17) is on 110 Welland Way – second turning right after the Shell. **Internet** facilities are at the town library or *Adrienne's Cafe* in Karratha City Shopping Centre and the Northwest's regional **CALM** office is based in the SGIO Building, Welcome Road, Karratha (☏08/9186 8288) – a good place to pick up information and maps on all the national parks of northern WA.

Roebourne, Cossack and Port Samson

ROEBOURNE, established in 1864 (and once the capital of the Northwest), is the oldest existing settlement between Port Gregory and Darwin. The renovated **Old Gaol** is perhaps the most significant survivor in the small town, housing the **tourist office** (Mon–Fri 9am–5pm, Sat 9am–4pm; ☏08/9182 1060) and **museum**. Nowadays the town is a centre for the Aboriginal population displaced by the pastoral settlement of the Northwest. Other nineteenth-century institutional buildings are dotted around the town. Next to the *Victoria Hotel* is *Mount Welcome Motel* (℡08/9182 1282; ❸), and a **caravan park** (℡08/9182 1063; on-site vans ❸) on De Grey Street, at the town's east end, but with better options in Karratha there is little reason to stay here.

COSSACK, once simply known as "the Landing", was the small seaport which begat the town of Roebourne, and it's well worth a look. All early settlers to the Northwest came through Cossack: pastoralists, pearlers and prospectors heading for the goldfields of the East Pilbara. The original tin and timber buildings used to be chained to the ground so they could weather the occasional cyclones. At the end of the nineteenth century the inlet by the quay began silting up and the harbour was moved to nearby Point Samson until Port Hedland's became pre-eminent, and by the 1950s Cossack was all but abandoned, its tram lines to Roebourne long since uprooted for scrap.

This historic "ghost port" has been excellently restored in a matter of only a few years. The **courthouse**, with its museum of the settlement (donation), is the most impressive building, both inside and out, while the **post and telegraph office** is now a small art gallery displaying some fine local work. **Settler's Beach**, past the old cemetery at the end of Perseverance Street, is a sandy and sheltered swimming spot. Hostel **accommodation** is available at the *Cossack Backpackers* (℡08/9182 1190; dorms $19), housed in the old police barracks, but it's become more of a budget family place. Pick-ups can be arranged from the Wickham bus stop (see below). The building also has a **café**.

Beyond Robe River Iron's oddly anachronistic company town of **Wickham** (handy for facilities and services, and on the Perth–Darwin bus route), **POINT SAMSON** has a sharp, windswept, North Atlantic quality, even if it does happen to be 320km inside the tropics. The port, now a popular retirement and "wintering" centre, once had the ignoble distinction of shipping out the blue asbestos mined at Wittenoom, in the Hamersley Ranges. Close to town is **Honeymoon Cove**, which has fine swimming. Gastronomes will relish the **seafood** with a view at the *Trawlers Tavern* first-floor restaurant (daily 6–10pm), better value than the takeaway on the ground floor (daily 11am–2pm & 5–9pm). If you develop a taste for the food, then **places to stay** include *Point Samson Lodge*, 56 Samson Rd (℡08/9187 1052; ❹), which also runs **boat charters**, or the small *Solveig Caravan Park* (℡08/9187 1414; ❸) next to the *Trawlers Tavern*.

Millstream–Chichester National Park

Little more than a scenic drive and an inland oasis of palms and pools along the Fortescue River, the **Millstream-Chichester National Park** (CALM fee; see box on p.722) is only worth a visit if you're coming or going from the Hamersley Ranges. Note, however, that this can entail a three-hundred-kilometre fuel stage. Access from the north breaks off the coastal highway between Roebourne and Whim Creek, passing Pyramid Homestead soon after. Looking back north from the many lookouts atop the **Chichester Ranges** you'll see why the homestead is so named, if you haven't guessed already; the view across this ancient Pilbara landscape is stirring and timeless.

Just inside the park, **Python Pool** is a striking waterhole backed with black and orange cliffs, and cut by the shriek of birds – worth a photo stop. From this point it's a sixty-kilometre run to **MILLSTREAM**, 150km from Roebourne and 183km from Wittenoom, where an old homestead has been converted into an unusually good **visitors centre** (daily 8am–5pm; ☎08/9184 5144). A section describes the predictable rustic bliss of the Yinjibarndi Aborigines of Ngarrari (Millstream), but omits to mention that they were cleared out by pastoralists and ended up around Roebourne. **Chunderwarriner Pool**, a short walk from the homestead, is a lily-dappled pool surrounded by palm trees. The date palms, introduced by Afghan cameleers, have overrun the indigenous Millstream palm, but this does not detract from the unexpectedly luxuriant scene. Black flying foxes hang from the palms' fronds, and Millstream is also a haven for dragonflies and damselflies: 22 species have been recorded here. Walking trails up to 7km long follow the palm- and paperbark-lined Fortescue River to **Crossing** and **Deep Reach pools**, where you can **camp**.

Port Hedland and on to Broome

Whichever way you approach **PORT HEDLAND** you'll spot the dazzlingly white stockpile of industrial salt at the Dampier Salt Works. It's particularly striking as the BHP iron ore coats almost everything else in town in an orangey brown dust. Although the southern suburb of South Hedland is the favoured residential area, the **old port** has an unpretentious charm. The old **town centre** is set on an island surrounded by mangroves and sludge and if you're travelling by bus north along the coast to Broome (600km away) you should hop off at Port Hedland if you want to get to the Karijini gorges (see p.766).

The visitors centre (see below) runs a daily town tour if there are enough interested people, but more popular is the ninety-minute tour of the **BHP loading facility** (Mon–Fri 9.30am; $11) where ships load up with 250,000 tons of iron ore at a time. Whale- and turtle-watching tours are organized in the wet season (roughly Nov–March) by the tourist office, as well as fishing and diving charters and harbour cruises, as incentives to stop travellers leaving town on the next bus. You can also visit the **Royal Flying Doctor** base at the airport (Mon–Fri 10am–2pm; free). Other than that, *Dingo's* backpackers' (see below) arranges **tours** to the Karijini National Park.

Practicalities

The **visitors centre** is on Wedge Street (Mon–Fri 8.30am–5pm, Sat & Sun noon–4pm; ☎08/9173 1711, ⓦwww.porthedlandtouristbureau.com). Overland **buses** stop outside the visitors centre. The **post office** is opposite, as are most banks. Round the corner is the original *Port Hedland Backpackers* (☎08/9173 3282; dorms $18) on 20 Richardson St, looking rather dormant these days. *Dingo's Oasis Backpackers*, 59 Kingsmill St (☎08/9173 1000, ⓦwww.dingotrek.com.au; dorms $18), down the foreshore, may be the reason, offering Karijini tours and its own private "beach" to watch the ore ships glide in. Dingo Treks is planning monthly (May–Oct) six-day runs into the remote Rudall River National Park in the Great Sandy Desert, and waterholes along the way, unless the successful Mardu land claim of 2002 scuppers their plans. The *Pier Hotel* (☎08/9173 1488; ❸) on the Esplanade describes itself as "infamous", and is a safe bet for a beer, band and skimpies. Pricey **motels** are located out of the dust zone south of the port and include the *Hospitality Inn* (☎08/9173 1044 or 13 17 79; ❹) on Webster Street and the *Mercure Inn* (☎08/9172 1222; ❹) on the highway opposite the airport. *Dixon's Caravan Park* (chalets ❸), also on the highway, suits those who just want to crash out, while *Cooke Point Caravan Park* is on Athol Street by the ocean, 8km from town.

Iron-ore dust can't do much for the taste buds, judging by Port Hedland's eateries. Good **restaurants** are confined to the motels. Otherwise, try *Kath's*

The strike that never ended

In 2002 a sculpture was unveiled in Port Hedland's Leak Park to commemorate the Aboriginal stockman's strike of the 1940s. It acknowledged that Australia's once-legendary pastoral wealth was built on the backs of the Aboriginal people, on whose land and cheap labour it depended. Even John Forrest, WA's turn-of-the-twentieth-century premier, pastoralist and former explorer, conceded that "many of us could not be in the position we are today without native labour on our stations".

By the 1940s Australia was producing a sixth of the world's mutton and a quarter of its wool. In the Northwest, two million sheep grazed vast tracts of meagre land into the dustbowls of today, a marginal enterprise made economical by the employment of black stockmen paid barely $2 a week. The archaic **Native Administration Act** of the time protected the interests of rural industry by hampering mobility and sanctioning low or nonexistent pay for black workers.

Around this time **Don McLeod**, a white prospector encouraged **Clancy McKenna** and **Dooley Binbin** to defy their conditions and, after several years of painstaking preparation, eight hundred black workers simultaneously walked off the stations in the Port Hedland/Nullagine region on May 1, 1946. Police were instructed to harass the two camps established near Port Hedland and east of Marble Bar, and arrested McKenna and Binbin for communist subversion. Postwar food coupons were withheld, so the strikers returned to traditional ways of feeding and trading among themselves. Port Hedland was at this time a small town with an "official" (white) population of just 150 and a "mob" of 400 strikers down the road. Jittery police arrested a visiting mediator, Padre Hodge, for being "within five miles of a congregation of natives", adding further support to the strike, coverage of which was largely censored from the national press.

In 1949 things came to a head, and a **station-to-station march** was organized calling all remaining workers to join the strike. Arrest for such defiance was certain, and the strikers cheerfully offered to fill up the jail at Marble Bar and others throughout the Northwest. Only when the Seamen's Union banned the handling of "slave station" wool did the government hastily concede to McLeod's proposals – though they swiftly reneged on the deal. All through the 1950s McLeod employed and assisted the strikers in mining ventures around Marble Bar until the big mining companies began taking an interest in the Pilbara's mineral wealth and pushed them off their claims. The strikers never returned to the stations, demonstrating black assertion long before the 1960s civil rights campaigning in the USA or the indigenous Australian land claims of the 1970s.

Kitchen, a **snack bar** on Wedge Street, or the *Esplanade Hotel* on the Esplanade, where you might be served by a skimpy.

   Internet facilities are at the visitors centre on Wedge Street or in the laundromat nearby.

Port Hedland to Broome

The six-hundred-kilometre run from Port Hedland to Broome is one of world-class boredom, a dreary plain of spinifex and mulga marking the northern edge of the Great Sandy Desert. Halfway to Broome, the *Sandfire Roadhouse* (6am–midnight) provides a welcome fuel stop before the 286-kilometre stretch to *Roebuck Roadhouse*.

   Despite your proximity to the ocean, beach access is only possible at the promisingly named **Eighty Mile Beach**. There is nothing to do at the palmy caravan park there (shop, fuel; cabins ❸), ten corrugated kilometres off the highway, but a drive along the beach at low tide (possible in an ordinary car if you're careful) is always exhilarating. The next beach access and a similar caravan park is 180km east of Sandfire, at **Point Smith**.

If you're coming from Broome and heading for Karijini there's an interesting dirt-road alternative that bypasses Port Hedland. One hundred kilometres after Sandfire, turn south onto the sandy Borehole Road, climb into the ranges at Shay Gap and then cross the De Grey River near Muccan station. From here work your way through to **Marble Bar**, 270km from Sandfire, where you'll find motels and a service station. After Marble Bar, head southwest to Hillside station and then west to Woodstock Community, where you soon rejoin the tarmac heading down to the *Munjina Roadhouse*, 250km from Marble Bar and 42km from Wittenoom (see p.768). You save only 20km, but it's a lovely, if lonely, drive through the ochre ranges of the East Pilbara.

Inland to the Pilbara

About a thousand kilometres north of Perth are the ancient, mineral-rich highlands of the **Pilbara**, a geographical area north of the twenty-sixth parallel and including the highest point in WA. The world's richest surface deposits of **iron ore** were developed here in the 1950s by the legendary Lang Hancock (see p.744). Rich discoveries continue to be made today as several mining companies go about reducing mountains into pits while their private railways cart the ore to the coast for shipping to Japan's steel-hungry industries. Surrounding the huge open-cast mine sites are vast and arid pastoral properties, recovering from early over-grazing and in the centre of this region is the underplayed grandeur of the **Karijini National Park**, mile for mile, WA's most spectacular national park. Offering dramatic scenery, the main attraction is the **gorges** cut deep into the Hamersley Range's north-facing escarpment. Here the former mining town of **Wittenoom** sits at the mouth of the main gorge and, although not officially approved, makes a lovely place to park up and enjoy the region.

The Great Northern Highway

Scenically, there's precious little to commend the **Great Northern Highway**'s 1635-kilometre inland section from Perth to Port Hedland – most people shoot through in two long days and, with the honourable exception of the Hamersleys, they miss very little. Overland buses operate a service three times a week between Perth and Port Hedland, stopping at the few places along the highway, including the *Munjina Roadhouse* (see p.767), 190km north of Newman and 260km south of Port Hedland.

Among the half-dozen towns along this inland route, only the semi-abandoned **CUE**, 650km north of Perth, retains some character from the gold-drush era of the 1890s. A **tourist information centre** on Big Bell Road has details on the area's rich history.

MEEKATHARRA, 115km north of Cue, is a mining and pastoral centre, with a couple of century-old **hotels**; the *Royal Mail* on the main road still looks good but accommodation behind the facades is far from luxurious. You can listen to shunting road trains all night at the caravan park behind the *Ampol* or take cover in the *Auski Inland Motel* (☎08/9981 1433; ◑). On Saturday nights the Picture Gardens theatre at the top of town is the place to be. From Meekatharra, its 120km of dirt to forlorn Wiluna, then another 600km of dull bitumen to Kalgoorlie (for a description of this route, see p.746), while in the other direction Carnarvon (itself no paradise, see p.757) lies at the end of a good seven-hundred-kilometre dirt road. North of Meekatharra a road sign marks the **26th parallel** and welcomes you to the fabled "Nor'west". As if to underline the isolation and extremes symbolized by "the 26th", an unvarying 350-kilometre stretch leads to Newman, with only the **Collier Range National Park** – nothing more than a series of 4WD tracks – and a roadhouse or two along the way.

NEWMAN was built to serve what is now the world's largest open-cut iron-ore mine, and the **mine tours** (Mon–Sat 8.30am, plus Mon–Fri 1pm during peak season; 1hr 30min; $10; enclosed shoes necessary), departing from the **tourist information centre** (Mon–Sat 8am–5pm, Sun 9am–1pm; ☏08/9175 2964) on Newman Drive, are the main reason you might want to stop here. The tours clearly demonstrate the simplicity and scale of the operation as **Mount Whaleback** is gradually turned inside out and dispatched to the Far East to return as Toyotas and Mazdas. Local companies run **tours** (see box on p.768), lasting between half a day and three days, to local waterholes and the rarely visited Rudall River National Park to the east (see below). The town has a pair of swish **motels** (both ➍) that offer discounts if booked though the tourist information centre, and two **caravan parks** (on-site vans ➋), as well as a busy shopping centre.

Marble Bar and Rudall River National Park

From Newman a dirt road leads north for 300km through the scenic East Pilbara to **NULLAGINE** and **MARBLE BAR**, the latter notorious for being Australia's hottest town, in 1923–24 clocking up 160 days over 38°C. This is the sole reason many visitors come to "the Bar", misnamed after a colourful bar of jasper by the Coolingan River 5km south of town. For an overnight stay, there's a **caravan park**, a **motel** (☏08/9176 1166; ➌) and the town's famed, windowless *Ironclad Hotel* (☏08/9176 1066; ➌) – a good place to get some drinking done or, if you're a "sheila", be stared at.

Rudall River National Park, 300km east of Newman, is an undeveloped national park, designated more for reasons of conservation than recreation, and also the site of some ultra-remote Aboriginal communities including Jiggalong, as featured in the 2002 film *Rabbit Proof Fence*. Perhaps not by coincidence, in the same year the Mardu people won a long-fought land claim that gave them a huge chunk of the Great Sandy Desert, although the park was not included. The park is accessible only to self-sufficient 4WDs from Newman (easier) or via Telfer to the north (permit needed), or off the Canning Stock Route; tours from Newman or Port Hedland also visit the park.

Karijini National Park

The **Karijini National Park** (CALM fee; see box on p.722) is huge, with a vast unvisited section to the south, separated by the BHP Yandicoogina mine railway. Apart from the impressive gorges, it is the distinctive blend of white-trunked cadjiput gums and pale green spinifex spread across the ox-blood ranges which makes the Pilbara more resplendent than the better known Kimberley. Most of the roads in the park are dirt but usually kept in good condition and possibly on the way to being sealed; indeed, barring thunderstorms, the park remains accessible throughout the year.

The **gorges** themselves can be broadly divided into three groups: those in the east near the visitors centre, the central cluster – the Four Gorges area – and those in the far west. They offer some **spectacular lookouts** as well as adventurous walks that can evolve into exposed or slippery scrambles – you can still test your mettle in Karijini with nothing more than guard rails and emphatic warning signs. Take heed of these "Gorge Risk" warnings or take advantage of tours and their guides' experience. Deaths and several accidents have occurred, but **rangers** are rarely seen.

If you're driving through the park, note that distances can be deceptive: a full tour of all the gorges can involve over 250km. With Yampire Gorge now closed, it's easiest to appreciate most of the park while travelling via Parabardoo/Tom Price, *Munjina Roadhouse* or Karratha/Port Hedland.

The visitors centre and the eastern gorges

On the east side of the park, around 36km from the turn-off on the Great Northern Highway is the swish new **visitors centre** (daily 9am–4pm; ℡08/9189 8121), a witty construction of massive iron plate symbolizing the riches of the Pilbara. Inside, exhibits concentrate on the "Aboriginal care-of-the-land" theme – a subject that, unless new signs have been erected, is not actually pursued anywhere else in the park, even though evidence of Aboriginal occupation exists. Predictably, it's the selective view used by many national parks to underline a fashionable eco-message while leaving us clueless as to the bigger picture of Australian indigenous culture.

North of the visitors centre crossroads is the old exit from Yampire Gorge, while a right turn leads 10km to the **Dales Gorge** area (with camping). Here the idyllic Fortescue Falls makes a great lookout or a place to swim. With half a day to spare a visit to the falls can be joined with a great six-kilometre walk to Fern Pool and Circular Pool beyond, with plenty of water to cool off in along the way. If you're still feeling adventurous you can explore further up or down Dales Gorge, but remember you will be on your own.

West of the visitors centre, on the way to the Four Gorges area, **Kalamina Gorge** offers good walks along its bed without too much climbing and scrambling,

The Four Gorges area

Heading west from the visitors centre towards the **Four Gorges area** you reach a turn-off ending at an impressive lookout onto the tiered amphitheatre of **Joffre Falls** (usually just a trickle) which can be easily reached and crossed along a spinifex-fringed path. There is camping nearby and the track leads on to **Knox Gorge**. Here you'll find another dramatic lookout down through the gorge below. A loose rubbly track leads down into the gorge which gradually gets ever-narrower and slippier until its very hard to walk – bridging the walls is easier (allow 30min from the lookout). Progress ends looking down the exhilarating (to say the least) "Knox Slide", not something to even consider without skilled supervision and equipment as this one-way slide leading into the green waters of Red Gorge (see below) cannot be done in reverse.

Back on the main road from the visitors centre, a turning north passes a campsite and ends at a car park on the spur between **Hancock** and **Weano gorges**. From here, it's a five-minute walk to **Oxer's Lookout**, surveying an impressive view of the confluence of four gorges. The real Oxer's Lookout, with the original plaque, is ahead of the secure viewing platform, but has been deemed too perilous for day-trippers. Straight ahead is **Red Gorge**, which runs on into Wittenoom Gorge and the Settlement. Back a bit on the Hancock (south) side of the spur is a more impressive viewing platform which looks straight down to the mouth of Hancock Gorge as it runs into Junction Pool (see p.769) with its stand of tall cadjiput trees. The "Miracle Mile", with its

Tours of the Karijini

All Terrain Safaris (☎1800 633 456, ⓦwww.allterrain.com.au) runs four-day tours between Exmouth and Broome from May to October and includes the "Miracle Mile".

Dingo Trek (☎08/9173 1000, ⓦwww.dingotrek.com.au) runs three-day tours from Port Hedland deep into the park's gorges as well as the Pilbara region.

Karijini Day Tours (☎08/9188 1670) out of Tom Price offers an easy scenic day-tour to all the gorges' lookouts from around $80 (with lunch) as well as longer tours.

Newman Eco Tours (☎08/9175 2944) runs 4WD tours to beauty spots around Newman and into Karijini.

Snappy Gum Safaris (☎08/9185 2141, ⓦwww.snappygum.karratha.com), based in Karratha, runs two- to four-day tours through the Pilbara including the "Miracle Mile".

origins as a 1960s character-building exercise for Perth schoolboys, starts from the car park, descending over loose rock and a ladder into Hancock and returning up Weano Gorge. A thrilling couple of hours swimming, sliding and climbing, this should only be attempted with a guide, although it's quite easy and fun to reach **Kermit's Pool** (30min) where the main warning signs start. For the less adventurous, the short walk down the steps into Weano Gorge ending at **Handrail Pool** is popular but less impressive (30min return).

Mount Bruce, the western gorges and Tom Price

From the Four Gorges the road continues across the roof of the Pilbara to **Mount Bruce**, at 1235m WA's second-highest peak and climbable along a six-kilometre track from where you can survey the Marandoo mine. At this point you've rejoined the sealed road linking Tom Price with the Great Northern Highway.

Depending on where you're going, it's now quite a detour to visit **Hamersley Gorge**, just outside the northwestern corner of the park, 48km west of Wittenoom. With its spa-like pool and acutely folded beds of blue-grey and orange rock, it's unlike any of the other gorges and a bit of exploring up- and downstream could easily fill a day here. Just east of the Hamersley Gorge turn-off, the road passes through **Rio Tinto Gorge**, which bears an extraordinary resemblance to a box-canyon film set from 1950s westerns.

TOM PRICE is the government-approved base for exploring Karijini. The **tourist office** (Mon–Fri 8.30am–5pm; ☎08/9188 1112), on Central Road, organizes daily ninety-minute **tours** ($15) of Hamersley Iron's mine. The least expensive of the two **motels** is the *Mercure Inn* (☎08/9189 1101; ❹) on Central Road. Your other option is a caravan park (cabins ❸). Although it's not on the bus route, the town has all the services you'd expect, including a couple of nondescript cafés near the **supermarket**.

Wittenoom and Wittenoom Gorge

At each end of **WITTENOOM**, warning signs proclaim the possible health hazard incurred by entering the town as a result of the asbestos mining carried out here from 1937 to 1966, by – among others – the young Rolf Harris. It's estimated that one in ten ex-miners and former inhabitants have died of diseases associated with inhaling asbestos dust, so nowadays, for legal reasons the sole public call box is absurdly situated just outside the town's tainted limits.

In its natural state **blue asbestos** or crocidolite is a harmless and unusual fibrous mineral, readily found in Yampire and upper Wittenoom gorges; it's only the **dust** produced during crushing that can be lethal. Unfortunately, tailings from the mine were once used to grade the town's streets, leaving not only the millers but also all those resident at the time susceptible to disease and eligible for compensation. These days, resurfacing has long been completed and, unless you're kicking about in the tailings, the air contains no more harmful particles of asbestos than most urban centres. The emotional overreaction to the "Town of Death" is neatly summed up in the bumper sticker available at the Gem Shop that states "I've been to Wittenoom and lived". Wittenoom has been eliminated from government publications and maps, and some tourist offices have been misinforming visitors, claiming that the town no longer exists or the access road requires 4WD – none of this is true. Perhaps because of its tragic history, and certainly due to the intransigence of its remaining twenty inhabitants, the town, which successive governments wanted razed long ago, possesses an intangible ambience like few other places in WA. In the 1950s it was the biggest settlement in the Northwest but today the empty lots and roaming euros (a type of wallaby) speak of a ghost town not prepared to die.

Although a few years ago the government failed in court to have power and water services cut, the weather played into their hands in 2001 when the track up Yampire Gorge was destroyed by floods, cutting direct access to Karijini from the town. The track remains closed, though not actually blocked at either end, and a good 4WD can just get through the numerous creek crossings (up to a metre deep). Don't try it in a rental unless you want to risk a huge bill and possibly a fine.

Three times a week the Perth–Port Hedland **bus** stops at the *Munjina Roadhouse* (T08/9176 6988; ➍) on the Great Northern Highway, 42km from town. If you call in advance, the *Guest House* (see below) may pick you up. As far as services in town go, there's a **post office** at the Gem Shop on Sixth Avenue, which also dispenses **tourist information** (daily 8am–6pm; T08/9189 7096), including a detailed **mud map** of the national park as well as some basic groceries. If you're planning to stay a few days bring what you need.

There are two **places to stay** in Wittenoom, neither fancy but both cheap. *Wittenoom Holiday Homes* (T08/9189 7096; ➋; enquire at the Gem Shop) offers complete three-bedroom houses for rent and the *Wittenoom Guest House*, the green bungalow by the "church" (T08/9189 7060; dorms $20, rooms ➋), is a lovely old convent with a screened verandah and camping in the well-kept garden.

Wittenoom itself is at the mouth of **Wittenoom Gorge**, not in the park but with several pools inviting you for a cooling dip. At the end of the sealed road on which euros abound might still stand the cluster of buildings known as **Settlement**, 11km from town. Maintained by caretakers for thirty years for the former asbestos mining company, Hancock–Wright, it may now house the engineers who've been charged with dismantling the ageing **mill** on the west side of the gorge, surrounded by the lethal tailings. From the Settlement, it's possible to trek up to the dramatic entrance to **Red Gorge** (2hr), and then trek and swim (including some long stretches) for another hour, past the slender mouth of Knox Gorge to **Junction Pool** far below Oxer's Lookout (see p.767). From this apparent dead end, the two halves of the "Miracle Mile" meet to tempt the truly intrepid, but unless you've already been initiated, this should not be attempted without a guide. All in all, the above is a hard day's adventuring out of Wittenoom, with a vehicle best left as far up Wittenoom Gorge as you can get.

WESTERN AUSTRALIA | Inland to the Pilbara

Broome and around

"Slip into Broometime" is the well-worn local aphorism that captures the tropical charm of **BROOME**, a popular and unexpectedly classy town of fourteen thousand people, which clings to a peninsula hanging over Roebuck Bay. William Dampier, the English buccaneer-explorer, passed the area in 1699 while on the run from an irate Spanish flotilla, and nearly two hundred years later the Djuleun Aborigines repelled an early fleet of prospective pastoralists. However, the imminent discovery of literally heaps of pearl shell soon led to the "**Pearl Rush**" of the 1880s and firmly set Broome on the colonial map of Australia.

It was actually the nacre-lined shells, or **mother-of-pearl**, rather than the pearls themselves, which brought brief fortune to the town. By 1910, eighty percent of the world's pearl shell, used in the manufacture of buttons, came from Broome, whose rich (though not always harmonious) ethnic mix developed at this time. "Chinatown" teemed with raucous and sometimes rioting Filipinos, Japanese, Arabs, Malays and Kupangers (from Timor), servicing the four hundred luggers and their crews involved in the dangerous business of diving for shells. While Broome's cemeteries steadily filled, perhaps one shell in a thousand produced a perfect example of the silvery pearls unique to this area.

Stagnation followed both world wars, although the Japanese, masters in the art of culturing pearls, invested in pearl-farming ventures around Broome's well-suited coastal habitat. Things improved with the sealing of the coastal highway from Perth in the early 1980s and the philanthropic interest of the English businessman Alistair McAlpine, who fell for Broome and subsequently kicked off its renovation. Tasteful development and refurbishment increased the town's oriental and pearling mystique, enhanced by the sweeping expanse of **Cable Beach**, **Gantheaume Point**'s brick-red outcrops and the Indian Ocean's stunning turquoise hue. It's not all rosy however: residents suffer the same problems as in Carnarvon, though to a lesser degree and the town's remoteness and lack of company town subsidies make it expensive. But while many continue to be drawn in and the adjacent Kimberley's appeal catches on, Broome's prosperity looks set to continue.

Arrival, information and getting around

Buses arrive right by the tourist office on the corner of Bagot Street and Broome Road where minibuses and taxis meet all arrivals. The **airport terminal**, round the corner on McPherson Street, couldn't be more central, less than a kilometre west of Chinatown and a five-minute walk to the two main hostels. The well-organized **tourist office**, off Broome Road (Mon–Fri 8am–5pm, Sat & Sun 9am–4pm; ☎08/9192 2222, ⓕ9192 2063, ⓦwww.ebroome.com/tourism), dishes out local guides and town maps to help you find your way around the dispersed and sometimes confusing layout of Broome. The town's **bus service** ($3, day-passes $10) runs daily between the town and Cable Beach, via most of Broome's accommodation centres, and finally returns outside the super-swish *Cable Beach Inter-Continental Resort* at 6.15pm. Timetables are available at the tourist office or in the town guide.

Accommodation

Most of the **hotels** are in the southern part of town, and the **hostels** congregate around Chinatown, with self-contained apartments in resorts located on

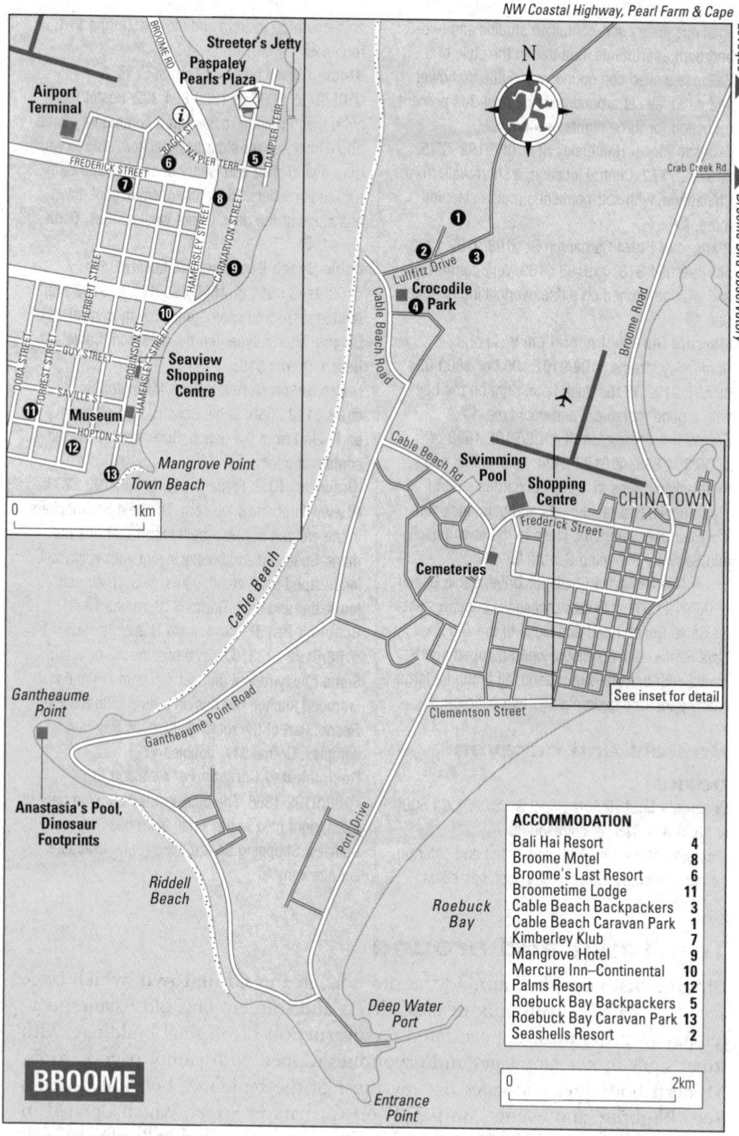
NW Coastal Highway, Pearl Farm & Cape Leveque
Crab Creek Rd
Broome Bird Observatory
N
Broome Road
Streeter's Jetty
Paspaley Pearls Plaza
Airport Terminal
BROOME RD
BAGOT ST
NAPIER TERR
DAMPIER TERR
FREDERICK STREET
HAMERSLEY STREET
CARNARVON STREET
HERBERT STREET
GUY STREET
ROBINSON ST
HAMERSLEY ST
DORA STREET
FORREST STREET
SAVILLE ST
HOPTON ST
Seaview Shopping Centre
Museum
Mangrove Point
Town Beach
0 1km
Lullfitz Drive
Crocodile Park
Cable Beach Road
Cable Beach Rd
Swimming Pool
Shopping Centre
CHINATOWN
Frederick Street
Cemeteries
Cable Beach
See inset for detail
Clementson Street
Gantheaume Point
Gantheaume Point Road
Anastasia's Pool, Dinosaur Footprints
Port Drive
Riddell Beach
Roebuck Bay
Deep Water Port
Entrance Point
BROOME
0 2km
ACCOMMODATION
Bali Hai Resort 4
Broome Motel 8
Broome's Last Resort 6
Broometime Lodge 11
Cable Beach Backpackers 3
Cable Beach Caravan Park 1
Kimberley Klub 7
Mangrove Hotel 9
Mercure Inn–Continental 10
Palms Resort 12
Roebuck Bay Backpackers 5
Roebuck Bay Caravan Park 13
Seashells Resort 2

Cable Beach. These resorts can represent good value if there's a group of you, but some don't have restaurants or bars. Prices are relatively expensive up here, but if you're down south and want to make a visit, it's possible to pick up a week's "flight and resort" aimed at the domestic market. Ask at travel agents.

Hotels and resorts

Bali Hai Resort 6 Murray St, Cable Beach ⓣ08/9191 3100 or 1800 807 061, ⓕ9191 3133, ⓦwww.balihairesort.com. Sumptuous and spacious luxury self-contained studios and two-bedroom apartments, outfitted in the style of a Balinese walled compound with outdoor shower and patio, all set around a shady pool. Ten percent reduction for three nights or more. **❻**

Broome Motel Hamersley St ☏ 08/9192 7775, ℻ 9192 7772. Central location, a short walk from Chinatown, with self-contained rooms sleeping three. **❹**

Mangrove Hotel Carnarvon St ☏ 08/9192 1303 or 1800 094 818, ℻ 9193 5169. Very comfortable and well positioned on a rise overlooking Roebuck Bay. **❺**

Mercure Inn–Continental Cnr Weld and Hamersley streets ☏ 08/9192 1002 or 1800 094 822, ℻ 9192 1715. Plush hotel right on the bay with a good restaurant and pool area. **❻**

Palms Resort Hopton St ☏ 08/9192 1898 or 1800 094 848, ℻ 9192 2424. Apartments and motel-style rooms in a tropical garden setting. Three pools, two restaurants and bars, including the *Beer and Satay Hut*, close to the town beach and Seaview Shopping Centre. **❺**

Seashells Resort 4 Challenor Drive, Cable Beach ☏ 08/9192 6111, ⓦ www.seashells.com.au. Just off Cable Beach Road and close to the *Old Zoo Café Restaurant*. Spacious, well-equipped apartments with balconies or a patio, all around a large shady pool. One bedroom **❻**, two bedroom **❼**

Hostels and caravan parks

Broome's Last Resort Bagot St ☏ 08/9193 5000 or 1800 801 918, ⓔ lastresortyha @smartchat.com.au. A bit congested and catering for party animals, with a small pool, bar, bikes,

coin-operated lockers and air-con. Dorms $18, rooms **❸**

Broometime Lodge 59 Forrest St ☏ & ℻ 08/9193 5067 or 1800 804 322. Hostel/motel hybrid with private rooms but a communal atmosphere, suitable for older backpackers able to wash their own dishes and weary of snorers and 6am rucksack rustlers. Big kitchen, small pool, town bus stops at the door. Offers weekly rates. Book ahead. **❸**

Cable Beach Backpackers Lullfitz Drive ☏ 08/9193 5511 or 1800 655 011, ℻ 9193 5532. A change from the sometimes rowdy central Broome alternatives. Ten minutes from Cable Beach. Dorms $18.

Cable Beach Caravan Park Millington Rd ☏ 08/9192 2066. Cable Beach's only caravan park, 2km from the beach. Bunkhouse $19, self-contained cabins **❻**

Kimberley Klub Frederick St, ☏ 08/9192 3233, ⓦ www.kimberleyklub.com. The best backpackers in the west; a purpose-built resort that hits the mark. Spacious and breezy layout with volleyball, landscaped pool, email, bikes, coin-op air-con, tours, bar and café. Dorms $18, rooms **❸**

Roebuck Bay Backpackers Napier Terrace ☏ 08/9192 1183, ⓔ roey@broome.wa.com.au. Some musty rooms (but several with TV) and a cramped kitchen put this on a level with the *Last Resort*. Part of the rocking *Roebuck Bay Hotel* complex. Dorms $17, doubles **❸**

Roebuck Bay Caravan Park Walcott St ☏ 08/9192 1366. The best-located caravan park in town, right next to the small town beach and Seaview Shopping Centre. Bike rental available. On-site vans **❸**

The Town and around

Broome first flourished around the old port area in **Chinatown**, which once accommodated a lively mix of pearl divers and seamen. This old Asiatic quarter has seen the most concentrated reconstruction of original buildings, with street signs in five languages and payphones topped with jaunty pagoda roofs. Modern boutiques and cafés occupy most of the buildings, but Sun Pictures (see "Nightlife and events" on p.774) on Carnarvon Street, which opened in 1916 (making it as old as Hollywood itself), is one of the oldest "walk-ins" still in use today. During the daytime you can take in the virtually unchanged interior and see photographs showing the segregated seating codes of the old days (tours Mon–Fri 11am & 2pm; $4). At the end of the street is the **post office** and the Paspaley Pearls Plaza **shopping centre**. The dilapidated Streeter's Jetty runs into the mangroves off Dampier Terrace where you'll find **Pearl Luggers** (daily 9am–5pm), a long-overdue free exposition of Broome's pearling heritage, offering a close look at a couple of luggers, as well as informative one-hour tours (11am; $20).

A walk down Hamersley Street, past the 1888 courthouse on the corner of Frederick Street, leads to what was the rich end of the old town, where masters and merchants once lived in splendid, airy bungalows such as **Captain Gregory's House**, now a brewery near the junction with Carnarvon Street. Next door, *Matso's Store* (daily 10am–5pm) displays local artwork and is a cool spot for an alfresco lunch.

Next to the old Seaview Shopping Centre (daily 8am–6pm), the Customs House is home to the local **museum** (May–Nov Mon–Fri 10am–4pm, Sat & Sun 10am–1pm; Dec–April daily 10am–1pm; $3). Naturally focusing on the town's maritime traditions, and with a pleasing "junk shop" appearance, it could easily occupy a couple of hours. Round the back, the old **Pioneer Cemetery** overlooks **Town Beach**, the nearest to the town centre. From the jetty, very low tides reveal the remains of Dutch sea planes bombed by the Japanese in 1942. This is also the best vantage point for observing the "**Staircase to the Moon**", the overrated lunar reflections in the mud flats, which occur for a few nights each month, around the full phase of the moon. Dates and precise times can be obtained from the tourist office.

Gantheaume Point, Cable Beach and Broome Bird Observatory

The outskirts of Broome offer a number of interesting attractions, and a full day could be spent cycling along the following route, which ends at Cable Beach, 6km from town on the ocean side of the peninsula. Alternatively you can take the bus or rent a car or scooter (see p.775).

Just past the turning for Cable Beach, off Frederick Street, is the old **cemetery** from the pearling years. The Japanese section's enigmatic headstones (refurbished by an anonymous philanthropic countryman) testify to the nine hundred lives lost in the hazardous search for mother-of-pearl. The 1908 cyclone alone cost the lives of over 150 men, five percent of the workforce at that time. The Chinese cemetery next door is less cared for, and the Muslim and Aboriginal graveyards at the back are barely distinguishable.

Continuing down Port Drive for 5km, a right turn onto the nine-kilometre part-dirt road section leads to **Riddell Beach**. Walk right along the shore, past the outcrops weathered by eons of wind and water, to **Gantheaume Point**, where the dark red-sandstone formations contrast sharply with the pearly-white expanse of Cable Beach stretching north. The old **lighthouse** is now a beacon, but the **pool** built by the former keeper for his disabled wife, Anastasia, remains among the tidal rocks. A cast of some 120-million-year-old **dinosaur footprints** is set in the rocks – the originals are out to sea and only visible at extremely low tides. Casts of the prints can be seen at the *Broometime Lodge* (see opposite). More dinosaur footprints were found on Aboriginal land north of Cable Beach in 1996, but were bizarrely cut out of the rock and still remain unfound.

Named after the nineteenth-century telegraph cable which came ashore here, **Cable Beach** extends for an immaculate 22km north of Gantheaume Point. Cars are permitted onto the beach north of the rocks, near the access ramp, as well as down a ramp just before Gantheaume Point. The area north of the rocks is also a nudist beach. The *Cable Beach Tea Rooms* overlooking the beach serves great meals, as does the *Diver's Camp Tavern* and bottle shop, on Cable Beach Road. Windsurfers and sailboards are available on the beach during the season.

Broome is loosely regarded as the very westernmost limit of saltwater **crocodiles**. The **Broome Crocodile Park** (April–Oct Mon–Sat 10am–5pm, Sun

2.30–5pm; Nov–March daily except Sat 3.30–5pm; guided tours at 3pm; $15), on Cable Beach Road, can show you hundreds of these fascinating beasts at close quarters.

Roebuck Bay, on Broome's eastern flank, is on the flight path for thousands of migratory wading birds – a third of Australia's species have been seen here. The **Broome Bird Observatory** (℡08/9193 5600; free; ❸) 25km from town (last 9km dirt) welcomes day and overnight visitors. There are walks through the bushland around the observatory, with tours and courses also offered for those interested in local fauna, feathered or otherwise.

Eating and entertainment

Not surprisingly, the food in Broome is distinctly oriental in flavour. The customary fast-food outlets and a couple of health-food shops are also prominent, while some hotels have their own very reputable restaurants.

Bloom's Café Restaurant (7.30am–late), on Carnarvon Street, is one of the town's best **cafés**, with an airy jarrah interior, great drinks, snacks, meals and vegetarian breakfasts. *Henry's* has coffee and meals with a view of the corner of Carnarvon and Short streets, while over the road there's the *Shady Lane Cafe*, off Johnny Chi Lane, featuring good lunch choices. Next to the Checkpoint Shell Service Station on Hamersley Street are a couple of **takeaways**: *Noodlefish* does Thai food and their soups are a meal in themselves. A further option, at 12 Napier Terrace, is the *Sheba Lane Garden Restaurant*, specializing in fish dishes. The *Beer & Satay Hut* at the *Palms Resort* (see p.772; entrance on Walcott Street) is a good outdoor alternative to the **pub food** at the *Roebuck Bay Hotel*.

For a proper **restaurant** meal, the hard-to-find *Carlotta* (Wed–Sun 4pm to late; ℡08/9192 7606), tucked away in Jones Place off Dora Street opposite Saville Street, serves great wood-fired pizzas and pasta, and you can BYO. With its verandah, *Murray's*, on Dampier Terrace, is a good place for Asian and seafood dishes. *Sanga's Thai Food* on Coghlan Street is better value and also does takeaway. Out at the fancy *Cable Beach Inter-Continental* resort there are no less than five classy restaurants to turn your wallet inside out; the least expensive is *Lord Mac's* which offers ocean views with your burgers, salad and pasta, or try the *Old Zoo Café Restaurant* by the Crocodile Park. Closer to town, *Charters*, at the *Mangrove Hotel* on Carnarvon Street is the best of the hotel restaurants and also has views of the ocean. Out by the Deep Water Port, Broome now has its own branch of Derby's acclaimed *Wharf Restaurant* and takeaway.

Nightlife and events

Broome's raging **pub** is the *Roebuck Bay Hotel* on Napier Terrace, with live entertainment and happy hours. The least rough of the three bars here is the *Pearlers' Rest*. The *Divers' Camp Tavern* at Cable Beach comes a close second and usually gets the bands after the "*Roey*". Two **nightclubs** in Chinatown are open until 2am: the *Nippon Inn* on Dampier Terrace and *Tokyo Joes* round the corner on Napier Terrace, with banks of pool tables. If you prefer **real ale** to tinned lager pay a visit to the Broome Brewery at *Matso's Store* at the end of Hamersley Street where all sorts of local fermentations await you. Alternatively, the *Sunset Bar* at the *Cable Beach Inter-Continental* has pricey **cocktails** but is worth the splurge at dusk.

For a uniquely "Broometime" experience, Sun Pictures **walk-in cinema** in Chinatown is a real treat: watch the latest movies while mosquitoes nibble your ankles and the odd light aircraft comes in low across the screen. The town also has a conventional new twin-screen on the corner of Weld Street and Napier Terrace.

The tourist office has information on various events, such as the **Broome Fringe Arts Festival**, usually held in early June, a celebration of local artiness and culture. However, the big one is the **Shinju Matsuri**, or Festival of the Pearl, in September – it lasts over a week and attracts people from all over the country. The town celebrates its ethnic diversity, and the pearl which created it, with the crowning of the Pearl Queen and a beach concert, finishing up with a huge fireworks display. Broome can get packed out for the Shinju, so unless you want to end up camping miles away, book your accommodation in advance. Exact dates for both festivals can be checked with the tourist office.

Listings

Bicycle and scooter rental Broome Cycle Centre, next to the Shell in Chinatown and also outside the zoo on Cable Beach. Scooters $40 per 24hr.
Buses McCafferty's (☎13 14 99 or 08/9321 6211) visits Broome on its Darwin–Perth run as does Integrity Coach Lines (☎08/9226 1399 or 1800 226 339, ⓦwww.integritycoachlines.com.au). You can book buses at the visitors centre.
Car rental Besides the big companies (which can offer relocation deals), try Broome Car Rentals, next to the Shell on Hamersley Street (☎08/9192 2110), or Woody's, Dampier Terrace (☎08/9192 1791); both do local runabouts and offer some of the cheapest 4WDs in town. Broome Discount Hire Car on McPherson St (☎08/9193 3100), has small cars from $65 per day, while at Just Broome (☎08/9193 6636) bangers start at just $35 a day.
Hospital Robinson St ☎08/9192 9222.
Internet access Best place overall is the Telecentre, at the top end of Dampier Terrace.
Police ☎08/9192 1212.
Post office Carnarvon St, WA 6725. Next to Paspaley Pearls Plaza.

Taxi ☎08/9192 1133 or 1800 880 330.
Tours Broome Day Tours (☎1800 801 068) organizes daily three-hour historic tours, plus trips out to Willie Creek Pearl Farm (see overleaf); Ships of the Desert (☎08/9192 6833) has sunset camel rides along Cable Beach, though Broome Camel Safaris (☎0419 916 101) may be a cheaper option; Broome Aviation (☎08/9192 1369) and King Leopold Air (☎08/9193 7155) offer scenic flights over the region; while Seair Broome (☎08/9192 6208) uses sea-planes. For more unusual jaunts on Harleys, helicopters, hovercrafts and hang-gliders, enquire at the tourist office (see p.770). For excursions to the Kimberley, Flak Trak Tours (☎08/9192 7778) has 4WD tours for small groups, including one-day Cape Leveque and up to eight-day West Kimberley/Gibb River Road tours; Over The Top Adventure Tours (☎08/9192 5211, ⓦ www.4wdtourswa.com) offers one- to five-day packages; and All Terrain Safaris (☎1800 633 456, ⓦwww.allterrain.com.au) does seven- to twelve-day tours including the Gibb River Road, Mitchell Plateau and the Bungles, leaving every Tuesday (May–Oct) at around $130 a day, using swags but a better bus than most.

The Dampier Peninsula and Cape Leveque

About 10km outside Broome, just after the turn-off for the Bird Observatory, a road leads north to the Aboriginal lands of the northern **Dampier Peninsula**. Continuing down this turn-off you soon come to the **Willie Creek Pearl Farm** but after this you're best off arming yourself with a 4WD campervan, or better still someone else's 4WD, as the 200-kilometre **Cape Leveque track** is as rough as they come. If you plan staying at any of the three Aboriginal communities on the Cape, booking in advance is essential.

Willie Creek Pearl Farm and the Western Peninsula

Thirty-five kilometres north from Broome (follow the signs), most of which is along a dirt track and tidal flat, the **Willie Creek Pearl Farm** (June–Sept daily 9.30am–12.30pm & 1.30–4.30pm; Oct–May Mon, Tues, Thurs, Fri & Sun same hours; $25) is housed in a beautiful building on Willie Creek. In the creek, racks of seeded oysters hang for two years at a time, building layers of pearlescent nacre over their implants as they feed from the tidal nutrients. The fact that this process takes half the normal time is what makes the Dampier Peninsula's environs so suitable for pearl cultivation. The mysteries of this fascinating and once highly secretive process are explained by informative **tours** (up to three daily). Bookings are essential, you can't just turn up, and Broome Day Tours (℡1800 801 068) runs visits to coincide with the guided tours.

Continuing past the Willie Creek turn-off leads to a dead end coastal track with a number of short turn-offs to basic beach campsites (three days maximum stay). Popular with fishermen, they can make for a few tranquil days camping to which you best come fully equipped as there are no facilities whatsoever. The first of these is **Barred Creek**, passing through a sandy section in which most 2WDs get stuck. Take your pick of the cleared spots dotted either side of the creek mouth. A few kilometres up the coast is **Quondong Point** overlooking the low red cliffs and a white rocky beach below. **Price Point**, after another 10km, is often considered the pick of the points. Continue a few hundred metres past the signed turn-off to the point and you'll find a ramp giving easy access to the beach and numerous coves below. Just be sure you know how far the tide is coming up if you spend the night. After Price Point the track continues close to the cliff edge with views to the ocean but appears still blocked a few kilometres before **Malari** or Coulomb Point as a result of erosion. From here it's around 55km back to the Cape Leveque road.

The road to Cape Leveque

By no means a scenic drive and an infamously vehicle-destroying track, the **Cape Leveque** road continues wide and corrugated to the Aboriginal community of **Beagle Bay** (entry $5), 120km from Broome. The highlight here is the **Sacred Heart Church**, built by German missionaries in 1917, a beautiful building with an unusual altar decorated with mother-of-pearl. After Beagle Bay the track gets narrower and sandier and once you've travelled a further 40km you'll reach the turn-off leading, after another 35km, to **Middle Lagoon** (℡08/9192 4002; bookings essential), a lovely white-sand cove with camping, basic shelters (❷) and four-berth cabins (❹). The bay offers sheltered swimming and good snorkelling over the reefs at each point. Up the road another 20km or so is the community of **Lombadina/Djarindjin** (℡08/9192 4936; entry $5), where you'll find dorms (❷), units (❺), fuel and 4WD access to the beach over banks of soft sand (follow the signs). The wide shallow bay before you is again ideal for safe swimming, and with Lombadina's mixed reputation, something you'll likely have to yourself when other places are busy.

A stay at the very popular **Kooljaman Resort** right at the tip of Cape Leveque (℡08/9192 4970, ℻9192 4978; beach shelters ❷, cabins ❹, units ❻) is the reason why you've endured the last 220km; as long as the car survived no one leaves here disappointed. You'll find fuel, a restaurant and a small kiosk selling basic provisions. Situated right on the "sunrise" beach, the paperbark

cabins and **beach shelters** (basically shade, a windbreak and a barbie) are the pick of the accommodation – fancier four-berth tent-based accommodation (**6**) is up the hill. Come well prepared, however, as despite the prices, Kooljaman is no upmarket wilderness experience.

From Kooljaman you can try fishing, mudcrabbing and bushtucker **tours** (ask a local) with the local Bardi people or follow the very sandy track down to Hunter Creek. You'll find the "sunset" beach on the western side of the point a bit exposed for swimming but usually deserted, and at dusk the low red-sandstone cliffs glow warmly. If you don't fancy driving up to Kooljaman there are tours available from Broome as well as **flights** – an experience in itself. The airstrip is a short walk from all accommodation. Ask at the Broome tourist office for a schedule.

The Kimberley

A region of tablelands, tropical woodland and big rivers and gorges that's about the size of Poland, the **Kimberley** is romantically described as Australia's last frontier. It's a wilderness dotted with unviable cattle stations and small, isolated Aboriginal communities, with a ragged, tide-swept coastline inhabited chiefly by crocodiles and a couple of exclusive get-aways. The extreme seasons and harsh terrain make access slow and difficult – for those who live here, light aircraft are a necessity rather than an indulgence.

With the difficulty of running cattle (most have gone feral) in a region racked by floods and bushfires, many stations are resorting to adventure tourism, though even this is not without its setbacks; one week of rain wiped out two properties in early 2002. Even the full exploitation of minerals known to exist in the region is made barely economical by the climate and isolation, and this alone says a lot about the Kimberley's remoteness. The road between Fitzroy Crossing and Halls Creek was the last section of the circumcontinental Highway 1 to be sealed, in the mid-1980s.

The region, particularly the barely accessible **Drysdale River National Park**, has many examples of the unusual Wandjina-style rock paintings, which depict rows of mouthless beings with owl-like heads, or the slender Bradshaw figures, thought to be much older. **Tours** of the Kimberley operate from Broome and Kununurra (see box on p.784), along the **Gibb River Road** and to the popular **Bungle Bungles**, south of the highway.

Derby to Fitzroy Crossing

Situated 36km north of the coastal highway on a spur of land jutting into the mud flats of King Sound, **DERBY** is a mineral exploration base and a centre for local Aboriginal communities. Although there are plans to build a Longreach-style "Stockman's Hall of Fame" for the Kimberley here, there's little appeal for tourists, short of overnighting or perhaps taking a **scenic flight** over the West Kimberley coastline (from \$170; ask at the tourist office). Without your own transport you'll find the spread-out town hard work to navigate.

If it hasn't yet moved into the planned Stockman's museum, the **tourist office** (Mon–Fri 8.30am–4.30pm, Sat 8.30–11.30am; ☎08/9191 1426, Ⓦwww.derbytourism.com.au) is on Clarendon Street, where **buses** also arrive. **Places to stay** include the *Spinifex Hotel* (☎08/9191 1233), the town's main **pub** with ultra-basic dorms (\$17) and small, budget motel rooms (**3**).

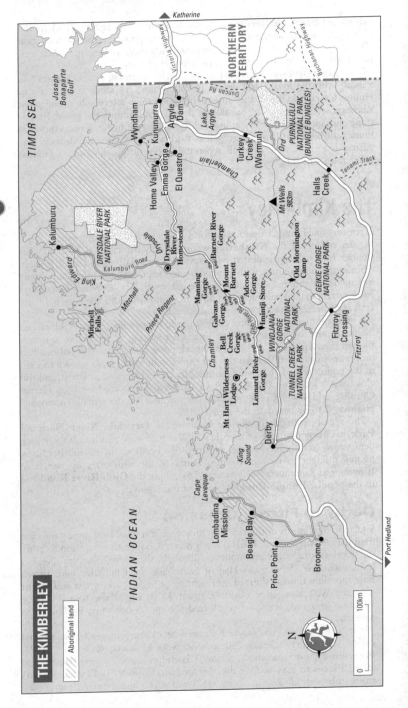

THE KIMBERLEY

Aboriginal land

0   100km

N

INDIAN OCEAN

TIMOR SEA

Joseph
Bonaparte
Gulf

NORTHERN
TERRITORY

Katherine

Victoria Highway

Duncan Rd

Buchanan Highway

Wyndham

Kununurra

Argyle
Dam

Lake
Argyle

Turkey
Creek (Warmun)

Ord

PURNULULU
NATIONAL PARK
(BUNGLE BUNGLES)

Tanami Track

Home Valley

Emma Gorge

El Questro

Chamberlain

Mt Wells
983m

Halls
Creek

Kalumburu

DRYSDALE RIVER
NATIONAL PARK

Edward

King

Drysdale

Kalumburu Road

Drysdale
River
Homestead

Mitchell

Prince Regent

Mitchell
Falls

Chamley

Manning
Gorge

Galvans
Gorge

Mount
Barnett

Barnett River
Gorge

Adcock
Gorge

Gibb River Rd

Imintji Store

Old Mornington
Camp

GEIKIE GORGE
NATIONAL PARK

Bell
Creek
Gorge

Mt Hart Wilderness
Lodge

Lennard River
Gorge

WINDJANA
GORGE
NATIONAL
PARK

TUNNEL CREEK
NATIONAL PARK

Fitzroy
Crossing

Fitzroy

Derby

King
Sound

Cape
Leveque

Lombadina
Mission

Beagle Bay

Price Point

Broome

Port Hedland

With your own transport you'll be much more comfortable at the *West Kimberley Lodge* (T08/9191 1031, F9191 1028; ❹), at 17 Sutherland St, a guesthouse with shared facilities; or the *Derby Boab Inn* on Loch Street (T08/9191 1044, F9191 1568; ❹). There's a good **restaurant** at the *Boab*, but for something special (and expensive) try the *Wharf* seafood restaurant, out by the wharf (Tues–Sun from 6.30pm; closed Jan & Feb), which also does take-aways.

The **Gibb River Road** (see p.785) starts just east of Derby and cuts straight across the Kimberley, rejoining the tarmac near Wyndham 667km further on. If you are heading east and want to see **Windjana Gorge** and **Tunnel Creek**, follow the Gibb River Road for 119km to the Windjana turn-off. From here you rejoin the Great Northern Highway after 123km. This section is OK in dry weather in a 2WD and is only 30km longer than following the highway to Fitzroy Crossing, 256km from Derby.

Since the pastoral expansion into the Kimberley in the late nineteenth century, **FITZROY CROSSING** has been a small travellers' rest stop and crucial crossing over the still-troublesome Fitzroy River. Today it's growing as a "welfare town" serving the Aboriginal communities strung out along the Fitzroy Valley to the southwest. Because of its large catchment and restricted run-off, the Fitzroy is thought to be one of the world's fastest flowing rivers; when in flood it pushes through two cubic kilometres of water a minute while getting up to 40km wide in places, before disgorging into King Sound.

As for the town, a Friday-night **drinking** session at the century-old *Crossing Inn* on Skuthorpe Road might give you the most memorable experience of the place. It's been brightly repainted by local kids into something of a tourist attraction. The *Fitzroy River Lodge* (T08/9191 5141, F9191 5142; ❻), on the highway east of the bridge, caters comfortably for passing tours. It has **motel rooms**, canvas bushland lodges and grassy campsites, as well as a pool, **restaurants** and a bar. The *Crossing Inn* (T08/9191 5080; cabins ❹) also has tent sites and the obligatory counter meals, while the *Tarunda Caravan Park*, next to the **supermarket/post office** on Forrest Road, has cheap tent sites and on-site vans (❷). The new **tourist office** (daily 9am–5pm; T08/9191 5355) is on Flynn Drive, by the roadhouse and can give you the lowdown on tours to the nearby national parks.

The Devonian Reef national parks

During the Devonian era, 350 million years ago, a large barrier reef grew around the then-submerged Kimberley plateau. The unusual limestone remnants of this reef are today exposed north of Kununurra and in the national parks of **Geikie Gorge**, **Tunnel Creek** and, most spectacularly, **Windjana Gorge**, sometimes misleadingly described as the "West Kimberley", of which they are just a dramatic and easily accessible fraction. All three parks are closed and periodically submerged from November to April.

Geikie Gorge National Park

Eighteen kilometres upstream from Fitzroy Crossing, the river has carved out the five-kilometre **Geikie Gorge** through the exposed reef, best seen by **boat** with Darngku Heritage Cruises (2–4hr; $50–110; T08/9191 5552). Water marks on the gorge's walls clearly show how high the river can rise, while below the surface harmless freshwater crocodiles jostle with freshwater-adapted stingrays and sawfish. Walking trails lead along the forested western banks, strategically dotted with picnic sites, barbecues and campsites.

Tunnel Creek and Windjana Gorge national parks

Along the highway, 42km west of Fitzroy Crossing, a dirt road turns north to follow the Napier Range (as the reef is known here) to **Tunnel Creek National Park** (no camping), 105km from Fitzroy. Here Tunnel Creek has burrowed its way under the range, creating a 750-metre tunnel hung with bats and with who-knows-what in the pools. Although the collapsed roof illuminates the cavern halfway, the wade through the progressively deeper and colder water to the other end still takes some nerve – you'll need a torch and shoes that you don't mind getting soaked.

A hundred years ago the caves were the hideout for a Bunuba Aborigine, Jandamarra (better known as **Pigeon**), and his gang of bushrangers. A police tracker for many years, one day he shot the officer at nearby Lillimoorla police station (now a ruin 2km south of Windjana Gorge) and released all the prisoners. A three-year spree of banditry followed before Pigeon was cornered and killed by fellow trackers in 1897.

The most dramatic remainders of the reef are the towering ramparts of **Windjana Gorge** (camping), 135km from Fitzroy and 140km from Derby. A walking trail leads through a limestone crevice into a wide gorge splitting the Napier Range, lined with paperbark and Leichhardt trees. Freshwater crocs share the pools with various birds and can be seen sunning themselves in the afternoons.

Halls Creek and around

There's recently been a bit of money spent on **HALLS CREEK**, 288km west of Fitzroy. The goldrush that begat the town in 1885 took place in the hills 17km south of town and in less than four years the thousand prospectors succeeded in exhausting the area's potential, before stampeding off to Kalgoorlie.

Today new gold mines and diamond mines are opening up, even if touristically the town seems to be facing facts: it's just another stop on the highway. However, the gold-bearing hills to the southeast offer a few diversions for those with their own transport. **China Wall** is a block-like vein of quartzite looming over a toxic pool, 6km from town; it appears even more impressive from the air where the vein emerges again and again. **Caroline Pool**, 15km from town, can be a bit fetid for swimming but **Palm Springs** about 25km on is well worth a splash even if camping by the track gets a bit dusty. You're better off spending the night by **Sawtooth Gorge**, a couple of kilometres further on; all but the final creek crossing just before the gorge is managable in a 2WD.

Practicalities

There's a new **information centre** (May–Sept daily 8.30am–4.30pm; ☎08/9168 6262), with a café, in the middle of town and **Internet access** next door in the library. For somewhere to **stay**, the *Halls Creek Caravan Park* (☎08/9168 6169), Roberta Avenue, has tent sites, grim single cabins ($18) and more spacious on-site vans (❷). The *Kimberley Hotel* (☎08/9168 6101, ℱ9168 6071), opposite the caravan park, has pokey bunkhouses (beds $18) and expensive motel units (❺). It's also the only **pub** in town. The *Halls Creek Motel* on Duncan Road (☎08/9168 6001; budget ❷, motel units ❹) is a better bet.

If you fancy flying over the **Bungle Bungles**, call Oasis Air (☎1800 501 462) a day or two in advance. The ninety-minute early-morning flights are the ones to go for, costing around $150.

Purnululu National Park (Bungle Bungles)

The spectacular **Bungle Bungle** massif (rarely referred to by its official name, the **Purnululu National Park**; closed Jan–March; $9) is one of Australia's greatest natural wonders and a couple of days spent exploring its chasms and gorges is well worth the effort and expense involved. Brought to prominence in the early 1980s, the Bungles have quickly attracted a mystique matching that of Uluru (Ayers Rock). The delicate nature of the banded rock domes, as well as the difficulty in patrolling the remote park, means that limiting land access to 4WDs saves money and the ecostructure of the park, while keeping numbers down to just 22,000 a year. The park was acquired in a severely over-grazed state (like much of the Northwest) but over the years CALM has worked hard to fix the soil, eliminate feral animals and reintroduce indigenous wildlife. Take note that the Bungles are always hot, with temperatures of 40°C possible in early September, so make sure you carry water and a wear a hat on the longer walks.

The **fly-drive tours** available from Kununurra (see box on p.784), which involve flying to the park's airstrip and then being driven around in a 4WD, offer the best of both worlds. But the half-hour doorless **helicopter flights** ($180; turn up at the airstrip or call ℡08/9168 1811), available in the park are permitted to fly much lower and will leave you grinning for hours – if you've ever wanted to fly in a chopper, save your money for the Bungles and you will not be disappointed. Less exhilarating flights are also available from Turkey Creek (see p.782).

From the highway it's a fun, 53-kilometre (two-hour) 4WD journey through station land to the **visitors centre** and entry station (daily 8am–1pm & 2–4pm; $9 per car; ℡08/9168 7300). Take it easy as the track is narrow and hilly with a couple of creek crossings. Expect people driving out in the morning.

From the entry station you can head to either of the two basic campsites on the north or south side of the park. **Kurrajong Camp** is the north site, 10km from the entry station and giving access to **Echidna Chasm**, a one-hour return walk into a slender chasm nearly a kilometre long and half as high. At times the cleft is less than half a metre wide and each time you think it's over, another chink opens up and you head further into the rock. **Frog Hole** (30min return) is a wider chasm, with a seasonal pool at the end, while **Mini Palms** is a longer walk along a creek bed to a palm-filled amphitheatre and then on over collapsed boulders to a viewing platform with a gorge below. At any point on these walks you can look up and see palms clinging to the rock walls hundreds of metres above you; the scale of the clefts is underlined when you realize the palms can be up to 20m high.

Wilardi Camp on the parks south side is a better laid-out campsite, 25km from the entry station with access to the classic Bungle vistas. From the main car park the short **Domes Walk** gets you among some bungles on the way to the half-hour walk into **Cathedral Gorge**, a huge overhanging amphitheatre with a seasonal pool whose rippled reflections flicker across the roof above.

Piccaninny Gorge is a tough, thirty-kilometre overnight walk for which you'll need to register and carry **large quantities of water**. Most people are understandably put off but it's quite possible to walk the seven kilometres along the creek to the **Elbow** and back in a day, following the creek. The rest of the park is currently inaccessible, the northeast being the ancestral burial grounds of the Djaru and Gidja people.

The geology of the Bungles

The weathered, beehive-like domes of the Bungles are a most unusual sight, exhibiting alternating strata of iron oxide (orange) and cyanobacteria (grey-green or black), forming a fragile crust over the sometimes powdery interior. The theory is that alternating deposition from different origins created sediments with varying mineral characteristics. The darker bands are marginally more porous (water bearing) and so support the lichen-like cyanobacteria – incidentally another name used for the stromatolite formations of pre-Cambrian (ie, very, very old) origin found at Shark Bay (see p.754).

You'll also notice the rocks on the higher, north side of the massif are conglomerate (stones set in a sand cement) and are actually older than the southern domes which were deposited on top of them. The whole range has been tilted to the south over the millennia, exposing the older conglomerate.

Meanwhile, back on the south side the maze of chasms dividing each "bungle" are being put down to an impact structure recently discovered on the roof of the plateau. At some stage a meteor is thought to have struck with such force that it sent fracture lines down through the rocks below. Over time the smashed upper strata have eroded exposing the splintered layers which were subsequently exposed and weathered into the well-known domes. The fact that there are "mini-bungle" formations elsewhere in the Kimberley, as well as the proven tilting of the massif and the current fashion for explaining epochal cataclysms with meteor strikes make this dramatic concept a little hard to swallow.

On to Wyndham

Halfway between Halls Creek and Kununurra is the roadhouse at **TURKEY CREEK** (bunkhouse $19, cabins ❹) next to the Warmun community, where a helicopter ($200; ☎08/9169 1300) offers **flights** into the Bungles. Compared to the smaller helicopters used in the park a faster, enclosed "Jetranger" is used, less exhilarating but still a memorable way of seeing the domes. Opposite the roadhouse is the Aboriginal Gidja Culture Centre displaying the art and books on the original occupants of the region; there is also **Internet access**.

From Turkey Creek the road continues directly north, passing a new roadhouse and the **Argyle Diamond Mine** (tours from Kununurra, see box p.784), source of most of the world's diamonds – although the majority end up in industrial use. The scenery hereabouts takes on a rugged turn as you pass the **Ragged** and **Carr Boyd ranges** to the junction with the Victoria Highway. Kununurra is 46km to the east and Wyndham 51km northwest.

Strung out in three built-up areas along the muddy banks of the Cambridge Gulf, **WYNDHAM** was the port established to serve the brief goldrush at Halls Creek in the 1880s. The town was then well positioned to process and export East Kimberley beef until the meat works closed in 1985, but with the expansion of mining in the area, the West Kimberley's only port ticks over quietly serving out Aboriginal welfare. On the way to Wyndham you'll pass a turn-off to the **Grotto**, where steps lead down to a small flooded gorge, and at the top of town is the **Crocodile Farm** (May–Nov daily 8.30am–4pm; feeding time 11am; $14). If you haven't been to one yet, here is your chance, but give the paltry croc sandwiches a miss. The biggest salties (more on p.635) make the in-house Komodo Dragon look rather lame although the pens full of hatchings draped across each other might be said to possess a kind of repulsive cuteness. You get a good aerial view of the farm and a whole lot more from the **Five Rivers Lookout** at the top of the 335-metre Bastion Ranges. With the tide out you'll see the intricate web of creeks feeding into the Cambridge Gulf.

The **tourist office** (daily 8am–5pm; ☎08/9161 1054) is on O'Donnell Street, and you can **camp** at the *Three Mile Caravan Park* (☎08/9161 1064; on-site vans ❷) on Baker Street. The *Gulf Breeze Guest House* (☎08/9161 1401; ❸) in the old post office on O'Donnell Street looks a bit of a sleazy long-termers' haunt although you could try the old hospital opposite which may be getting a makeover for accommodation. Opposite the *Gulf Breeze* is the *Wyndham Town Hotel* (☎08/9161 1202; ❺) with plenty of **rooms** plus the town's one **restaurant** – nothing special but better than the usual takeaways.

Kununurra and the Ord River

KUNUNURRA is the Kimberley's youngest town, built in the early 1960s to serve the **Ord River Irrigation Project**, fed by Lake Kununurra. The Diversion Dam Wall, an impressive sight as you come in from the west, created this lake, essentially the bloated Ord River. Fifty kilometres upstream is another dam, known as the Argyle Dam Wall, built in 1971 to ensure a year-round flow to the project, which has created **Lake Argyle**, the world's largest man-made body of water. In addition to early pest and wildfowl problems, the Ord River Irrigation Project was on the verge of expansion when it became mired by an inconclusive and expensive native title decision in 2002.

Perhaps enhanced by the copious amounts of fresh water nearby which lend themselves to recreational use, Kununurra manages to escape the resigned feel of older Kimberley towns. Besides being an ideal base from which to explore the adjacent Kimberley, the town is also a good place to seek out casual farming work from April to September – some of the hostels may be able to help in this respect.

A couple of kilometres from town is **Hidden Valley** or Mirima National Park (CALM fee; see box on p.722), where a road leads into a narrow valley of "mini-bungles" and terminates with some short trails – you couldn't ask for a better walking area so close to town. Another popular spot is **Ivanhoe Crossing**, 13km north of town on the Ord River. Officially the ford is closed to vehicles and you wouldn't want to try crossing it in anything less than a hefty 4WD. This is croc country and, although some locals still fish and bathe by the banks, it's inadvisable, being just the sort of habitual behaviour salties apparently go for. **Valentines Pool**, **Black Rock Falls** and **Middle Springs** are other waterholes on the far side of the Crossing (also accessible off the highway), though all three get pretty soupy towards the end of the Dry.

Triple J Tours (☎08/9168 2682) offers cruises up **Lake Kununurra** to **Argyle Dam** and Kimberley Canoeing & Bushwalking (☎08/9169 1257 or 1800 805 110) organizes one- to three-day self-guided canoeing trips down the Ord River from $110 to $230 (plus camping gear). One or two days is probably as much as you'll need here. The Zebra Rock Gallery (daily 8am–6pm; free), 6km out of town on Packsaddle Road, has examples of the unusually banded rock found on an island in Lake Argyle, as well as a small wildlife park.

Practicalities

The **tourist bureau** (daily 8am–5pm; ☎08/9168 1177), on Coolibah Drive, has displays and videos on the area's many attractions, and details of all the tours that can take you there. There is a perennially warm **swimming pool** ($2) over the road, and the **post office** is also on Coolibah Drive. You'll find a **tele-centre** around the corner. **Buses** arrive outside the BP 24-hour roadhouse, passing through daily for Katherine, Darwin and Broome.

The two better **hostels** in town are the central *Desert Inn* (℡08/9168 2702 or 1800 805 010; dorms $22) on Konkerberry Drive, close to the pub and supermarket with some twins, eight-bed air-con dorms and a shaded pool and terrace, and *Kununurra Backpackers* (℡08/9169 1998 or 1800 641 998; dorms $23), on 24 Nutwood Crescent, a quiet back street fifteen minutes' walk from town. The latter is more open plan and suits younger types, with a small pool, TV room and a farm workers' section. Of the town's five **caravan parks**, the *Town* (℡08/9168 1763), on Bloodwood Drive, is the most central, while the *Kona* (℡08/9168 1031), right by Lake Kununurra, is west of town. The *Mercure Inn* (℡08/9168 1455, ℻9168 2622; ➎), on the highway, is the town's best **motel**; you could also try the cheaper *Hotel Kununurra* (℡08/9168 0400, ℻9168 1946; ➎) on Messmate Way.

Places to eat include the *Kimberley in the Stars* on Cotton Terrace, *Valentino's* (daily 5–10pm) on Papuana Street for pizzas, or *Chopsticks Restaurant* (daily 6–9.30pm) at the *Country Club*, next to the *Hotel Kununurra*. *Gulliver's Tavern*, opposite the *Desert Inn*, gets the occasional band in the picking season, when the town gets fairly lively.

Lake Argyle

When the **Argyle Dam** was completed in 1972, the Ord River managed to fill **Lake Argyle** in just one wet season; along with the neighbouring Victoria and the Fitzroy, these rivers account for a third of Australia's freshwater run-off. Creating the lake was an engineer's dream: only a small defile needed damming to back up a lake, albeit shallow, of over a thousand square kilometres. The fish population has grown over the years to support commercial fishing, as well as numerous birds and crocodiles, both estuarine and freshwater. When the lake was proposed, the Durack family's Argyle Homestead was moved to its present site, 2km from the tourist village (see below), and is now a **museum** (May–Oct daily 8.30am–4.30pm; $3) of early pioneering life in the Kimberley, as described in Mary Durack's droving classic, *Kings in Grass Castles*.

Close to the dam wall, 70km from town, the old construction workers' camp has been turned into *Lake Argyle Tourist Village* (℡08/9168 7361; ➍), offering camping and cabins. Lake Argyle Cruises (same number) runs cruises from two

Regional tours from Kununurra

Although prices are as high per day as anywhere in Australia, Kununurra is in the best position to offer a range of tours to the **Bungles** as well as the **Kimberley**, and many operators are based or pass through here. The *Desert Inn* (℡1800 805 010) offers two- to three-day Bungles and five-day Gibb River Road adventures, costing around $150 a day and leaving from both Broome and Kununurra. Kimberley Adventures is run by *Kununurra Backpackers* (℡1800 641 998) and offers pretty much the same deals. East Kimberley Tours (℡08/9168 2213) has a whole raft of options from one day in the Bungles to an eleven-day see-it-all tour for over $2000 (including some flights). Slingair (℡1800 095 500) visits the diamond mine in a day by road, air or with the Bungles thrown in from $255. Alligator Air (℡1800 632 533) has two-hour Bungle flights in high-wing aircraft for around $190 (no minimum numbers). Their six-hour Kimberley "The Works" flight ($420) includes a stop on the Mitchell Plateau and is one of the best scenic flights over the Kimberley but needs a minimum of four passengers; call in advance if you're heading for Kununurra.

to six hours (about $20 an hour) to show you wallaby caves, jabirus and other birds, as well as freshwater crocs and **Zebra Rock Island**.

The Gibb River Road

On the way to Wyndham you pass the start of the mostly unsealed **Gibb River Road** (or "GRR") with its attendant warning sign. Originally built to transport beef to Wyndham and Derby, it cuts through the heart of the Kimberley, offering just a slice of this vast and rugged expanse. At around 670km to Derby, it's 230km shorter than the Great Northern Highway, but no one uses the "Gibb River" as a short cut. The route's notorious corrugations depend partly on the quality of your suspension (letting a little air out of the tyres helps) but it's rare to get across without something breaking or falling off, and punctures are common. The attractions that make the route interesting – mostly gorges and their pools – are off the road and some are accessible only to robust, high-clearance vehicles, although unless stated a 4WD is not necessary in the places listed below. At times when your vehicle is shaking like a pile-driver you may wonder if the trip is worth it. To absorb the experience it's best to plan to stop for a couple of days somewhere along the road at some of the places listed below; you'll probably only be here once. The Derby tourist office produces a comprehensive and annually updated guide to the GRR (including accommodation prices), available at local tourist offices for a couple of dollars. Distances given in brackets below are to destinations off the GRR.

If you're traversing the GRR west to east and want to spare your car, turn back from Manning Gorge and head down to the highway via Windjana Gorge; the best GRR gorges are in the western half. Tours are available from Broome (see p.775) and Kununurra (see box opposite).

The Karunjie Track and the eastern Gibb River Road

If you're starting the GRR from Wyndham consider taking the **Karunjie–King River Track** which starts just out of town (follow signs for King River and Drovers Rest). The track is on El Questro station land and is more varied than the easternmost section of the GRR which you bypass, but you'll need a 4WD to get through the deep bull dust as you near the GRR at the Pentacost River crossing, 85km from Wyndham – allow about three hours. If you can get hold of the leaflet on the route (at the El Questro homestead) so much the better – without it follow the small, numbered but intermittent "ELQ" signs on the gates; the numbers diminish in the direction described below.

The track starts by heading out across a causeway to follow the King River, crossing it (usually dry) 30km from Wyndham by a Boab Prison Tree. Here the track divides: left intercepts the GRR east of the Emma Gorge turn-off (see overleaf); right leads west slowly round to the Cockburn Ranges, at one point crossing smooth, hardened mud flats before the going gets rough again as the track nears the Pentacost River. There are some washed-out sections and deep patches of bull dust that need to be churned through slowly. You join the GRR at the Pentacost crossing about 57km from the Great Northern Highway.

The GRR proper starts halfway between Wyndham and Kununurra, the scenically impressive 250-kilometre eastern section up to the Kalumburu junction crosses many ranges and is crossed in turn by big rivers, the first of these being the **King River**, 17km from the sealed highway.

The turn-off for the plush mini-resort at **Emma Gorge** (1km; $12.50 day-use; T & F08/9169 1777; ⑤–⑥), part of *El Questro Station*, leads to an "executive" bushcamp with shared facilities and a restaurant, bar and pool. It's popular with coach parties, but there's a forty-minute walk along Emma Creek to the beautiful, fern-draped **gorge** which is worth the entry fee.

Further down the road, *El Questro Station* (16km; $12.50 day-use; T & F08/9169 1777, W www.elquestro.com.au) is developing itself into a private national park. Uniformed rangers assist you in all sorts of activities, including heli-fishing, gorge cruises and various walks, waterholes and drives all over the million-acre property; the three-hour slog up to **El Questro Gorge** is recommended. Affordable **accommodation** includes secluded camping (with distant washing facilities; $12.50 per person), and bungalows with shared kitchens (⑥). There's also a bar, shop, fuel and restaurant.

From the *El Questro Station* turn-off, the Cockburn Range's cliffs lead you to the stony **Pentecost River** crossing. Eight kilometres on is *Home Valley Station* (1km; T08/9161 4322; ①), the polar opposite of snazzy El Questro but with a breezy barn-like homestead that's a more authentic Kimberley experience. As well as camping, they offer half-board for $100 per person. The same family also runs *Jack's Waterhole* ($5 entry fee; half-board ④, camping available), 57km down the GRR just after the steep sealed rise at Gregory's Jump Up. *Jack's* has been rebuilt a little higher up the slope after the nearby Durack River rapidly rose 24km in 2002 and washed the whole joint out into the Cambridge Gulf. From here the GRR has been extensively rebuilt following the 2002 flood, passing wide-open Kimberley countryside recovering from the last bushfire. On the way, *Ellenbrae station* (5km; camping) might still be operating, but don't count on it.

The Northern Kimberley

Though a common destination for four-wheel drivers in the Dry, the Northern Kimberley is a remote part of the region where a self-sufficient 4WD is essential. You'll find the **Kalumburu Road** about as rough as the GRR, with a store and fuel at *Drysdale River Homestead* (59km; April–Nov daily 8am–noon & 1–5pm; T08/9161 4326; units ④), which also has dinner and B&B at $80 per person, and scenic flights. The **Drysdale River National Park** is tantalizingly inaccessible by private vehicle but the determined should call Darwin-based Willis Walkabouts (T08/8985 2134), which operates bushwalking tours that sometimes include the park – access is by light plane, 4WD and helicopter, so it won't be cheap.

The main destination up here is the beautiful, five-tiered **Mitchell Falls**, 240km off the GRR and 70km off the Kalumburu Road. This once remote spot is getting less so by the year: you'll find campsites at King Edward River just off the Kalumburu Road and at Mitchell Falls car park (both June–Oct; half-board ④). From the car park it's a three-kilometre walk to the falls themselves where a helicopter stands by to offer scenic flights in season from around $150.

Kalumburu (276km; T08/9161 4300; $25 vehicle permit) has the languorous feel of a dispersed African village, where ancient cars lie rusting and palms flap and sway in the tropical breeze; buy your permit on arrival from the community office (if there's anyone there). As well as being able to get (expensive) fuel and basics from the store here, you can visit a mission set up in the nineteenth century by Benedictine monks (tours available). North of town along sandy tracks there are basic campsites at pretty **McGowans Beach** (22km) and **Honeymoon Beach** (26km), the latter situated on a small bay and the better of the two. There are a couple of other sites up here on the remote Kimberley coast, mostly exclusive, all-inclusive resorts costing around $500 a day and only accessible by air or sea.

Mount Barnett to Derby

About eighty kilometres after the Kalumburu Road junction is a turn-off for **Barnett River Gorge** (5km; basic camping), nothing too spectacular but with a couple of places you can camp for free and swim in a billabong. Another 20km down the GRR is *Mount Barnett Roadhouse* (May–Oct daily 7am–6pm; ☎08/9191 7007; bungalows ❹). Assuming they've re-opened the track you can camp at **Manning Gorge** (7km; $7), or take an hour's walk to the even nicer, multi-tiered **Upper Manning Gorge** (follow the beer-can markers on the far side of the pool). Further down the road both **Galvans** (700m) and **Adcock** (if re-opened, 5km) gorges are less impressive by comparison,

A possible detour off the GRR leads you 100km south to **Old Mornington Camp**, with camping, a bar, and by the time you read this, some cabins. Initially the access track uses the western end of the Tablelands Track (which, though closed to passing traffic, eventually leads down to near Halls Creek), the going is relatively smooth compared to the GRR, apart from the final 15km after Glenroy Homestead where you'll have a few creeks to cross. Another property washed out in 2002, *Old Mornington Camp* is being redeveloped. At the time of writing the camping facilities were basic but if plans are carried out successfully it will be a great place to stay for a few days. From the camp you can access two gorges on the Fitzroy River: **Sir John Gorge** (14km; 30min) has broad pools ideal for swimming; exploring upstream leads to greater grandeur. To appreciate **Dimond Gorge** (23km; 1hr) you'll have to rent a paddle from the camp to make use of the on-site canoes to downstream beyond the sheer walls.

Back on the GRR, the **Imintji Store** (☎08/9191 5761) has fuel, ice and a good supply of groceries. Seven kilometres on is the access track to **Bell Creek Gorge** (30km; camping). Well worth some extra corrugations, this is the loveliest gorge along the Gibb River Road, although perhaps becoming a bit too popular because of this. Twenty-three kilometres further down the GRR, on the far side of the King Leopold Ranges is **Lennard River Gorge** (8km; last 3km 4WD), a dramatic cleft carved through tiers of tilted rock. Even in a 4WD you may find it quicker and certainly easier to walk the last two kilometres which, unless they've been repaired, are very rough in parts.

A few kilometres on further down the GRR is the turning for *Mount Hart Wilderness Lodge* (50km; ☎08/9191 4645, ⓦ www.mthart.com.au; half-board ❹, reductions and lunch included on subsequent nights, no camping or day visits). You need to book ahead but you can call from the Imintji Store or even use the HF radio at the GRR turn-off to the lodge. The former homestead has been cultivated into a cozy shaded retreat with a bar, comfortable indoor areas and a waterhole, as well as private gorges to explore a few kilometres away. Scenic flights use the lodge's airstrip to stop for lunch, but at other times it could be all yours.

Back on the GRR you wind your way through the impressive **King Leopard Ranges** and presently come to the **Napier Ranges** composed of the Devonian Reef where a rock-chiseled profile of Queen Victoria's Head is evident as you pass through the gap. Nine kilometres from here a turn leads southeast to Windjana Gorge National Park (21km; see p.779) and Fitzroy Crossing (165km; see p.779). The last 62km to Derby is a sealed avenue of portly boab trees with the local expression "gorged out" possibly on the tip of your tongue.

Travel details

Trains

Perth to: Bunbury (2–3 daily; 2hr); Kalgoorlie (1–2 daily; 7hr 30min); Adelaide/Sydney (2 weekly; Adelaide 50hr, Sydney 60hr).

Buses

Kalgoorlie to: Adelaide (1 daily; 36hr); Esperance (3 weekly; 5hr); Leonora (2 weekly; 11hr); Perth (5 weekly; 8hr).

Perth to: Adelaide (1 daily; 35hr); Albany (3 daily; from 6hr); Augusta (6 weekly; 6hr); Broome (daily; 32hr); Bunbury (1–2 daily; 2hr); Carnarvon (daily; 11hr); Dampier–Karratha (5 weekly; 21hr); Darwin (daily; 56hr); Denham (for Monkey Mia; daily; 12hr); Derby (3 weekly; 37hr); Esperance (4 weekly; 10hr); Exmouth (6 weekly; 6hr); Fitzroy Crossing (3 weekly; 40hr); Geraldton (2–4 daily; 6hr); Halls Creek (daily; 44hr); Hyden (for Wave Rock; 2 weekly; 5hr); Kalbarri (daily; 8hr); Kalgoorlie (5 weekly; 8hr); Kununurra (daily; 49hr); Margaret River (3 daily; 5hr); Meekatharra (2 weekly; 10hr); Newman (2 weekly; 13hr); Port Hedland (1 daily; 25hr).

Flights

Perth to: Adelaide (6 daily; 4hr 15min); Alice Springs (5 weekly; 4hr); Ayers Rock Resort (3 weekly; 3hr 45min); Brisbane (3 weekly; 6hr 15min); Broome (1 daily; 2hr 30min); Darwin (1 daily; 6hr 15min); Esperance (2 daily; 1hr 50min); Kalgoorlie (1 daily; 1hr); Kununurra (6 weekly; 3hr 15min); Melbourne (12 daily; 5hr 15min); Sydney (12 daily; 6hr); Tom Price (1 daily; 2 hr).

8

South Australia

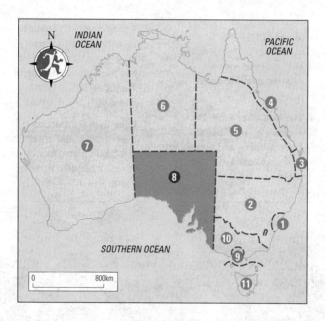

CHAPTER 6   # Highlights

✷ **Adelaide Festival of Arts**
The country's best-known
and most innovative arts
festival. See p.812

✷ **Barossa Valley** A popular
day-trip from Adelaide, the
Barossa Valley is home to
some of Australia's finest
wineries. See p.822

✷ **Kangaroo Island** Spectacular
scenery and a huge range of
wildlife. See p.837

✷ **Murray River** Stay in a
houseboat on the beautiful
Murray River, lined with
majestic river red gums. See
p.854

✷ **The Nullarbor Plain** Drive
across – or, even better,
catch a train – and appreciate
how vast Australia is. See
p.870

✷ **Coober Pedy** Surrounded by
desert, the inhabitants of
scorching Coober Pedy live
underground to escape the
heat of summer. See p.872

✷ **Wilpena Pound** The main
attraction of the rugged
Flinders Ranges National
Park is the huge natural basin
of Wilpena Pound, with its
fantastic bushwalks and great
views. See p.879

✷ **The Strzelecki, Birdsville
and Oodnadatta tracks** Fill
up your tank and head off
into the Outback on one of
Australia's fabled journeys.
See p.881, p.884 & p.886

✷ **Lake Eyre** Surrounded by
desert, this massive salt lake
has filled up only four times
in over a hundred and thirty
years. See p.883

South Australia

South Australia, the driest state of the driest continent, is split into two very distinct halves. The long-settled southern part, watered by the Murray River, and with **Adelaide** as its cosmopolitan centre, has been thoroughly tamed; the northern half, arid and depopulated, most definitely has not.

Most of southern – which is to say southeastern – South Australia lies within three hours' drive of Adelaide. Food and especially **wine** are among its chief pleasures: this is prime grape-growing and wine-making country. As well as its wineries the **Fleurieu Peninsula**, just south of Adelaide, has a string of fine beaches, while nearby **Kangaroo Island** is a fine place to see Australian wildlife at its unfettered best. Facing Adelaide across the Investigator Strait, the **Yorke Peninsula** is primarily an agricultural area, preserving a little copper-mining history and some great fishing. The superb wineries of the **Barossa Valley**, originally settled by German immigrants in the nineteenth century, are only an hour east from Adelaide on the **Sturt Highway**, the main road to Sydney. This crosses the Murray River at Blanchetown and follows the fertile **Riverland** region to the New South Wales border. Following the **southeast coast** along the Princes Highway, you can head towards Melbourne via the extensive coastal lagoon system of the Coorong and enjoyable seaside towns such as Robe, exiting the state at **Mount Gambier**, with its crater lakes. The inland trawl via the **Dukes Highway** is faster but far less interesting. Heading north from Adelaide, there are old copper-mining towns to explore at Kapunda and Burra in the area known as the **mid-north**, which also encompasses the **Clare Valley**, a quieter, more down-to-earth wine centre than the Barossa Valley.

In contrast with the gentle and cultured southeast, the remainder of South Australia – with the exception of the relatively refined **Eyre Peninsula** and its strikingly scenic west coast – is unremittingly harsh desert, a naked country of vast horizons, salt lakes, glazed gibber plains and ancient mountain ranges. Although it's tempting to scud over the forbidding distances quickly, you'll miss the essence of this introspective and subtle landscape by hurrying. For every predictable, monotonous highway there's a dirt alternative, which may be physically draining but enables you to get closer to this precarious environment. The folded red rocks of the central **Flinders Ranges** and **Coober Pedy**'s post-apocalyptic scenery are on most agendas and could be worked into a sizeable circuit, but overall the Outback lacks any real destinations. Making the most of the journey is what counts – the fabled routes to **Oodnadatta**, **Birdsville** and **Innamincka** are still real adventures, and not necessarily only for 4WDs.

Rail and **road** routes converge in Adelaide before the long cross-country hauls west to Perth via Port Augusta or north to Alice Springs and Darwin. The

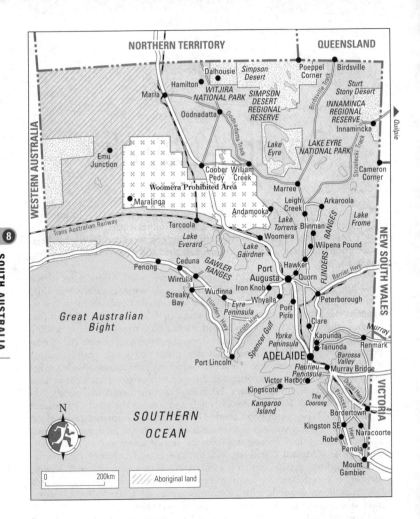

trip on the Ghan to Alice Springs is one of Australia's great train journeys, as is the ride on the Indian Pacific, which passes through Adelaide en route between Perth and Sydney.

Adelaide and the surrounding gulflands, cooled by the Gulf St Vincent, enjoy a Mediterranean **climate** that makes them tremendously fertile. As you head further north the temperature hots up to such an extreme that by Coober Pedy people live underground to escape the searing summer temperatures.

Some history

When South Australia was first settled by Europeans in 1836, it was home to as many as fifty distinct **Aboriginal groups**, with a population estimated at 15,000. Three distinct cultural regions existed: the Western Desert, the Central Lakes, and the Murray and southeast region. It was the people of the comparatively well-watered southeast who felt the full impact of white settlement, those who survived being shunted onto missions controlled by the government. Some Aboriginal people have clung tenaciously to their way of life in the Western Desert, where they have gained title to some of their land, but most now live south of Port Augusta, many in Adelaide.

The coast of South Australia was first **explored** by the Dutch in 1627. In 1792 the French explorer Bruni d'Entrecasteaux sailed along the Great Australian Bight before heading to southern Tasmania, and in 1802 the Englishman Matthew Flinders thoroughly charted the coast. The most important expedition, though – and the one which led to the foundation of a colony here – was **Captain Charles Sturt**'s 1830 navigation of the Murray River from its source in New South Wales to its mouth in South Australia.

South Australia was planned from the start: in the idealistic scheme of the English entrepreneur Edward Wakefield, there were to be no convicts here – instead, free settlers would be sold small units of land (rather than given large free land grants) in a state guaranteeing them civil and religious liberty. The success of the scheme was guaranteed when George Fife Angas formed the **South Australia Company** to finance it. In 1836, **Governor John Hindmarsh** landed at Holdfast Bay, now the Adelaide beachside suburb of Glenelg, with the first settlers; the next year Colonel William Light planned the spacious, attractive city of Adelaide, with broad streets and plenty of parks and squares. By 1839, Angas was assisting persecuted Lutheran communities from the eastern provinces of Prussia to settle in South Australia.

Early problems caused by the harsh, dry climate and financial incompetence (the colony went bankrupt in 1841) were eased by the discovery of substantial reserves of **copper**. The population of Adelaide boomed over the following decades, while the state's tradition of **libertarianism** continued; in 1894, South Australia's women were the first in the world to be permitted to stand for parliament and the second in the world to gain the vote (after women in New Zealand). Social improvement through slum clearances began after World War I, though of all the mainland states, the depressions and recessions of the interwar period hit South Australia the hardest. The situation eased following World War II, when new immigrants arrived, boosting the output of industry and injecting fresh life into the state.

The 1970s were the decade of **Don Dunstan**. The flamboyant Labor Premier was an enlightened reformer who had a strong sense of social justice: he abolished capital punishment, outlawed racial discrimination and decriminalized homosexuality. The state has been a duller place since his retirement in 1979, and a poorer one since the recession started to bite at the end of the 1980s. During recent years the largely unsuccessful privatizations of public utilities have added to South Australia's economic woes, while the state's image has been dominated by arguments over the siting of nuclear waste disposal facilities and the detention of asylum seekers, much to the chagrin of South Australians themselves, who feel that their state's attractions are being unfairly eclipsed by the lure of other Australian destinations.

Adelaide and the southeast

Adelaide is the state's transport hub, with good **bus** connections throughout the southeast, though there are more rewarding alternatives is you fancy travelling under your own steam. Much of the country is flat and great for **cycling**. The principal route is the **Mawson Trail**: 800km specifically planned for cyclists, extending from the Mount Lofty Ranges through the Barossa Valley and Flinders Ranges to the Outback town of Blinman. **Walkers** can follow a parallel route along the 1500-kilometre **Heysen Trail**, starting at Cape Jervis and running up the coast of the Fleurieu Peninsula before heading north over the Mount Lofty Ranges to the Flinders. The Heysen trail is closed between December and April – partly due to the high risk of fire, and partly as a result of an agreement with private landowners, through whose property some of the trail passes. Further information and maps for the trails are available from Information SA in Adelaide (see p.796).

Adelaide

ADELAIDE is always thought of as a gracious city and an easy place to live in, and despite a population of around one million and a veneer of sophistication, it still has the feel of an overgrown country town. It's a pretty place, laid out on either side of the **Torrens River**, ringed with a green belt of parks and set against the rolling hills of the **Mount Lofty Ranges**. During the hot, dry summer the parklands are kept green by irrigation from the waters of the Murray River on which the city depends, though there's always a sense that the rawness of the Outback is waiting to take over.

The original occupants of the Adelaide plains were the **Kuarna people**, though their traditional way of life was destroyed within twenty years of the landing of Governor John Hindmarsh at Holdfast Bay in 1836. The colony's surveyor general, **Colonel William Light**, had visionary plans for the new city. After a long struggle with Hindmarsh, who wanted to build around a harbour, Light got his wish for an inland city with a strong connection to the river, formed around wide and spacious avenues and squares. Postwar immigration provided the final element missing from Light's plan: the human one. Italians now make up the city's biggest non-Anglo cultural group, and in the hot, dry summers, Mediterranean-style alfresco eating and drinking lend the city a vaguely European air. Not surprisingly, one of Adelaide's chief delights is its **food** and **wine**, with South Australian vintages in every cellar, and restaurants and cafés as varied as Sydney and Melbourne's, only much cheaper.

Outwardly conservative, Adelaide nonetheless takes advantage of South Australia's liberal traditions, with a nudist beach, relaxed drug laws and 24-hour hotel licences. It's the free and easy **lifestyle** within an ordered framework that's so appealing; Adelaide may not be an obvious destination in itself, but it's a great place for a relaxed break on your way up to the Northern Territory or across to Western Australia.

Arrival, information and city transport

Buses from out of town, including the airport bus, will drop you off at the basic **Central bus station**, on Franklin St. The international **airport**, 7km southwest from the centre, is small and modern, and has a currency exchange and information booth. The domestic terminal is about half a kilometre southwest. Both are serviced by the Skylink **airport bus** (daily 6am–9pm; 1–2 departures hourly; $7 one-way; to book a return trip or ask for a hotel pickup, ring ☏08/8332 0528), which will drop you off at most city accommodation on request; the bus also stops at Victoria Square and North Terrace, as well as the Central bus station.

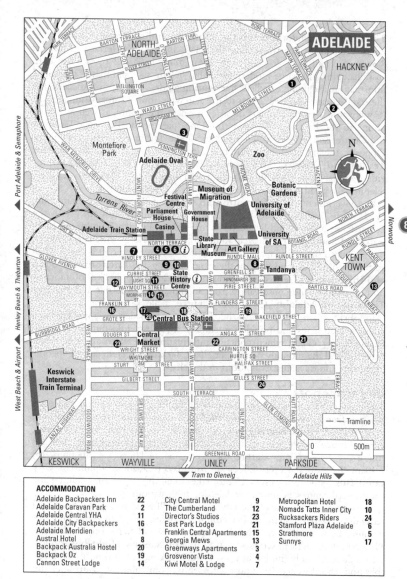

ADELAIDE

NORTH ADELAIDE

HACKNEY

Montefiore Park

Adelaide Oval

Zoo

Botanic Gardens

Festival Centre
Parliament House
Government House
Museum of Migration
University of Adelaide

Adelaide Train Station
Casino

State Library
Museum
Art Gallery

University of SA

KENT TOWN

State History Centre

Tandanya

Central Bus Station

Central Market

KESWICK
WAYVILLE
UNLEY
PARKSIDE

Keswick Interstate Train Terminal

Port Adelaide & Semaphore

Henley Beach & Thebarton

West Beach & Airport

Norwood

— — Tramline

0   500m

Tram to Glenelg

Adelaide Hills

SOUTH AUSTRALIA | Adelaide

ACCOMMODATION

Adelaide Backpackers Inn	22	City Central Motel	9	Metropolitan Hotel	18
Adelaide Caravan Park	2	The Cumberland	12	Nomads Tatts Inner City	10
Adelaide Central YHA	11	Director's Studios	23	Rucksackers Riders	24
Adelaide City Backpackers	16	East Park Lodge	21	Stamford Plaza Adelaide	6
Adelaide Meridien	1	Franklin Central Apartments	15	Strathmore	5
Austral Hotel	8	Georgia Mews	13	Sunnys	17
Backpack Australia Hostel	20	Greenways Apartments	3		
Backpack Oz	19	Grosvenor Vista	4		
Cannon Street Lodge	14	Kiwi Motel & Lodge	7		

The airport bus also stops at the **Keswick Interstate** train terminal, about 1km from the city centre, from where it costs $3.50 to the city or airport; alternatively, walk across to the suburban platform and catch a train into **Adelaide train station**, situated on North Terrace in the city centre. A **taxi** from the airport costs around $17 to either the city or the beachside suburb of Glenelg; taxis to the city from the Keswick Interstate Terminal charge about $10.

Information

The first stop for information is the **South Australian Travel Centre**, at 18 King William St, between Rundle Mall and North Terrace (Mon–Fri 8.30am–5.30pm, Sat & Sun 9am–2pm; ℡1300 655 276, ⓦwww.south australia.com). This large modern office has helpful staff and masses of general information, including excellent free touring guides and maps of Adelaide and the state. There's also free access to the statewide tourist information website (ⓦwww.touristvision.com.au) on a terminal in the centre, as well as a freephone to the Passenger Transport InfoLine (part of the Passenger Transport InfoCentre; see below); you'll need to queue for more specific enquiries. Opposite the bus station at 110 Franklin St, the bright pink **Backpacker Transit and Travel Centre** (daily 8.30am–6pm; ℡08/8410 3000) can provide free maps and book all domestic tours; there's also a currency exchange, telephone, a good notice board, and Internet access ($3 for 1hr).

The government-run **Information SA**, 77 Grenfell St (Mon–Fri 9am–5pm, Wed from 9.30am; ℡08/8204 1900, ⓦwww.info.sa.gov.au), sells the Department of Sport and Recreation's maps of the Heysen Trail, Mount Lofty walks and South Australian cycle routes (these can also be purchased online); there are also some free maps and brochures, and free Internet access for half an hour. On the ground floor of the same building, the **Environment Shop and Information Centre** (same hours; ℡08/8204 1910) has lots of information on national and conservation parks in and around Adelaide and the state. The **City of Adelaide Customer Centre**, a block south on 25 Pirie St (Mon–Fri 8.30am–5.30pm; ℡08/8203 7203, ⓦwww.adelaide.sa.gov.au), has a range of free maps and booklets, including the glossy fold-out *Art in Public Places Walking Guide*, which contains information on art throughout South Australia, and the monthly newspaper *About Adelaide*, which details all upcoming events and travelling exhibitions in the city.

City transport

The city centre is compact and flat, making walking an easy option. There are also two **free buses**. The **Bee Line** (#99B) is a handy alternative that cuts out a lot of the legwork, running from Victoria Square via King William Street, North Terrace and the train station to Hindley Street, then back again. Services run every five minutes during the week (Mon–Thurs 7.40am–6pm, Fri 7.40am–9.20pm) and every fifteen on Saturdays (8.30am–5.30pm). The **City Loop Bus** (same times; every 15min) takes in all the city's major cultural and commercial centres, beginning at Adelaide train station.

To explore further out of the city centre, you'll need to use the integrated **Adelaide Metro** system, which comprises buses, suburban trains and one tramline from the city to Glenelg. Metro buses and trains run until about 11.30pm, with reduced services at night and on Sundays. **Night buses** operate on Saturday only (midnight to 4am; $6.60). A night bus timetable is available from the Passenger Transport InfoCentre. Four suburban **train** lines run from Adelaide train station. The **tram** to seaside Glenelg (30min) leaves from Victoria Square every fifteen to twenty minutes. The **O-Bahn** is a fast-track bus which runs on concrete rails through scenic Torrens Linear Park, between the city (Grenfell St) and Tea Tree Plaza in Modbury, 12km northeast. Free timetables and transport info are available from the **Passenger Transport InfoCentre** on the corner of King William and Currie streets (Mon–Sat 8am–6pm, Sun 10.30am–5.30pm; ⓦwww.adelaidemetro.com.au); staff also sell tickets and hand out copies of *The Metroguide*, a free information booklet including a handy map of the system. You can also get transport info on

$\textcircled{T}$08/8210 1000 (daily 7am–8pm) or via the freephone at the South Australian Travel Centre. Services on less popular bus routes can be infrequent, so check the relevant timetables before setting out.

Tickets for the Metro system come in single-trip, multi-trip and day-trip permutations, and can be used on buses, trains and the tram; if you need to use more than one form of transport for a single journey, one ticket will suffice. Single tickets range in price from $1.90 to $3.20, depending on the time of day, and are valid for two hours. You can buy single-journey tickets from machines on board trains, buses and trams, as well as from train station ticket offices and the Passenger Transport InfoCentre. Other types of ticket, including the day-trip ticket ($6), can be bought from the Passenger Transport InfoCentre, train stations, post offices and some newsagents.

Cycling is a popular and excellent alternative to public transport: the flat city area and its wide streets make riding a breeze, and there are several good cycling routes – including the **Torrens Linear Park track**, which goes from the sea at Westbeach to the hills at Athelston, weaving along the river. A map of this and other cycling routes is available from Information SA (see p.796), and several other cycling route maps from the City of Adelaide Customer Centre (see p.796); for bike rental outlets, see "Listings", p.815.

Accommodation

Adelaide has loads of **hostels**, and competition keeps prices low. Those on Gilles or Carrington streets, about ten minutes' walk southwest from the city centre, are generally cheaper than those closer to the city centre, and will pick you up from the bus or train station if you call ahead (several also send minibuses to scout for custom); some hostels will even come to the airport if you call in advance. Otherwise, buses #171 or #172 from Victoria Square stop close to Gilles Street. There are cheap **hotel** rooms on Hindley Street, Adelaide's nightclub area and its tame answer to a red-light district, but some women may find it threatening. The swankiest accommodation is along North Terrace. The only time you may have difficulty finding accommodation is during Womadelaide in late February (annually) and the Arts Festival at the end of February and beginning of March (even years only) – book ahead. Rooms also fill up quickly at weekends, especially at the more popular hostels around the Central Bus Station on Franklin Street and adjacent Waymouth Street. The seaside suburb of **Glenelg** and the nearby beach resorts (see p.807), about half an hour away from Adelaide by public transport, are good alternatives to the city centre, with plenty of self-catering apartments and one of Adelaide's liveliest hostels.

The most central **campsite** is at the *Adelaide Caravan Park*, Bruton Street, Hackney, on the Torrens River 2km northeast of the centre ($\textcircled{T}$08/8363 1566, $\textcircled{F}$8362 1989, $\textcircled{W}$www.adelaidecaravanpark.com.au; cabins ❸, two-bed holiday units ❹, villas with spas ❺); it's right on the Torrens Linear Park cycling route and can be reached by bus #281 or #282 from North Terrace, or on foot through parkland and along the river. For a beachfront setting, head to *Adelaide Shores Caravan Park*, Military Road, West Beach ($\textcircled{T}$08/8356 7654, $\textcircled{E}$adelaideshores@senet.com.au; bus #278 from Currie St; cabins and on-site vans ❸), or the *Adelaide Beachfront Tourist Park*, 349 Military Rd, Semaphore ($\textcircled{T}$08/8449 7726 or 1800 810 140, $\textcircled{F}$8449 5877; cabins ❸–❹), which has a swimming pool, recreation room, playground and a free shuttle bus service to West Lakes Mall and Ethelton train station. Both sites get very busy during summer. You could also pitch your tent on the rooftop of *Backpack Australia* (see overleaf) in the centre of the city.

City centre

Hotels, motels and pubs

Austral Hotel 205 Rundle St ☎08/8223 4660, ⓦwww.theaustral.com. Basic rooms in one of Adelaide's best pubs on this "arty" street. Bands or DJs nearly every night, so it can be noisy. ❸

City Central Motel 23 Hindley St ☎08/8231 4049, ⓕ8231 4804. Centrally located budget motel. ❸

Director's Studios 259 Gouger St ☎08/8213 2500 or 1800 882 601, ⓕ8213 2519, ⓦwww.savillesuites.com.au. Modern and very good-value hotel, with pleasant, well-furnished self-catering studio apartments and standard rooms. A five-minute walk to Chinatown and the Central Market. 24hr reception and free parking. ❹–❺

Franklin Central Apartments 36 Franklin St ☎08/8221 7050, ⓦwww.ihm.com.au/franklin.html. Fully serviced one-, two- and three-bedroom apartments in a central location ideal for business or extended stays. 24hr reception. ❻

Grosvenor Vista 125 North Terrace ☎08/8407 8888 or 1800 888 222, ⓦwww.grosvenorvista hotel.com.au. Genteel establishment dating from 1918, complete with potted palms in the foyer. Spacious, modern en-suite rooms with air-con. 24hr room service, gym and sauna, bar and bistro and undercover parking. Breakfast included. ❺–❼

Kiwi Motel & Lodge 262–266 Hindley St ☎08/8231 9524, ⓔprincesarcade@one.net.au. Motel-cum-hostel in a converted arcade, with spacious rooms – some en suite and with kitchenette – and quiet four-bed dorms with their own TV. Helpful tour desk, laundry and Internet access. Rates include linen and a filling breakfast. Dorms $15, rooms ❷

Metropolitan Hotel 46 Grote St ☎08/8231 5471, ⓕ8231 0633. Rather tacky locals' pub but with basic clean rooms upstairs at bargain prices. Good-value bistro meals. Light breakfast included. ❶–❷

Stamford Plaza Adelaide 150 North Terrace ☎08/8461 1111, ⓦwww.stamford.com.au /adelaide/adpla1bar.html. This central, high-rise luxury five-star hotel has all you'd expect: swimming pool, sauna, three restaurants, room service and views of the Festival Centre. Room rates are in excess of $200, though cheaper weekend packages are available. There's also a beachside equivalent, the *Stamford Grand Hotel*, at Glenelg. ❼

Strathmore 129 North Terrace ☎08/8212 6911, ⓦwww.strath.com.au. Smart, small hotel in a desirable location. The en-suite, motel-style rooms are small and have no views, though they come with all mod cons from air-con to room service; free undercover parking. Breakfast included. ❹

Hostels

Adelaide Backpackers Inn 112 Carrington St ☎08/8223 6635 or 1800 247 725, ⓦwww.tne.net.au/abackinn. Set in a converted pub, this place is shabby, but has a friendly ambience and helpful staff. There are six- to twelve-bed dorms here and annexe accommodation across the road with plenty of singles and doubles in a brighter, more modern air-con building. Generous breakfast thrown in. Internet access. Reception doubles as a travel agency, selling bus and train tickets. Dorms $20, rooms ❷

Adelaide Central YHA 135 Waymouth St ☎08/8414 3010, ⓔadlcentral@yhasa.org.au. Modern, rather ugly but extremely efficient youth hostel with over 200 beds in a convenient location in the heart of the city – though don't expect a lively atmosphere. Accommodation is in dorms (four- to eight-bed; all have lockers), doubles (some en suite) and two family rooms ($87). There are also well-equipped kitchens, a large laundry room, lockers, a comprehensive travel centre and Internet access next door. Some off-street parking spaces can be reserved. Dorms $23, rooms ❸

Adelaide City Backpackers 239 Franklin St ☎08/8212 2668, ⓦwww.citybackpackers.com.au. Family-owned hostel set in a beautifully restored Victorian house with charm and character throughout, including a country-style kitchen and breakfast room, small bar and cosy plant-filled courtyard. If you can put up with a ten-bed dorm, or can get one of the immaculate double rooms, this place is the closest you'll get in Adelaide to a home away from home. Courtesy pick-up, free night tour and hearty continental breakfast included. Dorms $20, rooms ❷

Backpack Australia Hostel 128 Grote St ☎08/8231 0639 or 1800 804 133, ⓕ8410 5881. Friendly, clean and modern, with colourful murals decorating the entrance area, this is one of Adelaide's more sociable hostels. You can even pitch your tent on the roof terrace, making this the cheapest spot in town. Travel agent service, BBQs, free bikes and an excellent notice board. Light breakfast and linen included. Dorms $18, rooms ❶

Backpack Oz 144 Wakefield St, cnr Pulteney St ☎ & ⓕ 08/8223 3551, ☎1800 633 307, ⓦwww.backpackoz.com.au. Converted from a nineteenth-century hotel, this low-key hostel has light, spacious rooms and dorms (four-, six- and ten-bed). There's a comfortable common room downstairs; plus bar (summer only), laundry and a small kitchen. Pick-ups from bus, train and airport available, and tours booked. Linen and a light breakfast included. Dorms $18, rooms ❷

Cannon Street Lodge 11 Cannon St, entrance on Franklin St opposite the bus station ☏ 08/8410 1218 or 1800 069 731, ⓦ www.cannonst.com.au. One of the best hostels in town, this huge, warehouse-style place has a groovy young feel and is very clean and well run. The big foyer has a travel centre, Internet access and a funky licensed bar complete with pinball, pool table and cheap meals. While there's lots of noise and action downstairs, it's peaceful upstairs. Free light breakfast, plus cheap day-membership at the gym around the corner, undercover parking and bed linen. Dorms $17–20, rooms ❷

The Cumberland 205 Waymouth St ☏ 08/8231 3577, ⓕ 8231 3578. Nomad hostel in a delightful, recently renovated Victorian hotel. But don't expect much peace and quiet: rooms are above a wine bar/dance club that's open 24 hours a day, seven days a week. Dorms $18, rooms ❷

East Park Lodge 341 Angas St ☏ 08/8223 1228 or 1800 643 606, ⓦ www.eastpark.com.au. Huge three-storey mansion with singles, doubles and four-bed dorms, all with air-con. The atmosphere is peaceful, with views of the hills from balconies and rooftop, and an outdoors pool to cool off in. Bus and train pick-ups if pre-booked; airport buses drop off here. Limited on-street parking. Tours booked. Free breakfast. Dorms $22, rooms ❸

Nomads Tatts Inner City 1st Floor, 17 Hindley St ☏ 08/8231 3225, ⓔ tattscity@hotmail. Small, centrally located hostel above a heritage-listed hotel. A bit noisy, but has good facilities, including a sunny verandah overlooking the main street, a well-equipped kitchen, pool table, Internet access, games and videos. Dorms $17–20, rooms ❷–❸

Rucksackers Riders 257 Gilles St ☏ 08/8232 0823. The small dorms here are the cheapest in Adelaide; not surprisingly, there are few facilities and even the pay showers (20¢ for 5min) are a drag. Popular with Japanese cyclists and motorbike riders, hence the name. Dorms $15, rooms ❷

Sunnys 139 Franklin St ☏ 08/8231 2430 or 1800 631 391, ⓦ www.sunnys.com.au. A friendly place in an old house next to the bus station. Facilities include a pool table, sound system, TV and video. Six- to eight-bed dorms (bunks), plus one twin and a double, all with ceiling fans. Train, bus and plane tickets sold and tours booked, and plenty of useful information on hand as well as free Internet access. Off-street parking. Rates include linen, tea and coffee and a pancake breakfast. Dorms $17, rooms ❶

North Adelaide and Kent Town

Adelaide Meridien 21 Melbourne St, North Adelaide ☏ 08/8267 3033, ⓦ www .adelaidemeridien.com.au. Located on fashionable Melbourne St, though the modern brick building is an eyesore and the 1980s decor is rather outdated. Creature comforts include a sauna, spa and outdoor pool. Undercover parking is included in the rates. ❼

Georgia Mews 31–33 Wakefield St, Kent Town ☏ 08/8362 0600, ⓦ www.georgiamews.com.au. Just east of the city centre, and close to the restaurants and cafés of The Parade in Norwood. Beautifully decorated, light and spacious one-bedroom apartments, with a shady, flower-filled courtyard, telephone, TV, laundry and car parking. Fully self-catering, and supplies for a hearty breakfast included. ❺

Greenways Apartments 41–45 King William Rd, North Adelaide ☏ 08/8267 5903, ⓦ www.green ways.auz.net. One-, two- and three-bedroom fully furnished self-catering units in an excellent location. ❹

Beach suburbs

Glenelg Beach Resort 1–7 Moseley St, Glenelg ☏ 08/8376 0007 or 1800 066 422, ⓦ www.glenelgbeachresort.com.au. Award-winning hostel near the beach. Lots of doubles (with fridge and sink) and some singles and self-contained units available, as well as five- to six-bed dorms (no bunks). The lively common area downstairs has a bar open to the public, with loud music and activities ranging from bands, karaoke and comedians to pool comps and theme nights. Lots of extras, including Internet access, free breakfast, bikes, videos and free weekly tours of the city and the Fleurieu Peninsula. No parking. Dorms $16–20, rooms ❷–❸, self-contained units ❹–❺

Glenelg Jetty Hotel 28 Jetty Rd, Glenelg ☏ 08/8294 4377, ⓕ 8295 4412. Friendly, homely pub accommodation popular with country people

The beachfront **Semaphore Hotel**, 17 Semaphore Rd (℡08/8449 4662, ℻8449 4626), in Semaphore (see p.807), a beach suburb about 15km northwest of the centre, is lesbian-run but also welcomes gay male guests and straights. The pleasant pub rooms share bathrooms (❷–❸, weekly rates available), and there's a comfortable common room with a wood stove and pool table. The pub itself serves inexpensive meals and hosts live bands and DJs (Wed–Sun until 2am). Other, more central gay-friendly establishments include self-catering apartments at **Gurny Lodge**, 190–194 Gover St, North Adelaide (℡ & ℻ 08/8239 2301; ❻) and **Greenways Apartments** (see p.799); and deluxe hotel rooms at the **Stamford Plaza Adelaide** (see p.798). Parkside Travel (℡08/8274 1222) has an accommodation service, or check the ads in *Blaze* (see box on p.814).

visiting the city. Rooms are en suite or with shared bathroom. ❸–❹

Glenelg Seaway Apartments 18 Durham St, Glenelg ℡08/8295 8503. Four basic and slightly run-down apartments in a quiet location close to the beach. ❷–❹

Meleden Villa 268 Seaview Rd, Henley Beach ℡08/8235 0577. Good-value B&B one street back from the beach in a lovely old two-storey building with a pool and outdoor terrace. Downstairs rooms

share a bathroom, while upstairs rooms, with balconies and sea views, are en suite. ❸–❹

Taft Motor Inn 18 Moseley St, Glenelg ℡08/8376 1233, ⓦwww.taftmotorinn.citysearch.com. Well-equipped motel units and one- and two-bedroom self-catering apartments near the beach; all have air-con and slightly dreary old-fashioned decor. Good for families, with a playground, garden and swimming pool (and toddler pool); baby-sitting available. 24hr reception. ❹–❺

The City

Adelaide's city centre is laid out on a strict grid plan surrounded by parkland: at the heart of the grid is **Victoria Square**, and each city quarter is centred on its own smaller square. **North Terrace** is the cultural precinct, home to the city's major museums, two universities and the state library. **Hindley Street** is the liveliest in town, and the focus of the city's nightlife, while **Rundle Mall**, its continuation, is the main shopping area; **Rundle Street**, further east, is home to the city's arty café strip. West of Victoria Square between Grote and Gouger streets is the lively **Central Market** and the small **Chinatown**. The **Torrens River** flows to the north of North Terrace, while the Botanic Gardens and zoo are set on its south bank. Three main roads cross the river to the distinctive colonial architecture and café culture of **North Adelaide**.

Adelaide suffered numerous economic setbacks and built up its wealth slowly, and its well-preserved **Victorian architecture** has a reassuring permanence quite unlike the over-the-top style of 1850s Melbourne, with its grandiose municipal buildings funded by easy goldrush money. The bourgeois solidity of Adelaide's streets is enhanced by the fact that virtually every building, public or domestic, is made of **stone**, whether sandstone, bluestone, South Australian freestone or slate.

The Botanic Gardens and Ayers House

There's really only one place to start your tour, and that's tree-lined **North Terrace**, a long heritage streetscape perfect for exploring on foot. At the eastern extremity of North Terrace is the main entrance to the **Botanic Gardens** (Mon–Fri 8am–dusk, Sat & Sun 9am–dusk; free guided tours from the kiosk by the main lake Tues, Fri & Sun at 10.30am; ⓦwww.environment.sa.gov.au /botanicgardens). Opened in 1857, the lovely gardens boast ponds, fountains, wisteria arbours, statues and heritage buildings – just like a classic English-style garden, but with plenty of native trees too. The elegant glass and wrought-iron **Palm House**, completed in 1877, was based on a similar building in Germany. Its role of displaying tropical plant species has been taken over by the stunning **Bicentennial Conservatory** (daily 10am–4pm, summer until 5pm; $3). This, the largest glasshouse in Australia, houses a complete tropical rainforest environment with its own computer-controlled cloud-making system. Make sure you pick up the leaflet *Walk with the Plants*, which gives detailed information about the glasshouse's contents. Other attractions include a fragrant herb garden, a rose garden and **Simpson House**, a pleasantly cool thatched hut containing palms and ferns beside a stream. When you've had enough, you can sit under shady trees by the duck-filled main lake outside the excellent licensed **kiosk** and have a beer or snack. At the northern entrance to the gardens, **North Lodge**, once the caretaker's residence, is now a shop (daily noon–4pm) that sells books on botany and gardening, plus other souvenirs.

Heading away from the gardens on North Terrace, the first notable building you come to is the National Trust-owned **Ayers House** (Tues–Fri 10am–4pm, Sat & Sun 1–4pm; $6). Home to the politician **Henry Ayers** who was premier of South Australia seven times between 1855 and 1897 and after whom the Rock was named, it began as a small brick dwelling in 1845: the fine bluestone mansion you now see is the result of thirty years of extensions. Inside, it's elaborately decorated in late-nineteenth-century style, with portraits of the Ayers family.

The universities and the Art Gallery of South Australia

Between Frome Road and Kintore Avenue, a whole block of North Terrace is occupied by the University of Adelaide, and the art gallery, museum and state library. The **University of Adelaide**, the city's oldest, was established in 1874 and began to admit women right from its founding – another example of South Australia's advanced social thinking. The grounds are pleasant to stroll through: along North Terrace are **Bonython Hall**, built in 1936 in a vaguely medieval style, and **Elder Hall**, a turn-of-the-twentieth-century Gothic-Florentine design now occupied by the Conservatorium of Music (concerts Fri 1.10pm; $4; ☎08/8303 5925 for details). The highly decorative, Gothic-inspired **Mitchell Building** beside it constituted the entire original university; on the first floor is the **Museum of Classical Archaeology** (Mon–Fri noon–3pm, term time only; free).

Overbearing Victorian busts of the upright founders of Adelaide line the strip between Bonython Hall and Kintore Avenue until you reach the two contemporary abstract sculptures outside the **Art Gallery of South Australia**, established in 1881 (daily 10am–5pm; free; guided tours Mon–Fri 11am & 2pm, Sat & Sun at 11am & 3pm; talks at 12.45pm most Tuesdays; Ⓦwww.artgallery.sa.gov.au). The gallery itself has an impressive collection of **Aboriginal art**, including many non-traditional works with overtly political content; major works by the Western Desert school of Aboriginal artists are on permanent display in Gallery 7. There's a fine selection of **colonial art**, too, and it's interesting to trace the development of Australian art from its European-inspired beginnings up to the point where the influence of the local light, colours and landscape begins to take over. The collection of **twentieth-century Australian art** has some good stuff – Sidney Nolan, Margaret Preston, Grace Cossington-Smith – but a lot of dross too. There's also a large collection of twentieth-century British art, including paintings by Roger Fry and Vanessa Bell (Virginia Woolf's sister). The gallery also has a good bookshop and coffee shop.

The South Australian Museum and State Library

Next to the art gallery, a huge whale skeleton guards the entrance to the **South Australian Museum** (daily 10am–5pm; free; tours Sat & Sun at 2pm; Ⓦwww.samuseum.sa.gov.au). The museum's east wing houses the engrossing **Australian Aboriginal Cultures Gallery** (40min guided tours Wed–Sun; $10; book at the museum shop or on Ⓣ08/8207 7370), home to the world's largest collection of Aboriginal artefacts. Amongst the exhibits are a 10,000-year-old boomerang and the *Yanardilyi (Cockatoo Creek) Jukurrpa*, a huge painting by a collection of artists from across the continent recalling four important dreaming stories. The west wing focuses on **natural history and geology**, including an extensive collection of minerals from around the world (on level 3), amongst them local malachites, quartz and opals. There's also a permanent exhibition on local geologist **Sir Douglas Mawson** (1852–1958), who was commissioned by the museum to explore much of Australia in the early 1900s and who also undertook the historic Australasian Antarctic Expedition in 1911. Some of the animals he brought back from this expedition are still on display, along with others from around Australia. There's also a section on **Australian dinosaurs**, including a skeleton of Diprotodon, the largest marsupial ever to walk the earth, plus the **Normandy Nugget** (at the east wing entrance on the ground floor), the second-largest gold nugget in the world, weighing 26kg.

Next door to the museum, on the corner of Kintore Avenue, the 1884 **State Library** (Mon–Wed & Fri 9.30am–8pm, Thurs 9.30am–5pm, Sat & Sun noon–5pm; Ⓣ08/8207 7200, Ⓦwww.slsa.sa.gov.au) has everything from archives to newspaper and magazine reading rooms and free Internet access. The State Library also encompasses the **Bradman Collection** (Mon–Fri 10am–5pm, Sat & Sun noon–5pm; free; Ⓦwww.bradman.sa.com.au), housing Sir Donald Bradman's personal collection of cricket memorabilia, including his own memoirs of the infamous Bodyline series with England. A large screen shows interviews and footage of his finest moments.

Around the corner on Kintore Avenue is the **Migration Museum** (Mon–Fri 10am–5pm, Sat & Sun 1–5pm; free; Ⓦwww.history.sa.gov.au), which takes you on a journey from port to settlement in the company of South Australia's settlers, through innovative interactive displays and reconstructions – the "White Australia Walk", for example, has a push-button questionnaire giving you the red, green or amber light for immigration under the guidelines of the White Australia policy, which was in force from 1901 to 1958. One writer called it a "museum of grief", no doubt affected by its focus on the grim individual struggles of everyday lives, though it does celebrate cultural diversity too. The museum is housed in a former **Destitute Asylum**, where the city's poor and homeless were hidden away in the nineteenth century.

Government buildings and arts spaces

Continue west along North Terrace, past the War Memorial, to reach **Government House**, Adelaide's oldest public building, completed in 1855: every governor except the first has lived here. Across King William Road, two parliament houses, the old and the new, compete for space. The current **Parliament House**, begun in 1889, wasn't finished until 1939 because of a dispute over a dome, and while there's still no dome (and only half a coat of arms), it's a stately building all the same, with a facade of marble columns.

Alongside is the modest **Old Parliament House** (closed to the public), built between 1855 and 1876.

On the corner of North Terrace and Morphett Street, the **Lion Arts Centre** is home to theatres, bars, a cinema, galleries and the **Experimental Art Foundation,** which houses artists' studios upstairs and provocative exhibitions in the gallery downstairs (Tues–Fri 11am–5pm, Sat 2–5pm). The **Jam Factory Craft and Design Centre** (Mon–Fri 9am–5.30pm, Sat & Sun 10am–5pm, Ⓦ www.jamfactory.com.au) displays beautiful objects (all of them for sale) made of leather, glass, wood and clay. A blue metal spiral staircase leads to a viewing platform above the **glass-blowing centre** (demonstrations Mon–Fri 9am–4pm, Sat & Sun 10am–4pm). A block west of here is the latest addition to Adelaide's contemporary art scene, the **Light Square Gallery** (Mon–Fri 10am–5pm; free) in the basement of the Roma Mitchell Arts Education Centre on Light Square. The focus here is on techno art and the digital age.

Along the Torrens River

The **Torrens River** meanders between Adelaide and North Adelaide, surrounded by parklands. Between Parliament House and the river is the **Festival Centre**: two geometric constructions of concrete, steel and smoked glass, in a concrete arena scattered with abstract 1970s civic sculpture. The main auditorium, the Festival Theatre, has the largest stage in the Southern Hemisphere, hosting opera, ballet and various concerts; the foyer is often the venue for free Sunday afternoon concerts (2–4pm). The smaller Playhouse Theatre is the drama theatre, while the Space Theatre is often used for cabaret and stand-up comedy. Call ☎13 12 46 for details of specific events.

A short walk across **Elder Park** is the river with its large fountain and black swans. **Popeye Cruises** to the zoo leave from here (Mon–Fri 1–3pm hourly; Sat & Sun 11am–5pm every 20min; $4 one-way, $7.50 return), and you can also rent paddleboats ($8.80 per 30min). Nearby, the green shed at **Jolleys Boathouse**, across King William Road, is an Adelaide institution, housing a restaurant (see p.810) and a cheaper kiosk, both with river views.

The most pleasant way to get to the **Zoological Gardens**, whose main entrance is on Frome Road (daily 9.30am–5pm; $14.50, children $8; free guided walks at 11am and 2pm; call ☎08/8267 3255 for feeding times and keeper talks), is to follow the river, either by boat (see above) or on foot – a fifteen-minute stroll. Alternatively, walk from the Botanic Gardens through Botanic Park, entering through the children's zoo entrance on Plane Tree Drive, or take bus #272 or #273 from Grenfell or Currie streets. Opened in 1883, the country's second-oldest zoo (after Melbourne's) is more of a botanical garden than a zoo, with century-old European and native trees, including a huge Moreton Bay fig, and grounds full of picnic tables. The Victorian architecture is well preserved, and a few classic examples of the old-fashioned animal houses have survived, such as the **Elephant House**, built in 1900 in the style of an Indian temple. Adelaide Zoo is best known for its extensive collection of **native birds**, and there are two large walk-through aviaries. The zoo's newest section is the Southeast Asian Rainforest exhibit, whose naturalistic settings are home to sixteen animal species, including the endangered Malaysian tapir.

King William Street and Victoria Square

The city's main thoroughfare, **King William Street**, is lined with imposing civic buildings and always crowded with traffic. Look out for the **Edmund Wright House** at no. 59, whose elaborate Renaissance-style facade is one of

Adelaide's most flamboyant. Inside the building, the **State History Centre** sometimes hosts free travelling exhibitions. On the other side of the street, and a couple of blocks south, the **Town Hall** (1866) is another of Edmund Wright's Italianate designs. The **General Post Office**, on the corner of Franklin Street, is yet another portentous Victorian edifice, this time with a central clock tower: look inside at the main hall with its decorative roof lantern framed by opaque skylights. Opposite, on the corner of Flinders Street, the **Old Treasury Building** retains its beautiful facade, although it now houses apartments.

Halfway down King William Street lies pleasant **Victoria Square**, a favourite Aboriginal meeting place and home to the Catholic **Cathedral of St Francis Xavier** (1856) and the imposing **Supreme Court**, on the corner of Gouger Street. Just to the west, the covered **Central Market** (Tues 7am–5.30pm, Thurs 11am–5.30pm, Fri 7am–9pm, Sat 7am–3pm) has been a well-loved feature of Adelaide for over a hundred years. Here you can find delectable European and Asian produce in a riot of smelly stalls and lively banter, as well heaps of shops (open Mon–Sat), cafés, sushi and noodle bars and restaurants. Surrounding Gouger and Grote streets are also filled with lively restaurants and cafés.

Rundle Mall and Rundle Street

The main shopping area in the central business district is the pedestrianized **Rundle Mall**, which manages to be bustling yet relaxed, enhanced by trees, benches, alfresco cafés, fruit and flower stalls, and usually a busker or two. The two main shopping centres are the **Myer Centre**, with over 120 specialty stores over five floors, and the **Adelaide Central Plaza**, dominated by the upmarket David Jones Department Store and a fantastic foodmart in the basement. Towards the east end of the mall is the decorative **Adelaide Arcade** and the Regent Theatre. By night, Rundle Mall is eerily deserted, a strange contrast to Hindley and Rundle streets on either side, which really come to life after dark.

Rundle Street was once the home of Adelaide's wholesale fruit and vegetable market, but was later appropriated by the alternative and arty, and by university students from the nearby campuses on North Terrace. It's now home to over fifty cafés and restaurants, many of them alfresco, several slick wine bars and two of the best pubs in town (*The Austral* and *The Exeter*, see p.811). The disused **Adelaide Fruit and Produce Exchange** (1903) is worth a peek: a classically Edwardian building built of red brick with curved archways decorated with yellow plaster friezes of fruit, vegetables and wheat. The facade has remained, but the interior has been transformed into pricey serviced apartments.

Tandanya: the National Aboriginal Cultural Institute

Tandanya, the National Aboriginal Cultural Institute, is situated opposite the classic old market buildings at 253 Grenfell St (daily 10am–5pm; $4; ☎08/8224 3200 for details of exhibitions and events; ⓦwww.tandanya.com.au). The centre is managed by Aboriginal people, with the major focus on the visual arts, with temporary exhibitions of national significance and a permanent display of work called the "Desert Dream", created by Aboriginal communities from the Northern Territory. Displays cover Dreamtime stories, history and contemporary Aboriginal writing, while political paintings confront black deaths in custody and other issues. There are even a few scattered sand paintings around the floor representing the mortality of traditional art. The shop is an excellent place to buy Aboriginal products, original paintings, didgeridoos, tapes and books, as well as T-shirts and other souvenirs. There's also a 160-seat theatre for live performances – daily **didgeridoo** or **dance performances** are held at noon – and a café (Mon–Fri only) where you can try some bush tucker.

North Adelaide

North Adelaide, a ten-minute walk from the city centre, makes for an enjoyable stroll past stately mansions and small, bluestone cottages, or a good pub crawl around the many old hotels. There are three ways of getting there. The best walking route to North Adelaide is up King William Road past the Festival Centre (nearly every bus from outside the Festival Centre also goes this way). From Elder Park you cross the pretty 1874 Adelaide Bridge over the river to Cresswell Gardens, home of the **Adelaide Oval** cricket ground (guided tour Tues & Thurs except match days at 10am, Sun 2pm; 2hr; $8), which has a small **museum** of cricketing memorabilia (Tues 10am–noon & Thurs 10am–1pm; $2) and affords superb views of **St Peter's Cathedral** (daily 9am–5pm; free guided tours Wed 11am & Sun 3pm) on Pennington Terrace opposite Pennington Gardens. This Anglican cathedral was built in 1869 in French Gothic-Revival style, with an entrance suggestive of Notre-Dame in Paris. The *Cathedral Hotel* opposite, built in 1850, is Adelaide's second-oldest hotel. At the top of King William Road, the peaceful and shady **Brougham Gardens** boast palm trees set against the backdrop of the Adelaide Hills. If you continue straight up, you'll come to North Adelaide's main commercial strip, **O'Connell Street**, whose restaurant scene rivals that of Rundle Street.

The district's best range of early **colonial architecture** lies a block west of here along **Jeffcott Street**. Just south of the street in Montefiore Park is **Light's Vision**, a bronze statue of Colonel William Light pointing proudly to the city he designed. On Jeffcott Street itself is the neo-Gothic 1890 mansion **Carclew**, with its round turret, and the **Lutheran Theological College**, a fine bluestone and red-brick building with a clock tower and cast-iron decoration. Halfway up Jeffcott Street, on peaceful **Wellington Square**, lies the pretty 1851 *Wellington Hotel*, complete with its original wooden balcony. Turning into tree-lined **Gover Street** you'll find rows of simple bluestone cottages; in contrast, **Barton Terrace West**, two blocks west, has grand homes facing the parklands.

East of O'Connell Street is **Melbourne Street** (buses #204 and #209 from King William Street, #272 and #273 from Currie and Grenfell streets), an upmarket strip of good cafés, antique stores, restaurants, designer clothing boutiques and speciality shops. The **Banana Room**, at no. 125 is probably the best retro-chic clothes store in Australia, with an immaculate range of designer dresses from the 1920s through to the 1950s. Don't expect bargains – most things are over $100, but it's fascinating to browse.

The suburbs

Adelaide's **suburbs** spread a long way, and though they remain little visited, some of the inner suburbs – such as **Norwood** and **Thebarton** – have plenty of local character, inexpensive restaurants and out-of-the-ordinary shopping that's worth venturing out of the city centre for. West of the city lies a string of beaches, from **Henley** via **Glenelg** to **Brighton**, sheltered by the Gulf St Vincent. Further north, **Port Adelaide** has some excellent museums to set off its dockside atmosphere.

Norwood and Thebarton

Norwood, just east of the city, has two interesting streets: **Magill Road** (bus #106 from Grenfell or Currie streets), with its concentration of antique shops, and **The Parade** (bus #123 and #124 from Grenfell or Currie streets), a lively shopping strip with some great cafés and pubs and good bookshops. At weekends the small **Orange Lane Market** (Sat & Sun 10am–5pm), at the corner of Edward Street and The Parade, is a sedate place to browse among second-hand and new clothes, books and bric-a-brac, or eat from Asian and fry-up food stalls.

In **Thebarton**, west of the city, the lively **Brickworks Market** (Fri–Sun 9am–5pm; bus #110, #112 or #113 from Grenfell or Currie streets) spreads out from the 1912 Brickworks Kilns at 36 South Rd. There are plaza shops and indoor and outdoor stalls, mostly selling new clothes, and it's always busy with buskers and crowds of people.

Immediately south of the city, **Unley Road** (buses #190–198 from King William Street) is known for its antique shops and expensive boutiques. The parallel King William Road at **Hyde Park** (bus #203 from King William Street) is shaded by lots of trees, plants and vine-covered awnings, and has some good cafés to relax in.

Port Adelaide and Torrens Island

The unfortunate early settlers had to wade through mud at Port Misery when they arrived; nowadays, **Port Adelaide** takes the strain. Established not far from Port Misery in 1840, by 1870 it was a substantial shipping area with solid stone warehouses, wharves and a host of pubs. The area bounded by Nelson, St Vincent and Todd streets and McLaren Parade is a well-preserved nineteenth-century streetscape; several ships' chandlers and shipping agents show that it's still a living port, a fact confirmed by the many corner pubs (with pretty decorative iron-lace balconies) still in business. The **Port Adelaide Tourist Visitor Information Centre**, near the waterfront on the corner of Commercial Road and St Vincent Street (daily 9am–5pm; ☎08/8447 4788, Ⓦwww.portenf.sa.gov.au), provides up-to-date details of attractions and information about local history.

To get here, take a train from the Adelaide train station or bus #151 (Mon–Sat daytime only) or #153 (evenings and Sun) from North Terrace, or #340 from Glenelg (Mon–Fri only). The best day to visit is Sunday or public holiday Monday, when the **Fishermen's Wharf Markets** (9am–5pm) take over a large waterfront warehouse on Queens Wharf and several **cruises** are available on the water. The market (mainly bric-a-brac) adds some life to the waterfront, but the once-varied food stalls are now dominated by purveyors of meat pies and steak sandwiches. Outside is the quaint, red-painted metal **lighthouse** (daily 10am–4pm), dating from 1869, which can be climbed as part of a visit to the South Australian Maritime Museum (see below), as can the museum's two floating vessels moored 300m away, the steam tug *Yelta* and the coastal trader *Nelcebee*. There are Sunday afternoon trips from the lighthouse with Adelaide Cruises Ltd (☎08/8447 2366) and Port Adelaide River Cruises (☎08/8341 1194).

The pick of Port Adelaide's several museums is the **South Australian Maritime Museum** on Lipson Street (daily 10am–5pm; Ⓦwww.history.sa.gov.au; $8.50, combined ticket with the Port Dock Station Railway Museum $15). Located in the old Bond Store, with its massive timber posts and wooden floors, the museum describes the story of the migrants who came through the port and the South Australian **coastal ketch trade**. Starting from the basement, the migration section has faithfully reconstructed three typical steerage or economy cabins from 1840, 1910 and 1950; you can wander through them, lie on a bunk, listen to sails creaking or hear "new Australians" remembering their journey. Level two explores South Australia's connections with the sea, from seaside scenes (with a working penny arcade), to pleasure cruises on the gulf, fishing and making model ships. On the ground floor you can board a real ketch; upstairs is a more traditional collection. Further along Lipson Street, the **Port Dock Station Railway Museum** (daily 10am–5pm; $9; combined ticket with the South Australian Maritime Museum $15) is a trainspotter's delight, with a collection of over twenty steam and diesel locomotives. A free train ride runs on demand.

A few kilometres north of Port Adelaide is **Torrens Island**. Apart from a lively fresh fish and produce market on Sunday (7am–2pm), its main attraction is its intricate **mangrove forests**, a tranquil habitat rich in marine life that can be explored on foot in the **St Kilda Mangrove Trail** (Mon–Fri 10am–3pm, Sat & Sun 10am–5pm; $6.90; ℡08/8280 8172), which has an interpretive centre and a 1.7-kilometre boardwalk for self-guided tours; or by kayak with **Blue Water Sea Kayaking** (weekends and school holidays only; $40; booking essential; ℡08/8295 8812), giving the chance to spot Port River dolphins along the way.

Semaphore to Henley Beach

On the coast just east of Port Adelaide, **Semaphore**, with its picturesque jetty and fine old buildings, was important as the site of Adelaide's signal station from 1856 until the mid-1930s, before becoming a desirable holiday spot. Its current incarnation is as a popular lesbian area (see box on p.814) with several gay- and lesbian-run cafés and a pub on **Semaphore Road**, a charming street running perpendicular to the beach, with awnings, stained-glass shop and café windows, and an old-fashioned cinema. A Sunday steam train runs from Semaphore Jetty to **Fort Glanville** at 359 Military Rd (Sept–May every third Sun 1–5pm; $4), the only complete example of the many forts built in Australia in the mid-nineteenth century, when fear of Russian invasion reached hysterical heights after the Crimean War. To get to Semaphore by public transport, take a bus to Port Adelaide (see p.806) and then bus #333.

About 8km south of Semaphore, **Grange** is a charming beachside suburb, with a row of Victorian terraced houses facing the sands (bus #112 or #135 from Grenfell Street, 30min; Grange line train, 20min) and a popular pier with an upmarket kiosk. The next beach along is atmospheric **Henley Beach** (Mon–Sat bus #137, Sun #130, both from Currie Street, 20min; #286 or #287 from North Terrace, 35min), where the focus is **Henley Square**, opposite the long wooden pier. The square is lined with classic Federation-style buildings housing several popular restaurants and cafés. South of here, on the way to Glenelg, **West Beach** (#278 bus from Currie Street; 25min) is a rather soulless spot with a caravan park. It does have a good, long, sandy **beach** though.

Glenelg and Brighton

The most popular and easily accessible of the city's beaches is at **Glenelg**, immediately south of West Beach, and 11km southwest of the city. The thirty-minute tram ride here from Victoria Square is part of the experience: the beautiful 1929 trams have original fittings – red leather seats and leather hanging straps, and wood-panelled compartments. Glenelg was the site of the landing of Governor John Hindmarsh and the first colonists on Holdfast Bay; the **Old**

Gum Tree where he read the proclamation establishing the government of the colony still stands on McFarlane Street (bus #167 or #168 from Currie or Grenfell streets), and there's a re-enactment here every year on Proclamation Day (Dec 28).

Nowadays, Glenelg is busy even off season. **Jetty Road**, the main drag, is crowded with places to eat (for the obligatory seaside fish and chips, *Bay Fish Shop* at no. 27 is the best) and there's lots of accommodation (see p.797). The tram terminates at **Moseley Square**, with its elegant town hall and clock tower. On the opposite corner, the original Victorian *Pier Hotel*, now part of the imposing seafront *Stamford Grand Hotel*, is crowded with drinkers on Sunday, when Glenelg is at its most vibrant. From Moseley Square, the jetty juts out into the bay, and in summer the beach on either side is crowded with people swimming in the calm waters; it's also a popular windsurfing spot year-round. Facing the shore, **Glenelg Tourist Information** (daily 9am–5pm; ☏08/8294 5833, Ⓦwww.holdfast.sa.gov.au) can help with the booking of accommodation, tours and rental cars; there's also a 24-hour touch-screen information terminal outside. Next door, **Beach Hire** (☏08/8294 1477) rents out deck chairs, umbrellas, bikes, surf skis, body-boards and snorkel sets. Rollerblading and cycling are other popular activities in Glenelg, with a **bike track** south of the square – you can rent mountain and touring bikes from Beach Hire for $35 per day. The foreshore is also overlooked by a new marina development, a huge, but tastefully designed complex comprising apartments, waterfront restaurants and upmarket cafés, including *Cybersurfer*, a licensed Internet cafe.

South of Glenelg, **Brighton** has an old-fashioned, sleepy air, dominated by the stone Arch of Remembrance, flanked by palm trees, which stands in front of the long jetty. Running inland from the beach, Jetty Road has a string of appealing one- and two-storey buildings shaded with awnings that contain an assortment of art, craft and secondhand stores, and two popular alfresco cafés: *A Cafe Etc* and *Horta's*. Brighton is reached by train from Adelaide (25min) or bus #266 from Grote Street. For beaches further south, see p.832.

Eating and drinking

Adelaide has roughly one restaurant for every thirty people, so not surprisingly **eating out** is a local obsession, and it's incredibly inexpensive compared to Sydney or Melbourne. One of the city's most popular places for a meal out is **Gouger Street** – many of the restaurants here are alfresco and at their busiest on Friday night, when the nearby Central Market stays open until 9pm. **Moonta Street**, right next to Central Market, is the home of Adelaide's small **Chinatown**, and has several Chinese restaurants and supermarkets, while the excellent **food plaza** off Moonta Street (daily 11am–4pm, Fri until 9pm) serves Vietnamese, Indian, Singaporean, Thai and Malaysian food, as well as Chinese *yum cha* and Cantonese BBQ. **Café** society is based around **Rundle Street** in the city, and **O'Connell Street** and the decidedly chic **Melbourne Street** in North Adelaide. Finally, eating in **pubs** in Adelaide doesn't just mean the usual steak and salad bar but covers the whole spectrum, from some of the best "contemporary" Australian food in town to bargain specials in several pubs along King William Street.

As for drinking, South Australian **wine** features heavily – which is just as well, since, by general consensus, **tap water** in Adelaide tastes dreadful, although it's perfectly safe. There's usually only a small charge for spring water. And thanks to the state's liberal licensing laws, even most cafés are licensed.

City centre

Cafés and cheap meals

Al Fresco Gelateria & Pasticceria 260 Rundle St. If you go to only one café in Adelaide, make it this one. Packed every night, the young Italian community have made it their own, and it's *the* place to people watch and be seen, plus great coffee, *biscotti*, delicious home-made *gelati* and focaccia and calzone. Daily 6.30am until late.

Cowley's Pie Cart An Adelaide institution, this mobile pie cart takes up its position each night outside the GPO on Franklin St. It's famous for its pie floaters. Mon–Thurs & Sun 6pm–1am, Fri & Sat 6pm–3.30am.

Eros Ouzeri 275–277 Rundle St. Greek meze-style dining in a smart and airy setting in a renovated old building with high metal ceilings; the attached café serves Greek pastries and coffee. Licensed.

Fasta Pasta 131 Pirie St and 465 Pulteney St. Part of a chain which serves authentic and inexpensive fresh pasta with unusual sauces. Other branches at Glenelg and Brighton (see p.807).

Govinda's 79 Hindley St. Small vegetarian restaurant with Indian sweet cakes and an all-you can-eat lunch for $8.50. Lunch Mon–Sat 11.30am–3pm, dinner Tues–Sat 5.30–8.30pm.

Hawkers Corner 141 West Terrace, cnr Wright St. Something of an Adelaide cheap-eats institution, with Chinese, Thai, Malaysian and North Indian stalls. Try the Malay seafood laksa. Unlicensed and no BYO allowed. Tues–Sat 5–10pm, Sun 11.30am–8.30pm.

Jerusalem Sheshkebab House 131B Hindley St. Dimly lit Lebanese BYO that serves fresh and tasty Middle Eastern dishes. Daily noon until midnight.

Marcellina Pizza Bar 273 Hindley St. This all-night pizza, steak and pasta bar is always full of people who have spilled out from the area's clubs and pubs. The pizzas are among the best in town; deliveries too (call ☎08/8211 7560). Mon–Thurs & Sun 11.30am–2am, Fri & Sat 11.30am–5am.

Roma's 200 Hutt St. Deli-style café with gleaming counters and displays packed with cosmopolitan but reasonably priced edibles. Great breakfasts and excellent coffee too. Licensed and BYO. Mon–Fri 7.30am–5pm, Sat & Sun 7.30am–6pm.

Scoozi Caffe Bar A few doors east of *Al Fresco*. This popular licensed café does great Italian food – try the excellent wood-fired pizzas.

Zuma Caffe 56 Gouger St. Locals flock here for the huge breakfasts, big salads, and filo parcels, bruschetta, focaccia and quiche baked on the premises. Mon–Thurs 7am–6pm, Fri 7am–10pm, Sat 7am–4am.

Pubs and wine bars

Ambassadors Hotel 107 King William St. Slightly sleazy pub, but does a cheap, simple pub lunch, put on to attract people to play the pokies here.

Austral Hotel 205 Rundle St. Excellent, inexpensive bistro meals, Malaysian, Thai, Mexican and Italian dishes, and good old Aussie steaks, burgers and seafood. There's also a pricier restaurant with an extensive wine list sourced from boutique wineries.

Bull and Bear Ale House 91 King William St. This snazzy bar in the basement of the State Bank Centre offers a cool retreat on hot days for sticky stockbrokers, with imported ales and sophisticated, expensive meals.

Earl of Aberdeen 316 Pulteney St, Hindmarsh Square ☎08/8223 6433. Set in a gazebo full of greenery and serving huge portions of moderately priced, imaginatively cooked pasta, steak, fish and kangaroo. Attentive service.

Oostende Ebeneezer Place, off Rundle Street. Busy Belgian café, with loads of different Belgian beers (bottled and on tap) and Belgian food. Daily 10.30am until late.

Universal Wine Bar 258 Rundle St ☎08/8232 5000. Stylish bar run by a winemaker which aims to educate people about South Australia's wines, with vintages by the glass or bottle, plus a small menu of delicious, moderately priced bistro food with a provincial French and Mediterranean slant. Mon–Sat 11.30am–late. Live jazz on Sundays from 3.30pm.

Restaurants

Amalfi Pizzeria Ristorante 29 Frome St ☎08/8223 1948. Upbeat, jazzy and young with a variety of moderately priced vegetarian dishes, innovative pasta sauces and traditional ones given a hot edge. Crowded, and open very late. Licensed. Closed Sat lunch & Sun.

Garage 163 Waymouth St ☎08/8212 9577. Funky, moderately priced restaurant and bar in a converted garage warehouse with original brick walls. Great breakfasts and a lively lunch menu plus snacks served throughout the evening, when the focus turns to socializing, dancing and DJ music. Restaurant Mon–Fri 9.30am–3pm, Sun 11am–4pm, also dinner Mon 5.30–9.30pm.

Gaucho's 91 Gouger St ☎08/8231 2299. If you're after red meat, this Argentinian place serves some of the best steaks in town: name your weight. Licensed and BYO. Moderate prices. Closed Sat & Sun lunch.

The Grange At the *Adelaide Hilton*, 233 Victoria Square ☎08/8217 2000. European-style fine dining prepared by one of Australia's best chefs,

SOUTH AUSTRALIA | Adelaide

8

Cheong Liew, who brings an Asian angle to already adventurous dishes. Very expensive. Dinner Tues–Sat, closed Dec & Jan.

Irodori 291 Rundle St ⑦08/8232 6799. Modern, moderately priced Japanese restaurant specializing in sushi and *teppanyaki*. Some alfresco seating. BYO and licensed. Lunch Mon–Fri, dinner nightly.

Jolleys Boathouse Jolleys Lane, off Victoria Drive next to City Bridge ⑦08/8223 2891. Converted boathouse serving mouthwatering but pricey contemporary Australian cuisine. A popular venue for Sunday lunch. Licensed. Closed Sun night.

The Oyster Bar 14 East Terrace ⑦08/8232 5422. This contemporary bar with alfresco seating overlooking Elder Park dishes up oysters ($12 per dozen) and a range of moderately priced bistro meals. Daily noon–late.

Star of Siam 67 Gouger St ⑦08/8231 3527. Extremely popular, award-winning Thai restaurant with a superb, reasonably priced menu, including a good range of vegetarian dishes. Licensed. Lunch Mon–Fri, dinner Mon–Sat.

T-chow 68 Moonta St ⑦08/8410 1413. Huge, popular and reasonably cheap Chinese restaurant serving Teochew regional specialities such as Teochew tender duck, shark's fin soup and green peppercorn chicken, plus quick noodle lunches for $5.

Ying Chow 114 Gouger St ⑦08/8211 7998. Unpretentious place, always crowded, serving inexpensive northern Chinese cuisine, including specialities such as aniseed tea duck or scallops cooked with coriander and Chinese thyme. Vegetarians can enjoy delicious dishes such as bean curd with Chinese chutney. Licensed and BYO. Lunch Fri only, dinner nightly.

North Adelaide, Norwood and Unley

Cafés and cheap meals

Café Paradiso 150 King William Rd, Hyde Park, near Unley. A long-established Italian favourite, with great coffee and *biscotti* and alfresco dining out front. Food ranges from pasta to *fritto misto*. Licensed. Daily 8.30am–11.30pm.

Caffe Buongiorno 145 The Parade, Norwood. Large, always lively café serving a wide variety of Italian food and drink which reaches a crowded and noisy crescendo on Sunday night. Daily 8am–1am or later.

Elephant Walk Coffee Lounge 76 Melbourne St, North Adelaide. Lively but intimate place, with small private lounge areas divided by carved wooden elephants and bamboo screens. Daily 8pm–late.

The Oxford Deli Bar At the *Oxford Hotel*, 101 O'Connell St, North Adelaide. Groovy and good-value pub, with plenty of meals around for $8 – try the Oxburger and fries.

Red Rock Noodle Bar 48 Unley Rd, Unley ⑦08/88357 3888. Stylish restaurant serving generous and inexpensive servings of all sorts of delicious noodle dishes – the $6 lunch specials are good value. Other branches include 125 The Parade, Norwood, and 141 O'Connell St, North Adelaide.

Restaurants

Bacall's 149 Melbourne St, North Adelaide

⑦08/8267 2030. Cajun specialist with authentic oven-baked dishes and a lively New Orleans-style atmosphere. Book early if you want one of the few streetside tables. Moderate. BYO and licensed. Tues–Sat 6–10pm.

Kwik Stix 42 O'Connell St, North Adelaide ⑦08/8239 2023. Spacious modern Asian restaurant with good-value meals, including excellent char-grilled and sizzling dishes from Laos, Korea and Malaysia (dinner only). Daily noon–2.30pm & 5–10pm.

The Melting Pot 160 King William Rd, Hyde Park, near Unley ⑦08/8373 2044. One of the best modern French restaurants in Adelaide, with fantastic veal, spiced duck and seasonal fish, plus good wines and champagnes. Lunch Thurs & Fri, dinner Mon–Sat.

Shibata 131 Melbourne St, North Adelaide ⑦08/8267 3381. Japanese restaurant specializing in moderately priced *nabe mono* (one-pot dishes). BYO and licensed. Dinner Tues–Sun.

The Snake Charmer 60 Unley Rd, Unley ⑦08/8272 2624. Upmarket North Indian place. BYO and licensed. Closed Sun.

Zambracca 94–98 Melbourne St, North Adelaide ⑦08/8239 1345. A lively, licensed bistro crowded with Adelaide's smart set and dishing up superb, moderately priced Mediterranean food in slick, spacious surroundings. Daily 8am–late.

Beach suburbs

Cafés and cheap meals

Fasta Pasta 16 Jetty Rd, Glenelg, and 430 Brighton Rd, Brighton. Inexpensive pasta chain.

Henley on Sea Immediately south of Henley Square, opposite the Henley Beach Life Saving Club ⑦08/8235 2250. Relaxed café-brasserie – it was used as the location for *Moby Dick's* piano bar in the film *Shine* – with a summery atmosphere and views of the jetty and water, plus shaded tables outside. Food comprises light contemporary dishes with an emphasis on seafood. Licensed. Lunch & dinner daily from 11am; closed Tues.

Horta's 75–77 Jetty Rd, Brighton. Pretty licensed beachside place with pavement tables and a fish mosaic out front. Popular for lunch, with dishes ranging from pasta to Thai. Closed Mon. If it's full try the neighbouring *A Cafe Etc*, which does great all-day breakfasts and big salads.

The Lovin' Spoonful 69A Semaphore Rd, Semaphore. Gay- and lesbian-friendly café/restaurant with rich cakes, light vegetarian meals and Aussie bush tucker on the menu, plus cocktails in the quaint courtyard. Daytime only (opening hours change with the weather).

Sarah's 85 Dale St, Port Adelaide ☎08/8341 2103. Popular vegetarian restaurant. Lunch Mon–Fri, dinner Wed–Sat.

Stamford Grand Hotel The Foreshore, Glenelg ☎08/8375 0622. There are several good cafés and places to eat in this hotel, including the excellent café-style *Rickshaw's* restaurant, divided by an open kitchen where you watch the chefs at work: one side serves spicy Indian meals, the other a variety of Asian dishes. There's also a more upmarket contemporary restaurant, *The Promenade*, with great sea views.

Restaurants

Estias Henley Square, Henley Beach ☎08/8353 2875. Fun seaside place for casual dining on Greek meze amongst a playful modern Hellenic-themed decor, with reproduction classical sculptures and columns supporting the bar. Also serves more substantial, moderately priced dishes such as moussaka, and daily specials. Licensed and BYO. Closed Mon.

Lido On the Marina Pier Promenade at Glenelg. Reasonably priced Mediterranean-style restaurant, right on the water, with great views and an excellent atmosphere. Daily lunch & dinner.

Mama Carmella 4 Jetty Rd, Glenelg ☎08/8331 2288. Very popular, gleaming Italian café-pizzeria which is good for moderately priced lunches, a late meal or just coffee. Outside tables overlook the square. Daily 8am–late.

Entertainment and nightlife

Adelaide may appear dead at night, but there's actually quite a lot going on – bands, clubs, film and theatre – if you know where to look. The best place to find out **what's on** is *The Guide*, which comes with Thursday's *Advertiser* and has film and theatre listings and reviews. There's also a thriving **free press**: top of the culture stakes is *The Adelaide Review*, a highbrow monthly covering the visual and performing arts, dance, film, literature, history, wine and food, available from bookshops such as Imprints on Hindley Street, museums, galleries and just about everywhere else. At the more populist end of the scale, *Rip It Up* is a gig listings magazine, out every Thursday, with film, theatre, club and music reviews and interviews; *db Magazine*, in the same vein, is published every two weeks on Wednesdays – both can be picked up at Rundle Street record stores such as B# Records, at no. 240, and Verandah Music at no. 182. Most big music events can be booked through Bass (☎13 12 46, ⊛www.bass.sa.com.au), which has an outlet at Verandah Music; B# Records sells tickets for underground events around town.

At night, the two spots to head for are **Rundle Street**, which boasts the most fashionable pubs and bars, and the more mainstream and rather sleazy **Hindley Street**, where you'll find several funky clubs and live-music venues east of Morphett Street catering for the nearby university crowd. For something a bit different, try the **Adelaide Casino** (Mon–Thurs & Sun 10am–4am, Fri & Sat 10am–6am; neat dress required), near the train station, complete with stunning domed marble entrance, glitzy gaming rooms and jaw-dropping Austrian crystal chandeliers.

Pubs and bars

Austral Hotel 205 Rundle St ☎08/8223 4660. More consciously arty and music-oriented than the *Exeter* (see overleaf), the *Austral* is frequented by students for the independent local bands on Fri

The Adelaide Festival of Arts and Womadelaide

The huge **Adelaide Festival of Arts**, which takes over the city for three weeks from late February to mid-March in even-numbered years, attracts an extraordinary range of international and Australian theatre companies, performers, musicians, writers and artists. An avant-garde **Fringe** has grown up around the main festival, which for many people is more exciting than the main event. The official festival began in 1960 and has been based since 1973 at the purpose-built **Festival Centre** (see p.803). In addition, free outdoor concerts, opera and films are held outside the Festival Centre and at various other locations during the festival, while other venues around town host an "Artists' Week", "Writers' Week" and a small film festival. The 2004 Festival of Arts runs from February 27 to March 14 (ⓦwww.adelaidefestival .org.au).

The **Fringe Festival** begins with a wild street parade on Rundle Street a week before the main festival. The festival is based in **Rundle Street**, but events are held at venues all over town, with bands, cabaret and comedy at the Fringe Club, plus free outdoor shows and activities, while full use is made of the 24-hour licensing laws. The 2004 Fringe Festival runs from February 20 to March 14 (ⓦwww .adelaidefringe.com.au). **Advance programmes** for both the main and the fringe festival and further information is available from the offices of Tourism South Australia, or from all Bass outlets.

The annual **Womadelaide** world music weekend began in 1992 as part of the Arts Festival but has now developed its own separate identity, attracting over 30,000 people. Womadelaide is held in early March in the Botanic Park – four stages, two workshop areas, multicultural food stalls and visual arts – and is a great place to hear some of Australia's local talent, with a broad selection of Aboriginal musicians as well as internationally acclaimed contemporary and traditional artists from around the world. The full weekend (Fri night–Sun night) costs $150, but day and session passes are also available. Tickets are available from Bass (☎13 12 46, ⓦwww.bass.sa.com.au). For advance information check out the website of Womadelaide (ⓦwww.womadelaide.com.au).

and Sat nights, and DJs Tues–Thurs & Sun nights. DJs are free, as is most of the music – when there's a cover charge, it's around $5. Fri & Sat open until 3am.

The Daniel O'Connell 165 Tynte St, North Adelaide ☎08/8267 4032. Huge Irish pub with a lovely beer garden set around an old pep-pertree plus a large restaurant. Live bands – sometimes Irish folk musicians – play on Friday and Saturday nights, when the place is heaving.

Exeter Hotel 246 Rundle St ☎08/8223 2623. This spacious old pub with an iron-lace balcony is a long-established hangout for Adelaide's artists, writers and students, yet remains totally unpreten-tious. Good lunches served, and music nightly; no cover charge.

Governor Hindmarsh 59 Port Rd, Hindmarsh ☎08/8340 0744, ⓦwww.thegov.com.au. The Gov, as this Adelaide institution is affectionately known, is one of Adelaide's leading live venues (it survived a recent threat of closure after five thousand people marched to Parliament House to voice their con-cern). It currently hosts a broad range of live music and cabaret, with gigs on Wed, Thurs & Sat from 9pm, and jam sessions and Irish music Fri from 9pm.

Grace Emily 232 Waymouth St ☎08/8231 5500 Relaxed atmosphere and a range of local acts to suit everyone. Nightly until late.

Worldsend 208 Hindley St ☎08/8231 9137. Large, multi-functional pub popular with the nearby university crowd and boasting two bars, a restaurant, cocktail bar, lounge, beer garden and live music at weekends. Licensed till 4am.

Clubs, comedy and live music

Café Tapas 147 Hindley St ☎08/8211 7446. Spanish tapas bar hosting arty events including flamenco music and dancing on Friday and Saturday. Closed Sat lunch & Mon.

Cargo Club 213 Hindley St ☎08/8231 2327. Laid-back club featuring live jazz, spoken word, cabaret, soul, Latin, African and reggae acts and local and international DJs; the decor is a mix of classic cool and 1990s postmodernism, and there's something on most nights.

Church 9 Synagogue Place, off Rundle St ℗08/8223 4233. This industrial-chic club venue in a converted temple is the enduring focus for Adelaide's rave scene, with local and international DJs. Wed–Sat 9pm–5am.

Crown and Sceptre 308 King William St ℗08/8212 4159. A heritage-listed pub with original leadlighting that's been groovified into one of Adelaide's best venues, complete with sparkly bar stools, cosy couches in the intimate band area and a busy espresso machine. Local bands Tues–Fri & Sun (usually free); Saturday is club night (until 5am; around $5), alternating weekly from *Comfy Club* (funk-beat oriented) to jungle and techno. Plays and poetry readings are sometimes held in the lounge.

Enigma 173 Hindley St ℗08/8212 2313. Hip venue for the alternative university crowd. The small bar spills out into the street at weekends, and there's either funk or live grunge music upstairs. Wed–Sat till late.

Heaven 2 1 West Terrace ℗08/8211 8533. Huge dance club with a trashy teenage feel hosting resident DJs as well as visiting international acts and one-off events. Wed–Sat 9pm–5am.

The Planet 77 Pirie St ℗08/8359 2797. There's a whole world of entertainment crammed into this place, with a dance club hosting the best of local and international DJs, as well as a pool room, cocktail bar, wine bar and several cafés.

Rhino Room Upstairs at 13 Frome St ℗08/8227 1611. Underground club venue with an intimate lounge atmosphere: come casual or get glammed up, no one cares, though the regular clientele may make you feel as if you've barged into a private party. Comedy and poetry on Wed, local bands Thurs, funk on Fri and techno DJ on Sat. The cosy little bar provides a retreat from the performance. Wed–Fri 9pm–1am, Sat & Sun until 3am. Standard charge $5.

Royal Oak 123 O'Connell St, North Adelaide ℗08/8267 2488. Popular North Adelaide bar and restaurant with arty decor and a young crowd. Live jazz/Latin Sun and Wed, local bands Tues and Fri.

Gay and lesbian nightspots

Edinburgh Castle Hotel 233 Currie St ℗08/8410 1211. Friendly gay and lesbian-only venue with a dance floor Thurs to Sun, plus jukebox, bistro and beer garden with drag shows on Sun. Mon–Thurs 11am–midnight, Fri 11am–1.30am, Sat 11am–1am, Sun 2pm–1am.

Mars Bar 122 Gouger St ℗08/8231 9639. This Adelaide institution has been around for years and hosts rag acts and a big, friendly mixed crowd. Wed–Sat 9pm–late.

Film

As well as several city and suburban mainstream film complexes, Adelaide now has four art-house/retro cinemas. The main **discount day** for mainstream cinemas is Tuesday. In the summer, you can watch films outdoors at the **Moonlight Cinema** in the Botanic Gardens; bookshops around town have programmes (or check out Ⓦwww.moonlight.com.au); tickets ($13) are available at the gate from 7.30pm onwards or through Bass (℗13 12 46, Ⓦwww.bass.sa.com.au).

Capri 141 Goodwood Rd, Goodwood ℗08/8272 1177. Alternative and arty films complete with pre-show Wurlitzer organ on Tuesday, Friday and Saturday evenings.

Chelsea 275 Kensington Rd, Kensington Park ℗08/8431 5080. The latest releases and a "crying room" for parents and babies.

Cinema Nova 251 Rundle St ℗08/8223 6333. New arts cinema complex with three screens. Substantial backpacker discounts (with the relevant card); discount day is Tuesday.

Mercury Cinema Lion Arts Centre, 13 Morphett St ℗08/8410 1934, Ⓦwww.mrc.org.au. A great art-house cinema showing short and foreign films.

Odeon Star Cinema 65 Semaphore Rd, Semaphore ℗08/8341 5988. Quaint local beach-side cinema showing mainstream films.

Palace East End 274 Rundle St ℗08/8232 3434. Alternative venue showing foreign-language and art-house and other new releases. Cheap day Tuesday. Discounts for backpackers.

Trak Cinemas 375 Greenhill Rd, Toorak Gardens ℗08/8332 8020. Good alternative cinema with two screens. Cheap day Tuesday. Bus #145 from North Terrace to stop 10.

Gay and lesbian Adelaide

South Australia was the first state to legalize gay sex and remains one of the most tolerant of lesbian and gay lifestyles, although Adelaide's gay scene remains more modest than Sydney or Melbourne. Apart from the city's more mainstream annual festivals, there are a few strictly gay and lesbian fiestas. The biggest and best is **Feast** (T08/8231 2155), launched in 1997, which runs for three weeks from late October to mid-November; events include theatre, music, visual art, literature, dance cabaret, historical walks and a **Gay and Lesbian Film Festival** at the Mercury Cinema (see p.813). The festival culminates in **Picnic in the Park**, an outdoor celebration in the parklands which surround central Adelaide, which has been a feature of the Adelaide scene for over a decade. Entertainment includes a very camp dog show. Earlier in the year, June's **Stonewall Celebrations** are less flamboyant, featuring serious talks and exhibitions in a number of venues. A popular gay hangout is **Pulteney 431 Sauna**, 431 Pulteney St (Wed–Fri noon–1am, Fri & Sat noon–3am; T08/8223 7506), with a spa, sauna, steam room, pool and snack bar.

To find out where the action is, pick up a copy of *Blaze* or check out other possibilities in the listings below. See p.800 for gay- and lesbian-friendly **places to stay**, and p.813 for gay and lesbian nightspots.

Useful organizations and publications

Blaze 213 Franklin St T08/8211 9199, Wwww.blazemedia.com.au. Fortnightly gay and lesbian newspaper, with news, features and listings. Free from venues and bookshops (you'll definitely find it at Imprints, 80 Hindley St). Blaze also publishes the handy free *Lesbian & Gay Adelaide Map*.

Darling House Gay and Lesbian Community Library 64 Fullarton Rd, Norwood T08/8362 3106. Fiction, non-fiction and newspapers. Mon–Fri 9am–5pm, Sat 2–5pm.

Liberation Monthly newsletter for lesbians – good for contacts and local happenings.

Murphy Sisters Bookshop 264 Portrush Rd, Beulah Pk T08/8332 7508. Gay/lesbian bookshop with a handy notice board. Wed–Sat only.

Parkside Travel 70 Glen Osmond Rd, Parkside T08/8274 1222 or 1800 888 501. Gay owned and operated. Hotel reservations, information and travel services.

Theatre and the performing arts

Out of festival time, mainstream theatre, ballet, opera, contemporary dance, comedy and cabaret continue to thrive at the **Festival Centre**. Classical concerts are held at the **Adelaide Town Hall** (usually performed by the Adelaide Symphony Orchestra) and at **Elder Hall** at the Conservatorium of Music on North Terrace. Almost anything that's on can be booked through Bass T13 12 46, Wwww.bass.sa.com.au.

Doppio Teatro Based at the Lion Arts Centre T08/8231 0070, Wwww.doppio-parallelo.on.net. This bilingual company promotes cultural diversity in the arts as well as exploring new media in its performances at various venues around Adelaide.

Festival Centre King William Rd T08/8216 8600. Three major auditoriums and free music events in the foyer (Sun 2–4pm, winter only). See p.803 for more details.

Music House Lion Arts Centre, cnr Morphett St and North Terrace T08/8218 8400. The Lion Theatre is the main venue here, and there's always lots going on, from interstate performers and jazz bands to comedy line-ups. An irregular programme, so watch out for flyers.

Theatre 62 145 Burbridge Rd, Hilton T08/8234 0838. Two venues under one roof: the larger auditorium hosts mostly pantomime and sometimes a theatre-restaurant; the smaller Chapel theatre is used for more experimental productions.

Shopping

You can find most things you'll need in **Rundle Mall** (see p.804), which has three department stores, plus a handy Woolworths at no. 86 with a small supermarket attached. There's also a Coles supermarket at 21 Grote St (open daily), next to the Central Market. For **alternative fashion**, Rundle Street and, particularly, Miss Gladys Sym Choon at no. 235 is the place to go. For retro clothing visit Mabs, 207 Grenfell St, or The Banana Room (see p.805). For **Aboriginal arts and crafts** try Tandanya (see p.804) or the Otherway Shop at 185 Pirie St. B# Records at 240 Rundle St and Krypton Discs, at 34 Jetty Rd, Glenelg, are both good for **records**.

There are several good **bookshops** around the city: Imprints, 80 Hindley St, is a good highbrow shop; the excellent Unibooks, at Adelaide University, provides an excuse to nose around the university; Angus & Robertsons, 138 Rundle Mall, is a large mainstream store; while the huge Borders, in Rundle Mall, has an excellent range of international newspapers and magazines and an in-store café. Adelaide Booksellers, 6A Rundle Mall sells good secondhand titles, as does O'Connell's Bookshop at 62 Hindley St – they also buy and exchange books.

Markets include Central Market (see p.804), Orange Lane Market, Brickworks Market, Port Adelaide Market and Torrens Island Fish and Produce Market (see p.806). East End Cellars, 22–26 Vardon St, tucked away in a lane behind the excellent *Universal Wine Bar* (see p.809) on Rundle Street, is an excellent **bottle shop** if you want to buy some choice South Australian wines to take away.

Shopping hours are Monday to Saturday 9am to 5 or 6pm, with late-night shopping until 9pm on Friday in the city and Thursday in the suburbs, plus Sunday trading (11am–5pm) in the city only.

Listings

Airlines (domestic) Airlines of South Australia (☎08/8234 3000, ⓦwww.asa.mtx.net), flies to Port Augusta, Leigh Creek, Port Lincoln. Hawker Regional Express (☎13 17 13) flies to Broken Hill, Ceduna, Mount Gambier, Port Lincoln, Whyalla, Coober Pedy, Olympic Dam and Kangaroo Island. Emu Airways (☎08/8234 3711, ⓦwww.emuair.mtx.net) flies to Kangaroo Island. Virgin Blue (☎13 67 89) now flies out of Adelaide to major cities countrywide.

Airlines (international) Air New Zealand ☎13 24 76; Alitalia ☎08/8306 8411; British Airways ☎08/8238 2000; Garuda ☎1300 365 330; Japan Airlines ☎08/8212 2555; Lufthansa ☎08/8212 6444; Malaysia Airlines ☎08/8231 6171; Qantas ☎08/8407 2233; Singapore Airlines ☎08/8203 0800.

Airport bus Skylink (☎08/8332 0528) has pick-up points at various locations, including the *Hilton Hotel* on Victoria Square and the Central bus station, but will pick you up at other city locations if you pre-book; it also services Keswick Interstate train terminal. See p.794 for details.

American Express Shop 32, Citi Centre, Rundle Mall (Mon–Fri 9am–5pm, Sat 9am–noon; ☎1300 139 060); 120 Jetty Rd, Glenelg (Mon–Fri 9am–5pm, Sat 9am–noon; ☎08/8376 7731).

Banks and foreign exchange All the major banks are located on King William St. Exchange services are available at the international airport, at American Express (see above) and at Thomas Cook, 45 Grenfell St (Mon–Fri 9am–5pm; ☎08/8211 7037) and 4 Rundle Mall (Mon–Fri 9am–5pm, Sat 10am–4pm, Sun 10am–2pm; ☎08/8231 6977). Outside these hours, the casino (see p.811) or international hotels on North Terrace can help, but obviously the exchange rates will be poor.

Bikes and bike rental Flinders Camping, 187 Rundle St (☎08/8223 1913), rents bikes for $15 per day and offers weekly rates; Linear Park Mountain Bike Hire at Elder Park (☎08/8223 6271), situated near a section of the River Torrens Linear Park bike track, rents bikes by the hour or day at competitive prices; Bicycle SA, 1 Sturt St (☎08/8410 1406), is a nonprofit cycling organization providing information and cycling maps and organizing regular touring trips.

Buses *The State Guide*, available from South Australian Travel Centre has route maps and timetables of all South Australia's bus routes. Most long-distance buses leave from the Central Bus Station, Franklin St. Greyhound Pioneer (℡1800 801 294) has a nationwide service that includes Alice Springs and Broken Hill in its destinations, while Firefly Express (℡08/8231 1488) and McCafferty's (℡08/8212 50 66, reservations ℡13 14 99), runs to Melbourne and Sydney. V/Line (℡08/8231 7620 or 13 61 96, ⓦ www.vline.vic .gov.au) also runs to Melbourne from Adelaide and Mount Gambier. State services are dominated by Premier Stateliner Coach Service (℡08/8415 5544, ⓦ www.premierstateliner.com.au), which goes to the Riverland, Whyalla, Port Lincoln, Ceduna, Woomera, Roxby Downs and Olympic Dam, Wilpena Pound via Port Augusta, the Yorke and Fleurieu peninsulas and to Mount Gambier either inland or along the coast. Other local operators include the Barossa–Adelaide Passenger Service (℡08/8564 3022), which stops at the main towns in the Barossa Valley en route to Angaston; the Yorke Peninsula Passenger Service (℡1800 625 099), which runs from Adelaide to Yorketown, down the east coast via Ardrossan, Port Vincent and Edithburgh, and down the centre via Maitland and Minlaton; the Mid North Passenger Service (℡08/8823 2375) via the Clare Valley and/or Burra to Peterborough; and the Murray Bridge Passenger Service (℡08/8415 5555) to Pinnaroo via Murray Bridge and to Murray Bridge via Mannum and Meningie. Tickets can be purchased at the Central bus station; the Bus Booking Centre at Station Arcade, 52 Hindley St (℡08/8212 5200), can arrange travel on any bus service.

Camping equipment and rental Rundle St is the place: for rental, try Flinders Camping at no. 187 (℡08/8223 1913), who can kit you out for the Flinders Ranges given 24hr notice – they are also the only place in town that repairs backpacks; Paddy Pallin at no. 228 sells a range of high-quality gear, plus maps; or there's Scout Outdoor Centre at no. 192.

Canoe rental and tours Try Canoe & Kayak Hire, 29 Angus St, Goodwood (℡08/8271 6354), which also offers canoe trips to the Torrens Island mangroves, an area frequented by dolphins.

Car rental Avis (℡1300 367 227), Hertz (℡13 30 39) and Thrifty (℡08/8211 8788) have desks at the airport. Otherwise, try the recommended small and friendly Access, 121 Currie St (℡08/8212 5900 or 1800 812 580, ⓔ access@tne.net.au), which does free airport deliveries and is one of the few companies which allows you to take their cars to Kangaroo Island; they also rent out sports cars.

Also try Action (℡08/8352 3044, ⓦ www.action-cars-australia.com) or Excel (℡08/8234 1666, ⓦ www.excelrentalcar.com.au). Older, cheaper cars can be obtained from Cut Price Car Rentals (℡08/8443 7788, ⓦ www.cutprice.com.au), which also does one-way rentals and buy backs, or Rent-a-Bug (℡08/8443 3313). Campervans Australia NQ Rentals, 151 Burbridge Rd, Hilton (℡08/8443 3002, ⓕ 8443 3656), has two-berth campervans, sometimes on stand-by deals.

Disabled travellers Disability Information and Resource Centre, 195 Gilles St ℡08/8223 7522; Access Cabs ℡1300 360 940.

Environment and conservation The Conservation Council of South Australia, 120 Wakefield St (℡08/8223 5155), is a good place to find out what's going on; there's a notice board and reference library. The Environment Shop, 77 Grenfell St (℡08/8204 1910, ⓦ www.parks.sa.gov.au) has good free maps of the national parks and other useful brochures. The Wilderness Society has its campaign office at 116 Grote St (℡08/8231 6586) and a shop in Victoria Square Arcade, Victoria Square (℡08/8231 0625).

Hospital Royal Adelaide Hospital, North Terrace ℡08/8222 4000; Dental Hospital, North Terrace ℡08/8222 8222.

Internet access Ngapartji, 211 Rundle St (Mon–Thurs 8.30am–7pm, Fri 8.30am–10.30pm, Sat 10am–10pm, Sun noon–7pm) is a snazzy multimedia centre whose Aboriginal name means "community skills brought together". A couple of computer terminals out front can be used for free; the cybercafé inside charges $8 per hour. There's limited-time free access at the State Library (see p.802; book in advance), and cheap access at Talking Cents, 53 Hindley St ($2 per 30min). Many of the backpackers' now have Internet access for guests, including the *Adelaide YHA*, *Canon St Lodge*, *Backpack Australia*, *Sunny's* and *Glenelg Beach Resort*.

Laundries Adelaide Launderette, 152 Sturt St (daily 7am–8pm; service washes 8am–5pm); City Laundromat, cnr Gilles & Hutt St (daily 7am–9.30pm; unattended), is handy for hostels.

Left luggage Adelaide Train Station has 24hr lockers. There are also facilities at the Central Bus Station: Premier Stateliner ($2 per 24hr); Greyhound/McCafferty's (from $6 per 24hr).

Maps The Map Shop, 16A Peel St, between Hindley and Currie streets, has the largest range of local and state maps; if you're a member of an affiliated automobile association overseas, you can get free regional maps and advice on road conditions from the Royal Automobile Association, 41 Hindmarsh Square (℡08/8202 4540, ⓦ www.raa.net).

Medical centre City Centre Medical Clinic, 29 Gilbert Place ☏08/8212 3226.

Motorbike rental Show & Go Motorcycles, 236 Brighton Rd, Somerton Park ☏08/8376 0333.

Newspapers Adelaide's *The Advertiser* is very provincial and doesn't have good coverage of national and international news, but is useful on Thursday for entertainment listings, and Wednesday and Saturday for classifieds if you're looking for a car or other travel equipment. Alternatively, Melbourne's *The Age* is widely available. The best place to buy foreign and interstate newspapers is Rundle Arcade Newsagency, off Gawler Place or Borders in Rundle Mall.

Pharmacy Midnight Pharmacy, 13 West Terrace (Mon–Sat 7am–midnight, Sun 9am–midnight). In Glenelg try Walker & Stevens Chemmart, cnr Jetty Rd and Gordon St (daily 8.30am–10pm).

Police For emergencies call ☏000.

Post office GPO, 141 King William St, cnr Franklin St (Mon–Fri 8am–6pm, Sat 8.30am–noon); poste restante, Adelaide GPO, SA 5000.

Swimming pool Adelaide City Swim, 235 Flinders St (Mon 5.30am–8pm, Sat 6am–5pm, Sun 9am–1pm; $6 per hour). Adelaide Aquatic Centre, cnr Jeffcott Rd and Fitzroy Terrace, North Adelaide (daily 5am–10pm; swimming $5.10), is an indoor centre with pool, gym, sauna and spa; take bus #231 from North Terrace.

Taxis Adelaide Independent ☏13 22 11; Suburban Taxi Service ☏13 10 08; Yellow Cabs ☏13 22 27. There's a taxi rank on the corner of Pulteney and Rundle streets.

Telephones Rundle Mall has lots of phones, including ones that take credit cards. For peace and quiet, try the Phone Room in the GPO.

Tours The hop-on hop-off Adelaide Explorer City Sights Tour, in a bus dolled up as a tram, covers the city, Glenelg and West Beach, with departures from the Travel Centre, 14 King William St, daily at 9am, 10.30am, noon, 1.30pm & 3pm (☏08/8364 1933; $35; 3hr). Further afield, the majority of tours from Adelaide head for the Barossa Valley (see p.822), Kangaroo Island (see p.837) and the Fleurieu Peninsula (see p.830). General operators include Gray Line (☏1300 858 687, ⊛www .grayline.com), for upmarket tours to Cleland Wildlife Park, Adelaide Hills and Hahndorf, the Barossa Valley, McLaren Vale, Clare Valley and Kangaroo Island; Premier Day Tours (☏08/8415 5566, ⊛www.premierstateliner.com.au); and Adelaide Sightseeing (☏08/8231 4144, ⊛www .adelaidesightseeing.com.au), all of which also arrange trips further afield to the Murray River, Coorong and Flinders Ranges. Adelaide is also the home base for the excellent Wayward Bus, 115

Waymouth St (☏08/8410 8833 or 1800 882 823, ☏8410 8844, ⊛www.waywardbus.com.au), which does a good one-way, small-group tour from Adelaide to Melbourne (or vice versa) via the scenic coastal route (three and a half days; $290 including breakfast, lunch and hostel accommodation). Wayward also runs one-way tours to Alice Springs taking in the Clare Valley, Flinders Ranges, Oodnadatta Track, Lake Eyre, Coober Pedy, Uluru, Kata Tjuta and Kings Canyon (eight days; $770 all-inclusive); plus a five-day option taking in Coober Pedy, Oodnadatta Track, Lake Eyre, Maree, Wilpena Pound and the Flinders Ranges ($460). Heading Bush 4WD Adventures (☏08/8648 6655, ⊛www.headbush.mtx.net) does ten-seater camping tours to the Flinders Ranges (three days; $299); while Camp Wild Adventures (☏08/8132 1333, ⊛www.campwild.com.au) offers an adventurous 4WD camping tour to Kangaroo Island (two and a half days; $260 all inclusive), and another tour to Alice Springs via the Flinders Ranges, which continues to the Simpson Desert, Uluru, Kings Canyon, Devils Marbles and Kakadu (ten days; $985 all inclusive).

Trains The Great Southern Railway Travel Pty (☏13 21 47, ⊛www.gsr.com.au) produces a glossy brochure with current timetables. The Australian National Travel Centre, Station Arcade, North Terrace (Mon–Fri 8.30am–5.30pm; ☏08/8231 4366), deals with interstate train enquiries and sells tickets; alternatively, call in at the Australian Rail Travel Centre, 18–20 Grenfell St (Mon–Fri 8.30am–5.30pm, Sat 9am–1pm; ☏08/8231 4366).

Travel agents Adelaide YHA Travel, 135 Waymouth St ☏08/8414 3000, ⓔtravel@yhsa.org.au; City Centre Travel, 75 King William St ☏08/8221 5044, domestic travel specialists; Flight Centre, 54 King William St ☏08/8211 7246; Jetset, 23 Leigh St, off Hindley St ☏08/8231 2422; Peregrine Travel, upstairs at 192 Rundle St ☏08/8223 5905; STA Travel, 235 Rundle St ☏08/8223 2426; Thor Adventure Travel, upstairs at 228 Rundle St ☏08/8232 3155.

Vaccinations Travellers Medical and Vaccination Centre, 27–29 Gilbert Place ☏08/8212 7522, ⊛www.traveldoctor.com.

Work Employment National, 55 Currie St ☏13 3444. Information on work rights is available from the Department of Immigration and Multicultural Affairs ☏13 18 81, ⊛www.immi.gov.au /employers. Unemployment is high in Adelaide itself, but it's a good place to find out about casual fruit-picking work in the Riverland. Hostels can help with finding work, and often provide a source of employment for young travellers.

Around Adelaide

Escaping Adelaide for a day or two is easy and enjoyable, with a tempting range of beaches, hills and wineries to choose from. Closest at hand are the **Adelaide Hills**, southeast of the city, which are popular for weekend outings and have numerous small national and conservation parks that are great for walking. To the south, the **Fleurieu Peninsula** extends towards Cape Jervis and has plenty of fine beaches and several small wineries. If wine is your priority, though, head for the **Barossa Valley**, Australia's premier wine-producing region, with over thirty excellent wineries within 50km of Adelaide. The valley is easily visited in a day from the city, but is also a great place to stop over and unwind. The **Yorke Peninsula**, across the gulf from Adelaide, is far less known, though many locals holiday here: as well as beaches, it has the remains of an old copper-mining industry and an excellent national park.

The Adelaide Hills

The beautiful **Adelaide Hills** are the section of the **Mount Lofty Ranges** which run closest to the city, just thirty minutes' drive away, and largely accessible by train and the Hills Transit bus service (℡08/8339 1191); several tours heading for the Fleurieu Peninsula also take in the area (see p.830). Many people have set up home in the hills to take advantage of the cooler air, and there are some grand old summer houses here. The **Heysen Trail** long-distance walk cuts across the hills, with four quaint YHA hostels along it; most are run on a limited-access basis and you'll have to pick the key up first from the Adelaide office at 135 Waymouth St (℡08/8414 3010). Due to the high fire risk in midsummer, the trail is closed from mid-December to April. The **Adelaide Hills Visitors Information Centre** in Hahndorf (see p.820) is a good source of information about the area, and can also make accommodation bookings.

Leaving the city by Glen Osmond Road you join the **South Eastern Freeway**, the main road to Melbourne. This was the traditional route to Melbourne – there's an old tollhouse not far out of the city at Urrbrae and several fine old coaching hotels such as the *Crafers Inn*. At **CRAFERS** itself you can leave the freeway for the scenic Summit Road, which runs along the top of the hills, past the western side of the extensive **Mount Lofty Botanic Gardens** (daily 10am–4pm) to the **Mount Lofty Lookout**, the highest point of the range (727m). There's an **information centre** here (Mon & Tues 9am–5pm, Wed–Sun 9am till late; ℡08/8339 2600, Ⓦwww.parks.sa.gov.au) with fantastic views and a café-restaurant and bar. Hills Transit buses #820, #821 and #822 run from Adelaide bus terminal or Currie Street via Crafers and up Piccadilly Road, from where you can access the eastern side of the Botanic Gardens. The free *Adelaide Hills Monthly* has information about local events and is available from the South Australia Travel Centre in Adelaide (see p.796) and other regional tourist information centres.

The turn-off to **Cleland Wildlife Park** (daily 9.30am–4.30pm; $9.50; Ⓦwww.cleland.sa.gov.au) is the first on the left after the lookout. Here you can cuddle a koala and see other Australian fauna in enclosures, and there are several good walking trails through native bush leading from the park into the surrounding Cleland Conservation Area. You can get up here as part of a tour with Gray Line (℡1300 858 687, Ⓦwww.grayline.com; $38), Adelaide Sightseeing (℡08/8231 4144, Ⓦwww.adelaidesightseeing.com.au; $38) or Premier Day Tours (℡08/8415 5566, Ⓦwww.premierstateliner.com.au; $37). Otherwise, take Hills Transit bus #822.

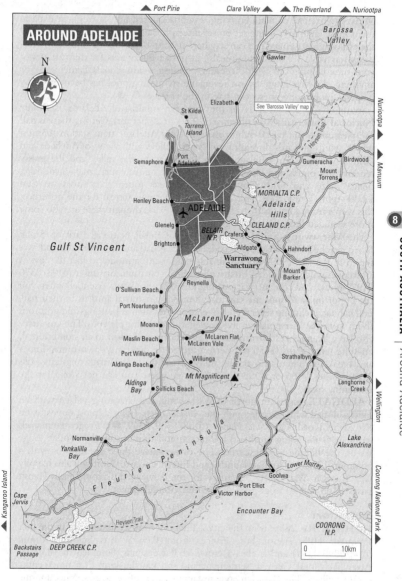

AROUND ADELAIDE

N

Barossa
Valley

Gawler

Elizabeth ●

St Kilda ●

Torrens
Island

See 'Barossa Valley' map

Semaphore ●   Port
Adelaide ●

Gumeracha ● ● Birdwood

Mount
Torrens

Henley Beach ●

MORIALTA C.P.

ADELAIDE

*Adelaide
Hills*

Glenelg ●   *BELAIR*   CLELAND C.P.
N.P. Crafers

Brighton ●   Aldgate ●   ● Hahndorf

**Warrawong
Sanctuary**

Mount
Barker ●

Gulf St Vincent

O'Sullivan Beach ●   ● Reynella

Port Noarlunga ●

Moana ●   *McLaren Vale*

Maslin Beach ●   ● McLaren Flat
McLaren Vale

Port Willunga ●

Aldinga Beach ●   ● Willunga

Strathalbyn ●

Aldinga
Bay   ● Sellicks Beach

Mt Magnificent ▲

Langhorne
Creek

Normanville ●

Yankalilla
Bay

F l e u r i e u   P e n i n s u l a

*Lake
Alexandrina*

Lower Murray

Goolwa ●

Cape
Jervis

Port Elliot
Victor Harbor ●

Encounter Bay

*COORONG
N.P.*

Heysen Trail

Backstairs
Passage   DEEP CREEK C.P.

0   10km

8

SOUTH AUSTRALIA | Around Adelaide

The **Morialta Conservation Park**, north of here, is easily reached by taking the #105 bus from Grenfell Street (35min), which goes right into the park along the scenic Morialta Falls Road; from the entrance it's a two-kilometre bushwalk into the park to a lovely waterfall. By car you can approach the park along the equally impressive Norton Summit Road; the *Scenic Hotel*, clinging to the side of the hill at **Norton Summit**, is a great place to stop for a drink. Running off here, Colonial Drive leads to **Fuzzies Farm** (☏08/8390 1111,

©fuzzyt@ozemail.com.au; bookings essential; closed July & Aug), an experiment in co-operative living set on seventeen hectares of bush and overseen by the philosophical Fuzzy. You can stay here in four-bed cabins (a minimum one-week stay costs $88 including meals); in return Fuzzy asks for thirty hours of your time helping out with carpentry, building, tending goats, gardening – or anything else that interests you (even the swimming pool has been made by helpers). Holidaying guests can stay in the cottage (❷–❺).

South of Crafers, virtually in the southern suburbs of Adelaide, is **Belair National Park** (daily 8am till sunset; $2.50, or $7 per car). Getting there is half the pleasure – you take a suburban train from Adelaide train station (35min) which winds upwards through tunnels and valleys with views of Adelaide and Gulf St Vincent. From Belair station, steps lead to the valley and the grassy recreation grounds and kiosk. With its joggers, tennis courts, man-made lake, hedge maze and **Old Government House** (open to visitors on Sun 12.30–4pm), a residence built in 1859 as a summer retreat for the governor, this seems more like a garden than a national park, though there are also some more secluded bush trails through gum forests.

The **Warrawong Sanctuary**, southeast of Belair National Park on Stock Road, reached by Sturt Valley Road, Heather Road and Longwood Road, was set up in the late 1960s as a sustainable conservation model to halt the loss of Australian wildlife. Guided **bushwalks** starting at dawn or sunset (☏08/8370 9197, ⓦwww.esl.com.au/warrawong.htm; $22; bookings essential) offer you the opportunity to spot the sanctuary's mostly nocturnal animals in their natural habitat, including several endangered species such as bettongs and potoroos (both from the marsupial family) as well as the elusive platypus. The sanctuary also has a licensed **restaurant** as well as **accommodation** in air-conditioned, en-suite tent-cabins ($150 per person including dusk and dawn tours, dinner and breakfast). There's no public transport or tours to Warrawong, but Hills Transit buses #166 or #193 go to Stirling, where you can get a taxi for the remaining 5km.

ALDGATE, just 3km north of Warrawong, is a charming village with an old-fashioned white-washed pub, the *Aldgate Pump House*. Almost opposite, on Kingsland Road, *Geoff and Hazels* (☏08/8389 8360, ⓦwww.geoffandhazels .com.au; ❷ including breakfast) has accommodation in a lovely wooden lodge set on the hillside amongst trees. The owners have three guestrooms with a communal kitchen/lounge, laundry and Internet access. Geoff will also happily take guests to Warrawong Sanctuary for the dawn or dusk tours. Hills Transit buses #163 and #165 go to Aldgate from Grenfell Street.

Hahndorf

HAHNDORF, 28km from the city, is the most touristy destination in the hills (frequent Hills Transit bus services from Central Bus Station; 40min; ☏08/8399 1191) and is always crowded at weekends. Founded in 1839, it's Australia's oldest German settlement and still has the look of a nineteenth-century village. The Bavarian-style restaurants and coffee houses, crafts, antique and gift shops are thoroughly commercial, but it's still enjoyable, especially in autumn when the chestnuts and elms lining the main street have turned golden. The **Adelaide Hills Visitors Information Centre**, 41 Main St (daily 9am–5pm; ☏08/8388 1185 or 1800 353 323, ⓦwww.visitadelaidehills .com.au), has lots of information on B&Bs and other accommodation in the hills (no charge for bookings) and can provide information about the entire area, though you won't need much help in the village itself: there's basically just one street and all the buildings have blue plaques recounting their history. The

Hahndorf Academy (Mon–Sat 10am–5pm, Sun noon–5pm; free) is a working artists' studio with a small collection of photographs, prints, displays and well-written interpretive boards that shed light on the lives of early German settlers, plus a few sketches by the town's most famous resident and one of Australia's best-known artists, **Hans Heysen**, who settled here in 1908. There's a more comprehensive collection of Heysen's paintings on display at his old home, **The Cedars**, about 2.5km northwest of the village, off Ambleside Road (daily except Sat 10am–4pm; guided tours 11am, 1pm & 3pm; $8 studio and house; shop and garden free).

For a glass of authentic locally brewed pilsner, head for the lovely wooden bar of the *German Arms Hotel*, which has a log fire and photos of old Hahndorf, a reasonably priced bistro, and a more expensive **restaurant**. There are dozens of other places to eat, all with filling meals for around $8: *Zarnows*, a licensed, child-friendly café on the main street serves light meals (and also has Internet access for $2 for 20min), while *The German Cake Shop*, near the tourist office, just off the main street on Pine Avenue (daily 8.30am–6pm), is a crowded bakery and coffee shop where the speciality is *bienenstich*, a yeast cake topped with honey and almonds and filled with cream, butter and custard. For a picnic, the Hahndorf Showcase Inn at the other end of the main street, stocks a tasty range of local produce.

Torrens River Gorge

Further north in the upper valley, the 27-kilometre **Gorge Scenic Drive** beside the Torrens River Gorge is one of the loveliest areas in the Adelaide Hills, but you'll need your own car to get there: take the Gorge Road off the A11 from Adelaide, a few kilometres past the suburb of Cambelltown. Fourteen kilometres along this road is the **Gorge Wildlife Park** (daily 8am–5pm; koala cuddling 11.30am, 1.30pm & 3.30pm; $9), a private park with mainly native birds and animals housed in walk-through enclosures. A few kilometres past the park, at Cudlee Creek, the Gorge Scenic Drive turns southeast away from the river and passes through picturesque valleys and vineyards to Mount Torrens. If you want to stick with the river, turn north before Cudlee Creek towards the Chain of Ponds, where the road connects after a few kilometres to the equally stunning **Torrens Valley Scenic Drive**.

GUMERACHA, the first town east of here, is home to **The Toy Factory**, 389 Birdwood Rd (daily 9am–5pm; ⊚www.thetoyfactory.com.au), which sells wooden toys, games and puzzles and has a tacky eighteen-metre-high rocking horse which children (and adults) can climb up for good views of the countryside. At the eastern end of the Torrens Valley Scenic Drive is **BIRDWOOD**, home to the **National Motor Museum** on Shannon Street (daily 9am–5pm; $9) – Australia's largest collection of veteran, vintage and classic cars, trucks and motorcycles.

The Barossa Valley

The **Barossa Valley**, only an hour's drive from Adelaide, produces internationally acclaimed wines and is the largest **premium wine** producer in Australia. Small stone **Lutheran churches** dot the valley, which was settled in the 1840s by German Lutherans fleeing from religious persecution: by 1847 over 2500 German immigrants had arrived and after the 1848 revolution more poured in. German continued to be spoken in the area until World War I, when the language was frowned upon and German place names were changed by an act of parliament. The towns, however – most notably Tanunda – remain thoroughly German in character, even without the large doses of oompah tourist hype, and the valley is well worth visiting for the vineyards, wineries, bakeries and butcher's shops, where old German recipes have been handed down through generations. With up to 800,000 visitors per annum, the valley can seem thoroughly touristy and traffic-laden if you whizz through it quickly; the peaceful back roads are more interesting, however, with a number of small, family-owned wineries to explore, many of which provide picnic areas and barbecues, and even children's playgrounds.

The first vines were planted in 1847 at the Orlando vineyards, an estate which is still a big wine producer. There are now over fifty **wineries**, from multinationals to tiny specialists. Because of the variety of soil and climate, the Barossa seems able to produce a wide range of wine types of consistently high quality; the white rieslings are among the best. The region has a typically Mediterranean climate, with dry summers and mild winters; the best time to visit is autumn (March–May), when the vines turn russet and golden and the harvest has begun in earnest. Much of the grape-picking is still done by hand and **work** is available from February. This is also the time of the week-long **Vintage Festival**, beginning on Easter Monday in every odd-numbered year (☎08/8563 0600 for more information). Another local celebration is the **International Barossa Music Festival**, held annually for two weeks in early October and featuring mostly chamber music. Its headquarters are at Richmond Grove Winery on Para Road near Tanunda; other wineries act as venues, as do some of the area's pretty Lutheran churches.

Getting around the valley

The principal route from Adelaide to the Barossa Valley follows the Main North Road through Elizabeth and Gawler, and then joins the **Barossa Valley Highway** to Lyndoch. A more scenic drive takes you through the Adelaide Hills to Williamstown or Angaston, while from the **Sturt Highway** you can turn into the valley at Nuriootpa. Getting to the valley by **bus** is also reasonably easy: the Barossa–Adelaide Passenger Service (Mon–Sat 2 daily, Sun 1 daily; ☎08/8564 3022) stops at the main Barossa towns en route to Angaston, while the daily Premier Stateliner (☎08/8415 5555) service to Riverland can drop you at Nuriootpa on request. The exclusive tourist **Barossa Wine Train** runs from

Adelaide all the way into Tanunda (Thurs, Sat & Sun 8.50am, returning 5.20pm; $65 return; bookings essential on ☎08/8212 7888, ⓦwww.barossawinetrain .com.au; tour packages also available). If you're **cycling**, you might want to consider taking your bike on the standard train to Gawler, 14km from Lyndoch.

Driving isn't the ideal way to explore the Barossa, particularly if you want to enjoy tasting wines – once here, you can always rent a bike or take a tour. If you decide you do need a **car** to get around, you can rent one from the Caltex service station, 8 Murray St, Tanunda (☎08/8563 2677; $50 per day). A better way to experience the area is to **cycle**; there's a sealed bike track avoiding the busy highway between Tanunda and Nuriootpa and bike rental (around $10 a day) is available at *Zinfandel's*, 58 Murray St, Tanunda (☎08/8563 2822), *The Bunkhaus*, Barossa Valley Way, Nuriootpa (☎08/8562 2260), and *Barossa Caravan Park*, Barossa Valley Way, Lyndoch (☎08/8524 4262). Alternatively, you can take a two- to five-day **cycling tour** with *Ecotrek* (☎08/8383 7198, ⓦwww.ecotrek.com.au), with an emphasis on wine-tasting, gourmet food and heritage accommodation. There's also a range of **sightseeing tours** from Adelaide offered by all the big commercial tour operators (see "Listings", p.817). For something different, try the small-group day-tour with Groovy Grape Getaways (☎1800 661 177, ⓦwww.groovygrape.com.au; $46), which

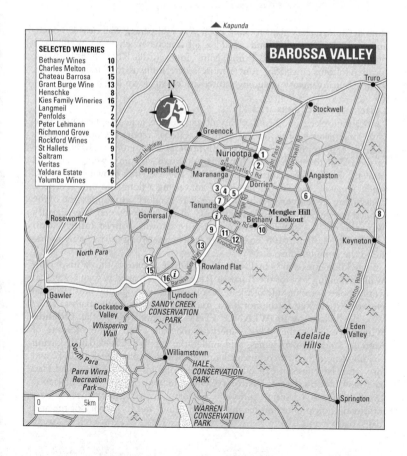

SELECTED WINERIES

Bethany Wines	10
Charles Melton	11
Chateau Barrosa	15
Grant Burge Wine	13
Henschke	8
Kies Family Wineries	16
Langmeil	7
Penfolds	2
Peter Lehmann	4
Richmond Grove	5
Rockford Wines	12
St Hallets	9
Saltram	1
Veritas	3
Yaldara Estate	14
Yalumba Wines	6

BAROSSA VALLEY

▲ Kapunda

Truro

Stockwell

N

Greenock

Nuriootpa

Sturt Highway

Seppeltsfield

Marananga

Dorrien

Angaston

Tanunda

Mengler Hill
Bethany Lookout

Roseworthy

Gomersal

Bethany Rd

Krondorf Rd

Keyneton

North Para

Rowland Flat

Barossa Valley Way

Gawler

Lyndoch

Cockatoo
Valley

SANDY CREEK
CONSERVATION
PARK

Whispering
Wall

South Para

Eden
Valley

Adelaide
Hills

Williamstown

HALE
CONSERVATION
PARK

Parra Wirra
Recreation
Park

WARREN
CONSERVATION
PARK

Springton

0   5km

Smaller wineries tend to have more charm and intrinsic interest than the larger commercial operators and it's here you'll often get to talk personally to the wine-maker. Groups are welcomed by most wineries but are encouraged to book in, although some wineries are too small to accommodate them. A few charge an **entry fee**, but for this expect extra staff and a more personalized tasting experience. You're under no obligation to buy any wine, but coming away with a few of your favourite taste sensations of the day – often only available at the cellar door – and a few fruity adjectives to describe them is part of the fun.

For a novice, wine-tasting can be an intimidating experience. On entering the **tasting area** (or cellar door) you'll be shown a list of wines that may be tasted, divided into reds and whites, all of which are printed in the order that the winemaker considers best on the palate. Unless you know what you're doing, it's not acceptable to alter this order, though by all means concentrate on red or white if you prefer. To get the full taste, sniff the wine first to appreciate the aroma or bouquet, and then take a sip, rolling it around on your tongue before swallowing; there's usually a spittoon if you don't want to swallow. Don't be shy about discussing the wines with the person serving – their purpose is to dispense chat and wisdom, and even wine snobs are down-to-earth Australians at heart.

stops at Gumeracha's giant rocking horse, the Whispering Wall near Lyndoch, and four large wineries, and includes a barbecue lunch – it's particularly popular with backpackers. Prime Mini Tours (☎08/8293 4900, ⓦwww.primeminitours.com; $55) runs a more sedate minibus tour from Adelaide, with a similar itinerary including a three-course sit-down lunch.

Lyndoch and around

"A beautiful place, good land, plenty of grass and its general appearance open with some patches of wood and many kangaroos," reported Colonel William Light in 1837 on first sighting the **LYNDOCH** area; settled in 1839, it's one of the oldest towns in South Australia. Although vineyards were established from the outset, the primary activity until 1896 was the growing of wheat, when someone had the bright idea of converting a flour mill into a winery. Today there are ten wineries in the immediate Lyndoch area, from some of the smallest to one of the largest in the Barossa, all still family-owned. **Kies Family Wineries** on Barossa Valley Way, provides free informal **tourist information** (daily 10am–4.30pm; ☎08/8524 4110); their wine-tasting cellars (same hours) are in the same building.

Eight kilometres south of Lyndoch, off **Yettie Road**, is the **Whispering Wall**, a retaining wall for the **Barossa Reservoir**; it's shaped in such a way that words spoken on one side of the reservoir can be heard plainly on the opposite side 140m away. To the northeast, four kilometres along the Barossa Valley Way, the village of **ROWLAND FLAT** is dominated by the **Orlando Winery** complex, the oldest winery in the valley and home of some of Australia's best-known wines, sold under the **Jacob's Creek** label. Johann Gramp planted the first commercial vines at nearby Jacob's Creek in 1847, and forty years later his son expanded the winery and moved it to Rowland Flat. The new **Jacob's Creek Visitor's Centre**, located on the banks of Jacob's Creek itself, has a tasting centre and restaurant with a gallery that includes information on production techniques, viticulture and the history of the area (daily 10am–5pm).

Four kilometres north of Rowland Flat, the peaceful **Krondorf Road/Hallet Valley** area runs east of the Barossa Valley Way, with three charming wineries – Rockford, St Hallets and Charles Melton – each with its own philosophy of wine-making and tasting. Next to St Hallets Winery you can watch skilled coopers at work at the **Keg Factory**, St Hallet Road (Mon–Sat 8am–4.30pm, Sun 10.30am–4.30pm); the huge stainless steel fermentation tanks you'll see around the valley aren't suitable for all wines, many of which still need to be aged in wood to impart flavour.

Parallel to Krondorf Road to the north, Bethany Road runs east off the Barossa Valley Way to **BETHANY**, the first German settlement in the Barossa. The land is still laid out in the eighteenth-century Hufendorf style, with long, narrow farming strips stretching out behind the cottages, and the creek running through each property. Pretty gardens set off the old stone cottages, which remain well cared for. At dusk each Saturday the bell tolls at **Herberge Christi Church**, keeping up a tradition to mark the working-week's end, and Bethany – without even a pub or shop – retains its peaceful, rural village feel. The common where cattle grazed is now the Bethany Reserve, with a picnic spot by the creek.

Tanunda

TANUNDA is the Barossa's most quintessentially German town. The tree-lined main drag, **Murray Street**, boasts several old and beautiful buildings and proclaims its pedigree with German music wafting out of small wooden kegs above the shops. There's a more authentic atmosphere in the narrow streets on the western side of town, towards the river. Here, **Goat Square** was the site of the first town market and is bordered by the original cottages; the early market is re-enacted during the Vintage Festival (see p.822). Many **wineries** dot the town, the largest concentration being along **Para Road**, beside the Para River, including Stanley Brothers, Peter Lehmann, Richmond Grove, Langmeil and Veritas, all of which can be visited in the course of a pleasant stroll along the road and river.

For a good introduction to the wine-making industry, head for the **Barossa Wine and Visitor Centre**, 66–68 Murray St (Mon–Fri 9am–5pm, Sat & Sun 10am–4pm; wine centre daily 10am–4pm; $2; ☎08/8563 0600 or 1300 852 982, ⓦ www.barossa-region.org). The centre tells the history of the Barossa in an original way, on three tiers of cylinders, which you roll to read. Each group of cylinders represents a different historical period: spin the top tier for a background on world events, the middle tier for a specific Barossa chronology, and the bottom tier for Australia-wide happenings at the time to examine the Barossa's wine industry in the context of Australian and world history – it's quite engrossing. There are also engaging interpretive displays about wine making, and you can pick up some additional tips on wine-tasting etiquette. There are also lots of visitor information racks with brochures to thumb through. The low-key **Barossa Valley Historical Museum**, 47 Murray St (Mon–Sat 11am–5pm, Sun 1–5pm; $2), crams local history into a small quaint building which it shares with an antiques shop.

Three kilometres out of town, **Norm's Coolies**, at "Breezy Gully" off Gomersal Road (Mon, Wed & Sat 2pm; $8, children $2), could only be in Australia: 28 sheepdogs are put through their paces by Norm and a herd of sheep. **Mengler's Hill Lookout**, east of Tanunda along Basedow Road and then the Mengler's Hill Road Scenic Drive, provides an unmatched view of the valley and its vineyards: there's a **sculpture garden** with white marble sculptures on the slopes below, and at night you can see the lights of Adelaide.

Barossa wineries

It's hard to choose between so many wineries, as almost all of them are worth a look. However, this selection should start you off.

Bethany Wines Bethany Rd, Bethany. A hillside winery set in an old quarry, with views over Bethany village (see p.825); five generations of the Schrapel family have grown grapes here. The ports are worth trying, especially the unusual white variety. Mon–Sat 10am–5pm, Sun 1–5pm.

Charles Melton Krondorf Rd, Tanunda. Small, friendly winery concentrating on a limited range of full-bodied reds that sell out fast. Informal tasting area in a wooden shed, where you sit at a long wooden table, with the door open to the vineyards and a friendly dog at your feet. Daily 11am–5pm.

Grant Burge Wines Barossa Valley Way, Jacob's Creek. Small, quality winery, established in 1988 to process wine from the area's oldest vineyards. Daily 10am–5pm.

Henschke Moculta Rd, Keyneton, 14km southeast of Angaston. Fifth-generation winemakers, the Henschke family's wines have won many international prizes. It's set in a peaceful setting off the beaten track and you'll need to ring the bell to rouse the amiable staff and start tasting. Mon–Fri 9am–4.30pm, Sat 9am–noon.

Langmeil Winery Langmeil Rd, near Tanunda. This was the original Langmeil village, built in the 1840s; the little vineyard you can see from the tasting area was planted in 1846. Prints of nineteenth-century photos on the walls document the local wine industry. With a slow and thoughtful approach to tasting and a small range (four reds, five whites and two tawny ports), you really get to know the wines – try the very peppery Grenache. Daily 10am–4.30pm.

Peter Lehmann Para Rd, near Tanunda. Another pleasant spot for a bit of tasting in a homestead with vine-entwined verandahs surrounded by flowerbeds, gum trees and palms, overlooking a lawn leading down to the Para River; you're welcome to picnic here. Lehmann is as well known for his art collection as for his red wines, whose labels feature paintings by South Australian artists which are displayed here. Mon–Fri 9.30am–5pm, Sat & Sun 10.30am–4pm.

Richmond Grove Para Rd, near Tanunda. Large, historic winery sourcing grapes from around the Barossa and from other premier wine-growing areas in Australia – good if you want to compare the different regional characteristics of Australian wine. There's a lovely picnic area alongside the North Para River. Mon–Fri 10am–5pm, Sat & Sun 10.30–4.30pm.

Rockford Wines Krondorf Rd, Tanunda. No-nonsense approach and big unfussy wines by Robert O'Callahan, produced using old-fashioned techniques and including a good Basket Press Shiraz and an amazing fizzy Black Shiraz at around $50 a bottle. Tasting in an 1850s stone barn. Mon–Sat 11am–5pm.

St Hallets Winery Krondorf Rd, Tanunda. Medium-size, quality producer. Its star wine is Old Block Shiraz, sourced from vines eighty to a hundred years old, with an intense flavour and a velvety softness. Daily 10am–5pm, lunch Sat & Sun.

Veritas Corner Stelzer Rd and Seppeltsfield Rd, near Tanunda. Established in the 1950s and known for its Hungarian-style wines, this family operation is a good place to come during harvest, around April, with tastings and sales in an unpretentious shed. Mon–Fri 9am–5pm, Sat & Sun 11am–5pm.

Yaldara Wines Gomersal Rd, Lyndoch. The ruins of a nineteenth-century flour mill have been transformed into a Baroque-style chateau complete with wine cellar and café (see p.829). Mon–Fri 8.30am–5pm, Sat 9am–5pm.

Yalumba Wines Eden Valley Rd, Angaston. Largest and oldest family-operated Barossa winery, established in 1849, set in a lovely building and gardens. Mon–Fri 8.30am–5pm, Sat 10am–5pm, Sun noon–5pm.

Seppeltsfield, off the highway 4km northwest of Tanunda, must be the most spectacular of the wineries (tastings Mon–Fri 10am–5pm, Sat & Sun 11am–5pm). During the Great Depression the Seppelt family paid their workers in food to plant an avenue of date palms from Marananga to Seppeltsfield. On a hill halfway along the palm-lined avenue is the **Seppelt family mausoleum**, resting place of the male members of the family. The estate itself was founded in 1851 when Joseph Seppelt, a wealthy merchant, arrived from Silesia with his workers: he turned to wine making when his tobacco crop failed, establishing the largest winery in the colony, with everything from a port-maturation cellar to a distillery, vinegar factory and brandy bond store. All have been preserved in their original condition, and can be seen on a **tour** (Mon–Fri 11am, 1pm, 2pm & 3pm, Sat & Sun 11.30am, 1.30pm & 2.30pm; $3).

Nuriootpa, Angaston and Springton

Just 7km from Tanunda, **NURIOOTPA** is the valley's commercial centre: as the place where local Aborigines gathered to barter it takes its name from the word for "meeting place". It's not the most attractive of towns, dominated as it is by **Penfolds**, the Barossa's largest winery, which churns out mass-produced wines made with grapes from across South Australia. The finest building here is **Coulthard House**, a gracious, two-storey edifice commissioned by the area's first settler, William Coulthard. The town grew around his red-gum slab hotel, now the site of the *Vine Inn* community hotel. Together with the community store (where co-op members purchase shares and share in the profits), this finances many developments in the town, such as the excellent **swimming centre** in Coulthard Reserve by the shady, gum-lined North Para River. There's free **Internet access** at the public library, 10 Murray St (Mon–Fri 9am–5pm, Sat 9am–noon, Sun 2–4pm).

ANGASTON, southeast of Nuriootpa, is a pretty little town situated in the Barossa Ranges, an area of predominantly grazing land, red gums and rolling hills, although a few of the Barossa's oldest winemakers have been here for more than a century. This is the side of the Barossa that attracted the British pioneers, including George Fife Angas, the Scotsman after whom the town is named. The **Collingrove Homestead** (Mon–Fri 1–4.30pm, Sat & Sun 11am–4.30pm; $5; ⑱ www.colgrove.mtx.net), 6km from town on Eden Valley Road, was one of his homes. Owned by the National Trust, it's surrounded by lush gardens and offers accommodation (see overleaf). Angas also lived at nearby Lindsay Park, now the private **Lindsay Park Stud**, Australia's leading racehorse breeding and training complex.

The major attraction at **SPRINGTON**, 20km south of Angaston, is the **Herbig family tree**, a hollowed-out gum tree in which a pioneer German couple lived for five years from 1855; they began their married life in the tree and had two of their sixteen children in it. Inevitably, Springton's old buildings have undergone the "boutiquing" process: the blacksmith shop is now a winery, and the old post office has been transformed into an arts and crafts gallery.

Barossa accommodation

There's comfortable accommodation in B&Bs and caravan parks throughout the valley, and you shouldn't have a problem finding somewhere decent to stay. Listed below are some of the better-value places.

Barossa Brauhaus Hotel 41 Murray St, Angaston ☏ 08/8564 2014. Good-value basic rooms and cheap singles in a pub first licensed in 1849. Central location. Light breakfast included. ❸

Bunkhaus Travellers Hostel and Cottage Barossa Valley Way, 1.5km south of Nuriootpa ☏ & ⑲ 08/8562 2260. A comfortable, friendly, family-run hostel set in vineyards, with a cosy

△ Chateau Yaldara Winery

common room for winter and a swimming pool for summer. Bike rental. Dorms $20, self-contained cottage ❷

Caithness Manor 12 Hill St, Angaston ☎ 08/8564 2761, ⓦ www.dove.net.au/~hillview. A former girls' grammar school whose lower storey has been transformed into a gracious guesthouse run by a friendly family. There's a sitting room complete with open fires, a stereo and bar, plus a swimming pool and spa. Each of the two spacious guest rooms has its own bathroom and antique furnishings. Gourmet breakfast included. ❼

Collingrove Homestead Eden Valley Rd, 6km from Angaston ☎ 08/8564 2061, ⓦ www .colgrove.mtx.net. National Trust-listed B&B accommodation in old servants' quarters, set in English-style gardens. ❼

Langmeil Cottages Langmeil Rd, Tanunda ☎ 08/8563 2987, ⓦ www.langmeilcottages.com. German-style stone cottage with cooking facilities, peaceful setting and views of the Barossa Ranges; extras include champagne on arrival, breakfast provisions, free use of bicycles, BBQ, heated pool and laundry facilities. ❻–❼

Lawley Farm Krondorf Rd, south of Tanunda ☎ 08/8563 2141, ⓦ www.lawleyfarm.com.au. Restored stone cottages shaded by pepper trees on a quiet road ideal for walking and cycling and within walking distance of the best wineries. A full breakfast (included in rooms rates) is served in the farmhouse kitchen, and there's a hot spa in the garden. ❻–❼

Seppeltsfield Holiday Cabins Seppeltsfield Rd ☎ 08/8562 8240, ⓕ 8562 8563. These well-equipped log cabins, with wood fires, offer some of the best-value accommodation in the valley, set on a rural hillside overlooking the Seppelt winery. Standard rooms ❸, deluxe cabins with spa ❺

Tanunda Caravan and Tourist Park Murray St, Tanunda ☎ 08/8563 2784, ⓦ www.tanunda caravantouristpark.com.au. Set in parkland among beautiful waratah trees. On-site vans ❶, cabins ❷

Tanunda Hotel 51 Murray St, Tanunda ☎ 08/8563 2030 or 8563 2165. Built from local stone and marble in 1845, with Edwardian additions and decor inside. All rooms have TV, air-con, fridge, tea and coffee; some are en suite. ❸

Vine Inn Hotel Motel 14 Murray St, Nuriootpa ☎ 08/8562 2133, ⓦ www.vineinn.com.au. Spacious, modern motel-style units with air-con and queen-size beds; continental breakfast included. Spa and heated pool. ❹–❺

Vineyards Motel cnr Stockwell and Nuriootpa roads, Angaston ☎ 08/8564 2404, ⓦ www.mdt.net.au/~vinmot. Good location opposite the *Vintners Bar and Grill*, just a short walk away from Saltram Winery and its bistro. Modern units; facilities include room service, swimming pool and spa. ❸

Barossa eating and drinking

There are excellent restaurants throughout the valley, as well as plenty of picnic spots and barbecue areas.

1918 Bistro and Grill 94 Murray St, Tanunda ☎ 08/8563 0405. Fresh food and local ingredients cooked with a Mediterranean twist. Eat outside on the wide, plant-shaded verandah, or inside the beautiful old house, built in 1918, and with a variety of nooks and corners for intimate dining. Local wines or BYO. Expensive.

Barossa Bistro 37 Murray St, Angaston ☎ 08/8564 2361. Casual dining nightly with affordable, filling main courses including some interesting kangaroo dishes; lighter, cheaper meals at lunchtime. Licensed.

Barossa Wurst Haus and Bakery 86A Murray St, Tanunda. Specializing in traditional Barossa *Mettwurst*, this delicatessen offers cheap but very tasty food. Good cappuccino. Daily 8am–5.30pm.

Cafe "Y" (Yaldara) Gomersal Rd, Lyndoch. Affordable prices aimed at families, with a children's menu too; pasta dominates, and they also do morning and afternoon tea. Daily 10am–4pm.

Harvesters Cafe 29D Murray St, Nuriootpa ☎ 08/8562 1348. Spacious, contemporary-style café with a nice courtyard serving great cooked breakfasts, homemade soups and a variety of vegetarian dishes. Tues–Sun 9am–5.30pm.

Lyndoch Bakery & Restaurant Barossa Valley Highway, Lyndoch. The best German bakery in the Barossa. The adjoining licensed restaurant serves hearty, moderately priced traditional dishes. Daily 8.30am–5.30pm.

The Park Restaurant/Café 2A Murray St, Tanunda ☎ 08/8563 3500. Affordable modern Australian cuisine in an 1840s stone villa set in a park, with either alfresco dining or indoor seating by the fire if it's cold.

Rendezvous House 22 Murray St, Angaston ☎ 08/8564 3533. Set in an old cottage with a small garden overlooking the pretty main street, this friendly organic café and restaurant serves vegetarian and meat dishes for under $10 and plenty of delicious tapas as well. Wed–Sun lunch, Fri–Sun dinner.

Salters Saltram Winery, Nuritoopa Rd, Angaston ☎08/8564 3355. Elegant bistro serving modern Australian cuisine with an Italian twist – all fresh, deliciously prepared and reasonably priced. The attached nineteenth-century winery specializes in full-bodied reds – try them at the cellar door before eating. Lunch only.

Vine Court Restaurant 49 Murray St, Nuriootpa. Serving simple but good Australian dishes and a few German specials, this place has the best-value meals in the valley: three courses for $15. Open daily for lunch and dinner.

Vintners Bar and Grill Cnr Stockwell and Nuriootpa roads, Angaston ☎08/8564 2488. A winemakers' hangout with Mediterranean-style regional produce on the menu and a suitably impressive wine list. The decor is a mix of cool contemporary plus old stone walls, fireplaces and wooden beams, and there's a vine-covered courtyard for warm days. Expensive. Tues–Sun lunch, Wed–Sat dinner.

Zinfandel Tea Rooms 58 Murray St, Tanunda. Popular place for hot, cooked breakfasts, German and Australian dishes for lunch and a delicious choice of strudels and cakes. You can sit inside the cosy cottage or out on the verandah. Daily 8.30am–6pm.

The Fleurieu Peninsula

The **Fleurieu Peninsula** (ⓦwww.fleurieupeninsula.com.au), thirty minutes south of Adelaide by car, is bounded by Gulf St Vincent to the west and the Southern Ocean to the south, the two connected by the Backstairs Passage at **Cape Jervis** (where the ferry leaves for Kangaroo Island, see p.837). There are fine beaches on both coasts and, inland, more wineries in the rolling **McLaren Vales**. It's pleasantly undeveloped: many of the towns were settled from the 1830s and there's a lot of **colonial architecture**, much of it now housing restaurants or B&Bs. For a round trip, leave the city via the Adelaide Hills and cut down through Mount Barker to well-preserved Strathalbyn and Goolwa, on the south coast, circling round through Victor Harbor, Yankalilla, Willunga and McLaren Vale. The peninsula is a good place to **cycle** – in addition to its roads it has two sealed bike paths: the 24km Encounter Bikeway (see box on p.834) follows the coast from Goolwa to just beyond Victor Harbor; another (shorter) path runs between Willunga and McLaren Vale. For **walkers**, the **Heysen Trail** starts at the southern tip of the peninsula at Cape Jervis and winds its way across the hilly countryside north to the Adelaide Hills and beyond. Although the trail is meant for long-distance walking, there are a number of well-signposted short walks along the way, including the 3.5-kilometre Deep Creek Waterfall Trail, just east of Cape Jervis with its wild coastal scenery. The Heysen Trail also passes through the Mount Magnificent Conservation Park, which contains a number of shorter walks offering excellent panoramic views.

If you're relying on **public transport**, Premier Stateliner (☎08/8415 5555) makes four daily trips from Adelaide to Goolwa via McLaren Vale, Willunga, Victor Harbor and Port Elliot. There's also a sporadic service provided by the Southern Encounter and The Highlander **steam trains** (occasionally replaced by a diesel locomotive) which chug from Mount Barker to Victor Harbor and Strathalbyn respectively (first Sun of month June–Nov; ☎08/8231 4366, ⓦwww.steamranger.org.au). Adelaide Sightseeing Tours run **tours** of the area (Mon, Wed & Sat 9.30am–5.30pm; ☎08/8202 8688, ⓦwww.adelaidesight seeing.com.au; $60), visiting Goolwa, Victor Harbor and McLaren Vale, connecting with Coorong Pelican cruises from Goolwa, with optional overnight stays at Victor Harbour to see the penguins returning to Granite Island.

The McLaren Vales

The fifty wineries of the **McLaren Vales**, in the northwest of the peninsula, are virtually in Adelaide, and the suburban fringes of the city now push right up to **REYNELLA**, where the first vineyards were planted in 1838. Among the earliest was Hardy's Reynella Winery on Reynell Road (Mon–Fri & Sun 10am–5pm, Sat 10am–4pm), where the tasting room occupies the original ironstone and brick building, set in botanical gardens. There are several other wineries in Reynella, but the largest concentration – often in bush settings, though only an hour's drive from Adelaide – is around the small town of **McLAREN VALE**, which has about fifty wineries, mostly small and family-run. Since the 1960s there's been a trend for grape growers to switch from supplying winemakers to producing their own wine, and there's a swath of "boutique" wineries here as a result. More recently, the area has gained a reputation for its **olives**, and a number of shops have opened for tastings and sales. *The Olive Grove* (daily 9am–5pm), opposite the D'Arenberg winery (see below), is the best, with excellent olives, oils, pestos and other sauces.

McLaren Vale is itself a "boutique" town, with many B&Bs and restaurants catering for the wine-buff weekend crowd. The liveliest time is in October, when the **Bushing Festival** celebrates the new wines, and the Bushing King or Queen, the winemaker who has produced the wine judged to be the best of the vintage, is crowned. A big part of the festival is the **craft market** held during the last weekend at Kay's Amery Vineyards (see box below), where there are fifty stalls manned by the artisans themselves, as well as food and entertainment. Information on this, and on the area's wineries, can be found at the **McLaren Vale and Fleurieu Visitor Centre** on Main Road, about 2km from the centre (daily 10am–5pm; ℡08/8323 9944, ⊛www.visitorcentre.com.au) – it even has its own vineyard with a café and wine bar where you can sample wines here from across the vale, including those wineries without cellar doors.

McLaren Vale wineries

Listed below are half a dozen favourites from a wide choice of excellent wineries.

Chapel Hill Chapel Hill Rd, McLaren Vale, adjacent to the Onkaparinga Gorge. A small but very civilized winery in an old stone chapel with nice views over the vineyards. Winemaker Pam Dunsford was McLaren Vale's first Bushing Queen, and her wines have won several prizes. Daily noon–5pm.

D'Arenberg Osborn Rd, McLaren Vale. A family winery set up in 1928 and well known for its prize-winning reds. Daily 10am–5pm.

Hoffman's Ingoldby Rd, McLaren Flat. Smallest of the wineries with only three labels to choose from, and these only available through the cellar doors or by mail order. A great place to sit in a peaceful setting and chat about wines with the friendly owners. Daily 11am–5pm.

Kay's Amery Vineyards Kays Rd, McLaren Vale. A wonderful family winery established in 1890; old photos of the family and the area cover the oak casks containing port. It's renowned for its Block 6 Shiraz from vines planted in 1892, though it sells out quickly. Also has a picnic area set amid towering gum trees. Mon–Fri 9am–5pm, Sat & Sun noon–5pm.

Scarpantoni Scarpantoni Drive, McLaren Flat. Small, prize-winning winery run by an Italian family, with a contemporary cellar more akin to a city wine bar. Mon–Fri 9am–5pm, Sat & Sun 11am–5pm.

Wira Wira McMurtie Rd, McLaren Vale. A large, classic ironstone building provides the setting for an impressive range of reds, whites and award-winning tawny ports, not forgetting the fortified Shiraz. Daily 9am–5pm.

8

SOUTH AUSTRALIA | Around Adelaide

831

The centre can also book **accommodation**. Among the town's B&Bs are the historic *Claddagh Cottage*, Lot 8, Caffrey St (☎08/8323 9806; ❺–❻), within walking distance of the town centre; *Southern Vales*, 13 Chalk Hill Rd (☎08/8323 8144; ❺), a more modern and hotel-like place with vineyard views; and *Samarkand*, Branson Road (☎ & ⓕ08/8323 8756; ❻), set in a large log cabin on a peaceful property complete with its own alpacas. Most **places to eat** in town are fairly fancy, and some of the wineries also have restaurants attached. Simpler meals can be had at *Koffee 'n' Snax*, an unpretentious coffee shop at 150 Main Rd. The award-winning *Magnum Bistro* in the *Hotel McLaren*, 208 Main Rd (☎08/8323 8208), has delicious main courses, all reasonably priced. Across the road, at no. 201, the stylish *Oscar's* serves pizzas and Mediterranean salads (daily 11am–11pm; BYO). Restaurants include *The Barn*, on the corner of Main and Chalk Hill roads (☎08/8323 8618), where you can dine on moderately priced contemporary cuisine accompanied by local wines. On the corner of McMurtie Road, in the direction of Willunga, the award-winning *Salopian Inn* (☎08/8323 8769; lunch daily, dinner weekends only) is set in an atmospheric 1851 stone inn with a seasonally varying menu.

Gulf St Vincent beaches

A series of superb swimming beaches, often known as the **wine coast**, runs along the Gulf St Vincent shore roughly parallel to the McLaren Vales, from **O'Sullivans Beach** down to **Sellicks Beach**. All are easily accessible from Adelaide on public transport: take the train from Adelaide to Noarlunga Centre and bus #750 or #751 to the various beaches. Alternatively, Premier Stateliner (☎08/8415 5555) runs a coach to Victor Harbor which stops at Willunga, while Public Coach Service (☎08/8231 1744) has a daily service from Adelaide to Cape Jervis via Aldinga and Normanville.

PORT NOARLUNGA is the main town, surrounded by steep cliffs and sand hills: its jetty is popular with anglers and with wetsuit-clad teenagers who dive-bomb from it; at low tide a natural reef is exposed. Lifesavers patrol the local beaches, and you can rent surf and snorkelling gear at Ocean Graffix Surf and Skate Centre, 21 Salt Fleet Point. For the latest **surf report** call ☎1902 241 018 (75¢ per min). **Moana**, two beaches south, has fairly tame surf that's perfect for novices. The southern end of **Maslins Beach**, south again, broke new ground by becoming Australia's first legal **nude** beach in 1975. The wide, isolated beach is reached by a long, steep walking track down the colourful cliffs from the Tait Road car park, deterring all but the committed. **Port Willunga**, the next stop down, offers interesting diving around the wreck of the *Star of Greece*, while just further south is **Aldinga Beach**, reached by the daily Adelaide–Cape Jervis Public Coach Service. From here there's a connecting bus to **Sellicks Beach** where, if you have your own car, you can drive along 6km of firm sand.

The coastal region south of here is more rugged, although there are some nice secluded beaches as well as the popular Heritage-listed sand dunes at **NORMANVILLE**. You can camp at *Normanville Beach Caravan Park* (☎08/8558 2038; en-suite cabins ❸). A few kilometres inland, the **Yankalilla District Visitor Information Centre**, 106 Main Rd (daily 9am–5pm; ☎08/8558 2999, ⓦwww.fleurieupeninsula.com.au), has a complete list of caravan parks and B&Bs along the coast. Cape Jervis is at the end of the Main South Road; ferries for Kangaroo Island (see p.837) depart from here.

Victor Harbor

The old resort of **VICTOR HARBOR**, on Encounter Bay, is currently experiencing a resurgence in its fortunes, thanks principally to whales and penguins.

In the 1830s there were three whaling stations here, hunting **southern right whales**, named because they were the "right" ones to kill: slow-moving because of their high oil content, which fortuitously also meant that they continued to float even after being killed. The whales came to Encounter Bay to mate and breed between June and September, heading close to shore, where they became easy targets. Not surprisingly, their numbers began to decline, and by 1930 they had been hunted almost to extinction. Half a century later there were signs of recovery: in 1991, forty were spotted in the bay and eighty thousand people flocked to see them, while in 1998, sixteen females stayed in the bay to calf, and a dozen humpback whales were also spotted. A Heritage-listed former railway goods shed on Railway Terrace now houses the **South Australian Whale Centre** (daily 11am–4.30pm; $5.50), with excellent interpretive displays, exhibits and screenings on whaling and on the natural history of whales, dolphins and the marine environment. The centre also acts as a monitoring station, locating and tracking whales, and confirming sightings, which are most likely in June, July or August (call the hotline on ☏1900 931 223, calls cost 75¢ per min; ⓦwww.webmedia.com.au/whales). Two-hour whale cruises depart from Granite Island daily (June–Sept; ☏0427 102 387; $55).

As well as whales, **Little penguins** come to nest, roost and moult on **Granite Island**, which is linked to the esplanade by a narrow causeway. At dusk they come back from feeding – this is the best time to see them, on one of the ranger-led **penguin walks** run by Granite Island Nature Park (daily at dusk; 1hr; $10; booking essential on ☏08/8552 7555, ⓦwww.granite island@chariot.com.au). Before exploring the island you can visit the **Penguin Interpretive Centre**, which houses an audiovisual holographic display with a 3D park ranger giving the lowdown on daily penguin life (opens an hour before the start of a walk). You can walk across the 600-metre causeway to the island at any time, or get there on a traditional holiday ride with the Victor Harbour Horse Tram (daily 10am–4pm, after which a shuttle bus takes over until 8.30pm; $6 return). The Granite Island Nature Park also has a small shark aquarium ($10), just offshore from the Penguin Interpretive Centre, and runs several cruises, including one to the West Island to spot the largest **sea-lion colony** in South Australia (minimum twelve people; $75; bookings essential on ☏08/8552 7555).

Other local attractions include the **Cockle Train**, a Sunday steam train (sometimes diesel-hauled) which runs on the otherwise disused line along the coast to Goolwa via Port Elliot and back (every Sun & daily during school holidays; $20 return). If you're travelling with restless children, **Greenhills Adventure Park**, Waggon Road, alongside the Hindmarsh River (daily 10am–5pm, 6pm in summer; $18 adult or child), has activities from canoeing to waterslides. The **Urimburra Wildlife Experience** (daily 9am–6pm; $8, child $4.50), 5km north on Adelaide Road, is an open-range park with native animals from all over the continent.

Practicalities

For further information, head for the Victor Harbor **Tourist Information Centre** next to the causeway (daily 9am–5pm; ☏08/8552 5738, ⓦwww.tourismvictorharbor.com.au); in the same building, the **Fleurieu & KI Booking Centre** (☏1800 088 552, ℮genesis@granite.net.au) can book accommodation and tours. The best **place to stay** is the *Anchorage*, 21 Flinders Parade (☏08/8552 5970, ⓦwww.anchorage.mtx.net; ❸–❺), a lovingly restored beachfront guesthouse with en-suite and spa facilities, a good restaurant attached (see overleaf) and an adjoining backpackers' hostel (dorms $18).

The Encounter Bikeway

The **Encounter Bikeway** follows a scenic 24-kilometre stretch of coast between Victor Harbor and Goolwa. Parts of the route are on-road and slightly inland, but mostly it follows the coastline and is for cyclists and walkers only. The return trip can be completed comfortably in a day; the most scenic, and hilliest, section is between Dump Beach in Victor Harbor and the town of Port Elliot. **Mountain bike rental** is available at Goolwa Cycle Hire, Ampol Service Station, Cadell Street, Goolwa (T08/8555 1000; $22 per day), or Victor Harbor Cycle, 73 Victoria St, Victor Harbour (T08/8552 1417; $20 per day); alternatively, take your pick from a unique selection of brightly painted **tandem bikes**, some side-by-side and some with trailers, from Victor Bike Hire, 12 Flinders Parade, Victor Harbor (T08/8552 4458; from $10 per hour). Unfortunately, none offers a drop-off service for one-way journeys, but on Sundays you can take your bike on the Cockle Train (see opposite) between Victor Harbor and Goolwa and cycle back.

Alternatives include the *Villa Victor Bed and Breakfast*, 59 Victoria St (T08/8552 4258; ❹–❺); and the *Family Inn Motel*, 300 Port Elliot Rd (T08/8552 1941, F8552 8645; ❸–❹).

Good **places to eat** abound. The super *Cafe Bavaria* at 11 Albert Place is a gleaming venue with delicious fresh-baked German cakes and savouries at reasonable prices (closed Mon). The *Blackfriars Bookshop and Coffee Bar*, 157 Hindmarsh Rd, also has good cakes, coffee and **Internet access** ($4 per 30min) If you're after Italian food, head for *Nino Solari's Pizzeria*, nearby at no. 16 (closed Mon), where you can plough into some generous portions of pasta and home-made *gelati*; for seafood, try the *Anchorage Café* on the beachfront Flinders Parade, a lively city-style café with an eclectic menu that's good for vegetarians. The best place to **drink** is on the Esplanade at the *Hotel Crown* which serves cheap bar meals, has streetside tables and big-name bands on Thursday and Friday and DJs on Saturday.

Port Elliot

PORT ELLIOT, just 5km east of Victor Harbor, is a pleasant little town with some good **coastal walks** along the cliffs at Freeman Knob and an attractive sandy beach with safe swimming at Horseshoe Bay. Campers can enjoy the beachside setting at the award-winning *Port Elliot Caravan & Tourist Park* (T08/8554 2134, W www.portelliotcaravanpark.com.au; cabins ❸, cottages ❹). A short stroll inland on the main Victor Harbor–Goolwa road, *Arnella by the Sea* (T08/8554 3611; dorms $22, rooms ❶) is a charming nine-bedroom guesthouse in a National Trust-listed building retaining its original wooden floorboards. From here you can explore the coastal Encounter Bikeway (see box above), or learn how to **surf** at nearby Middleton. For experienced surfers, Waitpinga Parsons and Chiton offer more thrills. Boards, wetsuits and fins can be rented from Southern Surf, 36 North Terrace (T08/8554 2375). For the latest surf report, call T08/8554 2047.

Goolwa

GOOLWA lies 14km east of Port Elliot, and 12km upstream from the ever-shifting sand bar at the mouth of the Murray River. Boaties love its position adjacent to vast Lake Alexandrina, yet with easy access to the Coorong (see p.845) and the ocean. Although so close to the coast, Goolwa feels like a real river town, and it thrived in the days of the Murray paddle-steamer trade, when it was the steamer's final offloading port – a rip-roaring place with almost a hundred taverns and the biggest police station in South Australia. The **railways** brought the good days to an end, and today only a few reminders of the boom times remain along Railway Terrace, with its old buildings painted in Federation colours. Steam trains make a comeback on Sundays, however, when the **Cockle Train** heads along the coast to Victor Harbor and back (every Sun & daily during school holidays; $20 return); and the **Southern Encounter** runs from the Adelaide Hills to Goolwa via Strathalbyn and Victor Harbor (see p.832). There are also frequent **coaches** from Adelaide to Goolwa run by Premier Stateliner (Mon–Fri 5 daily, Sat 2 daily, Sun 1 daily; ☏08/8414 5555).

Overlooking the wharf beside the Hindmarsh bridge is **Signal Point Interpretive Centre** (daily 10am–5pm; $5.50), an innovative exhibition telling the story of the Murray and its river trade. The centre houses a small souvenir shop and café, as well as the helpful **Goolwa Tourist Information Centre** (daily 10am–4pm; ☏08/8555 1144, ⒲www.visitalexandria.sa.gov.au), which can book local river tours but not accommodation. The PS *Murray River Queen* (☏08/8555 1733, ⒲www.fleurieupeninsula.com/MurrayRiver Queen.htm; ❸), an old paddleship moored at the wharf, has a wide range of **accommodation** from tiny backpacker cabins to stateroom suites. For B&Bs, Cottages of Goolwa (☏08/8555 5880, ⒲www.cottagesofgoolwa.com) has a selection of self-catering cottages, including *Josephs* (❺), a luxurious historic cottage near the centre of town. *Riverport Motel* (☏08/8555 5033, Ⓕ8555 5022; ❹), on Noble Avenue 3km northeast of Goolwa, has motel units in a quiet setting beside the Lower Murray River, plus a pool, tennis court, bar and inexpensive dining room. Alternatively, try the *Corio Hotel* on Railway Terrace (☏08/8555 2011, Ⓕ8555 1109; ❹), which is also a popular **eating** place, along with the *Whistlestop Café* in Hays St and *Woks 2 Eat*, an excellent licensed noodle bar in the centre of town. **Campers** can head for *Goolwa Caravan Park*, Noble Ave (☏08/8555 2737; cabins ❷–❸).

Strathalbyn

The pretty town of **STRATHALBYN** sits quietly amongst rolling hills about 25km north of Goolwa and an hour's drive south of Adelaide. Settled in 1839 by Scottish immigrants, the historic town is the market centre for the surrounding farming community, but is also renowned for its antique shops, Heritage-listed buildings and serene atmosphere. Strathalbyn comes alive during its irregular but well-publicized **horse-racing** meetings and for a few traditional **festivals**: an antiques fair held in the third week of August, and an agricultural show and duck race in October. For a self-guided walking

---

Cruises from Goolwa

Cruises to the mouth of the Murray and as far as Coorong National Park (see p.845) leave from the end of the wharf. Spirit of the Coorong Cruises (☏08/8555 2203, ⒲www.coorongcruises.com.au) runs three trips: **MV Aroona** heads to the river mouth, passing through the barrages which keep saltwater out of the freshwater system, and into the Coorong wetlands (Tues & Sat summer only; 2hr 45min; $28); the **Discovery Cruise** goes to the dune-covered Younghusband Peninsula, where passengers can alight and walk to the Southern Ocean (Mon & Thurs; 4hr; $67, or $110 from Adelaide); the **Adventure Cruise** consists of a 30-kilometre trip right into the national park (Wed & Sun; 6hr; $80, or $124 from Adelaide). Coorong Cruises (☏08/8555 1133) offers a day-long trip focusing on bird-watching and looking at Aboriginal sites on the Younghusband Peninsula (Oct–June Tues, Thurs & Sun; $85).

brochure of the town, head to the **Strathalbyn Tourist Information Centre** at the Old Railway Station, on South Terrace (daily 9am–5pm; ☎08/8536 2478).

The best of the town's many **B&Bs** are *Watervilla House*, 2 Mill St (☎08/8536 4099, ✉watervillahouse@triplei.net.au; ❺), a beautiful 1840s cottage overlooking landscaped gardens and the River Angas Park; and the equally charming *Hamilton House*, 23 Commercial Rd (☎08/8536 4275; ❹). Alternatively, the historic *Victoria Hotel* has quality motel rooms and a reasonable bistro (☎08/8536 2202; ❹–❺) For **eating**, *Café Ruffino*, on the High Street, serves excellent home-made pastries and cakes, while *Jacks Cafe*, on the other side of the High Street, has excellent coffee and an interesting gourmet menu. The only regular **public transport** is from Adelaide on Transit Bus #843 via Adelaide Hills (Mon–Fri only); alternatively, if your timing's right, the Southern Encounter steam train chugs in from Mount Barker and Goolwa on selected Sundays (see p.835).

The Yorke Peninsula

The **Yorke Peninsula** was almost the last section of the Australian coastline to be mapped by Matthew Flinders in 1802, and it still seems a bit of an afterthought: flat plains stretch out to the sea, so extensively cleared for farming that only tiny areas of original vegetation remain – in the Innes National Park at the very tip of the peninsula and in a couple of conservation parks. Much is now made of the northern peninsula's **Cornish heritage**, but the miners from Cornwall who flocked to the area when **copper** was discovered in 1859 have left behind little but their names and the ubiquitous Cornish pasty. The three towns of the Copper Triangle or "**Little Cornwall**" – Kadina, Wallaroo and Moonta – make the most of it at the Kernewek Lowender (Cornish Festival), held over the long weekend in May of every odd-numbered year, though in fact the mining boom ended seventy years ago, and they've been plain country towns ever since.

Just two hours' drive from Adelaide, the peninsula offers a peaceful weekend break as well as good **fishing**. The east coast ports of Ardrossan, Port Vincent and Edithburgh on the Gulf St Vincent were visited first by ketches and schooners, and later by steamers transporting wheat and barley to England. Now the remaining jetties are used by anglers. They're all pleasant to visit, but **EDITHBURGH** offers the most facilities: once a substantial salt-production town and grain port, it still has a few fine old buildings and a long jetty. There's a tidal swimming pool set in a rocky cove, and from Troubridge Hill you can see across to the Fleurieu Peninsula and to **Troubridge Island Conservation Park**, with its 1850s iron lighthouse, migrating seabirds and Little Penguin population: guided tours are available (groups of four or more only; 2hr; $25; ☎08/8852 6290 for bookings and details). Accommodation is available here in the lighthouse-keeper's cottage, which sleeps up to ten – if you stay here you'll have the whole island to yourself, but it doesn't come cheap (arrange through the tour guide; minimum two-night stay; ❼).

In Edithburgh itself, more affordable **accommodation** options include foreshore motel units and comfortable two-bedroom apartments at *The Anchorage Motel and Holiday Units*, 25 O'Halloran Parade (☎08/8852 6262, ℻8852 6147; holiday units and rooms ❸) and *Edithburgh Caravan Park* (☎08/8852 6056) further along the foreshore, which has vans (❷) and en-suite cabins (❸–❹). There are also motel units at the back of the *Troubridge Hotel* on Blanche Street (☎08/8852 6013, ℻8852 6323; ❸); this faces the 1878 *Edithburgh Hotel*

(☎08/8852 6263), which is the best place for **meals** including local oysters. The *Edithburgh Café* on Edith Street (8am–4.30pm, closed Tues) does good simple meals, from baked potatoes to quiche and salad.

At the tip of the peninsula lies the **Innes National Park**, with its contrasting coastline of rough cliffs, sweeps of beach and sand dunes, and its interior of mallee scrub. The park is untouched except for the ruins of the gypsum-mining town of **Inneston**, near **Stenhouse Bay**. The **visitor centre** (☎08/8854 4040) in the park sells entry permits ($6.50 per car) and **camping** permits ($6.50–15.50 per car depending on which campsite you choose) and offers facilities such as hot showers. The main camping area is at **Pondalowie Bay**, which has some of the best **surf** in the state; there are several other good surfing spots around the park and north towards Corny Point. Other more sheltered coves and bays are good for **snorkelling**, with shallow reef areas of colourful marine life, while on land you might see emus, western grey kangaroos, pygmy possums and mallee fowl. The NPWS also operates five self-contained lodges around Inneston (☎08/8854 3200, ℱ8854 3299; ❸–❹; a minimum two-night stay). Alternatively, for a taste of luxury surrounded by wildlife, try the *Wilde Retreat* (☎08/8854 6500, ⓦwww.wilderetreat.info; ❺), a tastefully designed and secluded cottage sleeping up to eight.

Premier Stateliner (☎08/8415 5555) has a daily **bus** service from Adelaide to Moonta, via Kadina and Wallaroo. The Yorke Peninsula Passenger Service (☎08/8823 2375) runs from Adelaide to Yorketown, alternating daily between the east coast via Ardrossan, Port Vincent and Edithburgh and the centre via Maitland and Minlaton. There's no transport to the national park itself.

Kangaroo Island

As you head towards **Cape Jervis** along the west coast of the Fleurieu Peninsula, **KANGAROO ISLAND**, only 13km offshore, first appears behind a vale of rolling hills. Once you're on the island, its size and lack of development – there's only one person for every square kilometre – leave a strong impression. This is actually Australia's third-largest island (after Tasmania and Melville Island, north of Darwin), with 450km of quite spectacular and wild coastline, and so takes some time to explore. To see all the island's unusual geological features and wildlife habitats, you'll need at least three days, though most people only visit the major attractions on the south coast – Seal Bay, Little Sahara, Remarkable Rocks and Flinders Chase National Park.

Although the island is promoted as South Australia's premier destination for tourism, it's still very unspoilt; only in the peak holiday period (Christmas to the end of Jan, when most of the accommodation is booked up) does it feel busy. Once out of the island's few small towns, there's little sign of human presence to break the long, straight stretches of road as they run through undulating fields, dense gum forests or mallee scrub. There's often a strong wind off the Southern Ocean, so bring something warm whatever the season, and take care when **swimming**: there are strong rips on many of the beaches. Safe swimming spots include Hog Bay and Antechamber Bay, both near Penneshaw; Emu Bay, northwest of Kingscote; Stokes Bay, further west; and Vivonne Bay, on the south side of the island.

Kangaroo Island is possibly the best place in Australia to see an astonishing range of **wildlife**, largely untroubled by disease or natural predators, and a third of the island is now protected in some form. When Matthew Flinders first

KANGAROO ISLAND

sighted the island in 1802, "black substances" seen on shore in the twilight turned out to be **kangaroos**, prolific and easily hunted. Kangaroos still abound, as do wallabies. **Koalas** were introduced at Flinders Chase National Park in 1923 as a conservation measure. They have remained free of chlamydia, which is common in the mainland population, and have spread so widely that they are killing off many of the gum trees – calls for culling in the mid-1990s caused national controversy, so fertility control and relocation to other parts of Australia are being tried instead. Other animals found here include echidnas, platypuses, Little penguins, fur seals, sea lions and, in passing, southern right whales. The island is also home to over two hundred kinds of **birds**, as well as snakes.

Wild pigs and feral goats, the descendents of those left here by early seafarers, can also be found, while a pure strain of **Ligurian bees** brought by early settlers now forms the basis of a local honey industry. There are also over a million **sheep** on the island, most of them merino, while a sheep dairy here makes delicious Continental-style cheeses. The latest local craze is for **marron farming**, with about 140 licensed producers of the freshwater crustacean, a bit like a cross between a lobster and a yabbie. Other diverse new industries include abalone farming, oyster and mussel production, olive-oil pressing and the revival of eucalyptus-oil distilling.

Getting to the island

Kangaroo Island Sealink **ferries** ply across the Backstairs Passage **from Cape Jervis to Penneshaw** – often a rough journey, though mercifully short. Two large vehicle ferries make the journey at least four times daily, and up to seven times during peak holiday periods, taking about forty minutes to cross: buses connect the service with Adelaide twice daily ($64 ferry return, $96 including bus from Adelaide, cars $138, motorbikes $44, bikes $11; ☎13 13 01, ⓦ www.sealink.com.au). At Penneshaw, connecting Sealink buses run to American River ($8 one-way) and Kingscote ($11), though they'll need to be booked in advance.

In addition, it's worth checking out various cheap **packages**, including accommodation and tours or car rental, often with special backpackers' rates. At one end of the scale, Sealink does a whirlwind $179 one-day coach tour leaving Adelaide at 7am and returning at 10.30pm, but it's pretty exhausting. A more leisurely option aimed at independent-minded budget travellers is with Kangaroo Island Ferry Connections (☎08/8553 1233 or 1800 018 484,

@ www.ki-ferryconnections.com.au), which offers two-day, one-night small-group packages from Adelaide for about $220 per person, staying in the Penneshaw hostels. Camp Wild Adventures (☎08/8332 6615 or 1800 444 321, @ www.campwild.com.au) has an excellent, more laid-back two-day 4WD tour from Adelaide, camping overnight in a secluded spot on the southern coast ($350 per person). The Wayward Bus's two-day tour from Adelaide also takes advantage of an overnight stop near the Flinders Chase National Park, giving more time for viewing the spectacular sights there ($310 per person, or $365 to upgrade from dorm to twin or double room; ☎08/8410 8833 or 1800 882 823, @ www.waywardbus.com.au).

It takes thirty minutes to **fly** to Kingscote on Kangaroo Island from Adelaide and costs about $160 return. The two relevant airlines are Regional Express (☎13 17 13, @ www regionalexpress.com.au; 2 daily) and Emu Airways (☎08/8234 3711, @ www.emuair.mtx.net; 6 daily). There are **car rental** offices at Kingscote Airport, and a bus to town for about $11 with Airport Shuttle Services (☎08/8553 2390).

Getting around, tours and activities

If you don't have your own transport you can buy a **KI Bus Pass** (☎13 13 01; @ www.kibuspass.com.au; $139 from Adelaide, $107 from Cape Jervis, $45 on the island; runs daily; valid for 14 days) and explore the island on a shuttle bus which links up with tours and hostels. Alternatively there are three **car rental** firms. It's best to book to be sure of a vehicle – that way you'll also be met with the vehicle off the ferry or plane. In Kingscote try Budget Rent a Car, 57A Dauncey St (☎08/8553 3133; $96 per day, $595 per week), or Kangaroo Island Rental/Hertz, on the corner of Franklin Street and Telegraph Road (☎08/8553 2390 or 1800 088 296, @ hertzki@kin.net.au; $90 per day, $490 per week or $150 per day for 4WD); Penneshaw Hire, run by the *Penneshaw Youth Hostel* (☎08/8553 1284; $80 per day, $150 per two days), rents out new-model cars.

Roads to most major attractions are bitumen-sealed, including the scenic eighty-kilometre **South Coast Road** from Cygnet River to the Flinders Chase National Park, Remarkable Rocks and Admirals Arch. The main drag is the **Playford Highway** from Kingscote through Cygnet River and Parndana to the western tip of the island at Cape Borda, although the last part of the highway along the northern edge of Flinders Chase National Park is not sealed and can be rough. At the eastern end of the highway, sealed roads feed off to the airport, Emu Bay and American River and Penneshaw. Most other roads are constructed of ironstone rubble on red dirt and can be very dangerous; the recommended speed on these roads is 60kph. Driving at night on all roads is best avoided due to the high risk of collision with kangaroos and wallabies. You'll see the carnage of animal remains alongside the road at depressingly short intervals – most are hit by speeding trucks. Cars have far less protection from impact and insurance excesses are often a mandatory $2000 for animal collision. The main roads are all good for **cycling**. For the island's best mountain and tandem bikes, go to Bob's Bikes, 1 Commercial Rd, Kingston (☎08/8553 2349; $27.50 per day).

Most people opt to visit the island on a **tour**, which can be good value if bought as part of a package (see opposite). There are several small-group tour companies based on the island: Adventure Charters of Kangaroo Island in Kingscote (☎08/8553 9119, @ www.adventurecharters.com.au), led by an ex-park ranger, offers 4WD tours with an emphasis on fine food, wine and accommodation as well as nature. There are also a couple of **dive** tour

SOUTH AUSTRALIA | Kangaroo Island

operators: Kangaroo Island Diving Safaris (℡08/8559 3255, ⊛www
.kidivingsafaris.com), based at Telhawk Farm on the north coast, offers diving
charters and residential dive courses with special backpackers' rates; and
Adventureland Diving, based at *Penneshaw Youth Hostel* (℡08/8553 1284,
ⓔadvhost@kin.on.net), has three-day residential scuba courses and certification ($275 includes hostel accommodation), as well as half-day **snorkelling** at
Kangaroo Head ($50) and abseiling at Cape Willoughby ($66).

Information and park entrance fees

With about one third of the island deemed a national or conservation park area,
many of the parks charge entry fees and extras for guided tours. However, a
one-year **Island Pass** ($32 per person) covers virtually all these costs (except
for camping and the night-time penguin tours from Penneshaw and Kingscote,
see below and p.842 respectively), and is worth it if you're here for a while. The
entry fees and tour prices quoted in the following accounts apply only if you
don't have a pass – add up the cost of what you want to see and work out which
is cheaper. Passes can be bought from the parks themselves or from the NPWS
office on Dauncy Street, Kingscote (Mon–Fri 8.45am–5pm; ℡08/8553 2381,
⊛www.environment.sa.gov.au); this office can also arrange camping permits
and cottage accommodation in most of the national parks around the island.
Passes can also be purchased from the **Kangaroo Island Gateway Visitor
Information Centre**, at the edge of Penneshaw on the main road to Kingscote
(Mon–Fri 9am–5pm, Sat & Sun 10am–4pm; ℡08/8553 1185, ⊛www
.tourkangarooisland.com.au), which also has an interpretive display on the
island's history, geology and ecology and dispenses free maps.

The island

Coming by boat, you'll arrive at Kangaroo Island's eastern end at the small settlement of **Penneshaw** with its Little penguin colony. **Kingscote**, to the west,
is the island's administrative centre and also South Australia's second-oldest
colonial settlement, though little remains to show for it. Between Penneshaw
and Kingscote, sheltered **American River** is another good base. The airport
is situated near **Cygnet River** – a quiet spot inland from Kingscote. From
here, the **Playford Highway** and **South Coast Road** branch out to traverse
the island, entering **Flinders Chase National Park** in the north and south
respectively. The national park and surrounding wilderness protection area
cover the entire western end of the island. The rugged **south coast** provides
more wildlife-spotting and fine scenery: running west to east you can visit the
aptly named Remarkable Rocks and Admirals Arch, both within the national
park; go bushwalking in Hanson Bay; tour the limestone caves of Kelly Hill;
camp at Vivonne Bay Conservation Park; play Lawrence of Arabia among the
impressive sand dunes of Little Sahara; or roam amongst sea lions at Seal Bay.
The quieter **north coast** has a series of sheltered beaches, including Emu Bay
and Stokes Bay, and wild coastal cliff walks around Scotts Cove.

Penneshaw

Most people arrive by ferry at **PENNESHAW**, set on low, penguin-inhabited
cliffs. This is a popular base, with comfortable accommodation and plenty of
places to eat (see opposite). Penneshaw's crescent of sandy beach at Hog Bay
curves from the rocks below the wharf, where the ferries come in, around to
a wooded headland. The bay provides safe **swimming** and even a shady shelter on the sand; above, there's a grassy picnic reserve with barbecues and the

Penguin Centre. A national park guide (daily: April–Sept 7.30pm & 8.30pm; Oct–March 8.30pm & 9.30pm; $6) provides an informative commentary on the antics of the **Little penguins** from the centre at dusk. This is the time they return from feeding in the unpolluted sea and cross the beach at Hog Bay to their cliffside burrows – a specially lit **boardwalk** provides a rookery viewing area.

Antechamber Bay, 10km southeast of Penneshaw, also has good, safe swimming. If you drive or cycle a further 10km along the unsealed dusty road you'll come to **Cape Willoughby Lighthouse**, at the eastern end of the island. Guided tours are offered by the NPWS (daily every 30min 10am–4pm; $7), and you can even stay in the sandstone homes of the original keepers (see below). You'll find more safe swimming at **American Beach**, southwest from Penneshaw along the scenic road that hugs Eastern Cove.

The **Dudley Peninsula**, on which Penneshaw stands, is attached to the rest of the island by a narrow neck of sand; at the isthmus 511 steps lead up to **Mount Thisby** (Prospect Hill), a 99-metre hill of sand with views across to the mainland, to Hungry Beach, Pelican Lagoon and American River on the island's north coast, and in the opposite direction to **Pennington Bay**. Here there are sponge-textured weathered rocks to clamber over, and some good surf, but a dangerous undertow.

Practicalities

Penneshaw's Sealink office is at 7 North Terrace (Mon–Fri 8am–6pm, Sat & Sun 8am–1pm & 3–6pm; ☎08/8553 1122). There's no bank, but the **post office** (Mon–Fri 9am–5pm, Sat 9am–11pm) acts as an agent, and there's EFTPOS at Grimshaw's, the town's **general store** opposite the hotel (daily 8am–7pm, summer until 8pm). Penneshaw has the island's widest range of accommodation: there are two **hostels**, the modern and lively (but non-YHA) *Penneshaw Youth Hostel* (☎08/8553 1284, ✉advhost@kin.on.net; dorms $19, rooms ❷), which also rents out cars and runs a diving school, and the more spacious and relaxed *Penguin Walk YHA* (☎08/8553 1233, ⓦwww.ki-ferryconnections.com.au; dorms $19, rooms ❸); both also run their own tours (see p.833). The upmarket alternative is the friendly *Kangaroo Island Seafront Hotel* (☎08/8553 1028, ⓦwww.seafront.com.au; ❻–❼), set in landscaped gardens with motel-style rooms and fully equipped cabins, plus a heated pool, spa, sauna and tennis court, bar and restaurant. There's **camping** at the small, shady *Penneshaw Caravan Park* on Talinga Avenue, to the left of the Sealink terminal overlooking the beach (☎ & ⓕ08/8553 1075; on-site vans ❸, cabins ❺). You can also stay in the two lighthouse-keepers' cottages at **Cape Willoughby** (☎08/8559 7235, ⓕ8559 7268; BYO linen; ❸–❹).

The best **restaurant** in town is *Sorrento's*, in the *Seafront Hotel*, specializing in seafood, steaks and local wines (☎08/8553 1028). *Wildfish Cafe*, overlooking the Sealink wharf, serves pizza and pasta, while the tin-roofed bungalow of the *Penneshaw Hotel* is a small and friendly place to drink, with a verandah overlooking the water; counter meals include cheap daily specials. *Dolphin Rock Takeaway* (daily 7.30–11am & 5–7.30pm), attached to the *Penneshaw Youth Hostel*, does fast food and a breakfast fry-up and sells a small range of groceries, but you'd be better off going to Grimshaw's, which sells virtually everything and has a takeaway service and seating area in the adjoining *Ruby Joe's Café*.

American River and Cygnet River

Facing Penneshaw across Eastern Cove, **AMERICAN RIVER** is actually a sheltered bay, where many small fishing boats moor, aiming to catch some of its abundant whiting. It's a peaceful place to stay, with a concentration of accommodation along the hilly shoreline and a general store. American River Rendezvous, the kiosk at the wharf (⊤08/8553 7150), provides a bit of a spectacle here with its raucous **pelican feeding** (daily 4.30pm; free). Boats can be chartered for local **fishing and sailing** from the kiosk or direct from Cooinda Charter Services (⊤ & ⒻO8/8553 7063). *Matthew Flinders Terraces* (⊤08/ 8553 7100, Ⓦwww.falconweb.net.au/~matthewflinders; ⑤–⑥) is a beautifully situated **motel** with pool, spa and a good licensed restaurant (reservations only), or try the *Wanderers Rest* (⊤08/8553 7140, Ⓦwww.wanderersrest .com.au; ⑦), an upmarket B&B where each room has a patio. Holiday units include the budget *Casuarina Units* (⊤08/8553 7020; ③) and the more expensive *Ulonga Lodge* (⊤ & ⒻO8/8553 7171; ④), which also has a café.

CYGNET RIVER, at the junction of Playford Highway and the road from Penneshaw, boasts one of the best places to stay on the island: *Koala Lodge* (⊤ & ⒻO8/8553 9006; ⑤), set amidst large gum trees, has personalized en-suite units near the river bank.

Kingscote and the north coast

It's a 45-minute drive on a sealed road from Penneshaw to **KINGSCOTE** (60km), the island's main town, with banks, shops, Internet access, a hospital, library and the only high school. The coast here has been the scene of several **shipwrecks** – interpretive boards on the foreshore provide details. For more history, you can walk north along the Esplanade to the **Reeves Point Historic Site**, where more boards commemorate the South Australia Company's first landing of settlers in July 1836, before they headed off to establish nearby Adelaide. The settlement never numbered more than three hundred people, and folded in 1839. Less than a kilometre up the hill above, on Seaview Road, is **Hope Cottage Folk Museum** (daily 1–4pm, Sat only in Aug), the restored 1859 home of a pioneering family. Kingscote has a small colony of **penguins** that were transported from Penneshaw during the building of the boardwalk there; not as impressive as Penneshaw's, they're best seen on the **guided ranger talks** that leave from the Marine Centre underneath the *Ozone Hotel* (April–Sept 7.30pm & 8.30pm; Oct–March 9pm & 9.40pm; $7.50). There's also **pelican feeding** around the Fisherman's Jetty with a small talk about their habits and habitat (daily 5pm; $2).

Established in 1907, the waterfront *Ozone Hotel* (⊤08/8553 2011 or 1800 083 133, Ⓦwww.ozonehotel.com; ⑤) is a local institution and the best place in town to eat. For a quieter meal, the 1950s-style *Island Resort Motel* on Telegraph Street (⊤08/8553 2100, Ⓔisland@kin.net.au; ⑤–⑥), houses the *Seafood Platter Restaurant*. Both these places also have rooms. Back from the beach on Dauncy Street is the *Queenscliffe Family Hotel* (⊤08/8553 2254, Ⓕ8553 2291; ③), another old pub offering rooms and meals; next door is the *Blue Gum Cafe*, which has a varied menu, with vegetarian dishes and real coffee (closed Sun). Upmarket motel accommodation, with sea views, is found at *Wisteria Lodge*, Cygnet Road (⊤08/8553 2707, Ⓦwww.kigateway.kin.on.net /wisteria; ⑤–⑥). For the budget-conscious there's the *Kangaroo Island Central Backpackers Hostel*, 21 Murray St (⊤08/8553 2787, Ⓕ8553 2694; dorms $19, rooms ②), which has large clean dorms, a kitchen and common room. *Nepean Bay Caravan Park* (⊤ & ⒻO8/8553 2394; on-site vans, cabins and cottages ②–③) at Brownlow Beach, 3km away, is the only place for **campers**.

The **beaches** on the north coast are more sheltered than those on the south. **Emu Bay**, 21km along a sealed road from Kingscote, is a secluded and quiet spot with a clean, sandy beach, a small penguin community, no shops, a few holiday homes and a couple of B&Bs. Wintersun Holiday Units (℡08/8553 5241, ℮dmorris@kin.net.au) manages several self-contained cottages (❷–❹) along the bay and in the nearby hills. About 30km further west, secluded **Stokes Bay** is reached along a dirt road passing through a natural tunnel between overhanging boulders. There's a delightful calm rock pool – a perfect semicircle of rounded black stones which conveniently provides protection from the dangerous rip in the bay. Outside the tunnel, the overpriced *Rockpool Cafe* (summer only, daily 10am–5.30pm; ℡08/8559 2277) looks after the beachfront **campsites** and also sells milk and bread to campers.

The south coast

There are several conservation parks strung out along the exposed south coast. The largest is **Cape Gantheaume**, an area of low mallee scrub supporting prolific birdlife around **Murray Lagoon**, the largest freshwater lagoon on the island (this is where you'll find the ranger station: daily 8am–5pm). The adjacent **Seal Bay Conservation Park** is home to almost six hundred **sea lions**, the third-largest breeding population in Australia. They are unusually tolerant of humans and you can walk quietly among the colony on the beach at Seal Bay, accompanied by a national park guide (9am–4.15pm, until 7pm during summer holidays; every 15min in summer, every 45min in winter; $10.50), or take a stroll on the boardwalk ($7).

    Vivonne Bay, with its long, sandy beach and bush setting, is a great place to camp. The beachside **campsite** (toilets, water, barbecues) is privately run ($4), and there's a well-stocked store and bottle shop 1km away on the main South Coast Road. It's safe to swim near the jetty or boat ramp or in the Harriet River, but the bay itself has a dangerous undertow. Between Seal Bay and Vivonne Bay, **Little Sahara** comprises 15km of perfect white-sand dunes rising unexpectedly out of mallee scrub.

    The main features of the **Kelly Hill Conservation Park** are the **Kelly Hill Caves**, extensive limestone cave formations (NPWS guided tours daily: 10am–3.30pm; in summer until 4.30pm; $7.50). The tour explores only the largest cave – not the usual damp, bat-filled cavern, but very dry, with a constant temperature of 16°C. The NPWS runs adventure caving tours of three other caves ($24–35 depending on the cave; ℡08/8559 7231 for details and booking). The eighteen-kilometre return **Hanson Bay Trail** goes from the caves to the sea, passing freshwater lagoons and dune systems: allow at least eight hours – or longer, if you're tempted to stop for a swim. *Hanson Bay Cabins* (℡08/8553 2603, ℠www.esl.com.au; ❻–❼), just west of the Kelly Hill Conservation Park, is situated in a lovely secluded spot surrounded by bushland with excellent walking trails.

Flinders Chase National Park

Flinders Chase National Park, South Australia's largest, occupies the entire western end of the island. It became a park as early as 1919, and in the 1920s and 1930s koalas, platypuses and Cape Barren geese from the Bass Strait islands (see p.1121) were introduced. The land is mainly low-lying mallee forest, with occasional patches of taller sugar gum trees. The **Flinders Chase Visitors Centre** (daily 10am–5pm; ℡08/8559 7235, ℮kiparksaccom @sau.gov.au; park entry fee $6.50 per person) is surrounded by open grasslands where large numbers of kangaroos and wallabies graze. Koala signs lead to a glade of trees where you can see the creatures swaying overhead, within binocular range. Follow the **Platypus Waterhole Walk** for 3km to a platypus-viewing area, but be warned that to get a glimpse of the creatures requires endless patience. The winding sealed road through the park will take you to its most spectacular features, the huge and weirdly shaped, rust-coloured **Remarkable Rocks** on Kirkpatrick Point, and the impressive natural formation of **Admirals Arch**, where hundreds of fur seals bask around the rocks. At the northern corner of the park, you can go on a guided tour of the 1858 **Cape Borda Lighthouse** (4–7 tours daily; $7; ℡08/8559 3257, ⓦwww.environment.sa.gov.au/parks/flinderschase/visit).

The main **camping** area is at Rocky River. There are various **cottages** (❶–❹) throughout the park, bookable through the Flinders Chase Visitors Centre. There are several other good places to stay along the South Coast Road just outside the park. *Kangaroo Island Wilderness Resort* (℡08/8559 7275, ⓦwww.austdreaming.com.au; dorms $35–40, rooms ❻–❼) has large wood cabins set amidst bushland, plus an excellent restaurant – at dusk you can watch the nocturnal animals coming out to feed. Nearby, the *Western KI Caravan Park* (℡08/8559 7201, ⓕ8559 7298, ⓔbeckwith@kin.net.au; cabins ❹) is set in an expansive wildlife reserve, where you can camp under the tall gum trees and try to spot koala bears. By staying this end of the island you'll also see the spectacular coastal sights at their best – particularly Remarkable Rocks, which turn a deep orange with the setting and rising sun.

The southeast

Most travellers en route between Adelaide and Melbourne pass through southeast South Australia as quickly as possible. From Tailem Bend, just beyond Murray Bridge some 85km out of Adelaide, three highways branch out. The first, the **Ouyen Highway**, is the quintessential road to nowhere, leading through the sleepy settlements of Lameroo and Pinnaroo to the insignificant town of **Ouyen** in Victoria's mallee country (see p.1015). The second, the **Dukes Highway**, offers a fast and boring route to Melbourne via the South Australian mallee scrub and farming towns of **Keith** and **Bordertown**, birthplace of former prime minister Bob Hawke, before continuing in Victoria as the Western Highway across the monotonous Wimmera (see p.1013). It is, however, well worth breaking your journey to visit **the Coonawarra** and **Naracoorte**, in between the Dukes Highway and the coastal route: the former is a tiny wine-producing area that makes some of the country's finest red wine; the latter is a fair-size town with a freshwater lagoon system that attracts prolific birdlife, and a conservation park with impressive World Heritage-listed caves.

The third option, the **Princes Highway** (Highway 1), is much less direct but far more interesting. It follows the extensive coastal lagoon system of **the Coorong** to **Kingston SE**, and then runs a short way inland to the lake craters of **Mount Gambier**, before crossing into Victoria. There's another possible route on this last stretch – the **Southern Ports Highway** – which sticks closer to the coast, plus a potential detour along the Riddoch Highway into the scenic Coonawarra wine region. Premier Stateliner (℡08/8415 5555) serves two routes between Adelaide and Mount Gambier, one inland via Keith, Bordertown, Naracoorte, Coonawarra and Penola; the other along the coast via Meningie, Kingston SE, Robe and Millicent. If you're coming from Melbourne, V/Line (℡08/8231 7620 or 13 61 96, ⓦwww.vline.vic.gov.au) has a daily service which terminates at Mount Gambier. The NPWS free newspaper, *The Tatler*, gives practical details relating to the southeastern coastal parks –

pick up the latest copy from the Adelaide office (see p.796), or regional offices en route. More information can be found at the regional visitor information website at ⓦ www.thelimestonecoast.com.

Coorong National Park

From Tailem Bend, the Princes Highway skirts Lake Alexandrina and the freshwater Lake Albert before passing the edge of the **Coorong National Park**. The coastal saline lagoon system of the Coorong (from the Aboriginal *Karangk*, meaning long neck) is separated from the sea for over 100km by the high sand dunes of the **Younghusband Peninsula**. This is the state's most prolific **pelican breeding ground**, and an excellent place to observe these awkward yet graceful birds – there's a shelter with seating and a telescope focused on the small islands where some birds breed at Jacks Point, 3km north of Policemans Point on the Princes Highway. Without your own **transport**, one way to see the Coorong is to head off in a 4WD with a local naturalist from Coorong Nature Tours (day-trip $150 from Meningie, $200 from Adelaide; longer two- and three-day trips available; ☏ 08/8574 0037, ⓦ www.coorongnaturetours.com). You can also get to the park on a **cruise** from Goolwa (see box on p.834).

There are several designated **camping areas** with shelters, barbecues, toilets, running water (but no showers) and marked walking trails. The Coorong is also good for beach camping: with a permit (see below) you can camp anywhere along the beach between high and low watermark, but cars must be parked in designated places, and you must bring your own drinking water, which can be collected outside the seldom-manned **Salt Creek NPWS ranger station** on the edge of the park. Elsewhere, **information** and **camping permits** ($6 per car) and maps of the park and campsites can be obtained at the national park **headquarters** at 34 Main St, Meningie (Mon, Wed & Fri 9am–5pm; ☏ 08/8575 1200), the Melaleuca Information Centre, 76 Princes Highway (Mon–Fri 9am–5pm, Sat & Sun 10.30am–2.30pm; ☏ 08/8575 1259), and most petrol stations on the way to the park including Salt Creek's Shell petrol station, which has an outside notice board and a **café** serving delicious grilled Coorong mullet. There are **caravan parks** at Long Point, Parnka Point, Gemini Downs and 42-Mile Crossing – the only land access to the Younghusband Peninsula. If you're passing by, park your car at the 42-Mile Crossing information area and walk 1km along a sandy 4WD track for great views of the sand dunes and the wild Southern Ocean. This track runs alongside the beach all the way up the peninsula to Barkers Knoll and down to Kingston SE, with camping along the way. If you want to stay in more comfort, there are plenty of motels at the popular fishing centre of **Meningie**, by Lake Albert.

Camp Coorong, run by the Ngarrindjeri Lands and Progress Association, is 10km south of Meningie. This cultural centre attempts to explain the heritage and culture of the Ngarrindjeri Aborigines, once one of the largest groups in South Australia, occupying the land around the Coorong and the lower Murray River and lakes. There's a fascinating **museum** (Mon–Fri 9am–5pm; donation), and you can camp here or in the nearby Bush Reserve ($5 per group) or stay in the well-outfitted **cabins** (booking required on ☏ 08/8575 1557, ⓔ nlpa@lm.net.au; ❸). A few kilometres further north is the Ngarrindjeri owned *Coorong Wilderness Lodge*, designed in the shape of a fish (☏ 08/9575 6001, ⓔ kurangk@lm.net.au; camping $10 per car, en-suite cabins ❸). The restaurant serves indigenous meals (booking essential), and if you want to learn more about Ngarrindjeri culture, the owners offer short tours, plus a comprehensive three-day wilderness and cultural tour.

Southern Ports Highway

KINGSTON SE, on Lacepede Bay, is the first town past the Coorong: here the Princes Highway turns inland, while the **Southern Ports Highway** continues along the coast before rejoining the main road at Millicent. As the **Big Lobster** on the highway in Kingston suggests, Kingston has an important lobster industry: you can buy them freshly cooked at *Lacepede Seafood* by the jetty (daily 9am–6pm) for around $40 a kilo.

Lobsters apart, you're better off continuing down the coast. **ROBE**, on the south side of Guichen Bay, 44km from Kingston, was one of South Australia's first settlements, established as a deep-water port in 1847. After 1857, over sixteen thousand Chinese landed here and walked to the goldfields, 400km away, to avoid the poll tax levied in Victoria. As trade declined and the highway bypassed the town, Robe managed to maintain both dignity and a low-key charm, and during the busy summer period the population of less than eight hundred expands to over eleven thousand. Adelaidians love the place, with its well-preserved nineteenth-century streetscapes and its beach setting surrounded by lakes and bushland; some even drive the 366km for a weekend. Summer is also the season for Robe's other major industry: **crayfishing**. **Tourist information** is available inside the library on the corner of Smiley and Victoria streets (Mon–Fri 9am–5pm, Sat & Sun 10am–4pm; ☎08/8768 2465, ⊛www.robe.sa.gov.au); they have walking and driving maps, and free limited-time Internet access.

There are dozens of places to **stay**, most of which double up as places to eat. *Robe Hotel*, Mundy Terrace (☎08/8768 2077, ℱ8768 2495; ❸–❺), is an old stone beachfront hotel with modern budget accommodation and en-suite motel-style rooms with views and spa units; the downstairs bars serve good bistro meals – lots of fish and a vegetarian dish of the day. The charming, ivy-covered *Caledonian Inn* on Victoria Street (☎08/8768 2029, ℮caled@seol.net.au; ❹–❻ including breakfast) was first licensed in 1858 and wouldn't look out of place in an English village – it offers B&B accommodation upstairs or in homely cottages, and serves excellent food. Also on Victoria Street, *Guichen Bay Motel* (☎08/8768 2001; ❸) has good-value, spacious rooms, some with kitchenette, as well as the licensed *Robetown Cottage Restaurant*, which has special crayfish dishes in season. *Sea Vu Caravan Park*, 1 Squire Drive (☎08/8768 2277; cabins ❸–❹), is family-run and close to town, with a swimming beach right by it. The excellent *Bushland Cabins*, set in bushland southeast of the centre on Nora Creina Road (☎08/8768 2386, ℮bushland@seol.net.au; dorm $18, cabins ❷–❸), has walking trails into the surrounding bush, including a one-kilometre clifftop track into Robe. There's also the award-winning *Robe Long Beach Holiday Park*, on the Esplanade (☎08/8768 2237, ⊛www.robelongbeach.com.au; cabins ❷–❹). For **meals**, there's excellent café fare, all-day breakfasts and Italian coffee at *Wild Mulberry Cafe*, 46 Victoria St, opposite the Shell garage (Mon–Fri 9am–4pm, Sat & Sun 8am–5pm). For self-caterers, Foodland Supermarket, opposite the Ampol petrol station, is open daily 7.30am–6.30pm, later in summer.

Between Robe and Beachport are four lakes: for part of the way you can take the Nora Criena Drive through **Little Dip Conservation Park**, 14km of coastal dune systems. The drive provides views of Lake Eliza and Lake St Clair before returning to Southern Ports Highway and the former whaling port of

Lobster · For
Sale..

COLD
BEER

△ Larry the Giant Lobster, Kingston

BEACHPORT, which boasts one of the longest jetties in Australia and many lobster-fishing boats at anchor on Rivoli Bay. Beachport has plenty of **accommodation**. *Bompas*, overlooking the bay at 3 Railway Terrace (T08/8735 8333, Wwww.beachportaustralia.com; dorms $18.50, en-suite rooms ❹), was the town's first licensed hotel in 1879, and is now a pleasing B&B guesthouse with a coffee bar, bistro and **restaurant** downstairs, with Thai, Malay, Italian and Australian dishes. There's also the *Beachport Caravan Park*, opposite the beach on Beach Road (T & F08/8735 8128; on-site vans ❷, en-suite cottages ❹–❺). For a snack, try *The Green Room* on Railway Terrace, which does great *giros* and also rents out surf gear and golf clubs.

Continuing south on Southern Ports Highway, there are several turn-offs to **Canunda National Park** which has giant sand dunes, signposted coastal walking trails, an abundance of birdlife and camping facilities ($6 per vehicle honesty box). The best place to explore the park is from **SOUTHEND** – you can pick up leaflets detailing the walks from the **National Park Headquarters** just beyond the town (Mon–Fri 8.30am–5pm; T08/8735 6053). The only **place to stay** apart from the campsites is the *Southend on Sea Tourist Park* (T08/8735 6035, F8735 6034; on-site vans ❷, cabins ❸–❹). More accommodation is available in the rather ordinary town of **MILLICENT**, 15km to the south, which also has its own **Visitor Information Centre**, 1 Main St (Mon–Fri 9am–5pm, Sat & Sun 9.30am–4.30pm; T08/8733 3205) and access to the park. The Southern Ports Highway rejoins the Princes Highway at Millicent.

Mount Gambier

Set close to the border with Victoria, **MOUNT GAMBIER** is the southeast's commercial centre. The small city sprawls up the slopes of an extinct volcano whose three craters – each with its own lake surrounded by heavily wooded slopes and filled from underground waterways – are perfect for subterranean diving. The **Blue Lake** is the largest of the three, up to 204m deep and 5km in circumference. From November to March it's a stunning cobalt blue, reverting to duller grey in the colder months. There are lookout spots and a scenic drive around the lake, and guided tours are offered by Aquifer Tours (Nov–Jan: daily on the hour 9am–5pm; Thurs also 7pm; Feb–Oct: daily on the hour 9am–3pm; 45min; $5.50). The second-largest crater holds **Valley Lake** and a Wildlife Park (daily 7am–dusk; free), where indigenous animals range free amid native flora; there are lookouts, walking trails and boardwalks. West of the centre, on Jubilee Highway West, is the extensive complex of underground caverns at **Engelbrecht Cave** (guided tours hourly 11am–3pm, check times in winter; 45min; $6). You can **dive** here in limestone waterways under the city, though you'll need a CDAA (Cave Divers Association of Australia) qualification to tackle these dark and dangerous waters. Contact the Mount Gambier NPWS office at 11 Helen St (T08/8735 1177, Wwww.adelaide.net .au/~ecave) for further information.

The centrepiece of the city itself is **Cave Gardens**, a shady park surrounding a deep limestone cavern with steps leading some way down; the stream running into it eventually filters into the Blue Lake. At the rear of the park the municipal offices contain the Civic Centre, library and a small theatre. Fronting the park is the former Town Hall and the **Riddoch Art Gallery** (Tues–Fri 10am–4pm, Sat 10am–2pm; free) whose focus is the impressive Rodney Gooch collection of Aboriginal art from Utopia, Central Australia. In the same building, Studio One sells the work of local artists (Mon–Fri 10.30am–4pm,

Sat 9.30am–11.30am). For more information on Mount Gambier's attractions, head for the excellent **Lady Nelson Victory and Discovery Centre**, on Jubilee Highway East (daily 9am–5pm; exhibition $9; ☎08/8724 1730, ⓦwww.mountgambiertourism.com.au), where the ecology, geology and history of Mount Gambier are explored from Aboriginal and European perspectives. Highlights include a ten-minute narration by the ghostly holographic image of missionary Christina Smith, the short wetlands boardwalk and a demonstration of a volcanic eruption complete with steam – quite scary when it booms.

The CDAA (see opposite) issue permits for snorkelling in the crystal-clear waters of **Piccaninnie Ponds Conservation Park** and **Ewans Pond Conservation Park**, both south of Mount Gambier near Port Macdonnell. At Piccaninnie Ponds, a deep chasm with white-limestone walls contains clear water that is filtered underground from the Blue Lake – it takes five hundred years to get here. East of the city is **Umpherston Sinkhole** (open access), also known as the Sunken Garden, since it contains Victorian-era terraced gardens – they are floodlit at night when possums come out to feed.

Practicalities

Mount Gambier has heaps of places to **stay**, with motels lining the highway either side of town. The pick of them is the *Barn Motel & Apartments*, on Nelson Road (☎08/8726 8366, ⓦwww.barnmotel.com; motel ❸, apartments ❺). *The Jail*, on Margaret Street (☎08/8723 0032, ⓦwww.adelaide.net.au/~turnkey; dorms $20), was built in the 1860s and is now a Heritage-listed building. The last inmates left in 1995 and you can stay in the original cells behind locked doors (some even have a solitary loo in the corner) or in the simple three-bed dorms. Meals are provided in the large common room, which also has a bar, and there are laundry facilities and Internet access. The central *Jens Hotel*, 40 Commercial St (☎08/8725 0188, ⓔjens.town.hall.hotel@alhgroup.com.au; ❸), is a classic, wide-balconied old boozer with cheap bar and bistro meals, late opening hours and en-suite accommodation. The best places to **eat** are the licensed *Café Capri Restaurant*, 53 Gray St (Mon–Sat 8.30am–10 or 11pm), and the award-winning *Belejorno*, serving classic Italian pizza and gourmet pasta. The town's **cinema** is next door in the Oatmill Building. There's **Internet access** at the Cave Internet Lounge, 15–17 Commercial St ($2.50 per 30min), and – free of charge – at the public library at the end of Watson Terrace (Mon–Fri 9am–4pm).

Heading on to Melbourne from Mount Gambier, V/Line (☎13 61 96) has a daily **bus** service via Portland, Warrnambool, Geelong and Ballarat.

The Coonawarra wine region

Directly north of Mount Gambier, the **Riddoch Highway** heads through the low-key and pretty **Coonawarra wine region**, and past some World Heritage-listed caves at Naracoorte, eventually linking up with the Dukes Highway at Keith. Most wineries are located on a ninety-kilometre stretch of highway between Penola and Padthaway. The region is renowned for the quality of its reds, which have been compared to those of Bordeaux. The soil and drainage is ideal, classic Terra Rossa over limestone, and the climate is perfect – and as the weather is not really variable from year to year, the wines are consistently good. Premier Stateliner (☎08/8415 5555) stops daily at Penola and Naracoorte on its Adelaide to Mount Gambier inland service. Penola Coonawarra Tour Service (☎08/8737 2779) offers restaurant transfers and winery tours around the area.

Penola

Twenty-two kilometres north of Mount Gambier, **PENOLA**, gateway to the Coonawarra wine region, is a simple but dignified country town of well-preserved nineteenth-century architecture. For information, head for **Penola Coonawarra Visitor Centre** in the old Mechanics Institute Building (Mon–Fri 9am–5pm, Sat 10am–5pm, Sun 9.30am–4pm; ☎08/8737 2855, ⓕ8737 2251), which also houses a display featuring John Riddoch, pioneer of Coonawarra's vineyards, and hands out the free *Historic Penola and Coonawarra* map with details of the region's wineries.

Beside the 1857 Cobb & Co booking office (now a restaurant), **St Joseph's Catholic Church** looks like something out of an Italian village, a world away from the very modern **Mary MacKillop Interpretative Centre** (daily 10am–4pm; ☎08/8737 2092, ⓦwww.penola.mtx.net.au/~mackillop; $3.50) next door. Sister Mary MacKillop (1842–1909) was Penola's most famous resident, and Australia's first would-be saint – in 1995 Pope John Paul II pronounced her "Blessed", the last stage before full sainthood. MacKillop set up a school, created her own teaching method and, with Father Julian Tennyson Woods, co-founded the Sisters of St Joseph of the Sacred Heart, a charitable teaching order that spread throughout Australia and New Zealand. Dramatic episodes of alleged disobedience and excommunication give her story a certain oomph. There's an informative display in the centre, with Barbie-doll lookalike "nuns on the run" and dressed-up dummies in the original school room. Across the fields stand the National Trust-listed cottages of **Petticoat Lane**, where many of Mary's poverty-stricken students lived. One of the buildings now houses a craft shop (daily 10am–5pm), while a display in another and an interpretive board in the garden tells the story of the seventeen-member Sharam family.

There are backpacker **beds** at the comfortable and centrally located *McKay's Trek Inn*, 38 Riddoch St (☎0407 391 886 or after hours on ☎08/8725 4308; dorms $20), which caters to the Oz Experience crowd and long-stay grape-pickers, so it's worth booking ahead. *Penola Caravan Park* on South Terrace (☎08/8737 2381) has good-value on-site vans (❷) and en-suite cabins (❸). The focus of the town is the friendly, National Trust-listed *Heywood's Royal Oak Hotel*, 31 Church St (☎08/8737 2322, ⓕ8737 2825; ❹), with four-poster doubles and some twin rooms. Out of town, on the Riddoch Highway, is the upmarket motel complex of *Chardonnay Lodge* (☎08/8736 3309, ⓦwww.chardonnaylodge.com.au; ❺–❻), set amongst lawns and rose gardens, with a swimming pool and an attached café-restaurant.

The best place to **eat** is *Heywood's Royal Oak Hotel*, which has a beautiful beer garden and an excellent bistro. Otherwise, *Sweet Grape*, 48 Church St (daily 8.30am–4.30pm), dishes up affordable café favourites and international dishes. On the Riddoch Highway, *Hermitage Café and Wine Bar*, attached to Wetherall Winery (daily 11am–9pm; ☎08/8737 2122; bookings advised for dinner), focuses on local and organic produce. The vineyard setting is very pleasant, with a little pond for yabbies and a native garden out back, filled with banksias and big gum trees.

Coonawarra Township

There isn't much to what is called **COONAWARRA TOWNSHIP**, a settlement which developed to house and service the adjacent Wynns Coonawarra Estate (see box opposite), but it does make a good base if you're touring local vineyards. Cottage **accommodation** here includes *Skinner Cottage* (☎08/8736 3304, ⓕ8736 3016; ❻), a quaint tin-roofed bungalow just around the corner from the old Coonawarra school, now *Nibs Bistro and Grill* (☏08/8736 3006; licensed and BYO; bookings on Sat night recommended), which is a fun place to **eat** – choose from a display of marinated meats and grill them yourself.

Naracoorte Caves

Midway between Penola and Padthaway, the **Naracoorte Caves Conservation Park** protects a World Heritage-listed system of limestone caves. The **Wanambi Fossil Centre** (daily 9am–5pm, summer until sunset; ☏08/8762 2340) gives an insight into the area's archeological siginnficance – important fossils of extinct Pleistocene megafauna, including giant kangaroos and wombats, were discovered here in the Victoria Fossil Cave in 1969. Another notable feature is the **Bat Centre**, the only place in the world where you can watch bats inside a cave with the help of infrared remote control cameras.

The caves are spread out over the Conservation Park: **Alexandra Cave** has the prettiest limestone formations (tours at 9.30am & 1.30pm; 30min), while **Victoria Fossil Cave** is popular for its fossils (10.15am & 2pm; 1hr). You can guide yourself through the **Wet Cave** (9am and 5pm), named after the very wet chamber at its deepest part; an automatic lighting system switches on as you walk through. **Admission fees** are $10 for one cave, $18 for two or $28 for all of them. There are also **adventure caving** tours in several other caves (2hr novice tours $25; 3hr advanced tours $200 per party, maximum six people; overalls can be rented for $5; lights and helmets supplied).

You can **camp** within the park ($18 per car), where facilities include powered sites, hot showers and even a free laundry, or stay in **dorms** at *Wirreanda Bunkhouse* (☏08/8762 2340; $13). More comfortable is the rural tranquillity at the *Cave Park Cabins* (☏08/8762 0696; ⓕ8762 0693; ❸), only 1.5km from the caves. There's a basic campsite at nearby **Bool Lagoon Conservation Park** ($15 per car; water and toilets only), which is a magnet for birds; camping permits are issued at the Wanambi Fossil Centre. For **meals**, the licensed *Bent Wing Cafe* at the centre is surprisingly sophisticated, dishing up everything from Greek salads to char-grilled kangaroo fillets with native plum chutney.

On the highway 12km west of the caves, the town of **NARACOORTE** is a small regional centre with a supermarket (open daily) and several places to eat and stay. *Naracoorte Hotel Motel*, 73 Ormerod St (☎08/8762 2400; ❷–❸) has motel rooms and cheap meals; *Naracoorte Backpackers* (☎08/8762 3835, ⓦwww.nctebackpackers.mtx.net; dorms $17) offers tours to the caves, has bikes for rent and 24-hour Internet access. A ten-minute walk north of town at 81 Park Terrace, *Naracoorte Holiday Park* (☎08/8762 2128; cabins ❸) is set in a shady spot by a creek, close to a swimming lake.

The Riverland

The **Riverland** is the name given to the long irrigated strip on either side of the **Murray River** as its meanders for 300km from Blanchetown to Renmark near the Victorian border. The Canadian Chaffey brothers had already developed successful irrigation settlements in California when they were invited to Australia to look into possibilities for the Murray, establishing a colony at **Renmark** in 1887. The Riverland's deep red-orange alluvial soil – helped by extensive irrigation – is very fertile, making the area the state's major supplier of oranges, stone fruit and grapes. Fruit stalls along the roadsides add to the impression of a year-long harvest, and if you're after **fruit-picking work** it's an excellent place to start; contact the Harvest Labour Office on Riverland Drive in Berri (☎1300 720 126). The area is also Australia's major **wine-producing** region, though the hi-tech wineries here mainly make mass-produced wines for casks and export. Many are open to visitors, but their scale and commercialism make them less enjoyable than, say, the McLaren Vales (see p.831).

The **Sturt Highway**, the major route between Adelaide and Sydney, passes straight through the Riverland. Leaving Adelaide, it bypasses Gawler and cuts across the northern end of the Barossa Valley, reaching the Murray at Blanchetown, about 130km from the city. Premier Stateliner runs a twice-daily service along the highway from Adelaide to Renmark via Blanchetown, Waikerie, Barmera and Berri, and also goes daily (except Sat) to Loxton. Between Waikerie and Renmark all the **towns** feel pretty much the same, with a raw edge, little charm or sophistication, and a yobbo culture (most apparent on drunken Friday nights). Each town has only one hotel, and these huge and mostly graceless **community hotels** are a feature of the Riverland: owned and run by the town, their profits are ploughed back into the hotel or channelled into the community, generally into sporting groups.

Blanchetown to Waikerie

BLANCHETOWN, 130km from Adelaide, is the first Riverland town, and the starting point of the Murray's lock and weir system, which helps maintain the river at a constant height between the town and Wentworth in New South Wales (see p.361). Eleven kilometres west of town, **Brookfield Conservation Park**, a gift to South Australia from the Chicago Zoological Society, is home to the endangered **southern hairy-nosed wombat**; the creatures also thrive at nearby *Portee Station* (☎08/8540 5211, ⓦwww.portee.com.au; ❸), a 200-square-kilometre sheep-grazing property where, if you can afford it (rates are $224 per person), you can stay in the 1873 riverfront homestead. A range of tours (enquire for details) include river trips in a small boat to look at the prolific birdlife, and a 4WD station tour where you'll see wombats close up.

A forty-kilometre drive from Blanchetown, between Sedan and Swan Reach, is the fascinating **Yookamurra Sanctuary** (☎08/8562 5011, ⓦwww.flinders .com.au/yookam.htm). Surrounded by the world's largest feral-proof fence, 14km long, the property is home to some of Australia's most endangered species – including ant-eating numbats and large-eared bilbies – which, protected from predators, thrive on the mallee scrubland. Accommodation ($65 per person) is on a half-board basis in air-conditioned lodges; rates include dusk and dawn animal-spotting tours.

Following the river from Blanchetown, it's 36km directly north to **MORGAN**, one of the most attractive of the Riverland towns. At the height of the river trade between 1880 and 1915 Morgan was one of South Australia's busiest river ports, transferring wool from New South Wales and Victoria onto trains bound for Adelaide; parts of its mainly red gum and jarrah **river wharf** remain intact. You can wander through the riverfront park, past the old train station and the stationmaster's building, now a **museum** (Tues 2–4pm, on other days knock on the caretaker's door at the back of the museum or call ☎08/8540 2136), and up onto the wharves overlooking moored houseboats on the river to bushland beyond. The well-preserved nineteenth-century streetscape of **Railway Terrace**, the main street, sits above the old railway line and wharf, dominated by the huge Landseer shipping warehouse. There's standard **accommodation** in two adjacent old pubs: the *Terminus Hotel* (☎08/8540 2006; ❷) and the *Commercial* (☎08/8540 2107; ❸). You can also stay at the *Morgan Riverside Caravan Park* (☎08/8540 2207, ⓔmorgancp @riverland.net.au; cabins ❷–❸), in a great spot right in town by the river. For **food**, try the pubs or *Morgan Pizza Bar*, 17 Railway Terrace (☎08/8540 2103; pizzas Fri–Sun from 5pm only, fish and chips from 5pm all week).

From Morgan the river takes a sharp bend east, meandering south to **WAIK-ERIE**; it's 32km from Morgan to Waikerie on a riverside road, with a free ferry crossing at Cadell. A less attractive drive from Blanchetown bypasses the river loop, reaching Waikerie directly by heading 42km northeast along the Sturt Highway. Waikerie is at the heart of the largest citrus-growing area in Australia; the first thing you notice is a huge complex owned by **Nippies** that takes up both sides of a street, allegedly the largest fruit-packing house in the southern hemisphere. A good base for **fruit-picking** work is the *Kingston-on-Murray Backpackers* (☎08/8583 0211 or 1800 737 378; dorms $18, rooms ❷), on the Sturt Highway about 30km east of Waikerie.

Loxton

Some 35km east of Waikerie, the Murray makes another large loop away from the Sturt highway, with **LOXTON** at its southernmost reach, before twisting back north to Berri (see p.856). Leaving the highway at Kingston-on-Murray, you pass the **Moorook Game Reserve**, a large swamp fringed with river red gums and home to many waterbirds. In Loxton itself, the **Tourist & Art Centre**, at Bookpurnong Terrace (Mon–Fri 9am–5pm, Sat 9.30am–12.30pm, Sun 1–4pm; ☎08/8584 7919, ⓦwww.riverland.net.au/~loxinfo), acts as an agent for Stateliner and can fill you in on local attractions such as the riverside **Loxton Historical Village** (Mon–Fri 10am–4pm, Sat & Sun 10am–5pm; $8), a replica of a turn-of-the-twentieth-century Riverland town. Altogether more compelling is the **Katarapko Game Reserve**, opposite Loxton, where Katarapko Creek and the Murray have cut deep channels and lagoons, creating an island. Access from Loxton is by water only – perfect for canoeing and observing birdlife; to **camp**, you need a permit from the NPWS, 28 Vaughan Terrace, Berri (☎08/8595 2111). *Loxton Riverfront Caravan Park*, Packard Bend

The **Murray River** is Australia's Mississippi – or so the American author Mark Twain declared when he saw it in the early 1900s. It's a fraction of the size of the American river, admittedly, but in a country of seasonal, intermittent streams it counts as a major river and, like the Mississippi, the Murray helped open up a new continent, first to explorers, later to trade. Fed by melting snow from the Snowy Mountains, and by the Murrumbidgee and Darling rivers, the Murray has enough volume to flow through the arid plains, eventually reaching the Southern Ocean southwest of Adelaide near Goolwa (see p.834). Together, the Murray and the Darling and its tributaries make up one of the biggest and longest watercourses in the world, giving life to Australia's most important agricultural region, the **Murray–Darling basin**. For much of its length the Murray forms the border between New South Wales and Victoria, slowing as it reaches South Australia, where it meanders through extensive alluvial plains and irrigation areas. Almost half of South Australia's water comes from the Murray: even far-off Woomera in the Outback relies on it.

Historically, the Riverland was densely populated by various **Aboriginal peoples**. They navigated the river in bark canoes, the bark being cut from river red gums in a single perfect piece; many trees along the river still bear the scars. Nets and spears were used to catch fish, duck and emu, and mussels were also an important food source. The Ngarrindjeri people's Dreamtime story of the river's creation explains how Ngurunderi travelled down the Murray from its confluence with the Darling, looking for his two runaway wives. The Murray was then just a small stream. As Ngurunderi searched, a giant Murray cod surged ahead of him, widening the river with swipes of his tail. Ngurunderi tried to spear the fish, which he chased right through to the ocean: the thrashing cod carved out the pattern of the Murray River during the chase.

The explorers **Hume** and **Hovell** came across the Murray at Albury in 1824. In 1830 **Sturt** and **Mitchell** navigated the Murray and Darling in a whale boat, Sturt naming it after the then Secretary of State for the Colonies (coincidentally, *Murrundi* was the Aboriginal name for part of the river). Their exploration opened up the interior, and from 1838 the Murray was followed as a **stock route** to South Australia by drovers or "overlanders" taking sheep and cattle to newly established Adelaide. In 1853 the first **paddle steamer** on the Murray, the *Mary Ann*, was launched near

(T08/8584 7862, @loxtoncp@hotkey.net.au; cabins ❷–❸), is a peaceful spot opposite the game reserve, with canoes for rent ($11 per hour, $55 per day).

Back in town, the only **accommodation** option is the rather too glitzy *Loxton Hotel-Motel*, East Terrace (T08/8584 7266, Wwww.loxtonhotel.com; ❹), where you can get good bistro **meals** (noon to 2pm & 6–8pm only) and all-day breakfasts on Sundays. Alternatively, cheap meals and free **Internet access** are available at the friendly *Loxton Club* (T08/8584 7353) at 27 Bookpurnang Terrace.

Barmera

If you haven't followed the river to Loxton, **BARMERA**, on the shores of Lake Bonney, is the next major stopping point along the highway. Its claims to fame are varied and dubious: at **Pelican Point**, on the lake's western shore, there's an official **nudist beach** (and a nearby nudist resort with camping, and on-site vans ❸; T08/8588 7366, bookings essential), while every June, the **South Australian Country Music Festival and Awards** are held in the lovely old Bonney Theatre. For more about the music awards, and **tourist information** in general, contact the Barmera Visitor Information Centre,

Mannum. Goods were transported far inland, opening up new areas for settlement; in return, wool was carried to market. River transport reached its peak in the 1870s, but by the mid-1930s it was virtually finished, thanks to the superior speed of the railways.

Seeing the river

The best way to appreciate the calm brown beauty of the Murray – lined with majestic river red gums and towering cliffs that reveal the area's colourful soils – is to get out on the water. Several old **paddle steamers** and a variety of other craft still cruise the Murray for pleasure, and you can spend a weekend or more on board the *Murray Princess* (Fri 6.30pm to Sun 2pm; $395 per person; 7-day package $1365 per person also available; ℡08/8569 2511, ⓦwww.captaincook.com.au), based at **Mannum**, one-hour's drive east of Adelaide (or take the Murray Bridge Passenger Service; Mon–Fri daily; ℡08/8532 2633). Other cruises from Mannum include sporadic trips on the restored paddle steamer *Marion* (book at Mannum Tourist Information Centre, 67 Randell St; ℡08/8569 1303), and regular outings on the MV *Proud Mary* (morning tea cruises Mon 11am; 1hr 15min; 2-, 3- or 5-night cruises also available; ℡08/8231 9472, ⓕ8212 1520, or book at Mannum Tourist Information Centre). You'll find details of other cruises in the Riverland town accounts.

Renting a **houseboat** is a relaxing and enjoyable way to see the river. All you need is a driving licence, and the cost isn't astronomical if you can get a group of people together and avoid the peak holiday seasons. A week in an eight-berth houseboat out of season should cost around $1200, in a four-berth $900. The South Australian Tourism Commission (℡1300/655 276, ⓦwww.southaustralia. com) has pamphlets giving costs and facilities; they can also book for you; alternatively, contact the Houseboat Hirers Association (℡08/8395 0999, ⓦwww.houseboat-centre.com.au).

A more hands-on way to explore the wetlands and creek systems is in a **canoe**, while the flat country, short distances between towns and dry climate are perfect for cycling – **bikes** can be rented at various hostels along the way.

For other Murray River accounts, see Goolwa (p.834), and the Victoria and New South Wales chapters (p.1015 and p.360 respectively).

Barwell Avenue (Mon–Fri 9am–5.15pm, Sat 9am–noon, Sun 10am–1pm; ℡08/8588 2289). The pokie-packed *Barmera Hotel/Motel* (℡08/8588 2111; ❷–❸) is not the most attractive of the big Riverland community hotels. Better is the *Barmera Lake Resort Motel*, Lakeside Drive (℡08/8588 2555, ⓔlakeresor@riverland.net.au; ❸), overlooking the lake, with a pool, laundry, games room, barbecue and *Cafe Mudz*, a bright and attractive café–wine bar serving breakfast, lunch and evening meals in an Australian country style. The extensive *Lake Bonney Holiday Park*, is close by on Lakeside Drive, (℡08/8588 2234, ⓔlbhp@sa.ozland.net.au; cabins ❷, cottages ❸). Eating options include the *Pagoda Chinese Restaurant* (℡08/8588 3167; closed Tues). Riverland Leisure Canoe Tours, Thelma Road (℡08/8588 2053), rents out **kayaks** for $15 per day, two-person **canoes** for $25 per day, and arranges day and overnight guided tours (phone for details).

Just under 20km from town towards Morgan, you pass a bend in the river dubbed **Overland Corner**, the former crossing point for the overland cattle trade heading to New South Wales. Opened in 1859, the restful and delightfully isolated *Overland Corner Hotel* (℡08/8588 7021, ⓔochotel@dodo.com.au; ❷ including continental breakfast), serves food (Tues–Sun) and has basic, old-fashioned **accommodation** – look, too, at the flood level from the incredible 1956 flood, practically up to the roof. You can camp and bushwalk in the adjacent **Herons Bend Reserve**, where an eight-kilometre trail (around 3hr) takes you past old Aboriginal campsites; a pamphlet detailing sites on the walk is available from the pub.

Berri

The **Big Orange** sets the scene in **BERRI**, announcing the fact that this is the town where the trademark orange juice comes from, and many travellers are drawn here between October and April by the prospect of **fruit-picking work**. The river is the main attraction, of course, with scenic river walks above coloured sandstone cliffs, as well as the **Wilabalangaloo Flora and Fauna Reserve** (Mon & Thurs–Sun 10am–4pm, daily during school holidays; $4), a native animal enclosure and a local history museum on the waterfront. You can also climb up the Big Orange for a good view of the Riverland, or watch the juice itself being produced in vast quantities at Berri Ltd. For more information, head for the **tourist office** on Riverview Drive (Mon–Fri 9am–5pm, Sat & Sun 10am–4pm; ☎08/8582 5511).

In terms of places to **stay**, in town the *Berri Resort Hotel*, Riverview Drive (☎08/8582 1411, ⓦwww.berriresorthotel.com; pub rooms ❸–❺, motel units ❺), is a huge riverfront pub that grows ever tackier and ritzier – though it's not a bad place to stay, with a swimming pool, tennis courts and good food. The excellent *Berri Backpackers* (☎08/8582 3144; dorms $18, rooms ❶), 1km out of town towards Barmera on the Old Sturt Highway opposite the *Berri Club*, is the place to stay if you're fruit-picking, but is popular, so book ahead. Amenities include free bikes, Internet access, a sauna, swimming pool, gym, tennis and volleyball courts, plus two tree houses and a houseboat. For **food**, *Berri Canton Palace*, 1 Worman St (☎08/8582 2818; closed Tues lunch), is a good Chinese restaurant; while the *Mallee Fowl Restaurant*, on the Sturt Highway 4km west of Berri (☎08/8582 2096; lunch and dinner Thurs–Sat) serves excellent barbecue-style meals in a busy and characterful setting of Australiana.

Renmark

RENMARK, on a bend of the Murray 254km from Adelaide, is the last major town before the border with New South Wales. There's not a great deal to see in the town apart from **Olivewood**, an interesting National Trust property on the corner of Renmark Avenue and 21st Street (Mon & Tues 2–4pm, Thurs–Sun 10am–4pm, closed Wed; $4) which was the former home of the Chaffey brothers, the Canadians who pioneered the irrigation and settlement of the Murray region. A palm-lined drive leads through a citrus orchard and olive trees to the house, which is a strange hybrid of Canadian log cabin and Australian lean-to. The attached museum is the usual hotchpotch of local memorabilia, unrelated to the Chaffeys or their ambitious irrigation project. The **Chaffey Theatre** on 18th Street (☎08/8582 1800) has an impressive performing arts centre hosting amateur and professional plays, films and concerts. The main attraction of Renmark, however, is the river and its surrounding wetlands.

The riverfront **Renmark Paringa Visitor Centre** on Murray Avenue (Mon–Fri 9am–5pm, Sat 9am–4pm, Sun 10am–4pm; ☎08/8586 6704, ⓦwww.riverland.info) can book **river cruises**. The PS *Industry* – one of the few wood-fuelled paddle steamers left on the Murray – is moored outside and cruises once a month (1hr 30min; $15; contact the tourist centre for times and bookings). Daily cruises are run by Renmark River Cruises (☎08/8595 1862, ⓦwww.riverland.net.au/renrivcruises), which offers both motorized dinghy expeditions through the local backwaters (2hr; $49) and trips aboard the *Big River Rambler* (daily 2pm; 2hr; $25), which leaves from Renmark wharf and heads upstream for 7km past colourful river cliffs. The UNESCO-backed **Bookmark Biosphere Reserve**, a few kilometres from Renmark, manages nine thousand square kilometres of land. To explore this region by land or river, Bookmark Guides (details from the visitor centre) offer a variety of day and overnight tours from 4WD bush safaris to wine tasting.

The obvious **place to stay** in Renmark is the landmark *Renmark Hotel/Motel* (℡08/8586 6755, ⊛www.renmarkhotel.com.au; ❸–❺), overlooking the river. Built in 1897 and given its facade in the 1930s, the hotel has been thoroughly modernized and has a large bistro, outdoor swimming pool and spa. The *Renmark Riverfront Caravan Park*, on Patey Drive 2km east of town (℡08/8586 6315; on-site vans ❷, en-suite cabins ❹), has an idyllic setting along 1km of riverfront. *Renmark Kebab & Pizza* (Tues–Sun 11am to 8 or 9pm) at 31 Renmark Avenue is good for Greek-style food and pizzas; for Chinese, try *The Golden Palace*, 114 Renmark Ave (closed Tues).

The mid-north

Stretching north of Adelaide up to Port Augusta (see p.863) and the south Flinders Ranges is the fertile agricultural region known as the **mid-north**. The gateway to the region is the town of **Kapunda**, only 16km northwest of Nuriootpa in the Barossa Valley (see p.822), which became the country's first mining town when copper was discovered there in 1842. Kapunda can also be reached as a short detour from the **Barrier Highway** en route to Broken Hill in New South Wales, a route that continues through the larger mining town of **Burra**, and then to **Peterborough**, the self-proclaimed "frontier to the Outback". The centre of the mid-north's wine area, **Clare**, is 45km southwest of Burra, on the **Main North Road**, the alternative route to Port Augusta. Heading north to Port Augusta on **Highway 1** for the Northern Territory or Western Australia, you'll pass through the ugly lead-smelting city of **Port Pirie**, and thence on to the south Flinders Ranges.

Getting around the area by **bus** is problematic: while most of the major towns have transport links to Adelaide, there are virtually no buses between towns, however close they might be. The Greyhound Pioneer Adelaide to Broken Hill service goes via Burra, while the Mid North Passenger Service (℡08/8826 2346; no service Mon & Sat) from Adelaide takes in Burra, Peterborough and the main Clare Valley settlements. In addition, the Barossa to Adelaide Passenger Service (℡08/8564 3022) has a weekday service from Gawler – which can be reached by train – to Kapunda. All interstate buses to Darwin or Perth take Highway 1 through Port Pirie.

Kapunda and Burra

At the beginning of the 1840s South Australia was in serious economic trouble, until the discovery of **copper** at Kapunda in 1842 rescued the young colony and put it at the forefront of Australia's mining boom. The early finds at Kapunda were, however, soon overshadowed by those at **Burra**, 65km north: the Burra "**Monster Mine**" was the largest in Australia until 1860, creating fabulous wealth and attracting huge numbers of Cornish miners. The boom ended as suddenly as it began, as resources were exhausted – mining finished at Burra in 1877 and Kapunda in 1878.

Heading to **KAPUNDA** from the Barossa, the landscape changes as vineyards are replaced by crops and grazing sheep. As you come into town, you're greeted by a colossal sculpture of a Cornish miner entitled *Map Kernow* – "son of Cornwall". A place that once had its own daily newspaper, eleven hotels and a busy train station township is now a rural service town, pleasantly undeveloped and with many old buildings decorated with locally designed and manufactured iron lacework.

If you have your own transport, you can follow a ten-kilometre **heritage trail** that takes in the ruins of the Kapunda mine, with panoramic views from the mine chimney lookout; details are available from the **Kapunda Information Centre** on Hill Street (Mon–Fri 9am–5pm, Sat 10am–1pm, Sun noon to 3pm; ☏08/8566 2902, ⓦwww.light.sa.gov.au/community/kapunda/visitor.htm). On the same street, the **Kapunda Museum** (June–Aug Sat & Sun 1–4pm; Sept–May daily 1–4pm; $4; ☏08/8556 2286) occupies the mammoth Romanesque-style former Baptist church. The best time to come to Kapunda is during the **Celtic festival**, held on the first weekend before Easter, when Celtic music, bush and folk bands feature at the four pubs.

For **accommodation**, there's a colonial-style B&B at *Ford House*, 80 Main St (☏ & ⓕ08/8566 2280; ➍); the *Sir John Franklin Hotel*, also on Main Street (☏08/8566 3233, ⓕ8566 3873; ➋), has simple, clean rooms and is the most popular pub for inexpensive **meals**. Campers are catered for at *Dutton Caravan Park*, 11 Montefiore St (☏08/8566 2094; cabins ➌).

Burra

In 1851 the mine at **BURRA** was producing five percent of the world's copper; when the mines closed in 1877, it became a service centre for the surrounding farming community, though it nowadays also takes advantage of its mining heritage to attract visitors. Plenty of money has been spent restoring and beautifying the place (even to the extent of topping up pretty, gum-shaded **Burra Creek** to ensure that it's always flowing), and the town's well-preserved stone architecture, shady tree-lined streets, great country pubs and upmarket home stores, art-and-craft and antiques shops, make it a popular weekend escape between March and November, before it gets too hot. The creek divides the town in two: the mine is in the north, while the southern section has the shopping centre, based around **Market Square**, where you'll also find the **Burra Visitors Centre** (daily 9am–5pm; ☏08/8892 2154, ⓦwww.weblogic.com.au/burra). Its main function is to issue the **Burra Passport Key** to people driving the eleven-kilometre **heritage trail** ($15 per person, plus $5 deposit); the key gives you access to eight sites en route – and for an extra $9 you gain entry to all four museums (see below).

Heading north along Market Street you come to the **Burra Monster Mine** site, where there are extensive remains and interpretive walking trails, as well as the **Morphetts Enginehouse Museum** (Mon, Weds & Fri 11am–1pm, Sat & Sun 11am–2pm; $4.50). Continuing north, the **Bon Accord Mine Complex** on Linkson Street (Tues, Weds & Thurs 1–3pm; Sat & Sun 1–4pm; $4.50) was a short-lived failure compared to its hugely successful neighbour; there's a scale model of the monster mine and a shaft and mining relics on view. Other key-pass places in the northern section of the town are the old **police lock-up and stables**, **Redruth Gaol**, and **Hampton**, a now-deserted private township in the style of an English village. Back in the main part of the town, the pass gets you entry to the **Unicorn Brewery Cellars** (1873) and the fascinating two remaining **miners' dugouts**: by 1851, because of a housing shortage nearly two thousand people were living in homes clawed out of the soft clay along Burra Creek. There are two further museums: the **Market Square Museum** (Sat & Sun 1–3pm; $3.50) was a general store, post office and home from 1880 to 1920; the **Paxton Square miners' cottages** on Kingston Street (Sat 2–4pm, Sun 2–4pm; $4.50) are decorated in 1850s style.

You can **stay** in other miners' cottages in Paxton Square, all overseen by the office in the former Methodist Chapel at the end of the row (☎08/8892 2622, ℻8892 2555; ❸–❹). There are 32 in all, although on weekends from mid-March to October they get quickly booked out by Adelaidians on short winter breaks. It can get very cold in the winter, but the cottages have fireplaces (free wood provided) and plenty of blankets, as well as modern kitchens, though breakfast is available at the office. Other accommodation in town includes *Burra View House*, Mount Pleasant Road (☎08/8892 2648, ℻8892 2150; ❹–❺), and the tree-surrounded *Burra Motor Inn*, Market Street (☎08/8892 2777, ℻8892 2707; ❹), with contemporary-style rooms backing onto a creek, an indoor swimming pool and a well-priced restaurant. All the **hotels** in town have rooms, and most provide breakfast; for down-to-earth accommodation, try the *Commercial Hotel*, 22 Commercial Rd (☎08/8892 2010; ❶–❷ including breakfast). If you have a **tent** you could try the *Burra Caravan Park*, Bridge Terrace (☎08/8892 2442; on-site vans ❷), in a pretty spot beside the creek, a couple of minutes' walk from the shops. *The Burra Hotel*, 3 Market St, does excellent **meals**, and there are several good cafés in town: try *Polly's Kitchen* (daily 9am–5.30pm), Commercial Road, which has good coffee and a range of light meals, including a credible version of an authentic Cornish pasty.

The Clare Valley

The wine industry in the **Clare Valley**, west of the Barrier Highway between Kapunda and Burra, was pioneered by Jesuit priests at **Sevenhill** in the 1850s. There's no tourist overkill here: bus trips are not encouraged, and because it's a small area with just over thirty wineries, you can learn a lot about the local styles of wine; the area is especially recognized for its fine Rieslings. Often, too, you'll get personal treatment, with the winemaker presiding at the cellar door. In the cool uplands of the North Mount Lofty Ranges, Clare Valley is really a series of gum-fringed ridges and valleys running roughly 30km north from **Auburn** to the main township of **Clare**, on either side of the Main North Road. Huge sheep runs were established here in the nineteenth century and the area, which is prime merino land, still has a pastoral feel; several stations can be visited. There are also beautiful old villages and some well-preserved mansions, plenty of charming B&B accommodation and some superb restaurants attached to wineries. The big event of the year is the **Clare Valley Gourmet Weekend**, held in May at local wineries.

Between Clare and Auburn, the old railway line has been transformed into the **Riesling Trail**, a 27-kilometre cycling path; to cycle one way takes about two hours. Mountain **bikes** can be rented from Clare Valley Cycle Hire, 32 Victoria Rd, Clare ($22 per day; ☎08/8842 2782), which will deliver to anywhere in the valley.

Auburn to Watervale

Heading north through the valley, **AUBURN**, 120km from Adelaide, is the first settlement, small and village-like, which began life as a halfway resting point for wagons carrying copper ore from Burra to Port Adelaide. The *Rising*

Sun Hotel (℡08/8849 2015, ✉rising@capri.net.au; ❹ including breakfast) is one of many great **pubs** in the valley, first licensed in 1850. It has small bedrooms in the hotel and mews-style accommodation in old stone stables, as well as a very affordable modern Australian menu and an appropriately long wine list. A more luxurious place to stay is *Dennis Cottage* (℡08/8277 8177, ⓦwww.denniscottage.com.au; ❺), which has a spa, as well as paraphernalia associated with C.J. Dennis, the popular poet who was born here in 1876. *Tatehams*, on the Main North Road (℡08/8849 2030, ✉tatehams@ capri.net.au; ❺) is a very distinguished dining/guesthouse combination. There are two small **wineries** nearby: **Grossets** (Wed–Sun 10am–5pm) and **Mount Horrocks** (Sat & Sun 10am–5pm).

The next small village is **LEASINGHAM**, where you can camp or stay at *Leasingham Village Caravan & Cabins* (℡08/8843 0136; cabins ❸), a popular place for **grape-pickers** from March to May. An attached restaurant serves simple, inexpensive weekend lunches (Thurs–Sun lunch and dinner; licensed or BYO). You can taste wines nearby at **Tim Gramp Wines** (Sat & Sun 10.30am–4.30pm). There are four small wineries at **WATERVALE**, 2km north: **Crabtree of Watervale**, North Terrace (daily 11am–5pm, occasionally closed midweek), is one of the most enjoyable in the valley.

Mintaro

From Leasingham, you can turn off east to **MINTARO**, a village whose tree-lined streets and cottages are beautifully preserved from the 1850s, when it was a resting place for bullock teams travelling from the Burra copper mines. There's no general store or petrol supply here: the emphasis is on upmarket cottage accommodation, popular with Adelaide weekenders. The focus of the village is the *Magpie and Stump Hotel*, which is particularly lively on Sunday afternoons. Opposite, at **Reilly's Wines** (daily 10am–5pm), housed in an 1856 Irish bootmaker's building, you can taste vintages produced since 1994 from Watervale grapes; the **restaurant** here serves Italian food, with mains around $20 (dinner Mon & Fri–Sun; ℡08/8843 9013), and can also book **accommodation** in the nearby *Mintaro Pay Office Cottages* (❺–❻ including breakfast). *Mintaro Mews*, on Burra Street (℡08/8843 9001, ℻8843 9002; ❺), has upmarket B&B accommodation (no children) with an indoor heated pool and spa; Saturday nights are package only ($110 per person), including a four-course meal in the atmospheric restaurant. Southeast of the town lies the Georgian-style *Martindale Hall* (Mon–Fri 11am–4pm, Sat & Sun noon–4pm; $6; ℡08/8843 9088, ℻8843 9082, ✉marthall@chariot.net.au; ❼ including breakfast); the mansion featured in the 1975 film *Picnic at Hanging Rock*. For $190 per person you can stay overnight and enjoy a four-course meal, cooked breakfast and the full run of the place – but it's freezing in winter.

Heading northwest from Mintaro to Sevenhill (see below) takes you through the rolling hills of the Polish Hill River area. About 8km along, **Paulett Wines** (daily 10am–5pm) has fabulous views, its verandah overlooking the "river" – a dry creek for eleven months of the year.

Sevenhill and the Spring Gully Conservation Park

The village of **SEVENHILL** has the valley's oldest winery, **Sevenhill Cellars**, on College Road (Mon–Fri 9am–4.30pm, Sat 9am–4pm). This is still run by a religious order and mainly makes sacramental wine, though the brothers have diversified into table wines, sweet sherry and port, doing everything from growing the grapes to bottling. The sandstone building has a tasting room with lots of character and history, and there's an old Catholic church in the grounds.

Nearby, on College Road, *Thorn Park Country House* (☎08/8843 4304, ⓦwww.thornpark.com.au; ❼) occupies an 1850 stone and slate building in a gorgeous setting; it offers **B&B** and a beautifully indulgent dinner – but at a price ($220 per person; B&B only costs $160 per person). *Sevenhill Hotel*, on the Main North Road, is a classic country pub serving popular inexpensive meals (daily except Sun).

To the west of the Main North Road, **Spring Gully Conservation Park** has the last remnant of red stringybark forest in South Australia. There are steep gullies, waterfalls, wildlife and, in spring, lovely wild flowers; free camping is allowed outside the fire-ban season. Nearby, attached to boutique wineries signposted from Sevenhill, are two excellent restaurants serving gourmet meals from deliciously fresh local produce; both are moderately priced. **Eldredge Wines**, Spring Gully Road (tastings daily 11am–5pm; lunch Thurs–Sun; restaurant bookings ☎08/8842 3086) is located in a small farmhouse fronting a dam; **Skillogalee Winery** (daily 10am–5pm; ☎08/8843 4311; lunch bookings advised) occupies a wonderful spot set against the backdrop of a clunking windmill, bushclad hill and vineyards, with meals and tastings by the fire in the 1850s cottage or on the verandah.

Clare

CLARE itself is a surprisingly ordinary town, with few concessions to the weekend visitors who pour in from Adelaide: it consists primarily of Main North Road, and everything is closed on Sunday. The **tourist information** office, in the town hall at 229 Main North Rd (Mon–Sat 9am–5pm, Sun 10am–4pm; ☎08/8842 2131, ⓦwww.clarevalley.com.au), provides an excellent free visitors' guide and can book accommodation and restaurants. **Wineries** around town include Knappstein Wines, 2 Pioneer Ave (Mon–Fri 9am–5pm, Sat 10am–5pm, Sun 11am–4pm), an ivy-covered sandstone building with a verandah and an open log fire in winter; Jim Barry, a friendly, family-run place on the Main North Road (Mon–Fri 9am–5pm, Sat & Sun 11am–4pm); and Leasingham, 7 Dominic St (Mon–Fri 9am–5pm, Sat & Sun 10am–4pm), a large commercial winery established in 1893.

Some local sheep stations are open for tours, and **farmstays** are also available: pick of the bunch is *Bungaree Station* (☎08/8842 2677, ⓕ8842 3004; BYO-bedding shearers' quarters $16.50, cottages B&B ❹), a working merino station 12km north of Clare on the Main North Road; one of the oldest and largest properties in the district, it has its own church as well as a swimming pool. *Geralka Rural Farm* (☎08/8845 8081, ⓕ8845 8073; on-site vans ❷, units ❹) is a sheep and cereal property 25km north of Clare which offers weekend **farm activity tours** aimed at families (Sun & daily during school holidays 1.30pm, or by appointment; 2hr; $8, children $4).

Places to **stay** in Clare itself are all along Main North Road. Overlooking the hills, 2.5km south of the centre, is *Clare Valley Motel* at no. 74 (☎08/8842 2799, ⓕ8842 3121; ❹); the *Clare Central Motel* is at the north end of town at no. 325 (☎08/8842 2277, ⓕ8842 3563; ❹ including breakfast); both have pools. The best of the hotels are the friendly family-run *Bentleys*, 191 Main North Rd (☎08/8842 1700, ⓕ8842 3474; motel rooms ❸–❹), which also has a bistro; and the *Taminga Hotel* (☎08/8842 2808; ❷), offering basic pub rooms. You can **camp** 4km south of town at *Clare Caravan Park* on Main North Road (☎08/8842 2724, ⓔclarpark@rbe.net.au; on-site vans ❶, cabins ❷), which also has a swimming pool. Besides the pubs, you can **eat** well during the day at *Clare Fine Foods*, 279 Main North Rd (closed Sun), a small deli serving gourmet rolls and sandwiches and dishes such as Caesar salad or pasta; the espresso coffee here is the best in town. There's **Internet access** at Caprice Clare ($5 per 30min) in the Village Plaza on the Old North Road.

Port Pirie

From Clare, the Main North Road heads to Jamestown, 65km north. To the west, a road branches off towards Crystal Brook, where there's a hikers' lodge at Bowman Park providing basic overnight shelter for hikers on the Heysen Trail. From here it's not far up Highway 1 to **PORT PIRIE**, the fourth-largest urban centre in South Australia. An ugly industrial city, its skyline is dominated by smelters' chimneys: as the nearest seaport to Broken Hill, the lead and zinc smelting industry here dates back to the discovery of the rich vein of lead-silver-zinc found there in 1883. The **Port Pirie Tourism and Arts Centre** on Mary Elie Street (Mon–Fri 9am–5pm, Sat 9am–4pm, Sun 10am–3pm; ☎08/8633 0439 or 1800 000 424) has interpretive brochures and self-guided walking tours of the town if you're interested in **historic buildings** and the smelting industry. If not, there's little else to keep you here. Beyond Port Pirie, Telowie Gorge and Mount Remarkable National Park, in the southern stretches of the Flinders Ranges (see p.876), are within easy reach.

Outback South Australia

. . . a country such as I firmly believe has no parallel on earth's surface.

The explorer Charles Sturt, 1844.

All routes in the Outback radiate from **Port Augusta** and, with few connecting roads, interstate destinations will probably dictate which direction you leave town. Buses cover the highways, but elsewhere you'll need to have your own transport or take a tour. To the west, the **Eyre Highway** runs 950km to the border of Western Australia, with desert scenery all the way unless you detour around the coast of the Eyre Peninsula. The rail line west runs further inland, through even more extreme desolation. North, the **Stuart Highway** and **New Ghan rail line** link Port Augusta with the Northern Territory through 890km of progressively drier scenery, where regular markers along the roadside record the distance covered, as well as how far there is to go. The railway is currently being extended a further 1410km from Alice Springs right through to Darwin, due for completion in 2004 (see p.665 for more details). **Prohibited zones** surround much of the highway, though about the only places you'd want to leave it anyway are at **Woomera** and **Coober Pedy**, both outside military areas and the boundaries of Aboriginal land.

All other roads north head from Port Augusta along the route taken by the legendary but now defunct **Old Ghan** to the country towns of **Quorn** and **Hawker**, where routes diverge: northeast through the **Flinders Ranges** and along the **Strzelecki Track** to **Innamincka**; or due north to **Marree**, at the head of the **Birdsville** and **Oodnadatta tracks**. Sealed roads end at Lyndhurst on the way to Marree, and Wilpena Pound in the central Flinders.

Check conditions if you plan to go any further – in dry weather 2WD vehicles often make it to Innamincka and Oodnadatta, but none of the north's remoter tracks should be attempted during the searing summer months. **Buses** run the length of the Stuart Highway between Woomera and Andamooka, and from Port Augusta to Marree and Arkaroola in the northern Flinders.

A **Desert Parks Pass** is required for legal entry into Innamincka Regional Reserve, Lake Eyre National Park, Witjira National Park and the Simpson Desert: $85 per vehicle allows twelve months' unlimited access and use of campsites, with copies of the detailed NPWS *Desert Parks Handbook* and Westprint Heritage Maps' surveys thrown in. Passes are available from agencies throughout the north, or by post from the Port Augusta NPWS (PO Box 78, Port Augusta 5700; ☏ 1800 816 078). To find out about **road conditions** in these regions, call ☏ 1300 361 033, or check out the Desert Access **website**, ⓦ www.desertaccess.com.au.

Many roadhouses and fuel pumps have **EFTPOS** facilities. **Water** is vital: with few exceptions, lakes and waterways are dry or highly saline, and most Outback deaths are related to dehydration or heatstroke – bikers seem particularly prone. As always, stay with your vehicle if you break down. Summer **temperatures** can be lethally hot, winters pleasant during the day and subzero at night; rain can fall at any time of year, but is most likely to do so between January and May. RAA **road maps** are good but lack topographical information. If you're spending any time in the north, pick up the excellent Westprint Heritage Maps and the cluttered *Landsmap Outback: Central and South Australia*. The South Australia Tourist Association issues a road map of the Flinders Ranges, but it's inadequate for walking; **hikers** traversing the Flinders on the Heysen Trail need topographic maps of each section and advice from the nearest NPWS office. Conditions of **minor roads** are so variable that maps seldom do more than indicate the surface type; local police and roadhouses will have current information.

Port Augusta and the west

How you see **Port Augusta** depends on where you've come from. Arriving from the Outback, the town's trees, shops and hotels can be a real thrill, but compared with the southeast of the state, it's pretty basic. However, being a transport hub has saved the town from destitution, and plans are afoot to make more of its seaside location. While you're deciding where to head next, there are a few things to see in town and some good **bushwalking** country around **Mount Remarkable**, at the tail end of the Flinders Ranges. The direct route west from Port Augusta, the **Eyre Highway**, begins its daunting journey towards Western Australia across the top of the **Eyre Peninsula**, but going this way you'll see virtually nothing. An alternative route detours around the peninsula's coastline (via the Lincoln and Flinders highways) before rejoining the highway at **Ceduna** on the brink of the **Nullarbor Plain**, while the rail line parallels the coast some 100km inland.

Port Augusta

Unkindly dubbed "Porta Gutter" by Adelaide's smart set, who paint dire pictures of a town rife with petty crime, **PORT AUGUSTA** sits at the tip of the Spencer Gulf and on the edge of everywhere else. Despite the name, the docks closed long ago and more recent employment mainstays such as the power station and railways were drastically scaled down during the 1980s – the former rail buildings have been converted to Employment Service offices.

During summer, you should make the most of the small **swimming beach** at the end of Young Street to escape the dust and heat – the old wooden pile crossing, now a footbridge, and a hundred-year-old jetty, all that remains of the port, make good perches for fishing. The chief source of **information** is the **Wadlata Outback Centre**, at 41 Flinders Terrace (Mon–Fri 9am–5.30pm, Sat & Sun 10am–4pm; ☎08/8641 0793, ⓦwww .portaugusta.sa.gov.au). This has a very helpful visitor information centre, an attractive café and an interesting permanent **exhibition** ($8.95). Audiovisual technology, didgeridoo loudspeakers and a giant model of Akurra, the Dreamtime snake, are deployed to explain Aboriginal bushcraft and Flinders Ranges' creation myths, while geological and mining displays give a scientific perspective. Human interest is provided by tales of the hardships suffered by nineteenth-century explorers Eyre and Sturt, plus short films (shown in continuous loops) which give a compelling account of early European settlement. You can also book a wide variety of **tours** from the centre including plane trips, fishing expeditions, 4WD tours and even golf. Internet access is also available ($5 for 30min).

The **Homestead Park Pioneer Museum**, east of the town centre on Elsie Street (daily 9am–5pm; $2.50), is centred around a log-built sheep station building. The 135-year-old homestead has been moved 100km from Yudnapinna and is filled with period furnishings, heaps of farm and railway machinery, plus animals, birds and a photographic museum in a vintage railway carriage. Nearby, the **School of the Air**, at 59 Power Crescent (10am on school days; $2.50 for a 30min tour), allows you to listen in to a lesson conducted over the airwaves. The interaction is pretty lively and might help explain the better-than-average academic record for students in remote areas who use the school. You could also take a look at the **Electricity Power Station** (free tours Mon–Fri; ☎08/8641 0793), which produces forty percent of all South Australia's electricity or watch the sunset illuminate the Flinders mountains from the **water tower lookout** on Mildred Street.

Flanking the north side of town on the Stuart Highway is the new and ambitious **Australian Arid Lands Botanic Garden** (Mon–Fri 9am–5.00pm, Sat & Sun 10am–4pm; free entry, but it's worth taking the 1hr guided tour for $5.95, which starts at 11am in winter and 9.30am in summer), a showcase and research centre for regional and international desert flora, the slow-growing nature of which means that the garden's full splendour has yet to be realized, although a closer look will reveal a surprising wealth of species. The rain-gathering, solar-powered information centre, shop and café underline the ideals of the garden as an ongoing ecological project.

Practicalities

The centre of town overlooks the east side of the Spencer Gulf, more like a river where it divides the town. The **airport** (☎08/8642 3100) is down Caroona Road, 5km west of the centre – you'll need to get a taxi in if arriving by plane (☎08/8642 4466). The **bus terminal**, serving McCafferty's, Greyhound Pioneer and Stateliner, is at 21 Mackay St (all services ☎08/8642 5055); **trains** pull in at Stirling Road (☎08/8642 6699). Shops, banks and the post office are clustered along narrow Commercial Road. If you need **maps and information** beyond what's available at the Outback Centre, try the helpful **NPWS** at 9 Mackay St (☎08/8648 5300) for park maps, info and permits; if you're a member, the RAA, at 91 Commercial Rd (☎08/8642 2576),

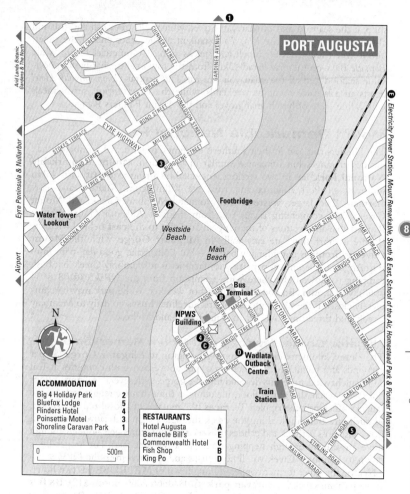

PORT AUGUSTA

Footbridge

Water Tower
Lookout

Westside
Beach

Main
Beach

Bus
Terminal

NPWS
Building

Wadlata
Outback
Centre

Train
Station

N

ACCOMMODATION

Big 4 Holiday Park	2
Bluefox Lodge	5
Flinders Hotel	4
Poinsettia Motel	3
Shoreline Caravan Park	1

0 — 500m

RESTAURANTS

Hotel Augusta	A
Barnacle Bill's	E
Commonwealth Hotel	C
Fish Shop	B
King Po	D

provides very good road maps. **Cars** can be rented from Budget, at 16 Young St (℡08/8642 6040).

There are two central budget places to **stay**: *The Bluefox Lodge*, on National Highway One (℡08/8641 2960, ⓦwww.bluefoxlodge.com; dorms $16.50, rooms ❸); and the friendly *Flinders Hotel,* 39 Commercial Rd (℡08/8642 2544; dorms $14, rooms ❶–❸). Alternatively, there are several **motels**, such as the comfortable *Poinsettia*, 24 Burgoyne St (℡08/8642 2411; ❸), along the highway just across the gulf. The town's closest **campsites** are near here too, including the *Shoreline Caravan Park* at the end of Gardiner Avenue (℡08/8642 2965; cabins ❷–❸) and the *Big 4 Holiday Park*, junction of Eyre and Stuart highways (℡08/8642 6455; cabins ❷–❹).

Hotels are the place for **meals and entertainment**, but opening hours are vague and often depend on demand, which can be almost nonexistent during the week. The *Transcontinental*, Port Augusta's weekly rag, will have details of anything happening around town. Seafood addicts should head for the fish shop at the seaward end of Marryatt Street, which sells fresh fish and fish and chips; for Chinese, try the *King Po* restaurant at the other end of the street. You'll find a few cafés for lunch and snacks along Commercial Road, while *Barnacle Bill's*, on Victoria Parade 3km from the town centre, has pretty good-value seafood and all the salad you can eat. The central *Commonwealth Hotel* boasts an à la carte menu at weekends, while the *Hotel Augusta* serves meals with a fine view of beach, mangroves and the distant Flinders Ranges.

Mount Remarkable National Park

The Flinders run low in their southern extremes, more heavily timbered than the desert ranges but otherwise similar in formation. **Mount Remarkable National Park** lies in two sections, encircled by a ring road that starts 45km southeast of Port Augusta and runs via Wilmington, Melrose and Port Germein. The larger **western** slice contains Mambray Creek and Mount Cavern, and connecting tracks run from them to Alligator Gorge; Mount Remarkable and sections of the Heysen Trail rise to the **east** behind Melrose. If time is short, there are easy walks in **Alligator Gorge**, while the **Mount Cavern circuit** is considerably harder – but both make good day-trips from Port Augusta. The only **campsite** with facilities is at Mambray Creek, but bush camping is allowed elsewhere with permission from the NPWS (℡08/8634 7068); you should also consult them in hot weather, as the park may be completely closed if there's a high risk of fire. Stateliner **buses** go daily to Mambray Creek, and three times weekly to Wilmington and Melrose.

Alligator Gorge, Melrose and Mount Remarkable

The eleven-kilometre dirt road from Wilmington to **Alligator Gorge** ($6 per car) ends at a picnic area perched on a spur above two bush campsites at Teal and Eaglehawk dams. Stairs descend into the gorge, with several walking options once you reach the gorge floor, including a three-hour circuit north to the ranger's office past the rippled **Terraces** (the remains of a fossilized lake shore), or an hour's trek south along the creek through a tight red canyon alive with frog calls, moss gardens and echoes (this section sometimes gets flooded, though there are usually enough stepping stones to avoid wet feet). For longer hikes down to Mambray Creek you'll need maps and approval from the NPWS.

Nearby, the quiet former copper-mining town of **MELROSE** has two hotels and a pleasant creekside **caravan park** (℡08/8666 2060; dorms $12). **B&B** is available at *Bluey Blundstone's Blacksmith Shop* (℡08/8666 2173; ❹), carefully restored to its original 1865 condition. When the proprietor isn't producing decorative wrought-ironwork he serves cakes in a coffee shop at the back of the forge. The unremarkable summit of **Mount Remarkable** can be reached in three hours via the **Heysen Trail**, starting a couple of kilometres north of town from the showground.

Telowie Gorge, Mambray Creek and Mount Cavern

The small and appealing **Telowie Conservation Park** lies to the south off the Port Germein to Murray Town road. A very short path leads between the gorge walls, but, unless you're properly equipped for a long hike over to Wirrabara Forest and the Heysen Trail, you'll get more of a flavour of the area by camping along the creek and looking for rare wallabies at dawn and dusk.

The access track to **Mambray Creek** is east off the highway, halfway between Port Germein and the Wilmington road. Here you'll find a **campsite** (with water and toilets) and the national park headquarters. Mambray Creek is the start of some serious walks, either into the north part of the park along the **Battery Track** and **Alligator Creek**, or on the tough but shorter **Mount Cavern** circuit, which follows the path anticlockwise along the Black Range, giving spectacular views. The descent is down a loose stone slope held together by grasstrees, then entering cool woodland at Mambray Creek Gorge, where you might be able to get close to large groups of emus.

The Eyre Peninsula

Far from the rigours of the true Outback, and long appreciated by Adelaidians as an antidote to city stress, the **Eyre Peninsula**'s broad triangle is protected by the **Gawler Ranges** from the arid climate further north. The area began to be farmed in the 1880s; fishing communities sprang up at regular intervals and iron ore, discovered around 1900, is still mined around **Whyalla**. The detour **around the coast** passes imposing scenery and superlative **surfing** and **beach fishing**, especially where the Great Australian Bight's elemental weather hammers into the western shore – a chance to give your senses a workout before dealing with the Nullarbor's deadening horizons. Stateliner **buses** from Port Augusta run either across the top of the peninsula to Ceduna, or via Whyalla down the east coast to **Port Lincoln** at the southern tip, so you'll need your own transport to tackle the west side. Major **car rental** companies have outlets at both Whyalla and Port Lincoln which, if time is limited, are only fifty minutes by air from Adelaide. Note that locals don't rate Eyre Peninsula **tap water** as worth drinking; bottled water and filters are readily available in supermarkets.

Whyalla and the east coast

First visible an hour from Port Augusta as a smudge of grey over Long Sleep Plain, **WHYALLA**, the state's second most important city and headquarters of its heavy industry, isn't the prettiest of places. One Steel has its massive "long products" **steelworks** here (tours Mon, Wed & Sat 9.30am; 2hr; $8; book through the information centre, see below) and tankers queue offshore to fill up at Santos' oil and gas refinery. Until it closed in 1978, the **shipyard** produced a few famous vessels, the first being the *Whyalla*, which now guards the northern entrance to town, having been dragged 2km from the sea in a complicated and expensive manoeuvre. The accompanying **information centre** and **maritime museum** (☎08/8645 8900, ✉visitor.centre@whyalla.sa.gov.au; daily 10am–4pm; $7.50 including ship tour) is largely occupied by a huge model of the oil refinery, as well as more relevant displays of shipping history. From the southwest, Whyalla presents a much greener aspect. You can cuddle a koala – or a python – at the **Wildlife and Reptile Sanctuary** (daily 10am–dusk; $7.50), while at the junction of Broadbent Terrace and Playford Avenue an old aerodrome site has been landscaped into a series of ponds to recycle stormwater.

The highway curves through the old town under the name of Darling Terrace; you'll find a **post office**, **banks**, a **bus station** (☎08/8645 9911), hotels and shops around the junction with Forsyth and Patterson streets, all periodically covered in (harmless) red fallout from the steelwork's mysterious pellet plant. **Accommodation** options include the *Foreshore Caravan Park* on Broadbent Terrace (☎08/8645 7474; cabins ❶–❷) and *Derham's Motel* on Watson Terrace (☎08/8645 8877; ❹), both a ten-minute walk from the centre along a surprisingly attractive beach, with Hummock Hill mercifully obscuring the view of the steelworks; people and pelicans find good fishing off the jetty. Otherwise, try your luck at one of the hotels: *Spencer* on Forsyth Street (℗08/8645 8411; ❷–❸) has rooms, good food and weekend music. For **food**, seafood at *Spagg's*, 30 Patterson St, makes a welcome change from counter meals; after eating, walk past the rows of fifty-year-old workers' homes to the top of Hummock Hill for a view of the industrial complexes by night.

Beyond Whyalla, the east coast is an unassuming string of sheltered beaches and villages nestled beneath towering grain silos, the sort of places you could drive through without a second glance or else get waylaid beachcombing for a week. **COWELL** is known for its whiting and as the world's largest source of black "nephrite" jade, though not much of it is in evidence, since it's largely exported rough. **Arno Bay**, **Port Neil** and the larger **Tumby Bay** all boast clean, quiet beaches, good fishing and a range of accommodation – diversions include sundry museums and even a worm farm.

Port Lincoln

A tuna port and resort town built on a hillside above Boston Bay, **PORT LIN-COLN** has the busiest atmosphere of anywhere on the peninsula. Its harbour is dotted with trawlers, and the main seafront streets of Tasman Terrace and Liverpool Street are full of eateries and far-from-genteel taverns. There's a **tourist information centre** here too (daily 9am–5pm; ℗08/8683 3544 or 1800 629 911, ⓔplvic@dov.net.au), between the post office and shopping mall; Stateliner **buses** (℗08/8682 1288) terminate a couple of streets away on Darling Terrace.

Porter Bay, until recently a swamp just south of town, has been transformed into a **marina** which has drawn many of the boats and some of the life away from the old town. The development includes a large, modern **leisure centre** (Mon–Fri 6am–9pm, Sat, Sun & holidays 9am–6pm; ℗08/8682 3833). Entering town from the north, the Lincoln Highway (which later becomes Tasman Terrace and then London Street) affords splendid views of Boston Bay and presents you with myriad motel **accommodation** options, such as the luxurious *Limani Motel* (℗08/8682 2200, ℗8682 6602; ❹–❺), at the far end of which lie the terraced tent sites of *Kirton Point Caravan Park* (℗08/8682 2537, cabins ❶–❸).

Most of Port Lincoln's attractions are underwater. You can get bait and tackle from any service station and **fish** off the town jetty; for heavier game fishing contact Sea Charters (℗08/8682 2425), which can also take you on a cruise to **Dangerous Reef** for spotting seals, birdlife and sharks. The seas off Lincoln were once rated as the best place in the world to see **great white sharks** – footage for *Jaws* was filmed here – but trawling and hunting since the mid-1970s have placed this little-understood fish on the endangered species list. If this doesn't put you off **diving** – or if you just need advice on good places to fish or arrange a boat charter – contact Got One at 80 Tasman Terrace (℗08/8683 0021).

Around Port Lincoln

Lincoln National Park, just south of Port Lincoln, covers a rough peninsula of sandy coves, steep cliffs and mallee scrub, which is home to the discreet rock parrot. The NPWS at 75 Liverpool St (℗08/8688 3111) can supply maps and advice on road conditions. There's similar scenery 32km south at **Whalers Way** you'll need to collect a permit and key from the information centre in Port Lincoln ($17, plus $3 key deposit); the name derives from the whaling station which once operated at Cape Wiles – relics are stacked up around the gate. The power of the Southern Ocean is memorably demonstrated at **Cape**

Carnot, in the southern section of the park, where giant waves and frosty blue surf force their way through blowholes which sigh as they erupt in sync with the swell.

Coffin Bay National Park, an hour's drive west from Port Lincoln, comprises a landscape of dunes and saltmarsh, mostly only accessible by 4WD, though parts are open to other types of vehicle – consult the NPWS in Port Lincoln before visiting. You'll be rewarded by isolation, sand sculptures at Sensation and Mullalong beaches, and the quality of the fishing. Semicircular stone walls on the northern shore are **Aboriginal fish traps** – fish were chased in at high tide and then the gaps in the side blocked with nets as the water receded. If you don't have your own 4WD, Great Australian Bight Safaris (℡08/8682 2750) offers various day-trips ($60–$150), as well as longer camping and fishing adventures.

The picturesque setting of the town of **COFFIN BAY** is worth a look, though perhaps not during school holidays, when the caravan park (℡08/8685 4170; on-site vans ❷, cabins ❷–❸) and abundant holiday cottages are full to bursting. A stroll along the coastal "Oyster Walk" takes you past the original fishermen's shacks, now mostly summer houses, and reveals a wealth of bird and plant life – a taste of Coffin Bay National Park to the west.

The west coast

To catch the best of the west coast and the townships along the way, you'll need to detour off the main road between Coffin Bay and Ceduna. The region's coastal communities are an unlikely mix of conservative farmers and "alternative" surfies who come to ride the endless succession of strong, hundred-metre-long crests rolling into Waterloo Bay at **ELLISTON**, one of the state's most highly regarded **surf beaches**. Bold **murals** at the Community Hall between the café and campsite address local themes – including a long-suppressed incident when Aboriginal people were driven over the cliffs. South of Venus Bay, rocks have been hollowed by the sea to form the **Talia Caves**, but the lengthy beach is more compelling, though camping is prohibited. Turning to the coast about 20km north of Port Kenny, you pass the strangely flared **Murphy's Haystacks**, a group of low granite monoliths that look like giant mushrooms. Push on to **Point Labatt** for a look at mainland Australia's only colony of **fur seals**. Binoculars or a telephoto lens help to distinguish mother seals teaching pups to swim from the torpid, bulkier males basking on the rocks. Then it's back to the highway at **Streaky Bay** – the only place on the west coast that has a real centre – and then to drier country as you approach Ceduna and the Nullarbor.

The Eyre Highway and Gawler Ranges

Taking the **Eyre Highway** directly across the top of the peninsula from Port Augusta ensures an easy crossing to Ceduna, speeding past the mines at **Iron Knob** and dry scrub populated by green ring-necked parrots. Unusual geology appears around Wudinna in the form of isolated granite mounds (inselbergs) of various shapes and sizes. The largest, **Mount Wudinna**, 10km to the northeast, is second only to Uluru (Ayers Rock; see p.690) in monolithic magnitude, while 30km southwest lies **Ucontichie Hill**, whose curved natural formations include a **wave rock** similar to Hyden's in Western Australia (see p.742).

Iron Knob can be the start of forays along dirt tracks into the **Gawler Ranges**, before rejoining the highway at Wirrulla. While you might not need a 4WD, it's a remote area that requires advance preparation and advice from the

NPWS. The ranges are low, rounded volcanic ridges coloured orange by dust, with occasional speckled boulders poking through a thin grass cover; it's worth frightening the sheep and pink Major Mitchell cockatoos by walking up one of the peaks for a closer look. The centrally located *Mount Ive Homestead* (℡08/8648 1817; ❶–❷) has fuel, information and **accommodation** in basic rooms, plus camping space, but don't turn up unannounced. The track into the ranges passes **Lake Gairdner**, largest of the Gawler's **salt lakes**, with the ruins of Pondanna Homestead on a lonely plain at its southern end.

Ceduna and the Nullarbor Plain

You know where you are in **CEDUNA**: all the shops from camping store to supermarket are unambiguously named and a large signpost in the centre gives distances to everywhere between Perth and Port Augusta. Despite being small enough to walk around in twenty minutes, there's no lack of **caravan parks**, **banks** or **service stations**, with almost every brand of fuel on offer – some places even hand out discount cards for use at their pumps along the way. The *Foreshore Van Park* on South Terrace (℡08/8625 2290; cabins ❷) and the *Community Hotel/Motel* on O'Loughlin Terrace (℡08/8625 2008 or 1800 655 300; ❸) are right next to the jetty – you can fish for whiting on the turn of the high tide – and *Ceduna Greenacres Backpackers* is also not far from the sea at 12 Kuhlmann St (℡08/8625 3811; dorms $16.50). Before your early-morning start – it's a long way to anywhere – call in at the **information centre** on Poynton Street (Mon–Fri 9am–5.30pm, Sat & Sun 10am–4pm; ℡08/8625 2780) and the NPWS on McKenzie Street (℡08/8625 3144) for the latest on the Nullarbor's attractions. Incidentally, it almost never rains on the plain, and there's always a charge for **water**, which has to be distilled from underground reserves – so carry your own.

The Nullabor Plain

Nullarbor may not be strictly correct Latin for "treeless", but it's an apt description of the plain which stretches flat and infertile for over 1200km across the Great Australian Bight. Taking the **train** brings you closer to the dead heart than does the **road**, which allows some breaks in the monotony of the journey to scan the sea for southern right whales and visit at least one Aboriginal site. From Ceduna to the Western Australian border it's 480km, which you can easily cover in under five hours if you want; Daliesque fridges standing along the highway in the early stages of the drive are actually makeshift mailboxes for remote properties. The last chance to catch some waves is at **Cactus**

Beach/Point Sinclair south of **Penong**, though its popularity took a dive after a surfer was killed by a great white here in 2000. Even for non-surfies it's worth the drive through white dunes, green shrubbery and blue lagoons to watch the extraordinary wave formations; there's a **campsite** with firewood provided (but no drinking water) and a basic store (12.30–2pm), while the nearest civilized **accommodation** is at the *Penong Hotel* (T08/8625 1050; ➋).

Two hours from Penong you arrive at **Yalata Community**, settled by the Maralinga peoples cleared off their ancestral land by the British atomic bomb tests at Maralinga in the 1950s. At the roadhouse and **whale–watch centre** (T08/8625 6986) you can obtain permits to cross community borders and reach the **Head of the Bight**, the best place to see whales when they migrate up here between June and October. The Head is a stirring setting, where powdery dunes rise to absurdly melodramatic cliffs over just a couple of kilometres – you can't help feeling that this is how early cartographers must have envisaged the edge of the world. The southern right whales (see p.833) sport idly with their calves in the water below. Twenty minutes away is the **Nullarbor Roadhouse** (T08/8625 6271; ➊–➍), which has budget **beds**, motel rooms and a campsite, and is the last place to get fuel before Border Village. The famous triple yellow sign on the highway warning of camels, wombats and kangaroos marks the beginning of the run, which has absolutely no trees. Ironically, rabbits – no longer controlled by farmers now that the area is a national park – have almost crowded out the wombats.

Curiously enough for a land with minimal rainfall, the Nullarbor is undermined by partially flooded limestone **caverns**. From the outside, **Koonalda Cave** (just north of the *Nullarbor Roadhouse*) is a large hole with recently planted fruit trees growing in the mouth; inside, a tremendously deep network of tunnels leads to an underground lake, the shafts grooved by fingers being dragged over their soft walls. Although the patterns are clearly deliberate, their meaning is unknown. The cave is closed off to protect the engravings, but the Ceduna NPWS (see overleaf) might be able to arrange a visit.

Border Village is just another roadhouse (T08/9039 3474; ➊–➍) with a natty fibreglass kangaroo in the car park – certainly the largest one between here and Antarctica. **Eucla** (see p.747) and the rest of the Nullarbor lie 16km over the border in Western Australia on a noticeably worse road and in a considerably earlier time zone.

The Stuart Highway: Woomera and beyond

Heading north of Port Augusta along the **Stuart Highway**, the first place of any consequence is **WOOMERA**, an uncharismatic but well-appointed barracks town two hours north of Port Augusta. The town has been in the news recently on account of its harsh **detention centre**, which houses political asylum seekers while their cases are being decided. In fact, the whole town was closed to the public until 1982, as it sits at the southeast corner of a five-hundred-kilometre corridor known locally as "the Range", ominously highlighted on maps as **Woomera Prohibited Area**. Don't expect to find out why at the mostly military **Heritage Centre** (daily 9am–5pm; $5), at the crossroads of Dewrang and Banool avenues. Models, rocket-relics and plenty of pictures detail the European Launcher Development Organisation's

(ELDO) unsuccessful efforts to launch satellites here in the 1960s, but the reasons for the creation of the Prohibited Area – weapons-testing and the British-run 1950s **atomic bomb tests**, contaminated dust from which is still being scraped up and vitrified – are not mentioned. For a first-hand account, read Len Beadell's *Outback Highways*, cheerful tales of the bomb tests and the construction of "some sort of rocket range – or something" by the chief engineer. Currently, Australian, UK and US rocket prototypes are once again being tested here in the hope of turning Woomera into a launching centre.

There are two **places** to stay: the *Eldo Hotel* on Kotara Crescent (℡08/8673 7867, ℻8673 7226; ➊–➌), which also provides **meals** and booze; and the welcoming *Woomera Travellers Village* on Wirruna Avenue (℡08/8673 7800; ➊–➌) – **camping** on the lawn is preferable to the beds in the dreary ex-barracks. The **shopping centre** has banks and other facilities, while next door **The Oasis** houses a small leisure centre with a café, bar and bowling alley. Greyhound buses travelling on the Stuart Highway don't go into Woomera but will drop you off at the roadhouse at Pimba, 7km away; Stateliner services do, however, call in to the town.

Roxby Downs, Andamooka and Lake Torrens

Instead of returning to the highway, you might want to carry on past Woomera to the strangest two companion towns in Australia (a Stateliner **bus** goes from Woomera six nights a week). The first, **ROXBY DOWNS**, 80km away, is completely modern, a service centre built in 1986 for miners working the copper, gold, silver and uranium deposits at the nearby Olympic Dam Mine (tours Mon, Thurs, Sat 9am; 2hr; donation; bookings on ℡08/8671 2001). The friendly **Roxby Downs Cultural Precinct** on the main street (daily 9am–5pm; ℡08/8671 2001, ⓦwww.roxbydowns.com), has local information and a café. Another thirty minutes on along an unsurfaced road lies **ANDAMOOKA**, an opal-mining shantytown of block and scrap-iron construction whose red-earth high street becomes a river after rain. The soil proved to be too loose for the underground homes which became *de rigueur* at Coober Pedy (see p.872), but mud lean-tos, built in the 1930s, are still standing opposite the post office. **Facilities** include fuel, a supermarket, the *Tuckerbox Restaurant* (11am–late), two hotel/motels, two campsites, and the Opal Creek Showroom, which distributes maps and advice. If you fancy your luck "noodling", head to **German Gully**. Opals here are more strongly coloured than Coober Pedy's, but few have been found for years.

Another thirty-minute 4WD ride away is **Lake Torrens**, a sickle-shaped salt lake related to the Acraman meteorite (see box on p.871) which gets popular with bird-watchers in wet years. The lake is also renowned in paleontological circles for traces of the 630-million-year-old **Ediacaran fauna**, the earliest-known evidence of animal life anywhere on the planet, which was first found in Australia, and possibly wiped out by the meteorite. Delicate fossil impressions of jellyfish and obscure organisms are preserved in layered rock. The South Australian Museum in Adelaide (see p.802) has an extensive selection, but rarely issues directions to the site, which has been plundered by collectors since its discovery in 1946 by the geologist Reg Sprigg.

Coober Pedy

COOBER PEDY is the most enduring symbol of the harshness of Australia's Outback and the determination of those who live there. It's a place where the

SOUTH AUSTRALIA | The Stuart Highway: Woomera and beyond

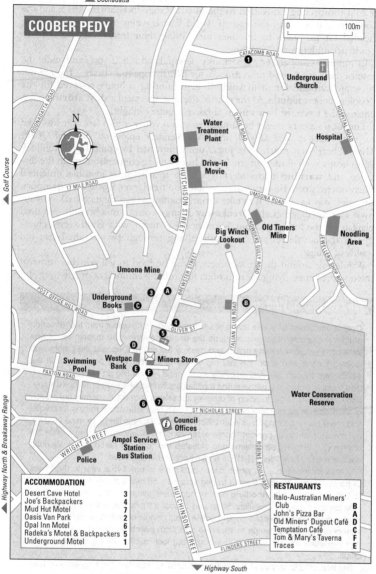

COOBER PEDY

▲ Oodnadatta

0 ——— 100m

CATACOMB ROAD ①

Underground Church

Water Treatment Plant

Drive-in Movie

Hospital

② (Oasis Van Park)

17 MILE ROAD

UMOONA ROAD

Big Winch Lookout

Old Timers Mine

Noodling Area

Umoona Mine

POST OFFICE HILL ROAD

③ Ⓐ

Underground Books Ⓒ

④

⑤ OLIVER ST

Ⓑ

Ⓓ

Swimming Pool

Westpac Bank Ⓔ

Miners Store Ⓕ

PAXTON ROAD

⑥ ⑦

ST NICHOLAS STREET

ⓘ Council Offices

WRIGHT STREET

Ampol Service Station Bus Station

Police

Water Conservation Reserve

HUTCHINSON STREET

BREWSTER STREET

O'NEIL ROAD

CROWDERS GULLY ROAD

ITALIAN CLUB ROAD

JEWELLERS SHOP ROAD

HOSPITAL ROAD

ROBINS BOULEVARD

FLINDERS STREET

▼ Highway South

◀ Golf Course

◀ Highway North & Breakaway Range

8

SOUTH AUSTRALIA | The Stuart Highway: Woomera and beyond

ACCOMMODATION	
Desert Cave Hotel	3
Joe's Backpackers	4
Mud Hut Motel	7
Oasis Van Park	2
Opal Inn Motel	6
Radeka's Motel & Backpackers	5
Underground Motel	1

RESTAURANTS	
Italo-Australian Miners' Club	B
John's Pizza Bar	A
Old Miners' Dugout Café	D
Temptation Café	C
Tom & Mary's Taverna	F
Traces	E

terrain and temperatures are so extreme that homes – and even churches – have been built underground, yet which has managed to attract thousands of opal prospectors. In a virtually waterless desert 380km from Woomera, and considerably further from anywhere else, the most remarkable thing about the town – whose name stems from an Aboriginal phrase meaning "white man's burrow" – is that it exists at all. **Opal** was discovered by William Hutchison on a gold-prospecting expedition to the Stuart Range in February 1915, and the town itself dates from the end of World War I, when returning servicemen headed for the fields to try their luck, using their trench-digging skills to construct underground dwellings.

In summer Coober Pedy is seriously depopulated but, if you can handle the intense heat, it's a good time to look for bargain opal purchases – though not to scratch around for them yourself: gem-hunting is better reserved for the "cooler" winter months. At the start of the year, spectacular **dust storms** often enclose the town for hours in an abrasive orange twilight.

The local scenery might be familiar to you if you're a film fan, as it was used to great effect in *Mad Max III* and Wim Wenders' epic *Until The End Of The World*. There's not much to it, just a plain disturbed by conical pink mullock (slag) heaps, with clusters of trucks and home-made contraptions off in the distance, and **warning signs** alerting you to treacherously invisible, unfenced thirty-metre shafts. Be very careful where you tread: even if you have transport, the safest way to explore is to take a tour, examine a map, then go back on your own. Past the diggings, the **Breakaway Range** consists of a brightly coloured plateau off the highway about 11km north of town, with good views, close-ups of the hostile terrain, and bushwalking through two-hundred-year-old stands of mulga.

Wandering around the dusty streets, it can be hard to tell whether some of the odd machinery lying about is bona fide mining equipment or left-over film

Finding and buying an opal

Opal is composed of fragile layers of silica and derives its colour from the refraction of light – characteristics that preclude the use of heavy mining machinery, as one false blow would break the matrix and destroy the colour. Deposits are patchy and located by trial and error: the last big strikes at Coober Pedy petered out in the 1970s, and though bits and pieces are still found – including an exceptional opal-ized fossil skeleton of a pliosaur (the reptilian equivalent of a seal) in 1983 – it's anybody's guess as to the location of other major seams (indeed, there may not be any at all). Because so much depends on luck, you'll hear little about mining technique and more about beating the system. For instance, it's now illegal to mine in town, but there's nothing to prevent "home extensions"; similarly, non-mining friends are often roped in to register claims and sidestep the "one per person" rule. Working another's claim (the "night shift") is a less honourable short cut.

Unless you're serious (in which case you'll have to pay $45 a year to the Mines Department for a **Miner's Permit** to peg your 50 x 50 metre claim), the easiest way to find something is by **noodling** over someone's diggings – ask the owner first. An area on the corner of Jewellers Shop and Umoona roads has been set aside as a safe area for tourists to poke about freely without danger of finding open mineshafts. Miners use ultraviolet lamps to separate opal from **potch** (worthless grey opal), so you're unlikely to find anything stunning – but look out for shell fossils and small chips.

The best time to **buy opal** is outside the tourist season, but don't expect wild bargains and don't deal through grizzled prospectors in the hotels unless you're very clued in. There are three categories: **cabochon**, a solid piece; **doublet**, a thin wafer mounted on a dark background to enhance the colour; and **triplet**, a doublet with quartz lens. While cabochons are most expensive and triplets least valuable, it takes some experience to price accurately within each category, as size, clarity, strength of colour, brightness and personal aesthetics all contribute. With about fifty dealers in town, it's up to you to find the right stone; reputable sources give full written guarantees.

props. The **Big Winch Lookout** in the centre gives a grandstand view of the mix of low houses and hills pocked with ventilation shafts. The welded metal "tree" up here was assembled before any real ones grew in the area, though in the last few years there have been some attempts to encourage greenery with recycled waste water. For more on mining, there are several mine displays and museums in town: try **Old Timers Mine**, Crowders Gully Road (☎08/8672 5555; $7.50), or **Umoona** on Hutchison Street (☎08/8672 5288; entrance free, tours $6). There are numerous **tours** on offer for around $30: all feature a town drive, a spot of noodling and a visit to an underground home – which you might find embarrassingly like visiting a zoo. Book through your accommodation, or try Radeka's five-hour tour (☎08/8672 5223), which includes a look at the Breakaway Range.

Coober Pedy has lately achieved a bit of a reputation for **violence**, which is perhaps not surprising given its extreme climate and the fact that most people have access to explosives. However, signs warning "no parking unless your car is dynamite-proof" are really for amusement-value only, and visitors are unlikely to be the object of any discord.

Practicalities

Just about everything you'll need in Coober Pedy lies around the 500-metre strip between the *Opal Inn Hotel* and the water-treatment plant on **Hutchison Street** (also known as Main Street), which leads north off the highway. **Buses** drop you off either at the Ampol service station (Greyhound Pioneer and Stateliner; ☎08/8672 5151) or at *Radeka's Motel* (McCafferty's; ☎08/8672 5223). From the **airport** you may be able to get a lift with one of the hostel buses that meet most flights, or make an advance reservation to ensure that someone meets you. *Desert Cave Hotel* (see below) is agent for Territory Rent a Car; book well in advance.

The council offices on Hutchison Street (Mon–Fri 9am–5pm; ☎1800 637 076, ⓦwww.opalcapitaloftheworld.com.au), opposite the Ampol service station, are a mine of local **information**. Underground Books (☎08/8672 5558), on Post Office Hill Road opposite the Mobil service station, is a good alternative source – it stocks packs of local sketch maps which are a useful back-up to road maps. The Miners Store supermarket on Hutchison Street (☎08/8672 5051) is also the **post office** and Commonwealth **bank** agent (there's a Westpac branch opposite). The **hospital** is on Hospital Road, at the north end of town (☎08/8672 5009), and there's a **pharmacy** at the Medical Centre in the middle of Hutchison Street. Everyone shops on Thursday, as fresh meat and veggies arrive in a refrigerated lorry on Wednesday night and are scarce by the weekend. The **swimming pool** at the school on Paxton Road gives a welcome chance to cool down; it's open to the public for a few hours daily.

Accommodation

Coober Pedy relies heavily on tourist income, so finding **lodgings** shouldn't be a problem. To some people, the idea of sleeping underground is disturbing but, while not all accommodation is subterranean, it's worth spending at least one night in naturally cooled tunnels for the experience.

Desert Cave Hotel Hutchison St ☎08/8672 5688, ⓦwww.desertcave.com.au. Offers a choice of below- or above-ground four-star accommodation. There's a swimming pool, and scenic flights, tours and car rental can be arranged. ⑥

Joe's Backpackers Hostel and Motel Oliver St ☎08/8672 5163. Above-ground motel rooms sleep up to three people; backpackers go under-ground. Dorms $17.50, rooms ②.

Mud Hut Motel Next to the council offices ☏08/8672 3003, ⊛www.mudhutmotel.com.au. The bare, rammed-earth construction of this well-furnished motel gives a flavour of the subterranean without losing out on daylight. ④

Oasis Van Park Opposite the water-treatment plant, Hutchison St ☏08/8672 5169. The only place to camp under trees. Cabin rooms ②

Opal Inn Motel Hutchison St ☏08/8672 5054. A standard motel block behind the hotel of the same name. ④

Radeka's Downunder Motel and Backpackers Inn Oliver St ☏08/8672 5223, ⓔradekadownunder@ozemail.com.au. The best budget option in town. There are snaking tunnels downstairs with alcoves holding two to six beds – though it can be a long trek upstairs to the well-appointed kitchen and toilets – and a bar and pool table provide evening entertainment. Dorms $19, motel rooms ②–④

Underground Motel Catacomb Rd ☏08/8672 5324. Clean tiled rooms with views over the desert from the front porch. ④ including break-fast.

Eating, drinking and entertainment

Restaurants in town are good value and portions are huge – beware of over-ordering; all those listed below are on the main street. The drive-in **cinema** on Hutchison Street shows a double bill most Saturday nights.

Italo-Australian Miner's Club ☏08/8672 501. Big Italian dinners on Thursdays and Fridays.

John's Pizza Bar Takeaway fast food and coffee.

Old Miners' Dugout Café Kangaroo dishes and budget specials.

Temptation Café Upmarket place with pavement tables, excellent pastries and coffee.

Tom and Mary's Taverna ☏08/8672 5622. Souvlakia morning to midnight.

Traces ☏08/8672 5147. Greek grills, plus danc-ing. Daily 4pm–late.

Beyond Coober Pedy

The Stuart Highway ploughs 350km north from Coober Pedy to the state border. From **Marla** township (shop, post office and Commonwealth Bank at the roadhouse) you could head east to Oodnadatta across the **Painted Desert** at Arkaringa Hills, a larger version of the Breakaway Range, or 35km west into Aboriginal land to the state's newest opal strike at Mintabie – seek permission from Marla's police. If you want to get to **Oodnadatta**, there's also a direct two-hundred-kilometre dirt road from Coober Pedy across the pan of Giddi-Gidna (the **Moon Plain**), covered by the **mail run** which departs from Underground Books (☏1800 069 911; $110) on a roughly twelve-hour trian-gular route to William Creek and Oodnadatta every Monday at 9am (anti-clockwise) and Thursday (clockwise).

Australia's hottest 4WD journey has to be west from Coober Pedy to the **atomic bomb sites** at **Emu Junction**: concrete slabs cap pits where contam-inated equipment lies buried, and sand fused into sheets of glass by the blasts covers the ground – the area is still highly radioactive and you'd be advised to pass through quickly. Beyond lies the virgin **Unnamed Conservation Park** and routes across the sand-dunes and Aboriginal land to the **Warburton Road** in Western Australia (see p.746). The NPWS at 11 McKenzie St in Ceduna (☏08/8625 3144) supplies practical details and permits to 4WD convoys only.

The Flinders Ranges and northeast

If you're heading north from Port Augusta but want to avoid the Stuart Highway, an adventurous alternative route leads up to the spectacular **Flinders**

Ranges National Park and beyond to the remote settlements of **Maree** and **Innamincka**. The first stop between Port Augusta and the Flinders Ranges National Park is 50km northeast at **QUORN**, whose stone buildings and village atmosphere offer a last taste of the pastoral south before the austerities of the Outback set in. Best known for the **Pichi Richi railway**, the sole operational section of the old Ghan, Quorn was a major rail centre until the line was re-routed through Port Augusta in the 1950s. Enthusiasts restored the service twenty years later and started taking passengers on a two-hour return haul to Woolshed Flats through the **Pichi Richi Pass** – whose name has been variously attributed to a medicinal herb or an Aboriginal word for "gorge". Punctuated by a break at Woolshed Flats for a cream tea, it makes a relaxing and mildly scenic journey. Trains run only on a few weekends and holidays April–October; call ahead to check and book (☎08/8658 6598, Ⓦwww.prr.org.au).

There's a **caravan park** in Quorn (☎08/8648 6206; cabins ❸), but a night spent at the *Transcontinental Hotel* (☎08/8648 6076; ❶–❷) is much more congenial, with an easy-going crowd of truckies and drovers from the north for company. A good alternative is the *Andu Lodge* (☎8648 6655; dorms $19, rooms ❷), which has excellent dorms and double rooms; they also run a host of one- to three-day **tours** into the different sections of the Flinders for between $99 and $299.

The main road through town is Railway Terrace, where you'll find the town's post office and hotels, which all do good-value **meals** but are quite strict about serving times. First Street and the block between it and Railway Terrace contain a few art-and-craft and secondhand shops to poke about in. The **tourist information** centre is at 3 Seventh St (☎08/8648 6419). If you want to explore some of the country round here, Intrepid Tours, 17 Sixth St (☎08/8648 6277), runs a 4WD tour any day they can fill a vehicle.

There's good local bushwalking off the back road to Hawker along a string of ridges and cliffs, outrunners from the main body of the central Flinders, 100km north. Closest to Quorn is **Dutchmans Stern**, a solid day's hike for the reasonably fit from the car park to various lookouts. Less dedicated walkers will find **Warren**, **Buckaringa** and **Middle gorges** an easier proposition; Buckaringa's steep face is the most reliable place in the ranges to see the rare and ravishingly pretty **yellow-footed rock wallaby**, with its bushy, ringed tail and yellow paws – climb to the top at around 4pm and sit still until they appear. Closer to Hawker, it's also worth taking in the well-preserved remains of **Kanyaka Homestead**, abandoned after a drought in the 1880s, and **Yourambulla Cave**, which has some unusual charcoal symbols in a high overhang, reached by a ladder. Both are signposted from the road.

HAWKER itself, some 100km from Port Augusta, is somewhere to fuel up, make use of the last banks and shops, have a meal at the *Old Ghan Restaurant*, organize a **flight over the Flinders** through *Hawker Caravan Park* on the Wilpena exit (☎08/8648 4006), and acquire **Desert Park Passes** and advice about road conditions from the NPWS office at 60 Elder Terrace (Mon–Fri 8.30am–4pm; ☎08/8648 4244). Once in Hawker, you'll have to decide whether to press on into the Flinders and the northeast or continue following the former Ghan line north towards Marree; the bitumen on the latter route extends past the Leigh Creek coalfields to Lyndhurst, at the start of the Strzelecki Track. Stateliner **buses** pass through Sunday, Wednesday and Friday, continuing to Wilpena, with a connection (Mon & Fri) to Arkaroola in the Northern Flinders. On Sunday, Thursday and Friday the buses return to Port Augusta and Adelaide.

Flinders Dreaming and geology

The almost tangible spirit of the Flinders Ranges is reflected in the wealth of Adnyamathanha ("hill people") **legends** associated with them. Perhaps more obvious here than anywhere else in Australia is the connection between landscapes and Dreamtime stories, which recount how scenery was created by animal or human action – though, as Dreamtime spirits took several forms, this distinction is often blurred. A central character is **Akurra**, a gigantic maned serpent (or serpents) who guards waterholes and formed the Flinders' contours by wriggling north to drink dry the huge salt lakes of Frome and Callabonna. You may well prefer the Aboriginal legends to the complexities of geology illustrated on boards placed at intervals along the Brachina Gorge track, which explain how movements of the "Adelaide Geosyncline" brought about the changes in scenery over hundreds of millions of years.

Flinders Ranges National Park

The procession of glowing red mountains at **Flinders Ranges National Park**, folded and crumpled with age, produces some of the Outback's most spectacular and timeless scenery, rising from flat scrub to form abrupt escarpments, gorges and the famous elevated basin of **Wilpena Pound**. The hard contrast between sky and ranges is softened by native cypresses and river red gums, and in spring the plains are burnished by **wild flowers** of all colours. Bushwalkers, photographers and painters flock here in their hundreds, but with a system of graded **walking tracks** ranging from a few minutes' length to several days – not to mention roads of varying quality – the park is busy without being crowded.

Nestling up against the edge of Wilpena Pound, **WILPENA** is a good place to orient yourself: it has a motel, campsite, gas, diesel and petrol pumps and an overpriced store. The NPWS **information centre** (daily 8am–6pm) is situated at the end of the bitumen where the main routes start into Wilpena Pound. Wilder places further into the park to set up camp for a few days include the national park campsites at **Bunyeroo** and **Brachina Gorge** in the west, **Trezona** and **Oraparinna** in the centre, and **Wilkawillana Gorge** in the extreme northeast, all accessible on unsealed roads. Even the more formal **lodgings** tend to be basic: for a longer stay you might consider renting a holiday cottage, which can be a bargain during the summer – Flinders Ranges Accommodation Booking Service (☎1800 777 880, ⓦwww.frabs.com.au) offers a range of cabins (❸–❹) in the region.

Back at Wilpena, *Wilpena Pound Motel* (☎08/8648 0004 or 1800 805 802, ⓦwww.wilpenapound.com.au; ❺–❻) provides comfortable but expensive **accommodation**: there's a good, surprisingly exotic restaurant, however, and the chalet-like bar makes an atmospheric setting for an après-hike drink. Four-wheel-drive tours and flights over the Pound can also be arranged here. If you've a tent, the adjacent *Wilpena Campsite* (☎08/8648 0008) is wooded and well equipped, and has standing tent accommodation. Other places to stay are dotted around the park: about 15km back towards Hawker *Rawnsley Park* (☎08/8648 0030, ⓦwww.rawnsleypark.com.au; cabins ❸–❹, plus tent spaces) is beautifully located below Rawnsley Bluff, and has its own fuel, store, mountain bike rental, and 4WD trips; *Willow Springs* (☎08/8648 6282, ⓦwww.frabs.com.au/willowsprings.htm; ❶–❸), 17km north of Wilpena before the Wilkawillana Gorge junction, is a working sheep station with blockhouse dormitories and cottage.

Most **walking tracks** lead into Wilpena Pound, though you can also pick up the Heysen Trail and follow it north from Wilpena for a couple of days around the ABC Range to **Aroona Ruins** on the northern edge of the park. The Wilpena NPWS offers booklets, maps (sometimes the 1:50,000 topographical series) and the latest information on routes; you're required to log out and back with them on any walk exceeding three hours. Realistically, hiking is restricted to the cooler winter months between May and October, as scant shade and reflective rocks raise summer temperatures above 40°C. Don't underestimate conditions for even short excursions: you'll need good footwear, a hat, sunscreen and **water** – at least half a litre per hour is recommended. **Camping out**, a waterproof tent, groundmat and fuel stove are essential, and note that the **weather** is very changeable; wind-driven rain can be a menace along the ridges and heavy downpours can make tracks dangerous.

Wilpena Pound

Wilpena Pound's two major hiking destinations are **St Mary's Peak** on the rim and **Edowie Gorge** inside the Pound – from Wilpena, allow nine hours for Edowie Gorge, eight hours for the ascent of St Mary's. Alternatively, an **overnight** trip through the Pound allows you to see all its major attractions. Leave the peak until last and head off across the Pound's flat, grassy bowl to the remains of **Hill's Homestead** – further evidence of the region's unsuitability for farming – then follow the track northwest to **Cooinda Camp**, about two hours from Wilpena. Assuming you left early enough, there's time to pitch a tent and spend the rest of the day following the creek upstream past **Malloga Falls** to **Glenora Falls** and views into Edowie Gorge before heading back to Cooinda – there might be places to swim after rain. Next morning it's a steep climb to **Tanderra Saddle** below the peak, followed by the last burst up to the summit of St Mary's Peak itself. The effort is rewarded by unequalled views west to Lake Torrens and north along the length of the ABC Ranges towards Parachilna; on exceptional mornings the peak stands proud of low cloud inside the Pound. The direct descent from the saddle back to Wilpena is initially steep, but shouldn't take more than three hours.

Shorter routes lead up **Mount Ohlssen Bagge** (a not-too-tiring four hours) and **Wangara Lookout** (2hr) for lower vistas of the Pound floor, and southwest across the Pound to **Bridle Gap** (6hr) following the Heysen Trail's red markers. Things to look out for are euro wallabies, emus and parrots inside the Pound, and cauliflower-shaped fossil **stromatolites** – algal corals – on the Mount Ohlssen Bagge route, similar to those still living at Hamelin Pool in Western Australia (see p.754).

Arkaroo Rock, Sacred Canyon and nearby gorges

Two **Aboriginal galleries** worth seeing are Arkaroo Rock and Sacred Canyon, both a short drive from Wilpena. **Arkaroo** is back off the main road towards Rawnsley Park and involves an hour's walk up the outside of Wilpena Pound to see mesh-protected rockfaces covered in symbols relating to an initiation ceremony and the Pound's formation, some dating back six thousand years. Snake patterns depict St Mary's Peak as the head of a male Akurra coiled round the Pound. To reach **Sacred Canyon**, briefly take the road from Wilpena into the north of the park, past the **Cazneaux Tree** – a river red gum made famous by Harold Cazneaux's prize-winning 1930 photograph *Spirit of Endurance* – before turning right and following a bumpy track to its end. Rock-hop up the narrow, shattered gorge to clusters of painted swirls covered in a sooty patina and clearer engraved emu prints and geometric patterns; the best examples are around the second cascade.

The main road through the park heads straight out to Blinman, but another track detours to **Bunyeroo** and **Brachina gorges** on the western limits. The gorges make good campsites: you have to walk into Bunyeroo but the track passes through Brachina on its way to the surfaced Hawker to Marree road. If you're pressing directly on to the Northern Flinders, you can avoid Blinman by turning right off the main road about 20km from Wilpena, heading to **Wirrealpa Homestead**.

The Northern Flinders

The Wilpena–Blinman road passes through a low group of hills, thin in timber but still swarming with wallabies, emus and galahs. **BLINMAN** comprises a few houses with well-tended gardens, three fuel pumps, and a hotel (℡08/8648 4867, ℮blinman@senet.com.au; ❷–❹) with log fires, games room, pool and campsite; the keys to everywhere else in town are kept at the bar. The main track winds west through beautiful Parachilna Gorge, in the middle of which you could stay at **Angorichina** *Tourist Village* (℡08/8648 4842; dorms $18), which also has a campsite. The track meets the Hawker–Marree road at **Parachilna**, where there's great bush tucker at the *Prairie Hotel* (℡08/8648 4895, ⓦwww.prairiehotel.com.au).

According to the Adnyamathanha, **coal** was made by Yoolayoola the kingfisher man, who built fires at Leigh Creek, halfway between Hawker and Marree. Today, 2.6 million tonnes of it are scooped out of the ground annually to be sent by rail and burnt at the power station in Port Augusta. At a car park just off the road you can climb around an old dragline crane and look over the edge of an open-cast mine; there are free **tours** daily (℡08/8675 2723). Coal-workers live either in the well-planned modern township of **Leigh Creek South** or at more traditional **Copley**, where *Tulloch's Bush Bakery* does a very civilized cappuccino and quandong pie. Fuel and camping sites are available at both towns.

The route into the Northern Flinders lies east, joining up with the direct road from Wilpena and then running north to the **Gammon Ranges National Park** and Arkaroola.

Chambers Gorge and Big Moro

On the road to the Gammon Ranges are the remote and little-visited sites of **Chambers Gorge** and **Big Moro**, worth every groan and twang of your vehicle springs for their stark beauty and Aboriginal significance. The ten-kilometre access track east into **Chambers Gorge** (28km after Wirrealpa) is decidedly dodgy after rain when you'll need a 4WD, but at other times 2WD vehicles – with care – should reach the natural campsite at the foot of **Mount Chambers**, within twenty minutes' walk of the gorge mouth. In a Dreamtime story, Yuduyudulya, the Fairy Wren spirit, threw a boomerang which split Mount Chambers' eastern end and then circled back to form the crown. An indistinct left fork before the gorge leads to a dense gallery of **pecked engravings**; most are circles, though a goanna stands out clearly on the right, facing the main body of art. Chambers Gorge itself is huge and silent, the broad stony entrance guarded by high, perpendicular cliffs and brilliant green waterholes; it would take days to explore properly.

Big Moro is sacred to the Adnyamathanha as the residence of an Akurra. The creek trickles through a crumbling gorge into two clear green pools; limestone outcrops on the south side conceal miniature caves. The gorge lies west down an exceptionally tortuous fifteen-kilometre 4WD track opposite **Wertaloona Homestead**, 60km from the Mount Chambers junction. Pay attention to any signs and leave the three gates as you found them.

The Gammon Ranges

Arid and bald, the **Gammon Ranges** are the Flinders' last fling, a vicious flurry of compressed folds plunging abruptly onto the northern plains. Balcanoona is the NPWS headquarters for the otherwise undeveloped **Gammon Ranges National Park**, a thick band of sandstone cliffs – check with the Hawker NPWS (see p.877) for current conditions. There are two ways to experience the area: either carry on to Arkaroola (outside the park), or take the road west across the park through **Italowie Gorge** to Copley on the Hawker–Marree road. The steep red walls of the gorge are home to iga – native orange trees which symbolize the Adnyamathanha as a people. There are **bush campsites** here and shearers' quarters at **Balcanoona** (book through the Hawker NPWS; $12).

On the northern edge of the park, **Arkaroola** (Mount Painter Sanctuary) is a private wildlife sanctuary and **resort** (☎08/8370 8454 or 1800 676 042, ⓦ www.arkaroola.on.net; ❷–❺) and a source of fuel, provisions, meals, rooms and a campsite. Scene of Australia's most recent volcanic activity, the area is a geologist's dream: **Paralana Hot Springs** (two hours away by 4WD) bubble out radioactive radon gas, and walks into the shattered hills surrounding the resort turn up fossils and semi-precious minerals. According to Aboriginal legend, the springs mark the site where a Dreamtime warrior extinguished his firestick after using it to kill a rival. The area is so rugged that conventional mining isn't really a profitable venture – drilling rigs are airlifted in, then ferried around on the lower half of a Chieftain tank. The resort's **Ridgetop Tour** ($66 per person) brings you closest to the heart of the scenery: four hair-raising hours in an open 4WD (wear something warm) following precipitous contours to **Sillers Lookout** and views east to the shimmering salt lakes of **Frome** and **Callabonna**. Remains of the hippopotamus-sized marsupial diprotodon have been found at Callabonna; the diprotodon survived well into Aboriginal times, but died out as the climate changed after the last Ice Age.

Arkaroola marks the limit of public transport, running its own connection to meet the Stateliner bus at Hawker on Monday and Friday. Some vehicles (with either high clearance or very careful drivers) can continue directly north to join the **Strzelecki Track** at Mount Hopeless, a little under half the distance to Innamincka. If you're unsure, the track can also be reached via Lyndhurst on the Hawker–Marree road, but this involves a three-hundred-kilometre detour from Arkaroola.

The Strzelecki Track

The 460-kilometre **Strzelecki Track** between Lyndhurst and Innamincka was pioneered in 1870 by **Harry Redford**, better known as Captain Starlight, who stole a thousand cattle from a property near Longreach in Queensland and drove them south across the Strzelecki Desert and down to Adelaide (see p.569 for more). Later used for more orthodox purposes, the track had a reputation as one of the roughest stock routes in the country, a serious obstacle for transport. Much of its epic nature has since been flattened, along with the road surface, by companies draining the **Moomba gas and oil fields**, and it's negotiable in any sound vehicle when dry.

Start at Lyndhurst by filling the tank – the next **fuel** is at the other end – and heading off around the northern tip of the Flinders; once past them, the journey becomes flat and pretty dull. At around the 105-kilometre mark you cross the 4850-kilometre-long **Dog Fence** (or Great Dingo Fence), designed to keep dingoes away from southern flocks, which stretches from the Nullarbor Plain east into New South Wales. Although its value is debatable, you do frequently see desiccated canine corpses poisoned by "1080" bait lying nearby. The road from Arkaroola connects within sight of **Mount Hopeless** (a pathetic hill, appropriately named); the next place to stop and perhaps camp is at the hot outflow from **Montecollina Bore**, 30km on. From here the scenery improves slightly as the road runs between dunes, and it's hard to resist leaving footprints along one of the pristine red crests.

At **Strzelecki Crossing** there's a choice of routes: you could abandon the track and head east to where Queensland, New South Wales and South Australia meet at **Cameron Corner**, where there's a store with **fuel**, a campsite (☎08/8091 3872) and a small bar; alternatively, you could continue to Innamincka either via Moomba or by following the direct but less-frequented **Old Strzelecki Track**. Cameron's Corner and the old track are 4WD only, and all of the routes are crossed by straight **seismic test lines** which run off to dead ends in the bush – you risk becoming permanently lost if you accidentally follow one, so take care. **Moomba**'s jumble of pipes and lick of flame are sometimes marked as a township on maps but, though visible from the road, the refinery is closed to the public. Within an hour you've crossed into the **Innamincka Regional Reserve** and are approaching Innamincka's charms.

Innamincka

Cooper Creek, which runs through Innamincka, is best known for the misadventures of explorers Burke and Wills, who ended their tragic 1861 expedition by dying here (see box on p.575). **INNAMINCKA** was later founded on much the same spot as a customs house to collect taxes on stock being moved between Queensland and South Australia. Never more than a handful of buildings, it found fame mainly because John Flynn's Flying Doctor Service ran a mission here and because the hotel piled up decades of empties into a legendary 180-metre-long bottle dump before the town was abandoned in 1952. Recreational four-wheel driving has led to a renaissance: the new *Innimincka Hotel* (☎ & ℻08/8675 9901; ❹) has weekend barbecues, a video jukebox and impromptu dance sessions on Friday and Saturday nights; the Innamincka Trading Post (☎08/8675 9900) has a couple of comfortable **cabins** (❹), and stocks provisions and fuel; the mission was rebuilt in 1994 as a **museum** (for opening hours ask at the Trading Post); there's a solar-powered telephone and spotless toilet/shower block opposite. Pelicans, parrots and inquisitive dingoes will be your companions if you camp out for free along the creek.

It only takes an hour to look around the museum and hunt for evidence of the bottle dump before you're ready for other distractions: taking a walk, **fishing** for yellowbelly, bream and catfish, swimming in the creek, or renting a canoe from the hotel or the Trading Post. With a vehicle you could strike out 20km west to **Wills' grave** or 8km east to where **Burke** was buried (both bodies were removed to Adelaide in 1862). Another 8km beyond Burke's cairn is **Cullyamurra waterhole**, the largest permanent body of water in central Australia, and a footpath to rock engravings of crosses, rainbow patterns and bird tracks. With a 4WD you can also tackle the 110-kilometre track north to the shallow **Coongie Lakes**, where you can swim and watch the abundant birdlife. An hour's drive east of Innamincka along a rather poor track is Queensland, the Dig Tree and a fuelless route to Quilpie (see p.574).

The far north: Marree and beyond

MARREE is a collection of tattered houses which somehow outlived the old Ghan's demise in 1980, leaving carriages to rust on sidings and rails to be used for tethering posts outside the hotel. Although it was first a camel depot, then a staging post for the overland telegraph line, and finally the point where the rail line skirted northwest around **Lake Eyre**, today all traffic comes by road and is bound for the **Birdsville Track** into Queensland or the **Oodnadatta Track**, which follows the former train route to Oodnadatta and beyond into the Northern Territory or Simpson Desert.

Accommodation is limited to the hotel on the main street (☎08/8675 8344; ❸), which is also good for lunch or dinner, and the caravan park run by the *Oasis Café* (☎08/8675 8352; cabins ❸), a fairly well-stocked shop, fuel and fast-food outlet which was originally the telegraph relay station. The General Store (☎08/8675 8360), across the railway track towards Oodnadatta, doubles as a Commonwealth Bank agent and post office with fuel and EFTPOS. If it's open, visit the **Arabana Community Centre**, whose friendly staff will explain the uses of different types of boomerang.

Lake Eyre

Lake Eyre is a massive salt lake caught between the Simpson and Strzelecki deserts in a region where the annual evaporation rate is thirty times greater than the rainfall. Most years a little water trickles into the lake from its million-square-kilometre catchment area, which extends well into central Queensland and the Northern Territory, but floods have filled the basin only four times since white settlement of the region – most dramatically in 1974, when the lake expanded to a length of 140km. A hypnotic, glaring **salt crust** usually covers the southern bays, creating a mysterious landscape whose harsh surrounds are paved by shiny gibber stones and walled by red dunes – the crust was thick enough in 1964 to be used as a range for Donald Campbell's successful crack at the world land-speed record. Some **wildlife** also manages to get by in the incredible emptiness. The resident Lake Eyre dragon is a diminutive, spotted grey lizard often seen skimming over the crust, and the rare flooding attracts dense flocks of birds, wakes the plump water-holding frog from hibernation and causes the plants to burst into colour.

While you can **fly** over the lake (make bookings through the *Oasis Café* in Marree), only 4WDs can reach the shore 95km north of Marree, though the track to the campsite at a gum-shaded waterhole, just over halfway at **Muloorina Homestead**, is good. Timber at the lake is sparse and protected, which means that there's little shade and no firewood. There's no one to help you if something goes wrong, so don't drive on the lake's crust – should you fall through, it's impossible to extricate your vehicle from the grey slush below.

The Birdsville Track

Assuming there's been no rain, the 520-kilometre **Birdsville Track** is no obstacle to careful drivers during the winter: the biggest problem is getting caught in dried wheel ruts and being pulled off the road. Tearing north from Marree, the distant tips of the Flinders Ranges dip below the horizon behind, leaving you on a bare plain with the road as the only feature. Look for the **MV Tom Brennan**, a vessel donated to the area in 1949 to ferry stock around during floods, but now bearing an absurd resemblance to a large grey bathtub.

Before the halfway house at Mungeranie Gap, a scenic variation is offered by the **Natterannie Sandhills** (150km), once a severe obstacle which has now been graded by digging out the soft sand and replacing it with clay. The **Mungeranie roadhouse** (☎08/8675 8317; ❷) provides the only services on the track (fuel, beds and snacks), but seems to be unattended on Sundays, when you'll have to slog up the hill to the manager's house. In a 4WD you can head west from the roadhouse to **Kalamurina campsite** near Cowarie Homestead (58km) for the thrill of desert fishing on Warburton Creek.

Back on the track, a windmill at **Mirra Mitta bore** (37km from the road-house) draws piping-hot water out of the ground beside long-abandoned buildings; the water smells of tar and drains into cooler pools, providing some-where to camp. By now you're crossing the polished gibber lands of the **Sturt Stony Desert**, and it's worth going for a walk to feel the cold wind and watch the dunes dancing in the heat haze away to the west. The low edge of **Coonchera Dune** to the right of the track (190km from the roadhouse) marks the start of a run along the mudpans between the sandhills; look for desert plants and dingoes. In two more hours you should be pulling up outside the Birdsville pub (see p.576).

The Oodnadatta Track

The road from **Marree to Oodnadatta** is the most interesting of the three famous Outback tracks, mainly because abandoned sidings and fettlers' cottages from the old Ghan provide frequent excuses to get out of the car and explore. Disintegrating sleepers lie by the roadside along parts of the route; otherwise, embankments and rickety bridges are all that remain of the line. As with the roads to Birdsville and Innamincka, with care, any sound vehicle can drive the route in dry winter weather.

About 100km into the journey, near **Curdimurka ruins**, the road runs within sight of **Lake Eyre South**, giving a flavour of its bigger sister if you can't get out there. In alternate Octobers (even-numbered years) the **Curdimurka Outback Ball** (⊛www.curdimurka.3000.it) is organized by the Ghan Railway Preservation Society, which maintains a few buildings, relics and 5km of track. Three thousand souls from everywhere between Alice Springs and Sydney pay $66–$80 a head, donning their finest threads for a night of mayhem under the stars; eagles and crows pick over the debris for a couple of weeks afterwards. Twenty-five kilometres later, a short track south ends below three conical hills – two of which have hot, bubbling **mound springs** at the top, created when water escaping from the artesian basin deposits heaps of mud and minerals. The perfectly symmetrical **Blanche Cup** looks out across a plain – stripped of every shred of greenery by rabbits and cattle – to **Hamilton Hill**, an extinct spring, while further south the **Bubbler** gurgles a verdant stream into the desert where it evaporates after a couple of hundred metres. Important to the Arabana, these springs were used by Sturt in the 1850s and later by the telegraph and rail depots, but tapping the artesian basin for bore water has greatly reduced their flow.

One of these bores is not far up the road at **Coward Springs**, where a cor-roded pipe spilling into ponds beside the track has created an artificial envi-ronment of grasses and palms behind a **campsite**, with toilet blocks and cabins built from sleepers. The ground can be boggy after rain but it's still a tempting stop; a $2 donation is requested for overnight stays. **WILLIAM CREEK**, 75km further, has a resident population of just ten – and is a source of fuel, camping and relaxation in the **hotel** (☎08/8670 7880). Bar, walls and ceiling are heavily decorated with cards and photographs of 4WD disasters, and it also serves as a hangout for stockmen from **Anna Creek Station**, the world's largest cattle property, covering an area the size of Belgium. A solar-powered phone outside faces the battered remains of a Black Arrow **missile** dragged off the Woomera Range, just a few minutes' drive away. Off-road drivers can take a seventy-kilometre track from here to Lake Eyre's western shore; in the other direction is a more passable road to Coober Pedy, though there's almost nothing to see on the way except **Lake Cadibarrawirracanna**, a salt lake with permanent water and birdlife, at the halfway mark.

After William Creek the track gets rougher, crossing sand dunes and then moving into stony country cut by frequent creeks – shallow for most of the year. Hardy mulgas line the banks, their soft yellow blooms giving off a distinctive acrid scent. On the last stretch to Oodnadatta, look out for a sight of the extraordinary red and black crescent petals of **Sturt's desert pea**, the state emblem, growing by the roadside.

Oodnadatta

Unless you stay long enough to meet some locals, you'll probably feel that, like Marree, **OODNADATTA** survived the Ghan's closure with little to show for it. A few logically arranged but untidy streets lacking atmosphere or purpose, Oodnadatta was founded as a railhead in 1890, and mail and baggage for further north had to make do with camel trains from here until the line to Alice Springs was completed in 1928. Now that has gone, the town has become a base for the Aranda community – *utnadata* ("mulga blossom") is the Aranda name for a local waterway – and 4WD crews heading into the Simpson Desert. After rain you'll even need a 4WD for the last slippery kilometre into town, past the racecourse. If your visit coincides with the **race weekend** in May, helicopters will be circling the track on the left, trying to dry it out, and the town will be deserted, so stop at the track, buy a pass and join in. With neat clothes and some sort of tie, you'll even get into the "formal" ball afterwards.

You can camp at the **Pink Roadhouse** (⊕08/8670 7822, ⓦwww .biziworks.com.au/pink), unless the relative luxury of a bed at the *Oodnadatta Hotel* appeals (⊕08/8670 7804; ❸). The roadhouse acts as a store, bank, post office and café (home of the famous Oodnaburger), and sells detailed sketch maps of the area. The hotel holds the key to the **Railway Museum** opposite, where you'll find a strangely timeless photographic record of the town – scenes are hard to date because so little seems to have changed. Stock up with provisions and then check at the **police station** (⊕08/8670 7805) for a report on the roads and next fuel supplies if you plan to head north towards Dalhousie Springs and the Simpson Desert (4WD only), or west to the Stuart Highway at Coober Pedy or Marla.

Dalhousie Hot Springs and desert crossings

Apart from the track out to the Stuart Highway, the area north of Oodnadatta is strictly for 4WDs, with **Dalhousie Hot Springs** in the Witjira National Park a worthwhile destination, or the **Simpson Desert** for the ultimate challenge. The route directly north, initially towards Finke and the Northern Territory, is relatively good as far as **Hamilton Homestead** (110km), though Fogarty's Claypan, around halfway, might present a sticky problem. From Hamilton the direct route east to Dalhousie Springs, shown on some maps, is now closed; take the longer route via **Eringa ruins** (160km) and **Bloods Creek bore** on the edge of **Witjira National Park**.

The Simpson Desert crossing

Crossing the approximately 550km of steep north–south dunes through the **Simpson Desert** between Dalhousie in South Australia and Birdsville in Queensland is the ultimate challenge for any off-roader; in June, 4WD groups are joined by bikes attempting to complete the punishing **Simpson Desert Cycling Classic**. In winter, a steady stream of vehicles moves from west to east (the easier direction since the dunes' eastern slopes are steeper and harder to climb), but there's no help along the way, so don't underestimate the difficulties. Convoys need to include at least one skilled mechanic and, apart from the usual spares, a long-handled shovel and a strong tow-rope. While keeping weight to a minimum, you'll also need more than adequate food and water (six litres a day per person), and of course fuel – around a hundred litres of diesel if you take the shortest route, or two hundred litres of petrol. **Dune-ascent techniques** start with reducing tyre pressures to around 15psi to increase traction; select the gear and build up revs before starting. Don't attempt a gear change on the way up, and beware of oncoming vehicles on blind dune crests. If you don't make it over, slide down and try again; lighter vehicles may end up towing overburdened trucks. If all else fails, detours bypass many dunes.

The most testing, direct route follows the **French Line**, with the **Rig Road** detouring around the worst section but adding substantial distance (and fuel requirements) to the crossing. The enjoyment is mostly in the driving, though there's more than sand to look at: trees and shrubs grow in stabilized areas and at dusk you'll find dune crests patrolled by reptiles, birds, small mammals and insects. Photographers take advantage of clear skies at night to make timed exposures of the stars circling the heavens. **Purni Bore**, 70km from Dalhousie, is another uncapped spout (though this may change with growing concerns over diminished ground water), where birdlife and reeds fringe a 27°C pool; camping facilities here include a shower and toilet. A post battling to stay above shifting sand at **Poeppel Corner** (269km) marks the junction of Queensland, South Australia and the Northern Territory; salt lakes here vary in their water content and sometimes have to be skirted around. After the corner the dunes become higher but further apart, separated by claypans covered in mulga and grassland; you'll have to negotiate some of **Eyre Creek**'s channels too, which can be very muddy. **Big Red**, the last dune, is also the tallest; once over this it's a clear 41-kilometre run to Birdsville.

Note: A large area of the Simpson Desert outside the Witjira National Park and the Simpson Desert Conservation Park is now a Regional Reserve under the control of the NPWS, from whom you should seek advice and a **Desert Parks Pass** before setting out. Contact the NPWS at Port Augusta (☏1800 816 078), Hawker (☏08/8648 4244) or Birdsville (☏07/4656 3272).

From there you can detour 30km north to **Mount Dare Homestead** (fuel, accommodation, food and provisions; ☏08/8670 7835, ⓔbraithwaite10@hotmail.com; ❶–❹). In winter the homestead is busy with groups of 4WDs arriving from or departing for the desert crossing; it's at least 550km to the next fuel stop at Birdsville in Queensland. From the homestead it's a rough and bleak drive to Dalhousie Hot Springs.

The explorer Giles passed through this way in the 1870s, before the artesian basin had been extensively tapped by pastoralists, and described the scene:

> The ground we had been traversing abruptly disappeared, and we found ourselves on the brink of limestone cliffs. . . From the foot of these stretched an almost illimitable expanse of – welcome sight – waving green reeds, with large pools of water at intervals, and dotted with island cones topped with reeds or acacia bushes.

Though reeds and water are less abundant today, Giles' account still rings true. The collection of over one hundred **mound springs** form Arabian-like oases, an impression enhanced by the green circle of date palms clustered around many of the pools. The largest spring, next to the **campsite** (which has showers and toilets), is cool enough to swim in and hot enough to unkink your back. What survives of the vegetation simmers with birdlife: budgerigars, galahs and the eye-catching purple, blue and red fairy wren. As nothing flows into the springs, the presence of **fish** – some, like the Dalhousie hardyhead, unique to the system – has prompted a variety of improbable explanations. One theory is that fish eggs were swept up in dust storms and later fell with rain at Dalhousie, but it's more likely that fish were brought in during an ancient deluge or that the population survives from when the area was an inland sea.

While the main springs area is flat and trampled by years of abuse from campers and cars – please stay on the marked paths here to avoid causing further erosion – trudging out to other groups over the salt and samphire-bush flats armed with a packed lunch and camera gives you an idea of what Giles was describing, and a good overview of the region from the top of well-formed, overgrown mounds. More views can be had from the stony hills to the west, and from **Dalhousie Homestead**, 16km south of the springs along the Pedirka road. The homestead was abandoned after the Ghan line was laid down, and today the stone walls, undermined by rabbit burrows, are gradually falling apart in the extreme climate.

Travel details

Trains

Adelaide to: Alice Springs (Ghan, 2 weekly; 20hr); Melbourne (Ghan, 1 weekly, 10hr 20min; Overlander, 4 weekly; 12hr 30min); Perth (Indian Pacific, 2 weekly; 38hr); Peterborough (Indian Pacific, 2 weekly; 4hr); Port Augusta (Ghan, 2 weekly; 4hr); Sydney (Ghan, 1 weekly, 23hr; Indian Pacific, 2 weekly; 26hr). For all trains contact Great Southern Railway ☎ 13 2147, ⓦ www.gsr .com.au.

Buses

Further details of bus services can be found at ⓦ www.bussa.com.au.
Adelaide to: Alice Springs (2–3 daily; 18hr 30min); Ayers Rock Resort (1 daily; 20hr); Barossa Valley (2–3 daily; 1hr 30min); Broken Hill (1 daily; 7hr); Ceduna (2 daily; 12hr); Clare (1 daily except Mon & Sat; 2hr 15min); Coober Pedy (4–5 daily; 10hr 30min); Goolwa (2–4 daily; 1hr 55min); Loxton (1 daily except Sat; 3hr 30min); Mannum (1 daily except Sat & Sun; 2hr 10min); McLaren Vale (4 daily; 50min); Melbourne (6 daily; 9hr 30min–14hr); Mount Gambier (2–4 daily; 6hr); Perth (1 daily; 34hr); Port Augusta (6–8 daily; 6hr);

Port Lincoln (1–2 daily; 10hr); Renmark (2 daily; 4hr); Sydney (3 daily; 21–24hr); Victor Harbor (4 daily; 1hr 30min); Whyalla (4–6 daily; 5hr); Woomera (1–2 daily; 6hr); Yorke Peninsula (1–2 daily; 3–4hr).
Ceduna to: Adelaide (2 daily; 9hr 30min); Kalgoorlie (6 weekly; 26hr); Penong (6 weekly; 50min); Perth (6 weekly; 47hr); Port Augusta (2 daily; 5hr); Port Pirie (2 daily; 5hr 30min).
Coober Pedy to: Adelaide (at least 1 daily; 11hr); Alice Springs (at least 1 daily; 7hr); Oodnadatta (2 weekly; 5hr); Port Augusta (at least 1 daily; 6hr 10min).
Port Augusta to: Adelaide (at least 3 daily; 4hr 15min); Alice Springs (at least 1 daily; 14hr); Arkaroola (2 weekly; 7hr); Blinman (2 weekly; 3hr 15min); Ceduna (2 daily; 5hr); Coober Pedy (at least 1 daily; 6hr 10min); Hawker (3 weekly; 1hr 30min); Mambray Creek (for Mount Remarkable; several daily; 1hr); Marla (at least 1 daily; 10hr); Marree (2 weekly; 5hr); Melrose (2 weekly; 1hr); Port Lincoln (1–2 daily; 4hr 30min); Quorn (3 weekly; 40min); Roxby Downs (5 weekly; 3hr); Wilmington (2 weekly; 45min); Whyalla (1–2 daily; 50min); Wilpena Pound (3 weekly; 2hr 15min); Woomera (5 weekly; 2hr).
Port Lincoln to: Adelaide (1–2 daily; 10hr); Port

Augusta (1–2 daily; 4hr 30min); Whyalla (1–2 daily; 3hr 30min).

Flights

Adelaide to: Alice Springs (2 daily; 2hr); Ayers Rock Resort (2 daily via Alice; 3hr 45min); Brisbane (5–9 daily; 4hr); Broken Hill (1–2 daily; 1hr 40min); Cairns (1 daily; 4hr); Canberra (3 daily; 3hr 10min); Ceduna (1 daily except Sat; 1hr 30min); Coober Pedy (1 daily; 1hr 30min); Darwin (2 daily; 5hr); Kangaroo Island (8 daily; 30min); Leigh Creek (1 daily Mon–Fri; 2hr), Melbourne (11 daily; 1hr); Perth (3 daily; 5hr); Port Augusta (2–3 daily Mon–Fri; 1hr); Port Lincoln (5–7 daily; 30min); Sydney (9 daily; 2hr 10min); Whyalla (1–3 daily; 45min); Woomera (1 daily Tues, Wed & Thurs; 2hr).

Ceduna to: Adelaide (8 weekly; 1hr 20min).
Coober Pedy to: Adelaide (1 daily; 2hr).
Port Lincoln to: Adelaide (6 daily; 45min).
The **Channel Mail Run** is a weekend in a light aircraft taking in 47 stops between Port Augusta and Boulia in southwestern Queensland – check latest prices at ⓦwww.asa.mtx.net/mailrun.htm, or contact Port Augusta Airport (☏08/8642 3100).

9

Melbourne and around

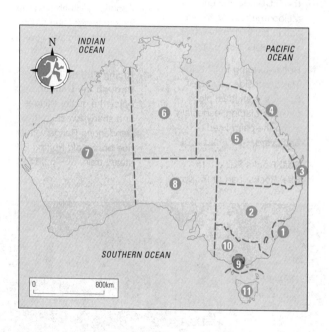

CHAPTER 9

Highlights

* **Chinatown** The low-rise, narrow streets of Melbourne's Chinatown haven't changed much since the nineteenth century, when a goldrush brought every corner of the world to this cosmopolitan city. **See p.906**

* **Aussie Rules match at the MCG** Join the cheering Melbourne crowds for an action-packed footy game at the MCG. **See p.909**

* **Roller-blading in St Kilda** The beachside suburb of St Kilda is an ideal place for roller-blading, especially along the palm-lined boulevard. **See p.921**

* **Seal Rocks** Sail out to Seal Rocks, part of Phillip Island Reserve, to see the largest known colony of Australian fur seals. **See p.950**

* **Yarra Valley** Victoria's answer to South Australia's Barossa Valley boasts pretty scenery and some great wineries. **See p.952**

* **Healesville Sanctuary** Beautifully situated wildlife sanctuary for injured and orphaned animals. **See p.953**

* **Riding Puffing Billy through the Dandenongs** Enjoy the quaint villages and shady forests of the Dandenong Range with a ride on the old Puffing Billy steam train. **See p.954**

9

Melbourne and around

MELBOURNE is Australia's second-largest city, with a population of 3.4 million, around half a million less than Sydney. Rivalry between the two cities – in every sphere from cricket to business – is on an almost childish level. In purely monetary terms, Sydney is now clearly in the ascendancy, having stolen a march on Melbourne as the nation's financial centre. However, as Melburnians never tire of pointing out, they have the incredible good fortune to inhabit what is often described as "one of the world's most liveable cities", and while Melbourne may lack a truly stunning natural setting or in-your-face sights, its subtle charms grow on all who spend time here, making it an undeniably pleasant place to live, and enjoyable to visit, too.

In many ways, Melbourne is the most European of all Australian cities: magnificent landscaped gardens and parks in the English style provide green spaces near the centre, while beneath the skyscrapers of the Central Business District (CBD), an understorey of solid, Victorian-era facades ranged along tree-lined boulevards present the city on a more human scale. The European influence is perhaps most obvious in winter, as trams rattle past warm cafés and bookshops, and promenaders dress stylishly against the chill. Not that Europe has supplied the city's only influences: large-scale immigration since World War II has shaken up the city's formerly self-absorbed, parochial WASP mindset for good. Whole villages have come here from Lebanon, Turkey, Vietnam and all over Europe, most especially from Greece, furnishing the well-worn statistic that Melbourne is the third-largest Greek city behind Athens and Thessaloniki. Not surprisingly, the immigrant blend has transformed the city into a **foodie mecca**, where tucking into a different cuisine each night – or new hybrids of East, West and South – is one of the great treats.

Melbourne's strong claim to being the nation's **cultural capital** is well founded: laced with a healthy dash of counterculture, Melbourne's artistic life flourishes, culminating in the highbrow Melbourne Festival in the last two weeks in October, and its slightly more offbeat (and shoestring) cousin, the Fringe Festival. The city also takes pride in its leading role in Australian literary life, based around the Writers' Festival in August. Throughout the year, there are heavyweight seasons of classical music and theatre, a wacky array of small

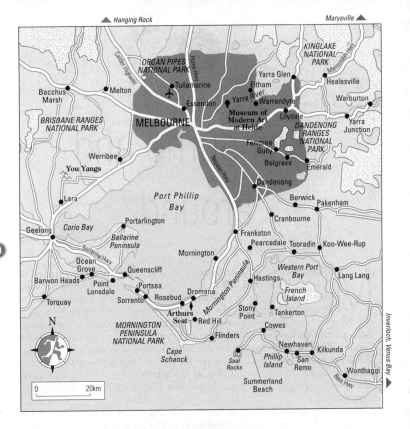

KINGLAKE
NATIONAL
PARK

ORGAN PIPES
NATIONAL PARK

Yarra Glen

Healesville

Eltham

Tullamarine

Warburton

Bacchus
Marsh

Melton

Yarra River

Warrandyte

Essendon

BRISBANE RANGES
NATIONAL PARK

MELBOURNE

Museum of
Modern Art
at Heide

Lilydale

Yarra
Junction

DANDENONG
RANGES
NATIONAL
PARK

Ferntree
Gully

Werribee

Belgrave

Emerald

You Yangs

Dandenong

Lara

Port Phillip
Bay

Berwick

Pakenham

Geelong

Corio Bay

Portarlington

Cranbourne

Frankston

Bellarine
Peninsula

Pearcedale

Tooradin

Koo-Wee-Rup

Bellarine Hwy

Mornington

Ocean
Grove

Queenscliff

Western Port
Bay

Lang Lang

Barwon Heads

Point
Lonsdale

Portsea

Dromana

Hastings

French
Island

Torquay

Sorrento

Rosebud

Mornington Peninsula

Stony
Point

Tankerton

Arthurs
Seat

Red Hill

Cowes

MORNINGTON
PENINSULA
NATIONAL PARK

Flinders

Newhaven

Kilkunda

N

Cape
Schanck

Seal
Rocks

Phillip
Island

San
Remo

Wonthaggi

0   20km

Summerland
Beach

Bass Hwy

9

MELBOURNE AND AROUND

galleries, and enough art-house movies to last a lifetime. **Sport** too, especially
Australian Rules Football, is almost a religion here, while the Melbourne Cup
in November is a public holiday, celebrated with gusto.

Melbourne is an excellent base for day-trips out into the surrounding countryside. Closest to Melbourne are the quaint villages of the eucalypt-covered
Dandenong Ranges, while the scenic **Yarra Valley**, in the northeast, is
Victoria's answer to South Australia's Barossa Valley, and one of many wine-
producing areas around Melbourne. To the south, huge **Port Phillip Bay** is
encircled by the arms of the Bellarine and Mornington peninsulas.
Mornington Peninsula offers more opportunity for wine-tasting, and in
addition to bucolic scenery there are beaches galore, the windswept ones at the
ocean coast popular with surfers, while the placid waters of the bay are good
for swimming and messing about in boats. While **Geelong** and most of the
Bellarine Peninsula are not quite so captivating, Queenscliff near the narrow
entrance to Port Phillip Bay, with its beautiful, refurbished grand hotels from
the Victorian era, is enjoying something of a comeback as a stylish (and expensive) weekend getaway.

Melbourne boasts a reasonably cool **climate** (although January and
February are prone to barbaric hot spells when temperatures can climb into
the forties).

Arrival and information

Melbourne's **Tullamarine Airport** is 22km northwest of the city; the **Skybus** service (every 15min from 7am to 7pm, 1–2 hourly at other times; $14; ☎03/9670 7992) will take you to Spencer Street railway station and bus terminal, where you can board their complimentary minibus service (Mon–Fri 7.30am–4.30pm, Sat 8.30am–4pm, Sun 9am–5.30pm), which drops passengers off at hotels in the city centre and the adjacent suburbs of Carlton, East Melbourne and South Melbourne. Travelling time between the airport and Spencer Street bus terminal is about thirty minutes. A **taxi** from the airport costs around $35 to the city centre, $45 to St Kilda.

Greyhound and McCafferty's **buses** arrive at the **Melbourne Transit Centre** on the north side of the city centre at 58 Franklin St; Firefly and V/Line buses use the **Spencer Street bus terminal** on the west side of the city. **Spencer Street railway station** nearby handles country and interstate **trains**. Some hostels pick up from these terminals, as well as from the Tasmanian ferry terminal. About 4km southwest of the city centre, the Tasmanian **ferry terminal** at Station Pier in Port Melbourne is served by the #109 tram to Collins Street in the CBD.

Information

The **Victoria Visitor Information Centre**, housed in brand-new offices at Federation Square (daily 9am–6pm; ☎03/9658 9658), has tourist pamphlets galore (including self-guided walking tours), multimedia touchscreens and information about public transport and major events. There's also a tour and accommodation telephone-booking service here: **Best of Victoria** (same hours; ☎03/9650 3663), which runs a free **Greeter Service** matching up visitors with local volunteers for half a day, giving them an unparalleled insider's view of the city – book at least three days in advance (☎03/9658 9658, ✉greeter@melbourne.vic.gov.au). **Information Victoria**, at 356 Collins St (Mon–Fri 8.30am–5.30pm; ☎1300 366 356), has free maps and brochures, as well as a notice board of city events and a shop selling the city's largest range of local maps. **Victoria Tourism** (daily 8am–6pm; ☎13 28 42, ⓦwww.visitvictoria.com) is a phone and Internet service providing information on attractions, accommodation and upcoming events.

Volunteers in red uniforms – so-called **Melbourne City Ambassadors** – roam the CBD between Elizabeth, Russell, La Trobe and Flinders streets. They'll try to assist with all kinds of tourist enquiries, and at the very least can point you in the right direction. There's also a **Visitor Information Booth** in the middle of Bourke Street Mall (Mon–Thurs 9am–5pm, Fri 9am–7pm, Sat 10am–4pm, Sun 11am–4pm). Alternative sources of information include the **DSE Information Centre**, 8 Nicholson St, East Melbourne, run by the Department of Sustainability and Environment (Mon–Fri 8.30am–5.30pm; ☎03/9637 8325, ⓦwww.nre.vic.gov.au); and **Parks Victoria** (phone and Internet information service only: ☎13 19 63, ⓦwww.parkweb.vic.gov.au). Both dispense information about national parks and conservation areas in Victoria. Another good resource is the **National Trust** office, Tasma Terrace, 6 Parliament Place (Mon–Fri 9am–5pm; ☎03/9654 4711, ⓦwww.nattrust .com.au), which sells several historical walking-tour guides. *Melway,* available from all newsagents, is the city's best **street directory**. The Friday edition of *The Age* contains an excellent pull-out **listings** section, "EG", detailing the

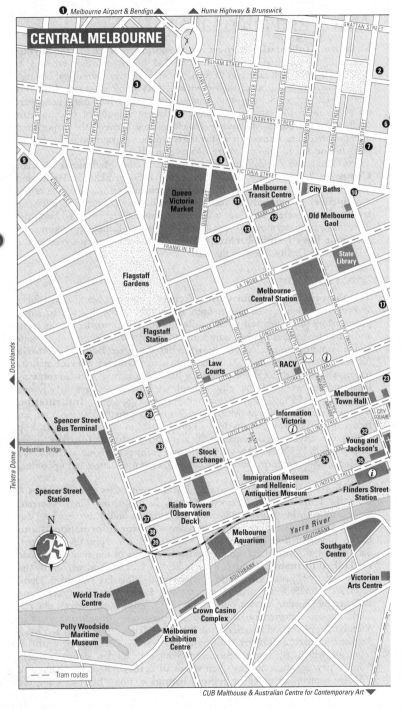

① , Melbourne Airport & Bendigo ▲   ▲ Hume Highway & Brunswick

GRATTAN STREET

PELHAM STREET

②

③

ELIZABETH STREET

LEICESTER STREET

BOUVERIE STREET

SWANSTON STREET

CARDIGAN STREET

LYGON STREET

⑤

QUEENSBERRY STREET

⑥

ERROL STREET

LEVESON STREET

CHETWYND STREET

HOWARD STREET

CAPEL STREET

PEEL STREET

⑦

⑧

VICTORIA STREET

⑨

KING STREET

Queen
Victoria
Market

QUEEN STREET

Melbourne
Transit Centre

City Baths

⑩

⑪

FRANKLIN STREET

Old Melbourne
Gaol

⑫

⑬

⑭

State
Library

FRANKLIN ST

LA TROBE STREET

Flagstaff
Gardens

Melbourne
Central Station

SWANSTON STREET WALK

⑰

LITTLE LONSDALE STREET

QUEEN STREET

Flagstaff
Station

LONSDALE STREET

ELIZABETH STREET

HARDWARE STREET

WILLIAM STREET

LITTLE BOURKE STREET

Law
Courts

RACV

(i)

BOURKE STREET MALL

CAUSEWAY

ROYAL ARCADE

㉓

⑳

Docklands ◀

㉔

KING STREET

Melbourne
Town Hall

CITY
SQUARE

Spencer Street
Bus Terminal

SPENCER STREET

㉙

Information
Victoria

(i)

LITTLE COLLINS STREET

BANK PL

COLLINS STREET

Young and
Jackson's

㉜

Telstra Dome ◀

Pedestrian Bridge

㉝

Stock
Exchange

㉞

㉟

Spencer Street
Station

㊱

㊲

Immigration Museum
and Hellenic
Antiquities Museum

FLINDERS STREET

(i)

N

Rialto Towers
(Observation
Deck)

㊳

㊴

Melbourne
Aquarium

Flinders Street
Station

Yarra River

SOUTHBANK

Southgate
Centre

World Trade
Centre

SOUTHBANK

Victorian
Arts Centre

Polly Woodside
Maritime
Museum

Crown Casino
Complex

Melbourne
Exhibition
Centre

– – Tram routes

CUB Malthouse & Australian Centre for Contemporary Art ▼

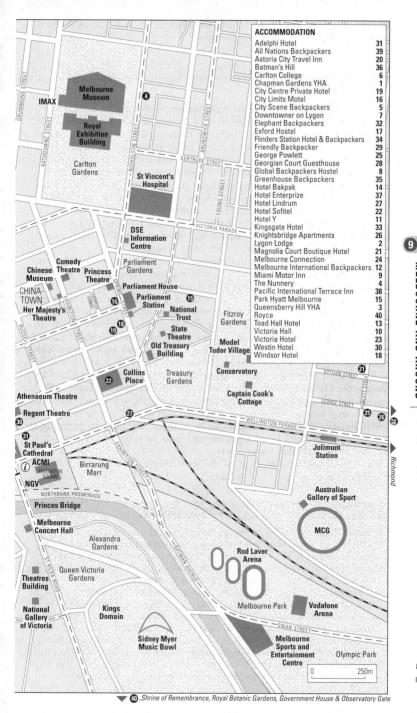

ACCOMMODATION

Adelphi Hotel	31
All Nations Backpackers	39
Astoria City Travel Inn	20
Batman's Hill	36
Carlton College	6
Chapman Gardens YHA	1
City Centre Private Hotel	19
City Limits Motel	16
City Scene Backpackers	5
Downtowner on Lygon	7
Elephant Backpackers	32
Exford Hostel	17
Flinders Station Hotel & Backpackers	34
Friendly Backpacker	29
George Powlett	25
Georgian Court Guesthouse	28
Global Backpackers Hostel	8
Greenhouse Backpackers	35
Hotel Bakpak	14
Hotel Enterprize	37
Hotel Lindrum	27
Hotel Sofitel	22
Hotel Y	11
Kingsgate Hotel	33
Knightsbridge Apartments	26
Lygon Lodge	2
Magnolia Court Boutique Hotel	21
Melbourne Connection	24
Melbourne International Backpackers	12
Miami Motor Inn	9
The Nunnery	4
Pacific International Terrace Inn	38
Park Hyatt Melbourne	15
Queensberry Hill YHA	3
Royce	40
Toad Hall Hotel	13
Victoria Hall	10
Victoria Hotel	23
Westin Hotel	30
Windsor Hotel	18

9

MELBOURNE AND AROUND

895

Shrine of Remembrance, Royal Botanic Gardens, Government House & Observatory Gate week's entertainment, as well as fairs and markets, art and craft exhibitions, sport, and other events in and around town.

City transport

Melbourne has an efficient public transport system of trams, trains and buses, called **The Met**. Unless you're going on a day-trip to the outer suburbs, you can get anywhere you need to, including St Kilda and Williamstown, on a **zone 1 ticket** ($2.70); this is valid for two hours (or all evening if bought after 7pm) and can be used for multiple trips on trams, buses and trains within zone 1. Alternatively, a **short-trip ticket** ($1.80) is valid for a single trip on buses and trams within two sections of any particular transport line (sections are clearly marked on the timetable at stops, or ask the driver). A **day-ticket** ($5.20 for zone 1; $8.50 for zones 1 and 2; $11.40 for zones 1–3) is better value if you're making a few trips in zone 1, or if you are planning a trip to the outer suburbs. For longer stays, a **weekly ticket** ($22.90 for zone 1; $38.80 for zones 1 and 2; $47.40 for zones 1–3) is an even better bargain.

You'll need to **validate** your ticket by machine every time you board a new vehicle. Short-trip, two-hour and day-tickets are available from **vending machines** on board trams and at train stations. Those on trams accept coins only, but change is given. You can't buy tickets from the tram driver. The reverse applies on buses: there are no vending machines, so buy your ticket from the driver (exact change preferred). Major train stations (including Flinders St, Spencer St, Flagstaff, Melbourne Central and Parliament, South Yarra and North Melbourne) have staffed ticket offices; other stations are equipped with coins-only vending machines. You can also buy Met Tickets and get travel advice at the Visitor Information Centre at Federation Square, the City Met Shop at the Melbourne Town Hall on the corner of Swanston and Little Collins streets, and at other shops, including most newsagents, a few milk bars and pharmacies – look for the flag with the green Met logo.

Met services operate Monday to Saturday from 5am until midnight, and Sunday from 8am until 11pm, supplemented in the early hours of Saturday and Sunday by **NightRider buses** (every 60min 12.30–4.30am; $6), which head from the City Square (in front of the new *Westin Hotel* – see p.899) on Swanston Street to the outer suburbs of Frankston, Dandenong, Belgrave,

---

Melbourne's vintage trams

Some of Melbourne's trams are vintage wooden vehicles dating back as far as the 1930s (though none is quite as old as the system, which dates from 1885). Vintage **City Circle trams** (free) run in a loop along Flinders Street, Spring Street, Nicholson Street, La Trobe Street and Spencer Street (daily every 10min 10am–6pm, Nov–March Thurs–Sat until 9pm). The **Colonial Tramcar Restaurant** (☎03/9696 4000, ⓦ www.tramrestaurant.com.au) is a converted 1927 tram offering traditional silver- and white-linen restaurant service as you trundle around Melbourne. The service starts at Normanby Rd near the Crown Casino, South Melbourne; the restaurant (non-smoking) offers a three-course early dinner (daily 5.45–7.15pm; $66) and a five-course dinner ($104.50 Fri & Sat, $93.50 Mon–Thurs & Sun), plus a four-course lunch (Sun 1–3pm and other days subject to demand; $71.50). All drinks are included. You'll need to reserve at least two to three weeks ahead, or up to three or four months in advance for Friday and Saturday evenings.

Lilydale, Eltham, Epping, Craigieburn, St Albans, Werribee and Melton ($8.20), more or less in the same direction as the suburban train routes. Each bus has an onboard mobile phone, on which the driver can book a taxi to meet you at a bus stop (free call), or you can call a friend ($1) to meet you. For further information, call the **Met Transport Information Centre** (daily 6am–10pm; ☎13 16 38). For a range of public transport information including timetables and disability services, visit Ⓦwww.victrip.com.au.

Trams

Melbourne's **trams** give the city a distinctive character and provide a pleasant, environmentally friendly way of getting around: the **City Circle** (see box opposite) is particularly convenient, and free. Trams run down the centre of the road, and stops are signposted (the "Central Melbourne" map on pp.894–895 shows the main routes in the centre); they often have central islands where you can wait, but if not, take care crossing the road. It can be uncomfortable waiting in the middle of a busy road, especially for a woman alone at night – you may feel less vulnerable waiting on the footpath, where there's often a shelter anyway. Some trams can be boarded only at the front; others also have access via middle and rear doors.

Trains

Trains are the fastest way to reach distant suburbs. An underground loop system feeding into seventeen suburban lines connects the city centre's five train **stations**: **Spencer Street**, which also serves as the station for interstate and country trains; **Flagstaff**, on the corner of La Trobe and William streets; **Melbourne Central**, on the corner of Swanston and La Trobe streets; **Parliament**, on Spring Street; and **Flinders Street**, the main suburban station. Bikes can be carried free, except during peak periods (Mon–Fri 7–9.30am & 4–6pm), when an extra adult concession fee has to be paid. Surfboards can also be brought on board, for which an extra adult concession fee is payable.

Buses

Regular **buses** often run on the same routes as trams, as well as filling gaps where no train or tram lines run. In general, they are the least useful mode of public transport for visitors, with the exception of the city's double-decker **explorer buses**. These are operated by four different companies, all working along the same lines: they start from Swanston Street (usually outside the Melbourne Town Hall) and do a circuit of the city and adjacent suburbs, stopping at, or near, major attractions; passengers buy a ticket on board which allows them to get on and off the bus as often as they want within 24 hours. The **Melbourne Explorer,** a red double-decker operated by London Transport Bus Tours (daily every 30min 10am–4pm; $32; ☎03/9650 7000), runs past the Rialto Observation Deck and the Polly Woodside Maritime Museum to the Arts Centre south of the CBD, then back up the eastern side of the city to Lygon Street, the Zoo, Queen Victoria Market and Melbourne Central. Confusingly, **Gray Line** (daily every 30min 10am–4pm; $32; ☎1300 858 687, Ⓦwww.grayline.com) operates a white double-decker bus with the same name and covering more or less the same route, though it takes in the sports arenas precinct (Melbourne Park, Vodafone Arena, MCG) but leaves out the zoo. **Melbourne On The Move** (daily every 30min 9.45am–3pm; $32; ☎1300 558 686, Ⓦwww.melbourneonthemove.com.au) covers the city and East Melbourne; while the brightly painted **Melbourne Tour** double-decker buses, operated by City Sightseeing (☏0500 505 012, ⓦwww.citysightseeing.com.au), depart from City Square and offer two separate circuits. The so-called "Grand Tour" takes in Melbourne city centre, East Melbourne and Carlton (every 30min 9.30am–1pm, then hourly until 5pm); the "South Melbourne Tour" takes in Albert Park Lake, St Kilda, Beaconsfield Parade, Port Melbourne, Crown Casino and the Shrine of Remembrance (at least three departures daily). The 24-hour ticket ($30) is valid for both circuits.

Accommodation

When looking for somewhere to stay in Melbourne, the most obvious areas to head for are the **city centre** (and the adjoining suburbs of **North Melbourne**, **Carlton**, **Fitzroy**, **East Melbourne and Richmond**) and down by the sea around **St Kilda**. Some of the cheap accommodation areas on the fringes of the city centre are fairly dead at night, though they're within easy reach of all the action. St Kilda is very lively, if a bit rough around the edges, with a few hostels and an abundance of inexpensive motels and apartments. South of the CBD, **South Melbourne**, **Albert Park**, **South Yarra and Windsor** (see the "Melbourne Suburbs" map on p.917) offer a good compromise, handy for both the city centre and the beach, and with lots of good eating options.

The most exclusive **hotels** are downtown, particularly around Collins Street and the leisure precincts of Southgate and the Crown Casino, while there's a collection of large and recently revamped hotels around Spencer Street station. Melbourne has plenty of **backpacker accommodation**, ranging from fairly basic, even scruffy places to salubrious Victorian-era mansions with dorms attached. During winter, most hostel beds cost around $20, rising to around $24 in summer (the prices given in the listings below are for summer). Most hostels have separate dorms for males and females on request. Standard facilities include a kitchen, TV room, laundry, luggage storage and Internet access.

Campsite cabins and vans are an alternative worth considering for those with their own transport (see p.904). You can book last-minute **discounted accommodation** in the city at ⓦwww.wotif.com. Note that Melbourne accommodation is packed out during the Grand Prix (see p.921).

Hotels and motels

Adelphi Hotel 187 Flinders Lane ☎03/9650 7555, ⊛www.adelphi.com.au. Stylish hotel with a striking exterior and a sparse, ultramodern interior design that extends to the large guest rooms, all topped with a huge pool on the roof. ❼

Astoria City Travel Inn 288 Spencer St ☎03/9670 6801, ⊛www.astoriainternational .com. Pleasant motel three blocks north of Spencer Street station with spacious and bright units and an undercover car park; amenities include a saltwater pool and laundry. ❹

Batman's Hill 66 Spencer St ☎03/9614 6344 or 1800 335 308, ⊛www.batmanshill.com. An elegant Edwardian exterior belies a functional and modern interior. The wide range of facilities includes bars, a restaurant and 24hr room service, and it's handy for Spencer Street station and the Casino Entertainment Complex just south of the river. ❺–❻

City Limits Motel 20 Little Bourke St ☎03/9662 2544 or 1800 808 651, ⊛www.citylimits.com.au. Motel-style units with en suite and the usual mod-cons on a quiet street just around the corner from Parliament station. Rates include continental breakfast. ❺

Hotel Enterprize 44 Spencer St ☎03/9629 6991 or 1800 033 451, ⓔentrpriz@ozemail.com.au. Solid hotel in central location opposite Spencer Street station. Good, no-frills singles and doubles (en suites available). Room service and undercover parking ($5 per day) available. ❹

Kingsgate Hotel 131 King St ☎03/9629 4171 or 1300 734 171, ⊛www.kingsgatehotel.com.au. Huge, renovated old private hotel. En-suite rooms with colour TV, heating, air-con and telephone are good value; there are also inexpensive no-frills budget rooms with shared facilities and a few rooms for small groups or families (up to four beds). Facilities include a laundry, Internet access, a pleasant TV lounge and a bar and café (but no kitchen). Cheap breakfast available. ❸–❹

Hotel Lindrum 26 Flinders St ☎03/9668 1111, ⊛www.hotellindrum.com.au. Intimate five-storey boutique hotel named after legendary Australian billiards player Walter Lindrum, and featuring a billiard table and lots of Lindrum memorabilia. Rooms come complete with huge beds, fax, CD player and complimentary in-house movies. ❽

Miami Motor Inn 13 Hawke St, off the north end of King St ☎03/9329 8499 or 1800 132 333, ⊛www.themiami.com.au. Renovated en-suite rooms with TV, wardrobe and ceiling fan, as well as simple, clean, standard rooms with shared facilities – good-value rates include a cooked breakfast. Facilities include a TV lounge, pool table, laundry and free off-street parking, but no kitchen. ❸

Pacific International Terrace Inn 16 Spencer St ☎03/9621 3333 or 1800 816 168, ⊛www .pacifichotels.com.au. Popular with business people, this very pleasant, well-maintained and good-value hotel has en-suite rooms plus bar, restaurant and Internet access. Breakfast included. ❺

Park Hyatt Melbourne 1 Parliament Square, off Parliament Place ☎03/9224 1234, ⊛www .melbourne.hyatt.com. This opulent bunker for business travellers and Melbourne's junior moguls has deluxe rooms and suites with lush trimmings, such as open fireplaces and spa baths with TV. The service, naturally, is first class. ❼

Royce Hotel 379 St Kilda Rd ☎03/9677 9900, ⓔreservations@roycehotels.com.au. This luxury boutique establishment is usefully positioned within walking distance of the CBD, Royal Botanic Gardens, Shrine of Remembrance and Arts Centre. There's a variety of room types available, from mezzanines with a ground-level lounge to deluxe spa rooms and rooms with balconies. All have the usual trimmings, plus there are dataport connections and ISDN. ❼

Hotel Sofitel 25 Collins St ☎03/9653 0000, ⊛www.sofitelmelbourne.com.au. I.M. Pei-designed hotel, set on the top floors of a fifty-storey building, with marvellous views across Melbourne and surrounds, gloriously comfortable rooms and a good spread of cafés and restaurants, including the airy and reasonably cheap *Cafe La* (see p.924) and *Le Restaurant* (see p.925), a formal dining place with sensational vistas. ❼

Victoria Hotel 215 Little Collins St ☎03/9653 0441 or 1800 331 147, ⊛www.victoriahotel .com.au. Huge old refurbished hotel in an unbeatable central location, with its own café and bar; all rooms – with or without their own bathrooms – have telephones, heating, tea- and coffee-making facilities. Undercover parking available ($9.50 per day). ❹–❻

Westin Hotel 205 Collins St ☎03/9635 2222, ⊛www.westin.com.au. Plonked squarely on the City Square, the monstrously huge and hideous exterior of this new 260-room hotel hides surprisingly glamorous interiors and elegantly understated rooms. ❼

Windsor Hotel 103 Spring St ☎03/9633 6000 or 1800 033 100, ⊛www.thewindsor.com.au. This luxurious, landmark Victorian-era hotel has 180 spacious, lavishly decorated rooms and suites, though even the cheapest will cost you $500. ❼

Hostels and budget accommodation

All Nations Backpackers 2 Spencer St, at the corner of Flinders St ☎1800 222 238, ⓦwww .nomadsworld.com. Big, rambling hostel renovated to a rather mediocre standard, though an in-house employment agency, bar and lots of freebies (including free tea and coffee) seem to keep the guests happy. There's 24hr reception and good security. dorms (4–12 beds) $15–22, rooms ❷

Hotel Bakpak 167 Franklin St ☎03/9329 7525 or 1800 645 200, ⓦwww.bakpakgroup.com. Around six hundred beds in a converted former school building brightened up with colour co-ordinated paintwork, carpets and polished timber floors. Facilities include an in-house employment agency, travel shop, Internet access, café, bar, a small in-house cinema with free screenings and a large rooftop terrace with great views of the city. All dorms (4–12 beds) have fans and lockers; separate men and women's dorms available on request. There are also some spartan doubles. Rates include light breakfast. Dorms $22–25, rooms ❸

City Centre Private Hotel 22 Little Collins St ☎03/9654 5401, ⓕ9650 7256. Good position on a quiet street 100m from Parliament station. Inexpensive doubles, singles and a few dorms (four beds, usually separate for males/females), all sharing bathrooms. Most rooms have fridges; other facilities include heating, basic kitchens, a TV lounge, laundry and car parking. Dorms $21, rooms ❷–❸

Elephant Backpacker 250 Flinders St ☎03/9564 2616 or 1800 002 616, ⓦwww.elephant backpackers.citysearch.com.au. Very clean, well-equipped, secure and inexpensive hostel in converted school buildings in an unbeatable central location. Singles and doubles are especially good value; the only drawback is a lack of complete privacy, as the walls between the rooms don't reach the ceiling. Dorms $17–20, rooms ❷

Exford Hotel 199 Russell St ☎03/9663 2697, ⓦwww.exfordhotel.com.au. Secure, clean and good-value hostel set in an extremely central position above a refurbished pub, with friendly and helpful staff and the usual amenities, plus a tiny sundeck with BBQ. Accommodation is in two- to four-bed dorms, twins and doubles. Dorms $20–25, rooms ❸

Flinders Station Hotel & Backpackers 35 Elizabeth St ☎03/9620 5100, ⓦwww .flindersbackpackers.com.au. Reasonably well-organized hostel, centrally located a few hundred metres from Flinders Street station. Basic twins and doubles, and two en-suite doubles for wheelchair users. Dorms have lockers and are mainly four-bed, though a few have up to ten beds. Dorms $20–22, rooms ❸

Friendly Backpacker 197 King St ☎03/9670 1111 or 1800 671 115, ⓔfriendlybackpacker @optusnet.com.au. This clean and secure hostel in a refurbished office building has bright rooms with air-con and heating. Each floor has a cosy sitting area with TV, and there's a good kitchen and common room in the basement. Dorms (mainly 4-bed) $24.

Greenhouse Backpackers 228 Flinders Lane ☎03/9639 6400, ⓔfriendlybpacker @optusnet.com.au. Clean, friendly and well-equipped place in a superb sixth-floor location amidst the characterful alleys and laneways of Melbourne's CBD. Sleeping is in dorms, singles and doubles, and there's a big kitchen and lounge and a nice rooftop garden with a BBQ; staff can assist with finding work. Dorms (4–8 beds) $26, rooms ❸

Melbourne Connection Travellers Hostel 205 King St ☎03/9642 4464, ⓦwww.melbourne connection.com. Convenient location close to Spencer Street station and Victoria Market. Rooms and dorms (3–12 beds) are clean; facilities include laundry, kitchen and lounge with satellite TV and Internet access. Dorms $22–27, rooms ❸

Melbourne International Backpackers 450 Elizabeth St ☎03/9662 4066, ⓔmelbbackpackers @hotkey.net.au. Located just a few metres away from the Franklin Street bus terminal, this is yet another hostel set in refurbished former offices. It's clean and secure, with rooms and dorms (mainly 4-bed), big kitchen and common room, Internet access. Reception 24hr. Dorms $18–20, rooms ❷

Toad Hall Hotel 441 Elizabeth St ☎03/9600 9010, ⓦwww.toadhall-hotel.com.au. Excellent choice, close to Melbourne Transit Centre: friendly, cosy, secure and clean, with a good kitchen, TV room, and a lovely, shaded courtyard out the back. Dorms $25, rooms ❸

Victoria Hall 380 Russell St ☎03/9662 3888, ⓦwww.victoriahall.com.au. Centrally located international student accommodation, but accepts budget travellers from the end of November until the end of February. Great-value twins and singles (all with wardrobes, desks and phone) plus dorms(2–4 beds). Dorms $25–30, rooms ❷

Hotel Y 489 Elizabeth St ☎03/9329 5188 (or call central YWCA reservations on ☎1800 249 124), ⓦwww.ywca.net. Close to Melbourne Transit Centre and Victoria Market, with simple en-suite standard rooms, and deluxe rooms with fridge, telephone, air-con and colour TV. The few dorms are overpriced. Limited kitchen facilities in a bright, spacious common room; laundry available. Dorms $28, rooms ❹

North Melbourne, Carlton and Fitzroy

Carlton College 101 Drummond St, Carlton ☎03/9664 0664 or 1800 066 551, ⓦwww .carltoncollege.com.au. Ideally located near the Lygon St cafés and shops, this student hostel also accomodates backpackers, turning into a fullblown backpackers from mid-December to the end of February. The small dorms, singles, twins and doubles are simple, but excellent value; especially at weekly rates. Dorms $16–20, rooms ❷–❸

Chapman Gardens YHA 76 Chapman St, North Melbourne ☎03/9328 3595, ⓦwww.yha.com.au. More intimate than its sister hostel, the *Queensberry Hill YHA*, but further away from the city centre (3km) – take tram #50, #57 or #59 north from Elizabeth St. Mainly twins, a few singles, doubles and dorms (4 beds); car parking and free use of bicycles. Skybus drops off and picks up 50m from here. Dorms $22, rooms ❷

City Scene Backpackers 361 Queensberry St ☎03/9348 9525, ⓦwww.cityscene.com.au. Small friendly hostel next to a pub; the rooms and dorms (4 beds) come with heating and air-con; rates include breakfast. Ring for airport pick-up. Dorms $17–19, rooms ❷

Downtowner on Lygon 66 Lygon St, Carlton ☎03/9663 5555 or 1800 800 130, ⓦwww.down towner.com.au. Attractively refurbished rooms with all mod cons (some with spa) in the heart of Carlton. Undercover parking. ❺–❻

Global Backpackers Hostel 238 Victoria St, North Melbourne ☎03/9328 3728 or 1800 700 478, ⓔglobalhostel@bigpond.com. Set in a renovated Art Deco hotel in an unbeatable location opposite Queen Victoria Market, this small, simple but pleasant hostel has dorms (mainly 4-bed), rooms, a TV lounge, big kitchen, Internet access and a tiny courtyard. Dorms $19, rooms ❷–❸

Lygon Lodge 220 Lygon St, Carlton ☎03/9663 6633, ⓕ9663 7297. Good motel in central Carlton with attractive rooms, some with small kitchenette. Undercover car parking. ❺

The Nunnery 116 Nicholson St, Fitzroy ☎03/9419 8637 or 1800 032 635, ⓕ9417 7736; take #96 tram from Bourke St. The hostel section here has rather crammed dorms (4–12 beds), but the atmosphere is busy and friendly; there's also a big, cosy TV lounge, a kitchen and Internet access. The much more spacious guesthouse section next door has private rooms with shared facilities, plus a kitchen and lounge. There's a great pub just two doors away, and the Brunswick Street cafés are close to hand. Breakfast included. Dorms $23–27, hostel rooms ❸, guesthouse rooms ❹

Queensberry Hill YHA 78 Howard St, off Victoria St ☎03/9329 8599, ⓦwww.yha.com.au. An easy ten-minute walk from Melbourne Transit Centre, this huge ultramodern hostel – really more like a smart hotel – has family rooms, double rooms and dorms (4–8 beds), kitchen, Internet lounge, free bicycles and car parking, plus a licensed cafeteria, currency exchage and an in-house travel agent. Skybus drops off and picks up here every half-hour. Dorms $23, rooms ❸–❹

East Melbourne

The George Powlett Powlett St, cnr George St ☎03/9419 9488 or 1800 689 948, ⓦwww.georgepowlett.com.au. Motel-style units off two central courtyards in a central location. All mod cons, plus parking. ❹

Georgian Court Guesthouse 21–25 George St ☎03/9419 6353, ⓕ9416 0895. Standard rooms with shared facilities, and en-suite rooms equipped with colour TV, fridge and radio; all are bright, tastefully furnished and serviced daily. Rates include light breakfast. Quiet yet very central location. ❺–❻

Knightsbridge Apartments 101 George St ☎03/9419 1333, ⓦwww.knightsbridgeapart ments.com.au. Bright, serviced self-catering studio apartments 1km from the centre, on a quiet street running off the east side of Fitzroy Gardens. Laundry and off-street parking. Excellent value. ❺–❻

Magnolia Court Boutique Hotel 101 Powlett St ☎03/9419 4222, ⓦwww.magnolia-court.com.au. Elegant hotel in a quiet street, but within walking distance of Fitzroy Gardens, the CBD, MCG and the Rod Laver Arena in Melbourne Park. Very tastefully furnished rooms with all facilities in two older, lovingly restored buildings and in a motel section. Breakfast available. ❺–❻

Richmond

Boutique Backpackers 337 Highett St, ☎03/9428 7821 or 0410 320 730. More of a family home than a hostel, this very small and pleasant place, set in a modern townhouse, is mainly used by people on a working holiday visa; weekly bookings are therefore preferred. Centrally located near Bridge Rd, a few tram stops (or a 20min walk) from the MCG and Melbourne Park. Owners can help finding work. Dorms $18, or $100 per week, rooms ❸

Central Accommodation 21 Bromham Place, Richmond ☏ 03/9427 9826, ⓦ www .centralaccommodation.net. Another homely atmosphere, with dorms (4-bed) and doubles in a super-central location close to the lively pubs and shops of Bridge Rd, and within walking distance (15min) of the MCG and Melbourne Park. Owners have good employment contacts in the area. Take tram #75 or #48 from Spencer St or Flinders St to stop no. 18. Dorms $99 per week (weekly bookings only).

Hillside Court Womens Accommodation 155–159 Hoddle St ☏ 03/9428 6698, ⓕ 9428 7698. Extremely good-value rooms in a rambling old Victorian mansion; guests are mainly working or studying in Melbourne, so weekly bookings are preferred. There's a kitchen and lounge, plus a

small pool in the back yard. Near West Richmond station and Bridge Rd. Dorms $20, or $120 per week, rooms ❶

Richmond Hill Hotel 353 Church St (between Bridge Rd and Swan St) ☏ 03/9428 6501 or 1800 801 618, ⓦ www.richmondhillhotel.com.au. Set in a stately Victorian mansion in a pretty garden, with spacious and cosy dining and sitting rooms. The guesthouse section offers B&B rooms with en-suite or shared facilities; the budget section small, very clean dorms and good-value singles and twins (bunks), all with shared facilities and a kitchen. Tram #75 or #48 from Spencer St or Flinders St. Dorms $22–30, budget rooms ❷–❸, guesthouse rooms ❹–❺

Wild Bunyip 153 Hoddle St ☏ 03/8430 2978. Recently and thoroughly renovated place, with well-equipped rooms and dorms (maximum 4 beds). It's just around the corner from West Richmond station, within walking distance of Bridge Rd. Dorms $16, rooms ❷

South Melbourne, Albert Park , South Yarra and Windsor

Beach House Hotel 97 Beaconsfield Parade, Albert Park ☏ 03/9690 4642, ⓔ beach.house@alhgroup.com.au. Pub accommo-dation in renovated, bright and clean rooms. Front rooms have great views over the beach and Port Phillip Bay, but get a bit of traffic noise. Shared facilities. Next to a tram stop (take #1 or #2 from Swanston St to South Melbourne Beach) and very close to the Tasmania ferry terminal. ❸–❹

Chapel Street Backpackers 22 Chapel St, Windsor ☏ 03/9533 6855 or 1800 613 333, ⓦ www.csbackpackers.com.au. Small and very clean non-smoking hostel at the southern, quieter end of Chapel St. Some of the dorms (4–6 beds) and doubles are en suite, and all rates include continental breakfast. Opposite Windsor station (Sandringham line). Dorms $19–25, rooms ❸

The Como 630 Chapel St, South Yarra ☏ 03/9824 0400, ⓦ www.hotelcomo.com. Very upmarket accommodation with spacious suites in unusually bold colours and with all the amenities you'd expect in a five-star hotel, including indoor heated pool, sauna, spa, gym, valet parking, restaurant and a jazz bar. ❼

Gunn Island Brew Bar 102 Canterbury Rd, cnr Armstrong St, Middle Park ☏ 03/9690 1882, ⓕ 9645 8928. Dorms and simple but pleasant rooms with shared facilities above a refurbished pub. Take tram #96 from Spencer St. Close to the Aquatic Centre, beach and lots of restaurants and delis. Dorms $19, rooms ❷–❸

The Hatton Hotel 65 Park St, South Yarra ☏ 03/9868 4800, ⓦ www.hatton .com.au. Modern boutique hotel with 32 rooms, all immaculately appointed. ❽

Lords Lodge Backpackers 204 Punt Rd, cnr Greville St, South Yarra ☏ 03/9510 5658, ⓦ www.lordslodge.com. Small, family-run hostel in an old mansion, centrally positioned in fashionable South Yarra, with dorms (4–8 beds) and rooms, all with fridge and lockers. Owners have good local work contacts. Take tram #3, #5, #6 or #16 from Swanston St and get off at stop no. 26, or take the Sandringham line train to Prahran. Pick-up from airport and bus terminals on request. Dorms $18–22, rooms ❷–❸

Nomads Hotel Claremont South Yarra 189 Toorak Rd, South Yarra ☏ 03/9826 8000 or 9826 8222, ⓦ www.hotelclaremont.com. B&B rooms with shared facilities; modestly priced, given the location in the heartland of chic South Yarra. ❸

Nomads Market Inn 115 Cecil St, South Melbourne ☏ 03/9690 2220 or 1800 689 948, ⓕ 9690 2544. Small hostel with lots of atmos-phere, above a pub opposite South Melbourne Market. Pick-up from bus terminals in the city, and lots of freebies, including BBQs on Sunday, bicy-cles, and a welcome beer. Breakfast included. Dorms (4–6 beds) $20–24, rooms ❸

Pint on Punt 42 Punt Rd, Windsor ☏ 03/9510 4273 or 1800 835 000, ⓦ www.pintonpunt.com.au. Hostel set above a

British-style pub at the southern end of Windsor, within walking distance of Chapel St cafés and St Kilda nightlife, with dorms (4–6 beds), singles, twins and doubles. There's a common room with cable TV and cheap pub meals are available; rates include a continental breakfast. Take the train to Windsor (Sandringham line) or tram #3, #5, #16, #64 or #67 from Swanston St to St Kilda Junction. Dorms $25, rooms ❸

Victoria Hotel 123 Beaconsfield Parade, South Melbourne ☎03/9690 3666, ℻9699 9570. Grand hotel dating from 1888: choose between stylish en-suite doubles and cheaper rooms with shared facilities; the bright front rooms have good views of the waterfront, but some traffic noise. Great house music from some of Melbourne's best DJs is played every Sunday from 2pm till late downstairs. ❹–❼

West End Hotel 76 Toorak Rd West, South Yarra ☎03/9866 3135. An old-fashioned B&B overlooking a shady park and close to the heart of exclusive South Yarra, with doubles and singles with shared facilities. Take tram #8, or the train to South Yarra. ❹–❺

St Kilda

Coffee Palace 24 Grey St ☎03/9534 5283 or 1800 654 098, ⓦwww.coffeepalace.com.au. Very busy hostel in an old, rambling building. Some of the dorms are women-only, and there are plenty of basic twins and doubles, some en suite. There's an in-house travel agent and job agency; rates include breakfast. Dorms $18–23, rooms ❷

Easystay Bayside 63 Fitzroy St ☎03/9525 3833 or 1300 301 730, ⓦwww.easystay.com.au.Good, secure budget motel in the thick of the action and within a ten-minute walk of the beach. If you want quiet, book one of the units facing the car park out the back (which is locked at night). ❹

Enfield House 2 Enfield St ☎03/9534 8159 or 1800 302 121, ⓦwww.bakpakgroup.com. Set in a stately, Victorian-era mansion and surrounding buildings, with a bewildering number of very basic dorms and rooms out the back. There's a smallish central kitchen, a courtyard, notice boards, employment contacts and lots of activities,

including cheap tours to the Great Ocean Road, Phillip Island and Ramsay Street – the latter is very popular with British backpackers. Prearranged pick-up from the bus terminals and airport. Rates include breakfast. Dorms $21–24, rooms ❷–❸

Jacksons Manor Travellers Hostel 53 Jackson St ☎03/9534 1877, ⓔjacksonsmanor @optusnet.com. Pleasant hostel in a renovated old mansion with dorms and doubles; facilities include off-street parking. Dorms $20–22, rooms ❸

Olembia 96 Barkly St ☎03/9537 1412, ⓦwww.olembia.com.au. Very comfortable budget guesthouse in a fine old building with open fireplaces, a cosy lounge and dining room and a well-equipped kitchen. All the rooms are very appealing, and the singles are particularly good value. Off-street parking available. Dorms $24, rooms ❸

The Prince 2 Acland St ☎03/9536 1111, ⓦwww.theprince.com.au. This boutique hotel is one of Melbourne's most elegant places to lay your head. The minimalistic bedrooms come with TVs

---

Gay and lesbian accommodation

For further accommodation possibilities other than those listed below, ring **Gay Share** (☎03/9691 2290), which arranges house shares for gays and lesbians, or visit ⓦwww.galta.com.au.

169 Drummond Street 169 Drummond St, Carlton ☎03/9663 3081, ⓦwww .169drummond.com.au. Non-smoking B&B set in a refurbished Victorian mansion with en-suite rooms. ❺–❻

California Motel 138 Barkers Rd, Hawthorn ☎03/9818 0281 or 1800 331 166, ⓦwww.californiamotel.com.au. Gay-friendly motel accommodation close to the city; parking available. Take tram #109 or #42 from Collins St. ❼–❽

Heathville House 171 Aitken St, Williamstown ☎03/9397 5959, ⓔheath@jeack .com.au. B&B in a pretty weatherboard house. Non-smoking. ❻–❼

Laird Hotel 149 Gipps St, Abbotsford ☎03/9417 2832, ⓦwww.lairdhotel.com. Rooms for gay men only. ❺–❻

Palm Court B&B 22 Grattan Place, Richmond ☎03/9427 7365. Spacious, moderately priced bedrooms in a Victorian mansion. Non-smoking. ❸

and DVD players, Bose stereo radios, and a data connection for modem and fax. Other facilities include a day spa and relaxation centre, the elegant *Circa* restaurant (see p.929),the *Mink* bar (see p.933), and a club/band room. ❻
Hotel Tolarno 42 Fitzroy St ℡03/9537 0200, ⓦwww.hoteltolarno.com.au. Boutique hotel set in a restored building right in the thick of things. Rooms are pleasant and good value, with en-suite bathrooms, polished timber floors and all

mod cons. ❺–❼
Warwick Beachside St Kilda 363 Beaconsfield Parade ℡03/9525 4800 or 1800 338 134, ⓦwww.warwickbeachside.com.au. Just around the corner from the cafés and pubs of Fitzroy St, the studio, one- and two-bedroom units here come with colour TV, phones and kitchen facilities. Some are better than others, but all are excellent value, particularly at weekly rates. ❸–❹

Camping and caravan parks

There are no **campsites** anywhere close to the centre; the nearest is the *Melbourne Holiday Park*, with scenic *Hobsons Bay* not much further on.

Crystal Brook Holiday Centre Cnr Anderson's Creek and Warrandyte roads, East Doncaster ℡03/9844 3637, ⓕ9844 3342. Modern campsite and holiday park with tennis courts and a pool, 21km northeast of the city centre (20min via the Eastern Freeway). On-site vans and cabins ❸–❺
Hobsons Bay Caravan Park 158 Kororoit Creek Rd, Williamstown ℡03/9397 2395. Pitch your tent

facing St Kilda across Hobsons Bay, 13km west of the city. Cabins ❹
Melbourne Big 4 Holiday Park 265 Elizabeth St, Coburg East ℡03/9354 3533 or 1800 802 678, ⓕ9354 4550. Ten kilometres north of the city, with kitchen and a swimming pool. Take bus #526 to the city (daytime only, no service Sun). Cabins ❹–❻

The City

Melbourne is a city of few sights but plenty of lifestyle, and you'll get to know the city just as well by sitting over a coffee or strolling in the park as by traipsing around museums or tourist attractions. At the heart of the city lies the **Central Business District** (CBD), bounded by La Trobe, Spring, Flinders and Spencer streets, dotted with fine public buildings and lots of shops. Sights here include the ghoulish **Old Melbourne Gaol** and a new museum in the **Old Customs House** dedicated to Victoria's immigration history. The CBD is surrounded by gardens on all sides (save the downtown west): few cities have so much green space so close to the centre. To the north a wander through lively, century-old **Queen Victoria Market** will repay both serious shoppers and people-watchers, while the newly built **Melbourne Museum** in tranquil Carlton Gardens draws on the latest technology to give an insight into Australia's flora, fauna and culture. In the east, the CBD rubs up against **Eastern Hill**, with its government buildings and landscaped **Fitzroy Gardens**, from where it's a short walk to the venerable **Melbourne Cricket Ground (MCG)**, a must for sports fans.

Bounding the south side of the CBD, the muddy and much-maligned **Yarra River** lies at the centre of the massive ongoing developments which are slowly transforming the face of the city, with high-rises and new developments popping up like mushrooms. The shift towards the Yarra river kicked off in the mid-1990s with the waterfront development of **Southgate**, **Crown Casino** and the **Melbourne Exhibition Centre**, while the latest addition to Melbourne's cityscape is the new **Federation Square**, on the north bank of the Yarra opposite Flinders Street station. South of the river, the **Victorian Arts Centre** forms a cultural strip on one side of St Kilda Road, while on the other, Government House and the impressive Shrine of Remembrance front the soothing **Royal Botanic Gardens**.

The CBD

Seen from across the river or from the air, Melbourne's **Central Business District** presents a spectacular modern skyline; at ground level, however, what you notice are the florid nineteenth-century facades, grandiose survivors of the great days of the goldrushes and after. The former Royal Mint on William Street near Flagstaff Gardens is one of the finest examples, but the main concentrations are on **Collins Street** and along **Spring Street** to the east. At the centre of the CBD, trams jolt through the busy but run-down **Bourke Street Mall**. A stone's throw from these central thoroughfares, narrow lanes, squares and arcades with quaint, hole-in-the-wall cafés, small restaurants, shops and boutiques add a cosy and intimate feel to the city.

Collins Street

Collins Street is *the* smart Melbourne address – especially if you're an international banker – becoming increasingly exclusive as you climb the hill from the Spencer Street end. At the western end of Collins Street the Stock Exchange squares up to the **Rialto Building** opposite, an Italianate Gothic complex built in the 1890s which now houses the luxury *Meridien* hotel. The massive **Rialto Towers** is Melbourne's tallest structure, the reflective surface of its twin towers lending the skyline a bit of oomph. On clear days, especially in the evening, a trip up to the **Rialto Towers Observation Deck** on the 55th floor is a must (Mon–Thurs & Sun 10am–10pm, Fri & Sat 10am–11pm; $11.80; Ⓦ www.melbournedeck.com.au). The admission fee includes the use of high-powered binoculars, and a twenty-minute film at the Rialto Vision Theatre on street level that highlights the best parts of Melbourne and Victoria. Nearby, at 333 Collins St, the former **Commercial Bank of Australia** has a particularly sumptuous interior, with a domed banking chamber and awesome barrel-vaulted vestibule which you're welcome to admire during business hours.

Further up Collins Street, beyond the worthwhile diversion down William Street to the new museums in the Old Customs House (see overleaf), shops become the focus of attention. The 1890s **Block Arcade**, at nos. 282–284, is one of Melbourne's grandest shopping centres, its name appropriately taken from the tradition of "doing the block" – promenading around the city's fashionable shopping streets. Restored in 1988, the L-shaped arcade sports a mosaic-tiled floor, ornate columns and mouldings, and a glass-domed roof. **Australia on Collins**, a modern alternative next door, has set its sights firmly on the street's glitzy shopping crown, with an upmarket food court and adjacent licensed restaurants and bars in its basement. Beyond this, on the corner of Collins and Swanston streets, Neoclassical **Melbourne Town Hall** faces the new *Westin Hotel* (see p.899), squatting on **City Square**, a beleaguered space that never achieved the intended purpose of providing Melbourne with a focal point. There is, however, an unmissable landmark on the south side of the square: the splendid **St Paul's Cathedral**, built in the 1880s to a Gothic-revival design by English architect William Butterfield (who never actually visited Australia). Across from the cathedral on Swanston Street, the restored *Young and Jackson's Hotel* is now protected by the National Trust, not for any intrinsic beauty but as a showcase for a work of art which has become a Melbourne icon: **Chloe**, a full-length nude which now reclines upstairs in *Chloe's Bar and Bistro*. Exhibited by the French painter Jules Lefebvre at the Paris Salon of 1875, it was sent to an international exhibition in Melbourne in 1881 and has been here ever since.

Back on Collins Street, the pompous **Athenaeum Theatre** next to the Town Hall is an important ingredient in the rising streetscape leading up past **Scots Church**, whose Gothic-revival design merits a peek, though it's famous mainly as the place where Dame Nellie Melba first sang in the choir. Further up, beyond expensive boutiques and even more expensive souvenir shops, **Collins Place** shopping centre and the towering **Hotel Sofitel** next door dominate the upper part of Collins Street, known as the "Paris end". The (male) toilet of *Le Restaurant* on the 35th floor of the *Sofitel* is known as the "loo with a view", but the **view** from the tables by the window isn't bad, either – though it doesn't come cheap (see p.925). Opposite, overshadowed by the *Sofitel* tower, stands one of the last bastions of Australian male chauvinism: the very staid, men-only **Melbourne Club**.

The Immigration Museum and Hellenic Antiquities Museum

At the corner of Flinders and William streets, just off the western stretch of Collins Street, the **Immigration Museum** (daily 10am–5pm; $8; Ⓦ www.immigration.museum.vic.gov.au) is dedicated to one of the central themes of Australian history. Housed in the beautifully restored **Old Customs House**, the museum builds a vivid picture of immigration history and personal stories using the spoken word, music, moving images, light effects and interactive screens, evoking the experiences of being a migrant on a square-rigger in the 1840s, a passenger on a steamship at the turn of the twentieth century, or a post-war refugee from Europe. In the **Tribute Garden**, the outdoor centrepiece of the museum, a film of water flows over polished granite on which are engraved the names of migrants to Victoria, symbolizing the passage over the seas to reach these faraway shores. The names of all the Koorie people living in Victoria prior to white settlement are listed separately at the entrance to the garden.

The **Hellenic Antiquities Museum** on the second floor of the same building, is currently empty, its contents having been sent to Athens in honour of the Olympics in 2004.

Bourke Street, Chinatown and the State Library

Run-down **Bourke Street Mall** extends west from Swanston Street to Elizabeth Street. The mall is in desperate need of an overhaul, scheduled to be completed in time for the Commonwealth Games in 2005, though sadly plans are afoot to turn the wonderful Victorian-era **General Post Office**, at the corner of Elizabeth Street and Bourke Street, into a shopping complex. Running off the mall, the lovely **Royal Arcade** is Melbourne's oldest (1839), paved with black and white marble and lit by huge fanlight windows. A clock on which two two-metre giants, Gog and Magog, strike the hours adds a welcome hint of the grotesque. As you climb the hill east of here, Bourke Street keeps up the interest, with several cafés and bars that put out pavement tables at night – including *Pellegrini's*, Melbourne's first espresso bar and still buzzing – as well as late-opening book and record stores.

North of Bourke Street, and running parallel to it, is **Little Bourke Street**, with the majestic **Law Courts** by William Street at the western end, and **Chinatown** in the east between Exhibition and Swanston streets. Australia's oldest continuous Chinese settlement, Melbourne's Chinatown began with a few boarding-houses in the 1850s (when the goldrushes attracted Chinese people in droves, many from the Pearl River Delta near Hong Kong) and grew as the gold began to run out and Chinese fortune-seekers headed back to the city. Today the area still has a low-rise, narrow-laned, nineteenth-century character, and it's packed with Chinese restaurants and stores. The **Chinese Museum**, in an old warehouse on Cohen Place (daily 10am–4.30pm; $6.50), is concerned particularly with the Chinese role in the foundation and development of Melbourne. The museum organizes two-hour guided tours of the building and Chinatown ($16.50, or $33 including lunch). Tours require a minimum of six people, and bookings two or three days in advance are preferred (℡03/9662 2888).

Three blocks north of Little Bourke Street lies the **State Library** (Mon–Thurs 10am–9pm & Fri–Sun 10am–6pm; ⓦwww.statelibrary .vic.gov.au), dating from 1856 and still the state's largest research and reference library accessible to the public; the Queen's Hall and its domed reading room are splendid examples of Victorian architecture. Opposite the State Library, the modern shopping complex of **Melbourne Central** skilfully incorporates an old red-brick shot tower under its pointed glass dome.

Old Melbourne Gaol

The **Old Melbourne Gaol** (daily 9.30am–4.30pm; $12.50; ⓦwww .nattrust.com.au), on Russell Street, a block north of the State Library, is probably the most worthwhile of all the downtown sights. It's certainly the most popular, largely because Australian folk hero and bushranger **Ned Kelly** was hanged here in 1880 – the site of his execution, the beam from which he was hung and his death mask are all on display (for more on Ned Kelly's exploits, see p.1040), as is assorted armour worn by the Kelly Gang. The "Melbourne Gaol Night Tour" (Wed, Fri, Sat & Sun: April–Oct 7.30pm, Nov–March 8.30pm; $20; advance bookings required on ℡13 28 49) uses the spooky atmosphere of the prison to full effect.

The bluestone prison was built in stages from 1841 to 1864 – the goldrushes of the 1850s caused such a surge in lawlessness that it kept having to be expanded. A mix of condemned men, remand and short-sentence prisoners, women and "lunatics" (often, in fact, drunks) were housed here; long-term prisoners languished in hulks moored at Williamstown, or at the Pentridge Stockade. Much has been demolished since the jail was closed in 1923, but the entrance and boundary walls at least survive, and it's worth walking round the building to take a look at the formidable arched brick portal on Franklin Street.

The gruesome collection of death masks on show in the tiny cells bears witness to the nineteenth-century obsession with phrenology, a wobbly branch of science which studied how people's characters were related to the size and shape of their skulls. Accompanying the masks are compelling case histories of the murderers and their victims. Most fascinating are the women: Martha Needle, who poisoned her husband and daughters (among others) with arsenic, and young Martha Knorr, the notorious "baby farmer", who advertised herself as a "kind motherly person, willing to adopt a child". After receiving a few dollars per child, she killed and buried them in her backyard. The jail serves up other macabre memorabilia, including a scaffold still in working order, various nooses, and a triangle where malcontents were strapped to receive lashes by the cat-o'-nine-tails. Perhaps the ultimate rite of passage for visitors is the "Art of Hanging", an interpretive display that's part educational tool and part setting for a medieval snuff movie.

Queen Victoria Market and Melbourne Museum

Opened in the 1870s, **Queen Victoria Market** (Tues & Thurs 6am–2pm, Fri 6am–6pm, Sat 6am–3pm, Sun 9am–4pm; ⓦwww.qvm.com.au) remains one of the best loved of Melbourne's institutions. Its collection of huge, decorative open-sided sheds and high-roofed halls is fronted along Victoria Street by restored shops, their original awnings held up with decorative iron posts. Although undeniably quaint and tourist-friendly, the market is a boisterous, down-to-earth affair where you can buy practically anything from new and secondhand clothes to fresh fish at bargain prices. Stallholders and shoppers seem just as diverse as the goods on offer: Vietnamese, Italian and Greek green-grocers pile their colourful produce high and vie for your attention, while the huge variety of deliciously smelly cheeses effortlessly draws customers to the old-fashioned deli hall. Saturday morning marks a weekly social ritual as Melbourne's foodies turn out for their groceries, while Sunday is for clothing and shoe shopping. The guided **Foodies Dream Tour** takes in all the culinary delights of the market (10am Tues & Thurs; $22 including food sampling, bookings essential). The market also runs regular day, evening and weekend cooking classes. For programs and tour bookings call ☎03/9320 5835; details of the Cooking School program are shown on the market's website.

At the CBD's northeast corner is **Carlton Gardens**, home to one of Melbourne's most significant historic landmarks – the **Royal Exhibition Building**. Built by David Mitchell (father of Dame Nellie Melba) for the International Exhibition of 1880, this is where Australia's first parliament sat in 1901 and where the Victorian State Parliament resided in 1901–27. It was also used as a sporting venue for the 1956 Melbourne Olympics. Buildings origi-nally covered the whole of the park, but only the magnificent Neoclassical Main Hall remains, dwarfed by the mammoth **Melbourne Museum** (daily 10am–5pm; $15; ⊛www.melbourne.museum.vic.gov.au). Opened in 2000, this state-of-the-art museum makes a dramatic contrast to its nineteenth-century neighbour, with its geometric forms, vibrant colours, immense blade-like roof and a greenhouse accommodating a lush fern gully flanked by a canopy of dozens of tall forest trees. The museum, which also houses a 400-seat amphitheatre, touring hall for major exhibitions and a museum shop, has been designed with the Internet generation in mind – glass-covered display cabinets are few and far between; instead, there's a greater emphasis on digital culture and multimedia, with exhibition spaces exploring the way science and tech-nology are shaping the future.

Spread over six huge levels (half of which are below ground level), the museum's highlights include the **Science and Life Gallery**, which explores the plants and animals inhabiting the southern lands and seas; the **Bunjilaka Aboriginal Centre**, showcasing an extraordinary indigenous collection of Aboriginal culture (curving for 50m at the entrance is "Wurreka", a wall of over seventy zinc panels etched with Aboriginal artefacts, shells, plants and fish); and the **Australia Gallery**, focusing on the history of Melbourne and Victoria, and featuring the legendary racehorse Phar Lap (reputedly Australia's most popular museum exhibit) and the kitchen set from the TV show *Neighbours*. Also of interest is the **Evolution Gallery**, which looks at the earth's history and holds an assortment of dinosaur casts, and the **Children's Museum**, where the exhibition gallery, "Big Box", is built in the shape of a giant, tiled cube painted in brightly coloured squares. One of the most strik-ing exhibits is the **Forest Gallery**, a living, breathing indoor rainforest con-taining over 8000 plants from more than 120 species, including 25-metre-tall gums, as well as birds, insects, snakes, lizards and fish. Also part of the museum, the **IMAX Melbourne** boasts the world's biggest movie screen. Up to seven different IMAX films (daily on the hour 10am–10pm, plus Fri & Sat midnight & 1am; $15, 3D films $17; ☎03/9663 5454, ⊛www.imax.com.au/melbourne)

are projected each day; for some you need to don special liquid-crystal glasses for 3D action.

Eastern Hill and the MCG

The **Eastern Hill** area beyond Spring Street has many fine public buildings, centred around **Parliament House**. Erected in stages between 1856 and 1930, the parliament buildings (guided tours on non-sitting days Mon–Fri 10am, 11am, noon, 2pm, 3pm & 3.45pm; free; ☏03/9651 8568) have a theatrical presence, with a facade of giant Doric columns rising from a high flight of steps, and landscaped gardens either side. Just below, the Old Treasury Building from 1857 and adjacent State Government office, facing the beautiful Treasury Gardens, are equally imposing. In the old gold vaults deep in the basement of the **Old Treasury Building** (Mon–Fri 9am–5pm, Sat, Sun & public holidays 10am–4pm; $7) an audiovisual presentation, *Built on Gold*, illustrates the impact of the Victorian goldrushes on the fledgling colony. A permanent exhibition on the social and architectural history of Melbourne shares the ground floor with temporary shows.

East of Parliament House, the broad acres of **Fitzroy Gardens** run a close second to Carlton Gardens as a getaway from the CBD. Originally laid out in the shape of the Union Jack flag, the park's paths still just about conform to the original pattern, though the formal style has been fetchingly abandoned in between. The flowers, statuary and fountains are best appreciated on weekdays, as at the weekend you'll spend most of your time dodging the video cameras of wedding parties. The gardens' much-touted main attraction is really only for kitsch nostalgists: **Captain Cook's Cottage** (daily: April–Oct 9am–5pm; Nov–March 9am–5.30pm; $3.30) was the supposed home of Captain James Cook, the English navigator who explored the southern hemisphere in three great voyages and first "discovered" the east coast of Australia. The cottage was purchased in 1933 by Russell Grimwade, a wealthy Melbourne businessman, who had it shipped over piece by piece from its original location in Whitby, Yorkshire, and presented as a gift to the state of Victoria for its 1934 centenary. The red-brick and creeper-covered cottage with period fittings attempts to re-create the atmosphere of eighteenth-century England, reinforced by worthy displays about the explorer himself. Elsewhere in the gardens, a tacky open-air **model Tudor village** continues the "olde worlde" theme, but you'll probably find the **Conservatory**'s flower displays (daily 9am–5pm; free) more interesting.

Federation Square and around

Back in the city centre, sandwiched between the southern edge of the CBD and the Yarra, lies the huge orange-and-brown **Flinders Street station**, the city's main suburban railway station, its entrance faced with a row of clocks detailing the times of all train departures on various lines ("under the clocks" is still a traditional Melbourne meeting place). This famous old city landmark is now faced by **Federation Square** (or "Fed Square", as it's generally known), officially opened in October 2002, which occupies an entire block between Flinders Street and the Yarra. By linking the CBD and the river, Federation Square has provided Melbourne with the single, central unifying focus it had always previously lacked. The development consists of a huddle of buildings, with a huge open space, the Plaza, at its core. The design is irregular and complex – nothing about Fed Square is actually square. Viewed from the northern side, the square's buildings present a jumble of odd angles, jagged edges, oddly shaped windows in improbable places, and facades covered by a bewildering

MELBOURNE AND AROUND | The City

array of zinc, glass and sandstone panels, like the pieces of some giant but only half-completed puzzle. Although the various buildings are very differently shaped, their "fractal facades" of sandstone, zinc and glass triangles provide something of an architectural leitmotif, creating an impression of unity within diversity.

The **Plaza** is paved with sandstone cobblestones in soft hues of ochre, siena and iron, rising from St Kilda Road in a gentle incline towards the east, where it narrows into a horseshoe-shaped space hemmed in by buildings including the Australian Centre for the Moving Image and Ian Potter Centre (see below). Narrower buildings provide passageways: the "**Atrium**" between the Plaza and Flinders Street, and the "**Crossbar**" between the Plaza and the Ian Potter Centre: NGV Australia. The new underground **Melbourne Visitor Centre** is located at the northeastern end of the Plaza, directly across from Flinders Street station.

Housed in the Alfred Deakin Building on the north side of the Plaza, the **Australian Centre for the Moving Image** (daily 10am–6pm; free; Ⓦ www.acmi.net.au) is devoted to exploring the moving image in all it forms: film, television, games, video and digital media. A large underground gallery features changing exhibitions of screen-based art; two state-of-the-art multi-format cinemas screen special themed film programmes and host film festivals and special events.

Ian Potter Centre: NGV Australia National Gallery of Victoria

Walk from Flinders Street through the **Atrium** – a unique passageway of glass, steel and zinc – or from the Plaza through the similar **Crossbar** to reach the striking new home of the National Gallery of Victoria's collection of Australian art, the **Ian Potter Centre: NGV Australia** (Mon–Thurs 10am–5pm, Fri 10am–9pm, Sat & Sun 10am–6pm; free, except for special exhibitions; Ⓦ www.ngv.vic.gov.au), named in honour of Sir Ian Potter (1902–1994), a local financier, philanthropist and patron of the arts. Occupying three floors, the centre showcases one of the best collections of Australian art in the country, with some seventy thousand works, of which about 1800 are usually on display (exhibits are rotated regularly). Traditional and contemporary indigenous art is displayed in four galleries on the ground floor; historic and modern Australian collections are housed on level two; the galleries on level three are reserved for special temporary exhibitions. The artworks are complemented by interactive videos which feature an overview of artists' works, with biographies and even interviews.

The **building** itself is as much a work of art as its exhibits, constructed from two overlapping wings forming a slightly crooked X and offering constantly shifting views, with glimpses of the Yarra and the parklands beyond through the glass walls in the southern part of the building. The best way to get a handle on the collection, as well as the building, is to participate in a free **guided tour** (Mon–Fri at 11am, noon, 2pm and 3pm, Sat & Sun at 11am and 2pm).

Galleries 1–4 on the ground floor give an excellent overview of the art produced in Australia's **indigenous communities**, showcasing artworks in both traditional and contemporary styles. Traditional art is respresented by carved and painted figures from Maningrida, masks from Torres Straits Island, Pukumani Poles from the Tiwi Islands north of Darwin, the Wandjina paintings from the north of Western Australia and bark paintings from Yirrkala and other places in Arnhem Land. One of the highlights is undoubtedly *Big Yam Dreaming* (1995), an enormous canvas by **Emily Kam Kngwarray** (c.1910-

1996) showing tangled, spidery webs of white against a black background, representing the pencil yam that grows along the creek banks at the artist's birthplace northeast of Alice Springs. In her brief career – she didn't take up painting until she was in her mid-70s – Emily produced a staggering three thousand-plus works, transcending the Western Desert-style dot paintings and developing a uniquely personal style, whose seemingly abstract, vibrantly coloured style is sometimes reminiscent of late Monet or Jackson Pollock.

On the **second floor**, galleries 5–11 contain paintings, sculptures, drawings, photographs and decorative arts from the mid-nineteenth century to the 1980, displayed in chronological order. One recurrent leitmotif is the harsh beauty of the Australian landscape, and (European) peoples' place in it. The **early colonial paintings** – with works by artists such as John Glover, Henry Burn, Frederick McCubbin and Tom Roberts – are particularly interesting, showing European artists struggling to come to terms with an alien land, as well as offering pictorial records of the growth of new cities and the lives of immigrants and pioneers.

Highlights of the **twentieth-century collection** include paintings by Albert Tucker, Russell Drysdale, John Perceval and, especially, **Sidney Nolan**. Dissatisfied with his Eurocentric art training at Prahran Technical College, Nolan (1917–1992) strived to express the Australian experience in a fresh style, exploring new ways of seeing and painting the nation's landscapes, as in his *Wimmera* painting of the 1940s; Nolan also showed a unique interest in the histories of convicts, explorers and bushrangers, resulting in pictures such as his well-known *Ned Kelly* series (1946–48). Another highlight is the gallery dedicated to the overwhelming *Pilbara* collection of **Fred Williams**, painted in 1979 in the Pilbara region of Western Australia.

Biarrung Marr

East of Fed Square sits Melbourne's newest park, **Birrarung Marr**, created from land previously up by railway lines, a swimming pool and a road. Located opposite Alexandra Gardens, the park forms a green link between Federation Square and the sports precinct of Melbourne Park, giving striking views of the city skyline, the sports arenas, river and parklands. The park consists of grassy slopes, intersected by a long **footbridge** that crosses the entire park from the southeast to the northwest. The footbridge starts at a small, artificially created wetland area in the southeast by the river called the **Billabong**, leads over Red Gum Gully to the park's centrepiece, the **Federation Bells**, a collection of 39 bells, ranging in size from a small handbell to a one weighing a tonne, created to commemorate the Centenary of Federation in 2001. The bells are computer controlled and ring daily at 8am, 9.10am, 12.30pm, 1.30pm, 5pm and 6.10pm.

The MCG and around

East of Birrarung Park lies **Yarra Park**, containing the hallowed **Melbourne Cricket Ground (MCG)** – also easily reached by tram along Wellington Parade or train to Jolimont station. Home to the Melbourne Cricket Club since 1853, the MCG is now a vast and rather ugly slab of concrete, as only the historic members' stand survived the complete reconstruction that made the ground the centrepiece for the 1956 Olympic Games. As well as hosting state and international cricket matches and some of the top Aussie Rules football games, the MCG contains the **Australian Gallery of Sport and Olympic Exhibition**, and the **Australian Cricket Hall of Fame** (daily 9.30am–4.30pm; $17; ⓦ www.mcg.org.au). One-hour tours of the ground itself (hourly 10am–3pm; no tours on event days) are included in the admission fee; the highlight is the members' pavilion – home of the most traditional and elitist club in Australia – packed with fascinating cricketing memorabilia. The Olympic Exhibition covers all the Olympiads, and incorporates an audio tour of the museum.

From the MCG, three pedestrian bridges over Brunton Avenue lead to **Melbourne Park**, home to a further cluster of sporting venues. **Rod Laver Arena** and **Vodafone Arena** in Melbourne Park are home of the Australian Open tennis championship in January – the latter can seat up to 10,500 people and has a retractable roof and moveable seating that allows for fully enclosed or open-air events such as cycling, tennis, basketball and concerts. On the other side of Swan Street lies the **Melbourne Sports and Entertainment Centre**, or "Glasshouse", as it's known locally; next door, **Olympic Park** is where the Melbourne Storm rugby league team play their matches.

The Yarra River and the south bank

Despite its nondescript appearance, the muddy **Yarra River** was – and still is – an important part of the Melbourne scene. Traditionally home to the city docks, tidal movements of up to two metres meant frequent flooding, a problem only partly solved by artificially straightening the river and building up its banks – this also had the incidental benefit of reserving tracts of low-lying land as recreational space, which are now pleasingly crisscrossed by paths and cycle tracks. Four **bridges** cross the river from the CBD: Spencer Street Bridge at the end of Spencer Street; Kings Bridge on King Street; Queens Bridge, not quite at the end of Queen Street; and Princes Bridge, which carries Swanston Street across. There's also a pedestrian bridge from the bank below Flinders Street station to the Southgate Centre. The best way to see the Yarra is on a **cruise** – see the box opposite.

On the south side of Princes Bridge you can rent **bikes** to explore the river banks (see "Listings", p.938); on fine weekends, especially, the Yarra comes to life, with people messing about in boats, cycling and strolling. **Southgate**, immediately west of Princes Bridge, is a highly successful development: once dingy and industrial, it's now an upmarket shopping complex with lots of smart cafés, restaurants, bars and a huge food court with very popular outdoor tables; at lunchtime and weekends it's very hard to find a table, even indoors.

The Crown Casino, Docklands and Telstra Dome

Providing the Yarra's unavoidable focal point, the **Crown Casino** is Australia's largest gambling and entertainment venue, stretching across 600m of riverfront west of Southgate between Queens Bridge and Spencer Street Bridge. Next door, the **Melbourne Exhibition Centre** (known locally as "Jeff's Shed", a reference to Jeff Kennett, the former state premier behind its construction) is a whimsical example of the city's dynamic new architectural style: facing the river is an immense, 450-metre-long glass wall, while the street entrance has an awning resembling a ski jump propped up by wafer-thin pylons. The interesting **Polly Woodside Maritime Museum** (daily 10am–4pm; $9.90) is tucked into a small old dock next to the Exhibition Centre. The focus is the *Polly Woodside* itself, a small, barque-rigged sailing ship, built in Belfast in 1885 for the South American coal trade and retired only in 1968, when it was the last deep-water sailing vessel in Australia still afloat.

The squat building facing the Exhibition Centre and the museum across the Yarra is the **World Trade Centre**. Next to it, opposite the Crown Casino on

River cruises on the Yarra

The main departure points in the city for cruises along the Yarra are **Northbank Promenade**, at the southern end of Federation Square (sometimes still referred to as Princes Walk), **Southgate** and, further west, **Williamstown** at the mouth of the Yarra (see p.922). You can choose between short trips and longer journeys towards the sea and the bird colonies at Port Phillip Bay and Herring Island.

Melbourne River Cruises depart from Northbank Promenade near Princes Bridge. You can buy tickets at the sales kiosk at Northbank Promenade or call ⑦03/9629 7233. The Scenic River Garden Cruise (1hr 15min; $16.50) heads upriver past affluent South Yarra and industrial Richmond to Herring Island. The Port and Docklands Cruise (1hr 15min; $16.50) runs downriver past the Crown Casino and Melbourne Exhibition Centre to the Westgate Bridge. Combined up- and downriver cruises cost $29.70. In additon, cruises to Williamstown and back leave on the hour between 10.45am and 3.45pm daily, stopping at Scienceworks on demand ($13.70, return $ 24.20)

Williamstown Bay and River Cruises (⑦03/9682 9555; ⓦwww.williamstown ferries.com.au; $10, or $18 return) ply the lower section of the Yarra between Williamstown and Southgate in the west of the city, passing the Crown Casino, Melbourne Exhibition Centre, the docks and the Scienceworks museum. There are daily departures (weather permitting) at 11am, 1pm, 3pm & 5pm, returning from Williamstown at noon, 2pm, 4pm and 6pm. Advance bookings aren't required; tickets can be bought on board. The company also runs a ferry service from St Kilda Pier to Williamstown on Saturdays, Sundays and public holidays.

the corner of Queenwharf Road and King Street, is the **Melbourne Aquarium** (daily: Jan 9am–9pm; Feb–Dec 9am–6pm; $19; ⓦwww .melbourneaquarium.com.au). Resembling a giant fish-and-chip shop, the aquarium harbours thousands of creatures from the Southern Ocean. Part of it is taken up by the Oceanarium tank, which rests seven metres below the Yarra, holding over two million litres of water and containing 3200 animals from 150 species (there are over 550 species, or 4000 creatures, in the aquarium in total), as well as a sting-ray-filled beach with a wave machine and a fish bowl turned inside out where you can stand in a glass room surrounded by shark-filled water. The curved, four-storey building also houses a hands-on learning centre where children get a fish-eye view of life underwater, "Ride the Dive" platforms that simulate an underwater roller-coaster, lecture halls, an amphitheatre, cafés, shop and a restaurant.

Further downstream lies the **old dock area**, earmarked for grand-scale commercial, residential and leisure development as part of the **Docklands project**. Of all the city's new developments, this is likely to have the biggest impact on the look and feel of Melbourne: if all goes to plan, in ten to twelve years an entire new city district will stand by the waterfront here. For the time being, the area is still mostly an urban wasteland of warehouses, old docks and new roads cutting through empty open spaces. Squat in the middle of it all sits another of Melbourne's giant sporting venues, **Telstra Dome** (originally known as Colonial Stadium when it opened in 2000), a 54,000-seater venue for AFL, cricket, and international soccer and rugby union matches, as well as concerts by big-name artists. A wide pedestrian footbridge crosses the railway tracks at Spencer Street station, connecting Telstra Dome and the Docklands district-in-the-making with Spencer Street and the older part of the city. The only completed waterside development to-date, **New Quay**, near the extension of La Trobe Street, was opened in December 2002 and now provides the setting for

△ Footbridge over River Yarra, Melbourne

a few restaurants and cafés. The area hasn't quite come to life yet, but given New Quay's unique waterside location – within walking distance of the city centre, and with gorgeous panoramic views of Bolte Bridge to the west and the city's skyline to the east – it probably won't be long before the place is buzzing.

Victorian Arts Centre

The **Victorian Arts Centre**, just off St Kilda Road, comprises the older building of the National Gallery of Victoria, the Melbourne Concert Hall and the Theatres Building, topped by a 162-metre-tall **spire**, whose curved lower sections are meant to evoke the flowing folds of a ballerina's skirt; the mast at its peak turns an iridescent blue at night. There are guided **tours** (Mon–Sat noon & 2.30pm; $11; the backstage tour allows visitors to get a look behind the stages; Sun 12.15pm; $13.50; ⓦ www.artscentre.net.au) of the **Melbourne Concert Hall** and **Theatres Building**. Exhibits from the collection of the former Performing Arts Museum are on view in the small **George Adams Gallery** and the basement, alternating with exhibits from the collection of visual arts (Mon–Sat 9am–11pm, Sun 9am–5pm; free). The **National Gallery** is currently closed for major refurbishment until late 2003; the refurbished gallery will house works from the international collection. Further south, on Sturt Street, the **Australian Centre for Contemporary Art** (ACCA; daily 11am–6pm; free) has consistently challenging exhibitions of contemporary international and Australian art.

On Sunday between 10am and 6pm the stalls of a good **arts and crafts market** line the pavement outside the Arts Centre, extending onto the footpath under the Princes Bridge.

Kings Domain

Across St Kilda Road from the National Gallery of Victoria, the grassy open parkland of **Kings Domain** encompasses the **Sidney Myer Music Bowl**, which serves as the outdoor music arena for the Victorian Arts Centre. South of the Bowl, and behind imposing iron gates with stone pillars and a British coat of arms, you can glimpse the flag flying over **Government House**, the ivory mansion of the governor of Victoria, set in extensive grounds. The National Trust runs **guided tours** of the house (Mon, Wed & Sat, times by appointment; ⓣ 03/9654 4711; closed Dec 16–Jan 25; $11), the highlight being the state ballroom, which occupies the entire south wing and includes a velvet-hung canopied throne, brocade-covered benches, ornate plasterwork and three huge crystal chandeliers.

La Trobe's Cottage (Mon, Wed, Sat & Sun 11am–4pm; $2.20) has been re-erected on Dallas Brooke Drive as a memorial to Lieutenant-Governor La Trobe, who lived in this tiny house throughout his term of office (1839–54). The whole thing was sent over from England in prefabricated form, and makes a telling contrast to the later governor's residence. Inside there are interesting displays on La Trobe and the early days of the colony.

The **Shrine of Remembrance**, in formal grounds in the southwestern corner of the Domain, is aligned with St Kilda Road – which describes a gentle arc around it – so that its forbidding mass looms ahead as you enter or leave the city from the south. Completed in 1934, it's a rather Orwellian monument, apparently half Roman temple, half Aztec pyramid, given further chill when a mechanical-sounding voice booms out and calls you in to see the symbolic light inside. The shrine is designed so that at 11am on Remembrance Day (Nov 11) a ray of sunlight strikes the memorial stone inside – an effect that's simulated every half-hour.

Royal Botanic Gardens

The **Royal Botanic Gardens** (daily: May–Aug 7.30am–5.30pm; April, Sept & Oct 7.30am–6pm; Nov–March 7.30am–8.30pm; free; ⓦwww.rbgmelb .org.au) contain twelve thousand different plant species and over fifty thousand individual plants, as well as native wildlife such as cockatoos and kookaburras, in an extensive landscaped setting. Melbourne's much-maligned climate is perfect for horticulture: cool enough for temperate trees and flowers to flourish, warm enough for palms and other subtropical species, and wet enough for anything else. The bright and airy **visitors centre** (daily 9am–5pm) at Observatory Gate on Birdwood Avenue has displays, maps and brochures and is the best place to start your wanderings.

Highlights include the **herb garden**, comprising part of the medicinal garden established in 1880; the **fern gully**, a lovely walk through shady ferns, with cooling mists of water on a hot summer's day; the large ornamental **lake** full of ducks, black swans and eels; and various hothouses where exotic cacti and fascinating plants such as the Venus flytrap thrive. The *Observatory Gate Café* next to the visitors centre has indoor and outdoor sitting under sun sails and sells coffee, scrumptious cakes and sandwiches as well as light meals. The *Terrace Tearooms and Reception Centre* (daily 10am–4pm) by the lake is licensed and serves meals, or there's a snackbar next door. On summer evenings, plays are often performed in the gardens. Cinema buffs can also swap popcorn for picnic baskets each year from mid-December to mid-March when art-house, cult and classic films are projected onto a big outdoor screen at the **Moonlight Cinema** ($14; recorded information about screenings on ☎1900/933 899, or visit ⓦwww.moonlight.com.au). Enter at D Gate on Birdwood Avenue; films start at sunset. Don't forget to take an extra layer of clothing, a rug and, most importantly, insect repellent.

Guided walks (Mon–Thurs & Sun; 11am & 2pm; bookings on ☎03/9252 2300; $4.40) through the gardens start at the visitors centre; alternatively, the Aboriginal Heritage Walk (Thurs 11am & second Sun of month 10.30am; $15.40) explores the traditional uses of plants for foods, medicine, tools and ceremonies. The painstakingly restored **Observatory Gate** complex, a group of Italianate buildings (originally built 1861–63) next door to the visitors centre can be visited on a self-guided tour (Mon & Fri–Sun 9am–4pm), or join a "Night Sky Experience tour" from the visitors centre (Tues 7.30–9.30pm; during daylight-saving time 9–10.30pm; $15.40; booking required on ☎03/9525 2300).

Melbourne suburbs

Far more than in the city centre, it's in Melbourne's **inner suburbs** that you'll really get a feel for what life here is really all about. Many have quite distinct characters, whether as ethnic enclaves or self-styled artists' communities. What's more, all can easily be reached by a pleasurable tram ride from the centre. Café society finds its home to the north among the alternative galleries and secondhand shops of **Fitzroy**, while the Italian cafés on Lygon Street in nearby **Carlton** fuelled the Beat Generation with espresso, though there are now as many boutiques as bookshops. Grungy **Richmond**, to the east, can claim both Vietnamese and Greek enclaves, and a diverse music scene in its many pubs. South of the river is the place to shop until you drop, whether at wealthy **South Yarra**, self-consciously groovy **Prahran** or snobby **Toorak**. To the

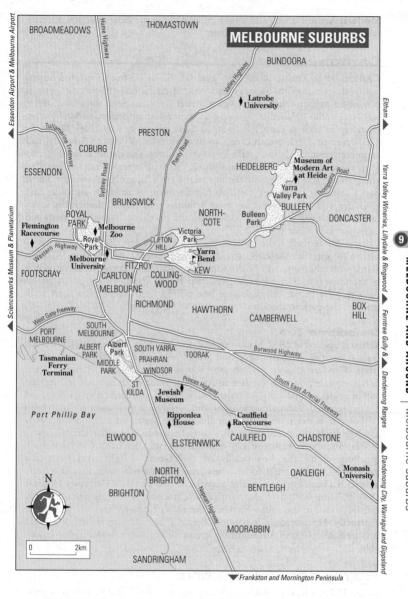

south, **St Kilda** has the advantage of a beachside location to go with its trendy but raucous nightlife.

Browsing through markets and shops, cruising across Hobsons Bay, sampling the world's foods and, of course, sipping espresso are the primary attractions of the suburbs. To firm up your itinerary with something more concrete, make for the well-designed **Zoo** in Carlton, or **Scienceworks**, a hugely enjoyable interactive museum in Spotswood. Also of interest is the **Heide Museum of**

Modern Art in Bulleen and, a bit further along in the same direction, Eltham, with its artists' colony of **Montsalvat**.

Carlton

Carlton lies just north of the city (tram #1, #3 or #5 from Swanston Street) but, with its university presence and its long-established Italian café scene, it could be a million miles away. **Lygon Street** is the centre of the action, and it was here, in the 1950s, that espresso bars were really introduced to Melbourne; exotic spots such as the *Caffe Sport*, *La Gina*, *University Caffe*, *Don Basilio*, *La Cacciatora* and *Toto's* (which claims to have introduced pizza to Australia) had an unconventional allure in staid Anglo-Melbourne, and the local intelligentsia soon made the street their second home. Victorian terraced houses provided cheap living, and this became the first of the city's "alternative" suburbs. These days Carlton is no longer particularly bohemian; its residents are older and wealthier, and Lygon Street has gone definitively upmarket, though the smart fashion shops still jostle with bookshops, and excellent ethnic restaurants and cafés like *Tiamo* (see p.927).

Lygon Street itself is the obvious place to explore, but the elegant architecture also spreads eastwards to Drummond Street and, flanking Carlton Gardens, Rathdowne and Nicholson streets. Running along the western side of the university, Royal Parade gives onto **Royal Park**, with its memorial to the explorers Burke and Wills (see box, p.575), from where it's a short walk through the park to the Zoo.

Melbourne Zoo

When it opened in 1862, **Melbourne Zoo** (daily 9am–5pm; $15.80; Mon–Sat tram #55 from William Street, Sun tram #68 from Elizabeth Street, or train from Flinders Street station to Royal Park on the Upfield line; Ⓦ www.zoo.org.au) was the first in Australia. Some of its original features are still in evidence, including Australian and foreign trees, landscaped gardens, and a few restored Victorian-era cages, but almost all the animals have been rehoused in better, more natural conditions. The Australian area contains a central lake with waterbirds, open enclosures for koalas and other animals, and a bushland setting where you can walk among emus, kangaroos and wallabies. Strolling along the boardwalks of the **Great Flight Aviary** (daily 10.30am–4.30pm) you'll come across areas of rainforest, wetland, and a scrub area with a huge gum tree where many birds nest. The dark **Platypus Habitat** (daily 9.30am–4.30pm) is also worth a look, since the mammals are notoriously difficult to see in the wild – even here there's no guarantee you'll be lucky. The **Butterfly House** (daily 9.30am–4.30pm), a steamy tropical hothouse with hundreds of colourful Australian butterflies flitting about, is also highly enjoyable.

Fitzroy and Collingwood

In the 1970s, **Fitzroy** took over from Carlton as the home of the city's artistic community, and every year at the beginning of October, the colourful Fringe Parade and a street party on Brunswick Street usher in the **Fringe Festival**, the alternative scene's answer to the highbrow Melbourne Festival. The **International Comedy Festival** (April) and the **Next Wave Festival** (May, even-numbered years), two other notable arts events, also take place mainly in Fitzroy. The district's focus is **Brunswick Street** (tram #11 from Collins St), especially between Gertrude Street, home to Turkish takeaways, and

Johnston Street, with its lively Spanish bars and restaurants. In the shadow of Housing Commission tower blocks, welfare agencies and charity shops rub shoulders with funky secondhand clothes and junk shops, ethnic supermarkets and restaurants, cafés full of students and equally grungy artists, writers and musicians, and thriving bookshops that stay open late and are often as crowded as the many bars and music pubs. Most of the rough old hotels have been done up to match the prevailing mood: the *Provincial* is a good example, with its distressed paint-job and deli/café/bar inside.

Fitzroy's fringe art leanings are reflected in wacky "street installations" such as mosaic chairs, and sculptures like *Mr Poetry*. The eye-catching wrought-iron gate at the entrance to the Fitzroy Nursery at 390 Brunswick St, with its fairytale motif, sets the theme for the Artists Garden above the nursery, which exhibits sculptures and other decorative items for garden use. Small **galleries** worth looking out for are Goya Galleries, 95–105 Victoria St; Moor Street Gallery, at 5/108 Moor St; and Gertrude Contemporary Art Spaces, at 200 Gertrude St, all of which present works by emerging artists. The Centre for Contemporary Photography, 205 Johnston St (Wed–Sat 11am–5pm) is also worth a look. Fitzroy also boasts its own **arts and crafts market** (third Sun of the month 10am–3.30pm) at the old Fitzroy Town Hall on the corner of Napier and Moor streets. The **Fitzroy Pool**, in the north of the suburb on the corner of Young and Cecil streets, is a summer meeting place where people occasionally swim between posing sessions.

While not as trendy as Brunswick Street, formerly shabby **Smith Street** (tram #86 from Bourke St), which forms the boundary between Fitzroy and **Collingwood** to the east, is catching up. You'll still find many charity shops, ethnic butchers and cheap supermarkets, but New Age bookshops, quirky little cafés and revamped pubs are edging in. Collingwood and the adjacent suburb of Abbotsford have a large **gay** population, with a clutch of gay bars and clubs, particularly on Peel and Glasshouse streets.

South Yarra, Toorak and Prahran

South of the river, the suburbs of **South Yarra**, **Prahran** and, to the east, **Toorak**, are home to the city's biggest **shopping** area, both grungy and upmarket. **Chapel Street** is the main drag: in South Yarra it extends for a Golden Mile of trendy shopping and *very* chic cafés; heading south beyond Commercial Road through Prahran and Windsor it gradually moves downmarket. Crossing Chapel Street at right angles in South Yarra, Toorak Road boasts equally ritzy designer boutiques and, if that's possible, becomes even more exclusive east of Grange Road, as it enters Toorak, a suburb synonymous with wealth. **Trams #5, #6 and #72** from Swanston Street will get you from the city centre to Chapel Street.

South Yarra and Toorak

The **South Yarra** stretch of **Chapel Street** is awash with boutiques and speciality shops, bistro bars full of beautiful people and cooler-than-thou nightclubs. Amongst the wall-to-wall chic, it's worth making a beeline for the **Jam Factory** shopping complex, named after its former incarnation, as well as **Como Historic House and Gardens**, overlooking the river from Lechlade Avenue in South Yarra (daily 10am–5pm; $11). This elegant white mansion, a mixture of Regency and Italianate architectural styles, is a good example of the town houses built by wealthy nineteenth-century landowners. To reach the house, walk east along Toorak Road from Chapel Street, and then north on Williams Road; from the city centre, take tram #8 from Swanston Street.

Toorak has never been short of a bean: when Melbourne was founded, the wealthy built their stately homes here on the high bank of the Yarra, leaving the flood-prone lower ground for the poor; in addition, many European Jews who made good after arriving penniless in Australia celebrated their new wealth by moving to Toorak in the 1950s and 1960s. There's little to see or do in the suburb: the hilly, tree-lined streets are full of huge mansions in extensive private gardens, while so-called Toorak Village is stuffed with wickedly expensive designer boutiques.

Prahran and Windsor

Beyond Commercial Road in **Prahran** proper, Chapel Street still focuses on fashion, but in a more street-smart vein, becoming progressively more downmarket as it heads south. Landmarks include **Prahran Market** (Tues & Thurs dawn–5pm, Fri & Sat dawn–6pm), round the corner on Commercial Road, an excellent though expensive food emporium (fish, meat, fruit, vegetables and delicatessen) plus cafés and a few clothes shops. **Chapel Street Bazaar**, on the western side of Chapel Street, has good secondhand clothes, Art Deco jewellery, furniture and bric-a-brac. Just opposite, tucked away in Little Chapel Street, a lane off Chapel Street, **Chapel off Chapel** provides a venue for an eclectic mix of theatre performances, music and art exhibitions. Heading a further 100m south along Chapel Street brings you to **Greville Street**, in the heart of Prahran, a fantastic pocket of eccentric bohemia – young, brash and full of freewheeling brio – which has now taken over from Chapel Street as the corridor of cutting-edge cool, with retro and designer boutiques, music outlets, bookshops, and groovy bars and restaurants. Things really hot up over the weekend, and every Sunday the small **Greville Street Market** has arts, crafts and secondhand clothes and jewellery on the corner of Gratton Street in Gratton Park (noon–5pm).

As Chapel Street crosses High Street the suburb changes to **Windsor** and becomes more interestingly ethnic. Discount furniture and household appliance shops sit cheek by jowl with inexpensive Asian noodle bars, organic produce shops and a few up-and-coming café-bars. Busy Dandenong Road marks the boundary of Windsor and **St Kilda East**. Just across Dandenong Road on Chapel Street lies the **Astor Theatre**, a beautifully decorated cinema in an Art Nouveau building.

South Melbourne and Albert Park

If it's the bay you're heading for, then St Kilda is the obvious destination; the quickest and most interesting way there is on the #96 tram from Bourke or Spencer streets, which runs on a light rail track via South Melbourne and Albert Park, past the Aquatic Centre with its five swimming pools (see "Listings", p.938). **South Melbourne**'s focus is the **South Melbourne Market** on the corner of Coventry and Cecil streets (Wed 8am–2pm, Fri 8am–6pm, Sat & Sun 8am–4pm), an old-fashioned, value-for-money place where you can browse stalls selling everything from fruit and vegetables to clothes and continental delicacies. Opposite here, a number of cafés and upmarket retail stores line **Coventry Street**; at no. 399, three portable iron houses (Sun 1–4pm; viewing by appointment on ☎03/9822 4369), prefabricated residences constructed in England and shipped to Melbourne during the goldrush, have been preserved by the National Trust. At the other end of Coventry Street, **Clarendon Street** is South Melbourne's main shopping precinct, and a fine example of a nineteenth-century streetscape, with original Victorian awnings overhanging numerous cafés, clothing shops and restaurants.

Exclusive **Albert Park** has the feel of a small village, with many lovely old terraced houses and Dundas Place, a shopping centre of mouthwatering delis and bakeries. In the shadow of the St Kilda Road office buildings lies Albert Park itself, the home of the **Australian Grand Prix** (held in March), which Melbourne snatched from Adelaide in 1996.

St Kilda and around

The former seaside resort of **St Kilda** has an air of shabby gentility, which enhances its current schizophrenic reputation as a sophisticated yet seedy suburb, largely residential but blessed with a raging nightlife. Running from St Kilda Road down to the Esplanade, **Fitzroy Street** is Melbourne's red-light district – usually pretty tame, though late at night not a comfortable place for women alone – and epitomizes this split personality, since it's lined with dozens of thoroughly pretentious cafés and bars from which to gawp at the strip's goings-on. On weekend nights these and others throughout St Kilda are filled to overflowing with a style-conscious but fun crowd. During the day there's a very different feel, especially on **Acland Street**, with its wonderful continental cake shops and bakeries. Ogling the mouthwatering window displays is a favourite way of passing the time on Sunday. Also on Sunday, the **St Kilda Craft Market** (10am–4pm) lines the waterfront on Upper Esplanade. It's mainly arts and crafts, and not really good enough to justify the hordes of strollers, but going there is part of the ritual that includes taking a look at the beach, feeding your face, ambling into a few shops, listening to a busker, and perhaps calling at the covered market on Albert Street.

St Kilda's most famous icon, **Luna Park** (Easter to Sept Sat & Sun 11am–6pm; Oct to Easter Fri 7pm–11pm, Sat 11am–11pm, Sun 11am–7pm; Ⓦ www.lunapark.com.au), is located on the Esplanade, entered through the huge laughing clown's face of "Mr Moon". Despite a couple of new attractions, there's nothing very high-tech about this 1912 amusement park: the Scenic Railway – the world's oldest operating roller-coaster – runs along wooden trestles, the dodgem cars could do with a lick of paint and the Ghost Train wouldn't spook a toddler – but then that's half the fun. Wandering around is free, but you pay $6.50 for individual rides, or $32.95 for a day's unlimited rides. You can sit under the palm trees of **O'Donnell Gardens** next door, or nearby **St Kilda Botanical Gardens**, and eat your Acland Street goodies. The **beachfront** is a popular weekend promenade all year round, with separate cycling and walking paths stretching down to Elwood and Brighton, and a long pier thrusting out into the bay. Near the base of the pier are the **St Kilda Sea Baths**. Redevelopment of the historic site, which dates back to 1931, has dragged on for years, but work on this cement blunder (a heroically bad mix of shopping complex and function centre with a Moorish twist) is now complete, with a seawater pool, food shops, and various health facilities like a spa and gym.

On Saturday, Sunday and public holidays, **boat trips** from the pier across Hobsons Bay to Williamstown (Williamstown Bay and River Cruises; departures hourly between 11.30am and 3.30pm – last departure one-way only; 20min; $6, $10 return; ℡03/9397 2255) give lovely views of St Kilda and the city. An alternative is a ninety-minute cruise with Penguin Waters Cruises (daytime $23, sunrise and sunset cruises $33; bookings on ℡03/9645 0533), with a barbecue lunch or dinner thrown in. On the evening cruises – with a little luck – you'll catch a glimpse of **Little penguins** coming ashore at a certain spot 4km from the mouth of the Yarra. As the exact location isn't publicized, you can see them without the crowds that congregate on Phillip Island (see p.948).

Elwood and Elsternwick

The next stop south along the bay, **Elwood**, is a quieter version of St Kilda, still with a faintly alternative air. Ormond Road's original shopfronts conceal a health-food store and an alternative-therapies centre, but more-yuppified cafés and bars have edged their way in. Ormond Esplanade runs past parkland through which occasional paths run down to the beach.

East of Elwood, **Elsternwick** (train to Ripponlea) is a largely Orthodox Jewish area. The original 1918 fittings and facade of Brinsmead Chemist at 73 Glen Eira Rd are protected by the National Trust, as is **Ripponlea House** at 192 Hotham St (daily 10am–5pm; $11), which shows how Melbourne's wealthy elite lived a century ago. The 33-room mansion has magnificent gardens, complete with ornamental lake and fernery, and a way-over-the-top interior. The grounds are popular for picnics at weekends, when the tearoom is also open (11am–4pm). Ten- to fifteen-minutes' walk away in East St Kilda, at 26 Alma Rd opposite the St Kilda Synagogue, is the **Jewish Museum of Australia** (Tues–Thurs 10am–4pm, Sun 11am–5pm; $7; tram #3 or #67 to stop 32 from Swanston Street in the city or from St Kilda Road). The museum's permanent exhibitions focus on Australian and world Jewish history, plus displays on Jewish beliefs and rituals, with a focus on festivals and customs.

Spotswood and Williamstown

Docks and industry dominate the area west of the city centre, reached by sub-urban train, by the *Williamstown Seeker* ferry (11.10am, 1.10pm & 3.10pm) from the Southbank jetty at the Melbourne Exhibition Centre, or by heading out on the Westgate Freeway across the huge Westgate Bridge. A good reason for visiting **Spotswood**, the first suburb across the Yarra, is **Scienceworks**, at 2 Booker St (daily 10am–4.30pm; $9.50, or $14.50 for combined Scienceworks and Planetarium ticket; ⓦwww.scienceworks.museum.vic.gov.au). Inside a Space Age building, set in appropriately desolate wasteland, the displays are ingenious, fun and highly interactive. Part of the exhibition consists of the original Spotswood Pumping Station, an unusually aesthetic early industrial complex with working steam pumps. The Planetarium features state-of-the-art digital technology, taking visitors on a virtual journey through the galaxy (Mon–Fri 2pm, Sat & Sun on the hour 11am–3pm; the 11am and noon shows are aimed at younger children).

On a promontory at the mouth of the Yarra, **Williamstown** is a strange mix of rich and poor; of industry, yachting marinas and working port. Expensive cafés ring Nelson Place, but the down-to-earth *Yacht Club Hotel* here offers the cheapest meal in town – prices have been fixed since the 1970s and it's always packed on Sunday, especially when the **Williamstown Market** is held along the waterfront (third Sun of each month). The most enjoyable way to get to Williamstown is by **boat** from St Kilda (see p.921), or you can take a trip into the city with Williamstown Bay and River Cruises ($10); for more, see the box on p.913.

Bulleen and Eltham

Further afield in the northeastern suburbs lie two further attractions: the Museum of Modern Art at Heide in **Bulleen** and Montsalvat in **Eltham** – you could make a day of it and visit them en route to the Yarra Valley wineries and the Healesville Sanctuary (see p.953). The **Heide Museum of Modern Art** (Tues–Fri 10am–5pm, Sat & Sun noon–5pm; Heide I $7, Heide II $10, combined ticket $15) on Templestowe Road at Bulleen was the home of Melbourne art patrons **John Reed** (1901–1981) and **Sunday Reed** (1905–1981), who in the mid-1930s purchased what was then a derelict dairy farm on the banks of the meandering Yarra River. During the following decades the Reeds fostered and nurtured the talents of young unknown artists and played a central role in the emergence of Australian art movements such as the Angry Penguins, the Antipodeans and the Annandale Realists; the painters Sidney Nolan, John Perceval, Albert Tucker and Arthur Boyd were all members of the artistic circle at Heide at one time or another. The museum consists of two parts. **Heide I**, set in the farmhouse where the Reeds lived from 1934 until 1967, houses a selection of works from the museum's extensive collection of paintings and other works purchased by the Reeds over four decades, including works by famous Australian artists of the mid- to late twentieth century, including Nolan, Tucker, Perceval and Boyd. Exhibits change every six months. **Heide II**, set in an attractively modernist 1960s building, houses the Reeds' Gallery, which shows consistently interesting temporary exhibitions of contemporary Australian art, including paintings, installations, sculptures and photographs. There's a good licensed café in the courtyard adjacent to Heide II, and you can ramble through the extensive gardens, which feature sculptures and a kitchen garden (free entrance). The museum is about 14km from the city centre; take the suburban train to Heidelberg station (Eltham line) then bus #291 to Templestowe Road (frequent services).

Eltham, a bushy suburb further northeast, about 24km from the city, is known as a centre for arts and crafts. Its reputation was established in 1935 when the charismatic painter and architect Justus Jorgensen moved to what was then a separate town and founded **Montsalvat**, a European-style artists' colony. Built with the help of his students and followers, the colony's eclectic design was inspired by medieval European buildings with wonderful quirky results; Jorgensen died before it was completed and it has deliberately been left unfinished. He did, however, live long enough to see his community thrive, and to oversee the completion of the mud-brick Great Hall, whose influence is evident in other mud-brick buildings around Eltham. Today Montsalvat, a two-kilometre walk from Eltham station, contains a gallery and is still home to a colony of painters and craftspeople (daily 9am–5pm; $6.50; Ⓦ www.montsalvat.com.au).

Eating and drinking

Melbourne is Australia's premier city for **eating out**. Sydney may be more style-conscious and Adelaide cheaper, but Melbourne has the best food and the widest choice of it – and almost all of it is exceptionally good value. In the **city centre**, Greek cafés line Lonsdale Street between Swanston and Russell streets, while Little Bourke Street is the home of Chinatown. Lygon Street, in inner-city **Carlton**, is just one of many places across the city with a concentration of Italian restaurants. Johnston Street in **Fitzroy** is the Spanish strip, while nearby Smith Street and arty Brunswick Street both have a huge variety of international cuisines and smart cafés. Greek restaurants fill Swan Street in inner-city **Richmond**, and Vietnamese places dominate Victoria Street. Fitzroy and **St**

Kilda, another gastronomically mixed bag, are the centres of café society; St Kilda also has great restaurants, bakeries and delis, as does Jewish **Balaclava**. In March each year, the city celebrates all this culinary diversity with a **Food and Wine Festival**, with food-themed street parties in the city's various different ethnic areas.

Most licensed restaurants still allow you to **bring your own drink**, though check first, and note that sometimes you're only allowed to bring in wine – in addition, a corkage fee ($1–2 per person) often applies. If you're going to be around for a while, *The Age Cheap Eats in Melbourne*, and its more upmarket companion, *The Age Good Food Guide*, are worthwhile investments.

City centre

There are still plenty of old-fashioned **coffee lounges** in the city – the type of place where you can get a milky cappuccino and grilled cheese on toast, with a mini-jukebox at your table – but stylish **cafés** with smarter decor and more diverse menus are edging in. In the department stores, both the Myer and David Jones **food halls** are excellent for upmarket picnic ingredients, while Melbourne Central has several good eating places.

Cafe La 35th Floor, *Hotel Sofitel*, cnr Collins and Exhibition streets ☎03/9653 7744. The café with the best views in Melbourne, and much more affordable than the exclusive *Le Restaurant* on the same floor (see below). Open daily for breakfast, lunch, dinner and afternoon teas.

Cafe Segovia 33 Block Place, off Little Collins St. One of the oldest of the cafés in this fashionable laneway between Little Collins St and Block Arcade, this Spanish-style place serves good coffee, breakfasts and light meals. Occasional live music on Friday nights. Licensed.

Campari 25 Hardware St. Casual and characterful spot which pulls in lawyers from the nearby courts with excellent southern Italian food, including pasta (around $15) and steaks and fish ($19). Breakfast is also available. Licensed and BYO. Mon–Thurs 7am–5.30pm, Fri 7am–8.30pm.

Crossways Food for Life 123 Swanston St. Dirt-cheap, Indian-style vegetarian food prepared by Hare Krishnas. Mon–Sat 11.30am–2.30pm.

Curry Bowl 250 Elizabeth St. Sri Lankan fast food to eat in or take away. Closed Sun.

Dish 379 St Kilda Rd ☎03/9677 9933. Cavernous modern restaurant nestled in the Heritage-listed *Royce Hotel* a few minutes by tram south of Melbourne's CBD. Food runs from salmon fish cakes, panfried fish and veal shanks to vegetable tarts and a reasonable choice of desserts. It's fairly expensive, unless you go for the lunch set menu ($25). Licensed. Mon–Fri 6.30am–11am, noon–2.30pm & 6–10pm, Sat 6–10pm.

ezard at the Adelphi 187 Flinders Lane ☎03/9639 6811. This hip, dimly lit place is one of Melbourne's coolest eateries, with a tasty range of

East meets West favourites. Expensive. Licensed. Mon–Fri noon–2.30pm & 6–10.30pm, Sat 6–10.30pm.

Gopals 139 Swanston St. *Crossways'* sister restaurant – another very cheap, Hare Krishna-run veggie place. Mon noon–3pm, Tues–Fri noon–8.30pm, Sat 5–8.30pm.

Grand Hyatt Foodcourt 123 Collins St ☎03/9653 4549. Spacious, airy place with various stalls and bars dishing up a range of cakes, imaginative salads and other dishes. Friday night happy hour (5pm–7pm) is popular with the office crowd.

Grossi Florentino 80 Bourke St ☎03/9662 1811. A Melbourne institution. Choose between the cellar café-grill-restaurant, serving inexpensive, home-style pasta dishes, drinks and good coffee, and the very pricey, elegant Italian–French restaurant upstairs. Licensed. Mon–Sat 3pm & 6–11pm, upstairs restaurant closed Sat morning.

Gust Cofetarie 174 Queen St ☎03/9602 4846. Moderately priced European menu with a slight Eastern European slant – try the debrzin sausages with mash. Bookings essential for lunch. Licensed. Mon–Tues 7am–7pm, Wed–Fri 7am–11pm.

Hopetoun Tea Rooms Block Arcade, 282 Collins St ☎03/9650 2777. Tea, scones and delicious cakes have been served in these elegant surroundings for more than one hundred years, but new-fangled delicacies such as focaccia with pesto sauce have now wheedled their way onto the menu. Mon–Thurs 9am–5pm, Fri 9am–6pm, Sat 10am–3pm. Moderate.

Il Solito Posto Basement, 113 Collins St (off George Parade) ☎03/9654 4466. Charming basement location, casual atmosphere and good, no-fuss Italian food make for one of Melbourne's best dining experiences. Prices are moderate to expensive. Licensed. Mon–Fri 7.30am–11pm, Sat 9am–11pm.

Kappo Okita 17 Liverpool St ⊤03/9662 2206. Modest Japanese café with good, inexpensive food, especially sushi and sashimi. Best to reserve for weekend evenings. BYO. Mon–Fri 2.30pm & 6–10pm (Fri until 11pm), Sat 6–10pm.

Kenzan 45 Collins St ⊤03/9654 8933. More upmarket than *Kappo Okita*, this sushi bar is renowned for the freshness of its sushi and sashimi. Licensed. Mon–Fri noon–2.30pm & 6–10pm, Fri & Sat 6–11pm.

Laurent Patisserie 306 Little Collins St (between Collins and Elizabeth streets). Mouthwatering breads, cakes and pastries, as well as filled baguettes, croissants, soups for lunch. Licensed. Mon–Sat 8am–6pm, Sun 9am–5pm.

Le Restaurant 35th Floor, *Hotel Sofitel*, cnr Collins and Exhibition streets ⊤03/9653 0000. Luxurious restaurant with silver service and fantastic views over Melbourne and Port Phillip Bay. Serves carefully prepared seasonal dishes, together with Australian produce such as barramundi and yabbies. Expensive. Tues–Sat 7pm till late.

Medallion Cafe & Cakes 209 Lonsdale St. Popular Greek café, once shabby, now with an over-the-top, disco-style interior, but still serving authentic, cheap food. Daily 8am until late (3am Fri & Sat).

Mekong 241 Swanston St. Small Vietnamese café specializing in *pho* (beef or chicken noodle soup). Excellent-value food (dishes about $5), but packed at lunchtime. Mon–Sat 9am–10pm, Sun 10am–10pm.

Ong International Food Court Basement of the *Welcome Hotel*, 256 Little Bourke St. Authentic Asian food court with stalls selling Chinese, Vietnamese, Malaysian/Singaporean and Thai food. Licensed. Daily 10am–10pm.

Pellegrini's Espresso Bar 66 Bourke St. Melbourne's first espresso bar, and still an institution, with classic 1950s interior and great cheap pasta. Mon–Sat 8am–11.30pm, Sun noon–8pm.

Radii *Park Hyatt Melbourne*, 1 Parliament Square ⊤03/9224 1211. Part of the swanky *Park Hyatt Melbourne*, this monstrously large and expensive restaurant seats close to 150. If you can take your eyes off the over-the-top decor (all marble and mirrors), you'll discover enough waiters to serve a small island state, as well as some of the most imaginative Mediterranean-style dishes in the city. Food fit for a king and an ideal place for marriage proposals and assorted special occasions. Licensed. Daily noon–2.30 & 6–10.30pm.

Satay Inn 250 Swanston St. Excellent, affordable Malaysian place, close to the big department stores. BYO. Daily 11am–11pm.

Southgate Across the river from Flinders Street station. With fine views of the river and the city skyline, this centre has developed into a very popular place to dine and drink – advance booking is essential for the restaurants on Friday and Saturday nights. Some of the best places are *The Blue Train Café* (⊤03/9696 0111), which attracts a young, hip crowd and serves drinks and tasty and very inexpensive light meals; *Egusto* (⊤03/9690 9819), which does moderately priced "modern Australian" cuisine with an Italian slant; and the more upmarket *Walter's Wine Bar* (⊤03/9690 9211) and *Simply French* (⊤03/9699 9804), the latter serving superb but pricey French food – leave some space for the brilliant desserts.

Swiss Rosti Bar 87 Flinders Lane, between Exhibition and Spring streets ⊤03/9654 0088. Tasty, well-presented and moderately priced Swiss–German fare, along with a few international dishes. Try *kassler* (pickled pork) with sauerkraut or bratwurst, fried onions and mushrooms, all served with *rosti* (fried grated potatoes), a Swiss speciality. Licensed. Mon–Fri 9am–late.

Syracuse 23 Bank Place ⊤03/9670 1777. Mouthwatering tapas (served from 3pm) and lamb and leek sausages, along with fantastic cheeses, panforte and coffee, all at moderate prices. There's also an extensive wine list, a good selection of cigars and seductive atmosphere. Licensed. Mon–Fri 7.30am–11pm.

Tsindos 197 Lonsdale St ⊤03/9663 3194. All the Greek classics from taramasalata to moussaka and souvlakia at reasonable prices, plus live bouzouki music every night except Sunday. Licensed and BYO. Daily noon–3pm & 5–10pm (Fri & Sat till 11pm).

VIS 245 Swanston St ⊤03/9662 9995. Stylish café-restaurant underneath *The Lounge* with food to match – check the blackboard menu for unusual, moderately priced dishes such as prawn and basil ravioli and smoked rack of lamb *harissa*. Licensed. Daily 10am till late (Sat from noon).

Waiters Restaurant 20 Meyers Place, off Bourke St between Exhibition and Spring streets ⊤03/9650 1508. Long-established Italian place on the first floor above a bar, once a waiters' favourite for its late hours. No frills, simple food and low prices. Licensed and BYO. Mon–Fri noon to 2.30pm plus Mon–Sat 6pm–midnight.

William Angliss College La Trobe St ⊤03/9606 2111. Owned by a catering college, this cheap restaurant aims to dish up fine food and service, and usually succeeds, though occasional hiccups may occur. Bookings essential.

Zukini 310 Flinders Lane. Stylish, moderately priced two-level canteen and restaurant renowned for its mix of chemical-free food and Zen-like decor. If you can decipher the verbose menu, you'll find a big range of seasonally fresh produce, plus meat dishes, a large wine list and a superb variety of teas. The canteen menu is also available downstairs in the more formal dining area. Licensed. Mon–Fri 7am–1am, Sat 10am–1am.

Chinatown

Yum cha (elsewhere known as dim sum, a series of small delicacies served from trolleys) is available at lunchtime almost everywhere; on Sunday it's a crowded ritual.

Camy Shanghai Dumpling and Noodle Restaurant Tattersalls Lane, between Little Bourke and Lonsdale streets, close to Swanston St. An extremely cheap, partly self-service place, dishing up very simple but delicious dumplings and noodles. No alcohol. Mon–Fri 11am–10pm, Sat & Sun 11am–9.30pm.

Chez Phat 7 Waratah Place ☎03/9663 0988. First-floor hideaway with a marvellous 1970s atmosphere. The interesting menu includes Jerusalem artichoke soup, porterhouse steak, and roast beetroot and duck neck sausages; tapas are served on Sunday. Licensed. Tues–Sat 6pm–midnight (Fri from noon, Sat from 10am), Sun 4–11pm.

China Bar 235 Russell St. Cheap chain with lots of Malaysian–Chinese noodle or rice fast-food classics such as won ton soup, char kway teow (fried rice noodles), nasi lemak (coconut rice); plus assorted claypot dishes and desserts. BYO. Other branches at 747 Swanston St, Carlton; and 500 Chapel St, South Yarra.

Empress of China 120–122 Little Bourke St ☎03/9663 1883. Expensive but good value, with lots of lesser-known dishes on offer. Licensed. Closed Sat lunchtime.

Flower Drum 17 Market Lane, between Bourke and Little Bourke streets ☎03/9662 3655. Outstanding Cantonese cuisine, including exquisite seafood and fish, an extensive wine list, excellent service and luxurious ambience. Naturally, this all comes at a price: expect to pay at least $70 per person for three courses. Licensed. Mon–Sat 2pm & 6–10pm, Sun 2pm.

King of Kings 209 Russell St. Simple, inexpensive Hong Kong-style food, including *congee* and lots of dishes with pork and offal. BYO. Lunch and dinner daily; open until 2.30am.

Little Malaysia 26 Liverpool St. Cheap and good Malaysian hawker fare. Licensed and BYO. Daily 11.30am–3pm & 5.30–11pm.

Shark Fin House 131 Little Bourke St ☎03/9663 1555. Converted warehouse with three storeys devoted to about fifty kinds of *yum cha*. Very busy at lunchtime, especially at weekends. There's another branch at 50–52 Little Bourke St (☎03/9662 2681). Licensed and BYO. Daily noon–3pm (Sat from 11.30am, Sun from 11am) & 5.30pm–1.30am.

Carlton and North Melbourne

As well as an Italian strip of restaurants and cafés on Lygon Street, between Gratton and Elgin streets, Carlton is home to several good Asian restaurants. To the south of Carlton, North Melbourne harbours an excellent Balinese restaurant.

Brunetti 198–204 Faraday St ☎03/9347 2801. An array of display cases filled with a mouthwatering selection of chocolates, pastries, biscuits and cakes, plus coffee. Licensed restaurant next door. Cakes and café daily 7am–10pm; restaurant Mon–Fri noon–3pm (Sat from 12.30pm); dinner Mon–Sat 6–10pm.

Jimmy Watson's 333 Lygon St ☎03/9347 3985. This Lygon St icon features very good bar meals (modern Australian cuisine) in convivial, atmospheric surroundings, and a super wine list.

Moderate prices. Licensed. Mon 10am–6pm, Tues–Sat 10am–9.30pm.

Lemongrass 174–176 Lygon St ☎03/9662 2244. Royal Thai cuisine in stylishly subdued surroundings. Moderate to expensive. Licensed. Daily noon–2.30pm & 5.30–10pm.

Shakahari 201–203 Faraday St ☎03/9347 3848. Excellent and imaginative Asian-influenced vegetarian food at moderate prices. Licensed. Mon–Sat noon–3pm & 6.30–9.30 (Fri & Sat until 10pm), Sun 6.30–9.30.

Tiamo 1 303 Lygon St ☎03/9347 5759. One-time beatnik hangout and still popular with students, with layers of browning 1950s posters and a good-value blackboard menu. Next door is its sibling, *Tiamo 2*, which is more upmarket but still excellent value. Licensed and BYO. Mon–Sat 7.30am–11pm, Sun 9.30am–10pm.

Toofey's 162A Elgin St ☎03/9347 9838. Considered Melbourne's best seafood restaurant. The extremely fresh fish and seafood are prepared in a light, Mediterranean or Middle Eastern style.

Expensive. Licensed. Tues–Fri noon–3pm & 6–10pm, Sat & Sun 6–10pm.

Toto's Pizza House 101 Lygon St ☎03/9347 1630. Melbourne's first pizzeria, dating from the 1950s – cheap, cheerful and noisy. Licensed. Daily 11am–11pm.

Warung Agus 305 Victoria St ☎03/9329 1737. Authentic Balinese restaurant with superb, affordable food. Licensed and BYO (wine only). Tues–Sat 6.30 till late.

Fitzroy and Collingwood

Adjacent Fitzroy and Collingwood probably have the widest choice of cuisines in the city, and are good places to finish off a night on the town, as there's always lots going on. There's a smallish Spanish centre with a few tapas bars on Johnston Street, between Brunswick and Nicholson streets.

Brunswick Street

Afghan Gallery 327 Brunswick St ☎03/9417 2430. Cheap and authentic Afghan food, popular with students, served up amidst Afghan hangings and rugs. Licensed and BYO. Daily 6–11pm.

Babka Bakery Cafe 358 Brunswick St ☎03/9416 0091. A deservedly popular place: the home-made bread and cakes are divine, and dishes from the changing blackboard menu are equally enticing. Try Russian blintzes for breakfast or borsch (a tangy, beetroot-based soup) and sourdough bread for lunch. Cheap. Licensed and BYO. Tues–Sun 7am–7pm.

Mario's 303 Brunswick St ☎03/9417 3343. European-style café where you can eat breakfast (until midnight), lunch and dinner or just have a coffee or a drink. Dauntingly smart staff and decor, but not expensive or dressy. The clientele is an interesting mixture of poseurs, celebrities and scruffs. Mon–Wed & Sun 7am–midnight, Thurs–Sat 7am–1am.

Rhumbaralla's 342 Brunswick St ☎03/9417 5652. The neon sign in the window is one of the street's landmarks, and the inside of this stylish café is just as vibrantly coloured. Breakfast until noon – the eggs Benedict are popular – then it's anything from focaccia to steak. Licensed and BYO. Daily 9am–1am.

Shanti 285 Brunswick St ☎03/9416 2170. Moderately priced tandoori dishes, southern Indian specialities cooked in coconut milk, plus lots of vegetarian options and seafood. Licensed and BYO (wine only). Mon–Fri noon–2pm & 6–10.30pm, Sat & Sun noon–2pm.

Thai Thani 293 Brunswick St ☎03/9419 6463. One of Melbourne's best Thai restaurants, on two crowded levels, with moderate prices. Licensed

and BYO (wine only). Daily 6–10.30pm.

The Vegie Bar 380 Brunswick St ☎03/9417 6935. Cheap, popular and hip (rather than hippie) place with simple, fresh vegetarian and vegan food. Licensed and BYO (wine only). Daily 11am–10pm.

Johnston Street

Carmen Bar 74 Johnston St ☎03/9417 4794. The best-value tapas bar in the area, usually full of Spanish people, and with live flamenco Thursday to Saturday. Tues–Sun 6pm–1am.

Guru da Dhaba 240 Johnston St ☎03/9486 9155. Cheap and always packed Indian restaurant specializing in Punjabi cuisine – advance bookings are advised. BYO. Daily 5.30–11pm, Sat & Sun noon–3pm also.

Kahlo's 36 Johnston St ☎03/9417 7810. Smallish, cosy tapas bar. Wed–Sat 6pm–1am.

Smith Street

Breizoz 123 Smith St ☎03/9415 758. Savoury and sweet crepes galore. Licensed. Tues–Sat 6pm till late, also Fri noon–3pm, Sat & Sun noon–5pm.

Cafe Coco 129 Smith St ☎03/9417 39370. Cosy spot, with a regularly changing menu of inexpensive light meals, excellent cakes and good coffee. Licensed and BYO (wine only). Mon–Fri 11am–10.30pm, Sat & Sun 9am–10.30pm.

Gluttony – It's a Sin 278 Smith St ☎03/9419 2949. Good cakes, cooked breakfasts and meals. Popular with locals. Licensed and BYO. Tues–Sat 7am–11pm, Sun 10am–11pm.

Soulfood Cafe 273 Smith St ☎03/9419 2949. Comfortable cafeteria-style vegetarian café with wooden trestle tables. Daily 10am–4pm.

Richmond

Swan Street, running from Church Street towards Wattle Park, is home to Melbourne's best Greek restaurants. On the north side of Richmond, **Victoria Street** is lined with Vietnamese supermarkets, clothes shops and dozens of cheap, authentic restaurants.

Fenix 680–682 Victoria St ☎ 03/9427 8500. Great views over the Yarra, especially in summer on the deck. As for the food, you can dive into steak, fish and steamed pudding, all of it decently priced and well presented. Mon–Fri 9am–11pm, Sat & Sun 8am–11pm.

Salona 262A Swan St ☎ 03/9429 1460. Long-established Greek restaurant – one of four in this block – serving good, plain and very reasonably priced dishes. Licensed and BYO. Daily noon–11.30pm.

Tho Tho's Bar-Restaurant 66 Victoria St ☎ 03/9428 5900. Usually packed and noisy, this place looks a bit more stylish than the other no-frills restaurants in this "Little Saigon" section of Victoria Street. Inexpensive food – the lunch specials are especially good value. Licensed and BYO.

Daily 11am–midnight.

Thy Thy 1 Upstairs at 142 Victoria St ☎ 03/9429 1104. The most popular Vietnamese restaurant on Victoria St – there's always a queue to get in – offering simple but tasty, inexpensive food BYO. Daily 8am–10pm.

Thy Thy 2 116 Victoria St ☎ 03/9428 5914. A slightly more upmarket version of *Thy Thy 1*, but also very popular. BYO. Daily 10am–11pm.

Vao Doi 120 Victoria St ☎ 03/9428 3264. Another much-frequented Vietnamese place, with set lunch menus for the uninitiated. BYO. Daily 10am–11pm.

VV 86 Victoria St ☎ 03/9429 8328. Stylish bar and restaurant attracting a mixed clientele of local Vietnamese, Australians and students from Malaysia, Singapore and Thailand. Inexpensive food. Licensed and BYO. Daily 11am–11pm.

South Yarra, Prahran and Windsor

Borsch, Vodka and Tears 173 Chapel St, Windsor ☎ 03/9530 2694. Hearty Eastern European cuisine – beetroot-based, deep red borsch soup, pierogi (dumplings), cabbage rolls and potato blintzes (pancakes) – plus a bottomless list of vodkas (plain, sweet, flavoured any which way). Inexpensive. Daily 10am till late.

Caffe e Cucina 581 Chapel St, South Yarra ☎ 03/9827 4139. Still one of Melbourne's coolest eating spots, attracting a smart clientele and dishing up fantastic pasta. Licensed. Mon–Sat 7am–midnight.

Candy Bar 162 Greville St, Prahran. Funky joint popular for eating, drinking, bopping into the early hours or just lounging around on comfy sofas; food ranges from noodles and curries to polenta. Licensed. Mon–Fri noon till late, Sat & Sun 10am till late.

Chinta Ria Jazz 176 Commercial Rd, Prahran ☎ 03/9510 6520. Smart Malaysian eatery serving excellent curry laksa, nasi lemak, curry puffs and other Malaysian favourites. Very moderately priced. BYO. Daily except noon–2.30pm & 6–10.30pm.

Falafel House 196 Toorak Rd, South Yarra. Middle Eastern takeaway, perfect after pubbing or clubbing. Daily 9am–5am.

Greville Bar 143 Greville St, Prahran. Small bar and eatery with comfortable, dark-wood interior; there's a daily specials board as well as a tapas-style menu featuring things like char-grilled polenta fingers and duck spring rolls with hoisin sauce – great for sharing. Licensed. Daily 5pm–11pm.

Tamani Bistro 156 Toorak Rd, South Yarra. Dimly lit, crowded Italian cheapie. BYO. Daily 9am–10.30pm.

South Melbourne, Albert Park and Port Melbourne

There's not much of a night-time scene in these suburbs, but cafés and delicatessens dish up a mouthwatering selection of food during the day.

Albert Park Deli 129 Dundas Place, Albert Park ☎ 03/9699 9594. Superb delicatessen takeaway, specializing in delicious breads and *arancini* (Italian rice balls). Daily 5am–9pm.

Arkibar 27 Coventry St, South Melbourne ☎ 03/9690 6688. Modern café serving good

Italian food. Licensed. Mon–Wed 7.30am–4.30pm, Thurs & Fri 7.30am–10pm, Sat 9am–1pm.

Cafe Sweethearts 263 Coventry St, South Melbourne. Good for breakfast, and also has numerous (and some very exotic-sounding)

varieties of sandwiches and eggs. Mon–Fri 7am–3pm, Sat & Sun 8am–3pm.

Coventry Blue 313 Coventry St, South Melbourne. Set in a terrace house opposite the South Melbourne market, this café has an alternative feel and cheap vegetarian grub. BYO. Tues–Thurs 7am–3pm, Fri & Sat 7am–5pm, Sun 8am–5pm.

Montague Hotel Cnr Park and Montague streets, South Melbourne ☏ 03/9690 9044. Atmospheric old pub with a good restaurant out the back serving hearty, moderately priced pub grub.

Montague Park Foodstore 406 Park St ☏ 03/9682 9680. Delicious dishes and desserts to take away or eat in – it's particularly pleasant in summer when tables are set out on the footpath. Daily 8am–5pm.

Ruby Ruby 321 Bay St, Port Melbourne. Popular meeting place for the seaside set, this part-bar, part-café is a great place for a meal, snack, wine or coffee. Licensed. Tue–Fri noon–3pm & 5pm till late, Sat & Sun 9am till late.

Sushi Chef 193 Clarendon St. Inexpensive sushi bar relying mainly on the takeaway trade, but you can also eat in. Mon–Sat 11am–8pm.

Villagio Continental Delicatessen Dundas Place, Albert Park. Gleaming shop full of all kinds of Italian food, with tables outside where you can eat your selections and drink coffee. Closed Sun.

Vista Bar & Bistro Cnr Bridport and Montague streets, Albert Park. Eclectic international mix of dishes and a good selection of wines by the glass. Tues–Fri & Sun noon–3pm & 6–10pm, Sat 6–10pm.

St Kilda

Although **Acland Street** is still very popular – especially for late breakfasts and pigging out on cakes – **Fitzroy Street** has taken over as St Kilda's liveliest area, especially the block from Grey Street to the waterfront – stylish new cafés and restaurants (with prices to match) seem to open almost every day.

Bala's 1D Shakespeare Grove, just off Acland St near Luna Park. Excellent, cheap Asian takeaway food, including lots of stir-fried dishes with ultra-fresh ingredients, plus samosas, curry puffs and lassis. There are a few tables if you want to eat in, though it gets very busy at lunch and dinner. Mon–Sat 4–10.30pm, Sun noon–10.30pm.

Big Mouth 201 Barkly St ☏ 03/9534 4611. A great spot for people-watching. The café downstairs is open for breakfast and light meals from 10am until late, while the upstairs restaurant (modern Australian cuisine) is open Monday to Friday 5pm–1am, Saturday 11am–late, and Sunday 10.30am till late. Licensed.

Birdcage 129 Fitzroy St ☏ 03/9534 0277. In a corner of the *George Hotel* foyer, this tiny bar-cum-bistro does a great line in Japanese food – choose from sashimi, noodles and rice dishes. Doesn't take evening bookings. Licensed. Tues–Fri noon–10.30pm, Sat 5–10.30pm, Sun noon–midnight.

Cafe Ninety Seven 97 Fitzroy St ☏ 03/9525 5922. Cosy little café; in warm weather you can sit in the pleasant courtyard next to the café. The back of the courtyard is framed by palm trees and the columned facade of a stately house. Cakes and light meals like risotto and soups. Moderate. Licensed. Daily 7.30am–midnight.

Cafe Racer 15 Marine Parade ☏ 03/9534 9988. Ocean-facing café that provides excellent coffee and snacks to posses of cyclists and bikers, their

Harley Davidsons and Vespas parked at the kerbside. Daily 6am–6pm.

Chinta Blues 6 Acland St ☏ 03/9534 9233. Breezy, airy Malaysian eaterie, part of well-known restaurateur Simon Goh's string of restaurants, with very moderately priced food. There's another small branch at 94 Acland St (bookings on ☏ 03/9525 4664). BYO. Both open Mon–Sat noon–2.30pm & 6–10.30pm, Sun noon–10pm.

Cicciolina 130 Acland St ☏ 03/9525 3333. Friendly staff and moderately priced Italian food with an interesting twist keep this restaurant going from strength to strength, despite the number of tables crammed into the small space. Licensed. Mon–Sat noon–11pm, Sun noon–10pm.

Circa At *The Prince St Kilda*, 2 Acland St ☏ 03/9534 5033. Big on style and price, this is one of Melbourne's best spots for fine dining, boasting a magnificently theatrical fit-out, excellent food and wine and top service. More casual dining can be found at *Circ*, its slightly younger offshoot downstairs, where you can breakfast or lunch in a gorgeous courtyard filled with olive trees and massive terracotta urns. Licensed. Tues–Thurs & Sat 6–11.30pm, Fri & Sun noon–3pm & 6–11.30pm.

The Espy Kitchen at the Esplanade Hotel 11 Upper Esplanade ☏ 03/9534 0211. The veggie restaurant at the back is casual and slow, with slapdash decor to match, but the excellent food is worth the wait. Daily noon–3pm & 6–8pm.

Galleon Cafe 9 Carlisle St ☎03/9534 8934. Breakfast, served until 4pm, is the big attraction here, especially popular at weekends. Licensed and BYO. Mon–Fri 9am–11pm, Sat & Sun 8.30am–11pm.

Greasy Joe's 68 Acland St ☎03/9525 3755. Good greasy breakfast until 6pm, and a range of burgers both meaty and veggie, which you can eat at pavement tables. Licensed. Daily 7am–1am.

Lip 133 Fitzroy St ☎03/9593 6133. Cheapish restaurant serving flavoursome nosh from all points of the globe. Good wine list too, with lots of by-the-glass selections. Licensed. Mon–Thurs & Sun noon–midnight, Fri & Sat noon–1am.

Luxe 15 Inkerman St ☎03/9534 0255. Cool minimalist decor, an extensive wine list and moderately priced European bistro-style food that satisfies rather than stupefies. If it seems too busy try the *Luxe Cellar*, a snug bar/café next door, for first-rate wine and nibbles. Licensed. Mon–Sat 6pm-10.30pm, Sun 1pm til late.

The Melbourne Wine Room In the *George Hotel*, cnr Fitzroy and Grey streets ☎03/9525 5599. Swanky restaurant, bar and café with full meals (such as Sicilian-style ocean trout; barramundi with roasted tomatoes) and snacks (salad of seared crab meat and baby leeks; duck ravioli with pea purée), plus a wine list offering three hundred vintages. Moderate to expensive. Daily noon–11pm.

One Fitzroy Street Corner of Fitzroy St and The Esplanade ☎03/9593 8800. Hard-to-beat location, with a café and bar downstairs serving cheap to moderately priced café food (pizza, pasta, salads) and a more expensive, ultramodern restaurant upstairs sporting a balcony with stupendous views over Port Phillip Bay. The menu here features East-meets-West dishes such as spaghetti with mussels, pan-fried chicken with Asian vegetables and Sichuan pepper mudcrab. Licensed. Daily noon–midnight.

Stokehouse 30 Jacka Blvd ☎03/9525 5555. Right by the beach (it gets packed in warm weather), this restaurant has two sections: a very affordable downstairs section with lots of unusual pizzas and pastas, fantastic cakes, coffee and wines; and a pricier upstairs section with superb views of the bay and excellent Italian-inspired food. Moderate to expensive. Licensed. Downstairs open Mon–Sat 11am–1am, Sun 10am–1am, upstairs daily noon–2.30pm & 6pm–10pm.

Termini 60A Fitzroy St ☎03/9537 3465. *Termini* subscribes to the what-do-they-know-about-food style of dealing with customers. Luckily, they know one end of a pot from another: the main courses, from pasta to pork, are simple and rustic, while desserts, such as rich chocolate *sfomato*, are sensational. The business card – designed like a train ticket – is also a nice touch – as befits the restaurant's location in the old St Kilda Railway Station. Licensed. Tues–Fri 9am–11pm, Sat & Sun 10am–11pm. Moderate.

Topolinos 87 Fitzroy St ☎03/9534 4856. A dimly lit, noisy and smoky St Kilda institution, which churns out cheap pizzas, generous portions of pasta and good cocktails until very late. Licensed. Mon–Thurs noon–3am, Fri–Sun noon–6am.

Wild Rice 211 Barkly St ☎03/9534 2849. Vegan macrobiotic café with a lovely courtyard garden. Daily noon–10pm.

Elwood and Balaclava

Elwood's easy-going haunts are similar to St Kilda's, while **Balaclava**, to the east along Carlisle Street, specializes in inexpensive kosher food.

Beach House 63A Ormond Esplanade, Elwood ☎03/9531 7788. Friendly, if somewhat chaotic café next to the car park at Elwood Beach. Very good for breakfast, but *very* crowded on weekends, so book ahead. Licensed. Daily 9am–5.30pm.

Cafe Tarrango 15 Ormond Rd, Elwood ☎03/9531 7151. Indian-run café, with delicious organic, bio-dynamic vegetarian food at cheap prices, though there's not much atmosphere. Licensed and BYO. Mon 5–11pm, Tues–Sun 10am–11pm.

Glicks 330A Carlisle St, Balaclava ☎03/9527 2198. Friendly bakery renowned for bagels and traditional Jewish savouries: try the kreplach, *latkes* or gefilte fish. Mon–Thurs & Sun 6am–9pm, Fri until sunset. Closed Sat.

Jerry's Milk Bar 345 Barkly St, Elwood ☎03/9531 3078. Cornershop milk bar-cum-café brimming with old-fashioned trappings and locals who come for the cheap delicious soups, pasta and risotto. Daily 7am–6pm.

Turtle Cafe 34 Glenhuntly Rd, Elwood ☎03/9525 6952. Relaxed old corner café that attracts a faithful crowd for breakfast and light meals and snacks including bagels, foccacia, soups, salads. Cheap. Daily 7am–7pm.

Zartowa 114 Ormond Rd, Elwood ☎03/9531 1700. More upmarket than the *Turtle*, this popular café-restaurant at the yuppie end of Ormond Rd features a varied à la carte menu of Australian, Mediterranean and Asian-inspired dishes. Lots of foccacias and salads for brunch, plus good coffee. Licensed. Daily 9am–11pm.

Nightlife and entertainment

Melbourne has a rich arts and music scene, and there's always plenty to do in the evening. To find out **what's on**, check out *The Age* on Friday, when the newspaper publishes a comprehensive entertainment guide, "EG". *Melbourne Events* is a handy free monthly guide to all sorts of happenings, available at tourist information outlets. Also check out the free magazines *Beat* and *Inpress*, which you can pick up at most record shops, cinemas and cafés.

Annual festivals further enliven the scene: the **Melbourne International Festival** (ⓦwww.melbournefestival.com.au) in October concentrates on mainstream visual and performing arts, with a sprinkling of good concerts and opera. The much more experimental and innovative **Melbourne Fringe Festival** (ⓦwww.melbournefringe.org.au) happens more or less at the same time, as does the **Melbourne Writers' Festival** (ⓦwww.mwf.com.au). The heavily promoted **Moomba Festival**, held during the first half of March, has events including firework displays and dragon boat races on the banks of the Yarra River in Alexandra Gardens, but is actually rather drab and commercial. Three music festivals take place in the first half of the year: the **Melbourne Jazz Festival** in the last week of January, at venues in the city centre; the **Melbourne Music Festival** in February, one of the largest Australian festivals of contemporary music; and the **Brunswick Music Festival** in the third week of March, concentrating on folk and world music. The **Next Wave Festival**, held over two weeks in the second half of May, celebrates Victoria's young artists, writers and musicians.

Tickets for most venues can be booked through Ticketmaster (ⓣ13 61 66, ⓦwww.ticketmaster.com.au) or Ticketek (ⓣ13 28 49, ⓦwww.ticketek .com.au); both take credit-card bookings only. You can buy tickets half-price on the day of performance from the HalfTix booth, on the Bourke Street Mall (Mon & Sat 10am–2pm, Tues–Thurs 11am–6pm, Fri 11am–6.30pm; cash only; ⓣ03/9654 9420).

Bars and pubs

Melbourne's fondness for a drink or three is reflected in its plethora of excellent **bars and pubs** – from places so obscure and cutting-edge you'll only know they exist by word of mouth to large establishments catering to broader and louder tastes. The push to revive Melbourne's once staid CBD has seen many older watering holes transformed into lively, youth-oriented venues, while cheap bar licences have meant that new spots are popping up each week. In addition, the relaxing of Melbourne's once draconian licensing laws has produced enlightened opening hours, meaning that it's now possible to drink from noon until dawn. The distinction between restaurant, bar, café and nightclub is often blurred, but not at the handful of pub breweries, where a range of beers is made on the premises. A number of drinking places are also listed under "Live music", overleaf.

City Centre

Bridie O'Reilly's 62 Little Collins St. Above-average theme pub, with lots of Irish gewgaws and hearty grub like stews, steaks and Guinness pies. There's another *Bridie*'s in South Yarra (see p.919). **Charles Dickens Tavern** Downstairs at Block Court, 290 Collins St. Comfy place for homesick Brits, with bitter and Guinness on tap, pint glasses, and live soccer and rugby on big-screen TVs.

The Elephant and Wheelbarrow 96 Bourke St. A popular Friday night spot, this English theme pub has timber booths, a photograph of Big Ben on the wall, plus simple, wholesome and inexpensive food.

Gin Palace 190 Little Collins St (entry via Russell Place). Glamorous subterranean joint with an upmarket drinks list specializing in cocktails – not cheap, but delicious and generous. Yummy food and good lounge music, too.

Glowbar 422 Queen St. Opposite the Victoria Market, this sci-fi-style bar is flooded with blue neon lighting and attracts a very fashion-savvy crowd.

Hairy Canary 212 Little Collins St. This modern and stylish bar is a real people-puller, especially later in the week. An extensive menu is available most of the day, with a wide range of local and imported beers, wines by the glass and cocktails.

Khokolat 43 Hardware Lane. Attracts a laid-back crowd in search of cool retro style, sophisticated sounds and simple but tempting food.

The Lounge 243 Swanston St. Genuine all-rounder, attracting an arty-grungy crowd. The bar and nightclub have live music (see "Clubs" on p.934), and there's good food in the upstairs restaurant – eat alfresco on the terrace.

Meyers Place 20 Meyers Place, off Bourke St. This swish, dimly lit hole in the wall has proved a massive hit with Melbourne's trendy office workers and is the grooviest place to fall down in town on a Friday night, bar none.

Pugg Mahone 106–112 Hardware St. Another Irish theme pub, with a great party atmosphere on Fridays and Saturdays, fuelled by house bands playing a mixture of folk and R&B.

Stork Hotel 504 Elizabeth St. Phlegmatic watering hole, located in a historic hotel from the goldrush era, featuring lovely Art Deco fittings, emphysemic regulars and superb artwork on the walls from some of Australia's finest cartoonists, including Melbourne-based Michael Leunig.

Tony Starr's Kitten Club 267 Little Collins St. Sleek and stylish interior tricked out with slightly Oriental furnishings, conducive to lolling on comfy sofas and ottomans while cradling a cocktail and nibbling on Asian-inspired food from the grill.

Young & Jackson's Cnr Swanston and Flinders streets. Victoria's oldest and most famous boozer has undergone a massive renovation, but it's still as good a place as anywhere to start drinking your way around town.

North Melbourne, Carlton and Fitzroy

Builders Arms 211 Gertrude St, Fitzroy. Groovy pub with guest DJs on weekends, when it's easily identifiable by the punters queuing to get in. Meals and snacks are available, and the atmosphere is laid-back and unpretentious. The "No Pokies" sign above the door has become a Melbourne land-mark.

Gypsy Bar 334 Brunswick St, Fitzroy. Intimate bar crammed with Brunswick St's finest, especially for jazz on Sunday night. Great coffee and food.

Lemon Tree 10 Grattan St, Carlton. Upmarket bar that often features live jazz and has a fine beer garden.

Lord Newry 543 Brunswick St, North Fitzroy. The cosy front bar with an open fire is a good place for conversation, while delicious food is served upstairs, where there might be anything from poetry readings to jazz.

Pumphouse Hotel 128 Nicholson St, Fitzroy. Pub brewery, very popular with backpackers from the nearby hostel, *The Nunnery*.

Punters Club Hotel 376 Brunswick St, Fitzroy. Legendary knees-up drinking hole boasting a rough-and-ready band scene each night and obscenely cheap pool tables.

The Redback Brewery 75 Flemington Rd, North Melbourne. Slick boutique brewery packed out on Friday and Saturday with the striped-shirt brigade. Redback, the house beer, is one of the tastiest around.

Richmond, Prahran and South Yarra

All Nations Hotel 64 Lennox St, off Swan St, Richmond. Old-style Aussie pub with exceptional bar meals and a relaxing beer garden.

Bridie O'Reilly's 462 Chapel St, South Yarra. Irish-themed pub incongruously housed in an old church and saved from terminal tackiness by the pleasant front patio. Has meals and plenty of memorabilia from the Emerald Isle. Can get rau-cous on weekends, but it's fun if you're desperate for a Guinness or British beer.

Candy Bar 162 Greville St, Prahran. Roomy bar populated with couches, fireplaces and, at night, Melbourne's twenty-something, party-going dance crowd. Dress up, however, or you may have trou-ble getting past the fashion police at the door.

Fawkner Club 52 Toorak Rd, South Yarra. Swanky pub with a great beer garden, though it's hard to get a seat on a sunny day.

Revolver 229 Chapel St, Prahran. Electronic beat DJs and artists create a cool vibe every night, bands play most weekends, while it's the perfect place on a Saturday afternoon, when DJs spin throbbing reggae and dub sounds. You can grab a snack in the Thai restaurant, lounge around with a drink in the spacious, comfortable main area, or boogie in the back room.

St Kilda

Dog's Bar 54 Acland St. Chic setting attracting a dedicated clientele. The wine list is terrific (although there's a surprisingly small range of beers) and there's great tucker like bangers and mash, steak, pizza, pasta and chips.

The Esplanade Hotel 11 Upper Esplanade. Famous for its beachside views, this hotel is the epicentre of St Kilda's drinking scene and shouldn't be missed. Bands play every night and there are inexpensive meals from *The Espy Kitchen* at the rear, plus pool tables and pinball machines.

The George Public Bar 127 Fitzroy St. Very cool underground bar with an upbeat design. Favoured by locals, it has a large range of beers on tap, plus a pool table and free live music on Saturday afternoons. The service is friendly and the kitchen is open until late each night, serving a wide range of snacks and good-value meals. Table seats outside.

Mink Bar *The Prince St Kilda*, 2B Acland St. This subterranean space has back-lit refrigerated shelves stacked high with an astonishing array of Russian, Polish, Swedish, Finnish, Lithuanian and – gulp – Japanese vodka. There are also private booths for intimate tête-à-têtes and a portrait of Karl Marx hanging from the wall. A great place for convivial quaffing and mellowing, it also has film nights (free) most weeks on a big screen.

The Prince St Kilda 29 Fitzroy St. Defiantly local and no-frills, the downstairs public bar has an air of stubborn resistance in the face of St Kilda's freewheeling gentrification. Frequented in equal parts by colourful local identities and desperadoes, this hotel is not for the faint-hearted.

Veludo Bar 175 Acland St. Magnet for St Kilda fashion plates, *Veludo* sports a bar downstairs with interesting and cheap food, and a smart restaurant upstairs overlooking Acland St. Spacious and stylish, it really gathers steam on the weekends.

Live music

Melbourne has a thriving **band** scene, and just about every pub puts on some sort of music – often free – at some time during the week. The pubs listed below are also good places for a drink, and always have at least two bars, so you can escape the din if you want to. Grungy Richmond has a big concentration of **music pubs**, with several putting on African and reggae music; Fitzroy and St Kilda are the other areas to head to for a range of live music. Free **listings** magazines such as *Beat*, *Inpress* or *Zebra* are good sources of information about the local music scene, while local FM stations Triple R (102.7) and PBS (106.7) air alternative music and tell you what's on and where.

City centre and the northern suburbs

Bennetts Lane 25 Bennetts Lane, off Little Lonsdale St in the CBD, between Exhibition and Russell streets. One of Melbourne's most interesting jazz venues, now expanded to include a larger back room to complement the original cramped, 1950s-style cellar.

Dan O'Connell's 225 Canning St, between Rathdowne and Nicholson streets, Fitzroy. Irish music from Wednesday to Sunday; no cover charge.

Grace Darling Hotel 114 Smith St, Collingwood. Pleasant watering hole, which sometimes hosts live jazz and R&B.

The Punters Club 376 Brunswick St, Fitzroy. One of the nerve centres of the Melbourne band scene, with well-known independent bands nightly; usually $5. Licensed until 3am.

The Rainbow 27 St David St, Fitzroy. Mellow atmosphere, interesting crowd and decor in an intimate bar with free music – R & B, funk and fusion – every night.

The Stage 1st Floor, 231 Smith St, Collingwood. Live African and Latin American music (Thurs–Sun from 8 or 10pm; cover charge) and a dance floor. Come earlier and have a two-course dinner for an additional $15.

The Tote 71 Johnston St, Fitzroy. Hardcore thrash.

Richmond and the southern suburbs

Bridge Hotel 642 Bridge Rd, Richmond. Jazz, reggae and African music.

Continental Cafe Greville St, Prahran. Smart venue for established and up-and-coming artists.

Corner Hotel 57 Swan St, Richmond. Alternative independent bands.

The Esplanade Hotel 11 Upper Esplanade, St Kilda. The "Espy" is the soul of St Kilda and of Melbourne's eclectic band scene (huge bouncers make it look rougher than it actually is), hosting an interesting nightly line-up of bands in the front bar (free) and Gershwin Room (small admission charge).

Molly Bloom's 39 Bay St, Port Melbourne. Irish music most nights; no cover charge.

The Palace Lower Esplanade, St Kilda (next to the *Palais*). Entertainment complex with big-name bands in the main room, smaller bands in the pool room, and a club at the rear.

The Prince St Kilda Fitzroy St, St Kilda. Another St Kilda icon, which has undergone a facelift to fit in with the smart cafés and restaurants at this end of Fitzroy St. Late-night venue with good bands.

Clubs

Promoters hand out flyers, on the corner of Bourke and Russell streets, for reduced or free admission to a rapidly changing array of **clubs**, or you can pick up the passes in record shops such as Gaslight, further up Bourke Street. King Street, in the CBD between Collins Street and Flinders Lane, has a handy concentration of clubs. Most clubs have a **cover charge** of between $5 and $10.

The Bull Ring 95 Johnston St, Fitzroy. The best place to dance to Latin rhythms. The band starts at 10.30pm, the dance-floor show at 11pm.

Carousel Aughtie Drive, Albert Park. Dance venue playing good acid jazz and funk.

Chasers 386 Chapel St, South Yarra. Veteran of the Melbourne club scene, with a regular focus on accessible house, retro and electronic beats, presented in the spacious main room and two snug lounges.

Club UK 169 Exhibition St, city centre. Retro and mainstream pop and rock, with an emphasis on the UK scene.

Heat, Mercury Lounge and Odeon Crown Casino Entertainment Complex, south of the Yarra. Clubs on level 3 of the complex, playing mainstream pop from the 1980s onwards; occasional live bands.

Lizard Lounge *The Union Hotel*, 90 Chapel St, Windsor. Alternative indie club.

The Lounge 243 Swanston St, city centre. Upstairs club with bands, films, pool, dance floor and a cool-off balcony.

The Metro 20 Bourke St, city centre. Huge old theatre on three floors with eight bars and three dance floors, all very lavish. Enormous queue of spivved-up kids on Friday night.

Monsoon Russell St. Upmarket club at the *Grand Hyatt*. *daFunk Club* for R&B, funk and soul.

Viper Room 373 Chapel St, Prahran. Popular spot with Melbourne's dancing crowd.

Gay and lesbian nightspots

Diva Bar 153 Commercial Rd. Cocktail and dance bar with a mixed crowd.

DT's Hotel 164 Church St, Richmond. Mixed crowd and popular pool competitions.

Fox Hotel 27 Weston St, Brunswick. Lady Bird Lounge for women only, first Saturday of each month. Cover charge.

Greyhound Hotel 1 Brighton Rd (corner of Carlise St), St Kilda. Drag shows (Wed, Fri and Sat).

Laird Hotel 149 Gipps St, Collingwood. Well-equipped men-only venue, with two bars, DJs, a beer garden and games room; popular with the leather crowd. Cheap drinks until 10pm.

The Market 143 Commercial Rd, South Yarra. Excellent dance club with weekly menu of top-notch drag shows, karaoke nights and talent quests. No cover charge.

Peel Dance Bar 113 Wellington St (corner of Peel St), Collingwood. Dance floor, music videos and shows, drawing a large and appreciative crowd, mainly of men.

The Prince St Kilda 29 Fitzroy St, St Kilda. Hosts a gay night, *Homosexualle*, every Sunday, and *Girl Bar*, a lesbian night one Friday per month.

Star Hotel 176 Hoddle St, Collingwood. Sociable pub hosts a mixed crowd with a strong Asian presence.

Trade Bar 9 Peel St, Collingwood. Gay bar with drag shows.

Xchange Hotel 119 Commercial Rd, South Yarra. Mainly men.

Comedy

Melbourne is the comedy capital of Australia, home of the madcap Doug Anthony All Stars, Wogs Out of Work and comedians from TV shows such as *The Big Gig* and *The Comedy Company*. The highlight of the comedy year is the **Melbourne International Comedy Festival** (Ⓦ www.comedyfestival .com.au) in April, based at the Town Hall in Swanston Street, with performances

Gay and lesbian Melbourne

Melbourne's gay and lesbian scene may not be as in-your-face as Sydney's, but it's almost as big, and is also less ghettoized than in Sydney. Fitzroy, Collingwood and Carlton, north of the river, and St Kilda, South Yarra and Prahran, to the south, boast a strong **gay** presence; Fitzroy, Northcote and Clifton Hill are the city's recognized stomping grounds for **lesbians**. There are three free gay and lesbian **papers**: the *Melbourne Star Observer*, *Bnews* (Ⓦ www.bnews.net.au), *MCV* (Melbourne Community Voice), all published weekly.

Big **events** are mostly organized by the ALSO (Alternative LifeStyle Organisation) Foundation, including one over the Australia Day weekend at the end of January: **Red Raw Resurrection**. The scene's annual highlight, however, is the fabulous **Midsumma Festival** (late Jan to early Feb; Ⓣ 03/9415 9819, Ⓦ www .midsumma.org.au). Already in its twelfth year, Midsumma provides an umbrella for a wide range of sporting, artistic and theatrical events. The queen's birthday in June is celebrated at the **Winterdaze** party, while Melbourne Show Day in September is marked by the **Show Off** dance party.

Organizations, support groups, bookshops and radio station

ALSO Foundation 1st Floor, 6 Claremont St, South Yarra Ⓣ 03/9827 4999, Ⓦ www.also.org.au. Organizes events and publishes the *ALSO Directory*, free from community outlets, which lists everything from gay vets to lesbian psychologists.

Beat Books 157 Commercial Rd, Prahran Ⓣ 03/9827 8748. Gay bookshop with a large range of magazines, books, sex toys and leather goods.

Gay and Lesbian Switchboard Ⓣ 03/9827 8544 or 1800 631 493 (Mon, Tues & Thurs–Sun 6–10pm, Wed 2–10pm) for counselling, referral and information.

Joy 94.9 FM Ⓣ 03/9699 2949, Ⓦ www.joy.org.au. Gay and lesbian radio station, with 24hr music ranging from classical to R & B and world music, plus news and updates about the arts and club scene.

Hares and Hyenas 135 Commercial Rd, Prahran Ⓣ 03/9824 0110. Gay and lesbian bookshop.

Cafés and meeting places

189 Espresso Bar 189 Acland St, St Kilda Ⓣ 03/9534 8884. Huge *pides*, pizza, cakes and expertly made coffees, while outside tables make this a good place for crowd surveillance.

Globe Cafe 218 Chapel St, Prahran Ⓣ 03/9510 869. Good choice for a well-deserved treat after a hard morning's browsing on Chapel St.

Jackie O 204 Barkly St, St Kilda Ⓣ 03/9537 0377. Comfy, atmospheric surroundings complemented by relaxed service and value-for-money food.

Red Orange 194 Commercial Rd, Prahran Ⓣ 03/9510 3654. Cosy, inexpensive café in the heart of gay Prahran. Licensed.

See also p.903 for gay- and lesbian-friendly places to stay and opposite for gay and lesbian nightspots.

⑨

MELBOURNE AND AROUND | Live music

at several other venues around town. As well as local and interstate acts, you're likely to see some of the best stand-up comedians from overseas. For one-off performances and other venues, check out the "EG" supplement to *The Age* on Fridays.

Comedy Club 380 Lygon St, Carlton. Slick, cabaret-style space, which features largely mainstream comedians.

Comedy Lair *Prince Patrick Hotel*, 135 Victoria Parade, Collingwood. Shows each Wednesday.

The Esplanade Hotel 11 Upper Esplanade, St Kilda. Stand-up shows each Tuesday and Sunday from 8pm.

Theatre

Melbourne offers a rich array of dramatic productions, from fringe to mainstream, with venues everywhere. Watch out for **outdoor performances** in summer, including alfresco Shakespeare and shows for children in the Royal Botanic Gardens from December until the end of February (℗03/9650 1500 for details; credit-card bookings with Ticketmaster7 ℗1300 136 166.

Athenaeum Theatre 188 Collins St, city centre ℗03/9650 1500. One of numerous small Victorian theatre buildings in the city, hosting guest performances – mainly plays and concerts.
Comedy Theatre 240 Exhibition St, city centre ℗03/9209 9000. Not a comedy venue, but a small theatre hosting events similar to the Athenaeum (see above).
CUB Malthouse 113 Sturt St, South Melbourne ℗03/9685 5111. A renovated malthouse containing two venues – the Beckett Theatre and the larger Merlyn Theatre – hosting guest performances, opera, dance, concerts and readings. The resident Playbox company produces contemporary Australian plays.
Her Majesty's Theatre 219 Exhibition St, city centre ℗03/9663 3211. Lavish musicals in a fabulously ornate old theatre.

La Mama 205 Faraday St, Carlton ℗03/9347 6142. Plays by new writers, as well as poetry and play readings.
Playhouse Theatre Victorian Arts Centre, 100 St Kilda Rd ℗03/9281 8000. Mainstream productions, mainly from the Melbourne Theatre Company.
Princess Theatre 163 Spring St, city centre ℗03/9299 9500. Small but lavish old-fashioned theatre which stages musicals and mainstream plays.
Regent Theatre 191 Collins St, near City Square, city centre ℗03/9299 9500. This lovingly restored old theatre puts on productions of big-name musicals.
Theatreworks 14 Acland St, St Kilda ℗03/9534 4879. Ground-breaking new Australian plays.

Classical music, opera and dance

The **Melbourne Symphony Orchestra** has a season from February to December based at the Melbourne Concert Hall and the Melbourne Town Hall, while the **State Orchestra of Victoria** performs less regularly at the Concert Hall, often playing works by Australian composers. If you can't afford the ticket prices – expect to pay $40–80 for classical music performances, $60–130 for opera – you can listen to the Symphony Orchestra concerts on Tuesday at 7pm on Radio 3MBS (103.5FM).

George Fairfax Studio Victorian Arts Centre, 100 St Kilda Rd ℗03/9281 8000. Modern dance and plays.
Her Majesty's Theatre 219 Exhibition St, city centre ℗03/9663 3211. Occasionally hosts some of the great foreign ballet companies.

Melbourne Concert Hall Victorian Arts Centre, 100 St Kilda Rd ℗03/9281 8000. Big-name concerts.
State Theatre Victorian Arts Centre, 100 St Kilda Rd ℗03/9281 8000. Venue for the Victoria State Opera and the Australian Ballet Company.

Film

Mainstream **cinemas** are concentrated on Bourke Street, where discount day is usually Tuesday. The Crown Casino has a number of cinemas showing blockbuster movies. In summer, watching a film under the stars at the Moonlight Cinema in the Botanic Gardens (see p.916) or at the Cinema at the Bowl (Sidney Myer Music Bowl) nearby can be a real treat (details from local press; bookings through Ticketmaster7 ℗1300 136 166). The city's independent cinemas screen less obviously commercial US films and foreign-language films; these cinemas tend to offer discounts on Monday. The **Melbourne**

International Film Festival in July (☏03/9417 2011, ⓦwww.melbourne filmfestival.com.au) has been going for over forty years, based at a number of cinemas around the city.

ACMI Federation Square ☏03/9651 1515. Film-buff's cinema; often shows Australian movies.

Astor Theatre Cnr of Chapel St and Dandenong Rd, St Kilda ☏03/9510 1414, ⓦwww.astor-theatre.com. Classic and cult movie double bills in a beautiful Art Deco cinema.

Brighton Bay Twin Cinemas 294 Bay St, Brighton ☏03/9596 3590. Comfortable sitting. Part of the Palace Cinemas chain, showing new Hollywood releases and arthouse films. Cheap day Monday.

Chinatown Cinema 200 Bourke St, city centre ☏03/ 9662 3465. Chinese films with English subtitles.

Cinema Europa Jam Factory, 500 Chapel St, South Yarra ☏03/9827 2440. Opulent movie house showing the latest mainstream, mainly American, movies.

Cinema Nova Lygon Court Plaza, 380 Lygon St, Carlton ☏03/9347 5331, ⓦwww .cinemanova.com.au. A rabbit warren of small, recently refurbished and comfortable cinemas showing the latest Hollywood releases, as well as arthouse movies. Cheap day Monday.

Classic 9 Gordon St, off Glenhuntly Rd, Elsternwick ☏03/9523 9739. Near Elsternwick station. Latest releases and arthouse.

Como Gaslight Gardens, cnr of Toorak Rd and Chapel St, South Yarra ☏03/9827 7533. Belongs to the Palace Cinemas chain, which shows latest releases of Hollywood movies as well as arthouse films.

George Cinema 133–137 Fitzroy St, St Kilda ☏03/9534 6922. Another Palace Cinema, showing the latest Hollywood releases plus arthouse films.

IMAX Theatre Melbourne Museum complex, Rathdowne St, Carlton ☏03/9663 5454. Part of the Melbourne Museum complex (see p.907), with kitsch interiors and awesome technology, including a gigantic screen and film reels so big they require a fork-lift to move them. Shows both 2D and 3D films, usually lasting from 45min to 1hr, mostly documentaries on inaccessible places or anything involving a Tyrannosaurus Rex.

Kino Dendy 45 Collins St, city centre ☏03/9650 2100. In the Collins Place atrium, with several cafés and bars in the complex. Cheap day Monday.

Lumiere 108 Lonsdale St, city centre ☏03/9639 1055, ⓦwww.lumiere.com.au. The city's only independent cinema, screening a wide range of world cinema, with films from everywhere from Tunisia to Taiwan. Cheap day Monday.

Rivoli Camberwell Rd, Camberwell Junction ☏03/9882 1221. Two theatres in a beautifully renovated Art Deco building showing first releases of arthouse films.

Westgarth Theatre 89 High St, Northcote ☏03/9482 2001. Art Deco period piece, decorated by the planner of Canberra, Walter Burley Griffin, showing quality mainstream films, cult classics and late shows. Cheap day Monday.

Shopping

Melbourne's big two **department stores**, David Jones and Myer, are located off the Bourke Street Mall. **Shopping hours** are generally Monday to Friday 9am to 5.30pm, with late-night shopping on Thursday and Friday evenings; many places also open at weekends from noon to 5pm.

Clothes

Dangerfield (branches in the CBD at 224 Flinders St, the Sportsgirl Centre on Collins St, and Melbourne Central, and on Greville St, Prahran; and Brunswick St, Fitzroy) has modern funky clothes, including lots of great hats and jewellery. Chapel Street in South Yarra is home to interesting upmarket **fashion** outlets, getting younger and less expensive towards Prahran. Greville Street, Prahran, has lots of big-name **clearance centres**. In Richmond, Bridge Road between Punt Road and Church Street is home to clothes and shoe shops selling seconds, samples and end-of-season stock – lots of cheap rubbish, but also brand names such as Country Road, Sportsgirl, Jag and Witchery. In the city, Little

Bourke Street (from no. 349 upwards) and Hardware Street, round the corner, are the places to go for **travel clothing** and equipment. Brunswick Street in Fitzroy is the best spot for **secondhand clothes**.

Books

Mainstream bookshops include Angus & Robertson (cnr of Bourke and Elizabeth streets, 35 Swanston St, and 379 Collins St, all in the CBD); Border's (500 Chapel St, Prahran, and Lygon Court Plaza, Carlton); Collins Booksellers (104 Elizabeth St, 86 Bourke St and 401 Swanston St, all in the CBD); Bookcity (205 Swanston St, CBD); Readers Feast (Midtown Plaza, cnr of Bourke and Swanston streets, CBD); the small but well-stocked Hill of Content Bookshop (86 Bourke St, CBD); and Readings Books & Music, one of Melbourne's best bookshops (309 Lygon St, Carlton).

In Fitzroy, Brunswick Street has the very good Brunswick Street Bookstore, at no. 305, and Grub Street Bookshop at no. 379 for **secondhand books**. Other good secondhand bookshops include the Academic and General Bookshop (259 Swanston St, CBD; 196 Elgin St, Carlton); Book Affair (200–202 Elgin St, Carlton). St Kilda also has several good bookshops, including Chronicles Bookshop (91 Fitzroy St) and Cosmos Books and Music (112 Acland St). Metropolis (160 Acland St) specializes in **art**, photography, design and architecture, while Map Land, in the city at 372 Little Bourke St, has a good stock of **travel books and maps**. Black Mask Books (78 Toorak Rd, South Yarra) and Kill City (226 Chapel St, Prahran) specializes in **mystery and crime**.

Music

Gaslight, at 85 Bourke St, has a superb range of everything except classical; Thomas's Records nearby at no. 31 is small but very good; Au-go-go, at 2 Somerset Place, sells independent and rare recordings, and displays notices for room shares and what's on. Discurio, 113 Hardware Lane, sells classical music, jazz, blues and folk; while Basement Discs, 24 Block Place, off Little Collins St, also has a great range of jazz and world music. Blue Moon records at 54 Johnston St, Fitzroy, spezializes in world music, particularly Latin and Spanish. In the southern inner city suburbs Border's, at the Jam Factory, South Yarra, has a big CD department, while the funky Rhythm and Soul Records in Prahran at 128 Greville St, is where you'll find the latest funk, electronic, trance and techno grooves. Readings and Cosmos bookshops (see above) also have a small, but good selection of CDs.

Markets

Melbourne's best-loved **market** is the venerable Queen Victoria Market (see p.907), though the Sunday Victorian Arts Centre crafts market (p.915) is also popular, and there are good local markets at Prahran (p.920), South Melbourne (p.920) and an arts and crafts market in St Kilda (p.921). Camberwell Market, Station Street (Sun 7am–3pm; train to Camberwell), is a large flea market with lots of good secondhand clothes, books, records, bric-a-brac, and plenty of food vans and cafés.

Listings

Airlines (domestic) Air New Zealand ☎13 24 76; Qantas ☎13 13 13; Virgin Blue ☎13 67 89.
Airlines (international) Alitalia ☎03/9920 3799;

British Airways ☎03/9656 8133; Canadian Airlines ☎1300 655 767; Garuda Indonesia ☎1300 365 330; Japan Airlines ☎03/9654 2733; KLM

⊕1300 303 747; Lauda Air ⊕1800 642 438; Malaysia Airlines ⊕13 26 27; Olympic ⊕03/9629 5022; Qantas ⊕13 13 13; Singapore Airlines ⊕13 10 11; Thai Airways ⊕1300 651 960; United ⊕13 17 77.

Airport bus Skybus (⊕03/9662 3066) departs roughly every 30min from Spencer Street bus terminal (see also "Arrival and information", p.893).

American Express 233 Collins St and 260 Collins St (Mon–Fri 9am–5.30pm, Sat 9am–noon).

Banks and foreign exchange All major banks can be found on Collins St. Standard banking hours are generally Mon–Fri 9.30am–4pm (Fri until 5pm), although some branches of the Bank of Melbourne, including the one at 142 Elizabeth St, are open on Saturday (9am–noon). Most banks have 24-hour ATMs, which accept a variety of cash, credit and debit cards. Thomas Cook is at 257 Collins St (Mon–Fri 9am–5pm, Sat 10am–5pm); other branches are at 188 Swanston St, 99 William St and 261 Bourke St (also Sun 9am–5pm). The Thomas Cook desks at the international and domestic terminals of Tullamarine Airport open to meet all international arrivals.

Bike rental Hire a Bicycle, a stall at Princes Bridge (daily 11am–5pm, weather permitting; ⊕0412 616 633) has basic bicycles, mountain bikes and tandems ($9–12 per hour; helmets, locks, maps and backpacks are provided). In St Kilda, try the helpful St Kilda Cycles, 11 Carlisle St (Mon–Fri 9am–6pm, Sat 9am–5pm, Sun 10am–4pm; ⊕03/9534 3074; full day $20, or $15 per half-day after 1pm), or the stand next to the cycle path near St Kilda Pier, which rents out bicycles on weekends, and daily during the summer holidays.

Buses You can buy last-minute tickets at the bus company offices in the Spencer Street and Franklin Street terminals. Operators include V/Line (daily 7am–9pm; ⊕13 61 96); Greyhound/McCafferty's (Franklin St terminal reservation desk daily 6.30am–10.30pm; ⊕13 20 30); Firefly, Spencer St coach terminal (reservations daily 7am–8.30pm; ⊕03/9670 7500). For advance bookings, it's easier to go to the Bus Booking Centre, 24 Grey St, St Kilda (Mon–Sat 10am–6pm, ⊕03/9534 2003), or Backpackers Travel Centre, Shop 1, 250 Flinders St (Mon–Fri 9am–6pm, Sat 10am–4pm; ⊕03/9654 8477). They will shop around for you to find the cheapest deals, and they also sell bus passes and make bookings for tours around Melbourne and one-way to Sydney or Adelaide (see "Tours", overleaf). City bus information is available from the Met Transport Information Centre on ⊕13 16 38.

Car rental All the following do one-way rentals, subject to availability: Avis, 20 Franklin St ⊕03/9663 6366; Budget, 398 Elizabeth St ⊕13 27 27; Delta, cnr Franklin and Elizabeth streets ⊕03/9600 9025 or 13 13 90; Hertz, 97 Franklin St ⊕03/9663 6244 or 13 30 39; National, cnr Queensberry and Peel streets ⊕13 10 45; Thrifty, 390 Elizabeth St ⊕1300 367 227. Used-car companies with cheaper rates include Rent-A-Bomb, 507 Bridge Rd, Richmond ⊕13 15 53; and Ugly Duckling, 108 St Kilda Rd, St Kilda ⊕03/9525 4010 or 1800 335 908. Campervans are available from Backpacker Campervan & Car rentals ⊕03/8379 8768 or 1800 670 232; Britz Australia ⊕03/8379 8890 or 1800 331 454; Kea Campers Australia ⊕1800 252 555; and NQ Australia Campervan Rentals ⊕1800 079 529.

Consulates Canada, 1st Floor, 123 Camberwell Rd, Hawthorn East ⊕03/9811 9999; USA, 553 St Kilda Rd ⊕03/9526 5900.

Disabled travellers Disability Information Victoria ⊕1300 650 865; Paraquad Victoria, 208 Wellington St, Collingwood ⊕03/9415 1200, @www.paraquad.asn.au. Assistance is available at metropolitan, suburban, country and interstate stations, while relevant information for people with disabilities can be obtained by calling the Met Transport Information Centre on ⊕13 16 38. Buses are progressively being replaced with low-floor wheelchair accessible models; however, passengers in wheelchairs still need to contact local bus operators for information. The Melbourne City Council produces a free mobility map of the CBD showing accessible routes and toilets in the city centre, available from the front desk of the Melbourne Town Hall. For wheelchair-accessible taxis, call Central Booking Service (⊕1300 364 050). TADAS (Travellers Aid Disability Access Service), at Level 2, 169 Swanston St, near Bourke St Mall (Mon–Fri 9am–5pm, Sat & Sun 9am–4pm; ⊕03/9654 7690), provides personal care and various services, including wheelchair rental; to get to the lifts, enter via alcove 2 shops south of Bourke St Mall.

Diving Underwater Victoria – Dive Industry Victoria Association (⊕1800 816 151) has a list of members in the Greater Melbourne area who rent equipment, organize diving trips and offer dive courses.

Emergency ⊕000 for fire, police or ambulance.

Employment Backpackers Resource Centre, at Hotel Bakpak (Mon–Fri 9am–5pm, Sat 9am–1pm; ⊕03/9329 7525, @www.bakpak.com). Traveller's Contact Point, Ground Floor, 29–31 Somerset Place, off Little Bourke St between Elizabeth and

Tours from Melbourne

Melbourne can be used as a base for a wide variety of **tours** to the interior of Victoria or along the coast. Popular destinations – both as **day-trips** and **one-way tours** – are to the Grampians, Phillip Island and the Mornington Peninsula, and along the Great Ocean Road. For **longer trips**, there are a number of two- to four-day excursions offered by various operators.

Autopia Tours ☎03/9326 5536 (from outside Victoria ☎1800 000 507), ⓦwww.autopiatours.com.au. Long-established outfit running very popular day-trips by minibus along the Great Ocean Road ($70) and to Phillip Island ($75), plus longer tours, including combined visits to the Great Ocean Road and Phillip Island (2 days; $120), and the Great Ocean Road and Grampians (3 days $150). They also offer one-way tours between Melbourne and Adelaide (3 days; $170) and Melbourne and Sydney (4 days; $190).

Bunyip Bushwalking Tours ☎03/9531 0840, ⓦwww.bunyiptours.com. Tours to Wilson's Promontory National Park (1–4 days; $90–390) with – as their name implies – lots of bushwalking; for the longer trips you need to be reasonably fit and able to carry a pack with your own tent and supplies. The one- and two-day tours can be combined with the Phillip Island penguin parade on the way back to Melbourne. A two-day tour to the Grampians departs every Saturday ($190).

Duck Truck Tours ☎03/5952 2548, ⓦwww.promcountry.com.au/ducktrucktours. Day-trips from Melbourne to Phillip Island ($69), plus combination trips to Mornington Peninsula and Phillip Island (3 days; $255), Phillip Island and Wilson's Promontory National Park (2–3 days; $185–270), and the Great Ocean Road and Grampians ($129). They also do day-trips along the Great Ocean Road ($70).

Echidna Walkabout ☎03/9646 8249, ⓦwww.adventures.com.au. Upmarket eco-tours, with very small groups and enthusiastic, knowledgeable guides, focusing on native wildlife and local Koorie culture. Day-tours go to the Brisbane Ranges and You Yangs, west of Melbourne, while longer trips head along the Great Ocean Road and to remoter parts of East Gippsland, and include bushwalks; accommodation is in B&Bs or very comfortable camps.

Eco Platypus Tours ☎1800 819 091, ⓦwww.ecoplatypustours.com. Two-day trips to the Great Ocean Road and Grampians, with overnight stays at a family-run farm west of Hamilton ($140 plus $20–25 for accommodation and food).

Go West ☎03/9826 2008, ⓦwww.gowest.com.au. One of the very few companies

---

Queen streets (Mon–Fri 8.30am–5.15pm, Sat 10am–4pm, ☎03/9642 2911).

Environment and conservation Australian Trust for Conservation Volunteers ☎03/5333 1483 or 1800 03 2501, ⓦwww.atcv.com.au; Department of Sustainability and Environment (DSE) Information Centre, 8 Nicholson St, East Melbourne ☎03/9637 8080; Parks Victoria telephone information service ☎13 19 63; Wilderness Society Shop, 247 Flinders Lane ☎03/9639 5455. The Victoria Visitor Information Centre at Federation Square also has a range of brochures on national parks.

Ferries *Spirit of Tasmania I* and *II* run between Melbourne and Devonport in Tasmania, taking nine to ten hours. There's a daily departure from Station Pier, Port Melbourne, at 9pm, plus additional departures at 9am (daily from mid-Dec to mid-

Jan; then every weekend from mid-Jan to April). The cheapest one-way fares range from $100 off-peak to $140 peak. Cars and motorbikes are free from February to November; from early December until late January the one-way fare is $55 for a car or campervan, $45 for a motorbike. Reservations with TT Line, Station Pier, Port Melbourne ☎13 20 10, ⓦwww.spiritoftasmania.com.au. To get to Station Pier take tram #109 from Collins Street in the city or catch the Skybus (departing the Skybus Terminal at Spencer Street coach station at 6.30am and 6.30pm for the day and night sailings respectively; $5)

Flat-hunting and sharing Check the Saturday edition of *The Age*, as well as the notice boards of hostels, cafés along Brunswick St in Fitzroy, the *Galleon Café* at 9 Carlisle St, St Kilda, and Readings bookshop, 309 Lygon St, Carlton.

offering a day-trip to the Dandenong Ranges and Yarra Valley, in addition to the usual destinations, such as the Great Ocean Road and Phillip Island (all trips $70).

Groovy Grape ☎1800 661 177, ⓦwww.groovygrape.com.au. One-way tour specialist offering regular trips between Melbourne and Adelaide via the Great Ocean Road and the Grampians (3 days; $300).

High Spirit Adventures ☎03/9391 8188 or 1800 212 020, ⓦwww .highspirit.com.au). Three-day Great Ocean Road plus Grampians tours ($240), and two-day combined Mornington Peninsula, Phillip Island and Wilson's Promontory tours ($180), both geared to the backpacker market, with lots of activities such as (for an additional fee) canoeing, mountain biking and horse riding.

Let's Go Bush ☎03/9640 0826, ⓦwww.letsgobush.com.au. Two-day tours to the Great Ocean Road ($130) and "Penguin Express" tours to Phillip Island via Ramsay Street ($70 including admission fee and pizza dinner).

Otway Discovery ☎03/9654 5432. Day-tours from Melbourne to the Great Ocean Road ($70, with a hop-on, hop-off option available), and Phillip Island ($75 including BBQ dinner and wine-tasting).

Oz Experience ☎1300 300 028. Backpacker bus service which does runs three times weekly along the south coast to Adelaide and four times weekly to Sydney, with visits to all major sights along the way. Attracts a very young, party crowd.

Parktrek Walking Tours Australia ☎03/9486 7070, ⓦwww.parktrek.com. Catering to bushwalking and nature enthusiasts, with three- and four-day hikes in national parks all over Victoria and further afield; a three-day trip to Wilson's Promontory costs $370. Prices include full guiding, transport to and from the parks, camping gear and meals.

Wayward Bus ☎1800 020 007, ⓦwww.waywardbus.com.au. Long-established one-way specialist, with regular tours between Melbourne and Adelaide via the Great Ocean Road, Mount Gambier and The Coorong (3.5 days; $320).

Wild-Life Tours ☎03/9534 8868, ⓦwww.wildlifetours.com.au. One-way tours between Melbourne and Adelaide (2–4 days; $160–215) and Melbourne and Sydney (2–4 days; $160–220), as well as various round trips from Melbourne (1–3 days; $70–150). Depending on the length of the trip, the tours take in the Great Ocean Road, the Grampians and Phillip Island; longer stopover options are available.

Hospitals and medical centres Alfred Hospital, Commercial Rd, Prahran ☎03/9276 2000; Royal Children's Hospital, Flemington Rd, Parkville ☎03/9345 5522; Royal Melbourne Hospital, Grattan St, Parkville ☎03/9342 7000; and St Vincent's Hospital, Victoria Parade, Fitzroy ☎03/9807 2211. Melbourne Sexual Health Centre, 580 Swanston St, Carlton ☎03/9347 0244 or 1800 032 017 offers a free service. For vaccinations, anti-malaria tablets and first-aid kits contact the Travellers Medical and Vaccination Centre (TMVC), 2nd Floor, 393 Little Bourke St ☎03/9602 5788, ⓦwww.tmvc.com.au.

Internet access There are plenty of cybercafés throughout Melbourne; most charge around $5–7 per hour online. Most backpacker hostels have Internet access, such as Backpackers World at *Hotel Bakpak* (see p.900; daily 8am–9pm; about

$3 for 30min). Alternatively, try Traveller's Contact Point (see "Employment", p.939); Global Gossip, 440 Elizabeth St (Mon–Fri 8am–midnight; Sat & Sun 8am–9pm); e:FIFTYFIVE, 55 Elizabeth St (Mon–Fri 8am–3am, Sat 10am–3am, Sun 10.30am–11pm): Internet Café, 429 Elizabeth St (Mon–Sat 9am–11.30pm; Sun 10am–11.30pm); Hubway Internet Café, 9 Grey St, St Kilda (daily 9.30am–11pm).

Laundries Most hostels and hotels have their own laundry. Commercial laundries include City Edge Laundrette, 39 Errol St, North Melbourne (daily 6am–11pm); *The Soap Opera Laundry & Cafe*, 128 Bridport St, Albert Park (Mon–Fri 7.30am–7.30pm, Sat 8am–6pm, Sun 10am–6pm); and Blessington Street Launderette, 22 Blessington St, St Kilda (daily 7.30am–9pm).

Left luggage Spencer Street station has lockers

(daily 6am–10pm; $2; emptied nightly); luggage can be left overnight at the cloakroom ($3.50 per item). Flinders Street station has lockers (8am–8pm; $2). The lockers at the Greyhound/McCafferty's terminal at Franklin St are accessible 24hr ($6–10). Traveller's Contact Point also stores luggage (see "Employment", p.939).

Library The General Reference and Information Centre at the State Library of Victoria, 328 Swanston St, keeps popular Australian and overseas magazines; the Newspaper Room has foreign papers (Mon–Thurs 10am–9pm, Fri–Sun 10am–6pm).

Motorbikes The northern end of Elizabeth Street in the city centre has a string of motorbike shops. Garner's Motorcycles, 179 Peel St, North Melbourne ℡03/9326 8676, ⓦwww.garners motorcycles.com.au, and Victorian Motorcycles, 606 High St, East Kew ℡03/9817 3206, both do rentals and may sell secondhand machines with buy-back deals.

Newspapers Melbourne's *The Age* is one of Australia's better papers; the pulpy *Sun-Herald* is the city's only other daily. Foreign newspapers can be perused at the State Library (see p.907) or bought from McGill's Newsagency, 187 Elizabeth St.

Pharmacies Australian Unity Pharmacies, 286 Little Bourke St, next to the Myer department store (Mon–Wed 9am–5.45pm, Thurs 9am–6.30pm, Fri 9am–9pm, Sat 10am–5pm); Leonard Long, cnr of Williams Rd and High St, Prahran (daily 9am–midnight); Mulqueeny's Pharmacy, cnr Swanston and Collins streets, opposite the Town Hall (Mon–Fri 8am–8pm, Sat 9am–6pm, Sun 11am–6pm).

Police Melbourne City Police Station, 637 Flinders St; ℡03/9247 6491; emergency ℡000.

Post office The old General Post Office at the cnr of Bourke and Elizabeth streets is currently closed for long-term renovation. The GPO retail shop is located at 250 Elizabeth St (Mon–Fri 8am–6pm, including the poste restante counter). Other post offices are open Mon–Fri 9am–5pm. For voicemail and mail forwarding, contact Traveller's Contact Point. ("see Employment", p.939).

RACV The two RACV outlets in the city are at 422 Little Collins St and 123 Queen St; both have good maps of Melbourne, Victoria and the rest of Australia (free for RACV members and members of affiliated overseas motoring associations; ⓦwww.racv.com.au). They also book accommodation listed in their guides and package holidays; members get special rates.

Skiing Skiman, 295 Clarendon St ℡03/9696 4955, and AUSKI Ski Hiring & Information Centre, 9–11 Hardware Lane ℡03/9670 1412, can advise on skiing conditions at Baw Baw, Buffalo, Mount Hotham, Buller, Falls Creek and at Thredbo in NSW.

Swimming pools City Baths, cnr of Swanston and Franklin streets (Mon–Thurs 6am–10pm, Fri 6am–8.30pm, Sat & Sun 8am–6pm; $3.80 for a swim plus $4.50 for use of sauna and spa; $15 for use of gym plus pool, sauna and spa; ℡03/9663 5888), has a 30-metre heated indoor pool for swimming, plus a pool for water-aerobics and a gym. In the state-of-the-art Melbourne Sports & Aquatic Centre, Aughtie Drive, off Albert Park Rd in Albert Park there's a choice between a wave pool, a 50-metre pool, a dive pool, a 25-metre lap pool, a 20-metre multi-purpose pool and a toddler area, plus a giant curling waterslide, spa, sauna and steam rooms (Mon–Fri 6–10pm, 50-metre pool Mon–Fri 5.30–8pm, Sat & Sun 7am–8pm; admission $5.30 plus $3.40 for spa, sauna and steam room; ℡03/9926 1555). Take tram #112 from Collins St or #96 from Bourke St in the city.

Taxis Taxi rank on Swanston St outside Flinders Street station, and plenty to flag down. Call Black Cabs Combined ℡13 22 27; Embassy Taxis ℡13 17 55; or Silver Top ℡13 10 08.

Telephones Melbourne is well stocked with public telephones. Some backpacker hostels and a lot of shops in the city sell discount phonecards (such as ezycom, Unidial, iprimus and Apple) which can be used in any payphone for cheap international calls. The official Telstra rate for a call from a public phone to the UK is about $1.60 per minute during peak hours (Mon–Fri 7am–7pm) and about 80¢ per minute off-peak. With one of the phonecards mentioned above, calls are markedly cheaper: expect to pay about 6–10¢ per minute, plus a small connecting fee (less than $1).

Trains Spencer Street station has a staffed information desk where you can get hold of all V/Line train (and bus) timetables; buy your ticket at the V/Line booking desk opposite or on ℡13 61 96 (6am–10pm). If you're travelling with a bicycle, come at least thirty minutes earlier to book it on the train. Suburban train information is available from the Met Transport Information Centre (see p.897).

Travel agents Backpackers Travel Centre, Shop 1, 250 Flinders St ℡03/9654 8477, ⓦwww.back packerstravel.net.au; Flight Centre, 19 Bourke St, 53 Elizabeth St and many other branches (℡13 16 00); STA Travel, 273 Little Collins St, 142 Acland St, St Kilda, and many other branches (book and pay over the phone ℡1300 360 960; or for nearest branch ℡1300 851 414; ⓦwww.statravel .com.au); Student Uni Travel, Shop 4, 440 Elizabeth St ℡03/9662 4666, ⓦwww.sut.com.au; Traveller's Contact Point, Ground Floor, 29–31 Somerset Place (off Little Bourke St between

Elizabeth and Queen streets) ☏ 03/9642 291, ⓦ www.travellers.com.au; YHA Travel, 83 Hardware Lane ☏ 03/9670 9611, ⓦ www.yhavic.org.au.

Travellers aid centres Lower ground floor, Spencer Street station (Mon–Fri 7.30am–7.30pm, Sat 7.30am–11.30am; ☏ 03/9670 2873), and 2nd

Floor, 169 Swanston St (Mon–Fri 9am–5pm, ☏ 03/9654 2600): both provide nappy-changing facilities, showers (for a fee), toilets, lounge rooms, wheelchairs for rent, assistance for disabled and frail persons, and information. There are also tea-rooms and lockers ($1) at the Swanston Street centre.

Around Melbourne

There are many possible day-trips out of Melbourne, mainly around the shores of the huge **Port Phillip Bay**, encircled by the arms of the Bellarine and Mornington peninsulas. The **Mornington Peninsula** on the east side has farmland and wineries on gently rolling hills and is home to some of the city's most popular beaches and surfing spots, packed on summer weekends. **Western Port Bay**, beyond the peninsula, encloses two fascinating islands – little-known **French Island**, much of whose wildlife is protected by a national park, and **Phillip Island**, whose nightly "Penguin Parade", when masses of Little penguins waddling ashore each night, is among Australia's biggest tourist attractions. Inland to the east, the **Yarra Valley** and the **Dandenong Range** offer beautiful countryside, wine-tasting and bushwalking. The **Bellarine Peninsula** and the western side of Port Phillip Bay are less exciting, but they do give access to the west coast and the Great Ocean Road.

The Mornington Peninsula

The **Mornington Peninsula** curves right around Port Phillip Bay, culminating in Point Nepean, well to the southwest of Melbourne. The shoreline facing the bay is beach-bum territory, though the well-heeled denizens of the main resorts, **Sorrento** and **Portsea**, might well resent that tag. On the largely straight, ocean-facing coast, **Mornington Peninsula National Park** encompasses some fine seascapes, with several walking trails marked out. Interspersed among the peninsula's bushland, grazing land and orchards are about 170 **vineyards**, which produce superb, if pricey, Pinot Noir and Shiraz wines, as well as good whites. As in the Yarra Valley, good restaurants, especially winery restaurants, have proliferated on the peninsula in recent years, some of them in truly spectacular settings. Two of the best are the Dromana Estate, Harrison's Road, Dromana (☏ 03/5987 3800), which serves light lunches daily; and Red Hill Estate, 52 Red Hill–Shoreham Road, Red Hill (☏ 03/5931 0177), which has views over the hills and Western Port Bay; they serve lunches daily and dinners during the summer (Nov to Easter Thurs–Sat from 6pm). You could also try the pricey but excellent Vines of Red Hill, 150 Red Hill Rd, Red Hill (lunch and dinner Fri–Sun, daily in January; ☏ 03/5989 2977); or the Hickinbotham Winery, 194 Nepean Highway, Dromana (daily 10am–5pm; ☏ 03/5981 0355), whose bakery-café serves soups, antipasto platters, foccacia and other breads. For more details, see the *Peninsula Wine Country Annual*, published by the Mornington Peninsula Vignerons Association; or *Wine Regions of Victoria*, available at tourist information centres.

As well as the beaches, the peninsula's **community markets**, selling local produce and crafts, attract many city dwellers: most are monthly affairs, so there's usually one every weekend. One of the biggest and best is the Red Hill Community Market, held on the first Saturday of every month (Sept–May 8am–1pm), at Red Hill Recreation Reserve, Arthurs Seat Road, 10km east of Dromana; others include the Balnarring Racecourse Market on the third Saturday of every month (Sept–May 8am–1pm) at Colaart Rd, Balnarring, and the Sunday Mornington Racecourse Market (year round 9am–2pm) at Racecourse Road, Mornington.

You can get to the peninsula by **public transport** from Melbourne to Frankston and from there to the main beach resorts and towns along the Nepean Highway on the northern side, but for a sightseeing trip taking in wineries, beaches and Arthur's Seat you'll need your own vehicle. Take a Met train to Frankston and change there for Stony Point, or connect with a Portsea Passenger Service bus #788 from Frankston to Sorrento ($7.80) and Portsea ($8; for timetable information call ☎1800 115 666). From Sorrento there's a community bus to Dromana via Blairgowrie, Rye and Rosebud (4 daily Mon–Fri), but no transport to Arthur's Seat. The *Bayplay Adventure Lodge* (see opposite) in Blairgowrie runs the **Bayplay Bus**, which goes to and from Melbourne once daily, picking up at various locations in the CBD early in the morning before heading to the lodge, then taking in various activities in the area before returning to the lodge and then Melbourne in the evening (☎03/5988 0188; $25 one-way or $50 for the day). The YHA hostel in Sorrento also operates a transfer service from Melbourne for guests.

The western coast

The peninsula starts at suburban **Frankston**, 40km from central Melbourne. From here on down, the western coast, flanked by the Nepean Highway, sports beach after beach, all crowded and traffic-snarled in summer. Twelve kilometres beyond Frankston, the fishing port of **Mornington** preserves some fine old buildings along Mornington Esplanade; there's a produce and craft market on Main Street every Wednesday. Five kilometres further on, near Mount Martha, **Briars Park** (daily 11am–4pm; $3.50) comprises an 1850s homestead complete with a collection of furniture and memorabilia given to the owner by Napoleon Bonaparte, and an enclosed wildlife reserve comprising woodlands and extensive wetlands (daily 9am–5pm; free). The **visitor's centre** near the homestead has an audiovisual display giving you an overview of how the affluent upper crust lived in early pioneering days, as well as a rundown on the present-day facilities of the park. Two walkways through the woodlands start near the visitor's centre; the adjacent **wetlands** are visited by more than fifty species of waterbirds, which can be observed at close distance from two bird-hides, accessible via a boardwalk from the visitor information centre.

Inland from Dromana, where seaside development begins in earnest, the granite outcrop of **Arthur's Seat State Park** rises 305m, providing breathtaking views of Port Phillip Bay. The chairlift up is currently closed, perhaps for good, following safety scares, but the views from the winding road and the top are well worth the detour, if you've got your own car. There are some tearooms and a restaurant at the summit, while the nearby **Arthur's Seat Maze** (daily 10am–6pm; $11) combines traditional hedge mazes with theme gardens and giant tree sculptures.

Sorrento

Beyond Arthur's Seat, the peninsula arcs and narrows: the sands around

Sorrento and Portsea offer a choice between the rugged surf of the ocean ("back" beaches) or the calmer waters of the bay ("front" beaches). With some of the most expensive real estate outside the Melbourne CBD, **SORRENTO** is the traditional haunt of the city's rich during the "season" from Boxing Day to Easter. Well-heeled outsiders also make it their playground in January and on summer weekends, flocking here to swim, surf and dive at the bay and ocean beaches. Exploring beautiful rock formations and low-tide pools, and swimming with bottlenose dolphins add to the attraction. The smell of money is everywhere – in the wide, tree-lined residential streets, the clifftop mansions boasting million-dollar views, and the town-centre cafés, restaurants, galleries and antique shops, running along Ocean Road down to the beach.

Sullivan Bay, 3km southeast, was in 1803 the site of the first white attempt to settle in what is now Victoria; the settlers struggled here for four months before giving up and moving on to what is now Tasmania. One of the convicts in the expedition was the infamous William Buckley, who escaped, was adopted by the local Aborigines and lived with them for 32 years. When the "wild white man" was seen again by settlers he could scarcely remember how to speak English; his survival against all odds has been immortalized in the phrase "Buckley's chance". You can walk along the cliffs and around the pioneer cemetery; there's a signposted turn-off from the main road.

Swimming with dolphins and seals is becoming one of Port Phillip Bay's prime attractions. Operators include the environmentally conscious Polperro Dolphin Swims (℡03/5988 8437 or 0428 174 160; ⓦwww.polperro.com.au), which takes the smallest groups; and Moonraker (℡03/5984 4211 or 0418 591 033; ⓦwww.moonrakercharters.com.au), which, weather permitting, runs several four-hour trips daily during the season (Sept/Oct to April/May; $90 for swimmers, including wetsuit and snorkelling equipment; $40 for sightseers).

Practicalities

Accommodation options in Sorrento include the charming 1871 limestone *Hotel Sorrento*, 5 Hotham Rd (℡03/5984 2206, ⓕ5984 3424; ❺–❻), located in a secluded spot on a hill above the jetty; *Carmel*, 142 Ocean Beach Rd (℡03/5984 3512, ⓕ5984 0146; ❻–❼), a charming, sandstone B&B (non-smoking) smack in the middle of town; *Tamasha House*, 699 Melbourne Rd (℡03/5984 2413, ⓕ5984 0452; ❻), a modern B&B halfway between ocean and bay beaches; and *Sorrento Hostel YHA*, 3 Miranda St (℡ & ⓕ03/5984 4323; dorms $20, rooms ❸), a modern, comfortable place with small dorms (some en suite), double and twin rooms and stacks of local information. They also do three-day packages featuring activities like horse riding, surfing, golf, dolphin swims and walks ($160–220, including transfers from Melbourne). The small, family-run *Peninsula Backpackers*, 17–19 Mitchell St, Rosebud (℡03/5982 0488; dorms $22, rooms ❷–❸) is set in two timber cottages close to the beaches. The owner can arrange lots of activities, and has good local employment contacts. Some 4km away in **Blairgowrie**, the well-organized and comfortable *Bayplay Adventure Lodge* is set in bushland near the beach at 46 Canterbury Jetty Rd (℡03/5988 0188, ⓦwww.bayplay.com.au; dorms $25, rooms ❸). Facilities include free bicycles, a licensed café serving budget meals, and camping space – the lodge is also a PADI dive resort and offers **diving courses** (all levels). Diving and other activity packages including transfers from Melbourne are available, as well as straight transfers. **Caravan parks** tend to be either closed (out of season) or completely booked up, and cost twice the normal price: a reasonable place is *Nautilus* (℡03/5984 2277; on-site vans ❹); the *Foreshore Reserve* (℡03/5984 2797) has tent sites.

There are also plenty of fancy **eating places**. The venerable *Continental Hotel*, 21 Ocean Beach Rd, has food, plus live music and a disco at weekends. In the moderate price range, *Buckley's Chance*, 174 Ocean Beach Rd, is a relaxed pancake parlour, which also serves burgers and steaks; and the century-old former *Sorrento Tearooms* at 3278 Nepean Highway now houses the *Sandpiper Licensed Restaurant* which is open for breakfast, lunch and dinner (international cuisine) and has great views of the bay. The *Continental Hotel*, 21 Ocean Beach Rd, has a good café serving Mediterranean cuisine and Mornington Peninsula wines. More modest options include the **takeaways** along Ocean Road or on the beach: try the *Sorrento Village Bakehouse*, 29 Ocean Beach Rd.

Ferries run across the mouth of the bay from Sorrento to **Queenscliff** on the Bellarine Peninsula. The *Peninsula Searoad Ferry* (℡03/5258 3244, Ⓦwww.searoad.com.au) carries passengers and vehicles year-round (hourly 6am–6pm, summer until 8pm; one-way fares: pedestrians $7; cars $38 plus $3 for each passenger; motorbike plus rider $18; advance car bookings recommended). The pedestrian-only *Sorrento Passenger Ferry* runs a spring and summer service ($8 single, $14 return; ℡03/5984 1602, Ⓦwww.sorrento ferry.com.au), calling at Portsea en route.

Portsea and Point Nepean

PORTSEA, just beyond Sorrento, is a mecca for divers, with excellent **dives** of up to 40m off Port Phillip Heads; trips operate from the pier throughout the summer and there are a couple of good dive shops. Portsea Front Beach, on the bay by the pier, is wall-to-wall beautiful people, as is Shelley Beach, which also attracts playful dolphins. On the other shore, Portsea Ocean Beach has excellent surfing, and a hang-gliding pad on a rock formation known as London Bridge. Back on the bay side, the extensive lawns of *Portsea Hotel*, a hugely popular drinking spot which features bands at weekends, overlook the beach.

The tip of the peninsula, with its fortifications, quarantine station and former army base is now privately operated under the name **Park at Point Nepean**, part of a patchwork of parks sprinkled over the southern end of the peninsula, collectively known as Mornington Peninsula National Park. The visitor centre is 1km west of Portsea (daily 9am–5pm; ℡03/5984 4276), and there is a car park. Because of its fragile sandy environment, visitor numbers are limited, so you'll need to book to visit: entrance to this part of the park costs $7. To get to **Point Nepean**, 6km from the visitor centre, you can either rent a bike ($12 for 3hr) or board the Transporter "train" – actually a few carriages pulled by a tractor ($10.50 one-way; $12.40 return; these fares include the park admission fee). The Transporter departs from the visitor centre daily between 10.30am and 3pm. Alternatively, you can drive to Gunners car park, 2.5km into the park, and walk the rest of the way to Point Nepean.

The Transporter runs to the fortifications at Point Nepean, with four optional drop-offs for walks: the first, the **Walter Pisterman Heritage Walk** (1km), leads through coastal vegetation to the Port Phillip Bay shoreline; the second (1km) leads to the top of Cheviot Hill, where you can look across to Queenscliff, then continues to **Cheviot Beach** where on December 17, 1967, **Harold Holt**, Australia's then prime minister, went for a swim in the rough surf of Bass Strait and disappeared, presumed drowned: his body was never found. The third walk, the **Fort Pearce and Eagle's Nest Heritage Trail** (2km), crosses through defence fortifications. A fourth walk takes you around **Fort Nepean**, right at the tip of the peninsula. Built at the same time as Fort

Queenscliff opposite to protect wealthy post-goldrush Melbourne from the imagined threat of Russian invasion, the fort comprises two subterranean levels, whose tunnels lead down to the Engine House at water level.

South and east coast

The rest of Mornington Peninsula National Park, which spreads along the ocean coast, is freely open to the public. An enjoyable two-day walk (27km) runs from London Bridge along the coast to **Cape Schanck**, site of an 1859 lighthouse. Here walkways lead down to the sea along a narrow neck of land, providing magnificent coastal views. The three **lighthouse keeper's cottages** offer the most scenic accommodation on the peninsula (℡03/9568 6411; ❻), each with a cosy lounge and kitchen. There's a small maritime museum ($8) at the lighthouse, which is open daily for tours (10am–4pm; $10).

The nearby **Bushrangers Bay Nature Walk** (6km; 2hr) heads from the cape to Main Creek, beginning as a leisurely walk along the clifftop, then leading down to a wild beach facing Elephant Rock. More energetic activities in this part of the peninsula include **horse rides** along Gunnamatta Beach or through bushland, organized by the Gunnamatta Equestrian Centre, Trueman's Rd, Rye (℡03/5988 6755), and **surfing** lessons, offered by the East Coast Surf School at various spots near Point Leo (bookings essential on ℡03/5989 2198 or 0417 526 465; $30 per hour, equipment provided).

Set in bushland 15km southeast of Frankston, near the northern end of Westernport Bay, **Pearcedale Conservation Park**, at 55 Tyabb–Tooradin Rd (Wed–Sun noon–late; $8; ℡03/5978 7935, ⓦ www.pearcedale.com) is home to lots of kangaroos, wallabies, emus and waterbirds. However, the park's emphasis is on rare nocturnal Australian animals, so it's well worth coming late in the day to take part in their guided **Moonlit Sancuary tour** (90min; $18; reservations essential). Starting at dusk, this tour offers the chance to see rare nocturnal Australian creatures such as eastern quolls, eastern bettongs, pademelons, gliders and tawny frogmouths in bushland enclosures.

French Island

FRENCH ISLAND, on the eastern side of the Mornington Peninsula, is well off the beaten track. A former prison farm, about two-thirds of the island is a national park, with the remaining third used as farm land. The island is renowned for its rich **wildlife**, especially birds of prey, and a flourishing koala colony. Virtually vehicle-free, it's a great place to cycle, an activity which is encouraged, with all walking tracks open to bikes. In the national park, the small and basic *Fairhaven Campground* has a pit toilet and tank water, but no showers. Camping is free, but must be booked in advance – two weeks ahead is advised during the summer school holidays and at Easter; at other times booking one or two days in advance will suffice (℡03/5986 9100). Also in the national park is the *McLeod Eco Farm and Historic Prison* (℡03/5678 0155, ⓕ5678 0166; ❷–❸), where you can stay in former prison cells converted into twins with bunk beds, or in the former officer's quarters with queen-size beds – all have shared facilities. The farm is surrounded by national park and has 8km of beach frontage; the very reasonable rates include organic meals and transfer from the ferry jetty 29km away. Near the jetty, the small *Tortoise Head Guesthouse* (℡03/5980 1234; ❺) offers B&B accommodation in guest rooms with shared facilities and four en-suite cabins with water views. Moderately priced lunches and dinner are also available. The general store, 2.5km from the jetty (℡03/5980 1209) offers B&B accommodation in a cottage with two bedrooms (❹); moderately priced lunches and dinners are also available. The *Bayview Chicory Kiln Tea Room* (10km from the jetty) has a private campsite with toilets and shower. In addition, scrumptious lunches and Devonshire Teas are served here, and the owner Lois Airs runs a free information centre (☎03/5980 1241).

Two ferry companies provide transport for passengers and bicycles to French Island. **Inter Island Ferries** (☎03/9585 5730, ⓦwww.interislandferries.com.au) connects the Mornington Peninsula with French Island and Phillip Island; there are departures daily at 8.30am and 4.15pm (and additional departures Tues & Thurs at noon, and Sat & Sun at 10am & noon) from **Stony Point**, on the eastern side of the Mornington Peninsula, departing from **Tankerton jetty** on French Island thirty minutes later for Cowes on Phillip Island ($9, bikes $4, one-way from Stony Point to Tankerton, or from Stony Point to Cowes via Tankerton – provided you don't get off the ferry at Tankerton). To get to Stony Point from Melbourne, take the Frankston train from Flinders Street station and a bus to Stony Point. **Bay Connections** (☎03/5952 3501, ⓦwww.bayconnections.com.au) runs a seasonal service from Cowes on Phillip Island to Stony Point, then on to Tankerton jetty on French Island and back to Cowes (Sept–July; departing Cowes Wed & Sun at noon, Stony Point at 12.30pm, and Tankerton at 12.45pm; fares for each leg of the trip are around $10).

For a brief visit to French Island, it's best to book one of the afternoon tours covering the island's natural attractions and the historic prison. The **French Island Bus Tour** (☎03/5980 1241; $17 including Devonshire Tea), operated by Lois Airs from the *Bayview Chicory Kiln Tea Room*, runs on Tuesdays, Thursdays and Sundays. Take the Interisland Ferry from Stony Point at noon. Lois will meet this ferry at Tankerton Jetty on French Island and drop passengers off at the end of the tour at 4.30pm for their trip back to Stony Point. Alternatively, **French Island Eco Tours** (☎03/5997 1822 or 03/5980 1210; $60 including ferry and organic, buffet-style lunch at McLeod Eco Farm) runs tours on Wednesday and Sunday. Take the Bay Connections ferry at 12.30pm from Stony Point.

Phillip Island

The hugely popular holiday destination of **PHILLIP ISLAND** is famous above all for the nightly roosting of hundreds of Little penguins at Summerland Beach – the so-called "**Penguin Parade**" – but the island also boasts some dramatic coastline, plenty of surfing (for more information, call the Phillip Island Surf Report on ☎1902 243 082), fine swimming beaches, and a couple of well-organized wildlife parks. **Cowes**, on the sheltered bay side, is the main town and a lively and attractive place to stay. Other, smaller, communities worth a visit are **Rhyll**, to the east, and **Ventnor**, just west of Cowes.

A daily **V/Line bus** to Cowes departs from Melbourne in the afternoon, but there's no public transport on the island itself, so it can be tricky getting to the Penguin Parade, over 10km from Cowes. Joining a **tour** solves the transport problem. Some tour operators offer the option of combining a visit to Phillip Island with tours to other tricky-to-reach places, such as the Mornington Peninsula and Wilson's Promontory National Park. Duck Truck Tours, based at *Amaroo Park YHA* in Cowes (see overleaf), does a full-day tour of Phillip Island ($69) from Melbourne and also runs a three-day tour from Melbourne to

Phillip Island which also takes in Sorrento on the Mornington Peninsula ($245 inclusive); both these tours can also be combined with a one- or two-day bush-walking trip to Wilson's Promontory National Park. Autopia Tours (☎03/9326 7910, ⊛www.autopiatours.com.au) runs a one-day tour ($70 including entrance fees and dinner) of the island, which also takes in the Wonthaggi State Coalmine on the South Gippsland coast.

If you're **driving**, head southeast from Melbourne on the Princes Highway to Dandenong, then follow the South Gippsland Highway to Lang Lang and from there the Bass Highway to Anderson where the road heads directly west to San Remo and the bridge across to the island, a drive of approximately three hours in total. The scenic lookout about 3km before San Remo is worth stopping at, for fantastic views of Western Port Bay and the surrounding countryside. **SAN REMO** itself has lots of motels, a picturesque fishing fleet by its wharf and a co-operative selling fresh fish and crayfish. Not surprisingly, you can get delicious fish and chips; the best are served at the building at 121 Main St.

NEWHAVEN, the first settlement you come to after crossing the bridge, has a large **tourist information centre** (daily 9am–5pm; ☎1300 366 422), where you can book accommodation, pick up a free map and buy tickets for the Penguin Parade ($14), Churchill Island ($7.70), the Koala Conservation Centre ($5.60), or a combined ticket for all three ($22.40), as well as ferry cruises. **Churchill Island** (daily 10am–5pm; $7.70), 1km north of town, is occupied by a working farm. A leisurely walk leads around the island, with views of the unspoilt coastline; there's also a historic homestead and cottage in English-style gardens, surrounded by ancient moonah trees which are home to abundant birdlife.

Phillip Island Reserve and the Penguin Parade

The **Phillip Island Reserve** includes all the public land on the **Summerland Peninsula**, the narrow tip of land at the island's western extremity. The reason for the reserve is the **Little penguin**, smallest of the penguins, which is found only in southern Australian waters and whose largest colony breeds at Summerland Beach (around 2000 penguins in the parade area, and 20,000 on the island altogether). The **Penguin Parade** (nightly after dusk; $14; ☎03/5956 8300, ⊛www.penguins.org.au) sounds horribly commercial – and with four thousand visitors a night at the busiest time of the year (around Christmas, when bookings are essential), it can hardly fail to be. Spectators sit in concrete-stepped stadiums looking down onto a floodlit beach, with taped narrations in Japanese, Taiwanese and English. But don't be too hard on it: eco-logical disaster would ensue if the penguins weren't managed properly, and vis-itors would still flock here, harming the birds and eroding the sand dunes. As it is, all the money made goes back into research and looking after the pen-guins, and into facilities such as the excellent **Penguin Parade Visitor Centre** (open from 10am; admission included in the parade ticket): the "Penguin Experience" here is a simulated underwater scene of the hazards of a penguin's life, and there are also interactive displays, videos and even nesting boxes to which penguins have access from the outside, where you can watch the chicks.

The parade itself manages to transcend the setting in any case, as the penguins come pouring onto the beach, waddling comically once they leave the water. They start arriving soon after dark; fifty minutes later the floodlights are switched off and it's all over, at which time (or before) you can move on to the

MELBOURNE AND AROUND | Phillip Island

extensive boardwalks over their burrows, with diffused lighting at regular intervals enabling you to watch their antics for hours after the parade finishes – they're active most of the night. If you want to avoid the worst of the crowds, the quietest time to observe them is during the cold and windy winter (you'll need water- or windproof clothing at any time of year). Remember too that you can see Little penguins close to St Kilda Pier in Melbourne (see p.921) and at many other beaches in southern and southeastern Australia, perhaps not in such large numbers, but with far fewer onlookers.

The Nobbies and Seal Rocks

At the tip of the Summerland Peninsula is **Point Grant**, where **The Nobbies**, two huge rock stacks, are linked to the island at low tide by a wave-cut platform of basalt, affording views across to Cape Schanck on the Mornington Peninsula. From the Point, a boardwalk leads across spongy greenery – vibrant in summer with purple and yellow flowers – along the rounded clifftops to a lookout over a blowhole. This is a wild spot, with views along the rugged southern coastline towards Cape Woolamai, a granite headland at the eastern end of the island. From September to April you may see muttonbirds (shearwaters) here – they arrive in September to breed and head for the same burrows each year, after an incredible flight from the Bering Strait in the Arctic Circle. Further off Point Grant, **Seal Rocks** are two rocky islets with the largest known colony of Australian fur seals, estimated to number around 16,000. It's possible to see seals here all year round, though their numbers peak during the breeding season between late October and December. **Cruises** to Seal Rocks are available from Cowes (see below).

Phillip Island Wildlife Park and the Koala Conservation Centre

Two further parks complete Phillip Island's rich collection of wildlife attractions. **Phillip Island Wildlife Park**, on Thompson Avenue just 1km south of Cowes (daily 10am–10.30pm; $12.50), provides a shady sanctuary for Australian animals. Highlights include the beautiful pure-bred dingoes, Tasmanian devils, fat and dozy wombats, which you can hold and feed if they're awake (but watch out, they bite), as well as an aviary and a koala reserve. There are also freely ranging emus, Cape Barren geese, wallabies, eastern grey kangaroos and pademelons.

The **Koala Conservation Centre**, on Phillip Island Tourist Road between Newhaven and Cowes (daily 10am–5.30pm; $5), aims to keep the koala habitat as natural as possible while still giving people a close view. A treetop boardwalk through a part of the bushland park allows visitors to observe these marsupials at close range. At 4pm the rangers provide fresh gum leaves – a very popular photo opportunity. You can learn about koalas in the excellent interpretive centre.

Cowes

Phillip Island's main town, **COWES**, is situated at the centre of the north coast, where the sandy bays are sheltered enough for good swimming. Several good places to eat and stay can be found here on **The Esplanade**, a lively strip facing the jetty. Based in the old Rotunda, Bay Connections (℡03/5952 3501; ⊛www.bayconnections.com.au) offers various **cruises** from the jetty, the best being the trip to Seal Rocks (2hr; $45) to see the Australian fur seals close up.

The same company runs transfers from Cowes to Stony Point and French Island (Wed & Sun Sept–July; ferry service plus a tour of French Island.

Accommodation

Out of season you shouldn't have any trouble finding somewhere **to stay**, but during the peak Christmas to Easter season accommodation nearly doubles in price and some places require weekly bookings. The Phillip Island tourist information centre in Newhaven handles accommodation bookings for the island; in addition, a private agency in Melbourne, Island Retreats (℡ 1800 629 319) can also arrange accommodation and packages.

Abaleigh on Lovers Walk 6 Roy Court ℡ 03/5952 5649, ⓦ www.babs.com.au/abaleigh. Four very nicely furnished, cosy apartments (1, 2 and 3 bedrooms) in a two-storey house in a quiet location near the beach and ten minutes' walk from the town centre. Breakfast included. ❻–❼

Amaroo Park Cnr Church and Osborne streets ℡ 03/5952 2548, ⓔ phillipisland@yhavic.org.au. Good YHA hostel offering free transport (Tues & Fri) to and from Melbourne. Facilities include a convivial bar, heated swimming pool, cheap meals and bike rental. Dorms $20, rooms ❷–❸

The Castle – Villa by the Sea 7–9 Steele St, Cowes ℡ 03/5952 1228. Delightful B&B in a pleasant location. ❼

Coachman Motel 51 Chapel St ℡ 03/5952 1098, ⓕ 5952 1283. Luxurious town house with motel units and suites. Facilities include a heated pool and spa for communal use. ❸–❻

The Continental Phillip Island 5–8 The Esplanade ℡ 03/5952 2316, ⓕ 5952 1878. A conveniently central hotel with en-suite rooms, some with seafront balconies, and a heated pool. ❹–❼

Kaloha Holiday Resort Cnr Chapel and Steele streets ℡ 03/5952 2179, ⓕ 5952 2723. Motel units with cooking facilities, plus cabins, camping sites and facilities for on-site vans. Located in shady grounds giving onto a quiet swimming beach. ❸–❹

Narrabeen Guesthouse 16 Steele St ℡ 03/5952 2062, ⓕ 5952 3670. A delightful guesthouse; the owners can arrange gourmet dinners. ❺

Penguin Hill Country House B&B Cnr of Ventnor and Back Beach roads, Ventnor ℡ & ⓕ 03/5956 8777. A rural B&B with good ocean views. ❻

Rothsaye on Lover's Walk 2 Roy Court ℡ & ⓕ 03/5952 2057. A cosy, comfortable B&B. ❺–❻

Seahorse Motel 29–31 Chapel St, Cowes ℡ 03/5952 2003, ⓕ 5952 3775. An above-average, centrally located motel. ❸–❺

Eating and drinking

Boyle's at the Castle 7–9 Steele St, Cowes ℡ 03/5952 1228. Sophisticated, small and cosy restaurant in the upmarket *The Castle – Villa by the Sea* guesthouse. The set menu costs $50–60. Licensed. Bookings recommended.

Carmichael's Restaurant 17 The Esplanade, Cowes ℡ 03/5952 1300. Breakfast, lunch and dinner (mains $25–32) daily, with views from the wide balcony over the water.

The Clock Cafe 1 Findlay St, Cowes. Near the western end of the Esplanade. Small cosy café with a view of the pier and a small sundeck. Open

daily for breakfast, light lunches and dinner.

Fountain Place Ice Cream & Pancake Parlour 29 Thompson Ave, Cowes. Delicious ice cream.

Isle of Wight Hotel The Esplanade, Cowes. Good-value bistro with sea views, a couple of bars, a lively beer garden and entertainment at summer weekends.

The Jetty The Esplanade, Cowes ℡ 03/5952 2060. Relaxed restaurant specializing in fresh local seafood. Licensed.

Praha Coffee House 92 Thompson Ave, Cowes. Simple café serving excellent food, plus great coffee.

The Yarra Valley and the Dandenongs

Northeast of Melbourne, the **Yarra Valley** stretches out towards the foothills of the Great Dividing Range, with **Yarra Glen** and **Healesville** the targets for excursions into the wine country and the superb forest scenery beyond. To the east, and still within the suburban limits, the cool **Dandenong Range** is as pretty as anywhere in Australia, with quaint villages, fine old houses, beautiful flowering gardens and shady forests of eucalypts and tree ferns.

To get to all these destinations and to have a good look round, you really need your own vehicle. From Monday to Saturday it's possible, although not exactly easy, to see the Dandenongs by **public transport** – for further details, enquire at the Met Transport Information Centre (☎13 16 38) in Melbourne. Trains run via Ferntree Gully to Belgrave, starting point of the **Puffing Billy** steam train (see p.954). **Bus #694** runs from Belgrave via Mt Dandenong Tourist Road to Olinda township in the Dandenong Ranges. **Bus #688** runs from Olinda via the northern part of Mt Dandenong Tourist Road to Croydon railway station, where you can catch a Met train back to Melbourne. **Healesville** comes within the orbit of the suburban transport system: take a train from Melbourne to Lilydale and then bus #685 (to visit the Healesville Sanctuary, it's best to take the daily bus departing from Lilydale). There's a daily V/Line service from Melbourne to **Eildon** via Healesville and Marysville; the V/Line service to **Mansfield** passes through Lilydale and Yarra Glen daily (for further information, call V/Line on ☎13 61 96). There are local buses from Belgrave to **Emerald**.

The Yarra Valley

Just half an hour's drive from Melbourne, the **Yarra Valley** is home to around thirty of Victoria's best small **wineries**. The combination of good wine and fine food is really taking off in the valley, and in recent years quite a few winery restaurants have made a name for themselves in culinary circles. Wine country starts in outer suburbia north of the Maroondah Highway just before Lilydale (turn-offs are signposted). North of Lilydale, you can check out wineries (again, all signposted) along or near three routes – the Warburton Highway to the east, the Maroondah Highway to Healesville, and the Melba Highway, heading north past Yarra Glen. The brochure *Wineries of the Yarra Valley* contains a complete list of all local wineries and a map. Even better is the detailed booklet *Wine Regions of Victoria* – both are available at tourist information centres. If you intend to take a few swigs (and can't find a teetotal driver) it's best to join a **winery tour**: Backpacker Winery Tours (☎03/9877 8333, ⓦwww.backpackerwinerytours.com.au) picks up from three locations in central Melbourne and two in St Kilda, visiting four wineries in the Yarra Valley ($79 including transport, tastings and lunch).

The following are just a few of the wineries and restaurants in the Yarra Valley worth a visit. **Yering Station** (☎03/973 1107; daily 10am–5pm), 32 Melba Highway, just south of Yarra Glen, is located on the site of the first vineyard planted in the area in 1838 (the cellar door operates from the original brick building) and has a glass-walled restaurant offering views across the valley, plus a wine bar and a shop selling regional produce. On the same property is **Chateau Yering Historic House** luxury hotel. For real comfort and luxury, wine and dine at the hotel's more casual *Café Sweetwater* or the very posh *Eleonore's Restaurant*, then sink into a four-poster bed in one of the period-style rooms (☎03/9237 3333, ⓦwww.chateau-yering.com.au; ⑥–⑦). Lovers of gourmet cheeses might want to drop in at the **Yarra Valley Dairy** (daily 10.30am–5pm) at McMeikans Road, just south of Yering station, where you can buy or sample handmade hard and soft cheeses washed down with a glass of local wine. **De Bortoli** (bookings for the restaurant advisable on ☎03/5965 2271) occupies an unbeatable location at Pinnacle Lane, off the Melba Highway at Dixon's Creek north of Yarra Glen, with views over gently rolling hills. This was one of the first places in the valley to offer gourmet food along with its wine – both cuisine and decor betray Italian influences.

Domaine Chandon, on the Maroondah Highway near the town of Coldstream, produces fine *méthode champenoise* sparkling wine, which you can sample ($7–9 per glass) in a modern, bright and airy tastings room with brilliant views. Free thirty-minute tours depart hourly from 11am to 4pm. **Eyton on Yarra** winery and restaurant, further up towards Healesville at the corner of Maroondah Highway and Hill Rd (☏03/5962 2119), is a relative newcomer, known for its sparkling Pinot Chardonnay and specializing in locally produced food. There are four more wineries off the Warburton Highway, including **Yarra Burn** on Settlement Road at Yarra Junction; the restaurant here serves hearty Australian country cuisine (lunches daily; dinner Fri & Sat), and B&B accommodation is available in the homestead.

From Yarra Junction it's not far to **WARBURTON**, a pretty, old-fashioned town on the Upper Yarra River, and starting point for the **Upper Yarra Track**, which follows old timber tram and vehicle tracks upstream for over 80km. The track can be covered as a series of short walks or as a continuous five- to seven-day trek, finishing in the **Baw Baw National Park**, where it joins the Alpine Walking Track. For more information contact the DSE Information Centre in Melbourne (☏03/9637 8080) or the telephone information service run by Parks Victoria (☏13 19 63).

Wineries apart, **YARRA GLEN** also boasts the splendidly restored *Grand Hotel* and, not far away on the Melba Highway, the National Trust **Gulf Station** (Wed–Sun & public holidays 10am–4pm; $7), a collection of ten 1850s slab farm buildings set in a large area of farmland.

Healesville and beyond

HEALESVILLE is a small, pleasant town nestled in the foothills of the Great Dividing Range; there's a **visitor information centre** in the old courthouse building at the southern end of town, just off the Maroondah Highway (daily 10am–5pm). The town's main attraction is the renowned **Healesville Sanctuary** (daily 9am–5pm; free guides 10am–3pm if booked in advance; ☏03/5957 2800, ⊛www.zoo.org.au; $15.80), which cares for injured and orphaned animals, some of which are subsequently returned to the wild; those that stay join the sanctuary's programmes for education and the breeding of endangered species. It's a fascinating place in a beautiful setting, with a stream running through park-like grounds, dense with gum trees and cool ferns, and 3km of walking tracks. Many of the animals are in enclosures, but there are paddocks of emus, wallabies and kangaroos you can stroll through. The informative "meet the keeper" presentations are worth joining, especially the one featuring the birds of prey (noon, 2.30 & 3.30pm, weather permitting).

Continuing north on the Maroondah Highway over the Black Spur and Dom Dom Saddle towards Alexandra, the scenery becomes progressively more attractive. The **Maroondah Reservoir Lookout**, just off the highway 3km north of Healesville, is worth a brief stop, with picturesque views across the forest-fringed dam. There are very popular **picnic grounds** and **gardens** in the park on the southwest side of the reservoir. Soon after the reservoir, the highway meanders along bush-clad mountain slopes and enters luxuriant wet eucalypt forest with incredibly tall mountain ash, moss-covered myrtle beech, manna gum, tree ferns, gurgling creeks and waterfalls. The **Fernshaw Reserve and Picnic Ground** is a good place to stop and view the scenery. After the Dom Dom Saddle, 509m above sea level and 16km past Healesville, the highway descends towards Narbethong, where it enters drier country. Three kilometres past Narbethong there's a worthwhile detour down a turn-off to scenic **MARYSVILLE**, 9km off the highway. The village nestles in the foothills of the Great Dividing Range, with **Lake Mountain** (1400m), a very popular area for cross-country skiing and tobogganing, 20km further west. In summer, Marysville makes an excellent base for **bushwalking**, being surrounded by wet mountain ash forests with many creeks and waterfalls. The best-known, **Steavensons Falls**, can be reached from the village by a walking trail or by road and is floodlit at night until 11pm. Just out of Marysville, the unsealed **Lady Talbot Forest Drive** turns off the Lake Mountain road and then winds 46km through the forest, past picnic areas and walking tracks (suitable for conventional vehicles, though after heavy rainfall it's best to check in Marysville for road conditions). Return to Marysville via the Buxton Road, or turn right and head straight north to Buxton, where you rejoin the highway. Further up, the Maroondah Highway passes the drier **Cathedral Range State Park**: west of the road here the mighty sandstone cliffs of Cathedral Mountain seem to rise almost vertically behind the paddocks, overlooking the Acheron Valley.

⑨ The Dandenongs

As in the Blue Mountains of New South Wales, the **Dandenong** hills are enveloped in a blue haze rising from forests of gum trees which cover much of the area. Abundant rain ensures the area stays cool and lush, while fine old houses and gardens add to the scenery. Easy bushwalks in the **Dandenong Ranges National Park** start from Ferntree Gully, accessible by train or by car via the Burwood Highway. A pleasant way to enjoy the forests and fern gullies is to take a ride on the **Puffing Billy** steam train (☎03/9754 6800, Ⓦwww.puffingbilly.com.au), which runs for 13km from the Puffing Billy station in Belgrave to Lakeside ($27.50 return) on Lake Emerald, stopping at Menzies Creek and Emerald: one train a day continues a further 9km from Lake Emerald to Gembrook ($38 return). The Puffing Billy station is a short, signposted walk from **Belgrave** station (suburban trains). The train has run more or less continuously since the early twentieth century, though its operation now depends on dedicated volunteers; on total fire ban days, diesel locomotives are used. Timetables vary seasonally but there are generally several services daily until late afternoon.

Just outside Emerald, man-made **Emerald Lake** has paddle-boats to rent and a swimming pool, as well as trails through bushland which continue into the nearby state reserve. *Emerald Backpackers*, 2 Lakeview Court (☎03/5968 4086; dorms $16, rooms ❷) caters mainly for people seeking farm work; the owners have local contacts. On weekdays and Saturday morning, bus #695 runs from the Belgrave train station to Emerald.

Geelong and the Bellarine Peninsula

Heading west towards Geelong – for the Bellarine Peninsula and Great Ocean Road – it's just a short detour off the Princes Freeway to **WERRIBEE**, home to the restored **Mansion at Werribee Park** (Mon–Fri 10am–3.45pm, Sat & Sun until 4.45pm, $10.60; ☎03/9741 2444 or 13 19 63), located on K Road. Built in 1874–77 by Scottish squatters Thomas and Andrew Chirnside, who struck it rich on the back of sheep, the sixty-room mansion is the largest private residence in Victoria. Guides in period costume show you around the ornate homestead and the Victorian-era gardens; alternatively, free audioguides are available at the entrance. Beyond the mansion's gardens are the extensive grounds of **Victoria's Open Range Zoo**, where animals from Africa, Asia and Australia (giraffes, cheetahs, rhinoceroses, hippopotamuses, monkeys and other creatures) roam in large open enclosures. A fifty-minute **safari bus**, included in the admission price, takes visitors through the property (daily 9am–5pm; bus tours 10.30am–3.40pm; $15.80; ℡03/9731 9600, ⓦwww.zoo.org.au). **Werribee Park Shuttle**, a private bus service to Werribee Park (mansion and zoo) operates from Melbourne, departing from St Kilda Road behind the taxi rank at Flinders Street station at 9.30am and 11.30am ($15 return; advance booking required on ℡03/9731 9600). Southeast of here is the recently built **Shadowfax Winery**, an impressive box-like structure that offers cellar-door sales (Sat & Sun from 10am), glimpses of the wine-making process and gourmet food.

Continuing along the freeway, you can detour west again through Little River to the **You Yangs**, small but rugged volcanic peaks which rise sharply out of the surrounding plains. Scramble to the top of the highest, **Flinders Peak** (348m), and you're rewarded with fine views of Geelong and Port Phillip Bay. The You Yangs, as well as the nearby **Brisbane Ranges**, are excellent places for spotting kangaroos, wallabies, koalas and possums at dusk. Alternatively, you can observe kangaroos, wallabies and emus, as well as numerous waterbirds, in their natural habitat at the little-known **Serendip Sanctuary**, 20km north of Geelong at 100 Windermere Rd, Lara (daily 10am–4pm; ℡03/5282 1584; free), which occupies a square kilometre of bush, marsh and wetlands. A refuge for threatened birds of the Western Plains of Victoria, the sanctuary is renowned for its captive breeding programme of brolgas, magpie geese and Australian bustards.

Geelong

The industrial town of **GEELONG**, en route to the Bellarine Peninsula, doesn't have much to offer visitors: the fact that the **National Wool Museum** (daily 10am–5pm; $7.30) is the main attraction gives you some idea of the place. The museum is housed in the Geelong Wool Exchange, a National Trust-listed building at the corner of Brougham and Moorabool streets (wool is still auctioned off thirty days a year on the top floor of the exchange); the well set-up exhibition concentrates on the social history of the wool industry, with reconstructions of typical shearers' quarters and a millworker's 1920s cottage. Many of the town's best Victorian buildings are on **Little Malop Street**, including the elegant **Geelong Art Gallery** (Mon–Fri 10am–5pm, Sat & Sun 1–5pm; free, but donation appreciated), which has an extensive collection of paintings by nineteenth-century Australian artists such as Tom Roberts and Frederick McCubbin, plus twentieth-century Australian paintings, sculpture and decorative arts. From Little Malop Street and Malop Street, Moorabool Street leads down to **Corio Bay** and Geelong's waterfront, with its recently renovated promenades, rotunda, fountains and lovely nineteenth-century carousel featuring over thirty sculpted wooden horses. There's a swimming enclosure at Eastern Beach. New waterfront eating places have also emerged, notably the large restaurant complex at the end of new **Cunningham Pier**, which comes into its own at night. Nestled among the lawns and trees of Eastern Park around ten minutes' walk from the city centre are Geelong's historic **Botanic Gardens** (Mon–Fri 7.30am–5pm, Sat & Sun 7am–7pm; free). Begun in the late 1850s, the gardens boast rare and endangered plants, fountains, a geranium conservatory, sculptures and the *Tea House* (daily 11am–4pm), where you can take refreshments or pick up brochures and other material about botanical subjects

On the way to Torquay, **Narana Creations**, an Aboriginal arts, crafts and cultural centre at 410 Torquay Rd (Surfcoast Highway) in Grovedale is worth a brief stop. Paintings and various arts and crafts are sold here, and visitors can sometimes listen to Dreamtime stories or didgeridoo playing (Mon–Fri 9am–5pm, Sat 10am–4pm; free).

Practicalities

In addition to the **visitor information centre** (daily 9am–5pm; ℡1800 620 888) at the Wool Museum, there's a helpful **tourist information stall** (Mon–Sat 9am–5pm) in the Market Square Shopping Centre at the corner of Moorabool and Malop streets. Both provide lots of brochures and free maps. The main **shopping** strip is just a block south of the Wool Museum along Malop Street. Places to **stay** include *National Hotel Backpackers*, above a pub at 191 Moorabool St (℡03/5229 1211 or 0410 529 935; dorms $17–19); *Kangaroo Motel*, The Esplanade South (℡03/5221 4365; ❹), which has reasonably priced units in a central location; the *Lucas Innkeepers Motor Inn*, 9 Aberdeen St (℡03/5221 2177; ❺–❻), just west of the town centre; and the reasonably priced *Ardara House B&B*, 4 Aberdeen St (℡03/5229 6024; ❹). At the other end of the price scale, the *Sundowner Geelong*, 13 The Esplanade (℡03/5222 3499; ❺–❻), has water views, a restaurant and bar, sauna and a pool. If you want to **camp**, try the *City Southside Caravan Park* on Barrabool Road, south of the Barwon River at Barwon Valley Park (℡03/5243 3788; cabins ❸–❹), or the nearby *Riverview Tourist Park* (℡03/5243 6225; cabins ❸–❹).

To check out what's going on, pick up a copy of the free **listings magazine** *Forte*, available at CD and record shops, and sometimes also at the visitor information centre. It covers the whole of southwest Victoria, and also has information on surfing, diving and other activities. There's a surprisingly healthy local **band** scene: check out *Irish Murphy's*, 30 Aberdeen St; the *Wool Exchange Hotel*, 59 Moorabool St; *The Barwon Club Hotel*, 509 Moorabool St; *Lamby's Bar*, downstairs at the Wool Museum; and the *Scottish Chief's Tavern & Restaurant* at 99 Corio St, which has its own microbrewery.

To get to the Bellarine Peninsula from Geelong, take the Bellarine Transit **bus** from the Busport on Brougham Street (next to the Wool Museum) for Ocean Grove and Barwon Heads, Point Lonsdale via Queenscliff, St Leonards via Portarlington, and Grovedale via Torquay.

Eating

There's plenty of choice when it comes to **eating**, especially along the foreshore.

Beach House Restaurant Eastern Beach Reserve ℡03/5221 8322. The café downstairs serves breakfast all day as well as other cheap fare, while the upmarket restaurant upstairs offers eclectic East-meets-West cuisine. Great views, especially from the restaurant. Moderate to expensive. Licensed.

Bazil's Café Cunningham Street ℡03/5229 8965. Small, cosy café serving superb, moderately priced Mediterranean-inspired food – try the bouillebaisse. Licensed. Wed–Sun breakfast and lunch only; Thurs–Sat also open for dinner.

Cats Bar Restaurant Lounge 90 Little Malop St ℡03/5229 3077. Big place with a polished cedarwood bar and moderately priced food – gets packed in the evenings. Licensed. Daily 10am–midnight.

Fishermen's Pier Seafood Restaurant Yarra Street ℡03/5222 4100. Fish and seafood prepared in a range of styles, from Thai to Tuscan. Expensive. Licensed.

Sailor's Rest Tavern 3 Moorabool St ℡03/5224 2241. Pleasant family restaurant with a menu of cheap to moderately priced warm and cold salads, risotto, pasta, steak and fish. Licensed. Daily 9am–9pm.

Sempre Caffe e Paninoteca 88 Little Malop St. Excellent range of fish, pasta and meat dishes, plus good desserts, all at moderate prices. Licensed. Tues–Sat 10am–midnight.

Tonic 5 James St ☎03/5229 8899. This restaurant-bar just around the corner from Little Malop St goes for cool, minimalist chic. The menu has a bit of everything: Cajun chicken salad, risotto, linguini, Thai green chicken curry, crispy lime battered fish, all available either as an entrée or main course. Moderate. Licensed. Mon–Sat lunch and dinner.

Queenscliff and around

From Geelong, the Bellarine Highway runs 31km southeast to **QUEENS-CLIFF** through flat and not particularly scenic grazing country. Queenscliff is essentially a quiet fishing village on Swan Bay – with several quaint cottages on Fishermens Flat – which became a favourite holiday resort for Melbourne's wealthy elite in the nineteenth century, then fell out of favour, and has only recently begun to enjoy something of a revival as a popular place for a weekend away or a Sunday drive. Queenscliff's position near the narrow entrance to Port Phillip Bay made it strategically important: a **fort** here faces the one at Point Nepean. Now the home of the Australian Army Command and Staff College, the fort can be visited on guided tours (Sat & Sun 1pm & 3pm; $4.40).

Full details of other things to do are available from the Queenscliff **Visitor Information Centre**, 55 Hesse St (daily 9am–5pm; ☎03/5258 4843). During school holidays and in summer, **Queenscliff Historical Tours** (☎03/5258 3403) rents out bicycles ($15–20), as well as providing a map and audioguide to the town; you can either pick up a bike near the pier at the end of Symonds Road, or have it delivered to your accommodation. Other activities include kayaking ($24 for 2hr; ☎03/5258 2166; rentals from the marina on Larkin Parade) along the coast or further offshore, or diving among wrecks and marine life with the **Queenscliff Dive Centre** (☎03/5258 1188).

Among the attractions is the **Queenscliff Maritime Museum**, Weerona Parade (Mon–Fri 10.30am–4.30pm, Sat & Sun 1.30–4.30pm; ☎03/5258 3440; $4.40), which concentrates on the many shipwrecks caused by The Rip, a fierce current about 1km wide between Point Lonsdale and Point Nepean. Outside, a tiny fisherman's cottage is set up as it would have been in 1870, and there's a shed where an Italian fisherman painted, in naive style, all the ships he'd seen pass through from 1895 to 1947 (imaginatively including the *Titanic*). Next door, the **Marine Discovery Centre** has a small aquarium stocked with local marine life (daily 10am–4pm during school holidays, other times by appointment; ☎03/5258 3344; ⊛www.DSE.vic.gov.au/mafridiscovery; $5); it also organizes a range of activities, mainly during the summer holidays, such as marine biology cruises, rock pool rambles and snorkelling tours. Every Sunday, the **Bellarine Peninsula Railway** operates steam trips from the old Queenscliff Railway Station to Drysdale, 20km northwest (11.15am & 2.30pm; ☎03/5258 2069, ⊛www.bpr.org.au; $14).

The **Queenscliff Music Festival** (☎1900 930 060, ⊛www.qmf.net.au), held annually on the last weekend of November, features an eclectic mix of Australian contemporary music (folk, blues, world music, fusion) and draws ever-growing crowds.

Practicalities

Three grand **Victorian-era hotels** in Queenscliff are popular settings for romantic (but very expensive) breaks: the *Vue Grand*, 46 Hesse St (☎03/5258

1544, ℱ5258 3471; ❼) has a Spanish-style exterior and a fabulously ornate Victorian interior with a very expensive restaurant; the clifftop *Ozone Hotel*, 42 Gellibrand St (☎1800 804 753, ⓦwww.ozonehotel.com.au; ❻–❼ including breakfast), has sea views from its iron-lace verandahs and a gorgeous dining room; while the refined *Mietta's Queenscliff Hotel*, 16 Gellibrand St (☎03/5258 1066, ℱ5258 1899; ❽), is perhaps the best of all. **Budget alternatives** include the *Queenscliff Inn YHA*, 59 Hesse St (☎03/5258 3737, ℱ5258 3737; dorms $20, rooms ❷–❹), a pleasant Victorian guesthouse offering B&B – the single rooms are particularly good value; and *Beacon Resort Holiday Park & Motel*, 78 Bellarine Highway (☎03/5258 1133, ℱ5258 1152; ❸–❺), which has tent sites, cabins, holiday units, motel rooms and a heated pool.

Among the town's **eating places**, the best fish and chips are at *Queenscliff Fish and Chips*, 77 Hesse St. Among the cafés there are *Queenscliff Hotel Shop & Bar* (daily 11am–5pm) in the *Queenscliff Hotel*, which does light lunches, coffees and drinks, and *38 South*, a café at the car ferry terminal with a fantastic view of the heads of the bay and the Mornington Peninsula. The *Royal Hotel* in 34 King St has two moderately priced restaurants: *Zara's* upstairs does breakfasts, lunches and dinners (seafood, pasta, and meat from the grill), and there's a pizzeria downstairs. More pricey options include the outstanding *Harry's*, an excellent BYO seafood restaurant at the foreshore at Princes Park (open Thurs–Sun, daily in January; ☎03/5258 3750) and the gorgeous, though pricey, restaurants at the *Vue Grand* and the *Queenscliff Hotel* (the latter also has a cheaper courtyard restaurant). All are licensed and serve lunch and dinner daily.

Ferries run from Queenscliff across the mouth of Port Phillip Bay to Sorrento (see p.944).

Point Lonsdale and Portarlington

From Queenscliff it's about 5km to peaceful **Point Lonsdale**, whose most noticeable feature is its magnificent 1902 lighthouse, 120m high and visible for 30km out to sea. Below the lighthouse, on the edge of the bluff, is "Buckley's Cave" where William Buckley is thought to have lived at some stage during his thirty-year sojourn with the Aborigines. At **PORTARLINGTON**, which sits on Port Phillip Bay about 14km north of Queenscliff, there's a beautifully preserved steam-powered flour mill, four storeys of solid stone, owned by the National Trust (Wed, Sat & Sun noon–4pm; ☎03/5259 3847; $2.50).

Travel details

Trains

Melbourne to: Adelaide (5 weekly; 10hr); Alice Springs (1 weekly; 36hr); Ballarat (6–10 daily; 1hr 30min); Bendigo (5–11 daily; 2hr); Geelong (12–20 daily; 1hr); Perth (2 weekly; 60hr); Sydney via Albury (2 daily; 11hr); Warrnambool (1–3 daily; 3hr 15min).

Buses

Melbourne to: Adelaide (4 daily; 10hr); Brisbane (1 daily; 25hr); Perth via Adelaide (3 weekly; 47hr);

Sydney via Bega (1 daily; 17hr); Sydney via Canberra (5–6 daily; 12–14hr)

Ferries

Melbourne to: Devonport, Tasmania (1–2 daily; 9–10 hr).

Flights

Qantas flies from **Melbourne** to: Adelaide (10–13 daily; 1hr 15min); Alice Springs (2 daily; 3hr 30min); Ayers Rock Resort (1–3 daily; 3hr 30min); Brisbane

(12–15 daily; 1hr 55min); Cairns (7–11 daily; 3hr 15min direct); Canberra (5–7 daily; 1hr 5min); Coolangatta/Gold Coast (6–12 daily; 2hr); Darwin (3 daily; 4–5hr with one stopover); Hobart (4–7 daily; 1hr); Launceston (4 daily; 50min); Mackay (3–4 daily; 4hr 15min with one stopover); Perth (5–7 daily; 4hr); Rockhampton (6–7 daily; 3hr 30min with one stopover); Sydney (16–22 daily; 1hr 20min); Townsville (3–5 daily; 5hr with one stopover). Virgin Blue flies from **Melbourne** to: Adelaide

(10–13 daily; 1hr 15min); Brisbane (8–9 daily; 2hr); Cairns (3–4 daily; 3hr 20min with one stopover); Canberra (2 daily; 1hr); Darwin (1 daily; 7hr with one stopover); Coffs Harbour (2 daily; 3hr 50min with one stopover); Gold Coast (6–8 daily; 2hr); Hobart (4 daily; 1hr 10min); Launceston (3 daily; 1hr); Mackay (1 daily; 4hr 10min with one stopover); Perth (4 daily; 4hr 15min); Sydney (13–18 daily; 1hr 20min); Townsville (3–4 daily; 6hr 30min with one stopover).

Victoria

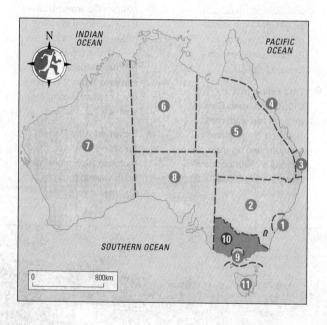

CHAPTER 10

Highlights

* **Great Ocean Road** Wait until the sun is down and the crowds are gone and watch the fairy penguins come out to play at the Twelve Apostles. **See pp.966–986**

* **Goldfields** Mining memorabilia and grandiose architecture grace the old gold towns of Ballarat and Bendigo. **See pp.986–1003**

* **Trail riding in the Gippsland bush** Canter through the wilderness, watched by goannas in the surrounding trees, in Victoria's "high country". **See pp.1025–1033**

* **Wilson's Promontory National Park** There's great bushwalking and fantastic coastal scenery – once you escape the crowds – at Victoria's favourite national park. **See p.1028**

* **Milawa Gourmet trail** Excellent local produce washed down with great wines from the Brown Brothers winery – all sampled against a backdrop of stunning Alpine scenery. **See p.1041**

* **Victorian Alps** Perfect for skiing in winter, the Victorian Alps make ideal bushwalking territory in summer. **See p.1044**

10

Victoria

ustralia's second-smallest state, **Victoria** is the most densely populated and industrialized, and has a wide variety of attractions packed into a small area. It may not be a state to tour comprehensively, but Australians, at least, lap up the legends of their history that are thick on the ground: you're never too far from civilization, but everywhere there's a wild past of **gold prospectors** and **bushrangers**. All routes in the state radiate from **Melbourne**, bang in the middle of the coastline on the huge Port Phillip Bay, and no point is much more than seven hours' drive away. Yet all most visitors see of Victoria apart from its cultured capital is the **Great Ocean Road**, a winding 280km of spectacular coastal scenery. Others may venture to the idyllic **Wilsons Promontory National Park** (the "Prom"), a couple of hours away on the coast of the mainly dairy region of **Gippsland**, or to the **Goldfields**, where the nineteenth-century goldrushes left their mark in the grandiose architecture of old mining towns such as **Ballarat** and **Bendigo**.

There is, however, a great deal more to the state. Marking the end of the Great Dividing Range, the massive sandstone ranges of the **Grampians**, with their Aboriginal rock paintings and dazzling array of springtime flora, rise from the monotonous wheatfields of the **Wimmera** region and the wool country of the western district. To the north of the Grampians is the wide, flat region of the **Mallee** – scrub, sand dunes and dry lakes heading to the **Murray River**, where **Mildura** is an irrigated oasis supporting orchards and vineyards. In complete contrast, the **Victorian Alps** in the northeast of the state have several winter **ski slopes**, high country that provides perfect bushwalking and horse-riding territory in summer. In the foothills and plains below, where bushranger **Ned Kelly** once roamed, are some of Victoria's finest **wineries** (wine buffs should pick up a copy of the excellent hundred-page brochure, *Wine Regions of Victoria*, available from the visitor information centre in Melbourne and other towns). Beach culture is alive and well on this **coastline** with some of the best **surfing** in Australia.

The only real drawback is the frequently cursed **climate**. Winter is mild, and the occasional heatwaves in summer are mercifully limited to a few days at most, but the problem is that of unpredictability. Cool, rainy "English" weather can descend in any season, and spring and autumn days can be immoderately hot. But even this can be turned to advantage: as the local saying goes, if you don't like the weather, just wait ten minutes and it'll change.

Public transport, by road and rail, is with **V/Line** and subsidiary country bus lines. After the restructuring of recent years, however, using your vehicle is definitely a more convenient transport option, as train and bus services are fairly infrequent and quite a few places of interest can be reached only with difficulty, if at all.

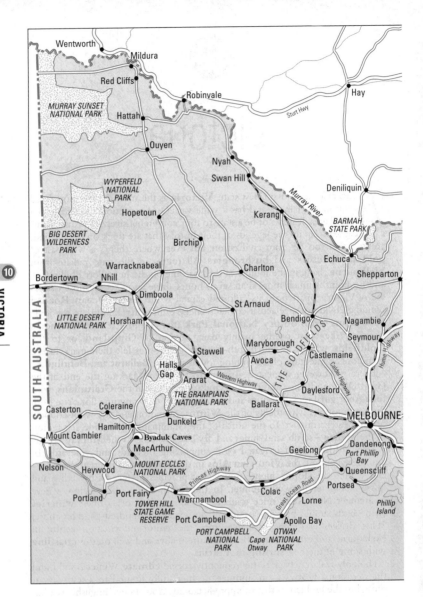

Some history

Semi-nomadic **Koories** have lived in this region for at least forty thousand years, and from earliest times developed sophisticated hunting and gathering methods, creating rock art, weaving baskets, making possum-skin cloaks to protect against the cold, and establishing semi-permanent settlements such as those of circular stone houses and fish traps found at Lake Condah in western Victoria.

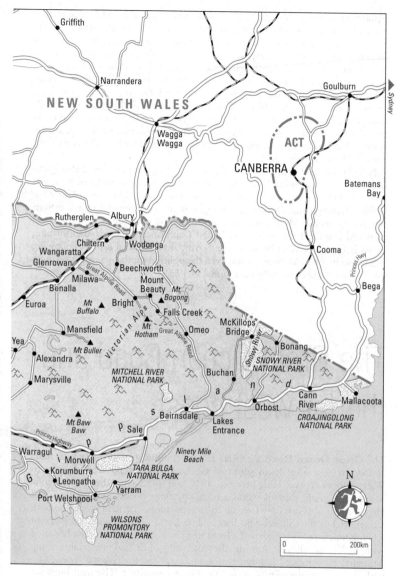

For the colonists, Victoria did not get off to an auspicious start: there was an unsuccessful attempt at settlement in the **Port Phillip Bay** area in 1803 but Van Diemen's Land (Tasmania) across the Bass Strait was deemed more suitable. It was in fact from Launceston that Port Phillip Bay was eventually settled, in 1834; other Tasmanians soon followed and **Melbourne** was established. This occupation was in defiance of a British government edict forbidding settlement in the territory, then part of New South Wales, but squatting had already begun the previous year when Edward Henty arrived with his stock to establish the first white settlement in **Portland** on the southwest coast. A pattern was created of land-hungry settlers – generally already men of means – responding to Britain's demand for wool, so that during the 1840s and 1850s what was to become Victoria evolved into a prosperous pastoral community with squatters extending huge grazing runs.

From the beginning, the Koories fought against the invasion of their land: 1836 saw the start of the **Black War**, as it has been called, a bloody guerrilla struggle against the settlers. By 1850, however, the Aborigines had been decimated – by disease as well as war – and felt defeated, too, by the apparently endless flood of invaders; their population is believed to have declined from around 15,500 to just 2300.

By 1851 the white population of the area was large and confident enough to demand separation from New South Wales, achieved, by a stroke of luck, just nine days before **gold** was discovered in the new colony. The rich goldfields of Ballarat, Bendigo and Castlemaine brought an influx of hopeful migrants from around the world. More gold came from Victoria over the next thirty years than was extracted during the celebrated Californian goldrush, transforming Victoria from a pastoral backwater into Australia's financial capital. Following federation in 1901, Melbourne was even the political capital – a title it retained until Canberra became fully operational in 1927.

The Great Ocean Road and the far west coast

The **Great Ocean Road**, Victoria's famous southwestern coastal route, starts at Torquay, just over 20km south of Geelong, and extends 285km west to Warrnambool. It was built between 1919 and 1932 with the idea of constructing a scenic road of world repute, equalling California's Pacific Coast Highway – and it certainly lives up to its reputation. The road was to be both a memorial to the soldiers who had died in World War I, and an employment scheme for those who returned. Over three thousand ex-servicemen laboured with picks and shovels, carving the road into cliffs and mountains along Australia's most rugged and densely forested coastline; the task was speeded up with the help of the jobless during the Great Depression. The road hugs the coastline between **Torquay** and **Apollo Bay** and passes through the popular holiday towns of **Anglesea** and **Lorne**, set below the Otway Range. From Apollo Bay the road heads inland, through the towering forests of the **Otway National Park**, before rejoining the coast at Princetown to wind along the shore for the entire length of the **Port Campbell National Park**. This stretch from Moonlight Head to Port Fairy, sometimes referred to as the "Shipwreck Coast", is the most spectacular – over eighty ships have been sunk here, victims of the rough Southern Ocean and dramatic rock formations such as the

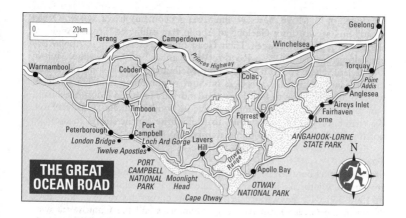

Twelve Apostles, which sit out to sea beyond the rugged cliffs. The often windy and stormy weather enhances the jagged coastline, and even at the height of summer you can't rely on it being sunny here. Information on all the villages and sights on the Great Ocean Road can be found on the area's website, ⓦwww.greatoceanroad.org.

If you're in a hurry to get from Melbourne to Warrnambool, the **Princes Highway** is a much faster route – and a much duller one. The only place you might consider stopping briefly is Colac, where **Lake Colac** and the vast **Lake Corangamite** support a profusion of birdlife, with botanical gardens and a bird sanctuary.

From **Warrnambool**, the small industrial coastal city where the Great Ocean Road ends, the Princes Highway continues along the coast, through quaint seaside **Port Fairy** and industrial **Portland**, before turning inland for the final stretch to the South Australian border. If you're determined to stick to the coast, you can continue along the Portland–Nelson road, with Mount Richmond National Park and Discovery Bay Coastal Park on the coastal side, and Glenelg National Park on the other, to end up at the unspoilt little town of **Nelson** on the peaceful Glenelg River, with the spectacular Princess Margaret Rose Caves nearby.

The **Great Southwest Walk**, a 250-kilometre circuit starting from just outside Portland, going on to the Glenelg River and Nelson, and then back through the two coastal parks to Portland, is magnificent. There are campsites all along the route; for further information, and to obtain maps, contact the DSE Information Centre, 8 Nicholson St, East Melbourne (☏03/9637 8325, ⓦwww.dse.vic.gov.au), or **Parks Victoria** (☏13 19 63, ⓦwww.parkweb.vic.gov.au).

Transport

If you don't have your own car or can't get a **lift** (it's always worth checking hostel notice boards), you might want to consider one-way **car rental**, usually available from the big-name companies in Melbourne. There are plenty of parking spots where you can pull over and admire the view, but even so the unfortunate driver will miss out on a lot of the scenery; with narrow roads, steep cliffs and incessant hairpin bends you need to keep your eyes glued to the road. In summer the road is filled with **cyclists**, and although the routes are exhilarating they are really only suitable for the experienced and adventurous.

V/Line (☎13 61 96, ⓦwww.vlinepassenger.com.au) has a "Great Ocean Road" **bus** service from Geelong to Apollo Bay, calling at Torquay, Anglesea, Lorne and points in between. Their Coast Link bus service from Apollo Bay goes along the Great Ocean Road to Warrnambool on Friday (plus Mon in Dec & Jan). There's a **train** service from Melbourne, via Geelong and Colac, to Warrnambool (3 daily, 2 services on Sun are combined train/bus services), with connecting buses to Port Fairy, Portland and Heywood (Mon–Sat 2 daily, Sun 1 daily) and on to Mount Gambier in South Australia (1 daily). From Warrnambool you can also return to Melbourne on the inland road, or go north to Ballarat. There's no public transport to Nelson.

Tours

One-way tours between Melbourne and Adelaide, via the Great Ocean Road, are a good way to take in the scenery. The backpackers' busline Oz Experience (☎1300 330 044, ⓦwww.ozexperience.com) covers this route in four days, taking in the Great Ocean Road, the Grampians and the Coonawarra wine region in South Australia ($260, transport only), while Wayward Bus (☎1800 020 007, ⓦwww.waywardbus.com.au) sticks to the coast all the way to the Coorong in South Australia on its three-and-a-half-day tour (from $310, including hostel accommodation breakfasts and lunches). With both you can get off the bus and continue your trip a few days later (booking required). The small and friendly Groovy Grape covers the route in an all-inclusive three-day tour (☎1800 661 177, ⓦwww.groovygrape.com.au; $295) with overnight stops at the Aboriginal-run *Brambuk Hostel* in the Grampians and Port Campbell.

A few other reliable tour operators do **one- or two-day round-trips** from Melbourne to the Great Ocean Road, some with an extra Grampians option and/or possible transfer to Adelaide – note that prices given below don't include food and accommodation costs. Autopia Tours (☎03/9326 5536 or 1800 000 507, ⓦwww.autopiatours.com.au) does one-day tours (daily; $70), a three-day tour adding on a visit to the Grampians (Mon, Wed & Sat; $160), and a one-way tour to Adelaide, via the Great Ocean Road and the Grampians in three days (Mon, Wed & Fri; $175).

Let's Go Bush Tours (☎03/9662 3969) is a smaller, long-established tour operator that offers a two-day tour of the Great Ocean Road staying overnight in Apollo Bay (Wed & Sat, plus extra trip Mon Nov–May; $99 for transport plus $25 for food and accommodation kitty). A similar outfit, Eco Platypus Tours, runs a two-day tour including a full day in the Grampians (☎1800 819 091, ⓦwww.ecoplatypustours.com; $120 plus meals and accommodation), with a choice of dorm or twin/double room accommodation at their own lodge on the Wannon River between Warrnambool and the Grampians. Try also Go West, which runs a one-day trip (☎03/9828 2008; daily; $70).

Torquay

TORQUAY is the centre of **surf culture** on Victoria's "surf coast", which extends from Point Lonsdale, on the Bellarine Peninsula, to Lorne; two local beaches, **Jan Juc** and **Bells Beach**, are solidly entrenched in Australian surfing mythology. If you're not here for the surf, then there's not really a lot happening: in hot weather the place is boisterously alive, but out of season it's somnolent and low-key. The big event here is the Rip Curl Pro & Sun Smart Classic, held at Bells Beach in Easter, which draws national and international contestants and thousands of spectators (call SurfVictoria on ☎03/5261 2907 or see ⊛www.ripcurlpro.com.au for details). Local **buses** run between Geelong and Torquay via Jan Juc – call Bellarine Transit (☎03/5223 2111) for the latest information.

As you come into Torquay along the Great Ocean Road (Geelong Road in town), you'll see the **Surfcity Plaza** shopping centre, by far the best place to rent surf gear. The **Surfworld Museum** (daily 9am–5pm; $6.50; ⊛www .surfworld.org.au) at the rear of the plaza is devoted to Torquay's main industry – and a prosperous one it is, taking in at least $200 million a year. Surfworld features a wave-making machine, interactive videos that explain how waves are created, and displays about the history of surfing. The museum also functions as the **Torquay Visitor Information Centre** (☎03/5261 4219), handing out a few leaflets and brochures. Many of the biggest surfing businesses are based in Torquay, and every surf accessory conceivable is sold here. The biggest and oldest is Rip Curl, 101 Surf Coast Highway (daily 9am–5.30pm), which started making surfboards here in 1969 and now stocks all the major brands, as well as its own boards and gear. Based at the same shopping centre are showcase outlets for other big names, such as Billabong, Piping Hot and Quiksilver. Bargains can sometimes be found at Baines Beach Surf Seconds, around the corner on Baines Street (fourth factory on the right). The **Mary Elliott Pottery**, 80 Surfcoast Highway (open daily), is worth a look; it supplies tourist information as well.

A grassy public reserve shaded by huge Norfolk pines (with electric barbecues and picnic tables) runs along rocky **Fisherman's Beach** and **Front Beach**. The **Surf Beach** (or "back beach"), south of Cosy Corner (a headland separating Front and Surf beaches), is backed by rugged cliffs and takes a full belting from the Southern Ocean; it's patrolled in summer. **Jan Juc**, just south of Surf Beach across Torquay Golf Club, is also patrolled in season and has better swimming and surfing. The **South Coast Walk** to Aireys Inlet via Anglesea begins from here (25km; 8hr); the sector to **Bells Beach** is a one-hour, three-kilometre walk.

Practicalities

For **surfing lessons**, call the Westcoast Adventure & Surf School in Torquay (☎03/5261 2241), or Go Ride a Wave (☎1300 132 441), an outdoors activities company based in neighbouring Anglesea which also does day-trips from Melbourne in summer, including a two-hour surfing lesson ($90). If you feel like taking to the air, turn to **Tiger Moth World Adventure Park**, a family amusement park on the Bellarine Peninsula halfway between Geelong and Queenscliff (daily 10am–5pm; $9.50; ☎03/5261 5100, ⊛www.tigermothworld.com), which has lots of fun and sports facilities, most of them water-based. They also offer skydives and **scenic flights** aboard vintage Tiger Moths, biplanes and modern aircraft – the latter fly as far west as the Twelve Apostles, following the rugged coastline (1hr 20min return, $180 per person, min 2 passengers).

Accommodation

Accommodation in Torquay consists of two hostels, a couple of motels, several B&Bs, and a few caravan and camping parks.

Anita's at Torquay 17 Anderson St ☎03/5261 4732. Budget cabins with shared facilities, as well as more upmarket rooms with en-suite bathrooms and a self-contained cottage with two bedrooms. Budget cabins ❸, en-suite rooms and cottage ❹

Bells Beach Backpackers 51–53 Surfcoast Highway ☎03/5261 7070, ⓕ5261 3879, ⊛www.bellsbeachbackpackers.com.au. Painted with beach-house murals, this place is hard to miss. Boasts dorms with lockers, Internet access

($5/hr), bikes, boards and wetsuits for rent, and a courtesy bus to the beaches. Dorms $19–23, rooms ❷–❸.

Bernell Holiday Park Surfcoast Highway ☎03/5261 2493. Features tent and caravan sites, cabins and good facilities, including a heated salt-water pool, beach volleyball court and tennis courts. ❸–❹.

Pointbreak Backpackers 185 Addison Rd, Bells Beach ☎03/5261 5105, ⓦwww.pointbreakback packers.com.au. Smallish dorms in a converted

stable, located on a ten-acre property. The owners pick up from Torquay and run shuttles, as well as organizing surfing lessons, bushwalks and other activities. Dorms $18–20.

Torquay Hotel 36 Bell St ☎03/5261 2001, ⓕ5261 4065. Very centrally located and serves good bistro fodder. ❹–❺.

Zeally Bay Caravan Park On the Esplanade ☎03/5261 2400. Few facilities and no pool but water views instead, including from some of their cabins. ❷–❹.

Eating

When it comes to **food**, there are a few excellent, typically casual places designed to satisfy a surfer's hunger: *Micha's Restaurant*, 23 The Esplanade (☎03/5261 2460; licensed or BYO wine), is a long-time favourite dinner spot serving Mexican food and cheap drinks – you'll need to book on summer weekends. *Spooners* and *Kuzies*, both in the Plaza, are good for filling fare, and the *Nocturnal Donkey* on Bell Street is popular for munchies late into the night. Good ice cream is sold at *The Great Australian Ice Creamery*, Shop 4, 57 Surfcoast Highway, and *The Scandinavian Ice Cream Company*, 34 Bell St. Gilbert Street in the heart of Torquay is lined with cafés, such as *Sandbah* at no. 21 (7.30am–6pm), and *Tapas* at no. 9 (8am–6pm), a light and airy licensed café-bar with polished floorboards. For **entertainment**, surfies head for the *Torquay Hotel*, 36 Bell St, where live bands play at weekends. At Jan Juc, both *Pabs Tavern* and the *Birdrock Bar* on Stuart Avenue are popular hangouts day and night.

Anglesea and Aireys Inlet

On the way to Anglesea from Torquay, you can make a short but worthwhile detour to **Point Addis**; turn left just beyond Bells Beach. The road goes right out to the headland where, from the car park, you look down on the waves crashing onto the point. Steps lead down to an even better vantage point, with surf heaving below you and Bells Beach stretching to the northwest. Just before the headland, there's another car park from where an access track leads to the **Point Addis Koori Cultural Walk**. Interpretive signs along this one-kilometre trail point out the use of plants and other aspects of the traditional lifestyle of the Wathaurong clan who inhabited the Geelong region.

ANGLESEA itself is a pleasant place for a holiday, with the Anglesea River running through to the sea, and picnic grounds along its banks; its main claim to fame is a large population of **kangaroos**, which graze on the golf course. Despite tourist development, the beach has managed to retain its sand dunes and untouched aspect. Children can swim safely here, as the surf is fairly gentle, but the waves are high and powerful enough for body-surfers to enjoy. The small and very clean *Anglesea Backpackers Hostel* on 40 Noble St (☎03/5263 2664, ⓦhome.iprimus.com.au/angleseabackpacker; dorms $23, room ❸), located between the river and the golf course, has two six-bed dorms and an en-suite double, and the owner can arrange lots of activities in the area. Phone for a pick-up from the bus stop. There are a few **cafés**: *Heathlands Teahouse* on the Great Ocean Road also has a gallery exhibiting photographs and other work by local artists (Wed–Sun, holidays daily from 10am).

From Anglesea the road goes inland for a few kilometres through scrubby bush. Beyond, a pretty white lighthouse with a red cap overlooks the small town of **AIREYS INLET**. There's a general store, a café and craft shop near the lighthouse in what used to be the former lightkeeper's stables (7 Federal St; daily 9am–5pm). For accommodation try the *Aireys Inlet Caravan Park* on the Great Ocean Road (☎03/5289 6230, ⓦwww.aicp.com.au; cabins ➌–➎) and Split Point Cottages at 40 Hopkins St (☎03/5289 6566; ➎–➏), which features self-contained accommodation in four mud-brick cottages with two bedrooms. *Airey's By the Light*, on the way out of town (☎03/5289 6134; ➏–➐), is a very upmarket B&B with private decks and stunning sea views, in keeping with the huge and ritzy houses that jostle for ocean views on the way to Lorne. A little further down the road in **FAIRHAVEN**, the small *Surfcoast Backpackers* (☎03/5289 6886 or 0419 351 149; dorms $25) has very clean en-suite dorms and a cosy kitchen/common room with a piano – it's located at 5 Cowan Ave, a prime location 100m away from the main road and the long, sandy Fairhaven Beach, which is patrolled. The owner books horse rides through the bush and along the beaches. Ask the bus driver to stop at the Yarringa Road bus stop – there's a signpost on the Great Ocean Road pointing towards the hostel.

Lorne and around

Picturesquely set at the foot of the heavily forested **Otway Range**, on the banks of the Erskine River, **LORNE** has long been the premier holiday town of the Great Ocean Road. Only two hours' drive from the city, it's hugely popular with Melbourne weekenders who relish its well-established café society and whiff of 1960s counterculture overlaid on an essentially middle-class 1930s resort. To complete the picture, the **Angahook–Lorne State Park** (see overleaf), with its walking tracks, plunging falls and fern gullies, surrounds the town.

About a thousand people live in Lorne, but from Christmas until the end of January twenty thousand more pour in; if you arrive unannounced, you'll have no hope of finding even a camping spot. The **Falls Festival** (ⓦwww.falls festival.com) on New Year's Eve is celebrated with a big rock concert that attracts droves of teenagers, followed eight days later by the Mountain to Surf Run and one day later by the highlight of the peak season, the **Pier to Pub Swim**. It's the largest blue-water swimming event in the world and attracts as many as two and a half thousand competitors who race the 1200m from Lorne Pier to the main beach. The atmosphere surrounding these events is a lot of fun, but generally Lorne is much more enjoyable when it's less crowded, which means avoiding weekends and the peak summer season.

The main beachfront promenade, Mountjoy Parade, is enlivened by the restored *Grand Pacific Hotel*, with its 1870s facade, and the modern, very pink, terraced *Cumberland Resort*. Between the street and the beach is a foreshore with trampolines and a pool. The **surf beach** itself is one of the safest in Victoria, protected from the Southern Ocean by two headlands, but in summer it gets very crowded. Ten minutes east of Lorne is the secluded beach of Cathedral Rocks, a very popular **nudist beach**.

Practicalities

Lorne's **tourist office**, at 144 Mountjoy Parade (daily 9am–5pm; ☎03/5289 1152), is very helpful and has a good stock of leaflets packed with local information, including several free driving maps and details of walks in the state park. Mocean Surfboards on Mountjoy Parade (daily 9.30am–5.30pm), rents out quality surf- and boogie-boards and wetsuits. Other services, such as banks, a post office and shops, are clustered primarily along Mountjoy Parade and parallel Smith Street.

Accommodation

Lorne has a mix of old **guesthouses** and modern **holiday apartments** – often side by side. There's plenty of motel, hotel and self-catering accommodation, but most of it is in the upper price bracket, and in December and January most places rent by the week, with even B&Bs insisting on a three- or four-night minimum stay. If you want to keep costs down (but don't fancy the dorms at the *YHA* or *Great Ocean Road Cottages*), contact the Lorne Foreshore Committee, Ocean Road by Erskine Bridge (℡03/5289 1382, ⓦwww.lfcmd.asn.au), which runs four **caravan parks** in the vicinity.

Anchorage Motel and Villas 32 Mountjoy Parade ℡03/5289 1891, Ⓕ 5289 2988. Motel units and two-storey villas with two bedrooms. Pool and common spa. Units ❹–❺ villas ❺–❻

Cumberland Lorne Resort 150 Mountjoy Parade ℡03/5289 2400 or 1800 037 010, Ⓕ5289 2256, ⓦwww.cumberland.com.au. Luxurious but very pricey one-bedroom apartments, some with ocean views. Lots of facilities, including tennis and squash courts, an indoor pool, spa, sauna, and rental of windsurfers, boogie-boards and bikes. ❼

Erskine Falls Cottages Cora-Lynn Court, off Erskine Falls Rd 4.5km north of town ℡03/5289 2666, Ⓕ5289 2247, ⓦwww.lornecottages .com.au. Spacious timber cottages (2–3 bedrooms) in a bushland setting in the hills near Erskine Falls, with views of the ocean over the treetops, big verandahs, fireplaces, a solar-heated pool and a tennis court. ❺–❼

Erskine on the Beach Mountjoy Parade ℡03/5289 1209, Ⓕ5289 1185, ⓦwww.erskine-house.com.au. A huge country house with guest lounges and open fires, decorated in Art Deco style and with magnificent gardens out the back, facing the ocean. In addition to the traditional rooms, there are twenty new apartments. Facilities include tennis, croquet and bowls. Rooms ❺–❻, apartments ❻–❼

Grand Pacific Hotel 268 Mountjoy Parade ℡03/5289 1609, Ⓕ5289 2279. A restored Victorian building whose grandeur conceals motel-style accommodation. ❻

Great Ocean Road Backpackers YHA 10 Erskine Ave ℡03/5289 1809, Ⓕ5289 2508, ⒺLorne@yhavic.org.au. Excellent, attractive hostel with wooden verandahs and balconies, in a central location beside the Erskine River. Dorm bed $20 for YHA members; rooms ❷–❸

Great Ocean Road Cottages 3 Erskine Ave ℡03/5289 1070, Ⓕ5289 2247. Well-designed, comfortable, self-catering cottages in a lovely forest setting beside the Erskine River. Also some dormitories. Dorms about $22, cottages $1500 per week.

Lemonade Creek Cottages 690 Erskine Falls Rd ℡ & Ⓕ 03/5289 2600. Self-contained weatherboard cottages with a heated pool and tennis court, in a bushland setting, but not far from the beach and town. ❺–❻

Lorne Hotel 176 Mountjoy Parade ℡03/5289 1409, Ⓕ5289 2200. Very large rooms, some with balconies and sea views, but noisy at weekends. ❺–❻

Sandridge Motel 128 Mountjoy Parade ℡03/5289 2180, Ⓕ5289 2722. The standards of the motel units range from "simple" to "deluxe"; the latter feature private balconies facing the sea. ❺–❼

Eating and entertainment

There are great places to **eat** and **drink** everywhere in town. Most licensed places allow you to BYO wine but charge a hefty corkage fee, up to $6 per bottle. *Kosta's* often has music in the evenings, while the *Lorne Hotel* has bands on Friday and Saturday nights, and its public bar, with pool table and pinball machine, is a favourite with the young crowd. The *Lorne Theatre*, 78 Mountjoy Parade (℡03/5289 1272), screens films all week during summer.

The Arab 94 Mountjoy Parade. An original beatnik hangout, which opened two weeks before the Olympic Games in 1956 and has been going strong ever since. It now sports minimalist decor but is still good for daytime snacks and fancier meals at night.

Erskine Falls Café Off Erskine Falls Rd, in the hills above town (about 4.5km north). Open daily from 9am; they serve breakfast all day and light lunches.

Kafé Kaos 54 Mountjoy Parade. Huge, delicious, healthier-than-thou sandwiches, salads and wraps with extensive (and much less healthy) breakfast options. Licensed and BYO wine. Mon–Thurs & Sun 8.30am–6pm. Fri & Sat until 11pm.

Kosta's 48 Mountjoy Parade ⊕03/5289 1883. A popular, Greek-style bar and eating place, serving up good seafood as well as grilled meats. Licensed or BYO wine. Daily 9am–1am; closed mid-June to mid-July.

Lorne Hotel 176 Mountjoy Parade. Best pub meals in town, and has a dining room overlooking the ocean.

Lorne Pier Seafood Restaurant On the pier at Point Grey. Excellent seafood. Licensed or BYO.

Mark's 124 Mountjoy Parade ⊕03/5289 2787. A modern restaurant with a menu featuring a large variety of dishes, from marlin steak to home-made potato gnocchi. Licensed and BYO wine. During summer holidays daily noon–3pm & 6pm–late; other times only evenings and Sat afternoon; closed in May.

Moon's Espresso Bar 108 Mountjoy Parade. A little taste of city life by the sea, this ultra-modern establishment serves excellent coffee and Mediterranean lunches and even has an attached cocktail bar.

Qdos Allenvale Rd ⊕03/5289 1989. Tucked away in the eucalypt-clad hills above Lorne, this art gallery-cum-café serves light lunches, dinners and tasty home-made cakes and coffee in a relaxed atmosphere. Bookings advisable. Summer daily 9am–1am, winter closed Weds 10am–6pm.

Reifs Restaurant & Bar 84 Mountjoy Parade ⊕03/5289 2366. Serves a wide range of dishes, including seafood and vegetarian, with Asian and Mediterranean influences. A large outdoor area overlooks Loutit Bay. Licensed and BYO wine. Oct–April Mon–Fri 11am–4pm & 6pm–late, Sat & Sun 9.30am–4pm; May–Sept Tues–Fri 6pm–late, Sat 9.30am–4pm & 6pm–late, Sun 9.30am–4pm.

Angahook-Lorne State Park

Angahook–Lorne State Park extends along some 50km of coastline, from Aireys Inlet to Kennett River. Pockets of temperate rainforest, towering blue-gum forests, cliffs and waterfalls characterize the Lorne section of the park, south of the Erskine River. The **Erskine Falls**, one of the most popular attractions, drops 30m into a fern-fringed pool – you can reach them along a winding eight-kilometre road which ends with a short descent on a very steep but sealed section. From the car park the falls are a few minutes' walk through majestic trees and tall umbrella ferns; another 150m takes you down to the quiet, rocky Erskine River. It's also possible to walk through the bush from Lorne to the falls (7.5km one-way; 4hr), starting from the *Erskine River Caravan Park* and following the river; after 1km you'll pass the Sanctuary, a natural rock amphitheatre, then Splitter Falls and Straw Falls, before reaching Erskine Falls.

Closer to Lorne, **Teddy's Lookout**, in Queens Park, is either a quick drive from the Great Ocean Road (up Otway Street, turn left at the roundabout into George Street), or a three-kilometre walk. You end up high above the sea, with a view of the St George River below and the Great Ocean Road curving around the cliffs. On the way back to Lorne, the **Qdos Arts centre** (daily 11am–11pm) on Allenvale Road, with an art gallery, sculpture gardens and a very good café-restaurant, merits a visit – just turn left at the roundabout and go up the hill.

Apollo Bay and the Otway Ranges

Beyond Lorne, wooded hills fall away steeply into the ocean. The road snakes along the coastline, becoming very narrow in places where it was literally gouged out of the rockface. On a fine, sunny day the views are glorious, but best admired from one of the many scenic lookout points as you need to drive with care.

The road descends to small bays at the mouths of the **Wye** and **Kennet** rivers. The small hamlets named after these rivers provide an idyllic setting for a few days of lazing around, fishing and bushwalking. There's **camping** at the *Wye River Foreshore Camping Reserve* (☎03/5289 0412), *Wye River Valley Caravan Park* (☎03/5289 0241) and *Kennett River Caravan Park* (☎03/5289 0272), plus motel units at the *Rookery Nook Hotel* in Wye (☎03/5289 0240; ❹) – their bistro serves good pub food. You'll also find a host of self-contained cottages (bookings handled by Wye & Kennet River Getaways ☎03/5289 0486, ⓦwww.wyeriverget aways.com.au). The most impressive, though pricey, option is "the deckhouse" on 5 Sturt Court, Wye – it's perched right above the ocean, with stunning views and an equally stunning colour scheme inside the bright studio apartment (☎03/5289 0222, ⓦwww.thedeckhouse.com.au; B&B ❻–❼).

Apollo Bay

APOLLO BAY enjoys a picturesque setting between pounding surf and gently rounded green hills. **Fishing** – commercial and recreational – is the main activity here. If you're interested in doing a bit yourself, enquire at Apollo Bay Fishing and Adventure Tours (☎0418 121 784), which offers fishing trips and scenic boat cruises (from $25 per hr). The town has an enjoyably alternative feel – a lot of musicians live here and both local pubs often have music at weekends. The annual Apollo Bay Music Festival takes place over a weekend at the end of March and features jazz, rock, blues and country, plus many workshops (information and bookings ☎03/5237 6761, ⓦwww.apollobaymusicfestival.com). For information on local activities, head for the Great Ocean Road Visitor Information Centre on the foreshore at the eastern end of town (daily 9am–5pm; ☎03/5237 6529, ⓕ5237 6194), which has very helpful staff and an informative display on the rainforest and local history.

Practicalities

Flying is becoming increasingly popular here: the Wingsports Flight Academy (☎0419 378 616) offers courses in hang-gliding and paragliding and allows those with no prior experience to fly with a fully qualified pilot along the coast in a powered hang-glider. Twelve Apostles Airtours (☎03/5237 7370) and Cape Otway Aviation (☎0407 306065) do scenic flights to a variety of destinations, including nearby Cape Otway and the Twelve Apostles (from $70 for 10min), and as far afield as King Island, Tasmania; prices are per person and based on a minimum of three passengers. If you're interested in **horse riding**, book a trail ride with Wild Dog Trails (☎03/5237 6441; 1hr 30min $40/3hr $60); **cycling** enthusiasts can enquire about mountain-bike tours run by Otway Expeditions (☎0419 007 586; minimum of two people required). Sunroad Tours picks up people from their accommodation at dusk and takes them to view glow-worms on a private property near Apollo Bay (☎03/5237 6080; 1hr 30min; $20) while Otway Natural Wonders operates out of the Otway town of Forrest, 37km northwest of Apollo Bay, and runs night waterfall walks and "paddle with a platypus" **canoe trips** in the densely forested hinterland at dawn and dusk (from $75 per 2–3hr). For other sightseeing **tours** (4WD or normal vehicle) enquire at the Visitor Information Centre.

Accommodation

Apollo Bay has a wide variety of **accommodation**. Numerous holiday apartments, cosy B&B cottages, guesthouses and farmstays are to be found in the area, many of them picturesquely located in the hills and valleys surrounding the town – a scenic location is the **Barham River Valley** 8km west of town which has a few accommodation places in a lush rainforest setting. Apollo Bay's main street is lined with **motels**, most of them rather drab affairs dating from the 1970s.

There are several **caravan parks**, the closest to town being the *Waratah Caravan Park* at 7 Noel St (Ⓣ03/5237 6562; cabins ❸–❹). *The Pisces Caravan Resort*, 2km north of the town centre, also has cabins, some with en-suite facilities (Ⓣ03/5237 6749; ❸–❺). For foreshore **camping** in more secluded surroundings, try the *Marengo Camping Reserve* on Marengo Crescent (Ⓣ03/5237 6162; closed May–Oct), or *Skenes Creek Camping Reserve*, 6km back along the Ocean Road.

Apollo Bay Backpacker Hostel 400m up from Apollo Bay's main street on 47 Montrose Ave Ⓣ03/5237 7360 or 0419 340 362. Located in a small weatherboard house with dorms and cheap doubles, some out the back in an extension to the house; the hostel has Internet access. Dorms $20, rooms ❸

Arcady Homestead B&B 925 Barham River Rd, Barham River Valley Ⓣ03/5237 6493. An old-fashioned, friendly guesthouse with four rooms and a guest lounge. ❹

Beachfront Motel 163 Great Ocean Rd Ⓣ03/5237 6437, Ⓕ5237 7197. One of the newer and better motels in town. ❹–❻

Marriner's Falls Cottages 1090 Barham River Rd, Barham River Valley Ⓣ03/5237 7494. Cosy and well equipped, with spa and open fire. ❻

Otway Paradise Cottages 935 Barham River Rd, Barham River Valley Ⓣ03/5237 7102, Ⓦwww.otway-paradise-cottages.com.au. Five

fully equipped, spacious cottages (1, 2 & 3 bedrooms) with wood heaters, in a rainforest setting on 40 acres of land. ❺

A Room with a View 280 Sunnyside Rd, Wongarra Ⓣ03/5237 0218. Cosy, aptly named B&B accommodation 14km east of town, with magnificent views of green rolling hills and the ocean. ❺–❻

Surfside Hostel Corner of Great Ocean Rd and Gambier St Ⓣ03/5237 72630. A friendly place with dorms and cheap doubles in a scenic location on a hill at the western side of town. All beds have electric blankets; other facilities include a fully equipped bathroom for the disabled, outdoor BBQs and a large record collection. Dorms $17–20, rooms ❷

Wongarra Heights Guesthouse 65 Sunnyside Rd, Wongarra Ⓣ03/5237 0257. Five comfortable guest rooms in Wongarra, 12km east of town, with stunning ocean views. ❹

Eating

In town, the **eating** places are strung along the Great Ocean Road. *Buffs Bistro* at no. 51 serves light snacks, seafood and pasta. The atmospheric *Bay Leaf Café* (Ⓣ03/5237 6470; daily) at no. 131 does good egg breakfasts, as well as simple but well-presented lunches and dinners such as zucchini fritters, pumpkin risotto and roti with marinated lamb. Moving more upmarket, there's cosy *La Bimba* (Ⓣ03/5237 7411; closed Mon & Tues May–Nov) on the first floor of no. 125 with an imaginative, eclectic menu, and the more austere *Chris's Sea-Grape Wine Bar & Grill* (Ⓣ03/5237 6610; closed Mon May–Aug) at no. 141, which does good but more predictable grilled meat-and-salad combinations in the evening and standard brekkie and lunch fare during the day. Vegetarians and wholefood junkies will like the *Sandy Feet Café*, a tribute to all things healthy next door at no. 139. The *Apollo Bay Hotel* on Collingwood Street has good seafood, and also cheaper counter and bistro meals.

Outside town, *Chris's Beacon Point Restaurant*, 2km up Skenes Creek Road in the hills up the coast above **Skenes Creek**, while not cheap (mains

$26–32; ☎03/5237 6411), is renowned for its Mediterranean cuisine, especially seafood. The *Tanybryn Tea House and Gallery*, on the corner of Skenes Creek and Wild Dog roads, is also worth the fifteen-minute drive for its well-stocked craft shop, café and fine panorama (10am–5pm; closed July to mid-Sept).

Otway National Park

From Apollo Bay, the Great Ocean Road soon enters **Otway National Park**, curving and bending upwards through temperate rainforest and offering occasional glimpses of cleared hilltops and grazing sheep in the distance. From Maits Rest car park, 17km west of Apollo Bay, you can take an easy stroll through a lovely fern gully, which gives a feel of the dense rainforest that once covered the entire Otway Ranges. A little further down the road, towards Lavers Hill, you'll see a turn-off to the **Cape Otway Lighthouse**, 14km away, where there's a small café (daily 9.30am–4.30pm) and pleasant accommodation in refurbished lighthouse keepers' residences, simply but tastefully decorated and fully equipped. The main building is a Heritage sandstone house with four bedrooms and two open fireplaces (only the entire house is rented out), there are also an older cottage and a modern studio unit, both with one bedroom, kitchen, lounge and electrical heating (☎03/5237 9240; ❹–❻). The lighthouse and the grounds are open to the public (daily 9am–5pm; $9); guided tours are scheduled at 11am, 2pm & 3pm daily ($11).

The only **caravan park** actually within the national park is *Bimbi Park* (☎03/5237 9246; cabins ❸), about halfway along the road to the lighthouse. The facilities and some of the cabins are quite basic but the setting is gorgeous – on a small farm with paddocks surrounded by bushland – and the caravan park offers excellent **horse-riding** excursions, including a ride to Station Beach (1hr 30min; $40), a three-kilometre-long stretch of sand with freshwater springs and waterfalls. The Oz Experience Bus calls at the caravan park for an overnight stop.

Back on the Great Ocean Road, you momentarily return to the ocean at **Castle Cove**, a good lookout point across green, undulating dairy country. As you turn inland again, stepped hills rise sharply from the road as it passes turn-offs to **Johanna**, one of Victoria's best-known surf beaches, and winds up towards **LAVERS HILL**, high in the Otway Range. The tiny town is characterized by its fern nursery and two cosy tearooms: the *Gardenside Manor* and the *Blackwood Gully Tea Rooms & Tourist Centre*, both of which serve light snacks and Devonshire teas daily from 10am. The *Otway Junction Motor Inn* offers more solid meals as well as motel-style accommodation (☎03/5237 3295; ❹–❺). Much cheaper, especially for single travellers, are the cabins at the *Lavers Hill Roadhouse* (☎03/5237 3251; ❷). Three kilometres out of town is **Melba Gully Conservation Park**, one of the wettest spots in Victoria. It's the location of the Big Tree, a three-hundred-year-old Otway messmate, its base covered in moss; at night glow-worms are a common sight.

From Moonlight Head to Peterborough

The 130-kilometre stretch of coast between lonely, windswept Moonlight Head and Port Fairy is known as the **Shipwreck Coast**, all of it protected within Otway National Park and **Port Campbell National Park**. In 150 years of maritime history, more than 180 ships came to grief in these treacherous waters. The **Historic Shipwreck Trail**, which links the sites of dozens of shipwrecks with informative plaques and signed walking paths, also runs between these two points. The stretch from Princetown to Peterborough is the most obviously hazardous to shipping, with its sheer limestone cliffs and massive eroded stacks. Beyond Princetown, the first worthwhile stop is the steep and slippery **Gibsons Steps**, where you walk down to a kelp-covered beach beneath towering cliffs.

From here on, the spectacle gets more and more extraordinary, with plenty of convenient stopping points from where you can admire the amazing formations. The most stupendous are the **Twelve Apostles** – gigantic limestone pillars, some rising 65m out of the ocean, which retreat in rows as stark reminders of a wasting coastline (the cliff faces erode at a rate of about 2cm a year). The recently built (unstaffed) Twelve Apostles Centre at the car park on the northern side of the road provides clean toilet facilities and welcome shelter from the rain and bone-chilling winds blowing off the Southern Ocean. It features wall-length panels of sailcloth with scripted poems about the Shipwreck Coast's awesome, dangerous beauty. Covered walkways lead through a tunnel under the road, to the lookout points and a short walk along the clifftop. Sunset here (summer around 9pm, winter around 5.45pm) is a popular time for photographers and, unfortunately, crowds. Wait ten minutes or so after dusk, however, when the tourists have jumped back on their coaches and left, and you'll be treated to another fantastic spectacle, as hordes of fairy penguins waddle into shore in their droves.

Next stop is **Loch Ard Gorge**, where a small network of coastal walks gives you the chance to view the fantastic rock formations all around. It was here that the *Loch Ard*, an iron-hulled square rig, hit a reef and foundered while transporting immigrants from England to Melbourne in the spring of 1878. Of fifty-three people on board, only two survived: Eva Carmichael and Tom Pearce, both in their late teens. They were swept into a long gorge that had a narrow entrance, high walls and small beach, and Tom dragged Eva into a cave in the western wall of the gorge before going for help. A walkway leads down to the beach, covered with delicate pink kelp, and you can scramble over craggy rocks to the cave where Eva sheltered, now a nesting site for small birds. The Loch Ard cemetery, where the ship's passengers and crew are buried, is on the clifftop overlooking the gorge. As you drive further, you pass more scenic points, with resonant names such as the Blowhole and the Thundercave, before reaching Port Campbell.

Port Campbell and around

PORT CAMPBELL is a small and companionable settlement on the edge of the Port Campbell National Park. The **Port Campbell Information Centre** on Morris Street (daily 9am–5pm; ☏03/5598 6089 or 1800/620 888) has displays and information about the area and its national parks, and can also book accommodation. Ask here too about the self-guided **Port Campbell Discovery Walk** (90min), which will take you along a clifftop to a viewpoint above Two Mile Bay.

Port Campbell **beach** is a small sandy curve, safe for swimming and patrolled in season – the town climbs the hill behind the beach. Port Campbell Trading Company at 27 Lord St is a small **art gallery** which displays works by local artists and craftspeople, as does Neptune's Realm opposite at no. 34.

If you're really fascinated by shipwrecks, Port Campbell Boat Charters (☏03/5598 6411) offers **diving** to some wreck sites and can rent out snorkelling or diving gear to those who want to go it alone.

△ The Grotto, Port Campbell National Park

Practicalities

The town itself is a pleasant place to while away an evening, and with two hostels in town, **accommodation** needn't be prohibitive. Port Campbell *Ocean House Backpackers* (℡03/5598 6223, ℱ03/5598 6471; dorm bed from $20) is a brand-new homely place in a lovely old house on the main street. It's run by the more upmarket *Comfort Inn Port Campbell* (℡03/5598 6231, ⓦwww .great-ocean-road.com; ❺–❻), which boasts a café with Internet access and a good licensed restaurant, *Napiers* (same phone number) There's also a rather commonplace hostel, *Port Campbell YHA*, on Tregea Street (℡ & ℱ 03/5598 6305; dorms $18, rooms ❸, with four large dorms, a huge kitchen and a TV lounge with wood-fired heater. *Port O'Call* at 37 Lord St (℡03/5598 6206; ❸–❹) is an attractive, inexpensive motel on the main street, while the *Port Campbell National Park Cabin & Camping Park* on Morris Street (℡03/5598 6492, ℱ5598 6493; ❸–❹) offers beachside cabins.

Port Campbell offers plenty of choices as far as **eating places** go – they all sit cheek by jowl on Lord Street. For regular Aussie fare, go to the good-quality bistro at the *Port Campbell Hotel* (daily lunch and dinner) or the no-frills *Port Campbell Take Away Café* at no 15. *Timboon Fine Ice Cream* next to the Mobil petrol station sells delicious home-made ice cream, fruit sorbets and good coffee. More sophisticated eating places include *Waves* at no. 29, an upmarket licensed café/restaurant serving tasty breakfast, lunch and dinner daily (booking advised on ℡03/5598 6111); *Kooh Aah* at no. 26 which operates a café on the ground floor open for breakfast, lunch and dinner and a restaurant on the upper floor (daily from 6pm; ℡03/5598 6408); and *20ate*, a wine bar-café at, you guessed it, no. 28 which has a big terrace and serves snacks and light meals as well as steaks and fish dinners (summer daily, otherwise Wed–Sun noon till late; ℡03/55986142)

Port Campbell's **general store** (daily: winter 8am–6pm; summer 7am–7pm) also has a bottle shop and functions as the post office and newsagent, and has an EFTPOS system that takes every type of card. It's expensive, though, and has limited stock, so if you're planning to stay you'd be advised to shop on the way in Warrnambool or Lorne.

London Bridge, the Grotto and Timboon

Tourists could once walk across the double-arched rock formation known as **London Bridge**, a short distance west of Port Campbell, to the outer end facing the sea. In mid-January 1990, however, the outer span collapsed and fell into the sea, minutes after two very lucky people had crossed it – they were eventually rescued from the far limestone cliff by helicopter. As fate would have it, the couple were conducting an extra-marital affair, and fled from the waiting media as soon as the helicopter arrived. Another good place to stop, just before Peterborough, is the **Grotto**, where a path leads from the clifftop to a rock pool beneath an archway.

Moving on, you pass through undulating dairy country on the last stretch of the Great Ocean Road from Peterborough, on Curdies Inlet, to Warrnambool. There's little to detain you along the route, although if you're a cheese fan you might consider a detour to **TIMBOON**, 18km inland from Port Campbell: at **Timboon Farmhouse Cheese** on the corner of Ford and Fells roads (daily 10am–4pm), you can taste and buy excellent cheese and wine.

Warrnambool and onwards

WARRNAMBOOL seems unable to decide whether it's an industrial city or a charming, seaside agricultural town. Coming into town on the Great Ocean Road you see the more pleasant aspects: the city's lovely coastal setting, with **Allansford Cheeseworld** (Mon–Fri 8.30am–5pm, Sat & Sun 8.30am–4pm) indicating that this is the centre of rich **dairy country**. As well as selling cheese, it has cheese and wine tastings, a café serving teas and light meals, and a local history museum. However, if you approach Warrnambool from the west along the Princes Highway, you'll pass car lots, motels and an ugly factory belching smoke.

Lady Bay, where Warrnambool is sheltered, was first used by sealers and whalers in the early nineteenth century and was permanently settled from about 1839. **Southern right whales**, hunted almost to extinction, have begun to return in the last decade. Every year between June and September, female whales come to the waters off **Logans Beach** to calve. Often the whales swim very close to the shore and can be viewed from a specially constructed platform at Logans Beach.

The perils of shipping in the treacherous waters of the bay are the theme at **Flagstaff Hill** at 23 Merri St (daily 9am–5pm; $14). It features a re-created nineteenth-century coastal village, arranged around the original fort, erected in 1887 when the fear of a Russian invasion was widespread in Australia. The Gravesend Theatre screens a multimedia presentation about the history of the coast, featuring extracts from a diary written by the migrant Edward Charlewood in 1863, and the Grand Circle Gallery has displays about nineteenth-century shipbuilding and navigation. Flagstaff Hill's piece de resistance, however, is the multi-million-dollar sound and laser show **Shipwrecked** ($20; 70min, book at least 2 days in advance; ☎1800 556 111). Screened nightly after dusk, it recounts the story of the *Loch Ard* disaster (see p.977). Spectators are taken through the museum village to the new Wharf Theatre where they can graphically relive *Loch Ard's* last voyage in 1878. The film is partly projected onto an "aquascreen" – a wall of water pumped in from a nearby lake.

Warrnambool has a bustling downtown, with a major shopping centre on Liebig Street, several galleries and museums, and some fine old churches. Perhaps the best of the sights is the **Warrnambool Art Gallery** on Liebig Street (Mon–Fri 10am–5pm, Sat & Sun noon–5pm; $4), a fine provincial gallery with collections of Western District colonial paintings and contemporary Australian prints. The **Botanic Gardens** on Botanic Road, designed in 1877 by William Guilfoyle, then Director of the Melbourne Botanic Gardens, are also worth visiting if you happen to have some spare time. The classically designed, ornamental gardens are filled with winding paths and hills, and provide glimpses of the sea. There's also a fernery, a water-lily pond and a small rotunda.

Practicalities

The well-organized **Warrnambool Visitor Information Centre** (daily 9am–5pm; ☎03/5564 7837 or 1800 637 725, ⓦwww.warrnambool.info.com.au) has been relocated to Flagstaff Hill at 23 Merri St. **Internet** access is available at the hostels (residents only) and at *Hotspot*, 200 Timor St. *Rogers Bar*, around the corner from *Balena's*, is a slick, modern-looking place where Warrnambool's young and trendy go to **drink**. It's only rivalled by the basement bar attached to *Café Regal*, itself a cheap but stylish lunch spot at 163 Timor St, near the art gallery.

Accommodation

Backpackers Barn at the Victoria Hotel Corner of Lava and Liebig streets ☎03/5562 2073. Centrally located, with three-bed dorms, very cheap singles and doubles and a fully equipped kitchen. Dorms $20, rooms ❶

Girt By Sea B&B 52 Banyan St ☎03/5561 3162. In a restored historic house (built 1856) – a convenient location between the town centre and the beach. ❺

Port Warrnambool Village Apartments 14A Pertobe Road, near the foreshore ☎03/5562 8063. Has brand-new three-bedroom apartments with direct beach access. ❺–❻

Stuffed Backpacker Operated by Flaherty's Chocolate Shop, 52 Kepler St ☎ & ☎ 03/5562 2459, ⓦ www.stuffed.axs.com.au. A pleasant place just around the corner from the busy end of Liebig Street, offering lodgings in a renovated old building with simple dorms ($20) and twin rooms. ❷

Hotel Warrnambool Corner of Koroit and Kepler streets ☎03/5562 2377. Upmarket, refurbished place offering good B&B pub accommodation in the town centre. ❸–❹

Warrnambool Beach Backpackers 17 Stanley St ☎03/5562 4874, ⓦ www.beachbackpackers.com. Less than ten minutes' walk from the beach. The hostel has doubles and comfy dorms with lockers, and you can phone for a pick-up from the bus stop in town. They also do cheap meals, have a licensed bar, free mountain bikes and canoes. Enquire at the hostel about trail rides along the beach (1hr; $28) and to locate the spot where penguins waddle ashore at dusk. Dorms $20, en-suite rooms ❷–❸

Warrnambool Surfside Holiday Park Pertobe Rd, opposite Lake Pertobe and near the foreshore ☎03/5561 2611. Self-contained one- to three-bedroom cottages and cabins as well as camping right on the beach. Cabins ❹–❻

Warrnambool Whale View B&B 11 Logan Beach Rd, 5km southwest, on the way to the beach and whale-watching platform ☎03/5562 2484. A good choice in whale-watching season (May–Aug). ❹

Eating

There are plenty of good places to **eat** on Liebig Street. Out of town, two eating places near the water are worth seeking out: the licensed *Fishsails Café* near the southern end of Pertobe Street at the breakwater (a branch of the *Fishtales Café* on Liebig Street), and *Proudfoots on the River* at 2 Simpson St, in a refurbished historic boathouse on the Hopkins River, with tearooms, a smoke-free bistro and a tavern bar.

Balenas *Whalers Inn*, corner of Liebig and Timor streets. A trendy restaurant serving mod Oz cuisine.

Beach Babylon 72 Liebig St. Serves pizza and pasta.

Black Olive Bar Restaurant & Cafe *Hotel Grand*, 158 Liebig St ☎03/5561 6106. The dinner menu features Mediterranean-inspired dishes and there's a good wine list. Open daily noon–late.

Figsellers Café 89 Liebig St. A simple, pleasant joint with a tree-lined courtyard serving sandwiches, quiches and other snacks from 8.30am.

Fishtales Café (BYO) 63 Liebig St. Funky place with an open courtyard and good coffee. Open daily 7.45am until late.

Freshwater Café 78 Liebig St ☎03/5561 3188. A renowned restaurant featuring modern Australian cuisine, using regional produce, especially seafood. Try the scallop wantons with native lemon myrtle sauce (daily lunch & dinner).

Pippies by the Bay 23 Merri St ☎03/5561 2188. The new restaurant at the redeveloped Flagstaff Hill has views over Flagstaff Hill Maritime Village (see opposite), and of Lady Bay. Licensed. Open daily for breakfast, lunch and dinner. Enquire about packages for the sound and laser show plus dinner at the restaurant.

Puds Pantry and Deli 60 Kepler St. Sells excellent home-made bread and pastries, as well as soups, pasta and curries to take away or eat in. Closed Sun.

Restaurant Malaysia 69 Liebig St. Inexpensive Southeast Asian cuisine.

Rios Deli 142 Liebig St. Dishes up sandwiches, bagels and cakes.

Seafoods 126 Liebig St. Freshly cooked fish and chips.

Slessars Café Bar Restaurant 168 Koroit St ☎03/5560 5522. Stylish café-restaurant with balcony and pavement seating; out the back is a tapas bar and music venue. The excellent cooking betrays a strong Mediterranean/Middle Eastern influence, with plenty of local seafood on the menu. Very good coffee. Moderate, licensed. Open Mon–Sat 10am–1am, Sun 10am–5pm.

Victoria Hotel Corner of Liebig and Lava streets. Bar meals and all-you-can-eat pasta, soup and casseroles for $9 on Wednesday nights.

Tower Hill State Game Reserve and Koroit

About 13km west of Warrnambool along the Princes Highway, **Tower Hill State Game Reserve** is located in the crater of a volcano which last erupted about 25,000 years ago. In the nineteenth century, pioneer settlers stripped Tower Hill of its trees and used it as grazing land, but since the 1960s it has been reforested and wildlife has gradually returned. If you visit the island in the middle of the crater lake at dusk, you'll encounter **emus**, **koalas** and loads of **kangaroos** and **wallabies**. The game reserve is accessible all the time; the **Natural History Centre** (daily 10am–4pm) on the island has displays about the area's geological history and the re-vegetation programme, while a bird hide nearby enables you to spy on the abundant birdlife. There are also five self-guided short **walks** around the reserve (30min–1hr). Port Fairy-based Moonbird Tours (☎03/5568 1374) specializes in nature and Aboriginal culture; their extensive programme includes guided walking tours (day and night) in the reserve – they are pretty good at spotting birds and elusive nocturnal animals such as sugar gliders.

KOROIT, 7km to the north, is a tiny, old-fashioned town with Australia's largest concentration of people of Irish descent. The Catholic church is impressive, but the building that really dominates the town is the elegant two-storey **Koroit Hotel** on the main street, run by the same family since 1922. If you cut north from here to the Hamilton Highway you'll know you're getting into wool country when you see sheep walking down the main street of Woolsthorpe.

Port Fairy and Mount Eccles

PORT FAIRY, the next stop along the coast, was once an early port and whaling centre but is now a quaint crayfishing town with a busy jetty, a harbour full of yachts, and over fifty National Trust-listed buildings. Heavy southern breakers roll into the surrounding beaches, and on **Griffiths Island**, poised between the ocean and Port Fairy Bay, there's a **muttonbird** rookery with a specially constructed lookout where between September and April you can watch the birds roost at dusk. For a historic town, it's also quite a happening place, hosting numerous events: in summer the four-week-long **Moyneyana Festival** focuses on outdoor activities with events such as a raft race on the Moyne River, reaching its climax with the Moyneyana New Year's Eve procession, and at Easter the annual Queenscliff to Port Fairy **yacht race** ends here, with a huge party. **Music** is big here, too, with the Spring Music Festival on a weekend in mid-October which is centred on classical music (chamber music and symphony orchestras), with a bit of opera and jazz thrown in for good measure, and the huge **Port Fairy Folk Festival** over the Labour Day long weekend in March, which takes over the entire town, with Australian and overseas acts playing world, roots and acoustic music. Tickets are sold in early November, and usually sell out in less than a day. Up to twenty thousand people pour into town for the festival, and even a tent site is hard to get. For more information and festival bookings call the **visitor information centre**, on Bank Street (daily 9am–5pm; ☎03/5568 2682, ℻5568 2833, ⓦwww.myportfairy.com). The centre also produces an excellent 20¢ map of the Port Fairy Heritage Walk, which takes you on a route around town to admire the many fine buildings. **The History Centre**, in the old courthouse on Gipps Street by the river (Wed, Sat & Sun 2–5pm, daily during holidays; $3), displays costumes, historic photographs, shipwreck relics and other items relating to the town's pioneer history.

Port Fairy practicalities

With its village-like atmosphere and variety of excellent **accommodation** options, as well as good pubs, tearooms and restaurants, Port Fairy makes a good place to break your journey between Melbourne and Adelaide. The *Port Fairy YHA*, at 8 Cox St (℡03/5568 2468, ℱ5568 2302; dorm bed $18 for YHA members, rooms ❸), is in a lovely old house right in the town centre. More luxurious is the *Comfort Inn* (formerly known as Seacombe House) at 22 Sackville St (℡03/5568 1082, ⓦwww.seacombehouse.com.au; ❹–❼), one of many National Trust-listed buildings in the town, with gorgeous but pricey modern motel units and historic cottages and a good restaurant. Another upmarket and stylish place to stay and eat is the beautifully renovated *Victoria Hotel* at 42 Bank St (℡03/5568 2891, ⓦwww.vichotel.com; ❻). There are also a number of B&Bs in quaint colonial cottages, amongst them *The Douglass*, by the river at 85 Gipps St (℡03/55668 1016; ❹–❺); the *Merrijig Inn* at 1 Campbell St (℡03/5568 2324; ❹–❻); and *Lough Cottage* at 216 Griffith St (℡03/5568 1583; ❹). Full details of all cottages and B&Bs, and of Port Fairy's six caravan parks, can be obtained from the visitor information centre.

Arguably the best **food** in town can be found at the above-mentioned *Victoria Hotel* (℡03/5568 2891) which has a highly recommended atmospheric restaurant and a cheaper – but equally good – café (try the brunch for a real treat). Other upmarket licensed restaurants are the *Merrijig Inn* at 1 Campbell St (daily 6pm till late; ℡03/5568 2324), and the *Stag Inn* at 22 Sackville St (Mon–Sat 6pm till late; ℡03/5568 3058). *Rebecca's,* 70 Sackville St, serves breakfasts and light lunches, cakes and good coffee, and next door at no. 72 there's delicious home-made ice cream. *Culpepper's,* a healthfood shop at 24 Bank St, serves healthy soups and light meals, and the *Glass Onion* is a newish licensed café-restaurant on 19 Bank St specializing in wines from Western Victoria. The best place to **drink** is the *Caledonian Inn* ("The Stump"), on the corner of Bank and James streets – it's the oldest continually licensed pub in Victoria (since 1844).

Mount Eccles National Park

Just over 50km north of Port Fairy is **Mount Eccles National Park**. Mount Eccles (though it hardly deserves to be called a mountain) is an extinct volcano with lava caves, channels and a crater lake set in rugged, stony country; there used to be a quarry here and you can see the various layers of different lava flows where the mountain has been cut. **Lake Surprise** is the delightful crater lake, shimmering blue in summer. **Walks** – all of which begin from the picnic ground at the end of the entrance road – include a two-kilometre stroll around the rim of the crater, or you can descend and walk around the shoreline (with a chance to swim in the lake); there's also a two-hour walk along a lava canal leading to a cave.

Birdlife around the lake includes wedge-tail eagles, kookaburras, tawny frogmouths, dog birds, barn owls and boobooks. The trees are loaded with koalas, seen at any time of the day. There are also eastern grey kangaroos, echidnas, bats, tiger snakes, copperhead snakes and blue-tongued lizards. Mid- to late spring is a good time for **wild flowers** – from orchids to native geraniums – and wattle. Look out for a tree in the southwest corner of the park that has had an Aboriginal shield cut out of it with a sharpened stone tool. You can **camp** in the park: there are toilets, hot showers, picnic tables and fireplaces (BYO wood; $12.60 per site per night; bookings required, ℡03/5576 1338).

Portland to Nelson

PORTLAND, the last stop on the Victoria coast going west on the Princes Highway, is a large industrial and fishing port. There's a smattering of historic buildings, but they don't form a coherent townscape. Despite the best efforts of the local tourist industry to promote Portland, there's nothing in town that merits an extended stay. However, the wild coastal scenery to the southwest around Cape Nelson and Cape Bridgewater is well worth a detour.

Huge ships dock in **Portland Bay**, where a vast heap of sandy brown bauxite sits beside the Alcoa smelter, in full view of the Esplanade. **Aluminium** is one of Australia's largest exports, and in 1980 big business was met with **Aboriginal resistance** here, when a legal battle developed over the siting of the smelter on land that had great importance for the Gunditj Mara. There were traces of over sixty Aboriginal campsites and workshop areas on the proposed site, and sacred places including a burial ground. Plans for building the smelter eventually went ahead, but Alcoa was forced to pay the Gunditj Mara $1.5 million in compensation, which was used to buy back land in the area of the Lake Condah mission (see opposite).

Before the area was permanently settled by whites – it's the oldest settlement in Victoria – there had been conflict between whalers and Aborigines that resulted in massacres and the decimation of an entire tribe. The first squatters in Victoria, the Hentys, came to the Portland area in 1834 to pasture sheep on vast landholdings, and they, too, soon came into conflict with the Koories – from 1838 clans began to use their traditional burning-off process in an attempt to drive the Hentys away. During the 1840s a sustained guerrilla war, known as the Eumeralla War, was fought against settlers occupying land around Port Fairy, Mount Napier and Lake Condah. In the end it was only the deployment of the Aboriginal Native Police Corps in 1842 that finally broke the resistance – and even they took four years.

The seafront Esplanade is lined with fish-and-chip shops and cafés. The **visitor information centre** is located in the **Portland Maritime Discovery Centre** (daily 9am–5pm; ☎03/5523 2671 or 1800 035 567), and gives out information on the numerous museums and historic buildings around town, which mainly celebrate white settlement.

A restored and modified vintage **cable tram** (daily 10am–4pm; $10) carts sightseers along the foreshore on a round trip of 7.5km, from the depot at Henty Park past the **Powerhouse Vintage Car Museum** (daily 10am–4pm plus weekends during school holidays; $5) to Fawthrop Lagoon, then back through the Botanic Gardens, past the Maritime Discovery Centre to a lookout tower, and back the same route.

Very cheap **accommodation** is available at *Portland Backpackers*, a small hostel in an old two storey-bluestone house in the centre of town at 14–16 Gawler St (☎03/5523 6390; dorm bed $15, rooms ❶) which has off-street parking and Internet access ($5/hr). More expensive but very scenic accommodation can be found at the **Cape Nelson Lightstation**, 20km southwest of Portland (☎03/5523 5100, ⊛www.lightstation.com.au; rooms ❺, plus four-bedroom house which sleeps 11: $400). The licensed **café** is open daily 10am–5pm.

Along the coast to the southwest, around craggy **Cape Nelson** and stormy **Cape Bridgewater**, the scenery is stunning: caves, freshwater lakes close to the cliff coast, blowholes, a petrified forest of limestone columns where ancient trees used to stand, and the beach at **Bridgewater Bay**, which extends in a wide, sandy arc from one cape to the other. The best way to explore these features is along the walking tracks that start from the blowholes car park, sign-posted left off the road to Cape Bridgewater. Bring good walking shoes, as the volcanic rocks can be very sharp, and carry food and drink.

Lake Condah Mission

Lake Condah Mission lies about 50km northeast of Portland, on the western edge of Mount Eccles National Park. A mission was established in 1867 in this traditional Aboriginal area, with its plentiful game and fish, and surviving Aborigines were brought here but were forbidden to speak their own language or practise their culture. At its height in 1880 there were over twenty buildings of timber and stone. Although the mission was officially closed in 1919, a large community remained until the 1950s, when they were gradually dispossessed as land was given to returned soldiers under the soldier settlement scheme. Perhaps the greatest injustice occurred when several Aboriginal returned soldiers, who had lived on Lake Condah, applied for land, only to be refused. With the money paid in settlement of the Alcoa dispute (see opposite), the land was finally bought back in the 1980s, and the government has since pledged $50,000 towards uncovering some of the original rock art here.

Lower Glenelg National Park and Nelson

From Portland, the Princes Highway makes its uneventful way, via Heywood, to Mount Gambier in South Australia. After 120km it crosses the **Glenelg River** (which has its source in the Grampians) at Dartmoor, a popular point to begin a four-day canoeing trip down to the river's mouth at Nelson; ask about canoe rental at the Nelson Parks & Visitor Information Centre (see below). For most of the journey, the clear blue river flows through the unspoilt **Lower Glenelg National Park** in a sixty-kilometre gorge cut through limestone. The spectacular **Princess Margaret Rose Cave** (guided tours daily at 10am, 11am, noon, then hourly from 1.30pm to 4.30pm; $7.50; ☎08/8738 4171) lies beside the river as it loops round by the South Australian border, and can be reached by canoe, car (unsealed roads from both sides of the border lead to the caves) or on a cruise from Nelson.

NELSON is at the end of the coastal road and virtually on the Victorian/South Australian border, less than 40km from Mount Gambier – it's well worth an overnight stay. A peaceful, friendly little hamlet, it feels caught in a time warp, and there's little to do but wander along the coast, read on the beach, and **fish** or **canoe** on the Glenelg. Paestan Boat Hire 2km out of town on the Nelson–Winnap road (☎03/5528 1481) and Nelson Boat Hire on Kellet Street (daily 8.30am–6pm; ☎08/8738 4048) rent out canoes and kayaks. The latter also sells bait; you'll need a fishing licence, obtained from the Nelson Kiosk (daily 8am–6pm; ☎08/8738 4220), the local service station or post office. Fishing shelters line the river. Glenelg River Cruises on Old Bridge Road on the opposite bank operates **cruises** to the Princess Margaret Rose Caves (Tues–Thurs, Sat & Sun, daily during holidays; departs 1pm; 3hr 30min; $20; ☎08/8738 4191, ⊛www.glenelgrivercruises.com.au).

The **Nelson Parks & Visitor Information Centre** (daily 9am–5pm; ☎08/8738 4051) is signposted just off Leake Street; it also covers the Discovery Bay Coastal Park, which protects the shoreline almost all the way from Portland to the border. Here you can get camping permits for this and the Lower Glenelg National Park (book in advance in peak season) and information on walks and activities. A gorgeous **place to stay** in Nelson is the *Motel Black Wattle* (☎08/8738 4008, ⊛www.bwattle.mtx.net; ❸), situated in a lovely garden setting on the crest of Mount Gambier Road, overlooking the river and ocean. The on-site restaurant serves delicious modern Australian cuisine, with an emphasis on local seafood, and excellent wines. Alternatively, the one-storey *Nelson Hotel* on Kellet Street (☎08/8738 4011; ➌) is a classic and untouristy pub that has budget accommodation and very inexpensive counter meals. Other options include the *Nelson Cottage B&B* on the corner of Kellet and Sturt streets which has particularly cheap singles (☎08/8738 4161; ➌); *Nelson Kywong Caravan Park* on North Nelson Road (☎08/8738 4174), which has cheap vans (➊) and cabins (➋); and the four-bunk cabins at the Margaret Rose Caves (☎08/8738 4171; cold water only & BYO linen; ➋).

Central Victoria: the Goldfields

Central Victoria is classic Victoria: a rich pastoral district, chilly and green in winter and parched a brownish yellow in summer, with two grand provincial cities, **Ballarat** and **Bendigo**, whose fine buildings were funded by gold. Nowadays both are major tourist centres on the gold trail. The many surrounding country centres such as **Maryborough** and **Castlemaine**, once prosperous gold towns in their own right, now seem too small for their extravagant architecture.

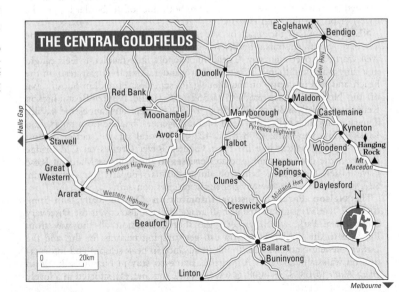

Melbourne ▼

The goldrushes

The Californian goldrushes of the 1840s captured the popular imagination around the world with tales of the huge fortunes to be made gold-prospecting, and it wasn't long until Australia's first goldrush took place – near Bathurst in New South Wales in 1851. Victoria had been a separate colony for only nine days when gold was found at Clunes on July 10, 1851; the **goldrush** began in earnest when rich deposits were found in Ballarat nine months later. The richest goldfields ever known soon opened at Bendigo, and thousands poured into Victoria from around the world. In the golden decade of the 1850s, Victoria's population increased from eighty thousand to half a million, half of whom remained permanently in the state. The British and Irish made up a large proportion of the new population, but over forty thousand Chinese came to make their fortune too, along with experienced American gold-seekers and other nationalities such as Russians, Finns and Filipinos. Ex-convicts and native-born Australians also poured into Victoria, leaving other colonies short of workers; even respectable policemen deserted their posts to become "diggers", and doctors, lawyers and prostitutes crowded into the haphazard new towns in their wake. The goldfields were a great equalizer; all you needed was a shovel and perseverance, and a fortune was as likely yours as the next man's.

In the beginning, the fortune-seekers panned the creeks and rivers searching for **alluvial gold**, constantly moving on at the news of another find. But gold was also deep within the earth, where ancient riverbeds had been buried by volcanoes; in Ballarat in 1852 the first **shafts** were dug, and because the work was unsafe and arduous, the men joined in bands of eight or ten, usually grouped by nationality, working a common claim. For deep mining, diggers stayed in one place for months or years, and the major workings rapidly became stable communities with banks, shops, hotels, churches and theatres, evolving more gradually, on the back of income from gold, into grandiose towns.

Interstate buses don't service this area any more, but there's fairly good **transport**, with regular V/Line trains and buses to Bendigo, Ballarat and the other major centres in the Goldfields, and a few local buses fill some gaps. However, in order to get around and really see the area you need your own means of transport. The easiest way to tour is to follow the **Goldfields Tourist Route**, whose chocolate-brown signs are marked by a distinctive circled capital G. The route links the major cities and towns – Bendigo, Castlemaine, Ballarat, Ararat and Stawell – with many smaller places in between.

Towards the Goldfields: the Calder Highway

Though you could take the Western Freeway or the train directly to Ballarat, the route **towards Bendigo**, 150km northwest of Melbourne along the Calder Highway, is much more interesting. The railway to Bendigo, which continues to Swan Hill, follows the same route, calling at the main towns. At Diggers Rest, 22km from Melbourne, a short detour to the east will take you to the tiny **Organ Pipes National Park** (Mon–Fri 8.30am–4.30pm; Sat & Sun & public holidays until 6pm), designated a national park for its outstanding geological interest. The rock formations here form a series of basalt columns, created by lava cooling in an ancient riverbed, and rising up to 20m above Jacksons Creek. The park can be explored along walking tracks and has picnic areas with tables. Back on the highway you'll come to **Gisborne**, 50km from Melbourne, developed as a coaching town for travellers on their way to the Bendigo and Castlemaine goldfields; it's dominated by **Mount Macedon**, an extinct thousand-metre volcano.

Fifteen kilometres or so from Gisborne, **WOODEND** is the jumping-off point for **Hanging Rock**, in a reserve 6km northeast (daily 8am–6pm; $8 per car). The rock became famous because of the eerie film *Picnic at Hanging Rock*, about a group of schoolgirls who mysteriously go missing here after a picnic – a story which many people falsely believed to be true, though the rock itself is not at all spooky. You can walk around the base or climb to the summit with its massive boulders and crags in around an hour. Encounters of a more freaky kind can be had at the **Insectarium of Victoria** near the train station at the southern end of town (Sun 10am–4pm; during school holidays daily 10am–4pm; $9; Ⓦwww.insectarium.org); a gruesome collection of oversized cockroaches, spiders, giant snails, deadly (dead) snakes, and other scuttly beasts. The admission fee includes a guided tour by the very knowledgeable entomologist owner who may let you touch some of his exhibits.

KYNETON, 15km further north, features **Piper Street**, a historic strip lined with several fine historic bluestone buildings and the **Botanic Gardens**, scenically located above the Campaspe River, but lacks Woodend's inviting, friendly buzz. There are, however, a few eating places along Piper Street that merit a detour off the Calder: *Kyneton Provender*, a lovely café-cum-bookshop at no. 30; *The Great Ronaldo's Café* at No 62; *The Cottage* at no. 91 (Ⓣ03/5422 6944; dinner only); and in particular *Gonellas* at no. 72 (Ⓣ03/5422 2022; lunch Fri–Sun, dinner Wed–Sun), which is renowned for its excellent Tuscan cuisine. If you happen to be around you can step into the local history museum which is housed in a two-storey 1850s building at no. 67 (Fri–Sun & public holidays 11am–4pm; $3). The **tourist information office** (daily 9am–5pm; Ⓣ03/5422 6110) is located on the High Street. For **accommodation**, the *Kyneton Country House*, at 66 Jennings St (Ⓣ03/5422 3556; B&B ❻), is a wonderful weekend hideaway in a restored National Trust mansion surrounded by a beautiful cottage garden; it has a good reputation for its traditional cooking.

Bendigo

Rich alluvial gold was first discovered in **BENDIGO** in 1851, and once it was exhausted shafts were sunk into a gold-bearing quartz reef. Bendigo became the greatest goldfield of the time, and had the world's deepest mine. Mining continued here until 1954, long after the rest of central Victoria's goldfields were exhausted, so it's a city that has developed over a prosperous century: the nationwide department store Myer began here, as did Australia's first building society in 1858. Although in many ways more magnificent than Ballarat (see p.998), Bendigo is considerably lower key, never having turned itself into a purely tourist town. Its most visited sights are legacies of the mining days – the **Chinese Joss House** and the **Central Deborah Mine**.

At the heart of Bendigo is the vast **Rosalind Park**, and three important religious buildings constructed through money from gold-digging – All Saints Church, St Pauls Cathedral and **Sacred Heart Cathedral**. Local Catholics imported stonemasons from Italy and England, and their craftsmanship can be seen in the design and details of Sacred Heart, begun in 1897 in English Gothic style. The interior has beautiful woodcarvings of the Twelve Apostles, and the crypt is the burial place of local bishops. Wanting to give Bendigo a sophisticated air reminiscent of London, the newly prosperous citizens called its central crossroads **Charing Cross**. Pall Mall runs off to the east, while View Street, with its many fine old buildings, climbs north off Pall Mall. Mitchell Street

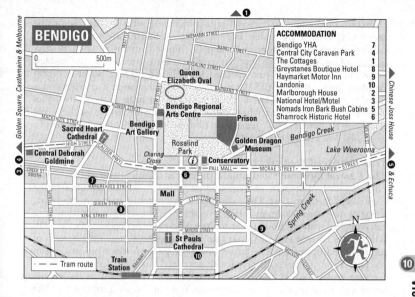

BENDIGO

0   500m

NIEMANN STREET
BARKLY STREET
ROSALIND STREET
BARNARD STREET

Queen Elizabeth Oval

WATTLE ST
ROWAN STREET
MACKENZIE STREET

Bendigo Regional Arts Centre

Prison

Sacred Heart Cathedral

Bendigo Art Gallery

Central Deborah Goldmine

HIGH STREET
CALDER HWY

Charing Cross

Rosalind Park

Golden Dragon Museum

Bendigo Creek

Lake Weeroona

INDIAN ST

Conservatory

PALL MALL — MCRAE STREET — NAPIER STREET

CREEK ST SOUTH

HARGREAVES STREET

BULL ST

CHAPEL STREET

Mall

MYRTLE STREET
QUEEN STREET

KING STREET

WILLIAMSON STREET
LYTTLETON
MITCHELL STREET

MUNDY STREET
TERRACE

Spring Creek

MYERS STREET

MCIVOR

St Pauls Cathedral

RAILWAY PL

HIGHWAY

· — — · Tram route

Train Station

N

ACCOMMODATION

Bendigo YHA	7
Central City Caravan Park	4
The Cottages	1
Greystanes Boutique Hotel	8
Haymarket Motor Inn	9
Landonia	10
Marlborough House	2
National Hotel/Motel	3
Nomads Iron Bark Bush Cabins	5
Shamrock Historic Hotel	6

leads south to the **train station** and High Street (the Calder Highway) is the main exit west out of the city. The other important street is Hargreaves, parallel to Pall Mall one block south, with its impressive town hall and a bland shopping mall, about to be refurbished at the time of writing.

The City

Many of Bendigo's finest goldrush buildings are along **Pall Mall**, including the law courts (1896) and the ornate Italianate (1887) edifice which now houses the visitor information centre – neither of which would seem out of place in a capital city. The amazingly decorative **Shamrock Hotel** stands opposite, four storeys of gold-boom architecture at its most extreme. **View Street**, climbing the hill beside Rosalind Park, has a few more elaborate goldrush buildings. The **Bendigo Regional Arts Centre** here is a massive Neoclassical pile, joined to the much more homely red-brick fire station which now serves as the Community Arts Centre. The **Art Gallery**, in another beautifully restored nineteenth-century building at no. 42 (daily 10am–5pm; gold coin donation appreciated), has an extensive collection of Australian painting from Bendigo's goldfield days to the present, as well as nineteenth-century British and European art acquired with all that gold. Several antique shops, restaurants and bars add to the arty feel of the street. The **Queen Elizabeth Oval**, with its old red-brick stadium, backs onto Rosalind Park, and you can watch Aussie Rules football here on winter weekends.

    Bridge Street, one of the oldest in Bendigo, was once **Chinatown**, home to the Chinese who came by the thousands in the 1850s and who knew Bendigo as *dai gum san* ("big gold mountain"); when the gold ran out, many turned to market gardening in the area. Until as late as the 1960s old shops sporting faded Chinese signs were still in evidence, but now Chinese customs and ways of life are best seen in the **Golden Dragon Museum and Classical Chinese Gardens** (daily 9.30am–5pm; $7), where there is an impressive collection of Chinese processional regalia including what are supposed to be the world's longest and oldest Imperial dragons, Sun Loong and Loong. An exhibition tells the full story of Bendigo's Chinese community since the days of the goldrush, whilst the attached gardens feature a temple to the goddess Kuan Yin. The National Trust-operated **Joss House**, on Finn Street in North Bendigo (daily 10am–5pm; $3), was built by the Chinese in the 1860s and is the oldest Chinese temple still in use in Australia. The route to the shrine passes man-made Lake Weeroona, whose picnic grounds are the setting for the lovely *Boardwalk Restaurant & Café* (daily 7am till late) in an old Chinese teahouse. To get to the Joss House, take bus #7 (approximately hourly Mon–Fri).

The Central Deborah Goldmine

The Central Deborah Goldmine, at the corner of Violet Street and the Calder Highway (daily 9am–5pm; underground tour $16.90), was the last mine in the Central Goldfields to close. The sixty-minute underground tour is worth taking if you've never been down in a mine; everybody is issued with a reassuring hard hat, complete with torch and generator. You go down to a depth of 60m in a lift, which takes 85 seconds – it would take thirty minutes to reach the bottom of some of the deepest shafts. The further down you go the hotter it gets, but at 60m it's quite warm and airless, dripping with water and muddy underfoot.

Above ground, you're free to wander about and take a look at the engine room with its steam-driven air compressor. You can also see a room set up like a modest miner's house from the 1840s, a model of the mine itself, and a museum installed in the old changing rooms.

Practicalities

The **visitor information centre** on Pall Mall (daily 9am–5pm; ℡03/5444 4445 or 1800 813 153, ⓦwww.bendigotourism.com) provides lots of brochures and maps, including the free *Bendigo & Region* booklet, complete with walking map (you'll also find "Heritage Walk" panels outside significant buildings). A good way to get an impression of Bendigo is to take the **Talking Tram Tour** (daily 10am–3pm; departures every 1hr, or every 30min Sat & Sun, from the Central Deborah Goldmine; 1hr; $13; combined ticket for the mine and tram tour $26.50). The tram tour ticket includes entrance to the Bendigo Tram Museum, located on Hargreaves Street at the opposite end of the route. Bendigo had electric trams even before Melbourne, but they ceased operation in 1972. **Buses** (Christians Bus Company ℡03/5447 2222) have since replaced trams as a means of everyday transport – they all leave from the corner of Mitchell and Hargreaves streets and charge a flat fare of $1.65, valid for two hours. Bendigo Airport Service provides a link to Melbourne's Tullamarine Airport (3 daily; $34 one way; booking essential on ℡03/5447 9006).

Accommodation

In terms of atmosphere and style, the **B&B guesthouses** and **cottages** throughout Bendigo and the whole goldfields area are a much better option than the average, somewhat sterile motel room.

Bendigo YHA 33 Creek St South ℡03/5443 7680 or 0438 437 680, ⓔbendigo@yhavic.org.au. Small, cheery hostel right in the centre of town with dorms ($18), and two twin and two family rooms. Open fire in the lounge, and Internet access. ❶

Central City Caravan Park 362 High St, Golden Square, 2.5km south ℡ & ⓕ 03/5443 6937. Hostel-type accommodation in three cabins with separate kitchen and common room, plus camping, vans and cabin units. Dorms $16, on-site vans ❸, cabins ❹

The Cottages Cnr Niemann and Anderson streets ⓣ03/5441 5613, ⓕ5444 4313. B&B in two small, self-contained weatherboard cottages. ❺

Greystanes Boutique Hotel 57 Queen St ⓣ03/5442 2466, ⓕ5442 2447, ⓔgreystanes@netcon.net.au. Centrally located, beautifully appointed rooms in an elegant Victorian mansion with separate bar/lounge and open fires. ❺–❻

Haymarket Motor Inn 5 McIvor Highway ⓣ03/5441 5654, ⓕ5441 5655. Ultramodern motel with one unit accessible to the disabled, a swimming pool and sauna; some rooms with spas. ❺–❻

Landonia 87 Mollison St ⓣ03/5442 2183. A centrally located B&B in a Federation-style home, with separate guest entrance and an open fireplace in the lounge. ❻

Marlborough House 115 Wattle St ⓣ03/5441 4142. B&B in a goldrush-era mansion near the cathedral, with stained-glass windows, marble fireplaces and a covered balcony. ❺

National Hotel/Motel 182 High St, 1km south ⓣ03/5441 5777, ⓕ5441 5890. Facilities include a pool and spa, as well as a bar and bistro. Units ❹–❻, suite ❽

Nomads Iron Bark Bush Cabins Watson St ⓣ03/5448 3344 or 1800 737 378, ⓦwww.nomadsworld.com. Shared accommodation ($20) in self-contained cabins in a bushland setting a few kilometres out of town. Free pick-ups and drop-offs, lockers and linen. Horse riding available. ❶

Shamrock Historic Hotel Cnr of Pall Mall and Williamson St ⓣ03/5443 0333, ⓕ5442 4494. Fabulous Victorian hotel that has a wide range of accommodation from budget-priced rooms to executive suites. ❹–❼

Eating, drinking and nightlife

The town offers a fairly good choice when it comes to eating and drinking, and there's plenty of student-influenced nightlife during term time. Entertainment facilities at the LaTrobe University campus are open to all – call ⓣ03/5444 7988 to find out what's happening. Several pubs have **bands** playing on Friday and Saturday nights, including the *Old Crown Hotel* at 238 Hargreaves St and *The Vine* at 135 King St, which also has an open-stage night on Mondays. Of the **Irish bars** in town, the Celtic-run *Brian Boru* on McIvor Road is by far the best, serving up decent Guinness and real Irish *craic* without the four-leaved clovers, while the *Shamrock Hotel* may not be Irish but is certainly popular for balcony drinking in the late afternoon. A young crowd congregates at the *Rifle Brigade Hotel* at 137 View St, a brewery pub with great food and beer and a wrought-iron verandah and moves on to the *Eclipse* nightclub at the corner of Hargreaves and Williams streets. Other **nightclubs** include Hargreaves Street's hipper-than-thou techno haven *The Tonic Bar*, and alternative rock hangout *The Icon* at 2–4 Howard Place. Thirty-somethings might prefer *Studio 54* on Queen Street, playing three floors of mainstream pop from the last three decades.

Bath Lane Café Next to Green Olive at 13 Bath Lane. Local artwork is featured on the brightly painted walls. They serve good coffee, excellent breakfast, soups and other tasty snacks. Mon–Sat 7am–late.

Bazzani Howard Place ⓣ03/5441 3777. Cosy restaurant at the end of the mall, renowned statewide for the interesting, aesthetic and downright tasty dishes on the menu. Licensed. Daily noon–late.

Café Tram 76 Violet St ⓣ03/5443 8255. Modelled after Melbourne's *Tramcar* restaurant: wine and dine while trundling around the streets of Bendigo. Bookings essential. Dinner Fri & Sat, lunch Sun, afternoon tea Sat & Sun.

Colonial Bank Gallery and Mully's Cafe 32 Pall Mall. In a grand, historic bank building from the 1880s, with an art gallery upstairs. Good breakfasts, brunches and afternoon teas. Licensed or BYO. Mon–Sat 10am–5pm, Sun from 9am.

Green Olive Delicatessen 11 Bath Lane. Fantastically cosy Italian-run café with outdoor seating, serving excellent coffee and desserts as well as gourmet deli fare to go. Open daily.

The Match Bar & Bakehouse 58 Bull St. Stylish café-restaurant with lots of pasta, focaccia and pizza. Dinner daily, lunch daily except Sat.

Shamrock Hotel Café Cnr Pall Mall and Williamson St. This café-restaurant in the lovely, refurbished former public bar serves good breakfasts (home-baked bread) and has interesting, mainly Modern Australian cuisine for lunch and dinner. Open daily.

Whirakee Restaurant and Wine Bar 17 View Point, at the beginning of View St, just opposite the fountain ☎03/5441 5557. By now an old-timer, but still serving outstanding modern Australian cuisine, with an excellent wine list featuring local wines. The lunch set menu for $22 (2 courses plus coffee) is particularly good value. Lunch Wed–Fri, dinner Tues–Sat.

Castlemaine and around

CASTLEMAINE is at the centre of the area once known as the Mount Alexander Goldfields. Between 1851 and 1861, when its gullies were among the richest in the world, 105,000kg of gold were found here (more modest quantities are still found at Wattle Gully mine at nearby Chewton, the oldest working gold mine in Australia). Castlemaine became the headquarters of the Government Camp for the area in 1852, and its impressive buildings were all built during the following ten years. With no deep mines to sustain it, however, Castlemaine has developed little since then.

The town's finest building is the **Old Castlemaine Market** on Mostyn Street, a wonderfully over-the-top piece of Neoclassical architecture. The **Theatre Royal** on Hargraves Street, one of the oldest theatres in Australia, is also quite magnificent; it's said that when the famous Lola Montez performed here, miners threw nuggets of gold at her in appreciation. It's now a **cinema** (☎03/5472 1196) incorporating a cabaret-style section and a licensed bistro downstairs, and more traditional movie-house seating upstairs. Theatre groups and live bands sometimes perform here, and there's even a sporadic disco.

Another unusual attraction, a short distance from the centre, is **Buda**, at 42 Hunter St (Wed–Sat noon–5pm, Sun 10am–5pm, Mon & Tues by appointment only; $7; ☎03/5472 1032), a gracious nineteenth-century home and garden originally built in 1861 by a retired Baptist missionary in the style of an Indian villa. It was added to by its subsequent owner Ernest Leviny, a Hungarian silversmith, in the 1890s. The house and gardens give an insight into the good life enjoyed in the goldrush days, and much work by Leviny and his family is on display, including lampshades, carved woodhangings and embroidery made by his daughters, as well as early photography and the family's art and silverware collection. The **Castlemaine Art Gallery and Museum** on Lyttleton Street (Mon–Fri 10am–5pm, Sat & Sun noon–5pm; $5) is also worth a visit. It specializes in Australian photographs and paintings, featuring many works by the Heidelberg School, notably Frederick McCubbin and Tom Roberts. Partly because of the big **Castlemaine State Festival** (✇www.castlemainefestival.com) which takes place over ten days in March and April in odd-numbered years, this is quite an arty place, and there are several other galleries around town. In odd-numbered years lots of gardens in the Castlemaine district open their doors to visitors during the **Festival of Gardens**, which takes place during the Melbourne Cup week in November.

If you're here on a Saturday, trek the 2km out along the Melbourne Road to **Wesley Hill Market**, a giant flea market selling local produce and crafts (7.30am–1pm). Another tourist attraction is the **Dingo Farm** (daily, but call to confirm times and prices on ☎03/5470 5711) between Castlemaine and Chewton, where around a hundred dingoes are kept in fenced-in enclosures on bushland; signs along the Pyrenees Highway will direct you there.

Practicalities

The very helpful **Castlemaine Visitor Information Centre** is in the Market Building at Mostyn Street (daily 9am–5pm; ☎03/5470 6200 or 1800 171 888, ⓦwww.mountalexander.vic.gov.au/tourism or www.maldoncastlemaine.com) and can arrange accommodation in the area.

Places to stay include *Campbell Street Motor Lodge* in a historic building at 33 Campbell St (☎03/5472 2377; ④–⑤), which has motel-style rooms in a National Trust-listed house, and the *Old Castlemaine Gaol* on Bowden Street (☎03/5470 5311, ⓕ5470 5097; ⑤), converted into an unexpectedly cosy B&B guesthouse, with beds in former prison cells and a restaurant/wine bar (Wed–Sun). Two centrally located B&Bs are the very popular late-Victorian *Clevedon Manor*, 260 Barker St (☎03/5472 5212; ⑤), and the *Coach and Rose*, 68 Mostyn St (☎03/5472 4850; ④–⑤). The *Botanic Gardens Caravan Park* (☎03/5472 1125; vans ②) is ideally situated between the botanic gardens and the open-air swimming pool (Dec–March only).

Food in Castlemaine is excellent, with a wide variety of places to choose from. The best café is *Saff's* at 64 Mostyn St (breakfast and lunch daily, dinner Wed–Sun; ☎03/5470 6722), which serves up great breakfasts, smoothies and other feelgood fodder, and hosts special night-time events, including recitals and poetry readings, as well as live jazz most Sunday afternoons. *Togs Place Café* (dinner Sat & Sun; ☎03/5470 5090) at 58 Lyttleton St provides good food in a peaceful atmosphere, and has a courtyard where you can sit out in summer. The lovely *Chambers Café and Gallery* in the historic Oriental Bank Chambers (1860) at 155 Barker St also has a courtyard and exhibits local arts and crafts (Tues–Sun & public holidays 9am–5.30pm; ☎03/5472 3300); while the licensed *Globe Restaurant*, 81 Forest St (☎03/5470 5171), has a courtyard and an attached cheaper bistro serving a seasonally varied menu. Or go for cheap pub meals at the local hangout, the *Criterion Hotel* at 163 Barker St, which has pool tables and bands at weekends, or the *Cumberland Hotel* on the corner of Barker and Lyttleton streets.

Maldon

MALDON, closely surrounded by low hills, is a tiny, peaceful town of tea-rooms, antique shops and B&Bs, a popular weekend getaway where you can simply relax and unwind. In 1965 the National Trust declared it the best-preserved gold-era settlement in Victoria. Gold was found here in 1853 and the rich, deep alluvial reefs were mined until 1926, almost rivalling Bendigo for longevity. The main shopping street largely preserves its original appearance, with single-storey shopfronts shaded by awnings and decorated with iron-lace work. During the long weekend before the Melbourne Cup (first weekend of November), things get a bit busier than usual as people head to town for the four-day **Maldon Folk Festival** (ⓦwww.penscape.com.au/maldon, ☎03/5475 2166). In its thirtieth year in 2003, it has steadily grown, especially in the last five years. Apart from traditional folk, it also features blues, bluegrass and world music as well as some theatre and dance. The main performance space is at the Tarrangower Reserve at the base of Mount Tarrangower, just out of town, but throughout the weekend there are also lots of things happening in the streets, the pubs and cafés in town where you can listen for free. The weekend ticket for the festival is about $70 and includes bushcamping at the Tarrangower Reserve; a day ticket (Sunday only) is $30. Discounted "early bird" tickets are available two months in advance.

Practicalities

It's best to come to Maldon in your own vehicle, as **public transport** from Melbourne operates only on weekdays, and to a very limited timetable; take a train from Melbourne (Mon–Fri 8.35am & 3.50pm) to Castlemaine where you catch the connecting private Castlemaine Bus Lines service to Maldon. Return buses leave from Maldon post office to connect with trains back to Melbourne (Mon–Fri 9am; ⓣ03/5472 1455).

The Victorian Goldfields Railway, a tourist **steam train** (or diesel locomotive on days of total fire ban) runs from Maldon to Castlemaine (Sun, during school holidays also Wed & Sat; in the summer holidays daily 11.30am, 1pm & 2.30pm; $14; ⓦwww.vgr.com.au).

Apart from the town's architecture, there aren't many other points of interest: you can take an underground tour at the stunning candlelit **Carman's Tunnel Goldmine**, off Parkin's Reef Road, 3km south of town (Sat, Sun, school & public holidays every 30min 1.30–4pm; 30min; $4). To find out about other activities, check with the **Maldon Visitor Information Centre** in the Shire Gardens, High Street (daily 9am–5pm; ⓣ03/5475 2569, ⓦwww.maldoncastlemaine.com).

An excellent place to **stay**, if you're hankering for a little luxury, is *The Barn*, at 242 Barker St (ⓣ & ⓕ 03/5475 2015; ❺), which offers self-catering amongst whitewashed stone walls, an open fire and French windows. *Mount Hawke of Maldon B&B*, 24 Adair St (ⓣ03/5475 1192; en-suite rooms ❹) is a very cosy guesthouse and the *Heritage Cottages*, 25 Adair St (ⓣ03/5475 1094; ❼), has a selection of ten historical cottages, most with period furnishings and open fires; there's a minimum stay of two nights. Much cheaper yet still a treat is *Agatha Panthers Cottages*, on Church Street (ⓣ03/5475 1066, ⓦwww.apcottages.com.au; ❹).

Eating places include *Café Maldon* at 52 Main St and *Berryman's Café* in an old bowling alley at 30 Main St. *McArthur's Restaurant*, further up at no. 45, is quainter and has a very pleasant courtyard (Wed–Sat morning & afternoon teas & dinner ⓣ03/5475 2519). On the High Street you'll find the *Royal Wine Bar & Café Restaurant* at no. 18, where music is sometimes played in the courtyard (Wed–Sun 5.30pm till late & Sun lunch; ⓣ03/5475 1223), and *Ruby's Restaurant at Calder House*, at no. 44 (Sat & Sun lunch, Fri–Sun dinner; ⓣ03/5475 2912) for good food and local wines.

Maryborough and around

MARYBOROUGH was relatively late getting on the gold bandwagon – the first find here was in 1853, but it didn't take long to exploit it. The town is now a large, solid and rather dull country place, interesting only for remnants of architecture far too pompous for this quiet setting. The **train station** is exceptional: when Mark Twain visited Maryborough he described it as a train station with a town attached. The restored building houses an antiques and collectables emporium as well as an arts and crafts **gallery** (daily except Tues 10am–6pm). Another newly restored historic – if much less ornate – building is the Old Flour Mill at the corner of Inkerman and Albert streets which is now used by a timber workshop, a gallery which exhibits paintings, fine handmade furniture and other crafts, and a coffee shop. The Civic Centre at the heart of town is a classic nineteenth-century square with an elegant post office and gracious town hall and courthouse. For more information, turn to the

Central Goldfields Information Centre at the corner of Nolan and Alma streets (daily 9am–5pm; ☎03/5460 4511 or 1800 356 511, Ⓦwww.central goldfields.com.au or www.cgoldshire.vic.gov.au).

The *Bull & Mouth Hotel* at 119 High St (☎03/5461 1002; ❷) has inexpensive pub **accommodation** and the bistro downstairs serves equally inexpensive **meals** (Mon–Sat); for B&B accommodation try *Maryborough Guesthouse*, 44 Goldsmith St (☎03/5460 5808; ❹–❺) or *Bella's Countryhouse*, 39 Burns St (☎03/5460 5574; ❹–❺).

Twenty-one kilometres north of Maryborough is **DUNOLLY**, an attractive town filled with many distinctive old buildings and with kurrajong trees lining the main street. The goldfields here produced more nuggets than any in Australia, including the largest ever found: the 65-kilogram "Welcome Stranger" nugget was found in 1869 by two Cornish miners just 3cm below the surface as they were working around the roots of a tree, and valued at £10,000. Fourteen kilometres south of Maryborough, **TALBOT** is a tiny settlement consisting of little more than a restaurant, a pub and a corner store. It's hard to believe now that the town once had 56 hotels and a population of 33,000. The licensed *Bull and Mouth Restaurant and Guesthouse* (lunch Sun, dinner Thurs–Sun; ☎03/5463 2325), located in an 1859 bluestone hotel on Ballarat Street, serves hearty but sophisticated country fare and also has five timber miners' cottages for rent (❺ including breakfast). **AVOCA**, 26km southwest of Maryborough on the Pyrenees Highway, was another rich source of alluvial gold, and today boasts a collection of nineteenth-century buildings, including a chemist's shop established in 1854 and believed to be the oldest in Victoria. These days, the area around Avoca, known as the **Pyrenees region**, is increasingly known for its **vineyards**. A cluster of them is located in or near Moonambel, a hamlet 17km northwest of Avoca: one to aim for is the *Warrenmang Vineyard Resort* on Mountain Creek Road (daily 9am–5pm; ☎03/5467 2233, ⒻY5467 2309, Ⓦwww.bazzani.com.au/warrenmang), which has a picturesque setting, an excellent restaurant, and offers accommodation in a homestead and timber lodges (full board from $160 per person).

Daylesford and Hepburn Springs

The attractive, hilly country around Daylesford and Hepburn Springs is known as the "spa centre of Australia", with a hundred **mineral springs** within a fifty-kilometre radius. Daylesford grew from the Jim Crow gold diggings of 1851, but the large Swiss-Italian population here quickly realized the value of the water from the mineral springs, which had been bottled since 1850. People have been taking the waters at Hepburn Springs for almost as long – the spa complex was built in 1895. The **Daylesford Visitor Information Centre**, servicing the whole area, is next to the post office on Vincent Street in Daylesford (daily 9am–5pm; ☎03/5348 1339); it has loads of brochures for the many places offering bed and breakfast and a board listing the vacancies at weekends, when places tend to fill up. You can get a local **bus** to Hepburn Springs from Little's bus depot at 45 Vincent St (Mon–Fri 4 daily). To get to Daylesford from Melbourne, take a **train** to Woodend, then a connecting bus to Daylesford (Mon–Sat 2 daily, Sun 1 daily). You can also take a train from Melbourne to Ballarat (Mon–Fri 1 daily) and then get the connecting bus to Daylesford. There's also a bus service between Geelong and Bendigo (Mon–Fri 1 daily), via Ballarat, Daylesford and Castlemaine.

Daylesford

The town of **DAYLESFORD**, a popular weekend retreat for Melburnians, has a New Age, alternative atmosphere, with a large gay community. As a result, the town has several gay-friendly guesthouses, and in the second weekend in March it is the venue for **ChillOut**, Australlia's largest rural gay and lesbian festival, featuring a street parade, music and cabaret, dance parties and a carnival at Victoria Park.

Daylesford's well-preserved Victorian and Edwardian streets rise up the side of Wombat Hill, where you'll find the Botanical Gardens, between Hill Street and Central Springs Road, whose lookout tower has panoramic views. Not far away, on the corner of Daly and Hill streets, is the **Convent Gallery** (daily 10am–5pm; $3.50), a rambling former convent which now has seven galleries selling high-quality arts, crafts and antiques, plus the *Bad Habits Café*, a Mediterranean-style café open for lunch and coffee, and the *Altar Bar* for light meals, wines and cocktails (Mon–Thurs & Sun 11am–5pm, Fri & Sat 11am–midnight). There's a great Sunday market (8am–2pm) just nearby, on the main road to Castlemaine. All your esoteric needs are taken care of at places like the Yasodhara Spiritual Resource Centre, 107 Vincent St, which sells crystals and offers tarot readings and meditation sessions.

Lake Daylesford, a short distance south from the town centre on Vincent Street, is the location of the Central Springs Reserve, which has several walking tracks and old-fashioned water pumps from which you can drink from the mineral springs. The **Lake Daylesford Book Barn** here (open daily) is a picturesquely situated bookshop, with an extensive range of secondhand books. The charming *Boathouse Café* (breakfast & lunch daily, dinner Sat & Sun; ℡03/5348 1387) has lakeside dining, as well as dinghies, canoes and paddle-boats for rent. With your own transport there are two more options further afield: the **Lavandula Swiss Italian Farm** (daily 10.30am–5pm; $3) in nearby Shepherds Flat, 5km north of Hepburn Springs, where you can walk among the historic stone farmhouses, in the extensive gardens and lavender fields, and then sit down for lunch or coffee and cake at *La Trattoria*, the farm's renowned Italian restaurant (℡03/5476 4347); and **Tuki trout farm** (℡03/5345 6233, ⓦwww.tuki.com.au) in Smeaton, 23km west of Daylesford via Creswick, where you can catch your own lunch and have it boned and cooked for you while you wait.

Practicalities

Internet access is available at the Hepburn Hub at 96 Vincent St, near the visitor information centre ($2 per 30min; Mon, Tues, Thurs & Fri 11am–5.30pm, Wed until 9pm, Sat until 3pm). You must book well in advance if you want **to stay** in Daylesford at the weekend. Bookings are handled by Daylesford Accommodation Booking Service (℡03/5348 1448, ⓦwww.dabs.com.au), or try Daylesford Getaways (℡03/5348 4422, ⓦwww.dayget.com.au).

35 Hill Street ℡03/5348 3878. Early Victorian brick cottage just below the Botanical Gardens, much-loved for its casual, friendly attitude. ❹

Ambleside on the Lake 15 Leggat St ℡03/5348 2691. Meticulously renovated Edwardian guesthouse overlooking Lake Daylesford. ❻–❼

The Balconies 35 Perrins St ℡03/5348 1322, ⓦwww.spacountry.net.au/balconys. A rambling mansion with several balconies overlooking the lake: a favourite with gay visitors. ❺

Bergamo 51 Woolnoughs Rd ℡03/5348 7572, ⓦwww.daylesford.net.au/bergamo. Two enchanting mud and timber cottages situated 12km north-east from town at Porcupine Ridge (travel along the Daylesford–Glenlyon Rd, and after 3km turn off to Porcupine Ridge). ❺–❻

Royal Hotel corner of Vincent and Albert streets ℡03/5348 2205. Refurbished Victorian pub with

10

ten pleasant, centrally heated rooms with en-suite facilities, some with spa bath. B&B. ❹
Wildwood YHA 42 Main Rd, Hepburn Springs ☎03/5348 4435, ✉daylesford@yhavic.org.au. The best deal in town: a small and lovely reno-

vated guesthouse with a homely kitchen and a deck overlooking a great garden area; if you're arriving by bus, phone ahead for a pick-up. Dorm bed from $21 for YHA members, rooms ❸

Eating

Cliffy's Emporium 30 Raglan St. In a town of good cafés, this delightful deli-café/winebar rates a special mention for food and atmosphere. Mon–Thurs 10am–6pm, Fri–Sun till late.
Farmers Arms Hotel 1 East St. A great place to go for a drink (try a local ale) or a drink and dinner (Wed–Sun 6–9pm) – the cuisine is modern Australian and the servings are generous.
Frangos & Frangos Restaurant and Koukla Café Both at 82 Vincent St ☎03/5348 2363. The café serves excellent breakfasts and slightly simpler and cheaper lunches and dinners than the fine restaurant. Mediterranean-inspired food.
Harvest Café 29 Albert St. A friendly, noncon-

formist haven that has an extensive menu (vegetarian, vegan and seafood), plus folk and acoustic music on Sunday night. Thurs–Mon 9am–9pm.
Hill End Café and Gallery 123 Vincent St. Serves good breakfasts until 5pm.
Himalaya Bakery 73 Vincent St. Heavy but nutritious dark rye bread and delicious cakes.
Lake House King Street near the lake ☎03/5348 3329. For a real splurge, try this outstanding but expensive restaurant; as well as dinner they do coffees and brunch.
Sweet Decadence at Locantro 87 Vincent St. Chocolates, coffee and cake served up in a characterful old building.

Hepburn Springs

HEPBURN SPRINGS is not really a town at all, but a collection of guesthouses and a wonderful Art Deco **resort hotel** in a green, hilly and peaceful spot only 4km north of Daylesford. From the bus stop, walk through the shady Soldiers Memorial Park to the Mineral Springs Reserve, where you can taste three kinds of mineral water from old pumps and take advantage of the facilities at the ultraposh **Hepburn Spa Resort** (Mon–Thurs 10am–7pm, Fri 10am–8pm, Sat 9am–10pm, Sun 9am–7pm; ☎03/5348 2034, ℱ5348 1167, ⓦwww.hepburnspa.com.au). You can spend as long as you like here in the relaxation pool (34°C) and mineral-water spa (38°C; both Mon–Fri $11; Sat, Sun & public holidays $14). Otherwise, indulge yourself with twenty minutes in your own aero-spa bath, with essential oils (Mon–Fri $27; Sat, Sun & public holidays $30). The southern wing has massage, saunas, flotation tanks, and therapy and couch pools. Bookings must be made at least three (preferably six) weeks in advance, especially for weekends.

Practicalities

The Springs Retreat at the corner of Main Road and Tenth Street (☎03/5348 2202; ❺–❼) is a classic 1930s Art Deco resort with tastefully renovated en-suite rooms. There's a good-value buffet lunch in the dining room and a more expensive dinner menu; tasty counter meals are also available in the bar. *Dudley House*, at 101 Main Rd (☎03/5348 3033, ⓦwww.netconnect.com.au/~dudley; ❼, weekends ❽), is a lovely Federation-style weatherboard house with bed and breakfast and a fine restaurant. At the budget end of the scale is *Continental House*, 9 Lone Pine Ave (☎03/5348 2005; ❷), a guesthouse with an alternative feel, in a lovely garden setting on a hill above the Mineral Springs Reserve. The rambling house contains doubles, twins and small dorms (bed $20–25; BYO linen for all), a kitchen (vegetarian only), and several lounge rooms. A vegetarian café is open on Saturday night.

Another good choice for vegetarian **food** is the *Cosy Corner Café* at 3 Tenth St (breakfast and snacks daily, lunch and dinner Thurs–Mon). Back on Main Street, there's *Jasmine Thai* at no 114 for traditional Thai food (dinner daily except Tues; ☎03/5348 1163) and *Misto* at no. 70 for interesting East-meets-West cuisine (dinner Mon & Thurs–Sun, lunch Sat & Sun; ☎03/5348 2843). The Art Nouveau *Palais* at no. 111 is a restaurant and bar (Wed–Sat evening): the adjacent ballroom is used for dance classes and as an entertainment venue – quite a few top-notch names from the Melbourne music scene and further afield make their appearance here.

Ballarat and around

BALLARAT is a grandiose provincial city that makes a lasting impression from whichever direction you approach it. From the west, you enter via the Western Highway along the **Avenue of Honour**, lined on either side with over 22km of trees and dedicated to soldiers who fought in World War I. It ends at the massive **Arch of Victory**, through which you drive to enter Sturt Street and the city. Coming from the east, you approach the city on the Western Highway (Victoria Street), flanked by lawns, trees and colourful flowerbeds. Trains pull in to the elegant 1889 **station**, topped by a domed clock tower.

The Ballarat area was already settled before gold was discovered, and thus preserves a rural life for which the city is the supply centre. Nonetheless, it's gold which has marked the place indelibly: over a quarter of all **gold** found in Victoria came from Ballarat's fantastically rich reef mines before they were exhausted in 1918. Nowadays, in addition to the more obvious tourist attractions – especially Sovereign Hill – and fine **architecture**, the town is interesting in its own right, with a fairly large student population that lends some cultural presence and gives the city a reasonably active nightlife. Most people don't stay here overnight, however, as it's only little more than an hour's drive from Melbourne.

The centrally located Ballarat Visitor Information Centre, on the corner of Sturt and Albert streets (daily 9am–5pm; ☎03/5320 5741 or 1800 44 66 33, ⓦwww.ballarat.com), has free **information** and maps of the town and can make accommodation bookings. Public **transport** in Ballarat and surrounding areas is handled by Davis Buslines (☎03/5331 7777); they charge a flat two-hour fare of $1.60. Buses to Sovereign Hill and Eureka Street depart from the bus stop on Lydiard Street, near the corner of Sturt Street; to get to Lake Wendouree take bus #15 from Sturt Street near the Myer department store, going to Sturt Street West. The system extends as far as Creswick (see p.1003), 18km north.

Accommodation

There's an abundance of **accommodation** in all price ranges in Ballarat, from hostels to grand hotels, so you shouldn't have a problem finding a room to suit. Bear in mind that many places will be more expensive at weekends.

The Ansonia 32 Lydiard St ☎03/5332 4678, ⓕ5332 4698, ⓦwww.small-hotel.com/ansonia. Lovely boutique hotel with restaurant, library and guest lounge in the historic precinct. ⑤–⑦
Ballarat City Apartments 225 Lydiard St North ☎03/5332 6992, ⓔbca@cbl.com.au. Five centrally located, self-contained apartments with one or two bedrooms, all with spas. ④–⑥
Craigs Royal Hotel 10 Lydiard St South ☎03/5331 1377 or 1800 648 051, ⓕ5331 7103.

BALLARAT

ACCOMMODATION	
Ansonia	4
Ballarat City Apartments	1
Craigs Royal Hotel	6
Eastern Station Hotel	2
George Hotel	3
Goldfields Caravan Park	7
Miners Retreat Motel	5
Sovereign Hill Lodge YHA	8

The accommodation at this grand Victorian-era hotel ranges from traditional pub rooms to luxurious suites – go for the wonderful two-level North Tower suite if your budget will allow it. ④–⑦

Eastern Station Hotel Cnr Humffray St and Scott Parade ☎03/5338 8722. Reasonably priced comfortable doubles with shared kitchen and bathroom facilities. ③

George Hotel 27 Lydiard St ☎03/5333 4866, ☎5333 4818. Three-storey 1850s hotel with colonial-style decor, an inexpensive bistro and rooms, some with four-poster beds. ③–④

Goldfields Holiday Park 108 Clayton St ☎03/5332 7888 or 1800 632 237. Well located, right next to Sovereign Hill. Good facilities for campers, including a camp kitchen. Cabins ③–④

Miners Retreat Motel 602 Eureka St ☎03/5331 6900, ☎5331 6944. Standard motel units, just 100m from the site of the Eureka Stockade; light breakfast included. ③

Sovereign Hill Lodge YHA Magpie St ☎03/5333 3409, ☎5333 5861, ☎ballarat@yhavic.org.au. This small hostel –part of a motel as well as part of Sovereign Hill theme park – has drab rooms but a pleasant kitchen/dining area and a bar on site. Dorms from $20, rooms ③, B&B in motel rooms ⑤

The City

Sturt and Victoria streets terminate on either side of the Bridge Mall, the central shopping area at the base of quaint **Bakery Hill** with its old shopfronts. Southeast of the city centre, Eureka Street runs off Main Street towards the site of the **Eureka Stockade**, with several museums and antique shops along the

The Eureka Stockade

The **Eureka Rebellion** is one of the most celebrated events of Australian history, regarded as the only act of white armed rebellion the country has seen. It was provoked by conditions in the goldfields, where diggers had to pay exorbitantly for their right to prospect for gold (as much as thirty shillings a month), without receiving in return any right to vote, to have decent roads, transport or police protection, or to have any chance of a permanent right to the land they worked. Checks for licences were ruthless and brutal, and corruption rife. Protest meetings calling on diggers to refuse to pay drew huge crowds at Ballarat, Bendigo and Castlemaine; in response, in November 1853 the government made a small reduction in the fee.

The administration at Ballarat was particularly repressive, and in November 1854 local diggers formed the **Ballarat Reform League**, demanding full civic rights and the abolition of the licence fee, and proclaiming that "the people are the only legitimate source of power". At the end of the month a group of two hundred diggers gathered inside a **stockade** of logs, hastily flung together, and determined to resist further arrests for non-possession of a licence. They were attacked at dawn on December 3 by police and troops; thirty died inside, and five members of the government forces also lost their lives.

The movement was not a failure, however: the diggers had aroused widespread sympathy, and in 1855 licences were abolished, to be replaced by an annual **Miner's Right** which carried the right to vote and to enclose land. The leader of the rebellion, the Irishman Peter Lalor, eventually became a member of parliament.

The **Eureka Flag**, with its white cross and five white stars on a blue background, has become a symbol of the Left – and indeed of almost any protest movement: shearers raised it in strikes during the 1890s; wharfies used it before World War II in their bid to stop pig-iron being sent to Japan; and today the flag is flown by a growing number of Australians who support the country's transformation to a republic. On a deeper level, all sorts of claims are made for the Eureka Rebellion's pivotal role in forming the Australian nation and psyche. The diggers are held up as a classic example of the Australian (male) ethos of mateship and anti-authoritarianism, while the goldrush in general is credited with overthrowing the hierarchical colonial order, as servants rushed to make their fortune, leaving their masters and mistresses to fend for themselves.

way. Main Street becomes Ballarat–Buninyong Road, and six blocks down is crossed by Bradshaw Street, where you'll find Sovereign Hill, the recreated gold town. Northwest of the centre, approached via Sturt Street, are the **Botanical Gardens** and Lake Wendouree.

The most complete **nineteenth-century streetscape** is probably along Lydiard Street, which runs from the centre up past the train station; there are several two-storey terraced shopfronts, with verandahs and decorative iron-lace work, mostly dating from the mid- to late nineteenth century. The former **Mining Exchange** (1888) has been recently renovated to its former splendour, and the architecture of Her Majesty's Theatre (1875) also proclaims its goldrush-era heyday. The **Ballarat Fine Art Gallery** at 40 Lydiard St (daily 10.30am–5pm; free guided tours daily 2pm, $5), another superb building, is the oldest provincial art gallery in Australia, established in 1884. The gallery had a recent facelift when a modern, cutting-edge extension was added. The original frayed **Eureka Flag** (see box above) is on display there in a purpose-built space, with subdued lighting to protect the precious relic. The gallery's extensive collection is particularly strong on colonial and Heidelberg School paintings; displayed alongside are the watercolours of S.T. Gill, a self-taught artist who painted scenes of goldrush days in Ballarat. In another part of the gallery is a reconstruction of the drawing room of the famous Lindsay family (whose best-known members are the artist Norman and the writer Jack), from nearby Creswick, complete with several of their paintings. The new wing of the gallery, a striking structure with a curved zinc roof and a glass-encased staircase, extends out to former Camp Street, now re-named Alfred Deakin Place, and stands cheek by jowl with an 1880s red-brick building, a police station in its previous incarnation and now the *Gallery Café*. The visual and performing arts faculties of Ballarat University have been relocated to Deakin Place and are housed in new quarters of equally striking modern design. Walking from the Art Gallery along Lydiard Street to Sturt Street you'll see more nineteenth-century goldrush architecture: check out the imposing Classical-revival **town hall** on Sturt Street, which dominates the centre of the city.

There are still over fifty **hotels** in Ballarat – survivors of the hundreds that once watered the thirsty diggers. Some of the finest are on Lydiard Street: *Craig's Royal Hotel* at no. 10 and the *George Hotel* at no. 27 are an integral part of Ballarat's architectural heritage. Sadly, during the 1970s, the council forced most of the old pubs to pull down their verandahs on the grounds that they were unsafe, so very few survive in their original form. One that does is attached to the *Golden City Hotel*, 427 Sturt St, which took the council to the Supreme Court to save its magnificent wide verandah with original cast-iron decoration; the hotel is now open at weekends as a bar and is appreciatively packed out in summer.

The Botanical Gardens

The **Botanical Gardens**, laid out in 1858, cover about half a square kilometre alongside **Lake Wendouree**, just to the northwest of the city centre (#15 bus from Sturt St, by Myer). Begonias grow so well in Ballarat that a **Begonia Festival** runs for ten days in March. The new **Conservatory** at the Botanic Gardens, an impressive glass house whose design was inspired by origami, is used to showcase them, and other floral displays, throughout the year (conservatory daily 9am–5pm; $3).

Other highlights are the **Avenue of Big Trees**, with a Californian redwood among its monsters, and the classical statuary, donated by rich gold miners, scattered about the gardens. Pride of place goes to Benzoni's *Flight from Pompeii*, housed in the Statuary Pavilion. Along Prime Minister Avenue you can see a bust of every prime minister of Australia.

Eureka and York streets

As you head towards Eureka Street and the Eureka Stockade (bus #8 from outside the ANZ Bank on Sturt St), take a look at the unique shop facades on Main Street. The site of the Eureka Stockade (see box opposite) is in Eureka Memorial Park, and the nearby **Eureka Stockade and Interpretation Centre** (daily 9am–4.30pm; $8) gives detailed background information on the Eureka story. On the same street further toward the town centre, **Montrose Cottage** at no. 111 (daily 10am–5pm; $6.50) is the last original miner's cottage in Ballarat – it's furnished in 1850s style and fitted out with a social history display.

Parallel to Eureka Street is York Street, where you'll find the free-range **Ballarat Wildlife Park**, on the corner of Fussell Street (daily 9am–5.30pm, $14.50). There are guided tours daily at 11am; and feeding times are also worth attending (weekends, daily during the school holidays: koalas 2pm, wombats 2.30pm, crocodiles 3pm, Tasmanian devils 3.30pm).

Sovereign Hill and the Gold Museum

The re-created gold-mining township of **Sovereign Hill** is located 1.5km from the city centre, on Bradshaw Street (daily 10am–5pm; $27 also includes admission to the Gold Museum; ☎03/5331 1944, ⓦwww.sovereignhill.com.au; bus #9 from outside the ANZ Bank on Sturt St). Seventy buildings and shops here are modelled on those that lined Ballarat's main street in the 1850s, with a cast of characters wandering about in the dress of the period. The township was planned around an actual mine shaft from the 1880s, where guided underground tours are available. There are diggings where you can learn how to pan for gold (and perhaps get a small memento) and a mining museum filled with steam-operated machinery. Sovereign Hill puts on a spectacular outdoor **sound and light show**, "Blood on the Southern Cross" (nightly during school holidays, Mon–Sat rest of the year; 1hr 20min; $32, or joint ticket for show and Sovereign Hill $55; ☎03/5333 5777), which makes use of the whole panorama of Sovereign Hill to tell the story of the Eureka Stockade.

Opposite Sovereign Hill, the **Gold Museum** (daily 9.30am–5.20pm, in summer until 6pm; $6.80) offers a good overview of the recreated settlement. It has an outstanding display of real gold, and a large collection of coins that are arranged in displays exploring the history and uses of gold. The museum's **Eureka Exhibition** details life on the goldfields and explains the conditions that provoked the Eureka Stockade. Central to the exhibition is a large painting of the rebellion by George Browning, a mid-nineteenth-century artist: it's interesting to see quite a few black faces portrayed in the stockade, which is generally labelled as the only white armed uprising to have taken place in Australia.

Eating and drinking

For its size, Ballarat has an astonishing number and variety of **eating places**, ranging from European coffee bars established by postwar immigrants to upmarket gourmet restaurants, not to forget more than forty **pubs**.

The Ansonia 32 Lydiard St ☎03/5332 4678. Restaurant in refurbished building that also houses a swish boutique hotel. The eclectic cuisine betrays influences from the Mediterranean to Southeast Asia. Licensed; open daily for breakfast, lunch and dinner (book for dinner).

Boatshed Restaurant 27 Wendouree Parade. Have a coffee or meal on the deck fronting Lake Wendouree. Licensed, open daily till late.

Cafe Pazani 102 Sturt St. Slick Italian café serving expensive food and excellent coffee. Licensed. Tues–Sat 9am–1am, Sun & Mon 9am–5.30pm.

Da Vincis 29 Sturt St. The best place for pasta in town: a lively atmosphere and generous, good-value servings, plus vegetarian options. Licensed. Open daily.

Europa Café 411 Sturt St. A pleasant café serving good coffee, cakes and breads, and light meals. Mon–Wed & Sun 9am–6pm, Thurs–Sat 9am until late.

Game Keeper's Secret Humffrey and Mair streets ☎03/5332 6000. African-themed restaurant run by South Africans. The place for fun-loving thirty-somethings in search of good, interesting cuisine. Open daily for lunch and dinner.

Golden City Hotel 427 Sturt St. This historic 1896 hotel packs them in with an all-you-can-eat lunch, and a varied dinner menu. Relaxed bar with espresso machine, pool tables, music videos and locally brewed Ballarat Bitter.

Irish Murphys 36 Sturt St. Big food at small prices, decent beer and frequent live music with minimal Irish kitsch combine to make this bar one of the most popular in town.

L'Espresso 417 Sturt St. European-style, hip place for coffee and eclectic breakfasts; the mains are good too, and very moderately priced. Daily 7.30am–6pm, also Thurs–Sun 6.30pm until late.

The Pancake Kitchen 2 Grenville St South. Pancakes on order all day and night in a cosy goldrush building.

Sebastiaans Coffee Bar 58 Lydiard St. Café-bar with cool minimalist decor opposite the Regent Multiplex cinemas. Open daily from 11am.

Tokyo Grill House 109 Bridge Mall ☎03/5333 3945. Specializes in *teppanyaki* cooking, which means it's prepared on hotplates in front of you.

Expensive. Open daily for lunch and dinner. The Views Bar & Café 22 Wendouree Parade.

Excellent location overlooking Lake Wendouree, open daily from 7am till late.

Entertainment and nightlife

The **music** scene in Ballarat is more lively than you might expect; for up-to-date information about what's on, check *The Courier* on Thursday, or log on to Ⓦ www.ballaratunderground.com.au. Located in an old church at 102 Dana St, *The Chapel* is the best of the **clubs**, popular with students, or there's the bustling *21 Arms*, at 21 Armstrong St, Ballarat North, which has six bars. There are **live bands** on Friday and Saturday nights at the *Grand Hotel Ballroom*, 120 Lydiard St, while *Sturt Street Blues*, 404 Sturt St (℡03/5332 3676), occasionally showcases excellent live jazz and blues.

The elaborate Victorian-era Her Majesty's Theatre, at 17 Lydiard St (℡03/5333 5800), stages all types of touring **productions**, and there's a three-screen **cinema** on the same street at no. 49 (℡03/5331 1399).

Around Ballarat

Rich alluvial **gold** was found at **CRESWICK**, 18km north of Ballarat, in 1851, which made it an important mining centre. It's now a quiet little town, where the only reminder of earlier days is the grandiose Victorian architecture. The *American Hotel* and the *British Hotel* face each other across the main street, a hangover from mining days when miners of different nationalities stuck to their segregated groups. **CLUNES**, just beyond Creswick, to the northwest, was the site of the first worthwhile Victorian goldfield in 1851. The reefs here were too deep for small-scale mining, and the Port Phillip Company took over operations. The only profitable British gold mine in Australia, it was most productive between 1857 and 1881. The main street has many solid old buildings and rows of original shopfronts which are sadly vacant – entrepreneurial attempts to attract the tourist trade with antique and craft shops have foundered. The **Clunes Museum** (Sat 10am–4.30pm, Sun & school holidays 11am–4.30pm; $2) details the gold-mining era of the town. *The Club Hotel*, at 34 Fraser St (℡03/5345 3250; ➍), has inexpensive **accommodation**, with a buffet breakfast included, and rustles up cheap rump steaks for lunch and dinner.

Western Victoria and the Mallee

Several roads run west from the goldfields to the South Australian border through the seemingly endless wheatfields of **the Wimmera**. To the west of the farming centre of **Ararat** is the major attraction of the area, **The Grampians (Gariwerd) National Park**, the southwestern tail-end of the Great Dividing Range. Stawell and **Horsham** – the latter regarded as the capital of the Wimmera – are good places to base yourself, but **Halls Gap**, inside the park, is even better. North of Horsham are **Nhill** and **Dimboola**, close to **Little Desert National Park** and, like **Warracknabeal** further north, wheat centres. Beyond here is the least populated part of the state, the wide, flat **Mallee** with its twisted mallee scrub, sand dunes and dry lakes. This region, with several state and national parks, extends from **Wyperfeld National Park** in the south, right up to Mildura's irrigated oasis on the Murray River. South of the Grampians is sheep country; following the Hamilton Highway from Geelong you'll end up at **Hamilton**, the major town and wool capital of the western district, also accessible via **Dunkeld** on the southern edge of the Grampians.

Transport

V/Line (℡13 61 96) has a **bus service** from Ballarat to Hamilton via Dunkeld (Mon–Sat 2 daily, Sun 1 daily; Mon–Fri the morning service continues to Mount Gambier in South Australia), and a bus service from Warrnambool (Mon–Fri & Sun 1 daily). The Grampians Link consists of a **train service** from Melbourne to Ballarat and a connecting bus to Halls Gap, via Ararat and Stawell (1 daily). The Overland train service between Melbourne and Adelaide departs Melbourne Sun, Mon, Thurs & Fri at 9.30pm, Wed at 10.30pm, and arrives in Adelaide 10hr later (for details call Trainways Australia ℡13 21 47). The Daylink connection (train from Melbourne to Ballarat, and from there a connecting bus via Horsham and Dimboola to Adelaide) departs Melbourne daily in the morning. Greyhound-McCafferty's and Firefly buses to Adelaide travel the Western Highway via Ballarat, Ararat, Stawell, Horsham, Dimboola and Nhill.

Hamilton and around

Three highways converge at **HAMILTON**, where you can see the Grampians from the edge of the main street. It's a civilized little city whose main claim to fame is that it's the "Wool Capital of the World". The only reason you're likely to be here is if you're a traveller passing through, en route from the Goldfields to South Australia, or from the mountains to the coast. There's plenty to distract you, however, and the friendly **Hamilton Visitor Information Centre** on Lonsdale Street (daily 9am–5pm; ℡03/5572 3746 or 1800 807 056) can book accommodation if you decide to stay.

The most worthwhile of the town's five museums and galleries is the **Hamilton Art Gallery**, on Brown Street (Mon–Fri 10am–5pm, Sat 10am–noon & 2–5pm, Sun 2–5pm; donation), one of the finest provincial art galleries in the state. Its collection of eighteenth-century watercolours of English pastoral scenes by Paul Sandby is the largest outside Britain; among other gems are ninety engravings by William Hogarth and several pieces of eighteenth-century English furniture. The influence of the wealthy local Ansett family (of airline fame) is obvious; many of the excellent contemporary paintings were acquired through the Ansett Hamilton Art Awards.

Also in the town centre, but of marginal interest, is the **Hamilton History Centre** (2–5pm; closed Sat; $1), located in the Mechanics Institute Building at 43 Gray St. East of town, on the Ballarat Road, is the **Sir Reginald Ansett Transport Museum** (daily 10am–4pm; $2), charting the history of the now defunct Ansett flight network which began here, while **The Big Woolbales** (daily 9.30am–4pm) on Coleraine Road contain a small exhibition telling you about the wool industry of the Western district. There's also some refreshing greenery in the town centre: the Botanical Gardens are on the corner of French and Thompson streets, just one block from Gray Street, the main thoroughfare, while the banks of the **Grange Burn** are home to the eastern barred bandicoot, the only known population in mainland Australia. Grange Burn flows into man-made **Lake Hamilton**, which has a safe, sandy swimming beach and is filled with trout.

Practicalities

Hamilton features a wide variety of **accommodation**. Budget travellers can stay at the pleasantly sited Lake Hamilton Caravan Park, 8 Ballarat Rd (℡03/5572 3855; cabins ❷–❸) or the *Peppercorn Lodge* next door at 10 Ballarat Rd (℡03/5571 9046; dorms $19, rooms ❶, BYO linen or rent for a fee), which has backpackers' accommodation and comfortable, heated rooms. On the same road at no. 142 is the luxurious *Comfort Inn Grange Burn* (℡03/5572 5755; ❺). The relaxed *Grand Central Hotel*, 141 Gray St (℡03/5572 2899; ❸), is a good place both to eat and sleep: breakfast is included in the price of the motel-style rooms, there's an unpretentious bistro and bands play here at weekends.

One of the best eating places is the *Hamilton Strand* at 56 Thompson St (Mon–Sat 11am until late; BYO; ℡03/5571 9144), which serves coffee, cakes and light snacks out the front, and more substantial meals in the rooms behind. Other good options include the pleasant *Gilly's Coffee Shop & Grill*, 106 Gray St (daily from morning till late); the *Meeting Place* at the corner of French and Thompson Streets (daily lunch and dinner; licensed and BYO; ℡03/5572 1855); and *Georgies Restaurant* at the *George Hotel*, 213 Gray St (daily lunch and dinner; ℡03/5572 1844).

Around Hamilton

Hamilton is situated on the fringe of an extensive volcanic plain that runs across western Victoria and into South Australia. Mount Napier (439m) to the south and Mount Rouse at Penshurst to the east were the sources of most of the lava flow covering the Hamilton area. Byaduk Caves Road, going towards MacArthur, has a very good view of Mount Napier, directly ahead as you drive. Lava flows are still clearly visible here, with black wattle trees flourishing on many of them. The **Byaduk Caves** are actually fern-filled lava tubes; three of the twelve are easy enough to get into, but the others have restricted access – call the ranger at Mount Eccles (℡03/5576 1338) for further information. As you explore, watch out for stinging nettles and rough terrain, with frothy textured lava rocks scattered around, porous and covered in moss.

At Wannon on the Glenelg Highway, 15km west of Hamilton, there's a signposted turn-off to **Wannon Falls**, which are at their most impressive after a good winter rainfall season. A further 17km on, **COLERAINE** is picturesquely sited in the Wannon River Valley, between two tablelands. The Peter Francis Point Aboretum and Eucalypt Discovery Centre here (open 24hr; free) is the nation's official eucalypt collection, and has the largest number of species in the world. At **CASTERTON**, 29km further west on the Glenelg River, the 1843 **Warrock Homestead** (daily 10am–5pm; $6) is one of the most interesting in the country: more than thirty buildings are still used by the descendants of the original settlers and are open to visitors. From here it's less than an hour's drive to South Australia and the Coonawarra wine region (see p.851).

Ararat and the Western Highway

ARARAT, some 90km west from Ballarat, is still very much a goldfields town, with an overabundance of grandiose Victorian architecture and a main street laid out to show off the best profiles of the nearby mountains: **Mount Ararat** in the west and the **Pyrenees Range** with **Mount Cole** in the east. The town was founded in 1857, when a group of seven hundred hopeful Chinese from Guangdong province in southern China, making the slow trudge from the South Australian ports to the central Victorian goldfields, stumbled across a fabulously rich, shallow alluvial goldfield, the **Canton Lead**. The new multi-million-dollar **Gum San Chinese Heritage Centre** (daily 10am–4.30pm; $8; @www.gumsan.com.au) pays homage to the fact that Ararat is the only town in Australia founded by the Chinese. It was designed by a Melbourne architect of Chinese origin and is a recreation of a two-storey southern Chinese temple set in traditional Chinese garden. The exhibits recount the tale of the founding of the city and familiarize Western visitors with aspects of Chinese culture.

These days Ararat is the commercial centre for a sheep-farming and wine-producing area; local **wineries** include the Montara Winery, 3km south along the Chalambar Road (Mon–Sat 10am–5pm, Sun noon–5pm), and Mount Langi Ghiran on Vine Road north of Buangor (turn north from the Western Highway towards Warrak; Mon–Fri 9am–5pm, Sat & Sun noon–5pm), renowned for its superb white and red wines.

Next door to the town hall, with its clock tower and fountain, is the **visitor information centre** on High Street (Mon–Fri 9am–5pm; ☎03/5355 0281 or 1800 657 158, @www.ararat.asn.au), which provides information on the Grampians and can book accommodation in the area. The **Langi Morgala Museum** nearby (Sat & Sun 1–4pm; $2.20) occupies an old brick building banded with bluestone at the base and around the huge arched windows and doors. Along with the usual pioneering displays, there's an important collection of Aboriginal artefacts.

For **food**, go to Barkly Street, where you'll find a healthfood store, a bakery, a decent delicatessen; and two good cafés: *Vines Café & Bar* at no 74, which serves classy sandwiches, good-value meals and wine, and *Sicilian's Café-Bar-Restaurant* at no. 102. For bar meals head to the *Ararat Hotel* at 130 Barkly St or the *Blue Duck Hotel* at no. 257. A good value-option is the bistro at the Ararat RSL club, 74 High St, which serves inexpensive meals daily.

Great Western and Stawell

Between Ararat and Stawell is the small settlement of **GREAT WESTERN**, the centre of a wine-producing area whose most famous historic **wineries** are right in town, on the Moyston Road. **Seppelt Great Western** (daily 9am–5pm), established in 1865, and **Best's Great Western** (Mon–Sat 10am–5pm, Sun 11am–4pm) established in 1866, are both renowned for their sparkling *méthode champenoise* wines but they also produce a range of other wines (Best's in particular): Shiraz, Cabernet Sauvignon, Riesling and Chardonnay. Best's has a timber winery building and an old underground cellar whereas Seppelt's boasts 1.5km of underground tunnels dug by miners in the late nineteenth century to aid sparkling-wine maturation. A **winery tour** includes these tunnels (Mon–Sat at 10.30, 1.30pm & 3pm, during school holidays also on Sun). A much-respected newcomer on the wine circuit is **Garden Gully** on the Western Highway in Great Western (Mon–Fri

10.30am–5.30pm, Sat & Sun 10am–5.30pm), whose sparkling reds and innovative whites have won over ninety awards in recent years.

STAWELL (pronounced "stall") is most famous for the **Stawell Gift**, a sprint race offering big prize money that has been held here every Easter since 1877. It's also the closest major town to the Grampians and the departure point for the **bus** to Halls Gap. The helpful **Stawell & Grampians Visitor Information Centre** is at 52 Western Highway (☎1800 246 880); the **Stawell Gift Hall of Fame** on Main Street (Mon–Fri 9–11am or by appointment; $2; ☎03/5358 1326) charts the history of the race itself. The town, with its winding main street, has a pleasant, old-fashioned feel, and it's a much less expensive place to stay than Halls Gap. The many motels along the highway all charge much the same (❸–❹) for similar facilities. More expensive B&Bs and two caravan parks are the only real alternatives: *Walmsley B&B* at 19 Seaby St (☎03/5358 3164; ❸–❺) is reasonably priced, and has a pleasant lounge and a verandah, while the *Stawell Grampians Gate Caravan Park* on Burgh Street 400m south of the Western Highway (☎03/5358 2376; cabins ❷–❸), is the closest camping area to town.

The Grampians National Park

Rising from the flat plains of western Victoria's wheat and grazing districts, the sandstone ranges of the **Grampians**, with their weirdly formed rocky outcrops and stark ridges, seem doubly spectacular. In addition to their scenic splendour, in the **GRAMPIANS NATIONAL PARK** you'll find a dazzling array of **flora**, with a spring and early summer bonanza of wild flowers; a wealth of **Aboriginal rock art**; an impressive **Aboriginal Cultural Centre**; **waterfalls** and **lakes**; and over fifty **bushwalks** along 150km of well-marked tracks. There are also several hundred kilometres of road, from sealed highway to rough track, on which you can make exciting **scenic drives** and **4WD** tours.

HALLS GAP, 26km from Stawell, on the eastern fringes of the Grampians, is the only settlement actually in the national park. Its setting is gorgeous, in the long flat strip of the Fyans Valley surrounded by the soaring bush and rock of the Mount Difficult and Mount William ranges; koalas are frequently seen in the surrounding trees. Packed with accommodation (see p.1012) and other facilities catering to park visitors, this is the obvious place to base yourself, especially if you don't have your own transport. The Mobil service station has an ATM for the Commonwealth Bank; the newsagent and a lot of other shops in town have EFTPOS facilities.

Just over 2km south of Halls Gap along the Grampians Road (also known as the Dunkeld Road or the Dunkeld–Halls Gap Road) is the **National Park Visitor Centre** (daily 9am–5pm; ☎03/5356 4381, ⓦwww.parkweb.vic.gov.au), the best place to start your visit; it has a fascinating display and videos which trace the development of the Grampians over four hundred million years. Here you can buy books, including the excellent *Grampians Touring Guide* (ideal for short walks) and more detailed topographic maps. Although most walking tracks are clearly defined and well signposted, it's a good idea to buy Vicmap, or the walking maps published by the NPWS, and carry a compass if you're planning an

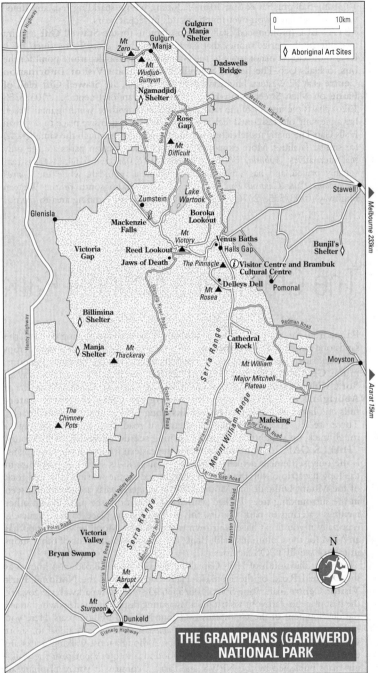

Gulgurn
Manja
Shelter

Mt
Zero

Gulgurn
Manja

Dadswells
Bridge

Mt
Wudjub-
Gunyun

Ngamadjidj
Shelter

Western Highway

Rose
Gap

Mt
Difficult

Stawell

Lake
Wartook

Zumstein

Boroka
Lookout

Glenisla

Mackenzie
Falls

Mt
Victory

Venus Baths

Halls Gap

Bunjil's
Shelter

Victoria
Gap

Reed Lookout

Jaws of Death

The Pinnacle

Visitor Centre and Brambuk
Cultural Centre

Delleys Dell

Mt
Rosea

Pomonal

Billimina
Shelter

Serra Range

Cathedral
Rock

Manja
Shelter

Mt
Thackeray

Mt William

Major Mitchell
Plateau

Moyston

Mount William Range

Mafeking

The
Chimney
Pots

Victoria
Valley

Bryan Swamp

Serra Range

Mt
Abrupt

Mt
Sturgeon

Dunkeld

Glenelg Highway

Henty Highway

Mount Zero Road

Mount Difficult Road

Smiths Road

Rose Gap Road

Glenelg River Road

Green Creek Road

Grampians Road

Victoria Valley Road

Victoria Valley Road

Victoria Point Road

Mount Abrupt Road

Yarram Gap Road

Moyston Dunkeld Road

Redman Road

Jimmy Creek Road

Henty Highway

Melbourne 233km

Ararat 15km

0   10km

Aboriginal Art Sites

N

THE GRAMPIANS (GARIWERD)
NATIONAL PARK

It's estimated that **Koorie** Aborigines lived in the area known to them as **Gariwerd** at least five thousand years ago. The area offered such rich food sources that the Koories didn't have to spend all their time hunting and food-gathering, and could therefore devote themselves to religious and cultural activities. Evidence of this survives in rock paintings, which are executed in a linear style, usually in a single colour (either red or white), but sometimes done by handprints or stencils. You can visit some of the rock shelters where Aborigines camped and painted on the sandstone walls, although many more are off-limits. In the northern Grampians one of the best is **Gulgurn Manja** (also known as Flat Rock), 5km south of the Western Highway near the Hollow Mountain campsite; from Flat Rock Road it's a signposted fifteen-minute walk. The name means "hands of young people", as many of the handprints here were done by children. In the southern Grampians is **Billimina** (Glenisla Shelter), a fifteen-minute walk above the Buandik campsite; it's an impressive rock overhang with clearly discernible, quite animated red stick figures. **Guided rock-art tours** are organized by the Brambuk Cultural Centre (see below).

overnight trek. Details of bushwalks are posted and there are masses of free-leaflets; before beginning an extended walk, call into the visitors centre and register. Some **walks** start from the campsite at Halls Gap, while others branch off the Victory and Grampian roads, making them difficult to get to without a car.

The **best times to come** are in autumn, or in spring and early summer when the waterfalls are in full flow and the wild flowers are blooming (although there'll always be something in flower no matter when you come). Between June and August it rains heavily and can get extremely cold; at that time many tracks are closed to avoid erosion. Summers are very hot, with a scarcity of water and the ever-present threat of bushfires. If you're undertaking extended walks in summer, carry a portable radio to get the latest information on the fire risk: on **total fire ban days** no exposed flames – not even that from a portable gas stove – are allowed.

Brambuk Aboriginal Cultural Centre

Located behind the National Park Visitor Centre, **Brambuk Aboriginal Cultural Centre** (daily 10am–5pm; ☎03/5356 4452) grew from an idea for a rock-art facsimile centre that would draw the tourist traffic away from the actual art sites, which are very fragile. From that beginning, it developed into a full-blown cultural centre for western Victorian Aboriginal culture – a place where visitors could learn and Koories could find employment, with a management committee composed entirely of Koories. The centre's building, with its undulating red-ochre tin roof, blends in wonderfully with the backdrop of bush and rocky ridge; it was designed in consultation with the five Koorie communities responsible for the centre and incorporates many symbolic features.

A small **exhibition** inside features a poignant photographic history of the area's Aborigines, and there's a visual display on traditional Aboriginal foods and lifestyles, plus a section devoted to Central Australian land rights. Downstairs, a shop sells Aboriginal music, books and souvenirs, while the Gariwerd Dreaming Centre presents the Gariwerd creation story with a multimedia sound and light show ($5) The small **Bushtucker Café** upstairs sells snacks and light meals, with, as its name implies, an emphasis on bushtucker – try possum-tail soup with damper, a rooburger or emu kebab, followed by a "wattlecino" (a cappuccino-style drink made from wattle seeds); for the less

10

VICTORIA | The Grampians National Park

adventurous, more familiar fare is available too. The café also offers **Internet access** ($4/hr) – the only one in Halls Gap apart from the backpacker hostels which cater to guests only. Outside, the landscaped grounds are planted with examples of the major plant species found in the park.

There are short **rock-art tours** from the centre, as well as half- and full-day walks to other Aboriginal art sites in the national park. All tours are on demand only, must be booked at least a week in advance, and require a minimum of four people.

Bushwalks, scenic drives and tours

The scenery and wildlife of the Grampians is tremendously varied, and the diversity of **vegetation** in the park is enhanced by the fact that this is the meeting place of the ecosystems of the forested areas in the south and east of Victoria and the dry mallee country in the north. It's significantly warmer in the northern Grampians, an area of arid bushland filled with bent and twisted trees and scrubby undergrowth. In the cooler south, the vegetation ranges from stringybark forests and red-gum woodland in the wet Victoria Valley to luxuriant fern gullies such as Delleys Dell in the Wonderland Range. There are also subalpine communities of plants in exposed sites such as Mount William, as well as areas of stunted heaths on the Major Mitchell Plateau.

You can **drive** on roads through the park to major points and then get out and walk. Take care, though, as animals are often killed by drivers, especially on the Grampians Road south of Halls Gap and the Mount Abrupt Road north of Dunkeld. The most popular section for visitors is the **Wonderland Range**, immediately to the west of Halls Gap. From the Halls Gap campsite you can head directly to **Venus Baths** (2km), **Mackeys Peak** (1km) or **The Pinnacle** (10km), the most popular lookout in the Grampians with a narrow rock ledge nearby – the **Nerve Test** – that many try out. **Delleys Dell** is another Wonderland walk (5km), through canopies of tree ferns: start at the Rosea picnic area. The other major features are the Balconies, Mackenzie Falls and Zumstein, all accessible via the Mount Victory Road northwest of Halls Gap. The walk to the **Balconies** (1.6km return), also known as the **Jaws of Death**, begins from the Reid Lookout car park and goes through a stand of lichen-covered tea trees. The weird formation consists of one ledge above another, and if you're brave enough you can stand right on the edge of the lower jaw and be enthralled by splendid views over the forested Victoria Valley. The much-photographed formation can also be seen at a distance from the **Reid Lookout** itself.

The Major Mitchell Trail

The first Europeans to reach the Grampians were **Major Thomas Mitchell** and his exploration party in 1836. Mitchell was the Surveyor General of New South Wales, and his glowing reports of the explorations subsequently attracted many squatters in the early 1840s. The **Major Mitchell Trail**, a signposted 1700-kilometre "long-distance cultural trail" along backroads and sometimes bush tracks, allows you to follow his route through Victoria, from Mildura along the Murray River to Swan Hill, then south to Horsham, detouring into the Grampians to ascend Mount William, and thence to the coast at Nelson and Portland. Heading back, it runs inland via Hamilton and Dunkeld on the southern edge of the Grampians, through central Victoria via Castlemaine, and then across the northeast part of the state via Benalla and Wangaratta, crossing back into New South Wales at Wodonga. A **handbook** of the walk is sometimes available at the DSE Information Centre or Information Victoria in Melbourne (see p.893), or enquire at the visitor information centres along the trail.

△ The Grampians, Victoria

At **Zumstein** (5km east of Mount Victory Road) there's a picnic area and car park where western grey kangaroos stand passively, waiting for food. They're tame enough to pet, but can be a serious nuisance when you get out your food; don't encourage them by feeding them. A three-kilometre walk runs along the Mackenzie River Gorge from here to the base of thundering **Mackenzie Falls**, which you can also reach more directly from the Mount Victoria Road. There's parking above the falls, and it's a short but strenuous walk to the base.

If you're reasonably fit, consider tackling the walk to the peak of **Mount William** (1168m; 3.5km return), the highest point in the park. This starts from the Mount William Road car park, for which you turn off 16km south of Halls Gap. More challenging overnight walks include one to the **Major Mitchell Plateau**, starting from the same car park but involving a difficult five-hundred-metre climb to the plateau, and the **Mount Difficult** walk, which starts from Rose Gap and goes across a large, undulating, rocky plateau.

Information, tours and activities

The friendly staff at the **Halls Gap Visitor Information Centre**, at the Centenary Hall on Grampians Road next to the Mobil service station, book accommodation, tours and activities (daily 9am–5pm; ℡03/5356 4616 or 1800 065 599). A few tour operators have banded together to form the **Grampians Central Booking Office** at the Halls Gap newsagency (daily 9.30am–6pm; ℡03/5356 4654), which also does bookings for activities and tours. Grampians Scenic Flights (Dec–June only) gives the definitive overview of the mountain range ($150–200, depending on the number of passengers ℡03/5358 3822; or book via the visitor information centre).

Accommodation

During school holidays, particularly in January and at Easter, the Grampians are packed, and although Halls Gap has lots of **accommodation** of every kind, you'll need to book in advance. Note that many places will insist on long stays, and prices also rise at weekends.

A permit is required for the **campsites** in the National Park which must be obtained at the National Park Visitor Centre. After hours you fill in a form and put your money into the box outside the centre. The fee is $10.40 per site per day. **Bushcamping** is allowed in the park, except in the Wonderland Range and within 100m of a dam, river or creek, or within 50m of a road; but the staff at the National Park Visitor Centre will want to be informed about where and when you are going to pitch your tent. Besides the basic park campsites, there are dozens of **caravan parks** in the vicinity. The most convenient, *Halls Gap Caravan Park* (℡03/5356 4251, ℻5356 4421; cabins ❹, on-site vans ❸), is right opposite the shopping centre and so a bit noisy, but it's well equipped, and at the start of many walks. *Grampians Gardens Caravan Park* (℡03/5356 4244, cabins and vans ❸, motel units ❹), 3km out of town at the corner of the Ararat and Stawell Roads, is another good option. At the northern end of the park is *Roses Gap Recreation Centre* (℡03/5359 5264; ❸–❹), which has cabins, a camp kitchen and sheltered BBQ.

Brambuk Backpackers Grampians Rd ℡03/5356 4250. Run by the Aboriginal Cultural Centre, this hostel is clean, comfortable and friendly, making judicious use of natural space and light. Backpacker busline Groovy Grape stops here.

Dorms $20, rooms ❷–❸
Grampians Wonderland Cabins Ellis St, just off the Grampians Tourist Rd on the way to Brambuk ℡ & ℻ 03/5356 4264, ⊛www.grampians.net.au/wonderland. Beautiful

two-bedroom timber cabins in a bushland setting; good for a splurge. ❼–❽

Grand Canyon Motel Less than 1km north of Halls Gap on Grampians Rd ☎ 03/5356 4280, ℻ 5356 4513. The cheapest motel accommodation in the park. ❹–❺

Hall's Gap YHA Grampians Rd ☎ 03/5356 4544, ℮ grampians@yhavic.org.au. New hostel built according to environmentally friendly principles, recycling waste water and using solar electricity and wood-heating stoves. It's a huge place with excellent facilities, but a little too functional to be welcoming. Dorms $20, rooms ❸

Kingsway Holiday Flats Grampians Rd ☎ 03/5356 4202. Spartan, but cheap and clean self-catering accommodation, with TV and fully equipped kitchens. ❹

Kookaburra Motor Lodge 14 Heath St ☎ 03/5356 4395, ℻ 5356 4490. One of the better motels in town, with rooms facing a patio hung with plants, and a well-kept garden. ❺–❻

Mountain Grand Grampians Rd, Halls Gap ☎ 03/5356 4232, ℻ 5356 4254, ⓦ www .mountaingrand.com.au. Elegant, friendly guesthouse with a licensed restaurant and a jazz café cum bar downstairs. ❻–❽

Tim's Place Grampians Rd ☎ 03/5356 4288, ⓦ www.timsplace.com.au. Small, cosy, centrally located hostel with dorms, three doubles and a single which is particularly good value. The rates include continental breakfast with plunger coffee or good tea. Extras include cheap Internet access ($3/hr) and free use of mountain bikes. Dorms $22, rooms ❷

Eating, drinking and entertainment

There's no shortage of places to **eat** in Halls Gap, and you may want to venture beyond the rather touristy Stony Creek Stores complex on the main road which comprises the *Stony Creek Bakery* (daily 8am–5pm); the *Flying Emu Café* for cakes, snacks and light meals; the *Black Panther Café and Bar*, a relative newcomer, for coffee and cake; and *Coolas* which sells delicious home-made ice cream.

Away from the stores, the *Halls Gap Tavern*, Lot 5, Dunkeld Road (daily 5pm till late), is a pleasant, moderately priced **restaurant** and bar, while the *Kookaburra Restaurant* on Grampians Road (☎ 03/5356 4222) comes highly recommended for its inexpensive café-style dishes – mainly pasta and salads – and for its restaurant food, including venison and home-made ice cream. *Darcy's* at the *Colonial Motor Inn* on Grampians Road (daily from 6.30pm, bookings advisable on ☎ 03/5356 3440) is a motel restaurant dishing up good grub including emu. Both restaurants have local wines on their wine list.

For entertainment, there's Saturday night **jazz** at the *Mountain Grand Guest House* from 10pm; they also have a cocktail bar. An alternative **film festival** comes to town at the beginning of November, and there's a jazz festival in mid-February.

The Wimmera

The Wimmera, dry and hot, relies heavily on irrigation water from the Grampians for its vast wheatfields; before irrigation and the invention of the stump jump plough, the area was little more than mallee scrub, similar to the lands beyond **Warracknabeal**, the northernmost wheat-growing centre.

HORSHAM, capital of the wheatfields, makes a good stop-off point en route to Adelaide; it has an idyllic picnic spot, complete with barbecues, by the Wimmera River. However, there's little else to attract you here, though the Grampians National Park (see p.1007) is within striking distance to the southeast, and **Mount Arapiles**, 40km west, is one of the most important **rock-climbing** centres in Australia – if you're interested contact The Climbing Company in Natimuk (☎ 03/5387 1329), which can also organize

abseiling. The Horsham Visitor Information Centre, at 20 O'Callaghan Parade (daily 9am–5pm; ☎03/4382 1832 or 1800 633 218, ⓦwww.grampians.org.au), books both accommodation and **tours**. One central **place to stay** is the *Royal Hotel*, 132 Firebrace St (☎03/5382 1255; ❸), a grand old place established in 1881, which has retained many of its original features. The *Fig Tree Café*, 59 Firebrace St, serves coffee and snacks, while *Café Bagdad* at 48 Wilson St has a very local, slightly arty alternative feel and serves espresso, cakes and ice cream, as well as big portions of cheap soups, salads and focaccia.

Continuing on the Western Highway, you come to **DIMBOOLA**, deep in the dreary flatlands; it's the sort of place that runs to its own dusty clock, frustratingly closing down for lunch just as interstate buses stop for a break. The *Dimboola Motel* (☎03/5389 1177; ❹) and *Dimboola Hotel* (☎03/5389 1380; ❹) are both on Horsham Road. **NHILL** and **Kaniva**, further along the highway, are similarly undistinguished. All three towns are within a few kilometres of **Little Desert National Park**, with Nhill being the best starting point if you plan to explore. *Little Desert Lodge* (☎03/5391 5232; dorms $20, B&B rooms ❸), 16km southeast of the town on the Harrow Road, lies on the fringe of the park and runs good 4WD **tours**; it has camping, motel units and bunk rooms for groups. Far from being a desert, the national park has a great variety of plants, with colourful wild-flower displays in spring; much of the vegetation is low mallee scrub, among which the now rare mallee fowl can be spotted. There are three **campsites** within the national park: one on the Kiata South Road 13km from Kiata, east of Nhill – the others are at Horseshoe Bend and Ackle Bend, south of Dimboola (call Parks Victoria for more information on ☎03/5391 1255).

The Mallee

The Mallee, the most sparsely populated area of Victoria, begins north of Warracknabeal, from where the **Henty Highway** heads up to join the Sunraysia Highway and forge its way to Mildura, on the border with New South Wales. This is an area worth visiting only in winter, when it's drier and warmer than the rest of Victoria, but not too hot to make bushwalks unbearable. You really need your own transport to see anything; just about the only **public transport** is the small Henty Highway Coach that runs between Horsham and Mildura which mainly carries freight (departs Horsham BP service station Mon, Wed & Fri 7.45am, & Mildura train station Tues & Thurs at 9.15am; 5hr; $56. For bookings call ☎03/5382 4260 or 0427 865 379). Along the way are small dusty towns such as Brim, Bealah and **HOPETOUN** ("gateway to the Mallee"), whose shops still have their old awnings and apparently their original window displays too.

Fifty kilometres west of Hopetoun is **Wyperfeld National Park**, which at 3500 square kilometres is Victoria's third largest, with a chain of normally dry lake beds, mallee scrub, river red gum and black box woodlands, and rolling sand plains, with emus, kangaroos and mallee fowl among its wildlife. A sealed road leads from Hopetoun via Yampeet to the *Wonga Campground*, where there's shady camping ($10.40 per site per night, max 6 people; payable by self-registration) and a picnic area with water and toilets. Bushcamping is not allowed in the park. The Big Desert Wilderness is directly west of Wyperfeld but can be reached only by the Nhill–Murrayville track that runs between

Broken Bucket, northwest of Nhill, and Murrayville, on the Mallee Highway west of Ouyen; there are no tracks, roads or facilities in the park, just more sand dunes, mallee scrub and lots of wildlife. You'll need a 4WD and considerable dedication to get the most out of it.

Beyond Hopetoun, the Henty Highway merges into the Sunraysia Highway. Heading north on the Sunraysia, you come to the small town of **SPEED** – which could hardly have a less appropriate name; tourist information is available at the general store here. From here the mallee scrub tenaciously clings to the edges of the highway, threatening to invade the red soil of cleared fields on either side, and the equally red dust of the unsealed road. **OUYEN**, the "heart of the Mallee", is another small, undistinguished town where two highways meet. Heading west on the Mallee Highway, the access track to the picturesque **pink salt lakes** of the **Murray–Sunset (Yanga–Nyawi) National Park** leads north from Linga. Continuing north on the Calder Highway from Ouyen, you pass the **Hattah–Kulkyne National Park**, just east of the highway; the park consists of dry mallee scrub, native woodland, and a lakes system lined with gums. Lake Hattah is reached by turning off the highway at Hattah, 34km north of Ouyen, onto the Hattah–Robinvale Road. From Hattah it's less than 70km to Mildura and the Murray River.

The Murray region

From its source close to Mount Kosciuszko high in the Australian Alps, the **Murray River** forms the border between Victoria and New South Wales until it crosses into South Australia (someone got a ruler out for the rest of the border to the coast); although the actual watercourse is in New South Wales, the Victorian bank is far more interesting and more populous. After the entire length was navigated in 1836, the river became the route along which cattle were driven from New South Wales to the newly established town of Adelaide, and later in the century there was a thriving paddle-steamer trade on the lower reaches of the river, based at Wentworth on the New South Wales side (see p.361). In 1864, **Echuca** was linked by railway to Melbourne, stimulating the river trade in the upper reaches, and thus became a major inland port, the furthest extent of the navigable river. At the height of the paddle-steamer era, **Mildura** was still a run-down, rabbit-infested cattle station, but in 1887 the Chaffey brothers instituted irrigation projects that now support dairy farms, vineyards, vegetable farms and citrus orchards throughout northwestern Victoria. Between Mildura and Echuca, **Swan Hill** marks the transition to sheep, cattle and wheat country; the **Pioneer Settlement** here explores the extraordinarily hard lives of the early settlers. Above Echuca the Murray loses much of its magic as it flows through the more settled northeast.

Nowadays **paddle steamers** cruise for leisure, and are the best way to enjoy the river and admire magnificent **river red gums** lining its banks, as well as the huge array of birds and other wildlife that the Murray sustains. Renting a **houseboat** is also a relaxing (if expensive) way to travel.

Mildura and around

MILDURA has a mirage-like aura, its vineyards and orange orchards standing out from a hot, dry landscape. To the southwest is the evocatively named **Sunset Country**, with nothing but gnarled mallee scrub, red sand and pink salt lakes (reached via Linga on the Mallee Highway). Mildura makes a good winter getaway, but summer can be stiflingly hot – the green grape vines in the surrounding countryside and the flowers and towering red gums that line Deakin Avenue, the main thoroughfare, offer some relief, but you'd do best to avoid the area at this time if you can.

Deakin Avenue runs northwest through town to the river, with 7th Street and the train station facing the parklands that run along the river. Like any self-respecting small city, Mildura has a couple of malls, one running parallel to Deakin Avenue between 8th and 9th streets, and another, smaller one out of town at Deakin Avenue and 15th street. The **Mildura Visitor Information and Booking Centre** is situated in the state-of-the-art Alfred Deakin Centre at Deakin Avenue and 12th Street (Mon–Fri 9am–5.30pm, Sat & Sun 9am–5pm; ℡03/5021 4424 or 1800 039 043, ⓦwww.mildura tourism.com), which also houses a pool ($4.40) and gym, a decent café and a modern library, where you can check your email ($2/30min). The visitor centre will book accommodation and supply free town maps: they also have particularly good information on the Murray–Sunset (Yanga–Nyawi) and Hattah–Kulkyne national parks.

Down on the river the seventy-year-old **Mildura Weir** system, designed to provide stable pools for irrigation and to enable navigation throughout the year, makes a pleasant place to while away an hour or so. There's a pretty picnic spot by lock 11 (the trickiest), just beyond the art gallery at the arts centre. Alternatively, wander down to the **Mildura Arts Centre**, 199 Cureton Ave (daily 10am–5pm; gallery \$.2.50), which consists of a historic home, Rio Vista, the Mildura Regional Art Gallery, a theatre and a sculpture park. **Rio Vista** was built in 1890 for William Chaffey, who lived here with his first and second wives (both called Hattie Schell, the second the niece of the first) until he died in 1926. It's a lovely house, though rather ill-suited to the climate, and inside are various displays about the Chaffeys and the development of Mildura. The art gallery's most important piece is *Woman Combing Her Hair at the Bath*, a pastel by Edgar Degas; it also has some excellent sculpture by Australian artists.

Practicalities

Mildura is 555km from Melbourne, about as far as you can go in this small state; right on the border of New South Wales, and little over 100km from South Australia, it's ideally located for **onward transport** to either. Buses on the Sturt Highway, the major route between **Adelaide** and **Sydney**, pass through several times daily, with a McCafferty's/Greyhound Pioneer service to Adelaide at 8.50am and a service to Sydney at 5.30pm, and a 4am Countrylink service to Sydney via Cootamundra. From Melbourne, there's also a V/Line train-bus connection via Bendigo or Swan Hill at least twice daily (call ☎13 61 96 to book). **Broken Hill**, north up Silver City Highway, can be reached by bus via Wentworth (departing Mildura train station Mon, Wed & Fri 9am; 3hr 30min; book at the visitor information centre). **Ballarat** is served once a day (except Sat) by V/Line, whilst you can get to **Albury**, via Swan Hill, Echuca and Rutherglen, on Tuesday, Wednesday, Friday and Sunday. In terms of **local transport**, Coomealla Buslines runs a service across the river to Wentworth via Buronga (see p.1019), while the very regular Sunraysia Buslines (☎03/5023 0274) services the centre from 7th to 15th streets, and to suburban areas further to the east and west, and to the south as far as Red Cliffs. Alternatively, you can **rent a car** from, among others, Budget at 7th Street and Etiwanda Avenue (☎03/5021 4442).

Mildura has a good reputation as a place to obtain **work** as a fruit-picker; the only guaranteed time is in February, when the grape harvest takes place. Unfortunately, this is also the time when the heat is most intense. If you think you can handle it, come around the end of January, the beginning of the eight-week season. Otherwise, there's a chance of picking up work during the citrus harvest in June and August, and possibly vine pruning. For details, phone or call in at the Mildura and District Harvest Labour Office (corner of Deakin and 10th streets ☎03/5022 1797) or Employment National (Shop 2, corner of Ninth St & Lime Ave ☎1300 720 126). Most of the town's hostels have contacts with a wide range of employers. Some growers have accommodation, but normally you'll need your own transport and a tent.

Accommodation

Mildura has lots of reasonably priced **accommodation**, and an ever-increasing amount of hostels to cater to the hordes of hard-up backpackers that drift here looking for work. There's also a number of houseboats based in Mildura or across the river in Buronga or Wentworth. Weekly rates range from \$900–1900 for a luxurious boat. If you get a group together, the expenses can be quite reasonable. You'll need a driver's licence and must supply your own food. Ring the visitor information centre for information and bookings.

Adventure Houseboats Buronga ☎03/5023 4787, ⓦwww.adventure.ozland.net.au. Self-contained houseboat with laundry, CD player, TV and BBQ. Sleeps up to ten. ❺

Aquavilla Houseboats Wentworth ☎03/5027 3396 or 1800 039 094, ⓦwww.aquavilla.com.au. Three well-equipped boats with laundry, TV, radio-cassette player, and gas BBQ, one sleeping up to six, the other two boats up to ten people.

Carn Court Apartments 826 15th St ☎03/5023 6311 or 1800 066 675. Good, inexpensive choice if you want self-catering; also has an outdoor pool but is a bit out of town. ❺

Mildura Grand Hotel 7th St, opposite the train station ☎03/5023 0511, ⓕ5022 1801, ⓦwww.milduragrand.com. Recently restored hotel, complete with guest ballroom, bistro, games room, spa, sauna and outdoor swimming pool. Accommodation ranges from basic to luxurious, with breakfast included. The hotel's chef is very respected and an ABC TV star; see below. ❹–❼

Mildura International Backpacker 5 Cedar Ave ☎03/5021 0133, ⓔmibpackers@ncable.com.au. Work-oriented hostel with air-conditioning, recreation area, cable TV and laundry. The operators have work contacts, do all the paperwork required and organize transport to work. Rooms are twin-, three- and four-bedded. Only weekly stays accepted; $120 per person per week.

Nomads Juicy Grape International

Backpackers Block 446, Calder Highway, Sunnycliffs ☎03/5024 2112, ⓦwww.nomadsworld .com. Located 5km out of town, but there are free pick-ups from the bus stop and transport to jobs. Dorms $18, rooms ❷

River Beach Camping Ground Cureton Ave, Chaffey Bend ☎03/5023 6879. Well-equipped site 4km west of the centre, right on the Murray by the beach. Cabins and on-site vans ❷–❺

River Gardens Tourist Park Corner of Sturt Highway and Punt Road, Gol Gol, east of Buronga on the NSW-side of the river ☎03/5024 8541 or 1800 816 326. Well-equipped and right on the water. Cabins and on-site vans ❷–❺

Riverboat Bungalow 27 Chaffey Ave ☎03/5021 5315, ⓦwww.backpackers.com.au. This shambolic 1891 house is a work-and-play oriented place with work registry, Internet access, cable TV and a swimming pool in a large backyard near the river. Weekly rates available. Dorms $20, rooms ❷

Riverview B&B 115 Seventh St ☎03/5023 8975. Two rooms with en-suite in 1950s-style house overlooking the river; central location ❹

Zippy Koala Backpackers 206B 8th St ☎03/5021 5793 or 0412 185 150. Central work-oriented hostel, with small dorms, cable TV, air-conditioning, two kitchens, a beer garden and transport to work for guests. Weekly rates available. ❶

Eating and drinking

Healthy food abounds in Mildura's **cafés and restaurants**, most of which are clustered on Langtree Avenue, just south of the mall. If you have your own transport, you can make an enjoyable outing to buy fruit and vegetables from surrounding farms. Otherwise, there are three excellent supermarkets, including a 24-hour Coles, surrounding Langtree Mall. In the upmarket bracket, there's the renowned restaurant *Stefano's* – resident chef Stefano de Pieri put Mildura on the culinary map of Australia with his cooking show on ABC TV.

27 Deakin 27 Deakin Ave. This gorgeous shrine to food serves eclectic breakfasts and delicious frittata, salads and soups, as well as excellent coffee and cakes. Gourmet foodie haven/picnic shop inside. Mon–Fri 9am–7pm, Sat & Sun 9am–3pm.

Hudak's Bakery Café Langtree Mall, 8th St & Central Plaza. Good continental breads and delicious zucchini slices. Daily from 7am.

Mildura Grand Hotel *The Grand*, as it's known, incorporates three eateries: tucked away in the cellar its crowning glory, *Stefano's* (dinner

Mon–Sat; bookings essential ☎03/5023 0511) where there's no menu but the northern Italian banquets are excellent. The *Grand Pizza Caffe and Wine Bar* serves cakes, coffees, pasta and wood-fired pizzas (Mon–Thurs & Sun 10am–midnight, Fri & Sat 10am–1am) while the *Grand Bistro* does surf'n'turf (lunch Mon–Sat, dinner daily).

The Rendezvous 34 Langtree Ave ☎03/5023 1571. Cheap lunches and other meals served in the bistro. There's also an upmarket restaurant, as well as a bar and courtyard seating. Lunch Mon–Fri, dinner Mon–Sat.

Sunraysia Wine Centre Next to the *Restaurant Rendezvous* at 34 Langtree Ave (☎03/5023 1571) does cellar door sales. You can also sample local wines by the glass and have coffee and cake or snacks in the courtyard or on the terrace.

Taco Bills Langtree Ave. Cheap, substantial Mexican fare in cheery surroundings near the river. All main meals half-price on Tues. Tues–Sun from 6pm.

Nightlife

Mildura's nightlife may not be the world's greatest, but there's enough to keep you occupied. Perhaps the best thing to do is to try out one of the **clubs**, where you can be signed in as a visitor; as an incentive to get you to the gambling machines, there's lots of inexpensive food and drink. The *Mildura Workingman's Club*, on 90 Deakin Ave between 9th and 10th streets, is one of many in town. Established in 1895, the club reputedly has the world's longest bar – 91 metres. Another good place for a drink is the vibrantly coloured, youth-oriented *Sandbar* at 43 Langtree Ave (nightly until 1am; light meals until 10pm; happy hour Mon–Fri 5–8pm), which has a courtyard and puts on live music weekly in the summer and at weekends the rest of the year. *Dom's Nightclub*, upstairs from the restaurant of the same name at 32 Langtree Ave, is open Thursday to Saturday. If all else fails, *Malley's Irish Pub* on Deakin Avenue in the centre of town has regular drink promotions and live music Wednesday to Saturday; there's a $5 cover charge after 9.30pm at the weekends.

Around Mildura

The easiest excursion from Mildura is to **RED CLIFFS**, some 15km south, with its vineyards and tree-lined streets. The huge **Lindemans Karadoc Winery** (daily 10am–4.30pm) is one of the largest **wineries** in Australia, where fifty thousand tonnes of grapes are crushed every year. The range of wines for tasting is extensive, prices are very reasonable and there's a café serving light lunches, coffee and cake (Mon–Fri 10am–3pm).

Across the Murray from Mildura at **BURONGA** (actually in NSW but more readily accessible from the Victorian side of the river), Boatmen Hire Boats next to the bridge (☎03/5023 5874) rents out fishing boats for $25 per hour and canoes for $20 per hour. The nearby *Floating Café* (daily 10am–6pm) is a colourful pontoon moored in a lovely spot where there are lots of pelicans and ducks. Also at Buronga is the **BRL Hardy wine company** (Mon–Fri 10am–4pm, Sat 10.30am–4pm, Sun noon–4pm; ☎03/5023 4341), the largest cask winery in New South Wales, their most famous brand being Stanley Wines – you can taste the wine here or just pose for photos in front of the big wine cask outside. On a much smaller scale, **Trentham Estate Winery**, 10km down the Sturt Highway in an idyllic setting overlooking the river, has cellar door sales (Mon–Fri 9am–5pm, Sat & Sun 9.30am–5pm; and an upmarket restaurant (lunch Tues–Sun; dinner Sat; for bookings ☎03/5024 8888, ⓦwww .trenthamestate.com.au).

Swan Hill and around

Heading for Swan Hill, you can go south down the Calder Highway, turning east at Hattah onto the Hattah–Robinvale Road and continuing past the Hattah Kulkyne National Park (see p.1015). Alternatively, you can cross the Murray into New South Wales and follow the Sturt Highway, re-crossing the river at **ROBINVALE**, a small, rather characterless fruit-growing town, but idyllically situated within a great loop of the river. Wine buffs should make a stop at the **Robinvale Winery**, Sea Lake Road (Mon–Sat 9am–6pm, Sun 1–6pm ☏03/5026 3955, ⓦwww.organicwines.com.au), where a wide range of wines, including some Greek varieties, are biodynamically produced.

Twenty-five kilometres from Swan Hill you reach the highly productive stone-fruit and vegetable-growing area of **NYAH**. Bushcamping (no water or facilities) is allowed in the nearby Nyah and Vinefera **state forests** along the Murray; contact Parks Victoria (☏13 19 63). Eight kilometres beyond Nyah is the **Tyntynder Homestead** (open by appointment only on ☏03/5037 2754; $8), a classic 1846 bungalow furnished in wealthy squatter style and set amid flowering gardens. Part of the homestead is a museum containing, among other things, a collection of Aboriginal artefacts.

As you approach **SWAN HILL** itself, the landscape changes – this is cattle and sheep country, with wheatfields further north. The Murray here is shallow and tricky to navigate, so there's not much river traffic. Swan Hill is a service centre for the pastoral industry and has a typically solid, conservative atmosphere. Surprisingly, it's quite a multicultural place, having ten percent of Victoria's Aboriginal population, and a large Italian community. The Pioneer Settlement (see below) is undoubtedly Swan Hill's main attraction, but while you're here, you could also visit the **Swan Hill Regional Art Gallery** (Tues–Fri 10am–5pm, Sat & Sun 11am–5pm; donation of $2 appreciated; free guided tour Sun 1.30pm), which specializes in folk and Aboriginal art, or take a guided tour to the **Murray Downs Homestead**, an impressive Victorian mansion at the heart of a forty-square-kilometre station – it's over the bridge in New South Wales, but barely 1km from town (tour bus leaves the Kookaburra booking office at 2pm on Tues–Thurs & Sat–Sun; $8.50; ☏03/5032 0003). The town's **swimming pool** on Monash Drive (Nov–March Mon, Wed & Fri 6am–8pm, Tues, Thurs, Sat & Sun 11am–7pm; $2.50), has several pools and a waterslide, while the leisure centre has an indoor pool and a gym (Mon & Fri 6am–11am & 3.30–8pm, Tues–Thurs, Sat & Sun 6am–9am & 3.30–8.30pm; $3.50)

Pioneer Settlement

Swan Hill's **Pioneer Settlement**, a reconstruction of a pioneering community at Horseshoe Bend about 1km south of the train station, was the first of its kind in Australia and is still one of the best (daily 9am–5pm; $16; combination ticket for settlement, sound and light show and Pyab Cruise $34). The settlement may be closed for a short period every February; enquire on ☏03/5036 2410. The buildings are all authentic, having been transported from various sites near and far. One of the most interesting is the **Iron House**, an example of a nineteenth-century "kit home", many thousands of which were shipped out from Britain during the housing crisis that accompanied the gold-rush – cities and towns in Victoria had whole streets of them, and they were stiflingly hot in summer and freezing cold in winter. This particular example came from south Melbourne, where it was inhabited until 1967.

In the settlement's streets many of the **shops** are functional – the baker, the printer, the haberdashery and the porcelain doll shop – with assistants dressed in vaguely period costume. Generally, though, it's low-key and peaceful: buildings such as the barber's shop and the stock and station agents are open for you to wander around undisturbed. The pharmacy has a large collection of old medicines, with a gruesome dentist's surgery out back; the church is made from old bricks of the original courthouse; and there's even a rather creepy Masonic

Lodge, which is still in use. The **Mechanics Institute** has a traditional collection of books and a wonderful working "Stereoscopic Theatre" from 1895: the wooden cylinder has 25 viewfinders, each with a leather seat from which you can admire the 3D scenes. You can go on rides around the settlement in a 1924 Dodge or a horse-drawn carriage. In the evening, the **sound and light show** (nightly from dusk; $10) is strikingly effective.

The settlement is situated on the banks of the Marraboor River, a branch of the Murray. A wooden bridge spans the river to Pental Island, which has an assortment of native flora and fauna. Meanwhile, an old **paddle steamer**, the *Pyap*, cruises from the settlement upriver past Murray Downs every day at 10.30am and 2.30pm (1hr; $12), while the MV *Kookaburra* offers a longer luncheon cruise (1hr 30min; $29), departing at 12.30pm (Tues & Thurs-Sun).

Practicalities

The **Swan Hill Visitor Information Centre**, 306 Campbell St (daily 9am–5pm; ☎03/5032 3033 or 1800 625 373, ⓦ www.swanhillonline.com), has a free map of the town giving detailed information on local attractions; it also sells tickets for the Pioneer Settlement, its sound and light show and the MV *Kookaburra* and MV *Pyap* cruises. **Parks Victoria** at 1 McCallum St (Mon–Fri 8.30am–5pm; ☎03/5033 1290) can provide you with information on camping in the nearby Nyah and Vinefera state forests.

There's a strip of **motels**, all with swimming pools, along Campbell Street, where almost all the town's facilities are located. The most luxurious of the lot is the *Sundowner Swan Hill Resort* at no. 405 (☎1800 654 576, ⓕ03/5032 9109; ④–⑥) which has an indoor and outdoor pool and spa, gym and other sports facilities; it's easily located because of its restaurant, the *Silver Slipper*, which has a huge rotating stiletto outside and even tackier decor inside. The *Padddle Steamer Motel Holiday Resort* on the Murray Valley Highway, 3km south of the centre, has very good facilities and is much cheaper (☎03/5032 2151 ③). Also good value and much closer to the centre is *Jacaranda Holiday Units* at 179 Curlewis St (☎03/5032 9077; ③). The *Riverside* at 1 Monash Drive (☎03/5032 1494; on-site vans ②–③, cabins ③–④) is a good, centrally located **caravan park** right on the riverfront.

Swan Hill **restaurants** still demonstrate a culinary Italian influence. *Bartalotta's Hot Bread Kitchen*, at 178 Campbell St, is excellent, as is *Quo Vadis*, an authentic pizzeria at 255 Campbell St serving pasta and ribs as well as pizza; a branch of the pizza-pasta restaurant chain *La Porchetta*, a newcomer in town, serves its very inexpensive pizza and pasta at no. 423. Next door is *Teller's Café Restaurant & Bar* at no. 22, a slick-looking, city-style brasserie in an old bank, open daily for lunch and dinner. *Café 202*, at 202 Beveridge St, serves tasty lunch-time options and good, strong coffee.

Swan Hill to Gunbower Island

From Swan Hill, the Murray Valley Highway heads southeast, away from the river, and follows the rail line past a series of about fifty freshwater lakes. At the first of these, **Lake Boga**, 16km from Swan Hill, you'll find Lake Boga Jet Ski Hire and Parasailing. Also by the lake – follow the signs – is Best's at St. Andrew's Winery, a large, commercial **winery**, the oldest in the Swan Hill region (Mon–Fri 10am–5pm, Sat 10am–4pm, Sun noon–4pm during holidays; tours Mon–Fri 11am–3pm; ☎03/5037 2154). The lakes peter out at Kerang, a sizeable town in a citrus-growing area on the Loddon River. Nearby Lake Reedy is one of the largest ibis-breeding grounds in Australia and has a viewing hide; the birds are widespread in the area, though, so you probably won't have any trouble seeing some.

From Kerang, the Murray Valley Highway continues east to Cohuna, in a rich dairy-farming area, and from there towards **Gunbower Island**, a further 23km. The "island", encircled by the Murray River and Gunbower Creek, is a state forest of huge red gums and Gunnawarra wetlands, with 160 species of birds and a lot of wildlife. It's most easily approached from Cohuna (follow the signs on the Kerang–Koondrook road); for details of walks and camping contact Parks Victoria (☎13 19 63).

Echuca and around

ECHUCA, a lively and progressive place, is the most easily accessible river town from Melbourne – it's only three hours or so by bus or car, making it a popular weekend getaway. Echuca became the largest inland port in Australia after the railway line connected it with Melbourne in 1864. When the **missions** began to close in the 1930s, many Aboriginal families, especially Yorta Yorta people from Cummeragunja mission, and Wemba Wemba from Moonacullah mission, migrated to the Echuca area. Since they weren't made welcome in the towns, the migrants were forced to live on the fringes in badly constructed, flood-prone housing, just close enough to be able to get to work and school. Women commonly worked in the canneries and hospitals, and the men packed fruit, sheared sheep and did other labouring jobs.

Nowadays, **Port of Echuca**, with its massive wharves and collection of old buildings, is a major tourist attraction, and several cruises ply along the river from here. The town itself, however, is not too touristy, and has retained much of its charm. There are two principal streets: High Street, the former main street, leads to Murray Esplanade and the wharf, and is the centre of tourist activity, with lots of cafés and boutiquey shops; while Hare Street, the present-day main street, is lined with more commercial buildings.

Port of Echuca

To enter the old wharf area, dubbed the **Historic Wharf** (daily 9am–5pm), you'll need to pay a $10 entrance fee, which also allows entry to the *Star Hotel* and the *Bridge Hotel*. Alternatively, you can combine a tour with a cruise on the *Pevensey* or the *Alexander Arbuthnot* (see opposite) for $20. The **Star Hotel** was first licensed in 1867 and is a typical pioneer pub, a tiny one-storey building with a tin roof and verandah. As the river trade declined, the *Star* was delicensed (in 1897), along with many of the other 79 hotels in town. Drinking on the premises became illegal, so the loyal clientele dug a tunnel to the street through which they could escape at the first hint of a police raid – you can examine this, along with the cellar and a small museum.

The magnificent red-gum **wharf** was nearly a mile long in its prime and is still fairly extensive. Three landing platforms at different levels allowed unloading, even during times of flooding, and there are wonderful views from the top, high over a bend in the river. Goods were transferred from train to steamer via this top level, and old train carriages sit on sidings here, piled high with trunks of red gum. You can wander below to the other levels, through a network of thick river-red-gum piles standing 12m high. At the lowest level, several **old boats** are moored, including the *Pevensey*, a 1911 steam-driven cargo boat which you can wander aboard; **cruises** are available on either the *Pevensey* or

A wide choice of **cruises** is on offer, departing from berths just beyond the old wharf, best approached from High Street. One-hour port cruises are available on the PS *Pride of the Murray* (daily 9.45am, 11am, 12.15pm, 1.30pm, 2.30pm & 3.45pm; $13.50; ☏03/5482 5244). The PS *Canberra* which usually does one-hour cruises was being refurbished at the time of writing (enquiries ☏03/5482 2711). The PS *Emmylou*, a wood-fired paddle steamer, has a variety of cruises ☏03/5480 2237, ⓦwww.emmylou.com.au), while the MV *Mary Ann* does lunch cruises (12.30pm; 2hr; $44) and dinner cruises (7pm; 3.5hr; $65). Kingfisher Wetland Cruises (☏03/5480 1839) offers a two-hour eco-cruise through the Barmah wetlands some 30km upstream of the Murray, which contain the world's largest single stand of river red gums (see overleaf).

the similar *Alexander Arbuthnot* daily (☏03/5482 4248; $16.50). In the wharf cargo shed there's a scale model of the working port and a ten-minute audio-visual presentation.

Back outside the wharf complex, along Murray Esplanade opposite Hopwood Gardens, is the **Bridge Hotel**, opened in 1858 but delicensed in 1916. It was built by the founder of Echuca, Henry Hopwood, an ex-convict who also started a punt service across the Murray; the story goes that if the pub wasn't doing well he'd close the ferry down for a few hours, leaving prospective passengers with little else to do but drink. Other attractions in the area include the **Red Gum Works** (daily 9am–5pm; free), housed in a large loading shed which is wonderfully scented by the wood as it's transformed from tree-trunk to souvenir; there's also a steam-operated sawmill and a blacksmith at work. The **Movie House & Penny Arcade** screens silent movie classics continuously, and visitors can work the old gambling machines of the "penny arcade", all for a rather steep admission fee of $12. The **World in Wax Museum**, 630 High St (daily 9am–5pm; $9), displays sixty wax figures of "famous personalities" which include Charles and Di, Paul Hogan and Dame Nellie Melba, as well as a diorama depicting various murderers.

Practicalities

The **tourist information centre**, 2 Heygarth St (daily 8am–5pm; ☏03/5480 7555 or 1800 804 446, ⓦwww.echucamoama.com), sells tickets to the port complex and for cruises, books accommodation and is an agent for V/Line and Countrylink **bus** tickets. V/Line runs up to six services between Melbourne and Echuca (train-bus and one direct train); there is also one daily connection with Sydney via Albury, and two to Adelaide (one direct, one via Bendigo).

Accommodation

As well as the **accommodation** options listed below, ask at the tourist office about the many **houseboats** available to rent in the area.

Echuca Caravan Park Crofton St, Victoria Park ☏03/5482 2157. A well-equipped caravan park right on the riverfront. Cabins ❸–❹
Echuca Gardens YHA 103 Mitchell St ☏03/5480 6522 (8–10am & 5–10pm), ⓔechuca@yhavic .org.au. Offers budget accommodation in a restored Victorian worker's cottage – very atmospheric, but the tiny dorms are cramped. The location on the edge of the Banyule Forest is very scenic, though, and it's a ten-minute walk through red gums to sandy river beaches where it's safe to swim on the inner bends. Dorms $20, rooms ❷–❸

Echuca Hotel 571 High St ☎ 03/5482 1087. The town's first pub, which still has some of its original features and offers simple accommodation in large pleasant rooms. ➍

Nomads Oasis Backpackers 410–424 High St ☎ 03/5480 7866, ⒺΓnomads@river.net.au. Centrally located, air-conditioned dorms as well as twins/doubles at an affordable price; has a small kitchen and a courtyard. The owner has outdoor employment contacts and can provide transport to places of work. Dorms $20, rooms ➋

River Gallery Inn 578 High St ☎ & Ⓕ 03/5480 6902, Ⓔ inn@echuca.net.au. Upmarket B&B accommodation in a pretty, historic home: seven of the eight self-contained rooms here have open fireplaces, and five have spas. ➎–➐

River Valley Nudist Resort ☎ 03/5482 6650, Ⓦ www.rivervalley.com.au. A thriving nudist resort, near Echuca in a bushland setting along the Goulburn River. ➌

Steam Packet Inn Corner of Leslie St and Murray Esplanade ☎ 03/5482 3411. A National Trust-listed motel in the heart of the old port area. ➎

Eating and drinking

With hungry Melburnians to feed, there's no shortage of decent **eating places**.

American Hotel Corner of Heygarth and Hare streets. Inexpensive, old-fashioned pub meals.

Beechworth Bakery 513 High St near the Campaspe River. Sells a variety of breads baked in a wood-fired oven, sandwiches, pastries and other snacks. It has a sun deck which is a good spot for breakfast or lunch. Daily 6am–7pm.

Black Pudding Delicatessen 525 High St near the Campaspe and Murray rivers. Does lots of deli snacks like frittata, baguettes, bruschetta, French onion tarts, plus black pudding and good coffee. Specials change daily. Licensed, lovely courtyard. Tues–Fri 9.30am–6pm, Sat & Sun 9.30am–3pm.

Bridge Hotel Hopwood Place. This coffee shop, bar and restaurant in the historic port area serves good coffee, cakes and desserts, light lunches and mainly traditional Aussie dishes in the restaurant. Open daily for breakfast, lunch and dinner; the bar is open daily 7.30am–1am, Sun till 11.30pm.

Echuca Dock Café, Bar & Restaurant Heygarth St opposite the American Hotel. Cosy café and bar with a more upmarket restaurant. Daily from 10am.

Fiori 554 High St ☎ 03/5482 6688. Rustic trattoria serving very good, authentic northern Italian food. Licensed. Daily from 6.30pm.

Giorgio's on the Port 527 High St ☎ 03/5482 6117. Another Italian restaurant with a good reputation. Licensed. Daily from 6pm.

La Porchetta 196 Annesley St ☎ 03/5480 1130. Inexpensive pizza and pasta chain restaurant. Good-value meals. Licensed. Open daily.

Oscar W Murray Esplanade ☎ 03/5482 5133. This restaurant serves excellent, superbly presented food to match the scenic setting next to the old Echuca Wharf, overlooking the Murray River. The cuisine is Mediterranean-inspired "mod Oz". Moderate to expensive. Licensed.

Suttons 216 Hare St. Old-fashioned Aussie bakery selling a variety of breads as well as pies and pasties.

Top of the Town High St, opposite the Aquatic Centre. Does excellent-quality, freshly cooked fish, including river fish, and chips.

Wistaria Tearooms High St opposite the Shamrock Hotel, or enter from the port. In a lovely Victorian house. Breakfast and light meals, coffee and cakes. Licensed. Daily 8am–6pm.

Nightlife

There's enough going on to keep you occupied. The **clubs** serve very cheap meals and drinks, presumably as an incentive to get you to their gambling machines – non-members can sign in as visitors. The bistro restaurant at the Echuca Workers and Sports Club, 165 Annesley St, is open for lunch and dinner daily (☎ 03/5482 3140); there are more clubs across the river in Moama.

The small and friendly *American Hotel* is a good place to head for a **drink**. The *Harvest Hotel*, 183 Hare St, draws a youngish crowd and plays host to live bands at weekends, likewise the *Red Dog Saloon Bar* at the corner of Nish and Darling streets. The OPT Entertainment Complex at 273 Hare St has a restaurant, bar and pool tables; the nightclub there is open Friday and Saturday also Sunday on long weekends. The brand new Paramount Cinemas & Performing

Arts Centre at 392 High St has an auditorium and four cinemas with state-of-the-art facilities (℡03/5482 3399, Ⓦwww.echucaparamount.com). If you happen to be around in mid-February, visit Echuca for the **Jazz, Food and Wine Weekend**.

Around Echuca

Thirty kilometres southeast of Echuca, Kyabram's main attraction is **Kyabram Fauna Park** (daily 9.30am–5.30pm or 8.30pm in summer; $8.50), a community-owned wildlife park divided into grassland for free-ranging kangaroos, wallabies, emus and other animals, and a huge wetland area. You can wander around the grassland area and through several aviaries. A two-storey observation tower affords views of the more than eighty species of native birdlife. Diamond pythons, tiger snakes, crocodiles and other not-so-pleasant creatures can be viewed from a safe distance at the Reptile House.

BARMAH, some 30km upstream on the Murray, is most easily reached by crossing into NSW at Echuca and heading north on the Cobb Highway, then turning east. This small river town is associated with red-gum milling, and with sleeper-cutting in the early railway days. The *Barmah Caravan Park* (℡03/5869 3225; ❶–❸) has a great site on the banks of the river among red gums, with a small, sandy beach for swimming. **Barmah State Park**, 10km out of town, has Australia's largest stands of **river red gum**, some of them 40m tall and five hundred years old. The forest runs along the Murray for over 100km and stands in an extensive flood plain – **canoeing** among the trees at flood time (July–Nov) is a magical experience; you can arrange transport and rent canoes from Echuca Boat and Canoe Hire (℡03/5480 6208, Ⓦwww.echucaboatcanoehire.com). During the wet season more than two hundred species of waterbird come here, and there's plenty of other wildlife; you might even see brumbies (wild horses). When it's dry you can use several well-established walking tracks: the place was of special significance to the Yorta Yorta Aborigines and you can still see fish traps, middens and scars on trees where the bark was used for canoes. During the **Barmah Cattle Muster** every April, two thousand head of cattle that are grazed in the forest are mustered in a frenzied, exciting atmosphere.

Yorta Yorta culture and lore are explained in the park's **Dharnya Centre** (daily 10.30am–4pm; ℡03/5869 3302), which also has archeological information and artefacts. A **cruise** in the MV *Kingfisher* leaves from the bridge near the centre (Mon, Wed, Thurs, Sat & Sun, plus other days during busy times; 2hr; $20; booking essential on ℡03/5840 1839) – a flat-bottomed boat that glides over Barmah Lake and through stands of red gum. Bushcamping is permitted in the park; contact Parks Victoria (℡13 19 63) for details.

Gippsland

GIPPSLAND stretches southeast of Melbourne from Western Port Bay to the New South Wales border, between the Great Dividing Range and Bass Strait. Green and well watered, it's been the centre of Victoria's dairy industry since

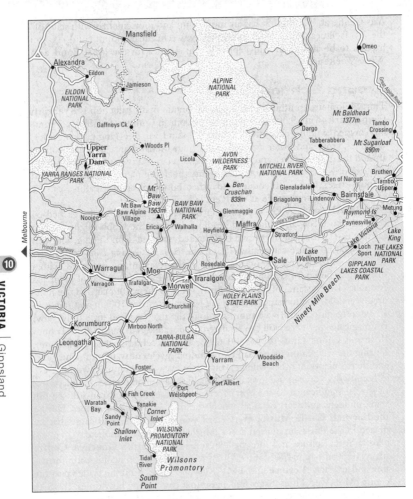

the 1880s. **South Gippsland** is also, in contrast, the site of vast brown-coal deposits between Moe and Traralgon in the Latrobe Valley, where power stations generate more than 85 percent of the state's electricity while, offshore, Bass Strait wells exploit natural gas and crude oil reserves with several gas-processing and oil-stabilizing plants disfiguring the coastline. South Gippsland also has Victoria's most popular national park, **Wilsons Promontory**, or "The Prom", a hook-shaped landmass jutting out into the strait, with some superb scenery and fascinating bushwalks. In the east, around the **Gippsland Lakes** and **Ninety Mile Beach**, the region is unindustrialized; and just beyond Orbost–Marlo the unspoilt coastline of the **Croajingolong National Park** – with its rocky capes, high sand dunes and endless sandy beaches – stretches to the New South Wales border.

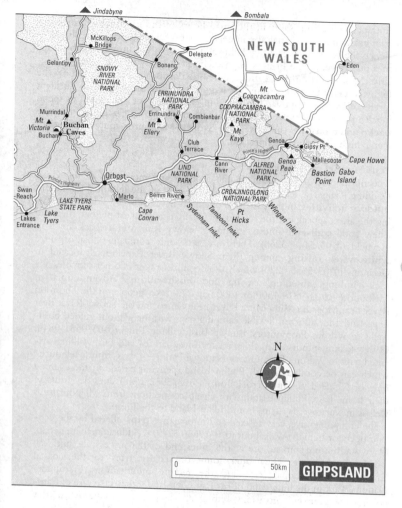

GIPPSLAND

Transport

V/Line **trains** run from Melbourne to Sale, basically following the Princes Highway through South Gippsland. From Sale, **buses** leave for Orbost, stopping at Lakes Entrance. The Sapphire Coast Link is a daily train–bus connection between Melbourne and Narooma on the south coast of New South Wales: take the train to Sale, then a connecting bus along the Princes Highway via Lakes Entrance, Orbost, Cann River and Genoa. Similarly, the Capital Link train/bus service heads to Canberra via Sale on Monday and Thursday mornings, returning Tuesday and Friday afternoons. Bookings for all the above should be made through V/Line (☎ 13 61 96, ⓦ www.victrip.com.au). There's also a daily McCafferty's/Greyhound Pioneer service along the coast from Melbourne to Sydney, but it's not very convenient if you want to get off at stops in East Gippsland: the bus leaves Melbourne at 10pm and gets to Lakes

Entrance and Cann River in the small hours of the morning. Having your own **car** is almost essential, as you need to get off the highway to really experience the region's diverse highlights and to get to the unspoilt bush campsites on the coast. The Princes Highway itself is a very boring drive, particularly the stretch from the Latrobe Valley to Bairnsdale, but after Orbost the highway becomes more scenic as it goes through the tall, dense eucalypt forests of Far East Gippsland. If you don't have a car, or don't want to spend much money, you might want to consider travelling on Oz Experience, the **backpacker bus** line that covers the Sydney–Melbourne route via the very scenic high country and Gippsland.

Tours and activities

The north part of Gippsland, in the foothills and mountains of the Great Dividing Range, is Victoria's "high country" – and it's ideally suited for a lot of **outdoor activities**. In the past, local operators have been a bit slow in exploiting the area's appeal, but the scene is gradually changing. At present, there are a few good **trail-ride** outfits, including Snowy Range Horseback Tours in Heyfield (℡03/5148 3268). There are also some companies that organize **white-water rafting**, among them Snowy River Expeditions, located in Gelantipy (℡03/5155 0220) which also organizes a host of other activities like rock-climbing, abseiling, caving and **bushwalking**. Adventurama in Melbourne (℡03/9819 1300 or 1300 652 277) takes people on the Thomson River near Moe, the Mitta Mitta River near Omeo and the Snowy River near Gippsland; they also run flexible camping trips with or without guided bushwalks to Wilsons Promontory. Bunyip Bushwalking Tours (℡03/9531 0840, Ⓦwww@bunyiptours.com) does inexpensive, nature- and bushwalking-oriented trips to Wilson's Promontory National Park (1–4 days) from Melbourne which can be combined with Phillip Island (penguin parade in the evening only, or whole day). Duck Truck Tours (℡03/5952 2548) does day-tours of their home base, Phillip Island, with cheap connections from Melbourne, as well as inexpensive day-trips from Phillip Island to the Prom.

The comprehensive, very relaxed and informative **trips** offered by the eco-tour operator Echidna Walkabout (℡03/9646 8249, Ⓔekidna@netcore.net.au, Ⓦwww.adventure.com.au) are at the other end of the price scale, but well worth the expense. They offer four- or six-day trips to the coastal Croajingolong National Park and the remote mountainous Errinundra National Park in the hinterland of Far East Gippsland – they take care of transporting the gear and provisions, setting up camp and cooking. Most tour companies don't operate during the winter months.

Wilsons Promontory and Tarra Bulga

WILSONS PROMONTORY, the most southerly part of the Australian mainland, was once joined by a land bridge to Tasmania. Its barbed hook juts out into Bass Strait, with a rocky coastline interspersed with sheltered sandy bays and coves; the coastal scenery is made even more stunning by the backdrop of granite ranges. It's understandably Victoria's most popular **national park**. Though the main campsite gets totally packed in summer, there are plenty of walking tracks and opportunities for bushcamping; the park's big enough to allow you to escape the crowds, with about 130km of coastal scenery, and inland areas covered with tall forests, heathlands and salt marshes.

You can swim at several of the beaches and even **surf**: Wilsons Prom Surf School, based at Tidal River, operates courses for all ages and abilities, with all equipment provided (T03/5680 8512).

There's no public transport to Wilsons Promontory; the nearest you can get to it is with the evening V/Line bus from Dandenong to Yarram. You need to get off at **FOSTER** on the South Gippsland Highway where you can stay overnight at the intimate and idiosyncratic *Foster Backpackers Hostel* (T03/5682 2614), either in small dorms in a cosy house ($20), or in a self-contained cottage on the same grounds ($50 sleeps 3–4); check in at the office on 17 Pioneer St. The hostel runs a transport service to Tidal River in the national park (daily; $15 per person one-way, min 2 passengers), and rents out camping equipment. If you're coming from Phillip Island, Duck Truck Tours based at *Amaroo Park YHA* in Cowes (T03/5952 2548) has good trips to Wilson's Promontory, including bushwalking (1 day; $75) and camping ($175; all gear provided). Melbourne-based Bunyip Bushwalking Tours (T03/9531 0840, Wwww .bunyiptours.com) offers an array of nature-focused trips to the Prom: a one-day "Escape" ($90; daily), a two-day Bushwalking Tour ($230; 3 times weekly) and a three-day Coastal Circuit Hike ($300; twice weekly). All of these can be combined with the penguin parade or a longer tour of Phillip Island; all food and camping gear provided – sleeping bags and backpacks can be rented. Detailed information on all sorts of accommodation within touring vicinity of Wilsons Promontory is available from Wwww.promaccom.com.au.

With your own vehicle, the easiest way to get here from Melbourne is to follow the **South Gippsland Highway** to Meeniyan, where you turn right onto Route 189 which takes you all the way to the park entrance. Once you get into the park, it's 30km to **Tidal River** on a good sealed road. At the entrance you pay $9 per car – if you stay overnight, this is deducted from the cost. The **information centre** (daily 8.30am–4.30pm; T03/5680 9555 or 1800 350 552, Wwww.parkweb.vic.gov.au) at Tidal River is an obvious first stop. They have plenty of information, though not all of it is on display, so ask: the small booklet *Discovering the Prom on Foot* ($14.95) is invaluable if you're attempting any of the overnight **walks**. Tidal River, situated by a small river on Norman Bay, is the park's main camping and accommodation centre; colourful rainbow lorikeets fly around and land to be fed from people's hands. There's also a general store here open daily, with a pricey supermarket section, takeaway food, fuel pumps and LP gas. Accommodation is arranged through the information centre, although from Christmas until the end of April – especially during public and school holidays – it's virtually impossible to get somewhere to stay; many places are booked up to a year in advance. **Accommodation** in the very basic motor huts (use of the campsite's facilities; linen not supplied) works out at $13 per person if you're in a group of four to six people. The camping area has about 480 non-powered campsites ($18.50 per night for 3 adults and 1 car; additional cars and people extra; max 8 people per site). Facilities include ablution blocks with hot showers, a laundry and a summer outdoor cinema. There are also some very spruce and comfortable self-contained holiday units sleeping up to six people (6 for two adults, plus $18.50 each extra adult).

Many short walks begin from Tidal River, including a track accessible to wheelchairs. One of the best is the **Squeaky Beach Nature Walk** (1hr return), which crosses Tidal River, heads uphill and through a tea-tree canopy, finally ending on a beach of pure quartz sand that is indeed squeaky underfoot. **The Lilly Pilly Gully Nature Walk** (3hr return) is very rewarding, as it affords an excellent overview of the diverse vegetation of "the Prom", from low-growing shrubs to heathland to open eucalypt forest, as well as scenic views. The walk starts at the Lilly Pilly Gully car park near Tidal River, follows a small valley and returns to the car park along the slopes of Mount Bishop. For **overnight camping** ($6.20 per person per night), you need to obtain a **permit** from the information centre at Tidal River (see p.1029), as there is a restriction on the number of people allowed on the campsites. Half the sites at each camping area are reserved for advance bookings (at least 21 days in advance for holidays and long weekends; credit-card phone bookings accepted), while the remaining sites can be booked on arrival in the park. From September until the end of April, restrictions to the length of stay apply to the southern section of the park: only one night at each campsite, two at the *Roaring Meg* campsite. Hikers must use a gas-fuel stove as open fires are not allowed anywhere, and absolutely all rubbish must be carried out. Water from creeks is usually okay but the rangers recommend sterilizing it.

The tracks in the southern section of the park are well defined and not too difficult; the campsites here have pit toilets and fresh water. The most popular walk here is the two- to three-day (37km) **Sealers Cove–Refuge Cove–Waterloo Bay** route, beginning and ending at the Mount Oberon car park. Crowds are much thinner in the remote north of the park, where there are no facilities (except for pit toilets at Tin Mine Cove) and limited fresh water: this is the province of experienced, properly equipped bushwalkers. However, during summer holidays and at long weekends between November and the end of April, all tracks become extremely busy, so book well in advance or show up early.

Tarra Bulga National Park

Another good national park can be reached from Yarram, 50km beyond Foster on the South Gippsland Highway. **Tarra Bulga National Park**, in the heart of the Strzelecki Ranges, is dominated by forests of mountain ash and myrtle beech with a lower canopy of ferns – a cool green environment alive with colourful lyrebirds, crimson rosellas and yellow-breasted robins among the rich birdlife. The **visitors information centre** (Sat & Sun, daily in summer and Easter holidays, usually 10am–4pm; ☎03/5196 6166) at Balook on the Grand Ridge Road, between the two separate sections of the park, has information about the park (geology, history, flora and fauna) and the walks. The Grand Ridge Road (mostly unsealed) winds along the top of the Strzelecki Ranges through fern gullies and towering trees, affording gorgeous views of South Gippsland. The *Tarra Bulga Guest House* (☎03/5196 6141; ❹), on a beef and lamb property on Grand Ridge Road just 50m from the visitors centre, has every amenity, including a library and games room.

The Gippsland Lakes region

The **Gippsland Lakes**, Australia's largest system of inland waterways, are fed by the waters of the Mitchell, Nicholson and Tambo rivers, and are separated from the sea by Ninety Mile Beach. East of Yarram, the beach stretches long and straight towards **Lakes Entrance**, the tacky focal point of the area and one of Victoria's most popular holiday spots, with the foothills of the high country within easy reach to the north.

SALE, at the junction of the South Gippsland Highway and the Princes Highway, is a good point from which to head off to explore the coastal park and

Ninety Mile Beach. From Seaspray, 35km south, a coastal road hugs the shore for 20km to Golden Beach, from where a scenic drive heads through the Gippsland Lakes Coastal Park to Loch Sport; here you're faced with the enviable dilemma of lakes on one side and ocean beaches with good surfing on the other. An unsealed road then continues on to Sperm Whale Head in the Lakes National Park. Sale's **tourist information centre** (daily 9am–5pm; ☎1800 677 520, Ⓦwww.gippslandinfo.com.au), on the Princes Highway, can provide you with all the details. They can also give information about the **Bataluk Cultural Trail**, which starts in Sale and links sites of cultural and spiritual significance to the Gunai people, the original inhabitants of the Gippsland coast. The first stop on the trail, the Rahmayuck Aboriginal Corporation at 117 Foster St in Sale, sells arts and crafts, paintings and T-shirts (usually Mon–Fri 9am–5pm).

BAIRNSDALE is the next major town on the highway east of Sale and serves as another departure point for the lakes to the south. The efficient staff at the **tourist office** on Main Street (daily 9am–5pm; ☎03/5152 3444 or 1800 637 060, Ⓦwww.lakesandwilderness.com.au) will provide all the local information you'll need. The well set-up exhibition at the Krowathunkoolong Keeping Place, parallel to the Princes Highway at 37–53 Dalmahoy St (Mon–Fri 9am–5pm; $4), explains the history of the Gunai people. Bairnsdale Air Charter (☎03/5152 4617) arranges cheap scenic flights from the Bairnsdale Aerodrome over the extensive waterways of the Gippsland Lakes (10min; from $25 per person; min 2 people). In Bairnsdale itself, try the *Grand Terminus Hotel* at 98 McLeod St for budget accommodation (☎03/5152 4040; ❷–❸). A gorgeous – if very pricey – option is the luxurious *Lake Gallery B&B* (☎03/5156 0556 or 0409 560 448, Ⓦwww.lakegallerybedandbreakfastcom; ❼) in **Paynesville**, 16km south of Bairnsdale, which has two designer-decorated guest suites at the water's edge and its own jetty.

A short ferry ride away across the McMillan Straits from Paynesville is **Raymond Island** which, with its prolific birdlife, kangaroos and koalas, is an idyllic place to stay. The Raymond Island Ferry runs every half-hour throughout the day (Mon–Thurs 7am–10.30pm, Fri & Sat 7am–midnight, Sun 8am–10.30pm; $6 return; ☎03/5150 9100. Accommodation options on the island include two cabins at *espas*, sleeping a maximum of six people each (☎03/5156 0983, Ⓦwww.espas.com.au; ❹) – there's a courtyard kitchen for guests, and the licensed *café espas* does very good breakfasts, lunches and dinners on Fridays and Saturdays 10am–late (Sun till 5pm) by the waterfront. Otherwise, you can stay at *Currawong Cottage* (☎03/5156 7226, Ⓦwww.visitvitoria.com; ❹), a cute timber cottage with two bedrooms and full kitchen facilities.

Forty-five kilometres northwest of Bairnsdale is another site on the Bataluk Cultural Trail, the **Den of Nargun** in the **Mitchell River National Park**. According to a Gunai legend, the small cave here was inhabited by a large female creature, a *nargun*, who would abduct people who wandered off on their own. As the Den of Nargun was a special place for Gunai women and may have been used for initiation ceremonies, the story served the purpose of keeping unauthorized people away. The cave is located in a small, beautiful valley; follow the loop track from the park picnic area via a lookout to the Mitchell River (30min), then take the track along Woolshed Creek to the cave and climb up the steep path back to the starting point (40min).

Lakes Entrance and Metung

The sandy barrier between the Gippsland Lakes and the sea was formed about six thousand years ago; when first seen by white men in the 1840s the outlet to the sea was a seasonal, intermittent gap, unsuitable for reliable trade. In 1889 the present stable entrance was opened 6km east of the old one: the artificial entrance effectively cuts off the town's access to the length of **Ninety Mile Beach**, and means that it's no longer really ninety miles either.

As you might expect from the area's popularity, **LAKES ENTRANCE** is a big, rather tawdry, tourist town, with loads of motels at either end of town as you enter from the highway. There are all sorts of attractions aimed at keeping holidaying children happy – from Fun Park to minigolf – on the Esplanade, which fronts onto an arm of Lake King. The **Griffiths Sea Shell Museum** at 125 Esplanade (daily 9am–5pm; $5), with its rather off-putting 1950s-style facade, has a huge collection of shells and marine life, as well as an aquarium containing an intriguing assortment of fish from the Gippsland Lakes. Lakes Entrance is also a big **fishing port**; the Fishermans Cooperative Wharf has a viewing platform where you can watch the catch being unloaded, as well as a tantalizing fish shop.

Beaches are obviously the big attraction here. Lakes Entrance Surf Beach, a substantial stretch of white sand patrolled in season by surf lifesavers, can be reached via a footbridge across the lake to Hummocks Reserve. Of the many **lake cruises** on offer, one of the most popular is the trip from the *Club Hotel* jetty at the western end of town, up North Arm to the Wyanga Park Winery – the most famous local winery – on the fringe of the Colquhoun Forest, in the winery's own boat, the *Corque* (daily lunch cruise $40, Fri & Sat dinner cruise $62, Sun brunch cruise $32; book at Lakes Entrance Tourist Information, or through the winery on ☎03/5155 1508). Other lake activities include environmentally friendly, electric-powered cruises on Lake Tyers, just east of Lakes Entrance, with MB *Rubeena* (boats leave from Fisherman's Landing; from $20; ☎03/5155 1283), and three-hour **fishing** trips, including morning or afternoon tea, with Mulloway Fishing Charters (☎0427 943 154). Those who prefer less watery pursuits could try the excellent Lakes Entrance Wilderness Trail Rides, offering **horseback treks** for all levels through bushland replete with all sorts of wildlife ($25 per hour, call for longer or overnight rates; ☎03/5156 3288).

Practicalities

Lakes Entrance Tourist Information (daily 9am–5pm; ☎1800 637 060), on the Esplanade, provides local advice and tickets for cruises on the lakes, and can also book accommodation, a useful service in summer when the place gets very crowded.

Accommodation

The two town **hostels** are both excellent, while most of the motels are as tacky as their names suggest – better, and usually cheaper, options are **cabins** or **cottages**.

Coastal Waters Motel Esplanade ☎03/5155 1792. Probably the best of the motels, with its own heated saltwater pool. ❺–❻

Deja Vu Out of town at 17 Clara St ☎03/5155 4330, ℉5155 3718, ⋓www.dejavu.com.au. A rather special B&B in a pleasant location, with spacious en-suite units overlooking the waterway of North Arm. ❻–❼

Kalimna Woods Kalimna Jetty Rd ☎03/5155 1957. Fully self-contained timber cottages, some with spas and log fires. ❺

Lazy Acre Log Cabins 35 Roadknight St ☎03/5155 1323, ℉5155 1212, ℮lazy-acre@net-tech.com.au. A good bet, with a pool, BBQ, adventure playground, spa and facilities for the disabled. ❺–❼

Riviera Backpackers YHA 5 Clarkes Rd ☎03/5155 2444, ℉5155 4558. In the east end of town just 50m from the McCafferty's/Greyhound Pioneer bus stop, this is a friendly place situated close to a beautiful stretch of lake. It has 24-hour reception, dorms and good en-suite rooms, a large kitchen/common room with Internet access, a library, a laundry and a small pool with spa. They also rent out bikes. Dorms $18, rooms ❷

Sand Bar Motel 637 Esplanade ☎03/5155 2567. Boasts a heated pool and a communal spa. ❸–❹

Silver Sands Backpackers (VIP) Myers St ☎03/5155 2343, ℉5155 3134, ⓦwww.back-packers.com.au. Part of a small, well-maintained caravan and camping park in a quiet location a block behind the Esplanade, with en-suite cabins and on-site vans, plus a camp kitchen, barbecue area, laundry, table tennis and pool with spa. Dorms $20, rooms ❷

Eating

There's no shortage of places to **eat** in Lakes Entrance and they're easy to find too, as most are lined up along The Esplanade.

At the **budget** end you'll find fish and chip shops such as the excellent *Fish-a-Fare* at no. 509 and *L'Ocean Fish & Chips* at 19 Myer St, just off The Esplanade, which serves its fish with gluten-free and wheat-free batter. For coffees, breakfasts and light meals, go for *Clearwater Café* at 23 Myer St and, back on The Esplanade, *Café Pelicano* at no. 171, *The Boathouse Licensed Café* at no. 213, *Lakes Patisserie Bakery* at no. 307, *Shell's Harbour Deli Café* at no. 477 and the wonderfully named *A Moose on the Loose* at no. 567. Inexpensive restaurants include *Egidios Wood Oven* at no. 573 for Italian, and backpackers' favourite *Tres Amigos Mexican* for super-cheap stodge at no. 521.

Moving **upmarket**, try *Skippers Cocktail Bar and Restaurant* (☎03/5155 3551) and *The Nautilus* (☎03/5155 1400), a floating restaurant specializing in local seafood – arguably the best (and the most expensive) food in town. In addition to **wine-tasting**, the popular *Henry's Winery Cafe* at Wyanga Park Winery, 3km from town near North Arm (follow the signposts), also serves cakes and Devonshire **teas**, cheese platters and other meals; wines are available by the glass at cellar door prices (daily lunch & snacks noon–2.30pm, dinner Fri–Sat, in January and during the Easter holidays daily dinner from 6pm; bookings preferred on ☎03/5155 1508).

Metung

If the commercialism of Lakes Entrance turns you off, head for the more refined charms of **METUNG**, a pretty, upmarket boating and holidaying village just 10km west along the shoreline. To get there, take the highway towards Bairnsdale, then turn south on the side road at Swan Reach.

A typically civilized **accommodation** option in Metung is *Maeburn Cottages*, 33 Mairburn Rd (☎03/5156 2736; ❹–❺), where you stay in three-to four-person cabins (BYO linen). *McMillans of Metung*, at 155 Metung Rd, has very comfortable, fully equipped cottages of different sizes in a garden setting, with a solar-heated pool, tennis court and a private jetty (☎03/5156 2283; ❻–❼). *The Moorings at Metung*, 28 Main Rd (☎03/5156 2750, ⓦwww.themoorings.com.au; ❺–❼), are luxury apartments with sun decks and BBQs overlooking Bancroft Bay; their bistro menu offers everything from champagne brunch to coffee and cake. Cheaper is the *Metung Hotel* (☎03/5156 2206; ❸), which also offers bistro meals. The pleasant BYO *Little Mariners Café* at 57 Metung Rd serves breakfast, light **meals** and local seafood daily, while *Marrillee at Metung* on the same road at no. 50 (☎03/5156 2121) is pricier, licensed and specializes in local wines and fish. Both offer alfresco dining.

Buchan and the Snowy River Loop

Nowa Nowa is the inauspiciously named town where you turn north off the Princes Highway for the small town of **BUCHAN**, in the foothills of the Victorian Alps, and take a satisfying loop through the Snowy River National Park. Buchan boasts over six hundred **caves**, the most famous of which – the Royal Cave and the Fairy Cave – can be seen on **guided tours** (daily: April–Sept 11am, 1pm & 3pm; Oct–March 10am, 11.15am, 1pm, 2.15pm & 3.30pm; $11; booking advised on ☎03/5155 9264). In the extensive park surrounding the caves there's an icy, spring-fed swimming pool, a playground, walking tracks and a campsite, plus lots of wildlife.

The delightfully idiosyncratic *Holloways Colonial Tea Rooms and B&B* (☎03/5155 9329; ❹), tucked away in a valley near Buchan South, serves excellent Devonshire teas, light lunches and hearty dinners – call for bookings and directions. In Buchan itself, on the north bank of the Buchan River, is the wonderful independent backpackers' **hostel** *Buchan Lodge* (☎ & ℱ03/5155 9421; ❶), where people have been known to come for a night and stay half a year. Dorms are in a wooden home with log fire and resident dog, and facilities include a volleyball court, country-style kitchen, BBQ, garden and laundry. The owner, Dick, will happily advise about local activities, including caving, trail riding and rafting, and the village itself boasts the lovely *Willow Café*, serving all manner of drinks, grub and live music to a friendly, welcoming crowd.

The road continues north from Buchan through hilly country, following the Murrindal River and slowly winding its way up to the plateau of the Australian Alps. The sealed road ends at Wulgumerang, just before the *Seldom Seen Roadhouse*, where you can get fuel and supplies, and the turn-off to McKillops Bridge. You can continue straight up to Jindabyne in the Snowy Mountains of New South Wales – a spectacular drive – but about two-thirds of the road is unsealed and can be rough; check road conditions before setting out.

Snowy River National Park

Turning right at Wulgumerang, about 55km north of Buchan, enables you to make a scenic arc through part of the **Snowy River National Park**, following the road towards Bonang (check road conditions in advance, as this is an unsealed road that can deteriorate badly in adverse weather conditions). **Little River Falls** are well worth a stop on this stretch: a short walk leads from the car park past snow gums to a lookout with breathtaking views of Little River Gorge and the falls. Equally stunning is the view from the second lookout from the top of the northeastern cliff face of **Little River Gorge** (about 10min from the car park).

Further on, you descend to the valley of the Snowy River, which you cross at **McKillops Bridge**, set in the landscape that inspired "Banjo" Paterson's famous ballad, "The Man from Snowy River". The river's sandy banks are a favourite swimming spot, and are also the place to set out on a **rafting** trip through deep gorges, caves, raging rapids and tranquil pools; Snowy River Expeditions in Buchan (☎03/5155 0220) offers good-value river expeditions, as well as horse riding, rafting, abseiling and rock-climbing adventures. They also run the *Karoonda Park YHA* (☎03/5155 0220, ℱ5155 0308, ℮gelantipy@yhavic.org.au; dorms $20, two double rooms ❸), a small country hostel situated in a beef and sheep farm in Gelantipy. The manager can arrange transfers from *Riviera Backpackers* YHA (see p.1032), 100km south. Oz Experience buses pass through Gelantipy.

Bonang to Orbost

The road through the Snowy River National Park continues until it meets the Bonang–Orbost road. The general store (℡02/6458 0265) at **BONANG**, a former goldrush town, sells takeaway food, groceries and fuel and has some information about the area. The rustic *Delegate River Tavern*, on the Monaro high plains about fifteen minutes' drive north from Bonang across the NSW border, is open daily for counter **meals** and has good-value B&B **accommodation** in log cabins (℡02/6458 8009; ❸).

The road down from the plateau to the coast, still mostly unsealed, leads past the **Errinundra National Park**, which protects magnificent wetland eucalypt forests containing giant, centuries-old specimens, as well as Victoria's largest surviving stand of **rainforest**. At **Errinundra Saddle**, in the heart of the park, there's a delightful picnic area and a self-guided boardwalk through the forest (about 40min). Take special care while driving, as all the roads in the area are heavily used by logging trucks.

The road from Bonang eventually leads to the old-fashioned town of **ORBOST**, on the Princes Highway where it crosses the Snowy River. There's a tranquil picnic spot opposite the *Snowy River Orbost Camp Park*, on the corner of Lochiel and Nicholson streets (℡03/5154 1097; on-site vans ❷), with huge gums lining one bank and cows roaming the paddocks on the other. The **Orbost Visitors Centre** on Lochiel Street (daily 9am–5pm; ℡03/5154 2424) books accommodation and tours.

Lind and Croajingolong national parks

From Orbost to **Cann River**, the Princes Highway continues well inland, not to reach the coast again until Eden, across the border in New South Wales. For a drive through the warm temperate rainforest of **Lind National Park**, take the turn-off to the north (in the direction of Club Terrace and Combienbar) about 55km east of Orbost. After 4km along this road, and just 1km before the hamlet of Club Terrace, turn right onto the **Euchre Valley Nature Drive** which leads through a lush valley lined by tree ferns, following the Euchre Creek for about 6km until you get back to the Princes Highway. One third along the way, the **Growler picnic area**, equipped with tables, benches and a fireplace, is a very pleasant place to stop for a while.

The **Parks Victoria ranger office**, on the Princes Highway in Cann River (Mon–Fri 9am–noon & 12.30–3.30pm; ℡03/5158 6351), provides information on the **Croajingolong National Park**, which begins southeast of the town at Sydenham Inlet and continues for 100km along the coast to the state border. Within the park, foothills cloaked in warm temperate rainforest drop down to the unspoilt "Wilderness Coast". There's a good two-hour **hike** to Genoa Peak (access is from the Princes Highway a few kilometres west of Genoa; drive 8km to the car park and picnic spot which is the start of the walking track) which gives stupendous views over the forest and bay. There are several scenic camping spots in the park, which are very popular in summer and allocated way in advance by a ballot system. You can also stay in the lighthouse-keeper's cottage at *Point Hicks Lighthouse* at Point Hicks (℡03/5158 4268; sleeps eight ❻). If you want to break your journey, Cann River itself offers very good-value accommodation at three motels – the cheapest being the *Cann River Motel* on the Princes Highway (℡03/5158 6255; ❸ including breakfast) – and at the *Cann River Rainforest Caravan Park* at the junction of Princes and Cann Valley highways (☏03/5158 6369; ❷), which has on-site vans for rent.

In summer, OzStyle Adventures (☏1800 000 824, ⓦwww.ozstyle.net.au) runs good-value **bushwalking safaris** (minimum 6 people) in the Croajingolong National Park, with other activities (such as snorkelling and canoeing) thrown in. They pick up from Cann River, Lakes Entrance and Bairnsdale, and accommodation is in tents or at the Point Hicks lighthouse.

Mallacoota and around

MALLACOOTA is an unspoilt village in a gorgeous location surrounded by Croajingolong National Park, on the lake system of the **Mallacoota Inlet**. During the summer and Easter holidays the tranquil place turns into a bustling holiday resort. It's approached via Genoa, 47km east from Cann River along the Princes Highway. About 10km from Genoa, a turn-off to the left leads to **Gipsy Point**, an idyllic spot near the confluence of the Genoa and Wallagaraugh rivers on the upper reaches of the Mallacoota Inlet; it's a fine place to spend a blissful day or two.

There is no tourist office in Mallacoota, but the people at the *Mallacoota Caravan Park* (see below) will do their best to help any visitors with enquiries. **Activities** in the area range from 4WD tours to guided walks and kayaking on the lakes and rivers of Croajingolong National Park and the ocean offshore. Rankins Hire Cruises (☏03/5158 0555) is a top-class operation arranging leisurely cruises via Bottom Lake and Top Lake and Wallagaraugh River up to the New South Wales border, or you can explore on your own by renting a boat or canoe from Buckland's Jetty Boat Hire (☏03/5158 0660). The **Parks Victoria office**, on the corner of Allan and Buckland drives (daily 9.30am–3.30pm; ☏03/5158 0219, ⓦwww.parkweb.vic.gov.au), has details of secluded camping spots and local bushwalks.

During the summer, Mallacoota, although seemingly remote, teems with avid holiday-makers. The population of just over a thousand trebles again for the Easter **Festival of the Great Southern Ocean**, which includes all sorts of music, theatre and comedy, a community market, and fascinating sand sculptures.

Practicalities

Several **accommodation** options are located outside Mallacoota (and away from the summer crowds): try the friendly B&B *Mareeba Lodge*, 59 Mirrabooka Rd (☏03/5158 0378, Ⓕ5158 0050, ⓦwww.mallacoota.net/mareeba; ❹–❺), or the cosy mud-brick apartments at *Adobe Flats*, 17 Karbeethong Ave, Karbeethong, 4km northwest of town (☏03/5158 0329, ⓦwww.mallacoota.net/adobe; BYO linen; ❹), which boast beautiful views of Bottom Lake and are located in an area teeming with birdlife. In Mallacoota itself, just behind the *Mallacoota Hotel*, is the subdued but serviceable YHA hostel, *Mallacoota Lodge* (☏03/5158 0455, Ⓕ5158 0453; dorms $19, rooms ❷), which has accommodation in renovated motel units. Alternatively, you can pitch your tent at *Mallacoota Caravan Park*, right on the shores of the lake (☏03/5158 0300, Ⓔcamppark@vicnet.net.au; unpowered sites $14–21, powered sites $18–26 for two people).

Choices for **food** are very limited. The deli next to the newsagent on Allan Drive serves brunch, light meals and good coffee, while the *Tide Restaurant & Cocktail Bar* on Maurice Avenue is the best place in town for dinner. Otherwise, counter meals are served at the *Mallacoota Hotel* nearby. Other distractions include

bands at the *Mallacoota Hotel* every night in January, and a summer cinema at the Mallacoota Community Centre, Allen Drive. There's an **ATM** machine at 58 Maurice Ave, another in the supermarket, and a small Commonwealth Bank branch inside the post office next door. Additionally, EFTPOS facilities are available at the Mobil service station and the supermarket.

Gipsy Point, about 20km northwest, has another good accommodation option: *Gipsy Point Lakeside Luxury Apartments*, set in a garden by the Wallagaraugh River (℡03/5158 8200 or 1800 688 200, ℻5158 8308; ❺), has attractive new apartments, some with spa, and there is also a heated pool. The *Gipsy Point Lodge*, nearby on MacDonald Street, has B&B rooms and cottages (℡1800 063 556, ℻03/5158 8205, Ⓦwww.gipsypoint.com; rooms ❼, cottages ❺), and arranges bird-watching and bushwalking excursions.

The northeast

The **Hume Highway**, the direct route between Melbourne and Sydney, cuts straight through Victoria's northeast – an area that has become known as **Ned Kelly Country**. **Euroa**, **Benalla** and **Glenrowan** (where he was finally seized after a bloody shoot-out) all have traces of the masked bushranger's activities, with Glenrowan wholeheartedly cashing in on his fame. West of the Hume, **Rutherglen**, right up against the state border, is Victoria's oldest established wine-producing region. There are also vineyards in the rich fruit-growing region of the **Goulburn Valley**, north along the Goulburn Valley Highway from **Seymour**. **Bushwalking** in the Alpine region is most easily organized through outdoor tour operators such as Ecotrek Bogong Jack Adventures (℡08/8383 7198, ℻8383 7377).

V/Line runs several **train and bus routes** through the northeast. The Melbourne–Albury train service goes via Seymour, Euroa, Benalla, Glenrowan, Wangaratta, Chiltern and Wodonga (at least 4 daily). There are also trains and buses from Melbourne to Shepparton, with connections to Cobram and Tocumwal in NSW (2–3 daily). Buses depart from Albury to Bendigo via Wangaratta and Benalla (Mon, Wed & Fri morning). The Murray Link bus service connects Albury with Mildura and runs via Rutherglen, Yarrawonga, Shepparton, Echuca, Kerang and Swan Hill (departing Albury Mon, Wed, Thurs & Sat mornings). There's a bus service from Wangaratta to Rutherglen (Mon–Fri), and one to Wahgunya and Corowa on the Murray. From Melbourne, you can catch a late afternoon train to Wangaratta (Wed, Fri or Sun) and take the connecting bus to Corowa via Rutherglen. For bookings and timetables call ℡13 61 96.

The Goulburn Valley

The **Goulburn River** rises at Lake Eildon and flows through Seymour, Nagambie and Shepparton to join the Murray just east of Echuca. The rich plains of the Goulburn Valley yield much **fruit**, and there's an important fruit-canning industry based at Shepparton, as well as several **wineries**.

Seymour is the first major stop on the Hume Highway out of Melbourne; an important train interchange, it's an uninspiring place for the visitor. The Goulburn Valley Highway begins here, heading north to **NAGAMBIE** on the shores of the man-made Lake Nagambie. The town itself is uninteresting, but two prominent **wineries** nearby add some welcome flavour. **Chateau Tahbilk** (Mon–Sat 9am–5pm, Sun 11am–5pm, ☎03/5794 2555, ⒲www.tahbilk.com.au), 6km southwest, is the oldest continually operating winery and vineyard in Victoria; it opened in 1860, and the Shiraz and Marsanne are still made from vines that have seen more than 130 harvests. The whitewashed buildings have been well preserved and there are extensive grounds to explore. In complete contrast is the ultramodern **Mitchelton Winery** (daily 10am–5pm; ☎03/5736 2222, ⒲www.mitchelton.com.au), 14km southwest of Nagambie in Mitchellstown, off the Goulburn Valley Highway: its distinctive sixty-metre observation tower features on the Mitchelton label. The extensive riverside grounds have a pool and barbecues, which draw the crowds on Sunday. At the *Mitchelton Restaurant & Winebar*, overlooking the river, the wines are matched with outstanding food, using regional produce (daily 10.30am–3pm).

Goulburn River Cruises ply the Goulburn River between Chateau Tahbilk and the Mitchelton Winery (summer only; ☎03/5794 2877, ⒺIjjr@mcmedia.com.au). The **Nagambie Lakes Visitor Information Centre**, at 145 High St (daily 9am–5pm; ☎03/5794 2647 or 1800 444 647), also deals with bookings for V/Line – or get your tickets at the newsagent at 310 High St. As few people stopover in town, **accommodation** is very inexpensive: try the *Nagambie Goulburn Highway Motel*, 143 High St (☎03/5794 2681; ❷–❸), or the *Nagambie Caravan Park* next door (☎03/5794 2681; on-site vans ❷).

The small city of **SHEPPARTON** is the operations centre for the SPC and Ardmona canned fruit companies, with peaches, pears, apples and plums tinned and exported worldwide; with its pleasant riverside picnic spots, it also makes a good place to stop for a while on the way to Echuca. The Greater **Shepparton Visitor Information Centre** is located beside Victoria Park Lake in the south of town, at 534 Wyndham St on the Goulburn Valley Highway (daily 9am–5pm; ☎03/5831 4400 or 1800 808 839, ⒲www.shepparton.vic.gov.au).

The Hume Highway and Kelly Country

Forty-seven kilometres beyond Seymour, **EUROA** is a small, friendly town with many fine red-brick buildings. The **Euroa Visitor Information Centre** is located on the Hume Highway (daily 9am–5pm; ☎03/5795 3677 or 1300 134 610). Binney Street has a pleasant, old-fashioned feel, with the colourful and airy *Blue Dorset Deli* serving fresh coffee, gourmet sandwiches and other goods. For accommodation, try the *Euroa Caravan Park*, Kirkland Avenue (☎03/5795 2160; on-site vans ❶, en-suite cabins ❷), which sits by the creek among huge gum trees; or the *Castle Creek Motel*, on the Old Hume Highway (☎03/5795 2506; ❸), which has inexpensive units, a pool, large garden and laundry.

BENALLA, 45km northeast of Euroa on the Hume Highway, is a civilized town on the lake of the same name, formed by the Broken River which runs through town and occasionally floods it. There's a rose festival held here every November, which transforms the town's picnic spots and gardens. The helpful

Benalla Visitor Information Centre, 14 Mair St (daily 9am–5pm; ☏03/5762 1749), has lots of pamphlets and information on the region, and can also book accommodation. In the same building, the **Costume and Pioneer Museum** ($3) displays a collection of women's dresses from the 1930s and a range of Ned Kelly relics, including the green silk cummerbund he was awarded as a child for saving a friend from drowning, and which he proudly wore when captured. The renovated **Benalla Art Gallery**, in a lovely setting across the lake (daily 10am–5pm; free), has a fine collection of early twentieth-century and contemporary Australian art. Benalla is Australia's main centre for **gliding** and is home to the biggest gliding club in the southern hemisphere; contact the Gliding Club of Victoria (☏03/5762 1058, ⓦwww.gliding-benalla.org.au) to find out about flights.

If you want **to stay**, there's a new hostel, the well-equipped *Trekker's Rest* (☏03/5762 3535, ⓦwww.trekkersrest.com.au; dorms from $22, rooms ❷), 1km out of town on the Kilfeera Road. For something to **eat** during the day, there's the new *Raffety's Gallery Café* in a serene location at the Art Gallery by the lake (licensed; daily 10am–4pm). In town, *Hides Bakery* at 111 Bridge St prepares excellent vegetarian pies, salads and sandwiches and serves good coffee; in the evening two good choices are the very reasonable *Brigall's Restaurant* at the *Commercial Hotel* on Bridge Street, for interesting wood-fired pizza; and the excellent contemporary Australian cuisine at *Raffety Café*, 92 Nunn St (lunch Mon–Fri, dinner Mon–Sat; ☏03/5762 4066).

Glenrowan and Kelly's last stand

GLENROWAN, 29km on from Benalla, was the site of the **Kelly Gang's last stand**. You're never allowed to forget it: a gigantic effigy of Ned Kelly, in full iron-armour regalia, greets you as you enter town, and there are lots of other tawdry attractions along the highway, such as the **Last Stand Show** (daily 9.30am–4.30pm; every half-hour; 40min; $16), a "computerized animated theatre" using dummies shuffling around on cue to dramatize the story of the siege – your money's better spent elsewhere. The last stand itself took place in Siege Street near the train station. Along the rail lines north of town, a small stone monument marks the spot where Kelly forced railworkers to rip up a section of the track, to try to derail the trainful of troopers he had lured to the town – though visitors are asked to stay away as the site is dangerous. Overlooking the town to the west is Mount Glenrowan, which the bushrangers used as a lookout.

More interesting and far better value than the Last Stand Show is **Kate's Cottage and Ned Kelly Memorial** (daily 9am–5.30pm; $2.50), a replica of the Kelly home. With its bare earth floor, bark roof and newspaper-lined walls, it speaks volumes of the deprivation that drove the family towards crime. An evocative audiotape narrates Ned's story from childhood and is interspersed with folk songs inspired by his life. The original homestead, 9km west along Kelly Gap Road, is now nothing more than rubble and a brick chimney.

Wangaratta

The small city of **WANGARATTA**, at the junction of the Ovens and King rivers, 16km from Glenrowan, is a convenient overnight stop between Sydney and Melbourne, but there are few reasons to linger unless you're here for the famous four-day **Wangaratta Festival of Jazz** (☏03/5722 1666, ⓦwww.wangaratta-jazz.org.au). Beginning on the Friday prior to the Melbourne Cup (the last weekend in Oct or the first weekend in Nov), this is

The Ned Kelly story

Even before Ned Kelly became widely known, folklore and ballads were popularizing the free-ranging bush outlaws as potent symbols of freedom and resistance to authority. By the time he was 11, **Ned Kelly**, son of an alcoholic rustler and a mother who sold illicit liquor, was already in constant trouble with the police, who considered the whole family troublemakers; constables in the area were instructed to "endeavour, whenever the Kellys commit any paltry crime, to bring them to justice . . . the object [is] to take their prestige away from them".

Ned became the accomplice of the established bushranger **Harry Power**, and by his mid-teens had a string of warrants to his name. Ned's brother, Dan, was also wanted by the police – hearing that he had turned up at his mother's, a policeman set out, drunk and without a warrant, to arrest him. A scuffle ensued and the unsteady constable fell to the floor, hitting his head and allowing Dan to escape. The following day warrants were issued for the arrest of Ned (who was in New South Wales at the time) and Dan for attempted murder; their mother was sentenced to three years' imprisonment.

From this point on, the **Kelly gang**'s crime spree accelerated and, following the death of three constables in a shoot-out at Stringybark Creek, the biggest manhunt in Australia's history began, with a £1000 reward offered for the gang's apprehension. On December 9, 1878 they robbed the bank at Euroa, taking £2000, before moving on to Jerilderie in New South Wales, where another bank was robbed and Kelly penned the famous **Jerilderie Letter**, describing the "big, ugly, fat-necked, wombat-headed, big-bellied, magpie-legged, narrow-hipped, splay-footed sons of Irish bailiffs or English landlords which is better known as Officers of Justice or Victoria Police" who had forced him onto the wrong side of the law.

After a year on the run, the gang formulated a grand plan: they executed Aaron Sherritt, a police informer, in Sebastopol, thus attracting a trainbound posse from nearby Beechworth; this train was intended to be derailed at Glenrowan with as much bloodshed as possible before the gang moved on to rob the bank at Benalla and barter hostages for the release of Kelly's mother. In the event, having already sabotaged the tracks, the gang commandeered the *Glenrowan Inn* and, in a moment of drunken candour, Kelly detailed his ambush to a schoolteacher who escaped, managing to save the special train. As the armed troopers approached the inn, the gang donned the home-made **iron armour** that has since become their motif. In the ensuing gunfight Kelly's comrades were either killed or they committed suicide as the inn was torched, while Ned himself was taken alive, tried by the same judge who had incarcerated his mother, and sentenced to hang.

Public sympathies lay strongly with Ned Kelly, and a crowd of five thousand gathered outside Melbourne Gaol on November 11, 1880 for his execution, believing that the 25-year-old bushranger would "die game". True to form, his last words are said to have been "**Such is life**".

one of the premier jazz events in the country, attracting national stars and international legends. Much of the city's accommodation is booked out two years in advance, so reserve ahead if you're planning to attend. The highway on either side of "Wang" is lined with motels, and the staff at **Wangaratta Tourist Information**, on the corner of Handley Street and Tone Road (daily 9am–5pm; ☏03/5721 5711 or 1800 801 065, ⊛www.visit.victoria), can book local tours and accommodation and give out stacks of leaflets about the area. The **Wangaratta Exhibitions Gallery**, in a fine old red-brick building on Ovens Street, has a changing programme of exhibitions (Mon, Tues, Sat & Sun noon–5pm; Wed–Fri 10am–5pm; free but donation appreciated).

There is a vast range of **accommodation**. Good choices include the *Wangaratta Central Motel*, 11 Ely St, next to Merriwa Park (℡03/5721 2188; ❸); the *Billabong Motel*, 12 Chisholm St (℡03/5721 2353; ❷), with good-value singles; and the modern *Hermitage Motor Inn,* corner of Mackay and Cusack streets (℡03/5721 7444, ❹), which has a pool. In terms of **food**, *Scribbler's Cafe*, at 66 Reid St, serves good cakes and lunchtime fodder, while *Coffee.com*, at 84 Ovens St, has similar fare and Internet access. For dinner the renowned *Café Martini* at the *Bull's Head Hotel*, 87 Murphy St, has great but pricey wood-fired pizza, while the bistro at the *Vine Hotel* on Detour Road serves excellent local food and wine in a congenial setting (℡03/5721 2605).

V/Line operates a daily bus service from Wangaratta to Bright via Beechworth, and a bus service six times a week to Rutherglen.

Beechworth

Thirty-five kilometres east of Wangaratta, off the Ovens Highway (also known as the Great Alpine Road), is **BEECHWORTH**, once the centre of the rich **Ovens gold-mining region**. Sited picturesquely in the foothills of the Victorian Alps, the entire town has been acknowledged by the National Trust as being of historic significance, and the surrounding area has been designated a **historic park** by the Department of Conservation and Natural Resources. The **visitor information centre** is located in the fine old shire office on Ford Street (daily 9am–5pm; ℡03/5728 3233 or 1300 366 321, ⓦwww .beechworth.com/bworthinfo), and can book accommodation as well as provide you with pamphlets on places of interest, including the Gorge Scenic Drive (see overleaf). They also have Internet access.

The Milawa Gourmet Region

The high country area of Victoria – and in particular the small town of **MILAWA** – is renowned amongst foodies for the excellent quality of its locally produced food and wine, so much so that it has been dubbed the **Milawa Gourmet Region**, and even the most urban Melburnians have been known to make the two-hour trip just to stock up on dinner party supplies.

If it's a tipple of something special you're after, try a tour of the **Brown Brothers Winery** (daily 9am–5pm; ℡03/5720 5500, ⓦwww.brown-brothers.com.au), situated about 2km from Milawa; there's also a great café-restaurant here, the *Epicurean Centre* (daily 11am–3pm), which specializes in complementing Brown Brothers wines with unusual local foods. Back in the town, there's the **Milawa Cheese Company** (daily 9am–5pm) on Factory Road, where you will find award-winning cheeses and another excellent café. At the crossroads nearby, **Milawa Mustards** (10am–5pm, closed some Wednesdays) offers seventeen home-made seed varieties, while **Whitehead's Mead** (daily 9am–4.30pm) on the Snow Road sells a variety of meads made from Australian honey, a wide array of sticky, sweet honeys that put commercial brands to shame, candles and other honey products. The *King River Café* (Wed–Sun 10am–late; ℡03/5727 3461) on Snow Road is a popular eatery specializing in local wines and good food, using regional products; cakes and coffee are excellent, too.

Milawa is situated around 15km southeast of Wangaratta on the Snow Road, which heads off east from the Hume Highway towards the Victorian Alps. Grapevine Getaways (℡02/6023 2599, ⓦwww.grapevinegetaways.com.au) operates a Milawa Meander **tour**, leaving Albury/Wodonga at 10am and returning about 4.30pm (Thurs–Sun only). The $60 price includes transport, all tastings and a two-course gourmet lunch, and includes visits to the Brown Brothers Winery, Milawa Cheese Factory and Milawa Mustards.

As is true in so many other towns in the northeast, Beechworth is rich in **Ned Kelly** history. The **government buildings** on Ford Street house the imposing HM Training Prison, where he and his mother were incarcerated before the 1880 trial, and the **courthouse** (daily 9am–5pm; $4) is where the fatal trial was held. Opposite, underneath the town hall, is the grim cell where he was imprisoned as a teenager (daily 10am–4pm; free). Other sights of interest in town include the **Burke Museum** on Loch Street (daily 10am–5pm; $5.50), which displays relics of the goldrush and tells the story of the Chinese miners who flocked here. The museum is dedicated to the explorer Robert O'Hara Burke, one-time Superintendent of Police in Beechworth, who perished with William John Wills on their historic journey from Melbourne to the Gulf of Carpentaria (see box on p.575). On Last Street the century-old **Murray Breweries** (daily 10am–4pm; free) is well worth a visit, not only for its free tastings and sales, but also for its National Trust display of twenty beautifully restored old carriages, including a Cobb & Co stagecoach.

The five-kilometre, one-way route of the **Gorge Scenic Drive** begins at Sydney Road and ends at Bridge Street, along the western edge of the town. It includes the famous Spring and Reid creeks, which supported eight thousand diggers in 1852, and an old storehouse for blasting powder known as the powder magazine, as well as natural features such as Flat Rock, Telegraph Rock and Woolshed Falls.

Practicalities

There's a very good choice of B&B **accommodation** in Beechworth: try *Rose Cottage*, 42 Camp St (☎03/5728 1069; ⓦwww.hotkey.net.au/~rose-cot; ❺); Swiss Cottages, 22 Malakoff Rd (☎03/5728 2435, ⓦwww.swisscottages.com.au; ❺–❼); or *Apple Tree Cottage* on Frederick Street (☎03/5728 1044, ⓔappletree@hotkey.net.au; ❺). A good-value place is *The Old Priory*, on Priory Lane (a continuation of Loch St), almost at the corner of Church Street (☎03/5728 1024, ⓕ5728 2035; ❸), a historic B&B with very reasonably priced singles. If you want peace and quiet, it's best to come at the weekend, when the school groups have gone. The *Empire Hotel*, on Camp Street (☎03/5728 1030; ❸), and *Tanswells Commercial Hotel*, 30 Ford St (☎03/5728 1480; ❸), are historic pubs that also offer B&B accommodation. The latter has been continuously licensed since 1853 and has pleasant bars and bistro food.

The *Beechworth Bakery*, 27 Camp St (daily 6am–7pm) is famous all over Australia for its delicious pies, bread, cakes and pastries, and on sunny days you can have breakfast on the balcony. *Gigis* at 69 Ford St is a very good Italian restaurant whose owner/chef worked in Melbourne institutions such as *Pellegrini's* (licensed; daily except Wed 9am–late, Sun until 6pm; ☎03/5728 2575). Even better – but also pricier – is The *Bank*, in the Bank of Australia building at 86 Ford St (licensed; daily from 6.30pm; ☎03/5728 2223).

V/Line has a **bus service** from Wangaratta to Beechworth (1 daily Mon–Fri) and an additional service to Bright via Beechworth (1 daily), and during school terms Beechworth Buslines has a service twice daily (☎03/5728 2182; Mon–Fri) from Beechworth to Albury and Wodonga.

Chiltern

CHILTERN, a sleepy former gold-mining centre with a well-preserved, mid-nineteenth-century streetscape, lies just off the Hume Highway about 40km from Wangaratta. The setting – with a bit of recent architectural licence on Conness Street – has been used in several period films. Although no longer licensed, the **Star Hotel** is still set up with the original bar and taps, an authentic background to a rather more ordinary souvenir and craft shop. For $2 you can gain access to the back (daily except Thurs) to look at a **monster vine**: planted in 1867 and reputedly Australia's largest, it once produced a single yield of over 6kg of grapes. The 1866 **Athenaeum** (Wed, Sat, Sun & public holidays 10am–4pm; $2) is now a local-history museum that features a collection of paintings by the obsessive local artist Alfred Eustace, who would use any available medium to paint on: paper, cardboard, even large gum leaves. **Dows Pharmacy Museum**, also on Conness Street (Sat & Sun 10am–4pm or by appointment, (℡03/5726 1490; $2), has an extensive collection of old pharmaceutical equipment. Chiltern's most interesting attraction, however, is the National Trust-owned **Lake View Homestead** (most weekends 1–4pm or by appointment' ℡0427 003 013; $2), on the shores of Lake Anderson, near the train station. Built in 1870, it was for a short period the home of the writer Ethel Florence Lindesay (1870–1946), who, under the pseudonym **Henry Handel Richardson**, immortalized the house in the novel *Ultima Thule*, the last book in *The Fortunes of Richard Mahoney* trilogy. For **refreshment**, stop in at the *Mulberry Tree Restaurant and Tearooms* on Conness Street.

Rutherglen

RUTHERGLEN, 18km west of Chiltern and 32km west of Wodonga on the Murray River Highway, is at the heart of Victoria's oldest wine-producing region, renowned for its excellent fortified wines, Rutherglen Muscat and Tokay. Thirteen **wineries** are situated in the area, most of them third- or fourth-generation establishments with cellars full of character. The landscape is rather disappointing, consisting largely of flat paddocks of cattle and sheep where you'd expect undulating vineyards. In fact, winemaking has always been just one of a range of farming activities in this area, where diversification remains the key to survival. The weather partly accounts for the quality of Rutherglen's fortified wines: the long, mild autumns allow the grapes to stay on the vines for longer, producing higher levels of sugar in the fruit. All the wineries are open for free **tastings** and cellar-door sales (Mon–Sat 10am–5pm – Sun hours differ from place to place).

The **Wine Experience Centre** at 57 Main St (daily 9am–5pm; ℡02/6032 9166 or 1800 622 871) is local history museum, shop, café and visitor information centre all in one – it has informative displays about the goldrush and agricultural history of the district, including winemaking. The shop sells local wines and arts and crafts, and there are stacks of brochures, including the informative *Rutherglen Touring Guide and Map* published by the winemakers of Rutherglen. They also rent mountain bikes ($22/day). On the Queen's Birthday weekend in June the town hosts the **Winery Walkabout** – one of Australia's biggest wine-tasting festivals, when the new season's releases are presented to the public. Another festive event, the **Tastes of Rutherglen**, is held over the Victorian Labour Day weekend in mid-March, and sees some of the best local restaurants guest-starring at the wineries.

Rutherglen is a popular weekend getaway from Melbourne, so **accommodation** can be hard to find at that time; during the week you'll have no problem. The focus of the small town is the excellent, National Trust-listed *Victoria Hotel*, 90 Main St (℡02/6032 9610, ℻6032 8128; ❷–❹), where you can both eat and sleep well. On the walls of the bar is a framed cover of the June 28, 1880 *Melbourne Herald* chronicling the capture of the Kelly Gang, which makes for fascinating reading. Alternatively, a good-value B&B is *Country Cottage*

Accommodation (☎02/6032 8328; ❺), or there's the *Walkabout Motel* (☎02/6032 9572, ⓕ6032 8187; ❸–❺), both on the Murray Valley Highway. The wineries all offer delicious, if expensive, gourmet **food**.

The Snowfields and the High Country

The **Victorian Alps**, the southern extension of the Great Dividing Range, bear little resemblance to their European counterparts; they're too gentle, too rounded, and above all too low to offer really great **skiing**. Nonetheless in July and August there is usually plenty of snow, and the resorts are packed out. Most people come here for the downhill skiing, though the **cross-country skiing**, which is rapidly growing in popularity, is excellent: **Lake Mountain**, 21km from Marysville, is the region's premier cross-country destination. **Snowboarding** was first encouraged at Mount Hotham and is now firmly established almost everywhere. **Falls Creek**, **Mount Hotham** and **Mount Buller** are the largest and most commercial skiing areas, particularly the last which is within easy reach of Melbourne; smaller resorts such as **Mount Baw Baw** are more suited to beginners. While you wouldn't come to Victoria especially to ski, you might as well give it a go if you're here at the right time of year, though be warned that accommodation is very pricey.

In summer, when the wild flowers are in bloom, the alps are ideal **bushwalking** territory with most of the high mountains (and the ski resorts) contained within the vast **Alpine National Park**. The most famous of the walks is the four-hundred-kilometre **Alpine Trail**, which begins in Baw Baw National Park, near Walhalla in Gippsland, and follows the ridges all the way to Mount Kosciuszko in the Snowy Mountains of New South Wales. If you are doing any serious bushwalking, you'll need to be properly equipped. Water can be hard to find, and the weather can change suddenly and unexpectedly: even in summer it can get freezing cold up here, especially at night. After prolonged dry spells, **bushfires** can also pose a very real threat, as in early 2003, when fires, most likely ignited by a flash of lightning, blazed across a large chunk of the high country in Victoria and southeastern New South Wales. They burned for six weeks, leaving behind a wasteland of blackened tree stumps, dead animals and the skeletal ruins of quite a few farm homesteads. Partly because of lucky wind and weather changes, but mainly owing to the efforts of firefighters, the towns of Bright and Mount Beauty as well as the ski resorts of Falls Creek, Dinner Plain and Mount Hotham – all of them surrounded by fires at some stage or another – were spared and nobody came to grief. Just months after the fires were extinguished, new shoots sprouted from blackened tree branches and ashen soil, the resilient Aussie bush beginning its process of recovery.

Mansfield and **Bright** are good bases for exploration of the Alps, and are great places to unwind. In summer the ski resorts can be ugly and only half the facilities are open, but there are often great bargains to be had on rooms. If you're **driving**, you'll need snow chains in winter (they're compulsory in many parts), and you should heed local advice before venturing off the main roads.

Mansfield and Merrijig

MANSFIELD is located at the junction of the Maroondah and Midland highways, just a few kilometres north of Lake Eildon, 140km east of Seymour and 63km south of Benalla. As the main approach to Mount Buller, it's a lively place with good pubs, restaurants and a cinema. The annual highlight is the **Mountain High Country Festival** in early November, which begins the weekend prior to the Melbourne Cup in Nov; activities include a picnic race known as the "Melbourne Cup of the bush". In the middle of April hundreds of hot-air-balloon pilots flock here for the three-day **Mansfield Balloon Festival**.

V/Line has a year-round **bus** service from Melbourne to Mansfield (Mon–Sat 2, Sun 1 daily; 3hr). The helpful **Mansfield Visitor Information Centre** on the Maroondah Highway (daily 9am–5pm; ☎03/5775 1464 or 1800 060 686 for accommodation bookings, ⓦwww.mansfield-mtbuller .com.au), has complete information on all sights and activities, including skiing and walks in the surrounding country. Out of the snow season, you have a choice of horse riding, hiking, climbing, abseiling, hang-gliding, rafting, canoeing or 4WD tours. Among the many local outfits are Stirling Experience (☎03/5775 3541, ⓦwww.stirling.au.com) and Alpine 4WD Tours (☎03/5777 3709) for 4WD tours around Mount Buller and Mount Stirling (see p.1047).

The *Alzburg Inn Resort*, 39 Malcolm St (☎03/5775 2367 or 1800 033 023, ⓦwww.alzburg.com.au; self-contained units ❺, suites ❺–❼), is a resort **hotel** with all mod cons, popular with skiers, while the neat and friendly *Mansfield Traveller's Lodge*, 116 High St (☎03/5775 1800, ⑤5775 2396; has motel rooms (❸–❹), and a backpackers' hostel in a separate building next door ($22). The managers organize all sorts of activities and also have good contacts for fruit-picking in summer and for work at the Mount Buller ski resort in winter. The area around Mansfield is renowned for **luxurious B&Bs**, the most famous of which is the extremely expensive *Howqua Dale Gourmet Retreat*, south of town near Howqua (☎03/5777 3503, ⑤5777 3896; one night $770, all inclusive), which is run by two chefs and is renowned for its outstanding food; aspiring chefs might be tempted to attend one of their weekend cooking courses. On a much more modest scale, *Willawong Bed & Breakfast and Cottage* at Lot 12, Mount Buller Road, Merrijig (☎03/5777 5750, ⓦwww.willawongbnb .com.au; rooms B&B ❹ cottage ❻), offers Bavarian-style accommodation in a gorgeous wooden house and a separate cottage set in a lovely garden at the foot of the Alps, or there are four cottages with private spas at *Alpine Country Cottages*, 5 The Parade, Mansfield (☎03/5775 1694, ⑤5775 1586, ⓦwww .alpinecc.com.au; B&B ❼).

In winter, Mansfield–Buller Bus Lines runs frequent **bus services** for skiing from Mansfield to Mount Buller in conjunction with the V/Line bus service from Melbourne to Mansfield. In summer there are two services a day with Mansfield–Buller Bus Lines from Mansfield to Mount Buller via Merrijig (booking essential on ☎0417 307 504).

Merrijig

The small town of **MERRIJIG**, a little under halfway to Mount Buller from Mansfield, is largely responsible for the great number of **riding** outfits in the area. The breathtaking high-country scenery nearby was used as the location for the film *The Man from Snowy River*, and visitors have been trying to live out their fantasies ever since. If you want to combine riding with lodge **accommodation**, try *Merrijig Lodge and Trail Rides*, Mount Buller Road (☎03/5777 5590; ❷).

Mount Buller and Mount Stirling

To reach **MOUNT BULLER ALPINE VILLAGE**, 48km from Mansfield, you ascend gradually upwards on the smooth, sealed Summit Road. With 7000 beds, 24 modern ski lifts and 80km of runs, the village has the greatest capacity of any Australian ski resort. In **winter**, during the ski season, the Central Reservation Service books **accommodation** and dispenses information about all things ski-related (℡03/9809 0291 or 1800 039 049); in summer, call the Mansfield Visitor Information Centre on ℡03/5775 1464 or 1800 060 686, Ⓦwww.mtbuller.com.au).

ABOM Hotel & Bistro, on Summit Road (℡03/5777 6091 or 1800 810 200; ❸), is the hub of the Alpine Village when it is open in winter. There are great views from here, and further up, on the **summit** of Mount Buller, there's an even more spectacular panorama west to Lake Eildon, north to farmlands and east to Falls Creek and Mount Hotham. The huge *Arlberg Hotel*, 53 Summit Rd (℡03/5777 6260 or 1800 032 380; summer ❺, winter ❻), provides entertainment in ski season, and has everything from fast food to an expensive restaurant; alongside its rooms there are some six-person, self-contained apartments (summer $250, winter $750). More reasonably priced, although still excellent, is the B&B *Duck Inn* (℡03/5777 6326; summer ❹, winter ❻). In winter the truly budget-conscious can stay at the *YHA Lodge*, on The Avenue right in the centre of the village (℡03/5777 6181, Ⓔmountbuller@yhavic.org.au; open June–Sept; dorms $50–60), which has self-catering facilities; advance booking

Skiing practicalities

The official start of the **ski season** is the Queen's Birthday long weekend in June (though there may not be enough snow cover until August), lasting through to October. Day-trip or weekend **packages** are the best way to go, and are far cheaper than trying to do it yourself. The best value for money are the day-trips organized by the *Alzburg Inn* Resort at Mansfield (℡1800 033 023, Ⓦwww.alzburg.com.au), as they leave Melbourne at 4am in the morning and arrive at Mount Buller at about 9am, giving the opportunity for a full day's skiing ($135, including entrance fees, a limited lift pass and a two-hour beginner's ski lesson or, for more advanced skiers, an Unlimited Day Lift Ticket). It's also worth checking out the area around Hardware Street in Melbourne, where such companies as Ski Haus at no. 17 (℡03/9670 2855), Auski at no. 9 (℡03/9670 1412), and Mountain Designs at 377 Little Bourke St (℡03/9670 3354) can advise on skiing conditions at the resorts, and sell or rent equipment. In South Melbourne at 295 Clarendon St, Ski Man (℡03/9696 4955) also sells and rents out equipment.

During the snow season, an entry fee of $19–22 per car applies, depending on the resort. For **weather** and snow conditions, call the **Snow Reports Line** (℡1900 912 990; $1.93 per min); or Snow Reports Updates (℡1900 912 207; $1.05 per min). Accommodation bookings are organized by **Alpine Reservations Australia** (℡03/9455 1277), or phone the central reservation hotlines of each mountain resort. The free *Australian Alpine News* is available at the visitor information centre in Melbourne as well as in the Alpine region. As a rough guide to **costs**, a lift ticket at Mount Buller is $75 per day, while **lessons** cost $75 for beginners (1-day limited lift and a 2hr lesson) and $110 for lower intermediate (1-day lift and a 3hr lesson). Full equipment rental is about $60 per day.

During the season, Mansfield–Mount Buller Bus Lines, 133 High St, Mansfield (℡03/5775 2606), operates a **ski transport service** to Mount Buller about six times daily; and Stirling Experience (℡03/5777 3541) runs a daily service from Mansfield and Merrijig to Mount Stirling (prebooking essential; $40 return). In Bright, Adina Ski Hire, 15 Ireland St (℡03/5755 1177, Ⓦwww.adina.com.au), and Bright Ski Centre, 22 Ireland St (℡03/5755 1093), rent out skiing and snowboarding equipment, offer package deals including off-mountain accommodation and transport to Mount Hotham, and have up-to-date snow reports and information on road conditions. There's no transport to Mount Buffalo.

(available from March 1) is essential. The *Avalanche Chalet and Apartments* (℡03/9894 7375; **❼**) has self-contained apartments and B&B rooms. There's a two-night minimum stay at weekends.

Mount Stirling, a few kilometres northeast, has more than 60km of maintained trails and is a good place for **cross-country skiing**. The only facility here is Mount Stirling Alpine Resort, a large complex at Telephone Box Junction, 9km from the turn-off left at Mirindah along Mount Stirling Road (℡03/5777 6441, ⓦwww.mtstirling.au.com); within the complex there's a visitor centre, a bistro, a ski school and ski rental is also available. As it's a day-resort, there's no accommodation in the complex itself, but the owners do have bunkroom and loft dormitories on a nearby farm, *Wairere Lodge* (℡03/5777 3541, ⓦwww.stirling.au.com), about 45 minutes from the mountain; in summer (Oct–June) there's a minimum booking of four people allowed ($20 per person); in winter, you'll have to rent out the whole place (sleeps 24; $300 first night, $220 thereafter). All roads beyond Telephone Box Junction are open only from the beginning of November until the beginning of June, weather permitting. The fifty-kilometre **Circuit Road** from Telephone Box Junction circumnavigates Mount Stirling, and a 4WD access track from this road leads to **Craig's Hut**, which was used as a film set for *The Man from Snowy River*. As sections of Circuit Road are very rough for 2WD vehicles even in good weather conditions, you'll really need a 4WD for this route. In summer, Stirling Experience (℡03/5775 3541; ⓦwww.stirling.au.com) does 4WD **tours** to Craig's Hut and other destinations around the Mount Buller/Mount Stirling area.

Bright

BRIGHT is at the centre of the picturesque Ovens Valley, between Mount Buffalo and Mount Beauty about 75km southeast of Wangaratta on the Ovens Highway. It began life as a gold-mining town in the 1850s and today still has a faintly elegant air, with tall European trees lining the main street and filling the parks. A clear stream flows through Centennial Park, opposite the tourist information centre, and in autumn the glorious colours of the changing leaves make for a very un-Australian scene.

As the ski fields of Mount Hotham, Mount Buffalo and Falls Creek are less than an hour's drive away, the town is popular as a **ski base** in winter. In summer **outdoor activities** are on offer – such as paragliding, hang-gliding, bushwalking, horse riding and cycling. Alpine Paragliding, 6 Ireland St (℡03/5755 1753), organizes tandem flights for novices, and introductory and full courses leading to a licence. You could also take to the air in a powered hang-glider from Bright Micro-Light Centre (℡03/5750 1555) or with the Eagle Flying School (℡03/5750 1174 or 0428 570 168), which also does very enjoyable instructor-accompanied tandem flights. Freeburgh Trail Rides, on Harrietville Road in Freeburgh, about 4km north of Bright (℡03/5755 1370), does very good short horseback rides for beginners; they also have longer rides and can arrange overnight safaris with bushcamping.

For a change of pace, visit Boynton's of Bright, a **winery** 10km northwest of Bright at Porepunkah, on the northeast slopes of the Ovens River Valley, which specializes in cool-climate wines (daily 10am–5pm; ℡03/5756 2356). There's a café here (Thurs–Sun in summer, weekends only in winter 11am–4pm) and a picnic area on its lawns, with spectacular views of Mount Buffalo. Alternatively, head south to nearby **WANDILIGONG**, a beautiful village that's entirely owned by the National Trust, where you'll find the *Wandiligong*

Café and **maze** (Wed–Sun 10am–5pm; $8). The maze itself is a lot of fun but the café, serving salads, freshly squeezed juices and home-made treats, and set in a tranquil garden at the end of a six-kilometre bushwalk from Bright, is a truly wonderful find.

Practicalities

V/Line operates a **bus** service to Bright from Wangaratta (1–2 daily; 1hr 15min). To **get around**, you can rent a mountain bike from the Sports Centre, 47 Gavan St (℡03/5755 5159) or Cyclepath, 9 Camp St (℡03/5750 1442) – both outfits also arrange biking tours. The **tourist information centre**, at 119 Gavan St (daily 9am–5pm; ℡03/5755 2275, accommodation bookings 1800 500 117, ℮bright@dragnet.com.au), has complete information on what's happening around town and also books accommodation. There's also an excellent **Internet café** in the same building.

Accommodation

Alpine Hotel 7 Anderson St ℡03/5755 1366. Charming century-old place which is the focal point of town, with a rowdy bar, good-value bistro meals and excellent breakfasts; the back bar has bands on Friday night, and outside there's a sunny beer garden. ❸

Bright Hikers Hostel 4 Ireland St ℡03/5750 1244, ℉5750 1246, ⓦwww.backpackers.com.au. One of the best budget places to stay, right in the centre of town. Its wide range of facilities includes a games room and an Internet lounge. Dorms $22, rooms ❸

Buckland Valley B&B 23A Devils Creek Rd, Porepunkah, 4km west of Bright ℡03/5756 2656. Offers meals, meditation and massage in a gorgeous bush setting. ❺

Ellenvale Holiday Units East of town at 68 Delany Ave ℡03/5755 1582. This excellent place has a solar-heated pool and spa, tennis court and barbecues. ❹–❻

Elm Lodge Holiday Motel 2 Wood St ℡1800 245 845, ℉03/5755 2206. Good-value and centrally located motel in a beautiful garden with a pool. Evening meals available in dining room ❸–❺

Knox Farm School Rd, 4km northeast from Bright in the beautiful Wandiligong Valley ℡0417 367 494. A terrific B&B which has just one fantastic room – self-contained, with a spa and a wooden balcony with beautiful mountain views. ❺

Mystic Valley Cottages 9 Mystic Lane, 2km southeast on the way to Wandiligong ℡03/5750 1502. A good-value option, situated on a hill overlooking the beautiful Wandiligong Valley. ❹–❺

Eating

Simone's, at the *Ovens Valley Motor Inn*, at the corner of Ovens Highway and Ashwood Avenue (open daily for dinner; licensed; ℡03/5755 2022) is one of the top Italian **restaurants** in Victoria. Its offshoot is the equally reputable *Cafe Bacco* at 2D Anderson St (Wed–Sun lunch and dinner; ℡03/5750 1711).

Other good **places to eat** are the *Liquid Am-Bar Restaurant Cafe*, opposite the *Alpine Hotel*, which (besides the amber fluid alluded to in its name) also serves good coffee; the *Riverdeck Café* at the tourist information centre, which sells great deli sandwiches; and the *Bright Bakery* at 80 Gavan St. Two cheap, casual family restaurants are *Tin Dog Café & Pizzeria* at 94 Gavan St, and the *Cosy Kangaroo* across the street. For a treat head to *Poplar's Restaurant*, at 4/7 Star Rd (open daily for dinner; licensed and BYO; ℡03/5755 1655).

Mount Hotham and around

Heading southeast out of Bright on the Alpine Tourist Road, it's 18km to **HARRIETVILLE**, tucked just below **Mount Hotham** and Mount Feathertop. Originally a gold-mining town, it's now a pretty little village of wide, tree-lined streets, and is also a popular skiing base: there are outlets to rent skis and chains, a seasonal shuttle-bus service up to the resorts, and several places to stay and eat. Beyond Harrietville, it's a steep ascent to Mount Hotham in the Alpine National Park, the "powder snow capital of Australia". Because this is the state's highest ski area, the snow here can be marginally less sticky than elsewhere. **Dinner Plain**, a resort 8km from the summit and about 1500m above sea level, has much more of a cosy, alpine village feel – complete with architect-designed timber houses that are meant to resemble cattlemen's mountain huts – than the somewhat unsightly Hotham "village". Cross-country trails lead from Hotham to Dinner Plain. Hotham is also considered the home of Victorian **snowboarding**, with special facilities, rental and lessons available. During the ski season, tractor-driven carts ferry you around the village and to the start of cross-country trails and skiing areas (all day until late; free), and helicopter shuttle flights in winter link Mount Hotham with Falls Creek, only a few minutes away by air. A few lodges and pubs stay open in summer, including the *General Hotel*, which has a bar, bistro, bottle shop and fantastic mountain views, and in summer Dinner Plain Trail Rides (℡03/5159 6661, ⓦwww.horsetreks.com) offers fully inclusive overnight horse treks from $160 per day. Following the establishment of a fully fledged airport at Horsehair Plain, 20km south of Mount Hotham where seventy-seater jets from Melbourne and Sydney can land, it's now easier than ever to get to Hotham and surrounding areas.

A few centres handle bookings for the mainly lodge-style **accommodation**: Mount Hotham Reservation Centre ℡1800 35 45 55; Mount Hotham Central Reservations ℡03/5759 3522 or 1800 657 547, ⓦwww.mthotham-centralres.com.au; Mount Hotham Accommodation Service ℡03/5759 3636 or 1800 032 061; and Alpine Accommodation ℡1800 246 462, ⓦwww.explore.skihotham.com.au; and Dinner Plain Central Reservations ℡1800 670 019, ⓦwww.dinnerplain.com.

Falls Creek

Thirty kilometres east of Bright, in the Upper Kiewa Valley, the town of **Mount Beauty** lies at the base of the state's highest peak, **Mount Bogong** (1986m). **FALLS CREEK**, 32km further along, on the edge of the Bogong High Plains, has a much more villagey feel than its sister resort at Mount Hotham. It also has probably Victoria's **best skiing**, with the largest snow-making system in Victoria to supplement any shortage of the real stuff, a wide variety of downhill pistes, and good cross-country trails. A park for **snowboarders** has been established, too, in the Vertigo Valley near the Scott's Chair ski lift. For **accommodation** bookings and information, contact Falls Creek Central Reservations (℡1800 033 079), or ask at the **Mount Beauty Visitor Information Centre** (daily 9am–5pm, ℡03/5754 4531 or 1800 808 277, ⓦwww.mtbeauty.com) on the Kiewa Valley Highway in the town. The budget-conscious would do best to stay in Mount Beauty and travel to Falls Creek for their skiing: enquire about packages at the Mount Beauty Accommodation Service (℡03/5754 1267). Accommodation options in the valley include *Mountain Creek Lodge* in Tawonga (℡03/5754 4247, ⓕ5754 4860; motel units ❺–❻); the wonderful *Braeview B&B* in Mount Beauty (℡03/5754 4746, ⓦwww.braeview.com.au; ❺–❼), which has two luxurious guest rooms, one self-contained studio apartment and a separate cottage built from rammed earth, stone and timber, all in an established garden setting; and the well-designed and very nicely furnished cottages at *Dreamers Luxury Accommodation* (℡03/5754 1222, ⓦwww.dreamers1.com; ❺–❼).

Many of the pubs, **restaurants** and lodges in Falls Creek stay open in summer: some of the best are *The Cock 'n' Bull*, a pleasant old-English-style pub on the corner of Christie and Slalom streets; *The Man Hotel*, a cosy pub on Telemark Street; and the *Milch Café and Wine Bar* on Schuss Street.

Apart from **bushwalks**, nature lovers can join Alpine Nature Rambles for informative short walks, studying the Alpine flora (T 03/5758 3492, W www.rambles.com.au/rambles; $100–120 per walk for a minimum of 4 people). From December until the end of April, Bogong Horseback Adventures (T 03/5754 4849, F 5754 4181, W www.bogonghorse.com.au), a very professional and experienced operator based on a farm at Tawonga near Mount Beauty, organizes three- to seven-day **packhorse tours** across the high plains ($825–1925 per person), traversing country that is otherwise only accessible to the most experienced and hardy bushwalker, while still providing creature comforts such as comfortable camps, good food and wine sourced from the region. They also run half-day ($70) and day rides ($140) through the Kiewa Valley and the lower levels of the Alpine National Park. As for **festivals**, the entire village of Falls Creek, plus visitors, get together to celebrate the Food, Wine and Wildflower Weekend ("A Taste of Falls Creek") in mid-January.

Mount Buffalo National Park

Six kilometres northwest of Bright, back along the Ovens Highway, you can turn off into **Mount Buffalo National Park** ($9 per car in summer, $12.50 in winter), which encompasses a huge plateau around Mount Buffalo. **Skiing** here is for beginners to intermediates – and it's a gorgeous place to learn, among surreal-looking, snow-covered gum trees. Relatively inexpensive packages, including accommodation at the *Mount Buffalo Chalet* (see below), ski lessons and other fees, can be arranged through Mount Buffalo Reservations (T 1800 037 038). The *Mount Buffalo Lodge*, a tiny resort at the ski slopes of the Cresta Valley (T 03/5755 1988) has motel units (summer ❺, winter ❻), lodge rooms (❺) and bunkhouse dorm-beds – all subject to a two-night minimum stay. There are also kitchen facilities, a bistro and restaurant.

The park looks at its best in summer, though, when there are wild flowers and waterfalls, and it's a great place for walking, water sports and other outdoor activities. Among the main attractions is the *Mount Buffalo Chalet* (T 03/5755 1500, F 5755 1892, W www.mtbuffalochalet.com.au; ❽ full board), a forty-minute drive on a sealed road from the Ovens Highway turn-off. Built by the Victorian government in 1910, it's very Australian in appearance, with a bottle-green tin roof, but is European in feel, and surrounded by flowers and magnificent views. You can play croquet on the lawn, and there's a sauna, billiard room, games room and tennis court, plus horse riding (summer only), and canoes and mountain bikes for rent. There are two **eating places**: the *Chalet Café* (daily 9.30am–4.30pm), a no-frills, no-views cafeteria – if you want to have a proper meal, reserve a place in the main dining room (T 03/5755 1500). On the way to the chalet, you'll pass Lake Catani, where there's the only camping in the park (Nov–April; booking essential on T 03/5755 1466, or through Parks Victoria on T 13 19 63), as well as swimming, canoeing, kayaking and trout-fishing; the chalet rents out equipment. Bent's Lookout, opposite the chalet, has tremendous views over the Ovens Valley, with small stone cabins doing duty as winter picnic areas. There's a hang-gliding ramp near here: if you're experienced and want to leap into the void, contact one of the operators in or near Bright (see p.1047). Beyond the chalet a sealed, not too steep road continues to Mount Buffalo itself (1721m).

Mount Baw Baw

The ski village at **MOUNT BAW BAW**, near the edge of the Baw Baw National Park, is considerably south of all the resorts and is, strictly speaking, in Gippsland. It's a quiet little place, commanding magnificent views south over much of Gippsland and consisting mainly of private lodges (reservations on ☎ 1800 629 578). Otherwise, try the *Cascades Apartments* (☎ 1800 229 229). The entry fee is $21 per vehicle per day or $10 overnight and $10 each extra day. There are five ski lifts here, and a lift day-pass costs about $50, a much more reasonable price than at other resorts. As at Mount Buffalo, the ski runs are mainly for beginners and intermediates. In addition to downhill skiing, you can ski cross-country on 10km of groomed trails.

Getting to the resort is a major problem. There's no public transport to the mountain, and the closest town is Noojee, 48km west. The road between the town and the resort is narrow, steep and winding. To make matters worse, there are lots of logging trucks thundering along, so take care. For more on Mount Baw Baw, see ⓦ www.bawbaw.com.au.

Travel details

V/Line monopolizes transport within Victoria, with a comprehensive combination of **train** and **bus** services; Melbourne, Ballarat and Geelong are the main interchanges. Following are the main V/Line Victorian services; local buses are detailed in the text. Timetables are subject to frequent change – call V/Line on ☎ 13 61 96 or consult ⓦ www.vline passenger.com for the latest information.

Trains

Melbourne to: Albury (4 daily; 3hr–3hr 40min) via Euroa (3 daily; 1hr 30min–2hr), Benalla (4 daily; 2hr–2hr 30min); Ballarat (6–10 daily; 1hr 30min); Bendigo (5–11 daily; 2hr) via Castlemaine (1hr 35min); Echuca (Fri and Sun 1 daily; 3hr 20min) via Bendigo (2hr); Geelong 12–20 daily; 1hr); Sale (2–3 daily; 2hr 35min); Shepparton (1–2 daily; 2hr 10min); Swan Hill (1 daily; 4hr 15min) via Castlemaine (1hr 35min) and Bendigo (2hr); Wangaratta (4 daily; 2hr 30min–3hr); Warrnambool (1–3 daily; 3hr 15min) via Geelong (1hr) and Colac (1hr 50min).

Buses

Apollo Bay to: Geelong (2–3 daily; 2hr 30min); Lorne (2–3 daily; 55min); Warrnambool (Fri only; 3hr 20min) via Twelve Apostles (1hr 25min), Port Campbell (1hr 55min); Torquay (2–3 daily; 2hr). **Ballarat** to: Bendigo (5 weekly; 2hr); Castlemaine (5 weekly; 1hr 30min); Daylesford (5 weekly; 45min); Geelong (2–4 daily, 1hr 25 min); Hamilton via Dunkeld (1–2 daily; 2hr 15min); Horsham (3–4

daily; 2hr 20min); Maryborough (5 weekly; 1hr), Mildura (2 weekly; 7hr 10min) via Castlemaine (1hr 35min) and Swan Hill (2hr 50min); Warrnambool (5 weekly; 3hr). **Beechworth** to: Bright (1–2 daily; 1hr); Wangaratta (1–4 daily; 30min). **Bendigo** to: Echuca (1–3 daily; 1hr 20min); Geelong (5 weekly; 3hr 55min); Horsham (daily; 3hr 15min); Mildura (1–2 daily, 6hr); Swan Hill (1–3 daily; 3hr 10min). **Bright** to: Beechworth (1–2 daily; 1hr); Wangaratta (1–3 daily; 1hr 25min). **Castlemaine** to: Ballarat (5 weekly; 1hr 30min); Maryborough (1–4 daily; 55min). **Cowes** to: Melbourne (1–4 daily; 3hr 15min). **Echuca** to: Albury (1–2 daily; 3hr 45min–4hr 20min); Bendigo (1–3 daily; 1hr 20min); Melbourne (4–6 daily; 3hr); Mildura (4 weekly; 5hr 55min); Rutherglen (4 weekly; 3hr 35min); Shepparton (5 weekly; 1hr 10min); Swan Hill (daily; 1hr 55min). **Foster** (closest to Wilson's Promontory NP) to: Melbourne (daily; 2hr 40min). **Geelong** to: Apollo Bay (2–4 daily; 2hr 55min); Ballarat (2–4 daily; 1hr 25min); Bendigo (5 weekly; 4hr); Lorne (2–5 daily; 1hr 50min); Maryborough (4 weekly; 3hr 5min); Mildura (6 weekly; 9hr); Torquay (2–4 daily; 45min); Warrnambool (Coastlink via Apollo Bay; Fri only; 7hr). **Halls Gap** (Grampians) to: Stawell (daily; 35min). **Hamilton** to: Ballarat (1–2 daily; 2hr 15min); Warrnambool (1–2 daily except Sat; 1hr 40min). **Horsham** to: Ararat (3–4 daily; 1hr 35min); Ballarat

(3–4 daily; 1hr 50min); Stawell (3 daily; 55min).

Lakes Entrance to: Bairnsdale (1–4 daily; 35min); Canberra (2 weekly; 6hr 15min); Cann River (daily; 1hr 45min); Orbost (daily; 45min); Sale (1–3 daily; 1hr 40min).

Mansfield to: Melbourne (daily; 3hr); Mount Buller (snow season only; 2–3 daily; 1hr).

Maryborough to: Ballarat (5 weekly; 1hr); Castlemaine (1–4 daily; 55min).

Mildura to: Bendigo (1–2 daily, 6hr); Ballarat (6 weekly; 7hr 50min); Geelong (6 weekly; 9hr); Swan Hill (1–2 daily; 3hr 10min).

Mount Beauty to: Melbourne (2 weekly; 5hr 35min).

Mount Buller to: Mansfield (snow season only; 1 daily; 1hr).

Portland to: Mount Gambier (1–3 daily; 1hr 30min); Port Fairy (1–3 daily; 1hr); Warrnambool (1–3 daily; 1hr 30min).

Sale to: Bairnsdale (1–3 daily; 1hr); Canberra (2 weekly; 7hr 40min); Cann River (daily; 3hr 10min); Lakes Entrance (1–3 daily; 1hr 40min); Orbost (daily; 2hr).

Shepparton to: Albury (1–3 daily; 2hr 20min); Melbourne (1–2 daily; 3hr).

Stawell to: Ballarat (daily; 1hr 40min); Halls Gap (Grampians; daily; 35min); Horsham (3 daily; 55min).

Swan Hill to: Albury (1–2 daily; 5hr 45min–6hr 20min); Bendigo (1–3 daily; 3hr); Echuca (1–2 daily; 1hr 55min); Mildura (1–2 daily; 2hr 30min–3hr).

Wangaratta to: Beechworth (1–3 daily; 30min); Bendigo (3 weekly; 4hr 25min); Bright (1–2 daily; 55min–1hr 25min); Mount Beauty (2 weekly; 2hr 30min); Rutherglen (6 weekly; 1hr 20min).

Warrnambool to: Apollo Bay (Fri only; 3hr 10min); Ballarat (5 weekly; 2hr 55min); Casterton (1–2 daily except Sat, 2hr 25min); Geelong (Coastlink via Apollo Bay; Fri only; 7 hr); Hamilton (1–2 daily except Sat; 1hr 40min); Mount Gambier (1–3 daily; 3hr); Port Fairy (1–4 daily; 40min); Portland (1–3 daily; 1hr 30min).

Flights

Albury to: Melbourne (2–8 daily; 50min).
Mildura to: Melbourne (3–8 daily; 1hr 10min).
Portland to: Melbourne (1–3 daily; 40min).

Tasmania

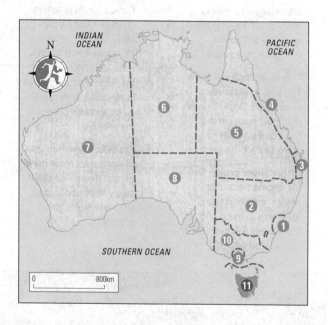

CHAPTER 11

Highlights

* **Salamanca Market**
  Lined with old stone warehouses and characterful old pubs, Hobart's Salamanca Place comes alive for its colourful open-air Saturday market. **See p.1071**

* **Port Arthur** The infamous old penal settlement is the biggest draw on the wild, scenic Tasman Peninsula. **See p.1093**

* **Freycinet National Park** The hike to exquisite Wine Glass Bay is one of the finest walks in the glorious Freycinet National Park. **See p.1099**

* **Arthur River cruise** See the largest tract of temperate rainforest found anywhere in the world on the five-hour Arthur River cruise. **See p.1137**

* **Gordon River cruise** A cruise up the dark, brown Gordon River is the best way to get a glimpse of the World Heritage-listed wilderness. **See p.1144**

* **Cradle Mountain–Lake St Clair National Park** Famed for its gruelling Overland Track bushwalk, Cradle Mountain–Lake St Clair National Park is one of the most glaciated areas in Australia, with many lakes and tarns. **See p.1146**

* **Franklin River** Raft one of Australia's most dangerous rivers – or see it safely from above on a seaplane flight. **See p.1152**

Tasmania

There's an otherworldly quality to **Tasmania**, with its gothic landscape of rain clouds and brooding mountains. This was a prison island whose name, Van Diemen's Land, was so redolent with horror that when convict transport ended in 1852 it was immediately changed. Yet the island has another, friendlier side to it too, with distances comprehensible to a European traveller – it's roughly the size of Ireland – and resonant echoes of England: cream teas, old-fashioned B&Bs and amiable, homespun people. In winter, when the grass is green, the gentle and cultivated midlands, with their rolling hills, dry stone walls and old stone villages, are reminiscent of England's West Country. Town names, too, invariably invoke the British Isles – Perth, Swansea, Brighton and Somerset among them. It's a "mainlander's" joke that Tasmania is twenty years behind, and it's true that in some ways it is very old-fashioned, a trait that is by turn charming and frustrating. However, things are changing fast: with a new state-wide arts festival, accolades from top US magazines such as *Condé Nast*, booming real estate, and cheaper and more frequent ferries and flights. Tasmania is certainly capturing imaginations, with a recent list of internationally lauded novels set here, from Chloe Hooper's *A Child's Book of True Crime* to Matthew Kneale's *English Passengers*.

Tasmania is the closest point in Australia to the Antarctic Circle, and the west coast is wild, wet and savage, bearing the full brunt of the Roaring Forties. Inland, the southwest has wild rivers, impassable temperate rain-forests, buttongrass plains, and glacially carved mountains and tarns that have been linked to create a vast World Heritage Area. This region – crossed only by the Lyell Highway – extends from the South West National Park, through the Franklin Lower Gordon Wild Rivers National Park, and across to the Cradle Mountain–Lake St Clair National Park, providing some of the world's best wilderness walking and rafting. The stage for frequent and dramatic conflicts between conservationists and the logging and mining communities, it's still one of the cleanest places on earth: a wilderness walk, breathing the fresh air and drinking freely from tannin-stained streams, is a genuinely bucolic experience.

A north–south axis divides the settled areas, with the two major cities, **Hobart**, the capital, in the south, and **Launceston** in the north. The **northwest coast**, facing the mainland across Bass Strait, is the most densely populated region, the site of Tasmania's two other cities, **Devonport** (where the Bass Strait ferries docks) and **Burnie**. Tasmania's **central plateau**, with its thousands of lakes, is sparsely populated, though full of weekender fishing shacks. The sheltered, mostly flat **east coast** is the place to go for sun and watersports activities; it has plenty of deserted beaches, safe for swimming, set against a backdrop of bush-clad hills.

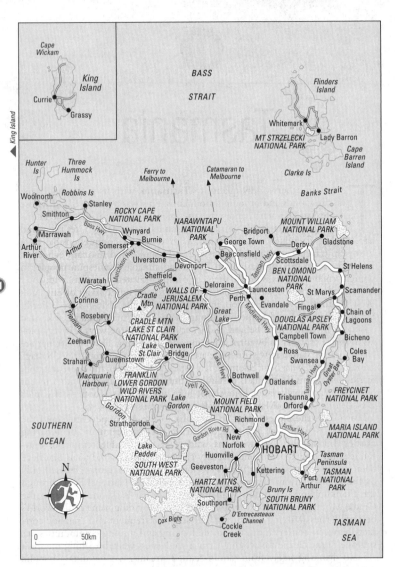

It rarely gets above 25°C in Tasmania, even at the height of summer, and the weather is notoriously changeable, particularly in the uplands, where it can sleet and snow at any time of year; the most stable month is February. However, with the ozone layer thinning every year the UV rays are particularly strong: wear plenty of sunscreen and a hat. Winter (June–Aug) is a bitterly cold time to visit unless you choose the more temperate east coast; wilderness walks are best left to the most experienced and well-equipped at this time of year.

Some history

The Dutch navigator **Abel Tasman** sighted the west coast of the island in 1642. Landing a party on its east coast, he named it **Van Diemen's Land** in honour of the governor of the Dutch East Indies. Early maps show it connected to the mainland, and several eighteenth-century French and British navigators, including William Bligh and James Cook, who claimed it for the British, did not prove otherwise. It was not until 1798 that Matthew Flinders circumnavigated the island, and his discovery of the **Bass Strait** reduced the journey to Sydney by a week. In 1803, after the French had been observed nosing around the island's southern waters, it was decided to establish a second **colony** in Australia (the first was Sydney Cove) and Lieutenant David Bowen was dispatched to Van Diemen's Land, settling with a group of convicts on the banks of the Derwent River at Risdon Cove. In the same year, Lieutenant-Colonel John Collins set out from England with another group to settle the Port Phillip district of what would become Victoria; after a few months they gave up and crossed the Bass Strait to join Bowen's group. **Hobart Town** was founded in 1804 and the first **penal settlement** opened at Macquarie Harbour in 1821, followed by Maria Island and Port Arthur; they were mainly for those who had committed further offences while still prisoners on the mainland. Van Diemen's Land, with its harsh conditions and repressive, violent regime, became part of British folklore as a place of terror, a prison-island hell. Collins was Lieutenant-Governor of Van Diemen's Land until his death in 1810, but it is Lieutenant-Governor **George Arthur** (1824–36) who has the most prominent position in the island's history. His ideas were an influence on the prison settlement at Port Arthur and he was in charge at the time of the **Black Line** (see box, p.1058), the organized white militia used against the Aboriginal population.

Tasmania did not experience the postwar industrialization that transformed the mainland. A small, isolated and neglected state, it even missed out on postwar immigration and consequently remains predominantly Anglo-Saxon in character, with an insular, often conservative, population. Its **natural resources** include forests – covering forty percent of the island – and water, and the mountainous terrain and fast-flowing rivers meant that hydroelectricity schemes began early here, under the auspices of the huge Hydro Electricity Commission (HEC). The flooding of **Lake Pedder** in 1972 led to the formation of the **Wilderness Society**, a conservation organization whose successful **Franklin Blockade** in 1982 managed to save one of the last wild rivers. Controversy over these issues still divides the state into "Greens" and a pro-logging, pro-dam working class worried about their jobs. By voting for the **Tasmanian Greens** in 1989, enough ordinary Tasmanians showed they didn't want Tasmania's natural assets destroyed, and the party held the balance of power in the state's parliament until 1992; in early 1996 the Greens again had the power balance, with a Liberal state government. Before the 1998 state elections, the two major opposing parties, Labor and Liberal, conspired together to change the electoral structure, voting to reduce the number of members in the House of Assembly from 35 to 25, purposefully making it more difficult for the Greens to win seats. The Labor government was voted in, and the sole Green Member of Parliament in the House of Assembly, Peg Putt, had little chance of exercising any influence. However, the Tasmanian Greens set about widening its range of policies, and in the 2002 state elections, they increased their toehold by three seats, though Labor, with fourteen seats are still the majority. The Tasmanian Green party is represented federally by one senator, the Tasmanian environmental activist **Dr Bob Brown**.

The attempted genocide of the **Aboriginal peoples of Tasmania** is one of the most tragic episodes of modern history. Ironically, if it were not for American and British sealers and whalers who had operated from the shores of Van Diemen's Land since 1793, abducting Aboriginal women and taking them to the Furneaux Islands in the Bass Strait as their slaves and mistresses, the Tasmanian Aborigines would have disappeared without trace. Until recently, it was stated in school books that the last Aboriginal Tasmanian was **Truganini**, who died at Oyster Cove, south of Hobart, in 1876. However, a strong Aboriginal movement has grown up in Tasmania in the last thirty years.

The Aboriginal people of Tasmania appear to have been **racially distinct** from those of the mainland, although their beliefs and rituals were similar. About twelve thousand years ago, the thawing of the last Ice Age brought rising ocean levels, which separated these people from the mainland and caused their genetic isolation; it's thought that on the mainland new cultures probably entered ten thousand years ago. This isolation was also evident in **cultural development**: they couldn't make fire but kept alight smouldering fire sticks; their weapons were simpler – they didn't have boomerangs; and although seafood was a main source of food, eating scaly fish was taboo. In **appearance**, the men were startling, wearing their hair in long ringlets smeared with grease and red ochre, while women wore theirs closely shaved. To keep out the cold, they coated their bodies with a mixture of animal fat, ochre and charcoal; women often wore a kangaroo-skin cloak. Men decorated their bodies with linear scar patterns on their abdomens, arms and shoulders. Their **art** consisted of rock carvings of geometric designs, still to be seen in areas on the west and northwest coasts.

When the first **white settlement** was established in the early years of the nineteenth century there were reckoned to be about five thousand Aboriginal people in Tasmania, divided into nine main **tribes**. A tribe consisted of bands of forty to fifty people who lived in adjoining territory, shared the same language and culture, socialized, intermarried and – crucially – fought wars against other tribes. They also traded such items as stone tools, ochre and shell necklaces, and bands moved peaceably across neighbouring tribes' territory along well-defined routes at different times of the year to share resources: the inland Big River tribe, for example, would journey to the coast for sealing. Once they realized the white settlers were not going to "share" their resources in this traditional exchange econ-

Ongoing campaigns have been aimed at stopping old-growth logging in particularly sensitive areas, and ending **woodchipping** (pulping trees for paper) for export to Japanese paper manufacturers; currently some ninety percent of the wood taken from Tasmania's forests ends up this way, with Tasmania the only state in Australia that woodchips **rainforests**. It's claimed that the state government is subsidizing the industry, selling woodchips off at a third of the going rate to keep Tasmanians employed. There is an ongoing campaign to stop a woodchip-fuelled power station, Southwood, being built just south of Hobart, in forest near Huonville; the station has been approved but political and public pressure, plus current lack of financial funding, may see it stopped in its tracks. After much campaigning, the Tasmanian government defied the rest of Australia and announced a one-year moratorium on **GE crops**, which has recently been extended for another year. The majority of the Tasmanian people want this moratorium extended indefinitely and many would like to see Tasmania market itself as a clean, green, organic state.

omy but were instead stealing the land, the nomadic people displayed a determination to defend it – by force, if necessary. Confrontation was inevitable, and by the 1820s the white population was in a frenzy of fear – though for every settler who died, twenty Aborigines met a similar fate. In 1828 Governor Arthur declared martial law, expelling all Aboriginal people from the settled districts and giving settlers what was, in practice, a licence to shoot on sight. Alarmed by these events, the British government planned to round up the remaining Aborigines and confine them to **Bruny Island** (see p.1086), south of Hobart Town. In 1830 a mass militia of three thousand settlers formed an armed human barrier, the **Black Line**, which was to sweep across the island, clearing Aborigines before them, in preparation for "resettlement".

The line failed; but unfortunately the final tactic was "divide and rule", in which the Aboriginal people themselves, with their superb tracking skills, were enlisted to help ensnare their tribal enemies. The 135 Aborigines who survived the Black Line were moved in 1834 to a makeshift settlement on exposed and barren Flinders Island (see pp.1123–1125). Within four years most of these people died of disease, or as a result of harsh conditions. In 1837 the 47 survivors were transferred to their final settlement at Oyster Cove, near Hobart, where – no longer a threat – they were often dressed up and paraded on official engagements. The skeleton of the last survivor, "Queen" Truganini (see p.1069 and p.1087), originally from Bruny Island, was displayed in the Tasmanian Museum until 1976, when her remains were finally cremated and scattered in the D'Entrecasteaux Channel, according to her final wishes.

The descendents of the original Aboriginal Tasmanians were given a voice with the establishment of the **Tasmanian Aboriginal Centre** (TAC) in the 1970s. The TAC's push for land rights has included the handing over of Wybalenna in Flinders Island. In the 1981 census, 2700 Tasmanians ticked the Aboriginal box; 16,000 did so in 2001. But this huge increase of people proclaiming Aboriginal heritage has ironically not pleased the TAC, whose sympathies lie with the long-documented and distinct Bass Strait communities. Many of those now identifying themselves as Aboriginal are from mainland Tasmania, but of these only descendents of Aborigines such as Fanny Cochrane (see p.1069) and Dolly Dalrymple can produce documents that trace a genealogy back to the time of white settlement, part of the tight selection criteria for the establishment of a controversial Tasmanian indigenous electoral roll by the national Aboriginal body ATSIC (see p.1175) in 2002.

Tasmanian practicalities

Although it's small in Australian terms, make sure you give yourself enough **time** to see Tasmania; if you want to see only its cities you need no more than a few days, but to get a flavour of the countryside – the great outdoors is the real reason to come here – a couple of weeks or longer is necessary. **Tasmanian Travel Centres**, in Sydney at 60 Carrington St and in Melbourne at 259 Collins St (☎1300 655 145, ⓦwww.tastravel.com.au), can provide **information** and also book all transport, tours and accommodation; their free information paper, *Travelways* (ⓦwww.travelways.com.au), is extremely useful, filled with detailed, reliable and comprehensive information on accommodation, attractions, bus timetables, car rental, adventure tours and national parks. It can also be picked up at local tourist offices in Tasmania. For general tourist information check out the goverment-run **Tourism Tasmania** site ⓦwww.discovertasmania.com.au.

It's easy to find **Internet access** in Tasmania, as most towns have an Online Access Centre. The Tasmanian Communities Online website (ⓦwww.tco.asn.au)

gives locations of all the 64 centres as well as access to local town sites, often useful sources of information on local attractions and businesses.

Getting there

If you plan to be in Melbourne, or have a car you want to take over, a good way to get to Tasmania – if a potentially rough, (usually) ten-hour overnight trip doesn't worry you – is across the Bass Strait on the TT Line *Spirit of Tasmania* **ferries**. Departures are from Port Melbourne and Devonport (daily Port Melbourne and Devonport departing 9pm, arriving 7am; also day sailings daily mid-Dec to mid-Jan and 3–4 times monthly Sept–Nov & April–May, departing 9am, arriving 7pm; ☎1800 634 906, ⓦwww.spiritoftasmania.com.au). Peak fares operate early December to late January, shoulder fares late January to late April and early September to early December, and off-peak fares late April to late August. On board, there are restaurants, bars and entertainment, and you can choose to sit up on reclining cruise seats (one-way: $99/$105/$130) or take a private en-suite cabin (pricier with portholes) ranging from basic twins (one-way per person: $200–$207/$210–220/$249–$261) and four-bunk cabins ($178–$190/$187–200/$206–$234) to luxury suites ($283/309/$369). **Book in advance** in summer, especially if you want to take a vehicle. Standard-sized cars travel free in off-peak and shoulder seasons; in peak season the charge is $55 (bicycle $6; motorbike $38). Cheaper Apex return fares (21-day advance purchase) are available.

Prices are very competitive for **flights** to Tasmania from the mainland with Virgin Blue (☎13 67 89, ⓦwww.virginblue.com.au; direct flights from Melbourne to Hobart and Launceston from $190 return; flights via Melbourne including Sydney to Hobart $330 return) and Qantas (☎13 13 13, ⓦwww.qantas.com.au; direct flights from Melbourne to Burnie, Devonport, Launceston; Sydney to Hobart; Adelaide to Launceston; cheapest flight is Melbourne to Launceston at $390 and a booked-in-advance Apex return at $247). **Island Airlines** (☎03/6231 6330 or 1800 645 875), based at Essendon, just outside of Melbourne, flies to Launceston via Flinders Island (one-way: Essendon–Flinders $199; Flinders–Launceston $139). Tasmania's regional airline, Tasair (☎03/6248 5088 or 1800 062 900, ⓦwww.tasair.com.au) flies daily to King Island from Burnie and Devonport ($170 one-way), and from Hobart to Burnie. **Fly-drive packages**, which include accommodation, can be particularly good value: ask at travel agents.

Getting around

Six local **bus companies** and one charter service reach most destinations on the island. You cannot use a mainland bus pass with any of these, and services are limited, often not running at weekends, especially on the east and west coasts; in winter and spring services are even further reduced. The largest operator, **Tasmanian Redline Coaches** (☎03/6336 1446 or 1300 360 000, ⓦwww.tasredline.com.au), offers frequent scheduled services between Hobart and Launceston ($23.40) via the east coast or direct via the Midland Highway, from Devonport to Hobart ($39.80) via Deloraine and Launceston, and along the northwest coast from Devonport to Burnie and on to Smithton. **TassieLink** (☎03/6272 6611 or 1300 300 520, ⓦwww.tigerline.com.au), specializes in scheduled regional transport and bushwalkers' "Wilderness Link" services to some of the more remote destinations from November to the end of April. Scheduled services run from Hobart to Queenstown via Lake St Clair, with a connecting service to Strahan; Hobart south to Dover via Huonville, Franklin and Geeveston; Queenstown to Launceston via Cradle Mountain and

Devonport; from Hobart up the east coast as far as St Helens; and from Launceston east to Bicheno. "Wilderness Link" services (minimum of four people) include routes running west from Hobart to Mount Field National Park and Scotts Peak, and south to Cockle Creek, and from Launceston to the Walls of Jerusalem National Park and to Cradle Mountain via Deloraine and Devonport. Their fares are rather high, considering the short distances – for example, Strahan to Launceston costs $70.20 one-way, and Hobart to Mount Field costs $23.50. **Hobart Coaches** (☎03/6233 4232), head north out of Hobart to Richmond and New Norfolk, and south to Kingston, Snug, Kettering, Woodbridge and Cygnet. Several smaller local operators on the east coast, such as **Bicheno Coach Service** (Coles Bay–Bicheno; ☎03/6257 0293), **Peakes Coaches** (St Marys–Swansea; ☎03/6372 5390) and **Suncoast** (Derby–St Helens; ☎03/6376 3488), help to fill in the gaps. **Maxwell's** (☎03/6492 1431) provides a charter service based on a minimum of four passengers from Devonport and Launceston to and around the Cradle Mountain–Lake St Clair area and the Walls of Jerusalem National Park.

Buying a local **bus pass** can be one way of cutting costs, but study time-tables carefully before you buy. Redline's **Tassie Pass** comes in seven-, ten-, fourteen- and 21-day versions ($135/$160/$185/219) starting from the first day of use. TassieLink's **Explorer Pass** combines scheduled and "Wilderness Link" services (except for the Cockle Creek and Scotts Peak services, which cost an extra $30 return each; seven-day pass valid for travel in ten days $160, ten-day for fifteen days $190, fourteen-day for twenty days $220, 21-day for thirty days $260). A YHA or VIP membership will give you substantial savings on all bus tickets and tours (see Basics, p.35).

Renting a car is a sensible option, considering the vagaries of the transport system. Local operators offer reasonable weekly rates including basic insurance (see "Listings" in city accounts); as Tasmania is such a small island kilometres are usually unlimited, and you don't need a lot of petrol. Though distances seem short compared to the mainland, roads are often winding and mostly two-laned – there are few freeways, except some short stretches on the outskirts of large cities – so **driving** can be slow and tiring. At dusk and night-time you have to be especially careful of animals darting in front of your car, as evidenced by the high number of dead native animals you'll see by the roadsides. But with few cars, it's easy to relax and enjoy the scenery, also making **cycling** an attractive option, especially in summer, and on the flatter midlands and east-coast routes (otherwise, plenty of gruelling hills will keep you in shape). Several operators in Hobart, Launceston and Devonport rent bikes for touring.

Another option is a **tour of the island** with Under Down Under Tours (☎03/6369 5555 or 1800 064 726, ⓦwww.downunder.com.au), a small-group outfit aimed at independent-minded travellers. Their five-day tour (departing Launceston, Devonport, Deloraine or Hobart; $430 including breakfast and lunch but not accommodation) does a loop of the island and includes plenty of bushwalking and some wildlife-spotting; the two-day tour (departing Devonport or Launceston; $220) of the northwest includes the Arthur River cruise. Both can be combined into a seven-day trip ($620).

National parks and bushwalking

All **national parks** in Tasmania charge daily (24hr) **entry fees**, often on an honour system, of $3.50 per pedestrian or cyclist, or $10 per vehicle (including up to eight passengers); if you plan to go bush for long periods, then a **Parks Pass** will be better value. On offer are a two-month holiday pass (person, cyclist or motorcyclist $13.50, vehicle $33) or an annual pass for longer-stayers (car $20 for one park, $46 for all parks); camping fees are not included (though many sites are free anyway). Tasmania's wilderness has always attracted thousands of **bushwalkers**, and many of the churned-up tracks are gradually being boardwalked; keeping to set paths to avoid further erosion is just one of the national park's minimum-impact guidelines, available in a leaflet from the **Tasmania Parks and Wildlife Service**, 134 Macquarie St, Hobart or downloadable from their website (☎03/6233 6191, ⓦwww.parks .tas.gov.au), which also supplies detailed maps. It must be emphasized that walking in the wilderness can be dangerous if you're ill-prepared: you should never go by yourself and you should always register your plans with a park ranger or inform others of your intentions. The free *Bushwalking Trip Planner for Tasmania's World Heritage Area* gives information about the clothing and equipment needed in these parks, where the weather can change rapidly – even on a warm summer day hail, sleet or snow can suddenly descend in the highlands, and walkers who have disregarded warnings have died of hypothermia. As a minimum, you'll need wet-weather gear, thermal clothing, walking boots, a sturdy tent, warm sleeping bag, a fuel cooking stove, maps and a compass (which you should know how to use). Gear can be rented from outdoor shops in Hobart, Launceston and Devonport.

Festivals

The **Ten Days on the Island** festival, inaugurated in 2001, is Tasmania's first international arts festival, held biennially in March/April in venues around Tasmania (☎03/6233 5700, ⓦwww.tendaysontheisland.org); a celebration of island cultures, it combines the cream of local arts with the best from island cultures throughout the world. Also hosted state-wide is the **Tasmanian Writers' Festival** each August (☎03/6224 0029, ⓦwww.tasmanianwriters.org). The big music event is the **Cygnet Folk Festival** (see p.1083). See also the festival listings for Hobart (p.1079) and Launceston (p.1105).

On the sports front, the big event is the finale of the **Sydney–Hobart yacht race** (see p.1079), while **Targa Tasmania** is a car rally for GT and sports cars which takes over 2000km of the state's tarmacked roads for six days in April or May of each year (ⓦwww.targa.org.au).

Hobart and the east

From Lake St Clair in central Tasmania, the **Derwent River** flows past **Mount Field National Park**, Tasmania's oldest and most popular national park, through well-preserved **New Norfolk**, and towards **Hobart**, Tasmania's capital. Here, the river estuary widens to form a fine harbour before flowing into the waters of **Storm Bay** and out to the Tasman Sea. Hobart is Australia's most southerly city, battered by winter winds roaring in from the Antarctic, and surrounded by a jagged coastline. The hook-shaped **South Arm**, at the entrance to Storm Bay, is echoed on a larger scale by the **Tasman Peninsula**, with its infamous convict settlement at **Port Arthur**. To the south, the two tenuously connected halves of **Bruny Island** protect the waters of the **D'Entrecasteaux Channel**. On the mainland opposite Bruny Island is the fertile and cultivated **Huon Valley**, but as you head further south the coastline becomes increasingly wild: there are caves and thermal springs, the **Hartz Mountains National Park** inland, and the **Picton River**, where there's good rafting. The last settlement in this direction is **Cockle Creek**, the starting point for the South Coast Track which takes you towards the South West National Park (see p.1153), the great mass of wilderness forming Tasmania's southwest corner.

North of Hobart, the **east coast** of Tasmania is the tamest and most temperate part of the island, providing a popular cycling route past numerous sandy and deserted beaches and some lovely national parks. The **Tasman Highway** follows this coastline from Hobart to Launceston, heading inland through the northeast at **St Helens**, the east coast's largest town. The northeast corner is virtually unpopulated, and the **Mount William National Park** here is a haven for the Forrester kangaroo. Inland are some old tin-mining towns, and superb rainforest remnants and mountain scenery at **Weldborough Pass**, beyond which you pass through rich agricultural and forestry country to Launceston.

Hobart

HOBART is small but beautifully sited, and approaching it from any direction is exhilarating: speeding across the expressway on the Tasman Bridge over the wide expanse of the Derwent River, or swooping down the Southern Outlet with hills, harbour, docks and houses spread out below. The green- and red-tin-roofed timber houses climb up the lower slopes of Mount Wellington, snow-topped for two or three months of the year, and look down on the expansive harbour. It's a city focused on the water: the centre is only a few minutes' walk from the waterfront, where fresh seafood can be bought directly from fishing boats in Sullivans Cove, and yachties hang out at old dockside pubs or head for fish and chips served from the punts moored in Constitution Dock. South of Constitution Dock is Salamanca Place, a well-preserved streetscape of waterfront stone warehouses which is the site of a famous Saturday market, a Hobart highlight. Yacht races and regattas are held throughout the year, while at weekends the water is alive with boats; you can choose any type of craft for a harbour cruise – perfect in the summer when it's dry and not too hot. In winter, though, the wind roars in from the Antarctic and temperatures drop to 5°C and below.

Australia's second-oldest city after Sydney, Hobart has managed to escape the clutches of developers, and its early architectural heritage is remarkably well preserved – more so than any other antipodean city. In 1803 **Lieutenant John Bowen** led a party of 24 convicts from Sydney to settle on the eastern shores of the Derwent River at Risdon Cove. A year later **Lieutenant-Colonel David Collins** arrived, with about three hundred convicts, a contingent of marines to guard over them, and thirty or more free settlers including women and children, and founded Hobart Town on Sullivans Cove, 10km below the original settlement and on the opposite shore. Collins went on to serve as Lieutenant-Governor of the colony for ten years. For the first two years, food was scarce, and settlers had to hunt local game, creating an early culture based on guns that was later to have terrible effects on the Aboriginal population. The fine deep-water port helped make the town prosperous, and a merchant class became wealthy through whaling, shipbuilding and the transport of crops

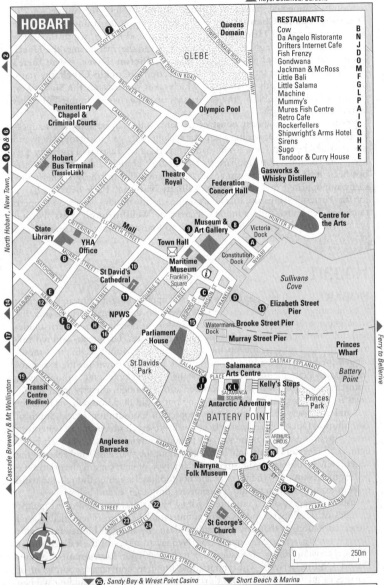

HOBART

Royal Botanical Gardens

Queens Domain

GLEBE

Olympic Pool

Penitentiary
Chapel &
Criminal Courts

Hobart
Bus Terminal
(TassieLink)

Theatre
Royal

Federation
Concert Hall

Gasworks &
Whisky Distillery

Centre for
the Arts

State
Library

YHA
Office

Mall

Museum &
Art Gallery

Victoria
Dock

Town Hall

Maritime
Museum

St David's
Cathedral

Franklin
Square

Constitution
Dock

Sullivans
Cove

NPWS

Elizabeth Street
Pier

Parliament
House

Watermans
Dock

Brooke Street Pier

Murray Street Pier

Princes
Wharf

St Davids
Park

Transit
Centre
(Redline)

Salamanca
Arts Centre

Kelly's Steps

Battery
Point

Antarctic Adventure

Princes
Park

BATTERY POINT

Anglesea
Barracks

Narryna
Folk Museum

Arthurs
Circus

St George's
Church

N

North Hobart, New Town,

Cascade Brewery & Mt Wellington

Ferry to Bellerive

Sandy Bay & Wrest Point Casino

Short Beach & Marina

0   250m

and wool. The period between the late 1820s and the 1840s was a golden age for building, with the government architect **John Lee Archer** and the convict **James Blackburn** responsible for some of Hobart's finest buildings. There's a wealth of colonial Georgian **architecture**, with more than ninety buildings classified by the National Trust, sixty of which are on Macquarie and Davey streets. **Battery Point**, a village of workers' cottages and grand houses set in narrow, irregular streets, has hardly changed in the last 150 years.

Arrival, information and transport

Hobart **airport** is 17km northeast of the city outside of Cambridge. Tasmanian Redline Coaches runs an airport **shuttle bus** to the city ($9 one-way, $15 return; bookings ☏0419 383 462), dropping off at central accommodation, as well as the *Adelphi Court YHA* and *Allport's* in New Town; a **taxi** costs around $32–37. Redline **coaches** arrive at the **Transit Centre**, 199 Collins St (☏1300 360 000; showers $5; left-luggage $1.50 per item per day), which has hostel accommodation upstairs (see p.1067). TassieLink disembarks at the **Hobart Bus Terminal**, 64 Brisbane St (☏1300 300 520) where there's a free left-luggage service for passengers and a cafeteria. If arriving by **car**, be aware that most of the streets are one-way.

Information

The first stop for general information is the **Tasmanian Travel and Information Centre** at 20 Davey St, corner of Elizabeth Street (Mon–Fri 8.30am–5.15pm, Sat & Sun 9am–4pm; ☏03/6230 8233), though it functions mainly as a travel, car-rental and accommodation-booking agency. The **National Trust Shop**, in the Penitentiary Chapel at the corner of Brisbane and Campbell streets (Mon–Fri 10am–2.30pm; ☏03/6231 0911), has inexpensive architectural guides detailing the bewildering range of listed buildings. On a more alternative note, the **Tasmanian Environment Centre**, 102 Bathurst St (Mon–Fri 9am–5pm; ☏03/6234 5566, ⓦwww.tased.edu.au/tasonline/tec), is a relaxed resource space with lots of books and information and notice boards featuring environmental events, rooms to let and items for sale; the centre operates a programme of talks and bushwalks throughout the year. For **bushwalking information** and a full range of Tasmaps, head for the Service Tasmania Shop at 134 Macquarie St (Mon–Fri 8.15am–5.30pm; ☏1300 135 513). Upstairs, the Parks and Wildlife Service (same hours and number) has information sheets and can refer you to a parks officer for advice; other general and bushwalking maps are stocked at the Tasmanian Map Centre, 96 Elizabeth St (☏03/6231 9043).

City transport

Hobart's public transport system, the **Hobart Metro** (information ☏13 22 01, ⓦwww.metrotas.com.au), is useful for getting to less central accommodation and some more distant points of interest. The Metroshop, inside the GPO on Elizabeth Street sells Metro Tens (a pack of ten tickets giving a twenty percent saving) and provides timetables; the area outside – Elizabeth Street, Franklin Square and Macquarie Street – is the bus interchange. The handy yellow-painted **Busy Bee bus** does a circuit from Franklin Square through Battery Point and up Sandy Bay Road to the casino and back again. Single **tickets** cost from $1.40 (valid 1hr 30min); off-peak day-rover passes are $3.60. The *Wrest Point Wanderer*, a Roche O'May Cruises **ferry** (see box on p.1071), runs to the Botanical Gardens, Bellerive, on the eastern shore, and Wrest Point

Casino in Sandy Bay from Brooke Street Pier on a one-and-a-half-hour circuit (departs Mon–Fri 11am, 1.30pm, 3pm; Sat & Sun 10.30am, noon, 1.30pm & 3pm; $4 per stop or $15 day-pass). You can hail a **taxi** on the street, or there are taxi stands around the city; the major one is outside the Town Hall on Elizabeth Street (for phone numbers, see "Listings" p.1080).

Accommodation

There's plenty of **accommodation** in Hobart, but during the peak season from Boxing Day and throughout the first week of January, when the yachties hit town, prices can shoot up and places are hard to find. City and dockside **hotels** are the best option for clean, affordable private accommodation, and there's an increasing number of **hostels**; in the summer, student rooms are available at the excellent *Jane Franklin Hall* in South Hobart (℡ 03/6223 2000). Battery Point is full of (sometimes pricey) **B&Bs**, and the area has several good **self-catering** holiday apartments, with costs comparable to a motel. Most **motels** are situated in Sandy Bay, about 3km south of the centre, or along the Brooker Highway, but B&Bs and guesthouses tend to offer better value.

Hotels and motels

Astor Private Hotel 157 Macquarie St ℡ 03/6234 6611, ⓦ www.astorprivatehotel.com.au. Central, old-fashioned, family-run hotel; rates include breakfast. The elegant *Astor Grill* at street level specializes in fine Tasmanian beef and seafood. ❸–❹

Blue Hills Motel 96A Sandy Bay Rd, Battery Point ℡ 03/6223 1777 or 1800 030 776, ⓦ www.blue hillshobart.com. Pleasant motel with fantastic views of Mount Wellington from one side of the building – ask for one of these rooms. Also one-bedroom apartments (sleeping four) with kitchen. ❺

Customs House Hotel Cnr Murray and Morrison streets, opposite Watermans Dock ℡ 03/6234 6645. Old-style waterfront hotel opposite Parliament House with great views. Recently extended and renovated, its accommodation is now all en suite. ❺

Grand Chancellor 1 Davey St ℡ 03/6235 4535, ⓦ www.hgchobart.com.au. Hobart's five-star hotel, in a great waterfront spot (but with a very ugly exterior itself). Facilities include two restaurants, two bars and a health club. ❻–❼

Hadley's Hotel 34 Murray St ℡ 03/6223 4355 or 1800 131 689, ⓦ www.hadleyshotel.com.au. National Trust-listed hotel close to the waterfront, with an old-fashioned feel but modern facilities; in-house restaurant, café, bistro and bar. Room service, 24hr reception, and free parking. ❻

Harringtons 102 Harrington St ℡ 03/6234 9240, ⓔ harringtons@harringtons.com.au. Small – only ten rooms on two floors – friendly and very modern hotel, handily located close to a concentration of cafés and restaurants. Good-value, small but colourful, nicely decorated and very clean

rooms, plus some larger, more luxurious ones with marble bathrooms. ❹–❺

Hobart Tower Motel 300 Park St, off the Brooker Highway, New Town ℡ 03/6228 0166, ⓔ hobtower@southcom.au. Clean, comfortable accommodation 2km north of the city, with a walk-up tower giving fantastic city and mountain views. Budget-priced, though traffic can be heard from the highway. Rooms are modern and pleasantly decorated, several with views. Family rooms sleep five. ❸–❹

Kingston Beach Motel 31 Osborne Esplanade, Kingston ℡ 03/6229 8969. Older-style beachfront motel that looks unpromising from the outside, but has comfortable, homey rooms with handy kitchen areas. Run by a friendly family. Bus #61. ❸–❹

Macquarie Motor Inn 167 Macquarie St ℡ 03/6234 4422, ⓦ www.leisureinns.com.au. Very central high-rise, friendlier than it looks; under-5s stay for free. Facilities include a pool, sauna and spa. ❺

Prince of Wales 55 Hampden Rd, Battery Point ℡ 03/6223 6355, ⓔ princeofwaleshotel @bigpond.com. Ugly modern pub but in a great heritage location, with good motel-style rooms (but no phones) which either have views of the water or of Mount Wellington. Bathrooms all have tubs. Light breakfast in the bistro included. Guest laundry; parking. Bands (Wed, Sat & Sun) don't play too near rooms, so noise isn't a problem. ❹

Theatre Royal 31 Campbell St ℡ 03/6234 6925, ⓕ 6231 1773. A basic hotel, but in a great position across from the Theatre Royal, with plain but presentable rooms; some singles available, and light breakfast included. Excellent bar and bistro downstairs. ❹

Wrest Point Hotel-Casino 410 Sandy Bay Rd, Sandy Bay ☎03/6225 0112, ⓦwww.wrestpoint.com.au. Upmarket four-star hotel with riverside rooms. Heated indoor pool, sauna and 24hr room service. Luxury tower or cheaper motel section. ⑤–⑦

B&Bs and guesthouses

Colville Cottage 32 Mona St, Battery Point ☎03/6223 6968, ⓦwww.colvillecottage.com.au. Peaceful Victorian weatherboard B&B, with en-suite rooms and a pleasant garden. ⑤

The Lodge on Elizabeth 249 Elizabeth St, cnr Warwick St ☎03/6231 3830, ⓦwww.thelodge.com.au. Delightful guesthouse in an elegant National Trust-listed 1829 mansion; guest lounge with fireplace, games and compli-mentary port. All rooms en suite, some with spa. Also offers a self-contained cottage with spa. Light buffet breakfast included. ④–⑤, cottage ⑥

Wellington Lodge 7 Scott St, Glebe ☎03/6231 0614, ⓦwww.view.com.au/wellodge. A weather-board B&B classified by the National Trust, close to Queens Domain park and the city centre. All rooms en suite and nonsmoking. ⑤

Hostels and budget accommodation

Adelphi Court YHA 17 Stoke St, New Town ☎03/6228 4829, ⓔadelphi@yhatas.org.au. Modern, motel-like hostel and guesthouse arranged around a courtyard, on a quiet suburban street, with the usual facilities. Two-and-a-half kilometres north of the city centre, and a 10min walk to the Elizabeth Street restaurant strip in North Hobart, but with plenty of parking. Bus #15 or #16 from Argyle Street to Stoke St, or #25–42, #100 or #105–128 from Elizabeth Street. Dorms $20–$22, rooms ③–④

Allport's 432 Elizabeth St, North Hobart ☎03/6231 5464, ⓦwww.tassie.net.au/~allports. Heritage-listed 1850s mansion is now a very clean and comfortable hostel away from the centre but close to bars, cafés, restaurants and a cinema. Dorms and rooms are brightly painted with colour-ful duvets, simple pine furniture and telephones. Good private showers. The usual facilities plus loads of common areas, disabled access, Internet, free storage and help-yourself veggie garden. Plenty of parking. Dorms $20, rooms ③

Central City Backpackers 2nd Floor, 138 Collins St, entrance off Imperial Arcade ☎03/6224 2404 or 1800 811 507, ⓦwww.centralbackpackers .com.au. One of Hobart's best hostels, in the spa-cious quarters of a once grand hotel. Friendly, effi-cient management. Dorms, singles, twins or dou-bles; all heated; linen rental $2 extra. Well set-up kitchen, pleasant dining area, TV and games rooms, storage room and bike rental. No parking. Dorms $18–$22, rooms ②

Montgomery's Private Hotel & YHA Backpackers 9 Argyle St ☎03/6231 2660, ⓔmontys@southcom.com.au. Centrally located in a renovated old warehouse, this feels more imper-sonal hotel than friendly hostel. The tastefully dec-orated en suites have everything you'd get in a motel, including a phone but dorms (up to twelve-bed) have nowhere to put or hang stuff (even the lockers are in the hall). Very small kitchen/dining room, small lounge with TV. Bus and tour booking facilities, Internet, bike rental. Bag storage $2 per day. No parking. Some disabled-access rooms downstairs (no lifts). Dorms $20–22, rooms ④

Narrara Backpackers 88 Goulburn St ☎03/6231 3191, ⓦwww.narrara.com.au. Attractive turn-of-the-twentieth-century house turned into a friendly, secure hostel, with an amiable live-in manager. The common room downstairs has pretty leadlight win-dows, a big table and comfy sofas; decent, well-equipped kitchen. Free Internet access. Dorms, twins and doubles, all very clean. Parking; bikes for rent. Free storage. Dorms $18–21, rooms ②

New Sydney Hotel 87 Bathurst St ☎03/6234 4516, ⓦwww.newsydneyhotel.com. Clean, central backpackers' above a pub, with kitchen facilities and guest lounge. Noisy bands play downstairs six nights. Always lively, though, and budget pub meals are available. Dorms $18, rooms ②

The Pickled Frog Backpackers 281 Liverpool St ☎03/6234 7977, ⓦwww.thepickledfrog.com. Pub-turned-hostel, with young staff and a sociable, lively feel. Downstairs is a fantastic, extensive com-munal area: within its several rooms are a bar sell-ing cheap beers and meals, an espresso machine, comfortable sofas, a pool table, booths, a wood-combustion fire, computers and a huge industrial kitchen. Simple clean dorms (ranging from four- to ten-bed), singles, doubles and triples all have sinks and heating, though no storage. Linen included but bedding $3 for length of stay. Light breakfast included. Bike rental. Parking available. Free lug-gage storage. Dorms $18–21, rooms ②

Transit Centre Backpackers 199 Collins St, above the Transit Centre ☎ & ⓕ 03/6231 2400, ⓦwww.salamanca.com.au/backpackers. Modern, central, well-equipped and spacious, but lacking in atmosphere. Dorms $18; rooms ②

Caravan parks and self-catering apartments

Crelin Lodge 1 Crelin St, Battery Point ☎03/6223 1777, ⓦwww.bluehillshobart.com. Pleasant apartments with up to five beds, in a great spot. Most have views down the river. ❹

Graham Court Apartments 15 Pirie St, New Town ⓉU03/6278 1333, Ⓦwww.grahamcourt .com.au. Comfortable, well-equipped and good-value one- to three-bedroom self-contained apartments, but 2.5km north of the city centre. Disabled access. ❹–❺

St Ives Hotel Apartments 67 St Georges Terrace, off Sandy Bay Rd, Battery Point ⓉU03/6224 1044. Two-level apartments with two bedrooms and full kitchen, TV/dining room and neutral decor; sleep five. Others are like standard motel rooms, but with full kitchen. All have bathrooms with tubs, and balconies with water views.

On four floors; luggage lift only. Rooms ❹, apartments ❺–❻

Somerset on Elizabeth Pier Elizabeth St Pier ⓉU03/6220 6600 or 1800 620 462, Ⓦwww .the-ascott.com. Waterfront apartment hotel – gorgeous studio, family studio (sleeping four) and one-bedroom apartments; all are split level, spacious and flooded with light. Some have balconies, all have kitchen and laundry, and there's a gym and sauna. From $220 for a studio to $320. ❼

Treasure Island Caravan Park 671 Main Rd, Berriedale ⓉU03/6249 2379, ⒻU6249 1420. Large park 14km northwest of the city centre on the banks of the Derwent River; camp kitchen and pool. Vans ❷, en-suite cabins ❸

The City

Hobart is small and easy to find your way around, with the streets arranged in a grid pattern running southeast towards **Sullivans Cove**. You can walk anywhere in the city centre, which is mostly flat, although surrounded by some steep hills. The civic centre is **Franklin Square**, bounded by **Macquarie** and **Davey** streets, which between them have a concentration of listed buildings. The main shopping area is **Elizabeth Street Mall**, roughly in the centre of the **CBD** (the City Business District); Elizabeth Street slopes down from **North Hobart**, known for its many fine restaurants, to the Elizabeth Street Pier on **Franklin Wharf**. Here, at the harbour, fishing boats and yachts are moored, and cruises leave from Brooke Street Pier. **Salamanca Place**, with its row of Georgian warehouses, is on the waterfront on the south side of the cove; a steep climb up Kelly's Steps brings you to **Battery Point**, to the south. Following the Derwent River around from Battery Point, you reach salubrious **Sandy Bay**, with its casino and Royal Yacht Club. To the north of the centre are the parklands of the **Queens Domain**, with the **Royal Botanical Gardens** along the waterfront; from the Domain, the **Tasman Bridge** crosses the river to the residential eastern shore.

There are relatively few sights in Hobart other than the streets themselves, but these are enough to keep you wandering around for hours, stopping at a few museums and parks along the way. While walking through the city, it's worth glancing up occasionally to observe the **street signs**; the streets are often named after important local figures and the signs have portraits and biographies. Around the docks area, and in Battery Point, interpretive boards point out historic and architectural features. Get self-guided walking maps from the Travel and Information Centre or go on one of the good historical walking tours (see p.1072). There are also many other coach and bike tours and cruises; see p.1071 and p.1080.

Franklin Square and the Tasmanian Museum and Art Gallery

Starting from **Franklin Square**, you can walk south past many of the fine old buildings on Davey Street to **St Davids Park**, originally the graveyard of St Davids Cathedral (at the corner of Murray and Macquarie streets but converted to a park in the early twentieth century. It's a quiet spot containing some important monuments, among them a huge memorial to the first governor,

David Collins. Other gravestones have been removed and set into two undulating sandstone walls at the bottom of the park.

Just north of Franklin Square is the excellent **Tasmanian Museum and Art Gallery** at 40 Macquarie St (daily 10am–5pm; free but charge for some special exhibitions; free guided tours Wed–Sun 2.30pm; Ⓦ www.tmag.tas.gov.au). The collection is, as the building's name suggests, a mixed bag. Much space is devoted to exploring Tasmania's tragic history, dwelling on penal cruelty, near genocide and the extinction of animal species.

As you enter, there's a collection of photographs of the **Tasmanian tiger** (thylacine), thought to have been extinct since 1936 – including a 1920s photo of a proud-looking family posing with their Tasmanian tiger rug spread out before them. The museum has recently acquired a unique, eight-skinned **thylacine rug** made by a Tasmanian family of similar, avid tiger-hunting ilk in the late 1890s, in a collaborative purchase with the Queen Victoria Museum in Launceston and Federal Hotels; the three are making arrangements to take turns exhibiting the rug (the latter in Strahan, see p.1141). The peculiar, flesh-eating, dog-like marsupial, which had a rigid tail, stripes and a backwards-opening pouch, was hunted out of existence by farming families who were fearful for their stock – although unconfirmed sightings of them still occur from time to time, and the Australian Museum in Sydney is attempting a long-term, ambitious project to resurrect them using DNA from pickled specimens. A stuffed example is part of the unexciting taxidermy exhibition in the adjoining room, though the life-size reconstructions of the **megafauna**, giant marsupials that once roamed Australia, on the same level, are far more riveting.

On the next level above, an **Aboriginal room** displays cultural artefacts of the island's indigenous people, including some examples of the kind of exquisite shell necklaces that would have adorned "Queen" Truganini, reputed to be the last Aboriginal Tasmanian (see box on p.1058). The display gives a comprehensive account of the Aboriginal people, from their tragic near-extermination to recent events involving land rights campaigns. Particularly poignant is the recording of the voice of **Fanny Cochrane** (1834–1905) singing traditional songs; it is she who was probably the last full-blooded Aboriginal Tasmanian rather than Truganini as the myth relates. The **art gallery** section has a display of colonial art featuring several 1830s and 1840s portraits of the well-known "final" Aborigines, including Manalargenna and Truganini, as well as superb landscape paintings of Tasmania by the nineteenth-century Tasmanian **W.C. Piguenit**. There's also an excellent section on **convicts**: if you can't get to Port Arthur, Richmond Gaol or any of the other convict ruins, this display will convince you of the brutality of the regime.

Opposite the Museum and Art Gallery, the small, modest **Maritime Museum of Tasmania** (daily 10am–5pm; $6; Ⓦ www.maritimetas.org), in the red-brick Carnegie Building on the corner of Argyle and Davey streets, houses memorabilia, photographs and exhibits dominated by models of boats – the most impressive is a third-scale model of an open whaling boat.

Northwest of Macquarie Street

There are several worthwhile sights along the straight streets that run northwest of Macquarie Street (running alongside Franklin Square), particularly Murray and Campbell streets. Three blocks northwest of Macquarie Street, on Murray Street at the corner of Bathurst Street, the **State Library** (Mon–Thurs 9.30am–6pm, Fri 9.30am–8pm, Sat 9.30am–12.30pm; Ⓦ www.statelibrary.tas.gov.au) holds the **Allport Library and Museum of Fine Arts** (Mon–Fri 9.30am–5pm; free), a private collection of eighteenth- and nineteenth-century furnishings, ceramics, silver and glass, paintings, prints and rare books relating to Australia and the Pacific.

Zest, the great little contemporary café at ground level, is very popular for Saturday brunch (closed Sun).

The **Theatre Royal**, on Campbell Street at the corner of Sackville Street (bookings ☏03/6233 2026), is Australia's oldest surviving theatre, built in 1837. It has an intimate interior decorated in Regency style, best seen while attending a performance (see p.1077); otherwise, the staff might let you in for a peek. Further up, at the corner of Brisbane Street, the **Penitentiary Chapel and Criminal Courts** (daily tours except Aug 10am, 11.30am, 1pm & 2.30pm; 1hr; $7.70) comprise a complex of early buildings with two court-rooms, underground tunnels and cells. There's also a rather spooky ghost tour (nightly 8pm; $8.80; bookings essential on ☏0417 361 392).

The Waterfront

The focus of **Sullivans Cove** is busy **Franklin Wharf**, the first commercial centre of Hobart, where merchants erected large warehouses as the colony grew wealthier. In the 1830s, Hobart was one of the world's great whaling cen-tres, and to cater for the growing volume of shipping, the New Wharf – **Princes Wharf** – was built, featuring a row of handsome sandstone ware-houses on Salamanca Place. As the new wharf became the focus of port activ-ity, the old wharf developed into an industrial centre of flour mills and facto-ries. Part of the the Henry Jones Jam Factory, between Victoria and Macquarie docks on Hunter Street, is now the **Centre for the Arts**, the University of Tasmania's art school. Beyond the original facade in a courtyard there are sev-eral large pieces of sculpture and the high-tech face of the art school. Inside, the **Sir James Plimsoll Gallery** (daily noon–5pm when there is an exhibi-tion; free) has several shows a year featuring the work of contemporary Australian artists. The rest of the old jam factory is being redeveloped and extended into a complex made up of a luxury hotel, restaurant, bar and shops – an indication of the direction the area is now taking. Beyond this, is the ren-ovated old **Gasworks** on Macquarie Street in the former red-light slum dis-trict of **Old Wapping**. Its restored stone buildings are attractive enough, but the slick shops, restaurants and enterprises within – many are part of chains – try too hard to attract tourists; one of these is the **Tasmanian Distillery and Museum** (daily 9am–7pm; $5.50 including tasting). Opposite is the new **Federation Concert Hall** (see p.1077), attached to the *Grand Chancellor* hotel and home to the Tasmanian Symphony Orchestra. The brass-clad building is oval shaped, in keeping with the original gas cylinder in the old gasworks, and its accoustics are supposedly the best in Australia.

The old docks along Franklin Wharf are also thriving: at **Victoria Dock** lob-ster boats are moored, at **Constitution Dock** boats sell fresh and cooked seafood, and alongside is the Mures Fish Centre, a two-level complex of restaurants and cafés (see "Eating and drinking", p.1075). The stylish development on Elizabeth Street Pier has a slew of trendy bars, eateries and luxury hotel apartments. From Brooke Street Pier and Watermans Dock, any number of **cruises** depart (see box opposite), while Murray Street Pier has been jazzed up with several restaurants. In summer, huge international cruise ships berth at the harbour, creating a rather glamorous backdrop to the waterfront pubs. Just behind the Travel and Information Centre, is **Mawson's Place**, completed in January 2001. Named after the Antarctic explorer Sir Douglas Mawson (see p.1072), this public space uses wooden benches, glass screens and light towers to evoke a strong maritime theme sympathetic to its dockside location. In the square the **Waterside Pavilion** retains the dimensions and facade of the original 1930s building, but the interior is a light, minimalist modern space designed for use as a display area.

Harbour cruises

The Cruise Company Brooke Street Pier ☎03/6234 9294. Fast catamaran cruises. Their Cadbury's Cruise heads upriver to the chocolate factory at Claremont; it's essential to book in advance as chocaholics treat this as a pilgrimage (Mon–Fri 10am; 4hr; $40 includes factory tour).

Fell's Historic Ferries Brooke Street Pier ☎03/6223 5893. A range of particularly good-value harbour cruises on the MV *Emmalisa*, all of which include meals of some kind ($13–28).

Lady Nelson Elizabeth Street Pier ☎03/6234 3348 or 0412 846 639, Ⓦwww.tased.edu.au/tasonline/ladynel. This replica of the brig in which Matthew Flinders made his exploratory journeys is a sail-training vessel, but also offers bargain pleasure trips most weekends year-round (call for times; 1hr 30min; $6). When the ship leaves Hobart at the end of summer for longer four- to five-day journeys on the eastern seaboard, you can join as a paying passenger (about $100 per day).

Port Arthur Cruises Brooke Street Pier ☎03/6224 0033, Ⓦwww.portarthur-cruises.com.au. Cruises along the stunning, rugged coastline north to Port Arthur on the brand-new MV *Marana*, a 25-metre fast catamaran (departs 8am Sun, also Wed 26 Dec–May, no service Aug; 2hr 30min cruising, 3hr 30min at Port Arthur; Port Arthur Historic Site entry fee and return coach to Hobart leaving at 4pm included plus morning tea; $120, without return coach $85).

Roche O'May Cruises Brooke Street Pier ☎03/6223 1914. Several cruises on an eighty-year-old boat, the MV *Cartela*, that used to bring apples from the Huon; offered are a breakfast cruise (daily 10am; 2hr; $18), a two-course lunch cruise (Mon–Thurs & Sat & Sun; 12.10pm; 2hr; $26), a shorter, cheaper Friday lunch cruise (12.10pm & 1.10pm; 50min; $12), an afternoon tea cruise (2pm & 3.15pm; 45min; $12) as well as dinner cruises (Mon, Wed, Thurs & Sat 6pm; 2hr 30min; $26 includes a main course). Their *Wrest Point Wanderer* offers a commuter ferry service to the Botanical Gardens, Bellerive and Wrest Point Casino as well as a cruise to the Cadbury Factory and Moorilla Estate Winery (Mon–Fri 10.30am; 4hr 30min; $45 includes morning tea, wine- and cheese-tasting and Cadbury tour).

On **Salamanca Place** the old warehouses, shipping offices and storerooms are now full of arts-and-crafts galleries, speciality shops and cafés, interspersed with characterful waterfront pubs. At the end of Salamanca Place, on Castray Esplanade, the old silos have been converted into upmarket apartments. Salamanca Place comes alive for the open-air **Salamanca Market** (Sat 8am–3pm), an event with an alternative feel and wonderful local food, including colourful fruit and vegetable stands, and buskers; stalls focus on local crafts, particularly woodwork using distinctive Tasmanian timber (often recycled), and there's lots of bric-a-brac and secondhand books and clothes. Several of the narrow lanes and arcades in the area are worth exploring – with shops devoted to books, fairies and secondhand clothes and crafts – as is the **Salamanca Arts Centre** (☎03/6234 8414, Ⓦwww.salarts.org.au), a former jam-canning factory that's now home to a diverse range of arts-based organizations, from the Tasmanian Writers' Centre to the Terrapin Puppet Theatre. Downstairs, the Peacock Theatre is the performance venue, and there are several galleries (daily 10am–5pm); upstairs, emerging contemporary artists show at the Long Gallery, with smaller displays in Side Space. Outside the Peacock Theatre, the great little *Foyer Espresso Bar* (Tues–Sat 8.30am–5pm) doubles as an installation venue.

Through the Arts Centre, Woobies Lane leads to lively **Salamanca Square**, a large public square with a fountain at its centre. The former is now filled with cafés, restaurants and bars with outside seating, and some interesting shops including a great bookstore. Here you'll find **Antarctic Adventure** (daily 10am–5pm; $16; ⓦwww.antarctic.com.au), an overpriced tourist attraction which cashes in on Hobart's obvious links with the Antarctic. Australia has the oldest continuously operating Antarctic station, Mawson, established in 1954, and has considerable claims under the Antarctic Treaty. Organizations based in Hobart include the Australian Antarctic Division and the Australian National Research Expedition (ANARE); the latter was the brainchild of the legendary Australian explorer, **Sir Douglas Mawson**, who led an Australian expedition from 1911 to 1914. Part-theme park, part-museum, the centre has everything from a "cold experience" room and a mock Antarctic field camp to a planetarium, but a free visit to the foyer exhibition at the Antarctic Division Headquarters at Kingston (see p.1074) is more informative and compelling in its authenticity.

A **guided walk** explores Sullivans Cove and Salamanca Place, starting from outside the Travel and Information Centre (daily 10am; 2hr; $19; bookings ⓣ03/6230 8233).

Battery Point

Kelly's Steps lead up from Salamanca Place to **Battery Point**, a district with an enduring village atmosphere. With the building of the new wharf in the 1830s, a working-class community grew up behind Salamanca Place, transforming what had been farmland into a residential area; it takes its name from the battery of guns that were once sited on present-day **Princes Park**, protecting the harbour below. The newly developing area was first home to small cottages for waterfront workmen and, later, fine merchants' houses: the old pubs, with names such as the *Shipwright's Arms* and *Whalers Return,* leave no doubt about the nature of the population. Narrow streets, closely packed cottages, the flower-filled green of **Arthurs Circus** and the "corner-store" nature of the shops (such as the delightful Bahr's Chocolate Shop, 95 Hampden Rd), enhance the nineteenth-century village feel.

There's a particular concentration of early buildings on De Witt and Cromwell streets. **St George's Church**, on Cromwell Street, is the joint work of John Lee Archer (responsible for the nave, completed in 1838) and James Blackburn (the tower, added in 1847), the early colony's two best-known architects. **Hampden Road** has more fine nineteenth-century mansions, including one at no. 103 known as **Narryna** (Tues–Fri 10.30am–5pm, Sat & Sun 2–5pm; $5), a house museum furnished with period antiques.

If you want to become really acquainted with the history and architecture of the area, take the **Battery Point Walking Tour** (Sat 9.30am–noon, departing from the Wishing Well, Franklin Square; $10 including morning tea; bookings on ⓣ03/6223 7570), led by admirably knowledgeable National Trust volunteers.

Queens Domain and Royal Tasmanian Botanical Gardens

The **Queens Domain**, just north of the city centre, looks attractively green on the map but is considerably less inviting in reality: a sparse, bush-covered hill traversed by walking and jogging tracks but positioned between two very busy highways. At the base of the hill on the Derwent, where the trees suddenly become lush and green, are the **Royal Tasmanian Botanical Gardens** (daily 8am–4.45pm), a formal collection of flower displays and orderly trees. Pick up a leaflet outlining the features of the garden at any entrance, or from the **Botanical Discovery Centre** at the main entrance on the west side of the park (daily 10am–4.30pm, until 5pm Sept–April; free), where you'll find interactive games and exhibits as well as the **information centre**, café and restaurant. It's easy enough to walk to the Domain, following Davey Street or Liverpool Street from the city centre, but the gardens are quite far inside the grounds: from the city centre to the gardens should take you about thirty minutes. Bus #17 or any of the many buses to the Eastern Shore will drop you at Government House, in the centre of the Domain near the gardens, but there's no transport back. A more interesting way of getting to the gardens is to take the *Wrest Point Wanderer* ferry from Brooke Street Pier (see box on p.1071).

North and east around the harbour

The estuary of the **Derwent River** is the deepest (and second-busiest) natural port in Australia. Just north of the Queens Domain, at **Cornelian Bay** in **New Town** you'll find cute fishing shacks and the well-regarded *Cornelian Bay Boat House Restaurant* (☎03/6228 9289) which also has a kiosk for coffees. A bike track runs here from the end of the Queens Domain below the Aquatic Centre (see "Listings" p.1080). Heading upstream, the scenery becomes increasingly industrial, with a huge zinc-processing plant, but by Berriedale the setting is more unspoilt. Here, the **Moorilla Estate Winery**, off Main Road, has gorgeous river views from its landscaped grounds and from the huge windows of the wonderful **antiquities museum** whose collection includes African, Egyptian, Mesopotamian and pre-Columbian galleries as well as Roman mosaics (daily 10am–4pm; free; Bridgewater bus #X1). It's one of Tasmania's oldest wineries, established in 1958; you can taste some of its fine cool-climate wines or eat lunch in the restaurant (bookings ☎02/6249 2949, Ⓦwww.moorilla.com.au). Beyond Berriedale is Claremont, and the riverfront **Cadbury's Factory** on Cadburys Rd. The understandably popular factory tours include lots of chocolate-tasting (every 30min Mon–Fri 9am–1.30pm; 2hr; $12.50; booking essential on ☎03/6249 0333); from the city centre, take bus #37, #38 or #39 direct to the factory. Alternatively, you can cruise here (see the box on p.1071) or go on a guided coach tour with Tigerline (Mon–Fri 9.30am; 3hr; $35; ☎03/6272 6611).

The eastern side of the river is more residential, and looking across you'll see swelling, bush-clad hills with a modest line of homes below. The **Tasman Bridge** connects the eastern shore with the city: it was put out of action for over two years from January 1975, when the 20,000-tonne tanker *Lake Illawarra*, heading for the zinc-smelting works, crashed into it and destroyed two pylons. The ship is still at the bottom of the river, with its cargo of zinc concentrate, as are the bodies of seven crew members and five people in four cars.

The **Kangaroo Bluff Battery** at Bellerive, on the eastern shore – along with its counterparts at Sandy Bay (Alexandra Battery) and Battery Point (Mona Street Battery) – was erected in response to a Russian scare in the late nineteenth century, but it never saw active service. **Bellerive**, which you can reach by ferry from Brooke Street Pier (see box on p.1071), has a long, sandy beach at the Esplanade; some swim from it, although the water is somewhat polluted. The beach suburb is host to international test cricket at the modern **Bellerive Oval** on Derwent St (details on ☎03/6211 4000). There's cleaner water and surf beaches across the promontory from Bellerive at **Opossum Bay** (bus #296 or #300); while **Seven Mile Beach**, on Frederick Henry Bay, offers calmer swimming (bus #292 or #293). Ten kilometres north of Bellerive is **Risdon Cove**, site of the first European settlement of Van Diemen's Land; interpretive boards explain its early history (bus #267, #269 or #270).

Sandy Bay

Leafy, well-heeled **Sandy Bay**, a suburb south of Battery Point, is home to a busy shopping centre on Sandy Bay Road. Near the shops, the Royal Yacht Club (where visitors can take a drink) fronts a marina, beside a beach and waterfront park. Further around the bay is the **Wrest Point Casino** on Sandy Bay Road. An ugly 1970s high-rise, the casino strives hard to be glamorous, but a rather downmarket tone is set by groups of pensioners and swarms of tour groups wearing name tags. More glamorous is the annual weekend **Sandy Bay Regatta** in January, when yachts are moored all around Sandy Bay's marinas, the river is filled with boats, and a funfair is held on the waterfront. At weekends throughout the year, too, hundreds of yachts are out on the water. Several buses go to Sandy Bay from the city centre, among them the yellow Busy Bee bus, and buses #52–56 and #60, #61 and #94. You can reach Sandy Bay over water from Brooke Street Pier on the *Wrest Point Wanderer* (see box on p.1071).

South around the harbour

South of the centre, what are defined as Hobart's suburbs terminate at beachside Kingston, reached speedily after 13km on the inland **Southern Outlet** or by a scenic, winding coastal drive via Sandy Bay Road (see above) and the **Channel Highway**. En route, at **Taroona**, 10km south of Hobart, the 48-metre-high **Shot Tower** (daily 9am–5pm; $4.50), built in 1870 to make lead shot, gives wonderful views of Hobart and the Derwent Estuary. **Kingston** is a residential suburb with wide, sandy **Kingston Beach**, which is 1km down Beach Road from the large and busy shopping centre. The sheltered beach makes a great spot for boat-watching, as all craft coming by sea into Hobart have to go past; it's also a particularly good place to catch the end of the Sydney–Hobart yacht race. At the beach there's a cluster of accommodation (see p.1066), takeaways, a pub serving good bistro meals, and a great café, *Citrus Moon*, at 23 Beach Rd (daily 9/10am–5pm, Fri to 9pm). Heading south on the Channel Highway, Australia's **Antarctic Division Headquarters** (Mon–Fri 9am–5pm; free), on the town's southern edge, can fill you in on Antarctic exploration; there's also a decent canteen. You can continue from here to **Blackmans Bay**, a long sandy beach on the promontory below Kingston; it has a stylish new waterfront café-restaurant-bar, *The Beach* (Mon–Fri 11am–midnight, Sat & Sun 9am–midnight). To get to Taroona, take bus #60 or #61; bus #61 continues on to Kingston; bus #67, #70 and #80 service Kingston and Blackmans Bay.

Inland to Mount Wellington and Mount Nelson

Heading inland, the route southwest towards Mount Wellington via Davey and Macquarie streets takes you through **South Hobart**, on to Cascade Road and past the pretty **Cascade Gardens** and the nearby **Female Factory Historic Site** on Degraves Street. The sandstone walls here are all that remain of a prison built in 1827 to house recidivist convict women who were set to work washing and sewing; fascinating interpretative boards tell their story. It's free to visit, but the fudge factory and café beside it (daily 8am–4pm) run guided tours (Mon–Fri 10.30am; $6.60; 1hr 15min); all profits go back into site conservation. Beyond Cascade Gardens, at 140 Cascade Rd, the magnificent seven-storey **Cascade Brewery** is the oldest in Australia, still using traditional methods and taking advantage of the pure spring water that cascades – of course – down Mount Wellington. **Tours** (Mon–Fri 9.30am & 1pm; 2hr; $12; bookings essential on ☎03/6221 8300) are at a fairly gruelling pace, but you're rewarded with a glass of draught beer at the end of the tour in the brewer's original residence. The small **museum** of brewing paraphernalia (Mon–Fri

9.15am–4pm; free) includes a few childhood pictures of the Hollywood actor Errol Flynn, who was brought up in the South Hobart area. If you miss the tour, you can visit the souvenir shop and museum and have a drink at the bar or in the beer garden. Take bus #43, #44, #46 or #49 to the brewery. Alternatively, you can walk or cycle all the way to Cascades Gardens and past the Female Factory along the pathway following the peaceful **Hobart Rivulet** (platypus are often seen here), starting from just behind the Village Cinema on Collins Street near the corner with Molle Street.

In any image of Hobart, **Mount Wellington** (1270m) is always looming in the background, sometimes snow-covered. Access is up winding Huon Road lined with houses as far as **Fern Tree**, from where Pillinger Drive turns into the steep and winding Pinnacle Road to the summit; the nineteen-kilometre drive provides several lookout points. The *Fern Tree Tavern* offers teas, meals and views; it's near the bottom of a walking track which goes right up the mountain (13km; 2hr up, 1hr down). There are picnic grounds with barbecues, shelters and information boards at the beginning of the track at Fern Tree, and about halfway up at The Springs. Pure, drinkable water cascades from rocks as you climb and the thick bush begins to gradually thin; by the top it's bare and rocky. Here, the stone **Pinnacle Observatory Shelter** (daily 8am–6pm) has details of the magnificent panorama spread before you, which includes vast tracts of uninhabited bush and grass plains. Metro buses #48 or #49 run to Fern Tree, or The Mount Wellington Shuttle Bus Service can get you to the summit (3 daily; $25; 2hr tour includes 30min on top; ☎0417 341 804), leaving from the Travel and Information Centre (see p.1065), or picking up from accommodation. Brake Out Cycling Tours' trip includes a visit to the summit, and then a twenty-kilometre downhill mountain-bike ride to Salamanca Place (year-round, subject to demand; $48; ☎03/6239 1080).

The views are also terrific from the Old Signal Station on **Mount Nelson** (340m) above Sandy Bay. The station was established in 1811 to announce the appearance of ships in Storm Bay and the D'Entrecasteaux Channel; the signalman's residence has been converted into tearooms (daily 9.30am–4.30pm), from where you get a panorama of the city below. To get to Mount Nelson, take bus #57 or #58.

Eating and drinking

Hobart's fare can't compare with the mainland cities' ethnically eclectic range of cuisines, but its food is becoming more cosmopolitan; the greatest diversity of restaurants and cafés is found along the Elizabeth Street strip in North Hobart including Turkish, Indian, Sudanese, Indonesian, Mexican, Thai, and several Italian places. Superlative **seafood** can be had throughout the city, but especially in the restaurants by Victoria Dock and Elizabeth Street Pier, and from the permanently moored punts selling fresh and cooked fish and seafood in Constitution Dock. In the city centre, there's a concentration of great places to eat near the junction of Collins and Harrington streets. On Saturdays, the fresh produce and food stalls at **Salamanca Market** are excellent. Also see listings in "Bars, clubs and live music".

Cafés, pubs, bars and takeaways

Cool Thai 384 Elizabeth St, North Hobart. Tiny, bright Thai takeaway with seating for ten. Good noodles, curries and soups; fresh ingredients and low prices (average $8).

Cow 112 Murray St. Nonsensically titled former (rough) pub is a cross between a bar, café and restaurant. The small modern menu does have a few steaks, but the feature is the woodfired pizzas, plus Asian dishes, risotto, fish, chicken, and kangaroo (mains around $19); food is served in a big stylish atrium-lit space, with sofas as well as tables and chairs, an open fire and a tiny courtyard beer garden. Closed Sun and Sat lunch.

Drifters Internet Cafe 33 Salamanca Place, off Montpellier Retreat. Cosy long nook of a café, its walls covered with Errol Flynn paraphernalia (tours showing where he grew up are organized from here – 1hr; $40), has several computers with Internet access ($3 per 30min, $5 per hour). Simple menu of soups, toasted sandwiches, nachos, and jacket potatoes; nothing over $8.50. Mon–Sat 10am–6pm, Sun 11am–6pm.

Jackman & McRoss 57–59 Hampden Rd, Battery Point and 32 Cross St, New Town. Two stylish eat-in bakeries. Excellent pastries and baked savouries, gourmet baguettes and rolls. Mon–Fri 7.30am–6pm, Sat & Sun 7.30am–5pm.

Kaos Cafe 237 Elizabeth St, North Hobart. Trendy, gay-friendly coffee spot, with groovy music and magazines to read. Focaccia, real fruit muffins and cakes plus delicious all-day breakfast. BYO. Mon noon–8pm, Tues–Fri noon–midnight, Sat 10am–10pm.

Little Bali 84 Harrington St. Cute, popular, inexpensive Indonesian café. Lunch Mon–Fri, dinner nightly.

Little Salama 82 Harrington St. Inexpensive Middle Eastern food. Lunch & dinner Mon–Fri.

Machine 12 Salamanca Square. Quirky combination café-laundry. Mon–Sat 8am–6pm, Sun 9am–6pm.

Macquarie Street Foodstore 356 Macquarie St, South Hobart. Colourful relaxed café, close to the Hobart Rivulet, is a great place to stop for their legendary all-day breakfast – served until 3pm – en route to the Cascade Brewery or Mount Wellington. Big portions, free-range eggs, and huge and fluffy pancakes. Mon–Fri 7.30am–6pm, Sat & Sun 8.30am–5pm.

Mummy's 38 Waterloo Crescent, Battery Point. A bright and funky licensed café serving excellent coffee and offering Internet access ($6 per hour). Snacks, such as $5 polenta wedges, are available all day and the good-value breakfast is served until 3.30pm. Simple lunches plus some more substantial main-course specials. Tues–Sun 8am–7pm.

Renown Milkbar 337 Elizabeth St, North Hobart. A Hobart institution whose windows are full of local and imported chocolates. Good for a coffee, milkshake or snack before or after a movie at the nearby cinema. Daily 8am–10pm.

Retro Café 31 Salamanca Place. Relaxed, light and airy place serving the best espresso in town, plus wonderful breakfasts. Often full of politicians from the nearby State Parliament and other high

flyers meeting over coffee mid-week. Outside tables popular on market day (Sat). A good place to find out what's on – notices and flyers cover one wall. Mon–Sat 8am–6pm, Sun 8.30am–6pm.

Shipwright's Arms Hotel Cnr Colville and Trumpeter streets, Battery Point. Old pub, popular with the yachtie crowd. Dishes up a legendary fresh seafood platter.

Sugo Shop 9, Salmanca Square. Trendy café, with a dramatic, inviting interior and big glass windows giving a view of the action-packed square. Despite appearances, it's not at all expensive. The excellent coffee and food is Italian-style: very reasonably priced gourmet pizza (from $5), foccacia, salads, pasta and risotto ($12–$14). Breakfast, served until 11.30am, costs up to $10. Mon–Fri 9.30am–5pm, Sat & Sun 9am–5pm.

Trout Bar and Cafe Eagle Hawk Inn, Elizabeth St, cnr Federal St, North Hobart ☎ 03/6234 4921. Pub which feels and focuses more as an arty café. Small menu of pasta, salads, steaks, chicken and Asian curries plus very popular Tuesday night Sudanese food cooked and served up by former refugees; bookings essential. Music, usually free, Thursday to Sunday nights in a friendly, chatty atmosphere. Lunch Wed–Fri, dinner nightly.

Restaurants and bistros

Annapurna 305 Elizabeth St, North Hobart ☎ 03/6236 9500. Popular, casual restaurant serving North and South Indian food. Great curry-and-rice lunch specials for under $9. BYO. Closed lunch Sat & Sun.

Da Angelo Ristorante 47 Hampden Rd, Battery Point ☎ 03/6223 7011. A great village spot for an upmarket, tasty Italian meal including gourmet pizzas; generous portions and good service. Licensed and BYO. Dinner nightly.

Fish Frenzy Elizabeth Street Pier. A stylish modern fish café – order your food at the counter and find a seat. The food is cheap and terrific, the staff are friendly, and it's always packed. Open daily for lunch and dinner, continuously at the weekend from noon to 9pm. Licensed.

Gondwana Cnr Hampden Rd and Francis St, Battery Point ☎ 03/6224 9900. In an old cottage with village views, this is one of Hobart's best restaurants; the creative and innovative cuisine is sourced from quality fresh, local ingredients. Tasmanian wines available by the glass. Dinner bookings essential. Expensive. Lunch Tues–Fri, dinner Tues–Sat.

Marti Zucco 364 Elizabeth St, North Hobart ☎ 03/6234 9611. Italian restaurant serving imaginative dishes, including fish, schnitzels and thick-crust pizzas. Large and very popular, with a casual atmosphere. Licensed and BYO. Dinner nightly.

Mit Zitrone 333 Elizabeth St, North Hobart ☎03/6234 8113. Funky café-restaurant: bright citrus-coloured walls, several intimate rooms, an innovative, cosmopolitan menu and extremely trendy staff. Delicious mains (around $21 at dinner, $16.50 at lunch), a superb but pricey cake and dessert selection ($9.50) and excellent coffee. BYO. Tues–Sat 10am until late.

Mures Fish Centre Victoria Dock. Set among yachts and fishing boats, this two-level food centre (open daily) houses three restaurants, a fishmonger, a bakery (great scallop pies) and a café. *Mures Upper Deck* (☎03/6231 1999) is an upmarket restaurant which has lovely harbour views; *Mures Lower Deck* (☎03/6231 2121) has bistro food, with cheaper prices; *Orizuru* (☎03/6231 1790; closed Sun) serves authentic sushi – their salmon is delicious – and is the best Japanese in Hobart.

Sirens 6 Victoria St ☎03/6234 2634. Upmarket vegetarian/vegan restaurant serving subtle Middle Eastern/North African-inspired food in a lovely plant-filled, high-ceilinged space. The interior crosses Gothic with Ottoman Empire, and there are private booths. Licensed. Lunch Mon–Fri, dinner Tues–Sat.

Sisco's Murray Street Pier ☎03/6223 2059. Waterfront Spanish-Mediterranean restaurant guarantees a fine, though pricey, feast. Licensed. Lunch Fri, dinner Mon–Sat.

Tandoor & Curry House 101 Harrington St ☎03/6234 6905. Good authentic Indian; all the favourites and accompaniments. Mains around $13. Licensed. Closed Sat lunch & Sun.

Vanadol's 353 Elizabeth St, North Hobart ☎03/6234 9307. A popular veteran, this casual, affordable place serves Thai, Indian and Indonesian food. BYO. Dinner Tues–Sun.

Entertainment and nightlife

Nightlife – what there is of it – is focused around the waterfront. The focal point is *Knopwood's Retreat* (see p.1078), which attracts a large crowd on Friday and Saturday nights, and has a popular nightclub upstairs. The more conservative *Wrest Point Casino*, at 410 Sandy Bay Rd in Sandy Bay, is open late every night for gambling, drinking and dancing (☎03/6225 0112; casino Mon–Thurs & Sun 2pm–2am; Fri & Sat 2pm–3am, *Regine's* nightclub Wed–Sun 10pm–4am).

If you want to know **what's on**, Thursday's *Mercury* has a gig guide, and you could also check its Friday and Saturday entertainment sections. A local website with details about the the **live music** scene is ⓦ www.nakeddwarf.com.au, sponsored by Aroma Records, 323 Elizabeth St, North Hobart, which has lots of flyers and info plus a great little café. Tasmania is too small to attract many bands, so the ones that play the pubs are mainly local. The few big events that do occur attract an extraordinarily varied audience, as everybody goes to everything. For more interesting gigs, keep an eye on what's happening at the University of Tasmania campus at Sandy Bay (☎03/6220 2861). There's usually free live music on Salamanca Square on Friday nights, enjoyed from the tables outside the several cafés and bars. **Concerts** are staged by the Tasmanian Symphony Orchestra at the Federation Concert Hall (see p.1078) and by the Tasmanian Conservatorium of Music at the Conservatorium (5–7 Sandy Bay Rd; ☎03/6226 7306); the Conservatorium also performs at churches around town (free or $3–15). You'll find traditional and touring **theatre** at the Theatre Royal, and more contemporary local shows at the Peacock Theatre in Salamanca Place; in February and March there's a season of outdoor Shakespeare in the Royal Botanical Gardens. Most **tickets** can be booked via Centretainment, at 132 Liverpool St (☎03/6234 5998).

Bars, clubs and live music

Bar Celona 24 Salamanca Square. Renovated sandstone warehouse turned into a slick and spacious café (by day) and bar on two levels. The light lunches (from $7 to $14) can also be eaten at tables on the square. On Friday and Saturday nights DJs play laid-back lounge music on the mezzanine level (9pm–12.30am). Daily 9am–midnight, till 1am Fri & 2am Sat.

Isobar 11 Franklin Wharf. Young and packed, the stylish *Isobar* (Wed, Thurs & Sun 5pm–midnight, Fri & Sat 5pm–2am) is a weekend favourite (expect to queue and be vetted) with live music on Friday and Saturday. At *The Club* upstairs (Fri & Sat 10pm–5am; $5/$6 or free before 11pm; cheap drinks to midnight) DJs play commercial dance on the main floor and there's also an R&B room and the quieter *Back Bar*.

Knopwood's Retreat 39 Salamanca Place. Pub that's a favourite with students, yachties and just about everyone else, with a relaxed coffee parlour/bar feel; plenty of magazines and newspapers, plus outside tables. Open until midnight on Friday, when the pavement outside is packed. Closed Sun.

Lark Distillery 14 Davey St. A handy spot to recharge, with outside tables overlooking Mawson Place. A range of spirits made on the premises can be tasted for free (the single malt whiskey has a $3 charge). Also a huge range of whiskey and bourbon, and an all-Tasmanian wine list. Cheese platters to snack on (and soup in winter). Live folk music on Friday nights (free) . Mon–Thurs & Sun 9am–6pm, Sat 10am–6pm, Fri 9am–10pm.

Möbius 7 Despard St ☎03/6224 4411. This funky basement lounge bar is Hobart's alternative club. There's live original music on Wednesdays from 9pm ($4), attracting a big student crowd, and DJs on Friday and Saturday from 10pm (free). Call to find out about the one or two extra events each month. Wed 9pm–1am, Fri & Sat 9pm–4am.

New Sydney Hotel 87 Bathurst St (☎03/6234 4516). Hobart's Irish pub, featuring live music nightly except Monday – from traditional Irish to blues and folk.

O2 7 Watchorn St. Recently renvovated, barn-like, late-opening bar-cum-nightclub. R&B and mainstream dance music; a couple of pool tables. Wed–Sat 8pm–6am, Fri from 4pm.

Prince of Wales 55 Hampden Rd, Battery Point ☎03/6223 6355. Lively, friendly pub, attracting a mixed crowd. Local bands Wednesday and Saturday nights (two bands; 9pm to midnight; $4); Sunday is more laid-back, featuring a funky jazz trio (6pm–9pm; free). Inexpensive bistro too.

Republic Bar & Café 299 Elizabeth St ☎03/6234 6954. Laid-back lounge atmosphere, funky decor and free music, usually blues and jazz, five nights a week; attracts a good crowd, including plenty of uni students. Excellent meals too – with lots of seafood on the menu.

Gay and lesbian Hobart

Acts of male homosexuality were still a criminal offence in Tasmania until 1997. Founded in 1988, the **Tasmanian Gay and Lesbian Rights Group** (TGLRG) put persistent pressure on the government. Led by spokesperson **Rodney Croome**, their rally cry "We're here, we're queer, and we're not going to the mainland" certainly shook up conservative Tasmania; thousands signed the petition to urge the reform of the law. Backlash across Tasmania included the infamous anti-gay rally in Ulverstone on the northwest coast in 1988. The federal government and the UN Human Rights Committee also pressed for change, and Tasmania's anti-gay upper house finally cracked, changing the law on May 1, 1997. Ironically, Tasmania now has the best legislation of any state to protect gay and lesbian rights.

The TGLRG office is at 82 Hampden Rd, Battery Point (☎03/6224 3556), and there's a Gay and Lesbian Community Centre (GLC) in North Hobart (PO Box 152, North Hobart, TAS 7002; ☎0500 808 031; ⓦwww.gaytas.org). GLC publishes a monthly newsletter, *CentreLines*, which is sold from the TGLRG stall at Salamanca Market and details events and occasional dance parties around town. There are **gay and lesbian club nights** at *Cruze*, 60 Argyle St (Fri & Sat from 10pm; $7/$8) and at *Lalaland Bar & Dance Club*, above *Bakers*, cnr Macquarie and Barrack streets, on the second and fourth Saturday of the month (9am–5pm; $8) playing progressive house and trance. *T-42°* and *Syrup* (see opposite) are popular alternatives. The **Gay Information Line** (☎03/6234 8179) is a five-minute recorded message that provides pointers for gay and lesbian visitors, details of events and meeting places and numbers for further information; there's also a specifically **Lesbian Line** (Thurs 6–10pm; ☎03/6231 4228).

Rockerfeller's Café & Bar 11 Morrison St ☎03/6234 3490. Cocktails, live jazz Sunday nights and a contemporary Australian menu. Lunch Mon–Fri, dinner nightly.

St Ives Hotel 86 Sandy Bay Rd, Sandy Bay. "Boutique" brewery hotel (opens 4pm) with popular club nights (Wed, Fri and Sat). Good range of Tasmanian wines at its bottle shop.

Syrup Above *Knopwood's*, 39 Salamanca Place ☎03/6224 8249. The first floor of this trendy club doubles as a restaurant; at midnight the nightclub takes over this and the floor above (Wed–Sat). Different nights and floors have changing sounds and themes: anything from Sixties theme nights, techno, house, drum'n'bass, 1980s retro, to live disco and funk. Often international guest DJs. Open till 6am on Fri & Sat; $7–10.

T-42° Elizabeth Street Pier ☎03/6224 7742. Stylish lounge bar in a great waterfront location – some tables on the pier – attracting a cross-section of trendies and young professionals. Half the place is an eating area serving well-priced modern meals at lunch and dinner. A good place to try Tasmanian wines, with many available by the glass. Daily 11.30am–1.30am.

Temple Place 121 Macquarie St ☎03/6223 2883. Sophisticated jazz venue, with restaurant, cocktail bar and cigar lounge. Open nightly and Sun afternoons.

Theatre Royal Hotel 31 Campbell St. Despite its trendily upmarket renovations, the public bar is as down-to-earth as ever. People spill in here after the theatre. Recommended bistro too. Open until midnight, closed Sun.

Film, theatre, concerts and cabaret

Federation Concert Hall 1 Davey St, bookings ☎1800 001 190. Home to the Tasmanian Symphony Orchestra, with regular concerts.

Playhouse Theatre 106 Bathurst St ☎03/6234 1536. Home to an amateur theatrical society that regularly puts on plays. Premises are also rented out to travelling shows.

Salamanca Arts Centre 77 Salamanca Place ☎03/6234 8414. Base of several performance companies, including the Terrapin Puppet Theatre, which puts on touring shows – including a puppet picnic at the end of December in St Davids Park. Puppeteers are welcome to come in and look around. The theatre venue here is the Peacock Theatre which specializes in contemporary works, performed by various local theatre companies.

State Cinema 375 Elizabeth St, North Hobart ☎03/6234 6318. Art-house and foreign films; reduced ticket prices Wednesday ($8). Licensed bar.

Theatre Royal 29 Campbell St ☎03/6233 2299. This lovely old place (see p.1070) is not too expensive or stuffy, offering a broad spectrum of entertainment from comedy nights to serious drama. The ancillary Backspace is smaller and more experimental – often hosting very entertaining Theatresports (improv) on Friday nights.

Village Cinema Centre 181 Collins St ☎03/6234 7288. Seven screens showing mainstream new releases; discount day is Tuesday.

⑪

Festivals and events

Hobart's premier event is the last part of the **Sydney–Hobart yacht race** (see also p.60). The two hundred or so yachts, which leave Sydney on December 26, arrive in Hobart around December 29, making for a lively New Year's Eve waterfront party. **Taste of Tasmania** (Dec 28–Jan 5), a festival promoting Tasmanian food, wine and beer, is held at Princes Wharf to coincide with the arrival of the boats; stalls sell samples of Tasmanian products at around $5 a plate, and there's lots of entertainment. The **Australian Wooden Boat Festival** runs over three days in early February in odd-numbered years, marked by a host of boats moored around the docks; activities include theatrical and musical performances, and there's even a School of Wooden Boat Building offering courses to visitors (☎03/6266 3486, ⓔinfo@awoodboatfest.com).

The week-long **Hobart Fringe Festival** in mid-March has visual arts and performance components; check cafés for flyers (ⓦwww.hobartfringe.com; ticket sales at the door only). The whole city shuts down on October 24 during the **Royal Hobart Show** (Oct 23–26), an agricultural festival.

Listings

Airlines Par Avion, Cambridge Airport ☎03/6248 5390, ⓦwww.paravion.com.au; Qantas ☎13 13 13, or their travel centre at 77 Elizabeth Street Mall ☎03/6237 4900; Tasair, Cambridge Airport ☎03/6248 5088 or 1800 062 900; Virgin Blue ☎13 67 89.

American Express 74A Liverpool St ☎03/6234 3711.

Banks Branches of all major banks on Elizabeth Street.

Bike rental and tours Several hostels rent bikes; see p.1067. Derwent Bike Hire (☎03/6234 2910; $7 per hour, $20 per day) has mountain bikes to rent at the beginning of the bike track to Cornelian Bay (see p.1073), by the Cenotaph in the Regatta Grounds at the south end of the Queens Domain.

Bookshops Ellison and Hawker Bookshop, 90 Liverpool St, is the best in Hobart, with an excellent travel section upstairs. Fullers Bookshop, 140 Collins St, and Hobart Bookshop, 22 Salamanca Square, are also good. For a fine range of second-hand books, try Rapid Eye Books, 36–38 Sandy Bay Rd, Battery Point.

Bus companies Tasmanian Redline Coaches, Hobart Transit Centre, 199 Collins St ☎1300 360 000; TassieLink Hobart Bus Terminal, 64 Brisbane St ☎1300 300 520.

Campervan rental Tasmanian Campervan Hire, Cambridge Airport (☎03/6248 9623 or 1800 807 119, ⓦwww.tascampervanhire.com.au), from $110 per day, minimum five-day rental.

Camping and outdoor equipment Jolly Swagman Camping World, 107 Elizabeth St, has a big range of camping gear; Paddy Pallin, 119 Elizabeth St, has quality outdoor equipment, and provides bushwalking information; Mountain Creek Great Outdoors Centre, 75–77 Bathurst St, has a big selection, from cheap to top of the range, and also rents out gear.

Car rental Autorent-Hertz, 122 Harrington St (☎03/6237 1111 or 1800 030 222, ⓦwww.autorent.com.au), has rates from $70 per day, also campervans; Avis, at the airport (☎03/6248 5424), has similar rates; Lo-Cost Auto Rent, 225 Liverpool St (☎03/6231 0550 or 1800 647 060, ⓦwww.locostautorent.com) has rentals from $59 per day; Advance Car Rentals (☎03/6224 0822 or 1800 030 118), offers free delivery and YHA and VIP discounts, also 4WDs; Marquee Car Rentals, 248 Argyle St (☎03/6231 3820), offers very cheap weekly rates; Rent-A-Bug, 105 Murray St (☎03/6231 0300, ⓦwww.rentabug.com.au), has low-priced VW Beetles from $35 per day.

Disabled travellers The Aged and Disability Care Information Service, 181 Elizabeth St (☎03/6234 7448, ⓦwww.adcis.org.au), is an excellent source of information, providing free mobility maps of Hobart. Maxi Taxis (☎03/6227 9577) has specially adapted vehicles.

Diving Southern Tasmanian Divers, 212 Elizabeth St (☎03/6234 7243), organizes dive charters and rents out equipment; The Dive Shop, 42 Bathurst St (☎03/6234 3428), runs PADI certification courses.

Environment To find out about or volunteer for any environmental conservation programmes, the Wilderness Society's campaign office is at 130 Davey St (☎03/6224 1550, ⓦwww.wilderness.org.au/tas); its shop is at 33 Salamanca Place.

Hospitals Royal Hobart Hospital, 48 Liverpool St ☎03/6222 8308.

Internet access There's free drop-in access at the Service Tasmania Shop at 134 Macquarie St (Mon–Fri 9am–4.45pm; max 30min), and paid access at the State Library (see p.1069; $5.50 per 30min for overseas visitors) but the best rates are at hostels ($2–3 per hour) and at *Drifters Internet Cafe* ($5 per hour; see p.1076).

Laundrette *Machine*, 12 Salamanca Square, is a combined café/laundry (see p.1071).

Pharmacy Macquarie Pharmacy, 180 Macquarie St (daily 8am–10pm; ☎03/6223 2339); North Hobart Pharmacy, 360–362 Elizabeth St (daily 8am–10pm; ☎03/6234 1136).

Post office GPO, cnr Elizabeth and Macquarie streets (Mon–Fri 8am–6pm). Poste restante: Hobart GPO, TAS 7000.

Swimming pool Tattersall's Hobart Aquatic Centre, cnr Liverpool St and Davies Ave (Mon–Fri 6am–10pm, Sat & Sun 8am–6pm; $4.60). Heated swim centre with waterslides and bubblejets.

Taxis City Cabs Co-op ☎03/6234 3633; Combined Services ☎13 22 27.

Tours Tigerline (☎03/6272 6611, ⓦwww.tigerline.com.au) runs large-group bus tours: their Mount Wellington and Hobart Great Sights Tour covers the city, the dock area, Battery Point, Mount Wellington and the Royal Botanical Gardens (Tues & Thurs 2pm; 3hr 30min; $45). Tigerline also offers day-trips to Port Arthur, Richmond, the Huon Valley, Bruny Island and the Derwent Valley. The other big tour operator, Experience Tasmania (☎03/6234 3336), has a wide range of city tours; their *Hobart Explorer*, a bus dolled up as a tram, does a three-hour sightseeing tour (Jan–April Mon–Fri & Sun 10am, daily 1pm; May–Dec

Mon–Fri & Sun 10am, Sat 1pm; $26), plus trips to Mount Field National Park. The best tour to Bruny Island is with Bruny Island Ventures (book through Tigerline), which does a small-group day-tour led by a knowledgeable guide (8.30am, returning 5.30pm; $125 including meals). The Bottom Bits Bus (ⓣ03/6234 5093 or 1800 777 103, ⓦwww.bottombitsbus.com) offer a range of great small-group tours from Hobart (all $75), including Port Arthur and the Tasman Peninsula, Bruny Island and Mount Field National Park, Mount Wellington and the Tahune Forest AirWalk, and Freycinet National Park.

Women Women Tasmania, 140 Macquarie St (03/6233 5485), provides information services. Hobart Women's Health Centre, 326 Elizabeth St, North Hobart ⓣ03/6231 3212.

YHA Tasmania Head Office, 28 Criterion St ⓣ03/6234 9617, ⓦwww.yha.com.au (Mon–Fri 9am–5pm).

Around Hobart

South of Hobart is picturesque channel, orchard and island country. The D'Entrecasteaux Channel region and the Huon Valley form Tasmania's premier **fruit-growing** district, which once exported millions of apples to England; since the UK joined the European Community, however, two-thirds of the apple orchards have been abandoned. The region is also heavily forested, and around **Geeveston** magnificent forests are still logged. **Hartz Mountains National Park** and the **Picton River** are easily accessible to the west of Geeveston and you can get wonderful views of both, and of old-growth forests, from the wonderful new **Tahune Forest AirWalk**. As you head down the coast, caves, thermal springs and an operational railway are all accessible en route to **Cockle Creek**, the southernmost point you can drive to in Australia, with foot access along a track into the South West National Park. Offshore, across the D'Entrecasteaux Channel from **Kettering**, **Bruny Island** – Truganini's birthplace – has deserted beaches and coastal bushwalks. To the north, you can head inland to **New Norfolk** and on to **Mount Field National Park**, while to the east lies historic **Richmond** and, on the Tasman Peninsula, the old penal settlement at **Port Arthur**.

South: the D'Entrecasteaux Channel, Huon Valley and beyond

The **Channel Highway** (B68) hugs the coastline south from Hobart and makes a lovely drive around the shores of the **Huon Peninsula**, circling back beside the Huon River to Huonville: heading to Huonville directly, it's a much shorter 37km on the **Huon Highway** (A6), which then heads south for 64km, terminating at Southport. An excellent free fold-out guide map, "The Huon Trail", is available from tourist offices; it outlines the **Huon Discovery Trail**, a series of signs and interpretative boards detailing points of interest off the Channel and Huon highways.

The Channel Highway

On the Channel Highway beyond Taroona and Kingston (see p.1074), **KETTERING**, 34km south of Hobart, is a thriving fishing port, with an attractive marina. It's from Kettering that you catch the ferry for Bruny Island (see p.1086). The unpretentious *Oyster Cove Inn* (ⓣ03/6267 4446; **B&B** ❸–❹) is right on the water, not far from the ferry terminal, and has fantastic views from its restaurant, and a quirky sculpture-cum-beer garden; it specializes in seafood and local produce. More upmarket is *Herons Rise Vineyard* on Saddle Road (ⓣ03/6267 4339, ⓦwww.heronsrise.com.au; ❺), which has luxury self-contained cabins gazing

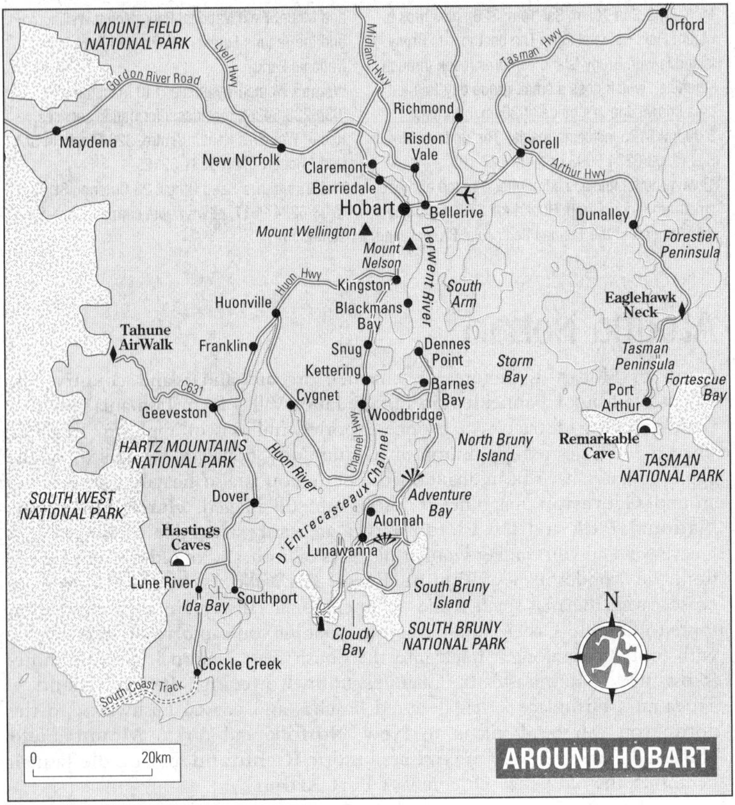

across the marina. Inside the excellent **visitors centre** at the ferry terminal (see p.1087), the *Mermaid Cafe* has good food and great coffee (daily 9am–5pm; licensed); the centre has **Internet access**. Roaring 40s Ocean Kayaking, based at the marina (Ⓣ03/6267 5000, Ⓦwww.roaring40skayaking.com.au), has **sea kayaks** for rent (from $15 per hour, $55 per day), and also organizes day-trips (Mon–Fri; $120) and longer tours.

The pretty village of **WOODBRIDGE**, 4km further south, with its quaint general store and wooden meeting hall, won't be so picturesquely unspoilt for much longer: its popular old waterfront *Woodbridge Hotel* was demolished in April 2003 to make way for the $10 million *Peppermint Bay Hotel* development, which is to include accommodation, an upmarket restaurant and fast catamaran service to link it to Hobart. For now, you can **stay** in the *Old Woodbridge Rectory* (Ⓣ03/6267 4742, Ⓦwww.rectory.alltasmanian.com; B&B ④), an attractive B&B with disabled access. Woodbridge's **Online Access Centre** is at the West Winds Community Centre. You can get to Kettering and Woodbridge with Hobart Coaches on weekdays (4 daily).

From Woodbridge, you can continue around to the other side of the peninsula to Cygnet on the Channel Highway via **Verona Sands**, a pretty, sheltered beach, undeveloped except for a general store; you can **stay** at the simple two-bedroomed *Verona Sands Holiday Units* (☎03/6297 8177; ❸). You could also take the gorgeously scenic inland route to Cygnet from Woodbridge on the C627 through hilly, rural countryside, detouring after 5km for free wine-tastings at the **Hartzview Wine Centre** (daily 9am–5pm; ☎03/6295 1623, ⓦwww.hartzview.com.au; luxury three-bedroom house ❺), a further 2km along a well-graded dirt road.

  CYGNET, at the centre of a major fruit-growing region, is a good spot to look for **fruit-picking work** in the very busy apple-harvest season (March–May), but there is also the chance of finding work strawberry-(Nov–May) or blueberry-picking (Dec–Feb) and also flower and vineyard work at other times. The town itself is very pleasant, backed by bush-covered hills and with the main thoroughfare, Mary Street, dominated by an imposing Catholic church; the appearance is sweetly old-fashioned but the town has quite an alternative cultural scene, the focus of which is the laid-back *Red Velvet Lounge Cafe*. It has a warm, communal atmosphere, sofas, a piano, affordable wholefood meals (nothing over $10), great cakes, an in-house healthfood shop and useful notice board. Behind the café *fire bird bakehouse* serves pizzas cooked in a beautiful old wood-fired oven (Thurs–Sun from 6pm). The more tradi-tional, cosy *School House Coffee Shop* across the road does great scones, while all three pubs offer counter meals and you can also **stay** in clean rooms at the *Cygnet Hotel* (☎03/6295 1267; ❷) or in more comfort at the *Cygnet Guest House* (☎03/6295 0080, ⓕ6295 1905; ❺), in an elegant converted Edwardian-era bank. Out of town, *Nomads Huon Valley Backpackers*, at 4 Sandhill Rd just off the Channel Highway, 4km north at Cradoc (☎03/6295 1551, ⓕ6295 0875; dorms $19, rooms ❷–❸; pick-ups available if arranged in advance), on several rural acres, with river views, has all the necessary contacts for fruit-pick-ing work. It has a family suite as well as several doubles, some with en suites. The weekend-long **Cygnet Folk Festival** (ⓦwww.cygnetfolkfest.south com.com.au), established in 1982, is the state's major folk, world and roots music event, and takes over the town in early January. Hobart Coaches runs a service from Hobart to Cygnet Monday to Saturday.

The Huon Highway: Huonville and around

HUONVILLE, on the Huon River, is a commercial centre, the focus of the region's apple industry, and another likely place to find work in the apple-harvest season (March–May). The once rather redneck town is developing a more alternative and upmarket edge, suited to its picturesque position on the Huon River. It now has a handy **Parks and Wildlife Service information centre** and shop, at 24 Main Rd (Mon–Fri 9am–4.30pm; ☎03/6264 8460) with information on all parks and reserves, park passes, books, maps, gifts, some walking gear, and there's also a community-based **Environment Centre** at 17 Wilmot Rd (Tues–Fri 9.30am–4.30pm, Sat 10am–3pm; ☎03/6264 1286), northwest of the roundabout near the Parks shop. There's real café culture too, at *Cafe Moto* (closed Tues) opposite the centre. Another good place to **eat** is *Huon Manor Bistro* (☎03/6264 1311; lunch daily, dinner Mon, Tues & Thurs–Sat), a cosy, reasonably priced restaurant-cum-bar in a big federation-style riverfront homestead, just by the bridge into town.

  There are opportunities to get onto the river at Huonville with Huon River Cruises (☎03/6264 1838), based with the **Huonville Visitor Information Centre** (daily 9am–5pm; same phone) on The Esplanade, as the Channel Highway is called coming into town from Cygnet. They offer cruises on the *Southern Contessa*, which visits Atlantic salmon fish farms (Mon–Fri 10am; 2hr; $32), and **jet-boat rides** through the rapids (40min; $52), or you can rent a pedal boat (30min; $12). Huonville's **Online Access Centre** is at 23 Wilmot Rd. TassieLink runs a service from Hobart to Huonville.

At **GROVE**, 6km back towards Hobart on the Huon Highway, is the **Huon Valley Apple and Heritage Museum** (daily 9am–5pm; $5), which celebrates the local produce; the museum is surprisingly interesting, with hundreds of varieties of apples and assorted apple paraphernalia from what was once a huge export industry.

Three kilometres northwest of Huonville via Wilmot Road, at the picturesque hamlet of **RANELAGH** is the lauded *Matilda's of Ranelagh* at 44 Louisa St (☎03/6264 3493, ⊛www.matildasofranelagh.com.au; ❻ including cooked breakfast), a B&B in an 1850 National Trust-listed mansion within English-style gardens with a characterful outhouse on the grounds. Just out of Ranelagh, the sleek, architect-designed, vineyard-set winery/restaurant, **Home Hill**, at 38 Nairn St (free tastings daily 10am–5pm; lunch Wed–Sun, dinner Fri & Sat, morning and afternoon tea daily; bookings ☎03/6264 1200), has a stunning backdrop of Mount Wellington. It's always booked out for Sunday lunch.

Southwest beyond Huonville, the road follows the west bank of the Huon to **FRANKLIN**, a handsome riverside community with several fine old buildings and cute weatherboard homes facing the river and set against green hills. At the **Wooden Boat Centre Tasmania**, on the riverfront, you can see traditional wooden boat building and restoration (daily 10am–5pm; $5.50; ⊛www.woodenboatschool.com). You can stay in the swanky *Franklin Lodge* (☎03/6266 3506; ❺). Franklin is also a good stop-off point for a **meal**. There's good-value bistro food at the *Franklin Tavern* and great coffee at the waterfront *Southern Providore* (closed Wed; licensed), which has a small blackboard menu of freshly baked dishes. *Franklin Tea Gardens*, inside a plant nursery, serves great home-made food. In the evening, offerings at the licensed *Franklin Grill* include fresh Bruny Island oysters (dinner Wed–Sun; ☎03/6266 3645) while *Cafe Purple* does great wood-fired pizza (from 5pm Wed–Sun).

Geeveston and around

GEEVESTON, 18km south of Franklin, is a sleepy but solid town at the centre of the Southern Forest, a traditional logging centre, with two huge upright logs acting as an entrance to the town. Confrontation between conservationists and the timber industry here led to the so-called "Battle of Farmhouse Creek" in 1986, a dispute won by the conservationists, after which some of the forests were awarded World Heritage listing. The Forestry Commission was awarded millions of dollars in compensation, to be used on special forestry projects, one of which is the **Forest and Heritage Centre** in the town hall on Church Street (daily 9am–5pm; ⊛www.forestandheritage centre.com.au; $4; ☎03/6297 1836), which also has a **visitor information** centre. Displays explain how the Southern Forests grow and look at the history of logging in the area – including the Farmhouse Creek dispute. There's also a gallery of local woodwork and a woodturner in residence (lessons are available if you're keen). A related Forestry Tasmania project, the Tahune Forest AirWalk (see opposite), is 26km southwest along the now-sealed Arve Road; tickets are meant to be purchased here first and you can buy a combined ticket for the heritage centre costing $11. En route to the must-see AirWalk, on the drive along Arve Road, several boardwalks have been constructed through magnificent swamp gum and eucalypt forests – they're detailed on the free leaflet that's handed out.

Twenty-four kilometres southwest along Arve Road is the rugged **Hartz Mountains National Park**, with its glacial lakes, rainforests and alpine moorlands; a day-walk map is available from the Forest and Heritage Centre. From Arve Road, a stony, unsealed track winds up for 12km, with several stopping-off points; at the end of the track it's a couple of minutes' walk to Waratah Lookout, with great views over the Huon Valley and the Southern Forests. Another walk (4km) heads off to the sometimes snowcapped Hartz Peak (1255m); most of the walk is boardwalked, but parts are wet and boggy under-foot and there's the potential for fog to settle and icy winds and snow to sweep in at any time – recommended for well-prepared walkers only.

The **Picton River** skirts the Hartz Mountains from its source deep in the South West National Park; with its bouncy rapids, intermittent gentle sections and magnificent wilderness scenery, it's a popular, short (and affordable) **rafting** alternative to the Franklin River. Rafting Tasmania (℡03/6239 1080) runs year-round day-trips from Hobart for $115. The river continues towards the **Tahune Forest Reserve**, at the junction with the Huon River, just north of Hartz Mountains National Park. Here, the impressive new $4.5 million **Tahune Forest AirWalk and Visitor Centre** (daily: April–Nov 9am–4.30pm; Dec–Mar 9am–8.15pm; $9; ℡03/6297 0068, Ⓦwww.forestry-tas.com.au) was opened in mid-2001. The 597-metre-long, steel-framed walk-way is supported by twelve towers and suspended 25–48m in the air at the level of the tree canopy of the surrounding old-growth forest and, thrillingly, above the confluence of the rivers, with magnificent views across to the Hartz Mountains. Below, the riverside Huon Pine boardwalk provides an easy twenty-minute return to huge and ancient Huon Pines. The visitor centre has a Forestry Tasmania interpretative display, while the attached licensed café focuses on local gourmet products. If you're picnicking, there are great shelters with roaring fires and gas barbecues for even the wildest day.

You can **stay** at *The Geeveston Forest House*, a cottage hostel on the edge of town at 24 Arve Rd (℡03/6297 1102, Ⓦwww.tassie.net.au/~ldillon; dorms $14, room ❶). TassieLink has a Hobart–Geeveston service (4 daily Mon–Fri, 1 daily Sat) but there's no transport to the AirWalk. Otherwise, Experience Tasmania's full-day Huon Valley tour includes the AirWalk (℡03/6234 3336; $95).

Dover and around

DOVER, 21km from Geeveston, is a scenic fishing village on a large bay – **Port Esperance**. It's very pretty, with trees everywhere, and lush hills sur-rounding the village, backed by the clear, virtually triangular, outline of **Adamsons Peak** (1226m), snowcapped in winter. Boats moor off a pictur-esque jetty in the bay, where two tiny tree-covered islets are silhouetted against the sky at dusk.

The hub of Dover is the *Dover Hotel*, on the Huon Highway (℡03/6298 1210, Ⓔdoverhotel@bigpond.com; dorms $16, rooms ❸, motel units ❹), which has an old-fashioned dining room overlooking the water, and a back-packers' lodge beside an apple orchard and rolling fields. The *Dover Beachside Caravan Park* on Kent Beach Road (℡03/6298 1301; vans ❷, cabins ❸) is scenically sited near the jetty, beside a creek. Back up towards Geeveston, 12km north near Police Point, the picturesque waterfront cottage *Huon Charm* (℡03/6297 6314, Ⓦwww.huoncharm.com; ❹) is a more secluded alternative. A great place to eat is the excellent *Dover Woodfired Pizza* (℡03/6298 1908; Wed–Sun from 4pm; BYO), in a characterful cottage with tables overlooking the water. Although you can find fuel and supplies 20km south at **Southport** (the last place to get either), there's more choice and better value in Dover. TassieLink runs a limited summer service to Dover (Nov–April Mon, Wed & Fri).

Thirty-one kilometres from Dover are the Hastings Caves, in the foothills of Adamsons Peak, with the **Thermal Springs State Reserve** en route. The springs (late Sept to end April daily 9am–5pm, end Dec to end Feb until 6pm, end April to early Sept 10am–4pm; $4.40; ℡03/6298 3209) are in a lush setting, and there are several walks in the grounds, though the pool itself is very disappointing – small, shallow and tepid (ranging from 20–30°C); the café and visitor centre are open the same hours as the springs. At the time of writing, self-contained cabin accommodation was being built at the site; call for details. **Hastings Caves**, a few kilometres further on from the springs, are more worthwhile: Newdegate Cave, the best, is open daily for tours (hourly 11am–3pm, with extra tours Oct–March; 45min; $14.50); it's always wet and cold inside, so bring something warm to wear. Also on offer are **adventure tours** of King George V Cave (6hr including BBQ and swim; $149), and a Caves, Formation and Wildlife Tour (3hr; $76); the tours need to be booked a week ahead (℡1300 368 550 or 03/6298 3209).

Other attractions in the immediate area include the **Ida Bay Bush Tram** (Wed & Sun 12.30pm & 2.30pm, daily Dec 26 to end April; 1hr 20min; $20; bookings essential on ℡03/6223 5893). This vintage, narrow-gauge bush railway, in operation since 1914, runs 16km along the southern edge of Southport to the beautiful beach at Deep Hole Bay.

Cockle Creek

Beyond Ida Bay, the unsurfaced Cockle Creek Road takes you past picturesque sheltered bays and scenic coastal forests, where wild flowers bloom in summer, to **COCKLE CREEK** on the lovely, **Recherche Bay** (pronounced "research" by locals). It's an unspoilt place for the moment, but there are controversial plans to develop the area for tourism. There are lots of free camping spots along the shore, as well as fishing shacks and old buses inhabited semi-permanently by mainly fishing-obsessed retirees after the abundant crayfish, cockles and fish in the bay. Pit toilets and water are the only facilities. The pleasant and easy Fishers Bay Walk takes you around the coast (4km round-trip), but the most popular walk is the muddy but boardwalked first part of the **South Coast Track** to the beach at South Cape Bay and back (4hr); the entire length of the track is for the very experienced only, but this portion gives you a small taste (see p.1155 for details of the whole walk). TassieLink has a "Wilderness Link" service to Cockle Creek (Nov–April Mon, Wed & Fri).

Bruny Island

For beautiful lonely beaches and superb bushwalking, one of the best places in Tasmania is **Bruny Island**. Almost two distinct islands joined by a narrow isthmus (where you can sometimes see Little penguins from a specially constructed viewing platform), it's roughly 71km from end to end and has a population of only four hundred. The cost of taking a car across on the ferry deters casual visitors, so the island is never very full. The ferry from Kettering goes to substantially rural North Bruny, although most of the settlements, and places to stay and eat, are on South Bruny – the more scenic half, with its state forests and reserves.

Information, getting there and getting around

The **ferry from Kettering** (see p.1081) sails at least eight times daily (Mon–Sat 6.50am–6.30pm, till 7.30pm Fri, Sun 8am–6.30pm; 20min; ℡03/6267 4494 for times; $21 per car return or $26 public holidays, motorbikes $11, bikes $3, foot passengers free). The **Bruny D'Entrecasteaux Visitor Centre** at the Kettering ferry terminal on Ferry Road off the Channel Highway (daily 9am–5pm; ☏03/6267 4494, ⓦwww.tasmania holiday.com) books island accommodation, much of which is in self-catering cottages (it's best to stock up on groceries and petrol in Kingston, p.1074, as island prices are high and choice limited) and must be arranged in advance. The centre can also supply you with **information** on the island, including a good free fold-out map. As there is no public transport on the island, you'll need your own car or bike to get around unless you come on the excellent small-group day-tour from Hobart with Bruny Island Ventures (see p.1081), or Bruny Island Charters, which does very popular three-hour **wildlife cruises** exploring the south, around Fluted Cape, following the spectacular cliff line, to a seal colony; if you're lucky you'll see dolphins and maybe even a southern right whale, as well as the abundant birdlife in the area (Oct–April daily except Sat 11am from the jetty at Adventure Bay; $70, lunch extra $30; ☏03/6234 3336, ⓦwww.brunycharters.com). They also offer the cruise as part of a return trip from Hobart (Hobart pick-up 8.30am, returning 5/5.30pm; $130 including lunch). There are also great nature tours offered on the island by *Inala* (see p.1088).

If you're driving or riding yourself, be aware that many of the island's roads are unsealed, so expect some discomfort; even the stretch of speedy highway will suddenly become a dusty unsealed road for kilometres at a time. Petrol is only available at Dennes Point, Adventure Bay, Alonnah and Lunawanna. Hobart Coaches operates services from Hobart to Kettering that connect with a couple of the ferries (see p.1156).

Around the island

There's no town at **Roberts Point**, where the ferry docks on the north of the island, just a phone box, some public toilets, a post box and a fast-food van that takes advantage of cars arriving too early for the ferry. The main settlement on **North Bruny** is **DENNES POINT** at the northern extreme of the island, which has a general store (petrol sold) and attached café, and a jetty. This is a popular spot for weekend getaway 'shacks' for Hobart citizens fond of fishing. A detour off this route, 3km off the main road along an unsealed road, is the secluded settlement of **Barnes Bay**, where pretty Shelter Cove was the first "Black station" to be established for the forced resettlement of Aboriginal people (see box on p.1058). There's a small jetty which is a peaceful spot to contemplate the boats bobbing in the cove, and a pebbly beach, but no facilities.

At the northern end of the isthmus connecting the two islands, the **Neck Game Reserve** (free) acts as a sanctuary for Little penguins and mutton-birds who inhabit rookeries in the sand dunes here. A wooden boardwalk (with stairs) descends over the burrows to the beach and an interpretative board provides information on the birds, best sighted between September and February as they return to their burrows after dusk. Atop the tallest sand dune here, reached by a high wooden stairway, is a small monument to **Truganini** (the "last" Tasmanian Aborigine, who was born here), and you can take in superb views of the southern part of the island, where three former reserves have been turned into **South Bruny National Park** (for permits, see p.1062). You can see the Fluted Cape State Reserve region to the east of Adventure Bay; here, a steep climb to the top of the Cape (2hr 30min return) offers still better views. The Labillardiere State Reserve area occupies the western "hook" of South Bruny Island; a winding, bumpy road leads to the **Cape Bruny Lighthouse**, built in 1836 and manned until 1996; beyond this a seven-hour walking trail explores the peninsula. East of the hook, across **Cloudy Bay** is the final chunk of the national park, with its great sweep of surf beach. You can do a spot of bushcamping here (pit toilet only, no water), and at Neck Beach about 1.5km from the isthmus viewing point (pit toilet, water, shelter with barbecue). For considerably more comfort, there's the secluded, self-catering beachfront *Cloudy Bay Cabin* (℡03/6293 1171; ❻), powered by solar energy and gas. You can also stay just north of Cloudy Bay in the comfortable self-contained cottage at *Inala* (℡03/6293 1217, ⓦwww.inalabruny.com.au; ❺), which also serves as the base for Inala Nature Tours. These nature-based guided tours – from half-day to extended trips – are run by a qualified biologist and are customized to suit the interests and size of the group. A typical tour will take in Adventure Bay, Cloudy Bay and Cape Bruny.

ADVENTURE BAY is the main settlement on the east coast of South Bruny, and the main tourist centre; you can swim from the beautiful sandy sweep of beach, and there's a general store (petrol sold) and several accommodaton choices. The **Bligh Museum of Pacific Discovery** (daily 10am–3pm; $4) charts Bruny's links with early explorers and seafarers (including captains Cook and Bligh), for whom it provided a safe refuge after the arduous journey across the Southern Ocean, and the museum displays maps, documents, paintings and artefacts relating to landings there. The *Penguin Tea Rooms* (daily 10am–5pm) serves freshly baked food, while a good place to **stay** is the *Lumeah*, in a charming homestead on Quiet Corner, off Main Road (℡ & ⓕ03/6293 1265; ❻); you have the run of a spacious, yet homey and comfortable, wing of a homestead to yourself (sleeps up to ten) with an outside spa and pretty garden. You can **camp** next to the beach at the *Captain James Cook Caravan Park* (℡03/6293 1128; vans ❷), which is closer to the shops but less attractive than the *Adventure Bay Holiday Village* (℡03/6293 1270, ⓕ6293 1485; dorms $18, vans ❷, cabins ❷–❸, cottages ❹), a couple of kilometres further on, which has a range of cabins, some en suite, and cottages, plus bunk rooms; both are on Adventure Bay Road. Just north of town, also on Adventure Bay Road, *Morella Island Retreats* (℡03/6293 1131, ⓦwww.morella-island.com.au; ❻–❼) has several secluded, individual retreat cabins in their 25 acres of gardens; their *Hothouse Cafe* (bookings essential after 5.30pm) offers exotic dining in a hothouse amongst peacocks and parrots, surrounded by an abundant vegetable garden, with panoramic views across Neck Beach and all the way to Mount Wellington.

ALONNAH, is the main settlement on the west, D'Entrecasteaux Channel coast. As well as a general store here (petrol sold), you'll find the basic *Hotel Bruny*, on Bruny Main Road (℡03/6293 1148; basic motel-style units ❸), which also offers good-value counter meals (except Sun), and has the island's only bottle shop. Near the town, *The Tree House* (℡03/5255 5147; Ⓔthetree house@iprimus.com.au; ❻) is a gorgeous all-wood, open-plan studio apartment (sleeps up to four) with wonderful water views; it's a fifteen-minute walk from here along the coast to the shop and pub. Bruny Island's **Online Access Centre** is on School Road. Five kilometres south at **LUNAWANNA**, the Mangana Store (daily 8am–8pm) sells petrol, groceries and great veggie-, fish- and hamburgers; the bakery next door bakes **pizzas** (Thurs only). You can stay at *Bruny Island Explorer Cottages* on Light House Road overlooking Daniels Bay (℡03/6293 1271, ⓦwww.brunyisland.com; linen supplied; ❹). From Lunawanna, it's a scenic drive south to Cloudy Bay (see above).

New Norfolk and Mount Field National Park

Heading inland from Hobart through the Derwent Valley towards Mount Field National Park, the A10 hugs the Derwent River for the 50km to the well-preserved colonial buildings of **NEW NORFOLK**. It was to here that the original settlers of Norfolk Island (see p.388) were moved between 1806 and 1814. The sizeable town has been at the centre of the hop-growing industry for 150 years, and there are still oast houses in the surrounding hop fields. The broad stretch of the Derwent here is clean, beautiful and swimmable, disturbed only by thrillseekers in jet boats: Devil Jet runs high-speed rides through the rapids (daily 9am–4pm; on the hour; 30min; $50 per person, minimum 2 people; ☎03/6261 3460), leaving from the Esplanade. The river-facing *Bush Inn* at 49 Montagu St, the main road, claims to be Australia's oldest continuously licensed **hotel** (☎03/6261 2011; B&B ❸), and with its stained wooden floorboards, huge stone fireplaces and a small ballroom with chandeliers and piano, it's a lovely place to stay; as is the antique-furnished *Old Colony Inn*, a simple, whitewashed building on the same street at no. 21 (☎03/6261 2731; B&B ❹). From New Norfolk, you can visit the **Salmon Ponds** (daily 9am–5pm; $5.50), 18km west on the Glenora Road in Plenty; established in 1864, this is Australia's oldest trout hatchery, set in beautiful formal gardens, with six display ponds and a restaurant.

Hobart Coaches has six **buses** on weekdays from Hobart to New Norfolk and three on Saturday; the buses leave from Metro Hobart's Elizabeth Street terminus. TassieLink also runs to New Norfolk (5 weekly) on their scheduled year-round service to Queenstown. New Norfolk's **Online Access Centre** is on Charles St.

Mount Field National Park

It's 37km through pretty rolling countryside full of hop fields from New Norfolk to **Mount Field National Park**, a high alpine area with tarns created by glacial activity where, in winter, there's enough snow to create a small ski field. At the base, the magnificent stands of **mountain ash** known locally as swamp gum (the tallest species of eucalypt and the tallest hardwood in the world), along with the many **waterfalls**, help make this Tasmania's most popular park. Most people come here to see the impressive **Russell Falls**, which cascades in two levels. It's close to the park entrance and can be reached on an easy thirty-minute circuit walk. Longer walks continue on to **Horseshoe Falls** (1hr) and **Lady Barron Falls** (3hr return). The best short walk is the **Tall Trees Track** (1hr 30min), where huge swamp gums dominate; the largest date back to the early nineteenth century.

To get away from the tour-group mob, several shorter walks leave from various spots along the Lake Dobson Road, which leads high up to **Lake Dobson**, 16km into the park in the area of the alpine moorlands and glacial lakes. From the lake car park, you can go on plenty of longer walks, including treks along the tarn shelf that take several days, with huts to stay in along the way. The walk to **Twilight Tarn**, with its historic hut, is one of the most rewarding (4hr return), or you can continue on for the full tarn shelf circuit (6hr return). A shorter option is the **Pandani Grove Nature Walk** (with an accompanying leaflet available from the ranger station – see over), a forty-minute circuit of the lake, including a section of tall **pandanis** – the striking heath plant which, with its crown of long fronds, looks like a semi-tropical palm. You'll need your own transport to reach these higher walks, or you could come with the friendly **Close to Nature Tours**, based at the Possum Shed, Westerway (☎03/6288 1477, ✉closetonature@bigpond.com.au) with Hobart pick-ups. Tigerline also operates day-tours from Hobart, visiting the Salmon Ponds (see p.1080) en route and allowing several hours to explore the park (Mon, Wed & Fri 9am–5.30pm; $125 including meals).

For information on the walks, to register for overnight hikes and to talk to the ranger, drop in to the **Mount Field Ranger Station** at the entrance to the park (daily 9am–4.30pm; ☎03/6288 1149), a complex also housing a café, shop and interpretive centre. An excellent range of free pamphlets detail the natural environment alongside several of the walks in the park. There's also information here about walks in the South West National Park, several of which can be started from Scotts Peak Road, which runs off the Gordon River Road to the west of Mount Field (see p.1089). If you want to **stay** in the vicinity, head for the tiny settlement of **NATIONAL PARK** on Maydena Road, a ten-minute walk from the park, where there's basic ground-floor **pub** accommodation at the friendly *National Park Hotel* (☎03/6288 1103; ❸ including breakfast), and dorms at the easy-going *National Park Youth Hostel* opposite (☎03/6288 1369; dorms $16–17); there's plenty of interaction between the two, including pool tournaments, and the pub **meals** are also popular with travellers. The pub has an EFTPOS facility, but the nearest fuel is 7km further on at Westaway. Just outside the entrance to the park are spacious 1950s style self-contained units at *Russell Falls Holiday Cottages* (☎03/6288 1198; ❹); while within the park itself, there's a well-equipped **campsite** near the entrance.

Nearby **Junee Cave State Reserve** is prime platypus-spotting territory; to get there head 11km southwest to **Maydena**, then right onto the narrow, winding Junee Road for 3.5km. A ten-minute walk from the reserve entrance through lush rainforest will bring you to **Junee Cave**, popular with cave divers. In Maydena you can stay at the friendly *Tyenna Valley Lodge* which has a guest kitchen and lounge (☎03/6288 2293, ⓦwww.tvlodge.com; rooms ❸, self-contained cabins ❹). Their characterful, licensed *Cockatoo Cafe* serves delicious organic **meals**. The lodge offers personalized 4WD ecotours of the surrounding area, as well as pick-ups and drop-offs for bushwalking. Maydena's **Online Access Centre** is in the Maydena Kindergarten on Holmes Street.

Out of Maydena, you can see the world's tallest Christmas tree (80m) in the **Styx Forest**, a large remnant of old-growth forest that's suffered damage from logging activities. A campaign is currently underway to protect 150 square kilometres of this forest as the Styx Valley of the Giants National Park; contact the Wilderness Society for details and to get hold of a self-guided drive leaflet. Island Escape Tours (☎1800 133 555, ⓦwww.islandescapetours.com) visits Mount Field National Park and does an overnight camping trip to the Styx as part of their three-day "Wild West Escape" ($345).

Richmond

RICHMOND, on the Coal River about 25km north of Hobart and surrounded by undulating countryside, scattered with wineries, is one of the oldest and best-preserved towns in Australia. Settlers received land grants in the area not long after the fledgling colony had been set up in 1803, and in 1824 Lieutenant-Governor Sorell founded the town, on the route between Hobart and the east coast. Soon, traffic to the new penal settlement at Port Arthur began to pass through, and Richmond's strategic location made it an important military post and convict station when Richmond Gaol was built in 1825;

by the 1830s it was the third-largest town in Tasmania. In 1872, however, the **Sorell Causeway** was opened, bypassing Richmond, which became a rural community with little incentive for change or development. Most of the approximately fifty buildings – plain and functional stone dwellings – date from the 1830s and 1840s, and many are now used as galleries, craft shops, cafés, restaurants and guesthouses; the gorgeous village green is still intact. A free leaflet and map, *Let's Talk About Richmond*, is available at the gaol and details the buildings. Attractions along Bridge Street include the wooden **Richmond Maze** (daily 10am–5pm; $3.50) and the **Old Hobart Town Model Village** (daily 9am–5pm; $7.50), a large-scale outdoor model of Hobart in the 1820s.

Richmond's most authentic attraction, however, is the sandstone, slate-roofed **Richmond Gaol** (daily 9am–5pm; $4.50), an intact example of an early prison. The prison's function was mostly to house prisoners in transit or those awaiting trial, and to accommodate convict road gangs working in the district; the east wing was designed to hold female convicts, who could not be accommodated at Port Arthur. Informative signs explain the various features of the gaol, which now seems incongruously pretty, set around a leafy central square. Richmond also has the distinction of having both Australia's oldest Roman Catholic church – that of **St John**, which dates in part from 1837 – and its oldest bridge. The graceful arched stone **Richmond Bridge** was constructed in 1823 under harsh conditions using convict labour; legend says that it's haunted by the ghost of the brutal flagellator, George Grover, who was beaten to death by the convicts and thrown into the river during its construction. The scene is positively idyllic today: green lawns stretch beside the bridge and river and the stone steeple of St John's rises above.

Practicalities

Hobart Coaches runs four **bus** services a day from Hobart (Mon–Fri; buses leave from Metro Hobart's Elizabeth Street terminus) and TassieLink also drops off on their Hobart to Swansea service (1 daily Mon–Fri, plus Sat during school holidays). Richmond's **Online Access Centre** is on Torrens Street. One of the nicest **places to stay** is *Prospect House* (℡03/6260 2207, Ⓦ www.Prospect-House.com.au; ❺), a Georgian country mansion set in extensive landscaped grounds, with its own licensed restaurant; it's on your left as you come into town on Cambridge Road. Further out, 6km from Richmond along Prossers Road, is *Richmond Country Bed and Breakfast* (℡03/6260 4238, Ⓕ6260 4423; ❹), a comfortable, reasonably priced, non-smoking homestead in a quiet rural setting. The central pretty *Richmond Arms Hotel*, 42 Bridge St (℡03/6260 2109, Ⓦ www.richmondarms.com; ❹), has characterful, self-catering accommodation in its converted mid-nineteenth-century stone stables; a light breakfast is included and the hotel also serves affordable meals. The cheapest place to stay is the *Richmond Cabin and Tourist Park*, on Middle Tea Tree Road on the outskirts of town (℡03/6260 2192; vans ❷, cabins ❸), which provides shady grounds for camping and has an indoor heated pool.

For **food**, there's an upmarket café-restaurant in the *Richmond Food & Wine Centre*, opposite the *Richmond Arms Hotel* in an old weatherboard cottage set in pretty gardens with outside tables (Mon, Tues & Sun 10am–6pm, Wed–Sat until 8pm; bookings ℡03/6260 2619), where just about everything served is Tasmanian, including the wine. The *Richmond Bakery* on Edward Street, just off Bridge Street, has a Swiss baker who continues to win awards and makes delicious pastries; with an attached café, you can eat in the courtyard or take away and eat at picnic tables in the village green.

The Forestier and Tasman peninsulas

The fastest route from Hobart to the **Tasman Peninsula** heads northeast along the Tasman Highway and then across the **Sorell Causeway** to the small town of **Sorell**, your last chance for shopping and banking; on the huge expanse of Pittwater, windsurfers are out in force on a sunny day. From Sorell, the Arthur Highway heads 34km southeast to **Dunalley** (fuel available), where a bridge crosses the narrow isthmus to the **Forestier Peninsula**. The bridge regularly opens to let boats through, which can cause delays. Once across, it's a further 42km to the infamous **Eaglehawk Neck**, the narrow point connecting the two peninsulas, once guarded by vicious dogs that in effect turned the Tasman Peninsula into a kind of prison island.

Port Arthur, at the very bottom of the Tasman Peninsula, is the major attraction, but the hardly developed **peninsula** has several good **bushwalks**, and some impressive rock formations on the rough ocean side. Some of the finest coastal features are around Eaglehawk Neck: just to the north, there's the **Tessellated Pavement**, onto which you can climb down at low tide; and to the south, off the highway, a fierce **blowhole**, the huge **Tasman Arch**, and the **Devils Kitchen**, a sheer rock cleft into which the sea surges. The **Tasman Trail** is an exhilarating sixteen-kilometre coastal walk starting from the Devils Kitchen and ending at **Fortescue Bay**, which has a good camping area (otherwise, the bay is 12km down a dirt road east off the Arthur Highway). South of Port Arthur, several walking tracks begin from **Remarkable Cave**: to Crescent Bay (5hr return), Mount Brown (5hr return) and Maingon Blowhole (3hr return). Much of this area has recently been declared the **Tasman National Park**; you can get information and advice from the ranger (☎03/6250 3497) or from the Officers Mess, a privately owned shop with an information centre at Eaglehawk Neck. Otherwise, to get details on the walking trails, look for a copy of *Tasman Tracks*, by Shirley and Peter Storey, in a Hobart bookshop.

Eaglehawk Neck Backpackers (☎03/6250 3248; dorms $12), at 94 Old Jetty, 1km west of the Arthur Highway on the Forestier Peninsula side of Eaglehawk Neck, is the perfect **place to stay** to explore these areas – friendly, nonsmoking and green (in both senses of the word). Bunks are in two spacious, self-contained cabins; bikes are loaned (for a small donation) and there are canoes too. Also in the area is *Wunnamurra Waterfront Bed and Breakfast* (☎ & ℱ03/6250 3145; ❻), which offers more luxury in its en-suite rooms. For something to **eat**, try the French-run *Eaglehawk Cafe Restaurant*, on the Arthur Highway near the turn-off to the blowhole (open daily for breakfast, lunch and dinner; licensed; ☎03/6250 3331), in a two-storey house overlooking Norfolk Bay; the food is tasty and reasonably priced, utilizing local produce with a menu ranging from vegetarian to traditional meat dishes, plus coffee and cakes. The nearby Eaglehawk Dive Centre (☎03/6250 3566, Ⓦwww.eaglehawk dive.com.au) offers **dive-boat charters** (equipment included) at low rates to caves, shipwrecks, kelp forests and nearby seal colonies with an underwater visibility of 15–30m. If you're interested in any other outdoor activities, **Hire it with Dennis** (☎03/6250 3103) can deliver canoes, kayaks, dinghies, fishing lines, tents, sleeping bags and bicycles to the area, including Port Arthur.

Southwest of Eaglehawk Neck, in the middle of the Tasman Peninsula at the small settlement of **KOONYA**, **Cascades Historic Site** is a well-preserved 1840s Probation Station that has been owned by a farming family for five generations; one of the old red-brick buildings has been converted into a small museum (open by arrangement), while several officers quarters and the old workshop and convict cell block have been converted into self-catering cottages, most with open fires and one with a spa (*Cascades Colonial Accommodation*; ⓣ03/6250 3873, ⓕ6250 3013; no children under 5; ❺–❼). The peaceful, rural site, complete with apple orchard, has a half-hour waterfront walk. Nearby is the friendly *Seaview Lodge* (ⓣ & ⓕ03/6250 2766; dorms $15; rooms ❶). The TassieLink Port Arthur service can drop you off near either acccommodation.

Port Arthur

The most unceasing labour is to be extracted from the convicts . . . and the most harassing vigilance over them is to be observed.

Governor Arthur

PORT ARTHUR was chosen as the site for a **prison settlement** in September 1830, as a place of secondary punishment for convicts who had committed serious crimes in New South Wales or Van Diemen's Land itself, men who were seen to have no redeeming features and were treated accordingly. The first 150 convicts worked like slaves to establish a timber industry in the wooded surroundings of the "natural penitentiary" of the Tasman Peninsula, with narrow Eaglehawk Neck guarded by dogs. The regime was never a subtle one: **Governor George Arthur**, responsible for all the convicts in Van Diemen's Land, believed that a convict's "whole fate should be ... the very last degree of misery consistent with humanity". Gradually, Port Arthur became a self-supporting industrial centre: the timber industry grew into shipbuilding, there was brickmaking and shoemaking, wheat-growing, and even a flour mill. There was also a separate prison for boys – "the thiefs prison" – at Point Puer, where the inmates were taught trades. From the 1840s until transport of convicts ceased in 1853, the penal settlement grew steadily, the early timber constructions later replaced by brick and stone buildings. The lives of the labouring convicts contrasted sharply with those of the prison officers and their families, who had their ornamental gardens, drama club, library and cricket fields. The years after transport ended were in many ways more horrific than those that preceded them, as physical beatings were replaced by psychological punishment. In 1852 the **Model Prison**, based on the spoked-wheel design of Pentonville Prison in London, opened. Here, prisoners could be kept in tiny cells in complete isolation and absolute silence; they were referred to by numbers rather than names, and wore hoods whenever they left their cells. The prison continued to operate until 1877, by now incorporating its own **mental asylum** full of ex-convicts, as well as a geriatric home for ex-convict paupers. The excellent **interpretive centre**, housed in the new visitors centre (daily 9am–5pm), provides much more detail on the prison's sad history through artefacts and texts, and there's more fascinating information in the older museum, housed in what was the asylum.

In 1870 Port Arthur was popularized by Marcus Clarke's romantic tragedy, *For the Term of his Natural Life*. The public became fascinated by its buildings and the tragedy behind them, and soon after the prison closed, guided tours were offered by the same crumbling men who had been wrecked by the regime. In the 1890s the town around the prison was devastated by bushfires that left most buildings in ruins. A major conservation and restoration project began in the 1970s and today the **Port Arthur Historic Site** covers a huge area (office and most buildings daily 8.30am–dusk, grounds until about 11pm; $22 for a 48hr pass, including 40min guided tour and 20min harbour cruise on the MV *Marana* to Piont Puer Prison – except July & Aug; $10 for a pass after 4pm; for an extra $3 the pass lasts 2 years). The ticket office area houses a vis-

△ Flour Mill, Port Arthur Historic Site

itor information centre (☎03/6251 2371). For an extra $7.50 you can also take a trip across the bay with Port Arthur Cruises to the **Isle of the Dead**, Port Arthur's cemetery from 1833 to 1877, where you can view the resting places of 1100 convicts, asylum inmates, paupers and free men; the same company also run a longer two-and-a-half-hour Tasman Island Wilderness Cruise from here to see the island's sheer cliffs and its sea birds and fur seals (☎03/6224 0033, Ⓦwww.portarthurcruises.com.au; Mon 8am, also Thurs 26 Dec–May, no service Aug; $49).

The Port Arthur Historic Site houses more than sixty buildings, some of which – like the poignant **prison chapel** – are furnished and restored. Others, like the ivy-covered **church**, are picturesque ruins set in a landscape of green lawns, shady trees and paths sloping down to the cove. The beautiful setting makes it look more like a serene, old-world university campus than a prison, and indeed, the benign feeling of the place seems to have a capacity to absorb tragedy: another horrific chapter in Port Arthur's history occurred in April 1996, when the massacre of 35 tourists and local people by a lone gunman made international headlines. The café where most of the people were killed has been partially dismantled and a memorial has been built – a garden and reflecting pool laid out around the remaining walls. Visitors are requested to act sensitively and not ask the staff about the tragedy.

If you're staying overnight in Port Arthur (see p.1093 for accommodation), join the nightly lantern-lit **Historic Ghost Tour** (1hr 30min; $14; bookings on ☎03/6251 2310), which features lovingly researched and hauntingly retold tales of the settlement's past as you wander through the ruins.

Practicalities

If you don't have your own transport, and want to get to Port Arthur from Hobart on a **regular bus**, you'll usually have to stay overnight. TassieLink has a single afternoon service (Mon–Fri during school terms; Mon, Wed & Fri school holidays) and also a morning service in summer (Nov–April Mon, Wed & Fri 10am), stopping en route at Eaglehawk Neck, Koonya and other places on the Tasman and Forestier peninsulas. However, there are plenty of **bus tours** that take in some of the Tasman Peninsula sights along the way. Tigerline offers a good one-day tour (avoid the option with the Bush Mill Experience; $75; ☎03/6272 6611), and Experience Tasmania has a similar trip ($60; ☎03/6234 3336). Port Arthur Cruises also offers a pricey but spectacular cruise from Hobart (see box on p.1071) with an optional return coach trip.

There are various **places to stay** on the outskirts of Port Arthur. The *Port Arthur Motor Inn* (☎03/6250 2101, Ⓦwww.portarthur-inn.com.au; ❺), overlooking the ruined church, is a pleasant place, with a bar open to the public – the only place nearby to drink – and reasonable counter meals. Somewhat less expensive, the spacious *Port Arthur Villas* (☎03/6250 2239, Ⓦwww.wwt.com.au/portarthurvillas; ❹) has the amenities of a motel and kitchens in the units. Both are just across the road from the site on Safety Cove Road. Opposite the *Port Arthur Motor Inn* is the popular *Roseview YHA*, on Champ Street, in a former 1890s guesthouse (☎03/6250 2311, Ⓔroseview@southcom.com.au; booking essential Jan & Feb; dorms $18–19, rooms ❷–❸). If it's full, 1km from the site, there are bunkhouse rooms and camping (including an excellent enclosed camp kitchen) at the tree-filled *Port Arthur Caravan and Cabin Park* at Garden Point (☎03/6250 2340, Ⓦwww .portarthurcaravan-cabinpark.com.au; dorms $15, en-suite cabins ❹).

Within the Port Arthur Historic Site, in the visitors centre, you can **eat** at the cafeteria-style *Port Arthur Cafe* (daily 9am–5pm), or spend more at the good *Felons*

Restaurant; otherwise, there's the *Museum Tea Rooms* in the old asylum. There are also several eating options in **Taranna**, 10km before Port Arthur on the A9; the best of these, serving fresh seafood, is *The Mussel Boys Cafe* (Thurs–Sun).

The east coast: the Tasman Highway

For much of its length along the sunny **east coast**, the **Tasman Highway** gently rises and falls through grazing land and bush-covered hills. In summer there's something of an unspoilt Mediterranean feel about this coast, with its long white beaches, blue water stretching to a cloudless sky, scenic backdrop of hills, and a thriving local fishing industry. Because the east coast is sheltered from the prevailing westerly winds and is washed by warm offshore currents, it has one of the most temperate climates in Australia. This, and the mainly safe swimming beaches, mean that it's a popular destination for Tasmanian families in the school holidays – prices go up and accommodation is scarce from Christmas to the middle of February. Even so, it's still relatively undeveloped and peaceful; there are four national parks, which include a whole island – **Maria Island** – and an entire peninsula – the glorious **Freycinet National Park**.

The east coast is also Tasmania's best **cycling route**: it's relatively flat, and the winter climate is mild enough to tackle it in colder months, too. Distances between towns are reasonable, there's a string of youth hostels so you don't need to camp, and there are few cars. **St Helens** is the largest town on the east coast, with a population of just over a thousand; situated on **Georges Bay**, it makes a good base to explore the northeast corner and **Mount William National Park**. The oldest town, **Swansea**, lies sheltered in **Great Oyster Bay**, facing the Freycinet Peninsula. To the north, **Bicheno** is a small fishing town with fantastic diving, and it's a convenient place from which to visit both the Freycinet National Park (and its tiny settlement of **Coles Bay**) and the **Douglas Apsley National Park** inland. The highway detours inland at **St Marys**, although there's a more recently built road that allows you to follow the coast and enjoy spectacular views without having to tackle any hills.

Because the east coast is not heavily populated, **banking facilities** are rather inadequate, with no ATMs. Only St Helens and Scottsdale have banks (both Westpac), while small settlements have post offices that are also Commonwealth Bank agents. EFTPOS facilities are widely available in shops and service stations, but it's important to make sure you always have enough cash.

Transport services don't run to daily schedules either, with big transport gaps on weekends – another good reason to cycle or drive – and the various bus services may need to be interchanged to get from one place to another. From Hobart, Tasmanian Redline Coaches has one service to Bicheno via Swansea (Mon–Fri 1 daily), which continues on to St Marys and St Helens on Tuesday and Thursday; one Sunday St Helens service goes via St Marys. From Launceston, Redline has services to Derby via Scottsdale (Mon–Fri 3 daily, Sun 1 daily), to Bicheno and Swansea (Mon–Fri 1 daily), and a Sunday service to St Helens via St Marys. TassieLink has scheduled year-round services up the east coast from Hobart to Launceston and vice versa via the Coles Bay turn-off for Freycinet National Park, Bicheno and St Helens (Wed, Fri & Sun 1 daily in both directions; also Nov–April Mon 1 daily). Five local bus companies also operate: Suncoast (Mon–Fri 1 daily ; ☎03/6376 3488) runs between St Helens and Scottsdale; Stan's Coaches (Mon–Fri 2 daily; ☎03/6356 1662) between Scottsdale and Bridport; Peakes (Mon–Fri 1 daily; ☎03/6372 5390) takes you from Bicheno to Derby; Broadby's (☎03/6376 3488) operates the postal bus between Derby, St Helens and St Marys; and the Bicheno Coach Service (daily; out of season you often need to book; ☎03/6257 0293) takes you to Coles Bay and the Freycinet National Park. If you don't fancy getting stuck somewhere for a couple of days, check timetables carefully.

Another option is to go on a **tour**: Island Escape Tours offers an active small-group (max 12) four-day "East Coast Escape" departing from Launceston, which takes in Mount William National Park and the Bay of Fires walk, Freycinet National Park, Maria Island, and the Tasman Peninsula and Port Arthur ($460; youth hostel/bunkhouse accommodation and most meals provided; ☎1800 133 555, ⓦwww.islandescapetours.com).

Maria Island National Park

As the Tasman Highway meets the sea at **ORFORD**, a small holiday resort on the estuary of the Prosser River, you get your first views across to **Maria Island**. The entire island, 15km off the east coast, is a national park, uninhabited save for its ranger. Its wide tracks are ideal for mountain biking, an activity encouraged here – because no other vehicles are allowed, you can ride in perfect safety. The island's coastal road has no gradient, but inland there are a few hills to climb. **Birdlife** is prolific, with over 130 species; it's the only national park containing all eleven of the state's endemic bird species. The old airstrip is covered with Cape Barren geese, which you'll see if you walk to the **fossil cliffs**, a twenty-minute stroll from Darlington.

The ferry lands at **DARLINGTON**, where the structures of the former **penal settlement** still stand, including the commissariat store with its visitor information boards, the convict barn, the cemetery, the mill house and the penitentiary. The last of these is now a **bunkhouse** ($22 per unit, sleeping six, or $8.80 per person in the "backpackers" bunkhouse); the basic units have wood stoves, table and chairs and bunks with mattresses, but you'll need to bring your own cooking equipment and bedding. The units are always in demand and are often booked up six months in advance, so call the ranger (see below) before turning up. The **campsite** here ($4.40 per person) is the island's best, with a public phone, toilets, fireplaces, cold water taps and tank water for drinking. As there is little water elsewhere on the island, free-range camping is best done at **Frenchs Farm** or **Encampment Cove**, two campsites with a rainwater supply and fireplaces; the latter, on Shoal Bay, is the more picturesque.

You can take many short **walks** on the island, as well as longer bushwalks (though watch out for cyclists); free pamphlets are available from the ranger's office at Darlington (Mon–Fri 4.15–5pm; ☎03/6257 1420; ⓦwww.parks .tas.gov.au). With a couple of days to spare, you can walk past the narrow isthmus to the rarely visited **southern end** of the island, which has unspoilt forests and secluded beaches. As there's no water here, be sure to bring supplies with you. Freycinet & Strahan Adventures offers four-day **sea-kayaking and walking tours** of the island, departing from Hobart ($890; ☎03/6257 0500, ⓦwww.tasadventures.com).

Getting there: Triabunna
Ferries leave for Maria Island from the main fishing wharf on the Esplanade at **TRIABUNNA**, reached by TassieLink from Hobart, Bicheno or St Helens. The *Derwent Explorer* catamaran takes 45 minutes (ex-Triabunna daily 10.30am & 1pm; ex-Maria Island 11.30am & 4pm; extra trips Nov–April; return $25, bikes and kayaks $2; bookings ☎0427 100 104).

The **visitor information centre** on the Esplanade in Triabunna (daily 10am–4pm; ☎03/6257 4090) is staffed by helpful volunteers and has information on the island. Triabunna's **Online Access Centre** is on the corner of Vicary and Melbourne streets. A good base for day-trips to Maria Island is the friendly, relaxing and cosy *The Udder Backpackers YHA* on Spencer Street, 1km west of Triabunna (☎03/6257 3439; dorms $16, rooms ❷). It's well set-up for, and popular with, cyclists and as it's set on a farm, fresh organic fruit, vegetables and herbs, are picked daily and sold cheaply to guests; other food is sold in small amounts at the office and there's also a take-away liquor license. There are a couple of free bicycles if you've come without your own, and tents and sleeping bags for rent to take over to Maria Island (free pick-ups and drop-offs to the ferry). East Coast Ecotours (☎03/6257 3453) offers **boat trips** to local seal colonies and you might see dolphins, whales and sea eagles along the way.

Swansea

From Triabunna it's a fairly uneventful 50km drive north to **SWANSEA**, overlooking **Great Oyster Bay**, with views across to the Freycinet Peninsula. If you're lucky, you might see dolphins frolicking in the bay from Franklin Street, the main street that runs along the waterfront. One of Tasmania's oldest settlements, Swansea is an administrative centre, fishing port and seaside resort, with well-preserved architecture dating from the 1830s to the 1880s. The focus of town has always been **Morris's General Store**, on Franklin Street, run by seven generations of the family since 1868. Further evidence of Swansea's past can be found at the **Community Centre** (Mon–Sat 9am–5pm; $3), also on Franklin Street, a former school now housing a miscellaneous collection including a billiard table built from a single log of blackwood ($2 for a game), and at the restored **Swansea Bark Mill & East Coast Museum**, 96 Tasman Highway (daily 9am–5pm; $5.50), once used to produce leather tanning agents from native blackwattle bark. Swansea's **Online Access Centre** is on Franklin Street.

Accommodation options include the *Swansea Motor Inn*, at 1 Franklin St (☎03/6257 8102, ☏6257 8397; ❸–❹), a fine old hotel with a pricier red-brick motel addition and a bistro. *Freycinet Waters*, at 16 Franklin St (☎03/6257 8080, ⓦwww.freycinetwaters.com.au; ❹), is a light, refreshingly uncluttered seaside B&B in the old post office building; each en-suite room has its own private verandah overlooking the bay. Other B&B options include the *Oyster Bay Guest House* at 10 Franklin St (☎ & ☏03/6257 8110; ❹), and *Meredith House*, 15 Noyes St (☎03/6257 8119, ☏6257 8123; en suite ❺–❻), an antique-filled guesthouse on a hill overlooking the bay. On the waterfront are two **caravan parks** with excellent facilities: *Swansea Holiday Park* on Shaw Street, opposite the Old Bark Mill (☎03/6257 8177; cabins ❷–❸), and the friendly *Kenmore Caravan Park*, 2 Bridge St (☎03/6257 8148; vans ❷, cabins ❸).

As for **food**, Swansea has a wide choice. The *Shy Albatross Restaurant* (dinner nightly; licensed), downstairs at the *Oyster Bay Guest House*, serves reasonably priced Italian food and local seafood. There's a very smart, award-winning restaurant specializing in seafood and game in the atmospheric 1846 *Schouten House*, 1 Waterloo Rd (☎03/6257 8564), with alfresco dining in summer. The *Left Bank Coffee & Food Bar*, behind the red door on the main street (closed Tues), has a great atmosphere, outdoor dining, excellent coffee and fresh, simple food. *Kabuki By the Sea* (open daily for morning and afternoon tea and lunch; May–Nov Fri & Sat dinner, Dec–April Tues–Sat dinner; dinner bookings ☎03/6257 8588) is a fine Japanese-style restaurant 12km south on the Tasman Highway with stunning views; it also has some Japanese-style guest cottages (❺).

The Freycinet Peninsula

Heading for Coles Bay and **Freycinet National Park**, you turn off the Tasman Highway 33km north of Swansea, following the Coles Bay Road. The drive from Swansea onwards is winding, with fantastic views of rural country-side contrasted with dramatic mountain- and sea-scapes. After about 8km along Coles Bay Road, you can turn left down a side road (3km unsealed) to the **Friendly Beaches**, part of the national park, taking in a length of unspoilt shoreline backed by eucalypt forest. If you're **cycling**, you can cut 40km from your journey by riding along Nine Mile Beach Road, at the end of which a ferry (book the night before on ☎03/6257 0239; $12; no service May–Sept) crosses the Swan River to **SWANICK**, about 6km northwest of Coles Bay.

COLES BAY, on the north edge of the Freycinet National Park, is a shel-tered inlet with fishing boats moored in the deep-blue water, all set against the striking backdrop of **The Hazards**, three pink-granite peaks – Amos, Dove and Mayson – rising straight from the sea. Since the 1930s the hamlet of Coles Bay has been the base for the park, and for fishing and recreation. As a result, there are numerous fishing shacks and **holiday houses** available to rent: call Freycinet Rentals (☎03/6257 0320), which also rents just about anything you might need for watersports, camping and walking. Just 3.5km west of Coles Bay, *The Edge of the Bay* (☎03/6257 0102, ⓦwww.edgeofthebay.com.au; cot-tages ❺–❻, suites ❻–❼) has secluded, self-catering two-bedroom cottages set in bushland, or elegant Japanese-style suites with water views; rates drop con-siderably for a second and subsequent night's stay. There's also a restaurant and bar (dinner nightly). The *Iluka Holiday Centre*, in a great spot on the Esplanade across from Muirs Beach (☎03/6257 0115 or 1800 786 512, ⓦwww.iluka holidaycentre.com.au; dorms $18.50, vans ❷–❸, units ❹–❺), has a wide vari-ety of accommodation, including a **YHA hostel** section. Nearby is a small supermarket, a tavern with bistro meals and the popular *Freycinet Cafe & Bakery*, an eat-in bakery selling European-style breads, pastries, pizza from 4pm, and decent coffee (daily 8am–7pm). The café has outside tables looking across to the beachfront park. One kilometre from the *Iluka Holiday Centre*, over-looking The Hazards, supplies of all sorts are available at the **general store**, Coles Bay Trading, on Garnet Avenue (daily 8am–6pm, til 7pm Dec 26 to end Feb; ☎03/6257 0109), which also serves as the post office, service station and official tourist **information** centre; you can book accommodation, buy park passes, rent bikes ($11 half-day, $17 day) and use the public phones. Its coffee shop has great views. Next door you can get a seafood dinner at *Madge Malloy's* (dinner Tues–Sat; licensed; ☎03/6257 0399).

Redline and TassieLink drop off 31km away from Coles Bay, at the turn-off on the Tasman Highway, connecting with the Bicheno Coach Service to Coles Bay (up to 3 daily; booking for off-peak times on ☎03/6257 0293), which can also take you right to the start of the walking tracks.

Freycinet National Park

The brand-new **national park office** (daily 9am–5pm; ☎03/6256 7000) is just 1km from Coles Bay, and sells maps and booklets on day-walks and has an interpretative display on the park. The gravelled, disabled-access Great Oyster Bay path leads down to the beach (10min return). Opposite the centre, the powered national park **campsite**, with water and toilets but no showers, is in a sheltered location among bush and dunes behind Richardsons Beach; it's packed in holiday season, when you'll need to book well in advance through the park office. At the other end of Richardsons Beach, *Freycinet Lodge*

TASMANIA | The east coast: the Tasman Highway

(☎03/6257 0101, ⊛www.freycinetlodge.com.au; ❼) has luxurious wooden cabins spread through bushland and offers guided bushwalks; there's a bistro and a more upmarket restaurant with fabulous views overlooking the bay, both open all day and available to non-guests, and a tennis court. You can also stay at the basic *Coles Bay YHA* (no hot water) in the park itself, but only if you've booked in advance through the Hobart YHA office (see p.1081; dorms $10); it's very popular during the summer months and Easter.

Tracks into the park begin at the **Walking Track Car Park**, a further 4km from the office. **Water** is scarce, so you must carry all you'll need, although the ranger can advise if there are any streams where the water is safe to drink. The shorter walks are well marked: the strenuous, gravelly walk up to the look-out to exquisite **Wine Glass Bay**, with its perfect curve of white beach, is where most walkers head, and many continue on down to the beach itself (2.6km return to the lookout, 1–2hr; 5km return to the beach, 2hr 30min to 3hr 30min). The 27-kilometre **peninsula circuit** is a wonderful walk (10hr), best done over two days; it makes a good practice run for the big southwest hikes. There's a **campsite** at **Cooks Beach**, with a pit toilet, water tank, and a rough hut where you can stay.

Schouten Island, off the tip of the peninsula, is part of the national park: it's perfect for really secluded camping, as you're quite likely to have it all to yourself. Freycinet Sea Charters, in Coles Bay (☎03/6257 0355 or 0417 355 524), will drop you off there for around $110 per person return. They also offer a couple of small-group cruises: a two-hour sunset cruise around the island ($55) and a four-hour cruise to Wine Glass Bay (daily 10am; $88), or you could charter the boat for a day-trip which could take in a walk on the island and a visit to a nearby seal colony. There are campsites with pit toilet, a hut and two water tanks at **Moreys Bay**, and the creek at **Crocketts Bay** has reliable upstream water. Although there are no proper tracks on the island, walking is easy.

Freycinet & Strahan Adventures (☎03/6257 0500, ⊛www.tasadventures.com) offers **sea-kayaking tours** on Coles Bay (2hr $50; half-day $80), which can be extended to include overnight camping in the national park; they also run **abseiling** and **rock-climbing** trips. A couple of operators offer **4WD tours** of the park: All Four Adventures (☎03/6257 0018) and Naturally Freycinet (☎03/6257 0293).

Bicheno

Halfway up the east coast, **BICHENO** (pronounced "bish-eno"), sheltered in **Waubs Bay**, is a busy crayfishing and abalone port. The same conditions that make Bicheno ideal for fishing also make it a perfect spot for diving. Don't let the unattractive inland town centre on the Tasman Highway put you off; it has a beautiful bay setting and there's lots to do.

The 3.5-kilometre, one-way **Bicheno Foreshore Footway** runs from Redbill Point (reached via Gordon Street off the Tasman Higway at the western edge of town) and follows several points, bays and beaches, with views of **Governor Island Marine Nature Reserve**, and past the Blowhole. The usually clear waters are rich with a variety of marine life, and the reserve has spectacular large caves and extraordinary vertical rockfaces with swim-throughs and drop-offs. Bicheno Dive Centre, opposite the Sea Life Centre at 2 Scuba Court (☎03/6375 1138), offers dive courses and rents out gear. One of the most popular activities in Bicheno are the evening tours to a local **penguin** rookery with Bicheno Penguin and Adventure Tours based in the East Coast Surf Shop on the highway shopping strip (☎03/6375 1333; nightly; $16); by day, they also offer one-hour, glass-bottom-boat **tours** of the marine reserve ($15), plus 4WD, fishing, walking and cycling tours, and scenic flights. Opposite, the French-owned Le Frog Trike Rides (℡03/6375 1777) runs a range of fun and thrilling three-wheeler tours; among the offerings is a day-trip ($200) complete with wine and frog's legs sampling and a visit to a local oyster farm. The **Sea Life Centre** (daily 9am–5pm; $5), on the Tasman Highway, has a rather dingy aquarium but an excellent seafood restaurant (daily 9am–9pm; dinner bookings ℡03/6375 1311). Bicheno's **Online Access Centre** is at The Oval, Burgess Street.

With a wide choice of **accommodation**, Bicheno makes a pleasant stopover. You can camp at the *East Coast Caravan Park* at 4 Champ St (℡03/6375 1999; vans ❶, cabins ❸) or stay at the small, tidy and well-equipped *Bicheno Backpackers*, 11 Morrison St (℡03/6375 1651, dorms $17). For something really special, head for the *Bicheno Hideaway*, at 179 Harveys Farm Rd (℡03/6375 1312, Ⓦ www.bichenohideaway.com; ❺), 3km south of Bicheno, where uniquely designed oceanfront self-contained chalets are set on six acres of natural bushland teeming with wildlife. Other options include the central *Beachfront Family Resort*, on the Tasman Highway (℡03/6375 1111, Ⓕ6375 1130; ❹), which has a swimming pool, and the *Bicheno Gaol Cottages*, on the corner of James and Burgess streets (℡03/6375 1430; ❺), which offers accommodation in the old prison and its converted stables. **Food**, too, is good in Bicheno. The formal *Cyrano French Restaurant*, at 77 Burgess St (dinner nightly; ℡03/6375 1137), is in the classic French vein, while the *Beachfront Tavern*, on the Tasman Highway, has the best counter meals: big servings and a great salad bar. The eat-in *Freycinet Bakery* (daily 8am–4pm) is an excellent café, while next door the *Cod Rock Cafe* cooks up fresh fish and other seafood (daily 11am–7.30pm). To sample some gourmet Tasmanian products, head for *Mary Harvey's Restaurant* in the gardens of the *Bicheno Gaol Cottages* (daily 10.30am to 5pm).

The Bicheno Coach Service (℡03/6357 0293) to Freycinet National Park leaves from the *Bicheno Takeaway* at 52 Burgess St.

The Douglas Apsley National Park and the Elephant Pass

Just 4km north of Bicheno on the Tasman Highway there's a turn-off to the **Douglas Apsley National Park**. Proclaimed in 1990, it's the location of the state's only remaining large dry sclerophyll forest. Because of the temperate weather of the east coast, the park's two-day walk, the **Leeaberra Track** – undertaken north to south – is a good one at any time of the year. Although facilities are being improved, this is a low-maintenance, untouristy park, so be prepared for basic bushcamping. You can buy the *Douglas Apsley* map and *Notes* ($9.10) from the Land Information Bureau, 134 Macquarie St, Hobart.

Thirty kilometres north of Bicheno, just past Chain of Lagoons, the coastal Tasman Highway continues north to St Helens; turn off to the left for a spectacular climb with views of the surrounding coastline on a detour inland to **St Marys**, 17km away. You can stop at the dramatic Elephant Pass for pancakes, views and atmosphere at the *Mount Elephant Pancake Barn* (daily 8am–6pm), though the menu prices are high.

St Marys and St Helens

From Elephant Pass the road heads on to **ST MARYS**, a picturesque little town surrounded by state forest and waterfalls; there are some fine bushwalks in the area. The place has a quiet, old-fashioned feel to it, but a bit of an alternative edge focused around the great licensed café, bar and theatre, *Todd's Hall*, on Story Street (Ⓣ03/6372 2066; Tues–Sun 10am–5pm), which shows films every Wednesday night at 7.30pm ($5.50; movie-and-dinner deals available). St Mary's **Online Access Centre** is at 23B Main St. The best place to stay is *Seaview Farm* (Ⓣ03/6372 2341, Ⓦwww.seaviewfarm.com.au), in an idyllic setting 8km uphill from St Marys on German Town Road; it has hostel accommodation in a cottage (dorms $17.50, linen extra) or private accommodation in en-suite cabins (❸). Meals aren't provided, so bring provisions; you can arrange a pick-up in advance if you don't have your own transport.

Heading downhill back to the coast, **ST HELENS** is the largest town on the east coast and the last before the Tasman Highway turns west and inland. It's situated on **Georges Bay**, a long, narrow bay with two encircling arms, and the surrounding coastline has plenty of interest. Local **information** is available from the St Helens History Room, at 55 Cecilia St opposite the post office (Mon–Fri 9am–4pm & Sat 9am–noon, plus Sun 10am–2pm in summer; $4; Ⓣ03/6376 1744), which details the area's mining history and provides maps and walk information.

The southern arm of Georges Bay is the site of **St Helens Point Recreation Area**, where there's a large lagoon – Diana's Basin – which the highway skirts as it enters town. On the ocean side the **Peron sand dunes** stretch for several kilometres, and at the point there's good surfing at **Beer Barrel Beach**. **Binalong Bay**, 10km north of Georges Bay, has a beach of bright sugary sand and is an easy bike ride away, with only a couple of small climbs. It's another popular surf spot (with a strong current, so beware); there's safer swimming in the large lagoon tucked behind, where people boat and waterski. You can **camp** here, as well as further along at the **Bay of Fires Coastal Reserve**.

To get to the southern half of **Mount William National Park** take the road running inland north for 54km from St Helens to the pink-granite tower of the Eddystone Lighthouse. The northern end of the park is reached via Gladstone, by taking an unsealed track to **Great Musselroe Bay**, where there's a free basic **campsite**. There are no real tracks within the park itself, but plenty of beach and headland walking, and lots of Forrester kangaroos. The excellent **Bay of Fires Walk** (Ⓣ03/6331 2006, Ⓕ6331 5526, Ⓦwww.bayoffires.com.au; $1465) is a four-day guided coastal walk through Mount William National Park; packs and waterproof jackets are provided and accommodation is in luxury "ecotents" and a superbly designed ecolodge 40m above the sea with stunning views up and down the coast. Island Escape Tours does a five-hour walk in the Bay of Fires as part of their good-value, four-day east-coast tour (see p.1114).

St Helens practicalities

There's a good range of **accommodation** to choose from in town. The *St Helens YHA*, at 5 Cameron St (Ⓣ03/6376 1661; dorms $16–$17, rooms ❷), is clean and friendly. There are also a number of B&Bs: best value is *Artnor Lodge*, at 71 Cecilia St, with share-bathroom or en-suite rooms (Ⓣ03/6376 1234; ❸), or you could try the salubrious *Warrawee Guest House* (Ⓣ03/6376 1987, Ⓕ6376 1012; ❻) on the Tasman Highway. The *Bayside Inn*, at 2 Cecilia St (Ⓣ03/6376 1466; ❸–❹), is a modern hotel/motel with a restaurant, pool and drive-in bottle shop; or there's the much cheaper *Anchor Wheel Motel* at 59 Tully St (Ⓣ03/6376 1358; ❸), which also has its own restaurant. For self-contained accommodation, best value is the spacious, well-equipped *Kellraine Units* (Ⓣ &

ⓕ03/6376 1169; ➋). *Tidal Water*, facing Georges Bay at 2 Jason St (ⓣ03/6376 1100; dinner only, closed Sun), is an award-winning **restaurant** serving Asian-influenced contemporary cuisine. For all-day breakfasts, excellent coffee and a great menu featuring local organic produce, head for the cute *Milk Bar Cafe* at 57B Cecilia St (Mon–Sat 9am–5pm). Next door the reasonably priced, trendy *Wok Stop* (lunch Mon–Fri, dinner Mon–Sat), does Indian curries, wok-fried noodles, fresh juices and excellent coffee. St Helens' bank is Westpac, at 41 Cecilia St, and its **Online Access Centre** is in the library at no. 61.

St Helens to Scottsdale: the Tasman Highway

From St Helens, the **Tasman Highway** cuts across the northeast highlands towards Launceston, 170km away. This is mostly dairy country, although there's the odd patch of surviving rainforest and the remnants of a tin-mining industry, based around the **Blue Tier**, a mountain that experienced a mining boom in the 1870s. Many **ghost towns** were left after the mines finally closed in the 1950s.

Twenty-six kilometres out of St Helens is the turn-off south for **PYENGANA** (1km) and St Columba Falls (a further 4km). In Pyengana it's worth touring **Healey's Pyengana Cheese Factory** (daily 9am–5pm; free), where you can watch the stuff being made (except Fri & Sat) and buy all the ingredients for a picnic at the falls. Further along, *St Columba Falls Hotel* (ⓣ03/6373 6121; ➋) – the "Pub in the Paddock" – looks like a farmhouse; it's a real country local, serving huge steaks (meals daily). At the end of the road (the last bit on dirt) is the **Columba Falls State Reserve**, an area of cool, temperate rainforest. The short walk to the viewing platform at the base of **St Columba Falls** is easy, passing through a forest of manferns and under a canopy of sassafras and myrtle. At 110m, the falls are among the highest in Tasmania, pouring with tremendous force over the cliffs – truly thunderous in winter.

Back on the main road approaching the Blue Tier, **Goshen** is the first of the ghost towns, little more than an old school and the ruins of the *Oxford Arms Inn*. A little further on is the turn-off for **Goulds Country**, with the remaining buildings – all wooden – of what was once a town. The **Weldborough Pass** (595m) is probably the most beautiful part of the drive, with views across the valleys to the sea; it's worth taking the twenty-minute walk through the **Weldborough Pass Scenic Reserve**, predominantly myrtle forest with manferns and occasional tall blackwoods. **WELDBOROUGH** itself, once the centre of a Chinese mining community, now consists of the isolated, characterful *Weldborough Hotel* (ⓣ & ⓕ03/6354 2223; ➋), where you can get a **meal** (Mon–Sat) and a basic pub **room** for the night; there's also a campsite. **DERBY**, on the Ringarooma River, was made prosperous by the profitable **Briseis Tin Mine** between 1876 and 1952. The **Derby Tin Mine Centre** (daily: June–Aug 10am–4pm; Sept–May 10am–5pm; $4.50) is now the only sign of development in a town that's been closing down since the 1950s: it has some interesting relics connected with the Chinese miners. **SCOTTSDALE**, 99km from St Helens, is a large, pleasantly situated town servicing the agricultural and forestry industries of the northeast. The new **Scottsdale Eco Centre** (Mon–Fri 9.30am–5pm, Sat & Sun 10am–3pm) is yet another Forestry Tasmania public relations exercise; the unique, energy-smart building looks like a wooden spaceship that has landed and half-sunk into the ground. Inside, an "eco-walk" winds up the circular building, putting the local forest and forestry industry into historical and ecological context, and there's a pleasant café (daily

⑪

TASMANIA | The east coast: the Tasman Highway

10am–3pm) and a **visitor information** centre (☎03/6352 6520). Scottsdale has good facilities, including banks, supermarkets and an **Online Access Centre** in the library at 51 King St. There are some beautiful areas to visit nearby; Pepper Bush Peaks 4WD Adventure Tours (☎03/6352 2263, ⓦwww.tasadventures.com/pepperbush) offers a range of **tours** which take you off-road to visit magnificent waterfalls, old-growth forests – including the tallest white gum trees in the world – and lookouts, as well as giving you the opportunity to catch your own fish. Tours include fine food and wine and range from a nocturnal wildlife tour with BBQ ($109) to a full-day tour ($259); they pick up from Launceston.

Twenty-one kilometres northwest, the fishing town and holiday spot of **BRIDPORT** has several places to **stay** including the modern, purpose-built *Bridport Seaside Lodge YHA Backpackers*, at 47 Main St (☎03/6356 1585, ⓔseasidelodge@bigpond.com.au; dorms $19–22, rooms ❷). There's camping at *Bridport Caravan Park* (☎03/6356 1227; sites only), which stretches for about a kilometre along Anderson Bay. The **beaches** in the area are lovely, especially the wide, sandy expanse where the Bird River flows among sand dunes and into the sea. *Bridport Seafoods* (daily 10am–7pm), attached to the fish-processing plant on Main Street, does excellent sit-down meals.

North and central Tasmania and the Bass Strait

The **north** of Tasmania is rich and settled agricultural country, and the fertile soil of the **Tamar Valley** in particular made this a prosperous area during the early colonial period. **Launceston** quickly grew as a port and city, 30km inland at the confluence of the Tamar and the North and South Esk rivers; gracious early houses and well-preserved villages are still found around the area. Also settled early, due to its fine and open land, was the mostly flat, gently undulating **midlands** area between Launceston and Hobart; the **Midland Highway** more or less follows the old coaching route between the two cities. With its stone walls, hedgerows, haystacks and small villages and towns, this rural stretch from the Tamar Valley to Hobart is softly appealing but not particularly exciting. In contrast, the area around **Deloraine**, 45km west of Launceston, is spectacular: the early colonial town is surrounded by rich farmland and dramatically located in hilly country below the crest of the **Great Western Tiers** – a mecca for bushwalkers. From Deloraine, the **Lake Highway** heads steeply south up over the Western Tiers and on to the **Central Plateau**, a sparsely populated lake-filled region dominated by the **Great Lake** and its shambolic fishing shacks.

Lying off the northern coast, in Bass Strait, are two islands worth visiting for their bushwalks and historic associations: **Flinders Island** in the northeast, largest of the Furneaux Islands, and **King Island** to the far northwest, part of the Hunter Island group. Both are reached by plane only, with flights from Victoria or Tasmania.

Launceston and around

LAUNCESTON is dominated by the **Tamar River**, and approaching from the north along the Tamar Highway, zooming through haystack-filled countryside, it's a lovely sight, with grand Victorian houses nestling on hills above the banks. Approaching from the south on the dreary Southern Outlet, however, gives a slightly more accurate picture of the dull but worthy provincial town. However, Tasmania's second-largest city, with a population of around 68,000, is currently undergoing a bit of a shake-up, with a young female mayor, Janie Dickenson, at the helm; a former furniture designer, she was voted in, in 2002, aged just 27.

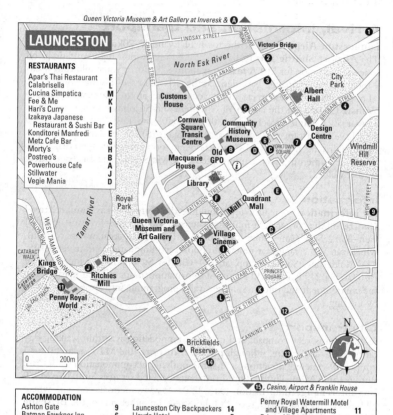

Queen Victoria Museum & Art Gallery at Inveresk & Ⓐ ▲

LAUNCESTON

RESTAURANTS

Apar's Thai Restaurant	**F**
Calabrisella	**L**
Cucina Simpatica	**M**
Fee & Me	**K**
Hari's Curry	**I**
Izakaya Japanese Restaurant & Sushi Bar	**C**
Konditorei Manfredi	**E**
Metz Cafe Bar	**G**
Morty's	**H**
Postreo's	**B**
Powerhouse Cafe	**A**
Stillwater	**J**
Vegie Mania	**D**

LINDSAY STREET
CHARLES STREET
INVERMAY ROAD
Victoria Bridge
North Esk River
ESPLANADE
WILLIAM STREET
City Park
Albert Hall
BRISBANE STREET
TAMAR STREET
CIMITIERE ST
Customs House
Cornwall Square Transit Centre
Community History Museum
CAMERON ST
Design Centre
YORKTOWN SQUARE
Windmill Hill Reserve
Old GPO
Macquarie House
ⓘ
YORK STREET
Library
CIVIC SQUARE
PATERSON STREET
CHARLES STREET
Royal Park
Quadrant Mall
Mall
HIGH STREET
Queen Victoria Museum and Art Gallery
BRISBANE STREET
Village Cinema
GEORGE STREET
ST JOHN STREET
Tamar River
WEST TAMAR HIGHWAY
TREVALLYN ROAD
CATARACT WALK
Kings Bridge
River Cruise
Ritchies Mill
WELLINGTON STREET
YORK STREET
ELIZABETH STREET
PRINCES SQUARE
Cataract Gorge
JIG ZAG TRACK
Penny Royal World
MARGARET STREET
BATHURST STREET
FREDERICK STREET
BOURKE STREET
Brickfields Reserve
CANNING STREET
BALFOUR STREET
N

0   200m

▼ Ⓑ, Casino, Airport & Franklin House

ACCOMMODATION

Ashton Gate	**9**	Launceston City Backpackers	**14**	Penny Royal Watermill Motel and Village Apartments	**11**
Batman Fawkner Inn	**6**	Lloyds Hotel	**5**	Prince Albert Inn	**3**
The Edwardian	**12**	The Maldon	**7**	Sandors on the Park	**4**
Glebe Cottages	**1**	Metro Backpackers	**8**	Sportsman's Hall Hotel	**13**
Irish Murphy's Backpackers	**10**	No. 1 Backpackers	**2**	Treasure Island Caravan Park	**15**

As the third-oldest city in Australia, first settled in 1804, Launceston has hung on to disappointingly little of its elegant colonial Georgian architecture. Existing examples are mainly utilitarian structures such as merchant warehouses and mills, now converted into museums, galleries or tourist attractions. What the city does have in abundance, however, are many fine examples of colonial **Victorian architecture**: the 1870s and 1880s were prosperous times for Launceston, years of mineral exploration spurred on by the mainland goldrush, and a number of massive, dignified public buildings date from this boom period.

Launceston's real attractions, though, are its natural assets. It's situated at the confluence of the narrow **North Esk** and **South Esk rivers**, with the breathtaking **Cataract Gorge** only fifteen-minutes' walk from the centre, where the South Esk has carved its way through rock to reach the Tamar River. Yachts and outboard motors ply the 50km of river, and the surrounding countryside of the **Tamar Valley**, with its wineries, strawberry farms and lavender plantations is idyllic; beyond the western suburbs bush-covered hills fold back into the distance to **Ben Lomond**, a popular winter skiing destination just an hour's drive away.

Arrival, information and transport

Launceston Airport is near the town of Evandale, 20km south of the city. The **Airport Shuttle Bus** (☎0500 512 009) meets most flights and drops off at accommodation for $10. A **taxi** costs about $28–30, or you could **rent a car** – the main car companies have desks at the airport, or see "Listings" on p.1113.

Long-distance **buses** arrive in the city centre at the **Cornwall Square Transit Centre**, on the corner of Cimitiere and St Johns streets, where both Tasmanian Redline Coaches (☎1300 360 000) and TassieLink (☎1300 300 520) have ticket offices; Redline has left luggage ($1.50 per 24hr) and there is a café. If driving, note that most streets operate on a **one-way system** and the length of Cameron Street is interrupted by Civic Square, and Brisbane Street by the Mall.

Information

For **information**, your first stop should be the **Gateway Tasmanian Travel Centre**, on the corner of St John and Paterson streets (Mon–Fri 9am–5pm, Sat 9am–3pm, Sun 9am–noon; ☎03/6336 3133, ⓦwww.gatewaytas.com.au), which can also arrange car rental and book accommodation and travel tickets. The Wilderness Society Shop, at 174 Charles St, opposite Princes Square (☎03/6334 2499), is a good source of information about wilderness issues and the environment and offers a summer walks programme into areas under threat by logging.

City transport

Launceston is very compact and most accommodation is within walking distance of the city centre, although **public transport** (the MTT) is useful for a couple of scattered attractions and some outlying accommodation (buses run until 6.15pm Mon–Thurs, 10pm Fri & Sat; restricted services Sun). The **MTT bus interchange** (information ☎13 22 01, ⓦwww.metrotas.com.au), where all buses arrive and depart, is on St John Street, on either side of the **Brisbane Street Mall**. Single fares are inexpensive, but it may be worth buying a Day Rover ($3.60) for unlimited off-peak travel (buy on board) or a ten-trip ticket (from $11.20; buy at Teagues Newsagency, opposite the post office.

Accommodation

Accommodation in Launceston is very good value, and rates don't tend to hike up in the busy December-to-February period, though **hostel** beds can be scarce then. There's a concentration of **motels** along Brisbane Street and an abundance of **B&Bs** and self-catering accommodation.

Hotels, motels, B&Bs and self-catering

Ashton Gate 32 High St ☎03/6331 6180, ⓦwww.view.com.au/ashtongate. Classified by the National Trust, this weatherboard B&B has been taking guests for over forty years. Bedrooms are large and light; all are en suite, with TV and hot drinks. ❺–❻

Batman Fawkner Inn 35–39 Cameron St ☎03/6331 7222, ⓕ6331 7158. Established in 1822, and offering bargain, single en-suite rooms with TV and phone ($45); larger, more attractive rooms have similar facilities. Light breakfast included. ❹

The Edwardian 227 Charles St ☎03/6334 7771, ⓦwww.theedwardian.com.au. Lovely, two-storey red-brick Edwardian house near Princes Square, with self-contained self-catering suites. Breakfast provisions provided. Handy for the supermarket. No children. ❹–❺

Glebe Cottages 14A Cimitiere St ☎0500 500 581, ⓦwww.glebecottages.com.au. Good-value, spacious two- and three-bedroom self-contained cottages, in a convenient location near City Park. ❺

Lloyds Hotel 23 George St ☎03/6331 4966, ⓕ6331 5589. Solid, rather drab old-fashioned pub but with good-value en-suite rooms. Hot drinks and TV in the guest lounge. Economical pub meals downstairs. Closed Sun. ❷–❸

The Maldon 32 Brisbane St ☎03/6331 3211, ⓕ6334 4641. Elegant Victorian-era B&B, featuring iron-lace verandahs, chandeliers, engraved glass and a carved wooden staircase; en-suite rooms with modern facilities. ❹

Penny Royal Watermill Motel and Village Apartments 145–147 Paterson St ☎03/6331 6699, ⓔpennyroyal@leisureinns.com.au. Built in 1840, this motel has a comfortable old-world charm, while the more modern self-contained apartments are spacious and reasonably priced. Close to the city centre and a short walk to the gorge and Cliff Grounds. ❺–❻

Prince Albert Inn Cnr William and Tamar streets ☎03/6331 7633, ⓦwww.princealbertinn.com.au. Refurbished nineteenth-century inn near City Park, with spacious en-suite rooms furnished in Heritage style. The dining room, where you have breakfast, is full of stuffed animals, while old photographs and colonial prints cover the walls. Nonsmokers only. ❺–❼

Sandors on the Park 3 Brisbane St ☎03/6331 2055 or 1800 030 140, ⓕ6334 3910. The best of a bunch of motels on this strip overlooking City Park – but not the most expensive –and just a short walk from the centre. Friendly professional service; guest laundry. Its bistro-style *Monkey Bar Café* opens noon–10.30pm. ❸–❹

Sportsman's Hall Hotel 252 Charles St ☎03/6331 3968, ⓕ6334 4227. Pleasant pub with well-furnished, comfortable rooms (shared bathrooms). Breakfast included. Excellent, café-style bistro downstairs serving up very reasonably priced meals. ❸

Hostels and caravan parks

Irish Murphy's Backpackers 211 Brisbane St ☎03/6331 4440, ⓦwww.irishmurphys.com.au. Hostel accommodation above a lively, centrally located pub. Facilities include TV lounge and a fully equipped kitchen. Bedding $3 extra for dorms. Dorms $17, rooms ❷

Launceston City Backpackers 103 Canning St ☎03/6334 2327, ⓦwww.launceston backpackers.com.au. A good hostel in a newly decorated, clean and well-equipped old house. Friendly managers and a great atmosphere. Tours and bus tickets can be booked here. Single rooms available ($38). Book ahead in summer. Dorms $17, rooms ❷

Metro Backpackers 16 Brisbane St ☎03/6334 4505, ⓦwww.backpackersmetro.com.au. Friendly, very central YHA hostel in a 1930s Art Deco building. Great facilities, including a pool table, Internet access, satellite TV and a BBQ rooftop area off the kitchen. Knowledgable staff and informative noticeboards; tours can be booked. Free luggage storage; bikes for rent. One en-suite family room (sleeps 4). Linen and towels included. Dorms $23, rooms ❸

No. 1 Backpackers *Tamar Hotel*, 1 Tamar St, by Victoria Bridge ☎03/6334 9288. Renovated former pub with an all-you-can-eat restaurant downstairs, and clean and well-run backpacker accommodation upstairs. Facilities include a free

laundry; BYO linen. Dorms $16, rooms ❷
Treasure Island Caravan Park 94 Glen Dhu St,
South Launceston, 2km south of the centre
ⓣ03/6344 2600. A small park, sloping up a hill-

side and looking right over a noisy freeway. Hard,
uneven ground; crowded in summer. Camp kitchen
with TV. Bus #21 or #24 to Wellington Street (stop
8). Vans ❷, en-suite cabins ❸

The City

The **Brisbane Street Mall** marks the centre of the city, which is arranged in
a typical grid pattern around it. **Brisbane Street**, with the mall as its focus, is
the main shopping precinct; heading east along the street, two other pedestrian
shopping areas branch off it: **Quadrant Mall** and **Yorktown Square**. The city
is small and easy to get around, but if you want some background information,
join Launceston Historic Walks (departs Mon–Fri 9.45am; 1hr 15min; $15;
bookings ⓣ03/6331 3679) outside the Gateway Centre on Paterson Street.

City Park and the old wharf area

City Park (daily 8am–5pm), with its entrance of impressive wrought-iron
gates on Tamar Street, is a real treasure. Established in the 1820s, the impression
of a formally organized, very English park is reinforced by the **John Hart
Conservatory**, full of flowers and ferns, and by the wrought-iron drinking
fountain erected here for Queen Victoria's Diamond Jubilee in 1897. Referred
to by the locals as "Monkey Park", it's the closest thing Launceston has to a
zoo: its Japanese macaques (over twenty of them), romp around their small,
moat-surrounded island. The **City Park Train** (11am–4.30pm) whizzes children and adults twice around the park for around a dollar a ride.

Within City Park, on the corner of Tamar and Brisbane streets, is the **Design
Centre of Tasmania** (Mon–Fri 10am–6pm, Sat 10am–1pm, Sun 2–5pm;
free), established in 1976 to support and encourage Tasmanian designers. In a
state that's always been perceived by the mainland as lagging behind, it's a
source of pride that Tasmanian designers helped furnish the New Parliament
House in Canberra; "Furniture Focus", a permanent display of contemporary,
innovative furniture made from native Tasmanian woods, includes some of
their work. Pieces are regularly sold and shipped overseas; prices are beyond the
range of most visitors, but the centre is also one of the best places to buy more
portable **craft** items, such as woodwork, leatherwork and jewellery. Backing
onto City Park, near the corner of Tamar and Cimitiere streets, is **Albert Hall**,
a grand building in the ornate High Victorian style, built for the Tasmanian
Industrial Exhibition of 1891. You can go up the steps and look inside at the
restored Great Hall; the Brindley water-powered organ, imported from
England in 1861, is the only one of its kind in the world.

The wharves on the North Esk River have disappeared, but the massive
Neoclassical **Customs House** is still there on The Esplanade, just east of the
Charles Street Bridge. The **old wharf area**, around William Street and the
Esplanade, has several interesting old industrial buildings, including the 1881,
still-operational **J. Boag & Son** brewery. Its popular brewery tours start in the
Boag's Centre For Beer Lovers, opposite at 39 William St, which includes
a **museum** (Mon–Fri 8.45am–4.30pm; free) and giftshop, and finish with a
small tasting of four beers (Mon–Thurs 9am, 11.45am & 2.30pm; Fri 9am &
11.45am; 1hr 30min; $12; bookings ⓣ03/6332 6300, ⓦwww.boags.com.au).

The North Bank and Heritage Forest

Opposite the Esplanade, reached by Victoria Bridge from Tamar Street, and
then a boardwalk along the river, is the new **Queen Victoria Museum and**

Art Gallery at Inveresk (daily 10am–5pm; $10 includes admission to the Royal Park site – see overleaf), part of a multimillion-dollar redevelopment of the complex of old railway yards here. Opened in late 2001, the new building has an incredible interior sense of space. Two-thirds of it is home to the **Academy of Arts**, part of the University of Tasmania. The art gallery is well worth visiting for its "Aspects of Tasmanian Art" exhibition, which notably contains landscapes by the nineteenth-century painter W.C. Piguenit, and "Strings Across Time – Tasmanian Aboriginal Shell Necklaces", which displays beautiful examples of the ancient women's art, including recent examples from the tradition of Cape Barren Islanders. From the art gallery you walk through to the former **Railway Workshops**, now transformed into a social history museum; the history of railways in Tasmania is hardly compelling stuff (though the Playzone for kids is great), but the walkway through the old Blacksmith Shop, complete with soundscape of machinery and voices, is eerie, and the exhibition on migration to the state, based on personal stories including those of people from Kosovo, El Salvador, Afghanistan, Somalia and Vietnam gives a different angle on contemporary Tasmania. The sedate licensed café in the Railway Workshops has part of its seating in an old train carriage (simple menu, nothing over $12).

The railway yards site spans a large expanse of riverfront land dubbed by the council as the **Northbank Experience**. It includes the Tasmanian Conservation Workshops, the Exhibition Centre and the York Park Sports and Entertainment Centre, which has finally brought live AFL football to Launceston. Still to come is a visitor information centre and a clutch of cafés, restaurants and stores. The boardwalk to the art gallery continues along the North Esk River to **Heritage Forest**, parkland with walking, bike-riding and horse-riding trails.

Civic Square and around

Shady, grassy **Civic Square**, closed to traffic, does convey a tidy spirit of civic-mindedness. Here, **Macquarie House** was built as a warehouse in 1830 for Henry Reed, a wealthy merchant. These days it's the home of the **Tasmanian Wood Design Collection** (Mon–Fri 10am–1pm; $2.20), which showcases Tasmanian wood pieces of some of the state's superb designers, wood-workers and furniture-makers. **Cameron Street** was one of the first streets laid out after the city's settlement in 1806, and the stretch from Civic Square to Wellington Street is an almost perfectly preserved nineteenth-century streetscape, including the imposing Supreme Court building and, opposite, a row of fine Victorian red-brick terraced houses adorned with beautiful wrought-iron work.

South of Civic Square is the main shopping thoroughfare, the pedestrianized **Brisbane Street Mall**, a modest precinct taking up one small city block. Just off here is the arc of the **Quadrant Mall**, bounded by Brisbane and St John streets, with several lanes and an arcade off it. Gourlay's Sweet Shop here is a Launceston institution – for something really local, try the leatherwood honey drops. **Yorktown Square**, designed to re-create the atmosphere of the nineteenth century, can be reached by cobbled lanes off Cameron, George and Brisbane streets; cafés and restaurants – most with outdoor tables – range around the square where a Sunday "village market" (9am–2pm), selling mainly crafts, is held. Nearly opposite the square's George Street entrance is The Old Umbrella Shop at no. 60 (Mon–Fri 9am–5pm, Sat 9am–noon; ☏03/6331 9248), a **National Trust information centre** housed in a rare example of a mid-Victorian shop, built in the 1860s and lined with Tasmanian blackwood.

The Queen Victoria Museum and Art Gallery at Royal Park

The **Queen Victoria Museum and Art Gallery**, on Wellington Street (daily 10am–5pm; $10 includes entry to the Inveresk site – see p.1108; Ⓦ www.qvmag.tas.gov.au), was opened in 1891 to mark half a century of Queen Victoria's reign. Its most valued possession is the Chinese joss house from Weldborough (see p.1103), constructed in the 1870s by Chinese workers introduced to the east-coast tin mines to provide cheap labour. Elsewhere, other permanent **museum** exhibitions include: a history of mining in Tasmania; displays about the state's fauna, with big sections on the Tasmanian Tiger and the Tasmanian devil; accounts of the geology of Launceston and the local area; a **Planetarium** (Tues–Fri 3pm, Sat 2pm & 3pm; $5); and the "Discovery Plus" room, containing microscopes and specimen trays, as well as a display of live spiders and puzzles to play with. The **art gallery** section includes traditonal and contemporary Aboriginal works, and decorative arts including costumes, textiles and ceramics, but most of the art collection has moved to the Inveresk site. The *Queen Vic Café* is one of the best in Launceston.

Royal Park to Ritchies Mill Arts Centre

Behind the museum, and across Bathurst Street, **Royal Park** has extensive formal parklands running down to the Tamar River; there's even a croquet lawn here, if you were in any doubt about its English character. Between Royal Park and Cataract Gorge is a concentrated tourist area. **Ritchies Mill Arts Centre**, at 2 Bridge Rd on the Tamar River, has been converted from a nine-teenth-century flour mill and millers' cottage and now contains two galleries and an alfresco café, *Stillwater* (see p.1112). Tamar River Cruises depart from the landing stage behind the arts centre and head along the Tamar and into the mouth of beautiful Cataract Gorge, allowing a close-up view of the Launceston Yacht Club, as well as the wealthy suburb of **Trevallyn**, filled with classic Victorian mansions strung along the tree-covered hillside (Mon–Fri 3pm; 2hr 30min; $32). A longer trip continues north up the Tamar as far as the Rosevear vineyards (see p.1115; Mon–Sat 10am, Sun 11am; 4hr; $60 including lunch; bookings ☏03/6334 9900).

Opposite Ritchies Mill, the overpriced **Penny Royal World** (daily 9.30am–4pm; $15) is a sort of historical funfair, developed on the site of an old bluestone quarry and based around an 1840 ironstone water mill and farm-house – transferred to the site – and a replica of an 1825 wooden corn mill.

Cataract Gorge and beyond

Few cities have such a magnificent natural feature within fifteen minutes' walk of the centre as Launceston. For a beautiful view of **Cataract Gorge**, turn left out of Penny Royal World and walk to the decorative wrought-iron **Kings Bridge**, fabricated in Manchester and transported to Launceston in 1863, which has a span of 60m. From the bridge the cliffs rise almost vertically from the smooth water of the South Esk River as it empties into the Tamar. The nat-ural spectacle is even more dramatic when floodlit after dusk.

The **Zig Zag track** (25min one-way), on the Penny Royal World side of the bridge, is the more strenuous of the two walking routes along the gorge. The rock-stepped path shrouded by bush is satisfyingly secluded (due to recent sexual assaults women should be careful not to walk here alone). The track runs steeply along the top of the gorge, from Kings Bridge to the **First Basin**, a large, deep canyon worn away by the river and filled with water. Across the Kings Bridge, is the easier but busier **Cataract Walk** (40min one-way), which begins by the small tollhouse; the stroll is suitable for prams or wheelchairs, and offers spectacular views of the gorge. From the trail, particularly at weekends, you'll see people canoeing, abseiling or even jumping off the cliffs into the water; Tasmania Expeditions offers abseiling trips here (see "Tours", p.1114).

The Cataract Walk leads to the gardens of the **Cliff Grounds**, on the shady northern side of the gorge – genteel, English-style gardens with parading peacocks, they make for a startling contrast with the gorge's wild beauty. The garden's native and exotic plants are artfully arranged around a lovely 1896 rotunda, which contains an interpretive centre detailing the gorge's history and botany. *The Gorge Restaurant* (closed Mon; ℡03/6331 3330) in the grounds has stunning views over the First Basin. Less expensive Devonshire teas are served from the kiosk at the back of the restaurant. If you enter the grounds from the First Basin end (where there's a car park; or take bus #51B), you'll find an enormous, unattractive **swimming pool**, built mainly to discourage people from swimming in the basin itself, where some have died. However, people still continue to swim there, despite prominent signs warning them of the dangers of hypothermia and submerged rocks and logs.

To get across the First Basin to the Cliff Grounds, the **Launceston Basin Chair Lift** (daily 9am–4.30pm weather permitting; $6.60) takes an exhilarating six minutes to cover 457m – it's supposed to have the longest single span (308m) of any chair lift in the world. The views are wonderful, but if you're afraid of heights you might want to cross on foot via the **Basin Walk** directly underneath, although this route is impassable when the river is in flood. The other alternative, the narrow **Alexandra Suspension Bridge**, is fairly alarming, too. Called the "swinging bridge" by locals, it's even shakier when crowded with joggers.

Several other walks and lookouts in the grounds are all well signposted. It's even possible to undertake longer bushwalks: a track starting from the Alexandra Suspension Bridge follows the river through unspoilt bush to the narrower **Second Basin** and the disused **Duck Reach Power Station** (90min return). From the station you could continue a bit further to the large **Trevallyn State Recreation Area** (daily 8am–dusk; no camping), on the South Esk River, and the **Trevallyn Dam**, 6km west of the city centre. To reach the area by road, go via the suburb of Trevallyn, following Reatta Road. In the recreation area at Aquatic Point, there's an **information centre** (which can advise about renting canoes and windsurf boards in the summer), a children's playground, toilets and barbecues. The rest of the reserve consists of open eucalypt forest, with marked bushwalks and nature trails shared with horse riders.

The Waverly Woollen Mills and Franklin House

Waverly Woollen Mills, on Waverly Road, 5km west of the city centre, (Mon–Fri 9am–4pm; tours $4; bus #34 or #38 to the Waverly Road turn-off then a 500m walk), is the oldest woollen mill in Australia, established in 1874, and much of the cloth is still manufactured on old-fashioned machinery.

Franklin House, at 413 Hobart Rd, 6km towards Hobart on the Midland Highway (daily 9am–5pm, till 4pm June & Aug, closed July; $7.70; bus #21 from the city), was built in 1838 for Britton Jones, a prosperous local brewer. Furnished as an early Victorian home, it became a leading school for boys four years after it was built, a role it retained for half a century. Beautifully furnished and restored by the National Trust, its most outstanding feature is the woodwork of the interior, made entirely of unusual cedarwood from New South Wales.

Eating

Eating out in Launceston is a predominantly Anglo-Saxon affair, with **pubs** in particular offering decent meals. However, there are also a few excellent **cafés** and the odd ethnic place.

Arpar's Thai Restaurant Cnr Charles and Paterson streets ☎03/6331 2786. Thai restaurant with a good reputation. Licensed and BYO. Lunch Fri, dinner nightly.

Calabrisella 56 Wellington St ☎03/6331 1958. A crowded, noisy, atmospheric and affordable Italian restaurant. BYO. Dinner nightly except Tues.

Cucina Simpatica Cnr Margaret and Frederick streets, opposite Brickfields Reserve ☎03/6334 3177. Hip café with a colourful Mediterranean feel. Becomes a restaurant in the evening, with an eclectic, "contemporary" menu: delicious food (though pricey and small portions) and an emphasis on fresh local and organic produce. Licensed and BYO. Daily 10am until late.

Fee & Me 190 Charles St ☎03/6331 3195. Award-winning restaurant serving up regional cuisine with an international flavour. Expensive. Licensed. Dinner Mon–Sat.

Hari's Curry 152 York St ☎03/6331 6466. Very cheap, well-recommended Indian place. BYO. Closed lunch Sat & Sun.

Izakaya Japanese Restaurant and Sushi Bar Yorktown Square ☎03/6334 2620. Serves all the usual Japanese dishes: *ramen*, sushi, tempura, *bento*. Licensed (sake) and BYO. Lunch Tues–Fri , dinner nightly.

Konditorei Manfredi 106 George St ☎03/6334 2490. German cakes and pastries accompanied by delicious coffee; also a full menu of contemporary meals served on the smart upper level with its polished wood floors, licensed bar and outside courtyard. Mon–Sat 8.30am–5.30pm.

Metz Cafe Bar 119 St John St, cnr York St. Cosmopolitan combination of café and wine bar with music videos playing day or night. Typical café fare plus wood-fired pizzas and all-day breakfasts. Licensed. Daily 8am–midnight, Fri & Sat until 3am, Sun until 2am.

Morty's Cnr Brisbane and Wellington streets. Popular foodcourt near the cinema, with lots of Asian kitchens including Thai and Chinese. *Dave's Noodles* – which are freshly cooked – is the best choice. Also fish and chips, pancakes, a juice bar. Licensed. Daily 10am–9.30pm.

Postreo's Cnr St John and Cameron streets. Built in 1889, the rather grand, red-brick former General Post Office is now home to a great café. It has a wonderful Victoriana setting under a domed atrium, with decorative brickwork and leadlighting. A small, well-chosen menu with mains around $16.50, features fish, scallops and Hokkien noodles etc, plus more affordable gourmet salads, Italian sandwiches and wraps. Licensed. Mon–Fri 8am–5pm, plus dinner Fri.

Powerhouse Cafe Inveresk Railyards, off Invermay Rd. This art college student association café/bar/restaurant, in a round and sunny former powerhouse, is a young, lively hangout, with music pumping. Classic, café meals for under $8, plus more substantial mains up to $14.50 (from a seafood curry to an oven-roasted chicken breast). Outside tables prove very popular for the Sunday brunch. Blues bands every Friday night and ambient DJs Saturday night (both from 7pm) while dinner is served. Upstairs is used for film festivals, exhibitions and performances. Licensed. Mon–Sat from 10am (dinner Wed–Sat only), Sun 11am–3pm.

Stillwater Ritchies Mill Arts Centre, Paterson St ☎03/6331 4153. Very popular riverside café/restaurant and wine bar with a great atmosphere. During the day it's an alfresco café, with generous all-day breakfasts and board specials. At night it becomes a fine-dining establishment. Licensed and BYO. Daily 10am to late (book for dinner).

Vegie Mania 64 George St, next door to the Old Umbrella Shop ☎03/6331 2535. Highly recommended Singapore-Chinese vegetarian restaurant. Mains around $14. BYO. Dinner nightly, lunch Mon–Fri.

Entertainment and nightlife

The *Examiner*, based in Launceston, is the newspaper for the north of Tasmania – Thursday's edition contains an entertainment section. However, there's never very much going on in this quiet city, and there's no particularly lively area. The **Princess Theatre**, 57 Brisbane St (☎03/6323 3666), stages regular drama, opera, ballet and concerts, usually touring from interstate. Behind the theatre is the Earl Arts Centre, 10 Earl St (☎03/6334 5579), which has fringe theatre productions, while the **Silverdome**, out of town on the Bass Highway at Prospect (☎03/6344 9999), is the venue for big entertainment events, exhibitions and sports events. AFL matches are held in **York Park Sports and Entertainment Centre** just near the new Inveresk development (details and bookings ⓦwww.aflintasmania.com), and you can gamble at the **Country Club Casino**, 9km out of town, off the Bass Highway at Prospect Vale (daily noon–1am, Fri & Sat until 4am; bus #61, #64, #65 ☎03/6335 5777). The only **cinema**, the four-screen Village 4, at 163 Brisbane St (☎03/6331 5066), shows mainstream films. Launceston's only **gay** bar is *Mickey D's Nightclub*, part of the *New St James Hotel*, 122 York St, with DJs and dancing on Friday and a fortnightly drag show.

Pubs and clubs

Irish Murphy's 211 Brisbane St. Lively Irish pub with Guinness on tap, live music Wednesday to Sunday, and pub meals.

Launceston Saloon 191 Charles St ☎03/6331 7355. Always packed out on event nights with a young studenty crowd. The huge main *Saloon Bar* is Wild West-themed and has pool tables, local bands (Wed) nights and irregular interstate and international band events, and DJs nights on Friday and Saturday (9.30pm–3.30am; $5–7) when the mezzanine-level becomes a karaoke bar. Big-screen TV and typical pub food served in the *Sports Bar*.

The Lounge Bar 63 St John St. Imposing corner stone building in a former bank is now a sophisticated bar with lots of sofas. Wed & Thurs 6pm to late, Fri & Sat 5pm–5am.

Royal Oak Hotel 14 Brisbane St ☎03/6331 5346. Popular, genial watering hole with live blues and jazz Thursday to Saturday nights. Crowded bistro serves Greek dishes as well as counter meals. Mon–Sat until midnight, Sun until 10pm.

Royal on George 90 George St ☎03/6331 2526. Renovated glass-fronted, light and colourful pub with an emphasis on food (from 8.30am for breakfast). A modern café-style menu – gourmet sandwiches and salads, pasta and risotto, plus classic but meaty mains. Live rock, jazz or acoustic music Friday and Saturday. Mon–Thurs & Sun until midnight, Fri & Sat to 3am.

Star Bar Café 113 Charles St. Sophisticated bar with slick, modern decor; brasserie-style Mediterranean food available. Daily 11am until late.

Listings

Banks and foreign exchange Commonwealth Bank, 97 Brisbane St; Thomas Cook, 98 St John St (Mon–Fri 9am–5.30pm, Sat 10am–1pm).

Bike rental Metro Backpackers (see p.1107) rents bikes: $10 half-day, $15 full day, $70 per week including panniers.

Books Fullers Bookshop, 93 St John St.

Camping equipment A good option for renting or buying gear is Allgoods, with stores at 71–79 York St and 60 Elizabeth St. Paddy Pallin, 110 George St, focuses on the top end of the market; also rents gear and sells a wide range of freeze-dried foods, guidebooks and maps.

Car rental Europcar, airport and 112 George St (☎03/6331 8200 or 1800 030 118), has daily rates from $70; also 4WDs, from $105 per day. Autorent-Hertz, airport and 58 Paterson St (☎03/6335 1111), charges from $70 per day, and has campervans; Economy Car Rentals, 27 William St (☎03/6334 3299), from $65 per day; Lo-Cost Auto Rent, 152 Cimitiere St (☎03/6334 3437),

from $59 per day; Ryan's Minicar Rentals, 22 Wellington St (☎03/6344 3600), has old Leyland minis from $44 for one day to $27.50 per day for five days and over.

Hospital Launceston General, Charles St (☎03/6332 7111).

Internet access Launceston's Online Access Centre is on the ground floor of the State Library, Civic Square; there's free access next door at the Service Tasmania Centre (max 30min).

Motorbike rental Tasmanian Motorcycle Hire, 17 Coachmans Rd, Evandale (☎03/6391 9139, ⓦwww.tasmotorcyclehire.com.au; from $100 per day, helmets included).

Pharmacy Amcal Centre Pharmacy, 84 Brisbane St (daily 9am–10pm; ☎03/6331 7777).

Post office 170 Brisbane St, Launceston, TAS 7250.

Swimming The Launceston Swimming Centre, Windmill Hill Reserve (☎03/6323 3630), has an outdoor 50m pool, a diving pool, children's pool and waterslides. Aquarius Roman Baths, 127–133 George St (☎03/6331 2255), are a very popular, self-indulgent complex of therapeutic warm, hot and cold baths, sauna, steam rooms, gym, massage and solarium; admission to baths and saunas $20 (or $33 per couple).

Taxis There's a taxi rank on George Street between Brisbane and Paterson streets, and one on St John St outside Princes Square. Central Cabs ☎13 10 08; Taxis Combined ☎13 22 27.

Tours Coach Tram Tour Company (☎03/6336 3133) offers city sights tours ($26; 3hr; Jan–April daily 10am & 2pm; May–Dec 10am) leaving from the Gateway centre. Tigerline Coaches (☎03/6272 6611 or 1300 653 633) has a programme of big commercial coach tours: Launceston city sights (half-day; $49); Mole Creek caves and the wildlife park (full day $99); Seahorse World at Beauty Point and Hillwood Strawberry Farm (half-day; $69); and Cradle Mountain tour (full day $109), which gives

3hr 30min at the park. Tiger Wilderness Tours has the most interesting day-trips (☎03/6394 3212, ⓦ www.tigerwilderness.com.au); Tamar Valley Trekking, with a morning of four short walks (half-day; $50); Cradle Mountain including Mole Creek caves and Sheffield, and a walk around Dove Lake (full day $95); Mole Creek caves and the wildlife park, including a walk to Alum Cliffs (full day $95). Tasmanian Expeditions, 110 George St (☎03/6334 3477, ⓦ www.tasmanianexpeditions.com.au), offers cycle tours (half-day $55; full day $99), rock-climbing at Cataract Gorge (Wed, Sat and on demand; half-day $90, full day $150) and canoeing, as well as longer trekking, cycling and rafting tours to the state's wilderness areas. Island Escape Tours, 16 Brisbane St (☎03/6334 4505; ⓦ www.islandescapetours.com), offers small-group active participation tours; ex-Launceston is a four-day east-coast tour ($460); and an overnight Bay of Fires excursion ($150; see p.1102).

⑪ Around Launceston

Before launching yourself into the beauty of the Tamar Valley, there are several local destinations worth visiting **around Launceston**, most notably the well-preserved town of **Evandale**, just 20km from the city. If you're here in winter, you might consider joining the ski crowd who descend upon **Ben Lomond National Park**, southeast of Launceston; out of season, this is fine bushwalking country.

Evandale

Twenty kilometres southeast of Launceston is **EVANDALE**, a National Trust-classified town from the 1830s, where the principal attraction is the Sunday market. At the **Evandale Tourism and History Centre**, on High Street (daily 10am–3pm; ☎03/6391 8128), pick up a free *Heritage Walk* brochure. Otherwise, the map opposite the Ingleside Bakery, also on High Street, points out notable features – many of the old buildings bear descriptive plaques. **Solomon House** (1836), on the corner of High and Russell streets, operated as Clarendon Stores for about 130 years; the bakehouse at the rear once supplied the early settlers, though now it's an excellent tearoom. Another good place for refreshment is the *Dalmeny Bookcafé & Gallery* at 14 Russell St (closed Mon & Tues). The **Clarendon Arms Hotel**, on Russell Street (☎03/6391 8181; ❷), was built in 1847 on the site of the former convict station; its interior walls are covered in murals depicting the early history of Tasmania.

Further down Russell Street is the **Evandale Market** (Sun 10am–2pm), which attracts large crowds to its 140 stalls. A lot of local vegetable-growers – particularly those who grow organically – bring their produce here. You'll also find a flea market, and some food stalls that are rather exotic for Tasmania. Once a year, running over three days in late February, Evandale hosts the **National Penny Farthing Championships** as part of its Village Fair; the races using the old bikes are quite a sight. There's no public transport to Evandale.

Ben Lomond National Park

The plateau of the **Ben Lomond Range**, over 1300m high and 84 square kilometres in area, lies entirely within **Ben Lomond National Park**, 50km southeast of Launceston. A small ski village sits below **Legges Tor** (1572m), the second-highest point in Tasmania, and can be reached in an hour from Launceston; above it the bumpy outline of the range's steep cliffs dominates the horizon. The **ski season** runs from mid-July to the end of September, and although **accommodation** is limited, the region's accessibility means there's no real need to stay. If you're determined, try the *Ben Lomond Creek Inn* (℡03/6372 2444; bunk rooms ❷–❸, half-board rooms ❺–❻), which is usually booked out at weekends. Meals are available here, or there's fast food from the ski resort kiosk.

An all-day pass on the **ski lifts** costs around $35. Some ski rental is available on the mountain but there's a better range at Launceston Sports Centre, 88A George St (℡03/6331 4777). The Gateway centre (see p.1106) can advise on ski packages. During the season, Starline (℡03/6331 1411) offers a **bus service** from Launceston. If you're driving, be warned that the final 20km to the ski village is unsealed and the last leg, **Jacobs Ladder**, is very steep, with hairpin bends, sheer drops and no safety barriers. You must carry wheel chains, which can be rented from the snowline. Outside the ski season, all services cease and the businesses close down, but **bushwalkers** are lured by the magnificent scenery and the alpine vegetation. There's a 12.5-kilometre track from Carr Villa, on the slopes of Ben Lomond, to Legges Tor. Bush **camping** is permitted anywhere in the national park, but Carr Villa is an informal camping area with a pit toilet. For more information, contact the ranger (℡03/6230 8233).

The Tamar Valley

To the north of Launceston is the beautiful **Tamar Valley**, where – for 64km – the tidal waters wind through orchards, vineyards, strawberry farms, lavender plantations, forested hills and grazing land. Only the Batman Bridge, near Deviot, and the APPM Wood Mill and Bell Bay Power Station, near the river's mouth, spoil the idyllic scenery.

West of the Tamar

The West Tamar Highway (A7) follows the line of the Tamar River from Launceston to Beauty Point, passing through the absurdly tacky **Grindlewald Swiss Village**. Further along, **Brady's Lookout State Reserve** provides magnificent views of the Tamar Valley and Ben Lomond; you can see as far as Low Head, 34km away. Rather than head straight along the highway, you can detour for a stretch through **ROSEVEARS**, on a picturesque sweep of road along the riverbanks that's popular with cyclists. Along the way, stop at the **St Matthias Vineyard** (daily 10am–5pm) for some wine-tasting, Tasmanian cheeses and great views. In the village itself there's the **Waterbird Haven Trust** (daily 9am–dusk; $4), extending for half a kilometre along the waterfront, and the 1831 **Rosevears Tavern**, where you can have a drink. A few kilometres west of Rosevears is **Notley Gorge State Reserve**, a beautiful fern gorge with a number of walking tracks, reached by turning west off the highway at Legana. Back on the highway, **EXETER** has the useful **Tamar Visitor Centre** (daily 9am–5pm; ℡1800 637 989, ⓦwww.tamarvalley.com.au), an **Online Access Centre** on Main Road, and the excellent *Exeter Bakery*. Further north, **BEACONSFIELD** was once at the centre of Tasmania's former **gold-mining** area, and the mining ruins are still visible; two former mine buildings house the interesting, interactive **Grub Shaft Gold & Heritage Museum** (daily 10am–4pm; $8).

At gorgeous **BEAUTY POINT**, the fascinating **Seahorse World** ($15; tours 9.30am–3.30pm, every 30min; 45min–1hr; ⓦwww.seahorseworld.com.au) is the world's only commercial seahorse farm. By successfully harvesting the difficult-to-breed creatures for aquariums and the Chinese market, the farm is helping save those in the oceans from further depletion. The **Australian Maritime College** (AMC), established in Beauty Point in 1978, has developed the interpretative material at the farm, and there is also an interesting display about the AMC on the top floor, beside a café with stunning water views. The AMC lends Beauty Point bags of atmosphere, with a big busy training ship moored at the marina by the *Beauty Point Hotel*. From the jetty here, the **Shuttlefish Ferry** crosses the Tamar to George Town (2–4 daily; $6 one-way, $10 return; 15–20 min; 2hr, $26 cruise to George Town, Mon–Sat 11am & 2pm, Sun noon & 2.30pm; bookings ☎03/6383 4479). You can **stay** in attached motel units at the *Beauty Point Hotel* (☎03/6383 4363, ⓔbeautypointhotel@bigpond.com.au; ❸–❹), which have seen better days but have fantastic river views. The pub itself is more upmarket, with tables outside on the water and views from the dining room, which has an excellent menu featuring lots of seafood. For somewhere really special to stay, head for *Pomona* (☎03/6383 4073, ⓦwww.pomona bandb.com.au), just across the road on a rise above the river; there's B&B accommodation (❺) in a charming federation-style house with great views from the verandah-cum-breakfast nook, or luxurious timber self-catering cottages (❻ includes breakfast hamper).

East of the Tamar: George Town and Low Head

Leaving Launceston and heading north along the East Tamar Highway, it's only a few minutes before you're zooming through scenic countryside, passing through Dilston where cows graze in paddocks at the base of bush-covered hills. After Hillwood and its famous strawberry farm, you're headed for the port of **GEORGE TOWN**, the third-oldest town in Australia, where Colonel Paterson landed in 1804 to begin settlement of northern Tasmania. The **George Town Visitor Information Centre**, is on Main Road on the way into town (daily 10am–4pm; ☎03/6382 1700), George Town's **Online Access Centre** is on Macquarie Street.

Despite its history, George Town isn't particularly old or interesting, with only one colonial building to look at, **The Grove**, an elegant stone Georgian mansion at 25 Cimitiere St (daily 10am–5pm; $5.50). More appealing is **LOW HEAD**, 5km north, with 24 National Trust-listed buildings, whitewashed cottages and rambling houses, all set amid extensive parkland. The original convict-built **Pilot Station** now houses a **museum** (daily 9am–9pm; $5), which has a display of maritime memorabilia. There's also a **Little penguin colony** at Low Head; guided tours are offered each evening at sunset (1hr; $12; bookings on ☎0418 361 860). Cruises to a nearby **fur seal** colony on Tenth Island are also on offer with Seal and Sea Adventure Tours (3–4 hours; $121; bookings ☎0419 357 028, ⓦwww.sealandsea.com). You can catch a ferry to Beauty Point from George Town with the Shuttlefish Ferry (see above).

George Town **accommodation** includes *Gray's Hotel*, at 77 Macquarie St (☎03/6382 2655; ❹), the oldest pub in town but with few discernible traces of its early-nineteenth-century heritage. The *Pier Hotel*, at 5 Elizabeth St (☎03/6382 1300; rooms ❺, apartments ❻), is a pretty wooden hotel on the waterfront with rooms upstairs in the old part, modern motel rooms on the waterfront, and self-catering units; the **food** here is very good, from pasta to

Asian curries. Opposite, at 4 Elizabeth St, is the *Traveller's Lodge YHA* (⊕03/6382 3261; dorms $18–19, rooms ❷) in a pretty 1870 home, with a clean, modern interior.

In Low Head, you can stay in good-value Heritage cottage accommodation at the Pilot Station (see opposite; ⊕ & ⊕03/6382 1143; ❸–❹), and at *Belfont Cottages*, at 178 Low Head Rd (⊕03/6382 1841; ❺, with breakfast provisions supplied), or **camp** at *Low Head Caravan Park*, 136 Low Head Rd (⊕03/6382 1573; vans ❷, cabins ❸).

Around George Town: the Pipers River wine region

Heading **east** of George Town, a pleasant day can be spent exploring the **vineyards** around the **Pipers River area**, which produce distinctly flavoured, crisp and fresh cool-climate wines. The *Tamar Valley Wine Route* brochure, available from the information centres in Launceston (p.1106) and Exeter (see p.1115), covers sixteen vineyards in the Tamar Valley and Pipers Brook area (virtually all open daily 10am–5pm). One of the best known is **Pipers Brook Vineyard,** on the sealed C818, 2km off the B82. Established in 1974, the winery is housed in a modern, architect-designed complex, with tastings and self-guided tours. It also has a café (mains around $15) and vine-covered courtyard. Nearby, also on the C818, lake-fronted **Janz** makes premium sparkling wines; there are tastings, and information on the wine-making process in the interpretive centre. The friendly, small-scale **Delamere Vineyard** on the B82, specializes in Pinot Noir and Chardonnay and also has tastings. Wine tours operate from Launceston (see "Tours", p.1114).

The Midland Highway

The **Midland Highway** is a fast three-hour route between Hobart and Launceston, more or less following the old coaching road, although you'll have to detour if you want to visit some of the towns on the way. Tasmanian Redline Coaches have several daily **bus** services between Hobart and Launceston, stopping at the major midland towns.

Campbell Town and Ross

Beyond **Campbell Town** – a rather plain community originally settled by Scots but the midlands' major centre with an **Online Access Centre** on Bridge Street – you drive south through sheep-grazing countryside, eventually turning off the highway to **ROSS**, 2km east. Also settled by Scots, this has a very secluded, rural feel; elm trees line the main Church Street, creating a beautiful avenue, while paddocks with grazing cattle stretch alongside. Old stone buildings along the idyllic street are well preserved, including the characterful sandstone *Man O'Ross Hotel*. As you walk through the grounds of St Johns Church of England, just one of the town's three pretty churches, there are views of the Macquarie River, spanned by the sandstone **Ross Bridge**, designed by John Lee Archer and built by convicts in 1836; the intricate stone carvings on its three arches earned the convict stonemason a free pardon. A melancholy walk in the other direction from the church, leads down to the original Ross burial ground and past the site of the **Female Factory**, actually a prison, where women convicts were held before being sent to properties or assigned servants. You can **stay** in several of the old cottages dotted about town: *Colonial Cottages of Ross* (⊕03/6381 5354, ⊕6381 5408; ❼ including breakfast provisions) has four to pick from. The *Man O'Ross Hotel* (☎03/6381 5445, ℱ6381 5440; ❸ including breakfast) has several intimate rooms in which to **eat or drink**, and shared-bathroom accommodation upstairs. You can **camp** at a pleasant caravan park on Bridge Street (☎03/6381 5462; cabins ❶). Another good eatery is the *Bakery Tea Rooms* (daily 8.30am–5.30pm). The Tasmanian Wool Centre on Church Street (daily 9am–5pm; ☎03/6381 5466) acts as an **information centre** and also houses a wool exhibition and history museum (entry by donation) and has **Internet access**.

Oatlands

Back on the Midland Highway, it's 88km south from Ross to **OATLANDS**, which has Australia's greatest concentration of colonial **Georgian buildings**: 140 in two square kilometres, most built by convicts. Many are now occupied by antique and bric-a-brac shops, B&Bs and guesthouses. The most striking building is the **Callington Mill** and its outbuildings; the partly restored **windmill** was built in 1837 and remained in operation until 1892. From the top there are fine views of the town and the surrounding countryside; ask to go up to the adjacent **Dolls At The Mill** (daily 10am–4pm; $2), an extensive doll collection in the old mill residence. The best way to see the town is to go on one of Peter Fielding's guided **heritage walks** (☎03/6254 1135; $5), which visit several other buildings, including the Old Gaol and courthouse. His spooky evening **ghost tour** commences outside the mill (9pm during daylight savings, 8pm rest of year; $8).

For **food**, the cosy *Blossom's Georgian Tea Rooms*, 116 High St (☎03/6254 1516), serves scones and light lunches. The **Central Tasmania Tourism Centre**, 85 High St (daily 9am–5pm; ☎03/6254 1212) can book **accommodation** from the many colonial-style B&Bs in the town; a good choice is the central *Oatlands Lodge*, at 92 High St (☎03/6254 1444, ℱ6254 1492; ❺). Oatlands **Online Access Centre** is in the library at 68 High St.

The Great Western Tiers and Central Plateau

Deloraine, on the **Meander River**, is nestled in a valley of rich farmland dominated by **Quamby Bluff** (1256m) and the **Great Western Tiers**, where the Central Plateau drops abruptly to the surrounding plains. On the Bass Highway, it's roughly equidistant from Devonport (51km) and Launceston (48km). From Deloraine the **Lake Highway** begins, rising up over the Western Tiers to the Central Plateau, with its thousands of lakes. To the west of Deloraine are the extensive **cave systems** around **Mole Creek**, while **Walls of Jerusalem National Park** is accessed from **Western Creek**, 32km southwest of Deloraine.

Deloraine and around

DELORAINE is a delightful hilly town, often shrouded in mist, even on summer mornings, and divided into two parts by the bubbling **Meander River**. Although the area was settled by Europeans in the 1830s, Deloraine didn't really begin to develop until after 1846, and today it's a National Trust-classified town. **West Parade** follows the river, facing the park; at no. 17 is the

Georgian **Bonney's Inn** (1830), the town's oldest remaining building (now a B&B; see overleaf). At the next block, Westbury Place rises up steeply from West Parade; if you climb the hill you'll reach **St Marks Church** (1860), with its tall spire. At the top of the hill there's a scenic **lookout** that gives a panoramic view over the town and the Western Tiers to the south. Deloraine has a café culture, plenty of secondhand and antique shops, and a small, alternative arts-and-crafts scene, witnessed regularly at the **market** on the first Saturday of every month across the river opposite the *Apex Caravan Park*, and at the annual **Tasmanian Craft Fair**, a huge event held over four days in early November (contact the information centre for details – see below).

Close to prime **bushwalking** areas in the Western Tiers, Deloraine is an established base for walkers. Popular tracks are the short walk to **Alum Cliffs**, overlooking the Mersey River Gorge (40min return), signposted on the road between Mole Creek and Chudleigh; a difficult walk to **Quamby Bluff**, renowned for its myrtle rainforest (6.5km; 6hr; beginning at Brodies Road, off the Lake Highway); the track to **Liffey Falls** (8km; 3hr; beginning at the picnic ground 5km west of the tiny community of Liffey), and the day-walk to **Meander Falls** through the Meander Forest Reserve, about 25km south of Deloraine, reached via the small settlement of Meander and Meander Falls Road (10km; 6–7hr; beginning from the picnic ground). There's a walker registration and information booth at the Meander Falls car park. A free leaflet issued by Forestry Tasmania, *Visiting the Great Western Tiers*, has a map of the Meander Forest Reserve and tracks; you can pick it up from the Deloraine information centre (see below). Tiger Wilderness Tours includes a walk to Alum Cliffs in one of their tours from Launceston (see "Listings", p.1114).

The western end of the Great Western Tiers overlooks **MOLE CREEK**, 24km southwest of Deloraine. Here, you can get up close to some Tasmanian devils at **Trowunna Wildlife Park** (daily 9am–5pm; $12.50), or buy delicious local honey from **Stephen's Leatherwood Honey Factory** (Mon–Fri 8am–5pm). Surrounding the town, the **Mole Creek Karst National Park** has a network of over two hundred underground caves. About 20km west of Mole Creek, are two rather spectacular ones: **Marakoopa Cave**, with huge caverns, streams, pools and glow-worms (daily 10am, 11.15am, 1pm, 2.30pm & 4pm; 50–80min; $11); and the smaller but more richly decorative **King Solomons Cave**, with stalactites and stalagmites (daily 10.30am, 11.30am, 12.30pm, 2pm, 3pm & 4pm; 40–60min; $11). Wild Cave Tours (℡03/6367 8142, ⊛www.wildcavetours.com), offers excellent $75 half-day and $150 full-day caving tours of the Mole Creek caves, underground streams and subterranean systems. Places to **stay** in **Mole Creek** range from an excellent campsite (℡03/6363 1150) to the congenial *Mole Creek Guest House* (℡03/6363 1399; B&B ❹–❺), with its own restaurant and tourist information.

Deloraine practicalities

The two major **bus** companies both make regular stops in Deloraine. Tasmanian Redline Coaches on its Launceston–Devonport service (2 daily), and its Launceston–Deloraine service (4 daily Mon–Fri, 2 daily Sat & Sun) which continues on to Mole Creek once daily on weekdays; and TassieLink on its Launceston–Queenstown service (1 daily Tues, Thurs & Sat, plus Dec–April 1 daily Mon). The depot for Redline is the video shop by the roundabout at 29 West Church St (℡03/6362 2046); TassieLink is based at *Sullivans Restaurant*, at 17 West Parade. The **Great Western Tiers Visitor Information Centre**, at 98 Emu Bay Rd (daily 9am–5pm; ℡03/6362 3471), has maps, details on walking times and conditions, and makes free accommodation bookings; the centre is housed in an old inn with an attached folk museum ($7), which features a series of vast woven silk wall hangings, made by the local community. The **Online Access Centre** is behind the library at 21 West Parade.

Operators leading **outdoor activities** in the area include Cradle Wilderness on the Edge 4x4 Tours (℡03/6363 1173; half- and full-day tours; $75/$120); Jahadi Indigenous Experiences (℡03/6363 6172, ⓦwww.jahadi.com.au; 4WD tours), and the Tasmanian Fly Fishing School (℡03/6362 3441, ⓦwww .tasmanianflyfishing.com.au).

For budget **accommodation**, it's about a ten-minute walk from the information centre to the well-run, clean *Highview Lodge YHA Hostel*, at 8 Blake St (℡03/6362 2996; dorms $18, rooms ❷; bike rental available), set on a hill commanding unparalleled views of Quamby Bluff. There are cheap pub rooms and good value singles ($20) at the *Bush Inn*, 7 Bass Highway (℡03/6362 2365; ❷), plus economical counter meals. In the centre of town, the big old *Deloraine Hotel* faces the river on the corner of Emu Bay Road, and has shared-bathroom and en-suite rooms upstairs (℡03/6362 2022; ❸). Virtually next door, old-fashioned *Bonney's Inn*, 17 West Parade (℡ & ℻03/6362 2974, ⓦwww.bonneys-inn.com; B&B ❹–❺), has spacious suites suitable for families. A good motel on the outskirts of town is *Mountain View Country Inn*, 144 Emu Bay Rd (℡03/6362 2633, ℻6362 3233; ❹) – though it's on the main road, the row of units afford great Tiers' views. You can **camp** at the riverside *Apex Caravan Park*, 51 West Parade (℡03/6362 2345). *Bonney's Farm*, off Weetah Road, 4km northwest of Deloraine (℡03/6362 2122, ℻6362 3566; ❹), has a guesthouse (B&B) and self-contained two- or three-bed units. For something very special, however, head for the exquisite French-run guesthouse *Calstock*, on the Lake Highway just outside Deloraine (℡03/6362 2642, ⓦwww.calstock.net; B&B ❼), where French country-style meals are created from local organic ingredients.

In Deloraine there are plenty of informal **places to eat** on the main street, Emu Bay Road. The best is the *Deloraine Deli* at no. 36 (Mon–Fri 9am–5pm, Sat 9am–2.30pm), a combination deli counter and tearoom. The *Emu Bay Brasserie* at no. 21 (Mon–Sat 9.30am–2.30pm & dinner from 6pm; licensed; ℡03/6362 2067) has a casual café atmosphere but serves upmarket meals. The best pub meals are at the *Deloraine Hotel*.

Walls of Jerusalem National Park

The **Walls of Jerusalem National Park** is on the western side of the Central Plateau, a series of five mountain peaks that enclose a central basin, an isolated area noted for its lakes, pencil pines and the biblical names of its various features. The best time to visit is November through to April; people have died of exposure here, so make sure you're well prepared. You'll need the *Walls of Jerusalem National Park Map and Notes* ($9.10), which has walking notes on the reverse.

The Walls of Jerusalem is the only national park that you can't drive into, so the walk in begins outside the park boundaries. From King Solomons Cave (see p.1119), head south, following the Mersey River and the unsealed road east of Lake Rowallan; the car park is at Fowells Bluff. You walk through wilderness into the park, which is isolated and lacking even basic facilities, without a ranger (although rangers do patrol). However, the track is well kept, with boardwalks laid down over boggy areas, and there's plenty of clean water to drink from the streams and lakes. The few small leaky huts are really for emergencies only – bring your own tent. If you just want to walk into the park to the central basin (through **Herods Gate**, with views of Barn Bluff and Cradle Mountain to the northwest), set up camp and then walk back, it's a fourteen-kilometre return hike, which takes seven or eight hours altogether, going at a steady pace over two days. The walk begins with a steep climb then levels out on the plateau. There are numerous routes to the various peaks and lakes – from **Damascus Gate** you get stunning views of Cradle Mountain–Lake St Clair National Park immediately west – and an experienced, well-equipped walker could spend a couple of days here. If you can afford the prices, you can always go on an **organized walk**: Tasmanian Expeditions (☎03/6334 3477) has a three-day, two-night trip for $540, departing from Launceston (Oct–April). TassieLink can bring you to the beginning of the walk into the park on their summer-only service from Launceston to Lake St Clair via Deloraine, Mole Creek and Marakoopa Cave (Nov–April 3 weekly), while Maxwell's (☎03/6492 1431) operates on demand from Devonport ($180 1–4 people; $45 per person 5 or more people) and Launceston ($240/$60).

The Central Plateau

At its northern and eastern edges, the **Central Plateau** is rimmed by the long crest of the Great Western Tiers (1440m). At over a thousand metres above sea level, the plateau is often covered in frost and subject to sleet and snowstorms in winter. The **Great Lake** lies on the plateau about 8km from the escarpment, and only 40km from Deloraine, along the Lake Highway that continues to **BOTHWELL**, the plateau's only town, ending at Melton Mowbray, where it joins the Midland Highway. The major lakes can be reached from roads leading off the Lake Highway. To the west, between Cradle Mountain–Lake St Clair National Park and below the Walls of Jerusalem National Park, is the inaccessible "Land of Three Thousand Lakes".

The Central Plateau has few inhabitants – the permanent population is only around eight hundred – but it's full of **fishing shacks**, and on a fine weekend the population sometimes swells to 25,000. It's also the base for the **Hydro Electricity Commission** (HEC): the countless high-altitude lakes are used as water storage for the generation of electricity. Temporary HEC villages are set up for hydroelectrical workers, and once abandoned they're often transformed into lodge-style accommodation. One is the *Bronte Park Highland Village* (☎03/6289 1126, ⓦwww.bronteparkhighlandvillage.com.au; dorms $20, cabins ❹, lodge ❹, spa cottages ❻), which also has a campsite, EFTPOS facilities, a dining room and bar, a store selling groceries and fuel, and is ideally situated for **Lake St Clair** (25km) and **Lake Big Jim**, popular trout-fishing spots. Ausprey Tours (☎03/6330 2612, ⓦwww.gotroutfishtasmania.com.au) offers **fly-fishing tuition** (1–5 days), trout-fishing day-tours from Launceston or extended camping treks to fish in the Western Lakes.

To reach the *Bronte Park Highland Village*, take the bone-shattering Marlborough Highway (B11), which runs southwest off the Lake Highway as it curves around the bottom of the lake to Miena. TassieLink drops off at the *Bronte Park* turn-off on the Lyell Highway on their Hobart–Queenstown scheduled service (1 daily Tues, Thurs, Fri, Sat & Sun). Call in advance to be met for *Bronte Park*.

The Bass Strait Islands

Located in the rough waters of the Bass Strait, battered by the Roaring Forties, are two groups of islands: the Hunter group, dominated by **King Island** off the northwest tip of Tasmania, and the Furneaux group, the largest of which is **Flinders Island**, lying just beyond the northeast corner of the state. In the nineteenth century, sealers roamed the Bass Strait, but the two main islands now consist of low-key rural communities, while several tall lighthouses, and many shipwrecks offshore are testimony to the turbulence of the sea at King Island. Details of **flights** to King and Flinders Island are given on p.1156, or you can go by **ship** to Flinders Island from Bridport (see p.1104) on the northeast coast of Tasmania: Southern Shipping Co (ex-Bridport Mon, ex-Flinders Tues; departure times depend on tides; ☎03/6356 1753) operates a car and passenger ferry. Car costs are prohibitive, but the return passenger fare of $79 is good value, if you can put up with a possibly rough, eight-hour trip.

King Island

KING ISLAND, smaller but more heavily populated than Flinders Island, is chiefly known for its rich dairy produce, with crayfish and kelp as secondary industries; green, low and windswept, it can't offer anything like Flinders Island's dramatic landscape, nor its history, though it did witness around sixty **shipwrecks** between 1801 and 1995, and there are several working light-houses – **Cape Wickham Lighthouse** in the north is one of the tallest in the southern hemisphere. Many of the wreck sites can be dived with King Island Dive Charters (☎03/6461 1133, ⓦwww.kingislanddivecharter.com.au).

The island's main town is **CURRIE**, which has a simple museum (daily 2–4pm, closed July & Aug; entry by donation). The bleak former tungsten mining village of **GRASSY** is on the eastern side of the island. The best thing about King Island is the food, with free-range lamb and pork and local beef and wallaby, as well as seafood and delicious creamy milk, which you can drink unpasteurized while on the island – a rare treat. Indeed, top of the list of things to do on the island is a visit to the **King Island Dairy** (Mon–Fri 8am–5pm, Sun 12.30–4pm; free), 8km north of Currie, for free tastings of the rich local dairy produce; the brie and the thick cream in particular have legendary gourmet status around Australia. The island's **kelp factory** is near Currie's golf course; the bull kelp is gathered from the surrounding shores and left to dry outside the factory on racks – you'll see it as you pass by. After drying, the kelp is milled into granules and shipped to Scotland to be processed into alginates, used as a gelling agent in products like toothpaste and ice cream.

Practicalities

King Island Coach Tours, 95 Main St, Currie (☎1800 647 702), does pre-booked **airport transfers** to Currie, which is less than 10km away ($20 for 1–4 passengers), and Grassy. They also run various coach, bushwalking and wildlife **tours**; the best is the short evening tour to see the **Little penguin** community at Grassy (Tues & Thurs; $35). Otherwise, to **get around**, Cheapa Island Car Rentals (☎03/6462 1603, ⓔkimotors@kingisland.net.au; $68 per day) and Howells Auto Rent (☎03/6462 1282, ⓔkicars@bigpond.com; $70 per day) both do airport drop-offs, or you can rent a **mountain bike** from The Trend, 26 Edward St, Currie ($16.50 per day). The Trend also provides **tourist information** (daily 8.30am–6.30pm; ☎03/6462 1360) or you can contact **King Island Tourism Inc** (☎1800 645 014, ⓦwww.kingisland.org.au).

The most obvious **places to stay** are around Currie. *King Island Gem Accommodation* (☎03/6462 1260 or 1800 647 702, ⓦwww.kingislandgem .com.au) incorporates several styles and standards on North Road, 1.5km from town: *King Island Gem Motel* (❹), *A-Frame Holiday Homes* (❺), *King Island Cosy*

Cabins (④) or **camping** at *Bass Caravan Park* (vans ②, cabins ④). Right in the centre, *Parers Hotel* (☎03/6462 1633, ⓔparers@kingisland.net.au; ④), has en-suite, motel-style rooms and serves excellent meals in its bistro. Near the golf course, there's the immaculate *Wave Watcher Holiday Units*, 18 Beach Rd (☎ & ⓕ03/6462 1517; ⑨). Nearby, the rooms at *Boomerang By the Sea* (☎03/6462 1288; ⓦwww.bythesea.com.au; ⑤) have stunning sea views – even better from the motel's glass-walled **restaurant**. Back in town, *King Island Bakery* makes delicious pies, *Nautilus Coffee Lounge* is Currie's best café and there's a super-market (open daily), a bottle shop, a Westpac bank with an ATM, and an **Online Access Centre** at 5 George St.

Flinders Island

With a population of just under one thousand, **FLINDERS ISLAND** is nonetheless the largest of 52 named islands which make up the Furneaux group, first mapped by Tobias Furneaux in 1770. The islands became a base for seal hunters, who slaughtered seals in their tens of thousands and, so legend goes, lured many ships to their demise for a spot of piracy. These rough men provided a vital link in the continuing survival of the Tasmanian Aboriginal people, ironically by stealing women to work for them on the islands. When sealing ended, the communities survived by **muttonbird harvesting**, a seasonal industry that continues today (with land rights claims in 1995 giving title to several outlying islands).

Flinders Island itself played a large part in the attempted genocide of the Tasmanian Aboriginal people; between 1831 and 1834 the remnants of the Tasmanian tribes were persuaded or forced to accept relocation here. Settled at windswept **Wybalenna** on the west coast of the island, the Aborigines were without adequate food and shelter, and were forcibly Christianized, as their culture was expunged and their numbers dwindled. All that remains of the period of enforced Aboriginal settlement is the **chapel**, built in 1838 at Wybalenna, and the cemetery where only the white graves bear headstones. Of the 135 tribespeople who were sent here, only 47 were still alive when the settlement was abandoned in 1847 and moved to Oyster Cove, near Hobart. The chapel has been restored by the National Trust, but the Aboriginal people of Flinders Island succeeded with their land rights claim on Wybalenna, which was handed over in early 1999, and it is now up to them to decide how they'll run It. Due to political in-fighting, it's presently abandoned but can be visited. There's a walk to Settlement Point, where a viewing platform looks over an extensive **muttonbird** rookery, where you can experience the extraordinary sight and sound of hundreds of thousands of birds flying to the nesting islands each evening at dusk during the breeding season (Oct–March); otherwise, you can go on a dusk boat tour with Flinders Island Adventures (2hr 30min–3hr; $30 per person; ☎03/6359 4507, ⓔjamesluddington@bigpond.com). They also offer several other half- or full-day trips, including cruises to the outer islands, fishing and diving trips and 4WD tours.

For more history, it's just a few kilometres northwest to the **Emita Museum** (Sat & Sun: summer 1–5pm; rest of year 1–4pm; $2), where there's a display of shell necklaces made by the Aboriginal people of nearby Cape Barren, plus exhibits relating to sealing and shipwrecks. In the grounds there's a replica of a **muttonbirding shed**, with magazines covering the walls and a dirt floor lined with tussock grass; most professional muttonbirders are Aboriginal.

History aside, isolated Flinders Island is very much a mecca for **bushwalkers**. Only about half of the island is cultivated, and you can walk its entire length in about six days on the partially signposted north–south **Flinders Trail**, a route designed to provide a sampling of the various terrains. The best-known walk, however, is to the distinctive summit of **Mount Strzelecki**, in the **Strzelecki National Park** in the south. The climb to the top starts about 10km south of Whitemark, signposted on Trousers Point Road – look out for a brown national park sign. Though navigation is easy, it's a strenuous walk – about 5km return (3–5hr). The wind can be fierce at the summit, and mists roll in, so take something wind- and waterproof. **Trousers Point** itself, also near the park, is a good introduction to the delights of the island's deserted beaches. The site, with its fine, white sand and rust-coloured rock formations, is particularly spectacular, with Mount Strzelecki rising up behind the granite headland; there's a free camping area here, with water available. The **Flinders Island Ecology Trail** is a circuit designed to be followed in a car, with five stopping-points where interpretive material is provided. **Walkers Lookout**, in the Darling Range, is a good starting point, offering the best panorama of Flinders and the surrounding islands, with signs pointing out all the landmarks; the other four points on the route highlight bird habitats. You can see the endemic protected **Cape Barren goose** everywhere and likewise the island's wombats.

Practicalities

There are two main bases on Flinders Island: **WHITEMARK**, the administrative centre on the west coast, and **LADY BARRON** in the south, the main fishing area and deep-water port; both places have shops, fuel and accommodation. The post office in Whitemark houses the island's only **bank** – Westpac (Mon–Thurs noon–3pm, Fri noon–3pm & 4–5pm) – with EFTPOS, but no ATM facilities. As there's no public transport, the best option is to **rent a car** and arrange to pick it up at the airport on arrival. Prices are quite reasonable: from around $60–70 per day with Flinders Island Car Rentals (T03/6359 2168, F6359 2293), Flinders Island Transport Services (T03/6359 2060) or Bowman Lees Car Hire (T03/6359 2388).

For **information** on **activities** such as cruises, scuba diving, fishing, bird-watching and scenic flights, or just for general enquiries, head for the Area Marketing and Development Office, as you come into Whitemark on Lagoon Rd (Mon–Fri 8.15am–5pm; T1800 994 477, Wwww.flindersislandonline.com.au); *Flinders Island Naturally*, a free visitors' guide with map, can be picked up here and at Tasmanian travel centres before you arrive on the island. Flinders Island's **Online Access Centre** is just opposite. The General Store in Whitemark also publishes a free leaflet full of useful contacts.

There's a **campsite** with water and showers (T03/6359 8560) at Killiecrankie Bay in the northwest of the island – where you can also fossick for topaz – or you can camp for free at the coastal reserves, or on any crown land as long as it's 500m from the road: designated sites are at Allports Beach, Lillies Beach, North East River and Trousers Point, and all have toilets and fireplaces, though only the last has water and a gas barbecue. In Whitemark you can **stay** at the *Interstate Hotel* in the centre of town (T03/6359 2114, F6359 2250; B&B ❸–❹), which has some en-suite rooms and serves meals (except Sun); it also offers showers and laundry facilities to nonresidents. *Sweet Surprises Coffee Shop* is a decent place for a daytime snack (closed Sun); or try the *Flinders Island Sports Club* at the end of the Esplanade for a reasonable meal in pleasant surroundings. Lady Barron is a far nicer place to stay than Whitemark, however. The *Furneaux Tavern* overlooking the picturesque Furneaux Sound, has spacious and attractive motel units (T03/6359 3521,

@6359 3618; ❹), **meals** are served here in the *Shearwater Restaurant*. You could also try the self-catering accommodation at *Yaringa Holiday Cottages* (☎03/6359 4522; ❹), or the excellent cabins with beautiful views at *Partridge Farm*, a ten-minute drive from Lady Barron at the end of the road to Badger Corner (☎03/6359 3554; ❺).

The West

Except for the rich beef, dairy and vegetable-growing land along the north-west coast, the western half of Tasmania is an untamed area. The wild **west coast**, densely forested and battered by the rough Southern Ocean and the Roaring Forties, its shores strewn with huge dead trees washed down from the southwest's many rivers, would probably still be uninhabited if it weren't for the **logging** and **mining** industries. This part of the island is very densely populated (by Tasmanian standards), and the **Bass Highway**, which skirts the northwest coast, passes through two unattractive industrial cities, **Devonport** and **Burnie. Rocky Cape National Park** and the town of **Stanley** (originally built by the Van Diemen's Land Company – VDL – which still owns the northwest corner of the state) are the most interesting places for visitors.

Just south of Stanley the highway turns inland to **Smithton**, marking the beginning of a thickly forested region and a logging heartland. The Bass Highway ends at the tiny settlement of **Marrawah**, on the west coast (popular with surfers), where it meets the **Western Explorer** road, which runs south to sleepy **Arthur River** and then through the Arthur Pieman Protected area to **Corinna**, where the road heads east via Savage River and Waratah onto the A10 (Murchison Highway). Alternatively, you can continue southwards, taking a barge across the Pieman River and then heading on to Zeehan (on the C249) and **Strahan** (on the B27), on the vast **Macquarie Harbour**. To reach Strahan on sealed roads, you have to go back to Marrawah and then to Somerset on the northwest coast, from where the Murchison Highway heads south through a copper- and lead-mining backwater. On the way you pass **Queenstown**, which has been subject to an ecological disaster; its surrounding rainforest has been destroyed, and in its place are bare and chalky hills.

Strahan sits on the edge of the **southwest wilderness**, an area of rugged coastlines, wild rivers, open plains, thick rainforest and spectacular peaks – the wettest part of Australia after the tropical lowlands of north Queensland. It's mostly inaccessible, except to very experienced and well-prepared bushwalkers, but **cruises** leave from Strahan to go up the **Gordon River**, offering a glimpse of its magnificent scenery. Some years ago, a plan to dam the Gordon River below the point where it joins the **Franklin River** put Strahan at the centre of a struggle between environmentalists and the state government. Eventually the federal government stepped in, and – following a landmark High Court ruling in 1983, the whole of the southwest – including the **South West National Park**, the **Franklin Lower Gordon Wild Rivers National Park** and the adjoining heavily glaciated **Cradle Mountain–Lake St Clair National Park** – became a vast, protected **World Heritage Area**, occupying twenty percent of the the the state's land area. From Queenstown, en route to Hobart, the **Lyell Highway** provides limited access to the mainly inaccessible Franklin Lower Gordon park, and to Lake St Clair at **Derwent Bridge**.

The northwest coast

A succession of Tasmania's larger towns dot the conservative, agricultural **northwest coast**, including the cities of **Devonport** and **Burnie**, and the smaller community of older **Stanley**, on a peninsula jutting into the Bass Strait. The **Bass Highway**, which connects them, becomes spectacularly beautiful beyond Wynyard, passing Table Cape, Boat Harbour Beach and Rocky Cape National Park, though it skirts the very northwest tip (privately owned by the Van Diemen's Land Company). At the end of the highway is **Marrawah**, from where you can head to Arthur River for a cruise. Tasmanian Redline Coaches runs daily services from Devonport to Burnie, and from Burnie to Smithton, stopping at all towns along the Bass Highway; there is no public transport to Marrawah or Arthur River.

Devonport and around

The industrial port of **DEVONPORT**, which in 1959 replaced Launceston as the terminal of the **Bass Strait ferry**, the *Spirit of Tasmania*, is not the most inspiring first point of contact with Tasmania. As the ship makes its slow progress up the Mersey River, you might almost think you're arriving at a 1950s English seaport, but for the tin-roofed weatherboard bungalows, the brittle quality of the light, the bush-covered hills to the east and a *McDonald's* on the waterfront. As a jumping-off point for Cradle Mountain, the Overland Track and the rugged west coast, Devonport has developed a significant tourism infrastructure – car-rental companies, bus companies, camping stores and backpacking information – and though it's hardly a destination in itself, it makes a good **base** for trips into the surrounding countryside.

Arrival and information

Up to 1400 people arrive in Devonport at 7am each morning on the **Bass Strait ferry** (see p.1156), and more in the evening when day-sailings are in operation; the ferry docks at the terminal in East Devonport, just across the Mersey River from the city centre. As the boat has its own tourist information and booking centre, you might have made all your arrangements on board. If not, there are company representatives in the terminal, and you can buy bus passes and tickets here. Most passengers head immediately for the waiting Tasmanian Redline Coaches **express buses** to Launceston ($16.40) and Hobart ($39.80) or the Tassielink Spirit Shuttle to Launceston ($16.50) and Hobart ($40.50). Other bus routes leave from the depots in town (see p.1129). If you decide to stay, you can get to the city centre by walking north for a short distance to the bottom of Murray Street, where the ferry *Torquay* crosses the river (on demand Mon–Sat 7.45am–6pm; $2, bikes $0.50).

Devonport Airport is 10km east of the city; taxis into Devonport cost about $18 and it's a good idea to prebook (Taxis Combined ☎03/6424 1431). In town, staff at the **Tasmanian Travel and Information Centre**, 92 Formby Rd (daily 7.30am–5pm and until 9pm when day-sailings arrive; ☎03/6424 4466), book accommodation, tours and travel, and sell all types of bus passes. For maps, bushwalking tips and local knowledge of the area visit the

ACCOMMODATION

Abel Tasman Caravan Park	2
Alexander Hotel	5
Gateway Motor Inn	4
MacFie Manor	7
Macwright House YHA	8
Molly Malone's	3
River View Lodge	1
Tasman House Backpackers	6

RESTAURANTS

Banjo's	C
Chinese Garden	E
Mason and Mason	F
Mauritz	B
The Old Rectory	G
Spurs Canteena	D
Taco Villa	A

excellent **Backpackers Barn**, 10–12 Edward St (Mon–Sat 9am–6pm; ☎03/6424 3628), which specializes in planning itineraries, booking tours (including some good-value, small group tours to Cradle Mountain) and renting and selling equipment for bushwalkers and backpackers; it also offers travellers a day-room, showers ($2) and huge lockers ($1 per day, $5 per week) and there's a vegetarian café. Allgoods, at 10 Rooke St (☎03/6424 7099; closed Sun), sells and rents out gear, too. The Tasmanian Redline Coaches depot is opposite Backpackers Barn; TassieLink leaves from the tourist information centre, which sells tickets for both. Devonport's **Online Access Centre** is at the library at 21 Oldaker St.

Accommodation

Devonport has plenty of **accommodation**, mainly intended for ferry passengers. Hotels, motels and B&Bs take advantage of the summer trade to raise their prices.

Abel Tasman Caravan Park 6 Wright St, East Devonport ☎03/6427 8794. Campsites on East Devonport Beach, just a short walk from the ferry terminal. Vans ❷, cabins ❸

Alexander Hotel 78 Formby Rd ☎03/6424 2252, ℗6424 1046. Neat, well-furnished, shared-bath rooms, all with sinks and some with views of the port. TV room, plus tea and coffee room; light breakfast served in the dining room. ❷

Gateway Motor Inn 16 Fenton St ☎03/6424 4922, ℗6424 7720. Devonport's best hotel, a quiet, centrally located, three-storey place offering views over the port and river mouth. Rooms are spacious and tastefully decorated. Bar, restaurant and room service. ❺

MacFie Manor 44 MacFie St ☎03/6424 1719. A rambling, two-storey, turn-of-the-twentieth-century B&B that has distant views of the water from its wrought-iron balcony. ❹

Macwright House YHA 115 Middle Rd ☎03/6424 5696. A large, barracks-like hostel with loads of rules and regulations. More than half an hour's walk from the city centre and not close to any shops, but the local Mersey Bus will get you

from the city on weekdays. On the plus side, there's access to a heated pool next door and a big garden. Dorms $13, rooms ❶

Molly Malone's 34 Best St ☎03/6424 1898, ℮mollymalones@vantagegroup.com.au. Convenient backpackers' accommodation, with dorms and comfortable rooms – some en suite – well away from the noise of the Irish theme-pub downstairs, which has live bands (Thurs–Sat). Good facilities and security. Dorms $15, rooms ❷

River View Lodge 18 Victoria Parade ☎03/6424 7357. A waterfront guesthouse with a convivial atmosphere. Serves generous cooked breakfasts. All rooms share bathroom. ❸–❹

Tasman House Backpackers 169 Steele St ☎03/6423 2335, ⓦwww.tasmanhouse.com. Recommended, secure hostel in a large, former nurses' residence. Mostly well-furnished twins, a couple of en-suite doubles and some dorms. Affordable tours available to places such as Cradle Mountain. Fifteen minutes' walk from the city centre, but free pick-ups on request. Dorms $15, rooms ❷

The City

Central Devonport is bounded by the Mersey to the east; Formby Road runs alongside it, while Stewart Street, at right angles, is dominated by a view of the bulky *Spirit of Tasmania*, when it's in port, and sometimes other colourful freighters. The **Devonport Art Gallery** at 45 Stewart St (Mon–Sat 10am–5pm, Sun 2–5pm; free), is a converted church with changing exhibitions and a small permanent collection of Tasmanian ceramics. The city centre is a **shopping** focus for departing tourists in need of last-minute souvenirs, with big-name chain stores on **Rooke Street Mall** and tasteful gift shops on Stewart Street.

The **Tasmanian Maritime and Folk Museum**, north of the city centre at 47 Victoria Parade, near the river's mouth (Tues–Sun 10–4pm; $3), has an extensive display of model ships ranging from sailing vessels to modern passenger ferries. The **Imaginarium Science Centre**, 19–23 MacFie St, near the *YHA*, is Tasmania's hands-on science discovery centre (Mon–Thurs 10am–4pm, Sat & Sun noon–5pm; $7.50). The only really compelling place to visit, though, is the **Tiagarra Tasmanian Aboriginal Culture and Art Centre** (daily 9am–5pm; $3.30), located at the dramatic **Mersey Bluff**, 1.5km northwest of the Maritime and Folk Museum, near the end of Bluff Road. The centre has preserved around 270 Aboriginal rock engravings (11 of which are on show), and a **Display Centre** provides generalized (and rather rushed) taped background information on how the Tasmanian Aborigines lived.

The **Don River Railway** runs excursions from Don Recreation Ground, west of town, along the Don River to the popular surfing spot of **Coles Beach** (hourly 10am–4pm; 30min; $8 return). On Sunday, public holidays and from Christmas to the end of January the carriages are pulled by steam locomotives; otherwise, diesel power is used.

Eating, drinking and nightlife

Alexander Hotel 78 Formby Rd ☎03/6424 2252. Refurbished riverfront pub, popular with the young crowd. A good jukebox in the lounge bar, from where you can gaze out at the ships; excellent bistro menu.
Banjo's Rooke Street Mall. One of a Tasmanian chain of early-opening, eat-in bakeries offering inexpensive fresh-baked goods and unlimited tea and coffee. Daily 6am–6pm.
Chinese Garden 33 King St ☎03/6424 4148. Popular Cantonese restaurant. Licensed.
Mason and Mason Interiors & Fine Coffee 38 Steele St. Upmarket interiors shop with an attached café serving soup, Italian sandwiches and gourmet pies. Mon–Sat 9am–5pm.
Mauritz 105 Rooke Street Mall. Big, popular mall café opposite the bookshop; serves good coffee.

Molly Malone's Irish Pub 34 Best St. Characterful and extensive Irish theme-pub with a great bistro. Lots of meaty pub favourites – including a roast of the day for $12 – and fish as well as some Italian, Thai and vegetarian choices.
The Old Rectory 71 Wright St, East Devonport ☎03/6427 8037. Located in a Heritage church building with an old English garden, on the ferry side of town. Daytime alfresco menu; evening menus specialize in game and local seafood. Licensed. Lunch Thurs–Sun, dinner Wed–Sun.
Spurs Canteena 18 King St. Lively bar, bistro and nightclub with a Wild West decor. Wed–Sun 4pm–late.
Taco Villa Kempling St ☎03/6424 6762. Good Mexican food. BYO. Dinner Tues–Sun.

Listings

Bookshop Angus & Robertson Bookworld, 43 Rooke St Mall ☎03/6424 2022.
Buses Tasmanian Redline Coaches and TassieLink both have ticket desks at the ferry terminal. Redline's depot is at at 9 Edward St (☎1300 360 000; left luggage $1 per item); TassieLink (☎1300 300 520) services leave from the tourist office at 92 Formby Rd. Backpackers Barn (see p.1127) is the collecting point for Maxwell's Coaches on-demand service to Cradle Mountain, Frenchmans Cap and Walls of Jerusalem (☎03/6492 8093).
Car rental Firms located at the airport and ferry terminal, with cars from about $70 per day, include Autorent-Hertz ☎03/6424 1013,

ⓦwww.autorent.com.au, Avis Tasmania ☎03/6427 9797 and Budget ☎03/6427 0650; among cheaper alternatives are Lo-Cost Auto Rent, 23 King St ☎03/6424 9922, ⓦwww.locostautorent.com (from $59 per day, 4WDs from $110 per day), and the popular Rent-A-Bug, Murray St, near the ferry terminal, East Devonport ☎03/6427 9304, ⓦwww.rentabug.com.au (VW Beetles from $35 per day).
Cinema C-Max Cinemas, 5–7 Best St (☎03/6240 2111), is a four-screen cinema complex.
Post office Cnr Stewart St and Formby Rd, TAS 7310.
Taxi Taxis Combined ☎03/6424 1431.

Around Devonport

East of Devonport are some particularly rewarding spots on the **Rubicon River estuary**, where you'll find the seaside resort of **PORT SORELL**, roughly 19km from Devonport and across the river from the Narawntapu National Park (see p.1130).You can **stay** here in a self-catering three-bedroom house at *Heron on Earth Organic Farm* (☎03/6428 6144, ⓦwww.heronon earth.com; ❹), which lends out canoes for you to paddle across to the national park, and also bikes. More luxurious accommodation is provided 4km north-east at **HAWLEY BEACH**, at the well-regarded *Hawley House* (☎03/6428 6221; B&B ❻), which has a fine restaurant and a rooftop bathtub for soaking under the stars. From Hawley Beach there's a ten-kilometre return walk to Point Sorell.

To reach the western edge of the **Narawntapu National Park** (formerly Asbestos Range National Park, on the east side of the Rubicon River estuary, it's a meandering, forty-kilometre drive from Devonport. The remote park is worth the trip – particularly at dusk – for the chance to spot some wildlife. Introduced **Forrester kangaroos** come down to feed at **Bakers Beach** at that time, and it's the best place in Tasmania to see **wombats**. The park is renowned for its occasional spectacular storms, accompanied by strong winds roaring along the beach. There's a self-registering **campsite** here, for which you pay a small fee (ranger ☎03/6428 6277), and the beach is good for swimming, and for oyster-hunting from the rocks at low tide. You'll need your own transport to get out here.

SHEFFIELD, 30km **south of Devonport**, is a popular stop en route to Cradle Mountain; the cute, old-fashioned town, set amongst farmland made fertile by red volcanic soils, is situated near the base of **Mount Roland** (1231m) which provides a scenic backdrop. The town's rural economy was ailing when the community decided to reinvent itself through the medium of visual art; since the mid-1980s over thirty **murals** in various styles have been painted by several local artists, showing the history and folklore of the town. In late-March, 2003, the town hosted the inaugural **Murals Fest** to coincide with the Ten Days on the Island Festival; the results are displayed for a year in Mural Park, in Pioneer Crescent just adjacent to the very efficient council-run, **Sheffield Visitor Information Centre** (daily 9am–5pm; ☎03/6491 1036), near the post office. The centre hands out a free pamphlet detailing the history of the murals project and a self-guided walking tour, which should take about an hour; they also book **accomodation** for free and offer **Internet access** ($2 per 10min, $5 per 30min); the **Online Access Centre** itself is in the high school on Henry Street. A good **place to stay** is *Sheffield Backpackers*, 82 Main St (☎03/6491 2611, ⓦwww.sheffieldbackpackers.com.au; dorms $19, linen extra), in one of four dorms in a modern home-style hostel, with fresh veggies and eggs available from the owner, a former adventure guide who can impart lots of knowledge (and has maps) of nearby Mount Roland, Cradle Mountain and Walls of Jerusalem. The best **eating** option is the *High Country Bakehouse* on Main Street, which serves coffee and bakery goods – including great scallop pies (Mon–Sat from 6am, Sun from 8am).

Sixteen kilometres southwest of Sheffield at **GOWRIE PARK** at the base of **Mount Roland**, you can **stay** at *Weindorfers Budget Backpacker Rooms* (☎03/6491 1385, ⓦwww.weindorfers.com; dorms $10), which has bunk-style quarters, sleeping eight, plus one double room (❷), as well as some en-suite cabins (❸), and is a good base for walks up and around the summit (2hr return) with great views of Cradle Mountain. The attached **café-restaurant**, *Weindorfers Great Food & Real Coffee* (daily 10am–9/10pm; closed Sept), is recommended for its delicious meals cooked with fresh Tasmanian produce.

You can get to Sheffield and Gowrie Park with TassieLink on their scheduled Launceston–Queenstown service via Cradle Mountain (daily Tues, Thurs & Sat).

Ulverstone to Burnie

Tasmanian Redline buses follow the unremarkable coast from Devonport west to industrial Burnie, stopping at Ulverstone and Penguin. **ULVERSTONE**, 20km west of Devonport where the **Leven River** flows into the sea, is a popular family holiday centre with unpolluted **beaches**. A population of Little penguins comes to breed on the beach here between September and April, and the responsible *Penguin Point Twilight Tours* takes small groups out from dusk to see the penguins and their habitat (1hr 30min; $10; bookings ☏03/6437 2590). **Accommodation** possibilities include B&B in the pleasant, two-storey *Ocean View Guesthouse* at 1 Victoria St (☏ & ℱ03/6425 5401; ❻), and the splendid 1903 red-brick *Furners Hotel* at 42 Reibey St (☏03/6425 1488, ℱ6425 5933; B&B ❹), the latter complete with carved blackwood staircase and an excellent **bistro**; or try the waterfront *Ulverstone Caravan Park*, 1km east of the centre (☏03/6425 2624; vans ❷, cabins and units ❸). You can pick up free maps and information from the volunteer-run **Ulverstone Visitor Information Centre**, behind the post office (Mon–Fri 9.15am–3.30pm, Sat & Sun 10am–3pm; ☏03/6425 2839).

In the picturesque hop-growing countryside south of Ulverstone, the **Gunns Plains Caves** (hourly tours daily 10am–4pm; 50min; $10), part of a state reserve, are worth visiting for their remarkable limestone formations which, when lit from behind, glow a succulent red. A permanent stream feeds an underground lake, and platypuses and possums enjoy the cool temperatures. You'll need your own transport to get here.

The best route west from Ulverstone follows the old Bass Highway along the coastline, passing the Three Sisters and Goat Islands bird sanctuaries, and Penguin Point where Little penguins roost. **PENGUIN** itself, 12km along the highway, is a neatly tended town with three safe swimming beaches. Tacky blue-and-white, penguin-shaped garbage bins line the main street, culminating in the two-metre-high "big penguin" in the foreshore park. Five kilometres outside town, there are walking trails in the **Dial Range State Forest**.

BURNIE, on Emu Bay 15km west of Penguin, is an industrial and paper-manufacturing centre that's undergone something of a transformation in recent years. Situated amid rich farmland and beautiful rocky coves, tourism is being actively developed in the town and Burnie port is attracting passenger ships for the first time in decades. The Tasmanian Redline Coaches depot is at 117 Wilson St and TassieLink departs, from outside the **Tasmanian Travel and Information Centre** at the Civic Square precinct, off Little Alexander Street (Mon–Fri 8am–5pm, Sat & Sun 10am–4pm; ☏03/6434 6111). The Civic Centre on Wilmot Street is home to both the **Pioneer Village Museum**, with its reconstructed turn-of-the-twentieth-century street (Mon–Fri 8.30am–5pm, Sat & Sun 9am–4pm; $6), and the **Burnie Regional Art Gallery** (Tues–Fri 10.30am–5pm, Sat & Sun 1.30–4.30pm; free). In complete contrast to the region's industrial base, the large-scale **Australian Paper Mill**, check out the wonderful community-based, non-profit **Creative Paper Mill**, on old Surrey Rd, 100m off the Bass Highway on the eastern side of Burnie (Mon–Fri 9am–4pm, plus Nov–April Sat & Sun 10am–4pm; tours Mon–Fri 11am & 1pm; 35–40min; $8). The paper here is handmade and there's a product showroom, plus an art gallery.

Just 1km from the centre is **Fernglade**, a unique platypus reserve on a peaceful, forested stretch of the Emu River; a steep bank on one side of the river gives the wild platypus a feeling of safety. The platypus are easy to spot, particularly at dawn and after dusk. Burnie also has a free **penguin interpretative centre**, reached via a one-kilometre-long boardwalk from the town centre; the long, thin building, the size of a bus, is open to the Little penguins who, lit by infra-red light, can be observed through little windows via a periscope-style mirrored tunnel; the best time to view the penguins is after dusk between September and April. Conservationist William Walker (☏ & ℱ03/6435 7205, ✉wagwalker@bigpond.com) runs personalized nature-based scenic and cultural interpretive tours, visiting Fernglade and the penguins and other local points of interest, and specializing in day-walks with local gourmet food. It's also worth stopping at **Lactos**, a prize-winning speciality **cheese factory**, 3km from Burnie on the Old Surry Road (tastings Mon–Fri 9am–5pm, Sat & Sun 10am–4pm; free), where you can sample and buy blends and variations of European cheeses.

There's plenty of **accommodation**, should you decide to stay in Burnie. The cheapest hotel is the very basic *Regent Hotel*, 26 North Terrace (☎03/6431 1933; rooms ❶–❷), which has inexpensive singles ($21, en-suite $30), bunk twins and an en-suite double. The least expensive motel is the *Ocean View Motel*, 253 Bass Highway, at Cooee on the pleasant, non-industrial side of town towards Wynyard (☎03/6431 1925; vans ❷, cabins ❸, motel ❹), with an attached campground and caravan park. For more character, *Glen Osborne House*, at 9 Aileen Crescent (☎03/6431 9866, ☎6431 4354; ❺), is a stylish Victorian-era B&B with en-suite rooms and a lovely garden of lawns, roses and fruit trees. **Food** choices include the veteran *Rialto Gallery*, an affordable Italian at 46 Wilmot St (BYO; ☎03/6431 7718), and a decent Indian, *Renusha's* at 28 Ladbrooke St (☎03/6431 2293; dinner Tues–Sat; BYO). *Kinesis*, at 53 Mount St (closed Sun & Mon), is a mainly vegetarian café focusing on healthy specials and gourmet bakes and muffins, plus organic coffees and teas. They also serve dinner on Friday nights when they have free live acoustic music. Just around the corner, is the licensed *Cafe Europa*, at 23 Cattley St (Mon–Thurs 8.30am–9pm, Fri & Sat 8.30am–midnight, Sun 10am–6pm). Burnie's **Online Access Centre** is at 2 Spring St.

Wynyard and around

WYNYARD, another 19km along the old Bass Highway from Burnie, snuggles into the lush pasturelands between the **Inglis River** and the sea. Most of the action in the town centres on the wharf area off Goldie Street – the main street that parallels the river – with its fishing boats and fresh fish shop, but the adjacent coastline has much to entice visitors. At **Fossil Bluff**, an easy three-kilometre walk along the Bicentennial Track from the riverfront park in front of the tourist information office (see opposite), layers of sedimentary rock containing fossilized seashells can easily be examined at low tide, and the beach itself has good views of the 170-metre seaface of **Table Cape**. A drive up to Table Cape will reward you with magnificent views of the coast and hinterland, particularly pretty when the cape's **tulip fields** are in bloom around October.

Eleven kilometres west of town, a turn-off from the Bass Highway winds down to **Boat Harbour Beach**, the prettiest on the northwest coast, with pale-blue water, white sand and very gentle waves. It's perfect for **diving**, too; equipment can be rented from the Scuba Centre at 62 Bass Highway in Wynyard (☎03/6442 2247), which also organizes excursions. The milk bar on the beach does takeaways and rents **boogie-boards** and **wave skis**, and there are a few restaurants on the Esplanade. The luxurious *Boat Harbour Beach Resort* (☎03/6445 1107, ☎6445 1027; ❹–❺), has a restaurant, indoor heated pool and spa, but you can enjoy the area just as much by camping at the *Boat Harbour Beach Caravan Park* (☎03/6445 1253; vans ❷, en-suite cabins ❸), which also has a general store. Nearby **Sisters Beach** is also attractive.

Rocky Cape National Park

Stretching for a mere 12km along the coast, from Sisters Beach to Rocky Cape, are the rugged hills and cliffs of **Rocky Cape National Park**, Tasmania's smallest national park, created in 1967 for the purpose of preserving some remarkable **Aboriginal archeological finds**. The mainly quartzite hills are pockmarked with caves, of which the two major ones, North Cave and South Cave, contain huge shell middens, bones and stone tools dating back as far as eight thousand years, when the sea was several fathoms below its current level.

Although North Cave can be visited – it's a fifteen-minute walk there and back from the road, reached by driving 5km into the park and taking the left fork at the lighthouse – most people prefer just to walk along the various easy tracks. It takes seven hours to traverse the whole length of the park; there's no water, no toilets and camping is not allowed. Rocky pools, safe swimming beaches and picnic areas are scattered along the route, while in spring and summer there's a profusion of wild flowers on the scrubby heathland, including some unique native orchids. At dusk you may see wallabies, echidnas and various species of bird.

Practicalities

Wynyard may well be the first place you see in Tasmania, since "Burnie" **airport** is actually just 800m from the town centre. You can **rent a car** at the airport with Autorent-Hertz (☎03/6442 4444), Avis (☎03/6442 2512) or Budget (☎03/6442 1777). MTT **public transport buses** connect Wynyard with Burnie, departing from 38 Jackson St. Tasmanian Redline Coaches call at Gale's Auto Service, 28 Saunders St (☎03/6442 2205), en route from Burnie to Smithton via the turn-offs to Table Cape, Boat Harbour Beach and Rocky Cape.

Wynyard Tourist Information, in front of the riverfront park on the corner of Goldie and Hogg streets (April–Sept Mon–Fri 10am–4pm, Sat noon–3pm; Oct–March Mon–Fri 9am–4pm, Sat & Sun 1–4pm; ☎03/6442 4143), has information on local activities and **accommodation**. There's camping at *Wynyard Caravan Park*, at 30B Old Bass Highway (☎03/6442 1998; dorms $15, vans ❷, cabins ❸), and dorms for backpackers. Rates at the homely *Federal Hotel*, at 82 Goldie St (☎03/6442 2056, ℱ6442 1545; ❸), include a cooked breakfast. The *Inglis River Hotel-Motel*, 4 Goldie St (☎03/6442 2344; ❷), offers the best value of the few motels, while the *Alexandria*, on Table Cape Road (☎03/6442 4411, ℮alexandria@ozemail.com.au; ❺), is a classy B&B. For **places to eat**, try the pubs for cheap fare. *Cafe Ricardo*, 8 Inglis St, serves Italian pasta dishes (☎03/6442 1755), while *Buccaneers Restaurant*, nearby at no. 4 (☎03/6442 4104) offers fresh fish and seafood. Wynyard's **Online Access Centre** is at 21 Saunders St.

Stanley

The tiny fishing village of **STANLEY**, 6km off the Bass Highway (A2) and 32km west of Rocky Cape, was the first settlement in northwest Tasmania, being the original 1826 headquarters of the **Van Diemen's Land Company** (see box, overleaf). It occupies a scenic setting on a small, foot-shaped peninsula, right at the base of an unusual rock formation – **The Nut**, described by Matthew Flinders as a "cliffy round lump in form resembling a Christmas cake" – that rises directly out of the ocean to a height of nearly 150m. **Circular Head**, as it's officially called (the name also for the surrounding municipality), is thought to be a volcanic plug, with the softer sediments around it having eroded away.

Although it's still possible to do the strenuous ten-minute walk up the grassy Nut itself, you can get to the top more comfortably by means of an exhilarating

The Van Diemen's Land Company

. . . how is it that an absentee owner across the world got this magnificent and empty country without having paid one glass bead?

Cassandra Pybus

The **Van Diemen's Land Company (VDL)** was the brainchild of a group of prominent and well-connected individuals, who in 1824 managed to obtain by Royal Charter 250,000 acres of the mainly thickly forested, unexplored northwest corner of Tasmania. Their plan was to create their own source of cheap wool in the colonies, which could be relied upon even if Europe was subject to political upheaval; the *Tranmere* arrived at Circular Head in 1826, with the personnel, livestock, supplies and equipment to create the township of Stanley.

The first flocks were grazed at Woolnorth on Cape Grim, a plateau of tussock grass and trees that might have been made for the purpose but, in fact, was prime Aboriginal hunting land. When hunting parties began to take sheep, whites killed Aborigines in retaliation, and a vindictive cycle of killings began. The most tragic incident (a version of events denied by Woolnorth) was supposed to have occurred around 1826 or 1827: a group of Aboriginal men, seeking revenge for the rape of their women, speared a shepherd and killed one hundred sheep. These deaths were ruthlessly avenged when a group of thirty unarmed Aborigines, hunting for muttonbirds near the same spot, were killed by shepherds and their bodies thrown over a cliff (now euphemistically called "Suicide Bay"). Ultimately, the Aboriginal people of the northwest were systematically hunted down, the last one being captured near the Arthur River in 1842.

In the 1840s the company changed its emphasis from wool production to the sale and lease of its land, and it now holds just a fifth of its original land. Still registered on the London Stock Exchange, it is the only remaining company in the world operating under a Royal Charter; its major shareholder is a New Zealand public company based in Dunedin.

chair lift, reached via the ramp opposite the post office (daily 9.30am–5pm, weather permitting; call ☏03/6458 1286 to check; $4 one-way, $7 return). A short walk around the windy **Nut State Reserve** at the top affords views over the town and port, and southeast as far as Table Cape. Directly below is the exquisitely deserted **Godfrey's Beach**, with its calm and translucent blue waters.

Stanley's main street, **Church Street**, runs below the foot of the Nut, and its restaurants and crafts shops are high enough above the beach, wharves and the rest of the town to command excellent views. On the foreshore area is Stanley Artworks, an art gallery housed in the slate-roofed **Van Diemen's Land Company Store**, designed in 1844 by John Lee Archer, whose work can be seen notably in Hobart (see p.1065). From the nearby **port area**, at low tide, you can see the remnants of a 1923 **shipwreck**, a victim of the "furies" of the Bass Strait. Two kilometres north of the town, the headquarters of the Van Diemen's Land Company, with superb views over Half Moon Bay, have been restored as the **Highfield Historic Site** (daily 10am–4pm; grounds $2, house $6).

Practicalities

For **tourist information** visit the Stanley Visitor Centre on the way into Stanley at 45 Main Rd (Mon–Fri 9.30am–4.30pm, Sat & Sun 10am–4pm; ☏03/6458 1330), which also has **Internet access** ($2 per 15min, $8 per hour). The visitor centre serves as Stanley's Tasmanian Redline Coaches **depot** and sells tickets; Stanley is reached on the Redline route between Burnie and Smithton (Mon–Fri 2 daily). Wilderness to West Coast Tours (T & F 03/6458 2038, W www.wildernesstasmania.com), based in Stanley, offers a variety of **tours**, including a platypus-viewing tour, which leaves an hour before dusk (2hr; $25); a penguin tour (1hr; $10), following on from the platypus tour (both tours combined: 3hr; $30); and trout fishing (half-day $125). They also offer a wilderness 4WD tour which explores the northwest tip of Tasmania, taking you through farm country, temperate rainforest, gum forests and button-grass plains (6hr; $125); a longer version also visits the wild west coast (8.5hr; $159) and both include home-made resfreshments and gourmet lunch. Stanley Seal Cruises will take you to view the rare Australian fur seal, weather permitting (daily 10am, 1.30pm & 4.30pm; 1hr 10min; $35; T 03/6458 1312).

In keeping with its historic ambience, Stanley has several "colonial" **B&Bs**, actually self-contained cottages with breakfast provisions supplied, such as *Touchwood Cottage*, at 33 Church St (T & F 03/6458 1348; ❺), and *Bayside Colonial Cottage* at 44 Alexander Terrace, which rises above Church Street (T 03/6458 1209; ❹–❺). As you come into town, you'll see the signpost for the *Dovecote Motel*, 1km along Dovecote Road (T 03/6458 1300, F 6458 1448; W www.dovecote.com.au; ❹–❺), which has spacious, well-appointed units (some self-catering), plus one for disabled guests; facilities include a bar, and a restaurant open to the public. From the motel you have the best views of the Nut, across the green fields of the Dovecote Estate. For budget travellers, **simple rooms** are available at the sprawling, three-storey *Union Hotel* on Church Street (T 03/6458 1161; ❷), with good single rates ($25), or the *Stanley YHA*, at the caravan park on Wharf Road opposite Marine Park (T 03/6458 1266; dorms $18, cabins ❸), where you can also **camp**.

Probably the best place to **eat** in Stanley is *Hurseys Seafoods*, next to Marine Park, considered to be one of the best fish-and-chip shops in Tasmania. Inside are huge holding tanks from which you select live fish and crayfish; as well as around twenty kinds of fish, they may have freshly cooked local muttonbirds in season – not to everyone's taste, as they're very oily. The café downstairs opens daily for lunch, while evening meals are available in the upstairs restaurant (restaurant bookings T 03/6458 1103). Among other eating options are *Stanleys on the Bay*, a seafood and steak restaurant on the foreshore (T 03/6458 1404; dinner nightly); the *Dovecote Restaurant*, at the *Dovecote Motel* (see above; dinner nightly); and the *Union Hotel* on Church Street, serving fresh seafood in its lounge bar. Also on Church Street, the relaxed *Stranded Whale Coffee Shop* (daily 9am–4pm, plus Fri night when bookings are preferred on T 03/6458 1202) has walls covered with photographs depicting various attempts to rescue pygmy right whales, which occasionally get stranded on the beaches around Stanley. The licensed *Nut Rock Cafe*, next door to the chairlift on Nut Reserve, with fantastic views, specializes in lobster and local produce (lunch daily).

Woolnorth and Smithton

Until recently, the only way to see Tasmania's rugged northwest tip, which remains under the control of the Van Diemen's Land Company, was by tour. Now, it's possible to stay at **WOOLNORTH**, the original VDL cattle and sheep property, in a variety of accommodation: the old shearers' quarters, self-contained cabins or the 1970s-built Directors Lodge (T 03/6452 1493, W www.woolnorthtours.com.au; rates include breakfast and dinner; shearers' quarters ❺, cabins ❻, lodge ❼). Alternatively, you can stay nearby in the unattractive logging town of **SMITHTON**, at the mouth of the Duck River 22km west of Stanley, and visit Woolnorth on a full-day **tour** (daily; $86 including morning tea and lunch in the Directors Lodge; bookings as for Woolnorth accommodation); tours also take in **Cape Grim**, where the air is reputed to be the cleanest in the world – it's the site of one of only six baseline air-monitoring stations, and Tasmania's largest **wind farm**. A couple of kilometres east of Cape Grim, you can stand at the point where Bass Strait meets the Southern Ocean and walk along the spectacular, rugged coastline.

What Smithton lacks in aesthetics it makes up for by its usefulness as a service centre, with supermarkets, fuel and banking facilities and an **Online Access Centre** on Nelson Street; the Redline **depot** is at 27 Victoria St (Mon–Fri 2 daily from Burnie via Wynyard and Stanley). The *Bridge Hotel-Motel* on Montague Road (☎03/6452 1389, ⓦwww.view.com.au/bridge; ❷–❹) has a range of **accommodation** options, a reasonably priced restaurant and counter **meals**. South of Smithton ten **forestry reserves**, ranging from rainforests to blackwood swamps and giant eucalypt forests, are all accessible from a circular route, via Kanunnah Bridge and Taytea Bridge on the C218 (90km return). **Julius River Forest Reserve** and the **Milkshakes Hills Forest Reserve** are the most rewarding. The Forestry Commission, at the corner of Nelson and Smith streets (☎03/6452 1317), provides maps and route information.

The tiny and remote **Three Hummock Island**, is just 20km north of Woolnorth; charter flights ($160 return) leave from Wynyard. Flights, accommodation and tours are organized through Three Hummock Island Escape (☎03/6452 1554, ⓦwww.threehummockisland.com.au), run by the island's two inhabitants. The range of terrains, from rainforest to white-sand beaches and open heathland, provides a variety of walks, and opportunities to see some of the island's abundant wildlife – including muttonbirds, fairy penguins, Cape Barren geese and Forrester kangaroos; all of which can be seen on a **tour** (half-day $60, full day $99). The **accommodation** at *Eagle Hill Lodge* is either shared-bathroom rooms or in one of two wooden yurts in self-catering, en-suite cottages which sleep eight (self-catering ❹–❺, full board ❼); mountain bikes and sea kayaks are available for rent. There are no shops on the island, so if you plan to stay in the self-catering accommodation, take all your supplies with you.

Marrawah

From Smithton the Bass Highway cuts across the northwest corner to the rich farming settlement of **MARRAWAH** on the west coast. Thirty kilometres along the way, a 1500-metre trail leads through a swamp at the grumpily named **Dismal Swamp Nature Reserve**. Marrawah itself has a small store, and the *Marrawah Tavern* serves plain but filling meals. **Greenpoint Beach**, which has been voted one of the three best **surfing** beaches in Australia, is 2km from Marrawah and has a small **camping area** as well as the stylish *Ann Bay Cabins* (☎03/6457 1361; ❹), decorated by artists. There's also excellent, spacious self-contained **accommodation** at *Glendonald Cottage* on the Arthur River Road, 3km south of Marrawah (☎03/6457 1191, ⓦwww.redpa.tco.asn.au/glenking; ❹); the owner, Geoff King, is a passionate conservationist who is working to regenerate the coastal land and preserve its Aboriginal sites. Geoff knows just about everything natural, local and Aboriginal history and runs **specialist bird and wildlife tours**, as well as fascinating nocturnal viewings of Tasmanian devils in the wild. The curve of Ann Bay here is shrouded by the hump of Mount Cameron West to the north. Three kilometres north of this bluff, at the end of a long exposed beach, is the most complex

Aboriginal art site in Tasmania: rock carvings of geometric or nonfigurative forms cover slabs of rock at the base of a cliff.

Arthur River and the Arthur Pieman Protected Area

Just over 20km south of Marrawah, the scattering of holiday homes at **ARTHUR RIVER** marks the start of one of the Tasmanian coast's last great **wilderness areas**, where mighty trees that have been washed down the Arthur River have crashed and battered against the windswept shoreline. At one time the entire west coast looked like this, but the progressive damming of its rivers has left the **Arthur Pieman Protected Area** as a unique reminder, complete with a spectacular array of birdlife, such as black cockatoos, Tasmanian rosellas, orange-breasted parrots, black jays, wedge-tail eagles, pied heron and azure kingfishers. Trees on the steep banks of the river include myrtle, sassafras, celery-top pines, laurels and giant tree ferns. It's dangerous to swim in the protected area, due to extremely wild conditions and occasional freak waves – even walking along the beach, where you have to pick your way over scattered bits of lumber, can be an obstacle course. It's therefore essential to get the latest information on conditions from the Parks and Wildlife office on Arthur River Road (daily 9am–5pm; ☎03/6457 1225).

The small **shop** on Gardiner Street is the only source of supplies in Arthur River; attached is *Arthur River Holiday Units* (☎03/6457 1288; ❸–❹). *Ocean View Holiday Cottage* (☎03/6452 1278; ❸–❹) and the excellent *Sunset Holiday Villas* (☎03/6457 1197; ❸) are on the same street. **Camping** at Arthur River is a truly pleasurable experience, with facilities that range from a fully serviced caravan park near the base office, to secluded areas among shady trees in the dips and hollows behind the dunes, equipped merely with water taps.

If you want to get out on the river, take a **cruise** (see below) or contact Arthur River Canoe Hire (☎03/6457 1312), which has canoes and boats available for rent (one-person canoes $8 per hour or $40 per day, two-person canoes $10 or $50, boats which can be used for overnight camping $18 per hour or $110 per day).

The Arthur River Cruise

Perhaps the biggest attraction of the entire northwest coast is the five-hour **Arthur River Cruise** on the MV *George Robinson* (daily 10am, returning 3pm; no trips June–Aug; $55; bookings ☎03/6457 1158, ⓦ www.tasadventures.com

---

The Western Explorer route

It is possible to drive from Arthur River all the way south to Zeehan on the controversial **Western Explorer**, the "tourist road" crossing the wild **Tarkine area** on the west coast. Ignoring the protests of conservationists, the road was constructed hastily and finished in January 1996. A year before, an incredibly vast and ancient Huon pine was found in the area, as big as a city block and thought to date from around 8000 BC. Conservationists are apprehensive that "the road to nowhere", as they've called it, is being used as a cover to open up the area (currently state forest) to logging, thereby degrading it and reducing the likelihood of World Heritage listing in the future. If you choose to drive this route, pick up the *Western Explorer, Travel Guide* – issued by the Department of Infrastructure and available in information centres – and remember that the road is rough and Marrawah is the last fuel stop before Zeehan.

/arthurcruises), which sails 14km upriver to the confluence of the Arthur and Frankland rivers at Turks Landing. En route you cruise past a white-breasted sea eagle's nest, see a pair of enormous sea eagles being fed and experience the transition from coastal scrub woodland to the edge of the Tarkine – the largest tract of temperate rainforest found anywhere in the world. After a barbecue lunch in a clearing, there's an optional bushwalk. Alternatively, AR Reflections River Cruises offers a slightly shorter – and not so appealing – cruise, from which you return early for a barbecue lunch in the operator's back garden (daily 10.30am–2.30pm; $53; bookings ☏03/6457 1288).

The A10 route to the west coast

From Somerset, a suburb of Burnie on the shores of Emu Bay, the A10 (called the Murchison Highway between here and the Zeehan turn-off) heads to **Queenstown**, in the heart of Tasmania's west-coast mining area. This major route to the west coast is relatively recent; prior to 1932 the coast was accessible only by sea. Following the highway, after 10km you pass **YOLLA**, a picturesque little town surrounded by rich farming country; you can get fuel here. A few kilometres past the Tewkesbury turn-off, the rural landscape ends and the road rises and winds through temperate rainforest to the **Hellyer Gorge State Reserve**. A walk leads through spicy ferns and dense myrtle forest to the Hellyer River and back on a wide and easy track (20min return). Once through the reserve, there's the shocking spectacle of a landscape ravaged by logging, but by the B23 turn-off west to Waratah, on the way to the Pieman River, the forest is beginning to reassert itself.

West to Waratah and the Pieman River

Tiny, windswept **WARATAH**, set in mountain heathland 8km off the A10, reached its peak in the early twentieth century after thirty years of tin-mining at **Mount Bischoff**, when it was linked to Burnie by the **Emu Bay Railway**, built to facilitate access to the silver fields of Zeehan and Rosebery. Though the mine closed in 1935, Waratah is still a miners' town, with recent mining developments at the Que River. Little more than a scattered collection of scruffy weatherboard cottages, it's a pretty soulless place, but you can stop off for a **meal** at the big old two-storey pub on the hill. Beyond Waratah, the last fuel stop on the road is the former mining town of **Savage River**, 45km along the B23.

The beautiful, unspoilt **Pieman River**, within the **Pieman River State Reserve**, is reached from the old gold-mining settlement of **CORINNA** on an unsealed road (C247) 26km south of Savage River. It's hard to believe that 2500 people once occupied what's now just a few shacks surrounded by dense bush. Corinna even had its own port, despite the difficulties of getting through the narrow **Pieman Heads** from the coastline. The river here is too dangerous for swimming, with an average drop of nearly 20m from the banks, and very cold water. The reserve used to be a logging area and it still holds one of the biggest stands of remaining Huon pine – saved because the water here was too deep to allow a dam to be built.

You can take a **cruise** on the river, all the way to the west coast, with MV *Arcadia II* (daily 10.30am; 4hr; $40 including morning tea, $47.70 with lunch; bookings essential ☏03/6446 1170). The boat was built in Hobart (from Huon pine) as a luxury pleasure cruiser, but during World War II saw active service off the Philippines and has since been put to other uses. From its deck you can see Huon pine, leatherwood and pandanus ferns among the **temperate rain-forest** of the river's north bank; the drier southern bank has mainly brown stringybark eucalypts. The trip allows you an hour and a half to wander on your own along the west coast; by the landing are several intriguing **holiday shacks**, ramshackle affairs with tin verandahs variously propped up by raw tree posts and an old bus.

The brothers who run the cruise virtually run Corinna too. They open the **kiosk** daily whenever they have time, but bring food along if you intend to use the **campsite** (no showers) or the cabins at the *Getaway Resort* (❸, plus $8.80 per person for linen or BYO). From the car park there's a walking track leading to a huge 600-year-old **manfern**, one of only four of such antiquity known to exist in Tasmania.

The brothers also operate the **barge** that takes you across the Pieman River from here (daily 9am–7pm; $11 car, $5.50 bike), to continue on the C249 to Zeehan, and then on the B27 to Strahan.

South to Zeehan

Back on the A10, there's no fuel until tiny **TULLAH**, 40km south of Waratah, where you'll find a pub, tearooms and cottage accommodation. Fourteen kilometres further on, the comparatively large zinc-mining town of **ROSEBERY** is a good place to stock up on supplies, with **an** ANZ bank (Mon, Tues & Fri 9.30am–noon, Wed 2–4pm) and an ATM. There's comfortable motel-style B&B **accommodation** at *Mount Black Lodge* on Hospital Road (☎03/6473 1039, ⓦwww.mountblacklodge.com; ❸–❹), which has both a guest kitchen and a licensed restaurant.

From Rosebery, it's 23km to the turn-off to **ZEEHAN**, 6km southwest off the A10. The town became prosperous from the silver-lead mines that opened in the 1880s, and at its height boasted a population of eight thousand. However, the mines had already begun to fail by 1908, and the town was not to see a revival until the 1970s, when the Renison Bell tin mines were opened. Several boom-period buildings are still standing, including the elaborate facade of the **Gaiety Theatre**, once the largest theatre in Australia. The **West Coast Pioneer Memorial Museum** on Main Street (daily 8.30am–5pm; $5.50) has displays on mining history and its own café. **Accommodation** is expensive, as Zeehan catches Strahan's overflow, and includes the *Heemskirk Motor Inn* (☎03/6471 6107; ❹–❺), and basic pub rooms at the *Hotel Cecil* on Main Street (☎03/6471 6221; ❸–❹), where you can get decent counter **meals**. The *Mount Zeehan Retreat Bed and Breakfast* provides evening meals on request (☎03/6471 6424; B&B ❹). By far the cheapest option is the friendly **caravan park**, nicely situated 1km from the centre on Hurst Street (☎03/6471 6633; vans ❷, cabins ❷–❸). The ANZ **bank** has restricted opening hours (Mon & Tues 2–4pm, Wed 9.30am–noon, Thurs 9.30am–4pm & Fri 2–4pm), but there's an ATM at Vickers General Store on the main street (open daily).

From Zeehan it's possible to go straight to Strahan (47km) on a sealed road (B27), bypassing Queenstown and visiting the Henty Dunes (see p.1145) en route; or you could head back to the A10 (called the Zeehan Highway until Queenstown) and reach Strahan via Queenstown, another 32km along the highway. You can get to Rosebery and Zeehan on TassieLink's scheduled Launceston–Queenstown service via Cradle Mountain (1 daily Tues, Thurs & Sat).

Queenstown

QUEENSTOWN is worth a visit, but not for normal reasons. Its infamous "**lunar landscape**" is chilling evidence of the devastation that single-minded commercial exploitation can wreak in such a sensitive environment. If you approach the town from Strahan you're confronted by the hideously ugly **Mount Lyell Copper Mine**; from Hobart, the road winds down to the town around bare, reddish-brown rock.

Queenstown has been a mining centre since 1883, when gold was discovered at Mount Lyell, and it looks like a typical mining town, with its wide streets, two-storey hotels and identical, pokey tin-roofed weatherboard houses. In 1893 the **Mount Lyell Mining and Railway Company** was formed and began to mine copper at Mount Lyell, which it has continued to do ever since. The weird-looking mountains here, chalky white and almost totally devoid of vegetation, are the result of a lethal combination of tree-felling, sulphur, fire and rainfall. Since the smelters closed in 1969 there has been some regrowth on the lower slopes, but it's estimated that the damage already done has had an impact that will last some four or five hundred years. In late 1994 the Mount Lyell mine closed down, but the lease was taken over by Copper Mines of Tasmania, which foresees another ten years of operation with the remaining ore. Tailings from the mine are now dumped into a multimillion-dollar dam instead of the town's **Queen River**, where aquatic life is beginning to return. The Queen eventually flows into the King River, however, and the moonscaped banks of the **King River** delta near Strahan attest to the lasting and wide-ranging environmental damage of the past century.

The West Coast Wilderness Railway

Queenstown, whose infamous "lunar landscape" was touted by the Tasmanian tourist board as a major attraction in the 1970s, is currently putting itself back on the tourist map for very different reasons, with the opening of the **West Coast Wilderness Railway**, a $25-million redevelopment of the old **Abt Railway**. The railway was completed in 1896 to connect the Mount Lyell Mining Company with the port of Teepookana, and in 1899 the line was extended to Regatta Point in Strahan. The railway closed in 1963, when it became more economical to transport by road, but years of lobbying finally led to the federal government financing its redevelopment.

The West Coast Wilderness Railway will be fully completed by the end of 2003 including the restoration of forty bridges. Two of the four surviving locomotives from 1963 have been restored and each carriage – replicas of old timber and brass models – has been designed using different Tasmanian woods; using steam and diesel engines (the locomotives shunt halfway at Double Barrell, where there is a 1hr lunch stop; BYO or buy from the kitchen carriage), they travel the 34km from **Queenstown to Strahan** on restored 1896 rack and pinion track, passing en route some of Tasmania's most scenic wilderness – crossing bridges spanning wild rivers (and the sadly polluted King River), and climbing over 200m up a 1:16 rack gradient. On the way, historic settlements are passed, such as Lynchford Station – where passengers can alight for some gold panning – and Rinadeena, and there are stops at forest and riverside walkways. The train leaves from Queenstown at the original station on Driffield St, opposite the *Empire Hotel* (see opposite), and at Strahan from the original station there at Regatta Point (see p.1143). There is a daily service in both directions but you have to choose whether you want to go one way and pay extra for a return coach and use up more time, or reach the halfway point and then return (departs Queenstown 10am, departs Strahan 10.15am; one-way 4hr; return 4hr 30min; $65, extra $10 for return coach).

Underground tours of the **Mount Lyell Mine** run daily (10am, 1pm & 7pm; 2hr 30min; $58); it's hard to stifle a lingering cynicism, even though the plans for reforestation are explained. Bookings and departures are from Lyell Tours (℡03/6471 1472), based at the *Empire Hotel* (see below); the tour office also provides **tourist information**. Queenstown's **Online Access Centre** is on Driffield Street.

Next door to the mine is the **Parks and Wildlife Service office** (℡03/6471 2511), the base for the Franklin Lower Gordon Wild Rivers National Park and the place to pick up the department's rafting and bush-walking guidelines. While in town, you could also check out the old photographic displays in the **Galley Museum** (Mon–Fri 10am–5pm, Sat & Sun 1–5pm; $4), housed in the old *Imperial Hotel*. There's also a rather joyless **chair lift** just outside town on the Lyell Highway (daily April–Sept 9am–5pm; Oct–March 9am–6pm; $8), to help you get an even better view of those frightening hills.

If you're **staying** in Queenstown, try the *Empire Hotel*, at 2 Orr St (℡03/6471 1699, ⓔempirehotel@tassienet.au; ❷), a lovely, old-fashioned building noted for its blackwood staircase; it has a good range of reasonably priced rooms, including some en suites and several budget singles ($25), plus good-value meals. *Mountain View Holiday Lodge*, at 1 Penghana Rd (℡03/6471 1163, ⓕ6471 1306; dorms $15, motel units ❸), across the river from the town centre, has been converted from the mine's single men's lodgings. For something special, *Penghana*, on The Esplanade at no. 32, provides B&B-style accommodation in an imposing stately mansion set in rainforest overlooking Queenstown (℡03/6471 2560, ⓕ6471 1535, B&B ❺–❻). There are **banking** facilities at the Trust Bank, but no ATM. From Queenstown you can drive to Strahan on the B24 (40km), which starts as a steep, winding road through bare hills, or you continue along the A10 (called the Lyell Highway from Queenstown to Hobart) 86km east to the first fuel at Derwent Bridge, surrounded by the World Heritage Area (Franklin Lower Gordon Wild Rivers National Park, p.1050, and Cradle Mountain–Lake St Clair National Park, p.1146).

Strahan and around

STRAHAN is easy-going, relaxed and even progressive. The only town and port on the west coast, it sits in the huge **Macquarie Harbour**, site of **Sarah Island**, a harsh secondary convict settlement in use between 1822 and 1830, which can be visited on a Gordon River cruise (see box p.1144). The entrance to Macquarie Harbour, named **Hells Gates** by arriving convicts, is only 80m wide. **Huon pine**, perfect for shipbuilding, grows abundantly in the area – logging and boatbuilding became the convicts' trade. After 1830 the timber continued to attract loggers, but it wasn't until 1882 that Strahan began life as a port for the nearby copper and lead fields. Although it was Tasmania's third-largest port in 1900, its unreliability led to its closure by 1970 and the population dwindled to three hundred. It's now a small **fishing village** for abalone, crayfish and shark, and commercial fish farming of rainbow trout and Atlantic salmon, though the main industry is tourism. The basing of the **Franklin Blockade** campaign here in 1982 shook up the town and brought the Australian media here for two months. **Cruises** on the **Gordon River** had already been running before this event, but the declaration of a **World Heritage Area** has meant that busloads of tourists now regularly descend upon Strahan to see the river, creating a hectic atmosphere for a short time, after which the town rapidly reverts to its usual peaceful state. You would be mad to come all this way and not take a cruise; though they may seem expensive, it's the best way to get to see the wilderness, and well worth the money.

Transport and services

The place to make enquiries and bookings for TassieLink **bus** services is the visitor centre (see opposite). There's a scheduled service from Launceston and Devonport via Cradle Mountain (Tues, Thurs & Sat), connecting with a Queenstown–Strahan service (Tues, Wed, Thurs, Fri & Sun), which connects with the service to Hobart via Lake St Clair. The Strahan General Store on The Esplanade (Mon–Fri 7.30am–7pm, Sat & Sun 8am–6pm) has EFTPOS facilities and is an ANZ **bank** agent; there is an **ATM** outside. At the far end of The Esplanade, the old **Customs House** contains the **post office** (also a Commonwealth Bank agent), and there is a **Parks and Wildlife** office (daily 8am–5pm; ⓣ03/6471 7122), where park passes are available, and an **Online Access Centre**.

If you want to **shop** for food, the Strahan General Store houses a small supermarket selling a decent range, including fresh vegetables. There's also a supermarket on Reid Street and *Banjo's Bakery* on The Esplanade.

Accommodation

If you've got your own transport to get there, you can **camp** for free at Ocean Beach and Henty Dunes (see p.1145); there are no facilities, but free hot showers can be had in town in the toilet block opposite the post office. **Accommodation** is expensive and gets booked up in the summer; to be safe, **book ahead** or bring a tent – otherwise you might have to head back to Zeehan or Queenstown. *Strahan Village* has virtually overtaken the town – with pub and motel accommodation and several restaurants along The Esplanade, and a rather impersonal reception/booking office (ⓣ03/6471 7160 or 1800 628 286, ⓦwww.strahanvillage.com.au) in a corner building. Another accommodation booking agency is run by Strahan Central (ⓣ03/6471 7612, ⓔstrahancentral@trump.net.au), which books for the YHA and several B&Bs. The Strahan Visitor Centre (see opposite) has a free accommodation hotline – you call and book a room yourself from the list provided.

Franklin Manor The Esplanade ⓣ03/6471 7311, ⓦwww.franklinmanor.com.au. Sedate and elegant two-storey weatherboard B&B, surrounded by trees and flowers. The interior is attractively decorated and lovingly maintained; classical music plays in the guest lounge, always filled with fresh flowers, and there's a classy restaurant. ❺–❼

Gordon Gateway Chalet Grining St, Regatta Point ⓣ03/6471 7165, ⓔggc@tassie.net.com.au. Peaceful harbourfront spot looking across to the town and its fishing boats. Spacious rooms with kitchenettes. ❹–❻

Hamers Hotel The Esplanade ⓣ03/6471 7191 or 1800 628 286, ⓦwww.strahanvillage.com.au. Renovated 1930s hotel with clean, modern rooms with basins, TV and sea views; light breakfast included. Also stylish modern motel units attached to the ground floor of the pub. The café-style lounge bar serves seafood and good salads. ❸

Ormiston House The Esplanade ⓣ03/6471 7077, ⓦwww.ormistonhouse.com.au. This magnificent 1899 stately house was originally the home of Frederick Ormiston, the founder of Strahan; now it's a five-star guesthouse and restaurant. B&B ❼

Risby Cove The Esplanade ⓣ03/6471 7572, ⓦwww.risby.com.au. An old sawmill, fully renovated using corrugated iron and Huon pine salvaged from the harbour, now houses upmarket one- and two-bedroom accommodation suites with kitchenette area, a restaurant/café, gallery and theatre. ❺–❻

Strahan Caravan & Tourist Park The Esplanade ⓣ03/6471 7239. Good-value camping and cabins near the foreshore. Vans ❷, cabins ❸

Strahan Colonial Cottages Reid St ⓣ03/6471 761. Three beautifully renovated and well-equipped cottages, one a renovated church. ❻

Strahan Village Motor Inn Jolly St ⓣ03/6471

7160 or 1800 628 286, ⓦ www.strahanvillage
.com.au. Motel complex on a hill overlooking the
town, with some wheelchair-accessible units; the
restaurant/bar has sea views. ❹–❻
**Strahan Wilderness Lodge & Bayview
Cottages** Ocean Beach Rd ⓣ & ⓕ 03/6471 7142.
The best-value place in Strahan, set in spacious
grounds crisscrossed by walking tracks, just out of
town. Old homestead B&B, plus private self-
catering cottages. B&B ❸, cottages ❹

Strahan YHA Harvey St ⓣ 03/6471 7255,
ⓔ strahancentral@trump.net.au. Located in two
separate buildings beside a bush-lined stream
with its own resident platypus, this modern hostel
has spacious but slightly neglected common
kitchens, eating areas, and lounge. There are well
cared-for timber bedroom cabins with double or
twin beds, which share the hostel bathroom and
kitchen. Buses drop off here. Dorms $20, rooms
❷, cabins ❸

The Town

Your first stop should be the innovative wooden and iron **Strahan Visitor
Centre**, on The Esplanade (daily: Oct–March 10am–6pm, till 9pm Jan;
April–Sept 11am–6pm; 24hr ticket $2; ⓣ 03/6471 7622, ⓔ strahan@tas
visinfo.com.au), whose exterior design aims to echo the area's boatbuilding and
timber industries. The interior features a waterfall, and a huge glass wall
providing views of the harbour. The centre sets out its exhibits in a provocative and challenging way, under seven main themes: the Aborigines, convicts,
logging, ecology, economy, wilderness and conflict – all making a satisfyingly
radical departure from the usual displays in a local museum. You can enter the
foyer free of charge to pick up leaflets and information and take advantage of
the **Internet access** ($3 per 30min). Outside, an **amphitheatre** is the early-
evening venue for an entertaining two-man show, *The Ship That Never Was*,
which retells – in slapstick vein, with plenty of audience participation – the
true story of an 1834 convict escape from Sarah Island (daily 5.30pm plus
8.30pm performance in Jan; $12).

Adjacent to the visitor centre is the **Strahan Woodworks**, in a large,
corrugated-iron shed (daily 8am–5pm), selling well-designed and crafted
woodwork; you're also welcome to roam around Morrison's Saw Mill next
door, and watch the Tasmanian timbers being processed. Also worth a visit
is the **Forestry Tasmania Office** (Mon–Fri 9am–noon & 1–5pm;
ⓣ 03/6471 7176), which has leaflets describing the trees in the area, as well
as other information. You should also check out the amazing window display which features a Huon pine log transforming itself into the bow of a
boat.

The **Strahan Historic Foreshore Walkway** is a pleasant gravel track
following the shore of the harbour around to **Regatta Point** and its 1899
train station. Once used by the Mount Lyell Railway and Mining Company
to transport ore to the port, it has been renovated and is in use again for the
newly opened **West Coast Wilderness Railway** (see box on p.1140). En
route you pass the **People's Park**, from where you can take the rainforest walk
to **Hogarth Falls** (40min; 2km return).

Eating and drinking

Strahan's best **restaurant** is the dining room of the stylish *Franklin Manor* (see
opposite). The cheaper, less formal *Hamers Hotel* (see opposite), is the focus of
the town's social life; it has a fine bistro which serves up a varied selection of
seafood, and is always a lively place for a **drink**. For snacks, there's *Banjo's
Bakery*, or the *Strahan Central Café*, just off The Esplanade on Harold Street – a
young, city-style and funky café with waterviews, an outdoor deck and excellent coffee. Alternatively, the general store on Innes Street serves cheap breakfasts and takeaways.

The **Gordon River** is deep, its waters dark from the tannin leaching out of button-grass plains – even the tap water in Strahan is brown (though perfectly fine to drink). Cruise boats used to travel as far as Sir John Falls, 30km upriver, but the speed at which the boats had to go was causing the river banks to erode. Boats now travel only the 14km to **Heritage Landing**, where there's a chance to see a section of real **rainforest**: a boardwalk above the rainforest floor allows you to get close without disturbing anything. Trunks and branches of ancient myrtles and Huon pines provide homes for mosses, lichens and liverworts on their bark, and ferns and fungi grow from the trunks – even the dead trees support some forms of life, however lowly. The wet and swampy conditions are ideal for **Huon pines**, a threatened tree species found only in Tasmania: they're the second-oldest living things on earth after the bristlecone pines of western North America, with some trees found to be more than ten thousand years old. The massive pines, which may reach a height of 40m, can grow from seed but more often regenerate vegetatively, putting down roots where fallen branches touch the soil. The vast tree at the landing, reckoned to be around 2000 years old, split in two during 1997 – one half fell to the ground – but the trunk won't rot for up to one hundred years as it contains methyl eugenol oil which slows fungal growth. The oil content of the wood helps explain why it was so highly sought after as one of the few green Tasmanian timbers that floats: Huon pine logs were floated down to the boom camp and there fashioned into huge rafts to be rowed across Macquarie Harbour. The **boom camp** is still set up, and anyone can stay for free – all you need to bring is bedding and food – and you need to rent a kayak (from Hell's Gate Wilderness Tours; ☎03/6471 7576) to be dropped off near the mooring by the *Wanderer II*.

Two operators offer **river cruises**; both visit Sarah Island and make a thirty-minute stop at Heritage Landing. To make the most of the experience, turn up early to bag a good seat and bring water- and windproof gear so you can brave the prow of the boat – much the most exhilarating spot when you whizz through Macquarie Heads (Hells Gates). The larger operator, **Gordon River Cruises** (cruise departs 8.30am, returns 2pm, Nov–April extra cruises departs 2.30pm, returns 8pm; $50 including morning tea, bow-atrium seat $55, window seats $75, upper-deck seats including smorgasboard lunch $129; includes 1hr at Sarah Island; ☎03/6471 7187, ⓦwww.strahanvillage.com.au), has two boats and is located on the waterfront in a spacious complex, where there's a photographic display of Strahan's history and interpretive material relating to the unique thylacine rug (see p.1069) bought by the federal group and two museums, to be shared between Strahan, Launceston and Hobart. When it's in Strahan, the delicate rug is displayed at 12.30pm and 4.30pm with an acccompanying talk (free). **World Heritage Cruises**, the smaller friendlier company, also has two boats (the *Wanderer II and III*), and offers a slightly cheaper cruise, with a one-hour tour of the prison settlement Sarah Island, led by an actor telling convict tales (daily 9am–3.15pm; $65; snacks and $12 buffet meal available on board; licensed; ☎03/6471 7174, ⓦwww.worldheritagecruises.com.au). They also offer a similar afternoon cruise in summer (Jan–April; 2pm–8pm; $65), and a shorter morning cruise in the warmer months which doesn't stop at Sarah Island (Oct–April; 9am–1.30pm; $60).

Around Strahan

Six kilometres east of town, **Ocean Beach** is, at 30km, the longest beach in Tasmania. In the early 1990s – and again in 1998 – dozens of **pilot whales** from Antarctica were stranded here: unfortunately, attempts to rescue them were unsuccessful and their skeletons, half-buried in the sand, can still be seen. Come at dusk to observe the marvellous sunsets and to watch – from

November to February – the migratory **muttonbirds** roost. It's an eleven-kilometre drive on a gravel road, south off the road to Ocean Beach, to **Macquarie Heads** (Hells Gates). The extensive **Henty Dunes**, 12km north of town on the Zeehan Road (B27), are also worth seeing; you can **camp** at the picnic area.

To get around, you can rent **mountain bikes** from *Risby Cove* (see p.1142; half-day $15, full day $25). 4Wheelers offers popular guided four-wheel motorbike tours of Henty Sand Dunes (40min; $35; bookings essential ☎03/6471 7622 or 0419 508 175). In addition to the Gordon River cruises (see box opposite) there's a wide choice of water-based tours. West Coast Yacht Charters, on The Esplanade (☎03/6471 7422, ⓦwww.tasadventures.com.au), runs evening **crayfish dinner sails** on Macquarie Harbour on a twenty-metre ketch, *Stormbreaker* (daily 6–8.30pm except May–Aug; $55 including dinner), plus morning fishing trips (on demand 9am–noon; $40) and longer cruises (1 night $275, 2 nights $390) up the Gordon River; you can even stay on board the ketch for a waterborne B&B experience (❸). With Wild Rivers Jet (50min; $50; ☎03/6471 7174) you can explore the **King River**, which, like the Gordon, flows into Macquarie Harbour, just south of Strahan. Strahan Marine Charters (☎0418 135 983) offers private fishing (3hr; $55) or sightseeing tours (3hr 30min; $55) for up to twelve people; or you can rent the whole boat (1hr; $135; minimum four people).

Wilderness Air, on Strahan Wharf, runs spectacular **seaplane flights** over Macquarie Harbour and the wilderness area (daily from 9am; 1hr 20min; $132; bookings ☎03/6471 7280, ⓔwildernessair@tasadventures.com), providing the unforgettable image of the smooth dark ribbon of the pristine Gordon River easing through dense forest. The highlight of the trip is the dramatic landing at **Sir John Falls Landing**, further upriver than the cruise boats can reach. They also have longer flights for viewing the rugged scenery around Frenchmans Cap. Seeair Adventure Charters (☎03/6471 7718) offers **helicopter flights** over Hells Gates and Macquarie Harbour ($75; 15min), and the Teepookana Forest ($140; 1hr). Freycinet and Strahan Adventures (☎03/6257 0500 or 0419 321 896) does a range of kayaking tours.

The World Heritage Area

If we can revise our attitudes towards the land under our feet; if we can accept a role of steward, and depart from the role of conqueror; if we can accept the view that man and nature are inseparable parts of the unified whole – then Tasmania can be a shining beacon in a dull, uniform, and largely artificial world.

Olegas Truchanas, conservationist, 1971

It's the lure of the **wilderness** that attracts a certain type of traveller to Tasmania, to commune with nature at its most unspoilt. The state's vast wilderness areas of the South West National Park, Franklin Lower Gordon Wild Rivers National Park and the adjacent Cradle Mountain–Lake St Clair National Park make up the **World Heritage Area**, recognized by UNESCO.

The future of the parks could have been very different had it not been for the bitterly fought battle waged by the environmentalists in the 1980s. In 1972 the flooding of the beautiful and unique **Lake Pedder** led to the formation, in 1976, of the **Wilderness Society**, which began a relentless campaign against the next plan for the southwest by the Hydro Electricity Commission (HEC), which was to build a huge dam on the Lower Gordon River that would efface Tasmania's last wild river, the Franklin. Pro-HEC forces included the then Tasmanian Premier Robin Gray. Years of protests and campaigns ensued, but in 1981 the whole southwest area was proposed for the World Heritage List. The **Franklin Blockade**, organized by the Wilderness Society and led by **Dr Bob Brown**, began on December 14, 1982, the day the southwest officially joined the list – a fact the Tasmanian government was choosing to ignore.

For two months, blockaders from all over Australia travelled upriver from their base in Strahan to put themselves in front of the bulldozers at the site, in nonviolent protest. The **blockade** attracted international attention, notably when the British botanist David Bellamy joined in the protest and was among the twelve hundred or so arrested for trespassing. During the course of the campaign, Bob Hawke's Labor government was voted in, and in March 1983, following a trailblazing High Court ruling, the federal government forbade further work by the HEC. Though the blockade itself had failed to stop the preparatory work on the dam, it had changed, or at least challenged, the opinion of many Australians. Particularly on Tasmania's west coast, communities and families were split over the Franklin issue; local people who supported the "Greenie" protesters faced a lot of antagonism within the community, and resentment grew towards the mainlanders, who were regarded as denying potential employment to Tasmanians. Recent Wilderness Society campaigns have only added to these tensions.

Cradle Mountain–Lake St Clair National Park

This must be a national park for the people for all time. It is magnificent, and people must know about it and enjoy it.

Gustave Weindorfer, botanist and mountaineer, 1910

Cradle Mountain–Lake St Clair National Park is Tasmania's best known, its northern **Cradle Mountain** end easily accessible from Devonport, Deloraine or Launceston, and its southern **Lake St Clair** end from Derwent Bridge on the Lyell Highway between Queenstown and Hobart. A popular route from Devonport is via Sheffield (see p.1130) on the B14, then the C132 via Wilmot, and for the final stretch to Cradle Valley, the C136. One of the most glaciated areas in Australia, with many lakes and tarns, the park covers some of Tasmania's highest land, with craggy mountain peaks such as **Mount Ossa** (1617m), the state's highest point. At its northern end, **Dove Lake**, backed by the jagged outline of Cradle Mountain, is one of the state's most breathtaking sights, and at the park's southern end, Lake St Clair is the country's deepest freshwater lake at over 200m, occupying a basin gouged out by two glaciers. Between Cradle Mountain and Lake St Clair, the eighty-kilometre **Overland Track**, attracting walkers from all over the world, is the best way to take in the stunning scenery – spread over five or more mud- and leech-filled days of physical, albeit exhilarating, exhaustion. However, you can do just part of the walk, or make several other satisfying day-walks around Cradle Mountain or Lake St Clair (see pp.1144–1150).

Transport to the park

TassieLink services both ends of the national park on two year-round **scheduled routes**, while The Overland Track Summer Service provides more frequent transport from November to the end of April. A scheduled service from Launceston and Devonport to Queenstown goes via Cradle Mountain (Tues,

△ Cradle Mountain–Lake St Clair National Park

The Overland Track

In summer, hundreds flock here to walk the **Overland Track**, probably Australia's greatest extended bushwalk: 80km, unbroken by roads and passing through buttongrass plains, fields of wild flowers, and forests of deciduous beech, Tasmanian myrtle, pandanus and King Billy pine, with side-walks leading to views of waterfalls and lakes and starting points for climbs of the various mountain peaks. Much of the track is boardwalked, but you'll still end up thigh-deep in mud. Along the route are nine basic stove-heated huts (not for cooking – bring your own stove), with composting toilets outside. There's no guarantee there'll be space, so you should carry a good tent; a warm sleeping bag is essential even in the heated huts in summer.

The direct walk generally takes six days – five, if you catch a boat from Narcissus Hut across Lake St Clair; if you want to go on some of the side-walks, allow eight to ten days. On average, most walkers go for six to eight days. You should take enough food and fuel, plus extra supplies in case you have an accident or bad weather sets in; there's always plenty of unpolluted fresh water to drink from streams. Around 8000 people walk the track each year; most people come between November and April, but the best time is during February and March when the weather has stabilized, though it's bound to rain at some point, and may even snow. The track is at its most crowded from Christmas to the end of January. Most people walk north to south, which is more downhill than up, but you can register at either end in the **national park offices** (see below and p.1150), where you receive an obligatory briefing and have your gear checked to make sure it's sufficient; if you haven't already got some sort of park pass, you'll have to purchase one. The office sells last-minute camping gear and supplies: fuel stoves, meths, water bottles, trowels, warm hats and gloves. The *Cradle Mountain–Lake St Clair National Park* **map** and notes ($4.40) is an essential purchase, and the *Overland Track Walkers Notebook* ($9.90) is a handy reference. Once you end up at Derwent Bridge, exhausted and covered in mud, you can use the hot showers at the campsite, for which there's a small charge.

The logistics of doing a one-way walk are smoothed by a couple of operators: Maxwell's Coaches can do **transfers** to get you back to your car, while TassieLink has special Overland Track fares that include transfers from Launceston to Cradle Mountain, and then back from Lake St Clair to Launceston ($95) or Hobart ($66). They can provide baggage transfer for an extra charge. **Guided tours** are available, the best offered by Craclair Tours (Oct–April; 8 days $1350, 10 days $1630; ☎03/6424 7833, ⊛www.southcom.com.au/~craclair); you'll still have to camp (except for comfortable cabin accommodation at the start and end) and carry a six-kilo pack, however. The easiest option is to go on a guided walk staying along the track at *Cradle Huts*, **private lodges** with hot showers, beds and delicious meals (6 days $1895 full board departing and returning Launceston; ☎03/6331 2006, ⊛www.cradlehuts.com.au).

Thurs & Sat; connecting with a Queenstown to Strahan service), while the scheduled Hobart–Strahan service takes the Lyell Highway to Lake St Clair (Tues, Thurs, Fri, Sat & Sun). A daily Launceston to Cradle Mountain summer service runs via Deloraine, Sheffield and Devonport. A Hobart to Lake St Clair summer service via Mount Field National Park runs daily. You can also try Maxwell's Coaches charter service (☎03/6492 1431), which connects Devonport and Launceston to Lake St Clair ($70), and Launceston and Devonport to Cradle Mountain ($40).

Cradle Mountain

At **Cradle Mountain**, the impressive modern **Cradle Mountain Visitor Centre** (daily 8am–5pm, later in summer; ☎03/6492 1133) provides information on the many day-walks available in this area of the park, and acts as a registration point for the Overland Track; it's worth buying the *Cradle Mountain Day Walk Map* ($4.05) for more information. You can start here with a gentle ten-minute boardwalk circuit through rainforest and overlooking **Pencil Pine Falls**, ideal for wheelchairs or strollers. There's also the "Enchanted Walk" that follows the creek through rainforest to *Cradle Mountain Lodge* (1km one-way; 20min). Five kilometres into the park from the visitor centre, **Waldheim** ("Forest Home" in German), is the King Billy pine chalet built by the Austrian-Australian **Gustave Weindorfer** in 1912, and now a museum (open 24hr; free) devoted to the man who loved this wilderness area and helped to have it declared a national park; a fifteen-minute forest walk from the hut shows examples of ancient King Billy pine. Near the hut, there's a cosy heated day shelter where you can also picnic. From **Dove Lake car park**, 2.5km on from Waldheim, you can take the Dove Lake circuit (2–3hr), an easy all-weather walk around the shore of the lake, or a popular, but steep and strenuous, day-walk from here to the summit of **Cradle Mountain** (6hr return; get advice from the ranger first). If you're feeling lazy, you can opt for a **scenic flight** (weather permitting) over the area with Seaair (from $110 for 25min, minimum 3 people; helicopter from $150 for 50min with a landing at Fury Gorge with 20min on the ground, minimum 4 people; ⊤03/6492 1132, ⓦwww.seaairac.com.au), which is based by the *Cradle Wilderness Cafe* (see below). Further on from the café, at *Doherty's Cradle Mountain Hotel* (see overleaf), the $2-million, nine-room **Wilderness Gallery** (daily 10am–5pm; $5) opened in early 2003; it features landscape photography – of Tasmania, Antartica and the Pacific – from well-known and emerging local and international nature photographers, including the late, great Tasmanian, **Peter Dombrovskis**.

Just on the edge of the national park, and within walking distance of the visitor centre, the wonderful *Cradle Mountain Lodge* (⊤03/6492 1303, ⓦwww.poresorts.com; cabins ❼) is the focus for **accommodation**, eating and drinking. It's definitely worth considering staying here as a treat after finishing the Overland Track. Scattered through the bush around the lodge are 96 luxurious serviced timber cabins, all with log fires and bathrooms (no cooking facilities but microwaves on request). At the lodge itself, guest facilities include lounges, a sauna – with a window providing bush views – a massage room ($50 for 30min) and free movies shown each night. Guided walks into the national park are available daily (1.30pm; $25, shorter walks $6) Nonguests can book in to eat at the classy **restaurant** (the buffet-style breakfast is well worth the cost – $24.50 full buffet and is included in the guest rate), or drop in to eat or drink at the cosy tavern **bar**. You can rent **bicycles** from the lodge ($15 half-day) and there's a **general store** selling expensive groceries. In the national park there are eight basic self-catering **huts** (❹–❺) at Waldheim (see above), which sleep four to eight people with generator electricity, pot-bellied stoves, no fridge or power points, and a shared amenities block – these are looked after by the National Park Visitor Centre. There's more accommodation at the cute *Cradle Mountain Highlander Cabins*, 1.5km from the park entrance on Cradle Mountain Road (⊤03/6492 1116, ⓕ6492 1188; ❺–❻). The newer *Cradle Mountain Wilderness Village*, next door, has a more antiseptic feel (⊤03/6492 1018, ⓦwww.cradlevillage.com.au; ❻). Nearby, the licensed fast-food/bistro-style *Cradle Wilderness Cafe* also sells petrol and diesel (daily 8.30am–8pm, to 10.30pm in summer). *Cradle Mountain Tourist Park* (⊤03/6492 1395, ⓦwww.cosycabins.com/cradle), another half-kilometre back along Cradle Mountain Road, has a **campsite**, two hostel-style heated **bunkhouses** (dorms $22; bedding $6) sharing kitchen, toilet and washing facilities with the campers, and some basic huts (**❸**), plus well set-up cabins sleeping up to six (**❹**), complete with TV and air conditioning. The campsite has a small **shop** and is linked to the lodge in summer by a shuttle bus. A little further on, the brand-new, four-and-a-half star *Doherty's Cradle Mountain Hotel* (℡03/6492 1404, ⓦwww.dohertyhotels.com.au; **❻–❼**), has ground-floor rooms in two adjoining guest wings, casual and upmarket restaurants, a bar serving snacks, a billiard room, tour desk, and an impressive photographic gallery directly opposite (see p.1149).

Lake St Clair and Derwent Bridge

You can register to walk the Overland Track in the opposite direction at the ranger station at **CYNTHIA BAY** on **Lake St Clair** (daily 8am–5pm; ℡03/6289 1115), which houses an informative interpretive centre and an attractive bistro restaurant with views over the lake. Short and long **walks** around Lake St Clair are detailed on a board in the centre. You can go on a **cruise** on the MV *Idaclair*, which will drop you off at Narcissus Hut to begin the Overland Track from the southern end, or you can walk back to the centre (5–6hr); alternatively, get off at Echo Point and return on a three-hour bushwalk (summer: Cynthia Bay 9am, 12.30pm & 3pm; Narcissus Hut 9.30am, 1pm & 3.30pm; in winter the ferry runs on demand; round-trip 1hr 30min; $20 oneway, $25 return). Tickets (bookings essential) are sold at the restaurant, where you can also rent dinghies with outboard motors, canoes, kayaks and bicycles.

The restaurant also takes bookings for **accommodation**. *Lakeside St Clair Wilderness Holidays* (℡03/6289 1137, ⓦwww.view.com.au/lakeside; **❺–❻**) has several expensive lodges, and also a backpackers' lodge (dorms $25). Compared to Cradle Mountain, the **campsite** here is poor – there's no kitchen and there's a $0.50 fee to use the showers. For supplies (and takeaway alcohol), you have to go to **DERWENT BRIDGE**, 5km away on the Lyell Highway, served by Maxwell's Coaches (℡03/6289 1125), whose shuttle service ($9) runs on demand. At Derwent Bridge you can stay in luxurious, self-catering units sleeping four to eight at *Derwent Bridge Chalets* (℡03/6289 1000, ⓦwww.view.com.au/dbchalets; B&B **❺**), where you'll be greeted by a welcoming fire, complimentary port and a friendly, considerate host. The focus of the small community is the *Derwent Bridge Wilderness Hotel* (℡03/6289 1144, ⓕ6289 1173; **❹**), where you can stay in old-fashioned, lodge-style accommodation or very basic hostel rooms (dorms $22; no kitchen) out back; there's excellent **food** and drink here too. Derwent Bridge is close to **Lake King William**, equivalent in size to Lake St Clair and popular with anglers.

Franklin Lower Gordon Wild Rivers National Park

The **Franklin Lower Gordon Wild Rivers National Park** was declared in June 1980 and by 1982 had been included with the adjoining parks on the World Heritage List. The park exists for its own sake more than anything, most of it being virtually inaccessible. You can cruise up the Gordon, or fly over it, but the really adventurous can explore by **rafting the Franklin** (see box on p.1152) and walking the **Frenchmans Cap Track**, both accessible from the **Lyell Highway**, which extends from Strahan to Hobart and runs through the park between Queenstown and Derwent Bridge. Plenty of short **walks** also lead from the highway to rainforest, rivers and lookouts.

The **Franklin River** is one of the great rivers of Australia, and the only major wild river system in Tasmania that's not been dammed. It flows for

120km from the Cheyne Range to the majestic **Gordon River**, from an altitude of 1400m down to almost sea level. Swollen by the storms of the Roaring Forties and fed by many other rivers, it can at times become a raging torrent as it passes through ancient heaths, deep gorges and rainforests. The discovery in 1981 of stone tools in the **Kutikina Cave** on the lower Franklin has proved that during the last Ice Age southwest Tasmania was the most southerly point of human occupation on earth.

A **seaplane** from Strahan flies over the national park (see p.1145), and from it you can see the confluence of the two rivers – the planned site of the ill-fated dam – surrounded by thick forest, much of it impenetrable and probably never traversed by humans. The Gordon appears wide and slow compared to the narrow, winding Franklin.

Along the Lyell Highway

Heading east from Queenstown, the Lyell Highway enters the Franklin Lower Gordon Wild Rivers National Park, reaching Nelson River bridge after 4km, from where **Nelson Falls** is an easy twenty-minute return walk through temperate rainforest. From here, the road begins to wind and rise up to **Collingwood River**, the starting point for raft or canoe trips down the Franklin (see box overleaf), with some basic camping facilities.

In fine weather, the white-quartzite dome of Frenchmans Cap, looking a little like snow, can be seen from the highway. For a more spectacular viewpoint that takes in the Franklin River Valley, **Donaghy's Hill Wilderness Lookout Walk** begins further along the highway on the right. Walk from the parking area along the old road to the top of the hill, where a sign marks the beginning of the forty-minute return track. Further along the highway, the **walking track to Frenchmans Cap** (see below) begins with a fifteen-minute stroll to the suspension bridge over the river. Continuing on the Lyell, you have another opportunity to see the Franklin on a ten-minute **Nature Trail**, at a point where the river is tranquil, as it flows around large boulders; there's also a longer 25-minute circuit. At the start of the trail there's a picnic area and a wooden shelter with an **interpretive board** about the river. Beyond this point, open buttongrass plains take over, huge uninhabited expanses fringed with trees. This is **Wombat Glen**, which looks as though it's been cleared into grazing country until you step out into it and discover its bog-like nature.

At the foot of **Mount Arrowsmith**, the highway begins to ascend, winding around the mountain's southern side above the U-shaped glacial Surprise Valley. The **Surprise Valley Lookout** offers a good view of the valley and, across to the southwest, another excellent aspect of Frenchmans Cap. Continuing down, you come to King William Saddle, another fine lookout point with views of the **King William Range** to the south and **Mount Rufus** to the north.

The Frenchmans Cap Track

The most prominent mountain peak in the Franklin Lower Gordon Wild Rivers National Park is the white-quartzite dome of **Frenchmans Cap** (1443m). Its southeast face has a sheer five-hundred-metre cliff and from its summit there are uninterrupted views of Mount Ossa in the Cradle Mountain–Lake St Clair National Park, Federation Peak, Macquarie Harbour and, on a fine day, the whole of the southwest wilderness. It takes three to five days to do the 54-kilometre return trip to the summit, best done between December and March, though you'll be in the company of another nine hundred or so people. Frenchmans Cap

One of the most rugged and inaccessible areas left on earth, the surrounds of the Franklin River can't really be seen on foot – few tracks lead through this twisted, tangled and wet rainforest. **Rafting** is the only way to explore the river and even this is possible only between December and early April. The Franklin is reached by rafting down the Collingwood River from the Lyell Highway, 49km west of Derwent Bridge. The full trip takes eight to fourteen days, ending at the Gordon River, where rafters head finally to Strahan by yacht from Heritage Landing or by seaplane from Sir John Falls Camp.

One of the most dangerous Australian rivers to raft, with average **rapids** of grades 3 to 4 – and up to grade 6 in places – the Franklin requires an expedition leader with great skill and experience (though even guides have died in the rapids). It's also very remote, and in the event of an accident help can be days away. However, this haunting isolation is part of the attraction for most visitors. The weather, too, can be harsh – and the water is cold. It's inadvisable to attempt the trip **independently** unless everyone in the party has white-water experience and the group leader has made a previous Franklin River trip; groups are required to have at least two rafts and to stay in contact with the **ranger** at Queenstown. Bear in mind that there's nowhere to rent rafting equipment in Tasmania. The **tour operators** don't require you to be experienced – just fit, with lots of stamina and courage. Prices are high, but this is an experience of a lifetime, with the seaplane flight back to Strahan included in the price. The one Tasmanian-based licensed operator is **Rafting Tasmania** (☎03/6239 1080, ⓦ www.tasmanianadventures.com.au). The others are based in Melbourne: Peregrine Adventures (☎03/9662 2800); and Sydney: World Expeditions (☎02/9264 3366). For the shorter four-day trip from Propsting Gorge to the Gordon, expect to pay around $1045; for the full ten-day trip from the Collingwood to the Gordon prices start at $1800.

The sketchy *Franklin River Rafting Notesheets* are available free from the Queenstown Ranger Station, PO Box 21, Queenstown, TAS 7467 (☎03/6471 2511) or you can download a copy from the internet (ⓦ www.parks.tas.gov.au). There are **campsites** all along the Franklin, but most have room for only two or three tents.

The route

From the **Collingwood River**, it takes about three days to raft to the **Frenchmans Cap Track**. This is the **Upper Franklin**, alpine country with vegetation adapted to survive snow and icy winds. Watch out for two endemic pines, the **Huon pine** and **celery top pine**. There are lots of intermediate rapids along this stretch and a deep quartzite ravine and large still pool at Irenabyss.

The **Middle Franklin** is a mixture of pools, deep ravines and wild rapids as the river makes a fifty-kilometre detour around Frenchmans Cap. Dramatic **limestone cliffs** overhang the **Lower Franklin**, which involves a tranquil paddle through dense myrtle beech forests with flowering leatherwoods overhead. The best raftable white water is here at Newlands Cascades. It's a short distance to **Kutikina Caves** and **Deena-reena**; only rafters can gain access to these Aboriginal caves.

is much more demanding than the relatively straightforward Overland Track, as it has some very steep extended climbs and sections of mud, and should be attempted only by skilled bushwalkers – preferably with experience of other Tasmanian walks. The weather is temperamental: it rains frequently, and it can snow even in summer. Beyond Barron Pass, the track is above 900m and at any time of the year is subject to high winds, mist, rain, hail and snowfalls.

The track begins at the Lyell Highway, 55km from Queenstown, served by TassieLink's scheduled Hobart–Queenstown service (1 daily Tues, Thurs, Fri,

Sat & Sun), or you can charter Maxwell's Coaches (☏03/6492 1431) for $65 from Lake St Clair. A fifteen-minute walk from the road brings you to the suspension bridge across the river for the start of the walk. Record your plans in the registration book here and again in the logbook at the two **huts** at Lake Vera and Lake Tahune that provide basic accommodation (though this is usually full and you must bring tents and stoves with you); Frenchmans Cap is a proclaimed "Fuel Stove Only Area". There are composting toilets at both huts and plenty of camping spots along the way; water along the track is safe to drink. From the Franklin River to Lake Vera the well-defined track crosses plains and foothills, then becomes steep and rough as it climbs to Barron Pass – where there are magnificent views – becoming easier again on the way to Lake Tahune, close to the cliffs of Frenchmans Cap. From here it's a steep one-kilometre walk to the summit, before returning the same way.

For further **information**, get the free *Frenchmans Cap Track Bushwalker Notes* from Service Tasmania, 134 Macquarie St, Hobart 7000; you can also buy the *Frenchmans Cap Map and Notes* ($9.10) there; or contact the Queenstown Ranger Station (☏03/6471 2511). If you don't feel equipped to tackle the walk independently, contact Craclair Tours (see box on p.1148), which organizes seven-day guided treks (ex-Devonport $1260), or Tasmanian Expeditions offers a five-day trip (see p.1114; ex-Launceston; $860).

The South West National Park

Tasmania's **southwest** is an area of contrast: arrow-sharp, crested ranges of white quartzite cut across buttongrass plains. The isolation, rough terrain and unpredictable weather, even in summer – the southwest has more than two hundred days of rain a year – means that this is an area for experienced bushwalkers only. Being able to use a compass and read a map are important, but so is a tolerance for trudging through deep mud and swampy buttongrass while heavily laden with supplies and plagued by leeches.

The map *South Coast Walks* ($9.10) covers the southern gateways to the World Heritage Area: Cockle Creek through Port Davey to Scotts Peak, as well as Moonlight Ridge and South West Cape, including notes on track conditions, weather and campsites. For the rest of the area you'll need to purchase Tasmap topographic **maps**.

Two airlines operate **flights** into the national park from Cambridge aerodrome, 15km from Hobart. **Par Avion** (☏03/6248 5390, ⊛www .paravion.com.au) runs eighty percent of flights to the southwest, with a twice daily service to Melaleuca, weather permitting (45min; $145 one way, $265 return); you can register your walk at the airstrip. They also offer a scenic flight over the southwest ($135), a combined scenic flight and cruise on Melaleuca Inlet (4hr; $170) or Bathurst Harbour (full day; $275 including lunch). Par Avion also owns a luxury boat, the MV *Southern Explorer*, based on Bathurst Harbour with on-board accommodation, which cruises the harbour, Port Davey and the Davey River (2 days, 2 nights from $1155). You can also stay overnight at the **Wilderness Camp** on kayaking expeditions with Roaring 40s Ocean Kayaking (details ☏03/6267 5000, ⊛www.roaring40skayaking.com.au). **TasAir** (☏03/6248 5088, ⊛www.tasair.com) flies to Melaleuca or Cox Bight (both $150 one-way, $300 return), which can cut out the trudge from Melaleuca, and also offers joyrides over the whole of the World Heritage Area for $176 (2hr 30min, includes a landing and refreshment at Cox Bight). If you're planning an extended walk, you can arrange for either airline to drop food supplies for you ($2.20 per kilo).

The flooding of Lake Pedder

To Senator Bob Brown, Tasmania's foremost Green activist, **Lake Pedder** "was one of the most gently beautiful places on the planet". The glacial lake, in the Frankland Range in Tasmania's southwest, had an area of 9.7 square kilometres until 1972, when it and the surrounding valleys were flooded as part of a huge hydroelectric scheme, creating a reservoir covering a massive 240 square kilometres and reached by the Lake Gordon Road via Maydena. Before then, the lake was so inaccessible that it could only be visited by light aircraft, which used to land on the perfect sand of the lake beach. In late 1994 a scientist revealed that, beneath the water, the sandy beach remained; in 1995 divers filmed underwater, revealing the still-visible impressions of light-aircraft tyre tracks. Certain scientists and conservationists, backed by the Wilderness Society, believe if Lake Pedder were drained it would revert to its former state, though it might take up to thirty years.

Unless you're flying in, or beginning a walk at **Cockle Creek** (see p.1086), south of Hobart, access to the South West National Park is via the **Gordon River Road,** which passes to the south of Mount Field National Park. The ranger for this (northern) end of South West National Park is based at Mount Field (see p.1089) and you should drop in or call to ask about conditions and to check that you're adequately prepared. The good sealed road heads through state forest and the South West Conservation Area, where the amazing craggy landforms of the **Frankland Range** loom above and signposts helpfully point out the names of the features, and past the drowned **Lake Pedder** (see box, above) and the Gordon Dam's power station. The Hydro Tasmania-run **Gordon Dam Visitors Information Centre** is at the end of Gordon River Road, above the dam (Nov–April daily 10am–5pm; May–Oct 11am–3pm; ☎03/6280 1134). The Gordon Dam lookout here is breathtaking, and if you're after a thrill you can **abseil** down it with Aardvark Adventures (☎0408 127 714, ⓦwww.aardvarkadventures.com.au), which runs day-tours from Hobart ($165 including lunch).

You can **stay** at Lake Pedder at the recently refurbished *Lake Pedder Chalet* (☎03/6280 1166, ⓕ6280 1145; shared-bathroom or en-suite rooms ❷–❹), a former staff house for the HEC that has lake views; facilities include a bar and bistro. Alternatively there are a number of free **campsites** in the area: just down the road on the shore of Lake Pedder, *Ted's Beach* has a sheltered kitchen area, electric barbecues, water and toilets; or there are two more campgrounds at Scotts Peak at the southern end of Lake Pedder, where the Port Davey walk begins (see opposite). TassieLink runs a "Wilderness Link" service to Scotts Peak and to Condominium Creek from Hobart, via Mount Field (Dec–April).

Western Arthurs Traverse and Federation Peak

The most spectacular bushwalk in Tasmania, only 20km in length and 5km in width, **Western Arthurs Traverse** contains 25 major peaks and 30 lakes. The last glacial period gouged into this range, leaving sharp quartzite ridges, craggy towers and impressive cliffs, and carving cirque valleys that are now filled by dark, tannin-stained lakes, surrounded by contrasting buttongrass plains. Violent storms, mists and continuous rain can plague the route in summer since it's in the direct path of the Roaring Forties. Crossing these ranges makes for a superb but difficult walk. Though there's no man-made track, the route, starting at Scotts Peak Road, is not difficult to follow; it involves scrambling over roots and branches and making short descents and ascents into gullies and cliff lines, and you'll need to use a rope at some point. The whole walk takes between nine and twelve days, and camping areas are limited.

The **Eastern Arthur Range** is the location of the major goal for intrepid southwest walkers – **Federation Peak**, often considered the most challenging in Australia, with its steep, almost perfectly triangular outline rising starkly above the surrounding rugged peaks and ridges. It was named by a surveyor in 1901, the year of federation, when most of the major landmarks in the southwest were still unvisited; in fact, the peak was not successfully scaled until 1949, its thick scrub, forests and cliffs having kept walkers at bay. Although the walk is now easier since the terrain has been "broken in", each year many walkers are turned back by the worst weather in Tasmania, and one person has died tackling the route. All the ascents are extremely difficult, and most parties take between seven and ten days to reach the peak and return; minor rock climbing is required to get to the summit. The walk begins at the same point as the Port Davey Track (see below).

Mount Anne Circuit

The highest peak in the southwest, **Mount Anne** (1423m) is part of a small range capped with red dolerite – a contrast to the surrounding white quartzite. Views from the summit are spectacular in fine weather, but even in summer the route is very exposed and prone to bad weather. It's suitable only for experienced walkers carrying a safety rope. The three- to four-day walk begins 20km along Scotts Peak Road at Condominium Creek (where there are basic camping facilities) and ends 9km south at Red Tape Creek; a car shuttle might be advisable, or you can arrange with TassieLink to be picked up and dropped off from Hobart.

Port Davey Track

Going straight through the heart of the World Heritage Area, from Scotts Peak Dam south to Melaleuca (where you fly out, see p.1153), is the 54-kilometre **Port Davey Track**, a wet, muddy four- to five-day trek over buttongrass plains, with views of rugged mountain ranges along the way. Only around 200 people walk the track each year. It's less interesting than some of the other walks in the area and most groups combine it with the **South Coast Track** (see below) for a ten- to sixteen-day wilderness experience, which requires a drop-off of food supplies. This combined walk is often called the **South West Track**. Contact TassieLink if you want to arrange drop-offs.

South Coast Track

The **South Coast Track** is known for its magnificent **beaches** and spectacular coastal scenery of Aboriginal **middens**, rainforest and buttongrass ridges. At 80km, it's one of the longest tracks in the South West National Park – a five-to ten-day moderate to difficult walk, usually done from Melaleuca east to Cockle Creek. Since the route is mostly along the coast, the climate is milder than in many parts of the World Heritage Area; however, you'll still need wet-weather gear as it tends to rain frequently. Though the track is regularly maintained, you do need to plough through sections of mud and across the exposed Ironbound Range (900m), which should be attempted only in fine weather. There are no huts along the way, except at the Melaleuca airstrip. Around 2000 people do the walk each year, 75 percent of them between December and March. The best **approach** is to fly direct to Cox Bight with TasAir, cutting out the boring buttongrass plains walk from Melaleuca, then head for Cockle Creek. Alternatively, you can begin at Cockle Creek and fly out at Melaleuca with TasAir or Par Avion, or arrange for extra food supplies to be flown in at Melaleuca and continue along the Port Davey Track across the water, using the rowboats provided.

Tasmanian Expeditions (☎03/6334 3477, ⓦwww.tasmanianexpeditions .com.au) runs an extended **organized walk** of the South Coast Track (Nov–March; $1450). You need to be very fit for the nine-day trip, as each party member (maximum of ten) carries a share of the food and tents, a weight of 18–20kg.

South West Cape

The granite South West Cape juts out for 3km into the wild Southern Ocean. **Walking** is fairly easy here, though the rough unmarked tracks across open countryside require sound navigation, and some high windy ridges have to be crossed. All routes start and end at Melaleuca or Cox Bight but there are a variety of ways to the cape and beyond, taking in different beaches and bays. Depending on which you choose, a simple route will take from three to seven days, and the full circuit between six and nine. Because of the growing popularity of the walks, they may be overcrowded in the summer months.

Travel details

Between Tasmania and the mainland states

Ferries

Spirit of Tasmania I & II Bass Strait ferry from Port Melbourne to Devonport (daily 9pm arriving 7am, either direction; extra peak-period day sailings depart 9am and arrive 7pm; 10hr).

Flights

Mainly through Sydney's Mascot or Melbourne's Tullamarine airports, with smaller companies operating from Essendon airport, on the fringes of Melbourne.

Flinders Island to: Launceston (2–4 daily; 45min); Melbourne (Essendon 4 weekly; 50min).
King Island to: Burnie (3 daily Mon–Fri, 2 daily Sat & Sun; 45min); Devonport (4 daily Mon–Fri, 2 daily Sat & Sun; 45min); Melbourne (Tullamarine 5 weekly; 45min).
Melbourne to: Burnie (4 daily; 1hr); Devonport (4 daily, 1hr); Flinders Island (Essendon 4 weekly; 50min); Hobart (10 daily; 1hr); King Island (Tullamarine 5 weekly; 45min); Launceston (10 daily; 1hr).
Sydney to: Hobart (4–7 daily; 2hr 20min); Launceston (1–3 daily; 2hr 35min).

Transport on the island

Buses

We have only included scheduled services in this list. Extra "Wilderness" services, which need a minimum of four people to depart, are provided by TassieLink to all bushwalking destinations, and some operate in the summer only. These are all detailed in the text of the Guide.
Burnie to: Smithton via the northwest coast (1–3 daily Mon–Sat, 1 daily Sun; 1hr 30min).
Deloraine to: Devonport (3 daily; 40min); Hobart (2–4 daily; 4hr); Launceston (3–5 daily; 45min).

Devonport to: Burnie (3–6 daily; 50min); Cradle Mountain (3 weekly; 2hr 15min); Deloraine (3 daily; 40min); Hobart (2–4 daily; 5hr 30min); Launceston (3–5 daily; 1hr 30min); Queenstown (3 weekly; 7hr).
Hobart to: Bicheno (3–6 weekly; 4hr); Burnie (3–6 daily; 4hr 45min); Cygnet (3 on Thurs, 1 daily rest of week; 55min); Deloraine (2–4 daily; 4hr); Devonport (2–4 daily; 5hr 30min); Dover (2 daily Mon–Fri; 55min); Geeveston (4 daily Mon–Fri, 1 daily Sun; 1hr 15min); Kettering (Mon–Fri 4 daily; 40min); Lake St Clair (4 weekly; 3hr); Launceston

(3–7 daily; 2hr 30min); New Norfolk (1–7 daily; 30min); Port Arthur (2 daily Mon–Fri; 2hr); Queenstown via New Norfolk, Lake St Clair and Frenchmans Cap with connections to Strahan (5 weekly; 7hr 45min); Richmond (5 daily Mon–Fri; 25min); St Helens (1–2 daily except Sat; 3hr); St Marys (1–2 daily except Sat; 3hr); Swansea (1–2 daily except Sat; 2hr 30min–3hr 30min).

Launceston to: Bicheno (3 daily except Sat; 2hr 40min); Burnie (3–6 daily; 3hr); Cradle Mountain (3 weekly; 4hr); Deloraine (2–5 daily; 45min); Derby (1–2 daily except Sat; 2hr 40min); Devonport (3–5 daily; 1hr 30min); Hobart (3–7 daily; 2hr 30min); Mole Creek (1 daily Mon–Fri;

1hr 30min); Queenstown (3 weekly; 7hr); St Helens via St Marys (1 daily except Sat; 2hr 45min).
Queenstown to: Strahan (5 weekly; 45 min).
Scottsdale to: Bridport (2 daily Mon–Fri; 30 min).

Ferries

Beauty Point to: George Town (2–3 daily Mon–Sat, 2 daily Sun; 15–20min).
Bridport to: Flinders Island (1 weekly; 8hr).
Kettering to: Bruny Island (10–11 daily Mon–Sat, 8 daily Sun; 20min).
Triabunna to: Maria Island (2 daily; 45min).

11

Contexts

Contexts

History

The first European settlers saw Australia as *terra nullius* – empty land – on the principle that Aborigines didn't "use" the country in an agricultural sense, a belief which remained uncontested in law until 1992. However, decades of archeological work, the reports of early settlers and oral tradition have established a minimum date of forty thousand years for human occupation, and evidence that Aboriginal peoples shaped, controlled and used their environment as surely as any farmer. Even so, it's difficult for visitors to form a unified idea of pre-colonial times, as two centuries of European rule shattered traditional Aboriginal life, and evidence of those earlier times mostly consists of cryptic art sites and legends – though if you're lucky enough to get beyond the tourist image, you'll realize that Aboriginal culture, though being redefined, is far from confined to the past. The very simplified outline of Aboriginal history below is intended mainly as a background to accounts given in the Guide, followed by a fuller description of the years since European colonization.

From Gondwana to the Dreamtime

After the break-up of the supercontinent **Gondwana** into India, Africa, South America, Australasia and Antarctica, Australia moved away from the South Pole, reaching its current geographical location about fifteen million years ago. Though the mainland was periodically joined to New Guinea and Tasmania, there was never a land link with the rest of Asia, and the country developed a unique fauna – most notably the marsupials, or pouched mammals, but also a whole range of giant animals, the megafauna – which flourished, along with widespread rainforests, until about fifty thousand years ago. Subsequent Ice Ages dried out the climate, and though some of the megafauna survived into Aboriginal times, by six thousand years ago the seas had stabilized at their present levels and Australia's environment was much as it appears today: an arid centre with a relatively fertile eastern seaboard.

Humans had been in Australia long before then, of course, most likely taking advantage of low sea levels to cross the Timor Trough into northern Australia, or island-hop from Indonesia onto what is now the Cape York Peninsula via New Guinea. Exactly when this happened, how many times it happened and what the colonists did next are debatable. There's no direct evidence for either distinct or continuous migrations from Asia, but since the earliest dated sites are found in the south of Australia, it seems reasonable that human occupation goes back further than scientists' current forty-thousand-year estimates. The oldest known remains from central Australia are only 22,000 years old, so it's also fairly plausible that initial colonization occurred around the coast, followed by later exploration of the interior – though it's just as likely that corrosive rainforests, which covered the centre until about twenty thousand years ago, obliterated all trace of earlier human habitation. The presence of the dingo and disappearance of the **thylacine** (Tasmanian tiger) on the mainland but not (until recently) in Tasmania indicates that there was a further influx of people and **dogs** more recently than twelve thousand years ago, after Tasmania had become an island.

The earliest inhabitants used crude **stone implements**, gradually replaced by a more refined technology based around lighter tools, **boomerangs**, and the use of core stones to flake "blanks" which were then fashioned into spearheads, knives and scrapers. As only certain types of stone were suitable for the process, tribes living away from quarries had to trade with those living near them. **Trade networks** for rock, **ochre** (a red clay used for ceremonial purposes) and other products – shells and even wood for canoes – eventually reached from New Guinea to the heart of the continent, following river systems away from the coast. **Rock art**, preserved in an ancient engraved tradition and more recent painted styles, seems to indicate that cultural links also travelled along these trade routes – similar symbols and styles are found in widely separated regions.

It's probable that the disappearance of the megafauna was accelerated by Aboriginal hunting, but the most dramatic change wrought by the original Australians was the controlled use of **fire** to clear areas of forest. Burning promoted new growth and encouraged game, indirectly expanding grassland and favouring certain plants – cycads, grasstrees, banksias and eucalypts – which evolved fire-reliant seeds and growth patterns. But while the Aborigines modified the environment for their own ends, their belief that land, wildlife and people were an interdependent whole engendered a sympathy for the natural processes, and maintained a balance between population and natural resources. Tribes were organized and related according to complex kinship systems, reflected in the three hundred different **languages** known to exist at that time. Legends about the mythical **Dreamtime**, when creative forces shaped the landscape, provided verbal maps of tribal territory and linked natural features to the actions of these Dreamtime ancestors, who often had both human and animal forms. This spiritual and practical attachment to tribal areas was expedient in terms of use of resources, but was the weak point in maintaining a culture after white dispossession: separated from the lands they related to, legends lost their meaning – and the people their sense of identity.

The first Europeans

Prior to the sixteenth century, the only regular visitors to Australia were the **Malays**, who established seasonal camps while fishing the northern coasts for trepang, a sea slug, to sell to the Chinese. In Europe, the globe had been carved up between Spain and Portugal in 1494 under the auspices of Pope Alexander VI at the **Treaty of Tordesillas**, and all maritime nations subsequently kept their nautical charts secret to protect their discoveries. Therefore it's likely, but not certain, that the inquisitive **Portuguese** knew of **Terra Australis**, the Great Southern Land, soon after founding their colony in East Timor in 1516.

But while contemporary politics later confused the issue of "discovery", various nations were making forays into the area: the **Dutch** in 1605 and 1623, who were appalled by the harsh climate and inhabitants of Outback Queensland, and the **Spanish** in 1606, looking for plunder, and pagans to convert to Catholicism. Guided by the Portuguese **Luis Vaes de Torres**, they blithely navigated the strait between New Guinea and Cape York as if they knew it was there. Torres probably did; there's evidence that the Portuguese had **mapped** a large portion of Australia's northern coastline as early as 1536.

Later in the seventeenth century the Dutch navigators **Dirk Hartog**, **Van Diemen** and **Abel Tasman** added to maps of the east and north coasts, but eventually discarded "New Holland" as a barren, worthless country. British interests were first stirred in 1697 by **William Dampier**, a buccaneer who wrote popular accounts of his visit to Western Australia, but it wasn't until the British captured the Spanish port of Manila in the Philippines in 1762 that detailed maps of Australia's coast fell into their hands; it took them only six more years to assemble an expedition to locate the continent. Sailing in 1768 on the *Endeavour*, Captain **James Cook** headed to Tahiti, then proceeded to map New Zealand's coastline before sailing west in 1770 to search for the Great Southern Land – unsure whether this was New Holland or an as yet undiscovered landmass.

The British sighted the continent in April of 1770 and sailed north from Cape Everard to **Botany Bay**, where Cook commented on the Aborigines' initial indifference to seeing the *Endeavour*. When a party of forty sailors attempted to land, however, two Aborigines attacked them with spears and had to be driven off by musket fire. Continuing on up the Queensland coast, they passed Moreton Bay and Fraser Island before entering the treacherous passages of the Great Barrier Reef where, on June 11, the *Endeavour* ran aground off Cape Tribulation. Cook managed to beach the ship safely at the mouth of the Endeavour River (present-day Cooktown), where the expedition set up camp while the ship was repaired.

Contact between Aborigines and whites during the following six weeks was tinged with a mistrust that never quite erupted into a serious confrontation, and Cook took the opportunity to make notes in which he tempered romanticism for the "noble savage" with the sharp observation that European and Aboriginal values were mutually incomprehensible. The expedition was intrigued by some of the wildlife but otherwise unimpressed with the country, and were glad to sail onwards on August 5. With imposing skill, Cook successfully managed to navigate the rest of the reef, finally claiming possession of the country – which he named **New South Wales** – on August 21 for King George III at Possession Island in the Torres Strait, before sailing off to Timor.

Convicts

The expedition's reports still didn't arouse much enthusiasm in London, where echoes resounded of the Portuguese and Dutch opinions of the previous century. The outcome of the **American War of Independence** in 1783, however, saw Britain deprived of anywhere to transport convicted criminals; they were temporarily housed in prison ships or "hulks", moored around the country, while the government tried to solve the problem. Sir **Joseph Banks**, botanist on the *Endeavour*, advocated Botany Bay as an ideal location for a **penal colony** that could soon become self-sufficient. The government agreed (perhaps also inspired by the political advantages of gaining a foothold in the Pacific), and in 1787 the **First Fleet**, packed with over 700 convicts, set sail for Australia on eleven ships under the command of Captain **Arthur Phillip**. Reaching Botany Bay in January 1788, Phillip deemed it unsuitable for his purposes and instead founded the settlement at **Sydney Cove**, on Port Jackson's fine natural harbour.

Early years at Sydney were not promising: the colonists suffered erratic weather and starvation, Aboriginal hostility, soil which was too hard to plough and timber so tough it dented their axes. In 1790, supplies ran so low that a third of the population had to be transferred to a new colony on **Norfolk Island**, 1500 kilometres east. Even so, in the same year Britain dispatched a second fleet with 1000 convicts – 267 of whom died en route. To ease the situation, Phillip granted packages of farmland to marines and former convicts before he returned to Britain in 1792. The first **free settlers** arrived the following year, while war with France reduced the numbers of convicts being transported to the colony, allowing a period of consolidation.

Meanwhile, **John Macarthur** manipulated the temporary governor into allowing his **New South Wales Corps**, which had replaced the marines as the governor's strong arm, to exercise considerable power in the colony. This was temporarily curtailed in 1800 by **Philip King**, who slowed an illicit rum trade, encouraged new settlements, and speeded production by allowing convicts to work for wages. Macarthur was forced out of the corps into the wool industry, importing Australia's first **sheep** from South Africa; but he continued to stir up trouble, which culminated in the **Rum Rebellion** of 1808, when merchant and pastoral factions, supported by the military, ousted Governor **William Bligh** of "Mutiny on the *Bounty*" fame. Britain finally took notice of the colony's anarchic state and appointed the firm-handed Colonel **Lachlan Macquarie**, backed by the 73rd Regiment, as Bligh's replacement in 1810. Macquarie settled the various disputes – Macarthur had fled to Britain a year earlier – and brought the colony eleven years of disciplined progress.

Labelled the "Father of Australia" for his vision of a country that could rise above its convict origins, Macquarie implemented enlightened policies towards former convicts or **emancipists**, enrolling them in public offices. He also attempted to educate, rather than exterminate, Aboriginal people, and was the driving force behind New South Wales becoming a productive, self-sufficient colony. But he offended the landowner **squatters**, who were concerned that emancipists were being granted too many favours, and also those who regarded the colony's prime purpose as a place of punishment. In fact, conditions had improved so much that by 1819 New South Wales had become the major destination for voluntary emigrants from Britain.

In 1821 Macquarie was replaced as governor, and his successor, Sir Thomas Brisbane, was instructed to segregate, not integrate, convicts. To this end, New South Wales officially graduated from being a penal settlement to a new British colony in 1823, and convicts were used to colonize newly explored regions – Western Australia, Tasmania and Queensland – as far away from Sydney's free settlers as possible.

Explorers

Matthew Flinders had already circumnavigated the mainland in 1803 (suggesting the name "**Australia**") in his leaky vessel, *Investigator*, and with the colony firmly established, expeditions began pushing inland from Sydney. In 1823 John Oxley, the Surveyor General, having previously explored newly discovered pastoral land west of the Blue Mountains, chose the **Brisbane River** (in Queensland) as the site of a new penal colony; this opened up the fertile Darling Downs to future settlement. Meanwhile, townships were being founded elsewhere around the coast, eventually leading to the creation of **separate colonies** to add to that of Van Diemen's Land (Tasmania), settled in 1803 to ward off French exploration: Albany (1827) and Fremantle on the west coast (1829), the Yarra River (Melbourne, Victoria) in 1835, and Adelaide (South Australia) in 1836.

But it was the possibilities of the **interior** – which some maintained concealed a vast inland sea – that captured the imagination of the government and squatters. Setting out from Adelaide in 1844, **Charles Sturt** was the first to attempt to cross the centre. Forced to camp for six months at a desert waterhole, where the heat melted the lead in his pencils and unthreaded screws from equipment, he managed to reach the aptly named Sturt's Stony Desert before scurvy forced him back to Adelaide. At the same time, **Ludwig Leichhardt**, a Prussian doctor, had more luck in his crossing between the Darling Downs and Port Essington (near Darwin), which he accomplished in fourteen months. Unlike Sturt, Leichhardt found plenty of potential farmland and returned a hero; he vanished, however, in 1848 while again attempting to cross the continent. In the same year the ill-fated **Kennedy** expedition only just managed the trek from Tully to Cape York in northern Queensland, but with the loss of most of the party – Kennedy included – as a result of poor planning, starvation and attack by Aborigines. Similarly, **Burke and Wills'** successful 1860 south-to-north traverse between Melbourne and the Gulf of Carpentaria in Queensland was marred by the death of the expedition leaders (see box on p.575 for the full story of their trek). Finally, Australia's centre was located by **John MacDouall Stuart** in 1860, who subsequently managed a safe return journey to Adelaide from the north coast the following year. Hopes of finding an inland sea were quashed, and the harsh reality of a dry, largely infertile interior began to dawn on developers.

Aboriginal response

European advances had been repulsed from the very first year of the colony's foundation, when Governor Phillip sadly reported that "the natives now attack any straggler they meet unarmed". Forced off their traditional hunting grounds, which were taken by the settlers for agriculture or grazing, the Aborigines began stealing crops and spearing cattle. Response from the whites was brutal; a relatively liberal Lieutenant-Governor George Arthur ordered a sweep of Tasmania in 1830 to round up all Aboriginal people and herd them into **reserves**, a symbolic attempt to clear "the uncivilized" from the paths of progress (see box on p.1058). More direct action, such as the **Myall Creek Massacre** in 1838 (see box on p.333), when 28 Aborigines were roped together and butchered by graziers, created public outcry, but similar "**dispersals**" became commonplace wherever indigenous people resisted white intrusion. More insidious methods, such as poisoning waterholes or lacing gifts of flour with arsenic, were also employed by pastoralists angered over stock losses.

Aboriginal peoples were not a single, unified society, and Europeans exploited existing divisions by creating the notorious **Native Mounted Police**, an Aboriginal force that aided and abetted the extermination of rival groups. By the 1890s, citing a perversion of Darwinian theory which held that Aboriginal people were less evolved than whites and so doomed to extinction, most states had followed Tasmania's example of "**protectionism**", relocating survivors into reserves which were frequently far from traditional lands: in Queensland, for instance, Rockhampton Aborigines were moved to Fraser Island, 500km away.

Gold

The discovery of **gold** in 1851 by Edward Hargraves, fresh from the Californian fields, had a dramatic bearing on Australia's future. The first major strikes in New South Wales and Victoria saw an immediate rush of hopeful miners from Sydney and Melbourne and, once the news spread overseas, from the USA and Britain. The British government, realizing the absurdity of spending taxes on shipping criminals to a land of gold when there were plenty of people willing to pay for their passage, finally **ended transportation** in 1853. Gold also opened up Australia's interior far more thoroughly than explorers had done; as returns petered out in one area, prospectors moved on into uncharted regions to find more. Western Australia and Queensland (which was saved from bankruptcy by gold in 1867) experienced booms up until 1900 and, while mining initially followed in the path of pastoral expansion, rushes began to attract settlements and markets into previously uncultivated regions.

A new "level society", based on a work-and-mateship ethic, evolved on the goldfields, where education had little bearing on an ability to endure hard work and spartan living conditions. Yet the **diggers** were all too aware of their poor social and political rights in other arenas. At the end of 1854, frustrations over mining licences erupted at **Eureka** (see box on p.1000), on the outskirts of Ballarat in Victoria, where miners built a stockade and ended up being charged by mounted police. Twenty-two of the miners were killed in the event, which is commonly regarded as a turning point in Australian history. The surviving rebels, put on trial for high treason, were vindicated and rights, including the vote, were granted to miners. The Victorian goldfields also saw **racial tensions** directed against a new minority – the Chinese – who first arrived there during the 1850s. Disheartened by diminishing returns and infuriated by the Chinese ability to find gold in abandoned claims, diggers stormed a Chinese camp at **Lambing Flat** in 1861. Troops had to be sent in to stop the riots, but the ringleaders were acquitted by an all-white jury. Throughout the country, goldfields became centres of **nationalism** (despite the fact that the Chinese improved life by running stores and market gardens in mining towns), peaking in Queensland in the 1880s where the flames were fanned by the importation of **Solomon Islanders** to work on sugar plantations. Ostensibly to prevent slavery, but politically driven by recession and growing white unemployment, the government forced the repatriation of Islanders, taxed the Chinese out of the country, and passed the 1901 Immigration Act – also known as the **White Australia policy** – greatly restricting non-European immigration.

Federation and war

Central government was first mooted in 1842, but new states were not keen to return to being controlled by New South Wales, lose interstate customs duties, or share the new-found mineral wealth which had consolidated separation in the first place. But by the end of the century they began to see advantages to **federation**, not least as a way to control indentured labour and present a united front against French, German and Russian expansion in the Pacific. A decade of wrangling by the states, to ensure equal representation irrespective of population, saw the formation of a High Court and a two-tier parliamentary system consisting of a House of Representatives and Senate, presided over by a Prime Minister. Each state would have its own premier, and Britain would be represented by a Governor-General. Approved by Queen Victoria shortly before her death, the **Commonwealth of Australia** came into being on January 1, 1901.

It's notable that the Immigration Act (see opposite) was the first piece of legislation to be passed by the new parliament, and reflected the nationalist drive behind federation. Though the intent was to create an Australia largely of European – and preferably British – descent, the policy also sowed the seeds for Australian independence from the "Mother Country". The first pull away came as early as 1912, when the **Commonwealth Bank** opened; Australia was trying to become less financially reliant on Britain. Centred entirely on white interests, the White Australia policy ensured that Aboriginal people were not included in the national census, or even allowed to vote until 1967. The new government did, however, give **women** the vote in 1902, and the Australian Labor Party, which had grown out of the Depression and union battles with the government during the 1890s, established the concept of a **minimum wage** in 1907.

Defence had also been a moving force behind federation. But, even forewarned by the war between Japan and Russia in 1904, Australia was largely unprepared for the outbreak of hostilities in Europe a decade later, owning little more than a navy made up from secondhand British ships. Promising to support Britain to "the last man and the last shilling", there was a patriotic rush to enlist in the army, and an opportunistic occupation of German New Guinea by Australian forces. Surprisingly, the issue of compulsory conscription raised by Prime Minister **Billy Hughes** was twice defeated in referendums during World War I.

From the Australian perspective, the most important stage of the war occurred when Turkey sided with Germany in 1915. **Winston Churchill** formulated a plan to defend British shipping in the Dardanelles by occupying the **Gallipoli Peninsula**, and diverted Australian infantry bound for Europe. Between April and December 1915, wave after wave of Australian troops were mown down below Turkish gun emplacements as they attempted to take control of the peninsula. By the end of the year it became clear that Gallipoli was not going to fall, and the survivors were "evacuated" to fight on the Western Front. The long-term effect of the slaughter was the first serious questioning of Anglo-Australian relations: should Australia have committed and sacrificed so much to help a distant country further its European policies? Conversely, Gallipoli, as Australia's debut on the world stage, still remains a symbol of national identity and pride.

1918–39

After World War I, the Nationalist Party joined forces with the **Country Party** to assume government under the paternalistic and fiercely antisocialist guidance of **Earle Page** and **Stanley Bruce**. The Country Party was formed due to the widening divisions between a growing urban population and farmers, who felt isolated and unrepresented politically. Under the coalition, pastoral industries were subsidized by overseas borrowing, allowing them to compete internationally, and technology began to close the gap between the city and the Outback: radio and aviation developments saw the birth of **Qantas** – the Queensland and Northern Territory Aerial Service – and the **Royal Flying Doctor Service** in Queensland's remote west. Development occurred in the cities: work started on the Sydney Harbour Bridge, and the new Commonwealth capital, **Canberra**, was completed.

On the social front, the USA stopped mass immigration in 1921, deflecting a flood of people from depressed **Southern Europe** to Australia – which the government countered by encouraging British immigrants with assisted passages. While progressive in some areas – for example, proposing a dole for the unemployed, sick, pensioners and mothers – the government overreacted to opposition, as exemplified by the **seamen and dockers' strike** of 1928. Citing the arch-villain "communism" as behind the dispute, they attempted to stretch the scope of the Immigration Act to allow action to be taken against disturbances that were politically motivated. However, the implications that the law could be altered against anyone who disagreed with the government contributed to the downfall of Bruce and Page the following year. The themes of their rule – differences between rural and urban societies, questions of Australian identity, union disputes, and the effects of heavy borrowing to create artificially high living standards, unsupported by Australia's actual capabilities – are still current issues.

As the **Great Depression** set in during the early 1930s, Australia faced collapsing economic and political systems, with all the parties divided; pressed for a loan, the Bank of England forced a restructuring of the Australian economy. Adding to national embarrassment, politics and sports became blurred during the 1932 "**body-line**" cricket series: the loan was virtually made conditional on Australian cricket authorities dropping their allegations that British bowlers were deliberately trying to injure Australian batsmen during the tour.

Meanwhile, worries about communism were succeeded by the rise of fascism, as Mussolini and Hitler took power in Europe and Japanese forces invaded Manchuria – the **Tanaka memorial** in 1927 actually cited Australia as one of Japan's future conquests. Although displaying a certain ambivalence to fascism, Australia assisted the immigration of refugees from central Europe, and after a prolonged union battle, halted iron exports to Japan. When Prime Minister Joseph Lyons died in office, **Robert Menzies**, a firm supporter of British notions of civilization, was elected to the post in time to side with Britain as hostilities were declared against Hitler in September 1939.

World War II and after

As happened in World War I, Australia developed its identity in World War II through participation in global affairs, but this time without Britain's help. Menzies' United Australia Party barely lasted long enough to form diplomatic ties with the USA – in case Germany overran Europe – before internal divisions saw the government crumble, replaced by **John Curtin** and his Labor Party in 1941.

Curtin, concerned about Australia's vulnerability after the Japanese attack on Pearl Harbor, made the radical decision of shifting the country's commitment in the war from defending Britain and Europe to fighting off an invasion of Australia from Asia. After the **fall of Singapore** in 1942 and the capture of sixteen thousand Australian troops, Curtin succeeded in ordering the immediate recall of Australians fighting in the Middle East, despite opposition from Churchill, who wanted them for the Burma campaign. In February the Japanese unexpectedly bombed Darwin, launched submarine raids against Sydney and Newcastle, and invaded New Guinea. Feeling abandoned and betrayed by Britain, Curtin appealed to the USA, who quickly adopted Australia as a base for co-ordinating Pacific operations under General **Douglas MacArthur**. Meanwhile, Australian troops in New Guinea halted Japanese advances along the **Kokoda trail** at Milne Bay, while the Australian and US navies slowed down the Japanese fleet in the **Battle of the Coral Sea** – which, thanks to modern cannons, was notable as the first naval engagement in which the two sides never even saw each other.

Australia came out of World War II realizing that geographically, the country was closer to Asia than Europe, that it could not count on Britain to help in a crisis (Churchill had been ready to sacrifice Australian territory to protect British interests elsewhere), and that it was able to form political alliances independent of the mother country. From this point on, Australia began to look to the USA and the Pacific, as well as Britain, for direction. Another consequence of the war was that immigration was speeded up, fuelled by Australia's recent vulnerability. Under the slogan "Populate or Perish", the government reintroduced assisted passages from Britain – the "ten-pound-poms" – also accepting substantial numbers of European refugees; even Torres Strait Islanders, previously banned from settling on the mainland, were allowed to move onto Cape York in northern Queensland.

With international right-wing extremism laid low by the war, the old bogey of **communism** returned. When North Korea, backed by the Chinese, invaded the south in 1950, Australia, led by a revitalized Menzies and his new Liberal Party, was the first country after the USA to commit troops to counter communist forces. Menzies also sent soldiers and pilots to Malaya (as it was known at the time), where communist rebels had been fighting the British colonial administration almost since the end of World War II, under the anti-communist SEATO (Southeast Asia Treaty Organization) banner. At home, he opened up central Australia to British **atomic bomb tests** in the 1950s, because – echoing the beliefs of the first European colonists – "nobody lived there". A number of Aborigines were moved to reserves; others – along with British troops involved in the tests – suffered the effects of fallout and had their traditional lands rendered uninhabitable for the foreseeable future. Wrangles with the British government over compensation and the clearing of the test sites at **Maralinga** and **Emu Junction** were finally settled in 1993.

Menzies was still in control when the USA became involved in **Vietnam**, and with conflict in Malaya all but over, Australia volunteered "advisers" to Vietnamese republican forces in 1962. Once fighting became entrenched, the government introduced conscription and, bowing to the wishes of the American president **Lyndon B. Johnson**, sent a battalion of soldiers into the fray in 1965, events that immediately split the country. Menzies quit politics the following year, succeeded by his protégé **Harold Holt**, who, rallying under the catchphrase "All the way with LBJ", willingly increased Australia's participation in the Vietnamese conflict. But as the war dragged on, world opinion shifted to seeing the matter as a civil struggle rather than as a fight between

Western and communist ideologies, and in 1970 the government began scaling down its involvement. In the meantime, Aboriginal people were finally granted **civil rights** in 1967, and Holt mysteriously disappeared while swimming in the sea off the coast of Victoria, leaving the Liberals in turmoil and paving the way for a Labor win under **Gough Whitlam** in 1972.

Whitlam's three years in office had far-reaching effects: he ended national service and participation in Vietnam, granted independence to **Papua New Guinea**, and instituted free health care and higher education systems. In doing so, however, he alienated the mostly conservative Senate, and when the government attempted to finance mining interests with an illicit overseas loan in 1975, the opposition prevented the Senate from functioning. In an unprecedented move, the Governor-General **John Kerr** (until then, a largely decorative representative of the Crown overseeing Australian affairs) dismissed the government – a move that shocked many into questioning the validity of Britain's ultimate hold on Australia – and called an election, which Labor lost. By contrast, the following eight years were uneventful, culminating in the return of Labor in 1983 under the charismatic Bob Hawke, a former trade union leader. Labor's subsequent thirteen years and record four terms in office, which produced surprisingly little lasting legislation, were suddenly brought to a close by the arrogant antics of Hawke's successor and former treasurer, **Paul Keating**. He was already widely unpopular for his scornful rhetoric and general lack of concern for the country's woes – particularly the effects of a massive foreign debt and crippling drought in eastern Australia – when news of a secret military agreement with Indonesia created a public backlash, resulting in a landslide victory for the **Liberal–National coalition**, led by **John Howard**, in 1996.

Current events

Formerly considered an ineffectual character, Howard has shown consummate – though often unpopular – political skills. One of his first actions was to cut government costs by announcing a reduction of the civil service, replacing the redundant departments with private enterprise. His stand against automatic firearms in the wake of the Port Arthur Massacre in 1996 (see p.1093) also reduced his feeble image, after he pushed through his legislation despite stiff opposition from gun lobbies and several state premiers. Indeed, Howard's political position was so secure by 1998 that the coalition managed to be **reelected** on what some considered a suicidal platform of **tax reform** through the implementation of a **GST**, or Goods and Service Tax. By mid-2001, however, Howard's prospects of winning the impending election were slipping away. A GST-inspired rise in fuel costs had driven many farmers – traditional National Party supporters – to bankruptcy; businesses were reeling under the effects of the tax, while consumers were having to pay more for their goods; and the Liberal-National coalition had been soundly trounced in state elections in Western Australia and Queensland. Then, on August 27, 2001, the *Tampa* came to Howard's rescue; when the Norwegian freighter requested permission to land on Christmas Island, northwest of Darwin, with 433 **refugees** on board (rescued from a sinking boat in international waters near the island), Howard used it as a chance to turn public opinion around. Contrary to international practice, he steadfastly refused to let the refugees ashore, even temporarily. After a long stand-off, the tiny, almost bankrupt Pacific island state of Nauru agreed to house most of the asylum seekers in Australian-built detention centres while their refugee status was being assessed, while a few luckier others were ferried off to New Zealand. Despite the so-called "Pacific Solution" costing $20 million of Australian taxpayers' money, Howard successfully played on the time-honoured Australian fear of being "swamped" by hordes of immigrants and his political status strengthened; the government's popularity soared, and the tribulations of the GST and the not-so-perfect shape of the economy were all but forgotten. The terrorist attacks in New York on September 11 did nothing to assuage xenophobic fears, and when Australian soldiers were sent to Afghanistan to join the "war on terrorism" in mid-October 2001 this was also considered a show of appropriate strength. Buoyed by his good ratings in the opinion polls, Howard called a federal election for November 10. Predictably, it was a comfortable win for his coalition, he returned to office for the third time, and the opposition Labor party was further diminished. The refugee question remained in the media spotlight for a few more months until Australia's possible involvement in the US/UK-led war on Iraq dominated the headlines. The carnage of the **car bomb in Kuta, Bali,** on October 12, 2002 – terrorist action targeted at Westerners but in particular, some argued, Australians – added urgency to the debate. Opinion polls taken in mid-January 2003 showed that about three quarters of the Australian population were against their country's involvement in a war on Iraq without backing from the UN, and from mid-January until mid-February anti-war rallies in major Australian cities attracted protesters in numbers not seen since the street marches against the Vietnam war in the late 1960s.

Defying public opinion, Howard vociferously supported a US-led war in Iraq, UN-backed or not, and subsequently joined the "coalition of the willing" in the military attack on Iraq. In contrast to the government's emphatic rhethorical support, Australia's physical contribution to the war was actually quite small: 2000 troops, plus some warships and aircraft. The political gamble paid off for Howard. By mid-April public opinion in Australia had swung around and opinion polls indicated record popular support for his government.

During the early Nineties, Australia focused more than ever before on its neighbours in the region, seeing itself more as **part of Asia** than of Europe or the United States. An Asian bias makes good economic sense, but has led in the past to an often appallingly conciliatory attitude to some Asian countries' more dubious actions against each other, and the response to regional human rights abuses has been pitifully weak. Nor, with its European heritage, is Australia accepted as "Asian" by other nations in the area, and Malaysia seems to harbour particular antipathy towards it, as shown by its continual vetoing of Australia's attempts to join ASEAN, the regional trading bloc. The rough-hewn right-wing outbursts by former chip-shop owner **Pauline Hanson** and the (short-lived) rise of her **One Nation** party in 1996, which capitalized on widespread dissatisfaction with the major political groups, did nothing to enhance Australian credibility in the region. By 2001, One Nation had disappeared from the political scene but Howard's own attitudes, exemplified by remarks made in the aftermath of the "Bali bombings" about his support for pre-emptive strikes against suspected terrorists in neighbouring countries, caused a furore across Southeast Asia. Resentment and distrust of Australia were expressed to such a degree that the Howard government made conciliatory noises about Australian involvement with its partners in the region. Howard, had, in fact, since becoming prime minister focused Australia's foreign policy on forging closer links with the US. Despite diplomatic gestures to the contrary, Australia's participation in the war on Iraq represented a continuation of this shift in political priorities away from Asia and towards the West. Postwar, Australia will have to handle relations with its Asian neighbours very carefully. A perception of Australia as the United States' deputy sheriff in the region could alienate countries Australia can't afford to offend, Indonesia in particular, jeopardizing long-term commercial relationships as well as mutual cooperation to combat the terrorist threat.

In the domestic arena there have been some advances under both Labor and the coalition in the field of **Aboriginal rights**. An ineffective inquiry into Aboriginal deaths in custody was overshadowed in June 1992 when the High Court handed down the landmark **Mabo Decision**, legally overturning the concept of *terra nullius*. The Mabo claim, set around Murray Island (Mer) in the Torres Strait, acknowledged the Merriam as traditional landowners and sparked furious debate as to interpretation. Nor was there any less of a reaction when Mabo itself was forced into the background in December 1996 by the **Wik Decision**, which stated that native title and pastoral leases could coexist over the same area. In an effort to test the implications of these rulings, Aboriginal groups across the country laid claim to everything from Brisbane city centre to cattle properties and Outback national parks, creating panic amongst developers, farmers and state governments, and something of a public backlash against Aborigines. Following the Wik decision, support for One Nation increased as the party exploited people's fears to the hilt, contributing to Australia's racist image overseas.

While Mabo and Wik are gradually beginning to have an effect – such as in the handing back of the **Silver Plains** property on Queensland's Cape York to its traditional owners in 2000 – few similar land claims are likely to succeed. A **Native Title Tribunal** has been set up to consider each case, but, given former resettlement policies, claimants have an uphill struggle as they need to prove constant association with the land in question since white occupation. Nonetheless, a growing perception that Aboriginal people will eventually be re-enfranchized has seen mining companies and farmers ignoring the political and legal wrangles by making private land-use agreements with local communities. In this sense, Mabo and Wik have finally confirmed that Aboriginal people have land rights, even if it takes years formally to establish exactly what these are.

Australia's indigenous peoples

White Australians are coming to recognize that grouping Aborigines under that overarching term, which simply means indigenous peoples, is similar to discussing as a whole the diverse but inter-related cultures of Europe. Today these cultures include urbanized Koorie communities in Sydney and Melbourne, semi-nomadic groups such as the Pintupi, living in the western deserts, and the Yolngu people of eastern Arnhemland, an area never colonized by settlers. If there is any thread linking these groups, it is the island continent they inhabit and, particularly in the north, the worsening state of health, education and opportunities they experience, despite the apparent revitalization of Aboriginal culture.

Colonization

In 1788, the estimated 750,000 indigenous people of Australia were unilaterally dispossessed of their lands and livelihoods by the British colonists who failed to recognize them as inhabitants and owners. Australia was annexed to the British Empire on the basis that it was *terra nullius*, or uninhabited wasteland. This legal fiction persisted until the High Court judged in the 1992 **Mabo** case that native title to land still existed in Australia unless it had been extinguished by statute or by some use of the land that was inconsistent with the continuation of native use and ownership. The **Wik Decision** of 1996 went a step further, acknowledging that native title continues to exist on pastoral leases, though with the proviso that "pastoral interest will prevail over native title rights, wherever the two conflict". (For more on the Mabo and Wik decisions, see "History", opposite)

Upon deciding that the country was unoccupied, successive waves of new settlers hastened to make it so. Violent conflicts between indigenous and recently arrived Australians resulted in the decimation of Aboriginal groups. The most widely known of these conflicts was the **unofficial war** waged against Tasmania's Aboriginal peoples, which resulted in the near-destruction of indigenous Tasmanians (see also box on pp.1058–1059). Grisly souvenirs of this war, including skeletons and preserved body parts, still shame the collections of museums throughout the world. Historians estimate that twenty thousand Aborigines may have died in these mostly unrecorded battles. Measuring the impact of colonization on the indigenous population has been hampered by a lack of information about conditions prior to colonization, as well as the failure of successive governments to record indigenous people as part of the population until quite recently.

Disease has also been a powerful, if unintentional, weapon in the war against indigenous Australians, and has proved more effective than shooting or poisoning. Australia's geographical isolation ensured that there were very few communicable diseases on the continent prior to the arrival of Europeans, and successive generations of indigenous Australians had developed resistance to these. The arrival of colonists and their diseases posed an almost insurmountable immunological challenge. Whole populations were wiped out by smallpox and malaria epidemics, and the diaries of officers of the First Fleet record the rapid destruction from smallpox of the Aboriginal camps in the Sydney hinterland within four years of the establishment of the colony of New South Wales. Those who didn't die fled the area, unwittingly infecting neighbouring groups as they went. When Governor Hunter made the first exploratory expedition to western New South Wales in the 1820s, he recorded evidence of prior smallpox epidemics among Aboriginal groups who had not previously come into contact with European settlers. As recently as the 1950s, desert peoples were severely affected by outbreaks of influenza and measles. The lack of immunity to these introduced diseases was exacerbated by the trauma of dispossession, the lack of availability of traditional food and water supplies, and the unhygienic results of being required to wear European-style clothing.

The **interruption of traditional food and water supplies** became progressively worse through the nineteenth and twentieth centuries as the pastoral industry expanded in rural Australia, and vast areas were stripped of vegetation to provide for grazing land. Grazing animals competed with local animals for food, fouled established water sources, and their hard hooves damaged the integrity of surface soil, contributing to substantial erosion and salinity problems. Other European animals, originally introduced to make the countryside seem more like "home", rapidly multiplied and have now become ubiquitous throughout Australia. Cats and foxes, both vicious predators, have been blamed for the near extinction of small to medium-size mammal species throughout arid Australia. Rabbit populations have expanded to fill the niche the other mammals vacated, and their destructive grazing habits have contributed to the increasing desertification of Australia's arid rangelands. Aboriginal tribespeople in central Australia have witnessed this ecological disaster within the last sixty years, and have lamented the loss of many animal species that sustained them in the past.

Australia's Aboriginal peoples have also been subjected to various forms of **incarceration**, ranging from prisons to apartheid-style reserves. Much of this systematic incarceration was instigated between 1890 and 1950 as an official policy of **protection**, in response to the devastating impact of colonization. Missionaries and other well-meaning people believed that Aborigines were a dying race, and that it was a Christian duty to "soothe the dying". Parliamentary records of the time reveal a harsher mentality. Aborigines were often viewed as a weak and degenerate people, little better than animals, who exposed white settlers to physical and moral disease. To "protect" the Aborigines and settlers from each other, various state governments enacted legislation for the protection of Aborigines, appointed official **Protectors of Aborigines**, established reserves in rural areas and removed Aboriginal people to them. In some parts of Australia these reserves were established on traditional lands, allowing people to continue to live relatively undisturbed. In other parts of the country, notably Queensland, people were forcibly removed from their home areas and relocated in reserves throughout the state. Families were brutally broken up and the ties with the land and religion shattered. The so-called protectors had virtual life and death powers over those they allegedly protected. In Queensland, for example, Aboriginal people required permits to marry and to move from one reserve to another. They were forced into indentured labour, and their wages collected and banked on their behalf by the State government. If they fell ill with a notifiable disease, they could be arbitrarily removed from home and family to a lock hospital, including the notorious Fantome Island, off the coast from Townsville. This treatment persisted in some areas until the late 1960s. Aboriginal people are still ridiculously over-represented in Australia's prison population, a situation which led to a **Royal Commission into Aboriginal Deaths in Custody**, which reported to the Federal Parliament in 1991. It called for wide-ranging changes in police and judicial practice, and substantial changes to social programmes aimed at improving the lot of Aboriginal peoples in the areas of justice, health, education, economics and empowerment. Although there has been considerable government lip-service to the recommendations of the Royal Commission, this has not resulted in any substantial change to incarceration rates.

Also since the 1920s, Aboriginal children had been legally removed from their black mothers and given into the care of state institutions and white foster parents as part of a policy of **assimilation**. The practice began in Victoria in 1886 and continued until remarkably recently (1969). This period of "taking the children away" still haunts the lives of many Aboriginal Australians who have lost contact with their natal families and their culture. The policy was the subject of a major government inquiry in 1997, bringing the issue to wider attention for the first time. The trauma suffered by the people now known as the **Stolen Generation** has received considerable media attention since the release of the report of the inquiry, and led to calls for a national **apology** to Aboriginal people. Prime Minister John Howard has consistently refused to acknowledge that the Australian people have anything for which to apologize, but his government has made funding available for link-up and counselling services for those who were affected. He has been publicly criticized for his stance by a number of influential Australians, and many people have expressed their personal regrets to the Aboriginal community.

The result of two centuries of brutal mistreatment and three decades of mismanagement, characterized by "throwing money" at the problem, is that, by almost every statistical indicator, the Aboriginal population is highly **disadvantaged** in both absolute terms and compared to non-Aboriginal groups.

Revitalization

The **revitalization** of Aboriginal peoples effectively began in 1967, when a constitutional referendum recognized indigenous Australians as voting citizens, and gave the federal government the power to legislate for Aboriginal people. Prior to this referendum, Aboriginal people had the status of wards of each of the states – the Letters Patent, documents which established the states, often referred to them, amongst the flora and fauna, as things to be protected and preserved. The referendum ushered in a new era of **self-determination** for Aboriginal people, evidenced by the establishment of the first Ministry for Aboriginal Affairs in the Whitlam Labor Government of 1972–75. After more than a hundred years of agitation, **land rights** were accorded to Aboriginal groups in the Northern Territory in 1976 under federal legislation. Since then, other states have legislated to vest title over various pieces of state-owned land to their traditional Aboriginal owners. All the mainland states and territories have now made provisions for Aboriginal land rights. Various representative bodies were set up by successive federal governments throughout the 1970s and 1980s, culminating in the **Aboriginal and Torres Strait Islanders Commission** (ATSIC), established in 1990. This statutory authority gives elected Aboriginal representatives effective control over many of the federal funding programmes directed at Aboriginal organizations and communities.

Along with ownership of land and control over funding have come opportunities for economic self-sufficiency and expansion previously unavailable to Aboriginal groups. In many parts of the country, this has allowed Aborigines to buy the cattle stations on which they worked without wages for many years. In central Australia, Aboriginal enterprises include TV and radio stations, transport companies, small airlines, publishing companies, tourist businesses and joint-venture mining operations.

Co-operative agreements with the Australian Nature Conservation Agency have led to Aboriginal ownership and joint management of two of Australia's most important conservation reserves, **Uluru–Kata Tjuta** and **Kakadu** national parks in the Northern Territory. These arrangements recognize that Aboriginal owners retain an enormous understanding about the ecology of their traditional lands that can be of great assistance in the development of land-management plans.

Since the late 1980s, substantial funds have been directed towards training for employment and improved health education. Running at around $2 billion per annum, this should, in theory, see Aboriginal people thriving right across Australia. The reality is very different.

Citizenship and its problems

Despite some successes, Australia's indigenous peoples are struggling against considerable disadvantages. Along with citizenship in 1967 came a new-found unemployability (station owners could not face paying Aborigines award wages) along with the legal right to purchase **alcohol**, a disastrous combination. Since that time institutionalized welfarism has compounded feelings of futility as well as shame towards one's Aboriginal origins, and substance abuse including petrol sniffing is heavily implicated in the destructive spiral often observed by visitors to Outback towns (and some inner cities). For Aborigines today the negative repercussions are evident in sickness and death, violence and despair, exclusion from education and meaningful employment, as well as families and communities in disarray. The vast over-representation of Aboriginal people in the criminal justice system is directly attributable to alcohol.

On the **positive** side, many families and communities are confronting the problems that alcohol is causing. This is possible because although some Aboriginal people equate drinking rights with racial equality, most have a negative view of alcohol abuse. A large proportion of Aborigines, particularly **women** (who collectively suffer the worse excesses of male violence), abstain altogether. Furthermore, Aboriginal people themselves are beginning to put pressure on problem drinkers to limit their drinking, and are now able to implement new laws to reduce the damage that alcohol is doing to their families and communities.

A **case study** illustrates these efforts and complications. Imanpa is a small Pitjantjatjara community between Alice Springs and Uluru (Ayers Rock). Seeing their community racked by alcohol-related violence and death, Imanpa residents looked at ways to limit availability of alcohol to residents. With neighbouring communities, they successfully lobbied the Northern Territory Liquor Commission to limit the amount of takeaway alcohol that could be purchased at highway roadhouses to six cans of beer. They reached co-operative agreements with the licensees of these roadhouses that they would not serve take-away alcohol to anybody travelling to, or living on, Aboriginal communities. And yet ironically, a couple of hundred kilometres down the road, the white owner of the Curtin Springs roadhouse was taken to court for attempting to enforce similar measures.

Poor health continues to reduce substantially the life expectancy of Aborigines. Aboriginal women have a life expectancy thirty years less than that of their white counterparts and in some places this gap is increasing. As with most areas of social service, health services for Aboriginal peoples have been the province of white professionals until very recently; an essential focus of the new strategy is to empower Aboriginal people by giving resources to them directly.

The future

Aboriginal people remain at a considerable and growing **disadvantage**, a national disgrace that was exposed in Rosemary Neill's forthright book *White Out: How Politics is Killing Black Australia* (see p.1204). In early 1999 the Australian government was censured twice about its Aboriginal policies by key international bodies. The government's Wik legislation, which attempts to effectively extinguish native title on pastoral leases, received sharp criticism from the United Nations Committee on Elimination of Racial Discrimination, which judged that the provisions of the legislation are inconsistent with the international convention to which Australia is a signatory. The continuing adversarial or lazy stance of the current government ensures that Aboriginal lives continue to be wasted. Walking past the many Aboriginal art galleries in Alice Springs may give the impression of a thriving Aboriginal culture but just beyond the tidy quarter-acre blocks are rubbish-strewn slums, while out in the desert communities teenage boys are dying in their sleep, hands clawed around a tin of petrol; this is a disparity of opportunity that knows little equal even in the world's poorest nations and reveals the contemporary scandal of the "lucky country's" indigenous underclass.

Wildlife

D espite forty thousand years of human pressure and manipulation, accelerated in the last two centuries by the effects of introduced species, Australia's ecology and wildlife remain among the most distinctive on earth. Nonetheless, they are also some of the most endangered: in the last two hundred years, more native mammals have become extinct here than on any other continent, and land clearing – particularly in Queensland – kills an estimated 7.5 million birds a year, bringing several species to the edge of extinction.

Australians love to tell stories about the **dangers** that the bush holds for the inexperienced (see the "Health" section of Basics, p.26, for general advice on coping with hazardous wildlife). In reality, fearsome "drop bears" lurking in gums, fallen tree trunks that turn out to be giant snakes, bloodthirsty wild pigs and other rampaging terrors are mostly confined to hotel bars, the product of suburban paranoia laced with a surprising naivety about the great outdoors. Apart from a couple of avoidable exceptions, there's little to fear from Australia's wildlife, and if you spend any time in the bush at any stage you'll undoubtedly end up far better informed than the yarn-spinners.

Marsupials and monotremes

In the years after the demise of the dinosaurs, Australia split away from the rest of the world, and the animals here evolved along different lines to anywhere else: as placental mammals gained the ascendency in South America, Africa, Europe and Asia, it was the marsupials and monotremes which took over in Australia, alongside the megafauna (see box, opposite). These orders may not be exclusive to Australia (they're also found in New Guinea and South America), but it's here that they reached their greatest diversity and numbers.

Marsupials are mammals that give birth to a partially formed embryo which itself then develops in a **pouch** on the mother; this allows a higher breeding rate in good years. Easiest to find because they actively seek out people, **ringtail** and **brushtail possums** are common in suburbs and campsites, often hard to avoid if they think there's a chance of getting some food. With a little persistence, you should encounter one of the several species of related **glider possums** on the edges of forests at dusk. **Kangaroos** and **wallabies** are the Australian answer to deer and antelopes, and range from tiny, solitary rainforest species to the gregarious two-metre-tall red kangaroo of the central plains – watching these creatures bouncing effortlessly across the landscape is an extraordinary sight. The arboreal, eucalyptus-chewing **koalas** and tubby, ground-dwelling **wombats** are smaller, less active and more sensitive to disturbance, and this has made them more elusive, and has placed them on the endangered list as their habitat is cleared. Carnivorous marsupials are mostly shrew-sized today (though a lion equivalent probably survived into Aboriginal times, and fossils of meat-eating kangaroos have been found); two of the largest are spotted native cats or **quolls**, and Tasmania's indigenous **Tasmanian devil**, a terrier-sized scavenger.

Platypuses and echidnas are the only **monotremes, egg-laying mammals** that suckle their young through specialized pores. Once considered a stage in

Ancient Australian wildlife

Australia has a **fossil record** which makes up in range what it lacks in quantity. Imprints of invertebrates from South Australia's **Ediacaran fauna**, dated to over 600 million years, are the oldest evidence of animal life in the world. On a larger scale, footprints and remains of several **dinosaur** species have been uncovered, and **opalized marine fossils** are unique to the country. Perhaps most intriguing is evidence of the **megafauna** – giant wildlife which included the twenty-metre-long constricting snake montypythonides, flightless birds bigger than an ostrich, a rhino-sized wombat, carnivorous kangaroos, and thylacaleo, a marsupial lion – which flourished until about thirty thousand years ago, overlapping with Aboriginal occupation. Climatic changes were probably responsible for their demise, but humans definitely wiped out the **thylacine**, a dog-like marsupial with an oversized head, which vanished from the mainland after the introduction of dingoes but survived in Tasmania until 1936 – the year it received government protection.

the evolution of placental mammals, they're now recognized as a specialized branch of the family. Neither is particularly rare, but being nocturnal, shy and, in the case of the platypus, aquatic, makes them difficult to find. Ant-eating **echidnas** resemble a long-nosed, thick-spined hedgehog or small porcupine, and are found countrywide; **platypuses** are confined to the eastern ranges and look like a blend of duck and otter, having a grey, rubbery bill, webbed feet, short fur, and a poison spur on males. This combination seemed too implausible to nineteenth-century biologists, who initially denounced stuffed specimens as a hoax assembled from pieces of other animals.

Introduced fauna

Of the **introduced mammals**, **dingoes** are descended from dogs, introduced to Australia by Aboriginal people in the last twelve thousand years. To keep them away from flocks, graziers built "vermin fences", which were finally connected by the Australian government to form a 5400-kilometre-long, continuous fence, allegedly the world's longest. The **Dingo Fence** stretches from South Australia into northwest Queensland and down again to New South Wales. **Camels** have also become acclimatized to Australia since their introduction in the 1840s; they are doing so well in the central deserts that they are becoming a pest. Australia is the only place where dromedaries still occur in the wild, and they are regularly exported to the Middle East. The blight that **hoofed mammals** – horses, cows, sheep and goats – have perpetrated on Australia's fragile fauna is horrendous. Much of the country has been prematurely desertified by their eating habits, abrasive hooves and demand for water; once extracted from below ground, it is not replenished, which alters the mineral balance and kills remaining plant life. The damage caused by **rabbits** is equally all-pervasive, especially in the semi-desert areas where their cyclic population explosions can strip every shred of plant life from fragile dune systems. In an attempt to control the problem, the myxoma virus was introduced in the Fifties, and although a large part of the rabbit population was inititally wiped out, the rabbits eventually developed a resistance and their numbers increased again in the following decades. Since 1996, another viral disease affecting the European rabbit, the rabbit calicivirus disease (RCD), has been released all over

Australia, resulting in a dramatic reduction of rabbit numbers. It remains to be seen, however, whether the unsuccessful story of the myxoma virus is being repeated.

Feral **cats**, which hunt for sport as well as necessity, are currently seen as one of the greatest threats to the indigenous fauna, primarily small marsupials and birds, but an introduced amphibian has turned out to be the most insidious and rapacious invader of all. The highly poisonous **cane toads**, brought in to combat a plague of greyback beetles, have no natural enemies and for thirty years have been on a relentless march from the north Queensland sugar-cane fields southwards along the coast and across northern Australia. In late 2002 they were about to invade the lush Top End floodplains which have more wildlife per square kilometre than the richest parts of Africa, Asia and the Americas. For more on the cane toad see p.520.

Reptiles, birds, bats and marine life

Australian **reptiles** come in all shapes and sizes. In the tropical parts of the country, the pale lizards you see wriggling across the ceiling on Velcro-like pads are **geckos**, and you'll find fatter, sluggish **skinks** – such as the stumpy blue-tongued lizard – everywhere. Other widespread species are **frill-necked lizards**, known for fanning out their necks and running on their hind legs when frightened; and the ubiquitous **goanna** family, which includes the monstrous perentie, third-largest lizard in the world. In central Australia, look out for the extraordinary **thorny devil** or moloch, an animal that seems part rock, part rosebush.

Crocodiles are confined to the tropics and come in two types. The shy, inoffensive **freshwater crocodile** grows to around 3m in length and feeds on fish and frogs. The larger, bulkier, and misleadingly named saltwater or **estuarine crocodile** can grow to 7m, ranges far inland (often in freshwater), and is the only Australian animal that constitutes an active threat to humans. Highly evolved predators, they should be given a very wide berth (see box on p.635 for specific precautions to take while in crocodile country). Despite their bad press, **snakes** are generally timid and pose far less of a problem, even though Australia has everything from constricting pythons through to three-quarters of the world's most venomous species.

With a climate that extends from temperate zones well into the tropics, Australia's **birdlife** is prolific and varied. Little **penguins** and **albatrosses** live along the south coast, while **riflebirds**, related to New Guinea's birds of paradise, and the **cassowary**, a colourful version of the ostrich, live in the tropical rainforests. The drabber **emu** prefers drier plains further west. Among the birds of prey, the countrywide **wedge-tail eagle** and the coastal **white-bellied sea eagle** are most impressive in their size. Both share their environment with the stately grey **brolga**, an Australian crane, and the even larger **jabiru stork**, with its chisel beak and pied plumage. **Parrots**, arguably the country's most spectacular birds, come in over forty varieties, and no matter if they're flocks of green budgerigars, outrageously coloured rainbow lorikeets or white sulphur-crested cockatoos, they'll deafen you with their noisy song. Equally raucous are **kookaburras**, giant kingfishers found near permanent water. The quieter **tawny frogmouth**, an incredibly camouflaged cousin of the nightjar, has one of the most disgruntled expressions ever seen on a bird.

Huge colonies of **bats**, in orange, ghost and horseshoe varieties, congregate in caves or fill entire trees all over Australia. The **fruit bat**, or flying fox, is especially common in the tropics, where evenings can be spent watching colonies of the one-metre-winged monsters heading out from their daytime roosts on feeding expeditions.

In addition to what you'll see on the Barrier Reef (covered in the Tropical Queensland chapter), **whales**, **turtles**, **dolphins**, **seals** and **dugongs** (sea cows) are part of the country's marine life, with humpbacked and southern right whales recently making a welcome return to the coasts after being hunted close to extinction.

Flora

Australia's most distinctive and widespread **trees** are those which developed a **dependence on fire**. Some, like the seemingly limitless varieties of **eucalypts** or gum trees, need extreme heat to burst open button-shaped pods and release their seeds, encouraging fires by annually shedding bark and leaves to deposit a thick layer of tinder on the forest floor. Other shrubs with similar habits are **banksias**, **grevillias** and **bottlebrushes** with their distinctive bushy flowers and spiky seed pods, while those prehistoric survivors, palm-like **cycads** and **grasstrees**, similarly depend on regular conflagrations to promote new growth. Aborigines possibly enhanced these fire-reliant traits by organizing controlled burn-offs.

Despite the country's extensive arid regions, there is no native equivalent to the cactus, although the dry, spiky **spinifex**, or porcupine grass, the succulent **samphire** with its curiously jointed stem, and the aptly named **saltbush**, come closest in their ability to survive extreme temperatures. After a rain, smaller desert plants rush to bloom and seed, covering the ground in a spectacular blanket of colour, a phenomenon for which Australia's Outback regions are well known.

On a larger scale, the Outback is dotted with stands of hardy **mulgas** and **wattles**, which superficially resemble scrawny eucalypts but have different leaf structures, as well as scattered groups of bloated, spindly branched **bottle trees**, whose sweet, pulpy, moisture-laden cores can be used as emergency stock feed in drought conditions. The similar but far larger **boab**, found in the Kimberley and northeastern Northern Territory, is thought to be an invader from East Africa. **Mallee scrub** is unique to the southeastern Outback, where clearing of these tangled, bush-sized eucalypts for grazing has endangered both scrub and those animals who rely on it – the mound-building **mallee fowl** being the best known.

Mangrove swamps, found along the tropical and subtropical coasts, are tidal zones of thick grey mud and mangrove trees, whose interlocked, aerial roots make an effective barrier to exploration. They've suffered extensive clearing for development, and it wasn't until recently that their importance to the estuarine life-cycle won them limited government protection; Aboriginal people have always found them a rich source of animal and plant products.

Rainforest once covered much of the continent, although today it survives in only a small portion of its former abundance. Nevertheless, you'll find pockets everywhere, from Tasmania's richly verdant wilderness to the monsoonal examples of northern Queensland and the Top End in the Northern Territory. Trees grow to gigantic heights, as they compete with each other for light, supporting themselves in the poor soil with aerial or buttressed roots. The extraordinary **banyan** and **Moreton Bay fig** trees are fine examples of the two types. They support a superabundance of plant species, with tangled **vines** in the lower reaches and **orchids**, **elkhorns** and other epiphytes using larger plants as roosts. **Palms** and **tree ferns**, with their giant, delicately curled fronds, are found in more open forest where there's regular water.

Some forest types illustrate the extent of Australia's prehistoric flora. **Antarctic beech** or nothafagus, found south of Brisbane as well as in South America, along with native pines and **kauri** from Queensland, which also occur in New Zealand (the similarly-named Western Australian **karri** is also huge but unrelated), are all relict evidence of the prehistoric supercontinent Gondwana. Other "living fossils" include primitive marine **stromatolites** – algae corals – still found around Shark Bay, Western Australia, or in fossilized form in the central deserts.

As long as you don't eat them or fall onto the pricklier versions, most Australian plants are harmless – though in rainforests you'd want to avoid entanglement with spiky **lawyer cane** or wait-awhile vine (though it doesn't look like it, this is a climbing palm). However, watch out for the large, pale-green, heart-shaped leaves of the **stinging tree**, a scraggly "regrowth" plant found on the margins of cleared tropical rainforest. Even a casual brush delivers an agonizing and prolonged sting; if you're planning on bushwalking in the tropics, learn to recognize and avoid this plant.

Australian film

No visitor to Australia these days will be unaware of the popularity and respect for the Australian film industry since the early 1970s. It is generally agreed (with deference to a 1900 Salvation Army promo, *Stations of the Cross*) that *The Story of the Kelly Gang*, made by Charles Tait in 1906, was the world's first feature-length film. Australians' well-known antagonism towards figures of authority soon led to a hugely popular series of bushranger movies, eventually to be banned in 1912 by the New South Wales police on the grounds that their unsympathetic portrayal in these pictures was corrupting youngsters.

This **early heyday** of Australian film-making predated that of Hollywood and persisted with the production of various World War I morale boosters, despite the creation of a distribution duopoly (known as the "combine") which showed little interest in independent Australian films outside its control. With the ending of the war and its many cinematic testaments to the heroic disaster of Gallipoli, Australian silent cinema reached a creative peak. **Raymond Longford** was Australia's Spielberg of silents at this time, and his 1919 production of *The Sentimental Bloke* and its sequel, *Ginger Mick*, a year later, were popular and notably naturalist dramas about a woman's taming of her larrikin husband's proclivities. Along with the already established contempt for authority, Longford's films featured a distrust of sophistication and formality and, even then, the mythic spell of "the bush" began to make its mark on Australian productions.

Hollywood domination

The combine gradually squeezed the life from Australian cinema, which continued to decline as the powerful Hollywood studios got into their stride and entered the Golden Age of talkies. In 1933 the mildly reformed wild boy from Tasmania, **Errol Flynn**, starred in his first feature film, *In the Wake of the Bounty*, directed by **Charles Chauvel**, a leading figure in Australian film-making until the late 1950s.

During World War II there was a return to newsreels and documentaries, with the legendary cameraman, Damien Parer, earning **Australia's first Oscar** for his account of the fighting in New Guinea (*Kokoda Front Line*, 1942). Following the war, however, Hollywood's global domination of cinema was unassailed, and Australian cinema just about perished. Nevertheless, **Chips Rafferty** turned up as Australia's answer to John Wayne, appearing in an unremarkable series of formula films, such as the scenically superb epic of bovine migration, *The Overlanders* (1946).

In the 1950s the British Ealing Studios and the American MGM set up production companies in Australia, turning out the odd Outback drama which was watered-down for international consumption (but not success). This era produced few notable Australian films other than Cecil Holmes' return to the bushranger format in *Captain Thunderbolt* (1953), and his similarly leftist study of mateship, *Three In One* (1957). Chauvel's remarkable *Jedda, the Uncivilized* (1955) was more unusual in that it tackled the tricky issue of an Aboriginal girl's white upbringing, sexual temptation and subsequent abduction back to tribal life, where a tragic death inevitably awaited her. If there is one subject Australian cinema still has difficulty in dealing with (the New Wave having finally come to grips with women as individuals), it is that of the Aborigines.

Australia was by now nothing more than an exotic, marsupial-speckled location for "**kangaroo westerns**" and other dramas where British and American actors could exercise their skills. In 1959 Stanley Kramer directed *On the Beach*, Nevil Shute's post-Holocaust drama, with Ava Gardner, Gregory Peck and Fred Astaire tiptoeing through the fallout. A year later Fred Zinnemann directed Deborah Kerr and Robert Mitchum in *The Sundowners*, an affectionate classic of Outback itinerant labour.

The New Wave

The birth of the **New Wave** was a response to the burgeoning counterculture of the late 1960s. Among the many notable reforms of Gough Whitlam's Labor government was support for the long-neglected arts. Film-makers in particular were given a shot in the arm with the introduction of extremely generous grants to more than cover the cost of production. While in its early years this financial support helped produce some of the crassest male-fantasy "sex romps" ever seen (Tim Burstall's 1973 *Alvin Purple* and Terry Bourke's *Plugg* are matchlessly dire), the opening of the **Australian Film School** in 1973 allowed genuine talents such as Gillian Armstrong, Bruce Beresford and Paul Cox to flourish.

Two years later, the **Australian Film Commission** evolved from previous similar organizations to help produce and market Australian films, and although the grants have been regularly reduced ever since, their introduction kick-started the moribund industry so that there presently exists a diverse pool of directors and technicians to keep things going.

Peter Weir's unsettlingly eerie *Picnic at Hanging Rock* (1975) remains an early jewel, and the decade ended with further acclaim for his *Gallipoli*, Phillip Noyce's extraordinary *Newsfront* and Gillian Armstrong's first feature, *My Brilliant Career*. Auspicious futures were launched for Armstrong, and actors Sam Neill, Judy Davis and Mel Gibson, whose post-apocalyptic *Mad Max* trilogy saw a gradual stylistic evolution to suit the huge American market.

Contemporary Australian cinema is perhaps most exceptional for establishing a number of **women directors** and **producers** and providing a handful of strong women's roles. Inevitably, only the mainstream hits, such as the uplifting *Strictly Ballroom* and *Death in Brunswick*, have achieved wide overseas release, while many equally fine "small" films remain largely unseen. It is these quirky, uniquely Australian films of which the rejuvenated industry can be most proud. The prestige of numerous and consistent awards at the Cannes Film Festival and others proves that Australia's long-established cinematographic heritage has, more than any other art form, helped rid the country of its former philistine reputation. Confident and uncompromising films such as *Malcolm*, *Celia*, *Sweetie* and *The Year My Voice Broke* are just a few that complement their better-known siblings, with 1994 seeing a media-led "renaissance" in Australian film. Stephan Elliot's sartorially outrageous *Adventures of Priscilla, Queen of the Desert* was the country's biggest box-office success up to that time and won international acclaim, while P.J. Hogan's wonderful *Muriel's Wedding* perfectly encapsulated the indigenous film-making idiom and proved that Australia still could make financially viable and idiosyncratic films.

Recent developments

By 1996, Australian film critics had grown weary of the trend in making "quirky, offbeat romances", such as Shirley Barratt's *Love Serenade* and Emma-Kate Croghan's 1996 Cannes hit *Love and Other Catastrophes*, although few would have much to complain about with Scott Hicks' globally acclaimed *Shine*. Since then, talented young writer-directors have focused on **crime stories**, often blackly comic, such as Gregor Jordan's first feature, the Sydney-set *Two Hands* (1999), which launched the career of Heath Ledger; Scott Roberts' *The Hard Word* (2002), with international stars Guy Pearce and Rachel Griffiths; or Andrew Dominik's more graphic *Chopper* (2000), based on the autobiography of the very scary "Chopper" Read. Another trend is towards telling **Aboriginal stories**, with three major films coming out in the space of two years: Rolf de Heer's *The Tracker* (2002) and Phillip Noyce's *Rabbit-Proof Fence* (2002) both look back critically to the attitudes and atrocities of the 1920s and 1930s (respectively), dealing with the difficult subject matter of massacres (de Heer) and the "Stolen Generation" (Noyce); Stephen Johnson's *Yolngu Boy* (2001), set in Arnhemland, confronts contemporary indigenous adolescent experience, including graphic scenes of petrol sniffing. While other contemporary Australian films, such as the high-finance thriller *The Bank* by Robert Connolly (2001), starring American-based Anthony LaPaglia, could be set and told in any Western country, films such as *Rabbit-Proof Fence* and Ray Lawrence's bleak but brilliant *Lantana* show a distinctly Australian sensibility and landscape without exoticization, kitsch suburbia or cute and quirky characters, and reveal a new level of profundity and maturity in Australian cinema.

While the Liberal government has slashed funding to the Australian Film Commission and Film Finance Corporation, Australia's phenomenally successful actors now work mostly overseas where the pay, recognition and opportunities are much greater. These **actors** include Oscar-winners Russell Crowe (*L.A. Confidential*, *The Insider*, *Gladiator* and *A Beautiful Mind*), Nicole Kidman (*To Die For*, *Portrait of a Lady*, *Eyes Wide Shut*, *Moulin Rouge*, *The Others* and *The Hours*) and Geoffrey Rush (*Shine*, *Elizabeth* and *Quills*), and other major actors such as Judy Davis (*Naked Lunch*, *Husbands and Wives* and *Celebrity*), Mel Gibson (*The Bounty*, *Braveheart* and *The Patriot*), Rachel Griffiths (*Divorcing Jack*, *Hilary and Jackie* and the TV series *Six Feet Under*), Toni Collette (*The Sixth Sense*, *About a Boy* and *The Hours*), Cate Blanchett (*Elizabeth*, *The Talented Mr Ripley* and *The Lord of the Rings*), Sam Neill (*The Piano* and *Jurassic Park*), Anthony LaPaglia (*29th St* and *Sweet and Lowdown*), Guy Pearce (*L.A. Confidential* and *Memento*), Richard Roxburgh (*Mission Impossible II* and *Moulin Rouge*), Hugh Jackman (*X-Men* and *Swordfish*), David Wenham (*Moulin Rouge* and *The Lord of the Rings*), Heath Ledger (*10 Things I Hate About You* and *The Patriot*), Rose Byrne (*The Goddess of 1967*, *I Capture the Castle* and *Star Wars Episode II: Attack of the Clones*), and Naomi Watts (*Mulholland Drive*). These actors do occasionally return home to star in films such as Gregor Jordan's 2003 *Ned Kelly* (featuring Geoffrey Rush, Naomi Watts and Heath Ledger), but this won't necessarily attract the locals: Australian films usually have short runs at home. In 1998 box office receipts hit a record A$629.2 million yet Australian films made up only two percent of that – and almost all lost money.

However, a low Australian dollar, skilled crews and Sydney's Fox Studios (see p.143), which opened in 1998, have attracted major productions such as *Dark*

c

CONTEXTS | Australian film

City, The Matrix, Mission Impossible II, Star Wars Episode II, Moulin Rouge and *The Quiet American* to Australia. Melbourne's developing docklands project (see p.913) includes a Paramount-backed studio which will also boost the Australian film industry's facilities, skillbase and reputation. Queensland, too, is getting in on the act, with the Warner Roadshow Studios on the Gold Coast (see p.427), set for a huge expansion which will make it the same size as Sydney's Fox Studios.

Films to watch out for

While you'd be lucky to catch all the recommendations below on the big screen (although keep an eye on the programmes of art-house, or repertory, cinemas in the major cities), many of the titles can be found in video-rental stores.

Humour, black comedy and satire

The Adventures of Priscilla, Queen of the Desert (Stephan Elliot, 1994). A queer romp across the Outback, prying into some musty corners of Australian social life along the way.

Babakiueria (Julian Pringler, 1988). A culture-reversing spoof beginning with Aborigines invading Australia during a roadside barbie and continuing with an anthropological-style study of white Australia. Rare, but well worth the search.

The Castle (Rob Sitch, 1997). A family's struggle to defend their home in the face of a trinity of sub-urban horrors: toxic-waste dumps, overhead power lines and airport developers.

Death in Brunswick (John Ruane, 1990). A black comedy about the misfortunes of a hapless dishwasher

who becomes embroiled in a gang-land killing.

The Hard Word (Scott Roberts, 2002). Three bank-robbing brothers (one played by Guy Pearce) are in cahoots with corrupt cops and a crooked lawyer. Their target: $100 million in cash held by Melbourne Cup bookies. Double and triple crossing has them on the run from everyone. Also stars Rachel Griffiths.

Malcolm (Nadia Tass, 1985). A charming, offbeat comedy about a slow-witted tram driver in Melbourne.

Muriel's Wedding (P.J. Hogan, 1994). Kleptomaniac frump Muriel wastes away in an Abba-and-confetti dreamworld until ex-schoolchum Rhonda masterminds Muriel's escape from her awful family and ghastly seaside suburb of Porpoise Spit. Great performances.

Adolescent and misfit romance

Better Than Sex (Jonathan Teplitzky, 2000). Josh, played by David Wenham (*The Boys*), has only

three days left until he goes back to London, so a one-night, after-party fling with Cin (Susie Porter, *Mullet*)

Hot spots for film buffs and soap groupies

The majestic scenery of the Northern Territory has featured in many films. **Kakadu National Park** provided the setting for many of the scenes in *Crocodile Dundee*: familiar spots are possibly Anbangbang Billabong (see p.640) and Waterfall Creek (see p.641). *We of the Never Never* was set in the **Mataranka** region, which, predictably, has been rechristened "Never Never" country (see p.656); some costumes worn in the film are on display in the Old Courthouse and Residency in **Alice Springs** (see p.663).

Desolation and Outback grandeur have a stranglehold on the science-fiction and post-apocalyptic genres. Locations for *Mad Max II* include the **Silverton** area of New South Wales (see p.376); as his parting shot, Mel Gibson upscuttled the semi-trailer on the nearby **Mundi Mundi Plains**. In nearby **Broken Hill**, scenes from *Priscilla, Queen of the Desert* were filmed at the kitsch *Mario's Palace Hotel* (see p.375). In South Australia, the pockmarked scenery of **Coober Pedy** (see p.872) has found favour with many film-makers, including Wim Wenders, who made his epic *Until the End of the World* here, while the lunar-like landscape was also an invaluable element in creating the atmosphere of *Mad Max III*. And *that* Outback pub in *Crocodile Dundee* was none other than the *Walkabout Hotel*, at **McKinlay** in Queensland (see p.588).

More lush surroundings have also caught the imagination: in Victoria the eponymous **Hanging Rock** (see p.988), which featured in *Picnic at Hanging Rock*, is within striking distance of **Woodend** (though the imposing mansion-school is actually in South Australia, the visitable Martindale Hall in the Clare Valley – see p.860).

Since Fox Studios' production of big-budget international films began in **Sydney**, location-spotting in movies made there is fun for the locals: *Mission Impossible II* provided the best haul, including scenes filmed at the **Bare Island** fortifications (see p.162). The soapy teenage angst and surfie bonhomie of *Home and Away* has long revolved around **Palm Beach** in Sydney's northern beaches (see p.435), with the **Barrenjoey Lighthouse** and headland regularly in shot. **Melbourne** is famous for being the filming location of *Home and Away*'s competitor, the veteran soapie *Neighbours*; Ramsay Street, Erinsborough is actually Pin Oak Court in Vermont South, while the cool international-hit TV series, *The Secret Life of Us* is filmed around St Kilda. Desperate fans can find details of tours to both filming locations at ⊛ www.backpackvictoria.com.

---

shouldn't hold any complications. A very sexy, warm and hilarious romantic comedy.

Flirting (John Duigan, 1989). This sequel to *The Year My Voice Broke* follows a young boy's adventures in boarding school. Superior coming-of-age film.

Lonely Hearts (Paul Cox, 1981). Following the death of his mother, 50-year-old Peter buys a new toupee and joins a dating agency. A sensitive portrayal of the ensuing, at times awkward, relationship. Other Paul Cox features include *Man of Flowers*, *My First Wife* and *Cactus*.

Looking for Alibrandi (Kate Woods, 2000). Light yet surprisingly layered story of a teenage Sydney girl dealing with suicide, high school, new love and immigrant cultural identity.

Mullet (David Caesar, 2001). A slow-motion plot set in a New South Wales' south-coast fishing town where nothing happens until a mysterious prodigal son (Ben Mendelsohn) returns to mixed receptions from his family, former friends and fiancée.

Strictly Ballroom (Baz Luhrmann, 1991). Mismatched dancers who, together, dare to defy the prescribed routines. A feel-good hit at Cannes and the box office, and the first feature from the highly successful director of *Moulin Rouge* (2001).

Urban dysfunctionals

The Boys (Rowan Woods, 1998). This tense drama follows Brett, played by rising star, David Wenham (*Better Than Sex*) as an ex-prisoner who terrorizes his dysfunctional family and coerces his unemployed brothers into a violent crime.

Careful, He Might Hear You (Carl Shultz, 1982). An absorbing tug-of-love drama set in 1930s Sydney.

Chopper (Andrew Dominik, 2000). Eric Bana brilliantly plays notorious, nihilistic Melbourne criminal Mark "Chopper" Read who ruthlessly dominates prison inmates and underworld associates alike. Based on Read's autobiography.

The Devil's Playground (Fred Schepisi, 1975). Burgeoning sexuality oozes between pupils and their tutors in a Catholic seminary.

Head On (Ana Kokkinos, 1998). Unemployed Ari (Alex Dimitriades) escapes living with his strict Greek parents by spending a hectic 24 hours nightclubbing, drug taking and graphically exploring his homosexuality.

Lantana (Ray Lawrence, 2001) A sometimes bleak but thought-provoking tale of trust and secrecy in marriage, set in lush but wintry Sydney. Coincidences and consequences bind lives of strangers together in ways that are as twisting, tangled and tough as the Australian plant that provides the film's title. The strong cast includes Geoffrey Rush and Anthony LaPaglia.

The Last Days of Chez Nous (Gillian Armstrong, 1991). A middle-aged woman slowly loses her grip on her marriage and family.

Romper Stomper (Geoffrey Wright, 1991). A bleak and pointless account of the violent disintegration of a gang of Melbourne skinheads, notable only as Russell Crowe's big-screen debut.

Sweetie (Jane Campion, 1988). Part black comedy, part bleakly disturbing portrait of a bizarre suburban family.

Ockerdom

The Adventures of Barry McKenzie (Bruce Beresford, 1972). Ultra-ocker comes to England to teach the "pommie sheilas about real men". Ironically, Barry Humphries' satire got beer-spurting ovations from the very people he despised and also set Beresford back a couple of years.

Crocodile Dundee (Peter Faiman, 1985). The acceptable side of genial, dinky-di ockerdom saw Paul Hogan sell Australian bush mystique to the mainstream and put Kakadu National Park firmly on the tourist agenda. Enjoyable once, but don't bother with the sequels.

Wake in Fright aka Outback (Ted Kotcheff, 1970). A horrifying gem in its uncut, 114min version; a real *Deliverance* Down Under. A coast-bound teacher blows his fare in Outback Hicksville and slowly degenerates into a brutal, beer-sodden nightmare.

Gritty and defiant women

Celia (Ann Turner, 1988). A wonderful allegory that mixes a 1950s rabbit-eradication programme with a communist witch-hunt. Stubborn Celia is determined to keep her bunny.

Dance Me To My Song (Rolf de Heer, 1998). A unique and moving film written by and starring cerebral palsy sufferer, Heather Rose as she is abused by her carer and falls in love.

The Getting of Wisdom (Bruce Beresford, 1977). Spirited Laura rejects the polite sensibilities and snobbery of an Edwardian boarding school.

My Brilliant Career (Gillian Armstrong, 1978). An early feminist questions and defies the expectations of 1890s Victoria.

Puberty Blues (Bruce Beresford, 1981). Two teenage beach girls refuse to accept their pushchair-and-shopping-trolley destiny.

We of the Never Never (Igor Auzins, 1981). A good-looking version of Jeannie Gunn's autobiographical classic of turn-of-the-twentieth-century station life in the Top End.

Men in rugged circumstances

The Dish (Rob Sitch, 2000). Light-hearted take on how Australia saved NASA during the broadcasting of the 1969 Apollo 11 moon landing from New South Wales' Parkes Space Observatory (see p.342), and an aside on how the country's technological skills are often overlooked. Starring Sam Neill.

Gallipoli (Peter Weir, 1980). A deservedly classic buddy movie in which a young Mel Gibson strikingly evokes the Anzacs' cheery idealism and the tragedy of their slaughter.

The Last of the Knucklemen (Tim Burstall, 1978). Tensions build up in a remote Outback mine and explode in bare-fisted punch-ups.

The Man from Snowy River (George Miller, 1981). Men, horses and the land from A.B. ("Banjo") Paterson's seminal and dearly loved poem caught the overseas' imagination. A modern kangaroo western.

Plains of Heaven (Ian Pringle, 1982). A spookily atmospheric story of two weathermen in a remote meteorological station slowly losing their minds.

Sunday Too Far Away (Ken Hannam, 1973). A simple tale of macho shearers' rivalries in Outback South Australia.

Outback nightmares

Cunnamulla (Dennis O'Rourke, 2000). Controversial documentary of malaise in an isolated Outback town, 800km west of Brisbane, shot in a laconic style befitting Queensland, and featuring inhabitants' own stories of teen sex and hopelessness,

frontier redneckery, racial tension, social dysfunction, and desperate longings for escape to distant cities.

Evil Angels (*A Cry in the Dark*) (Fred Schepisi, 1987). A dramatic retelling of the Azaria Chamberlain story; Ayers Rock (Uluru) and dingoes will never seem quite the same again.

Picnic at Hanging Rock (Peter Weir, 1975). A richly layered tale about the disappearance of a party of schoolgirls and its traumatic aftermath.

Razorback (Russell Mulcahy, 1984). Dark, comedy exploiting

urban paranoia of the Outback and featuring a remote township, a gigantic, psychotic wild pig, and some bloodthirsty nutters who run the local abattoir.

Walkabout (Nicolas Roeg, 1971). Following their deranged father's suicide during a bush picnic, two children wander through the wilderness until an Aboriginal boy guides them back to civilization.

About Aboriginal people

The Chant of Jimmie Blacksmith (Fred Schepisi, 1977). Set in the 1800s, when a mixed-race boy is forced onto the wrong side of the law. Based on the novel by Thomas Keneally.

Dead Heart (Brian Brown, 1996). A long-overdue and regrettably overlooked thriller, set on an Aboriginal community near Alice Springs. Bravely gets its teeth into some juicy political and social issues.

The Fringe Dwellers (Bruce Beresford, 1985). An aspiring daughter persuades her family to move from the bush into a suburban white neighbourhood, with expected results.

Jedda, the Uncivilized (Charles Chauvel, 1955). An orphaned Aboriginal girl brought up by a "civilized" white family cannot resist her "tribal" urges when she is semi-voluntarily abducted by a black outlaw.

Manganinnie (John Honey, 1980). Set during the time of the "black drives" of 1830s Tasmania, a young Aboriginal girl gets separated from her family and meets a white girl in similar straits.

Rabbit-Proof Fence (Phillip Noyce, 2002). Very moving film, with beautiful cinematography, set in 1930s

Western Australia and based on a true "Stolen Generation" story. Three girls aged 8 to 14 , daughters of absent white fathers – construction workers of the fence itself – and black mothers, are taken from their families according to the policy of the all-powerful A.O. Neville, Chief Protector of Aborigines (Kenneth Branagh) to a settlement at Moore River, but manage to escape. The girls – Outback-cast unknowns giving emotive, natural performances – make their way over 2000km home following the fence, suspensefully pursued by a tracker (David Gulpilil).

The Tracker (Rolf de Heer, 2002). Set in 1922, this is something of a fable told in an experimental way. Each character is a type: "The Fanatic", a police officer who will stop at nothing including cold-blooded massacre, leads "The Tracker" (the film is a star-vehicle for David Gulpilil), "The Follower" (a young green policeman), and "The Veteran", all in search of "The Accused", an indigenous man wanted for a white woman's murder. Violent massacre scenes are replaced by landscape paintings but with a painful soundtrack, while songs (performed by Aboriginal musician Archie Roach) and narration mostly convey the themes, creating a disturbing impression.

Yolgnu Boy (Stephen Johnson, 2001). In Yolgnu country in Arnhemland, Lorrpu, Milika and Bortj have always been an inseparable trio. But when adolescence hits, 15-year-old Bortj's petrol-sniffing rampages land him in jail; as Lorrpu and Milika become tribally initiated, Bortj finds himself outside his own culture and unable to become a man, and friendships and loyalties are tested. When the three embark on a – beautifully shot – 500-kilometre overland trek to Darwin, living off the land, distress gives way to joy ... until they hit the city.

Portents of doom

Cane Toads: an Unnatural History (Mark Lewis, 1988). A very eccentric, original and amusing documentary about the mixed feelings Queensland's poisonous amphibians arouse and the real threat they may pose to Australia's ecology.

The Last Wave (Peter Weir, 1977). An eerie chiller about a lawyer defending an Aborigine accused of murder – and the powerful, elemental forces his people control.

Mad Max II (George Miller, 1981). The best of the trilogy, set in a near future where loner Max protects an oil-producing community from fuel-starved crazies. Great machinery and stunts.

Australian music

For a geographically isolated, sparsely inhabited island with a tiny market for its own recorded music, Australia has, with ever-more assurance, shouldered its way in to occupy a distinguished place in the international pop music hierarchy. In contrast with its fifty-year rock music heritage, the country's Aboriginal music boasts a creative presence of thousands of years. With a strong influence on contemporary Australian music, its importance in the ongoing reconciliation between black and white Australia can hardly be overstated.

Rock music

The story of Australian contemporary music closely parallels that of Britain and the US – rock'n'roll arrived in the 1950s, and each decade since has offered up its own revolutionary shift in the popular music landscape. Given the ubiquitous nature of Western popular culture, this is hardly surprising. Less predictable, however, has been the impact of Australian music on the global music scene, beginning in the 1970s with AC/DC, continuing in the 1980s with Midnight Oil and INXS, through to the more recent multimillion record sellers silverchair, Kylie Minogue and The Vines.

The early years

Australia's very first rock star emerged in 1957 in the form of a lean, throaty, stage-strutting powerhouse named **Johnny O'Keefe**. All snake-hips and sex appeal, "The Wild One", as he became known, was one of the few early rock performers who could very nearly out-Elvis Elvis. Concert footage of his live performances is largely taken up by shots of women screaming, passing out and being carried from concert venues by sweaty police and exhausted security people. O'Keefe discovered early on that all the big players in the industry – performers, managers, promoters and record companies – were expert manipulators, and he quickly set about becoming one himself: legend has it that he bullied his way into his first recording contract by calling a press conference and announcing that the deal was done, guessing correctly that the publicity would leave the record company no option but to sign him.

Johnny O'Keefe was, to Australians, the embodiment of the defiant new brand of music that was then sweeping the world. He was to become synonymous with 1960s TV programmes that showcased Australian rock'n'roll talent, even as his own recording efforts were gradually swamped by the peace-love-hair movement of the time. O'Keefe remained a presence on television and radio until his death of a heart attack in 1978, aged just 43. In keeping with the requirements of rock god-dom, his last years were characterized by a series of breakdowns, bouts of depression and problems with alcohol. His rendition of the classic crowd-anthem **Shout** (1959) remains, to this day, an integral part of early rock'n'roll's global legacy (video footage of O'Keefe performing live also constitutes the opening sequence of the ABC's late-night music video programme *Rage*).

Surviving the Sixties

In company with the rest of the world, Australian music rode out the 1960s hanging onto the coat-tails of the massive British rock invasion. Overwhelmed by the omnipresent Beatles and Rolling Stones, Australia was to produce little ground-breaking rock music, beyond the efforts of Billy Thorpe and the Aztecs, The Easybeats and Russell Morris, each of whom left behind a signature song forever embedded in the Australian psyche, and still played on commercial radio today: *Most People I Know (Think that I'm Crazy)* – Billy Thorpe and the Aztecs (1968); *Friday on My Mind* – The Easybeats (1966); *The Real Thing* – Russell Morris (1969).

The Seekers, however, were operating well clear of the crowded rock music mainstream, creating their own musical niche by building three-part harmonies around chords strummed on acoustic guitars, the two male voices cushioning the pristine power of lead vocalist Judith Durham. Songs such as *If I Had a Hammer* (1965) might sound like hippie anthems today, but The Seekers' brand of idealism appealed to millions of record-buyers, and several successful comeback tours show that their popularity has barely waned.

It was in 1967, however, that millions of Australians witnessed the decade's most significant music industry event – and not a single one of them even knew it. A young man named **Johnny Farnham** had appeared on television, performing a cute but innocuous ditty entitled *Sadie (the Cleaning Lady)* (1967). Good-looking and with a superb voice, as well as charming beyond his years, Farnham endeared himself immediately to Australian audiences; it was a promising debut, but nobody could have predicted how far he'd go. His name shortened these days to John, Farnham is now into his fifth decade as a performer, and continues to shift with apparently effortless ease between roles as rock star, stage-musical lead and TV personality. From 1982 to 1986 he was a popular frontman for the hugely successful Little River Band (having replaced Glen Shorrock), but it was in 1987 that his career peaked, with the release of his album *Whispering Jack*, which sold millions of copies worldwide, driven, appropriately enough, by the success of the single *You're the Voice* (1987).

Livin' in the Seventies

Having emerged from the shadows of the 1960s, Australian music began to find a voice of its own in the mid-1970s. For no obvious reason, **Glam Rock** was a phenomenon Australian bands not only embraced, but excelled at. Sherbet and **Skyhooks** pulled off the satin-jumpsuits-and-crazy-make-up combo with singular style. The "Mighty Hooks" were at all times the cheekier and sexier of the two. Singer "Shirley" Strachan famously performed in only a pair of tight satin trousers with a large, bright-red hand painted over the crotch; the other band-members were equally indulgent of their penchants for self-expression. There was no sacrifice of substance for style, however, with the band recording several of Australia's finest and most enduring pop songs, including such irresistible numbers as *You Just Like Me 'cause I'm Good in Bed* (1974), *Horror Movie* (1974), *Ego (Is Not a Dirty Word)* (1975), and *Women in Uniform* (1978).

Sherbet seemed almost serious by comparison, doing without the make-up and looking as though they only wore the satin pants, silly shoes and poncy scarves because that was what fashion dictated. It was a highly accomplished band no matter what they were wearing, and led by virtuoso pop vocalist Daryl Braithwaite, they recorded several standout tracks, including *Child's Play*

(1976), *Howzat* (1976), *High Rolling* (1977) and *Summer Love* (1975). Although both bands flirted with overseas success, touring the US (and subsequently expressing bitterness at not having cracked the big time), history has conferred upon them the honour of having kicked open the rock music establishment's door, on behalf of an Australian music fraternity that had simply been waiting around for someone to show them "we're just as good as those bands from overseas".

Proof perhaps of the depth of talent concentrated in these two bands is the continued presence of individual members in Australian music and media today. Trivia buffs can still track down various Skyhooks alumni: former guitarist Red Symons is now a Melbourne radio announcer and is regularly cast as the villain on some of TV's nastier game shows, while Greg Macainsh is in high demand still as a bass player and songwriter; former lead singer Graeme "Shirley" Strachan was tragically killed in a helicopter crash in 2001, having enjoyed almost twenty years as a popular TV presenter. Stalwarts of Sherbet have likewise soldiered on: Daryl Braithwaite, the lead singer, is now a successful solo performer; Harvey James, one of the first Australian guitar-heroes, graduated to session musician and guitar-ace-for-hire; and Garth Porter, former keyboardist, who has gone on to assume the unlikely mantle of producer/guru for many of Australia's top country music performers.

But even as Glam Rock was fading from cool to kitsch, a clannish group of young Scottish immigrants were beginning to play their own version of Chuck Berry-inspired blues-rock, only three times as loud and with heavily distorted guitars. **AC/DC** not only had the skills, the songs and the "muscle" to back it all up, they also boasted two figures who were destined to become universal icons of rock'n'roll rebellion: guitarist Angus Young's delinquent schoolboy persona had to share the adulation of wannabe rock rebels with singer Bon Scott, who was possessed not only of a genuine, self-destructive, live-hard-die-young ethos, but also sported the most mischievous grin ever seen in tandem with a microphone. It's unlikely anyone besides Bon could have delivered songs such as *Highway to Hell* (1979), *Whole Lotta Rosie* (1978), and *Dirty Deeds...Done Dirt Cheap* (1976) with the required sass to make them acceptable in a 1970s commercial market.

True to form, Bon died a rock star's death in London in 1980, poisoned by alcohol in the back seat of a car. It was, ironically, smack in the middle of a golden age for Australian music, when, during the period 1977–83, bands Men at Work, Midnight Oil, Cold Chisel, INXS, Air Supply and Little River Band were lining up right alongside AC/DC to take the pop music world by storm.

Top ten great Oz rock albums

1) *Livin' in the Seventies* Skyhooks. Mushroom Records, 1974.
2) *Howzat!* Sherbet. Sherbet Records, 1976.
3) *Goodbye Tiger* Richard Clapton. Infinity Records, 1977.
4) *Back in Black* AC/DC. Albert Records, 1980.
5) *East* Cold Chisel. WEA, 1980.
6) *Business As Usual* Men At Work. CBS, 1981.
7) *Kick* INXS. WEA, 1987.
8) *Diesel and Dust* Midnight Oil. CBS, 1987.
9) *Songs From the South: Paul Kelly's Greatest Hits* Paul Kelly. Mushroom Records, 1997.
10) *Highly Evolved* The Vines. Capitol Records, 2002.

Oz music grows up

Even as AC/DC managed – in the space of a year following Bon's death – to recruit a new singer (Brian Johnston), settle permanently into life in Britain, and record the most acclaimed and successful heavy rock album of all time, *Back in Black* (1980), bands back in Australia suddenly found that the world was interested in them, too. **Little River Band's** sound was so West Coast USA that commercial success in North America had long seemed inevitable; **Air Supply**, meanwhile, had the sort of stranglehold on the American easy listening love-song market to which Michael Bolton was perhaps, even then, beginning to aspire. More surprising was the impact made by **Men at Work**, a band whose well-crafted songs were invariably, if unfashionably, punctuated by arresting melodies played on a flute, and whose style came to be described as "white reggae". They announced their arrival in 1981 with the ska-ish *Who Can it Be Now?*, followed by *The Land Down Under*, both of which bombarded radio airwaves and shifted by the million.

During this period, Midnight Oil, Cold Chisel and INXS stayed closer to home, recognizing perhaps that their styles were less easily translatable from an Australian to a global audience. It is surely no coincidence that among these bands (all highly accomplished, and equally revered at home) the least identifiably "Australian" act – **INXS** – was the first to experience worldwide fame and fortune, when in 1987 their album *Kick* plundered the US charts. (This wave of success held tragic implications for singer Michael Hutchence; he would struggle to make the transition from rock star to rock superstar, suffering depression until his death by suicide in 1997.) Of the other two, most needs to be said about the band that had the biggest impact at home, and the least impact abroad – Cold Chisel. If the period three years either side of 1980 was to be remembered as the grand era of Oz "pub rock", then Chisel was the band that owned it, lock, stock and smoking barrel.

From Chisel to The Church

Formed in Adelaide in 1975, **Cold Chisel** was, like every great band from the Rolling Stones to U2, the sum of its parts. Steve Prestwich (drums) and Phil Small (bass) made a compact and classy rhythm team, variously casting light and shadow about the more illustrious members of the group. Ian Moss's blues–rock guitar virtuosity and awesome soul voice made him a natural star on any stage, in lethal combination with lead singer Jimmy Barnes, Australia's self-styled wild man of rock and working-class hero. A great band must have great songs, and these were duly delivered by the immensely tall and serious man at the piano, Don Walker, arguably Australia's greatest songwriter.

Among hundreds of examples of **Des Walker's** craftsmanship in capturing the times/places/people/events poignant to Australians, *Khe Sanh* (1978) – a treatise on the Australian experience of surviving the war in Vietnam – remains a work without peer, while *Star Hotel* (1980) captures, in three verses and a chorus, the mood and events of September 19, 1979, when, in the working-class steel-town of Newcastle, police came to close down the city's main pub-rock venue, *The Star Hotel*, only to find themselves confronted by an angry crowd spoiling for a fight. Police cars were overturned and set alight in the course of a civil disturbance that echoed convict rebellions of two centuries earlier. The hotel was finally closed down, but the punters had made their point – and Chisel weren't going to let the police forget it.

Cold Chisel not only recorded the boozy summer nights, the trips up the coast, the girls, the fights, the pubs, the streets, the cities and towns, they sang it all back to the faithful in sweaty pubs and heaving stadiums night after night. When they called it a day in 1984, Chisel were Australia's greatest ever rock band, bar none. "Mossy" and "Barnesy" went on to fame and fortune as solo performers, but the band's long-awaited return did not come until 1998, when they released their first studio album in fourteen years *The Last Wave of Summer*; predictably, they failed to capture the power of the band in its heyday.

During this period, **Midnight Oil** by no means played second fiddle to Cold Chisel; rather, they had a different agenda, and their commitment and energy in delivering it live were never in question. Always highly political (lead singer Peter Garrett narrowly missed out on a Senate seat while he was leader of Australia's Nuclear Disarmament Party), "the Oils" brought Aboriginal land rights into the forum of pop culture, even as their uncompromising album *Diesel and Dust* (1987) brought them worldwide success. Twenty-five year veterans with fourteen albums to their credit (and often bracketed by critics with bands like Queen and U2 as the most powerful live act in the world), Midnight Oil's rage against the machine appears to have ended, with Peter Garrett leaving the band in late 2002, allegedly to resume his political career.

Among the distinguished musicians of the 1970s and 1980s, two songwriters stand (alongside Don Walker) above the rest as chroniclers of their culture and environment: **Richard Clapton** and **Paul Kelly**. Clapton's 1977 album *Goodbye Tiger* is unmatched as a celebration of the very fact of life in Australia – riding the city tram, searching for the perfect wave, soaking up the streetscapes of Oxford Street and Kings Cross. Paul Kelly is a more contemporary presence, and his songs go unerringly to the heart of the matter: *Have You Ever Seen Sydney From a 727 at Night?* (1985), *From St Kilda to Kings Cross* (1985) and *Adelaide* (1985) capture their respective subjects better than any photograph, while his ode to *Bradman* (1987) – written in homage to Australia's greatest Test cricket batsman Sir Donald Bradman ("The Don"), is the stuff of a true bard, a composition in verse honouring the glorious return from battle of a people's champion.

But in order to appreciate the depth and diversity of Australian music as it reached **maturity**, one needs to take a stroll out to the fringes. With a well-established canon of "major" Australian bands now in place, others were finding looser creative environments in which to operate. The Triffids, The Birthday Party (with star alumnus Nick Cave), The Church and the Go-Betweens seemed tied to weirder and more eclectic influences (such as The Velvet Underground, David Bowie and Bob Dylan) than their "mainstream" counterparts. Although musically diverse, they held several characteristics in common: their songs seemed more poetic, or just more sensitive to light-and-shade; they were also far less commercially successful in Australia, yet all made a big impact in Britain and Europe. Among all of these, The Church alone continue to record and tour from various bases in Europe, while Nick Cave remains intent upon perfecting the art of the murder ballad; his album *Murder Ballads* (1996) features a duet with Kylie Minogue. Australia could boast, too, a white-hot outfit schooled in the nasty traditions of 1970s British punk: The Saints. Although known for their Sex Pistols-ish two-minute thrash exercises, The Saints were nevertheless real musicians, and survivors Chris Bailey and Ed Kuepper continue to record and perform songs of the highest quality.

The Nineties and beyond...

Strangest perhaps of all the facets of Australia's music industry has been its propensity for throwing up TV **soap stars** who mutated into pop stars. At last count there were no less than five ex-Neighbours cast members at large within the music industry: Kylie Minogue, Danii Minogue, Natalie Imbruglia, Holly Valance and Delta Goodrem. Australians have never known what to make of this, but both Natalie Imbruglia and Kylie Minogue have earned their stripes by recording fine pop albums; Holly Valance, meanwhile, has been widely dismissed as just another in a long line of soft-porn pop wannabes.

The roaring success of these soap-star singers goes some way to explaining the listlessness that afflicted the music community during the late 1980s to early 1990s. It seemed the moment **Kylie** was formally adopted by an adoring British public, Australian musicians breathed a collective sigh of relief, and got straight back to work. You Am I, The Whitlams, Powderfinger and The Cruel Sea had always been likely to show the way by writing and recording with passion and originality. By the mid-1990s, quality Australian bands were once again jostling for position in local and overseas markets, this time led by three scruffy-looking, fifteen-year-old schoolboys.

In 1994, Newcastle high-school trio Innocent Criminals sent a demo tape to radio station Triple J in response to a band competition, the prize for which was use of the station's recording facilities. The song, *Tomorrow*, had the Seattle grunge sound all over it, and an awesome rock vocal performance from singer/guitarist Daniel Johns. He didn't sound like a fifteen-year-old, although the band's written entry should have given some kind of clue; their "twenty-five-words-or-less" were written in green felt marker-pen on yellow cardboard: "We're not rap or hip-hop, we're rock and we love to play". *Tomorrow* arrived atop the Australian singles charts where it stayed for several weeks, and with the band renamed **silverchair**, their 1995 album *Frogstomp* took them into league – and onto a stage – with grunge giants like Pearl Jam and Soundgarden, even as the three "boys" were negotiating their last year of high school. Subsequent silverchair albums *Freak Show* (1997), *Neon Ballroom* (1999) and *Diorama* (2002) have all met with solid sales and critical approval, confirming their standing among the world's premier bands.

Not to be left out of the latest shift in the music biz, Australia has recently seen the emergence of another group of precocious young rockers – The Vines. Having tapped into the retro-rock mood that reared its head in 2002 with bands like The Strokes, The White Stripes and The Hives (each of which mined the raw and rampant sound of The Who, The Stooges and The Ramones), The Vines exploded onto the world scene with such a rush that they scored both a recording deal and a hit album (*Highly Evolved*, 2002) after having played only a handful of live shows.

As the musical culture of a new millennium takes shape, Australian music looks set to continue punching well above its weight. From The Vines and other rock outfits Powderfinger and Grinspoon, to the thrashier Jebediah and The Living End, stylish and witty The Whitlams, and the rock/techno crossover work of Regurgitator, the latest array of talent is dizzying.

Aboriginal music

Aboriginal music is an increasingly powerful and invigorating seam in the fabric of world music. Its instruments and rhythms have a strong influence on contemporary Australian music, and there's probably no better example of the musical crossing of cultural boundaries, than in the story of Australia's most recognizable instrument, the didgeridoo. Known also as a *yidaki*, or simply a "didge", this hollowed-out tree branch, when blown into, produces a resonant hum, punctuated by imitations of animal and bird noises. Its sound is evocative, to many, of the Australian landscape.

The big surprise for many visitors to Australia is the sheer **diversity** of Aboriginal music. From the big rock sound of the Warumpi Band to the heart-felt guitar ballads of Archie Roach, the cruisey island reggae of Saltwater, and the echoes of an ancient culture in the work of Nabarlek (who sing mostly in their own language) there is no way of pigeonholing the music. The latest indigenous talent to hit the radio airwaves in 2002 was a hip-hop group called the Wilcannia Mob, whose simple lyrics about days spent fishing and swimming are delivered by boys whose average age is 11. It's no problem to see Aboriginal bands playing live, doing everything from metal to hip-hop and performing in all parts of the country, but there's really no better way to immerse yourself than by attending an indigenous music festival.

Festivals

Biggest of all the festivals is the **Barunga Sports & Cultural Festival**, which showcases up to forty bands, along with sports events, spear-throwing and didge-playing competitions. It's held at Barunga Community, 80km south of Katherine in the NT, over the first weekend in June (campsites with facilities are available); for information, phone the Barunga Community direct on ☏08/8975 4504. Also in the Top End, the **Milingimbi Cultural Festival** is purely a music event and, being harder to get to than Barunga, gets fewer white visitors. Dates for this one are hard to nail down, although it's always held sometime mid-year, on Milingimbi Island in the Crocodile archipelago. There are flights from Darwin, otherwise you need permission from the Northern Land Council (Darwin Head Office ☏08/8920 5100) to drive across Arnhemland to Ramingining to catch a barge. Traditional music and dance are featured, along with gospel bands and lots of Arnhemland rock.

The festival held every odd-numbered year at **Laura**, in far north Queensland, attracts high profile performers like the Warumpi Band and Christine Anu, plus all the local Murri bands. Held in either May or June (it varies from year to year), there are usually quite a few backpackers and hippies about, as well as the local Murri community. It's roughly two hours' drive (on sealed roads) north from Cairns to Laura, a small town 60km west of Cooktown. Otherwise, another intriguing possibility on the west coast is the **Stompem Ground** Festival. First staged in Broome, Western Australia, in 1992, and then again in 1998 and 2001, it drew on the strong and highly independent Aboriginal communities of the Kimberley region, attracting singers, dancers and bands into the incomparable beauty of Western Australia's far north. Although it is not really an "established" event, it can be well worth checking out. (Triple J, which broadcasts Australia-wide, is a good source for music festival information.)

Even if you find yourself stranded in the Big Smoke, you need not miss out; if you're in **Sydney** over summer, there's no better place to be on the Australia Day holiday (January 26) than at "Survival", Waverley Oval, Bondi. This festival began as a highly political event, deliberately juxtaposed with the Australia Day festivities which mark the arrival of the First Fleet of "white invaders". It continues as a celebration of the survival of indigenous people and cultures in the face of white oppression, and draws many of the biggest names in indigenous music.

Artists

Most of the **bands** mentioned opposite have work available on CD, while other outstanding artists whose albums are widely available include Yothu Yindi, No Fixed Address, Tiddas, Kev Carmody and Coloured Stone. Compilation albums are worth looking into also, particularly those that cover a wide range of styles: *Meinmuk – Music from the Top End* (1996) is a Triple J compilation of songs by 24 different Arnhemland bands, covering rock, reggae, gospel and metal; *Demarru Hits* is another good one, available through CAAMA (Central Australian Aboriginal Media Association) in Alice Springs, and some music retailers. CAAMA is an excellent source for the latest indigenous CDs and videos, all of which are available online at ⊛www.caama.com.au.

Cameron Wilson

Books

A ustralian writing came into its own in the 1890s, when a strong nation-
alistic movement, leading up to eventual federation in 1901, produced
writers such as Henry Lawson and the balladeer A.B. "Banjo" Paterson,
who romanticized the bush and glorified the mateship ethos, while outstanding women writers, such as Miles Franklin and Barbara Baynton, gave a
feminine slant to the bush tale and set the trend for a strong female authorship.
In the twentieth and twenty-first century, Australian novelists came to be recognized in the international arena: Patrick White was awarded a Nobel Prize
in 1973, Peter Carey won the Booker Prize in 1988 and again in 2001, and
Kate Grenville scored the 2001 Orange Prize for Fiction. Other writers who
have made a name for themselves within Australia, such as David Malouf, Julia
Leigh, Tim Winton, Thomas Keneally, Richard Flanagan, Chloe Hooper and
Robyn Davidson have aroused curiosity further afield. Some of the best were
recently collected together in the international literary magazine, *Granta,* in
Granta 70: Australia: The New New World. Literary journals such as *Meanjin,*
Southerly, Westerly and *Heat* provide a forum and exposure for short fiction,
essays, reviews and new and established writers. The big prizes in Australian fic-
tion include the Vogel Prize for the best unpublished novel written by an
author under the age of 35, and the country's most coveted literary prize, the
Miles Franklin Award.

Many of the best books by Australian writers or about Australia are not available overseas, so you may be surprised at the range of local titles available in
Australian **bookshops**. A good website to check is that of Gleebooks
(ⓦwww.gleebooks.com.au), one of Australia's best literary booksellers, with a
whole host of recent reviews; you can also order books online, to be posted
overseas.

Travel and travel guides

Bill Bryson *Down Under.*
Characteristically dry humour in this
outsider's view of national character,
though Australians will find Bryson
relies too much on stereotypes.

Bruce Chatwin *Songlines.* A semifictional account of an exploration
into Aboriginal nomadism and
mythology that turns out to be one
of the more readable expositions of
this complex subject, though often
pretentious.

Sean Condon *Sean and David's
Long Drive.* Australia's answer to
Kerouac's *On the Road*, with humour
in overdrive: Melbourne-based
Condon and his friend David are
fully fledged city dwellers when they

set off on a tour around their own
country, to come face to face with
the dangers of crocs, tour guides and
fellow travellers.

Robyn Davidson *Tracks.* A compelling account of a young woman's
journey across the Australian desert,
accompanied only by four camels
and a dog. Davidson manages to
break out of the heroic-traveller
mould to write with compassion and
honesty of the people she meets in
the Outback and the doubts, dangers
and loneliness she faces on her way.
A classic of its kind.

Neal Drinnan (ed) *The Rough
Guide to Gay & Lesbian Australia.*
Well-reviewed and comprehensive

manual listing gay-friendly hotels, bookshops, bars, cafés, restaurants and beaches, plus info on support groups and specialist travel services, and the lowdown on gay and lesbian events countrywide.

Howard Jacobson *In the Land of Oz.* Jacobson focuses his lucidly sarcastic observations on a round-Australia trip in the late 1980s that gets rather too close to some home truths for most Australians' tastes.

⭐ **Mark McCrum** *No Worries.* Knowing nothing of the country except the usual clichés, McCrum arrives in 1990s Australia and makes his way around by plane, train, thumb and Greyhound, meeting a surprising cast of characters along the way. As he travels, the stereotypes give way to an insightful picture of modern Australia.

Ruth Park *Ruth Park's Sydney.* Prolific novelist Park's 1973 guide to the city was fully revised and expanded in 1999. A perfect walking companion, full of personal insights, anecdotes and literary quotations.

Alice Thomson *The Singing Line.* The great-great-granddaughter of Alice Todd, the woman after whom Alice Springs was named, retraces her ancestor's journey to central Australia. Nice change from the usual male-centric view of the early pioneers.

Mark Whittaker and Amy Willesee *The Road to Mount Buggery: a Journey Through the Curiously Named Places of Australia.* Australia certainly has some unfortunate, banal and obscure place names, which Mark and Amy seek out on their journey, from Lake Disappointment to Cape Catastrophe. This entertaining, well-informed travelogue gives the fascinating stories behind the names.

Autobiography and biography

Julia Blackburn *Daisy Bates in the Desert.* For almost thirty years from 1913, Daisy Bates was Kabbarli, "the white-skinned grandmother", to the Aboriginal people with whom she lived in the desert. Blackburn's beautifully written biography interweaves fiction with fact to conjure up the life of one of Australia's most eccentric and misunderstood women.

Jill Ker Conway *The Road from Coorain.* Conway's childhood, on a drought-stricken Outback station during the 1940s, is movingly told, as is her battle to establish herself as a young historian in sexist, provincial 1950s Australia.

⭐ **Robert Drewe** *The Shark Net.* Accomplished novelist and journalist, Drewe has written a transfixing memoir of his boyhood and youth in Perth which segues into a literary true-crime story. Against a vividly drawn 1950s middle-class backdrop, Drewe shows how one man's random killing spree struck fear into the 'burbs of sunny, friendly and seemingly innocent Perth.

⭐ **Albert Facey** *A Fortunate Life.* A hugely popular autobiography of a battler, tracing his progress from a bush orphanage to Gallipoli, through the Depression, another war and beyond.

Eddie Mabo and Noel Loos *Edward Koiko Mabo: His Life and Struggle for Land Rights.* Mabo spent much of his life fighting for the autonomy of Torres Strait Islanders and in the process overthrew the concept of *terra nullius*, making his name a household word in Australia. Long interviews with the late black hero form the basis of this book and affectionately reveal the man behind the name.

David Malouf *12 Edmondstone Street*. An evocative autobiography-in-snatches of one of Australia's finest literary novelists, describing, in loving detail, the eponymous house in Brisbane where Malouf was born, life in the Tuscan village where he lives for part of each year, and his first visit to India.

Laurie Moore and Stephan Williams *The True Story of Jimmy Governor*. A powerful telling of the life of the real Aboriginal outlaw who Thomas Keneally based his character on in his famous novel *The Chant of Jimmie Blacksmith* (see p.1190).

Leah Purcell *Black Chicks Talking*. In an effort to overcome Aboriginal stereotypes, indigenous actor and writer Purcell gives insight into the lives of contemporary black women with this collection of lively, lengthy interviews, conducted with nine young females (all under 35), including the first Aboriginal Miss Australia (and now politician) Kathryn Hay, dancer Frances Rings, and actor Deborah Mailman; spin-offs from the book include a documentary, art exhibition and a play.

Hazel Rowley *Christina Stead: a Biography*. Stead (1902–83) has been acclaimed as Australia's greatest novelist. After spending years in Paris, London and New York with her American husband, she returned to Australia in her old age.

Daryl Tonkin and Carolyn Landon *Jackson's Track*. Ghostwritten autobiography of Tonkin, a bushman who fell in love with an Aboriginal woman, Euphemia Mullet, who worked on his timber-milling property in East Gippsland in the 1930s. The cross-cultural couple overcame prejudices to create their own life and family, living amongst a wider Aboriginal community at Jackson's Track.

Society and culture

Richard Baker *Land is Life: From Bush to Town – the Story of the Yanyuwa People*. The Yanyuwa people inhabited the Gulf of Carpentaria before the Europeans arrived, but most now live in the town of Borroloola, 1600km southeast of Darwin. Historian Baker, assigned a "skin" in the Yanyuwa kinship system, gathered the people's oral history and produced this fascinating story told from the Yanyuwa point of view and time.

★ **Geoffrey Blainey** *Triumph of the Nomads*. A fascinating account portraying Aboriginal people as masters and not victims of their environment. One of the best books on the subject.

Frank Brennan *Sharing the Country*. Both lawyer and Jesuit priest, and a former Aboriginal Affairs advisor to Australia's Catholic Church, Brennan sets out his legal and social solutions for reconciliation between black and white Australians.

Monica Furlong *Flight of the Kingfisher: a Journey Among Kukatja Aborigines*. Furlong lived among the Aboriginal people of the Great Sandy Desert; this is her account of Kukatja perceptions and spiritual beliefs.

Roslynn Haynes *Seeking the Centre: The Australian Desert in Literature, Art and Film*. The geographical and metaphorical impact of the desert on Australian culture is explored in this illustrated book, as is the connection Aboriginal people have with the desert.

David Headon *North of the Ten Commandments.* An anthology of Northern Territory writings from all perspectives and sources – an excellent literary souvenir for anyone who falls for the charms of Australia's "one percent" territory.

Donald Horne *The Lucky Country.* Although over twenty years old, this seminal analysis of Australian society, written in 1976, has yet to be matched and is still often quoted.

Margaret Simons *The Meeting of the Waters: the Hindmarsh Island Affair.* In the early 1990s a plan to build a bridge from South Australian Murray River town Goolwa to Hindmarsh Island was interrupted by a group of Aboriginal women who applied to the federal government for the bridge to be stopped because of undisclosed "secret women's business". A year later a group of dissenting women claimed this wasn't true, leading to a 1995 Royal Commission which concluded, perhaps wrongly, that it was indeed a fabrication, and the bridge was built. Journalist Simons' book follows in incredible detail and with a huge cast of characters, the ins and outs of the complex case.

History and politics

Patsy Adam-Smith *The Anzacs.* Gleaned from diaries, letters and interviews, this is a classic account of Australia's involvement in World War I, with a special focus on the campaign that has become part of the Australian legend, Gallipoli, where thousands of "Anzacs" lost their lives.

Robyn Annear *Nothing But Gold.* With an eye for interestingly obscure details and managing to convey a sense of irony without becoming cynical, this is a wonderfully readable account of the goldrushes of the nineteenth century, a period in Australia's history which perhaps did more than any other to shape the country's national character.

Len Beadell *Outback Highways.* Extracts from Len Beadell's half-dozen books, cheerfully recounting his life in the central Australian deserts as a surveyor, and his involvement in the construction of Woomera and the atomic bomb test sites.

⭐ **John Birmingham** *Leviathan: the unauthorised biography of* Sydney. This Birmingham 1999 tome casts a contemporary eye at the dark side of Sydney's history, from nauseating accounts of Rocks' slum life and the 1900 plague outbreak, through the 1970s traumas of Vietnamese boat people, now Sydney residents, to scandals of police corruption.

Michael Cannon *Black Land White Land: Who Killed the Koories?* An account of the violent 1840s in New South Wales, as colonists and pioneers moving inland clashed with the local Aboriginal tribes.

Paul Carter *The Road to Botany Bay.* A fascinating and original analysis of "discovery" as cultural imperialism, and the metaphysics of exploration.

Manning Clark *A Short History of Australia.* A condensed version of this leading historian's multivolumed tome, focusing on dreary successions of political administrations over two centuries, and cynically concluding with the "Age of Ruins".

Ann Curthoys *Freedom Ride: A Freedom Rider Remembers*. Now in her fifties and a history professor, Curthoys was one of the busload of young idealistic white university students who accompanied Aboriginal activist Charles Perkins (only 29 himself) on his revolutionary trip through northern NSW in 1965, to look at Aboriginal living conditions and root out and protest against racial discrimination – memorably gaining Moree's black kids entry to the local pool.

David Day *Claiming A Continent: A History of Australia*. A recent, general and easily readable history, concluding in 1996. Day looks at Australia's history from a contemporary point of view, with the possession, dispossession and ownership of the land – and thus issues of race – central to his narrative. Excellent recommended reading of recent texts at the end of each chapter will take you further.

Bruce Elder *Blood on the Wattle: Massacres and Maltreatment of Aboriginal Australians Since 1788*. A heart-rending account of the horrors inflicted on the continent's indigenous peoples, covering infamous nineteenth-century massacres as well as more recent mid-twentieth-century scandals of the "Stolen Generation" children.

Tim Flannery (ed) *Watkin Trench 1788*. One of the most vivid accounts of early Sydney was written by a twenty-something captain of the marines, Watkin Trench, who arrived with the First Fleet. Trench's humanity and youthful curiosity shine through the pages of "A Narrative of the Expedition to Botany Bay" and "A Complete Account of the Settlement of Port Jackson", and the characters who peopled the early settlement, like the Aboriginal Bennelong, come alive.

Ross Gibson *Seven Versions of an Australia Badland*. Travel on the long and lonely stretch of the Bruce Highway above the Tropic of Capricorn in Queensland, prompts dissection of a present-day nation's unease. Gibson's stories of diverse cultural histories, genocide, murder and exile reveal a "'badland" hiding under silence and denial.

Harry Gordon *Voyage from Shame: the Cowra Breakout and Afterwards*. Excellent account of the breakout of Japanese prisoners of war from a camp in New South Wales during World War II.

★ **Robert Hughes** *The Fatal Shore*. A minutely detailed epic of the origins of transportation and the brutal beginnings of white Australia.

Alan Moorehead *Cooper's Creek*. A historian's dramatic retelling of the ill-fated Burke and Wills expedition that set out in 1860 to make the first south-to-north crossing of the continent. A classic of exploration.

Rosemary Neill *White Out: How Politics is Killing Black Australia*. Journalist Neill asserts in this outspoken book that the rhetoric of self-determination and empowerment excuses the wider society from doing anything to reduce the disparity between black and white Australian populations. Busting taboos about indigenous affairs, she criticises both left and right ideologies.

Cassandra Pybus *Community of Thieves*. Attempting to reconcile past and future, fourth-generation Tasmanian Pybus provides a deeply felt account of the near-annihilation of the island's Aboriginal people.

Henry Reynolds *The Other Side of the Frontier* and *The Law of the Land*. A revisionist historian demonstrates that Aboriginal resistance to colonial invasion was both considerable and organized. *The Whispering in Our Hearts* is a history of those settler Australians who, troubled by the treatment of Aboriginal people, spoke out and took political action. His latest book, *Why Weren't We Told?*, is his most personal, an autobiographical journey showing how he, like many generations of Australians, imbibed a distorted, idealized Australian history, and describing his path to becoming an Aboriginal history specialist; includes a moving story about his friendship with Eddie Mabo.

Portia Robinson *The Women of Botany Bay*. After ten years of painstaking research into the records of every woman transported from Britain and Ireland between 1787 and 1828, as well as the wives of convicts who settled in Australia, Robinson is able to tell us, with conviction and passion, just who the women of Botany Bay really were.

Eric Rolls *Sojourners and Citizens* and *Flowers and The Wide Sea*. The first and second volumes of farmer-turned-historian Rolls' fascinatingly detailed history of the Chinese in Australia. The first volume of his latest work, the ambitious *Australia: A Biography*, describes the continent before the arrival of humans; the second will tell of those first inhabitants and what befell them.

Anne Summers *Damned Whores and God's Police*. Stereotypical images of women in Australian society are explored in this ground-breaking reappraisal of Australian history from a feminist point of view, updated in 1994.

Ecology and environment

★ **Tim Flannery** *The Future Eaters*. Palaeontologist Flannery here poses that as the first human beings migrated down to Australasia, the Aborigines, Maoris and other Polynesian peoples changed the region's flora and fauna in startling ways, and began consuming the resources needed for their own future; the Europeans made an even greater impact on the environment, continuing this "future eating" of natural resources.

Josephine Flood *The Riches of AncientAustralia*. An indispensable and lavish guide to Australia's most famous landforms and sites. The same author's *Archaeology of the Dreamtime* provides background on the development of Aboriginal society.

Drew Hutton and Libby Connors *A History of the Australian Environmental Movement*. Written by a husband-and-wife team, Queensland academics and prominent in Green politics, this well-balanced book charts the progress of conservation attempts from 1860 to modern protests.

Peter Latz *Bushfires and Bushtucker: Aboriginal Plant Use in Central Australia*. Handbook with photos, published by an Aboriginal-owned press.

Tim Murray (ed) *Archeology of Australia*. The last thirty years have seen many ground-breaking discoveries in Australian archeology, with three sites in particular of great significance: Kakadu in the Northern Territory, Lake Mungo in NSW, and South West Tasmania; a range of specialists contribute essays on the subject.

Mary White *The Greening of Gondwana*. Classic work on the evolution of Australia's flora and geography.

Contemporary fiction

Thea Astley *The Multiple Effects of Rainshadow*. On an Aboriginal island reserve in 1930, a white woman dies in childbirth, and her husband goes on a shotgun and dynamite rampage. The novel traces the effects over the years on eight characters who witnessed the violent events, ultimately exploring the brutality and racism in Australian life.

Murray Bail *Eucalyptus*. This beautifully written novel has a fairy-tale-like plot: NSW farmer, Holland, has planted nearly every type of eucalyptus tree on his land. When his extraordinarily beautiful daughter Ellen is old enough to marry, he sets up a challenge for her legion of potential suitors, to name each tree.

John Birmingham *The Tasmanian Babes Fiasco*. Hilarious cult classic, about flat-share hell in contemporary Brisbane, and a follow up to *He Died With A Felafel In His Hand*, a collection of squalid and very funny tales emerging from experiences with the 89 people who the dissolute author had the misfortune of sharing house with in the 1980s.

Anson Cameron *Tin Toys*. The Aboriginal "Stolen Generation" issue explored through the tale of Hunter Carolyn, an unintentional artist who can change skin colour at will.

⭐ **Peter Carey** *Bliss*. Carey's first and perhaps best novel is the story of a Sydney ad executive who drops out to New Age New South Wales. Other novels by Carey to look out for include his two Booker Prize winners *Oscar and Lucinda* and *The True History of the Kelly Gang*, about the bushranger Ned Kelly. Also worth a read are his bizarre short stories, *The Fat Man in History*, with which he launched his career.

Peter Corris *The Empty Beach*. Australia's answer to Raymond Chandler. Corris's hard-boiled novel is set in a glittering but seedy Sydney, where a soft-centred private eye investigates murder and exploitation in an old people's home.

Robert Drewe *The Savage Crows*. This first novel, from one of Australia's best writers, is among his most powerful. A writer, whose own life is falling apart in a cockroach-ridden Sydney of the 1970s, sets out to discover the grim truth behind Tasmania's "final solution".

Richard Flanagan *Death of a River Guide, The Sound of One Hand Clapping*. Thoughtful writings about landscape, place, migration and the significance of history in these two novels, both set in Tasmania. In *Death of a River Guide*, the novel's narrator, Aljaz Cosini, goes over his life and that of his family and forebears as he lies drowning. His second novel, *The Sound of One Hand Clapping*, follows 38-year-old Sonya Buloh as she returns to Tasmania to confront her alcoholic father and her past. In his latest, a historical novel, Tasmania is once again the brutal penal settlement of Van Dieman's Land in the nineteenth-century-set *Gould's Book of Fish: a novel in Twelve Fish*, which won the 2002 Commonwealth Prize.

Tom Gilling *Miles McGinty*. Gilling is known for his colourful historical fables. Nineteenth-century Sydney comes alive in this riotous, entertaining love story of Miles, who becomes a levitator's assistant and begins to float on air, and Isabel, who wants to fly.

Kate Grenville *Lillian's Story*. The tragicomic tale of Lillian Singer is loosely based on the life of Bea Miles, the eccentric, Shakespeare-spouting, taxi-hijacking Sydney bag lady. Grenville's latest novel, *The Idea* *of Perfection*, set in the tiny, fictional NSW town of Karakarook, and about two unlikely characters who fall in love, won the 2001 Orange Prize for Fiction.

Sarah Hay *Skins*. The 2001 Vogel Prize-winning novel is based on the true story of a young female ship-wreck survivor marooned on Middle Island, off Western Australia's south coast. She, her brother and sister and other survivors are at the mercy of the gang of brutal seal hunters who have already subjected three kid-napped Aboriginal women to slavery and sexual abuse.

Chloe Hooper *A Child's Book of True Crime*. A lot of hype surrounds Hooper's first novel, picked up by a famous literary agent, published in fifteen countries, and commanding huge sums. Set in Tasmania, which gives it a wonderful sense of claus-trophobia, the perverse, chilling novel is narrated by a young primary school teacher having an affair with the married father of her smartest pupil. His writer-wife's true-crime book, about a love triangle that dis-integrates into murder, leads the anxious teacher into imagining a child's classic-Australian-literature-style version, with characters like Kitty Koala and Wally Wombat.

Janette Turner Hospital *Oyster*. Disquieting novel set in the literally off-the-map, opal-mining, one-pub Queensland town of Inner Maroo, whose inhabitants are either rough-as-guts mining people, or religious fundamentalists.

David Ireland *City of Women*. Ireland creates weird visions of Sydney: a futuristic, violent place from which men have been ban-ished. Also keep an eye peeled for his first novel, *The Glass Canoe*, and *Archimedes and the Seagle*, the latter a delightful philosophical discussion between a dog and a bird as they

roam The Domain and Woolloomooloo.

Linda Jaivin *Eat Me*. A successful first novel billed as an "erotic feast"; opens with a memorable fruit-squeezing scene (and this is only the shopping) as three trendy Sydney women (fashion editor, academic and writer) swap stories of sexual exploits.

Elizabeth Jolley *Woman in a Lampshade*. This is an excellent collec-tion of short stories to introduce you to Jolley's original and quirky work, which thrives on black humour. *The Sugar Mother* examines what happens to a faithful husband when his wife goes on sabbatical and a young woman and her mother turn up on his doorstep demanding shelter.

Douglas Kennedy *The Dead Heart*. A best-selling comic thriller made into a film; an itinerant American journalist gets abducted by man-eating hillbillies in Outback Australia.

Matthew Kneale *English Passengers*. British author Kneale won the Whitbread Prize for Best Book in 2000 for his cleverly structured novel about an 1857 voyage to Tasmania, where the Reverend Geoffrey Wilson is sure he will discover the Garden of Eden. A cast of twenty narrate the tale, including an Aboriginal boy and his white sealer father.

Julia Leigh *The Hunter*. Intriguing, internationally acclaimed first novel about the re-discovery and subsequent hunt of the Tasmanian tiger; a bit obvious in places – a faceless biotech company after thylacine DNA plays the bad guy – but well written.

David Malouf *The Conversations at Curlow Creek*. One of Australia's most important contemporary writers charts the developing rela-tionship between two Irishmen the night before a hanging; one is the officer appointed to supervise the execution and the other the outlaw facing his death. Also look for Malouf's *Dream Stuff* a collection of short stories which far outshines much of his output over the last decade.

Christos Tsiolkas *Loaded*. A gritty debut novel set in suburban Melbourne: caught between the traditional Greek world of his family and his emerging gay identity,

19-year-old Ari is unemployed and self-destructing in his milieu of drugs, clubs and anonymous sex. The 1998 film *Head On* (see p.1188) was based on the novel.

Tim Winton *Cloudstreet*. A wonderful, faintly magical saga about the mixed fortunes of two families who end up sharing a house in postwar Perth. His latest, *Dirt Music*, was shortlisted for the 2002 Booker Prize.

Australian classics

Barbara Baynton *Bush Studies*. A collection of nineteenth-century bush stories written from the female perspective.

Rolf Boldrewood *Robbery Under Arms*. The story of Captain Starlight, a notorious bushranger and rustler around the Queensland borders.

Marcus Clarke *For the Term of his Natural Life*. Written in 1870 in somewhat overblown prose, this romantic tragedy is based on actual events in Tasmania's once notorious prison settlement.

Miles Franklin *My Brilliant Career*. A novel about a spirited young girl in turn-of-the-twentieth-century Victoria who refuses to conform.

May Gibbs *Snugglepot and Cuddlepie*. A timeless children's favourite: the illustrated adventures of two little creatures who live inside gumnuts.

Barbara Hanrahan *The Scent of Eucalyptus*. This first novel by the late South Australian writer captures the essence of Adelaide in the 1960s.

Xavier Herbert *Capricornia*. An indignant and allegorical saga of the brutal and haphazard settlement of the land of Capricornia (tropical Northern Territory thinly disguised).

George Johnston *My Brother Jack*. The first in a disturbing trilogy set

in Melbourne suburbia between the wars, which develops into a semifictional attempt to dissipate the guilt Johnston felt at being disillusioned with, and finally leaving, his native land.

Thomas Keneally *The Chant of Jimmie Blacksmith*. A prize-winning novel that delves deep into the psyche of an Aboriginal outlaw, tracing his inexorable descent into murder and crime. Sickening, brutal and compelling.

Henry Lawson Ballads, poems and stories from Australia's best-loved chronicler come in a wide array of collections. A few to seek out are: *Henry Lawson Bush Ballads*, *Henry Lawson Favourites* and *While the Billy Boils – Poetry*.

Norman Lindsay *The Magic Pudding*. A whimsical tale of some very strange men and their grumpy, flavour-changing and endless pudding; a children's classic with very adult humour.

Ruth Park *The Harp in the South*. First published in 1948, this first book in a trilogy is a well-loved tale of inner-Sydney slum life in 1940s Surry Hills. The spirited Darcy family's battle against poverty provides memorable characters.

A.B. ("Banjo") Paterson Australia's

most famous bush balladeer, author of *Waltzing Matilda* and *The Man from Snowy River*, who helped romanticize the bush's mystique. Some of the many titles published include *Banjo Paterson's Favourites* and *Man From Snowy River and Other Verses*.

Henry Handel Richardson *The Getting of Wisdom*. A gangly country girl's experience of a snobby boarding school in turn-of-the-twentieth-century Melbourne; like Miles Franklin (see opposite), Richardson was actually a female writer.

★ **Nevil Shute** *A Town Like Alice*. A wartime romance which tells of a woman's bravery, endurance and enterprise, both in the Malayan jungle and in the Australian Outback where she strives to create the town of the title.

Christina Stead *For Love Alone*. Set largely around Sydney Harbour, where the late author grew up, this novel follows the obsessive Teresa Hawkins, a poor but artistic girl from a large, unconventional family, who scrounges and saves to head for London and love.

Randolph Stow *The Merry-go-round in the Sea*. An endearing tale of a young boy growing up in rural Western Australia during World War II.

Kylie Tennant *Ride on Stranger*. First published in 1943, this is a humorous portrait of Sydney between the two world wars, seen through the eyes of newcomer Shannon Hicks.

Patrick White Considered dense and symbolic – even visionary (though some claim misogynistic) – White's novels can be heavy going, but try and plough through *Voss*, *A Fringe of Leaves* or *The Twyborn Affair*, the last a contemporary exploration of ambiguous sexuality.

Poetry and anthologies

Phillip Adams and Patrice Newell *The Penguin Book of Australian Jokes*. An excellent introduction to the Australian sense of humour, divided into twenty sections close to the nation's heart, among them "A Sporting Chance", "The Work Ethic" and "History and the Yarts". You'll probably need a local to explain a lot of the references.

Graeme Aitken (ed) *The Penguin Book of Gay Australian Writing*. Published in 2002, the editor's original aim was to collect together new gay writing, but nowadays such narrow definitions aren't fashionable. Aitken was forced to trawl back over seventy years and has widened his scope to include gay and bisexual authors or subject matter, non-fiction and fiction, including novel extracts from the late Patrick White

as well as contemporary novelists Christos Tsiolkas and Neal Drinnan.

Don Anderson (ed) *65–95 Contemporary Classics*. One of the country's most eminent literary critics chooses the best of recent Australian short writing, from Glenda Adams to Tim Winton.

Carmel Bird (ed) *The Penguin Century of Australian Stories*. One hundred and thirty years of short-story writing, from Henry Lawson to Helen Garner and beyond. Ideal interstate bus companion.

Les Murray *Subhuman Redneck Poems*. A collection by the outspoken, larger than life and internationally recognized Australian poet, who lives on a farm in the New South Wales bush.

Dale Spender (ed) *The Penguin Anthology of Australian Women's Writing*. A brick-sized book containing all the best of Australian women's writing, from Elizabeth Macarthur to Germaine Greer.

John Tranter and Philip Mead (eds) *The Penguin Book of Modern Australian Poetry*. Poetry has a popular and active appeal Down Under; the twentieth century's best are collected in this anthology.

Aboriginal writing

Faith Bandler *Welour, My Brother*. A novel by a well-known black activist describing a boy's early life in Queensland, and the tensions of a racially mixed community.

John Muk Muk Burke *Bridge of Triangles*. Powerful, landscape-driven images in this tale of a mixed-race child growing up unable to associate with either side of his heritage, but refusing to accept the downward spiral into despair and alcoholism adopted by those around him.

Evelyn Crawford *Over My Tracks*. Told to Chris Walsh, this oral autobiography is the story of a formidable woman, from her 1930s childhood among the red sandhills of Yantabulla, through her Outback struggles as a mother of fourteen children, to her tireless work, late in life, with Aboriginal students, combating prejudice with education.

Nene Gare *The Fringe Dwellers*. A story of an Aboriginal family on the edge of town and society.

Ruby Langford *Don't Take Your Love to Town*. An autobiography demonstrating a black woman's courage and humour in the face of tragedy and poverty lived out in northern New South Wales and the inner city of Sydney.

Sally Morgan *My Place*. A widely acclaimed and best-selling account of a Western Australian woman's discovery of her black roots.

David Mowaljarlai and Jutta Malnic *Yorro Yorro*. Starry-eyed photographer Malnic's musings while recording sacred Wandjina sites in the west Kimberley and, more interestingly, Mowaljarlai's account of his upbringing and Ngarinyin tribal lore.

⭐ **Mudrooroo** *Wildcat Falling*. The first novel to be published (in 1965) by an Aboriginal writer, under the name Colin Johnson, this is the story of a black teenage delinquent coming of age in the 1950s. *Doctor Wooreddy's Prescription for Enduring the Ending of the World* details the attempted annihilation of the Tasmanian Aborigines. Mudrooroo's three latest novels – *The Kwinkan* (1995), *The Undying* (1998) and *Underground* (1999) – are part of his magic-realist Master of Ghost Dreaming series.

Oodgeroo Noonuccal *My People*. A collection of verse by an established campaigning poet (previously known as Kath Walker).

Paddy Roe *Gularabulu*. Stories from the west Kimberley, both traditional myths and tales of a much more recent origin.

Kim Scott *Benang*. Infuriated at reading the words of A.O. Neville, Protector of Aborigines in Western Australia in the 1930s, who planned to "breed out" Aborigines from Australia, author Scott wrote this powerful tale of Nyoongar history using Neville's own themes to overturn his elitist arguments.

Archie Weller *The Day of the Dog*. Weller's violent first novel came out in an angry burst after being released, at 23, from incarceration in Broome jail. The protagonist, in a similiar situation, is pressured back into a criminal world by his Aboriginal peers and by police harassment. Searing pace and

forceful writing. His second novel, *Land of the Golden Clouds*, is an epic science-fiction fantasy, set 3000 years in the future, which portrays an Australia devastated by a nuclear holocaust and populated by warring tribes.

Specialist and wildlife guides

Jack Absalom *Safe Outback Travel*. A recent edition of the bible for Outback driving and camping, full of sensible precautions and handy tips for preparation and repair.

Jean-Paul Bruneteau *Tukka: Real Australian Food*. This chef, who arrived in Australia in 1967 as a child from France, is passionate about the use and understanding of native Australian foods. More than just a cookbook, this is a wide-ranging combination of well-researched history and botany too.

Ben Canaider and Greg Duncan Powell *Drink Drank Drunk*. Fun, no-nonsense 2003 guide to Australian wine by an irreverent duo.

Catherine de Courcey and John Johnson *River Tracks: Exploring Australian Rivers*. A practical and up-to-date motoring guide to six river journeys, providing lots of insider insight and history too.

The Great Barrier Reef A Reader's Digest complete rundown on the Reef, lucid and lavishly illustrated. Available in coffee-table format and in a slighter, more portable, edited edition.

Leigh Hemmings *Great Australian Bike Rides*. A detailed illustrated guide, with gradient profiles and maps plus sections on packing and maintenance.

Tim Low *Bush Tucker: Australia's Wild Food Harvest* and *Wild Food Plants of Australia*. Guides to the bountiful supply of bushtucker that was once the mainstay of the Aboriginal diet; the latter is pocket-sized and contains clear photographs of over 180 plants, describing their uses.

Greg Pritchard *Climbing Australia: the Essential Guide*. The most up-to-date, comprehensive guide for rock-climbers. Covers everything from the major climbing sites to the best websites, with easy-to-understand route descriptions.

Mark Shields and Huon Hooke *The Penguin Good Australian Wine Guide*. Released every year in Australia, this is a handy book for a wine buff to buy on the ground, with the best wines and prices detailed to help navigate you around the bottle shop.

Peter and Pat Slater *Field Guide to Australian Birds*. Pocket-sized, and the easiest to use of the many available guides to Australian birds.

Tyrone Thomas Regional bush-walking guides by local publisher Hill of Content. A series of ten local guides (often updated), which make excellent trail companions.

Mark Warren *Atlas of Australian Surfing*. A comprehensive guide to riding the best of Australia's waves.

Australian English

The colourful variant of Australian English, or strine (which is how "Australian" is pronounced with a very heavy Australian accent), has its origins in the archaic cockney and Irish of the colony's early convicts as well as the adoption of words from the many Aboriginal languages. For such a vast country, the accent barely varies to the untutored ear; from Tasmania to the northwest you'll find little variation in the national drawl, with its curious, interrogative ending to sentences – although Queenslanders are noted for their slow delivery. One of the most consistent tendencies of strine is to abbreviate words and then stick an "-o" or, more commonly, an "-ie" on the end: as in "bring your cozzie to the barbie this arvo" (bring your swimming costume to the barbecue this afternoon). This informality extends to the frequent use of "bloody", "bugger" and "bastard", the latter two used affectionately. Attempting to abuse someone by calling them a bastard will most likely end up in an offer of a beer. There's also an endearing tendency to genderize inanimate objects as, for example, "she's buggered, mate" (your inanimate object is beyond repair) or "do 'im up nice and tight" (be certain that your inanimate object is well affixed).

The popularity of dire Australian TV soap operas has seen strine spread overseas, much as Americanisms have pervaded the English-speaking world. Popular strinisms such as "hang a U-ey" (make a U-turn) and the versatile and agreeable "no worries" are now commonly used outside Australia.

The country has its own excellent Macquarie Dictionary, the latest edition of which is the ultimate authority on the current state of Australian English. What follows is our own essential list.

Akubra Wide-brimmed felt hat; a brand name.

Anzac Australia and New Zealand Army Corps; every town has a memorial to Anzac casualties from both world wars.

Arvo Afternoon.

Back o' Bourke Outback.

Banana bender Resident of Queensland.

Barbie Barbecue.

Battler Someone who struggles to make a living, as in "little Aussie battler".

Beaut! or you beauty! Exclamation of delight.

Beg yours? Excuse me, say again?

Beyond the Black Stump Outback; back of beyond.

Billabong Waterhole in dry riverbed.

Billy Cooking pot.

Bitumen Sealed road as opposed to dirt road.

Blowies Blow flies.

Bludger Someone who does not pull their weight, or a scrounger – as in "dole bludger".

Blue Fight; also a red-haired person.

Blundstones Leather, elastic-sided workmen's boots, now also a fashion item in some circles. Often shortened to "blundies".

Bonzer Good, a good thing.

Bottle shop Off-licence or liquor store.

Brumby Feral horse.

Buckley's No chance; as in "hasn't got a Buckley's".

Bugs Moreton Bay bug – type of crayfish indigenous to southern Queensland.

Bunyip Monster of Aboriginal legend; bogeyman.

Burl Give it a go; as in "give it a burl".

Bush Unsettled country area.

Bushranger Runaway convict; nineteenth-century outlaw.

Bushwhacker Someone lacking in social graces, a hick.

BYO Bring your own. Restaurant which allows you to bring your own alcohol.

Chook Chicken.

Chunder Vomit.

Cocky Small farmer; cow cocky, dairy farmer.

To come the raw prawn To try and deceive or make a fool of someone.

Coo-eee! Aboriginal long-distance greeting, now widely adopted as a kind of "yoo hoo!"

Corroboree Aboriginal ceremony.

Cozzies Bathers, swimmers, togs; swimming costume.

Crim Criminal.

Crook Sick or broken.

Crow eater Resident of South Australia.

Cut lunch Sandwiches.

Dag Nerd

Daggy Unattractive.

Daks or strides Trousers/pants.

Dam A man-made body of water or reservoir; not just the dam itself.

Damper Soda bread cooked in a pot on embers.

Dekko To look at; as in "take a dekko at this".

Deli Delicatessen, corner shop or sandwich bar.

Derro Derelict or destitute person.

Didgeridoo Droning musical instrument made from a termite-hollowed branch.

Digger Old-timer, especially an old soldier.

Dill Idiot.

Dilly bag Aboriginal carry-all made of bark, or woven or rigged twine.

Dinkum True, genuine, honest.

Disposal store Store that sells used army and navy equipment, plus camping gear.

Dob in To tell on someone; as in "she dobbed him in".

Drizabone Voluminous waxed cotton raincoat, originally designed for horse riding; a brand name.

Drongo Fool.

Drover Cowboy or station hand.

Dunny Outside pit toilet.

Esky Portable, insulated box to keep food or beer cold.

Fair dinkum or **dinky di** Honestly, truly.

Fossick To search for gold or gems in abandoned diggings.

Galah Noisy or garrulous person.

Galvo Corrugated iron.

Garbo Garbage or refuse collector.

G'day Hello, hi.

Gibber Rock or boulder.

Give away To give up or resign; as in "I used to be a garbo but I gave it away".

Grog Alcoholic drink, usually beer.

Gub, gubbah Aboriginal terms for a white person.

Gutless wonder Coward.

Hoon A yob, delinquent.

Humpy Temporary shelter used by Aborigines and early pioneers.

Jackeroo Male station hand.

Jilleroo Female station hand.

Joey Baby kangaroo still in the pouch (also, less familiarly, a baby koala).

Koorie Collective name for Aboriginal people from southeastern Australia.

Larrikin Mischievous youth.

Lay by Practice of putting a deposit on goods until they can be fully paid for.

Lollies Sweets or candy.

Manchester Linen goods.

Mate A sworn friend, as essential as beer to the Australian stereotype.

Mexicans Residents of New South Wales and Victoria.

Milk bar Corner shop, and often a small café.

Moleskins Strong cotton trousers worn by bushmen.

Never Never Outback, wilderness.

New Australian Recent immigrants; often a euphemism for Australians of non-British descent.

No worries That's OK; It doesn't matter; Don't mention it.

Ocker Uncultivated Australian male.

Op shop Short for "Opportunity Shop"; a charity shop/thrift store.

Outback Remote, unsettled regions of Australia.

Paddock Field.

Panel van Van with no rear windows and front seating only.

Pashing Kissing or snogging, often in the back of a panel van.

Perve To leer or act as a voyeur; as in "What are you perving at?"

Piss Beer.

Piss head Drunkard.

Pissed Drunk.

Pokies One-armed bandits; gambling machines.

Pommie or Pom Person of English descent – not necessarily abusive.

Rapt Very pleased, delighted.

Ratbag An eccentric person; also a term of mild abuse.

Ratshit or **shithouse** How you feel after a night on the piss.

Rego Vehicle registration document.

Ridji Didge The real thing or genuine article.

Ripper! Rather old-fashioned exclamation of enthusiasm.

Rollies Roll-up cigarettes.

Root Vulgar term for sexual congress.

Rooted To be very tired or to be beyond repair; as in "she's rooted, mate" – your [car] is irreparable.

Ropable Furious to the point of requiring restraint.

Rouseabout An unskilled labourer in a shearing-shed.

Sandgroper Resident of Western Australia.

She'll be right or she'll be apples Everything will work out fine.

Shoot through To pass through or leave hurriedly.

Shout To pay for someone, or to buy a round of drinks; as in "it's your shout, mate".

Sickie To take a day off work due to (sometimes alleged) illness; as in "to pull a sickie".

Singlet Sleeveless cotton vest. The archetypal Australian singlet, in navy, is produced by Bonds.

Skivvy Polo neck.

Slab 24-can carton of beer.

Smoko Tea break.

Snag Sausage.

Speedo Famous Australian brand of athletic swimming costume; speedos (or sluggos) commonly refers to men's swimming briefs, as opposed to swimming trunks.

Spunk Attractive or sexy person of either gender; as in "what a spunk!" Can also be used as an adjective: spunky.

Squatter Historical term for early settlers who took up public land as their own.

Station Very large pastoral property or ranch.

Sticky beak Nosy person, or to be nosy; as in "let's have a sticky beak".

Stockman Cowboy or station hand.

Stubby Small bottle of beer.

Swag Large bedroll, or one's belongings.

Tall poppy Someone who excels or is eminent. "Cutting down tall poppies" is to bring overachievers back to earth – a national pastime.

Thongs Flip-flops or sandals.

Throw a wobbly Lose your temper.

Tinnie Can of beer, or a small aluminium boat.

Ute Short for "utility" vehicle; pick-up truck.

Wacko! Exclamation of enthusiasm.

Walkabout Temporary migration undertaken by Aborigines; also has the wider meaning of a journey. **Gone walkabout** To go missing.

Warm fuzzies Feeling of contentment.

Waxhead Surfer.

Weatherboard Wooden house.

Whinger Someone who complains – allegedly common among Poms.

Wog Derogatory description for those of Mediterranean descent.

Wowser Killjoy.

Yabber To talk or chat.

Yabbie Freshwater crayfish.

Yakka Work, as in "hard yakka".

Yobbo Uncouth person.

Index

and small print

Index

Map entries are in colour.

INDEX

INDEX

I

INDEX

Twenty Years of Rough Guides

In the summer of 1981, Mark Ellingham, Rough Guides' founder, knocked out the first guide on a typewriter, with a group of friends. Mark had been travelling in Greece after university, and couldn't find a guidebook that really answered his needs.There were heavyweight cultural guides on the one hand – good on museums and classical sites but not on beaches and tavernas – and on the other hand student manuals that were so caught up with how to save money that they lost sight of the country's significance beyond its role as a place for a cool vacation. None of the guides began to address Greece as a country, with its natural and human environment, its politics and its contemporary life.

Having no urgent reason to return home, Mark decided to write his own guide. It was a guide to Greece that tried to combine some erudition and insight with a thoroughly practical approach to travellers' needs. Scrupulously researched listings of places to stay, eat and drink were matched by careful attention to detail on everything from Homer to Greek music, from classical sites to national parks and from nude beaches to monasteries. Back in London, Mark and his friends got their Rough Guide accepted by a farsighted commissioning editor at the publisher Routledge and it came out in 1982.

The Rough Guide to Greece was a student scheme that became a publishing phenomenon. The immediate success of the book – shortlisted for the Thomas Cook award – spawned a series that rapidly covered dozens of countries. The Rough Guides found a ready market among backpackers and budget travellers, but soon acquired a much broader readership that included older and less impecunious visitors. Readers relished the guides' wit and inquisitiveness as much as the enthusiastic, critical approach that acknowledges everyone wants value for money – but not at any price.

Rough Guides soon began supplementing the "rougher" information – the hostel and low-budget listings – with the kind of detail that independent-minded travellers on any budget might expect. These days, the guides – distributed worldwide by the Penguin group – include recommendations spanning the range from shoestring to luxury, and cover more than 200 destinations around the globe. Our growing team of authors, many of whom come to Rough Guides initially as outstandingly good letter-writers telling us about their travels, are spread all over the world, particularly in Europe, the USA and Australia. As well as the travel guides, Rough Guides publishes a series of dictionary phrasebooks covering two dozen major languages, an acclaimed series of music guides running the gamut from Classical to World Music, a series of music CDs in association with World Music Network, and a range of reference books on topics as diverse as the Internet, Pregnancy and Unexplained Phenomena. Visit **www.roughguides.com** to see what's cooking.

Rough Guide credits

Text editor: Sally Schafer
Managing Director: Kevin Fitzgerald
Series editor: Mark Ellingham
Editorial: Martin Dunford, Jonathan Buckley,
Kate Berens, Ann-Marie Shaw, Helena Smith,
Olivia Swift, Matthew Teller, Geoff Howard,
Claire Saunders, Gavin Thomas, Alexander
Mark Rogers, Polly Thomas, Joe Staines,
Richard Lim, Duncan Clark, Peter Buckley,
Lucy Ratcliffe, Clifton Wilkinson, Alison
Murchie, Andrew Dickson, Fran Sandham,
Matthew Milton, Karoline Densley (UK);
Andrew Rosenberg, Yuki Takagaki, Richard
Koss, Hunter Slaton (US)
Design & Layout: Link Hall, Helen Prior, Julia
Bovis, Katie Pringle, Rachel Holmes, Andy
Turner, Dan May, Tanya Hall, John McKay,
Sophie Hewat (UK); Madhulita Mohapatra,

Umesh Aggarwal, Sunil Sharma (India)
Cartography: Maxine Repath, Ed Wright,
Katie Lloyd-Jones (UK); Manish Chandra,
Rajesh Chhibber, Jai Prakash Mishra (India)
Cover art direction: Louise Boulton
Picture research: Sharon Martins, Mark
Thomas
Online: Kelly Martinez, Anja Mutic-Blessing,
Jennifer Gold, Audra Epstein, Suzanne
Welles, Cree Lawson (US); Manik Chauhan,
Amarjyoti Dutta, Narender Kumar (India)
Finance: Gary Singh
Marketing & Publicity: Richard Trillo, Niki
Smith, David Wearn, Chloë Roberts, Demelza
Dallow, Claire Southern (UK); Geoff Colquitt,
David Wechsler, Megan Kennedy (US)
Administration: Julie Sanderson
RG India: Punita Singh

Publishing information

This sixth edition published October 2003 by
Rough Guides Ltd,
80 Strand, London WC2R 0RL
345 Hudson St, 4th Floor,
New York, NY 10014, USA.
Distributed by the Penguin Group
Penguin Books Ltd,
80 Strand, London WC2R 0RL
Penguin Putnam, Inc.
375 Hudson Street, NY 10014, USA
Penguin Books Australia Ltd,
487 Maroondah Highway, PO Box 257,
Ringwood, Victoria 3134, Australia
Penguin Books Canada Ltd,
10 Alcorn Avenue, Toronto, Ontario,
Canada M4V 1E4
Penguin Books (NZ) Ltd,
182–190 Wairau Road, Auckland 10,
New Zealand
Typeset in Bembo and Helvetica to an
original design by Henry Iles.
Printed in Italy by LegoPrint S.p.A

1232pp includes index
A catalogue record for this book is available
from the British Library

ISBN 1-84353-067-8

The publishers and authors have done their
best to ensure the accuracy and currency of
all the information in **The Rough Guide to
Australia**, however, they can accept no
responsibility for any loss, injury, or incon-
venience sustained by any traveller as a
result of information or advice contained in
the guide.

1   3   5   7   9   8   6   4   2

Help us update

We've gone to a lot of effort to ensure that the
sixth edition of **The Rough Guide to
Australia** is accurate and up-to-date.
However, things change – places get
"discovered", opening hours are notoriously
fickle, restaurants and rooms raise prices or
lower standards. If you feel we've got it wrong
or left something out, we'd like to know, and if
you can remember the address, the price, the
time, the phone number, so much the better.
     We'll credit all contributions, and send a
copy of the next edition (or any other Rough

Guide if you prefer) for the best letters.
Everyone who writes to us and isn't already a
subscriber will receive a copy of our full-
colour thrice-yearly newsletter. Please mark
letters: "**Rough Guide Australia Update**"
and send to: Rough Guides, 80 Strand,
London WC2R 0RL, or Rough Guides, 4th
Floor, 345 Hudson St, New York, NY 10014.
Or send an email to **mail@roughguides.com**
     Have your questions answered and tell
others about your trip at
www.roughguides.atinfopop.com

Acknowledgements

Margo Daly In Tasmania I'd like to thank Rod Parish, Jan Dale, Tim Dub and Rosie Waitt, Mark Mooney, Sha Sha Kwa and Caleb Gardner, Mark Hannam, Michelle Grima from Tourism Tasmania, and Mike Callinan from YHA Tasmania. In Sydney, thanks to Silke Kerwick of YHA NSW, and Adrian Proszenko for bars, clubs and music research. In Newcastle thanks to the Parkhouse brothers Nick and Damien, and Pam Gibbs of Tourism Newcastle. Thanks to Linden Hyatt for Blue Mountains hospitality, Janine Daly for kindness, support and extra Sydney research, Michael Bicknell for the last-minute film reviews, Caroline Nesbitt and Franca Morelli for fabulous help with childcare, and above all my travelling companions and fellow Tasmania-lovers Margaret and Arthur Daly and Lila.

Anne Dehne A big thank you to my friends for assistance, advice, support and companionship, especially to Julie Gittus and Ashley Mckeon. Also thanks to helpful staff at visitor information centres all over Victoria, particularly at Echuca, and last but not least to the editor Sally Schafer for her patience and understanding.

Rosie Waitt and Tim Dub Our thanks to the South Australian Tourist Commission and to Chris Burchett in Goolwa for their cheerful assistance, and to all those other South Australian individuals and businesses who made our stay in the Festival State so enjoyable.

In addition the editor would like to thank all those involved in producing this book, including Umesh Aggarwal for expert typesetting and layout; Sharon Martins for excellent picture research; Manish Chandra, Jai Prakash Mishra, Rajesh Chhibber and Sam Kirby for their cartographic expertise; Louise Boulton for the superb cover; Jo Mead for meticulous proofreading; Helena Smith and Gavin Thomas for additional editing; and especially Claire Saunders and Clifton Wilkinson for all their advice.

SMALL PRINT

Readers' letters

We'd like to thank all the readers who wrote in with comments and updates for this new edition (and apologies to anyone whose name we've misspelt or omitted):

Nick Adams, David Alldridge, Carla Ambrose, Sally Attwood, N.A. Baker, Roy and Audrey Bradford, Wendy Bradley, Tim Burford, C.W. Callister, Katie Carew, Jean Cartwright, Julie Clayton, Richard Crighton, Kelly Cross, Tom Crow, Emma Cutler, Chris Davis, Dietrich De Roeck, Lucinda Deacon-Davis, Ian Dickson, Tara Doheny, Bruce Doig, Alison Donnelly, John Donovan, Stephen Drewe, Kenny Dryburgh, Sonya Duck, Ruth Evans and Alan Gairey, Ian T. Farley, Michael Farley and Emma Stokes, Lisa and, Dulcie Foster, Christine Fowler, Geoff Freeman, Matt Gage, Suzanne Genever, Jennifer Gold, Tony Green, Max Greenhalgh, Sam Griggs, Lucy Hammon, Sharon Harris, Sally Hart, B. Hartmann, Annelies van't Hof, Elizabeth Hogan, Jo Hunt, Susan Jackson, Lesley-Anne Kinnon, Irma Kooistra, Helen Lambie, Katie Lester, Mark Little, Emma Livingston, Michael Low, Ingrid K. Lund, Tracy Lynch, Frank Maas, Becky Marley, Lisa Marriott, Sally Martin, P.D. Masters, Steven McDonald, Cara McEvoy, Richard Middlebrook, Nicole Miran, Mike Mordue, Katherine Moxhay, Yvonne Murphy, Mark Neill, James Newbery, Drew Noon, Larissa Norman, Amy O'Brien, Akiko Okamoto, Anna Pak Poy, Moyra Pierce, Hilton Purvis and Loretta Jakubiec, Christina Rae, Silvia Ranawake, Paraic Reddington, P. Michael Rhodes, Sally Robbins, Liam Rooney, Kerstin Rupprecht, Tony and Ayleen Sands, Tim Sass, Russell Seeney, Kirsty Sheppard, Sarah Smerdon, Jenny Smith, Stu Smith, Ben Snell, Pascal Sommacal, Heidi van Spaandonk, Kyran Speirs, Gary Spinks, Colinda Suthjerland, Dan and Vicky Temple, Kerrie Thomson, Tim Thurbin, Barbara and Beverly Tyler, Erika R. Vogel, Nicola Warburton, Ros Warburton, Rob Wavatt, Jeff Weeks, Jody Williams, Sadie Wilson, Shane Witham, Emilia Wojanczyk, K. Woltesing, Janet and Brian Wright, Alison Yeardley.

Photo credits

Cover

Front cover (small image, top) Rainforest, Queensland © Getty

Front cover (small image, bottom) Sydney Harbour Bridge © Getty

Back cover (top) Whitehaven Beach © Getty

Back cover (bottom) The Pinnacles © Robert Harding

Colour introduction

The Kimberley © WA Tourism

High tide at Whitehaven Beach © Yann Arthus-Bertrand/CORBIS

Kata Tjuta © O. Alamany & E. Vicens/CORBIS

Outdoor dining © South Australia Tourism

Backpackers hiking in the Adelaide Hills © South Australia Tourism

The Big Merino, Goulburn, NSW © Rosie Waitt

River Red Gums on the Murray River, NSW © Jerry Dennis

Surf lifesaving contest near Perth © Tony Yeates

Ferry races, Australia Day festivities, Sydney Harbour © Tourism New South Wales

Kangaroo Crossing © Paul A. Souders/CORBIS

Dream painting, Walpiri tribe © Claire Leimbacht/Robert Harding

Things not to miss

01 Uluru (Ayers Rock) framed by trees © Theo Allofs/CORBIS

02 Wilpena Pound © Courtesy of South Australia Tourism Commission

03 Mardi Gras, Sydney © John Miles

04 Humpback whales © David Lomax/Robert Harding

05 Water lily at sunrise, Kakadu National Park © Theo Allofs/CORBIS

06 Magnetic anthills © David Leffman

07 Performance at the Sydney Opera House © Courtesy of Tourism New South Wales

08 Bondi Beach © Jerry Dennis

09 Geelong vs Melbourne, AFL match, MCG © Jerry Dennis

10 Difficult river exit, Gunshot Creek, Cape York © David Leffman

11 Waterfall, Kimberley © WA Tourism

12 Sea lion, Kangaroo Island © Paul A. Souders/CORBIS

13 View up tree, Tall Timber Country © Chris Scott

14 Kings Canyon under thundery sky © Richard T. Nowitz/CORBIS

15 Crocodile, Northern Territory © Northern Territories Tourism

16 Climbing Sydney Harbour Bridge © K. Gillham/Robert Harding

17 Vineyards, Fleurieu © South Australia Tourism Commission

18 Skiing in the Snowy Mountains © Courtesy of Tourism New South Wales

19 Junction Mine, Broken Hill © Jerry Dennis

20 Atherton Tablelands © Dave King/Dorling Kindersle y

21 Manly Ferry, Sydney © Courtesy of Tourism New South Wales

22 Mutawintji National Park © Jerry Dennis

23 The Twelve Apostles © Max Alexander/Dorling Kindersley

24 Outback track, South Australia © Anne Dehne

25 North Queensland tribes, Aboriginal Dance Festival © John Miles

26 Horse racing, Melboure Cup © Photolibrary.com

27 The Sanctuary Retreat, Mission Beach © K. Gillham/Robert Harding

28 4WD vehicles on 75 Mile Beach, Fraser Island © Tourism Queensland

29 Forest pool, Carnarvon Gorge © David Leffman

30 Witchetty grub in root of Acacia Kemeana plant © John Miles

31 Birdsville Races © Julia Thorne/Robert Harding

32 Tree kangaroo and joey © Anne Dehne

33 Paddlesteamer on the Murray River © Peter Wilson/Dorling Kindersley

34 Beercan croc, Darwin Beer Can Regatta © Chris Scott

35 Coober Pedy © John Miles

36 Joffre Falls, Karijini National Park © Tony Yeates

37 Anemone fish © Stuart Westmorland/CORBIS

38 Cradle Mountain–Lake St Clair National Park © John Miles

39 View from seaplane flight over the Franklin River, Tasmania © Margo Daly

40 Sailing in the Whitsundays © Lisa Nellis

41 Three Sisters, Blue Mountains © John Miles

42 Salt lakes, Yorketown © Peter Wilson/Dorling Kindersley

43 Katherine Gorge © Michael S. Yamashita/CORBIS

44 Walkers at Norman Bay, Wilsons Promontory © Anne Dehne

Black and white photos

Sydney Opera House © Lisa Nellis (p.86)

Terrace house, Paddington, Sydney © Jerry Dennis (p.141)

Surfer at Manly © Alamy (p.157)

Scenic Skyway ride over the Blue Mountains, Katoomba © Rob Reichenfeld/Dorling Kindersley (p.224)

Byron Bay, NSW © John Miles (p.248)

Lake Burley Griffin, Canberra © Penny Tweedle/CORBIS (p.257)

Sub-tropical rainforest, Nightcap National Park, NSW © Rosie Waitt (p.325)

Desert sculptures, Broken Hill, NSW © Jerry Dennis (p.372)

Bushwalking © Courtesy of Australian Tourist Board (p.396)

Castlemaine Brewery, Brisbane © Neil Setchfield (p.411)

Boat to Great Barrier Reef, Port Douglas © Jerry Dennis (p.466)

Tropical beach, Dunk Island © Jerry Dennis (p.518)

Outback pub on the way to Townsville © Lisa Nellis (p.560)

Kookaburra © John Miles (p.586)

Mereenie Loop Road, NT © Courtesy of Northwest Territories Tourist Commission (p.612)

Going hunting, Melville Island © Jerry Dennis (p.631)

Putjamirra Camp croc warning © Jerry Dennis (p.648)

Lone Bungle © Chris Scott (p.696)

Surfer on Cottesloe Beach, Perth © Alan Keohane/Dorling Kindersley (p.718)

Pinnacles Desert, Nambung National Park © Alan Keohane/Dorling Kindersley (p.750)

Womadelaide © Ian Osborn (p.790)

Chateau Yaldara Winery © Neale Clark/Dorling Kindersley (p.828)

Larry the Giant Lobster, Kingston, SE Australia © Lisa Nellis (p.847)

Chapel Street tram, Melbourne © Christine Osbourne/Alamy (p.890)

Footbridge over River Yarra, Melbourne © James Davies/Alamy (p.914)

Great Ocean Road © Anne Dehne (p.962)

The Grotto, Port Campbell National Park, Great Ocean Road © Jerry Dennis (p.978)

The Grampians, Victoria © Jerry Dennis (p.1011)

Wine Glass Bay and wallaby, Freycinet National Park © Jerry Dennis (p.1054)

Flour Mill, Port Arthur Penitentiary © John Miles (p.1094)

Cradle Mountain–Lake St Clair National Park, Tasmania © Tony Yeates (p.1147)

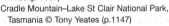

key ⊕ map   ▣ phrasebook   ⊙ cd

Rough Guides publishes new books every month

Rough Guides music & reference

Pocket History Series

"Solidly written, immaculately researched, Rough Guides
are as near as modern guides get to essential"
Sunday Times, London

www.roughguides.com

Rough Guide Reference

The Outback is our Territory

Nobody knows an outback adventure like Britz.

We'll give you the means for independent travel

so you can go where you want, when you want...

No hotels, No itineraries, No boundaries.

- Quality 2WD & 4WD campervan and rental car fleet
- 10 branches Australia-wide
- Half-day 4WD training courses, available Australia-wide
- Outback Safety Kits for rental, including EPIRBS
- Complimentary travel maps & caravan park guide
  including 10% discount off all Big 4 Holiday Parks
- Super Saver discount voucher booklet

So if you want to experience the real Australia, contact
Britz for a quote.

DARWIN

CAIRNS

BROOME

ALICE SPRINGS

BRISBANE

SYDNEY

PERTH   ADELAIDE   MELBOURNE

HOBART

Phone: (+61 3) 8379 8890

Freecall: 1800 331 454 (within Australia)
Website: www.britz.com
Email: ausinfo@britz.com

No Boundaries

Campervan, Car & 4WD Rentals